W9-ADG-948

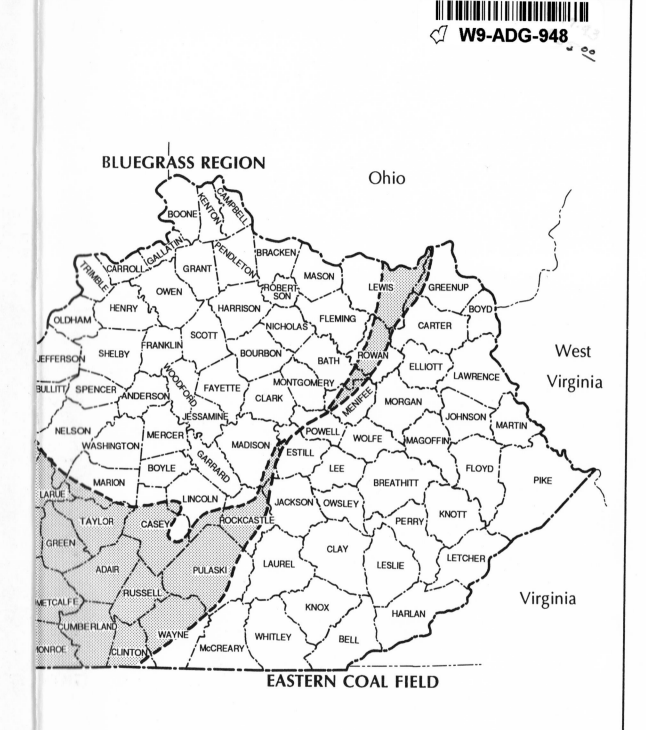

BLUEGRASS REGION

Ohio

West Virginia

Virginia

EASTERN COAL FIELD

jmh

The
Kentucky
Encyclopedia

The Kentucky Encyclopedia

JOHN E. KLEBER

Editor in Chief

THOMAS D. CLARK
LOWELL H. HARRISON
JAMES C. KLOTTER

Associate Editors

THE UNIVERSITY PRESS OF KENTUCKY

Second Printing

Copyright © 1992 by The University Press of Kentucky

Scholarly publisher for the Commonwealth,
serving Bellarmine College, Berea College, Centre
College of Kentucky, Eastern Kentucky University,
The Filson Club, Georgetown College, Kentucky
Historical Society, Kentucky State University,
Morehead State University, Murray State University,
Northern Kentucky University, Transylvania University,
University of Kentucky, University of Louisville,
and Western Kentucky University.

Editorial and Sales Offices: Lexington, Kentucky 40508-4008

Library of Congress Cataloging-in-Publication Data

The Kentucky encyclopedia / John E. Kleber, editor-in-chief; Thomas
D. Clark, Lowell H. Harrison, James C. Klotter, associate editors.

   p. cm.
Includes bibliographical references and index.
ISBN 0-8131-1772-0 (alk. paper)
   1. Kentucky—Civilization—Encyclopedias. I. Kleber, John E.,
1941-
F451.K413 1992   91-26146
976.9'003—dc20

This book is printed on recycled acid-free paper meeting
the requirements of the American National Standard
for Permanence of Paper for Printed Library Materials. ∞

AUTHORS

The following authors have contributed entries to this encyclopedia:

Michael C.C. Adams
Roger C. Adams
Constance Alexander
Virginia T. Alexander
Wendell Allen
R. Gerald Alvey
Eugene J. Amaral
James Anderson
Linda Anderson
Nathalie Taft Andrews
Lindsey Apple
Thomas H. Appleton, Jr.
Philip Ardery
Susan Arthur
Ernie R. Bailey
Robert Bailey
Nancy D. Baird
Jean H. Baker
Thomas P. Baldwin
Frances Keller Barr
Lon Carter Barton
Lee Bash
Carolyn Terry Bashaw
A. Goff Bedford
Mary Margaret Bell
Ted Franklin Belue
Mary Jane Benedict
James D. Bennett
James R. Bentley
Raymond F. Betts
Ann Bolton Bevins
James D. Birchfield
Ira ("Jack") Birdwhistell
Terry Birdwhistell
Barbara N. Bishop
William C. Black
Wilford A. Bladen
R. Charles Blair
George T. Blakey
Paul Blanchard
Gaye Keller Bland
Mary Ann Blankenship
Charles L. Bloch
John H. Blunk
David K. Blythe
Gifford Blyton
Barry W. Bobst
Charles Boewe
John H. Boh
John B. Boles
James Duane Bolin
Jim Bolus

George Street Boone
Joy Bale Boone
William R. Booth
Marquis Boultinghouse
William S. Bowmer
Carl B. Boyd, Jr.
Daniel F. Bradshaw
John B. Briley
Peggy M. Brock
Charles W. Brockwell, Jr.
Ann Brown
Daniel Brown
Emma C. Brown
Richard C. Brown
Gwynne Bryant
Jane C. Bryant
Ron D. Bryant
William S. Bryant
David F. Burg
John E. Burns
Jacqueline Burnside
James G. Burrow
Marlow G. Burt
Emma Cecilia Busam
Charles J. Bussey
Lee Button
Robert A. Bylund
Jean W. Calvert
B. Edward Campbell
Edward D.C. Campbell, Jr.
John A. Campbell
Tracy A. Campbell
Douglas E. Cantrell
Jerry H. Carpenter
Kenneth C. Carstens
Charles B. Castner
Harry M. Caudill
Tom Chaffin
Donald R. Chesnut, Jr.
Eric Howard Christianson
Kathleyne D. Christopherson
Thomas D. Clark
R. Berle Clay
James C. Claypool
Kevin Clay Cockrell
David Cohen
David H. Cole
John Collis
Carl B. Cone
Molly M. Cone
Betty Carolyn Congleton
Anna Marie Conklin

Joan W. Conley
Glen Conner
Beth Cooke
William Cooke
William Cooper
Miriam C. Corcoran
Judy Cornett
William Terrell Cornett
Vincent J. Cotton, Jr.
Madeline C. Covi
Bonnie Jean Cox
Dwayne Cox
Gary S. Cox
Berry Craig
Charles J. Crail
Byron Crawford
Hubert V. Crawford
Paul L. Crawford
Mary Michael Creamer
Clyde F. Crews
Helen B. Crocker
Alvin M. Cross
Carol Crowe-Carraco
Bill Cunningham
J.C. Currens
Leonard P. Curry
Donald Curtis
Dennis Cusick
Robert E. Daggy
Ronald Daley
C. David Dalton
David L. Davies
Bernard Davis
Roy Davis
Wayne H. Davis
Nelson L. Dawson
J.H. DeBerry
Hettie Delong
Carolyn Luckett Denning
David Deskins
Garland R. Dever, Jr.
Aloma Williams Dew
Lee A. Dew
Alan De Young
William K. Dickinson
George A. Dillingham
Jerry Parrish Dimitrov
Michael Bigelow Dixon
Felix Donahue
Michael J. Donahue
Everett Donaldson
Adron Doran

Richard B. Drake
John R. Duncan
William G. Duncan
Anthony L. Dunnavant
C.M. Dupier, Jr.
Gale Edwards
William D. Ehmann
Michael Ellis
William E. Ellis
Betty B. Ellison
T. Kyle Ellison
Fred Engle, Jr.
Sam English, Jr.
Florence Estes
Todd Estes
Frank R. Ettensohn
Will D. Evans
H.E. Everman
Charles F. Faber
Sara L. Farley
Jo M. Ferguson
Michael Flannery
William Barrow Floyd
Philip K. Flynn
Thomas R. Ford
Nancy Forderhase
R.E. Forderhase
Lawrence E. Forgy, Jr.
Harriet W. Fowler
Olivia Frederick
Robert Bruce French
Denver Fugate
Thomas W. Fugate
Paul E. Fuller
Frank M. Gaines
John W. Garden
Morris M. Garrett
William C. Garriott, Jr.
Charles L. Gartrell
Robert J. Gates
John Spalding Gatton
Mary Ann Gentry
Victor B. Gerard
William Gibbons
James M. Gifford
John S. Gillig
Lyman V. Ginger
John M. Glen
Marty Godbey
Joel Goldstein
Lester Goldstein
J.T. Gooch
Cecil E. Goode
James B. Goode
Betty Mitchell Gorin

Janet S. Graff
Karen R. Gray
Lloyd Graybar
Stephen F. Greb
William Green
James S. Greene III
Thomas A. Greenfield
Corinne T. Gregory
Joanne Kurz Guilfoil
Charles Snow Guthrie
Kenneth A. Hafendorfer
David H. Hall
Wade Hall
Martha Hall-Quigley
James W. Hammack, Jr.
Neal O. Hammon
Stratton Hammon
Hunter M. Hancock
Donald C. Haney
Gretchen M. Haney
Richard R. Hannan
Kay Harbison
Mary W.M. Hargreaves
Donald F. Harker, Jr.
Greg Harper
Keith Harper
James Russell Harris
Elaine M. Harrison
Lowell H. Harrison
Richard L. Harrison, Jr.
J.H. Havens
Julie Haviland
Elizabeth C. Hawes
Charles C. Hay III
Melba Porter Hay
Charles Hayes
Richard P. Hedlund
Keith Heim
Donald F. Hellmann
William L. Hendricks
Ed Henson
Gail Henson
Douglas E. Herman
Jerry A. Herndon
George C. Herring
John W. Hevener
Dixie Hibbs
O. Bruce Hinton, Jr.
Patricia M. Hodges
Alicia M. Hoerter
James J. Holmberg
David A. Holt
James F. Hopkins
Katherine L. House
Thomas M. House

H. Fred Howard
Charles D. Howes
J. Blaine Hudson
John W. Hudson, Jr.
Micheal A. Hudson
Nicky Hughes
Susan Lyons Hughes
William J. Hurley
Stephen P. Imhoff
Robert M. Ireland
Evelyn Scyphers Jackson
John Jackson, Jr.
Richard W. Jefferies
Judith Jennings
Malcolm E. Jewell
Virginia Honchell Jewell
Bruce K. Johnson
Leland R. Johnson
Joellen Tyler Johnston
Loyal Jones
Michael E. Jones
Tami Jones
Dennis Karwatka
Arthur L. Kelly
Daniel C. Kelly
Rick Kennedy
Roy C. Kepferle
Bettie L. Kerr
Clara Keyes
Clara Sue Kidwell
Thomas J. Kiffmeyer
George Kilcourse
Charles D. King
Gail King
Robert W. Kingsolver
Mary Jean Kinsman
Ed Klee
John Klee
James C. Klotter
Carl E. Kramer
William R. Kreuger
Joseph Krislov
Lavinia H. Kubiak
Richard La Brecque
D. Warren Lambert
Clay Lancaster
Herman Landau
Arthur B. Lander, Jr.
Anita Lawson
Ruby Layson
Allan R. Leach
Charles R. Lee, Jr.
Laura Harper Lee
Mary Latta Lee
Mimi C. Lewis

James K. Libbey
Z.L. Lipchinsky
Thomas Llewellyn
Milton Lomask
Kathleen Loomis
Richard C. Lovegrove
Marion B. Lucas
James O. Luken
William E. Lyons
Vaughn McBride
Ed McClanahan
Mark McFerron
Preston McGrain
Sue McGuire
Anthony A. McIntire
Ella MacLean
Mary Lou Madigan
Margaret H. Mahoney
Lorie A. Maltby
John P. Marcum
William Marshall
Galen Martin
James B. Martin
William H. Martin
Martyne Mason
Joseph L. Massie
Donna M. Masters
Susan M. Matarese
Frank F. Mathias
Thomas D. Matijasic
Henry C. Mayer
Porter Mayo
Andy Mead
Max E. Medley
Margaret L. Merrick
Boynton Merrill, Jr.
Danny L. Miller
Jim Wayne Miller
Mary Ellen Miller
Rena Milliken
Constance A. Mills
John D. Minton
Charles R. Mitchell
William Ray Mofield
Edward C. Monahan
Burt L. Monroe, Jr.
William Lynwood Montell
William J. Morison
William R. Morley
Trisha A. Morris
Lee Mueller
Kevin Mullen
Mike Mullins
Frederick I. Murphy
Carolyn M. Murray-Wooley

Flaget M. Nally
David A. Nash
Francis M. Nash
Alan Naslund
Humbert S. Nelli
James A. Nelson
Paul David Nelson
Mark E. Nevils
Anthony L. Newberry
David S. Newhall
Joe Nickell
Martin C. Noger
James B. North
Mary E. Nossek
Bradley Nystrom
James H. O'Donnell III
Anthony O'Keeffe
Durward Olds
Nettie Oliver
Lynn Olympia
Nancy O'Malley
William Sherman Oxendine
D. Gene Pace
Tom Pack
Charles E. Parrish
Frances Patridge
John Ed Pearce
James H. Peden
Ron Pen
Charles Allen Perry
L. Martin Perry
John C. Philley
James S. Pope, Jr.
James C. Powers
O. Leonard Press
James M. Prichard
Lester F. Pross
Karl Raitz
James A. Ramage
John M. Ramsay
James R. Rebmann
Sherrill Redmon
Milton Reigelman
Jim Reis
Lynn Renau
Robert M. Rennick
Jerry L. Rice
Otis K. Rice
Russell Rice
Evelyn B. Richardson
H. Edward Richardson
Thomas L. Riley
Anne Ritchie
Gerald F. Roberts
Thomas G. Roberts

John E.L. Robertson
George W. Robinson
Diane Nichols Rogers
Charles P. Roland
John Kelly Ross, Jr.
Dale Royalty
David Eugene Rule
Adam Ruschival
Dorothy C. Rush
Lois Russ
Carl G. Ryant
Dag Ryen
Anita J. Sanford
Charles Scaravilli
Martin F. Schmidt
Robert Schulman
William B. Scott, Jr.
Richard Sears
Sherry G. Sebastian
Scott A. Seiber
Robert F. Sexton
Allen J. Share
Warren J. Shonert
Stanley D. Sides
F. Kevin Simon
J. Allen Singleton
Karen O. Skaff
Deborah Skaggs
Lucy Brent Slater
Margaret Luther Smath
Albert P. Smith, Jr.
Gerald L. Smith
Kim Lady Smith
Bruce Smith-Peters
Richard Smoot
Patrick A. Snadon
Robert Snyder
Thomas W. Spalding
Dennis L. Spetz
Stuart S. Sprague
Helen Price Stacy
Frank B. Stanger, Jr.
Will Frank Steely
Samuel Steger
Richard G. Stone
Ronald L. Street
Marsha Tanner Strein
James G. Strohmaier
Daniel G. Stroup
Ronald L. Stuckey
Jeffrey Scott Suchanek
Jackie Swigart
Thomas H. Syvertsen
Kristin Layng Szakos
Mary K. Bonsteel Tachau

Charles G. Talbert
Harold D. Tallant
Roger Tate
Glen Edward Taul
Richard Taylor
Gene Teitelbaum
Thomas E. Templin
Paul A. Tenkotte
Jack W. Thacker
Janice Theriot
John W. Thieret
Frank C. Thomas
Gladys Cotham Thomas
James C. Thomas
Louis R. Thomas
Ronald Thomas
Samuel W. Thomas
Wendell C. Thomas
Anne Armstrong Thompson
E.I. ("Buddy") Thompson
Milton H. Townsend
Mary Philip Trauth
Vance H. Trimble
Richard L. Troutman
John M. Trowbridge
Ernest Martin Tucker

Daniel G. Tudor
Carolyn C. Turner
William T. Turner
Sandra F. Van Burkleo
R.R. Van Stockum
Robert C. Vitz
Andrew Vorder Bruegge
Robert F. Wachs
Frank H. Walker
Joseph Frazier Wall
H. Lew Wallace
James E. Wallace
Gregory A. Waller
M. Concetta Waller
Michael E. Walters
Riley Rogers Walton
Darold D. Wax
Lynn P. Weatherman
Ross A. Webb
Paul J. Weber
Louis Weeks
Joanne Weeter
Verona Weidig
Lee Shai Weissbach
Kit W. Wesler
Mary E. Wharton

Ronald F. White
Thomas W. White
Charles Whitlock
Joan Whitlow
Clarita B. Whitney
S. Mont Whitson
Bill D. Whittaker
Doris Wilkinson
David Williams
Michael Ann Williams
N. David Williams
Edward Senn Wilson
Richard G. Wilson
Shannon H. Wilson
Stephen Douglas Wilson
Stephen V. Wise
William A. Withington
Florence Wolff
George Wolfford
George C. Wright
John D. Wright, Jr.
George H. Yater
Jeanne Yates
Sarah Yates
Ivan L. Zabilka

INDEX

indi-indexers, Mary and George Neumann, Bloomington, Indiana

MAPS

John M. Hollingsworth, Bloomington, Indiana

CONTENTS

FOREWORD

The Kentucky Bicentennial Commission was formed in 1986 to plan a celebration to commemorate Kentucky's admission as the fifteenth state in the Union. The commission determined that this would be a true celebration of Kentucky—its history, its culture, and most important, the strength, character, and stories of its people.

At its initial meeting, the commission recognized the need for a comprehensive reference work on the commonwealth. Since that time, the commission has dedicated itself to producing *The Kentucky Encyclopedia* as the cornerstone of the bicentennial celebration. This project would not have succeeded without the devotion of our commission members and more than 650 other people who gave their time, talent, and energy. The commission would like to extend its sincere appreciation to all those involved.

As in all projects of this magnitude, certain individuals and organizations recognize the importance and necessity of such a work. Without the generous support of Mary Bingham and the Mary and Barry Bingham, Sr., Fund at its inception, *The Kentucky Encyclopedia* would not exist.

The dedicated efforts of John E. Kleber of Morehead State University guided this encyclopedia to completion. In addition, the determination of George Street Boone, Thomas D. Clark, and the University Press of Kentucky was the driving force behind the production of this book. Lastly, the commission would like to thank the James Graham Brown Foundation, the Knight Foundation (*Lexington Herald-Leader*), W.T. Young, George Street Boone, Joy Bale Boone, the Elkton Bank and Trust Company, the James N. Gray Construction Company, the IBM Corporation, Morehead State University, University of Kentucky, the *Louisville Courier-Journal*, and the *Kentucky Post* of Covington for their generous support.

The Kentucky Encyclopedia is the essence of the state's bicentennial celebration of Kentucky's past, its culture, and its traditions. The book shows that two hundred years of history have brought us to a point where Kentucky is a diverse and wonderful place to live. Most important, it provides the proper perspective for those who will lead Kentucky into the third century of statehood.

David K. Karem, Chairperson
Kentucky Bicentennial Commission

PREFACE

The Kentucky Bicentennial Commission, appointed by Gov. Martha Layne Collins (1983-87) and reappointed by Gov. Wallace G. Wilkinson (1987-91) to plan the celebration of the bicentennial of Kentucky's admission to the Union, acknowledged as part of its mandate "to help Kentuckians better know and understand their history, traditions, and overall contribution to the evolving American culture." To this end, the commission sponsored the preparation and publication of this encyclopedia, under the general oversight of a subcommittee chaired by George Street Boone of Elkton. The committee recruited the principal editor and found housing for the project in an ideal location—at the Margaret I. King Library of the University of Kentucky. A three-year leave of absence was arranged with Morehead State University to acquire the services of the editor in chief. With a generous grant from the Mary and Barry Bingham, Sr., Fund, the work began in the summer of 1988.

The editor, working with an advisory board, selected consulting editors in a variety of specialties, who were to recommend entries for inclusion, suggest writers, read entries for accuracy, and prepare bibliographic citations. The editor then sought the services of the writers—university professors, journalists, artists, businesspeople, lawyers, physicians, local historians, and many others. Altogether, some six hundred people helped to compile the text.

As *The Kentucky Encyclopedia* took shape, it seemed to bespeak the nature of the commonwealth itself. Our more than five hundred authors, possessed of diverse educational backgrounds and social and cultural experiences, represented every region. The sum of their contributions reflects the voice of Kentucky, its strengths and weaknesses at the end of two hundred years of statehood. The encyclopedia is a gift Kentuckians have prepared and given to themselves. The gift should provide the citizens of the commonwealth a sense of who they are, where they are, and from where they came.

SCOPE

A concerted effort was made to reflect more than two hundred years of Kentucky as a commonwealth. We have emphasized the twentieth century, about which fewer works had been published. Geographical balance was sought as well, and entries were selected partly to reflect regionalism and urban-rural diversity. Although history is the backbone of the book, we have included entries about such subjects as the arts, communications, economics, education, folklife, literature, politics, religion, sciences, sports, and transportation.

A real effort was made to identify and include women and minorities as subjects. The obvious preponderance of white males in the entries reflects a traditional social system that has provided fewer opportunities of leadership to others and has failed to record many of their contributions. *The Kentucky Encyclopedia* represents Kentucky as it has been, rather than as it should be. It is to be hoped that the record of the tercentenary will reflect the ideal.

The approximately 2,000 entries were selected by the editor in consultation with the consulting editors. All governors and U.S. senators are included, but not all U.S. representatives or members of the Kentucky General Assembly. To keep the encyclopedia from becoming too quickly outdated, some living people have been included; these are persons whose accomplishments will, we believe, be remembered in the future. Native Kentuckians who achieved fame elsewhere may be included; persons born elsewhere who became famous here may also be included. Among the entries on geographical places are all counties and county seats, and localities with a population of at least 2,500 as recorded in the 1980 census. (Figures from the 1990 census were added when they became available, during the final editing.)

Space limitations excluded some topics. Others we had hoped to include are missing because we were unable to find an appropriate contributor or because a promised contribution did not materialize.

Because of strict space limitations, entries could include little more than basic facts. In general, entries vary in length from one hundred to 2,500 words. Writers were asked to be brief and factual and to keep interpretation to a minimum; thus, little latitude was allowed for variation of writing styles. Somewhat more freedom was enjoyed in a few subject overviews, most of which were written by consulting editors; even these, however, are necessarily brief.

The Kentucky Encyclopedia was compiled and published in four years. To accomplish this, all resources had to be funneled into the work of identifying, assigning, acquiring, and editing entries. For this reason, and to keep the price of the volume as modest as possible, it was decided not to include photographs or other illustrations. We regret in particular the inability to include more maps. It is recommended that the user see P.P. Karan and Cotton Mather, eds., *Atlas of Kentucky* (Lexington, Ky.: University Press of Kentucky, 1977) and Thomas D. Clark, *Historic Maps of Kentucky* (Lexington, Ky.: University Press of Kentucky, 1979).

COMMENTARY

The Kentucky Encyclopedia has been published to fulfill a need for an accessible reference tool. It brings together the latest research, based upon both primary and secondary materials and prepared by capable scholars. This is particularly important in a state with such a heavy reliance upon oral tradition, and where gaps in documentation, conflicting data, and the wide dispersal of research institutions are so prevalent.

It became abundantly clear in our work just how many areas of research have been neglected and await the attention of young scholars. It is hoped that the inclusion here of topics of an obscure yet important nature will resurrect these aspects of Kentucky's past and foster new research. If this is done, the work of editors a century hence will be facilitated.

The editor is solely responsible for the selection of entries, and is aware that his bias may be evident. The criteria of chronological, regional, racial, and social representation, as well as a diversity of subject areas, were based upon a desire to fairly and accurately represent the contributions of Kentucky to the nation through two hundred years of statehood.

The editor is cognizant that factual error will more quickly destroy the integrity of an encyclopedia than any other single factor. For this reason, checks for accuracy were built into our procedure. Every entry was read by the editor, associate editors, and the appropriate consulting editor, as well as by at least two other members of the staff. Hundreds of facts were checked by our staff and many mistakes were corrected, but in general we were forced to rely upon the integrity of the author and the reliability of the sources. For the errors that escaped us, the editor assumes full responsibility and encourages the user to make note of these. It is hoped that the encyclopedia will be revised and kept up to date.

ACKNOWLEDGMENTS

No work of this kind is the accomplishment of one or a few. *The Kentucky Encyclopedia* is the result of a joint effort. Failures may be chargeable to the editor, but virtues of the encyclopedia are shared by the collective authorship. Space permits recognition of only a few who assisted me.

First and foremost, I am grateful to Thomas D. Clark, Kentucky's historian laureate, for asking me to undertake this task. At every stage of development, he was there offering support and encouragement, guiding with a gentle hand, while sharing his years of accumulated knowledge. So great was Dr. Clark's commitment to see this encyclopedia published that he donated freely of his time to read all the entries and to write both the historical overview and nearly one hundred entries. Except for his advocacy to the Bicentennial Commission, there would be no encyclopedia. To say thank you seems slight compensation to one who gave so much.

President C. Nelson Grote and the administration of Morehead State University saw the value of this project and arranged for a three-year leave of absence from all teaching responsibilities. Without that leave and the significant monetary support the university provided, I would have been unable to come to Lexington.

In Lexington, the University of Kentucky agreed to house the project. Paul Willis, director of libraries, supplied office space in the Margaret I. King Library, and for more than three years the good people in Special Collections tolerated our hectic search for the elusive "fact." William Marshall and Terry Birdwhistell and the entire staff were genuinely interested in making our task lighter. They provided resources, understanding, encouragement, and comradeship to a group of interlopers.

From the ranks of the university were recruited several students, most of them graduate students, who worked part-time with me doing the essential daily tasks of researching, fact-checking, writing and rewriting, word processing, mailing, duplicating, filing, and record keeping. All were delightful. They were given a unique opportunity to make a lasting contribution, and not one failed me or acted in any way not professional. To them I express my appreciation, affection, and regret that there will be no more of those late Friday afternoon get-togethers.

In Lexington, IBM not only lent us two PTS computers but put graduate student John Forgy and me through a one-week training session. Without those machines, which never failed us, we would have been unable to perform the editorial task in the allotted time.

I am grateful to the twenty-nine consulting editors who advised me. One editor, historian Mary K. Bonsteel Tachau, died before completing her services. Her scholarship was greatly missed. Raymond F. Betts, director of the Gaines Humanities Center, was the first person to propose the idea of an encyclopedia, and he remained a constant friend who ever provided a sympathetic ear. Philip P. Ardery of Louisville opened doors for us in our search for funds. Historian Robert M. Ireland took on additional editing responsibilities by checking problem entries.

To the three associate editors—Thomas D. Clark, Lowell H. Harrison, James C. Klotter—I must apologize. No one should be asked to do what they did, namely to read the entire manuscript of thousands of pages and make comments. Yet each undertook the task with an enthusiasm that reflected his commitment to the project. Always on schedule with their assignments, they identified hundreds of problem areas, thus enabling us to correct errors and strengthen our prose. Through it all, they never lost patience or a sense of humor, no small feat.

Evalin Douglas served as the liaison between the University Press of Kentucky and *The Kentucky Encyclopedia*. In her warm manner, she advised me on every aspect of book production. After her retirement from the press, she served as one of our staff. Evalin became both friend and confidante who helped me through the difficult times. Sharon Ihnen, managing editor, brought her vast experience to the project. Her diligent efforts, attention to detail, organizational skills, and commitment to the cause kept us on schedule and produced a much improved manuscript.

To many others, I owe much. The resource people at several libraries were always helpful, particularly the Kentucky Historical Society, the Filson Club, and the Kentucky State Libraries and Archives. Many of the staff at these institutions prepared entries for us. At the Filson Club, Nettie H. Oliver answered dozens of our inquiries. They housed one of our researchers for a summer and as a result enabled us to finish our Louisville entries quickly. Ron D. Bryant of the Kentucky Historical Society prepared many county and town entries. George Street Boone and Joy Bale Boone supported me with advice and friendship. Clay Campbell and Sherry Sebastian assisted ably in providing a liaison between the Bicentennial Commission and the encyclopedia. I grew dependent on their abilities, and they never disappointed me. George H. Yater, Herman Landau, and Lon Carter Barton joined me for lunches combined with good advice and encouragement. Vincent J. Cotton, Jr., my attorney, convinced me to undertake the project when remaining at Morehead State University seemed the easier choice. Hettie Delong always understood. Finally, to my family, who saw me through a second book, I am grateful for always being there in the good times and the bad.

John E. Kleber

KENTUCKY: A HISTORICAL OVERVIEW

The area later to become Kentucky was politically undefined at mid-eighteenth century. Its first white visitors found a region of diverse geographical and geological areas, a condition that in later years would have a profound bearing on the history of Kentucky. For convenience' sake, geologists and geographers early subdivided the Kentucky region into five major physical areas with numerous subdivisions. All of these have had a bearing upon the course of human life, and upon flora and fauna distribution as well.

Just as the physiographical regions have borne upon the course of Kentucky history, so have the layers of human occupation. Prehistoric peoples inhabited the stream valleys, mountain ridges, and coves. Archaeologists in the present century have begun to trace the cultural history of these peoples from scattered artifacts, gravesites, and other enigmatic remains.

In the era of the modern Native Americans—known to the Europeans as Indians or "red men"—the historical record is much clearer. The relationships of these people with the land of Kentucky reflected the border nature of the territory. None actually occupied with any permanence the present geographical pale of Kentucky, although Indians from both north and south visited the region on hunting and warring expeditions. Yet their presence and their often fiercely defended claims upon the land lay heavily upon early Kentucky history.

An attempt to identify the European who, probably at some time in the first half of the eighteenth century, first entered the area of present-day Kentucky would be a futile exercise in historical investigation. The documented history of Anglo-colonial Kentucky began with the explorations of Dr. Thomas Walker and his scouting party in April 1750. His journal is an enlightening description of the land and of the party's experiences. The next year Christopher Gist, in the employ of the Ohio Company, visited the area and kept a journal of his travels. Before the arrival of these visitors, there were identifiable visitations by John Lederer, Gabriel Arthur, Abraham Woods, Thomas Batts, Robert Fallam, and others.

Both French and Spanish explorers had traveled along the western rivers. By the fourth decade of the eighteenth century, a considerable trade had developed with the Indians, the source of a vigorous rivalry between the French and British traders. Culminating this rivalry at mid-century was the French and Indian War (1754-63). This international conflict was worldwide in scope, but its American phase was to have a fundamental bearing upon the future of Kentucky. It opened the Ohio River to settler access, created unrest among the Indians above the Ohio, produced active speculation in land, and involved the western country in major international diplomatic negotiations. Most important, however, it in large measure assured the establishment of an Anglo-American pattern of life and culture in the country that would become Kentucky.

The Treaty of Paris in 1763 was as important an incident in Kentucky history as if it had been composed and signed on the soil of the western country. It wiped away many of the political barriers to Anglo-colonial expansion in the land beyond the Appalachian highlands. The attempt to stem that tide, by King George III and the British Board of Trade in the Proclamation of 1763, was a diplomatic blunder. In simplest terms, the proclamation was aimed at placating the Indians and so gaining time in which to work out a policy for dealing with them. But in the eyes of American colonial borderers, who were poised on the Appalachian dividing line, it became a dare line to be violated at will.

The decades 1763 to 1783 were significant ones; these were years of decision, in which large blocks of land were explored and claimed and the cultural patterns of American pioneering were developed. All across the region personalities emerged who in time would be enshrined as American frontier heroes. The pattern of pioneering life, with only slight variations, that developed on the Kentucky frontier prevailed across the spreading western American empire. This was an era when Long Hunters, some named and many others nameless, wandered in the Kentucky wilderness hunting, trading with Indians, and spying out the land. Historians may never fully assess the role of these early visitors in feeding the human network of communication and gossip about the Kentucky frontier.

The Daniel Boone–John Finley hunting party of the spring of 1769 was essentially a band of Long Hunters. Certainly the lonely wanderings of Daniel Boone in the western country (1769-71) made him one of the longest hunters in the region. Thus by 1775 the land west of the Appalachians was no longer one of mystery, and it had already begun to assume the legendary aura of a new Eden.

Just as the French and Indian War opened the way for further Anglo-colonial expansion into the western lands, the Revolutionary War (1775-81) was to have a phenomenal impact upon American expansion in the western country. Settler footholds were established in the Kentucky backwoods in 1774 and 1775. James Harrod and his party of thirty-seven men arrived near the head of the Salt River to establish Harrod's Town, the first permanent settlement in the region. But they were by no means alone in the region. There were the McAfee brothers, Thomas Bullitt and Hancock Taylor, surveyors, Simon Kenton, George Yeager, John Strader, Michael Holsteiner, and others who came as adventurers. The outbreak of Dunmore's War (1774) interrupted the initial settlement of Kentucky, but at the same time helped to bring important leadership figures to the fore.

In 1775 Harrod's company returned to Harrod's Town to build their fort and begin settling on the land. Up the Kentucky River Richard Henderson and the Transylvania Land Company were busy after March of that year in establishing Boonesborough. Across the way Benjamin Logan was establishing his St. Asaph station and settlement. In February 1775 a party headed by Daniel Boone was dispatched to blaze a trail from Sycamore Shoals in eastern Tennessee through Cumberland Gap to the south bank of the Kentucky River. In time, the general course of this trail was to become the Wilderness Road, the great artery of immigrant travel.

During the decade 1775-85, forts, blockhouses, and stations were built in many places in central and south-central Kentucky. With the outbreak of the Revolutionary War and British actions in the Ohio Valley, both the Virginia back country and that west of the mountains were sorely beset by Indian attacks from above the Ohio. Immigrants moving along the Wilderness Road were attacked by the Cherokee from the south. The movement of population to the Kentucky country during the Revolution involved a complexity of social, cultural, economic, political, and folk issues; it was motivated by all the forces and circumstances that would propel westward population movements in later years.

Why did people come to Kentucky? Some came to escape the religious and political discrimination of British rule, some to avoid the ardors of the Revolution, many to shuck off the burden of debt, and some, no doubt, to escape the clutches of the law. The tug of adventure was ever strong. The lodestone attraction, however, was the availability of abundant and cheap virgin land, for many lands east of the mountains had been worn thin by primitive modes of cultivation and management. Above all of these was a less tangible lure; scores of settlers were drawn to the new country by fascinating rumors of a New World Eden, in which a person could settle, free of old legal and institutional entanglements, on bounteously productive soil.

For more than two centuries Kentuckians have based their domestic economy and culture upon the land and its natural resources. The Kentucky statutes are filled with laws pertaining to the land, laws as revealing of the turn of the Kentucky mind as of the legal developments they represent. The reports of the early court of appeals reflect eloquently the course of Kentucky history in this area, as do the hundreds of depositions in the offices of the Kentucky circuit court clerks.

Virginia governors and assemblymen struggled constantly to create a workable western land policy and administrative authority to control it. In this connection it may have been unfortunate that the settlement of Kentucky got under way before the adoption of the Northwest Ordinance created an orderly system of land surveys and distribution. Some of the major conditions of Virginia's consent to a separation of its western counties had to do with Virginia's own land laws.

Four major challenges in the decade of the 1780s put the western counties on the road to seeking separation from Virginia and the establishment of a new state. First was the Indian menace from both north and south, which needed to be dealt with promptly and decisively. There were mounting land disputes, which multiplied with the arrival of every new wave of settlers and had to be resolved locally. The presence of a growing and highly fluid population created all the social and domestic problems to which mankind is heir, and these also demanded quick resolution at the local level. The petitions the Kentucky inhabitants sent back to Richmond, Virginia, reflected the complexities of planting an Anglo-American civilization and culture in a virgin region sealed off from the source of central authority by an almost impenetrable range of mountains. Finally, there was the urgent matter of opening a dependable artery of trade and transportation to prevent economic strangulation of the region. This necessity involved dealing with Spain, the fickle international power that controlled the mouth of the Mississippi River and the downriver trading ports.

All of these pressures led to the organization of local governments. On December 7, 1776, the Virginia General Assembly created Kentucky County out of the vast county of Fincastle. On December 31 it defined the boundaries of the new county, which in general were those of modern Kentucky. Within four years the inrush of settlers demanded the creation in 1780 of the three counties of Fayette, Lincoln, and Jefferson. The new entities set a precedent for county proliferation that was to become a major problem in modern Kentucky.

In the early 1780s, some of the basic issues that led to the separation from Virginia were revealed and discussed in the so-called separation conventions in Danville (1784-92), in the Danville Political Club, and in the columns of the newly formed *Kentucke Gazette*. These were landmark moments in American history; there was no precedent for the creation of a new noncolonial state out of virgin western territory. Reflected in the debates and public comments in Kentucky during this era was a distinct shift away from the old frontier leadership of Daniel Boone, Simon Kenton, James Harrod, George Rogers Clark, John Bowman, John Floyd, and others. Only Benjamin Logan, among the old pioneers, remained active in public affairs. Leadership shifted to the more sophisticated George Nicholas, John Brown, Harry Innis, Samuel McCowell, Isaac Shelby, Thomas Marshall, Caleb Wallace, and James Wilkinson. Generally these new leaders were conservative landowning or professional men. The future state of Kentucky was to recruit much of its leadership talent from their ranks.

The Commonwealth of Virginia on two occasions had previously enacted legislation permitting the separation of its western counties. The act of 1789, known as the Virginia Compact, assured the extension of Virginia influence into the future of the new state of Kentucky. The constitution drafted in the tenth Danville convention in April 1792, despite all of the debating and discussion, reveals remarkably little originality on the part of the delegates. It outlines the divisions of government and defines the duties and responsibilities of the three divisions. The document provides for the selection of a governor, to whom it gives "supreme powers," but it makes no provision for a lieutenant governor. One of the constitution's distinguishing features is the extensive Bill of Rights. This section, reflective of all the British and American struggle to guarantee the rights and freedom of the individual, was adopted almost bodily from the second constitution of Pennsylvania (1790).

The government of the Commonwealth of Kentucky was organized in a ceremonial meeting in Lexington on June 4, 1792. Isaac Shelby of Lincoln County was appointed governor. The first constitution provided for the selection of a governor and senators by members of the House of Representatives, reflecting a distinct distrust of the citizens' ability to make wise choices of these officers. Isaac Shelby, a hero of the battles of King's Mountain and the Cowpens, had an impeccable reputation of integrity and leadership capability.

It was not the intention that Lexington would become the capital of Kentucky. A committee of five, including Robert Todd, John Edwards, John Allen, Henry Lee, and

Thomas Kennedy, was appointed on June 6, 1792, to select a permanent site. Frankfort was chosen principally because of a contribution of land and building materials and the town's location on the Kentucky River and near the center of population. The forty-seven members of the General Assembly met for the first time in Frankfort on November 1, 1793, in the farmhouse of Maj. James Love. They began the tasks of adapting a considerable volume of Virginia statutes to the needs of the new state, establishing the administrative offices of government, and enacting a body of local domestic laws.

A truly startling fact in Kentucky history was the phenomenal rush of people into the region in so brief an interval of time. Much has been made of the hardships and perils of settling the Kentucky frontier, but the eagerness with which settlers pushed westward seems almost to deny these deterrents. In 1790 there were estimated to be 61,133 whites, 12,430 slaves, and 114 free persons of color—73,677 persons in all. By 1800 this number had increased to 220,955, of whom 40,343 were slaves. The Kentucky frontier may have been a political and economic safety valve as some historians have asserted. But the rapid increase in population created its own peculiar problems and pressures. In this respect, the challenges of the raw frontier of Kentucky were distinctly different from those of most of colonial Virginia or the Carolinas, and meeting them required resolute local action. The Ohio River and Wilderness Road arteries of travel were crowded with immigrants who came west to seek ownership of land and to make new starts in their lives. From the beginning of settlement there were an appreciable number of slaves in the region; by 1800 they accounted for almost 18 percent of the population. Slaves proved to be sturdy pioneers, contributing substantially to the clearing of lands and the building of homes and to the establishment of a rural agrarian culture.

Within the first decade after the organization of the commonwealth, the farmlands of central Kentucky had become highly productive of field crops of corn, wheat, hemp, and tobacco, in approximately that order of importance. The meadows and forest yielded rich returns in livestock. Before the eighteenth century ended, a flourishing downriver trade was established. The Wilderness Road through Cumberland Gap to central Kentucky became a drover's path over which an almost endless procession of farm animals, including cattle, hogs, horses, mules, and sheep were driven to the eastern Atlantic coastal markets. The internal rivers and streams and the Ohio and Mississippi rivers became commercially and politically vital to the welfare of Kentucky. The state's economy depended upon these streams for access to markets for bulky and heavy goods.

The era of the flatboat trade was one of the colorful chapters in Kentucky history. This type of boating was serious business engaged in by hardy men. It developed rugged personalities whose rowdiness and belligerence colored the early popular image of Kentucky. The western rivers were beset by both natural and human perils to be reckoned with by boatmen. At the foot of the Mississippi there was the fickle Spanish authority, which could close the depot of deposit at will. The purchase of the Louisiana Territory, April 30, 1803, freed the western rivers to trade, but not before Kentuckians threatened to go to war against Spain for the release of the southern territory. The impact of the western river system on the course of Kentucky history was not confined to commerce. In both the flatboat and subsequent steamboat eras, the state's social, cultural, economic, and political interests became aligned with those of the lower South rather than the developing Old Northwest.

From that moment in March 1775 when Daniel Boone and his party set out from Sycamore Shoals to blaze a trail northward, transportation became a central issue in state history. The General Assembly in December 1793 enacted a law creating a commission to survey and improve a section of the Wilderness Road, and in 1795 it authorized the opening of the old pioneer trail to wagon traffic. During the first half of the nineteenth century an amazing body of laws was enacted applying to the opening of roads, the chartering of toll road, bridge, and ferry companies, and the maintenance of all these. At the local level, every meeting of a county court in this period dealt in some fashion with the location, relocation, and maintenance of roads.

During the interval 1811-50, both legislative and public attention was focused upon improvement of the navigable streams. The arrival in Louisville in December 1811 of Nicholas Roosevelt's steamer *New Orleans* marked the opening of a new and revolutionary era in Kentucky's economic and social history. In the following years, Louisville superseded Lexington as the urban center of Kentucky and the Falls of the Ohio became the scene of a rising commerce.

The Kentucky General Assembly in January 1825 granted the Louisville and Portland Canal Company a charter to construct a bypass around the Falls of the Ohio and on December 5, 1830, the steamer *Uncas* was the first vessel to pass through the canal. The clear navigational channel that was thus opened from Pittsburgh to New Orleans brought trade to Louisville from the north and south and established the town as Kentucky's major urban and commercial center.

The Lexington & Ohio Railway was chartered by the General Assembly on January 27, 1830. The promoters of this road hoped to bypass Louisville and connect with some point down the river near West Point. It was not until March 1850 that Kentucky entered the interstate railway age, when the General Assembly granted a charter to the Louisville & Nashville Railroad Company.

By many historical criteria, the first half of the nineteenth century was the state's most eventful period. In this era came to the fore a new generation of leaders including Henry Clay, Richard M. Johnson, Humphrey Marshall, George Robertson, William T. Barry, Cassius M. Clay, James Guthrie, John C. Breckinridge, John Jordan Crittenden, and others. By birth and later by family and educational associations, Kentucky claimed Abraham Lincoln and Jefferson Davis. Aside from these, Kentucky fed onto the expanding American frontier a stream of mountain men, trail breakers and guides, military personnel, and territorial officials.

Kentuckians were to play active roles in the War of 1812. Henry Clay and Richard M. Johnson were War Hawks, Isaac Shelby left the governor's chair to lead troops to the Michigan battlefield, and Kentucky troops were engaged in all the western battles and at New Orleans. Politically and financially, the war was to exert tremendous influence on Kentucky for years to come. A runaway period of speculation and financial inflation and a wholly irresponsible system of local state banking left Kentucky in a precarious situation

in the biting panic of 1819. In true western frontier style, Kentucky during the decades 1800-60 engaged in all but uncontrolled expansion of local government. In 1860 there were 110 counties, which ranged in population from 1,568 in the hill country of Jackson to 39,751 in Jefferson. There was an average of approximately 4,000 people per county. It took little political pressure in this era to create a new county and to name it for a military hero or a politician.

The first half of the nineteenth century was also an era of social and cultural developments. A state hospital was established to take care of the mentally dependent. The state penitentiary went through at least two stages of managerial philosophy. In the field of medicine, genuine progress was made in inoculation against smallpox and the removal of ovarian tumors and of bladder and kidney stones. The Transylvania Medical School trained doctors for both Kentucky and the lower South.

As the central Kentucky farmlands increased production of field crops and blooded livestock and landowners became established, artists were able to secure patronage. Among them were portrait painters, silversmiths, and sculptors. Matthew Harris Jouett, Asa Blanchard, Samuel Woodson Price, Joseph H. Bush, Oliver Frazier, and Louis Morgan painted scores of portraits of famous and not-so-famous Kentuckians during the first half of the nineteenth century. Edward Troye created an equally famous portrait gallery of Kentucky horses and purebred cattle. At the same time, Joel T. Hart carved busts of Kentucky's statesmen and portrayed such subjects as Maidenhood and the Triumph of Chastity. Gideon Shryock, a native architect, led the state out of the log cabin–Georgian colonial age. He created for Kentucky a Greek Revival state capitol in Frankfort, Morrison Hall in Lexington, the School for the Blind, and a bit of the Jefferson County courthouse in Louisville. He also influenced home building. In time, Greek Revival architecture became a symbol of the commonwealth.

From the appearance of the first issue of the *Kentucke Gazette* on August 11, 1787, the newspaper has been an important institution in Kentucky. The nineteenth century history of Kentucky journalism included George D. Prentice's *Louisville Daily Journal*, the *Lex-*

ington Observer, the *Lexington Reporter*, Albert Gallatin Hodges's *Frankfort Commonwealth*, and a host of country weeklies. Following the Civil War there were the *Louisville Courier-Journal*, the Lexington *Herald* and *Leader*, and a dozen smaller daily papers. Throughout Kentucky history, the newspaper has been the state's most consistent opinion-forming and literary force.

No institution in the state, however, has a more impressive history than organized religion. There were lay ministers among the earliest pioneers, and in the last quarter of the eighteenth century the new country was a magnet for missionaries. In 1781 from Virginia came the Traveling Church, of Baptist faith, led by Lewis and Elijah Craig. Bishop Francis Asbury and a host of Methodist circuit riders crossed and recrossed Kentucky establishing societies and churches. Roman Catholic missionaries came early to south-central Kentucky and land along the Ohio River. Presbyterians were on hand to wield considerable influence in the framing of the first constitution and the formation of the state.

At the turn into the nineteenth century occurred one of the most interesting religious movements in American history. Revival meetings along the Muddy and Gasper rivers in south-central Kentucky created a fervor that spread to Cane Ridge in Bourbon County. There, in August 1801, were assembled thousands of persons who responded to preaching and crowd psychology with wild outbursts of emotion. This meeting was to be followed by a spread of revivalism across Kentucky and into the lower South that continued for years. In 1805 missionaries of Mother Ann Lee's New England Shaker community came to Kentucky seeking converts; they organized a western community on the Isaiah Thomas farm in Mercer County. Thus religious denominations with numerous social and spiritual philosophies early became driving forces in human affairs in the commonwealth.

Educational beginnings in the commonwealth were left largely to the mercies of charity or to dependence upon limited public land grants. The act of establishing a civilization in a virgin country required the expenditure of an enormous amount of physical energy, but little or no educational training was necessary to wield the ax and hoe, to roll logs, or to build pole cabins and log houses. The economic base in Kentucky in its pioneering days was too thin to permit establishment of a supportive tax income.

Nevertheless, in 1780 the Virginia General Assembly chartered the Transylvania Seminary and assigned to it the escheated western lands of three Tories. The most important precedent, however, was the enactment by the Kentucky General Assembly of the Academy Act of 1798, which granted to each newly formed county 6,000 acres of undeveloped public lands for the organization and operation of a public academy. This was an inefficient and escapist process for organizing and supporting a public school system. After the War of 1812, Kentuckians were too deeply involved in financial panic and bitter partisan politics to take part in the general national movement to establish and maintain public schools. The General Assembly in 1820 made a gesture in that direction by appointing a committee to make both a state and national survey of opinion relating to public education. In 1822 William T. Barry submitted the report of the committee to the General Assembly; that body, torn by partisan strife, proceeded to file the report away. No doubt this action set public education back several decades. There was some public pressure in the early 1830s for the organization of public schools, a movement given considerable impetus by the return to Kentucky of more than $1 million of surplus funds by the U.S. Treasury. In 1849 the public school concept was for the first time given constitutional sanction.

Legal provision for the establishment of a public school system in Kentucky was one thing; the securing of public and fiscal support was more difficult. Fortunately, Robert Jefferson Breckinridge was superintendent of public instruction in 1850, and with tenacity he was able to give the constitutional mandate a practical application. The challenges at midcentury were many. A minimal tax base for school support had to be established; school districts had to be organized, along with county offices of superintendents; improvements were called for in teacher employment and training; and, most important of all, a public will to support schools had to be generated.

Too many social and political controversies raged in this era to permit the movement for public schools to gain momentum. Especially disturbing was the existence of slavery in the commonwealth. From the outset there were opponents of slavery in Kentucky, and especially so in the formative year of 1792. As the decades passed, the opposition became more vocal. Slavery never became a universal institution in the state; it scarcely existed in many of the counties, and in others the numbers were small. Slaves were concentrated largely in the more productive agricultural counties of central Kentucky and in the southern middle tier of counties. But opening of the cotton lands of the lower South after the successful introduction of the gin had a marked impact on slavery in Kentucky; between 1820 and 1860 an active interstate slave trade developed from Kentucky southward. This inhumane business subjected Kentucky to the bitter criticisms of foreign and domestic travelers, abolitionists, emancipationists, and contemporary authors. Blatant slave dealer advertisements in Kentucky newspapers, the conduct of public slave auctions, and the existence of slave jails eloquently documented the evils of the institution of slavery.

After 1820 there were active antislavery movements in Kentucky, which advocated various plans of emancipation. The American Colonization Society, which established a colony in Africa to receive free blacks, enlisted active support from many Kentuckians, including Henry Clay, in the 1820s and 1830s. The period of the most intensive opposition to slavery in Kentucky, however, occurred during the decades 1830-60. In 1833 the General Assembly attempted to reduce the infamous interstate slave trade by enacting an anti-importation law, which restricted the bringing in of slaves from other states. At the opening of the interstate slave trade in 1820, there were 126,732 slaves in Kentucky; this number grew to 248,809 in 1850, then dropped to 225,483 by the outbreak of the Civil War.

In slavery as in geography, politics, and economy, Kentucky was a border state, and in the nineteenth century it was on the "grand tour itinerary" of Europeans who wanted to see America. Visitors to the region often compared social and economic conditions with those across the river in Ohio. For many travelers, Kentucky was the first view of the institution of slavery, and they became more critical of the state as the century advanced. By the late 1830s slavery had become a burning issue in Kentucky, fed by the ardor of abolitionist publications. In 1839 Theodore Weld published his *American Slavery as It Is: Testimony of a Thousand Witnesses*. Much of its contents were garnered from Kentucky newspapers, personal interviews, slave auction handbills, and personal observations.

One of the most dramatic barbs aimed at Kentucky slavery was Cassius M. Clay's *True American* newspaper (1845). The editor, a son of one of the state's largest landowners and slaveholders, aroused great indignation. His printing office was destroyed in an act that violated the First Amendment in most flagrant fashion, and a few years later a court ordered damages paid to Clay.

In the drive of 1845-49 to revise the 1799 constitution, slavery became a central issue in the election of delegates, leading to impassioned controversy and occasional violence. Delegates in 1799 who revised the first constitution had written into the second an ironbound guarantee of the preservation of slavery in the state; the Kentucky slavery article of 1799 had been adopted verbatim in constitutions drafted for the new states in the lower South. During the convention of 1849, delegates ultimately included the 1799 slavery article in the new constitution.

Enactment of the Fugitive Slave Law by the U.S. Congress in 1850 had an important bearing on Kentucky. It was not too difficult for escaping slaves to reach free territory by crossing the Ohio River, and many runaway slaves took this route. In 1851-52 Harriet Beecher Stowe, wife of a Cincinnati Lane Seminary professor, began publishing chapters of her forthcoming book in the *National Era*, an abolitionist journal, under the title "Uncle Tom's Cabin, or Life Among the Lowly." Much of the setting and many of the characters were drawn from her visits to Kentucky. Published in book form, her stories were a powerful indictment of American slavery in general, and of the Kentucky institution in particular. Stephen Collins Foster's popular song "My Old Kentucky Home, Good-night!" is essentially the central theme of *Uncle Tom's Cabin* set to music; in fact Foster first titled it "Den Poor Old Uncle Tom, Good-night." Little could Foster have imagined in 1853 that his song would be so cherished by Kentuckians in future years, nor do modern Kentuckians, perhaps, sense the implications of the song.

Despite the increasing opposition to slavery and the emerging sectional controversies, in the decade 1850-60 Kentucky experienced one of the most prosperous periods in its history. For most of the years agricultural production was on the rise and cash returns from crops and livestock were at an all-time high. The cash value of farms showed a phenomenal increase. Trade along the rivers flourished; in fact, the possible disruption of trade was one of the biggest issues for Kentuckians in the approaching sectional crisis.

Left to their own local interests in 1860, most Kentuckians no doubt would have vigorously supported the stability of the Union and peace. In the presidential election that year, when 67.1 percent of the potential voters cast a ballot, sixty of the 110 counties gave a plurality of votes to John Bell and the Constitutional Union Party. John C. Breckinridge, a native son and vice-president of the United States, lost all the heavily slaveholding counties except Scott. He carried only forty-three counties, and in them the vote counts were low. Abraham Lincoln garnered less than 1 percent of the vote and carried no county.

The interval from December 1860 to December 1862 was one of the most stressful in Kentucky history. Caught between the two sections in the breakup of the Union, the state was confronted with major decisions. The state government was in the hands of a leadership incapable of taking bold measures for the preservation of Kentucky's peace and security. Gov. Beriah Magoffin's loyalty to the Union was questioned, despite his diligent efforts to find some compromise between the sections. The General Assembly was torn by a diversity of views, and public opinion was sharply divided and poorly informed as to the depth of the national crisis.

In 1860 Kentucky was in the very heart of the expanding Republic. For half a century its political leadership had played major roles in resolving explosive sectional issues, and again in 1860 it was called upon to make further efforts at preserving the peace. Governor Magoffin at the state level sought means of resolving the sectional issues that threatened dissolution of the Union, and at the national level John Jordan Crittenden, Garrett Davis, and others sought to effect a compromise. In Kentucky itself, the newspaper press was strong in its pro-Union views. No voice was more emphatic on this subject than that of George D. Prentice and the *Louisville Journal*.

The rapidity with which the southern states seceded forced Kentucky to formulate a policy in too short a time. During the first six months of 1861, the General Assembly faced complexities for which it could call on no precedent. Fortunately, cooler heads in the state saw clearly that Kentucky had everything to lose by seceding and nothing to gain by engaging in a civil war; eloquent proof was visible in the interference with trade on the Ohio River and the prospect of losing the southern market for Kentucky products. Too, the prospect of Kentucky's becoming a battleground was grim. Perhaps no one early in 1861 believed that true neutrality could be maintained for Kentucky. Gaining access to Kentucky was vital to both the Union and the Confederacy. Abraham Lincoln is reported to have said that he hoped God was on the side of the Union, but that he must have Kentucky. He added that to lose Kentucky was nearly the same as to lose the whole game—meaning that if Kentucky, a major border state, left the Union, the others would go as well.

On April 15, 1861, President Lincoln issued his famous call for 75,000 state troops, and Secretary of War Simon Cameron called upon Governor Magoffin to supply four regiments. The request was refused on the ground that it violated Kentucky's neutrality. In May of that year the War Department made an initial assignment of 5,000 guns, ostensibly to be issued to persons for protection of their homes and to the Kentucky Home Guards. The Kentucky militia at this point had followed Simon Bolivar Buckner and John Hunt Morgan into the service of the Confederacy. By this time there was little or no observance by either government of Kentucky's neutral position.

In August 1861, Gen. William Nelson established Camp Dick Robinson in Garrard County as a Union post. The Union forces in the area were under the command of Gen. Robert Anderson of Fort Sumter fame. Later Gen. William T. Sherman was made the general commander in Kentucky, with George H. Thomas and William Nelson in divisional commands. By early fall there was considerable recruiting activity by both sides in the state, producing a highly visible division of sentiments among the population. There is historical merit in the often repeated phrase that in Kentucky the war pitted brother against brother, as personified in the divisions of such prominent families as the Breckinridges, Crittendens, and Clays. But it was even more true among less well-known families. In his novel

Little Shepherd of Kingdom Come, written while memories were still vivid, John Fox, Jr., dealt effectively with the divisions of loyalties in Kentucky.

Kentucky's neutrality was violated on September 4, 1861, when Gen. Leonidas Polk's command occupied Columbus on the Mississippi River. After this date, events almost daily drew Kentucky more deeply into the conflict.

On June 1, 1866, a federal report credited Kentucky with supplying 76,355 troops to the Union Army; of this number 14,918 were black. It was estimated that approximately 34,000 Kentuckians fought with Confederate forces. No one knows precisely the latter number because of a laxness of record keeping by many of the Confederate commands.

Kentucky was invaded by both the Union and Confederate armies. A major early effort was made by the Confederates to establish a line of operation from Columbus on the Mississippi to Cumberland Gap on the east, with Bowling Green as a concentration point. This line was broken when Gen. Ulysses S. Grant's army pushed up the Tennessee and Cumberland rivers and forced the withdrawal of the Confederate forces under the command of Albert Sidney Johnston and Simon Bolivar Buckner.

In the fall of 1861 Gen. Felix Zollicoffer's Confederate command attempted to penetrate central Kentucky by way of the Wilderness Road but was thwarted on October 21-22, in a skirmish in the Rockcastle Hills at the Wildcat point, overlooking the crossing of the Rockcastle River. Zollicoffer undertook a second invasion from eastern Tennessee by way of Wayne and Pulaski counties. The Confederates were defeated in the Battle of Mill Springs, and Zollicoffer lost his life in the engagement.

Central Kentucky was harassed in the early years of the war by John Hunt Morgan's cavalry command, which disrupted railway traffic and skirmished at several points. In September 1862, Gen. Edmund Kirby-Smith led a successful invasion into central Kentucky up the Wilderness Road, winning the Battle of Richmond en route. Gen. Braxton Bragg led his army out of Tennessee and up through the southern counties to Perryville. He was followed by Gen. Don Carlos Buell's Union command. The two armies engaged in the furious and bloody Battle of Perryville on October 8, 1862. The defeat of the Confederates in this battle left Kentucky largely in the control of the Union forces, and the war drew away from the state.

There were to be no more pitched battles on Kentucky soil. But throughout the remainder of the Civil War after October 1862, Kentucky was harassed by hit-and-run raids that destroyed railroads, some property, courthouses, and a considerable amount of peace of mind. In the latter years of the war, the state was plagued with marauding guerrillas who owed allegiance to neither side.

For Kentucky there were marked paradoxes in the era of the Civil War, the greatest of which was the role of Louisville in the struggle and the fact that it escaped any real damage. Another was the impact of the war on Appalachian Kentucky and its political alliances. For all of Kentucky, the period of the war can be said to have been a distinct political, social, cultural, and economic watershed. Not a single aspect of Kentucky life was left untouched. Slaves became freedmen, with all the problems accompanying their change of status. What had been a slave issue now became a racial one. In the field of state politics, the central issue was restoring government to its former function and erasing the scars left by mismanagement during the interval of military control.

The Civil War brought about a drastic revision of Kentucky's commercial relationships with both the North and the South. It was forced to face a future of powerful competition from the rising new industrial America. Much of Kentucky's local economy was little more advanced than it had been in 1820. Its infant railway system was left in shambles by neglect and wartime raids. With the exception of the Louisville & Nashville Railroad, no interstate railway had been completed through Kentucky. On the rivers Kentucky lost ground to other states in the rising competition in steamboat traffic. The traditional southern market for Kentucky products had been bankrupted, and merchants and farmers from the North competed for the limited trade that remained.

In the immediate postwar years, vast areas of Kentucky remained largely in a virginal state, and most of the rural agrarian population lived little if any above a bare subsistence level. The mechanization of agriculture in the northwestern states offered serious competition to Kentucky farmers. Along with vast areas of unexploited lands, most of Kentucky's virgin timber was still standing, and only a small portion of its mineral resources had been tapped.

Urban expansion in Kentucky before 1865 was limited. Only Louisville had shown genuine signs of growth in population and business. In 1865 that city was in a rather good position to grow, but Lexington, the old pioneer urban center, was locked in a stagnant agrarian stage. Throughout the rest of the state, the county seat towns were small and their fortunes were tied to their agricultural territories.

A major sociological-demographic revolution revealed itself to Kentuckians after 1870; their state was no longer in the path of American migration. Kentucky was now a bypassed state, as foreign immigrants moved onto the opening frontiers of the Old Northwest and beyond the Mississippi. Not only was the state being bypassed, it was losing its own population to the new westward movement. In an effort to stem this tide of population loss, Kentucky joined the southern states in the 1870s and 1880s to attract western European immigrants to its vacant lands. Through the State Geological Survey and the newly created Bureau of Agriculture, Labor, and Statistics, a campaign was begun to entice Europeans to settle in Kentucky. Bundles of broadsides, statistical pamphlets, and even agents were sent abroad describing the bright future prospects of the state. This effort, however, met with only minimal success. A Swiss colony was established in Laurel County, a German one in Lincoln County, and the Ohio River towns received some immigrants, but Kentucky as a whole continued to lose population.

No Kentucky institution suffered greater disruption from the Civil War than education. A system of public schools, following the adoption of the educational clause in the constitution of 1849, was still in the preliminary organizational stage at the outbreak of the war. No properly sustaining tax base had been instituted, no provisions for teacher training had been made, and no sweeping public sentiment for the organization and conduct of schools had been generated. Kentucky was a land without an effective system of public schools and burdened with an inordinate rate of illiteracy. Perhaps no single statement could

better sum up the condition of Kentucky schools in the postwar years than that of Superintendent of Public Instruction Z.F. Smith, who wrote, "I assumed the duties of my office in September last [1867], under the prejudicial conviction of the popular mind, that the Common School System of Kentucky, no longer worthy of the grave consideration of our men of public trust, had been discarded from the politics of state legislation and abandoned to whatever fate fortune might hold in reserve for it."

The decades 1865-1915 were years of courageous and persistent struggle on the part of a few to persuade both the public and the General Assembly to assume fiscal and civic responsibility for the support of public education, to devise some method of teacher training, to break out of the bondage of short school terms geared to the rhythms of crop seasons, to organize a uniform statewide system of public schools, and to break the hold of the insidious local school trustees. There was an extremely fine line, if any, between partisan politics and education in late nineteenth century Kentucky.

In Kentucky's post–Civil War years, the control of state government fell into the hands of an extremely conservative pro-Confederate group of "brigadiers." These men were most reluctant to join the modern age of American economic and social change. The shortsightedness of the Radical Reconstructionists and the adoption of the Reconstruction amendments to the federal Constitution had fundamental bearings on political attitudes. For more than a decade the General Assembly was involved in revising and revoking laws enacted under Radical domination.

In the years immediately after 1865, a bitter partisanship developed in Kentucky that was to linger throughout the following years. Essentially, three political parties came to exist in the state, the Republican and two factions of the Democratic. Carried over from the antebellum years was a tendency toward personal factionalism rather than a focus on the demands of public issues.

During the half century 1865-1915, there were issues enough that were vital to Kentucky. First was the restoration and advancement of the state's economy. Many areas of the commonwealth were still geographically isolated, yet to be reached by either highway or railroad. The railroads in existence in 1870 served only portions of the state, and only one had interstate significance. Not until this condition changed was it possible to exploit the rich timber and mineral resources of both eastern and western Kentucky. Unfortunately a bitter fight arose between Louisville and central Kentucky over rail expansion. Louisville would no longer be able to control or monopolize trade once additional roads were built. In 1869 the city of Cincinnati proposed building a railroad south to bypass Louisville and tap the southern market by way of Chattanooga. From 1869 to 1872 the chartering of the new railroad company was caught up in a vigorous legislative conflict. Finally, in 1872, the dispute was settled and the road was chartered. The company began construction in 1873 and the Cincinnati-Southern Railway was opened to traffic to Chattanooga in March 1880, giving Kentucky a second vital connection with the South.

Local railways were chartered and built to connect most of the counties. In the 1880s the Louisville & Nashville built a line across southeastern Kentucky to Knoxville, with a line branching off into the developing Eastern Coal Field. Railway progress in the latter half of the nineteenth century greatly improved transportation in the state, but it also introduced new problems. Responding to public pressures, the General Assembly created the Kentucky Railroad Commission to oversee the chartering, building, operation, and freight charges of the intrastate railroads.

Contemporary with railway expansion was the opening in the 1880s of a major chapter in Kentucky industrial and social history: the first mining of the rich coal deposits in the Eastern Coal Field and the expansion of operations in the Western Coal field. For a century and a quarter, coal mining has had profound impact, both positive and negative, on Kentucky: extracting prodigious tonnages of coal, beset by troubled labor relations and strife, displacing from its traditional moorings a large proportion of the Appalachian population, subjecting the commonwealth to extraregional capitalism, injuring the land and the environment, and heavily influencing state government. In the latter half of the twentieth century, new complications have arisen with the rise of strip mining and the increasing mechanization of underground operations. All of these matters continue to have a direct relationship to Kentucky history.

Nature itself wielded a strong hand in the course of human affairs in Appalachian Kentucky. From the entry of the earliest settlers to the present, the area has been set apart by rugged topography; a heavy forest cover; social, cultural, and political isolation; and possibly by human limitations. Throughout the years 1865 to 1910, blood feuds in the region soiled Kentucky's image abroad. Lawlessness, violent incidents, and shady politics arose from a multiplicity of causes, none of which was more influential than geographical and cultural isolation. The persistence of these conditions reflected both the state of the commonwealth's economy and its lack of imaginative and courageous political leadership. In the latter half of the nineteenth century, there were other challenges for the commonwealth, including reform of its medieval prison system, advancing the cause of education, and revising an antiquated constitution. During the last quarter of the century, there was considerable unrest over marketing of farm products, depressed financial conditions, discriminatory freight rates, and the inadequacy of rural roads. But most crippling of all was political demagoguery.

After the Civil War, the adoption of the so-called Reconstruction amendments to the U.S. Constitution invalidated much of the 1849 Kentucky constitution. Aside from these developments, a general desire arose in Kentucky to extend the powers of government to reflect changes in economic and political conditions. Only after two tries at calling a convention, and a purging of voter rolls, did the voters endorse calling a convention in 1890. Represented in the convention were all the elements of conflict and political divisiveness of the age, in which an essentially populist-agrarian Kentucky was pitted against an industrially dominated one. The new constitution framed by that convention represented the social philosophy of control by the corporation; it attempted to fix and guarantee the status quo for a long span of time into Kentucky's future. This constitution was to cast a long shadow. Looking back over a century of American history, one is led to wonder if the framers of the 1890 constitution had any sense of the technological and social changes that were occurring in America.

One could hardly imagine an American state facing a more troubled future than did Kentucky in 1900. In the election of 1899 William S. Taylor, the Republican attorney general, sought to succeed the first Republican governor, William O. Bradley. The election was a hotly contested one between Republicans and two factions of the Democratic party. William Goebel trounced the dissident Democrat, John Y. Brown, but Taylor was the announced winner. The Democrats challenged the election on technical grounds that votes in some counties had been cast on "tissue-paper" ballots (old-style country newspaper stock), or citing other irregularities. An emotional storm verging on civil war arose in the state. Armed protesters from the eastern Republican counties descended on Frankfort, and the governor's office came under siege.

On January 30, 1900, as Goebel and two companions approached the capitol building, an assassin fired on Goebel and he was mortally wounded. The next day Goebel (dead or alive) was sworn in as governor as a result of legislative action, and J.C.W. Beckham was installed as lieutenant governor. After a bitter contest in both the federal and state courts, Goebel was declared to have been the legally elected candidate, and Beckham was sworn in as governor to succeed him. Taylor left the state, a commonwealth badly injured by the tragedy. The Goebel assassination sullied Kentucky's image for decades, coming as it did on the heels of miserable publicity about the blood feuds.

On a broader scale, the closing decade of the nineteenth century was by no means the happiest time in Kentucky history. Its people could look back on the century that had passed since the commonwealth was created with a mixture of pride and serious misgivings. The period had been colored by moments of triumph and unsettling acts of political and social disruption and conflict. For three decades, 1860-90, the rate of population growth had been almost stagnant, and even by 1900 growth was no more than modest. More than 12 percent of the population in 1890 was illiterate (statisticians then did not assess the rate of functional illiteracy).

Kentucky in 1900 epitomized the condition of an intensely rural-agrarian state with a distinctly regional mind-set. Only 21.8 percent of the population was considered urban, and most of this sector was concentrated in Louisville. A third of the land area was still undeveloped, and the rest was largely included in the 234,667 farms of less than one hundred acres in size. Farmlands and properties were estimated to be worth $292 million.

In 1890 Kentucky coal mines had produced 2,412,050 long tons; a decade later annual production was only 4,758,005 tons. Fewer than 70,000 Kentuckians in 1900 were engaged in manufacturing, mainly in operations with only four or five employees. Income from merchandising, except for the large wholesale houses in Louisville, was modest and diversified. This was the era in Kentucky when the crossroads country store was a central commercial and social institution. Kentucky's mail was still delivered largely through fourth-class post offices in villages and country stores. Community activities for the great mass of Kentuckians centered in rural churches, and entertainment was largely of the folk variety. With all of this, it would challenge human imagination to conceive of an American state facing a stormier transition from one century into a new one.

As Kentucky pitched headlong into the 1900s, blood feuds still raged in Appalachia. In the closing decades of the nineteenth century, a bitter dispute arose in the expanding burley tobacco belt in Mason and its neighboring counties. In the dark-tobacco belt of western Kentucky bitter dissatisfaction turned into violence. The Black Patch War, 1905-9, provoked disgruntled farmers into actions reminiscent of the Ku Klux Klan excesses after the Civil War. The source of dissatisfaction was the oppressive and monopolistic practices of buyers for the great tobacco syndicates and of the local pinhookers, or private buyers, who were able to hold prices for tobacco at starvation levels. The conflict lingered through two gubernatorial administrations and a series of court trials before it was, after a fashion, resolved.

While night riders galloped through the countryside scraping tobacco beds and intimidating farmers who would not cooperate with them in resisting the tobacco monopoly, a crusade was begun to modernize Kentucky's public school system. Under an aggressive superintendent of public instruction, John G. Crabbe, public opinion was sufficiently aroused to provoke the enactment of an omnibus law to re-structure the entire system of public schools. The Sullivan Law of 1908 was a shining landmark in Kentucky educational history. It finally spelled out in clear terms the forms of an orderly and universal system of public schools for the commonwealth, including a mandate for the creation of a tax base to support them. The law sought to eliminate the time-worn political abuses in school operation, to create a modern curriculum, to institute compulsory attendance, and to improve physical facilities. Two years earlier the General Assembly had enacted legislation creating teacher training schools, Eastern in Richmond and Western in Bowling Green, in addition to that at State College in Lexington.

The "Education Legislature" and the enactment of the Sullivan Law were followed by intensive "whirlwind" campaigns to alert an indifferent public to the importance of improved public schools. The crusades brought about the beginnings of school consolidation, the offering of a richer curriculum, the improvement of teaching conditions, and, finally, a mortal blow at the insidious three trustee—one room blight that had beset the commonwealth since 1838. But in 1918, only 533,355 of Kentucky's 707,766 school-age children were enrolled in classes, and fewer than half of them attended school an average of at least 150 days a year. Such a state of affairs was hardly what the writers of the educational clause in the 1890 constitution had in mind when they inserted the word "efficient."

The success of school consolidation and compulsory attendance hinged upon the condition of the public roads. The General Assembly sensed this urgency in 1912 when it created the offices of road commissioner and county road engineers. On July 11, 1916, the U.S. Congress enacted the first of a series of laws creating a national system of "good" roads. These advances had just begun to have an impact on the way of life in Kentucky when World War I began in 1914.

In the war era large volumes of Kentucky's forest resources were harvested and shipped abroad or used at home in the construction of military installations. Tragically, thousands of feet of prime Kentucky lumber were sunk in the North Atlantic in the submarine war. Kentucky lived up to its proud military tradition of filling its quota of men in the armed forces, a good proportion of them volunteers, and at home Kentucky civilians were diligent in support of the war effort. The Great War brought revolutionary changes in the state's economic and social affairs. Agriculture and industry flourished, as did general business. The coal mining industry experienced its most prosperous period to date during 1915-18. There was a major shifting of the Appalachian population from the old subsistence farms to mining camps, severing people from their ancient traditions and folkways. An outflow of Kentuckians to the industrial centers of the Great Lakes and northwestern states began during the war and would quicken during the Great Depression.

The era of World War I was also to have its ugly side in Kentucky. From the mid-nineteenth century into the 1880s, German immigrants had flowed into the Ohio River towns, especially around Covington and Louisville. The inflow of Europeans had brought talents of all kinds to the commonwealth and an infusion of new blood into the general population. At the outbreak of the war, the country was flooded with anti-German propaganda, and anyone with a German name was immediately suspected of disloyalty. In the hysterical reaction, personal freedoms were trampled and innocent people were discriminated against and even subjected to physical injury. Once the hysteria was calmed and a sane perspective reestablished, there was a realization of the shameful injustices done people who had committed no more serious crime against the Republic than that of having a German name.

No single influence in all Kentucky history was to have a greater revisionary impact on the state than the arrival of the automobile and motor truck age after 1918. The opening, improving, and maintenance of roads became mandatory, and after 1916 and the stimulus of the federal highway act, Kentucky was set on the road to a social and economic revolution. People became more acutely aware of barriers of isolation that had shaped the lives of their forebears. Promises to build "good roads" and bridges and to remove annoying tolls became central political themes. To pay for highway improvements, legislators turned to taxing motor fuels and levying licenses upon automobiles and trucks.

The war years inflated personal incomes in Kentucky, and at the same time inflated prices. In building the great war machine after 1914, advances were made in the mechanics of goods production, in the application of chemistry and technology, and in the distribution of and demand for products. Kentucky's tobacco farmers and whiskey distillers enjoyed a phenomenal period of prosperity. Golden burley tobacco came into its own in these years. The adoption of the Eighteenth Amendment to the U.S. Constitution on January 15, 1919, was a serious blow to the bourbon industry and gave new impetus to the state's traditions of moonshining and bootlegging.

Following a period of erratic prosperity during the 1920s, Kentucky was plunged into the depths of the Great Depression. The financial and economic panic had both negative and positive effects. The negative effects were stifling unemployment and stunted economic growth, but New Deal programs brought the restoration of antiquated schools and other public buildings and the construction of new ones. The Civilian Conservation Corps did much to lower barriers of isolation in many sections of Kentucky by opening roads and stringing telephone lines. In the field of conservation, its work was especially helpful in the newly organized Cumberland (Daniel Boone) National Forest. The creation of this preserve across a broad swath of southeastern and northeastern Kentucky was a delayed fulfillment of the Weeks Law of 1911 and subsequent public forest legislation.

In the midst of the Great Depression, the General Assembly enacted, in 1936, a far-reaching government reorganization law that brought the commonwealth a long step out of the nineteenth century. A weakness in the law, however, was its failure to create an adequate tax base to yield sufficient institutional support.

During the decade 1931-41, New Deal legislation had a marked impact upon Kentucky in the fields of public building and services, in agriculture, and, to a limited extent, in education. Aside from the physical accomplishments, the Federal Writers Project and the Historical Records Survey made lasting contributions. The Writers Project produced a more or less faithful account of Kentucky life of that time in its *Guide to the Bluegrass State*.

Passage of the Tennessee Valley Authority law in 1933 had an enormous effect on economic development in western Kentucky. The creation of the great Kentucky Dam and the vast lake behind it materially increased the water surface of the commonwealth. When the hydroelectric plant was constructed at the dam, it supplied an abundance of cheap electrical power to all sorts of users in its area. The dam and power plant, at the foot of the Tennessee Valley Authority System, gave new social and economic stimulation to the towns of Paducah, Murray, Mayfield, and other Jackson Purchase communities.

Nowhere in the Tennessee Valley were the three TVA purposes of flood control, transportation, and the generation of electricity more fully accomplished than in the Purchase region of Kentucky. To these must be added the development of a vast recreational area. The Tennessee River was opened more fully to use by heavy boat tows, and Paducah became a major port of entry. Just across the narrow dividing neck of land, the construction of the Barkley Dam on the Cumberland River created a second lake and opened that stream more fully to barge traffic. In 1963 President John F. Kennedy signed the law creating the 170,000-acre area to be known as the Land Between the Lakes. The lightly populated peninsula was set aside as a national conservation and recreation preserve that has served 100 million people.

Aside from the transportation and recreational advantages created by the Tennessee Valley Authority, the industrialization of western Kentucky was hastened by the availability of abundant electrical power and water. Chemical and paper industries located in the region gave economic momentum to the neighboring towns and counties. Up the Ohio River, Henderson and Owensboro grew into river and industrial centers that balanced agriculture with industry on the outer edges of the Western Coal Field. The southern and western counties of Kentucky began to contribute materially to the improved agricultural fortunes of the state.

If World War I began a deep-seated change in Kentucky's way of life, World War II finished the task. Every area of life in the commonwealth was affected by the war and its stirring aftermath. The new age of technology brought new ways of performing what had been arduous physical tasks, the reduction of the capital importance of agriculture, and the rise of industrial income. New efforts to attract industry to the state generated more intense demands for higher standards of education; Kentucky's chronically low rating on national statistical scales now became a more pressing issue.

The latter half of the twentieth century saw the building of five interstate limited-access highways, east and west, north and south, across Kentucky. The state system of highways was both improved and extended, so that no section of the commonwealth was left wholly isolated. Railroads, which had been so vital to the Kentucky economy in earlier years, ceased to have any intrastate function, and river traffic, which transported staggering tonnages of freight, landed little if any of it within the state. Where once the chartering and regulation of railways was a central issue, the building and expansion of airports, location of new industries, and expansion of public services characterized a new age.

The dawn of the television age brought drastic changes in that favorite of all Kentucky interests and pastimes, political campaigns. Television increased several hundredfold the cost of elections. By the closing decades of the twentieth century the old-style Kentucky political orator had vanished from the county courthouse squares, and his less eloquent descendants indulged in so-called television debates or in dull thirty-second "sound bites." These plastic changes left in Kentucky at the end of the century little that was definable of the old Jeffersonian republican ideal of nurturing the grass-roots constituency with discussions of fundamental issues. The age of the common man had ended.

Since the education reforms of 1908, there had been sporadic drives to improve the state of public education, but Kentucky's responses were not significant enough to overcome its past failures. Two or three gubernatorial administrations during the twentieth century sought to change conditions, but their efforts were never successful enough to bring Kentucky abreast of the post-Sputnik age. In 1988 sixty-four school districts filed suit in the Franklin County circuit court, contending that the commonwealth had not carried out its constitutional commitment of maintaining an "efficient" system of public schools. The court held this to be a valid complaint, and it was upheld by the Kentucky supreme court, which declared the entire public school system to be unconstitutional. In its 1990 session the General Assembly responded by enacting the far-reaching law embodied in House Bill 940, which promised to set Kentucky on a new educational course to meet the challenges of the twenty-first century.

Looking back from the historical perspective of two centuries, Kentuckians must view their commonwealth's past as one marked by ridges and valleys of public experience. Three times they have rewritten their basic law of 1792. They have developed contrasting images of their society, often sullied by political chicanery if not criminality. Their politics have often been more rowdy than constructive, a condition largely accepted by the populace. Kentuckians have gloried in their plenteous natural resources and at the same time wasted and despoiled them. In war and peace they responded, sometimes with a romanesque militant pride. Remarkably, in the past half century they have made phenomenal progress in developing and supporting their social and cultural institutions, in generating a public awareness of the fragility of the environment and the exhaustibility of their precious natural and human resources. As the contents of this volume so eloquently reflect, Kentuckians over two centuries have established their place in history, decade by decade, and incident by incident, always with the winds of change blowing strongly in their faces.

Thomas D. Clark

The
Kentucky
Encyclopedia

GUIDE FOR READERS

Entries in *The Kentucky Encyclopedia* are representative of many others that could as easily have been included. The entries were written during the period 1989 through mid-1991 (printing deadlines dictated exclusion of events after this point, except for death notices). Unsigned entries were written by the staff.

Entries are presented in alphabetical sequence. Many topics not treated in separate entries are included in more general articles and can be located by means of the index. Within an entry, small capitals indicate a cross reference to another entry containing additional information that is directly pertinent to the subject.

Biographical sketches include date and place of birth, parents' names, educational background, accomplishments, marriage and children, date of death, and place of burial. The information on places includes location and origin of the site, development, identities of notable residents, geographical features, economic development, and population figures for 1970 through 1990. In some cases, some of these facts were not available.

Many entries are followed by bibliographic citations. These do not necessarily reflect the author's sources; their purpose here is to direct the user to additional information on the specific topic of the entry. General histories of the state or other subject are usually not cited; a selection of these is listed in the bibliographic essay. The number of references that could be cited in individual entries was strictly limited, and we tried to cite those that would be most readily available to the user. For that reason, we have named few unpublished works or primary source materials in the text, although some are listed in the bibliographic essay following the body of the work.

Many towns have no published history, but facts about a town are often included in a history of its county. In seeking more information about a town, the reader should turn first to the entry for the county and then to the books on local history listed in the bibliographic essay.

The names of the *Register of the Kentucky Historical Society* and the *Filson Club History Quarterly*, the principal journal references, have been shortened to *Register* and *FCHQ*, respectively.

A

ABELL, IRVIN. Irvin Abell, surgeon, was born on September 13, 1876, to William Irvin and Sarah Silesia (Rogers) Abell in Lebanon, Kentucky. He attended St. Augustine's Parochial School in Lebanon (1882-89) and graduated from St. Mary's College at St. Mary, Kentucky, in 1892. After graduating from the Louisville Medical College in 1897, he studied in Germany at the University of Marburg and the University of Berlin. Abell joined the Louisville Medical College faculty in 1900; when the school merged with the University of Louisville in 1908, he became professor of surgery and in 1923 clinical professor of surgery. Abell's professional associations included the American Medical Association, of which he was president in 1938-39, the American College of Surgeons (president, 1944), the Southeastern Surgical Association (president, 1926), and the Kentucky State Medical Association (president, 1927). Abell was named to the board of trustees at the University of Louisville in 1935. At the beginning of World War II, he headed the national committee that consulted with the Defense Commission on matters of public health.

Abell married Carrie C. Harting of Lexington, Kentucky, on October 19, 1907; the marriage produced four sons: William Irvin, William Harting, Jonathan Rogers, and Joseph Spaulding. Abell died on August 28, 1949, and was buried at the Cave Hill Cemetery in Louisville.

See Burlyn Pike, "You Can't Pin a Prodigy Tag on Irvin Abell," *Louisville Courier-Journal Magazine*, Nov. 23, 1941.

ACTORS THEATRE OF LOUISVILLE. Actors Theatre of Louisville (ATL), a professional nonprofit organization, was founded by Richard Block in 1963 under the name Theatre Louisville. A year later, after merging with Ewel Cornett's Actors, Inc., it became Actors Theatre of Louisville, at 617 South Fourth Street. In 1965 ATL moved to the abandoned Illinois Central Railway Station, which had been renovated as a theater that seated 250. Several years later a balcony was added to increase the seating capacity to 350. In 1969 Jon Jory was named producing director and opened his first season with a successful production of *Under Milkwood*. Two years later Jory's musical *Tricks*, an adaptation of Moliére's *Scapin*, opened ATL's last season in the railway station, toured the Arena Stage Theatre in Washington, D.C., and opened on Broadway in 1973. Jory has earned worldwide recognition for ATL by directing more than eighty plays, producing more than five hundred plays and musicals, and establishing three festivals.

In 1972 ATL moved to its current two-theater complex on Main Street, which originally housed the Louisville Bank of Kentucky and is now designated a NATIONAL HISTORIC LANDMARK. This complex includes the 637-seat Pamela Brown Auditorium, the 159-seat Victor Jory Theatre, and the adjacent Arts and Commerce Building, which houses ATL's administrative staff and rehearsal halls. A campaign was announced in 1990 to enlarge the complex by adding a flexible 150/350-seat theater and a parking structure.

In the 1970s and 1980s, ATL gained international recognition for its production of new plays. Initiated in 1976 under the title Play Faire, the annual Humana Festival of New American Plays has premiered more than 150 works by one hundred playwrights. Many of these plays received major awards and have subsequently been produced on Broadway, published, televised, and adapted for film, including Marsha Norman's *Getting Out*, Beth Henley's *Crimes of the Heart*, D.L. Coburn's *The Gin Game*, William Mastrosimone's *Extremities*, John Pielmeier's *Agnes of God*, and Emily Mann's *Execution of Justice*. From 1980 to 1985 ATL's Shorts Festival premiered more than sixty one-act plays. Nearly two hundred short one-acts (called by ATL ten-minute plays) have premiered in the theater's festivals and biannual showcase productions for its apprentice company. Actors Theatre has sponsored several contests to encourage American playwrights: the Great American Play Contest for full-length scripts (1977-86); the National One-Act Play Contest (1979-90); and the National Ten-Minute Play Contest, beginning in 1990.

In 1986 ATL initiated the Classics in Context Festival. The festival presents works from world literature supported by films, lectures, and exhibits that illustrate the social, political, and biographical contexts of their creation. In 1988 ATL was joined by other arts and educational institutions as Classics in Context became a citywide event. In 1989 ATL presented a production by the Moscow Art Theatre as its part of "Arts and Revolution in Russia." Other Classics in Context festivals have focused on the Romantics, the Victorians, and the commedia dell' arte.

Actors Theatre of Louisville has toured internationally, performing in more than thirty cities in seventeen countries between 1980 and 1990. In 1974 ATL was designated the state theater of Kentucky. It has also been honored with the Tony Award for distinguished achievement and contribution to the development of professional theater, and the Margo Jones Award for new play production.

MICHAEL BIGELOW DIXON

ADAIR, JOHN. John Adair, Kentucky's governor during 1820-24, was born in South Carolina on January 9, 1757, to Baron William and Mary (Moore) Adair. He attended school in Charlotte, North Carolina. In 1784 he married Katherine Palmer, with whom he had twelve children. In 1787, after service in the Revolution, Adair moved to Mercer County, Kentucky. A political activist, he was a member of the constitutional conventions of 1792 and 1799, a state representative for many years after 1792, Speaker of the Kentucky House of Representatives in 1802 and 1803, and U.S. senator from November 8, 1805, to November 18, 1806. Arrested in 1807 on the order of Gen. James Wilkinson, Adair was accused of conspiring with Aaron Burr to disrupt the Union. His countersuit was successful, and Wilkinson was forced to apologize and pay damages. During the War of 1812, Adair was Isaac Shelby's aide and the commander of the Kentucky rifle brigade at the Battle of New Orleans. In 1820 he ran for governor on a pledge to provide relief for the state's debtors. Arrayed against three other Democratic Republicans, Adair won 20,493 votes, giving him a plurality victory over William Logan (19,947), Joseph Desha (12,418), and Anthony Butler (9,567). After leaving office in 1824, Adair spent most of his remaining years on his farm. His 1831-33 term in the U.S. House of Representatives was undistinguished. He died on May 19, 1840, and was buried in Frankfort Cemetery.

Governor Adair's priority was help for debtors who were in danger of losing their lands. Perhaps the most important relief measure created the Bank of the Commonwealth in 1820. A people's bank, it issued paper money and made generous loans; a creditor who refused to accept the inflated notes could not press his claim in state courts for two years. Several relief acts were declared unconstitutional by the Kentucky court of appeals on the grounds that they violated the U.S. Constitution's prohibition against "impairing the Obligation of Contracts." Adair, like a majority of the people, opposed such judgments, but neither the removal of the offending judges nor the calling of a constitutional convention was then possible. Adair also advocated state funding for education, a better penitentiary system, reform of the treatment of the insane, and improved navigation on the Ohio River, but other issues were subordinated to the relief question. It was certain to be the major issue in the 1824 election.

See Lowell H. Harrison, ed., *Kentucky's Governors 1792-1985* (Lexington, Ky., 1985); Arndt M. Stickles, *The Critical Court Struggle in Kentucky, 1819-1829* (Bloomington, Ind., 1929); Steven A. Channing, *Kentucky: A Bicentennial History* (New York 1977).   LOWELL H. HARRISON

ADAIR COUNTY. Adair County, in south-central Kentucky, is part of both the eastern Pennyroyal region and western Appalachia. Its 407 square miles of rolling countryside are drained by the Green River and its principal local tributary, Russell Creek. Over 40 percent of the land is covered with timber. Agricultural yields include dairy products, livestock, corn, and tobacco. In the late 1960s Adair County experienced a small oil boom.

The county, Kentucky's forty-fourth, was carved out of Green County in 1801 and named for Gen.

John Adair. In 1802 COLUMBIA was chosen as the county seat. Although the county lay along the Cumberland and Great Lakes Trail, the lack of modern transportation hindered its development as late as 1910, when travelers rode by stagecoach to Campbellsville to reach the Louisville & Nashville Railroad. Transportation became significantly easier in 1973, when the Cumberland Parkway was completed between Somerset to the east and Bowling Green to the west. The 8,200-acre Green River Lake, constructed in 1969, draws tourists to a state park in Adair and neighboring Taylor counties.

Located near the Tennessee border, Adair County saw action in the Civil War. The Battle of Gradyville, a minor skirmish, was fought there on December 12, 1861. Following his Christmas Raid of 1862-63, John Hunt Morgan passed through Columbia on his return to Tennessee. On July 4, 1863, Morgan fought Union soldiers at Tebb's Bend as he traveled north to Indiana and Ohio.

Noted residents include Thomas Bramlette, governor of Kentucky during 1863-67; Col. Frank Wolford, commander of the Union's 1st Kentucky Cavalry until dismissed for criticizing President Lincoln, and later a two-term Democratic representative (1883-87); James R. Hindman, Democratic lieutenant governor of Kentucky (1883-87); Colonel William Casey, for whom Casey County was named; Jane (Lampton) Clemens, mother of Samuel Clemens; Ed Diddle, noted Western Kentucky University basketball coach; and Janice Holt Giles, who wrote historical novels of the American frontier set in the Green River county.

Adair County's population was 13,078 in 1888 and climbed to a high of 18,566 in 1940; it was 13,037 in 1970; 15,232 in 1980; and 15,360 in 1990.

ADAMS, HENRY. Henry Adams, leader of black Baptists in Louisville, was born on December 17, 1802, of free parents in Franklin County, Georgia. Converted at eighteen and ordained at twenty-three, Adams first preached in the Southeast. He moved to Louisville in 1829 to become minister to the black members of the First Baptist Church. In 1842 Adams's forty-five-member congregation withdrew from the white church to form First African Baptist Church, renamed Fifth Street Baptist Church after the Civil War, and Adams served there as pastor until his retirement in 1871.

Largely self-educated, Adams established a reputation as a biblical scholar, and he dominated the religious scene in Louisville among black Baptists almost from his arrival. Conservative in race relations, the strong-minded Adams emphasized racial improvement through church-related educational and self-help programs. He began teaching the children of church members in the 1820s, and in the 1840s organized a church school that became the foundation for postwar public education for Louisville blacks. During the Civil War, Adams called for the organization of black Baptist churches, and later, as moderator of the General Association of

Colored Baptists, initiated the movement for an educated ministry that culminated in the founding of Kentucky Normal and Theological Institute (later SIMMONS UNIVERSITY) in 1879.

Adams married Margaret Corbin around 1842; they had two daughters and three sons. He died on November 3, 1872.

See George C. Wright, *Life Behind a Veil: Blacks in Louisville, Kentucky 1865-1930* (Baton Rouge, La., 1985).   MARION B. LUCAS

ADSMORE. Adsmore, on North Jefferson Street in Princeton, Kentucky, is a house built during the 1850s in the Greek Revival style by dry goods merchant John Higgins. Col. James B. Hewitt owned the house from about 1870 until 1900, when he sold it to John Parker Smith. At that time, the house was remodeled and enlarged in the popular Colonial Revival style by noted Louisville architect Brinton B. DAVIS. The house passed into the hands of Smith's daughter, Mayme, the wife of Robert Garrard, director of insolvent banks under Andrew Mellon. Their daughter, Katharine Garrard, was the last family member to own the house. At her death in September 1984, she left house and contents to the board of trustees of the George Coon Public Library. The house was listed on the National Register of Historic Places in July 1973, and was opened as a public museum in November 1986.

WILLIAM B. SCOTT, JR.

AFRO-AMERICAN CULTURE. Influenced by African customs and traditions, blacks in Kentucky created songs, music, recipes, folktales, and a style of religious worship somewhat different from that of whites. Black churches, organized before the Civil War in several Kentucky cities, including Lexington, Louisville, and Paducah, served as the social and educational centers of the black community. In 1866 the General Association of Negro Baptists in Kentucky was organized in Louisville. It later opened a school to train ministers and teachers. The Baptist Woman's Educational Convention and the Baptist Woman's Missionary Convention, concerned for the physical and moral conditions of the black community, collected money for scholarships, playgrounds, and teachers' salaries. In Lexington, the Colored Agricultural and Mechanical Association began sponsoring a black fair in September 1869. The fair attracted visitors from across the nation and remained a popular social event well into the twentieth century.

Afro-Americans organized several clubs, community organizations, and fraternal lodges during the era of racial segregation. Some of these groups were chapters of national organizations such as the Masons, the Odd Fellows, and the Knights of Pythias. The black Masons had established forty-eight lodges in the state by the early 1900s. The United Brothers of Friendship was founded in Louisville in 1861 and later became a national fraternal order. Afro-American fraternal lodges sponsored a mixture of benevolent and recreational programs within the black community. Similar to the fraternal organizations, black women's clubs sought to advance pride in the race and to improve the depressed conditions blacks faced. The Loyalty Charity Club and the Georgia A. Nugent Improvement Club of Louisville were among the state's altruistic female organizations. Several branches of the National Association of Colored Women were founded in the state.

The Plymouth Settlement House of Louisville was founded by the Rev. E.G. Harris, to offer a variety of social and cultural activities. After the building was completed in the fall of 1917, plays, movies, concerts, receptions, and parties were held in the auditorium. Harris and his assistants also organized Bible classes, girls' clubs, basketball teams, and a Boy Scout troop.

Among Afro-American newspapers, the editorial sections of the *American Baptist*, *Louisville Defender*, *Louisville Leader*, and *Louisville News* served as a forum for the black community. The papers also reported on social, political, and economic issues as they related to blacks.

During the 1960s, as racial barriers began to fall, Afro-Americans pressured white colleges and universities throughout the nation to develop black history courses and recognize black student organizations. Afro-Americans sought respect and appreciation for the culture that had evolved in their communities. The University of Kentucky's Martin Luther King, Jr., Cultural Center sponsors plays, lectures, films, seminars, and displays that focus on the Afro-American experience.

See Kentucky Commission on Human Rights, *Kentucky's Black Heritage* (Frankfort, Ky., 1971); Gerald L. Smith, "Blacks In Lexington, Kentucky: The Struggle for Civil Rights, 1945-1980," M.A. thesis, University of Kentucky, 1983.

GERALD L. SMITH

AFRO-AMERICANS. Though the contributions of Afro-Americans have often been ignored or minimized by scholars and other observers, they played a role, indeed often making significant contributions, in every period of Kentucky's past. Black people in the workforce aided the economic growth of the state. The status of blacks—as slaves, or as second-class citizens, or as people entitled to full equality—has been debated by Kentucky's politicians, meaning that by their very presence blacks have been part of the political process. Furthermore, in spite of racial discrimination that severely limited the opportunities available to them, blacks have made contributions in many fields, ranging from poetry and literature to the performing arts, education, athletics, business, and medicine.

The early pioneers—including Daniel Boone, who owned at least three slaves—brought their bondsmen to Kentucky to help clear the land, plant crops, and subdue the Indians. In addition to providing much of the labor force on farms and plantations—occupations associated with chattel slavery—early Kentucky Afro-Americans also worked in salt mines, iron works, and bridge and road construction. Slaves were trained for specialized work as blacksmiths, wagoneers, boot- and shoemakers, rope spinners, and carpenters. In Kentucky's urban areas, slaves worked as waiters and cooks in the better hotels and performed all of the household chores in the homes of the white elite. In Louisville and Lexington, several large business concerns relied entirely on slave labor for their workforce, entering into contracts with slave-owners for the use of the laborers. These contracts, usually running from January 1 to mid-December, generally ranged in price from $100 to $200 a year, but highly skilled slaves commanded prices beyond this range.

The ownership of slaves was profitable to Kentucky whites; the slave trade shipped approximately 80,000 Afro-Americans southward during 1830-60. The income from this trade constituted an appreciable part of the state's financial resources during these years. In antebellum Kentucky, the ownership of human beings who could be exploited as labor or sold in the marketplace was an important economic advantage.

Undoubtedly, if the family trees of most Afro-Americans were known, the vast majority would be seen to be descendants of slaves; yet the institutions and cultural traditions that started during slavery and remained a part of black life in the postbellum period—in fact, down to the present in many instances—were created by free blacks. Outside of scholarly circles, the story of free blacks is not widely known. Their plight in Kentucky and elsewhere grossly violated the concepts of democracy and equal protection under the law, beliefs supposedly greatly valued by Kentuckians. Kentucky's small number of free "people of color" (which peaked at no more than 11,000 in 1860, compared with 211,000 slaves) lived under severe legal restrictions. In 1807 the state enacted a law that prevented free blacks from other states from entering Kentucky and prohibited the return of those who left Kentucky for any reason. Under Kentucky law, they were required to carry "free papers," identifying them as free people of color. To obtain such papers required yearly registration and the payment of an annual fee.

Kentucky's free blacks could be arrested for allegations of numerous vague violations: for keeping a disorderly house, for engaging in no honest calling, for attending unlawful meetings with slaves, for having more than one firearm, and for selling alcohol. If unable to pay the fines, they risked being sold into slavery, a condition about which no white had to worry. In a state where people believed fervently in the right of self-defense, the law proclaimed it to be a criminal act for a free black to defend himself from attacks by whites. Whites could violate free blacks in almost any manner without fear, and acts that would have been illegal if other whites had been the victims would be sanctioned by the law. Kentucky law denied free blacks one of the most basic rights of citizenship, the right to vote, and they were denied also the right to legal redress. Whites in antebellum Kentucky could be sentenced to death for any one of four offenses; free blacks faced the death penalty for any of eleven criminal acts.

In spite of these incredible obstacles, free blacks created and sustained a life of their own. Starting first in Lexington, then Louisville, and even in several smaller communities, free blacks formed churches, which became much more than religious institutions. On the eve of the Civil War, there were seventeen black churches in Kentucky, nine of them located in Louisville, the site of the state's largest free black population. Since blacks were prohibited by law and custom from attending white schools, they organized their own schools, which usually operated in church buildings. By any present-day standard these schools were inadequate, but the small, church-supported groups became the foundation of Afro-American education in Kentucky and the rest of the South. Kentucky's handful of free blacks also created numerous societies that were a source of recreational and cultural activities. One such society, the United Brothers of Friendship, started in Louisville in 1864 and eventually formed branches all over the nation, becoming by the start of the new century the largest black fraternal order in America.

The Civil War and the Reconstruction years proved to be a particularly crucial period for Kentucky blacks. The Union's decision in 1863 to allow blacks to join the army and thereby gain legal freedom greatly undermined slavery in the state. Over 28,000 Kentucky blacks joined the Union army, gaining freedom for themselves, their wives, and children. This point is especially significant because for decades some scholars erroneously held that blacks gained their freedom without any effort on their part. John G. Fee provided opportunities for blacks to be educated at Camp Nelson, where they could also enlist.

The official end of slavery in Kentucky came with the ratification of the Thirteenth Amendment of the U.S. Constitution in December 1865. Slaves in most other states were freed from their bondage by the Emancipation Proclamation of January 1863 or by the end of the Civil War in the spring of 1865. But two states loyal to the Union, Kentucky (with 100,000 slaves) and Delaware (with fewer than 1,000), did not free their slaves until the Thirteenth Amendment (which the Kentucky legislature had overwhelmingly rejected) was finally ratified by action of the other states. Thus, human bondage, the most blatant contradiction of what America represents, ended last in Kentucky among all the states in the Union. (Not until 1970 did the Kentucky legislature ratify the Thirteenth Amendment.)

Afro-Americans took steps to uplift themselves in the weeks and months after their emancipation. A significant number of black churches were started, or existing buildings and programs were enlarged. With state officials unwilling to start public schools for blacks, a posture that was unchanged for years, Afro-Americans created, and supported through small tuitions, schools for blacks. Perhaps even more important at this time was the establishment of a number of welfare institutions (such as hospitals and orphanages) and organizations that provided assistance to the aged, the orphaned, and the infirm. These successful efforts at self-help were all the more remarkable in view of violence by whites during the first fifteen years of freedom, in which 140 or more lynchings took place; scores of blacks, especially veterans of the Union army, were forced to leave parts of the state; and countless numbers of black schools and churches were destroyed by white mobs. Although most blacks were poor, many whites adopted the irrational belief that the smallest efforts by blacks to better their lot would lead to "Negro domination" and therefore had to be suppressed swiftly and brutally.

The Reconstruction years foreshadowed two major themes relating to black existence in Kentucky for more than a hundred years: the consistent white belief that blacks must remain in their "place," and the determination of blacks to attain racial justice, ultimately to achieve equality in all areas of society. Beginning in the 1880s, Kentucky's black citizens faced racial discrimination on a number of fronts (see SEGREGATION). The state legislature grudgingly acknowledged that blacks had the right to public schools, but then segregated the schools by race and violated the law by refusing to appropriate equal funding for black schools. Laws were enacted segregating the races on interstate railroads and in state institutions for the insane and the blind. In 1904 the DAY LAW ousted blacks from Berea College, a private institution that had admitted blacks on an equal basis with whites for thirty years. A state law prohibited interracial marriage. City governments all over Kentucky enacted scores of discriminatory ordinances that excluded blacks from most areas of public accommodations, public parks, and libraries, and established segregation in housing. Lawmakers often applauded mob rule and refused to adopt stringent efforts to end lynchings; not surprisingly, the violence that started during the Reconstruction era remained a way of life. From 1880 to 1940 more than two hundred Kentucky blacks died at the hands of lynch mobs. Police brutality, a very effective form of violence, existed even in Lexington and Louisville. In western Kentucky during 1908-15, in Corbin in 1919, and in Estill, Bell, and Mercer counties in the 1920s, white gangs attempted to remove Afro-Americans from their homes and places of employment.

With the formation of statewide teachers' organizations and religious groups in the 1880s, the anti–separate coach movement in 1900, the Negro Outlook Committee in the early 1900s, the National Association for the Advancement of Colored People (NAACP) in the 1910s, and the National Urban League branches in the 1920s, black Kentuckians have a long tradition of challenging lawlessness and racial discrimination. Though the civil rights movements of the 1950s through the 1970s and the legislation enacted then are important accomplishments, they benefited greatly from the earlier efforts. The NAACP and its Louisville branch labored for three years, until 1917, to overturn the Louisville Residential Segregation Ordinance. This victory sustained the NAACP during its infancy. Efforts by the NAACP in the late 1910s prevented the showing of highly inflammatory films in several Kentucky cities, and the organization lobbied for the passage of "an act to suppress mob violence and prevent lynching." The antilynching law passed the Kentucky legislature in 1920 without a dissenting vote. For over twenty years, beginning in the mid-1930s, the NAACP and other organizations, most notably the Kentucky Negro Educational Association, worked consistently to improve race relations, to end segregation in the schools and public parks, and to convince both political parties that blacks deserved party backing when running for office. In the 1950s and 1960s blacks and concerned whites built on these successes and secured the passage of public accommodations ordinances, open housing laws, and new employment opportunities.

A definitive assessment of the full impact of the civil rights movement on the status of Kentucky blacks, through numerous pieces of legislation and increased educational and employment opportunities, has yet to be made. It seems that the civil rights movement has resulted in two distinct groups of Afro-Americans. One group benefited greatly from college attendance and technical programs and has what seem to be unlimited employment possibilities. This is the group that whites point to when proclaiming that racial discrimination no longer exists or that being black might be an advantage when competing for slots in professional schools and employment. Yet in Afro-American communities throughout the state, there still exist conditions that have changed little over the decades, and given the increasing presence of drugs and violent criminals, the problems have probably worsened. To be sure, not all of the problems of the poor are a result of racial prejudice. But compounding their plight is the attitude, which seems to be prevalent among whites, that race is no longer an issue in social policy, that laws of the 1960s eradicated completely the discrimination of the past. The plight of the black poor is not unique to Kentucky, but considering the relative poverty of the state and the unwillingness of its elected officials to adequately support social and educational programs, the situation seems to have remained without solution in the Bluegrass State.

See George C. Wright, *Racial Violence in Kentucky, 1865-1940: Lynchings, Mob Rule and "Legal" Lynchings* (Baton Rouge, La., 1990); Wright, *A History of Blacks in Kentucky* (Frankfort, Ky., 1992).   GEORGE C. WRIGHT

AGRICULTURAL AND MECHANICAL COLLEGE. The Agricultural and Mechanical College was founded on February 22, 1865, as a department of KENTUCKY UNIVERSITY, a denominational (Christian Church) university, which merged with TRANSYLVANIA UNIVERSITY, in Lexington, on February 28, 1865. John B. BOWMAN, president of Kentucky

University, raised $100,000 to establish the A&M College, as a condition for merging the university with Transylvania. Additional funds were obtained from the sale of land granted to the state by the Morrill Act, which had been signed into law by President Abraham Lincoln on July 2, 1862. Although part of a denominational institution, the A&M College was to be a secular state school.

Bowman purchased Henry Clay's former estate, Ashland, and the adjacent Woodlands farm, and on October 1, 1866, opened the A&M College with an enrollment of 190 students. Because agriculture and mechanics were new fields in American education at that time, no classes were offered in these areas. Courses were offered in the sciences and in liberal arts. Bowman believed that students needed a liberal and practical education, so he required students to take courses and to work on the college's experimental farm or at the mechanical works, built in 1868, where carpentry and blacksmithing were practiced.

The A&M College grew quickly at first and soon became the largest department of Kentucky University. Under the leadership of Dean James K. PATTERSON, who in 1869 became president of the university, the college reached a peak enrollment of 295 students in 1869-70. Unfortunately, this success was short-lived, and by 1875 enrollment was only ninety-four students, in large part because of the controversy that arose over denominational control of Kentucky University.

Believing that the state legislature, by placing the A&M College in Kentucky University, had favored one denomination, and that the school had become a religious institution, other denominations petitioned the state to remove the college from the control of the Christian Church. More important, however, may have been the doctrinal dispute in the 1870s within the Christian Church, which sharply divided the board of curators of Kentucky University. In 1873 Bowman offered to resign his post as regent of the university, hoping to ease the conflict, but the board responded with a vote of confidence. Nevertheless, in 1877 the curators abolished the office of regent and removed Bowman from the board. Hoping to save the A&M College from the dispute, the Kentucky General Assembly, on March 13, 1878, severed its connection with Kentucky University. The A&M College was renamed State College and remained on the Ashland and Woodlands land until 1882, when it moved to South Limestone Street. In 1908 it was renamed State University and in 1916 became known as the UNIVERSITY OF KENTUCKY.

See James F. Hopkins, *The University of Kentucky* (Lexington, Ky., 1951); Carl B. Cone, *The University of Kentucky* (Lexington, Ky., 1989); John D. Wright, *Transylvania: Tutor To The West* (Lexington, Ky., 1975).

AGRICULTURAL COOPERATIVES. Farmers operate cooperatives to increase their financial returns in two ways: through economies of scale in supply co-ops' purchases of large lots of agricultural inputs, and through co-ops' ability to compete with private firms in selling farm output. Dairy products and grain are the major commodities marketed by Kentucky agricultural cooperatives, which also handle some fruits, vegetables, and livestock. The BURLEY TOBACCO GROWERS COOPERATIVE ASSOCIATION is a specialized co-op that markets "pool" burley tobacco. Supply co-ops typically handle livestock feed, fertilizer, pesticides, fuels, and short- and long-term credit to farmers, but they seldom sell farm machinery. Co-ops have been popular since the early nineteenth century, particularly among tobacco farmers.

Agricultural co-ops' operating profits are distributed to members in proportion to the volume of business done with each member, a method of profit distribution that exempts co-ops from corporate taxes. In the election of officers, each member has one vote, irrespective of the member's volume of business or the number of shares of common stock owned.

See Charles E. French et al., *Survival Strategies for Agricultural Cooperatives* (Ames, Iowa, 1980); Ewell P. Roy, *Cooperatives: Today and Tomorrow* (Danville, Ill., 1969).   BARRY W. BOBST

AGRICULTURE. It defies reason that the Commonwealth of Kentucky has so long and so fervently boasted of its agricultural heritage, yet has no published history of the industry. Much of the story of agriculture still lies buried in original records, government reports, statistical tables, and obscure essays. Earlier authors of Kentucky histories either ignored the subject or gave it short shrift as being too commonplace. Nevertheless agriculture, economically and culturally, has been central to Kentucky's past, not only in the era of recorded history but even far back into the dim age of Paleolithic human presence in the region. The earlier history is eloquently documented in the generous finds of pipes and cultivating implements on the surface of the land and in excavations of burial places and kitchen areas.

It is almost a historical cliché to say that readily available virgin land was the lodestone that drew a phenomenal number of Anglo-American settlers who crossed the Appalachian ranges to the Kentucky country during the closing decades of the eighteenth century. They circulated by word of mouth and personal correspondence the concept of Kentucky as a new-found Eden; some contemporary viewers even promised pioneering souls eternal freedom from the frustrations and failures they experienced on the thin and exhausted soils of the eastern seaboard and Piedmont regions.

From the outset of settlement, the Kentucky country was designed to be pastoral and agrarian. This fact was recognized by the Virginia General Assembly in 1776 when it undertook to regulate the distribution of lands and the registry of claims. The land law of that year provided, among other things, "that no family shall be entitled to the allowance granted to settlers by this act, unless they have made a crop of corn in that country, or resided there at least one year since the time of their settlement." This legislation presupposed that settlers would from the start be rural dwellers extracting their livelihoods from the land, and that corn would become the new country's staple crop and the basic source of food and feed. Grain was highly transportable and could be readily consumed by both man and beast. It could be stored in primitive cribs, readily converted into several forms of edible products, or distilled into liquid form. From the moment of making the first clearings, corn could be grown with fair tolerance of shade and hardwood sproutings. No statistics are available for corn production before 1820, and even later they are little more than guesswork. Even so, it is safe to generalize historically that in Kentucky corn has been the mother crop from 1775 to date. In 1850 Kentucky was the second highest corn-producing state in the Union, after Ohio. A decade later, on the eve of the Civil War, it was exceeded in this category by only four states. Kentucky also produced small grains such as wheat, rye, and oats. Streams lateral to the Kentucky River were once lined with water mills to grind meal and flour for the downriver markets.

Largely dependent upon subsistence farming, Kentuckians grew abundant amounts of both food and fiber. Two field crops for fiber production figured prominently in the earlier way of life. Settlers brought overland both hemp and flax seeds, as well as metal parts for constructing the small wheels that would spin the coarse fibers into threads. The coarse cloths known as Kentucky jeans and linsey-woolsey became familiar throughout the South. HEMP early promised to be a substantial commercial crop, both for its production of abundant fiber and for its excellence in fallowing new ground. Until 1870 this field crop figured prominently in Kentucky agricultural statistics. The expanding cotton belt in the lower South created a growing market for bagging and rope to wrap cotton bales. The rise of the steamboat industry created a growing market for rope and caulking. Kentucky farmers, however, were at no point able to compete with eastern jute producers in capturing the naval cordage market. In the closing decades of the twentieth century, the growing of hemp once again became a capital enterprise—this time, however, not for its fiber but for its narcotic properties in the form of marijuana.

Since the arrival of the earliest settlers the cultivation of TOBACCO has had its own history. Of the crops adaptable to growth on Kentucky soils, no seeds could be more readily transported over the mountains than those of tobacco. An immigrant could bring along enough seeds in a jacket pocket to plant a sizable piece of land. That the use of tobacco reaches back many centuries is attested by ancient stone pipes of myriad designs. Both Paleolithic people and the later Indians no doubt smoked primitive forms of tobacco. The recorded history of tobacco opened with James Wilkinson's flatboat trading expedition downriver to New Orleans in 1787. Aside from the political double-dealing associated with this incident, it marked a search for a dependable market for Kentucky's agricultural products, including tobacco. In this moment tobacco became involved in international political intrigue and international commerce.

As Kentucky tobacco patches became more productive, Kentuckians had to construct special storage warehouses and provide more efficient transportation. These developments, often requiring special legislation, constitute an interesting chapter in Kentucky history. Because of the difficulty in transporting heavy hogsheads of tobacco in earlier years, cultivation of the crop was concentrated in areas bordering navigable streams. The appearance of the steamboat and the opening of somewhat improved roads greatly expanded the state's tobacco growing areas.

By the mid-nineteenth century tobacco had become Kentucky's central cash crop. In 1840 the state produced 53,436,909 pounds; in 1850, 55,501,196; and in 1860, 108,102,433 pounds. This upward trend continued to 1982, when the annual yield was 589,000,000 pounds; after that, tobacco cultivation and production began a downward trend. The limiting of acreage during and following the New Deal years, the health scare of the 1970s and 1980s, and competition from other burley tobacco-growing states have all played active roles in the fate of Kentucky's tobacco farmers. In the final decade of the twentieth century, tobacco growing in Kentucky, if not threatened with extinction, faces certain material reduction in importance.

Just as Kentucky pioneers became tillers of the soil, they also became herders and breeders of livestock. Frequent notes in contemporary documentary materials refer to domestic animals. Even before the Anglo-Americans penetrated the western wilderness, buffalo and other herbivorous animals grazed the cane lands and barrens. In the dawning of written history of the Kentucky country, Dr. Thomas Walker in 1750 noted the presence of horses and dogs in his exploration party. Later Daniel Boone and John Finley came mounted and accompanied by dogs in their historic journey westward, as did the famous Long Hunters and early surveyors. Subsequently, the avalanche of settlers that poured through Cumberland Gap and down the Ohio came mounted on horses, or floated the animals downstream aboard flatboats. For the settlers, the horse was both a vital means of transportation and a source of draft power and sport. Horses were also indispensable in breaking the land and in delivering its produce to market. In the earliest years of white settlement, the horse proved a dependable means of escape from Indian raids and was often the target of such raids.

Although no precise data are available for 1790, it is reasonable to suppose that the number of horses in Kentucky at that date equaled the human population. In 1840, in the first Kentucky state auditor's report, local assessors reported 362,690 horses and mules. In the same year, the U.S.

Census reported 395,853 horses in Kentucky, a number exceeded only in New York and Ohio. In 1840 the white Kentucky population totaled 590,253. By the latter date the number of mules was increasing as demand rose for them in the cotton belt of the lower South.

The cow was also an animal pioneer in Kentucky. Nearly every immigrant party that passed through Cumberland Gap herded in its wake cattle, hogs, and sheep. The cow signaled to Indian resisters the fact that settlement of the great hunting ground was imminent. This animal seems to have been especially sensitive to the presence of Indian raiders, and milking time was often a time for raids. Cattle were hardy pioneers that adapted readily to primitive woodland conditions. The cow was a slow but rugged traveler along the backwoods trails, and in later years was able to transport itself to the eastern and southern markets. Until the last quarter of the nineteenth century, hog, cattle, and horse and mule drovers traveled over the Wilderness Road to the east, and other roads to the south, driving animals to market (see TRAIL DRIVES).

Of all the farm animals entering Kentucky, none was more self-sufficient than the hog. It thrived in the great wilderness of mast-bearing deciduous trees, making its own living while reproducing its kind. The hog, like the cow, was a sturdy traveler to the Kentucky frontier, and in later years hog drovers crowded the roads herding thousands of head to eastern and southern markets. Aside from its commercial value, the hog supplied the Kentucky dining table with lard and pork. Although early Kentucky farmers grazed sizable flocks of sheep, it was pork, not lamb and mutton, that became the staple meat diet. Agrarian domesticity came to be symbolized by the farm triad of house, corn crib, and smokehouse. Cured pork products, especially hams, became a staple of external commerce from 1787 onward. Much less dramatic than the improvements in the breeds of cattle, horses, and sheep or the imports of breeding stock, the upgrading of swine types in Kentucky was nevertheless an important chapter in Kentucky's livestock history. Some central Kentucky hog breeders in the decades 1830-60 shared prestige with the more highly publicized breeders of horses and cattle. Consistently throughout Kentucky history, the hog has been an economic factor in the state's livestock production.

Kentucky became a pioneer state in the importation of highly bred livestock animals from England and continental Europe. In 1785 the three sons of Matthew Patton brought from Virginia to Kentucky three grade heifers from their father's herd. Their arrival, along with imports of blooded stallions, marked the beginnings of a major purebred livestock industry in Kentucky. On July 25, 1816, the first of scores of cattle and stock shows and fairs was held at Sanders's Garden just north of Lexington. In the first show, a Captain Smith exhibited his prize bull, Buzzard. Other owners showed good grade bulls and cows.

A second livestock show was held at Sanders's Garden in 1817, and from it stemmed numerous other shows and fairs, including the Kentucky State Fair itself. In 1838 the Kentucky Agricultural Society was formed, and in the 1840s and 1850s came a flood of petitions to the Kentucky General Assembly from counties seeking charters for local agricultural societies. In the period 1838-50, twenty-seven of these societies were created. Perhaps the most important was the Kentucky Agricultural and Mechanical Association in Lexington, chartered December 7, 1850. This organization was created by some of Kentucky's top farmers and livestock breeders, including Brutus J. Clay, Robert Aitcheson Alexander, William Warfield, W.R. Estill, Robert Wilmot Scott, and others. In 1856 the General Assembly chartered the State Agricultural Society as a quasi-official body that reported directly to the legislature. During the decade 1850-60, while local county petitioners sought charters for county or regional agricultural societies, not a single petition came from an Appalachian community.

The State Agricultural Society anticipated the creation of a state agricultural authority, the founding of an agricultural college, and the subsequent organization of the experiment station and extension services. Its annual reports contained essays on improved methods of farming and livestock management, descriptions of the activities of the local fairs, lists of prize winners, and brief reports from the county societies. During the decade 1850-60, the movement for improved farming in Kentucky gained a powerful momentum, only to be disrupted by the Civil War.

Numerous farm journals began publication in this era, discussing new sciences and offering solutions to old problems. All across the United States, agricultural societies began the publication of local farm journals, most of them patterned on the *American Farmer*, which began publication in Baltimore in 1818. Kentuckians published the *Franklin Farmer*.

In 1861 Kentucky was of vital strategic and supply importance to both the Union and Confederacy, not only politically and geographically but as a vital source of agricultural and livestock products. At that time the state was the fifth largest producer of horses and mules and a major breeder of cattle, hogs (exceeding Ohio in this category), and sheep. In an even more favorable position, Kentucky ranked fifth among the states in the value of its livestock and general farm products. Never again was Kentucky to attain such a high rating in the area of comparative agricultural statistics. Perhaps the most significant loss in the Civil War was that of momentum in agricultural husbandry. After 1865 Kentucky shorthorn and traditional Durham cattle had to compete with new breeds and with the great western cattle industry. Major hog production shifted to the expanding corn-growing states in the

Old Northwest, and Tennessee and Missouri came to dominate mule breeding and trade.

In agriculture, as in every other phase of Kentucky life, the Civil War was severely disruptive. The war shattered the rich southern market, which had been a growing and profitable one for Kentuckians. Military raiding across the state, especially during growing and harvest seasons, proved disastrous for many farmers. In numerous instances, both Union and Confederate forces commandeered livestock, especially horses and mules, and guerrillas proved even more menacing. Not only did the war upset demand and disrupt production, but it also bred competition. It was a catalyst for a rapid increase in production by farmers in the Old Northwest.

In 1858 the U.S. Congress enacted a law authorizing the states to establish agricultural and mechanical colleges. This law, however, was vetoed by President James Buchanan. The 1862 attempt was successful, as the land grant law sponsored by Rep. Justin N. Morrill of Vermont was enacted by Congress and signed by President Abraham Lincoln. Under the Morrill Act, each state was to be awarded 30,000 acres of public lands for each of its U.S. representatives and senators. Kentucky did not take advantage of the Morrill land grants until February 22, 1865, and it was not until the opening decades of the twentieth century that the AGRICULTURAL AND MECHANICAL COLLEGE was to have any appreciable impact on Kentucky agriculture as a whole. The state was niggard in the support of the institution, and the farmers were reluctant to make changes in their modes of farming. In other legislation to further the cause of agriculture in the nation, the 1887 Hatch Act provided for the establishment of state agricultural experiment stations, and the 1906 Adams Law modestly increased federal support for original research and experiments. For Kentucky, this marked the beginning of a fresh chapter in agricultural history.

While the U.S. Congress was enacting basic agricultural laws, the Kentucky General Assembly also gave some attention to the subject. On March 20, 1876, it enacted an all-embracing law creating a bureau of agriculture, horticulture, and statistics. This agency was to be directed by a commissioner appointed by the governor. The commissioner was instructed "to ascertain the agricultural, horticultural, mechanical, commercial, and educational condition of every county in the Commonwealth." Further instructions called for gathering statistics on field crops, orchards, gardens, dairies, and mines, with special attention to roads, railroads, streams, towns, villages, and schoolhouses. Not included in the commissioner's assignment was livestock. In 1891 the commissioner of agriculture was made a constitutional officer elected by the people, thus making the office a political one.

The depth of change in Kentucky agriculture can be documented in both an impressionistic view of the rural scene and an examination of the statistical data. After the 1930s discovery of the grass known as fescue 31, travelers saw large areas of the state transformed into hayfields and meadowlands. No more dramatic documentation of the changing crop patterns can be found than the literally thousands of ancient tobacco barns falling into shambles. Statistical data reveal the speed with which changes came. For instance, between 1982 and 1987 the state's farms fell in number from 101,642 to 92,453, or a 9 percent reduction. An even more telling comparison is the decline from 1954 to 1987, when the number of Kentucky farms fell from 193,487 to 92,453. Just as dramatically, the market value of farm equipment increased from $583,339 in 1969 to $2,091,558 in 1987. Even allowing for inflation, this comparison reveals that Kentucky farmers have gone a long way in mechanizing their operations. The average size of farms increased from ninety-three acres in 1954 to 152 acres in 1987, including an average increase of twelve acres in the five years from 1982 to 1987. The value of farm lands and buildings, based on a sampling of farms, declined from $144,427 in 1982 to $135,696 in 1987, reflecting a dramatic lowering of land prices, from a per-acre value of $1,049 in 1982 to $896 in 1987.

In 1987 a total of 78,463 farms were operated by family or individual farmers, while 12,717 were operated by "partnerships." Full-time farmers operated the 1987 total of 78,463, as compared with 49,062 in 1982. The 1982 figure represented a 15.5 percent reduction in full-time farmers as compared with 58,055 in 1974. In all, 14,012,700 of Kentucky's 25,862,400 acres were classed as farmed land in 1987. The amount of acreage has remained fairly stable over several years. There have been some changes in the leading crops produced, which in 1987 were tobacco, corn, hay, and soybeans, in that order. The value of farm products was about equally divided between crops and livestock.

A highly revealing factor in the changing picture of agrarian Kentucky is to be found in rural population statistics. In 1900, 1,679,500 Kentuckians lived in the country, as compared with an urban population of 467,668. In 1980 rural population was 1,798,000, or almost fifty percent of the total Kentucky population.

Since 1940 every segment of agricultural activity in Kentucky has been reflected in some sort of statistical table. The increased use of modern machines, the scientific advances in the fields of plant breeding and chemistry, and the rising emphasis on agribusiness all reveal the inefficiencies of the old agrarian system. Changing social and cultural mores since World War II have threatened the existence of the traditional FAMILY FARM with serious contraction, if not extinction. Already, old institutions such as the country store, post office, school, and church have either disappeared from the Kentucky rural scene or have been greatly reduced in importance. Among the specialists in service to agriculture, the extension service, seed dealers, manufacturers of fertilizers, bankers, and machine manufacturers have sought their own objectives, but in doing so they have wrought a social and economic revolution. Plant breeders have brought their own kind of change, as have other agencies that have a bearing on the rural agrarian way of life in Kentucky. At the closing of the twentieth century, it takes more than a piece of land, a strong will, and a stout back to successfully enter the business of farming—as a matter of fact, much of Kentucky farming has become a quasi-commercial enterprise.

See Lewis C. Gray, *History of Agriculture in the Southern United States to 1860* (Washington, D.C., 1933); Thomas D. Clark, *Agrarian Kentucky* (Lexington, Ky., 1977). THOMAS D. CLARK

AKEMAN, DAVID. David ("Stringbean") Akeman, comedian and banjoist, was born in Jackson County, Kentucky, on June 17, 1914. After meeting Asa Martin in 1935, he toured with Martin and Doc Roberts, appeared on radio station WLAP in Lexington, and joined the "Grand Ole Opry" with Bill Monroe in 1942. As a comedian, he was known for dressing in short pants and a striped shirt that reached his kneecaps. In 1950 he became an "Opry" regular. In 1968 he became a charter member of the television show "Hee Haw." He and his wife, Estelle (Stanfield), were murdered by burglars who ransacked their home on November 11, 1973.

See Charles K. Wolfe, *Kentucky Country* (Lexington, Ky., 1982). CHARLES F. FABER

ALBANY. Albany, the seat of Clinton County, is located on U.S. 127. In 1837 an election was held to determine the location of the seat of government, and Benjamin Dowell's tavern on the site of present-day Albany was chosen as the county seat. Legend relates that during the course of the voting, patrons of Dowell's tavern enthusiastically shouted, "All for Benny," a rough equivalent of the name Albany. But it is generally accepted that the town, incorporated January 27, 1838, was named for Albany, New York.

During the Civil War, Albany was attacked by Confederate guerrillas and a portion of the town, including the courthouse, was burned along with the early records of Clinton County. A new courthouse was constructed in 1870-73. By the 1870s, Albany had recovered from the destruction of the Civil War. In 1873 the town's businesses included dry goods establishments, grocery stores, and drugstores, in addition to a confectionery. In 1895, a third courthouse was built at a cost of $15,000. This structure burned August 2, 1980.

During the twentieth century, Albany began to build a small industrial base. The production of clothing, timber, and agricultural items, as well as the manufacture of stereo tapes, employed many residents of the area.

The population of the fifth-class city was 1,891 in 1970; 2,083 in 1980; and 2,062 in 1990. RON D. BRYANT

ALBRIGHT, ARNOLD DEWALD. Arnold Dewald Albright, a leader in Kentucky higher education, was born in Washington, D.C., on March 6, 1913. He was the son of Earl J. and Elizabeth (Welch) Albright. He attended Depauw University (Greencastle, Indiana) and graduated from Milligan College in Tennessee in 1937. Albright received an M.S. degree from the University of Tennessee the following year. He earned a Ph.D. from New York University in 1950.

Following a series of positions in public education in Tennessee, Albright became a professor of education at George Peabody College in Nashville. While at Peabody, from 1950 to 1954, he also served as associate director of the Southern States Cooperative Program in Educational Administration. In 1954 Albright became director of the Bureau of School Services and professor of education at the University of Kentucky. In 1957 he became executive dean of extended programs, beginning an administrative career at the University of Kentucky that also included terms as provost (1960-62) and executive vice-president of institutional planning (1970-73).

Albright was appointed executive director of the KENTUCKY COUNCIL ON HIGHER EDUCATION in 1973. During his four-year tenure he introduced long-range planning for Kentucky higher education. In 1976 he was selected to be the second president of NORTHERN KENTUCKY UNIVERSITY, a post he held until 1983. In 1986 Albright was asked to become president of MOREHEAD STATE UNIVERSITY, during a period of declining enrollments and institutional upheaval. During his brief tenure (1986-87) he brought stability to, and restored confidence in, the university.

In 1987 Albright was appointed to fill a vacant at-large position on Lexington's Urban County Council. His term expired in December 1989. Albright has served as an education and management consultant and has written prolifically in the area of educational administration.

Albright married Grace Carroll on June 23, 1939. They have two sons, Carl Wesley and Earl Thomas.

See Truman Mitchell Pierce and A.D. Albright, *A Profession In Transition: A Nine Year Study of Improving Educational Administration in the South* (Nashville 1960). TERRY BIRDWHISTELL

ALCORN, SOPHIA KINDRICK. Sophia Kindrick Alcorn, teacher, daughter of James W. and Sophie Ann (Kindrick) Alcorn, was born on August 3, 1883, in Stanford, Lincoln County, Kentucky. A graduate of Ward Seminary (now Belmont College) in Nashville, she received training in teaching the deaf at Clark School in Northhampton, Massachusetts. She earned her M.A. degree from Wayne University in Detroit, where she assisted in training teachers and served as a principal in the deaf school system. Alcorn devoted her life to teaching deaf and blind students at North Carolina School for the Deaf (1908-9); Kentucky School for the

Deaf (1909-20); South Dakota School for the Deaf (1920); Day School in Des Moines, Iowa (1924-25); Oral School in Cincinnati (1927-29); New Jersey School for the Deaf (1930); and the Detroit School for the Deaf (1930-53). Following retirement, she worked actively with the American Foundation for the Blind.

Alcorn invented the Tadoma method, named for two of her deaf-blind students, Tad Chapman and Oma Simpson. This system, still used internationally, teaches the deaf-blind to speak through the feel of sound vibrations from the lips and cheeks. She also created the Alcorn symbols, written characters used to help deaf students develop their speech. Alcorn died on November 28, 1967, in Stanford and was buried there in the Buffalo Springs Cemetery.

ALE-8-ONE. Ale-8-One, Kentucky's own soft drink, has been bottled in Winchester since 1926. A closely guarded family secret, the Ale-8-One formula was developed by G.L. Wainscott in the 1920s, after experimentation with ginger-blended recipes he acquired during extensive travels in northern Europe. He sponsored one of America's first name-the-product contests, and "A Late One" was the winning name for the latest thing in soft drinks. A pun turned the name into Ale-8-1.

Wainscott had been in the soft drink business in Winchester since 1902, bottling several flavored drinks in a plant on North Main Street. In 1906 he introduced Roxa-Kola, a popular rival to the cola drinks then available. By 1935 Wainscott had converted a livery stable on West Broadway and moved his growing bottling operation there. Jane (Rogers) Wainscott inherited half of her husband's bottling stock at his death in 1944; the other half was divided among the company's employees. At her death in 1954, Jane Wainscott left her interest to her brother, Frank A. Rogers. Rogers bought out his partners in 1962, and incorporated the Ale-8-One Bottling Company. His son, Frank A. Rogers, Jr., became manager and was later named president, and the rapid growth of the new corporation began.

In 1965 the company built a new plant on Carol Road. Production of Roxa-Kola had been discontinued in 1964, and by 1974 the remaining Wainscott flavored drinks had been eliminated in order to concentrate on Ale-8-1. At that time, Frank A. Rogers III joined the company's management. In 1976 a warehouse was constructed on an adjacent lot, and in 1980-81 a two-story syrup room was added to the main building. In 1989 the company, which remains in the Rogers family's hands, built two-story offices as part of an extensive addition that tripled warehouse space.

RILEY ROGERS WALTON

ALEXANDER, DAVID C. David C. Alexander, journalist and mystery writer, was born in Shelbyville, Kentucky, on April 21, 1907, to David Catlin and Effie (Buckner) Alexander. He grew up in Louisville. After spending the years 1926-28 at the University of Kentucky, and 1928-29 at Columbia University, Alexander joined the news staff of the *Lexington Herald*. He became interested in thoroughbred breeding and racing and in 1930 became managing editor of the *New York Morning Telegraph*, a leading racing publication. After more than ten years with that publication, he returned to Lexington, where he wrote for the *Blood-Horse* and the *Thoroughbred Record*.

Alexander's writing career was interrupted when he served in the U.S. Army during 1943-45. He then became racing editor for the *New York Herald-Tribune*, a post he held until the paper's demise in 1966. After graduating from the New York Institute of Criminology in 1950, he began writing murder mysteries; the first, *Murder in Black and White*, appeared in 1951. By 1962, Alexander had published fifteen mysteries, the best of them related to the Broadway theater, including *Die, Little Goose* (1956), *Death of Humpty Dumpty* (1957), and *Hush-a-Bye Murder* (1957). His *History and Romance of the Horse* (1963) was winner of the Boys' Club of America Juvenile Book Award. He received the Ellery Queen Award for mystery writing in 1956 for his short story "The Man Who Went to Taltavul's."

Alexander married Alice LeMere in 1930. He died on March 21, 1973, in New York City and was buried there. DAVID F. BURG

ALEXANDER, GROSS. Gross Alexander, Methodist theologian and author, was born to Charles Holliday and Eliza (Drane) Alexander in Scottsville, Kentucky, on June 1, 1852. The family moved to Louisville in 1867. Alexander graduated from Louisville's Male High School in 1871 and was a faculty member there until 1873. From the fall of 1873 to the spring of 1875, he taught Latin and Greek at Warren College in Bowling Green. In 1875, Alexander entered the Drew Theological Seminary at Madison, New Jersey, receiving his bachelor of divinity degree in June 1877. As a minister in the Methodist Episcopal Church, South, he served in the Louisville Conference in the Portland area during 1877-79.

After a year spent in touring Europe, Alexander became chaplain at Vanderbilt University in Tennessee in September 1884. In June 1885, he became an instructor in New Testament Greek at Vanderbilt and taught there as a professor until 1902. Returning to Louisville in that year, Alexander served as presiding elder to the Louisville Conference of the Methodist church until 1906, when he was elected editor of the *Methodist Quarterly Review*. He held that position until his death in 1915. Alexander translated from the Greek *Chrysostom's Homilies on Galatians and Ephesians* (1889) and *The Son of Man* (1889); edited *The Doctrines and Discipline of the Methodist Episcopal Church* (1914); and was a member of the commission that prepared the 1911 *Authorized Version of the English Bible*, a commemorative tercentenary edition. Gross's other works included *The Son of Man: Studies of His Life and Teaching* (1900), and *Steve P. Holcombe, the Converted Gambler: His Life and Work* (1888).

Alexander married Helen M. Watts of Louisville in August 1875; they had two children, Edith and Clay. Helen died in November 1885. Alexander married Arabel Wilbur of Chicago in 1887; they had two children, Gross, Jr., and Ruth. Alexander died on September 6, 1915, while on a trip to Los Angeles. He was buried at Cave Hill Cemetery in Louisville.

ALEXANDRIA. Alexandria, one of the two county seats of Campbell County, lies eight miles south of NEWPORT, the other county seat. Newport was the county seat from 1794 through 1840 except for a year-long move to Visalia in 1827 to be near a proposed railroad. When part of Campbell County went to create Kenton County in 1840, legislators designated Alexandria the county seat of Campbell because it was close to the center of the county, and a courthouse was built in Alexandria. Frustrated residents of Newport, however, built their own courthouse in 1884. An arrangement was worked out under which the county's fiscal court and judicial offices are located in the Newport courthouse, and the Alexandria court building houses other administrative offices.

The Alexandria area is believed to have been settled around 1793 by Frank Spilman and his family, who came from King George County, Virginia, and may have named the location for Alexandria, Virginia. By September 1819 Spilman began developing the town and selling lots. The city was incorporated in 1834.

Because the road between Newport and Winchester built by the state in 1836 was little more than a trail, Campbell County residents formed a turnpike association to construct a better road. The road, completed in 1856, came to be known as the Alexandria Pike. It was owned by the Newport and Alexandria Turnpike Company and had two tollgates in Alexandria. By the 1900s farmers and other residents wanted a free road for access to markets in Newport, Covington, and Cincinnati. The county bought the road in 1921, and it soon became part of US 27. Because of Alexandria's location near the center of the county, away from the Ohio River, the rapid commercial growth and industrial development that affected other northern Kentucky cities did not occur there. It remains largely a middle-class residential city surrounded by farmland. The rural tradition is annually celebrated by the Alexandria Fair and Horse Show, which began in 1856.

The fourth-class city had a population of 3,844 in 1970; 4,735 in 1980; and 5,592 in 1990.

ALI, MUHAMMAD. "Float like a butterfly, sting like a bee, Ali's World Champion for time number three": So said Muhammad Ali, probably the quickest heavyweight boxer who ever fought, at the same time bringing style and showmanship to the ring. Ali held the World Heavyweight Championship during 1964-67, 1974-78, and 1978-79.

Cassius Marcellus Clay—as Ali was known before he joined the Nation of Islam in 1964—was born on January 17, 1942, in Louisville, to Marcellus and Odessa (Grady) Clay. The Clay family lived at 3302 Grand Avenue in the West End of Louisville. To help his family financially, Ali took up boxing at age twelve. His first trainer was Joe Martin at Columbia Gym, who paid Ali four dollars each time one of his fights appeared on a local television program, "Tomorrow's Champions." Ali then switched to trainer Fred Stoner, joining Stoner's camp at the Grace Community Center. He attended Central High School in Louisville, where his studies suffered because of his intense involvement with boxing.

Ali won six Golden Gloves tournaments in Kentucky in weight classes from light to welter to heavy; the total number of his amateur fights is unknown. In 1959 and again in 1960 he won the Light Heavyweight National Golden Gloves and National AAU tournaments. As AAU champion he was invited to the Olympic trials, and became the light heavyweight entry for the United States. He defeated "Ziggy" Pietrzykowski of Poland for the gold medal in 1960.

On October 29, 1960, Ali made his first professional appearance, winning over Tunney Hunsaker by a decision. Needing money to repair his parents' home, he had signed for the fight himself. Ali then contracted to be managed by a group of Louisville millionaires led by William Faversham and remained with them until 1967. His promoters had scheduled training with fighter Archie Moore, but Ali quickly left and hired Angelo Dundee to manage and train him as a professional. Ali worked his way up the ranks, and on February 25, 1964, he scored a seventh-round knockout against Sonny Liston to win the world heavyweight championship.

After a swing through Europe, where he defeated all contenders, Ali received an army induction notice. Although Ali was offered both a commission and a support services assignment, he refused induction for religious reasons. He was sentenced to five years in prison and a $10,000 fine. The World Boxing Association then stripped him of his title on April 28, 1967, and awarded it to "Smokin' " Joe Frazier, the beginning of a bitter feud between the two fighters. Although Ali did not serve jail time, he was barred from boxing, his livelihood.

During his three-year exile from the ring, Ali toured colleges and universities making speeches about civil rights. On June 20, 1970, the U.S. Supreme Court decided in his favor in the army induction case, and Atlanta gave him his first boxing license, which effectively ended the exile. In his first return bout, held amidst protest on October 26, 1970, Ali knocked Jerry Quarry out in three rounds. The feud with Frazier festered, and the first Ali-Frazier bout was scheduled—Ali's first million-dollar purse and his chance to win back the world heavyweight title. The fight, outstanding in boxing history, was held in New York City on March 8, 1971. Frazier won the fifteen-round decision and retained the championship. Ali suffered his second loss, as well as a broken jaw, at the hands of Ken Norton on March 31, 1973.

Ali met George Foreman, then the champion, on October 30, 1974. This fight, called the "Rumble in the Jungle," took place in Kinshasa, Zaire, and featured a $5 million purse for each man. Ali changed from his famous shuffle, dance, and rope-a-dope style, and stood toe-to-toe with the hard-punching Foreman. The result was a worn-down Foreman whom Ali knocked out in the eighth round to reclaim the championship. The hard-driven Frazier, however, was still there to challenge for the title. Perhaps the greatest heavyweight fight in history was the "Thrilla in Manila" between Ali and Frazier on September 30, 1975. The fight was an action-packed brawl that finally ended when Frazier could not answer the bell for the fifteenth round. Ali lost the title on February 15, 1978, by decision to Leon Spinks, then regained it from him on September 15, 1978, by unanimous decision, becoming world heavyweight champion for the third time. Ali last fought on October 2, 1980, when he was knocked out by Larry Holmes in the eleventh round. The fights took their toll, as Ali developed Parkinson's syndrome.

Ali has been married four times, first to Sonji Rei. He then married Belinda Boyd (Kalilah Tolona) in April 1967; they had three daughters and a son. In June 1977, he married Veronica Porshe; in November 1986, Yolanda Williams. On occasion, Ali returns to Louisville to visit parents and friends. His autobiography, *The Greatest* (1975), was written with Richard Durham.

See Robert Hoskins, *Muhammad Ali* (Los Angeles 1980); Gary Smith, "A Celebration of Muhammad Ali," *Sports Illustrated*, Nov. 15, 1989.

JOEL T. SATTERLY

ALICE LLOYD COLLEGE. Cofounded in 1923 by social reformers Alice LLOYD and June BUCHANAN, Alice Lloyd College has provided higher education to generations of Kentucky mountain youth. Located in the Knott County community of Pippa Passes, the institution was created and initially maintained as a joint effort between the two founders and the residents of the Caney Creek community.

The college evolved from the Caney Creek Community Center, established in 1916 as Lloyd's vision of a model community in Appalachia. By the early 1920s, however, she and Buchanan, along with community members, decided to concentrate on mountain leadership training, and they founded Caney Junior College in 1923. Students performed chores to earn tuition and their room and board. Once they completed their studies, they were encouraged to return to lifelong service in the Kentucky mountains.

The school survived the economically difficult decades of the 1930s and 1940s and registered steady gains in both buildings and enrollment. Most of the new buildings constructed in this period were designed by Caney graduate Commodore Slone.

The institution reached a number of milestones in the 1950s, including a new science building, accreditation by the state board of education, and the creation of a nationwide donor network. For these and other achievements, Lloyd was honored on the nationally televised show "This Is Your Life" on December 7, 1955. The aging Lloyd gradually turned over many of her duties to Dean William S. Hays and Buchanan, and began work on an endowment fund to ensure the survival of the college. After Lloyd's death in 1962, the school was renamed Alice Lloyd Junior College. Hays became the school's first official president; Buchanan assumed the leadership of the community center. During Hays's fifteen-year presidency, he emerged as a spokesman for Appalachian educational concerns and also carried out an extensive modernization and building program.

In 1977 the board of trustees appointed Jerry C. Davis president. Under Davis and Buchanan, the school became a four-year college in 1982, completed a long-range endowment plan, founded the June Buchanan School (a model school for kindergarten through twelfth grade), and further expanded the campus physical plant.

At the end of the 1988 school year, the leadership of the institution changed dramatically. Davis resigned to accept another position and June Buchanan died. M. Fred Mullinax, a former Alice Lloyd vice-president, became the college's third president and the leader of the community center. Alice Lloyd College enrollment for the 1980s averaged five hundred students per year.

See Jerry C. Davis, *Miracle on Caney Creek* (Lexington, Ky., 1982).

STEPHEN DOUGLAS WILSON

ALLEN, HENRY TUREMAN. Henry Tureman Allen, career army officer, was born in Sharpsburg, Kentucky, on April 13, 1859, the son of Sanford and Susan (Shumate) Allen. He attended Peeks Mill Military Academy and graduated from Georgetown College in 1878. He graduated from the U.S. Military Academy at West Point in 1882 and was sent to the western frontier, where he explored and mapped part of Alaska in 1885. From 1888 to 1890, Allen was an instructor at West Point. He spent five years, 1890 to 1895, as a military attaché in St. Petersburg and the next two years as an attaché in Berlin. Allen served briefly in Cuba in the Spanish-American War (1898) and then commanded the Philippine constabulary from 1901 to 1907. After service as a military observer in the first year of World War I, he was placed in command of a cavalry regiment in the Mexican expedition in 1916. Allen was promoted to brigadier general in 1917 and commanded the 90th Division in 1918, taking part in both the St. Mihiel and Meuse-Argonne offensives. From 1919 to 1923 he served as commander of the American army of occupation, receiving his promotion to major general in March 1921. He retired from the army on April 13, 1923, and lived in Washington, D.C., where he wrote two books, *My Rhineland Journal* (1923) and *The Rhineland Occupation* (1927), about his experiences in the military. Allen died on August 29, 1930, in Buena Vista Springs, Pennsylvania. He was buried at Arlington National Cemetery.

See Heath Twichell, Jr., *The Biography of an Army Officer, 1859-1930* (New Brunswick, N.J., 1974).   JACK W. THACKER

ALLEN, JAMES LANE. James Lane Allen, whose books achieved both popular success and critical acclaim, was Kentucky's first important novelist. Born December 21, 1849, near Lexington, Kentucky, the seventh and last child of Richard and Helen (Foster) Allen, "Laney" (as he was known in childhood) grew to manhood near Lexington and did not leave Kentucky until he was twenty-two years old.

Though of sound heritage, the Allens never had the financial standing of the upper class, and Laney worked hard as a youth. His mother—to whom Laney dedicated six of his first eight books—nevertheless brought him up in an idealistic, romantic world filled with stories of honor and chivalry, where gallant and noble gentlemen courted women of spotless virtue. Yet, in adulthood, Allen saw around him a new industrial America where, it seemed to him, ethics were replaced by greed, honor by corruption, purity by vulgarity. Allen was over six feet tall, slim and handsome, an immaculately dressed, reserved Victorian gentleman. He gave many the impression of being cold, repressed, and formal. His sensitivity to anything he perceived as a slight caused him to strike out at even his few friends. Nor did he have any close female attachments, except within his family. He cared for his mother until her death, when Allen was nearly forty, as well as for his reclusive sister Anne.

Educated in local schools, Allen received a degree from what is now Transylvania University in 1872 and as the salutatorian delivered his address in Latin. In 1877 he earned a master's degree from the same institution. For a dozen years after earning his first degree, Allen taught in Missouri, West Virginia, and Kentucky before turning to full-time writing. The subject for fourteen of his ensuing nineteen books was Kentucky. Allen's Victorian Age readers were hungry for local color, and he immersed them in the atmosphere of the old commonwealth, a vanishing world of romantic ideals and genteel traditions. After publication of numerous short stories in the 1880s in the leading magazines of the day, Allen collected some of them, including the well-known "King Solomon of Kentucky," for his first book, *Flute and Violin and Other Kentucky Tales and Romances* (1891). Other works followed quickly: *The Blue-Grass Region of Kentucky* (an 1892 collection of articles that form a kind of travelog); *John Gray* (1893); his popular and well-written *Kentucky Cardinal* (1894); and its thin sequel *Aftermath* (1895). The next year, Allen's *Summers in Arcady*, with its realism and focus on lower-class subjects, aroused some controversy because of passages dealing with sexual matters. No such outcry greeted Allen's enormously popular *The Choir Invisible* (1897), which sold almost a quarter-million hardback copies within three years and was translated into several languages. An accurate historical novel set in frontier Lexington, it deals with the conflict of honor, love, and duty as schoolmaster John Gray realizes his forbidden love for a married woman.

Acclaimed as one of America's great writers, Allen chose to depart from the formula that had given him so much recognition. *The Choir Invisible*, together with *Two Gentlemen of Kentucky* (1899), marked the end of his first phase, as he tried to write more about the questions troubling modern America. But in so doing, he left behind the audience faithful to his earlier books. His next work, produced at age fifty in 1900, was *The Reign of Law: A Tale of the Kentucky Hemp Fields*. Dealing with religious doubt and Darwinism, the work proved popular but angered churchmen in Kentucky. Allen's success continued with his complex *The Mettle of the Pasture* (1903), another national best seller. Allen sought new themes, but as he tried to change, he never again was so successful. Even when he returned to romantic themes, the criticisms continued and sales dropped. The cold and humorless *Bride of the Mistletoe* (1909) scandalized reviewers with what they perceived as the vulgar frankness of its descriptive passages. Although some of his later work had real merit, only cursory public and critical attention was given to *The Doctor's Christmas Eve* (1910), *The Heroine in Bronze* (1912), *The Last Christmas Tree* (1914), *The Sword of Youth* (1915), *A Cathedral Singer* (1916), *The Kentucky Warbler* (1918), *The Emblems of Fidelity: A Comedy in Letters* (1919), *The Alabaster Box* (1923), and the posthumous *The Landmark* (1925).

Allen lived in New York after 1893, and his literary output declined. He died on February 18, 1925, and was buried in the Lexington Cemetery. His will specified that his royalties and estate go to the city of Lexington, to be used for the young.

Allen's writing often seems romantic and sentimental, but so was his time. He met perfectly the reading tastes of his age, wrote some outstanding literature, and made America aware that the Bluegrass State could produce fine writers.

See Grant C. Knight, *James Lane Allen and the Genteel Tradition* (Chapel Hill, N.C., 1935); William K. Bottorff, *James Lane Allen* (New York 1964).   JAMES C. KLOTTER

ALLEN, JOHN. John Allen, legislator and officer in the War of 1812, was born in Rockbridge County, Virginia, on December 30, 1771, eldest son of James and Mary (Kelsey) Allen. In 1779

the Allens migrated to Kentucky, to John Dougherty's (or Daugherty's) station in Boyle County; they settled in Nelson County in 1784. First educated at home, Allen entered school in Bardstown in 1786, studying with James Priestly. In 1791 he went to Stanton, Virginia, where he read law with Col. Archibald Stewart. Allen returned to Kentucky in 1795 and established a successful law practice in Shelby County. He married Jane Logan, daughter of Benjamin and Ann Logan, on December 21, 1798.

In 1800 Allen was elected to represent Shelby County in the General Assembly. He served in the House until 1807, when he was elected to the Kentucky Senate, a position he held until 1812. In December 1806 he and Henry Clay acted as defense attorneys for Aaron Burr in the Burr Conspiracy trial held in Frankfort. Allen ran for governor in 1808, losing to Gen. Charles Scott by a vote of 20,050 to 8,430. On June 5, 1812, he was commissioned a colonel in the 1st Rifle Regiment of the Kentucky militia, the first raised in the commonwealth to fight the War of 1812. Allen was killed on January 22, 1813, while rallying his troops at the Battle of RIVER RAISIN, and was buried in Frankfort Cemetery. Three states—Ohio, Indiana, and Kentucky—named counties in his honor.

See Anderson C. Quisenberry, *Kentucky in the War of 1812* (Baltimore 1969).

ALLEN, JOSEPH. Joseph Allen, son of James and Mary (Kelsey) Allen, was born in Augusta County, Virginia, on August 20, 1774. In 1779 the family migrated west to John Dougherty's (Daugherty's) Station in Boyle County, Kentucky, and in 1784 to a farm in Nelson County. Allen studied law with a Mr. Shackleford in Bardstown. After completing his studies, Allen moved to William Hardin's fort with his sister Margaret and brother-in-law Joseph Huston, who were among the first settlers of what became Hardinsburg. When Breckinridge County was formed in 1799, Allen became county clerk and circuit clerk, holding both positions until 1857. During the War of 1812, Allen served as a captain in the 8th Company of the Kentucky Mounted Volunteer Militia, declining a colonelcy on the ground that he lacked military training. Under the command of Gen. Samuel Hopkins, the company marched toward Vincennes, Indiana, in October 1812, only to return when the soldiers' enlistments expired.

Allen married Margaret Crawford of Botetourt County, Virginia, in 1803. They had five children who survived to maturity. Allen died on April 28, 1862, and was buried in the Hardinsburg Cemetery.

See Mary Allen Goodson, "Captain Joseph Allen," *Register* 43 (Oct. 1945): 345-59; Anderson C. Quisenberry, *Kentucky in the War of 1812* (Baltimore 1969).

ALLEN, JULIA FRANCES. Julia Frances Allen, educator, was born in Burkesville, Kentucky, to John Edward and Laura Owsley (Baker) Allen on April 14, 1896. She attended the Kentucky College for Women in Danville and graduated from Mt. Holyoke in 1920. Allen then went to China, studying Chinese at Nanking University and teaching in the Christian Girls' School at Nanking in 1922. She earned a master of arts degree from the University of Chicago in 1928. From 1931 to 1935 Allen served as dean at Hamilton Junior College in Lexington, Kentucky, then became assistant to the dean of women at Berea College. She served as dean of women at Berea from 1948 to 1959. A committed activist, Allen participated in sit-ins and other demonstrations protesting U.S. involvement in Vietnam. In 1970 Centre College presented her with its Alumni Recognition Award. Allen died in Berea on January 23, 1974.

CAROLYN TERRY BASHAW

ALLEN, ROBERT McDOWELL. Robert McDowell Allen, chemist, was born in Grundy County, Missouri, on October 29, 1879, to the Rev. Nelson McDowell and Caroline Josephine (Pelley) Allen, both native Kentuckians. In 1883, the family moved to Versailles, Kentucky, where Robert began his education at Henry Academy. He received a B.A. (1900) and an M.A. (1913) in chemistry from Kentucky State College (now the University of Kentucky) and briefly studied law at Transylvania University in Lexington (1905-06).

Allen was deeply committed to the ideas of the new Progressive movement in the United States and was a leading Progressive in Kentucky. Concentrating his efforts on food and drug controls, he began working as a chemist in 1902 at the Lexington Experiment Station, where he took charge later that year. His work at the experiment station and his position as secretary (1902-9) of the Association of State and National Food and Dairy Officials were influential in the passage of the federal Pure Food and Drug Law in 1906. As a special assistant to the U.S. attorney general (1908-9), he worked primarily on cases related to food and drug laws. A state leader in food regulation, Allen headed the Kentucky Food and Drug Control Committee (1902-16) and drafted many state laws in that area, including the Kentucky Pure Food and Drug Act of 1908 and the Kentucky Food Sanitary Act of 1916.

In 1916 Allen obtained a leave of absence to study progressive health operations in New York City. During World War I, he provided baking supplies to the government and shipped dried brewer's yeast throughout the South to treat the pellagra epidemic. When the war ended, Allen stayed in New York City, where he worked as director and president of Vegex, Inc., Vitamin Food Company, and Marmite Inc. of America for the remainder of his life. He was the author of more than fifty official and private publications on food and drug control, vitamins, and nutrition.

Allen, a direct descendant of Daniel Boone, was related to several prominent Kentucky, Virginia, and Rhode Island families, including the McDowells, Nelsons, Greenes, and Dawsons. He married Fanniebelle McVey on December 23, 1909; they had one daughter, Fanniebelle McVey. Allen died on March 28, 1948, and was buried in the Lexington Cemetery.

See Margaret Ripley Wolfe, "The Agricultural Experiment Station and Food and Drug Control: Another Look at Kentucky Progressivism, 1898-1916," *FCHQ* 49 (Oct. 1975): 323-38.

ALLEN COUNTY. Allen County, in south-central Kentucky, is bordered on the north and east by the Barren River, on the west by Warren and Simpson counties, and on the south by Tennessee. SCOTTSVILLE is the county seat. Allen County's 338 square miles of hilly terrain are a source of hardwood lumber and minor amounts of petroleum and natural gas. Tobacco and livestock are the chief agricultural products. The Port Oliver Dam on the Barren River, completed in 1964, created the 2,187-acre Barren River Lake State Resort Park, which draws tourists to the area.

Allen County, Kentucky's fifty-seventh county, was formed in 1815 by combining parts of Warren and Barren counties. It was named for Colonel John Allen, a hero of the War of 1812. The first settlers arrived in the area in 1797, and in 1816 the county seat was created and named in honor of Gov. Charles Scott. A trail through the county between Lexington and Nashville developed into a postal route by 1820. Scottsville lay on a stagecoach line between Louisville and Nashville that in the twentieth century became U.S. Highway 31E. In 1886 the Cumberland & Ohio Railroad built a line from Scottsville to Gallatin, Tennessee. This line, purchased by the Louisville & Nashville Railroad in 1906, was later abandoned.

Its strategic location on a north-south road brought Allen County into the Civil War. On June 11, 1863, the Union's 11th Kentucky was driven from Scottsville. On December 8, 1863, Confederate Col. John M. Hughes of the 25th Tennessee Infantry occupied the town and took eighty-six Union soldiers prisoner.

Noted residents of the county include Emma Guy Cromwell, the first woman elected to a statewide office when she became secretary of state in 1924. Opie Read, a regional writer and humorist, edited the *Scottsville Argus* in the 1890s. Mordecai Ham and his son of the same name were leaders of the Southern Baptist Church in Kentucky. Ham, Jr., was a nationally known evangelist and temperance leader in the early twentieth century.

An oil boom pushed Allen County's population to a high of 16,761 in 1920. Although oil had been discovered there in the 1850s and 1890s, the 1915-20 boom eclipsed earlier finds, and by 1920 more than two hundred drilling rigs were in operation.

The population was 12,598 in 1970; 14,128 in 1980; and 14,628 in 1990.

See H.H. Patton, *A History of Scottsville and Allen County* (N.p., 1974).

ALLEN DALE FARM. In 1795 Robert Polk Allen founded Allen Dale, a historic 473-acre farm about four miles south of Shelbyville, Kentucky, on the Zaring Mill Road. His descendants have owned Allen Dale continuously since its establishment, aided by several court decisions favorable to the family. Ann (Polk) Allen, his widowed mother, was buried on the property; Robert Allen died in Frederick County, Virginia, and was buried there. During the period 1907-28, Sue Thornton (Meriwether) Henning, wife of J.W. Henning and great-great-granddaughter of John and Ann (Polk) Allen, was owner and breeder of a prize-winning herd of registered Jersey cattle at Allen Dale. In 1914 the farm produced the national grand champion Jersey bull. Henning was the first woman to serve on the board of the American Jersey Cattle Club.

See R.R. Van Stockum, *Kentucky and the Bourbons* (Louisville 1991).   R.R. VAN STOCKUM

ALLIN, THOMAS. Thomas Allin, early civic and political leader who fought in the Revolutionary War, was born in Hanover County, Virginia, on May 14, 1757, the son of William and Frances (Grant) Allin. He was raised on a farm in Granville County, North Carolina, where the family moved in 1758. During the Revolutionary War Allin served various terms of enlistment with the North Carolina militia and was a member of the staff of Gen. Nathanael Greene in several southern campaigns in 1780-81. Allin first visited Kentucky in the spring of 1780. In the early fall of 1781, he moved to Lincoln County, Kentucky, and settled near Harrodsburg. In August 1782 Allin enlisted in the Kentucky militia and served as commissary and quartermaster during the ensuing Indian campaign, achieving the rank of major.

Soon after moving to Kentucky, Allin was appointed deputy surveyor (November 20, 1781–ca. 1786) and deputy sheriff (June 18, 1782–ca. 1786) for Lincoln County. Allin remained active as a surveyor through at least 1811, the year he was elected Harrodsburg's town surveyor. He also served as surveyor of the Transylvania Company, laying out Henderson, Kentucky, in 1797 and helping to lay out Harrodsburg and other Kentucky towns as well. On September 24, 1785, Allin was appointed deputy clerk for the Supreme Court for the District of Kentucky and served until ca. 1792. When Mercer County was established from Lincoln County on August 1, 1786, Allin was appointed county court clerk, a post he held until his resignation on February 7, 1831. He also served as clerk of the Mercer County circuit court (originally the court of quarter sessions), from its establishment on September 25, 1792, until his resignation in 1825. He was clerk of the Harrodsburg board of trustees from March 24, 1786, to May 4, 1816.

Allin also operated a farm, a mill, and a distillery. He was a substantial landholder and owned slaves. During the existence of the DANVILLE POLITICAL CLUB (1786-90), he served as treasurer, secretary pro tempore, and president on occasion.

He was a Mercer County delegate to Virginia's constitutional convention in June 1788, voting with ten of the Kentucky delegates against ratification (three voted for and one abstained). He was a charter member of the Kentucky Society for the Promotion of Useful Knowledge (1787–ca. 1788), Mercer County delegate to Kentucky's second constitutional convention (August 1799), and a Harrodsburg town trustee (ca. 1790–ca. 1815).

Allin married Mary Jouett in February 1789, in Mercer County; they had ten children. Allin died in Harrodsburg of cholera on June 26, 1833. He was buried in the Springhill cemetery in Harrodsburg.

See Norma Carter Miller and George Lane Miller, *Allens of the Southern States* (Baltimore 1989).   JAMES J. HOLMBERG

ALLISON, YOUNG EWING. Young Ewing Allison, writer and editor, was born in Henderson, Kentucky, on December 23, 1853, to Young Ewing and Susan Speed (Wilson) Allison. His father served Henderson County as both judge and clerk. Allison's partial deafness limited his formal education to less than three years, for which he compensated by extensive reading. By age fourteen, he was setting type for the *Henderson News* and a year later became its editor. Between 1873 and 1880, he worked for two newspapers in Evansville, Indiana, first as a typesetter and then as editor. He returned to Kentucky in 1880, to become city editor of the *Louisville Courier-Journal*. In 1888 he founded and edited an insurance trade newspaper called the *Insurance Herald*. He sold this in 1899, and started the *Insurance Field* and remained its editor until his death.

Allison is remembered for his epic poem *Derelict* (1891), which includes the lines from Robert Louis Stevenson's *Treasure Island* (1882): "Fifteen men on the dead man's chest, / Yo-ho-ho and a bottle of rum! / Drink and the devil had done for the rest, / Yo-ho-ho and a bottle of rum!" The poem is a favorite of readers of pirate lore. In cooperation with Henry Waller, Allison wrote many songs and four operas—*The Ogallallos* (1893), performed by the Bostonians, a leading opera company of the time; *Brother Francisco* (1893), performed in Berlin in 1896; and *The Scout* (1891) and *The Mouse and the Garter* (n.d.), which were never performed. Allison was a member of the first Old Kentucky Home Commission and wrote articles and pamphlets on Federal Hill and Stephen Foster. He was a frequent contributor to the state's historical journals and wrote for many literary periodicals.

Allison married Maggie Yeiser on March 27, 1883; they had two children, George S. and Young Ewing III. Allison died on July 7, 1932, and was buried at Cave Hill Cemetery. Many of his writings and private papers were donated to the Filson Club in Louisville.

ALMANACS. John BRADFORD published the first state almanac, the *Kentucky Almanac*, in 1788. On the title page, Bradford promised his patrons "A Variety of Entertaining Pieces in Prose and Verse." Between 1788 and 1811 Bradford distributed the slender pamphlet, containing astronomical data based on the approximate latitude and longitude of Lexington; a calendar of days and the risings and settings of the moon and the sun; and miscellaneous sections of anniversaries, pithy observations, and anecdotes.

The *Kentucky Almanac* was not long without a rival. Joseph Charless of Philadelphia, who moved west to establish a printing office and bookstore in 1803, published *Charless' Kentucky, Tennessee, and Ohio Almanac* in Lexington in 1805 and 1806. This publication not only contained the standard astronomical information, but was also a Lexington directory of court sessions.

In 1814 William Worsely printed and sold the first issue of the *Kentucky Farmers' Almanac*, by far the most important of the Kentucky almanacs. Each page in later issues quoted a folk proverb, and the information sections covered agriculture, literature, travel, politics, medical advice, and anecdotes. One issue in the early 1850s contained an accurate table of the landmarks and travel distances on the Oregon Trail. This almanac ceased publication in 1865.

After the Civil War the old-style Kentucky almanac with its astronomical tables and folksy data gave way to almanacs published by the patent medicine industry and a flood of travel guides. Once agricultural societies began publishing journals, their publications supplanted almanacs as guides to farming.

See Charles R. Staples, *The History of Pioneer Lexington, 1779-1806* (Lexington, Ky., 1939).   THOMAS D. CLARK

ALTSHELER, JOSEPH ALEXANDER. Joseph Alexander Altsheler, author of popular boys' books, was born on April 29, 1862. His father, Joseph, had come to Three Springs, Kentucky, from Bergen on the Rhine in Germany in 1849 and had married Lucy Curd Snoddy of Glasgow, Kentucky, in 1853. They built a red brick home and general store in what is now Metcalfe County. Altsheler and his brothers helped in the store as well as with crops, but young Altsheler was more interested in books and tales of travels. He graduated from Liberty College in Glasgow in 1880 and entered Vanderbilt University in Tennessee with scholarships in Latin and Greek. His father's death forced him to leave college for employment in Louisville in 1882.

He worked briefly as a clerk at John P. Morton Bookshop, then joined the *Louisville Courier-Journal* as a reporter, city editor, and editorial writer. He left in 1892 to become a feature writer for the *New York World*.

In 1900 Altsheler was named editor of the *World*'s magazine section, a position he held until his death. Altsheler also wrote historical fiction for teenage boys. D. Appleton & Company published forty-one of Altsheler's books, most of them in series based on the major historical events during the exploration, founding, and development of America. *The Young Trailers* series was the most popular and reflected the author's love of Daniel Boone's country.

In 1888 Altsheler married Sallie Boles, of Glasgow; they had one son, Sydney. After several years of poor health, Altsheler died on June 5, 1919, and was buried in Louisville's Cave Hill Cemetery. The *New York Times* obituary observed that a poll of large libraries had shown Altsheler to be the most popular writer of boys' books in the nation.

See Ora Belle Demaree, "Joseph A. Altsheler: His Contribution to American History for Boys," M.A. thesis, University of Louisville, 1938; Annie Carroll Moore, "Joseph A. Altsheler and American History," *Bookman* (Nov. 1918): 469-76.

LUCY BRENT SLATER

AMERICAN PRINTING HOUSE FOR THE BLIND. The American Printing House for the Blind was founded in Louisville in 1858 as an extension of the KENTUCKY SCHOOL FOR THE BLIND. When Kentucky in 1842 became the third state in the country to establish such a public school for the blind, its founders recognized the need to print its own materials. The efficiency to be gained by a central printing house for all public schools for the blind led the Kentucky General Assembly to establish the American Printing House for the Blind as a private, nonprofit institution. The founding board members were James Guthrie, a prominent lawyer who was president of the printing house in its first eleven years; William F. Bullock, founder of the Kentucky School for the Blind; Dr. Theodore S. Bell, medical professor at the University of Louisville; and Bryce M. Patten, first superintendent of both the School for the Blind and the American Printing House.

The printing house initially operated within the school itself; funding was expected from other southern states, but in the end they remanded their donations for their own schools. Between 1860 and 1865, funding came from Kentucky citizens. The school was commandeered as a Union hospital during the Civil War; nevertheless, a printing press was purchased, and in 1866 the first book for the blind was published. Nine years later, the state legislature voted to donate five dollars to the printing house for every student at the school, funds that were used to erect the main building of the printing house on the school property on Frankfort Avenue. Contributions came from across the country. Another source of funds was the National Association for Publishing Literary and Musical Works for the Blind, which joined the printing house in May 1871. Grants from the U.S. Congress, which began in 1879, were increased periodically, and the American Printing House became the world's largest manufacturer of materials for the education of the blind. By the early twentieth century it was not only producing books in braille but was also manufacturing writing utensils, mathematical aids, and phonograph recordings of books. In 1928 the printing house began reproducing each edition of *Reader's Digest* in "talking book" form and in 1959 it made *Newsweek* available in this format. Other magazines were soon reproduced as recordings. By 1960 the American Printing House had joined with IBM Corporation to computerize its braille printing; it also established printing operations around the world to serve the blind.

See William C. Dabney, "American Printing House for the Blind, Inc. (1858-1961)," *FCHQ* 36 (1962): 5-17.

AMERICAN PROTECTIVE ASSOCIATION. The American Protective Association (APA), a secret, anti-Catholic, nativistic organization, was founded in Clinton, Iowa, in March 1887, by Henry F. Bowers. Nativism and anti-Catholicism grew during the last quarter of the nineteenth century. At that time, a large influx of immigrants, many of them Roman Catholics from southern and eastern Europe, settled in urban areas along the Ohio River. Strongest in the Midwest, the APA spread throughout the United States and reached Kentucky by 1890. During the 1890s, the APA was the most prominent nativist organization and the term APA was applied to any anti-Catholic activity. The panic of 1893 heightened antagonism over economic competition between native-born Kentuckians and immigrants. Membership in the APA was restricted to males (although women's auxiliary groups were formed) but did not exclude blacks, a policy that limited its growth in the South.

The APA used existing political parties, especially the Republican party, to propagate its policies through law. Its statement of purpose included promotion of nonsectarian schools and exclusion of Catholic teachers.

The number of APA members nationwide is unknown. Membership in Kentucky was an estimated 20,000 to 30,000, strongest in Louisville, where two APA newspapers, *Freedom's Banner* and *Justice*, circulated. In 1891 Louisville's APA dominated the city council and attempted to change the names of streets named for saints. They succeeded in appointing an APA physician and head nurse to a city hospital where the Sisters of Charity did volunteer nursing, thus causing the nuns to resign. In 1894 the APA was instrumental in Walter Evans's defeat of Irish Catholic Edward J. McDermott in the congressional election. APA influence was also felt in Covington, Ashland, Frankfort, and Paducah. In Frankfort in 1895, Charles Weitzel was not allowed by the APA-controlled Republican party to run for local office because of his religious affiliation; three APA members were placed on the ticket. In Paducah, the APA moved into power in the Democratic party. In 1897 the APA dominated the school board in Stanford, Kentucky, which fired five Roman Catholic teachers. In the gubernatorial election of 1895, it endorsed Republican candidate William O. Bradley, who quietly supported the APA, more for political gain than ideological reasons, and who was supported by many Democrats sympathetic to APA. Bradley won the election by a narrow margin, 172,436 to 163,524.

APA influence reached its peak both in Kentucky and nationally between 1893 and 1896. It split in 1896 over presidential candidate William McKinley, and membership had rapidly dwindled by 1900. It ended as a national organization in 1911.

See John E. Wiltz, "APA-ism in Kentucky and Elsewhere," *Register* 56 (April 1958): 143-55.

AMERICAN SADDLEBRED HORSE ASSOCIATION. The American Saddlebred Horse Association, the first horse breed association in the United States, was founded in Louisville in 1891 as the National Saddle Horse Breeders Association. The rules for registration required that a horse perform five distinct gaits or be traceable to recognized bloodlines. The first registry volume was published in 1892. Initially, seventeen stallions were designated foundation sires. In 1908 the thoroughbred stallion Denmark, foaled in 1839, was named the single foundation sire because more than 60 percent of the horses in the first four volumes of the registry were directly traced by male line to him.

Gen. John B. CASTLEMAN was the first president of the association, and Col. I.B. Nall was secretary and registrar. Castleman resigned the presidency in 1895 in a dispute with some of the stockholders, nonhorsemen who wanted a dividend. Will Gaines succeeded him and paid off the disgruntled stockholders, but the settlement left the association too short of funds to publish another registry volume until 1900. Castleman reassumed office in 1897. In 1899 the group's name was changed to American Saddle Horse Breeders Association. In 1908 the annual election was disputed and two groups claimed victory. Mat S. Cohen, a professional horseman and later Kentucky commissioner of agriculture, led the dissidents. The Jefferson County circuit court found in favor of the established officers and directors. The next year the Missouri Saddle Horse Breeders Association threatened to bolt, charging that policies favored Kentucky breeders and were biased against the interests of other states. Castleman journeyed to Mexico, Missouri, where he made an impassioned speech that kept the organization intact.

Claude M. Thomas succeeded Castleman as president in 1918. Allie G. Jones assumed the presidency when Thomas died in 1936, and Jones in turn was followed by Thomas W. Wilson in 1948, William B. Belknap in 1958, and Thomas J. Morton, Jr., in 1979. The biggest changes in the history of the association came about with the election of James W. Aikman of Indianapolis to the presidency in 1980. The corporate structure was changed to open membership, breed promotion became a responsibility, and the name was changed to American Saddlebred Horse Association (ASHA), to describe the animal and to encompass all saddlebred enthusiasts. In 1984 Judith Werner became the first woman in the United States to head a major horse breed association when she became president of ASHA.

In 1985 ASHA moved its headquarters to the American Saddle Horse Museum at the Kentucky Horse Park in Lexington. According to a survey by the Chamber of Commerce, the museum is Lexington's second leading tourist attraction, after the Horse Park itself. Chartered as a charitable, nonprofit corporation in 1962, the American Saddle Horse Museum was first located in the carriage house at Spindletop Farm outside Lexington, then moved to downtown Louisville, and to the Kentucky Horse Park in 1986. The multimillion-dollar facility is a state-of-the-art museum dedicated to the history and uses of the American saddlebred, considered by Kentucky its only native breed of horse. The highlight of the museum is a multi-image show. At the entrance to the museum is a heroic-sized statue marking the grave of the stallion Supreme Sultan.   LYNN P. WEATHERMAN

AMERICAN SYSTEM. The heightened spirit of nationalism that arose during the War of 1812 with Britain motivated an elaborate plan by Henry CLAY for developing a profitable home market. He called his program the American System. It was to include a protective tariff behind which northeastern manufacturing would flourish; revenues obtained from the tariff would provide funds for canals and roads, particularly in the fast-developing West. Through these new conduits of transportation would flow foodstuffs and raw materials from the South and the West to the East and the North. A stream of manufactured goods would flow in the return direction.

New England's factory owners, who thought of the Atlantic as the font of their economic life, feared that a developed West would attract their own workers. Clay held that northeastern industrialists had no grounds to fear the consequences of internal improvements in the West. He argued that a populous West, joined to the Northeast by good roads, would provide an impressive domestic market for the manufactured goods of New England and the Middle Atlantic states. Clay proposed that revenues from western land sales pay the greater portion of the costs of internal improvements.

The weak link in Clay's plan was the South. Southerners had historically based their economic life on the export of tobacco or cotton to European markets and the easy import of European goods in exchange. A tariff would force them to sell cotton in American markets for lower prices and to pay higher prices for American manufactured goods. In the end, Clay had to be content with seeing only bits and pieces of his American System enacted by Congress. Many of his victories were limited or repealed when his political enemies captured Congress and the White House, yet the American System made Clay immensely popular and helped to secure his nomination for president on three occasions.

See Clement Eaton, *Henry Clay and the Art of American Politics* (Boston 1957).

DENVER FUGATE

AMES BUGGY COMPANY. Ames Buggy Company, organized in Owensboro, Kentucky, in 1887 by Frederic A. Ames of Washington, Pennsylvania, had become the largest privately owned buggy manufacturer in the nation by 1905. The factory employed 250 workers, with peak output of 125 buggies daily, some of them destined for Germany, South Africa, the West Indies, and parts of Latin America. Ames Buggy manufactured forty specific types and styles of passenger vehicles, many with silver and gold trim. During the period 1910-20 it built the Ames automobile, and from 1915 to 1925 it made bodies for Ford Model T vehicles. In 1922 Ames Buggy entered the furniture business and eventually was sold to Whitehall Furniture, Owensboro.   LEE A. DEW

ANDERSON, CHARLES W., JR. Charles W. Anderson, Jr., lawyer and legislator, was born May 26, 1907, in Louisville, the son of Dr. Charles W. and Tabetha (Murphy) Anderson. He attended what is now Kentucky State University. He earned a bachelor's degree from Ohio's Wilberforce University (1927) and a law degree from Howard University (1931) and was admitted to the Kentucky bar in 1933. Howard awarded him a doctor of laws degree in 1936. Having established a Louisville legal practice, Anderson quickly won election to the Kentucky House in 1935. For the next twelve years he fought for desegregation of public facilities and equality of opportunity for blacks. Because Kentucky law excluded blacks from the state's professional colleges, he successfully proposed the Anderson-Mayer State Aid Act, requiring the legislature to appropriate funds, initially $7,500 a year, to assist Kentucky blacks studying in other states (originally funded at $175 per student per year). Although other civil rights issues went unresolved during his legislative tenure, Anderson's gains included a law allowing public school teachers (white and black) to marry and retain their teaching positions; enhanced rural high school educational facilities for students of both races; and the requirement that counties lacking high schools grant a minimum of $100 for annual tuition and transportation to each student forced to seek a diploma in another county. He is credited, too, with repeal of Kentucky's public hanging law.

Anderson's service on the city-county Republican party policy committee (1935-58) was rewarded by his 1949 nomination for judge of the 3d Municipal Court. In the general election, he was narrowly defeated. A decade later President Dwight D. Eisenhower appointed him an alternate delegate to the United Nations. Anderson, a Methodist leader (Quinn Chapel), served two terms (beginning in 1943) as president of the National Negro Bar Association. He received the Lincoln Institute Key (1940) for outstanding service to blacks and an honorary LL.D. from Wilberforce (1947), and was elected president of the Louisville National Association for the Advancement of Colored People. Gov. A.B. Chandler (1955-59) awarded a Kentucky

Colonel's commission to Anderson, the first black to receive this honorary designation. In May 1946 he was named an assistant commonwealth's attorney for the 30th Judicial District.

Anderson died in Shelbyville in a car-train accident on June 14, 1960. He was survived by his second wife, Victoria McCall Anderson, and their two children, Charles III and Victoria.

See John Benjamin Horton, *Not Without A Struggle* (New York 1979).   THOMAS H. SYVERTSEN

ANDERSON, LUCIAN. Lucian Anderson, a U.S. congressman, was born in Mayfield, Kentucky, on June 23, 1824, to John and Nancy (Davenport) Anderson. A lawyer, Anderson served as Graves County attorney, as a Kentucky state representative (1855-57), and as a Whig presidential elector in 1852. Elected as the Unconditional Unionist candidate from the 1st District in 1863, he served in the U.S. House of Representatives from March 4, 1863, to March 3, 1865. He was a delegate to the 1864 Republican National Convention, which renominated Abraham Lincoln. Anderson declined to run for a second congressional term.

Anderson married Ann R. Lockridge in 1846; the couple had nine children. Anderson died on October 18, 1898, and was buried in the family cemetery in Mayfield.

See James Larry Hood, "For the Union: Kentucky's Unconditional Unionist Congressmen and the Development of the Republican Party in Kentucky 1863-1865," *Register* 76 (July 1978): 197-215.   BERRY CRAIG

ANDERSON, MARY. Mary Anderson, Shakespearean actress, was born in Sacramento, California, on July 28, 1859, to Charles Henry and Marie Antoinette (Leugers) Anderson. The following year the family moved to Louisville. Anderson's father died in 1863 while serving in the Confederate army, and in 1867 her mother married Dr. Hamilton Griffin, a Louisville physician, whose love of Shakespeare influenced the developing theatrical ambitions of his stepdaughter. She attended Ursuline Academy and Presentation Academy in Louisville, but at fourteen she persuaded her mother to let her study at home—mainly by memorizing lines from her favorite plays. Despite opposition from her mother's strict Catholic family, Anderson's enthusiasm for the theater grew, particularly after Charlotte Cushman and John McCullough, two of the best-known actors of the day, encouraged her.

At sixteen—with only two days' notice—Anderson made her debut as Juliet in Shakespeare's *Romeo and Juliet* at MACAULEY'S THEATRE at Fourth and Walnut streets in Louisville. On November 27, 1875, she launched a career that soon made her the toast of the American stage. When she retired fourteen years later, at age thirty, she had earned praise for her talent and beauty throughout the United States, Britain, and Ireland. Although she played many of the popular female roles of the nineteenth century stage, her favorites were

Shakespearean: Desdemona, Lady Macbeth, Rosalind, Perdita, and Juliet.

In March 1889 Anderson gave her final performance as Perdita in Shakespeare's *A Winter's Tale* in Washington, D.C. At the peak of her career she retired and sailed to England to recover from exhaustion. In June of 1890 she married Antonio de Navarro, a New Yorker living in England; the couple had two children, Maria Elena and José. She spent the remainder of her life in the small English village of Broadway, where she entertained friends including Henry James, Lord Tennyson, Sir James Barrie, Sir Edward Elgar, John Masefield, and A.E. Housman. Throughout her life she maintained close ties with her Louisville family and friends. She gave property she owned in Floyd Knobs, Indiana, for the Mount St. Francis Seminary—now the Mary Anderson Center for the Arts. She died in Broadway, Worcestershire, England, on May 30, 1940, and was buried there.

See Mary Anderson, *A Few Memories* (New York 1896).   WADE HALL

ANDERSON, RICHARD CLOUGH. Richard Clough Anderson, Revolutionary War officer and Kentucky land surveyor, was born at Goldmine, Hanover County, Virginia, on January 12, 1750, the son of Robert and Elizabeth (Clough) Anderson. He was a charter member of the Society of the Cincinnati, founded in June 1783 at Fishkill, New York, for officers of the Continental Army. A lieutenant colonel in the Continental army, Anderson was wounded in the Battles of Trenton and Savannah. Anderson came to Kentucky in 1784 and lived in Jefferson County for the rest of his life, as chief surveyor of the lands allotted to Virginia patriots. He was a delegate to the Kentucky convention of 1788, and a presidential elector in 1793. He became the first master of Lexington Masonic Lodge No. 25 in 1788. Anderson married Elizabeth Clark in 1787; they had one son and three daughters. Elizabeth died in 1795 and in 1797 he married Ann Marshall; they had eight sons and four daughters. Anderson died on October 16, 1826, and was buried in the family cemetery on Hurstbourne Lane in Louisville.

See Edward Lowell Anderson, *Soldier and Pioneer: A Biographical Sketch of Lt.-Col. Richard C. Anderson of the Continental Army* (New York 1879); W.P. Anderson, *Anderson Family Records* (Cincinnati 1936).   CHARLES SNOW GUTHRIE

ANDERSON, RICHARD CLOUGH, JR. Richard Clough Anderson, Jr., legislator and diplomat after whom Anderson County was named, was born on August 4, 1788, at Soldier's Retreat in Jefferson County, Kentucky, to Richard Clough ANDERSON and Elizabeth (Clark) Anderson. He was a graduate of William and Mary College. After studying law in Virginia, Anderson practiced law in Louisville and served in the Kentucky legislature in 1815. He was then elected to two terms in the U.S. House of Representatives (1817-21), where he chaired the

Committee on Public Lands. He was returned to the Kentucky legislature in 1821 and chosen Speaker of the House in 1822. Anderson was appointed U.S. minister plenipotentiary to Colombia on January 27, 1823, and in 1826 he was confirmed as a delegate to the Panama Congress of Nations. While on his way to Cartagena, he died of yellow fever on July 24, 1826, in Turbaco, Panama.

Anderson married Elizabeth Gwathmey in 1810; they had three daughters and one son. Anderson was buried in the family cemetery on Hurstbourne Lane in Jefferson County.

See Alfred Tischendorf and E. Taylor Parks, eds., *The Diary and Journal of Richard Clough Anderson, Jr., 1814-1826* (Durham, N.C., 1964).
                                          CHARLES SNOW GUTHRIE

ANDERSON, ROBERT. Robert Anderson, the commander of Fort Sumter in Charleston harbor at the outbreak of the Civil War, was born in eastern Jefferson County, Kentucky, on June 14, 1805, at his family's plantation, Soldier's Retreat. His parents were Richard Clough ANDERSON, a Revolutionary War officer, and Sarah (Marshall) Anderson. An 1825 graduate of the U.S. Military Academy at West Point, Anderson served in the Black Hawk War (1832) and the Seminole War (1837-38). In the Mexican War (1846-48), he was wounded and breveted major.

In December 1860, when South Carolina seceded, Major Anderson was sent to Charleston to command the island forts in the harbor. Anticipating attack, he moved his seventy-man command from Fort Moultrie to Fort Sumter as more defensible. There they held out for nearly four months without supply shipments from the North. On April 11, 1861, after word that the newly installed Lincoln administration was sending a shipload of provisions, the Confederate army in Charleston demanded Anderson's surrender. He refused and the bombardment of Fort Sumter began on April 12. After thirty-four hours of almost continuous shelling, when food supplies had reached the vanishing point, Anderson surrendered to Gen. P.G.T. Beauregard, and his command was evacuated by ship to New York. Anderson immediately became a hero in the North. Commissioned a brigadier general, he was placed in charge of recruiting Union troops in Kentucky, but ill health forced him to retire from active duty in October 1861.

Anderson married Eliza Bayard Clinch of Georgia in 1845; they had four children: Robert, Eba, Maria, and Sophie. Anderson died in Nice, France, October 26, 1871, and was buried at West Point.

See Eba Anderson Lawton, *An Artillery Officer in the Mexican War, 1846-47: Letters of Robert Anderson* (New York 1911); Thomas McArthur Anderson, *Monograph of the Anderson, Clark, Marshall and McArthur Connection* (n.p., 1908).
                                          GEORGE H. YATER

ANDERSON, ROBERT BALL. Robert Ball Anderson, farmer and Civil War volunteer, was born a slave on March 1, 1843, in Greensburg, Kentucky. He was a field hand on the property of Robert Ball when the Civil War began. In 1864 Anderson fled behind Union lines and enlisted in the U.S. Army. His unit, the 125th Colored Infantry, was training for combat when the war ended; he spent the remainder of his three-year enlistment at military posts in the Southwest.

Following his discharge at Louisville, he went west, eventually acquiring an eighty-acre farm in Butler County in eastern Nebraska. Poor economic conditions caused Anderson to move on to the panhandle of western Nebraska, where he obtained a quarter section of land under the provisions of the 1873 Timber Culture Act. In 1922, at the age of seventy-nine, he married twenty-one-year-old Daisy Graham. She encouraged him to write his memoirs, which were published in 1927. Anderson died in an automobile accident near Lincoln, Nebraska, on December 3, 1931. At the time of his death, his 2,080 acres made him the largest landowner among blacks in the state. He was buried at Hemingford, Nebraska.

See Robert Anderson, *From Slavery to Affluence: Memoirs of Robert Anderson, Ex-Slave*, 2d ed. (Steamboat Springs, Colo., 1967); Darold D. Wax, "Robert Ball Anderson, A Kentucky Slave, 1843-1864," *Register* 81 (Summer 1983): 255-73.

DAROLD D. WAX

ANDERSON COUNTY. Anderson County, the eighty-second county in order of formation, is located in the Bluegrass region of central Kentucky. The county is bounded by Spencer, Shelby, Franklin, Woodford, Nelson, Mercer, and Washington counties and covers 204 square miles. LAWRENCE-BURG, incorporated in 1820 as Lawrence, is the county seat. Most of the area is rolling hills. The most rugged terrain is near the Kentucky River, which borders the county on the east. The other major waterway is the Salt River, which flows north and then west through the county's center. There are deposits of limestone, clay, sand, and gravel in the county. A variety of agricultural commodities are produced, including burley tobacco and livestock. The county was established on January 16, 1827, from parts of Franklin, Washington, and Mercer counties. It was named for Richard Clough Anderson, Jr., a Kentucky legislator, U.S. congressman, and minister to Colombia.

What later became Anderson County was settled in the late 1770s and early 1780s. Many of the early settlers had spent time at James Harrod's Fort (now Harrodsburg) and had come north to take up land claims. Among them were Richard Benson, Nathan Hammond, William Brayer, and Thomas Baker. Jacob Kaufman (or Coffman), a German immigrant, established Kaufman's Station around 1780. He owned 1,400 acres on the future site of Lawrenceburg. Another early settlement was John Arnold's Station, built around 1783 on the Kentucky River just above the mouth of the Little Benson Creek. In 1798 the Salt River Baptist Church was built two miles south of Lawrenceburg. Its first pastor was John Penney, great-grandfather of J.C. Penney, who founded the chain of retail stores.

A network of trails connecting the pioneer settlements, which came together at Kaufman's Station, later developed into a road system that made Lawrenceburg the dominant city in the county. Trails led northward to settlements that became Frankfort and Shelbyville, southward to Harrodsburg, west to Bardstown, and east to where the Woodford Road forded the Kentucky River and connected with Lexington. Beginning in the 1830s, some of the county's roads were improved to turnpikes. Hemp, tobacco, and corn were important early crops, and distilling became a major local industry. Bond's Mill was erected in 1831 on Salt River and operated on that site until well into the twentieth century. In 1833 a cholera epidemic killed eighty-nine residents of the county.

During the Mexican War (1846-48), Anderson County furnished Company C, 2d Kentucky Infantry Regiment, known as the Salt River Tigers. Led by Capt. John H. McBrayer, it fought at the Battle of Buena Vista. During the Civil War, approximately four hundred county residents fought for the Confederacy, and two hundred entered the Union army. On October 8, 1862, while the Battle of Perryville was being fought to the south, some of Maj. Jones M. Withers's Confederates skirmished with a rear-guard Union force under the command of Gen. J.W. Sill near Fox Creek, five miles west of Lawrenceburg. The next day, the battle-weary Confederate army of Maj. Gen. Edmund Kirby-Smith encamped at McCall's Spring near the Mercer County line before withdrawing from Kentucky. In the later years of the war, there were numerous skirmishes in the county between partisan guerrillas and local Union Home Guard units.

A boon to the county's prosperity was the coming of the Southern Railway (now Norfolk Southern) to Anderson County in 1888. With the completion of Young's High Bridge over the Kentucky River at Tyrone, Anderson County was connected by rail with Louisville and Lexington. The cantilever bridge was named for Col. Bennett H. Young, a former Confederate officer and Louisville railroad promoter. The bridge and the railroad helped to speed Anderson County's best known product, bourbon whiskey, to market. Among the larger distilleries was one operated at Tyrone by the Ripy family (now Boulevard Distillers) and one on Salt River at Bond's Mill (now Joseph E. Seagram's and Son).

The Eighteenth Amendment to the U.S. Constitution, which prohibited the production and sale of distilled spirits, had a drastic effect upon the local economy. Tyrone, especially hard-hit, declined from an incorporated town of more than nine hundred to a quiet unincorporated village along the river. Although the distillery reopened after the end of prohibition in 1933, the town never regained its size.

The economy of Anderson County is based on industry centered around Lawrenceburg and on agriculture. Many county residents commute north to state government jobs in Frankfort. The Bluegrass Parkway, which provides rapid access to Versailles and Lexington, made the county one of the fastest-growing areas in the Bluegrass region during the 1980s. The population of the county was 9,358 in 1970; 12,567 in 1980; and 14,571 in 1990.

See Lewis W. McKee and Lydia K. Bond, *A History of Anderson County* (Frankfort, Ky., 1936).

ANSHUTZ, THOMAS POLLOCK. Thomas Pollock Anshutz, painter and teacher, was born October 5, 1851, in Newport, Kentucky, to Jacob and Jane Abigail (Pollock) Anshutz. In 1868 his family moved to Wheeling, West Virginia. Anshutz studied art at the National Academy of Design in New York City (1872-75); under Thomas Eakins at the Pennsylvania Academy of Fine Arts until 1881; and in Paris at the Académie Julien. He succeeded Eakins as teacher of painting at the Pennsylvania Academy in 1896 and became head of the faculty there in 1909. Among Anshutz's pupils were John Sloan, John Marin, and Charles Demuth. His landscape *On The Ohio* is based on boyhood memories and impressions of Kentucky. Anshutz was a member of the Philadelphia Water Color Club and National Academy of Design. In September 1892 Anshutz married Effie Schriver Russell of Wheeling, West Virginia. He died at his home in Fort Washington, Pennsylvania, on June 16, 1912.

ANTIEVOLUTION BILLS. Kentuckians who believed in the biblical account of creation opposed Charles Darwin's theory of evolution of organisms by natural selection, and by 1917 a movement had emerged to ban Darwinism from Kentucky schools. By the fall of 1921, many Protestant fundamentalists were calling for antievolution legislation to be adopted by the next General Assembly. Because Kentucky's was one of only six state legislatures that met in even-numbered years, it became the first battleground in one of America's most famous cultural clashes of the 1920s.

On January 23, 1922, Rep. George W. Ellis of Barren County introduced a bill listed in the House Journal index as the "Monkey Bill," which sought "to prohibit the teaching in public schools and other public institutions of learning, Darwinism, atheism, agnosticism or evolution as it pertains to the origin of man." Teachers who violated the ban would be subject to fines and/or jail sentences, and an offending institution would forfeit its charter and be fined up to $5,000. Two days later, in the other chamber, Sen. James R. Rash of Madisonville introduced a similar bill. The original Senate measure was tabled; one of three substitute bills was referred to the Rules Committee, where it died. After an emotional five-hour debate, the House voted on Ellis's bill on March 9. Passage required forty affirmative votes; the bill received only thirty-eight on the first roll call. Absentees were sought, and a second roll call produced forty affirmative votes. A recapitulation ended in a 41-41 tie, which Bryce Cundiff of Breathitt County broke in the negative. In later attempts, two antievolution bills and a resolution were defeated in the General Assembly in 1926, and the agitation ended in 1928, when the final bill on the subject was introduced too late in the session to be considered.

See Robert Halliburton, Jr., "Kentucky's Anti-Evolution Controversy," *Register* 66 (April 1968): 97-107; Frank L. McVey, *The Gates Open Slowly: A History of Education in Kentucky* (Lexington, Ky., 1949).   DOUGLAS E. HERMAN

ANTI-SEMITISM. Jewish families have lived in many Kentucky towns since the early nineteenth century. Between 1834 and 1850 the first significant numbers of Jewish families settled in Kentucky, especially in Louisville, Owensboro, Henderson, Madisonville, and the smaller towns of Hartford, Marion, Hickman, and Eddyville. There are, however, areas of the state—Appalachia in particular—where the residents have had little contact with Jews. Such lack of experience reinforces prejudicial stereotypes, as do lack of education, ignorance about religion in general, even Christian evangelistic misunderstanding. Nevertheless, cases of overt anti-Semitism have been rare in Kentucky. The Anti-Defamation League of B'nai B'rith in 1988 listed Kentucky fortieth among the fifty states in number of incidents of anti-Semitism, with only one recorded act of vandalism and only two assaults against individuals.

Although recorded instances of violence are rare, Kentucky has shown an undercurrent of anti-Semitism. As late as the 1920s some classified newspaper ads stated explicitly that Jews and Catholics need not apply. There were similar restrictions on property deeds, and many clubs excluded Jews. On December 17, 1862, Gen. Ulysses S. Grant issued an order expelling Jews from Kentucky, Tennessee, and Mississippi "as a class violating every regulation of trade established by the Treasury." Cesar Kaskel, a haberdasher from Paducah, was among those who personally protested to President Abraham Lincoln. Lincoln revoked the order in January 1863. In the mid-1920s George Colvin, president of University of Louisville, ended tenure for professors by offering one-year contracts. One of the leading opponents of this policy was Louis Gottschalk, who later became one of the nation's outstanding historians at the University of Chicago. There were charges of anti-Semitism when Gottschalk was fired rather than given a leave to teach for a year at the University of Chicago. The one Jewish member of the university's board of trustees, however, supported Colvin in his attempt to assert the power of the central administration over the faculty. Alumni said that the medical school at the University of Louisville had an unofficial 10 percent limit on admitting Jewish students. Louisville's Jewish Hospital was founded in 1905 because Jewish physicians were not admitted to the staffs of other hospitals.

Louisville elected Jerry Abramson in 1985 as its first Jewish mayor. He proved so popular that after the law had been changed to allow mayors to succeed themselves, the Republican party did not field a candidate and Abramson was reelected with minimal opposition.

The main organizations aligned to fight anti-Semitism in Kentucky are the Kentuckiana Interfaith Community, Kentucky Chapter of the National Conference of Christians and Jews, Anti-Defamation League of B'nai B'rith, the American Jewish Committee's Louisville chapter, and the Jewish Community Federation's Community Relations Council.

See Herman Landau, *Adath Louisville: The Story of a Jewish Community* (Louisville 1981); Dwayne Cox, "The Gottschalk-Colvin Case: A Study in Academic Purpose and Command," *Register* 85 (Winter 1987): 46-68.   HERMAN LANDAU

APPALACHIA. The Appalachian Mountains extend 1,600 miles from Quebec into northern Georgia and Alabama. The name Appalachia, however, is commonly applied only to the central and southern highlands, which extend for a distance of six hundred miles across a nine-state area. Appalachia includes the mountainous parts of Maryland, Virginia, Kentucky, North and South Carolina, Tennessee, Georgia, Alabama, and all of West Virginia, the only one of the nine states situated totally within the region.

The boundaries of Appalachia have been variously drawn. In 1894 William G. Frost, president of Berea College, designated 194 mountain counties in nine states as Appalachian America, and saw this region as Berea College's service area. In *The Southern Highlander and His Homeland* (1921), John C. Campbell identified as the Southern Highlands 254 counties in the same nine-state area. *The Southern Appalachian Region: A Survey* (1962), edited by Thomas R. Ford, a sociologist at the University of Kentucky, defines Appalachia as an area consisting of 190 mountain counties in seven states (Maryland and South Carolina are excluded). The Appalachian Regional Commission, established in 1965, expanded the definition of Appalachia to include 397 counties in thirteen states from New York to Mississippi, a region with a population of more than 21 million. In all these definitions, Appalachian Kentucky consists of forty-nine of the state's 120 counties, or the eastern third of the state.

No matter how its boundaries are drawn, Appalachia has always been a problem to those attempting to describe or interpret the region and its people. In 1921 John C. Campbell wrote that Appalachia was a region of America about which there was more misinformation than any other part of the country. Appalachia's inaccessibility and isolation from the rest of the country have been overemphasized, for example. Residents of the lowland South in fact visited the mountains throughout the pre–Civil War period. Tourism was a mountain industry from the time of George Washington and Berkley Springs. Travelers published numerous reports on the Appalachian region and its people, one of the best-known being Frederick Law Olmsted's *A Journey in the Back Country* (1860). William Barton

Rogers, founder and first president of the Massachusetts Institute of Technology, called attention to Appalachia's mineral resources in 1882, the same year the U.S. Geological Survey began to map the region.

Appalachia has been difficult to describe and interpret because the region is an American borderland characterized by diversity, complexity, and contradiction. It is not only a geological and geographical borderland, but also a historical borderland where wilderness and civilization met to form America's first and longest-lived frontier. The Appalachian Mountains shaped and impeded westward movement in America as did no other geographical influence on the continent. In the eighteenth century Appalachia became a political and cultural borderland, where aristocratic traditions of the Tidewater East met with egalitarian traditions of the frontier West. Appalachia was also an economic, ideological, and military borderland between the Union and Confederacy during the Civil War.

According to Henry Shapiro in *Appalachia on Our Mind* (1978), there is a basic misconception about Appalachia: the idea that "the mountainous portions of eight or nine southern states form a coherent region inhabited by a numerous population possessing a uniform culture." Since the mid-nineteenth century the idea of Appalachia has varied according to the needs, motives, and perspectives of abolitionists, social workers, missionaries of various Protestant denominations, local color writers, industries, and entrepreneurs. Abolitionists found allies in the mountain South in their struggle against the institution of slavery. After the Civil War, local color writers sought publishable quaintness in the highlands. During the same period, church leaders in the Northeast declared the Appalachian South a missionary field and by the 1920s had established over two hundred church-related schools in Appalachia.

Although the idea of Appalachia did not exist prior to the Civil War, a self-awareness on the part of people in the highland South predates the conflict. According to historian Carl Degler in *The Other South* (1974), the highlanders' sense of separateness and difference from the planter culture of the lowland South translated itself into strong Union sentiment as the Civil War approached, and thousands of whites from Appalachia served in the Union Army.

Topography and settlement patterns dictated by topography account for the complexity of social and economic conditions. Plantation culture, established in Virginia in the seventeenth century and based at first mainly on tobacco, expanded westward toward the Blue Ridge. For the most part small farmers, later immigrants tended to occupy the highlands. But the plantation culture also penetrated the highlands; the result was a mixed economic and social situation. Furthermore, the settlers were a diverse group described by one traveler as a "motley set of Germans, Irish, Scots and Anglo-Americans."

The presence in the upland South of both planters and new immigrants of diverse origins was of great significance to the course of American history. While each group lost something by contact with its neighbors, it also contributed something. This mix of cultures made Appalachia what the historian Thomas Jefferson Wertenbaker called "a test laboratory of American civilization" (*The Old South*, 1963).

The postbellum idea of Appalachia as a kind of separate South came to be well established during the next half-century. In *Human Geography of the South* (1935), Rupert Vance portrayed Appalachia as a distinct region of the South and of America, whose "significance is obscured by the fact that it is divided among eight different commonwealths," and whose area, were it brought together into one political unit, "would doubtless constitute America's one unique commonwealth."

However the boundaries are drawn, the definition of Appalachia appears to rest on a distinction between the upland and lowland South, or the upper South and the Deep South, a distinction now generally assumed. In a series of books inspired by John Gunther's *Inside U.S.A.*, Neil Peirce distinguishes between the Deep South and the border states, devoting separate volumes to each region. Forty years later, Peirce presents Vance's obscure mountainous zone as "the Border States' common territory and most unifying force." Since the late nineteenth century, the idea of Appalachia and the practice of designating the region's people as a distinct subset of the American population have gained increasing acceptance.

Perceptions of Appalachia differ sharply. One view is of a place of poverty, backwardness, problems, and peculiar people. Another is of a place of promise and a preserve of all those virtues and values that are, or should be, at the heart of American life. Some students of Appalachia have described the region as an economic colony where the people and natural resources have been exploited for the benefit of other parts of the country. Others see Appalachia as an American borderland, complex, diverse, with a mixed economy, culture, and political life. These varying perceptions can be found in the work of writers who have depicted the region and its people, from Mary Murfree (known by the pseudonym Charles Egbert Craddock) in the late nineteenth century to those twentieth century writers of both fiction and nonfiction concerned with Appalachian Kentucky: Elizabeth Madox Roberts, Jesse Stuart, Harriette Simpson Arnow, James Still, Cratis Williams, Harry Caudill, and others.

JIM WAYNE MILLER

APPALACHIAN COMPUTER SERVICES, INC.
Robert McReynolds founded Appalachian Computer Services, Inc., in Harlan, Kentucky, in 1965 to provide data processing services to three clients in the area. ACS has since relocated to London, Kentucky. The company faced lean years at first, but after 1978 it became the second fastest growing

corporation in Kentucky, averaging 31 percent annual growth. It has more than 2,500 employees at installations in California, Illinois, Nebraska, Texas, Vermont, and Jamaica. The company provides information management services to federal and state agencies as well as private enterprises; it secured a contract with the U.S. Justice Department to administer the Naturalization Service amnesty program. Late in 1988, First Financial Management Corporation of Atlanta acquired ACS.

ANTHONY A. MCINTIRE

APPALACHIAN REGIONAL COMMISSION.
President Lyndon B. Johnson signed the law that created the Appalachian Regional Commission (ARC) in 1965, fulfilling John F. Kennedy's promise in the 1960 West Virginia presidential primary to help solve the region's problems. Per capita income in Appalachian Kentucky in the early 1960s was less than half the national average; 57 percent of family incomes were below $3,000 (compared with a national average of 20 percent); only 17 percent over age twenty-five had at least four years of high school education. Besides eastern Kentucky, Appalachia as defined by the ARC includes all of West Virginia and parts of eleven other states. About 20 million live in the region's 397 counties, 9 million of them in rural areas.

By 1990, twenty-five years after it was created, ARC had spent $712 million in Kentucky's forty-nine Appalachian counties, including $517 million on 349.2 miles of highways and 13.2 miles of industrial access roads. The rest of the money went for health care, sewer and water lines, low-cost housing, vocational schools, airport facilities, childhood development, dropout prevention, and research and technical assistance. In the twenty-five-year period, the commission picked up about 18 percent of the administrative costs of its nine districts and spent about $7 billion in the entire Appalachian region.

The ARC's critics charge that it has been wasteful, overly responsive to courthouses and city halls dominated by politicians allied to the coal industry, and insensitive to environmentalists and community activists. The agency's friends—elected officials, and some business people and educators—say it has made investments in the infrastructure essential for progress. The road-building program alone justified the cost, they claim. Under the commission's "first dollar" policy, poor communities may use the money it dispenses to help qualify for other federal aid programs. In other words, each one of the commission's dollars becomes a magnet to draw three to four dollars more from other Washington sources.

Under the presidency of Ronald Reagan, starting in 1980, the commission's aid to Appalachia dropped sharply. The $1.2 billion that Congress gave the commission between 1981 and 1988 was 44 percent less than during 1974-80. When Reagan went back to his California ranch in 1989, however, the agency was still in business, rescued by a coalition of politicians from the mountains and Deep South.

See *Appalachia, Journal of the Appalachian Regional Commission* 18 (March 1985); Stuart Seely Sprague, *ARC from Implementation to Payoff Decade and Beyond* (Morehead, Ky., 1986).

AL SMITH

APPALACHIAN VOLUNTEERS. Founded in 1963 under the auspices of the Council of the Southern Mountains, the Appalachian Volunteers was a major force in eastern Kentucky during the War on Poverty. Originally a self-help operation, the organization recruited college students from schools in the region to take part in community improvement projects. The first school improvement project took place in Harlan County in January 1964. Projects included physical improvements to mountain schoolhouses and curriculum enhancement through such activities as science demonstrations and talks by foreign exchange students. With federal funds the Council of the Southern Mountains expanded the Appalachian Volunteers, which had operated initially during weekends and school vacations, into a year-round program. The small, mostly volunteer staff was succeeded by paid professionals conducting long-term community action projects.

In 1966 the Appalachian Volunteers split from its parent organization and became an independent corporation. It abandoned the council's apolitical stance and focused on controversial issues, attacking coal companies and local power structures and turning county, state, and federal governments against it. Officials in Pike County arrested an Appalachian Volunteer worker on August 11, 1967, and charged him with sedition. Though the law under which he was indicted was ultimately declared unconstitutional by a federal district court ruling that federal courts had exclusive jurisdiction in such matters, the case seriously hurt the effectiveness of the organization. A hearing in Pikeville by the Kentucky State Un-American Activities Committee, formed by the state legislature on March 27, 1968, did irreparable damage. Gov. Louie Nunn (1967-71) rejected a grant request on February 25, 1969, and the Appalachian Volunteers closed down in 1970 for lack of funds.

See David E. Whisnant, *Modernizing The Mountaineer* (Boone, North Carolina 1980).

THOMAS J. KIFFMEYER

APPALSHOP. Appalshop, a worker-operated arts and education center in Whitesburg, Kentucky, is dedicated to documenting and preserving cultural traditions and improving the understanding of social and economic issues in Appalachia. It was founded in 1969 as the Community Film Workshop of Appalachia, a federal War on Poverty program to teach vocational skills to poor and minority youth. The first students, who made films and television programs about local people and issues, were joined by other young people from eastern Kentucky and western Virginia who added art forms like storytelling and music. The operations have grown to include Appalshop Films, Roadside Theater, Headwaters Television, June Appal Records, WMMT-FM radio, and a variety of educational programs.

An ongoing film history examines the development of stereotypes about Appalachian residents, migration into and out of the region, and the area's economic development. Headwaters Television programs focus on how individuals and groups in the region deal with such issues as the environment, work, education, and social justice. Roadside Theater's plays are based on regional oral history and storytelling traditions. Records and radio preserve the work of traditional mountain musicians and present the best young artists. Appalshop films, television, plays, and music are presented throughout the nation and around the world. In 1990 Appalshop won the Alfred I. du Pont Award for Broadcast Journalism from Columbia University.

JUDI JENNINGS

ARCARO, GEORGE EDWARD. The jockey that *Sports Illustrated* called the most famous man to ride a horse since Paul Revere, George Edward ("Eddie") Arcaro is the winner of 4,779 races, including five Kentucky Derbies and two Triple Crowns. He was born on February 19, 1916, in Cincinnati, the son of Pasquale and Josephine (Giancola) Arcaro. He grew up in Covington, Kentucky, and at age fourteen began riding thoroughbreds as an exercise boy at the old Latonia Race Track in northern Kentucky. On May 18, 1931, at Bainbridge Park near Cleveland, he rode his first race and forty-five races later, on January 14, 1932, at Caliente, Mexico, he won for the first time. Arcaro won his first Kentucky Derby in 1938 riding Lawrin, then in 1941 on Whirlaway, in 1945 on Hoop Jr., in 1948 on Citation, and in 1952 on Hill Gail. His Triple Crown victories came with Whirlaway and Citation. During his career as a jockey (1931-63), Arcaro rode 24,092 mounts, finished in the money 11,888 times, posted 554 stakes victories, and won $30,039,543 in purses. He was inducted into the Jockey's Hall of Fame at Pimlico in 1955 and the National Museum of Racing Hall of Fame in 1958. After retiring, he and Ruth, his wife since 1937, moved to Miami, where he does race consulting and commentary. His wife died in 1988, survived by their two children, Carolyn and Robert.

See Eddie Arcaro, *I Ride to Win* (New York 1951).

ARCHAEOLOGY. Early European settlers in Kentucky believed that mounds and other archaeological remains they observed were not built by the "savage Indians" who regularly harassed them, but by "white Indians" who were possibly descendants of the Lost Tribes of Israel, the Egyptians, or the Romans. Collectively, these groups were referred to as the Mound Builders. It was only through the exhaustive efforts of archaeologists that these myths about the Kentucky Indians and their prehistoric forebears were finally dismissed.

By the mid-nineteenth century, emphasis was placed on describing and classifying some of the more interesting archaeological materials found in the New World. *Ancient History, or Annals of Kentucky* (1824), by Constantine Rafinesque, a professor at Transylvania University in Lexington, described archaeological sites that he had visited in forty-one Kentucky counties. The first professional archaeological investigation in Kentucky was part of an extensive study by E.G. Squier and E.H. Davis, under the auspices of the Smithsonian Institution, of major archaeological sites in the Ohio and Mississippi valleys. They produced detailed maps of many of Kentucky's mounds and earthworks previously reported by Rafinesque. Many of these sites were later destroyed by crop cultivation or by urban expansion, so these drawings are the only surviving record of the once large and impressive sites.

Many archaeological sites were reported first by geologists conducting surveys of the state. This information, much of which was collected between 1854 and 1885, still serves as an important source for archaeologists. In a letter written to the Smithsonian Institution in 1881, William Linney identified thirty-seven archaeological sites in Boyle and Mercer counties.

During the 1880s and 1890s Cyrus Thomas of the Smithsonian Institution's Bureau of Ethnology recorded hundreds of mounds scattered throughout the eastern United States, including many in Kentucky. Although at first a believer in the Mound Builder hypothesis, Thomas gradually changed his ideas. By the 1890s he was one of the leading proponents of the idea that the ancestors of living Native Americans had built the mounds. (See PREHISTORIC PEOPLES.) Although this proposition was accepted by archaeologists rather quickly, the term Mound Builders is still used by some nonprofessionals when referring to Kentucky's prehistoric inhabitants.

In the first quarter of the twentieth century, many archaeological sites were described in Union, Barren, Allen, Edmonson, Boyle, Mercer, Hopkins, and other Kentucky counties. Harlan I. Smith's 1910 publication on Fox Farm Village in Mason County was the first professional archaeological report on a Kentucky site. Smith classified the artifacts according to the activities for which they were used, then compared them with artifacts found at other sites. During much of the early twentieth century, archaeologists attempted to determine the age of cultures and materials they had defined and described during the preceding eighty years. In Kentucky their attention focused on the large shell mounds, consisting of deep deposits of mussel shell and artifacts, found along the Green River in Butler, Ohio, Henderson, McLean, and Edmonson

counties. At least ten of the Green River shell mounds were investigated by Clarence B. Moore. Moore's 1916 publication on the Green River sites, the first widely distributed report on a Kentucky site, contained many photographs and drawings of the shell mounds and their artifacts.

In 1917 Nels C. Nelson reported on his excavations at Mammoth Cave and other caves in the Edmonson County vicinity. This study was one of the first to use stratigraphy in archaeology. Nelson recognized the remains of a culture that was less complex than the widely known agriculture-based groups of the Late Prehistoric period. He proposed that the earlier groups subsisted on naturally available foods and that the later group evolved from the earlier one. Nelson's description of this hunter-gatherer way of life appears to be the first mention of what is now known as the Archaic tradition.

Two men who exerted a profound influence on Kentucky archaeology were University of Kentucky professors William S. Webb and William D. Funkhouser. Webb was professor of physics during the 1920s; Funkhouser was a professor of zoology. Both had keen interest in Kentucky archaeology, and when the University of Kentucky established the Department of Anthropology and Archaeology in 1927, they were appointed professors in the new department. In 1928 Funkhouser and Webb published *Ancient Life in Kentucky*, summarizing Kentucky prehistory. During the late 1920s and early 1930s, Webb and Funkhouser visited numerous Kentucky archaeological sites and published several reports on what they found. Much of this effort focused on Green River shell mounds, eastern Kentucky rockshelters, and central Kentucky Adena mounds and enclosures. Their *Archaeological Survey of Kentucky* (1932) was the first compilation of Kentucky archaeological sites.

The economic and social consequences of the Great Depression were devastating in Kentucky, but a combination of events during that time served to benefit archaeology. In 1935 the U.S. Congress passed the Emergency Relief Act, and the Works Progress Administration (WPA) was established to create jobs for the unemployed. The large pool of unemployed Kentucky workers, the newly established University of Kentucky Department of Anthropology and Archaeology, and the labor-intensive nature of archaeology made excavations of archaeological sites excellent projects for the newly established federal relief program. For the first time, large-scale excavation of sites was possible using standard field and laboratory techniques under the direction of professional archaeologists. Within a few years, Webb and his colleagues had investigated dozens of sites and accumulated thousands of artifacts, drawings, excavation forms, and photographs. Some of the more famous of these were Indian Knoll (Ohio County), the Wright Mound (Montgomery County), Jonathan Creek Village (Marshall County), McLeod Bluff (Hickman County), and the Robbins Mound (Boone County).

World War II brought this period of intensive field-work to an end. In many cases, artifacts were not processed and reports not written until many years after the war's end. The tempo of Kentucky archaeology has never returned to the furious pace of the 1930s.

Archaeological research after World War II was greatly influenced by the intensive activity of the preceding decade. Drawing on the great volume of new information that had accumulated, Webb and Charles E. Snow wrote *The Adena People* (1945), a synthesis of Adena culture based on a comparison of the traits of the many Adena mounds and artifacts excavated in Kentucky and surrounding states. A year later, Webb's *Indian Knoll* summarized ten years of shell mound excavations. The development of radiocarbon, or C-14, dating in the early 1950s made these syntheses easier. Dates produced by this new technique indicated that many of the excavated sites were thousands of years older than originally thought. The realization of the true length of the prehistoric period provided a new temporal framework for studying the development of Kentucky's prehistoric cultures.

The 1960s saw an increase in archaeological activity in Kentucky, much of it associated with federally funded reservoir construction projects. Funding was allocated for limited archaeological investigation before construction was to begin, which made it possible to study some of the more important sites. Reservoir projects initiated during the 1960s included Green River, Fishtrap, Cave Run, Eagle Creek, and a proposed reservoir on the Red River. Other archaeological projects included Douglas Schwartz and Martha Rolingson's study of the Green River Archaic groups, using excavation records and artifacts collected thirty years earlier by WPA crews. Donald Janzen, then a University of Michigan graduate student, addressed similar questions about Archaic groups living near the Falls of the Ohio. Schwartz and R. Berle Clay investigated the Late Prehistoric Tinsley Hill site on the lower Cumberland River.

Passage of federal legislation for the protection of environmental resources, including archaeological sites, greatly influenced the character of Kentucky archaeology during the 1970s and 1980s. The increased demand for archaeologists to conduct environmentally related projects created or enlarged archaeological programs at several state universities, the traditional employer of archaeologists. In addition, numerous private businesses specializing in archaeological investigations flourished.

The increased sophistication of modern archaeological research has altered the kinds of information needed, as well as the ways in which it is collected. Studies have examined questions about the distribution of sites over the landscape, the diet and health of prehistoric peoples, social distinctions within and between groups, the ways tools were made and used, and long-distance exchange and trade. In the most productive archaeological projects, scientists from a number of different disciplines (botany, geology, soil science, zoology, and others) have studied the relationships between sites within a geographic region. Such an approach has provided new insights into how prehistoric societies adapted to different habitats and how the landscape influenced the culture. The regional research approach contrasts sharply with that of the earlier days of Kentucky archaeology, which usually focused on a specific site and its artifacts. One of the projects applying the regional approach was the western Kentucky project of the University of Illinois, which studied Late Woodland and Mississippian communities along the Mississippi River. University of Kentucky archaeologists studied Adena mounds and earthworks in the Bluegrass region; late prehistoric and early historic Native American sites in northern and eastern Kentucky; and the historic settlement of central Kentucky. Archaeologists from Simon Fraser University (Canada) analyzed how Archaic period hunter-gatherers adapted to the rich riverine habitats of the lower Tennessee and Cumberland rivers.

See George R. Milner and Virginia G. Smith, *New Deal Archaeology in Kentucky: Excavations, Collections, and Research* (Lexington, Ky., 1986); Douglas W. Schwartz, *Conceptions of Kentucky Prehistory: A Case Study on the History of Archaeology* (Lexington, Ky., 1967).

RICHARD W. JEFFERIES

ARCHITECTURE. Settlers from Pennsylvania, Maryland, Virginia, and the Carolinas between 1775 and 1800 brought with them traditional building methods that employed the plentiful construction materials native to Kentucky—log and stone (see FOLK ARCHITECTURE).

Stone soon became the building material of preference for those who could afford it. Stone construction was most popular in central Kentucky, where residences typically took the form of a two-story gable-ended structure. Such construction was the work of a skilled craftsman—the mason. Thomas ("Old Stone Hammer") METCALFE, who was Kentucky's governor during 1828-32, is popularly credited with a number of central Kentucky buildings, including courthouses.

By the mid-1780s, brick had become an optional building material in Kentucky. This medium allowed a much higher degree of stylistic workmanship. Members of Kentucky's upper class, who wanted residences that reflected the contemporary design of former residences in the East, quickly began to execute houses in the Georgian-Federal styles. They had symmetrical layouts, elaborate classical doorways, and complex cornices. Kentucky's first statehouse, built in Frankfort during 1793-94, is the earliest structure to reflect such advanced design, followed in 1796 by Sen. John Brown's residence, Liberty Hall.

The amateur designer relied heavily on architectural treatises and builders' guides. Immigrants brought these books with them, and as commerce between Kentucky and other areas increased, so did the availability of such publications. John Bradford's Lexington bookstore offered such literature as early as 1795.

Thomas Jefferson promoted Roman and Renaissance classical forms to reflect the ideal, utopian image of the early Republic. Known as Monumental Classicism, the form is based on that of the classical Roman temple. Jefferson County's third courthouse, built during 1810-12, is a temple-form structure, fronted by a portico of four Doric columns. In 1814 Matthew KENNEDY designed the state's second capitol in this style. A similar design of his was chosen for the Transylvania College main building. Kennedy was the first to develop a distinctive building type in the Bluegrass region. The 1816 Roman Catholic Proto-Cathedral of St. Joseph in Bardstown is of this style.

The Greek Revival style evolved from Monumental Classicism, but it was inspired by Greek monuments rather than Roman and Renaissance forms. The Greek Revival, an academic style, required trained architects. Gideon SHRYOCK, credited with the introduction of the Greek Revival style in Kentucky, was only twenty-five years old in 1827 when he created the design chosen for Kentucky's third statehouse, one of the first Greek Revival capitol buildings in the United States. In 1831, the year after completion of the Portland Canal set off rapid growth in Louisville, Nashville architect Hugh Roland moved to the city, becoming its first resident architect. The Louisville Hotel in the Greek Revival style, on Main Street, was his most important commission. Designed in 1831, it is the first modern hotel erected in the state. A talented English architect, Maj. Thomas LEWINSKI, is best known for the grand Greek Revival–style houses he designed for the Bluegrass aristocracy. The epitome of residential architecture of this style is his 1854 design for WARD HALL in Scott County.

Contemporary with the Greek Revival was the Gothic Revival. Although most popular for churches, the style was adapted to residences that featured steep roofs, with one to three front gables having decorative bargeboards. The pointed Gothic arch was used in windows and verandas. Most architects worked interchangeably between Greek and Gothic. John Rogers built the first Gothic church at St. Thomas farm in Nelson County in 1816. Hugh Roland designed the 1831 Roman Catholic Chapel of St. Louis in Louisville, the city's earliest Gothic structure. Nathaniel Cook, of Frankfort, is best known for two Gothic structures, the 1849-50 Kentucky Arsenal and the 1849 Good Shepherd Church, both in Frankfort.

The 1840s and 1850s in Kentucky must have been an exciting period for architects. The rapidly developing building technology of this period brought numerous changes in construction methods, making the need for architects increasingly apparent. The introduction of mass-produced machine-sawed lumber and inexpensive machine-made wire nails resulted in the "balloon frame." During the early 1850s, cast iron and terra cotta were applied to architecture. Buildings rose from the common two stories to as many as five stories.

An alternative architectural style, the Italianate, became increasingly popular in Kentucky in the 1850s. Typical features include a low-pitched roof with widely overhanging eaves, supported by decorative brackets and tall, narrow, round-arched windows, sometimes with elaborate hood molds. Roofs often sported a cupola. Samuel Sloan's *The Model Architect* (1852) and *City and Suburban Architecture* (1859) widely encouraged the style's popularity. Significant Italianate buildings are E.E. Williams's 1853 Customs House in Louisville and Lewinski's 1854 Deaf and Dumb Asylum in Danville.

Isaiah Rogers, a major national figure during the period, arrived in Kentucky in 1852. He produced several early Italian-influenced (Renaissance) buildings, including the 1852 Capital Hotel in Frankfort and the Louisville Hotel of 1854. In 1854 he designed the Newcomb and Alexander buildings on Main Street, Louisville, the first five-story buildings in the state. Henry Whitestone, Rogers's partner, took over the office in 1857 and remained the city's major practitioner until the 1880s.

Cast-iron-front buildings appeared in the state during the 1850s. John McMURTRY is credited with designing the 1854-57 Elliott & Craig building in Lexington, the front of which consisted of an iron and glass Gothic design. Adjoining was the Italianate Melodeon Hall, for which Miles Greenwood of Cincinnati manufactured the iron front in 1858. This period saw the arrival of the last of the English immigrant architects in Kentucky. Henry Platt Bradshaw, who came to Louisville in 1859, is remembered for his designs for the City Hall and the Louisville Steam & Power Company. Arriving in 1865, John Andrewartha by 1873 had designed twenty business blocks on Main Street in Louisville, and was credited with the first iron structure in the city.

During the period from the 1857 depression through the end of the Civil War, construction and design slowed in the United States and eventually came to a virtual halt. The succeeding period showed little carryover from the previous years. The clear-cut Greek and Gothic Revival styles were no longer in vogue, having been replaced by Victorian eclecticism, which combined Gothic with Italianate and the French Second Empire. Later came Eastlake, Queen Anne, and Jacobean; the French Baroque and Rococo; and Moorish, Flemish, and Venetian Gothic styles. The highly decorative phases saw an integration of architecture and sculpture.

The first major Victorian style in Kentucky was the classical Second Empire. The primary influence was the 1852-57 additions to the Louvre in Paris for Napoleon III, based on French seventeenth century or Baroque sources. The style is recognized by horizontal lines, division of building into pavilions, and mansard roofs. The earliest Kentucky building in the Second Empire style is the Bourbon County courthouse of 1873-74, designed by Albert C. Nash of Cincinnati. Phelix L. Lundin, a native of Sweden practicing in Lexington, designed the Woodford County courthouse of 1880-83 and several central Kentucky residences in this style.

The period from 1885 until the end of the century saw less eclecticism in architecture and a rise in the influence of the Chicago school of architects. Three styles dominated the period: Richardsonian Romanesque, High Victorian Gothic, and after the 1893 Columbian Exposition, the Beaux Arts and the Colonial Revival. These styles were popularized by the growing circulation of architectural periodicals such as the *American Architect and Building News* and the Chicago-based *Inland Architect*. Most Kentucky architects aligned with the latter journal.

The Romanesque Revival style in the United States, commonly known as Richardsonian Romanesque, was developed by Boston architect Henry Hobson Richardson and became particularly popular after his death in 1886. Characteristics include round-topped windows and entrances; rough masonry walls, occasionally broken by smooth surfaces; and large towers. Mason MAURY, a Louisville architect, is credited with the introduction of Richardsonian Romanesque in Louisville for the Judge Russell Houston residence of 1886. The Fayette County courthouse of 1898, designed by the Cleveland architectural firm of Lehman & Schmitt, represents the most advanced Romanesque design in Kentucky.

The High Victorian Gothic was developed in England and popularized in the United States shortly after the Civil War as a counterpart of the Second Empire style. It found its theoretical basis in books by English writer John Ruskin advocating the Gothic style, noted for its rich exterior and interior surface polychromy. The first American architect to promote the style was Peter Bonnett Wight of New York, who introduced it to Kentucky in 1867 in his design for the Thomas P. Jacobs house in Louisville. The style's major representative in Kentucky is the Federal Post Office and Customs House of 1875-76 at Covington, designed in the office of the supervising architect of the U.S. Treasury Department.

The courthouses of Nelson County (1891) and Hopkins County (1892) are unique designs that synthesize the Richardsonian Romanesque and High Victorian Gothic styles. Both were designed by the Louisville architectural firm of Maury & Dodd, perhaps the most talented architects in the state during the Victorian period. William J. Dodd was trained under William Le Baron Jenney, the founder of the Chicago school and first to introduce skeletal building construction to the United States. He came to Louisville in 1885 and formed a partnership with Maury in 1891. In its first year, the firm won the competition for the Louisville Trust Company Building, the first steel-frame, fireproof structure in Kentucky.

The Colonial Revival was prevalent in Kentucky from 1893 until at least World War II. The main catalyst for this trend was the World Columbian Exposition of 1892-93 in Chicago, where millions of Americans saw buildings of classic style. The Ecole des Beaux-Arts in France is credited as the international leader of this movement. Colonial Revival exteriors tended to be smooth stone or brick, in contrast to the rough stone of the earlier Renaissance and Romanesque structures. Symmetry, monumental scale, and raised foundations were its ideals, and it used columns, balustrades, and cupolas.

During the Great Depression, the Public Works Administration (PWA) branch of President Franklin D. Roosevelt's New Deal programs was in charge of construction of public buildings and engineering projects. In Kentucky it erected more than one hundred schools, courthouses, city halls, community centers, and the like. PWA projects commenced soon after passage of the National Recovery Act in 1933 and continued through the beginning of the second World War. The PWA, somewhat like a large building and loan association, underwrote 100 percent of a project, granted a county up to 45 percent of construction costs, and lent the balance.

Many buildings of the New Deal were designed by the public buildings branch of the Procurement Division of the Treasury Department, but through the efforts of Kentucky's architects, most of the state's buildings were designed by its own architects. PWA courthouses are of numerous diverse styles, including the Colonial Revival, Art Deco, and Art Moderne. The earliest and the most numerous PWA buildings were built in the Colonial Revival style prominent prior to the Depression, including five New Deal courthouses: Hopkins County (1937), Grant County (1937-39), Grayson County (1937-38), Lewis County (1939-40), and McCracken County (1939-40). Art Deco features smooth walls with chevrons, zigzags, and other geometric motifs as decorative elements, which often rise above the roof line. The only two examples are the Caldwell County courthouse of 1938-40 and the larger Webster County courthouse of 1939-40. Both buildings are the work of Lawrence Casner, an architect of Madisonville, Indiana. Art Moderne, a very rare style, featured smooth walls; curved corners; a flat roof, usually with a small ledge at the roof line; and horizontal bands, contributing to an overall horizontal effect. The only Art Moderne style courthouse was the last built under the New Deal, in Ohio County (1940-43). Walter Scott Roberts of Owensboro designed this courthouse.

One of the most unusual courthouses of the New Deal is the Knott County courthouse, remodeled during 1935-36 in the Mission style. Hispanic in inspiration, the Mission style is primarily associated with California and is common only in the southwestern states. A typical feature of this style is the curved dormer above the entrance. The Louisville architectural firm Joseph and Joseph introduced the style to Kentucky in the early 1910s in their designs for the Kentucky State Fair grounds in Louisville and the J.T.S. Brown Distillery at Lawrenceburg.

The period since World War II has seen a predominance of styleless, or functional, architecture. During the 1960s the destruction of buildings in the heart of the larger cities, especially Louisville and Lexington, by urban renewal and the high-rise replacements completely changed the urban character. Featureless shafts of steel and glass created a new scale in downtown areas. The first in Lexington was the First Security Bank (1972) on the corner of High and South Upper streets. It was followed a few years later by the Lexington Center at Broadway and Main Street, a large complex consisting of Rupp Arena (a vast gymnasium-auditorium), the seventeen-story Hyatt Regency Hotel, the Civic Center shopping mall, and ample convention facilities. The area to the east soon sprouted similar buildings. They were complemented by the restoration of Victorian Square, a block of eclectic buildings of the 1880s on the north side of Main Street at Broadway. Restoration of Woodward Heights, southwest of Lexington Center, a neighborhood of residences contemporary with the business houses of Victorian Square, represented a trend of the 1980s.

The notable structure of this period in Kentucky is the Humana Building in Louisville, the object of an international design competition. The twenty-seven-story Postmodern building, designed by Michael Graves and Associates of Princeton, New Jersy, breaks from rectangularity. It has recessed and advanced planes, a bowed-front projection supported on exposed steelwork near the top, and a bowed-roof superstructure.

WILLIAM B. SCOTT, JR.

AREA DEVELOPMENT DISTRICTS. Kentucky's fifteen Area Development Districts are regional organizations of counties and municipalities that identify and address area-wide problems and assist local governments with technical matters. Each district has a board of directors; members are county judge-executives, mayors, and private citizens. The board employs an executive director and a professional staff to provide administrative assistance to local governments, coordinate state and federal grant programs within the district, and prepare regional plans.

The federal government was primarily responsible for the rapid development of substate regionalism. The Economic Development Administration and the Appalachian Regional Commission, both created in 1965, promoted the organization of multi-county development districts. In 1967 Kentucky became the first in the nation to establish a statewide system of regional organizations; it created the fifteen districts. In that year, seventeen federal programs contained provisions to encourage regional planning. Legislation in 1972 gave the Kentucky districts statutory authority. By that time, forty-three of the other states had adopted similar regional systems.

Because their boundaries are based on geographic, social, and economic criteria, the Area Development Districts vary widely in size and in population. Financing comes from both state and federal sources and is administered by the Kentucky Department of Local Government, which oversees their activities. The 1972 statute prohibits the districts from dealing with public education. Otherwise, they have considerable discretion in their programs and priorities. Economic development tops the list; other concerns of the districts are transportation, housing, social services, and environmental protection. The fifteen districts are: Purchase area, Pennyrile, Green River, Barren River, Lincoln Trail, Kentuckiana, Northern Kentucky, Buffalo Trace, Gateway, FIVCO, Big Sandy, Kentucky River, Cumberland Valley, Lake Cumberland, and Bluegrass.

See John Clements, *Kentucky Facts* (Dallas, Texas, 1990).   WILLIAM C. GARRIOTT, JR.

ARGUS OF WESTERN AMERICA. The *Argus of Western America*, for twenty-five years an influential newspaper published in Frankfort, Kentucky, was founded by William Gerard in 1806. Gerard sold it to Moses G. Bledsoe and Elijah C. Berry. In October 1816, Amos KENDALL bought half interest in the *Argus* and became editor; under his editorship its circulation became the largest in the state.

Kendall's style as a political journalist included sometimes controversial editorials, filled with appeals to prejudice and characterized by redundancy and unrestrained metaphors. In 1818 a series of articles criticized the Bank of the United States, and after the panic of 1819 Kendall supported the New Court party and debtor relief policies. In late 1826, Kendall's editorials stopped favoring Henry Clay and his fiscal policies and began to support Andrew Jackson's campaign for the presidency. Recognizing the readership potential of a strongly pro-Jackson paper, Kendall made the *Argus* one of the most partisan papers in the West. Kendall left the *Argus* in 1829 for posts in Jackson's administrations, first as fourth auditor of the treasury, then as postmaster general.

Francis P. BLAIR, Sr., who succeeded Kendall as editor of the *Argus*, resigned in 1830 to go to Washington, D.C., as editor of the *Washington Globe*. R.A. Ferguson published the *Argus* until 1835, when Gerard Russell edited the paper for a year, followed by B.J. Knott. Kendall returned briefly to Kentucky in 1838 in an unsuccessful attempt to revive the *Argus*, which ceased publication that year.

See Carl E. Kramer, *Capital on the Kentucky* (Frankfort, Ky., 1986); W.R. Jillson, *The Newspapers and Periodicals of Frankfort, Kentucky, 1795-1945* (Frankfort, Ky., 1945).

ARISTIDES. Aristides was the golden-red chestnut, barely fifteen hands high, that in 1875 won the first Kentucky Derby. He defeated fourteen of the best three-year-old thoroughbreds, including his stablemate, Chesapeake, the favorite. Aristides ran the fastest mile and a half (the initial derby distance) run by a three-year-old up to that time. The little colt also won several important races in New York at Saratoga and Jerome Park and in

Baltimore, and broke several records: the fastest race for 2 miles and a furlong, and the fastest 2½-mile-race.

He was sired by imported Leamington; his dam was Sarong, a daughter of LEXINGTON, America's leading sire for fourteen straight years. He was bred and raced by Price McGrath, who made a fortune in gambling and entertained lavishly at his Mc-Grathiana Farm on Newtown Pike in Fayette County. After one race at age six, Aristides was retired to stud, where he was a failure. He died in St. Louis at age twenty-one.

See Peter Chew, *The Kentucky Derby: the First 100 Years* (Boston 1974).   MARY E. WHARTON

ARNOW, HARRIETTE LOUISE (SIMPSON). Harriette Louise (Simpson) Arnow, author, was born to Elias and Mollie Jane (Denney) Simpson, on July 7, 1908, in Wayne County, Kentucky. She graduated from Burnside High School in Pulaski County, attended Berea College during 1924-26, then taught school in rural Pulaski County. She received her B.A. in science from the University of Louisville in 1930. For the next four years, she was a teacher and then principal at a high school in Pulaski County. In 1934 she taught junior high school in Louisville, then moved to Cincinnati to devote time to writing, including several short stories and her first novel, *Mountain Path* (1936), the first of her Kentucky trilogy. In 1936 one of her best short stories, "The Washerwoman's Day," was published in *Southern Review*.

Harriette Simpson married Harold B. Arnow in 1939, and they moved to a farm near Keno, Pulaski County, where she and her husband divided their time between farming and writing. In 1944 they moved to a housing project in Detroit, where he took a job with the *Detroit Times*. Arnow's second novel, *Hunter's Horn* (1944), was a best seller and brought her national acclaim as a novelist. This work portrays the life of a Kentucky hill farmer obsessed with the capture of an elusive red fox that he calls King Devil. In 1950 the Arnows moved to a farm near Ann Arbor, Michigan, where she finished her most popular novel, *The Dollmaker* (1954). This story, which completed her Kentucky trilogy, chronicles a Kentucky family's difficult World War II move from the mountains to a Detroit housing project, where they encounter economic uncertainty and social prejudices. *The Dollmaker* was made into a TV movie in 1983 starring Jane Fonda. Arnow's *Seedtime on the Cumberland* (1960), *Flowering on the Cumberland* (1963), and *Old Burnside* (1977) are social histories. The fictional *The Weedkiller's Daughter* (1970) was followed by *The Kentucky Trace: A Novel of the American Revolution* (1975). *The Kentucky Trace* reflects Arnow's concerns about contemporary problems such as the destruction of the environment.

Arnow received the Kentucky Woman of the Year Award in 1954, the Berea College Centennial Award and the Friends of American Writers Award in 1955, an Award of Merit from the American As-sociation for State and Local History in 1960, and the Milner Award from the Kentucky Arts Council in 1983. In 1955 *The Dollmaker* won the National Book Award. Arnow was inducted into the Michigan Women's Hall of Fame and received the Mark Twain Award for Midwestern Literature from Michigan State University. She also received honorary doctorates from Albion College in Michigan, Transylvania University, and the University of Kentucky. From 1978 until her death in 1986, she participated in the Hindman Settlement School's annual two-week writing workshop in Hindman, Kentucky.

Arnow and her husband had two children, Marcella and Thomas. On March 21, 1986, Arnow died at her Washtenaw County farm near Ann Arbor, Michigan, and her ashes were buried beside her husband's grave in Keno.

See Wilton Eckley, *Harriette Arnow* (New York 1974).

ART AND ARTISTS. Kentucky's first settlers left their homes, but not their cultural heritage, behind them. From that heritage, they quickly recreated on the frontier a domestic environment that was familiar to them, as Ann Clark, mother of George Rogers Clark, did in bringing her English sterling teapot when she arrived in Louisville in 1785 to live in a log house. Within a decade, her daughter, Lucy (Clark) Croghan, was mistress of a three-story brick home with French wallpaper on the ballroom walls. When William Whitley built his brick home at Stanford in 1792, he set his monogram in the facade as if to proclaim that the Kentucky frontier was neither uneducated nor anonymous. The spacious, high-ceilinged rooms of homes such as these, which sprang up rapidly in cities and towns across Kentucky, demanded suitable decoration.

Even before the conclusion of the War of 1812, both the money and the desire for likenesses, or portrait art, were evident. Antebellum Kentuckians did not take to the collection of landscape art as their eastern contemporaries did. All around them was too much nature, sometimes unwelcome, killing any desire to decorate their homes with it. In portrait art, they could record themselves and preserve the faces of loved ones, whose lives, without benefit of modern hygiene and medicine, might be brief in Kentucky's uncertain environment. It was no accident that, before the development of a reliable camera, Kentucky's successful painters were portrait artists. The English artist George Jacob Beck, who spent the last decade of his life in Lexington, depended on portraiture for his income. He supplemented it by teaching at the Lexington female seminary established by his wife, Mary, also an accomplished artist.

Foremost among portrait painters was Matthew Harris JOUETT. Trained as a lawyer, he opened a Lexington studio in 1815. Jouett was a much sought-after artist, but he could not support his family solely on his Kentucky commissions. Every winter he traveled south to paint the wealthy families of Louisiana and Mississippi. His total outputwas substantial, but as he did not sign his work, only his distinctive style and an occasional surviving document substantiate the claims that he produced more than three hundred pieces.

Contemporaries of Jouett who worked successfully in the Bluegrass region were miniaturists Benjamin Trott and Samuel H. Dearborn and portraitists Asa Park, John Grimes, Patrick Henry Davenport, Alexander Bradford, and Thomas Jefferson Wright. Each had a unique style, not always pleasing. Park's subjects, for instance, have a consistently hard, glassy-eyed stare. A chronicler of Mercer and Boyle counties' history documented an abundance of "coarsely painted family portraits by an itinerant artist who sometimes made marvelous hits of likeness, mainly, however, caricaturing the unfortunate subjects of his art." Perhaps the writer referred to Danville-born Davenport, whose female subjects were, it is hoped, not as plain, dour, and lacking in grace as he portrayed them.

Joseph H. BUSH and Oliver FRAZER, gifted Bluegrass-born pupils of Thomas Sully, returned to Kentucky, filling the void left by Jouett's death in 1827. In 1820 Bush headquartered himself in Louisville and advertised regularly in the local newspapers. Many of his portraits, which he did not sign, survive, having descended in the families of the subjects. His favorite work, a portrait of George Rogers Clark, painted from life around 1817, hangs at Locust Grove. It is a stark portrayal of the sixty-five-year-old invalid general who spent his last decade in his sister's home. Frazer, a pupil of Jouett who spent two years studying with Sully in Philadelphia, returned to Lexington in 1830. For the next thirty years, until his eyesight failed, he recorded the visage of the Bluegrass. He taught Samuel Woodson PRICE, best remembered for his portrait of the Lexington vagrant "King" Solomon, the hero of the 1849 cholera epidemic.

No history of Kentucky's arts heritage would be complete without mention of Edward TROYE, the Swiss-born equine portraitist who came to Lexington in the early 1830s. There he began his career as America's preeminent thoroughbred bloodstock artist. The primary market for his work was in the East, but he regularly returned to Kentucky, where A. Keene Richards was his foremost patron and lifelong friend.

The Bluegrass produced and encouraged more early nineteenth century art and artists than any other part of the commonwealth. Not until late in the nineteenth century did Louisville have a cohesive artistic output to rival Lexington's, although Louisville's growing population attracted itinerant artists throughout the century.

Edna Talbout Whitley, in her book *Kentucky Ante-Bellum Portraiture* (1956), records almost two hundred artists who had studios or temporary residences in the state. Almost half of the itinerants were Louisville-based. Chester Harding, a Massachusetts-born, untrained itinerant artist was drawn to Paris, Kentucky, in 1819 by stories of Jouett's financial success. He is said to have charged twenty-five dollars apiece for the one hundred portraits he completed during his stay there. Harding went on to become a portraitist of international renown but he returned to the Jefferson-Franklin-Fayette County area in the 1830s and 1840s to pick up lucrative commission work.

Eastern artists such as John Wesley Jarvis, George Peter Alexander Healy, and John Neagle occasionally came to the commonwealth, especially to paint the affluent and the politically prominent. Their total output was not large but all of it is museumworthy.

John James AUDUBON, a Louisville and Owensboro resident, kept his family from starvation during the financial panic of 1819 by drawing profiles for five dollars. While he is best known for his birds, the portraits that he did whenever he was short of funds were no small part of his work. He was especially adept at drawing the features of the dead. A Louisville clergyman had the body of his child disinterred so that Audubon could draw a likeness for the child's grieving mother.

Thomas Campbell was a miniaturist who worked in Louisville during 1836-51 before moving on, and Richard T. Clark advertised in the Louisville papers during 1859-67 that he painted portraits from life or "copied from photographs." Clark's work has not been identified but his ad portends the end of an era. The camera and the Civil War would change the face of art forever.

By the 1880s, wealthy Kentuckians traveled to the East Coast or Europe for their portraits. The agricultural Bluegrass declined as an arts center as newly monied Louisville industrialists sought art, and artists, to decorate their urban palaces. European romanticism, with its emphasis on landscape art of often heroic proportion, was the fashion. Louisvillian John Botto advertised himself as a landscape painter in the mid-1880s, then left to study abroad, where he died. Carl Christian Brenner, a native of Germany, first exhibited his work at Louisville's Southern Exposition of 1883. He is the most famous of the Louisville Tonalists, a group that included Harvey JOINER, a prolific artist who produced more than 5,000 paintings, primarily of nature.

Women artists in nineteenth century Kentucky were few. Young women studied art but did not make a career of it. Magdalen Harvie McDowell was a self-taught painter and draftsman whose remarkable portrait of her kinsman, scholar R.C. Ballard Thruston, hangs at the Filson Club in Louisville. Ruth Whittier Schutte Tarbell was a New England artist who came to eastern Jefferson County with her second husband in 1841. Portraits from her Kentucky period have descended in the families of the subjects. The century closed with Patty THUM, a Louisvillian who studied in New York in the 1870s and 1880s and produced landscapes and flower paintings, taught art, illustrated books, and served as art critic for the *Louisville Herald*. She was probably the only woman artist in nineteenth century Kentucky whose talent actually supported her throughout her life.

Of twentieth century Kentucky artists, the most well known within the state is Paul SAWYIER, a Frankfort-based landscapist who worked at the very beginning of the century. Barely able to support himself during his lifetime with the sale of his work, Sawyier pursued his own brand of American Impressionism and Tonalism, styles that have proved extremely popular with late twentieth century audiences. Working primarily in watercolor, occasionally in oils, Sawyier concentrated on Frankfort area scenes, sometimes using photographs to compose his subjects. His works, nostalgic reinterpretations of a bygone era in Kentucky history, have a strong sentimental appeal to modern audiences. Issued in reproduction form by the thousands, his work turns up in commercial buildings and private homes all over the state.

Sawyier, like many Kentucky artists at the beginning of the century, received training from Frank DUVENECK, among others. Duveneck must figure prominently in any discussion of Kentucky art of the twentieth century. This Covington-born artist achieved national success in his lifetime for his own work and for the superb training he offered to numerous other artists, both during his years abroad and in the United States, at the Cincinnati Art Museum, the Cincinnati Art Club, and later the Cincinnati Art Academy. Such Louisville artists as John Bernard Alberts studied with Duveneck and, taking his example, traveled abroad to further their education. Alberts reflects such international trends as Art Nouveau, Symbolism, and Post-Impressionism in his work, and, in fact, relates to the growing arts and crafts movement throughout the country in the early years of the century. Louisville's Paul Plaschke, who studied with George Luks, was one of the founders of the Louisville Art Academy and an active member of the Louisville Art Club. Dixie SELDEN, another Duveneck pupil, studied with William Merritt Chase and made numerous trips abroad throughout her career.

Following World War I, a number of Kentucky artists went to Europe to study. One of the most notable, William Welsh, was a Frank Duveneck student who received additional training in Paris at the Académie Julien and the Atelier Delecluse. Like many serious artists, Welsh, a muralist, illustrator, and portraitist, had to earn his living in the commercial field. While a number of his accomplished portraits are well known in the central Kentucky area, some of his finest works are commercial designs of the 1920s and 1930s. His travel posters, in particular, show Welsh's familiarity with European Art Nouveau design.

The lure of European study for Kentucky's artists, which goes back to the early nineteenth century with such artists as William Edward West, became very powerful in the early decades of the twentieth century, for Kentucky artists as for artists all over America. The 1913 Armory show in New York City had an extraordinary impact on American artists, establishing the dominance of European avant-garde styles that so dazzled—often shocked—American audiences. Prior to World War II many European intellectuals and artists came to America to escape Nazi persecution or the general climate of unrest, including Austrian-born Victor HAMMER, who settled in Lexington. He produced extraordinary artistic works in a variety of media, including paintings, sculpture, hand-printed books, and mezzotints.

During the 1930s federal art programs, the state's artists participated in a number of projects for the Public Works of Art Project, the fine arts project of the Works Progress Administration, and the Section Division of the U.S. Treasury. These artists' works, especially the many MURALS to be seen in the state's post offices, courthouses, and other public buildings, reveal great pride in Kentucky's history. Harlan HUBBARD's library murals at Berea, Louisville, and Morehead were commissioned for federal arts programs. Two of his murals at the University of Kentucky were also done in the 1930s, although not federally funded.

A strong characteristic of Kentucky art is a kind of native, untutored expression. Varying much too widely to be classified as any kind of school, this strain can be traced throughout much of the remarkable folk art of the region, a visual expression that flowered in rural isolation and has achieved national prominence in recent decades. Kentucky's most well-known folk artist is Edgar Tolson, whose simple, powerfully carved biblical figures have been widely emulated by contemporary folk artists throughout the southeastern United States. The concept of a hand-wrought object, frequently religious in subject matter, is a constant throughout this style of art. Henry FAULKNER, dramatically different from any other mid-twentieth century Kentucky artist, pursued an idiosyncratic, flamboyant style of painting. His expressive, heavily impassioned landscapes and still lifes are related to the unschooled, intensely personal individual artifact.

Kentucky art is as diverse as the inhabitants of the state. All varieties of media are explored and exhibited, from the most primitive amateur efforts to the most sophisticated avant-garde styles. There are persistent themes of landscape and craft in much of the state's late-twentieth century visual expression. The remarkable, diverse beauty of the natural terrain has entranced Kentucky's artists since they first enjoyed it, after the rigors of frontier life had eased into a more comfortable environment for them. The reliance on an inspiration of handcrafts marks some of Kentucky's most accomplished contemporary art, which often restates and reinterprets such traditional media as quilts, weavings, or pottery.

See Arthur F. Jones and Bruce Weber, *The Kentucky Painter from the Frontier Era to the Great War* (Lexington, Ky., 1981).

LYNN RENAU AND HARRIET FOWLER

ARTHUR, ALEXANDER ALAN. Alexander Alan Arthur, entrepreneur, eldest son of Alexander and Catherine (Allen) Arthur, was born August 30, 1846, in Glasgow, Scotland. The family immigrated to Montreal, Canada, when he was a child. In 1867 Arthur joined the 104th Highland Regiment in Scotland and married Mary Forrest there. After living in Sweden and Norway, they immigrated to the United States in 1879, settling in Boston, where Arthur worked as a representative for an English-owned steel company. After the death of Arthur's first wife, he married Nellie Goodwyn, of Boston, whose family had many business connections. In 1886, as an agent for the Richmond & Danville (R&D) Railroad Company, Arthur went to the Cumberland Gap area to research the possibility of a railroad extension into the region.

The coal, iron ore, and limestone deposits of the Yellow Creek Valley in Bell County impressed Arthur, who decided to find financial backers for the iron and steel production he planned. In August 1886 he and five other businessmen formed the Gap Association and purchased 20,000 acres in Bell County. With additional capital acquired in London, the company became the American Association, Ltd., in 1887. The American Association purchased additional coal land and ultimately owned 120,000 to 150,000 acres, at an investment of more than $20 million.

To secure access to the coal and iron fields, Arthur formed the Knoxville, Cumberland Gap & Louisville (KCG&L) Railroad. The sixteen-mile spur into Yellow Creek Valley included a tunnel through Cumberland Mountain. On August 23, 1889, the inaugural KCG&L train derailed, killing six and injuring Arthur.

Arthur established the town of Middlesborough in 1889, forming the Middlesborough Town Land Company to sell lots in Yellow Creek Valley. The company went bankrupt after a major London investor failed on February 14, 1890, at the same time that the iron ore in Yellow Creek Valley was found to be of low grade. Both the Land Company and the American Association collapsed, ruining Arthur's prospects early in 1891. He then spent time in eastern Tennessee, where he founded the town of Harrogate, and left for Alaska during the gold rush of 1897-98. Arthur later moved to New York City, where he suffered a stroke. He died in Middlesborough on March 4, 1912, and was buried in the Middlesborough Cemetery.

See Charles B. Roberts, "The Building of Middlesborough," *FCHQ* 7 (Jan. 1933): 18-33; Henry H. Fuson, *History of Bell County Kentucky* (New York 1947).

ASBURY, FRANCIS. Francis Asbury, the pioneer leader of the Methodist movement for whom Asbury College in Wilmore, Kentucky, is named, was born to Joseph and Elizabeth (Rogers) Asbury near Birmingham, England, on August 21, 1745. He was converted to Christianity at the age of four-teen, began to preach locally, and at twenty-one went to London, where he was admitted to the Wesleyan Conference. After five years as an itinerant preacher, Asbury volunteered as a missionary to North America, arriving in Philadelphia in 1771. The following year John Wesley, the founder of Methodism, appointed him superintendent of missionary work in America.

Wesley ordered him back to England in 1775 for insubordination, but Asbury took refuge in Delaware during the hostilities in the colonies, eventually becoming a U.S. citizen. After his role in reconciling northern and southern Methodists over the administration of the sacraments, in December 1784 he was chosen joint superintendent of the Methodist movement in America. During the next twenty years, despite frequent complaints about his autocratic exercise of power, Asbury directed the missionary work that sent circuit riders to the remote areas of the seaboard states and across the Appalachian Mountains into frontier regions.

Asbury first visited Kentucky in 1790 for an annual conference at Masterson's Station, five miles northwest of Lexington, where the first Methodist church in Kentucky was erected. He returned to Kentucky eighteen times over the next twenty-five years. Asbury died near Fredericksburg, Virginia, on March 31, 1816, and was buried in Mt. Olivet Cemetery in Baltimore.

See Elmer T. Clark et al., eds., *The Journals and Letters of Francis Asbury* (Nashville 1958).

RICHARD L. TROUTMAN

ASBURY COLLEGE AND THEOLOGICAL SEMINARY. Asbury College in Wilmore, Kentucky, is named for Francis ASBURY, a circuit rider who became the first Methodist bishop in the American colonies and who pioneered in education. At the end of the nineteenth century, the preaching of Henry Clay Morrison, a young Methodist minister, helped generate a religious revival in Wilmore. The Rev. John Wesley Hughes collected sufficient funds to establish the college there in 1890.

Asbury College is held in trust by a self-perpetuating board of thirty trustees, who are bound to operate the school according to the doctrines of "entire sanctification" and "scriptural holiness," developed and taught by Hughes and his immediate successors. The college, though essentially Wesleyan in its confessional position and predominantly Methodist in enrollment, is officially nondenominational and receives neither governmental nor denominational financial support for its institutional programs or facilities.

Asbury Theological Seminary, an outgrowth of Asbury College, was founded in 1923, after several members of the college faculty met with Morrison, who was then president, to discuss evangelical theological education in the region. Asbury Theological Seminary opened as a department of Asbury College. In 1931 separate articles of incorporation were drawn up, and the seminary became an independent educational and administrative unit. It moved to a campus adjoining the college in 1939.

See Joseph A. Thacker, *Asbury College, Vision and Miracle* (Nappanee, Ind., 1990).

FRANK B. STANGER, JR.

ASHER, THOMAS JEFFERSON. Thomas Jefferson Asher, entrepreneur, was born in Clay County, Kentucky, on May 21, 1848, the son of Jackson Davis and Margaret (Hendrickson) Asher. In 1870 he moved to Bell County, where he worked at logging, first at Calloway and then at Wasioto. In 1890 he bought a sawmill, which he operated under the name T.J. Asher & Sons, selling lumber on the international market. After acquiring significant coal and timber holdings in the upper Cumberland River valley, he built the Wasioto & Black Mountain Railroad. The Louisville & Nashville Railroad bought the line in 1909, but it continued to operate under Asher's management until 1915. The extension of this line from Bell County into Harlan County in 1911 opened coal deposits there to commercial development. Asher formed the Asher Coal Company in 1914 but soon found leasing land to others more profitable than mining, and real estate became his principal business activity. A Republican, he served as county judge of Bell County during 1914-18. He married Varilla Howard on March 3, 1870; they had five children: Hugh, Robert, George, Andrew, and Verdie. Asher died in Pineville on May 26, 1935, and was buried in the Pineville Cemetery.

See J.C. Tipton, *The Cumberland Coal Field and Its Creators* (Middlesborough, Ky., 1905).

JAMES S. GREENE III

ASHLAND. Ashland, the largest city in eastern Kentucky, is located on the banks of the Ohio River in Boyd County. This second-class city, when first incorporated by act of the legislature in 1856, was located in Greenup County. Boyd County was created four years later.

Ashland, first known as Poage Settlement, was settled by the Poage family of Virginia. Robert Poage and his sons Robert, Jr., and George, along with Maj. George Poage and his son John, held title to thousands of acres obtained by assignments from the William Bell patent and treasury land warrants. The first recorded land grant in the area was made to Gen. James Wilkinson in 1783, from whom Robert Poage purchased a 5,000-acre grant. It was from these early families that land was acquired by industrialists later on. The area was rich in the timber, coal, and limestone needed for production of pig iron, making the area attractive to early iron producers, who used the Ohio River for transport. The first iron furnace was established in 1818 by Richard Deering in Greenup County. The Ashland furnace opened in 1869, the largest of its kind, and was one of sixty at that time located in the area known as the Hanging Rock iron region. The furnaces later converted from charcoal fuel to coal.

Early industrialists formed the Kentucky Iron, Coal and Manufacturing Company, incorporated in 1854. The town they laid out on land they had purchased was named Ashland after Henry Clay's home in Lexington. Martin Toby Hilton, an engineer, was hired to lay out the town, with streets running parallel to the river to be one hundred feet wide and those at right angles to be eighty feet wide. Among the early families that iron and coal attracted to the area were the Means, Coles, Peebles, and Seatons. During the Civil War the Aldine Hotel was used as a government hospital. The building, several stories tall with fifty rooms, had been built by a promoter who hoped to give Ashland an air of permanence.

The region's furnace towns were linked through Ashland, and transportation of coal and raw materials was centered there. The first railroad, the Lexington & Big Sandy, reached Princess, ten miles away, by 1857. Other rail lines, such as the Ashland Coal & Iron railroad and the Chattaroi, developed to meet the demands of industry. In 1924 the Chesapeake & Ohio Railway acquired the rights to most of the lines and became the major railway through Ashland. The steamer lines on the Ohio River transported the iron to ports as far away as Cincinnati and Pittsburgh and returned with goods for the city. Among these lines were the Cincinnati, Portsmouth, Big Sandy & Pomeroy Packet Company, and the Pittsburgh & Cincinnati Steamboat line.

The government of Ashland started as a council of five trustees. Ashland incorporated as a city in 1876, with H.B. Brodess as its first mayor. The first postmaster was H.B. Pollard (1847), the first police chief was John Casebolt (1868), and the first fire chief was Jack Spicer (1885). Today the city has a city manager with a mayor and four city commissioners.

Ashland's lumber industry flourished from the 1880s until the turn of the century. The period of greatest growth was the decade of the 1920s, when the population increased from 14,729 to 29,074. The American Rolling Mill Company (Armco) headquartered in Middleton, Ohio, bought the Ashland Iron and Mining Company in 1921 and Norton Iron Works in 1928. The company continued to grow; it started up the first continuous sheet rolling mill in 1934 and a hot strip mill in 1953. In May 1989 Armco entered into a partnership with Kawasaki Steel that brought $350 million into the company, then known as Armco Steel. Ashland Oil, the thirteenth largest petroleum refining company in the United States, was founded in 1924, when it was headed by Paul G. Blazer.

In 1981 it became legal to sell liquor in downtown Ashland. The Simeon Willis Memorial Bridge opened in May 1985, followed by the Ashland Plaza Hotel in September 1985. The business district extended west to the $42 million Ashland Town Center shopping mall.

Former residents of Ashland include Ben Williamson, U.S. senator (1930-31); Simeon Willis, governor of Kentucky (1943-47); Fred Moore Vinson, chief justice of the United States (1946-53); and Stanley Foreman Reed, associate justice of the U.S. Supreme Court (1938-57).

The population was 29,245 in 1970; 27,064 in 1980; and 23,622 in 1990.

See Ashland Centennial Committee, *A History of Ashland, Kentucky, 1786-1954* (Ashland, Ky., 1954).

JAMES POWERS

ASHLAND. Henry CLAY, a major figure in national politics during the first half of the nineteenth century, lived at his estate, Ashland, in Lexington, Kentucky, from 1811 until his death in 1852. Clay, his wife Lucretia, and their eleven children lived in an elegant brick Federal-style country residence built ca. 1806-11. The one-story wings, designed by Benjamin H. Latrobe, were added by 1814. Clay took great pride in the six-hundred-acre farm at Ashland, where he raised imported livestock in addition to crops, and where thoroughbreds trained on one of the first private racetracks west of the Appalachians.

In 1855-57 Clay's son James rebuilt the house to rectify structural defects in the original. Noted architect Thomas LEWINSKI redesigned the house, retaining but modernizing the original Federal floor plan and adding decorative motifs of the Italianate style popular at the time.

Ashland was associated with the Clay family until the death of Nanette (McDowell) Bullock, a great-granddaughter of Clay, in 1948. Administered by the Henry Clay Memorial Foundation as a museum since 1950, the estate includes approximately twenty acres of woodlands around the house, several dependencies, and a large formal garden.

See Clay Lancaster, *Antebellum Houses of the Bluegrass* (Lexington, Ky., 1961).

BETTIE L. KERR

ASHLAND OIL, INC. In 1990 Ashland Oil, Inc., headquartered in Ashland, was one of the hundred largest industrial companies in the United States and was the largest corporation based in Kentucky. From its beginnings in 1924 as a $212,000 refinery operation, the company expanded into petroleum production, transportation, refining, and marketing, and later diversified into coal mining, chemicals, architectural engineering, road construction, and other business activities.

The company, a relatively small outsider compared with the international oil giants, has thrived in competition with them through its unconventional approaches to doing business: an informal, nonhierarchical organization where employees are highly motivated (similar to operations of Japanese companies recognized by American management experts in the 1980s); flexibility, as in its refinery production and service station affiliations; emphasis on refining and marketing rather than oil exploration and production; a small-town headquarters location, distant from financial centers; a marketing strategy aimed at niches overlooked by other com-

panies; and major use of inland waterways to serve its refineries.

Ashland Oil is an offshoot of Swiss Oil Corporation, a 1918 oil exploration and production company in Lexington, Kentucky, managed by J. Fred Miles of Oklahoma and financed by Chicago money. In 1924 the financially shaky Swiss Oil formed Ashland Refining Co. as a subsidiary and hired Paul G. BLAZER as president. The small refinery in Ashland quickly prospered, stabilizing the parent firm. Even during the depths of the Great Depression in the 1930s the refinery showed an annual profit. In 1936 Ashland Refining Company completed the purchase of its parent, Swiss Oil, and formed Ashland Oil & Refining Company.

Blazer's success as a manager, recognized by major stockholders, gave him the power to run Ashland as his own operation, although at no point during his tenure as chief executive officer (1936-57) did he own a controlling interest in the company. The liberally educated Blazer, with his impressive mathematical and analytical skills, set the tone of the informal organization. He seldom used his office to discuss matters with subordinates and visited them instead in their offices during his regular walks around the company.

Ashland Oil & Refining grew rapidly, through both internal expansion and acquisitions, including Union Gas & Oil Co. (1925), Tri-State Refining Co. (1930), Cumberland Pipe Line Company (1931), Allied Oil Company (1948), Aetna Oil Company (1949), Freedom-Valvoline Oil Company (1950), Frontier Oil Refining Co. (1950), and National Refining Corporation (1950).

Paul Blazer was succeeded as chief executive officer by his nephew, Rexford S. Blazer (1957-65), who had joined Ashland in the Allied Oil merger. As CEO, he was followed by Orin E. Atkins, an attorney (1965-81), and John R. Hall, a chemical engineer (1981-).

In 1970, when the company's name was changed to Ashland Oil, Inc., it acquired Northwestern Refining of St. Paul, Minnesota, adding a refinery and the SuperAmerica retail marketing concept. During the following decade, in response to the shocks of OPEC oil prices increase, Ashland Oil diversified into other sources of energy and into other industries, as well as emphasizing international oil exploration. It purchased the Archer Daniel Midland Chemical Company, took a 50 percent interest in Arch Mineral Corporation, formed Ashland Coal, Inc., and acquired both U.S. Filter and the Integon Corporation, an insurance company. In cooperation with government agencies and other private energy companies, Ashland operated a pilot plant to produce synthetic fuels. Ashland Oil Canada's producing properties were sold in 1978.

During the 1980s the company spun off unprofitable operations acquired in the 1970s, expanded its marketing through the SuperAmerica and Valvoline Oil outlets, and broadened the range of its chemical operations. During the period when the takeover campaigns of corporate raiders were very successful against other companies, Ashland, supported by the Kentucky General Assembly, successfully resisted an unfriendly bid by the Belzbergs of Canada. Beginning in the 1970s and continuing into the 1990s, the company has faced a variety of legal problems, including Atkins's guilty plea to conspiracy charges, fines for illegal activities in crude oil purchasing, oil spills in the Ohio River, and civil suits against pollution from refinery operations at Cattlettsburg.

Ashland Oil has made major financial contributions to secondary and higher education in Kentucky, including support of the Governor's Scholars Program. The company led in a state program for development of the Ohio River Basin and has contributed to numerous other public projects.

See Joseph L. Massie, *Blazer and Ashland Oil* (Lexington, Ky., 1960); Otto J. Scott, *The Exception: The Story of Ashland Oil & Refining Company* (New York 1968).   JOSEPH L. MASSIE

ASHLAND TRAGEDY. The Ashland tragedy is a story of retribution for violent murder in Boyd County in 1881. Teenagers Robert and Fannie Gibbons and Emma Carico, staying alone in the Gibbons home in Ashland, were beaten to death on the night of December 23. When the killers set the house ablaze to hide the crime, Emma's mother, next door, saw the fire and sounded an alarm. Neighbors found the three victims inside. George Ellis, a bricklayer, soon confessed and implicated fellow workers William Neal and Ellis Craft. The three were moved from the jail at Catlettsburg to avoid a lynch mob but were returned for trial on January 16, 1882. Neal and Craft were convicted in a ten-day trial and sentenced to death; they appealed the verdict. Ellis was tried May 30, convicted, and given a life term, but a mob removed him from the jail the next night and lynched him in Ashland.

On November 1, the steamboat *Granite State* with two hundred state guards picked up Neal and Craft at Catlettsburg to evade a lynch mob traveling by train from Ashland. As the steamer passed Ashland, a crowd formed on the riverbank; eighteen young males commandeered a ferry and approached the boat, firing two pistol shots. Guards returned some 1,500 shots in a two-minute hail of lead, killing four on shore. Investigation but no legal action followed.

Craft and Neal were found guilty in separate trials at Grayson. Craft was hanged there on October 12, 1883, and Neal on March 27, 1885.

GEORGE WOLFFORD

ATCHER, ROBERT OWEN. Robert Owen Atcher, country-western singer, was the son of George Christopher and Mary Agnes (Ray) Atcher. He was born in Hardin County, Kentucky, on May 11, 1914. In 1918 the family moved to North Dakota, where they lived until 1926. Atcher started performing on radio station WHAS, Louisville, in 1928. He enrolled at the University of Kentucky but left for WBBM, Chicago, in 1931. He went on to star on the WLS "National Barn Dance" and in three western movies for Columbia Pictures. Atcher also made several dozen records. In 1947 he married Maggie Whitehill; they have three children, Chris, Cecily, and Robert. Atcher performed on radio for forty-two years and on television for twenty-two. During 1961-75 he was mayor of Schaumburg, Illinois.   CHARLES F. FABER

ATCHISON, DAVID RICE. David Rice Atchison, U.S. senator, was born on August 11, 1807, in the part of south Lexington, Kentucky, then known as Frogtown. After graduating from Transylvania University in 1825, he studied law. He soon moved to Liberty, Missouri, where he entered the state legislature in 1834, served as general in the militia, and in 1841 became a state judge at Platte City. Thomas Reynolds, the governor of Missouri who appointed Atchison to a vacant U.S. Senate seat in 1843, was also a native Kentuckian. Atchison, whose appointment took effect on October 14, 1843, was then elected to the Senate and served until March 3, 1855; he was president pro tem during 1846-50 and 1852-54. Atchison led the successful effort to make Kansas open to slavery; his "Border Ruffians" interfered in elections and intimidated antislavery settlers who moved into Kansas. He campaigned for Southern Democrat John C. Breckinridge in the 1860 presidential election, then accompanied the secessionist governor of Missouri, Claiborne Fox Jackson, through his skirmishes in Missouri and sojourn in Texas. Atchison died in Clinton County, Missouri, on January 26, 1886, and was buried in Greenlawn Cemetery, Plattsburg, Missouri. The towns of Atchison in Kansas and Missouri were named for him.

See William E. Parrish, *David Rice Atchison of Missouri, Border Politician* (Columbia, Mo., 1961); Alan Nevins, *Ordeal of the Union* (New York 1947).   R.E. FORDERHASE

ATHLETIC CONFERENCES. All the state colleges and universities in Kentucky are members of athletic conferences—four major conferences (Southeastern, Metro, Sunbelt, and Ohio Valley) and three minors (Great Lakes Valley, College Athletic, and Kentucky Intercollegiate). Because of the revenue generated by big-time college athletics, exclusive television contracts and penetration of markets have replaced the conferences' more traditional role in governing competing schools, fostering competition, and sponsoring championships.

The Kentucky Intercollegiate Athletic Conference (KIAC), consisting solely of Kentucky schools, was formed in 1923. Its programs include baseball, golf, tennis, and women's basketball and softball. Entering the 1990s, member colleges were Alice Lloyd, Berea, Campbellsville, Cumberland, Georgetown, Lindsey Wilson, Pikeville, and Union. Unlike other conferences, the KIAC is governed by the National Association for International Athletics.

The national athletic conference best known for its association with Kentucky schools is the Southeastern Conference (SEC), headquartered in Birmingham, Alabama. Noted as a National Collegiate Athletic Association (NCAA) football power, it claims the University of Kentucky, notable for its basketball, as a member. Member institutions compete in men's and women's basketball, cross country, indoor/outdoor track, golf, swimming, and tennis; men's baseball and football; women's gymnastics and volleyball. The top teams compete in NCAA tournaments.

The Metro Conference, formed on June 13, 1975, has been gaining recognition in basketball, especially through the University of Louisville. It sponsors championships in men's and women's basketball, cross country, golf, swimming and diving, track and field, and tennis, as well as men's baseball and women's volleyball. Also an NCAA member, the conference is based in Atlanta.

Another non-football, basketball-oriented conference is the Sunbelt, formed in 1976 in Tampa, Florida, and first joined by a Kentucky school in 1982 when Western Kentucky University became a member. An NCAA member, the Sunbelt offers men's and women's basketball, cross country, tennis, men's baseball and soccer, and women's golf and volleyball.

Originally an all-Kentucky organization, the Ohio Valley Conference (OVC) was formed in 1948 and by 1955 had joined the SEC as a major conference. Its membership in 1990 included Eastern Kentucky University, Morehead State University, and Murray State University. Besides football, it includes men's and women's basketball, cross country, tennis, men's baseball and golf, and women's volleyball.

The Great Lakes Valley Conference, a NCAA division II member, was formed in 1978 exclusively for basketball competition. Among the six 1978 charter members were Bellarmine College and Kentucky Wesleyan College. Northern Kentucky University and Kentucky State University joined in 1985 and 1989, respectively. In 1983 women's basketball was added to softball, tennis, volleyball, and cross country. The men's program includes basketball, tennis, golf, soccer, and cross country.

Kentucky's Centre College is a member of the College Athletic Conference (NCAA division III), based at the University of the South in Sewanee, Tennessee. It offers competition in football, basketball, baseball, cross country, track, golf, swimming, soccer, and tennis.

ATTORNEY GENERAL, OFFICE OF. Under the first and second Kentucky constitutions (1792 and 1799), the attorney general was appointed by the governor, but the third constitution (1850) provided for election by the people. The attorney general is the chief law officer of the commonwealth and is entitled to represent Kentucky before all courts, state and federal. The office is active in litigation in the areas of civil and environmental law and consumer protection. Over 1,000 criminal appeals from throughout the state are handled each year by the office. Special prosecution and investigation units can be used independently or in assisting local efforts. The office also issues "Opinions of the Attorney General" on a wide variety of legal subjects and cooperates with the federal government in the prosecution of Medicaid fraud, welfare fraud, and food stamp trafficking.

Originally the attorney general acted as the sole legal representative of the commonwealth. In 1948 the General Assembly allowed the executive departments to hire their own attorneys, thus limiting the attorney general's role. The trend since 1960 has been for the General Assembly to give the attorney general statutory authority in specific areas. New duties, combined with the explosive growth of criminal appeals, have required additional staff. In 1908 the attorney general had only three assistant attorneys general; by 1962 the number had grown to eight, and in 1990 there were sixty-two.

See Robert L. Montague III, "The Office of Attorney General in Kentucky," *Kentucky Law Journal* 49 (Winter 1960-61): 194-224.

JOHN S. GILLIG

ATWOOD, RUFUS BALLARD. Rufus Ballard Atwood, educator and civic leader, was born on March 15, 1897, in Hickman, Kentucky, the youngest child of Pomp and Annie (Parker) Atwood. Raised in a family that emphasized the importance of education, Atwood graduated from Fisk Academy in Nashville in 1915 and then enrolled at Fisk University there. He left Fisk in 1918 to volunteer for service in the army. As a member of the Negro Signal Corps, he received a Bronze Star for gallantry in action. Atwood held bachelor's degrees from both Fisk and Iowa State University, as well as a master's degree in administration from the University of Chicago.

Atwood served as dean of agriculture at Prairie View State College in Texas during 1923-29. In 1929 he became the sixth president of KENTUCKY STATE UNIVERSITY in Frankfort, serving until 1962. During his presidency, Kentucky State was accredited as a four-year college, and educational and administrative programs were revised and expanded. His work to improve black education statewide and nationwide and his contributions to numerous civic organizations brought Atwood numerous awards. The University of Kentucky honored him with the Algernon Sydney Sullivan Citizen Medallion at its commencement ceremonies in 1962. Atwood was the first black to receive the award, established in 1925 and conferred by twenty-five colleges and universities in the South.

Atwood married Mabel Campbell on June 28, 1921. Atwood died on March 18, 1983, and was buried in the Frankfort Cemetery.

See Gerald L. Smith, "Mr. Kentucky State: A Biography of Rufus Ballard Atwood," Ph.D. diss., University of Kentucky, 1988.

GERALD L. SMITH

AUDITOR OF PUBLIC ACCOUNTS, OFFICE OF.

The auditor of public accounts is elected to a four-year term, as provided by the third constitution of the Commonwealth of Kentucky in 1850. Under the state constitutions of 1792 and 1799, the position was appointed annually by both houses of the General Assembly.

The auditor of public accounts is responsible for auditing the state's general accounts and the accounts of all state agencies and county governments; all private and semiprivate agencies receiving or handling any state funds; and all state revenue collections. The auditor also examines the management and condition of all institutions and public works in which the state has any financial interest or legal power and ensures the safe custody and proper accounting of all property of the state.

The auditor conducts special audits and investigations at the request of the governor, as well as monthly audits of the accounts of the state treasurer, the Department of Finance, and county budgets and expenditures. The office also handles annual audits of the county clerk's motor vehicle and motorboat registration fees, licensing, and tax receipts.

State law specifies that a scholarship program for economically disadvantaged students majoring in accounting is to be administered by the auditor. Up to four students annually can receive a full scholarship of up to four years at a Kentucky institution of higher learning. Upon receiving an accounting degree, graduates are then required to serve a year for the auditor's office for each year of scholarship.

See Bennet H. Young, *History and Texts of the Three Constitutions of Kentucky* (Louisville 1890).

JAMES STROHMAIER

AUDUBON, JOHN JAMES. America's foremost naturalist and illustrator of birds, John James Audubon was born April 26, 1785, in St. Dominque (now Haiti) on Les Cayes, his father's plantation. His father, Jean Audubon, was a French naval officer, merchant, and slave trader who had served under General LaFayette in the American Revolutionary War. Audubon's natural mother is thought to have been Jeanne Rabbine, his father's mistress, who died shortly after his birth. Audubon grew up in France under the affectionate care of his father's wife, Anne Moynette Audubon. He preferred roaming the woods and sketching birds to academic studies.

In 1803 Audubon arrived in America to manage his father's farm in Norristown, Pennsylvania. He led an active social life, with enough time to study and draw the abundant birds of his new country. His outgoing nature and accomplishments as a musician and dancer attracted Lucy Bakewell, daughter of a neighbor, who became his wife on April 5, 1808.

Audubon and Ferdinand Rozier, his fellow-Frenchman and business partner, had left Pennsylvania in 1807 to become storekeepers in Louisville. Both were aware of the frontier town's reputation as a gathering point for trappers and traders. The following year, Audubon brought his new bride to "temporary" quarters in Louisville's Indian Queen Hotel, which was to be their home for more than two years. In 1809 their first son, Victor Gifford, was born. As before, Audubon spent a great deal of his time in the woods, observing and drawing birds.

By 1810 Audubon's collection of bird portraits had grown to more than two hundred drawings. At that time, noted Scottish ornithologist Alexander Wilson arrived in Louisville to draw birds and to sell subscriptions to a published portfolio of his works. After seeing Wilson's drawings, Audubon confided that he, too, had been working for years in an effort to draw all the birds of America. Until that meeting, he had considered his efforts merely a personal pastime. However, he could see that his own drawings were superior to Wilson's.

Later that year, believing more profits could be made where there was less competition, Rozier convinced Audubon to move their business 120 miles downriver to Henderson, Kentucky. Along with Rozier, the Audubon family moved into a log cabin, setting up their store in the front room. By 1811 the ambitious Rozier suggested moving farther west, to the Mississippi River outpost of St. Genevieve, Missouri. After seeing St. Genevieve, Audubon decided that it lacked potential, and he and Rozier amicably agreed to end their partnership.

The first years in Henderson brought the Audubons relative prosperity and happiness. A second son, John Woodhouse, was born there on November 30, 1812. Audubon took advantage of frequent business trips to increase the number of drawings in his portfolio. Victor and John took an interest in their father's avocation, later becoming accomplished artists and playing roles in the successful completion and publication of Audubon's books on birds.

By 1818 Audubon had fallen into serious debt. Embittered by his misfortunes and grieving at the death of his two-year-old daughter, Lucy, in 1817, Audubon sold the family's belongings and they returned to Louisville, where he earned his living by painting portraits and giving art lessons. He was jailed briefly for his debts, and he filed for bankruptcy in the panic of 1819. The final sad note of his time in Kentucky came with the birth and death, in Louisville, of his daughter Rosa, who was buried in an unmarked pauper's grave. Audubon and his family left Kentucky in 1819, moving first to Ohio, where he became a taxidermist for Daniel Drake's new Western Museum in Cincinnati, and in 1820 to Louisiana.

Audubon's four-volume *Birds of America* was published in 1827-38, ensuring his place in history. His artistic renderings of America's birds and animals are unsurpassed in their accuracy and beauty. The work was followed by the five-volume *The Viparous Quadrupeds of America* (1842-45) and portfolios (1846-54). Audubon also wrote *Ornithological Biography* (1831-39), the text of the fifth volume of *Birds of America*, and *Synopsis of Birds of North America* (1839), which cataloged the birds.

Audubon spent several years of increasing senility. He died on January 27, 1851, at Minnie's Land, his home on the Hudson River (now Audubon Park in New York City), and he was buried there.

Many of Audubon's engravings, paintings, personal artifacts, and one of the few remaining complete, four-volume sets of the double-elephant *Birds of America* portfolios are on view at the John James Audubon Memorial Museum at Audubon State Park, Henderson, Kentucky.

See Lucy Bakewell Audubon, ed., *The Life of John James Audubon, the Naturalist* (New York 1894); Mary Durant and Michael Harwood, *On the Road with John James Audubon* (New York 1980).

CONSTANCE ALEXANDER AND ROY DAVIS

AUDUBON, LUCY (BAKEWELL). Lucy (Bakewell) Audubon, teacher, was born in Burton-on-Trent, England, on January 18, 1787, to William and Lucy (Green) Bakewell. Her father, a wealthy Englishman, brought the family to America in 1801, and they settled near Norristown, Pennsylvania, on land adjoining the family farm of John James Audubon, the naturalist. Lucy Bakewell married Audubon on April 5, 1808.

The couple lived first in Louisville, then in Henderson, Kentucky. The store that Audubon opened there failed, and he declared bankruptcy in the Panic of 1819. The couple lost everything they owned, including Lucy's inheritance. The Audubons moved to Ohio, then Louisiana, and to New York in 1839. Lucy supported their family financially as a tutor while Audubon traveled in search of birds for the drawings that would make him famous. "If I were jealous," she once said, "I should have a bitter time of it, for every bird is my rival."

In 1830 Lucy went with Audubon on his second trip to England, where she helped arrange for the engraving and publication of *The Birds of America* (1827-38). Audubon died in 1851. Lucy edited *The Life of John James Audubon, the Naturalist* (1869), which included a good bit of Audubon's own writing. In 1863 she sold the original studies for *The Birds of America* to the New York Historical Society.

The Audubons had four children: Victor, John, Lucy, and Rosa. Lucy (Bakewell) Audubon died June 13, 1874, at the home of her sister-in-law in Shelbyville, Kentucky. Her ashes were buried beside Audubon's remains at Minnie's Land, their home in New York.

See Francis Hobart Herrick, *Audubon the Naturalist* (New York 1938); Carolyn E. DeLatte, *Lucy Audubon, A Biography* (Baton Rouge, La., 1982).

GAIL KING

AUGUSTA. Augusta is a city in northeastern Bracken County on KY 8 along the Ohio River. It is eighteen miles downriver from Maysville and forty-two miles upriver from Cincinnati. Because an abundance of prehistoric artifacts have been found there, it is believed that Augusta was once the site of a large permanent Native American village.

The area was part of a Revolutionary War grant by Virginia to Capt. Philip Buckner, who first visited there in 1781. Buckner returned in 1796 with forty Virginia families and found that ten Pennsylvania families had settled there. They purchased lots from Buckner, and in 1797 the city was named Augusta, after the Virginia county, and incorporated as the county seat. Augusta was the county seat of Bracken County from 1797 to 1800. From October 1800 until March 1802, county court was held in the town of Oxford on the plantation of Andrew Morrow. A courthouse built on the public square in Augusta in 1802 served the court until 1839, when the legislature moved the seat to the more central location of Brooksville. The old court building at Augusta burned on April 20, 1848.

In 1798 a private school, the Bracken Academy, was established in the city. AUGUSTA COLLEGE, which was founded in 1822, absorbed the school. The college became a center of antislavery activity; a declining enrollment led to revocation of its state charter in 1849.

The river and the railroad were commercial lifelines to the city, stimulating economic growth during the nineteenth and early twentieth centuries. Keelboats and flatboats landed and unloaded at Augusta. Around 1800 John Bouche established ferryboat service to Brown County, Ohio, which has operated continuously since then except for periods of high water or ice jams. The arrival of the Chesapeake & Ohio Railroad in the area in 1888 brought freight and passenger service to Augusta. The competition caused river traffic to decline.

Augusta prospered during the 1800s in spite of numerous disastrous events. Floods periodically inundated the town, causing widespread damage, and a cholera epidemic claimed lives there in 1849. A Civil War skirmish nearly destroyed the town on September 27, 1862, when Confederate cavalry led by Col. Basil Duke defeated a group of local Union Home Guards. Duke's forces looted and burned part of the city, which caused an estimated loss of $100,000 in property. Violence returned to Augusta in 1908 when local farmers, angry over low tobacco prices, damaged warehouses operated by the American Tobacco Company and by night harassed fellow farmers who sold to the company. To quell the night riders, the state militia was called to Augusta.

Augusta, a city of beautiful old homes, has attracted television filming. Scenes for the miniseries *Centennial* and the Public Broadcasting Service's *Huckleberry Finn* were filmed on the city's riverfront. The major employers in the city are the F.A. Neider Corporation, which produces metal stampings, and the town's largest business, the Copay Corporation, which manufactures plastic parts. In the early 1990s, the town's major highway, KY 8, will be supplemented by the completion of the nearby AA Highway, which will provide residents with easier access to Cincinnati to the west and Maysville and Ashland to the east.

The population of this fourth-class city was 1,434 in 1970; 1,455 in 1980; and 1,336 in 1990.

AUGUSTA, BATTLE OF. In the Confederate invasion of Kentucky in 1862, Gen. Edmund Kirby-Smith divided Col. John Hunt Morgan's brigade into two groups. While Col. Basil Duke led one contingent of about 350 men to northern Kentucky, Morgan marched to southeastern Kentucky in an effort to delay Union Gen. George Morgan in reaching Ohio. Duke, who was to threaten Ohio in an effort to draw Federal troops out of Kentucky to protect Cincinnati, approached Augusta, Kentucky, on September 27, 1862. As the Confederates occupied the high ground south of the town, about a hundred members of the pro-Union Home Guard, led by Col. Joshua Bradford, barricaded themselves in houses along the main road into town. Two Federal gunboats on the Ohio River commanded the Confederate approach. Setting up artillery, Duke fired on the gunships, forcing them to flee upriver. Without the protection of the boats, Duke believed, the Home Guard would surrender immediately.

As the Southern forces entered Augusta, however, the Home Guard opened fire, killing many Confederate soldiers. Hearing the gunfire, the Confederate artillery fired on the town, causing more harm to their own soldiers than to the Home Guard. Organizing his forces, Duke moved from house to house, setting them aflame for two city blocks to drive out the defenders. During the fighting, which lasted only twenty minutes, the Confederates suffered twenty-one deaths and the Home Guard probably fifteen. Though the pro-Union forces were defeated, the Battle of Augusta could hardly be considered a Confederate victory. The resistance mounted by the Home Guard exhausted Duke's ammunition supplies and forced him to retreat south toward Falmouth, thus preventing him from threatening Cincinnati.

See Basil Duke, *A History of Morgan's Cavalry* (Bloomington, Ind., 1960 reprint); James Ramage, *Rebel Raider: The Life of General John Hunt Morgan* (Lexington, Ky., 1986).

AUGUSTA COLLEGE. Augusta College, at Augusta in Bracken County, the first Methodist college in Kentucky and only the third in the United States, was chartered by the legislature on December 7, 1822. It opened in 1825 after the construction of a three-story building in the center of Augusta, absorbing the Bracken Academy, founded in 1798. Financial support came from the state and Methodist Episcopal Church conferences of Ohio and Kentucky. The curriculum included classic and modern foreign languages, English, mathematics, and sciences, and it awarded both the bachelor of arts and master of arts degrees.

During the 1830s the enrollment at Augusta College approached two hundred men and women, from both free and slave states. Its status as a ranking institution was jeopardized by its dual support—split between the Ohio and Kentucky church conferences, neither of which was ultimately responsible. A decline in enrollment was precipitated by the controversy over slavery, as well as the desire of the Ohio conference to have its own college and the preference of the Kentucky conference for a more centrally located school. The college also faced local hostility over the transfer of Bracken Academy endowments to Augusta College. Uncertainty over endowment funding and the disposition of its financing led the Kentucky church conference to transfer its financial support to Transylvania University in 1842. In 1844 the Ohio conference terminated its funding, and the school was left with insufficient operating money. The Kentucky legislature revoked Augusta's charter on February 26, 1849, and it ceased to function on June 1, 1849.

Augusta College's faculty included Joseph S. Tomlinson, uncle of Stephen Collins Foster, who visited Tomlinson there in 1833; Henry Bascom, president of Transylvania University; and John P. Durbin and Herman Johnson, presidents of Dickinson College. Among the prominent alumni were Randolph S. Foster, president of Northwestern University; Sen. Alexander W. Doniphan; Gov. Robert Wickliffe of Louisiana; Gen. William Preston; John Gregg Fee, cofounder of Berea College; George Robertson, chief justice of the Kentucky court of appeals; and William S. Groesbeck, Democratic nominee for vice-president in 1872.

AVERY, BENJAMIN F. Benjamin F. Avery, businessman, was born in Aurora, New York, on December 3, 1801. He was raised on his father's New York farm and studied law at Union College in Schenectady, N.Y., where he graduated in 1822. Avery moved to Clarksville, Virginia, where he opened a small business in 1825. He also lived in Milton, North Carolina, and Meadeville, Virginia. In 1847 Avery moved to Louisville to help his nephew, Daniel H. Avery, start up an agricultural foundry at Preston and Main streets. The business was successful, supplying much of the South with farm equipment, including the so-called Avery plow. Operations were suspended during the Civil War, when the Union sought to halt the flow of supplies to the Confederacy, and the foundry building was used as a Union hospital. Benjamin Avery took over the business in 1868, when his nephew died, and soon established a partnership with his two eldest sons, Samuel and George. He ran the business until late in his life and helped make Louisville a major supply center for most of the South. Avery also served as director of the Bank of Louisville, and he owned the Talmadge Lake Ice Company.

Avery and his wife, Susan, who were married in 1843, had six children: Lydia, Samuel, Gertrude, George, Nelly, and William. Avery died in Louisville on March 2, 1884, and was buried in Cave Hill Cemetery in Louisville.

B

BACON COLLEGE. Bacon College was founded in Georgetown, Kentucky, in the first half of the nineteenth century. The institution was the product of a religious conflict between the Baptists of the Georgetown College administration and three professors at the college who were members of the Disciples of Christ. Resigning from the faculty of Georgetown College in 1836, the three, led by Thornton Johnson, founded their own institution of higher learning, Bacon College, which received a state charter on February 23, 1837. Named in honor of Francis Bacon, English philosopher and statesman, Bacon College had no source of revenue except tuition; the expected contributions from fellow church members did not materialize, and because of the hostile environment created by Georgetown College, Bacon College openly sought a new location. Mercer County pledged $50,000 toward its support and in the spring of 1839 Bacon College moved to Harrodsburg, where classes resumed that September.

In 1843 a two-story Georgian building was erected, and in 1847 enrollment reached 180 students. But pledges of financial support were easier to obtain than the actual funds. Mercer County paid the college only about $18,000 of the promised $50,000, and tuition payments fell short, forcing Bacon College to close on June 14, 1850. John Bryan Bowman (class of 1842), a Mercer County attorney and Bacon trustee, refused to let his alma mater die; in 1855 he embarked on an extensive fund-raising campaign. Bowman, aided by Harrodsburg attorney James Taylor, raised $180,000 for what he hoped would become a major educational center in Kentucky. In 1857 he petitioned the state legislature to amend the Bacon College charter and on January 15, 1858, the legislature established "a first class university," known as KENTUCKY UNIVERSITY, where classes first met on September 19, 1859. Kentucky University operated in Harrodsburg until a fire on February 10, 1864, destroyed the building. In February 1865 it merged with Transylvania and relocated to Lexington.

See Dwight E. Stevenson, *The Bacon College Story* (Lexington, Ky., 1962).

BADIN, STEPHEN THEODORE. Born in Orleans, France, July 17, 1768, Stephen Theodore Badin attended college in Paris, later studying for the Roman Catholic priesthood in the seminary of his hometown. A religious exile in the French Revolution, he went to Baltimore, where on May 25, 1793, he became the first Catholic priest ordained in the United States. Assigned by Bishop John Carroll to missionary work in Kentucky, Badin reached his new post by walking from Baltimore to Pittsburgh and then taking a flatboat to Limestone (Maysville) in 1793. He then served the Catholics of Scott County for one year. Late in 1794 Badin moved to St. Stephen's farm near Pottinger's Creek

in Marion County. The LORETTO Motherhouse was later built on this property, and Badin's 1816 cabin is preserved there.

Until the arrival of Benedict FLAGET as Kentucky's first bishop in 1811, Badin was the leader of Kentucky Catholicism. By the mid-1790s he was ministering to three hundred Catholic families scattered among ten pioneer settlements. An earnest man with rough edges, Badin was severe in his morality and Federalist in his politics. He quarreled with the Catholics of central Kentucky over control of the parishes, and with Bishop Flaget over land titles. The land dispute caused Badin to leave Kentucky in 1819 for France. When he returned to America, he acted as missionary to Potawatomi Indians and later to Irish workers building the Wabash Canal. Badin purchased the land in Indiana on which the University of Notre Dame stands. He died in Cincinnati on April 19, 1853, and was buried at Notre Dame.

A prolific writer of letters, Badin also kept historical notes, later vital in recording early Kentucky Catholic history. He was an occasional poet, and he wrote *The Principles of Roman Catholics*, published at Bardstown in 1805.

See J.H. Schauinger, *Stephen T. Badin* (Milwaukee, Wis., 1956).   CLYDE F. CREWS

BAILEY, CLAY WADE. Clay Wade Bailey, journalist, was born at Little Sandy in Elliott County, Kentucky, on September 22, 1905, to George W. and Rebecca (Weddington) Bailey. He was raised at the Masonic Widows and Orphans Home in Louisville. He lived with an uncle in Kansas while attending high school and later took courses at Sue Bennett College in London, Kentucky. As a reporter, he covered Kentucky's capital for forty-six years, mainly for Covington's *Kentucky Post*. He also wrote for the *Lexington Herald* and the *Evansville Press*. Bailey was a well-known, respected newsman, and many political figures in Frankfort sought him out for advice and for his vast knowledge of the political intrigues of past administrations. Bailey married Ann Josephine Robinson in Frankfort on May 12, 1939; they had one son, Logan. Bailey died on February 19, 1974, and was buried in the Frankfort Cemetery.

RICHARD G. WILSON

BAIN, GEORGE WASHINGTON. A prominent figure on the chautauqua lecture circuit, George Washington Bain was born in Lexington, Kentucky, on September 24, 1840, the son of George W. and Jane E. (West) Bain. He was educated at several academies in rural Fayette and Bourbon counties. Brought up in the Methodist Church, South, Bain at an early age became an ardent advocate of temperance. In 1869, at a Fourth of July temperance picnic in Winchester, Kentucky, he was a last-minute substitute for the scheduled speaker, and his eloquent, stirring polemic against the liquor traffic immediately propelled him to the front ranks of the temperance movement in Kentucky. Within two years he was elected grand worthy chief templar, the presiding officer of the Order of Good Templars, the leading temperance organization in the state. For several years he traveled throughout Kentucky establishing Good Templar lodges and pledging thousands to total abstinence. From 1871 to 1874, he also edited a newspaper, the *Temperance Advocate*.

By 1880 "Colonel" Bain had become a popular fixture on the chautauqua and lyceum circuits in various states. His customary speaking schedule kept him away from home for eight months of the year. During a forty-year career, he delivered more than 10,000 temperance messages throughout the United States and Canada. With his national following, the attractive, mustached Bain would have been a logical candidate for public office, yet he declined even a suggestion of nomination, declaring that he could more effectively serve the temperance cause at the lectern. On one occasion in 1904, his decision not to accept the presidential or vice-presidential nomination of the Prohibition party led the *New York Voice*, a temperance newspaper, to write: "Formally some other must be looked to as our leader, but in essential leadership no man in the history of the Prohibition movement will ever walk ahead of George W. Bain."

On August 31, 1860, Bain married Anna Maria Johnson, who shared his devotion to the antiliquor crusade. In addition to raising five children, she served as president of the Kentucky Women's Christian Temperance Union during its formative years in the 1880s. Bain died at his home on March 28, 1927, and was buried in the Lexington Cemetery.

See George W. Bungay, *Pen Portraits of Illustrious Abstainers* (New York 1881); George W. Bain, *Wit, Humor, Reason, Rhetoric, Prose, Poetry, and Story Woven into Eight Popular Lectures* (Louisville 1915).   THOMAS H. APPLETON, JR.

BAKER, ABNER, TRIAL. Although clearly insane, Dr. Abner Baker was convicted and hanged for murder in Clay County, Kentucky, in 1845, in a case that represents Kentucky criminal justice at its worst. Baker believed most women were whores, and he repeatedly accused his young wife of sexual misconduct with Daniel Bates, one of the richest and most powerful residents of Clay County. Acting under this delusion, Baker shot Bates on September 13, 1844, and he died the next day. The murder occurred at Bates's salt works, where Baker approached him from the rear and shot him once in the back.

At first the authorities refused to prosecute Baker because they believed him insane, but the Bates faction obtained an indictment and an order for Baker's arrest. Although public opinion in Clay County was clearly prejudiced against Baker, his lawyers agreed for him to be tried there. Throughout the trial, members of the Bates faction menaced

the judge and jury with prominently displayed weapons and loud commentary on the testimony. The judge showed a lack of understanding of the current law on legal insanity, and the main defense attorney, George Robertson, failed to cite the most important American case on the subject (*Commonwealth v. Rogers*, 1844). The jury convicted Baker and the judge imposed the mandatory death sentence. Although Baker's family and his lawyers tried to secure a pardon, Gov. William Owsley (1844-48) not only refused to grant a pardon but even declined to convene a medical panel to determine whether Baker was sane enough to be hanged. As there was no right of appeal from a felony conviction in Kentucky until 1854, Owsley's decision doomed Baker to the gallows and he was hanged on October 3, 1845.

See Robert M. Ireland, "The Judicial Murder of Abner Baker," *Register* 88 (Winter 1990): 1-24.
                    ROBERT M. IRELAND

BALLARD, BLAND W. Bland W. Ballard, pioneer and early legislator, was born October 16, 1761, in Spotsylvania County, Virginia. He was the third child and the eldest son of Bland Ballard and his wife. In 1779 father and son moved to Kentucky, where young Bland joined the militia and defended the western frontier. On March 31, 1788, fifteen or twenty Delaware Indians killed Ballard's father, stepmother, two brothers, and a half-sister at Tyler Station, on Tick Creek in what is now Shelby County. (Another half-sister was tomahawked but recovered.) Lyman C. Draper, a collector of early Kentucky history, quoted Ballard as claiming to have killed thirty to forty Indians in battle to avenge the murder of his family, as well as to punish horse theft. In 1792 Ballard helped to mark the road that is now U.S. 60 from Shelbyville to the Falls of the Ohio. In 1798 he was appointed a trustee for Shelby Academy. Although uneducated, Ballard had a remarkable gift for speaking fluently and graphically, and he was elected to represent Shelby County in the General Assembly in 1800, 1803, and 1805.

The six-foot-tall, outspoken pioneer died at his home, four miles west of Shelbyville, on September 5, 1853, and was buried there. His body was later reinterred in the Frankfort Cemetery, along with that of his first wife, Elizabeth Williamson. The couple had seven children: James, Mary, Dorothy ("Dolly"), Susan, Sally, Martha ("Patsy"), and Nancy. Ballard's second wife was Diane Matthews; his third, Elizabeth Weaver Garrett. Ballard County was named in his honor in 1842.

See E.D. Shinnick, *Some Old Time History of Shelbyville and Shelby County* (Frankfort, Ky., 1974); Margaret Morris Bridwell, "Notes on One of the Early Ballard Families of Kentucky, Including the Ballard Massacre," *FCHQ* 13 (Jan. 1939): 1-20.   MARY LOU MADIGAN

BALLARD COUNTY. Located in extreme western Kentucky at the confluence of the Ohio and Mississippi rivers, Ballard County is part of the region known as the Jackson Purchase. Comprising an area of 254 square miles, Ballard County, the ninety-third county in order of formation, was established on February 15, 1842, out of parts of Hickman and McCracken counties and named in honor of Capt. Bland Ballard, a participant in the battle of Fallen Timbers (1793) and the River Raisin (1813), and a member of the Kentucky General Assembly. Ballard County is bordered by the Ohio River on the north and the Mississippi River on the west, and Carlisle and McCracken counties share its southern and eastern boundaries, respectively. WICKLIFFE is the county seat.

Ranging from flatland to moderately rolling hills, the topography of the county is fairly uniform. Bluffs along the Ohio and Mississippi rivers from Barlow southward are among the main geographic features of the area. Extending at certain points about five miles inland, the Ohio River floodplain creates numerous swamps, sloughs, ponds, and lakes. With about 65 percent of the land occupied by farms in 1987, the county has remained a highly agricultural area. Crops such as tobacco and soybeans, along with corn and wheat, made the county forty-eighth in agricultural receipts among Kentucky counties in 1987.

Prehistoric Indians first inhabited the Ballard County area about 800-1350, as the Wickliffe mounds, the remains of an ancient village, testify. This culture had long since disappeared by the time Europeans visited the region. While looking for the mouth of the Mississippi River, French explorer La Salle stopped near the site of present-day Wickliffe about 1682, but the first attempt at white settlement did not come until nearly a century later. In 1780 Gen. George Rogers Clark established FORT JEFFERSON at the mouth of Mayfield Creek. In 1781, following a five-day siege by Chickasaw Indians, the fort was abandoned. With the cessation of Indian threats and the inclusion of the area in the Jackson Purchase of 1818, settlers returned to the Ballard County region and Fort Jefferson. Although these new settlements outlasted the original settlement on Mayfield Creek, the county remained sparsely populated for some time.

During the Civil War, though Southern sympathizers predominated, Ballard County was a Union stronghold. After reactivating old Fort Jefferson and building a second military installation just north of Wickliffe called Fort Holt, Union Gen. Ulysses Grant used these defenses as supply stations for his campaigns along the Mississippi River. Despite this heavy Federal presence, about four hundred Ballard County men joined the Confederate forces, whereas only about one hundred enlisted in the Union army.

Following the war, Ballard County residents resumed their mostly agricultural way of life. The courthouse, located in Blandville since the creation of the county in 1842, burned in 1880, setting off a heated debate over the location of the county seat. Because Wickliffe was a river port and was served by two railroads, the Illinois Central and the Mobile & Ohio, many citizens favored it as the county seat. A public election held in May 1880 approved Wickliffe, but proponents of Blandville disputed the fairness of the vote. Nevertheless, the county seat was moved to Wickliffe, and in 1882 the court of appeals upheld the election results. In 1884 voters again chose Wickliffe as the Ballard County seat. The county reached its highest population of 14,378 in 1880; it lost population in 1886, when Carlisle County was created out of the portion of Ballard County below Mayfield Creek.

As the county entered the twentieth century, its location on the rivers and the Illinois Central Railroad made Ballard County one of western Kentucky's leading trading centers. Towns such as Barlow, Cairo, and Wickliffe all prospered. Nonetheless, agriculture has remained the most important feature of the economy. Although no major highway serves it (the Purchase Parkway and I-24 both bypass the county), industry has come to Ballard County, the most important being the Westvaco Corporation, a pulp and paper producer, which was established in 1970. The largest industrial employer in the county, Westvaco employed 639 people in 1990.

The Peal and Ballard County Wildlife Management Areas, purchased in 1954, attract hunters and fishermen throughout the county to a superior wildlife habitat. The wildlife management areas are nationally famous for waterfowl hunting.

The population of Ballard County was 8,276 in 1970; 8,798 in 1980; and 7,902 in 1990.

See J.H. Battle, *Histories and Biographies of Ballard, Calloway, Fulton, Graves, Hickman, McCracken and Marshall Counties, Kentucky* (Louisville 1885).

BANKING. The system of commercial banking in Kentucky today dates from the National Banking Act of 1865, which established the dual, national-state chartering provision, and from the Federal Reserve Act of 1913. The first bank in Kentucky was approved by legislation in 1802 as the Kentucky Insurance Company. The company, which survived until 1820, had the right to issue paper money, an authority that, in effect, gave it banking powers. The BANK OF KENTUCKY was incorporated by the legislature in 1806 and was partly owned by the state. The bank was based in Frankfort and had branches in other towns. In 1818 the legislature permitted the chartering of forty-six independent banks around the state, from Owingsville to Henderson and from Maysville to Barbourville. These banks could issue their own paper money totaling up to three times their capital stock. The result was almost as many values for bank notes as there were banks. In many cases the national bank in Kentucky, the Second Bank of the United States, with branches in Louisville and Lexington, refused to accept the Kentucky banknotes. After the financial PANIC OF 1819, it was almost impossible to redeem the notes of any Kentucky bank. On February 10, 1820, the independent bank law was repealed, leaving only the thirteen branches of the Bank of Kentucky and the two branches of the Second Bank of the United States. To relieve the shortage of money, the legislature chartered the Bank of the Commonwealth in November 1820 with a branch in each judicial district. This bank's legality was questioned but it survived.

In 1834 the Louisville Bank of Kentucky was chartered for thirty years, to have six branches around the state. In 1835 the legislature chartered the Northern Bank of Kentucky in Lexington, with four branches. These acts set the stage for a more conservative and dependable banking system in Kentucky despite a financial panic in the early 1840s. Today's Bank of Maysville was originally one of the branches of the Louisville Bank of Kentucky. Other banks were also established during this period. The National Banking Act of 1865 had the effect of eliminating bank notes issued by the state-chartered banks.

In 1989 there were 331 banks in Kentucky, 84 of them having no branches. The remaining 247 banks operated 796 branches, giving Kentucky a total of 1,127 banking offices. The number of banks in Kentucky has declined slightly since the end of World War II, but the number of banking offices has expanded. Kentucky banks fall into two of the twelve Federal Reserve Bank districts in the nation. Banks that lie east of a line that runs from the Indiana-Ohio border on the north to the western edge of McCreary County on the south are served by the Federal Reserve Bank's Cleveland branch in Cincinnati. Banks that lie to the west of the line are served by the Louisville branch of the Federal Reserve Bank in St. Louis.

To guarantee liquidity, a bank must maintain on deposit at the Federal Reserve Bank, or in its vault, a certain percentage of demand and time deposit liabilities. This requirement applies to all depository institutions that hold checkable accounts—commercial banks, savings and loans, and credit unions—whether or not they are Federal Reserve members. Prior to federal legislation in 1980 and 1982, only Federal Reserve member banks were subject to the reserve requirements. Since the same reserve requirements now apply to both commercial banks and other depository institutions, there is less distinction between them than there was prior to 1980. A deposit in a checkable account at a Kentucky savings and loan or a credit union is from the viewpoint of the depositor the same as funds in a checking account at a commercial bank.

Kentucky banks are either national banks, chartered by the U.S. comptroller of the currency, or state banks, chartered by the Kentucky commissioner of financial institutions. If a bank has a national charter, it must include "national" in its name. Such a bank is subject to supervision by the Federal Reserve System to ensure liquidity and safety of the bank's assets. A state-chartered bank is subject to Kentucky banking laws governing liquidity and safety of assets. Some state-chartered banks are also members of the Federal Reserve System. All banks in Kentucky, national or state-chartered, are members of the Federal Deposit Insurance Corporation, which insures all deposit accounts up to $100,000.

To meet basic economic goals, the banking system must be able to handle a large volume of payments and transfers of funds. Most Kentucky banks have a check clearing arrangement whereby they trade checks drawn on each other. If payments on receipt originate in other parts of the country, the check clearing function involves a larger bank in another city or the Federal Reserve System. Automated check clearinghouses in Cincinnati and St. Louis provide for the continuous clearing of checks. Many Kentucky banks keep deposits there to facilitate the check clearing process. In addition to accepting deposits and making loans, Kentucky banks provide many other services vital to a healthy, growing economy. Since real goods and services are the basic measure of economic health, banks must remain responsive to the changing needs of members of the economy by offering services such as trust accounts, safe-deposit boxes, certified checks, traveler's checks, credit cards, equipment leasing, or international trade.

Before a new bank can be chartered in Kentucky, an investigation is made of the financial standing, moral character, and capability of each of the incorporators, and the bank must have enough prospective business to make it a success. A new bank must also meet the test of adding to public convenience and advantage.

Kentucky banking laws restrict the asset size of many local banks by permitting branch banking outside a bank's home county only in an adjoining county where no bank has its home office. Kentucky legislation in 1984, for all practical purposes, negated this limited branching law by permitting a multibank holding company to own banks in different counties, thus reducing geographic barriers. Kentucky's 1984 bank holding company law also permitted national, reciprocal interstate banking. To prevent monopolization of banking markets, acquisitions in Kentucky are prohibited if the acquiring bank holds more than 15 percent of total bank deposits in the state. After the 1984 bank holding company legislation was enacted, several Kentucky banks changed hands. Some of Kentucky's largest banks were acquired by regional multibank holding companies: Citizens Fidelity Bank and Trust Company of Louisville by PNC Financial Corporation; First National Bank of Louisville and Commerce National Bank of Lexington by National City Corporation of Cleveland; and Citizens Union Bank by Banc One Corporation of Columbus, Ohio, which renamed it Bank One Lexington. A total of thirty Kentucky banks were owned by out-of-state bank holding companies at the end of 1988, representing about 36 percent of total bank assets in the state.

Banks within Kentucky also were busy forming multibank holding companies and buying out other banks. At the end of 1988, thirty-nine Kentucky multibank holding companies had been formed, including Liberty National Bancorp of Louisville, with eight affiliates in Kentucky; First Security

Corporation in Lexington, with four affiliates; Farmers Capital Bank Corporation of Frankfort, with six affiliates; and Pikeville National Corporation, with five affiliates.

See Carolyn Donnella Beauchamp, "Banking in Kentucky," *Kentucky Banker* 37-47 (Dec. 1986-Oct. 1987); Randolph McGhee, *Kentucky Banking Structure and Economic Development* (Frankfort, Ky., 1979).   BERNARD DAVIS

BANK OF KENTUCKY. The Bank of Kentucky was chartered in 1806 by the state legislature as part of a compromise that ended the political controversy over private banking. Modeled on the Bank of the United States, it had a capital of $1 million, with one-half the stock reserved for the state. The bank was governed by a president and a twelve-member board of directors. Six directors and the president were elected annually by the legislature, and the other six directors were elected annually by private stockholders. Robert Alexander of Versailles was chosen president in 1807 and served in that capacity for the next fourteen years. During Alexander's tenure the Bank of Kentucky was a sound, profitable, and conservatively administered institution.

To fend off political pressures for inflation in the turbulent times following the panic of 1819, the Bank of Kentucky suspended specie payments in 1820 and established new branches. A total of thirteen were ultimately opened, but these measures were not sufficient to satisfy popular demands for financial relief. In 1820 the legislature enacted an extensive relief program designed to force devaluation of debts by inflating the currency. To ensure the cooperation of the state bank, Alexander was replaced as president by John Harvie. When Harvie proved only marginally more receptive to inflation than Alexander, the legislature chartered the politically controlled Bank of the Commonwealth and flooded the state with the paper currency of the new bank. The runaway inflation and collapse of property values that followed led to a conservative backlash and the election of a hard-money legislature, which repealed the charters of both state banks in 1822. For several years after that, the Bank of Kentucky was active in winding up its affairs, but it no longer engaged in banking.

See Dale Royalty, "Banking and the Commonwealth Ideal in Kentucky, 1806-1822," *Register* 77 (Spring 1979): 91-107; Bray Hammond, *Banks and Politics in America from the Revolution to the Civil War* (Princeton, N.J., 1957).   DALE ROYALTY

BANK OF THE COMMONWEALTH. The Bank of the Commonwealth was chartered in 1820 as part of the debtor relief program enacted by the legislature in response to the economic depression of 1819-23 (see RELIEF CRISIS). Its first president was John J. Crittenden and its board of directors included Amos Kendall and Francis Blair, Sr. As stated in its charter, the bank's purpose was to discount paper and make loans for the relief of the

community—up to $1,000 for every Kentuckian who applied. Not surprisingly, the paper of the Bank of the Commonwealth deteriorated to approximately 20 percent of its face value within a year of its opening. Kentuckians reacted sharply against all banks as a consequence of this paper fiasco, and the General Assembly repealed the Bank of the Commonwealth charter in 1822.

The bank was an integral part of the effort by Relief politicians to create a state economic system separate from that of the rest of the United States. Its failure convinced many Kentuckians that they shared in the economic fate of the rest of the nation. The experience also helped shape the financial views of Kendall and Blair, and through them U.S. economic policy during the administration of Andrew Jackson.

See Dale Royalty, "Banking and the Commonwealth Ideal in Kentucky, 1806-1822," *Register* 77 (Spring 1979): 91-107; Bray Hammond, *Banks and Politics in America from the Revolution to the Civil War* (Princeton, N.J., 1957).

DALE ROYALTY

BANKS, NANCY (HOUSTON). Nancy (Houston) Banks, author, was born around 1850 to George and Sarah (Brady) Houston and raised in Morganfield, Kentucky. Following her marriage to James N. Banks, she worked for the *Cincinnati Enquirer* and her first book, *Stairs of Sand*, appeared in 1890. During the 1890s she was a member of the staff of the *Bookman* in New York City, which aided in creating recognition for fellow Kentuckian James Lane Allen by printing her favorable reviews of his works. Thereafter she lived in England and wrote for *Vanity Fair*, serving as correspondent in South Africa during the Boer War. Banks's best-known novel, *Oldfield: A Kentucky Tale of the Last Century* (1902), depicted life in frontier Kentucky. It and *'Round Anvil Rock* (1903), which presented life in early Union County, made use of historical persons and events. Banks died on April 5, 1934, in Washington, D.C., and was buried in Morganfield in the Masonic Cemetery.   DAVID F. BURG

BAPTISTS. Baptist Christians first appear in Kentucky's historical records in 1776, when William Hickman from Virginia preached a sermon on an April Sunday in Harrodstown (now Harrodsburg). Hickman soon returned to Virginia, however, and there was no Baptist congregation until June 1781, when the Severns Valley settlement (now Elizabethtown) was established. There remains a persistent traditional belief among Baptists that Daniel Boone's brother, Squire Boone, was at least an occasional preacher among the Baptists of North Carolina and Kentucky. The earliest congregations clustered around the Elizabethtown-Bardstown area, forming the Salem Baptist Association in 1785. In central Kentucky, the Elkhorn Association was made up of Baptist immigrants from Virginia, including the preachers of the Craig family: Lewis, pastor of the TRAVELING CHURCH, Elijah, and

Joseph. These Baptist settlers were fairly well-to-do, many arriving with slaves to help till the land. Among them were John Taylor, John Gano, Ambrose Dudley, and James Garrard, a landowner and Baptist preacher who served as governor of the commonwealth from 1796 until 1804.

In the last two decades of the eighteenth century, the Baptist congregations were scattered and small, most of them meeting only once a month for preaching services. Many of the log, brick, or stone church buildings had balconies or galleries for the slaves of the members of the congregations. The Baptists of Kentucky were categorized as either Regulars, north of the Kentucky River, who were orderly in their worship and practices, or Separates, south of the Kentucky, whose worship was emotional and unstructured. Both groups were divided internally over such issues as slavery, Unitarianism, and the pay of ministers.

The nineteenth century brought great change in the form of an unprecedented outbreak of emotional religious fervor, known as the GREAT REVIVAL, or Second Great Awakening. The participants were mostly Methodists and Presbyterians, but the excitement spilled over into meetings of local Baptist churches and associations, and the number of Baptist churches in Kentucky doubled between 1800 and 1803, while the number of Baptists tripled. The revival also resulted in the union of most of the Regulars and Separates in Kentucky into one fellowship (1801). The influx of new converts, mainly the less affluent new arrivals in the commonwealth, heightened the need for church discipline. Records of early churches are filled with references to members, including slaves, who were expelled for a wide variety of offenses, often for drunkenness.

The missionary Luther Rice, a native of Massachusetts who preached often in Kentucky after 1815, encouraged Baptist churches and individuals to support the causes of missions overseas and education at home. Partly inspired by Rice, the Baptists of Kentucky began to contemplate a statewide organizational institution and other cooperative ventures. Silas Mercer Noel, a minister in the Frankfort area, was one of the leaders of these early efforts.

While the Baptists of Kentucky have generally united around tenets of Biblical authority, congregational independence, and baptism by immersion, they have tended to divide over such issues as the extent of organizational structure, the importance of education, the need for a professional ministry, and the structure of worship. The majority of Kentucky's Baptists have favored organization for the purpose of missions, education, and other causes. These Baptists founded the organization now known as the Kentucky Baptist Convention, commonly known as Southern Baptists. By 1989 the nearly 2,370 congregations of the Kentucky Baptist Convention claimed a total of 765,578 members—nearly one of every five Kentuckians.

The first group known as the Kentucky Baptist Convention, organized in 1832 in Bardstown, dissolved from lack of support in June 1837. It was succeeded by the General Association of Baptists in Kentucky, organized in Louisville in October 1837. The gradual acknowledgement of Louisville as the organizational center for Kentucky Baptists during the nineteenth century made many Kentucky Baptists, most of whom were rural people, feel uneasy. During the third decade of the nineteenth century, Baptists in Kentucky lost nearly a third of their numbers to the religious movement tied to the ministry of Alexander CAMPBELL of Bethany, Virginia, who opposed the centralizing tendencies at work among the Baptists. Many Baptists joined the denominations known as the Christian Church, Church of Christ, and Disciples of Christ.

In addition to the General Association of Baptists in Kentucky, other forms of Baptist cooperation included the Kentucky Baptist Missionary Society, which operated a school for American Indians near Georgetown in the 1830s and 1840s; Baptist denominational publications, the most successful being the *Baptist Banner*, which later evolved into the present-day state Baptist paper, the *Western Recorder;* and Georgetown College, founded in 1829 by the Kentucky Baptist Education Society, with the support of local citizens. Less successful cooperative ventures were the American Indian Mission (Louisville) and the Western Baptist Theological Institute (Covington).

In a step toward regional cooperation, Kentucky Baptists began to support the work of the Southern Baptist Convention, organized in 1845 in Augusta, Georgia. Baptist identity was also strengthened by a doctrinal emphasis known as Old Landmarkism, extremely influential among Baptists of southern and western Kentucky. The Landmarkers emphasized Baptist uniqueness and superiority to other Christian groups, an emphasis hardly conducive to ecumenicism.

During the Civil War, Baptists in central, southern, and western Kentucky tended to support the Confederacy, while Baptists in Louisville, northern Kentucky, and eastern Kentucky were mostly Unionists. Church and denominational life suffered throughout the state except in Louisville, where Baptist strength actually increased during the war years. After the war, the Baptists of Kentucky bore much of the financial burden for the missionary work of the Southern Baptist Convention, owing to the plight of the Baptists in states farther south.

The Louisville Baptist Orphans' Home (now Spring Meadows), founded in 1869, enjoyed the support of Baptists throughout the state. Schools operated by groups of Baptists sprang up all over Kentucky, the most notable being Georgetown Female Seminary (1845); Bethel College, Russellville (1856); Bethel Female College, Hopkinsville (1858); Clinton College (1874); Lynnland Institute, Glendale (1866); Williamsburg Institute, now Cumberland College, (1889); Oneida Baptist Institute (1899); Magoffin Baptist Institute, Salyersville (1905); and Russell Creek Academy, now Campbellsville College (1907).

The Southern Baptist Theological Seminary, which relocated from Greenville, South Carolina, to Louisville in 1877, had a major influence on Kentucky Baptists. A host of seminary students over the years have traveled from the seminary campus on weekends to serve as pastors of small churches within a 150-mile radius of Louisville, raising the educational level of the congregations served—but not without controversy. A distrust of too much education among Kentucky Baptists resulted in periods of attack on Southern Seminary in the 1890s. A central committee of Baptist women's missionary societies was formed in 1878, and a women's meeting was held as part of the Southern Baptist Convention in Louisville in May 1887. The Kentucky Baptist Woman's Missionary Union, auxiliary to the General Association of Baptists in Kentucky, was organized on June 16, 1903, in the First Baptist Church of Winchester. Between 1830 and 1910 the number of Baptist churches in Kentucky tripled, from 574 to 1,774, and the church membership increased over fivefold, from 39,957 to 224,237.

Before World War I, the General Association of Baptists in Kentucky adopted a plan under which several independent societies and agencies cooperated in solicitation for state and national Baptist causes. This sort of collective effort later developed into the "75 Million Campaign" of the Southern Baptist Convention. During the nearly two decades of economic recession and depression after 1920, many of the agencies and institutions of the Kentucky Baptists fell deeply into debt, and there was no relief until the later years of World War II. Membership and financial contributions from Kentucky Baptists grew rapidly after World War II. Church membership, 437,160 in 1945, grew to 888,000 by 1986. The number of churches increased from 2,149 to 2,244.

Since 1961 cooperative Kentucky Baptists have been called the Kentucky Baptist Convention. By 1965 it was operating three senior denominational colleges— Georgetown College, Cumberland College, and Campbellsville College—as well as hospitals in Louisville, Lexington, and Paducah; Clear Creek Baptist Bible College in Pineville; Oneida Baptist Institute (a residential high school); Cedarmore Baptist Assembly and Jonathan Creek Baptist Assembly; and the Kentucky Baptist Board of Child Care. A new building was erected in Middletown to house administrative offices. Among the leaders of the cooperative movement were W.C. Boone (1946-61), Harold G. Sanders (1961-72), and Franklin Owen (1972-83). Under the leadership of William Marshall (1983-) the convention has emphasized world missions in Kenya and Brazil.

Not all Baptist churches in Kentucky are associated with the Kentucky Baptist Convention. The most numerous of the smaller groups in Kentucky are the black Baptists. In the earliest days of Kentucky Baptist history, slaves worshiped along with their masters in the frontier churches, often while seated in a separate balcony, or gallery. In many churches, in fact, black members outnumbered white. A handful of black Baptist churches existed in Kentucky before the Civil War. The largest of these was in Lexington, where the pastor was the slave Peter DUERETT, known as Old Captain. Another large black congregation gathered in Louisville around the ministry of the freedman Henry Adams. For years these were two of the largest congregations of any kind in Kentucky. Emancipation hastened the establishment of the black Baptist churches. By 1870 congregational separation of black and white Baptists was virtually complete, and a statewide black Baptist organization had been formed.

Black Baptists in Kentucky have developed their own denominational enterprises, notably the State Mission Board; a newspaper, *The American Baptist*; and Simmons Bible College (later Simmons University), as well as other works at the district and local levels. Among their outstanding leaders were London Ferrill, long-time pastor in Lexington; George Dupee, pastor in Georgetown, Lexington, and Paducah; William J. Simmons, first president of the school that would later bear his name; and C.H. Parrish, president of Simmons during 1918-30. Over the years, a spirit of greater cooperation has developed between black and white Baptist groups in Kentucky, leading to joint meetings at the state and local levels.

By 1990 the 650 congregations affiliated with the black Baptists, now called the General Association of Baptists in Kentucky, claimed a membership of nearly 170,000, divided among sixteen district associations.

Of the other smaller Baptist groups in Kentucky, those with a strong Appalachian identity are the Old Regular Baptists, the Primitive Baptists, and the Free Will Baptists. Their traditional practices include foot-washing services and baptisms in creeks, and they tend to spurn modernity. Primitives and Old Regulars are Calvinist in theology, holding firmly to the doctrine of predestination. Free Will Baptists, on the other hand, believe in free grace and free will, known as the Arminian theology.

The Old Regular Baptist movement began with the formation in 1825 of the New Salem Association. Their Calvinist theology disavows mission efforts and eschews revival meetings and Sunday schools. Worship in the Old Regular tradition is emotional and impassioned, especially at the annual communion and foot-washing services in the spring. Most Old Regular congregations meet for worship once a month. Since they have no state organization, their numbers are very difficult to ascertain. They probably number several thousand in eastern Kentucky.

Primitive Baptists began in the 1830s and 1840s as a reaction against the rise of missionary societies, colleges and seminaries, and Sunday schools. Like the Old Regulars, the Primitives have neither revival meetings nor outreach campaigns, but their style of worship is more solemn. Like other

Baptists, the Primitives join into associations with nearby congregations, and yearly association meetings are major events. The fewer than one hundred Primitive Baptist churches in Kentucky claim a total of 2,000 to 3,000 members.

In contrast to the Old Regulars and Primitives, the Free Will Baptists are decidedly non-Calvinist in theology and decidedly evangelistic and missionary in method. Like their Calvinistic relatives, however, they emphasize foot-washing in worship. In the 1870s and 1880s they organized several associations in Kentucky, and by 1935 a National Association of Free Will Baptists had been formed. A Kentucky State Association was formed in 1939. Free Will Baptist membership appears to be growing slowly in Kentucky. In 1989 the nearly two hundred churches had a total of nearly 24,000 members. A much smaller group of Free Will Baptists, known as the John Thomas Association, is clustered near Jenkins, Kentucky.

Two other small Baptist groups, the Separate Baptists in Christ and the United Baptists, also trace their origins to the earliest days of church life in Kentucky. The Separate Baptists, descendants of the early settlers from Virginia and the Carolinas, remained distinct after the union between most Separates and Regulars following the Great Revival of 1801. The Separate Baptists are loosely organized, emotional in worship, and practice foot-washing. These Baptists have fifty-five churches in Kentucky with a total of 5,900 members in two district associations, South District and No-Lynn District.

Following the Union of 1801, many Kentucky churches took the name United Baptists. Gradually, this name was dropped among those who became part of the cooperative General Association of Kentucky Baptists after 1837. Many churches in eastern Kentucky, however, opposed to what they saw as unnecessary and unscriptural cooperation, retained the name. They are organized into district associations, claiming several thousand church members.

Another group of Baptists in Kentucky, the General Baptists, was founded by Benoni Stinson. Born in Montgomery County, Kentucky, in 1789, and converted in Wayne County in 1820, Stinson became a pastor and moved to south-central Indiana, where he started a church that rejected Calvinism and preached free salvation for all. Two of the first three associations of the General Baptists were located mainly in Kentucky. They favor revivals, missions, and education, and sponsor a college in Oakland City, Indiana. In Kentucky they had 196 churches and 23,864 members in 1990.

In addition, there are independent Baptist congregations scattered throughout Kentucky that are not linked with any specific group.

Taken as a whole, the Baptists of Kentucky in 1990 were the state's largest denominational family, making up nearly one-half of the total church membership. Prominent Kentuckians associated with the Baptist denomination include: Govs. James Garrard (1796-1804), Preston H. Leslie (1871-75), Bert T. Combs (1959-63), John Y. Brown, Jr. (1979-83), Wendell H. Ford (1971-74), and Martha Layne Collins (1983-87); Reps. Eugene Siler, Emmet O'Neal, Tim Lee Carter, Carl Perkins, and Carroll Hubbard; Sen. John Sherman Cooper; U.S. Vice-President Richard Mentor Johnson; artist Paul Sawyier; architect Gideon Shyrock; and scientist J. Lawrence Smith.

See Leo T. Crimson, ed., *Baptists in Kentucky, 1776-1976: A Bicentennial Volume* (Middletown, Ky., 1975); Howard Dorgan, *Giving Glory to God in Appalachia: Worship Practices of Six Baptist Subdenominations* (Knoxville, Tenn., 1987); Ira ("Jack") Birdwhistell, *Kentucky Baptists: 150 Years on Mission Together* (Middletown, Ky., 1987).

IRA ("JACK") BIRDWHISTELL

BARBECUE. Kentucky barbecue is a variation of one of the South's more distinctive foods. The word is derived from *barbacoa*, the conquistadors' word for the green wood frame on which the Carib Indians roasted meat over open fires. Barbecue today means meat, fowl, or fish roasted over coals of wood from nut-bearing trees, usually hickory. The wide variety of seasonings, bastings, and sauces for the food are also called barbecue, as is the social event that takes place while the food is roasted. Cuts of meat or chicken are roasted slowly on racks suspended over hardwood coals, then served with a seasoned sauce that is peppery to a greater or lesser degree. To make a sandwich filling, the meat is pulled from the bone and coarsely chopped or sliced, and sauce is then added. Pork and beef are the most common ingredients of barbecue in Kentucky except in the western part of the state, where the numerous sheep farms make mutton the meat of choice. Cooks typically serve BURGOO or brunswick stew along with barbecue.

The earliest settlers from Virginia brought the cooking and social tradition of barbecue to Kentucky. During the nineteenth century, barbecues were a major form of social entertainment at religious, fraternal, and charitable gatherings and they became a fixture of political campaigns. Although not confined to the South, barbecues were more common there because of the availability of slave labor to do the extensive work required, starting with excavation of a pit for the coals. Barbecue cooking became a part of black tradition, and even today a great many of the pit men—those who tend the roasting—are black. The term "pit-cooked," too, is still in use to signify authenticity, even when the coals are heaped in a metal container in the kitchen.

As restaurants became common early in the twentieth century, barbecue made a transition from food at social events to an entree on menus. In 1890 Henry Green, a black, opened a commercial barbecue stand in Owensboro—one of Kentucky's first: Today, the Moonlight Inn in Owensboro is well known for pit-cooked barbecue, and in the 1980s Owensboro initiated its annual International Barbecue Festival to keep the tradition alive in western Kentucky.

See Janet Alm Anderson, *A Taste of Kentucky* (Lexington, Ky., 1986); John Egerton, *Southern Food: At Home, on the Road, in History* (New York 1987).

BARBOURVILLE. Barbourville, the county seat of Knox County in southeastern Kentucky, is located in the center of the county on the bank of the Cumberland River. US 25E and KY 11 intersect at the city, thirty-two miles northwest of the Cumberland Gap and fifteen miles southeast of Corbin. The area was explored by Dr. Thomas Walker and a surveying party who built a small log cabin in the spring of 1750 near the city's present site. The Dr. Thomas Walker State Shrine, established in 1938, houses a replica of the original structure. The future site of Barbourville was close to Richard Ballinger's tavern, established around 1795 on the Wilderness Road. It was regarded as the best inn between Cumberland Gap and Crab Orchard to the north; among the many visitors was Methodist Bishop Francis Asbury, who served in the region.

Barbourville was named after landowner James Barbour, a Virginia-born pioneer who offered the county thirty-eight acres for the site of the city. On October 27, 1800, the city was selected over Flat Lick as the seat of Knox County. The county has had five courthouses since the first was built in 1802. The most substantial of these were the fourth courthouse, built in 1875 and Italianate in style, and the fifth one, a brick structure completed in 1964.

For much of the nineteenth century, Barbourville was the largest and most progressive city in southeastern Kentucky. The Barbourville Debating Society, organized in 1837, polished the talents of Joseph EVE, Samuel F. MILLER, and others who debated the issues of the day. Eve was circuit judge of the area from 1817 to 1841 and a member of the state Senate from 1817 to 1821. Miller was appointed to the U.S. Supreme Court by President Abraham Lincoln in 1862.

During the Civil War, Barbourville's predominantly Union sympathies and its proximity to the Cumberland Gap led to the foundation of Camp Andy Johnson, a recruiting station that attracted over a thousand pro-Union soldiers from east Tennessee. In the war's first skirmish in Kentucky, Confederate Gen. Felix Zollicoffer attacked Barbourville on September 19, 1861, removing the last remnants of the camp. In August 1862 Confederate Gen. Edmund Kirby-Smith camped for several days in Barbourville before moving north to occupy Lexington. On January 7, 1864, Union Gen. Ulysses S. Grant spent a night in the city after inspecting the road to the Cumberland Gap.

The town experienced a boom in the post–Civil War era. UNION COLLEGE was incorporated there in 1879 and the Louisville & Nashville Railroad (now CSX Transportation) reached the town in 1888, during a period of great speculation over southeastern Kentucky's mineral and timber re-

sources. A second boom came near the turn of the century, when oil was discovered in Knox County.

James D. Black, governor (1919), was born near Barbourville, and Flem D. Sampson, governor (1927-31), lived most of his life in Barbourville. Sampson's law partner in Barbourville was Caleb Powers, secretary of state, who was charged with complicity in the assassination of William Goebel.

Barbourville is expanding its business district south along U.S. 25E and has tied its destiny to a developing tourist industry in the region. The city celebrates its frontier heritage with the annual Daniel Boone Festival, which has been held since 1948. The population of the fourth-class city was 3,549 in 1970, 3,333 in 1980; and 3,658 in 1990.

CHARLES REED MITCHELL

BARDSTOWN. Bardstown, the county seat of Nelson County, is located at the intersection of U.S. 31E and U.S. 62, thirty-two miles southeast of Louisville and twenty-six miles northeast of Elizabethtown. The area was part of a 1,000-acre tract granted to David Bard by Gov. Patrick Henry of Virginia. Settlers from Maryland, Pennsylvania, and Virginia, who began arriving in the area from the Falls of the Ohio in 1780, were sold lots by a lottery organized by developers David and William Bard and John C. Owings. The area was first named Salem but was commonly referred to as Bard's Town. It became the county seat in 1784, when Nelson County was formed from Jefferson County.

Craftsmen, educators, lawyers, and political leaders helped the county prosper. Known beyond the state boundaries for its boarding schools and its lawyers, Bardstown attracted both intellectuals and investment. The 150 log houses built in 1789 were soon replaced by brick mansions built in the Federal, Greek Revival, and Georgian styles, reflecting the success of the Bardstown tradesmen and attorneys.

The Civil War divided the community. Because of the city's central location on major north-south and east-west roads, armies of both sides passed through Bardstown. During the Confederate invasion of the state in the autumn of 1862, Gen. Braxton Bragg's army of 28,000 camped in Bardstown from September 20 to October 3. The day after Confederates evacuated the city, Union forces occupied it. Gen. Don Carlos Buell and much of his Union army passed through Bardstown on the way to engage Bragg's army at Perryville, Kentucky, on October 8, 1862. John Hunt Morgan's Confederate cavalry passed through Bardstown on three occasions during the war. On October 20, 1862, they captured and burned a Union wagon train six miles north of Bardstown at Coxes Creek, and they camped in the city on December 29, 1862, after destroying railroad trestles at MULDRAUGH HILL. On July 6, 1863, Morgan was delayed at Bardstown by a night-long skirmish with twenty-five Union cavalrymen.

Bardstown was incorporated in 1788 and governed by a board of trustees until 1894, when a mayor and six councilmen were elected. In the next twenty-five years, water, electricity, and public sewers were installed, and sidewalks and streets were paved. After the war, the mainstays of the local economy were agriculture and whiskey distilling. The Bardstown branch of the Louisville & Nashville Railroad (now CSX Transportation) was completed in 1860 and was extended to Springfield in 1887.

The centennial of ST. JOSEPH PROTO-CATHEDRAL in 1916 and the state's purchase and preservation of FEDERAL HILL in 1922 focused media attention on the town. The negative impact of prohibition on the city's economy, which depended on whiskey production, was somewhat offset by the tourist trade. Repeal of prohibition in 1933 brought distilleries back into business, and 60 percent of the world's supply of bourbon whiskey is now manufactured in this area. Tourism helped to support the town through the Great Depression and World War II and has become the major industry in the city. Stately brick and frame structures of the eighteenth century are part of its charm. Two hundred and twenty Bardstown buildings are listed on the National Register of Historic Places. Since 1959, the outdoor drama *The Stephen Foster Story* has been enjoyed by more than 1 million people. In the last two hundred years, Bardstown has hosted millions of visitors, including President Jimmy Carter, who held a town hall meeting there in 1979.

The population of the fourth-class city was 5,816 in 1970; 6,401 in 1980; and 6,801 in 1990.

See Dixie Hibbs, *Nelson County Kentucky, A Pictorial History* (Norfolk, Va., 1989).

DIXIE HIBBS

BARDWELL. Bardwell, a fifth-class city located 190 miles southwest of Louisville, twenty-nine miles north of Fulton and sixteen miles southeast of Cairo, Illinois, is the county seat of Carlisle County. It is 390 feet above sea level. The principal manufactured products include ready-mix concrete, water tanks, and lumber.

The name Bardwell may have originated during construction for the Illinois Central Railroad. One story relates that in the 1870s a well was drilled to provide water for the construction crew. Through use and time the term bored well evolved into "Bardwell." Another story is that Bardwell was the name of the superintendent of the construction crew. The town was incorporated in 1879 and became the county seat when Carlisle County was formed in 1886. The first courthouse, built in 1886, was destroyed by an arsonist on October 22, 1980. A second courthouse was completed in July 1982. The population has been slowly dropping; it was 1,049 in 1970, 988 in 1980, and 930 in 1986.

BARKLEY, ALBEN WILLIAM. Alben William Barkley, U.S. congressman, senator, and vice-president, was born in a log house on November 24, 1877, near Lowes in Graves County, Kentucky. His parents, John Wilson and Electra Eliza (Smith) Barkley, were tenant farmers who raised dark tobacco. Barkley attended common school in Lowes between fall harvest and spring planting. In 1891 the family settled on a wheat farm near Clinton in Hickman County, where Barkley enrolled in Marvin College in 1892. Within five years he earned a bachelor of arts degree.

After Marvin, Barkley enrolled at Emory College of Atlanta, a Methodist school connected with Marvin. He spent the 1897-98 academic year studying classics and participating in the school debating society, but his poverty sent him back to Clinton, where he taught in the Marvin College intermediate department. Unable to afford to rent a room and pay for meals, Barkley resigned in December 1898 and joined his parents in Paducah, where his father had found regular employment. Barkley obtained access to the library of Democratic Rep. Charles K. Wheeler, and in the summer of 1899 barristers William S. Bishop and John K. Hendrick hired Barkley as their law clerk. After two years of study and clerking, he passed the bar examination and opened an office in 1901. Hendrick's friend Judge L.D. Husbands appointed him circuit court reporter.

In Paducah, Barkley joined the Broadway Methodist Episcopal Church and numerous local organizations and attended dances and socials. He was a talented speaker and his rich baritone could be heard preaching lay sermons or telling jokes. He married Dorothy Brower of Tiptonville, Tennessee, on June 23, 1903. They had three children: David Murrell, Marion Frances, and Laura Louis.

In 1904 Barkley entered the Democratic primary for county attorney, establishing in this campaign a successful style and pattern for future runs. He announced his candidacy in December 1904, well before the March primary, because the primary rather than the general election was the key to gaining office in the heavily Democratic region. He was solely responsible for the organization and leadership of the campaign. He overwhelmed the voters with personal appearances, which appealed to his gregarious nature and showed off his talent in speechmaking and debating.

As county attorney, Barkley prosecuted three hundred wrongdoers and saved the county thousands of dollars by challenging overcharges against the local government. In 1907 the Democratic State Central Committee invited him to serve on the speakers' bureau and he was elected president of the State Association of County Attorneys. The local Democratic club looked to save the party from its scandal-ridden image by nominating Barkley for county judge. The 1909 election was the most vicious campaign in Barkley's career, and his victory marked him as a formidable political force.

The new judge repaid his staunchest supporters, farmers, by nearly bankrupting McCracken County with a massive project of road improvements. But he also inaugurated a number of progressive measures, such as appointing a purchasing agent and auditing the county books. Barkley announced late in 1911 that he planned to run for 1st District representative to the U.S. Congress. In the primary, Barkley faced three strong contenders, including his former employer Hendrick.

Barkley quickly took two positions most important to the farmers: lowering taxes and reducing the influence of the railroads through stricter regulation by the Interstate Commerce Commission. He also advocated federal support for highway construction, and his opponents tagged him a socialist. Midway through the 1912 campaign the national Democratic delegates selected Woodrow Wilson as the party's presidential nominee and adopted a progressive platform favorable to Barkley, who with the support of the district farmers won a large plurality in the primary and a secure victory in the general election.

During his seven terms in Congress (March 4, 1913, to March 3, 1927), Barkley served on the Interstate Commerce Commission. Barkley enlisted in Wilson's New Freedom program to bolster economic stability by eliminating financial privilege, and he strongly supported the Clayton Anti-Trust Act of 1914. Barkley moved beyond the New Freedom, however, by seeking governmental solutions to a variety of social problems, including child labor in interstate commerce. He was coauthor of a bill to ban liquor sales in the District of Columbia, which laid the foundation for future prohibition measures; though the initiative eventually failed, it gave Barkley national prominence and put him in the forefront of the Progressive movement. He gave hundreds of talks to aid fellow Democrats in their election bids between 1916 and 1922.

On November 11, 1922, Barkley announced his candidacy in the 1923 Kentucky gubernatorial race. His campaign was spirited, and he earned the nickname "Iron Man." He supported the immediate completion of the state highway network and substantial improvement in the educational system, but he also attacked coal-mining and horse-racing interests. He narrowly lost the primary but gained the future support of Democrats, and when he announced for the U.S. Senate in 1926, no Democrat opposed him.

Barkley defeated Republican incumbent Richard P. Ernst in 1926, and his Senate committee appointments reflected a status far beyond that of a newly elected junior senator. In 1928 he was considered for the vice-presidential nomination; in 1932 he was selected temporary chairman and keynote speaker for the party's national convention. With the onset of the Great Depression, Barkley played a national role as spokesman and policy-shaper during Franklin Roosevelt's terms. Barkley assisted Senate majority leader Joseph T. Robinson in the enactment of much New Deal legislation, defending Roosevelt's policies on national radio. Roosevelt chose him to deliver the keynote address at the 1936 party convention, and when Robinson died in 1937 Roosevelt urged Democratic leaders to make

Barkley his successor. The new majority leader was defeated in the management of the president's court-packing plan, but Barkley later impressed his colleagues with his legislative insight and persuasive rhetoric.

Roosevelt's focus on foreign affairs during World War II gave Barkley extraordinary power on domestic programs. Occasionally Barkley disagreed on issues of internal interest, and he slipped uneasily between the roles of administration cheerleader and watchdog. He attacked inequities in the War Production Board's contracting practices and successfully led the passage of a tax bill that Roosevelt vetoed as insufficient. Though Barkley resigned his majority leadership, he was quickly reelected, setting a precedent of autonomy for future congressional leaders. In 1944, however, as Roosevelt chose Harry S. Truman over Barkley as his vice-presidential candidate, perhaps in retribution for legislative defeats at Barkley's hands. Though his wife, Dorothy, died of heart disease in 1947, Barkley continued his career and his popularity soared. He received numerous awards, was ranked as the most popular Democrat, and vied with Gen. Dwight D. Eisenhower as *Look* magazine's most "fascinating" American.

In 1948 Truman asked Barkley to serve again as the convention keynote speaker, and later as his running mate. As the Democrats had seemed ripe for a presidential loss, their victory was a major upset. On January 20, 1949, Barkley took the oath as the nation's thirty-fifth vice-president, the oldest man to do so. He became the only vice-president to wed in office when he married Jane Rucker Hadley on November 18, 1949, after a cross-country courtship. Barkley was the first working vice-president in U.S. history. Because of his legislative expertise, Truman insisted on Barkley's inclusion in all cabinet-level meetings and on the National Security Council. His extraordinary speaking abilities made him the administration's principal spokesman, and Truman commissioned a vice-presidential seal and flag from the army's heraldic branch.

Barkley's age in 1952 prevented his candidacy for president. After leaving office he hosted a national political television show and then retired to write his memoirs. Finding retirement unsatisfactory, he entered the Senate race in 1954, handily defeating incumbent John Sherman Cooper; his colleagues appointed him to the prestigious Senate Foreign Relations Committee. On April 30, 1956, Barkley traveled to Lexington, Virginia, to give a keynote speech before a mock convention conducted by students of Washington and Lee University. There he observed that he "would rather be a servant in the house of the Lord than to sit in the seats of the mighty." At the conclusion of the address, he suffered a fatal heart attack. He was buried in Paducah.

See Alben W. Barkley, *That Reminds Me* (Garden City, N.Y., 1954); Polly Ann Davis, "Alben W. Barkley: Senate Majority Leader and Vice President," Ph.D. diss., University of Kentucky, 1963;

James K. Libbey, *Dear Alben: Mr. Barkley of Kentucky* (Lexington, Ky., 1979).   JAMES K. LIBBEY

BARLOW, THOMAS HARRIS. Thomas Harris Barlow, inventor, was born in Nicholas County, Kentucky, in 1789 or 1791 to William and Sarah (Kimbrough) Barlow. During the War of 1812, he fought under Richard M. Johnson at the Battle of the Thames. He married Keziah West in 1816. He moved to Lexington in 1824, and for many years operated a foundry and machine shop where he manufactured sawmill equipment. Barlow developed a small steam locomotive in partnership with Joseph Bruen in the winter of 1825-26. It operated on a small circular track and was capable of carrying two adults. Barlow and Bruen's attempt to build a full-sized locomotive to pull passenger cars on the Lexington & Ohio Railroad was not successful.

In 1845 Barlow received a patent for a steam-powered hemp-retting mechanism to separate the fiber from the stalk of the plant. Although the device worked well, it was too expensive for general use. Barlow's most widely used invention was a mechanically operated orrery, or model of the solar system. The remarkably accurate apparatus showed the location of the planets on any given day of the nineteenth century. Many of the "planetariums" were sold to schools, and they were purchased by the U.S. government for use at the Naval Academy and the U.S. Military Academy at West Point. The invention was demonstrated by Barlow's son, Milton, at the world exposition in Paris in 1867 and at exhibitions throughout the United States. A few Barlow planetariums have been exhibited in museums in the United States.

Many of Barlow's inventions were devised with the aid of his son, Milton. Among them were a cradling harvester, a mechanical device for cutting nails and tacks, and a cannon with a rifled barrel that greatly improved accuracy. It was undoubtedly someone from this ingenious family who invented the Barlow knife, the sturdy, single-bladed jackknife that has become a treasured keepsake for many people. Barlow's numerous inventions did not bring financial success, and on more than one occasion he was forced to mortgage his personal property to satisfy his debts. In 1861 he suffered a stroke and spent the last years of his life with a daughter in Cincinnati. He died on June 22, 1865, and was buried in Cave Hill Cemetery in Louisville.

BARREN COUNTY. Barren County, the thirty-seventh in order of formation, lies in south-central Kentucky, midway between Louisville and Nashville, and covers an area of 482 square miles. It is bounded by Hart, Edmonton, Warren, Allen, Monroe, and Metcalfe counties. The Kentucky General Assembly created it on December 20, 1798, from parts of Warren and Green counties. Barren County then totaled some 1,500 square miles, but parts of it have gone into the creation of surrounding counties. Originally it extended from the Green River on the north to the Tennessee line on the south. Although the county now is only about a third of its original size, only ten counties today are larger.

The county was named for the barrens, the meadowlands that cover the northern third. Many of the early settlers were Revolutionary War veterans who received grants of land south of the Green River reserved for that purpose by Virginia. Seventy percent of the original settlers came from Virginia; more than 80 percent of the early settlers were English, Scottish, Welsh, or Irish in background. The county seat was named GLASGOW to honor the large number of Scottish settlers. Other principal towns in the county include Cave City, Park City (formerly Three Forks), and Hiseville (formerly Goose Horn); many of the hamlets of the early days have disappeared.

Perhaps the first explorers to spend time in what is now Barren County were Long Hunters led by Henry Skaggs, who camped on Beaver Creek in 1769. Many pioneers traveled the Cumberland Trace, which passed through the northern part of the county, connected with Daniel Boone's Wilderness Road at Hazel Patch, and went on to Lexington and Limestone (now Maysville). Stage lines later linked the area to Nashville, Louisville, and Lexington. A well-known stage line of the last half of the nineteenth century ran from Park City through Glasgow to Burkesville.

Mammoth Cave lies outside Barren County, but visitors to the cave in the 1800s reached it by way of Park City or Cave City; a railroad to the cave ran from Park City (then Glasgow Junction). The spur railroad from Park City to Glasgow that opened in 1870 and connected with the Louisville & Nashville (now CSX Transportation) was a boon to economic development of the county.

During the early decades, most of the county residents were small farmers. Tobacco has been the main cash crop since early days. Livestock and dairying have replaced row crops to a great extent. Hay is another major farm product. A new industrial growth has recently taken place in the county, especially in Glasgow.

Two governors of Kentucky, Preston H. Leslie (1871-75) and Louie B. Nunn (1967-71), have come from Barren County. During the bicentennial celebration in 1976, three of the county's modern greats were recognized: Gen. Russell E. Dougherty, then the commanding general of the Strategic Air Command; Billy Vaughn, band leader and musician; and Julian Goodman, who was then chairman of the board of the National Broadcasting Company. Arthur Krock, a writer for the *New York Times*, was a native of Glasgow.

The population of the county in 1970 was 28,677; 34,009 in 1980; and 34,001 in 1990.

See Cecil E. Goode and Woodford L. Gardner, Jr., eds., *Barren County Heritage* (Glasgow, Ky., 1980); Goode, *Heart of the Barrens* (Glasgow, Ky., 1986).   CECIL E. GOODE

BARREN RIVER. The Barren River, known earlier as the Big Barren, is the largest tributary of the Green River, rising in Monroe County to join the

Green River at the northeast corner of Warren County, across from Butler County. It also touches Allen and Barren counties. Bowling Green is the largest city on the river. Along its banks, Barren River State Resort Park includes an impounded lake. The Barren River and the Green River carried steamer passengers and freight traffic from the mid-nineteenth century until 1965, when the dam at Woodbury and Lock No. 4 broke, ending commercial navigation. Traffic from Evansville, the point where the Green River meets the Ohio, to Bowling Green via the Barren River was a major factor in the development of both cities. The first steamer to reach Bowling Green was the *United States* in 1828.

Among the series of locks built by the state of Kentucky in the nineteenth century, Lock and Dam No. 3 on the Green River, completed in 1838, effectively opened the Green and Barren River valleys to river transportation. Maintenance of the river and the system of locks was taken over by the U.S. government in 1888. By 1890, navigation on the Green and Barren rivers exceeded that on the Kentucky River and nearly equaled that of the Cumberland and Tennessee rivers. The Barren River was the principal means of transportation to market for chickens, turkeys, and other farm products, as well as timber from the western Kentucky woodlands destined for Evansville.

See Agnes Harralson, *Steamboats on the Green* (Berea, Ky., 1981); Helen Bartter Crocker, *The Green River of Kentucky* (Lexington, Ky., 1976).

CECIL E. GOODE

BARRENS. Kentucky's barrens are a grassland relatively free of trees that covers the southern part of Hart County, the northern part of Metcalfe County, the eastern part of Warren County, and the northern third of Barren County. According to geologist Willard Rouse Jillson, the grassland at one time extended southwestward across Warren, Logan, Todd, and Christian counties. Among early travelers in the barrens, French naturalist F.A. Michaux wrote his impressions in 1802: "I was agreeably surprised to meet with a beautiful meadow, the abundant grass of which was from two to three feet high, and afforded excellent food for cattle; amongst it I saw a great variety of plants, but particularly gall of the earth, white plantain, and Rudbekia purpura. . . . I, however, collected and sent to France upwards of ninety species."

The barrens have few watercourses; water flows mostly underground or runs into sinkholes of this karst area. The pioneers, thinking the land was infertile, settled the wooded, hilly areas first. Later, however, they found the barrens to be a very fertile region.

See Franklin Gorin, *The Times of Long Ago* (Glasgow, Ky., 1974); Cecil E. Goode, *Heart of the Barrens* (Glasgow, Ky., 1986).

CECIL E. GOODE

BARROW, DAVID. David Barrow, Baptist minister and early abolitionist, was born in Brunswick County, Virginia, on October 30, 1753, to William and Amy Lee Barrow. In 1772 he was ordained a minister and preached in Virginia and North Carolina. He joined the Revolutionary army in 1776. When he resumed his ministry after the war, Barrow was persecuted for his abolitionist and religious teachings. On June 24, 1798, he became minister for the Mt. Sterling, Goshen, and Lulbegrud (Lullebegrud) Baptist churches in Montgomery County, Kentucky, and he established a school near the Lulbegrud church in January 1801. In 1803, he published a pamphlet on the Trinity designed to stop the growth of Unitarianism, and he was one of the committeemen appointed by the Elkhorn Baptist Association to dissuade Gov. James Garrard (1796-1804) from his Unitarian beliefs.

As an abolitionist, Barrow published the work of the British scholar, Thomas Clarkson, whose *Essay on Slavery and Commerce of the Human Species* (1785) profoundly influenced the American abolitionist movement. In 1806 the Bracken Baptist Association prosecuted Barrow for emancipationist teachings, and he lost his seat on the North District Baptist Association. Barrow responded in 1807 by organizing a confederation of emancipationist Baptist churches: the Baptist Licking-Locust Association, Friends of Humanity, whose membership included Thomas Lincoln, father of the future president. An offshoot of this organization was the Kentucky Abolition Society, founded in 1807, of which Barrow was president for several years. In 1808 Barrow's antislavery essay, *Involuntary, Absolute Hereditary Slavery Examined*, was published.

Barrow married Sarah Gilliam of Sussex County, Virginia, in 1772. He died on November 14, 1819, and was buried at his home near the Lulbegrud church.

See Asa C. Barrow, "David Barrow and His Lulbegrud School, 1801," *FCHQ* 7 (April 1933): 88-94.

BARROW UNIT. Good Samaritan Hospital Unit No. 40 (Barrow Unit), organized by Dr. David Barrow of Lexington during World War I, was staffed by Kentucky doctors, nurses, and soldiers in Europe. As a member of the American expeditionary forces, Barrow accompanied the unit to England in July 1918 and set up the hospital at a large country estate near Southampton; it became one of the largest American hospitals in Europe. In March 1919, when the Barrow Unit returned, many Kentuckians assembled on the Lexington courthouse grounds to pay tribute to it. In 1957 a new Army Reserve Training Center in Lexington was named for Dr. Barrow.

See William Barrow Floyd, *The Barrow Family of Old Louisiana* (Lexington, Ky., 1963).

WILLIAM BARROW FLOYD

BARRY, WILLIAM TAYLOR. The son of John and Susannah (Dozier) Barry, William Taylor Barry, politician and jurist, was born in Lunenberg County, Virginia, on February 5, 1784. The Barry family migrated to Kentucky in the mid-1790s, settling in Fayette County. Barry attended the Pisgah Academy, the Kentucky Academy in Woodford County, and Transylvania University. In 1803 he graduated from William and Mary College and began to study law with Judge John Rowan, one of Kentucky's finest attorneys and legal scholars; two years later, Barry was admitted to the Fayette County bar.

Shortly after Barry commenced law practice in Lexington, he was appointed commonwealth attorney. In 1807 Lexingtonians elected him to the Kentucky House; he was returned in 1809. The physically diminutive, extroverted Barry quickly developed a reputation for splendid oratory and considerable political savvy. He served in the U.S. House of Representatives from August 8, 1810, to March 3, 1811. After a brief period of military service in the War of 1812, he was reelected to the Kentucky House in 1814. His fellow assemblymen sent him to the U.S. Senate, but Barry resigned and returned to his home in Kentucky after serving one uneventful session, from December 16, 1814, to May 1, 1816. He was a Jeffersonian Republican.

Between 1817 and 1821, Barry served in the Kentucky Senate; simultaneously, he worked with Judge Jesse Bledsoe to establish a new law curriculum at Transylvania University. After mid-1818, as Kentuckians confronted a bank panic, Barry quickly emerged as a spokesman for the Relief party, which sought currency enhancement, expanded bank credit, and debtor relief legislation (see RELIEF CRISIS). In the stormy elections of 1820, Barry soundly defeated William Blackburn for lieutenant governor and served with pro-Relief Gov. John Adair (1820-24) throughout Kentucky's crisis over relief for debtors. Anti-Relief legislators often said that without Barry's fiery Senate and stump speeches, the Relief party's legislative achievements—especially the establishment of the state-funded Bank of the Commonwealth—would have been fewer; his critics also said that Barry had been instrumental in shattering both the state's economy and national reputation. As lieutenant governor, Barry headed a committee investigating other states' public school systems. The committee's BARRY REPORT recommended that Kentucky establish a system of free public schools for all children.

When the Relief party dismantled Kentucky's court of appeals (OLD COURT) in 1824, Barry became chief judge of the New Court. Voters routed New Court candidates in 1826, however, and in 1828 Barry was narrowly defeated for governor by Thomas Metcalfe (1828-32). Old Court partisans predicted Barry's demise as a politician, but they were wrong. By March 1829 his support for Andrew Jackson during the 1828 presidential elections bore fruit, in the form of the office of postmaster general. Within two years, however, accusations of corruption and favoritism within the Jackson administration led to congressional investigations in 1834-36. Although Barry hotly denied the charges

leveled against him, abuses and neglect in the Department of the Post Office were well documented, if not always attributable to Barry himself; the harrowing experience ruined his physical and emotional health. He resigned his office in April 1835 and accepted the position of minister to Spain. On August 30, 1835, Barry died suddenly in Liverpool, England, en route to his new assignment. He was buried in the Frankfort Cemetery.

SANDRA F. VANBURKLEO

BARRY REPORT. The Barry Report on free public education in Kentucky contained the recommendations made in 1822 by an investigative committee headed by Lt. Gov. William T. BARRY (1820-24). On December 18, 1821, the Kentucky General Assembly took the initial steps toward a public school system by creating a literary fund for education and appointing the committee to investigate other states' systems and recommend a system for Kentucky. The other committee members were David R. Murray, John R. Witherspoon, John POPE, David White, and William Roper. The Barry report, submitted December 2, 1822, carried only the first four names. The actual writing was probably done by Amos KENDALL, editor of the *Frankfort Argus.*

The committee studied the school systems of Massachusetts, New York, Connecticut, Virginia, and South Carolina and surveyed the schooling then available in Kentucky. The committee also sought opinions from prominent men, including former presidents John Adams, Thomas Jefferson, and James Madison, and attached their responses to the report. No Kentuckian responded to the request.

The committee's primary recommendation was that Kentucky provide a system of free schools for the education of all children, which could be done for about the same amount that wealthy Kentuckians were spending on private academies. The committee recommended that the schools be supported not only by a literary fund—which was to receive half the profits of the Bank of the Commonwealth, or about $60,000 a year—but also by a school tax that was optional for local districts. No state money would go to any district that refused to tax itself. A state superintendent would be named to oversee the schools. In reality the Bank of the Commonwealth was struggling for survival, and the literary fund was temporarily suspended in 1824. Money from the literary fund was diverted to turnpikes and other uses, and the only amount that went for education was a $3,000 donation to the School for the Deaf at Danville in 1829.

The Barry Report went to the General Assembly with Gov. John Adair's (1820-24) approval. Unfortunately, the move to establish a school system came at a time of political and economic upheaval in Kentucky. Adair and Barry had been elected as Relief candidates who favored a moratorium on indebtedness resulting from the bank failures of the economic panic of 1819. Angered by an unfavorable appeals court decision on this issue, the legislature created the rival New Court (see OLD COURT-NEW COURT), of which Barry became chief justice in 1825.

The General Assembly ordered 5,000 copies of the Barry Report printed but took no further action on it, because of both the political turmoil and the reluctance to provide money for schools. The report's chief influence was in the wide circulation it gained and the interest it aroused, partly through the letters of opinion from prominent leaders.

RUBY LAYSON

BASEBALL, PROFESSIONAL. Baseball was played in Kentucky before the Civil War, and the LOUISVILLE COLONELS figured prominently in the development of the game as a professional sport in the nineteenth century. In 1867 Louisville's baseball club hosted the touring Washington Nationals, and by that time games between Louisville and Cincinnati were being reported in the *Cincinnati Commercial*. In the 1870s, several amateur and semiprofessional teams had strong local support.

Kentucky has not been represented by a major league team in the twentieth century, but minor league baseball has flourished in the state. At least thirty-one Kentucky cities have had minor league teams, most of them members of two Class D leagues: the Blue Grass League (1908-12, 1922-24), which operated in central Kentucky, and the KIT (Kentucky-Illinois-Tennessee), or "Kitty" League, which existed for more than half a century after it was formed in 1903. The KIT League included several western Kentucky cities, such as Paducah, which won the championship in 1913, Henderson, and Owensboro. Louisville has had an AAA team, the highest level of minor league baseball, throughout most of the century, first as a member of the American Association (1902-62), then the International League (1963-72), and the restructured American Association since 1982.

In 1887 the Louisville team known as the Falls City joined the first league for black players, the League of Colored Baseball Clubs, but the club failed within a week. Before the formation of the Negro National League in 1920, several independent semiprofessional black teams in Kentucky played in exhibition and barnstorming tours. Louisville was also the home of the Negro National League's White Sox (1931), Black Caps (1932), and Buckeyes (1949). Two Kentuckians who had outstanding Negro League careers were Pat Dougherty of Summer Shade, who pitched for several Chicago teams between 1909 and 1915, and Clint Thomas of Greenup, an outfielder who played for Hilldale in Philadelphia, the New York Black Yankees, and several other teams from 1920 to 1937.

More than two hundred Kentucky natives have played major league baseball, and three Kentuckians have been elected to the Baseball Hall of Fame: Earle Combs, a native of Pebworth, in 1970; A.B. CHANDLER, of Corydon, in 1982; and Harold ("Pee Wee") Reese, of Ekron, in 1984. Combs was the centerfielder on the great Yankee teams of 1924-35.

Chandler, who served as commissioner of baseball from 1945 to 1951, was instrumental in bringing about the racial integration of the major leagues in 1947. Reese, who played from 1940 to 1958, was the shortstop and captain of the Brooklyn Dodgers teams that won six National League pennants and a World Series between 1947 and 1956. Eight other Kentuckians have been named on Hall of Fame ballots: pitchers Jesse Tannehill (who was born in Dayton, and played from 1894 to 1911), Howie Camnitz (Covington, 1909-15), Carl Mays (Liberty, 1915-29), Paul Derringer (Springfield, 1931-45), and Jim Bunning (Southgate, 1955-71); infielders Bill Sweeney (Covington, 1907-14) and Ray Chapman (Beaver Dam, 1912-20); and outfielder Bobby Veach (Island, 1912-25).

See John Thorn and Peter Palmer, eds., *Total Baseball* (New York 1989); A.H. Tarvin, *75 Years on Louisville's Diamonds* (Louisville 1940).

WILLIAM C. GARRIOTT, JR.

BASKETBALL. Just four years after James A. Naismith invented the game in 1891 at the Young Men's Christian Association (YMCA) Training School in Springfield, Massachusetts, basketball arrived in Kentucky. The first games were played at the Louisville YMCA. By February 1903 basketball reached the collegiate level as Kentucky University (KU) in Lexington played the Lexington YMCA. The first women's game was played the following year between KU and Hamilton College in Lexington. Women's basketball at both high school and collegiate levels was discontinued in 1932, but was reinstated by the General Assembly in 1974.

While basketball was developing on college campuses, it engulfed the social life of many rural towns through high-school competition. The first Kentucky State High School Basketball Tournament, an invitational affair for eight teams, was held in 1916 at Danville. The event was moved to the University of Kentucky campus two years later under the newly formed Kentucky High School Athletic Association (KHSAA). The university managed the event until 1938, paying the bills and turning over the remainder to the KHSAA for division among the teams as partial payment. Through the years, the boys' state basketball tournament has been played in Lexington and Louisville.

The larger schools won most of the early championships, but in the era before consolidation of city and county high schools the tournament gained much of its flavor from a steady procession of fine players and teams from little-known hamlets in all reaches of the commonwealth. One of the most famous basketball games in Kentucky prep history was Ashland's four-overtime victory over Carr Creek in the 1928 state championship final. (The Carr Creek student body totaled forty-one, eighteen of them boys.) Both teams advanced to the National High School Basketball Tournament in Chicago. Although Ashland won the tournament, the "barefoot boys" from Carr Creek established a small-town tradition that was continued by such state tournament champions as Heath (1929), Corinth (1930), Midway (1937), Sharpe (1938), Brooksville (1939), Hazel Green (1940), Inez (1941 and 1954), Hindman (1943), Brewers (1948), Cuba (1952), and Carr Creek (1956).

The University of Kentucky (UK) was an early beneficiary of the steady stream of fine players produced in high schools throughout the state. In addition to the 1922 Lexington Senior High champions, who attended UK as a group, the Wildcats also secured the services of such outstanding local players as Bill King, who sank the free throw after time expired to beat Georgia for the championship of the first Southern Intercollegiate Athletic Association Tournament in Atlanta in 1921, and Burgess Carey and Carey Spicer, who were accorded All-American honors.

Basil Hayden, a native of nearby Paris and a member of the 1921 championship team, was named UK's first All-American. The state high school system also gave UK such early All-Americans as Paul McBrayer and Forest ("Aggie") Sale of Kavanaugh; John ("Frenchy") DeMoisey of Walton; Ellis Johnson, star of Ashland's national championship team; and such later stars as Lee Huber of Louisville St. Xavier, Jack Tingle of Bedford, Ralph Beard of Louisville Male, Wallace ("Wah Wah") Jones of Harlan, Cliff Hagan of Owensboro, Frank Ramsey of Madisonville, Vernon Hatton of Lexington Lafayette, Johnny Cox of Hazard, Jack Givens and Melvin Turpin of Lexington Bryan Station, and Rex Chapman of Owensboro Apollo.

Adolph RUPP, a member of the 1923 national champion team at the University of Kansas, was coaching basketball at Freeport High School in Illinois when he was hired as UK coach prior to the 1931 season. Rupp and the Wildcats emerged on the national scene in January 1935, when they appeared in a collegiate basketball doubleheader played in Madison Square Garden. After the Wildcats, featuring sophomore All-American center Leroy Edwards, lost to New York University 22-21 on a controversial call by an official, they became regular visitors to the big New York City arena.

In the 1947-48 season, Rupp blended talented young players with war veterans in the FABULOUS FIVE, which won the National Collegiate Athletic Association (NCAA) championship. UK's Cliff Barker, Ralph Beard, Alex Groza, Kenny Rollins, and Wallace Jones—and alternates Dale Barnstable and Joe Holland—competed in the Olympic Games in London, England, where the U.S. team won the gold medal.

The Wildcats repeated as national champions in 1951 and 1958. They were undefeated in 1954 after a one-year suspension for violating NCAA and conference regulations, including recruiting violations and the involvement of five players in point-shaving scandals and bribery. Six years after the Wildcats lost to Texas Western in the championship game of the 1966 NCAA tournament, Rupp retired as the winningest coach of all time, compiling a record of

879 wins and 190 losses. In addition to four national championships that his teams achieved, they won a National Invitational Tournament (NIT) championship in 1946, five postseason Sugar Bowls, and twenty-seven Southeastern Conference championships.

During the same era, Ed DIDDLE compiled a record of 789 wins and 302 losses during his forty-two years at Western Kentucky University in Bowling Green. Diddle's HILLTOPPERS won thirty-two conference championships, played in three NCAA tournaments and eight NITs. Thirteen of his players were named All-Americans.

Paul McBRAYER, a former UK All-American, coached Eastern Kentucky University in Richmond from 1946 to midseason in 1962, compiling a record of 214 wins in 355 games. Another former UK star, ELLIS JOHNSON, amassed a record of 176 victories, 158 losses during fifteen years at Morehead State University. Harlan Hodges coached sixteen and a half years (1926-41, 1948) at Murray State University, which produced Joe Fulks, who took Kuttawa High School in Lyon County to its only state tournament appearance in 1940. Fulks returned from serving with the U.S. Marines in World War II to become the National Basketball Association's first great scorer. Bernard ("Peck") Hickman, who had starred for Diddle at Western, took over a weak University of Louisville program in 1944 and retired twenty-three years later with a record of 443 wins and 183 losses. His Cardinals won the National Association of Intercollegiate Athletics championship in 1948 and the NIT in 1956. Kentucky Wesleyan College in Owensboro was the "little UCLA." They won the NCAA division II national championships in 1966, 1968, 1969, 1973, 1987, and 1989 and made tournament runs during other years. Coach Lucias Mitchell of Kentucky State University in Frankfort led KSU to three consecutive National Association of Intercollegiate Athletics championships. They were paced by seven-foot, one-inch Elmore Smith and Travis ("The Machine") Grant, the leading scorer in collegiate basketball history.

The color barrier in the state tournament was broken in 1957, when three black players were on Goebel Ritter's Hazard team. Lexington Dunbar and Covington Grant were the all-black teams in the Sweet 16 the following year. The first black player to play in a championship game was James Ricketts of Louisville Manual in 1959. Two years later, Dunbar became the first all-black team to advance to the finals, losing to Ashland.

Mike Redd and Wesley Unseld led Louisville Central to the tournament championship over Dunbar in 1963. The Redskins repeated as champions the following year, defeating Breckinridge County in the final game. Unseld scored 105 points and pulled down eighty-eight rebounds during the tournament in one of the finest individual efforts in state tournament history. He enrolled at the University of Louisville, where he was joined the following year by Butch Beard, also black, who had led

Breckinridge County to the 1964 championship. Both earned All-American honors with the Cardinals and had outstanding professional careers.

The UK program remained segregated, but Western acquired the services of future All-Americans Clem Haskins (later to coach at WKU and the University of Minnesota in Minneapolis), star of the 1963 Taylor County team, and Allen County's Jim McDaniels. Cincinnati successfully recruited Tom Thacker of Covington Grant; Louisville Central's Ron King cast his lot with Florida State. UK finally broke the color barrier in 1969 with Tom Payne, a seven-footer out of Louisville Shawnee. Payne, the only black to play for Rupp, made All-Southeastern Conference in his single season at UK before turning pro with the Atlanta Hawks.

Rupp was succeeded in 1972 by his No. 1 assistant coach, Joe B. Hall, who had played briefly for UK in 1949. Lexington natives Jack Givens and James Lee were key members of Hall's UK teams, which advanced to the championship game of the 1975 NCAA tournament against UCLA and were champions of the 1976 NIT, defeating the University of North Carolina at Charlotte, and of the 1978 NCAA tournament, defeating Duke University. The year after the Wildcats lost to Georgetown University in the 1984 NCAA Final Four, Hall retired, with a record of 297 games won and 100 games lost in thirteen years at UK. He was succeeded by Eddie Sutton from the University of Arkansas in 1985. Sutton compiled an 88-39 record at UK before he was forced to resign in 1989 by university president David Roselle in the wake of an NCAA investigation. The investigation also resulted in the resignation of athletics director Cliff Hagan and the loss of two scholarships, no postseason play for two years, and no television appearances for one year. Rick Pitino, coach of the New York Knicks of the NBA, was named UK basketball coach in 1989, and C.M. Newton, a former UK player under Rupp, resigned as Vanderbilt basketball head coach to become UK athletics director the same year. With a squad depleted by transfers, Pitino compiled an amazing 14-14 received in his first season, 1989-90, at UK. The next year a 22-6 record placed the school in the top ten, and it was first in the SEC with 14-4.

The new coach at Louisville in 1971 was Denny CRUM, who had played for John Wooden at UCLA. Entering the 1990-91 season, Crum had a record of 459 wins, 156 losses. His Cardinals teams had appeared in the Final Four six times. They were arguably the dominant team during the 1980s, winning two national championships (1980 and 1986) and sending an unmatched four teams to the Final Four. The Cardinals also appeared among the final sixteen seven times and posted the highest NCAA Tournament winning percentage.

The Kentucky Colonels were Louisville's entry in the new American Basketball Association in 1967. Their first coach, Johnny Givens, was a former Western Kentucky player; their first player, Louie Dampier, was an All-American guard on the 1966 "Rupp's Runts" team. Charles ("Cotton") Nash, another former UK All-American, played briefly the first year. As a rookie center in 1970, UK's all-time scorer Dan Issel averaged 29.9 points a game, leading the Colonels to the seventh and decisive game of the league championship, which they lost to Utah. Under the ownership of John Y. Brown, Jr., and his first wife, Ellie, the Colonels won the league championship in 1975. Issel later had a long and distinguished career with the Denver Nuggets of the NBA. Louisville lost its franchise when the ABA folded in 1976-77 and four of its teams were merged into the National Basketball Association.

As basketball entered its second century, the sport had established itself as a way of life throughout the commonwealth, especially in the rural areas where the wintertime social structure often centered on the local high school teams, both boys and girls. The ultimate goal of players, coaches, and fans alike was the state tournament.

See Dave Kindred, *Basketball: The Dream Game in Kentucky* (Louisville 1976); Mike Embry, *Basketball in the Bluegrass State* (New York 1983); Russell Rice, *The Wildcat Legacy* (Virginia Beach, Va., 1982).   RUSSELL RICE

BATES, MARTIN VAN BUREN. Martin Van Buren Bates, known as the "Giant of Letcher County" for his extreme height, was the son of John W. and Sarah Bates, born on November 9, 1845, in Whitesburg, Kentucky. Although none of his family members was above average height, Bates at age fifteen was already six feet tall, and by twenty-eight he had reached his maximum height of seven feet, eleven and a half inches, and weighed 478 pounds.

Bates was attending Emory and Henry College in Virginia when the Civil War broke out. On September 15, 1861, he joined the 5th Kentucky Infantry under the command of John S. Williams. He was promoted to first lieutenant of Virginia State Line Troop's Company A and was later raised to the rank of captain, serving until the end of the war. Bates moved to Cincinnati and on July 18, 1865, began to use his size for monetary gain by touring in exhibitions throughout the United States and Canada. In November 1870 Bates went to Elizabeth, New Jersey, to meet with his manager, Judge H.P. Ingalls, who was making plans for a group exhibit in Europe. In New Jersey Bates met Anna Hanen Swan, the "Giantess of Novia Scotia," equal to him in height, who had recently toured Europe with P.T. Barnum. The two were married on June 17, 1871, in London while on tour. They were received by Queen Victoria on three occasions. Returning to the United States in July 1874, the couple purchased a farm in Seville, Ohio, where they custom-built a house with fourteen-foot-high ceilings, eight-and-a-half-foot doorways, and specially made furniture. Bates used Norman-bred draft horses to farm and a pair of Clydesdales pulled their carriage.

On several occasions the couple returned to the road, traveling with W.W. Cole's Circus, Menagerie and Museum. Throughout his life, Bates never

60

toured with Barnum, and rarely traveled with tent circuses, preferring instead to hold receptions where he and his wife could meet with guests. He wrote an autobiography, *The Kentucky River Giant* (probably published posthumously), which described the couple's life. The Bateses had two children, both of whom died at birth. Their daughter was born on May 19, 1872, in London. A son, born on January 18, 1879, in Seville, was thirty inches long, and weighed twenty-three and three-fourths pounds; it was claimed to be the largest human baby born up to that time.

Anna Bates died on August 5, 1889, and was buried in Seville's Mound Hill Cemetery, where Martin built a memorial to her. He married Lavonne Weatherby in 1900. The giant died on January 14, 1919, and was buried next to his first wife.

See Capt. Martin Van Buren Bates, *The Kentucky River Giant* (Hazard, Ky., n.d.); Lee Cavin, *There Were GIANTS on the Earth!* (Loudonville, Ohio, 1970).

BATH COUNTY. The fifty-fifth county in order of formation, Bath County is located in the northeastern part of the state. Bordered by Fleming, Menifee, Montgomery, Nicholas, and Rowan counties, Bath County was created by the General Assembly on January 15, 1811, out of part of Montgomery County, an area of 277 square miles. Bath County was named for the many medicinal springs within its borders. OWINGSVILLE is the county seat.

Topographically the county is divided roughly in half. The northwestern part of the county lies within the Bluegrass region, but the southern and eastern portions are hilly to mountainous. Agriculture is the dominant feature of the county. In 1987, about 74 percent of the land was devoted to farms. Burley tobacco, hay, and grain, as well as beef and milk cattle, are the major farm products from Bath County, which ranked fifty-second among Kentucky counties in agricultural receipts in 1987. Nearly 18,000 acres of land in the extreme southeastern section of the county lie within the Daniel Boone National Forest. The forest, of mixed hardwoods such as walnuts, oaks, and buckeyes, and softwoods such as cedars and pines, offers hiking, camping, and hunting. Along the border with Rowan County lies Cave Run Lake, completed in February 1974. This impoundment on the Licking River is one of the most productive eastern U.S. muskie fisheries.

Settlers were living in the area as early as 1775, when a certain Elias Tolin made improvements on some land on Slate Creek. It is likely that the region's rich deposits of iron ore induced many pioneers to make Bath County their home. In 1790 the Old State iron furnace was built in the county. In the late eighteenth and early nineteenth centuries Bath County supplied most of the iron needs of Kentucky and other regions west of the Blue Ridge Mountains. Originally Catlett's Flat was the county seat, but because a number of prominent families had established residence in the Owingsville area by 1811, the seat was moved that same year.

Bath County was home to OLYMPIA SPRINGS, one of Kentucky's most popular resorts in the nineteenth century and destination of the first stagecoach line out of Lexington in 1803.

During the Civil War, the county witnessed limited military activity. In October 1863, members of the 1st Kentucky Federal Cavalry skirmished with about 250 rebel troops at Olympia Springs. The results were indecisive and both sides claimed victory. On March 21, 1864, when Confederate troops attempted to force Federal troops out of quarters in the county courthouse, an overheated stove started a fire that destroyed the building. The federal government paid for the construction of a replacement, which was completed in 1868.

In 1872 the first two common school districts were created, signifying the beginning of organized public education in the county. Railroads entered the region in 1880 when construction began to extend the Elizabethtown, Lexington & Big Sandy Railroad eastward from Mt. Sterling through Bath County. In 1882, this road was made part of the Chesapeake & Ohio Railroad system, which soon linked Bath County with the rest of the state as well as the East Coast. In the 1980s, the Chesapeake & Ohio (then the Chessie Systems) ceased running through the county. In the early twentieth century two spurs, one from Salt Lick to Blackwater (in Morgan County) called the Licking River line, and another, the Owingsville & Olympia, were built off the main line. By the 1920s both these narrow-gauge lines had shut down.

In the late twentieth century, despite the completion of I-64 through Bath County, it has remained overwhelmingly agricultural. Nevertheless some industry has come to Bath County, although most nonfarm income is still generated by the service and retail trade industries. The Donotech Electrical Manufacturing Corp., a producer of circuit boards, opened in Owingsville in 1982. Reeves Lumber Co., in Salt Lick, a producer of wood flooring and paneling, which opened in 1984, also provides jobs for Bath County residents.

The population of Bath County was 9,235 in 1970; 10,025 in 1980; and 9,692 in 1990.

See Van B. Young, *An Outline History of Bath County, Kentucky* (Lexington, Ky., 1886); J.A. Richards, *A History of Bath County, Kentucky* (Yuma, Az., 1961).

BEARD, ALFRED, JR. Alfred ("Butch") Beard, Jr., basketball player and coach, son of Alfred and Mable (Moorman) Beard, was born on May 4, 1947, in Hardinsburg, Kentucky. He played basketball at Breckinridge County High School and entered the University of Louisville in 1966. Joining the varsity team in 1967, Beard, along with Wes Unseld, led U-of-L in several outstanding seasons, including two National Collegiate Athletic Association tournament appearances. In 1969 Beard was named an All-American. During his playing years at Louisville (1967-69), the high-scoring guard netted 1,580 points, which in 1990 placed him tenth on the U-of-L career scoring list. His average of 19 points per game was second-best in Louisville basketball history. He was selected in the first round of the 1969 National Basketball Association (NBA) draft by the Altanta Hawks. Beard played for five NBA teams—Hawks (1969-70), Cleveland Cavaliers (1971-72 and 1975-76), Seattle Super Sonics (1972-73), Golden State Warriors (1973-74) and New York Knicks (1975-79)—and was an NBA All-Star in 1972. Following his playing career, Beard became an assistant coach with the Knicks from 1979 to 1982, then moved into the broadcast booth, serving as a commentator for both the Knicks and the Hawks. In 1988 he returned to coaching as an assistant with the New Jersey Nets. In June 1990 he was named head basketball coach at Howard University in Washington, D.C.

Beard married Ruth Hackett on April 18, 1969; they have four children: Alfred III, Cory, Samantha, and Jan.

BEARD, DANIEL CARTER. Daniel Carter Beard, one of the founders of the Boy Scouts of America, was born June 21, 1850, in Cincinnati, Ohio, to James Henry and Mary Caroline (Carter) Beard. The family moved to Covington, Kentucky, where he was educated in local schools and studied civil engineering at Worrall's Academy, graduating in 1869. He went to work as a surveyor for the Cincinnati city engineer and in 1874 joined Sanborn Maps and Publishing Company of New York. For the next four years, Beard traveled extensively throughout the country, surveying land and drawing animals, a talent inherited from his father, one of the best-known portraitists of his time. In 1878 Beard joined his brothers James, Harris, and Thomas as an illustrator in New York City. His first book, *What to Do and How to Do It: The American Boy's Handbook*, was published in 1882. Fifteen other handicraft books followed over the next fifty years.

Beard became editor of *Recreation*, a sportsmen's monthly, in 1905 and under his direction the magazine began supporting wildlife and environmental concerns. In the same year he organized the Sons of Daniel Boone, the earliest forerunner of the Boy Scouts of America, to encourage conservation, love of the outdoors, and the pioneer spirit. In 1909 he founded the Boy Pioneers of America, which had some influence on the formation of the Boy Scouts movement in England, headed by Sir Robert Baden-Powell, and the Boy Scouts of America, founded in 1910. Although Beard did not himself form the Boy Scouts, he is often credited as its founder, and he served as a charter member of the Boy Scouts of America executive committee and as national Scout commissioner for thirty years. He designed and created the Scout hat, shirt, neckerchief, and many of the merit badges. He was associate editor of *Boy's Life*, the Scouting magazine, in which he wrote a monthly column until his death. In 1922

he received the only gold eagle badge ever awarded by the Boy Scouts. He was awarded the first medal for outstanding citizenship by the state of Kentucky.

On August 15, 1894, Beard married Beatrice Alice Jackson of Long Island, New York. They had two children, Barbara and Daniel Bartlett. Beard died at Brooklands, his home near Suffern, New York, on June 11, 1941, and was buried at Brick Church Cemetery in Rockland County, New York, near his estate. One of the honorary pallbearers at his funeral was President Franklin D. Roosevelt.

BEARD, FRANK. Professional golfer Frank Beard, whose game has been typified by remarkable consistency, was born on May 1, 1939, in Dallas, Texas, the son of Ralph, Sr., and Pauline (Sherman) Beard. His half-brother was University of Kentucky basketball star Ralph Beard, Jr. He grew up in Louisville and later entered the University of Florida, where he earned a B.A. in accounting in 1961. Beard returned to Kentucky to play amateur golf, and won the state championship in 1961 and 1962, turning pro in 1962. On the professional tour, he quickly gained the reputation of being a cool, steady player with exceptional putting ability who did not take undue risks. In 1969 he was the tour's top money winner. He transformed his tour diary into the book *Pro: Frank Beard on the Golf Tour* (1970). At age fifty he joined the senior tour.

Beard married Pat Roberts on October 30, 1965; they have four children: Danny, Randi, Jennifer, and Rachel.

BEARGRASS CREEK. Beargrass Creek, a major tributary of the Ohio River, has three major forks, which run across most of Jefferson County. The Muddy Fork runs generally parallel to the Ohio in eastern Jefferson County before turning from the river toward Westport Road. The Middle Fork flows straight through the central part of the county away from the Ohio, toward Anchorage, traversing both Cherokee and Seneca Parks. The South Fork, largest of the three, runs past the Audubon Bird Sanctuary before branching off and flowing toward Houston Acres and Buechel. The three forks meet only a short distance before Beargrass Creek empties into the Ohio River near Towhead Island.

The name is generally considered to be derived from the nickname of the yucca plant that the first pioneers found growing abundantly on the creek's banks; the yucca was called beargrass because it was eaten by bears. Some historians believe that early French explorers named it La Barre Grosse Crique, in reference to the sand bar that formed in the Ohio River near mouth of the creek. However, the earliest known maps of the creek, drawn by British settlers Lewis Evans (1775) and Thomas Hutchins (1778), label it Beargrass Creek or Rotten Creek. The name Rotten Creek would seem anomalous, since the creek was clear drinking water, and unpolluted when discovered. Some speculate that that name was in fact derived from the French word *rotin*, meaning cane growth.

Several settlement stations were built along the creek, the first being Floyd's Station (or Bear Grass Station) built along the Middle Fork in 1779. Beargrass Creek originally joined the Ohio River between what came to be Third and Fourth Streets in Louisville, just a few hundred feet above the Falls of the Ohio, at the lower end of a small peninsula. The creek was untouched by Louisville development until 1854, when flooding and the need to improve river traffic caused it to be rerouted so that it emptied into the Ohio approximately two miles upstream, across from Towhead Island, near River Road. The filling of the original lower channel of the creek obliterated the peninsula, known as the POINT.

Early in the twentieth century, flooding caused frequent evacuation of populated areas and halted freight transportation by blocking the railways. Under a 1909 plan, sewer interceptors and drainage channels were built to catch waste and relieve flooding, and the creek was slightly rechanneled. The plan called for the City of Louisville to buy land adjacent to the creek where it could impose waste disposal regulations. Similar projects were undertaken in 1956 (when the world's second-largest pumping station, the Beargrass Creek Pumping Plant, was built between Story Avenue and Brownsboro Road), and in 1975, as more people moved out into the county and were affected by the threat of flooding.

See Otto A. Rothert, "Origins of the Names Beargrass Creek, The Point, and Thruston Square," *FCQH* 2 (July 1927): 19-21.

BEATTY, NED. Ned Beatty, motion picture, television, and stage actor, was born on July 6, 1937, in St. Matthews, Kentucky, a Louisville suburb. His parents were Charles William Beatty, a salesman, and Margaret (Fortney) Beatty. He won a $100 prize as Louisville's "best breast-fed baby" of 1938 in a contest sponsored by the city Department of Health with a bequest from the will of a local bachelor. Beatty grew up in St. Matthews and attended Eastern High School in Middletown. After a year at Transylvania University in Lexington, Beatty began his professional career as a singer in the 1957-58 production of *Wilderness Road* in Berea. He was a member of repertory stage companies at the Barter Theatre, Abingdon, Virginia; the Arena Stage in Washington, D.C.; and his hometown's Carriage House Players, Children's Theatre, and Actors Theatre of Louisville. Beatty made his Broadway debut in *The Great White Hope* in the 1960s.

In 1972 Beatty began his movie career with a featured role as a rape victim in *Deliverance*. He had roles in *Nashville* (1975), *Silver Streak* (1976), *Superman* (1978), *Hopscotch* (1980), and *The Big Easy* (1987). Beatty received an Academy Award nomination for best supporting actor for the movie *Network* in 1976 and an Emmy nomination for best actor for the television movie *Friendly Fire* in 1979. He starred in the television series *Szyszynk* in 1977-78. Beatty has worked with the Kentucky

Film Office to attract location shooting to the commonwealth and has served as an adviser to Appalshop Productions in Whitesburg. He is the father of eight children from three marriages: Douglas, Lennis, Wally, Charles, John, Blossom, Thomas, and Dorothy.   MARY MARGARET BELL

BEATTYVILLE. The county seat of Lee County, Beattyville is located at the junction of KY 11 and KY 52, at the fork of the Kentucky River. Originally called Taylors Landing, the town was established by the General Assembly on March 15, 1851, as Beatty, in honor of Samuel Beatty, on whose lands a portion of the town was built. After the village was incorporated as Beattyville on March 28, 1872, the county seat was moved there from the nearby hamlet of Proctor. The first courthouse in Beattyville was completed in 1873.

Beattyville experienced steady growth, primarily based on coal, during the first decade of its existence. In the 1870s, the town had three churches, one school, four taverns, and about twenty mining companies. In November 1902 the Louisville & Atlantic Railroad, which had taken over the "Riney B" railroad running from Versailles to Irvine, completed the line from Irvine into Beattyville. When the Louisville & Nashville Railroad (now CSX Transportation) acquired the Louisville & Atlantic in 1909, it built a line from Beattyville through Irvine to Winchester. The route to Versailles was closed in 1932. Beattyville's early development was promoted also by its location on the Kentucky River. Major industries based in Beattyville through the years have produced lumber, concrete, shoes, and Fiberglass boats.

A disaster occurred in Beattyville on September 24, 1977, when the brakes of a gasoline truck carrying 8,200 gallons of fuel failed, and the truck careened into a section of the downtown business district. The resulting explosion and fire destroyed two blocks of the main street and killed seven people.

The population of the fifth-class city was 923 in 1970; 1,068 in 1980; and 1,131 in 1990.

See Bernice Calmes Caudill, *Remembering Lee County* (Danville, Ky., n.d.).   RON D. BRYANT

BEAUCHAMP, EMERSON. Emerson ("Doc") Beauchamp of Russellville, Kentucky, kingmaker in the Barkley-Clements-Combs wing of the Democratic party and the heir to the Logan County Democratic organization headed for forty years by Thomas S. Rhea, was born in Logan County on June 14, 1899, to Isaac and Ella (Offutt) Beauchamp. There were physicians in his family, so his father, thinking to incline him in that direction, began to call him "Doctor." The strain of politicians in the family won out, however. Both grandfathers had served in the Kentucky legislature, and Beauchamp himself began as a thirteen-year-old page in the legislature. He held various clerkships in the House and Senate; was Logan County clerk and sheriff; served on the state Tax Commission; was director of personnel and rural highway commissioner under Gov. Earle Clements (1947-50); and was secretary of the state Democratic central committee. Beauchamp was elected lieutenant governor on a ticket with Lawrence Wetherby (1950-55) in 1951; state agriculture commissioner in 1959; and state treasurer in 1963. His other occupation was farming. In World War II, he volunteered and served overseas as an overaged army captain.

Beauchamp had hoped his elevation to lieutenant governor would lead to the governor's chair, but his gravel voice, short, stocky figure, and slightly disheveled appearance conspired against his other assets— a shrewd, affable nature, good-humored wit, and a natural talent for "working" small groups. He decided to support Bert Combs for governor in 1955 instead of running himself, and although Combs lost the race to A.B. Chandler, Beauchamp was ready to back him again in 1959. Beauchamp was a welcome addition to the two successful statewide tickets fielded by the Democrats in the next eight years: Combs in 1959 and Edward T. Breathitt in 1963.

Beauchamp's desire to be rural highway commissioner collapsed with the 1967 defeat of Henry Ward, the Democratic nominee for governor. The old warrior then went back to Russellville to wait out the Louie Nunn (1967-71) Republican years. By that time, his own political base was being eroded by the addition of 3,000 manufacturing jobs in agrarian Logan County, lessening the traditional dependence on patronage. In 1969 his county ticket lost the sheriff's and county judge's office. Beauchamp died on March 26, 1971, as he was again backing Combs in a race for governor. Two months later, Combs lost to Wendell Ford, and three years later Beauchamp's friend Frank Albert Stubblefield lost the congressional seat that Beauchamp more than any other had won for him. The Rhea-Beauchamp machine had run out of gas and there was no one left to fill the tank.

Beauchamp was buried in Maple Grove Cemetery, Russellville. He was survived by his wife, the former Elizabeth Orndorff, whom he had married in 1924, and their sons, Russell Clark Beauchamp and Emerson, Jr.

See John Ed Pearce, *Divide and Dissent, Kentucky Politics 1930-1963* (Lexington, Ky., 1987); George T. Blakey, *Hard Times and New Deal in Kentucky 1929-1939* (Lexington, Ky., 1986).

AL SMITH

BEAUCHAMP, FRANCES (ESTILL). Frances (Estill) Beauchamp, temperance advocate, was born in 1857 in Madison County to James W. and Nancy (Scott) Estill. An only child, Fannie was educated locally and later at Science Hill Academy in Shelbyville. In 1875 she married James H. Beauchamp, an attorney, and lived in Taylorsville for five years, then moved to Lexington in 1880. A devout Presbyterian, Beauchamp embraced the temperance cause at an early age. She became active in the Women's Christian Temperance Union (WCTU) in 1886, when a local chapter was formed in Lexington. As president of the Lexington union, she worked to establish chapters throughout the state. In 1894 Beauchamp was elected assistant recording secretary of the national WCTU, an office she held for ten years. Beauchamp became president of the Kentucky WCTU in 1895, a position she retained until her death. Under her leadership, the organization flourished; as many as three hundred chapters were founded throughout the state. The WCTU was principally devoted to antiliquor agitation, but Beauchamp broadened her group's agenda to include prison reform and the establishment of separate facilities for juvenile offenders.

A polished, graceful orator, Beauchamp carried the temperance message to chautauquas, women's clubs, revivals, and other forums across the nation. Although women were then denied the vote, she rose to elective leadership positions in the Prohibition party at the state and national level. She chaired the state Prohibition party for ten years, and she served as secretary of the Prohibition National Committee from 1912 until her death. She was widely credited for the ratification of the prohibition amendment to the state constitution in November 1919.

Beauchamp died in Geneva, New York, on April 11, 1923, and was buried in the Lexington Cemetery. She and her husband brought up seven boys from disadvantaged circumstances.

See Thomas H. Appleton, Jr., " 'Like Banquo's Ghost': The Emergence of the Prohibition Issue in Kentucky Politics," Ph.D. dissertation, University of Kentucky, 1981. THOMAS H. APPLETON, JR.

BEAUCHAMP-SHARP TRAGEDY. On November 7, 1825, Col. Solomon P. Sharp, a former attorney general of Kentucky, was murdered at his home in Frankfort. At approximately 2:00 a.m., he was awakened by a knock on the door. When Sharp answered the door, he was stabbed in the chest, severing his aorta and killing him almost instantly. The killer fled. Initially, political enemies were suspected, but Sharp's two major rivals, Patrick Darby and John V. Waring, had alibis for the time in question. During the 1824 election contest, Waring had conducted a smear campaign against Sharp by printing handbills accusing him of seducing Ann Cook of Bowling Green and fathering an illegitimate child born to her in 1820. Suspicion in the Sharp case turned to Ann's husband, Jereboam O. Beauchamp, a young Simpson County law student who had married Ann Cook in 1824 and who had been infuriated by the accusations in the handbills. It was learned that Beauchamp had arrived in Frankfort the evening of November 5 and had taken a room at the home of Joel Scott.

Beauchamp was arrested in Bowling Green and brought to trial in Frankfort on May 8, 1826, charged with Sharp's murder. He was found guilty and sentenced to death by hanging. Ann did not want to be separated from her husband, and the jailer permitted her to remain in Beauchamp's cell. On July 5 the couple attempted double suicide with an overdose of laudanum, but the attempt failed, and a guard was placed in the cell to watch them.

On July 7, the morning of her husband's execution, Ann asked the guard for privacy while she dressed. When he left, the couple again attempted suicide with a knife that Ann had smuggled into the cell. Ann was taken to the jailer's home and doctors were summoned in an effort to save her life. Beauchamp was taken to the gallows to be hanged before he could die of his wounds. When he proved too weak to stand, he was supported by two men as the rope was placed around his neck. To the strains of "Bonaparte's Retreat," as he had requested, Beauchamp was executed. Ann died at approximately the same time.

The two were buried in a joint grave in Maple Grove Cemetery at Bloomfield, Kentucky. The tombstone was engraved with an eight-stanza poem written by Ann. The Beauchamp-Sharp tragedy has been recorded in many writings and has influenced many melodramas.

See J. Winston Coleman, Jr., *The Beauchamp-Sharp Tragedy* (Frankfort, Ky., 1950); Carl E. Kramer, *Capital on the Kentucky* (Frankfort, Ky., 1986).

BEAUMONT INN. The Beaumont Inn, a three-story brick structure of Federal design in Harrodsburg, Kentucky, near Old Fort Harrod State Park, is known for its antique furnishings, traditional Kentucky cooking, and elegant accommodations. The main building was constructed ca. 1845, and a succession of women's schools—Greenville Institute (1835-1856), Daughters College (1856-1893), and Beaumont College (1894-1914)—operated on the grounds. In 1917, two alumnae of Daughters College, Annie Bell Goddard and May (Mary) Pettibone Hardin, purchased the building. Goddard, who became sole owner of the property, opened the Beaumont Inn in 1918 to accommodate former students who returned to visit their alma mater. Goddard's daughter, Pauline Dedman, later took over ownership of the popular establishment, and Dedman's son, T.C. Dedman, Jr., and his son, Charles, were operating the Beaumont Inn in 1990.

BEAVER DAM. Beaver Dam is a city in Ohio County at the intersection of U.S. 231 and U.S. 62, between BOWLING GREEN and OWENSBORO. The town's name came from Beaver Dam Creek, which flows into Muddy Creek, a tributary of the Rough River. The creek was named by Martin Kohlmann (Coleman), a German immigrant, who was impressed by the numerous large beaver dams on the creek near his farm in 1795. Settlers from nearby Fort Hartford (now Hartford) came to the area for church services, and on March 5, 1798, they established the Beaver Dam Baptist Church. The church building was completed in 1807. The earthquakes in 1811-12 contributed to a wave of religious revivalism in western Kentucky that caused the Beaver Dam church to grow rapidly and led it to establish numerous other congregations.

Around 1870 an east-west railroad, the Elizabethtown & Paducah (now Paducah & Louisville) Railroad was built through Beaver Dam, heralding an era of rapid growth. The railroad bypassed HARTFORD, the county seat (whose citizens did not enthusiastically invest in the railroad) and the track was laid in the valley of Beaver Dam Creek because of the existence of coal reserves near Beaver Dam.

Beaver Dam was incorporated in 1873 and soon became a major trading center, with tobacco warehouses and stockyards supplementing coal mines and railroad as major industries. The city's location, near the junction of the Green River Parkway and the Western Kentucky Parkway, has attracted several manufacturers, including Royal Crown Cola Bottling Company and Thomas Industries, which makes lighting fixtures. Other major employers include Young Manufacturing Company, makers of machinery parts, and the Greene Coal and Pyramid Coal surface mines. The population of the fourth-class city was 2,622 in 1970; 3,185 in 1980; and 2,904 in 1990.

BECK, JAMES BURNIE. James Burnie Beck, who served several terms in the U.S. Senate and House of Representatives, was born in Dumfriesshire, Scotland, on February 13, 1822, the son of Ebenezer P. Beck. When his parents immigrated to the United States, Beck remained in Scotland with his maternal grandparents to complete his education. In 1838 he joined his parents in Wyoming County, New York. He moved to Lexington, Kentucky, in the spring of 1842, and began reading law with Gen. Leslie Combs while working for Drummond Hunt as plantation overseer. In the fall of 1845 Beck matriculated in the senior class at Transylvania University, receiving a law degree on March 21, 1846. Beck practiced law with John C. Breckinridge, a partnership that lasted through Breckinridge's term as U.S. vice-president (1857-61). Beck was also involved in land speculation and by 1860 owned 7,000 acres in Kentucky, as well as land in Arkansas and Illinois. He was a slaveholder.

Beck was a Whig until that party's dissolution, then became an intensely partisan Democrat. He was a member of the 1860 Democratic convention in Charleston, South Carolina, in April, when the party split over the issue of slavery. Delegates from seven southern states withdrew before a candidate was selected, and a second convention met in Baltimore in June. Beck was one of the 105 delegates to withdraw from the Baltimore convention when errant southern delegates were not allowed to reclaim their seats. During the Civil War, Beck was an adamant Southern sympathizer and believed strongly in states' rights.

In 1861 Beck was defeated in his bid for the Kentucky General Assembly. He was elected to the U.S. House of Representatives for four consecutive terms, serving from March 4, 1867, to March 3, 1875. He was then elected three times to the U.S. Senate, where he served from March 4, 1877, until his death in 1890. In Congress Beck served on the commission that defined the boundary line between Maryland and Virginia and on the Select Committee on Woman's Suffrage. During Reconstruction, Beck was a defender of the white South and consistently challenged legislation supported by the radical wing of the Republican party. In 1872 he was a member of the Senate committee that toured the South to gather testimony on accusations of Ku Klux Klan violence. Beck voted against legislation to suppress Klan activities, believing that the charges of violence were overstated and that the Klan was simply a political organization intended to protest the rule of the Radical Republicans. An influential member of the Senate Finance Committee, Beck was spokesperson for the Democratic party on tariff and revenue issues.

Beck married Jane Washington A. Thornton, stepdaughter of Kentucky Gov. James Clark (1836-39), on February 3, 1848. They had five children: Margaret, Sophy, Bettie, George, and James, Jr. Beck died in Washington, D.C., May 3, 1890, and was buried in the Lexington Cemetery.

See T. Ross Moore, "The Congressional Career of James B. Beck, 1867-1875," M.A. thesis, University of Kentucky, 1950.

BECKHAM, JOHN CREPPS WICKLIFFE. John Crepps Wickliffe Beckham, governor during 1900-1907, was born to William Netherton and Julia Tevis (Wickliffe) Beckham on August 5, 1869, in Bardstown, Kentucky. He was the grandson of Gov. Charles A. Wickliffe (1839-40). He attended Central University in Richmond, Kentucky, and then became Bardstown's principal of public schools (1888-93). Admitted to the bar in 1889, he opened a law practice in 1893. Beckham was elected to three terms in the state House of Representatives as a Democrat (1894-1900). In 1899 William GOEBEL, with some reluctance, accepted Beckham as his running mate for lieutenant governor. They lost, and Republican William S. Taylor was elected. But the Democratic majority in the General Assembly reversed the decision, and when Goebel died of an assassin's bullet a few days after being declared governor, Beckham succeeded to the office. In a special election held on November 6, 1900, to determine who should fulfill Goebel's term, Beckham defeated Republican John W. Yerkes, 233,052 to 229,363. Anxious to reunite his party and to calm the state, Beckham stressed noncontroversial issues and the need for compromise. In 1903 he was easily nominated for a full term as governor; he defeated Republican M.B. Belknap by 222,014 to 202,764.

As governor, Beckham called for improved roads, greater attention to penal and charitable institutions, and improvement of the state's educational system, all consensus positions. The governor did not display strong leadership, and the legislature showed little inclination to initiate reforms. Beckham was able to reduce the public debt, and under his leadership a uniform textbook law was passed in 1904 and two state normal schools

were created in 1906, at Bowling Green and Richmond. Beckham's ideas about railroad regulation were considerably more moderate than Goebel's, and he did little to stop the violence of the tobacco farmers' Black Patch War. During his term, work was begun on an imposing new state capitol.

Denied the nomination for the U.S. Senate in 1908, Beckham returned to his law practice, but in 1914 he defeated another former governor, Augustus E. Willson (1907-11), in Kentucky's first popular election to the Senate and served from March 4, 1915 to March 3, 1921. When he sought reelection to the Senate in 1920, his support of President Woodrow Wilson and of prohibition cost him the election, which he lost to Republican Richard P. Ernst by fewer than 5,000 votes. He was the Democratic candidate for governor in 1927, but a number of his own party rejected him, and he lost to Republican Flem D. Sampson, 382,306 to 350,796. In return for his support of Gov. A.B. Chandler (1935-39, 1955-59) in 1935, Beckham was appointed to Kentucky's Public Service Commission in 1936. He also served as the chairman of the Government Reorganization Commission. Beckham made one further attempt to gain the Democratic nomination for the U.S. Senate in 1936, but was unsuccessful.

In 1900 Beckham married Jean Raphael Fuqua; they had two children. Beckham died on January 9, 1940, and was buried in the Frankfort Cemetery.

See Nicholas C. Burckel, "From Beckham to McCreary: The Progressive Record of Kentucky Governors," *Register* 76 (Oct. 1978): 285-306; Glenn Finch, "The Election of United States Senators in Kentucky: the Beckham Period," *FCHQ* 44 (Jan. 1970): 38-50; Lowell Harrison, ed., *Kentucky's Governors 1792-1985* (Lexington, Ky., 1985).

LOWELL H. HARRISON

BECKHAM, JULIA TEVIS (WICKLIFFE). Julia Tevis (Wickliffe) Beckham, the daughter, sister, and mother of state governors, was born in the family home, Wickland, in Bardstown, Kentucky, in 1835. She was the youngest daughter of Charles Anderson Wickliffe, governor of Kentucky during 1836-40, and Margaret (Crepps) Wickliffe. She was named for teacher Julia A. Tevis, who had established Science Hill School for girls in Shelbyville, Kentucky, which Julia Wickliffe attended along with her four older sisters. Her sister Nannie married David L. Yulee, who was elected a U.S. senator from Florida; her brother Robert C. Wickliffe was governor of Louisiana from 1856 to 1860. On October 16, 1855, Julia Wickliffe married William Netherton Beckham, a Kentucky legislator who represented Nelson County for one term. The couple's son, John Crepps Wickliffe Beckham, served as governor of Kentucky during 1900-1907.

Julia Beckham died at Wickland on August 1, 1913, and was buried in Bardstown Cemetery.

BECKHAM COUNTY. Beckham County, an eighty-day wonder that was abolished by state courts, was carved out of Carter County in northeastern Kentucky, along with corners of Lewis and Elliott, as Kentucky's 120th county. Beckham County was created by the legislature on February 9, 1904, during a period of rapid growth, in a mix of local pride and political ambition. First envisioned as being named Hardscrabble, then Goebel, it was in the end named for the sitting governor, J.C.W. Beckham (1900-1907), with Olive Hill as county seat. Disputing a seventy-dollar debt judgment, C.V. Zimmerman filed suit against the new county judge, Capt. C.C. Brooks, claiming the county was unlawful because it left the parent counties with fewer than four hundred square miles of area each and had less area than that itself. Carter County joined the suit, claiming that Beckham County's boundary ran too close to Vanceburg and Grayson, both county seats, violating a ten-mile minimum set by the state constitution. The suit also claimed that Beckham County would rob Carter of rightful taxes. The court of appeals dissolved Beckham County on April 29, 1904. Postal orders and marriage licenses remain the only official records of its existence.

See George Wolfford, *Carter County, a Pictorial History* (Ashland, Ky., 1985).

GEORGE WOLFFORD

BEDFORD. The county seat of Trimble County, Bedford is located at the junction of U.S. 42 and U.S. 421. The first settler was Richard Ball, who constructed a house around 1805 on a hill above Bedford Springs. The town established at this location on February 16, 1816, and incorporated on March 5, 1850, was named for Bedford, Virginia, Ball's former home. The first Trimble County courthouse was erected in Bedford in 1837 and was replaced in 1884.

Bedford grew slowly during the nineteenth century. The population began a marked decline in the post–Civil War era; in the 1870s, the population was approximately two hundred. The community did have some industrial development, however, in the form of a wool carding factory and a steam-powered gristmill. The industrial base of Bedford remained small throughout the nineteenth and twentieth centuries. The manufacture of plastics is one of the primary industries.

One of the popular spas of nineteenth century Kentucky was Bedford Springs, where many southerners came to sample the waters and escape the heat of the summer months. The historic resort building was destroyed by fire in 1967. Fire had destroyed another Bedford landmark on March 5, 1952, gutting the Trimble County courthouse. Most of the county records were saved by local volunteers and firemen from neighboring Carrollton. The historic structure was rebuilt using the original walls of the remaining first floor.

The population of this sixth-class city was 780 in 1970; 835 in 1980; and 761 in 1990.

RON D. BRYANT

BEDINGER, GEORGE MICHAEL. George Michael Bedinger, soldier and politician, was born in York County, Pennsylvania, on December 10, 1756, to Henry Bedinger and Magdalene (Slagle) Bedinger. He saw extensive Revolutionary War service in the East before settling at Boonesborough in the spring of 1779. He then served under Gen. Anthony Wayne. Bedinger was elected to two terms in the Kentucky General Assembly and two terms as a Jeffersonian Republican in the U.S. Congress (March 4, 1803-March 3, 1807).

Bedinger was married to Nancy Keene on December 25, 1786; they had one child. On February 11, 1793, he married Henrietta Clay, with whom he had nine children. A farmer, he died on December 7, 1843, and was buried in the family cemetery near Lower Blue Lick Springs, Kentucky.

See Danske B. Dandridge, *George Michael Bedinger: A Kentucky Pioneer* (Charlottesville, Va., 1909).

CHARLES G. TALBERT

BEE ROCK. Bee Rock is a 355-foot-high cliff at the narrows of the Rockcastle River near the conjunction of Rockcastle, Pulaski, and Laurel counties, not far from the site of the Sublimity Spring resort, popular in antebellum years. The sandstone face of the cliff, one hundred feet above sea level, is pockmarked by numerous cells that formed natural hives for vast swarms of honeybees—the origin of the name Bee Rock. Tradition has it that swarms of bees were so vast that they cast a heavy shadow on the river. Both Indians and white settlers believed the rocky pockets harbored untold quantities of honey. The hives, however, could not be reached from the base of the cliff. Sometime after 1882, vandals lowered explosives from the top, killing the bees.

See Russell Dyche, *History of Laurel County* (N.p., 1975).

THOMAS D. CLARK

BEHRINGER-CRAWFORD MUSEUM. William Behringer, a resident of West Covington, Kentucky, who collected natural history specimens, gave his collections to the city of Covington when he died in 1948. City manager George Lyon and archaeologist Ellis Crawford developed the William Behringer Memorial Museum to house the collection in the 700-acre Devou Park in Covington. The museum opened on July 5, 1950. One of the last operating trolley parlor cars in the United States is part of the permanent exhibit. Ellis Crawford, the first curator, added to the collection through archaeological work at Big Bone Lick and other prehistoric sites in northern Kentucky. In 1972 the facility was renamed the Behringer-Crawford Museum in honor of Crawford's twenty years of service. A board of trustees administers the museum as a repository of northern Kentucky's natural and cultural heritage. A complete renovation started in 1980 and is due for completion by 1995.

GREG HARPER

BELKNAP, MORRIS BURKE. Morris Burke Belknap, businessman and civic leader, was born in Louisville on June 7, 1856, the younger son of William Burke and Mary (Richardson) BELKNAP.

He received his primary education in Louisville. After graduating from the Sheffield Scientific School of Yale University in 1877, he did graduate work there in mechanical engineering. He returned to Louisville in 1879 and went to work for Thomas Mickle and Co., which manufactured plows. Four years later he became vice-president of his father's firm, W.B. Belknap and Co., later known as the Belknap Hardware and Manufacturing Company.

Belknap enlisted in the 1st Regiment, Kentucky State Guard (Louisville Legion), in 1879 and was promoted to the rank of lieutenant colonel in 1893. He served with his unit in Puerto Rico during the Spanish-American War and was discharged in December 1898. Belknap joined Gov. Simon B. Buckner's (1887-91) staff in 1887. In 1903, as the Republican candidate for governor, he lost to incumbent Gov. J.C.W. Beckham (1900-1907) by 202,764 to 222,014.

On June 14, 1883, Belknap married Lily Buckner, Governor Buckner's daughter; they had four children: Walter, Morris, Gertrude, and Lilly. Lily (Buckner) Belknap died on December 29, 1893. Belknap's second wife was Marion Stewart Dumont, whom he married on July 16, 1900. Belknap died in Louisville on April 13, 1910, and was buried at Louisville's Cave Hill Cemetery.

BELKNAP, WILLIAM BURKE. William Burke Belknap, businessman, was born in Brimfield, Massachusetts, on May 17, 1811, to Phoebe Locke (Thompson) and Morris Burke Belknap. In 1816 his father moved the family to Pittsburgh, where they lived until 1827. Belknap's education began at the academy of the Rev. Joseph Stockton in Allegheny, Pennsylvania, and he subsequently attended Cannonsburg College, but left before completing his studies, when his family moved to Tennessee. There Belknap was employed in investigations of the coal and iron deposits along the Tennessee and Cumberland rivers. At age seventeen, he started working in his father's company, and soon the family moved to the Cumberland Valley of Kentucky. Unhappy there, Belknap left home in 1830, taking up residence in Hickman, Kentucky, near the junction of the Ohio and Mississippi rivers. He began a merchandising business there that shipped goods as far as Vicksburg, Mississippi.

Belknap sold his interest to his partners in 1839, traveled for a year, then settled in Louisville. He opened a store that sold iron nails and other small hardware, and he soon expanded into heavy hardware, shipping supplies across the South and Southwest. He built large warehouses for his property on Main Street in Louisville and purchased Louisville's first iron factory, Louisville Rolling Mill.

Belknap married Mary Richardson on May 30, 1843; they had five children: Fanny, Caroline, William Richardson, Lucy, and Morris Burke (BELKNAP). Belknap died on February 24, 1889, and was buried in Cave Hill Cemetery in Louisville.

See William B. Belknap, *Memorandum of the Family of William Burke Belknap* (Louisville 1870); C.J.F. Allen, "William B. Belknap," *Iron Age* (March 1889); James Speed, *1840-1940: Belknap Welcomes Another Century* (Louisville 1940).

BELL, JAMES FRANKLIN. James Franklin Bell, educator and military hero, was born to John Wilson and Sarah Margaret Venable (Allen) Bell in Shelby County, Kentucky, on January 9, 1856. He attended public schools in Shelbyville and worked as a bookkeeper before attending the U.S. Military Academy at West Point between 1874 and 1878. Graduating thirty-eighth in a class of forty-three, Bell received his command as second lieutenant in the 9th Cavalry, a black regiment. Bell's attempts to resign his commission failed, and he was transferred in August 1878 to the 7th Cavalry at Fort Abraham Lincoln in the Dakota Territory.

From 1886 to 1889, Bell was an instructor in military science and tactics at Southern Illinois University at Carbondale, where he also taught mathematics. During his tenure, Bell read law and passed the Illinois bar examination. In 1889 Bell returned to the 7th Cavalry. He was on personal leave when the regiment participated in the Indian massacre at Wounded Knee in December of 1890. Bell was promoted to first lieutenant on December 29, 1890, and participated in the Pine Ridge, South Dakota, campaign in 1891. When the 7th Cavalry was posted to Fort Riley, Kansas, later that year, Bell joined the staff at the newly opened Cavalry and Light Artillery School, and soon became adjutant, then secretary of the school. In November 1894 Bell became aide-de-camp to Gen. James Forsyth and was posted to the Department of California; in July 1897 to Fort Apache, Arizona Territory; and to Vancouver Barracks, Washington, in February 1898.

With the outbreak of the Spanish-American War, Bell was made head of the Office of Military Information of the Philippine Expeditionary Force. He received a promotion to temporary major of the Engineers, U.S. Volunteers, on May 17, 1898, and the rank of captain of the regular army in March 1899. On April 17, 1899, he became temporary major assistant adjutant general, U.S. Volunteers. On July 5, 1899, he was promoted to temporary colonel and assembled the 36th Regiment, which became known as the "Fighting 36th" and the "Suicide Club." Bell became a specialist in guerrilla warfare, receiving the congressional Medal of Honor for "most distinguished gallantry in action" for his bravery on September 9, 1899, at Luzon. In December 1899, Bell was promoted to brigadier general in the volunteers while retaining his regular army rank of captain and was given command of the 3d Brigade. Among his duties in the Philippines were those of provost marshal general of Manila. In February 1901, when the regular army was reorganized, Bell was promoted to brigadier general.

In July 1903 Bell was transferred to Fort Leavenworth, Kansas, where he headed the Command and General Staff School until April 14, 1906. In his efforts to raise the professional standards of the army, Bell established the Staff College at Fort Leavenworth in 1905. In April 1906 Bell was appointed U.S. Army chief of staff and, unlike his predecessors, served his full four-year tour of duty. His subsequent post, 1911-14, was commanding general of the Philippine Department. During 1914-15 he commanded the 2d (Tactical) Division, then the Western Department from 1915 to 1917. Bell was then put in command of the Eastern Department, with a brief training assignment to the newly formed 77th Division in 1917.

The University of Kentucky conferred the degree of LL.D. upon him in 1907. Bell married Sarah Buford on January 5, 1881. Bell died while in command at New York City on January 8, 1919, and was buried in Arlington National Cemetery.

See Edgar F. Raines, Jr., "Major General J. Franklin Bell, U.S.A.: The Education of a Soldier, 1856-1899," *Register* 83 (Aug. 1985): 315-46.

BELL, JOSHUA FRY. Joshua Fry Bell, politician, was born on November 26, 1811, in Danville, Kentucky, to David and Martha (Fry) Bell. He attended public school and graduated from Centre College in Danville in 1828. Bell studied law at Transylvania University in Lexington, then traveled through Europe, returning to Danville in 1833 to set up a law practice. He was elected to the U.S. House of Representatives as a Whig and served from March 4, 1845, to March 3, 1847. He declined renomination. Gov. John J. Crittenden (1848-50) appointed Bell secretary of state in 1849 and he served until July 31, 1850, when Crittenden resigned. After the collapse of the Whig party, Bell considered himself part of the Opposition party. He ran for governor on that ticket in 1859, but was defeated by Beriah Magoffin, 76,187 to 67,283. Bell served as commissioner to the Peace Conference held in Washington, D.C., in February 1861, in an attempt to prevent civil war. During his service in the Kentucky House of Representatives (1863-67), he was responsible for the creation of the 112th county, which was named for him. Originally Josh Bell County, the name was officially changed in 1872 to Bell County. Bell declined nomination for governor in 1863 by Union Democrats. In 1867 he returned to his law practice in Danville.

Bell married Mary M. Helm on October 20, 1836; they had four children. He died August 17, 1870, at his home and was buried in Bellevue Cemetery in Danville.

See Maria T. Daveiss, *History of Mercer and Boyle Counties* (Harrodsburg, Ky., 1924).

BELLARMINE COLLEGE. Bellarmine College, located on Newburg Road in Louisville, is a coeducational liberal arts institution with undergraduate and graduate programs. It opened its doors on October 3, 1950, as a Roman Catholic archdiocesan liberal arts college for men. It was established by Archbishop John A. Floersch, who named the Rev. Alfred F. Horrigan as first president and academic dean, the Rev. Raymond Treece as vice president

and financial officer, and John T. Loftus as registrar and dean of students. The college was named after the seventeenth century Italian Jesuit cardinal Robert Bellarmine. The school's motto, *In veritatis amore* (in the love of truth), was taken from the collect of the mass that celebrates his feast day. Bellarmine opened in 1950 with 115 male students, but only sixty-five returned for the second semester because of the Korean War. In 1954 the first graduating class had forty-two members.

The Bellarmine campus is on property that was part of a royal land grant from King George III to James McCorkle for his service in the French and Indian War. During the antebellum period, the land was a plantation owned by the Griffin family, who sold it to Bishop William George McCloskey for a seminary. Preston Park Seminary opened in 1871 and operated, with interruptions, until 1909. The SISTERS OF CHARITY OF NAZARETH staffed two orphanages that operated on the property: St. Vincent's for girls (1892-1901) and St. Thomas for boys (1910-38). As Kentucky's segregationist DAY LAW had been invalidated, Bellarmine in 1950 became one of the first schools in the commonwealth open to all races. The college began its work in affiliation with the Catholic University of America, Washington, D.C., and was accredited by the Southern Association of Colleges and Secondary Schools in December 1956.

In fall 1968 Bellarmine College merged with Louisville's Ursuline College for women, established by the Ursuline Sisters in 1938. The student body became coeducational and the college's governing board became independent of the archdiocese, although the archbishop remained chancellor of the college. For three years it was called Bellarmine-Ursuline College; in 1971 the name Bellarmine College was restored. In 1973 Dr. Eugene V. Petrik succeeded Horrigan as president of Bellarmine and in 1984, under Petrik's leadership, the institution was reorganized into three colleges: the College of Arts and Sciences, the Allan and Donna Lansing School of Nursing, and the W. Fielding Rubel School of Business. The following year, five new buildings were added to the existing ten on the 120-acre campus.

Bellarmine began to present the Bellarmine Medal to persons of civic and moral excellence on the national or international level in 1955. Recipients have included Carlos P. Romulo, former president of the Philippines; Henry Cabot Lodge; Mother Theresa of Calcutta; William F. Buckley, Jr.; Jesse Jackson; Philip Habib; and Lech Walesa. In 1963 Bellarmine opened the Thomas MERTON studies center to preserve the works of Merton, a Trappist monk who lived at the nearby Abbey of Gethsemani in Nelson County. The International Thomas Merton Society based itself at Bellarmine in 1989.

Inaugurated in 1984 through a gift of Dr. John Guarnaschelli and his wife, Marty, the Guarnaschelli lecture series brings leading arts and humanities speakers to Bellarmine students and the

Louisville community. The Wilson and Anne Wyatt Annual Lectures, endowed in 1989, bring outstanding national and international speakers in the field of public service or public affairs to the campus. Publications housed at Bellarmine College include the *Kentucky Poetry Review*, the *Kentucky Journal of Economics and Business*, and the *Merton Seasonal*. The Small Business Development Center offers various services in the seven-county region around Louisville.

Bellarmine grants the bachelor of arts degree in twenty-two departments and the bachelor of science degree in six areas, as well as associate of arts and associate of applied science degrees. Bellarmine began its first graduate program, the master of business administration, in 1975 and a graduate-level program in education was added in 1981. It also offers an M.S. in nursing, M.A. in social administration, and M.A. in teaching. Enrollment in 1989 was 2,054 undergraduate and 616 graduate students. The number of alumni totaled over 9,000 men and women.   MARGARET MAHONEY

BELL COUNTY. Bell County, 112th county in order of formation, lies in the southeastern section of Kentucky. It was created on August 1, 1867, from portions of Harlan and Knox counties, and has an area of 361 square miles. It is bordered by Clay, Harlan, Knox, Leslie, and Whitley counties and the states of Tennessee and Virginia. It was named for Kentucky congressman Joshua Fry Bell, who worked in the legislature for the creation of the county, which was originally called Josh Bell County. The county seat is PINEVILLE.

The topography of Bell County is mountainous, rugged, and picturesque. Over 80 percent of the county is covered by forestland, much of it in Kentucky Ridge State Forest, Pine Mountain State Resort Park, and CUMBERLAND GAP NATIONAL HISTORICAL PARK. The national historical park, an area of over 20,000 acres in and around the Cumberland Gap, is one of the largest of its kind. The principal waterways in the county are the Cumberland River and its tributaries, which include Yellow Creek, Clear Creek, and Greasy Creek.

The first explorers in the area are believed to have been Dr. Thomas Walker (great-grandfather of Joshua Fry Bell) and his party, who passed through the Cumberland Gap in 1750. Between the 1770s and early 1800s, thousands of settlers entered Kentucky through the Cumberland Gap. During the Civil War, both Confederate and Union armies recognized the strategic value of the Cumberland Gap, and it was fortified and occupied by one or the other army at various times during the conflict.

The land had rich mineral resources. Crude iron furnaces were erected early, including the Clear Creek, Owings, and Bourbon iron works. By the 1880s the timber and mineral resources of the region attracted the attention of foreign investors, who established MIDDLESBOROUGH.

The Great Depression hit hard in Bell County. As early as 1927, overproduction of coal crippled the industry and many of the mines closed. In 1929 a series of flash floods inundated the Yellow Creek Valley of Bell County early in the year, and in early March, after days of steady rainfall, flood waters destroyed $500,000 worth of property. In May 1988 a tornado struck Middlesborough, damaging thirty-eight businesses, twenty-four homes, and two churches. One person was killed and sixteen others were injured.

Not until World War II did the coal industry recover. The coal industry has remained an economic mainstay of Bell County; in 1988 1,700 men were employed in producing roughly 5.4 million tons of coal. The industrial output of the county includes lumber, coal, clothing, leather goods, steel, and plastics. In tourism, the *Book of Job* attracted thousands of visitors each year, and the Mountain Laurel Festival remains popular.

The population of Bell County was 31,087 in 1970; 34,330 in 1980; and 31,506 in 1990.

See Henry Harvey Fuson, *History of Bell County, Kentucky* (New York 1947).   RON D. BRYANT

BELLE OF LOUISVILLE. The *Belle of Louisville*, an excursion boat operating from the Fourth Street Wharf of the Ohio River at Louisville, is one of only two sternwheel river passenger boats still operating under steam. Originally christened the *Idlewild*, the vessel was built as a multipurpose transport, excursion, and ferry boat in 1914 at the James Rees and Sons Yard in Pittsburgh. She is 191.5 feet long, 40 feet wide, and has a 5-foot draft. The oak and steel paddlewheel weighs 17.5 tons. During her first ten years, the *Idlewild* operated primarily as a ferry between Memphis, Tennessee, and Arkansas. After 1925 she served as a day packet carrying freight and passengers, then as an excursion boat carrying tourists, and during World War II as a towboat pulling barges filled with oil along the Mississippi and Ohio rivers. Renamed the *Avalon* in 1948, she tramped the western rivers system for over fifteen years after the war, searching for excursion business.

In May 1962 the boat was purchased at auction by Jefferson County Judge Marlow Cook for $34,000. After reconditioning, the boat was rechristened the *Belle of Louisville*. Representing the city of Louisville since that time, she has carried over 5 million passengers on the Ohio River. A highlight of each season is the *Belle*'s annual race with Cincinnati's *Delta Queen* during the Kentucky Derby Festival celebrations. On June 30, 1989, the *Belle of Louisville* was named a national historic landmark by the National Park Service.

See Alan L. Bates, *The Western Rivers Steamboat Cyclopoedium* (Leonia, N.Y., 1968).
          OLIVIA FREDERICK AND KEVIN MULLEN

BELLEVUE. Bellevue is a city with a working-class population in northern Campbell County, situated between Dayton to the east and Newport on the west. The area was once part of the hilltop property of Gen. James Taylor, whose home in

Newport was called Bellevue. In 1866 the area was laid off into town lots by developer A.S. Berry and named in honor of the old Taylor estate. Berry, a moving force behind Bellevue's development, served as a four-term U.S. congressman from the area (1893-1901).

Bellevue was incorporated as a city on March 15, 1870. Its elevation kept most buildings above water during the floods of 1884, 1891, and 1937. At the turn of the century, Bellevue's beaches were popular for swimming, canoeing, and dining at clubhouses. By the late 1920s, river pollution and the number of lawsuits over accidents had closed most of the beaches. During the 1930s Bellevue was known for the Horseshoe Gardens, an entertainment club that featured big-band music. Among the entertainers who performed there were the Mills Brothers. The Horseshoe Gardens was destroyed by the 1937 flood.

The population of the fourth-class city was 8,847 in 1970; 7,678 in 1980; and 6,997 in 1990.

BENEDICT, JENNIE CARTER. Jennie Carter Benedict, restaurateur and author, was born near Harrod's Creek, eight miles east of Louisville, on March 25, 1860, to John C. and Mary C. (Richards) Benedict. She was educated in the Louisville public schools and took cooking classes at the Boston Cooking School with Fannie Farmer. In 1893 she began a career as chef and caterer; she created benedictine cheese (a spread made of cucumbers and cream cheese) and thus the benedictine sandwich. In 1900 she opened Benedict's, a restaurant and tearoom, on South Fourth Street. She became editor of the *Louisville Courier-Journal*'s Household Department in 1894, and helped to start Louisville's Businesswoman's Club in 1897. In 1902 the first edition of Benedict's *The Blue Ribbon Cook Book* was published, and in 1903 she was invited to join the Louisville Board of Trade. In 1925, she sold her successful enterprise for $50,000, retiring to her home, Dream Acre, overlooking the Ohio River. Her autobiography, *The Road to Dream Acre*, was published in 1928.

Business was not Benedict's only area of success. An active humanitarian, she served as superintendent of the Training School for Nurses (1887-1912) and devoted time to the King's Daughters' Home for Incurables and the Woman's Club of Louisville. Benedict, affectionately known to the public as "Miss Jennie," died on July 24, 1928. She was buried in Cave Hill Cemetery in Louisville.

BENTON. Benton was designated the seat of Marshall County when the county was formed on February 15, 1842. The site for Benton, on land belonging to John H. Bearden and Francis H. Clayton, was chosen by John Wortham of Graves County, Alfred Boyd of Trigg County, Charles B. Davidson of McCracken County, and Hugh McCracken of Caldwell County. It was named for Thomas Hart Benton, U.S. senator from Missouri. The town was not incorporated until January 11, 1845. In 1893, an addition was made to the town, giving it 113 lots around a public square. The East Fork of Clark River, named for George Rogers Clark, runs through Benton.

The first courthouse, a log structure, was built in 1843-44 by Francis Clayton. The second courthouse, built in 1847, was destroyed by fire in 1888; the next structure, built that year, burned in 1914. The current courthouse, of Beaux Arts–influenced design, was built in 1915. The Marshall County Seminary opened in Benton in 1868 and was the major educational institution until it consolidated with the public school system in 1888.

During the Civil War, detached forces of Confederate Gen. Nathan B. Forrest's cavalry met by accident a force of Union troops at Benton on March 23, 1864. In the two resulting clashes, seven men were killed. The Confederate force continued toward Paducah in search of supplies and horses.

Benton's economy evolved from that of a small industrial town to one based on the tourism industry. In 1890, the Paducah, Tennessee & Alabama Railroad came through Benton to accommodate a flour mill, a planing mill, carding factory, and tobacco warehouse as well as providing passenger service. In 1896, the Louisville & Nashville Railroad (now CSX Transportation) took over the line. In 1923 the Nashville, Chattanooga & St. Louis Railroad served Benton, which between 1930 and 1949 was a loading point for a Paducah produce firm that shipped strawberries from the region. In 1988, ten manufacturing firms employed fewer than two hundred persons.

With the completion of Kentucky Dam in 1944, the impoundment of the Tennessee River created a lake, of which Marshall and Calloway counties form the western boundary; Benton's economy has since been increasingly influenced by tourism. The 1966 impoundment of the Cumberland River, which formed Lake Barkley and created the federal recreation area Land Between the Lakes, and the development of Kentucky Dam Village and Kenlake State Resort Park increased the travel numbers. Benton, in the center of the county, is between the two parks and depends heavily upon tourist revenue, which in 1988 exceeded $56.5 million.

Marshall Countians celebrate their heritage and culture with two long-running annual events at Benton. Tater Day started in 1843, the first crop year after the city's founding, as farmers came to town to buy seeds and fertilizers for the upcoming planting season. On the fourth Sunday in May, lovers of shaped-note singing, based on William Walker's tunebook *Southern Harmony* (1835), crowd the courthouse to sing the songs of their ancestors. Known as Big Singing Day, the homecoming event spawned the Society for the Preservation of Southern Harmony Singing, incorporated in 1973.

Benton is a transportation crossroads in the county. The Purchase Parkway passes through Benton to connect with I-24 in the northern part of the county. U.S. 641 goes through the town to U.S. 68 above Benton. The L&N abandoned the rail line in

1950, and in 1982 the J&J Railroad, which serves the Hardin Grain Elevator, bought six miles of track from Benton to Murray to ship grain.

The Joe Creason Community Center in Benton is named for the late *Louisville Courier-Journal* columnist, who was a native.

Benton, a fourth-class city, had a population of 3,652 in 1970; 3,700 in 1980; and 3,899 in 1990.

RAYMOND MOFIELD

BEREA. Berea, the second largest city in Madison County, is located between the foothills of the Cumberland Mountains and the Bluegrass plains. The city is fourteen miles southeast of the county seat, Richmond, at the intersection of U.S. 25 and KY 21, one mile east of I-75. Berea was so named by its abolitionist founder, the Rev. John Gregg FEE, after a town in the New Testament. Fee organized a church for nonslaveholders and a school. The school became BEREA COLLEGE in 1858. In 1859 he and several abolitionist followers were forced out of Berea by an armed mob from Richmond. During the Civil War, Fee returned to Kentucky, working as a Union army chaplain, teacher, and advocate for black soldiers and their refugee slave families at Camp Nelson (Jessamine County).

When the war ended, Fee invited black veterans to settle in Berea, where his school and church were dedicated to interracial brotherhood. Hundreds of blacks found their way to "Feetown," and most settled in the valley nearby. Others settled along the Berea ridge, where Fee, as a Berea College trustee, arranged purchases of large land tracts, which were resold in small lots to create interracial neighborhoods around the church and school. Along with the boom in housing construction, the town's economy was bolstered by construction projects associated with Berea College. The coming of the railroad in 1883 made Berea a transit station for timber hauled from the mountains for shipment to urban markets.

When Berea was incorporated in April 1890, its population exceeded five hundred. Of that number, approximately one-fourth were blacks. All interracial aspects of the town, including its interracial council, thrived until 1904, when the Kentucky legislature enacted the Day Law, which prohibited Berea College from educating blacks and whites together. The Day Law symbolized the antiblack sentiments in the town, state, and region, and brought about a decline in the town's black population. Whites continued to move in for the college's educational and economic opportunities.

This fourth-class city's population was 6,956 in 1970; 8,600 in 1980; and 9,126 in 1990.

See Richard D. Sears, *Day of Small Things: Abolitionism in the Midst of Slavery, Berea, Kentucky, 1854-1864* (Lanham, Md., 1986).

JACQUELINE BURNSIDE

BEREA COLLEGE. Berea College in Berea, Kentucky, which was founded to educate former slaves and the children of the Appalachian poor, obtained its charter in 1859. Before the school could open, however, the Civil War broke out, and no classes were held until 1866. Berea College was established as an independent nonsectarian Christian school; at various times it was closely associated with the Presbyterian, Congregational, and Baptist churches. It was the creation of the Rev. John G. FEE, an evangelical abolitionist minister from Bracken County, Kentucky, who moved to land in Madison County that Cassius M. Clay had given him. From 1855 to 1859, Berea was the name of the mission school from which Fee and his fellow workers, mostly students from Oberlin College in Ohio, campaigned against slavery.

As early as 1856 the abolitionists proposed a college at Berea as an integrated school where men and women, blacks and whites could study together. However, before Berea College could open in 1859, John Brown led his attack on Harper's Ferry in Virginia. Slaveholders in Madison County, especially those in Richmond, decided that the abolitionist Fee represented a similar threat, and a band of sixty wealthy, prominent citizens from Richmond rode to Berea on December 23, 1859, and told the Bereans to leave the state within ten days. Although the Bereans appealed to Gov. Beriah Magoffin (1859-62) for help, Fee and his colleagues were forced to abandon their homes, their livelihoods, and their plans for a colony and a college. Not until late in the Civil War did Fee and some of his most dedicated workers return to Kentucky.

During the war Fee lived in New Richmond, Ohio, preaching against slavery and eventually calling for slave men to be drafted into the Union Army as a way to emancipate them immediately. In July 1864 Fee volunteered as a missionary at Camp Nelson in Jessamine County, the primary military camp for blacks in Kentucky. It became a refugee camp, housing black families who had fled their owners when the slave men enlisted, and Fee became their ardent defender. At the end of the war, Fee invited many of the blacks to settle in Berea, promising them a supportive community, an integrated church, and an interracial school.

Berea College opened as an elementary school in 1866 and became integrated on March 6 of that year, when three black girls enrolled. The first class attended by black students at Berea was conducted by Ellen P.T. Wheeler, the wife of a missionary whom Fee had met at Camp Nelson. Along with those who had met Fee at Camp Nelson came settlers from Jackson and Rockcastle counties and from the East and North, especially from Oberlin, Ohio. In 1869 seven students became Berea's first college class, and Edward Henry Fairchild, an Oberlin College graduate, was invited to become the first president of Berea College. Under Fairchild, the college gained endowment funds from the American Missionary Association, an affiliate of the Congregational church, and from private donors. Three-story Gothic buildings were constructed, including Fairchild Hall and Lincoln Hall.

The goal at Berea College—in reality a school with classes from kindergarten through college—was interracial education and social equality among the races. During almost all of Berea's first two decades, from 1866 to 1889, at least half the student body was black. At Fairchild's death in 1889, William B. Stewart became president, but he left two years later after disagreements with the college trustees.

William Goodell Frost, who became president in 1892, almost immediately began changing Berea's mission. Although Fee was still living, his ideas about black equality and the importance of balanced integration had fallen victim to the system of legalized discrimination across the United States. Frost decided that Berea should concentrate on the poor whites of Appalachia, and Berea's emphasis on nondiscrimination began to disappear, both from the college's promotional material and from its campus. The separation of races in classes and dormitories was encouraged and, in some cases, legislated; white students were actively recruited, but not blacks. During Frost's tenure, the proportion of blacks fell until only one-seventh of the student body was of African descent, a figure that Frost claimed reflected the percentage of blacks in Appalachia, Berea's exclusive constituency.

Berea College operated as the only integrated school in Kentucky until 1904, when passage of the DAY LAW, making it unlawful to educate black and white students together, forced it to abandon its original goals. The college challenged the law, but it was upheld both in state courts and, in 1908, in the U.S. Supreme Court. Having exhausted its legal options, Berea completed its plan for building a school for black students, LINCOLN INSTITUTE, near Shelbyville, Kentucky. Assisted by a gift of $200,000 from Andrew Carnegie, Berea divided part of its endowment in establishing the new school, which opened to black students in 1910.

After that point, Berea College became known as an Appalachian school that recruited poor students, charged no tuition, and required all students to work in a college industry while attending Berea. Its former incarnation, unique in the American South, was virtually forgotten. Not until 1950 was Berea College reintegrated, and the former high ratio of black students has not been restored, although college administrators are focusing recruitment on black students and faculty.

William J. Hutchins, who succeeded Frost as president in 1920, developed new programs for training teachers and agricultural and home demonstration agents. His son, Francis S. Hutchins, took over the presidency in 1939, followed by Willis D. Weatherford in 1969 and John B. Stephenson in 1984. During their terms, Berea College has become well-known not only for its educational fare and student industries, but also as a center for preservation of mountain crafts and traditions and a tourist attraction.

See John A.R. Rogers, *The Birth of Berea College: A Story of Providence* (Philadelphia 1903); Edward Henry Fairchild, *Berea College, Ky.: An Interesting History* (Cincinnati 1875); Elisabeth S. Peck and Emily Ann Smith, *Berea's First 125 Years, 1855-1980* (Lexington, Ky., 1982).

RICHARD SEARS

BERNHEIM, ISAAC WOLFE. Isaac Wolfe Bernheim, distiller, was born in Schmieheim, Germany, on November 4, 1848, to Leon Solomon and Fanny (Dreyfuss) Bernheim. He came to the United States in 1867, worked for a time as a peddler and later as a bookkeeper, and settled in Paducah, Kentucky. He and his younger brother Bernard established a distillery in Paducah in 1872, which they moved to Louisville in 1882, and the firm expanded further. In 1903 they incorporated the $2 million Bernheim Distilling Company.

Bernheim was a philanthropist whose most impressive legacy is the 10,000-acre BERNHEIM FOREST in Kentucky, a nature preserve opened to the public in 1950. Among his other gifts were the first library building at the Hebrew Union College in Cincinnati, an addition to Louisville's Jewish Hospital in 1918, and civic statuary—of Thomas Jefferson at the Jefferson County Courthouse (1899), of Abraham Lincoln at the Louisville Free Public Library (1922), and a Lincoln bust in Frankfort (1910). Although Bernheim was active in several Jewish organizations, serving as treasurer of the American Jewish Committee from 1906 until 1921, he was a staunch assimilationist and an opponent of Zionism. He advocated the adoption by the Jews of a Sunday Sabbath, and in 1918 he urged the establishment of the Reform Church of American Israelites. Bernheim wrote two autobiographical works, *The Story of the Bernheim Family* (1910) and *Closing Chapters of a Busy Life* (1929), and the brief *History of the Settlement of the Jews in Paducah and the Lower Ohio Valley* (1912). In the 1920s Bernheim moved to Denver, Colorado.

Bernheim married Amanda Uri in 1874. They had seven children: Leon, Morris, Bertram, Elbridge, Amelia, Helen, and Marguerite. He died while wintering in Santa Monica, California, on April 1, 1945.

See Herman Landau, *Adath Louisville: The Story of a Jewish Community* (Louisville 1981); Frank H. Bunce, "Dreams from a Pack: Isaac Wolfe Bernheim and Bernheim Forest" *FCHQ* 47 (1973): 323-32.

HERMAN LANDAU AND LEE SHAI WEISSBACH

BERNHEIM FOREST AND ARBORETUM. Bernheim Forest and Arboretum, twenty-five miles south of Louisville, Kentucky, in Bullitt and Nelson counties, totals approximately 10,000 acres of Kentucky woodlands and park area, created and maintained for the conservation of nature and the enjoyment of the public. The creator of the forest was Louisville philanthropist Isaac W. BERNHEIM (1848-1945), who in 1928 bought 14,000 acres of "knobland" for this purpose from the United States Trust Company. The forest was developed over former iron and salt works within a scenic backdrop of knobs, ridges, and rugged terrain. The entrance to the forest is one mile east of I-65 on KY 245.

Bernheim, a native of Germany, formed the private nonprofit Isaac W. Bernheim Foundation on May 10, 1929, to hold title to the land, and he set up the Bernheim Trust to manage the endowment he gave the foundation. A board of trustees governs the foundation, and an executive director is in charge of daily operations. The foundation also owns an adjoining, undeveloped 4,000-acre tract called Knobs Forest, which is scheduled for inclusion as part of the Bernheim Research Forest.

Between 1929 and 1947, the majority of the area was returned to a natural state, conservation measures were enacted, and public use projects were completed. Three small lakes were completed by 1939. After Bernheim's death in 1945, his associates Robert Paul and Charles King McClure III oversaw the project. In 1949 the thirty-two acre Lake Nevin was impounded. On May 19, 1951, the 10,000-acre expanse was officially named Bernheim Forest, which is open to the public from March 15 through November 15 each year.

Bernheim Forest, similar to the ones settled by the first pioneers in the region, has more than 300,000 annual visitors. The nature museum and arboretum have educational programs about birds, wildflowers, geology, and history. The park contains 1,800 species of trees and shrubs, labeled along floral trails. Under state refuge status, the park is restoring species of wildlife, such as grouse, quail, wild turkey, and Virginia whitetail deer, that were indigenous to Kentucky when it was wilderness. The park's sole wildlife sport, fishing, is allowed in only one of the four lakes. There are also picnic areas. Only 1,500 acres of the forest have any structural development, leaving the rest to remind visitors of the Kentucky of old.

See Frank H. Bunce, "Dream from a Pack: Isaac Wolfe Bernheim and Bernheim Forest," *FCHQ* 47 (Oct. 1973): 323-32; Jack Harrison, "Bernheim: A Gift of Nature," *Louisville Magazine*, Jan. 1979.

JAMES J. HOLMBERG

BERRY, WENDELL ERDMAN. A native of Henry County, Kentucky, Wendell Erdman Berry, writer of poetry, fiction, and essays, was born on August 5, 1934, the eldest son of John M. and Virginia (Perry) Berry. He was educated at Millersburg Military Institute in Kentucky and at the University of Kentucky, where he received a B.A. in 1956 and an M.A. in 1957.

Berry began writing both fiction and poetry as a student at the university, and his poems appeared in *Poetry: Chicago* and *Prairie Schooner* as early as 1957-58, while he was teaching at Georgetown College in Kentucky. In 1958-59, he held a Wallace Stegner Fellowship in Creative Writing at Stanford University, where he stayed on during 1959-60 as E.H. Jones Lecturer in Creative Writing. While at Stanford, he finished *Nathan Coulter* (1960), the first of his ongoing cycle of novels and stories chronicling the history of the fictional community of Port William, Kentucky. In the summer of 1960, Berry returned to Kentucky to live and work on his family's farm, near New Castle. In 1961 he was awarded a Guggenheim Foundation Fellowship and spent the winter of 1961-62 in Italy, where he concentrated on poetry. His work appeared in magazines and journals as diverse as *Contact* and *Library Journal.*

He taught English and was director of freshman composition for two years (1962-64) at City College of New York University. In the fall of 1964 he returned to the University of Kentucky to teach there. The following year, acting out of concern for the conservation of natural resources and the preservation of the small farm, he moved with his family to Henry County, where he purchased and began to restore a small farm on the bank of the Kentucky River, near Port Royal.

Berry's first book of poems, *The Broken Ground*, appeared in 1964; it was followed by ten others, including *Collected Poems* in 1985, and he became one of the most widely read poets in America. His poetry won numerous awards, including the Borestone Mountain Award, *Poetry* magazine's Vachel Lindsay Prize and Bess Hokin Prize, and the *Virginia Quarterly Review's* Emily Clark Balch Prize. In fiction, his Port William cycle includes four novels and *The Wild Birds*, a collection of short stories published in 1986. His *A Place on Earth*, which brings the story of Port William to the brink of the twentieth century, is an American pastoral. The novel *The Memory of Old Jack* won the first-place award of the Friends of American Writers for 1975 and was praised by *Library Journal* as "worthy of a place among the best pieces of prose written by American writers of this century."

It is perhaps as an essayist that Berry's voice has been most influential. Between 1969, when *The Long-Legged House* appeared, and 1990 he published almost a dozen books of nonfiction on a formidable range of subjects—environmental and ecological concerns, agricultural practices, racism in American life, public policy, literary and philosophical matters, the role of technology in modern society, and the like. His *The Unsettling of America: Culture and Agriculture*, published in 1977, was called by the *Los Angeles Times* "one of the most important books of the decade." The novelist Ken Kesey likened Berry to "Sergeant York charging unnatural odds across our no-man's-land of ecology." *Publisher's Weekly*, praising his *Recollected Essays, 1965-1980*, called him "a prophetic conscience of the nation." In 1989 his work won the prestigious Lannan Foundation Award for nonfiction.

William S. Ward, writing of *The Wild Birds* in his *A Literary History of Kentucky* (1989), assessed Berry's contribution to both contemporary letters and contemporary thought: "He is still the traditionalist, a latter-day romantic celebrating the importance of the individual, the need for a sense of community in the natural and social order, and the centrality of our relationship to the land and through it to the universe. These are the matters he writes about, and perhaps no one today does it better."

Berry married Tanya Amyx, of Lexington, in 1957; they have two children, Mary Dee and Den. Berry left the University of Kentucky in 1978 to devote his energies full-time to writing, lecturing, and farming but rejoined the permanent faculty in 1987.   ED McCLANAHAN

BETHEA, RAINEY. The execution of Rainey Bethea at Owensboro, Kentucky, on August 14, 1936, was the last legal public hanging in American history. Bethea, a black who was twenty-three years old at the time of his death, was a native of Roanoke, Virginia, who had lived in Owensboro for five years. He had served time in Eddyville prison for housebreaking. Bethea was sentenced on June 25 to die for the rape and murder of an elderly white woman, Eliza Edwards, on June 7, 1936. A crowd estimated at 10,000 packed downtown Owensboro for the hanging. The event received media coverage by reporters from throughout the country, with newsreel cameras and chartered airplanes to deliver photographs to major dailies. The national reaction was a great outcry against public executions, and in 1938 the Kentucky General Assembly modified the law to require that all executions "take place within the walls of the state penitentiary."

See Lee A. Dew, "The Hanging of Rainey Bethea," *Daviess County Historical Quarterly* 2 (July 1984): 51-59.   LEE A. DEW

BETHEL ACADEMY. Bethel Academy was the second chartered educational institution of American Methodism. Bishop Francis ASBURY and others in 1790 drew up plans for the school, to be located on a bluff overlooking the Kentucky River, four miles southeast of Wilmore. The school opened in 1794 and was chartered by the Kentucky General Assembly in 1798, but in 1805 lack of funds shut down operations at that site. The academy moved to Nicholasville, where it was successively housed in several private dwellings and later in a brick structure built for the purpose. After 1893 Bethel Academy functioned for a time as a public school.

FRANK B. STANGER, JR.

BETHEL COLLEGE. Bethel College in Hopkinsville, Kentucky, a coeducational college when it closed in 1964, was established by the Bethel Baptist Association as a high school for young women in the spring of 1854. At that time, it was known as Bethel Female Institute. The school acquired a five-acre lot, and Maj. N.B. Kelley drafted plans for a three-story brick structure in Greek Revival style. The building was completed in March 1857, at a cost of around $30,000. In 1890 the school was rechartered as Bethel Female College, with the authority to grant degrees. The school was designated a junior college and the name was changed to Bethel Woman's College in 1917. It conferred the associate in arts degree until it closed. In 1928 Bethel became the first junior college in Kentucky to be admitted to the Southern Association of Colleges and Secondary Schools. The name Bethel College was adopted in 1951, when the school became coeducational. Student enrollment peaked in the fall of 1963 at 209 students.

The college was closed twice during wartime. In 1861-62 Confederate forces used the structure as a hospital for soldiers suffering from black measles and pneumonia. During World War II the rooms were rented to military personnel and their families from nearby Fort Campbell.

Bethel trustees voted to close the financially troubled school in the spring of 1964, after the Kentucky Baptist Association diverted operating funds from Bethel for the support of the new Kentucky Southern College in Middletown. The historic main building, auditorium, and dormitory wings were razed in the spring of 1966.

WILLIAM T. TURNER

BEVERLY HILLS NIGHTCLUB. The Beverly Hills nightclub in Southgate, Kentucky, was destroyed in a disastrous fire in 1977 in which 165 people perished. The club had a colorful history. From 1940 to 1961 the club, operated by organized gambling interests, featured sophisticated (and illegal) casinos and Hollywood entertainment. The club's fortunes declined in the 1960s with the demise of ORGANIZED CRIME in northern Kentucky. In 1970 real estate developer and businessman Richard Schilling bought, expanded, and reopened the Beverly Hills as an elegant supper club that again featured popular entertainers. On May 28, 1977, when the supper club was packed with more than 2,000 patrons, a fire started in the Zebra Room around 9:00 p.m. It spread rapidly and sent deadly black smoke through the building. More than five hundred firemen, policemen, emergency squad members, nightclub employees, and other volunteers fought the fire. It was attributed to faulty wiring, improper insulation, and the absence of a sprinkler system. Only the 1942 Cocoanut Grove fire in Boston, which killed 491, was a worse nightclub disaster. The total amount recovered by plaintiffs in settlements was $55.4 million.

See Robert G. Lawson, *Beverly Hills: The Anatomy of a Nightclub Fire* (Athens, Ohio, 1984).

H. LEW WALLACE

BIBB, GEORGE MORTIMER. George Mortimer Bibb, jurist and U.S. senator, was born in Prince Edward County, Virginia, on October 30, 1776, to Richard and Lucy (Booker) Bibb. Bibb received an A.B. degree in 1792 from Princeton College and was also a student at Hampden-Sydney College and William and Mary College. Bibb studied law and may have practiced for a short time in Virginia before moving to Lexington, Kentucky, where he set up a practice in 1798. Bibb was defeated for the U.S. Senate in 1806 by Henry Clay.

On November 26 of that year he was elected to the Kentucky House of Representatives. He resigned to be commissioned a judge on the Kentucky court of appeals on January 31, 1808, and he became chief justice of the court on May 30 of the following year. He resigned in March 1810 and was again elected to the state House.

In 1811 Bibb was elected by the legislature to the U.S. Senate, serving from March 4, 1811, until August 23, 1814, when he resigned to return to private law practice. During this period Bibb, along with Henry Clay and John C. Calhoun, was a supporter of the War of 1812. Bibb moved his law practice to Frankfort in 1816. The following year he served another term in the state House. Bibb and Henry Clay represented Kentucky before the U.S. Supreme Court in a land dispute case with Virginia known as *Green v. Biddle*. In the battle between OLD COURT-NEW COURT factions in Kentucky, Bibb was a proponent of the New Court. On January 4, 1827, he was once again appointed chief justice of the Kentucky court of appeals. He resigned on December 23, 1828, to serve another term in the U.S. Senate, from March 4, 1829, to March 3, 1835.

Bibb, elected to the Senate as a Jacksonian Democrat, supported President Andrew Jackson by voting against the Maysville Road bill and the rechartering of the Bank of the United States. He criticized Jackson's use of patronage, however, and considered the president's so-called Force Bill, emphasizing federal power, to be unconstitutional. Bibb was a supporter of states' rights and the constitutional rights of minorities. He believed in a strict interpretation of the Constitution, opposed a high protective tariff, and defended the institution of slavery. After Bibb's Senate term ended, he was appointed to the Louisville chancery court, and he served as secretary of the Treasury under President John Tyler in 1844-45. He practiced law in Washington, D.C., for the rest of his life.

Bibb married Martha Scott, the daughter of Kentucky Gov. Charles Scott (1808-12), on May 19, 1799; they had ten children. Martha (Scott) Bibb died on April 12, 1829. In 1832 Bibb married a Mrs. Dyer of Washington, D.C.; they had four or five children. Bibb died in Washington on April 14, 1859, and was buried in the Frankfort Cemetery.

See John S. Goff, "The Last Leaf: George Mortimer Bibb," *Register* 59 (Oct. 1961): 331-42.

BIBB, HENRY WALTON. Henry Walton Bibb, a self-educated slave who escaped to write and lecture against slavery, was born in Shelby County, Kentucky, in May 1815 to Mildred Jackson, a slave, and James Bibb, a landowner and politician. In his youth, Bibb was often hired out to other planters. In 1833 he learned to read from a Bible and then to write as well. In 1834 he married another slave, Malinda, who belonged to William Gatewood of Trimble County. Gatewood bought Bibb when his owners moved to Missouri. In December 1837 Bibb escaped to Perrysburg, Ohio. In June 1838 he attempted to return to Kentucky to rescue Malinda

and his daughter, Mary Frances, but was captured in Cincinnati. The following day he escaped and returned to Perrysburg. In July of 1839 he made another attempt to reach his wife, but this time he was captured and returned to Gatewood, who sold the entire family to a slave trader in Louisville. The family was taken to New Orleans and sold at auction to Francis Whitfield. After another failed attempt to run away, Bibb was sold to Indians; he fled them in 1842 and traveled to Detroit.

In May 1844 Bibb made his first antislavery speech, and for a number of years he toured the Northeast giving abolitionist lectures. In 1845 he received word that Malinda had taken another husband. In June 1848 he married Mary E. Miles. Bibb's story of slavery, *Narrative of the Life and Adventures of Henry Bibb, an American Slave*, was published in 1849. In 1850 he moved to Windsor, Ontario, upon passage of the Fugitive Slave Act. Bibb founded and edited the black semimonthly newspaper the *Voice of the Fugitive*. He also organized and worked with the Refugee Home Society, which assisted runaway slaves in relocating and purchasing farms in Canada. Bibb died in 1856.

See Gilbert Osofsky, *Puttin' on Old Massa: The Slave Narratives of Henry Bibb, William Wells Brown, and Solomon Northup* (New York 1969).

BIBB, JOHN B. John B. Bibb, horticulturalist, the youngest son of Richard and Lucy (Booker) Bibb, was born on October 27, 1789, in Prince Edward County, Virginia. The Bibb family moved to Fayette County, Kentucky, in 1798, then to Bullitt County, and to Logan County. Bibb received his early education from Joshua Fry of Mercer County and studied law under Judge H.P. Broadnax of Daviess County. In August 1813 Bibb answered Gov. Isaac Shelby's (1812-16) call to arms for the War of 1812, joining the 4th Kentucky Volunteer Brigade as a private. He was promoted to major after the American victory at the Battle of Thames on October 15, 1813. When discharged on November 4, 1813, Bibb returned to Russellville in Logan County, was admitted to the bar in 1814, and practiced law until 1816, when he gave up the practice because of poor health. Bibb was elected to the Kentucky House as a Whig from Logan County in 1827 and 1828, and to the Kentucky Senate for the period 1830-34.

In 1856 Bibb built Gray Gables (now the Bibb-Burnley house), a Gothic-style house on Wapping Street in Frankfort. In a large garden and greenhouse at the rear of his home, Bibb, an amateur horticulturalist, developed a new variety of lettuce some time after 1865. Originally called limestone lettuce, it was later named for Bibb. This variety of lettuce has a compact head, with leaves of single-serving size. Although tender and easily bruised, it is resistant to plant lice. Bibb did not market the lettuce but often gave it away, and it was grown regionally by truck farmers who had received seeds from Bibb. The lettuce was widely marketed after 1919 by the Grenewein greenhouse in Louisville.

Bibb married Sarah P. (Hopkins) Horsley on August 24, 1831. Bibb died April 13, 1884, and was buried in the Frankfort Cemetery.

See Camille Glenn, "Lettuce Rejoice," *House and Garden* 162 (Mar. 1990): 84-86; John S. Goff, "The Last Leaf: George Mortimer Bibb," *Register* 59 (Oct. 1961): 331-42.

BIBB, RICHARD. Richard Bibb, emancipationist, was born in Virginia in 1752, the son of John and Susana (Bigger) Bibb. He was first intended for the ministry, but he instead entered the Continental army, where he attained the rank of major during the Revolutionary War. After serving in the Virginia legislature, he moved to Kentucky in 1779. In 1803 he represented Bullitt County in the General Assembly. Major Bibb, one of the wealthiest men in western Kentucky, owned approximately one hundred slaves, of whom he freed fifty-two in 1829 at his home, at Eighth and Winter Streets in Russellville, while thirty-two consented to go to Liberia. At his death, the remaining slaves were freed by his will, which also provided for their care. His son Richard, Jr., was active in the American Colonization Society. Bibb's home was restored and endowed as a museum.

Bibb and his first wife, the former Lucy Booker, had eight children: John B., George, Robert, Mary, Lucy, Susannah, Florence, and Richard, Jr. After the death of his first wife, Bibb married Alice Young Jackson. Bibb died in Russellville on January 25, 1839, and was buried in the Bibb family burying ground at Echo Valley in Logan County, seven miles east of Russellville.

See M.B. Morton, *Kentuckians Are Different* (Louisville 1938); Lowell H. Harrison, *The Antislavery Movement in Kentucky* (Lexington, Ky., 1978). GEORGE STREET BOONE

BIG BONE LICK. Fifteen to twenty thousand years ago, in the Pleistocene Epoch, a great ice sheet covered an area from northern Canada to the Ohio River. South of the ice sheet, elephant-like woolly mammoths and mastodons, giant ground sloths, giant bison, and other animals came to a salt lick twenty-two miles southwest of what is now Covington, in Boone County, Kentucky. Many of the animals became trapped in the surrounding bogs and died, their big bones buried and preserved around the lick named for them.

In 1739 French Canadian Capt. Charles Lemoyne de Longueil collected some of the fossils while exploring the Ohio River Valley and sent them to King Louis XV of France. Benjamin Franklin studied some of them and concluded that elephants had once lived in America. In 1807 Capt. William Clark was commissioned by President Thomas Jefferson to excavate bones from Big Bone Lick for scientific study. Specimens from these collections made their way to museums throughout the world, and it was determined that the abundant elephant-like bones were not those of any surviving type of elephant, but of a distinctly different type, the mastodon. In all, twenty-two distinct species of

Pleistocene mammals have been documented at Big Bone Lick.

To preserve this historical area, the Boone County Historical Society and schoolchildren of Boone County raised enough money to purchase the land around Big Bone Lick, and in 1960 the area was transferred to the commonwealth and became a state park. Big Bone Lick State Park offers a museum, historical and nature trails, camping, and recreational activities.

See Willard Rouse Jillson, *Big Bone Lick—an Outline of Its History, Geology, and Paleontology* (Louisville 1936). STEPHEN F. GREB

BIG CROSSING STATION. Big Crossing Station was the first permanent settlement in Scott County, Kentucky, located along the North Elkhorn, about two miles west of Georgetown. It was founded by Robert JOHNSON during the winter of 1783-84 and named for the buffalo path that crossed the stream. McClelland's Station had been founded in Scott County eight years earlier, in 1775, but was abandoned from 1777 until 1782 because of fears of Indian attack. After completing the stockade and moving his family there in late 1783, Johnson continued making improvements. A mill was built in early 1784, but a spring flood destroyed it before it could be used. As more settlers entered the area, the need for a fortified station diminished, and by 1789 it had become a private residence. By 1811 a small town called Great Crossing was established around the former station. Johnson left Great Crossing in 1815 and moved to Gallatin County, where he helped found the town of Warsaw.

See Nancy O'Malley, *Stockading Up* (Lexington, Ky., 1987).

BIG SANDY–GREENBRIER ROAD. After the Wilderness Road, the Big Sandy–Greenbrier Road was the next to be improved in Kentucky with the aid of state funds. On December 13, 1802, the General Assembly authorized the establishment of "a good way . . . from Mt. Sterling or Paris to Big Sandy River, in a good direction to communicate with the Greenbrier Road in Virginia." The opening of the road was indicative of the General Assembly's awareness of the need for public communication and transportation networks within the state. The legislature made sporadic efforts to improve and maintain the road during the first half of the nineteenth century; after 1850, the work was undertaken by the counties through which the road passed.

BIG SANDY RIVER. Some twenty-seven miles in length and formed by the junction of the Levisa and Tug forks at Louisa in Lawrence County, Kentucky, the Big Sandy River flows northward and empties into the Ohio River at Catlettsburg. Big Sandy's LEVISA FORK, 164 miles in length, rises in southwestern Virginia as Russell Fork. TUG FORK, 154 miles in length, rises in southwestern West Virginia. The headwaters of the two forks are about twenty miles apart, and both flow on parallel lines, often no more than twenty-five to forty miles apart, until their confluence at Louisa. In 1954 the Kentucky General Assembly adopted a resolution specifying that what constituted the Big Sandy River was the Levisa Fork from Millard in Pike County to Louisa, a distance of one hundred miles. However it is measured, the Big Sandy River, with its Levisa and Tug forks and maze of tributaries, drains a land basin area of 4,283 square miles in Kentucky. Its valley encompasses the counties of Boyd, Floyd, Johnson, Lawrence, Martin, and Pike and the eastern edges of Magoffin, Knott, and Letcher.

Settled later than the rest of Kentucky because of Indian hostilities from the North and the geographical barriers, the Big Sandy valley long had an isolated, frontier aspect. Settlers came overland through the gaps or down the Ohio by riverboat. For generations the river served as the only practical means of transportation and contact with the outside world, yet navigation on the narrow, crooked Big Sandy was uncertain and frequently interrupted by low water or floods. The Civil War divided the valley as it did the rest of Kentucky. The local authorities were unable to prevent soldiers and guerrillas alike from robbing and killing at will.

The colorful steamboat era, which lasted from the 1830s to the eve of World War I, did much to shape the culture of the Big Sandy valley. Entrepreneurs, like Orlando Bowles, Walter Harkins, John C.C. Mayo, and Jay H. Northrup, as well as the Big Sandy Valley Improvement Association, advocated river improvement projects to expand the navigation possibilities. In 1878 the U.S. Army Corps of Engineers undertook the improvement of the Big Sandy River. In 1897 a unique movable needle dam and lock opened just below Louisa, and by 1905 two additional locks and dams had been built on the river's main channel. Engineers completed a lock and dam on each of the river's forks by 1910. Even with the system of locks and dams, navigation was uncertain because of low water. The colorful steamboat era came to an inevitable close when railroads paralleled the river and sent branch lines up many of the formerly isolated hollows. With the exploitation of vast timber and mineral resources by outside capital, changes came to the Big Sandy valley.

The history of the Big Sandy valley and that of Kentucky's bituminous coal industry are irrevocably intertwined. While the Big Sandy River itself has not played a major role in coal transportation, the railroad that moves the coal to market traverses the region only by following the course of the Big Sandy and its tributaries. The economic fortunes of the coal industry play a critical role in the lives of all residents of the valley and govern the economic health of the region. In contrast to labor problems in Harlan in southeastern Kentucky, the United Mineworker of America unionized the valley and established headquarters at Pikeville by 1933.

Since 1945 the Big Sandy River valley's natural resources have attracted national attention as the cycle of booms and busts in the coal industry has repeated itself. The valley produces almost one-third of Kentucky's total coal output and one-half of the preferred low-sulfur, high-carbon coal of eastern Kentucky. In the late 1940s and 1950s, out-migration of residents to urban centers drained the area's human resources, and public assistance programs became a way of life for many. In the 1960s the New Frontier–Great Society legislation brought federal assistance programs to the area. The Big Sandy Area Development District planned the future growth of the river valley, and community action groups began to appear. In opposition to national energy demands, the voices of environmentalists cried out against the ruthless exploitation of the land by surface mining and advocated the preservation of the mountains and streams.

In the late twentieth century, the Big Sandy River is navigable in a nine-foot channel for six miles upstream from its junction with the Ohio River and in a six-foot channel for an additional nine miles. Over 500,000 tons per year of freight, mostly petroleum products to and from a major oil refinery at Cattletsburg, move along this limited route. Despite the construction of Dewey, Fishtrap, and Paintsville lakes, floods still bring disaster to the valley. The Big Sandy is a river, a watershed, and a place where yesterday, today, and tomorrow coexist in haunting harmony.

See Harry M. Caudill, *Night Comes to the Cumberlands: A Biography of a Depressed Area* (Boston 1963); Carol Crowe-Carraco, *The Big Sandy* (Lexington, Ky., 1979); Henry Scalf, *Kentucky's Last Frontier* (Pikeville, Ky., 1966).

CAROL CROWE-CARRACO

BIG SOUTH FORK NATIONAL RIVER AND RECREATION AREA. The Big South Fork National River and Recreation Area was established by an act of Congress in March 1974. The U.S. Army Corps of Engineers was designated responsible for planning, acquisition, and development, and the National Park Service is responsible for management of the finished project. By 1990 more than $100 million had been spent on acquisition and development. The recreation area includes over 100,000 acres of land, one-third of it within McCreary County, Kentucky, and the rest in Tennessee. The Big South Fork of the Cumberland River runs for eighty-six miles through the center of the park, making white-water sports a popular pastime. Hunting and trapping are also authorized in the park. The re-created Blue Heron mining camp and the Big South Fork Scenic Railway are on the north end of the park. Visitors can view waterfalls and large natural stone arches along the 170 miles of hiking trails, one hundred miles of horseback riding trails, and three hundred miles of old logging roads. Developed campsites are available to visitors.

WILLIAM K. DICKINSON

BILL OF RIGHTS. Knowing that Kentucky was to be admitted to the Union as a state, delegates to the tenth statehood convention, held in Danville in 1792, spent April 2-18 drafting a constitution that included a twenty-six-point bill of rights. There is little or no documentation describing the actual process of adding these sections or identifying their origins. Without question, however, George Nicholas was the predominant drafter of the bill of rights. Nicholas was fully informed on the subject of constitutions and the rights they guaranteed states and individuals. He had come to Kentucky from Virginia in 1788, fresh from the great debate over that state's ratification of the U.S. Constitution. He was familiar, too, with George Mason's *Virginia Declaration of Rights* (1776).

One or more of the delegates in Danville in April 1792 obviously had copies of the Massachusetts constitution of 1780 and the second Pennsylvania constitution of 1790. Both of these documents contain extensive statements of the rights of citizens; though they use differing phraseology, they express precisely the same guarantees. It seems certain that the framers of the Pennsylvania document were influenced by the earlier Massachusetts document. Delegates to the tenth convention in Danville simply copied the Pennsylvania bill of rights, making only a few minor changes.

Whatever the immediate sources of the Kentucky bill of rights, some of the guarantees were clearly derived from the centuries-old struggles of Englishmen to gain personal freedoms. The basic freedoms of speech, the press, and assembly grew out of an extended legal fight by British publishers against the restrictions of the Crown, a battle that extended to the American colonies in the well-known John Peter Zenger case of 1735. In his *New York Weekly Journal,* Zenger had been critical of the administration of New York's colonial governor, William Cosby, and other colonial officials. The Crown charged him with seditious libel. Represented by the able Philadelphia lawyer Andrew Hamilton, Zenger won his case, which became a landmark of freedom both in colonial America and in England.

Delegates who revised the Kentucky constitution in 1799 left the bill of rights intact. Those in 1849, however, engaged in rather extensive debate about modifying some sections and adding others. One delegate even advocated curbing the freedoms of speech and press. Minor changes were made, and a new section concerning property rights (section 2) was added. But, in the main, the bill of rights was left essentially intact in the 1849 constitution.

When delegates to the fourth constitutional convention (1890) came to consider the bill of rights, they engaged in a veritable orgy of old-fashioned Kentucky oratory, rich with eloquence and appeals to the classical past. The convention spent twenty-one days debating possible changes in and additions to the statement of rights, and their speeches took up 512 pages of the massive journal of proceedings. However, changes made were largely of an editorial nature, except for section 25, which declared: "Slavery and involuntary servitude in this state is forbidden, except as a punishment for crime, whereof the party shall have been duly convicted."

Adoption of the Thirteenth, Fourteenth, and Fifteenth amendments to the U.S. Constitution had a fundamental bearing on the Kentucky bill of rights in several areas, especially in the case of the due process clause of the Fourteenth Amendment. The state bill of rights has been affected in many ways by changing political and social conditions, as reflected in the massive body of court decisions and legislation in the field of civil rights. The cases contesting segregation of races in public education and accommodations and those dealing with voting, especially, have had a bearing on the interpretation of the Kentucky bill of rights.

In the field of public education, the decisions in *Johnson v. University of Kentucky* (1949) and *Brown v. Board of Education* (1954) had great impact in Kentucky. The enactment by the U.S. Congress of the civil rights laws of the 1960s fundamentally influenced the course of state legislation. In the case of Kentucky's bill of rights, the result has been the invalidation of all references, stated or implied, to race and gender. Perhaps the establishment of civil rights will ultimately lead to substantial rephrasing of many of the sections of the bill of rights to ensure equality of treatment under the laws without regard to race or gender.

Whatever changes may be made in the future to the Kentucky bill of rights, the statement made in the first constitution in the tenth convention in Danville in 1792 has endured intact for two centuries except for additions of the section on property rights in 1799 and the section forbidding slavery in 1890, and modification of several others.

See Joan Wells Coward, *Kentucky in the New Republic: The Process of Constitution-Making* (Lexington, Ky., 1979); Patricia Watlington, *The Partisan Spirit: Kentucky Politics, 1779-1792* (New York 1972); *A Citizen's Guide to the Constitution of Kentucky* (Frankfort, Ky., 1977).

THOMAS D. CLARK

BINGHAM, GEORGE BARRY, JR. George Barry Bingham, Jr., editor and publisher, son of newspaper magnate George Barry and Mary Clifford (Caperton) BINGHAM, was born September 23, 1933, in Louisville. A member of one of Louisville's most prominent families, he attended private boarding schools and graduated from Harvard in 1956 with a B.A. in history. He served in the U.S. Marine Corps in 1956-58, rising to the rank of captain.

Bingham, who had spent summers working at the family's newspapers and WHAS, in 1959 took a one-year training program with the Columbia Broadcasting System in New York. He remained in New York, becoming a general assignment researcher for the National Broadcasting Company in 1960. He transferred to NBC's Washington, D.C., bureau in 1961 and served as field producer and researcher for such documentaries as "The River Nile" and "Shakespeare: Soul of an Age." Bingham returned to Louisville in 1962 to begin his long career in the family businesses. His domain was to be the WHAS stations; his older brother Worth was in charge of the newspapers. After Worth's untimely death in 1966, however, Bingham became more involved in running the *Courier-Journal* and *Louisville Times*. After his father retired in 1971, he was made editor and publisher and held this position until 1986, when the interests were sold to Gannett. Bingham was also vice-chairman of the boards of WHAS and Standard Gravure Corporation. He raised eyebrows in March 1984 when he restructured the family's businesses, removing from the boards of directors his wife, his mother, and both sisters, setting in motion the events that led to sale of the family's interests. In April 1989 Bingham became publisher of *Fine Line*, a newsletter on media ethics. He has served on many local and national boards and commissions.

Bingham married Edith Wharton Stenhouse on November 30, 1963; they have four children: Emily Simms, Mary Caperton, Philip John, and Charles Wharton.

BINGHAM, GEORGE BARRY, SR. George Barry Bingham, Sr., became president of the company that published the *Louisville Courier-Journal* and the *Louisville Times* at the death of his father, Robert Worth BINGHAM, in 1937. Later he also headed WHAS radio and television stations and Standard Gravure Corp. He was chairman of the board when the Bingham companies were sold in 1986. His newspapers had won six Pulitzer prizes.

He was born February 10, 1906, in Louisville. His mother, Eleanor (Miller) Bingham, died in 1913 after an automobile accident in which he was involved. He attended schools in Louisville, Asheville, North Carolina, and Concord, Massachusetts. After graduating magna cum laude from Harvard in 1928, he traveled and wrote a novel. On June 9, 1931, he married Mary Clifford Caperton (BINGHAM) of Richmond, Virginia. They had five children: George Barry (BINGHAM), Jr., Sarah ("Sallie") Montague (BINGHAM), Eleanor Miller, Robert Worth III, and Jonathan Worth.

After working at WHAS radio in 1930, Bingham became a police reporter for the *Louisville Times*, then a general assignment reporter, Washington correspondent, and editorial writer before holding managerial positions. He went on active duty as a lieutenant in the U.S. Naval Reserve in May 1941. He was on special assignment in London in 1942 and served as public relations officer for U.S. Naval Forces in Europe until being transferred to the Pacific theater in 1945. He was present at the Japanese surrender, and received two Bronze Stars. Bingham traveled to Germany, Austria, and Trieste in 1946 and again in 1947 at the behest of the secretary of the army. He was chief of the mission of the Economic Cooperation Administration to France in 1949 and 1950, when harbors were reopened, dams and factories constructed, and railroads put back in operation under the Marshall Plan. He toured Asia with his friend Adlai Stevenson in 1953 and served as cochairman of volunteers in Stevenson's presidential campaign in 1956.

During Bingham's reign, the newspapers and radio and television stations championed many causes—civil rights, military preparedness, mental health, ethics, and the environment, while supporting educational and cultural activities in the region. Bingham's philanthropy included the Crusade for Children, company contributions of 5 percent of pretax earnings, and more than $50 million through the Mary and Barry Bingham, Sr., Fund.

Bingham was a longstanding participant in the affairs of Berea College, Harvard University, the University of Louisville, Pine Mountain Settlement School, American Press Institute, American Society of Newspaper Editors, International Press Institute, Asia Foundation, English-Speaking Union, National Portrait Gallery, various preservation and mental health groups, and several presidential commissions. He was an accomplished speaker, a facile and precise writer. He wrote poetry and was a devotee of Shakespeare and theater in general.

He received the Algernon Sidney Sullivan Award from the University of Kentucky, the William Allen White Award from the University of Kansas, and the Roger Williams Straus Award from the National Conference of Christians and Jews, as well as the titles Commander of the Order of the British Empire and Commandeur de la Legion d'Honneur.

Bingham died on August 15, 1988, and was buried in Louisville's Cave Hill Cemetery. His personal papers were given to the Filson Club.

SAMUEL W. THOMAS

BINGHAM, GEORGE CALEB. George Caleb Bingham, painter of the western frontier, was born on March 20, 1811, on a South River plantation in Augusta County, Virginia, to Henry and Mary (Amend) Bingham. In 1819 the family moved to Missouri, where Bingham was to reside intermittently until his death. By 1830 he was subsisting as a portrait painter and in 1837 studied for three months at the Philadelphia Academy of Fine Arts. During the winter of 1850-51, Bingham painted *Daniel Boone Coming through the Cumberland Gap*, a historical composition said to be based upon the account given in Humphrey Marshall's *History of Kentucky* (1824). In 1852 he sent letters dated May 2 and July 5 from Lexington, Kentucky, seeking subscriptions for engravings of his painting *County Election*, the purpose of his tour of the surrounding area's principal towns (Danville, Harrodsburg, Frankfort, Richmond). The painting was sold for $1,000 to Robert J. Ward of Louisville in 1853. In July 1856 in Louisville, Bingham sold $400 worth of prints of his painting *Verdict of the People*. In February 1859 he was commissioned to paint portraits of Henry Clay to be placed in the Hall of Representatives in Jefferson City, Missouri. A fire destroyed both paintings in 1911. In 1873, at the request of J.D. Osborne of Louisville, Bingham sent his paintings *Order No. 11* and *Washington Crossing the Delaware* to be exhibited in an exposition there. Bingham died in Kansas City, Missouri, on July 7, 1879, and was buried in Union Cemetery there.

See Albert Christ-Janer, *George Caleb Bingham of Missouri* (New York 1940).

BINGHAM, MARY CLIFFORD (CAPERTON).
Mary Clifford Caperton Bingham was from 1942-1985 vice president and a director of the Courier-Journal and Louisville Times Company, which also owned WHAS radio and television stations and Standard Gravure Corporation. As editor of the respected Sunday feature page "World of Books," she particularly championed children's books.

Mrs. Bingham was born December 24, 1904, the daughter of Helena Lefroy Caperton and Clifford Randolph Caperton of Richmond, Virginia. She received an A.B. degree in 1928 from Radcliffe College and studied in Athens, Greece. She married Barry Bingham on June 9, 1931, and is the mother of five children.

Mrs. Bingham has remained concerned with liberal thought and politics. Her tireless efforts and considerable philanthropy have been directed toward improving education and the environment. She was instrumental in extending library services to rural counties through the Kentucky Bookmobile project. She has been an active director and president of the Council for Basic Education and has served on several national education commissions. She was a trustee of Radcliffe College and has received four honorary degrees.

She has led efforts against stripmining, crusaded to save the American elm, and helped preserve Lilley Cornett Woods in Letcher County, as well as being active in the Garden Club of America, Nature Conservancy, River Fields, Inc., and the State Environmental Quality Commission. Mrs. Bingham has served the Kentucky Arts and Bicentennial commissions, The Filson Club, the Louisville Free Public Library, and Shakertown at Pleasant Hill. She has sought to preserve the 1928 Book of Common Prayer and is a member of St. James Episcopal Church, Pewee Valley.

The Mary and Barry Bingham, Sr. Fund has been her most ardent concern. The fund has given more than $50 million to countless projects that enhance, stimulate, and improve the arts, education, and medicine.

SAMUEL W. THOMAS

BINGHAM, ROBERT WORTH. Robert Worth Bingham, a Louisville lawyer and newspaper publisher who served as U.S. ambassador to the Court of St. James's, was born November 8, 1871, in Orange County, North Carolina, to Delphine Louise (Worth) and Col. Robert Bingham. In 1888 he graduated from his father's Bingham Military School in Asheville. He attended the University of North Carolina, where he was captain of the first football team, and the University of Virginia. From 1892 to 1896, he taught Latin and Greek in his father's school. He moved to Louisville after his marriage on May 20, 1896, to Eleanor Miller.

Bingham received a law degree from the University of Louisville in 1897, and began practice with Pryor, O'Neal & Pryor before forming a firm with W.W. Davies, an old friend. Bingham was appointed, then elected Jefferson County attorney. In 1907, when the election of 1905 was overturned, he was appointed mayor of Louisville. Even in a brief period, he was able to institute many reform measures. He ran unsuccessfully on the Republican ticket for the Kentucky court of appeals in 1910 and as a Democrat for Jefferson fiscal court in 1917. He was appointed chancellor of the Jefferson circuit court in 1911.

In 1913, Bingham's wife, Eleanor, died as a result of an automobile accident. They had three children: Robert Norwood (later changed to Worth), Henrietta Worth, and George Barry (BINGHAM). Bingham married Mary Lily (Kenan) Flagler, widow of Henry Flagler, on November 15, 1916. She died eight months later of a heart condition. Under a codicil to her will, Bingham received $5 million. In 1918 he purchased the *Louisville Courier-Journal* and the *Louisville Times*, to which he later added a printing firm, Standard Gravure Corporation, and a radio station, WHAS.

Bingham was member of the law firm of Bingham, Peter, Tabb and Levi, a forerunner of the present Wyatt, Tarrant, and Combs. He was also a director of the American Creosoting Company, Liberty National Bank and Trust Co., and Louisville & Nashville Railroad (now CSX Transportation), and he served as trustee of Berea and Centre colleges. He was instrumental in the establishment of the Burley Tobacco Growers Cooperative Association in 1921. In the 1920s his newspapers made him a force in Democratic politics throughout the state. The editorial page supported better public education and help for blacks and the rural poor.

Bingham married Aleen Lithgow (Muldoon) Hilliard, widow of J. Byron Hilliard, in London, England, on August 21, 1924.

Bingham was appointed ambassador to England in 1933. He promoted understanding of Roosevelt's policies in England, while working for Anglo-American cooperation to foster international peace. He took part in the London Economic Conference, chaired the International Wheat Advisory Committee, and participated in the Naval Arms Limitation Conferences and the preliminary discussions of the Anglo-American trade agreement.

Bingham was an avid hunter and fisherman, a member of the Juniper Club, and raised bird dogs. He died of abdominal Hodgkin's disease at Johns Hopkins University Hospital, Baltimore, on December 18, 1937, and was buried in Cave Hill Cemetery. His papers were given to the Filson Club and the Library of Congress.

SAMUEL W. THOMAS

BINGHAM, SARAH ("SALLIE") MONTAGUE. Sarah ("Sallie") Montague Bingham, author, the daughter of George Barry, Sr., and Mary (Caperton) BINGHAM, was born January 22, 1937, in Louisville. Her father was editor and publisher of the *Louisville Courier-Journal* and *Louisville Times*. She graduated magna cum laude from Radcliffe College in 1958. Bingham's first novel, *After Such Knowledge*, was published in 1960. It was followed by two collections of short stories, *The Touching Hand* (1967) and *The Way It Is Now*

(1972); both include penetrating portrayals of children and adolescents.

After the sale of the Bingham communications empire in 1986, Sallie Bingham devoted part of her share of the proceeds to establishing the Kentucky Foundation for Women which supports original work by women as well as other programs for women. It also publishes the *American Voice*, a literary quarterly that has been a forum for local, unknown writers as well as the nationally and internationally famous.

Thrice married, Bingham has three sons, Barry Ellsworth and Will and Chris Iovenko, and a stepson, Doug Peters.

See Alanna Nash, "The Woman Who Overturned an Empire," *Ms* 14 (June 1986): 44-46.

BONNIE JEAN COX

BIPARTISAN COMBINE. The bipartisan combine, a powerful political coalition, exerted tremendous influence on the politics of Kentucky during the first three decades of the twentieth century. The coalition's influence grew during the 1920s, but diminished when the Great Depression and the New Deal changed the political environment. Statewide urban political bosses from both parties, along with wealthy Bluegrass farmers, worked to protect the railroad, coal mining, liquor, and racetrack interests in the state by supporting like-minded candidates regardless of party affiliation. The control of large blocs of votes by the urban bosses, and substantial campaign contributions from the special interests, ensured election victories. Combine members did not hesitate to bolt their party and support a candidate from the other party. In 1923 Alben Barkley, running for governor on a reform platform, was defeated by a combine candidate in the Democratic primary, and in 1927 the Republican Flem D. Sampson, with combine support, defeated the reform-minded former governor, J.C.W. Beckham (1900-1907), in the general election.

Bipartisan combine members included Billy Klair, the Democratic boss of Lexington, the Republican Maurice Galvin from Covington, Louisville's Michael Brennan, Allie Young of Morehead, and Ben Johnson of Bardstown, who later became prominent as a member of the state highway commission. The activities of the bipartisan combine illustrated the factionalism within the state's Democratic party, and indicated the power of special interests in state politics during the first thirty years of the twentieth century.

See Malcolm E. Jewell and Everett W. Cunningham, *Kentucky Politics* (Lexington, Ky., 1968); John H. Fenton, *Politics in the Border States* (New Orleans 1957).   JAMES DUANE BOLIN

BIRD, ROBERT MONTGOMERY. Robert Montgomery Bird, writer, was born to John and Elizabeth (Van Leuvenigh) Bird in Newcastle, Delaware, on February 5, 1806. In April 1827 Bird graduated from the University of Pennsylvania's medical school and set up a medical practice in Philadelphia. Within a year he turned to writing fiction and he became a prolific writer of novels, short stories, and poems. His best known novel, *Nick of the Woods; or the Jibbenainosay, a Tale of Kentucky* (1837), described an Indian battlefield. Bird was a resident of Kentucky for an unknown period. His *Peter Pilgrim, or a Rambler's Recollection*, published in 1838, includes studies of Kentucky, notably Mammoth Cave. Bird spent much of his adult life in Delaware. In 1847 he moved to Philadelphia, where he became an editor for the *North American Gazette*. He married Mary Mayer of Philadelphia on July 13, 1837. On January 23, 1853, Bird died in Philadelphia and was buried there in Laurel Hill Cemetery.

See Clement E. Foust, *The Life & Dramatic Works of Robert Montgomery Bird* (New York 1919).

BIRDS. As early as 1780, Col. William Fleming reported sighting an ivory-billed woodpecker—now extinct—at Logan's Fort (now Stanford, Lincoln County). Bird study in Kentucky began in earnest in 1807 with the advent of the renowned bird artist John James AUDUBON. The ornithologist Alexander Wilson, much less well known than Audubon but undoubtedly a much better scientist, spent part of 1810 in Kentucky. He met Audubon in Louisville and trekked with him across the barrens of southwestern Kentucky and from Louisville to Nashville, recording the sight of the now-extinct Carolina parakeet and passenger pigeon, as well as the now rare whooping crane and greater prairie chicken—species that have not been found in Kentucky for over a century. A third accomplished ornithologist from the early nineteenth century was Constantine RAFINESQUE, a botanist associated with Transylvania University, whose ornithological writings are a major part of Kentucky's history of birds.

Late in the nineteenth century, C.W. Beckham emerged as the leading ornithologist in Kentucky. He made the first major scientific collection of Kentucky birds: some 1,000 specimens, now housed at the University of Louisville, Department of Biology. Beckham lived at Bardstown, and most of his material is from Nelson County.

The modern period of ornithology in Kentucky began with the formation of the Kentucky Ornithological Society in 1923 by L. Otley Pindar, Gordon Wilson, and Brasher C. Bacon. This society has many local chapters throughout the state; its journal, the *Kentucky Warbler*, is the only specialized publication of scientific articles on bird study in the state. Two other ornithologists have been responsible for most of the additional collected specimens and scientific data on Kentucky birds: Burt L. Monroe, Sr., and Robert M. Mengel; their specimens are also housed at the University of Louisville. Mengel produced *The Birds of Kentucky* (1965), the only thorough scientific treatise on the birds of the state. The *Annotated Checklist of the Birds of Kentucky* (1988), by Burt L. Monroe, Jr., Anne L. Stamm, and Brainard L. Palmer-Ball, Jr., was published through the Kentucky Ornithological Society.

Considering that it is an interior midwestern state, Kentucky is rich in bird life. A total of 340 species of birds have been recorded within its boundaries. In addition to birds typically found in the midwestern states, other species are found in the southwestern portion of Kentucky (the Jackson Purchase), which is an extension of the Gulf coastal plain up the Mississippi River. Species occur here that are found nowhere else in the state, including the fish crow. This area is also the site of several heron rookeries and contains nesting bald eagles in the eastern part, which extends to the Land Between the Lakes. Located on the eastern edge of the central flyway for waterfowl, the area has large goose and duck concentrations, especially in the Ballard Wildlife Management Area in Ballard County.

As the southern extension of the northerly transition zone in the Appalachian Mountains, the Cumberland Mountains have unique nesting arrays, especially on top of Big Black Mountain; birds found breeding in Kentucky only in this zone include the veery, golden-winged warbler, chestnut-sided warbler, black-throated blue warbler, blackburnian warbler, Canada warbler, rose-breasted grosbeak, and dark-eyed junco. The Outer Bluegrass area of north-central Kentucky also has its array of nesting species that breed nowhere else in the state: upland sandpiper, vesper sparrow, Savannah sparrow, Henslow's sparrow, and bobolink. Perhaps the most unusual bird native to Kentucky is the red-cockaded woodpecker, a federally protected endangered species that has known nesting sites in pine trees in the southern portion of Daniel Boone National Forest, near Cumberland Falls.

In the city of Louisville, the Falls of the Ohio below McAlpine Dam is the site of exposed coral beds that are stopping place during migration for numerous herons, egrets, waterfowl, shorebirds, gulls, and terns. This area was a rapids in the days of Audubon and is mentioned several times in his work. The falls area also contains an extensive black-crowned night heron nesting colony—one of the few left in the state—and is the site of Kentucky's only known breeding specimens of the cattle egret, a species that has entered the United States only in the last half-century.

BURT L. MONROE, JR.

BIRNEY, JAMES GILLESPIE. James Gillespie Birney, abolitionist, the only son of James and Martha (Read) Birney, was born at Danville, Kentucky, on February 4, 1792. After his mother died in 1795, James and an infant sister, Anna Maria, were cared for by a Mrs. Doyle, their father's widowed sister. At the age of eleven, Birney enrolled at Transylvania University for two years. In 1806 he entered the newly opened Priestly's Seminary at Danville and in 1808 entered the sophomore class of the College of New Jersey (Princeton), where he graduated in 1810. He studied law in the office of Alexander Dallas in Philadelphia before returning to Danville to begin practice in 1814.

Elected to the Kentucky House of Representatives in 1816, Birney opposed a resolution to enlist the aid of Indiana and Ohio in returning runaway slaves. Although a slaveowner, his father had advocated a free-state constitution for Kentucky. Young Birney had also heard many antislavery sermons delivered by David RICE and David BARROW. On February 1, 1819, Birney married Agatha McDowell, the daughter of William McDowell, a U.S. district judge. Two years later they moved to a plantation near Huntsville, Alabama. Within a few years, however, financial reverses forced Birney to sell the plantation and slaves and move into Huntsville to resume the practice of law.

Birney became a trustee of Centre College in Danville upon its founding in 1819 and timed his annual visits to Kentucky so as to attend board meetings. Nevertheless, in 1834 his appointment as professor of ancient languages in the college was rejected—because of his abolitionist views, he believed.

After serving as an agent of the American Colonization Society, which advocated removal of blacks to Africa, Birney relocated his family to Danville in late 1833. In 1834 he resigned from the society and published his "Letter on Colonization," which called for immediate abolition and gave him a national reputation. In the same year he broke with Henry Clay after a discussion of slavery; Birney wrote in his diary that Clay had no conscience about this matter, and would swim with the popular current.

Instrumental in the founding of the Kentucky Anti-Slavery Society in 1835, Birney announced plans to publish a weekly abolition newspaper, the *Philanthropist*. Opponents, however, bought out the local printing firm. Birney moved to Cincinnati, where the paper continued to be published by Gamaliel Bailey after Birney moved to New York City in September, 1837, to become a secretary of the American Anti-Slavery Society. Once asked why he did not remain in the South to fight slavery, Birney replied that a man who was hired to kill a den of venomous snakes would be insane to jump into the den. The apex of Birney's antislavery career was reached in 1840 and 1844 when he was a candidate for president of the United States on the Liberty party ticket.

Birney's first wife died in 1839 and two years later he married Elizabeth Fitzhugh. Six Birney children survived to adulthood: James, William, David, Dion, Fitzhugh, and Florence. In 1853 the Birneys moved to Eagleswood, near Perth Amboy, New Jersey, where he died on November 25, 1857.

See William Birney, *James Birney and His Times* (New York 1890).   WILLIAM COOPER

BISHOP, STEPHEN. One of the most celebrated guides in the history of Mammoth Cave, Stephen Bishop was born into slavery in 1821; his owner was Glasgow, Kentucky, native Franklin Gorin. Gorin purchased the Mammoth Cave property around 1838 and brought Bishop there to be an explorer and guide; Bishop proved an excellent choice. While guiding tours in 1838, he encountered the deep chasm known as the Bottomless Pit, where all tours were forced to turn back because no one had found a way around or across it. With the aid of one of the visitors, Bishop suspended a log pole (possibly a log pole ladder) over the chasm and shinnied across.

This single act was probably enough to secure him a prominent place in the history of guided tours, but it was not the last of his exploits. Bishop continued to delight the public with his wit and charm. In the published travel logs of the 1840s and 1850s, he is the Mammoth Cave guide most written about. Other slaves served as guides during this period—including the Bransford Brothers, Matt and Nick—but Bishop appealed to the public in a way that others did not. Bishop is still regarded by historians as having explored more of Mammoth Cave than any other person. He died in 1857 and was buried in the Guides' Cemetery near the Mammoth Cave entrance.

See Samuel W. Thomas, Eugene H. Conner, and Harold Meloy, "A History of Mammoth Cave, Emphasizing Tourist Development and Medical Experimentation under Dr. John Croghan," *Register* 68 (Oct. 1970): 319-41.

BLACK, JAMES DIXON. James Dixon Black, governor during 1919, was born to John C. and Clarissa (Jones) Black in Knox County, Kentucky, on September 24, 1849. After attending local schools, he graduated from Tusculum College, Greeneville, Tennessee, in 1872. He taught school in Knox County for two years while studying law and in 1874 was admitted to the bar. After serving a term in the Kentucky House of Representatives (1876-77), Black helped establish Union College in Barbourville; he was its president during 1910-12. Deeply interested in education, Black served as superintendent of the Knox County schools in 1884-85, before resuming his law practice. In 1912 he became the state's first assistant attorney general, and in 1915 he won the Democratic nomination for lieutenant governor. A "dry" on the issue of prohibition, he balanced the ticket with "wet" A.O. Stanley. They won, and when Gov. A.O. Stanley resigned in 1919 to take a seat in the U.S. Senate, Black became governor for the last seven months of the term (May 19-December 9).

Black secured the Democratic nomination for governor in 1919 over Judge John D. Carroll. His Republican opponent, Edwin P. Morrow, made the alleged misdoings of the Stanley administration the main issue of the campaign. The General Assembly did not meet during the few months Black was in office, and much of his time was spent defending the Stanley administration against partisan charges, including criticism concerning the State Textbook Commission and special tax arrangements for the estates of L.V. Harkness and Mrs. Robert Worth Bingham. Black's failure to take decisive action contributed to his defeat in 1919. Days before the election, Morrow revealed details of an excessive

cloth purchasing contract approved by the Board of Control that appeared to prove his charges of serious mismanagement. Morrow won easily, 254,490 to 214,114.

One of Black's last official acts was to pardon parolee Henry Youtsey, who had served eighteen years for conspiracy in the assassination of Gov. William Goebel (1900). After leaving office Black was appointed chief prohibition inspector in Kentucky in 1920. Later he resumed his law practice, then became president of the Barbourville National Bank. He married Nettie Pitzer in December 1875; they had three children. Black died on August 5, 1938, and was buried in Barbourville.

See Lowell H. Harrison, ed., *Kentucky's Governors 1792-1985* (Lexington, Ky., 1985).

LOWELL H. HARRISON

BLACKBURN, JOSEPH CLAY STILES. Joseph Clay Stiles Blackburn, U.S. Senator, was born to Edward and Lavinia Blackburn on October 1, 1838, in Spring Station, Woodford County, Kentucky. He attended Frankfort Academy and graduated from Centre College in Danville in 1857. He read law under George B. Kinkead and was admitted to the bar in 1858. After practicing law in Chicago for two years, he returned to Kentucky in 1860 to work in the presidential campaign of John C. Breckinridge. In 1861 Blackburn joined the Confederate army as a private. He volunteered as aide de camp to Brig. Gen. William Preston, receiving the rank of captain, and fought with distinction in the September 1863 Battle of Chickamauga. He later was a lieutenant colonel under Gen. Leonidas Polk along the Mississippi River and in 1864 was given the command of a cavalry battalion in the District of Mississippi and East Louisiana under Maj. Gen. Franklin Gardner.

Blackburn moved to Arkansas at the end of the war, practicing law and engaging in farming in Desha County. In 1868 he returned to Kentucky and opened a law office in Versailles. He was elected to the Kentucky House in 1871, serving two terms. As a Democrat, he served in the U.S. House of Representatives from 1875 until 1885. He was then elected and reelected to the U.S. Senate (March 4, 1885, to March 3, 1897). Blackburn's support for William Jennings Bryan and the free silver issue defeated his 1896 bid for reelection, but he regained the Senate seat four years later (March 4, 1901, to March 3, 1907). On April 1, 1907, President Theodore Roosevelt appointed Blackburn governor of the Panama Canal Zone; he resigned on November 20, 1909. In 1914 President Woodrow Wilson appointed him resident commissioner of the Lincoln Memorial.

Blackburn was married to Therese Graham in 1858. She died in 1899 and he married Mary E. Blackburn in 1901. He died on September 12, 1918, in Washington, D.C., and was buried at the Frankfort Cemetery.

See Leonard Schlup, "Joseph Blackburn of Kentucky and the Panama Question," *FCHQ* 51 (Oct.

1977): 350-63; H. Levin, *The Lawyers and Law-makers of Kentucky* (Chicago 1897).

BLACKBURN, LUKE PRYOR. Kentucky's only physician-governor, Luke Pryor Blackburn (1879-83) was born to Edward and Lavinia (Bell) Blackburn in Woodford County on June 16, 1816. He received his medical degree from Transylvania University in 1835, and began his practice in Versailles. He served in the House of the General Assembly in 1843-44 as a Whig. After moving to Natchez, Mississippi, in 1846, Blackburn earned acclaim in 1848 and again in 1854 for establishing effective quarantines in the Mississippi River valley against yellow fever. He served the Confederacy in several ways, including an unsuccessful attempt to infect Northern cities with yellow fever. Charged with conspiracy to commit murder, Blackburn did not return to Kentucky until 1872. His efforts to combat yellow fever in Memphis, Tennessee (1873), in Florida (1877), and in Hickman, Kentucky (1878) enhanced his reputation. In 1879 he won the Democratic nomination for governor and easily defeated Republican Walter Evans, 125,790 to 81,882. In 1883 he returned to his medical practice.

Blackburn's administration accomplished the first important reforms of the postwar period. His major accomplishment as governor was a genuine improvement in the penal system. He issued pardons generously to alleviate overcrowding, and a commission on which he served supervised a number of changes at the Frankfort penitentiary. The governor's persistent efforts resulted in the belated funding for a new facility at Eddyville in 1884. Blackburn had sought an institution aimed at rehabilitation rather than punishment, but that concept was limited to hiring out convicts to work on public projects. His achievements included an increase in the property tax to fund needed programs; extensive changes in the judicial system; reorganization of the Agricultural and Mechanical College; and appointment of Joseph McCORMACK to the Board of Health.

Blackburn married Ella Gist Boswell and they had one son. After her death in 1856, Blackburn married Julia Churchill. He died on September 14, 1887, and was buried in the Frankfort Cemetery.

See Nancy Disher Baird, *Luke Pryor Blackburn: Physician, Governor, Reformer* (Lexington, Ky., 1979).   LOWELL H. HARRISON

BLACK FISH. Black Fish, subchief of the Chalahgawtha (Chillicothe) Shawnee, was successor to the principal chief, Cornstalk, after the latter was killed by whites in 1777. In February 1778 Black Fish led 120 Shawnee into Kentucky and captured Daniel Boone and approximately thirty other Kentuckians at the Lower Blue Licks. Black Fish adopted Boone and named him Shel-to-wee, meaning Big Turtle. Following Boone's escape back to Kentucky on June 16, 1778, Black Fish led more than 440 warriors in an ineffective nine-day siege of Fort Boonesborough in September of 1778. In the spring of 1779, during Col. John Bowman's campaign against the Shawnee at Old Chillicothe (three miles north of present-day Xenia, Ohio), Black Fish was severely wounded in the thigh. Within six weeks he died of gangrene.

TED FRANKLIN BELUE

BLACK JACK CORNER. Black Jack Corner in the Kentucky-Tennessee state line is located in Simpson County, Kentucky, and Sumner County, Tennessee, where U.S. 31W now crosses the BOUNDARY. This jog in the state line was created on November 14, 1780, when a survey party wandered off course from a marked beech tree on the bank of Drakes Creek. When Thomas Walker arrived from Nashville and discovered the error, the surveyors reset their compass rather than go back and correct their error. A black jack oak was marked at the apex of the jog.

See James W. Sames III, *Four Steps West* (Versailles, Ky., 1971); Thomas D. Clark, *Historical Maps of Kentucky* (Lexington, Ky., 1979).

THOMAS D. CLARK

BLACK MOUNTAIN. The highest elevation in Kentucky, 4,145 feet above sea level, is the crest of Black Mountain in eastern Harlan County. It is an unmarked point immediately north of a benchmark at 4,139 feet above sea level, which is shown on the topographic map of the Benham quadrangle.

GARLAND R. DEVER, JR.

BLACK PATCH WAR. The Black Patch War over low prices paid to tobacco farmers began in 1904 in the tobacco fields of western Kentucky and western and middle Tennessee. It was the product of two economic realities that hit tobacco farmers after Reconstruction: the steady price declines in all agricultural products following the return to the gold standard, and the formation of one of the largest industrial U.S. monopolies, the American Tobacco Company. By 1900 tobacco prices were severely depressed and the company controlled the industry. Competing buyers had disappeared.

Having gained experience in the 1880s during the rather short-lived FARMERS' ALLIANCE in Kentucky, growers throughout the Black Patch—the dark-tobacco region—had tried to form cooperative marketing groups in the late 1890s, but lack of organization doomed these efforts. In 1904 a new group, the Planters' Protective Association, gave farmers a definite strategy for combating the controlled market and low prices. It was based on the Tobacco Growers Association organized in Robertson County, Tennessee, by farmer and attorney John M. Foster to withhold tobacco until satisfactory prices were offered. Foster, along with Black Patch grower Felix G. Ewing, and others organized the Black Patch.

At a meeting in Guthrie, Kentucky, on September 24, 1904, more than 5,000 farmers participated in the official creation of the Planters' Protective Association. A charter was drawn up, and Ewing was selected as chairman. The annual meeting in

Guthrie the next year was a festive, often emotional occasion. The final Guthrie meeting, in 1906, drew more than 25,000 farmers. The Planters' Protective Association enlisted approximately one-third of the Black Patch tobacco growers. To defeat their tobacco pool, the American Tobacco Company began offering higher prices to growers who refused to join the group. The Planters' Protective Association's attempts to recruit these noncooperators were mostly futile. Frustrated by the company's boycott of the Protective Association's tobacco and by the high prices paid to nonpoolers, some tobacco farmers resorted to violence in 1905.

Armed, hooded vigilantes on horseback known as NIGHT RIDERS destroyed plant beds, barns, and machinery of nonpoolers, as well as administering numerous whippings and committing occasional murders. Tobacco warehouses in Trenton, Princeton, and Hopkinsville were set on fire. The association's officials disavowed violence and any link with night riding, but there was no doubt that most riders were sympathetic to the group's aims.

By 1907 the Planters' Protective Association's leaders had become quite authoritarian. They paid themselves salaries, which were expressly forbidden by the association's charter. A second charter was drawn up that gave Ewing virtual control of the group. Many farmers expressed dissatisfaction at local meetings, but it was soon squelched by local leaders appointed by Ewing. He also forbade members to sell their tobacco in public, which produced further outrage. By 1909 the organization had virtually no democratic input. From 1910 to 1913, membership declined dramatically. Those farmers who remained loyal to the principles of cooperation found themselves powerless against both the group's hierarchy and the American Tobacco Company's control of the market. When World War I closed major foreign shipping lanes, the Planter's Protective Association no longer had a market for what was essentially an export crop. The association officially collapsed in 1914.

See James O. Nall, *The Tobacco Night Riders of Kentucky and Tennessee, 1904-1909* (Louisville 1939); C. Vann Woodward, *Origins of the New South, 1877-1913* (Baton Rouge, La., 1951).
                                        TRACY A. CAMPBELL

BLACKS. See Afro-Americans

BLAIR, FRANCIS PRESTON, JR. Francis Preston Blair, Jr., Missouri legislator, was born on February 19, 1821, in Lexington, Kentucky, to Eliza Violet (Gist) and Francis Preston BLAIR, Sr. In 1830 the family moved to Washington, D.C., where his father established the *Globe*, a newspaper that supported the Andrew Jackson administration. Blair graduated from Princeton University in 1841. He returned to Lexington to study law, received a law degree from Transylvania University in 1843, and was admitted to the Kentucky bar. In the same year, he moved to St. Louis, where he set up a law practice.

Blair served two terms in the Missouri legislature, from 1852 to 1856. An outspoken opponent of slavery, he was one of the leaders of the Free Soil movement in St. Louis. Blair served in the U.S. House of Representatives during 1857-59, 1861-62, and 1863-64. The Missouri legislature appointed him to the U.S. Senate to fill the unfinished term of Charles Drake; he served from January 20, 1871, to March 3, 1873. Blair married Appoline Alexander of Woodford County, Kentucky, on September 8, 1847. He died on July 8, 1875, and was buried in Bellefontaine Cemetery in St. Louis.

See George Baber, "The Blairs," *Register* 14 (Sept. 1916): 37-49.

BLAIR, FRANCIS PRESTON, SR. Francis Preston Blair, Sr., political leader and newspaper editor, was born at Abingdon, Virginia, in 1791, the eldest of seven children of James and Elizabeth (Smith) Blair. His father, at one time a member of the Virginia legislature, moved his family to Kentucky in the early 1790s and beginning in 1796 held long tenure as attorney general of the commonwealth. Blair was educated for law at Transylvania University and graduated with honors in 1811. In 1812 he suffered a lung hemorrhage, a problem that was to recur intermittently throughout his life.

Blair was appointed circuit court clerk of Franklin County, a position he held for eighteen years. The salary was meager and fee collection erratic. Blair speculated in real estate, and when economic depression developed in 1818, he was heavily in debt. Out of this experience he became, as clerk of the New Court of Appeals, a leader in the Kentucky controversy over debtor RELIEF. When the New Court system collapsed, Blair wrote for Frankfort editor Amos Kendall in the *Argus of Western America*, advocating the election of Andrew Jackson.

As President Jackson neared a break with John C. Calhoun in 1830, Kendall arranged for Blair to edit a Washington, D.C., newspaper that supported the president's views. In November Blair established the *Washington Globe*, which he edited as the voice of the Democratic party for fifteen years; John Rives was his partner and financial manager after 1834. When James K. Polk assumed the presidency in 1845, Blair was replaced because Polk believed that Blair had opposed his personal advancement and that Blair's longstanding controversy with Calhoun was damaging to party unity.

Widely influential through his writing and patronage connections, Blair then went to live on a farm at Silver Spring, Maryland, just outside Washington, where he entertained extensively, and retained close political contacts. He helped organize the Republican party in 1854, served as convention chairman in 1856, and campaigned for John C. Frémont. Although he was not originally a backer of Abraham Lincoln for the presidential nomination in 1860, Blair quickly became a confidant and supporter of the Illinoisan. A slaveowner, Blair believed that emancipation must be accompanied by colonization but shared the view that extension of slavery threatened the survival of the Union. He counseled delay in issuing the Emancipation Proclamation and moderation in Reconstruction. Maintaining strong White House ties during the administration of Andrew Johnson, Blair promoted a coalition of moderate Republicans and Democrats in the congressional elections of 1866. In 1869 Blair, who had not endorsed the economic measures of the Republican party, issued a lengthy attack on the banking legislation of that decade. Thereafter his support remained with the Democrats.

In 1812 Blair married Eliza Gist Scott, daughter of the well-to-do Indian trader and planter Nathaniel Gist, and stepdaughter of Gov. Charles Scott (1808-12). Eliza bore six children, of whom two died in early childhood; Montgomery, James, Elizabeth, and Francis Preston (BLAIR), Jr., grew to adulthood. Blair died on October 19, 1876, and was buried in Rock Creek Cemetery in Washington, D.C.

See Elbert B. Smith, *Francis Preston Blair* (New York 1980); Arthur M. Schlesinger, Jr., *The Age of Jackson* (Boston 1945).

MARY W.M. HARGREAVES

BLAIR V. WILLIAMS. The court case of *Blair v. Williams*, October 8, 1823, began in the Bourbon County, Kentucky, circuit court as a simple piece of unpaid note litigation. Its timing, however, gave it political importance. According to the court records, persons named Blair, Ingles, and Barr had executed a note to Williams in the sum of $209.67, one-half due in sixty days. When the note came due, it was not paid. Under the provisions of the replevin law of February 11, 1820, Blair and his associates had the option of offering to redeem the note in Bank of Kentucky notes or staying the execution for two years. Williams contended that this would impair the obligation of a contract and Judge James Clark so ruled. Judge Clark held that the replevin law violated section 10 of the first article of the federal Constitution.

The Kentucky court of appeals affirmed Judge Clark's decision. Reacting to the appellate court decision, which invalidated the state's debt relief law, the Kentucky General Assembly, then dominated by Relief partisans, committed one of its most irresponsible acts by attempting to replace the OLD COURT with a new one.

See A.M. Stickles, *The Critical Court Struggle in Kentucky, 1819-1829* (Bloomington, Ind., 1929).

THOMAS D. CLARK

BLANCHARD, ASA. Asa Blanchard was a prominent silversmith and clock- and watchmaker in Lexington, Kentucky, during the first half of the nineteenth century. His date and place of birth are unknown, but he may have been descended from a Thomas Blanchard of England who settled in Braintree, Massachusetts, in the mid-seventeenth century.

Blanchard's early silver pieces have a typical English shape and monogram style, and he may have been sent to England to learn his craft as a young man. There is also a record of an Asa Blandchard, listed as the head of household in the 1790 and 1800 censuses of Wildersburgh Town, Orange County, Vermont.

The first record of Blanchard in Kentucky is in Fayette County Order Book II of May 9, 1808, stating that "William Grant . . . be bound apprentice to Asa Blanchard." He is known to have taken on several more apprentices over the years, including Simon Bradford, Andrew (Alex) Anderson, James I. Lemon from Scott County, Eli Garner, and George Easley, some of whom went on to become renowned silversmiths.

On June 30, 1809, Blanchard purchased a lot fronting on Mill Street in Lexington from Samuel Wilkinson. The following year he bought the lot on the corner of Mill and Short streets, where he later located his shop. His business must have prospered, for an ad in the *Reporter* of March 1816 lists "a large assortment of gold and silver work" in his shop outside the Lexington Branch Bank. Blanchard's silver pieces were owned by some of the most prominent families in Kentucky. A silver beaker made by him was presented to Henry Clay by the Kentucky Agricultural Society for the "Best Saxon Ram." A pair of candlesticks now in the J.B. Speed Art Museum in Louisville were made for Kentucky's first governor, Isaac Shelby (1792-96, 1812-16). A silver christening bowl monogrammed "Letitia Dallam Coleman" is now in the Harned Collection, Frankfort. Gen. Green Clay owned a tea service and the Filson Club has three of his silver cups. Blanchard also made a tall case clock that is in the collection of the Metropolitan Museum of Art in New York City.

Blanchard was married twice, the first time to Rebecca, whose maiden name is unknown. Matthew Harris Jouett painted the couple's portraits around 1818. They had two children, Mary L. and Horace F. Rebecca died in 1836. Blanchard's marriage to Hester Harris, a widow, took place on March 7, 1838. Blanchard died at an advanced age in Lexington on September 15, 1838.

See Margaret M. Bridwell, "Asa Blanchard, Early Kentucky Silversmith," *Antiques* 37 (March 1940): 135-36; Marquis Boultinghouse, *Silversmiths, Jewelers, Clock and Watch Makers of Kentucky, 1785-1900* (Lexington, Ky., 1980).

BLANDA, GEORGE F. George F. Blanda, professional football player, was born in Youngwood, Pennsylvania, on September 17, 1927, the son of coal miner Joseph Blanda and his wife. He entered the University of Kentucky in 1945, finished his eligibility in 1948, and graduated in 1951, two years after being signed by the Chicago Bears to his first professional football contract. At UK he played football for Bernie Shively and Paul ("Bear") Bryant. Blanda was drafted in the twelfth round in 1949. He was quarterback for the Bears through 1958, except for one game when he was traded to the Baltimore Colts. He sat out the 1959 season but was signed by the Houston Oilers as a free agent in 1960. He was traded to the Oakland Raiders in 1967 and was their quarterback and field goal kicker until his retirement in 1976.

Blanda is recognized as one of football's greatest players. He was the No. 1 passer, with 362 attempts and 187 completions, for a total of 3,330 yards and thirty-six touchdowns, in the American Football League (AFL) in 1961 and was the AFL's player of the year in 1963. He led the AFL in scoring in 1967 and played in the AFL All-Star games of 1962, 1963, 1964, and 1968. The AFL merged with the National Football League in 1970, and Blanda was named that year's American Football Conference player of the year. He played more seasons (26), in more games (340), made more consecutive appearances (224), scored more lifetime points (2,002), made more lifetime field goals and attempts (335 out of 638), and scored in more consecutive games (40, from December 11, 1960, through November 10, 1963) than any other player. He was named the Associated Press male athlete of the year in 1970 and the NFL man of the year in 1974, and he was elected to the Professional Football Hall of Fame in Canton, Ohio, in 1981.

Blanda married Betty Ruth Harris on December 18, 1949. He was named to the University of Kentucky Hall of Distinguished Alumni in 1987.

BLANDING, SARAH GIBSON. Sarah Gibson Blanding, educator, the daughter of William DeSaussure and Sarah Bison (Anderson) Blanding, was born on November 22, 1898, in Lexington, Kentucky. In 1919 she graduated from the New Haven Normal School of Gymnastics and joined the staff of the University of Kentucky as an instructor in physical education. Blanding earned an A.B. degree from the University of Kentucky in 1923 and in 1926 a master's degree in political science from Columbia University; she spent a year in further study at the London School of Economics. Between 1915 and 1921, Blanding served as director of playgrounds for the city of Lexington. In 1925, after two years as acting dean of women at the University of Kentucky, she accepted the position on a permanent basis. During her sixteen years as dean of women, Blanding greatly expanded the influence and prestige of the position. She left Lexington in 1941 to head the School of Home Economics at Cornell University. Five years later, Blanding became Vassar College's first woman president and held that position until her retirement in 1964.

The recipient of eighteen honorary degrees, Blanding was also a member of the University of Kentucky's Hall of Distinguished Alumni. In 1968 the university named a new woman's dormitory, Blanding Tower, in her honor. Blanding died March 3, 1985, in Newtown, Pennsylvania, and was buried in Lakeville, Connecticut.

CAROLYN TERRY BASHAW

BLANDVILLE COLLEGE. Blandville College, incorporated by the Kentucky General Assembly in 1866, was a private school in the county seat of Ballard County, Kentucky. Its purpose was to promote liberal arts and science education. The school had nearly a hundred students in 1875 and in 1885 it was said to have one of the finest school buildings. West Union Baptist Association purchased the facilities in 1886 for educating young men as ministers and young women as missionaries. The school changed presidents often. Its main building burned on October 24, 1904; a new building opened in 1905, but was sold for a county school in 1910.

R. CHARLES BLAIR

BLAZER, PAUL GARRETT. Paul Garrett Blazer, oil company executive, was born in New Boston, Illinois, on September 19, 1890, the son of David N. and Mary Melinda (Jones) Blazer. His father was the owner and publisher of regional newspapers. He studied at William and Vashti College in nearby Aledo, Illinois, and the University of Chicago. While in college he was national distribution manager of Curtiss Publishing Company of Philadelphia. When the United States entered World War I, he volunteered to serve in the U.S. Army but a back injury resulted in his discharge.

In 1920 Blazer moved to Kentucky as vice president of the Great Southern Oil & Refining Company in Lexington. In 1924 he joined the Swiss Oil Corporation of Lexington, in charge of constructing and managing the operations of ASHLAND Refining Co., of Ashland. Managing the company was more than a vocation for Blazer; from 1924 to 1957 he was regarded as head of the "Ashland family." He did not use his office at company headquarters extensively, but conferred with employees in their offices or his office at home. Blazer was a striking figure (six feet, four inches tall), hardworking, and unusually effective in expressing himself in business correspondence.

Blazer served as chairman of a campaign for a Kentucky constitutional convention (1946-47) and as chairman of the Cincinnati Branch, Federal Reserve Bank of Cleveland (1949-50). He received honorary degrees from Centre College in Danville (1950), University of Kentucky (1952), Marshall University in Huntington (1958), and Pikeville College (1959), as well as the Sullivan Medallion Award from the University of Kentucky (1948). He was elected Kentuckian of the year (1954) by the Kentucky Press Association. Blazer, a strong supporter of education, was a member of the board of trustees of Centre College, and a high school in Ashland was named for him. The Blazer family funded a lecture series at the University of Kentucky in memory of a son of Blazer's who was killed in the Korean War.

In April 1917 Blazer married Georgia Monroe, whom he had met at the University of Chicago. She was active in her own right in promoting education in Kentucky, serving successive terms as a member of the board of trustees of the University of Kentucky from 1939 to 1960. The Blazers had three children: Paul G., Jr., Doris Virginia, and Stuart

Monroe. Rexford Blazer, later chief executive officer of Ashland Oil, was a nephew. Paul Blazer died on September 9, 1966, and wås buried in the Ashland Cemetery.

See Joseph L. Massie, *Blazer and Ashland Oil* (Lexington, Ky., 1960); Otto J. Scott, *The Exception: The Story of Ashland Oil & Refining Company* (New York 1968).   JOSEPH L. MASSIE

BLEDSOE, JESSE. Jesse Bledsoe, member of both the Kentucky Senate and the U.S. Senate, was born in Culpeper County, Virginia, on April 6, 1776, the son of the Rev. Joseph and Elizabeth (Miller) Bledsoe. At an early age, Jesse and an older brother migrated to Kentucky. He was educated at Transylvania University in Lexington, where he was considered an excellent classical scholar. During 1795-97 he was a tutor at Transylvania. Bledsoe later studied law and was admitted to the bar around 1800; he became an associate and close friend of Henry Clay. Bledsoe represented Bourbon and Fayette counties in the General Assembly in 1812, and between 1808 and 1812 he was Kentucky's secretary of state.

Bledsoe served as U.S. senator from March 4, 1813, until his resignation on December 24, 1814; he was a member of the state Senate from 1817 to 1820. Gov. John Adair (1820-24) appointed him a judge of the circuit court in Lexington in 1822. The same year Bledsoe became a law professor at Transylvania University, holding that position until 1825. In 1823 the university awarded him an honorary LL.D. degree. He retired from the legal profession to become a minister in the Christian Church (Disciples of Christ). In 1833 he left Kentucky to settle in Mississippi and in 1835 moved to Texas. He died in Nacogdoches, Texas, on June 25, 1836, survived by his wife Sarah, daughter of Col. Nathaniel Gist, granddaughter of Christopher GIST, and stepdaughter of Gov. Charles Scott (1808-12).

See H. Levin, *The Lawyers and Lawmakers of Kentucky* (Chicago 1897).

BLOCH, CLAUDE CHARLES. Claude Charles Bloch, four-star U.S. admiral, was born July 12, 1878, in Woodbury, Butler County, Kentucky, the son of Adolph and Bellvina (Pendleton) Bloch. He attended public schools and Ogden College in Bowling Green. Bloch entered the U.S. Naval Academy in 1895. He volunteered for active duty in the Spanish-American War, serving aboard the U.S.S. *Iowa*, before he graduated in 1899. During the Boxer Rebellion in 1900, he was a member of the China Relief Expedition. In World War I Bloch served as navigator on the U.S.S *Arizona*, and he was in command of the U.S.S. *Plattsburg*, transporting troops to France. He received the Navy Cross in 1918. From 1923 to 1927 Bloch was chief of the bureau of ordnance at the gun factory of the Washington naval yard. He was promoted to rear admiral, and from 1927 to 1929 he was at sea, commanding the U.S.S. *California*. In 1930-31

Bloch was stationed at the Newport, Rhode Island, torpedo station.

In 1933 Bloch was judge advocate of the navy. From 1937 to 1940 he was commander-in-chief of the U.S. fleet and was promoted to admiral. Bloch was commandant of the Hawaiian Sea frontier, 14th Naval District, at Pearl Harbor when the Japanese attacked in December 1941. In investigating the Japanese attack, the Roberts committee cleared him of any dereliction of duty. He remained commandant until April 1942. During World War II, Bloch served as chairman of the Navy Board for Production Awards. He retired in 1945 with the rank of four-star admiral.

Bloch married Augusta Kent on March 3, 1903, and they had one daughter, Ethel. He died October 6, 1967, and was buried in Arlington National Cemetery.

See Gordon W. Prange, *At Dawn We Slept* (New York 1981).   CHARLES L. BLOCH

BLOODY MONDAY. The antiforeigner and anti-Catholic riot in Louisville on the election day of August 6, 1855, gave it the name Bloody Monday. At least twenty-two people were killed. The riot was an ugly manifestation of the national tensions arising from rapidly mounting German and Irish immigration, the collapse of the Whig party, and the escalating debate over the extension of slavery into "free-soil" territory west of the Mississippi River.

After 1848, the failed German revolution and the Irish potato famine swelled the influx of immigrants to the United States, fleeing political and economic misery. By 1850 these newcomers numbered nearly 11,000 of the total white population of 36,224 in Louisville. They added a new and exotic element to the city, where the white population was predominantly Protestant and of English and Scotch-Irish ancestry. Many of the Germans and Irish were Catholic.

The influx threatened the dominance of the Whigs in Louisville, since most of the newcomers, once naturalized, joined the Democratic party. Meanwhile, the Whig party was torn internally over the slavery-extension issue, and many Whigs joined the new American, or KNOW-NOTHING, party. Antiforeigner and anti-Catholic, the party fanned the fear that immigrants threatened both Protestantism and democracy. By 1854 it claimed a million members nationwide and was well entrenched in the Ohio Valley. As early as the mid-1840s, the *Louisville Daily Courier* began to comment on what its editor and publisher, Walter N. Haldeman, saw as the immigrant threat. By 1854, when the American party gained control of Jefferson County government, Haldeman had abandoned the Whigs and openly supported the Know-Nothings. At the same time the city's foremost editor, Whig stalwart George D. Prentice of the *Louisville Daily Journal*, sadly watched his party fall apart. On January 15, 1855, he wrote, "It is evident that this foreign question is to override all others, even the slavery question, as we see men of the most opposite views on slavery, forgetting their differences and acting together." By that summer he was lending his vitriolic pen to all-out support of the Know-Nothings. To Prentice, this was apparently a way of defusing the slavery issue that threatened the Union.

The violence against immigrants that had been sporadic in 1854 became frequent in 1855. The election for Louisville mayor and city councilmen on April 7 produced turbulence and a Know-Nothing victory. Violence increased at the May 5 election for members of the county court, which resulted in another Know-Nothing victory. It was enough to shock even Haldeman, who soon abandoned the nativist cause and began to support the Democrats. As the August 6 election for governor, other state officers, and congressmen approached, the Know-Nothing rhetoric became ever more intense. The *Louisville Daily Democrat* of August 1 advised its readers to go to the polls with "unblanched cheek and unfaltering step, relying on no official protection." Those who followed the advice found that the American party controlled the polls, admitting its members while keeping naturalized citizens waiting in long lines in sweltering heat. Fights broke out between waiting voters and taunting Know-Nothing bullies. By noon the Germans and Irish had given up trying to vote.

Precisely what set off the riots, arson, and murder during the afternoon and night of August 6 is impossible to determine. The disorder began east of downtown Louisville, where most Germans lived. Know-Nothing mobs howled through the streets, ransacking shops, taverns, and homes, beating hapless passers-by, and setting fires on Shelby Street. There were exchanges of gunfire, and the new St. Martin's Church was saved only by the intercession of Know-Nothing Mayor John Barbee. The rioters burned the William Armbruster brewery near Beargrass Creek after helping themselves to the establishment's product.

The mob next turned its attention to the heavily Irish area, west of downtown, setting fires and bludgeoning residents. Quinn's Row, a group of twelve buildings near Main and Eleventh streets, owned by longtime Irish resident Patrick Quinn, went up in flames. As it burned, several Irish people attempting to escape (including Quinn) were shot to death. Firemen were warned not to extinguish the blaze. The fires and rampages continued into the early hours of August 7, and ugly scenes occurred for several more days. Needless to say, the Know-Nothing slate swept Louisville and Jefferson County.

The spasm passed relatively quickly, however, as a chastened city counted the toll in lives and property and as the American party itself foundered on the slavery issue. The former Know-Nothings drifted to the Democratic party or the newly founded Republican party. It took the Civil War to wash the last vestiges of the Know-Nothing phenomenon from Louisville and Jefferson County, but as early as January 3, 1857, the *Louisville Daily Courier* could report, "The 'Know-Nothing' headquarters on Jefferson Street has been turned into a German theater."

See Agnes Geraldine McGann, *Nativism in Kentucky to 1860* (Washington, D.C., 1944); George H. Yater, *Two Hundred Years at the Falls of the Ohio: A History of Louisville and Jefferson County* (Louisville 1979).   GEORGE H. YATER

BLUEGRASS. Bluegrass (*Poa pratensis* L.) is a cool-season, sod-forming grass that thrives in the rainy climate and limestone-based soils of Kentucky. Healthy bluegrass is dark green, not blue. The name bluegrass may have arisen from confusing it with orchard grass or other species that are more blue-green in color. Bluegrass is not tolerant of deep shade, but it does stand up well to mowing and foot traffic, and the species spreads vegetatively in closely clipped lawns or grazed pastures. Its roots are too shallow to pull moisture from the subsoil during hot, dry weather; two weeks without rain are sufficient to send it into dormancy in midsummer. Unless extensively irrigated, it turns brown in August, but new green shoots appear with the fall rains, and bluegrass stays green through all but the most severe Kentucky winters.

Because its grains are usually formed apomictically (without sexual reproduction), seedlings normally inherit all of their genes from the maternal parent. This characteristic simplifies maintenance of distinct genetic lines, which are adapted to different growing conditions. About fifty varieties of this adaptable species have been named and classified on the basis of seed characteristics. Its variability has made this species economically valuable as a lawn and pasture grass across a broad geographic range, including North America, northern Europe, the Soviet Union, and New Zealand.

Although it is known throughout the world as Kentucky bluegrass and lends the Bluegrass State its nickname, this plant is in fact native to Eurasia. In England it was traditionally called smooth-stalked meadow grass. English settlers brought *Poa pratensis* to the Atlantic seaboard as early as 1625, then introduced the species a number of times, either intentionally or accidentally, as seed mixed with grain or livestock feed. The French traders brought it to the Great Lakes region and down the Ohio and Mississippi river valleys. Bluegrass spread so extensively in European-American settlements that American Indians named it "white man's foot-grass." By the time Daniel Boone arrived in Kentucky, bluegrass had already invaded the meadows he found so attractive. Elsewhere, dense stands of cane originally predominated, but cattle brought over the Appalachians rapidly devoured the tall, succulent cane stalks. Bluegrass turf, which is much more tolerant of heavy grazing, then replaced the canebrakes.

The fortuitous establishment of bluegrass as the forests were cleared from central Kentucky fostered a livestock industry unparalleled anywhere in the world. Cattle and sheep could be overwintered with no food or shelter other than bluegrass growing in open woods. Peter Robert noted in 1882 that cattle matured a year sooner on bluegrass than did similarly bred animals reared in the mountains or the Western Coal Field. He also attributed the robust bone and muscle development of the renowned Kentucky thoroughbred horses to their nourishing diet.

Conservationist Aldo Leopold singled out the development of Kentucky as an excellent example of history forged not solely by human enterprise, but by biotic interactions between people and the land. It was, he said, an ecological accident "that the cane-lands, when subjected to the particular mixture of forces represented by the cow, plow, fire and axe of the pioneer, became bluegrass. What if the plant succession inherent in this dark and bloody ground had, under the impact of these forces, given us some worthless sedge, shrub, or weed? Would Boone and Kenton have held out? Would there have been any overflow into Ohio, Indiana, Illinois, and Missouri? Any Louisiana Purchase? Any transcontinental union of new states? Any Civil War?"

See Aldo Leopold, *A Sand County Almanac* (New York 1966); Peter D. Walton, *Principles and Practices of Plant Science* (Englewood Cliffs, N.J., 1988).   ROBERT W. KINGSOLVER

BLUEGRASS BLADE. The *Bluegrass Blade*, a maverick newspaper with a wide circulation, was founded in 1884 by Charles Chilton Moore in Lexington, Kentucky. Moore, a one-time Christian Church minister, ran into financial difficulties, and the paper's publication was sporadic until 1890, when weekly distribution began. Its offices at that time were located at 155 West Short Street. Following Moore's death on February 7, 1906, the publisher, James Edward Hughes, assumed the duties of editor until the paper ended publication in 1910.

Throughout its existence, the *Bluegrass Blade* was controversial, championing such causes as agnosticism, women's suffrage, and prohibition. Headlines from the July 2, 1905, edition are indicative: "He Assails Bible for the Young" (Sunday School seen as "farce, dull, weak and cheap"); "Sunny Side" (a discussion of the existence of God in view of the problems that humans face); "Sunday Baseball and Prohibition" (parallel ways of wasting time) and "Bible Stories Are Myths." Two of the *Bluegrass Blade's* mottoes over the years indicate to some extent the controversy that surrounded it: "The Only Prohibition Paper Printed by A Heathen," and "Edited by a Heathen in the Interest Of Good Morals." Its controversial nature may help to explain the paper's wide circulation, reaching from Kansas to Boston and the Gulf States.

See Charles C. Moore, *Behind the Bars: 31498* (Lexington, Ky., 1899).

BLUEGRASS MUSIC. Bluegrass, as a category of music, dates from the popularity of William Smith ("Bill") MONROE's radio shows in the late 1940s, although the term was not common until much later, when fans used it to distinguish their favorite music from the "new" Elvis-style country music. Bluegrass music has its foundation in ancient ballads that came into the Appalachian Mountains with the earliest European settlers.

Since the time of Monroe and his Blue Grass Boys band, bluegrass has meant acoustic music (as opposed to electric, commercial country music), played by groups using various combinations of stringed instruments. The mandolin, guitar, and banjo are considered basic to any bluegrass combination, but most bands add the sounds of fiddle, dobro (a specially designed acoustic guitar with a metal resonator), and bass. Innovative or novelty bands use drums, harmonicas, and other instruments. The bluegrass repertoire includes ballads and fast-paced traditional tunes with high-pitched, "lonesome" tenor vocals.

Bobby and Sonny Osborne, Hylo Brown, Cliff Carlisle, Grandpa Jones, Don Parmley, J.D. Crowe, and Ricky Skaggs are among the many good bluegrass musicians born or reared in Kentucky. These performers—along with Monroe's allegiance to his home state, and bluegrass songs such as "Blue Moon of Kentucky," "My Rose of Old Kentucky," and "Kentucky Waltz"—have perpetuated the idea of bluegrass as Kentucky music. But its progenitor, mountain string band music, was very popular in the Carolinas and Tennessee as well during the earliest days of radio, and some of the best bluegrass musicians have come from the Carolinas.

The Scotch-Irish who settled the Appalachians brought with them old Scottish and English folksongs and ballads. In remote, isolated mountain communities, these songs stayed unadulterated until the end of the nineteenth century. The fiddle was the main instrument for playing the tunes and accompanying traditional songs. Then the mountain people began hearing the music of black workers and touring minstrel shows, and gradually the blacks' five-string banjo became an instrument of mountain music. As mail-order catalogs made five-string banjos, guitars, and mandolins easy to obtain, mountain musicians began to add these instruments to tunes traditionally played on the fiddle. After World War I, radios and phonographs brought jazz and the music of Latin America and Hawaii to the mountains. Radio and movies popularized cowboy songs as western swing. String bands incorporating all these sounds became immensely popular throughout the mountain states during the 1920s and 1930s. The mandolin did not become vital to this music until Bill Monroe began playing it as a crisp, quick accompaniment to his high-pitched tenor voice.

Monroe started singing in Chicago and Detroit during the Great Depression. Later, playing on radio stations in North and South Carolina, he evolved the sound that became bluegrass, a combination of mountain folk tunes, blues, gospel from his days at church SHAPE-NOTE SINGING schools, and instrumental techniques of the musicians who played the radio circuit of the Tennessee-Carolinas mountains. Those musicians often named their groups in honor of their native locale and Monroe, wanting to announce to all that he was from Kentucky, named his band the Blue Grass Boys. They began to perform on the "Grand Ole Opry" radio program in Nashville in 1939. By 1945 Monroe had assembled what was considered the all-time classic bluegrass band: Monroe on mandolin; Lester Flatt, guitar; Earl Scruggs, banjo; Chubby Wise, fiddle; and Howard Watts, upright bass. Scruggs's three-finger banjo picking style, popular in his native North Carolina, became an important part of bluegrass. Flatt and Scruggs broke away from Monroe in 1948 to form the Foggy Mountain Boys band. The new group played the same music they had played with Monroe, while other country music performers were beginning to tilt toward what would become the country-rock avalanche. There was a large audience for the older style music that Flatt and Scruggs had helped Monroe to popularize. Rumors of ill feeling between the two bands made people hesitate to ask Flatt and Scruggs for "Monroe music," so they began to request "bluegrass" music. The name stuck. Flatt and Scruggs added the dobro, which gave their group a slightly Hawaiian sound, and it proved a lasting contribution to the bluegrass genre.

Bluegrass musicians place a high value on improvisation, playing with flying fingers, so they generally learn by ear and do not depend on written music. Traditionally, bluegrass groups have emphasized close instrumental interplay, story songs, and high-harmony singing. As mountain people migrated to Ohio, Indiana, and Michigan, the story songs tended to glorify "our old mountain home." When homesick mountaineers congregated in nightclubs around Cleveland and Detroit, the lyrics began to include honky-tonks and city lights. Trains and diesel trucks and "the girl I left behind" got more and more attention as little cabins and close-knit, isolated mountain communities became mostly a thing of the past.

Modern bluegrass falls into several categories. Monroe's hard-core bluegrass remains as he developed it in the 1940s. Although purists insist that this is the only true bluegrass, the genre has expanded and has influenced other kinds of music. Some groups perform bluegrass heavily tinged with blues or gospel or honky-tonk styles. Bluegrass bands are generally acoustic, meaning that they do not rely on electrified instruments. Most of them, however, use an amplification system. Monroe and a few others made bluegrass a career, but far more have made it an avocation, performing mainly at bluegrass or folk festivals.

The International Bluegrass Music Association has its headquarters in the RiverPark Center in Owensboro, Kentucky. The complex there includes a performing arts center and a bluegrass music museum.

See Neil V. Rosenberg, *Bluegrass, A History* (Urbana, Ill., 1985); Charles K. Wolfe, *Kentucky Country* (Lexington, Ky., 1982).   GAIL KING

BLUEGRASS REGION. The Bluegrass region occupies the broad rolling area of east-central Kentucky, from the Ohio River south to the encircling, hilly Knobs zone. It is one of the state's three largest regions; only the extensive Pennyroyal to the south and west and the Eastern Coal Field to the east are larger or about as large in total area (see GEOGRAPHY). Throughout most of Kentucky's history, the Bluegrass region has been the focus of settlements. In recent years the region has been home to slightly more than one-half of Kentucky's population. Although cities of considerable size are spread throughout the Bluegrass region, most of the inhabitants are concentrated in three large urban clusters sometimes referred to as the Golden Triangle. Greater Louisville lies at the western edge. To the north, immediately south of Cincinnati, are Covington, Newport, Florence, and other cities and towns within Campbell, Kenton, and Boone counties. The third and most central urban cluster is that of greater Lexington and a number of sizable cities ten to thirty miles away. Frankfort, the state capital, lies about thirty miles northwest of Lexington.

Physiographically, the Bluegrass spreads across Ordovician limestone, the oldest surface rocks in Kentucky. The Bluegrass region is on a low upland created as the Cincinnati Arch rose, and streams, including the Kentucky River, cut into the arch's higher rocks. Today the rolling surface rises to just over 1,000 feet in the Lexington area. Immediately to the south, the most distinctive physical feature of the Bluegrass region is the Kentucky River Gorge, incised as much as three hundred feet below the upper level. This gorge has as one of its manmade features the High Bridge carrying the Norfolk Southern Railroad tracks across the Kentucky River; farther upstream and more recent are the twin high bridges for highway I-75, carrying traffic between Lexington to the north and Richmond to the south.

The region takes its name from the bluegrass plant (*Poa pratensis*), which for at least two centuries has been a major pasture grass on the region's phosphatic limestone soils. This region of Ordovician limestone is subdivided into the fertile, highly prosperous Inner Bluegrass region, around Lexington; the uneven hills of the Bluegrass, or Eden Shale Belt; and the broad Outer Bluegrass zone, extending to the fringing hilly Knobs, underlain by Devonian and Silurian shales and other rocks.

The Bluegrass region is highly accessible by a variety of transportation means. The Ohio River carries sizable volumes of coal and other freight along the northern edge of the region. Kentucky's three largest airports in size and frequency of daily flights are found in the region: the Cincinnati–Northern Kentucky Airport in northern Boone County; Standiford Field on Louisville's south side; and Blue Grass Airport on Lexington's western edge. While large volumes of freight still are moved along a series of railway lines, in recent decades the major and lesser highways have been the principal routes for transporting people and goods.

Interstates 75 and 65 provide north-south service through Lexington and through Louisville, respectively. Interstate Highways 471 and 275 are feeder and bypass routes serving northern Kentucky and adjacent Cincinnati; I-71 provides an northeast-southwest route connecting the northern Kentucky-Cincinnati area with Louisville. Interstate 64 is the primary east-west artery, passing through both Lexington and Louisville. The oldest of Kentucky's state parkways, the Mountain, or Bert T. Combs, Parkway, has its western anchor at I-64 near Winchester, east of Lexington; the Bluegrass Parkway cuts across the region west of Lexington to the edge of Elizabethtown. In addition, the Bluegrass has an extensive network of federal, state, and county highways.

The Bluegrass region of Kentucky is best-known for its rolling acres of horse farms and the annual Kentucky Derby at Churchill Downs in Louisville. The region is also the nation's principal producer of burley tobacco. High-grade livestock, such as beef and dairy cattle, are raised in Outer Bluegrass farms.

The Bluegrass region is also Kentucky's principal manufacturing area. The Louisville area dominates in industrial employment and numbers of manufacturing plants, but Lexington and nearby cities of the Inner Bluegrass and the northern Kentucky areas within the Bluegrass region also are manufacturing centers. Lexington's post-1950 industrial development has continued in recent years, bringing a Toyota automobile assembly plant to nearby Georgetown, for example. Most cities of the Bluegrass and their outskirts have at least small manufacturing plants.

The state's institutions of post–high school education also are concentrated in the Bluegrass region. The principal centers for medical services in Kentucky are in Lexington and Louisville. In each city the major university has a medical school and hospital facilities. Each city has also many general and specialized hospitals and other health support services.

Tourist and recreation activities focus on breeding and racing horses (Churchill Downs and Louisville Downs in Louisville, Turfway in northern Kentucky, and Lexington's Keeneland for thoroughbred racing and Red Mile for standardbred pacing and trotting). The Kentucky Horse Park, north of Lexington, draws visitors from across the country and around the world. Football and basketball games at both the University of Kentucky and the University of Louisville draw very large crowds. General Butler State Resort Park, which has lodging for guests, lies near Carrollton, immediately east of the Ohio River's juncture with the Kentucky River.

Trends within the Bluegrass region as a whole indicate a growing commercial and information-oriented economy, rather than earlier agricultural and manufacturing activities. The continuing population density in this Kentucky region suggests that centrality, soil fertility, and accessibility, which drew settlers to Harrodsburg and Boonesborough, the state's first major settlements, are still key regional assets.

See Wilford A. Bladen, *Geography of Kentucky* (Dubuque, Iowa, 1984); P.P. Karan and E. Cotton Mather, eds., *Atlas of Kentucky* (Lexington, Ky., 1977).   WILLIAM A. WITHINGTON

BLUE GRASS TRUST FOR HISTORIC PRESERVATION. In 1955 Joseph C. Graves founded a society for the immediate purpose of saving the John Wesley Hunt house (1814) on Gratz Park in Lexington, Kentucky. It was threatened by demolition, which had already befallen the John Bradford house across Second Street. The society, first known as the Foundation for the Preservation of Historic Lexington and Fayette County, was intended to promote interest in the area's cultural history and to preserve its monuments. It saved the log-frame Adam Rankin house (1784), for example, and Benjamin Latrobe's sophisticated John Pope house (1811-12). In 1957 the society changed its name to Blue Grass Trust for Historic Preservation. It sponsors meetings, lectures, exhibitions, tours, recitals, and benefits; it issues books, maps, a news journal, and announcements of general interest. It also maintains the Hunt house as the Hunt-Morgan House Museum.

CLAY LANCASTER

BLUE LICKS, BATTLE OF. The Battle of Blue Licks, known to generations of Kentuckians as "the last battle of the American Revolution," was fought August 19, 1782, at a site just north of the Lower Blue Licks crossing of the Licking River, in what is now Robertson County. The battle was, in fact, but one of a series of frontier skirmishes that took place between the 1781 defeat of the main British army at Yorktown and the 1783 conclusion of the final peace agreement. Fortunately for the United States, this remote encounter had no influence on the Revolutionary War's outcome, as it was one of the worst military disasters suffered by Americans on the Kentucky frontier.

In early August 1782, the British and their Indian allies amassed a force at Old Chillicothe, Ohio, for another foray, this one larger than usual, in a long series of raids upon the frontier settlements. They set out to attack Wheeling (now West Virginia), but while on the march received word of a possible offensive on the Shawnee home territory led by Kentucky commander George Rogers Clark. Most of the Shawnee in the eleven-hundred-man force went home. Capt. William Caldwell, the British officer in command, pressed on with about sixty Canadians, mostly men of Butler's Rangers, and perhaps three hundred Indians, mostly Wyandot. Their target changed to BRYAN'S STATION, an outpost just north of Lexington. They surrounded the Bryan's Station stockade on August 15 and harassed its occupants for a couple of days. Unable to overcome the defenders quickly, the Indians tired of the attack, and the raiders began a slow march back to the north.

Word of the attack on Bryan's Station spread quickly. Detachments of Kentucky militiamen gathered to go to the settlement's defense, but most arrived after the attackers had withdrawn. By early morning on August 18, Col. John Todd, commander of the Fayette County militia, had assembled about 180 men at Bryan's Station, but no enemy was in sight. Although Todd and his men knew that Col. Benjamin Logan was on the way with many reinforcements, they feared that any delay might allow the Indians to escape. Soon they rode off in pursuit.

The raiding party had made no effort to conceal its route and by August 19 the Kentuckians caught up with them. From a rise just south of the Lower Blue Licks crossing, the pursuers saw a few Indians disappear over a hill on the other side of the river. Daniel BOONE, an officer in the militia, feared an ambush from ravines he knew to be beyond the opposite hilltop, and he advised a flanking maneuver to another crossing. But the Kentuckians pressed on to the Lower Blue Licks ford. They paused again on the riverbank, and several officers urged the group to await the arrival of Logan's men. A few began crossing the river, however, led by Hugh McGary, as legend would have it, and soon the entire little army splashed over to the north shore. There they stopped long enough to take up an attack formation. An advance party, probably mounted, under Silas Hardin and William McBride led the way up the hill. Behind them came the main body in three rough divisions—the center probably under John Todd, the left commanded by Boone, and the right led by Col. Stephen Trigg. Most of the men advanced on foot. When the advance party came within fifty yards of the ravines Boone had warned of, the British and Indians waiting there opened fire, bringing down several of the scouts. Boone led his men forward and pushed back the Indians opposite them. The fire against Trigg's detachment was more effective, and when their leader fell, the Kentuckians' right began a confused retreat. Some of the Indians followed and quickly outflanked Todd's men in the center, who also began a general run back toward the river. Boone's men pulled away to the left, and most of them swam the Licking farther downstream.

While the militiamen ran back toward the crossing or tried to mount their horses, the Wyandot closed with their tomahawks. In a few minutes close to seventy Kentuckians were killed, and a few others were captured. Fast-riding Benjamin Netherland organized a party of Kentuckians who stood briefly on the south bank and gave covering fire to allow a few of their comrades time to escape. Most of the militiamen fled with hardly a pause back toward Bryan's Station. The Wyandot pursued for only a couple of miles, then returned to the battlefield to strip, scalp, and mutilate the bodies. The British and the Indians had suffered two dozen casualties—fourteen wounded and perhaps ten killed.

Logan's force, meanwhile, had assembled at Bryan's Station and started north after the first Kentucky pursuers. Within five miles they met the fleeing survivors and turned back. On August 24 Logan finally arrived at the battle site at the head of a five-hundred-man army. All his men could do was bury the remains of their comrades.

The bloody defeat stunned the residents of frontier Kentucky. Many community leaders were among the dead, including Todd, Trigg, McBride, and Daniel Boone's son Israel. A time of fear and mourning followed, and arguments broke out over responsibility for the disaster. George Rogers Clark was a favorite target of accusations, many blaming him for failure to prevent the raid in the first place by properly fortifying and patrolling the northern approaches to central Kentucky. Clark soon mounted a retaliatory attack against the Indian homelands in Ohio.

The Battle of Blue Licks was but one tragic episode in the warfare between Kentucky settlers and Indians that raged off and on from the earliest pioneer days until the conclusion of the War of 1812.

See Bennet K. Young, *History of the Battle of Blue Licks* (Louisville 1897); Samuel W. Wilson, *Battle of the Blue Licks* (Lexington, Ky., 1927).

NICKY HUGHES

BLUE LICK SPRINGS. Blue Lick Springs was a thriving health resort of the mid-nineteenth century in Nicholas County, Kentucky, on the south bank of the Licking River across from Robertson County. In the late 1770s, the saline water from the springs was used in SALT MAKING. With the development of more productive salt works, such as Bullitt's Lick in 1779, salt manufacturing ceased. In the early 1880s one of the owners of the springs, William Bartlett, began to bottle and sell the water as medicinal. He also began construction of the Blue Lick Springs resort. Meeting with only moderate success, the spa passed from Bartlett through several other owners. John and L.P. Holladay bought the resort in the early 1840s and built the luxurious, three-hundred-room Arlington Hotel in 1845. Blue Licks Springs, only twenty-four miles from Maysville, along a major stage route between Ohio and Tennessee, became one of Kentucky's most popular spas.

During cholera outbreaks in the state between 1833 and 1849, the resort was completely free of the dreaded disease. Not only was the hotel filled at this time, but there was also a boom in bottled Blue Lick water, which until that time had only a limited local market. Bartlett emphasized the medicinal qualities of the water, and it became nearly as popular as the resort.

During the Civil War, the spa virtually closed down because of lack of patronage, and the Arlington Hotel was destroyed by a fire in 1862. The bottled water, however, continued to be profitable.

Companies such as Pierce and Stanton of Maysville, Kentucky, and the Blue Lick Water Company of Covington, Kentucky, marketed the water from the late 1850s through the 1870s. After the Civil War, Blue Lick Springs was renovated by its new owner, Capt. D. Turney, and by 1888 was again a popular resort. In 1889 the Lower Blue Lick Springs Company was incorporated and began to bottle and sell the water. In 1896 the spring ceased to flow and a well that was dug produced too little water to support sales. Having lost its major attraction, the resort closed early in the twentieth century.

See Joan W. Conley, *History of Nicholas County* (Carlisle, Ky., 1976).

BOARD OF INTERNAL IMPROVEMENTS. The Board of Internal Improvements was created by the General Assembly in 1835, during the administration of Gov. James T. Morehead (1834-36), to oversee the improvement of Kentucky transportation routes; it was to be composed of the governor and three other members appointed by him. The board initiated a survey of Kentucky's rivers and $1 million was set aside to begin the work. Some improvements were made over the next several years, but the project suffered financially from the economic panic of 1837. The sum of $375,000, nevertheless, was spent on the Licking River, greatly facilitating trade between cities and towns on that river and Cincinnati.

Work began in July 1836 on a system of thirty-three dams on the Kentucky River. The five dams completed by 1842 created ninety-five miles of slack water on the river, referred to as the Kentucky River Navigation. Four locks and dams were built on the Green River and one on the Barren, so that by 1842 the river system was navigable as far as Bowling Green. The board was a result of the determination of the federal government (particularly after the presidency of Andrew Jackson) not to expend funds for internal improvements. Not until after the Civil War did the federal government begin to take up some of the financial burden for these improvements. Kentucky's rivers were eventually improved by the U.S. ARMY CORPS OF ENGINEERS.

See Mary Verhoeff, *The Kentucky River Navigation* (Louisville 1917).

BOARD OF WAR. The federal government granted frontier leaders the right to establish the Board of War in January 1791 to deal with the threat of attack by British-supported Indians from the Northwest Territory. In a military disaster the previous year, Gen. Josiah Harmar, commander of the federal troops on the Ohio frontier, had been forced to retreat October 22 after Indians soundly defeated his main force under John Hardin, a Kentucky militia colonel. Kentucky leaders including Gens. Isaac Shelby and Charles Scott, both Revolutionary War veterans, claimed that the federal troops knew nothing about fighting Indians and asked the federal government for authority over future expeditions. The Board of War, established under federal supervision, included Shelby; Scott; John Brown, a congressman from Virginia; U.S. District of Kentucky Judge Harry Innes; and Benjamin Logan, an experienced Indian fighter and pioneer. The board acted in conjunction with federal troops under the direction of the governor of the Northwest Territory, Gen. Arthur St. Clair.

The board quickly called for volunteers and planned two campaigns against their antagonists for the end of May 1791. Led by General Scott and Col. James Wilkinson, the Kentuckians attacked several Indian villages along the Wabash River, but the Indians had been forewarned and had abandoned their towns. In August Wilkinson led a third expedition into the Northwest Territory and destroyed the village of Kikiah, near the confluence of Wabash and Eel rivers. Although these forays against the Indians may have boosted the morale of the Kentuckians, the raids may also have united the tribes and precipitated even greater violence against the settlers. Hoping, like his predecessor General Harmar, to gain final victory over the Indians, General St. Clair began in October 1791 what he thought would be a sustained campaign along the eastern fork of the Wabash River. On November 4, 1791, St. Clair was surrounded by Indians and easily defeated. After news of the debacle reached President George Washington, St. Clair found himself relieved of command and replaced by Gen. Anthony Wayne, the commander in chief of the Army of the United States. Determined not to meet the same fate as St. Clair, Wayne prepared extensively for battle. His troops defeated the Indians decisively at FALLEN TIMBERS on August 20, 1794. With the threat of Indian attack removed from the Ohio Valley, the Board of War disbanded.

See Harry M. Ward, *Charles Scott and the Spirit of '76* (Charlottesville, Va., 1988); Paul D. Nelson, *Anthony Wayne* (Bloomington, Ind., 1985).

BODLEY, TEMPLE. Temple Bodley, lawyer and Kentucky historian, son of William Stewart and Ellen (Pearce) Bodley, was born on August 5, 1852, in Louisville. He attended the University of Virginia and the University of Louisville School of Law, where he graduated in 1875. He began practicing in Louisville with the firm of Bodley, Simrall, and Bodley and later with the firm of Simrall, Doolan, and Bodley. He served as city parks commissioner during 1893-97, the only political post he held. After retiring from law in 1903, Bodley turned to writing history. His first book, *Richard A. Robinson: A Memoir*, was published in 1903. His best-known works were *George Rogers Clark, His Life and Public Service* (1926) (a biography of his great-great-uncle), and the first volume of *A History of Kentucky* (1928). Bodley wrote the lengthy introduction for a reprint (1926) of William Littell's *Political Transactions*. In 1938 Bodley published *Our First Great West*, a history of the west in the Revolutionary War. He also served as the first president of the Louisville Art Association. Bodley married Edith Fosdick of Louisville on November

22, 1892; they had three children—Ellen, Edith, and Temple, Jr. Bodley died on November 23, 1940, in Louisville and was buried in Cave Hill Cemetery.

See *Proceedings of the Seventh Annual Meeting of the Kentucky Bar Association* (Louisville 1941).

BOILING SPRINGS SETTLEMENT. Boiling Springs Settlement—sometimes referred to as James Harrod's Station—was founded by James HARROD in 1774 in present-day Boyle County, Kentucky, about six miles south of Harrodsburg on the Mocks Branch of Dick's (now Dix) River. Harrod, a surveyor from Virginia who arrived in Kentucky in 1773, laid out the town of Harrodsburg in June 1774 and immediately traveled south with the hope of surveying his own private estate. Just south of his initial settlement, he located a fertile tract of land where a large pool was fed by an underground spring, and he named the site Boiling Springs. The outbreak of LORD DUNMORE'S WAR (1774) forced Harrod to return to the safety of Virginia after making only minor improvements on his claim. By March 1775 Harrod and several families had returned to Boiling Springs, which by 1779 had been fortified to protect the settlers from Indian attacks. No attacks occurred, and by 1784 Boiling Springs resembled an affluent neighborhood rather than a fortified station. In 1785 Harrod replaced his cabin with a large frame house that also served as a Latin school in 1786 and 1787, transforming his station into his much-desired estate. Harrod lived at Boiling Springs until 1792, when he embarked on an ill-fated hunting trip, during which he disappeared. Harrod was not seen again, and his body was not recovered.

See Nancy O'Malley, *Stockading Up* (Lexington, Ky., 1987).

BOND, JAMES. James Bond, minister, was born into slavery on September 5, 1863, in Lawrenceburg, Kentucky. His mother was named Jane Bond by her owner, Preston Bond. Bond was freed at the age of two, and his mother soon took him and his brother to Barbourville, Kentucky, where he was raised. In the early 1880s, Bond left home and walked seventy-five miles to Berea College to begin his education; he used a calf given to him by his mother to pay his expenses. At Berea College, Bond worked as the chapel janitor and bell ringer. At his graduation in 1892, Bond was one of about 2,000 blacks in the country to hold a college degree. Bond went to Oberlin College in Ohio, where he received his divinity degree in 1895.

Bond spent a good part of his life outside of Kentucky, moving first to Birmingham, Alabama, after receiving his divinity degree, then to Nashville, where he was the pastor of the Howard Congregational Church until 1906, when he returned to Kentucky at the request of Berea College. Kentucky's Day Law of 1904, which outlawed coracial education, led Berea to establish a separate college for black youths. Bond was asked to lead fund-raising for the new LINCOLN INSTITUTE. The campaign, which began in 1907, was a success, and the institute opened near Simpsonville in 1912. Bond sat on the first board of the institute but soon left for Atlanta. World War I marked Bond's return to Kentucky, this time to Louisville, where he volunteered for the army but was turned down because of his age (fifty-five). Bond served during the war as the YMCA camp service director at Camp Zachary Taylor near Louisville. After the war, Bond continued his work with the YMCA and was appointed Kentucky secretary for YMCAs for blacks. He also served as director of the newly formed Kentucky Commission on Interracial Cooperation, later known as the Kentucky Council on Human Relations. In both positions, Bond toured the state extensively, speaking out against segregation and urging interracial communication.

Bond met his wife, Jane Browne, at Oberlin. They had four children: Horace Mann, Max, Thomas, and Lucy. James Bond died on January 15, 1929, and was buried in the Louisville Cemetery.

See Roger M. Williams, *The Bonds: An American Family* (New York 1971).

BON HARBOR HILLS. Bon Harbor Hills in Daviess County, just west of Owensboro, is a series of low, rolling inclines of loess up to forty feet thick over Pennsylvanian sandstones, with glacial outwash of sand, gravel, and silt in the lowland areas. Several coal seams are found in the Pennsylvanian rock, and in 1811 the crew of the *New Orleans*, the first steamboat on the Ohio River, dug coal at an outcropping along the river bank. Industrial development of Bon Harbor began about 1820 with the arrival of Robert Triplett, a Virginian who mined coal at Bon Harbor for sale to steamboats. To haul coal from his mines to the river bank, he built one of the first rail lines west of the Appalachians. He pioneered the shipping of coal by flatboat to Louisiana for use in tugboats and the sugar industry, but this venture proved unsuccessful. Triplett, who envisioned Bon Harbor as a major factory town, branched out into a variety of enterprises. He established a small woolen factory for the making of linsey-woolsey and jean, two popular fabrics of the day that combined cotton warp threads and woolen fibers, and he built a small cotton mill to supply the warp threads. Bon Harbor became a town as workers' cottages surrounded the factories. However, the enterprises failed, and Triplett moved with his family to Philadelphia, where he died in 1853. Bon Harbor's settlement ended, and the homes and factories were abandoned.

A prison camp at Bon Harbor during the Civil War was used briefly for the internment of suspected Confederate sympathizers. Development of the coal reserves on a larger scale began about 1890, with the completion of a railroad through the area, and coal mining remained a major activity at Bon Harbor until the 1930s. It is now the site of the Ben Hawes State Park.

See Lee A. Dew and Aloma W. Dew, *Owensboro: The City on the Yellow Banks* (Bowling Green, Ky., 1988). LEE A. DEW

BOOKMOBILES. In 1887, Mrs. C.P. Barnes of Louisville started a traveling book project at a local literary club, the Monday Afternoon Club. The group sent books in wooden crates to rural areas with no libraries, and, once read, the books were repacked and returned. The project met with such success that Fannie Mae Rawson, a member of the club, was appointed to coordinate the work of the "traveling library." During the Depression of the 1930s, women on horseback delivered books to the remote areas of Kentucky. Mary Belknap Gray, one of the original organizers of the library, raised funds to buy vehicles to transport the books. The first bookmobiles were an ambulance, a hearse, a jeep, and several panel trucks. In 1954 the Friends of Kentucky Libraries raised funds to buy new bookmobiles. The vehicles were presented to Gov. Lawrence W. Wetherby (1950-55) and became the property of the Department of Libraries and Archives, which administered the bookmobile program. In September 1954 eighty-four bookmobiles on display at the old state fairgrounds in Louisville formed a parade through downtown Louisville that stretched for almost a mile.

The Kentucky Bookmobile Project of 1954 was a landmark in the expansion of Kentucky's public library system. Bookmobile service was extended to one hundred Kentucky counties, where bookmobile committees were formed and eventually became library boards. ED KLEE

BOOK THIEVES. Despite their name, the Book Thieves of Lexington, Kentucky, were not larcenous. The small group of authors and book collectors adopted the name as a bit of whimsical humor. The group originated in the fall of 1931, when J. Winston Coleman, Jr., Charles R. Staples, and Thomas D. Clark met on Saturday afternoons to talk books and book collecting. In time they were joined by William H. Townsend, Claude W. Trapp, John S. Chambers, Samuel M. Wilson, Frank L. McVey, and Herman Lee Donovan. All of them had collections of either Kentuckiana or Lincolniana, including first editions. By 1980 death had decimated the Book Thieves, who had assembled notable book and manuscript collections and had contributed generously to Kentucky library holdings.

See Thomas D. Clark, "The Book Thieves of Lexington, a Reminiscence," *Kentucky Review* 15 (Winter 1984): 27-45. THOMAS D. CLARK

BOONE, DANIEL. America's quintessential frontiersman was born November 2, 1734, in Berks County, Pennsylvania, the son of Quaker pioneers Squire and Sarah (Morgan) Boone. Little is known of his formative years, apart from some dubious anecdotes; the wife of an older brother reportedly taught him the fundamentals of the three R's, and

he is said to have aspired to be a woodsman rather than a farmer. When he was twelve or thirteen, his father gave him his first gun, with which he provided game for the family table.

Two family "scandals"—Boone's eldest sister's pregnancy before marriage and a brother's marriage to a non-Quaker—resulted in his father's expulsion from the Society of Friends. Squire Boone then moved his family from Pennsylvania to the Yadkin Valley of North Carolina, arriving in 1751 or 1752. There Daniel contributed to the family enterprise of transporting pelts and provisions to the town of Salisbury. Soon the young Boone engaged, unsuccessfully, in his first combat with Indians. Early in the French and Indian War (1755-63), he and his friend John Finley had signed on as wagon drivers in Gen. Edward Braddock's ill-fated campaign against Fort Duquesne. The march from Virginia began early in April 1755. Three months later, nearing the fort, Braddock's army was ambushed. In the resulting slaughter and the melee of fleeing troops, Boone wisely abandoned his loaded wagon and—leaping onto one of his team and cutting the traces—rode to safety. His fellow wagoners followed suit.

Back in the Yadkin Valley, Daniel resumed his courtship of Rebecca Bryan (see Rebecca BOONE). On August 14, 1756, they were married and subsequently settled on Sugar Tree Creek, where they lived for ten years and raised half of their children. Boone farmed and spent the fall and winter hunting. In 1760 he enlisted in a final campaign against the Cherokee and in 1765 he accompanied some fellow frontiersmen on a trip to explore Florida (which Britain had recently acquired from Spain).

In the fall of 1767, Boone—like many other white explorers before him—penetrated the Kentucky wilderness on a hunting expedition, accompanied by his brother Squire (BOONE) and another frontiersman. Soon after, in the winter of 1768-69, his friend Finley, then a fur trader and peddler, visited Boone and proposed that he serve as guide for a major hunting and trapping expedition in Kentucky. Finley was seeking the WARRIORS' PATH, a route the Cherokee had used against the Shawnee and other tribes, which led from a gap in the Cumberlands into Kentucky, teeming with game. Boone readily accepted, and Judge Richard HENDERSON probably agreed to finance the venture. On May 1, 1769, a party of six, including John Stuart (Boone's brother-in-law), left the Yadkin for the western wilderness.

After passing through the Cumberland Gap, the party camped on a branch of the Rockcastle River. While Finley went off in search of his former trading site, Boone ascended a knob that permitted him his first view of Kentucky's meadowlands. Just before Christmas, having stockpiled a great quantity of deerskins, the men were confronted by a party of Shawnee braves who confiscated the goods and warned their "brothers" not to return. As the frustrated hunters headed toward home, however, they encountered Boone's brother Squire and Alexander Neely proceeding into Kentucky, and Boone and

Stuart elected to join up with the newcomers, while the other four continued their retreat. This time a wiser Boone camped well away from the Warriors' Path. Near the beginning of February, Stuart was killed by Indians and Neely soon returned home, but the Boones remained to hunt and trap. Twice Squire went to market with their pelts and obtained fresh provisions, while Daniel remained alone to explore the Kentucky River and Licking River valleys and even along the Ohio. He kept a careful watch for Indians and slept away from his campfire. In 1771 the Boones joined a party of hunters who had braved the forbidden wilderness, but the brothers soon left for home. Along the way Indians again relieved them of their packload of skins, but Daniel, who now knew Kentucky better than perhaps any other white man, would return.

In 1773 Boone reexplored Kentucky with a small group of men and resolved to attempt a settlement. Hastened by the fact that other parties had similar intentions, and fearing that choice land would be lost, Boone set out with his own and five neighboring families on September 25. Two weeks later, a few of the group who had been sent to procure more flour were attacked in their sleep by a band of Indians. Most of the group were killed outright, but two, including Boone's oldest son, James, were tortured to death. After learning of the tragedy and burying their dead, the settlers held a council. Over Boone's protests, the expedition was abandoned. The following year Lord Dunmore, governor of Virginia, sent Boone and Michael Stoner into Kentucky to warn surveyors of the danger of Indian attacks. When he returned, Boone was made a lieutenant, then a captain, in the colonial forces and was given command of three frontier forts. Following the cessation of hostilities in Lord Dunmore's War, Boone was instrumental in urging the inhabitants of the Cherokee towns to agree to a treaty. Granting a vast area of wilderness land to Richard Henderson's Transylvania Company in return for the equivalent of 10,000 pounds sterling, the Sycamore Shoals treaty was signed on March 17, 1775. Subsequently Henderson employed Boone to organize a crew of thirty axmen to cut a suitable road into the territory. Known as BOONE'S TRACE, it extended through the Cumberland Gap to the newly founded Fort Boone—now Boonesborough—on the Kentucky River.

Ultimately, however, Henderson could not secure valid title to his land, and instead of becoming a fourteenth colony, Kentucky was made a county of Virginia. With the onset of the Revolutionary War, the Indians stepped up their hostilities at the instigation of the British. Several settlers were killed, and in 1777 Boone himself was shot in the ankle. A year later he and most of thirty others were captured while on a salt-making excursion at Blue Licks; Boone surrendered his men to spare their lives. The captives were taken north of the Ohio River to the Shawnee town of Old Chillicothe, where Boone shrewdly ingratiated himself with Chief Black Fish and—along with sixteen of his men—was adopted into the tribe. Boone became the "son" of Black Fish himself and was given the name *Shel-tow-ee*, or Big Turtle. Eventually, he was allowed to hunt alone and was able to hoard enough for his escape. Boone made his break on June 16, 1778—more than five months after his capture—upon learning of Shawnee plans to attack Boonesborough. Covering 160 miles in the next four days, he exhausted his pony, then continued on foot.

When the attack came in early September, Boonesborough was prepared. After a ten-day siege, the Indians finally withdrew. Just two settlers had been killed and only four wounded, whereas the Indians suffered many casualties. After the danger had passed, however, simmering anger over Boone's supposed collaboration with the enemy boiled over and Col. Richard Calloway brought formal charges. A full investigation vindicated Boone, who was even promoted to major because of his dedicated service.

From late 1778 through the autumn of 1779, Boone and his family were apparently in North Carolina. Soon, however, he hastened back to Kentucky to establish title to his otherwise invalidated land claims. He then sold his land, intending to use the proceeds to purchase new land warrants, but he and a companion were robbed of the entire amount while they slept at a Virginia inn. Having been entrusted with the money of several friends, Boone spent many years paying them back, one at a time. His troubles increased in 1781 at the British storming of Charlottesville, Virginia, while he was a legislator; he was captured and imprisoned for several weeks. In August, as a lieutenant colonel in charge of a division against the Indians, Boone was caught in the ambush at Blue Licks. Although he escaped, his son Israel was among the many killed, and Boone felt partially responsible for the massacre.

Probably in 1783, Boone moved with his family to Limestone (now Maysville), Kentucky. He opened a trading post and tavern and, on behalf of the state of Virginia, supplied food for Indian prisoners. Boone took part in one mission against Shawnee towns on the Miami River, and he helped make prisoner exchanges. He also served as a deputy surveyor for both Lincoln and Fayette counties. However, although he received as much as half the land that he located for claimants, he was to lose most of it under legal technicalities.

About 1790 he moved again, this time to Point Pleasant in Kanawha County, Virginia (now West Virginia). He served as a county representative to the Virginia Assembly, and contracted to supply ammunition to military outposts. Apparently he lived near Blue Licks in Kentucky around 1795. By 1798, however, the lawsuits over the old land claims had left him virtually bereft of property, and in September of 1799, nearing his sixty-fifth birthday, Daniel Boone left for Spanish-owned Missouri. The following year he was made magistrate of the Femme Osage District. After Missouri became part of the United States in 1804, however, Boone again lost most of his land. On March 18, 1813, Rebecca, his beloved wife of fifty-six years, died. A few years later, probably in 1817, Boone went on his last hunt, accompanied by a grandson. In 1819 the American artist Chester Harding sought out the old frontiersman to record his likeness, thought to be the only portrait of Boone painted from life.

Daniel Boone died on September 26, 1820, and was buried, as he had requested, in Marysville Cemetery at Defiance, Missouri, next to his wife, Rebecca. His death did not end the indignities. Twenty-five years later his remains and those of his wife (or, as a rumor would later claim, the remains of Rebecca and a slave, whose grave was supposedly mistaken for Daniel's) were removed to Kentucky. With military pomp and parade, tribute and taps, they were reinterred in the Frankfort Cemetery. It was not until 1862, however, that a monument was erected over the graves.

In the meantime, wags and hoaxers in several states were at work carving inscriptions on rifles and powderhorns, rocks, and trees ("D. Boon kilt a bar" was a favorite), which were enshrined by promoters of tourism. Ultimately, however, not even the demeaning caricatures of the backwoods bumpkin they evoke (complete, perhaps, with the coonskin cap he did not wear) can diminish the stature of Kentucky's great frontiersman. Nor can attempts to exaggerate his role as Indian fighter. (He told his son Nathan that he could be certain of having killed only a single Indian in all his years.) The true story of his accomplishments alone is sufficient to make Daniel Boone seem larger than life.

See John Bakeless, *Daniel Boone: Master of the Wilderness* (New York 1939); Michael A. Lofaro, *The Life and Adventures of Daniel Boone* (Lexington, Ky., 1978); Bayless E. Hardin, ed., "Daniel Boone and the Frankfort Cemetery," *Register* 50 (July 1952): 201-36.   JOE NICKELL

BOONE, JOY (FIELD) BALE. Joy (Field) Bale Boone, poet, was born October 29, 1912, in Chicago to William Sydney and Edith (Overington) Field. She was educated at the Chicago Latin School and the Roycemore School for Girls in Evanston, Illinois. Boone has resided in Kentucky for more than half a century, principally in Elizabethtown (1937-75) and in Elkton. She was married to physician Shelby Garnett Bale from 1934 until his death in 1972; they were the parents of six children. In 1975 she married George Street Boone, an attorney, and moved to Elkton.

Boone began her literary career in Kentucky as a reviewer for the *Louisville Courier-Journal* in 1945. She edited two collections of *Contemporary Kentucky Poets* (1964, 1967). In 1964 she founded the literary magazine *Approaches* and served as its editor for eleven years. Since relinquishing the editorship to Wade Hall, she has served on the editorial board for the journal now known as *Kentucky Poetry Review*. Boone's long narrative poem *The Storm's Eye: A Narrative in Verse Celebrating Cassius Marcellus Clay, Man of Freedom 1810-1903*,

was published in 1974 by the Kentucky Poetry Press, and was reprinted in the tenth anniversary issue of *Approaches*. Her *never less than love* was published in 1972. Individual poems have appeared in numerous poetry journals, and she is one of two Kentucky poets featured in the award-winning video *Poetry: A Beginner's Guide*, produced at Western Kentucky University in Bowling Green.

For several years, Boone served as president of Friends of Kentucky Libraries. She has chaired the Robert Penn Warren Committee at Western Kentucky University since its inception in 1987. In 1990 she was appointed to the board of the Gaines Humanities Center at the University of Kentucky, and she chairs the endowment committee for the University Press of Kentucky. Boone's awards include the Distinguished Kentuckian Award from Kentucky Educational Television in 1974 and the Sullivan Award from the University of Kentucky in 1969.

See Michael Lasater and Mary Ellen Miller, *Poetry: A Beginner's Guide* (Bowling Green, Ky., 1985); William S. Ward, *A Literary History of Kentucky* (Knoxville, Tenn., 1988).

MARY ELLEN MILLER

BOONE, REBECCA (BRYAN). Rebecca (Bryan) Boone, pioneer, daughter of Joseph and Alee (or Aylee) Bryan, was born June 9, 1739, probably near Winchester, Virginia. Her family settled on the Yadkin River in North Carolina several years after her grandfather moved to the area in 1748. Squire Boone moved his family nearby in 1750 and from that time the two families' histories were linked. Rebecca's life has been overshadowed by that of her husband, Daniel BOONE, son of Squire Boone. The two were married on August 14, 1756. Shortly thereafter they moved several miles north to Sugar Tree Creek, where they lived for ten years except when Indian attacks between 1758 and 1760 forced them to retreat to Culpeper County, Virginia. Scarcity of game prompted other moves between 1766 and 1768.

Rebecca had ten children: James (1757), Israel (1759), Susannah (1760), Jemima (1762), Levina (1766), Rebecca (1768), Daniel Morgan (1769), Jesse Bryan (1773), William (1775), and Nathan (1781). Jemima was said to be the offspring of Edward, Daniel's brother; she was conceived while Daniel was away from home fighting in the Cherokee War. Because Rebecca had thought him dead, Daniel forgave this infidelity and treated Jemima as his own.

The Boones moved to the Kentucky frontier in late September 1773. After Indians killed their eldest son few weeks later, the group decided to return to North Carolina. Daniel began work on the Wilderness Road in the early spring of 1775 and by April he and his brother Squire had chosen a location for Boonesborough and started building Fort Boone on the Kentucky River. In August 1775 the family headed back to Kentucky. In July 1776 Rebecca's daughter, Jemima, along with Betsey and

Fanny Callaway, was kidnapped by Indians after their canoe had drifted across the Kentucky River. Daniel, leading a group of men, caught up with the Indian party and, after several rounds of gunfire, scared them away and rescued the girls. In early 1778, Daniel himself was captured by Shawnee and was imprisoned from February through June. Believing her husband was dead, Rebecca moved her family back to North Carolina to live at her family's home on the Yadkin River. Daniel was taken north to the Indian villages in southern Ohio, after convincing his captors that an attack on Fort Boone would be unsuccessful. He escaped the camp, and arrived in Boonesborough on June 20. He joined his family in North Carolina in the fall of 1779 and they returned to Boonesborough. The family moved to Limestone (now Maysville), Kentucky, probably in 1783, where Daniel operated a tavern and store and served as surveyor for the area.

The Boone family moved from Kentucky to Missouri in 1799 after Daniel had lost most of his Kentucky acreage through legal technicalities. They first lived with their son Daniel Morgan in the Femme Osage District sixty miles west of St. Louis. They later established a community on the Missouri River five miles south of Augusta, where Daniel became magistrate of the Femme Osage District in July 1800. In Missouri the Boones again faced legal problems when the Louisiana Purchase was transferred to the United States in 1804. Although the U.S. Congress eventually approved a portion of his claim, Boone sold the land to appease his creditors.

Rebecca died on March 18, 1813, and was buried in Marysville Cemetery in Defiance, Missouri. Her remains and those of her husband were reinterred in the Frankfort Cemetery in Kentucky on September 13, 1845. On March 2, 1862, the state erected a monument there.

See Michael A. Lofaro, *The Life and Adventures of Daniel Boone* (Lexington, Ky., 1986).

BOONE, SQUIRE. Squire Boone, frontiersman, was born October 5, 1744, in Exeter Township, Berks County, Pennsylvania, the tenth of eleven children of Squire Boone, Sr., and Sarah (Morgan) Boone. The family lived briefly near Winchester, Virginia, then moved down the Valley of Virginia, settling on the east side of the South Yadkin River, near Wilkesboro, North Carolina. His older brother Daniel taught Squire woodcraft, and in 1759 he was apprenticed to his cousin Samuel Boone, a gunsmith on the Potomac River in Maryland. After five years, Squire became an expert gunsmith. He returned to North Carolina in 1765.

Squire and Daniel Boone explored Florida, and in 1767 Squire Boone went to Kentucky. He helped cut the Wilderness Road and build Boonesborough in 1775. A redoubtable Indian fighter, he was seriously wounded five times. A Baptist minister, he preached the first sermon on the site of Louisville, and August 7, 1776, he performed the first marriage in Kentucky. Boone was twice elected to serve in the Virginia legislature; he signed petitions in 1779 and 1780 requesting that the legislature charter Louisville. Encountering problems with Kentucky land titles, Boone moved to Vicksburg, Mississippi, then to New Orleans, where he opened a gun shop. He also lived in Florida and Missouri.

In 1765 Boone married Jane Van Cleave, daughter of Aaron and Rachael (Schenck) Van Cleave. Their children were Jonathan, Moses, Isaiah, Sarah, and Enoch Morgan. In 1806 Boone moved to Boone Township in Indiana. He died there in August 1815 and was buried in a cave near Corydon. Some accounts say that his son moved the body to Boone Cemetery on the Fort Knox Military Reservation.

See Hazel Atterbuy Spraker, *The Boone Family* (Rutland, Vt., 1922).   GEORGE STREET BOONE

BOONE COUNTY. Boone County, the thirtieth county in order of formation, is located in northern Kentucky, along the Ohio River. It is bordered by Gallatin, Grant, and Kenton counties and covers 252 square miles. Boone County was formed December 13, 1798, from a section of Campbell County and named in honor of the pioneer Daniel Boone. The county seat is BURLINGTON. A large portion of the hilly county is used for agriculture, producing tobacco, corn, cattle, and dairy products. The principal waterways are the Ohio River and numerous creeks, including Big Bone, Gunpowder, Middle, Mud Lick, and Woolper.

In 1729 Capt. Charles Lemoyne de Longveil discovered one of the largest concentrations of prehistoric fossils in the United States at BIG BONE LICK, near the Ohio River, where herds of mastodons and other Ice Age mammals came to the springs along Big Bone Creek seeking the salt that permeated the water and soil.

Christopher Gist, John Finley, and Robert Smith were among the explorers of what is now Boone County. The first permanent settlement in the county was made in 1785 by a group of settlers from Pennsylvania. About forty acres owned by John Tanner were cleared and a blockhouse was constructed in the site now known as Petersburg. During the Indian raids in the early settlement period, Tanner's son was abducted and lived among the Indians for the next twenty years.

In 1800 the population of the county numbered about 1,500, which had doubled by 1810 and doubled again by 1820. Incorporated towns are FLORENCE, Petersburg, Union, and Walton; unincorporated communities are Burlington, Beaverlick, Belleview, Constance, Hebron, Idlewild, Rabbit Hash, Sugartit, and Verona.

River trade nourished the growth of Boone County. Steamboats began to ply the Ohio River in ever increasing numbers by the 1830s and 1840s. In heavy river traffic on January 28, 1859, the steamers *David Gibson* and *Nat Holmes* collided and sank at Petersburg. Boone County was a stopover on the underground railroad, and slave patrollers guarded the river as closely as possible to prevent escape.

During the Civil War, Boone County was the scene of several skirmishes. Between July 28 and August 11, 1864, Gen. Stephen Burbridge of the Union army ordered the arrest of several Boone County residents on charges of disloyalty to the federal government.

In the twentieth century Boone County has felt the urban influence of Cincinnati. Located in the county six miles north of Florence is the Cincinnati-Northern Kentucky Airport, one of the largest in the nation. Boone County has one weekly newspaper, the *Boone County Recorder*, and one radio station, WMLX (Florence). The largest religious denominations are the Southern Baptist, Catholic, and Christian churches.

The population of the county was 32,812 in 1970; 45,842 in 1980; and 57,589 in 1990.

See Ann Lutes, *A Brief History of Boone County, Kentucky* (Florence, Ky., 1958).

RON D. BRYANT

BOONESBOROUGH. One of the most celebrated sites in Kentucky's pioneer history, Boonesborough was established by Judge Richard Henderson, Daniel Boone, and members of the TRANSYLVANIA COMPANY in the spring of 1775 on the Kentucky River in what is now Madison County. Henderson, a native Virginian who practiced law in North Carolina, and his financial backers—John Williams, Leonard Henley Bullock, James Hogg, Nathaniel, David, and Thomas Hart, John Luttrell, and William Johnstone—envisioned Boonesborough as the center of government for the proposed colony of Transylvania. The colony was to be established on a huge land tract covering northern, central, and western Kentucky, which they purchased in March 1775 from the Cherokee Indians at Sycamore Shoals on the Watauga River, in North Carolina (now east Tennessee). Despite the opposition of the Virginia government, they proceeded to gather and stock two settlement parties, one headed by Daniel Boone, who had scouted out a location on the Kentucky River earlier, and another led by Judge Henderson himself. Boone's party set out on March 10, 1775, to cut a trail to the proposed site of the colony's capital. Henderson followed with additional settlers and supplies on March 20. The venture encountered many problems and threats from its inception. Boone's party lost three of its members from Indian attacks on the way, and most settlers in both parties turned back and abandoned the endeavor after learning of the dangers.

The more intrepid members of the two parties reached the proposed site of Boonesborough in April. Boone's party, which arrived first, immediately began building a small camp (usually referred to as Boone's first fort, although it was unfortified) and surveyed numerous two-acre lots. They were already in possession of these lots when Henderson arrived on April 20, leaving him with land on the opposite (south) side of a large mineral-water lick called Sycamore Hollow. A series of town lots were surveyed April 21 and 22 on the bank of the Kentucky River and were distributed by drawing to the settlers. Henderson obtained four lots for a garden and the fort he proposed to build. Building began soon after, a powder magazine being one of the first completed structures. Richard Henderson left a plan of the fort as he envisioned it: a rectangle with four corner blockhouses, eight cabins and a central gate on each of two long sides, and five cabins along each of the short sides. Stockading filled in gaps between the cabins, blockhouses, and gates. Accounts of visitors in subsequent years indicate that the fort was not completed before Henderson's departure. A few cabins and two of the corner blockhouses were completed but most, if not all, of the stockade, the southeast and southwest blockhouses, and other features of the fort were not built until shortly before the siege of 1778.

Henderson's journal chronicles his difficulty in inducing the settlers to cooperate in building defensive facilities for their common protection. He also encountered resistance from one of his own land company partners, Nathaniel Hart, who withdrew from active involvement in the fort construction and established himself on land nearby on which a fine, permanent freshwater spring was located. This site became known as White Oak Spring Station. Adding to Henderson's troubles was the questionable validity of the title to his colony. Periodic food shortages and wastefulness in preserving game left many settlers in dire straits. Many lost heart and returned east during the late spring and early summer of 1775.

Henderson continued to develop his plans for Boonesborough as the capital of the Transylvania colony, drawing together a plan of government by popular representation, and organizing an election of members for a House of Delegates of the Colony of Transylvania. On May 8, the colony and its capital were formally named Transylvania and Boonesborough, respectively. The House of Delegates met at Boonesborough on May 23, 1775, under a huge tree called the Divine Elm to draw up laws and sign a compact between the proprietors and the settlers. All of Henderson's plans were dashed, however, when the Virginia legislature acted to nullify the company's right to the Kentucky lands; by 1778 the purchase was officially declared null and void. Henderson probably knew his enterprise was doomed by 1776, and by 1778 he ceased to have any active role in Boonesborough history.

After Henderson's departure, settlers continued to use Boonesborough as a stopping place, sanctuary, and communication point during the tumultuous years of the Revolutionary War. Kentucky history books relate many hair-raising events there. Indian raids, the kidnapping of the Boone and the Callaway girls, and the murder of prominent settlers such as Richard CALLAWAY kept life at Boonesborough in a state of uncertainty. In September of 1778 the fort was besieged for ten days by Indians led by

Black Fish, a famous Shawnee chief, and a French Canadian unit under British command. Although this event accounted for only a few days of Boonesborough's history, it probably has received more published mention than any other incident at the site. At the time, Boonesborough had only about sixty men capable of fighting and a handful of women and children living at the fort.

In 1779 a group of settlers petitioned the Virginia legislature for a charter to establish a town at Boonesborough. The petition indicated that twenty acres had already been laid off into lots and streets, and fifty adjoining acres were planned for additional development. The charter was granted, although with some modifications in the list of trustees. As trustees, the final charter named Richard Callaway, Charles Mimms Thruston, Levin Powell, Edmund Taylor, James Estill, Edward Bradley, John Kennedy, David Gass, Pemberton Rawlings, and Daniel Boone. The fledgling town got off to a rocky start. Some of the trustees refused to serve, for various reasons, and at least one (Callaway) was killed by Indians. At various times, new trustees were appointed to revitalize plans for the town, with limited results.

Some gains were made, however, one of the most important being the establishment of a tobacco inspection point. A tobacco warehouse was built around 1788, and tobacco storage and inspection became an important economic activity at Boonesborough for the next twenty-five years. The town also served as a post office for many settlers in the area, and early newspapers regularly notified individuals of mail waiting for them there. Another important facility was the Boonesborough ferry, originally franchised to Richard Callaway, but granted to and operated by his heirs after his death in 1780.

Despite the flourishing economic activities, the town never grew to any substantial size. Although many people visited Boonesborough on their way elsewhere, relatively few people remained there for any length of time. Boonesborough's population was largely a transient, ever-changing one. After the war ended, even fewer people settled permanently in the main part of the town, although they were scattered in the surrounding area. Even when it became safer for settlers to establish permanent residences on their plantations and farms, Boonesborough did not grow much beyond a few houses, the tobacco warehouse complex, and buildings associated with the ferry. By 1810, when a federal census was taken, the town contained only eight households, totaling sixty-eight people. In the same year, an official town plan was filed in the Madison County clerk's office, but its ambitious layout of streets and lots belied the limited construction that had taken place. By the 1820 federal census, Boonesborough's population was not separately tabulated but subsumed under the county totals. During the 1830s and 1840s, the town claims were acquired by a few landowners and turned into farms. Part of the original town claims were devel-

oped into an early twentieth century watering place by a local doctor who capitalized on the mineral-water springs in Sycamore Hollow, but this spa was a short-lived enterprise.

An archaeological survey in 1987 of the part of the town claims along the Kentucky River documented several residences, the tobacco warehouse complex, the site of Henderson's stockaded fort, and remains of the ferry complex, which formed most of the man-made environment of the town. There probably were other residences in the uplands around the river where town outlots were laid out, but these areas have not been researched. Limited excavations at the fort site revealed the remains of a stone chimney base from one of the cabins and the remains of a fire where meat from white-tailed deer, buffalo, black bear, pig, cow, wild turkey, and channel catfish had probably been cooked. Artifacts such as gunflints, molded lead bullets, and English ceramics dating before 1800 were also recovered. An enigma during the excavations was the discovery of stains in the ground where two large wooden posts had once stood. They may have been gate supports or part of the stockade. The stockade filled in only short sections of open ground between cabins. It was probably built by sinking a few large posts, placing smaller upright logs on the surface of the ground between the posts, and pegging horizontal log members across the upright logs to hold everything together.

Despite the early decline and the lack of substantial development at Boonesborough, its role is assured as a place of sanctuary, communication, and defense during the tumultuous years when Kentucky was first being settled. This site fully deserves national recognition for its importance to the United States' westward expansion.

See Nancy O'Malley, *Searching for Boonesborough*, Archaeological Report 193, Department of Anthropology, University of Kentucky, 1989; Neal O. Hammon, "Pioneers in Kentucky, 1773-1775," *FCHQ* 55 (July 1988): 268-83.

NANCY O'MALLEY

BOONE'S TRACE. Boone's Trace was a trail blazed by Daniel Boone and his company of adventurers when they entered what is now Kentucky through the Cumberland Gap in March 1775. For the first part of the journey, Boone used the existing Warriors' Path, which had been traveled for centuries by the Indians, and Skaggs's Trace from Cumberland Gap into Kentucky. Upon reaching Hazel Patch in present Laurel County, Boone left the old trails and blazed a new one to the Kentucky River, proceeding north from Hazel Patch to the Rockcastle River, then over a hillside to the waters of Roundstone Creek in Rockcastle County. The men followed this creek through thick cane and reeds to the headwaters, then went through Boone's Gap into Rockcastle County.

The trail passed what is now Berea to the east, and passed near what was later called Boone's Blue Lick. Boone and his men then crossed the Hayes and Hart forks of Silver Creek in Madison County and camped for the night on Taylor's Fork near Richmond. There they were attacked by Indians, who killed two men, wounded another, and stole some horses. Afterward, Boone's party erected several small cabins for protection, which were later called Twitties Fort. A few days later the group continued, following Otter Creek to the Kentucky River, and began construction of another fort on April 1, 1775, at the site that became Boonesborough.

Later expeditions of pioneers using Boone's Trace established that wherever possible, Boone had followed buffalo roads and deer trails. In September 1775, when Boone brought his family to Kentucky, he did not use this trace, but followed Skaggs's Trace to Dick's (now Dix) River before turning northward to Boonesborough.

See Robert L. Kincaid, *The Wilderness Road* (Middlesboro, Ky., 1966); Neal Hammon, "Early Roads into Kentucky," *Register* 68 (April 1970): 91-131; Hammon, "The First Trip to Boonesborough," *FCHQ* 45 (July 1971): 249-63.

NEAL HAMMON

BOONEVILLE. Booneville, the seat of Owsley County in eastern Kentucky, is located in the north-central part of the county at the junction of KY 30 and KY 11, on the South Fork of the Kentucky River. The town was named to honor Daniel Boone, who is said to have camped by a spring near the present site of the courthouse in Booneville while on a surveying trip in 1780-81. The early settlement that grew up there was alternately known as Boone's Station and Moore's Station, after James Moore, Sr., who in the 1790s was one of the first permanent settlers. When Owsley County was formed on May 20, 1844, the town was known as Owsley Court House; two years later it was incorporated as Booneville.

In 1843 Elias Moore, son of James Moore, Sr., donated an acre of land on which to build the first courthouse. A log house served as a temporary court building until a permanent structure, probably of brick, was built. A large brick courthouse built in 1887 was destroyed by fire on January 29, 1929. A Colonial Revival–style brick courthouse completed in 1931 was consumed by fire on January 5, 1967. It was replaced in 1974 by a modern brick courthouse completed with a federal grant. Booneville has been the site of several fires, which destroyed a brickyard, the Booneville Hotel, a telephone exchange, and numerous homes.

During the Civil War most Booneville residents supported the Union, and many young men enlisted in the 7th Kentucky Infantry Regiment. On September 21, 1862, Gen. George W. Morgan's Union army retreated through the town on its way from the Cumberland Gap to Ohio, and on June 17, 1864, Col. C.H. Hanson and three hundred Union troops stopped there while pursuing Gen. John Hunt Morgan's Confederate soldiers. A more serious menace to the pro-Union citizens of Owsley County was pro-South guerrillas from neighboring counties who threatened their lives and property. On April 14, 1864, the Three Forks Battalion, a Home Guard unit of forty local citizens, drove off a force of seventy-five Southern guerrillas at Booneville.

Industries in Booneville around 1900 included a tanyard, a mill, and a brickyard. Hiram Hogg, Jr., built the tanyard, which operated from the early 1880s until around 1917. One of the largest mills in the county, built around 1900 by Charlie Minter, was operated after 1907 by Pleas Abshear. A few years after Abshear's death in 1957 the mill was destroyed in a flood. A brickyard processed locally dug clay around 1850; a larger brickyard was destroyed by fire in 1905.

In the early 1900s, Court Day, the first Monday of each month, was a festive occasion for trading and swapping. Chatauquas, religious and social gatherings, and shooting matches were popular summer activities.

Booneville's city limits have never been enlarged. Most residents who are employed are service workers or are employed by state or local government. The population of the sixth-class city was 126 in 1970; 191 in 1980; and 232 in 1990.

MORRIS M. GARRETT

BOUNDARIES. For many years, the external boundaries of the Commonwealth of Kentucky were as imprecisely defined as the irregular METES AND BOUNDS within the state and, like them, necessitated numerous surveys and gave rise to much litigation. In 1776 the Virginia House of Delegates defined the northern boundary of Kentucky District as the low-water mark at the mouth of the Big Sandy, on the northern shore of the Ohio River. The boundary followed the Big Sandy River from that point to the junction of the Tug Fork, and from there up to the Laurel Ridge of the Cumberland Mountain to the point where it crossed the Virginia-North Carolina line (a spot later known as "seven pines and two black oaks"). When Virginia agreed to the separation of Kentucky in the Compact of 1789, that earlier territorial description was accepted.

In 1779-80 the Virginia–North Carolina dividing line was extended westward to the first crossing of the Cumberland River. From this point west to the Mississippi, Thomas Walker surveyed the line for Virginia, following generally the established eastern course of 36°30'. The Walker survey was by no means a thorough or efficient one. Most of the boundary had to be located through dense virgin forests and much of it over rugged mountainous terrain. The rest followed stream courses, where it was equally difficult to establish precise boundaries.

To settle the boundary between Virginia and Kentucky, the Virginia House of Delegates in 1799 created a boundary commission and sought similar action from Kentucky. Kentucky appointed John Coburn, Robert Johnson, and Buckner Thruston as its commissioners, who were to meet with Virginia's delegation—Archibald Stewart, Gen. Joseph Martin, and Creed Taylor. The commissioners began their survey at the forks of the Big Sandy and followed eastward along the Tug Fork to the Breaks of Sandy. They surveyed in a northeasterly direction from the Walker line, at the point known as seven pines and two black oaks, up the watershed of the Cumberland Mountain to the crossing of the Russell Fork of the Levisa Fork. From that point the surveyors followed a straight magnetic line on the call 45° east longitude to the crossing of the Tug Fork and the line established earlier.

The 1799 joint commission settled Kentucky's eastern and northeastern boundaries, but left the other boundaries still not fully determined. Westward from the ridge top of the Cumberland Mountain, the boundary between Virginia and North Carolina (after 1796, Tennessee) remained in doubt from the Walker survey in 1779 until 1859. The statutory description of the landmarks of this boundary refers to some quaint place names, such as Left Hand Yellow Creek, Log Mountain, Roaring Paunch, Big South Fork, Little South Fork, and Kettle Creek. No doubt these names were given to the creeks and mountains by the Walker surveyors as they struggled through the wilderness.

Attempting to bring sense from the confusion, Tennessee in 1821 solicited Kentucky's cooperation in surveying that portion of the boundary from Cumberland Mountain to the first crossing of the Cumberland River. Gov. John Adair (1820-24) appointed William Steele, surveyor, to represent Kentucky, and Tennessee's governor appointed Absalom Looney. On May 1, 1821, the surveyors began their line on Cumberland Mountain, and on July 2 they concluded it at the crossing of the Cumberland River and a joining of the Walker line, at a point on the west bank 20° above John Kerr's house. The surveyors had marked 114 miles of the line. The Tennessee legislature approved the survey, but the line westward remained uncertain until the 1859 survey by Austin P. Cox and Benjamin Peebles, a Kentucky-Tennessee team.

Between January 9 and October 20, 1859, the Cox-Peebles survey party blazed a 320-mile path across the same terrain that Walker's party had traversed from New Madrid Bend to Cumberland Gap. They marked this boundary permanently, they hoped, by erecting three-foot-high stone slabs every five miles, beginning at Compromise on the Mississippi River and placing the final stone just below the point where the old Wilderness Road passed through Cumberland Gap. (See MIDDLETON OFFSET.) The establishment of the Cox-Peebles boundary ended three-quarters of a century of surveying controversy between Kentucky and Tennessee.

Aside from the southern boundary with Tennessee, the most confused Kentucky boundary has been that part along the Ohio River. When the Virginia General Assembly ceded to the U.S. government its claim to the Northwest Territory on March 4, 1784, it stipulated that it was surrendering "all rights, title, and claim, as well of soil as of jurisdiction, which the said commonwealth had to the territory within the Virginia Charter, situated, lying, and being to the northwest of the Ohio." This cession established the Virginia boundary on the northwest shore of the Ohio River at the low-water mark. No permanent monument was erected to indicate the level of the low-water mark at that date, a point that has been in contention almost continually since 1784.

On November 4, 1985, the U.S. Supreme Court ruled in *Kentucky v. Indiana* that the boundary between the states is "a series of straight lines between sequentially numbered geodetic points, 1927 North American Datum." The common boundary with Ohio was set in *Ohio v. Kentucky*, on April 15, 1985. On May 28, 1991, the Supreme Court ruled in *Illinois v. Kentucky* that the boundary between Kentucky and Illinois is the low-water mark on the northern shore of the Ohio River, but the Court had not defined the low-water mark as of this writing. The Kentucky-Missouri boundary is "a line drawn through the center of the Mississippi River." The KENTUCKY BEND, or New Madrid Bend, carved in the river by the earthquake of 1811, created a geographical quirk, leaving a portion of Kentucky's Fulton County an "island" accessible only by ferry or, by land, via Tennessee.

The boundaries of Kentucky in 1990 encompassed a land area of 39,650 square miles and a water area of 745 square miles, or a total of 40,395.

See James W. Sames, *Four Steps West* (Frankfort, Ky., 1971); Thomas D. Clark, *Historic Maps of Kentucky* (Lexington, Ky., 1979).

THOMAS D. CLARK

BOURBON. Nearly two hundred years after it was first distilled, bourbon whiskey was recognized as a distinctly American product by Congress on May 4, 1964, in a joint resolution that prohibited the import into the United States of any distilled spirits labeled "bourbon whiskey." The most distinctive of America's commercial whiskeys, bourbon is made from a fermented mash containing at least fifty-one percent corn and lesser amounts of wheat, rye, and barley, along with yeast and distilled limestone water; it is distilled at no more than 160 proof and aged in charred oak barrels, a process that gives the bourbon its reddish color and unique taste.

Settlers from Virginia, Maryland, and Pennsylvania began producing whiskey in 1775, when the first corn crops were harvested in Kentucky. It is doubtful that the name of the first distiller of bourbon whiskey will ever be known. Jacob Meyers and Jacob Froman of Lincoln County, Marsham Brashear of Jefferson County, Elijah Craig of Scott County, Jacob Spears of Bourbon County, or any of a number of other distillers may have produced the first bourbon.

The name of the whiskey probably came from Bourbon County, established on December 29, 1785, where there were a number of early distillers.

Twenty-five Bourbon County distillers were among those indicted for their failure to pay a federal excise tax on their product from 1791 to 1798. The first known newspaper advertisement for bourbon whiskey appeared in the *Western Citizen*, a Bourbon County newspaper, on June 26, 1821, and read "Bourbon whiskey by the barrel or keg." The advertisement was placed by the Maysville firm of Stout and Adams. The December 2, 1826, issue of the newspaper carried a notice from the Paris firm of Hughart and Warfield advertising "Spears and Williams' Best Old Whiskey," from the distillery of Solomon Spears and Samuel Williams. The stone structure that Jacob Spears built in 1790 as a warehouse for the distillery still stands on Clay-Kiser Road in Bourbon County. Other Bourbon County distilleries included the Bourbon County Distilling Company at Ruddles Mill, whose brands were "Pure Bourbon Whiskey" and "H.C. Bowen's Old Bourbon." The Chicken Cock Distillery at Paris had warehouse space for more than 30,000 barrels of its whiskey. The Edgewater Distillery, near the Harrison-Bourbon County line, also operated as a gristmill.

The term bourbon whiskey was in wide use in the 1840s to distinguish between Kentucky's corn whiskey and Pennsylvania's rye. By 1891 Kentucky had 172 distilleries with a daily mashing capacity of 36,265 bushels, the largest in the nation. The product, however, was not of uniform quality. The federal Bottle-in-Bond Act of 1897 specified the minimum number of years that bourbon and other whiskey must be aged, as well as setting a proof standard and specifying manufacturing processes.

The 1936 Federal Alcohol Administration Act established the current standards of identity for all American whiskeys. By 1960 European distillers and vintners granted American bourbon whiskey the same standing and protection awarded Scotch whiskey and French cognac. Over the past three decades, while consumption of distilled spirits in general declined, the demand for Kentucky bourbon whiskey has held. The state produces 70 percent of the nation's distilled spirits.

See Henry G. Crowgey, *Kentucky Bourbon, The Early Years of Whiskey-Making* (Lexington, Ky., 1971).   FLAGET M. NALLY

BOURBON COUNTY. Bourbon County, the fifth county in order of formation, is located in the central Bluegrass region, and has an area of 292 square miles. Its boundaries originally extended northward to the Ohio River and eastward to the Big Sandy, taking in land that has since been split into more than thirty counties. Virginia subdivided Fayette County in 1785 and honored the French royal family by naming the fifth western county Bourbon. It was rich in timber, cane, pasture grass, fertile soil, and limestone and had many creeks and springs. Early Bourbon settlers claimed choice farmland and built homes, mills, taverns, warehouses, businesses, churches, and a courthouse on the hill near the confluence of Houston and Stoner creeks. The county seat, Hopewell (renamed PARIS in 1790), became an economic center as the population grew in the early 1800s. Millersburg, North Middletown, Little Rock, Ruddles Mills, and Clintonville remained small villages.

Mainstays of the agrarian economy were corn, whiskey, hemp, tobacco, sheep, and horses. The Bourbon Agricultural Society dominated economics and politics into the twentieth century. The unique BOURBON whiskey, aged in charred barrels, led to the proliferation of distilleries and taverns in the antebellum era. Religion provided the primary social and cultural life into the Civil War. Rural churches, especially the CANE RIDGE Meeting House (1791), held frequent religious revivals. For decades before the Civil War, the Cane Ridge area endorsed emancipation. Slaves and citizens enjoyed harmonious relations and shared religious experiences in integrated churches until the 1870s.

By the 1830s the county court devoted most of its attention to local improvements. The powerful courthouse leadership sponsored turnpikes, bridges, macadamized county roads, and even railroad bonds in the antebellum period. Bourbon County adhered to the Virginia tradition of a natural aristocracy, and Gov. James Garrard (1796-1804) and his family dominated the early era. Planters and lawyers controlled local politics into the 1860s. Leaders were conservative, educated, and wealthy. The Civil War splintered families as brothers fought brothers. In the post–Civil War years, Bourbon County residents, who had generally been Unionists, joined the Democratic party and began electing former Confederates as leaders. Conflict between the county and city governments accelerated as blacks and businessmen developed a Republican alternative in Paris. The *Western Citizen*, founded in 1808, became the voice of the Democratic party but provided balance and moderation on most political and social issues. Although the war was the catalyst for a new society, the economy remained agrarian. Bourbon County continued to rank near the top in Kentucky in production of corn, tobacco, hemp, sheep, cattle, and horses, giving the wealthy citizens a high standard of living.

Political patterns remained constant into the twentieth century. Four generations of Patons served as county clerk for some seventy years. George Batterton was elected to a record eight terms as county judge (1917-49). John T. Hinton served five mayoral terms in Paris at the turn of the century, and George Doyle was elected Paris mayor six times (1929-53). New leaders emerged at mid-century as bitter political divisions reflected state politics. The *Kentuckian-Citizen*, successor to the *Western Citizen*, supported the regular Democratic machine, while the new *Paris Daily Enterprise* of the Republican Alverson family represented the A.B. Chandler faction. The death in 1965 of Paul Brannon, the wily *Citizen* editor, ended the most controversial newspaper war in county history.

Public education gained momentum when William Garth bequeathed to the county his estate, which became the base for one of the largest educational funds for disadvantaged children in the state. The Garth Fund still pays students' secondary and college expenses. The county's higher education institutions included North Middletown Classical and Business College, MILLERSBURG Female COLLEGE, Millersburg Male Methodist College (Wesleyan), and Bourbon Female College in Paris. Professor George Chapman promoted night school programs, bond issues, and a quality black high school (Paris Western). World War I and the 1920s ushered in the golden age of education in Bourbon County. Lee Kirkpatrick, superintendent of the Paris schools (1918-53), created a renowned educational system with his strong academic background, ethical emphasis, and administrative leadership. He hired high-quality faculty and attracted citizen participation. At Paris Western, black educator F.M. Wood tested policies and reforms put into effect when he became president of Kentucky State University. MILLERSBURG MILITARY INSTITUTE and the newly consolidated Bourbon County High School underscored the county's reputation for educational excellence.

Citizens repeatedly approved railroad expansion and bond issues in the postwar era. The Louisville & Nashville Railroad (now CSX Transportation) expansion of 1905 is estimated to have increased the local population by a thousand. The new wealth explained the success of eight local banks, five with half-million-dollar assets. In 1914 the old aristocratic Alexander Bank failed amid embezzlement charges, and thirty indictments ruined directors, depositors, and family names. This scandal forced banking reforms, and two leading million-dollar banks were formed by mergers: People's Deposit and Bourbon Agricultural.

The agrarian economy changed slowly in the 1900s, when horse breeding and burley tobacco became dominant. Arthur B. Hancock, Sr., of Claiborne Farm, became America's top horse breeder, having won many honors in the 1930s. Virgil Chapman, of Paris, was Kentucky's leading spokesman for tobacco interests while serving as a congressman (1925-29, 1931-49) and U.S. senator (1949-51). By the 1950s, however, industry began to challenge agriculture as a source of jobs in the rural county. School integration, a small industrial boom, the decline of both newspapers, agricultural problems, and new leadership seemed to point to dramatic change as Bourbon County celebrated its 1986 bicentennial. The population was 18,476 in 1970; 19,405 in 1980; and 19,236 in 1990.

See H.E. Everman, *The History of Bourbon County, 1785-1865* (Paris, Ky., 1977).

H.E. EVERMAN

BOURBON DEMOCRATS. Similar to the House of Bourbon in France, which held to royal tradition after the French Revolution, the namesake Bourbon Democrats hoped to continue antebellum politics in the post–Civil War era. Rejecting the Fourteenth and Fifteenth amendments to the U.S. Constitution, and believing that agriculture, not industry, would remedy the ravages of the Civil War, the Bourbon Democrats were centered in the rich Bluegrass region and led by Josiah Stoddard Johnston, a former Confederate officer from General John C. Breckinridge's staff.

Stoddard, editor of the Bourbon newspaper, the *Kentucky Yeoman*, managed to control the Democratic party's politics and machinery statewide throughout the latter half of the nineteenth century, despite the efforts of his rivals, the New Departure Democrats. Looking for a "new order," the New Departure Democrats faction, headquartered in Louisville, advocated the development of industry and improvement of transportation networks, such as railroads, rather than a return to plantation agriculture. By renouncing vehemently all tenets of the New Departure program, Kentucky Bourbons were unique among Southern Bourbon Democrats as a whole. Although they shared some basic convictions, such as white supremacy, oligarchical (ex-Confederate) rule, and retrenchment, most Southern Bourbons also favored industrial growth and better railroads.

In spite of their differences, Kentucky Democrats were united in their abhorrence of Republican rule, which they had experienced during Readjustment. This fear, which proved to be stronger than their differences, kept the Democratic party in control of the state. In 1895, the free silver issue, which called for an end of the gold standard, split the party more deeply than ever. The Democratic coalition broke down and Kentucky's first Republican governor, William O'Connell Bradley (1895-99) was elected. By the late 1890s, the era of Bourbon control of the organization had passed as Populism gained control of the Democratic party in Kentucky.

See Hambleton Tapp and James C. Klotter, *Kentucky: Decades of Discord, 1865-1900* (Frankfort, Ky., 1977).

GAYE KELLER BLAND

BOWERSOX, KATHERINE SOPHIA. Katherine Sophia Bowersox, educator, was born in Paxtonville, Pennsylvania, on August 24, 1869. She attended the State Normal School, Bloomsburg, Pennsylvania. Between 1893 and 1902, she taught at the Indian Industrial School, Carlisle, Pennsylvania. From 1902 until 1907, she served as principal of the school's Academy Department. Bowersox became dean of women in the Normal School at Berea College in 1907. Between 1918 and her retirement in 1939, she served as Berea's dean of women. She was a tireless advocate of the interests of women students and faculty. In 1950 Berea College presented her with an honorary doctorate. Bowersox died in St. Petersburg, Florida, December 24, 1961, and is buried there.

CAROLYN TERRY BASHAW

BOWIE, JAMES. There is evidence that James Bowie, frontiersman, was born in 1796 to Rezin and Elveria (Jones) Bowie on Terrapin Creek in Logan (now Simpson) County, Kentucky, although several other states claim to be his birthplace. A man named Rezin ("Reason") Bowie is on the Logan County tax lists of 1794-97 and 1799. After the time he sold his Logan County land in February 1800, his name appears on the 1800 Livingston County tax lists. On the 1810 census records, his name appears in the Catahoula Parish, Louisiana. James and his brothers grew up in pioneer Louisiana where they became proficient hunters, land speculators, and duelists. James and his father developed and refined the wide-bladed hunting and dueling knives later known as bowie knives. In 1827 Bowie dueled on a Mississippi sandbar with Norris Wright and others.

About 1828 Bowie moved to San Antonio, Texas. He was granted Mexican citizenship on October 5, 1830, and began acquiring land. On April 25, 1831, he married Ursula de Veramendi, daughter of San Antonio's vice-governor; in 1833 his wife and children died of cholera.

Bowie was among the first to take up arms in the war for Texas independence. He was a colonel in Sam Houston's forces. When General Santa Anna entered Texas with the Mexican army, the ailing Bowie was among the 150 men with Col. William Travis who defended the abandoned Alamo mission in San Antonio. They were overwhelmed after furious resistance, and Bowie was killed on his cot on March 6, 1836. Bowie's and other defenders' bodies were burned at Santa Anna's command.

LINDA ANDERSON

BOWLING GREEN. Bowling Green, the seat of Warren County, is located along the Barren River at the intersection of U.S. 31W, U.S. 68, and U.S. 231, just west of I-65. Bowling Green was founded in 1798 on two acres of land donated by Robert Moore and his brother George, who had arrived from Virginia in about 1794. They are credited with being the first settlers. The town was incorporated March 6, 1798, and its name (also spelled Bolin Green and Bowlingreen in early records) may have honored Bowling Green, Virginia. Some local historians maintain that the name referred to Robert Moore's "ball alley" near his home, where early residents played a game called bowling on the green.

By 1810 there were only 154 residents, but with the arrival of the steamboat era, Bowling Green began to prosper. The construction of a series of locks and dams on the Barren and Green rivers improved river travel, and a portage railroad was built in 1832, from the Barren River to what is now the site of the Warren County courthouse. Mules pulled the cars along the tracks, transporting goods from the river into the town. In the 1850s the Louisville & Nashville Railroad (now CSX Transportation) completed a rail line through Bowling Green, linking it to northern and southern markets.

In 1861 Bowling Green became an objective of both the Confederate and Union armies. Despite the declaration of state neutrality, the Confederate army invaded and occupied Bowling Green on September 18, 1861. While the residents were bitterly divided by the Civil War, a majority hoped that the Union would be preserved. Confederate forces began to fortify the surrounding hills of the town, thus securing the approaches to the river and the railroad for the Confederacy. In November 1861, the Confederate State of Kentucky chose the military stronghold as its capital. On February 14, 1862, after receiving reports that Union forces had taken two Confederate strongholds in the region—Fort Henry on the Tennessee and Fort Donelson on the Cumberland—Confederate forces evacuated Bowling Green without a fight, even though the town was well fortified. Before leaving, the retreating Confederates destroyed the bridges across the Barren River, the railroad depot, and numerous other buildings.

After the Civil War, the business district grew rapidly and many of the city's historic business structures were erected in the years between 1870 and 1890. In 1867-68 a new courthouse, the fourth, was completed. The first Warren County courthouse, built in 1797-98, had been replaced in 1805 by a building along the river in what was then the community of Jeffersonville. The third Warren County courthouse was built in Bowling Green, which became the county seat again in 1813. In 1868 the first waterworks system was constructed, and in 1889 the first mule-drawn streetcars began operating. The first electric-powered cars replaced them in 1895.

In 1884 the Southern Normal School was founded in Bowling Green. In 1889 Pleasant J. Potter established a women's college. It closed in 1909 and its property was bought by the Western Kentucky State Normal School, created in 1906 (now Western Kentucky University). Other schools of historical significance in Bowling Green were the Methodist Warren College; Ogden College, which became part of Western Kentucky University; and the Green River Female College, a boarding school for women. In 1862 St. Columbia's Academy was established in Bowling Green by the Sisters of Charity of Nazareth. In 1911 St. Joseph's School succeeded St. Columbia's.

In the nineteenth century one of the most successful business concerns in Bowling Green was the dressmaking establishment of Carrie Burnam Taylor, who by 1906 employed more than two hundred women in the production of Taylor-made dresses. In 1940 Bowling Green gained one of its largest industries with the completion of the Union Underwear factory. Between 1960 and 1970 the city grew rapidly, surpassing Ashland, Paducah, and Newport in size. After the completion of I-65 through the area in the late 1960s, Bowling Green attracted new industry. One of the city's largest employers, the General Motors Corporation, completed a plant in 1980 for assembling its Corvette automobile line.

Other major employers are Holley Automotive, which builds carburetors and other automotive parts, and the Eaton Corporation, which produces electronic parts.

Bowling Green is the largest city in southern Kentucky. The population of the second-class city was 36,253 in 1970; 40,450 in 1980; and 40,641 in 1990.

See Nancy D. Baird, Carol Crowe-Carraco, and Michael L. Morse, *Bowling Green, A Pictorial History* (Norfolk, Va., 1983).   RON D. BRYANT

BOWLING GREEN ACADEMY. Bowling Green Academy was established in 1902 and incorporated in 1904 as an educational institution for blacks. The school, operated by the Kentucky Synod of the Colored Cumberland Presbyterian Church, stressed the values of interracial cooperation and good will. It consisted initially of primary, secondary, and high school departments; a Bible department was later opened to provide religious training. The school eventually came to own more than $15,000 worth of property and for a while had an annual enrollment of over 150 students. The Rev. William Wolfe served as president of the academy. The school closed in 1933.

BOWMAN, JOHN BRYAN. John Bryan Bowman, lawyer and founder of Kentucky University, son of John and Mary (Mechum) Bowman, was born on October 16, 1824, in Mercer County, Kentucky. He grew up a devoted member of the Christian Church (Disciples of Christ) and graduated in 1842 from Bacon College in Harrodsburg. He read law, and married Mary Dorcas Williams of Bourbon County in 1846. Bowman farmed his estate near Harrodsburg until the collapse of Bacon College, of which he was then a trustee. He then took the lead in founding Kentucky University in 1858 on the old Bacon College site and under control of the Disciples of Christ. He moved it to Lexington in 1865 for a merger with Transylvania University, and to found at the same time the state's Agricultural and Mechanical College as a unit of the expanding institution, over which, with the title of regent, he was the chief administrative officer.

Bowman's vision of a great modern university offering practical as well as moral training to young men of all walks of life seemed attainable, but growing criticism, chiefly from within his church, brought it to an end. In 1878 the state withdrew its A&M College from the university, where the board of curators abolished the office of regent, and the Bowman era came to an end. He then lived in the Southwest. In his last illness, Bowman returned to Harrodsburg, where he died September 22, 1891, in the home of his brother-in-law, John Augustus Williams. He was buried in the Lexington Cemetery.

See John W. Wayland, *The Bowmans: A Pioneering Family in Virginia, Kentucky and the Northwest Territory* (Staunton, Va., 1943).

JAMES F. HOPKINS

BOWMAN FIELD. Bowman Field, Kentucky's oldest continuously operated public airfield, is located east of the center of Louisville on Taylorsville Road (KY 155). It has no commercial flight service. Col. John Floyd first owned the land in the 1700s and it remained in the hands of his family until the federal government seized it under the Alien Property Act of 1917. The property had passed to Floyd's descendant Mary Caldwell, who married a German, Baron Von Zedwitz. Both died before World War I, and the government seized the land from their heirs.

In 1919 Abraham H. Bowman leased fifty acres of the land from the federal government and established Bowman Field with his partner, aviator Robert Gast. Although he never learned to fly, Bowman was an aviation enthusiast and furnished the first plane for the airfield, a Canadian Jenny. In 1922 the federal government leased the airfield to the U.S. Army Air Corps Reserve for five years at $1 annually. Seven years later the army obtained a thirty-five-year lease for a portion of the field to be used as a depot.

The Aero Club of Kentucky, founded in 1922 by aviation enthusiasts, spearheaded the effort to make Bowman Field a municipal airport. Voters approved a parks bond issue of $750,000 to purchase the Von Zedwitz property. Seneca Park was created adjacent to the airfield with some of the unused land. Bowman Field acquired a weather station in 1930, and in 1938 the Works Progress Administration replaced the airfield's sod runways with concrete. On August 1, 1928, Continental Airlines (now American Airlines) initiated mail flights between Louisville and Cleveland, Ohio; in 1931 it started passenger service through Louisville. Eastern Airlines opened a Chicago-Miami route in 1934.

During World War II thousands of troops were housed and trained at Bowman, and the Glider Pilot Combat Training School was started there in 1943. After the war the airfield facilities were sold to either private owners or the Louisville and Jefferson County Air Board. It remained home to the 100th Division of the Army Reserve. On November 15, 1947, all commercial airline operations were moved to the larger Standiford Field.

Bowman Field serves the general aviation needs of corporate and private interests, providing fuel, maintenance, and flight instruction to the public. After World War II more than twenty-two flying services operated there, including Louisville Flying Service, Cardinal Aviation Inc., Kentucky Flying Service, and Central American Flying Service.

See R.C. Riebel, *Louisville Panorama* (Louisville 1960).

BOWMAN'S STATION. Col. John Bowman, first county lieutenant and military governor of Kentucky, established Bowman's Station on Cane Run in Mercer County in the fall of 1779. Crude log shelters initially housed at least seven families (those of Robert Bowmar, Stephen Collins, Joseph

Collins, Elisha and Robert Pruett, William Hall, James Cox, and Thomas Glass) during the severe winter of 1779-80. By the spring, when cabin-building began in earnest, the station's population grew to twenty-eight families, with a few more arriving in June. Though never stockaded, the cabins were built in a protected valley and formed a half-H plan, flanking a small tributary. John Bowman was frequently absent, participating in Kentucky's defense against the British during the Revolutionary War, but the station housed his family and served as his home base. Despite his reportedly irascible temper and opinionated character, Bowman was admired by his fellow pioneers for his bravery and daring. He died in 1784 at the age of 50. His son, John, later built a brick house that still stands near the station site.

See Nancy O'Malley, *Stockading Up*, Archaeological Report 127, Department of Anthropology, University of Kentucky, 1987; John Walter Wayland, *The Bowmans, A Pioneering Family in Virginia, Kentucky and the Northwest Territory* (Staunton, Va., 1943).   NANCY O'MALLEY

BOYD, LINN. Linn Boyd, who represented western Kentucky for seven terms in the U.S. Congress, was born in Nashville on November 22, 1800. Of Scottish descent, the Boyd family had been early settlers in Virginia. James Boyd, Linn's grandfather, and Linn's father, Abraham, both served in the Revolutionary War. Boyd grew up as a laborer and had little schooling. In 1826 he moved into the Jackson Purchase, settling on a farm in Calloway County, and the next year was elected to the Kentucky legislature. In 1828-29 he served as a representative of Calloway County at the same time that his father was representing Trigg County. In 1831 Boyd moved to Trigg County, which then sent him to the legislature. Boyd was defeated for the U.S. Congress as a Democrat in 1833 but was elected in 1835 and served from March 4, 1835 until March 3, 1837. He was unseated in 1837 when the Whigs swept Kentucky.

The Democrats regained control of the 1st Congressional District in Kentucky, and Boyd served continuously in the U.S. House of Representatives from March 4, 1839 to March 3, 1855, often running without opposition. Boyd was a staunch supporter of Andrew Jackson. Calling for the annexation of Texas after its separation from Mexico in 1836, Boyd took an active part in the maneuvers leading up to the successful joint resolution requested by President John Tyler on March 1, 1845. Boyd's role in working for Henry Clay's Compromise of 1850 in the House is often overlooked. Both Clay and Boyd were devoted to southern rights but insisted on preserving the Union. In the House, Speaker Howell Cobb, a close friend of Boyd, allowed him to preside in September during a critical debate on Boyd's "little omnibus" bill, which combined the measure for defining the Texas boundary and assumption of the Texas debt with a proposal to organize the New Mexico Territory.

Boyd became a prominent figure in Washington as a result of his efforts on behalf of the Compromise of 1850, and he was made Speaker of the House for the remainder of his congressional career (1851-55). In 1856 he was Kentucky's favorite son for the vice-presidency but was unsuccessful. In 1859, Boyd was elected lieutenant-governor of Kentucky but did not live to fill the position.

Boyd married Alice C. Bennett of Trigg County in 1832. In 1850 he married a widow from Pennsylvania, Anna L. Dixon. Boyd moved to Paducah in 1852 and built Oaklands, a spacious brick home. He died on December 17, 1859, and was buried in Oak Grove Cemetery at Paducah.

See Holman Hamilton, *Prologue to Conflict: The Crisis and Compromise of 1850* (Lexington, Ky., 1964).   JOHN E. L. ROBERTSON

BOYD COUNTY. Boyd County, the 107th county in order of formation, is located at the eastern edge of the state on the Ohio and Big Sandy rivers and totals 160 square miles. The county was created in 1860 from parts of Greenup, Carter, and Lawrence counties and named for Linn Boyd of Paducah, former U.S. congressman, who died in 1859 soon after being elected lieutenant governor of Kentucky. The first county judge of Boyd was John D. Ross; the first sheriff, William Williams; and the first clerk, J.W. Riely. The county seat is CATLETTSBURG.

Along the broad river bottoms, numerous mounds containing human skeletons, burial goods, and other artifacts give evidence that prehistoric Native Americans inhabited the area. In 1973 archeologists discovered a serpent-shaped mound built of rocks dating to 2000 B.C. It stretched for nine hundred feet along the top of a ridge parallel to the Big Sandy River south of Catlettsburg.

One of the early settlers in what is now Boyd County was Charles ("One-handed Charley") Smith, from Frederick County, Virginia. A veteran of the French and Indian War who had served under Col. George Washington in 1754, Smith received for that service some four hundred acres around Chadwicks Creek, where he built a cabin in 1774. This land was known as the Savage grant because it was part of 28,627 acres at the Ohio and Big Sandy rivers that had been granted to Lt. John Savage and his soldiers by Virginia Governor Dunmore on December 15, 1772. Smith died in 1776 and his land eventually passed into the hands of Alexander Catlett and his heirs, who came to the area in 1797 and for whom the town of Catlettsburg was named. Settlers began to arrive in increasing numbers after the Battle of Fallen Timbers in 1794, which had eased the danger of Indian predation. The Poages came from Staunton, Virginia, in October 1799 and formed Poage Settlement, now the city of ASHLAND. They founded the first church, Bethesda (Presbyterian), in 1819. Col. William Grayson's heirs came to what is now Carter County to claim his 70,000-acre grant, part of which helped form Boyd County.

The Poages acquired most of the land above and below Ashland and many tracts west of the city. George, William, Thomas, and Hugh Poage built the steam-powered Clinton iron furnace in 1832, the earliest industry in present-day Boyd County. In 1834 John C. and Jacob Kouns built Oakland furnace, which closed in 1849. As part of the Hanging Rock iron ore region, this area attracted German and Irish immigrant laborers, ironmasters from Pennsylvania, and wealthy investors from the South and East. Buena Vista furnace was built in 1847, Sandy furnace in 1853, Ashland furnace in 1869, Norton furnace in 1873, and Princess furnace in 1876. A total of twenty-nine charcoal-fueled iron furnaces operated on the Kentucky side of the Ohio River, seven of them in what is now Boyd County.

The Kentucky Iron, Coal and Manufacturing Company was incorporated on March 8, 1854, and it laid out the town of Ashland, then within Greenup County. The company purchased thousands of acres of coal, timber, and ore lands throughout the county. It invested $210,000 in bonds of the Lexington & Big Sandy River Railroad Company, with the stipulation that the eastern division of that line extend into Ashland instead of ending, as originally planned, in Catlettsburg. By 1857 the first ten miles of track had been opened from Ashland to Princess. The line was extended to Coalton in 1858 and to Rush in 1872. In 1880 the name of the line was changed to Ashland Coal & Iron Railroad. Chattaroi Railway Company was incorporated on March 11, 1873, and by 1882 its track reached up the Sandy River to the Peach Orchard mines in Lawrence County. The Ohio & Big Sandy Railroad was incorporated on August 20, 1889, and operated until 1892. The Chesapeake & Ohio Railroad eventually purchased these rail lines.

On December 21, 1921, Ashland furnace was sold to American Rolling Mill Company of Middletown, Ohio, which developed into Armco Steel Corporation, a major business in eastern Kentucky. In 1969 Armco constructed the Amanda furnace, one of the largest blast furnaces in the world.

Ashland Oil, Inc., the largest corporation headquartered in Kentucky, was started in 1924 at a small refinery at Leach Station, south of Catlettsburg.

Boyd County's population was 52,376 in 1970; 55,513 in 1980; and 51,150 in 1990.

See Donald E. Rist, *Iron Furnaces of the Hanging Rock Iron Region* (Ashland, Ky., 1974); Elmer G. Sulzer, *Ghost Railroads of Kentucky* (Indianapolis 1967).   EVELYN SCYPHERS JACKSON

BOYLE, JEREMIAH T. Jeremiah T. Boyle, lawyer, soldier, and railroad entrepreneur, was born in Mercer (now Boyle) County, Kentucky, on May 22, 1818, the son of John and Elizabeth (Tilford) Boyle. He was educated at Centre College in Danville, at Princeton University, and at Transylvania University law school in Lexington, Kentucky. He began the practice of law in Harrodsburg, but later moved to Danville. He married Elizabeth Ow-

sley Anderson, the daughter of Simeon Anderson, in 1842 and joined her brother in business. Although a slaveholder and a Whig, he advocated the abolition of slavery. He served as commonwealth's attorney in 1861.

With the outbreak of the Civil War, Boyle began recruiting volunteers for the Union army and received a commission as brigadier general. His conspicuous gallantry at Shiloh and his knowledge of his native state resulted in his appointment as military commander of Kentucky. Boyle was unable to suppress the guerrilla and Confederate forays into the state, especially John Hunt MORGAN's raid of July 1862. In an effort to stop support for the raiders, on June 1, 1862, Boyle ordered the arrest and punishment of known rebels, assessed Confederate sympathizers for damages done by the guerrillas, and used Union troops to influence elections. These actions alienated many Kentucky Unionists, who complained to President Abraham Lincoln, and Secretary of War Edwin M. Stanton cautioned Boyle. When Gov. Beriah Magoffin (1859-62) criticized Boyle's violation of the civil rights of Kentuckians, Boyle attempted to unseat the governor by questioning his Union loyalty.

Boyle failed in efforts to become governor and congressman from Kentucky. When the state authorized raising 20,000 troops to maintain order within Kentucky, Boyle was directed to enroll black soldiers for the purpose. Boyle protested; his reluctance to enlist blacks, his interference with the Kentucky corn trade, and his efforts to end fraud in securing horses for the army resulted in his being relieved of his command on January 2, 1864. Boyle resigned his commission two days later. He became president of the Louisville City Railway Company (1864-66), and later president of the Evansville, Henderson & Nashville Railroad Company. Boyle died in Louisville on July 28, 1871, and was buried in Bellevue Cemetery, Danville.   ROSS A. WEBB

BOYLE, JOHN. John Boyle, congressman and jurist, was born October 28, 1774, on the Clinch River near Tazewell in Botetourt County, Virginia. The family moved to Kentucky in 1779, settling first at Whitley's Station near Boonesborough and then in Garrard County. Boyle received no formal education, learning the basic subjects from a minister and law from a local lawyer. He began practicing law in 1797 in Lancaster and was elected to the U.S. House of Representatives in 1803, serving three consecutive terms, from March 4, 1803 to March 3, 1809. Boyle then accepted an appointment to the Kentucky court of appeals. In 1810 he became chief justice, a position he held until he resigned from the court in 1826.

Boyle's most significant opinions as chief justice concerned land titles and debt relief, the leading issues of the era. Boyle's court upheld Kentucky's land statutes in defiance of a ruling of the U.S. Supreme Court, holdings that delighted natives and distressed absentee claimants. Less popular was his opinion in *Blair v. Williams* (1823), which declared unconstitutional Kentucky's debt relief law, a decision that prompted the General Assembly in 1824 to abolish Boyle's court and to create a new court of appeals. For the next two years, Boyle's OLD COURT and the New Court operated as rivals. In 1826, when the anti-Relief party captured control of the legislature, it abolished the New Court. Shortly thereafter Boyle resigned from the court to accept an appointment by President John Quincy Adams as U.S. district judge, a position he held until his death. During the last year of his life, he was an instructor in law at Transylvania University.

Boyle married Elizabeth Tilford in 1797. He died on January 28, 1834, and was buried in Bellevue Cemetery in Danville. Formed in 1842, Boyle County was named in his honor.

See George Robertson, *Scrap Book on Law and Politics, Men and Times* (Lexington, Ky., 1855).

ROBERT M. IRELAND

BOYLE COUNTY. Boyle County, the ninety-fourth in order of formation, is located in the Bluegrass region. It is bordered by Casey, Garrard, Marion, Mercer, and Washington counties and has an area of 182 square miles. The county was formed from Lincoln and Mercer counties on February 15, 1842, and was named in honor of Judge John Boyle, former chief justice of the Kentucky court of appeals. The seat of Boyle County is DANVILLE, located in the eastern part of the county. The topography of Boyle County is gently rolling to hilly, with rich, productive soil. Tobacco, corn, and hay are the primary agricultural products. Beef and dairy cattle are also raised in large numbers on the farms of the county. The principal waterways in Boyle County are the Dick's (Dix), Chaplin, and Salt rivers, and many creeks flow through the area.

The area that became Boyle County was one of the first settled in Kentucky. In 1774 James Harrod erected a cabin in what is now Danville. In 1787 the town of Danville was established by an act of the Virginia legislature, making it one of the oldest communities in the commonwealth. Isaac Shelby, the first governor of Kentucky (1792-1796), made his home at Travelers Rest, six miles south of Danville.

Around 1781 James Harberson established a fort at PERRYVILLE, seven miles west of Danville on the Chaplin River. The town was laid out there in 1815 at the junction of roads leading from Danville to Springfield and from Harrodsburg to Lebanon. It was named in honor of Oliver Hazard Perry's victory on Lake Erie in 1813. On October 8, 1862, the largest Civil War battle in Kentucky was fought in the area surrounding the small crossroads village. About thirty buildings in and around the city are of historical interest for their association with the battle. Two miles northwest of the city is the Perryville Battlefield State Shrine, a museum and a cemetery that includes some of the battlefield.

Because Boyle County was a rich agricultural region, recovery from the war was rapid. Industrial growth took place after the coming of the railroads. In 1866 the Louisville & Nashville Railroad's Lebanon branch crossed the southern part of the county east-west. In 1882 the Cincinnati Southern Railroad (now the Norfolk Southern) made a north-south connection with the L&N four miles south of Danville. The city that grew along the railroad became known as Junction City and, along with Danville and Perryville, is one of the three incorporated towns in the county. Junction City, in which the major industry is the Penn Ventilator Company, is largely residential.

Throughout the twentieth century, most of Boyle County has remained primarily agricultural. Commercial and residential growth in and around Danville and along U.S. 127 increased during the mid-1960s and continued during the 1970s and 1980s. Nevertheless, in 1987 farms still occupied 89 percent of the county. Tourism is an important county industry and was directly or indirectly responsible for 430 county jobs in 1988.

The population of Boyle County was 21,090 in 1970; 25,066 in 1980; and 25,641 in 1990.

See Maria T. Daviess, *History of Mercer and Boyle Counties* (Harrodsburg, Ky., 1924).

RON D. BRYANT

BRACKEN, WILLIAM. William Bracken came to Kentucky with the survey parties of McAfee and Bullitt in 1773. He apparently accompanied George, Robert, and James McAfee down the Kentucky River as they surveyed the area around present-day Frankfort and Harrodsburg. He then went to the Falls of the Ohio, where Thomas Bullitt was surveying. Bracken settled along either the Big or the Little Bracken, two creeks that converge and empty into the Ohio River between Cincinnati and Maysville. Bracken was killed by Indians sometime during the early settlement of Kentucky. Bracken County, established in 1796, was named after him.

BRACKEN COUNTY. Bracken County, the twenty-third county in order of formation, is located at Kentucky's northern border, along the Ohio River. It is also bordered by Mason, Pendleton, Harrison, and Robertson counties. Bracken County has an area of 206 square miles. Mineral resources include limestone, residual clays, sands and gravels from the river, and small quantities of oil.

One of the earliest settlers of Bracken County, who arrived during the 1770s, was William Bracken, a trapper and Indian fighter for whom the county is named. Bracken County was formed in 1796 out of parts of Mason and Campbell counties. The county seat was established at AUGUSTA, an important commercial center on the Ohio River. Bracken County's economy was largely agricultural; its chief crops before the Civil War were tobacco and corn. White burley tobacco, a light, adaptable leaf that revolutionized the industry, was first produced in 1867 from Bracken County seed.

The county is often considered the seat of the white burley belt. Bracken County also achieved prominence in the 1870s as one of the leading wine-producing counties in the United States, with an annual production of 30,000 gallons. Agriculture remains vital to the economy, with farms occupying 83.8 percent of the land area in 1982. Commodities include wheat, hay, and milk. Burley tobacco production in 1988 amounted to 5,406,000 pounds. Agricultural receipts in 1986 totaled $19,158,000.

The county government moved from Augusta to Woodward's Crossing (now BROOKSVILLE) in 1833.

Bracken County's industrial and business sectors are rather small, with most interests concentrated in manufacturing and retail trade. One of the larger concerns is a plastics factory in Augusta. The county has been served since the nineteenth century by the Cincinnati-Ashland portion of the Chesapeake & Ohio Railroad. The population was 7,227 in 1970; 7,738 in 1980; and 7,766 in 1990.

See *Recollections: Yesterday, Today for Tomorrow 1969* (Brooksville, Ky., 1969).

BRADEN AFFAIR. Just past midnight on June 27, 1954, a time of high racial tensions, an explosion ripped through the Louisville home of black electrician Andrew Wade IV. Since the late 1940s, Louisville had integrated its libraries, city golf courses, amphitheaters, medical and bar associations, civil service, police department, and university. Rigid segregation still characterized Louisville's housing patterns, however.

When Wade, a Korean war veteran, had been unable to find a suitable home for his family, he sought the help of two white acquaintances, Carl and Anne Braden. Carl Braden, a copy editor at the *Louisville Courier-Journal*, was an avowed socialist and trade unionist; his wife, Anne, was a journalist and social activist. Native southerners and committed integrationists, the Bradens purchased a home in a previously all-white neighborhood, then transferred title to Wade. When the Wades moved in in May, they immediately became the victims of fierce harassment, including random gunfire and cross burnings. On May 18, the day after the U.S. Supreme Court, in *Brown v. Board of Education*, declared school segregation unconstitutional, the *Courier-Journal* carried two editorials, one endorsing *Brown*, the other lambasting the Bradens. The Bradens' attempts to "force the issue" of residential segregation, the paper said, threatened Louisville's "careful, steady effort" to improve "the standard of Negro life."

After the bombing on June 27, Commonwealth's Attorney A. Scott Hamilton seized on the theory that the incident was an "inside job," designed by the Bradens to prepare the way for a Communist takeover. Nationally, the recent Army-McCarthy hearings had undercut the credibility of unbridled anti-Communism. Yet in Louisville, in a highly charged atmosphere, the Bradens and five acquaintances were indicted for "criminal syndicalism"

against the governments of the United States and the Commonwealth of Kentucky. Carl Braden was the only "conspirator" brought to trial. No evidence was presented to connect him with the bombing, but the prosecution's allegations of Communist affiliation, though denied under oath and never proven, made objectivity difficult. Braden was convicted under a 1920 Kentucky sedition statute, serving seven months of a fifteen-year sentence at LaGrange State Reformatory before the Kentucky court of appeals invalidated the state's sedition law. In November 1956 all charges against Carl Braden and the other defendants were dismissed.

See Anne Braden, *The Wall Between* (New York 1958).   ANTHONY NEWBERRY

BRADFORD, JOHN. John Bradford, pioneer printer and journalist, son of Daniel and Alice Bradford, was born on June 16, 1749, in Fauquier County, Virginia. He served briefly in 1776 in the Revolutionary War. Bradford arrived in Kentucky in 1779 and in 1780 worked as a land surveyor under George May. He also participated in the campaign against the Indian towns of Chillicothe and Piqua.

At Kentucky's first separation convention, held in Danville in December 1784, it was agreed that a newspaper was needed to unite the citizens of Kentucky and to spread news of the struggle to separate from Virginia. Despite having no experience in the printing business, Bradford was assured public patronage by the 1786 convention in exchange for establishing a weekly newspaper. He and his brother, Fielding, procured the printing materials and machinery in Philadelphia. The first edition of the *Kentucke Gazette* (a spelling changed to *Kentucky Gazette* on March 7, 1789) was published in Lexington on August 11, 1787. Bradford became an accomplished printer and journalist, overcoming lack of skilled workers and at times a scarcity of paper. The *Gazette* published foreign, national, and local news, public announcements, advertisements, and the early volumes of the *Acts of the General Assembly*. A later popular feature of the newspaper was Bradford's *Notes on Kentucky*, a series of sixty-six articles appearing from August 1826 to January 1829, in which Bradford wrote about early Kentucky history.

From its inception until 1795, the *Gazette* was the only newspaper published within five hundred miles of Lexington. His son Daniel took over the newspaper in April 1802, but Bradford returned as editor from May 1825 until June 1827. Bradford's press also printed the *Kentucky Almanac*, an annual containing astronomical and meteorological data as well as general information, published between 1788 and 1807.

Bradford held the state contract as public printer from 1792 to 1798, excepting 1796. After losing the contract to Col. William Hunter, publisher of the *Palladium*, a Frankfort newspaper, Bradford and his son James began publishing the *Guardian of*

Freedom in Frankfort to compete with Hunter's newspaper. When the move to win back the state printing contract failed, Bradford resigned his position as editor in 1803, and James took control of the *Guardian*.

On April 11, 1792, Bradford was elected to the board of trustees of Lexington's Transylvania University. A year later he became chairman, a position he held with a few periods of absence until his death. He helped found Lexington's first public library in 1795. Bradford also was chairman of the board of trustees of the City of Lexington and sheriff of Fayette County. He served two terms as a representative in the state legislature, starting in 1797 and 1802.

Bradford married Eliza James of Fauquier County, Virginia, in 1771; they had five sons and four daughters. He died on March 20, 1830, in Lexington, and was buried at an early burial site where the First Baptist Church of Lexington was later built.

See Richard Miller Hadsell, "John Bradford and His Contributions to the Culture and the Life of Early Lexington and Kentucky," *Register* 62 (Oct. 1964): 265-77; J. Winston Coleman, "John Bradford and The Kentucky Gazette," *FCHQ* 34 (Jan. 1960): 24-34.

BRADLEY, WILLIAM O'CONNELL. The state's first Republican governor, William O'Connell Bradley (1895-99) was born in Garrard County, Kentucky, on March 18, 1847, to Robert McAfee and Nancy Ellen (Totten) Bradley. The family moved to Somerset, where Bradley attended school. Age thwarted his attempt to enlist in the Union army, and because of his youth a special legislative act was required to let him be examined for the bar in 1865. Bradley was elected county attorney in 1870, but as a Republican he suffered several defeats in elections for various offices. An excellent public speaker of an arresting appearance, "Billy O' B" became the leading Republican in the state, frequently attending national meetings. In 1887 he opposed Simon Bolivar Buckner for governor on a platform that emphasized improvements in education, a high protective tariff, development of mineral resources, and criticism of Democratic spending. Bradley received strong support from black voters, and although he lost to Buckner, 143,466 to 126,754, it was the best showing that had been made by a Republican candidate for governor. Nominated again in 1895, Bradley stressed the scandals and factionalism in the Democratic party. A number of Gold Democrats supported him as their party moved toward free silver, and poor economic conditions hurt the Democrats. Bradley was attacked for his party's alleged dominance by black voters, but he beat Democrat P. Wat Hardin, 172,436 to 163,524.

During Bradley's term as governor, the Democrats controlled the Senate, while the Republicans had a majority in the House; this deadlock, as well as infighting within the Democratic party, contributed to the making of one of the weakest administrations of the century. In 1898 the GOEBEL ELECTION LAW was passed over Bradley's veto, giving control in disputed elections to a three-man commission. Bradley continued efforts to curb violence in the eastern part of the state, and he also had to contend with the tollgate wars that were especially prevalent in central Kentucky. An ineffective compulsory school law was passed during his term, and two reform houses were established for minors. A pure food and drug act became law without the governor's signature. As his term ended in 1899, Bradley became an influential adviser to William S. Taylor in the gubernatorial election. In 1900 Bradley lost his bid for a seat in the U.S. Senate, but he won election in 1908, 64 to 60, over J.C.W. Beckham, with the vital aid of four "wet" Democratic votes.

Bradley married Margaret R. Duncan in 1867; they had a son and a daughter. Bradley died in Washington on May 23, 1914, before his term as senator expired, and was buried in Frankfort.

See Hambleton Tapp and James C. Klotter, *Kentucky: Decades of Discord, 1865-1900* (Frankfort, Ky., 1977); Maurice H. Thatcher, *Stories and Speeches of William O. Bradley* (Lexington, Ky., 1916); Lowell H. Harrison, ed., *Kentucky's Governors 1792-1985* (Lexington, Ky., 1985).

LOWELL H. HARRISON

BRAMLETTE, THOMAS ELLIOTT. Kentucky's governor from 1863 to 1867, Thomas Elliott Bramlette was born in Cumberland (now Clinton) County, Kentucky, on January 3, 1817. His parents, Ambrose S. and Sarah Bramlette, saw that he received a sound common school education. He studied law and was admitted to the bar in 1837. Bramlette was elected to the Kentucky House of Representatives in 1841. Appointed a commonwealth's attorney in 1848, he resigned in 1850 and moved to Columbia, Kentucky, where in 1856 he was elected judge of the 6th Circuit Judicial District. Commissioned colonel in the Union army in 1861, Bramlette raised the 3rd Kentucky Volunteer Infantry Regiment. He resigned in 1862 to accept President Lincoln's appointment as U.S. district attorney for Kentucky. Commissioned a major general in 1863, Bramlette resigned to accept the Union Democrats' nomination for governor. He defeated regular Democrat Charles A. Wickliffe by 68,422 votes to 17,503. While governor, Bramlette declined nomination to the U.S. Congress and the offer of nomination as vice-president on the national Democratic ticket in 1864. When he left office in 1867, he established a law practice in Louisville, where he was a patron of numerous public organizations. Bramlette married Sallie Travis in 1837; they had two children. After her death in 1872, he married Mary E. Graham Adams, a widow. Bramlette died on January 12, 1875, and was buried in Cave Hill Cemetery, Louisville.

An able politician, Bramlette provided strong leadership during one of the most traumatic periods in Kentucky's history. While devoted to preservation of the Union and the Constitution, he defended the state against what he saw as invasions of its rights. He responded angrily when the Union army began to enlist blacks and when President Lincoln on July 5, 1864, suspended the writ of habeas corpus in the state. Bramlette protested interference with elections by Gen. Stephen G. Burbridge and other military officers in the state, but took strong action against the guerrilla activities of Confederate sympathizers. Under his leadership, the Democrats swept the 1865 elections, and President Andrew Johnson soon ended martial law and restored the writ of habeas corpus. Bramlette issued a general pardon to most ex-Confederates who had been indicted in the state, as he sought to restore harmony. The General Assembly conferred some civil rights upon ex-slaves, but Bramlette and a majority of the legislators strongly opposed both the Fourteenth and Fifteenth amendments to the U.S. Constitution; the legislature had earlier refused to ratify the Thirteenth Amendment. The governor also protested when the Freedmen's Bureau was established in the state. Not preoccupied solely with the Civil War and its aftermath, Bramlette took pride in the reduction of the state's debt, an apparent decline in crime, and the establishment of the Agricultural and Mechanical College, the predecessor of the University of Kentucky, in Lexington. He was a supporter of immigration to secure adequate labor, the development of natural resources, and the construction of turnpikes financed by bond issues.

See E. Merton Coulter, *The Civil War and Readjustment in Kentucky* (Chapel Hill, N.C., 1926); Lowell H. Harrison, ed., *Kentucky's Governors 1792-1985* (Lexington, Ky., 1985).

LOWELL H. HARRISON

BRANDEIS, LOUIS DEMBITZ. Louis Dembitz Brandeis was one of eleven Kentuckians who have served as justices of the Supreme Court of the United States. Brandeis was also a leader in American reform movements for social and economic betterment of the working class and the leader of the American Zionist movement. Born in Louisville to Adolph and Frederika (Dembitz) Brandeis on November 13, 1856, Brandeis lived there until the age of sixteen, when he traveled to Dresden, Germany, to study at the Annen-Realschule. Brandeis entered Harvard Law School in 1875 and graduated in 1877 with an LL.B. degree, after achieving perhaps the highest academic record in the school's history. He stayed at Harvard for an additional year doing graduate work.

In 1878 Brandeis went to St. Louis to practice law, but returned in 1879 to Boston, where he practiced law until 1916. He and his first law partner, Samuel Warren, wrote "The Right to Privacy," published in the *Harvard Law Review* in 1890, an article that is the cornerstone of the legal concept of the right to be let alone. In arguing the case of *Muller v. Oregon* before the U.S. Supreme Court in 1908, Brandeis included an extensive amount of nonlegal materials, such as social science data, in a legal brief, in a format now called a Brandeis brief. The court accepted Brandeis's arguments in *Muller v. Oregon* and affirmed a state legislature's right to regulate the number of hours to be worked by women per day.

On January 28, 1916, President Woodrow Wilson nominated Brandeis to be an associate justice of the Supreme Court. A long and bitter confirmation struggle ensued in the U.S. Senate, which on June 1 confirmed Brandeis by a vote of forty-seven to twenty-two, with twenty-nine abstentions. He took his seat several days later. In his twenty-three years on the High Court, Brandeis generally supported the validity of social and economic legislation intended to regulate industry and protect individuals, but opposed governmental efforts to curb civil liberties such as freedom of speech and assembly. Many of his dissenting opinions in time became the majority view. Three of his most enduring judicial opinions are his concurrence (which is in fact a dissent) in the free speech case of *Whitney v. California* (1927), his dissent in the wiretapping case of *Olmstead v. United States* (1928), and his majority opinion in *Erie Railroad Co. v. Tompkins* (1938), a federal diversity of citizenship civil procedure case. He retired from the Supreme Court on February 13, 1939.

Although Brandeis left Louisville permanently in 1872, he materially supported the University of Louisville law school, its law library and the university library by donating money, books, and his personal papers to them.

On March 23, 1891, Brandeis married Alice Goldmark of New York City. They had two daughters, Susan and Elizabeth. Brandeis died in Washington, D.C., on October 5, 1941. His wife died four years later, on October 12, 1945. Both were cremated and buried at the University of Louisville School of Law Building.

See Alpheus Thomas Mason, *Brandeis, A Free Man's Life* (New York 1946); Samuel J. Konefsky, *The Legacy of Holmes and Brandeis: A Study in the Influence of Ideas* (New York 1956).

GENE TEITELBAUM

BRANDENBURG. Brandenburg, the county seat of Meade County, is located on the Ohio River. The town was built on 3,000 acres known as the Falling Springs Tract, which was purchased in 1804 by Solomon Brandenburg. Brandenburg later operated a tavern that was visited by Gen. James Wilkinson, Aaron Burr, and John James Audubon. The community grew around Brandenburg's tavern and by 1825 was made the county seat. During the 1820s it became a well-known shipping and trading port along the Ohio River. The town was named in honor of Solomon Brandenburg and incorporated on March 28, 1872.

The first courthouse, a single-room brick building, was constructed in 1825. The second courthouse, built in 1850-51 and severely damaged by Union troops during the Civil War, was repaired and the county collected $1,000 in damages from the federal government in 1894. A new structure was erected in 1872-73, on the original site of Brandenburg's home. This was destroyed by a tornado in 1974. A fourth edifice was completed in 1976.

On April 3, 1974, a tornado struck the town, killing thirty-one people and severely damaging both business and residential sections of the community. Many historic buildings were destroyed.

The population of the fifth-class city was 1,637 in 1970; 1,831 in 1980; and 1,857 in 1990.

RON D. BRYANT

BRASHEAR, WALTER. Walter Brashear, physician, a native of Maryland, was born on February 11, 1776. Brashear's family moved to Bullitt County, Kentucky, during his youth. He attended local schools and Transylvania University, studied medicine with physicians in Lexington and Philadelphia, and served as a surgeon on a China clipper. Returning to the United States, he practiced medicine in Bardstown, Kentucky, and then in Lexington, where he pioneered in a number of surgical procedures, including a successful amputation at the hip joint. In 1822 Brashear moved to St. Mary's Parish, Louisiana, where he combined his medical practice with politics. Brashear and his wife, the former Margaret Barr, were the parents of seven children: Robert, Walter, Darwin, Mary, Rebecca, Carolyn, and Frances. Brashear died in Louisiana on October 23, 1860.   NANCY D. BAIRD

BREAKS INTERSTATE PARK. The Breaks Interstate Park, at the Kentucky-Virginia border near Elkhorn City, Pike County, Kentucky, was jointly created by the Kentucky and Virginia legislatures in 1954. The 4,600-acre park is situated at the northeastern end of a 125-mile-long ridge of Pine Mountain. The ruggedness of the scenery is a product of the resistant Lee sandstone that was brought to the surface by displacement along the Pine Mountain Thrust Fault, which runs through the park. As the Russell Fork of the Big Sandy River breached Pine Mountain, it slowly eroded the sandstone, creating a 1,000-feet-deep gorge called the Breaks. Rapids were formed by sandstone boulders that collected at the bottom of the gorge. Lee sandstone and part of the Pine Mountain Thrust Fault can be seen in the canyon walls. The park has hiking trails, scenic overlooks, and a nature center staffed by a naturalist. It also has a lodge, cottages, restaurant, picnic areas, swimming pool, and camping area.

See Preston McGrain, "Breaks Interstate Park," *Scenic Geology of Pine Mountain in Kentucky* (Lexington, Ky., 1975).   DONALD R. CHESNUT, JR.

BREATHITT, EDWARD THOMPSON, JR. Edward Thompson Breathitt, Jr., governor during 1963-67, was born in Hopkinsville, Kentucky, on November 26, 1924, the son of Edward Thompson and Mary (Wallace) Breathitt. After high school, he

served in the air force during 1942-45. He graduated from the University of Kentucky in 1948 and received his law degree there in 1950. He married Frances Holleman in 1948; they had four children. Breathitt opened a law practice in Hopkinsville and in 1951 won the first of three consecutive terms in the Kentucky House of Representatives. He gained political experience in Adlai Stevenson's 1952 presidential campaign and Alben Barkley's 1954 bid for the U.S. Senate. Breathitt was president of the Young Democrats Club of Kentucky in 1952-54 and a national committeeman of the Young Democrats of America. As commissioner of personnel in Governor Bert T. Combs's administration (1959-63), he developed a new merit system, then moved to the Public Service Commission.

In the 1963 Democratic primary, which focused on the 3 percent sales tax enacted under Combs, Breathitt, backed by Combs, trounced former Gov. A.B. Chandler. Breathitt won a close race, 449,551 to 436,496, over Republican Louie B. Nunn. Nunn criticized as "rule by executive decree" Combs's executive order prohibiting racial discrimination in businesses licensed by the state. When he left office in 1967, Breathitt returned briefly to his Hopkinsville practice, serving as special counsel to the Southern Railway System. He also held executive positions in the Ford Foundation Institute for Rural America, the Coalition for Rural America, and American Child Centers. In 1972 he became vice-president of the Southern Railway System. He has remained active in Democratic politics from his home in Washington, D.C.

Governor Breathitt won voter approval of a $176 million bond issue that received matching federal funds and allowed him to carry out his plans for highways, public education on all levels, parks, and social services. A state vocational training program was established, an educational television system was started, and the community colleges were placed under the University of Kentucky. In a special 1965 legislative session, Breathitt won a reduction of property tax rates to counter a decision of the Kentucky court of appeals that property must be assessed at its full value. Despite the governor's efforts, voters overwhelmingly rejected a proposed constitution drafted by a thirty-eight-member special committee. In 1966 Breathitt secured a major civil rights bill to prohibit discrimination in employment and public accommodations, a tough strip mining act, a compulsory automobile inspection act, an agency to regulate the use of natural resources, a redistricting of congressional districts, and greater regulation of political contributions and expenditures. Tourism was promoted, and the industrial development program won national recognition. The 1966 budget was 27 percent higher than the previous one, and virtually all state programs and agencies benefited. Backed by federal programs, extensive funding went into the depressed Appalachian region.

See Kenneth E. Harrell, ed., *The Public Papers*

of Governor Edward T. Breathitt, 1963-1967 (Lexington, Ky., 1984); Allan Trout, "The Breathitt Years: 'You Have to Lead,' " *Louisville Courier-Journal*, Dec. 10, 1967.   LOWELL H. HARRISON

BREATHITT, JOHN. Kentucky's governor during 1832-34 and the second to die in office, John Breathitt was born to William and Elizabeth (Whitsett) Breathitt on September 9, 1786, near New London, Virginia. The family moved to Russellville in Logan County, Kentucky, soon after 1800, where Breathitt learned surveying and read law with Caleb Wallace. Admitted to the bar in 1810, Breathitt developed a successful practice and a taste for politics; he served in the Kentucky House of Representatives from 1811 to 1815. He married Caroline Whitaker and, after her death, Susan M. Harris. He was the father of four children. A Democrat, Breathitt defeated Joseph Underwood, the National Republican candidate for lieutenant governor, by 1,087 votes in 1828, although Underwood's running mate, Thomas Metcalfe, a National Republican, was elected governor. In 1831 the Democratic convention nominated Breathitt for governor, with little-known Benjamin Taylor as his running mate. They were opposed by National Republicans Richard A. Buckner and James T. Morehead. With no real state issue, the election was seen as a forerunner of the struggle for the presidency in 1832. Breathitt barely won, with 40,715 votes to Buckner's 39,473, and in the pattern of the previous election, Morehead defeated Taylor for the second spot. On this occasion, Oldham County voters set what may be Kentucky's all-time record for election fraud: 162.9 percent of those eligible participated in the election. Breathitt's illness with tuberculosis was complicated by his clashes with a hostile Whig (National Republican) majority in the General Assembly. He died on February 21, 1834, and was buried in Russellville.

During the South Carolina nullification controversy, Governor Breathitt put Kentucky in a strong Union position. He favored the Jacksonian proposals to terminate the Second Bank of the United States and to allow each state to use its public lands to finance internal improvements, but such moves were opposed by the Whig-dominated legislature. Breathitt tried to get several state banks chartered but he succeeded only with the Louisville Bank of Kentucky. He was involved in controversy over construction of the Lexington & Ohio Railroad, chartered in 1830. He favored its completion. When private investment proved inadequate, the Board of Internal Improvements ruled in 1832 that a state loan of $300,000 would not violate the constitutional restrictions. Rechartered in 1833, the railroad secured a state loan of $150,000, but it was not completed to Louisville until 1851. Breathitt displayed little concernfor public education, although there were signs of a rising interest in that issue in Kentucky. Plagued by a hostile majority in the legislature, Breathitt accomplished little.

See Frank F. Mathias, "The Turbulent Years of Kentucky Politics," Ph.D. diss., University of Kentucky, 1966; Lowell Harrison, ed., *Kentucky's Governors 1792-1985* (Lexington, Ky., 1985).
                                                    LOWELL H. HARRISON

BREATHITT COUNTY. Breathitt County, the eighty-ninth county in order of formation, is located in eastern Kentucky in the mountainous Cumberland Plateau. The county is bordered by Lee, Wolfe, Magoffin, Knott, Perry, Leslie, Clay, and Owsley counties, and has an area of 494 square miles. It was formed in 1839 from Clay, Perry, and Estill counties, and named for Gov. John Breathitt (1832-34). JACKSON is the county seat.

The rugged foothill county is located on the edge of the Eastern Coal Field, where resources include coal, iron, and timber. Major rivers are the North and Middle forks of the Kentucky River and numerous tributaries, which include Quicksand, Troublesome, Lost, and Frozen Creeks.

Stone artifacts found in the county indicate that prehistoric people lived there, often finding shelter under rock ledges and farming the Kentucky River bottoms. The first penetration of white settlers into the area began in the 1780s and included such family names as Haddix, Neace, Noble, Strong, Turner, and Watts. Most of them settled in the vicinity of Lost Creek. By the 1790s, the North Fork of the Kentucky River and sections near Quicksand and Frozen creeks were settled.

The isolated mountain county grew slowly. For most of the nineteenth century it was sparsely inhabited by subsistence farmers; the only industries were logging and salt making. In the 1860s the Civil War ignited a long-running tradition of violence in Breathitt County. No major battles were fought there, but bitter animosity between Northern and Southern sympathizers led to sixty-four deaths, mostly of Confederate and Union soldiers who had been discharged or were home on leave. Capt. Bill Strong led a pro-Union faction of guerrillas in cattle rustling. A dispute over the division of spoils led to the Strong-Amis feud, which lasted into the 1870s.

Feuding between the Little and Strong clans caused Gov. Preston H. Leslie (1871-75) to send sixty members of the state militia to Jackson on September 16, 1874. By the time the soldiers were withdrawn in December of 1874, their numbers had increased to five companies. A narrow margin in a local election in November 1878 rekindled hostilities and caused Gov. James B. McCreary (1875-79, 1911-15) to order troops to the county from mid-December 1878 to February 1879. In the early twentieth century, the Hargis-Marcum feud gave the county the tag "Bloody Breathitt."

The Kentucky Union Railroad (later the Louisville & Nashville) entered the county between 1888 and 1890, and on July 15, 1891, Jackson became the southern terminus of the road. The Ohio & Kentucky (abandoned in 1935) was extended from

Jackson up the valley of Frozen Creek. The railroads opened up the county's timber and coal resources, and the population rose from 8,705 in 1890 to 14,320 in 1900 and 17,540 in 1910.

By the 1920s, most of the timber had been cleared, and the last of the large companies, Mowbray and Robinson, left the county in 1925. Fifteen thousand acres of the Robinson property at Quicksand were donated to the University of Kentucky as the Robinson Agricultural Experiment Substation and Robinson Forest. In 1929 completion of KY 15 gave the county access to Winchester on the west and Virginia on the east. Other county roads were built during the Great Depression by the Public Works Administration.

Breathitt County once had a strong agricultural economy. By the 1930s, however, much of the land had been damaged by erosion or soil depletion. In 1987 farms occupied only 14 percent of the county land area, and a mere 22 percent of the farmland was under cultivation. Crops included hay, corn, and tobacco. The largest employers in 1990 were coal and mining-related industries.

The population of Breathitt County was 14,221 in 1970; 17,004 in 1980; and 15,703 in 1990.

See Writer's Program, Work Projects Administration, *In the Land of Breathitt* (Northport, N.Y., 1941); Green Trimble, *Recollections of Breathitt* (Jackson, Ky., 1916).　　CHARLES HAYES

BRECKINRIDGE, DESHA. Desha Breckinridge, newspaper editor and reformer, was born August 4, 1867, in Lexington, Kentucky, the son of U.S. congressman W.C.P. and Issa (Desha) Breckinridge. He attended State College in Lexington and graduated from Princeton University in 1889. After studying law at Columbia University and the University of Virginia, he joined his father's Lexington law firm.

In 1897 Breckinridge and his father bought the *Lexington Herald*, where Breckinridge served as managing editor and, after his father's death in 1904, as editor. A Democrat, Breckinridge was frequently at odds with both parties in championing such causes as regulation of business, child labor laws, improvements in education, prison reform, and women's suffrage. He married Madeline McDowell on November 17, 1898, and, largely through the pages of the *Herald*, the two became leaders of the Progressive movement in Kentucky.

Active in thoroughbred racing, Breckinridge by 1922 was ranked as one of the top twenty horsemen in the country. In 1906 Breckinridge was instrumental in creating a state racing commission, under which pari-mutuel betting replaced bookmaking. Madeline Breckinridge died in 1920, and, on July 27, 1929, the widower married Mary Frazer LeBus. Breckinridge died on February 18, 1935, and was buried in Lexington Cemetery.

See James Klotter, *The Breckinridges of Kentucky, 1760-1981* (Lexington, Ky., 1986).

MELBA PORTER HAY

BRECKINRIDGE, JOHN. John Breckinridge, one of the wave of leaders who came to the commonwealth after statehood and quickly rose to political power, was born December 2, 1760, near Staunton, Virginia, the son of Robert and Lettice (Preston) Breckinridge. By his marriage into the prominent Preston clan, the father had solidified his status as a member of the local gentry. The son, with his uncle William Preston's aid, became a surveyor, then entered the College of William and Mary in Williamsburg in 1780. While still at school, he learned of his election to the Virginia House of Delegates, where he attended the 1781 session. Breckinridge returned to the college, then in 1783 won reelection and served in 1784. He won election in Virginia to the U.S. Congress, but he did not take the seat, for by 1793 he had moved across the mountains to Kentucky.

Breckinridge's large farm, Cabell's Dale, near Lexington, became home for a stable of thoroughbreds, and its rich fields produced crops of hemp, corn, wheat, and rye (but never tobacco). The 30,000 acres he held elsewhere in Kentucky, plus his successful law practice, ensured his fortune.

Breckinridge's marriage to sixteen-year-old Mary Hopkins Cabell, called Polly, in June 1785 brought a sizable dowry from her prominent father, as well as ties to another influential family. Among their nine children were: Joseph Cabell, Speaker of the Kentucky House, secretary of state, and father of 1860 presidential candidate John C. Breckinridge; William Lewis, church leader and college president; and Robert Jefferson, father of the state's public school system.

In December 1793 Breckinridge was appointed attorney general of Kentucky. After four years in that part-time post, he won election in 1797 to the state House. The next year, his humanitarian reform of the criminal code was enacted by the General Assembly. After the 1798 enactment of the Federalist-inspired Alien and Sedition acts, Breckinridge visited his friend Thomas Jefferson and returned with a confidential draft, written by the man from Monticello, of what became known as the KENTUCKY RESOLUTIONS. Introduced by Breckinridge, with his own modifications, the resolutions passed in 1798. Only years later did Jefferson's role become public; in his lifetime, Breckinridge was seen as the author of the Kentucky Resolutions.

A student of political theory, Breckinridge was a delegate to Kentucky's 1799 constitutional convention. As the owner of sixty-five slaves, as a major landowner fearful of change, as a Democratic-Republican who distrusted the voice of the electorate, Breckinridge led a conservative faction that protected slavery, enacted a more oligarchical system of local government, and instituted voice voting, while compromising to allow popular election of the governor and state senators. Breckinridge received credit as the father of the state's second constitution (1799) and emerged as the acknowledged leader of his party in Kentucky.

In 1800 Breckinridge was elected U.S. Senator by a 68-13 General Assembly vote, serving from March 4, 1801, to August 7, 1805. He soon became a spokesman for President Jefferson, particularly regarding repeal of the 1801 Judiciary Act and the Louisiana Purchase question. In 1805 Breckinridge accepted the office of U.S. attorney general. In so doing, the Kentuckian became the first cabinet-level official from west of the Alleghenies. The post proved relatively minor, its powers few, and its satisfactions fewer. Breckinridge had little opportunity to expand the prestige and influence of the office. He died of tuberculosis on December 14, 1806. He was buried first at Cabell's Dale and later in the Lexington Cemetery.

See Lowell H. Harrison, *John Breckinridge, Jeffersonian Republican* (Louisville 1969); James C. Klotter, *The Breckinridges of Kentucky, 1760-1981* (Lexington, Ky., 1986).   JAMES C. KLOTTER

BRECKINRIDGE, JOHN BAYNE. John Bayne Breckinridge, political leader, was born November 29, 1913, in Washington, D.C., to physician Scott Dudley and Gertrude Ashby (Bayne) Breckinridge. Breckinridge graduated from the University of Kentucky in 1937, received a law degree there in 1939, and was admitted to the bar the next year. After service as an officer in World War II, he set up a law practice in Lexington. Breckinridge won election as a Democrat to the 1956 and 1958 Kentucky General Assembly, where he quickly gained his lifelong reputation as an independent-minded representative. In 1959 he won the first of two terms as attorney general, a post held again during 1968-72. Campaigns for lieutenant-governor twice ended in losses in the primary—in 1963 to Harry Lee Waterfield and in 1971 to Julian M. Carroll. In 1972, Breckinridge defeated Laban P. Jackson for a seat in the U.S. Congress. He served from January 3, 1973, to January 3, 1979, and took a moderate course. He was unexpectedly defeated in the May 1978 primary.

Breckinridge's first marriage, to Frances Knight Archibald, ended in divorce after producing two children, John and Knight. In 1954 he married Helen Congleton. Breckinridge died on July 29, 1979, of a heart attack and is buried in the Lexington Cemetery.

See James C. Klotter, *The Breckinridges of Kentucky, 1760-1981* (Lexington, Ky., 1986).
JAMES C. KLOTTER

BRECKINRIDGE, JOHN CABELL. By the time he was forty-five years old, John Cabell Breckinridge had served as state legislator, U.S. representative, vice-president, U.S. senator, major general, and Confederate secretary of war. His only political defeat came in the 1860 presidential race, when he lost to another native Kentuckian, Abraham Lincoln.

Breckinridge was born on January 16, 1821, the only son among the six children of Joseph Cabell and Mary Clay (Smith) Breckinridge. When John was two years old his father died; the widow, burdened by debt, moved to her mother-in-law's large farm near Lexington and then to a sister's home in Danville. Breckinridge's father was speaker of the Kentucky House and secretary of state for the commonwealth. His grandfather was John BRECKINRIDGE, and an uncle and close adviser was the Rev. Robert J. BRECKINRIDGE.

After graduating in 1838 from Centre College in Danville, he attended the College of New Jersey at Princeton. Breckinridge then studied law under future Whig governor William Owsley (1844-48) and at Transylvania University. After completing his studies in February 1841, Breckinridge began practicing law in Burlington, Iowa.

He returned to the commonwealth and married Mary Cyrene Burch on December 12, 1843; over the next eleven years, they had six children. In 1847 Breckinridge enlisted to fight in the Mexican War. He was elected to the Kentucky House of Representatives as a Democrat in 1849. Two years later he sought the congressional seat of the Ashland district, Henry Clay's old bailiwick. An extremely attractive campaigner, Breckinridge had a charming personal manner. His voice was that of an orator—clear, vibrant, expressive—and he had few peers as a stump speaker. A charismatic leader, the young Democrat swept the usually Whig district.

During Breckinridge's two terms in the U.S. House (March 4, 1851–March 3, 1855), he quickly became known as a supporter of the viewpoints of the South. Breckinridge argued that the states had created the federal authority and, as its creators, were supreme. The constitution he followed had specific, limited powers; groups that attacked slavery were, in his view, attacking property rights guaranteed by the highest legal authority of the land. (Though once a slaveholder, he apparently held no slaves by 1860.) To allow attacks on the "peculiar institution" would be to admit to a flexible constitution, one that could be changed to allow radical, despotic acts.

Declining to run for reelection, Breckinridge returned to Lexington, served as president of the Kentucky Association for the Improvement of the Breed of Horses, operated a small farm, and devoted time to the law. In 1856 his party nominated him to be vice-president of the United States on the James Buchanan ticket. When inaugurated at the age of thirty-six, in March 1857, he became the youngest vice-president in the nation's history.

In December 1859—long before the term began—the Kentucky legislators elected him to the U.S. Senate, with 81 votes to Joshua F. Bell's 53. In the presidential election year of 1860, when his party divided nationally over the initial nomination of Stephen Douglas, Breckinridge became the nominee of dissatisfied southern Democrats. With Lincoln's selection by the Republicans and with John Bell seeking election as a Constitutional Unionist, it became a four-way race. Perceived as a sectional candidate, Breckinridge expected to make few inroads in the North. Yet if he downplayed his Southern ties too much, he risked losing that area to Bell. A moderate tone resulted. Lincoln's 180 electoral votes overwhelmed Breckinridge's 72, Bell's 59 (including Kentucky's), and Douglas's 12.

Breckinridge was elected to the U.S. Senate and served from March 4, 1861, until December 4, 1861. For several months he hesitated in his course, as he tried to avoid a devastating war. He then joined the Confederacy, the most important Kentuckian to do so. Though involved in a bitter controversy with Gen. Braxton Bragg, Breckinridge, overall, performed ably. As a subordinate, he led forces at Shiloh, Murfreesboro, Chickamauga, and Chattanooga, then in 1864 was given independent command of the Western Department of Virginia. During the ensuing campaign, he fought his finest battle, winning a decisive victory at New Market in May, then joined Jubal Early's unsuccessful foray against Washington, D.C.

On February 7, 1865, Breckinridge was appointed Confederate secretary of war. With the end of the conflict in sight, it was a thankless position, but he was perhaps the most effective of those who held that office. Breckinridge fled southward following Appomattox. Fearing arrest, he and a few others made a heroic escape through Florida and across the waters to Cuba.

For the next four years, Breckinridge remained in exile, touring Europe and the Middle East and living in Canada. In December 1868 he received amnesty and the following March he returned to Kentucky. Serving as manager of an insurance company and as president of a local railroad, while still practicing law, Breckinridge remained out of the political arena, although he did speak out against the lawlessness of the Ku Klux Klan. Breckinridge died on May 17, 1875, and was buried in the Lexington Cemetery. A man of unlimited promise, he, like so many of his generation, never recovered from the Civil War.

See William C. Davis, *Breckinridge: Statesman, Soldier, Symbol* (Baton Rouge, La., 1974); James C. Klotter, *The Breckinridges of Kentucky, 1760-1981* (Lexington, Ky., 1986).

JAMES C. KLOTTER

BRECKINRIDGE, MADELINE (McDOWELL). Madeline (McDowell) Breckinridge, Progressive reformer and suffragist, was born on May 20, 1872, at Woodlake in Franklin County, Kentucky, the daughter of Henry and Anne (Clay) McDowell, and great-granddaughter of Henry Clay. At the age of ten she moved with her family to the Henry Clay estate, Ashland, in Lexington. She attended Mrs. Higgins's School in Lexington and in 1889-90 Miss Porter's School in Farmington, Connecticut. During 1890-94 she intermittently took courses at the State College in Lexington. At some time during these years, she contracted tuberculosis of the bone, and a portion of one leg was amputated. Before her illness, she had been devoted to sports and outdoor activities; afterward she immersed herself in intellectual pursuits, joining the Fortnightly Club in the 1890s and leading it in the study of subjects such as German literature and philosophy. She began to write book reviews for the *Lexington Herald*, and on November 17, 1898, she married the newspaper's editor, Desha BRECKINRIDGE.

In 1899-1900 she led the Gleaners of Christ Church Episcopal in establishing a social settlement at the Episcopal mission in Proctor, across the river from Beattyville in the mountains of eastern Kentucky. In 1900 Breckinridge became one of the founders of the Associated Charities and the Lexington Civic League. The former coordinated relief activities and attempted to administer "scientific" charity by the casework method; the latter initiated programs for civic improvement such as parks and playgrounds, public kindergartens, and manual training in the city's schools. For many years the moving spirit of these two organizations, she acquired both inspiration and practical information from her sister-in-law, Sophonisba P. BRECKINRIDGE, a pioneer in the professionalization of social work at the University of Chicago. Contacts made through Sophonisba enabled her to bring many of Chicago's leading Progressives to Lexington to speak on various reforms.

One of the first projects undertaken by the Civic League was development of a playground in Irishtown, the poorest section of the city. Beginning with a summer playground in 1901, the work soon encompassed a kindergarten and a four-grade elementary school. With cooperation between the league and the city, parks and playgrounds were soon added in other parts of town. Under Breckinridge's leadership the league advocated the introduction of manual training in the schools, compulsory school attendance, and child labor laws. In 1903 Jane Addams, the Hull House reformer, came to Lexington to speak on these subjects, and in 1907 the school board appropriated money to begin manual training in carpentry and domestic science. In 1908 the Civic League undertook, with the help of the school board, to build a model school in Irishtown. The school had a carpentry shop, a gymnasium, a laundry, showers, a swimming pool, and an assembly hall and was open to the community as a social and civic center. Breckinridge, as president of the Civic League, undertook to raise $35,000 to supplement the school board appropriation of $10,000. The cornerstone of the Abraham Lincoln School was laid on December 6, 1911, and the school opened the following year.

While spending the winter of 1903-4 in a sanatorium in Denver, Breckinridge observed the work of Judge Ben B. Lindsey's juvenile court. Upon her return, she led the Civic League in bringing Lindsey to Lexington and advocating a state law, passed in 1906, which established a juvenile court system.

In 1905 Breckinridge led the Civic League and the Associated Charities in initiating work against tuberculosis. A free dispensary was established in Lexington and a state sanatorium became her goal.

In 1909 she became a founding member of the Kentucky Association for the Prevention and Relief of Tuberculosis, and in 1916, working with the Fayette County Tuberculosis Association, she raised $50,000 to build the Blue Grass Sanatorium in Lexington. She also served from 1912 to 1916 on the state tuberculosis commission.

Breckinridge became best known for her work in behalf of woman suffrage. She frequently said she was forced into the suffrage movement by the indifference of politicians to women's pleas for social reform; she concluded that only when women had the vote would lawmakers pay attention to them. In 1908, 1910, and 1912, as legislative chairman for the Federation of Women's Clubs, she lobbied the General Assembly for a bill granting women the right to vote in school elections. When that bill was passed in 1912, she turned her attention to full suffrage for women, serving as president of the Kentucky Equal Rights Association from 1912 to 1915 and again in 1919-20. Also serving as a vice-president of the National American Woman Suffrage Association during 1913-15, she became a popular suffrage speaker and traveled in several states. Her gift for oratory was often compared to that of her great-grandfather Henry Clay. In 1919 she broke with Laura Clay, the founder of the KENTUCKY EQUAL RIGHTS ASSOCIATION and a distant cousin, over the issue of a federal (as opposed to a state) constitutional amendment for woman suffrage. While Clay opposed ratification of the Nineteenth Amendment, Breckinridge campaigned for it, and it was largely through her efforts that the Kentucky legislature ratified the federal amendment on January 6, 1920.

Breckinridge attended the International Women's Suffrage Alliance in Geneva, Switzerland, in 1920. Returning home, she embarked in October on a rigorous tour of several states in support of the Democratic presidential ticket and the League of Nations. She then began to prepare for a meeting to convert the Kentucky Equal Rights Association into the League of Women Voters. Before the scheduled meeting, however, she suffered a stroke and died two days later, on November 25, 1920. She was buried in the Lexington Cemetery.

See Sophonisba P. Breckinridge, *Madeline McDowell Breckinridge, A Leader in the New South* (Chicago 1921); James C. Klotter, *The Breckinridges of Kentucky, 1760-1981* (Lexington 1986); Melba Porter Hay, "Madeline McDowell Breckinridge: Kentucky Suffragist and Progressive Reformer," Ph.D. diss., University of Kentucky, 1980.

MELBA PORTER HAY

BRECKINRIDGE, MARY CARSON. Mary Carson Breckinridge, who founded the Frontier Nursing Service to provide infant and maternal care in the mountains of southeastern Kentucky, was born on February 17, 1881, in Memphis, Tennessee, to Clifton Rodes and Katherine (Carson) Breckinridge. Her grandfather was vice-president of the United States; her father served as minister to Rus-

sia. Breckinridge spent her childhood in Arkansas, Washington, D.C., and Europe and received her education at finishing schools in Switzerland and Connecticut. She earned a nursing degree from St. Luke's Hospital in New York City.

Twice married (widowed in 1906 when Henry Ruffner Morrison died; divorced from Richard Ryan Thompson in 1920, after which she resumed her maiden name), she lost two very young children (Clifton Breckinridge Thompson, 1914-18, and Mary Thompson, 1916). These misfortunes, combined with her strong sense of social obligation, caused her to devote the rest of her life to the causes of maternal and child welfare. After service in Europe with the American Committee for Devastated France, she took graduate courses in midwifery at London's British Mothers and Babies Hospital and at York Road Lying-In-Hospital and became a certified nurse-midwife.

In 1925, at the age of forty-four, Breckinridge introduced the concept of the professional nurse-midwife to Kentucky when she established the Frontier Nursing Service at Hyden in Leslie County. Riding on horseback, "Mrs. Breckinridge's nurses" provided midwifery and general nursing care to some 10,000 people in a seven hundred-square-mile area in the isolated mountains of southeastern Kentucky. Her experiment, which depended upon local community support, soon expanded into a family-centered health care organization staffed by professional nurse-midwives. To finance the medical care, Breckinridge sought philanthropic support outside the mountains. For forty years she edited the *FNS Quarterly Bulletin* and spent six to twelve weeks a year on fund-raising tours. By the time of her death she had raised some $6 million for her medical service.

When World War II brought the departure of most of Frontier Nursing's British staff and prevented American travel abroad for midwifery training, Breckinridge founded the Frontier Graduate School of Midwifery at Hyden, which expanded in 1970 to include a family nursing program to train students in primary-care nursing. In 1989, after sixty-four years of operation, the Frontier Nursing Service had served more than 90,000 patients and assisted at 22,477 births, with a loss of only eleven mothers in childbirth.

Breckinridge held memberships in the Royal College of Midwives (Great Britain), American Association of Nurse-Midwives, American Nurses Association, and the American Public Health Association, and was the recipient of numerous state and national awards. In 1982 she was posthumously elected to the American Nurses Association Hall of Fame.

Mary Breckinridge died May 16, 1965, at Wendover, her home in Leslie County, and was buried in the Lexington Cemetery.

See Mary Breckinridge, *Wide Neighborhoods: The Story of the Frontier Nursing Service* (New York 1952); Anne G. Campbell, "Mary Breckinridge and the American Committee for Devastated

France: The Foundations of the Frontier Nursing Service," *Register* 82 (1984): 257-76.

CAROL CROWE-CARRACO

BRECKINRIDGE, ROBERT JEFFERSON. Robert Jefferson Breckinridge, called the father of the public school system in Kentucky, was born March 8, 1800, near Lexington, Kentucky, to John and Mary Hopkins (Cabell) BRECKINRIDGE. His father, a U.S. senator and cabinet member under President Thomas Jefferson, died in 1806 when the boy was six; his mother ran their large plantation for nearly half a century.

After attending Princeton and Yale, Breckinridge graduated from Union College in Schenectady, New York, in 1819. He was elected to the Kentucky legislature in 1825 and served until 1830. A near-fatal illness, coupled with the death of his second child, then caused him to turn to religion. Breckinridge was ordained in the Presbyterian church in 1832 and held pastorates in Baltimore and Lexington. During 1853-69, he was a professor at Danville Theological Seminary. Although elected to the church's highest leadership position in 1841, he was often involved in religious controversy. Breckinridge took a leading role in the debates that split his church in the antebellum period, wrote numerous articles and books bitterly attacking Catholicism, and composed lengthy theological works that gained both praise and considerable criticism.

After serving as president of Jefferson College in Pennsylvania during 1845-47, Breckinridge returned to Kentucky, where he was soon appointed SUPERINTENDENT OF PUBLIC INSTRUCTION. After the office became elective, he was returned to the post in 1851 and served until 1853. He obtained legislative and voter approval for the first Kentucky property tax for educational purposes and secured that system in the 1850 constitution; attendance at public schools increased from 24,000 in 1848 to 195,000 four years later.

Although Breckinridge himself held slaves—thirty-seven in 1860—he supported gradual emancipation and colonization and spoke for those causes in state, national, and international forums. He was an eloquent orator, but his combative spirit led to bitter debates, such as the confrontation with Robert WICKLIFFE, a Lexington legislator and attorney, over slavery. Breckinridge followed a political path from Whig to Know-Nothing to Republican. Running unsuccessfully as an emancipation candidate for the 1849 Kentucky constitutional convention, he was one of the last elected public officials in the South to give the antislavery cause strong public support.

Breckinridge quickly sided with the Union when the Civil War started and became a major border state spokesman for that cause through the pages of the *Danville Quarterly Review*. His family sent two sons south, as well as two north, and his nephew John C. BRECKINRIDGE, a former vice president of the United States, was a Confederate general. Yet Breckinridge called for harsh measures against secession, and he eventually accepted Abraham Lincoln's emancipation of slaves.

In 1864 Breckinridge was chosen temporary chairman of the national convention that renominated President Lincoln. But with the war's end, Breckinridge and his supporters became outnumbered as the commonwealth turned antiadministration and even pro-Southern. Within his family, one of his daughters-in-law refused to let him see her children for two years after the war ended.

Breckinridge married his cousin, Ann Sophonisba Preston, in 1823; they had eleven children. Following her death in 1844, he married another cousin, Virginia Hart Shelby; they had three children. His second wife died in 1859, and in 1868 he married Margaret Faulkner White. Breckinridge died on December 27, 1871, and was buried in the Lexington Cemetery.

See James C. Klotter, *The Breckinridges of Kentucky* (Lexington, Ky., 1986).

JAMES C. KLOTTER

BRECKINRIDGE, SOPHONISBA PRESTON. Sophonisba Preston Breckinridge, lawyer, author, and sociologist, was born April 1, 1866, in Lexington, Kentucky, the second child of Issa (Desha) and William Campbell Preston BRECKINRIDGE. In 1882 Breckinridge was among the first women to matriculate at the high school preparatory academy at the University of Kentucky. In 1884 she enrolled at Wellesley College in Massachusetts, graduating in 1888 with a degree in mathematics. From 1888 to 1890, she taught mathematics at Washington (D.C.) High School, returning to Lexington in 1890 to study law in her father's law office. Breckinridge passed the bar examination in August 1892 and became the first woman admitted to the Kentucky bar. Unable to acquire a clientele in Lexington, she moved to Oak Park, Illinois, in 1895 at the invitation of a college friend. Breckinridge enrolled at the University of Chicago and received a master's degree (1897) and a Ph.D. (1901) in political science. She then attended the university's law school and in 1904 became the first woman to receive the degree of juris doctor there.

In 1902 Breckinridge became a part-time instructor in social work at the University of Chicago, advancing to assistant professor during 1909-20. During the years 1907-20, she also held the position of dean at the Chicago School of Civics and Philanthropy, which was incorporated into the University of Chicago in 1920 as the Graduate School of Social Service Administration. Breckinridge was professor there until 1925, dean of preprofessional social service students from 1925 to 1929, and Samuel Deutsch Professor of Public Welfare from 1929 to 1933. She retired in 1933 but remained active as professor emeritus until 1942. Breckinridge taught the first course in public welfare administration and introduced the case study method of social work. In 1927 she founded the *Social Service Review* and remained managing editor until her death.

She wrote and edited over thirty books on urban social problems. Her *Public Welfare Administration in the United States* (1927; second edition 1938) was a standard text for many years.

Actively involved in social work, Breckinridge investigated tenement housing conditions for the Illinois State Bureau of Labor. From 1907 to 1920 she lived at Hull House every summer. A member of the Women's Trade Union League since 1907, she participated in the Chicago women's garment workers' strikes in 1911 and 1915. In 1908 she helped organize the Chicago Immigrants' Protective League and was secretary until 1942. An early member of the National Association for the Advancement of Colored People and the Urban League, Breckinridge also served as adviser to the Illinois State Consumer League. As a social reformer, she advocated social work in the courts and the development of a juvenile court. She was a delegate at the White House Conference on Children in 1919, 1930, and 1940, and in 1925 she attended the Child Welfare Congress.

Breckinridge was also an active suffragist, concerned with women's rights and political equality. Among her many professional monographs was *Women in the Twentieth Century* (1933); her biography of her sister-in-law Madeline (McDowell) Breckinridge was published in 1921. In 1911 she was elected vice president of the National American Woman Suffrage Association. In 1915 she was a delegate to the International Congress of Women, where she participated in the organization of the Women's International League for Peace and Freedom, and she was active in the American Association of University Women. Breckinridge represented the United States at the 1933 Pan American Conference on Legal, Economic and Social Affairs in Montevideo, Uruguay.

On July 30, 1948, Breckinridge died in Chicago. Her ashes were buried in the family plot in the Lexington Cemetery.

See James C. Klotter, *The Breckinridges of Kentucky: 1760-1981* (Lexington, Ky. 1986); Anthony R. Travis, "Sophonisba Breckinridge, Militant Feminist," *Mid-America: An Historical Review* 58 (April 1976): 111-18.

BRECKINRIDGE, WILLIAM CAMPBELL PRESTON. William Campbell Preston Breckinridge, politician and journalist, was born August 28, 1837, in Baltimore to Robert J. BRECKINRIDGE and his wife, Ann Sophonisba (Preston). He came from a distinguished family: his grandfather John BRECKINRIDGE had been U.S. senator and cabinet minister; his cousin John C. BRECKINRIDGE ran for the presidency; his father, a renowned minister, was state superintendent of public instruction and a leader of the Union during the Civil War. Breckinridge attended school in Pennsylvania and Kentucky, graduated from Centre College in Danville in 1855, and became an attorney.

Breckinridge, unlike his father and two of his brothers, supported the Confederacy; he was colonel of the 9th Kentucky Cavalry. On his return from the conflict, he served as editor of the *Lexington Observer and Reporter* from 1866 to 1868 and became a spokesman for the New South and for the less conservative faction of his state Democratic party. Denied political office initially because of his then-progressive racial stand, Breckinridge became an influential lawyer and outstanding platform speaker. Known as "The Silver-tongued Orator," Breckinridge gave sought-after talks across the nation.

Elected to the U.S. House of Representatives in 1884, where he served from March 4, 1885, to March 3, 1895, he was recognized as one of his party's chief advocates of free trade and individual rights. In 1893 Madeline Pollard brought suit against him for breach of promise, saying that she had been his mistress since 1884, when she was seventeen, and that he had offered to marry her after his wife's death. When he married another, she sued. The sensational case received front-page national newspaper coverage and Pollard won a $15,000 judgment. Breckinridge, who admitted that she had been his mistress but not that he had offered to marry her, ran for reelection to the House in 1894 and lost by 255 votes out of 19,000.

His formal political career ended, Breckinridge became the chief editorial writer for his son's *Lexington Morning Herald*. From that forum, he led the Gold Democrats against the silver wing of the party, spoke out forcibly in 1899 against Democratic gubernatorial candidate William Goebel, and defended railroad interests. He also, however, took advanced stands on the race issue, on schools, and on political demagoguery.

Breckinridge's 1859 marriage to Lucretia Clay ended in thirteen months with her death; their child died soon thereafter. He married Issa Desha in 1861; after her death, he married Louise Scott Wing in 1893. Among the seven children of his second marriage were social reformers Desha and Sophonisba BRECKINRIDGE. On November 19, 1904, Breckinridge died in Lexington. After a funeral described as the city's largest since Henry Clay's, he was buried in the Lexington Cemetery.

See James C. Klotter, *The Breckinridges of Kentucky, 1760-1981* (Lexington, Ky., 1986).

JAMES C. KLOTTER

BRECKINRIDGE COUNTY. The thirty-ninth county formed, Breckinridge County is located in western Kentucky on the Ohio River. Bordered by the counties of Hancock, Hardin, Grayson, Meade, and Ohio, it has an area of 565 square miles. Breckinridge County was created from a portion of Hardin County on December 7, 1799, and was named in honor of Kentucky statesman John Breckinridge. The county seat is HARDINSBURG, named for Capt. William Hardin, one of the early settlers of the area.

The topography is undulating and well adapted to an agrarian economy. In 1987 farms occupied 74 percent of the land area, of which 56 percent produced tobacco, hay, corn, livestock, and vegetables. Breckinridge ranks twenty-sixth among Kentucky counties in agricultural receipts. It has deposits of limestone and dolomite.

Among the first settlers were Capt. William Hardin, an Indian fighter who built a fort in 1780, and Christopher Bush, the father of Sarah Bush Johnson, Abraham Lincoln's stepmother. A pioneer community, Joe's Landing, was established by Joe Huston in 1798 and renamed Cloverport in 1828. Huston operated a ferry across the Ohio, the first along this portion of the river, at the mouth of Clover Creek. Tar Springs, a fashionable nineteenth century spa, was located four miles from Cloverport. Settlement in the region grew steadily in the early nineteenth century. In 1821 the state legislature established an early toll road between Bowling Green and Cloverport.

By 1864 the residents of the county were strongly pro-Confederate. Guerrilla warfare became a serious problem. A major figure in the Civil War, Joseph HOLT, was born and is buried six miles north of Cloverport. Holt was postmaster general and briefly secretary of war under President James Buchanan and was President Abraham Lincoln's judge advocate general.

The county in 1870 produced 3.1 million pounds of tobacco and 509,058 bushels of corn. In 1920 Eleanor Beard Inc. began producing women's robes, comforters, and handmade quilts. The Galante Studios, established in 1929, manufactures fabric, pillows, and bedspreads and employs seventy-nine workers. Tourism revenues grew with the impoundment of Rough River Lake in 1959 and the opening of Rough River Dam State Resort Park in 1961. Other travel attractions include the Yellowband and Glen wildlife management areas, boating facilities on the Ohio River, and the Sacajawea Festival each August in Cloverport. In 1989 tourism spending was $7.1 million, a 10 percent increase over the previous year.

The three incorporated towns are Hardinsburg, Cloverport, and Irvington. The population of the county was 14,789 in 1970; 16,861 in 1980; and 16,312 in 1990.

See Margaret G. Smith, *Cloverport, Looking Backward* (N.p., 1977).   RON D. BRYANT

BRENNAN, MICHAEL JOSEPH. Michael Joseph ("Mickey") Brennan, Democratic party leader, was born in Louisville on February 19, 1877. His parents, Daniel J. and Lucy (Hyde) Brennan, were natives of Ireland, a heritage of which Brennan was extremely proud. He received his education in the public and parochial schools of Louisville. Coached by John and James Whallen, the controlling influences of the Democratic party in Kentucky at the turn of the century, Brennan rose rapidly in politics, as he had a sharp wit, a keen memory, a knack for organization, and ambition. He soon became the unchallenged leader of the Democratic party in Louisville. He built the Democratic machine that ruled Louisville politics for thirty years, beginning

when Joseph D. Scholtz won the 1933 mayoral election after sixteen years of Republican dominance.

Brennan was also active in state politics, and his organizational skills have been credited as the guiding light of Kentucky's Democratic party. On March 17, 1936, Brennan was honored for more than two decades of service to local politics at a testimonial dinner at the Kentucky Hotel attended by 1,600 people, including the mayor of Louisville, Neville Miller, and local officials of both political parties. He was appointed to the military staff of Gov. A.O. Stanley in 1918, and was known from then on as Colonel Brennan. He spent his entire life in Louisville, where he lived on Beechwood Avenue. Brennan died on November 25, 1938, and was buried in St. Louis Cemetery in Louisville.

BRENNER, CARL CHRISTIAN. Carl Christian Brenner, prominent landscape artist, was born on either August 1 or 10, 1838, at Lautereicken on the Rhine in Bavaria. From ages six to fourteen, he attended public school, where his teacher recognized his talent in drawing and applied to King Ludwig I for permission for Brenner to attend the Academy of Fine Arts in Munich. However, Brenner's father, Frederick, refused to consent to this.

Brenner's family emigrated to the United States in 1853, stopping for awhile in New Orleans, then moving to Louisville in the winter of 1853-54. Brenner found work as a glazier and house and sign painter while he pursued his interest in landscape painting. The Louisville 1866-67 city directory lists Brenner as having a studio at 103 West Jefferson, one of many he occupied until his death. In 1871 Brenner began painting and selling landscapes of beech trees and scenes in Cherokee Park, the work for which he is best known. In 1873 he exhibited at the Louisville Industrial Exposition and in 1876 at the Pennsylvania Academy of Fine Arts. He completed one of his better-known paintings, *Falls of the Cumberland River, Whitley County, Kentucky,* in 1881-82. Other paintings of his are in prominent collections throughout the country, including the Corcoran Gallery of Art in Washington, D.C.

In 1864 Brenner married Anna Glass, the daughter of an eminent musician. They had six children: Carl, Jr., Edward F., Nellie, Olivia, Maye, and Proctor Knott. Brenner died on July 22, 1888, at his home in Louisville, and was buried in St. Louis Cemetery there.

See Doris Ostrander Dawdy, *Artists of the American West* (Chicago 1974).

BRESCIA COLLEGE. Brescia College is a four-year liberal arts college in Owensboro, Kentucky, operated by the Company of St. Ursula (URSULINES). Brescia's origins can be traced to the arrival of the first Ursuline sisters at Maple Mount, in western Daviess County, in 1858. They founded an elementary school and academy there and by the early 1900s began offering postsecondary courses, leading to the establishment of Mt. St. Joseph College in 1925. The college began offering extension classes in Owensboro in 1946, expanding to both day and evening classes by 1947. The Ursulines began buying property around Seventh and Frederica streets in Owensboro, and in 1949 a joint commencement was held for graduates of both the Owensboro and Maple Mount campuses of Mount St. Joseph College.

The Owensboro campus became Brescia College in 1950, offering a full course of study, and its first baccalaureate degrees were awarded in 1953. The college received accreditation affiliation with the Catholic University of America in 1951, and in 1957 was first accredited by the Southern Association of Colleges and Secondary Schools. Governance of the college remained with the Ursuline administration at Maple Mount during the 1950s, but with the appointment of Joan Marie Lechner as president in 1960 the administration was moved to Owensboro, and in 1964 Brescia College was incorporated independently of Mount St. Joseph Convent and Academy. In 1968 the Ursuline board of directors merged with the board of community trustees, forming the Brescia College board of trustees. The campus grew rapidly, with construction of an administration building, library, and chapel-cafeteria-residence buildings, and a number of older buildings were remodeled. The Brescia-Owensboro Orchestra, a forerunner of the Owensboro Symphony, was organized in the mid-1950s. A five-story science building was completed in 1969.

Brescia College has offered unique programs in speech and hearing therapy, and it organized the first complete program in Kentucky for teachers of the educable mentally retarded. The music program adopted the Suzuki methods for teaching young musicians, and in 1980 the Weekend College program began. Intercollegiate athletics also began in the 1980s. In 1989 the college opened its flagship building, a campus center and gymnasium complex.

See Ruth Gehres, "History of Brescia College," *Daviess County Historical Quarterly* 6 (July 1988): 66-72. LEE A. DEW

BREWER, GAY ROBERT, JR. Gay Robert Brewer, Jr., golfer, was born in Middletown, Ohio, on March 19, 1932. Gay Robert Brewer, Sr., moved the family to Kentucky when the child was an infant. The family lived next to the Ashland Golf Club in Lexington, where young Brewer worked as a caddy. By the time Brewer played golf at Lafayette High School in 1947, he had developed an exceptional game. He won three straight high school championships, a state record, in 1949, 1950, and 1951. He began to make a name for himself around the country as one of the bright young stars of golf when he won the national junior title in 1949. In 1951, he became only the fifth amateur in thirty-two years to take the Kentucky Open, earning the title of man of the year in Kentucky golf. He won the state amateur title in June 1952 and was the first Kentuckian in forty-six years to claim the southern amateur title. Brewer won the thirty-first

Master's Tournament in 1967 and the Alcan golfer of the year championship in 1967 and 1968. In 1984, he won the Citizens' Union Senior Golf Classic and the Legends of Golf with Billy Casper, and in 1988 the BMW Senior Golf Classic. In his career, he has won more than ten Professional Golfers Association (PGA) events.

See Johnny Carrico, "Kentucky's Up-and-Coming Golf Star," *Louisville Courier-Journal*, August 17, 1952.

BREZING, MARY BELLE. Mary Belle Brezing, who operated a well-known brothel in Lexington, Kentucky, was born the illegitimate child of Sarah Ann Cox in Lexington on June 16, 1860. She took the name of the man her mother later married, George Brezing. At fifteen and pregnant, Belle Brezing married James Kenney on September 15, 1875. A few days later her boyfriend Johnny Cook either committed suicide or was murdered at the back gate of her home, and her new husband left her. Brezing's retarded daughter, Daisy May Kenney, was born on March 14, 1876. In 1879 Brezing became a prostitute in the brothel of Jennie Hill (in the house where Mary Todd Lincoln once lived, on West Main Street in Lexington).

In the early 1880s Brezing rented a row house and opened her own establishment. In 1894, with the backing of a wealthy Philadelphia client who came to Lexington during the trotting meets at the Red Mile, Brezing bought a house at 59 Megowan Street, which she filled with elegant furnishings. In contrast to other local houses of ill repute, Brezing's had strict standards of behavior for the employees; Brezing required them to be formally dressed while in the parlor. She and her prostitutes soon became widely known, and they entertained a local and international clientele.

Contributions to carefully selected officials allowed her to operate with little interference from the law. In 1882, when she was charged with operating a house of ill repute, she was pardoned by special executive order of Gov. Luke Blackburn (1879-83). In April 1917 Brezing's house, along with the other Lexington brothels, was closed by order of the army for the protection of the young soldiers stationed at Camp Stanley on the Versailles Road. She never reopened her business and lived a reclusive life until her death on August 11, 1940. She was buried in Lexington's Calvary Cemetery.

See Buddy Thompson, *Madam Belle Brezing* (Lexington, Ky., 1983).

E. I. ("BUDDY") THOMPSON

BRISTOW, BENJAMIN HELM. Lawyer, railroad entrepreneur, and national political figure, Benjamin Helm Bristow was born on June 20, 1832, at Elkton, Kentucky, the eldest son of Francis Marion (BRISTOW) and Emily Edwards (Helm) Bristow. Educated at the male academy in Elkton and at Jefferson College in Canonsburg, Pennsylvania, he studied law under his father and was admitted to the bar in 1854. With the outbreak of the Civil War,

Bristow joined the Hopkinsville Guards and helped to raise the 25th Kentucky Volunteer Regiment for the Union. As a lieutenant colonel he fought at Fort Donelson and at Shiloh. He helped raise the 8th Kentucky Cavalry, received the rank of colonel, and assisted in the capture of John Hunt Morgan in Ohio in July 1863.

Elected to the Kentucky Senate in 1863, Bristow served as chairman of the committees on military affairs and on federal relations. He helped form the Unconditional Union party and became its leader. Bristow was appointed assistant district attorney for Kentucky in 1865 and district attorney in 1866. He won a reputation for sustaining the Civil Rights Act of 1866 and upholding the federal revenue laws in Kentucky. As an active Republican, Bristow helped found the Louisville *Daily Commercial*. In 1870 he was appointed the first solicitor general of the United States and in this capacity argued many of the Reconstruction cases before the Supreme Court. Resigning in 1872, Bristow became president of the California and Texas Railway Construction Company, but returned to private practice when rumors began to circulate that he was to be appointed to the U.S. Supreme Court. Although President Ulysses S. Grant nominated him as attorney general, he asked that his name be withdrawn.

In 1874 Bristow became secretary of the Treasury, where he instituted civil service rules. He exposed a safe-burglary conspiracy, a seal-lock fraud, and the Williams, Delano, and Chicago Customs House scandals, but his most famous exposé was the so-called whiskey scandal, which defrauded the federal government of more than $300 million. More than 250 civil and criminal suits were instituted as a result of his two-year investigation, the government recovered $3.3 million, and the annual return to the Treasury was estimated at $2 million. When the trail led to President Grant's friends, Grant intervened. Bristow summarily resigned in 1876. As secretary, Bristow broke the fiscal hold of the House of Rothschild over the Treasury.

Because of his honesty and integrity, Bristow was one of the candidates for nomination for the presidency at the Republican convention in 1876. Bristow Clubs had been formed across the country, but he was not selected, as he had alienated too many party bosses as secretary of the Treasury. When Rutherford B. Hayes was nominated, Bristow campaigned on his behalf. Refusing an appointment as minister to the Court of St. James's, Bristow retired from politics and moved to New York City. His ambition to sit on the U.S. Supreme Court was frustrated when John M. Harlan received the appointment. He withdrew his support from the Republican party in 1884 and as a mugwump backed Grover Cleveland's candidacy for the presidency. Remaining in private practice, Bristow served as an adviser to Presidents Chester A. Arthur, Grover Cleveland, and Benjamin Harrison. He was legal counsel for many outstanding industrial concerns of his day: the Pullman Palace Car Company, Atlantic & Pacific Railroad, Northern Pacific Railroad, Louisville & Nashville Railroad, Westinghouse Electric Company, New York Life Insurance Company, and Carnegie Steel Company. Bristow was one of the founders and the second president of the American Bar Association. In 1876 he received an honorary doctor of law degree from his alma mater, Washington and Jefferson College.

Bristow married Abigail Slaughter Briscoe on November 21, 1854. He died in New York City on June 22, 1896, and was buried in Woodlawn Cemetery.

See Ross A. Webb, *Benjamin Helm Bristow: Border State Politician* (Lexington, Ky., 1967).

ROSS A. WEBB

BRISTOW, FRANCIS MARION. Francis Marion Bristow, legislator, was born on August 11, 1804, in Clark County, Kentucky, the son of Archibald and Philadelphia (Bourne) Bristow. He received a liberal education, studied law, and was admitted to the bar. He settled in Elkton, where he practiced law and farmed. He was elected as a Whig to one-year terms in the state House of Representatives in 1831 and 1833 and to the state Senate in 1846. A member of the state constitutional convention in 1849, Bristow opposed the further spread of slavery (before his death, he freed all his slaves capable of providing for themselves); he advocated an elective judiciary, universal male suffrage, and an equal and uniform tax. He served in the U.S. House of Representatives from December 4, 1854, to March 3, 1855, and there supported internal improvements, the limitation of immigration, and diplomatic and consular reform. At the dissolution of the Whig party, he and John J. Crittenden attempted to form a moderate political party acceptable to the border states as well as to the South. He was one of eleven Opposition Party candidates elected to the 36th Congress in 1859, serving from March 4, 1859, to March 3, 1861.

As a member of the Special Committee of Thirty-three, Bristow opposed the acquisition of new territory, supported the reestablishment of the Missouri Compromise line and, in an effort to prevent the South from becoming a minority in the Union, advocated the admission of New Mexico as a state. Bristow was also one of twelve Kentucky delegates to the border state convention held in May 1861 at Frankfort, where he urged the states to mediate the sectional controversy. Failing this, he helped formulate the Bowling Green Resolves of May 1861, which declared that Kentucky would remain in the Union and that "no just cause" existed for secession. Because of his strong Union sentiments, he and his family fled to Indiana during the war but later returned to Kentucky.

Bristow married Emily Helm in 1831; they had two daughters, Mary Margaret and Martha Maria, and two sons, Benjamin Helm (BRISTOW) and Frank H., who fought for the Union. Bristow died on June 10, 1864, and was buried at Elkton.

See Ross A. Webb, "Francis Marion Bristow, A Study in Unionism," *FCHQ* 37 (April 1963): 142-58.
ROSS A. WEBB

BRITTON, MARY E. Mary E. Britton, a social activist who provided medical care to Afro-Americans in Lexington, Kentucky, was born there in 1855. She attended Berea College and graduated from the American Missionary College in Chicago. Between 1904 and 1923 Britton practiced medicine from her home in Lexington. Britton, a specialist in hydrotherapy and electrotherapy, was a Seventh Day Adventist whose religious beliefs influenced her medical practice. Active in the post-Reconstruction movement to improve the lives of Americans of African ancestry, she participated in an 1895 Frankfort demonstration against separate railroad coaches. She also taught school and served as secretary to the board for the Colored Orphans Home, a major institution for orphaned children and the elderly. Britton retired after twenty years of practice. Her home at 545 North Limestone Street is a site of historic interest. She died in 1925 and is buried in Lexington's Cove Haven Cemetery.
DORIS WILKINSON

BROADBENT, SMITH D., JR. Smith D. Broadbent, Jr., agricultural developer and civic leader, was born to Smith D. and Anna (Hopson) Broadbent on February 8, 1914, in Trigg County, Kentucky. He received a B.S. degree in 1934 and a master's degree in agriculture in 1935 from the University of Kentucky. On his Trigg County farm, with the help of the University of Kentucky Experiment Station, Broadbent developed a hybrid seed corn, Kentucky 103, sold under the name Broadbent Hybrid. After completing work on a seed processing plant at Cadiz in 1946, he became a major supplier of corn throughout the south. Broadbent served as president of the Kentucky Farm Bureau in 1941-42.

Broadbent was appointed Trigg County Democratic chairman in 1952, holding this position into the 1990s. In 1960, he was state manager for Keen Johnson's senatorial bid and John F. Kennedy's presidential campaign. During 1952-68, he was a member of the executive committee of the University of Kentucky board of trustees. As chairman of the Kentucky State Fair board (1947-59), he supervised construction of the Kentucky Fair and Exposition Center in Louisville, which opened in 1956. A later addition, Broadbent Arena, built in 1977, was named in his honor.

In 1934 Broadbent married Mildred Holmes; they have four children: Sarah, Anne, Smith III, and Robert, who took over the family's farm operation in 1983.

See John Ed Pearce, "Trigg County's Main Man," *Kentucky Living* 43 (July 1989).

BROADCASTING. As early as 1892 Nathan Stubblefield, a Murray, Kentucky, melon farmer, performed radiotelephone experiments. His demonstrations of over-the-air voice transmissions did not evolve into full-scale broadcasting, but his work predates other documented experiments with wireless voice transmissions by a decade.

Amateur radio broadcasting began in the early part of the twentieth century. William J. Jordan, of Louisville, operated radio station 9LK as early as 1914. He is credited with installing headphone receivers in the Waverly Hills Hospital in early 1921 and was granted a license by the Department of Commerce on September 15, 1922, for WLAP radio in Louisville. Earlier that summer, on July 18, 1922, the state's first licensed station, WHAS, went on the air in Louisville. WHAS, the radiotelephone broadcasting station of the *Louisville Courier-Journal* and *Louisville Times*, was a cooperative effort of Robert Worth Bingham and Credo Harris. Local radio service followed at WCKY in Covington, which went on the air in 1929, and WPAD in Paducah, which was licensed in 1930. In 1932 WFIW was operating in Hopkinsville; it moved to Louisville in December of 1933, when it went on the air as WAVE. WLAP began broadcasting in Lexington in April 1934. WCMI brought radio into the eastern part of the state when it was built in 1935 in Ashland.

Early stations operated on limited schedules, usually at night, and offered a variety of live programming from local entertainers. Listeners tuned in on primitive crystal sets and were often hampered by interference from other signals until the federal government established the Federal Communications Commission in 1934 and improved service and regulation of the medium. During the so-called golden age of radio, listeners enjoyed local and network programming that included news, sports, drama, and music. Kentuckians also tuned in to WSM in Nashville, WLS in Chicago, and WLW in Cincinnati, stations that sent strong signals into the state. WLBJ in Bowling Green began operation in 1940. WOMI in Owensboro had gone on the air in 1938, and in the western part of the state the Lackey family started stations in Hopkinsville (WHOP) and Henderson (WSON). The people of eastern Kentucky got their own station when J. Francke Fox of West Virginia sought to start a station in Middlesborough. It was raining in that town on the day he arrived, so he drove on and settled in Harlan, where the sun was shining, and WHLN became a reality in May of 1941. All stations operated on the standard broadcast (AM) band.

A unique service developed in 1929 by WHAS and the University of Kentucky (UK) started a tradition of excellence in educational broadcasting in the state. The school, under the direction of president Frank McVey, began delivering daily programs through WHAS from a remote studio on the Lexington campus. Kentucky received national attention with the establishment of radio listening centers where people in remote areas of central and eastern Kentucky could gather to hear radio broadcasts. WHAS and the university worked together to begin the first listening post in Cow Creek, Owsley

County, in June of 1933. Eventually there were over eighty such centers in more than a dozen counties, under the supervision of Elmer Sulzer, the university's director of broadcasting. They remained in operation until the mid-1940s.

On October 17, 1940, UK started its own broadcast facility, with the first program over WBKY from a transmitter and studios at Beattyville in Lee County. The facility later moved to Lexington to operate on the new FM radio band. It is the oldest university-owned, noncommercial FM station in the nation. Several Kentucky stations experimented with the new high-fidelity FM service in the 1940s but had to discontinue operation. There were few FM receivers at the time, and FM broadcasting became prominent only in the mid-1960s and early 1970s. After World War II there was a large increase in the number of radio stations, and television broadcasting began.

The Kentucky Broadcasters Association was formed in 1945 as the professional group of the radio and television broadcasters of the state, with twice-yearly meetings, awards, programs, lobbying efforts, statewide campaigns, and a monthly newsletter. The postwar years saw radio move into the smaller cities of the state, with stations opening in Campbellsville, Corbin, Danville, Frankfort, Glasgow, Hazard, Madisonville, Mayfield, Maysville, Middlesborough, Newport, Pikeville, Paintsville, Somerset, and an all-religious station in Van Cleve. Before 1950 additional stations went on the air in Bowling Green, Lexington, Louisville, Owensboro, and Paducah.

Television in Kentucky began on Thanksgiving eve of 1948, when WAVE, channel 3 in Louisville, broadcast a program of local civic officials and entertainers from a set designed to resemble a Kentucky barn. George W. Norton, Jr., was founder and first president of WAVE. WHAS-TV went on the air in 1950, and Lexington had its first television station when WLEX inaugurated service in 1955 on the UHF band. The first public television station in the state was founded in Louisville as channel 15, WKPC, and started broadcasting in September of 1958. The Paxton family brought television to western Kentucky with WPSD in Paducah in 1957. WKYT in Lexington went on the air that same year, and by the mid-1960s a commercial station was operating in Bowling Green and additional stations entered the Louisville and Lexington markets. Border state stations in Huntington, Evansville, Knoxville, Nashville, and Cincinnati also served viewers in Kentucky. Cable television had its beginnings in eastern Kentucky in the late 1950s, when residents banded together to form a community antenna system to bring in distant signals. Cable television has grown to serve every major city and town with multichannel systems. Technological advances in communications, such as satellite delivery, digital audio, improved receivers, and video and audio enhancement, have improved service to Kentucky from radio and television stations.

Kentucky continued its leadership in noncommercial educational broadcasting when the KENTUCKY EDUCATIONAL TELEVISION network went on the air from Lexington on September 23, 1968. All of Kentucky's public universities and most private colleges in the state operate one or more public radio stations. Public radio and television provide the state's residents with a variety of cultural, educational, and informational programs.

Kentucky broadcast facilities offer a wide choice of programming services. Country music continues to be the most popular radio format and the state has served as a seedbed for the growth of many popular stars, beginning with Bradley KINCAID, known nationwide in the 1930s as the Kentucky Mountain Boy. Traditional country music known as bluegrass has its roots in Kentucky radio shows. The broadcasts from Renfro Valley in the 1930s were the start of many country music programs on the airwaves. Since the first games were aired in the 1930s, sports have been a popular offering of the UK sports network, which has become one of the nation's largest. In 1978 a radio news network was formed, and the Kentucky network continues to bring news, sports, and other programming to stations throughout the state. Television stations provide both network, syndicated, and independently produced programming to viewers, along with extensive local and state news coverage.

In 1990 Kentucky had more than three hundred radio licenses and forty-five television stations. Radio stations were found in 135 locations in the state, with more than twenty cities having four or more stations. Television, too, had spread throughout the state, and low-power stations being licensed will take local television into even small towns. Virtually every home had a television set and several radios, with more than 95 percent of the population being reached by the broadcast media in an average week.

See Credo Fitch Harris, *Microphone Memoirs of the Horse and Buggy Days of Radio* (Indianapolis 1937); Lewis Owens, *WLAP Through Sixty Years* (Lexington, Ky., 1982).

FRANCIS M. NASH

BROAD FORM DEED. The broad form deed derives its name from the complex, inclusive language used by purchasers cf mineral rights in Kentucky from the 1890s through World War I. Such purchases from surface owners allowed the use of the surface in any way appropriate to procure the minerals lying below, even if the result was the destruction of buildings on the land. Many of these deeds were acquired by entrepreneur John C.C. Mayo, who built a substantial fortune by buying mineral rights for relatively little investment. Broad form deeds are recognized in several other states, but only in Kentucky have the courts protected these deeds with such tenacity.

The broad form deed became a bitter issue after 1950, when modern technology was applied to surface mining, resulting in large areas being strip-mined. Despite the great damage done to the environment, the Kentucky court of appeals, at that time the highest state court, on at least five occasions beginning in 1956 protected the rights of the mineral owner, thus upholding the right of contract. The attack on broad form deeds began in the 1950s, and in each session of the legislature during the 1970s and 1980s, efforts were made to limit them. In 1988 an amendment to the state constitution was finally approved to require the consent of the surface owner before surface mining could occur.

See Richard B. Drake, "Documents Relating to the Broad Form Deed," *Appalachian Notes* 2 (1st Quarter 1974): 1-6.   RICHARD B. DRAKE

BROKE LEG FALLS. At Broke Leg Falls, the creek of the same name plunges nearly one hundred feet to the canyon below, a natural wonder that has long been a favorite picnic spot for families in eastern Menifee and southwestern Morgan counties. The falls lies within 100 yards of U.S. 460, approximately ten miles east of Frenchburg. Developed by its owner in the 1940s, Broke Leg Falls was a roadside attraction complete with restaurant through the 1950s. Early in the 1950s the *Louisville Courier-Journal* urged the state to adopt the area as a state park, but the pleas went unheeded. When the Bert T. Combs Mountain Parkway was built in the 1960s, it diverted traffic from the old highway and Broke Leg Falls lost its commercial appeal. The trees in the surrounding forest have been cut by logging companies, and the building that housed the restaurant is dilapidated beyond repair.

         KEVIN CLAY COCKRELL

BROOKS, CLEANTH. Literary critic and educator Cleanth Brooks was born on October 16, 1906, at Murray, Kentucky, son of Cleanth and Bessie Lee (Witherspoon) Brooks. He received a bachelor of arts from Vanderbilt University in Nashville in 1928 and a master of arts in 1929 from Tulane University in New Orleans. He was a Rhodes scholar at Oxford University during 1929-32.

At Louisiana State University (1932-47) he became associated with New Criticism, the most influential critical movement of its time, and worked closely for many years with Robert Penn Warren. Warren and Brooks together founded the *Southern Review* in 1935 and Brooks was its first editor. They also collaborated on a widely used series of college textbooks for the teaching of literature: *Understanding Poetry* (1938), *Understanding Fiction* (1943), and *Understanding Drama* (1948). Brooks's best-known works of criticism are *The Well-wrought Urn* (1947) and *Modern Poetry and the Tradition* (1939).

Brooks taught at Yale from 1946 to 1975. He now lives in retirement in New Haven, Connecticut. He married Edith Amy Blanchard on September 12, 1934. She died in October 1986.

See Lewis P. Simpson, *The Possibilities of Order: Cleanth Brooks and His Work* (Baton Rouge, La., 1976).

BROOKS, FOSTER. Foster Brooks, comedian and radio and television announcer, was born on May 11, 1912, in Louisville, one of eight children of Edna (Megowan) and Pleasant M. Brooks. At the age of thirteen he began his radio career at WHAS in Louisville, where his mother was a performer. During the 1937 Ohio River flood, Brooks and two other WHAS announcers maintained a twenty-four-hour vigil to provide news of the disaster. Brooks later broadcast for WAVE and WKLO radio in Louisville and worked at stations in St. Louis and in Rochester and Buffalo, New York. In the 1950s he moved into television and worked for WAVE-TV in Louisville. Brooks left local broadcasting for a career as a comedian and by the 1960s he was often seen in guest roles on television series. In the role of "Lovable Lush," he appeared frequently on stage in Las Vegas and Atlantic City. In the 1970s this character became a regular on television's "Dean Martin Show" and earned him an Emmy nomination. Brooks was a regular in the television series "New Bill Cosby Show" and "Mork and Mindy." Brooks returns to his native city annually as the sponsor of a celebrity charity golf tournament. The Baseball Hall of Fame recognized Brooks as the author of the poem "Riley On the Mound."   MARY MARGARET BELL

BROOKSVILLE. Brooksville, a fifth-class city and the county seat of Bracken County, was first settled sometime before 1800 by William and Joel Woodward. The settlement was known as Woodward's Crossroads, situated as it was at the intersection of the Augusta, Cynthiana, and Georgetown roads and the ancient Buffalo Trace. The county government was moved from Augusta to the more centrally located Woodward's Crossroads in 1833, and on February 16, 1839, the Kentucky legislature officially transferred the county seat. State Rep. David Brooks initiated the legislation that authorized the move, and the town was renamed Brooksville in his honor.

Bracken County's first courthouse had been built in Augusta in 1802. A new courthouse was built in Brooksville in 1839, and the first session was held in October of that year. The current Bracken County courthouse, the fourth, was built in 1915. Brooksville has suffered four major fires in its history—two in 1899, one in 1919, and one in 1921. Brooksville's population was 609 in 1970; 680 in 1980; and 670 in 1990.

BROWN, JAMES BUCKNER. James Buckner Brown, banker and politician, son of John Thornton and Paralee (McKee) Brown, was born in Lawrenceburg, Kentucky, on November 28, 1872. Educated in Shelbyville, Kentucky, public schools, Brown was a bookkeeper for the Southern Railway News Company in Louisville during 1889-97. He then became cashier in Louisville's tax receiver's office and in 1901 was elected tax receiver as a Democrat. After his four-year term, Brown became cashier at the First National Bank through his connections to city political boss John H. Whallen. By 1908 Brown was president of the bank and by 1911 was president of the Bank of Commerce as well. In 1919 Brown oversaw the merger of three Louisville banks into the National Bank of Kentucky and was elected its president. This institution was to dominate Kentucky banking during the 1920s. However, by 1929 Brown's lenient banking policies had resulted in overextensions on loans. With the onset of the Great Depression, the bank failed, closing its doors on November 17, 1930, and forcing the closure of other banks that had used the institution as depository. Brown declared bankruptcy on December 12, 1930. On February 27, 1931, federal and state indictments were handed down against Brown, including charges of willful misappropriations; he was acquitted of the charges.

Brown's political influence came not through elected office but as a supporter of the Democratic party's Sinking Fund Commission during 1908-19. In 1924 he was appointed chairman of the state Tax Commission by Gov. William Fields (1923-27); he resigned in December 1924 after his appointment was questioned. Brown purchased the *Louisville Herald* and the *Louisville Post* in January 1925 and used the consolidated *Herald-Post* as his forum of political expression. His editorials opposed the antigambling views of fellow Democrat and newspaperman Robert W. BINGHAM. The consequent split in the Democratic party caused it to lose the 1927 gubernatorial election.

Brown married Elizabeth (Barclay) Kennedy on September 9, 1901. Brown died on October 24, 1940, and was buried in Cave Hill Cemetery, Louisville.

See George H. Yater, *Two Hundred Years at the Falls of the Ohio* (Louisville 1979).

BROWN, JAMES GRAHAM. James Graham Brown, real estate developer, was born in Madison, Indiana, on August 18, 1881, to William Pool and Mary Craig (Graham) Brown. After attending a prep school (now Hanover College), he was a student at Purdue University for the 1899-1900 academic year. Brown then moved to Jackson, Kentucky, where he lived for four years while he worked in logging camps. In 1904 Brown went into business with his father and his brother, Thomas, in Louisville, where they opened W.P. Brown and Sons Lumber Company. James Brown took over as president of the company in 1918, and became the sole owner after his brother died in January 1920. He became the premier developer of Louisville and the surrounding area, constructing hotels, office buildings, and theaters in the downtown area along Broadway. In 1923 he built the famous Brown Hotel on the corner of Broadway and Fourth Street.

Brown opened the Brown Wood Preserving Company in Louisville and in Brownville, Alabama, in 1924 to support his development projects throughout the South. In 1925 the Brown Building, office space, joined the hotel and the next year the adjoin-

ing Brown Theatre was built. The Martin Brown Building (now the Commonwealth Building) was built across Fourth Street from the hotel, occupied by retail stores and business offices. In 1929 the Brown Garage and the Greyhound bus terminal were built on Broadway and Fifth Street. Twenty-three stories were added to the Martin Brown Building in 1955. On Bardstown Road, the Brown Suburban Motel (now the Brown Apartment Building) helped transform the area quickly from farmland into highly developed real estate. In 1966 Brown purchased ninety-seven acres of land in the east end of Louisville to develop Breckinridge Square. A horse breeder, Brown owned stables in Jefferson and Nelson counties. He served as president of the Thoroughbred Breeders Association of Kentucky and was a director of Churchill Downs.

Despite his fortune, Brown lived modestly, mostly in a suite in the Brown Hotel, while he was a generous benefactor of charitable organizations. He gave millions of dollars to Hanover College and the University of Louisville and donated $1.5 million to the development of the Louisville Zoological Garden. Many of his donations were anonymous. He is honored particularly for his gifts to the City of Louisville. Brown died on March 30, 1969, and was buried in Cave Hill Cemetery in Louisville. His assets were incorporated into the Brown Foundation, established in 1943, for the benefit of charities.

See Dorothy Park Clark, *Louisville's Invisible Benefactor: The Life Story of James Graham Brown* (Louisville 1978); Kay Gill, *The Brown Hotel and Louisville's Magic Corner* (Louisville 1984).

BROWN, JOHN. John Brown, U.S. senator, was born in Staunton, Virginia, on September 12, 1757, the son of the Rev. John and Margaret (Preston) Brown. He was educated first at his father's local grammar school, Liberty Hall Academy, then in 1774-76 served as James Waddell's assistant at his new academy in Augusta County, Virginia. Brown arrived at the College of New Jersey (now Princeton) in the late summer or early fall of 1776 but soon was forced to flee as the British army approached. Brown probably saw military service during the war, and later served as a private in his brother James's Kentucky militia company in the 1791 Indian campaign. By 1778 he had enrolled in the College of William and Mary in Virginia. Brown abandoned an initial inclination toward medicine and studied law instead because medical training in Williamsburg was inadequate. He studied law under Edmund Randolph (1779), George Wythe (1780), and Thomas Jefferson (1782) and became a practicing lawyer in 1782 or 1783.

Brown moved to Danville, Kentucky, in the late summer of 1783. He was selected as the Kentucky District's representative in the Virginia Senate in late 1783 and served until 1788, beginning an almost twenty-two-year legislative career. Brown served as a Virginia representative from the Kentucky District to the Continental Congress (1787-

88); Virginia member from Kentucky to the U.S. House of Representatives under the new U.S. Constitution (March 4, 1789-June 1, 1792); and U.S. senator from Kentucky (June 18, 1792-March 3, 1805), twice serving as president pro tempore of the Senate. He was defeated in his bid for a fourth term.

Brown, a Jeffersonian Republican, is noted for his behind-the-scenes work on many of the issues that came before Congress, particularly those regarding the West. He campaigned for the new Constitution in 1788 but failed to persuade a majority of the Kentucky delegates to vote for it. Brown worked tirelessly for Kentucky's statehood and its interests. Delays and frustrations in achieving statehood led Brown to enter into conversations with Spanish officials concerning navigation of the Mississippi River, trade, and other matters. In doing this, Brown did not consider himself disloyal to the United States and believed that even if Kentucky declared its independence it would eventually join the Union. Opinion is divided regarding Brown's involvement in the SPANISH CONSPIRACY. Brown also became embroiled in the Aaron BURR CONSPIRACY. His association with Burr in politics and in a canal project at the Falls of the Ohio led to accusations of his involvement in the former vice-president's schemes, but evidence to support this is lacking, and it is very unlikely that Brown would have supported or participated in such plans. Charges against Brown in both the Spanish and Burr conspiracies seem to have been politically motivated.

Brown was one of the first trustees of Harrodsburg, trustee of Transylvania University, founding member of the Danville Political Club, member of the Kentucky Society for the Promotion of Useful Knowledge, and member of the Kentucky Manufacturing Society.

Brown married Margaretta Mason on February 21, 1799. They returned to Frankfort and his home, Liberty Hall, which he had begun building in 1796. Five children were born to them: Mason, Orlando (BROWN), Alfred, Alfred II, and Euphemia Helm. Only Mason and Orlando lived to maturity. Brown died on August 28, 1837, and is buried in the Frankfort Cemetery. At the time of his death he had the distinction of being the last living member of the Continental Congress.

See Bayless Hardin, "The Brown Family of Liberty Hall," *FCHQ* 16 (Apr. 1942): 75-87.

JAMES J. HOLMBERG

BROWN, JOHN MASON. John Mason Brown, writer and drama critic, was born in Louisville on July 3, 1900, to John Mason and Carrie (Ferguson) Brown. Educated at Harvard (B.A., 1923), Brown is remembered primarily for the work he produced as drama critic for the *Theatre Arts Monthly* (1924-28), the *New York Evening Post* (1929-41), the *New York World-Telegram* (1941-42), and the *Saturday Review* (1944-55). Brown's more than two dozen books include memoirs and history. The dozen of them concerned with drama are, as his biographer George Stevens stated, a "comprehensive history of the American theatre for more than four decades—from the early 1920s to the mid-1960s."

In February 1933 Brown married Catherine Screvin Meredith; they had two sons, Preston and Meredith. Brown died in New York City on March 16, 1969, and was buried in Stonington, Connecticut.

See George Stevens, *Speak for Yourself, John: The Life of John Mason Brown, with Some of His Letters and Many of His Opinions* (New York 1974).

ANTHONY O'KEEFFE

BROWN, JOHN YOUNG. Kentucky's governor during 1891-95, John Young Brown was born in Elizabethtown, Kentucky, on June 28, 1835, to Thomas Dudley and Elizabeth (Young) Brown. After graduating from Centre College in 1855, Brown studied law and opened a practice in his hometown. His 1857 marriage to Lucie Barbee was ended by her death the next year. In 1860 he married Rebecca Hart Dixon, by whom he had eight children. Although underage for the office, Brown was elected to the U.S. House of Representatives in 1859. When he was elected again in 1866, the House refused to seat him because of alleged disloyalty during the Civil War. However, he later served two terms in the House, from March 4, 1873, to March 3, 1877.

In 1891 Brown won the Democratic nomination for governor as a compromise between the agrarian and corporate factions in his party. As the campaign neared its close, he finally announced support for the new constitution that was up for adoption. He won over Republican Andrew T. Wood, 144,168 to 116,087, and the constitution was ratified by a wide margin. As his term ended, Brown supported Cassius M. Clay, Jr., for governor, apparently hoping that a successful Clay would help him win a U.S. Senate seat in 1896. He lost interest in Clay's candidacy after a son was killed, and the anti-Brown forces nominated P. Wat Hardin. Brown practiced law in Louisville, failed to win a U.S. House seat in 1896, and in 1899 lost to William Goebel in a bid to become the Democratic candidate for governor. He was later a defense counsel for Caleb Powers in his first trial for the murder of Goebel. Brown died in Henderson, Kentucky, on January 11, 1904, and was buried there.

Governor Brown secured reforms in several areas: tax collection, control of foreign corporations, lotteries, and printing contracts. Some state functions were shifted to the counties, and the governor was empowered to fill vacant offices. However, he alienated some powerful figures and such influential interests as the Louisville & Nashville Railroad and the Mason and Foard Co., an extensive user of leased convict labor. Brown's frequent use of the veto and his caustic criticism of the state auditor and attorney general led to the formation of a hostile coalition within his party. Brown abolished the ongoing geological survey, and the legislature rejected his proposals to strengthen the railroad commission, to make extensive prison reforms, to abolish the parole board, and to create the offices of state bank inspector and superintendent of public printing. The governor angered the legislators by vetoing a number of major acts designed to implement the new constitution because they had not received the required majorities. The General Assembly passed several major acts without his recommendation: a separate coach law, a married women's property act, an act to prevent collusive tobacco bids, a coal mine safety act, an act to regulate grain warehouses, a "free" turnpike act, and a general common school law. Party factionalism gave Brown's administration more trouble than did the Republican opposition.

See John Edward Wiltz, "The 1895 Election—A Watershed in Kentucky Politics," *FCHQ* 37 (April 1963): 117-36.   LOWELL H. HARRISON

BROWN, JOHN YOUNG, JR. John Y. Brown, Jr., governor during 1979-83, was born in Lexington, Kentucky, on December 28, 1933, to John Young and Dorothy (Inman) Brown. He received his bachelor's degree (1957) and law degree (1960) from the University of Kentucky. Brown entered law practice with his father but soon turned to business, having dramatic success with the Kentucky Fried Chicken fast-food chain, which made him wealthy. Brown spent considerable time outside the state, and his jet-set, high-stakes life-style revealed little interest in state politics prior to March 27, 1979. On that day he surprised most Kentuckians, including the other candidates for the Democratic nomination for governor, by announcing his candidacy. Between that day and the May primary, he staged a media blitz that overcame his late start and his lack of a record in office.

Brown committed himself to few specific issues, saying instead that he would be a salesman for Kentucky and would run the government like a business. The primary was so close that runner-up Louisville Mayor Harvey Sloane did not concede for two days; Brown was a plurality winner with 29.89 percent of the vote. In the fall election he won an easy victory over former Gov. Louie B. Nunn, 554,083 to 376,809. After he left office, Brown engaged in various business activities, none of which has matched his earlier success. In 1984, just hours before the deadline, he filed for the U.S. Senate seat occupied by Walter ("Dee") Huddleston. Six weeks later, citing the effects of a serious operation and illness the previous year, Brown withdrew. In 1987 he joined another crowded field for the Democratic nomination for governor, but he came in second to Wallace Wilkinson, a political newcomer whose blitz tactics were similar to Brown's eight years earlier.

Governor Brown owed few debts to old-line politicians, and many of his top appointees were businessmen. His cabinet members, who included a woman (Jacqueline Swigart) and two blacks (William A. McAnulty and later George Wilson), had wide discretion in running their offices. Brown

surprised the General Assembly by not participating in the selection of legislative officers and by playing a much less active role in the legislative process than had been customary for governors. As a consequence, a number of his recommendations were not enacted. Among the failures were multicounty banking, a flat rate income tax, professional negotiations for teachers, and a constitutional amendment to allow a governor to be elected to successive terms. The governor proposed no innovative programs in the vital areas of public education and human resources. A sharp decline in anticipated state revenue and federal grants forced curtailment in the growth of most programs, and in keeping the state budget balanced, the number of state employees fell from 37,241 to 30,783. Under the direction of Frank Metts, the secretary of transportation, road construction was increased, and much of the traditional political influence was eliminated from that program.

Brown married Eleanor Bennett Durall in 1960; they had three children before their divorce in 1977. Two years later, during the campaign for governor, Brown married Phyllis George. They had two children. Brown and his second wife, a former Miss America, were highly visible both in and out of Kentucky as they endeavored to "sell the state." Reaction to the Brown administration varied widely, but few would dispute that he was unusual as both campaigner and governor.

LOWELL H. HARRISON

BROWN, MASON. Mason Brown, jurist, son of John and Margaretta (Mason) BROWN, was born on November 10, 1799, in Philadelphia. He was raised at his parents' home, Liberty Hall, in Frankfort, Kentucky, where he received his schooling from tutors. In 1820 he graduated from Yale University, then studied law. Brown was appointed to the Kentucky circuit bench in 1839, a position he held until 1849, when he returned to his law practice. He coedited with Charles S. Morehead *A Digest of the Statute Laws of Kentucky*, published in 1834. Brown served as secretary of state of Kentucky under Gov. Charles S. Morehead (1855-59). He was dedicated to the public interests of Frankfort, assisting in the creation of the Frankfort Cemetery in 1844.

Brown married Judith A. Bledsoe of Lexington in 1825; they had one son, Benjamin Gratz Brown. In 1835, after the death of his first wife, Brown married Mary Yoder of Spencer County. They had six children: John Mason Brown, Margaretta M. (Brown) Barrett, Mary Yoder (Brown) Scott, Yoder Brown, Knox Brown, and Eliza (Brown) Baily. Brown died on January 27, 1867, and was buried in the Frankfort Cemetery.

See Bayless Hardin, "The Brown Family of Liberty Hall," *FCHQ* 16 (April 1942): 75-87.

BROWN, ORLANDO. Orlando Brown, editor and confidant of Kentucky's Whig politicians, was born in Frankfort, Kentucky, on September 26, 1801. He was one of five children of John BROWN, Kentucky's first U.S. senator, and Margaretta (Mason) Brown. Orlando Brown attended Kean O'Hara's school in Danville and received an A.B. from Princeton in 1820 and a law degree from Transylvania University in 1823. He first practiced law in Alabama but returned to Frankfort in 1830, where he remained for most of his adult life.

His marriage to Mary Watts Brown, his first cousin, on July 29, 1830, produced three children: Euphemia, John, and Orlando, Jr. In 1833 he became joint proprietor and editor of the *Frankfort Commonwealth*, where his facile pen and Whig sentiments brought him fame. He was the first corresponding secretary of the Kentucky Historical Society at its founding in 1836.

Brown's wife died on August 17, 1841, and he resigned as editor early in 1842. Gov. John J. Crittenden (1848-50) appointed him secretary of state in 1848. Crittenden's ultimate purpose was to open his friend's path to Washington as patronage coordinator between the new federal administration and Kentucky. On June 30, 1849, President Zachary Taylor appointed Brown commissioner of Indian affairs, as a result of the patronage connections. Brown was unable to handle the confused Indian situation and resigned effective July 1, 1850.

He returned to private life in Frankfort, marrying Mary (Price) Brodhead, widow of Lucas Brodhead, on October 12, 1852. He returned as editor of the *Commonwealth* for seven months in 1862, venting his wrath on secessionists. He published thirteen chapters of a history, "The Governors of Kentucky," in his paper, but left it incomplete. Washington Irving stated that Brown could have produced works of long-lived literary merit but for his editorial tasks. Brown died on July 26, 1867, and was buried in Frankfort Cemetery.

See G. Glenn Clift, "The *Old Master*, Colonel Orlando Brown, 1801-1867," *Register* 49 (Jan. 1951): 5-24.   FRANK F. MATHIAS

BROWN, SAMUEL. Samuel Brown, physician, was born on January 30, 1769, in Augusta (now Rockbridge) County, Virginia, the eighth of eleven children of the Rev. John and Margaret (Preston) Brown. He earned a B.A. degree in 1789 at Dickinson College in Carlisle, Pennsylvania. He studied medicine under his brother-in-law, Dr. Alexander Humphreys; as a private pupil of Dr. Benjamin Rush at the medical school in Philadelphia for approximately two years; at Scotland's Edinburgh University for two years; and at the University of Aberdeen, graduating with an M.D. degree in 1794. He first practiced medicine at Bladensburg, Maryland, then moved to Lexington, Kentucky, in 1797 to join his family.

In 1799 Brown was named professor of surgery, anatomy, and chemistry and pharmacy at the newly established medical school at Lexington's Transylvania University. In 1806 he moved to New Orleans. On September 27, 1808, Brown married Catherine Percy and settled on a plantation near Natchez, Mississippi. They had three children: Susan Catherine, James, and Catherine. After his wife's death in 1813, he moved to a plantation near Huntsville, Alabama.

In 1819 Brown became professor of theory and practice of medicine at Transylvania. Brown, one of the foremost medical professionals of his time, had a wide range of interests and associates. He corresponded with Thomas Jefferson and partly through the influence of Jefferson, was elected a member of the American Philosophical Society. He is credited with being the first Kentucky physician to write a medical paper published in the *New York Medical Repository*, the only medical journal published in the United States at that time.

Brown was an early supporter and user of the cowpox virus for smallpox inoculation, and he vaccinated people in Lexington as early as 1802. He is credited with inventing an improved method of distilling spirits that used steam; with first suggesting the method for clarifying ginseng for the Chinese market; with playing a major role in establishing lithography in America (ca. 1819); and with helping to introduce lithotrity into the United States from France (1824). In an attempt to establish harmony and a code of ethics among doctors, Brown founded the Kappa Lambda Society of Hippocrates in Lexington around 1819.

After leaving Transylvania in 1825, Brown retired to his Alabama plantation. He died in Alabama on January 12, 1830.

See Bayless E. Hardin, "Dr. Samuel Brown, 1769-1830: His Family and Descendants," *FCHQ* 26 (Jan. 1952): 3-27.   JAMES J. HOLMBERG

BROWN, WILLIAM WELLS. William Wells Brown, novelist and historian, was born a slave in 1814 on the farm of Dr. John Young near Lexington, Kentucky. His mother, Elizabeth, is said to have been the daughter of Simon Lee, a slave soldier in the Revolutionary War, and his father may have been a cousin to his owner. At an early age, Brown moved to a farm near St. Louis with his owners' household. In 1834 Brown escaped to Ohio from the job he held on a river steamboat. He was aided by a Quaker named Wells Brown and in gratitude he adopted the Quaker's name as his own.

Brown made his way to Cleveland, where he worked at a variety of jobs, from barber to banker. As a steward on a Lake Erie steamboat, he was able to ferry sixty-nine fugitive slaves to freedom. Two years later Brown moved to Buffalo, New York, where he was active in temperance reform. In 1845 he moved to Farmington, Massachusetts, to take part in the strong abolitionist movement developing there.

After Brown wrote *Narrative of William Wells Brown, a Fugitive Slave, Written by Himself* (1847), his reputation as an abolitionist spokesman grew, along with fears that fugitive slave bounty hunters would carry him back to slavery. In 1849 he represented the American Peace Society at the world Peace Conference in Paris. He remained in Europe in voluntary exile for five years. During that time he was a regular speaker at abolition meetings and published his first novel, *Clotel; or, The President's*

Daughter: A Narrative of Slave Life in the United States, with a Sketch of the Author's Life (1853). This book was a fictional account of Thomas Jefferson's alleged long-term relationship with his slave mistress, Sally Hemmings, portraying the dehumanizing effects slavery had on her and their children. Considered too controversial for publication in this country, the book was first published in England and went through several printings and a number of changes before being published in the United States in 1864 with all references to Jefferson removed. Over the next thirty years, Brown wrote on the history of slavery, the black experience in America, and the role of black soldiers in the Civil War. He published a collection of slave songs and a five-act play based on his own escape from slavery. His writings, though not literary masterpieces, are significant because Brown was among the country's first and best-known black historians, authors, and playwrights.

Brown was married twice, first in 1834 to Elizabeth Schooner of Cleveland, then to Annie Elizabeth Gray of Cambridgeport, Massachusetts. He was survived by two daughters, Clarissa and Josephine. He died on November 6, 1884, and was buried in the Cambridge (Massachusetts) Cemetery.

See William Edward Farrison, *William Wells Brown: Author and Reformer* (Chicago 1969); J. Noel Heermance, *William Wells Brown and Clotelle: A Portrait of the Artist in the First Negro Novel* (Hamden, Conn., 1969).

BROWNE, JOHN ROSS. John Ross Browne, travel writer and essayist, was born in 1821 in Beggarsbush, a village on the outskirts of Dublin, Ireland, the third of seven children of Thomas Egerton and Elizabeth (Buck) Browne. Radical political views forced his father to emigrate after imprisonment. In 1834 the family settled in Louisville, where Thomas Browne operated a girls' school for seven years. When young Browne was eighteen, he attended Louisville Medical College for several months, just long enough to provide material for his first book, *Confessions of a Quack* (1841), a satire on the medical profession. He also began writing adventure tales, which were published in the *Southern Literary Messenger* and *Graham's Magazine*. After a year's sojourn in Washington, he shipped aboard a whaling vessel and began to collect material for his first major work, *Etchings of a Whaling Cruise* (1846), which exposed the harsh living conditions on whaling ships.

Browne's rambling instinct first manifested itself when he was seventeen and signed aboard a flatboat headed south from Louisville to New Orleans. Years later he wrote his wife, the former Lucy Anne Mitchell, whom he had married in 1844: "I sometimes wish I *could* stay home, but destiny seems to make me a wanderer." By boat, ship, horse, mule, stagecoach, train, and on foot, Browne traveled over much of the world. In addition to writing he worked as a customs house inspector, clerk, sailor, Indian agent, and for sixteen months

as ambassador to China. In 1849 he made his first trip to California, and although he continued to travel and live in many countries, he considered that state his home.

Browne's travel writing includes numerous sketches of western life, originally published in *Harper's Magazine*, and a seriocomic work about a tour of Palestine entitled *Yusef* (1853). "The Indians of California," an essay in *Crusoe's Island* (1864), protested the government's Indian policy. His technical studies include *Mineral Resources of the United States* (1867). Browne influenced two of the most important American authors of the nineteenth century, Herman Melville and Mark Twain, both of whom borrowed heavily from his books. Browne died on December 9, 1875, possibly of appendicitis, in Oakland, California.

See Lina Fergusson Browne, *J. Ross Browne: His Letters, Journals and Writings* (Albuquerque, N. Mex., 1969).   WADE HALL

BROWNING, CHARLES ALBERT. Charles Albert ("Tod") Browning, the so-called Edgar Allen Poe of the cinema, was born in Louisville, Kentucky, on July 12, 1881. His parents were Charles and Lydia J. (Fitzgerald) Browning. He attended Louisville Boys High School, and for several years worked as a stockboy and clerk at a wholesale saddlery. In late 1899 or early 1900, Browning left home to join a circus. Performing as a clown and contortionist, he later joined the World of Mirth vaudeville troupe. In 1913 Browning began working as an actor for cinema director D.W. GRIFFITH in New York. In October 1913 Browning followed Griffith to Hollywood, where he continued to act and began to write scripts and direct two-reelers. He played a crook in "The Modern Story" section of Griffith's *Intolerance* (1916), and was also one of Griffith's assistant directors on *Intolerance*.

In 1917 Browning and Wilfred Lucas codirected the feature film *Jim Bludso*. The following year Browning married Alice Houghton. In 1919 Browning, as director and screenwriter, collaborated with Lon Chaney, Sr., the actor, on *The Wicked Darling*. Working with Chaney on a total of ten films, including *The Unholy Three* (1925) and *The Unknown* (1927), Browning found his niche in atmospheric horror films. Browning was best known for directing *Dracula* (1931), starring Bela Lugosi, a classic of early horror films, and *Freaks* (1932). Now a cult classic, *Freaks* aroused such controversy after its original release that the studio withdrew it from general circulation, and it was rarely seen until it was honored at the 1962 Venice Festival.

After the commercial failure of *Freaks*, Browning made only four more films before he retired in 1939. Following his wife's death in 1944, he lived alone in their Malibu Colony home until his death on October 6, 1962. He was buried in Los Angeles.

See Rory Guy, "Horror: The Browning Version," *Cinema* (June/July 1963): 26-28; George Geltzer, "Tod Browning," *Films in Review* (Oct. 1953): 410-16.   THOMAS M. HOUSE

BROWNING, PETE-LOUIS RODGERS. The original "Louisville Slugger," with a career .343 batting average and three batting championships, was Pete-Louis Rodgers Browning, who was born on June 17, 1861, in Louisville. Playing primarily for the Louisville Colonels of the major league American Association, he led the league in hitting in both 1882, his rookie year, with a .382 average, and 1885, with .362. After he first used custom-made bats from Louisville woodworker John Hillerich, demand for these bats quickly spread and launched the Hillerich & Bradsby Company. The bats became known as Louisville Sluggers.

Originally an infielder, Browning converted to outfield and although he was a fast runner (103 steals in 1887), he played weak defense. After his worst season, 1889, he left the Colonels for the Cleveland Infants of the New Players League, where he won a third batting title with a .387 average in 1890. The league folded after a year and Browning finished his career splitting seasons with five other teams. He retired in 1894 with 299 doubles, 89 triples, 47 home runs, and 956 runs scored, and ranked tenth in all-time batting averages.

Browning died in Louisville on September 10, 1905, and was buried in the city's Cave Hill Cemetery.

BROWNSVILLE. The county seat of Edmonson County, Brownsville is located at the junction of KY 70 and 259, along the Green River. Established by the General Assembly on January 30, 1828, the town was probably named for Gen. Jacob Brown (1775-1828), commanding general of the U.S. Army from 1821 until 1828. A rural, agricultural community, Brownsville grew and prospered throughout the nineteenth century. After the Civil War upset the steady growth, prosperity returned. In 1872, the first Edmonson County courthouse, which was nothing more than connected old dwellings, was replaced after the first-story floor collapsed. The second courthouse, built in 1873, was a two-story, brick, Italianate-style edifice.

In the mid- and late twentieth century, recreation, in addition to agriculture, became important to the economy. The tourist dollars generated by Mammoth Cave National Park and Nolin River Lake, both within fifteen miles of the city, significantly benefit Brownsville. In the 1970s the Brownsville Manufacturing Company, producing womens' sportswear, came to town. It shut down in October 1987, but was replaced in July 1988 by the Brownsville Garment Company, a similar operation.

The population of the fifth-class city was 542 in 1970; 674 in 1980; and 897 in 1990.

RON D. BRYANT

BRUMFIELD, DONALD T. Donald T. Brumfield, jockey, son of Edgar and Viola (Morris) Brumfield, was born on May 24, 1938, in Nicholasville, Kentucky. His father was a horse trainer, and Brumfield's first win, at Monmouth Park, New Jersey, on August 2, 1954, came on a horse trained by his father. Brumfield became a racing fixture at Churchill Downs in Louisville (925 wins) and at Keeneland Race Course in Lexington (716 wins) and retired as the jockey with the most wins in the history of each track. In 1966 he was the second jockey to win both the Kentucky Oaks (on Native Street) and the Kentucky Derby (on Kauai King) in the same year. After racing in the Kentucky Derby twelve times, Brumfield retired in September 1989. He was fourteenth among jockeys with the most career wins—4,572, earning purses totaling $43,557,499. Brumfield became a racing official at Keeneland and later a racing steward at Hialeah in Florida. He maintains a home in Lexington but lives in Florida.

BRUNER, PETER. Peter Bruner, a slave who escaped to fight in the Civil War, was born at Winchester, Clark County, Kentucky in 1845. As a lad, he labored under harsh conditions in his owner's tannery and on occasion was hired out to others. His numerous failed escape attempts usually resulted in severe punishment. In July 1864 Bruner finally made good his escape, fleeing forty-one miles to CAMP NELSON, Kentucky, the largest black recruiting center in the commonwealth. There he enrolled in Company C, 12th Regiment, Heavy Artillery, U.S. Colored Troops. Bruner served primarily garrison duty in central and western Kentucky. Mustered out of service in 1866, Bruner moved to Oxford, Ohio, where in 1868 he married Fannie Procton. The couple had five children.

After struggling for several years as a farm laborer, handyman, and watchman, Bruner became the janitor and messenger at Miami University in Oxford. His memoirs, published in 1918, depict the difficulties bondsmen faced when fleeing slavery and contain one of the best accounts of black soldier life in Kentucky during the Civil War. Bruner died on April 6, 1938, and was buried in Woodside Cemetery, Oxford.

See John W. Blassingame, ed., *Slave Testimony: Two Centuries of Letters, Speeches, Interviews and Autobiographies* (Baton Rouge, La., 1977); Peter Bruner, *A Slave's Adventures Toward Freedom: Not Fiction, but the True Story of a Struggle* (Oxford, Ohio, 1918).   MARION B. LUCAS

BRYAN'S (BRYANT'S) STATION. In 1779 the Bryan brothers, William, Morgan, James, and Joseph, led settlers from North Carolina to a site five miles northeast of the Lexington fort. On the south bank of Elkhorn Creek, southeast of the present-day Lexington-Maysville road, they built a forty-four-cabin stockade and two-story blockhouse-style fort.

During the Revolutionary War, approximately six hundred Indians, Tories, and Canadian Rangers under the leadership of Alexander McKee, Simon Girty, and Capt. William Caldwell moved into Kentucky, arriving at Bryan's Station August 14-15, 1782. They secretly surrounded the station and prepared for an ambush, but seeing unusual activity in the fort, they feared discovery. On August 16 they planned a diversion to draw the men from the fort, enabling the larger hidden force to attack. The diversion failed and the fort's defenders prepared for battle, sending two messengers to Lexington. The fort was low on water, which came from a spring outside the fort. According to a popular story long believed true but now relegated to legend, twenty-six women and girls followed their regular procedure of going to the spring, believing the Indians would not risk revealing their larger force by attacking women. Once they had safely returned, the settlers opened fire. The fighting lasted until late afternoon, when part of a relief group from Lexington fought their way into the fort. Realizing that the fort could not be taken without artillery, the attackers became discouraged and withdrew during the night.

See George W. Ranck, *History of Lexington, Kentucky: Its Early Annals and Recent Progress* (Lexington, Ky., reprint 1970); Maude Ward Lafferty, *The Lure of Kentucky* (Detroit 1971).

ANITA J. SANFORD

BRYANT, EDWIN. Edwin Bryant, journalist and diarist, was born in 1805 in or near Pelham, Massachusetts, the son of Ichabod and Silence Bryant. His father was a ne'er-do-well who spent some time in a debtors' prison, and he grew up at the home of his mother's brother in Bedford, New York. Bryant's academic record is unclear; he may have attended Brown University. In the mid-1820s he founded and edited the *Providence Literary Cadet* in Rhode Island and went on to edit the *New York Examiner* in Rochester.

Bryant arrived in Louisville in the fall of 1830, and for a brief time wrote editorials for the *Louisville Journal* under the signature "B." Bryant departed Louisville for Frankfort by steamboat on January 27, 1831, to report on the doings of the General Assembly, and in May went to Lexington to become editor of the *Lexington Observer*. In 1832 this paper was consolidated with the *Reporter*, which Bryant edited for two years. In 1834-44 Bryant edited the *Lexington Intelligencer*.

In 1844 Henry Clay and John J. Crittenden persuaded Bryant to return to Louisville to establish a second Whig journal. Bryant then became associated with Walter N. HALDEMAN, who had acquired a failing newspaper called the *Daily Dime*, which he was able to transform into the successful *Louisville Courier*.

On April 26, 1844, Haldeman announced that Bryant and a party of other young Louisville men had departed for California in search of better health, with Bryant expecting to write a book when he returned. In Independence, Missouri, the Bryant party joined that of Missouri Gov. Lillburn Boggs, a native of Lexington, and Gen. William ("Owl") Russell, of Fayette and Nicholas counties. Between Independence and Fort Laramie dissension caused Bryant's party, along with William Russell, to mount themselves on Missouri mules and set off over Hastings Cut-off to the Great Salt Lake, the Humboldt River, and the Johnson Ranch on the Sacramento River. The party arrived in San Francisco on September 21, 1846.

In California Bryant became involved in the fight to wrest the region from Mexican control. He was also a figure in the dispute between Gen. Stephen Watts Kearny and John C. Frémont, leader of volunteer troops, over the command of the Los Angeles post. Active in establishing American control of San Francisco and the bay area, Bryant was appointed alcalde of the town, a position that favored his speculation in town lots on the bay front.

On June 2, 1847, Bryant joined General Kearny's party to return to Kentucky. In the return party was Frémont, a prisoner of General Kearny's command. Bryant's detailed overland journal, *What I Saw in California*, was published in 1848. It quickly went through seven editions and then through eleven further editions. The book came from the press just in time to become the cardinal guide book for gold rushers to California in 1849.

After Bryant's visit to Washington D.C., to testify in the Kearny-Frémont dispute, he returned to Kentucky and settled in the literary colony of Pewee Valley. Twice more he visited California, the last time making the journey by transcontinental train in June 1869. The sale of the San Francisco lots yielded a happy financial return. In December 1869 Bryant became seriously ill and was moved to the Willard Hotel in Louisville, where on December 16 he jumped to his death. His body was buried in Cave Hill Cemetery and reburied in Spring Grove Cemetery in Cincinnati.

See Edwin Bryant, *What I Saw in California: Being the Journal of a Tour* (New York 1848); Thomas D. Clark, "Edwin Bryant and the Opening of the Road to California," *Essays in Western History in Honor of T.A. Larson* (Laramie, Wyo., 1979).

THOMAS D. CLARK

BRYANT, PAUL WILLIAM. Paul William ("Bear") Bryant, football coach, son of Wilson Monroe and Ida (Kilgore) Bryant, was born on September 11, 1913, in Moro Bottom, Arkansas. He was one of eleven children in a poor family, and he remembered himself in his youth as feeling inferior, not doing well in school, and being lazy. But by the time he retired, Bryant was the college football coach with the most wins: 323 victories, 85 losses, and 17 ties. He compiled this record at four schools: University of Maryland (1945), University of Kentucky (1946-53), Texas A&M University (1954-57), and University of Alabama (1958-82). His teams won six national championships. Many of his former assistants became head coaches, including Jerry Claiborne, Jack Pardee, and Ray Perkins. He sent more than forty-five players to the pro ranks, including quarterbacks George Blanda,

Joe Namath, Ken Stabler, and Richard Todd. His coaching style stressed discipline and maximum effort. Some have said that he coached people more than football.

Bryant began his football career as a burly tackle at Fordyce (Arkansas) High School, where he received All-State honors. There he got his nickname when he wrestled a bear at a carnival. At the University of Alabama, he played football from 1932 to 1935 and helped the Crimson Tide to a 23-3-2 record and a victory in the 1935 Rose Bowl. Following graduation he remained at Alabama as an assistant football coach until 1939; he was at Vanderbilt University during 1940-41.

Bryant served in the navy as lieutenant commander (1941-45). After his discharge, Bryant became the head football coach at Maryland, leading the team to a 6-2-1 record, its first winning season in years. In 1946, following a clash with university president D.H. Byrd, who reinstated a player Bryant had suspended and who fired an assistant coach without consulting Bryant, he left to become the head coach at the University of Kentucky. In his first season Bryant's Wildcats posted a 7-3 mark. Overall at Kentucky, he had an impressive 60-23-5 record and led the Wildcats to four bowl games—Great Lakes 1948, Orange 1950, Sugar 1951, and Cotton 1952 (losing only the Orange Bowl)—as well as posting a Southeastern Conference championship in 1950. The highlight of his career at Kentucky came in the 1951 Sugar Bowl, when Bryant's Wildcats defeated the Oklahoma Sooners 13-7 and snapped their thirty-one-game winning streak.

Bryant brought charisma* to Kentucky football and made the Wildcats a national force. He had said he wanted to stay at Kentucky until he retired, but on February 4, 1954, he resigned as head football coach, after signing a twelve-year contract extension only a month earlier. Bryant attributed his decision to conflict with basketball coach Adolph Rupp. Both men, highly competitive, wanted top priority for their programs. Bryant, who had believed that Rupp would soon retire, resigned when he found out that Rupp had signed a ten-year contract extension. Bryant went to Texas A&M in College Station. He coached four years there, posting a 25-14-2 record.

Bryant returned to his alma mater in 1958 to become head football coach and athletic director. He led Alabama to twenty-four bowl appearances and six national championships. On November 28, 1981, he broke the collegiate coaching record with 315 career wins as Alabama defeated Auburn, 28-17. He was also instrumental in integrating the Alabama student body in 1971 by recruiting black athletes. Bryant retired following the 1982 season.

Bryant enjoyed duck hunting and fishing in Kentucky, occasionally in the company of his close friend Gov. Lawrence Wetherby (1950-55). In 1934 he married Mary Harmon Black; they had two children, Paul, Jr., and Mae Martin Tyson. Bryant died on January 26, 1983, and was buried at Elmwood Cemetery in Birmingham, Alabama.

See Mickey Herskowitz, *The Legend of Bear Bryant* (New York 1987).

BUCHANAN, JUNE. June Buchanan, a social reformer noted primarily for her contributions to Caney Creek Community Center and Alice Lloyd College in Knott County, Kentucky, was born in Moravia, New York, on June 21, 1887, the daughter of B. Frank and Julia (McCormick) Buchanan. She received a bachelor of arts degree in 1913 from Syracuse University and did graduate work at Wellesley College. In 1919, hoping to improve educational opportunities for mountain children, she joined Alice Lloyd at the Caney Creek Community Center in Pippa Passes, Kentucky. She devoted nearly seven decades of her century-long life to promoting education in eastern Kentucky in many ways, from teaching students and presiding over the community center to fund raising. Buchanan's service-oriented philosophy stressed such concepts as conscience, duty, and courage.

In 1933 Buchanan married D. Hollander Hall, a local lawyer, who died sixteen years later. By the time of her death on May 31, 1988, the Pippa Passes educational system supported all grades from kindergarten through grade twelve at the June Buchanan School, as well as four years of higher education at Alice Lloyd College, an institution that Buchanan helped establish. She was buried on the Alice Lloyd College campus.

See William Dutton, *Stay on Stranger!* (New York 1954).   D. GENE PACE

BUCHANAN V. WARLEY. A decision of the U.S. Supreme Court on November 5, 1917, held unconstitutional a 1914 Louisville ordinance prohibiting a person from moving into a block where a majority of the residents were of another race. William Warley, a black who headed the Louisville branch of the National Association for the Advancement of Colored People, tested the ordinance when he contracted to buy a lot on a predominantly white street from Charles Buchanan, a white realty agent sympathetic to the NAACP. Warley claimed that the ordinance invalidated their contract, and Buchanan sued for specific performance, arguing that the ordinance unconstitutionally deprived him of property. When the state courts upheld the ordinance in *Harris v. City of Louisville* (1915), Buchanan appealed to the U.S. Supreme Court.

The Supreme Court held that the ordinance denied members of both races the right to own and dispose of property as they saw fit, and thus violated the due-process clause of the federal Constitution, as well as the Civil Rights Act of 1866. States and municipalities, the Court conceded, should be accorded wide latitude in meeting the asserted objectives of the ordinance—protecting racial purity, preserving racial peace, and maintaining property values. However, such objectives could "not be promoted by depriving citizens of their constitutional rights and privileges." Nor, upon analysis, was the ordinance found to be reasonably related to the attainment of its stated objectives.

The court distinguished the *Buchanan* case from precedents like *Plessy v. Ferguson* (1896) and *Berea College v. Kentucky* (1908), which had upheld state segregation laws. The laws upheld in these cases merely limited the enjoyment of a right by "reasonable rules in regard to the separation of races." By contrast, the court asserted, the Louisville ordinance imposed absolute limitations on the disposal of property, and thus amounted to an unconstitutional taking. Although the *Buchanan* case did not overturn the precedents, its affirmation of federal civil rights laws and amendments and its recognition of limits on segregation were one of the first judicial steps away from Jim Crow.

See Paul A. Freund and Stanley N. Katz, eds., *History of the Supreme Court of the United States*, (New York 1984); George Wright, "The NAACP and Residential Segregation in Louisville, Kentucky, 1914-1917," *Register* (Winter 1980): 39-54.

DANIEL G. STROUP

BUCKNER, GEORGE WASHINGTON. George Washington Buckner, physician and diplomat, was born into slavery on the Stanton Buckner plantation in Green County, Kentucky, on December 1, 1855. Freed at the age of ten, he was educated in a freedmen's school and a private school at Greensburg. In 1870 he lived briefly in Louisville with an aunt and was a household servant for a white family. He became one of the first black teachers in Green County in 1871, and later moved to Indianapolis to reside with another aunt; there he attended public school and eventually graduated from the Terre Haute State Normal School. After teaching for several years in Indiana in Vincennes, Washington, and Evansville, he returned to Indianapolis to receive his medical degree from Eclectic Medical College. In 1890 he moved to Evansville and, except for a brief time out of the country, was a practicing physician there for fifty-three years.

Buckner, a member of the Democratic party, was interested in public affairs, and in 1913 President Woodrow Wilson appointed him minister and consul general to Liberia. He resigned the position in 1915 because of persistent bouts of African fever caused by the tropical climate, and returned to Evansville.

In 1879 Buckner married Estella White, who died of tuberculosis in 1889. In 1896 he married Anna Cowan; they had five children. Buckner died in Evansville on February 16, 1943. His son, Zack, donated many of the memorabilia Buckner had acquired in Liberia to the Evansville Museum.

BUCKNER, SIMON BOLIVAR. Simon Bolivar Buckner, governor of Kentucky during 1887-91, was born at Glen Lily, the family estate near Munfordville, Kentucky, on April 1, 1823. When his parents, Aylett Hartswell and Elizabeth Ann (More-

head) Buckner, moved to Arkansas, they left him behind to attend schools in Greenville and Hopkinsville before he entered the U.S. Military Academy at West Point in 1840. After graduation Buckner saw active duty with Gen. Winfield Scott during the Mexican War. In 1850 he married Mary Jane Kingsbury. In 1855 he resigned his commission to help his father-in-law with his extensive business interests. His wife died in 1874, and in 1885 Buckner married Delia Claiborne. He had a daughter by his first wife, a son by the second. He returned to Kentucky in 1858 from Chicago, and two years later became head of the state militia. Buckner tried to preserve the state's neutrality in 1861, but when that failed he rejected a Union commission, becoming a Confederate brigadier general.

He led troops to Bowling Green, Kentucky, in September 1861, and after a confused command situation left him in charge, he surrendered Fort Donelson to Gen. Ulysses S. Grant in February 1862. After a prisoner exchange, Buckner saw extensive duty in the western theater, including the 1862 Confederate invasion of Kentucky; he was promoted to major general and became involved in a bitter controversy with Gen. Braxton Bragg. Sent to the trans-Mississippi theater in 1864, Buckner was promoted to lieutenant general. On May 26, 1865, he surrendered Gen. Edmund Kirby-Smith's army. He was a New Orleans journalist and businessman until allowed to return to Kentucky in 1868. Lawsuits recovered most of his prewar property, and shrewd business deals made him moderately wealthy.

Nominated in 1887 as the Democratic candidate for governor, he defeated Republican William O'Connell Bradley in a relatively close race, 143,466 to 126,754. Buckner was a member of the 1890 constitutional convention. When his term expired in September 1891, he returned to Glen Lily. He failed to win the nomination for the U.S. Senate in 1895. He left the Democratic party in 1896 when it nominated William Jennings Bryan for the presidency, and became the vice-presidential candidate on the Gold Democrat ticket with Gen. John M. Palmer. Buckner died at home on January 8, 1914, the last surviving Confederate of lieutenant general rank, and was buried in the Frankfort Cemetery.

Buckner gave the state an honest, efficient administration. He vetoed numerous private-interest bills, and he rejected most requests for pardons. He secured reforms in tax equalization and the parole system for convicts, and he saw to the codification of school laws and completion of the Eddyville prison. A conservative legislature, however, rejected most of his progressive requests, such as the regulation of trusts, more local support for education, and the protection of forests. When an 1890 tax cut passed over his veto emptied the treasury, Buckner quietly lent the state enough to keep it solvent until tax revenue came in. A major scandal erupted in 1888, after Buckner ordered a routine audit that had been neglected for years. James W. ("Honest Dick") Tate, the state treasurer for twenty years, disappeared, leaving a shortage of $247,128.50.

See Arndt M. Stickles, *Simon Bolivar Buckner: Borderland Knight* (Chapel Hill, N.C., 1940); Lowell H. Harrison, ed., *Kentucky's Governors 1792-1985* (Lexington, Ky., 1985).

LOWELL H. HARRISON

BUCKNER, SIMON BOLIVAR, JR. Simon Bolivar Buckner, Jr., soldier, was born in Hart County, Kentucky, on July 18, 1886, to Simon Bolivar BUCKNER, Sr., the Confederate lieutenant general who became governor of Kentucky (1887-91), and Mary Jane (Kingsbury) Buckner. Buckner graduated from the U.S. Military Academy in 1908. He held a variety of peacetime army positions and served in the Washington, D.C., offices of the air service during World War I. Buckner graduated from the Command and General Staff School and the Army War College. He taught tactics at West Point and from 1933 to 1936 was commandant of cadets there, earning a reputation as an exacting drillmaster. Critics said, "Buckner forgets that cadets are born, not quarried." Confiscating the cadets' after-shave lotion, Buckner said, "Cadets should work and smell like men."

In July 1940 Buckner took command of the Alaska Defense Force and was brevetted to brigadier general in September. His diligence in fortifying Alaska against possible Japanese attack won him the Distinguished Service Medal. When war came with Japan in 1941, Buckner took part in the Aleutians campaign and urged an advance toward the enemy homeland from Alaska. Buckner feuded with the navy's northern Pacific commander, satirizing Adm. Robert Theobald in irreverent verse for what Buckner considered timid use of warships. By then sometimes called "The Old Man of the Mountains" or "Bull," Buckner enjoyed treating his friends with the toast, "May you walk in the ashes of Tokyo."

Buckner's proposed northern strategy was not adopted. In 1943 he became a lieutenant general and in the summer of 1944 received command of the 10th Army, assembling in Hawaii. In the assault on Okinawa, soldiers and marines first went ashore on April 1, 1945. After little opposition on the beaches, Buckner's men encountered heavily fortified Japanese positions inland, and the advance slowed. Losing ships to kamikaze attacks offshore, overall operations commander Adm. Chester Nimitz urged Buckner to speed up the pace of operations. Newspapers criticized Buckner's "ultraconservative" tactics and called the campaign a "worse example of military incompetence than Pearl Harbor." Nevertheless, in what Nimitz termed a "magnificent performance," Buckner's command broke through the main Shuri Japanese line on May 14. On June 18 Buckner visited a forward position "from which for the first time he could see the extreme southern tip of Okinawa," according to a war correspondent. When the Japanese began shelling the area, Buckner was killed.

Initially buried at Hagushi Beach on Okinawa, Buckner lies now in the Frankfort Cemetery.

See Lloyd J. Graybar, "The Buckners of Kentucky," *FCHQ* 58 (April 1984): 202-19.

NICKY HUGHES

BUELL, DON CARLOS. Don Carlos Buell, Civil War general, was born in Lowell, Ohio, on March 23, 1818. He graduated from the U.S. Military Academy at West Point on July 1, 1841, and on June 18, 1846 was promoted to first lieutenant. Distinguishing himself at the battles of Monterrey, Contreras, and Churobusco in the Mexican War, he rose to the rank of major. After the war he became assistant adjutant general (1848-49), then served in the Washington military bureaucracy as chief of several departments. On May 11, 1861, Buell was promoted to lieutenant colonel and in July was made brigadier general of volunteers.

Buell assumed command of the Department of the Ohio, which included Kentucky, on November 15, 1861. His actions were instrumental in keeping Kentucky in the Union. On February 14, 1862, Buell entered and took control of Bowling Green as a Confederate force under Gen. Albert S. Johnston retreated toward Nashville. The following September, Buell reached Louisville and prepared to advance against Confederate forces to the southeast. Buell's Federals surprised Gen. Braxton Bragg at Bardstown, forcing him to divide his army and withdraw south. Buell and others pursued and engaged the Confederates at Perryville on October 8, 1862. The following day, Bragg withdrew to Harrodsburg, while Buell moved to Danville, thus threatening Bragg's line of communication. With a superior cavalry force, Bragg completed his retreat from Kentucky through the Cumberland Gap.

Buell's failure to prevent Bragg's escape, along with his refusal to permit confiscation of property in Kentucky, Tennessee, and Alabama, precipitated questions about his loyalty and negated earlier commendation of his victory at Perryville. He was relieved of command on October 30, 1862, by Maj. Gen. William S. Rosecrans. On April 25, 1863, a commission hearing the allegations reported no serious misjudgements and recommended that Buell be returned to duty. The damage to Buell's reputation had been done, however, and his political enemies prevented his reassignment. He resigned his commission on June 1, 1864. Buell then moved to Kentucky, becoming president of the Green River Iron Company in Muhlenberg County. On March 9, 1880, Gov. Luke P. Blackburn (1879-83) appointed him one of twelve members of the first board of trustees of the Agricultural and Mechanical College (now the University of Kentucky) in Lexington. In 1885 Buell received a presidential appointment as state pension agent, a position he held until 1890.

Buell married Margaret (Hunter) Mason of Mobile, Alabama, and adopted her daughter by a previous marriage. He died on November 19, 1898, in Paradise, Kentucky, and was buried in Bellefontaine Cemetery in St. Louis.

See Hobert L. Sanders, "The Military Career of Don Carlos Buell during the Civil War," M.A. thesis, University of Kentucky, 1937.

BUFFALO. American buffalo, or bison, extended their range into Kentucky during prehistoric times (B.C. 10,000 to 1,000), probably because of overpopulation in the Great Plains. From Kentucky they migrated east and south through the Cumberland Gap to Virginia, Tennessee, and the Carolinas. By the time European explorers came to Kentucky, buffalo were abundant there. Simon Kenton estimated that he saw 1,500 at one time near a salt spring. Daniel Boone's reports from the Red River country in 1770 told of herds "more frequent than I have ever seen cattle in the settlements, browsing on the leaves of the cane, or cropping the herbage of those extensive plains, fearless because ignorant of man."

The concentrations of these game animals attracted many pioneer hunters. Buffalo served as an important source of food before the establishment of agriculture around the early settlements; Boone's settlement subsisted almost entirely on buffalo meat during the severe winter of 1780-81. In some areas, buffalo hunting so easily obtained food that there was little incentive to farm. In fact, the roving herds were considered pests, as they destroyed crops, fences, and even some buildings before extensive hunting reduced their numbers.

Buffalo trails that linked feeding areas in open valleys served as primitive roads during exploration. Pioneers following the ancient buffalo route through the Cumberland Gap claimed it as their own Wilderness Road. The buffalo trampled paths with banks up to six feet high and wide enough for two wagons to pass abreast. Around mineral springs such as Blue Lick Springs, the convergence of animal trails was compared to avenues leading into a city. Buffalo herds descending river banks over many years produced graded pathways that were the only ready access for people entering parts of the interior by boat. A "buffalo landing" on the high bank of the Ohio River near Yellowbanks Island determined the site of a settlement that grew into the city of Owensboro. Other cities in the region that owe their location to intersections of buffalo trails include Lexington, Louisville, Frankfort, and Cincinnati.

Buffalo had an ecological impact in Kentucky through grazing, which maintained meadows and the canebrakes, which were natural openings in the dense eastern forest. Later, cattle turned out in these clearings devoured the cane, which was replaced by plant species such as bluegrass. Explorers found in the western part of Kentucky a natural grassland. The so-called barrens were first thought to be insufficiently fertile to grow trees. In fact, this area was maintained as prairie by frequent fires set intentionally by Shawnee hunters to concentrate buffalo herds and to discourage the growth of woody vegetation.

Overhunting during the last thirty years of the eighteenth century exterminated the buffalo in Kentucky. The last confirmed reports of wild buffalo in the state came from Hart County, where a small herd was seen going down to the Green River as late as 1820. As the species neared extinction, some efforts were made to domesticate buffalo. George C. Thompson kept a herd on his farm at Shawnee Springs in Mercer County from 1825 to 1875. In 1810 Robert WICKLIFFE, of Lexington, was among the first livestock breeders to mate buffalo with domestic cattle and he kept "cattalo" stock for thirty years. Buffalo-cattle hybrids did not prove economically successful during the nineteenth century. Modern trends in low-fat meat production on marginal grazing lands, however, have renewed the interest of Kentuckians in buffalo as livestock, besides their value as a living reminder of the past.

See Francis Haines, *The Buffalo* (New York 1970); William D. Funkhouser, *Wild Life in Kentucky* (Frankfort, Ky., 1925).

ROBERT W. KINGSOLVER

BUFORD, JOHN. John Buford, Union cavalry general, was born in Woodford County, Kentucky, on March 4, 1826, and moved with his family to Illinois in the early 1840s. He received an appointment to the U.S. Military Academy at West Point and graduated in 1848 with a commission as a second lieutenant in the 2d Dragoons. Buford fought in the Mexican War and served on the frontier in Texas, New Mexico, and Kansas and on the Utah expedition of 1857-58 against the Mormons. After the Civil War began, Buford marched with his regiment to Washington, D.C., arriving there in October of 1861. He was assigned as a staff major to inspect the Washington defenses. On July 27, 1862, Buford was made brigadier general, in command of a cavalry brigade. He participated in the battles of Second Manassas, Antietam, Fredericksburg, and Stoneman's Raid. At the Battle of Gettysburg, Buford, then in command of a full division of cavalry, held off the vanguard of the Confederate army on July 1, 1863, until Union infantry support arrived. Buford was made major general shortly before he died of typhoid fever on December 16, 1863. He was buried at West Point.

BUILDING STONE INDUSTRY. High-quality building stone, one of the first MINERAL RESOURCES developed in Kentucky, was obtained from hand-dug quarries beginning in the late eighteenth century. Some quarries developed into large commercial enterprises that cut stone into tabular forms, known as dimension stone, and until the 1930s the state had a large building stone industry. The largest stone operations were around Bowling Green in the Pennyroyal region, producing limestone from the Mississippian-age Girkin Formation. This freestone can be readily cut and sculpted because it lacks a pronounced grain. It was both used in Kentucky and transported to surrounding states in the nineteenth and early twentieth centuries for use in building projects such as the Carnegie Library in Nashville and the Chamber of Commerce Building in Atlanta.

Inner Bluegrass quarries produced Ordovician dolomite and limestone, respectively, from the Oregon Formation and the Tyrone and Lexington limestones, all of which were used for construction. The Tyrone, called birdseye limestone, is easily recognized in buildings because it weathers to a distinctive white color. Oregon dolomite, known as Kentucky River marble for its ability to take a high polish, was commercially quarried as late as 1963 in Mercer County for veneer, window and door sills, and copings. It was polished to order for mantles, hearths, interior sills, tabletops, and storefronts. Kentucky River marble is denser and less permeable than other frequently used limestones, but its relatively greater weight makes it more costly to transport. Thin-bedded Lexington limestones were used extensively for rock fences in the Bluegrass region.

In the outcrop belt of Silurian rocks in the western part of the Bluegrass region, easily quarried Laurel dolomite lies at the surface. This formation has excellent properties as dimension stone, occurring in beds up to three feet thick and producing large golden-hued blocks. Nineteenth century buildings of Laurel dolomite are found in Nelson, Bullitt, Jefferson, and Oldham counties. The most widely used sandstone, the Farmers member of the Mississippian Borden Formation (also known as Kentucky bluestone, Rowan County freestone, and Buena Vista sandstone) occurs in northeastern Kentucky. In addition to its local use, large blocks of this sandstone were marketed in the 1800s for bridge construction, curbing, sills, steps, and columns in Cincinnati, Covington, and Newport.

Small quarries recently active in western and southeastern Kentucky have produced highly colorful red, brown, and gold-hued flagging and veneer from sandstones of Mississippian and Pennsylvanian ages. All other active quarries in the commonwealth produce only crushed stone at the present time. Kentucky still has substantial reserves of building stones, but dimension stone may be obtained only by special order.

See Preston McGrain, *Geology of Construction Materials in Kentucky*, Kentucky Geological Survey, Series 11, No. 13 (Lexington, Ky., 1982).

CAROLYN MURRAY-WOOLEY

BULLITT, ALEXANDER SCOTT. Alexander Scott Bullitt, pioneer political leader, in whose honor Bullitt County, Kentucky, is named, was born in Dumfries, Virginia, on an unknown date in 1762 to Judge Cuthbert and Helen (Scott) Bullitt. The young Bullitt was elected to the Virginia legislature in 1782. The following year, he came to Kentucky as a major in the militia of Prince William County. He soon became lieutenant in the Jefferson County militia, and on May 2, 1786, he was appointed one of the trustees of Louisville by the Virginia legislature. Bullitt first settled in Kentucky along Bull Skin Creek in Shelby County. He then moved to a thousand-acre farm east of Louisville, where he built the estate named Oxmoor, which was his home for the rest of his life.

Bullitt was a member of the Kentucky convention in Danville in 1788. In 1792 he served as a delegate to the constitutional convention, where he helped draft the first CONSTITUTION of Kentucky together with George Nicholas. Bullitt was elected one of the state's eleven original senators and on June 4, 1792, he was elected speaker of the Senate, a position he held until 1800. At the state's second constitutional convention in 1799, Bullitt presided at the drafting of the second constitution of Kentucky, which lasted until 1850. In 1800 Bullitt was elected Kentucky's first lieutenant governor. He was returned to the state Senate in 1804 and held the position until 1808, when he retired from public life.

Bullitt married Priscilla Christian on January 31, 1786; they had four children: Cuthbert, Annie, Helen, and William Christian. Priscilla died on November 11, 1806. Bullitt married Mary (Churchill) Prather on July 31, 1807; they had three children: Thomas, James, and Mary. Bullitt died April 13, 1816, and is buried at Oxmoor.

See Ella Hutchison Ellwanger, "Oxmoor: Its Builder and Its Historian," *Register* 17 (Jan. 1919): 9-21; Thomas Bullitt, *My Life at Oxmoor* (Louisville 1911).

BULLITT, HENRY MASSIE. Henry Massie Bullitt, physician and teacher, was born on February 28, 1817, in Shelby County, Kentucky, to Cuthbert and Harriet (Willis) Bullitt. He began studying medicine with Dr. Coleman Rogers, Sr., of Louisville in 1834, and graduated from the medical school of the University of Pennsylvania in 1838. Bullitt set up a medical partnership with Dr. Joshua B. Flint in Louisville. In 1845 he went to Europe for further medical study and the next year began teaching medicine at St. Louis Medical College. In 1848 he returned to Kentucky to teach for a year at Transylvania University. In 1850 Bullitt helped establish the Kentucky School of Medicine in Louisville, where he served as professor of physiology and pathology and dean of faculty until 1866. Bullitt then taught theory and practice of medicine (1866) and physiology (1867) at the University of Louisville. He left his chair in 1868 to help found the Louisville Medical College, where he remained until his death. The two private medical colleges that Bullitt helped establish later became part of the University of Louisville medical school. During his career, Bullitt served as coeditor of the medical journals of the various institutions where he taught: the *St. Louis Medical Journal*, the *Transylvania Journal of Medicine*, and the *Louisville Medical Record*, which he founded.

Bullitt married Julia Anderson on May 26, 1841; they had two children who survived to adulthood. After he was widowed, he married Sarah Crow Paradise on September 14, 1854; they had six children. Bullitt died on February 5, 1880, and was buried at Cave Hill Cemetery in Louisville.

BULLITT, THOMAS. Thomas Bullitt, surveyor and explorer, was born in Prince William County, Virginia, in 1730 to Benjamin and Elizabeth

(Harrison) Bullitt. He was a distinguished officer in the Virginia regiment during the French and Indian War, commanding companies under Col. George Washington between 1754 and 1758. He was honored for saving Washington's troops at the battle of Fort Duquesne. In 1773 Bullitt was commissioned by Lord Dunmore, the governor of Virginia, to lead a group of some forty pioneers into Kentucky to begin claiming and surveying the land. Bullitt undertook his expedition later that year, supported also by William and Mary College. Bullitt's party made early land claims in Kentucky. The first area explored extensively was the Big Bone Lick in Boone County. Bullitt then headed to the Falls of the Ohio River, where he surveyed and claimed the land that is now Louisville, where his nephew, Alexander Scott Bullitt, became a leading citizen. Bullitt left Kentucky in 1774 and did not return. He retired in 1776 and returned to his home in Fauquier County, Virginia, where he died early in 1778.

See Neal O. Hammon, "Pioneers in Kentucky, 1773-1775," *FCHQ* 55 (July 1981): 28-29.

BULLITT, WILLIAM MARSHALL. Scion of a family prominent in Kentucky since the 1780s, William Marshall Bullitt, U.S. solicitor general, was born in Louisville on March 4, 1873, to Thomas and Annie Priscilla (Logan) Bullitt. He was educated locally, at the Rugby School and Trinity Hall, and then at Lawrenceville School in New Jersey. He earned a B.A. degree at Princeton in 1894 and a law degree at the University of Louisville the following year. Admitted to the bar in 1895, he entered his father's firm, Bullitt and Shield, and became a specialist in corporation and insurance law. In 1912 President William Howard Taft named him solicitor general of the United States, a position he held for one year. In 1914 Bullitt ran unsuccessfully as Republican nominee for the U.S. Senate. During a long career, he argued more than fifty cases before the Supreme Court. At his death in Louisville on October 3, 1957, he was senior partner of Bullitt, Dawson & Tarrant, formed in 1948. He was survived by his wife Nora (Iasigi) Bullitt, whom he married in 1913; his son, Thomas; and daughters Nora Iasigi Leake and Barbara Watkins. He was buried at Oxmoor, the Bullitt ancestral home in Louisville.

See Willard R. Jillson, "William Marshall Bullitt," *Register* 56 (April 1958): 208-9.

THOMAS H. APPLETON, JR.

BULLITT COUNTY. Bullitt County, the twentieth in order of formation, is located in the far western Bluegrass region known as the Knobs. Bordered by Jefferson, Nelson, Spencer, and Hardin counties, it has an area of 300 square miles. The county was formed in December of 1796 from parts of Jefferson and Nelson counties and named for Alexander Scott Bullitt, Kentucky's first lieutenant governor (1800-1804) and the nephew of Capt. Thomas Bullitt. SHEPHERDSVILLE, founded in 1793

where the western leg of the Wilderness Road crossed Salt River, is the county seat. The first courthouse was built in 1804 of brick; the second, of Beaux Arts–influenced design, was constructed in 1900.

The county is hilly, with knobs covering most of its area. Salt River and its tributaries, the Rolling Fork and Floyd's Fork, drain to the west and empty into the Ohio River at West Point in Hardin County. Archaeological discoveries along parts of Salt River and Floyd's Fork indicate that Native Americans lived there 15,000 years ago. Settlers who arrived in the late 1770s and 1780s had numerous conflicts with Indians. Henry Crist, who later represented Kentucky in the U.S. House of Representatives (1809-11), was attacked by Indians in 1788 while attempting to navigate a boatload of salt kettles up Salt River. Of his party of thirteen, ten men were killed, a woman was captured, another man escaped, and Crist was badly wounded. Weakened by loss of blood, Crist crawled through the woods for three days, reaching safety among the salt makers at BULLITT'S LICK.

Salt licks attracted pioneers to the area. Furnaces to boil the salt-laden water were built at Bullitt's Lick, near what is now Shepherdsville. Named for surveyor Capt. Thomas Bullitt in 1779, they became the first commercial saltworks in Kentucky. Salt was manufactured also at Long Lick, Dry Lick, and Parakeet Lick. Iron ore is found in several places throughout the county, and smelting began at an early date.

MT. WASHINGTON, first called Mt. Vernon, was established in 1818. The city was an important stagecoach stop on the Louisville-to-Nashville turnpike and eventually became one of the largest cities in the county. In 1832 a town was established at the junction of the Salt River and Rolling Fork. The community, first called Pittstown and later Pitts Point, became a part of the FORT KNOX military reservation in the 1940s and no longer exists.

After the construction of the Louisville & Nashville Railroad (now CSX Transportation) in the mid-1850s, rail stops sprang up along the tracks on both the main line to Nashville and on the branch lines to Bardstown and Lebanon. They included Brooks Station, Hubers, Gap In Knob, Salt River, Bardstown Junction, Lebanon Junction, Clermont, and Hobbs. Lebanon Junction was selected by the railroad as a site for a railyard and a roundhouse for steam locomotives. As a result this rail stop became one of the county's largest cities. In 1895, when railroad expansion began, the city experienced rapid growth and prosperity. As the steam engine was gradually replaced by the diesel engine, demand for rail service diminished, the yard at Lebanon Junction became unnecessary, and the city declined. The construction of a full interchange on I-65 in the mid-1980s promised to revitalize Lebanon Junction. Lebanon Junction Press, a printing firm, opened in 1989.

Whiskey distilling, manufacturing, printing, and quarrying are the major industries in the county.

Agriculture is also important, and burley tobacco and soybeans are the major crops. Beef and dairy cattle and hogs are also raised there. Much of the county is wooded, including 10,000 acres of BERNHEIM FOREST and some of the 35,000 acres of county land that are part of the Fort Knox Military Reservation.

Among the prominent natives of Bullitt County was James Turner Morehead. Born near Shepherdsville on May 24, 1797, Morehead was elected lieutenant governor in 1832 and served as governor of Kentucky from 1834 to 1836.

After busing to further integration was instituted in the Louisville public school system, many people moved to Bullitt County, particularly the northern sector. The county became a commuter area, giving rise to several small incorporated cities. Among them are HILLVIEW, Pioneer Village, Hunters Hollow, Fox Chase, and Hebron Estates, all incorporated after 1965. By 1986 Hillview led all other cities in the county in population.

The population of Bullitt County was 26,090 in 1970; 43,346 in 1980; and 47,567 in 1990.

See Bullitt County Historical Commission, *History of Bullitt County* (N.p., 1974).   TOM PACK

BULLITT'S LICK. Bullitt's Lick, in Bullitt County, was discovered in 1773 by Capt. Thomas Bullitt while surveying a 1,000-acre land grant for Col. William Christian of Virginia. According to Robert E. McDowell, Bullitt's Lick was at one time the only place in what is now Kentucky where pioneer settlers could find salt. The SALT-MAKING operation there started up in 1779, preceding the Blue Licks salt works by five years and making Bullitt's Lick the first commercial industrial site in Kentucky. Salt produced there, and later from other licks in the area, was shipped by boat and pack train throughout Kentucky, as well as to the Illinois territory. The Bullitt's Lick salt works remained in full operation until the 1830s, when the development of the Kanawha salt works made production unprofitable.

See Robert E. McDowell, "Bullitt's Lick: The Related Saltworks and Settlements," FCHQ 30 (July 1956): 241-69.   TOM PACK

BULLOCK, JOSEPH JAMES. Joseph James Bullock, a Presbyterian minister who served as Kentucky's first head of education, was born on December 23, 1812, in Fayette County, Kentucky, the son of Waller and Marie O. (Burch) Bullock. He went to school near his home in Walnut Hills, attended Transylvania University, and graduated from Centre College in Danville in 1832. He first studied theology under Centre president John C. Young, then entered Princeton Theological Seminary in 1835. He was minister of the Frankfort Presbyterian Church during 1836-46.

Gov. James Clark (1836-39) appointed Bullock Kentucky's first superintendent of public instruction in February 1838. In a report to the General Assembly before his resignation in February 1839,

Bullock deplored Kentuckians' lack of learning and their apathy about education.

Bullock served on the Presbyterian church's domestic missions board (1846-48) and was pastor and president of the female seminary at Walnut Hills (1848-53). He received his D.D. from Centre College in 1850. He was pastor of Louisville's Second Church during 1853-55, and returned to head the Walnut Hills seminary during 1855-60. Bullock was employed at Danville Theological Seminary during 1860-61, was a pastor in Baltimore and in Alexandria, Virginia, in 1861-80, and served as chaplain of the U.S. Senate during 1879-84.

Bullock married Caroline Breckinridge in 1832. They had eight children: Waller, Mary, Cabell, Joseph, Letitia, John, Frances, and Sarah. Caroline died in 1867; Bullock married Elizabeth Lavender in 1869. He died on November 9, 1892, and was buried in Lexington Cemetery.

See Barksdale Hamlett, *History of Education in Kentucky* (Frankfort, Ky. 1914).

RUBY LAYSON

BUNNING, JAMES PAUL. James Paul Bunning, baseball pitcher and state senator and congressman, was born October 23, 1931, in Covington, Kentucky. His parents, Gladys (Best) and Louis Bunning, a ladder company executive, lived in nearby Newport. In 1949 Bunning graduated from St. Xavier High School in Cincinnati, where he played baseball, basketball, and football. Bunning entered Xavier University in Cincinnati on a basketball scholarship; a year later he signed a professional baseball contract with the Detroit Tigers. After six seasons in the minors, Bunning started pitching for Detroit in 1955, when his record was 3-5. The 1956 season, when Bunning posted a 5-1 record, was the start of a prolonged major league career with four teams (Detroit 1955-63; Philadelphia 1964-67; 1970-71; Pittsburgh 1968-69; Los Angeles 1969), winning recognition as one of baseball's best starting pitchers.

Bunning had a seventeen-year record of 224 wins, 184 losses, and a 3.27 earned run average. In 3,760 innings he allowed 3,433 hits, walked 1,000, and struck out 2,855, placing him ahead of Cy Young and, at the time, second only to Walter Johnson on the all-time strikeout list. Bunning made seven All-Star appearances, pitched a no-hitter for Detroit against Boston (July 20, 1958), and a perfect no-hit game in Philadelphia's 6-0 victory over the New York Mets on June 21, 1964. He was a central figure in the formation of the Major League Players Association. In 1991 he failed by three votes to enter the Baseball Hall of Fame. He entered politics in 1977 and was elected to a two-year term on the Fort Thomas, Kentucky, city council. In 1979 Bunning was elected as a Republican to the Kentucky Senate and was chosen minority floor leader. The Republican gubernatorial candidate in 1983, he lost to Democrat Martha Layne Collins, 561,674 to 454,650. In 1986 Bunning was elected to the U.S. House of

Representatives from Kentucky's 4th District, defeating Terry Mann by a vote of 67,626 to 53,906.

See Jim Bunning and Ralph Bernstein, *The Story of Jim Bunning* (Philadelphia 1965).

BURBRIDGE, STEPHEN GANO. Stephen Gano Burbridge, a Civil War military commander of Kentucky, was born on August 19, 1831, in Georgetown, Kentucky, the son of Robert and Elizabeth (Barnes) Burbridge. He was educated at Georgetown College and Frankfort Military Institute. Burbridge was a lawyer who at the outbreak of the Civil War owned a large plantation in Logan County and helped raise the 26th Kentucky Infantry. He was commissioned colonel on August 27, 1861.

Burbridge distinguished himself at Shiloh and was made brigadier general of volunteers on June 9, 1862. When Braxton Bragg invaded in 1862, Burbridge was sent to Kentucky and placed in command of federal troops in the state. He participated in the expedition sent against Vicksburg and was one of the first federal officers to enter Port Gibson, Mississippi, before laying siege to Vicksburg. For "gallant and distinguished services" in the repulse of John Hunt Morgan's June 12, 1864, invasion of Cynthiana, he was brevetted major general of volunteers on July 4, 1864, and received the thanks of President Abraham Lincoln. On August 7, 1864, he was placed in command of the Military District of Kentucky.

As military commander, Burbridge had the power to invoke martial law in the state. He was overzealous and antagonized much of the state. His job was to enforce the congressional act of 1864 that gave military courts jurisdiction over marauding guerrillas, and to uphold President Lincoln's suspension of the writ of habeas corpus. Burbridge was responsible for the infamous retaliation policy set forth in his Order No. 59, which commanded that four guerrilla prisoners be shot for each Union man killed. More than fifty executions resulted from this order, earning its author the epithet "Butcher" Burbridge. Some who were executed were Confederate prisoners of war. Burbridge later ruled that any Confederate sympathizer within five miles of a guerrilla raid was subject to arrest and banishment. His order on October 26, 1864, to shoot guerrillas on sight stirred up even more opposition. Burbridge also arrested several newspaper editors for treason and banished them to the Confederacy because of their criticism of Lincoln and of the war. Lincoln intervened in at least two of these cases on the ground that criticism of him did not constitute treason.

Burbridge was a part of the so-called GREAT HOG SWINDLE of 1864. He ordered that all surplus hogs in Kentucky be sold to the U.S. government and prohibited the shipment of hogs out of the state without a special permit. Lincoln reopened the markets at the end of November after a storm of protest over claims that Kentucky farmers had been cheated out of more than $300,000.

Efforts to remove Burbridge by many people, including Gov. Thomas Bramlette (1863-67), finally succeeded in February 1865, when Gen. John PALMER was named military commander. The *Louisville Journal* summed up many Kentuckians' feelings: "Thank God and President Lincoln." Burbridge resigned from the army on December 1, 1865, and left Kentucky. He moved to Brooklyn, New York, where he died on November 30, 1894.

ALOMA WILLIAMS DEW

BURDETT, GABRIEL. Gabriel Burdett, minister and educator, was born a slave on December 13, 1829, in Garrard County, Kentucky. Burdett in his twenties became a Baptist preacher at the Forks of Dick's River Church, where he held services on Sunday afternoons. He enrolled in the Union army on July 15, 1864. At Camp Nelson, Kentucky, Burdett began a twelve-year association with the Rev. John G. FEE and the American Missionary Association. After serving in the Union army with the 114th Regiment in Tennessee and Texas, Burdett returned to Kentucky in September 1866.

Burdett, who was married and had several children, became pastor of the Independent Church of Christ, which Fee founded at Camp Nelson in 1867. During the next decade, Burdett helped establish all-black congregations in surrounding counties. He participated in several postwar educational conventions, founded schools, and served twelve years as the first black on the Berea College board of trustees. He was instrumental in establishing Ariel Academy, a teacher training institution at Camp Nelson, by that time an all-black community. In the early 1870s, Burdett's interests became increasingly political. He supported the reelection of President Ulysses S. Grant in 1872, giving speeches throughout central Kentucky, and he attended state Republican conventions and served as a presidential elector. The violence associated with the disputed presidential election of 1876 convinced Burdett that future prospects for his family in Kentucky were poor, and in July 1877 he emigrated to Kansas. He died there on November 15, 1914.

MARION B. LUCAS

BURGOO. The word "burgoo" may have originated as burghul (now usually bulgur), the term for a Turkish wheat pilaf used for porridge by British sailors as early as 1740. Its use as the name of a Kentucky stew is traced to Gus Jaubert, of John Hunt Morgan's cavalry, who applied it to field rations he concocted and later prepared for political gatherings.

Lexington grocer James T. Looney, known as "the Burgoo King," carried on Jaubert's tradition with flair (a horse given Looney's nickname won the Kentucky Derby and the Preakness in 1932). Looney's recipe for 1,200 gallons of burgoo: lean meat (not game), fat hens, potatoes, onions, tomatoes, tomato puree, carrots, and corn, seasoned with red pepper and salt and his secret sauce. Family recipes often specify the type of meats for burgoo, with additional vegetables and seasonings, but few cooks would agree on the exact ingredients or proportions; burgoo is what you make it.

MARTY GODBEY

BURKESVILLE. The county seat of Cumberland County, Burkesville is located at the junction of KY 90 and KY 61. The site was originally called Cumberland Crossing. In 1798, Burkesville was established on land that belonged to Samuel Burkes, an early settler in the area from Virginia, and named for him. Burkesville was incorporated on February 23, 1846. The Cumberland River was an important economic link for Burkesville and Cumberland County in transporting goods to market. During the nineteenth and early twentieth centuries, Burkesville was an important riverboat landing. Much commerce was conducted in timber, tobacco, and farm produce. The first courthouse was built in Burkesville in 1800. The two-story log structure was destroyed by a flood in 1826. The second courthouse was burned by the Confederate forces of Gen. H.B. Lyons on January 3, 1865, when his troops ransacked the town. Cumberland County's third courthouse, constructed in 1867-68, was destroyed by fire on December 30, 1933. The fourth courthouse was completed in 1934.

A well in search of salt water was drilled near Burkesville in 1829. It hit oil, which gushed fifty feet into the air. The oil flowed onto the Cumberland River and ignited, and the river of fire produced a spectacular sight. The Cumberland County Oil Festival is held each September to commemorate this event. After experiencing slow industrial growth through much of the twentieth century, Burkesville in 1970 began to attract garment plants. Bole Evans of Kentucky, makers of work uniforms; Oshkosh B'Gosh, producers of jeans; and Sutton Shirt Corporation are the town's largest employers. Other manufacturing firms produce lumber, crushed stone, heat transfer products, and custom wood products.

The population of this fifth-class city was 1,717 in 1970; 2,051 in 1980; and 1,815 in 1990.

RON D. BRYANT

BURLEY TOBACCO GROWERS COOPERATIVE ASSOCIATION INC. The organization that administers the U.S. government's price stabilization program for burley tobacco is the second group known as the Burley Tobacco Growers Cooperative Association. Central Kentucky burley growers formed their first cooperative association in the early 1920s to withhold tobacco from the market until satisfactory prices were offered. In the aftermath of World War I, the new Federal Reserve Board had tried to end postwar inflation by nearly doubling the federal discount rate, and the tightening of the nation's economy had led to a significant decline in general prices within a year. In 1920 Kentucky burley markets opened with bids less than half those in 1919.

To counter the low tobacco prices, Robert W. Bingham, owner of the *Louisville Courier-Journal*, enlisted the help of organizers Aaron Shapiro and Joseph Passoneau in creating a marketing cooperative to pool Kentucky's burley crop. Bingham lent the cooperative $1 million of his own money, in addition to money made available by the War Finance Corporation. In 1922 the co-op claimed more than 77,000 members. As with earlier organizing efforts, however, the tobacco companies offered nonpoolers more than they did those who joined the pool, and the cooperative could not keep farmers signed to their contracts (see BLACK PATCH WAR). The organization collapsed in 1925.

In 1941, when the federal government's price support system was introduced, the current Burley Tobacco Growers Cooperative Association was formed. The federal government lends the association funds to stabilize burley prices. The 275,000 members of the association are burley growers in Kentucky, Indiana, Missouri, Ohio, and West Virginia.

See William E. Ellis, "Robert Worth Bingham and the Crisis of Cooperative Marketing in the Twenties," *Agricultural History* 56 (Jan. 1982); Reavis Cox, *Competition in the American Tobacco Industry, 1911-1932* (New York 1933).

BURLEY TOBACCO SOCIETY. The Burley Tobacco Society came into being in 1906 after a series of unsuccessful organizing drives by Bluegrass tobacco growers, who sought to raise prices for their product in a market controlled by the American Tobacco Company. With sound organization and financing, the society pooled over half of the region's 1906 burley crop, and had pledges for three-fourths of the 1907 crop. Boycotted by American Tobacco, the society in 1908 launched a successful large-scale agricultural strike, which was partly responsible for a cutback in planting to less than 10 percent of the previous year's crop. Another factor was armed NIGHT RIDERS who coerced many reluctant farmers into abandoning a crop. In November 1908, American Tobacco bought the pooled crops at the prices the Burley Tobacco Society demanded. Strained by the strike and facing internal conflicts, however, the society by 1910 was no longer a force, and it was dissolved in 1914.

See Theodore Saloutos, *Farmer Movements in the South* (Berkeley, Calif., 1960).

TRACY A. CAMPBELL

BURLINGTON. Burlington, the county seat of Boone County, is located on KY 18 and KY 338. Originally named Craigs Camp, the town was built on seventy-four acres of land donated by John H. Craig and Robert Johnson in 1799. In 1800 the site was renamed Wilmington, and in 1816 (some sources claim 1806) the name was changed to Burlington. The first Boone County courthouse, a log structure, was constructed in Burlington about 1800. Another building, made of brick, was erected in 1817. The third courthouse was built in 1889 and was placed on the National Register of Historic Places in 1979 as part of a historic district. The town was incorporated in 1824, and in 1870 the population was 277. Although Burlington was reincorporated in 1910, the charter was annulled in 1923. Today Burlington is one of the two unincorporated county seats in the state. Burlington's principal industry is the manufacture of boxes for washing machines.

The town's population was approximately six hundred in 1986.   RON D. BRYANT

BURMAN, BEN LUCIEN. Ben Lucien Burman (born Behrman), writer, was born in Covington, Kentucky, on December 12, 1895. His parents, Samuel N. and Minnie (Hurwitz) Behrman, were Jewish immigrants. Burman attended Miami University in Ohio during 1913-15. During World War I, he served in France, where he was wounded at Soissons in 1918. After graduating from Harvard in 1920, Burman taught in 1920-21 at Holmes High School in Covington, where he was accused of teaching bolshevism. In the early 1920s, Burman worked for the *Cincinnati Times-Star* and other newspapers, and for magazines including the *Nation, Reader's Digest,* and *Saturday Review.* His books about life on the river have been translated into numerous languages, and two of his novels were made into movies, *Mississippi* (1929) and *Steamboat Round the Bend* (1933), with Will Rogers. Burman received several literary awards, including the Southern Authors Award in 1938, and was given the French Legion of Honor in 1946 for World War II dispatches.

Burman married Alice Caddy on September 19, 1927. He died on November 12, 1984, in New York City and was cremated.   CHARLES D. KING

BURNETT, HENRY CORNELIUS. Henry Cornelius Burnett, lawyer, U.S. congressman, and Confederate senator, was born in Essex County, Virginia, on October 25, 1825, to Dr. Isaac and Martha (Garnett) Burnett. The family migrated to Cadiz, Kentucky, where Burnett attended local schools and a Hopkinsville academy. A Democrat, he served briefly as Trigg County circuit court clerk (1851-53) before 1st District voters sent him to the U.S. House of Representatives, where he began serving on March 4, 1855. Burnett succeeded the veteran Linn Boyd of Paducah, who had been Speaker of the House.

On June 20, 1861, Burnett, a three-term incumbent, was the only candidate elected to Congress from Kentucky on a Southern rights platform. In the House of Representatives, Burnett denounced Lincoln and voted against war measures. He was expelled from Congress on December 3, 1861, after he recruited for the Confederacy and presided in Russellville over secession conventions that formed a rump Confederate state government. He also recruited the 8th Kentucky Infantry Regiment, which was captured at Fort Donelson. Burnett escaped and became a Confederate senator, serving from February 19, 1862, to February 18, 1865.

After the Civil War, Burnett was charged with treason but not tried. He then resumed his Cadiz law practice. He died of cholera on September 28, 1866, and was buried in the East End Cemetery in Cadiz. In 1847, Burnett had married Mary A. Terry of Cadiz; they had three children, Mary, Muscoe, and Henry, the last a well-known Paducah attorney.

See Berry F. Craig, "Henry Cornelius Burnett: Champion of Southern Rights," *Register* 77 (Autumn 1979): 266-74.   BERRY CRAIG

BURNETT, MICAJAH. Micajah Burnett, Shaker architect, was born in Patrick County, Virginia, in 1791, the son of Benjamin and Elizabeth Burnett. In 1792 the Burnetts moved to present-day Wayne County, Kentucky, and in 1808 to Pleasant Hill, the SHAKER COMMUNITY founded in Mercer County two years earlier. Although Burnett had no formal training in architecture, he gained practical experience in his first assignment, at the age of seventeen, working as a framing carpenter for the 1809 Centre Family Dwelling at Pleasant Hill.

Burnett became the main architect and master builder for Pleasant Hill, where he expressed a creative genius in design, along with his personal experience in the building trades and his interpretation of builder's handbooks. He also held the responsibility of a Shaker trading deacon, traveling as far south as New Orleans to sell Shaker goods from Pleasant Hill. By 1860 Burnett was working in the community post office, perhaps as a concession to his advanced age and half century of service as an architect to Pleasant Hill. In 1872 he retired to enjoy his extensive library and the visits of other Shakers. Burnett died on January 10, 1879, and was buried in the Shaker village cemetery.

See Thomas D. Clark and F. Gerald Ham, *Pleasant Hill and Its Shakers* (Harrodsburg, Ky., 1968).   JAMES C. THOMAS

BURNETT, RICHARD DANIEL. Richard Daniel Burnett, musician, was born in Wayne County, Kentucky, in 1883. Orphaned at twelve and blinded during a holdup in 1907, he became a banjoist and ballad hawker. In 1927 he teamed up with fiddler Leonard Rutherford and made numerous phonograph recordings. A valuable link to country music's folk past, Burnett was a repository of material that he had preserved and/or rewritten. His most famous composition was the semiautobiographical "Man of Constant Sorrow." Burnett died in Somerset, Kentucky, on January 23, 1977, survived by his wife, Georgiana (Pratt), and five of their seven children.

See Charles K. Wolfe, *Kentucky Country* (Lexington, Ky., 1982).   CHARLES F. FABER

BURR CONSPIRACY. The Burr Conspiracy is the name historians have given to a decision by Aaron Burr, some months after his retirement from the vice-presidency of the United States in 1805, to lead an expeditionary force down the Ohio and Mississippi rivers in what may have been an effort to seize Mexico from its Spanish owners. Even before Burr had fully committed himself to this enterprise, segments of the U.S. press were accusing him of planning to withdraw from the Union the states and territories west of the Appalachians and to create an empire of his own by combining these with conquered Mexico. Burr claimed that he intended only to establish a colony.

Burr was at the Falls of the Ohio in Kentucky, supervising preparations for his trip down the rivers, when in December 1806 the judge of the U.S. district court in Frankfort, acting on the second such request from the district attorney, impaneled a grand jury to inquire into his activities. One of Burr's lawyers at this hearing was the twenty-nine-year-old Henry Clay of Lexington. The high point of the testimony came when both the coeditors of the *Western World*, a local newspaper, admitted that articles describing Burr as engaged in a plot to dismember the Union rested on nothing but hearsay. The grand jury brought in a verdict of "no true bill" and that evening Burr was the guest of honor at a giant ball.

It was his last taste of public adulation. A proclamation by President Thomas Jefferson, pronouncing Burr as "beyond question" guilty of treason, was slowly making its way westward. Authorities seized boats Burr had ordered built at Marietta, Ohio, and when on December 27 he joined his followers on the Ohio River near the Mississippi, he found not the small army he had hoped for but fewer than a hundred men, women, and children.

When Burr arrived in the Mississippi Territory on January 10, 1807, he learned that Gen. James Wilkinson, his supposed collaborator, had turned on him by sending Jefferson the translation of a cipher letter signed by Burr. The document was thought incriminating, though it is clear that little in the surviving copies of it was written by Burr. Burr was again summoned before a grand jury, this time in Washington, the capital of Mississippi Territory. He was again exonerated, but the presiding judge ordered him to continue reporting to the court. Fearful of arrest by federal agents, Burr fled the region, only to be seized by a federal military unit in what is now Alabama and sent east to Richmond, Virginia, to stand trial in the U.S. circuit court before Chief Justice John Marshall.

Though the government called almost 140 witnesses, it was unable to prove that Burr was guilty either of treason or of trying to grab the property of a foreign government.

His acquittal failed to alter public perception of him as a traitor and for at least a century most historians endorsed this view. Some have since concluded otherwise. Burr may have been a naif— "You do not know the world," his daughter Theodosia scolded him in one of her letters—but had he and his little band been left to their own devices, he surely would have had the good sense to terminate his expedition at the Bastrop Lands tract in what is now Louisiana, which he had purchased with the object of settling there.

See Milton Lomask, *Aaron Burr* (New York 1979 and 1982); Walter Flavius McCaleb, *The Aaron Burr Conspiracy* (New York 1966).

MILTON LOMASK

BUSH, JOSEPH HENRY. Joseph Henry Bush, known for his portraits of prominent Kentuckians and southern plantation owners, was born to Philip, Jr., and Elizabeth (Palmer) Bush sometime between 1794 and 1800, probably in Mercer County, Kentucky. Bush's father was an amateur portraitist. When Bush was seventeen or eighteen, his talent came to the attention of Henry Clay, who arranged for him to study painting with Thomas Sully in Philadelphia. By 1818 Bush was back in Kentucky, where he opened his first portrait studio in Frankfort. That year he painted a pair of portraits of Gen. George Rogers Clark and William Clark in Louisville. In 1819 Bush lived on Main Street in Frankfort in a house that doubled as his studio. At various times he also lived on Mill Street in Lexington, at the Galt House in Louisville, and in Cincinnati. In 1826 he occupied a studio in Cincinnati at the Academy of Fine Arts on Main Street between Third and Fourth streets.

Among his most notable portraits are those of Judge John Speed of Louisville; Henry Clay (ca. 1840); two renderings of Gen. Zachary Taylor (ca. 1848), one of which hangs in the White House; and Maj. William Preston Johnson (1854), founder of Tulane University in New Orleans. Many of Bush's paintings are owned by Transylvania University.

Around 1853 Bush was invited to Oak Hill in Woodford County to paint various members of the Meade and Woolfolk families. In 1861 he moved to the home of his brother, Dr. James M. Bush, in Lexington on North Mill Street. He died there on January 11, 1865, and was buried in Lexington Cemetery.

See William Barrow Floyd, *Jouett-Bush-Frazer: Early Kentucky Artists* (Lexington, Ky., 1968); Samuel Woodson Price, *The Old Masters of the Bluegrass* (Louisville 1902).

BUTLER, MANN. Mann Butler, who wrote the first generally reliable history of Kentucky, was born in July 1784 in Baltimore and spent eleven years of his childhood in England. He returned to the United States at age fourteen and studied at St. Mary's College in the District of Columbia, where he received degrees in both medicine and law. In 1806 Mann moved to Lexington, Kentucky, where he briefly practiced law. In the same year he began his lifelong career as an educator, founding an academy in Versailles. In August 1806 he married Martha Dedman. In 1810 he moved to Maysville, where he taught until 1811.

Butler later taught in Frankfort and accepted a professorship at Transylvania University. From 1831 to 1845 he taught in Louisville, where he helped found the University of Louisville and the Louisville Public Library.

Butler's history of Kentucky, published in 1834 and revised and enlarged in 1836, contains detailed descriptions of life on the frontier and is remarkably free of partisan political observations. His other writings include an unfinished history of the Ohio Valley, which was published in part in a contemporary magazine. In 1845 he moved to St. Louis and taught until his death on November 1, 1855, in a train wreck.   ROBERT M. IRELAND

BUTLER, WENDELL PACE. Wendell Pace Butler, state education official in several administrations, was born in Sulphur Well, Kentucky, on December 18, 1912, to Henry and Pearl (Pace) Butler. He received a bachelor of arts degree from Western Kentucky State College (now Western Kentucky University) in 1936 and a master of arts from the University of Kentucky in 1950. He was a teacher in the Metcalfe County public schools from 1931 to 1936, and served as superintendent of schools there from 1938 to 1942. After serving in the navy during World War II, he occupied a seat in the state Senate from 1947 to 1951, where he served as chairman of the Senate Education Committee. He was state superintendent of public instruction (1952-56) during the administration of Gov. Lawrence Wetherby (1950-55). That administration initiated the Minimum Foundation Program, designed to distribute school funding more equitably by providing minimum funding on the basis of attendance. Butler also served on an advisory commission to the governor that aided in the racial integration of Kentucky schools.

In 1956 Butler went into business as president and manager of the School Service Company in Frankfort, which sold school supplies and equipment in the state. He returned to public life in 1960 and for the following twenty years moved from one position to another in state government during successive gubernatorial administrations. He served as superintendent of public instruction in 1960-64 and 1968-72, as commissioner of agriculture in 1964-68 and 1972-76, and as secretary of education and humanities from 1976 until his retirement in February 1980.

Butler married Edna Pauline Ford on January 15, 1947. They have three children—Rendell, Kendell, and Wendell.

BUTLER, WILLIAM ORLANDO. William Orlando Butler, soldier and statesman, was born on April 19, 1791, in Jessamine County, Kentucky, the son of Percival and Mildred (Hawkins) Butler. He grew up on his father's estate at Port William (now Carrollton) at the confluence of the Kentucky and Ohio rivers. His father, who had served under Gen. George Washington during the Revolutionary War, was the first adjutant general of Kentucky. Butler graduated from Transylvania University in 1812, then studied law in Lexington for several months. With the outbreak of the War of 1812, Butler joined a company of the 5th Regiment of Kentucky Volunteers. In December 1812, Butler was appointed ensign and assigned to a company of the 17th Regiment, U.S. Infantry, which was attached to the northwest command of Gen. James Winchester. At the River Raisin in January 1813 Butler distinguished himself in battle, was wounded, captured, and then marched with other prisoners to Fort Niagara, where he was eventually paroled.

In 1814 Butler joined Andrew Jackson's army in the South and participated in the taking of Pensacola and in the Battle of New Orleans. As acting major of the 44th Infantry Regiment, Butler led a night attack against the British in New Orleans on December 23, 1814, and was stationed near the center of Jackson's line during the battle on January 8, 1815. Following the war, he replaced his brother Thomas as an aide to Jackson. In 1816-17 Butler was the commanding officer for the 1st U.S. Infantry Regiment and conducted surveying operations for the Jackson military road. He resigned from the army in 1817 with the rank of major.

Butler returned to Port William in 1817. He practiced law, served in the state legislature (1817-18), and wrote poetry. In the 1820s he gained recognition with the publication of his poem "The Boatman's Horn." In 1839 he was elected to the U.S. House of Representatives, serving from March 4, 1839, to March 3, 1843. A Jacksonian Democrat, Butler ran for governor of Kentucky against the Whig candidate William Owsley. Although defeated, Butler greatly reduced the Whig majority in the state.

When the Mexican War began, President James K. Polk appointed Butler a major general of volunteers. Butler was ordered to Mexico to support Gen. Zachary Taylor and at the Battle of Monterrey was Taylor's second-in-command. On September 21, 1846, while directing his men during an attack on the city, Butler was wounded in the leg and forced to quit the field. For his bravery at Monterrey, Butler was presented with a sword from the people of Kentucky and another from the U.S. Congress. In 1847 Butler was given a new division and joined Gen. Winfield Scott in Mexico City. After Scott's departure in February 1848, Butler was placed in command of all U.S. forces in Mexico and presided over the withdrawal of U.S. troops.

In 1848 Butler ran for the vice-presidency on the Democratic ticket with Lewis Cass, of Michigan, and in 1852 was a strong contender for the Democratic party's presidential nomination. His last public service was as a delegate to the Washington Peace Conference in 1861. Politically, Butler was a moderate. Although a slaveholder, he was opposed to the extension of slavery and favored gradual legal emancipation. He stood firmly for the preservation of the Union and was a Union Democrat during the Civil War. In April 1817, Butler married Eliza Todd, the daughter of Gen. Robert Todd of Lexington. He died in Carrollton on August 6, 1880, and was buried there in a private cemetery.

See G.F. Roberts, "William O. Butler, Kentucky Cavalier," M.A. thesis, University of Kentucky, 1962.   GERALD F. ROBERTS

BUTLER COUNTY. Butler County, the fifty-third county in order of formation, is located in the Western Coal Field region of Kentucky. Its 431 square miles are bordered by Muhlenberg, Ohio, Grayson, Edmonson, Warren, and Logan counties. The Green River flows through the southwest part of the state. The county was formed from parts of Logan and Ohio counties on January 18, 1810. It was named for Gen. Richard Butler, a Revolutionary War soldier from Pennsylvania, who was killed by Indians at St. Clair's Defeat in 1791.

Richard C. Dellium and James Forgy were the first to settle in what is now Butler County, near Berry's Lick in 1786. Salt was produced at Berry's Lick using horses to draw water from wells, some of which were over three hundred feet deep. The eleven justices of the peace who first governed the county recommended MORGANTOWN as the county seat. In the 1830s the state built locks and dams on the Green River to improve navigation. Barges and steamboats on the Green carried goods to market and provided mail service. Showboats brought entertainment to river towns. Slate mined at Indigo Bend on the Green River, eleven miles from Morgantown, was used to make school writing tablets. Rochester, Woodbury, and Morgantown became busy river towns and are still the largest communities in the county. In the late 1800s and early 1900s Morgantown and Rochester both had seminaries. At one time Brooklyn, Aberdeen, and Mining City were also sizable communities.

Although only a few skirmishes took place in Butler County, the Civil War slowed development and divided the citizenry. One of the first Union soldiers to be killed in western Kentucky was from Butler County. A stone monument on Big Hill, a short distance from Morgantown, marks the site where Granville Allen died in a skirmish on October 29, 1861. After the war, veterans from Confederate and Union forces joined to raise funds for a Civil War monument. The monument, dedicated on May 30, 1907, lists the names of Butler County citizens who fought in the war. It stands in front of the courthouse and is one of the few monuments in the state that honors both Confederate and Union soldiers.

After the war, Butler County again experienced growth. But riverboats were replaced by railroads, and as Butler County had no railways, access to markets was limited. In the early 1920s the U.S. Army Corps of Engineers moved its Green and Barren River Maintenance Corps from Woodbury to Owensboro, causing the decline of the economy in Woodbury. In 1965 Lock and Dam No. 4 at Woodbury washed out and in early 1980 Lock and Dam No. 3 at Rochester was abandoned by the Corps of Engineers. Thus, the Green River was closed to traffic.

In 1926 a hard-surface road (KY 403) was built from Morgantown to Borah's Ferry at Logansport. In 1949 the Morgantown-Aberdeen bridge across the Green River and a straighter, paved highway to Beaver Dam and Owensboro (US 231) were constructed. The Butler County High School was completed in 1952. In 1953 the county's economic outlook improved as the Kane Manufacturing Company, a clothing factory, brought three hundred jobs to Morgantown. The Green River Parkway linked Butler County to the nationwide interstate road system in 1970. A coal mining boom in 1974 gave a boost to the economy of the county by providing jobs and tax revenues. With the development of the industrial park in Morgantown during the mid-1970s, the county now has seven manufacturing businesses, including the Sumitoma Company and the Kellwood Company. The local economy is diversified among industry, mining, and agriculture.

Butler County's more notable citizens include: B.L.D. Guffy, chief justice of the Kentucky court of appeals; Claude BLOCH, one of only four Kentuckians to achieve the U.S. Navy rank of admiral; John M. Moore, Methodist bishop, one of three presiding bishops when the three Methodist denominations merged to form the United Methodist church, and one of the organizers of Southern Methodist University; and Gov. William S. Taylor (1899-1900). During the 1920s Maurice THATCHER was a U.S. representative from Louisville (1923-33), and John W. Moore a U.S. representative from Butler County (1925-29).

The population of the county was 9,723 in 1970; 11,064 in 1980; and 11,245 in 1990.

See Butler County Historical and Genealogical Society, *Butler County, Kentucky History* (Morgantown, Ky., 1987); Bennett F. Bratcher, *History of Butler County* (Morgantown, Ky., 1960).

LOIS RUSS

BYBEE POTTERY. Bybee Pottery, amid the hills of Madison County, Kentucky, in the small rural town of Bybee, may be the oldest continuously operating pottery west of the Alleghenies. Sales records date back to 1845, when the business was operated by the Cornelison family, but it may have been established as early as 1809. Walter Cornelison is the fifth-generation owner. The central log building where the clayware is made and sold has housed the business for over a century. The Bybee Pottery's success lies in the clayware's functionality, its good color, and its simple ruggedness. The production process is much the same today as it was over a century ago: mining the clay, mixing it with water, grinding it in the antique pug mill, throwing it on the wheel to shape it, trimming it by hand, and storing it in an antique vault to keep it moist. The clay deposits that were mined by the first settlers of Kentucky near Bybee are still the source of raw materials.

See William E. Ellis, H.E. Everman, Richard Sears, *Madison County: 200 Years in Retrospect* (Richmond, Ky., 1985).

BYCK, DANN CONRAD, SR. Dann Conrad Byck, Sr., was born in Atlanta, Georgia, on October 24, 1899, to Louis S. and Carrie (Dann) Byck. The family moved to Louisville in 1901, where Louis Byck and his brother opened Byck Brothers and Company, a retail shoe store that eventually became a women's and children's clothing store—one of the largest locally owned clothing stores in the city. Dann Byck was educated in the public grade schools and graduated from Male High School in 1917. He attended the University of Pennsylvania and graduated from the university's Wharton School of Finance with a degree in economics in 1921. Byck then spent a year in New York City working with a retail firm.

Upon his return to Louisville in 1922, Byck worked at various levels of merchandising in his father's company. He became vice-president of Byck Brothers and Company in 1925 and president in 1930. He incorporated the company, which had a store on South Fourth in Louisville and another on Lexington Road in St. Matthews. Byck contributed much of his time to charities, particularly Jewish welfare relief programs. He was as an active member of the Community Chest for years and a member of the board of the Adath Israel Temple. A political leader as well, he was elected to the Louisville board of aldermen in 1947 and served as president of the board from 1947 until 1953, when he decided not to seek reelection. As an alderman, Byck led the way in Louisville's expressway program, and was a leader in establishing the Louisville Orchestra as a part of the city's cultural revival. When Louisville Mayor Leland Taylor died suddenly in 1947, Byck was acting mayor for a month, until the board of alderman named Charles Farnsley to succeed Taylor. Byck also served on the city's board of education from 1955 to 1959, during the execution of the city's desegregation plan. President of the board in 1958, he was a strong advocate of the merger of city and county schools.

Byck married Mary Helen Adler on June 27, 1931; they had three children: Lucy, Elizabeth, and Dann, Jr. Byck died on May 30, 1960; his body was cremated.

C

CABBAGE PATCH SETTLEMENT. The Cabbage Patch Settlement was founded in Louisville in 1910 by Louise Marshall to alleviate urban poverty. The Christian social service project originally served those who lived in a truck-farming area known as the Cabbage Patch, south of Oak Street and west of Sixth Street. Alice (Hegan) Rice, who served on the settlement's first board of directors, used the area as the setting for one of her most popular novels, *Mrs. Wiggs of the Cabbage Patch*. The Cabbage Patch Settlement House, located at 1314 South Sixth Street, offers a total social service program to people of all ages in the Old Louisville area. GAIL HENSON

CABIN CREEK WAR ROAD. The Cabin Creek War Road was an entry into Kentucky from the east for early explorers and settlers. The trail began at the mouth of Cabin Creek on the Ohio River, five and a half miles above Limestone Creek in Mason County. (Cabin Creek was most likely named for the cabins that early explorers and survey crews built near the point where it enters the river.) The road cut across a corner of Lewis County into Fleming County, near present-day Orangeburg, where it split. One branch went to the Mt. Carmel area and the other toward Lewisburg. The two branches converged near present-day Flemingsburg and proceeded past the village of Battle Run before terminating at the Upper Blue Licks. The well-traveled trail was initially used by Indians who crossed the river from Ohio to hunt game near the Blue Licks. The trail was marked with Indian drawings of animals, the sun, and the moon.

See William M. Talley, "The Cabin Creek War Road," *Register* 63 (Jan. 1965): 17-23.

CADIZ. Cadiz, the county seat of Trigg County, is located on the Little River at the junction of U.S. 68 and KY 139. The origin of the town's name is unknown. One of the earliest settlers on the east bank of the Little River was Thomas Wadlington, who settled in the Cadiz vicinity as early as 1792. Like many others who settled there, he was from North Carolina. Large scale settlement began around 1814 and included Isaac McCullom, Marmaduke Ingram, William Husk, John Langley, and James Thompson. The town was laid off in 1820 on fifty-two acres of land deeded by Robert Baker for the establishment of the Trigg County seat and was incorporated in 1822. Early industries included several water mills and a number of small distilleries.

The location of Cadiz as the county seat did not meet with general approval in Trigg County, but in a March 6, 1822, election, Cadiz won over the rival cities of Canton, Warrington, and Center. The first official courthouse was a frame building built in 1821. It was replaced by a brick building in 1833, which in turn was replaced in 1843. The third courthouse was burned by the Confederates during the Civil War and was replaced by a fourth structure in 1865. The fourth and fifth courthouses were destroyed by fire as well. A sixth courthouse, a two-story brick building, was completed in 1922.

Cadiz grew as an agricultural, trading, merchandising, and shipping center. Tobacco was shipped by flatboat down the Little River to the Cumberland River and to downstream markets. The city was strategically located at a junction of the Clarksville (Tennessee)–Smithland road and the Columbus–Bowling Green stage and mail route established by the state legislature around 1820.

In 1830 the town had 168 residents and by 1860 had grown to a population of 706. During the Civil War most city residents were pro-Southern, but there were no major battles near the city. On December 13, 1864, a company of Confederates of Gen. Hylan B. Lyon's brigade routed a detachment of black Union soldiers who were bivouacked in the courthouse. One Union soldier who had smallpox was left behind and shot by the Confederates, who then burned the building.

In 1870 the town population had fallen to 680 and by 1880 had dropped again to 646. Cadiz had become a center for dark leaf tobacco and was a hotbed of NIGHT RIDER activism against the American Tobacco Company from 1906 to 1908. Many farmers turned to stock raising and by the 1930s Cadiz had become renowned as a ham shipping center.

In 1901 the Cadiz Railroad was built from the city to Gracey, where the ten-mile-long track connected with the Illinois Central (now Illinois Central Gulf). The railroad hauled hams, logs, and other freight. In 1966 a large interest in the railroad was sold to the Hoover Ball Bearing Company, which built a $3 million plant at Cadiz in that year. By 1990, Hoover was the town's largest employer, but it had abandoned the Cadiz Railroad.

Cadiz was profoundly affected by the creation of nearby Kentucky Lake and Lake Barkley and benefited from the tourist trade. Numerous retail stores were established there along with summer and retirement homes.

The population of the fifth-class city was 1,987 in 1970; 1,661 in 1980; and 2,148 in 1990.

CALDWELL, CHARLES. Charles Caldwell, physician and educator, named for his Irish immigrant father, was born in Caswell County, North Carolina, on May 14, 1772. He earned an M.D. degree (1796) from the University of Pennsylvania, where he studied under Benjamin Rush. Caldwell then practiced medicine in Philadelphia, taught at his alma mater, and edited the magazine *Port Folio* (1812), to which he also contributed. He moved to Lexington in 1819 at the invitation of the president of Transylvania University, where he developed the medical faculty into one of the nation's strongest, though his arrogant personality made opponents of many. In 1821, with $10,000 appropriated by the General Assembly and with other funds, Caldwell purchased in France a notable collection of rare scientific books, many of which are extant at Transylvania. Dismissed by the university's trustees in 1837, Caldwell helped to found the Louisville Medical Institute, one of the two forerunners of the University of Louisville; its success was the downfall of Transylvania's medical program.

Author of more than two hundred publications, Caldwell was advanced for the time in his study of fevers and in his teaching that nature tends to restore health without the physician's intervention. Yet he was also an early enthusiast of phrenology, and fought a rear-guard defense of the outmoded concept of vitalism. He was married twice. After his death on July 9, 1853, a stepdaughter edited his autobiography, which remains the principal source of information on his life. He is buried in Cave Hill Cemetery, Louisville.

See Charles Caldwell, *Autobiography* (Philadelphia 1855); Walter Wilson Jennings, *Transylvania: Pioneer University of the West* (New York 1955).

CHARLES BOEWE

CALDWELL, ISAAC. Isaac Caldwell, attorney and third president of the UNIVERSITY OF LOUISVILLE, was born on June 30, 1824, near Columbia, Adair County, Kentucky, the son of William and Anne (Trabue) Caldwell. He attended Georgetown College, studied law, and was admitted to the bar in 1847. He practiced law in Columbia, first with Judge Zachariah Wheat, then with his brother, U.S. Congressman George Alfred Caldwell. In 1852 they moved their office to Louisville, where Caldwell became one of the city's most successful criminal lawyers.

In 1870 Caldwell championed the LOUISVILLE & NASHVILLE Railroad and its business interests when the Kentucky legislature considered giving a central Kentucky right-of-way to the CINCINNATI SOUTHERN Railroad, a likely challenger of the L&N in the southern trade. In 1872 Caldwell opposed the primacy of federal authority in Kentucky civil rights matters when he argued the case of *Blyew v. United States* before the U.S. Supreme Court.

During Caldwell's service as president of the University of Louisville (1869-85), the university's medical department joined the American Medical College Association (founded in 1876) and raised its standards for admission and graduation. As he was seriously ill in his last year, he called meetings of the board of trustees at his home.

Caldwell married Catherine Smith of Louisville on January 20, 1857. He died November 25, 1885, and was buried in Louisville's St. Louis Cemetery. An editorial in the *Louisville Courier-Journal* on the day after his death stated that Caldwell left "no equal behind him at the bar whose recognized head he was [for] so long." WILLIAM J. MORISON

CALDWELL, JOHN W. John W. Caldwell, prominent in early Kentucky politics, was born in Prince

Edward County, Virginia, in 1757. He settled near the site of present-day Danville in 1781. He served under George Rogers Clark in the Indian campaign of 1786. In the conventions held in 1787-88 to prepare for separation from Virginia, Caldwell represented Nelson County. Following the constitutional convention in 1792, he was chosen as an elector to select Kentucky's first U.S. senators. He was elected as a state senator from Nelson County in 1792-93, and elected lieutenant governor as a Jeffersonian Republican on September 5, 1804, under Gov. Christopher Greenup (1804-08). On November 19, 1804, two months after assuming office, Caldwell died in Frankfort. Caldwell County, established in 1809 by the General Assembly, is named in his honor.

CALDWELL COUNTY. Caldwell County, the fifty-first county in order of formation, is located in the western part of the state in the Pennyroyal region. It is bordered by Crittenden, Webster, Hopkins, Christian, Trigg, and Lyon counties and has an area of 357 square miles. The county seat is PRINCETON.

In 1797 Capt. William Prince of South Carolina received a patent for a tract of land that surrounded Big Spring at the head of Eddy Creek. On a promontory above Big Spring, where many trails converged, he erected a large two-story limestone structure that served as both home and tavern. The building, Shandy Hall, was not only one of the earliest structures in this region but probably the first masonry building in all of western Kentucky. The settlement that developed there around Shandy Hall was originally known as Eddy Grove.

Prince's settlement originally lay within the part of Christian County from which Livingston County was created in 1799 and which ten years later was subdivided to form Caldwell County. It was named in honor of Gen. John Caldwell, who had served under Gen. George Rogers Clark in the Indian wars and who had been a prominent legislator and businessman in the Bluegrass region before he moved to western Kentucky. He was the first western Kentuckian to be elected to the Kentucky state Senate, and was the state's second lieutenant governor (1804). When it was formed, Caldwell County encompassed all of what are now Lyon and Calloway counties and portions of Trigg, Marshall, Hickman, Graves, and Fulton counties. Much to the dismay of the citizens living in the vicinity of Eddy Grove, EDDYVILLE was chosen the first county seat of Caldwell County.

After Prince died in 1810, his widow, Elizabeth Prince, donated fifty acres of land around Eddy Grove, where the new seat of Caldwell County would be established. The county court expressed its appreciation by renaming the town Princetown, soon changed to Princeton. When Caldwell County was created in 1809, it was one of two Kentucky counties that claimed land west of the Tennessee River in territory recognized by the federal government as Chickasaw tribal lands. After the Jackson

Purchase in 1818, the newly created town of Princeton became the staging area for the settlement of the Jackson Purchase region. In 1820 the Kentucky legislature approved legislation creating the Commonwealth Bank of Kentucky. The bank's westernmost branch was located in Princeton to serve those who settled in the newly opened Jackson Purchase. Two years later, the Register of the Kentucky Land Office opened a branch in Princeton to further encourage settlement of the Purchase.

Princeton's role in the western movement was enhanced when a state road was built in the late 1820s from Elizabethtown through Princeton to the Mississippi River crossing at Columbus. During the same period, another state road was built northward from Hopkinsville through Princeton to a number of crossings of the Ohio, to accommodate southerners migrating to the Midwest. Farriers, blacksmiths, wagon shops, harness and saddle shops, taverns, and all types of merchants whose wares were needed by settlers moving west, kept the young town of Princeton thriving for years.

Since early settlement, the economy of Caldwell County was based upon agriculture, and the principal crop was dark-fired tobacco. Western Kentucky was the most strategically located of all the regions for the export of tobacco through the port of New Orleans; in 1860 Caldwell County ranked sixth among Kentucky counties in the production of tobacco. In the early 1900s the county was at the center of a farmers' revolt against monopolistic tobacco processors and manufacturers, known as the BLACK PATCH WAR. David Amoss, of Cobb, Caldwell County, was one of those who organized farmers into vigilante bands.

Before the advent of railroads, Caldwell County produce was shipped to market through the Cumberland River ports of Eddyville, Dycusburg, and the Tradewater River port of Belleville. The Elizabethtown & Paducah (now the Paducah & Louisville) Railroad reached Princeton in 1872, and by the 1880s connections were made through the city to Nashville; Evansville, Indiana; and north-south routes at Fulton, Kentucky. Railroads played a dominant role in Princeton's growth. Train and maintenance crews were assembled there at the large railroad yard, and a roundhouse existed to maintain the steam locomotives. With the building of interstate highways, the Princeton area remained an important transportation center for western Kentucky as the Western Kentucky Parkway skirted the town and intersected I-24 just to the west of the town.

The population of the county was 13,179 in 1970; 13,473 in 1980; and 13,232 in 1990.

See Clauscine R. Baker, *First History of Caldwell County, Kentucky* (Madisonville, Ky., 1936); Samuel W. Steger, *Caldwell County, Kentucky History* (Paducah, Ky., 1987).   SAMUEL STEGER

CALHOUN. Calhoun, the county seat of McLean County, is located on the Green River and KY 81. The town was first laid out in 1785 by Henry Rhoads and called Rhoadsville. Solomon Rhoads, his brother, then built a fort. John Hanley, who took the Rhoads land by lawsuit in 1787, is said to have renamed the town Fort Vienna. On February 23, 1849, the town was named in honor of Judge John Calhoun, first circuit judge of Fort Vienna, who also served in the U.S. Congress during 1835-39. The town, incorporated January 7, 1852, became the county seat in 1854 when McLean County was formed. For many years the town of Calhoun was listed as Calhoon, a local spelling. In 1860 the population was 511 and by 1870 it reached 950.

The first McLean County courthouse was constructed in Calhoun around 1854-55. In 1870 a two-story brick Italianate building replaced the original structure and in 1904-8 was succeeded by a two-story brick building of classical design with Beaux-Arts influence.

During the Civil War the town was briefly captured on August 9, 1862, by a band of Confederate guerrillas. Later in 1862, Federal troops attacked and defeated a Confederate force near there. In the 1870s, the town had a steam sawmill and a flour mill, along with three hotels, three drygoods stores, and two drugstores.

In 1990 Calhoun was the site of several McLean County industries, including the manufacture of furniture. Agricultural products, in addition to the production of coal and timber, are part of the local economy.

The population of the fifth-class city was 901 in 1970; 1,080 in 1980; and 854 in 1990.

RON D. BRYANT

CALLAHAN, PATRICK HENRY. Patrick Henry Callahan, a spokesman for religious tolerance and racial justice, was born on October 15, 1866, in Cleveland, the only son of Cormac John and Mary Frances (Connolly) Callahan. He attended Roman Catholic schools in that city and studied at Spencerian Business College there for one year. In early 1886 he went to work for a Cleveland bank. Callahan wanted to play professional baseball, but became a salesman for the Glidden Varnish Company. He married Julia Laure Cahill on January 20, 1891. After a short time in Chicago, the Callahans moved to Louisville, where their three children—John, Edith, and Robert—were born. Callahan helped form the Louisville Varnish Company in 1895, and in 1908 he became its president, a post he held until his death. As the company prospered, Callahan turned to his fundamental concerns about religious, political, and social issues. In 1912 Callahan and Msgr. John A. Ryan of the Catholic University of America designed a profit-sharing plan that weathered even the Great Depression.

Callahan relished his Irishness and also took pleasure in using the title Kentucky Colonel, conferred on him by Gov. James B. McCreary (1911-15). During World War I Callahan organized the war-camp work of the Knights of Columbus, expanding his influence into the national sphere. After he clashed with the leaders of the Knights of

Columbus, Callahan took on an increasingly independent role as Catholic lay spokesman, becoming a national leader in the crusade for religious tolerance. Often reviled by Catholics, particularly by the *Kentucky Irish-American*, which was published in Louisville, Callahan was a vital mediary between Catholics and Protestants. Throughout his life he opposed the Ku Klux Klan, supported such groups as the National Conference of Christians and Jews, and pursued racial justice.

Callahan, who had had problems with alcohol in his youth, became a national spokesman for prohibition in the 1920s. His support of prohibition caused him to split with the Democratic party only once, in 1928, when he strenuously opposed the presidential bid of Alfred E. Smith, a fellow Catholic.

Callahan publicized his ideas through the "Callahan Correspondence," a mimeographed circular-letter that kept him in contact with hundreds of political, business, religious, and social leaders in America. He counted among his friends such diverse personalities as William Jennings Bryan and H.L. Mencken. A reformer at heart, he supported progressive causes from the 1890s through the New Deal. Callahan died on February 4, 1940, in Louisville and was buried there in Calvary Cemetery.

See William E. Ellis, *Patrick Henry Callahan (1866-1950): Progressive Catholic Layman in the American South* (Lewiston, N.Y., 1989).

WILLIAM E. ELLIS

CALLAWAY, RICHARD. Richard Callaway, pioneer settler, son of Francis Callaway, was born probably in Caroline County, Virginia, in 1722. After his parents died, he joined his brother, William, in Bedford County, Virginia, and fought in the French and Indian wars, attaining the rank of major. He moved to the Yadkin Valley area in North Carolina, then returned to Virginia before 1774. In 1745 Callaway married Frances Walton, daughter of Robert and Frances Walton; they had fourteen children. After her death, he married Margaret Wells in 1774; they had one child.

Judge Richard Henderson, owner of the Transylvania Company, asked Callaway to accompany Daniel Boone's party to Henderson's land in Kentucky, where they established the fort at what became BOONESBOROUGH in March 1775. Callaway, Boone, and twenty-eight other pioneers traced the WILDERNESS ROAD from the Clinch River to Boonesborough. Callaway returned to Virginia to get his family, and they arrived shortly after the Boone family. Callaway was elected one of six representatives from Boonesborough in the TRANSYLVANIA COMPANY on May 20, 1775. In the spring of 1777, Callaway was appointed one of five justices of the Kentucky County court, and he and John Todd were elected the first burgesses to the Virginia legislature from KENTUCKY COUNTY.

Callaway was promoted to colonel. During the summer of 1778, at the time of the Shawnee attacks on Boonesborough, he strongly disapproved of Boone's reconnaissance raid against the Indians' Paint Creek Town across the Ohio River. Callaway also had reservations about Boone's motives for a peace treaty during the Shawnee attack on the fort. After the attacks ended in September, Callaway brought charges of treason and conspiracy against Boone. Boone was court-martialed and acquitted.

In 1779 the Virginia legislature appointed Callaway and other trustees to lay off the town of Boonesborough. He was granted a franchise for a ferry across the Kentucky River at Boonesborough in October 1779. On March 8, 1780, while he and Pemberton Rawlings and a work party of two slaves were building a ferryboat near his home on Callaway's Creek, Indians attacked, killed, and scalped Callaway and Rawlings and took the two slaves captive. Callaway was buried at the fort. In 1822 Calloway County was created out of Hickman County and named, albeit with a different spelling, in his honor.

See William E. Ellis, H.E. Everman, Richard D. Sears, *Madison County: 200 Years in Retrospect*, (Richmond, Ky., 1985); R. Alexander Bate, "Colonel Richard Callaway, 1722-1780," *FCHQ* 29 (1955): 3-20.   JERRY PARRISH DIMITROV

CALLOWAY COUNTY. The seventy-second county in order of formation, Calloway County is located in western Kentucky on the Tennessee state line. Bordered by Graves and Marshall counties and by Kentucky Lake, the county has an area of 386 square miles. Formed on November 3, 1822, from a section of Hickman County, the county was named in honor of Col. Richard Callaway, a Kentucky explorer and pioneer who was a friend of Daniel Boone. (There is no explanation for the difference in spelling of the county's name.) MURRAY is the county seat.

The topography is mostly level, but the county has some hills and ravines. In 1987 farms occupied 78 percent of the land area, with 79 percent of farmland in cultivation. Calloway ranked thirty-fourth among Kentucky counties in agriculture receipts in 1987, from corn, soybeans, tobacco, livestock, fruits, and vegetables. Natural resources include limestone, clay, dolomite, and shale.

The Chickasaw Indians ceded their lands in western Kentucky under an 1818 federal treaty. Early pioneers included Samuel Watson, David Jones, and James Stewart. The first permanent settlement was built in 1820 by Banester Wade and called Wadesboro, which served as the county seat from 1822 to 1842. In 1842 Marshall County was created out of Calloway. In the 1840s, some residents moved westward into Missouri and beyond. Calloway County residents were strongly sympathetic to the Southern cause during the Civil War. About eight hundred joined the Confederate army, about two hundred the Union forces.

In 1862 Federal troops raided the Calloway County area, arresting citizens on charges of disloyalty. In 1863 a small force of Federal soldiers took Murray and occupied it for a brief period. The

Confederates erected FORT HEIMAN on the Tennessee River in the southeast section of the county in 1861 to help establish control of the area. By 1862, however, the Federal forces had captured the fort and they held it until 1864, when Gen. Nathan Bedford Forrest retook it and used it as a base for his successful assault on Johnsonville, Tennessee.

The Gerard iron furnace, built in 1854, closed before the beginning of the Civil War. In 1929 the Regan Milk Company, producers of dairy products, located in Murray. Fisher Price, producer of children's toys, which employed 825 in 1985, and Briggs and Stratton's lawn mower division are the county's largest manufacturing firms. Other industries include food, fabrics, wood, and safety apparel. The county is served by the Kentucky & Western Tennessee Railroad and U.S. 641. Tourism expenditures in 1988, mainly at Kentucky Lake and Kenlake State Resort Park, added $7.9 million to the economy.

The population was 27,692 in 1970; 30,031 in 1980; and 30,735 in 1990.

See E.A. Johnston, *History of Calloway County, Kentucky* (Murray, Ky., 1931).   RON D. BRYANT

CALMES, MARQUIS. Marquis Calmes, Revolutionary War soldier and one of the founders of Versailles, Kentucky, was born in Shenandoah County, Virginia, in 1755. He was the son of the Marquis de la Calmetz, a Huguenot nobleman who had fled France to escape religious persecution; the nobleman married Lucy Neville in Virginia and anglicized Calmetz to Calmes. When the Revolutionary War began, the younger Calmes was studying in Europe. He returned home, raised a company of soldiers at his own expense, and joined the 3d Regiment of Virginia. Calmes, who quickly rose to the rank of lieutenant colonel, led his regiment in the Battle of Brandywine. He participated in Washington's victory at Yorktown, Virginia, in 1781, where he was wounded. In 1785, along with many other veterans, Calmes migrated to Kentucky to settle land granted for service during the war. After settling briefly in what is now Clark County, he relocated to present-day Woodford County. At Caneland, Calmes's estate there, one of Kentucky's earliest brick homes was built. In 1788, present-day Woodford County was formed from Fayette County. In 1792 Calmes helped to establish the county seat at Versailles, named after the city in France. He served as a member of the Woodford County court and in 1795 he represented the county in the General Assembly. During the War of 1812, Calmes commanded the 1st Kentucky Brigade in the Northwest Territory. After the war he returned to Caneland, where he died on February 27, 1834. He was buried in the family cemetery at Caneland.

CAMDEN, JOHNSON NEWLON, JR. Johnson Newlon Camden, Jr., business developer, was born on January 5, 1855 in Parkersburg, Wood County, West Virginia, to Johnson Newlon and Anne (Thompson) Camden. His father mined coal and made some of it into coal oil. He joined John D. Rockefeller, Sr., in forming the petroleum combine that later became the Standard Oil Company.

Camden received his education at Phillips Academy, Andover, Massachusetts, and Virginia Military Institute, Lexington, Virginia, then attended Columbia Law School and the University of Virginia. In 1888 he was admitted to the bar but did not practice law, preferring to farm and breed thoroughbreds, Hereford cattle, and Hampshire sheep. He established the Hartland Stud on Spring Hill farm in Woodford County in 1888. He was director of the National Hereford Association and served as chairman of an agricultural committee under Gov. James B. McCreary (1911-15). In 1926 Camden was president of the Kentucky Jockey Club, which he had helped to organize, and he served as chairman of the Kentucky Racing Commission from 1920 to 1923. He was trustee at the University of Kentucky during 1914-1918.

After the death of his father in 1908, Camden was a representative of the coal, rail, and oil financiers and developers who entered the eastern Kentucky coal fields. Camden money helped finance railroads in the upper reaches of the Kentucky, Big Sandy, and Cumberland rivers. Camden served as a stockholder and director of various mining, banking, and railroad companies, including the Louisville & Nashville Railroad, the Consolidated Coal Corporation, the Kentucky River Coal Corporation, and the Elk Horn Coal Corporation.

As a Democrat, Camden served in the U.S. Senate from June 6, 1914, to March 3, 1915, to fill the vacancy caused by the death of William O. Bradley. He was Democratic national committeeman from Kentucky from 1920 to 1924.

Camden was married to Susanna Preston on October 16, 1888; they had two children: Tevis and Anne. After her death Camden married Agnes (McEvoy) Clay, on April 22, 1931. He died on August 16, 1942, and was buried in the Frankfort Cemetery.

See Harry M. Caudill, *Theirs Be the Power: The Moguls of Eastern Kentucky* (Urbana, Ill., 1983).

HARRY M. CAUDILL

CAMP BEAUREGARD. Camp Beauregard was a Confederate training center in Graves County approximately twenty miles east of Columbus, Kentucky. The camp, named for Gen. P.G.T. Beauregard, was established in September 1861 on the defense line of 1861-62 in western Kentucky-Tennessee. By year's end the camp had about 5,000 troops from seven states and was under the command of Missouri's Col. John Bowen. Severe weather and poor diet contributed to a devastating epidemic that killed about 1,000 men before the camp's evacuation on March 1, 1862. A large boulder monument, erected in 1920 by United Daughters of the Confederacy, memorializes those buried at the camp in mass graves, who were "denied the glory of heroic service in battle."

LON CARTER BARTON

CAMPBELL, ALEXANDER. Alexander Campbell was born September 12, 1788, near Ballymena, County Antrim, Ireland, the eldest of seven children of Thomas and Jane (Corneigle) Campbell. His paternal family were Scotch and Presbyterian, long resident in Ireland, while his mother's family were French Huguenots. Thomas Campbell immigrated to the United States in 1807, where he became pastor of a seceded Presbyterian congregation in Pennsylvania. His family followed in 1809.

In Pennsylvania the Campbells organized the Christian Association of Washington in 1809 as an independent church. Alexander Campbell, who had spent a year at the University of Glasgow preparing for the ordained ministry, preached his first sermon in 1810. In 1810 the Campbells and their followers formed a congregation of Disciples of Christ at Brush Run, Pennsylvania. The Redstone Baptist Association accepted the Disciples' application for membership in 1815, but relations soured and the Campbellite-Baptist affiliation ended in the 1820s.

Campbell's extensive travels brought him often to Lexington, Kentucky. His Disciples of Christ found sympathy among Barton Warren Stone's Christians. In Lexington in January 1832, the Disciples of Christ and Stone's group united. The movement flourished in Kentucky, southern and eastern Ohio, Indiana, western Pennsylvania, and Virginia in the 1830s through 1850s. It probably had 225,000 members at the time of the Civil War. [See CHRISTIAN CHURCH (DISCIPLES OF CHRIST).]

After his marriage in 1811 to Margaret Brown, Campbell made Bethany, Virginia (now West Virginia) his permanent home. He took part in formal public debates between 1820 and 1843, the most well-known taking place in Lexington against the Presbyterian champion, Nathan L. Rice (see CAMPBELL-RICE DEBATE). Among the doctrines Campbell emphasized were the supreme authority of scripture, weekly congregational celebration of the Lord's Supper, baptism of adults by immersion, and independence of the local congregation, complemented by cooperation between congregations.

Campbell was a member of the Virginia constitutional convention of 1829, where he tried unsuccessfully to have slavery made unconstitutional in Virginia. He did not consider slavery inherently wrong, because it was not condemned in scripture, but he viewed it as "inexpedient" and he freed his own slaves. As Campbell did not believe in military solutions to political problems, he was neutral in the Civil War.

Campbell died at Bethany, Virginia, on March 4, 1866, and was buried in the family cemetery near his home.

See Alexander Campbell, *The Christian System*, 2d ed. (Bethany, W.Va., 1839).

CHARLES W. BROCKWELL, JR.

CAMPBELL, ARTHUR. Arthur Campbell, political and military leader, was born in 1743 in southwest Virginia. After Campbell was given 2,000 acres in what is now Jefferson County, Kentucky,

for his service during the French and Indian War, he took part in the drive for Kentucky statehood. In 1776 Campbell served in the Virginia constitutional convention and in the legislature as a representative from Virginia's Fincastle County. Initially he opposed the division of that county into two; but when a third county was proposed, in which he was promised positions of authority by the Virginia governor, he supported the measure. In December 1776, Fincastle County was dissolved to form Kentucky, Montgomery, and Washington counties. Campbell became head of the Washington County court and militia. Influenced by Thomas Paine's *Public Good*, which held that Virginia's claim to lands west of the Allegheny Mountains was abrogated by the Proclamation of 1763 and perhaps also swayed by his own extensive land holdings in the region, Campbell became a leading advocate of Kentucky statehood. Returned to the Virginia General Assembly in 1782 and 1783, then again in 1786 and 1787, he continued his support of Kentucky's independence from Virginia. Little is known of his life after 1787. He died sometime in 1811, in what is now Middlesborough, Kentucky.

See James William Hagy, "Arthur Campbell and the Origins of Kentucky: A Reassessment," *FCHQ* 55 (October 1981): 344-74; Patricia Watlington, *The Partisan Spirit: Kentucky Politics, 1779-1792* (New York 1972).

CAMPBELL, JOHN. John Campbell was a frontier entrepreneur and land speculator born around 1735 in Ulster (Northern Ireland). He came to Pennsylvania, perhaps in 1755 with Gen. Edward Braddock's troops in the unsuccessful attempt to wrest Fort Duquesne (Pittsburgh) from the French during the French and Indian War. He is listed as a "trader" and the owner of a house there in 1761 after the French were ousted.

Campbell, with Philadelphia mercantile connections, became one of the more successful Indian fur traders on the frontier. He also was a backer of Virginia's claim to the Pittsburgh area. As a reward, he was made co-owner with Pittsburgher Dr. John Connolly of 4,000 acres at the Falls of the Ohio granted by Virginia Governor Dunmore in 1773 and encompassing much of the present city of Louisville.

As a partner in and agent for a speculative venture to acquire vast tracts of western Indian land, he came to Louisville in 1779. On his return river journey to Pittsburgh, his flotilla was attacked by Indians. He was taken prisoner and was held by the British in Montreal until late 1782. On his release, Campbell resumed his mercantile career and land speculation from his land at the falls. He became a leading citizen: a justice of the Jefferson County Court; a delegate to two of the Danville STATEHOOD CONVENTIONS (1784 and 1785); a Jefferson County representative in the Virginia legislature; a member of the convention that framed Kentucky's first constitution in 1792; and a state senator from Jefferson County that same year. In 1785 he founded Campbell Town (later Shippingport) at the lower end of the falls. About 1795 he moved to his land near Lexington. He kept "Bachelors Hall in a truly hospitable & genteel style [and] is very rich," according to *The Western Journals of Dr. George Hunter* (1963). He was elected to the state Senate in 1796 from Fayette County and died suddenly at his Senate seat in 1799. He was buried on his land near Nicholasville Pike, but his grave is unmarked. A county was named in his honor in 1794.

See Patricia Watlington, *The Partisan Spirit: Kentucky Politics, 1779-1792* (New York 1972).
GEORGE H. YATER

CAMPBELL COUNTY. The nineteenth county in order of formation, Campbell County is located in northern Kentucky. It is bordered by the Ohio River on the north and east, Kenton County on the west, and Pendleton County on the south. Covering 152 square miles, Campbell County was formed on December 17, 1794, from portions of Harrison, Mason, and Scott counties and named for Col. John Campbell, a Revolutionary War officer originally from Ireland. It has county seats at ALEXANDRIA and NEWPORT.

The topography of Campbell County is level to hilly. The rich river bottomlands produce large crops of burley tobacco, corn, hay, and vegetables. Pasture land is extensive, supporting large herds of beef cattle. The woodlands of the county are of mixed hardwoods, including ash, oak, hackberry, black walnut, and red cedar. The major watercourses are the Ohio and Licking rivers.

In early history of Campbell County, both Indians and pioneers moved along the Ohio River. Indian attacks were frequent during the settlement era. One of the first settlements in the area was Leitch's Station, built about 1789 by Maj. David Leitch, who fought in the Revolutionary War. In 1803 an army outpost (Newport Barracks) was established at the fledgling community of Newport to supply soldiers during the early Indian wars. This installation also served as a staging area for soldiers embarking on campaigns during the War of 1812, the war for Texas independence (1836), and the Mexican War (1846-48).

Campbell County prospered during the antebellum period. The town of Newport was a contender for the capture of the river trade, but was eclipsed by the rapid growth of Cincinnati. Newport, however, became an important river city, retaining its status well into the twentieth century. Though sentiments for both sides ran high, the Civil War did not severely affect Campbell County, located as it was far to the north. During the war, the county continued to prosper and grow. Industries such as steel, meat processing, and brewing were created, mostly in Newport, which gave residents steady employment.

In 1887, following the destruction of the Newport Barracks by a flood in 1884, the army post was moved to higher ground and Fort Thomas was founded. As the post expanded, it eventually absorbed the nearby community of District of Highlands, and in 1914 the town of FORT THOMAS was established. In 1933 and 1937, the 10th U.S. Infantry, which assisted in flood relief, was garrisoned at Fort Thomas. In the late twentieth century the post was maintained by the Brooks-Lawler Army Reserve Center and a Veterans Administration Hospital.

Though Newport was chosen as the county seat in 1794, the desire for a centrally located seat of government led to the creation of two county seats. Three courthouses, built in Newport in 1795, 1805, and 1814-15, respectively, served Campbell County until 1827, when the seat was moved to Visalia, along the Licking River. Visalia was located too far from the population center of Newport, however, and the next year the government returned to the river city. It remained there until 1840, when it was moved to Alexandria, the center of the county. Though a new courthouse, completed in 1842, was constructed in Alexandria, the people of Newport, still the population center, built another courthouse in their city in 1883. Since then the county offices have been housed in both locales.

In the late twentieth century, Campbell County has developed three fairly distinct regions. It is industrial along the Ohio River, residential in the highlands, and rural to the south. NORTHERN KENTUCKY UNIVERSITY at HIGHLAND HEIGHTS makes the county a regional education center.

Campbell County has one of the largest concentrations in Kentucky of residents of German descent. Some 26 percent of Campbell County's population claim German ancestry.

The population of Campbell County was 88,501 in 1970; 83,317 in 1980; and 83,866 in 1990.
RON D. BRYANT

CAMPBELL-RICE DEBATE. The Campbell-Rice debate on the comparative religious beliefs of the Christian Church and Presbyterian denominations took place in Lexington, Kentucky, from November 15 through December 1, 1843. It was held at the Main Street Christian Church, which had the largest auditorium in the city. Alexander CAMPBELL, president of Bethany College in West Virginia, represented the Christian Church, and the Rev. Nathan Rice, of Paris, Kentucky, spoke for the Presbyterian point of view. Henry Clay, who was between terms in the U.S. Senate and living at his Ashland estate, agreed to serve as moderator in the debate. J.M. Sandusky, a prominent Missouri lawyer formerly of Lexington, remarked, "I should have thought Clay could have made a much better judge of a horse race or good whiskey than a religious debate."

The forensic marathon, which took place from 10:00 a.m. to 2:00 p.m. each day, was a festive event that generated great excitement in Lexington. In 130 speeches, Campbell and Rice focused on baptism, the role of the Holy Spirit in conversion, and church creeds. Of the six propositions each day, four related to the mode and purpose of baptism and one each to the other two issues. The supporters of Campbell and Rice in the audience were emotionally expressive, and Campbell baptized many in the audience by immersion.

The debate with Rice was the last for Campbell, who had spent twenty-three years in debating such opponents as Robert Owen, the Welsh socialist and philanthropist who established the Owenite commune in New Harmony, Indiana. Rice, a noted polemicist, fluent of speech, had been chosen to represent the Presbyterians after Robert J. BRECKINRIDGE and several other prominent Presbyterians declined to participate. After the debate, Rice became pastor of churches in St. Louis and Chicago and of New York City's Fifth Avenue Presbyterian. A 912-page record of the debate was published by the Presbyterians.

See J.J. Haley, *Debates That Made History* (St. Louis 1920).   S. MONT WHITSON

CAMPBELLSVILLE. Campbellsville, the seat of Taylor County, is equidistant—eighty miles—from Louisville, Lexington, and Bowling Green. It is one of the more important manufacturing, medical, and recreational centers of south-central Kentucky. Campbellsville's industrial base provides employment for a region considerably larger than Taylor County.

The town was established by the General Assembly in 1817. The site was on the 10,000-acre Joseph Richeson survey. The town plat, registered in Green County records in 1820 (Taylor County was established in 1848), contained eighty-five lots and a public square, on which the courthouse was later built. Campbellsville was laid out by Andrew Campbell, one of five brothers who migrated from Augusta County, Virginia. He operated a gristmill on Buckhorn Creek in 1809, opened a tavern by 1813, and began selling lots in 1814. His brother James laid out the upper section of the town and built its first brick residence. Another brother, Adam, a landowner living on the western edge of the town, became a Green County justice of the peace in 1812 and sheriff in 1824. Their brother David was one of the first town trustees, a tavern keeper in the 1820s, and a Green County justice of the peace in 1825.

In 1817 the town's first postmaster was Pleasant Kirtley, and one of its first town marshals was Ferdinand J. Hiestand. When Taylor County was separated from Green County in 1848, the trustees of Campbellsville sold the public square to the county for a courthouse site to the county for one dollar. The first courthouse, a brick structure in the center of the Courthouse Square facing First Street, was erected in 1848. After Confederate forces burned it in 1864, a clerk's office was constructed in 1865-66 on the square. This served the court until the second brick courthouse was built in 1866-67. A second story and bell tower were added by 1910. This building was razed in 1965 to make way for the third courthouse, a brick structure of contemporary design.

In 1830 Campbellsville's population was 122; by 1850 it was 436, of whom 113 were slaves and eleven free blacks. The town had four attorneys, four physicians, and eight merchants by 1853. During the Civil War, Campbellsville was on the invasion routes of both the Northern and Southern armies. Federal Camp Andy Johnson was located in Campbellsville. Confederate Gen. John Hunt Morgan's men set fire to Union military stores on Main Street during one of their three raids through the county. After the Battle of Tebbs Bend on Green River in 1863, private homes and churches in Campbellsville were converted to hospitals. Confederate Gen. Hylan B. Lyon's troops, after permitting women to rescue the county records, burned the courthouse on Christmas Day in 1864.

Starting in the 1830s, Campbellsville served as a stagecoach stop on the National Mail Route between Zanesville, Ohio, and Florence, Alabama. The stage lines connecting Lebanon, Campbellsville, Columbia, and Greensburg became feeder lines to the railroad when it came to Lebanon in the 1850s. After a rail spur between Lebanon and Greensburg was opened by the Cumberland & Ohio Railroad in 1879, Campbellsville entered a new era of development. By 1890 Campbellsville's population reached 1,018, and by 1892, a flour mill, saw mill, and a woolen and carding mill were operating, as well as a lumber company, a bank, a newspaper, and two hotels. The Coca Cola Bottling Company plant was founded in 1905. By 1914 Campbellsville was served by an electric power company, a gas company, and a water works. Fires in 1911 and 1914 destroyed many of the town's early buildings.

From 1910 through 1950, Campbellsville's population grew by over 25 percent a decade and in the 1950s it registered a 100 percent increase. The coming of Union Underwear Company to Campbellsville in 1948 stimulated economic growth. In 1989 the plant, which manufactures Fruit of the Loom products, was the world's largest producer of men's and boys' underwear and the second largest textile plant in the United States: 4,200 jobs at one site, with a monthly payroll of $5 million. Elsewhere in the town, a thousand industrial jobs were supported by the manufacture of reproduction antique cherry furniture, church steeples, compressors, threaded fasteners, wood trim, cabinets, and caskets. The annual manufacturing income totaled nearly $85 million.

Public schools in the Buckhorn Creek area were holding classes as early as 1836. The Taylor County Academy, a private school on Lebanon Avenue, was established in 1884; it burned in 1891. Campbellsville High School, which opened in 1891, was replaced in 1904 by the Presbyterian-sponsored Buchanan Collegiate Institute, which operated until 1917. In 1906 the Baptists voted to establish Russell Creek Academy, which later became Campbellsville College.

The sixty-three-acre Robert L. Miller Park, established in 1967, together with the City-County

Park, and the nearby Green River Lake, with its marinas, make Campbellsville a recreational center for the area.

The population of this third class city was 7,598 in 1970; 9,259 in 1980; and 9,577 in 1990.

BETTY MITCHELL GORIN

CAMPBELLSVILLE COLLEGE. Campbellsville College is a private, four-year liberal arts and sciences college in Campbellsville, Kentucky, affiliated with the Kentucky Baptist Convention. In 1990 the college offered twenty-five academic majors and twenty-six academic minor programs; its enrollment was approximately eight hundred, and it employed about one hundred full-time faculty members and staff. It was accredited by the Southern Association of Colleges and Secondary Schools in 1963. Degrees conferred are the bachelor of arts, bachelor of science, bachelor of music, associate of arts, and associate of science.

Campbellsville College originated as Russell Creek Baptist Academy, established in Campbellsville in 1906 by the Russell Creek Association of Baptists. It began as a private elementary and high school, and its first principal was W.G. Welbourn. At a meeting of the General Association of Kentucky Baptists in November 1923, the trustees were given authority to raise Russell Creek Academy to the rank of junior college. While continuing the elementary and high school programs, Campbellsville College began operations as a junior college in 1924, with L.E. Curry as its first president. In 1938 the high school department was closed, and soon after that the elementary grades were discontinued. In November 1957 the General Association of Baptists in Kentucky authorized the trustees to develop the college into a four-year institution. In 1960 the college awarded the first degrees to graduates of the four-year program. John M. Carter, president of the college since 1948, was the first president of the expanded school. The president in 1990 was Ken Winters.

The administration building, the first building erected, was in use on the school's first day of classes in September 1907. It later burned and was rebuilt in 1939. The J.S. Stapp Dormitory was built soon after the school opened, and in 1918 another dormitory, now the music annex, was completed. In 1990 there were sixteen major buildings on the campus, including the Montgomery Library, which contained more than 100,000 volumes. Additions to the physical plant included a football stadium and the athletic complex, which contains both office space and training facilities.

DIANE NICHOLS ROGERS

CAMP BRECKINRIDGE. The Camp Breckinridge military installation, along U.S. 60 in northwestern Kentucky, between Morganfield and Henderson, was established as a training center during World War II. It covered 35,887 acres in Henderson, Webster, and Union counties. Named in

honor of John Cabell Breckinridge, Kentucky statesman and Confederate general, the camp trained 30,000 infantry recruits between September 1942 and February 1946. From 1943 to 1946, more than thirteen hundred captured German and Italian soldiers were interned there as prisoners of war. Those in the U.S. infantry who passed through the camp included baseball's Jackie Robinson, who played on the post team in 1944 before going on to break the color barrier in major league baseball in 1947, and Army Reserve Corps enlistee Robert Dole, an anti-tank gunner with the 75th Infantry Division in 1944, who was to become U.S. Senate minority leader.

In the postwar era, from July 1948 to July 1950, and during the Korean War, from September 1950 to January 1954, the camp trained infantry replacements and the 101st Airborne Division. After 1955 Camp Breckinridge trained both active and reserve army units and was available to numerous local civilian groups. Some of the land was leased for farms and oil exploration. The U.S. Army formally disposed of the camp on December 5, 1962. The lands of Camp Breckinridge were the basis for a failed class action suit in the federal court of appeals, *Higginson v. United States* (1965), initiated by Cyrus Higginson on behalf of former landowners forced to sell to the U.S. government in 1942.

In 1965 a Job Corps center was established on eight hundred acres of the land by the U.S. Department of Labor as a vocational training center. Skills in twenty-four areas, including automotive, computers, building trades, and culinary, are provided in the twelve-month program for resident students between the ages of sixteen and twenty-one. In 1965 the Job Corps center had 1,800 male students. Women students were first admitted in 1975. In 1990 the enrollment was 2,234. Primarily for students from the southeastern states, the center also admits students from other states and other countries. In 1980 the name was changed to the Earle C. Clements Job Corps Center, in honor of the former Kentucky governor and senator.

See Peyton Heady, *History of Camp Breckinridge* (Lexington, Ky., 1987); Ruby Higginson, *Land of Camp Breckinridge: Injustice to the Farmer*, 2d ed. (N.p., 1978).

LORIE A. MALTBY

CAMP DICK ROBINSON. Camp Dick Robinson, a recruiting station for the Union army in northern Garrard County, was the site of a popular stagecoach stop known in the early nineteenth century as Hoskins Crossroads. The Hoskins family had built a house on the property, which passed to Richard M. Robinson when he married Margaret Hoskins in 1848. In July 1861, Robinson, known for his staunch Unionist views, offered the use of his farm to federal authorities as a recruiting ground. Major Gen. William ("Bull") Nelson commissioned T.T. Garrard, Thomas Bramlette, and Speed S. Fry colonels of infantry and W.J. Landrum a colonel of cavalry and directed them to raise regiments in Kentucky. These regiments were to report to the Robinson farm on the first Tuesday after the August 6, 1861, elections. Nelson named the site Camp Dick Robinson. It was to this camp that the "Lincoln guns" designated for distribution to Home Guard units were sent.

By late August, Camp Dick Robinson was the residence of the 3d, 4th, and 7th Kentucky regiments of infantry, the 1st Kentucky Cavalry, the 1st and 2d Tennessee regiments of infantry, and Hewitt's artillery battery. The newly organized regiments learned artillery drill and received issues of clothing and arms, but battled only illness, not Confederate soldiers. By September 1, after an outbreak of measles at the camp, nearly one-third of the troops were unfit for duty. The epidemic overwhelmed the army's medical service, and many of the sick soldiers were cared for in the home of Robinson, where his niece, Eliza Hoskins, came to be known as the "Angel of Camp Dick" for her nursing.

Lack of uniforms, arms, and equipment was a major problem. Late in August 1861 a detachment of Col. Frank Wolford's 1st Kentucky Cavalry went to Lexington to escort a shipment of guns back to the camp. The hostility of secessionist Lexingtonians contrasted with the warmth accorded the soldiers in Garrard County. When the troops of the 7th Kentucky Volunteer Infantry left Camp Robinson on September 28, they still lacked proper uniforms.

Confederates viewed the establishment of Camp Dick Robinson as a blatant violation of the neutrality policy espoused by Kentucky Gov. Beriah Magoffin (1859-62). Alarmed by the numbers of Union soldiers enlisting at the camp, Confederate authorities hastened to establish camps in northern Tennessee to recruit Kentuckians for their cause. The presence of Union troops at Camp Dick Robinson gave Confederate Gen. Leonidas Polk an excuse to occupy Columbus, in far western Kentucky, with his Confederate force on September 3, 1861. A day later Ulysses S. Grant moved his Union troops into Paducah, and Kentucky's neutrality became a dead issue.

Throughout late 1861 and 1862, many Union movements in Kentucky originated at Camp Robinson. The campaigns of Camp Wildcat, Mill Springs, and Cumberland Gap were launched from the camp. The site remained an important depot for stores into late 1862, when it was replaced by a new camp on a more defensible site a few miles north beside the Kentucky River. The replacement, named Camp Nelson in honor of Maj. Gen. William Nelson, grew into a sprawling semipermanent installation. During the Perryville campaign, Confederate troops briefly occupied the site of Camp Robinson. SUSAN LYONS HUGHES

CAMP NELSON. Camp Nelson, located south of Nicholasville in Jessamine County, high on the palisades of the Kentucky River, was established in 1863 and named in honor of Maj. Gen. William Nelson. By August 1863 thousands of slaves from central Kentucky, impounded to build railroads for the Union army, were stationed there. When drafting of blacks began in Kentucky on March 10, 1864, Camp Nelson immediately became the most important recruiting station and training camp for blacks.

Many regiments formed at Camp Nelson, including the 5th and 6th U.S. Colored cavalries and the 114th and 116th U.S. Colored Heavy artilleries. As the number of soldiers increased, so did the number of refugees from slavery. But since Kentucky was a slaveholding state, Camp Nelson was not a legal refuge for the dependents of black soldiers who had been slaves. In November 1864 four hundred women and children were ordered from camp and driven out by armed soldiers; many of them, undernourished and ill clad for the subfreezing weather, died of exposure. The order was reversed and some refugees returned to camp, but 102 died within a few weeks.

Abolitionist minister John G. FEE, who arrived at Camp Nelson as a volunteer missionary in July 1864, founded schools for blacks, recruited workers from missionary societies, established a church that remained active at Camp Nelson for decades, and proposed and administered an official refugee home. Unfortunately, there were many deaths. Of 3,060 refugees who entered the camp, 1,300 died. Nevertheless, many men and women considered Camp Nelson their cradle of freedom because, when dependents of Kentucky's black soldiers were finally emancipated, Camp Nelson became the chief center issuing emancipation papers to former slaves. Designated a U.S. cemetery for Union dead in 1867, Camp Nelson remains a military cemetery.

See Richard Sears, *A Practical Recognition of the Brotherhood of Man: John G. Fee and the Camp Nelson Experience* (Berea, Ky., 1986).

RICHARD SEARS

CAMP ZACHARY TAYLOR. Camp Zachary Taylor was created in June 1917 for the purpose of training American troops after the United States entered World War I. It was in Jefferson County, Kentucky, southeast and south of Louisville, in what had been primarily a farming area. The camp was named for President Zachary Taylor, who grew up in Jefferson County. Construction began in June 1917 and was basically completed by mid-August. The first inductees arrived September 5. The camp was the home of the 84th, or Lincoln, Division (so named because its recruits came from Kentucky, Indiana, and Illinois), the 159th Depot Brigade, the Field Artillery Central Officers Training School, and other units. After the war the camp was used primarily as a demobilization center and hospital.

The camp covered approximately 2,700 acres and had some 2,000 buildings. As many as 10,000 people were employed in building the camp and providing services. The camp's highest population occurred in the summer of 1918, when about

64,000 soldiers were stationed there. More than 150,000 men were trained at the camp, and a total of 250,000 were housed there at some time. With its designation in June 1918 as a field artillery replacement depot, Camp Taylor soon became the largest artillery training camp in the United States.

The influenza epidemic of fall 1918 killed hundreds of soldiers; the camp was quarantined and training came to a halt. In September 1919 the U.S. House Military Affairs Committee recommended abandoning Camp Taylor, citing insufficient land as the reason. On July 27, 1920, the order was given to begin closing the camp around September 1. Its land, and all buildings and equipment not removed by the army, were to be sold at auction by June 30, 1921. The artillery school and adjunct artillery range at West Point, Kentucky, had already been transferred to Camp Henry Knox (Fort Knox). The auction of Camp Zachary Taylor began April 4, 1921, with the sale of the rifle range near South Park, and ended in June, when the hospital land and buildings were sold. Overall, the sale brought about $1 million. Most of the camp land reverted to crop and pasture use, but the part where the main camp had been became a residential area, which is still known as the Camp Taylor neighborhood.

See John P. Meyer, "History and Neighborhood Analysis of Camp Taylor," M.A. thesis, University of Louisville, 1981; Ella H. Ellwanger, "Camp Zachary Taylor," *Register* 16 (May 1918): 9-24.

JAMES J. HOLMBERG

CAMPTON. Campton, the county seat of Wolfe County, is located on KY 191 and KY 15, just south of the Bert T. Combs Mountain Parkway. According to tradition, the site was first called Camp Town after Nim Wills, the first settler, found the remains of an old camp there that he believed had been made by the legendary Jonathan SWIFT, of silver mine fame. The town that grew up on Swift Camp Creek became Campton.

In 1860 the isolated community was chosen as the seat of newly created Wolfe County because of its central location. A courthouse of logs was built about 1860 and served until destroyed by fire in 1884. The second courthouse, completed in 1885, was consumed by fire in 1913. The third courthouse, a two-story building of classical Beaux Arts-influenced design, was finished in 1917. Upon the pediment of the portico is a bas-relief of a wolf, as in the county name.

During the Civil War, Gen. George Morgan's Union army on September 23, 1862, passed through the small town on its way north to the Ohio River from the Cumberland Gap. Gen. John Hunt Morgan's Confederate cavalry passed through in June 1864. Because guerrillas were a threat to residents, a Home Guard unit occupied Campton for a time during the war.

Campton was incorporated in 1870, but the town's isolation inhibited growth until the advent of the railroads and the discovery of oil in the early 1900s. The Mountain Central Railway, a narrow-gauge logging track, entered the city in the fall of 1907 and made Campton its eastern terminus until abandoned in 1928. Oil was drilled one mile west of Campton in 1903 and by 1905 fifty-eight wells were operating in the field. Oil activity resumed in the 1950s.

In 1894 Kentucky Wesleyan College of Winchester opened a branch at Campton. The school was built by county judge Taylor Center, who built a kiln on the school site and made bricks from local clay. Kentucky Wesleyan withdrew its support in 1912, but the school remained open by charging tuition until 1934. It then became Wolfe County Grade School and High School.

Campton's isolation was relieved in May 1963 by the completion of the Mountain Parkway, which at that time made the city its eastern terminus. Some new industry was attracted there, including Campton Electric Manufacturing, Inc. in 1969.

The population of the sixth-class city was 419 in 1970; 486 in 1980; and 484 in 1990.

CANE. Cane (*Arundinaria gigantea*), a member of the grass family, is the South's only native bamboo species. It grows in canebrakes, dense evergreen colonies interconnected by a tough, extensive system of rhizomes, or underground stems. The plants reach heights of twelve to forty feet, with stems as much as two inches in diameter. In Kentucky, scattered patches are the only remnants of presettlement canebrakes, which covered hundreds of acres. John Filson's 1784 map of Kentucky is annotated with numerous references to "fine cane land." In 1771 Simon Kenton, an early explorer, came to what is now Kentucky specifically to view this unique plant community.

Canebrakes are no longer prominent features of Kentucky's natural plant communities. Many canebrakes on fertile bottomlands were destroyed to make way for cash crops such as corn and soybeans. Other cane, overgrazed by cattle, was gradually replaced by fast-growing pasture grasses. The plant colonies, however, did not yield willingly to hands or tools. Christian Schultz, an early traveler, noted in 1807 that the soil in canebrakes, "being so firmly bound together with roots, is almost impossible to drive a plow through." Early settlers also saw canebrakes as dangerous, since Indians launched bloody attacks from the camouflage of their dense growth.

Cane made a contribution to early technology as part of the framework of the first airplane constructed in Kentucky, the work of Matthew B. Sellers in 1908. The airplane was capable of speeds of twenty-one miles per hour. The strength and flexibility of cane stems are tested still, in the form of fishing poles. There is much interest in restoring canebrakes to their original habitats in Kentucky, in parks and nature preserves, and on roadsides, for both ecological and historical reasons.

See James O. Luken, "Canebrakes: Preserving Kentucky's Native Vegetation," *Kentucky Living*, Oct. 1989.

JAMES O. LUKEN

CANE RIDGE REVIVAL. The huge, highly emotional Cane Ridge revival of 1801, which led to the founding of the Christian Church and the Christian Church (Disciples of Christ) denominations, was part of the religious fervor that swept the western frontier at the turn of the century. During the GREAT REVIVAL of the summer of 1801, eighteen Presbyterian ministers, along with several Baptist and Methodist preachers, converged on the Presbyterian meetinghouse in the Cane Ridge area of Kentucky's Bourbon County. At times as many as seven ministers orated simultaneously from wagon beds or tree stumps before a crowd of perhaps 20,000. Listeners gathered near the wagons and among the tombstones, praying, weeping, screaming, moving in a jerking fashion, barking, singing, dancing, and fainting. Hundreds of revivalists were converted as the preachers expounded their gospel of love, harmony, union, and salvation for all.

Although the Cane Ridge revival was very emotional, several scholars also addressed an intellectual aspect, speaking on a variety of social and theological issues, including slavery. Many participants returned home and emancipated their slaves. Barton W. STONE, the Cane Ridge pastor, voiced regret at some of the fanaticism expressed at the revival, but he lauded the doctrinal debate for establishing a clear stand on universal salvation, a return to the Bible, baptism by immersion, open communion, local congregational rule, reunion of all churches, and the divinity of Christ.

See James R. Rogers, *The Cane Ridge Meeting House* (Cincinnati 1916); John B. Boles, *The Great Revival, 1787-1805* (Lexington, Ky., 1972).

H.E. EVERMAN

CANNON, JOHN W. John W. Cannon, riverboat captain, was born June 17, 1820, at Skillman Bottoms in Hancock County, Kentucky, near the present site of Cannelton Lock and Dam. He was captain of the famous racing steamboat the *Robert E. Lee* in the victory over the *Natchez* in the New Orleans-St. Louis race in 1870. Cannon spent most of his career in the Greenville-Vicksburg-New Orleans trade. Later he owned the *John W. Cannon*, built in 1878. He died on April 18, 1882, and was buried in the Frankfort Cemetery.   LEE A. DEW

CANTRILL, FLORENCE McDOWELL (SHELBY). Florence McDowell (Shelby) Cantrill, political leader, daughter of Wallace and Margaret (Bryan) Shelby, was born on June 13, 1888, at Waveland in Fayette County, Kentucky. Two of her great-great-grandfathers were prominent: Isaac Shelby, the first governor of Kentucky (1792-96, 1812-16), and Dr. Ephraim McDOWELL, an accomplished surgeon. She studied at Hamilton College in Lexington and Vassar College in New York.

Cantrill was an advocate of women's rights and encouraged women to vote. After campaigning for Franklin D. Roosevelt and attending his first inauguration in 1933, she decide to run for political office herself. She was the first woman to represent Lexington in the General Assembly, serving from January 2, 1934, until the end of December 1935. As the city's first woman commissioner (1936-40), Cantrill played a major role in the organization of Lexington's civil service and the establishment of the first community swimming pool. Cantrill served as mayor pro tem from 1936 to 1940. She was the first woman to serve on the governing board of Lexington's Christ Church Episcopal.

Florence Shelby married Cecil Edwards Cantrill; they had two children, Margaret and Cecil, Jr. She died on October 30, 1981, and was buried in the Georgetown Cemetery.

CANTRILL, JAMES CAMPBELL. James Campbell Cantrill, U.S. and Kentucky legislator, was born in Georgetown, Kentucky, on July 9, 1870. Educated at Georgetown College, Cantrill was elected to the Kentucky House in 1897. After serving two terms, Cantrill was elected to the Kentucky Senate in 1901. In 1907 he was named state chairman of the American Society of Equity, an agricultural organization that favored the cooperative pooling of crops to increase market prices. In that position, Cantrill gained the support of many central Kentucky tobacco farmers. Cantrill was elected to the U.S. House of Representatives in 1908 and served from March 4, 1909, until his death on September 2, 1923. Prominent in the Democratic party, he was President Woodrow Wilson's Kentucky campaign chairman in 1916. In the House, Cantrill opposed women's suffrage, believing it would do irreparable harm to the Democratic party. While stressing his regard for the "common man," Cantrill also consistently voted against any business regulatory legislation. In August 1923 Cantrill became the Democratic nominee for governor, on a platform calling for a primary election and for equal taxation for all classes. On September 2 Cantrill died of appendicitis. He was buried in Georgetown.

TRACY A. CAMPBELL

CAPITOL BUILDINGS. Frankfort was chosen as the capital of Kentucky (by act of the General Assembly on December 8, 1792) partly because of its central location on a site accessible to the Kentucky River. The legislature was also influenced by Andrew Holmes's offer to give the state a house formerly occupied by Gen. James WILKINSON, nine city lots, and the materials to build the statehouse, in exchange for making Frankfort the capital. The Wilkinson house, located at the southwest corner of Wilkinson and Wapping streets, was the first structure in Frankfort used by the legislature. They met there during the session beginning on November 4, 1793, and ending on December 21.

When General Wilkinson laid out Frankfort in 1786, he provided for a public square. These were the lots given to the state as the site of the capitol. In 1793 construction began on Kentucky's first permanent statehouse. The capitol was a one-hundred-foot-square stone building, three stories in height, covered by a hipped roof with a central cupola.

John Cape, a Lexington builder, is known to have produced several county courthouses in this style; it is likely that he was the designer and builder of this building.

The capitol was first occupied by the legislature on Monday, November 3, 1794. The first floor contained the offices of the state auditor, treasurer, registrar, and public printer; the second floor, the hall of the House of Representatives and committee rooms, along with courtrooms; and the third floor, the Senate chamber and offices of the secretary of state. On November 25, 1813, fire destroyed the statehouse.

The second statehouse was built on the same site, as authorized on January 31, 1814, by the legislature. The legislature appointed John Brown, Daniel Weisiger, Richard Taylor, William Hunter, and Jephthah Dudley commissioners to oversee all aspects of the new building's construction. One of the main stipulations was that the building be of fireproof construction. The commission was to collect subscriptions to underwrite the cost of the new building (eventually amounting to $19,607 of the $40,000 cost). The commission signed contracts with Matthew Kennedy for the design of the new capitol and with James Ware for all carpentry. The masonry work was done by Oliver Brown, who received three hundred acres in Woodford County as partial payment. Harrison Blanton was responsible for the brickwork.

The new capitol was a two-and-a-half-story brick building measuring 65 by 100 feet. A nine-bay structure of classical design, the building was fronted by a four-column pedimented portico, and a classical two-tiered cupola centered on the building. The first floor contained spaces for the courts and committee rooms and the second was divided between the houses of the General Assembly. On the interior walls, the artist M. Audin created allegorical murals. The chamber of the House of Representatives was a circular room covered by an arched ceiling. An image of Themis, goddess of justice, with the scales of justice and the sword of punishment, adorned its ceiling. Audin painted fourteen Corinthian columns, flanked by figures of the virtues and a figure of America, around the room. Fire consumed the capitol on November 4, 1824. A constant threat, fire also destroyed a temporary building where the House was in session on December 12, 1825.

It was not until January 12, 1827, that the legislature approved a bill to build the third capitol. The bill appropriated $20,000 in money and supplies and appointed John Brown, Daniel Weisiger, Peter Dudley, John J. Crittenden, John Harvie, Evan Evans, and James Shannon as commissioners. The commissioners advertised for building plans and estimates on January 31. They chose a plan by Gideon SHRYOCK, who had recently returned to Kentucky. His plan was one of the first in the United States to use the Greek Revival style.

Shryock moved to Frankfort to supervise construction of his design. The stone was furnished by Harrison Blanton and quarried by Humphrey Evans and Jack Holbert; it was cut to shape by a saw invented by Joel Scott, the keeper of the state penitentiary. Although the building was not complete, the legislature first met there in December 1829. When completed in 1830, the building cost about $85,000 and measured 70 by 120 feet. It was believed to be the most elaborate capitol building in the country at the time. The first floor contained committee rooms and a library, with federal courtrooms in the rear. The second contained the chambers of the House of Representatives and the Senate.

By the late 1860s, the capitol building had become overcrowded and the legislature decided to erect a new one. Designed by the Louisville architectural firm of Bradshaw and Vodges, the building was to resemble the U.S. Capitol, with a large central domed rotunda flanked by wings. It was to be built in three stages. The legislature authorized construction of the east wing on February 2, 1869. Local builder John Haly was primarily responsible for construction, which was completed in 1871. The $200,000 cost greatly exceeded that originally planned, and by 1873 plans for the two other stages were all but scrapped.

In 1902 the shortage of space had become critical and removing the capital from Frankfort was debated. This issue was settled in 1904, when the legislature appropriated $1 million, a debt collected from the U.S. War Department, to build a new capitol. The act also set up a state capitol building commission: Gov. J.C.W. Beckham (1900-1907); S.W. Hager, auditor; H.V. McChesney, secretary of state; H.M. Bosworth, treasurer; and N.B. Hays, attorney general. H.B. Ware of Frankfort served as secretary of the group. At its meeting on April 7, 1904, the commission elected C.M. Fleenor, of Bowling Green, superintendent of construction. On June 10, 1904, Frank M. Andrews, of Dayton, Ohio, was elected architect.

The commission soon decided that the public square was too small for a building of the scale proposed. In a special session, the legislature in 1905 appropriated $40,000 to purchase a new site in South Frankfort. The Kentucky Historical Society took over the Old State House in 1920; it is now a national historic landmark.

Preliminary clearing and excavation for the new capitol was begun on May 25, 1905. On August 10 the general contract for the construction of the building was let, and excavation for the foundation was begun four days later. The building was officially dedicated June 1, 1910. The total appropriation was $1,750,000. The capitol building proper accounted for $1,250,000; its furnishing and outfitting, $255,000; the power plant and equipment $90,000; the architectural terrace and landscape work on the grounds, $115,000; and the grounds themselves, $40,000.

Like many state capitols, the building is of French Renaissance architecture with a Neoclassic dome. It measures 402 feet, 10 inches east and west, and 180 feet through the central pavilion north and south; the terrace walls add some 30 or 40 feet each way. The base of the exterior of the building is Vermont granite; the rest of the face work, including the dome, is Bedford limestone. The 1906 legislature appropriated money for the handsome pediment and for finishing the interior—the corridors, nave, and the like—in Georgia marble and Vermont granite rather than Bedford stone. The difference is marked and it gives richness and tone to the general treatment. The sculptor Charles H. Niehaus of New York City did the work on the pediment. In the nave, generous in length and breadth, thirty-six great monolithic columns support massive cornices. The columns are of Vermont granite; the stairs, pilasters, and cornices of Georgia marble; and the floors of Tennessee and Italian marbles bordered with verde antique.

See C. Julian Oberwarth and William B. Scott, Jr., *A History of the Profession of Architecture in Kentucky* (Lexington, Ky., 1987); Bayless Hardin, "The Capitols of Kentucky," *Register* 43 (July 1945): 173-200.   WILLIAM B. SCOTT, JR.

CARDOME. Cardome, now a community center in Georgetown, Kentucky, was the monastery, academy, and farm of the Roman Catholic Sisters of the Visitation from 1896 to 1987. Located on U.S. 25 north of North Elkhorn Creek, the eighty-seven-acre property, including a brick mansion built in 1821, was purchased in 1844 by James Fisher Robinson, who later served as governor of Kentucky (1862-63). Robinson took the name Cardome from the Latin *carus domus*, meaning "dear home." The Sisters of the Visitation purchased the mansion and farm from Robinson's heirs in 1896, and constructed an Italianate academy building with a Romanesque central tower. Between 1896 and 1969, Visitation Academy, a boarding school, graduated 583 young women.

The Robinson house was demolished after a fire in late 1985. The remaining structures at Cardome include the academy building (1896); monastery (1900-1904); outbuildings, institutional, and agricultural buildings; dry-laid stone fences; tunnels with political, military, or underground railroad associations; and early road and mill sites along Elkhorn Creek. Toyota Motor Manufacturing, U.S.A. donated $1 million toward Georgetown's purchase of Cardome as a community center.

See Ann Bolton Bevins, *A History of Scott County as Told by Selected Buildings* (Georgetown, Ky., 1981); B.O. Gaines, *History of Scott County* (Georgetown, Ky., 1961).

ANN BOLTON BEVINS

CARLISLE, JOHN GRIFFIN. John Griffin Carlisle, U.S. senator and secretary of the Treasury, was born on September 5, 1835, in a log cabin in the small community of Key West, Campbell County (now part of Kenton County), Kentucky. He was the eldest of eleven children of Lilborn and Mary (Reynolds) Carlisle. Carlisle left home at age sixteen to work as a teacher in Covington and in 1853 became the main support of his family when his father died. He gave up teaching in 1856 to study law under John White Stevenson, a highly respected attorney in Covington. At age twenty-three, Carlisle joined the law firm of William Kinkead in Covington. Much later in his law career, Carlisle became a law partner of Gov. William Goebel (1900).

As a state legislator from 1859 to 1861, Carlisle voted with the majority to keep Kentucky in the Union during the Civil War, but his vote was based more on the preference of his district than on his personal choice. Carlisle remained neutral while others his age enlisted. His stand did not make him popular. Nevertheless, he ran for the state Senate in 1865. His Republican opponent collected the most votes, but the Senate threw out the results, saying the elections had been influenced by U.S. Army soldiers. In a special election, Carlisle won. He was reelected in 1869, and resigned two years later to run for lieutenant governor. The thirty-six-year-old Carlisle won the lieutenant governor's race, serving with Gov. Preston H. Leslie (1871-75). In 1870, while still in the Senate, Carlisle assumed another role—editor of the *Louisville Daily Ledger*. He promised to write "plainly and earnestly in support of the men and measures of the Democratic party."

When his term as lieutenant governor expired, Carlisle ran for the U.S. Congress, winning election in 1876. He was reelected six times, serving from March 4, 1877, to May 26, 1890. By 1880 Carlisle's popularity was such that the *Covington Daily Commonwealth* speculated that he might make a good Democratic presidential candidate. The article praised Carlisle's abilities as a constitutional lawyer and described him as a statesman with the "Jeffersonian qualities of honesty and capability." The national Democratic party convention passed over Carlisle, however, in favor of Winfeld Scott Hancock, a Union Civil War general, as the presidential candidate. Political writers said there were still too many hard feelings from the Civil War for a Southerner to be seriously considered. The stigma, however, did not prevent Carlisle from being named speaker of the U.S. House of Representatives in 1883. Carlisle was again considered a presidential candidate in 1884, but again the party passed him over, this time picking Grover Cleveland.

Carlisle moved from the House of Representatives to the U.S. Senate in 1890 and served until February 4, 1893.Carlisle's name once more came up in 1892 as the Democratic party discussed possible presidential nominees. This time, however, it was Carlisle himself who asked that his name not be considered at the convention. Grover Cleveland, again the Democratic candidate, picked Carlisle to be secretary of the Treasury. Carlisle is said to have dropped out of the race and accepted the secretary's job in return for party support for a future presidential bid. Carlisle served as secretary of the Treasury in the Cleveland administration (1893-97).

Back in Kentucky, Carlisle's popularity waned because of his opposition to strict trade tariffs and to anything but gold as the country's monetary standard. It was the hard money issue that brought Carlisle back to Covington in 1896. He was among those asked to speak at the Odd Fellows Hall at Fifth Street and Madison Avenue on the question of using silver as a monetary standard. A stacked crowd gave Carlisle a rough reception and some began throwing rotten eggs, forcing him off the speaker's platform. It was his last public speech in Covington. A year later he retired from public life.

After his death, Carlisle's enemies launched one final attack, distributing a circular stating that he had been a pauper and that public donations were needed to bury him. Carlisle, in fact, left an estate of about $40,000, but several out-of-town newspapers printed the pauper story. In recognition of Carlisle's work on whiskey taxes during his term as secretary of Treasury, his likeness was later added to the bottled-in-bond whiskey stamps found on bottles of bourbon.

On January 15, 1857, Carlisle married Mary Jane Goodson, daughter of Capt. John A. Goodson, of Covington. They had five children, all of whom died before Carlisle. In 1902 he severed his last ties with northern Kentucky by selling his home in Covington. A virtual exile, Carlisle died July 31, 1910, in New York City and was buried in Linden Grove Cemetery in Covington.

See James A. Barnes, *John G. Carlisle—Financial Statesman* (New York 1931).   JIM REIS

CARLISLE. Carlisle, the county seat of Nicholas County in the Outer Bluegrass, is located at the intersection of KY 36 and KY 32, three miles southeast of U.S. 68, between Lexington and Maysville. The city was founded in 1816 on what had once been a peach orchard belonging to John Kincart, who deeded fifty acres of land, laid off streets and town lots, and selected a number of choice sites for himself. The original 139 lots sold for a total of $13,830, and the town grew rapidly. The town was probably named by Kincart for Carlisle, Pennsylvania, the hometown of his father, Samuel.

The county seat, probably including the log cabin courthouse, was moved from Ellisville to Carlisle in 1816. The courthouse was replaced by a brick structure in 1818, which in turn was replaced by a third courthouse in 1844. The fourth courthouse, a brick structure that is an eclectic combination of architectural styles, was completed in 1893-94.

When the Maysville and Washington Turnpike Company began building a macadamized road in the 1830s to connect the Ohio River with Lexington, some prominent Carlisle residents, including Gen. Samuel Fulton, opposed the new road through the county seat. They feared that the turnpike would bring six-team express wagons, with which local wagon owners, who operated on a smaller

scale, would not be able to compete. The turnpike thus bypassed Carlisle by three miles, depriving the city of the economic advantages it brought to other communities. Nevertheless, by 1830 the population of the city exceeded six hundred and local businesses included three tanyards, two hatters, three cabinet shops, three tailors, three hotels, two carding factories, three saddle shops, three smiths, two shoemakers, and other shops and grocery stores. In 1830 Carlisle bought its first fire engine, which was first used in 1832 when a bagging and bale rope factory burned. The city suffered from fires throughout its history. Dwellings were destroyed by fire in 1838; stables and a granary in 1840; a hemp factory in 1843; and the Masonic Hall, a newspaper office, and several businesses in 1873. Cholera epidemics were also a threat, closing down all commerce in Carlisle during the epidemic of 1833, when many residents left the city.

The Kentucky Central Railroad (now the Trans Kentucky Terminal Railroad) was built into Carlisle in 1871 and helped to make the city a tobacco marketing center by 1900. The tobacco market thrived until 1921, when declining burley tobacco sales caused its closure. It was reopened for a time during the Great Depression but went out of business permanently in 1933.

Because Carlisle was settled early and the area remained rural, many buildings of historic and architectural interest have been preserved. Northwest of the city is Forest Retreat, a stone building constructed by Thomas Metcalfe, governor of Kentucky (1828-32). Built in 1893, the old railroad depot has been restored to serve as a museum and community center. The restored Forest Retreat Tavern was once a stagecoach stop, as was the Old Stone Tavern on U.S. 68, built around 1807. In 1989 Carlisle was listed on the National Register of Historic Places.

Carlisle is one of central Kentucky's smallest county seats. The city's largest employer is Jockey International, which manufactures undergarments. The weekly newspaper is the *Carlisle Mercury*, founded in 1867. The population of the fourth-class city was 1,579 in 1970; 1,757 in 1980; and 1,639 in 1990.

See Joan W. Conley, *History of Nicholas County* (Carlisle, Ky., 1976).   JOAN W. CONLEY

CARLISLE BROTHERS. The two popular musicians known as the Carlisle Brothers were born to Van Luther and Mary Ellen (Boes) Carlisle in Spencer County, Kentucky—Clifford Raymond on March 6, 1904, and William Tolliver on December 19, 1908. Cliff was among the first whites to play the Hawaiian guitar with a blues sound. His recordings ranged from children's ballads to hobo songs and raunchy blues. During the 1920s he toured with Wilbur Ball. In the 1930s and 1940s he and Bill teamed up as the Carlisle Brothers. After retirement in 1947, Cliff wrote songs and taught painting in Lexington. He died April 2, 1983, survived by his wife Alice Henrietta (Smith) and three children, Thomas, Violet, and Carolyn. In 1950 Bill joined the "Grand Ole Opry" and toured with his own band, which included his children, Bill and Sheila; his wife is the former Leona King.

See Charles K. Wolfe, *Kentucky Country* (Lexington, Ky., 1982). CHARLES F. FABER

CARLISLE COUNTY. Carlisle County, the 119th in order of formation, lies in the Jackson Purchase region of far western Kentucky. Bounded by Ballard, Graves, and Hickman counties, and by the Mississippi River, it has an area of 191 square miles. The area, originally Chickasaw tribal lands acquired by Isaac Shelby and Andrew Jackson in 1818, was part of Hickman County from 1821 to 1842, when it was included in the creation of Ballard County. Carlisle County was created on May 3, 1886. The county was named for John G. CARLISLE, a statesman who served at many levels of government. The county seat is BARDWELL, incorporated in 1879.

The mostly flat county has an abundance of fresh water in the many creeks and streams draining into the Mississippi River. In the late 1700s many islands lay offshore in the river, but erosion and the earthquake of 1811-12 along the New Madrid Fault destroyed most of the islands and others became part of the contiguous land mass. The county has sand, gravel, clay, rich fertile soil, and natural springs and artesian wells. Most of the area is farmland, growing mainly burley and dark-fired tobacco and livestock.

Among those who settled in the region after the Jackson Purchase was William Milburn of Maryland, who arrived in about 1822 and with a neighbor, William Reddick, established the town of Milburn. Another early landowner was George Reeves, who at about that time owned the site of the present village of Cunningham in the northeastern part of the county. Although fighting took place in the Jackson Purchase during the Civil War and horses were taken by Confederate cavalry led by Gen. Nathan Bedford Forrest and by local guerrillas, Carlisle County was not greatly affected by the conflict. One hundred and sixty-eight Carlisle County residents joined the Confederate army; only forty-four joined the Union cause.

After the war, the coming of two railroad lines linked the area with Chicago to the north and the Gulf Coast region to the south. The Illinois Central Railroad (now Illinois Central Gulf) was completed in 1874 through Arlington, Bardwell, and Winford Junction. The Gulf, Mobile & Ohio Railroad was completed in 1880 in the extreme western part of the county and passed through the communities of Berkley, Laketon, and Winford Junction. Bardwell became the first county seat. A Victorian-style courthouse survived until 1980, when it was destroyed by arson. A modern brick courthouse was completed in 1982.

Arlington grew as a business and banking center. By the mid-1880s the town numbered among its businesses the *Arlington Leader* newspaper; numerous stores; saw and gristmills; the Flegle Rolling Mill; and several hotels, including William E. Hall's combination hotel and coffin supplier. Berkley likewise grew to be a prosperous trading center on the railroad, while Milburn, site of a Methodist seminary, grew in spite of its location away from the rail line. By 1900 a flour mill, livery stable, plow factory, churches, hotel, and drugstore were operating. In 1925 work began on U.S. 51 through the county, and in 1928 U.S. 62, then a gravel road, connected Bardwell with Paducah.

Between 1940 and 1960 the population of the county declined from 7,600 to 5,600. Many residents were engaged in farming, but from 1954 to 1969 the number of farms fell while the average acreage grew, reflecting a statewide trend. Burley tobacco, dark-fired tobacco, soybeans, and corn were the major crops, and substantial numbers of hogs and cattle were raised there. The county has two factories that produce lamps and light fixtures. The population of the county was 5,354 in 1970; 5,478 in 1980; and 5,238 in 1990.

See Mary Ellen Thomason, *A History of Carlisle County, Kentucky For the Years 1820-1900: Celebrating America's Bicentennial 1776-1976* (Bardwell, Ky., 1976).

CARMICHAEL, OMER. Omer Carmichael, educator, was born in Hollins, Alabama, on March 7, 1893, to William Colin and Lucy (Wilson) Carmichael. The eldest of eight children, he grew up on his father's farm. Carmichael left home in 1909 to enroll at the University of Alabama, where he graduated in 1913. He began his career in education the following year, teaching in a secondary school in Selma, Alabama. Carmichael rose rapidly in the Alabama public school system, becoming superintendent of schools in Selma in 1919. In 1924 he received an A.M. from Columbia. He served as superintendent of schools in Tampa, Florida (1926-32), and in Lynchburg, Virginia (1932-45), before moving to Louisville in 1945 to take on the same responsibility there.

In the early 1950s Carmichael successfully led the change to coeducation in public schools, but it was not until 1954 that he began to receive attention as a leader among educators. That year, the U.S. Supreme Court, in *Brown v. Board of Education*, declared segregated public education to be unconstitutional. In response to that decision, Carmichael began a two-year program that resulted in the peaceful desegregation of Louisville's public schools on September 10, 1956. As other public school systems in the South faced violence and picketing, Louisville's transition to desegregation was cited as a model for the nation, resulting in Carmichael's being honored at the White House by President Dwight D. Eisenhower.

Carmichael married Elnora Blanchard on October 9, 1926; they had three children: Shirley, Carol, and Donald. Carmichael's term as Louisville superintendent of schools ended with his sudden death on January 9, 1960. He was buried at the Hatchett Creek Presbyterian Church Cemetery in Goodwater, Alabama.

See Omer Carmichael and Weldon James, *The Louisville Story* (New York 1957).

CARPENTER, JOHN HOWARD. John Howard Carpenter, motion picture director and writer, was born on January 16, 1948, in Carthage, New York, the son of Howard Ralph and Milton Jean (Carter) Carpenter. The family moved to Bowling Green, Kentucky, in 1953, where his father taught music at Western Kentucky University. The Carpenters lived in the log home behind Western's Kentucky Building, and Carpenter attended local schools. He began making home movies at the age of ten with an 8mm camera. After briefly attending Western, he enrolled at the University of Southern California to study film in 1968. Carpenter did not earn a degree but his student project, *The Resurrection of Bronco Billy*, won an Academy Award as 1970's best live-action short subject. Carpenter is best known as the director of several successful horror films of the 1970s and early 1980s, including *Halloween*, *The Fog*, and *The Thing*. He was a coproducer of the successful sequel *Halloween II*. He also directed the film *Escape From New York* and the television movies *Someone Is Watching Me* and *Elvis*. Carpenter is divorced from actress Adrienne Barbeau. He has a son, John Cody.

MARY MARGARET BELL

CARROLL, JULIAN MORTON. Julian Morton Carroll, governor during 1975-79, was born to Elvie B. and Eva (Heady) Carroll in McCracken County, Kentucky, on April 16, 1931. In 1951 he married Chariann Harting; they had four children. In 1952 he received an associate of arts degree from Paducah Junior College in Kentucky; two years later he graduated from the University of Kentucky with a political science major, and in 1956 he received his law degree there. After three years of military service as an air force attorney, Carroll joined a Paducah law firm. In 1961 he was elected to the first of five consecutive terms in the state House of Representatives and was Speaker of the House from 1968 to 1970. As well as participating in civic affairs and Democratic politics, Carroll, a Presbyterian, was a frequent lay speaker and in 1966-67 served as moderator of the Kentucky Synod of the Cumberland Presbyterian Church.

When Bert T. Combs sought a second term as governor in 1971, he selected Carroll as his running mate to give geographical balance to the ticket. Combs lost to Wendell H. Ford, but Carroll won the nomination for lieutenant governor and was elected. When Ford resigned on December 28, 1974, to go to the U.S. Senate, Carroll became governor for the remainder of the term. He won an easy nomination for a full term in 1975 and enjoyed a decisive victory over Republican Robert E. Gable, 453,210 to 274,559. When he left office in 1979, Carroll opened a law practice in Frankfort.

He tried to regain the governorship in 1987, but won only 7 percent of the votes in the Democratic primary, finishing a distant fifth in a crowded field.

Governor Carroll's term was blessed with unusual prosperity for Kentucky. The Arab oil embargo increased the demand for coal, and for a time the state unemployment rate was well below the national average. Revenues were curtailed in his last year in office. During one of Carroll's frequent trips outside the state, politically ambitious Lt. Gov. Thelma Stovall called a special legislative session that cut taxes over Carroll's objections. Carroll's major cause was improvement of public schools, and Kentucky's standing in national statistics went up sharply in most categories, including the vital area of teachers' salaries. The Minimum Foundation Program for education was enhanced, free textbooks were provided, and special attention was given to both weak and strong students. Higher education did not fare as well, and the regional universities bore the brunt of Carroll's curtailments. On both state and national levels, Carroll was a strong advocate of coal as an answer to the energy crisis. A state Department of Energy was established to give direction and coordinate efforts in that field. A series of disasters (floods, fires, mine accidents) focused state attention on safety regulations. As well as working to expand Kentucky's economic base, Carroll initiated an innovative matching grant program for the encouragement of the arts, and he pushed for the construction of a major performing arts center in Louisville.

See Charles Paul Conn, *Julian Carroll of Kentucky* (Old Tappan, N.J., 1970).

LOWELL H. HARRISON

CARROLL COUNTY. Carroll County lies in the north-central section of Kentucky on the Ohio River at the mouth of the Kentucky River. The eighty-seventh county established, it was formed in 1838 from parts of the adjoining counties of Gallatin, Trimble, and Henry. The county seat is CARROLL-TON; both were named for Charles Carroll of Maryland, the last surviving signer of the Declaration of Independence. Carroll County is Kentucky's third smallest, covering 130 square miles.

Prior to settlement, Indians hunted in the area. A military blockhouse built in 1790 by Gen. Charles Scott and his Kentucky Volunteers provided protection for early settlers from Virginia, Pennsylvania, and Maryland. The federal government's treaty with the Shawnee in 1794 lessened the danger of attack, and farmers began producing crops for marketing in Louisville and Cincinnati via riverboats on the Ohio.

Carroll County is watered and drained by the Kentucky River, as well as the Little Kentucky River, Eagle Creek, and McCool's Creek. Along the river bottoms the land is gently rolling, with the remainder of the county hilly. General Butler State Park, opened in 1933 and named in honor of General William Orlando Butler, features year-round outdoor recreation activities, including the state park system's only ski area. The 809-acre park also offers lodging, camping, fishing, and golf.

Carroll County's economy is based on both agriculture and industry, with farms productive in such crops as tobacco, corn, soybeans, garden vegetables, and fruit, as well as livestock. Combined agricultural receipts in 1986 were $10.29 million, including $8.27 million in crops and $2.02 million in livestock. In 1988 2.92 million pounds of burley tobacco were produced. Industrial manufacturers include Atochem, Dow Corning, Kentucky Ladder, North American Stainless, Teledyne, and Woodmaster Foundations.

The population of Carroll County was 8,523 in 1970, 9,270 in 1980; and 9,292 in 1990.

See M.A. Gentry, *History of Carroll County* (Madison, Ind., 1984). MARY ANN GENTRY

CARROLLTON. Carrollton, the seat of Carroll County, is located at the confluence of the Ohio and Kentucky rivers, thirty-nine miles northeast of Louisville. This fourth-class city, laid out by Benjamin Craig and James Hawkins, was named Port William by an act of the Kentucky legislature in 1794. When Gallatin County was formed in 1798, Port William served as the seat. In 1838, when part of Gallatin County was incorporated in Carroll County, Port William became Carrollton and the seat of the new county. Carrollton's riverfront location promoted growth until 1868, when the Louisville & Nashville Railroad was built ten miles from the city limits and river traffic waned. The Carroll County courthouse, built in 1841, was replaced by the present courthouse in 1884. It is listed on the National Register of Historic Places, along with twenty-five other Victorian buildings in the downtown area.

The population of Carrollton was 3,884 in 1970; 3,967 in 1980; and 3,715 in 1990. Carrollton's tobacco market usually ranks among the top five in the state. Manufactured items include furniture, silicones, chemical coatings, automobile parts, and wooden ladders.

See M.A. Gentry, *History of Carroll County* (Madison, Ind., 1984). MARY ANN GENTRY

CARSON, CHRISTOPHER. Christopher ("Kit") Carson, frontiersman and soldier, was born on December 24, 1809, in Million, Kentucky, four miles northwest of Richmond, to Lindsay and Rebecca (Robinson) Carson. His father, a North Carolinian, had moved to Kentucky in 1793 after serving in the Revolutionary Army, and his parents were married in 1793. Kit was the fifth of their ten children. In the spring of 1811, the Carson family moved to Howard County, Missouri.

At age fifteen, Carson was apprenticed to a saddler and two years later, in 1826, joined an expedition to New Mexico. He settled in Taos, where he became a trapper and hunter, supplying meat for nearby Bents' Fort. About 1836 he married an Arapaho whom he called Alice. They had one daughter, also named Alice, whom Carson took to live with relatives in Missouri after his wife died in 1842.

While preparing to return west, Carson met Lt. John C. Frémont and became Frémont's guide during his exploration of the West, distinguishing himself as a soldier. Carson's exploits in the war with Mexico (1846-48) made him a national hero. He crawled through Mexican lines at San Pascal and walked barefoot thirty miles to San Diego to obtain aid for Gen. Stephen W. Kearny's stranded troops. In 1853 he was appointed an Indian agent in New Mexico; he avoided paperwork connected with the job, but had considerable success dealing with Indian tribes, who trusted him. He resigned his post at the outbreak of the Civil War. On July 25, 1861, Carson was appointed lieutenant colonel of the New Mexican Volunteer Infantry, U.S. Army, directing actions against the Indians of the Southwest. He was promoted to general on March 13, 1865, and was given the command of Fort Garland in Colorado in 1866. He resigned from the army on March 22, 1867, because of declining health. Carson died at Fort Lyon, Colorado, on March 23, 1868, and was buried in Taos, New Mexico.

See Dewitt C. Peters, *Kit Carson's Life and Adventures* (Hartford, Conn., 1874).

CARTER, TIM LEE. Tim Lee Carter, physician and U.S. congressman, was born on September 2, 1910, in Tompkinsville, Monroe County, Kentucky, the son of James and Idru (Tucker) Carter. His father was circuit judge for Monroe County. The young Carter was educated in the public schools of Tompkinsville, graduated from Western Kentucky State Teachers College (now Western Kentucky University) in 1934, and received his M.D. from the University of Tennessee in 1937. Carter then set up a private medical practice in Monroe County. During World War II, he spent forty-two months as a captain in the 38th Infantry Division in the Philippines.

Carter was elected to the Monroe County School Board, where he served as chairman during 1952-64. He was elected as a Republican from Kentucky's 5th Congressional District to the U.S. House of Representatives during 1965-81, one of the few congressmen who were also practicing physicians. He was a major supporter of health and hospital legislation as well as vocational schools, sanitary water systems, libraries, recreational facilities, airports, and roads. He was an early advocate of national insurance against catastrophic illness and was instrumental in the passage of legislation that provided health care for the children of needy families.

In 1981 Carter returned to his farm and private medical practice at Turkey Neck Bend on the Cumberland River. His wife was the former Kathleen Bradshaw; they had one child, William. Carter died in Glasgow on March 27, 1987, and was buried in Evans Oak Hill Cemetery in Tompkinsville.

CARTER, WILLIAM GRAYSON. William Grayson Carter was a state senator from Lewis, Greenup, and Lawrence counties from 1834 to 1838. He was instrumental in the 1838 formation of Carter County, which was named in his honor. He donated the land for a courthouse when Grayson was chosen as the county seat and later donated land for building a Methodist church. The town of Grayson was named in honor of his wife, Hebe (Grayson) Carter, daughter of Col. William Grayson, aide de camp to Gen. George Washington. In 1847 Carter moved to Arkansas. He died while visiting Lexington in 1850.

CARTER AND CASCADE CAVES. Eastern Kentucky, especially Carter County, is well-known for its unique geological formations, among them deep gorges, cliffs, and underground passageways. Carter Caves and the nearby Cascade Caves were formed during the glacial period when this area was part of the Great Teays River drainage system (see GLACIERS). The present landscape, including the caves, is a result of inexorable erosion forces. Moving water and weather changes wore away limestone and earth, which in turn created deep chasms and labyrinthine caves. The caves and adjacent area are visited by thousands of people each year. Nearby Bat Cave still harbors a rare and endangered species of bat. Various caves have been temporary shelters for humans and animals, and signs of their habitation remain. Carter Caves became a state park in 1946. Kentucky Gov. William Jason Fields (1923-27), a native of Carter County, was the primary force behind the state's purchase of the several hundred acres of undisturbed land that constitute the Carter Caves State Resort Park. The Cascade Caves became part of the park in 1959.

HUBERT V. CRAWFORD AND
PAUL L. CRAWFORD

CARTER COUNTY. Carter County, the eighty-eighth county in order of formation, is located in northeastern Kentucky. The county is bounded by Lewis, Greenup, Boyd, Lawrence, Elliott, and Rowan counties, and has an area of 397 square miles.

Carter County was formed on April 10, 1838, from parts of Greenup and Lawrence counties and named for state Sen. William Grayson Carter. GRAYSON, incorporated in 1844, is the county seat. Boyd County was formed in 1860 and Elliot County was formed in 1869, each from a portion of Carter County. In 1904 the residents of Olive Hill made an attempt to create the county of BECKHAM from the western part of Carter County. Other communities in the county include Hitchins, Carter, Soldier, and Grahn. Carter County has deposits of limestone, fireclay, and coal.

Archaeological finds indicate that prehistoric Native American groups once lived in the area. Salt wells along the Little Sandy River drew pioneers in the late 1780s. Much of the area was part of a 70,000-acre tract that had been awarded by Virginia to Col. William Grayson for his services during the American Revolution. Other grants were the Robert Henderson tract and the Maylan tract, which included what would later be known as Carter Caves. In 1790 residents included Henderson, John Cox, John Rigs, and the Reaves family.

The Civil War divided residents of Carter County. Although there were 320 slaves in the county just before the war, many residents supported the Union and joined Companies D, H, I, and G of the 22d Regiment of Kentucky Volunteer Infantry. Many of the Confederate sympathizers joined the Fields Partisan Rangers, organized by county sheriff William Jason Fields (whose grandson and namesake, William Jason Fields, served as Kentucky governor during 1923-27). Although only minor skirmishes occurred in Carter County during the war, there was personal and property damage. In the 1870s the western portion of the county was the scene of the UNDERWOOD-HOLBROOK FEUD.

Salt extraction was a major industry in Carter County from the late 1700s until around 1850, and saltpeter was mined locally during the War of 1812. Five iron furnaces were built in Carter County, beginning with Pactolus in 1824; Mt. Savage and Star in 1848; Boone in 1856; and the largest, Iron Hills (later renamed Charlotte), in 1873. The last furnace to operate was Mt. Savage, which closed in 1882. Tobacco became the county's most important cash crop after 1883, when experienced growers from Owen, Henry, Carroll, and Grant counties emigrated to Carter County. Two sales warehouses and a chewing tobacco plant operated between 1890 and 1925. Clay was mined for use in steam locomotives and by the steel industry. Five brickyards produced fire bricks.

Commercial mining of coal began in 1850. The industry prospered during periods of peak demand in 1891, 1902, 1920, 1947, and 1974. Strip mining after 1960 had a profound impact on the land and the county economy. Limestone mining continues, although the former underground quarry at Lawton was converted for a short time into a mushroom farm. After World War II, there was an exodus of labor from the county, and by 1984 most local jobs were in service fields or government. The skilled blue-collar workers who remained commuted to Boyd and other counties for jobs.

The main highways in Carter County are US 60, KY 1, KY 2, KY 7, and I-64, which was completed through the area in 1973. The road system brought tourism to the area and led to the formation of two parks in the county: Carter Caves State Resort Park in 1947 and Grayson Lake State Park in 1970. Camp Cardinal, a Girl Scout camp near Carter Caves, and the Robert C. Webb Conservation Camp are used by schoolchildren during the summer. Christian Normal Institute, renamed Kentucky Christian College in 1944, was founded on December 1, 1919, by J.W. Lusby in Grayson.

Among former residents of the county are singer-songwriter Tom T. Hall; operatic singer Carol

Malone; and Matthew Bacon Benjamin ("King Benjamin") Purnell, who in 1894 began to preach throughout the Midwest. By the early 1900s, Purnell had a following, known as the House of David, in which members committed their worldly goods to a common fund and believed in arranged marriages. The group sponsored bearded basketball and football teams and a bearded baseball team that toured the country from 1908 until 1958.

The population of the rural county was 19,850 in 1970; 25,060 in 1980; and 24,340 in 1990.

See Carter County Bicentennial Committee, *Carter County History 1838-1976* (Grayson, Ky., 1976); George Wolfford, *Carter County: A Pictorial History* (Ashland, Ky., 1985).

GEORGE WOLFFORD

CARTWRIGHT, PETER. Peter Cartwright, a Methodist circuit rider, son of Peter and Christian (Garvin) Cartwright, was born on September 1, 1785, in Amherst County, Virginia. His father moved the family to Kentucky in 1790 and settled in Logan County in 1793.

Cartwright joined the Methodist church in 1801 after a camp meeting during the GREAT REVIVAL, which spread through the Green River vicinity of Logan County, near the Cartwright home. In 1802 he received a license to preach and moved his family to Livingston County, near the mouth of the Cumberland River. After briefly attending Brown's Academy, Cartwright established the Livingston preaching circuit. In 1803 he traveled the Red River circuit for three months, and was then assigned to the Waynesville circuit, stretching from north of the Green River to the Cumberland River, and south into Tennessee. In 1806 Cartwright was ordained a deacon, and he became a presiding elder in 1808.

Cartwright, known as "Kentucky Boy," was a powerful speaker and a popular figure on the circuits. He served principally in Kentucky and Tennessee until 1824, when he had himself transferred to Illinois because of his antislavery sentiments. He was elected representative of Sangamon County in the Illinois legislature in 1828 and 1832, defeating Abraham Lincoln in the latter election. Cartwright married Frances Gaines of Glasgow, Kentucky, on August 18, 1808; they had nine children, eight of whom reached maturity. Cartwright died on September 25, 1872, and was buried at Pleasant Plains in Sangamon County, Illinois.

See Edward Coffman, *The Story of Logan County* (Nashville 1962); W.P. Strickland, ed., *The Backwoods Preacher: An Autobiography of Peter Cartwright* (London 1858).

CASEY, WILLIAM. William Casey, pioneer, a native of Frederick County, Virginia, was born in 1754 to John and Margaret (Blackburn) Casey. He came to Kentucky in the winter of 1779-80 and camped on Dick's (now Dix) River. In 1782 he married Jane Montgomery, daughter of William Montgomery; they lived near Logan's Station until 1791. That year Casey, with a company of soldier settlers,

followed Green River, crossed it south of what was later called Casey's Creek, and erected a blockhouse and fort fifty miles from the nearest white settlement. The station was named for Casey. He was commissioned December 18, 1792, as a lieutenant colonel of the 16th Regiment of the Green County militia. Sincere, honest, and civic-minded, he employed a traveling tutor for the early settlements and assisted in the establishment of academies in Green and Adair counties. In 1795 he was a member of the state House of Representatives; in 1799 a member of Kentucky's second constitutional convention; in 1800 a member of the state Senate. Colonel Casey died in 1816 on his Russell Creek property in Adair County. He was buried in Johnston Cemetery under this inscription: "William Casey 1754-1816, Ensign Clark's Ill. Regiment, Revolutionary War." His will, recorded in Adair County, lists his heirs as his wife, Jane; son, Green Casey; and daughters Peggy Lampton (the grandmother of Samuel Clemens), Jenny Paxton, Mollie Creel, and Ann Montgomery. When Casey County was organized in 1806, it was named in his honor.

GLADYS COTHAM THOMAS

CASEY COUNTY. The forty-sixth in order of formation, Casey County was created on November 14, 1806, from Lincoln County, and named in honor of Col. William Casey, a Revolutionary War veteran from Virginia who explored the area in 1779. The 435-square-mile county is bordered by Russell, Pulaski, Lincoln, Boyle, Marion, Taylor, and Adair counties. LIBERTY, the county seat, was incorporated in 1830.

Topography varies from dissected uplands to broad valleys with flat-topped ridges. The headwaters of the Green River and the Rolling Fork of the Salt River are the main water sources. Casey's 1850 population of 5,863 included 634 slaves. In 1870 the county produced 95,750 pounds of tobacco and 332,779 bushels of corn. In 1989, 71 percent of the land area was in farms and half of those were in cultivation. Casey ranks thirty-eighth among counties in agricultural receipts from tobacco, corn, hay, livestock, and vegetables. The county's 30,000 apple trees produce one-sixth of the state's crop.

Early settlers arrived in 1779. Henry Quarles received a Virginia land grant for 1,000 acres in 1784. Prior to 1800, thirteen land grants for 3,022 acres were filed. While the population grew slowly, numerous travelers followed two trails across the county that connected Logan's Station at Stanford with settlements on the Green and Barren rivers to the west. The first county court met on May 4, 1807, and among other business, fixed rates on liquor, meals, and lodging at several taverns. Whiskey and brandy were eight cents and twelve cents a half-pint, respectively; breakfast was seventeen cents and dinner twenty-five cents; lodging was six cents a night.

One of the families who settled in the county around 1781 was that of Capt. Abraham Lincoln, the president's grandfather. The Lincolns lived for two and a half years on eight hundred acres on the Green River. The land was sold in 1803 to Christopher Riffe for 400 pounds sterling by Mordecai Lincoln, Captain Lincoln's heir. Another landowner, Enoch Burdett, accumulated 13,000 acres of timberland, and upon his death in 1875, his holdings were sold to Eugene Zimmerman, a Cincinnati businessman. Zimmerman employed three hundred at his mills. In 1879 he built a wooden train track from Kings Mountain to Staffordsville, and in 1884 he organized the CINCINNATI & GREEN RIVER Railway Company. In 1891 when the timber resources were exhausted, he liquidated his holdings. The timber boom and early railroad had little lasting economic impact on the county.

While there are no records of Civil War skirmishes in the county, Casey is credited with producing one-third of the 1st Kentucky Cavalry, recruited by Col. Frank Wolford and Col. Silas Adams, to serve in the Union army. The 1st Cavalry was active in the Battles of Mill Springs, Perryville, and Lebanon, Tennessee. Adams served as state representative and later in the 53d U.S. Congress (1893-95).

Lumber continues in the 1990s to be an important segment of the economy, with five manufacturing firms producing wood products. Eight firms manufacture metal farm gates. The largest employer is Oshkosh B'Gosh, producer of children's clothing. Tourism brought in $1 million in 1988. Crude oil production totaled 4,599 barrels in 1989. The Casey County Apple Festival each September features the baking of what is billed as the world's largest apple pie. Casey County's primary transportation route is U.S. 127.

Casey County's population was 12,930 in 1970; 14,818 in 1980; and 14,211 in 1990.

See Gladys C. Thomas, *Casey County, Kentucky 1806-1983* (Danville, Ky., 1983).

GLADYS C. THOMAS

CASTLEMAN, JOHN BRECKINRIDGE. John Breckinridge Castleman, military officer and horseman, was born June 30, 1841, at Castleton Farm, Lexington, Kentucky, to David and Virginia (Harrison) Castleman. Before the Civil War, he studied law at Transylvania University and was a member of the Lexington Chasseurs militia. In 1862 he recruited forty-one men from Lexington and after joining John Hunt Morgan at Knoxville, Tennessee, was made captain of Confederate Company D, 2d Kentucky Cavalry. He led his company at the Battle of Taylor's Crossroads, at the intersection of Newtown Pike and Iron Works Pike near Lexington in July 1862 during Morgan's first Kentucky raid.

Castleman rode with Morgan until after the second battle of Cynthiana on June 11, 1864. He was promoted to major in 1864 and participated in the Northwest conspiracy, an abortive attempt to free Confederate prisoners of war from Camp Douglas near Chicago. He then led a band of guerrillas who tried to burn U.S. supply boats at the St. Louis wharf. Castleman was captured by federal authori-

ties in October 1864 at Sullivan, Indiana, and was sentenced to death for spying. President Abraham Lincoln interceded on his behalf, writing, "Whenever John B. Castleman shall be tried, if convicted and sentenced, suspend execution until further notice from me and send me the record. A. Lincoln." After Lincoln's assassination and the end of the war, Castleman was banished from the United States. He went to France, where he studied medicine.

Castleman was pardoned by President Andrew Johnson and returned to Kentucky late in 1866. After graduating from the University of Louisville Law School in 1868, he married Alice Barbee and formed the insurance company Barbee and Castleman with his father-in-law. The firm was southern representative for the Royal Insurance Company of Liverpool. In 1878 Castleman revived the Louisville Legion of the Kentucky militia and in 1883 was appointed adjutant general of Kentucky.

In 1898, his militia unit volunteered for service in the Spanish-American War, becoming the 1st Kentucky Volunteers. Castleman was commissioned a colonel in the U.S. Army. The 1st Kentucky Volunteers participated in the bloodless invasion of Puerto Rico. Castleman was promoted to brigadier general in the U.S. Army and served as military governor of the island. He helped secure the nomination of Grover Cleveland for president at the Democratic convention of 1892. After the assassination of Gov. William Goebel in 1900, General Castleman was again appointed Kentucky adjutant general and was instrumental in averting civil war in Kentucky over the assassination.

Castleman was one of the founders of the AMERICAN SADDLEBRED HORSE ASSOCIATION and was elected its first president in 1891. The same year he founded the Louisville Park Department and was made park commissioner. He was also president of the Louisville Horse Show. In 1893 Castleman rode his five-gaited mare Emily to win the grand championship at the Chicago Columbian Exposition World's Fair. A statue of General Castleman riding his American Saddlebred mare Carolina was unveiled near Cherokee Park in Louisville in 1914.

Castleman died on May 23, 1918. He was preceded in death by two sons, David and Breckinridge, and survived by five daughters. He was buried at Cave Hill Cemetery, Louisville.

See John B. Castleman, *Active Service* (Louisville 1917).   LYNN WEATHERMAN

CATHEDRAL BASILICA OF THE ASSUMPTION. The Cathedral Basilica of the Assumption, located at Madison Avenue and Twelfth Street in Covington, Kentucky, is a building of French Gothic style. The interior draws its inspiration from St. Denis in Paris, and its main, or west, facade is based on Notre Dame in Paris. The principal architect was Leon Coquard of Detroit. A local architect, David Davis, designed the west facade. The sculptures at the portal are the work of Clement Barnhorn of Cincinnati.

Inside the church, the ribbed gothic vaults of the nave and apse, completed in 1901, rise eighty-one feet above the floor. Many of the stained glass windows were executed by Mayer and Company of Munich. The north transept window, sixty-seven feet high and twenty-four feet wide, is one of the largest stained-glass windows in the world. The Blessed Sacrament Chapel, adjoining the south transept, contains a gold-plated tabernacle inlaid with semi-precious stones and four large paintings by Frank Duveneck of Covington. The cathedral has three complete pipe organs; the oldest is the Mathias Schwab organ in the rear gallery, dating from 1859, which was originally installed in St. Joseph Church in Covington. The Cathedral of the Assumption also contains fourteen stations of the cross executed in mosaic by Venetian craftsmen.

The cathedral was built under the auspices of Roman Catholic Bishop Camillus P. Maes, third bishop of Covington. Construction began in 1894 and by 1901 the completed nave was opened for services. In 1910 the main facade was completed. The church, originally called St. Mary Cathedral, was designated a basilica by Pope Pius XII in 1953, the centenary of the formation of the diocese of Covington.

See Walter A. Freiberg, *A Guide to the Cathedral* (Covington, Ky., 1947).

MARY PHILIP TRAUTH AND
PAUL A. TENKOTTE

CATLETTSBURG. Catlettsburg, the seat of Boyd County, is located southeast of Ashland on U.S. 23 and U.S. 60, at the confluence of the Ohio and Big Sandy rivers in northeastern Kentucky.

The city was named for early settlers Alexander Catlett and his son Horatio, who arrived from Virginia in 1798. The town grew up around Horatio Catlett's tavern, which existed from 1808 to 1833. Because of its river location, the city became an active trading post and a steamboat landing, known as the Mouth of Sandy. The town was laid out by James Wilson Fry in 1849 and incorporated on February 11, 1858. Two years later it became the seat of newly organized Boyd County. The limestone courthouse is of Beaux Arts design.

Catlettsburg thrived during the steamboat era as the timber industry prospered and many related businesses moved in. Wharves were built along the shore for loading boats. The timber industry started around 1840 and peaked around 1900, when the city was one of the largest hardwood timber markets in the world. Virgin timber from eastern Kentucky was logged, pulled by oxen to creeks, and floated to the Big Sandy River and on to the Ohio in giant timber rafts. Of the several hotels, the Alger House (1879) was regarded as the finest. A race track (1890) and the Morse Opera House (1878) provided recreation for the influx of people. Front Street had twenty-one saloons and a restaurant.

Rail transportation began with the arrival of the Big Sandy Valley Railroad in 1873; the Chatteroi Railway Company in 1879; and the Elizabethtown, Lexington & Big Sandy Valley Railway Company

in 1879. The Chesapeake & Ohio, which arrived in 1911, tore down many city landmarks after it acquired right of way in 1929. Streetcars came in 1894, and the Interstate Camden Railway appeared in 1903. A fire on July 22, 1878, destroyed several of the businesses and homes in downtown Catlettsburg, at a cost of $300,000. Other fires, in 1884, 1919, and 1932, destroyed many businesses. Major floods occurred in 1884, 1913, 1937, and 1948.

During the Civil War, Gen. James A. Garfield with the Union 42d Division located briefly in Catlettsburg in December 1861. In 1902 a U.S. district court was established there and the federal courthouse was built in 1911. Federal court was held there until 1985, when it was moved to Ashland. Two U.S. senators, George Brown Martin (1918-19) and Ben Mitchell Williamson (1930-31); and one U.S. representative, Laban Theodore Moore (1859-61), lived for a time in the city. Mary Eliott FLANERY, first woman legislator in Kentucky (1922-23), also lived there.

Catlettsburg is surrounded by heavy industry. The city is on an Amtrak route and is one of the few Kentucky cities with an active rail passenger depot. Catlettsburg is part of the greater Huntington, West Virginia, metropolitan area. The population of the fourth-class city was 3,420 in 1970; 3,005 in 1980; and 2,231 in 1990.

See John L. Smith, *The Early History of Boyd County, Kentucky* (Catlettsburg, Ky., 1944).

JAMES C. POWERS

CATTLE INDUSTRY. "Wherever two blades of grass grow in Kentucky there are cattle," writes Thomas D. Clark in *Agrarian Kentucky* (1977). Cattle farming typifies the system of mixed farming and stock raising that differentiates Kentucky from other southern states. Domesticated animals were brought to Harrodsburg and Boonesborough in the mid-1770s. Abundant savannah lands, canebrakes, and forests offered excellent grazing. Ample water and relatively mild winters allowed for open range grazing, typical in pioneer days. Owners identified their animals with distinguishing earmarks or notches and permitted their stock to wander freely across the countryside in search of food. At the onset of winter, farmers collected their herds and slaughtered surplus animals for domestic consumption. Because of marauding Indians and limited access to distant markets, commercial cattle production probably did not commence in Kentucky with the earliest settlements.

The transition from subsistence to commercial livestock production began in the 1780s, when the diminished Indian threat and the ever-increasing influx of settlers led to increased production. By 1785 purebred cattle raised by Virginian Matthew Patton and his sons had entered Kentucky and launched the blooded cattle industry. After the Pattons' introduction of such famous foundation stock as the bulls Mars (1795) and Pluto (1803) and the cow Venus (1795), Kentucky came to be associated with excellence in the raising of SHORTHORN CATTLE.

Early nineteenth century agriculturalists wrestled with the problem of developing new markets, improving stock bloodlines, and increasing pasturage. Pioneer and early antebellum cattle marketing connected Kentucky to Atlantic coastal markets via the Wilderness Road and the Cumberland Gap. Professional cattle drovers herded cattle and other stock to markets in Charleston, South Carolina; Richmond, Virginia; Baltimore; Philadelphia; and Boston. Their journey to market usually started in midsummer, with animals grazing along the way. Small producers en route sold or acquired stock from the drovers and also supplied them with corn. Every effort was made to maintain the stock in good condition during the many weeks of the trip. After 1800 cattle drives were commonplace, and by 1828 stock worth over $1.1 million had passed through the Cumberland Gap (see TRAIL DRIVES).

Following 1814 and the defeat of the Creek Indians, southern markets increasingly opened to Kentuckians as the cotton frontier expanded southwest into Alabama and Mississippi. Roads connected Louisville to Nashville and branched southward to Memphis, Tennessee; Vicksburg, Mississippi; and New Orleans. Cattle were driven through the gap and on to Chattanooga in Tennessee and to Huntsville, Montgomery, and Mobile in Alabama. Southern planters, obsessed with cotton production, relied heavily upon Kentucky for stock and supplies. This reliance was strengthened by the introduction of steamboat shipping on the Mississippi and Ohio rivers in the 1810s.

The cotton boom of the lower South coincided with a radical shift in the type of farming conducted by Kentuckians. The national financial panic of 1819 and the collapse of international prices for tobacco led many farmers to abandon row crops for livestock. Landholders possessing the necessary capital to acquire pedigreed cattle, purchase seed, erect fences, and add acres of pasturage planted cover crops in their fields and clover and bluegrass in their pastures. By the mid-1830s the transition from a grain- to a livestock-based economy was largely complete; the change brought improved maintenance of soil fertility and the consolidation of smaller into larger landholdings, in addition to expanded production of cattle, both common and purebred, but especially the latter.

Until 1817 most improved cattle came from earlier Patton stock. That year Lewis Sanders, an enterprising Fayette County farmer, shipped English purebred stock—Bakewell longhorns, Holderness, Durham reds, Westmorelands, and other breeds—to central Kentucky. By the late 1830s shorthorn stock had grown in popularity among cattlemen and direct importation of European foundation stock began in earnest. Kentucky, especially the Bluegrass region, became the center of the shorthorn industry. Between 1852 and 1856, 10 percent of the registered shorthorns in America were to be found in the Bluegrass region.

The image of the aristocratic central Kentucky planter monopolizing cattle production is inaccurate. An exceedingly small minority of the wealthiest agriculturalists, those owning three hundred acres or more, raised 22 percent of all the state's cattle in 1850, but smaller producers accounted for the rest. The Appalachian region was also an important livestock center. In 1850 the mountain counties of Breathitt, Floyd, Harlan, Perry, and Pike surpassed Bourbon, Fayette, and Woodford in cattle production per capita. The Pennyroyal region also produced substantial numbers of animals.

New modes of transportation and the growing prominence of regional stockyards and slaughterhouses altered marketing patterns. Louisville's stockyards, which opened in 1834, quickly lured stockmen by attractive prices. By the 1840s the smaller community slaughterhouses were losing out to agribusiness centralization. The pace of this process increased with the coming of the railroads.

Only seventy-eight miles of railroad spanned Kentucky in 1850; over five hundred had been laid by 1860. Rail transportation gradually came to supplant the overland stock drive by the late 1850s. The Lexington & Covington, Louisville & Nashville, and Mobile & Ohio railroads eagerly sought this trade and in doing so sped the growth of Louisville and Cincinnati as livestock processing centers.

In 1860, 835,059 head of cattle were produced in Kentucky. The high demand for quality breeding stock seemed to assure cattlemen a prosperous future. Unfortunately, the 1860 level of production was not reached again until 1878 because the Civil War devastated the state's cattle industry. Occupying armies slaughtered animals for food and destroyed rail lines, bridges, and river locks. Guerrillas burned stock barns and fences. The state's agricultural labor system lay in ruins. These factors, coupled with diminished demand from newly bankrupt southern customers slowed recovery, which was further retarded by competition from ranchers west of the Mississippi.

During the late 1860s immense droves of Texas cattle stopped to fatten on Kentucky pastures while journeying to such emerging agricultural processing centers as Chicago's Union Stockyards. They lingered long enough to introduce ticks, parasites, and diseases, formerly unknown in the region, that were fatal to native stock. Dominance in cattle breeding and raising had shifted to the mid- and far-western regions of the nation. The older coastal markets gradually gave way to those of Chicago; St. Louis; Kansas City, Missouri; and Omaha, Nebraska, with their newly established railroads and facilities for processing, cold storage, and shipping of meat, which further strengthened the westerners' grip on Kentucky's traditional markets.

Kentucky livestock production, which had surpassed 1 million head by 1886, remained at that level for the next forty years. A threefold growth in the number of farms took place between 1860 and 1900, but livestock values rose only marginally. Western cattle breeders' preference for Herefords over other pedigreed shorthorn stock drove Kentucky from its commanding position in shorthorn production.

As the nineteenth century drew to a close, cattle drives had been replaced by rail shipping and county court days. Open range grazing, once so prevalent in pioneer Kentucky, existed only marginally in the more remote areas. New breeds such as the Hereford and Angus were gaining popularity. Kentucky's state government belatedly and tentatively moved to assist livestock producers and farmers by establishing the Kentucky Bureau of Agriculture, Horticulture, and Statistics. Agricultural education received increased emphasis with the founding of a university-based experiment station.

At the start of the twentieth century, cattle production averaged fewer than five head per farm: Over 230,000 farmers tended some 1 million animals. In eastern Kentucky fewer than 25 percent of the farmers raised as many as five animals. The 1900s also ushered in an era of increased agricultural education and government involvement. Scientists helped develop techniques to improve breeding stock, control diseases, and ensure the quality and purity of animal feed. State government appropriated funds to provide premiums at the annual state livestock and agricultural fair. Kentucky's slaughtering and meatpacking industries flourished during World War I. By 1920 Kentucky's cattle herds represented more than 25 percent of the total $85.5 million worth of livestock within the state.

The great southern drought of 1930-31 and the worsening national economic situation were serious setbacks to the industry. The number of beef cattle dropped to a record low in 1930. Prime animals selling for $5.90 per hundredweight in 1925 sold for $3.05 by December of 1933. Their fields and gardens scorched and lacking feed, farmers sacrificed stock for their hungry families. Not until the late 1930s and the impact of New Deal relief programs did the situation begin to improve. Cattle production by the end of the decade had increased from 990,000 to 1.5 million head.

The cattle industry in the late twentieth century has experienced dramatic gains and setbacks. From 1940 to 1975, the majority of southern states increased their cattle production fourfold. At its peak, Kentucky's production tripled, from 1.25 million head in 1940 to 3.75 million in 1975. During the same period, the number of Kentucky farms declined from 267,000 to 99,000. Fewer farmers, cultivating larger farms, produced more and better cattle. Average beef cattle prices increased almost without interruption between 1960 and 1973 and peaked in 1979. Improved rural roads meant more cost-effective marketing. Historically low interest rates, favorable international market conditions, and productivity gains all worked together to generate record production and price levels by the mid-1970s.

Kentucky's cattle industry by the 1970s had shifted westward within the state. Central Kentucky still possessed the largest concentration of registered purebred cattle, but the Pennyroyal, Jackson Purchase, and Western Coal Field regions had become the state's agribusiness centers. As an example, in 1870 the top seven cattle-producing counties were Bourbon, Madison, Clark, Fayette, Shelby, Pulaski, and Warren. A little over one hundred years later, the top five counties were Barren, Warren, Lincoln, Bourbon, and Pulaski. After 1975 production gradually dropped until it stabilized in 1987 at 2.45 million head—lower than at any time since 1967. Prices also declined until the latter half of the 1980s. Especially notable is the dramatic drop in the number of cattle farms. One-third of the 90,000 cattle farms operating during the prosperous mid-1970s had ceased production by 1987.

Retirement and economic opportunities have lured many farmers off the land, yet Kentucky still ranks tenth nationally in the total number of cattle and twelfth in the total of cows and calves. Livestock sales totaled $1.51 billion in 1987, with only the revenue from horse sales exceeding that from cattle. Not even tobacco, for all its acclaim as Kentucky's cash crop, produced receipts equaling cattle and calf sales that year.

See Kentucky Department of Agriculture, *Kentucky Agricultural Statistics, 1987-1988* (Louisville, n.d.).

JAMES E. WALLACE

CAUDILL, HARRY MONROE. Appalachian historian and social critic, Harry Monroe Caudill was born May 3, 1922, in Letcher County, Kentucky, the son of Cro Carr and Martha Victoria (Blair) Caudill, both of Scotch-Irish descent. After graduating from Whitesburg High School in 1941, Caudill joined the U.S. Army and was wounded in action during World War II. He graduated from the University of Kentucky Law School in 1948. Returning to Whitesburg, Caudill in 1954 was elected to the first of three terms in the state House of Representatives, a largely frustrating experience that led to the article "How an Election Was Bought and Sold" in the October 1960 issue of *Harper's Magazine*. The byline read "A Kentucky Legislator," and the article launched Caudill's career as a writer.

With his first book, *Night Comes to the Cumberlands* (1963), Caudill in effect made history by writing it. The book—"The story of how this rich and beautiful land was changed into an ugly, poverty-ridden place of desolation," wrote author Harriette Arrow—turned the nation's eyes toward Kentucky's hills. It described a sort of corporate feudalism in which coal operators bullied a neglected people through the use of the broad form deed to protect the mineral ownership of entrepreneurs. Caudill's book was generally credited with sparking the creation in 1964 of the Appalachian Regional Commission, a federal agency to assist Kentucky and twelve other states in the Appalachian Mountains. Some criticized the work's lack of footnotes or disagreed with its theory that Appalachia was populated by the "wretched outcasts" of British prisons, but Caudill himself emerged as a symbol of eastern Kentucky. For the next three or four years, Appalachia became a cause célèbre, bringing hundreds of volunteers, along with writers and government agencies, into the mountains.

Caudill became a beacon for the area's conservationists. He represented a roadblock for coal operators such as William Sturgill of Lexington, who maintained that Caudill did not support the economy or provide job opportunity, but rather made personal gain from advertising worldwide the misfortunes of his friends and neighbors. Nationally, Caudill became known as an eloquent and courageous spokesman for an exploited region and its people. He helped organize grass-roots opposition to strip mining and the broad form deed and fought them in the courts, in magazine and newspaper articles, in letters and speeches and appearances before legislative committees. He gained in the process a national reputation, many enemies, and some influential friends. Historian Thomas D. Clark has spoken of Caudill's voice as one of the most important in Kentucky's history.

After *Night Comes to the Cumberlands*, Caudill wrote nine books, fifty magazine articles, and eighty newspaper articles and he made hundreds of speeches. In *My Land Is Dying* (1971), he pleaded for a change in economic priorities to prevent the rest of the country from being strip-mined; *The Watches of the Night* (1976) updated his first book to include the 1974 coal boom; *Theirs Be the Power* (1983) is the story of coal barons and capitalists, including prominent Kentuckians, who industrialized eastern Kentucky and transformed its mineral wealth into personal fortunes.

A lawyer for twenty-eight years, Caudill retired and became a professor of history at the University of Kentucky between 1977 and 1985. During that time he wrote *The Mountains, the Miner and the Lord* (1980), lively stories he collected while practicing law.

Caudill married Ann Frye of Cynthiana, Kentucky, in 1946. They had three children, James, Diana, and Harry. Caudill died on November 29, 1990, and was buried in the Battle Grove Cemetery in Cynthiana.

See Calvin Tompkins, "The Seventeen-Year Locusts," *New Yorker*, June 10, 1972; Robert Coles, introduction in Caudill, *My Land is Dying* (New York 1971).　　　　　　　　　　　LEE MUELLER

CAUDILL, REBECCA. Rebecca Caudill, author, was born on February 2, 1899, on the Poor Fork of the Cumberland River, in Harlan County, Kentucky, to George and Susan (Smith) Caudill. When she was four, the family moved to a farm in Carter Valley, Tennessee, where she attended public schools, graduating from Sumner County High School in Portland, Tennessee, in 1916. In 1920 she graduated with a degree in history from Wesleyan College in Macon, Georgia. Caudill taught English and history at Sumner County High School for one year, then enrolled at Vanderbilt University, graduating in 1922 with an M.A. degree in international relations. She taught at Collegio Bennett, an all-girls' school in Rio de Janeiro, Brazil, during

1922-24 and then worked in Nashville at the Methodist Publishing House, editing a girls' magazine until 1930. Caudill was preparing to sign a contract to work in Turkey when she met James S. Ayers, whom she married on September 8, 1931. They moved to Urbana, Illinois, and had two children—James, Jr., and Rebecca.

Caudill's first book, *Barrie & Daughter* (1943), was based on her childhood memories of her father and life in Appalachia. Her writing for children and juveniles was set in Appalachia, the stories of ordinary people in everyday situations. Seven of her books were Junior Literary Guild selections; *Tree of Freedom* (1949) was runner-up for the Newbery Medal award; and *Susan Cornish* (1955) received the Nancy Bloch Memorial Award. During the 1960s, Caudill wrote four of what are considered her best books: *A Pocket Full of Cricket* (1964); *A Certain Small Shepherd* (1965); *Did You Carry the Flag Today, Charlie?* (1966); and a nonfiction, nostalgic look at her childhood home, *My Appalachia* (1967), which compares the Appalachian region as she remembered it with what it had become. Caudill wrote twenty-one books and numerous articles, as well as haiku poetry and two books of verse.

A Quaker, Caudill was active in the peace movement, cofounded the Champaign-Urbana Peace Council, and in 1951 attended a peace conference in Geneva, Switzerland. Caudill died on October 2, 1985, and was buried in Urbana, Illinois.

CAUTHEN, STEPHEN MARK. Stephen Mark Cauthen, jockey, son of Ronald ("Tex") and Myra (Bischoff) Cauthen, was born on March 1, 1960, in Covington, Kentucky. Through his father, a blacksmith who had been a trainer and breeder, young Cauthen had access to the inner workings of racetracks. He spent many days at Latonia (now Turfway Park) in Florence and River Downs in Cincinnati, where he learned everything from exercising thoroughbreds to timekeeping.

Cauthen received his jockey license at age sixteen, and in spring 1976 he was the leading rider at River Downs. Cauthen raced at two tracks in Chicago, then at Churchill Downs in Louisville in the fall of 1976. He rode in New York at Aqueduct in the winter of 1976-77, flying to Los Angeles to ride at Santa Anita on weekends. In 1977 Cauthen broke the New York record for victories in a year, 299, and became the first jockey in the world to win $6 million in purses. That year he was *Sports Illustrated*'s sportsman of the year, and he won the Seagram Seven Crowns of Sports Award as the year's top professional athlete. In 1978 he became the youngest jockey to win the Triple Crown, aboard Affirmed; Cauthen won his only Kentucky Derby victory that year.

Cauthen rode 110 races in 1978-79 without a winner. He went to England in March 1979 and became one of Europe's most successful jockeys, winning the English championship three times and becoming the first rider to win four derbies: the Kentucky (1977), the Epsom (1985), the Irish

(1989), and the French (1989). Cauthen races in England and returns to Kentucky only to visit his family, who live in Walton.

See Pete Axthelm, *The Kid* (New York 1978); Clive Gammon, "A Dandy Yankee Derby Double," *Sports Illustrated*, June 17, 1985.

CAVE ANIMALS. Kentucky is rich in cave life. More than two hundred species have been found in Mammoth Cave alone. Bats, crickets, and pack rats periodically leave their caves to find food; these trogloxenes, or cave visitors, leave droppings that provide food for more permanent cave dwellers. Dead plants and animals washed in through numerous sinkholes serve the same purpose. Animals such as turtles and salamanders that accidentally fall or wander into cave entrances may survive for a while, but they usually die of starvation. True cave animals (known as troglobites) live their entire lives underground, aided by special adaptations: supersensitive organs to help find food and low metabolic rates to help survive starvation. Most troglobites cannot survive outside caves because they have lost their sight, pigment, and ability to tolerate warm temperatures and low humidities. Kentucky's troglobites include fish, crayfish, flatworms, beetles, spiders, and many others.

See Dick Ruehrwein and Vickie T. Carson, *Mammoth Cave* (Cincinnati 1983); Charles E. Mohr and Thomas L. Poulson, *The Life of the Cave* (New York 1966).   JERRY H. CARPENTER

CAVE HILL CEMETERY. The City of Louisville planned a pesthouse and graveyard on the site of Cave Hill farm, at the head of Broadway, which the city purchased in 1835 for its stone quarries. Local civil engineer Edmund Francis Lee designed the grounds in the new American style called rural, or garden, cemetery, taking advantage of the terrain and picturesque setting. The Cave Hill Cemetery Company was chartered on February 5, 1848. Three hundred acres have been landscaped as an arboretum, containing over five hundred plant specimens. More than 112,000 people have been buried in the cemetery, including many of the first families of the city and state figures such as Gen. George Rogers Clark and Col. Harland Sanders. Monumental art includes examples by craftsmen of national reputation who made Louisville a regional monument center.

See Samuel W. Thomas, *Cave Hill Cemetery: A Pictorial Guide and Its History* (Louisville 1985).
SAMUEL W. THOMAS

CAVE-IN-ROCK, ILLINOIS. Cave-In-Rock is a large, natural cavern in a limestone bluff overlooking the Ohio River in Hardin County, Illinois, opposite Crittenden County, Kentucky. It is located approximately a half mile east of Cave-In-Rock Ferry, which links KY 91 and IL 1 highways. The cavern, believed to have been named by an early French explorer, extends into the bluff approximately 160 feet. The arched opening is about thirty feet high and fifty-five feet wide and the ceiling ranges in height from twenty to thirty feet. An early historian wrote that prehistoric drawings were once visible on the cavern walls.

In flatboating days, Cave-In-Rock was a lair for murderous outlaws who preyed on river travelers. The HARPE brothers, wanted for murder in Kentucky, took refuge in the cave but were driven away in 1799 when they proved too vicious even for the band of outlaws that lived there. Many of the victims were lured to the cavern by women who gestured to them from the shore, and by large signs such as the crudely written one seen in 1797 proclaiming the cavern to be a "Liquor Vault and House for Entertainment." By the late 1830s most of the crime had been put to an end. The site became a state park in 1929. Portions of the motion pictures *How the West Was Won* (1963) and *Davy Crockett* (1950) were filmed there.

See W.D. Snively, Jr., and Louanna Furbee, *Satan's Ferrymen, a True Tale of the Old Frontier* (New York 1968).   BYRON CRAWFORD

CAVES. Kentucky has over 765 miles of surveyed passages in caves that are more than one mile long. Many mapped caves are less than a mile long; they may total an additional one hundred to two hundred miles. The Flint-Mammoth-Roppel system in Edmonson, Hart, and Barren counties is the longest cave in the world; it has over 340 miles of surveyed passage, and mapping is still in progress. Four other caves in Kentucky are among the fifty longest caves in the world: Fisher Ridge Cave System (48 miles) and Hidden River Cave System (19.5 miles) in Hart County; Sloans Valley Cave system (25 miles) in Pulaski County; and Whigpistle Cave (22.5 miles) in Edmonson County.

Kentucky caves are concentrated in three major regions: the Inner Bluegrass, surrounding Lexington in central Kentucky; along the Pottsville Escarpment in the east, and along the Dripping Springs Escarpment in the west. The two escarpments border areas of Mississippian-age limestones and are subparallel to the Cincinnati Arch, a structural high extending from Ohio to Tennessee. The Inner Bluegrass area is centered on the crest of the arch, where older Ordovician-age limestones are exposed. There are two additional areas of cave occurrence in eastern Kentucky. The first and best-known is near CARTER CAVES State Resort Park in Carter County. There a large, broad, upward fold raises Mississippian limestones to the surface. The second area is Pine Mountain. There, the Cumberland overthrust, a huge sheet of rock pushed to the northwest along a nearly horizontal fault, has brought a band of Mississippian limestones to the surface along a line extending from Pike County to Whitley County.

Kentucky's setting meets many of the rather special conditions required for water-formed caves to develop. Only in exceptional cases will all of these factors combine to produce a truly gigantic cave system such as MAMMOTH CAVE. The first requirement for cave formation is a large region underlain by water-soluble rock such as limestone. Rainwater picks up carbon dioxide from the air and additional carbon dioxide from the soil as it seeps into the ground. This process forms a weak carbonic acid solution, which attacks the easily dissolved calcite (calcium carbonate) in limestone as it moves downward. The second requirement is that the limestone be placed in such a way that precipitation will eventually pass through the rock to reach a permanent surface stream (local base level). Water seeping downward first fills the joints and bedding planes in the limestone. These narrow fissures are enlarged by the slow-moving water as it dissolves the limestone, and some develop into solution conduits and caves. The caves carry an ever-increasing percentage of the precipitation until all of it flows underground. The third requirement for cave development is adequate precipitation. Around Mammoth Cave and Pulaski County, the state has its greatest average annual rainfall (fifty to fifty-two inches a year). Kentucky's humid climate also promotes dense plant growth. Decaying vegetation produces acids and carbon dioxide in the soil that contribute to the acidity of the groundwater. Other factors that influence cave development are the geologic structure, the purity of the limestone, the presence of an insoluble cap rock, and the development and spacing of faults, joints, and bedding plates.

In the Mammoth Cave area, the environment is ideal for cave formation. An area of limestone about 330 to 460 feet thick covers more than eighty square miles. The limestone is very pure, being nearly 95 percent calcium carbonate. The bedding planes are far enough apart to support large openings without being so widely spaced that groundwater flow is restricted. The rocks dip northwestward toward the Green River at a rate of thirty feet per mile, which promotes flow toward the river. Near the river, the limestone is protected by a sandstone caprock. Away from the river, the caprock has been eroded, and dissolution of the limestone has created a gently rolling surface riddled with sinkholes, known as the Sinkhole Plain. All precipitation that falls there and seeps into the ground must flow through the limestone to a permanent, base-level stream. The dip of the limestone toward Green River, combined with the tendency for solution rates to be the greatest near the top of the water table, has produced very long passages parallel to the bedding, called phreatic tubes.

During their development over geologic time, these passages remained almost filled with water and enlarged in all directions equally, creating a nearly elliptical cross section. When the water table fell, another type of passage was formed by free-flowing streams—tall, narrow, vadose canyons. The canyon passages began in the floors of the tubes but frequently diverged from the course of the older passages. As channel downcutting of the Green and Barren rivers alternately started and stopped in response to glacial activity to the north, multiple levels of passages were created. In the dry, upper parts of the cave as it now exists, abandoned tube passages join and diverge and are interconnected by the canyon passages, forming a labyrinth.

Cave development in the rest of the state follows the same principles; however, in most areas the conditions are not as favorable as at Mammoth Cave. The caves along the Pottsville Escarpment from Estill County to Wayne County are limited in size by the rugged relief and the unfavorable dip of the limestone away from, or parallel to, the major streams. The caprock has been eroded from the Pennyroyal Plain west of Mammoth Cave, allowing the caves to be destroyed by the solution process nearly as fast as they form. In the Inner Bluegrass region, many Middle Ordovician-age limestones are relatively impure, containing 20 to 60 percent insoluble material, and they are also thinly bedded, thus limiting the rate of cave development. Along the deep Kentucky River Gorge, thick sequences of purer, thicker-bedded Middle Ordovician limestones are exposed. Close to the river, the removal by erosion of shale near the top of these formations and the large topographic relief along the Palisades have allowed the formation of some vertical shafts as much as 160 feet deep, and caves with total reliefs of more than two hundred feet are known. On Pine Mountain, Cole Hill Cave in Letcher County has two vertical shafts in a stairstep configuration with a combined total depth of 180 feet, which is the record vertical drop in the state. The cave with the greatest overall vertical extent, more than 350 feet, is probably Mammoth Cave. Its natural upper entrances are at least as high as 771 feet elevation (the top of the manmade Snowball Dining Room elevator shaft is eight hundred feet), and lower levels of the cave have been explored to the level of the Green River at 421 feet.

Most speleothems, or cave decorations, in Kentucky are the common flowstone varieties composed of calcium carbonate, or calcite. Flowstone is formed from drips and films of water flowing down walls or falling from ceilings. When groundwater seeps into a well-ventilated cave, the carbon dioxide dissolved in the water escapes into the air. This reduces the acidity of the solution and calcite is precipitated on the cave walls. The shapes that flowstone takes range from the well-known stalactites, stalagmites, and massive draperies to elegant cave "pearls" and delicate helictites. Cave pearls are formed by the tumbling action of constantly dripping water. The thin, translucent sheet of calcite slowly built out from the wall by a trickle of water running down a narrow path is called bacon. The shapes of formations such as helictites, anthodites, and heligmites are controlled by the structure of the slowly growing calcite crystals. The color of flowstone is caused by impurities. Pure calcite is white to translucent. Various shades of red and yellow are caused by iron oxides, and black is caused by manganese oxides. Sulfate minerals form another type of speleothem found in Kentucky, common in the Mammoth Cave area: intricate snowballs, gypsum flowers, angel hair, cave cotton, cave grass, and translucent stalactites. These are most commonly of gypsum, but may also be other minerals, such as epsomite and mirabilite.

All speleothems form over the course of thousands of years. The removal or destruction of speleothems is considered unethical by cave explorers, and is illegal in Kentucky.

The history of cave exploration in Kentucky is longer than the written history of the state. Woodland Indians probed the long corridors of Mammoth Cave centuries before European explorers reached America. The early settlers explored and exploited caves for a variety of uses, including water, cooling, and SALTPETER, which was processed to make potassium nitrate, a key ingredient of gunpowder. The modern age of cave exploration began in the United States after World War II, when the National Speleological Society was organized, and better roads made it possible to travel longer distances. Routine mapping of caves began in the late 1940s but did not become a major activity until the 1960s, when access to computers made data processing easier. The decade of the 1970s, when numerous large caves were discovered and mapped, can be considered the golden age of cave exploration in Kentucky. The exploration of the Flint Ridge Cave System in Mammoth Cave National Park by the Cave Research Foundation reached its climax. The mapping of the Sloans Valley Cave System in Pulaski County was finished by Louis Simpson and others. Crumps Cave in Hart County was explored and mapped by Norman Pace, Joseph Saunders, Keith Ortize, and others. Ortize, Saunders, Daniel Crowl, and others began the massive exploration effort in the Fisher Ridge Cave System in Hart County. The Coral Cave System in Pulaski County was discovered by Michael Johnson and associates. Gradys Cave in Hart County was mapped by Joseph Saunders. James Quinlan, then park hydrogeologist at Mammoth Cave, conducted his intensive research on the hydrology of the Mammoth Cave area. Quinlan also supported cavers, including Sheri Engler and Don Coons, as they explored Whigpistle Cave in Edmonson County; they also explored Morrisons Cave in Barren County. James Currens and James Borden led the discovery and survey of the Roppel Cave in Hart County to fifty miles in length.

The most exciting exploration achievement was the integration of several vast cave systems into one. In 1972 cavers discovered a route from the Flint Ridge Cave System to Mammoth Cave. In 1979 Morrisons Cave was connected to Proctors Cave inside the park, and a few months later the two caves were connected to Mammoth Cave. In 1983 the Roppel Cave was connected to Mammoth Cave, yielding the surveyed length of more than 340 miles.

See P.H. Dougherty, ed., *Caves and Karst of Kentucky* (Lexington, Ky., 1985); R.W. Brucker and R.A. Watson, *The Longest Cave* (New York 1976).   J.C. CURRENS

CAWEIN, MADISON JULIUS. Madison Julius Cawein, poet, was born in Louisville, Kentucky, on March 23, 1865, fifth child of William and Christiana (Stelsly) Cawein. His father, who had emigrated from Germany in the 1840s, earned his living in Louisville as a confectioner and herbalist. His mother, daughter of German immigrants, was a spiritualist. In 1886 Cawein graduated from Louisville's Male High School and became assistant cashier at the Newmarket poolroom, where he remained until 1892, writing at night and in his spare time and paying for publication of his books. His poetic career was launched in 1887 when William Dean Howells favorably reviewed his first book, *Blooms of the Berry*. Thirty-six others followed, including *Kentucky Poems* (1902), solicited by the English critic Edmund Gosse, and a five-volume collected edition in 1907. Cawein's poetry shows the naturalist's lore he learned from his father and the creative imagination of his spiritualist mother. Literary influences on his work were the English poets, especially Spenser, Keats, Shelley, and Tennyson, and the German poets Goethe, Heine, and Geibel, a collection of whose works he translated (*The White Snake*, 1895).

Cawein's nature poetry preserves, like the paintings of Carl Brenner, a landscape that has all but disappeared. Accurate in terms of flora and fauna, the poems are yet visionary. One of them, "The Wasteland" (*Minions of the Moon*, 1913), which describes a barren site and an old man, looks forward to the landscape of loss that T.S. Eliot made real for his generation.

On June 4, 1903, Cawein married Gertrude Foster McKelvey; they had one child, Preston Hamilton (whose name was later changed to Madison Cawein II). Cawein died of an apoplectic attack on December 8, 1914, and was buried in Louisville's Cave Hill Cemetery.

See Otto A. Rothert, *The Story of a Poet: Madison Cawein* (Louisville 1921); John Rutledge, "Madison Cawein as an Exponent of German Culture," *FCHQ* 51 (Jan. 1977): 5-16.

MADELINE COVI

CENTRAL CITY. Central City is a fourth-class city in Muhlenberg County, in the Pennyroyal region of west-central Kentucky. A village had grown up there by 1870 on farmland owned by John Stroud and around a mill owned by Charles S. Morehead. The village, known as Morehead's Horse Mill, was incorporated in 1873 as Stroud City, while the local post office was named Owensboro Junction. In 1882 the town was reincorporated as Central City, named for the Central Coal and Iron Company, which by 1900 had become the largest producer of coal in the Green River Valley.

Among the railroads built in the region to haul coal to market, two intersected in Central City in 1882: the Owensboro & Russellville Railroad (later part of the Louisville & Nashville) and the Elizabethtown & Paducah (later part of the Illinois Central). Because of its strategic location for transportation in west-central Kentucky, Central City had become the largest city in Muhlenberg County by 1900 and it grew rapidly well into the 1900s. In addition to the railroads and the coal mines, businesses included a stave works, brick works, planing mill, marble shop, saw mill, gristmills, and a blacksmith and saddlery.

In 1892, in the city's first election for mayor, Dr. J.L. McDowell defeated Thomas Coleman du Pont, a mining engineer. Du Pont, who left the county in 1893, later served as U.S. Senator from Delaware (1921-22 and 1925-28).

Three miles east of Central City is the town of Brownie, the birthplace of Phil and Don Everly, who achieved international acclaim in the 1950s and 1960s as the Everly Brothers, a country and pop music duo. In 1988 the annual Everly Brothers Homecoming Festival was started, and a section of U.S. 62 was renamed Everly Brothers Boulevard.

Central City remains a transportation hub, served by the Western Kentucky Parkway, the Paducah & Louisville Railroad, and CSX Transportation. Surface mines operated by Peabody Coal Company in the Central City area provide employment for many residents. New technology for producing more coal with fewer mines led to a countywide unemployment problem in the 1980s. The economy received a boost, however, when it was announced in 1990 that Central City would be the site of a new $46 million state prison employing 250 people, to open in November 1992.

The population of Central City was 3,455 in 1970; 5,214 in 1980; and 4,979 in 1990.

CENTRAL UNIVERSITY. Central University, a nineteenth century institution in Richmond, Kentucky, had its origins in a schism within the Presbyterian church growing out of the Civil War. The Presbyterian synods of the Confederate states severed relations with the national organization, and in Kentucky, as a result of the Kentucky General Assembly's 1861 decision to support the Union cause, the Northern and Southern factions competed for control of Centre College in Danville. After the Southern faction lost several court appeals, it decided to form a separate institution, establishing Central University at Richmond on September 22, 1874. Of the $220,000 endowment, $101,000 was contributed by the citizens of Richmond and the rest of Madison County. A College of Letters and Science, a Preparatory Department, and a College of Law were located in Richmond, and a College of Medicine and Dentistry in Louisville. In 1901 financial considerations resulted in the merger of Central with Centre College on the Danville campus. The eight buildings and campus at Richmond became the property of what later became Eastern

Kentucky University. Two of Central University's more distinguished leaders during its quarter century of existence were chancellor Robert L. Breck (1874-80) and Lindsay Blanton (1880-1901).

See Fred A. Engle, Jr., "Central University of Richmond, Kentucky," *Register* 66 (July 1968): 279-305.

CENTRE COLLEGE. Centre College in Danville was founded by the Kentucky legislature on January 21, 1819, and was named for its location in the center of the state. It had a self-perpetuating board of thirteen members, including Isaac Shelby, the first governor of Kentucky (1792-96, 1812-16); Dr. Ephraim McDowell, who performed the first successful ovariotomy; and the Rev. Samuel K. Nelson. The state did not live up to its financial responsibilities, and on January 24, 1824, gave control of the college to the Presbyterian denomination of Kentucky. The state stipulated: "The college shall at all times be conducted upon liberal, free, and enlightened principles, and no student shall be excluded in consequence of his religious opinions, or those of his parents, guardians, or relatives," and "No religious doctrine peculiar to any one sect of Christians shall be inculcated by any professor in said college." For the Presbyterians, operating a college in Kentucky had been a goal since at least 1780.

The main building, now known as Old Centre, was completed in 1820. There were two students in the first graduating class of 1824 and five in 1829. The Rev. James McChord was president from 1820 to 1822, the Rev. Jeremiah Chamberlain from 1822 to 1824, and the Rev. Gideon Blackburn from 1827 to 1830.

John C. YOUNG, a twenty-seven-year-old minister, teacher, and administrator, became president in 1830. During his brilliant twenty-seven-year presidency, Young expanded the student body from barely thirty to 225, added to the endowment more than $100,000, attracted very able faculty members, including three future presidents of the college, and greatly enhanced the reputation of the institution. He also was the minister at the local Presbyterian church (1834-53) and founded the Second Presbyterian Church in Danville (1853-57). Young served as moderator of the Kentucky Synod twice, was moderator of the Presbyterian national General Assembly in 1853, and founded the Danville Theological Seminary in the same year. He was president until his death in 1857.

Lewis W. Green, a member of Centre's first graduating class of 1824, served as president from 1857 until his death in 1863. William L. Breckinridge, like Green a faculty member, was president from 1863 to 1868. During the Civil War, there was a dramatic decline in the size of the student body. There were only seven men in the graduating class of 1863. During the Bragg-Buell military campaign in Kentucky in the fall of 1862, Confederate soldiers occupied Old Centre before, and Union soldiers after, the Battle of Perryville on October 8.

Ormand Beatty was president (1868-88) during the strained period of Reconstruction. In 1871 Old Main building was completed, and in 1886 Beatty celebrated fifty years of service to the college as professor and president. Beatty was succeeded by William C. Young (1888-96), son of John C. Young. He raised $100,000 for the endowment, and he established the law department; J. Proctor Knott, former governor of Kentucky (1883-87), served as its first dean.

The average tenure of the eleven college presidents from 1898 until 1990 was about eight years. In 1901, under William C. Roberts (1898-1904), CENTRAL UNIVERSITY in Richmond and Centre College were united for financial, educational, and administrative reasons as the Central University of Kentucky. Centre was the undergraduate liberal arts college of the university until 1918, when the union was dissolved during the presidency of William A. Ganfield (1904-22). In 1921 the Centre football team defeated the national champion Harvard team in the upset victory of the half-century. Under Ganfield's leadership, the student body grew to 315, and the endowment reached $1 million.

In an era that lacked a formal system of schools leading from elementary to secondary to higher education, colleges often established preparatory schools to ensure a supply of well-prepared students. Centre College Academy, also known as Prep, began in 1820, when a Mr. Maury's grammar school was housed in Centre College's first building. Prep ended when circumstances changed: Kentucky improved public secondary schools; Danville viewed Prep as an obstacle to a public high school; and Centre decided to concentrate solely on collegiate education. After Danville bought Prep's building and hired Prep's principal, Centre College closed the academy in 1918.

Centre College became coeducational in 1926, when Kentucky College for Women (1913) became the women's department of the college. In 1962 the women students moved to the Centre campus on Walnut Street, during the presidency of Thomas A. Spragens (1957-81). During his presidency Spragens increased the size of the student body from 380 to seven hundred, more than doubled the size of the teaching faculty, led a major revision of the curriculum and calendar, virtually rebuilt the college physical plant, and increased the plant valuation from $1.8 to $21 million. He raised the endowment from $2.6 to $18 million and led a $30 million fund drive.

During the presidencies of Richard L. Morrill (1982-88) and Michael F. Adams (1988-), the percentage of alumni donating funds to the college has exceeded that at any other college or university in the United States. Centre's alumni include two U.S. vice-presidents, one U.S. chief justice, and one associate justice of the U.S. Supreme Court, as well as congressmen, governors, and leaders in education, business, law, journalism, and medicine.

See Hardin Craig, *Centre College of Kentucky, A Tradition and an Opportunity* (Louisville 1967).

CHARLES R. LEE, JR., AND BRADLEY NYSTROM

CENTRE-HARVARD FOOTBALL GAMES. The Centre College football team's record of 9-0 in 1919 encouraged Harvard to add the small Danville, Kentucky, college to its 1920 schedule. Coach "Uncle Charlie" Moran's team from Centre included three All-Americans—Alvin Nugent ("Bo") McMillin (quarterback), Jim ("Red") Weaver (center), and third team end James ("Red") Roberts. In Cambridge, the score was 14-14 at half-time and Bo McMillin gained more than 280 yards that afternoon, but Centre's Praying Colonels lost, 31-14. The Harvard Crimson, national champions and undefeated in five years, met the Praying Colonels for the second time in Harvard Stadium on Saturday, October 29, 1921, before 45,000 fans. The first half ended scoreless. Early in the third quarter on the Harvard 32-yard line, McMillin took the ball through the right side of the line, reversed his direction and crossed the goal line at the left sideline. At the end of the historic game, the score was Centre 6, Harvard 0. Many people that day believed that they had seen David defeat Goliath. The Associated Press in 1950 and the *New York Times* in 1971 agreed that the Centre victory was the football upset of the century.

See John Y. Brown, *Legend of the Praying Colonels* (Louisville 1970).   CHARLES R. LEE, JR.

CHAINED ROCK. In a community project in the midst of the Great Depression, a giant unstable rock on a cliff overlooking PINEVILLE, Kentucky, was secured by chaining it to the cliff. In 1933 Fred Chappell, Pat Caton, and Arthur Asher, with support from the local Kiwanis and others, launched the project to secure the rock. With no funds or grants available, all materials were donated and labor was unpaid. A one-and-a-half-ton chain from an antiquated power shovel was donated by Bert Paynter, Sr. The chain was trucked in two sections to the foot of Pine Mountain, where mules and numerous helpers pulled it along a primitive trail up to the overhanging rock. The chain was stretched between heavy steel rods secured deeply in the rock and in the anchoring cliff. Pineville thus became "The City of the Chained Rock."

EDWARD SENN WILSON

CHAMBERS, WALLACE. Wallace ("Wally") Chambers, football player and coach, son of Jimmie L. Chambers, was born on May 15, 1951, in Phoenix City, Alabama. During 1969-73 he attended Eastern Kentucky University, where he earned a B.S. in physical education and a B.A. in broadcasting. While a student, he received four letters in football, and was named an All-American in 1973. He was the first-round selection of the Chicago Bears in the 1973 National Football League draft and was named the NFL defensive rookie of the year by the Associated Press. He played defensive end with the Bears, 1973-78, and with the Tampa Bay Buccaneers in 1978. He was also named to the Pro Bowl in 1973, 1975, and 1976.

Following his playing career, Chambers coached at Northern Iowa University in Cedar Falls, at East

Carolina University in Greenville, North Carolina, and for the New York Jets.

CHANDLER, ALBERT BENJAMIN. A.B. ("Happy") Chandler, twice governor of Kentucky (1935-39, 1955-59), was born near Corydon, Kentucky, on July 14, 1898, to Joseph Sephus and Callie (Saunders) Chandler. After graduating from Corydon High School in 1917, he attended Transylvania University, then enrolled for a year at Harvard law school; he graduated from the University of Kentucky law school in 1925. That same year he married Mildred Watkins; they had four children. Chandler opened a law practice in Versailles, Kentucky, and coached high school sports. Deeply interested in Democratic politics, he won a seat in the state Senate in 1929. In 1931 he was elected lieutenant governor over Republican John C. Worsham, 426,247 to 353,573, while Ruby Laffoon became governor. Chandler and the governor split over the sales tax, which Chandler opposed, and some of Chandler's powers were removed by legislation. In 1935, while the governor was in Washington, D.C., Chandler called a special legislative session that passed a bill requiring party nominations to be made by a primary election and not by a convention, which Laffoon and his supporters might well control. Chandler trailed Tom Rhea in the first primary but won the runoff, then defeated Republican King Swope, 556,262 to 461,104, to become governor.

The "Boy Governor" had the new sales tax repealed. Then through reorganization, reform, frugality, and higher excise and income taxes, he financed far-reaching improvements in schools, roads, health and welfare programs, and penal institutions. A masterful politician, aided by such associates as J. Dan Talbott of Bardstown, Chandler dominated the legislature. He used radio effectively to win public support. The Government Reorganization Act of 1936 created a more efficient administration, and he was able to pay off much of the state's debt. Among the most significant innovations were the free textbook program, participation in the federal rural electrification program, establishment of a teachers' retirement system and an old-age assistance program, and the start of a special rural roads program. Although friendly to labor, Chandler opposed closed shops and sit-down strikes, and he sent the National Guard into Harlan County to curb labor-related violence there. Chandler's first administration was one of the most productive in the state's history.

In 1938 Chandler challenged Alben Barkley for his U.S. Senate seat. When President Franklin D. Roosevelt made a whistle-stop trip to Kentucky in support of the Senate majority leader, the governor boarded the train uninvited and appeared with the president whenever possible. Barkley won, and Chandler then took aim at the U.S. Senate seat vacated in October 1939 when M.M. Logan died. Chandler resigned as governor, and on October 10, 1939, when Lt. Gov. Keen Johnson succeeded him, Johnson appointed Chandler to the U.S. Senate. In 1940 Chandler won a special election for the rest of Logan's term, and in a controversial 1942 campaign he defeated John Y. Brown, Sr., and won a full six-year term. In Washington Chandler usually backed the administration although he opposed some of the New Deal fiscal policies and the decision to give priority to the war in Europe over the Pacific conflict. On November 1, 1945, Chandler resigned from the Senate to become national commissioner of baseball. During the next six years, black players entered the major leagues for the first time and a players' pension fund was established. As commissioner, Chandler alienated many of the owners, and when his contract was not renewed in 1951, he resumed his law practice in Versailles.

In 1955 he won the Democratic nomination for governor over Bert T. Combs, despite the opposition of many of the party's most powerful leaders. His smashing victory over Republican Edwin R. Denney, 451,647 to 322,671, was an anticlimax to the Democratic primary. Times had changed greatly in the twenty years since Chandler's first term, and he was opposed by many of the liberal elements in his party. In his second term, he achieved substantial improvements in the highway program (using a $100 million bond issue), the schools, and other public institutions. Additional funding went to the public schools' Minimum Foundation Program and the teachers' retirement system. His proudest accomplishment was the establishment of the University of Kentucky Medical Center, named for him. He attracted national notice in 1956 when he used state police and National Guardsmen to enforce desegregation in the public schools, yet his second administration lacked some of the reforming zeal of his first term.

Increasingly out of touch with the times, Chandler failed in bids for the nomination for governor in 1963, 1967, and 1971. In 1967 he supported the Republican nominee, Louie B. Nunn, for the office. He remained deeply interested in politics and was especially close to Gov. Wallace Wilkinson (1987-91), who restored voting rights to Chandler's lifetime honorary membership on the University of Kentucky board of trustees in January 1988. Two incidents in the late 1980s involving alleged racial slurs led to unsuccessful demands for Chandler's resignation or removal from the board. In 1989, in collaboration with Vance H. Trimble, Chandler published his autobiography, *Heroes, Plain Folks, and Skunks.*

Chandler died on June 15, 1991, at home in Versailles and was buried in the cemetery of Pisgah Presbyterian Church in Woodford County.

See J.T. Salter, ed., *The American Politician* (Chapel Hill, N.C., 1938).

LOWELL H. HARRISON

CHANDLER MEDICAL CENTER. Named for the former Kentucky governor, the Albert B. Chandler Medical Center is located at the University of Kentucky in Lexington. The Chandler Medical Center was the second of the many university-based medical centers established in the United States after World War II. Funding for the state-supported academic health sciences center originated with the 1956 Kentucky General Assembly during the governorship of Chandler (1955-59), and in 1960 the first matriculants entered the colleges of medicine and nursing. In 1962 the College of Dentistry and the University Hospital opened, and the Chandler Medical Center expanded further by adding the existing University of Kentucky College of Pharmacy in 1966 and creating the College of Allied Health Professions in 1970.

Missions of the Chandler Medical Center include education, research, and training in the health sciences. Innovative medical educators affiliated with the Lexington campus influence statewide and national health care policies, delivery, and practices. The Sanders-Brown Research Center on Aging opened in 1979 and is now a nationally recognized center for Alzheimer's disease research. With the 1985 dedication of the Lucille Parker Markey Cancer Center, the Chandler Medical Center moved to establish itself as one of the leading cancer care and research facilities in the United States. The center operates outreach programs and has links with the Veterans Administration Medical Center.

See John H. Ellis, *Medicine in Kentucky* (Lexington, Ky., 1977).   RICHARD C. SMOOT

CHAPMAN, VIRGIL MUNDAY. Virgil Munday Chapman, U.S. representative and senator, was born March 15, 1895, in Middleton, Simpson County, Kentucky, to James Virgil and Lily (Munday) Chapman. After attending the Franklin, Kentucky, public schools and graduating from Franklin High School in 1913, he studied law and was admitted to the bar in 1917. He was the editor in chief of the *Kentucky Law Journal* in 1917-18, when he graduated from the University of Kentucky law department. He established a law practice at Irvine, Kentucky, in June 1918 and until 1920 he served as the city attorney. In June of 1920 he moved to Paris, Kentucky, and practiced law in Lexington.

Chapman received state-wide attention in 1921 for aiding in the organization of tobacco cooperative marketing associations. In 1924 he was the Democratic candidate for the 7th Congressional District, ran unopposed in the general election, and served two successive terms in the U.S. House of Representatives (1925-29). He was defeated for reelection in the Hoover landslide of 1928. In 1930 he regained a congressional seat, defeating the incumbent, Robert Blackburn, and served eight successive terms (1931-49). He defeated the Republican candidate for the U.S. Senate, John Sherman Cooper, for the term that began on January 3, 1949. Chapman died on March 8, 1951, in Washington, D.C., following an automobile accident and was buried in the Paris Cemetery in Kentucky.

In the House, Chapman was a member of the Interstate and Foreign Commerce Committee, and he was chairman of the Democratic National Congressional Committee, but he was best known for his work on behalf of Kentucky's tobacco growers. In the Senate, Chapman served on the Armed Services Committee, and was a member of the Democratic Policy Committee.

Chapman married Mary Adams Talbott of Paris, Kentucky, on June 12, 1920. They had one child, Elizabeth.

CHAUMIERE DES PRAIRIES. Chaumiere des Prairies was the estate of David Meade (1740-1826), who in 1796 moved his wife, Sarah, their nine children, and forty slaves from Tidewater Virginia to 330 acres in present-day Jessamine County. There Meade dedicated the final third of his life to horticulture and landscape architecture. Chaumiere was renowned for its sloping lawns, walks, and winding drives within a park-like setting of trees, shrubbery, and gardens with man-made lakes. Interspersed through the grounds were alcoves with seats, fountains, statuary, and an artificial island reached by an arched bridge and containing a small building designed after a Greek temple. Enclosing the one-hundred-acre park was a low stone fence covered with rambling roses, honeysuckle, and other blooming vines. The grounds were patterned upon the English parks designed by Capability Brown. A crew of seven maintained the grounds, and slave children picked up rocks, sticks, and other clutter.

The residence, a cluster of one-story buildings connected by numerous passageways, was constructed of stone, log, and brick. In the dining room, which seated one hundred, the Meades lavishly entertained the Bluegrass aristocracy and other guests, including four presidents and other prominent politicians, among them Aaron Burr. In preparation for the visit of General Lafayette in 1825, Meade constructed an octagonal brick parlor. When the house was demolished, only this room was preserved, and a Greek Revival house was constructed adjoining it in 1840. So famous was the estate that it was included on the 1818 map of Kentucky, the first authorized by the General Assembly.

David Meade died in 1826 and his heirs sold the estate in 1832 to a "plain, practical farmer," William Robards. He filled the park with horses, cattle, and hogs; the trees were cut, the garden overrun, and the lakes drained. Distraught neighbors placed a sign, "Paradise Lost," over the entrance to the estate.

See Mary C. Oppel, "Paradise Lost: The Story of Chaumiere des Prairies," *FCHQ* 56 (April 1982): 201-10.

CHENOWETH MASSACRE. The Chenoweth Massacre in 1789 was the final major attack by the Indians in Kentucky against the settlers. It came as the family of Capt. Richard Chenoweth was sitting down to dinner at Chenoweth Station (located in what is now Middletown).

Captain Chenoweth had aided in construction of Fort Nelson in 1781, before settling at Chenoweth Station in the Beargrass settlement. Over the next eight years, Indian attacks killed a number of settlers and wounded others, including Chenoweth's son James; his son Thomas was kidnapped. Among the more famous battles were the Long Run Massacre (1781), Floyd's Defeat (1781), and the Battle of BLUE LICKS (1782). Throughout the first half of 1789, the Indians raided the Beargrass settlement. No longer were battles being fought, but periodic ambushes drove out every family except the Chenoweths, who hired several soldiers to guard their plantation. The hired protection was of no avail on the night of July 17, 1789, when the Shawnee killed three Chenoweth children, one of the guards, and all of the livestock. Capt. Chenoweth and his three other children were injured, and his wife, Peggy, was shot with an arrow, scalped, and tomahawked twice. She recovered and lived for twenty years. Chenoweth, one of the founders of Louisville, took his family back to Virginia when they were all strong enough to travel.

See Blaine A. Guthrie, Jr., "Captain Richard Chenoweth: A Founding Father of Louisville," *FCHQ* 46 (April 1972): 147-60; Alfred Pirtle, *James Chenoweth: The Story of One of the Earliest Boys of Louisville and Where Louisville Started* (Louisville 1921).

CHEROKEE INDIANS. The Cherokee are indigenous North Americans of Iroquoian lineage who inhabited the Southern Appalachian region, including areas in or adjacent to south-central and eastern Kentucky. Following a subsistence economy derived from Woodland and Mississippian cultures, the Cherokee lived in small river villages or towns. The men were primarily hunters and gatherers; women cultivated basic crops such as corn and gourds. They used stone implements, made pottery from local clay, and constructed log dwellings and public houses roofed with bark. Cherokee social and political organization was highly developed and they had a sophisticated spiritual belief system. Cherokee society was based on a matrilineal kinship system with seven clans. A family lived in the household of the mother and the mother's brothers or uncles served as primary role models for young boys. Village life was ruled by town council, where prominent villagers, men and women, debated issues until consensus was reached.

There may have been as many as a quarter-million Cherokee living in the southeastern United States at one time, but by 1650 diseases brought by early European explorers had reduced that number to about 25,000, who lived in Appalachian valleys from the Savannah River in Georgia to the Cumberland Gap. There were no permanent Cherokee settlements in Kentucky at the time of early European exploration and settlement. But Cherokee hunting parties frequented the region, venturing as far west as the Green River Valley and as far north as Great Salt Lick. There is some indication that the Cherokee maintained semipermanent hunting camps in the Cumberland River Valley and elsewhere in southeastern Kentucky.

During the French and Indian War (1755-63), the Cherokee first sided with the English and took part in a campaign against the French and their Shawnee allies in the Ohio River Valley. But the alliance ended with the 1760 massacre of twenty-nine Cherokee chiefs at Fort Prince George. A Cherokee war party captured Fort Loudon but was defeated by a combined force of British soldiers, Chickasaw, and Creek warriors. In the Treaty of Lochaber in 1770, the Cherokee were forced to cede all claims to hunting grounds in central and western Kentucky, and in 1775 the Treaty of Sycamore Shoals gave the Transylvania Land Company rights to Cherokee lands west of the Kentucky River.

During the Revolutionary War and sporadically through the 1780s, Cherokee war parties raided along Virginia's southern borders, harassing settlers crossing into Kentucky. By 1794, however, the last group of resisters, the Chickamauga, had been subdued and almost all Cherokee pushed back into the central Appalachians.

See Charles Hudson, *The Southeastern Indians* (Knoxville, Tenn., 1976).   DAG RYEN

CHERRY, HENRY HARDIN. Henry Hardin Cherry, educator, was born November 16, 1864, to George Washington and Frances Martha (Stahl) Cherry on a Warren County, Kentucky, farm. One of nine sons, Henry received little education until January 1886, when he started intermittent studies at the Southern Normal School in Bowling Green. He was soon on the faculty there, and in 1892 he and his brother Thomas Crittenden Cherry purchased the failing school. Thanks to Henry's promotional genius, enrollment grew from twenty-eight to nearly seven hundred by 1899, when he purchased Thomas's share of the school. The institution became known as the Southern Normal School and Bowling Green Business University.

Concerned over the condition of Kentucky's public schools, Cherry played a major role in getting the 1906 legislature to create state normal schools in Bowling Green and Richmond. In June 1906, he became the first president of the Western Kentucky State Normal School (later Western Kentucky University). Cherry spent the rest of his life in that position, and his dynamic leadership created one of the best teachers' colleges in the country. The school granted its first bachelor's degrees in 1924; the "Normal" designation was dropped in 1930. Cherry attracted and held some exceptionally able faculty members, and Western Kentucky University became known for its liberal arts as well as its education program; the premedical program was outstanding. By 1937 fourteen major buildings had been constructed and adjacent Ogden College had merged with Western. During Cherry's long tenure, the state provided $1,435,000 for capital construction; capital outlays during that time totaled $2,658,818. Cherry contended with such problems as the chronic shortage of funds, the Great Depression, and the unfavorable attitude of some toward regional state schools. Addressing students in

Western's chapel, he inspired generations of them to "do and be something." In 1915 and again in 1919 he sought the Democratic nomination for governor but withdrew both times when the expected support did not materialize.

Cherry married Bessie Fayne in 1896; their children were Josephine, Elizabeth, and Hardin. After a severe fall at his campus home, the seventy-two-year-old college president died on August 1, 1937, and was buried in the Fairview Cemetery in Bowling Green.

See Lowell H. Harrison, *Western Kentucky University* (Lexington, Ky., 1987).

LOWELL H. HARRISON

CHERRY, WENDELL. Wendell Cherry, president and chief operating officer of HUMANA, Inc., was born in Horse Cave, Kentucky, on September 25, 1935, to L.S. and Geneva (Spillman) Cherry. He earned a bachelor's degree in business from the University of Kentucky in 1957 and graduated first in his class from the university law school. He practiced law in Louisville and taught economics at the University of Louisville before he and David A. Jones founded Humana, a national investor-owned hospital corporation. An art connoisseur, Cherry served as the first chairman of the Kentucky Center for the Arts. *Art & Antiques* magazine in 1985 listed Cherry among the top one hundred American collectors. Cherry and his first wife, Mary Elizabeth (Baird), were the parents of four children: Andy, Angelia, Alison, and Hagan. Cherry married Dottie Morton, an interior designer, in 1977. He died in Louisville on July 15, 1991.

ALLEN J. SHARE

CHESAPEAKE & OHIO RAILWAY. The Kentucky operations of the Chesapeake & Ohio (C&O) Railway, which became part of CSX Transportation in 1986, were concentrated in the eastern half of the commonwealth. The main cargo was coal mined in the Big Sandy River counties. C&O's main line linked Virginia with the Midwest and Great Lakes; the Kentucky sector of the line paralleled the Ohio River from Ashland to Covington. The road's major coal artery ran south from Ashland along the Big Sandy and its tributaries to Elkhorn City; ancillary lines branched out to various coal mines.

Of the C&O's antecedents in Kentucky, the Lexington & Big Sandy line was the earliest, chartered in 1852 to join the Bluegrass region with the eastern counties. In the early 1870s only the Lexington–Mt. Sterling and Ashland-Coalton segments were open. In 1880 the C&O gained control of the Lexington line and finished the middle link in 1881, making it a prime candidate in the plans of the C&O's president, Collis P. Huntington, for a coast-to-coast rail empire. An arrangement with the LOUISVILLE & NASHVILLE RAILROAD gave C&O trains access from Lexington to Louisville, while cars for Cincinnati were sent up the KENTUCKY CENTRAL to Covington. Huntington also leased the former Elizabethtown & Paducah, which by then entered Louisville. By 1884 Huntington controlled roads reaching from Newport News, Virginia, C&O's eastern terminus, through Kentucky to the Pacific, and two leased lines in Tennessee and Mississippi gave C&O access all the way to New Orleans.

To reach Cincinnati and the much-sought midwestern markets, Huntington constructed the 143-mile Maysville & Big Sandy line along the Ohio River from Ashland to Covington. The road was finished in 1888, and a bridge over the Ohio at Covington was opened on Christmas Day that year. The operations became the C&O's Cincinnati Division. The antecedent of C&O's Big Sandy Division was the Chattaroi Railroad, built in the 1870s to tap coal deposits at Peach Orchard in Lawrence County. That line, which reached Richardson in 1883, came under C&O control in 1889.

Huntington's coast-to-coast empire did not last, as revenues fell far short of costs to assemble and run the network; the C&O was reorganized in 1888, and much of the remaining system was dismembered. The Lexington line became part of the parent C&O in 1892. The Big Sandy Division operations were upgraded as part of C&O's extensive plans to serve coal fields in the Big Sandy region.

After 1900 C&O built additional branches to serve Floyd, Johnson, Knott, Magoffin, and Pike county mines, which sent immense volumes of coal north to Russell, then east to tidewater or north to the Great Lakes. The massive, 1,550-foot-long Limeville, Ky., bridge was opened in 1917 as a C&O coal route across the Ohio River and north. After 1889 the C&O concentrated Ashland area operations at Russell. It greatly expanded the Russell yard in the 1920s, making it the major coal marshaling facility for the system in the East. A freight car repair shop was built nearby at Raceland in 1929.

The C&O was the dominant partner in a merger with the neighboring Baltimore & Ohio in 1963; that consolidation produced a new parent, Chessie System, in 1972. In 1986 the operations of Chessie System and the Seaboard Coast Line family of railroads were joined as a single system, CSX Transportation. CSX serves twenty states, the District of Columbia, and Ontario, Canada.

See Charles W. Turner, *Chessie's Road* (Alderson, W.Va., 1986).

CHARLES B. CASTNER

CHICKASAW INDIANS. The Chickasaw are indigenous North Americans of Muskogean lineage. Closely related in life and culture to the Creek and other southeastern Indians, the Chickasaw were a preliterate, seminomadic people who inhabited the middle Mississippi Valley, including portions of western Kentucky and Tennessee. Chickasaw society was organized around a matrilineal kinship system and a complex belief system based on maintaining purity and harmony in the world. The Chickasaw, numbering only a few thousand, lived in scattered dwellings along streams rather than in villages. At the time of earliest contact with European explorers, distinct Chickasaw chiefdoms had fortified ceremonial centers, containing council houses and other dwellings, where political conferences and rituals, including the annual green corn purification ceremony, were held.

Their first contact with Europeans came in 1540, when Hernando deSoto's expedition moved north along the Mississippi into Chickasaw territory. Chickasaw raiding parties, warned by neighboring Choctaw, harassed the explorers, killed many, and captured their horses. During European colonization, the Chickasaw sided with the British and helped instigate the Natchez conspiracy against French settlers and traders in the Mississippi Valley. They were not significantly involved in the French and Indian War and remained neutral during the Revolutionary War. Fort Jefferson, the outpost established by Gen. George Rogers Clark at the confluence of the Ohio and Mississippi rivers in 1780, was attacked by a band of Chickasaw under the leadership of British sympathizer James Colbert.

In 1786 the Chickasaw territory extended as far north as the Ohio River and included extreme western Kentucky. In 1805 James Robertson and Silas Dinsmoor negotiated a treaty for the ridge of land between the Tennessee and Cumberland rivers. During the same period, the Shawnee chief Tecumseh visited Chickasaw villages along the Mississippi in an effort to unite Indian opposition to settlement. Individual Chickasaw were recruited and others joined the Creek Red Sticks, who allied with the British during the War of 1812. An agreement securing release of all Chickasaw claims to land in Kentucky and Tennessee was concluded by Isaac Shelby and Andrew Jackson in 1818.

See James H. Malone, *The Chickasaw Nation: A Short Sketch of a Noble People* (Louisville 1922).

DAG RYEN

CHILTON, THOMAS. Thomas Chilton was born to Thomas John Chilton, a Baptist minister and spokesman for the Baptist Separatists, and Margaret (Bledsoe) Chilton on July 30, 1798, near Lancaster, Garrard County, Kentucky. After attending the common schools of Paris, Kentucky, he studied law and was admitted to the bar, beginning his practice in Owingsville, Bath County. He served one term in the Kentucky House of Representatives (1819-21), then returned to Owingsville, where he taught and preached. In 1823 he moved to Henry County to become minister of the Newcastle Baptist Church. He later established a law practice in Elizabethtown.

When U.S. Representative William S. Young died in 1827, Chilton, an early Jacksonian, was elected to fill the vacancy in Congress, where he served until March 3, 1831. He was known for his legislation of "retrenchment and reform." His policies, however, drove him from the Jacksonian party when in March 1830 he proclaimed himself a friend of Henry Clay. Chilton was defeated for reelection in 1830 by the Jacksonian, John Adair, and returned to

Elizabethtown to resume his law practice. Active in politics, he was chosen a Kentucky presidential elector in 1832, voting for Whig candidate Henry Clay. Chilton returned to Congress for one term (1833-35), when he collaborated with a fellow congressman, Davy Crockett, in writing *Narrative of the Life of David Crockett of the State of Tennessee*.

Chilton served briefly as pastor of the Baptist church in Hopkinsville, Kentucky, then moved to Alabama, where he served churches in Montgomery, Greensboro, and Newbern. He presided over the Alabama Baptist State Convention from 1846 until 1851. Chilton left Alabama with his wife Louisa and their sons to become pastor of churches in Houston and Montgomery, Texas. He died on August 15, 1854.

See Sharon Elaine Hannum, "Thomas Chilton, Lawyer, Politician, Preacher," *FCHQ* 38 (April 1864): 97-111; J.H. Spencer, *A History of Kentucky Baptists from 1769 to 1885* (Cincinnati 1886).

CHINN, GEORGE MORGAN. George Morgan Chinn, historian and soldier, was born in Mercer County, Kentucky, January 15, 1902, the son of George P. and Anna (Carlisle) Chinn. He attended Millersburg Military Institute and Centre College in Danville. In 1941 he entered the U.S. Marine Corps. An automatic weapons expert, Chinn served until 1961 and retired as a colonel. He was secretary-treasurer of the Kentucky Historical Society in 1959, its director from 1960 to 1973, and deputy director from 1974 to 1980. Chinn wrote several works on pioneer and local history and produced the five-volume work *The Machine Gun* (1951-87). He was the holder of several weapons patents. Chinn married Haldon Grimes on August 29, 1924; they had one child, Ann Hardin.

Chinn died on September 4, 1987, and was buried in Springhill Cemetery, Harrodsburg.

JAMES RUSSELL HARRIS

CHINN, JOHN PENDLETON. Equally at home in thoroughbred racing or politics, John Pendleton Chinn was born in Harrodsburg, Kentucky, on February 11, 1849, the second son of John and Elenor (Pendleton) Chinn. He attended local Mercer County schools and the University of Kentucky. As a teenager, he served briefly during the Civil War as a member of Jesse's Scouts, under the command of Confederate Gen. John Hunt Morgan. For almost half a century, "Colonel Jack" was perhaps the most colorful and influential figure in the state's thoroughbred industry. He bred or owned a number of stakes winners, including Leonatus, who won the Kentucky Derby in 1883. To honor his prized stallion, Chinn renamed his Mercer County stock farm Leonatus. There he delighted in yet another of his passions: fox hunting. Chinn became confidant and adviser to a number of the state's leading Democrats, most notably William Goebel. He remained a full-time farmer and horse breeder, however, and sought political office only late in his career. In 1906 and 1908, he represented Mercer County in the state Senate; in 1910, he served in the state House of Representatives. Chinn married Ruth Morgan on February 18, 1868. They were the parents of four sons: George, John, Philip, and Christopher. Chinn died on January 31, 1920, and was buried in Springhill Cemetery in Harrodsburg.

THOMAS H. APPLETON, JR.

CHOCTAW ACADEMY. The Choctaw Academy was established at Great Crossings (near Georgetown) in 1818 by the Baptist Mission Society of Kentucky. It opened in the spring of 1819 with eight Indian boys as students. In 1821 the school closed for lack of financial support but was revived in 1825 under the auspices of Richard M. Johnson, U.S. senator from Kentucky, who had received a request from Choctaw leaders that he start a school. The request was forwarded by his brother-in-law, William Ward, the government agent for the Choctaw nation in Mississippi. The Choctaws had ceded land to the government in 1820 and 1825 and wanted part of the money they received as a result of the treaties to go to the education of Choctaw youths.

Johnson set up the school near his home in Scott County and hired a teacher, Thomas Henderson. The first class was twenty-five Choctaw boys. The curriculum included reading, writing, arithmetic, grammar, geography, practical surveying, astronomy, and vocal music. The school later received financial support from the Creek and Pottawatomie tribes and enrolled students from those tribes as well as the Ottawa, Miami, Quapaw, Seminole, Sac and Fox, and Osage tribes. Its enrollment reached a high of 188 students in 1835 but slowly declined thereafter. The Choctaw tribe was moved to Indian Territory (now Oklahoma) after the Treaty of Dancing Rabbit Creek in 1830; mission schools in the territory then supplanted the Choctaw Academy in importance, and in 1841 the tribe voted to start its own school. Many Choctaw students left the academy and the tribe withdrew its financial support. The school closed in 1842.

See Carolyn Foreman, "The Choctaw Academy," *Chronicles of Oklahoma* 6 (Dec. 1928): 453-80; 9 (Dec. 1931): 382-411; 10 (March 1932): 77-114. Shelley D. Rouse, "Colonel Dick Johnson's Choctaw Academy; a Forgotten Educational Experiment," *Ohio Archaeological and Historical Quarterly* 25 (Jan. 1916): 88-117.

CLARA SUE KIDWELL

CHOLERA EPIDEMICS. During each of the four Asiatic cholera epidemics that struck nineteenth century America, Kentucky was among the states with the highest fatality rate; Asiatic cholera is usually fatal. Not until the late nineteenth century did the medical profession discover that Asiatic cholera is spread by the ingestion of food and water contaminated by the fecal discharges of other cholera victims. In some locales in the commonwealth in the 1800s, streams that fed private and public wells flowed through subterranean limestone caverns that also served as "sinks," and heavy rainstorms flooded wells with water that had washed through shallow privies, piles of refuse, and cemeteries. Whole communities might then be stricken within a brief period. At the first hint of cholera, panic ensued and the able-bodied fled. Many victims of the disease lay unattended during their last hours, and the dead, hastily abandoned at the cemetery gate, often shared unmarked, common graves. As frightened residents sought safety in neighboring communities, they spread the disease across the state.

During the 1832-35 epidemic, nearly every area of the commonwealth suffered disastrously. One-tenth of the populations of Lexington and Russellville died within a few weeks, and other communities suffered similar losses. The scourge devastated the state again during 1848-54, claiming thousands of victims from urban and rural communities. An outbreak in 1866 was relatively mild in Kentucky, but the 1872 epidemic claimed thousands of lives in Woodburn, Millersburg, Lebanon, Columbia, Lancaster, and hundreds of other communities that relied on wells and shallow streams for their water supply.

Because the malady struck Kentuckians of all ages and economic status, the commonwealth's leading physicians argued and wrote extensively about the disease. Those who saw a correlation between sanitation and cholera surmised that rotting vegetation and standing water produced airborne cholera pathogens. Some sought an explanation in diet, believing that the ingestion of raw fruits and vegetables caused the disease. One widely held opinion linked strong emotions, strong drink, and sinful ways to the onset of cholera. Much of the contemporary literature concerned cures, and favored remedies included draining the body's "diseased" fluids by means of the lancet and blister cup. Although many practitioners favored secret concoctions, calomel was the most frequently prescribed medicine. After the final epidemic of 1872, evidence seemed to prove that better sanitation could decrease the risk of cholera, and fear of the scourge led many Kentuckians to clean up their communities. An 1875 publication by the U.S. surgeon general emphasized the commonwealth's record of careless sanitation measures and high fatality rates, citing a relationship between drinking water, sewage disposal, and cholera. In 1882 German physician Robert Koch discovered the Asiatic cholera-causing bacillus, proving the link between the disease and contaminated water.

See Nancy D. Baird, "Asiatic Cholera's First Visit to Kentucky: A Study in Panic and Fear," *FCHQ* 48 (July 1974): 228-41; Baird, "Asiatic Cholera: Kentucky's First Health Inspector," *FCHQ* 48 (Oct. 1974): 327-42.

NANCY D. BAIRD

CHRISTIAN, WILLIAM. William Christian, statesman and soldier, was born in 1743, the son of Israel and Elizabeth (Stark) Christian, who lived in Staunton, Augusta County, Virginia. At the age of twenty, he was a captain in William Byrd's Virginia regiment during the French and Indian War. Later he studied law in the office of Patrick Henry and married Henry's sister, Anne.

Christian represented Fincastle County in the lower house of the Virginia legislature from 1773 to 1775, and in 1776 he represented Fincastle and Botetourt counties in the state Senate. In 1774, during Lord Dunmore's War, he commanded a regiment of the Fincastle militia. In 1775 he was a member of the Committee of Safety, formed in preparation for hostilities with Britain, and was commissioned a lieutenant colonel of the 1st Virginia Regiment, Continental Line, when fighting broke out. He then became colonel of the militia of the Virginia Council of Defense. Christian was sent to drive the Over Hill Cherokee from the Long Island region along the Holston River in eastern Tennessee. He was a member of the commission that in July 1777 negotiated the Treaty of Long Island of Holston, which ceded large areas of Tennessee and Kentucky to Virginia.

Following the Revolutionary War, Christian again represented Fincastle and Botetourt counties in the Virginia Senate, from 1780 to 1783. He received a large land grant near Louisville for his French and Indian War service and moved his family to Beargrass Creek in 1785. On April 9, 1786, he was killed near present-day Jeffersonville, Indiana, while chasing a band of Wabash Indians. When the Kentucky legislature created Christian County out of Logan County in 1796, it was named in his honor.

CHRISTIAN APPALACHIAN PROJECT. The Christian Appalachian Project was founded in 1964 by the Rev. Ralph W. Beiting, who was a Roman Catholic missionary, to care for Appalachians' immediate needs as well as work toward long-term solutions to the region's chronic poverty. It first operated summer camps, used-clothing stores, a dairy farm, a woodworking shop, and a greenhouse. It expanded into areas of economic development, family counseling, early childhood development, adult education, youth enrichment, and care of the elderly. It is headquartered in Lancaster, Kentucky.

GLEN EDWARD TAUL

CHRISTIAN CHURCH. The Christian Church denomination is a product of the Stone-Campbell movement, a background that it shares with the CHRISTIAN CHURCH (DISCIPLES OF CHRIST) and the CHURCH OF CHRIST. The Stone-Campbell movement, or Restoration movement, began as an attempt to restore the pattern of church life and doctrine reflected in the New Testament. Barton Warren STONE, one of the founders of the Stone-Campbell movement, was minister of the Cane Ridge Presbyterian Church when it hosted the Cane Ridge revival of 1801 in Bourbon County, Kentucky.

Stone saw in the Cane Ridge revival an opportunity to preach Christ without the restrictions laid down by Calvinism or by denominational identity.

In 1803 Stone and four other ministers separated from the Presbyterian Synod of Kentucky and formed their own Springfield Presbytery. In 1804 they dissolved their presbytery, believing they ought to exist only as individual congregations of believers, with no attachment to denominational structures or authority. Their congregations were known as the Christian Church or the Church of Christ, and sometimes as the New Light Church. Of the original five ministers who began this Christian Church movement in Kentucky, two soon joined the Shakers and two rejoined the Presbyterians in 1811, after the Christian Church refused to adopt a theological statement of faith. Stone was the only one of the original five who remained. By 1826 his group numbered about 15,000, including three hundred preachers.

The other part of the Stone-Campbell movement was led by Alexander CAMPBELL and his father, Thomas Campbell, who came from a Presbyterian background in western Pennsylvania. They emphasized the Bible as the only source of authority and a commitment to unity among all Christians, to form one body of Christ on earth—the same concerns the Stone movement had developed. In the 1820s the Campbells were identified with the Baptists because they shared a common commitment to baptism by immersion. By 1830, however, the Campbells and the Baptists had separated because of differing views on the purpose of immersion, the role of the Holy Spirit in conversion, and other implications of Calvinism.

Stone first made contact with Alexander Campbell in the mid-1820s, and the Stone and Campbell movements began to unite in 1831 in Kentucky. Congregations in Millersburg joined together in April, congregations in Georgetown united over Christmas, and on New Year's Day in 1832 a similar meeting was held in Lexington. Similar unions occurred throughout the Ohio Valley in communities where there were churches of both the Campbell and Stone movements. Alexander Campbell preferred to call the congregations Disciples of Christ; some congregations used the names Christian Church or Church of Christ.

The Christian Church groups were opposed to denominational structures, but a loosely organized meeting of their churches in Kentucky began in 1850. A national convention of Christian Church representatives was held in Cincinnati in 1849, but many felt that such a body was a threat to the independence of the local congregation, as well as a departure from the New Testament precedent. Another issue of dispute arose in 1859 when the church in Midway, Kentucky, became the first congregation of the movement to use a musical instrument to accompany congregational singing. Many thought this was unsanctioned by New Testament authority and corrupted the pattern of New Testament worship services. The issues of musical instruments and organization above the congregational level led to an increasing polarization within the congregations of the Christian Church. The real issue, however, was how restrictive the pattern of New Testament precedents was to be. Could the churches innovate applications without explicit New Testament instruction?

The disagreements on these issues became so intense that soon congregations were refusing fellowship with one another because of their differences in practice. The congregations that were opposed to instrumental music and organization beyond congregations came to refer to themselves uniformly as the Church of Christ, and that term took on a specific meaning it did not have earlier. The separation was finalized in 1906, when the U.S. Bureau of the Census distinguished between the Christian Church and the Church of Christ. Since then the Church of Christ followers have constituted a separate fellowship.

Meanwhile, other tensions were building in the Christian Church, as the concepts of religious liberalism entered America from European thought. Liberalism saw the Bible not as a divine revelation, but as the record of man's upward quest for religious certainty. Under the impact of an increasing confidence in Darwinian science, biblical accounts of miracles were questioned, and the Genesis account of creation was interpreted as poetry, myth, or folklore. The College of the Bible (now Lexington Theological Seminary), headed by J. W. McGarvey, became a bastion of defense of the traditional teachings of the Bible. When McGarvey died in 1911, however, a new administration brought in new teachers, and by 1917 the College of the Bible had adopted liberal positions. Conservative churches throughout Kentucky then created other institutions to train ministers: Kentucky Christian College in Grayson in 1919; McGarvey Bible College in Louisville in 1923; the College of the Scriptures, a school for blacks in Louisville, in 1945; and Louisville Bible College in 1948.

Similar tensions over religious liberalism influenced policies at the national level. Resolutions to stop the spread of liberal practices were adopted at the national convention, but were so loosely applied by the leadership that nothing changed. In 1927 the conservatives in the Christian Church formed the North American Christian Convention as a voluntary assembly of individual members of Christian Church congregations. The conservatives have no denominational structure or hierarchy; they maintain a fellowship of churches and numerous para-church organizations, but they acknowledge no structure above the local congregation.

The North American Christian Convention met in Lexington in 1931 and 1962; in Louisville in 1956, 1966, 1981, and 1989. Attendance at such gatherings is often above 20,000. The Christian Church in Kentucky in 1990 included 429 congregations, with a total of 84,575 members. One particular congregation in Louisville, listed as the eighth fastest growing church in the country, had over 5,000 members.

What began as a commitment to Christian unity now exists in three segments: the Christian Church (Disciples of Christ), a denominational structure strongly influenced by theological liberalism; the Christian Church, committed to a conservative evangelical view of Christianity; and the Church of Christ, whose members have an even more conservative view of Scriptures, insisting that the churches do nothing unless sanctioned by explicit New Testament teaching. The Church of Christ tends to be separatist in relationships toward other evangelical Christian groups. In recent years, there have been discussions between leaders of the Christian Church and the Church of Christ, exploring not only their differences but also the numerous beliefs they hold in common.

See Henry E. Webb, *In Search of Christian Unity: A History of the Restoration Movement* (Cincinnati 1990); James DeForest Murch, *Christians Only: A History of the Restoration Movement* (Cincinnati 1962).   JAMES B. NORTH

CHRISTIAN   CHURCH   (DISCIPLES   OF CHRIST). The American Christian denomination known as the Christian Church (Disciples of Christ) began with the Cane Ridge revival in Bourbon County, Kentucky, in August 1801. The host for that event, Presbyterian minister Barton Warren STONE, invited Methodists and Baptists as well as other Presbyterians to share the preaching responsibility during the revival. Stone came away from the revival convinced that if Christians were to be effective in teaching their faith, they must be united, and the only way to achieve unity was to tolerate a diversity of opinion. In 1803 Stone and four other Presbyterian ministers in Kentucky broke their church affiliation and created the Springfield Presbytery, which they soon dissolved in favor of becoming "simply Christians." They emphasized the Bible as the primary authority for matters of faith and practice.

Stone emerged as the leader of these congregations, which were part of a broad movement among Presbyterians called the New Lights. In general, they were pro-revival, evangelical Presbyterian churches with a tendency to criticize the concept of predestination, at least in its more rigid forms. Stone went even further, expressing a willingness to question any traditional doctrine in light of his reading of the Bible. In the atmosphere of the frontier, the emphasis on liberty of thought and acceptance of differences among believers found a positive response in many places, and these Christian congregations grew in number and size, expanding from Kentucky to other states.

A similar movement was underway in western Pennsylvania and what is now West Virginia under the leadership of Thomas and Alexander CAMPBELL, father and son. Their followers, who also came from a schism among Presbyterians, were concerned with individual freedom of interpretation, the authority of the Bible, restoration of the New Testament form of the church, and unity among Christians. Similar in practices to the Baptists, the Campbell churches were united with the Baptists from 1813 to about 1830, then separated because of sociological and theological differences.

Alexander CAMPBELL, who succeeded his father as leader, debated Presbyterian Nathan Rice in Lexington in 1843. The Campbell churches came to be called Disciples of Christ.

Campbell met Stone in 1824. On January 1, 1832, at a meeting at what is now Central Christian Church in Lexington, the two groups united, forming the basis of the rapid growth among the congregations. The Stone-Campbell churches focused on education. Many of the first-generation ministers were teachers who established schools as well as churches. Bacon College, founded in Georgetown in 1836, was the first venture of the Disciples in higher education. Midway College, which dates back to 1849, is a Kentucky Disciples institution. The Louisville Christian Bible School (1873-77), the Louisville Bible School (1892-1914), and the Christian Bible College in New Castle (1886-92) provided both general and theological education for blacks.

From the beginning, the Stone churches had held meetings in various parts of Kentucky for purposes of mutual support. They led to district cooperatives in the 1820s and 1830s and to a loose state organization in 1840. A state convention of Disciples held in Lexington in 1850 resulted in a formal structure for a state missionary society. These organizations evolved into what is now the Christian Church (Disciples of Christ) in Kentucky. The initial purpose of the state and district organizations was to assist the churches in evangelism. They quickly evolved into means of nurturing congregations, helping them to find ministers, and aiding ministers who wanted to move from church to church. The corresponding secretary, who kept the mailing list of churches and ministers, became the central figure. The office of the regional minister and president now serves that function.

When the Disciples developed their first national organization, the American Christian Missionary Society, Kentuckians were among the leaders. The first Disciples missionary to Africa was Alexander Cross, a slave from Christian County whom the Disciples had purchased, freed, and educated. Disciples were as divided over slavery as any other church. Both Stone and Campbell opposed slavery but refused to make it a test of fellowship. Each supported the work of the American Colonization Society. Because of the Disciples' modest national structure, the church was able to weather the Civil War without a formal schism.

After the Civil War, black Disciples began to exercise leadership over a growing number of Afro-American congregations. Although there was no formal division between black and white Disciples, Afro-Americans set up their own state and national structures. In 1872, Preston Taylor, a black minister in Mt. Sterling, led in organizing what is now the Kentucky Christian Missionary Convention, as well as the national black Disciples organization. A state Sunday school convention of black Disciples was formed in the 1880s.

The Christian Woman's Board of Missions began in 1874, and a Kentucky group of women Disciples, organized in 1875, brought new vigor to missions in Appalachia. Ida Withers Harrison of Lexington was one of the leaders of the state and national Disciples women. By 1880 black women Disciples in Kentucky had formed the Kentucky Christian Women's Board of Missions Convention. Disciples began ordaining women in the ministry in 1888, though none served a congregation in Kentucky until after 1900.

A schism among Disciples in the early part of the twentieth century paralleled the fundamentalist-modernist conflict that affected most American Christian denominations in that era. In 1917, at Lexington's College of the Bible (now Lexington Theological Seminary), conservatives called for an examination of faculty suspected of being modernists, or liberals, in their interpretation of the Bible. The trustees refused to conduct a heresy trial and vindicated the faculty. The conservatives then began to establish their own institutions of education and gradually their own church structures. The schism was essentially complete by the 1950s, and the conservative groups formed the Church of Christ.

By the 1990s, the Disciples had moved more directly into the mainstream of Protestantism, emphasizing Christian unity.

See Alonzo W. Fortune, *The Disciples in Kentucky* (Lexington, Ky., 1932); Lester G. McAllister and William E. Tucker, *Journey in Faith: A History of the Christian Church (Disciples of Christ)* (St. Louis 1975).   RICHARD L. HARRISON, JR.

CHRISTIAN COUNTY. Christian County, the twenty-first in order of formation, is located in southwestern Kentucky, a part of the Pennyroyal region. The county is bordered by Hopkins, Muhlenberg, Todd, Trigg, and Caldwell counties and by Tennessee. Covering 722 square miles, Christian County is the second largest in the state (forty-five miles long and twenty-five miles wide). The county seat is HOPKINSVILLE.

Christian County was formed from a portion of Logan County by the Kentucky General Assembly in 1796 and organized on March 1, 1797. The new county was named in memory of Col. William Christian, a native of Augusta County, Virginia, and a veteran of the American Revolution. He settled on Beargrass Creek near Louisville in 1785 and was killed by Indians in southern Indiana the following year. Originally, the county included all land north of the Tennessee line, west of Logan County and the Green River, south of the Ohio River, and east of the Tennessee River. All of the counties now in this area were formed out of Christian County between 1798 and 1860.

James Davis and John Montgomery made the first permanent settlement in the county around 1784. They brought their families by flatboat down the Ohio River and then up the Cumberland River to settle on Montgomery Creek, southeast of present-day Pembroke. There the settlers built a log blockhouse on land, where they hunted and farmed. In the next two decades, settlement concentrated in northern Christian County, which had abundant fresh water, wild game, and timber for building and for firewood. Poor road conditions, the struggle for existence, and the land's topography isolated the valley settlements.

The flat, fertile land in southern Christian County was settled in the first quarter of the nineteenth century. Rich clay soil with a foundation of limestone was well-suited for crops, especially dark tobacco. Most of the land was barren of trees and covered in prairie grass, with a few springs along Little River and West Ford of the Red River. Large farms supported by slave labor were patterned after those in the Tidewater and the Deep South. Both sections of the county were fully settled by 1830, when the population reached 12,684.

During the forced removal of the Cherokee Nation from Georgia to the Indian Territory in what is now Oklahoma, more than 13,000 Cherokee passed through western Kentucky on the so-called Trail of Tears between October 1838 and February 1839. Hundreds became ill and died en route, including two aged chiefs, Fly Smith and White Path, who died while camped in Hopkinsville.

In the four decades after settlement, the county population doubled and many farm communities were established. Rich farmland worked by slave labor produced livestock, corn, and wheat, but the heart of local agricultural success was the production of dark tobacco. Farmers specialized in dark-fired tobacco, popular in Europe for snuff, chewing, and cigars. The nearby Cumberland and Tennessee rivers carried the crops for large-scale marketing at New Orleans. Toll road construction began in 1837. Western State Hospital for the mentally ill was organized in 1848 near Hopkinsville.

The Civil War divided the county. Slave-owning farmers in the southern part were Confederates and those in Hopkinsville and the northern part who had no slaves were Unionists. Christian County (now Todd County) was the home of Union Gen. James S. Jackson, and birthplace of Confederate President Jefferson Davis. The rapid recovery after the Civil War is reflected in the stable labor market, the innovative methods used by farmers, and the investments in turnpikes, railroads, schools, houses, warehouses, and flour mills.

The first local tobacco market sale took place in 1870. During the 1870s county farmers joined the Grange movement, which all through the South promoted fraternal cooperation to better the farmer's lot, and the annual county fair drew large numbers of country and town people. The county was the scene of tobacco farmers' revolt against pricing in the early twentieth century. In 1913 Christian County had one of the first county agents in Kentucky. Geoffery Morgan, an Englishman, initiated a progressive agricultural program, which introduced burley tobacco and established the agricultural extension service. The Kentucky Farm Bureau was formed in 1920, 4-H clubs in 1921, and the first homemaker's club in 1924. Pennyrile Rural Electric Cooperative came to the county in 1938. Turnpike

construction progressed rapidly during the 1870s, and by 1901 county roads were free of all tolls. Rural free delivery of mail began the same year. The first federal highway, constructed of loose gravel between 1923 and 1927, was U.S. 41N and 41S, known as the Dixie Bee Line. In 1932 this highway, along with U.S. 68W, was the first paved road in the county.

A black school system was organized in 1872. In 1885 the first black served on a grand jury, and by 1898 blacks had occupied the political offices of coroner, jailer, constable, and pensioner. County political influence shifted after the Civil War. Christian County was a Republican stronghold in both national and local elections from 1865 through the 1928 election. Since that time the Democratic party has carried all but four presidential elections and has maintained control of county offices.

After 1940 mechanization transformed farming operation, and soybean production replaced tobacco as the principal cash crop. The county has a new public library and a historical museum, a community concert association, the expanded Western Kentucky State Fair, four radio stations, and a television station. County improvements include the Bassett Urban Renewal Project, the Riverfront Improvement Project, and the Pennyrile Parkway and I-24. Bethel College closed, Hopkinsville Community College and University Heights Academy opened, and the city and county school systems merged. The county health department and a mental health center were created when Jennie Stuart Medical Center was enlarged.

The population was 56,224 in 1970; 66,878 in 1980; and 68,941 in 1990.

WILLIAM T.TURNER

CHURCHILL DOWNS. Churchill Downs in Louisville has been the site of the world-famous Kentucky Derby since it was first run in 1875. Col. M. Lewis Clark, who founded the derby, raised $32,000 in capital to build the track and selected a site that was three miles south of the city center. A prime reason for this choice was that Clark could lease the land from two uncles, John and Henry Churchill, rather than buy it. After the land was cleared and the racing strip graded and constructed, there was no money left for a grandstand. W.H. Thomas, a leading Louisville merchant, lent the track enough money to build a small wooden grandstand on the east side of the track. That location proved to be a mistake, as it forced fans to look directly into the afternoon sun.

Clark served as president of the first twenty runnings of the derby (1875-94). The 1895 derby not only had a new president, William F. Schulte, in charge but the track had a new look as well. (Colonel Clark was retained as presiding judge.) Schulte's group built a 285-foot grandstand on the west side of the track. The grandstand, surmounted by imposing twin spires, had a seating capacity of 1,500, with standing room for approximately 2,000 on its stairways. Col. Matt J. WINN, a great promoter, came along early in the twentieth century to rejuvenate the race, which had fallen on hard times. Colonel Winn, who built the derby into "the greatest two minutes in sports," remained at the Downs until his death in 1949.

The derby has attracted more than 100,000 fans each year since 1969, the last year of southern gentleman Wathen Knebelkamp's reign as track president. He was succeeded by Lynn Stone, track president until Tom Meeker took over in the late summer of 1984. Under the leadership of Meeker, board chairman Warner L. Jones Jr., and vice-president Gerald Lawrence, the Downs changed its image, becoming a bright, upbeat track with an aggressive marketing strategy. A total of $25 million was spent in capital improvements, including a new paddock installed for the 1986 fall meeting and a turf course first used in the spring of 1987.

The main track, one mile in circumference, is famous for its long stretch, known as "Heartbreak Highway." The distance from the last turn to the finish line is 1,234½ feet. In 1990 the Downs had a seating capacity of 51,500 in its grandstand, bleachers, clubhouse, and terraces. With 1,404 stalls in its barn area, the Downs draws solid stables for its spring and fall meetings, with such trainers as D. Wayne Lukas, Jack Van Berg, Phil Hauswald, and Steve Penrod represented with horses.

Bill Mott is the Downs's all-time leading trainer in career wins, with 337 through the 1990 spring meeting. Van Berg is second with 324. The late Henry Forrest, who saddled Kentucky Derby winners Kauai King (1966) and Forward Pass (1968), is third with 271. Pat Day is the all-time leading jockey at the Downs with 937 wins, having overtaken the retired Don BRUMFIELD at the 1990 spring meeting. Brumfield, who won the 1966 Derby, retired with 925 wins at the Downs, including forty-six in stakes races. Day holds the record for most wins on a single card, triumphing with seven of his eight mounts on June 20, 1984.

In 1988 the Downs served as host for the Breeders' Cup, drawing a record crowd of 71,237. Alysheba, the popular 1987 Kentucky Derby winner, captured the Breeders' Cup Classic in the final start of his career.

Churchill Downs is a company with approximately 1,710 stockholders—but, of course, the old track is much more than a company. It is an institution, a source of great pride for Kentuckians, a track where such legendary horses as Hindoo, Regret, Exterminator, Citation, and Secretariat have run.

As the home of the Kentucky Derby, it belongs to all of Kentucky.

See Jim Bolus, *Run for the Roses* (New York 1974).   JIM BOLUS

CHURCH OF CHRIST. The New Testament Church of Christ had its beginning in the Restoration movement in Kentucky following the Great Awakening, which swept the frontier after 1800. In 1803 Barton Warren Stone, minister of the Cane Ridge Presbyterian Church in Bourbon County, and four other Presbyterian ministers expressed their belief in the Bible alone as the rule of faith and practice, rather than the Presbyterian denomination's Westminster Confession of Faith. They broke with the Presbyterian Synod of Kentucky and joined the Restoration movement. Stone and his associates preached and wrote about restoring New Testament Christianity as it had been established in Jerusalem following the death and resurrection of Jesus Christ. They insisted that all Christians renounce their affiliation with the various sects formed following the European Reformation and identify themselves only as the body of Christ. Eight Presbyterian congregations in Kentucky and seven in Ohio did so, forming the first congregations of the Church of Christ.

The eight congregations in Kentucky that joined the Stone movement were located at Cane Ridge; Concord (Nicholas County); Harrodsburg (Mercer County); Bethel, Mt. Tabor, and Republican (Fayette County); Indian Creek (Harrison County); and Cabin Creek (Lewis County). Stone established a congregation in Lexington in 1816 and purchased a lot on Hill Street in 1828 for a building to be erected by "trustees of the Christian Church." The names Church of Christ and Christian Church were used interchangeably to identify the congregations. However, most titles to church property were vested in trustees of "the Church of Christ." Stone gave the name Old Union Church of Christ to the congregation he organized in northern Fayette County on June 23, 1823, and when the Lexington Main Street Church was organized in 1842, the property was deeded to the "trustees of the Church of Christ."

Shaker missionaries who came into Kentucky in 1805 converted two of the ministers who had left the Presbyterian church with Stone, and in December 1811 the others left Stone's movement and returned to the Presbyterians. At the same time, Thomas and Alexander Campbell, father and son who had broken with the Presbyterians in Pennsylvania, preached and practiced the same beliefs in Pennsylvania, Ohio, and West Virginia as Stone in Kentucky. Baptist congregations in Kentucky joined the Campbell movement, just as the Presbyterians had joined the Stone movement. By 1827, associates of the two men had recognized that their beliefs were the same, and at a meeting at the Hill Street Church in Lexington on January 1, 1832, the two groups, each claiming to represent the restored Church of Christ, agreed to unite in teaching the Bible as the source of spiritual light.

Unity among the believers continued until the formation of the American Christian Missionary Society in Cincinnati in 1849 and the Kentucky Missionary Society in 1850. Some congregations objected to any form of organization above the local level, causing a major breach within and among the local congregations. A second division occurred in 1859 when the church in Midway, Kentucky, introduced organ music into the worship service, the first use of instrumental music by any of the congregations. By 1906 the U.S. Bureau of the Census recognized the distinct cleavage between the two groups and began to list both the Church of Christ and the Christian Church. In the main, the Church of Christ did not accept the missionary society or mechanical instruments of music in worship. The Christian Church accepted both. The more liberal element of the Christian Church came to identify itself as the Christian Church (Disciples of Christ). The three groups—Church of Christ, Christian Church, and Disciples of Christ—all have roots in the early efforts to restore New Testament Christianity in America.

Members of the Church of Christ have become segmented into various fellowships, dividing over such issues as cooperation among congregations to do mission and benevolent work, organization and support of widows' and orphans' homes, establishment and management of Christian colleges, the role of women in the church, the matter of divorce and remarriage, and methods of study and interpretation of the Scriptures.

See Alonzo Willard Fortune, *The Disciples in Kentucky* (Lexington, Ky., 1932); Leroy Garrett, *The Stone-Campbell Movement* (Joplin, Mo., 1981).

ADRON DORAN

CHURCH OF CHRIST, SCIENTIST. Organized in Boston in 1879, the Church of Christ, Scientist, was formed to "commemorate the word and works" of Christ Jesus, "which should reinstate primitive Christianity and its lost element of healing." An experience of healing in 1866 led the church's founder, Mary Baker Eddy, to what she considered the "science" of Christianity, on which Jesus's works were based. The first Christian Science services in Kentucky were held in Lexington in 1886 in the home of Josephine Lancaster, who studied with Eddy. In 1887 Lancaster and Dr. Francis J. Fluno, a physician who became a Christian Science practitioner, established the Kentucky Academy of Christian Science for the purpose of healing and teaching.

In Louisville the first Christian Science services were held in 1888. The group organized formally in 1895 as a branch of the First Church of Christ, Scientist, in Boston. By 1915, there were thirteen Kentucky congregations with a diverse membership. In 1990 there were Christian Science congregations in Bowling Green, Frankfort, Fulton, Hopkinsville, Lakeside Park, Lexington, Louisville, Madisonville, Murray, Newport, and Paducah.

JOHN H. BLUNK

CHURCH OF THE NAZARENE. The Pentecostal Church of the Nazarene denomination resulted from the merger of three independent churches: the Association of Pentecostal Churches in America and the Church of the Nazarene in 1907, joined by the Holiness Church of Christ in 1908. In 1919 the word Pentecostal was deleted from the name to avoid possible confusion with other groups who practiced speaking in tongues. The Nazarenes' background is decidedly Methodist; they espouse a Wesleyan theology. Members believe in the verbal inspiration of the Scriptures, in Christ's atonement for the entire human race, in redemption of all penitent believers, in baptism and the Lord's Supper, and in Christ's second coming. There is scarcely any information regarding the first Nazarene church in Kentucky, but the first district assembly was probably convened as early as 1916. In 1950 church officials divided the state into two districts, the east and the west. As of 1989 there were eighty-seven Nazarene congregations with a combined membership of 7,821 members in the west district; the east district had sixty-five congregations and 6,500 members. Local congregations are responsible for electing their pastors; district superintendents are elected by members of the district assembly.

See Timothy L. Smith, *Called Unto Holiness: The History of the Nazarenes* (Kansas City, Mo., 1962).

KEITH HARPER

CINCINNATI & GREEN RIVER RAILWAY. The Cincinnati & Green River Railway began in 1879 as a wooden rail line between Kings Mountain and Staffordsville, Kentucky, to haul trams loaded with timber. Sawmills had been built in Staffordsville and Walltown to handle the timber from 13,000 acres in Casey County that Cincinnati businessman Eugene Zimmerman purchased in 1877. The primitive wooden railway, its cargo pulled by oxen or mules, soon could not handle the great amount of timber being harvested. It was replaced in 1880 by a narrow-gauge steel railroad and extended to Grove. Zimmerman organized the Green River Lumber Company in 1883 and built the standard-gauge Cincinnati & Green River Railway in 1884. The railroad was extended to Yosemite, Kentucky, in 1886. Yosemite was a boom town until overharvesting and the panic of 1893 crippled the lumber industry. On August 6, 1896, Zimmerman's holdings were sold in small parcels at a sheriff's sale, and the railway was dismantled. Its connection with the Cincinnati, New Orleans & Texas Pacific Railroad at Kings Mountain and the location of the Yosemite terminal thirteen miles away, near the Green River, probably gave the railroad its name.

See Edgar B. Wesley, "The Cincinnati and Green River Railway Company," *Register* 24 (Jan. 1926): 59-63.

CINCINNATI ARCH. Sedimentary strata in central Kentucky are folded upward to form the Cincinnati Arch, a broad anticlinal structure that extends southward from Cincinnati through central Kentucky and into central Tennessee. One of the state's prominent geologic features, it separates the western Appalachian Basin in eastern Kentucky from the southeastern Illinois Basin in western Kentucky. Patterns of deposition and erosion in Paleozoic rocks indicate that the arch was present in the Silurian and Devonian periods (about 365 to 425 million years ago), and possibly existed as early as the Ordovician period (about 485 million years ago), but later subsided. The present arch resulted from renewed structural movement, probably around the close of the Paleozoic era (about 250 million years ago).

See Robert C. McDowell, ed., *The Geology of Kentucky—A Text to Accompany the Geologic Map of Kentucky* (Washington, D.C., 1986); Arthur C. McFarlan, *Geology of Kentucky* (Lexington, Ky., 1943).   GARLAND R. DEVER, JR.

CINCINNATI SOUTHERN RAILWAY. In the post–Civil War period, Cincinnati sought to recapture its lucrative antebellum trade with the South. Cincinnati's only rail connection south, the Kentucky Central Railroad, terminated at Nicholasville. In 1867, Cincinnati businessmen began to lobby for a southern railroad. In 1869, they secured passage of the Ferguson Bill in the Ohio General Assembly, which permitted Cincinnati to be the builder and sole owner of a railroad, thus circumventing an 1851 Ohio constitutional provision that prohibited cities from lending money to or investing in railroad companies.

Considering a number of possible routes, the city council of Cincinnati finally established Chattanooga, Tennessee, as the terminus, and called for a special election in June 1869 to consider the matter. A clear majority approved the measure, and the superior court of Cincinnati appointed a five-member board of trustees of the Cincinnati Southern Railway. In 1870 they obtained a railroad charter from the state of Tennessee, and in 1872 from the Kentucky legislature. In 1874 the trustees established the route of the road, crossing the Ohio River at Ludlow, Kentucky, and proceeding south through Walton, Williamstown, Georgetown, and Lexington. In July 1877 the route was completed from Ludlow to Somerset, and in December of that year the railroad's new Ohio River bridge at Ludlow was opened. In February 1880 the entire route of the Cincinnati Southern was finished. The 336-mile road was an engineering wonder. It passed through twenty-seven tunnels, including the 3,984-foot Kings Mountain tunnel, and crossed 105 bridges and viaducts.

The trustees of the Cincinnati Southern Railway leased the line to a couple of locally owned companies before arranging a more lucrative lease in September 1881 with the Cincinnati, New Orleans & Texas Pacific Railway Company (CNO&TP), the majority stock of which was controlled by Baron Frederick Emile d'Erlanger of Emile Erlanger and Co. Bankers, of London and Paris. With the introduction of Erlanger's interest in the railroad, the Cincinnati Southern became part of a larger railroad network, the Erlanger System, which embraced 1,165 miles of southern railroads, linking Cincinnati, the "Queen City," to New Orleans, the "Crescent City"—hence the name given the Erlanger System: the Queen and Crescent Route.

Baron Erlanger in 1890 sold his majority interest in the railroad to the Richmond & West Point Terminal Railway Company. Following financial difficulties, the Richmond & West Point and its holdings were reorganized as the Southern Railway Company, by the banker J.P. Morgan, of Drexel, Morgan and Company. It was chartered in 1894. The Southern, in conjunction with the Cincinnati, Hamilton & Dayton Railroad company, controlled the twenty-five-year leasehold (1881-1906) of the Cincinnati Southern Railway to Chattanooga. In 1901 early negotiations extended this lease for an additional sixty years—that is, until 1966. In 1928, however, the lease was renegotiated for a period of ninety-nine years, until December 31, 2026. In 1982 the Southern Railway merged with the Norfolk & Western Railway into a new parent organization called the Norfolk Southern Corporation, which holds the lease for the 336-mile Cincinnati Southern Railway, the right-of-way of which is owned by the City of Cincinnati.

See Burke Davis, *The Southern Railway: Road of the Innovators* (Chapel Hill, N.C. 1985).
     PAUL A. TENKOTTE

CIVIL RIGHTS ACT OF 1966. The Kentucky Civil Rights Act of 1966 was both the high-water mark of the civil rights movement in Kentucky and, as Martin Luther King, Jr., described it, "the strongest and most comprehensive civil rights bill passed by a southern state."

A precursor to the act, a bill banning discrimination in public accommodations, was introduced in the General Assembly in 1964 by Rep. Norbert Blume of Louisville. Drafted by the Kentucky Commission on Human Rights (CHR), a state agency established in 1960 with limited powers to promote improvements in the racial climate, the Blume bill had the support of the Allied Organizations for Civil Rights (AOCR), a statewide coalition. The head of the coalition was Frank Stanley, Jr., the son of the publishers of the *Louisville Defender* and a prominent student leader during protests against segregation in downtown Louisville in 1959 and the early 1960s.

At the start of the 1964 session, Gov. Edward T. Breathitt (1963-67) had called for passage of a strong public accommodations bill. Breathitt indicated, however, that he preferred to wait for enactment of the federal civil rights statute then making its way through Congress and in any case would not work actively for the cause until the last fifteen days of the session. In late February, with the Blume proposal locked in the House Rules Committee and the session drawing to a close, Breathitt announced his support of a less comprehensive measure introduced in the Senate by Shelby Kinkead of Lexington.

Disappointed with the governor's belated support of the weaker Kinkead bill, AOCR leaders organized a march on the state capitol. Late on a rainy Friday morning, March 5, 1964, 10,000 demonstrators demanded passage of a tough public accommodations measure. Several leaders of the march, including Martin Luther King, Jr., criticized Breathitt, both in speeches to the crowd and later in a private meeting with the governor.

Breathitt reiterated his commitment to civil rights and the next day the governor joined with AOCR and CHR members to hammer out a compromise bill, which exempted barber and beauty shops, taverns, and bowling alleys, as the Kinkead bill had done, but incorporated the stronger enforcement provisions of the Blume bill. The compromise bill ultimately received only 21 of the 29 votes needed to move out of committee and onto the floor, despite Breathitt's dramatic personal appeals before both the House and the Rules Committee and a hunger strike in the House gallery by thirty-two AOCR members throughout the session's last week.

After the defeat of the public accommodations bill, Breathitt pledged to call a special session of the General Assembly if he could be assured of legislative support. In May, at a conference of Kentucky mayors, the governor received a unanimous resolution for a strong civil rights bill. But in a spirited meeting with legislators in July, just weeks after President Lyndon Johnson signed the Civil Rights Act of 1964, only thirty-five of the 103 lawmakers present indicated that they would support an administration-drafted public accommodations measure in a special session.

Over the next eighteen months, Breathitt consolidated his administration's power over the legislative leadership, and he mended fences with state civil rights leaders. On December 16, 1965, at a major conference on civil rights in Louisville, where he shared the platform with King, Breathitt pledged that a forthright new civil rights bill, one addressing fair employment as well as public accommodations, would be a centerpiece of the upcoming legislative session.

Introduced as House Bill 2 on January 4, the session's first day, the civil rights bill remained nearly two weeks in the Rules Committee, where twelve amendments, most designed to preempt resistance from western Kentucky legislators, were attached. Once introduced on the House floor on January 17, the amended bill was substituted for the original by a voice vote. After a plea by Democratic floor leader John Y. Brown, a move to call the "previous question" passed 57 to 25, preventing the addition of further amendments. After only two hours of debate, HB 2 itself passed by a resounding bipartisan vote of 76-12. On January 25, as Democratic factions and Republicans competed for the mantle of most ardent defender of civil rights, the Senate endorsed the measure 36-1, with George Brand of Mayfield offering the only dissent. Soon after the Senate vote, in a little noticed but symbolically important action, Rep. Jesse Warders, a Louisville Republican who was the General Assembly's only black member, introduced legislation that purged from the statutes all the "dead letter" segregation laws that once authorized racial discrimination.

Signed by Governor Breathitt beneath the Lincoln statue in the capitol rotunda on January 27, 1966, the Kentucky Civil Rights Act of 1966 was stronger in some respects than the federal Civil Rights Act of 1964. Whereas the equal employment provisions of the federal law applied only to interstate commerce and initially only to firms of one hundred or more employees, the Kentucky statute prohibited racial discrimination in all businesses with eight or more workers and also applied to labor organizations and employment agencies. The accommodations section of the Kentucky law guaranteed "full and equal" access to public services except for barbershops, beauty parlors, and small, family-owned boardinghouses. The legislation significantly strengthened the Commission on Human Rights, granting CHR extensive authority to address complaints and issue regulations, and it gave cities and counties broad power to adopt and enforce civil rights ordinances.

The Civil Rights Act of 1966 provided criminal penalties only in cases of retaliation against individuals seeking protection under the law, and it explicitly rejected preferential hiring as a means of correcting racial imbalances in employment. The act did not address residential segregation, which became the focal point of the Louisville open housing demonstrations in 1967 and a new state civil rights act in 1968. Nor did it address educational inequities, the issue at the heart of the Louisville busing controversy of the mid-1970s. Thirty-five years after passage, in fact, full equality for blacks remained a dream deferred. The Civil Rights Act of 1966 stands nonetheless as a major blow against the legal foundations of discrimination in Kentucky life and the first significant civil rights law passed by a state south of the Ohio River.

See Kenneth E. Harrell, ed., *The Public Papers of Governor Edward T. Breathitt, 1963-1967* (Lexington, Ky., 1984).   ANTHONY NEWBERRY

CIVIL WAR. The 1861 rupture of the Union had a great impact upon the border slave state of Kentucky. Her citizens were deeply divided. Gov. Beriah Magoffin (1859-62) believed in the right of secession and was a firm defender of slavery, but he opposed immediate secession and hoped to avoid war. After the Civil War began in April 1861, Kentucky in May adopted an official policy of neutrality; that policy was to survive only until early September.

During the summer both North and South appeared to respect Kentucky's neutrality. The North established Camp Clay in Ohio, opposite Newport, and Camp Jo Holt in Indiana, opposite Louisville. The South stationed troops within fifty yards of Kentucky at Cumberland Gap and constructed Forts Henry and Donelson just over the state line on the Tennessee and Cumberland rivers. The greatest advantage to the Confederacy of Kentucky's neutrality was access to the Louisville & Nashville Railroad, which carried supplies to the South; all but 5 percent of the cars returning from Nashville were empty.

Meanwhile, both sides were receiving volunteers from Kentucky. The State Guards leaned to the Confederates and many made their way to Tennessee. Home Guards tended to support the Union.

Only in the 1st Congressional District, which included the Jackson Purchase, was there near-unanimity respecting the war; the Cumberland and Tennessee rivers drew the area economically into the orbit of western Tennessee, the most pro-Confederate section of the Volunteer State. After Kentucky's August election returns showed a decided Union majority, the neutrality policy lost credibility. Ignoring the protests of Governor Magoffin, Union agents established CAMP DICK ROBINSON in Garrard County to recruit Union troops, and thousands of so-called Lincoln guns were delivered there for distribution to the Home Guard and other Unionists.

Early in September Kentucky's fragile neutrality was finally shattered as the Confederates took Columbus. The Union replied by taking Paducah. The Confederates moved into Bowling Green and southeastern Kentucky near Cumberland Gap. While Confederate forces remained in southwestern Kentucky, Confederate sympathizers held a convention at Russellville and formed a provisional CONFEDERATE STATE GOVERNMENT with its capital at Bowling Green. The Kentucky theater remained quiet through autumn. Fortifying and building winter quarters or drilling raw recruits—not invading—was the order of the day. There were small-scale battles in November and December.

January 1862 brought more significant battles. Confederate Gen. Felix Zollicoffer and his soldiers were winning the Battle of MILL SPRINGS in Wayne County when he mistook Union troops for his own men, a mistake that cost Zollicoffer his life. His death turned the tide of battle. In eastern Kentucky James A. Garfield opened his Big Sandy campaign against Confederate Gen. Humphrey Marshall. They met in Floyd County at the Battle of Middle Creek. Had it not been for the Confederate artillery, which enabled a Union relief column from Paintsville to find the site of the battle just in time, the Confederates would have been victorious, but the reinforcements turned the tide. It was difficult to supply troops in the mountains, and both sides turned toward their bases of supplies. Garfield later moved on Pikeville but accomplished little in the area. Eastern Kentucky was poorly protected throughout the war and thus vulnerable to guerrilla attacks and bushwhackers.

In February boats loaded with Union troops of Gen. Ulysses S. Grant's army steamed up the Cumberland and Tennessee rivers to attack and capture Forts Donelson and Henry. Cumberland Gap did not fall into Union control until June. Kentucky was no longer a theater of war but instead an area from which supplies were forwarded. Soldiers were often sent to guard bridges along the state's railroads.

Such serenity was disturbed when John Hunt Morgan on July 4 commenced his first Kentucky raid, which covered more than a thousand miles in about three and a half weeks, capturing seventeen towns, destroying extensive amounts of government supplies, dispersing 1,500 Home Guards, paroling nearly 1,200 regular Federal troops, and returning south with three hundred more men than he had started with. Only once, at CYNTHIANA BRIDGE, did he meet heavy resistance.

Both Confederate and Union commanders thought they had learned the lesson of Morgan's raid. Morgan's ability to recruit troops in Kentucky encouraged the Confederates to invade Kentucky; Morgan's freewheeling raid convinced those in command in Kentucky that any invasion of the commonwealth would be merely another highly mobile Morgan raid. Both sides would pay dearly for drawing the wrong conclusions.

Union Gen. George W. Morgan was the first to understand that a troop movement, which included a substantial force advancing under Gen. Edmund Kirby-Smith on Morgan's location at Cumberland Gap, was a full-scale invasion, not a raid. Morgan refused to surrender or to budge. That obstinacy provided an excuse for Kirby-Smith to disobey orders. Kirby-Smith had been ordered to capture Morgan's position and then join Gen. Braxton Bragg, his superior, for the capture of Nashville. Only then, with their forces combined, were they to invade Kentucky.

But Kirby-Smith decided to head for the Bluegrass, leaving a sufficient force to handle the Union's Morgan. He believed this preferable to the inaction of a siege. Kirby-Smith's action forced Bragg to change his plans and join in the invasion before advancing on Nashville. Morgan's Union men remained at the gap far longer than the Confederates had expected and then completely surprised them by commencing a masterful retreat, traveling more than two hundred miles to Greenup, Kentucky, on the Ohio River, fighting frequent skirmishes, carrying off cannon and wagons. Morgan's loss was but eighty men.

At this time, Gov. Oliver P. Morton of Indiana believed Kentucky was doing too little to support the Union cause. Suspicious of the loyalty of Gov. James F. Robinson (1862-63), the hand-picked replacement for Magoffin, Morton sent newly formed Indiana regiments into Louisville, considering himself governor of both Indiana and Kentucky.

Union Gen. William Nelson, who commanded in the vicinity of Richmond, Kentucky, ordered Gen. Mahlon D. Manson, located near Richmond, not to engage the enemy. Nelson intended to meet Kirby-Smith and his Confederates on the palisades of the Kentucky River, taking advantage of the better terrain and of the delay, which would add to the number of regiments available to oppose Kirby-Smith.

Despite direct orders, Manson engaged in the Battle of RICHMOND, which after three separate stands led to a rout and the abandonment of much of Kentucky, including Lexington and Frankfort. Panic seized northern Kentucky. At one time Maysville was captured, and as a result of the Battle of AUGUSTA two squares of that Ohio River town burned to the ground. In Louisville it was rumored that Jeff Davis was in town and many fled to Indiana. In fact, it was Union Gen. Jefferson C.

Davis who was in town. Nelson had no use for either Davis or Governor Morton, and gave Davis a tongue lashing. Davis shot Nelson dead on September 29, 1862.

Meanwhile General Bragg began his belated advance into Kentucky. Had he kept his eye upon the prize, the chances are that he would have beaten Union Gen. Don Carlos Buell to Louisville and the Falls City would have fallen into Confederate hands. But an inexperienced Union colonel, John T. Wilder, withstood an assault by a large Confederate force at the Battle of Munfordville. The advance toward Louisville was delayed while an overwhelming force was brought to bear on Wilder. Wilder surrendered, but the delay saved Louisville.

Symbolically, the South's high-water mark was reached October 4, 1862, with the installation of Richard Hawes at Frankfort as Confederate governor of Kentucky. But nearly the first order of business was to skedaddle. As of October 1, Buell's army had fanned out to the south and east from Louisville. By then, too, regiments had begun to move southward from Cincinnati, including such unconventional troops as the Cincinnati Police Department, Cincinnati Fire Department, and folks called the Squirrel Hunters. Both Bragg and Smith were calling in their troops, who had earlier fanned out in a massive, unsuccessful recruiting effort and a search for supplies.

In the summer of 1862, perhaps the driest summer in Kentucky history, tramping armies raised dust, and thirst took its toll. The need for water led to skirmishing near Perryville on the night of October 7 and the following day the bloodiest fight in Kentucky took place, the Battle of PERRYVILLE. Union commander Buell, when no battle had commenced by early morning of October 8, told his corps commanders not to engage the enemy until the ninth. Buell did not consider the possibility of Confederate attack. His preconceptions, the locale of his headquarters, and the wind direction kept Buell unaware that a battle was going on until too late. Corps commander Gen. Thomas Crittenden was kept out of the main action by Confederate Gen. Joseph Wheeler and his cavalry, who by changing position constantly gave the impression of a much larger force. Most of the action was an attempt to turn the Union's left wing, and though Gen. Alexander McCook's men included raw recruits and were pushed back, they did not break. The Union artillery played an important role in holding the line as well. Darkness brought an end to the desperate struggle, which cost both armies heavily and changed nothing. The Confederates retired from the state and the Union pursuit was slow.

Kentucky was not massively invaded again during the war, yet Kentucky if anything became increasingly vulnerable, for as attention was drawn away from the commonwealth it became easier for small bands of renegades from both North and South to roam about, thieving, burning, creating panic. Gen. John Hunt Morgan did damage with his Christmas Raid of 1862-63, and the Ohio raid of 1863 led to a defeat at the Battle of Green River Bridge, or Tibb's Bend, and to the capture of Mt. Sterling in 1864.

On March 25, 1864, Confederate Gen. Nathan B. Forrest attacked Paducah and took control of a portion of the town; toward the end of the year, Gen. Hylan B. Lyon led cavalry through western Kentucky, burning a number of courthouses in the process. No year exceeded 1864 in the devastation by guerrilla bands. Gen. Stephen Burbridge responded by proclaiming that four guerrilla prisoners would be shot for every Union man lost at the hands of such cutthroats, but some of those shot were Confederate prisoners of war and the retaliation order earned Burbridge a reputation for brutality.

Intense hatred of the federal government followed the federal interference in state and national elections, extortion by Federal officers, suppression of the press, slave stealing, the use of black troops, the institution of martial law, and theft of all that was edible—treatment like that of a conquered province, although the state had supplied five Union soldiers for every two who joined the Confederacy. When given a chance, Kentucky citizens showed their animosity through the ballot box by voting overwhelmingly Democratic and later by voting often for former Confederates.

Gov. Thomas E. Bramlette (1863-67) fought federal excesses effectively and eventually issued a general pardon for ex-Confederates. Kentuckians were offended, however, by General Burbridge's successor, Gen. John M. Palmer, who gave freed slaves free rail passage ("Palmer passes") and with John G. Fee helped turn Camp Nelson into a refugee camp for freed black families.

Being treated like a conquered enemy proved far more damaging to Kentucky's future than the physical damage done to the commonwealth. Gone was the characteristic confidence and iron will. In its place came the romantic legend of the Lost Cause and a "Kentucky is a poor state" mentality.

See Lowell H. Harrison, *The Civil War in Kentucky* (Lexington, Ky., 1975); E.M. Coulter, *Civil War and Readjustment in Kentucky* (Chapel Hill, N.C., 1926).   STUART S. SPRAGUE

CLARK, FRANCIS. Francis Clark, planter and minister, was born around 1739. With John Durham, of Mecklenberg County, Virginia, he established the first Methodist society in Kentucky, in a cabin six miles west of Danville, Kentucky, about 1783. Well-instructed in the doctrines of Methodism, he was instrumental in forming several churches. An inventory of his estate showed that he owned a productive farm with a large number of slaves and reared a large family. He died in 1799 and was buried in Boyle County, Kentucky.

See Gladys Bosnell May, *The Story of Methodism in Danville, Kentucky* (Danville, Ky., 1964).
                                    WILLIAM J. HURLEY

CLARK, GEORGE ROGERS. George Rogers Clark, soldier and pioneer, was born into an Established church household on November 19, 1752, near Monticello, Albemarle County, Virginia. He was the son of John and Ann (Rogers) Clark. Donald Robertson, a renowned Scottish educator in King and Queen County, Virginia, tutored Clark, who became proficient in mathematics. He studied geography, history, and natural history as well. George Mason, a friend of the Clark family, tutored him informally. At the age of twenty, Clark purchased surveyor's instruments and a copy of *Euclid's Elements* and initiated his practice as a surveyor.

In 1774 Clark took part in Cresap's War, McDonald's expedition against the Shawnee, and Lord Dunmore's War, in which he was captain of the militia of Pittsburgh and its dependencies. Clark then returned to surveying for the Ohio Company in Kentucky. In 1775, in association with Col. Hancock Lee, Clark helped lay out the community of Leesburg, now a part of Frankfort, Kentucky. He was elected a delegate from Harrodsburg to go to Williamsburg, Virginia, in 1776 and promote the creation of KENTUCKY COUNTY out of Virginia's Fincastle County. Kentucky County came into being on December 31, 1776. Clark returned to Kentucky with five hundred pounds of gunpowder for the defense of the newly created county of Virginia.

Returning to Virginia in 1777 after the start of the Revolutionary War, Clark sought from Gov. Patrick Henry approval of a secret expedition against the British-held posts north of the Ohio River—Kaskaskia, Vincennes, and Detroit. Henry approved Clark's plans, appointing him lieutenant colonel and authorizing him to raise seven companies to carry out the secret mission. Clark moved down the Ohio River to the Falls of the Ohio, where he established a small post at Corn Island. After receiving a few additional soldiers, Clark left for Kaskaskia on June 24, 1778, shooting the falls during a full solar eclipse, "which caused various conjectures among the superstitious," according to Temple Bodley's biography. The small army of 175 men arrived at the mouth of the Tennessee River, proceeded overland on a northwesterly route for the remainder of the trip, and arrived undetected at the community of Kaskaskia on the evening of July 4, 1778. Kaskaskia was captured without the loss of a single life.

British Lt. Gov. Henry Hamilton subsequently left Detroit for Vincennes to counter Clark's move to Kaskaskia. Arriving late at Vincennes, on December 17, 1778, Hamilton decided he would not pursue Clark until the following spring. In the interim, Clark mounted an unexpected attack against Hamilton. Clark raised an army of 170 men (110 American and sixty French) and divided his forces into two groups. One accompanied him 240 miles across the flooded and partially frozen Illinois country. The other forty men traveled by boat with Capt. John Rogers down the Mississippi River and

up the flooded Ohio and Wabash rivers, to await Clark and his land party at the mouth of White River. Clark's party arrived at Vincennes before Rogers's company. Although Clark's men had suffered greatly from exposure to the elements and from the lack of food, Clark did not wait to attack. To the astonishment of Hamilton and his British soldiers, Clark's forces were victorious. On February 25, 1779, Hamilton agreed to the conditions of surrender. Clark was at the peak of his military career.

On April 19, 1780, Clark began the construction of Fort Jefferson, near the mouth of the Ohio River. In May he traveled north to Pancore (now St. Louis) and Cahokia to assist the Spanish in repelling attacking British and Indian forces. In August of that year Clark led a major assault against the Shawnee, who were firm allies of the British. The Shawnee had on many previous occasions crossed the Ohio River, raided Kentucky settlements, and returned north with scalps and prisoners. Clark, accompanied by regulars from Fort Jefferson and militia from the central Kentucky stations, traveled north to attack the Shawnee at their major village of Piqua, near present-day Springfield, Ohio. The Shawnee escaped unharmed, having had advance warning of Clark's approach, but Clark's army destroyed the Shawnee village and their winter's supply of corn.

On January 22, 1781, Clark was appointed brigadier general by Virginia Gov. Thomas Jefferson. Clark established a garrison, Fort Nelson, at the Falls of the Ohio. Late in 1782 he again led a retaliatory raid against the Shawnee for their part in the Battle of BLUE LICKS in central Kentucky. With the signing of the Treaty of Paris in 1783, the Revolutionary War was officially over. At that time, the state of Virginia owed Clark more than $20,000. Clark received 18,049 acres of land for his service, and 2,193 pounds sterling back pay for five years as a colonel and brigadier general. Most of that money, however, went to pay off debts to the Illinois battalion that he had organized to support Virginia's war effort. From that point on, Clark's career faltered. In 1783 reports circulated of Clark's overindulgence in liquor.

On August 7, 1784, Clark laid out the town of Clarksville, Indiana, and was granted the right to erect the first saw- and gristmill in the region. That privilege, however, was retracted by the Virginia Assembly. In September 1786, while leading a retaliatory raid against hostile Indians in the Wabash region, Clark confiscated supplies and boats from three Spanish merchants in Vincennes. This episode appeared to tie Clark to the SPANISH CONSPIRACY, and was rebuked by Virginia's Governor Randolph. Clark was innocent of the charge of conspiracy.

Clark was subsequently offered a military commission from France through Citizen Genet to attack Spanish-held New Orleans. He was given the title major general in the armies of France and commander-in-chief of the French Revolutionary

Legions on the Mississippi River. In June 1798 Clark was informed by the United States government that he must resign this position or be arrested.

In 1803 Clark moved to Clark's Point in Clarksville, which overlooks the Falls of the Ohio. In 1804 he proposed that a canal be made to circumvent the falls to facilitate trade and commerce. By 1805 Clark was described as "frail and helpless." In 1809 he had a stroke and fell unconscious in front of his fireplace, burning one of his legs so badly that it had to be amputated. Clark was then moved to Locust Grove, the home of his younger sister, Lucy (Clark) Croghan, near Louisville, where he remained for nine years. In 1813 a second stroke left him paralyzed. On February 13, 1818, Clark suffered a third stroke, which took his life. Clark was initially buried in the Croghan family cemetery at Locust Grove, but his remains were exhumed in 1869 and buried in Louisville's Cave Hill Cemetery.

See Temple Bodley, *George Rogers Clark: His Life and Public Services* (New York 1926); James Alton James, *The Life of George Rogers Clark* (Chicago 1929).   KENNETH C. CARSTENS

CLARK, JAMES. James Clark, governor of Kentucky during 1836-39, was born to Robert and Susannah Clark, in Bedford County, Virginia, on January 16, 1779. The family moved to a Clark County, Kentucky, farm when James was a child. After studying law with a brother in Virginia, he was admitted to the bar in 1797 and soon had an extensive practice. He married Susan Forsythe and, after her death, Margaret Buckner Thornton. Clark was the father of four children. He was elected to the Kentucky House of Representatives in 1807 and 1808 and was appointed to the court of appeals during 1810-12. In 1812 and 1814 he was elected to the U.S. House of Representatives. Appointed to the state circuit court in 1817, Clark rendered a major decision in *Williams v. Blair* in 1822, ruling that the state law for the benefit of debtors was unconstitutional. (The law allowed debtors to escape bankruptcy proceedings by imposing a moratorium on their debts.) The legislature passed a resolution of condemnation for this decision, but after Clark ably defended his position, the House vote of 59 to 35 fell short of the two-thirds majority needed to remove him from the court. In 1823 the state Supreme Court upheld his decision. The General Assembly then abolished the court of appeals (the Old Court) and replaced it with the New Court, setting off a major controversy. Clark returned to the U.S. House during 1825-31, but his role was passive. Elected to the Kentucky Senate in 1832, he became its speaker in 1835. A Henry Clay supporter, Clark helped organize the Whig party in the state. Rewarded by the Whig nomination for governor in 1836, Clark defeated Democrat Matthew Flournoy by 38,587 votes to 30,491. He died in office on August 27, 1839, and was buried in Winchester, Kentucky.

In his 1837 message to the legislature, Clark outlined an ambitious program: strengthen the auditor's office to encourage sound public finances; change the criminal code to combat rising crime; deal with the problem of fugitive slaves; and establish a public school system in every county. The General Assembly provided for a state board and a state superintendent of public education and for county school commissions, and it enacted several measures designed to make escape more difficult for slaves. It ignored most of the governor's other recommendations. During the 1838-39 session, the legislature followed Clark's advice by giving the sinking fund commission more discretion in handling funds and by adding a second auditor in that office. Clark asked for authority to prevent the spread of abolitionist propaganda within the state, but the legislature refused to restrict freedom of speech. Clark's administration was one of the most efficient during his era.

See Lowell H. Harrison, ed., *Kentucky's Governors 1792-1985* (Lexington, Ky., 1985).
                                LOWELL H. HARRISON

CLARK, THOMAS DIONYSIUS. Thomas D. Clark, historian, was born in Louisville, Mississippi, on July 14, 1903, to John Collinsworth and Sallie (Bennett) Clark. His parents were of pioneer families who had moved from South Carolina into Choctaw Indian lands that later became cotton country. In 1925 Clark entered the University of Mississippi, intending to study law. Instead, under the influence of historian Charles Sackett Sydnor, he turned to the study of history. Clark graduated from the University of Mississippi in 1928. He received his master's degree from the University of Kentucky in 1929 and his doctorate from Duke University in 1932. Duke professor William K. Boyd, a first-rate collector, had a profound influence on Clark's research skills. Clark said of Boyd that he had "both a genuine sense of the value of the original records, and the energy and imagination to collect them." These words apply equally well to Clark himself.

Clark began his teaching career at Memphis State University in 1930. In 1931 he moved to the University of Kentucky, which was then lacking in the quality of faculty and research that characterize first-rate institutions. University of Kentucky president Frank L. McVey (1917-40), who had high hopes for the school, personally hired Clark. The university was Clark's base for thirty-seven years, while at various times he taught at Harvard, Duke, North Carolina, Tennessee, Rochester, Chicago, Wyoming, Wisconsin, the Claremont Graduate School, Kent State, Stanford, Indiana, and at the Salzburg Seminar in American Studies in Austria. He lectured overseas for the Department of State, at Oxford University, and in Greece, India, and Yugoslavia.

At the University of Kentucky, Clark simultaneously taught fifteen-hour schedules and started the university library's Special Collections. He acquired a serial set of U.S. government documents from Centre College in Danville and the Kentucky State Library in Frankfort and a set of state documents for the law school. He also brought private collections to the university. For several years Clark taught extension courses, and quickly established himself as a popular lecturer, known for the humor and anecdotes with which he made his points. Clark became chairman of the UK's history department in 1942, and at the end of World War II he began to piece together a distinguished collection of faculty. He was in the vanguard of the movement that established the University of Kentucky Press in 1943 and the University Press of Kentucky in 1968.

Clark's own series of publications began in 1933 with *The Beginning of the L&N.* He followed with *A Pioneer Southern Railroad* (1936), *A History of Kentucky* (1937), *The Rampaging Frontier* (1939), and *Pills, Petticoats and Plows* (1944). In the last book, one of his most popular, Clark portrays the country store not as a homey institution but as a mirror of the basic images of the South. His next works on the region, *The Rural Press and the New South* (1948) and *The Southern Country Editor* (1948), reflect not only his affection for and sense of the South but also his tough-minded ability to look critically at his native land. His works, however, also reveal a universality that has made him not a regional specialist but an American historian of the first rank. As well as writing, Clark served as managing editor of the *Journal of Southern History* for four years and chief editor of two multivolume publications, a sixteen-year undertaking: *Travels in the Old South* and *Travels in the New South.*

In 1965 Clark's tenure as chairman of UK's history department ended. He was then Hallam Professor until 1968, when he retired. While teaching for a time at Indiana University, he wrote a multivolume history of that university and served as executive secretary of the Organization of American Historians. At seventy years of age, Clark left Indiana University in 1973 as Distinguished Service Professor Emeritus. He then taught at Eastern Kentucky University, at the University of Wisconsin as a visiting professor, and at Winthrop College in Rock Hill, South Carolina, as adjunct professor. His writing continued: *Indiana University in Mid-Passage* (1973), *South Carolina, the Grand Tour* (1973), *The Great American Frontier* (1975), *Off at Sunrise: The Overland Journal of Charles Grass Gray* (1976), *Indiana University: The Realization* (1976), *Agrarian Kentucky: That Far-Off Land* (1979), *A History of Laurel County* (1989), and *Footloose in Jacksonian America* (1990). Clark was the primary mover behind the founding of a state archives.

Clark's honors include a Guggenheim fellowship, a merit award from the Association of State and Local History, an Indiana author's award (1971), and eight honorary degrees. He lives in Lexington with his wife, the former Martha Elizabeth Turner,

whom he married in 1933; they have two children, Thomas Bennett and Ruth Elizabeth.

See Frank Steely and H. Lew Wallace, "Thomas D. Clark: A Biographical Sketch," *FCHQ* 60 (July 1986): 293-318; Bill Cunningham, *Kentucky's Clark* (Kuttawa, Ky., 1987); Thomas D. Clark Papers, Special Collections, Margaret I. King Library, University of Kentucky.   H. LEW WALLACE

CLARK, WILLIAM. William Clark, explorer and Indian agent, the youngest brother of Gen. George Rogers CLARK, was born in Caroline County, Virginia, on August 1, 1770, the ninth of ten children of John and Ann (Rogers) Clark. In 1784 the family moved to Louisville. Clark served in the Kentucky militia and was commissioned a lieutenant in the U.S. Army in 1792. He served with Gen. Charles Scott and Gen. Anthony Wayne in the Indian campaigns that took place along the Wabash, Maumee, and Miami rivers in the Northwest Territory, including the Battle of Fallen Timbers. In 1795 he was sent by Wayne to reconnoiter the Spanish post on the east bank of the Mississippi River at Chickasaw Bluffs (now Memphis, Tennessee).

President Thomas Jefferson appointed Clark co-leader of the Lewis and Clark exploration expedition (1803-06). Clark joined Meriwether Lewis in Louisville, and the expedition went to St. Louis and from there to the West. In 1807 Clark returned to St. Louis, where he served as Indian agent for the Louisiana Territory (1807-13) and superintendent of Indian affairs until 1838. Between 1813 and 1821 he also served as governor of the Missouri Territory. Clark died on September 1, 1838, in St. Louis. He was buried with full Masonic and military honors in St. Louis's Bellefontaine Cemetery.

See John Bakeless, *Lewis and Clark: Partners in Discovery* (New York 1947).

KENNETH C. CARSTENS

CLARK COUNTY. Clark County, the fourteenth formed, is located on the eastern edge of the Bluegrass region. It is bordered by Fayette, Bourbon, Montgomery, Powell, Estill, and Madison counties and has an area of 255 square miles. Clark County was formed from sections of Bourbon and Fayette counties in 1792 and was named for Gen. George Rogers Clark, Revolutionary War hero. The county seat is WINCHESTER.

The topography of the county is gently rolling. Tobacco is a major farm crop, and livestock are also raised there. Water sources include the Kentucky River, Red River, Lulbegrud Creek, and Boone's Creek.

Many pioneers passed through nearby Fort Boonesborough in Madison County before establishing permanent settlement in Clark County. At least nineteen pioneer stations or settlements are believed to have been established in the area. Among these were Strode's Station (1779), near Winchester; McGee's Station (ca. 1780), near Becknerville; Holder's Station (1781), on Lower Howard's Creek; and Boyle's Station (ca. 1785), one mile west of Strode's Station. Among the early settlers were a group of forty Baptist families led by Capt. William Bush, who settled on Lower Howard's Creek in 1785. In 1793 the group erected the Old Stone Meeting House. Another pioneer group was the Tracy settlement, founders in the 1790s of a church building that survived well into the twentieth century.

When the Indian threat ended, commercial and agricultural enterprises flourished. Facilities for loading flatboats sprang up along the Kentucky River and its tributaries. County farmers in the early 1800s began importing prime European livestock. Industries such as distilleries and mills thrived throughout the county until 1820, when they began to be concentrated around Winchester. Among the residents of Clark County were Gov. Charles Scott (1808-12); Gov. James Clark (1836-39); Jane Lampton, the mother of Samuel Clemens; and the sculptor Joel T. HART.

During the Civil War, approximately 1,000 men from the county joined either the Confederates or the Union army. In 1862 and again in 1864, Gen. John Hunt Morgan's Confederate cavalry passed through the county. The Elizabethtown, Lexington & Big Sandy Railroad reached Clark County in 1873, followed by the Kentucky Central in 1881, and the Kentucky Union (later abandoned) in 1883. The railroads helped make Winchester a transportation, commercial, and educational center, and gave rise to small service communities such as Hedges Station, six miles east of Winchester, and Ford, a once-prosperous mill town on the Kentucky River.

A number of agricultural changes occurred in the postbellum years through World War II. When Clark County shorthorn cattle were not able to compete with the vast numbers of western cattle being hauled to market by the railroads, several county fortunes were lost and many farmers turned toward burley tobacco as a substitute. Hemp, which was grown to make rope, suffered from foreign competition and vanished as a cash crop around World War I. The crop was brought back during World War II and a processing plant was built in the county. When the war ended, so did the revival of hemp.

In the 1950s and 1960s, industry began moving to the county, mostly around Winchester, aided by the completion of I-64 and the Mountain Parkway, which by the mid-1960s formed a junction near Winchester. By 1986 manufacturing positions accounted for 25 percent of the employed labor force while another 25 percent was employed in other counties, many in nearby Fayette. The county remains a rich agricultural area, with farms occupying 95 percent of the land.

The population of Clark County was 24,090 in 1970; 28,322 in 1980; and 29,496 in 1990.

See Kentucky Heritage Commission, *Survey of Historic Sites in Kentucky: Clark County* (Evansville, Ind., 1979); A. Goff Bedford, *Land of Our Fathers: History of Clark County, Kentucky* (Mt. Sterling, Ky., 1958).   A. GOFF BEDFORD

CLARKE, CHARLES JULIAN. Charles Julian Clarke was born in Franklin County, Kentucky, on December 16, 1836, the son of Joseph and Harriett (Julian) Clarke. He was Kentucky's fourth native architect, behind the Shryock brothers and John McMurtry. Clarke was educated in Kentucky. During the Civil War he worked in Louisville with Henry WHITESTONE and afterward with the Bradshaw brothers, eventually becoming a partner. After Whitestone's retirement in 1880, some considered Clarke Louisville's premier designer. In 1882 he became Kentucky's first architect to join the Western Association of Architects.

Arthur Loomis, a native of Massachusetts, entered the Clarke office in 1876 and became Clarke's chief draftsman in 1885. The 1890 Todd Office Building, designed principally by Loomis, was Louisville's tallest building at the time of its construction. In 1891 Clarke and Loomis established a partnership, which was one of the leading architectural firms in Louisville for the rest of the century. The Theophilus Conrad residence on St. James Court and the George A. Robinson residence are their best residential works; the 1893 Levy Brothers Store at Third and Market Streets is their most noted commercial structure. They also designed the Louisville Medical College of 1891 and the 1893 Manual Training School, both notable institutional buildings. Their Louisville churches include St. Paul's Evangelical, the German Reformed Evangelical, St. Matthew's, and the First Presbyterian at Fourth and York streets. Clark died on March 9, 1908, in Louisville and was buried in the Frankfort Cemetery.   WILLIAM B. SCOTT, JR.

CLARKE, MARCELLUS JEROME ("SUE MUNDY"). Marcellus Jerome Clarke, who under the nom de guerre Sue Mundy was the best known of the Kentucky guerrillas during the Civil War, was born near Franklin, Simpson County, Kentucky, on August 25, 1845 (possibly 1844). He was the son of Brig. Gen. Hector M. and Mary (Hail) Clarke. Both parents died before he was ten, and Clarke was raised by relatives and received a common school education. With his foster brother John Patterson, he enlisted in the Confederate army and was mustered into Company B, 4th Kentucky Infantry, 1st Brigade, at Camp Burnett near Clarksville, Tennessee, on August 25, 1861. Taken prisoner when Grant forced the surrender of Fort Donelson, he was sent to Camp Morton near Indianapolis. He and Patterson escaped and returned to Kentucky, where the Federals captured Patterson, who was wounded and lost his eyesight. Clarke was deeply affected by the incident and vowed never to take a Federal prisoner.

Clarke joined John Hunt Morgan's raiders and fought during many of Morgan's campaigns, first as a scout and later as an artillerist, rising to the rank of captain. After Morgan's death in September of 1864, Clarke returned to Kentucky, where he joined Sam ("One-Armed") Berry, Henry C. Magruder, and others in a guerrilla band that terrorized the state from mid-1864 until the war's end. The origin of the name Sue Mundy is uncertain, although Clarke's shoulder-length hair and almost feminine beauty gave rise to the tale that he was in fact a woman.

Though the band was guilty of shootings and train robberies, as well as the burning of bridges and at least one courthouse, the crimes attributed to the outlaws were exaggerated. Early in 1865, Clarke and his band joined Missouri's "Bloody" Quantrill for a raid in central Kentucky. Shortly thereafter, Clarke and three others were ambushed in Hancock County. The survivors took refuge in a tobacco barn near Webster in Meade County. When the news reached Louisville, troops were sent and on March 12, 1865, Clarke surrendered. He was taken to Louisville, where a military court found him guilty of guerrilla activities. The next day he was hanged at the old fairgrounds before a crowd of thousands, and his body was returned to Simpson County for burial.

See L.L. Valentine, "Sue Mundy of Kentucky," *Register* 62 (July 1964): 175-205; (Oct. 1964): 278-306.   RICHARD TAYLOR

CLARKS RIVER. Clarks River, a sixty-two-mile-long tributary of the Tennessee River, flows through the Jackson Purchase area in far western Kentucky. The East Fork of Clarks River, with its drainage area in Calloway County, flows north through the center of that county and northeast through Marshall County. The West Fork of Clarks River flows north through the western portion of Calloway County and the northeastern corner of Graves County. The East and West forks of the Clarks River merge in McCracken County and flow into the Tennessee River, approximately three miles east of that river's convergence with the Ohio.

See Bob Sehlinger, *A Canoeing and Kayaking Guide to the Streams of Kentucky* (Ann Arbor, Mich., 1978).

CLAY, BRUTUS JUNIUS. Brutus Junius Clay, U.S. congressman, was born July 1, 1808, in Madison County, Kentucky, the second son of Gen. Green and Sally (Lewis) CLAY. The brother of emancipationist Cassius Marcellus CLAY, he himself opposed emancipation. He graduated from Centre College in Danville and by 1837 had settled on more than 1,200 acres of choice land near Paris in Bourbon County. Clay was a member of the Kentucky House of Representatives in 1840 and 1860. For twenty-three years he was the president of the Bourbon County Agricultural Association, and for seven years was president of the Kentucky Agricultural Association. Clay was elected to the U.S. House of Representatives from the 7th Congressional District on the Union Democratic ticket and served from March 4, 1863, to March 3, 1865. He chaired the House Committee on Agriculture. He declared that he upheld the preservation of the Constitution and the Union and "the vigorous prosecution of the war to subdue the rebellion," yet he

consistently opposed abolition and the enlistment of slaves in the army, and in March of 1864 he spoke out against the Freedmen's Bureau bill. He opposed Abraham Lincoln in the 1864 presidential race and voted against the Thirteenth Amendment, which abolished slavery.

Clay married Amelia Field in 1831. They had four children—Martha, Christopher F., Green, and Ezekiel. Amelia died in 1843, and Clay then married her sister, Ann M. Field. They had a son, Cassius Marcellus. Clay died on October 8, 1878, and was buried on the grounds of Auvergne, the Clay home near Paris.

See James Larry Hood, "The Union and Slavery: Congressman Brutus J. Clay of the Bluegrass," *Register* 75 (July 1977): 214-21.

H. EDWARD RICHARDSON

CLAY, CASSIUS MARCELLUS. Cassius Marcellus Clay, emancipationist and diplomat, the son of Gen. Green and Sallie (Lewis) Clay, was born on October 19, 1810, in the Tate's Creek area of Madison County. After attending common schools and the Madison Seminary, he studied under the celebrated teacher Joshua Fry at his home in Garrard County and later enrolled at St. Joseph's College in Bardstown. From Transylvania University in 1831, Clay went to Yale, where in 1832 an antislavery speech by William Lloyd Garrison deeply impressed him and influenced his lifelong opposition to slavery.

Clay returned to Kentucky and completed a law degree at Transylvania. He embraced Henry Clay's American System and was elected state representative from Madison County in 1835. Opposing slavery interests, he was defeated the following year, but returned again in 1837 when, as a Whig, he backed the Bank of Kentucky and funds for public schools.

Clay's outspoken attacks on slavery aroused bitter hostility, especially among the pro-slavery faction of the Whig party, and occasionally involved him in violence. In 1841 he fought a duel with Robert Wickliffe, Jr.; neither was injured. In 1843, at a political meeting, he was attacked by Samuel M. Brown, reputed to be a hired assassin, who shot at Clay and in turn was severely wounded by Clay's bowie knife (a weapon that became part of Clay's colorful legend in Kentucky). Charged with mayhem, Clay was defended by Henry Clay and John Speed Smith and was acquitted on grounds of self-defense.

In the 1844 presidential race, Clay canvassed the North for his cousin Henry under the slogan "Clay, Union, and Liberty!" having by this time freed his unentailed slaves. The next year he began publishing an antislavery paper, the *Lexington True American*. A committee was organized to suppress the publication. Clay prepared to defend his office by force, but was stricken with typhoid fever; during his absence a posse including James B. Clay, Henry's son, packed the newspaper equipment and moved it to Cincinnati. Clay continued for a time to publish the paper in Cincinnati. Two years later he was awarded a judgment of $2,500 against the committee.

After serving as a captain in the Mexican War, Clay returned to Lexington in 1847 and continued to agitate on the slavery question, speaking frequently in the North. He corresponded with abolitionist John G. FEE, invited him to Madison County, donated a ten-acre tract of land, and encouraged Fee to begin the church-school community that became BEREA COLLEGE.

In 1856, Clay campaigned vigorously in the North for the first National Republican party ticket. By 1860 his picture had appeared in *Harper's Weekly* along with those of nine other likely presidential candidates. Clay supported Lincoln for the presidential nomination and after Lincoln's election was appointed minister to Russia in 1861. Before he sailed for Russia, Clay organized a battalion of volunteers to guard the Washington Navy Yard and protect government property in the capital until federal troops arrived.

In 1862 Clay was recalled from Russia and commissioned a major general; at Lincoln's request, he went to Kentucky to sound out opinion regarding the proposed emancipation proclamation and returned with a report that the loyal element would hold. About three weeks later, following the Union victory at Antietam, Lincoln released the historic proclamation.

Clay's second mission to Russia, 1863-69, was an extension of the first. His cultivation of amity between the two nations helped to bring about the U.S. purchase of Alaska.

After his return to the United States in 1869, Clay was a pioneer in the Liberal Republican movement and in 1872 helped to engineer the nomination of Horace Greeley. Later, his dislike of the Radicals led him to bolt the party. As a Democrat, he campaigned in Mississippi against Radical Republican Gov. Adelbert Ames; the famed emancipationist and hero of the North thus became a hero of the South.

Clay married Mary Jane Warfield of Lexington on February 26, 1833. Ten children were born to them: Elisha Warfield; Green; Mary Barr; Sarah Lewis; Cassius Marcellus, Jr. (died at three weeks); Cassius Marcellus, Jr.; Brutus Junius; Laura (CLAY); Flora; and Anne Warfield. After forty-five years of marriage the octogenarian divorced his wife and married Dora Richardson, many years his junior. He died on July 22, 1903, and was buried in Richmond, Kentucky.

See H. Edward Richardson, *Cassius Marcellus Clay: Firebrand of Freedom* (Lexington, Ky., 1976); David L. Smiley, *Lion of White Hall: The Life of Cassius M. Clay* (Madison, Wisc., 1962).

H. EDWARD RICHARDSON

CLAY, GREEN. Green Clay, pioneer and entrepreneur, son of Charles and Martha (Green) Clay, was born August 14, 1757, in Powhatan County,

Virginia, where his family had been prominent since the seventeenth century. He was a second cousin of Henry Clay and brother-in-law of Kentucky Gov. James Garrard (1796-1804). One of the first large-scale landowners in Kentucky, Clay prospered by speculating on the Virginia frontier, buying thousands of acres through agents who traveled into the wilderness at his behest. He moved to Madison County in the 1780s and established himself as one of the richest, most powerful men in the state. He held many political offices, served in the Kentucky legislature, and led a troop of volunteers in the War of 1812. He was a founder of Richmond, Kentucky. Clay's diversified empire included 40,000 acres of Madison County farmland, gristmills, distilleries, taverns, tobacco, slaves, tollroads, a resort, and two large warehouses.

On March 14, 1795, Clay married Sallie Lewis, by whom he fathered many children, including Brutus, Cassius, Elizabeth (wife of John Speed Smith), Sally Ann (wife of Col. Edmund Irvine), and Pauline (wife of William Rodes). Clay died October 31, 1826, and was buried in the Richmond Cemetery.

RICHARD SEARS

CLAY, HENRY. Henry Clay, U.S. senator under several presidents who is remembered for his devotion to the Union, was born in the Slashes section of Hanover County, Virginia, on April 12, 1777. He was the son of John and Elizabeth (Hudson) Clay. His father, a Baptist minister and farmer, died when the child was four years old, and his mother later married Henry Watkins. Clay had a rudimentary education at local schools. When he was fifteen, Clay's mother and stepfather moved to Versailles, Kentucky, leaving him in Virginia. Watkins had secured a place for his stepson as deputy clerk in Virginia's High Court of Chancery, where Clay attracted the attention of the chancellor, George Wythe, a classical scholar and law professor. Clay served as Wythe's copyist for four years while the chancellor directed his studies, giving Clay his mastery of the English language.

In 1796 Clay entered the law office of Robert Brooke, former Virginia governor, and after a year of study was licensed to practice law. In November 1797, Clay moved to Lexington, Kentucky, where he soon became a successful lawyer. On April 11, 1799, he married Lucretia Hart, daughter of Thomas Hart, a prominent Lexington merchant. The couple had eleven children: Henrietta, Theodore Wythe, Thomas Hart, Susan Hart, Anne Brown, Lucretia, Henry, Jr., Eliza, Laura, James Brown, and John Morrison.

In 1799, in the campaign for election for delegates to the Kentucky constitutional convention, Clay championed the cause of gradual emancipation of the state's slaves. In 1803 he was elected to the Kentucky legislature as a Jeffersonian Republican, serving there until 1806, when he was appointed to fill the unexpired term of John Adair in the U.S. Senate. During his short time in the Senate, from November 19, 1806, to March 3, 1807, Clay emerged as a spokesman for a system of federally funded internal improvements such as roads and canals. In 1807 he was again elected to the lower house of the Kentucky legislature and was chosen Speaker of the House on January 11, 1808, following the resignation of William Logan from that post.

Despite the Anglophobia aroused by British attacks on U.S. shipping, Clay successfully fought a bill that would have destroyed Kentucky's common law by forbidding the citation of any British legal decision in the state's courts. Clay devised a compromise by which only British decisions rendered after July 4, 1776, were excluded. In 1809 he introduced a resolution to require members of the state legislature to wear garments of domestic manufacture. A heated debate on this measure with Humphrey Marshall, a leading Federalist, led to a duel in which both men were wounded.

Clay was chosen in 1810 to fill the unexpired term of Buckner Thruston in the U.S. Senate, serving from January 4, 1810, to March 3, 1811. In the next Congress, he won a seat in the U.S. House of Representatives and was elected Speaker in 1811, a position he held for most of the next fourteen years. He quickly became known as a spokesman for the West and leader of the "war hawks"—a group of young men in the House who advocated war with Great Britain. Believing that the British were inciting Indian attacks on the frontier and outraged by their violations of neutral shipping, Clay strongly supported the declaration of war against Britain on June 18, 1812.

President James Madison named Clay as one of five U.S. peace commissioners sent to Ghent in 1814 to negotiate an end to the war. When Clay returned to Kentucky, he was reelected to the U.S. House and the speakership. A more confirmed nationalist as a result of the war and his European travels, he began to formulate the program known as the American System, which included federal aid for internal improvements, a protective tariff for industry, and a national bank. In fact, reversing his 1811 vote against a national bank, Clay in 1816 voted for a bill creating the Second Bank of the United States. The following year he attacked Andrew Jackson for his invasion of Florida, thereby making a lifelong enemy. When Missouri's application for statehood pointed up the question of the extension of slavery, Clay supported a compromise: allowing slavery to continue in Missouri but otherwise prohibiting it north of the 36° 30′ latitude. When the controversy again erupted over Missouri's attempt to prohibit the movement of free blacks into the state, Clay emerged in 1821 as the leader of the second Missouri Compromise, whereby the legislature of Missouri agreed not to deprive a citizen from another state of equal rights and privileges.

In 1821 Clay resigned from the House and returned to Kentucky to recoup financial losses caused by the bankruptcy of a brother-in-law whose notes Clay had endorsed. In 1823 Clay was returned to the House and was again chosen Speaker. His early successes in law, politics, and diplomacy had aroused an ambition to be president of the United States, and the Kentucky legislature, along with the legislatures of several other states, nominated him for that office. In the 1824 presidential contest, Clay ran fourth, after Andrew Jackson, John Quincy Adams, and William H. Crawford. Since no one received a majority, the election was decided by the House of Representatives, where Clay helped elect Adams.

Adams appointed Clay secretary of state, an office that often led to the presidency. Jackson and Crawford supporters immediately charged Clay and Adams with having made a "corrupt bargain," an accusation that dogged Clay for the rest of his political life. Despite their previous dislike of each other at the Ghent peace treaty negotiations, Adams and Clay worked well together. The U.S. State Department had few noted accomplishments under Clay, but he was proud of the commercial treaties negotiated and especially of his instructions to delegates to the 1826 Pan-American Congress.

In 1828 Clay worked actively for Adams's reelection to the presidency; he returned to Kentucky shortly after Andrew Jackson's victory. During the short retirement that followed, Clay maintained a vast political correspondence, with the expectation of being a presidential candidate in 1832. The Kentucky legislature nominated him for that office in 1830 and in 1831 elected him to the U.S. Senate, where his term began on November 10, 1831; reelected, he served to March 31, 1842. Clay led the opposition to the Jackson administration. Knowing the president's opposition to a national bank, he pushed through a bill to recharter the Bank of the United States. Jackson's veto of the measure became one of the main issues in the 1832 presidential campaign, in which Clay lost to his opponent by an electoral vote of 219 to 49.

Clay supported the highly protective tariff of 1832, which precipitated a nullification ordinance by South Carolina. Faced with the possibility of civil war, Clay in February 1833 led the passage of a compromise tariff that gradually lowered the tariff rates in exchange for South Carolina's repeal of the nullification ordinance.

As the various opponents of Jackson coalesced into the Whig party, Clay became their leader. He was able to block Senate ratification of many of the president's nominations for government office; he secured the passage of a bill to distribute to the states the surplus revenue from the sales of public lands, only to have the president pocket-veto it; he led a successful move in the Senate to censure Jackson for his removal of the government's deposits from the Bank of the United States; he opposed, unsuccessfully, the administration's Indian removal policy; and he was able to block congressional authorization for Jackson to make reprisals against the

French for nonpayment of indemnities. When petitions to Congress for the abolition of slavery were being tabled without being referred to a committee, Clay eloquently defended the right of petition, and he opposed a bill to forbid the dissemination of abolitionist literature in the U.S. mail.

The issue of slavery posed the greatest quandary in Clay's personal and political life. A slaveholder, he urged gradual emancipation and colonization in Africa, and he helped found and served for twenty-six years as president of the American Colonization Society. Yet Clay consistently argued that Congress had no right to interfere with slavery in the states where it already existed; his famous words "I had rather be right than be president" were uttered in 1839 in defense of a speech he was about to make in the Senate, attacking abolitionists. That speech and the political maneuvers of Thurlow Weed, editor of New York's *Albany Evening Journal*, cost Clay the presidential nomination at the Whig national convention in 1839. Though angered by this rejection, Clay campaigned for the successful Whig ticket of William Henry Harrison and John Tyler.

Apparently expecting to guide the new Whig administration from the Senate, Clay declined Harrison's offer of the office of secretary of state. He soon found himself in conflict with the president over patronage matters and the question of calling a special session of Congress. When Harrison died a month after taking office and Tyler became president, Clay was fearful of the reception the Whig party's program would receive from Tyler. Although Clay and Tyler had long been friendly, Clay recognized Tyler as a states' rights Democrat rather than a Whig. Clay was able to obtain repeal of the subtreasury system, a higher protective tariff, and a land distribution bill, but collided head-on with the president when Tyler twice vetoed national bank bills. Long before the election of 1844, it was generally conceded that Clay would be the Whig nominee. On March 31, 1842, he retired from the Senate and returned to Kentucky to begin his campaign. The Democratic nominee was James K. Polk, an ardent proponent of the annexation of Texas, a popular cause in the South and West; the North opposed annexation of Texas, where slaveholding was legal. Clay explained his position in three letters that differed in emphasis, one appearing to oppose annexation and the other two seeming to favor the addition of Texas to the Union if it could be done without dishonor or war and with the general consent of the states. The latter viewpoint alienated many opposed to slavery and cost Clay critical support in the North. In a campaign filled with slander and voting fraud, Polk won 170 electoral votes to Clay's 105 but had only a 38,000-vote popular majority.

In retirement, Clay opposed the declaration of war against Mexico that came soon after the annexation of Texas. His son Henry Clay, Jr., was one of the war's casualties. Although Clay still hoped for the presidency in 1848, he was defeated at the Whig nominating convention by Mexican War hero Zachary Taylor. In the crisis over the extension of slavery into the areas of California and New Mexico acquired from Mexico, Clay was returned to the Senate on March 4, 1849. To settle the controversy, he introduced a series of resolutions that became law as the Compromise of 1850, thanks to the efforts of Stephen A. Douglas. It made California a free state, opened the new territories of Utah and New Mexico to popular sovereignty, and redrew the Texas boundary. His health deteriorating, Clay returned to Washington, D.C., in December 1851 but made only one appearance in the Senate before his death in the city on June 29, 1852. He was buried in the Lexington Cemetery.

See Glyndon G. Van Deusen, *The Life of Henry Clay* (Boston 1937); Merrill D. Peterson, *The Great Triumvirate, Webster, Clay and Calhoun* (New York 1987).   MELBA PORTER HAY

CLAY, LAURA. One of the controversial figures in the national women's rights movement, Laura Clay was born at White Hall, her family's estate near Richmond, Kentucky, on February 9, 1849. Her parents were Cassius M. CLAY, the noted antislavery activist, and Mary Jane (Warfield) Clay, both of prominent Bluegrass families. Laura Clay was educated at Lexington's Sayre School, where she graduated in 1865. She then spent a year at Miss Hoffman's finishing school in New York City and later studied at the universities of Michigan and Kentucky for short periods. She supported herself and financed her long public career with her income as a "practical farmer," managing a three-hundred-acre farm in Madison County, which she leased from her father in 1873 and owned after his death in 1903.

Clay's commitment to women's rights arose from her parents' bitter separation in 1869 and divorce in 1878, when she became aware that the property and legal rights of Kentucky women, especially those married, were woefully unprotected. After considering careers in teaching, law, and the missionary field, Clay decided to devote her life to the woman's movement. In 1888 she took the leading role in organizing the KENTUCKY EQUAL RIGHTS ASSOCIATION (KERA), which she served as president until 1912. Although the growth of the association was slow, its lobbying in Frankfort by the mid-1890s had won a number of legislative and educational victories, including protection of married women's property and wages, a requirement for women physicians in state female insane asylums, and the admission of women to a number of male colleges.

As an officer in both the Women's Christian Temperance Union and the Kentucky Federation of Women's Clubs, Clay persuaded the groups to join the KERA in advocating additional benefits for women and children at the turn of the century. Their efforts secured legislation that provided for a women's dormitory at the University of Kentucky, established juvenile courts and detention homes, and raised the age of consent from twelve to sixteen years. Clay and other women activists saw the vote as the capstone of their movement. With the state legislature's grant of school suffrage in 1912, they won a partial victory.

During the 1890s, Clay became the best-known southern suffragist and the South's leading voice in the councils of the National American Woman Suffrage Association (NAWSA). Her efforts were largely responsible for the establishment of suffrage societies in nine of the former Confederate states. Clay addressed constitutional conventions in Mississippi and Louisiana and managed an unsuccessful NAWSA effort to add women's suffrage to the South Carolina constitution of 1895. In 1896 Clay was elected auditor of the NAWSA, a post she held for fifteen years. She maintained a position of moderation and conciliation on the NAWSA official board in matters of both race and personality clashes. As an unpaid NAWSA field worker, she also directed suffrage campaigns in Oregon, Oklahoma, and Arizona. While chair of the association's membership committee, she introduced recruiting innovations that almost tripled the number of members, from 17,000 in 1905 to 45,501 in 1907. In 1911 Clay lost her bid for reelection as auditor, following a dispute between the southern and western suffragists and those from the East over administrative and organizational matters. Contrary to some accounts, neither the race question nor the issue of the federal amendment versus the state route to enfranchisement figured in this dispute. Despite her removal from the official board of the NAWSA, Clay for a number of years chaired association committees, contributed to fund drives, and worked in state suffrage campaigns.

In 1916 Clay was elected vice-president-at-large of a new organization, the Southern States Woman Suffrage Association, founded to win the vote through state enactment. Clay saw this organization as an auxiliary, not a rival, of the NAWSA, whose activities she continued to support. It was not until 1919, when the U.S. Congress enacted the Nineteenth Amendment, that Clay withdrew from the NAWSA, turned her energies to securing a state suffrage bill in Kentucky, and began openly to oppose the federal bill. She based her opposition to it on states' rights, asserting that the Nineteenth Amendment was a vast and unneeded extension of federal power. A product of her time, Clay was a believer in Anglo-Saxon superiority but was paternalistic, rather than Negrophobic, in her attitudes.

After the ratification of the suffrage amendment, Clay continued to work for women's rights and the involvement of women in civic life. She helped organize the Democratic Women's Club of Kentucky, served as a delegate to the Democratic National Convention in 1920, and ran unsuccessfully for the state Senate in 1923. A firm believer in women's church rights, she was instrumental in winning vestry and synod eligibility for women in the Lexington diocese of the Episcopal church. In the 1928 presidential campaign, she made a number of speeches for the Democratic nominee, Alfred E. Smith, and vigorously condemned national prohibi-

tion. When Kentucky voted for the repeal of prohibition in 1933, Clay served as a member and temporary chair of the ratifying convention in Frankfort. Clay died on June 29, 1941, and was buried in the Lexington Cemetery.

See Paul E. Fuller, *Laura Clay and the Woman's Rights Movement* (Lexington, Ky., 1975).

PAUL E. FULLER

CLAY, LUCRETIA (HART). Lucretia (Hart) Clay, mistress of the ASHLAND estate for fifty years, was born in Hagerstown, Maryland, on March 18, 1781, the daughter of Col. Thomas and Susanna (Gray) Hart. She moved to Kentucky with her parents in 1784. She married Henry Clay on April 11, 1799. Hostess to many of the great figures of the time, she also superintended the large family farm in Fayette County, conducting its affairs with vigor and good judgment. The Clays had eleven children, five sons and six daughters, seven of whom reached adulthood. Lucretia Clay died on April 6, 1864, and is buried beside her husband in the family vault in the Lexington Cemetery.

See Rachael Sleasman Schwartz, *Lucretia Hart, the Hagerstown Girl Who Became the Wife of Henry Clay* (Hagerstown, Md., 1937).

FRANCES KELLER BARR

CLAYBROOK V. OWENSBORO. *Claybrook v. Owensboro*, a suit brought by black citizens of Owensboro in 1883, challenged the 1866 Kentucky law setting aside taxes collected from "negroes and mulattoes" for the support of black schools. The suit was touched off when the General Assembly in 1880 authorized the establishment of a black school in Owensboro to serve the five hundred black children of that town. A group of black parents, citing the equal protection clause of the Fourteenth Amendment to the U.S. Constitution, contended that the black school was inferior, thus denying equal educational opportunity to their children. The suit claimed that the black school operated for only "about three months each year," with "only one inferior school-house," and "facilities of every kind very inferior to those of the white children." Judge John W. Barr of the Federal District Court for Western Kentucky agreed with the plaintiffs, and enjoined the Owensboro school board from paying out the percentage of money in the common school fund equal to the percentage of black children in the system, thus threatening to shut down the white schools. Since many other towns in Kentucky had a similar arrangement, the decision threatened the entire state school system. The result was that the General Assembly, on March 18, 1884, repealed the act establishing the separate funding system and placed all tax money in the hands of the public school board. This law was the first step toward the improvement of black education in Kentucky, and a gigantic first step for blacks on the road to full equality.

See Lee A. Dew and Aloma W. Dew, *Owensboro: The City on the Yellow Banks* (Bowling

Green, Ky., 1988); Victor B. Howard, *Black Liberation in Kentucky* (Lexington, Ky., 1983).

LEE A. DEW

CLAY COUNTY. Clay County, the forty-seventh county in order of formation, is located in the foothills of the Cumberland Mountains of southeast Kentucky. The county is bordered by Jackson, Owsley, Perry, Leslie, Bell, Knox, and Laurel counties. Created from Madison, Floyd, and Knox counties on April 1, 1807, Clay County later ceded much of its land to form parts of Jackson, Owsley, Leslie, Lee, Breathitt, Knott, Perry, and Harlan counties. It reached its present size, 471 square miles, in 1880. It was named for Gen. Green Clay, a Madison County legislator and early Kentucky surveyor. Most of the heavily wooded county, approximately 61,000 acres, falls within the Redbird Purchase Unit of the Daniel Boone National Forest. Tobacco, timber, corn, and hay, are harvested. The county seat is MANCHESTER.

An early settler, James Collins, built a log cabin around 1798 at the headwaters of Goose Creek, a tributary of the south fork of the Kentucky River. Salt reserves and fertile grasslands attracted settlers to the area as they had attracted large game animals, making a bountiful hunting ground for prehistoric Native Americans and possibly the Cherokee during the early historic era. During the nineteenth century Clay County was the leading producer of SALT in the state. So vital was salt to frontier life and trade that Daniel Boone offered a plan to reroute the Wilderness Road to pass the Goose Creek salt works near Manchester. Boone did not get the contract, and the area was left without suitable roadways for the next century. In 1811 the Kentucky River was made navigable to the confluence of Clay County's Goose Creek and Redbird River (named for a Cherokee chief who, according to legend, was thrown into the river after being slain for his furs). A canal system proposed during the 1820s and 1830s to link the Ohio River to the Atlantic Ocean at Charleston and Savannah was to pass by the Goose Creek salt works to expand its market. Salt production peaked at more than 200,000 bushels per year between 1835 and 1845.

The Civil War divided Clay County, and control of the area shifted between the two sides. In September 1862 Union troops passed through on their retreat across Kentucky from the Cumberland Gap to the Ohio River. The following month, fearing that control of the valuable salt works would again fall to the Confederates, the Union ordered all production sites destroyed. Residents were permitted to take salt for their personal needs, and the owners were promised reimbursement for their losses. In 1873, however, President Ulysses S. Grant vetoed a bill for compensation, arguing that the destruction had been a military necessity. Only four salt facilities survived the war, the last of which finally closed in 1908. A series of feuds that followed the war created an impression of lawlessness.

Clay County lost contact with the outside world after the salt works closed. Transportation into the county was too poor to allow expansion. Logging of hard- and softwoods had started as early as 1810, but until 1925 the only means of transportation was rafting the logs. Several articles written in the late nineteenth century advertised Clay County's availability for industry and enterprise, but the stumbling block was lack of transportation. In 1827 Clay County granted public lands to construct highways, but roads were rough and often little more than expanded animal trails. Each landowner, however, was obligated to give six days of service each year to road maintenance, primarily on nearby roads. Gradually federal, state, and county roads crisscrossed the county. In 1971 the 68.5-mile Daniel Boone Parkway opened and linked Manchester to I-75 at London to the west and Hazard to the east.

In 1914 the Louisville & Nashville Railroad (now CSX Transportation) extended service to Clay County. Rail service to eastern Kentucky was not considered profitable until the region's extensive coal fields began to be developed, after the turn of the century. Rail service expanded in the early twentieth century, but has since been curtailed and now serves only a few of the remaining coal tipples.

Clay County has no urban areas. Manchester, the county seat, has only 1,634 persons. Other communities include Oneida and Burning Springs. Oneida Baptist Institute, founded in 1898 by a former instructor at Berea College, is patterned after Berea's work-study program. Among its former students is Bert T. Combs, Kentucky governor (1959-63). Burning Springs, discovered in 1798, was named for its ignitable release of natural gas. After commercial development in 1907, reserves there for several years supplied much of Lexington's natural gas needs.

Since the demise of salt making, Clay County has been mired in poverty. Over 40 percent of its 22,752 citizens lived beneath the poverty line in 1990, with a mean household income of $11,503. Employment opportunities in the area are limited; fewer than 3,000 persons held jobs for fifty weeks during 1980, and in 1986 the unemployment rate was 15 percent.

Although coal mining is not as extensive as in the 1970s, it still provides over a third of the local industrial jobs. Many residents recall the Hyden mining disaster of December 1970, which claimed twenty-nine Clay County lives. The county has some light industry, such as Mid-South Electronics and Kentucky Mountain Industries, and the Daniel Boone Development Council is active in employment promotion. The county anticipates an expanded economy when a medium-security federal prison opens in 1992.

As a corollary to the area's long years of isolation, education has suffered: only 27.7% of the residents over the age of twenty-five have finished high school and the median number of years of schooling is 8.5. This is an ironic turn in a region whose pioneering families brought extensive culture with them from Virginia and North Carolina. Attempts to treat the problem began with the MOON-LIGHT SCHOOLS of the early twentieth century. Recently the General Education Development program has been emphasized.

The population of the county was 18,481 in 1970; 22,750 in 1980; and 21,746 in 1990.

See Mr and Mrs. Kelly Morgan, eds., *History of Clay County, Kentucky, 1767-1976* (Manchester, Ky., 1978).   MARY LATTA LEE

CLAY INDUSTRY. Kentucky's argillaceous soils, clays, and shales, composed mainly of the clay minerals kaolinite, montmorillonite, and illite, have long provided the raw materials for the commonwealth's clay industry. The industry extracts raw source materials and makes ceramic and nonceramic clay products. Ceramic clays retain their molded shape on firing and are used in pottery, structural products, and refractory products.

Kentucky's aboriginal mound builders first used clay to fabricate pottery, 1,000 to 3,000 years ago. Small potteries established by European settlers during the nineteenth century were generally crude, short-lived facilities that produced earthenware and stoneware goods for local trade. Kentucky's commercial potteries in 1990 produced artware, dinnerware, and stoneware from a mixture of native and imported clays. BYBEE POTTERY, established in Madison County in 1809, is the oldest operating commercial pottery in Kentucky.

The first structural clay goods made in Kentucky were bricks, hand-formed and fired in Lincoln County in 1786. Small brick and tile plants utilizing a variety of local clay materials sprang up across Kentucky during the nineteenth century. Between 1890 and 1930, at least fifty structural clay firms created a diverse assortment of brick, pipe, tile, and terra cotta, generally fired in beehive kilns. The seven structural clay producers still operating in Kentucky fire their products in energy-efficient tunnel kilns. An innovative structural clay product—expanded shale lightweight aggregate, fired in rotary kilns—has been manufactured in Bullitt County since 1953 by Kentucky Solite Corp.

Refractory fire and flint clays, resistant to high temperatures, are composed almost exclusively of kaolinite. These clays often occur as the seatrock of coal beds and are best developed in the Olive Hill district of northeastern Kentucky; some ball clays in the Jackson Purchase are refractory. Fire clay was probably first used as mortar and hearth liner in the old iron furnaces of Kentucky, dating back to 1791. A fledgling fire brick and refractory clay mining industry existed in Boyd and Greenup counties before the Civil War. Following completion of the rail link between Louisville and Ashland in 1883, the industry gained a worldwide reputation among consumers of high-grade refractory products. As many as a dozen fire brick companies and seventy-five refractory materials producers operated during the 1920s. Refractory clay production peaked in the early 1950s and has since steadily declined, reflecting structural and technological changes in the steel industry. Three refractory clay

products establishments and a few clay mines were operating in northeastern Kentucky in 1990.

Ball clay, composed mostly of disordered kaolinite, is highly plastic and easily dispersible. It is an ivory-to-white-burning substance that enhances the workability and green strength of ceramic bodies. Because there are few ball clay deposits in the world, Kentucky's extensive reserves in the Jackson Purchase are significant. Mining of these deposits may date back to the 1820s, but major commercial extraction did not begin until 1890. Between 1890 and 1930 at least a dozen firms worked the clay pits, located primarily in Graves County; two major companies operated there in 1990. Production of Kentucky ball clay has shown steady growth, with rapid expansion during World War I. Used in minor amounts by the ceramic industries of Kentucky, it is mined and processed primarily for export purposes. Its versatility has given Kentucky ball clay wide use in the manufacture of artware, stoneware, whiteware, sanitary ware, tile, enamels, insulators, abrasives, and refractories.

Nonceramic clay materials form a small but important segment of Kentucky's clay industry. Alluvial clay deposits mined since 1906 by Kosmos Cement Company for manufacturing Portland cement are the most important of these. Ball clays are employed nonceramically as fillers in rubber, paper, and plastic products, and Devonian black shale is mined for highway subbase materials.

See Heinrich Ries, "The Clay Deposits of Kentucky," *Kentucky Geological Survey* Series 6, 1922; Joseph K. Roberts and Benjamin Gildersleeve, *Geology and mineral resources of the Jackson Purchase region, Kentucky*, Kentucky State Dept. of Mines and Minerals, Geological Div., Bulletin 8, 1945; Willard R. Jillson, *The Clays of Kentucky*, Kentucky Geological Survey Series 6, Pamphlet 9, 1926.   EUGENE J. AMARAL

CLAY'S FERRY BRIDGE. In 1792 Valentine Stone received a license from the Madison County government to operate Stone's ferry across the Kentucky River between Fayette County and Madison County. In 1798 Stone sold the ferry to Gen. Green Clay, who gave the crossing its name. In 1865, Brutus J. Clay and R.C. Rogers sold the ferry to the Richmond and Lexington Turnpike Company. In 1869 the company completed a low-level wrought iron toll bridge at Clay's Ferry. In 1897 Fayette and Madison counties bought out the turnpike company, but not the toll bridge. The company operated the bridge until 1906, when W.S. Moberly, James Erskine, and Thomas J. Smith purchased it at public auction for $4,755.

The three new proprietors organized the Clay's Ferry Bridge Company and operated the bridge until April 1, 1929, when the state purchased the bridge for $200,000. On December 24, 1930, the state government removed the toll gate on the bridge, which at that time was part of U.S. 25. In August 1946 the Kentucky State Highway Department completed a new bridge at Clay's Ferry, a steel and concrete three-span continuous deck-type bridge with Warren trusses. At the time of its completion, it was the seventh highest bridge in the United States. In 1963 a twin-span bridge was constructed to carry Interstate 75 traffic.

CLEAR CREEK BAPTIST BIBLE COLLEGE.
Clear Creek Baptist Bible College is the creation of L.C. Kelly, pastor of the First Baptist Church in Pineville, Kentucky. In 1923, when he discovered that only three of 125 Baptist preachers in his area had as much as a high school education, he was determined to set up a school for the clergy. With the help of a group of businessmen from Pineville and Middlesboro, Kelly bought four hundred acres of land at the union of Little Clear Creek and Big Clear Creek in Bell County. The first Bible school for mountain preachers was held there from July 18 to August 1, 1926, and for the next seventeen years Clear Creek hosted summer institutes for the preachers of southern Appalachia.

In 1943 the school first offered a three-year diploma program. On April 26, 1946, four of the fifty-six students became the first graduates of the Clear Creek Mountain Preachers Bible School. The school was chartered by the state in 1946 and became an educational institution of the Kentucky Baptist Convention in the same year. Kelly retired after twenty-eight years as president of the school, and was succeeded by D.M. Aldridge (1954-82), Leon D. Simpson (1982-88), and Bill D. Whittaker (1988-).

The school gained full accreditation from the American Association of Bible Colleges in 1986 and changed its name to Clear Creek Baptist Bible College to reflect its expanded program. The curriculum leads to a bachelor of arts degree with a major in Bible studies; other options are a three-year diploma, an associate degree in church secretarial work, and one- and two-year certificates in local church leadership. In 1990 the student body totaled approximately 175, averaging thirty-one years old; most were married, with children. The campus includes some fifty-five buildings on seven hundred acres adjoining Pine Mountain State Resort Park, five miles from Pineville. Many of the buildings were constructed of stones that students gathered from Clear Creek.

BILL D. WHITTAKER

CLEMENTS, EARLE CHESTER.
Earle Chester Clements, governor during 1947-50, was born October 22, 1896, in Morganfield, Kentucky, to Aaron Waller and Sallie Anna (Tuley) Clements. His study of agriculture at the University of Kentucky was interrupted in 1917 when he enlisted in the infantry. Promoted to captain, he was assigned to teach military science. After the war he worked in the Texas oil fields, then returned to Kentucky to farm, coach football at Morganfield High School, and to serve as deputy sheriff under his father's command. He received a thorough grounding in the Union County government, as sheriff (1922-26), county clerk (1926-34), and county judge (1934-42). In 1927 he

married Sara Blue; they had one daughter. In 1935 Clements refused to be A.B. Chandler's gubernatorial campaign chairman because he had already agreed to work in that capacity for Thomas S. Rhea. The resultant Clements-Chandler split helped shape Democratic politics in the state for decades.

Clements was elected to the state Senate in 1941; by 1944 he was majority leader. He virtually wrote the state budget that year, when the legislature was unable to pass a budget bill. Elected to two terms in the U.S. House of Representatives (1945-48), Clements usually voted as a liberal Democrat. In the 1947 Democratic primary for governor, he defeated Harry Lee Waterfield by some 30,000 votes, then won an easy victory over Republican Eldon S. Dummit, 387,795 to 287,756. Clements resigned as governor on November 27, 1950, to seek a U.S. Senate seat, which he won by defeating Republican Charles I. Dawson, 300,276 to 256,876. He served from November 27, 1950 to January 3, 1957. Soon he became assistant floor leader to Sen. Lyndon B. Johnson. Denied support from the Chandler faction in 1956, Clements lost a close race for reelection as senator to Republican Thruston B. Morton. During 1957-59, Clements was executive director of the U.S. Senate Democratic Reelection Committee. After serving during 1959-60 as state highway commissioner, Clements returned to Washington, D.C., as a maritime lobbyist, then held several executive positions with the American Tobacco Institute before his 1981 retirement to Morganfield, Kentucky. He died on March 12, 1985, and was buried at Morganfield.

As governor, Clements emphasized efficient administration, careful planning, and long-term economic development. During his administration, only New York spent more money on state park development, and only Texas spent more on its roads. The new Kentucky Agriculture and Industrial Development Board aggressively sought industries for the state and pushed construction of the State Fair and Exposition Center in Louisville. A nonpartisan Legislative Research Commission brought expert knowledge to the legislative process, and the Kentucky Building Commission gave central direction to the building program. A nonpartisan Kentucky State Police force replaced the patronage-riddled highway patrol, and the inefficient Insurance Commission was reorganized. Constitutional amendments raised to a more realistic level the maximum salaries for state employees and allowed a 15 percent increase in the Minimum Foundation Program to aid the poorest school systems. However, Clements was unable to do much to end segregation in the state's graduate and professional schools, and a conservative legislature blocked his attempts to control strip mining operations and to establish statewide pension and civil service programs. Overall, Clements's administration was one of the most progressive in the state's history.

See Malcolm E. Jewell and Everett W. Cunningham, *Kentucky Politics* (Lexington, Ky., 1968); Gary Luhr and Thomas H. Syvertsen, "The Governor Who Broke New Ground," *Rural Kentuckian* 37 (May 1983).   LOWELL H. HARRISON

CLIMATE. The middle latitude and interior location of Kentucky moderate its climate in comparison with that of coastal or deeply interior states. The occasional extremely hot or cold weather is usually short-lived, and snow cover of more than a few days is uncommon. Seasons are distinct and about equal in length.

The spatial variation in temperature is produced primarily by latitude. The annual mean temperature varies from 58° Fahrenheit in the Purchase area of Kentucky's western tip to 52° in the north. January's average temperature ranges from 36° in the south to only 29° in the north. There is less difference in July, with an average of 78° in the south and 75° in the north. Temperatures above 100° are uncommon in summer, and on only a few days does the temperature drop below zero in winter. The growing season (the period between the last freezing temperature in spring and the first one in fall) varies from an average of about 210 days in the southwest to about 170 in the eastern highlands.

The distribution of precipitation over Kentucky varies distinctly with latitude. The annual average rainfall diminishes from more than fifty-two inches in the south, along the Tennessee border, to less than forty-one inches in the north, along the Ohio River. There is considerable seasonality in Kentucky's precipitation patterns, amounts, and occurrence. During winter, polar air masses from the Northwest interact with tropical air masses from the Gulf of Mexico, the primary source of water vapor, to produce rain in typical frontal uplift patterns. The approaching cold air masses are usually well modified by the time they arrive; snowfall is common in winter, but the amounts are typically small. Spring, with March as the peak month, is the season of greatest precipitation over all but the Bluegrass region of central Kentucky. The Bluegrass has its heaviest rainfall during July, which for the other areas marks a secondary peak in a bimodal annual distribution. Most of the spring rains are produced by thunderstorms associated with cold fronts and squall lines, and as summer progresses, moist, unstable maritime tropical air masses often generate afternoon thunderstorms.

Fall is Kentucky's dry season, in terms of both the number of rain days and the amount of precipitation; this is caused by the westward expansion of the Bermuda high for extended periods. The driest month is October, with an average of less than three inches of precipitation. A drought of some duration and intensity occurs somewhere in Kentucky about one year out of ten, although the timing, intensity, and duration are unpredictable. Droughts hit Kentucky in 1854, 1881, 1894, 1901, 1904, 1930, 1931, 1936, 1954, 1986, and 1988. Kentucky endured its most prolonged period of below-normal water supply in 1930 and 1931, when Bowling Green had eighteen consecutive months of below-normal rainfall. There was no measurable rainfall in Mayfield in July 1930, when temperatures soared above 100° F. The 1930 heat wave peaked at 114° in Greensburg on July 28. Drought conditions exist independently of temperature and may occur even in winter, but higher temperatures compound the effects because evaporation rates increase with heat.

In the fall of 1930, Murray went forty-eight consecutive days without rain. That year the Bluegrass experienced the most severe drought recorded in the state. But as population growth puts greater demands on the water supply, droughts become more serious. The 1988 drought created serious problems in the rapidly growing Bluegrass region, and the need for alternate water sources for Lexington became apparent.

Flooding, generally a late winter or springtime occurrence, is often the result of slow-moving cyclones and remnants of hurricanes that move slowly inland from the Gulf of Mexico. Local flash flooding can occur from severe thunderstorms, particularly in mountainous eastern Kentucky.

Surface winds in Kentucky are light, with average speeds generally less than ten miles per hour. The prevailing wind direction during the year is from the south-southwest. Variations occurring as cold fronts during the winter cause temporary wind shifts to the north. During the late summer and early fall months, calm conditions dominate for as much as 20 to 30 percent of the time.

The moderate and favorable climate of Kentucky has affected economic development by allowing the production of a wide variety of crops and a range of industrial, commercial, and recreational activities.

See Thomas R. Karl, et al., *Statewide Average Climatic History, Kentucky 1889-1982, Climatology Series 6-1* (Asheville, N.C. 1983); Norman J. Rosenberg, *North American Droughts* (Boulder, Colo., 1978).   GLEN CONNER

CLINTON. Clinton, the county seat of Hickman County, in the Jackson Purchase region, is located in the center of the county at the intersection of U.S. 51 and KY 58 along the Illinois Central Gulf Railroad. The origin of the town's name is unknown, but it may have been named to honor a Capt. Clinton who was stationed there in 1826. The city, founded in 1828, became the county seat in the next year, succeeding Columbus, nine miles away. Stephen Ray donated the land for the public square, on which a log structure was built in 1830 to serve as the first courthouse. It was replaced in 1832 by a brick building, which at that time was the only brick courthouse in Kentucky west of the Tennessee River. In 1884 it was replaced by a Victorian-style brick courthouse. Although damaged by tornado in 1917, the building is still in use.

The city became an educational center for the area. One of the first high schools in the Jackson Purchase region, the Clinton Seminary, was established in 1846. Clinton Academy was incorporated in 1850; CLINTON COLLEGE, a Baptist school, existed from 1873 until 1913; and MARVIN COLLEGE, a Methodist school, existed from 1884 until 1922. Among the alumni of Marvin College was Alben W. Barkley, vice-president of the United States, who graduated from the school in 1897. Mid-Continent Baptist College was established as West Kentucky Baptist Bible Institute in Clinton in 1949 and operated for eight years before moving to Mayfield.

In 1873 the Illinois Central Railroad linked Clinton to commercial centers such as Mobile, Alabama, to the south and St. Louis to the west. The railroad brought jobs and culture, and by the turn of the century the city had an opera house and was on the chautauqua circuit. Telephones, water, and electricity had come to Clinton by that time as well. The *Hickman County Gazette*, a local newspaper founded in 1853, was bought in 1934 by Harry Lee WATERFIELD, who published the Clinton-based paper for over thirty-eight years. The newspaper helped launch his political career: Waterfield twice served as lieutenant governor of Kentucky (1955-59, 1963-67). The Hickman County Library was established in 1917 by the Clinton Woman's Club.

Clinton has an agrarian economy and some light industries, including Garan, Inc., and Harper's Country Hams. The sixth-class city has two banks, a savings and loan institution, and ten churches. The population of the city was 1,618 in 1970; 1,720 in 1980; and 1,547 in 1990.

VIRGINIA HONCHELL JEWELL

CLINTON COLLEGE. Clinton College was established in 1873 in the county seat of Hickman County. The college was to be a school for girls in the tradition of Clinton Female Seminary, which had operated there in the 1830s. Founder Willis ("Father") White was pastor of the First Baptist Church, a county judge, and moderator of West Union Baptist Association, which owned the school. The first president was T.N. Wells; Amanda Melvina Hicks, a cousin of Abraham Lincoln, was assistant principal. Hicks was president from 1880 to 1894. The school became coeducational in its early days, and enrollment often exceeded two hundred. Some graduates did advanced work at Wellesley College.

After the West Kentucky Baptist Association was formed in 1893, it took responsibility for the school. The trustees were from several Baptist associations in the Jackson Purchase. After Hicks's resignation in 1894, several men served one or two years each as president. Statistics reported to the General Association of Baptists in Kentucky after 1899 showed declining enrollment. In 1915 the school closed, and the property was sold to the county for public education. The original columns of a main building became part of a grade school built on the same site. R. CHARLES BLAIR

CLINTON COUNTY. The eighty-fifth county in order of formation, Clinton County is in the south-central portion of the state along the Tennessee line. Bordered by Cumberland, Russell, and Wayne counties, Clinton has an area of 196 square miles. The county was formed on February 20, 1835, from portions of Cumberland and Wayne counties, and is said to be named for New York's Gov. DeWitt Clinton. The county seat is ALBANY.

The county's topography is predominantly hilly with level, fertile bottomlands. Poplar Mountain has the highest elevation, 1,700 feet. Farms occupy 70 percent of the land area, with 54 percent of them in cultivation. Ten percent of the land is owned by the federal government. Clinton ranks fifty-fourth among counties in agricultural receipts from tobacco, hay, corn, and vegetables. Limestone and dolomite are found in the county, as are oil reserves. In 1819, Adam Beaty hit oil while drilling for salt water on the Little South Fork of the Cumberland River. Thirteen separate oil- and gas-producing strata are found in Clinton County. On September 10, 1945, the Lether Hay No. 1 well on Ill Will Creek came in as a gusher at 1,055 feet. Flames leaped three hundred feet into the sky. In 1989 the county's crude oil production was 71,952 barrels. Water sources for the county are the Cumberland and Wolf rivers and Lake Cumberland and Dale Hollow reservoirs.

Among the early settlers were Simon Barber and his family from Albany, New York, who settled where Albany, Kentucky, is now located. In 1798 Thomas Stockton was granted two hundred acres on Spring Creek. Harriette Arnow, in *Flowering of the Cumberland* (1963), wrote of a school in the Stockton's Valley section in 1796. Some of the agrarian settlers ran barges of rafts along the river to take out surplus goods and bring in supplies.

Champ Ferguson, a guerrilla with Confederate leanings, and Thomas Bramlette, the twenty-second Kentucky governor (1863-67), were natives of Clinton.

The county's leading industries are clothing manufacturers, Sutton Shirt and Winningham Apparel. Other industries include lumber, crushed stone, and cheese. Dale Hollow Lake attracts boaters and fishermen. In 1988, tourism expenditures totaled $17.8 million, a 4 percent increase over the previous year. Each October the week-long Foothills Festival is held. Clinton County is served by U.S. 127.

The population of Clinton County was 8,174 in 1970; 9,321 in 1980; and 9,135 in 1990.

See Jack Ferguson, *Early Times in Clinton County* (n.p., 1986). RON D. BRYANT

CLOONEY, ROSEMARY. Rosemary Clooney, singing star of radio, motion pictures, and television, was born on May 23, 1928, in Maysville, Kentucky, to Andrew Clooney, Jr. (son of the mayor of Maysville), and Frances (Guilfoyle) Clooney. The family moved to Cincinnati when Rosemary and her sister Betty were teenagers. The sisters began singing together on Cincinnati radio station WLW, and Tony Pastor, a popular band leader, hired them as featured vocalists. Paramount Studios offered Clooney a screen test; when her first movie, *The Stars Are Singing*, was produced in 1953, she arranged to have the premier showing in

Maysville. Always a booster of her hometown, where a street bears her name, she gave a benefit concert there in August 1983. In 1953 she married José Ferrer, the actor, and had five children: Miquel, Maria, Gabriel, Moncita, and Rafael. Divorced in 1962, Clooney suffered an emotional breakdown in 1968, but she fought her way back to a productive resumption of her career. Clooney and her brother Nick are co-chairs of the Betty Clooney Foundation for the Brain-Injured.

See Rosemary Clooney, *This for Remembrance* (Chicago 1977).   JEAN W. CALVERT

COAL MINING. Coal mining in Kentucky divides into five eras: 1790-1870, coal shipped by river; 1870-1900, extensive uses of coal, coming of railroads and unions; 1900-1932, increasing mechanization and challenges to safety through expanding production, decline of unionization, more outside control; 1933-69, dominance and then decline of unionization, loss of major markets, ascendancy of truck mines, growing mechanization, severe drops in employment; 1970- , growth of surface mining and its regulation, comprehensive federal safety laws, boom followed by leveling out and fewer mines, advent of computer.

Mining began in Lee County. Early concern for the navigability of rivers was tied to coal production, and failure to finance improvements crippled the industry's growth until the railroad arrived. By 1830, mining had spread to northeastern Kentucky and present-day Clay, McCreary, and Muhlenberg counties. The area that is now McCreary became the state leader up to the Civil War, employing 250 to 300 miners in 1833-34, with mining a seasonal activity. Coal was shipped on rafts to Nashville.

Coal became a legislative issue in the mid-1820s, and David Trimble, an operator from Greenup, chaired the first investigation of the state's mineral resources, leading to initial geological reconnaissance by William Mather of New York in 1838-39. Earlier there had been a limited investigation of the Cumberland River and other streams both by the U.S. Army Corps of Engineers and the state Board of Internal Improvements. However, the latter's ambitious plans to canalize rivers were thwarted by national economic difficulties and unwise local decisions.

In the antebellum period immigrant miners, mostly from the British Isles, arrived. The first known coal camp was built at Peach Orchard in Lawrence County. There was extensive talk of railroad construction, and some enabling bills were enacted by the legislature. Mather returned in 1852-53 to assist David Owen and others in publishing a four-volume geological inventory. Samuel Casey and associates began mining in Union County. An 1856 law incorporating the Hopkins County Mining and Manufacturing Company authorized the sale of $5 million in stock, but the Civil War frustrated the project. The leading Kentucky coal-producing county in the 1860 U.S. Census was Union, where 390 miners were paid a total of $168,000 in 1859.

Some miners were slaves, others immigrants, the latter including some involved in what appear to have been union activities. The Civil War seems to have restricted but not entirely stopped mining. After the war came construction of a railroad from Lexington to Ashland and from Crab Orchard to Livingston in Rockcastle County. Plans were beginning to be realized to bring the railroad into the western Kentucky coal field.

In the 1870s, railroads began to burn coal and to carry tonnage, and the St. Bernard Coal Co. opened its first mines in Hopkins County. At that time Cassius Crooke, said to be the first Kentuckian to ship coal by rail, was building a large mining operation at Pine Hill in Rockcastle. Union organization grew, and Crooke's mine experienced the longest nineteenth century strike (nineteen months). John B. Atkinson, head of St. Bernard Coal, became the leader of Kentucky's operators. The LOUISVILLE & NASHVILLE (L&N) Railroad extended service to the Tennessee line by 1883, opening up Laurel and Whitley counties, then built sideways to Bell through Knox all the way to Cumberland Gap. Its rival, the CINCINNATI SOUTHERN, had reached beyond Tennessee by 1880, carrying McCreary coal. The ILLINOIS CENTRAL (now Illinois Central Gulf) and the L&N operated in western Kentucky. Between 1870 and 1880, Kentucky coal production soared from 200,000 tons to 1 million and water transportation faded into the background.

After an unsuccessful attempt in 1879-80, Kentucky enacted its first mine inspection statute in 1884, which was amended several times. In the late nineteenth century, large-scale mining began in Knox and Bell, coinciding with the less than fully successful development of Middlesborough. In the mid-1880s some operators, notably Antoine Biederman DU PONT, tried unsuccessfully to contract for convict labor to defeat unionization. Kentucky was largely spared the violence that attended similar successful activities in Tennessee.

The 1890-91 constitutional convention discussed several coal-related issues including arbitration, convict labor, adequacy of inspection laws, and blacklisting, and voted to accept a provision requiring wages to be paid in lawful money. The leaders in the debates included William Goebel, then a senator from Kenton County, and William R. Ramsey from Laurel County. Ramsey had chaired the first legislative inquiry into mining conditions in 1886.

Between 1870 and 1900 the ever-growing number of purchases of mineral rights in eastern Kentucky led to controversies that are still alive. Several forms of option agreements were employed, including the BROAD FORM DEED. Purchasers included John C.C. Mayo, W.P. Horsley, and L.P. Trigg. Labor-related difficulties included the depression of 1893-97 and the increasing mechanization of the industry. Competition tended to drive the price of coal even lower and with it laborers' wages.

At the beginning of the twentieth century, railroad construction was completed, opening up more coal seams in far-eastern Kentucky. Ownership came to be largely in the hands of those living outside the state, leading to defeats for the union. Larger mines meant bigger workforces, more coal camps, and new problems. The quality of life in and around coal COMPANY TOWNS varied greatly, but towns like Jenkins, Benham, and Lynch were a distinct improvement over the dirty cabins of an earlier time. The Stearns enterprise came closest to one-company domination of a county (McCreary), and opinions are still divided as to how this company handled its resources and personnel. In western Kentucky, St. Bernard Coal's fight against organized labor split the coal field between union and nonunion workers until 1924.

Before World War I, a fairly steady flow of Eastern European immigrants came to the mountains, but it is uncertain whether they ever accounted for the majority of workers in any one county. After the overhauling of the mine safety law in 1914, there were no further amendments and no additional funds were put into this program. After 1913, eastern Kentucky became the state's leader in coal production. Some students of this era allege that this field overproduced, making recovery harder and adding to its human costs once the bubble burst. In 1929, two years after the boom ended, the stock market crashed and coal production dropped by a third, even more than it had done at the end of the war. Job time and job security were precarious in the 1920s and early 1930s in both coal fields.

A news analyst filing a report on the Kentucky coal fields between 1930 and 1932 probably would not have predicted almost complete victory for the union within several years. There was little in the start of JOHN L. LEWIS's career to indicate that he would so thoroughly organize labor in the mountains, let alone become a household name whose likeness was displayed in many homes. The struggle in Harlan County was not a complete victory, any more than in McCreary, but both achievements were close to total triumph.

Coal production accelerated only after war broke out in Europe in September 1939. After mines with six or fewer employees became subject to the inspection law, the fatality figures declined sharply, even though employment by the late 1940s, for example, was 17 percent higher than at the peak of the 1920s boom. After Kettle Island in 1930, there were no major disasters until the Duvin catastrophe in western Kentucky in 1939—the worst in that coal field since the record August 4, 1917, explosion, also in Webster County, took sixty-two lives.

The end of the war intensified the move to mechanization. Employment continued high after the war and just when it seemed that coal might level out or decline, involvement in the Korean War bolstered demand. With the end of that conflict in 1953, demand declined, precipitated by the railroads' change to oil and the large-scale conversion of domestic heating to oil and gas.

As smaller truck mines gradually outproduced rail mines, many of the three hundred coal camps either shut down or operated only in very limited fashion, and the company store disappeared in the 1950s. Surface mining, which had been only sporadic before the war, increased, and there was enough concern about its procedures in both coal fields that Gov. Lawrence Wetherby (1950-55) signed the first strip mine control bill in 1954.

One of the bill's sponsors was Rep. Harry CAUDILL, who later wrote *Night Comes To The Cumberlands* (1963), in which he described many ills of the eastern Kentucky coal fields. Some believed that, as one mountaineer alleged, "He's only talking about his holler," but there is ample evidence that the conditions Caudill described were widespread, if not universal. Not long before his book appeared, a 1959 strike failed in seeking organization of the workforce that operated the ramps and tipples to which truck miners brought their tonnage, as did John L. Lewis's attempts to organize workers in other jobs under the catchall organization he called District 50.

Western Kentucky did not have the eastern area's difficulties of underdevelopment and noncompetitive freight rates, and it gradually became a key source for the market that continues to buy Kentucky coal: the electric utilities. In 1966 Gov. Edward Breathitt (1963-67) signed what was then called the "toughest strip mine law in the country," (*New York Times*, July 16, 1967), but quality of enforcement was said to vary considerably. This period ended in 1969 with a double tragedy: a Christmas-week explosion at Hurricane Creek in Leslie County, which took thirty-eight lives, and the assassination of "Jock" Yablonski, his wife, and daughter after he sought the national presidency of the UNITED MINE WORKERS OF AMERICA (UMW). It was also in 1969 that the U.S. Congress enacted the most comprehensive mine safety and health measure yet considered.

After Mideastern oil-producing nations banded together into OPEC, changes in the crude oil market led to the energy crisis of the 1970s, and Kentucky coal experienced a boom somewhat similar to that of the mid-1920s. However, the earlier boom came in underground mining, while in the 1970s surface mining became the dominant means of extraction. In only a handful of Kentucky's coal-producing counties has underground tonnage remained primary, yet overall tonnage has reached all-time highs. The 1970s also witnessed a flurry of wildcat strikes. In western Kentucky, the workforce was 50-50 in terms of union membership. Throughout the state, the newly elected UMW international president, Arnold Miller, found relatively little support, unable to equal achievements of Lewis.

Since 1970 mechanization and technology have dominated the picture. In 1972 and 1976, the state revised its safety statute, while the Congress in 1977 amended the 1969 law and also enacted the first major federal surface mining regulation statute. However, the tendency toward deregulation by the federal government since 1981 has probably affected the degree and vigor of regulation. The demographics of mining employment has been changing and one of the more significant changes has been the entry of women into the active workforce.

By the 1980s, the boom had spent itself and the numbers of mines and miners were declining while mechanization was increasing. The decade saw a considerable decline in work-related fatalities, but the reasons for that may be multiple, including a more committed mine leadership, the provision in the union contract for work stoppage in a situation considered life-threatening, a more educated labor force, heightened uses of machinery, and informed, determined state inspection agency personnel. The Martin County Coal Company extracted more than 30 million tons in slightly more than ten years, with only one fatality—a unique achievement in the history of Kentucky coal.

As Kentucky begins its third century of mining, no new major markets are in sight, and successful marketing has emphasized long-term utility contracts. Other uncertainties include the extent of the union's presence and impact, the degree of solidarity among the miners, the impact of computerization, and ownership of the mines in the next century. The oil companies have entered the field of coal production, and the producers are larger and mostly from outside Kentucky. Almost the only certainties are that coal will be mined and that mining will be different. There are still questions about the accuracy of appraisals of the quantity and quality of reserves in each county. Transportation costs are another question mark, but it seems likely that entry into and successful operation of mining will continue to become a more expensive investment.

See Curtis Harvey, *Economics of Kentucky Coal* (Lexington, Ky., 1977); Curtis Harvey, *Coal in Appalachia* (Lexington, Ky., 1986); John Hevener, *Whose Side Are You On?* (Champaign, Ill., 1978).

HENRY C. MAYER

COAL OPERATORS' ASSOCIATIONS. In Kentucky, coal operators' associations have functioned at the local or regional and statewide levels. At one time, these organizations served as management's representatives in collective bargaining, or in some cases as the focus of their opposition to it, but this role no longer exists. Associations now exist chiefly for purposes of mutual consultation and joint action on such concerns as freight rates and other matters of common interest, such as lobbying.

The first known operators' organization was the Laurel Association, organized in 1882-83 with W.A. Pugh as its leader. For an undetermined time after 1884, the Jellico Field (Kentucky and Tennessee) Association functioned, led by M.E. Thornton and a Colonel Woolridge. The earliest statewide association was the Kentucky Coal Mine Operators Association, whose founder seems to have been Col. John B. Atkinson, for years president of the St. Bernard Coal Co., then the state's largest mining operation. Hywell Davies, a Welsh-born operator in both western and eastern Kentucky coal fields, and Frank D. Rash also served as presidents of this organization.

The oldest operators' organization still in existence is the Harlan County Coal Operators Association, which began in 1916 under the leadership of R.C. Tway and E.R. Clayton. Around that time, two organizations were emerging in western Kentucky, the West Kentucky Coal Operators Association and the Independent Coal Operators Association, whose leader was Percy D. Berry. Berry was a major force in the Ohio Valley Coal Operators Association, which may have been an interstate group. By the 1920s, the organizations included the Western Kentucky Conservation Association and the Hazard Coal Exchange, which soon changed its name to the Hazard Coal Operators Association; one of its early leaders was Joseph E. Johnson. Also around this time, operators from Pike County helped form the Operators of the Williamson Coal Field.

In the 1930s the Southern Appalachian Coal Operators, with L.C. Gunter as chief executive, came into being. Almost concurrently, in Floyd County, B.F. Reed, Harry La Viers, Sr., and Jack Price helped form the Big Sandy Elkhorn Coal Operators Association. In or around 1933, Percy Berry helped set up the Operators Association in western Kentucky.

In 1942, Reed, La Viers, and others, including George Evans and William Sturgill, organized the Kentucky Coal Association; one of its long-time leaders was Fred Bullard, who had been a leader of the Hazard group. The Kentucky Coal Association remains active, along with the Western Kentucky Coal Operators; the Harlan County Association; the recently formed Coal Operators and Associates, made up of operators around Pike County and vicinity; and the Knott, Letcher and Perry Independent Coal Operators Association.

HENRY C. MAYER

COBB, ANN. Ann Cobb, teacher and writer, was born in New England on September 15, 1885, into a family that emphasized both education and religion. She attended Wellesley College, studying history and classical languages. There she met May Stone, whom she visited in January 1906 at the HINDMAN SETTLEMENT SCHOOL in Knott County in southeastern Kentucky. Stone and Katherine Pettit had founded the school to educate mountain youth. During Cobb's visit to Hindman, a fire gutted the building in which she stayed, destroying her return ticket to Boston. Cobb remained at the school, where she taught, coordinated special programs and festivals, and wrote.

Cobb was one of five women on the staff who narrated mountain life in fiction and poetry, and her writing assumed a distinctly Appalachian flavor as she incorporated the mountain dialect into her work. Cobb's book, *Kinfolks: Kentucky Mountain Rhymes*, forty-eight poems in dialect describing local life, was published in 1922; among the poems are "Up Carr Creek," "The Hound," and "Far-'well Summer Flowers." Cobb was also published in *Saturday Evening Post, Mountain Life and Work*, and *St. Nicholas*. She died on January 12, 1960.

COBB, IRVIN SHREWSBURY. Irvin S. Cobb, journalist, fiction writer, and humorist, was born in

Paducah, Kentucky, on June 23, 1876, the oldest son of Joshua and Manie (Saunders) Cobb. A war injury made it difficult for his father to support the family, who lived with Irvin's maternal grandfather, Dr. Reuben Saunders, a prominent citizen of Paducah. Irvin alternated between public and private schools in the area. Irvin left school when he was sixteen to support the family as an apprentice reporter for the *Paducah Evening News*. When the paper was sold in 1896, he became managing editor. His youthful recklessness provoked several lawsuits, and after a year he returned to reporting for the *Louisville Evening Post*. In his three years there, Cobb developed a statewide reputation as a trial reporter, enhanced by his coverage of the trial of the accused assassin of Gov. William Goebel (1900). He also became known as a humorous essayist—the reporter's reporter.

In 1901 Cobb returned to Paducah as managing editor of the new *Democrat*. In 1904 he left the *Democrat* for New York City, to pursue his ambition of being a reporter on a major newspaper. He found work with the *Evening Sun*, and his successful reporting on the Portsmouth Peace Conference enabled him to move to Joseph Poultice's *Evening Herald*, where his reputation rose dramatically, bolstered by his coverage of the murder trials of socialite Harry Thaw in 1907 and 1908. Developing his natural talent for humor, Cobb published numerous articles, many in extended series such as "The Hotel Clerk." As Cobb's reputation grew, so did the stature of his byline and the number of his pieces that were syndicated nationally. His sociable demeanor gave him entry to the fashionable society of the day, from which he drew much of his material.

Cobb also began to write fiction, returning to the rural material of his Kentucky childhood. The *Saturday Evening Post* published his stories, and in 1912 he left newspaper journalism for the *Post* staff; shortly thereafter the *Post* published "Words and Music," the first of more than fifty short stories and novels of post–Civil War Paducah. Perhaps the best of these stories are in the early collection *Back Home* (1912). Sinclair Lewis wrote, "Cobb has made Paducah and all the other Paducah's—in Kentucky and Minnesota and California and Vermont—from which the rest of us come live in fiction."

In 1914 Cobb went to Europe to report on the war for the *Post*. The United States was still neutral, and Cobb's descriptions of Germany's strength and the war's devastation were the most vivid available to most Americans. Cobb and four companions slipped behind the German lines and were captured, but they were released unharmed.

On his return from Europe, Cobb embarked on a successful lecture tour of all states east of the Mississippi. Back in New York, he was honored by a banquet at the Waldorf-Astoria featuring a film biography, *From Paducah to Prosperity, or the Life of Irvin S. Cobb*. His plans to return to covering the war were interrupted by the illness that prompted his best-seller, *Speaking of Operations* (1915), which literary historian Norris Yates has characterized as a landmark in the development of twentieth century American humor.

A supporter and friend of President Woodrow Wilson, Cobb reluctantly supported the nation's entrance into the war in 1917, and he returned to the front to report on the American soldier for the *Post*—the most popular source of war information in America. Upon his return in 1918, Cobb took up the cause of racial tolerance. His admiring descriptions of black soldiers at the front made him a hero to black Americans, and he spoke at Carnegie Hall with Theodore Roosevelt in support of relief for black soldiers. He was honored by the blacks in Paducah in December 1918. Cobb became involved in activities to quell the Ku Klux Klan in the 1920s, even returning to Paducah in 1922 to edit the *Paducah News-Democrat* for one day, running a strong anti-Klan editorial.

In the meantime Cobb continued his prodigious output of fiction and humorous essays, and in 1923 he left the *Post* for a similar position with *Cosmopolitan*. Fascinated with the potential of cinema, Cobb sold several scripts to Hollywood in the 1920s. In 1934 he and his family moved to California, where Irvin advised his friend Will Rogers on a movie, *Judge Priest*, based on Cobb's stories of a wily small-town jurist. In Hollywood Cobb served as a consultant on several films with Old South settings, was master of ceremonies for the 1935 Academy Awards, and played the Mississippi riverboat captain in the 1935 film *Steamboat Round the Bend*. He appeared in five other movies. In 1936 he had his own radio show, "Paducah Plantation," and later served as a regular on other shows.

Cobb's autobiography, *Exit Laughing* (1941), brought him a resurgence of national acclaim. Between 1900 and 1950, Cobb shared with U.S. Vice-President Alben Barkely the distinction of being the American celebrity most widely associated with his home state of Kentucky.

Cobb married Laura Spencer Baker of Savannah, Georgia, in 1900; they had one child, Elizabeth. Cobb died on March 10, 1944, and was buried in Paducah's Oak Grove Cemetery under a granite boulder inscribed "Back Home."

See Irvin S. Cobb, *Exit Laughing* (New York 1941); Anita Lawson, *Irvin S. Cobb* (Bowling Green, Ohio, 1984).   ANITA LAWSON

COE RIDGE. Coe Ridge was a tiny black community in the foothills of southern Cumberland County, Kentucky, just north of Clay County, Tennessee, founded by ex-slaves. After the Civil War, Ezekiel and Patsy Ann Coe received from their former owner 1,200 to 1,500 acres of hill country at the rear of his plantation, where they lived with their children and extended family. An island of black culture, the Coe settlement withstood for almost a century the attempts of antagonistic white neighbors to remove this racial "scar" from their midst.

Coe Ridge, sometimes referred to as Zeketown, produced a belligerent group of residents whose defense of their homes made them legendary by the time the community died in the late 1950s. By then it had become a refuge for white women rejected by their families. Moonshining in Zeketown during the first half of the twentieth century eventually brought the downfall of the Coe enclave. After years of raids, arrests, and skirmishes, revenue agents won out. The residents of Coe Ridge headed for the industrial centers north of the Ohio River. Only a cemetery marks the site of the settlement.

See William Lynwood Montell, *The Saga of Coe Ridge: A Study in Oral History* (Knoxville, Tenn., 1970).   WILLIAM LYNWOOD MONTELL

COLE, WHITEFORD RUSSELL. Whiteford Russell Cole, railroad executive, was born on January 14, 1874, in Nashville to Col. Edmund William and Anna Virginia (Russell) Cole. His was one of the most prominent families in Tennessee; his father ran the Nashville & Chattanooga Railroad (later the Nashville, Chattanooga & St. Louis) and the East Tennessee, Virginia, & Georgia Railroad. Transportation and trade were part of Cole's early environment. As soon as he finished his education at Vanderbilt University (1890-94), he became a director of the Nashville, Chattanooga, & St. Louis Railroad, as well as president of iron and steel works in Sheffield, Alabama, and Bevier, Kentucky. In 1926 Cole moved to Louisville to become the president of the Louisville & Nashville Railroad, succeeding Wible Mapother, who had died. As president, Cole guided the railroad through the Great Depression without losing revenue. He was president of the Southeastern President's Conference, which represented railways before the federal government. At the same time, Cole held high positions on the Louisville Board of Trade, on the Vanderbilt Board of Trustees, and in numerous railroads, telephone companies, and banks.

Cole married Mary Conner Bass on April 21, 1901; they had one son, Whiteford Russell, Jr. Cole died suddenly while on a train returning from Nashville on November 17, 1934. He is buried in the Mt. Olivet Cemetery in Nashville.

See Jesse C. Bart, "Whiteford Russell Cole—A Study in Character," *FCHQ* 28 (Jan. 1954): 28-48.

COLEMAN, JOHN WINSTON, JR. John Winston ("Squire") Coleman, Jr., author and historian, eldest son of John Winston and Mary Shelby (Payne) Coleman, was born on November 5, 1898, in Lexington, Kentucky. He grew up on the family farm in Fayette County and received his early education in Lexington at Miss Ella M. Williams's Private School and at Morton High School, where he graduated in 1916. Coleman attended the University of Kentucky and received a bachelor of science degree in 1920 and a master's degree in mechanical engineering in 1929. Between 1920 and 1924 he worked in Louisville for American Telephone & Telegraph; in Albany, New York, for Fort Orange

Paper Co.; and in Hazard, Kentucky, for Green & Taylor Electric Company. He returned to Lexington in the spring of 1924 and, with John W. Davis, formed a residential construction company that functioned until 1936. Coleman then moved to Winburn farm on 240 acres in Fayette County he had inherited from his parents, and began farming. He sold the land in March 1966 and retired to the city of Lexington.

Coleman began researching, collecting, and writing Kentucky history in 1932 and became renowned for his work in state and local history, especially on the Bluegrass region. He wrote more than 150 pamphlets and articles on various Kentucky topics and more than twenty books; the first, *Masonry in the Bluegrass*, was published in 1933. His better known works are *Stage-Coach Days in the Bluegrass* (1935), *Slavery Times in Kentucky* (1940), *A Bibliography of Kentucky History* (1949), *The Springs of Kentucky* (1955), *Historic Kentucky* (1967), and *Kentucky: A Pictorial History* (1972). He belonged to an informal group of historians called the BOOK THIEVES that met monthly. Coleman's private collection on Kentucky history included approximately 3,500 books, pamphlets, manuscripts, maps, atlases, and more than two thousand photographs and negatives. Coleman donated most of his large collection of Kentuckiana to Transylvania University.

During his life, Coleman received numerous awards and honorary degrees, including doctor of letters from Eastern Kentucky University, doctor of literature from University of Kentucky (1949), and doctor of law from Transylvania University (1969).

Coleman married Burnetta (Zumwalt) Mullen on October 15, 1930. He died on May 4, 1983, and was buried in the Lexington cemetery.

See J. Winston Coleman, Jr., *The Squire's Memories* (Lexington, Ky., 1976).

COLEMAN, KELLY. "King" Kelly Coleman, a top basketball scorer, was born September 21, 1938, at Wayland, Kentucky, fifth among the eleven children of coal miner Guy Coleman and wife Rusha. A stout six-foot, two-inch guard, Kelly led the Wayland Wasps to third place at the 1956 state tournament while establishing two tournament records, total points (185) and single game points (68), playing against Bell County. In four seasons at Wayland (1953-56), he scored 4,263 points. Coleman became an All-American and holder of the school scoring record at Kentucky Wesleyan College. Drafted into the National Basketball Association in 1960 by the Knicks, Coleman was released after a preseason dispute with the coach.

See David Kindred, *Basketball: The Dream Game in Kentucky* (Louisville 1975).

JAMES C. CLAYPOOL

COLGAN, JOHN. John Colgan, pharmacist, was born in Louisville on December 18, 1840, to William and Elizabeth (Christopher) Colgan. His education began in the Louisville public schools and finished at St. Joseph's College in Somerset, Ohio, in 1860. Colgan then went into the pharmaceutical business. In 1879 Colgan developed a sweetened chewing gum, Colgan's Taffy Tolu, as a substitute for the sticky substance that children peeled from tree bark and chewed. The confection soon became a fad, appealing to all ages, and Colgan went into business with James McAfee to produce it. By 1890, he had disposed of his drugstores to concentrate on manufacturing the gum, which was one of Louisville's most extensively marketed products by the end of the nineteenth century. After Colgan's son William introduced the chewing gum at the 1893 World's Fair in Chicago, it began selling rapidly in the United States, Canada, and Australia.

Colgan married Mattie McCrory on November 30, 1867; they had five children: Bettie, William, Henry, Mabel, and Clifton. Colgan died on February 1, 1916, and was buried in Cave Hill Cemetery in Louisville.

See Jack Parks, "Chewing Gum is Louisville's Idea," *Louisville Courier-Journal Magazine*, June 18, 1989.

COLLIER, BLANTON LONG. Blanton Long Collier, football coach, was the son of O.H. and Eva (Long) Collier, born on July 2, 1906, in Millersburg, Kentucky. He played basketball and football at Paris (Kentucky) High School and received a bachelor of arts degree in 1927 from Georgetown College. He then began coaching at Paris High School, where he also taught mathematics. As a basketball coach, he was an innovator of the pressing man-to-man defense. He enlisted in the navy in 1943 and was assigned to Great Lakes Naval Station in Illinois as a swimming instructor. There he joined the staff of Paul Brown, who was coaching the navy's football team, and when Brown formed the Cleveland Browns in the American Football League in 1945, he hired Collier as a backfield coach.

In 1954 Collier became head football coach at the University of Kentucky, where he had earned a master of arts degree in 1947. During his eight years at UK he compiled a 41-36-1 record, second only to that of Bryant, and was Southeastern Conference coach of the year in 1956. He returned to the Browns in 1961 and the next year became Paul Brown's successor as head coach. Collier's record at Cleveland was 74-36-2, and he won the National Football League championship in 1964. He retired in 1970 and that year received an honorary doctor of laws degree from Georgetown College.

Collier married Mary Forman Varder of Paris, Kentucky in 1930; they had three daughters—Carolyn, Katherine, and Jane. Collier died on March 22, 1983, in Houston, Texas, and was buried in the Paris Cemetery.

See Kay Collier Stone, *Football's Gentle Giant: The Blanton Collier Story* (Lexington, Ky., 1985).

COLLINS, LEWIS. Lewis Collins, journalist and historian, was born in Fayette County, Kentucky, near Bryan's Station on December 25, 1797. His father, Richard Collins, who had fought in the Revolutionary War, came from Virginia. In 1813 Lewis Collins was orphaned, and he moved to Paris, Kentucky, to learn the printing trade from Joel R. Lyle, editor of the *Paris Citizen*. Collins went on to publish the *Maysville Eagle* from November 1820 to November 1847. Collins was Mason County school commissioner for nearly twenty years and was a lay leader of the Presbyterian Church. A Whig, he was the first Mason County judge, serving from 1851 to 1854.

Collins, a devotee of Kentucky history, wrote several articles of historical interest that he published in the *Maysville Eagle*. His major work was the extremely popular *Historical Sketches of Kentucky*, printed in 1847. He edited this compilation of articles by various contributors, including his brother-in-law, Henry Peers of Maysville. The most comprehensive Kentucky history of its time, the book has often been criticized for its lack of documentation, yet it contains a vast amount of information that would otherwise have been lost. Of particular value is the section "Annals of Kentucky," a daily chronology of major events from 1539 to the time of publication.

On April 1, 1823, Collins married Mary Eleanor Peers, daughter of Maj. Valentine Peers, who had been an officer in the Revolutionary War. Among their children was the historian Richard Henry Collins, who expanded on his father's *Historical Sketches*. Lewis Collins died in Lexington on January 29, 1870, and was buried in Maysville Cemetery.

See James P. Gregory, "Lewis and Richard H. Collins, A Chapter in Kentucky Historiography," *FCHQ* 21 (Oct. 1947): 309-23.

RON D. BRYANT

COLLINS, MARTHA LAYNE. Kentucky's first woman to hold the governorship (1983-87), Martha Layne Collins was born on December 7, 1936, in Shelby County, Kentucky, to Everett and Mary (Taylor) Hall. She spent a year at Lindenwood College in Missouri, then transferred to the University of Kentucky, where in 1959 she received a degree in home economics. Soon afterward Martha Layne Hall married William Collins; they have two children, Steve and Marla. While her husband completed his dentistry degree at the University of Louisville, she taught in area high schools. The couple moved to Versailles, Kentucky, in the mid-sixties, and Collins taught at Woodford County Junior High. She became interested in Democratic politics, showed a talent for organization, and became secretary of the Democratic Party and Democratic National Committeewoman after the election of Wendell Ford as governor in 1971.

Collins won the party's nomination for clerk of the court of appeals in 1975 and defeated Republican Joseph E. Lambert, 382,528 to 233,442, in the general election. In 1979 she was one of six major candidates who sought the party's endorsement for lieutenant governor. The vote was so divided that her 23 percent won the nomination. She then defeated Republican Harold Rogers, 543,176 to 316,798. In the John Y. Brown, Jr., administration (1979-83), Collins maintained close ties with the party machinery, which he tended to ignore. When she announced her candidacy for governor in 1983, she had the support of many party regulars and record campaign funds. The primary was a close race, in which Collins won the nomination with 223,692 votes to 219,160 for Harvey Sloane and 199,795 for Grady Stumbo. In the general election, she defeated state Sen. Jim Bunning, 561,674 to 454,650. Upon leaving office in December 1987, Collins became an international trade consultant; she taught at the University of Louisville in 1988 and at the Institute of Politics at Harvard University in 1989. She served on the boards of the Southern Baptist Theological Seminary, and Midway College and became president of St. Catharine College in Washington County in 1990.

During her campaign for governor, Collins promised to avoid new taxes and to give priority to educational reforms. However, recovering from the recession of 1982-83, Kentucky faced a revenue shortage even as demands for quick action on education became more insistent. Collins asked the General Assembly for $324 million in additional funds in 1984, most of it committed to public schools. When it became apparent that the House would not vote that sum in an election year for its members, she withdrew her tax proposals and substituted a continuation budget. Critics of the governor stressed her failure to control the newly independent legislature and the resultant defeat of major parts of her program during the first session. The legislature in 1984 enacted a tougher drunk-driving law and a measure that allowed state banking companies to purchase other banks in the state. Later that year Governor Collins chaired the Democratic National Convention and was one of the vice-presidential hopefuls interviewed by Walter F. Mondale.

Still committed to educational reform, Collins campaigned to win public support. This time she worked with the legislature, which enacted a number of changes during a special session in 1985. However, the increase in business taxes was not adequate to fund the proposed changes in full. She and the legislative leaders planned to increase revenue in 1987 by making the state income tax conform more closely with the federal tax, but that proposal was abandoned when Wallace Wilkinson, the Democratic nominee for governor, declared his opposition to it. In a special 1987 session, Collins's plan for financing the workers' compensation program was discarded in favor of one developed in the legislature. One of her major accomplishments came when the Japanese company Toyota decided to establish a large automobile plant near Georgetown. Some detractors, including Wilkinson, her successor, charged that the $125 million in incentives (with an ultimate cost of $300 million in bonds) was excessive, but criticism was blunted as dozens of Toyota suppliers set up plants across the state. A record number of new job opportunities were brought to Kentucky under Collins's national and international economic development program.

See "Governor Martha Layne Collins," *Register* 82 (Summer 1984): 211-13.

LOWELL H. HARRISON

COLLINS, RICHARD HENRY. Richard Henry Collins, historian, was born in Maysville, Mason County, Kentucky, on May 4, 1824, the son of Lewis and Eleanor (Peers) Collins. He was educated at Maysville Seminary; at Centre College in Danville, Kentucky, where he received bachelor's and master's degrees; and at Transylvania University in Lexington, Kentucky, where he obtained his law degree in 1846. From 1846 to 1850, Collins worked at the *Maysville Eagle*, serving initially as an assistant and eventually as editor. He practiced law in Maysville during 1851-53 and in Covington, Kentucky, during 1862-71.

Collins was very active in community affairs and a member of the Presbyterian Church. He was a founder of both the *Danville Review*, edited by Presbyterian minister Robert J. Breckinridge, and the Filson Club in Louisville. However, Collins's greatest contribution to Kentucky history came with the revision of his father's work, *Historical Sketches of Kentucky*, first published in 1847. From 1870 to 1874, he labored on the new edition of Lewis Collins's book. More than three hundred people were acknowledged as contributors to the new history. Collins himself did a great deal of original research and writing. He expanded his father's one-volume work of 560 pages to two volumes totaling 1,600 pages and covering the history of Kentucky from its beginnings to 1874. In March 1871 the Kentucky General Assembly voted to buy copies of Collins's history to be placed in the schools throughout the state. Later the decision was reversed. Collins became involved in a long and bitter legal struggle to hold the state to its initial agreement. Despite several appeals, the state did not honor the original contract, and the effort cost him $15,000.

Collins married Mary Cox in September 1846; they had seven children. Collins died on January 1, 1888, at the home of his daughter in Maryville, Missouri. His body was returned to Kentucky and buried in Maysville Cemetery.

See Jennie Chinn Morton, "Sketch and Picture of Richard H. Collins, Historian," *Register* 7 (Jan. 1909): 11-16; James P. Gregory, Jr., "Lewis and Richard H. Collins, A Chapter in Kentucky Historiography," *FCHQ* 21 (Oct. 1947): 309-23.

RON D. BRYANT

COLLINS, WILLIAM FLOYD. William Floyd Collins, whose ordeal while trapped in a Kentucky cave attracted worldwide attention, was born April 20, 1887, to Leonidas and Martha (Burnett) Collins on Flint Ridge in Edmonson County, Kentucky, just a few miles away from Mammoth Cave. Collins's

216

early childhood was spent working on the family's small, subsistence farm and occasionally venturing into the area's many caves.

In 1917 Collins made a discovery on the farm that he named Crystal Cave. The family constructed trails and opened Crystal Cave to tourists. Because the rough, winding local roads made access to the cave difficult, Collins decided to explore the cave for passages that might be connected to an entrance on the main road from Cave City to Mammoth Cave. During January 1925 a local farmer, Bee Doyle, agreed to allow Collins to explore a cave on his property on the main road, which Collins hoped might be used to reach Crystal Cave. On the Doyle property Collins blasted and cleared a passageway sheltered by a sandstone ledge. On the morning of January 30 he entered the excavation, dragging a length of rope and lighting his way with a lantern. It is here that stories of what happened begin to differ, but many believe Collins discovered a large cave on his journey downward, and in his haste to return to the surface dislodged a rock that pinned his legs in a narrow crawlway.

When Doyle learned the next day that Collins had not returned to his home, he discovered that Collins had been trapped in the passageway beyond reach. Collins asked Doyle to get his brothers to help him out. Collins's brothers and many others came to the entrance—so many in fact, that one of the biggest obstacles to freeing him was the throng of people. Though some rescuers, including his brothers Marshall and Homer, were able to reach Floyd, the rock that pinned him at the ankles was beyond their reach in the narrow passageway. Soon Collins's entrapment received national attention, and newspapers and radio stations sent reporters to cover the rescue efforts. Rescuers heard Collins coughing on February 13, but they could not finish digging a rescue shaft and lateral tunnel to reach him until February 16. At that point, Collins was dead.

Collins's body was removed in April 1925 and buried in a family plot near Crystal Cave. In 1927 the body was dug up and placed in a coffin inside Crystal Cave, against family wishes. In 1961 the National Park Service purchased the cave and closed it to the public. On March 24, 1989, Collins's remains were removed from the cave and buried in the Mammoth Cave Baptist Church cemetery.

See Robert K. Murray and Roger W. Brucker, *Trapped!: The Story of Floyd Collins* (Lexington, Ky., 1982); Homer Collins, *Floyd Collins in Sand Cave: America's Greatest Rescue Story* (Greenwich, Conn., 1958).　　NATIONAL PARK SERVICE

COLUMBIA. Columbia, seat of Adair County and a city of the fourth class, was settled in approximately 1800 on Russell Creek, a principal tributary of the Green River. It is located near the center of the county, along the Cumberland Parkway linking Somerset and Bowling Green. The name is thought to commemorate Christopher Columbus. The town was laid out by Daniel Trabue in 1802 and in that

year became the county seat. A courthouse was built in 1806; the present courthouse, of mid-Victorian architecture, was built on the same site in 1885, designed by the McDonald Brothers of Louisville. An attempt to bolster the town's tobacco market by bringing the Cincinnati & Southern Railroad through Columbia failed, and residents had to travel by stagecoach, first to Lebanon and then to Campbellsville, to reach the Louisville & Nashville Railroad. Five men reputed to be members of the Jesse James gang robbed the Bank of Columbia on April 29, 1872, killing the cashier and taking $4,000.

Columbia's first school, Robertson's Academy, was founded in 1812. Columbia College, the Male and Female College, and Christian College were nineteenth century attempts by various religious denominations to provide education beyond the local grade schools. In 1903 the Methodist Church founded LINDSEY WILSON College as a training school for students preparing to attend Vanderbilt University in Nashville. Lindsey Wilson became a junior college in 1923 and added a third year in 1986; its first senior class graduated in 1988.

Columbia's population was 3,234 in 1970; 3,710 in 1980; and 3,845 in 1990.

See Ruth P. Burdette, *Early Columbia* (n.p., 1974).

COLUMBUS-BELMONT, BATTLE OF. On September 3, 1861, Confederate forces under Gen. Leonidas Polk seized and fortified Columbus, Kentucky, the terminus of the Mobile & Ohio Railroad. To control river traffic, the Confederates stretched a ship's anchor chain across the Mississippi River from the Columbus side to Belmont, Missouri, on the opposite shore. In retaliation, Gen. Ulysses S. Grant left Cairo, Illinois, and his Union troops seized Paducah, the northern end of the New Orleans & Ohio Railroad. Each side worked to reinforce its position, in anticipation of a movement by the other. On November 5 Grant's superiors took the initiative, ordering him to make a demonstration against Belmont. The next day Grant sailed down the Mississippi with a force of 3,000, including five regiments of infantry, two companies of cavalry, and two cannons. He landed several miles above Columbus on the Missouri side of the Mississippi, putting out a few pickets on the Kentucky side to make contact with a Union force under Gen. C. F. Smith that was advancing overland from Paducah.

Grant decided to turn his demonstration into a raid on the Southern camp at Belmont. His army was elated at the prospect of action and he felt he could not maintain discipline much longer without giving his men the chance to fight. On the morning of November 7 Grant advanced against Belmont, defeating a Confederate force of five regiments under Gen. Gideon S. Pillow. The broken Confederates fled and huddled under the river bank, but Grant was unable to follow up his success because his ill-disciplined troops could not resist the opportunity to loot the abandoned rebel camp. General

Polk, across the river, ordered the Confederate guns there to fire on the Federals in the camp. At first Polk was reluctant to send reinforcements to Belmont, fearing an assault on Columbus from Paducah. But when Gen. Smith's attack failed to materialize, Polk sent three regiments of infantry across the river under Gen. Benjamin Cheatham. By that time, many of General Pillow's Confederates had rallied, and soon Grant was faced by an enemy force of 5,000, some of whom were threatening to cut his line of retreat to his transports. Some of Grant's officers advised that he surrender, but Grant, having cut his way into Belmont, was certain he could cut his way out again. The Federals did so, returning to their transports and retreating upriver. Grant himself narrowly escaped death during the retreat. He found himself alone at one point facing a large body of the enemy, but for whatever reason no one fired at him.

Grant accomplished his purpose at Belmont by taking the enemy camp, but some consider Polk the victor because his forces held the ground at day's end and suffered fewer casualties. At any rate, Grant obtained valuable experience as a battle commander on that day in 1861, experience that would aid the Northern cause greatly in the years to come.

Generations of tourists have posed for photographs at the deep-sea navy anchor and chain at the Columbus-Belmont Battlefield State Park in HICKMAN COUNTY. The anchor, which measures nine feet from fluke to fluke, weighs two tons. Each link of its chain measures eleven inches long by six inches wide and weighs twenty pounds. The chain, which the Confederates stretched from the bluffs above Columbus to Belmont to block river traffic, broke of its own weight before long, but Federals did not learn that fact until early 1862, after Grant had taken Forts Henry and Donelson.

See *War of the Rebellion, Official Records of the Union and Confederate Armies*, Washington, D.C., 1871; Ulysses S. Grant, *Personal Memoirs* (New York 1885-86).   JOHN E.L. ROBERTSON

COLVIN, GEORGE. George Colvin, educator, lawyer, and eighth president of the University of Louisville, was born September 7, 1875, near Willisburg, Washington County, Kentucky. He was the second of the eight children of William Arthur and Lucy Allen (Harris) Colvin. After attending public school in Willisburg, he entered Centre College in Danville in 1891 and graduated in 1895. He was captain and quarterback of Centre's noted football team of 1894. After a year spent studying law at Centre, Colvin went to Springfield, Kentucky, and taught school. In 1900 he joined the Louisville Title Company, where he did legal work. In 1903 he returned to Springfield, practiced law for a few months, then became the town's superintendent of public schools.

In July 1919 Colvin won the Republican party's nomination for SUPERINTENDENT OF PUBLIC INSTRUCTION, and in November was elected to office, along with the entire Republican ticket headed by gubernatorial candidate Edwin P. Morrow (1919-23). As state superintendent, Colvin worked for higher teacher salaries, a compulsory attendance law, health education, and an elected board of education for each county that would appoint the county superintendent. He was instrumental in the passage of the state's County School Administration Law in 1920. He urged the adoption of a longer school year for rural children and higher educational and professional standards for teachers and administrators, and he supported the Kentucky Education Association.

In May 1923 Colvin announced his candidacy for governor, but he failed to secure the Republican nomination. Colvin resigned his state post and returned to Louisville in November to accept appointment as superintendent of the Louisville and Jefferson County Children's Home. Formerly called the Louisville Industrial School of Reform, it was a city-owned facility for orphans and delinquent children on South Third Street. He instituted reforms and oversaw the institution's move to its new Ormsby Village site in February 1925.

After the death of University of Louisville president Arthur Y. Ford, the university's board of trustees appointed Colvin to that position on August 1, 1926. As president, Colvin resisted faculty efforts to strengthen graduate programs and concentrated on developing the undergraduate curriculum. When he limited faculty contracts to one year, he faced strong opposition. Louis R. Gottschalk, who taught history at the university from 1923 to 1927, resigned, called for an investigation by the American Association of University Professors, and issued a public statement critical of Colvin. Gottschalk's colleague, a professor of ancient history named Rolf Johannesen, who delayed signing the one-year contract, was dismissed. Although thirty-nine of the forty-seven liberal arts faculty members petitioned for Colvin's resignation, he was supported by most of the trustees and continued to serve as president until his death.

On January 20, 1904, Colvin married Mary McElroy of Springfield. They had a daughter, Lovey Mary, and two sons, George and Palmer. Colvin died on July 22, 1928, after surgery for appendicitis. He was buried in Springfield.

See Kitty Conroy, "George Colvin: Kentucky Statesman and Educator," *Bulletin of the Bureau of School Service, College of Education, University of Kentucky* 16 (March 1944): 5-57.

WILLIAM J. MORISON

COMBS, BERT T. Bert T. Combs, governor during 1959-63, was born August 13, 1911, in Clay County, Kentucky, to Stephen Gibson and Martha (Jones) Combs. After high school he spent a decade of intermittent study before receiving his law degree from the University of Kentucky in 1937. He married Mabel Hall that year; they have two children. After a divorce in 1969, he married Helen Clark Rechtin. Combs opened a law practice in Prestonsburg, Kentucky, but soon volunteered for army service in World War II. Discharged as a captain in

1946, he resumed his practice. He was city attorney in 1950 and commonwealth's attorney for the 34th District for a brief period in 1951. Appointed to a vacancy on the court of appeals in April 1951, he won election to a full eight-year term later that year. In 1955 he was a candidate in the Democratic primary for governor against former governor A.B. Chandler (1935-39). The exuberant Chandler outshone the inexperienced Combs; when Combs declared that the state needed $25 million in additional revenue, Chandler replied that an experienced governor would not need additional taxes. He defeated Combs, 259,875 to 241,754. When Chandler raised selected taxes, Combs was seen as an honest politician not afraid to face facts.

Combs won the 1959 Democratic gubernatorial primary by 25,000 votes over Harry Lee Waterfield, Chandler's choice, and then swamped Republican John Robsion, Jr., 516,549 to 336,456. When he left office, Combs became one of the state's best-known lawyers. He accepted an appointment on the federal 6th Circuit Court of Appeals (1967-70), then in 1971 sought another term as governor. He lost the Democratic primary to Wendell H. Ford, who had been his chief administrative assistant during his governorship. In the area of public service, Combs helped establish the Rural Housing and Development Corporation, and he was an active member of the Council for Higher Education. In 1988-89 he was lead counsel for the poor school districts that won the Kentucky Supreme Court decision that the Kentucky system of public schools was unconstitutional. Combs died in a flash flood near Stanton, Powell County, on December 4, 1991, and was buried in Beech Creek Cemetery, Lancaster, Clay County.

Governor Combs secured the funds for his ambitious programs by backing a 3 percent sales tax to pay a veteran's bonus. He knew that a 1 percent tax would have raised more than enough for this purpose, but the extra money paid for improvements in almost every other state activity—roads, education, parks, human resources, social services—as well as paying the veteran's bonus. Combs used every opportunity to let the people know that the sales tax had made the changes possible; he was determined that the state's belated progress would not be halted by another repeal of the tax. A merit system was installed for state workers, and the governor moved quickly against instances of misconduct. He appointed the state's first human rights commission and urged communities to set up similar bodies. In 1963 he issued an executive order that desegregated all public accommodations in the state. His was one of the most progressive administrations in Kentucky's history. Years later, politicians of his time would look back to Combs's term as their Camelot.

See George W. Robinson, Jr., *The Public Papers of Bert T. Combs, 1959-1963* (Lexington, Ky., 1979).   LOWELL H. HARRISON

COMBS, EARLE BRYAN. Earle Bryan Combs, professional baseball player, was born May 14,

1899, at Pebworth, Kentucky, one of the six children of farmer James J. and his wife Nannie (Brandenburg) Combs. A natural athlete, Combs was encouraged by his father, who supplied his children with homemade poplar bats and baseballs made by stitching cowhide around a core of rubber and tightly bound string.

Combs attended Eastern Kentucky University and received a teaching certificate in 1919. To pay for his education, he taught in one-room schools in Ida May and Levi, Kentucky. His athletic talents on the baseball field at college attracted much notice. He hit .591 during his senior year. During the summers Combs played semiprofessional baseball in Winchester, High Splint, and Lexington. While playing with the Lexington Reos of the Bluegrass League, Combs drew the attention of the Louisville Colonels. The American Association team offered Combs a contract that easily topped the $37 a month he had received for teaching. With the Colonels in 1922 and 1923, Combs played under manager Joe McCarthy and developed quickly, with batting averages for the two years of .344 and .380, respectively. Combs was a line-drive hitter, noted for driving the ball through the box. He had a reputation for speed and reckless base stealing.

In 1924 McCarthy convinced the New York Yankees to buy the young outfielder for $50,000—a huge sum at that time. In the summer of 1924, when Combs played in center field between Yankee greats Babe Ruth and Bob Meusel, he hit .400 before being sidelined by a broken ankle. The following season Combs was installed as the leadoff hitter in the Yankee lineup. During his career, he batted over .300 nine times and led the American League in at-bats (648) and hits (231) and in triples in 1927 (23), 1928 (21), and 1930 (22). His career average for twelve seasons was .325. As a fielder he was described as "swift, sure-handed, and coordinated." With his speed, Combs covered much of the outfield, leading the American League in putouts in center field with 411 in 1927 and 424 in 1928. Combs covered much of Babe Ruth's left field territory after the great slugger lost some of his mobility in his later years.

After hitting a full-season career high of .356 in 1927, Combs went on to score the winning run in the final game of the World Series. Combs was at his best at World Series time. In 1923 he had batted .357 and hit safely in all seven games, and in 1932 he had hit .375 as the Yankees swept the Chicago Cubs in four games. Combs became a Yankee fans' favorite, known by such nicknames as "Kentucky Greyhound," "Gray Fox," and "Kentucky Colonel." The introspective, religious Combs was considered one of the few real gentlemen on a series of great Yankee teams noted for their fun-loving boisterousness.

Combs's career was cut short in 1934 on an extremely hot day in St. Louis (110° F), when he crashed into a wall while chasing a towering fly ball, suffering a fractured skull, a broken shoulder, and a damaged knee. He was near death for several days and was hospitalized for over two months. He returned to play in 1935, but quit after breaking his collarbone in an outfield collision with another player. Signed as a coach, he trained his replacement, a young man from San Francisco. In a letter to Combs, Yankee general manager Ed Borrow wrote, "If this boy does as well as you, I'll be satisfied." The new center fielder was Joe DiMaggio.

Combs coached the Yankees from 1935 to 1944; St. Louis Browns, 1947; Boston Red Sox, 1948-52; and Philadelphia Phillies in 1954. After he retired, the former Yankee farmed, sold insurance, served as state banking commissioner during Gov. A.B. Chandler's second administration (1955-59), and was chairman of the Eastern Kentucky University board of regents. In 1970 he was elected a member of the Baseball Hall of Fame.

Combs married Ruth McCollum in 1922. They had three sons, Earle Jr., Charles, and Donald. Combs died on July 21, 1976, and was buried in the Richmond Cemetery.

See Dave Anderson et al., *The Yankees: The Four Fabulous Eras of Baseball's Most Famous Team* (New York 1981); Marty Appel and Burt Godblatt, *Baseball's Best: The Hall of Fame Gallery* (New York 1981).   WILLIAM MARSHALL

COMBS, LESLIE. Leslie Combs, youngest son among Benjamin and Sarah (Richardson) Combs's twelve children, was born in Clark County, Kentucky, on November 28, 1793. He attended a school operated by the Rev. John Lyle. Combs was a junior deputy clerk in the Jessamine County law office of S.H. Woodson when the War of 1812 began. Combs enlisted in the 1st Regiment Kentucky Volunteers under Gen. William Henry Harrison, then was transferred to Gen. Green Clay's command. In April 1813 Combs was promoted to captain of scouts. In the British attack on Fort Meigs, Combs commanded a detachment under Col. William Dudley. He was wounded and taken prisoner on May 5, 1813, during the battle known as the Second River Raisin. After his parole, Combs returned to Kentucky and settled in Lexington, where he read law under Samuel Q. Richardson. He was admitted to the bar in 1818. In 1827, Combs was elected as a Whig to the Kentucky House of Representatives and served until 1829. On January 27, 1830, when an act of incorporation for the Lexington & Ohio Railroad Company was passed by the General Assembly, he was one of the twenty incorporators. By 1855 he was president of the Lexington-Danville Railroad. Combs was reelected to the Kentucky House of Representatives in 1833 and served as chairman of the Committee on Internal Improvements.

In 1836 Combs, a colonel in the Kentucky militia, raised a regiment of volunteers in response to Stephen Austin's plea for assistance against Mexico while the Republic of Texas was being organized. President Andrew Jackson disbanded the regiment before it saw action. Combs was a Kentucky delegate-at-large to the 1840 Whig convention.

Originally a supporter of Henry Clay's bid for the party's nomination, Combs actively supported Gen. William Henry Harrison when he won the nomination. Combs was reelected to the Kentucky House of Representatives from 1845 to 1847, and served as Speaker of the House in 1846. At the outbreak of the Mexican War in 1846, Combs, promoted to general, raised another militia regiment. He resigned when he was not selected to command the regiment. In 1851 Combs was defeated by John C. Breckinridge in a bid for the U.S. House of Representatives. He was again elected to the Kentucky House from 1857 to 1859. During the Civil War, Combs was a staunch Unionist, and from 1860 to 1866 he was clerk of the state court of appeals. He went into retirement after declining to run for reelection.

On September 1, 1818, Combs married Margaret Trotter, daughter of George Trotter, Sr. They had eleven children. On April 11, 1849, after the death of his first wife, Combs married Mary Elizabeth (Brownell) Man, daughter of Episcopal bishop Thomas Brownell. They had three children. Combs died in his Lexington home on August 22, 1881. He was buried in Lexington Cemetery.

See James Wallace Hammack, Jr., *Kentucky and the Second American Revolution: The War of 1812* (Lexington, Ky., 1976).

COMMITTEE FOR KENTUCKY. Civic-minded citizens in Louisville organized the nonpartisan Committee for Kentucky near the end of World War II to help make Kentuckians aware of political issues. From 1945 to 1950 the committee published studies dealing with agriculture, education, health, housing, welfare, industry, labor, natural resources, taxation, and the Kentucky constitution. The committee's members were businessmen, lawyers, teachers, labor leaders, and other professionals, none of whom were ever candidates for public office. Though some efforts were made to promote a statewide operation, the group's strength originated in and remained primarily in Louisville. Harry Schacter, president and general manager of the Kaufman-Straus department store and president of the Kentucky Merchants Association, chaired the committee during its five-year existence.

Each committee report challenged Kentuckians to recognize what was wrong with the state and go to work to correct those problems. The reports had the approval of representatives from as many as eighty-eight state interest groups who served as delegates to the committee's central organization. The committee also sponsored a radio program "Wake Up Kentucky," later called "Kentucky on the March." Committee-sponsored speakers visited Kentucky communities and met with students on college campuses. The committee stirred up thought about state problems, awakened citizen interest, caused awareness of the need for cooperation, and prompted many to participate in improvement efforts.

See Harry W. Schacter, *Kentucky on the March* (New York 1949).   GEORGE W. ROBINSON

COMMONWEALTH. "Commonwealth" is a part of the official name of Kentucky, as decided by the first General Assembly on June 4, 1792. Kentucky is one of four commonwealths in the United States; Virginia, Pennsylvania, and Massachusetts are the others. The first use of the word commonwealth in official documents regarding Kentucky occurred in 1785, when the inhabitants of the Kentucky District petitioned Virginia to recognize Kentucky as a "free and independent state, to be known by the name of the 'Commonwealth' of Kentucky." Commonwealth is derived from the Anglo-Saxon word *wela*, meaning a sound and prosperous state.

RON D. BRYANT

COMMONWEALTH LIFE INSURANCE COMPANY. Commonwealth Life Insurance Company, Kentucky's oldest and largest insurer, was incorporated in May 1904 for $200,000. After raising the $100,000 deposit that Kentucky required of life insurance companies, Commonwealth introduced itself to the public in a *Louisville Courier-Journal* advertisement on June 4, 1905. Col. Joshua D. Powers, one of the principal organizers of the company, was elected its first president, and Darwin W. Johnson was elected secretary-treasurer. Louis G. Russell, who had experience in the life insurance business, was in charge of sales. Johnson succeeded Colonel Powers in 1922 and served as chief executive until his death in March 1936.

Commonwealth's failure to build financial reserves, together with a liberal dividend policy and unwise investments, brought the company to near-ruin by the mid-1930s. Homer Ward Batson, elected president in 1936, had little knowledge of the technicalities of life insurance, but from his law practice was experienced in dealing with critical financial problems. During his five-year tenure, Batson prevented the company from falling into bankruptcy, reduced the problems in the asset structure, and strengthened reserves. Morton Boyd, installed as president in 1941, engaged Benjamin N. Woodson, who expanded the sales operation, becoming executive vice-president in 1944.

At the end of World War II, Commonwealth hired many returning Kentucky veterans for its field force. The company entered the burial insurance business in 1947 in association with Kentucky Funeral Directors' Burial Association.

Boyd's eighteen-year tenure came to a close in 1958, when William H. Abell was elected to succeed him as president and chief executive. Abell and Homer D. Parker led Commonwealth for the next decade and a half. Commonwealth established Capital Holding Corporation in 1969 to aquire other life insurance companies. Capital Holding Corporation had $15.4 billion in assets and $45.1 billion of life insurance in force as of March 1990. It is Kentucky's largest public company in terms of assets and one of Louisville's largest employers, with 1,400 local employees.

Capital Holding sells a broad range of financial services in all fifty states. Its businesses include life, health, and property and casualty insurance; investment-type products for both institutional and retail customers; and consumer banking.

In 1981 Capital Holding acquired National Liberty, a marketer of life and health insurance. In 1984 the company acquired First Deposit, a consumer lending and credit card business, and in 1986 Worldwide Insurance, a property and casualty insurer. Meanwhile, Capital Holding consolidated a series of life and health insurers in the Southeast and Atlantic Coast states into three regional companies—Commonwealth Insurance in Louisville; Peoples Security Insurance in Durham, North Carolina; and Public Savings Insurance in Charleston, South Carolina. It created Capital Initiatives in 1986 to develop new markets and distribution channels for accumulation and investment-type insurance products.

The planned thirty-five-story Capital Holding Center at the corner of Fourth Avenue and Market Street, designed by John Burgee, will be Louisville's tallest building.

See Victor B. Gerard, *Commonwealth Life Insurance Company* (Louisville 1985).

VICTOR B. GERARD

COMMUNITY COLLEGE SYSTEM. The University of Kentucky Community College System comprises fourteen community colleges located throughout the state. All are public institutions under control of the board of trustees of the University of Kentucky. Transfer programs, career or technical programs, and continuing education and community service programs are offered. In the fall semester of 1989, 36,429 students were enrolled in credit courses. This figure represented over 25 percent of all Kentucky students taking college-level courses for credit and exceeded enrollment at any single college or university in the state. In the five-year period from 1984 to 1989, enrollment in the Community College System increased 53 percent. The colleges are fully accredited by the Commission on Colleges of the Southern Association of Colleges and Secondary Schools.

The legislation that authorized the formation of a community college system under the University of Kentucky was passed by the General Assembly in 1962 and the University of Kentucky board of trustees initiated the Community College System in 1964. Affiliation of a community college system with a major state research university is not a common organizational pattern. The relationship, however, has resulted in cost savings to the state, because a number of services and functions are shared with the Lexington campus of the university.

Five university extension centers, at Ashland, Covington, Cumberland, Fort Knox, and Henderson, became nuclei of the new system. Subsequently, the facilities of Northern Community College at Covington were transferred to Northern Kentucky University. Community colleges at Elizabethtown and Prestonsburg opened in 1964; Lexington Community College (formerly the Lexington

Technical Institute) and Somerset and Hopkinsville Community colleges in 1965; Jefferson Community College at Louisville and Maysville Community College in 1966; Hazard Community College in 1967; and Madisonville Community College in 1968. Paducah Community College, a municipally operated junior college, joined the system in 1968 and Owensboro Community College in 1986.

The Community College System is governed by the University of Kentucky board of trustees, but the administration of its academic programs is separate from that of the Lexington campus of the university. The chief administrative officer of the system is a chancellor who is directly responsible to the president of the University of Kentucky. Each community college is headed by a president who reports to the chancellor of the system. Each college has a dean of academic affairs, a dean of student affairs, and a dean of business affairs. Lay boards appointed by the governor serve in an advisory capacity to the president of the community college. Responsibility for the academic programs of the community colleges resides in the senate of the community college system. Each community college has representation on the senate and its committees, and a community college faculty member serves on the board of trustees of the University of Kentucky.

The ideal community college student body is a cross section of the area served by the college. Diversity is its chief characteristic. In the fall semester of 1989, 48 percent of students in the system were twenty-five years of age or older. Fifty-six percent were female. Six percent were Afro-American. Forty-four percent were enrolled in technical or career programs, 35 percent in transfer programs, and 21 percent were nondegree.

The General Assembly has charged the Community College System with three specific functions: 1) to offer career-oriented programs that prepare students for immediate employment upon graduation; 2) to offer the first two years of a baccalaureate degree; and 3) to offer general educational opportunities for citizens in the areas served by the colleges. To carry out the mission, the Community College System offers more than twenty-five career programs. These programs range from sixty- to seventy-two credit hours and are designed to be completed in two years. With the goal of maintaining high-quality programs, the system has initiated program review procedures to eliminate less productive programs while strengthening others, so that resources are directed toward the greatest needs and the largest number of students. Transfer programs in the community colleges are well established. Coursework taken in a transfer program is fully transferable to a four-year institution. Upon graduation the student receives either the associate in arts or associate in science degree. Continuing education or community service programs offered by the community colleges include credit and noncredit courses to meet reeducation and in-service needs of the community. In addition, workshops, seminars, short courses, concert series, lectures, and art exhibits are offered throughout the year.

In keeping with the student-centered philosophy, community college faculty are selected for both their expertise in a discipline and their interest in teaching. In the fall of 1989, 805 full-time faculty and 941 part-time faculty were employed systemwide.

Each of the community colleges is housed in facilities on campuses planned to accommodate growth. A number of the colleges have also developed off-campus centers to make college programs more accessible in the area served by the college. Jefferson Community College in Louisville has two campuses, one downtown and one in the southwestern part of the county. All of the community college campuses have collections of bound volumes, serials, government documents, audio-visual materials, journals and periodicals, and machine-readable materials. The LS2000 System is a computer communication network that links all community college libraries to each other and to the library on the Lexington campus of the University of Kentucky, as well as to other large information services.

See Judith E. Rozeman and Daniel G. Tudor, eds., *Compendium of Selected Data and Characteristics: University of Kentucky Community College System 1988-89* (Lexington, Ky., 1989); Patsy Stice and Margaret Smith, eds., *Community Colleges, Pathway to Kentucky's Future* (Lexington, Ky., 1989).

DANIEL G. TUDOR

COMPANY TOWNS. In Kentucky, the term company town is strongly identified with the coal industry. Other enterprises that owned the land and built the housing in the communities where their employees lived included the logging industry, railroads, and iron mines. The earliest company towns were established in Kentucky prior to the Civil War, but their origins are poorly documented.

American company towns are a British legacy that evolved from medieval antecedents. In the late seventeenth century coal became a marketable commodity, exported to cities from the hinterlands. Owners of manorial estates where coal deposits were found organized their laborers by erecting small cottages or row houses. The repetitiveness of architectural form in these complexes became the hallmark of American company towns. Company housing came to America as early as industrial processes themselves. New England mill towns date to 1791. Early company towns in Kentucky include Airdrie (1853), an iron town populated by Scots on the Green River near Paradise in Muhlenberg County, and Peach Orchard (1845), just north of Prestonsburg on the Big Sandy River's Levisa Fork.

For extractive industries such as iron, coal, and timber, the site of the resource determined the location of the company town. Company towns frequently were established where no community had existed before, isolated by underdeveloped lines of transportation and communication. Despite the presence of a county government, the company exercised local political control over all aspects of the workers' lives. For housing at the remote site, the company generally deducted rent from the employee's paycheck and it used its position as landlord to control the workforce. Given the transience of many resource-based operations, there was little incentive to make housing durable. Likewise, social structures such as schools, churches, stores, and entertainment facilities were provided only as company officials saw fit.

At the opening of the twentieth century, the oppression of company towns attracted national attention. Journalists publicized conditions, social scientists proposed model communities, and the federal government studied the problem. In response, a few companies constructed comfortable communities to showcase their economic strength and benevolence. The communities of Benham, Lynch (Harlan County), and Jenkins (Letcher County) stand as reminders of this unusual enlightenment.

Nearly all coal and railroad company towns in the Eastern Coal Field region after 1900 took advantage of low-cost precut homes available from companies such as Sears, Radford, Alladin, and Montgomery Ward. Dozens of identical featureless, factory-built houses stood side by side in company towns, while company officials lived in larger, more attractive, well-spaced structures on more desirable sites.

There was less need for company towns by the end of the 1920s, as a collapse in coal prices, the rise of strip mining, and improved technology had reduced the mining workforce, while railroad mainlines had largely been completed and timber resources had been depleted. Except for the unusual instance of Wheelwright (Floyd County), revived by Inland Steel in the 1930s and 1940s, company towns had outlived their usefulness by the close of World War II. Most of the towns have been sold and their structures dismantled for use at other sites, but vestiges of larger towns can yet be seen in the coal fields.

See Ronald Eller, *Miners, Millhands, and Mountaineers* (Knoxville, Tenn., 1982); Morris Knowles, *Industrial Housing* (New York 1920).

L. MARTIN PERRY

CONFEDERATE HOME. On March 17, 1902, the Kentucky legislature approved the establishment of the Kentucky Confederate Home for the care of infirm veterans. The Daughters of the Confederacy and Confederate veterans bought Villa Ridge, a Victorian-style summer resort in Pewee Valley, Oldham County, to house the former soldiers. Gov. J.C.W. Beckham (1900-1907) was host at its opening on October 23, 1902. By 1904 three hundred veterans resided at the health care facility. Perhaps the most famous gathering of veterans was that of twenty-five of Gen. John Hunt Morgan's former Raiders, many of whom lived there. On March 25, 1920, most of the facility burned. The remaining

one wing was large enough to house the few veterans who were still there.

More than seven hundred soldiers resided at the home at one time, but by 1934 only five veterans remained. Despite the high costs of operating the facility, the Daughters of the Confederacy successfully stopped its proposed sale on several occasions. On March 17, 1934, the legislature approved the sale of the property and allocated an annual allowance of $800 to the remaining veterans, who were transferred to the Pewee Valley Sanitarium. By the end of June 1934, the Confederate Home had closed.

Three hundred thirteen of the veterans who had lived on the grounds were buried there in the Pewee Valley Confederate Veterans Cemetery. In 1952 the state restored the cemetery, which had fallen into disrepair, and in 1957 Gov. A.B. Chandler (1955-59) rededicated it. The Kentucky State Parks Department has maintained the site since 1968.

CONFEDERATE STATE GOVERNMENT. Although Kentucky did not withdraw from the Union during the Civil War, Confederates in western Kentucky and portions of central Kentucky moved to establish their own government while Confederate forces under Gen. Albert Sydney Johnston held Bowling Green. After a preliminary meeting in October 1861, a formal convention met on November 18-20 in the Clark building in Russellville to form the provisional Confederate government of Kentucky.

An estimated 116 delegates claiming to represent sixty-eight counties met at the convention, where Henry C. Burnett of Trigg County presided. On the third day the convention moved to the tower of Bethel College for security reasons. George W. Johnson was elected governor and Bowling Green was designated as the capital. The Kentucky Confederate seal was a mailed arm with a star, extended from a circle of twelve other stars. Confederate Kentucky was admitted into the Confederate States of America on December 10, 1861.

Bowling Green served as the seat of the provisional Confederate government of Kentucky for less than three months. Governor Johnson fled Bowling Green on February 14, 1862, with the Confederate state records and headed south to join the Confederate forces. After Johnson was killed in the Battle of Shiloh on April 8, 1862, the provisional state government chose Richard Hawes of Paris to succeed him as governor. The two were the only ones to serve in that office. After 1863 the Confederate government of Kentucky existed only on paper, and it was disbanded when the Civil War ended in 1865.

See Edward Coffman, *The Story of Logan County* (Nashville 1962). RENA MILLIKEN

CONGRESSIONAL MEDAL OF HONOR WINNERS. The congressional Medal of Honor is the United States' highest military decoration, awarded for extraordinary personal heroism. The criterion of

CONGRESSIONAL MEDAL OF HONOR WINNERS

RECIPIENT	KENTUCKY CONNECTION	DATE AND PLACE OF ACTION
U.S. Army		
Col. J. Franklin Bell	Shelbyville	Sept. 9, 1899; Porac, Philippine Islands
Cpt. William P. Black	Woodford Co.	March 7, 1862; Pea Ridge, Arkansas
Pvt. John H. Callahan	Shelby Co.	April 9, 1865; Ft. Blakeley, Alabama
Corp. John W. Collier	Worthington	Sept. 19, 1950; Chindong-ni, Korea
Sgt. Morris Eugene Crain	Bandana	March 13, 1945; Haguenau, France
Lt. Thomas Cruse	Owensboro	July 17, 1882; Big Dry Fork, Arizona
Sgt. John S. Darrough	Mason Co.	Oct. 10, 1864; Eastport, Mississippi
Pvt. John Davis	Carroll Co.	June 17, 1865; Culloden, Georgia
Sgt. William L. Day	Barren Co.	April 12, 1875; Apache War
Lt. Carl Henry Dodd	Kenvir	Jan. 30, 1951; Subak, Korea
Lt. Don C. Faith Jr.	Fort Thomas	Nov. 27–Dec 1, 1950; Hagaru-Ri, Korea
Sgt. Charles Clinton Fleek	Petersburg	May 27, 1969; Binh Duong, Vietnam
Corp. John J. Given	Daviess Co.	July 12, 1870; Wichita River, Texas
Lt. Benjamin Franklin Hardaway	Benleyville	July 1, 1898; El Caney, Cuba
Pvt. William M. Harris	Madison Co.	June 25–26, 1876; Little Big Horn, Montana
Drummer William H. Horsfall	Newport	May 21, 1862; Corinth, Mississippi
Pvt. Aaron R. Hudson	Madison Co.	June 17, 1865; Culloden, Georgia
Corp. Oliver Hughes	Clinton Co.	June 26, 1864; Weldon RR, Virginia
Sgt. Don J. Jenkins	Quality	Jan. 6, 1969; Kien Phong, Vietnam
Corp. Charles E. Kelly	Louisville	Nov. 13, 1943; Altavilla, Italy
Cpt. John B. Kerr	Fayette Co.	Jan. 1, 1891; White River, South Dakota
Sgt. Ernest R. Kouma	Scottsville	Aug. 31–Sept 1, 1950; Agok, Korea
Lt. Darwin K. Kyle	Jenkins	Feb. 16, 1951; Kamil-Na, Korea
Pvt. Billy Lane Lauffer	Murray	Sept 21, 1966; Bon Son, Vietnam
Sfc. Gary Lee Littrell	Henderson	April 4–8, 1970; Dak Seang, Vietnam
Sgt. Donald Russell Long	Ashland	June 30, 1966; Republic of Vietnam
Pvt. Henry B. Mattingly	Marion Co.	Sept. 1, 1864; Jonesboro, Georgia
Pvt. Franklin M. McDonald	Bowling Green	Aug. 31, 1872; Ft. Griffin, Texas
Sgt. John James McGinty III	Louisville	July 18, 1966; Republic of Vietnam
Sgt. Francis M. McMillen	Bracken Co.	April 2, 1865; Petersburg, Virginia
Pvt. David P. Nash	Whitesville	Dec. 29, 1968; Dinh Tuong Prov., Vietnam
Pvt. James J. Nash	Louisville	July 1, 1898; Santiago, Cuba
Pvt. Oliver P. Rood	Frankfort	July 3, 1863; Gettysburg, Pennsylvania
Pfc. Wilburn K. Ross	Strunk	Oct. 30, 1944; St. Jacques, France
Sgt. Willie Sandlin	Jackson	Sept. 26, 1918; Bois-de-Forges, France
Pvt. Georg D. Scott	Lancaster	June 25–26, 1876; Little Big Horn, Montana
Sgt. Thomas Shaw	Covington	Aug 12, 1881; Cairezo Canyon, New Mexico
Pfc. David Monroe Smith	Livingston	Sept. 1, 1950; Yongsang, Korea
Sgt. Junior J. Spurrier	Russell Co.	Nov. 13, 1944; Archain, France
Sgt. John Charles Squires	Louisville	April 23–24, 1944; Padiglione, Italy
Pvt. William Steinmetz	Newport	May 22, 1863; Vicksburg, Mississippi
Pvt. Thomas W. Stevens	Madison Co.	June 25–26, 1876; Little Big Horn, Montana
Pvt. Thomas Sullivan	Covington	Oct. 20, 1870; Chirichua Mountains, Arizona
Saddler Otto Voit	Louisville	June 25, 1876; Little Big Horn, Montana
Pfc. Ernest Edison West	Wurtland	Oct. 12, 1952; Sataeri, Korea
Major John F. Weston	Louisville	April 13, 1865; Westumpka, Alabama
Col. James A. Williamson	Columbia	Dec. 29, 1862; Chickasaw Bayou, Mississippi
Lt. Samuel Woodfill	Fort Thomas	Oct. 12, 1918; Cunel, France
Sgt. Brent Woods	Pulaski Co.	Aug. 19, 1881; Cairezo Canyon, New Mexico
U.S. Marine Corps		
Cpt. William Earl Barber	Dehart	Nov 28–Dec 2, 1950; Chosin Reservoir, Korea
Pfc. William Bernard Baugh	McKinney	Nov. 29, 1950; Hagaru-Ri, Korea
Corp. Richard Earl Bush	Glasgow	April 16, 1945; Okinawa
Pfc. Leonard Foster Mason	Middlesborough	July 22, 1944; Marianas Islands, Guam
Corp. Joe Calvin Paul	Williamsburg	Aug. 18, 1965; Chu Lai, Vietnam
Pvt. Wesley Phelps	Neafus	Oct. 4, 1944; Peleiu Islands
Pfc. Luther Skaggs Jr.	Henderson	July 21–22, 1944; Marianas Islands, Guam
U.S. Navy		
Seaman Edward William Boers	Bellevue	July 21, 1905; U.S.S. *Bennington*
Watertender Edward Alvin Clary	Foxport	Feb. 14, 1910; U.S.S. *Hopkins*
Quarter Gunner George Holt	Kentucky	July 3, 1871; U.S.S. *Plymouth*
Landsman Daniel John Noble	Bath Co.	Aug. 5, 1864; U.S.S. *Metacomet*

"uncommon valour" in selecting the recipients, has kept the medal highly respected. It has been awarded to men and women since 1861. The sixty listed on page 223 won the award between 1861 and 1990 and were born or lived in Kentucky. (Merely to have enlisted in Kentucky is not sufficient ground for inclusion here.)

CONNOLLY, JOHN. John Connolly, the original owner of the property that became the downtown Louisville business district and West End, was born in Pennsylvania. He received a 2,000-acre grant by British proclamation on December 16, 1773, for service as a surgeon's mate in the French and Indian War. During the Revolutionary War, he was commissioned a British officer on November 5, 1775, and ordered to raise a Tory regiment in either Detroit or Pittsburgh and to form a coalition with the Northwestern Indians. Under his leadership, the group was to leave Detroit in 1775 to attack frontier settlements and then to join Lord Dunmore in eastern Virginia. Connolly was unable to complete the mission as he was captured at Hagerstown, Maryland, and imprisoned until April 1781. His Kentucky land claims were voided and seized in May 1780 by the Virginia legislature, and the city of Louisville was established. On July 1, 1780, an inquest of escheat in Lexington declared Connolly a British subject. The participants were John Bowman, Daniel Boone, Nathaniel Randolph, Waller Overton, Robert McAfee, Edward Cather, Henry Wilson, Joseph Willis, Paul Froman, Jeremiah Tilford, James Wood, and Thomas Gant.

Connolly appeared in Kentucky in 1788 under the pretense of recovering his lost lands. His real mission was to propagate a British plan to detach Kentucky from the Union. The British hoped that Kentucky would align itself with England in return for backing by troops from Canada and a British fleet in the Gulf of Mexico, which would guarantee Kentucky free navigation of the Mississippi River. Though free passage upon the Mississippi had become a divisive issue between Kentuckians and the U.S. government, Connolly found little support. Dissuaded by his principal confidant, Gen. James Wilkinson, an advocate of a similar Spanish plan, Connolly returned to Canada.

CONSTITUTIONAL UNION PARTY. In 1859 John J. Crittenden, then U.S. senator from Kentucky, took the first step toward forming the Constitutional Union party when he called a meeting of about fifty members of Congress who shared his weariness with the slavery controversy. Committees were appointed to confer with the American party, which Crittenden had joined, and remnants of the Whig party. From these elements the Constitutional Union party, so named by William C. Rives, was forged.

Various states supported the Constitutional Union party. On February 22, 1860, a gathering at Frankfort resolved that the people of Kentucky were "for the Union and the Constitution intact" and recommended Crittenden for president. The seventy-four-year-old Crittenden declined the nomination, but he campaigned actively for nominees John Bell of Tennessee and Edward Everett of Massachusetts. He delivered an address denouncing both Democrats and Republicans for their stands on slavery.

The Constitutional Union party was strongest in the border slave states, which hoped for compromise on slavery. The party platform declared that it would recognize "no political principles other than the Constitution of the country, the Union of the States and the enforcement of the laws." Crittenden accused Southern Democrats of nominating Kentuckian John C. Breckinridge for president in order to draw the state into a southern confederacy, but he declared that Kentucky was the very "heart of the Union" and would never secede.

Abraham Lincoln, the Republican nominee, won the 1860 election with 1,865,908 popular votes. Stephen A. Douglas, the Northern Democrat, received 1,380,202; Breckinridge, the Southern Democrat, 848,019; and Bell, 590,901. The electoral vote was Lincoln, 180; Breckinridge, 72; Bell, 39; and Douglas, 12. The Constitutional Unionists carried Kentucky, with its twelve electoral votes. Bell received 66,051, or 45 percent, of Kentucky's popular vote. Breckinridge followed with 53,143; Douglas with 25,638; and Lincoln with 1,364. Bell ran best in traditionally Whig counties, most of which had supported the American party in 1856. He won more than 60 percent of the popular vote in Logan, Clark, Boyle, Garrard, Lincoln, Todd, Boyd, Greenup, Knox, Whitley, Metcalfe, and Cumberland counties. He received between 50 and 60 percent in twenty-three others, including seven Bluegrass counties, six in the Pennyroyal and Western Coal Field, and four in the southeastern hill country, but only one in the Jackson Purchase. The vote indicated that in Kentucky the Constitutional Unionists were, indeed, generally old-line Whigs under a new name.

See Jasper B. Shannon and Ruth McQuown, *Presidential Politics in Kentucky 1824-1948* (Lexington, Ky. 1950); Albert D. Kirwan, *John J. Crittenden: The Struggle for the Union* (Lexington, Ky. 1962).   OTIS K. RICE

CONSTITUTIONS. The American people have lived under one Constitution since 1789, but Kentucky has had four charters since its admission to the Union: the constitutions of 1792, 1799, 1850, and 1891. In *McCulloch v. Maryland* (1819), John Marshall, chief justice of the United States, advised framers to write a constitution that would mark only the great outlines and designate only the important objects of a government, leaving that government to deduce "the minor ingredients which compose those objects . . . from the nature of the objects themselves." Order and change are the twin virtues of Marshall's constitution; it expresses an agreement on political fundamentals and grants the government flexibility in responding to future needs.

The first two Kentucky constitutions were influenced by the federal Constitution and by the spirit of a good constitution as described by Marshall. The constitution of 1792 was a brief document that established a tripartite government, a bicameral legislature, and a bill of rights. At the same time, the constitution limited popular control. Only the House of Representatives was chosen by direct popular election. The governor and Senate were chosen by a body of electors, and the judiciary was appointed by the governor. The framers of the 1792 constitution considered their work an experiment in government and provided for its reappraisal by the end of the decade. The constitution of 1799, however, retained the major features of the original document. Its principal change, reflecting an interest in greater democratic control, was the abolition of the electoral college in favor of direct election, by voice vote, of the governor and senators. It created the office of lieutenant governor. More power was given to local governments, and the counties became the most significant agencies of government, responsible for taxation, regulation of business, and patronage. Freed blacks lost the franchise they had had since 1792.

The commonwealth's two nineteenth century constitutions, like those of other states during this time, violate Marshall's *McCulloch* maxim by adding an increasing amount of statutory detail, reflecting a popular response to government misbehavior. The 1850 constitution, a lengthier and more detailed document, imposed more popular controls on government power. The judiciary were popularly elected to serve fixed terms. The major changes were, however, reserved for the General Assembly, which had abused its fiscal powers and amassed a debt of $4.5 million, largely for dubious internal improvements. The 1850 constitution limited legislative sessions to sixty days, unless two-thirds of the legislature agreed otherwise; protected the sinking fund (money set aside for debt repayment) against legislative misuse; and restricted to $500,000 the legislature's right to contract debt, unless it provided for taxes sufficient to meet interest payments each year, discharged the debt within thirty years, and received electoral majority approval. It also set up a system of public education, replaced annual elections with biannual ones, reaffirmed slavery, and required office holders to swear that they had not participated in a duel. The county judge, sheriff, and nearly all local officeholders were to be elected for fixed terms, rather than appointed.

The 1891 constitution held to statutory controls on the exercise of governmental power. The governor, unable to immediately succeed himself, lost further control over executive officials by the addition of two elective independent constitutional executive officials, bringing the total to eleven. These officials were, however, forbidden to serve terms of more than four consecutive years and their salaries were limited to $5,000. But the major restrictions, once again imposed upon the legislative branch, were motivated by its responsibility for the major public financial problems of the day. The General Assembly was limited to sixty-day sessions every two years unless extended by the governor; its special sessions and their agendas were also controlled by the governor; and its appropriations were subject to a gubernatorial line-item veto. Section 59 imposed twenty-eight curbs on special legislation for the benefit of local governments and corporations. Fiscal restrictions on local governments, almost entirely a creation of the 1891 constitution, severely limited their taxing and borrowing powers and prohibited them from granting franchises or privileges for more than twenty years. Corporate activity for the first time was restricted, by forty constitutional provisions.

At the same time, the 1891 constitution held to the pattern of making constitutional revision a tortuous process. The 1799 constitution had eliminated one of the original constitution's methods of calling a constitutional convention—a two-thirds legislative majority—while retaining the other method: legislative approval followed by two successive electoral majorities of "all the citizens of this State entitled to vote for Representatives" (article 9). The 1891 constitution altered this method, but did not weaken the barriers to constitutional revision. Section 258 requires that two successive legislative majorities enact a statute calling for a convention, that an electoral majority approve the call, and that "the total number of votes cast . . . equal one-fourth of the number of qualified voters who voted at the last preceding [state] general election."

As Thomas D. Clark has observed, the 1890 convention created a static document to protect its agrarian society from an emerging industrial order: "One gets the impression . . . that many of the delegates were, in fact, little Red Riding Hoods trudging alone and frightened through the perplexing forest of constitutional law, hoping that the big bad wolves of industrial and progressive changes were mere figments of their badly agitated imagination, and that a rigid constitution with static provisions would serve to dispel these threatening wraiths."

The framers of the 1891 constitution have, in fact, made it extremely difficult in the twentieth century for the state and its local governments to provide public services and to promote economic development. Moreover, the constitution has presented the commonwealth with an almost inescapable dilemma: how to change a document which, like the 1850 constitution, has abandoned the essentials of a good constitution and thereby made substantial change necessary, but which has made meaningful change virtually impossible by means of its restrictive constitutional convention provision.

The General Assembly, employing section 258, has issued four calls for a constitutional convention, but they were defeated in the elections of 1931, 1947, 1960, and 1977. The proponents of constitutional change, frustrated by the failure of the first three convention calls, devised an alternative method. The General Assembly created the Constitutional Revision Assembly in 1964, adopted its draft of a proposed revision, and then avoided section 258's laborious convention procedure by submitting the statute for direct popular approval pursuant to section 4 of the Bill of Rights, which provides, in part, that "the people . . . have at all times an unalienable and indefeasible right to alter, reform, or abolish their government in such manner as they deem proper." The court of appeals in *Gatewood v. Matthews* (1966) accepted the section 4 argument and upheld the statute, but the voters overwhelmingly defeated the revised constitution in the 1966 election.

The 1891 constitution also provides for change by amendment. Section 256 authorized the legislature by a two-thirds vote to propose no more than two amendments at a time (revised to four in 1979), which would become part of the constitution if ratified by a simple majority at the next state general election. As of November 1990, thirty amendments had been ratified, but almost all of them make only very limited changes. Ten minimally alter the General Assembly's taxing and spending powers. In a similar fashion, several other amendments change constitutional provisions governing the compensation of public officials, the legislative session, corporate behavior, local government, and the election process. Only two speak to the spirit of a good constitution. One extends the suffrage to eighteen-year-olds. The other, really an act of miniconstitutional revision, modernizes the judicial system. Overall, the amendment process has not meaningfully altered the 1891 constitution, nor has it adapted the constitution to the twentieth century, but merely modified its statutory detail.

If the 1891 constitution's revision and amendment provisions have not solved the dilemma it created, neither have the actions taken by the governor, General Assembly, and judiciary adapted the constitution to the realities of twentieth-century governmental life. Judicial legitimation of gubernatorial and legislative action has, however, been a significant—if subtle and fragmented—method of constitutional change, as in the Kentucky Supreme Court's decisions on governmental compensation, revenue bonds, and constitutional revision.

The 1891 constitution limited salaries of state officials to $5,000. A 1949 amendment raised the limit to $12,000, but a specific dollar limit, of course, cannot respond to the impact of inflation. In *Matthews v. Allen* (1962), the "rubber dollar case," the Kentucky Supreme Court remedied the situation by holding that circuit judges would not receive an adequate compensation for their services, as required by section 133, unless their nominal dollar salaries, as established by the amended section 246, were construed to enable the General Assembly to maintain their salaries—and, indeed, those of all constitutional officers—at the purchasing power of the 1949 dollar.

The constitution also severely limits the General Assembly's powers to finance public projects and economic development, but in a series of decisions, from *VanHooser v. University of Kentucky* (1936) to *Blythe v. Transportation Cabinet* (1983), the court held that legislation authorizing the use of revenue and moral obligation bonds to finance public buildings and roads does not violate the public debt limitations of sections 49 and 50. In *Hayes v. State Property and Building Commission* (1987), the Toyota incentive agreement case, the court upheld a further expansion of sections 49 and 50 and also sections 171 and 177, which limit the use of taxes for public purposes and forbid donations and loans of state credit to private corporations.

Creative judicial decisions, however, are not enough to make the commonwealth's basic law a good constitution. Piecemeal constitutional changes, whether by amendment or by judicial decisions, have had limited value in meeting the needs of a modern state. In this regard, the direct submission method of constitutional change has eliminated not only the almost insuperable barriers imposed by the 1891 constitution, but also the excuse, so frequently offered by Kentuckians and their elected representatives, that their constitution is to blame. If Kentuckians are interested, what changes need to be made to provide a good constitution?

Guidelines may be found in the National Municipal League's Model State Constitution; the Kentucky Constitutional Revision Assembly's proposed 1966 constitution; and the constitutional revision experiences of Illinois, Michigan, and Pennsylvania, which have rewritten their nineteenth century charters within the last quarter century to more closely comport with Marshall's maxim. At a minimum, the archaic constitutional material that should be deleted includes limits on the number of legislative employees, the dueling prohibition, and provisions concerning the Railroad Commission, temporary succession of the lieutenant governor, and racially based separate schools. Statutory provisions in the constitution, especially those governing taxation, finance, and corporations, should be substantially revised.

While these changes should occasion little opposition, other provisions, also essential to a good constitution, will be much more difficult to introduce, because of continuing popular distrust of government and preference for using the suffrage and the statutory detail of the constitution to control public officials. The changes needed, some of which have already encountered a hostile public response as the subjects of failed constitutional amendments, would include revisions in the salary limitations on public officials, the biennial legislative session, the prohibition of gubernatorial succession, the gubernatorial line-item veto of appropriation bills, and the method of filling the offices of eleven elective state executive officials. In any debate over a revised constitution, with these provisions at the core, Kentuckians should seriously reexamine the constitutional controls their forebears have imposed on the state and its local governments, as the commonwealth enters its third century.

See Charlie Bush, ed., *A Citizen's Guide to the Kentucky Constitution* (Frankfort, Ky. 1987); Joan W. Coward, *The Kentucky Constitutions of 1792 and 1799* (Evanston, Ill., 1971); Bennett Young, *History and Texts of the Three Constitutions of Kentucky* (Louisville 1890).   WILLIAM GREEN

COOK, MARLOW WEBSTER. Marlow Webster Cook, U.S. senator, son of Floyd T. and Mary Lee (Webster) Cook, was born on July 27, 1926, in Akron, New York. He moved to Louisville in 1943 and during World War II joined the U.S. Navy, where he served in submarines. In 1945 he enrolled at the University of Louisville, where he received a law degree in 1950. He practiced law in Louisville until 1957, when he was elected to the Kentucky House of Representatives. He was reelected in 1959. In 1961 Cook was elected Jefferson County judge and reelected in 1965. Cook was defeated by Louie Nunn in a bitterly fought 1967 Republican gubernatorial primary. In 1968 Cook was elected to the U.S. Senate as a Republican, winning with 484,260 votes to Democrat Katherine Peden's 448,960 and Independent Duane Olson's 9,645. Cook lost his bid for reelection to Wendell Ford, 399,406 to 328,982. Cook then set up a law practice in Washington, D.C. He moved to Sarasota, Florida, in 1989. Cook married Nancy Remmers of Louisville in 1947. They have five children.

COOPER, JOHN SHERMAN. John Sherman Cooper, U.S. senator and diplomat, was born on August 23, 1901, at Somerset, Kentucky, to John and Helen (Tartar) Cooper. His father, a prominent lawyer, farmer, and businessman, served as Pulaski County judge, a position also held by Cooper's maternal grandfather. Educated first in a private school but mainly in the Somerset public schools, Cooper in the fall of 1918 enrolled at Centre College. After one academic year, he transferred to Yale University, where he received an A.B. in 1923. Cooper entered Harvard Law School in the fall of 1923, but after his father's death the following summer he returned to Somerset to head the family.

Passing the Kentucky bar examination in 1928, Cooper began the practice of law in Somerset. In the same year he was elected to the Kentucky House of Representatives, where he was one of only three Republicans to oppose Gov. Flem Sampson's (1927-31) unsuccessful effort to politicize the state's Health Department. Cooper supported the governor's bill to provide free textbooks, and he introduced a bill to prohibit injunctions against labor strikes. After serving two terms as judge of Pulaski County (1930-38), he made a bid for the Republican gubernatorial nomination in 1939. Defeated by King Swope, he resumed the practice of law in Somerset. He had been appointed to the University of Kentucky board of trustees in 1935, a position he held until 1946.

At the age of forty-one, Cooper enlisted in the U.S. army as a private and was commissioned a second lieutenant in 1943. He served with Gen. George Patton's 3d Army in France, Luxembourg, and Germany. After the war, Captain Cooper headed the reorganization of the German judicial system in Bavaria and served as legal adviser for the repatriation of displaced persons in the 3d Army occupation zone.

While still in Germany, Cooper was elected circuit judge for Kentucky's 28th Judicial District. During his tenure, blacks were allowed to serve on trial juries for the first time in that judicial district. In 1946 Cooper was elected to the U.S. Senate to fill the unexpired term of A.B. Chandler, who had resigned to become commissioner of baseball. He won over John Y. Brown, Sr., by 42,000 votes, the largest majority given a Republican in Kentucky up to that time. As a freshman senator (November 6, 1946 to January 3, 1949), Cooper sponsored the first bill to provide 90 percent parity support for tobacco, and he quickly established a reputation for independence. His bid for reelection was thwarted by Democrat Virgil Chapman. In 1949 Cooper affiliated with the Washington law firm of Gardner, Morison and Rogers. President Harry S. Truman appointed him a delegate to the U.N. General Assembly in 1949, and he served as an alternate delegate in 1950 and 1951 and again in 1968 and 1981. He was an adviser to Secretary of State Dean Acheson at the London and Brussels meetings of the North Atlantic Treaty Organizations's Council of Ministers in 1950.

Cooper was again elected to the Senate over Thomas R. Underwood, to fill the vacancy created by the death of Virgil Chapman, starting November 5, 1952. However, in 1954 his bid for reelection was defeated by his good friend, former Senate majority leader and Vice-President Alben Barkley, and his term ended on January 3, 1955. President Dwight D. Eisenhower appointed Cooper ambassador to India and Nepal in January 1955; U.S.-Indian relations demonstrated a marked improvement during Cooper's tenure.

Cooper was elected over the Democratic candidate, Lawrence Wetherby, to fill the unexpired U.S. Senate term created by the death of Alben Barkley. In the senatorial election of 1960, Cooper won his first full six-year term, defeating Keen Johnson by 199,000 votes. In 1966 he won over John Y. Brown, Sr., by 217,000 votes. Cooper, who did not seek reelection in 1972, served from November 7, 1956, to January 3, 1973. He cosponsored with Sen. Jennings Randolph the Appalachian Regional Development Act. He vigorously opposed deployment of the antiballistic missile system (Cooper-Hart Amendment), and attempts to weaken the Tennessee Valley Authority. From his position on the Foreign Relations Committee, he was one of the earliest, most persistent, and influential critics of the Vietnam War.

A 1960 *Newsweek* poll of fifty Washington news correspondents named Cooper the ablest Republican in the Senate. President Lyndon B. Johnson in 1963 appointed him to the Warren Commission, which investigated the assassination of President John F. Kennedy. From 1973 to 1989 Cooper was a member of the law firm of Covington and Burling in Washington, D.C. He took leave from the firm in 1974 to accept President Gerald Ford's appointment as the first U.S. ambassador to the German Democratic Republic, serving in that post until late 1976.

In 1944 Cooper married Evelyn Pfaff. They were divorced in 1947. Cooper was married to Lorraine Rowan Shevlin from March 17, 1955, until her death on February 3, 1985. Cooper died on February 21, 1991, in Washington, D.C., and was buried in Arlington National Cemetery.

See Clarice James Mitchener, *Senator John Sherman Cooper: Consummate Statesman* (New York 1982); Robert Schulman, *John Sherman Cooper: The Global Kentuckian* (Lexington, Ky., 1976).

WILLIAM COOPER

CORBIN. Corbin is located at the juncture of Whitley, Laurel, and Knox counties in southeastern Kentucky on Lynn Camp Creek. The original settlement was named Lynn Camp after William Lynn, a Virginian who was lost in the area around 1800. It remained a scattering of small farms amid the wilderness until 1883, when the Louisville & Nashville (L&N) Railroad extended its main line to the rich coal fields of the Cumberland Valley. Two years later, Lynn Camp Station was renamed in honor of the Rev. James Corbin Floyd, a local minister.

Corbin began to grow when the L&N decided to build a roundhouse and other facilities there in 1891. By the 1930s, Corbin was a city of 8,070 people, and most of the city's 1,500 wage earners were dependent on the railroad in some way. When the town outgrew its original city limits in Whitley County, suburbs quickly formed in adjacent Knox and Laurel counties.

In 1990 Corbin was the leading railroad center of southeastern Kentucky. Its proximity to Cumberland Falls State Park and Laurel River Lake made tourism a vital part of the local economy. The first of Harland Sanders's Kentucky Fried Chicken restaurants opened in Corbin in 1930.

Corbin, incorporated in 1905, is a third-class city and the largest in Whitley County. Its population was 7,317 in 1970; 8,075 in 1980; and 7,419 in 1990.

CORN ISLAND. The small band of pioneers who established Louisville first settled on Corn Island in the Ohio River on May 27, 1778. During the following summer George Rogers Clark trained recruits for his Illinois campaign on the island, and the settlers planted corn and camped there until the fort on shore, Fort Nelson, was built in 1781. Part of Corn Island washed away and the rest was submerged when the dam at the Falls of the Ohio was built in the 1920s. Old maps show that it lay near what is now the foot of Twelfth Street in Louisville, above the falls.

See George H. Yater, *Two Hundred Years at the Falls of the Ohio* (Louisville 1979).   GAIL KING

CORN PATCH AND CABIN RIGHTS. In an effort to regularize western land distribution, the Virginia General Assembly in 1776 devised a clumsy, unworkable system known as "corn patch and cabin rights." The law provided that a settler on western lands could demonstrate a serious intent to establish a claim by erecting a cabin and planting a patch of corn prior to January 1, 1778. This procedure would establish a claim to four hundred acres if the claimant also procured a Virginia land warrant and registered a deed. The law said nothing of the cabin's size or construction nor of the size of the cornpatch, so even a token shelter and a few stalks of corn qualified.   THOMAS D. CLARK

COTTER, JOSEPH SEAMON. Joseph Seamon Cotter, poet and educator, was born on February 2, 1861, near Bardstown, Kentucky, to Micheil J. Cotter and Martha Vaugh. His father was a Scotch-Irishman and his mother the daughter of an African slave. Mother and infant moved to Louisville when Cotter was four months old. Cotter, who learned to read by the age of four, left the third grade in 1869 to help his mother support the family by such jobs as picking up rags, bricklaying, tobacco cutting, and prize fighting. He developed boxing skills in defending himself at work against older boys. William T. Peyton, a Louisville educator, discovered Cotter's ability to write poetry and persuaded him to quit boxing and return to school. Cotter attended Louisville's first black night school in 1883, and after taking two five-month courses earned a high school diploma and was qualified to teach. He taught at Cloverdale, outside Louisville, during 1885-87 and at a local private school during 1887-89. Cotter then began instructing in the Louisville public school system at Western Colored School. He became principal of the Paul Dunbar School, named for the poet who had visited him in 1894 and had become his close friend. He then served as principal at Samuel Taylor Coleridge School from 1911 until his retirement in 1942. Cotter became a member of the Louisville Board of Education in 1938.

Cotter's first volume of poetry was *A Rhyming* (1895). His *Links of Friendship* (1898) contained a variety of ballads, lyrics, and children's poems. It also contained his replies to the work of Paul Dunbar—"Answer to Dunbar's 'After a Visit' " and "Answer to Dunbar's 'A Choice' "—as well as one of Cotter's better-known poems, "Sequel to 'The Pied Piper of Hamelin'?" Cotter demonstrated his mastery of black dialect, learned from Dunbar, in the poems of *A White Song and a Black One* (1909), and in his one work of fiction, *Negro Tales* (1912). This book is thought to be one of only four works of fiction by black authors published between 1906 and 1922. Cotter had worked fifty years in the public school system when his *Collected Poems* (1938), which also used dialect, appeared in print.

His final collection was *Negroes and Others at Work and Play* (1947). Cotter also wrote *Caleb; A Play in Four Acts* (1903).

Cotter married Maria F. Fox on July 22, 1891; they had three children: Florence; Joseph, Jr., who was also a poet; and Leonides. Cotter died on March 14, 1949, and was buried in Greenwood Cemetery in Louisville.

COTTERILL, ROBERT SPENCER. Robert Spencer Cotterill, historian and educator, the son of Francis Marion and Jenny (Spencer) Cotterill, was born in Fleming County, Kentucky, on August 12, 1884, at the now forgotten village of Battle Run. Living near the Lower Blue Licks, young Cotterill was steeped in Kentucky's pioneer history. He received an A.B. degree from Kentucky Wesleyan College in Winchester (1904), a master's degree from the University of Virginia (1907), and a doctorate from the University of Wisconsin (1918). In the intervening years, 1904-18, Cotterill taught at Kentucky Wesleyan College and Western Maryland State College. At Wisconsin he was a student of and greatly influenced by historian Frederick Jackson Turner. His doctoral dissertation, *The History of Pioneer Kentucky*, was published in 1917.

Cotterill, one of the founders of the Southern Historical Association, was a member of the history department at the University of Louisville. He was a visiting professor at the Universities of Kentucky, Virginia, and Georgia. In 1928 he joined the history department of Florida State College for Women (now Florida State University at Tallahassee) where he remained until his retirement in 1951.

Cotterill was the author of *A Short History of the Americas* (1939) and *The Southern Indians* (1954). His book *The Old South* (1956) was a pioneering attempt to synthesize the subject. He served as president of the Southern Historical Association in 1948. In his presidential address that year, he contended that the Civil War was not a "mighty cataclysm engulfing the Old South or the chasm dividing the old from the new," but only an interruption in an established pattern of life; for the South the war marked no end, no beginning.

Cotterill established himself as an authority on southern Indians. At his death, on July 26, 1967, in Tallahassee, Florida, he had completed in draft form a well-researched history of Fleming County, Kentucky.

See Robert S. Cotterill, "The Old South to the New," *Journal of Southern History* 15 (Feb. 1949): 1-8.   THOMAS D. CLARK

COUNCIL OF THE SOUTHERN MOUNTAINS, INC. The history of the Council of the Southern Mountains exemplifies the shifting style, content, and direction of reform in Appalachia for most of the twentieth century. The expansion of industrialization into the region coincided with the arrival of hundreds of religious and philanthropic agents, who established "uplift" enterprises in mountain communities. In 1913 John C. Campbell of the Russell Sage Foundation invited more than one hundred of the Appalachian social workers to Atlanta, Georgia, where they formed the Southern Mountain Workers Conference. In 1954 the group's name became the Council of the Southern Mountains.

In 1925 the council opened an office at Berea College in Kentucky and began publishing *Mountain Life & Work* as part of a unified program to ameliorate Appalachia's ills. It formed standing committees on health, education, recreation, and spiritual life, and it created the Southern Highland Handicraft Guild, a cooperative marketing outlet for mountain artisans. Self-imposed operational limitations and severe financial constraints nearly doomed the organization. But under the leadership of Perley F. Ayer, appointed executive secretary in 1951, the council became the most well-known and influential voice in southern Appalachia. Ayer believed that the council should pursue a "partnership" ideal, encouraging various interests to develop a reform strategy based upon a consensus of regional opinion.

The council's scope of activities increased rapidly when national attention focused on the depressed areas of Appalachia in the early 1960s. The federal government's War on Poverty financed several new programs—the most publicized being the Appalachian Volunteers (AVs), college students who refurbished eastern Kentucky's one- and two-room schoolhouses. Tensions arose as some council staff members and AVs argued that the reform-by-consensus approach had been ineffective in ending Appalachian poverty and that what the poor needed was to organize themselves and challenge established institutions and groups.

A series of dramatic changes followed. The AVs declared their independence in 1966. Loyal Jones succeeded Ayer as executive director of the Council of the Southern Mountains and tried to bridge the council's divisions but in a takeover in 1969-70, the council was transformed into a strident advocate for the poor. From its new coal field headquarters in Clintwood, Virginia, the council supported various grass-roots economic, health, and environmental efforts. After several years of fitful activity, the council was officially dissolved in 1989.

See David E. Whisnant, *Modernizing the Mountaineer: People, Power, and Planning in Appalachia* (Boone, N.C., 1980).   JOHN M. GLEN

COUNTIES. Kentucky has 120 counties, making it third in the nation in the number of counties, after Texas and Georgia. Early in its history, Kentucky established counties to ensure that residents were within a single day's round trip of the county seat, but by the 1820s politics and land speculation began to figure in the process of county proliferation. Residents who became disenchanted with the politics and policies of the county government could, in effect, secede from the county if they could persuade the legislature to create a new county around them. The value of a farmer's land would be greatly enhanced if it became the site of the seat of a new county. After the Civil War, Kentuckians began to complain about the excessive number of counties, arguing that too many counties led to poor governmental services and even lawlessness. This concern prompted the framers of the constitution of 1891 to strictly limit the ability of the legislature to establish counties. Since the adoption of that constitution, only one additional county has been created. Modern observers complain that the excessive number of Kentucky counties compromises education and governmental services. Nevertheless, Kentuckians remain fiercely loyal to their counties, which because of their small size are like hometowns to many.

The county court has always been the nucleus of LOCAL GOVERNMENT in Kentucky. Until 1850 the justices of the peace, who individually had minor judicial and law enforcement powers, collectively formed the court and appointed most of the other officers of the county. The court levied local taxes, probated wills, oversaw guardianships and apprenticeships, regulated taverns, maintained the roads, provided for the poor, tried illegitimacy cases, and had charge of numerous other items of local business. The senior justice of the peace normally became the sheriff for a two-year period. Reforms in 1850 were a response to the tendency to sell that office in the more prosperous counties and the generally undemocratic, often partisan and unrepresentative nature of the antebellum courts.

The new constitution of 1850 created the office of county judge, who was to preside over the county court when it sat to transact nonjudicial business and to handle alone all judicial business, including probate matters. The justices of the peace continued to sit on the court of claims, although in the late nineteenth and the twentieth centuries a few counties replaced justices of the peace with county commissioners. The constitution of 1850 also provided that the voters would elect all of the county officers and that justices of the peace would represent individual districts, not the county as a whole, as had been the case previously. The sheriff continued to be a very important county officer, charged with a variety of duties. Sheriffs collected county and state taxes, served as the executive officers of the circuit courts, were the chief election officials, and conducted much of the local law enforcement. This latter function suffered, especially in the second half of the nineteenth century, because of the other burdens of the office, the dangers of law enforcement, the relatively poor pay, and the low caliber of some of the occupants of the office. Certain sheriffs in lawless counties were actually part of the leadership of feuding factions.

Of the other officers of the county, the county court clerk conducted the most important business. Because employment as the county clerk could be very lucrative in the more prosperous counties, the office was often bought and sold before the constitution of 1850 made the position elective. The coroner also had important duties, especially as lawlessness became a statewide problem. Well into the twentieth century, detractors complained that too often coroners lacked the necessary medical expertise to determine accurately the causes of suspicious deaths. By the twentieth century the office of county surveyor had become useless, seldom filled in most counties. Reformers called for the abolition of the surveyorship and the merger of the sheriff's office with that of the jailer. In 1975 Kentucky voters approved a constitutional amendment that stripped the county judge, usually not a lawyer, of judicial duties and transferred them to a newly created district judge.

For most of the nineteenth century, counties maintained an active interest in improving transportation and invested in turnpike and railroad ventures. The latter nearly bankrupted some counties after the Civil War. Too often railroad schemes would fail, leaving counties with nothing but a legal obligation to pay off an enormous debt. For much of the century, able-bodied male adults were obligated to work on the county roads when called into action by the local road overseer. The development of the modern road system in the twentieth century eliminated what was for most a highly unpleasant obligation, frequently evaded.

In antebellum Kentucky, a few counties sometimes engaged in serious rivalry with newly emerging towns and cities. Modified home rule gave municipal corporations judicial and fiscal power at the expense of county government. Smarting from this development, the leaders of the Fayette County government in 1836 launched a nearly successful campaign to revoke the recently issued charter of the City of Lexington. In the previous year, the city fathers of Louisville, resentful over their failure to convince the Jefferson County Court to make improvements in county buildings, attempted to arrange for Louisville to secede from Jefferson County by persuading the legislature to attach county-like status to the city. The legislature refused.

The counties of Kentucky have always had a close relationship with the General Assembly, as counties constitutionally are but units of the state and depend on the legislature for most of their power. During the first sixty years of Kentucky's history, many justices of the peace also served in the legislature. Increasingly in the nineteenth century, county courts and county officers found it necessary to petition the legislature for special statutes to solve very local and personal problems such as extensions of filing dates or waivers of maximum tax rates. By 1890 the legislature was so overwhelmed by such business that the constitutional convention of that year provided for strict limitations on the ability of future legislatures to enact special and local legislation.

Court day, the one day of the month when the county court conducted its most important business, was also the highlight of the month for many of the county residents. Farmers came to the county seat to sell livestock and produce and to buy items needed for the farm. County seat merchants enjoyed their most productive sales day. Politicians found a ready audience for their long-winded efforts to woo the voters. The tradition of court day continued into the twentieth century but gradually disappeared as transportation improved.

See Robert M. Ireland, *Little Kingdoms: The Counties of Kentucky, 1850-1891* (Lexington, Ky., 1977); Ireland, *The County in Kentucky History* (Lexington, Ky., 1976).   ROBERT M. IRELAND

COUNTRY LIFE MOVEMENT. In 1908 President Theodore Roosevelt appointed the Country Life Commission to study and advise on the nation's perceived crisis in rural life in the early twentieth century. A national nostalgia for America's agricultural and small-town past was prevalent at the time, as industrialization, urbanization, and immigration all accelerated rapidly. Most "country lifers" focused on a perceived loss of the agrarian values that rural living was assumed to teach, and sought some avenue for retaining what was left of such values in the countryside. Others, disturbed by the migration of rural residents to the cities, believed that a concerted effort to improve the daily lives of the remaining rural Americans was essential. Those concerned about food supplies necessary for continued urban economic growth wanted to ensure that enough capable farmers remained in the countryside.

The country life movement, like other social movements, is not easily defined. The Country Life Commission itself was not a policy group; rather, it completed a national survey and held public forums to discuss rural issues around the nation. However, specific rural improvement projects in Kentucky and elsewhere throughout the nation were the work of various philanthropic organizations and government agencies that were undoubtedly influenced (but not controlled) by advocates of improved country life. The quality of life of many rural Americans was no doubt enhanced in the early twentieth century through a number of economic infrastructure improvements, rural electrification programs, road construction, and sewage system projects. The country life movement might best be understood as the rural version of the larger Progressive movement in early twentieth century America, which viewed science, democracy, and technology as cornerstones of national progress and community health.

In addition to improving the rural infrastructure, believers in the message of improved country living sought to educate schoolchildren, adults, and civic organizations. Disseminating knowledge about scientific agriculture through county extension agents to farmers and farmers' organizations was one means of education. For women, strategies and techniques for better managing families and households were offered by home economics specialists under auspices of state and federal governments. Improving the education of children by consolidating small and costly one-room schools and by restructuring elementary school curricula toward

nature study became other agendas of some country lifers during the 1920s and 1930s.

                                                    ALAN DEYOUNG

COUNTRY MUSIC. Originally the music of rural America, country music continues to thrive in an urban-industrial society, especially among the blue-collar working class. Although it has always been nationwide in scope, it has been especially popular in the South. The term country music did not achieve universal usage until 1950; until then it was referred to as folk, old-time, old familiar, cowboy, western, or (sometimes derogatorily) hillbilly music.

The origins of country music are diverse: British ballads, music of European immigrants, jigs, reels, native American ballads, spirituals, gospel music, minstrel tunes, parlor songs, work songs, cowboy music, and especially the blues. Of all ethnic groups, none played a more important role in providing songs and styles for white country musicians than did blacks.

Commercial country music became important with the first country recordings and the development of the radio in the 1920s. Kentuckian William Houchens was among the earliest to record country music. As Uncle Jim Hawkins, he made his first recordings for Gennett on September 18, 1922, nine months before Fiddlin' John Carson made what some historians consider the first country recording. (Eck Robertson and Henry Gilliland, however, recorded some country fiddle tunes as early as June 1922.) In 1925 Welby Toomey became the first country singer from Kentucky to record. The first Kentuckians to appear on a major label were Dick Burnett and Leonard Rutherford. The most widely recorded of all Kentucky fiddlers was Philipine ("Doc") ROBERTS who is heard on nearly two hundred sides. In 1927 Roberts and two black brothers, John and Joe Buell KAZEE, the latter a Kentucky minister with a trained voice, played a major role in the transition from folk to country music. Dennis Taylor, one of the country music's first booking and recording agents, managed a biracial band called Taylor's Kentucky Boys and was responsible for the first recordings of Toomey, Roberts, and others.

The key event in country music during the late 1920s was a recording session in Bristol, Tennessee, in 1927, which led to the discovery of the Carter Family and Jimmie Rodgers (whose only joint recordings were made in Louisville in 1931). Kentuckians recording at Bristol included Alfred Karnes, Ernest Phipps and His Holiness Quarter, and B.F. Shelton.

Kentuckians were prominent on the nation's leading country radio programs—the "National Barn Dance" (WLS Chicago) and the "Grand Ole Opry" (WSM Nashville). The Kentucky Wonder Bean (Walter Peterson) and comic banjoist Chubby Parker were among the first to perform on WLS. They were eclipsed by Bradley KINCAID, the star of the show during 1926-30. Mac and Bob (Lester McFarland and Bob Gardner), who met as students at the Kentucky School for the Blind, joined WLS in 1931. In 1937 Kentuckian John LAIR became program director of WLS. He brought to the station numerous musicians from Kentucky, and organized the Cumberland Ridge Runners, which included Karl Davis, Harty Taylor, Red Foley, Doc Hopkins, Slim Miller, and Linda Parker. Another Kentucky string band on WLS was the Prairie Ramblers, consisting of Chick Hurt, Jack Taylor, Tex Atchison, and Salty Holmes. Kentucky's Bob ATCHER sometimes sang duets with his brother Randall or with one of a series of female singers, each known as Bonnie Blue Eyes.

In 1937 Lair moved to WLW Cincinnati, taking many WLS performers with him. He formed an all-female string band, the Coon Creek Girls, including Kentuckians Lily May and Rosie LEDFORD. In 1939 he opened the "Renfro Valley Barn Dance" in Rockcastle County. The show introduced many country music performers who went on to stardom, as well as bringing established stars to Renfro Valley for guest appearances. For several years the show was broadcast over WHAS (Louisville) and the NBC network.

Among the first Kentuckians to appear on the "Grand Ole Opry" were Asher Sizemore and his son, Little Jimmy, who started on WSM in 1933, at age five. Pee Wee King was an "Opry" headliner during 1937-47. Red Foley hosted the prime-time segment of the "Opry" on NBC radio during 1946-54. Bill Monroe, the "Father of Bluegrass Music," performed on the show during this era. Because of the prominence the "Opry" has enjoyed since World War II, most successful modern country music performers have appeared on it. Among them are Kentuckians David ("Stringbean") AKEMAN, Bill Carlisle, John Conlee, Skeeter Davis, the EVERLY BROTHERS, Tom T. HALL, Grandpa JONES (Louis Marshall), Loretta LYNN, the OSBORNE BROTHERS, Ricky SKAGGS, and Merle TRAVIS.

WHAS and WLAP (Lexington) became regionally important country music stations during the 1930s. Among Kentucky musicians not mentioned above who performed on these stations were Cliff Carlisle, Wilbur Ball, Lonesome Luke Decker's Farm Boys, Uncle Henry Warren's Original Kentucky Mountaineers, Cousin Emmy (Cynthia May Carver), Frankie Moore's Log Cabin Boys, Asa Martin, and Molly O'Day (LaVerne Williamson Davis). Promoter J.L. Frank brought much talent to WHAS, including King and Gene Autry. Leading bands in Louisville were those of Clifford Gross and Clayton McMichen.

Country music's highest honor is election to its Hall of Fame. Those with Kentucky connections so honored include Foley, Monroe, Travis, Jones, Autry, and Frank. Lynn, Hall, and Crystal Gayle have won Grammies. Lynn is the most honored female star in country music history. Kentucky is second to Texas in the number of country music stars produced, and the prominence of Kentucky musicians is demonstrated by the 1989 Music City News Awards. Winners included Skaggs (instrumental) and the Judds (vocal duo), and in the Star of To-

morrow category three of the five nominees were Kentuckians, with Patty Loveless winning over Dwight Yoakam and Keith Whitley. More important than numbers is the influence that Kentuckians have had in the preservation of old-time music and in the evolution of country music.

See Charles K. Wolfe, *Kentucky Country* (Lexington, Ky., 1982); Bill C. Malone, *Country Music U.S.A.* (Austin, Tex., 1985); Neil V. Rosenberg, *Bluegrass* (Urbana, Ill., 1985).

CHARLES F. FABER

COUNTRY STORE. Not until well into the twentieth century did Kentucky have within its borders what the U.S. Census Bureau classified as a standard metropolitan area. To satisfy the needs of its rural population, country stores for general merchandising came into existence after 1830, multiplying after the Civil War. For the most part, Kentucky's rural commerce took place at crossroads or at strategic sites on creek and river banks. To keep the subsistence farmer going, the country stores all carried the staples—salt, coffee, sugar, patent medicines, and farming supplies. Their shelves were stocked with bolts of coarse cloth rather than ready-made garments. The fully stocked country store sold everything a rural population needed, from swaddling clothes to burial shrouds and coffin fixtures.

The stores themselves were supplied with goods and credit by wholesale houses in Louisville, Lexington, and Cincinnati. Some in southern and western Kentucky bought goods in Nashville or St. Louis. Louisville merchants, especially solicitous of the country trade, sent swarms of drummers into the country to help set up stores, establish credit lines, and supply merchandise. At the same time itinerant salesmen traveled from one crossroads store to the next, lugging trunks of merchandise in hacks and farm wagons. These salesmen helped to set many of Kentucky's social and aesthetic tastes.

The country stores were market centers, exchanging merchandise for farm produce, eggs, chickens, furs, herbs, and even moonshine whiskey. Rural Kentuckians saw limited amounts of cash money, and the country store came close to being a complete barter center. Storekeepers in many cases acted as credit grantors and semibankers.

The Kentucky country store, however, was more than a commercial institution. It was a community center where people gathered to hear the news, to gossip, brag—even to fight. The store's traditional pot-bellied stove became as much a social and community gathering place as were the country church and school. Many country stores served as post offices. Often the storekeeper or a member of his family was postmaster, who served as both mail dispenser and public amanuensis for the lovelorn and illiterate who needed help in writing letters.

See Thomas D. Clark, *Pills, Petticoats, and Plows* (Indianapolis 1944).   THOMAS D. CLARK

COURIER-JOURNAL. On the first appearance of the *Louisville Courier-Journal* on November 8,

1868, its editor, Henry WATTERSON, wrote that the newspaper was "strong enough to go its own gait, regardless of the merchants and the politicians." In terms of nationwide editorial potency, Watterson's words proved strikingly apt through fifty years of his *Courier-Journal* editorship. By the time the paper was twenty-five years old in 1893, said Watterson biographer Joseph Frazier Wall, it had "an editorial page as widely quoted as . . . any . . . in the country. . . . Certainly, no inland city could boast of a paper as well known." In 1914 war in Europe was only thirty days old when Watterson editorially coined a battle cry: "To hell with the Hapsburgs and the Hohenzollern!" Despite the slogan's being what Wall called the work of "an unabashed jingoist," it won, with repetition, national attention and in 1917 brought Watterson and the *Courier-Journal* one of the first Pulitzer prizes awarded.

In 1918 Robert Worth BINGHAM bought the *Courier-Journal* and its sister afternoon daily, the *Louisville Times* from Watterson and from the embattled family of his business partner, Walter N. HALDEMAN. Under Bingham, the *Courier-Journal* earned respect for editorial policies supporting tobacco farmers, natural resource conservation, League of Nations–style internationalism, women's suffrage, and firm oversight of saloons—all at dramatic variance from Watterson's views. A 1925 exploit by *Courier-Journal* reporter William Burke ("Skeets") Miller, in interviewing trapped cave explorer Floyd COLLINS, brought a second Pulitzer Prize to Louisville.

In 1937 Robert Bingham's son, George Barry BINGHAM, took over the operations and employed Georgia journalist Mark ETHRIDGE as his top news and editorial director. At that point, the "true golden era" of the newspaper arrived, as the *Courier-Journal's* own historian, Joe CREASON, observed in the newspaper's 1968 centennial issue. Bingham and Ethridge added hard-driving news executives such as James E. Pope from Atlanta and Norman E. Isaacs from St. Louis to strengthen the two papers. They were so successful that the staff of 350 began attracting talent raids by the *Washington Post* and the *New York Times*. After a gap of forty years in producing work of Pulitzer Prize caliber, the year 1969 ushered in a twenty-year period during which staffers of the *Courier-Journal*, singly or jointly with *Louisville Times* colleagues, captured six Pulitzers for public service, domestic or foreign reporting, or photojournalism.

In 1946, in his *Inside U.S.A.*, John Gunther described the *Courier-Journal* as "one of the best newspapers in the country . . . the dominant newspaper in its state and a splendid liberal force." In 1955, as a candidate for governor, Bert T. Combs borrowed from John Ed Pearce, then a *Courier-Journal* editorial writer, what became a Kentucky axiom reflecting the newspaper's influence in a conservative state: "Only two things hold together the people of Kentucky—the University of Kentucky and the G.D. *Courier-Journal*." For almost twenty years, beginning in 1960, the *Courier-*

Journal was consistently included by journalistic peers in the lists of the ten best newspapers in the United States.

Both newspapers were sold to the Gannett conglomerate in 1986 and others bought the Bingham printing and radio-TV properties after Bingham failed to resolve hostility between his successor, son George Barry, Jr., and his daughter Sallie. The feud primarily concerned feminist issues, although Bingham, Jr., in 1974 had appointed a woman as managing editor—a first for any metropolitan newspaper in the country. The $306 million acquisition led the chairman of Gannett to observe that the *Courier-Journal* would be "the jewel" among the company's ninety-plus newspapers.

Fears that under Gannett the *Courier-Journal* would be milked of its news vigor proved unjustified. Nevertheless, even before the collapse of the Bingham family dynasty in 1986, rising transportation and newsprint costs had begun eroding the statewide circulation of the paper, which had peaked at 233,000 in 1973. Elimination of the afternoon *Times* had been contemplated even prior to the sale. After the takeover, Gannett retained the *Courier-Journal's* unusual pattern of regional bureau news coverage of Kentucky and southern Indiana. Gannett also kept personnel of the Bingham era in all news and management executive posts, including former *Courier-Journal* managing editor George Gill as publisher. The newspaper's ninth Pulitzer Prize came for reporting during the third year of the Gannett ownership, when *Courier-Journal* circulation climbed back to 235,000 after the *Times* was eliminated.

See Joseph Frazier Wall, *Henry Watterson: Reconstructed Rebel* (New York 1956).

ROBERT SCHULMAN

COURT OF OYER AND TERMINER. Under the Kentucky Constitution of 1792, the General Assembly on June 28, 1792, provided for the establishment of county courts, courts of quarter sessions, and courts of oyer and terminer. The phrase "oyer and terminer" means to hear and decide. Some form of court of this intermediate jurisdiction came to England from Norman France, and possibly from Rome, and the Kentucky court of oyer and terminer was brought across the mountains from Virginia. The Kentucky court of oyer and terminer, which met three times a year and had largely criminal jurisdiction, was presided over by three judges. The court of oyer and terminer was abolished on February 15, 1795.

See Mann Butler, *A History of the Commonwealth of Kentucky* (Louisville 1834).

THOMAS D. CLARK

COURT SYSTEM. Kentucky's courts have not escaped the colorful, sometimes violent struggles that have enlivened state history. If there is any single theme running through the history of the state judiciary, it is the struggle between the values of independence and responsiveness. Kentuckians have vacillated between wanting a judiciary adequately large and free of legislative pressures to provide prompt justice, and wanting a judiciary responsive to popular will and therefore subservient to the legislature and the voting public. The various reforms inaugurated from time to time have reflected that vacillation. The reforms ratified as a constitutional amendment in 1975 favor independence and have made Kentucky's courts among the most innovative and professional in the nation. There are two major components of the system—the one that the public sees and a collection of several less visible support groups under the Administrative Office of the Courts (AOC).

The Kentucky court system has four distinct layers: the supreme court, the intermediate court of appeals, circuit courts, and district courts. The supreme court is composed of seven justices, one elected from each of seven geographic areas. Justices are elected for eight-year terms, staggered among the areas so that no sudden political passion can instantly create a new supreme court. The chief justice is elected for a four-year term by fellow justices. The supreme court has appellate jurisdiction and ordinarily hears cases of constitutional or other high significance, on discretionary review from the court of appeals. Circuit court decisions imposing the death penalty, life imprisonment, or imprisonment of more than twenty years, however, are automatically reviewed. Traditionally, the supreme court has the final word on the admission of attorneys to the Kentucky bar and can discipline them as well. The supreme court has a great deal of discretion in determining the rules of practice and procedure for the entire court system.

The court of appeals was the one entirely new court created by the reforms of 1975. This court consists of fourteen judges, two elected from each appellate district for terms of eight years each. Unlike the supreme court, which traditionally sits in full in Frankfort, the court of appeals may divide itself into panels of three or more judges and move to various locations in the state. Panels are chosen on a rotating basis so that every judge sits with every other judge at least annually. A chief judge of the court of appeals is elected by his or her peers for a term of four years. The chief judge's duties are primarily the assignment of judges and cases to the various panels. The court of appeals hears cases on appeal from the circuit courts and it may be authorized by rule to review directly decisions of administrative agencies.

Circuit courts tend to be the workhorses of the system. All felony trials, contested probate, and cases involving monetary values of more than $4,000 begin in the circuit courts. Circuit courts also have jurisdiction over domestic relations and cases appealed from district court and administrative agencies. Circuit courts and district courts are trial courts, so it is at these levels that juries are impaneled. The ninety-one circuit judges are locally elected from fifty-six circuits for terms of eight years each. While these circuits follow county lines, some judges serve up to four counties, others serve

in one-county districts, and in the urban counties there are multijudge circuits. By law, circuit court must be held in each county, so some judges travel from county to county.

District courts round out the formal structure of the system. They have limited jurisdiction over felony preliminary hearings; mental inquest warrants; probate; and misdemeanors, including traffic violations, juvenile matters, and civil cases where the disputed amount is less than $4,000. Since the bulk of routine cases begin and end in district court, the district court system has the most judges. In 1990 there were 123 judges at this level, each elected for a four-year term. In sparsely populated counties where no district judge resides, a trial commissioner is appointed to handle routine legal matters.

An increasingly important part of district court is the small claims division. With an office in each county, the small claims court settles disputes involving money or property valued at $1,500 or less. Court procedures are purposely kept informal so that citizens can file a claim or defend themselves without the expense of an attorney. The parties at odds tell their stories to a judge, who may ask questions to clarify the facts, then make a decision based on the applicable law. Small claims court has no juries.

A remnant of a bygone era is the tradition of electing circuit court clerks in Kentucky on a partisan basis. While the supreme court and the court of appeals appoint their own clerks, a single circuit court clerk is elected in each of the 120 counties. Still a position of some power and patronage, the office of the clerk maintains court records, receives payment of fines, issues driver's licenses, schedules jury trials, and records trial proceedings for both circuit and district courts. Clerks are elected for six-year terms. Although candidates need have no particular training or expertise, candidates must pass a mandatory test, administered by the AOC. Clerks' duties are spelled out in a manual that has the force of law, and clerks are monitored by the AOC.

In 1976 the Kentucky General Assembly legislated that judges were to be elected from a nonpartisan ballot, on the theory that judges should be above party politics. Since judicial candidates are prohibited by the code of judicial ethics from discussing most substantive issues, judicial races have tended to become exercises in image building and name recognition. As a result, polls of local attorneys that rate the judicial candidates have had a significant impact on the outcome of at least some judicial races. Whether such polls accurately indicate who would be the better judge or simply who is the better attorney is still a matter of some dispute. Negative publicity over unpaid traffic tickets, for example, or for handing down a sentence considered too lenient, has also on occasion had a significant impact on voters.

Jury trials are held only at the circuit and district court levels. While federal courts require the unanimous decision of a twelve-person jury, Kentucky courts are much more flexible. In circuit court, juries may have six to twelve jurors, while district court juries have only six members. In criminal trials, jury verdicts must be unanimous, but in civil jury trials in circuit court, a three-fourths majority is sufficient to reach a verdict. A five-sixths majority is required in district court civil cases to reach a verdict.

The court of justice is supported by the AOC and a number of commissions, committees, and services. The most important of these are the Judicial Nominating Commission and the Judicial Retirement and Removal Commission. Although all judgeships in Kentucky are elective offices, the constitution provides that in the event of vacancies through death, disability, or retirement, the governor shall appoint a judge from a list of three names presented by a nominating commission. Each justice or judge so appointed must run for the office at the next regularly scheduled general election. There is one nominating commission for the supreme court and court of appeals and one for each circuit and district court jurisdiction—fifty-seven commissions in all. Each commission has seven members. The chief justice chairs all commissions; two commissioners are elected by the bar association of the jurisdiction in which the vacancy has occurred; and four are appointed by the governor, two from each of the two largest political parties. With the exception of the chief justice, all members serve four-year terms without compensation. Between elections as many as 10 percent of the judges may be appointed. For example, in 1983 the circuit court elections left twenty-three vacancies in district courts to be filled by appointment. The commissions are one way to balance local and partisan control with nonpartisan concern for judicial competence.

The Judicial Retirement and Removal Commission swings into action when elections or the appointive process fails to provide a high level of judicial competence. It is a watchdog with teeth. The commission has seven members and includes one judge of the court of appeals, one circuit judge, and one district judge, each elected by peers; one member of the bar association appointed by its governing body; and two persons not members of the bench or bar, appointed by the governor. Traditionally, judges have been removed from office only by impeachment, or in Kentucky, by defeat at the polls. Both are cumbersome, expensive, and ineffective. The commission has the authority to order the temporary or permanent retirement of any judge who has a physical or mental disability so serious that it interferes with the normal performance of judicial duties, to reprimand in private or in public any judge who is guilty of serious misconduct, and to remove that judge if appropriate. The commission can remove any judge who is elected without the proper qualifications.

If the four layers of formal courts are the backbone of the system, the AOC is the heart. For the most part it performs the duties of any governmental agency: budgeting, managing personnel and facilities, record keeping, auditing, planning judicial education, and informing the public. A unique and pioneering division of the AOC is Pretrial Services, which operates through fifty-seven field offices of various sizes. Pretrial Services has two major tasks; it provides objective information to the courts about persons arrested to ensure court appearance if they are released without posting bond (Kentucky is the only state that has outlawed commercial bail bonding), and it operates dispute-mediation programs in the five largest communities in the commonwealth. These programs, which resolve through voluntary mediation conflicts that might result in misdemeanor charges if pursued in district courts, save a considerable amount in time and money.

During the 1988-89 fiscal year, the supreme court handed down 1,038 final decisions and the court of appeals 2,836. The circuit courts decided roughly 68,869 cases. District courts issued final judgments in some 598,904 cases, nearly 4,791 per judge.

See Joel Goldstein, ed., *Kentucky Government and Politics* (Bloomington, Ind., 1984); Kentucky Court of Justice, *Annual Report 1985-1986*, Frankfort, Ky.   PAUL J. WEBER

COVERED BRIDGES. At one time there were more than four hundred covered wooden bridges in Kentucky, but most were destroyed by fire or allowed to deteriorate, leaving only thirteen still standing in 1990. Built by local woodworkers, most date from the 1800s, taking advantage of the abundance of timber in the state. The bridges were covered to protect their complex system of rigid trusses from the weather, as repair was a difficult and tedious task. Using local materials, each bridge was tailored to fit the stream and the traffic load it was expected to carry. Some of the bridges were partially assembled on the bank and rolled into place across the stream, and the roof and siding were then constructed. Bridges and roads were maintained by local residents over the age of sixteen who worked a specified number of days a year.

Except for Oldtown and Beech Fork, the thirteen bridges that remain are single-span structures. The bridges are located in the following counties:

Bourbon County. **Colville Bridge**, a double post and brace design, dates from 1877. The bridge has been painted several times by lawbreakers sentenced by a local judge to do so.

Bracken County. **Walcott Bridge**, also called **White Bridge**, dates back to the 1880s, when it probably replaced an earlier structure.

Fleming County. **Goddard Bridge** is a town lattice truss—the only one of this type remaining in Kentucky. There is no reliable source of the date of construction or the name of the builder. **Hillsboro Bridge**, constructed between 1865 and 1870, is of double post and brace design. Four flood marks are cut into the timber of this bridge, the highest—5 feet 9 inches above the floor—being dated January 25, 1937. **Ringos Mill Bridge** was built around

1869, near a gristmill. Of double post and brace design, it was built for the use of employees and customers living on or near the creek.

Franklin County. **Switzer Bridge** was built in 1855 by George Hockensmith and restored by Louis Bower in 1906. The bridge is a Howe truss, 120 feet long, 11 feet 6 inches wide, and 12 feet high.

Greenup County. **Oldtown Bridge**, a double post and brace design, was built around 1800. One of the two remaining two-span bridges, it has a long span of 145 feet and a short span of 41 feet, each built with a 6-foot shelter panel extension on the end. **Bennetts Mill Bridge** was built around 1856 by B. F. and Pramley Bennett to accommodate customers at their mill on Tygarts Creek. The longest single-span bridge in Kentucky—155 feet— it is still used for access to the lowlands.

Lewis County. **Cabin Creek Bridge**, built in 1873, is sometimes called the **Rectorville Bridge** or **Mackey-Hughes Bridge**. It is a single-span Burr truss, originally without arches.

Mason County. **Dover Bridge**, built as a toll bridge in 1835, is one of the oldest covered bridges still standing in Kentucky. The structure has a double set of queenpost trusses on each side. **Valley Pike Bridge**, a small privately owned structure built in 1864, is still in use. Most material in the bridge is original. A kingpost truss, it is 23 feet long, 15 feet wide, and 14 feet high.

Robertson County. **Johnson Creek Bridge**, built in 1874 by the Bower family, is a Smith truss design, 122 feet long.

Washington County. **Beech Fork Bridge** is the longest of Kentucky's covered bridges, each of its two spans being 102 feet in length. Sometimes called the **Mooresville Bridge**, it was built across the Beech Fork River in 1865 by L. H. and William Barnes and was part of the Springfield and Chaplin Turnpike. The two-span bridge is a Burr truss design with double arches at each truss.

See Vernon White, *Covered Bridges: Focus On Kentucky* (Berea, Ky., 1985); Robert A. Powell, *Kentucky Covered Wooden Bridges and Water-Powered Mills* (Lexington, Ky., 1984).

WENDELL C. THOMAS

COVINGTON. Covington, the largest city in northern Kentucky, is located in northwestern Kenton County at the confluence of the Licking and Ohio rivers. The city is built principally on a flat plain that is bordered on the south and west by hills. Covington lies across the Ohio River from Cincinnati and is connected to it by four bridges.

In the eighteenth century the area at the confluence of the Licking and Ohio rivers was known as the Point, a popular rendezvous place for explorers and pioneers. Christopher Gist, an agent for the Ohio Company, visited the area in 1751. Later, the Point served as a marshalling place for expeditions down the Ohio River to attack Indian settlements. On February 14, 1780, the site was presented as a two-hundred-acre military warrant to George Muse in recognition of his service during the French and Indian War. It then changed hands several times before Thomas Kennedy acquired it in 1791 and established a prosperous farm, a ferryboat service, and a tavern.

In 1814 Kennedy sold 150 acres of his land to John Gano, Richard M. Gano, and Thomas Carneal for the purpose of establishing a city. On February 8, 1815, the Kentucky legislature approved an act creating the town of Covington. The community was named in honor of Gen. Leonard Wales Covington, of Maryland, who had been mortally wounded at the Battle of Chrysler's Field in the War of 1812. Covington's growth was negligible during the years of the national depression following 1819, but by 1830 the town had a population of 715, a log church, several inns, and a schoolhouse where the town trustees met. In 1834 Covington received its charter as a city, and that year the voters elected New York-born Mortimer M. Benton as their first mayor.

Large numbers of Irish and German immigrants helped make Covington the state's second-largest city by 1850 and a recognized power in state politics by the time of the Civil War. Despite a highly vocal minority of Confederate sympathizers, the community remained overwhelmingly Unionist throughout the war. During the Confederate invasion of Kentucky in the late summer of 1862, southern troops commanded by Gen. Edmund Kirby-Smith threatened northern Kentucky, and martial law was declared in Covington by Union Gen. Lew Wallace. A pontoon bridge was laid over coal barges in the Ohio River to rush Cincinnati militia troops over to Covington to build and occupy earthen fortifications south of the city. The temporary bridge proved its value in connecting the two cities, and in 1867 the suspension bridge designed by John ROEBLING was opened. German and Irish immigration to the city continued after the Civil War, and the local economy grew rapidly. New industries, such as brewing and distilling, were established and existing ones, such as the manufacture of tobacco products, were enlarged.

In 1888 the bridge of the Chesapeake & Ohio Railway (now CSX Transportation) was opened, and the city was connected by rail with Cincinnati. The Covington & Lexington Railroad had connected it with Lexington as early as 1854. In the 1890s a city waterworks, an electric power plant, and a streetcar system were built. Local politics during this era was dominated by men such as John G. Carlisle, a lieutenant governor of Kentucky (1871-75) and U.S. senator (1890-93), and William Goebel, whose brief time as Kentucky governor in 1900 was ended by an unknown assassin.

In the early 1900s Covington expanded its boundaries. To the south it annexed the city of Central Covington (also known as Peaselburg) in 1906 and Latonia in 1909. To the west it annexed the city of West Covington in 1909, but failed in attempts to annex Ludlow. The annexations boosted Covington's population to more than 53,000 by 1910. That year, the Roman Catholic Cathedral Basilica of the Assumption was completed, patterned after Notre Dame Cathedral in France.

In 1930 the population of Covington peaked at 65,252 as many eastern Kentuckians flocked to the city in search of jobs during the Great Depression. In the decades that followed, the population of Covington declined as suburban cities began to grow in Kenton and surrounding counties. After World War II, a number of the city's well-established businesses and industries moved to the suburban outskirts.

To ease traffic congestion between northern Kentucky and Cincinnati, I-75 was built through the area during the 1960s. The highway construction razed one hundred homes in the city, and it divided Covington into east and west sections. The I-75 bridge across the Ohio River was completed in November 1963 and named for Brent Spence, a U.S. representative who served the northern Kentucky area from 1931 until 1963.

Both Independence and Covington are county seats of Kenton County. Although Independence maintains a courthouse, most county business has been transacted at Covington since the courthouse there was dedicated in 1843. The first Covington courthouse, of Greek Revival style, was replaced by a brick and stone Victorian building in 1902. The third courthouse is a modern ten-story city-county municipal building that replaced the old courthouse in 1970.

The population of the industrial, second-class city was 52,535 in 1970; 49,585 in 1980; and 43,264 in 1990.

See *Papers of Christopher Gist Historical Society*, vol. 6 (Covington, Ky., 1955).

JOHN E. BURNS

COWENS, DAVID WILLIAM. David William Cowens, named most valuable player by the National Basketball Association (NBA) in 1973, was born on October 25, 1948, in Covington, Kentucky, the son of Jack and Ruth (Atwood) Cowens. After leading Newport Catholic High School to the 1966 state basketball tournament, he entered Florida State University in Tallahassee. One of basketball's late bloomers, he was named All-American in 1970 and after graduating later that year, was drafted by the Boston Celtics. Although small for a center at six feet, nine inches, Cowens redefined the position's style of play by ferocious rebounding and fearless hustle.

After leading the Celtics to NBA titles in 1974 and 1976, Cowens left the team nine games into the 1976-77 season, citing burnout. Absent for sixty-five days, he returned to Kentucky and sold Christmas trees before rejoining the Celtics late in the season. His honors include rookie of the year in 1971, most valuable player in 1972-73, and All-Star most valuable player in 1973. He retired shortly before the 1980-81 season. In April 1981 he

became athletic director at Regis College in Weston, Massachusetts. In October 1982 he attempted a comeback with the Milwaukee Bucks but was stopped by injuries. He is chairman of the Sports Museum in Massachusetts. In February 1991 he was elected to the Basketball Hall of Fame. Cowens married Deborah Ann Cmaylo in 1978; they have two daughters.

COWGER, WILLIAM O. William O. Cowger, Louisville mayor and U.S. Congressman, was born in Hastings, Nebraska, on January 1, 1922, to Dr. R.H. and Catherine (Combs) Cowger. Cowger began his college education at Texas A&M in 1940 and received his bachelor's degree from Carleton College in Minnesota in 1944. He served in the navy for a year and in 1945 became president of the Thompson and Cowger Company, Inc., a mortgage realty firm. He ran unsuccessfully as a Republican candidate for the General Assembly in 1951. He was Republican campaign chairman in 1953 and has been credited with revitalizing the Republican party in Jefferson County. He was elected mayor of Louisville in 1961, the first Republican to hold the office since 1929, defeating William S. Milburn by 61,651 to 50,219. The issue of the campaign was the thirty-year dominance of Democrats in local politics, and Cowger almost singlehandedly dismantled the Democratic machine built by Mickey Brennan.

Through urban renewal projects, Cowger did much to rebuild Louisville's urban center. He had strong support from Louisville's black community and received national recognition for his backing of the first public accommodations act in any U.S. city south of the Mason-Dixon Line. Electoral laws did not permit Cowger to run for reelection as mayor in 1965. In 1966 he defeated Norbert Bloome by 66,577 to 46,240 for the position of U.S. Representative from Kentucky's 3rd District. He chaired the Republican Congressional Urban Affairs Committee. In 1970 he was narrowly defeated for reelection by Romano Mazzoli (49,361 to 49,305). Cowger was said to be considering running again for mayor in 1973, or contesting Mazzoli in 1972, when he died suddenly of a heart attack on October 2, 1971.

Cowger married Cynthia Thompson on March 19, 1945, and they had two children, Cynthia and David. Cowger was buried in Cave Hill Cemetery in Louisville.

COX'S STATION. For protection against the Indians, Cox's Station was built on Cox's Creek about five miles north of what now is Bardstown, Kentucky, on a one-hundred-acre preemption belonging to Col. Isaac Cox. Cox, along with Jonah Heaton, Daniel Holman, Thomas Jones, Richard and Samuel Richardson, Thomas Polke, William Chenoweth, and eleven other settlers, traveled by boat down the Ohio River to the mouth of the Kentucky River from Redstone, Pennsylvania, in April 1775.

They marched overland to Nelson County, suffering an Indian attack that caused two deaths. The group surveyed land tracts in what is now Nelson County but did not establish the station until 1780.

See Sarah B. Smith, *Historic Nelson County, Its Towns and People* (Bardstown, Ky., 1983).

NANCY O'MALLEY

CRABB, ALFRED LELAND. Educator, historian, and author, Alfred Leland Crabb was born on January 22, 1884, in Warren County, Kentucky, near Bowling Green, the son of James and Annie (Arbuckle) Crabb. He attended elementary school in the Girkin/Plum Springs community and later the Southern Normal School and the State Normal School in Bowling Green. He earned a bachelor's degree at Peabody College in Nashville, a master's degree at Columbia University, and a doctorate at Peabody.

Crabb's career as an educator included the positions of principal in Paducah and Louisville, and professor of history and education, as well as dean, at what is now Western Kentucky University in Bowling Green. From 1927 until his retirement in 1950, he was a professor at Peabody College, where he edited the *Peabody Journal of Education* for twenty-eight years. During a long and productive career, Crabb collaborated on a series of histories and textbooks, but he is best known for his eleven historical novels, which appeared in quick succession between 1942 and 1957. Five of Crabb's novels deal with life in Nashville and with historical figures and events such as Andrew Jackson and the Civil War. *Home to Kentucky* (1953) is a novel based on the life of Henry Clay. *Peace at Bowling Green* (1955), considered by many to be his best novel, chronicles the life of pioneer settler Jacob Skiles and his family and the growth of Bowling Green from a village into a thriving town between 1803 and the outbreak of the Civil War. Crabb's fictional characters mingle with historical figures in *Peace at Bowling Green* and in his other novels, which are lively, well-crafted, historically accurate accounts of people, places, and events in nineteenth century middle Tennessee and Kentucky.

In 1911 Crabb married Bertha Gardner, a Butler countian. They had one son, Alfred Jr. Crabb died in Lexington, Kentucky, on October 1, 1979, and was buried in the Mt. Olivet Cemetery in Nashville.   JIM WAYNE MILLER

CRAB ORCHARD SPRINGS. Crab Orchard Springs, eleven miles southeast of Stanford, Lincoln County, Kentucky, was the site of a popular nineteenth century resort. In pioneer days the springs marked one end of Logan's Trace of the Wilderness Road, which stretched from Cumberland Gap. The large orchard of crab apple trees that grew there gave the place its name. There are eight springs at the site: three chalybeate, or iron-impregnated, two saline, and one each red, white, and black sulphur. The first commercial development of the springs took place in 1827 under the ownership of Jack Davis, who built "A House of Entertainment" at the Sign of the Golden Bell Tavern. It changed hands many times before Jacob Harlan of Boyle County purchased the site in 1850; he sold it to Daniel W. Jones of Danville in 1861. During the summer of 1858, while Harlan owned the property, Col. John Hunt Morgan and his Lexington Rifles visited the springs. The resort was then at the height of its popularity, with four hundred to five hundred guests a day. For their medicinal value, the waters were advertised as being "resorted to with almost as much faith and certainty of cure as were the pools of Siloam and Bethesda." During the second cholera epidemic, in 1849, central Kentuckians flocked to the resort to escape the ravages of the disease.

The main building, including the dining room and ballroom, burned on February 4, 1871. The new owner, Isaac Shelby III, then built a hotel with more than 250 rooms, gaslight, and steam heat, at a cost of more than $115,000. The main floor of the hotel had coolers filled with fresh spring water to supply the guests. There were many forms of entertainment, including horse racing at the nearby Spring Hill course, horseback riding, fishing, golfing, boating—even cockfights and roulette. The hotel served as a girl's boarding school during the winter months. In 1882 a syndicate headed by W.N. Haldeman purchased the property, and its post–Civil War popularity reached a peak in the 1890s. Joe Willis and his wife purchased the site in 1897 and operated it until 1922, when the popularity of Crab Orchard Springs began to wane. It was sold in the early 1930s, and the hotel was remodeled to house a school, which burned on October 25, 1939. A high school was later built on the site.

See J. Winston Coleman, Jr., *The Springs of Kentucky* (Lexington, Ky., 1955).

CRAIG, ELIJAH. One of the most remarkable of the early Kentucky Baptist preachers, Elijah Craig was born in Orange County, Virginia, about 1743, the son of Taliaferro and Mary (Hawkins) Craig. Converted to the Baptist faith about 1764 and ordained a minister in 1771, Craig, like other Virginia Baptist preachers, was jailed at least once for preaching contrary to the beliefs of Virginia's Anglican establishment. Craig joined his older brothers Joseph and Lewis CRAIG in Kentucky by 1785 and became pastor at the church at the Great (Buffalo) Crossing in Scott County. He purchased a large area of land near the county's Royal Spring and laid off a town named Lebanon (now Georgetown). There he began to expand into businesses such as manufacturing paper, making rope from hemp, and distilling whiskey from Kentucky corn. The story of how Craig invented the process of making bourbon whiskey by accident is subject to debate, but the distilling industry has taken delight in pointing to a Baptist preacher as the inventor of its prime product.

Craig established a classical school near the Royal Spring, later linked to the Rittenhouse Academy and Georgetown College. He was active as a Baptist preacher at Great Crossing, Stamping Ground, Silas, and Marble Creek (now East Hickman), where he was involved in several church controversies. He died May 18, 1808, and was eulogized by the *Kentucky Gazette* on May 24, 1808: "He possessed a mind extremely active and his whole property was expended in attempts to carry his plans to execution—he consequently died poor. If virtue consists in being useful to our fellow citizens, perhaps there were few more virtuous men than Mr. Craig."

Craig was married in Virginia to Frances Smith, to whom were born Joel, Simeon, and Lucy. Upon her death, he married the widow Margaret (Kay) Gatewood; they had three children: Lydia, Polly, and John Dyer Craig.

See John Taylor, *A History of Ten Churches* (Frankfort, Ky., 1827).

IRA ("JACK") BIRDWHISTELL

CRAIG, LEWIS. Lewis Craig, minister and architect, was born in 1741 in Orange County, Virginia. He was the son of Toliver and Polly (Hawkins) Craig and the brother of Joseph and Elijah CRAIG. He was imprisoned in 1768, 1770, and 1771 for his Baptist beliefs while he was pastor of the Upper Spotsylvania Church. Craig led his TRAVELING CHURCH to Kentucky, establishing congregations along the way before settling in the Mason-Bracken County area. He was the guiding force behind the Bracken Association, and in 1793 built a substantial church in Minerva, where he was pastor. In 1794 he built Mason County's first courthouse, in Washington. Craig died in 1825 and was buried in a private plot near Minerva.

See Lewis N. Thompson, *Lewis Craig: The Pioneer Baptist Preacher* (Louisville 1910).

JOHN KLEE

CRAIG'S STATION (BURNT STATION). John Craig's Station, which housed Baptists seeking religious freedom, was established in 1779 along David's Fork, near present-day Winchester Road (U.S. 60), east of Lexington. Craig family members, including John, Joseph, Lewis, and Elijah, were associated with the TRAVELING CHURCH, a Baptist sect that moved an entire congregation from Virginia to Kentucky. Several Traveling Church families settled at Craig's Station on Christmas Eve in 1779 and lived in crude log shelters during one of the most severe winters on record. Four cabins, possibly with an enclosing stockade, were built the next year. When a planned Indian attack was reported in March of 1781, the inhabitants fled to Daniel Boone's Station near what is now Athens, Kentucky. Within hours after they abandoned Craig's Station, an Indian raiding party burned the settlement, which led to its second name.

See Nancy O'Malley, *Stockading Up*, Archaeological Report 127, Department of Anthropology, University of Kentucky, 1987.

NANCY O'MALLEY

CRAWFORD, JANE (TODD). Jane (Todd) Crawford, who survived abdominal surgery on the frontier, was the second of six daughters of Samuel and Jane Todd, born on December 23, 1763, in Augusta (later Rockbridge) County, Virginia. She grew up in Virginia and married Thomas Crawford in 1794. Eleven years later the Crawfords moved to Kentucky and settled on the Blue Spring Branch of the Caney Fork of Russell Creek. In 1809, Crawford traveled the sixty miles to Danville, Kentucky, where she permitted surgeon Ephraim MCDOWELL to remove a large ovarian cystic tumor. That feat established McDowell in the field of abdominal surgery, and it saved Crawford's life. She returned to her home, where she lived for thirty-two years. Crawford died on March 30, 1842, near Graysville, Indiana.   ALLEN J. SHARE

CREASON, JOE CROSS. Joe Cross Creason, one of Kentucky's best-known newspaper writers of the twentieth century, was born in Benton, Kentucky, on June 10, 1918, to Herman and Reba (Cross) Creason. He graduated from Benton High School and the University of Kentucky, became editor of the *Benton Tribune-Democrat* in 1940, worked briefly on the Murray, Kentucky, *Ledger & Times*, and late in 1940 joined the sports department of the *Courier-Journal* in Louisville. In 1944 he joined the navy, returning in 1946 to the *Courier-Journal*, where he was a feature writer until 1963. At that point he began writing "Joe Creason's Kentucky," a daily column about the state, its history and folklore and especially its people. Excerpts from the column were collected in *Joe Creason's Kentucky*, published in 1972, and in *Crossroads and Coffee Trees* (1975).

Creason married Shella Robertson, of Bethel, Kentucky; they had two sons, Joe Cross, Jr., and William Scott. Creason died of a heart attack while playing tennis on August 14, 1974, in Louisville and was buried in Longview Cemetery in Bethel, Kentucky.   JOHN ED PEARCE

CRIST, HENRY. Congressman and officer in the Kentucky militia, Henry Crist was born in Spotsylvania County, Virginia, on October 20, 1764. In 1779 he traveled to Kentucky with land speculator Jacob Myers and settled at the Falls of the Ohio in 1780. Crist's participation in land transactions made him aware of the potential for profit from the many salt licks in the area that is now Bullitt and Nelson counties. Crist, along with business partner Solomon Spears, acquired the Long Lick claim, near the Salt River in Nelson County, in 1784. In 1788 Indians attacked a small band of men led by Crist on a flatboat down the Salt River toward the Bullitt's Lick, near present day Shepherdsville. During the ensuing battle, referred to as the Battle of the Kettles because of the many salt-processing kettles on the flatboats, Spears was killed and Crist severely wounded. Crawling the remaining distance to Bullitt's Lick, Crist survived. Taking up permanent residence near Shepherdsville, Crist served in the Kentucky House of Representatives in 1795 and 1806 and in the Senate during 1800-4. He served also as a representative in the U.S. Congress from March 4, 1809, until March 3, 1811. On January 17, 1811, Gov. Charles Scott (1808-12) commissioned Crist a general in the Kentucky state militia. Crist died near Shepherdsville on August 11, 1844, and was buried in the Frankfort Cemetery.

CRITTENDEN, GEORGE BIBB. George Bibb Crittenden, soldier, son of John J. and Sarah (Lee) Crittenden, was born in Russellville, Kentucky, on March 20, 1812. He graduated from the U.S. Military Academy at West Point in 1832, served in the Black Hawk War, and in 1843 fought for the Texas Republic. Crittenden was captured and imprisoned in Mexico City for less than one year. In the Mexican War (1846-48), he commanded a mounted company in the occupation of Mexico City. He remained in the army and rose to lieutenant colonel in 1856. In 1861 he resigned and accepted a commission as brigadier general in the Confederate army. On November 9, 1861, Crittenden was promoted to major general. While commanding troops in eastern Kentucky, he lost the battle of Mill Springs on January 19, 1862, and was blamed for the collapse of the Confederate right flank. Although he was exonerated, he resigned his commission in October 1862 and served the remainder of the war as a colonel in subordinate positions. He was Kentucky state librarian from 1867 to 1874. Crittenden died in Danville on November 27, 1880, and was buried in the Frankfort Cemetery.

See C. David Dalton, "Zollicoffer, Crittenden, and the Mill Springs Campaign," *FCHQ* 60 (October 1986): 463-71. JAMES A. RAMAGE

CRITTENDEN, JOHN JORDAN. The best educated of the early Kentucky governors, John Jordan Crittenden (1848-50) was born on September 10, 1786, in Woodford County, Kentucky, to John and Judith (Harris) Crittenden. He attended Pisgah Academy in Woodford County and Washington College (later Washington and Lee) and graduated from William and Mary. After studying law with Judge George M. Bibb, he began practice in Russellville. The father of nine children, Crittenden married three times: Sarah O. Lee in 1811, the widow Maria K. Todd in 1826, and the widow Elizabeth Ashley in 1853. In 1809 Crittenden was appointed attorney for the Illinois Territory and aide de camp to Gov. Ninian Edwards. During the War of 1812 he served as an aide to Gen. Samuel Hopkins and then to Gov. Isaac Shelby (1792-96, 1812-16).

In 1811 Crittenden was elected to the state House of Representatives for the first of six consecutive terms; he served as Speaker in 1815, 1816, and 1817. In 1817 the General Assembly elected him to a vacancy in the U.S. Senate, where he promoted the interests of the underprivileged and the underrepresented. He served from March 4, 1817, until his resignation on March 3, 1819, when he moved to Frankfort to enlarge his law practice. He was defeated for a House seat in 1825, won a special election to the state House in 1829, then served three terms before retiring in 1832. Crittenden supported Henry Clay in the 1824 presidential race and switched to Andrew Jackson when Clay was eliminated, but then cooperated with President John Quincy Adams. His law practice flourished, and Crittenden became famous for his defenses in murder trials and for his oratory.

Crittenden became Kentucky's secretary of state in 1834. In 1835 he was elected to the U.S. Senate, where he opposed most Democratic measures. Taking office on March 4, 1835, he was reelected in 1840, but resigned on March 3, 1841, to become President William H. Harrison's attorney general. He resigned that position after John Tyler became president; Tyler broke with the Henry Clay faction of the Whig party. Elected in 1842 to an unexpired term in the U.S. Senate, Crittenden then won election to a full term in 1843 and served from March 31, 1842, to June 12, 1848. He surprised many Kentuckians, including Henry Clay, when he supported Zachary Taylor for president instead of Clay. In 1848 Crittenden again resigned from the Senate, probably because he believed his race for governor would help Taylor carry Kentucky. He defeated Democrat Lazarus W. Powell, 66,860 to 57,397. Crittenden added to his record of resignations by resigning as governor on July 31, 1850, to become attorney general in President Millard Fillmore's cabinet. In 1854 he was elected to the U.S. Senate for the fourth time (March 4, 1855, to March 3, 1861). Crittenden turned briefly to the Know-Nothings as the Whig party disintegrated, then helped form the Constitutional Union party in 1860. As the sectional crisis worsened, he introduced the CRITTENDEN COMPROMISE, proposals designed to preserve the Union. His proposals failed, as did the other peace attempts, including the border state convention over which Crittenden presided in May 1861. In the U.S. House (March 4, 1861, to March 3, 1863), he introduced the Crittenden resolution, which stated that the war was not being fought to interfere with the established institutions of the states. The resolution was passed in July 1861.

Crittenden died on July 26, 1863, and was buried in the Frankfort Cemetery.

Crittenden's major achievements as governor were in education. He gave strong support to Superintendent Robert J. Breckinridge, and considerable progress was made even though the property tax was woefully inadequate. In his first message the governor urged the General Assembly to provide for the constitutional convention the people appeared to want, and the state's third constitution was produced in 1849. He asked funding for a comprehensive geological survey that was expected to help economic development, and he pointed out the need to rebuild the penitentiary. He also requested a sinking fund that would ultimately pay off the state debt. His achievements might have been greater had he stayed to the end of his term.

See Albert D. Kirwan, *John J. Crittenden: The Struggle for the Union* (Lexington, Ky., 1962).

LOWELL H. HARRISON
AND FRANK F. MATHIAS

CRITTENDEN COMPROMISE. On December 18, 1860, U.S. Senator John J. Crittenden of Kentucky, following the tradition of his predecessor, Henry Clay, introduced into the Senate a set of compromise proposals that he hoped would alleviate sectional conflict. Referred to as the Crittenden compromise, these proposals sought to relieve concerns over the slavery issue in the North and South and reflected the senator's desire to preserve the Union. The Crittenden compromise consisted of six resolutions: 1) The Missouri Compromise line of 36° 30′ would be reestablished and extended to the Pacific. Slavery would be permitted south of this line in all states and territories thereafter acquired, but citizens of future states would decide whether they were to be free or slave states when they were admitted to the Union. 2) Slavery on public lands in the South was not to be prohibited by Congress. 3) Slavery in the District of Columbia could not be abolished as long as it existed in Maryland or Virginia, or until a majority of the district residents favored emancipation. 4) Congress could not interfere with the interstate transportation of slaves. 5) As a corollary to the Fugitive Slave Act, owners of slaves "rescued" by abolitionists would receive compensation should it prove to be impossible to return the slaves. 6) No future statutes would render these provisions null and void.

Crittenden's compromise was referred for discussion to the Committee of Thirteen, consisting of eight Democratic and five Republican senators, created to settle the disunion crisis. On December 22, 1860, two days after South Carolina seceded, the committee, with Crittenden as its chairman, met to deliberate the Kentuckian's resolutions. They first decided that any proposal had to be approved by a majority of both Republicans and Democrats. The Republicans, led by William H. Seward of New York, voted unanimously against the compromise. Two southern Democrats joined the Republicans in condemning the articles, seriously diminishing their chance of passage in the Senate. Still hoping for a settlement, Crittenden ignored the committee vote and, on January 3, 1861, introduced his compromise to the Senate as a whole. In a very close vote, 25-23, Crittenden was again defeated on January 16, ending any hope of settlement short of war.

See Albert D. Kirwan, *John J. Crittenden* (Lexington, Ky., 1962).

CRITTENDEN COUNTY. Founded April 1, 1842, Crittenden is the state's ninety-first county, named after John Jordan Crittenden, governor of Kentucky (1848-50), a native of Woodford County. The county, located in the western portion of the Pennyroyal region in the southwest part of the state, is bordered by the Ohio River and by Union, Webster, Caldwell, Lyon, and Livingston counties. The county seat in MARION.

The terrain is characterized by rolling hills and elevations ranging from 334 feet above sea level in the lowest areas on the Ohio River to 834 feet above sea level in the Ridgelands. The county is drained by the Crooked Camp, Hurricane, Livingston, and Piney creeks and by the Cumberland, Tradewater, and Ohio rivers. One-third to three-eights of the 360-square-mile county is wooded, with a wide variety of trees ranging from white oak to wild cherry. The county has valuable deposits of natural resources including fluorspar, zinc, oil, aluminum, porcelain, coal, limestone for gravel, and sand for glass making.

The county was crossed by the Chickasaw Road, a part of Old Saline Trace. The Indians used the road to hunt deer, elk, and buffalo that crossed the Ohio River on their way to the salt licks in Illinois. Even today Crittenden County is a rich hunting ground, with such game as wild turkey, squirrel, rabbit, quail, duck, fish, and a large number of deer. Flynn's Ferry was established at the intersection of the Chickasaw road and the Ohio River in the early 1800s.

The first settler to move into the region now known as Crittenden County was James Armstrong of South Carolina. He arrived in the Fredonia Valley area in 1786, where he built a cabin and was joined by his family in 1791. By then many other families had moved into the area, most being of English, Scotch, and Irish decent. The first county seat was the Crooked Creek community where the first court was held at the home of Samuel Ashley. In 1844 the county seat was moved a few miles south to Marion, where John S. Gilliam donated land for the public buildings. The first courthouse was finished in 1844 and the first court was held there on June 10 of that year. The courthouse was burned by Gen. Hylan B. Lyons on January 25, 1865, although the county saw little fighting during the Civil War. The second courthouse also burned, and the third was replaced by the present courthouse, dedicated in December 1961.

In the 1840s Marion was an industrial town with the largest fluorspar mine in the country. However, the fluorspar industry peaked in 1947 and has since greatly declined due to competition from imported fluorspar. Andrew Jackson owned land in Crittenden County, where he set up the first iron furnace in the area, near Tolu. Several other iron furnaces followed, including Crittenden furnace, built in Dycusburg in 1847 and run by the Cobb and Lyon families; Hurricane furnace, built by Andrew Jackson, Jr., in 1850, and known also as Jackson furnace; and the Deer Creek furnace, near Tolu. The private Crittenden Academy, the first school in the county, opened at Marion in 1849. The first public school was built on land donated to

Marion on August 8, 1868, by Nancy Gilliam. Other schools included Dycusburg Academy, Marion Academy and Normal School, N.M. Lloyd Private Academy, and the Fredonia Seminary.

The county has a strong agricultural economy, with 65.6 percent of the population living on farms and 44.5 percent claiming farming as their principal occupation. Total agricultural cash receipts for 1986 were $14,648,000. The major crops and livestock are corn, wheat, soybeans, alfalfa, cattle, and hogs. Among the 165 businesses in the county in 1985 were Frontier Spar, a subsidiary of Marathon Oil; Potter Brumfield, maker of electromagnetic relays; American Sportswear Inc., a clothing manufacturer; Marion Mining Bolt, producer of roofbolts and plates for the mining industry; and Cera-Tech Corporation, maker of ceramic products. Other products include lumber, modular homes, glass products, and the blue crystal made famous by Ball canning jars.

The population of Crittenden County was 8,493 in 1970; 9,207 in 1980; and 9,196 in 1990.

CROCKETT, JOSEPH. Joseph Crockett, pioneer, was born to Joseph Louis, Jr., and Jeanne (de Vignè) Crockett on May 7, 1742, in Botetourt County, Virginia. He served under Col. Andrew Lewis in the battle of Point Pleasant on October 10, 1774. In 1775 he was lieutenant in William Russell's company in the western part of Virginia, and in the winter of 1776 he enlisted in one of the newly formed companies of minutemen of the Continental army. He was appointed one of the captains in the 7th Regiment of the Virginia line and was ordered to defend the powder magazines in Williamsburg, Virginia.

Crockett's company remained in service around Blackwell's Island, Virginia, for the duration of the 1776 military campaign. In the winter of 1777, the company marched to Philadelphia, where Crockett was made a lieutenant in charge of raising the companies of Gen. Daniel Morgan's regiment. After the battle of Monmouth on June 28, 1778, he was promoted to lieutenant colonel. He remained in that position until the Continental Congress reorganized the army in October 1780, when his rank was reduced to captain. He was ordered to serve Gen. George Rogers Clark and was promoted to the rank of lieutenant colonel of the Illinois regiment, which became known as the Crockett regiment. Crockett's military service ended in February 1781.

In May 1784 Crockett traveled to Kentucky, arrived in Lexington, and was employed as a surveyor under Col. Thomas Marshall. He settled his family on a nineteen-hundred-acre farm on Hickman Creek in Jessamine County, five miles northeast of Nicholasville. He served as a representative in the Virginia Assembly in 1786 and 1790, during the debate over the independence of Kentucky, and was chosen as a member of the Kentucky House under the first Kentucky constitution in 1792, serving until 1795. On February 9, 1795, Gov. Isaac Shelby (1792-96, 1812-16) appointed him justice of

the court of quarter sessions for Fayette County, filling the vacancy created by the resignation of Robert Todd. In 1796 he was appointed by Governor Shelby to make improvements in the road cut through the Cumberland Gap in 1775, and on October 15, 1796, the *Kentucky Gazette* announced the completion of the Wilderness Road. In 1800 Crockett was elected to the Kentucky Senate and served until 1804. On June 26, 1801, he was appointed marshall for the District of Kentucky by President Thomas Jefferson. He was reappointed to the position by President James Madison.

Crockett was married to Elizabeth Moore Woodson from 1782 until her death on August 20, 1820. They had six children: Polly, Robert, Joseph, John, Martha, and Elizabeth. Crockett died in Georgetown, Kentucky, on November 7, 1829. He is buried in the family burial ground in Jessamine County.

See James Preston Collup French and Zella Armstrong, *Notable Southern Families: The Crockett Family and Connecting Lines* (Bristol, Tenn., 1928).

CROGHAN, JOHN. John Croghan, physician and entrepreneur, was born on April 23, 1790, at Locust Grove, Kentucky, east of Louisville, the son of Maj. William and Lucy (Clark) Croghan. His uncle George Rogers Clark was a member of his household. Croghan was educated at the College of William and Mary in Williamsburg, Virginia, and graduated in 1813 from the University of Pennsylvania School of Medicine, where his preceptor was Dr. Benjamin Rush. Croghan briefly practiced medicine and was involved in various business ventures, including drilling for salt along the Cumberland River, where in 1829 he made one of the earliest discoveries of oil in the United States. Croghan purchased Mammoth Cave on October 8, 1839, and set about making it into a tourist attraction and therapeutic resort for the treatment of tuberculosis. His promotion included publication of *Rambles in the Mammoth Cave During the Year 1844*. Those patients who agreed to live within the cave found that the cool, damp conditions only worsened their illness. After a short time, Croghan admitted the medical experiment to be a failure.

Croghan lived as a gentleman farmer at Locust Grove, where he entertained President Andrew Jackson in 1825, as well as Cassius M. Clay and Robert Wickliffe, Jr., who dueled near his mill in 1841. Croghan died on January 11, 1849, and was buried in the family graveyard in Locust Grove.

See Eugene H. Conner and Samuel W. Thomas, "John Croghan (1790-1849): An Enterprising Kentucky Physician," *FCHQ* 40 (July 1966): 205-34.

SAMUEL W. THOMAS

CROGHAN, WILLIAM. William Croghan, pioneer surveyor and settler, was born in Ireland in 1752. In 1771 he became an ensign in the 16th Foot Regiment, a British military unit serving in North America. He remained in America after he left the army in 1774 and migrated to western Pennsylvania, purchasing land in Washington County. Croghan joined the 8th Virginia Regiment in 1775 and served in the military throughout the Revolutionary War. In April 1776 Croghan was promoted to captain and by December of the same year became a major. On May 12, 1780, Croghan was captured; he was exchanged in the spring of 1782. He was stationed at Fort Pitt until the end of the war in 1783.

On February 9, 1784, Croghan and George Rogers Clark were commissioned by Virginia as principal surveyors of the public lands in Kentucky set aside for veterans of the Virginia militia. Although Clark was head of the survey, Croghan was in control of the office. In 1788 Croghan was commissioned to lay out a courthouse in the Jefferson County public square. He opened a land office in Louisville on April 26, 1791, and after statehood became a surveyor for the commonwealth.

Croghan established a mercantile partnership in 1788 with Richard Clough Anderson. Despite tight restrictions on trade with Spanish New Orleans, Croghan was able to procure a passport from the Spanish government and establish trade on the Mississippi River. The partnership was dissolved in 1822 at Croghan's death. A successful businessman who also dabbled in politics, Croghan was elected a representative of Jefferson County to the statehood convention that met for five days in July 1790 in Danville. He was elected a trustee of Louisville's city government in 1791.

Croghan married Lucy Clark, sister to George Rogers Clark, on July 14, 1789. He built a country residence, Locust Grove, on property in eastern Jefferson County, six miles from Louisville's center. The house was completed in 1790 and became home for the Croghans, their eight children, and George Rogers Clark during the last years of his life. Croghan died September 21, 1822, and was buried at Locust Grove in the family plot. The family's remains were reinterred at Cave Hill Cemetery, Louisville, in 1916.

See Samuel W. Thomas, "William Croghan, Sr.: A Pioneer Kentucky Gentleman," *FCHQ* 43 (Jan. 1969): 30-61.

CROMWELL, EMMA (GUY). Emma (Guy) Cromwell, Kentucky State government executive, was born in 1869 in Allen County, Kentucky, to Ashley D. and Alice (Quisenberry) Guy. She was educated at the Masonic Home in Louisville and at Howard Female College in Gallatin, Tennessee. In 1896, the Kentucky Senate elected her state librarian—the first woman in the commonwealth to hold a statewide office. In 1924 she was selected secretary of state and became the first woman to act as Kentucky governor during the chief executive's absence from the state. She also held the office of state treasurer, state park director, and state bond commissioner, and she served as state librarian several times. She became an authority on parliamentary law, often lectured on the subject, and wrote *Cromwell's Compendium of Parliamentary Law*

(1918). Her autobiography, *A Woman in Politics*, was published in 1939.

Emma Guy married Frankfort attorney William Cromwell in 1897; their only child, William, died in youth. Emma Cromwell died on July 19, 1952, in Frankfort, and was buried in the Frankfort Cemetery.

See Emma Guy Cromwell, *A Woman in Politics* (Louisville 1939).   CAROL CROWE-CARRACO

CRONAN, CHARLES J., JR. Charles J. Cronan, Jr., who was associated with the American Saddlebred Horse Association for more than half a century, was born in Louisville on September 6, 1895, to Charles Joseph and Anita (Hamel) Cronan. He was a graduate of the Jefferson School of Law (now part of the University of Louisville), and was admitted to the Kentucky bar in 1917. The next day he enlisted in the army. He remained in the 138th Field Artillery of the Kentucky National Guard after World War I and saw active service in World War II, attaining the rank of colonel. In 1918 he married Laura Virginia Ewing and established a general insurance company in Louisville.

In 1927 he founded the saddlebred Kentucky Futurity horse show, held annually at the Kentucky State Fair. The entries are selected at or before birth. In 1932 Cronan became secretary of the American Saddlebred Horse Association and held that post until 1979, when he was made executive vice president. He bred and raised American Model, the three-gaited "World Grand Champion" in 1936. When he retired in 1983, the association gave him a plaque officially designating him "Mr. Saddlebred."

Cronan died September 6, 1985, and was buried in St. Aloysius Cemetery, near Louisville. His survivors include a son, Charles III, and a daughter, Virginia Clarke.

See Lynn P. Weatherman, *American Saddlebred Magazine* (Lexington, Ky., 1985).

LYNN P. WEATHERMAN

CROWE, JAMES DEE. The son of Orval and Bessie Lee (Nichols) Crowe, James Dee Crowe, country banjoist and bandleader, was born in Lexington, Kentucky on August 27, 1937. He attended Nicholasville High School and received a general education development diploma from Lafayette High School in 1967. In 1951 Crowe received his first banjo and began learning to play it by watching Earl Scruggs, who was featured in the Kentucky Mountain Barn Dance at Clay Wachs Arena in Lexington. In 1956 Crowe joined Jimmy Martin's band and spent five years on the road before returning to Lexington. By 1964 Crowe had formed his own band, the Kentucky Mountain Boys, which included at various times Doyle Lawson, Bobby Sloan, Red Allen, Bob Morris, and Larry Rice. In 1971 Crowe changed the group's name to J.D. Crowe and the New South. When the group disbanded in 1975, members of the New South included Crowe (banjo), Bobby Sloan (bass), Tony

Rice (guitar), Ricky SKAGGS (mandolin), and Jerry ("Flux") Douglas (dobro). Crowe and the New South were instrumental in developing bluegrass music through the use of drums, steel pedal guitar, and an extended repertoire. Crowe retired from active playing in 1987.

See Charles K. Wolfe, *Kentucky Country* (Lexington, Ky., 1982). RON PEN

CROW'S STATION. Crow's Station was built by John Crow on 1,143 acres of land he claimed while accompanying James Harrod into central Kentucky in 1774. It was one of the crudely fortified places that served as temporary refuges for settlers flooding into Kentucky after the Revolutionary War. Crow's Station was a wooden palisade surrounding a log house and a spring, called the Town Spring when the station became part of the town of Danville. The supreme court of the District of Kentucky met briefly at the station while a courthouse was being built in pioneer Danville's town square. After the court moved to the town square in 1783, Crow's Station fell into disrepair. John Crow disposed of his remaining lands near Danville and took title to some wilderness land on the Green River, where one of his slaves murdered him.

See Calvin M. Fackler, *Early Days in Danville* (Louisville 1941). RICHARD C. BROWN

CROXTON, JOHN THOMAS. John Thomas Croxton, Civil War general and diplomat, was born to Henry and Ann K. (Redmon) Croxton on November 20, 1836, in Bourbon County, Kentucky. After graduating from Yale College in 1857, he studied law in Georgetown, Kentucky, and practiced law in Paris, Kentucky.

Croxton joined the Union army on October 9, 1861, with the rank of lieutenant colonel in the 4th Kentucky Mounted Infantry. On May 9, 1862, he was promoted to colonel of the 4th Kentucky. From August 15 through September 20, 1863, he commanded the 2d Brigade, 3d Division, 14th Corps, Army of the Cumberland. On July 30, 1864, he was promoted to brigadier general. From October 29, 1864, until June 26, 1865, he commanded the 1st Brigade, 1st Division, Cavalry Corps, Military Division of the Mississippi. During the war, Croxton took part in several major battles, including Mill Springs (January 19, 1862); Perryville (October 8, 1862); Murfreesboro (December 31, 1862-January 2, 1863); and Chickamauga (September 19-20, 1863), in which he was severely wounded. He fought in the Atlanta campaign (August 2-31, 1864) and the Franklin and Nashville campaign (November 29-December 27, 1864). During Gen. James H. Wilson's raid through Alabama, Croxton's brigade captured Tuscaloosa, for which he was brevetted major general of the Volunteers. Toward the end of the war, he commanded the Military District of Southwest Georgia. He resigned on December 26, 1865.

After the war, Croxton returned to Paris to continue his law practice and to farm. He was active in politics and helped establish the *Louisville Com-mercial*, a Republican newspaper. In 1873 Croxton accepted the position of U.S. minister to Bolivia. Croxton married Carrie A. Rogers on April 10, 1860; they had two children, Henry and Annie. Croxton died in La Paz, Bolivia, on April 16, 1874, and was buried in Paris, Kentucky.

See Rex Miller, "John Thomas Croxton," *Register* 74 (Oct. 1976): 281-300.

CRUM, DENZEL EDWIN. Denzel ("Denny") Edwin Crum, college basketball coach, was born on March 2, 1937, in San Fernando, California, to Alwin Denzel and June (Turner) Crum. Crum received his bachelor of arts degree from the University of California, Los Angeles (UCLA), in 1958 and a secondary teaching certificate from San Fernando Valley State College in 1960. He began his coaching career at Pierce Junior College in Los Angeles, serving first as assistant coach, then as head coach from 1962 to 1967. Crum spent the years 1967-70 as an assistant coach at UCLA under the legendary John Wooden.

He became the head basketball coach at the University of Louisville in 1971 and led the Cardinals to two National Collegiate Athletic Association (NCAA) national championships in 1980 and 1986. He made four appearances in the final four of the NCAA tournament during the 1980s. Through the 1990 season Crum posted a record of 463 wins and 156 losses at Louisville, and coached nine all-American players. He won the conference coach of the year award in 1973, 1975, and 1979, and the national coach award in 1974.

Crum lives on a fifty-five-acre farm in eastern Jefferson County, Kentucky. He married Joyce Elaine Lunsford in 1951; they have two children, Cynthia and Stephen. In 1977 Crum married Joyce Phillips; they have one son, Robert Scott.

See Billy Reed, "The Two Worlds of Denny Crum," *Louisville Courier-Journal Magazine*, Jan. 24, 1982.

CUMBERLAND. Cumberland, a fourth-class city that is the largest in Harlan County, is located at the foot of Pine Mountain on the Poor Fork of the Cumberland River. Settled in the early 1820s, the community was once known as Poor Fork. The rugged area remained isolated until the arrival of the railroads and mining interests in the early 1900s. In 1926 the town was renamed for the Cumberland River by local businessmen who sought a more fitting name.

Mines in the area, operated by U.S. Steel, Ford, and International Harvester, gave rise to company towns at nearby LYNCH and Benham.

Near Cumberland is Kingdom Come State Park, named after the book *The Little Shepherd of Kingdom Come* (1903), written by John Fox, Jr. Fox, who also wrote of the Harlan–Letcher County area in the *The Trail of the Lonesome Pine* (1908), lived in Cumberland for a time before his death in 1919. Within the state park, established in 1962, the Little Shepherd Trail begins and winds along the crest of Pine Mountain for more than 30 miles. Also near

Cumberland is Kentucky's highest point, Big Black Mountain, with an elevation of 4,145 feet. Southeast Community College, affiliated with the University of Kentucky, was established in Cumberland in 1960. The population of the city was 3,317 in 1970; 3,712 in 1980; and 3,112 in 1990.

CUMBERLAND, STATE OF. The state of Cumberland—a state of mind, not of government—was launched May 4, 1987, by an unusual combination of interstate and regional interests. Community and business leaders from southeastern Kentucky, southwestern Virginia, and eastern Tennessee, meeting to discuss regional tourism, created the new "state" by signing a "Declaration of Independence." This was the first of many tongue-in-cheek promotional events: constitutional conventions; the election of a governor, lieutenant governor, and cabinet officers; the establishment of a general assembly and legislative committees; an elaborate inaugural ball for the governor; and the production and distribution of an official State of Cumberland map, song, and flag. The first governor of Cumberland was Jackie Epperson of Middlesborough, Kentucky. Under the mock governmental veneer is a sound organizational structure, which has been incorporated as an interstate tourism agency. The board of directors and state membership hail from nine counties, including Bell, Harlan, and Knox (Kentucky); Lee, Scott, and Wise (Virginia); and Claiborne, Hancock, and Hawkins (Tennessee). Tourism brochures are distributed to publicize the area's mountain culture and natural beauty.

FRANCIS E. PATRIDGE

CUMBERLAND COLLEGE. Cumberland College is a Baptist institution in Williamsburg, Kentucky. It originated as the Williamsburg Institute, dedicated on January 1, 1889, the product of a fund-raising drive that began in 1887 at the urging of the Mt. Zion Association. The first students entered on January 7, 1889, with one administrator and two faculty members. In 1907 the institute purchased Highland College and much of the debt was paid by a local benefactor, Dr. A. Gatliff. In 1913 the institute was renamed Cumberland College. It had a four-year curriculum until 1918, when it became a coeducational junior college with vocational and professional programs. In 1959, at the behest of the General Association of Kentucky Baptists, in cooperation with the college board of trustees, a junior year was added, and in 1960 Cumberland College returned to a four-year curriculum. The college also began an expansion program, and the campus had twenty buildings by the late 1980s.

The location of Cumberland College in the southeastern region of Kentucky accentuated its initial purpose of providing higher education to the Appalachian people. In the 1980s the school enrolled more Appalachian students than any other private college in Kentucky. Approximately 70 percent of its graduates return to work in their home communities. Two governors, Edwin Morrow (1919-23) and Bert Combs (1959-63), were graduates.

CUMBERLAND COUNTY. The thirty-second county in order of formation, Cumberland County is located in south-central Kentucky along the Tennessee state line. It is bordered by Adair, Clinton, Metcalfe, Monroe, and Russell counties and has an area of 307 square miles. Cumberland County was formed on December 14, 1798, from a portion of Green County and named for the Cumberland River, which flows through the county. The county seat is BURKESVILLE.

The topography of Cumberland County varies from level river bottom to undulating and extremely hilly terrain. Over half the land is covered with timber. Beech, hickory, oak, and yellow popular are the predominant types of trees. The principal water sources in the county are the Cumberland River and the northern portion of the 27,000-acre Dale Hollow Lake.

The first settlers came into the region in the 1780s and early 1790s from Virginia, North Carolina, Pennsylvania, and Maryland. In 1769, Daniel Boone explored the area that later became Cumberland County. According to local legend, the first settlers fought an intense battle with the Indians in 1790 about ten miles north of what is now Burksville. A daring rescue of a young girl from the Indians took place at Little Renox Falls. A group of settlers attacked the Indian captors of the girl, killed them, and saved the girl, suffering no casualties.

When the Civil War began, Cumberland Countians for the most part were in sympathy with the Union cause. In the election of 1860, 67 percent of the voters cast their ballots in favor of the Constitutional Union Party, led by John Bell of Tennessee; Abraham Lincoln received seven votes. When war began in 1861, many joined the 5th Kentucky Cavalry under the command of Burkesville resident Col. David Haggard. The 3d Kentucky Volunteer and the 16th Kentucky Volunteer Infantry also received numerous Cumberland County men.

Cumberland County experienced several raids during the course of the war. Gen. John Hunt Morgan's cavalry crossed the Cumberland River at Burkesville in January, 1863. On February 12, 1863, two companies of Morgan's cavalry attacked and defeated Federal troops at Burkesville. Throughout 1862 and 1863, raids and skirmishes occurred in the county.

After the Civil War, Cumberland County's economy was in a state of disarray and for many years the county remained economically depressed, with poor roads and communications. By the 1940s, new roads had constructed in the area and the county became more accessible to the rest of the state.

The economy of Cumberland County is principally based on agricultural production of tobacco-,corn, and beef and dairy cattle. There are also lumber mills and clothing factories. The inlets and islands of Dale Hollow Lake attract boaters and fishermen. Marinas and resorts include Hendrick's

Creek, Sulphur Creek, Wisdom Dock, and Wolf River. Dale Hollow State Park provides swimming, camping, and horseback riding trails. Another recreational activity is a float fishing trip down the Cumberland River from Wolf Creek Dam in Russell County to Burkesville, a distance of seventeen miles.

The population of Cumberland County was 6,850 in 1970; 7,289 in 1980; and 6,784 in 1990.

See Joseph William Wells, *History of Cumberland County* (Louisville 1947).   RON D. BRYANT

CUMBERLAND FALLS. Cumberland Falls, located in Whitley County in the Cumberland Plateau area of southeastern Kentucky, is one of the largest waterfalls in the southeastern United States. The millions of gallons of water in the Cumberland River plunge over ledges of massive, resistant sandstone and conglomerate of Early Pennsylvanian age, carving a valley four hundred feet deep into the Cumberland Plateau. The drop from the lip of the falls to the pool below is fifty-five feet. The top ledge of the falls, from which water plunges when the river is at a high stage, is ten feet or more above the lip, making the total drop more than sixty-five feet in certain seasons. Published records indicate variations in stream flow from a minimum of 4 cubic feet (30 gallons) per second to a maximum of 59,600 cubic feet (445,800 gallons) per second. Cumberland Falls has not always been at the present location. It is thought to have originated on the Cumberland (Pottsville) Escarpment near Burnside and to have retreated upstream by typical stream erosion processes.

Cumberland Falls has been a tourist attraction for more than a century. Is is the focal point of a state park, first developed in the 1930s when private funds were donated to purchase the land to prevent industrialization of this scenic feature. The occasional moonbow or rainbow, produced by mists from the foaming cataract, adds to its scenic beauty.

See Preston McGrain, *Geology of the Cumberland Falls State Park Area*, Kentucky Geological Survey, Series 9, Special Publication 7 (1955).
PRESTON MCGRAIN

CUMBERLAND FORD. Cumberland Ford, also known as the Crossing of the Cumberland and the Old Ford, is the historically important shallow ford of the upper Cumberland River in Bell County in southeastern Kentucky, immediately downstream from the bridge serving highway KY 66. The Wilderness Road from the Cumberland Gap northward to Boonesborough and the Bluegrass area followed the west bank of the Cumberland River to Cumberland Ford, where it crossed the river. The ford is at an elevation of 1,000 feet. Nearby heights to the north, east, and southwest of the ford and narrow floodplains rise another 1,000 to 1,400 feet. The ford is about one-tenth of a mile downstream from the confluence of Straight Creek and the upper Cumberland River, and approximately fifteen miles north of Cumberland Gap. It seems to have been used by migrating animals as well as by Native Americans before the arrival of European settlers.

Cumberland Ford remained strategically important until after 1865. During the Civil War major army movements across the ford included those of the Confederate forces under Gen. Braxton Bragg after the Battle of Perryville in October 1862 and the troops of Gen. George Morgan in September 1862 as he retreated from Cumberland Gap to the Ohio River. Gen. John Hunt Morgan's Confederate forces also crossed the ford, which had been fortified to protect the crossing point.

In 1867 the act creating Josh Bell County (which became Bell County in 1873) directed the newly appointed commissioners to meet at Cumberland Ford to organize the county. As bridges, roads, and railroads were developed after 1867, the ford was no longer needed. Cumberland Ford was also the name for a small north bank settlement, which was absorbed in the incorporated limits of the city of Pineville.

See William Ayers, *Historical Sketches of Kentucky* (Pineville, Ky., 1925).
WILLIAM A. WITHINGTON

CUMBERLAND GAP. Cumberland Gap is a pass through CUMBERLAND MOUNTAIN in Bell County, on the border of Kentucky and Virginia, just northeast of Tennessee. For both animals and humans, the pass was on one of the most accessible routes to land west of the Appalachian Mountains. *Athawominee* (Path of the Armed Ones, or Warriors' Path) was the Shawnee name for the route. The first white person to pass through the gap is believed to have been Gabriel Arthur, who returned on June 18, 1674, to Fort Henry (Petersburg, Virginia) after spending nearly a year among the Indians. The Wilderness Road, used by the pioneers of the late eighteenth century, passed through the gap. Among the early hunters, explorers, and adventurers who crossed the gap were Thomas Walker (1750), Henry Scaggs (1764), Col. James Smith (1766), Daniel Boone and John Findlay (1769-71), and Col. James Knox and the Long Hunters. Settlers and land speculators followed in increasing numbers. Around 12,000 had passed through the gap by the time the colonies had won their independence in 1783. By 1800 more than 200,000 had headed west along the Wilderness Road.

During the Civil War, the area around Cumberland Gap was fortified and changed hands several times. It was a key access route for Confederate forces in a late 1862 invasion of Kentucky under Gen. Edmund Kirby-Smith and two retreating Confederate armies under Gens. Braxton Bragg and Kirby-Smith.

The elevation of the pass is between that of the pinnacle of Cumberland Mountain, on the northeast face of the gap, and those of the creek valleys on either side. Approaches to the gap are steeper on the west than on the east. This steepness has always been a hindrance to the movement of freight, in spite of the steady improvement of the overland trail, beginning in 1792. A railroad tunnel beneath the gap was completed in 1889 for more efficient movement west of the Appalachians, and its construction coincided with the development of coal mining in the area. Twin two-lane highway tunnels beneath Cumberland Mountain are planned, to replace U.S. Highway 25-E through the gap. This will promote an increase in traffic along the route and allow restoration of the surface of Cumberland Gap. The prehistoric origins of the gap have been confirmed by geologic studies on the surface and in the pilot tunnel driven through Cumberland Mountain for the highway relocation.

The physiographic features of Cumberland Gap and vicinity are the result of Paleozoic sedimentation; Late Paleozoic mountain building, folding, and faulting; and more than 200 million years of erosion. The less resistant shaley rocks have eroded and are now found mainly on lower hillslopes, recesses, and valley bottoms. The more resistant sandstone and limestone strata, now tilted, form the crests of Cumberland Mountain, PINE MOUNTAIN, and lower ridges. The Rocky Face Fault is the principal product of the geologic episode that led to the formation of Cumberland Gap.

One of the first to write an account of the geology of the gap was Walker, who noted the cave (Cudjo's Cave) and limestone on the north side of the gap, and coal along the creek three miles northwest of the gap. Other rocks exposed on Cumberland Mountain near the gap are sandstone and shale from the Late Silurian (410 million years ago) to the Pennsylvanian period (300 million years ago). When deposited, the rock strata were horizontal. Continental plate collision 250 million years ago caused one sheet of strata to break off from its adjacent equivalents, and slide several miles northwestward over these equivalents along a thrust fault. The leading edge of the nearly intact upper sheet tilted upward sharply to form Pine Mountain. The trailing, eastern part of this twenty-five-mile-long sheet was further warped upward into a long fold, of which Cumberland Mountain is a remnant. The strata of the otherwise unbroken upper sheet were later offset tens of feet along a tear fault. Movement along this offset (Rocky Face Fault) shattered the adjacent rocks and left them less resistant to forces of weathering than were the unbroken segments of the sheet. Traces of the fault pass directly through the lowest part of the saddle along the ancient route through Cumberland Gap.

See Robert L. Kincaid, *The Wilderness Road* (Middlesborough, Ky., 1973).

ROY C. KEPFERLE

CUMBERLAND GAP NATIONAL HISTORICAL PARK. In the 1920s a movement began to recognize the Cumberland Gap as a landmark in the westward expansion of the United States by making it a national park. Spearheaded by Robert Kincaid of Lincoln Memorial University, Harrogate, Tennessee, key local and state officials of Virginia and Kentucky founded an association in 1937 to campaign for creation of the park. After studies by the National Park Service, President Franklin D. Roosevelt on June 11, 1940, signed a law authorizing the creation of Cumberland Gap National Historical Park.

The states of Kentucky, Virginia, and Tennessee purchased land for the park over a period of fifteen years. Lands in Kentucky and Virginia were purchased by Howard J. Douglas of Middlesborough, who was appointed land buyer. The Tennessee Park Commission bought property in Tennessee. Douglas purchased more than 240 tracts, totaling 18,157.98 acres: 10,680 in Kentucky and 7,477.98 in Virginia. The Tennessee Park Commission acquired 2,027.06 acres. On September 14, 1955, the title deeds from the three states were formally presented to the U.S. secretary of the interior, and Cumberland Gap National Historical Park was formally established.

The official dedication ceremonies began with a visit by Vice-President Richard M. Nixon on July 3, 1959. On July 4 representatives of the Department of the Interior, National Park Service, and the three states assembled at the new visitor center for the ribbon cutting. The park, which attracts over 1 million visitors a year, has more than fifty miles of hiking trails, numerous campsites, and the Pinnacle Overlook, rising nearly 1,000 feet above Cumberland Gap. Within the park is the HENSLEY SETTLEMENT, containing the abandoned farmsteads of a once flourishing community.

See Charles A. Hanna, *The Wilderness Trail* (New York 1911).   DANIEL BROWN

CUMBERLAND MOUNTAIN(S). The Cumberland Mountains lie east of the Pottsville escarpment and adjacent knobs, covering all of upland eastern Kentucky. They were named in 1750 by explorer Thomas Walker in honor of the Duke of Cumberland. The Cumberland Mountains extend from the escarpment eastward to the Big Sandy River and its Tug Fork tributary, which form the boundary between Kentucky and West Virginia; northward to the Ohio River downstream from Ashland; and southeastward to the crests of Cumberland Mountain and Pine Mountain, where the boundary between Virginia and Kentucky was drawn.

One of the peaks in the chain is Cumberland Mountain, which is long, narrow, and ridge-like, with elevations along the crest ranging from 2,200 to 3,500 feet. Made up of resistant Lee (Pottsville) sandstone, it has a northeast-to-southwest axis. Cumberland Mountain's abrupt, steep southeast slope is the southern drainage divide between the Cumberland and Tennessee rivers. Northeast of Cumberland Mountain and essentially parallel to it lies Pine Mountain, 1,800 to 2,205 feet in elevation.

See Preston McGrain and James C. Currens, *The Topography of Kentucky* (Lexington, Ky., 1978); Wilford A. Bladen, *Geography of Kentucky* (Dubuque, Iowa, 1984).   WILLIAM A. WITHINGTON

CUMBERLAND PLATEAU.

Most of the eastern one-fourth of Kentucky lies within the Cumberland Plateau, which is the westernmost segment of the broader Appalachian Mountain system. The plateau's boundaries in Kentucky are the abrupt Pottsville Escarpment at its western margin; the Ohio River on the north; the Big Sandy River and its Tug Fork tributary on the east; and, on the southeast, Pine Mountain and Cumberland Mountain, which trend from northeast to southwest as far as the CUMBERLAND GAP.

Underlying the Cumberland Plateau are Kentucky's most extensive coal deposits, the source of 75 percent of the state's annual coal production. The considerable petroleum and natural gas resources beneath the plateau include Kentucky's largest gas field. The deciduous hardwood forest cover creates many scenic vistas, enhanced by lake impoundments.

Within Kentucky, the Cumberland Plateau is a highly dissected landform, cut by many rivers, but with a distinctive, nearly horizontal upper surface. Most of the rivers flow from southeastern sources to the northwest. The principal rivers are the Big Sandy and its upstream Levisa Fork and Russell Fork segments, as well as the Tug Fork; the Licking River; the Kentucky River with its northern, middle, and southern headwaters and Red River tributaries; and the upper Cumberland River, flowing southwest into Tennessee. The relatively narrow floodplains of the many rivers cutting below the plateau surface are the sites for most smaller cities and communities, including Hazard, Prestonsburg, Paintsville, Harlan, and Pineville.

From 1750 onward the Cumberland Plateau was explored and settled by pioneers traveling down the Ohio River from the east. Most Kentuckians now living in the Cumberland Plateau area, however, are descendants of those who entered through the broad, 1,600-foot-high saddle of the Cumberland Gap, or through one of several narrower gaps, such as Pound Gap or the gap at the Breaks of the Sandy along the Russell Fork. For many years residents of the area were almost exclusively subsistence farmers, lumber workers, or coal miners. The Cumberland Plateau has become more accessible and less isolated with recent improvements in transportation, including the Mountain Parkway, completed in 1958; I-64 west from Ashland, completed in 1973; the Daniel Boone Parkway (1974); and the widening of U.S. 23 to four lanes in the 1980s.

See Wilford A. Bladen, *A Geography of Kentucky* (Dubuque, Iowa, 1984); Joseph R. Schwendeman, *Geography of Kentucky* (Lexington, Ky., 1979). WILLIAM A. WITHINGTON

CUMBERLAND PRESBYTERIAN CHURCH.

In 1802, during the time of the GREAT REVIVAL, the Presbyterian Synod of Kentucky created a new presbytery—Cumberland—out of the southern portion of the Transylvania Presbytery. While the new presbytery included some of the most prominent revivalist ministers, about half the ministers opposed the revival, as well as the revivalists' loosening of requirements for ministerial candidates.

Between its creation in 1802 and the fall of 1805, there were twenty-seven irregular licensures and ordinations in the Cumberland Presbytery. In October 1805 the Kentucky Synod appointed a commission of seventeen ministers and elders to investigate the candidates' lack of educational qualifications and the presbytery's requirement that candidates adopt the confession of faith only so far as they believed it conformed to Scripture (allowing them to reject election). The synod commission declared that twenty-four of the men licensed or ordained by the Cumberland Presbytery were prohibited from preaching or administering the sacraments. The revivalist ministers of the presbytery attempted a reconciliation with the synod, to no avail. On October 21, 1806, the Kentucky Synod met in Lexington and dissolved the Cumberland Presbytery, transferring those ministers still in good standing to the Transylvania Presbytery.

From 1806 to late 1809 the revivalists unsuccessfully entreated the Kentucky Synod and general assembly to recognize the ordinations and licensures carried out by the former Cumberland Presbytery. In February 1810 the Revs. Samuel King and Finis Ewing rode more than eighty miles from Logan County, Kentucky, to Dickson County, Tennessee, where the Rev. Samuel McAdow had moved, and the three reconstituted the Cumberland Presbytery. Their first act was to ordain Ephraim McLean, a probationer who had ridden with King and Ewing to Tennessee. By all accounts their goal was not to create a new denomination, but their actions were rejected by Presbyterian synods. Presbyterian ministers in the region decided individually whether to align themselves with the new Cumberland Presbytery or remain with the parent body. The new independent presbytery grew swiftly and on October 5, 1813, it formed the Cumberland Synod, with three presbyteries: Cumberland, Logan, and Elk. In 1825 the Presbyterian general assembly decided that the Cumberland Presbytery should be viewed in the same light as other denominations.

In 1826 CUMBERLAND COLLEGE was opened near the Caldwell County town of Princeton to provide a liberal arts education for ministerial students and others. The school operated on a work-study principle that required all students to put in two hours of manual labor each day.

Continued growth of the new denomination led to convening of the first general assembly of the Cumberland Presbyterians on May 19, 1829, in Princeton. The former Cumberland Synod—the highest governing body until that point—was divided into four synods: Missouri, Green River, Franklin, and Columbia. The denomination had 120 ministers at that time.

In 1889 the Nolin Presbytery of the Cumberland Presbyterian denomination ordained Louisa M.

Woosley, perhaps the first ordained Presbyterian woman in America. Other Cumberland presbyteries began ordaining women in the 1910s and the practice was endorsed by the general assembly in 1921.

The 1989 yearbook of the Cumberland Presbyterian listed 168 Cumberland churches in Kentucky, with a total of 12,164 members. The denomination as a whole had 809 churches and 91,943 members that year.

See Ben M. Barrus, Milton L. Baughn, and Thomas H. Campbell, *A People Called Cumberland Presbyterians* (Memphis, Tenn., 1972); Louis B. Weeks, *Kentucky Presbyterians* (Atlanta 1983); Ernest T. Thompson, *Presbyterians in the South* (Richmond, Va., 1963).   MICHAEL E. JONES

CUMBERLAND RIVER. The extreme headwaters of the Cumberland River are in the southern part of Letcher County, Kentucky, near the small town of Oven Fork. Seven hundred miles downstream the Cumberland empties into the Ohio River in Livingston County near Smithland. The drainage basin covers 7,000 square miles of Kentucky and 11,000 square miles in Tennessee. The Cumberland is the only river in Kentucky that flows south, then changes course and flows north. Two of Kentucky's largest lakes are impoundments of the Cumberland: Lake Barkley, in western Kentucky, and Lake Cumberland, in southern Kentucky. One of the most popular recreation spots in Kentucky is CUMBERLAND FALLS, on the boundary between Whitley and McCreary counties.

Over the distance between Williamsburg, in Whitley County, and Lake Cumberland, the Cumberland has been designated a wild river, a classification that highly restricts land use within one-half mile of the river. This section of the river is popular with canoeists because of the many rapids and shoals. The descent of the river between Williamsburg and Cumberland Falls averages 2.61 feet per mile. Between Cumberland Falls and the mouth of Laurel River, a distance of 11.6 miles, the river falls an average of 11.75 feet per mile. The major tributaries of the Cumberland River in Kentucky are in the southern and southeastern parts of the state: Poor Fork, Martin's Fork, Clear Fork, Laurel, Rockcastle, and the Big South Fork of the Cumberland. Parts of the Big South Fork have been designated wild river areas (see BIG SOUTH FORK NATIONAL RIVER and Recreation Area).

The Cumberland River was named on April 17, 1750, by Dr. Thomas Walker, in honor of William Augustus, the Duke of Cumberland. Walker and his exploration party from Virginia first encountered the river at Pine Gap in Bell County. In the winter of 1780, Walker and Daniel Smith traveled down the Cumberland from the mouth of Pitman Creek in Pulaski County to what is now the Kentucky-Tennessee border in western Kentucky, while surveying the southern boundary of present-day Kentucky. Walker's men built a cabin along the river at Swan Pond, in Knox County.

See Joseph R. Schwendeman, *Geography of Kentucky* (Lexington, Ky., 1987).

C.M. DUPIER, JR.

CUMBERLAND TRACE. Cumberland Trace was a significant trail running through the wilderness of central Kentucky from 1779 or earlier. It branched westward off the Wilderness Road near Logan's Station in Lincoln County, crossed the South Fork of the Rolling Fork River, passed through a gap in the Knobs, and followed Robinson and Buckhorn creeks and the Trace Fork of Pitman Creek in Taylor County. The trail crossed the Green River at Pitman's Station in Green County, traversed the Barrens, crossed the Barren River near McFadin's Station in Warren County, and continued southwest to the Cumberland settlements near present-day Nashville. Among the noted travelers of this route were James Robertson and his band of men and boys. In 1779-80 they drove cattle on their way to settle at the French Salt Lick on the Cumberland River. John Donelson, co-founder of Nashville and father-in-law of Andrew Jackson, was killed on this trace in the mid-1780s.

See Katherine R. Barnes, "James Robertson's Journey to Nashville: Tracing the Route of Fall 1779," *Tennessee Historical Quarterly* 35 (Summer 1976): 145-51; Florence Merkley, "The Cumberland Trace Through Taylor County, Kentucky," *Register* 70 (July 1972): 219-24.

BETTY MITCHELL GORIN

CURRIER, MARY ANN. Mary Ann Currier, a Louisville realist known for her vivid oil pastel still lifes, was born on July 23, 1927, in Louisville, to Adolph and Gertrude (Bruehl) Ebert. She attended the Chicago Academy of Fine Art during 1945-47, and the Louisville School of Art during 1958-62, then taught at the Louisville art school from 1962 to 1982. On July 2, 1949, she married Lionel F. Currier, by whom she has three daughters. After eight years in Florida, Currier returned to Louisville in 1990. Galleries throughout the United States have exhibited her works, and they are a permanent part of the Twentieth Century Collection at the Metropolitan Museum of Art in New York City.

See Sarah McPhee, "Starting from Scratch," *ARTnews* 84 (Nov. 1985): 11.

CYNTHIANA. The county seat of Harrison County, Cynthiana is located at the junction of U.S. 27 and 62 and KY 32 and 36. Established as the county seat on December 10, 1793, the town was built on a 150-acre tract donated by Robert Harrison and named for his two daughters, Cynthia and Anna. Cynthiana was incorporated on March 2, 1860.

The Cynthiana area was first settled in 1775, by Capt. John Hinkston and a group of fifteen men from Pennsylvania. This site was soon abandoned but Isaac Ruddell reoccupied it in 1779 and named it RUDDELL'S STATION. In 1780 the British and

Indians attacked and forced it to surrender, killing several occupants and the taking the remainder captive. The settlement was later rebuilt by John Hinkston. The present-day site of Cynthiana is four miles south of Ruddell's Station.

As the center of a highly productive agricultural area, Cynthiana grew prosperous during the nineteenth century. During the antebellum period, distilling whiskey from the large quantity of grain produced by Harrison County farmers was probably the town's most thriving industry. Cynthiana's location on the South Fork of the Licking River made it the milling center for the county. Built in 1794, the first courthouse was a two-story log structure. A second structure was completed in 1816. This two-story brick edifice was destroyed by fire on January 24, 1851, and was replaced by a third building completed in November 1853.

Cynthiana was the scene on July 17, 1862, of the Battle of Cynthiana Bridge when attacked by Gen. John Hunt MORGAN. On June 11, 1864, Morgan again attacked Cynthiana and burned twenty-five houses to drive out Federal soldiers barricaded inside. Next day the Confederates in turn were driven out in a counterattack by Gen. Stephen BURBRIDGE.

Having an economy based on agriculture that was not seriously affected by the Civil War, Cynthiana quickly recovered. The small COVINGTON & LEXINGTON Railroad, which came to Cynthiana in 1856, merged with the Louisville & Nashville Railroad in 1891, tying Cynthiana to trading opportunities throughout the county. Through the remainder of the nineteenth century and well into the twenti-

eth, Cynthiana remained the marketing center for predominantly agricultural Harrison County. Tobacco, grain, and beef cattle are among the products traded there. In the latter twentieth century Cynthiana developed a substantial industrial base. Products such as stainless steel valves and fittings, steel tubing, refrigeration coils, and iron castings are manufactured in Cynthiana.

The population of the fourth-class city was 6,356 in 1970; 5,881 in 1980; and 6,497 in 1990.

RON D. BRYANT

CYNTHIANA BRIDGE, BATTLE OF. During the first Kentucky raid, on July 18, 1862, Gen. John Hunt MORGAN's brigade of eight hundred Confederate cavalry advanced to Cynthiana, where they met the strongest resistance of the expedition. At the covered bridge over the Licking River, 350 Union soldiers and Home Guards occupied houses on the northern shore. Morgan opened fire with his two cannon and ordered a dismounted frontal assault on the bridge. After three unsuccessful attacks, Company A waded the ford to the left of the bridge and was pinned down on the opposite bank. The artillery crossed the bridge but withdrew, abandoning the guns. Finally, the reserve attacked on horseback and the Union men retreated and surrendered. Morgan had about forty casualties and the Union about ninety. The railroad depot, part of the fledging Kentucky Central Railroad, and some weapons were destroyed, along with Camp Frazer, a Union encampment.

JAMES A. RAMAGE

D

DAILY INDEPENDENT. The *Daily Independent*, an Ashland, Kentucky–based newspaper, had a 1990 circulation of 26,000 through twelve northeastern Kentucky counties, focusing on Boyd and Greenup. Launched in 1895 in Catlettsburg by G.F. Friel as the *Tri-State Independent*, it was moved to Ashland in 1900 to compete with the *Ashland Daily News*. The first issue under the name *Daily Independent* was dated December 17, 1900. B.F. Forgey, another Catlettsburg publisher, bought a half-interest in 1902, and after 1921 J.T. Norris of Bracken County became a partner. By the mid-1920s, the *Daily Independent* had absorbed the *Catlettsburg Daily Press*, the *Ashland Daily News*, and the *Ashland Daily Commercial*. The Forgey and Norris families operated the paper under the name *Ashland Daily Independent* through 1979, when it was bought by the Ottaway Newspapers group, a subsidiary of Dow Jones Inc. The paper was hot-metal, linotype print through 1977, when computers and offset presses were adopted. The name Ashland was dropped from the masthead in 1982, emphasizing the regional scope of the paper.

GEORGE WOLFFORD

DAIRY INDUSTRY. The first cattle in Kentucky were driven through the Cumberland Gap or brought down the Ohio River. In 1787 cattle of the shorthorn milking variety were brought to central Kentucky. Pioneer families depended on their own cows for milk supply. Calving nearly always took place in the spring, and milk (perhaps a gallon a day) was available as long as pasture was good. The rolling land and the climate were well suited for forages.

When cities appeared, nearby farmers started producing milk, butter, and cheese to deliver to regular customers. Butter produced during the summer was packed in firkins (wooden bowls or buckets), covered with brine, and stored in cellars or spring houses. After this kind of preservation, it had a stale, rancid flavor. Cream separators became available after 1880 and farmers began selling cream to butter factories. In 1940 the cream business in Kentucky peaked at 201,709 producers, each having an average of 2.8 cows; they sold cream to 1,333 buying stations for twelve butter plants. Per capita consumption of butter began to decline, however, first because of competition from margarine and later because of public concern over fat content, particularly saturated animal fat. By 1950, nearly all of the cream stations had closed. In 1970, Kentucky had thirty-eight fluid milk plants, twenty-four cheese factories, eight evaporated milk plants, and one butter plant.

The number of Kentucky farms producing milk peaked in 1940 at 201,709 and fell to 63% of that number ten years later. Further declines brought the count as low as 7,000 in 1988. The average herd size increased from 2.8 cows in 1940 to 30.6 in 1988, while the total number of dairy cows in Ken-

tucky decreased from 600,000 in 1950 to 214,000 in 1988. Average production rose from 3,500 pounds per cow in 1940 to 10,684 in 1988. The improvement is no doubt due to better feeding and management, the dairy herd improvement program (which started in 1927), and the use of better sires through artificial insemination since 1946.

In 1988, Kentucky ranked twelfth among the states in number of dairy cattle, seventeenth in total production, and forty-ninth in average production per cow. Kentucky lags behind most other states in the percentage of cows on test under the dairy herd improvement program and in percentage of cows bred artificially.

See John B. Roberts, *Kentucky Dairy Industry*, University of Kentucky, College of Agriculture Progress Report 198, 1972; Robert L. Beck, *Kentucky's Manufacturing Milk Industry*, University of Kentucky, College of Agriculture Progress Report 263, 1982.

DURWARD OLDS

DANIEL BOONE NATIONAL FOREST. The Daniel Boone National Forest contains more than 660,000 acres of public land intermingled with privately owned land in portions of twenty-one eastern Kentucky counties. The topography is generally rugged, characterized by cliffs, steep slopes, and narrow valleys. The forest crosses portions of the drainages of the Licking, Kentucky, and Cumberland rivers. As it lies in the mixed mesophytic region of the eastern deciduous forest, it is characterized by an extremely wide variety of plant species. It was named the Cumberland National Forest when it was established on February 23, 1937, by a proclamation signed by President Franklin D. Roosevelt. The name was changed to honor Daniel Boone, the frontiersman who explored the area, by President Lyndon B. Johnson on April 13, 1966.

The forest is one of 156 national forests, managed by the Forest Service, an agency within the U.S. Department of Agriculture. Eastern national forests were originally established to protect headwaters of navigable streams and to provide a continuous supply of timber. Like all other national forests, the Daniel Boone is managed under the principles of multiple use and sustained yield, to supply the public with wood, water, wildlife and fish, recreation, livestock grazing, wilderness, and minerals. Twenty-five percent of the forest's total receipts are distributed to the counties in which it is located. By law, these funds must be used for roads and schools. Receipts are derived from timber sales, mineral extraction, recreation user fees, livestock grazing, and other land uses.

The forest supervisor administers the public lands within the Daniel Boone National Forest's boundary from headquarters in Winchester, Kentucky. The supervisor is assisted by a staff of professional foresters, engineers, landscape architects, geologists, wildlife biologists, soil scientists, watershed specialists, archaeologists, teachers, business managers, and clerks. The forest is divided into seven ranger districts, each administered by a forest ranger and staff, from offices in Morehead, Stanton, Berea, London, Somerset, Whitley City, and Big Creek. Two Job Corps Civilian Conservation Centers are located in the forest, in Menifee and McCreary counties. They are operated by the Forest Service in cooperation with the U.S. Department of Labor to educate and train disadvantaged youths sixteen to twenty-one years old.

The forest's attractions include the RED RIVER GORGE geological area, Pioneer Weapons hunting area, Cave Run Lake, Laurel River Lake, Beaver Creek and Clifty wilderness areas, Sheltowee Trace national recreation trail, Natural Arch scenic area, and the Gladie Cabin, a log boardinghouse used by loggers in the early 1900s.

See Robert F. Collins, *A History of the Daniel Boone National Forest, 1770-1970* (Washington, D.C., 1976). CHARLES J. CRAIL

DANVILLE. Danville, the county seat of Boyle County, is located at the junction of U.S. 150 and U.S. 127. The community began as Crow's Station, founded in 1782 by John Crow, a settler in the area. Danville was founded in 1783-84 by Walker Daniel, the first district attorney of Kentucky, and was named in his honor. The Virginia legislature granted a charter for the town in 1787, and Danville was incorporated on March 1, 1836.

In 1783 the legislature of Virginia created a supreme court for the District of Kentucky; the court met first in Harrodsburg but soon moved to Danville to hold its deliberations in a log courthouse built in the town square. Danville's convenient location, plus the presence of three hospitable taverns nearby, brought ten conventions to the log courthouse where the delegates discussed the future of Kentucky. The first convention met in December 1784 and the last in April 1792, producing an eighteen-page document that became the first constitution of the Commonwealth of Kentucky. Danville was the home of Dr. Ephraim McDowell, who performed the first successful ovariotomy in December 1809.

Danville was the first location of Transylvania University, established in 1783 and relocated to Lexington in 1789. Centre College in Danville, created in 1819, turned out a long and impressive list of graduates. In 1823 Danville was chosen as the site of the Kentucky School for the Deaf, the first institution of its kind to be operated at public expense. Danville Theological Seminary was founded in 1853 and Caldwell Institute for Young Ladies in 1860.

During the antebellum period, Danville was a prosperous and growing community in spite of two major disasters. In 1819 a tornado devastated a portion of the city and on February 22, 1860, a fire destroyed sixty-four businesses, churches, and homes and caused over $300,000 in damages. Among the structures destroyed was the 1844 courthouse. Its replacement, an Italianate-style

brick structure, was completed in 1862 and used as a military hospital following the Battle of PERRYVILLE on October 8, 1862. During the Civil War, the town was occupied by both Confederate and Union soldiers, and in October 1863 a large force of guerrillas passed through, causing damage.

James G. Birney, the presidential candidate for the Liberty party in 1840 and again in 1844, was born in Danville. Theodore O'Hara, a well-known author, poet, and soldier, was a native of Danville. O'Hara is best remembered for his poem "The Bivouac of the Dead."

With the coming of the Cincinnati, New Orleans & Texas Pacific Railroad (now Norfolk Southern) to Danville in the 1870s, the city prospered as a transportation and commercial hub as well as an educational center. The railroad built a large yard, a locomotive roundhouse, and repair shops there; Danville became an important division point on the north-south line. Industrial development proceeded steadily throughout the nineteenth and twentieth centuries. An out-of-the ordinary business in the 1870s distilled lubricating oil from hog fat. In 1891 an electrical clock company was built in Danville, along with three carriage factories, a hemp works, brick manufacturer, shoe factory, and a glassware plant.

In 1942 the state of Kentucky dedicated the John G. Weisiger Memorial Park in the center of Danville. Later known as Constitution Square State Shrine, the park celebrates the city's role in Kentucky statehood and contains log reproductions of an early courthouse, church, and jail, as well as an original log structure that is reputed have been the first post office west of Alleghenies. Because of its many old houses and nineteenth century appearance, Danville was chosen as the location for the motion picture *Raintree County* in 1956. The Civil War drama, featuring Elizabeth Taylor, Montgomery Clift, and Eva Marie Saint, employed many residents as extras.

During the 1960s new industry located on the western and southern edges of the city, while the population grew by over 2,500. Major employers are the Matsushita Floor Care Company, the ATR Wire and Cable Company, and the Matthews Conveyor Corporation. Products manufactured in Danville include clothing, shoes, furniture, chemicals, light bulbs, and tubing.

The population of the third-class city was 11,542 in 1970; 12,942 in 1980; and 12,420 in 1990.

See Calvin M. Fackler, *Early Days in Danville* (Louisville 1941). RICHARD C. BROWN

DANVILLE POLITICAL CLUB. The Danville Political Club was a short-lived private debating society, formed on the night of December 27, 1786, by seven men who met at the Danville, Kentucky, home of Judge Samuel McDowell. The other six were Harry Innes, John Brown, Thomas Todd, Robert Craddock, Christopher Greenup, and John Belli. As many as thirty men were members of the club at one time or another during the four years of its known existence, but it went unremarked for the next century. There is no mention of the club in the diaries, correspondence, or memoirs left by the distinguished men who were its members, and only one or two vague references in other contemporary documents.

Knowledge of the club's activities came to light nearly a hundred years later, when Thomas Speed II found in an old desk the minutes and other papers that his grandfather Thomas Speed had kept as the club's secretary. The Political Club met each Saturday in Danville, though no more than half its members were residents of that town. At each meeting the members present (never more than fifteen) debated a previously selected question of timely interest. The members spent several weekly meetings in discussing clause by clause the federal Constitution as printed in Philadelphia in September 1787. The result was a bulky document found among the old papers, titled and annotated as "The Constitution of the United States as Amended and Approved by The Political Club." They also debated several issues relating to separation from Virginia.

It is said that the collective biographies of the Political Club's members could be made into a history of Kentucky in the years when it was still part of Virginia and when it was a newly independent state. It is equally clear that the debates and the companionship offered by the club's meetings in Danville helped to shape the members' views and subsequent actions.

See Thomas Speed, *The Political Club*, Filson Club Publications No. 9 (Louisville 1894); Ann Price Combs, "Notes on the Political Club of Danville and Its Members," *FCHQ* 35 (Oct. 1961): 333-52.   RICHARD C. BROWN

DANVILLE THEOLOGICAL SEMINARY. In October 1853 the Danville Theological Seminary opened in Danville, Kentucky, with twenty-three students and four professors, established by the Presbyterian denomination. Enrollment rose to fifty-two in 1860, before the Civil War reduced the student body. The war and its aftermath divided Presbyterians into factions, southern and northern, the latter gaining control of both the seminary and Centre College in Danville. Adherents of the southern Presbyterian group organized Central College at Richmond and planned a seminary there as an alternative to the one at Danville. Neither seminary had the enrollment or the resources to stand alone, however, and in 1901 training of Presbyterian ministers for both the northern and the southern Presbyterian group was transferred from Danville and Richmond to the Louisville Presbyterian Theological Seminary.

See Walter A. Groves, "A School of the Prophets at Danville," *FCHQ* 27 (July 1953): 223-46; Louis B. Weeks, *Kentucky Presbyterians* (Atlanta 1983).   RICHARD C. BROWN

DARK AND BLOODY GROUND. The popular belief that the name Kentucky means "dark and bloody ground" is apparently without foundation. Yet the image persists in literary and oral tradition as a description of the Kentucky country. Its origin is unknown. One traditional explanation cites a Delaware legend in which the ancient tribe of the Lenni-Lenape, from the North and West, allied with the Iroquois to fight the Allegewi, the original inhabitants of Kentucky, who were virtually exterminated in a single bloody battle. The land where an entire nation had been eradicated became known as the "dark and bloody ground."

Violent confrontation between the Iroquois and the southern Indians reinforced the image. Richard H. Collins's *Historical Sketches of Kentucky* (1874) says that a northern Indian asked Indian fighter Joseph H. Daveiss how white men could live in a land that had witnessed so much bloodshed. The Indian said that the ghosts of those killed in Indian wars haunted the land, making it dangerous.

At the execution of the Treaty of Sycamore Shoals, the Cherokee chief Dragging Canoe is said to have told Col. Richard Henderson that the lands south of the Kentucky River were "bloody ground and would be dark and difficult to settle." Ruben T. Durrett said in *The Centenary of Kentucky* (1892) that the phrase was used to discourage Henderson from purchasing the land.

DAVEISS, JOSEPH HAMILTON. Joseph Hamilton Daveiss, a jurist in whose honor Daviess County was named in 1815, was born in Virginia in 1774 to Joseph and Jean Daveiss. (When Kentucky and Indiana named counties after Daveiss, neither state spelled the county the way he spelled his name.) The Daveiss family moved to Boyle County, Kentucky, when he was five years old. In 1793 Daveiss served in the Kentucky militia on an expedition against the Indians. After reading law with George Nicholas, he began his practice in June 1795 in Danville. In 1799, he became a U.S. attorney. He prosecuted the "Whiskey War" cases in 1799 and prosecuted Aaron Burr for treason in 1806. Daveiss was elected to the Kentucky legislature in 1800. Daveiss moved to Washington, D.C., in 1801, where he became one of the first attorneys from west of the Appalachians to argue a case before the Supreme Court. He was married in 1803 to Anne Marshall, the sister of Chief Justice John Marshall. The couple lived first in Frankfort, Kentucky, then at Cornland, a large farm just east of Owensboro. In 1809 Daveiss lived in Lexington, where he practiced law. In 1811, when Gen. William Henry Harrison raised an army against the Indians in the Wabash Valley, Daveiss joined him with the rank of major, later brevetted to colonel. A contemporary described Daveiss as a man of "high military genius." At the battle of Tippecanoe, Indiana, on November 7, 1811, Daveiss was mortally wounded while leading a charge; he died seventeen hours later and was buried at the battle site.

LEE A. DEW

DAVENPORT, GUY MATTISON, JR. Educator and writer Guy Mattison Davenport, Jr., was born November 23, 1927, in Anderson, South Carolina, the son of Guy Mattison and Marie (Fant)

Davenport. He graduated from Duke University in 1948, earned a bachelor of literature degree from Oxford University as a Rhodes scholar in 1950, and received his Ph.D. from Harvard University in 1961. He taught at Washington University in St. Louis during 1952-55 and at Haverford College in Pennsylvania during 1961-63. Davenport came to the University of Kentucky in 1963 as professor of English. He received the U.K. Alumni Distinguished Professor Award of 1976-77. In 1990 he received a MacArthur Fellowship, enabling him to write full time.

Davenport is known as one of the most original and versatile voices in American letters for his work as a poet, novelist, classicist, translator, critic, painter, and illustrator. He is the author of more than twenty books, including, in fiction, *Tatlin!* (1974), *Da Vinci's Bicycle* (1979) and *The Jules Verne Steam Balloon* (1987); in criticism, *The Geography of the Imagination* (1981) and *Every Force Evolves a Form* (1987); in poetry, *Flowers and Leaves* (1966); and in translation, *Sappho: Songs and Fragments, Herakleitos and Diogenes* (1979) and *Archilochos, Sappho, Alkman: Three Greek Poets* (1980).

See George Steiner, "Rare Bird," *New Yorker* 57 (Nov. 30, 1981): 196-204.   RICHARD TAYLOR

DAVENPORT, GWEN (LEYS). Gwen (Leys) Davenport, author, was born in Colon, Canal Zone, on October 3, 1910, to James Farquharson and Gwen (Wigley) Leys. In 1931 she received an A.B. from Vassar College. After her marriage to John Andrews Davenport in 1937, the couple lived in Louisville, where they reared three children: Christopher, John, and Juliet. During the 1940s and 1950s, she produced a number of witty novels, most of which satirize modern family life, especially from the point of view of the mother. Her novels include *Belvedere* (1947), which was produced as a motion picture called *Sitting Pretty* in 1948; *Candy for Breakfast* (1950); and *The Bachelor's Baby* (1958).   ANNA MARIE CONKLIN

DAVIESS COUNTY. Daviess County, the fifty-eighth county in order of formation, was formed from a part of Ohio County on January 14, 1815. The county's borders were altered in 1829 to form Hancock County, in 1830 to absorb a small area surrounding Whitesville, in 1854 to cede land to McLean County, and in 1860 to annex forty-four square miles from Henderson County. Daviess County measures 463 square miles, making it eighteenth in size in the commonwealth. The county seat is Owensboro.

William Smeathers (Smothers) settled at YELLOW BANKS, later Owensboro, in 1797 or 1798, about the time that Valentine Husk settled at Pup Creek. Other settlers were attracted to the healthy, well-drained hill country between Pup Creek and Blackford, especially along the many Indian trails that bisected this region, such as the Elizabethtown-Shawneetown trail. Another led from Iceland Landing on the Ohio to the town of Hartford in Ohio County. Yelvington, at the intersection of these two trails, became the first settlement in Daviess. The county was named to honor Col. Joseph Hamilton Daveiss, a major landowner and lawyer killed at the Battle of Tippecanoe. At the creation of the county, the enrolling clerk misspelled the county name, making it officially Daviess. Later the General Assembly passed an act making the spelling Daveiss legal, but the error persisted.

Originally most of the county was timbered, and woodworking industries thrived in the nineteenth century. Some timber remains as an exploitable resource, but with the draining of the Panther Creek bottoms in the 1920s, the main area for timber exploitation was clear-cut and converted to agricultural use. Coal mining began commercially in the 1880s, and Daviess County became a major producer with the development of strip mining technology in the 1950s. Production peaked in 1984 at 1,482,779 tons. Oil production, which began in 1925, topped out in 1958 at 1,835,526 barrels of crude oil. Sand and gravel from the bed of the Ohio River are other major resources of the county. From the settlement era, the primary source of income in Daviess has been agriculture. By 1870 Daviess County was a major producer of corn, tobacco, hogs and cattle, and soybean cultivation was introduced in the 1930s. By 1963 Daviess had become Kentucky's primary soybean producer, and two years later soybean acreage exceeded that of corn for the first time. By 1980 soybean acreage was nearly twice that of corn. By the 1970s Daviess also ranked in the top ten Kentucky counties in the production of hogs and cattle.

Early settlers stayed along the higher elevations to avoid the malaria-infested bottoms and swamps. The disease remained a problem until the draining of the Panther Creek bottoms in the 1920s. The rich soil made slave labor profitable, and by 1860 Daviess counted 3,515 slaves and seventy-six free blacks, accounting for more than 20 percent of the county's total population of 15,549.

Strong emotional ties to the South made many Daviess County residents supporters of the Confederate cause during the Civil War. The county gained a reputation as a hotbed of rebellion, although most residents preferred a neutral position and opposed only Lincoln and the prospect of emancipation. Lincoln and the Republicans could attract only seven votes in Daviess in the election of 1860, as a majority of voters maintained the county's former Whig allegiance by voting for the candidate of the Constitutional Union party. While guerrilla raids were common, only one formal battle took place in Daviess County: a skirmish at Panther Creek that drove a Confederate force south from Owensboro.

Daviess County's first industrial boom came in the 1870s from the distillery industry. Eighteen distilleries were erected in a period of a few years. Plenty of corn, adequate supplies of white oak timber for barrels, and cheap transportation by steamboat made Daviess the leading producer of sour-mash bourbon. The competition from cheap whiskeys and beer, however, coupled with a high federal tax on bourbon in bonded warehouses, quickly brought an end to the boom.

Railroads arrived in the 1870s and 1880s to link Daviess County to markets. Factories making products as diverse as light bulbs, wagons and buggies, and sewer tile provided employment for town dwellers and markets for foodstuffs, forest products, and other materials from clay to coal. In twentieth-century development, plants were built to process meat, dairy products, grain, and tobacco. The county was recognized by the U.S. Department of Agriculture as a part of the Corn Belt area, where most of the nation's corn is grown.

Today half of the county's population of nearly 90,000 lives in the suburban towns outside the city limits of Owensboro. Other towns in Daviess include the incorporated town of Whitesville and unincorporated communities such as Knottsville, Curdsville, Stanley, Utica, Sorgho, and Philpot. It was proposed in 1987 that city and county governments in Daviess consolidate, as the Lexington and Fayette County governments have done. Voters, however, overwhelmingly rejected the proposition in November 1990. The county is served by several county parks and recreation areas, including the Ben Hawes State Park. The Owensboro-Daviess County Airport is operated by both city and county governments. The county government also contributes to such facilities as the Owensboro Area Museum and Owensboro Museum of Fine Arts. The county is served by a daily newspaper, the *Owensboro Messenger-Inquirer*.

The decline in the number of manufacturing jobs brought a period of economic stagnation to Daviess County in the early 1980s. This trend was reversed with the creation of 1,500 new jobs in 1988-89 by reopening the Green River Steel plant and expanding other industrial sites.

The population was 79,486 in 1970; 85,949 in 1980; and 87,819 in 1990.

See Hugh O. Potter, *A History of Owensboro and Daviess County, Kentucky* (Montgomery, Ala., 1974).   LEE A. DEW

DAVIS, BRINTON BEAUREGARD. Brinton Beauregard Davis, architect, was born January 23, 1862, in Natchez, Mississippi, the son of Jacob Brinton and Mary (Gamble) Davis. A graduate of the Eustace Academy in Natchez, he trained with his architect father and with other architects in New York City, Chicago, and St. Louis before establishing a practice at Paducah, Kentucky, in 1892. After service in the Spanish-American War, he moved to Louisville about 1903. Among his important buildings are the Jefferson County Armory (1905, now Louisville Gardens), the Kentucky Home Life Building (1913), and the Kentucky Hotel (1925), all in Louisville. His designs include a major group of buildings for what is now Western Kentucky University in Bowling Green, the Ansley Hotel in At-

lanta, and buildings in Tennessee, Mississippi, and Indiana. Davis married Clara Benbrook on February 23, 1889; they had two daughters, Gladys and Mildred. He died in Louisville on June 27, 1952, and was buried in Cave Hill Cemetery.

See Jean Howerton Coady, "Brinton B. Davis: A Kentucky Name Written in Stone," *Louisville Courier-Journal*, Jan. 14, 1980.
                                          MARY JEAN KINSMAN

DAVIS, GARRETT. Garrett Davis, legislator, was born on September 10, 1801, at Mt. Sterling, Kentucky. He was the son of Jeremiah Davis, a blacksmith, who served one term in the legislature; his mother's surname was Garrett. Educated locally, Davis studied law and worked as a deputy to the clerk of the circuit court until 1823, when he was admitted to the bar and opened a law office in Paris, Kentucky.

In 1833 Davis was elected to represent Bourbon County in the state House of Representatives, where he served from 1833 to 1838. Elected to the U.S. House of Representatives, he served from March 4, 1839, to March 3, 1847. As a Whig, he supported Henry Clay's bid for the presidency in 1842. Returning to the practice of law and to his farm in 1847, he refused to run for lieutenant governor on the John J. Crittenden ticket in 1848. In 1849 Davis was elected to the state constitutional convention, where he urged the abolition of slavery and opposed an elective judiciary. Losing his arguments, he resigned and unsuccessfully opposed the new constitution. Concerned by the increasing influence of Roman Catholicism, he joined the American, or KNOW-NOTHING, party, but refused its nomination for governor in 1855 and for the presidency in 1856.

An outspoken critic of secession, Davis supported the Constitutional Union ticket of John Bell and Edward Everett in the 1860 presidential election. In April 1861 he met with President Abraham Lincoln, who assured Davis that the government had no intention of invading Kentucky if the state supported the Union. Davis relayed these sentiments to the legislature, which resolved that Kentucky should remain neutral. The legislature elected Davis to the seat in the U.S. Senate vacated by the resignation of John C. Breckinridge on December 10, 1861. An ardent supporter of the Union, Davis accused his Kentucky colleague, Lazarus W. Powell, of being a traitor, but his efforts to unseat Powell failed. A later attack upon President Lincoln and his "war party," in the form of eighteen resolutions, almost resulted in Davis's expulsion from the Senate, but his explanations of his criticisms saved his seat.

Both Republicans and Democrats hoped to capture the Senate seat in 1867. The Republicans nominated Benjamin H. Bristow and the Democrats chose Davis. Davis, more acceptable to the conservatives, won the election. When the Radical Republicans insisted on the need to reconstruct Kentucky, Davis consistently defended Kentucky against the charges of disloyalty. During the 1869 controversy between the Louisville & Nashville Railroad and the Cincinnati Southern Railroad over the right to build a road through central Kentucky to Tennessee, Davis prevented the Southern Railway Bill from passing the Senate, asserting that it was unconstitutional.

Davis was considered one of the ablest debaters of his day and lent his voice to many causes. Kentuckians respected his candor and honesty. Davis was married first in 1825; left a widower, he later married for a second time. He died near Paris on September 22, 1872, before the expiration of his second senatorial term, and was buried in the Paris Cemetery.

ROSS A. WEBB

DAVIS, JEFFERSON. Jefferson Davis, the only president of the Confederate States of America, was born at Fairview, then called Davisburg, in Christian (now Todd) County, Kentucky, June 3, 1808. He was the youngest of five sons and five daughters born to Samuel Emory and Jane (Cook) Davis. His father, a captain in the Revolutionary War, was of Welsh ancestry and his mother of Scotch-Irish descent.

The family had moved from Georgia to Nelson County, Kentucky, in 1793, and to Christian County in 1798. There the elder Davis built a double log house on the present site of Bethel Baptist Church. He was a farmer and served as postmaster of Davisburg. In 1810 the family moved to Louisiana and then to Mississippi. Davis attended St. Thomas of Aquin Catholic School, Springfield, Kentucky, from 1816 until 1818. While a student at Transylvania University, Lexington, in 1823-24, he developed a friendship with Albert Sidney Johnston, later a general in the Confederate army. Davis entered the U.S. Military Academy at West Point in 1824 and graduated twenty-third in his class, as second lieutenant, in 1828.

Lieutenant Davis was assigned to Jefferson Barracks, Missouri, and later to Fort Crawford, in Wisconsin Territory. He met and fell in love with Sarah Knox Taylor, daughter of Col. Zachary Taylor. Partly because of the colonel's opposition to their relationship, Davis resigned from the army in 1835. He married "Knox" in Louisville on June 17, 1835. She died three months later of malaria, at the plantation home of his brother. For eight years Davis lived alone at his Brierfield plantation in Mississippi, where he managed the farm operations. In February 1845 Davis married Varina Howell of Natchez, Mississippi. They had four sons and two daughters.

Davis was appointed to the U.S. House of Representatives and served from March 4, 1845, until he resigned in June 1846 to enter the Mexican War. He led the 1st Mississippi Volunteers Regiment and commanded staunch allegiance from his men. Deploying his men in the V formation, he led the storming of Monterrey, was wounded and emerged the hero of Buena Vista. Returning from the war,

Davis was appointed to the U.S. Senate on August 10, 1847, by the Mississippi legislature. In 1848 he was elected to complete the term, but resigned on September 23, 1851, in protest over Henry Clay's 1850 compromise. As a strict interpreter of the U.S. Constitution and a strong supporter of the states' rights leader, John C. Calhoun, Davis considered the compromise a constitutional violation. In 1851 Davis lost the election for governor of Mississippi as the Democrats' states' rights candidate.

President Franklin Pierce appointed Davis secretary of war in 1853. In this office he improved the system of infantry tactics, organized an engineers' company to explore railroad routes, and imported camels for use by the U.S. Army in the West. Davis was elected from Mississippi to the U.S. Senate for the term beginning March 4, 1857, and became a leading spokesman for strict constitutional interpretation. He resigned on January 21, 1861, after Mississippi's secession from the Union.

The provisional Confederate Congress, in a meeting in Montgomery, Alabama, named Davis president of the Confederate States of America on February 9, 1861. As an administrator, Davis acted with dignity and sincerity and portrayed a strict devotion to constitutional principle. When the Confederate military collapsed and Richmond fell, Davis and his family tried to flee to Mexico. They were captured by Union forces near Irwinsville, Georgia, on May 10, 1865. Davis's imprisonment at Fortress Monroe, Virginia, ended in May 1867.

After spending a year in Canada and another year traveling, Davis settled in Memphis, where he served as president of the Carolina Insurance Co. from 1869 until 1873. In 1879 he bought a six-hundred-acre plantation, Beauvoir, located on the Gulf Coast at Biloxi, Mississippi. Two years later Davis completed his two-volume *Rise and Fall of the Confederate Government*. The last years of his life were spent in traveling, making public appearances, and attending veterans' reunions.

Davis returned to his native county on two occasions. In 1875 he was invited to attend the Christian County Agricultural and Mechanical Association fair at Hopkinsville and there spoke before a crowd estimated at 10,000. In 1886 Davis attended the dedication of Bethel Baptist Church, built on the site of his birthplace at Fairview. The Confederate president died in New Orleans on December 6, 1889, and was buried there. His body was later removed to Richmond, Virginia.

See Clement Eaton, *Jefferson Davis* (New York 1977); Robert Penn Warren, *Jefferson Davis Gets His Citizenship Back* (Lexington, Ky., 1980).

WILLIAM T. TURNER

DAVIS, KARL, AND HARTY TAYLOR. Karl Davis and Harty Taylor, known professionally as the singers Karl and Harty, were both born near Mt. Vernon, Kentucky, in 1905 and were schoolmates there. Davis learned to play the mandolin at age twelve after hearing Doc Hopkins play, and

Taylor taught himself the guitar. After high school graduation the boys joined Hopkins in the Kentucky Krazy Kats. In 1930 Bradley Kincaid arranged an audition on the radio station WLS Chicago. The two sang duets and were members of the Cumberland Ridge Runners on the "National Barn Dance" radio program in the 1930s. More important than their singing style were the songs they introduced, including the composition "Kentucky." They moved to Chicago's WJJD "Suppertime Frolic" in 1937 and retired in the 1950s. Taylor died in 1963 and Davis in 1979.

See Charles K. Wolfe, *Kentucky Country* (Lexington, Ky., 1982).   CHARLES F. FABER

DAVISON, WILLIAM H. William H. Davison, Civil War guerrilla leader, was born November 3, 1839, in Hancock County, Kentucky, the son of Hardin Aurelius and Jane (Dupuy) Davison. In 1861 he enlisted in the 17th Kentucky Infantry and fought at Fort Donelson and at Shiloh. He resigned after the Emancipation Proclamation on the ground that he would not fight to free slaves. In 1864 he raised a company and joined Col. Lee Sypert's Confederate Partisan Rangers but was captured in August of that year. Davison escaped from the Union prison in Louisville and returned to Hancock and Daviess counties to reassemble a guerrilla troop called Davison's Hyenas. His activities centered around Daviess, Breckinridge, and Meade counties, where he rode with such colorful figures as Henry C. ("Billy") Magruder and Marcellus Jerome CLARKE ("Sue Mundy"). In January 1865 he and his men burned the Daviess County courthouse. On February 24, 1865, a Home Guardsman, Charles Hale, shot and wounded Davison, who was pursuing Hale through the woods on the road to Hardinsburg. In March a $5,000 reward was offered for Davison's capture. Davison died on March 7, 1865, was secretly buried in the backwoods of Hancock County, and later reburied in Hawesville.

ALOMA WILLIAMS DEW

DAVIS SISTERS. The duo known as the Davis Sisters started singing together while attending Dixie Heights High School in Kenton County. Betty Jack Davis, daughter of Tipp Davis, was born in Corbin, Kentucky, on March 3, 1932. Skeeter Davis was the stage name of Mary Frances Penick, the daughter of W.L. and Sarah Penick, born in Dry Ridge, Kentucky, on December 30, 1931. As the Davis Sisters, the two appeared on radio in Cincinnati and Lexington and had a radio-television show in Detroit. They popularized the pedal-steel guitar and had hits on both the country and pop music charts. Betty Jack was killed in an automobile accident on August 2, 1953, which seriously injured Skeeter. Skeeter resumed her career, joining the "Grand Ole Opry" in 1959. In 1973 she was suspended temporarily for criticizing Nashville police on the air.

See Charles K. Wolfe, *Kentucky Country* (Lexington, Ky., 1982).   CHARLES F. FABER

DAWSON, CHARLES I. Charles I. Dawson, jurist, son of Steven N. and Francis (Coleman) Dawson, was born on February 13, 1881, in Logan County, Kentucky. He attended public school in Russellville, and after one year at Bethel College attended what is now the University of Kentucky in 1898-99. He taught for three years in Logan County. In 1903 Dawson read law, first in the office of S.R. Crewdson and subsequently with Judge James Bowden in Russellville, and in 1905 he was admitted to the bar. In the same year Dawson was elected to one term as a Democrat to the Kentucky House of Representatives. He then changed his affiliation to the Republican party. In 1909 he was elected county attorney for Bell County as an independent, with the support of the Republican party. He was reelected twice, on the Republican ticket. In 1919 Dawson was elected the commonwealth's attorney general and held that office until May 1923, when he announced his candidacy for governor; William J. Fields defeated Dawson by 356,035 to 306,277.

President Calvin Coolidge appointed Dawson U.S. district judge for the Western District of Kentucky on February 2, 1925, a position he held until 1935, maintaining a strict interpretation of constitutional issues. Dawson blocked a $1.5 million low-cost housing project in Louisville in 1935 because he believed the government's rights to condemn private property were limited to projects for public use and did not extend to slum clearance. In February 1935 Dawson ruled the National Recovery Administration's codes regulating wages in the bituminous coal industry unconstitutional. On June 1, 1935, Dawson left the bench to practice law in Louisville with Bullitt, Dawson & Tarrant. In 1950 he was defeated in his bid for a U.S. Senate seat by Gov. Earle C. Clements (1947-50), by 334,249 to 278,368. In 1952 Dawson was a Kentucky delegate to the Republican National Convention in Chicago. He led the fight that influenced the Kentucky delegates to support Robert A. Taft. In 1968 Dawson was again a delegate to the convention. He retired from his law practice in January 1969.

Dawson married Eleanor Hobson, daughter of A.H. and Harriet (Stevenson) Hobson, in 1905. They had three children: Eleanor, Jean Maxwell, and Richard. Dawson received an honorary doctor of laws degree from the University of Kentucky in 1948. He died April 24, 1969, and was buried at Cave Hill Cemetery in Louisville.

DAWSON SPRINGS. Dawson Springs is a rural commercial city located in southwestern Hopkins County in western Kentucky. The city is situated on the west bank of the Tradewater River, at the junction of US 62 and KY 109, two miles south of the Western Kentucky Parkway.

An early Native American trading village may have been located on the site of the present-day city, known earlier as Tradewater Bend. The area was originally part of Lincoln County and later Henderson County. At the time of the formation of

Hopkins County in 1807, the Menser family held land that would become the west side of Dawson Springs and the Alexanders owned the east side. In 1869 a parcel of land on both the east and west banks of the Tradewater River owned by David Menser was jointly purchased by Mr. and Mrs. Riley P. Dawson and Bryant N. Dawson. The Dawsons relocated from Caldwell County and were followed by Whitfield Wright Dawson and his family, who were engaged in farming and the lumber business. Bryant Dawson also farmed and opened a general store. When the Elizabethtown & Paducah Railroad (now Illinois Central Gulf) was constructed in the early 1870s, the Dawsons proposed to establish a town and donate land for the railroad station. On September 6, 1872, the first train to make the trip between Elizabethtown and Paducah passed through the little settlement, then called Tradewater Station. The town grew rapidly and by 1874 was known as Dawson.

Washington I. Hamby, a veteran of the Confederate cavalry, was a prominent local merchant who kept a railroad eating house and hotel. In 1881 and again in 1893 he discovered mineral water while digging wells. The water was believed to have medicinal properties, and the city quickly developed as one of the most popular health resorts in the upper South. The population grew from 130 people in 1880 to more than 1,000 five years later. The town was incorporated as Dawson City in 1882 and renamed Dawson Springs in 1898. Between 1900 and 1920, thousands of visitors arrived annually by train to "take of the waters." Hotel and boardinghouse business boomed. Among the finest of the resort hotels were the Hamby House; the Summit House; the Arcadia Hotel; and the showplace New Century Hotel, a luxurious place said to be the envy of every town in western Kentucky. Traveling tent shows, boat rides, movie theaters, taverns, and baseball were summer highlights. The Pittsburgh Pirates held spring training in Dawson Springs from 1915 to 1917, and several other major and minor league baseball teams trained and played exhibition games there, including the Louisville Colonels in 1919, 1923, 1924, and 1934.

In the 1930s, coal mining began to play a major role in the prosperity of the city. Mining on a small scale had been in progress since 1910, and on May 27, 1936, the Dawson Colleries Mine began operations on the east side of the city. Numerous mines existed around the city in the 1940s and 1950s but most closed by the early 1960s. On March 6, 1960, the landmark New Century Hotel was destroyed by fire.

An industrial park was completed in 1962 and several manufacturers located there, including Mid-South Plastics in 1963 and Ottenheimer and Company, garment manufacturers, in 1968. One of the largest employers was the Outwood Hospital, a state-owned veterans' hospital. The city is also home to the West Kentucky 4-H Camp at the Dawson Springs State Park. Pennyrile Forest State Resort Park is located south of Dawson Springs.

The population of the fourth-class city was 2,830 in 1970; 3,275 in 1980; and 3,129 in 1990.

See Dawson Springs Centennial Celebration Committee, *Welcome to Dawson Springs, Kentucky; Centennial Celebration 1874-1974* (Dawson Springs, Ky., 1974).

DAY LAW. The Day Law, proposed by state Rep. Carl Day of Breathitt County, effectively segregated both public and private schools in the state of Kentucky. Aimed at Berea College, Day's bill proposed to make unlawful the operation of schools engaged in the coeducation of white and black students. Passed by 73 to 5 in the state House of Representatives and approved 28 to 5 by the Senate, the law took effect in July 1904. On October 8 a Madison County grand jury indicted the college for violation of the Day Law (*Commonwealth v. Berea College*), beginning a series of court cases that lasted until 1908. The college challenged the law in the state courts as abridging the liberty of contract and the freedom to engage in a lawful calling, in violation of the due process clause of the federal Constitution. The Kentucky court of appeals found the law to be a reasonable protection of the public welfare, asserting that "the purity of racial blood" was "deeper and more important than the matter of choice" (*Berea College v. Commonwealth*, 1906).

On appeal, the U.S. Supreme Court avoided the civil rights questions by holding that the commonwealth, in incorporating Berea College, had reserved the right to "alter or repeal" its charter. The Court ruled that the statute, as construed by the state court, did not "destroy the power of the college to furnish education to all persons," but simply required the two races to be educated at separate times or at places at least twenty-five miles apart (*Berea College v. Kentucky*, 1908). In dissent, Justice John Marshall Harlan, a Kentuckian, deplored that Americans had become so "inoculated with prejudice of race" as to tolerate governmental interference with the constitutionally guaranteed liberty of individuals to impart knowledge and to meet voluntarily for innocent purposes.

The Day Law remained in force until amended in 1948 to allow black physicians and nurses to take postgraduate instruction in public hospitals in Louisville. In 1950 the law was further amended to allow black students to attend an institution of higher learning if the governing body of that institution approved, and if no comparable courses were being taught at Kentucky State College (now Kentucky State University) in Frankfort. Berea College was the first institution to respond by admitting black students, primarily from the Appalachian region. The University of Kentucky and the University of Louisville quickly followed suit, as did many others. The U.S. Supreme Court invalidated the Day Law in June 1954, mandating integration for the nation "with all deliberate speed."

See Richard Allen Heckman and Betty Jean Hall, "Berea College and the Day Law," *Register* 66

(Jan. 1968): 35-52; Paul David Nelson, "Experiment in Interracial Education at Berea College, 1858-1908," *Journal of Negro History* 59 (Jan. 1974): 13-27.

SHANNON WILSON AND DANIEL G. STROUP

DAYTON. Dayton is a city with a working-class population in northern Campbell County on the Ohio River. Situated on KY 8 between Newport to the west and Fort Thomas to the east, Dayton is the result of the merger of two towns, Jamestown and Brooklyn. In 1796 Washington Berry and his family were the first to settle in the area, which grew quickly as a commercial center; Jamestown was incorporated as a city in 1848 and its neighbor Brooklyn in 1849. The two towns shared common economic pursuits related to river traffic, and thriving businesses included rope factories, sawmills, and hotels. Jamestown built wharves along the shore and in 1853 launched the ferryboat *John Hastings.*

After twenty years the two cities had grown into one and Dayton was formally established on March 12, 1867. The Newport and Dayton Turnpike was chartered in 1869, and in 1888 railroad service to Dayton was established by the Chesapeake & Ohio Railroad. In 1893 an electric streetcar service was inaugurated. The Wadsworth Watch Case Company moved to Dayton from Newport in 1900. The company made watch cases, compacts, and other jewelry items, and during World War II produced precision parts for the military.

Because of its location, Dayton suffered major damage from flooding in 1884, 1913, and 1937. Hundreds of homes were damaged and many completely destroyed in 1937, but no lives were lost. Instead of rebuilding, many residents relocated on higher ground at nearby Fort Thomas, and Dayton's population declined. A one-and-a-half-mile earthen flood levee was built in 1981; in the process many residences were torn down.

The population of the fourth-class city was 8,691 in 1970; 6,979 in 1980; and 6,576 in 1990.

DEBOE, WILLIAM JOSEPH. William Joseph Deboe, U.S. Senator, was born to Abraham and Mary Jane (Smith) Deboe on June 30, 1849, in Crittenden County, Kentucky. He received his education in the public schools, attended Ewing College in Illinois, and graduated from the medical department of the University of Louisville. He practiced medicine while reading law and was admitted to the bar in 1889. Deboe served as superintendent of schools of Crittenden County (1890-93) and as state senator (1893-97). In 1896 Deboe was elected to the U.S. Senate as a Republican, defeating J.C.S. Blackburn. In the Senate (April 28, 1897, to March 3, 1903), he presided over the committee on Indian depredations and the committee to establish the University of the United States. Choosing not to run for reelection, Deboe returned to his law practice in Crittenden County and engaged in mining. He served as postmaster of Mar-

ion (1923-27). Deboe was married to Victoria Larkin. He died on June 15, 1927, and was buried in Marion's Mapleview Cemetery.

DEMBITZ, LEWIS NAPHTALI. Lewis Naphtali Dembitz, attorney and writer, was born in the Prussian province of Posen in February 1833, to Sigmund Z. and Fanny (Wehle) Dembitz. He was educated in Poland, graduating in April 1848 from the gymnasium at Golgau in Silesia province. In the winter of 1849, Dembitz attended lectures on Roman law at Charles University in Prague. In May 1849 the family emigrated to the United States, where his parents settled in New Orleans, while Dembitz moved to Cincinnati. There he studied law with the firm of Walker and Kilber for two years. In 1851 he moved to Madison, Indiana, where he studied with the firm of Dunn and Hendricks. In 1852 he was admitted to the bar and moved to Louisville, where he spent the rest of his life. For a year Dembitz edited and wrote for the German daily *Der Beobachter am Ohio*, and he wrote one of the earliest known German translations of Harriet Beecher Stowe's classic novel, *Uncle Tom's Cabin.*

In 1853 Dembitz left the newspaper to practice law, quickly gaining recognition as perhaps the leading attorney in Louisville. His partners were Martin Bijur during 1856-64 and Otto A. Wehle during 1870-74. Dembitz was involved in virtually every important case involving land disputes in Louisville and Indiana. His two-volume *Dembitz on Land Titles* was published in 1885. In 1884 he drew up a tax law for Louisville that enabled the city to collect taxes that had been evaded. He was city attorney for tax collection during 1884-88. In 1888 Dembitz drafted the bill passed by the state legislature that required use of the Australian ballot (secret ballot) in Louisville elections. Known as the Wallach Law, it was the first of its kind in the United States. Dembitz wrote many scholarly works on American law, including *Kentucky Jurisprudence* in 1890. Dembitz was also a leading influence in the legal career of his nephew, Louis D. Brandeis, a liberal, who served on the U.S. Supreme Court from 1916 until 1939. Brandeis changed his middle name from David to Dembitz in honor of his uncle.

Dembitz served as a delegate to the Republican National Convention in 1860, where he was one of Abraham Lincoln's strongest supporters. He was just as well known in Kentucky for his writings on Jewish theology as for his legal works, his most famous work being *Services in Synagogue and Home*, published in 1892. Dembitz married his cousin, Minna Wehle, in 1852; they had eight children: Abraham L., Emily, Stella, Henry C., Annette, Milly, Ruth, and Martha. Dembitz died on March 11, 1907, and was buried in Brith Sholom Jewish Cemetery in Louisville.

See John J. Weisert, "Lewis N. Dembitz and *Onkel Tom's Hutte*," *American-German Review* 10 (February 1953): 7-8; Jewish Historical Society, *A*

History of the Jews of Louisville, Kentucky (New Orleans 1901).

DEMOCRATIC PARTY. Almost from the state's beginnings, Democrats have tended to dominate Kentucky's politics. In the early days of the commonwealth, Kentuckians divided their allegiance between the Whigs, who succeeded Alexander Hamilton's Federalists, and Thomas Jefferson's anti-Federalist Republicans, who became known as Democrat-Republicans, and eventually as Democrats. The tone of the party was set by the KENTUCKY RESOLUTIONS, written by Jefferson and John Breckinridge and adopted by the Kentucky and Virginia legislatures in 1798. The resolutions, written to protest the Alien and Sedition acts of 1798, charged the new federal government with violation of rights granted to the states by the Constitution. Enactment of the resolutions was the first step in the controversy over states' rights and led to the later claim that states had the right to nullify acts of the federal government they deemed unconstitutional.

Kentucky Democrats were greatly influenced in the early years by the state's planters, who were generally pro-slavery. They maintained that the least government was the best government, and that the government closest to people—that is, state government—was the soundest. Until the election of Andrew Jackson as president in 1828, the party was known as the Democrat-Republicans and supported Jefferson, Madison, and Monroe. With the election of Jackson, the party dropped the Republican portion of the name and became known simply as Democrats. Democrats followed Jackson's philosophy of states' rights, support for the agrarian economy, and curbs on the central government.

During the 1850s, as the Civil War loomed, Kentucky's Democrats and Whigs and their successors, the Know-Nothings, were divided on the question of slavery. Since the party's beginning in the 1830s, the Whigs had been a force in Kentucky politics largely because of Henry Clay, who was supported by many Democrats even when his path to the presidency was blocked by Andrew Jackson. In the U.S. Senate, Clay, like his colleague John Crittenden, pleaded in vain for compromise on the issue of slavery, which divided northern and southern Whigs and eventually brought about the dissolution of the party.

During the Civil War, state Democrats were again split. In western and southern Kentucky and parts of central Kentucky, pro-Confederate sentiment was strong, partly because of the traditional Democratic pro-slavery stand and the support of states' rights, but the pro-Southern forces could not muster enough strength in the state legislature for secession. At the same time, the new Republican party of Abraham Lincoln was gaining strength, especially in eastern and southeastern Kentucky and along the Ohio River, though the state never gave anything near a majority of its votes to Lincoln, its native son.

Following the war, Kentucky, which had remained loyal to the Union, erupted in sympathy for the lost Confederate cause, fed by the presence of federal officers in the state, sympathy for returning Confederate veterans, and resentment of Lincoln's Emancipation Proclamation, although this order freeing Southern slaves applied only to areas in rebellion. There was a great resurgence of Democratic strength in Kentucky after enactment of the Thirteenth Amendment, which ended slavery. Pro-Southern Democrats, most of them former Confederate officers, swept elections across the state, and for the next thirty years Republicans were able to win state elections only when the Democrats were divided.

Hardly had the fighting stopped when the Democrats split into two factions, the BOURBONS and the NEW DEPARTURES. The Bourbon Democrats had not entirely adjusted to postwar economic conditions, nor accepted the loss of slave labor. They were patrician in outlook, antiblack, antitax, anti-industry, and antiprogress. Since the Bourbons owned most of the turnpikes, they were opposed to state construction of free highways and unenthusiastic about the spread of railroads. The New Departure Democrats, behind such leaders as Henry Watterson, editor of the *Louisville Courier-Journal*, favored progress, closer ties to the markets of the industrial North, and development of industry within the state. They urged fairness to the newly liberated slaves and an end to prewar politics.

Even with competing factions, the Democrats dominated state elections from the Civil War until 1895, when they split, partly over the issue of currency, thus permitting the election of Republican William O. Bradley to the governorship. In 1899, when the governor's race between Democrat William Goebel and Republican W.S. Taylor ended in the only assassination of an American governor, the bitterness that followed almost boiled over into civil war.

Although the Goebel affair tended to weaken further the Republican party, factional strife among the Democrats helped to elect four Republican governors in the years between 1900 and 1932. The factional differences seemed to spring as often from personal reasons as from divisions over party policies or philosophy. For a generation the powerful Kentucky Jockey Club, though largely Democratic, worked to defeat candidates, Democrats or Republicans, considered hostile to horse racing interests. When Alben Barkley, of the 1st Congressional District, ran for governor in 1923 on a platform to repeal the state's Pari-Mutuel Act and levy a tax on coal, the club threw its weight behind his opponent, J.C. Cantrill. When Cantrill died before the campaign began, the state central committee chose William ("Honest Bill") Fields as his successor. The club then supported Barkley for the U.S. Senate, where no horse racing issues were at stake. It opposed J.C.W. Beckham for governor in 1927, helping to elect Republican Flem Sampson (1927-31). The Democratically controlled legislature then passed "ripper" legislation, which deprived Sampson of critical patronage control over highways and put much of the real power in the hands of a bipartisan highway commission, headed by Democrat Ben Johnson. Through his ruthless control of the expanding highway system, Johnson wielded great political power, and he helped to elect Ruby Laffoon governor in 1931. When Laffoon managed to enact a sales tax, Johnson turned against him and helped in 1935 to elect A.B. Chandler, Laffoon's lieutenant governor, who had turned against Laffoon over the 3 percent sales tax issue and who eventually got rid of the bipartisan highway commission.

Chandler won the Democratic nomination in 1935 by defeating Thomas Rhea, a western Kentucky political power who had helped to elect Laffoon. For years afterward the Democratic party was divided between the Chandler and Earle Clements factions. Both factions supported the successful 1939 campaign for governor of Keen Johnson, Chandler's lieutenant governor, but in 1943 the Democrats split over the candidacy of highway commissioner Lyter Donaldson, and Republican Simeon Willis was elected governor. Clements came back to win the governorship in 1947, along with his lieutenant governor, Lawrence Wetherby. Clements left the governor's office in 1950 to fill Vice-President Alben Barkley's Senate seat and Wetherby served out Clements's term and was his successor in 1951. Chandler, after having served in the U.S. Senate, then losing to Alben Barkley in the 1938 race for the Senate, served in the Senate later and returned to defeat Clements-backed candidate Bert T. Combs, winning a second term as governor in 1955.

Combs came back in 1959 to defeat Chandler's lieutenant governor, Harry Lee Waterfield, for governor, and became, in effect, the leader of the Clements faction. In 1963 Combs backed Edward T. Breathitt, who ended Chandler's long career by defeating him in the primary for governor. Chandler gained some measure of revenge, however, by backing Republican Thruston Morton in his successful race against Combs's lieutenant governor, Wilson Wyatt, for the U.S. Senate, and by supporting Republican Louie Nunn in his victory over Henry Ward, choice of the Combs-Breathitt faction, for governor in 1967. Combs ran for governor in 1971 but was defeated in the primary by Wendell Ford, his former administrative assistant and lieutenant governor under Nunn. With Combs's defeat, Democratic factionalism faded. Between 1971 and 1987 five consecutive Democrats were elected governor.

Ideology has generally been associated more with individuals than with the Democratic party or its factions. Broadly speaking, Goebel was for the common man, the laborer, and wage earner, and critical of big business, but he aroused almost as much antagonism among Democrats as among Republicans and probably did not represent a liberal swing by the party. Alben Barkley became identified with prohibition and opposition to the coal, racing, and whiskey interests while running for governor. In the U.S. Senate he became a firm supporter of Franklin D. Roosevelt and was generally regarded as a New Deal liberal. Chandler campaigned as the champion of the "little fella," and as governor won repeal of the Laffoon sales tax, which he called the "worst of all taxes, the most regressive," and imposed taxes on whiskey and tobacco. In his second term as governor he used state troops to enforce school integration, and claimed credit for breaking the color line in baseball while commissioner (1945-51). But in the Senate Chandler allied himself with such southern conservatives as Harry F. Byrd of Virginia and Richard Russell of Georgia and frequently opposed Roosevelt's liberal economic and foreign policies.

Clements was a cautious and often conservative governor, but he became identified with liberals in the Senate and was a leading supporter of Texas Sen. Lyndon Johnson. Combs won passage of a 3 percent sales tax, but enjoyed much support from labor, especially in eastern Kentucky, as well as from urban liberals. Yet these men, like most Kentucky candidates running for state rather than federal offices, seldom campaigned on issues that could be termed conservative or liberal, or that could be identified with Democratic rather than Republican philosophy. Instead, candidates of both parties have traditionally run on promises to oppose taxes, bring about economy and efficiency in government, and improve education.

Since the days of the Great Depression, Kentuckians have registered Democratic by a margin of almost two to one. The margin was increased during the Depression of the 1930s, thanks to President Franklin D. Roosevelt's New Deal policies, which made inroads into Republican strongholds in eastern and southern Kentucky. Miners in the economically depressed coal fields there were attracted by his pro-labor and relief programs.

Law requires that the state's political boundaries be redistricted every ten years, following the U.S. Census, into as many congressional districts as population dictates. Through their usual control of the legislature, which must approve the redistricting, the Democrats have greatly influenced the drawing of district lines, often gerrymandering boundaries to reduce potential Republican representation.

Kentuckians do not necessarily vote according to their registration. Between 1952 and 1988, Kentuckians voted for Republican presidential candidates in seven out of ten elections and sent four Republicans to the U.S. Senate. The state's population did not become more urban than rural until 1970, and the electorate still shows conservative agrarian and fundamentalist religious influence, repeatedly voting for conservative Republican presidential candidates over liberal Democrats.

See George Lee Willis, Sr., *Kentucky Democracy* (Louisville 1935); Malcolm Jewell, *Kentucky Politics* (Lexington, Ky., 1968).   JOHN ED PEARCE

DENHARDT, HENRY H. Henry H. Denhardt, military officer and lieutenant governor, was born March 8, 1876, in Bowling Green, Kentucky, to William and Margaret (Geyger) Denhardt. He was educated in the public schools and at Ogden College of Bowling Green and he obtained a law degree at Cumberland University, Lebanon, Tennessee. Denhardt was Bowling Green prosecuting attorney for ten years, followed by two terms as Warren County judge. With his brother he published the *Bowling Green Times-Journal*, and he was a regent of Western Kentucky University. He organized a volunteer company in the Spanish-American War and he was a part of the expedition into Mexico in 1916. In World War I he was cited for valor in the St. Mihiel offensive and promoted to lieutenant colonel. For service at the head of a national unit in controlling a riot in Newport, he was promoted to brigadier general in 1921.

In 1923 Denhardt, a Democrat, was elected lieutenant governor for the term 1923-27. He continually sparred with Warren County political figures and state Democratic leaders, and in 1927, when his gubernatorial candidacy gained no headway, he blamed factionalism within the party. On election day, 1931, he was shot in the back at a polling place by a Bowling Green political rival. At first given only an even chance of living, Denhardt survived, and Gov. Ruby Laffoon (1931-35) appointed him to the post of adjutant general. Denhardt led guardsmen into Harlan County to oversee a local election in 1935, and he was charged with vote-tampering by Harlan County authorities; he was pardoned by Laffoon before going to trial.

In 1935 Denhardt retired to his Oldham County farm; his marriage to Elizabeth Glaze in 1905 had ended in divorce in 1933. For several months in 1936, he had dated Verna (Garr) Taylor, a La-Grange widow, who died of a gunshot wound on a lonely country road on November 6, 1936, after being in his company that day. Circumstantial evidence pointed to Denhardt as the murderer. The first trial ended in a hung jury in late April 1937, and Denhardt was gunned down in Shelbyville by the woman's three brothers the night before the second trial was to start. The three brothers were acquitted of the charge of killing Denhardt. Denhardt was buried in Bowling Green's Fairview Cemetery.

The shooting of Denhardt is recounted in George A. Hendon's poem "Death of General Denhardt."

See William E. Ellis, "The Harvest Moon was Shinin' on the Streets of Shelbyville: Southern Honor and the Death of General Henry H. Denhardt, 1937," *Register* 84 (Autumn 1986): 361-96.

WILLIAM E. ELLIS

DENTISTRY. During the settlement of Kentucky, physicians provided dental care, as practicing dentists were found only in large communities east of the Appalachian Mountains. By 1820 nine dentists were practicing in Kentucky, and they probably sold toothbrushes and dentifrices of their own formulation. Retail stores carried toothache drops, gum stimulators, and poultices.

Preceptorship was the form of dental education. A student paid a fee to study with and observe the techniques of a practitioner. After a brief period of experience, the student received a certificate acknowledging the completion of instruction. Since there was no regulation of dentistry, however, even those who had no formal preparation could practice.

Chapin A. Harris, who practiced briefly in Frankfort in the 1830s, subsequently moved to Baltimore, Maryland, where in 1840 he founded and became dean of the nation's first dental school, the Baltimore College of Dental Surgery. Kentucky's first dental school, the Transylvania College of Dental Surgery (not associated with Transylvania University), was established in Lexington in 1850. Entrance to the school required "a good English education." The fee for the sixteen-week course of study was $125. The college closed after only three months of lectures, but not before four students had been awarded the degree doctor of dental surgery.

The Kentucky State Dental Association, formed in 1860, held its first meeting at the Phoenix Hotel in Lexington and elected W.D. Stone, a Frankfort dentist, as its president. The dental association temporarily disbanded during the Civil War; the state legislature chartered it as a professional organization in 1870. Kentucky's first dental practice act, passed by the legislature in 1878, set up the Kentucky State Board of Dental Examiners and prohibited "any person to practice dentistry in the State of Kentucky for compensation, unless such person has received a diploma from the faculty of a dental college, duly incorporated . . . or a certification of qualification issued by the Kentucky State Board." A total of 188 dentists in ninety-five communities registered with the state board.

The Louisville College of Dentistry was established in 1887 as a branch of the Hospital College of Medicine at Central University of Richmond, Kentucky. Dr. James Lewis Howell, dean of the medical college, also served as dean of the dental college. The college required two years of study before graduation. By the end of the 1891 session, sixty-seven students had graduated in dentistry. In 1890 the college occupied a new building at the corner of Brook and Broadway in Louisville. In 1918 the Louisville College of Dentistry reorganized as a school of the University of Louisville. The secretary of the State Board of Dental Examiners reported that there were 875 dentists in Kentucky in 1920.

In 1948, when prevention of dental problems became a concern, the University of Louisville established a training program for dental hygienists. In 1952 Kentucky's State Board of Dental Examiners began to license specialty disciplines approved by the American Dental Association. A decade later the University of Kentucky established a College of Dentistry in its newly created Medical Center. In 1970 the University of Louisville, which had been a private municipal institution, became part of the state system of higher education. The commonwealth's two state-supported colleges of dentistry enrolled and graduated record numbers in the 1970s.

Because Kentucky experienced a surplus of dentists in the early 1980s, the commonwealth's Council on Higher Education in 1984 considered closing one of the dental schools. Negative public response convinced the council to allow both institutes to remain open, while reducing the size of classes. In 1987 a major survey of the oral health of the citizens of Kentucky revealed that, even with the increased numbers of practitioners, the oral health of Kentuckians was significantly below that of the rest of the nation.

See Robert L. Sprau and Edward B. Gernert, *History of Kentucky Dentistry* (Louisville 1960).

DAVID A. NASH

DERRINGER, PAUL SAMUEL. Paul Samuel Derringer, All-Star pitcher, was born on October 17, 1906, in Springfield, Kentucky, the son of Samuel P. Derringer. While pitching for the Coalwood, West Virginia, baseball team, he signed a professional contract with Jack Ryan of the St. Louis Cardinals. In 1931 he posted an 18-8 record, the first rookie to lead the National League in winning percentage. In 1933 he was traded to the Cincinnati Reds for Leo Durocher. Derringer won twenty-two games for the sixth-place Reds in 1935, and during his prime, 1938-40, he posted marks of 21-14, 25-7, and 20-12, respectively.

Derringer was named to the All-Star team in 1935 and 1939-41 and pitched in four World Series, including the Reds' championship in 1940. He was traded to the Chicago Cubs in 1943 and closed out his career in 1945 with sixteen victories, which helped send the Cubs to the World Series. Over his fifteen-year career, Derringer pitched in 579 games and posted a 223-212 record, with 3,645 innings, 251 complete games, 1,507 strikeouts, 761 walks, and a 3.46 earned run average. After he left baseball, he was a sales representative for a plastics company. Derringer died on November 17, 1987, in Sarasota, Florida.

DESEGREGATION OF EDUCATION. Desegregation in Kentucky colleges began in 1950 when the General Assembly permitted schools to integrate. Berea, Bellarmine, Nazareth, Ursuline, and the University of Louisville did so quickly. Other schools soon followed. Graduate education had begun to desegregate on a limited basis in 1949, when the University of Kentucky was ordered to open its graduate and professional schools to black applicants. In this court case, Lyman Johnson had sued in federal district court in 1948 after being denied admission to graduate study.

Widespread desegregation of higher education and public schools in Kentucky followed the 1954 U.S. Supreme Court decision in *Brown v. Board of Education.* Kentucky black and white leaders for several years had been laying the groundwork for acceptance of school desegregation. After the Supreme Court decision, Kentucky leaders, most notably Gov. Lawrence W. Wetherby (1950-55), said

Kentucky would obey the law. Sens. Earle Clements and John Sherman Cooper both stated that Kentucky should abide by the ruling. Unlike many other Southern states, Kentucky never had a major party gubernatorial candidate running on a segregation platform.

By the fall of 1956, 75 percent of Kentucky's school districts had adopted desegregation plans, and soon nearly half of the school-age black students were enrolled in desegregated systems. The Louisville school district began desegregation in 1956 under a plan recognized as outstanding by President Dwight D. Eisenhower. The district changed the attendance areas for each school to serve students without regard to race. The district provided crucial leadership by notifying parents of the school their children would attend, with "freedom of choice" to request a transfer. Only 11 percent of the total school population requested such transfers in the first year. The Louisville plan included desegregation at all grade levels (many states used a grade-per-year plan).

Academic desegregation was challenged on many fronts in Kentucky, but the difficulties did not reach the levels of massive resistance experienced in Virginia and Alabama, nor the extensive opposition found as late as 1975 in Boston. When a white citizens' council blocked entry of eight black students into the desegregated Sturgis High School on September 4, 1956, Gov. A.B. Chandler (1955-59) ordered the state police and the National Guard to Sturgis. The black students attended classes for several days under the protection of two hundred guardsmen and twenty-eight state police.

At least a dozen suits were filed in federal courts to require individual schools to desegregate. Louisville attorney James Crumlin filed the first suit in December 1955 on behalf of the Legal Defense Fund of the National Association for the Advancement of Colored People (NAACP). This action was followed by a succession of cases during the next three years. Some suits were quietly invited by school officials who wanted to desegregate but sought full backing by the courts.

The possibility that black teachers might lose their jobs was obvious to leaders from the beginning of the desegregation movement. In 1956 the Kentucky Council on Human Relations began an extensive campaign "to insure that black teachers do not become victims of pupil desegregation." School desegregation leaders were critical of school officials who failed to desegregate teaching staff at the same time they desegregated students. Omer Carmichael, Louisville school superintendent, said the schools should first desegregate pupils, then desegregate teachers. Critics showed that 85 percent of black teachers had college degrees, while only 58 percent of white teachers did. Many whites were "emergency teachers," not qualified for Kentucky teacher certification. The trend was clear from the employment figures for 1970, when Kentucky had very few more black teachers (1,559) than in 1956 (1,439), while in the same period black students increased from 40,000 to 64,429. Thus the ratio of black teachers to black students declined substantially in fourteen years.

University employment of black faculty had much the same record. The 1951 merger of the Louisville Municipal College into the University of Louisville kept only one of four tenured professors. The hiring of black professors at Kentucky's other universities and colleges was no more encouraging. Kentucky was included in a national suit by the NAACP Legal Defense Fund to desegregate higher education, including faculty. Plans for desegregating university students and faculty were being revised in 1990, after years of limited successes.

Louisville schools underwent resegregation because they did not establish comprehensive desegregation plans, including teachers, and failed to fine-tune their desegregation plans from year to year. Between 1956 and 1965, the number of Louisville students attending integrated schools increased each year. By 1965, 20.3 percent of the city's pupils were in schools not predominantly either white or black. After 1965, however, this trend was reversed, and by 1968 90% of the city's students were attending schools predominantly black or white. A new integration plan went into effect in 1975 under a U.S. court order.

GIFFORD BLYTON AND GALEN MARTIN

DESHA, JOSEPH. Joseph Desha, Kentucky's governor during 1824-28, was born on December 9, 1768, in Monroe County, Pennsylvania, to Robert and Eleanor (Wheeler) Desha. The family moved to Fayette County, Kentucky, in 1781 and to Tennessee in 1784. Eight years later Joseph Desha and his wife Margaret (née Bledsoe) moved to Mason County, Kentucky, where he farmed. Desha served in the Indian war in 1794 and in the War of 1812. A Democratic Republican, he was a member of the Kentucky House of Representatives in 1797 and 1799-1802, the state Senate during 1802-07, and the U.S. House during 1807-19. Desha ran third in the 1820 gubernatorial race, with 12,418 votes to 20,493 for John Adair, 19,947 for William Logan, and 9,567 for Anthony Butler. Running as a relief candidate in the controversy over RELIEF to debtors in 1824, Desha defeated the conservative Anti-Relief candidate, Christopher Tompkins, 38,378 to 22,499. William Russell trailed badly, with only 3,900 votes. After four tumultuous years as governor, Desha retired to his Harrison County farm, where he lived until his death on October 12, 1842. He was buried in the Georgetown Cemetery.

Governor Desha and the pro-Relief majority in the General Assembly saw his victory as a mandate for change. Obstructive members of the court of appeals who opposed debt relief were questioned sharply, but the legislature could not muster the two-thirds majority necessary to remove them. In a wild legislative session on Christmas Eve in 1824, with the governor illegally lobbying on the House floor, the relief advocates passed a court reorganization bill that abolished the "Old Court" and created the "New Court." The Old Court judges re-

fused to quit their posts, but the New Court's clerk forcibly seized the court's records. Few issues have created as much excitement in the state as did this struggle. In 1825 the Old Court conservatives won control of the House, and in 1826 they gained a majority in the Senate. The legislature then repealed the court reorganization act and abolished the New Court, overriding Desha's veto. Although the court controversy dominated Desha's administration, two other issues also attracted much attention, one of them being the leadership of Transylvania University. Under the able guidance of Horace HOLLEY, a New England Unitarian, the university had earned a national reputation, but the president was thought too liberal by many Kentuckians, and he was attacked as an infidel with wicked personal habits. Desha joined in the attack in his 1826 annual message, and Holley was forced to leave the school the next year. The other controversy involved Desha personally. After two juries convicted his son Isaac of murdering a visiting Mississippian named Francis Baker in 1824, his father saved him from hanging with a pardon that drew extensive criticism.

See Lowell H. Harrison, ed., *Kentucky's Governors 1792-1985* (Lexington, Ky., 1985); Arndt M. Stickles, *The Critical Court Struggle in Kentucky, 1819-1829* (Bloomington, Ind., 1929).

LOWELL H. HARRISON

DESHA, MARY. One of the founders of the Daughters of the American Revolution (DAR), Mary Desha was born in 1850 or 1851. Her parents were Mary (Curry) and John Randolph Desha, a Lexington physician. The family's pro-Southern leanings during the Civil War caused young "Molly" (as she was known) and her mother to flee to Canada. On their return, the family suffered financial reverses and Molly contributed to their support by teaching in the private and public schools of Lexington. She briefly attended State College (University of Kentucky).

Fiercely Democratic and the sister-in-law of Rep. W.C.P. Breckinridge, Desha gained a minor post in Washington, D.C., in 1885. Three years later she accepted a government teaching position in Alaska. Soon back in the nation's capital, Desha worked there the rest of her life, first as a clerk in the pension office, then as a copyist in the Office of Indian Affairs.

On August 9, 1890, Desha and two companions organized what became the Daughters of the American Revolution. She served as one of the original vice-presidents general and as a member of the executive committee, suggested the DAR's seal, and signed the group's incorporation papers in 1891. The DAR congress of 1898 officially recognized her as one of the organization's founders. A controversy with another DAR vice-president general, who attacked Desha's suffragist sympathies, ended in the resignation of that official, and thereafter the strong-willed, energetic, and eloquent Desha focused her attentions on United Daughters of the Confederacy and DAR work. During the Spanish-American War, she served as assistant director of the DAR hospital corps. Desha died on January 29, 1911, and was buried in the Lexington Cemetery.

See James C. Klotter and Freda Campbell Klotter, "Mary Desha, Alaskan Schoolteacher of 1888," *Pacific Northwest Quarterly* 71 (April 1980): 78-86.   JAMES C. KLOTTER

DESHA-KIMBROUGH DUEL. The Desha-Kimbrough duel, fought on March 26, 1866, on a dueling ground along the Scott-Fayette county line near Donerail, was among the last Kentucky contests under the strict *code duello*. The participants were Alexander Kimbrough and Joseph Desha, grandson of the governor of the same name, both natives of Harrison County. The cause of the duel was probably personal animosity, although some accounts also cited political reasons, as Desha had been a major in the Confederate army and Kimbrough a Union sergeant.

The duel was the outcome of an encounter between the two in early February 1866 in the lobby of a hotel in Cynthiana, Kentucky. Desha approached Kimbrough, who refused to acknowledge Desha's hand extended for a handshake, and called Desha a scoundrel. Desha struck Kimbrough with a chair and a scuffle ensued, with no apparent victor. Kimbrough sent a note of challenge and Desha accepted, despite the illegality of dueling.

Kimbrough's second was William Long, a former major in the Union army, and Desha's second was his cousin Hervey McDowell, a former colonel in the Confederate army. The first shots were misses. In the second round, Desha wounded Kimbrough in the hip. Following the duel both men went to Canada to avoid prosecution. In 1875 Gov. James McCreary (1875-79) pardoned both, restoring their citizenship. Kimbrough, who limped for the rest of his life, settled in Texas, then Arizona, then Los Angeles. He died in Leavenworth, Kansas, at a home for disabled soldiers on August 22, 1921, and was buried in Battle Grove Cemetery in Cynthiana, Kentucky. After Desha's pardon, he raised livestock in Harrison County. He died in Cynthiana on May 8, 1902, and was buried in the same cemetery as Kimbrough.

See J. Winston Coleman, *Famous Kentucky Duels* (Lexington, Ky., 1969).

DIALECTS. The varieties of English spoken in Kentucky have drawn the attention of dialectologists since the late nineteenth century. Early treatments of Kentucky dialects were, however, generally unsystematic and tended to focus on what was perceived to be backward or archaic elements in the speech of the state. This tendency often led writers to use terms such as Elizabethan or Anglo-Saxon when describing Kentucky dialects, a practice that was misleading and failed to consider the great changes that had taken place in all dialects of American English since the colonial era. It was not until after World War II that dialectologists and linguistic geographers attempted a systematic and comprehensive survey of Kentucky dialects. Since 1950 Kentucky has been included in two major dialect projects, the *Linguistic Atlas of the North Central States* (LANCS) and the *Dictionary of American Regional English* (DARE). Although the complete results of these extensive projects have not yet been published, the data collected by the fieldworkers have provided the basis for several important studies.

According to researchers in the LANCS project, Kentucky lies within the midland speech area, an extensive region that includes most of the central United States and is characterized by pronunciations and vocabulary distinct from both northern and southern dialects. The LANCS researchers have further subdivided the midland area into distinctive north midland and south midland dialect layers, with Kentucky lying at the heart of the south midland layer. Other dialectologists prefer the terms upper south or inland south to describe the dialect area that includes Kentucky. These researchers, basing their arguments in part on results of the DARE survey, maintain that although Kentucky lies within an area of transition between northern and southern dialects, the varieties of English spoken in the state have more in common with southern than with northern dialects.

Whatever terms dialectologists may use to describe the speech of Kentucky, they agree that there is no single dialect for the state, but rather a complex group of social and regional dialects that are determined by a number of factors, ranging from the ethnic background of individual speakers to the early settlement history and geography of the state. Most of the regional Kentucky dialects reflect a blend of linguistic elements derived from the dialects of the state's early settlers, particularly those of Scotch-Irish, English, and German ancestry. This mixture of different dialects contributed to the development of new and distinctive pronunciations, as well as to the number and variety of words found in the folk vocabulary of the state. At the same time, the varied topography of Kentucky has contributed to the diversity among regional varieties of English within the state. Dialects in the mountains of eastern Kentucky, for example, tend to be somewhat conservative and are more likely to preserve the speech forms of the original settlers than dialects in other parts of the state. On the other hand, the Bluegrass region and areas along the Ohio River tend to be the least conservative, because of their proximity to major trade routes and centers of commerce, and also because of the greater social and ethnic diversity of the major urban areas in those parts of the state.

See Craig M. Carver, *American Regional Dialects, A Word Geography* (Ann Arbor, Mich., 1987); Ravin I. McDavid and Richard C. Payne, eds., *Linguistic Atlas of the North Central States, Basic Materials, Part Seven: Kentucky* (Chicago 1976).   MICHAEL ELLIS

DIDDLE, EDGAR A. Edgar Allen Diddle, basketball coach, was born near Gradyville, Kentucky, on March 12, 1895, to John Haskins and Mary Elizabeth (Hughes) Diddle. He was raised on his family's Adair County farm near Gradyville. He attended Centre College in Danville during 1915-17, entered the armed forces, then returned to Centre for a time. After coaching briefly at the high school level, Diddle arrived in Bowling Green in 1922, just as what is now Western Kentucky University was becoming a four-year teachers' college. He was initially athletic director and coach of all sports. As the Hilltoppers' men's basketball coach from 1922 to 1964, he compiled a career record of 759 victories and 302 defeats and took his teams to ten OVC championships, eight National Invitational Tournaments, and three National Collegiate Athletic Association tournaments.

Diddle was something of a beloved campus character, remembered for his malapropisms and the red towel he waved during games, as well as for his interest in and kindnesses to students and townspeople. The university's 12,000-seat E.A. Diddle Arena, dedicated November 7, 1963, is named in honor of the first man to coach 1,000 basketball games at a single college. Diddle is the fourth winningest coach in division 1, NCAA schools. From .ne ranks of his first girls' basketball team, Margaret Louise Monin became his wife in 1923; they had two children. Diddle died on January 2, 1970, and was buried in Fairview Cemetery in Bowling Green.

See C. Harvey Gardiner, *Coach Diddle—Mr. Diddle: Motivator of Men* (Nashville 1984).

DINSMORE. In 1838 James Dinsmore purchased approximately seven hundred acres of land near the Ohio River in Boone County, Kentucky. He and his family settled there after the construction of their farmhouse in 1842. Originally from New Hampshire, Dinsmore had moved to Kentucky from Louisiana to escape ill health and find a better opportunity to farm. He cultivated grapes and raised sheep, tobacco, corn, and wheat. Dinsmore farm was family-owned until 1988, when the Dinsmore Homestead Foundation purchased the residence and thirty acres of land to preserve the site, on KY 18, west of Burlington. The private, nonprofit corporation operates the site as a historic home, with emphasis on interpretation of the Dinsmores' family life. Nearly all the farm's contents survive.   WILLIAM R. KREUGER

DISTILLING. From the first Kentucky corn harvest in 1775 until the present time, distilling of whiskey has been an important ingredient of the state's economy. Corn was the staple crop for the early settlers, but had little cash value unless it was distilled into whiskey, which served as one medium of exchange in a specie-starved economy. In the beginning corn was as important to Kentucky as tobacco had been in eighteenth century Virginia or cotton would become in the Deep South. Since Kentuckians could not ship grain east because of the mountain barrier and lack of transportation routes, nor south because the Spanish controlled the Mississippi River below Natchez, they put together

their knowledge and the crude equipment they possessed to distill their corn into whiskey. A pack horse could carry only four bushels of corn as grain, but the equivalent of as many as twenty-four bushels after the conversion to whiskey.

William Calk, an early distiller who settled at Boonesborough in 1775 and later moved to Montgomery County, brought his equipment from Virginia. Stephen Ritchie was distilling whiskey on Cox Creek, in what is now Nelson County, in 1776. The "Old Pepper Whiskey" label listed 1780 as the year that James E. Pepper established his distillery in Lexington. The three distillers thus predate the year 1783 given by Reuben T. Durrett in *The Kentucky Centenary* (1893) as the time when the first whiskey was distilled in Kentucky, by Evan Williams in Louisville.

By 1790 distilling firms had proliferated; in that year the per capita consumption of distilled spirits by those fifteen years of age and older was 6.2 wine gallons. (The U.S. wine gallon is equal to 3.785 liters.) Kentucky distillers refused to pay the 1791 excise tax that the U.S. government had placed on their whiskey and distilleries. While the distillers obstructed efforts of revenue officials to collect the tax, they were protected to some extent by U.S. District Judge Harry Innes's legal maneuvers. The distillers were successful until 1800, when Joseph H. Daveiss, newly appointed U.S. attorney, filed 317 civil suits against them and succeeded in collecting the tax, which was repealed in 1802. The excise tax on distilled spirits, revived to assist in paying for the War of 1812, ended in 1817. It was not imposed again until 1862, when it was set at twenty cents a proof gallon, and came under the jurisdiction of the Internal Revenue Service. It reached a high of two dollars a gallon during the Civil War, was reduced to fifty cents per gallon in 1868, and increased to $1.10 per gallon in 1933, after Prohibition was repealed. It has not declined since. During World War II (1941-45) it climbed from four dollars to nine dollars. In 1985 it was raised to $12.50 a gallon, after thirty-four years at $10.50 a gallon. On January 1, 1991, it reached a high of $13.50 a proof gallon.

By 1810 approximately 2,200 distilleries were operating in Kentucky, producing 2.2 million wine gallons of whiskey annually. Harrison Hall in *The Distillers* (1812) gave high marks to Kentucky whiskey regardless of the absence of standardized production processes. Dr. James Crowe, an English chemist-physician, began experimenting in 1835 at his Glenn's Creek Distillery in Woodford County with a saccharimeter to measure sugar content. This litmus paper test to determine the mash acidity resulted in Crowe's decision to age his "Old Crow" whiskey before selling it.

Early distillers used the age-old methods of their forebears from Scotland and Ireland to produce their whiskey. Grains—corn, rye, and barley—were ground, and the meal was mixed with water or spent beer from an earlier run to produce sour mash. It was scalded in a tub or vat, then stirred with a paddle. The mixture was left overnight to ferment, and to the cooled, cooked grain was added malt, or germinated grain, which converted starch to fermentable sugar. Yeast was added, and the mixture was left to ferment seventy-two to ninety-six hours. When the fermentation was complete, the mixture was called beer or wash. The beer was placed in a still, often copper-lined, over an open fire to be distilled. The first distillation to be condensed through the "worm"—a twisted copper pipe or even hewn-out log—was known as head or foreshots and had to be boiled again to eliminate the impurities, the same process used for the end of the run, called tails. The worm spigot discharged a clear liquid that was 140 to 160 proof if the run was successful. Before the 1830s, distillers had few if any scientific instruments to determine the proof or strength of their whiskey. Instead, they mixed an equal amount of whiskey and gunpowder and applied a flame. If the powder failed to burn, the whiskey was too weak; if the flame burned too brightly, the whiskey was too strong; if the flame was blue and burned evenly, the whiskey was said to have been proved. Hence, the term "proof" was an indication the whiskey was drinkable in its best form—half alcohol and half water. The proof of the whiskey determined both its soundness and, after 1862, the amount of federal excise tax the distiller paid on the whiskey. The excise tax applied only to the alcoholic content.

In 1860 the 207 distilleries in Kentucky produced whiskey worth $1,446,216 annually. After the Civil War, the corporate structure changed and the distilling industry became more efficient in its production. Many distillers found themselves undercapitalized and unable to meet the postwar demands. Family operations were sold to large companies that were both distillers and distributors. Others, unable to withstand the powerful temperance societies and illegal distillers (moonshiners), closed their operations. With the Internal Revenue's excise tax in 1862 came government regulations supervising the distilling process and the storage and shipping of whiskey. By 1880, the number of distilleries had fallen to 153, but their more efficient production methods increased the annual worth of their output to $7.6 million. Kentucky distillers in 1891 produced 142,035 gallons of whiskey, or 34 percent of all the distilled spirits in the nation, and the collective mashing capacity of the 172 distillers—36,265 bushels of grain a day—made Kentucky No. 1 in the United States.

New production methods in the 1880s to increase output included roll mills to break the grain into uniform parts, copper-lined vats for fermentation, and cylindrical copper-lined condensers. The depression of 1893 hit the distillers hard, however, as they had to pay tax on whiskey stored in their warehouses after three years whether it was sold or not. The Wilson Act of 1890, which placed the interstate shipment of whiskey under state control, was a victory for temperance forces. After 1894 the distillers had eight years to pay taxes on their ware-

housed whiskey and could use the liquor as collateral for tax payments. After paying the taxes, the distiller sold whiskey in bulk to retailers and those who blended or mixed straight whiskey with other elements and thus watered or changed the nature of the production. Col. E.H. Taylor, Jr., and other Kentucky distillers worked for bottle-in-bond legislation. In 1897 the Bottle-in-Bond Act became federal law, specifying that bonded whiskey, distilled at the same place at the same time, had to be aged for four years in a government-supervised bonded warehouse, bottled at 100 proof, and the distiller identified. The 1907 Pure Food and Drug Act required whiskeys to be labeled as either blended, imitation, or straight. The Alcohol Administration Act of 1936 spelled out more precise classifications. (See BOURBON.)

By 1984 domestic consumption of distilled spirits had declined to 0.52 gallons per capita. Kentucky distillers diversified and produced brandy, gin, vodka, and cordials and liqueurs for both the domestic and growing export market. In October 1989, Kentucky distillers bottled for domestic use 32.2 percent of all bottled distilled spirits: 56.2 percent of the nation's domestic whiskey; 19.4 percent of the brandies; 28.9 percent of the gin; 20.7 percent of the vodka; and 21.6 percent of the cordials and liqueurs. For export use, distillers bottled 55.3 percent of the whiskey and 32.5 percent of all exported bottled distilled spirits.

See William L. Downard, *Directory of the History of the American Brewing and Distilling Industries* (Westport, Conn., 1980).

THOMAS H. SYVERTSEN

DISTRICT OF KENTUCKY. Created in March 1783 by the Virginia General Assembly, the District of Kentucky combined the counties of Fayette, Jefferson, and Lincoln into one judicial sphere. Before the district was established, land title disputes, caused by overlapping claims and grants that were not properly surveyed and marked, had required a legal solution from the distant courts at Richmond. In addition to jurisdiction over local property conflicts, the Kentucky district court had limited appellate jurisdiction from the local county courts and was empowered to try cases concerning treason and most felonies and misdemeanors; it was responsible to the Virginia high court. Many legal problems were solved by the creation of this new judicial district. With John Floyd and Samuel McDowell presiding, the supreme court of the District of Kentucky met at Harrodsburg on March 3, 1783 (a third judge, George Muter, joined the bench in 1785). In the summer of 1783 the court relocated to the recently established town of Danville.

See Thomas D. Clark, *A History of Kentucky* (New York 1937); Clark, *Historic Maps of Kentucky* (Lexington, Ky., 1979).

DIXON, ARCHIBALD. Archibald Dixon, political leader, was born to Wynn and Rebecca (Hart) Dixon near Redhouse, Caswell County, North

Carolina, on April 2, 1802. In 1804, the family moved to Henderson County, Kentucky, where Dixon received his limited education in the public schools. In 1822, Dixon started reading law in the office of James Hillyer and was admitted to the bar in 1824. In 1830 he was elected to the Kentucky House of Representatives, serving the terms 1830-33 and 1841-43. In 1836 he was elected to the state Senate, serving until 1840. On August 7, 1844, he defeated William S. Pilcher by 60,070 to 48,989, to become the fourteenth lieutenant governor of Kentucky. When his term ended in 1848, he was chosen as a Whig state elector-at-large in the presidential election.

Dixon represented Henderson County as a member of the 1849 state constitutional convention, losing the chairmanship to James Guthrie, 50 to 43. In an unsuccessful attempt to become governor of Kentucky, he was beaten by Lazarus W. Powell, 54,613 to 53,763, in 1851. When Henry Clay resigned his seat in the U.S. Senate, Dixon filled the vacancy from September 1, 1852, until March 3, 1855. During his tenure, he wrote the amendment that repealed section 8 of the 1820 Missouri Compromise in the Kansas-Nebraska bill. At the end of his Senate term, he returned to Henderson County, resuming his law practice and engaging in agricultural pursuits.

Before the Civil War, Dixon tried to stop disunion, serving in the Border State Convention in 1861 and the Frankfort Peace Convention in 1861. He retired from political life after the Civil War and returned to his home in Paducah. He was married to Elizabeth B. Pollit from 1834 until her death in 1851; they had six children. He married Sue Bullitt on October 29, 1853; they had three children. Dixon died on April 23, 1876, in Henderson County and is buried in Fernwood Cemetery, Paducah.

See Edmund L. Starling, *History of Henderson County, Kentucky* (Henderson, Ky., 1887).

DIXON. Dixon, the county seat of Webster County in western Kentucky, is located at the junction of U.S. 41A and KY 138. Revolutionary War veteran William Jenkins in 1794 established a stagecoach inn five miles north of the town's present site, on the old Indian trail between Nashville and St. Louis. When Webster County was formed in 1860, Dixon was platted from land owned by Ambrose Mooney. The town was incorporated on February 6, 1861, and named after Archibald Dixon, former lieutenant governor of the state (1844-48) and U.S. senator (1852-55).

The notorious HARPE brothers, murderous outlaws, once roamed the area. After Micajah ("Big Harpe") was slain on July 22, 1806, his head was cut off and impaled on a sharpened tree branch just north of Dixon, as a warning to other outlaws. Even such acts of lawlessness and "frontier justice" did not discourage settlers from coming into the area. Writer and poet Cale Young Rice was born in Dixon on December 7, 1872, and the town was the residence of Garrett L. Withers, U.S. senator (1949-50) and member of the U.S. Congress (1952-53).

Although Dixon is the county seat, both Providence and Sebree are larger. Pioneer Plastics, manufacturer of molding and custom injection parts, is Dixon's largest employer, and many residents work at local strip mines. The population of the residential sixth-class city was 572 in 1970; 533 in 1980; and 552 in 1990.   JAMES DUANE BOLIN

DIX RIVER. The 45-mile-long Dix River, a tributary of the Kentucky River, originates in Rockcastle County and flows northwest through Lincoln County, then through Boyle, Garrard, and Mercer counties. The river took its name, originally spelled Dick's, from a Cherokee chief called Captain Dick. Col. James Knox and his Long Hunters in the fall of 1769 were directed by the chief to "his" river, where there was plenty of game. Two miles south of where the Dix River empties into the Kentucky River, an impoundment forms Herrington Lake, near Burgin. The river drains part of the Inner Bluegrass physiographic region. Towns along the river include Marcellus and Highbridge. The river has one western tributary, Hanging Fork.

The Dix River has deeply dissected the limestone rock, forming walls that rise almost perpendicularly, to a height ranging from one hundred feet at the upper end to three hundred feet near the mouth of the river. The course of the river is very crooked. Maria T. Daviess describes it as having "no commercial nor much agricultural value, save the heavy mists which rise from it. . . . There is no scenery so wild and grand as borders this stream." Collins's *Historical Sketches of Kentucky* (1874) describes the scenery at the confluence of the Kentucky and the Dix as "among the grandest and most picturesque in the United States." Magnificent exposed rock palisades grace the river banks.

During his second trip to Kentucky, Thomas Walker in 1758 reportedly traveled as far as the Dix River. A ferry was established in 1786 on the land owned by John Curd at the mouth of the river, where the town of New-Market, now called Highbridge, grew up. In 1788 former Gen. James Wilkinson was authorized to purchase tobacco, butter, bacon, and other agricultural products at the mouth of the Dix and ship them to Louisville. From there the Kentucky products were shipped to New Orleans. In 1877 the Cincinnati Southern Railroad was opened to Somerset, crossing High Bridge, one of the highest, longest bridges of its time.

See Wilford A. Bladen, *A Geography of Kentucky: A Topical-Regional Overview* (Dubuque, Iowa, 1984); Maria T. Daviess, *History of Mercer and Boyle Counties* (Harrodsburg, Ky., 1924).
                              MICHAEL E. WALTERS

DONALDSON, J. LYTER. J. Lyter Donaldson, politican, was born in Carrollton, Kentucky, on

April 10, 1891, the son of Joseph and Susie (Giltner) Donaldson. He studied at Centre College and earned a law degree at Cumberland University in Lebanon, Tennessee. In 1913 he returned to Carrollton to practice law. Donaldson served as county attorney from 1921 to 1930 and succeeded his father as president of the First National Bank. He was a member of the Kentucky State Highway Commission from 1930 to 1936. In 1939 he managed the gubernatorial race of Gov. Keen Johnson (1939-43) and Johnson appointed him state highway commissioner. Donaldson resigned as commissioner to run for governor in 1943. In a bitter Democratic primary, Donaldson received 135,576 votes to Ben Kilgore's 81,027 and Rodes Myers's 34,077. He emerged tarnished, however, by allegations against his military record in 1918 and charges that he had accepted campaign contributions in 1939 from trucking interests in exchange for preferential legislation. In the general election, Republican candidate Simeon Willis, who made bossism an issue, defeated Donaldson by 279,144 to 270,525. Donaldson remained politically active, serving as chairman of the Democratic State Central Executive Committee (1944-48). In 1959 he cochaired a campaign advisory committee for the gubernatorial race of Bert T. Combs. He maintained a law practice in Carrollton.

Donaldson married Jessie Hill in 1913. He died in Louisville on March 27, 1960, and was buried in Carrollton.

DONOVAN, HERMAN LEE. Herman Lee Donovan, president of the UNIVERSITY OF KENTUCKY, was born on March 17, 1887, in Mason, County, Kentucky, the son of Arthur James and Arinda Ann (Shelton) Donovan. He attended schools in Mason County and graduated from Minerva College (a high school) in 1905. He was one of the first students to enroll at Western Kentucky State Normal School (now Western Kentucky University) in Bowling Green, from which he graduated in 1908. He was awarded an A.B. from State University (now University of Kentucky) in 1914. He earned an M.A. from Columbia Teachers College in 1920 and was awarded a Ph.D. from George Peabody College for Teachers, in Nashville, in 1925.

Donovan's career as educator began at the age of eighteen, when he taught and served as principal of a two-teacher school in Lewisburg, Kentucky, for one year. Later he taught in Wickliffe and Paducah, where he was principal of Franklin School in 1912. From 1914 to 1917 he was an administrator in the Louisville public schools, including one year as principal of the J.B. Atkinson School in 1916. He became assistant superintendent of the Louisville schools in 1918. In 1920-21 he was superintendent of the Catlettsburg schools, Boyd County.

In 1921 Donovan was appointed dean of faculty at Eastern Kentucky State Normal School (now Eastern Kentucky University), and served as professor of elementary education from 1925 to 1928. In 1928 he became the sixth president of Eastern Kentucky State Normal School (1928-41). In 1941 he assumed the presidency of the University of Kentucky (1941-56).

During Donovan's fifteen-year term of office at UK, he was an advocate for faculty rights and higher salaries. He helped to establish the medical college, developed international student exchange programs, built new facilities and student housing, expanded the sports programs, opened the campus to wartime training of officers and soldiers, and developed many programs in the arts, in agriculture, and in diplomacy. In 1956 he retired.

In 1959 Donovan published an extended report, *Keeping the University Free and Growing*, in which he underscored the importance of excellent instruction in elementary schools, where he believed the opportunity to spark intellectual curiosity was greatest. In 1960 he wrote a report for Gov. Bert T. Combs (1959-63) on the White House Conference on Aging, which recommended "that every college and university open its doors to all senior citizens sixty-five or older to register for courses free of cost." As a result, the University of Kentucky established a council on aging and the Herman Lee Donovan Senior Citizens Fellowship Program, later known as the Donovan Scholars Program.

Donovan married Nell Stuart, of Pembroke, Kentucky, in 1909. He died on November 21, 1964, and was buried in the Lexington Cemetery.

See Helen Deiss Irvin, *Hail Kentucky! A Pictorial History of the University of Kentucky* (Lexington, Ky., 1965); Carl B. Cone, *The University of Kentucky* (Lexington, Ky., 1990).

KAREN O. SKAFF

DORAN, ADRON. Adron Doran, educator, one of six sons of Edward Conway and Mary Elizabeth (Clemons) Doran, was born September 1, 1909, near Boydsville, Graves County, Kentucky. He distinguished himself in many fields, serving as a minister, educator, journalist, public servant, historical researcher, and author. He graduated from Cuba High School in Graves County and held an associate in arts certificate from Freed-Hardeman College in Henderson, Tennessee, bachelor of science and master of arts degrees from Murray State University in Kentucky, and the doctor of education degree from the University of Kentucky. Doran was elected to the Kentucky House of Representatives from Graves County in 1943 and served in the 1944, 1946, and 1950 sessions, during which time he both wrote and supported legislation that had a significant impact upon teacher education and funding for education. He served as Speaker of the House during the 1950 session.

Beginning his forty-five year career in education in 1932, Doran served twenty-two years as a teacher, coach, principal, and member of the Department of Education and twenty-three years (1954-77) as president of MOREHEAD STATE

UNIVERSITY. He served as president of the Kentucky Education Association (1946) and was also president of the education associations of the First District and the Eastern Kentucky District. He represented the National Education Association at the 1964 National Democratic Convention and was appointed by President Lyndon B. Johnson to the National Advisory Council on Education Professions Development.

Since his retirement from the presidency of Morehead State University, Doran has lectured, served as a minister to several Church of Christ congregations, and contributed articles to several publications. He coauthored the book *The Christian Scholar* (1985), a biography of Hall Laurie Calhoun, an influential educator and minister.

Many local, state, and national awards and honors were conferred upon Doran. In 1959 he was named Kentuckian of the year by the Kentucky Press Association and was the recipient of the Distinguished Kentuckian Award in 1966. September 1, 1970, was declared by the governor to be "Adron Doran Day in Kentucky." In 1971 he received the prestigious Horatio Alger Award. He was the world champion amateur walking horse rider in 1975.

Doran married Mignon Louise McClain on August 23, 1931.   EVERETT DONALDSON

DOUGLASS HILLS. Douglass Hills is a residential city in eastern Jefferson County; much of its city limits are within the area bounded by Shelbyville Road (U.S. 60) to the north, Watterson Expressway (KY 1819) to the east and south, and Moser Road to the west. The city is surrounded by Middletown on its east, Jeffersontown to the south, and Plainview to the west.

An early settler of what later became Douglass Hills was John Womack, who married Sarah Boone Bryan in 1813 and built for her an elegant brick house at what was then the west end of Middletown. Womack was a prominent citizen who helped to organize the Middletown Christian Church. The Womack property was later owned by Nicholas Finzer, a Swiss immigrant and Louisville tobacco merchant who established it as a stock farm. His widow, Agnes E. Finzer, sold the three-hundred-acre estate to Col. James J. Douglass, who moved there in 1896 and lived in elegant style until his death in 1917. Like Finzer, Douglass was an ardent racing patron and raised many fine horses on the estate, which was known then as Douglass Place.

After Douglass's ownership, the property passed through several owners, the house was demolished, and the farmland developed into a residential subdivision in the early 1970s. One of the original outbuildings of the old house, a stone spring-house on a hillside facing U.S. 60, remained standing in 1990. The subdivision, named Douglass Hills, was incorporated as a sixth-class city on June 18, 1973, and was upgraded to fourth-class status in 1976. The city consists of middle-class and upper-middle-class residences and several apartment complexes

and condominiums. The population of the city was 4,384 in 1980 and 5,549 in 1990.

DOWNS, LUCY (VIRGIN). Lucy (Virgin) Downs, thought to be the first white child born west of the Allegheny Mountains, was born in what is now Fayette County, Pennsylvania, on September 17, 1769, to Jeremiah and Lucy Virgin. In 1790 the family moved to Maysville, Kentucky. She relocated with a brother to Cincinnati in 1792 and was married there on September 20, 1800, to John Downs. She died in 1847 and was buried in Oldtown near the Little Sandy River in Greenup County, where she had resided for forty years.

See Diane Wells and Mary Lou S. Madigan, *Update: Guide to Kentucky Historical Highway Markers* (Frankfort, Ky., 1983).

DRAKE, DANIEL. Daniel Drake, a physician and founder of medical institutions, was born on October 20, 1785, near Bound Brook, New Jersey, the son of Isaac and Elizabeth (Shotwell) Drake. In 1788 his family moved to Mays Lick, Kentucky, and in 1800 his father apprenticed him to a physician in Cincinnati, Dr. William Goforth. In 1805-6 Drake studied medicine at the University of Pennsylvania in Philadelphia, where he became a student and friend of the noted American physician Benjamin Rush. He practiced medicine for a year in Mays Lick before assuming the Cincinnati practice of Dr. Goforth. In 1810, with his brother Benjamin, Drake established a Cincinnati general store and pharmacy, which he sold to complete his medical degree in Philadelphia in 1815-16.

Drake was a professor in the medical department of Transylvania University in Lexington, during 1817-18 and 1823-27 and at Louisville Medical Institute during 1839-49. He founded the Medical College of Ohio (now the University of Cincinnati College of Medicine) in 1819 and the Commercial Hospital and Lunatic Asylum in Cincinnati (now University of Cincinnati Hospital) in 1820-21, and he helped to establish the *Western Medical and Physical Journal in Cincinnati*.

Drake's publications include *Notices Concerning Cincinnati* (1810-11); *Natural and Statistical View, or Picture of Cincinnati and the Miami Country* (1815); *A Practical Treatise on the History, Prevention, and Treatment of Epidemic Cholera, Designed for both the Profession and the People* (1832); and *Systematic Treatise, Historical, Etiological, and Practical, on the Principal Diseases of the Interior Valley of North America, as They Appear in the Caucasian, African, Indian and Esquimaux Varieties of Its Population* (1850). He served as an editor of the *Western Journal of Medical and Physical Sciences* (1828-38), and of the *Western Journal of Medicine and Surgery* (1840-49). Drake's *Pioneer Life in Kentucky 1785-1800* (1870) is the basis of much information about early Kentucky social history.

In 1807 Drake married Harriet Sisson. They had three children who survived past infancy: Charles

Daniel, John Mansfield, and Harriet. Drake died on November 5, 1852. He was buried in Spring Grove Cemetery in Cincinnati.

See Emmet F. Horine, *Daniel Drake, M.D. (1785-1852): Pioneer Physician of the Midwest* (Philadelphia 1961).   PAUL A. TENKOTTE

DRAPER COLLECTION OF WESTERN AMERICANA. The Draper Collection is an extensive, unique assemblage of source materials on the American frontier, housed at the Wisconsin Historical Society in Madison. The collector, Lyman Copeland Draper, a native of western New York, was born September 4, 1815, the son of Luke Draper, a veteran of the War of 1812. He was educated in various elementary schools and in Granville College in Ohio. As a student he became an omnivorous reader of frontier history and began corresponding with many political and military figures of the time, including James Madison. His brother-in-law, Peter A. Remsen, aided Draper in the purchase of books. He early became fascinated with the American westward movement and its heroes and in the 1840s and 1850s Draper assiduously collected manuscripts and other source materials.

On at least six major collecting journeys into Tennessee, South Carolina, Kentucky, Indiana, and Ohio, Draper amassed five volumes of Daniel Boone manuscripts and notes, thirty-nine volumes relating to pioneer Kentucky generally, forty-five volumes relating to George Rogers Clark, and thirteen to Simon Kenton. All of these volumes contain original manuscripts, diaries, newspaper clippings, excerpts from published sources, and Draper's interview notes. The thirty-seven volumes of Kentucky papers contain the important John D. Shane papers, 1812-64, and those of other pioneers including Richard Henderson, the McAfees, William Whitley, and John Filson, as well as the James Weir letterbooks.

Draper was one of the earliest historians to make use of oral history. He patiently recorded reams of personal interviews with the aging pioneers, members of their families, and others who had known them. These interviews constitute an important portion of Draper's collection. He planned to write biographies of Daniel Boone, George Rogers Clark, and Simon Kenton, but never produced manuscripts. Failure to complete the Boone biography was a cause of lifelong regret, not only for Draper but also for Benson J. Lossing, who had hoped to be his coauthor. Draper perhaps never felt that he had sufficient data to begin writing, but in fact he was a collector rather than a writer. He seems to have lacked the skill to organize and produce a book-length manuscript and his writing lacks style and depth.

Draper was associated for some years with the Wisconsin Historical Society, which assisted him in his collecting projects. In his later years he arranged for the collection to be deposited at the Historical Society and maintained there. As its fame grew, jealousies arose among historians and others in the southern states, who believed the Draper Collection should be returned to the states where the documents originated. In the 1920s John Trottwood Moore of Tennessee undertook without success to persuade the Wisconsin legislature to order the return of the Draper manuscripts. Draper was even accused of pilfering papers. In his defense, some points must be made: He saved many valuable manuscripts from destruction, he supplemented the material with his extensive interview notes, he had the patience to travel afar to collect the papers, and he was careful to provide for their permanent housing and management. Kentucky and other pioneer states owe a heavy debt of gratitude to Draper. His vast collection is now available in microfilm form and is a basic source for writing about the history of the early westward movement in American history.

Lyman C. Draper died on August 27, 1891, leaving behind in the Wisconsin Historical Society a collection of 2,546 volumes of historical material and 478 volumes of manuscripts.

See William B. Hesseltine, *Pioneer's Mission, the Story of Lyman Copeland Draper* (Madison, Wis., 1954); Josephine L. Harper, *Guide to the Draper Manuscripts* (Madison, Wis., 1983).   THOMAS D. CLARK

DRENNON SPRINGS. Drennon Springs, like many of the springs in Kentucky, was once the site of a popular spa. The group of seven springs lies in northeastern Henry County on Drennon Creek, two miles upstream from its confluence with the Kentucky River and eight miles east of New Castle. The first settlers to discover the springs were Jacob Drennon, after whom the area is named, and Matthew Bracken in 1773. A land patent was first issued for the area in 1785 when Kentucky was still a part of the Commonwealth of Virginia and was granted by Gov. Patrick Henry to George Rogers Clark. In the late eighteenth and early nineteenth centuries, the springs were a source of salt. Settlers heard from Indians of the medicinal powers of the spring water and by the 1820s invalids were traveling to Drennon Springs. By the 1840s, it had become a popular summer resort, one of the most successful years being 1849, when more than a thousand guests visited the hotel and cottages.

In 1851 Western Military Institute moved to the springs, operating during the fall, winter, and spring months. During the Civil War, Union forces used the grounds and buildings as a recruiting station, and a number of skirmishes between Union and Confederate troops took place in the area. The main hotel and outlying cottages burned March 23, 1865.

See J. Winston Coleman, Jr., "Old Kentucky Watering Places," *FCHQ* 16 (Jan. 1942): 1-26.

DUDLEY, BENJAMIN WINSLOW. Benjamin Winslow Dudley, surgeon, was born in Spottsylvania County, Virginia, on April 12, 1785, to Ambrose Parson and Ann (Parker) Dudley. The couple and their seven children moved to Kentucky in the spring of 1786, settling at Bryan's Station. In 1797 the Dudleys moved to nearby Lexington and placed Benjamin Dudley under the tutelage of Dr. Frederick Ridgely. In 1804 Dudley enrolled in the medical school of the University of Pennsylvania in Philadelphia, and after graduating in the spring of 1806 he returned to Lexington.

By 1809 Dudley had allied himself with the Transylvania University's attempt to inaugurate a complete course in medicine, but the venture failed. In 1810 he flatboated down the Mississippi, sold the cargo, and bought a shipload of flour, which he then sold profitably in the European market. For four years he studied medicine, principally in Paris and London. From Napoleon's physician, the Baron Dominique Larrey, he learned basic principles of surgical management.

In 1816 Dudley returned to Lexington. By 1817 the medical department at Transylvania had been reorganized, and Dudley assumed the chair of anatomy and surgery. Dudley helped bring the university to nationwide prominence by the mid-1820s, becoming widely known throughout the western states for his surgical skills. Dudley performed the operation of lithotomy, or removal of bladder stones, 225 times with only three deaths, according to one report. He pioneered trephination in America in the treatment of traumatic epilepsy, and his surgical techniques were groundbreaking in the treatment of aneurysm in the first half of the nineteenth century.

Unlike his surgical contemporaries, Dudley did not rely solely on his skill and his instruments. Preparation, he emphasized, was even more critical. He insisted on cleanliness in every detail and did not permit any unsterilized water to touch a wound. *Annals of Medical History* lauded his grasp of "the essentials of modern surgical practice half a century before the principles underlying them had been revealed."

Dudley married Anna Maria Short in Lexington on June 9, 1821. They had three children: William, Anna Maria, and Charles. Dudley delivered his last lecture in 1850 and retired to his suburban home, Fairlawn. He died on January 20, 1870, and was buried in the Lexington Cemetery.

See Walter O. Bullock, "Benjamin Winslow Dudley," *Annals of Medical History* 7 (1935): 201-13; Bedford Brown, "Personal Recollections of the Late Dr. Benjamin W. Dudley, of Lexington, Kentucky, and His Surgical Methods and Work," *Transactions of Surgical and Gynecological Association* (1892): 11-28.   PORTER MAYO

DUDLEY, THOMAS UNDERWOOD. Thomas Underwood Dudley, Episcopal bishop of Kentucky, was born in Richmond, Virginia, on September 26, 1837, to Thomas and Maria (Friend) Dudley. He graduated from the University of Virginia in 1858. After serving as a major in the Confederate army, Dudley graduated from the Seminary of Virginia in Alexandria in 1867. He served the church in Virginia and Maryland, was made assistant bishop of

Kentucky in 1875, and became the second bishop of Kentucky in 1884. Dudley was widely respected for his vigor and piety, holding various community and national offices, including chancellor of the University of the South in Sewanee, Tennessee (1894-1904), and chairman of the House of Bishops (1901-04). His three principal interests were missionary expansion of the church among all the economic classes of Kentucky, education, and the free and unrestricted rights of black Americans. In "How Shall We Help The Negro?" Dudley, who was characterized by the bishop of South Carolina as "too much reconstructed," wrote that the "the negro is a man and a citizen; that the conditions of our life are all changed; that old things are passed away, and that the new things which are come to use demand . . . the uplifting of the negro."

Dudley married Fanny B. Cochran in July 1859, and they had four daughters before her death. In 1869 he married Virginia F. Rowland, with whom he had two sons and a daughter; his second wife died in 1877. In June 1881 he married Mary E. Aldrich, who survived him. Dudley died in New York City on January 27, 1904, and was buried in Louisville's Cave Hill Cemetery.

See Frances Keller Swinford and Rebecca Smith Lee, *The Great Elm Tree: The Heritage of the Episcopal Diocese of Lexington* (Lexington, Ky., 1969); Charles E. Wynes, "Bishop Thomas U. Dudley and the Uplift of the Negro," *Register* 65 (July 1967): 230-38.   RICK KENNEDY

DUELING. In the folklore of American history, dueling was the method honorable men used to resolve their most serious differences, especially during the first two-thirds of the nineteenth century. Although the formal duel did, in fact, resolve some of these disputes, the de facto duel, another name for a no-holds-barred fight, became in that century the most popular way for men to settle their most serious conflicts.

Forty-one formal duels were fought by Kentuckians, the first occurring in 1790 and the last in 1867, according to J. Winston Coleman, Jr. Sixteen died in these duels; no one was prosecuted successfully for the homicides. Distress over dueling prompted the legislature to enact a series of laws against formal duels, the first in 1799. The laws imposed a fine for each violation and a long period of disqualification from public office. Such legislation did little to temper Kentucky men's recourse to the duel, and the clamor for more effective legal restraint continued. In 1849 the delegates to the constitutional convention inserted a provision in the new charter that required all state officers to take an oath that they had never fought, issued a challenge, or acted as a second, in a duel. Although Kentuckians evaded that provision also, it did help to bring an end to formal dueling in the commonwealth shortly after the Civil War.

As some delegates to the constitutional convention of 1849 pointed out, the formal duel had positive as well as negative features. Elaborate rules known as the *code duello* required the would-be duelists to make a good-faith effort to settle their dispute peacefully and, if they fought, to do so fairly and as evenly balanced as possible. Such negotiations often avoided combat altogether. The rules of formal dueling thus included a life-saving safety valve.

No such rules governed the de facto duel, which, as opponents of the constitutional oath against dueling predicted, became after 1849 a much more popular form of combat than the formal duel. Often nothing more than street fights, de facto duels frequently allowed combatants to fight unfairly. This type of duel was thus much more likely to result in serious injury or death than the formal version.

See J. Winston Coleman, Jr., *Famous Kentucky Duels: The Story of the Code of Honor in the Bluegrass State* (Frankfort, Ky., 1953).

ROBERT M. IRELAND

DUKE, BASIL W. Basil W. Duke, lawyer and Confederate soldier, was born in Scott County, Kentucky, on May 28, 1838, the only child of Nathaniel W. and Mary Pickett (Currie) Duke. He studied at Georgetown College, Centre College in Danville, and Transylvania University in Lexington, where he earned a law degree in 1858. He was admitted to the bar in St. Louis, where he practiced law and served as police commissioner. An officer of the pro-secession Minute Men when the Civil War began, Duke burned bridges to delay a Federal advance and was indicted for arson and treason. He returned to Kentucky and on June 18, 1861, married Henrietta Hunt Morgan, a sister of John Hunt Morgan.

In October 1861 Duke enlisted in the Confederate army and was elected first lieutenant of Morgan's cavalry company. As second in command, he was, Morgan recorded, "wise in counsel, gallant in the field," and always "the right man in the right place." Duke was twice wounded, first at Shiloh and later near Muldraugh's Hill in Kentucky in the Christmas Raid on December 29, 1862. During the Great Raid, he was captured in Ohio and was held prisoner from July 19, 1863, to August 3, 1864. After Morgan was killed, Duke was brevetted brigadier general on September 15, 1864, and appointed commander of Morgan's men. At the close of the war he was attempting to unite with Gen. Joseph Johnston's army in North Carolina when he was assigned to the force escorting Jefferson Davis in his retreat from Richmond.

In 1868 Duke opened a law office in Louisville. The next year he was elected as a Democrat to the Kentucky House and served until 1870, when he resigned. In 1875 he was elected the commonwealth's attorney for the 5th Judicial District and served until 1880. He was chief counsel and lobbyist for the Louisville & Nashville Railroad for over twenty years and a founder of the Filson Club in Louisville. Duke, a historian interested in the Civil War and the development of transportation and banking, wrote *History of Morgan's Cavalry* (1867) and *History of the Bank of Kentucky 1792-1895* (1895). He died September 16, 1916, in New York City and

was buried in the Lexington Cemetery. His children were Johnnie ("Reb"), Basil, Thomas, Currie, Calvin, Henry, Julia, and Frances Key.

See Lowell H. Harrison, "General Basil W. Duke, C.S.A.," *FCHQ* 54 (Jan. 1980): 5-36; Basil W. Duke, *Reminiscences* (New York 1911).

JAMES A. RAMAGE

DULUTH SPEECH. James Proctor Knott, six-term member of the U.S. House of Representatives and Kentucky governor (1883-87), originally from Marion County, delivered his "Duluth speech" on January 27, 1871. Knott was well known for his oratorical skills, and the speech was a masterpiece of sarcasm attacking a piece of special-interest legislation on the House floor.

Knott's speech was directed against the railroad subsidies bill then pending in Congress. The bill provided for fifty-seven land grants and financial concessions from the federal government that would have enabled the railroads to further expand and develop their commercial enterprises. Ironically, Knott, who saw the bill as thievery, received his chance to speak through the efforts of a Bayfield & St. Croix Railroad lobbyist who was unaware of Knott's views. The agent guaranteed to secure time for Knott on the House floor if he would "go for Duluth" by backing the land grant in the railroad bill that proposed construction of a railroad in Minnesota from the St. Croix River to Duluth, on the western edge of Lake Superior. Knott took advantage of the remote location of the frontier town of Duluth to mock the efforts of the railroads, especially the Bayfield & St. Croix, to procure more land and money from the government.

With a map of Duluth in hand, provided by the unsuspecting agent, Knott elaborately described the "illimitable and inexhaustible" economic resources to be found in that part of Minnesota. Pointing out the true obscurity of the frontier town, he regularly asked, "But where was Duluth?" The halls of Congress rocked with laughter when Knott questioned whether Duluth was a "real, bona fide, substantial city" or just "one of those airy exhalations of the speculator's brain which I am told are ever flitting in the form of towns and cities along the lines of railroads built with government subsidies." After his speech, the railroad subsidies bill was dead, and Congress adjourned its business for the day.

Knott's Duluth speech was so popular that it brought him national acclaim and many copies were printed and sold. The people of Duluth, far from being insulted by Knott's speech, in fact, invited Knott to visit the city that he had publicized, and he did so in 1891.

See Hambleton Tapp, "James Proctor Knott and The Duluth Speech," *Register* 70 (April 1972): 77-93.

DUNCAN TAVERN. Maj. Joseph Duncan's tavern on the public square in Paris, Kentucky, was called the Goddess of Liberty. The name, associated with the French Revolution, suggests that it was constructed a year or two after the purchase of the property in 1788. The thick stone walls and ample accommodations seem all the more remarkable since Paris was a small community of log buildings at the time. Duncan's tavern is now a historical shrine housing a library and a museum. The two-and-a-half-story building has five bays; a transverse stair hall divides two assembly rooms from a parlor and dining room on the first floor. Four rooms for guests are on the second floor and smaller chambers make up the garret. Kitchen and service rooms occupied the basement. A Palladian window and lunette in the pediment may date from around 1800.

An old photograph in Ware's *The Georgian Period* (1903) shows a facade of stucco (since removed), the recessed Greek Revival doorway and a stoop, and twelve-over-eight-paved sashes in two dormer windows (now eight-over-eight). The rest of the windows were later enlarged and capped by metal hoodmolds. A brick wing has been added at the back. During renovations in the 1940s, parts from other buildings were installed inside, replacing original features. The adjoining clapboarded row was given a stone revetment that protrudes in front of the wall of the tavern.

See Rexford Newcomb, *Architecture in Old Kentucky* (Urbana, Ill., 1953); J. Winston Coleman, Jr., *Historic Kentucky* (Lexington, Ky., 1967).

CLAY LANCASTER

DUNNE, IRENE MARIA. Irene Maria Dunne, star of musical comedies, was born in Louisville on December 21, 1898, to Joseph and Adelaide (Henry) Dunn. (Their daughter added the final "e" to her name in Hollywood.) She spent the first eleven years of her life in Kentucky, attending the Louisville public schools and the Loretto Academy there. During that time, Dunne's mother gave her singing lessons at home. When Dunne's father died in 1910, the family moved to Madison, Indiana, where she attended the public high school. Her education was completed at Webster College in St. Louis, and she graduated in 1919 from the Chicago College of Music. Dunne made her professional acting debut in 1920 in Chicago in the touring company of the musical *Irene*. Her stage debut in New York City followed two years later, the start of a ten-year career on the stage that included one season with the Metropolitan Opera Company. While touring with the company of *Showboat* as Magnolia she first attracted the notice of Hollywood producers.

In 1930 Dunne appeared in her first movie, *Leathernecking*, and her performance in the film *Cimarron* the following year brought her the first of her five Academy Award nominations. Other nominations were for *Theodore Goes Wild* (1936), *The Awful Truth* (1937), *Love Affair* (1939), and *I Remember Mama* (1948). Dunne also starred in the movies *Showboat* (1936), *My Favorite Wife* (1940), and *Anna and the King of Siam* (1947). She retired in 1952 after her last movie, *It Grows on Trees*.

Dunne returned to Louisville on two notable occasions after becoming a celebrity, first to attend the premiere of *My Favorite Wife*, and in 1965 to receive the Bellarmine Medal for the contributions of her talent to the public. She was the first woman to receive the medal. Dunne received a Kennedy Center Honor in December 1985 for her contributions to the performing arts. President Dwight D. Eisenhower appointed her to serve as a delegate to the United Nations' 12th General Assembly.

Dunne married Francis D. Griffen on July 16, 1928; they adopted a child, Mary Frances. Dunne died September 4, 1990, and was buried in Los Angeles.

DUNNIGAN, ALICE (ALLISON). Alice (Allison) Dunnigan, journalist and civil rights leader, was born April 27, 1906, near Russellville, Kentucky, to Willie and Lena (Pittman) Allison. She graduated from the two-year Knob City High School and attended Kentucky State University in Frankfort. She taught in local rural schools and continued her education during vacations. Alice Allison married Charles Dunnigan in December 1931; they had one son, Robert. In 1942 Dunnigan went to work at the U.S. Labor Department in Washington, D.C., where she started her lifelong fight against discrimination.

Dunnigan became a reporter for the Associated Negro Press and in August 1947 was accredited to cover presidential press conferences. In the 1940s she reported the early Washington, D.C., sit-ins to desegregate restaurants. Dunnigan gained greater access for black journalists at even the highest level of government. As a reporter she came to know four presidents. The first black journalist to accompany a U.S. president when traveling, she covered Harry S. Truman's 1948 campaign trip up the West Coast. In the 1960s she was a member of the President's Committee on Equal Opportunity under both John F. Kennedy and Lyndon B. Johnson. Dunnigan was a world traveler, a well-known speaker, and a leader in the civil rights movement. She was inducted into the Kentucky Journalism Hall of Fame in 1982. For a time, she wrote a weekly column for the *Louisville Defender* on the achievements of Kentucky blacks. Her book *The Fascinating Story of Black Kentuckians: Their Heritage and Traditions* was published in 1982. She died May 6, 1983, and was buried in Maryland National Memorial Park.

See Alice Allison Dunnigan, *A Black Woman's Experience—From Schoolhouse to White House* (New York 1974). RENA MILLIKEN

DU PONT, ALFRED VICTOR. Alfred Victor du Pont, entrepreneur, was born in Wilmington, Delaware, on April 18, 1833, to Alfred Victor Philadelphe and Margaretta (Lammot) du Pont. He left Delaware in 1854 with his younger brother Antoine Bidermann (DU PONT) and a cousin. He and his cousin purchased a paper mill in Louisville, where they settled, for $37,500. The cousin soon sold his share to Alfred, who then took on his brother Bidermann as partner in the A.V. du Pont Company in 1857. Du Pont acquired holdings in various iron and coal companies; he owned Louisville's streetcar company and was vice-president and director of the First National Bank.

Du Pont lived in one room in the Galt House hotel. He built an estate, Central Park, which he gave to Bidermann. He gave great sums of money to local charities and served as guardian to the more than twenty children of his three brothers. He founded a technical school in Louisville for children of the poor, but, characteristically, refused to have his name associated with the gift. After his death, the school was renamed the A.V. du Pont High School.

Du Pont died on May 16, 1893, in Louisville. It was first reported that he had died of a heart attack, but it was then established that he had been shot by a woman said to be seeking financial support for a child she said was his. There is still some controversy about the events on the night du Pont died, but the family maintained that he was murdered. Du Pont was buried at the family estate along the Brandywine River near Wilmington.

See William H.A. Carr, *The duPonts of Delaware* (New York 1964).

DU PONT, ANTOINE BIDERMANN. Antoine Bidermann du Pont, businessman, was born in Wilmington, Delaware, on October 13, 1837, to Alfred Victor Philadelphe and Margaretta (Lammot) du Pont. In June 1854, at the age of sixteen, Bidermann (as he was known) and his brother Alfred DU PONT left Delaware and settled in Louisville. Bidermann worked as a clerk in the paper mill that his brother and a cousin had purchased. He became a partner in the business, which was established by Alfred as the A.V. du Pont Company when the cousin sold his shares and left Louisville in 1857. The brothers amassed a fortune, and Bidermann took up residence in a Central Park estate on Fourth Street at Park Avenue in Louisville, which his brother had built and given to him. Bidermann branched out into a variety of businesses, becoming president of both the Central Passenger Railway Company and the Central Iron and Coal Company. He also owned a newspaper, the *Louisville Commercial*, which later became the *Herald*.

Du Pont married Ellen Coleman of Louisville on April 18, 1861; they had seven children: Margaretta, Thomas, Antoine, Jr., Dora, Zara, Pauline, and Evan. Ellen died on May 10, 1876, in giving birth to their eighth child, who died the same day. Du Pont died on October 22, 1923, and was buried in Louisville's Cave Hill Cemetery.

See William H.A. Carr, *The duPonts of Delaware* (New York 1964).

DU PONT, THOMAS COLEMAN. Thomas Coleman du Pont, industrialist and U.S. senator, was born in Louisville, on December 11, 1863, to Antoine Bidermann DU PONT and his wife, Ellen Susan (Coleman). He attended Urbana University in Ohio and Chauncy Hall School in Boston and graduated with an engineering degree from the Massachusetts Institute of Technology in 1884. Du Pont moved to Central City in Muhlenberg County, Kentucky, in 1883 and began working at his family's Central Coal and Iron Company, where he became president. He left Kentucky in 1893 to manage the Johnson Steel Company in Pennsylvania. When he moved to Wilmington, Delaware, in 1900, he became president of several Kentucky interests, including the Jellico Mountain and McHenry Coal companies. From 1902 to 1915, du Pont served as president of the family's gunpowder business.

In 1916 du Pont received thirteen votes for the presidency of the United States on the second ballot at the Republican National Convention. Five years later Gov. William Denny of Delaware appointed du Pont to the U.S. Senate to fill the vacancy caused by the resignation of J.O. Wolcott, and he served from July 7, 1921, until November 7, 1922. Du Pont was later elected to a six-year term in the Senate, serving from March 4, 1925, until his resignation on December 9, 1928. When the Cumberland Falls area of Kentucky was threatened by commercial development, du Pont in 1928 donated $230,000 to buy 2,200 acres there for a state park.

Du Pont married Alice du Pont, a second cousin, in 1889. They had two sons and three daughters. He died November 11, 1930, in Wilmington and was buried in the family cemetery there.

See William H.A. Carr, *The duPonts of Delaware* (New York 1964).

DURRETT, REUBEN THOMAS. Reuben Thomas Durrett, historian, was born in Henry County, Kentucky, on January 22, 1824, the son of William and Elizabeth (Rawlings) Durrett. He attended Georgetown College and received a B.A. degree in 1849 from Brown University in Rhode Island. In 1850 he received an LL.B. degree from the University of Louisville. He was awarded the A.M. degree by Brown University in 1853. From 1850 until 1880, Durrett practiced law in Louisville. Durrett served on the city council in 1853. In 1857 he bought a half interest in the *Louisville Courier* and served as its editor from 1857 to 1859. For his pro-Southern leanings, he was confined briefly to Fort Lafayette in Indiana. In 1870 he helped found the Public Library of Kentucky in Louisville.

In the 1850s Durrett wrote poetry. After 1880 Durrett's articles on aspects of Kentucky history were published in magazines and newspapers. Durrett was one of those who established the Filson Club in 1884 to collect, preserve, and publish historic matter relating to Kentucky, and he was president of the club from 1884 to 1913. The club published five of Durrett's books on history.

Durrett's celebrated library at his home at Brook and Chestnut streets was the Filson Club's meeting place from 1884 until 1913. The library was used for research by many scholars, including Theodore Roosevelt while writing *Winning of the West* (1889-

96). When Durrett died in 1913, his collection, considered the finest and most comprehensive gathering of materials on Kentucky, was sold to the University of Chicago. It consisted of 20,000 volumes, 250 pamphlet boxes, 200 volumes of atlases and maps, hundreds of newspaper titles, and thousands of original manuscripts. The university still holds the Durrett Collection.

On December 16, 1852, Durrett married Elizabeth Humphreys Bates of Cincinnati. He died in Louisville on September 16, 1913, survived by his son, William. Durrett was buried in Louisville's Cave Hill Cemetery.

See Thomas D. Clark, "Reuben T. Durrett and His Kentuckiana Interest and Collection," *FCHQ* 56 (Oct. 1982): 353-78; Edward M. Walters, "Reuben T. Durrett, The Durrett Collection, and the University of Chicago," *FCHQ* 56 (Oct. 1982): 379-94.   JAMES R. BENTLEY

DUVENECK, FRANK. One of the most influential artists of the American Realist movement of the late nineteenth and early twentieth centuries, Frank Duveneck was born in Covington, Kentucky, on October 9, 1848, to Francis and Catherine Decker. His father, a cobbler, died of cholera in 1849, and his mother married Squire Joseph Duveneck, a grocer and justice of the peace whose name the artist adopted. The artist was descended from the German settlers who came to the Cincinnati and northern Kentucky area from Westphalia.

Duveneck's early training came at the Institute of Catholic Art in Covington, which produced religious artwork for Roman Catholic churches in North America. Duveneck worked with the Benedictine brothers who ran the institute from the age of fourteen until his twenty-first birthday, when his stepfather agreed to finance his study at the Royal Academy in Munich. During 1870, his first year in Munich, Duveneck won every prize given by the academy. When his paintings were exhibited in Boston in 1875, they were praised in critical essays by Henry James in *The Galaxy* and *The Nation* in 1875, and Duveneck was called the "greatest genius of the American brush" by John Singer Sargent. In 1877 Duveneck returned to Europe to teach, first in Polling, Bavaria, and later in Italy, having at times as many as one hundred students enrolled in his classes.

Duveneck was strongly influenced by the Dutch artists Franz Hals and Rembrandt as well as the contemporary French Realists Gustave Courbet and Edouard Manet. Alex von Saldern, director of the Kunstmuseum Landeshauptstadt Düsseldorf, described Duveneck as "the bridge between European and American Realism." Duveneck's influence as a teacher is his most important contribution to American art. His students were to be found in almost every art school and academy in American in the late nineteenth and early twentieth centuries, and his influence on Realism as a style of painting was significant. He achieved the distinction of being one of the first Americans to teach large numbers of American painters in Europe. A painter's painter, he had an appeal to human interest that extended beyond the boundaries of the studio.

Frank Duveneck married Elizabeth Otis Lyman Boott in Paris, France, on March 25, 1886; they had one son, Frank Boott. Elizabeth is thought to have been the model for female figures in Henry James's novels, according to James's biographer Leon Edel. Following his wife's death, Duveneck returned to Covington, Kentucky, where he opened a studio on Greenup Street. He began teaching at the Cincinnati Art Academy in 1900 and became the director in 1904, a position he held until his death. He was one of the founders of the Cincinnati Art Club, where he gave painting demonstrations. In 1915 Duveneck won a gold medal at the Panama-Pacific Exposition in San Francisco. He was awarded an honorable mention in sculpture in the Paris Salon of 1895, and as a printmaker, he ranked with James McNeil Abbott Whistler.

Following Duveneck's death in January 3, 1919, in Cincinnati, his works were acquired by most major museums in the Unites States and Europe. The largest collections of his paintings, sculptures, and prints are at the Cincinnati Art Museum and the Frank Duveneck Memorial Gallery in Covington, Kentucky. Duveneck was buried in the Mother of God Cemetery in Kenton County.

See Robert Neuhaus, *Unsuspected Genius: The Art and Life of Frank Duveneck* (San Francisco 1987).   WILLIAM R. BOOTH

E

EASTERN COAL FIELD. One of the five physiographic regions in Kentucky, the Eastern Coal Field occupies 10,500 square miles in the easternmost quarter of the state, and includes all or part of thirty-five counties. It is part of Appalachia and in 1990 was home to more than 800,000 persons, one-fourth of all Kentuckians. The region is bounded on the north by the Ohio River; on the east and south by the states of West Virginia, Virginia, and Tennessee; and on the west by the Bluegrass and Pennyroyal regions of Kentucky.

Within the Eastern Coal Field, three subregions are readily identifiable. The easternmost portion, about 60 percent of the total, is an area of creek bottoms and mountains, the only mountains in the state. In the extreme southeast, the Cumberland Mountain Range forms the boundary between Kentucky and Virginia. Big Black Mountain in Harlan County reaches an elevation of 4,145 feet. This subregion is drained by the Cumberland and Big Sandy rivers and their tributaries.

To the west of the Cumberland Mountains, the Pine Mountain Range forms the eastern edge of the Cumberland Plateau. The plateau area, which comprises about 20 percent of the Eastern Coal Field region, is deeply dissected by the Licking and Kentucky rivers and their tributaries. The plateau has been uplifted and tilted so that the higher elevations are to the southeast, with drainage generally toward the northwest. Valleys are V-shaped, with little level land. Most settlements in the plateau subregion are small and on floodplains. The westernmost subregion of the Eastern Coal Field is the Eastern Pottsville Escarpment. It is a heavily forested area of high cliffs, gorges, natural bridges, and waterfalls. It covers 2,000 square miles and is noted for its scenic beauty. The area is sparsely inhabited and has no major settlements.

The scarcity of level land in the Eastern Coal Field has been a drawback to settlement and economic development and to the construction of transportation facilities. Coal is found throughout the region, in varying amounts and quality. In some areas seams are too thin or the quality is too poor for profitable mining. Surface rock throughout the region is Pennsylvanian sandstone of the Carboniferous period, underlain by alternating layers of limestone, coal, and shale. Caves are found in the limestone. The region has oil and natural gas in relatively small deposits.

The Eastern Coal Field was the last region of Kentucky to be settled. Most early settlers were seeking good agricultural land and settled farther west in the Bluegrass and Pennyroyal regions. The Appalachian Mountains were a barrier. Pioneers seeking routes into the Kentucky Territory came down the Ohio River from the northeast or through Cumberland Gap in the southeast. In the northeast the cities of Ashland and Catlettsburg grew near the confluence of the Big Sandy and Ohio rivers. In the southeast, most settlers who came through Cumberland Gap continued west, following the Wilderness Road into the Bluegrass region, but some settled on level land in the river valleys along the way. Just north of Cumberland Gap lies the Middlesborough basin and the city of Middlesborough.

Kentucky is historically the top COAL producer in the United States. About 75 percent of all Kentucky coal comes from the Eastern Coal Field, and the economy of eastern Kentucky tends to revolve around coal mining. Mining towns were often named for coal company executives, their wives, or their girlfriends. In some cases the name of the town was an abbreviation of the company name, such as Seco for Southeast Coal, Vicco for Virginia Iron, Coal & Coke, or Kayjay (KJ) for Kentucky-Jellico Coal Company. In most counties the county seats became the largest communities. Catlettsburg and Pineville are exceptions. Corbin, a gateway city at the junction of Laurel, Knox, and Whitley counties, is larger than the county seat of any of those counties. Morehead, a county seat, is a gateway city in the northwest.

Other sectors of the Eastern Coal Field economy include agriculture, lumbering, tourism, manufacturing, and a variety of wholesale and retail trade and service industries. Agriculture is of relatively minor importance because there is little level land. Still, all but three counties—Pike, Letcher, and Harlan—produce saleable amounts of tobacco, although most acreages are small. Other crops include corn, hay, fruit, and vegetables. Small herds of beef and dairy cattle and a few hogs are raised.

The Eastern Coal Field was once a hardwood forest with great stands of oak, hickory, ash, walnut, cherry, and poplar. The trees were cut in the early part of the twentieth century, and most of the large forested areas today are at least second growth. Lilley Cornett Woods, a state-owned forest of about 550 acres in Letcher County, is the only remaining large stand of virgin timber in Kentucky. There are numerous sawmills in eastern Kentucky but most are small operations with few employees.

Eastern Kentucky has great potential for tourism but as an industry tourism is undeveloped. The state government has taken the lead, developing seven of the fifteen state resort parks in the region to make accessible lakes and streams, caves, waterfalls, natural bridges, and forest trails, and building lodges, cottages, and camping facilities.

There is little large-scale manufacturing in the Eastern Coal Field other than in the gateway cities of Ashland, Middlesborough, Morehead, and Corbin. There are no large cities and only one large manufacturer (American Standard at Paintsville). Large numbers of Eastern Coal Field workers are employed in construction, transportation, and a variety of service industries, but difficulty in accessing major highways and lack of level land hampers economic development.

See Wilford A. Bladen, *Geography of Kentucky: A Topical-Regional Overview* (Dubuque, Iowa, 1984).   W.A. BLADEN

EASTERN KENTUCKY RAILWAY. At the close of the Civil War, Nathaniel Thayer of Lancaster, Massachusetts, started the construction of the Eastern Kentucky Railway line in northeastern Kentucky, centered on the Ohio River at Riverton (now Greenup). The railroad into the Little Sandy Valley ran south to Argillite and Hunnewell, through several tunnels, and on to Grayson, Willard, and Webbville. It carried pig iron, lumber, coal, and passengers. The line was sold to local interests in 1928 and was abandoned in 1933.

See Elmer G. Sulzer, *Ghost Railroads of Kentucky* (Indianapolis 1968).   CHARLES D. HOWES

EASTERN KENTUCKY REGIONAL PLANNING COMMISSION. The Eastern Kentucky Regional Planning Commission was formed on August 13, 1957, by Harry Waterfield, acting governor, to address the Appalachian region's chronic problems of a weak economy, substandard education, inadequate roads and public services, and a meager per capita income. In 1959 the nine-member commission adopted executive director John Whisman's "Program 60," a ten-year plan to diversify eastern Kentucky's economy via development of industry, tourism, forestry, and agriculture; the plan also called for improvements in education and public services, and the construction of roads.

Although Gov. Bert Combs (1959-63) committed significant amounts of state resources to benefit the Appalachian region, the developmental nature of Program 60 required help from the federal government, which was not directly available to the commission. The strategy that Whisman and Combs followed led to the creation of the Appalachian Regional Commission to implement Program 60 on a regional basis. The commission's notable successes during ten years of activity included a modern four-lane highway connecting eastern and central Kentucky, as well as the creation of the Appalachian Regional Commission.

See Eastern Kentucky Regional Planning Commission, *Program 60: A Decade for Progress in Eastern Kentucky—1960-1970* (Hazard, Ky., 1960).   GLEN EDWARD TAUL

EASTERN KENTUCKY UNIVERSITY. In a series of educational reform measures, the General Assembly in 1906 approved the Normal School Bill (HB 112), introduced by Rep. Richard W. Miller, of Richmond. It called for the establishment of two normal schools, one in the Eastern district and the other in the Western district, for the purpose of training teachers for the classrooms of the state. The location of the schools was determined by a commission appointed by Gov. J.C.W. Beckham (1900-07).

Madison County civic leaders launched a successful campaign to locate the Eastern Normal School in Richmond, on the site of Walters Collegiate Institute, which had acquired forty acres and three buildings from the trustees of Central University. The trustees of Walters transferred title to the buildings and property of the institute to the commonwealth free of charge.

On May 9, 1906, the board of regents selected Ruric Nevel Roark, former director of the normal department at the University of Kentucky, to be Eastern's first president. Roark had a national reputation as an expert on public school management. He and his wife, Mary (Creegan) Roark, advocated progressive educational reforms. Eastern Normal School opened with seven faculty members. Roark faced many tribulations, but none greater than a challenge to the constitutionality of the normal school law. In 1908 the Kentucky court of appeals upheld the law, and the normal schools were saved. Shortly thereafter the legislature appropriated $150,000 for campus buildings.

In April 1909 Roark died and the regents appointed Mary Roark acting president of Eastern. She served in that capacity until March 1910, when John Grant Crabbe, Kentucky superintendent of public education, assumed the presidency. By the time he left in 1916, Crabbe had improved the curriculum, achieved financial solvency, and overseen the construction of an annex to Sullivan Hall dormitory.

Thomas Jackson Coates, former director of rural schools for the Department of Education, replaced Crabbe. The school experienced a small building boom during his tenure. Eastern acquired the 176-acre Stateland Farm and spent over $250,000 on new construction. In 1922 the legislature approved a change in the school's name to Eastern Kentucky State Normal School and Teachers College and granted the power to confer four-year teaching degrees. Like his predecessors, Coates faced constant competition for students from many public and private colleges in the region. Nevertheless, enrollment increased, despite inadequate dormitory space.

Coates died in office in 1928, and Herman Lee Donovan assumed leadership that year. Under Donovan's direction Eastern achieved regional accreditation for the first time, abolished the normal school, established academic ranks, created a division of graduate study in 1935 with the right to grant a master's degree in teaching, reorganized most academic departments, and expanded programs. Although severely hampered by the Great Depression, Donovan brought a spirit of innovation and activism to the campus. For several years in the midst of the Depression, faculty members received no salary increases and state appropriations decreased by 50 percent. Donovan, however, took advantage of several federal programs to secure funding for a much needed physical plant expansion. The Weaver Health Building opened in 1932, and almost immediately the Maroons, the basketball team coached first by Turkey Hughes and after 1934 by Rome Rankin, achieved a remarkable degree of success. Rankin coached football on the newly prepared Hanger Field (1936), and led his 1940 team through an undefeated season. By 1940 the Fitzpatrick Arts Building; Miller, Beckham, and McCreary halls; and the Keen Johnson Student Union had been constructed, in part with federal funding. Donovan resigned in early 1941 to accept the presidency of the University of Kentucky.

At the suggestion of Gov. Keen Johnson (1939-43), William Francis O'Donnell, the Richmond city school superintendent, was selected to replace Donovan as president. During World War II, the school experienced a significant decline in enrollment. Had there not been a sizable contingent of the Women's Auxiliary Army Corps and an army specialized training unit on campus in 1943 and 1944, Eastern would have had to close. After the war the return of the veterans brought stability and an increase in enrollment. The college's name was changed again in 1948, when it became known as Eastern Kentucky State College. At that time the legislature granted Eastern authority to offer non-teaching degrees. O'Donnell successfully implemented integration of the campus, and, in the summer of 1956, Andrew Miller, of Richmond, became the first black to enroll.

The years of fiscal conservatism ended when Robert Richard Martin assumed the presidency on July 1, 1960. Martin, the first Eastern alumnus to serve as president, led his alma mater into a period of unparalleled growth, using federal and state funds.

Martin first focused his attention on a building program, especially on the need for dormitories to house an anticipated increase in the number of students. Soon twelve new dormitories, classroom facilities, physical education and athletic structures, a new student center, an experimental farm, several natural areas and recreational facilities, and other administrative and academic buildings came into existence. Martin turned his attention next to academic development. Gov. Edward Breathitt (1963-67) had signed HB 238 into law on February 26, 1966; the legislation granted university status to the state's regional colleges, effective July 1, 1966. After 1967 Eastern began offering a variety of master's degrees and a joint doctoral program in education with the University of Kentucky. During Martin's tenure there was growth in several innovative academic programs, notably in law enforcement and in nursing. Eastern achieved a national reputation for developing career-oriented programs in technical and vocational education.

Martin's legacy continued under his successor and longtime associate, Julius Cherry Powell, who became president in 1976. Powell devoted himself to strengthening the academic programs and to raising money from the private sector. The opening in 1979 of the Carl D. Perkins Building, which provided meeting space for conferences, and of the unique Hummel Planetarium signaled the school's growing commitment to public service. In athletics Eastern fared well during Powell's tenure. Coach Roy Kidd's Colonels won the division I-AA national football championships in 1979 and 1982.

Powell retired on January 1, 1985, and was succeeded by Henry Hanly Funderburk, Jr., a native Alabamian with extensive experience in higher education administration.

See Jonathan T. Dorris, ed., *Five Decades of Progress: Eastern Kentucky State College, 1906-1957* (Richmond, Ky., 1957).

CHARLES C. HAY, III

EASTERN STATE HOSPITAL. In 1824, under the leadership of Gov. John Adair (1820-24), the state of Kentucky purchased the old Fayette Hospital in Lexington and nine acres of adjacent land to establish Eastern State Hospital, one of the oldest state-funded mental institutions in the country. In 1844, after years of external prodding by reformers in the East and members of the medical faculty at Transylvania University, the first full-time medical superintendent was appointed. Dr. John Rowan Allen, a graduate of the medical department of Transylvania University, attempted to bring Eastern State in line with other nineteenth century mental institutions, but much of his time was spent treating bodily diseases and a variety of epidemics. In 1854 Allen was replaced by another Transylvania graduate, Dr. William S. Chipley. The tradition of joint appointments at Eastern State and the medical department of Transylvania University lasted until 1859, when the medical department was dissolved. Although Chipley enjoyed considerable popularity and negotiated a major expansion and renovation of the hospital, he fell victim to post–Civil War politics and was forced to resign in 1869.

The history of Eastern State Hospital in the nineteenth century mirrored the rise and decline of asylum medicine (moral therapy) and the evolution of the medical superintendent from medical practitioner to administrator and advocate for the insane. With the rise of neurology near the end of the century, the optimism of early psychiatrists was replaced by a deeply rooted therapeutic nihilism— hence, the twentieth century practice of long-term confinement and the overcrowded conditions for most patients. One result was a proliferation of psychology, psychiatric nursing, and social work.

In the early 1950s, with the development of new antipsychotic drugs, the role of large state institutions like Eastern State changed. Recognized nationally as a model program, Kentucky's plan for deinstitutionalization made community-based mental health centers the principal providers of most mental health services, and long-term confinement in the state hospitals such as Eastern State became the exception rather than the rule.

See Ronald F. White, "A Dialogue on Madness: Eastern State Lunatic Asylum and Mental Health Policies in Kentucky, 1824-1883," Ph.D. diss., University of Kentucky, 1984, and "Custodial Care for the Insane at Eastern State Hospital in Lexington, Kentucky, 1824-1844," *FCHQ* 62 (July 1988): 303-35.

RONALD F. WHITE

EATON, W. CLEMENT. W. Clement Eaton, educator and historian, was born in Winston-Salem, North Carolina, on February 23, 1898, the son of Oscar Benjamin and Mary Gaston (Hough) Eaton. Eaton earned degrees at the University of North Carolina at Chapel Hill (A.B. 1919, M.A. 1920) and Harvard University (Ph.D. 1929). Before joining the University of Kentucky in 1946, he taught at Whitman College, Walla Walla, Washington; Harvard; Clark College, Atlanta; and Lafayette College, Easton, Pennsylvania. A distinguished historian, Eaton wrote ten major works about the South and many short pieces. Among his better known works are *Freedom of Thought in the Old South* (1940), *Henry Clay and the Art of American Politics* (1957), and *A History of the Southern Confederacy* (1954). Eaton married Mary Elizabeth Allis on June 12, 1933; they had three children: Allis, William, and Clifton. Eaton retired in 1968. He died in Lexington on August 12, 1980, and was buried in the Lexington Cemetery.

See Michael C.C. Adams, "Clement Eaton: Scholar and Gentlemen," *FCHQ* 60 (July 1986): 319-46.   MICHAEL C.C. ADAMS

ECKSTEIN NORTON UNIVERSITY. Eckstein Norton University at Cane Springs, Bullitt County, Kentucky, was a turn-of-the-century educational institution for blacks. The creation of William J. SIMMONS and Charles H. PARRISH, Sr., it opened on October 5, 1890, with an enrollment of twenty-four students and sixteen teachers. The university was named for Eckstein Norton, president of the Louisville & Nashville (L&N) Railroad, who helped to raise $3,100 from the railroad and its officials as a grant. The campus, including one brick building and six frame structures, was situated on seventy-five acres of land next to the L&N tracks at Cane Springs. Endorsed by the General Education Board of New York, the university offered academic and vocational training, with an option to pursue either a bachelor of arts or bachelor of science degree. By 1911 it had provided aid to 1,794 students and had graduated 189. One of the graduates, Juliet Carson Alvis of Henderson, Kentucky, was appointed by Governor Augustus E. Willson (1907-11) to represent the state at the Negro Educational Conference. In 1912 the university merged with the newly established Lincoln Institute at Simpsonville, Kentucky.

ECONOMY. From tobacco and bourbon to horses and coal, elements of the Kentucky economy evoke vivid images. But to describe the Kentucky economy only by its most famous products is to describe an elephant by its trunk; while interesting, it is but a small part of the whole animal. From its earliest days, Native Americans prized the land of Kentucky as a rich hunting ground. Later its game lured Long Hunters across the mountains; their reports of the Kentucky bounty and the availability of land encouraged thousands of settlers to stream through the Cumberland Gap on Daniel Boone's Wilderness Road or to journey down the Ohio

River. From 1774 to 1790, the population increased from a few dozen to 73,677. It tripled in the next ten years.

Agriculture was the engine driving the early Kentucky economy. Well before 1800, the rich Bluegrass region was producing grain, cattle, hogs, sheep, hemp, and tobacco. Rudimentary manufacturing flourished, too, at first because of the high cost of overland transportation and later because of the suspension of U.S. trade with Great Britain between 1807 and 1815, at the time of the War of 1812. As early as 1802, Lexington, the leading town, had two printing houses, two ropewalks, a nailery, two powder mills, and a number of skilled artisans. The prosperity attracted merchants selling china, fine fabrics, cutlery, and other items from the East, and it supported cultural institutions such as a public library and Transylvania University. The end of the War of 1812 brought a flood of inexpensive, high-quality manufactured goods into the United States. This supply and the beginning of steamboat service from New Orleans to Louisville combined to quickly shut down most Lexington factories and to shift the center of economic development to Louisville. From 1820 to 1860 Louisville went from being three-fourths the size of Lexington to being more than seven times as large.

With the steamboat to transport products on the state's extensive navigable streams, Kentucky became a center of agriculture. In 1820 it was first in production of flax and hemp, and second in tobacco and corn. By the 1830s it was first in wheat and second in hogs and mules. Hemp, the leading cash crop, was centered in the Bluegrass, while tobacco was predominant on the plantations of the Pennyroyal. The mountains remained isolated and poor—their few inhabitants engaged in hunting and subsistence agriculture.

Although Kentucky cash crops were not as well suited as cotton to gang labor, slavery was a predominant feature of the antebellum Kentucky economy. In tobacco-rich western Kentucky and the hemp-rich Bluegrass, the median slaveholder owned fourteen to nineteen slaves, fewer than in the cotton-growing South, but above the national average of six and constituting a considerable amount of wealth. Between 1810 and 1860 Kentucky's slaves comprised between 20 and 24 percent of the state's population, and in 1840 only Virginia and Georgia had more slaveowners. Slavery made Kentucky's economy more similar to that of the Deep South than that of northern states nearby. The capitalization of labor reduced the flow of savings available for investment in physical capital. Contemporary observers such as Cassius M. Clay attributed Kentucky's lagging industrial development to slavery.

Since so much of Kentucky's wealth was in the form of slaves—the owner of three slaves had a larger investment in labor than the average non-slaveholder had in all forms of wealth combined—and because slaves could be moved at will, there was little incentive for investments to improve the value of land, such as canals, roads, and railroads. While one in five Americans lived in urban places of 2,500 or more in 1860, only one in ten Kentuckians did. While northern states became crisscrossed with canals and railroads, Kentucky had only the short Portland Canal around the Falls of the Ohio and no rail link between its principal cities of Louisville and Lexington until 1854. The only state investment in infrastucture went into locks, dams, and other waterway improvements. Kentucky had a fairly extensive system of rudimentary, private toll roads by 1860.

The Civil War thrust Kentucky, like the rest of the South, into poverty. Agricultural and manufacturing income per worker fell behind the national average for the entire period between the Civil War and World War II. Kentucky's per capita income hovered around 60 percent of the national level from 1880 to 1920 and fell to about 54 percent by 1940. Its low income and wages stemmed in part from the high proportion of Kentuckians engaged in farming, and the small and shrinking size of Kentucky farms. Kentucky suffered significant physical damage during the Civil War, especially to its meager transportation network and its livestock. After the war, the number of Kentucky farms grew, but their average size decreased, as in the rest of the South but unlike the rest of the country. In 1860 the average Kentucky farm covered 211 acres, but by 1940 it had only 80.2 acres. The importance of agriculture steadily declined, although more slowly than in the North. Hemp declined rapidly after the war as cotton producers switched to jute and metal fasteners for their bales, but livestock, especially horses, became more important. In 1880 67.5 percent of Kentucky's labor force worked on farms, compared with 17.5 percent of all American workers.

Manufacturing employment grew steadily but slowly between 1869 and 1909, stagnated until 1929, and fell during the Great Depression. Factories employed 6.6 percent of the Kentucky workforce in 1880 and 11.9 percent in 1940. The proportion of the labor force in transport, trade, and finance grew more rapidly, from 8.2 percent in 1880 to 20.3 percent in 1940.

Much of the increase in nonagricultural activity occurred along the Ohio River. Spurred by its role as a major Union supply depot in the Civil War, Louisville grew from 68,033 in 1860 to 100,735 in 1870. After the war, it became a leading manufacturing center and freight depot for both water and rail traffic, supplying the South and other regions. It grew rapidly, attracting many Germans and other European immigrants, unlike most of the South. Its population went from 204,731 in 1900 to 307,745 in 1930. Ashland became a center of heavy industry, producing bricks and tiles, iron and steel, and refined petroleum products. Other cities on the Ohio, notably Covington, Owensboro, and Paducah, grew steadily but unspectacularly.

Although commercial coal production in Kentucky began in the 1850s, the lack of railroads hindered mining in the nineteenth century. In 1870 fewer than 1,200 Kentuckians worked in coal mines. With steady growth the number of miners reached 10,000 early in the twentieth century. Explosive growth came during and after World War I as rail lines reached new areas and the map became dotted with coal camps. In 1918 Kentucky coal production was more than double its 1910 level, two-thirds coming from the mountains and one-third from the Western Coal Field.

World War II and the decades since have transformed the Kentucky economy. Manufacturing dominates agriculture and mining in most of the state, while the share of services has increased significantly. The entire Kentucky economy, like the Southern economy in general, has become remarkably more integrated with both the national and international economies.

Agriculture. World War II began a precipitous decline in the relative importance of agriculture in Kentucky. In 1940 more than one-third of the labor force worked on the more than 250,000 farms in Kentucky. In 1990 there were fewer than 100,000 farms, employing less than 4 percent of the labor force. Farmers' off-farm income exceeded their net farm income and most farmers did not claim farming as their principal occupation. Farms produced about 3 percent of Kentucky's gross state product (GSP). Real farm earnings fell more than 4 percent per year from 1979 to 1988. As of 1990, agriculture was the largest single source of income in only five counties.

At the end of the 1980s, about half of farm cash receipts derived from livestock and half from crops. The three leading products were cattle, horses, and hogs, while the three leading cash crops were tobacco, corn, and soybeans. Because of the drop in demand and the rising cost of labor, tobacco has been declining in significance; beginning in the 1980s Kentucky farmers grew less burley than their quotas allowed.

In the late twentieth century some believed that hemp, or marijuana, was again Kentucky's leading, though illegal, cash crop. Most was grown in the mountainous Daniel Boone National Forest and in other isolated areas. Proceeds from marijuana sales were an important part of the economy in these areas, hard-hit by the decline of coal and tobacco.

The leading agricultural areas are the Bluegrass, the Pennyroyal, the Western Coal Field and the Jackson Purchase.

Manufacturing. The decline of agriculture has been mirrored by the rise of manufacturing. Between 1939 and 1947, the number of factories in Kentucky increased by 42 percent and the number of manufacturing workers increased by 69 percent. Manufacturing's relative importance in Kentucky grew until the 1960s. In 1963 it accounted for 35 percent of the GSP. Manufacturing grew less slowly than other sectors in the 1970s, and in 1980 it accounted for 25.4 percent of GSP. Recession and international competition in the 1980s hit Kentucky manufacturing hard. Employment decreased from its 1979 peak of about 300,000 to 269,000 in 1987, and real manufacturing earnings fell about 0.7 percent per year.

In terms of earnings, the principal Kentucky manufacturing industries are nonelectrical machinery, electric and electronic equipment, primary and fabricated metals, automobiles and related parts, food and kindred products, chemicals, printing and publishing, rubber and miscellaneous plastics, and tobacco manufactures.

The Louisville area remained the largest manufacturing center, with one-fourth or more of the state's manufacturing jobs. Its factories produce autos and trucks, home appliances, chemicals, tobacco products, and many other goods. Lexington emerged as a major center of light industry, producing typewriters, computer printers, various types of machinery, and tobacco products, among other goods. Ashland remained a heavy industry center, producing steel, chemicals, and petroleum products.

In the postwar era, manufacturing has spread to smaller cities and towns, aided by development of a good network of limited-access highways and other excellent roads. Bowling Green and Georgetown make cars; Calvert City, chemicals; Danville, vacuum cleaners and magazines. In 1985 only fourteen counties had fewer than five factories, and only one county had none.

Another notable trend has been a dramatic rise in Japanese investment in Kentucky manufacturing, especially in the automobile industry. From 1981 to 1987, the number of Kentuckians employed in foreign-owned businesses grew almost 44 percent, the fourteenth largest increase in the United States.

Mining. Kentucky emerged as the nation's leading producer of bituminous coal in the 1970s, spurred by the dramatic rise in the price of energy. Mining's share of GSP grew from less than 4 percent in 1963 to almost 8 percent by 1977. More than 90 percent of mining output in Kentucky is coal, but significant amounts of oil and gas are also produced, especially in the West.

The fall in oil prices in the 1980s and labor-saving technology have cut both employment and the value of coal produced, despite increases in production. Real earnings in mining fell almost 5.5 percent per year from 1979 to 1988, the steepest decline of any sector in the state. In the late 1980s, mining accounted for less than 6 percent of GSP and employment had dropped by more than one-fourth. Less than 3 percent of the labor force mined coal in 1990. Prolonged political instability in the Middle East or other disturbances to world energy markets could cause higher prices, production, and employment in the future.

Slightly more Kentucky coal comes from underground mines than from surface mines, with the western fields producing a bit more than one-fourth of the total. Strengthened federal restrictions on sulfur dioxide emissions in the 1990s could result in more production of low-sulfur eastern coal and less production of high-sulfur western Kentucky coal. Pike, Harlan, and Martin counties are the leading

eastern producers, while Hopkins, Muhlenberg, and Union counties are the leading western producers. More than one ton of every six in the United States comes from Kentucky mines.

Services. Employment and output in services have grown rapidly, though less so than in the nation as a whole. From 1980 to 1987 service jobs increased by more than 17 percent in Kentucky and 22 percent in the U.S. From 1979 to 1988, real earnings from services increased more than 4.7 percent per year. Services account for more than three-fifths of the GSP. The most rapid growth in service jobs has occurred in metropolitan counties, which have larger markets and greater access to the skilled and educated workers needed in service industries. A few nonmetropolitan counties with major tourist attractions or close proximity to metropolitan areas have also experienced rapid growth in service jobs.

Louisville and Erlanger, site of the Greater Cincinnati International Airport, have become important air service hubs, Louisville in freight and Erlanger in passengers. The other fastest-growing service sectors in Kentucky are retail trade, tourism, and other low-wage activities. Nationally, the fastest-growing have been high-wage service sectors such as finance, insurance, and medicine.

Kentucky has long been a low-income state. In per capita income it trails both the southeastern U.S. and the entire nation, ranking about fortieth nationwide in 1990. The proportion of Kentuckians receiving public assistance such as food stamps is much higher than the national average. Nevertheless, Kentucky has narrowed the income gap between itself and the rest of the nation. Since 1940, its per capita income has risen from 54 percent of the national average to almost 80 percent. The U.S. Department of Commerce predicts little change in Kentucky's relative standing before the year 2000.

But comparisons of Kentucky with the rest of the nation obscure important differences within the state. Kentucky's low ranking in per capita income is due in large part to its rural character. While more than 75 percent of all Americans live in metropolitan areas, less than half of Kentuckians do. Metropolitan areas benefit from better transportation and communication facilities and economies of scale. They are economically diverse and not heavily dependent on coal and tobacco, as are many rural Kentucky counties. Per capita incomes in Kentucky metropolitan areas are more than 90 percent of the national level and are about 40 percent higher than those in the rest of Kentucky. The richest counties are almost all metropolitan; the few that are not are close to metropolitan areas and are connected to them by excellent highways.

Because high-wage jobs increasingly require better-educated workers, the difference between rich and poor Kentucky counties may grow even larger. Kentucky's nonmetropolitan counties contain some of the highest percentages of adults in the nation lacking a high school education. Unless they change, economic growth and prosperity will become ever more concentrated in Kentucky's metropolitan areas. The results of educational reforms begun in 1990 remain to be evaluated in the area of economic development.

See Thomas D. Clark, *Kentucky: Land of Contrast* (New York 1968); Simon Kuznets, Ann Ratner Miller, and Richard A. Easterlin, *Population Redistribution and Economic Growth: United States, 1870-1950* (Philadelphia 1960); Carol M. Straus, ed., *1988 Kentucky Statistical Abstract* (Lexington, Ky., 1988).   BRUCE K. JOHNSON

ECUMENISM. The ecumenical Protestant movement produced the Kentucky State Sabbath School Association (1865-75) and its successor organizations. In 1910 the Louisville Men's Federation was founded "to unite men of the churches for the improvement of the religious, moral, and physical condition of the people of Louisville." The Kentucky Council of Religious Education, formed in 1926, became part of the KENTUCKY COUNCIL OF CHURCHES twenty years later. The Louisville Council of Churches, organized in 1926, became under George Stoll a model for local councils around the country. The Lexington Council of Churches was founded in 1950. In 1971 the Louisville Area Interchurch Organization for Service was founded with Stanley A. Schmidt as its first president. In May 1979 it opened to Jewish membership as the Kentuckiana Interfaith Community. The state's first chapter of the National Conference of Christians and Jews was founded by attorney Charles W. Morris of Louisville in 1936.

The United Church Women of Kentucky dates from February 1946. When the Kentucky Council of Churches was formally organized on December 11, 1947, its members were eighteen Protestant evangelical judicatories. By 1987 membership had expanded to every major Christian denomination, including the state's four Roman Catholic dioceses.

Ecumenism in Kentucky's broadcast industry began in May 1952 with WHAS Louisville's "Moral Side of the News," a radio panel of a rabbi, priest, and Protestant ministers. The panel, now televised, administers funding for the Crusade for Children, which assists physically and mentally handicapped children in Louisville and southern Indiana. From the late 1950s until his death in 1968, the Cistercian monk THOMAS MERTON held ecumenical meetings at the Abbey of Gethsemani for faculty and students from the Disciples of Christ's Lexington Theological Seminary and the Southern Baptist Theological Seminary in Louisville.

Networks of community ministries around the state provide services ranging from day care and food pantries to covenanting between congregations and parishes. The National Council of Churches has awarded recognition to the first such agency, Highlands Community Ministries in Louisville, founded in 1971 under Stan Esterle. At the University of Louisville campus, the construction of a jointly funded Ecumenical Center broke new ecumenical ground in 1974. Roman Catholic priests, Jewish

rabbis, and Protestant ministers collaborate on programming and budget. In the 1980s and 1990s the Ecumenical Center hosted a dialogue of Christian-Jewish-Islamic scholars. In 1980 Louisville's Council on Religion and Peacemaking began its political advocacy on issues of peace and justice.

Louisville was the site of the Consultation on Church Union's fifteenth plenary in 1971, the World Council of Churches 1979 consultation on baptism, and the 1983 National Workshop on Christian Unity. In 1988 the International Disciples of Christ–Roman Catholic Dialogue met at the Abbey of Gethsemani, Trappist, Kentucky, and the Presbyterian Church (USA) opened its national headquarters in Louisville. In September 1989 the North American Academy of Ecumenists held its annual meeting in Louisville.

See John B. Boles, *Religion in Antebellum Kentucky* (Lexington, Ky., 1976); George Voiers Moore, *Interchurch Cooperation in Kentucky* (Lexington, Ky., 1965).   GEORGE KILCOURSE

EDDYVILLE. Eddyville, the county seat of Lyon County, is located near Lake Barkley at U.S. 641 and U.S. 62, near I-24 and the Western Kentucky Parkway. The town was settled by David Walker, a Revolutionary War veteran who received a land grant surveyed in 1798 at 1,000 acres, sixty of which became the town of Eddyville. Lying on the north bank of the Cumberland River, the tract was divided by Walker into 120 lots. The village received its name from the large eddies that swirled in the passing stream. It was an attractive site, located in a fertile valley, fronting on the river, and flanked by hills filled with deposits of iron ore and timber. Eddyville was officially established as a town in 1798 and a year later was designated as the seat of Livingston County, which at that time took in a large portion of what is now far western Kentucky. One of the first settlers in the new town was Matthew Lyon, who in 1800 led a group of pioneers from Vermont. The town has served successively as the seat of three counties—Livingston, Caldwell, and Lyon County (since 1854).

During the Civil War, Eddyville sided heavily with the Confederate cause. Gen. Hylan B. Lyon, grandson of Matthew Lyon, led a band of Confederate guerrillas who burned eight courthouses in Kentucky during December 1864 and January 1865. Cobb's Battery, a Confederate artillery unit named for Robert Cobb of Eddyville, gained recognition for its exploits at the battle of Chickamauga. Cobb was the grandfather of well-known Kentucky humorist Irvin S. Cobb. During the war, Willis B. Matchen of Eddyville served as representative to the Confederate Congress in Richmond, Virginia.

A branch of the Kentucky State Penitentiary was opened in Eddyville in 1888 to relieve overcrowding at the penitentiary in Frankfort. When the latter institution closed in 1937, the Eddyville facility became the principal penitentiary. Eddyville was a center of much of the violence during the BLACK PATCH War in western Kentucky in the early

1900s, when farmers revolted against the monopoly of the American Tobacco Company.

In 1937 the devastating flood over the entire Ohio River valley inundated most of the town of Eddyville. Because of its location the little river town was vulnerable to flooding. In the late 1950s the Army Corps of Engineers bought most of the land in Eddyville, which lay in the floodplain of the planned Barkley Dam. By the time of the impoundment of Lake Barkley in 1965-66, most of Eddyville, including its business district, had been relocated to its present site a few miles to the northwest of the original town. There remains only a small portion of the original site, including an old cemetery and the Kentucky State Penitentiary on a ridge overlooking the lake.

Located in the heart of the west Kentucky lakes region, the fifth-class city has become a tourist center. The population of Eddyville was 1,981 in 1970; 1,949 in 1980; and 1,889 in 1990.

See Christopher R. Waldrep, "Tradition, Community, and Change: Barkley Dam and the Relocation of Eddyville and Kuttawa, 1950-1960," *Register* 88 (Spring 1990): 183-205.

BILL CUNNINGHAM

EDGEWOOD. Edgewood is a suburban community in the hills of north-central Kenton County immediately south of I-275, between KY 17 and Turkeyfoot Road; it is seven miles south of COVINGTON, three miles north of INDEPENDENCE, and is bounded by ERLANGER on the west, FORT MITCHELL on the north, and Taylor Mill on the west. The city is the result of a 1968 merger between three neighboring cities: Edgewood, which had incorporated on November 16, 1948; Summit Hills Heights, which had been formed on June 25, 1962; and Pius Heights, named for St. Pius X, which became a city on July 30, 1965. With the exception of a small retail center, a medical office center, and the St. Elizabeth Medical Center South Hospital, Edgewood is basically a residential area. The population of the fourth-class city was 4,139 in 1970; 7,243 in 1980; and 8,143 in 1990.

EDISON, THOMAS ALVA. Thomas Alva Edison, inventor, was born in Milan, Ohio, on February 11, 1847, to Samuel and Nancy (Elliott) Edison. Perhaps the best-known American inventor of the nineteenth century, he spent nearly two years in Louisville as a young telegrapher. He arrived in the city in late March or early April 1866 from Memphis, Tennessee, where he had been discharged as a telegraph operator. He found immediate employment in Louisville, handling the Western Union Telegraph Company's night press wire (newspaper stories). The office was then located in a shabby building on Main Street between Second and Third. He lived in a boardinghouse at Third and Guthrie streets, not far from the telegraph office, then in a room above a saloon (perhaps on Jefferson Street near Brook).

In June 1867 Western Union moved to a new building on the southwest corner of Second and Main streets. Constantly experimenting, Edison accidentally spilled several gallons of sulfuric acid on the third floor; the acid leaked through into the office of manager T.R. Boyle, which had new furnishings. Edison was discharged the next day, sometime in the late summer of 1867. One of his financial backers in the research that led to the first demonstration of the incandescent electric light bulb in 1879 was Dr. Norvin Green of Louisville, who had been involved in forming Western Union in 1866 and became its president in 1878. Green also became president of the Edison Company. It might have been this connection that led Louisville's SOUTHERN EXPOSITION, opened in 1883, to use Edison's light. The 4,600-lamp system was the world's largest at the time. Edison died on October 18, 1931.

See Reese V. Jenkins and others, eds., *The Papers of Thomas A. Edison* (Baltimore 1989); Frank L. Dyer and Thomas C. Martin, *Edison: His Life and Inventions* (New York 1910).

GEORGE H. YATER

EDMONSON, JOHN MONTGOMERY. John Montgomery Edmonson, son of William and Nancy Edmonson, was born in Washington County, Virginia, on February 21, 1764. From 1780 to 1782 he was a private in the Washington County militia, fighting in the Battle of King's Mountain, North Carolina, on October 7, 1780. For several years Edmonson served as clerk of the court at Abingdon, Virginia. In 1790 Edmonson purchased land in Fayette County, Kentucky, where he farmed. In the War of 1812 he formed a company of volunteer riflemen and joined Lt. Col. John Allen's 1st Rifle Regiment of the Kentucky militia. On June 12, 1812, Edmonson was elected captain of the company but resigned his commission on October 14, rejoining the company as a private. Edmonson was killed on January 22, 1813, at the Battle of River Raisin. His body was buried on his property in Fayette County. On January 12, 1825, the Kentucky General Assembly established Edmonson County, named in his honor. Edmonson was married to Margaret Robinson Montgomery; they had three children.

See G. Glenn Clift, *Remember the Raisin!* (Frankfort, Ky., 1961).

EDMONSON COUNTY. The seventy-ninth county in order of formation, Edmonson County is located in south-central Kentucky. Bordered by Barren, Butler, Hart, Grayson, and Warren counties, it has an area of 302 square miles. On January 12, 1825, the county was formed out of portions of Hart, Grayson, and Warren counties and named in honor of Capt. John Edmonson of Virginia, who was killed at the Battle of the River Raisin during the War of 1812. BROWNSVILLE is the county seat.

With a gently rolling terrain giving way to pronounced hills in some sections, the topography is markedly diverse. Green River meanders from east to west; Nolin River flows primarily south, meeting the Green River just north of Brownsville. When the river was dammed in 1963, the 5,800-acre No-lin River Lake was created in the northeastern part of the county.

The most noted feature of the county is MAMMOTH CAVE, the largest cave system in the world; it is a 51,000-acre national park (much of it in the county). The landmark has ensured economic prosperity for the region. In 1988 tourism in Edmonson County accounted for more than $39 million in revenue and generated more than 1,400 jobs.

Edmonson, from its earliest days, has been largely agricultural. Evidence of habitation in the county by prehistoric Indians exists. White settlement came slowly, and in the 1830s, the county's population reached 2,642. Early pioneers came to the region to hunt, but the abundance of good pasture and farmland encouraged many to stay.

Being near the Confederate stronghold of Bowling Green, Edmonson County was the scene of several Civil War skirmishes. On November 20, 1861, a Confederate detachment from Bowling Green raided Brownsville to obtain medical supplies and engaged a Union regiment in a small-scale battle. In August 1862 the Federals avenged their earlier setback when a company of Home Guards defeated a Confederate guerrilla force east of Brownsville, taking seventy-seven prisoners.

Following the war, Edmonson County continued to prosper to a remarkable degree despite the lack of a major railroad or interstate highway service. In 1987 it ranked seventy-fourth among counties in agricultural receipts, mostly from livestock production. The garment industry also found a home in the county.

The population of Edmonson County was 8,751 in 1970; 9,962 in 1980; and 10,357 in 1990.

RON D. BRYANT

EDMONTON. Edmonton, the county seat of Metcalfe County in south-central Kentucky, is located at the junction of U.S. 68, KY 80, and KY 163 on the Little Barren River. The city limits extend to the Cumberland Parkway, a mile north of the downtown district.

The town was named for Edmund Rogers, an early settler. Rogers, a Virginian who participated in the Revolutionary War, was a surveyor and a cousin of George Rogers Clark. In 1783 he surveyed Clark's land grant in Indiana. The next year he began surveying land south on the Green River and on the tributaries of the Barren River in the area that was known as the Green River Military District. Rogers claimed his own grant for military service rendered to Virginia and added other lands, eventually owning several thousand acres. He surveyed and laid off the town of Edmonton on his land in 1800 and is said to have offered a town lot to anyone who would build a house on it. Among the prominent families who settled in or around the city were the Pools, Stocktons, Clarks, Reids, Naylors, Shirleys, and Hardings. Edmonton was officially established by an act of the Kentucky legislature in 1836, but was little more than a trading post with a post office. The first church was

Presbyterian and was erected in 1838 on land donated by Rogers.

Edmonton remained a small village on the Greensburg-Tompkinsville Road until 1860, when it became the county seat of newly created Metcalfe County. A courthouse that was built soon afterward was burned by Confederate guerrillas in March 1865. According to legend, a quick-thinking county official saved the county funds from the looters and hid them in a nearby pile of wood shavings until they left. A general store operated by Edmund R. Beauchamp was also looted in the spring of 1865 by a guerrilla band. The courthouse was replaced in 1869 by a brick structure of Italianate design.

The town grew slowly during the late 1800s and early 1900s. The city government operated off and on in Edmonton between 1867 and 1920, and then not at all until 1945. The first industry in the city was a laundry soap factory that was operated for a time in 1901 by J.W. (Jake) Compton. A tile factory was operated in 1906-7 by Tilford Thompson and Henry Hoover, who abandoned the factory at considerable loss after they could not market the tile. The economy has been based mostly on tobacco farming. Oil was discovered in small amounts just east of the city around 1900, but the oil boom did not come until 1959, when wells northeast of the city were producing.

Edmonton High School was organized in 1910. In 1920 construction began of a road (now U.S. 68) between Edmonton and Glasgow. A livestock market was established in 1946, and in 1952 Edmonton Manufacturing Company, which produced men's clothing, was dedicated. It was the largest county employer until Sumitomo Electric Wiring Systems arrived in the early 1980s. The city's proximity to the Cumberland Parkway, which opened in 1973, helped to attract other industry in the 1980s. Nevertheless, Edmonton remains a small county seat in a rural area.

Annual events in Edmonton include the Metcalfe County Fair in July and the Pumpkin Festival in October. The population of the fifth-class city was 958 in 1970; 1,448 in 1980; and 1,477 in 1990.

JOAN WHITLOW

EDUCATION, AFRO-AMERICAN. Although a slaveholding state, Kentucky did not prohibit the education of slaves and free blacks as did many slave states before the Civil War. Educational opportunities were extremely limited, nonetheless, and available to blacks only through a few churches, the beneficence of sympathetic whites, or by clandestine means. Whites associated with the antislavery movement established short-lived schools for blacks in Louisville in 1827, 1833, and 1834, and in Lexington in 1839 and 1840. In 1841 the Rev. Henry Adams of Louisville's Fifth Street Baptist Church opened Adams's School, the first school that was black-sponsored. Others organized by newly emergent black churches provided elementary and some secondary instruction to small numbers of free blacks and slaves through the Civil War.

BEREA COLLEGE, chartered in 1854, was the only institution of higher education for Kentucky blacks during the antebellum period and the only biracial institution in any slaveholding state. The college closed after John Brown's Raid (1859) polarized public opinion in Kentucky. It reopened in 1865 and again admitted black students in 1866.

Following the Civil War, Kentucky faced the challenge of providing public schools for thousands of freedmen. Blacks held statewide conventions in Lexington (1867) and Louisville (1869) to petition for public schools. Rather than admit blacks to existing public schools, the General Assembly created a separate system of common schools for blacks in 1874. In 1891 the revised Kentucky constitution legalized segregated public education. The black schools were even more inadequate than those for whites. By 1899 only 13 percent of blacks under age twenty were attending school. According to the 1900 census, Kentucky had a school age population (ages five through twenty) of 104,512 blacks and 795,409 whites. The state in 1899 had appropriated $212,321 for black public education, supplemented by $110,000 in contributions from blacks, compared with $2,586,032 for schools serving whites.

The need for black teachers for common schools stimulated the development of public higher education for blacks after the Civil War. The Ealy Normal School opened in Louisville in 1868, jointly financed by the Freedmen's Bureau and the American Missionary Association. The State Normal School for Negroes, established in 1886 in Frankfort, evolved into Kentucky State University and became the state's black land-grant college under the second Morrill Act (1890).

In 1865 the General Association of Colored Baptists of Kentucky initiated plans to found a private black college. After many abortive efforts, the Kentucky Normal and Theological Institute opened in Louisville in 1879 and was renamed State University in 1882. The school offered academic, religious, and nursing training and provided professional education through its affiliation with two private black schools, the Louisville National Medical College and the Central Law School. In 1918 State University was renamed SIMMONS UNIVERSITY in honor of William J. Simmons, its president from 1880 to 1890.

In 1890 another private black institution, the ECKSTEIN NORTON INSTITUTE, was established at Cane Springs in Bullitt County. Under the leadership of Simmons and the Rev. Charles H. Parrish, Sr., the institute offered industrial and religious education until 1912. Both Simmons and Eckstein Norton were constrained by scarce financial resources. By 1900 most students enrolled in Kentucky's public and private higher institutions for blacks were actually doing only secondary-level coursework, and only Simmons University offered even a limited college curriculum.

After the U.S. Supreme Court upheld the DAY LAW in 1908, BEREA COLLEGE moved to create a sister institution for blacks. Through the efforts of the Rev. James M. Bond, the only black Berea trustee, Lincoln Institute of Kentucky opened in Shelbyville in 1912. Lincoln absorbed the Eckstein Norton Institute and was recognized, until it closed in 1966, as one of the outstanding secondary institutions in the South.

Following the passage of the Day Law, small black schools were established in Bowling Green, Hopkinsville, Glasgow, and Madisonville. Because of inadequate financial support, they closed soon after their establishment. Western Kentucky Industrial College was a noteworthy exception. Founded in Paducah as a private vocational school in 1910, the college began receiving state support in 1918 and merged with Kentucky State College in 1938. No institution had emerged by 1918 to replace what Berea had offered blacks in the field of liberal arts education.

In 1920 black residents of Louisville proposed that the University of Louisville admit black students. When this proposal was rejected, black and white citizens organized to defeat a $1 million bond issue designed to support the expansion of the university. Only after the university agreed to commit $100,000 to establish a college for blacks did the bond issue pass, in 1925, with widespread community support. On February 9, 1931, Louisville Municipal College for Negroes opened as a branch of the University of Louisville. Simmons University then discontinued all except its religious education programs. By 1936 the college was fully accredited, with a Class A rating, as a four-year institution. Kentucky State College, the only other accredited black institution, received a Class A rating in 1939.

The quality and conditions of black elementary and secondary schools improved gradually between 1900 and 1930. School facilities remained generally poor, and one-room schoolhouses were common in rural districts. By 1930 there were fifty-eight black public high schools in the state and 597 rural elementary schools, employing a total of 859 teachers. Black teachers received lower salaries than their white counterparts until 1941, when legal action eliminated a 15 percent salary differential in Louisville, which led, eventually, to salary equalization in other regions of the state. The school enrollment rate for black students increased from 31.1 percent (1900) to 68.4 percent (1940); white enrollment rose from 53.6 percent (1900) to 75.6 percent (1940). In 1930 Lexington Dunbar High School became the first black high school in Kentucky to gain full accreditation. Louisville Central High School was fully accredited in 1931.

After World War II, blacks pressed more vigorously for desegregation. In 1949 federal district Judge H. Church Ford ordered the University of Kentucky to admit Lyman T. JOHNSON, a Louisville educator and political activist, to its graduate school. The following summer, thirty black students enrolled in classes at the university. A lawsuit was filed to desegregate Paducah College in 1950 and the Louisville Chapter of the National Association for the Advancement of Colored People (NAACP) began working to desegregate the University of Louisville. After the General Assembly amended the Day Law in March 1950 to end segregation in higher education in the state, Berea, Bellarmine, Nazareth, and Ursuline colleges desegregated immediately. Most other Kentucky colleges and universities had desegregated by 1955. The University of Louisville desegregated its graduate and professional programs in 1950 and admitted black undergraduates in 1951. The university decided to close Louisville Municipal College at the end of the 1950-51 academic year. After a bitter controversy over the disposition of the college's four tenured professors, the university appointed Charles H. Parrish, Jr., to its faculty, the first appointment of a black person to the faculty of a historically white institution in the South.

Kentucky elementary and secondary schools remained segregated until after the U.S. Supreme Court's May 1954 *Brown v. Board of Education* decision. The Wayne and Fayette County school systems lifted their barriers in the summer of 1955. Louisville gained national recognition for implementing a "freedom of choice" desegregation plan in September 1956. Nevertheless, although 75 percent of Kentucky's school systems had desegregated by 1956, protests and lawsuits over the next decade were required to bring statewide desegregation.

The persistence of segregated residential patterns limited the effect of school desegregation across the state. In Louisville the issue of de facto segregation resulted in a September 1975 federal court order to bus 19,500 children to achieve racial balance in the Louisville and Jefferson County public schools. A majority of white Jefferson County residents opposed the court order and responded with community meetings, boycotts, and demonstrations. By the beginning of the 1977-78 school year, however, the school system was in compliance with the court order and community opposition had subsided.

In the late 1960s, the development of a statewide system of community colleges under the University of Kentucky made postsecondary education more accessible to many blacks, but the initial impact of desegregation on Kentucky's colleges and universities was limited. Comparatively small numbers of black students were admitted to historically white institutions, prompting black student protests at the University of Kentucky and the University of Louisville in 1968 and 1969 and the creation of special programs to increase black enrollment.

In 1980 the U.S. Office of Civil Rights determined that Kentucky had not ended segregation in its higher education system and imposed a court-ordered desegregation plan on the state. This plan required the elimination of all vestiges of segregation in historically white Kentucky institutions and the upgrading of Kentucky State University. Although the Office of Civil Rights mandate expired in 1987, the U.S. Department of Education continued evaluating Kentucky's progress in achieving the goals of the desegregation plan.

See James D. Anderson, *The Education of Blacks in the South, 1860-1935* (Chapel Hill, N.C., 1988); Lawrence H. Williams, *Black Higher Education in Kentucky 1879-1930: The History of Simmons University* (Lewiston, N.Y., 1987).

J. BLAINE HUDSON

EDUCATION REFORM ACT OF 1990. The Kentucky General Assembly passed House Bill 940, the Kentucky Education Reform Act, in 1990 to rectify gross inequities that had existed for a century among the 180 Kentucky school districts. In financing, in the nature of instruction, and in general support, such inequities clearly violated section 183 of the Kentucky constitution. In fact, in all of Kentucky educational history, equity had never been a reality.

The chain of events that led to the Reform Act of 1990 began in 1965, when the Kentucky Court of Appeals ruled in *Russman v. Luckett* that real property must be assessed at 100 percent of its fair market value; such an assessment would have increased the tax revenue for education. The General Assembly, however, enacted the Rollback Bill in 1965 to offset the increase in taxes by reducing the tax rate.

In 1985 the boards of education in sixty-six school districts banded together as the Council for Better Education, Inc. and, along with twenty-two public school students, filed suit through their attorney, former Gov. Bert T. Combs (1959-63), in the Franklin County circuit court, Judge Ray Corns presiding. Under the mandate in section 183 of the Kentucky constitution, the lawsuit sought equity for the plaintiffs' schools. In 1988 Judge Corns ruled that the General Assembly was required by the constitution to provide equal support to conduct an efficient educational effort in all Kentucky schools. This case was appealed to the Kentucky supreme court in *Council for Better Schools Inc. v. Wilkinson* and *Rose v. Council for Better Schools, Inc.* In a sweeping decision, the supreme court ruled in June 1988 that the existing system of public education in Kentucky was unconstitutional. Going far beyond the matter of technical constitutional issues, the court outlined a broad spectrum of negative findings and stated its perceptions of the nature of an efficient public school system.

Responding immediately, the General Assembly organized a task force consisting of three committees of legislators, educational specialists, and administrative officials. The task force held a long, intensive series of hearings and discussions in an attempt to devise new approaches to achieving equitable, efficient educational opportunities for every Kentucky schoolchild. The task force submitted its recommendations for reforming education to the General Assembly as House Bill 940 on March 9, 1990, and the bill was enacted on April 11.

The Reform Act of 1990 is a sweeping, complex piece of legislation—no doubt the most voluminous piece of single-purpose legislation presented to the General Assembly in its two centuries of existence. House Bill 940 called for a radical reconstruction of public education at every level; it set goals and outlined agendas for site-based decision-making within individual school systems, mandated financial equalization, and created the office of Kentucky school commissioner to replace the constitution's superintendent of public instruction. It was not within the General Assembly's power to destroy the century-and-a-half-old office of superintendent, but the legislature transferred the superintendent's duties, powers, and operations to the newly created commissioner.

The Reform Act essentially validated *Russman v. Luckett* and emasculated the Rollback Bill, setting a new course for the operation of public education in Kentucky. On February 27, 1991, newly appointed Commissioner of Education Thomas Boysen assembled, for the first time, the newly constituted State Board of Education. They began the long voyage of educational reform in Kentucky into the twenty-first century.

See *A Guide to the Kentucky Education Reform Act of 1990* (Frankfort, Ky., 1990).

THOMAS D. CLARK

EDWARDS, JOHN. John Edwards, U.S. senator, was born in Stafford County, Virginia in 1748 to Hayden and Penelope (Sanford) Edwards. He attended the Virginia common schools. In 1780 he moved to Kentucky, when land speculation secured him title to about 23,000 acres. Edwards settled in Lincoln County, one of the three original counties of the Kentucky District of Virginia, and represented the area in the Virginia legislature during 1781-83 and 1785-86. In 1783 he became a justice of the peace, which also placed him on the Lincoln County court. Edwards left Lincoln for Bourbon County, which separated from Fayette in 1785, and on May 16, 1786, he became the clerk of the first court held there.

Edwards attended the early statehood assemblies from 1785 to 1788 and participated in the drafting of the Kentucky constitution in 1792. In 1792 Edwards and John Brown were elected Kentucky's first U.S. Senators. Edwards served until March 3, 1795, then returned to Bourbon County and was elected to the state House. After serving briefly in the House, he was elected a member of the state Senate from 1796 to 1800. Edwards died on his Bourbon County plantation in 1837. He was buried in the family cemetery near Paris.

ELDERHOSTEL. Kentucky Elderhostel, an organization that offers education for older adults, held its first meeting in 1979, following the 1975 incorporation of the nonprofit international Elderhostel in Massachusetts. Director Alice W. Brown founded Kentucky Elderhostel with early help from Eastern Kentucky University and the University of Kentucky. These two universities, together with Union College and Morehead and Murray State universities, were the original Kentucky institutions offering the programs in 1980. By 1990 thirty-five

Kentucky institutions were participating. The state office for Elderhostel is located at the University of Kentucky. The courses are short-term, residential, and academic in nature. Their purpose is to provide intellectual stimulation and pleasurable experiences to older adults. Classes on aging are not offered.

JOY BALE BOONE

ELECTIONS. The Virginia legislature allowed free male inhabitants of Kentucky over twenty-one years of age to select the delegates who wrote the first Kentucky constitution in 1792, and the first Kentucky constitution continued this practice. It was not until 1799, when the second constitution was approved, that free "Negroes, mulattoes and Indians" (article 2, section 8) were denied the right to vote. Universal male suffrage came with the adoption of the Fifteenth Amendment to the U.S. Constitution in 1869. The second Kentucky constitution also limited enfranchisement to citizens, denying resident aliens the right to vote. No property qualification was included in either state constitution. The first constitution's residency requirements for voting—two years within the state and one year within the county—remained in effect until the U.S. Supreme Court ruled in 1972 that lengthy residency requirements were unconstitutional. In 1974 Kentucky reduced its residency requirement to thirty days within a precinct.

Women were not given the equal right to vote in Kentucky until the adoption of the Nineteenth Amendment to the U.S. Constitution in 1920. However, Kentucky was the first state to give women the right to vote in school board elections. The 1838 statute creating the common school system granted the right to vote in person or by proxy to any widow or unmarried woman more than twenty-one years of age residing in the school district and owning property there subject to taxation for school purposes. Later the basis for widows' voting rights changed from tax-paying to having children of school age. This was the only provision within the election statutes that permitted proxy voting. An argument that the right to vote was initially extended to widows in school board elections for the purpose of expanding the tax-payer base rather than the service-user faction is supported by the final portion of this section of the statute, which extended the right to vote to the guardians of infants residing in a school district and owning property subject to taxation for school purposes.

Kentucky was also one of the first states to extend the franchise to citizens between the ages of eighteen and twenty. This reform was enacted nearly two decades before the adoption of the Twenty-sixth Amendment to the U.S. Constitution in 1971.

The statute authorizing the election of delegates to the first Kentucky constitutional convention required that the elections be conducted over five days, including a Sunday. The first constitution enabled the presiding election official to hold the election over a maximum of three days. The second constitution changed this provision to allow any candidate to request a three-day electoral period. It was not until the third constitution (1850) that elections were limited to a single day.

The first constitution specified that ballots be used in the election process. The 1799 constitution changed the mode from ballots to *viva voce* voting, in which each voter told the election officials his choice of candidates, and the officials recorded that choice next to the voter's name. The election officials kept a running count of the support each candidate was receiving. The 1850 constitution gave the General Assembly the right to select the form of voting. In most cases, the legislature's choice was *viva voce* voting, although the 1872 legislature specified that members of the U.S. Congress were to be elected by ballot. Kentucky was one of the first states to adopt the Australian ballot (1888), in which the state prints and distributes the ballots and voting takes place in secret. School district elections continued to use the *viva voce* method of voting for more than a decade after the general adoption of the secret ballot for partisan elections. In the 1890s, school district elections were held between 1 and 6 p.m. on the first Saturday in October, while the general election was held in November.

The 1824 General Assembly authorized absentee ballots for the presidential election, allowing a voter to cast a vote for president in another county if he was absent from his home county on election day. A $10.00 fine was specified for voting twice.

The first constitution provided for the indirect election of the governor and the state Senate. Voters selected electors who voted for the Senate and the governor. The governor had the power to appoint county officials and the attorney general and the secretary of state. The second, third, and fourth constitutions expanded the number of officials that the people elected on both the local and state levels. After the adoption of the second constitution, the governor and the lieutenant governor were elected directly by the people for the first time. The third constitution extended direct election to the officials of the judicial branch, the treasurer, auditor, register of the land office, and the attorney general, and the fourth constitution (1891) did the same for the secretary of state and the superintendent of public instruction.

During the first century of statehood, there were several election days during each calendar year. Local, school, state, and national elections tended to be conducted separately. In addition, terms of office on the local level tended to be shorter. Politics played a greater role in people's lives during the nineteenth century. Frequent elections tended to give the political parties and their patronage workers something to do year-round. They likewise reduced the impact of national politics on state and local elections. Since most voters had a loyalty to their political party nearly as strong as their loyalty to their religious traditions, political victory depended upon the mobilization of voters. Frequent elections benefited the majority party; if specific issues or candidate personalities cost the party an election, it would most likely be able to regain its ground a few months later, when the unique conditions were no longer a factor.

Local elections tended to be held in April during most of the nineteenth century. School elections were held in June. State elections were held in August and federal elections in November.

During much of the nineteenth century, the political parties nominated their candidates for public office by a system of party meetings and conventions. Political parties were seen as private voluntary associations that were not subject to governmental regulation. Consequently, each party set its own membership requirements. The political bosses were able to control the nominating meetings, which operated without a secret ballot. Patronage workers and their families and friends, as well as associates of those who did business with the government, were expected to support the organization's proposed nominees.

A system of primary elections for the selection of party nominees began in the 1890s. The parties continued to use a convention process to name state-wide candidates until the mid-1930s. In primary elections the rank and file members of the political party selected their nominees by secret ballot. The primary was paid for by the state. It required a system for party (voter) registration to establish some control over who participated. The primary was designed to open the political process and to reduce the power of the political bosses. For most of its history, the Kentucky primary has awarded the nomination to the candidate with the most votes, even if fewer than a majority. In 1979, 1983, and 1987 the Democratic party's nominee for governor received less than 35 percent of the primary vote.

Kentucky used a presidential primary for the binding of its delegates to the Republican and Democratic national conventions in 1976 and 1980. In 1982 the legislature repealed this provision, and the method of selecting delegates to the 1984 conventions reverted to a series of party caucuses and conventions. In 1988 Kentucky participated in "Super-Tuesday," a southern regional presidential primary conducted on the second Tuesday of March. The 1990 General Assembly repealed the Super-Tuesday primary and replaced it with a presidential primary held with the regular primary in May.

The most common way for government to regulate the conduct of elections is regulation of campaign contributions and expenditures. The fourth constitution prohibited corporations from making donations to political campaigns. The Corrupt Practices Act of 1916 sought to further regulate campaigns by requiring candidates and their campaign committees to file public statements outlining the contributions to and expenditures for the campaign.

The 1916 statute also created expenditure limits, ranging from $10,000 for the election for governor to $750 for a seat in the state House of Representatives. The statute lacked an effective enforcement provision, however, and several loopholes allowed almost unlimited spending. In 1966 Kentucky repealed this statute and created the Registry of Election Finance to collect and disclose data on campaign contributions and expenditures. In 1974 the General Assembly passed a contributions limit of $3,000 per person for both the primary and the general election. There were no limitations on contributions from a Political Action Committee (PAC). The 1988 legislature limited PAC contributions to $4,000 per candidate per election and raised the individual contribution limit to $4,000. The law was also revised to forbid successful statewide candidates from raising money once they are in office. There are also limitations on the ability of candidates to raise money after the primary or general elections to repay campaign loans they have made to their own campaigns.

See Joel Goldstein, ed., *Kentucky Government and Politics* (Bloomington, Ind., 1984).

JOEL GOLDSTEIN

ELIZABETHTOWN. The county seat of Hardin County, Elizabethtown is located in Severn's Valley, on the southern slope of Muldraugh Hill. It was originally called the Severn's Valley settlement, after John Severns, an early explorer of the region.

On July 22, 1793, the first Hardin County Court was held at Isaac Hynes's house. Col. Andrew Hynes set aside thirty acres for the county buildings, dividing the acreage into fifty-one lots with streets and alleys. In 1797 Elizabethtown was established there, named after Col. Andrew Hynes's wife. In 1797 Thomas Lincoln, Abraham Lincoln's father, was a temporary resident of Elizabethtown and he moved there in 1803. Working in Elizabethtown as a carpenter, he built a sawmill for Denton Geoghegan and is said to have helped build several houses in the town. Elizabethtown was without a post office until August 10, 1820, when Isaac Mills became the first postmaster.

During the Civil War, John Hunt Morgan and his raiders approached Elizabethtown and burned two bridges of the Louisville & Nashville Railroad. The next day, December 27, 1862, Morgan and his men surrounded the town and set up their artillery on Cemetery Hill. At that point Lt. Col. Harry S. Smith and the 91st Illinois Volunteer Infantry were stationed in Elizabethtown. Although Smith and his 600 to 650 Federal troops were outnumbered, they demanded the surrender of Morgan and his raiders, who opened fire on the town with a parrott gun and several howitzers. Smith and his Federal troops, armed only with altered flintlock muskets, were no match for Morgan, and Div. Q.M. Maj. Llewellyn waved a white flag of surrender. The next day Morgan and his troops left Elizabethtown after destroying the trestleworks of the Louisville & Nashville

Railroad at Muldraugh Hill, disabling the railroad for several months.

Gen. George Armstrong Custer was ordered to report for duty at Elizabethtown on September 3, 1871. Custer and his two hundred men of the 7th Cavalry were stationed in Elizabethtown to put an end to illegal distilleries and to restrain the Ku Klux Klan and the bushwhackers. Custer and his men left in the spring of 1873, when they were restationed in the West.

The first Hardin County courthouse was built of yellow poplar by John Crutcher in 1796. The second courthouse, completed in 1806, was burned in 1864 by Gen. Hylan B. Lyons, a Confederate raider. The third courthouse, completed in 1874, was destroyed by fire in December 1932. The present courthouse, a three-story classical Beaux Arts design made of brick, was dedicated on March 8, 1934.

The diverse industries of Elizabethtown produce auto parts, highway guardrails and posts, electrical-mechanical devices, printed circuit boards, ceramic and alnico magnets, urethane roof insulation, silicon sealants, and cable, pipe, and other copper products, as well as cheese.

A fourth-class city, Elizabethtown has sometimes been called the Hub City. The Louisville & Nashville Railroad reached there in 1859, the Elizabethtown & Paducah Railroad was completed in the early 1870s, and the Hodgenville & Elizabethtown Railroad in 1888. Today I-65, Western Kentucky Parkway, Bluegrass Parkway, U.S. 31-W, U.S. 62, and KY 61 all pass through Elizabethtown. Its excellent recreation and parks system has helped it win the All-Kentucky City award seven times from the Kentucky Chamber of Commerce, on the basis of its education, recreation, industry, street improvement, downtown renewal, historic preservation, health services, and environmental programs. Elizabethtown Community College, a branch of the University of Kentucky, was established in the city in 1964. The population of Elizabethtown was 11,748 in 1970; 15,380 in 1980; and 18,167 in 1990.

See Samuel Haycraft, *A History of Elizabethtown, Kentucky* (Elizabethtown, Ky., 1921); Daniel E. McClure, Jr., *Two Centuries in Elizabethtown and Hardin County, Kentucky* (Elizabethtown, Ky., 1979).

ELKHORN CREEK. Elkhorn Creek is an eighty-six-mile-long stream in the Inner Bluegrass region. It flows west and northwest across Fayette, Scott, northeastern Woodford, and eastern Franklin counties and empties into the Kentucky River in northern Franklin County. It has two principal branches, North Elkhorn Creek and South Elkhorn Creek, which join at Forks of the Elkhorn immediately east of Frankfort. The short Town Branch of South Elkhorn Creek onced flowed through what is now downtown Lexington; its direction of flow was used to plot Main Street, parallel to it, and the right-angle streets. In the early 1930s most of Town

Branch was diverted into a subsurface conduit to eliminate flooding in central Lexington.

The many springs within Elkhorn Creek's drainage basin include McConnell's Spring, west of Lexington, and Royal Spring in Georgetown's center in Scott County. As it was in pioneer days, the drainage basin is an important water source for the central Bluegrass region.

WILLIAM A. WITHINGTON

ELKTON. The county seat of Todd County, Elkton is located on the Elk Fork of the Red River, which in post-settlement time was a watering place for elk herds, hence the name. The town was laid out by Thomas Garvin and Thomas Jameson in 1819 and was incorporated on May 18, 1820.

Todd County's first courthouse, built in 1821-22, was a two-story brick structure with cupolas. The land and labor were donated by Major Gray. As the county expanded, a larger courthouse, built of brick with Greek Revival details, was completed in 1836. The two-story brick structure still stands but is no longer in use as the courthouse. The current courthouse, constructed in 1975-76, is a one-story brick with a Doric order portico, keystone arches over the windows, and a dome on top of the building.

Thomas Garvin operated a mill in Elkton in 1817; early merchants were Charles Smith and William S. Logan. Samuel Hadley ran an early inn and in 1818 Maj. John Gray built the Nick and Will House, a hotel. Jesse Russell, a slaveowner and brickmason from Virginia, built many of the town's early houses. The Green River Female Academy, founded as a stock company by residents to educate their daughters locally, opened in 1835. The stock sold for $25 a share and $3,500 was subscribed. Most of the money was used to construct the school's two-story brick building on Goebel Avenue. In 1851 the school began accepting both male and female students. It remained in operation until the late 1870s.

Benjamin H. Bristow, secretary of the Treasury under President U.S. Grant, was a native of Elkton.

In 1988 eight manufacturers were located in Elkton, including a clothing plant, a maker of insulated glass doors, and a beef processing firm.

A fourth-class city, Elkton had a population of 1,612 in 1970; 1,815 in 1980; and 1,789 in 1990.

ELLENDALE FAIR. The Ellendale Fair was held at Ellendale farm, near Curdsville in Daviess County, Kentucky, from 1894 to 1898. Created by W.F. Rapier, born at Ellendale in 1869, to promote the family's livestock business, it attracted vast crowds to the area. Railroads offered special rates to fair-goers, and steamboats carried passengers to Curdsville on the Green River. The Ellendale Fair Company built a hotel, racetrack, exhibition halls, and other facilities, and in the winter months Rapier operated Ellendale Business College in the hotel building. Drought, storms, and unsettled economic conditions bankrupted the company in 1898, and Rapier worked for many years to pay

off the debts that had accumulated. He died in 1923, a respected Owensboro businessman, president of the Rapier Grain & Seed Company, and was buried in Owensboro.

See Lee A. Dew, "The Ellendale Fair," *Daviess County Historical Quarterly*, (Jan. 1987): 3-11.

LEE A. DEW

ELLIOTT, JOHN MILTON. John Milton Elliott, assassinated Kentucky jurist, was born on May 16, 1820, in Scott County, Virginia, the son of John Lisle and Jane (Ritchie) Elliott. The family settled in Kentucky, where his father, one of the most influential figures in early Morgan, Lawrence, and Carter counties, served two terms in the General Assembly. Elliott was educated in local public schools, studied law, and began to practice law at Prestonsburg, Floyd County, in 1843. On September 23, 1848, he married Sarah Jane Smith, the daughter of William Smith, in Johnson County.

A staunch Democrat, Elliott in 1847 was elected state representative from the district composed of Johnson, Floyd, and Pike counties. He subsequently represented Kentucky's 6th District in the 33rd, 34th, and 35th U.S. Congresses (March 4, 1853 to March 3, 1859). Not a candidate for renomination in 1858, he resumed the practice of law. He was elected state representative from Floyd County in 1861.

While not a member of the slave-owning gentry, Elliott occasionally acquired slaves, and he condemned northern abolitionists. A member of Kentucky's Southern Rights party, he initially advocated neutrality but cast his lot with the Confederacy after the adjournment of the General Assembly in the fall of 1861. According to one contemporary, Elliott was instrumental in organizing Confederate support in eastern Kentucky. Indicted for treason by the U.S. district court at Frankfort, he was expelled from the General Assembly on December 21, 1861. A member of the Russellville convention, which formed the Confederate state government, he served as a Kentucky representative in the 1st and 2d Confederate Congresses in Richmond, Virginia.

Elliott settled in Owingsville, Kentucky, after the war and served as circuit judge of the 13th Judicial District (1868-74) before moving to Catlettsburg. In 1876 he was elected judge of the court of appeals for the 1st Appellate District and was serving in that capacity when he was assassinated in Frankfort by Thomas Buford, an irate litigant, on March 26, 1879. Elliott's tragic death shocked Kentucky and the nation. The assassination, declared the *New York Times*, "could scarcely have taken place in any region calling itself civilized except Kentucky, or some other southern state." Indicted for murder by the Franklin County circuit court, Buford obtained a change of venue to Owen County. On July 23, 1879, he was found guilty and sentenced to life imprisonment. Buford's attorneys won an appeal for a new trial and based their defense on a plea of insanity. Buford's second trial, one of the most celebrated in Kentucky history, concluded in 1881 with a verdict of "not guilty by reason of insanity." Committed to the Central Kentucky Insane Asylum at Anchorage, Buford escaped in 1882 and fled to Indiana. He voluntarily returned to the asylum in 1884 and died on February 12, 1885.

Elliott was buried in the Frankfort Cemetery. His widow erected a statue to his memory at the Boyd County courthouse in Catlettsburg.

JAMES M. PRICHARD

ELLIOTT COUNTY. Elliott County, the 114th in order of formation, lies in the foothills of the Appalachian Mountains in northeastern Kentucky. The county was formed on April 1, 1869, from parts of Morgan, Lawrence, and Carter counties. Bounded by Carter, Lawrence, Morgan, and Rowan counties, it has an area of 234 square miles. The county seat is SANDY HOOK.

The land is characterized by rolling hills and mountainous terrain, much-eroded by early mining and logging operations. Reforestation by landowners, joined in 1955 by the Kentucky Division of Forestry, has been successful in revitalizing the deciduous hardwood forest. Farms, raising principally tobacco and corn, cover 47.7 percent of the land. The 2,712-acre Grayson Lake State Park lies on the northern edge of the county.

The majority of the families who settled in the region that became Elliott County came from southwestern Virginia or from the Rowan-Surry-Wilkes county section of North Carolina and professed a strong allegiance to the South during the war. Although no major battles were fought in the hills of eastern Kentucky during the Civil War, both sides raided, foraged in, and recruited from the area. Seven unknown soldiers, casualties of Confederate attacks on Union troops withdrawing from Cumberland Gap in September 1862, are buried just south of Sandy Hooks.

There is some disagreement whether the county is named for John Lisle Elliott or his son, John Milton Elliott. Both were staunch members of the Democratic party. The elder Elliott came to Kentucky from Scott County, Virginia, and served in the Kentucky legislature as a representative and a senator from Carter County.

At the time it was created, Elliott had neither the population nor the economic base to justify the authorization of a new county. The federal census of 1870 counted a population countywide of only 4,433, and in 1878 the report of the commissioner of the State Bureau of Agriculture noted that Martinsburg had only 125 to 150 residents. It therefore seems likely that Democratic party legislators were guilty of gerrymandering the Democratic precincts of Carter, Lawrence, and Morgan counties to create a Democratic county in what was then the Republican enclave of eastern Kentucky.

By 1900 Elliott County's population had grown to 10,387, and a decade later Sandy Hook had almost three hundred inhabitants. Nevertheless, from 1900 to 1990 the federal population schedules show a fairly steady decline in the county's population.

Although mining and logging businesses operated in the late nineteenth century, agriculture remained the principal means of support for most families. After 1900 agriculture was not enough to sustain the population. Some people followed the logging industry westward to Wisconsin, Washington, and Oregon, but most who left beginning around World War I moved to the industrialized communities along the Ohio River.

Some mining and logging still take place in the county. Surface mines extracted more than 140,000 tons of bituminous coal in 1987 and there is evidence of titanium deposits in the area. Commercial petroleum and natural gas production has served local needs, but the boom-and-bust nature of these industries, in a county that lacks a railway and easy access to the interstate highway system, has hindered development. Having failed to develop a strong economic base, Elliott County has a high unemployment rate, and it faces possible elimination of the tobacco subsidy as well as a declining coal market. The population of the rural county was 5,933 in 1970; 6,908 in 1980; and 6,455 in 1990.

See Elliott County History Book Committee, *The History of Elliott County, Kentucky, 1985* (Marceline, Mo., 1985); Elliott County Centennial Commission, *Historical Highlights of Elliott County, 1869-1969* (Sandy Hook, Ky., 1969).

MARTYNE MASON

ELLIS, JIMMY. A sparring partner of Muhammad Ali who went on to win the World Boxing Association (WBA) heavyweight championship, Jimmy Ellis was born on February 24, 1940, in Louisville, the son of Walter and Elizabeth (Roe) Ellis. Originally a middleweight trained by Angelo Dundee, Ellis won his first professional fight with a third-round knockout on April 19, 1961. Later he served as an Ali sparring partner for two years. After moving up in weight class, Ellis won the WBA heavyweight crown on April 27, 1968, with a fifteen-round decision over Jerry Quarry. In an effort to unify the heavyweight title, he faced World Boxing Council champion "Smokin' " Joe Frazier on February 16, 1970; Frazier knocked Ellis out in the fifth round. In 1987 he made a comeback in the sport, but as a trainer, not a fighter. Ellis and his wife, Mary Etta, have seven children.

ELMENDORF FARM. Elmendorf farm on Paris Pike in Fayette County has been producing top thoroughbreds continuously since 1874. In that year Milton Sanford, an eastern turfman, purchased 544 acres to establish the Preakness Stud, named for his horse Preakness, sired by Lexington. The horse farm was renamed Elmendorf in 1881 when it was bought by the premier horse breeder of his day, Daniel Swigert. James B. Haggin's purchase of Elmendorf in 1897 initiated the most famous phase of the farm's history. He constructed a palatial residence, added nearly 8,000 acres, built some of the finest barns in the country, bred many excellent thoroughbreds, and made the farm a model in the operations of its various departments. After Haggin's death in 1914, it took nearly ten years to disperse his vast holdings, the greatest expanse of Bluegrass land ever owned by one man.

In the 1920s Joseph E. Widener became the owner of a 1,200-acre Elmendorf. He placed great emphasis on landscape beauty, added barns that are architectural gems, and owned thoroughbreds of great renown. His grandson sold the land as three farms in the 1950s. Elmendorf, now 504 acres, was owned by Maxwell Gluck from 1952 until his death in 1984, and has since been owned by Jack Kent Cooke.

See James Gill, *Bloodstock* (New York 1977).

MARY E. WHARTON

ELSMERE. Elsmere is a suburban city in northwestern Kenton County along what is known as Dixie Highway (U.S. 25), between ERLANGER to the northeast and Florence to the southwest. The city was named in the 1890s by developer Lou Nolon, who once lived on Elsmere Street in Norwood, Ohio. Until the city was incorporated in 1896, the area was known as South Erlanger. Settlement in the area began around a stable on the Covington-Lexington turnpike around 1839. Black families moved to the area soon after emancipation, and again during the 1920s when the Southern (now Norfolk Southern) Railway needed workers to lay tracks through the area. German Catholics settled here during the late 1800s.

Woodside Park was a popular picnic site even before the city was established. Barbecues brought throngs of people and political hopefuls to the park. Land developers in the 1880s and 1890s arranged for excursion trains from Cincinnati to bring potential home buyers to Woodside Park, where they were wined and dined as lots were auctioned off.

In 1921 10,000 people in Elsmere celebrated as the paving of Dixie Highway was marked with a block party. In 1961, the construction of I-75 through Kenton County near Elsmere brought new business and rapid suburban growth. The population of the fourth-class city was 5,161 in 1970; 7,203 in 1980; and 6,847 in 1990.

EMIGRATION (IMMIGRATION) SOCIETIES. Emigration (Immigration) Societies were nonpolitical promotional organizations established by city and county residents in the nineteenth century to bring settlers to Kentucky. The societies' functions resembled those of today's chambers of commerce. Emigration societies published informational pamphlets and placed advertisements in eastern states' newspapers, giving details about a community's climate, topography, employment, agricultural yield, consumer product prices, and the mechanics of obtaining land. Charles Kerr's *History of Kentucky* (1922) cites organizations in existence as early as 1797 in Lexington and in Washington, Mason County. In 1885 the Bowling Green Immigration

Society published a relatively sophisticated fifty-four page booklet that greatly expanded on topics covered by earlier societies. Religious and educational institutions, white and "colored," were examined from a historical and structural perspective, with all religious denominations receiving equal attention. The booklet also discussed the community's systems of city and county government, road networks, geological wealth, and the manufacturing base and its potential.

See George Morgan Chinn, *Kentucky Settlement and Statehood, 1750-1800* (Frankfort, Ky., 1975).

EMINENCE COLLEGE. Eminence College was located in Eminence, Henry County, Kentucky, and began as a high school. In 1855 the citizens of Eminence organized a stock company to raise funds to build the high school, which opened in September 1857 under the direction of S.G. Mullen. The school soon became overextended, and in 1858 the facilities were sold to another stock company headed by the Rev. W.S. Giltner, a member of the Christian Church. As the major stockholder, Giltner became president of Eminence College, the name conferred by the Kentucky General Assembly on February 5, 1861. The college was one of the first coeducational institutions in the state. Programs were offered in Latin, Greek, mathematics, physics, and chemistry.

Lacking an endowment, Eminence College had to rely on the business acumen of its stockholders, particularly Giltner, for its survival. Under his leadership the school created a commercial department in 1880 and a normal school to train teachers in 1885. In spite of these advances, enrollment, which had seldom been greater than two hundred, began to decline. In 1893 Giltner retired. Unable to find an administrator of Giltner's ability, the college soon fell into debt and closed in 1895.

ENABLING ACTS. The four separate enabling acts that gave Virginia's consent for its Kentucky District to form an independent state foreshadowed Kentucky's later constitutional history. In the third Danville STATEHOOD CONVENTION on August 14, 1785, the delegates addressed the Virginia General Assembly on the subject of separation. In a garrulous and somewhat patronizing resolution, the Kentucky delegates finally got to the point of asserting, "We therefore with the consent, and by the authority of our constituents, after the most solemn deliberation, being warned of every consequence which can ensue, for them, for ourselves, and for posterity unborn,—do pray that an act may be passed at the ensuing session of the assembly declaring and acknowledging the sovereignty and independence of the district."

The Virginia General Assembly responded with the enabling act of January 1786. This act acknowledged the essential arguments for separation, namely: that the 500-mile distance between Kentucky and the Virginia capital at Richmond rendered impossible the timely application of executive power in public emergencies and made legislative representation difficult; that laws were enacted and expired before Kentuckians knew about them; that court appeals were so expensive that many were denied justice; that there were an unequal distribution of revenue and confusion in land laws; and that Virginia had not supplied troops to supplement the militia in repelling Indian raids. The Virginia legislature directed that, subject to congressional approval, Kentucky should be accepted into the Union by June 1, 1787.

It was impossible for the Kentucky District to meet that date, however. There was disagreement over taxes and over apportioning Kentucky's share in the Virginia Revolutionary War debt. The continuing Indian raids impeded negotiation, and there was a lack of concerted support in Kentucky for separation. The most divisive factor, however, was the proposal of James WILKINSON to ally Kentucky to Spain, which raised dissension in the fifth convention in September 1787, and also in the sixth and seventh conventions. The issues receiving the most attention in these conventions were those closely connected with Wilkinson—trade down the Mississippi, and the possible Spanish alliance. Wilkinson, who wrote the memorials to Virginia from the fifth, sixth, and seventh conventions, worded them in a manner that seemed to threaten an alliance with Spain, though the wording was ambiguous.

The second enabling act, passed in 1787, extended the time for Kentucky's admission to the Union, citing the hindrances encountered in completing arrangements, and made a few other minor changes.

Running through the first two enabling acts and those adopted in 1788 and 1789 were strong guarantees of land titles, ensuring that land grants issued by the new state would be subordinate to those previously issued by Virginia. The act of December 29, 1788, contains in addition the reservation that the entire channel of the Ohio River "shall remain within the limits of this commonwealth." Kentucky had to be safely in the Union before the laws of Virginia would cease to apply, and Kentuckians were to frame and adopt a constitution.

The fourth enabling act, adopted on December 18, 1789, became known as the VIRGINIA COMPACT. It expressed the hope that Kentuckians would draft a constitution and get their state admitted into the Union by November 1, 1791, at which date Virginia would cease to exercise dominion over the area. The act specifically authorized the Kentuckians to hold a convention and draft a constitution.

The enabling acts of Virginia are classic reflections of the difficulty Kentucky had in severing its ties with the mother state and beginning operation as an independent commonwealth. A certain amount of dilatoriness, the Indian menace, the Spanish Conspiracy, and the search for satisfactory terms of separation all delayed Kentucky's admission to the Union, and thereby denied it the honor of being the fourteenth state, a distinction that went to Vermont.

See John Mason Brown, *The Political Beginnings of Kentucky* (Louisville 1889).

THOMAS D. CLARK

ENDANGERED AND RARE ORGANISMS. More than two hundred years ago, when the first white settlers arrived, Kentucky's numerous rivers were rich in fish and mussels. The towering primeval forests and vast prairies were awash in colors from the 3,000 or so species of native plants. The landscape teemed with life: nearly seventy-five species of mammals, 105 species of amphibians and reptiles, and 340 species of birds.

The thousands of settlers who took the Wilderness Road across Cumberland Gap could not have foreseen that within two hundred years Kentucky's 24 million acres of original forest would be reduced to fewer than 1,000 acres of old growth. The nearly 2 million acres of prairie are now gone. No longer can we safely take a drink from the rivers, streams, and wetlands, because most have been polluted.

As we have taken our livelihoods from the Kentucky wilderness with ax and chain saw and plow and bulldozer, we have paid a heavy price. The hairlip sucker, Cumberland leafshell mussel, and Carolina parakeet—along with nineteen other native Kentucky species—have either become extinct or no longer exist in the state. Residents of the state for eons, these species were eradicated in only two hundred years. Thirty-seven species in Kentucky have been listed by the U.S. Fish and Wildlife Service as endangered or threatened, meaning that their continued existence is in jeopardy worldwide. An additional seventy-seven species are being considered for protection under the Endangered Species Act because of threats to their existence. In 1990, 114 species of the state's plants and animals were rare on a worldwide basis and the actions of Kentuckians will play a critical role in their survival. In the separate category of species that are rare within Kentucky, 543 species are in need of conservation action.

The roll call of species considered rare is not a meaningless list, for each species is an irreplaceable living organism resulting from genetic combinations millions of years in the making. All species have a right to exist, a right that humans do not have the moral authority to extinguish. Practically speaking, all species have the potential to help humans economically as sources of food, medicine, and raw material for industry. Kentucky's native plants and animals will not respond to rhetoric, nor will old wounds necessarily heal themselves. If the rich legacy of Kentucky that our pioneer ancestors discovered is not to be lost, Kentuckians must become better stewards of their natural inheritance.

RICHARD R. HANNAN

ENGINEERING. In a sense, Kentucky's first engineers and surveyors were prehistoric bison, mammoths, and Indians. The animals beat paths across Kentucky between salt licks, stamping grounds, and grazing fields. Indian hunting trails followed these paths and were used in turn by the earliest explorers and surveyors.

In Kentucky's earliest days, engineers educated in Europe, Virginia, and eastern states provided the engineering services for roads, bridges, furnaces, and gristmills. Before 1890 engineering education in Kentucky was available only at private colleges. The first graduate was a civil engineer from Bacon College in Harrodsburg (1840). Under the Morrill Land Grant Act, Kentucky's AGRICULTURAL AND MECHANICAL COLLEGE was founded in 1865 in Lexington, but it was not until 1890 that the A&M College produced its first engineering graduate. By 1990 the College of Engineering at the University of Kentucky had a strong alumni association with almost 10,000 alumni.

The other engineering college in Kentucky is Speed Scientific School at the University of Louisville, which started as a private school in 1925. It has a fully accredited cooperative program. The Colleges of Engineering at UK and Louisville have a joint Ph.D. graduate program in civil engineering and the deans of both are members of the State Registration Board. Over twenty colleges and universities in Kentucky have preengineering programs. Regional state and private universities, as well as the community colleges, provide one to two years of preengineering core curricula. Preengineers are usually enrolled in math and science classes with physics, chemistry, and mathematics majors.

To protect the health, safety, and welfare of the general public, the Kentucky legislature in 1938 passed the engineering registration law, which in 1966 was extended to include land surveyors. By 1990 almost 10,000 engineers and 3,600 land surveyors were registered; the Kentucky Society of Professional Engineers had 15,000 members; and the Kentucky Association of Professional Surveyors had 150 members.

In the late twentieth century engineering took on the new aspect of robotics. In Georgetown, Toyota Motor Company became a pioneer in the field, and the University of Kentucky soon expanded its engineering program to include automated technology for manufacturing in the twenty-first century.

See J. Winston Coleman, Jr., *The College of Engineering* (Lexington, Ky., 1965); Ruth L. Lockwood and W.R. McIntosh, *History of Progress in Engineering Education, Speed Scientific School, University of Louisville* (Louisville 1969).

D.K. BLYTHE AND J.H. HAVENS

EPISCOPAL CHURCH. The first recorded public service of worship in Kentucky was conducted by an Anglican clergyman, the Rev. John Lyth, at Boonesborough on May 28, 1775. Twenty years later a group of citizens of Lexington began to hold services on the farm of Capt. David Shely in a log cabin on Russell Cave Pike. The Episcopal Society, as it was called, became the nucleus of the first organized Episcopal congregation in Kentucky with a clergyman to minister to its members.

In 1796 the Rev. James Moore, a Virginian scholar and first president of Transylvania University, began to hold services in a small frame building on the corner of Market and Middle (now Church) streets in Lexington, the present site of Christ Church Cathedral. In 1803 a modest brick building replaced the little frame house. On July 2, 1809, the parish was organized and the first vestry chosen. The rector was supported by fees paid by pewholders each year.

Under its second rector, John Ward of Connecticut, the Lexington church agreed to the constitution of the Protestant Episcopal Church (USA). A delegate from the parish attended the general Episcopal convention held in Philadelphia in 1814. A new and commodious church building was erected on the same site that year.

Under the third rector, George Thomas Chapman of Massachusetts (1820-30), the diocese of Kentucky was organized. Four clerical and seventeen lay deputies represented the three parishes then organized in Kentucky: Christ Church, Lexington; Christ Church, Louisville, organized in 1822; and Trinity Church, Danville, founded by Chapman a month earlier.

Benjamin Bosworth Smith of Rhode Island became the fourth rector of Christ Church, Lexington, upon Chapman's resignation in 1830. Two years later Smith was elected first bishop of Kentucky, a territory covering 40,000 square miles, stretching from the Mississippi River into the Appalachians. He served as bishop of Kentucky for more than a half century (1832-84), becoming presiding bishop of the Protestant Episcopal Church for the last sixteen years. In 1867 George David Cummins of Chicago was elected assistant bishop of Kentucky. In 1875 Cummins abandoned the communion of the Episcopal church and founded the Reformed Episcopal denomination. During Bishop Smith's episcopate, parishes and missions sprang up throughout Kentucky. Among the antebellum parishes in the area that would become the diocese of Lexington were St. Peter's, Paris; Church of the Ascension, Frankfort; Trinity, Covington; St. Paul's, Newport; Church of the Nativity, Maysville; Advent, Cynthiana; St. John's, Versailles; St. Philip's, Harrodsburg; Holy Trinity, Georgetown; and Ascension, Mt. Sterling. An equal number were founded before the Civil War in the western half of the state.

Thomas Underwood Dudley, a Virginian, became bishop after Smith's death in 1884. During the two decades in which he was bishop, the Episcopal denomination enjoyed greater prosperity than at any other time in its history.

Edward Fairfax Berkley succeeded Smith as rector of Christ Church, Lexington. During his nineteen-year rectorate (1839-58), a gothic church was built (1848), the fourth building to occupy the same site. Henry Clay, long a supporter and pew-holder, was baptized by Berkley and confirmed by Smith in 1847. In Louisville, where Christ Church had languished for a number of years because of financial troubles, James Craik of Virginia in 1844 began an era of prosperity and growth. He served as rector for thirty-eight years. Gideon McMillan was the first rector of Trinity Church.

In Kentucky during the Civil War, no Episcopal parish was lost and none was split by internal dissension. In Lexington Jacob Shaw Shipman served as rector (1861-77) and, although a Unionist, his moderation held the parish together. Church expansion, begun under his predecessor and halted by the war, was completed by 1864, when chancel and transept were added.

In 1895 the diocese of Kentucky was split up to create the diocese of Lexington in the eastern half of the state, an area of 19,983 square miles. Dudley remained bishop of the diocese of Kentucky, with Christ Church, Louisville, as his cathedral. Lewis William Burton was elected bishop of the new diocese of Lexington, beginning his duties in January 1896, with Christ Church, Lexington, as his cathedral.

The bishops of the diocese of Lexington have been Lewis William Burton (1896-1929); Henry Pryor Almon Abbott (1929-45); William Robert Moody (1945-71); Addison Hosea (1971-84); and Don Adger Wimberly (1985-). Bishops of the diocese of Kentucky after the separation have been: Thomas Underwood Dudley (1884-1904); Charles Edward Woodcock (1904-36); Charles Clingman (1936-53); C. Gresham Marmion (1954-74); and David Benson Reed (1974-).

See Frances Keller Swinford and Rebecca Smith Lee, *The Great Elm Tree: Heritage of the Episcopal Diocese of Lexington* (Lexington, Ky., 1969); Frances Keller Swinford, *The Story of Christ Church, Lexington, Kentucky 1796-1976* (Lexington, Ky., 1976).   FRANCES KELLER BARR

EPISCOPAL THEOLOGICAL SEMINARY.

Benjamin Bosworth Smith, the first Episcopal bishop of the diocese of Kentucky, raised enough money to buy a two-acre lot on Second Street in Lexington for a seminary and hire Henry Caswell as professor of sacred literature. The state legislature chartered the Theological Seminary of the Protestant Episcopal Church in Kentucky on February 24, 1834, and its first class of two students graduated on November 9, 1834. As the result of an 1836 dispute concerning the election of vestry members, Smith was accused of misconduct, mismanagement of funds, and improper use of influence. Though he was exonerated in an ecclesiastical trial, the suit damaged the reputation of his church and his school, and Caswell left. In 1840 the seminary moved to Shelbyville, Kentucky, and became a department of the Episcopalian Shelby College. As such the seminary survived for thirty years, until August 20, 1870, when after years of mismanagement Shelby College closed.

The board of trustees of the seminary, using the proceeds from the sale of the Lexington property in 1844, had endowed the Rev. W.T. Elmer, of Louisville, to teach until 1896. When the diocese of Lexington was created in 1895, all remaining seminary assets were transferred to the bishop's fund of the new episcopate, and the seminary closed. In 1951 William R. Moody, bishop of Lexington, discovered that the seminary's charter had never been revoked and asked the diocese of Lexington to reestablish the school, where he had agreed to prepare two young men for the priesthood that fall. The assembly approved the petition and the seminary reopened in the fall of 1951.

See W. Robert Insko, "The Kentucky Seminary," *Register* 52 (July 1954): 213-32; Frances K. Swinford and Rebecca S. Lee, *The Great Elm Tree: Heritage of the Episcopal Diocese of Lexington* (Lexington, Ky., 1969).

ERIE SCHOOL–AIKEN HALL. The concept of Erie School–Aiken Hall originated at a meeting of the Methodist Church board of managers and Woman's Home Missionary Society in 1911. The purpose of the meeting was to develop a missionary school in Olive Hill, Kentucky, that would provide Appalachian children and their families with educational and religious leadership, training in home-making skills, industrial and crafts training, and academic studies. Another significant objective was to improve the quality of life in the local communities by involving citizens in educational, religious, and health-related activities. The school's outreach program promoted general health care in the community, and the school served as a temporary hospital during the influenza and smallpox epidemics of 1918-20. Several acres of land and building materials were donated by the General Refractories Company to erect Aiken Hall dormitory and later Erie School. Erie School–Aiken Hall served underprivileged mountain children and their families until the school closed in 1958.

See William Erastus Arnold, *A History of Methodism in Kentucky* (Louisville 1935).

HUBERT V. CRAWFORD AND
PAUL L. CRAWFORD

ERLANGER. Erlanger, a suburban city in northwestern Kenton County, is located on U.S. 25 one-half mile north of ELSMERE and one mile southwest of Crestview Hills. The area was first settled around 1807, when Barlett Graves built a log cabin on land that he had bought in 1802. Large-scale settlement occurred after the Covington-Lexington Turnpike was chartered in 1829, and the small community that grew up around a tollgate was originally known as Timberlake, in honor of William T. Timberlake, a local physician.

When the Southern (now Norfolk Southern) Railway arrived in the community in 1873, the depot was named Greenwood, after the first president of the railroad. In 1877 the depot was renamed Silver Lake to avoid confusion with five other cities along the rail line. When the post office was established in 1882, both the depot and the post office were named Erlanger in honor of Baron Frederic Emile D'Erlanger, a German-born English financier who headed a land syndicate organized to develop the city.

The land syndicate persuaded the railroad to make Erlanger a stop for all passenger trains and it offered one year of free rail transportation to anyone who located there. The town grew quickly and was incorporated on January 25, 1897. A business district grew along the Covington-Lexington road, which was paved on August 16, 1921. When the interstate highway I-75 came to northern Kentucky in the early 1960s, subdivisions and industrial areas were built up near the interstate, and Erlanger led the Cincinnati metropolitan area in new building for three years in the 1960s.

The population of the third-class city was 12,676 in 1970; 14,466 in 1980; and 15,979 in 1990.

ERNST, RICHARD PRETLOW. Richard Pretlow Ernst, U.S. senator, was born in Covington, Kentucky, on February 28, 1858, the son of William and Sarah (Butler) Ernst. He graduated from Centre College in Danville, Kentucky, in 1878 and in 1880 received a law degree from the University of Cincinnati; he subsequently practiced corporate law in Cincinnati and Covington. He was nominated by the Republican party for a U.S. Senate Seat in 1920. Amid charges of election fraud, Earnst defeated the incumbent, Sen. J.C.W. Beckham, by fewer than 10,000 votes. A heavy Republican vote in the 11th District ensured his victory. In the Senate Ernst served as chairman of the Committee on Revision of Laws and Patents, and was a member of the Judiciary, Finance, Privileges, and Elections committees. In 1926 he was defeated for reelection by the Democratic nominee, Alben W. Barkley, in another highly publicized and close race. Ernst served in the Senate from March 4, 1921, until March 3, 1927, when he returned to his law practice. He served as chairman of the board of the Covington Liberty National Bank, president of the local YMCA, and a member of the Covington town council. He was a trustee of the University of Kentucky, Centre College, and the Western College for Women.

Ernst married Susan Brent of Covington on September 28, 1886; they had two children, William and Sarah. Ernst died on April 13, 1934, in Baltimore and was buried in Covington's Highland Cemetery.

ESKIPPAKITHIKI. According to modern historians, Kentucky had only one relatively permanent Indian settlement in historic times: a one-acre palisaded village established around 1718 by a band of Shawnee on a 3,500-acre plain drained by the Upper Howard and Lulbegrud creeks in southeastern Clark County in the Bluegrass region. This place was called *Eskippakithiki*, a Shawnee word meaning "place of blue licks," for a salt lick at or near the present town of Oil Springs. Most of what is known of this settlement, inhabited by as many as two hundred families, is based on partially supported legend and on a 1736 French Canadian census.

Some anthropologists think the village occupied a site cleared earlier, possibly an Indian settlement and/or a seventeenth-century French outpost. The Shawnee occupants may have moved there from either the middle Cumberland Valley (in the vicinity of present-day Nashville) or the Savannah River country of what is now South Carolina. Other tribes in the area regarded the land that is now Kentucky as no one people's domain. Tecumseh's father lived at Eskippakithiki and the great chief Catahecassa (Black Hoof) claimed to have been born there. In 1752 John Findley of Pennsylvania built a cabin in the village, but early the following year, after an attack by a band of Ottawa, he abruptly left. By 1754 the village itself had been abandoned and it later burned. The inhabitants probably joined their Shawnee kindred across the Ohio River.

By 1780 white families began to settle on the same plain. They called it Indian Old Corn Fields, referring to the once-cultivated area that had returned to its sylvan state. Over the years this name was corrupted to Indian Old Fields and later to simply Indian Fields. On August 27, 1878, at the southeast corner of Indian Old Fields, Levi Goff established the Indian Fields post office, which served a village and station on the Lexington & Eastern Railway. The area is now farmland. Some historians have conjectured that the name Kentucky came from an Iroquois term applied to this plain: *kenta* (level) and *aki* (a locative), or "place of level land."

See Lucien Beckner, "Eskippakithiki: The Last Indian Town in Kentucky," *FCHQ*, 6 (Oct. 1932): 355-82.   ROBERT M. RENNICK

ESTILL, JAMES. Born in 1750 in Augusta County, Virginia, James Estill was an early settler in what is now Madison County, Kentucky. Little is known of his early life. He arrived in Madison County in 1775 and five years later founded, along with his brother Samuel, ESTILL'S STATION, a fort about three miles southeast of what is now Richmond. In March 1782 Estill, along with forty other men, reconnoitered the territory north and east of his station in anticipation of an Indian attack. In their absence on March 20, 1782, a band of Wyandot arrived at Estill's settlement, killed a girl who lived there, and captured MONK ESTILL, James Estill's slave. Under interrogation the slave persuaded his captors to evacuate the area, and subsequently was credited with saving the station from destruction. With the Indians in retreat, two boys, Samuel South and Peter Hackett, were dispatched from the station to inform Estill of the invaders' presence. When Estill received the news, he immediately set off in pursuit of the Wyandot, while five men returned to protect the station. On March 22, 1782,

Estill's party came in contact with the Indians at Little Mountain, near present Mt. Sterling, Montgomery County, Kentucky. In the ensuing bloody battle, known as ESTILL'S DEFEAT, Estill was killed. Estill County, Kentucky's fiftieth, formed in 1808, was named in his honor.

See Jonathan T. Dorris and Maud W. Dorris, *Glimpses of Historic Madison County, Kentucky* (Nashville 1955).

ESTILL, MONK. Monk Estill, a slave belonging to Capt. James Estill, arrived in Kentucky during the 1770s and in 1779 planted and maintained a nursery of apple trees in Boonesborough. In 1780 Monk moved to Estill's Station, established by Captain Estill southeast of present-day Richmond. On March 20, 1782, Wyandot Indians tomahawked fourteen-year-old Jennie Gass at Estill's Station and captured Monk Estill, whom they interrogated. By exaggerating the strength of the garrison, the slave convinced the Indians to postpone their planned assault. Two days later the Indians were attacked by James Estill and twenty-five Kentuckians at Little Mountain (now Mt. Sterling, Kentucky).

During the bloody conflict—known as the Battle of Little Mountain or ESTILL'S DEFEAT—Capt. James Estill was stabbed to death and thirteen of his men were either killed or gravely wounded. While the battle raged, Monk Estill escaped and carried James Berry, one of the wounded, nearly twenty-five miles back to Estill's Station. He later distinguished himself by manufacturing gunpowder for Boonesborough and Estill's Station. It is thought that he mined SALTPETER (potassium nitrate crystals) for the black powder mixture at Peyton Cave in Madison County.

Monk Estill was five feet five inches tall and weighed two hundred pounds. He had three wives, by whom he had thirty children. One of his sons, Jerry, was the first black child born in Boonesborough. In 1782, in recognition of his services, Monk Estill was given his freedom by James Estill's son Wallace, who provided for Monk until his death in Madison County in 1835. Monk Estill, who became a Baptist minister and lived in Shelbyville, is considered the first freed slave in Kentucky history.

See Robert S. Cotterill, *History of Pioneer Kentucky* (Cincinnati 1917).   TED FRANKLIN BELUE

ESTILL COUNTY. Estill County, the fiftieth in order of formation, was established on February 19, 1808, from parts of Clark and Madison counties. It was named in honor of Capt. James ESTILL, who was killed by Indians during Estill's Defeat on March 22, 1782. The county is located in eastern Kentucky and comprises an area of 256 square miles, bordered by Clark, Jackson, Lee, Madison, and Powell counties. The county seat is IRVINE.

Although mostly hilly, the fertile bottomlands are highly productive agricultural areas. Large crops of tobacco and alfalfa are grown, and there is limited livestock production. Extensive quantities of coal and smaller deposits of oil, iron ore, and lead are also found in the county. Approximately 75 percent of Estill County is forest, of which 4,458 acres lie within the Daniel Boone National Forest. Along with the Kentucky River, the principal streams of the county are the Red River and the Station Camp, Beech, Cow, Downing, and Miller's creeks.

Prior to pioneer settlement, Estill County was the site of a Shawnee village at Estill Springs, along the banks of Station Camp Creek. In the 1760s and 1770s, after John Finley, Daniel Boone, and Robert McAfee explored the area, many early settlers entered the region by way of an old buffalo and Indian trace that led to Boonesborough in what is now Madison County.

The mineral wealth of the region played an important role in the development of the county. The Shawnee mined lead in the area, and early settlers recognized the industrial potential of the region. The production of iron began in about 1810 and became one of the earliest industries. Evidence of the once-thriving iron industry can be found in the ruins of the Estill steam furnace, which operated from 1830 to 1874; the Cottage furnace; the Red River iron works; and the Fitchburg furnace. The iron industry declined after 1865 when iron deposits and timber to fire the furnaces were depleted, and innovations in the iron industry made charcoal furnaces obsolete.

The large hotel and landscaped grounds at Estill Springs drew many famous Kentuckians to the summer retreat before the Civil War. Henry Clay, who owned the springs, John Crittenden, and John C. Breckinridge were among the notables who summered there. The resort survived the Civil War and operated into the twentieth century.

Among the towns, villages, and communities in Estill County are the communities of Ravenna, Fitchburg, North Irvine, Sand Hill, South Irvine, and West Irvine. Estill County has one weekly newspaper, the *Citizen Voice and Times*, published in Irvine, and one radio station (WIRV). The population of Estill County was 12,752 in 1970; 14,495 in 1980; and 14,614 in 1990.

See Hallie T. Johnstone, *History of Estill County* (Irvine, Ky., 1974); Edward Puckett, *The Beginning of Estill County, Kentucky, 1808-1869* (Beattyville, Ky., 1987).   RON D. BRYANT

ESTILL'S DEFEAT (BATTLE OF LITTLE MOUNTAIN). On March 19, 1782, Col. Benjamin Logan sent messengers to Capt. James Estill, at ESTILL'S STATION, seeking his help because Wyandot Indians were in the Boonesborough area. From nearby stations, Captain Estill assembled a party of forty men and set out the same day to find the Wyandot party. On March 21, after learning that Indians had threatened his fort, he ordered five men to return to the station to protect the families living there. The rest of Estill's party, pursuing their original quarry, that night set up camp near Little Mountain, the present site of Mt. Sterling. The next morning, after leaving behind ten men whose horses were too worn to continue, the main group discovered fresh tracks and soon came upon the band of Indians.

The two sides, each with twenty-five men, were separated by Hinkston Creek, or Little Mountain Creek, about a mile and a half south of what is now Mt. Sterling. One account says the Wyandot had been in retreat when their leader, who was fatally wounded, ordered his men to stay and fight. Both parties fired shots across the creek at each other for several hours, with heavy casualties on both sides. Estill then divided his men into three groups and ordered one, under Lt. William Miller's command, to flank the rear of the Indian forces on the left, while Estill himself headed a group on the right and a third group held the center.

Miller's troops failed, one account holding that they panicked and fled the combat area. In any case, only four men remained in Estill's party when the Indians charged across the creek and overpowered them. Estill received three wounds, which left him too weak to continue fighting. It has been said that as Estill was leaving the battlefield a Wyandot attacked and killed him and that Joseph Proctor, who was uninjured, immediately shot and killed his captain's assailant. With only a handful of men left on each side and both commanders lost, the battle ended. The Wyandot, left in possession of the field, were considered victors.

See Bessie Taul Contwright, "Estill's Defeat or the Battle of Little Mountain," *Register* 22 (1924): 311-22.

ESTILL SPRINGS. Estill Springs was a large nineteenth century spa one-half mile from Irvine in Estill County, where the McAfee party, early explorers in Kentucky, had discovered five springs in 1773. Native Americans had used the springs for hundreds of years, and the site was a resting place along the Upper Blue Licks Prong of the Warriors' Path.

The property, first known as Sweet Springs at Estill Courthouse, was owned by Green Clay, who passed it on to his son Brutus. When William Chiles purchased the property in the 1840s, he constructed a large hotel, spacious enough to accommodate more than nine hundred guests. He also renamed the property Estill Springs. The waters were advertised as being "an elixir of nature" for invalids, and the resort as "a retreat where mirth and jollity reigns supreme." The Estill Springs resort was one of the more popular springs in Kentucky, every summer attracting visitors from throughout the state and region. During the Civil War, its grounds were used as the camp and recruiting station for the 8th Kentucky Federal Infantry. The resort's popularity began to fade in the early twentieth century. After the main hotel burned on December 16, 1924, the resort did not reopen.

See J. Winston Coleman, Jr., *The Springs of Kentucky* (Lexington, Ky., 1955); Ella H. Ellwanger, "Estill Springs: A Celebrated Summer Resort in Estill County," *Register* 9 (Jan. 1911): 45-53.

ESTILL'S STATION. Founded in 1780 by Capt. James ESTILL and his brother Samuel, Estill's Station was located approximately three miles southeast of what is now Richmond, Kentucky. Situated on the headwaters of Otter Creek, this settlement, along with Estill's New Station about two miles southeast of the original, represented one of the early population centers in Madison County. Established to aid and protect settlers in the region, Estill's Station was the temporary home of Green CLAY. Another of the station's residents, Monk Estill, James Estill's slave, probably saved the settlement from destruction. James Estill was killed at the Battle of Little Mountain, better known as ESTILL'S DEFEAT, on March 22, 1782. Samuel Estill, who lived in Madison County on his holdings on Little Muddy Creek, served in the Kentucky House of Representatives in 1795. Near the end of his life, he moved to his daughter's home in Tennessee, where he died in 1837. After Estill's Defeat, the station may have fallen into disuse as Kentucky became more settled and Indian threats diminished.

See William E. Ellis et. al., *Madison County: 200 Years in Retrospect* (Richmond, Ky., 1985).

ETHRIDGE, MARK FOSTER. Mark Foster Ethridge, general manager and publisher of the Louisville COURIER-JOURNAL and *Louisville Times*, was born in Meridian, Mississippi, on April 5, 1896. Ethridge began as a newspaper carrier and at the age of fourteen was spending leisure hours in the newsroom of the *Meridian Dispatch*, established by his father, William Nathaniel Ethridge, Sr., a local attorney. His mother, Mary (Howell) Ethridge, encouraged his interest, and in 1913, after high school graduation, he worked for a year at the *Meridian Star* before entering the University of Mississippi. In 1915, Ethridge went to Georgia as a reporter, first for the *Columbia Enquirer-Sun* and then the *Macon Telegraph*. After serving with the Navy during World War I, he returned to the *Telegraph* as city editor and in 1920 married Willie Snow (ETHRIDGE), a *Telegraph* staff writer. For the next fifteen years, Ethridge moved through a succession of key positions, including two years at the *New York Sun*, six years at the *Macon Telegraph*, brief stints with the Associated Press and the *Washington Post* and two years as president and publisher of the *Richmond Times Dispatch*. In 1936 Barry Bingham, Sr., brought Ethridge to Louisville as general manger of the *Courier-Journal* and the *Times*.

Ethridge arrived in Louisville an ardent New Dealer. He met Franklin D. Roosevelt in the early 1930s and by mid-decade the administration was consulting him often on southern policy matters. Like many native liberals, Ethridge embraced Roosevelt's 1938 declaration that the South was the "nation's Number 1 economic problem." His writings lamented the effects of farm tenancy, absentee ownership, illiteracy, and persistent poverty, placing much of the blame on the "colonial dependency" that the Northeast had "imposed" on the South after the Civil War. Ethridge's solution was an "aggressive liberalism" characterized by a dramatic expansion of the federal role in health care, rural housing, and a host of other areas. In 1944, disappointed by the apparent end of the New Deal, he lambasted Roosevelt for replacing Henry Wallace with Harry S. Truman as his vice-presidential running mate, a move Ethridge saw as a capitulation to southern reactionaries.

Ethridge's liberalism extended to racial issues. Throughout the 1930s and 1940s, he spoke out against the poll tax, denounced racial violence, and supported federal antilynching legislation. Yet, like many southern liberals, Ethridge believed that the South's system of racial segregation was unassailable; progress had to occur gradually within the framework of the "separate but equal" doctrine. When the U.S. Supreme Court repudiated this doctrine in *Brown v. Board of Education* (1954), Ethridge endorsed orderly desegregation, but remained critical of those, such as the Louisville activists Carl and Anne BRADEN, who called for a frontal assault against discrimination.

In 1941, Roosevelt appointed Ethridge the first chairman of the Fair Employment Practices Commission, an agency established to ensure equal job opportunities in war-related industries. Secretary of State James Byrnes asked Ethridge to report in 1945 on the status of new Communist governments in Romania and Bulgaria. Later, he made several official visits to Europe and the Middle East. A proponent of a vigilant anti-Communist foreign policy, Ethridge was also a critic of U.S. Sen. Joseph McCarthy and the anti-Communist hysteria of the early 1950s.

Ethridge retired from the *Courier-Journal* in 1963, but soon accepted a position as editor of *Newsday* in Garden City, New York. In 1965, he moved with his wife to Moncure, North Carolina, and until 1968 taught journalism classes at the University of North Carolina. Ethridge died on April 5, 1981, and was buried in Moncure, North Carolina.

ANTHONY NEWBERRY

ETHRIDGE, WILLIE (SNOW). Willie (Snow) Ethridge, a prolific author and humorist, was born December 10, 1900, in Savannah, Georgia. Her parents, William Aaron and Georgia (Cubbedge) Snow, moved the family to Macon, Georgia, while Willie was a child. In high school, she met Mark ETHRIDGE, a talented young reporter with the *Macon Telegraph*. During World War I, while Ethridge served in the navy, Snow became a *Telegraph* staffer, and she studied journalism and English at Georgia Wesleyan College and Mercer University in Macon. In 1920 she and Mark Ethridge were married.

Her earliest publications were in magazines, among them *Good Housekeeping* and the *New Republic*. The first of her seventeen books was *An Aristocracy of Achievement* (1929), a biography of Benjamin F. Hubert, a prominent black educator. Her first popular success was *As I Live and Breathe*, a spirited memoir published in 1937, the

year after Mark Ethridge became general manager of the *Louisville Courier-Journal*. During the family's twenty-eight years in Louisville, Willie Ethridge published ten additional books. Several, like *I'll Sing One Song* (1941), were engaging descriptions of life with her "roommate," Mark, and the four Ethridge offspring, Georgia Cubbedge, Mark Foster, Jr., Mary Snow, and William Davidson. "As American as cinnamon buns and as warm and spicy," the *New York Times* on March 7, 1937, said of Ethridge's domestic memoirs, which sometimes used gentle satire to dissect the male-controlled worlds of civic affairs and newspaper publishing. Critics praised her as a "vital new name in American humor" (*Christian Science Monitor*, February 11, 1948), a reputation that grew through five books, beginning with *It's Greek to Me* (1941), which recounted her husband's assignments in Europe and the Middle East as a United Nations commissioner and U.S. State Department troubleshooter.

Ethridge wrote serious works as well, including *Mingled Yarn* (1938), a prolabor novel about life in a southern mill town, and *Strange Fires* (1971), a study of Methodist cofounder John Wesley's love affair in colonial Georgia. It was her informal autobiographical volumes, however, that earned the respect of critics and the loyalty of a large readership. She moved from Louisville after her husband's retirement from the *Courier-Journal* in 1963, first to Garden City, New York, then in 1965 to Moncure, North Carolina. She died in Key West, Florida, on December 14, 1982; her body was cremated and the ashes scattered near Big Carpet and Cudjoe keys.

ANTHONY NEWBERRY

EVANS, HERNDON JULIAN. Herndon Julian Evans, journalist and publicist, the son of John G. and Roberta (Hamm) Evans, was born on December 22, 1895, in Morehead, Kentucky. When he was young his family moved to Frankfort, where he graduated from high school in 1914. Evans earned his degree in journalism from the University of Kentucky in 1921, after serving in the U.S. Army during World War I. He became state editor of the *Louisville Courier-Journal* in 1921 and worked for the Associated Press Bureau in Frankfort in 1922-23. Evans moved to Pineville, Kentucky, in November 1923, and in 1924 purchased the *Pineville Sun* with his partner Tilman Ramsey, remaining its editor until 1956.

Evans used the editorial page to promote the cause of eastern Kentucky, including conservation and reforestation projects, as well as the building of roads, lakes, state parks, and a tourist trade. During the spring of 1931, his articles documenting the coal miners' struggles in Harlan and Bell counties won Evans national recognition. Evans took the side of the mine owners and has been credited with presenting "the other side of the Harlan County coal strike." He wrote biting commentaries attacking outsiders who proposed solutions out of what Evans saw as a desire for publicity. Once he took critical aim at author Theodore Dreiser, who was interested in the miners' conditions in Harlan County and visited there.

In 1956 Evans moved to Lexington, Kentucky, where he became editor of the *Lexington Herald*. His column, "Thoughts of a Country Editor," was a popular feature. He wrote two books, *The Bluegrass Country* (1968) and *The Newspaper Press in Kentucky* (1976). Evans retired from journalism in 1967 and became director of public relations for the investment firm Dupree and Company, Inc.

In addition to journalism, Evans was involved in politics. He was director of publicity for the U.S. senatorial campaigns of Earle C. Clements in 1950 and Alben W. Barkley in 1954. In 1955 he worked with Bert T. Combs in Combs's unsuccessful gubernatorial bid in the Democratic primary. He is also known for helping organize the Kentucky Mountain Laurel Festival, held every May in Pine Mountain State Resort Park, where there is a lodge named in his honor.

Evans married Mary Elizabeth Downing in March 1923; they had one child, Mary. Evans died on February 25, 1976, and was buried in Louisville's Cave Hill Cemetery.

See Philip D. Supina, "Herndon J. Evans and the Harlan County Coal Strike," *FCHQ* 56 (July 1982): 318-35.

EVARTS, BATTLE OF. In February 1931 Harlan County coal operators made another in a series of many wage cuts, thereby further depressing already desperate living conditions and provoking a United Mine Workers (UMW) organizing drive in Harlan County; over 2,000 attended a rally in Pineville on March 1. Miners at the Black Mountain Coal Corporation and several other local mines were fired and evicted from company houses for joining the union. They congregated in the nearby noncompany town of Evarts, more than tripling that town's population. Starving miners looted several company commissaries and independent groceries. Some miners struck in sympathy with those dismissed. Numerous confrontations erupted between striking miners and mine guards and deputy sheriffs.

On May 5 ten deputies, riding in three cars, passed through Evarts to escort a nonunion miner from Verda to the Black Mountain mine. Two hundred yards beyond Evarts they were ambushed by perhaps three hundred concealed miners. Many shots were fired. One miner, Carl Richmond, and three deputies—Jim Daniels (the hated chief mine guard at Black Mountain), Otto Lee, and Howard Jones—were killed. On May 7 Gov. Flem D. Sampson (1927-31) dispatched 370 National Guardsmen to Harlan County. The strike then spread throughout the county and into Bell County. The National Guard halted all picketing, broke up miners' meetings, and arrested and charged forty-three miners with murder. By mid-June the strike had collapsed. Eight striking miners, including local UMW president William Hightower and local UMW secretary William B. Jones, were convicted

and imprisoned. Local coal operators, despite prounion federal legislation, prevented labor organization in Harlan County until 1938.

See John W. Hevener, *Which Side Are You On? The Harlan County Coal Miners, 1931-39* (Urbana, Ill., 1978).   JOHN W. HEVENER

EVE, JOSEPH. Joseph Eve, the U.S. chargé d' affaires to the Republic of Texas from 1841 to 1843, was born in Culpeper County, Virginia, on July 17, 1784. He first appeared on the Knox County, Kentucky, tax rolls in 1807. He made his home in Barbourville and eventually acquired land in Clay, Livingston, and Whitley counties as well. Eve served in the Kentucky House in 1810, 1811, and 1815, and as a state senator from 1817 to 1821. During the War of 1812, he earned the rank of colonel. In the presidential election of 1832, he was chosen as a presidential elector for the national Republican ticket and cast his vote for Henry Clay. He supported the Whig party in the elections of 1836 and 1840, and was rewarded after the election of William Henry Harrison in 1840 by being appointed chargé d' affaires to the Republic of Texas.

Eve favored annexation of Texas by the United States and was thus aligned with John Tyler, who had succeeded to the presidency after the death of Harrison. But this view also put him at odds with Secretary of State Daniel Webster. In 1843 Eve was recalled from his post in Texas for drawing on his future salary. On June 16, 1843, before he could return to Kentucky, Eve died in Galveston, Texas. He was married to Betsy Withers Ballinger.

EVERLY BROTHERS. The pop singers known as the Everly Brothers were born in Brownie, Kentucky—Donald Isaac on February 1, 1937, and Phil on January 19, 1939, the sons of country musicians Ike and Margaret (Embry) Everly. They made their radio debut as preteens on radio station KMA, Shenandoah, Iowa, working with their parents until they graduated from high school. In 1957 they joined the "Grand Ole Opry" in Nashville. The Everly Brothers sang close harmony in the style of Karl and Harty, but achieved their biggest hits with rockabilly numbers written by Felice and Boudleaux Bryant. Their records reached No. 1 on both country and pop charts. The brothers split up in 1973, but reunited ten years later.

See Douglas B. Green, *Country Roots: The Origins of Country Music* (New York 1976); Charles K. Wolfe, *Kentucky Country* (Lexington, Ky., 1982).   CHARLES F. FABER

EZELLE, SAMUEL. Samuel Ezelle, labor leader, son of Samuel and Augusta (Culley) Ezelle, was born July 16, 1920, in Evansville, Indiana. His parents, native Kentuckians, moved the family to Sturgis, Kentucky, in 1922, and to Madisonville in 1926. Ezelle graduated from Madisonville High School in 1938 and was a U.S. Air Force cadet during 1942-43. He received a bachelor of law degree from the University of Louisville in 1951.

In 1941 Ezelle became an iron worker, joining the union and working on the Kentucky Dam, the Pentagon, and many jobs in the Louisville area. In 1946 he was made research and education director for the Kentucky sector of the American Federation of Labor (AFL), and he became secretary-treasurer in 1952. After the merger of the AFL with the Congress of Industrial Organizations (CIO) in 1955, he became the executive secretary of the Kentucky State AFL-CIO. During 1952-72, he served as secretary-treasurer of the *Kentucky Labor News*. Ezelle was a vocal labor leader who helped defeat several local and state right-to-work laws that he believed would lower workers' wages. After twenty years as a union executive, he declined reelection.

Ezelle served as vice-president of American Health Profiles of Nashville, a provider of health examinations in mobile facilities, during 1972-76. In 1976 he became vice-president of Excepticon, Inc., a Kentucky-based corporation operating residential facilities for the mentally retarded in Indiana and Kentucky. From 1977 until his retirement in 1985, Ezelle was senior labor coordinator for the American Petroleum Institute in Washington, D.C.

Ezelle served on the board of trustees of the University of Kentucky and on the board of regents of Western Kentucky University in Bowling Green. He received over forty commissions from various Kentucky governors and two commissions from U.S. secretaries of labor. He worked for the U.S. State Department in Europe as labor education specialist for the Marshall Plan in 1952, and was guest and team leader for the Israeli union Histadrut on trips to Israel in 1956 and 1970.

Ezelle married Ruby Gordon Layman on September 16, 1939; they had one son, Sam IV. After a divorce, Ezelle married Dorothy Wheatley on December 16, 1967; they have two children, Kent and Dale.

F

FABULOUS FIVE. The 1947-48 University of Kentucky (UK) basketball team, perhaps the greatest Wildcat team in history, was known as the Fabulous Five. It posted a record of thirty-six wins and three losses, captured both the National Collegiate Athletic Association and Southeastern Conference (SEC) championships, placed seven members on the 1948 Olympic championship team, and was ranked first in the nation.

The starting lineup was Kenny Rollins and Ralph Beard at guard, Wallace Jones and Cliff Barker at forward, and Alex Groza at center. Their style of play was characterized by strong defense, tough rebounding, and a fast-break offense. Two guards who had been All-Americans in the 1945-46 season, Jack Parkinson and Jim Jordan (playing then for North Carolina), could not even make the starting lineup for the 1947-48 season. Nor could Joe Holland, an All-SEC forward in the 1946-47 season.

The Fabulous Five outscored opponents by an average of 69 to 44. During the regular season, they lost only to Temple University, by 1 point, and to Notre Dame University, by 9. They lost to the Phillips Oilers, an Amateur Athletic Union team, by four points in the finals of the Olympic trials.

It could be said that World War II helped make the Fabulous Five. Rollins, Groza, and Barker were military veterans, and they had improved their skills in competition in the armed services. Rollins, of Wickliffe, Kentucky, was the captain and the Fabulous Five's lone senior. Because of his navy service, he was twenty-four years old when the season began. Groza, who was born in Martin's Ferry, Ohio, was drafted into military service during his freshman season. He continued to play basketball while in the army, however, and was voted best service player in the nation. He returned from the army to become a three-time All-American and to lead the Fabulous Five in scoring. Coach Adolph RUPP called him the best rebounder he had ever seen. Barker, a native of Yorktown, Indiana, was twenty-seven, the team's oldest member. After playing one year, Barker enlisted in the Army Air Corps. His plane was shot down over Germany, and he spent sixteen months in a prisoner-of-war camp. During that time he played basketball and volleyball and developed his famous passing ability. When he returned to UK, he rejoined the basketball team.

Beard, who was born in Hardinsburg, Kentucky, in 1927, moved with his family to Louisville, where he led Male High School to the state championship in basketball. He went to UK on a football scholarship and only after several injuries tried out for basketball.

Wallace Jones, known as "Wah Wah," was born in Harlan, Kentucky. He got his nickname because his younger sister could not pronounce Wallace. In high school he set the national scoring record in basketball, starred in football, and was offered professional baseball contracts by the Chicago Cubs and the Boston Braves. At UK he lettered in baseball, basketball, and football, and earned All-SEC honors in football one year and in basketball three years. He also was an All-American in football his junior year and in basketball his senior year.

The Fabulous Five did not play as a unit until the twelfth game of the season, both because of injuries and because Jones was finishing the football season as the basketball season began. No other Wildcat team turned professional as a unit: Holland, a member of the Olympic team, replaced Rollins, and they formed the Indianapolis Olympians of the National Basketball League.

See Bert Nelli, *The Winning Tradition: A History of Kentucky Wildcat Basketball* (Lexington, Ky., 1984); Luke Walton, *Basketball's Fabulous Five: The Indianapolis Olympians* (New York 1950).

FAIRS. Fairs have been a part of the Kentucky cultural landscape since the nineteenth century. Derived from the English country fairs—themselves part of the tradition of itinerant, medieval European trade fairs—the Kentucky variety has generally been county-based, as is true across America. On a different scale are state fairs, such as Kentucky's, held annually since 1902, and the national or world's fairs in which Kentucky has participated since 1853. Louisville hosted the SOUTHERN EXPOSITION, a regional fair of impressive proportions held from 1833 until 1887. The first recorded fair held in Kentucky, which took place on Lewis Sanders's farm on Georgetown Road, north of Lexington, in 1816, may have been more a cattle show than anything else. Interest in livestock was a prime motive for the county-organized fairs, as indicated by the Kentucky Society for Promoting Agriculture, organized in 1816 in Lexington. In the late 1830s Kentucky fairs showcased other agricultural products and the fruits of homemakers' skills along with livestock.

A peak year was 1838, when fairs were held in twenty-one of Kentucky's eighty-eight counties. The number of fairs declined in the early 1840s, with only Bourbon County holding a fair in 1844 and 1845; an estimated 10,000 attended the 1845 three-day fair. By 1855, fairs were held in eleven communities, ranging from Crab Orchard to Paris. From 1850 to 1860, fifty-two agricultural associations were organized; one of them, the Mason and Bracken Farmers Fair Company, sponsored the Germantown Fair, which has been in continuous operation since 1854. The Civil War stopped Christian County's fair after 1860, but on October 20-23, 1869, the fair was back, with a balloon ascension and a fire department parade. In 1947, sixty-one local fairs were held in Kentucky; 1959, ninety-six; 1967, sixty; 1975, seventy-four; and 1989, eighty-seven.

Generated in the agrarian environment, the county and state fairs were the places and the occasions for judging outstanding agrarian development, with prizes given for the best livestock, the largest or best vegetables and fruit, the best preserves. The products of quilting contests were of particular renown in Kentucky.

Behind such county fairs was frequently a local agricultural association, such as the one that organized the first fair in Christian County in 1857, and the Henry Ridge Farmers Association, which in 1862 first held the Shelby County Fair, the second oldest in the state. Fayette County in 1870 chartered the Fayette Agricultural and Mechanical Association for Colored People to organize a fair. Similar organizations were formed in Shelby County in 1872 and Bourbon County in 1873.

Aside from the well-known eating delights—cotton candy being both the most easily consumed and the most enduring—fairs have offered a host of entertaining diversions, such as the ferris wheel (introduced at the 1893 Chicago World's Fair), "dodgem" cars, and other fast-spinning mechanical devices, largely fabricated out of American ingenuity. With the advent of television, shopping malls, and theme parks, county fairs and the state fair have lost some of their showcase value and economic purpose, but after reaching a low point in the 1960s they have bounced back as expressions of community pride and as annual occasions for pleasant, outdoor distraction.

See H. Clyde Reeves and Lawrence A. Cassidy, "Fairs in Kentucky," *FCHQ* 34 (Oct. 1960): 335-58; *Fairs and Fair Makers of Kentucky* (Frankfort, Ky., 1942).   RAYMOND F. BETTS

FALL, PHILIP SLATER. Philip Slater Fall, Protestant minister and educator, was born on September 8, 1798, in Brighton, England, the eldest son of James Slater and Katharine (Barratt) Fall. Fall's family emigrated to America in 1817, settling in Logan County, Kentucky. After the deaths of both parents, Fall moved to Franklin County in 1820 to teach. In the same year, he became a Baptist minister and married Anne (Nancy) Bacon of Franklin County. Their family eventually numbered ten children, but only six—James, Mary, Carrie, William, Elizabeth, and Albert—lived to maturity.

In 1823 Fall moved his family to Louisville, where he accepted responsibility for an academy and a small Baptist church. He began to study the teachings of the Rev. Alexander Campbell, ultimately leading to his conversion to the Campbellite movement, or Christian Church (Disciples of Christ) movement from the Baptist church. His congregation followed him and became the First Christian Church of Louisville. Fall established other Disciples churches (including the First Christian Church in Frankfort in 1832) and profoundly influenced the development of the new denomination in Kentucky and Tennessee. Sometime in the 1820s the Falls moved to Nashville. Returning to Frankfort in 1832, Fall took up farming and opened the Female Eclectic Institute. By the late 1850s, the

Falls were once more in Nashville. Southern sympathizers, they lost their son Albert in Confederate service. Fall retired in Frankfort in 1877. He died there on December 3, 1890, and was buried beside his wife in the Frankfort Cemetery. Philip's grandson Albert Bacon Fall was U.S. secretary of the interior and a figure in the 1920s Teapot Dome scandal.

See Martha Ann Burnley, "Philip Slater Fall," *Register* 7 (Sept. 1909): 62-68.

MARY MARGARET BELL

FALLEN TIMBERS, BATTLE OF. The Battle of Fallen Timbers on August 20, 1794, was a decisive engagement in which U.S. troops under Gen. Anthony Wayne defeated a force of Northwestern Indians on the Maumee River, near present-day Toledo, Ohio. The battle concluded two decades of Kentucky border warfare with the Indians. Wayne's army of more than a thousand regulars, augmented by 1,500 mounted Kentucky volunteers under Gens. Charles Scott and Thomas Barbee, was the third fielded by the United States since 1790 to overcome the Northwest Indians.

Hoping for a fight, the 1,300 Indians gathered at Fort Miami on the Maumee River, where they were being aided by British regulars and Canadian rangers. Wayne, having spent two years organizing and training his forces, took up the challenge and advanced against the Indians, who were positioned behind a mass of uprooted trees (hence, "Fallen Timbers"). Wayne ordered his regulars to charge with fixed bayonets, while directing the Kentucky mounted volunteers to carry out a flanking maneuver on his left. The Indians were routed in less than an hour, and the British in Fort Miami refused them aid. The British wanted to avoid war with the United States while locked in conflict with France in Europe, and to protect ongoing negotiations on the Jay Treaty.

For the United States, the Battle of Fallen Timbers led to agreements with the Indians, signed at Fort Greenville in 1795, to open the Northwest Territory for white settlement. The Jay Treaty provided for Britain to evacuate forts located within U.S. territory.

See Paul David Nelson, *Anthony Wayne: Soldier of the Early Republic* (Bloomington, Ind., 1985); Wiley Sword, *President Washington's Indian War: The Struggle for the Old Northwest, 1790-1795* (Norman, Okla., 1985).   PAUL DAVID NELSON

FALLS OF ROUGH. This small town in Grayson County, described by Robert M. Rennick's *Kentucky Place Names* as being "virtually extinct," is located on KY 110, seven miles below Rough River Dam State Park, on the south side of the Rough River. Named, in 1850, for the long steep rapids of the Rough, the village grew around a mill and farm built along the river. On June 9, 1821, Willis Green purchased the land at the falls from Benjamin Sebastian, who in 1790 had dammed the stream and built the first mill. Green built a new saw- and gristmill, along with a new dam in 1823. The mill, with submerged turbines and undershot wheel, was constructed around a frame building with stone burrs. Its horizontal gears were carved by hand from white hickory; the vertical gears were steel. A new stone dam was built in 1855 by Willis's nephew, Lafayette Green, but the original Green's Mill remained, and operations at the mill reached a height after a spur of the Elizabethtown & Paducah Railroad reached the falls in 1891. Employing two hundred people, nearly all the residents of the town, the Greens shipped cattle, hogs, poultry, Shetland ponies, cotton, and lumber on the new railroad. In the 1930s the farm began to cut back operations. After the timber on the land was depleted, the sawmill was dismantled and sold in 1941; employees bought the farm lands by 1945. Though the mill ceased to operate in 1965, the building, along with the general store and manor house, is still standing.

ELAINE M. HARRISON

FALLS OF THE OHIO. The Falls of the Ohio at Louisville, the only break in navigation on the Ohio-Mississippi rivers system between Pittsburgh and New Orleans, is actually a rocky rapids that falls some twenty-six feet over a two-mile distance. It is located between river miles 604 and 606 of the Ohio River as measured from Pittsburgh. Although river traffic at one time could navigate the falls during periods of high water, especially the spring and fall "rises," both goods and travelers had to be transported by land past this stretch of the Ohio during much of the year.

The falls is the result of an outcrop of resistant limestone in the riverbed, rich with fossil remains of the Devonian age (385 to 390 million years ago). The two main channels for navigating the Ohio through this outcrop were the Kentucky and Indiana (originally Indian) chutes. The original topography changed considerably in the nineteenth and early twentieth centuries when commercial interests removed limestone to pave streets and manufacture cement, as well as to improve navigation. Many boats traversed the falls even after it was bypassed by a canal in 1830, and wrecks were frequent. In 1881 the first of the dams that all but obliterated the falls was completed; an opening in the dam allowed vessels to pass through the Indiana chute. The McAlpine Dam of 1964 made no such provision and all traffic has since used the canal. The tamed falls now gives some hint of its former state only when high water spills over the dam. In 1981 Congress designated the falls and much land around it on both the Kentucky and Indiana shores a national wildlife conservation area.

See Richard L. Powell, *Geology of the Falls of the Ohio River* (Bloomington, Ind., 1970); Louis C. Hunter, *Steamboats on the Western Rivers: An Economic and Technological History* (Cambridge, Mass., 1949).

GEORGE H. YATER

FALMOUTH. Falmouth, the seat of Pendleton County in the Outer Bluegrass region of northern Kentucky, is located at the confluence of the main channel of the Licking River and its South Fork, at U.S. 27 and KY 22, near the center of the county. The town was settled around 1780 by Virginians who named it for their home town in Stafford County.

Until about 1830, the remains of a prehistoric earthen structure were visible in Falmouth, evidence of early Native American life at the site, strategically located at the river junction and surrounded by fertile fields. The river was a major thoroughfare into the Kentucky wilderness for the Shawnee, who traveled on it to raid Martin's and Ruddell's stations in 1780. According to unverified accounts, the Indian force, led by English Capt. Henry Bird, disembarked from their canoes at the river junction and traveled overland from that point to attack the settlements.

Once the Indian threat eased, the area proved attractive to settlement. John Waller, his brother-in-law John Cook, and William McDowell were the original landowners, having arrived from Virginia sometime after 1780. Waller, who named the town, received his land grant from Col. Holt Richardson, enrolling officer for Gen. George Washington. The city, which may originally have been called Forks of Licking, was chartered by the legislature as Falmouth on December 10, 1793. The exact location of Waller's grant was disputed and held up in litigation until after his death in 1823. The slow judicial process was probably responsible for holding back the growth of Falmouth in its early years.

As early as 1793 the town had a sawmill that shipped lumber regularly to the Cincinnati area, but Falmouth remained a small village with muddy roads until well after its founding. When the county was formed in 1798, construction was begun on a stone courthouse that was completed in 1800. Its replacement in 1848 was a two-story brick structure that was remodeled into a Victorian-style structure in 1884. The first church, a Baptist congregation, was organized by Alexander L. Monroe in 1792. By 1799 the first tavern, operated by James Wilson, was doing business. In 1814 the Pendleton Academy, a private school, was established. At several times in its history it united with the local public schools, and at the time of its closing in 1921 was known as the Falmouth Common School.

Until 1834 most of the merchandise brought into town was shipped down the Ohio River to Foster's Landing, brought overland by wagon to the Licking River, and then transported across the river on the Oldham Ferry to the Falmouth side. In 1834 the Kentucky General Assembly authorized the building of a suspension bridge, on which tolls would be collected to pay for its construction. By 1840 Falmouth had wool carding and packing establishments, as well as a hat factory. Pork was packed and shipped downriver. The Kentucky Central Railroad (later the Louisville & Nashville) from Covington in 1854 replaced the tedious overland route, and commerce developed with Covington. In the 1860s, it took only two hours to reach Covington from Falmouth traveling at a leisurely pace.

During the Civil War, eleven members of a local Union Home Guard unit fought a minor skirmish with twenty-eight Confederates at Falmouth on September 18, 1862. A larger Confederate contingent, led by Col. Basil Duke, returned to use Falmouth as a base of operations to attack the river town of Augusta on September 27, 1862. Stiff resistance by the Home Guard and heavier losses than expected caused the Confederates to return to Falmouth and withdraw to the Lexington area.

By the 1880s Falmouth was a flourishing trade center. The town had numerous businesses and was a major tobacco market. As tobacco depleted the soil, farmers diversified and many engaged in growing fruit or forage crops or keeping bees. The largest industry in Falmouth is the Fuller Manufacturing and Supply Company, which rebuilds automobile engines and parts.

The 1937 flood partially inundated the city, disabled the power plant, and interrupted rail service. Floods also caused extensive damage to the city in 1948, and on March 10, 1964, the Licking River flooded 75 percent of Falmouth and forced more than five hundred city residents to flee their homes. The town was struck by a tornado on April 23, 1968.

The population of the fourth-class city was 2,593 in 1970; 2,482 in 1980; and 2,378 in 1990.

WARREN J. SHONERT

FAMILY FARMS. The term family farm conjures up images of small subsistence patches on the sides of mountains in the eastern part of Kentucky, but it might just as well be represented by medium-size family-owned and -operated horse farms in the Bluegrass region or large grain farms in western Kentucky. Historically, the family farm has been the backbone of Kentucky, a cherished way of life for millions of Kentuckians whose descendants look back with misty eyes on the way things were and the way they feel things should have stayed. The small family farm in fact has not been preserved but has evolved into several forms, of which not all fully satisfy the family's economic needs as farms once did.

Writers on the subject, such as farmer-writer Wendell BERRY, agree that a family farm is one owned and operated by a family with the goal of making a good living for the family from the fruits of the farm. Like economist Marty Strange, many add that the family farm is a diversified operation, where there is no division between home and work, and the family is ultimately "responsible for and to its surrounding community." Family farming is not just a business. In these days when large farms are gobbling up smaller ones, Strange's test of a family farm asks whether the farmer feels pain at the loss of a neighbor rather than joy at the opportunity to acquire the neighbor's land. Berry and other writers see size, ownership, and historical continuity as part of the definition of the family farm. The definition must take into consideration the culture and values that have been handed down within farm communities. They make up the farmer's identity.

According to the 1987 farm census, Kentucky has nearly 93,000 farms. Of these, 75 percent were classified as small farms, ranging from one to 180 acres of land. These statistics suggest the persistence of small to medium-size farms. Since the 1982 census, however, Kentucky has lost 9,189 farms, most of them small to medium-size, a 40 percent decrease. At the same time, there has been a 30 percent increase in large, 1,000- to 2,000-acre farms. The large, single-crop farm seems to be gaining in Kentucky over the smaller, diversified farm.

Between 1940 and 1990 more than 4 million farmers nationwide quit farming for an assortment of reasons. Many farmers folded during the boom and bust years of the 1980s, when they were pushed toward buying more land than they could afford in response to promised world food markets that never materialized. When land prices inflated beyond everyone's imagination, the banks were left with the deeds to the land and the farmers had either to turn away from the land or work as tenants.

Wendell Berry thinks there are more fundamental reasons for the demise of the family farm. He says that Americans have fallen in love with materialism and the so-called dynamic economy, where bigger is always better, where cities are equated with culture, where work is considered drudgery, where people live for the weekend, where production is viewed as more important than the protection and conservation of the land, and where we would rather buy from a big, national company than revitalize our local communities. The trouble is that when small family farms buy into this version of the American dream, they find their expenses far outpacing their fluctuating, meager yearly incomes.

Does ownership by a family constitute a family farm? In 1990 more than 85 percent of Kentucky's farms were owned by individuals or families, with only 0.7 percent owned by corporations. However, more than half of Kentucky's 93,000 farms are operated on no more than a part-time basis; nearly 41 percent of the farmers spend more than two hundred days a year off the farm working other full-time jobs. These part-time farmers and their families, who work long hours to complete chores, are no longer able to work alongside each other. While juggling jobs and family schedules to keep the farm alive, they are deprived of the satisfaction that their ancestors derived from working the farm as a complete family operation. Conditions like these lead many to wonder why part-time farmers continue to farm. Despite these drawbacks, there still is something in the tradition and vision of the family farm that keeps thousands of them fighting the odds and hanging on "for one more year."

The tradition of the family farm in Kentucky has its roots in the Jeffersonian agrarian ideal, the needs of a new nation to settle and to develop the western frontier, and the diverse cultural backgrounds of the early settlers. Thomas Jefferson believed that agriculture was the fundamental employment of mankind and all other economic activities were secondary to it. He espoused the idea that the American nation ought to become and remain a nation of small husbandmen, with each family owning the farm it operated. Jefferson envisioned a landscape of small family-oriented farms clustered together, forming small communities. Within these communities, a way of life was to develop that defined the lifestyle and folkways of the Kentucky farmer.

Historically, Kentucky's family farms varied in size and design, depending on the cultural background of the farm family, the geography of the available farm land, the crops raised, and the stage of development of the particular farm. German-American families, for example, who settled the hills along the Ohio River near Maysville, Covington, and Louisville, tended small, fifteen- to thirty-acre farms as their ancestors did in the old country, where land was at a premium. These intensive-style truck farms used every part of the land to produce a variety of vegetables and fruits for the nearby urban markets.

The eastern mountains also produced small farms, but for different reasons. Lands that could be cleared for farming included mountain gaps, coves, hollows, ridges, and meadows where settlements predominated. Inadequate roads made transportation between neighbors and urban trading centers extremely difficult, but not impossible. Large surpluses of pork and corn were moved to markets in ingenious ways—pork through large hog drives up and over the mountains and corn through distillation as bottled spirits. Mountain herbs gathered during the late summer, before the crops were harvested, were bartered for products from outside communities. Subsistence farming, where nearly everything raised on the farm went to meet the needs of the family, was the rule for most mountain people. Families depended on their land, forest, and free-ranging livestock for their livelihoods.

In the early years of white settlement, small family farms were the norm. The rolling pasture and active culture of the Bluegrass region attracted another type of family farmer—the aristocratic second and third sons of Virginia family plantations. Men who had no prospect of inheriting their family's land established their own plantations in the Bluegrass. The early pioneer yeoman farmer predominated, however, typically owning from fifty to two hundred acres of land stocked with no more than a team of mules or horses, three or four low-grade milk cows, a sow and pigs, a few sheep, and an assortment of fowls. The early farmers depended on their family members, neighbors, and the community for help, guidance, and recreation. Local churches, country stores, post offices, and schools were the centers of the farm activities. Many people perhaps did not attend church on a regular basis, but the camp meetings brought in farmers from all over the county. Some came to worship but most came to visit with their fellow farmers.

The noun "neighboring," still used by farmers, refers not only to social visits but to the sharing of equipment and jobs with neighbors. Regional traditions encouraged sharing events such as barn raisings, quilting bees, butchering, threshing, clearing, log rolling, and brush burning. These activities were as much social occasions as work gatherings. The tradition continues to some extent in the sharing of some large equipment such as hay balers and other heavy, expensive machines, but the sense of community prevalent in the past is gone. With the advent of better transportation and communication systems, the consolidation of local schools, and increased migration of sons and daughters to urban centers, there has been a decline in the farmer's sense of community. Many part-time farmers report that the constraints of working two or more jobs leave little time for neighboring, and they consequently feel that they are out there trying to make it alone.

Many traditions continue, however, because they are relevant to the lives of people who practice them. The living traditions are a window into the values, concerns, and lifestyles of folk groups. The things a couple appreciated about their farm were being their own bosses, working where they lived, learning and doing a variety of chores during the yearly farming cycle, working side by side with each other and their children, raising their children in a safe and nurturing environment, and being able to continue the tradition of the family farm. Time after time, farmers referred to the earth as "she," with respect and admiration. Their stories and the photographs on their walls reflect the long-term commitment to their farm and the need to cherish it and pass it on within the family.

Old traditions persist and the new family folklore emerges to renew the family pride in the farming heritage: stories, jokes, names, games, music, celebrations, foods, buildings, quilts, carvings and other hand-crafted objects, garden and field design, yard art, and ritualized farm chores. A Kentucky tobacco stripping barn during stripping time becomes not a place of drudgery but a celebration by the whole family of the art of farming.

The expectations of farmers have changed. Older farmers considered it important not to be indebted, to buy equipment only when they had saved the cash for it. They believed in diversity instead of specialization, diversity as a hedge against blight and drought and as a way of naturally replenishing the soil. They also believed in maintaining and enjoying a quality of life not dependent on the mainstream popular culture. What a farm family sees as necessities has expanded, along with the American Dream. The rules of the game have changed, as they have for all Americans.

See W. F. Axton, *Tobacco and Kentucky* (Lexington, Ky., 1975); Wendell Berry, *The Gift of Good Land: Further Essays Cultural and Agricultural* (San Francisco 1981); Thomas D. Clark, *Agrarian Kentucky* (Lexington, Ky., 1977).

BOB GATES

FANCY FARM PICNIC. The Fancy Farm Picnic is an annual community gathering and political event held in the town of Fancy Farm, Kentucky. The town, approximately ten miles west of Mayfield in Graves County, was settled by Roman Catholics in the second quarter of the nineteenth century. The picnic, as an annual event, was initiated around 1880. Originally a local community affair, it gradually assumed significance as a speechmaking opportunity for state political figures. Kentucky politicians make a special effort to participate in this heavily publicized event.

The picnic takes place mainly on the grounds of Fancy Farm Elementary School, formerly the St. Jerome Parish School. Before 1956 the picnic was held on Wednesday in the last week of July, shortly before the August political primaries. Since 1956, when the General Assembly voted to hold the primary elections in May, the Fancy Farm Picnic has been held on the first Saturday in August, when politicians seek votes for the November elections. In addition to its political aspects, the picnic offers food, family activities, including popular bingo games, and raffle prizes. The picnic nets a substantial profit, which is used for community improvements in the Fancy Farm area. The consumption of 15,000 pounds of mutton, pork, and chicken at the 1982 Fancy Farm Picnic earned recognition in the 1985 *Guinness Book of World Records*.

FARISH, WILLIAM STAMPS, III. William Stamps Farish III, business magnate and horseman, was born in Houston, Texas, on March 17, 1939, to William S. and Mary Stovall (Wood) Farish, Jr. His father, an Army Air Corps pilot, was killed at an air show near Waxahachie, Texas, in 1942, and his mother married Hugo Neuhaus, in whose investment firm Farish worked after college. Farish attended St. John's School in Houston, St. Paul's in South Kent, England, and the University of Virginia at Charlottesville, where he studied history and political science.

Farish is president of the W.S. Farish Co. investment firm, which includes interests in oil and gas exploration, mining, cattle ranching, and television stations. The firm is named for his grandfather, who founded Humble Oil (now part of Exxon) and was president of Standard Oil. The Farish family is known for its thoroughbreds; Farish's aunt Martha Gherry owned and raced the champion Forego. Farish began buying thoroughbreds in 1965, and in 1979 he established Lane's End Farm in Woodford County, Kentucky, which in 1990 covered 2,000 acres. By 1990 Farish had bred eighty stakes winners, including Weekend Surprise, Clever Trick, Summer Squall (1972 Preakness winner), Bee Bee Bee, and 1987 Belmont winner Bet Twice.

Farish is a member of the boards of directors of Churchill Downs, Keeneland Race Course, and the Kentucky Derby Museum; a member of the executive board of the Breeder's Cup and chairman of the executive committee; vice-chairman and steward of the Jockey Club; and vice-chairman of the University of Kentucky Equine Foundation. Farish and his wife, the former Sarah Sharpe, have four children; they maintain homes in Florida, Texas, and Woodford County, where they have been the hosts of Queen Elizabeth II of England on her visits to Kentucky to inspect thoroughbreds.

See David L. Heckerman, "Will Farish: Kentucky Horseman," *Thoroughbred Record* 221 (July 1987): 1558-1559.

FARMERS' ALLIANCE. Farmers' Alliance was the general name for a number of kindred organizations that developed in the 1880s in response to falling prices for farm products and higher levels of farm debt and tenancy. In Kentucky the umbrella group was called the Farmers' and Laborers' Union, created in 1890 by merging groups sharing similar goals, notably the Agricultural Wheel and the Farmers' Alliance and Industrial Union, both of which had entered Kentucky in 1886. By 1891, the Farmers' and Laborers' Union had 125,000 members, most in the dark-tobacco belt of western Kentucky. The Farmers' Alliance advocated a number of reforms, including a graduated income tax, prohibition of monopolies, and government loans on nonperishable commodities stored in publicly owned warehouses. The Farmers' Alliance rapidly declined in the early 1890s after it became identified with the Populist party.

See Gaye Keller Bland, "Populism in Kentucky, 1887-1896," Ph.D. diss., University of Kentucky, 1979; Robert C. McMath, *Populist Vanguard: A History of the Southern Farmers' Alliance* (Chapel Hill, N.C., 1975); J.E. Bryan, *The Farmers' Alliances: Its Origin, Progress and Purposes* (Fayetteville, Ark., 1981). GAYE KELLER BLAND

FARMER'S LIBRARY. The *Farmer's Library*, Louisville's first newspaper, was established by Samuel Vail, who printed the first issue on January 19, 1801, under the title *Farmer's Library, or Ohio Intelligencer*, a name later shortened.

Vail, a twenty-two-year-old printer who had worked for the *Farmer's Library* newspaper in Fair Haven, Vermont, came to Louisville in 1800 to establish an anti-Federalist newspaper there. Vail relied heavily on the financial support of his longtime friend Matthew LYON, and money matters caused difficulty in printing at a time when Vail was becoming unpopular with readers for refusing to take part in the political fighting between parties in Kentucky. People turned to new competitors, such as the *Argus of Western America* (1806) and the *Louisville Gazette* (1807). When Vail became a supporter of Henry Clay and his "War Hawk" faction, he was politically alienated from Lyon, a pacifist, and funds became even shorter. Eventually Vail dissolved the *Farmer's Library*. Although the date of the final issue is not certain, the latest known copy is dated July 23, 1807.

Vail considered the possibility of starting a new newspaper and, in fact, advertised in St. Louis the coming of the *Missouri Correspondent & Illinois Gazette*; instead he joined the army.

FARMINGTON. Farmington is a brick, Federal-style residence built in 1810 by John Speed on his five-hundred-acre farm near Louisville. The one-story building on a raised English basement is thought to be an adaptation of a draft by Thomas Jefferson, although there is no evidence of any communication between Jefferson and Speed regarding the building of Farmington. The principal Jeffersonian elements are two octagonal rooms separated by a hall and flanked by square chambers. The outside dimensions of Farmington and the Jefferson plan are approximately the same. The source of the name Farmington was probably a house in Albemarle County, Virginia, owned by an uncle of Lucy Gilmer (Fry), wife of John Speed. One of their sons, Joshua Fry SPEED, was a close friend of Abraham Lincoln in New Salem, Illinois. Lincoln spent several weeks with the Speed family at Farmington in 1841, and he and Joshua often corresponded. Another son, James SPEED, was attorney general of the United States in Lincoln's cabinet.

The Speed heirs sold Farmington in 1865. In 1958 Historic Homes Foundation bought the house and five acres of surrounding land. The house, which was restored and opened to the public as a museum in 1959, is listed on the National Register of Historic Places.

See Janet Lowell Walker, "The Restoration of 'Farmington,' " *FCHQ* 33 (Oct. 1959): 287-95.

MARY JEAN KINSMAN

FARNSLEY, CHARLES P. Charles P. Farnsley, a lawyer who served as mayor of Louisville from 1948 to 1953, was born in Louisville on March 28, 1907, the son of Burrel H. and Anna May (Peaslee) Farnsley. He was one of the most innovative municipal officials of his era. The writer William Manchester in 1955 described Farnsley as "the most remarkable mayor in the city's history," as well as a "true eccentric" whose black string tie became his trademark. Farnsley also won election to the Kentucky House of Representatives in 1935 and 1937 and served in the U.S. Congress from January 3, 1965, to January 3, 1967. Farnsley studied political science and law at the University of Louisville and public administration at the University of Chicago, Columbia University, and the University of Kentucky. He was admitted to the bar in 1930.

As mayor of Louisville, Farnsley pioneered the use of an occupational tax to fund local projects, created the Louisville Fund (now the Louisville Fund for the Arts)—an umbrella organization that was among the first of its type in the country—and invigorated the Louisville Orchestra with new ideas and new programs. Farnsley turned admiration for the ideas of Thomas Jefferson, the French Physiocrats, and the Chinese philosopher Confucius into an array of innovative programs that earned him a national reputation. At his weekly "beef session," for example, citizens with problems or complaints could present them directly to the mayor and aldermen.

Farnsley understood earlier than most municipal officials that what would come to be called "quality of life" issues were related in significant ways to economic growth. In Manchester's words, Farnsley recognized that "culture, industry, and retail business are woven together—that the progress of one affects the progress of the others." With this insight, he paved streets, built small parks, installed street lights, raised city employees' salaries, and built community centers. He extended the city limits and put the city on a sound financial basis. Farnsley married the former Nancy Carter (whom he always called "Miss Nancy") in February 1937; the couple had two daughters and three sons. Farnsley died on June 19, 1990, and was buried in Cave Hill Cemetery.

See William Manchester, "Louisville Cashes in on Culture," *Harper's Magazine* 211 (August 1955): 77-83; George Kent, "Mayor Charlie Cuts Corners," *National Municipal Review* 38 (October 1949): 433-36, 442.   ALLEN J. SHARE

FAULKNER, HENRY LAWRENCE. Henry Lawrence Faulkner, painter, was born January 9, 1924, in Simpson County, Kentucky, to John Milton and Bessie Lee Faulkner. He was the tenth of thirteen children. After their mother's death, the children were sent to the Kentucky Children's Home in Louisville. In 1930 Faulkner went to live with foster parents Dan and Dora Whittimore near Falling Timber in Clay County. In 1939 Faulkner enrolled in the Louisville Junior Art School. In the fall of 1950 he enrolled in the writing program at Berea College for a few months. He won a scholarship to the Corcoran Gallery Academy in Washington, D.C., where he studied with Kenneth Stubbs, then spent three years at the Otis Art Institute in Los Angeles County. In 1955 Faulkner moved to Lexington, Kentucky, where he lived intermittently for the rest of his life. He spent most of his winters in Key West, Florida, where he became acquainted with Tennessee Williams, Bette Davis, James Herlihy, and Alice DeLamar, a wealthy heiress who became one of his principal patrons.

In July 1962 Faulkner purchased a small house on Arlington Avenue in Lexington and an eleven-acre farm eight miles south of the city. At a one-man exhibition at the Studio Club in Lexington in 1964, Faulkner acquired a new patron, Greene A. Settle, who eventually accumulated the largest collection of Faulkner's paintings. Inspired by the work of Chagall, Picasso, and Dali, Faulkner is best known for his oils and watercolors of fantasy still-lifes, landscapes, and animals, as well as for his poetry. His paintings have been exhibited in the High Museum of Art in Atlanta, Louisville's J.B. Speed Art Museum and Thor Gallery, Closson's in Cincinnati, and the Hemingway Gallery in New York City.

In 1968 Faulkner purchased a house at 462 West Third Street in Lexington. He died in an automobile accident two blocks from his home on December 5, 1981, and was buried in the Mt. Zion Missionary Baptist Church cemetery at Scottsville, Kentucky.

See Charles House, *The Outrageous Life of Henry Faulkner: Portrait of an Appalachian Artist* (Knoxville, Tenn., 1988).

FAYETTE COUNTY. Fayette is one of the three original counties formed by Virginia on June 30, 1780. With a land area of 280 square miles, the central Bluegrass County is bordered by Jessamine, Woodford, Scott, Bourbon, and Clark counties; the Kentucky River forms the southern boundary with Madison County. It was named for General Lafayette, who served in the Revolutionary War. The county's seat is LEXINGTON, created by Virginia on May 5, 1782.

The topography of the uplands is gently rolling until the three-hundred-foot limestone palisades of the Kentucky River are reached. Eighty-five percent of the land area is in farms, with 64 percent of farmland in cultivation. Fayette County is the center of the nation's thoroughbred industry. Equine sales in 1989 were $389 million, which represented 75 percent of all North American sales. The county ranks first in the state in agricultural receipts, derived from horses, tobacco, nursery and greenhouse crops, hay, and corn.

Fayette County was first inhabited by prehistoric Native Americans. Burial mounds were found in the vicinity of Hickman and Elkhorn creeks. Early pioneers arrived in 1774, when Jacob Baughman settled a claim on what was later known as Boone's Creek. Hancock Taylor, James Douglas, and John Floyd surveyed in the area in 1774. A party of explorers led by William McConnell arrived in 1775 and built one of the early stations. McConnell is credited with selecting the name for the settlement, Lexington, referring to the Massachusetts town's Revolutionary War activity. The Bryant family settled their station in 1776. Other early stations were those of Levi Todd, 1779, and William McGee, 1780.

The settlers brought horses with them and racing was both an occupation and recreation. The 1789 Fayette County tax rolls listed 9,607 horses and 56 stallions. By 1791 annual three-day race meetings were held in October over the Lexington course, and in 1797 Kentucky's first Jockey Club was organized at John Postlethwaite's Tavern. When wealthy Fayette Countians were not racing their horses, they were establishing farms and businesses, building fine homes, and constructing roads. Flatboats carried corn, oats, potatoes, whiskey, and tobacco down the Kentucky, Ohio, and Mississippi rivers to New Orleans. Many of these goods were produced by slave labor. The tax rolls in 1789 listed 2,522 slaves.

As early as 1785, farmers began importing shorthorn cattle to improve their herds. After the War of 1812, Spanish merino sheep were imported. Fairs and livestock shows were organized. The first fair was held in 1814 at Fowler's Garden near Lexington; the first cattle show at Sandersville on June 25, 1815. In 1870 there were 12,260 head of cattle and 7,843 hogs over six months of age. In the early 1900s the county was the site of the major livestock auction for central Kentucky. In 1990 Blue Grass Stockyards operated two sales rings, one on Lisle Road and the other on Angliana Avenue.

By the early 1780s, Fayette Countians were converting corn, wheat, and rye into whiskey. The business thrived for well over a hundred years. Among the early distilleries were the Ashland Distillery and Henry Clay Distillery, both on the Frankfort Turnpike; Stoll, Clay and Company at Sandersville; the Silver Springs Distillery on Yarnell Pike; Headley and Peck on Harrodsburg Pike; and Robert F. Johnson on Russell Pike where "Old Fashioned Hand-made Sour Mash Fire Copper Whiskey" was made. Manufacturing firms such as General Electric began operating plants in the county in 1947 and were followed by International Business Machines in 1956 and the Trane Company, manufacturers of air conditioning equipment, in 1963. In 1990 the county had more than fifty manufacturing plants.

Hemp was introduced at an early date. Nathan Burrowes, a county resident, invented a machine for cleaning it. The soil produced fine hemp and in 1870 the county grew 4.3 million pounds. The crop declined in the 1890s because of increased demand for tobacco and competition from imported hemp from the Philippines. In 1941, when the federal government saw a possible shortage of manila rope from the Philippines, farmers were encouraged to grow hemp once again for use in World War II. The crop declined again in 1945.

Tobacco, grown since the 1780s, replaced hemp as the major money crop in 1915. The amount of burley grown in Fayette and other central Kentucky counties led to the establishment of marketing facilities, and the first loose-leaf burley tobacco sale was held on January 9, 1905. By the 1940s the loose leaf burley market, with numerous warehouses, was among the world's largest. The demand for tobacco products has decreased, but the county is still the headquarters of the Burley Tobacco Growers Cooperative Association, an auction market, and tobacco plants such as Southwestern Tobacco Company, Inc., a processing plant since 1926, and C.F. Vaughn Company, Inc., since 1963 a stemming and redrying operation.

Transportation development began in 1797, when the legislature appointed Joseph Crockett to build a turnpike. The first stage route ran from Lexington to Olympian Springs in Bath County in 1803. Among the early turnpikes was the Lexington-Maysville, chartered in 1818 for sixty-four miles. It cost $426,400 to construct the macadamized road, thirteen tollhouses, and six covered bridges. Other turnpikes included the Lexington-Danville-Lancaster (1818), covering forty-two miles; and the Lexington-Harrodsburg-Perryville (1818), also covering forty-two miles. In 1817 Col. James Johnson established a stagecoach line from Lexington to Louisville, and Abner Gaines had a stagecoach running between Lexington and Cincinnati. In 1895,

Fayette County purchased the turnpikes. The state's first railroad, the Lexington & Ohio, extending from Lexington to Portland on the Ohio River, was chartered in 1830. In the 1850s, railroads connected the county both to adjoining counties and other areas of the state such as the Lexington–Big Sandy Railroad.

In 1990, the county continued to be a major transportation hub, served by two interstates (I-64 and I-75); U.S. 421, U.S. 60, U.S. 68, U.S. 27, and U.S. 25; KY 4 (New Circle Road), a four-lane beltline encircling the city; and Man O'War, a partial outer belt. Main line rail service is provided by CSX Transportation and thirty-seven inter- and intrastate common carriers.

In the early nineteenth century Fayette County became a center of culture and learning in the West. Its location and rich soil generated the wealth necessary to develop a landed aristocracy modeled after the Virginia Tidewater plantations. In 1784, Robert Boggs built a substantial stone house on the Athens-Walnut Hill Road. In 1787, Levi Todd built a twelve-room two-story brick home, Ellerslie, on the Richmond Pike. Other noteworthy early homes were Stoney Point, built in the 1790s on Parkers Mill Road; Hurricane Hall, still standing on the Georgetown Road, built before 1800 and known for its clothes presses and French wallpaper; Fairfield, John Bradford's home at the intersection of Iron Works Road and Russell Cave Pike; Winton, a brick residence built in 1823 for Samuel Meredith on Newtown Pike; Grasslands, between Walnut Hill and Jack's Creek roads, built in 1823 for Maj. Thomas Hart Shelby; and the Meadows, a sister house to Grasslands, built in the early 1830s for Dr. Elisha Warfield on Winchester Pike.

By the 1850s Italianate style had replaced the classical in home designs. Thomas LEWINSKI designed one of the nation's finest Italianate villas, Cane Run (later known as Glengarry), for Alexander Brand on Newtown Pike; it was completed in 1854. Five famous residences have been restored and are open to visitors: Ashland, Henry Clay's home on Richmond Road; the Mary Todd Lincoln House on West Main, the girlhood home of Abraham Lincoln's wife; the Hunt Morgan House in Gratz Park, built by John W. Hunt, Kentucky's first millionaire; Waveland, home of the Bryant family on Higbee Mill Road, and the Bodley-Bullock House in Gratz Park.

In 1988, tourism spending in the county was $372,330,211. Popular with tourists are the 1,030-acre Kentucky Horse Park on Iron Works Pike; the Red Mile, a historic standardbred track on South Broadway; Keeneland Race Course on Versailles Road; the Headley-Whitley Museum, a collection of jeweled bibelots on Old Frankfort Pike; and Raven Run Nature Sanctuary, off Old Richmond Road.

A number of federal installations are located in Fayette County. The Lexington Bluegrass Army Depot, established in 1942, covers 780 acres. The Federal Correctional Institute, on Leestown Road, is a medium-security prison with 519 inmates. The complex was built in 1934 as one of two federal narcotics hospitals in the nation and became a federal prison in 1974.

In 1974, the governments of the city of Lexington and the county of Fayette merged to form the Lexington-Fayette Urban County Government. The population of the county was 174,323 in 1970; 204,165 in 1980; and 225,366 in 1990.

See William H. Perrin, *History of Fayette County, Kentucky* (Chicago 1882).

WILLIAM WITHINGTON

FEDERAL AID TO SCHOOLS. Aid to Kentucky schools by the federal government began with a grant of $1,433,757 for its permanent school funds from a distribution of surplus funds to the states in 1836.

In 1862 Congress passed the Morrill Act, awarding land grants to states to promote the general welfare and national defense by establishing colleges that would teach agricultural and mechanical arts and military science and tactics. Kentucky had no federally owned land, so it received a grant of money in lieu of land. The University of Kentucky and Kentucky State University are land grant colleges. The Morrill Act land grants are the first examples of federal categorical (specific-purpose) aid to education. Grants to public schools for vocational education came with the passage of the Smith-Hughes Act of 1917, and aid has been extended through several subsequent acts, especially the Vocational Education Act of 1963. By the late 1980s, 479 institutions in Kentucky offered federally supported vocational training, including 252 public high schools and 72 area vocational centers.

Federal programs during the Great Depression of the 1930s are still in evidence throughout Kentucky in the form of school buildings constructed by the Works Progress Administration. The Civilian Conservation Corps (a forerunner of the Job Corps) and the National Youth Administration are other examples. A permanent outgrowth of the Depression is the school lunch program. Initiated in 1935, it has been expanded and serves virtually every school district in the nation. During the 1986-87 school year, Kentucky public schools received more federal dollars for school lunches than for any other program. Among federal programs surviving nearly fifty years after World War II is aid to areas where army bases or other federal activities have created special problems for school systems. (The Department of Defense operates two school systems in Kentucky, at Fort Campbell and Fort Knox.)

During the cold war the launching of the first Soviet Sputnik on October 4, 1957, led Congress to declare that "the security of the nation requires the fullest development of the mental resources and technical skills of its young men and women." Accordingly, it passed the National Defense Education Act, intended to identify talented students and encourage them to prepare for careers that would strengthen the defense capacity of the nation. Among other provisions, the act granted federal funds for strengthening science, mathematics, and language instruction and for promoting guidance counseling and testing services. This was the first categorical aid for academic school subjects. In Kentucky the most enduring effect of the act has been guidance counseling programs in secondary schools.

The Elementary and Secondary Education Act of 1965 (ESEA) was a part of President Lyndon Johnson's War on Poverty. Funds appropriated by this act were far greater than any previously set aside for elementary and secondary education. The most significant part of ESEA was title I, aimed at meeting the educational needs of poor children. States such as Kentucky with much poverty received substantial federal funding. ESEA title I became chapter 1 of the Educational Consolidation and Improvement Act of 1981 (ECIA). Twenty-eight other educational programs were consolidated into a block grant in chapter 2 of ECIA.

Civil rights legislation enacted to ensure equal treatment has had a significant impact on Kentucky schools since the mid-1960s. The Age Discrimination in Employment Act of 1967, as amended in 1986, prevents discrimination in employment based on age and invalidates compulsory retirement for age, negating provisions of the Kentucky tenure law by which teachers lose tenure upon reaching age sixty-five. The Bilingual Education Act protects children of limited English-speaking proficiency. Modest funding is available for bilingual programs. The only civil rights legislation carrying substantial funding is that prohibiting discrimination against the handicapped—section 504 of the Rehabilitation Act of 1963 and the Education of All Handicapped Children Act of 1975. The latter act distributes about $1 billion nationally each year to assist in the provision of educational services to various categories of handicapped schoolchildren. In accepting federal funds, school districts agree to a rigorous set of federal regulations and procedures to be followed in the testing, placement, and education of students with handicaps. These funds are making services available to thousands of Kentucky school children.

During the 1986-87 school year $171,475,187 in federal funding was allocated to elementary and secondary education in Kentucky and distributed as follows: school lunch, $75,836,100; chapter 1 (ECIA), $57,607,113; handicapped aid, $21,455,935; vocational education, $14,508,806; bilingual education, $1,736,149; impact aid, $331,084.

See James W. Guthrie and Rodney J. Reed, *Educational Administration and Policy* (Englewood Cliffs, N.J., 1986); Charles F. Faber et al., *School Law for Kentucky Teachers and Administrators* (Lexington, Ky., 1986).   CHARLES F. FABER

FEDERAL HILL. Federal Hill, the home of John Rowan, jurist and congressman, is located in Bardstown, Nelson County, Kentucky, on land given to him by his father-in-law. Construction of the Georgian-style mansion began in 1795 and was completed in 1818. It was named in honor of the Federalist party. Undocumented legend maintains that the house may have been the inspiration for Stephen Foster's song "My Old Kentucky Home, Good-Night!" published in 1852.

The main front wing of the house is built of native brick. It has a basement and three major rooms on each floor. A wide central passage ends in stairs in the rear, rising to a landing on the top floor, where a single room is finished under the roof slant. The back service wing is made up of two small chambers, with kitchen and smokehouse behind them. A covered walk from the kitchen gave access to the dining room by an outside door. The house is remarkable for its balanced front, impressive proportions, large windows, and subtle detail. The center entry portal is decorated with a flat-topped, Federal-style door surround, gouge-carved with swags and star medallions. The entryway's detached side lights and the matching three-part window at the second level, center, show the influence of Maryland examples of the early nineteenth century.

The house was extensively damaged by fire about 1839. The contract for repairs, dated 1840, stipulated that the master woodworker Alexander Moore was to make all repairs to the interior and exterior "in the fashion and manner in which it formerly existed . . . before it was burned." Moore may have been responsible for the original woodwork details and some design elements between 1815 and 1818, thus having intimate knowledge of the original finish.

Judge Rowan died in 1843 and left Federal Hill, in trust, to his son, John Rowan, Jr. At his death in 1855, John Rowan left his wife, the former Rebecca Carnes, with a family of ten children. She was mistress of Federal Hill until her death in 1897. Madge (Rowan) Frost, the granddaughter of Judge Rowan, sold the landmark to the state of Kentucky in 1921 to ensure "preservation forever as a State shrine of Home." A popular subscription raised the purchase funds. The legislature set up the eight-member My Old Kentucky Home Commission to take immediate possession and begin restoration of the house and grounds. The dedication took place on July 4, 1923, and the commission maintained and operated the estate as a state historical shrine until 1936, when the Division of State Parks took over.

See Randall Capps, *The Rowan Story* (Bowling Green, Ky., 1976).

FEE, JOHN GREGG. The Rev. John Gregg Fee, evangelical abolitionist, was born September 9, 1816, in Bracken County, Kentucky, the son of John and Sarah (Gregg) Fee, who were slaveholders. Fee received his B.A. from Augusta College near his home in Augusta, Kentucky, and in 1842 enrolled at Lane Theological Seminary in Cincinnati, scene of a rebellion in 1834 by abolitionist students who walked out to protest pro-slavery policies. There Fee formulated the religious principles of his lifelong fight against slavery and for social equality. As a worker for the American Missionary Association, he founded antislavery churches in Lewis and Bracken counties with the help of his wife, Matilda Hamilton, whom he had married on September 16, 1844.

Fee's attacks on slavery, from the pulpit and in print, attracted the attention of emancipationist Cassius Marcellus Clay, who regarded Fee as a useful political ally. Clay invited the minister to southern Madison County, where Fee was to be pastor of several new free churches. In 1854 Fee settled in Berea on ten acres of land that Clay gave him. Fee attracted many followers in his new ministry. But in 1856 his alliance with Clay was shattered when the two men, speaking at a Fourth of July Republican rally, disagreed publicly on the Fugitive Slave Law. Without Clay's protection, Fee was threatened by local mobs but continued to preach his "incendiary" views. By 1859 Fee proposed an abolitionist colony in Berea with a coeducational, integrated college.

John Brown's raid on Harper's Ferry frightened slaveholders all over the South, not least in Madison County, Kentucky, where, in December 1859, sixty planters banded together to drive Fee and his workers from the state. Although the Bereans appealed to Gov. Beriah Magoffin (1859-62), they were banished. Fee and his family settled near Cincinnati, but throughout the war he repeatedly tried to return to his native state. On several occasions he was mobbed by irate citizens—even in his hometown—and threatened with death if he continued his work. Suffering from ill health and despondent at the loss of his youngest child, who had died as a result of exposure during their exit from Kentucky, Fee persevered, holding immediate emancipation meetings and raising funds to purchase land for the college in Berea, even though his return to Kentucky was uncertain.

In 1864 Fee found a new missionary field at Camp Nelson, Kentucky's foremost military camp for black soldiers. Camp Nelson also attracted thousands of black women and children fleeing from slavery. Fee set up schools, founded a church, and administered a refugee camp for the dependents of black soldiers. Torn between his work at Camp Nelson and his mission at Berea, Fee finally opted for the latter, but he invited many people from Camp Nelson to settle in Berea, promising they could purchase land there. Again he proposed a school where men and women, black and white, could study together as equals. This plan was realized in Berea by 1866; by 1869 the new school became Berea College, and the town of Berea, colonized as part of Fee's total plan for integrated education in an interracial society, burgeoned. Throughout the 1860s, Fee labored for recognition of black equality, speaking in favor of black suffrage and advocating civil rights legislation. In Berea, Fee initiated a program of "interspersion," in which blacks and whites bought farm land and town lots in the same neighborhoods.

In his old age Fee's influence waned. Some of his followers repudiated his strict views on baptism by immersion and many more opposed his radical position on social equality, an anathema in America's Jim Crow era. Although Berea College flourished, the policies Fee had implemented were gradually phased out: During his presidency, beginning in 1892, William G. Frost completely revised the mission of Berea College. Nevertheless, Fee fought for social equality in Berea and across the nation until his death on January 11, 1901. He was buried in the Berea Cemetery.

See John G. Fee, *Autobiography of John G. Fee* (Chicago 1889); Richard Sears, *The Day of Small Things: Abolitionism in the Midst of Slavery* (Lanham, Md., 1986).   RICHARD SEARS

FERGUSON, CHAMP. Champ Ferguson, Civil War guerrilla, was born on a branch of Spring Creek near Albany, Clinton County, Kentucky, on November 29, 1821. He was the eldest of ten children and grew up along the Kentucky-Tennessee border in the Cumberland Mountains. In 1843 Ferguson married a woman named Ann, who died a few years later. In 1848 he married Martha Owens, also a native of Clinton County, and they had a daughter, Ann, in 1849.

Caught up in the fluid violence of the border region during the Civil War, Ferguson excelled as a guerrilla in the Kentucky-Tennessee area. Occasionally claiming respectability by riding with Gen. John Hunt Morgan's Confederate raiders, Ferguson spent most of the war commanding, with the self-commissioned rank of captain, an independent guerrilla company. He was declared an outlaw by the Federal authorities in Kentucky and threatened with summary execution if captured. Ferguson survived the war and returned to his prewar home in White County, Tennessee. Many other guerrillas were given amnesty, but Ferguson was arrested on May 26, 1865, and charged with fifty-three counts of murder before a military court in Nashville. The trial lasted from July to October 1865 and was reported daily in the Nashville newspapers. Ferguson was found guilty and on October 10, 1865, he was sentenced to be hanged. The sentence was carried out on October 20, and his body was turned over to his wife and daughter. Ferguson's last request was to be buried at his home in White County on a branch of Calfkiller Creek near Sparta, Tennessee.   JAMES MARTIN

FERGUSON, RICHARD BABINGTON. Richard Babington Ferguson, an early figure in medicine in Louisville, was born in 1769, in Londonderry, Ireland. When he arrived in Louisville in 1802, Ferguson intended to continue down the river to New Orleans but, at the urging of a friend and the flip of a coin, decided to remain in Louisville. There he married Elizabeth Aylett Booth on February 3, 1803. They had seven children.

In 1809 Ferguson, a practicing physician, assisted Drs. William Galt and John Collins in amputating the leg of Gen. George Rogers Clark, who survived despite the lack of anesthesia and antiseptics. A fife and drum band was assembled to play martial music outside the room where the surgery took place.

Ferguson helped organize Louisville's public health system and in 1817 became the only practicing physician on the board of Louisville Hospital, where he served in an administrative capacity until his retirement. In 1841 he become the first president of the Louisville District Medical Association, and he was named president of the boards of Jefferson Seminary and the Hibernian Benevolent Society. An active church member, he helped found Christ Church Cathedral in Louisville.

Ferguson died on April 9, 1853, and was buried in Cave Hill Cemetery.

See Evelyn Crady Adams, "Dr. Richard Ferguson (1769-1853), Pioneer Surgeon of Louisville, Attended General George Rogers Clark," *FCHQ* 36 (April 1962): 177-83.

FERRIES. While Kentucky was still part of Virginia, that state's legislature authorized the establishment of nine ferries in Kentucky, on the Ohio, Cumberland, and Kentucky rivers. The county courts were given control of ferries. They could exempt ferry keepers from county taxes, road duty, or any other public service, as well as authorize the operator to establish a tavern at the ferry. The ferry house served as a shelter in periods of high water, ice, or storms. Settlements often grew up around the ferry sites. Col. Richard Callaway put the state's first ferry into operation at Boonesborough on the Kentucky River in 1779.

Except for a few place names, ferries are not particularly well remembered in Kentucky history. Only a few have carved niches for themselves: Shryock's ferry, the St. Louis Transfer Train ferry, the ferry at Henderson, Clay's ferry, and the Valley View ferry across the Kentucky River between Fayette and Madison counties.

Except for those on the largest rivers, ferries were pulled across after attaching the boat with a sliding hitch to a rope or metal cable extending from bank to bank. This type was known as a current ferry because the rope or cable was used to counter the effect of the river's current. It was such an excellent solution for crossing smaller rivers that it was seldom replaced by steam power. At major river crossings, "teamboat" ferries, which relied on horse power, were developed. One to eight horses walked a treadmill or pushed a sweep around a capstan whose motion was used to move a wooden paddlewheel on the boat. This type of ferry was in operation at Covington in 1825 when the Marquis de Lafayette crossed the Ohio River during his grand tour of the western United States. The teamboat was introduced about 1815 and had virtually disappeared by 1835. It was replaced by the steam engine, which ultimately gave way to the gasoline- or diesel-powered ferry.

Early ferries were simple boxlike affairs designed to carry only one or two horses and their riders. Larger ferries had a ramp to facilitate loading of wagons and buggies. Typical nineteenth-century fares were: a person, 5 cents; a person and a horse, 10 cents; horse and buggy, 25 cents; buggy with two horses, 30 cents. The size of ferries grew along with the size of loads. A train transfer ferry in Kentucky operated across the Mississippi River from 1871 until 1911. The transfer ferry linked the St. Louis & Iron Mountain Railroad in Belmont, Missouri, with the Mobile & Ohio (M&O) Railroad in Columbus, Kentucky. A steam hoist lifted the cars, and the trucks (wheels) of the railcar were changed to fit the track gauge. After the M&O was extended to Cairo, Illinois, the train transfer ferry was used by the Nashville & Chattanooga (Green Line) until 1911.

In 1987 there were nine functioning ferries in Kentucky. The VALLEY VIEW ferry on the Kentucky River is generally acknowledged as the state's oldest continuously operating business, dating from 1785. A ferry has operated at Augusta, Kentucky, in Bracken County, since 1800. The Anderson ferry at Covington, Kentucky, is on the National Register of Historic Places.

The Buckeye, connecting Rabbit Hash, Kentucky, and Rising Sun, Indiana, was established in 1983. A barge pushed by a towboat on the Mississippi connects Hickman, Kentucky, and Dorena, Missouri. The Turkey Neck Bend ferry began operation across the Cumberland River in Monroe County in 1968. Two of the three Green River ferries operate in the Mammoth Cave National Park. Both the Mammoth Cave ferries and the Houchins ferry are sidewheelers. The ferry at Rochester, Kentucky, in Butler County also crosses the Green River.

See Sarah Bird Wright, *Ferries of America* (Atlanta 1987); J. Winston Coleman, *Stage Coach Days in the Blue Grass* (Louisville 1935).

J. ALLEN SINGLETON

FERRILL, LONDON. London Ferrill, Baptist minister, was born into slavery in Hanover County, Virginia, around 1789. Ferrill was apprenticed to a carpenter as a child. Converted at age twenty, he decided to become a Baptist minister despite a Virginia law forbidding slaves to be baptized or ordained. Though he possessed little formal education, he soon demonstrated an unusual gift for preaching. Awarded his freedom at his owner's death, Ferrill moved with his wife to Lexington, Kentucky, around 1815. There his exemplary lifestyle and conservative nature quickly won support among the white power structure. Invited to join First African Baptist Church, the oldest black church in Kentucky, Ferrill refused, citing its irregular relationship with white Baptists. Eventually called as pastor of First African and encouraged by white Baptists to accept the position, Ferrill received official ordination in 1821, and in 1824 his church entered the Elkhorn Baptist Association.

Over the next thirty years, Ferrill became the dominant black minister in central Kentucky, as First African Baptist grew to be the largest black congregation in the commonwealth, with 1,820 members. During his ministry Ferrill baptized more than 5,000 people. He started a school for children of church members in the early 1830s. The Ferrills set examples for the entire community, adopting two children to whom the couple eventually left their estate. During the famous 1833 cholera epidemic, when his wife became one of the victims, Ferrill selflessly nursed the sick of both races. He became known for his phrasing in conducting the marriage ceremony: realizing the tenuousness of slave marriages, Ferrill pronounced couples wedded until parted by "death or distance."

Ferrill died on October 12, 1854.

See J.H. Spencer, *History of Kentucky Baptists* (Cincinnati 1885).   MARION B. LUCAS

FEUDS. In the decade before the Civil War and the half-century following, a series of feuds swept through mountainous eastern Kentucky like a plague. In several instances county government came to a standstill and law enforcement became impossible. State troops were repeatedly called into the region to protect lives and to permit courts to operate, and on one occasion relations with neighboring West Virginia became so bitter because of a border feud that fighting between the two states was feared.

The feuds were not as violent, nor as bloody, as the national press reported at the time, and much of the resulting literature is based more on legend than fact. But the feuds were sufficient to reinforce Kentucky's unfortunate reputation as "the dark and bloody ground," and to paint a lasting and hurtful image of the eastern Kentucky mountaineer as an uncouth hillbilly with a slouch hat and overalls, full beard, rifle, whiskey jug, and a demeanor characterized as "dull when sober, dangerous when drunk."

Writers, historians, sociologists, economists, and psychologists have tried to explain why the feuds, pitting family against family, clan against clan, erupted only in the relatively limited area of eastern Kentucky. Some have attempted to trace the feuds to the Civil War and animosity between returning enemies, but there are notable exceptions to this time frame. The Hill-Evans feud flared in 1824 and sputtered out in 1852. The bloody Baker-White feud, sometimes called the Clay County war and probably the largest and longest of the feuds, began five years before the Civil War and lasted, in one form or another, until 1932.

Some sociologists have blamed the feuds on the isolation of the hill counties and the negligible influence of churches and schools. Yet neighboring western West Virginia, southwestern Virginia, western North Carolina, and eastern Tennessee had the same type of terrain and suffered similar isolation, and none fell victim to the feud virus as did eastern Kentucky. The settlers of all these regions shared a Scotch-Irish background, but there is no evidence that feuds sprang from clan rivalries brought from the old country. Nor did the return of

Rebel and Union veterans to other mountain regions spark the feuds that tore eastern Kentucky apart.

The mountaineer's fondness for firearms undoubtedly stemmed from a frontier dependence on rifles for food and protection against Indians. After the frontier had been tamed, families living far from the county sheriff often had to depend on their skill with a rifle for self-protection. The mountaineer also faced economic and cultural changes following the Civil War. Eastern land companies were buying up great tracts of the hills for timber. Coal mines were opening, and railroads were cutting into the heart of the mountains, bringing new manners and customs. In at least one instance (the Hatfields and McCoys), disputes over the title to land played a part in the feud. The mountaineer had to find methods to adjust to changing conditions without giving up familiar ways and traditions. The combination of these social and economic factors, the scarcity of schools and churches, the weakness of law enforcement, the pervasive influence of family, and the sensitive pride of people threatened with unfamiliar outside forces—all posed a potential for conflict that seemingly minor disputes could ignite. The Evans-Hill feud began when Dr. Hezekiah Evans allegedly mistreated a slave he had hired from Dr. John Hill. Hill got the slave back through trickery, Evans lashed out with angry words, and the thirty-year Hill-Evans feud was on. By some accounts, the Clay County war began when one man called another's dog a yellow cur. The French-Eversole feud of Perry County, fought between forces of rival merchants, began over a false story stemming from jealousy over a woman. According to some accounts, Harlan County's Turner-Howard feud flared when one of the Howards charged that a Turner "spoke badly to Mama."

Whatever the causes, the feuds took a bloody toll for half a century. At one point, the Hatfield-McCoy fray brought Kentucky and West Virginia into a legal battle settled only by the U.S. Supreme Court. Rowan County's Martin-Tolliver feud proved so destructive that a move was begun in the state legislature to abolish the county—but no surrounding counties wanted any part of it. For forty years local delegations periodically traveled to Frankfort to ask for state troops to rescue law and order from the feudists. When Governor-elect William Goebel was assassinated in 1900, some accused a feudist who was in Frankfort seeking a pardon for a murder he had committed in the Clay County war.

The results of the feuds were tragic, both for eastern Kentucky and for the state as a whole. Hundreds of people, including civic and political leaders, were killed, other hundreds injured. Education languished. Businesses were destroyed. The image of the Kentucky mountaineer in the eyes of the nation became that of a backward, drunken killer, an image that in turn tarnished the reputation of the entire state and earned for eastern Kentuckians the resentment and contempt of other Kentuckians. The influence of eastern Kentucky in state affairs was diminished, adding to the cultural isolation of the region, depriving it of state support for the roads and schools it needed, and perpetuating its reputation for violence.

See Altina L. Waller, *Feud: Hatfields, McCoys, and Social Change, 1860-1900* (Chapel Hill, N.C., 1988); Charles G. Mutzenberg, *Kentucky's Famous Feuds and Tragedies* (New York 1917); James C. Klotter, "Feuds in Appalachia: An Overview," *FCHQ* 56 (July 1982): 290-318.

JOHN ED PEARCE

FIELDS, WILLIAM JASON. William Jason Fields, governor during 1923-27, was born in Willard, Carter County, Kentucky, on December 29, 1874, to Christopher C. and Alice (Rucker) Fields. He attended the University of Kentucky, then farmed for several years and was a drummer for Crump and Fields, an Ashland wholesale grocery company. On October 10, 1893 he married Dora McDavid; they had six children. Running for a seat in the U.S. House of Representatives in 1910, as "Honest Bill from Olive Hill," Fields won the first of seven consecutive terms (1911-23). He served on the Military Affairs Committee.

In 1923 the Democrats were left without a candidate for governor of Kentucky when J. Campbell Cantrill suddenly died in early September, after besting Alben Barkley in a bitter fight for the Democratic nomination. Barkley refused the candidacy, and the Democratic Central Committee chose Fields to oppose Republican Charles I. Dawson. Fields resigned his House seat when he won a 1923 landslide victory, 356,035 to 306,277. After he left the governorship in 1927, he failed to regain his seat in the U.S. Congress. Admitted to the bar in 1927, Fields served as commonwealth's attorney for the 37th District during 1932-35 and practiced law in Louisville. Appointed to the Workmen's Compensation Board by Gov. A.B. Chandler (1935-39), Fields held the post until the Simeon S. Willis administration (1943-47). Fields moved to Florida in the 1940s, then returned to Carter County, where he farmed, was a realtor, and practiced law until his death at Grayson, Kentucky, on October 21, 1954. He was buried in Olive Hill Cemetery.

Fields kept both liquor and dancing out of the executive mansion. He was accused of nepotism in filling offices but allotted only lower power positions to his sons. In his 1924 message to the legislature, he called for a $75 million bond issue for highways, the upgrading of the Morehead and Murray normal schools, a tax increase of three cents per gallon on gasoline, and payment of the floating public debt. Opposition came from within his party, chiefly from the Percy Haly–Robert Worth Bingham faction, and one of Fields's few successes was passage of the bond issue—$50 million for roads, $25 million for education and penal and charitable purposes. In the 1924 general election, however, the voters killed the bond issue, despite a determined campaign by the governor.

Fields was more successful in the 1926 session, as the legislature passed a number of bills to implement his plans for reorganizing the state government. Creation of the state Purchasing Commission was perhaps his most notable accomplishment. The gasoline tax was raised to five cents per gallon to support the road fund, but Fields was not able to get approval of a bond issue for education. The state trade school for blacks at Paducah was established in the 1926 legislature, as was the Kentucky State Parks Commission. Unable to unite his factious party, Fields was blamed for corrupt practices and an excessive number of pardons.

See Paul Hughes, "William J. Fields," *Louisville Courier-Journal Magazine*, July 2, 1950.

FILMS. Of the hundreds of commercial films set in the South, Kentucky has been the subject of several score. In the earliest silent films, Kentucky's history as a border state divided by the Civil War provided an ideal plot for short features, such as the fifteen-minute *On Kentucky Soil* (1911), which required easily recognizable and highly dramatic material. The short film *Pauline Cushman—Federal Spy* (1913), dramatized wartime adventures. Most of the films, such as *Two Kentucky Boys* (1917) and D.W. Griffith's *In Old Kentucky* (1909), added the themes of sectional and familial reconciliation then so popular in literature. In numerous adaptations of *Uncle Tom's Cabin* (especially the productions in 1914, 1918, and 1927), Kentucky served in sharp contrast to the lower South as the setting for the protagonist's almost idyllic antebellum home, just as in the Harriet Beecher Stowe novel.

Interested in local color for the Depression era's escapist films, Hollywood studios in the 1930s produced several comic and musical films with Kentucky themes. The well-known team of Bert Wheeler and Robert Woolsey appeared with Willie Best in the midst of a stereotypical southern mountain feud in RKO's *Kentucky Kernels* (1935). *Kentucky Moonshine* (1938), perhaps one of the Ritz Brothers' best films, provided an irreverent look at hillbilly music. The horse-racing scene furnished a more prosperous setting for the B-picture *Kentucky Blue Streak* (1935) and the well-received *Kentucky* (1938), with Loretta Young and Walter Brennan. *My Old Kentucky Home* (1938) with the Hall Johnson Choir was another with a racing setting, as were the very successful *In Old Kentucky* (1939), featuring Will Rogers in a "glorious romance under Southern skies" (*Motion Picture Herald*, December 28, 1934), and *The Lady's From Kentucky* (1939), with Louise Beavers and George Raft.

Two other films are perhaps the period's best remembered depictions of the state: *Judge Priest* (1934), directed by John Ford, and the *The Little Colonel* (1935). *Judge Priest* featured one of humorist Irvin S. Cobb's most popular characters, played by Will Rogers. The film was remade in 1953 as *The Sun Shines Bright*, also directed by Ford. Although Ford remarked that the latter was his favorite picture, both are now dated, especially in their characterizations of southern blacks. Cobb and Rogers later appeared together in the nostalgic *Steamboat 'Round the Bend* (1935). In *The Little*

Colonel, Shirley Temple joined Lionel Barrymore (who refused a southern accent in playing his role as a Kentucky colonel) and Bill ("Bojangles") Robinson in a highly profitable film set in the 1870s.

The colonial frontier also proved popular. Both *The Great Meadow* (1931), a meticulous adaptation of Elizabeth Madox Roberts's 1930 novel, and *Daniel Boone* (1936) depicted the settling of the Kentucky wilds. The story was told again in *Daniel Boone, Trail Blazer* (1957), filmed in Mexico, and in the television series *Daniel Boone* (1964-70, and later syndicated).

Kentucky has repeatedly served as a shooting locale for stories set elsewhere, such as *Raintree County* (1957), *Flim-Flam Man* (1967), and *Steel* (1980). The state itself has been the subject of films less frequently. Among the exceptions are *The Little Shepherd of Kingdom Come* (1961), adapted from the 1903 novel by John Fox, Jr.; *In Country* (1989), which has a western Kentucky theme; and *Coal Miner's Daughter* (1980), based upon the life of Loretta Lynn.

Some productions, such as the European-made *Uncle Tom's Cabin* (1965) and *Slaves* (1969), have a Kentucky setting only as a brief introduction. Sometimes the state is tangential to the story, never actually depicted but serving as background flavor, as in the musical *Kentucky Minstrels* (1934) and the westerns *The Kentuckian* (1955) and *Kentucky Rifle* (1956), or merely as a brand name, as in the drive-in campus comedy *The Kentucky Fried Movie* (1977).   EDWARD D.C. CAMPBELL, JR.

FILSON, JOHN. John Filson, historian, surveyor, and cartographer, was born in East Fallowfield, Chester County, Pennsylvania, the eldest child of Davison Filson and his first wife, Eleanor (Clarke) Filson. According to family tradition, Filson was born on December 10, 1753. He was educated at the local schools and reputedly also at West Nottingham Academy in Colora, Maryland. Filson then taught school in the Chester County area of Pennsylvania. He is believed to have taught school during the Revolutionary War.

In the fall of 1783 Filson arrived in Kentucky. He acquired land, surveyed, taught school, interviewed early pioneers, and soon began writing a book about and drawing a map of Kentucky. The book was published in Wilmington, Delaware, in October 1784 as *The Discovery, Settlement, and Present State of Kentucke*. Filson's excellent map, the first to focus strictly on Kentucky, was engraved and printed in Philadelphia the same year. The purpose of both book and map, sold both separately and in combination, was to promote Kentucky and its settlement, from which Filson stood to gain through land investments. Both publications were very popular, and within a matter of years French and German editions appeared. An appendix to the book, "The Adventures of Colonel Daniel Boon," assured Boone's immortality and created the model of the American frontiersman.

Following brief residence in Philadelphia and Wilmington, Filson returned to Kentucky in the spring of 1785. He made two trips to St. Vincent (now Vincennes, Indiana), where he acquired property, engaged in business, and interviewed the inhabitants, apparently with the thought of using this information, along with his journals, to write a book about the Illinois country. He returned to Kentucky in June 1786 and made several trips to Pennsylvania's Chester County before the end of 1787. In January 1788 Filson proposed opening a seminary in Lexington, but it is doubtful that plans went any further.

In 1788 Filson traveled about Kentucky and surveyed a road from Lexington to the mouth of the Licking River, where he helped found the town of Losantiville (now Cincinnati). After Filson and two partners acquired eight hundred acres of Ohio land opposite the mouth of the Licking River, they publicized the proposed town and in September began surveying and laying it out. While exploring with a group north of the site, Filson disappeared and is believed to have been killed by Indians around October 1, 1788.

See John Walton, *John Filson of Kentucke* (Lexington, Ky., 1956).   JAMES J. HOLMBERG

FILSON CLUB. The Filson Club, of Louisville, was founded on May 15, 1884, by ten prominent citizens concerned that no institution was conserving Kentucky's past. It was named for John Filson, author of *The Discovery, Settlement and Present State of Kentucke* (1784). Col. Reuben T. Durrett was the guiding spirit of the club from 1884 until his death in 1913. In those years, the club met principally at Durrett's home for the presentation and discussion of papers on Kentucky history. In 1884 the club started producing books dealing with various aspects of Kentucky's past, publishing thirty-six volumes in the first series, which ended in 1938. A second series of publications began in 1964. The *Filson Club History Quarterly*, a journal of Kentucky history, has been published since 1926.

After 1913 the club was led by R.C. Ballard THRUSTON, president from 1923 until his death in 1946. Under his guidance the Filson Club acquired a headquarters at 118 West Breckinridge Street, which it occupied from 1928 until 1986. Thruston gave the club his substantial library of books on Kentucky and Virginia and manuscript holdings of family papers. He established a general endowment fund and a special endowment for acquisitions of historical materials. A staff was hired to conduct the activities of the society, and Otto A. Rothert, a local historian, served as secretary and editor.

The Filson Club is noted for its outstanding manuscript collection—approximately 1.2 million items, especially strong in the pioneer, antebellum, and Civil War periods of Kentucky history. The club has an excellent holding of original Kentucky newspapers, maps, photographs, prints, and ephemera (including broadsides, programs, menus, and sheet music). The book collection is one of the finest on Kentucky history and is strong on Virginia and regional genealogy. The club maintains a small museum of Kentucky art and works of craft, including some three hundred paintings, principally portraits, as well as textiles, firearms, silver, and other objects.

In 1986 the Filson Club moved to the finest example of residential Beaux Arts architecture in Louisville, the Ferguson mansion, at 1310 South Third Street. This facility has more room for reference services and better collection storage; it has enhanced the museum displays and made possible the creation of a department for photographs and prints.

The Filson Club, although privately supported, is open to the public. Its library is a noncirculating research collection, whose mission since 1884 has been "to collect, preserve, and publish historical material, especially that pertaining to Kentucky."

See Lowell H. Harrison, "A Century of Progress: The Filson Club, 1884-1984," *FCHQ* 58 (Oct. 1984): 381-407.   JAMES R. BENTLEY

FILSON CLUB HISTORY QUARTERLY. The Filson Club in Louisville, which initially published historic monographs, launched the *History Quarterly* in 1926 in conjunction with the history department of the University of Louisville. After the collaborative venture proved too eclectic to please anyone, the Filson Club in 1928 assumed sole control and renamed the publication the *Filson Club History Quarterly*. The *Quarterly* has become a respected regional history journal focusing on Kentucky. The editors have also maintained a broad perspective and have published articles and book reviews dealing with the surrounding states and the South generally. Over the years the *Quarterly* has also published news items and other features of particular interest to the club membership; in 1983 the Filson Club created the Otto A. Rothert Award for the best article published each year. The first editor of the *Quarterly* was Robert S. Cotterill (1926-28), followed by Otto A. Rothert (1928-45), Lucien Beckner (1946), Richard H. Hill (1947-71), Robert E. McDowell, Jr. (1971-75), and Nelson L. Dawson (1975-).   NELSON L. DAWSON

FINCASTLE COUNTY. Formed in 1772 out of Botetourt County, Virginia, Fincastle County included all the territory south and west of the Kanawha River, south of the Ohio River, and north of the unsurveyed dividing line with North Carolina. The borders were also to include all of Virginia's transmontane claims. In response to the growing population on the frontier, Virginia created the new county, named after its governor, Lord Dunmore, viscount of Fincastle, to extend governmental control in the West. To further consolidate control over western lands and to prevent recognition of Richard Henderson's TRANSYLVANIA COMPANY by the Continental Congress, Virginia in December 1776 divided Fincastle County into Kentucky, Montgomery, and Washington counties. Kentucky County was located west of the Big Sandy River, south of the Ohio River, and north of the

Virginia-North Carolina border. Granting Kentucky County representation in the Virginia General Assembly, meant that the claims of the Transylvania Company were denied. Richard Henderson, however, was granted 200,000 acres of land in what is now Henderson County, Kentucky, as compensation. On November 1, 1780, Kentucky County was divided into three local administrative units with the creation of Fayette, Jefferson, and Lincoln counties.

See Otis K. Rice, *Frontier Kentucky* (Lexington, Ky. 1975); Samuel M. Wilson, "West Fincastle—Now Kentucky," *FCHQ* 9 (April 1935): 65-94.

FINCASTLE SURVEYS. The Fincastle surveys were performed by surveyors from Fincastle County, Virginia. Most of the surveys were made in what is now Kentucky. Nearly all of the surveys that resulted in land grants were authorized by military warrants issued to veterans of the French and Indian War.

In April 1774 a company of deputy surveyors, including John Floyd, Hancock Taylor, James Douglas, and Isaac Hite, left Smithfield, Virginia, and traveled down the Kanawha and Ohio rivers, making surveys en route. Upon reaching the Falls of the Ohio on May 28, 1774, they conducted twenty-eight surveys of about 40,000 acres, which covered all of present-day Louisville as far south as the Watterson Expressway and east to Anchorage and Prospect. On June 3 the surveyors split into two groups. The one headed by Hancock Taylor visited Harrodsburg, then began surveying near Frankfort on June 17. The second party, headed by John Floyd, rejoined Taylor on July 1 at his camp near present-day Midway, Kentucky. Here they split into three parties, the third headed by James Douglas and Isaac Hite. Floyd surveyed along the North Fork of Elkhorn, Taylor along the South Fork of Elkhorn, and Douglas along Jessamine and Hickman creeks. In this area they made sixty-two surveys of about 113,000 acres.

The surveyors had intended to meet again at Harrodsburg, but an attack there by Indians on July 8 caused each of the surveying parties to return home by a different route. The Indians ambushed Taylor's company on July 27, killing the leader and another man. The survivors were escorted home by Daniel Boone and Michael Stoner, scouts who had been dispatched for that purpose. Floyd and his companions returned by an Indian trail that led up the North Fork of the Kentucky River and through Pound Gap. Douglas's company returned by paddling their canoe down the Ohio and Mississippi rivers to New Orleans and taking passage on a ship to Virginia.

Deputy Fincastle County surveyors continued to work in Kentucky during 1775 and 1776, and eventually surveyed a total of 206,250 acres on old military warrants within the central part of the state. (See also SURVEYING.)

See Neal Hammon, "Fincastle Surveyors in the Bluegrass, 1774," *Register* 70 (Oct. 1972): 277-94;

Neal Hammon, "Fincastle Surveyors at the Falls," *FCHQ* 47 (Jan. 1973): 268-83.   NEAL HAMMON

FINK, ALBERT. Albert Fink, bridge designer and railroad executive, was born October 27, 1827, in Lauterbach, Germany. He graduated in 1848 from the Polytechnic School of Darmstadt, where he studied architecture and engineering. He immigrated to the United States in 1849. Beginning as a draftsman for the Baltimore & Ohio (B&O) Railroad, he soon became principal assistant to the chief engineer. By 1852 his bridge truss design was being used by the B&O. In 1857 he was recruited by the Louisville & Nashville (L&N) Railroad as assistant engineer for bridges and buildings. His five-span Fink-truss bridge over Green River just south of Munfordville was the second-longest iron bridge in the nation. In 1859 he became L&N chief engineer and that same year completed the Jefferson County courthouse, which had stood unfinished for nearly twenty years.

After the outbreak of the Civil War in 1861, Fink and his engineering corps were kept busy repairing damage done to the L&N line by Confederate raiders. Repair gangs were sometimes on the scene so quickly that they themselves came under attack. At war's end Fink was named general superintendent of the L&N. He simultaneously designed and superintended construction of the first bridge across the Ohio River at Louisville. Opened in 1870, the Fink-truss bridge, one mile long, was at that time the longest in the United States. (It was replaced by a new bridge at the same location in 1918-19.)

After Fink was named a vice-president of the L&N in 1871, he made probably the first sophisticated analysis of railroad operating expenses, establishing freight rates on an accounting basis. His reputation in this new field brought him the commissionership of the newly organized Southern Railway and Steamship Association in Atlanta in 1875. Designed to stabilize rates, to bill through freight handled by several roads, and to solve similar problems, it was the model for the Trunk Line Association formed by northeastern railroads in 1877 with Fink as its head.

Fink married Sallie Moore Hunt of Louisville on April 24, 1865; they were parents of a daughter, Eleanor. In 1889 failing health caused Fink to resign the Trunk Line post and return to Louisville from New York City. He died April 3, 1897, and was buried in Louisville's Cave Hill Cemetery.

See Ellen Fink Milton, *A Biography of Albert Fink* (Rochester, N.Y. 1951).

GEORGE H. YATER

FINK, MIKE. Mike Fink, a colorful keelboatman on the Ohio and Mississippi rivers, was born near Fort Pitt (now Pittsburgh), Pennsylvania, around 1770. He took up keelboating once the Indian wars in the upper Ohio Valley ended, and he hauled freight in shallow covered barges until steamboats replaced keelboats. Fink then became a trapper for the Missouri Fur Company in the early 1800s.

Tall tales about Fink became part of American folklore. An inveterate braggart with a broad sense of humor, he boasted that he was "half horse, half alligator" and that he could "outrun, outjump, outshoot, outdrink, drag out and lick any man in the country." Fink's pleasant countenance belied a temperament notoriously cruel and cunning. Utterly fearless, he braved river hazards, hostile Indians, and dangerous bandits who infested the riverbanks, including the dreaded outlaws who gathered at Cave-in-Rock, Illinois.

Fink's reputation for marksmanship proved his undoing. He and his crony Bill Carpenter delighted in shooting tin cans filled with whiskey off each other's heads. In 1823, during one of these dangerous games, Fink "elevated a little two low" and killed Carpenter. Later, while drinking, the story goes, Fink boasted that the killing was intentional, whereupon one of Carpenter's friends, a man named Talbot, shot Fink through the heart. Before he died, Fink denied that he had intended to kill Carpenter. Both Fink and Carpenter were buried at Fort Henry, Montana, near the confluence of the Yellowstone and Missouri rivers.

See Walter Blair and Franklin J. Meine, *Mike Fink, King of Mississippi Keelboatmen* (New York 1933); Blair and Meine, *Half Horse, Half Alligator: The Growth of the Mike Fink Legend* (Chicago 1956).   OTIS K. RICE

FINLEY, JOHN. John Finley, pioneer and legislator, was born in Shippensburg, Pennsylvania, on July 7, 1748, to John and Martha (Berkley) Finley. During his early years, Finley was involved in the cattle trade with the French in the Great Lakes region. In July 1773, Finley joined an expedition, led by Capt. William Thompson, that floated down the Ohio River from Fort Pitt to Kentucky. Thompson led a group to the mouth of Cabin Creek, where they began surveying, while Finley joined a smaller group that traveled farther south to explore the Licking River at the Upper Blue Licks. The group spent a week clearing almost an acre of land to build a log cabin. They made only one survey, which covered about 1,440 acres, during which they discovered the Blue Lick Springs, farther south, that became the Lower Blue Licks. Hostile Indians forced Finley to rejoin Thompson and the main group at Cabin Creek in early August. When they left Kentucky, the expedition had marked lines along Cabin Creek, Salt Lick Creek, Johnson Creek, and the North Fork of the Licking River. All of the tracts of land adjoined, except for Finley's Upper Blue Licks survey, covering an area of about twenty square miles.

Virginia had refused to recognize the Thompson surveys since the expedition had not been commissioned by the colony. In 1779, however, the Virginia Land Act gave a preemption of 1,000 acres to any Virginian who had made a land improvement in Kentucky prior to January 1, 1778, which made Finley eligible for most of the land he had surveyed in the Upper Blue Licks. His military service had prevented him from filing his claim, but in 1789 he joined the expedition of Col. James GARRARD and marked his land in Fleming and Nicholas counties. For several years the danger of Indian attacks prevented him from moving, and not until 1796 was he able to settle along the banks of the Licking River with his family. His land was crossed by both the Warriors' Path to Cabin Creek and the main Washington Road, and he was appointed overseer of the main road in 1798.

Finley was perhaps Fleming County's most prominent citizen, serving as state legislator from that county during 1800-1804 and as justice of the peace during 1801-5. Indicating some dissatisfaction with his home, Finley in 1802 began leasing twenty-five acres of his land, his ferry on the Licking, and his salt works. In 1809 he built a tavern for people traveling down the river. That same year, relatives of John Durham (who had surveyed land in the same area) contested Finley's land, claiming it overlapped land that was rightfully theirs. Despite appeals, Finley lost between 250 and 300 acres of land in 1820, including the Washington Road and his new home. A son-in-law in 1828 bought back the land and sold it to Finley in 1836.

Finley married Hannah Duncan in Pittsburgh in 1790; they had seven children: Martha, David Duncan, Margaret, Samuel Berkley, Betsey Ann, Maria Jane, and Hannah.

Finley died on April 10, 1837, and was buried in the family graveyard near his first home on the Licking River.

See R.S. Cotterill, "John Finley, Pioneer of Fleming County," *Register* 42 (April 1944): 91-98.

FISH. Bounded on three sides by rivers, the Ohio on the north, the Mississippi on the west, and the Big Sandy on the east, and lying within several major river basins, including the Kentucky, the Tennessee, and the Cumberland, Kentucky is replete with favorable fish habitats. (It has been claimed that Kentucky has more miles of streams than any other state except Alaska.) Many of the state's rivers have been dammed, creating impoundments that further enhance Kentucky's fish environment. Inhabiting these waters, from the smallest of minnows to the larger silver muskellunge, are over two hundred species of fish representing twenty-six families.

Most sportsmen tend to place fish in one of three categories: forage fish, coarse fish, and sport fish. Although the proper classification may be subject to debate (some maintain that the bluegill, for example, is a forage fish, while others consider the bluegill to be a sport fish), these three categories are perhaps the most basic way to describe Kentucky's fish fauna.

Serving as food for larger predator fish, forage fish are the most numerous, inhabiting every lake and stream in the state. Rarely growing larger than five or six inches in length, these small creatures make up a vast majority of the fish found in Kentucky. In fact, the minnow family alone, consisting of minnows, chubs, shiners, and daces, is made up of more than fifty species.

Coarse fish are those species that have little or no sporting or food value. Made up mostly of carp, gars, and lampreys, they compete for food with the more popular sport fish; the coarse fish, more times than not, emerge victorious. As a result, the coarse fish type is regarded as a nuisance and is usually not protected by game laws.

Their fighting ability, as well as their desirability as table fare, make sport (or game) fish the most popular and most recognizable in Kentucky. Seeking them, sportsmen from all over the country visit such impoundments as Kentucky Lake, Lake Cumberland, and Dale Hollow Lake. Perhaps the most popular of the sport fish are the black bass—the largemouth bass, the smallmouth bass, and the spotted or Kentucky bass. Not true bass, but members of the sunfish family, they are present in every drainage in the state, except that the Kentucky bass is not found in the Little Sandy drainage. Other members of the sunfish family, the black crappie and the white crappie, are also very popular and are distributed statewide. Other important sport fish families in Kentucky are the salmonoids, represented by the rainbow, brook, brown, and lake trout; the perch family—the saugh and the walleye; the pike family, mainly the silver muskellunge; and the catfish family, represented by the flathead, blue, and channel catfish.

Kentucky is also home to the Mammoth Cave blindfish, a unique variety of aquatic marine life. In the dark recesses of Echo River, their habitat on the lowest level of Mammoth Cave, the eyes of this fish were useless, and eventually they became concealed beneath the skin. To compensate, the fish developed an acute sense of touch, and it tracks food by detecting disturbances in the water rather than by sight.

See William M. Clay, *The Fishes of Kentucky* (Frankfort, Ky., 1975); William M. Clay, *A Field Manual of Kentucky Fishes* (Frankfort, Ky., 1962).

FISHER, STEPHEN. Stephen Fisher was one of three brothers who were among the earliest and most influential settlers along Dick's (now Dix) River in what is now Lincoln, Boyle, and Mercer counties. Fisher was born in Culpeper County, Virginia, in 1736 to Lewis and Anna Barbara (Blankenbaker) Fisher. The Fisher brothers came to the frontier of Kentucky shortly after the death of their father in 1773. Stephen Fisher entered active military service in the Revolutionary War in 1777 and was returned to Kentucky under Col. John Bowman to help defend the interior settlements from British and Indian attacks. Fisher was wounded in the same year but recovered sufficiently to enable him to return to active duty. In 1782 he was wounded at the Battle of BLUE LICKS, but managed to escape to safety and, after a lengthy illness, recovered from his wounds. He was one of the few who survived that battle.

Fisher settled near CROW'S STATION, near what later became the city of Danville, in what was then Lincoln County. In 1779 or 1780, he built a blockhouse known as Fisher's Station, or more often as Fisher Garrison. The latter name suggests that Fisher's outpost may have had more military significance than did other early settlements in the area. Fisher later secured grant title to several hundred acres adjacent to his station.

With the conclusion of the Revolutionary War and the frontier struggle with the Indians, the Fishers began to settle away from the blockhouse on their own lands, all of which they had obtained through land grants. The Fisher brothers owned more than 2,000 acres north of Danville in the late 1780s and into the 1800s. Fisher's home was near his original station site.

Fisher may have been the first Revolutionary War soldier from Virginia to receive a pension. In his lifetime, he was associated with the early religious and educational development of Danville. Fisher was instrumental in the very early promotional efforts of Centre College. Fisher also served in a number of court-appointed positions. About 1759 he married Mary Magdaline Garr. Their children were Elizabeth, Elias, Benjamin, Jemima, Agnes, Stephen, Jr., Susannah, Rosannah, Elijah, and Mary Ann.

Fisher died in May 1817 and is believed to be buried at a family graveyard now lost, or at the First Presbyterian Church cemetery (McDowell Park) in Danville.

See Calvin Morgan Fackler, *Early Days in Danville* (Louisville 1941); Charles Heinemann, *Fisher Families of the Southern States* (Washington, D.C., 1934).   ALLAN R. LEACH

FISHING. Its climate and its geography make Kentucky a fisherman's paradise. The fish fauna of Kentucky is more diverse than that of any other inland state except Tennessee. As of 1990 there were 242 fish species in Kentucky, 226 of them native. At least forty of them are quarry for anglers. Four of the largest rivers in the United States—the Cumberland, Tennessee, Ohio, and Mississippi—conjoin in Kentucky. More than twenty major creeks and rivers drain the state, creating a mix of fish habitats that range from Appalachian mountain streams to cypress bayous. Over 8,000 miles of streams offer quality fisheries. The state's top game fish is the black bass, widely distributed in three species—the largemouth bass, the smallmouth bass, and the spotted bass.

The Kentucky Department of Fish and Wildlife Resources keeps weight records on thirty species of fish. Each year more than two hundred anglers receive citations for catching trophy-size fish, documented through the state's angler awards program. Kentucky's record largemouth bass—a 13-pound, 10¼-ounce lunker—was caught on April 14, 1984, from Woods Creek Lake by Dale Wilson, of London. Since Kentucky is one of the southernmost

states in the geographic range of the smallmouth bass, "bronzebacks" grow as big in Kentucky as anywhere else in the country. In fact Kentucky's state record smallmouth, which weighed 11 pounds, 15 ounces, is the current International Game Fish Association (IGFA) all-tackle world record for the species. The huge bass was caught from Dale Hollow Lake on July 9, 1955, by David L. Hayes, of Leitchfield.

Because of its abundance and distribution throughout Kentucky, the spotted bass is Kentucky's official game fish, posted as such on February 27, 1956, by the General Assembly. The spotted bass is thus commonly known as the Kentucky bass among anglers across the country.

Prior to the 1940s, most fishing in Kentucky was done in ponds, small lakes, creeks, and rivers. In the 1950s the emphasis began to shift toward fishing in large reservoirs. Herrington Lake, impounded in 1925 by Kentucky Utilities, was Kentucky's first major lake, but the 1,860-acre, privately-owned reservoir, thirty miles southwest of Lexington, is small compared with later projects. The first of the large federal flood control reservoirs was Dale Hollow Lake, 27,700 acres, created in 1943. A year later the Tennessee Valley Authority (TVA) finished Kentucky Lake, which has 160,300 surface acres (49,511 acres in Kentucky). Lake Cumberland was the only major lake created in the 1950s, followed by Rough River Lake in 1959, but the 1960s was a decade unparalleled in impoundment: Nolin River Lake, 1963; Barren River Lake, 1964; Lake Barkley, 1966; Green River Lake, 1969. Later impoundments are Cave Run Lake (1974), Laurel River Lake (1977), and Taylorsville Lake (1982).

The large reservoirs in Kentucky vastly increased opportunities for fishing and dramatically changed its character. The construction of modern marinas, resorts, parks, and campgrounds at the water's edge made fishing a major attraction for Kentucky's tourism industry. Each year fishermen in Kentucky spend about $262.8 million total, or about $309 per angler.

Panfish such as bluegill, shellcrackers, and channel catfish are favorites with anglers who fish in farm ponds and small state-owned lakes with live bait—crickets, nightcrawlers, red worms, meal worms, and wax worms. Sauger, blue and flathead catfish, white bass, and freshwater drum congregate in tailwater areas below locks and dams on major rivers. Anglers still fish with live minnows, or cast spoons, spinners, crankbaits, and jigs to catch schooling white bass and sauger in the spring. Large reservoirs appeal mainly to crappie and black bass anglers. Jigs and live minnows are the lures of choice for crappie fishermen, while popular artificial baits for bass fishing are plastic worms, jig and pork rind combinations, buzzbaits, crankbaits, topwater propeller baits, and spinner baits.

Tournament fishing for bass became popular in the 1970s and peaked in the mid-1980s. From spring through fall, anglers pay cash entry fees and the top finishers share in the purse money at hundreds of tournaments on lakes and rivers in Kentucky. An estimated eight hundred sanctioned bass tournaments of various sizes were held on Kentucky waters in 1985.

In 1990 158 lakes in sixty-five Kentucky counties were open to public fishing, including those owned and operated by various levels of government. The state's estimated 1 million anglers include 700,000 licensed fishermen and 300,000 persons who fish for free under exemptions for landowners, age (under sixteen or over sixty-five years), or disability.

The fisheries division of the Kentucky Department of Fish and Wildlife Resources operated two fish hatcheries, and employed a total of fifty-five biologists, fishery aides, researchers, and administrative personnel in 1990. Since modern fishery management began in the late 1940s, fishery scientists have reestablished native game fish populations in streams where they had been eliminated, and have introduced several nonnative species in suitable waters. "Put-grow-and-take" fisheries, where nonnative fish do not naturally reproduce, are stocked annually to maintain the populations. The landlocked striped bass and hybrid striped bass are the most notable of the nonnatives. On December 11, 1985, Roger Foster, of Somerset, boated Kentucky's state record landlocked striped bass from Lake Cumberland. The giant fish weighed 58 pounds, 4 ounces—just 7 pounds, 12 ounces less than the all-tackle world record.

Two other nonnative species widely introduced into Kentucky waters are the brown trout and rainbow trout. Among fish species reintroduced to waters where they once naturally occurred are the silver muskie and the walleye. Muskies are annually stocked in lakes and streams throughout the Kentucky and Licking River basins. The river strain of walleye native to Kentucky has all but disappeared, and the walleye stocked today in selected lakes and rivers throughout the state are a northern strain more suitable to lake environments. A wild trout program has reestablished self-sustaining populations of brook trout in some mountain streams where historical literature suggests they might have originally occurred. In the late 1980s volunteers helped start stream restoration projects in Daniel Boone National Forest, primarily aimed at improving trout habitat.

Kentucky's lakes and rivers may be threatened by toxic chemicals and metals, runoff from animal waste, municipal sewage, acid water from surface mining, and silt from timber cutting. An increase in oil and gas exploration could also pose a threat to water quality. By 1990 a fish consumption advisory had been issued for several rivers in the state. Channel catfish, carp, and white bass caught from the entire length of the Ohio River were not to be eaten because of health risks from polychlorinated biphenyl (PCB) contamination. Housing and business developments, and the push to locate heavy industry in rural areas to stimulate local economies,

are bound to have an adverse impact on fishing opportunities in Kentucky in coming decades.

See Brooks M. Burr and Melvin L. Warren, Jr., *A Distribution Atlas of Kentucky Fishes* (Frankfort, Ky., 1986); Arthur B. Lander, Jr., *A Fishing Guide to Kentucky's Major Lakes* (Hillsborough, N.C., 1984).   ARTHUR B. LANDER, JR.

FITCH, JOHN. John Fitch, steamboat inventor, was born at Windsor, Connecticut, on January 21, 1743. His parents were Joseph and Sarah Fitch. After serving in the Revolutionary War as a lieutenant in the New Jersey line, he journeyed to Kentucky in 1780 and surveyed and claimed three parcels of land in what is now Nelson County.

On the East Coast between 1781 and 1785, Fitch constructed models of boats propelled by steam. After successfully demonstrating a model on the Delaware River, he petitioned the U.S. Congress in August 1785 for funds to develop his invention. From the legislatures of Pennsylvania, New Jersey, Delaware, and New York, he obtained exclusive rights to navigate certain waters with boats powered by steam. Between 1787 and 1790, several of his boats operated commercially on the Delaware River. Congress granted him a patent in 1791, but it failed to grant the funds to support his invention, lacking the foresight to realize that Fitch's invention could make rivers the highways of the West. Discouraged and despondent, Fitch returned to Kentucky, hoping to form a company to build boats. Instead, he found people challenging his land claims. Although he was successful in defending his titles, his disappointments as an inventor reduced him to drink and depression. It is thought that an overdose of opium combined with whiskey ended his life in Bardstown in June or July of 1798.

Later investigation of the boats built by Robert Livingston and Robert Fulton proved that they were substantially the same in design as the one patented by Fitch. Through the efforts of Mrs. Ben Johnson of Bardstown, Congress appropriated $15,000 to erect a memorial in 1927 dedicated to the true inventor of the steamboat. His remains were moved from the Pioneer Cemetery to the site of the monument on the Court Square in Bardstown.

See Thompson Westcott, *The Life of John Fitch, the Inventor of the Steamboat* (Philadelphia 1857).
                                      DIXIE HIBBS

FITZBUTLER, HENRY. Henry Fitzbutler, physician, was born in Canada in December 1837 to slave parents who had escaped north. In 1872 Fitzbutler became the first black to graduate from the University of Michigan's medical school. Two years later he brought his family from Ontario to Louisville, where he helped fill a great need, for most of the town's physicians and hospitals refused treatment to the city's 15,000 blacks. Fitzbutler urged the General Assembly to open a medical school for blacks in Louisville. The result was the Louisville National Medical College, which opened in 1888 with no racial restrictions. The school operated until 1912, graduating 175 black students. Its adjoining hospital, on West Green Street (now Liberty Street) served blacks free of charge. Financial and other difficulties forced the college to close.

Fitzbutler and his wife Sarah, whom he married in 1865, had five children: Prima, Mary, James, Myra, and William. Fitzbutler died on December 27, 1901 and was buried in Louisville's Greenwood Cemetery.

FLAG, STATE. As authorized on March 26, 1918, by an act of the General Assembly, the Kentucky state flag is navy blue silk or bunting, with the seal of the commonwealth encircled by a wreath of goldenrod embroidered, printed, or stamped on the center. The dimensions of the flag may vary. Jessie Cox, an art teacher in Frankfort, designed the flag according to the specifications of the act. She and her sister made several of the early flags.

FLAGET, BENEDICT JOSEPH. The first Roman Catholic bishop of the West, Benedict Joseph Flaget was born at Contournat, France, on November 7, 1763. He entered the Society of Priests of St. Sulpice, attending the seminary at Clermont, and was ordained a priest in 1788. Because of the antireligious turn of events in revolutionary France, he emigrated in 1792 to Baltimore, a center of American Catholicism, voyaging on the same ship with Stephen BADIN. Flaget's first pastoral assignment was at Vincennes, Indiana. Recalled to the East in 1795 he taught at Georgetown College, Washington, D.C., and at St. Mary's Seminary in Baltimore. Three years in Havana as a teacher and tutor ended with a failed attempt to establish a Roman Catholic college in the Cuban capital.

At age forty-five, Flaget was appointed by Pope Pius VII as the first bishop of Bardstown, the first inland diocese in the United States. The diocese's jurisdiction extended from Michigan to Tennessee, and from the Allegheny Mountains to the Mississippi River. Flaget arrived at his new assignment in the spring of 1811. He took up residence with Badin in Marion County, Kentucky. In 1812 Flaget moved to St. Thomas Farm, south of Bardstown. He moved to Bardstown in 1819, after the completion of St. Joseph Proto Cathedral, the "Cathedral in the Wilderness," for which he assisted in fund raising. Flaget's Roman Catholic community exported its religious leadership—educators, bishops, nuns, and priests—throughout much of the South and Midwest. Flaget quickly became the friend of such leading Kentuckians as George Rogers Clark and Henry Clay, and he enjoyed easy relationships with Protestants on the frontier. A complex man, the bishop was himself a slaveowner who made the pastoral care of blacks a special concern.

In a personal report to Pope Gregory XVI in 1836, Flaget noted that in twenty-five years of his administration, the number of Roman Catholics in Kentucky had doubled; priests in service had increased sixfold; and a seminary, three communities of nuns, and two colleges had been established. On the national Catholic scene, the Kentucky bishop had been instrumental in the location of several new dioceses and the appointment of their bishops.

A hard-working missionary on horseback for many of his early years in Kentucky, Flaget returned to France in the late 1830s, at the pope's request, to lecture on the Kentucky church. On this tour, several French people attributed miraculous healing to his intercession.

Flaget left Bardstown in 1841, when the pope transferred the headquarters of the diocese to the growing city of Louisville. As first bishop of Louisville, the prelate lived at the rectory of the old St. Louis Church on Fifth Street. His last public act was the blessing of construction of a new cathedral on the same site in 1849. Flaget died February 11, 1850, and was buried in the crypt of the Cathedral of the Assumption in Louisville.

During his life Flaget was a prolific writer of letters, and he kept diaries in French during most of his career. A typical entry is that of April 19, 1812: "God is very good. I desire to love God and make Him loved."

See Clyde F. Crews, "Benedict Joseph Flaget, First Bishop of the West," *Patterns of Episcopal Leadership* (New York 1989).

CLYDE F. CREWS

FLANERY, MARY (ELLIOTT). Mary (Elliott) Flanery, journalist, legislator, and suffragist, born on April 27, 1867, in Carter County, Kentucky, was the daughter of Benjamin Franklin and Nancy (Kegley) Elliott. She received a public school education and attended Barboursville College (now University of Charleston) in West Virginia and the Agricultural and Mechanical State College (now the University of Kentucky). She married William Harvey Flanery on June 28, 1893, and lived briefly at Ann Arbor, Michigan, and in 1896 at Pikeville, Kentucky, before moving to Catlettsburg, Kentucky. While living in Pikeville, Mary Flanery became a journalist, and from 1904 to 1926, she wrote for the *Ashland Daily Independent*. She later served as correspondent for many regional newspapers. She also taught school in Elliot and Carter counties.

An active suffragist, Mary Flanery worked with Madeline McDowell Breckinridge and the Kentucky Equal Rights Association. In November 1921 she was elected representative from the 89th District (Boyd County) to the Kentucky General Assembly by a 250-vote plurality. She was the first woman elected to a state legislature south of the Mason-Dixon line. During her term, she successfully defended the act creating the teachers normal schools at Morehead and Murray. She lost a bid for Kentucky secretary of state in 1923 but remained active in politics. In 1924 she was a delegate to the Democratic National Convention in New York City.

The Flanerys had five children: Sue, Merle, Dawn, Dew, and John. After her death at Elliott Hall at Catlettsburg, on July 19, 1933, a bronze tablet was placed on Flanery's desk in the General Assembly, inscribed: "Mary Elliott Flanery, first woman legislator of Kentucky and the South, Boyd County 1922-1923, at this desk served her state with honor and distinction." She was buried in the Ashland Cemetery.   JAMES C. POWERS

FLATBOATS. In the early years of Kentucky settlement and statehood, before the rise of the steamboats in the 1820s, flatboats were the backbone of inland waterway navigation. The wooden flatbottom boats, built to go downstream only, were easy to build and operate. At journey's end, they provided timber for building a cabin—or for sale in New Orleans, where wood was scarce. Because of their importance to Kentucky trade and immigration, people in Pittsburgh and New Orleans often called them Kentucky boats, but they were also known as arks and broadhorns, or as Arkansas, Louisiana, tobacco, or family boats.

Flatboats ranged in size from twelve to twenty-five feet wide and from twenty to sixty feet long or more. They had a small box-like cabin for the family or crew. Steered with a thirty- to forty-foot rear oar called the gouger and two or four long side oars called side horns or sweeps, flatboats were at the mercy of river currents, floating debris, shallows, and floods. Their passengers were in danger from the ineptitude of builders and the inexperience of operators, as well as from pirates, Indians, and illness. Yet over a million immigrants floated into the Ohio River Valley on such boats, with furniture strapped atop the tiny cabins and livestock tied to the rails.

Glass and cabinetwork, chairs, millstones, nails, and imported goods came to the settlers from Pittsburgh on flatboats. The same settlers sent to New Orleans salt, cured pork, hemp, tobacco, corn, cherry and walnut planks, ginseng, flour, apples, cider, peach and apple brandy, and, perhaps most popular of all, whiskey, which aged on the trip. In the three years 1792 through 1794, ten flatboats landed 2,640 barrels of flour at New Orleans. By 1802 river shipments from Kentucky to New Orleans amounted to $1.2 million annually. In the 1820s steamboats took over most of the trade, but a few flatboats could be seen on Kentucky rivers as late as the Civil War.

See Gail King, *A Flatboat Hornbook* (Henderson, Ky., 1975).   GAIL KING

FLAT LICK. Flat Lick lies at the southeastern edge of Knox County, Kentucky, on a large level plain with numerous salt licks. It was one of the state's earliest settlements, at the junction of the Wilderness Road, which continued west, and the Warriors' Path, which went north up present-day Stinking Creek. Indians and Long Hunters camped here on their way north or south, since game animals were abundant. It is often mentioned in the writings of earlier travelers. During the Civil War, a Union army recruiting station was located at Flat Lick.

See John Fetterman, *Stinking Creek* (New York 1970).   SUSAN ARTHUR

FLATWOODS. Growing from the small town of Advance in the 1920s, the town of Flatwoods was incorporated in 1938. It may have been named for the terrain of the immediate area or for the Flatwoods District, the pre-1890s name for a hilly section of the city of Ashland. A third-class city, Flatwoods adjoins the town of Russell to the east and Raceland to the northwest; all are suburbs of Ashland. Much of the economy is dependent on Armco Steel, which operates a plant in the area. Other industrial production includes chemicals, refractories, and metals. The population of Flatwoods was 7,380 in 1970; 8,354 in 1980; and 7,799 in 1990.

FLEMING, JOHN. John Fleming, pioneer, was born to Sarah (Keith) Fleming in 1735. His father's given name is unknown. After his father died when Fleming was five, his mother remarried, and Fleming was raised by his grandparents. In 1750 Fleming moved to what is now Williamsport, Virginia, on the Potomac River, where he farmed and ran the Watkins ferry. In 1773 he sold his property and moved to Pennsylvania. In 1776 he traveled with a group to the area of Fleming County, Kentucky, to make "improvements" and "landmarks." In April 1780, under the May 1779 Virginia Land Act, Fleming secured the land from his first trip and moved to STRODE'S STATION near Winchester. He served as a deputy surveyor in Fayette County until January 23, 1786, when the county was divided to form Bourbon County, where he was a deputy surveyor from April 1786 until the spring of 1788. In 1790 he completed the construction of Fleming's Station near Martha's Mills in present-day Fleming County, which was named for him in 1798.

Fleming married Lucy Pettit Donaldson in 1782, bringing him six stepdaughters and two stepsons. From 1782 until his death in the spring of 1791, they resided at the Donaldson farm in Fayette County. He is thought to be buried in the Donaldson family graveyard.

See R.S. Cotterill, "John Fleming, Pioneer of Fleming County," *Register* 49 (July 1951): 193-202.

FLEMING COUNTY. Fleming County was the twenty-sixth formed in Kentucky, established in 1798 from part of Mason County in the northeastern portion of the state. In turn, some of the original area of Fleming County was taken to form Floyd County in 1800 and Rowan County in 1856. Fleming County is bordered by Rowan, Robertson, Mason, and Nicholas counties, along with the Licking River and its North Fork. FLEMINGSBURG, the county seat, and the county itself were named for Col. John Fleming, an early settler who built one of three forts in the county in 1790. John FINLEY, an associate of Daniel Boone's, settled in the county in 1796 on a 1,000-acre tract. The Civil War brought small skirmishes to Fleming County, including one in 1862 as Gen. John Hunt Morgan's raiders retreated from their attack on central Kentucky towns.

Fleming County is watered and drained by the Licking River and its tributaries. Its 351 square miles of terrain are rolling to almost level except for the western portion, which is hilly. The land is more than 25 percent wooded, mostly in hardwoods. Mineral resources include limestone, sandstone, and sand. A number of the mineral springs at one time were commercialized by resorts, including Fox Springs, an old spa site in the east-central portion of the county.

Fleming County's economy is based predominantly on agriculture; some industry clusters around Flemingsburg. Burley tobacco (5,935,000 pounds in 1988) and dairy products are among the most important agricultural commodities. Total receipts for agriculture in 1986 were $36.35 million, including $18.39 million in crop receipts and $17.96 million in livestock. The Louisville & Nashville Railroad (now CSX Transportation) cuts through the western part of the county. In the southern portion of the county, Maxey Flats was operated during 1963-77 as a nuclear waste disposal site; more than 4.5 million cubic feet of waste are stored there.

A Fleming County native was one of the World War II heroes memorialized in Associated Press photographer Joe Rosenthal's well-known image of the flag raising on Iwo Jima. Franklin R. Sousley, who helped raise the American flag on Suribachi on February 23, 1945, was killed later in the battle for the other islands of Iwo Jima; he is buried at Elizaville. Three covered bridges are still standing in the county: Hillsboro Bridge near Grange City, built in 1865; Ringo's Mills Bridge, built in 1867; and Goddard Bridge, built in 1867. One of the early schools in the area was Flemingsburg Christian Collegiate Institute (1863-1885).

Fleming County's population was 11,366 in 1970; 12,323 in 1980; and 12,292 in 1990.

See Wade Cooper, *Early Fleming County Kentucky Pioneers* (Ashland, Ky., 1974).

FLEMINGSBURG. Flemingsburg, the county seat of Fleming County in northeastern Kentucky, is located at the junction of KY 11, KY 32, and KY 57, 102 miles east of Louisville. The city was founded in 1796 by George P. Stockton of Virginia and was named for his half-brother, Col. John Fleming. It became the county seat in 1798, when Fleming County was formed from Mason County. A log structure built in 1798 or 1799 was probably the first courthouse, followed by a brick structure of Federal design completed in 1830 using skilled slave labor. The second courthouse was demolished in September 1951 and replaced in 1952 by the brick building that now stands.

Stockton and Fleming, who came down the Ohio River by canoe in 1776, were among the early explorers of the area. Indian hostility inhibited settlement, and Stockton returned to Virginia several times before founding a station near the site of Flemingsburg in 1786. In 1787 he brought his family from Virginia to settle what was called Stockton's Station. By 1793 the Indian threat had diminished and many settlers left the station to establish farms. In 1796 Stockton laid out Flemingsburg on land he owned near his station. By 1800 the population was 124. The first store in the county was established at Flemingsburg by Thomas Wallace and the first hotel by John Faris, both in 1804. The city was incorporated in 1812.

A cholera epidemic that swept the county in February 1833 killed sixty-six city residents. Flemingsburg's economy improved in 1836 when the Mt. Sterling and Maysville Turnpike was built through Flemingsburg. By the early 1840s stagecoaches traveled through the town. The population grew from 591 in 1840 to 759 in 1850, and the town was a bustling trade center for the county, with both wholesale and retail stores. Methodists built a brick chapel in Flemingsburg in 1799, as did the Presbyterians. A Christian church came in 1839, and the Baptists established a biracial congregation in 1840. A Catholic congregation held services in the *Democrat* newspaper office from 1850 until a church was built in 1859, and an Episcopal church was organized in 1857.

In the spring of 1859, James J. Andrews arrived in Flemingsburg and lived in the Fleming Hotel. As he was unable to find work as a teacher he painted houses, and he became engaged to a local woman, Elizabeth Layton. When the Civil War broke out, he enlisted in the Union Home Guard militia and eventually became a spy. He was the leader of Andrew's Raiders, a group of twenty-two Union men who stole a locomotive from the Confederates and precipitated the great locomotive chase across northern Georgia in April of 1862. Andrews was captured and hanged in Atlanta on June 7, 1862, ten days before his planned wedding date.

The post-Civil War economy was stimulated by the discovery of oil near Flemingsburg in 1865. The Covington, Flemingsburg & Pound Gap Railway was built in 1877. The narrow-gauge railroad was plagued by financial problems and operated under seven different names until its abandonment in 1955. On September 1, 1905, a fire swept Flemingsburg's business district and destroyed seven establishments. By 1908 the town had a high school, three banks, two hotels, two printing offices, seven churches, a roller mill, and an electricity and ice plant. For most of the twentieth century, Flemingsburg's economy has depended on the surrounding agricultural interests. Companies that moved to the city during the late 1950s and early 1960s include the U.S. Shoe Corporation and Randall-Textron, which manufactures automotive and appliance trim. In 1989 commercial development began along the KY 32 bypass, and business activity began to shift westward from the center of the city. The largest corporate employers in Flemingsburg are U.S. Shoe Corporation and Fleming Homes/Fleming Industries, which builds mobile homes.

The population of the fourth-class city was 2,483 in 1970; 2,835 in 1980; and 3,071 in 1990.

RONALD THOMAS

FLEXNER, ABRAHAM. Abraham Flexner, an educational reformer whose 1910 report critical of medical schools in the United States and Canada helped modernize medical education, was born in Louisville, on November 13, 1866, the son of Morris and Esther (Abraham) Flexner. He earned a B.A. degree from Johns Hopkins University in 1886, developing an admiration for the rigors of the German university system, which Hopkins had adopted. Flexner returned to Louisville in mid-1886 to teach at Male High School. Four years later he opened a college preparatory school that he operated for fifteen years; it drew the attention of many educators, including Harvard University president Charles W. Eliot.

In 1905 Flexner studied psychology at Harvard University, where he earned an M.A. degree in 1906. He then studied comparative education at the University of Berlin, from which he earned an M.A. in 1907. His book *The American College: A Criticism* (1908) reflected his belief that German universities were far superior to their U.S. counterparts. The book brought Flexner to the attention of Henry S. Pritchett, head of the Carnegie Foundation for the Advancement of Teaching, who asked Flexner to prepare a report on the state of medical education in the United States.

Flexner spent two years working on what has come to be called the Flexner Report, published in June 1910 by the Carnegie Foundation for the Advancement of Teaching as *Medical Education in the United States and Canada*. The report, which received much public attention, served as a catalyst for reform movements already underway. It also helped to speed the process by which the weaker, commercial/proprietary schools of medicine were phased out, a four-year standard curriculum was adopted, and the basic sciences achieved prominence in the nation's colleges of medicine.

After writing *Medical Education in Europe* (1912), Flexner joined the permanent staff of the General Education Board of the Rockefeller Foundation in 1913. He worked there in a variety of positions (including head of the Division of Studies and Medical Education) until 1928 and was instrumental in securing tens of millions of dollars for the advancement of scientific medical education and for the establishment of full-time research faculties in the basic sciences within U.S. colleges of medicine. In 1930 Flexner became the first director of the Institute for Advanced Study at Princeton University, a post he held until his retirement in 1939. The institute reflected his personal vision of educational excellence, and he brought a number of brilliant scholars—including Albert Einstein—to work in its ideal atmosphere for research. Flexner's autobiography, *I Remember* (1940), was revised and published posthumously as *Abraham Flexner: An Autobiography* (1960).

In 1898 Flexner married Anne Laziere Crawford; the couple had two daughters, Jean Atherton and Eleanor. When he died on September 21, 1959, the *New York Times* ran his obituary on the front page. Nearly twenty years earlier the *Times* had written that many recipients of medical care owed their lives to Abraham Flexner's pursuit of excellence. Flexner was buried in Louisville's Cave Hill Cemetery.

See Steven C. Wheatley, *The Politics of Philanthropy: Abraham Flexner and Medical Education* (Madison, Wis., 1988); Charles Vevier, ed., *Flexner: 75 Years Later: A Current Commentary on Medical Education* (Lanham, Md., 1987).

ALLEN J. SHARE

FLEXNER, MARION K. (WEIL). Marion K. (Weil) Flexner, author, daughter of Sidney and Adell (Kahn) Weil, was born in Montgomery, Alabama, on October 25, 1900. She attended Margaret Booth School for Girls in Montgomery and graduated from Wellesley in 1921. She married Morris Flexner, a Louisville native, on October 10, 1922, and moved to Louisville, where Morris Flexner practiced medicine. They had two children. Marion Flexner joined a Louisville women's writing group and with their encouragement began submitting articles to the *Louisville Courier-Journal*. Flexner's pieces were published in magazines including *Vogue*, *Woman's Day*, *House and Garden*, and *Gourmet*. She also wrote books on a variety of subjects, including a biography of the young Queen Victoria, a collection of plays for hand puppets, and a pamphlet for the American Cancer Society, *Cancer: I've Had It* (1946), relating her personal experiences. Best known for her six cookbooks, Flexner edited the first, *Food For Children and How to Cook It*, in 1929 with Isabella McLennon McMeekin, a friend from the writing group. Flexner's fourth cookbook, *Out of Kentucky Kitchens*, has been considered a classic. First published in 1949 and reprinted in 1989 by the University Press of Kentucky, it is a compilation of southern recipes interspersed with anecdotes about Kentucky's culinary history.

In 1957 Flexner opened a travel agency in Louisville. She retired in 1979.

FLEXNER, SIMON. Simon Flexner, a pathologist known for a serum against meningitis, was born in Louisville on March 25, 1863, the eldest of five sons of Morris and Esther (Abraham) Flexner. Abraham FLEXNER, his brother, revolutionized medical education in the United States and Europe. After graduating from the Louisville College of Pharmacy (now part of the University of Kentucky) in 1881, Simon Flexner received a medical degree at the University of Louisville in 1889. He later studied at the universities of Strasbourg, Berlin, and Prague, and at the Pasteur Institute in Paris. He was professor of pathological anatomy at Johns Hopkins University from 1888 to 1899 and then moved to the University of Pennsylvania. Flexner became director of the Rockefeller Institute of Medical Research in New York in 1903 and remained there until 1935. He achieved fame in 1905 for developing a serum that reduced the mortality rate from cerebrospinal meningitis to 25 percent from 75 percent in untreated cases. On August 19, 1911, he was awarded the Cameron Prize for this achievement.

Flexner wrote 350 scientific papers; his nonscientific works include *William Henry Welch and the Heroic Age of American Medicine* (1941), coauthored with his brother James Thomas Flexner, and the article "Scientific Careers for Women," published in *Scientific Monthly* in August 1921. He married Helen Thomas in 1903. Flexner died in New York City on May 2, 1946.

See James Thomas Flexner, *An American Saga* (Boston 1984).   HERMAN LANDAU

FLIPPIN, MANLIUS THOMPSON. Manlius Thompson Flippin, judge, legislator, and poet, was born July 29, 1841, in Monroe County, Kentucky, the son of James McAdoo and Phoebe (Wood) Flippin. Flippin received very little formal education and was largely self-taught. He studied law and was admitted to the bar in Monroe County in 1865. Flippin was elected to the Kentucky House of Representatives in 1867, 1871, and 1883. In 1874 he was elected county judge of Monroe County and was unopposed for reelection in 1878. As a Republican candidate from the 3d District in 1880, Flippin ran unsuccessfully for the U.S. Congress. He was chosen judge of Monroe County in 1884 after the resignation of Judge J.B. Evans. Flippin was an accomplished poet whose most popular works were "The Southland," "Evening Star," and "A Dream." Known for his eloquent prose and his oratorical ability, he was often asked to speak at political rallies and meetings of the Grand Army of the Republic.

In 1871 Flippin married Susan Maxey, daughter of Radford Maxey. Flippin died on January 1, 1899, and was buried next to his wife in the Flippin family cemetery in Tompkinsville, Kentucky.

RON D. BRYANT

FLOOD CONTROL. Heavy rains, sometimes in combination with melting snow, have often caused flooding along the Ohio River and its tributaries. Record flooding occurred in the Ohio Valley in 1936 and 1937 and caused devastation in many communities in Kentucky. The federal government responded by passing the flood control acts of 1936 and 1937, which created a nationwide comprehensive program for flood control. The program is administered by the U.S. Army Corps of Engineers.

Flood control programs lessen or prevent flood damage by regulating water flow with reservoirs, local protection projects, or combinations of the two. Channel improvements—deepening, widening, or straightening—may suffice to keep small streams from overflowing during flood seasons.

Reservoirs constructed for flood control may also be used for other purposes, including municipal and industrial water supply, navigation, development of hydroelectric power, conservation of fish and wildlife, and recreation. Reservoirs are located on tributary streams of the Ohio River. (The navigation dams on the Ohio do not provide flood control.) Local protection projects, usually levees and floodwalls, are built along the banks of rivers and are located both on the Ohio River and on tributary streams. Levees are wide-based earth structures used where land is neither expensive nor scarce, usually in rural areas. A floodwall is a relatively narrow concrete structure that is practical for urban areas.

In Kentucky, seventeen reservoir projects for flood control are operated by the Corps of Engineers districts at Louisville, Nashville, and Huntington, West Virginia. The Reservoir Control Center in the Ohio River Division, based in Cincinnati, coordinates the work. In addition, twenty-four local protection projects built by the corps have been turned over to local governments for management. The forty-one projects were constructed at a cost of $1.25 billion, and as of September 1989 they had prevented an estimated $1.4 billion in flood damage. Many small protection works that do not require specific congressional authorization have been built by the corps under its continuing authority program.

The Corps of Engineers fights Kentucky's flood problems also by providing detailed technical information on flood hazards, through its Flood Plain Management Services Program, to other federal agencies, state and local governments, and private citizens. This information is used in developing zoning regulations, building codes, sanitary codes, and other measures to reduce property loss and protect the environment by avoiding unwise development in flood-prone areas.

See *Water Resources Development by the U.S. Army Corps of Engineers in Kentucky* (Louisville 1987).   CHARLES E. PARRISH

FLOOD OF 1937. The extreme amount of precipitation in January 1937 remains unmatched in Kentucky's climate records. The average precipitation across the commonwealth that month was 15.77 inches, eleven inches above normal and four inches or more above the older record levels. Measurable precipitation was recorded somewhere in Kentucky every day during January. The number of days with measurable rainfall ranged from eighteen in Pikeville to twenty-one in Frankfort and Burnside. Rainfall exceeded one inch on ten days in Glasgow. Thunderstorms were recorded in Kentucky on eight days, compared with the January norm of just one thunderstorm. The heaviest rains totaled 7.36 inches at Taylorsville on January 24. By the end of the month, Earlington's total had reached 22.97 inches, which remains the record maximum monthly precipitation in Kentucky. Eleven other locations within the western and central areas had totals of twenty inches or more in January 1937. Only in the extreme eastern and southeastern border areas were amounts less than ten inches.

The heavy rains falling on saturated soils resulted in rapid runoff and severe flooding. All streams in the state were reported to have flooded. The Ohio River rose to 75.3 feet at Maysville, resulting in a declaration of martial law. All businesses in Carrollton were closed by flooding. The Kentucky River inundated more than half of Frankfort. The crest at Frankfort was 47.2 feet, which isolated the Old State House. All of the 2,900 prisoners from Kentucky State Prison in Frankfort were evacuated.

In Louisville the rising waters of the Ohio River damaged pumping stations and caused restrictions on water use. The Waterside Electric plant filled with water and ceased to operate on January 24. Power to the downtown area was not fully restored until February 12. Martial law was declared in Louisville on January 26 as 20,000 people became marooned in the downtown area. By the next day, 230,000 of Louisville's 350,000 residents had been evacuated to higher ground, many of them to towns throughout the state where they received food and shelter. The Great Flood crested at 57.1 feet on January 28, surpassing the old record set in February 1884 by more than ten feet. The flood did lasting economic damage to the city of Louisville. In Paducah, flood waters crested at 53.7 feet on February 1. Ninety-five percent of the city was flooded and by then Paducah was virtually abandoned.

The rivers were slow to recede. At Louisville, the Ohio River fell below flood stage on February 6 for the first time since January 15. Health agencies across the state waged a massive inoculation campaign to prevent typhoid fever. Flooded highways so disrupted transportation that burley tobacco markets closed for several days. Damage was estimated at $250 million. After the Great Flood, many river cities built flood walls and pumping stations.

FLORA. As well as an uncertain number of algae, Kentucky has about 3,500 kinds (species, subspecies, varieties) of native and naturalized flora, or regional plants. They include three hundred mosses, one hundred liverworts, ninety ferns, eight clubmosses, two spikemosses, two horsetails, three quillworts, one waterclover, and—by far the most numerous—the seed plants (spermatophytes). The seed plants comprise ten conifers (gymnosperms) and 3,000 flowering plants (angiosperms). Among the flowering plants—the emphasis of this article—about seven hundred kinds have been introduced from elsewhere, mostly Eurasia.

The smallest flowering plants in the world occur in Kentucky: the watermeals (*Wolffia*), freefloating, egg-shaped, pinhead-size aquatic plants. In their incredible abundance they cover ponds and sloughs with a green carpet made up of more individual plants than there are people on earth. At the other extreme is the tulip tree (*Liriodendron tulip-*

ifera), Kentucky's tallest tree species, which can grow to 190 feet tall and ten feet in trunk diameter. Tulip trees of this size are now rare, perhaps nonexistent.

Carnivorous plants, which trap and digest minute animals, are represented in Kentucky by several bladderworts (*Utricularia*), underwater plants that bear small sac-like structures acting as traps, and by two species of sundews (*Drosera*), which trap prey by means of sticky hairs on the leaves.

Of Kentucky's several parasitic flowering plants, perhaps the most easily recognized is mistletoe (*Phoradendron flavescens*), which grows on tree branches. Others are beechdrops (*Epifagus virginiana*), parasitic on roots of beech, and squawroot (*Conopholis americana*), on roots of oaks. Of agricultural concern are dodders (*Cuscuta*), which grow in tangled masses of orange-to-yellow threadlike stems on alfalfa and other cultivated and wild plants, and the introduced broomrape (*Orobanche ramosa*), parasitic on tobacco. Kentucky's two native broomrapes are *O. ludoviciana* and *O. uniflora*.

Some kinds of flowering plants occur only in Kentucky. The Cumberland rosinweed (*Silphium wasiotensis*) grows in Clay, Leslie, Perry, and Pike counties; the Kentucky gladecress (*Leavenworthia exigua* var. *laciniata*), in Bullitt and Jefferson counties; Short's goldenrod (*Solidago shortii*), in Fleming, Nicholas, and Robertson counties; and whitehair goldenrod (*Solidago albopilosa*), in sandstone rockhouses in the Red River Gorge area of Menifee, Powell, and Wolfe counties. Short's goldenrod was first found on an Ohio River island at Louisville but has been extirpated there.

Rock Island scrufpea (*Orbexilum stipulatum*), which has been found only on an Ohio River island at Louisville, has not been seen for many years, and is presumed to be extinct. It is the only known extinct species in Kentucky's modern flora—and one of the few in eastern North America.

The Kentucky plants considered poisonous range from various grasses and ragweeds that produce hay-fever-inciting pollen to plants deadly if eaten. The well-known poison ivy (*Toxicondendron radicans*) and nettles (*Laportea, Urtica*) can cause dermatitis. The introduced poison hemlock (*Conium maculatum*) is notorious among those that, when eaten, can cause illness or death. Plants poisonous to livestock include black locust (*Robinia pseudoacacia*), buckeyes (*Aesculus*), larkspur (*Delphinium tricorne*), mountain laurel (*Kalmia latifolia*), oaks (*Quercus*), rhododendron (*Rhododendron maximum*), squirrel corn (*Dicentra canadensis*), wild black cherry (*Prunus serotina*), and white snakeroot (*Eupatorium rugosum*).

Kentucky has its share of weeds—plants growing where they are not wanted—in cultivated fields, pastures, lawns, and home gardens. Among the most troublesome are cocklebur (*Xanthium strumarium*), crab grasses (*Digitaria*), giant foxtail (*Setaria faberi*), giant ragweed (*Ambrosia trifida*), Johnson grass (*Sorghum halepense*), morning-glories (*Ipomoea*), musk thistle (*Carduus nutans*), redroot (*Amaranthus hybridus*), and velvetleaf (*Abutilon theophrasti*).

Some of the edible plants that grow wild in Kentucky are as tasty as some cultivated food plants:
• Fruits—blackberries (*Rubus*), blueberries (*Vaccinium*), papaw (*Asimina triloba*), and persimmon (*Diospyros virginiana*).
• Nuts—black walnut (*Juglans nigra*), certain hickories (*Carya*), and pecan (*Carya illinoensis*).
• Seedlike fruits—American lotus (*Nelumbo lutea*).
• Greens—goosefoots (*Chenopodium*), purslane (*Portulaca oleracea*), and ramps (*Allium tricoccum*).

Even in these days of easy access to local pharmacies, people still use wild plants for medicine. Kentucky's best-known medicinal plant is ginseng (*Panax trifolius*), which has been exploited to the point that the plant is uncommon or even rare in many localities. Much ginseng from the Appalachians is exported to eastern Asia. Goldenseal (*Hydrastis canadensis*), often found growing with ginseng, is also highly regarded. Folk medicine also makes use of passion-flower (*Passiflora incarnata*), slippery elm (*Ulmus rubra*), and wild black cherry (*Prunus serotina*).

The timber trees of Kentucky—especially the hardwoods—contribute solidly to the economy. The best-known Kentucky namesake among plants is the KENTUCKY COFFEETREE (*Gymnocladus dioica*), the state tree, a species widely distributed in the eastern United States. The state's name is part of the scientific name of three Kentucky plants: a hybrid spleenwort fern (*Asplenium* x *kentuckiense*); a lady's-slipper orchid (*Cypripedium kentuckiense*); and one of the state's rare trees, the yellow-wood (*Cladrastis kentukea*).

See Earnest O. Beal and John W. Thieret, *Aquatic and Wetland Plants of Kentucky* (Frankfort, Ky., 1986); Ray Cranfill, *Ferns and Fern Allies of Kentucky* (Frankfort, Ky., 1980); Mary E. Wharton and Roger W. Barbour, *A Guide to the Wildflowers and Ferns of Kentucky* (Lexington, Ky., 1971).

MAX E. MEDLEY AND JOHN W. THIERET

FLORENCE. Florence is a middle-class city of eight square miles in eastern Boone County, located three miles south of the Greater Cincinnati International Airport and ten miles southeast of Cincinnati. Situated at the intersection of U.S. 25 and U.S. 42 near I-75, Florence is a manufacturing and commercial center of northern Kentucky. In the early 1800s the area was known as Crossroads because roads from Burlington to the northwest and Union to the southwest converged upon the north-south Ridge Road (now U.S. 25) near the future site of Florence. In 1821 the area became known as Maddentown after Covington attorney Thomas Madden, who owned a farm on the Burlington Pike. After Madden moved away, Jacob Conner, a local settler, assumed responsibility for the town in 1828

and it was named Connersville. Since there was already a town with that name in Harrison County, the name Florence was chosen in honor of Conner's wife, and it was incorporated on January 27, 1830. The city grew quickly with the completion of the Covington to Lexington Turnpike in 1836 and many new businesses were founded, including several hotels, blacksmiths, and carriage-makers.

During the Civil War and the Confederate invasion of Kentucky in the summer of 1862, elements of Brig. Gen. Henry Heth's Confederate troops threatened to attack Cincinnati and occupied Florence for a short while. After camping at Snow's Pond, a detachment of 101 Confederates was attacked at Florence on September 17, 1862, by a scouting party of fifty-three Union cavalrymen. In the ensuing skirmish, one Union soldier was killed and one wounded, five Confederates were killed and seven wounded, and one civilian was killed by a stray shot. As Union reinforcements arrived in Cincinnati, the Confederates withdrew to Lexington, then left the state after the Battle of Perryville on October 8, 1862.

John Uri LLOYD, who had grown up in Boone County, wrote a number of colorful novels that dealt with the divided loyalties of the area during the Civil War. His most popular book, *Stringtown on the Pike* (1900) drew heavily on the town of Florence as its inspiration. Sometime after 1900, Lloyd returned to Florence and restored the old town hall where his father had taught school in the 1850s.

Florence was described in 1950 as "a thriving community of law-abiding citizens," but its status as a quiet northern Kentucky suburb was rapidly changing. The Greater Cincinnati International Airport was built nearby in 1947, the Northern Kentucky Industrial Park was opened in 1959, and I-75 was completed through the area in 1963. In 1976 the Florence Mall was completed and became a regional business hub with an assortment of retail stores and shopping centers in the surrounding area. Commercial growth speeded up residential construction. Between 1985 and 1989 new commercial and residential construction in Florence exceeded $25 million in each year.

Industrial growth in Florence showed no signs of slowing in 1990, as announcements were made of a new $42 million manufacturing facility to be built by Sachs Automotive Corporation and a $60 million expansion by machine tool builder Mazak Corporation. Items produced by plants operating in the city include water meters, copying products, glass fiber panels, furniture, clothing, and building materials. The 4,200 manufacturing positions in Florence are the majority of Boone County's industrial jobs.

The third-class city is the largest in the county, with a population of 11,457 in 1970; 15,586 in 1980; and 18,624 in 1990.

See Boone County Historical Society, *Florence, Boone County, Kentucky* (Florence, Ky., 1958).

FLOYD, JOHN. John Floyd, an early surveyor and military figure in Kentucky, was born in 1750 in what is now Amherst County, Virginia, the son of William and Abadiah (Davis) Floyd. His father, of Welsh descent, was a small but apparently successful planter. Floyd's educational background is unknown, but his penmanship and spelling were above average for his time.

He was married at age eighteen to Burnell Burford, who died at the birth of their first child. Floyd became a deputy surveyor under William Preston, who in 1772 was named surveyor of newly formed Fincastle County, including most of present-day Kentucky. Floyd led a group into Kentucky in 1774 to survey tracts around the Falls of the Ohio and in the Bluegrass, which had been awarded to Virginia officers for service in the French and Indian War. Floyd led a group of settlers into Kentucky in 1775 and established St. Asaph Station on Dick's (now Dix) River, twenty miles from the Boonesborough headquarters of Richard HENDERSON's abortive Transylvania settlement. In his journal on May 3, 1775, Henderson described Floyd as a man "with a great show of Modesty and open honest countenance and no small share of good sense."

After an unsuccessful venture as partner in a privateer preying on British shipping, and a term in a British prison, Floyd returned to Virginia and in 1778 married Jane Buchanan, the ward of William Preston. In the fall of 1779 the couple, with an infant son and other family members, set out overland for the Falls of the Ohio, where Floyd had surveyed 2,000 acres in 1774 and had purchased the rights to it. There he established Floyd's Station, one of six fortified stations along the Middle Fork of Beargrass Creek, and in January 1781 was placed in command of all Jefferson County militia units. George Rogers Clark had recommended him for the post. He served with Clark in the 1780 and 1782 expeditions against the Shawnee in Ohio. Floyd was fatally wounded in an Indian ambush on April 9, 1783, on the way to a militia gathering at Bullitt's Lick, near Salt River in present-day Bullitt County. He was buried at the site of his station along Beargrass Creek, about one-half mile west of Breckinridge Lane. His children were a daughter, Mourning, born of his first wife; and sons William, George, and John, the last born twelve days after Floyd's death.

See Anna M. Cartlidge, "Colonel John Floyd: Reluctant Adventurer," *Register* 66 (Oct. 1968): 317-68; Hambleton Tapp, "Colonel John Floyd, Kentucky Pioneer," *FCHQ* 15 (Jan. 1941): 1-24.

GEORGE H. YATER

FLOYD COUNTY. Floyd County, the fortieth in order of formation, is located in eastern Kentucky and is bordered by Johnson, Martin, Pike, Knott, and Magoffin counties. It covers an area of 393 square miles. On December 13, 1799, the Kentucky General Assembly enacted the bill creating Floyd County from Fleming, Montgomery, and Mason counties, to become effective June 1, 1800. The county was named in honor of John Floyd, surveyor and pioneer explorer. Preston's Station, designated the county seat, was renamed PRESTONSBURG. The original 3,600-square-mile tract comprised the whole of the Big Sandy Valley and some adjacent territory, covering the entire eastern portion of the state. From 1806 to 1884 all or parts of fifteen other counties were formed from Floyd.

Located in the coal, oil, and natural gas fields of eastern Kentucky, Floyd County is part of the Cumberland Plateau of the Appalachian Mountain range. It is drained by the Levisa (Louisa) Fork of the Big Sandy River. The county's elevation ranges from 641 feet above sea level at Prestonsburg to more than 2,000. The other incorporated towns in the county are Allen, Wayland, Martin, and Wheelwright.

There is archeological evidence that the Adena culture, sometimes known as Mound Builders, once occupied the Big Sandy Valley. In the eighteenth century when pioneers pressed westward, the valley was defended by various tribes of Indians as their hunting grounds.

The earliest permanent settlement was founded on John's Creek in early 1790 by William Robert Leslie. The Leslies were followed by many other pioneer families: Damron, Auxier, Brown, Hammond, Weddington, Graham, Sellard, Mayo, Lackey, Layne, Martin, Leake, May, Ferguson, Spurlock, and others. Many early settlers have been honored in the names of the towns and waterways of the area.

With the act creating Floyd County, Gov. James Garrard (1796-1804) appointed John McIntire, James Young, and Jesse Spurlock as justices of the court of quarterly sessions. James Harris, Neely McGuire, Henry Stratton, Goodwin Lycan, James Ewington, and Bernet Wording were the first justices of the peace. The first courthouse burned on April 16, 1808, and the earliest available records of county activities date from September of 1808.

The first steamboat navigated the Levisa Fork of the Big Sandy River in 1837, opening a market for virgin timber in Catlettsburg at the mouth of the Big Sandy. After the Civil War, timber barons made it profitable for landowners to strip the area of hardwoods. Logging reached its peak on the Big Sandy between 1890 and 1910.

In the Civil War, Prestonsburg was a Confederate stronghold, but two battles fought in the area were Union victories: the Battle of IVY MOUNTAIN (November 8, 1861), in which Union Gen. William Nelson defeated the Confederates under Capt. Andrew Jackson May, and the Battle of Middle Creek (January 10, 1862), when Union Col. James A. Garfield's troops defeated a Confederate force under the command of Brig. Gen. Humphrey Marshall. During the Civil War, engineers recognized the signs of immense bituminous coal seams in the area and took the information to northern industrialists.

With the penetration of the railroad in 1903, coal soon became an important economic resource.

Some of the first companies to mine in Floyd County were the Northeast Coal Company of Auxier, the Middle Creek Coal Company, and the Colonial Coal and Coke Company of Prestonsburg. Deep mining became unprofitable in the late 1940s, and strip-mining took over. In the 1990s the county has struggled to diversify its economic base by adding wholesale and retail trade and service occupations.

Travelers arrived mostly on rutted wagon trails until 1920, when the hard-surfaced Mayo Trail ended a century and a half of isolation. The Mountain Parkway (completed in 1962) together with U.S. 23/460 and KY 114, further opened the area. Dewey Dam, completed on July 22, 1949, provided flood control and formed Dewey Lake. The lake is the focus of Jenny Wiley State Resort Park, completed in 1954. An outdoor amphitheater opened on July 11, 1964.

Education in the county was first provided by migratory teachers. The county received state money for education for the first time in 1843, and not until 1848 did Floyd County tax its citizens for the service. Today the Prestonsburg Community College of the University of Kentucky provides higher education, and the David School is a private, nonprofit alternative form of learning.

Among notable Floyd Countians are surgeon George P. Archer; Gov. Bert T. Combs (1959-63); educators Henry A. Campbell, Jr., and Danny Greene; historian Henry P. Scalf; newspaper publisher Norman Allen; merchant David Cooley; and authors Robert Rennick, Leonard Roberts, and Blaine Hall.

The population was 35,889 in 1970; 48,764 in 1980; and 43,586 in 1990.

See Henry P. Scalf, "Historic Floyd," *Floyd County Sesquicentennial* (Prestonsburg, Ky., 1950); Scalf, *Kentucky's Last Frontier*, 2d ed. (Pikeville, Ky., 1972).   TRISHA MORRIS

FLOYD'S STATION. Floyd's Station, one of the six stockaded, or fortified, stations on the Middle Fork of Beargrass Creek, was built in November 1779 by John FLOYD in the center of his 2,000-acre claim, in what became St. Matthews, a suburb of Louisville. Floyd claimed the land in 1774, when he was deputy surveyor for Fincastle County. He moved from his home in Amherst County, Virginia, to Kentucky to protect his claim from squatters, because immigration to that area had reached "floodlike proportions" by 1779. In so doing "Floyd was the first person to occupy land in what is now Jefferson County who had clear title to his property," according to George H. Yater. At first there was only a cabin housing Floyd, his wife, their child, three of his brothers, and two brothers-in-law. By February 1780 ten families had relocated to his settlement and a stockade had been built. As settlers continued to pour into the region, fear of Indian attacks increased, especially after the winter of 1779-80. In 1781, following a recommendation from Gen. George Rogers Clark, commander of the garrison at Fort Nelson (now Louisville), Floyd was appointed commander of the Jefferson County militia by Virginia Gov. Thomas Jefferson, and Floyd's Station became military headquarters. Floyd's tenure as militia commander, however, was short; on April 9, 1783, he was fatally wounded during an Indian ambush. Floyd's Station survived under the proprietorship of his wife, Jane Buchanan Floyd, who later married Alexander Breckinridge. She died in 1831 and was buried next to Floyd in Breckinridge Cemetery at the site of his station.

See George H. Yater, *Two Hundred Years at the Falls of the Ohio* (Louisville 1979).

FLUORSPAR INDUSTRY. Although fluorspar production in Kentucky is now minimal or nonexistent, the fluorspar industry—exploration, mining, and milling—had a significant impact on local and state-wide economies. Fluorspar is the industrial name for fluorite, the nonmetallic mineral calcium fluoride. The most important source of fluorine, fluorspar has wide application in the production of metals, ceramics, and chemicals.

In Kentucky, fluorite occurs primarily as veins or fracture-fill deposits in the complexly faulted western Kentucky fluorspar district and is associated with the Lexington and Kentucky River fault systems in the central Kentucky mineral district. The large deposits in the western district made it for many years the second largest producer of fluorspar in the United States. Most production in Kentucky has come from Crittenden and Livingston counties. A typical Kentucky fluorspar deposit is steeply dipping, pinches and swells erratically, and is a mixture of fluorite, calcite, and country rock fragments. The minerals barite, galena, and sphalerite, which commonly occur with fluorspar, are separated by milling operations. A commercial fluorspar deposit may be 3 to 10 feet wide, 200 to 400 feet long, and 100 to 200 feet high; most known Kentucky deposits are less than 800 feet below the surface. Kentucky has produced an estimated 3 million to 4 million tons of finished fluorspar, mostly from underground mines.

According to early reports, fluorspar was discovered in Kentucky by President Andrew Jackson, who sank a shaft in Crittenden County in 1835 for silver-bearing galena, or lead ore. However, the associated fluorspar that was discovered was discarded because of the lack of a market; it was not until 1873 that the first shaft was sunk for fluorspar. In the 1890s the market expanded when the basic open-hearth steel furnace was developed, since fluorspar proved to help remove impurities from iron ore. The aluminum and zinc industries took their share of fluorspar, as did new chemicals for refrigerants, heat-resistant plastics, and tooth-decay retardants.

Fluorspar production in Kentucky has varied greatly, reflecting wartime demand, economic depressions, steel industry strikes, foreign imports, technological improvements in metals industries, and environmental regulations. At peak production, during World War II and the years immediately following, fluorspar was even reclaimed from mill ponds, waste dumps, haul roads, and old workings of underground mines. With the big increase in imports of fluorspar ore, particularly from Mexico, Kentucky mining and production declined rapidly in the late 1940s and early 1950s. However, a number of fault structures that have not been completely explored may have some potential for a revival of the industry.

See Robert D. Trace, *Illinois-Kentucky Fluorspar District*, Kentucky Geological Survey, series 10, Special Publications 22, 1974.

PRESTON MCGRAIN

FLYNT, LARRY CLAXTON. Larry Claxton Flynt, nightclub owner and magazine publisher, was born November 1, 1942, near Salyersville in Magoffin County, Kentucky, the son of Larry Claxton and Edith (Arnett) Flynt. He attended public schools in Salyersville, not going beyond grade school. He served in the army in 1958 and in the navy during 1959-64. He then worked in a General Motors factory in Dayton, Ohio.

Flynt's controversial career began in 1970 when he opened the first Hustler Club in Dayton, followed by others in the Ohio cities of Columbus, Toledo, Akron, and Cleveland in the next four years. These establishments mixed a nightclub atmosphere with striptease shows and simulated performance of sexual acts. In 1974 Flynt started *Hustler*, a men's magazine specializing in female nudity and scatological and sexual humor, and *Chic*, a similar magazine for women, both published in Los Angeles. The publication of these two magazines resulted many times in his arrest on obscenity charges. On March 6, 1978, after testifying in his own defense at a trial on such charges in Lawrenceville, Georgia, Flynt was the victim of an assassination attempt that left him paralyzed from the waist down.

Flynt married Althea Leasure on August 21, 1976; they had four children: Tonya, Lisa, Teresa, and Larry Claxton III. Flynt's wife died on June 27, 1987.

FOLEY, CLYDE JULIAN. Clyde Julian ("Red") Foley, country music singer, was born at Blue Licks near Berea, Kentucky, on June 17, 1910, to Benjamin Harrison and Kathern Elizabeth (Haley) Foley. He attended Georgetown College, leaving after winning an Atwater-Kent talent contest in 1927. In 1930 he joined WLS radio's "National Barn Dance." After starring with John Lair's Cumberland Ridge Runners on Chicago's WLS, Foley helped him organize the "Renfro Valley Barn Dance" in 1939. During 1946-54 Foley hosted NBC's national radio segment of the "Grand Ole Opry." His "Peace in the Valley" was the first gospel record to sell a million copies, and his "Chattanoogie Shoe Shine Boy" was the first country record to reach No. 1 on the pop charts. Foley hosted the "Ozark Jubilee" on ABC-TV during 1956-62. In 1967 he became the first Kentuckian elected to the Country Music Hall of Fame. His first wife, Pauline Cox, one of the Three Little Maids singers, died in childbirth; he later married Eva Overstake. His third wife was Sallie Sweet. One of his daughters, Shirley, married singer Pat Boone. Foley died on a "Grand Ole Opry" tour on September 19, 1969, and was buried in Nashville.

See John Pugh, "The Late, Great Red Foley," *Country Music* 5 (June 1976): 53-56; Charles K. Wolfe, *Kentucky Country* (Lexington, Ky., 1982).

CHARLES F. FABER

FOLK ARCHITECTURE. The folk architecture of Kentucky is generally characteristic of traditional building throughout the Upland South. Folk architecture in this region is primarily a synthesis of British, Irish, and central European building practices brought to the area by settlers from the mid-Atlantic and upper Chesapeake regions. Debates still rage over the specific Old World antecedents of certain house types and construction techniques; it is evident, however, that the settlers exchanged building technologies, eliminated some Old World practices, and modified their architecture to fit economic, environmental, and social needs, thus creating a distinctly American folk architecture.

The most typical folk houses of the upland South are small one- or two-unit dwellings. The single-pen house is a single construction unit. At its smallest it may be a one-room cabin; it may also have an upstairs or a loft, and a partition may divide the unit into two rooms. Two equal-size units built around a central chimney form a saddlebag house. A related building form is the double-pen house with exterior end chimneys. If there is an open passage between the two pens, then the dwelling is a dogtrot house. Frequently, however, this open passage is later enclosed, creating a form of the central-passage house. A larger folk house form quite common in many parts of Kentucky is a central-passage dwelling two stories in height and a single room in depth, often dubbed an I-house by scholars. This form is found in many parts of the United States, but is particularly common in Kentucky and Tennessee. In the nineteenth century, these dwellings were often the homes of moderately prosperous people living in the rural parts of the state.

Folk architecture in Kentucky is most frequently associated with log construction, but folk builders used stone, brick, frame, and vertical plank construction. Some variations in preferred construction technique and house plans are due to the preponderance of certain ethnic groups in a particular area. In the Bluegrass, late eighteenth and early nineteenth century stone structures show the influence of Scotch-Irish or other British building traditions. Some remnants of Dutch building technology remain in the folk architecture of Mercer, Shelby, and Henry counties. Traditional buildings in the area near Covington and Newport exhibit a stronger German influence.

Variation in folk architecture within the state also reflects the availability of materials and particularly the economic base of the specific part of the state. Differences are found in the choice of house size, the detailing, and especially the continuance or abandonment of aspects of traditional building. In prosperous areas such as the Bluegrass, the proportion of folk houses to those based on elite and popular styles was smaller, and the majority abandoned traditional building at an earlier date. The most conservative folk architectural tradition is found in the Appalachian areas of eastern Kentucky, where the use of vertical log construction and the building of small traditional houses continued well into the early twentieth century. A relatively conservative tradition of folk building also survived in the rural parts of south-central and western Kentucky.

Although folk architecture is usually thought of as rural building, one form is more likely to be found in Kentucky's cities and towns: the long, narrow "shotgun" house, one room wide and several rooms deep. Some scholars have hypothesized that the shotgun house, influenced by African and Caribbean traditions, first appeared in New Orleans. In Kentucky, Louisville is particularly noted for its early forms of the shotgun house. In many parts of the state, the shotgun house is perhaps more commonly a popular rather than a folk house form, as builders constructed them as a form of speculative housing. As in much of the South, the shotgun house is often associated with African-American occupants.

See William Lynwood Montell and Michael Lynn Morse, *Kentucky Folk Architecture* (Lexington, Ky., 1976); Charles E. Martin, *Hollybush: Folk Building and Social Change in an Appalachian Community* (Knoxville, Tenn., 1984).

MICHAEL ANN WILLIAMS

FOLK ARTS AND CRAFTS. Folk arts and crafts are traditional forms of artistic expression that convey the values of a folk group and are usually learned through customary example. The distinction between art and craft is frequently arbitrary. In art, it is said, the aesthetic function predominates, while in craft the practical function is more important. However, in truth, most Kentucky folk art combines both aspects to varying degrees. The quilt may be a work of art, though it also has a practical function. More and more frequently, functional items such as baskets are displayed by owners as works of art, but their aesthetic dimension is present even when baskets are used to gather eggs or carry tobacco plants.

Kentucky is noted for the survival of traditional arts and crafts typically associated with the upland South: the crafting of white oak baskets, traditional musical instruments, handmade brooms, and wooden chains and toys. Creation sometimes occurs in traditional contexts, but the traditional craft forms have often changed in terms of how artists learn the skills and who inspires the creation of the piece. In the past century, a variety of groups and individuals in the state have promoted and revived traditional arts. In the early settlement schools and at Berea College, the marketing of traditional arts

and crafts was seen as a form of economic self-help for Kentucky residents. Such views have served to preserve, but also to change, many folk arts and crafts.

Some folk arts have always had a commercial aspect, of course. The traditional weaver or potter sold the products to make a livelihood. Even in the nineteenth century, craftspersons such as potters sometimes developed extensive trade networks. Economic changes have often forced craftspeople to adapt. For instance, southern potters who marketed utilitarian stoneware through much of the nineteenth century responded to the declining market for the wares in the early decades of this century by producing unglazed horticultural ware or glazed dinnerware. In Kentucky, the Cornelison family of Madison County, which has produced pottery in a family tradition since the early nineteenth century, produced garden wares in the early twentieth century and in the 1940s developed the glazed dinnerware for which the BYBEE POTTERY is famous.

The products of the arts at Kentucky's two SHAKER COMMUNITIES, Pleasant Hill and South Union, are relatively unadorned, while the Shakers lavished attention on the perfection of form. Every aspect of their lives was imbued with religious belief, and their values are reflected in the products they created. Shakers are best known for their architecture, furniture, and oval boxes, but Kentucky Shakers also produced iridescent silk kerchiefs from their own silk industry. Because their arts so appeal to modern aesthetics, craftspeople still replicate and sell Shaker products.

Although Shaker reproductions and the products of folk craft revivals are commercial objects, Kentucky's folk arts also survive within traditional contexts. Women's domestic arts are among the most enduring. Needlework, especially, expresses traditional values and is often learned in traditional ways. Even the preparation of food may be an artistic outlet. Canned vegetables or a chocolate pie may be judged aesthetically, in appearance, as well as taste. Folk arts are not stagnant; although the design may be traditional, a quilter may use polyester batting or do some of the sewing on a machine. Instead of using scraps from home sewing projects, the quilter may choose materials from the fabric store, or perhaps recycle in another way by using scraps from a local textile plant. New forms that express traditional values or concepts may also be considered folk art. The values and aesthetics of recycling are especially enduring. Homemade planters in the form of truck tires and whirligigs made of Clorox bottles dot the landscape in many parts of rural Kentucky.

Some folk artists go beyond the limits established by traditional aesthetics. Folklorist Michael Owen Jones studied a Kentucky chairmaker, for instance, who learned the craft in a traditional way but created eccentric forms such as rocking chairs with extra legs or built-in bookcases. Some artists are driven by a personal vision or aesthetic that is well outside the norms of either academic or traditional art. Sometimes labeled contemporary folk artists, they are perhaps better known as visionary or grass-roots artists.

See Michael Owen Jones, *The Handmade Object and its Maker* (Berkeley, Calif., 1975); Jan Arnow, *By Southern Hands: A Celebration of Craft Traditions in the South* (Birmingham, Ala., 1987).

MICHAEL ANN WILLIAMS

FOLK DANCE. Pioneer dances, both ballroom and backwoods kinds, are still alive in Kentucky. Various communities enjoy the older forms of folk dance, some of them dating back to the sixteenth century. Among the forms found in Kentucky are ancient circle dances, seventeenth century dances in rows, and nineteenth century dances in which couples move freely around the ballroom. Newer introductions, such as Western-style square dancing and ethnic dances brought to Kentucky by later immigrants, are part of the culture of the larger cities. In Louisville, for example, the active ethnic dance community includes Greek, Asian, Indian, Scottish, and English country and morris dancers, with several international dance clubs.

The heritage of folk dancing in Kentucky can be divided into at least four early types: 1) Kentucky set running, an early form of square dancing; 2) step-dancing, including clogging; 3) singing dances, sometimes called play-party games; and 4) country dances.

The Kentucky version of set running is a rare survivor of a form of dance dating back at least as early as the sixteenth century in the villages of the British Isles. In those villages, the dance died out during the Industrial Revolution of the eighteenth century. The patterns of set dancing as it survives in Kentucky reflect a cooperative society in which each person takes a turn. Dancers choose partners and each couple joins hands with the others to make a circle, stepping in an easy lope, with perhaps a shuffle added here and there. The first couple to lead out is the caller and his partner. They dance in turn with each of the other couples, in effect introducing them to the figure being called. After the first couple has introduced each of the others, there is a little promenade and the second couple then leads out. When the second couple completes its tour of the circle, the other couples lead out in turn until the last couple finishes the pattern. The dance concludes with a special figure involving the entire circle, or perhaps with a game.

Some of the figures in set running are the remnants of an ancient ring of pagan worshipers circling a well or a tree, or the magical serpentine winding in and out often found in prehistoric ceremonies. During the early seventeenth century, the British upper classes began to include the villagers' simple forms in their own social dances, calling them country dances. The country dances were soon exported to France, where they evolved from contre to cotillion and quadrille. All of these dances were in fashion in America during the colonial and Revolutionary War periods, and they are the foundation for the most popular forms of American folk

dance today. Country dances were regularly included in both public balls and private festivities in the larger plantation homes of the Bluegrass and western Kentucky. Dancing masters were hired by subscription in the months preceding the ball to prepare the participants for the event, where the dances were much more fashionable and sophisticated than Kentucky set running. During the late nineteenth century and the early twentieth, dance halls were built at Kentucky resorts.

Set running in its older form is still danced in a few eastern Kentucky communities. A more modern form of set running, called big set, big circle, or mountain square dancing, is popular in a wider section of the southeastern United States. Today's circles may include more than a hundred couples, making them too large for each couple to take a turn. This problem is resolved in the big circle variation by making every other couple the lead couple, so that all can begin dancing without delay. At a big circle, the caller, equipped with a microphone, does not dance. Bluegrass bands usually supply live music.

Step dancing in its old style was danced solo to live music and appeared to be improvised. Each community and each dancer developed a characteristic style—upper body rigid or loose, arms held down or flailing, a simple shuffle or complex footwork. The result might be called buck dancing, buck and wing, hoedown, jigging, foot stomping, or clogging. Old-style step dancers can still be found in most rural communities, but their talents often go unrecognized. In the more modern style of step dancing—precision clogging—skilled teams perform an intricate series of steps choreographed to a recorded tune. Precision cloggers perform for an audience, on television, or in competition with other cloggers.

The type of folk dancing called play-party games originated as a popular form of public courtship among young people before the days of television or videos. Some of the Kentucky play-parties from the past have British roots: skip-to-my-Lou, jubilee, jolly miller, going to Boston, Charlie, and old brass wagon. African roots show up in jump Josie, Jennie crack corn, and candy gal. The games of younger children pass on some very old play-parties in the form of ring around the rosy and the hokey pokey.

Cecil Sharp, a noted English folklorist who visited Kentucky in 1916-17, is perhaps the major figure in the history of folk dancing in the commonwealth. Having discovered a few villages in England where ancient morris dances and ritual sword dances were still being performed, Sharp was well able to appreciate the significance of Kentucky set running when he saw it danced at Pine Mountain Settlement School in Harlan County in August 1917. His scholarly description of set running is the earliest and best that is known. His appreciation of set running enhanced eastern Kentuckians' love for their own dance, and he created an interest in English folk dances by teaching three of them to the Pine Mountain staff while visiting there. He also started a revival of early country dances, based on notations first published by John Playford in 1651.

Thousands of Kentucky schoolchildren over the years have learned Kentucky set running and English folk dances as participants in BEREA COLLEGE's annual Mountain Folk Festival, organized in 1936. To train leaders for the festival, Berea College in 1938 instituted the Christmas Country Dance School, a week-long course during the Christmas holiday. Twenty-six representatives of schools and communities who appreciated the educational and social benefits of folk dancing attended the first course, often in spite of strong religious objections.

Two other annual festivals celebrate Kentucky's folk dance heritage: the Kentucky Dance Institute, where some of America's leaders in international folk dancing train participants from across the United States and other countries, and the Kentucky Summer Dance School, a family event that focuses on Kentucky and Anglo-American traditions. The Kentucky Dance Institute was organized in 1953 by Shirley Durham Fort, of the Louisville Recreation Department; M.G. Karsner, of the University of Kentucky; and Frank Kaltman, producer of Folkraft Records. After sessions at Hazel Green Academy in Hazel Green and at Lees Junior College in Jackson, the annual Kentucky Dance Institute moved to Morehead State University in Morehead, where it has been held since. The Kentucky Summer Dance School was organized in 1982 at Midway College in Midway by Leslie Trent Auxier and W. Donald Coffey. In 1986 it moved to Berea College, where it is now held annually.

See Frank H. Smith, *The Appalachian Square Dance* (Berea, Ky., 1955); Lloyd Shaw, *Cowboy Dances* (Caldwell, Ind., 1945).

JOHN M. RAMSAY

FOLK INSTRUMENTS. The instruments favored by Kentucky's folk musicians include the dulcimer; the mountain, or folk, banjo; the mandolin; the fiddle; the guitar; and the harmonica. With the possible exception of the dulcimer, none of these instruments is native to Kentucky; as part of a traditional folk process, however, Kentuckians have created homemade versions of all of them except the harmonica. For instance, banjos and guitars, and even fiddles, were made by stretching the skin of a groundhog or other animal over a makeshift box (often hand-carved or fashioned from tin cans, or an old cigar or dynamite box—or even a gourd), and using screen wire for strings and brass safety pins for frets. Employing similar folk ingenuity, Kentuckians have traditionally converted various other everyday objects into instruments to satisfy their desire to make music: bottles and jugs to blow into; old-fashioned washboards rubbed with a stick; a galvanized washtub pounded as a drum or converted into a huge stringed instrument by stretching a wire across it; bones, spoons, and other eating utensils beaten together; saws, both crosscut and hand, played like a bass fiddle; whittled and notched sticks rubbed together; pocket combs wrapped with waxed paper or cellophane to vibrate and hum with the mouth; or a simple piece of wire stretched between two electric wire insulators—or even between nails driven into a board or the side of a barn—to be plucked.

Indisputably one of the older of American folk instruments, the dulcimer was probably invented in the southern mountains, very likely by some unknown early settler from Pennsylvania German country who, not having been able to bring an instrument with him in the move to the southern mountains, created the dulcimer from memories of one or more similar European instruments, perhaps the German *sheitholt*. The invention, copied again and again by others, became the traditional Appalachian, or mountain, dulcimer (some even call it the Kentucky dulcimer). The most common shape is an elongated figure eight; most dulcimers have three or four strings over a fretboard, based on a diatonic scale. Played in a seated position by holding it on the lap and strumming it, sometimes with a feather quill, the instrument produces a soft sweet sound that is the source of the name (*dolce* means "sweet"). Some scholars believe the dulcimer may be a Kentucky invention, as many of the early known dulcimer makers were Kentuckians. The best known is J.E. THOMAS, born in 1850 in Letcher County, who lived in Bath County.

See R. Gerald Alvey, *Dulcimer Maker: The Craft of Homer Ledford* (Lexington, Ky., 1984); Gene Bluestein, "America's Folk Instrument: Notes on the Five-String Banjo," *Western Folklore* 23 (1964): 241-48. R. GERALD ALVEY

FOLKLIFE. The early folk culture strains in Kentucky were of European and African ancestry, largely from the British Isles and West Africa. The content of older folk songs, folk tales, and legends among both white and black Kentuckians attests to this heritage, and language survivals from both Europe and Africa are still discernible in some parts of the state. The vast but more recent repertory of folk songs and family stories from two centuries of Kentucky's own life and thought reveal a real flair for folk creativity and ingenuity.

Although Kentucky's Anglo and African heritages tend to dominate the folklife scene, other Euro-Americans have left their mark as well. Scattered colonies of later-arriving Swiss, Italian, and Welsh are found in Kentucky, mainly in the eastern portion. Germans left their cultural imprint on northern Kentucky, the Louisville area, and western portions of the state. Fancy Farm, a Graves County settlement founded by Germans in the nineteenth century, is known for the traditional picnic that kicks off every statewide political race. In more recent times, Kentucky has become home to Asian nationals, largely from Japan, Vietnam, Laos, and Cambodia. Kentucky's folk heritage is a patchwork of traditional cultures.

Folklorists have long been interested in Kentuckians' folk beliefs, superstitions, ballads, lyric songs, dance forms, and folk narratives. The study of folklife, however, has a much broader range, extending to all forms of expression that are derived from traditional patterns of living. Verbal utterances—proverbs, nicknames, stories of all varieties—are one category of folklife, as are customs, ranging from debutante balls to agricultural practices, and material objects shaped or made by hand (arts and crafts, architecture, landscapes, and ways with food). Contemporary Kentucky folklife scholars are thus interested in the lifestyles of all Kentuckians—young and old, rural and urban, black and white—who treasure and maintain cultural stability in the face of social change. For this reason, folklife field workers seek out urban artisans who make the Louisville Slugger baseball bats (or apply wax seals to whiskey bottles) with the same intensity with which they seek traditional basketmakers and quilters throughout the state. Making baseball bats or baskets, like banjo frailing, story telling, or folk dancing, is enduring evidence of artistry and craftsmanship.

Traditional cooking habits are one such practice, in evidence at family reunions, community picnics, gospel singings, and dinners-on-the-ground observed by many rural Kentucky church groups. The butter, home-butchered meats, deviled eggs, pastries, and home-grown vegetables cooked according to time-honored recipes are just as much a part of the folk process as the nine-patch quilt or the handmade comforter. Of course, not all folk traditions persist indefinitely. Some exist today only in the form of revivalisms, staged to depict the roles they played at a precise time in Kentucky's history: the shivaree, for example—the traditional dangerous frolicking that followed a wedding in the family or community. The shivaree has passed from the scene, along with social institutions such as the Friday afternoon ciphering matches in rural small town schools, the party games played instead of square dancing, and the candy breakings or corn huskings. Other traditions grow up to take their place, however, as times and social conditions change. Among the folklife forms of the last half of the twentieth century are teen cruising, slumber parties, tailgate picnics at athletic events, and drag racing.

In this age of rapid technological change, Kentuckians can find continuity in a rich heritage of family and community traditions.

LYNWOOD MONTELL

FOLK MEDICINE. Folk medicine is defined as medical beliefs and practices that lie for the most part outside the realm of scientific medicine. The methods are largely traditional, not learned in schools of medicine. To aid in home treatment, medical manuals for laymen became widely available in the late nineteenth and early twentieth centuries. Typically, they provided detailed descriptions of diseases and outlined treatments, usually with herbs and minerals, to be followed in the home.

Much folk medicine made use of plants and plant products. In Kentucky, over two hundred types of plants were used. For example, boiled poke root, strained and poured into the bathwater, was an effective, though painful, treatment for "the itch," or scabies. Hickory bark, white pine needles, and mullein boiled together, with sugar added, made a pleasant cough medicine. For poison ivy, the watery sap of the common jewel weed might be rubbed on the blisters to relieve the itching. The inner bark of willow trees contains salicin, which was used as a kind of natural aspirin.

Some folk remedies seem to defy any classification other than strange and mysterious. To cure shingles, painful little blisters that form along the paths of nerves in the skin, you might wring the head from a "coal-black chicken in the dead of the night" and rub the blood on the blisters. For sties, go to the fork of a road, decide which fork to take, and say, "Sty, sty, leave my eye, catch the next one passes by," then walk down the road you've chosen "and don't look back." An ax or knife placed under the bed with the sharp edge upward would "cut the pain" of childbirth.

In the realm of folk medicine, there is a special role for "healers." There were—and still are—people with the reputation of being able to stop bleeding, even serious arterial bleeding, without tourniquets, pressure bandages, or poultices. Others could take the "fire," the searing pain, out of a burn, and many healers are reputed to have been able to remove warts by "buying" them or "charming" them off. "Thrash doctors," also part of Kentucky folk medicine lore, appear to be particularly tied to superstitious belief, usually belief in "the seventh son of a seventh son." A baby suffering from "thrash" (thrush), a usually mild inflammation of the mucus membranes of the mouth, could be treated by having the folk doctor blow into its mouth seven times.

Veterinary folk medicine followed the same general patterns as medicine for human beings. Herbs, minerals, and mysterious cures were the rule in treating animals too. For example, powdered bracket fungi was prescribed for worms in dogs, as was finely powdered limestone for abrasions in livestock. For swollen udder, also called milk fever, a flat rock, taken from the running water of a creek and rubbed on the udder three times, could effect a cure.

Folk medicine survives in Kentucky, but mainly among the elderly, as tales to be told, and among the few who have learned to accept it as an alternative to costly modern medical practices. Most Kentuckians, however, when facing even the most minor illnesses, place their trust in the latest medical treatments. As Kentucky urbanizes, traditional medical practices seem quaint or are simply being forgotten—not to mention that the gathering of herbs to make folk medicines has proved to be too inconvenient in the Kentucky of the late twentieth century.

ERNEST MARTIN TUCKER

FOLK NARRATIVE. Throughout their history, Kentuckians have cultivated an oral narrative tradition. Even before the state's boundaries were fixed, stories about the area's untamed beauty lured settlers in search of a wilderness paradise. The Kentucky frontier was fertile ground for tall tales about men who successfully wrestled bears and wildcats. As character types they became national heroes dubbed "Kaintucks." Some of the tales found their way into nineteenth century fiction.

As Scotch-Irish and English settlers moved into the area, fairy tales with formulaic beginnings like "once upon a time" and happy endings became part of the state's oral traditions. Also called *märchen* (a German word), these stories are predominantly associated with the Appalachian region and include versions of such tales as "Cinderella," "Sleeping Beauty," and "Rumpelstiltskin." In another well-known Appalachian cycle of tales, the "Jack tales," the hero, Jack, outwits the devil and slays giants, among a host of other adversaries. As settlements were planted and the people adjusted to their new physical and social environments, so did their narratives. Passed from one generation to the next in the idiom of the Appalachian people, stories reflected the mountain way of life.

In *The Harvest and the Reaper: Oral Tradition of Kentucky* (1974), Kenneth and Mary Clarke trace the chronological development and study of the state's folk narratives, including those collected in remote sections of eastern Kentucky by Leonard Roberts. Roberts's *South from Hell-fer-Sartin* (1950) introduces more than a hundred tales of giants, ghosts, and magical objects, with descriptions of the folklife where they are told. He recalled a storytelling session in a mountain cabin where the grandmother of the family was persuaded to share some of her tales around the fireplace; one tale led to another and the session lasted most of the night. Roberts wrote with regret about the changes rapidly coming to the mountains that would mean the end of such scenes. Even at the time Roberts was collecting stories, Old World *märchen* were highly localized, and as roads and electricity pushed deeper into remote areas, storytelling was displaced by travel, radio, and television as the primary form of entertainment.

While Roberts was focusing on the traditional narratives of Appalachia, folklorists in other regions of the state were collecting other types of stories. At the University of Kentucky, William Hugh Jansen conducted an extensive collection project covering the Bluegrass area. Herbert Halpert and Mildred Hatcher, both of Murray State University, bagged a number of older narrative forms from Purchase storytellers, but their publication revealed a paucity of Old World stories. They, along with D.K. Wilgus and Lynwood Montell, who worked southern Kentucky by and large, recorded numerous belief tales, stories about local characters, and folk legends.

Tales that are told as true are called belief tales and are found in all regions of the state. A belief tale that enjoys wide popularity in the state is the ghost story. One story collected in a small town in the western part of the state describes the image of a young girl etched into the glass of a dormer window. Dressing for a very special social event when a storm struck, she prayed for good weather, but the storm continued. When the angry girl cursed God, lightning struck the house, killing the girl and etching her image in the windowpane forever. Attempts to cover the image or to remove it have repeatedly failed. Similar folktales of persistent images or bloodstains are very old, and various versions of them can be found in communities throughout the state.

The Saga of Coe Ridge: A Study in Oral History (1970) by Lynwood Montell is a landmark work in oral history and a study of folk narratives as well. It focuses on a small black Cumberland County community on the Tennessee border that was formed shortly after the Civil War. Virtually inaccessible, Coe Ridge sheltered black moonshiners and white fugitives until the 1930s. From interviews with the people of Coe Ridge, Montell reconstructed many events that had produced folk legends. In one such account a man is murdered and the murderer confesses, but local people claim to have known before the confession that the man was guilty, saying the murdered man's corpse oozed blood as the killer approached. As narratives about people, places, or events that are told as true, folk legends circulate widely throughout the commonwealth. They tend to focus on unusual circumstances surrounding an event, the eccentricities of a well-known local personality, or the antics of a group of pranksters. Such legends provide explanations for many of Kentucky's unusual place names, and they often supply details of unique or historical events at sites around the state.

Also of interest to later folklorists are family stories, narratives that people make up in response to real-life experiences, and contemporary legends that typically have an urban setting. Family stories describe the history and folklife of family members and usually include narratives about grandparents, cousins, aunts and uncles, in-laws, and nieces and nephews as well as parents and children. Their telling may be inspired by such things as a walk through a cemetery, a box of old photographs, a keepsake passed from one generation to another, a homecoming, or personal memories of happy and sad times.

Contemporary legends describe current concerns and beliefs about our fast-paced culture, and Kentucky like all other parts of the country has its share of such stories. Legends about worms in hamburgers and spider eggs in bubble gum reflect misgivings about our hurried, anonymous, consumer-oriented society. Stories about saving pull-tabs from soda pop cans to aid a desperately ill person reflect our need to turn an essentially useless item into something that will help someone and provide us with the sense that, despite our anonymity, we are caring people.

Folk narratives in the commonwealth have changed over the years to reflect current concerns, customs, and beliefs. A strong feeling for oral tradition persists even today, and anyone with the time to listen reaps a bounty of information and entertainment from the stories to be heard.

LAURA HARPER LEE

FONTAINE FERRY PARK. From 1905 to 1969, Fontaine Ferry Park was Louisville's foremost amusement park and family recreation center. Located at 230 South Western Parkway, Fontaine Ferry's sixty-four acres offered fifty-one rides and riverside attractions, including Hilarity Hall, the Racing Derby, Gypsy Village, and a hand-carved 1910 Dentzel carousel. Generations of families enjoyed swimming, roller skating, picnicking, and entertainment from Sousa to Sinatra.

The park evolved from Capt. Aaron Fontaine's Ohio River ferry landing and estate, originally called Carter's Ferry, purchased in 1814 from William Lytle. Fontaine, a Virginia militiaman, settled in Kentucky at Harrods Creek in Jefferson County in 1798. The twenty-six children in the combined families of Fontaine and his second wife, Elizabeth Thruston, included daughters who married names prominent in Louisville's early history: Cosby, Floyd, Jacob, Pope, Prather, and Todd. In 1887 Tony Landenwich purchased Fontaine's Ferry and established a riverside hotel, outdoor restaurant, bandstand, and world-class bicycle racetrack. Hopkins Amusements of St. Louis entered in 1903 with plans to build a grand-scale amusement park, which opened as Fontaine Ferry Park in May 1905. Misspellings and mispronunciations such as "Fountain" Ferry were common throughout its history.

Racially integrated in 1964, Fontaine Ferry Park was heavily vandalized during racial unrest of May 4, 1969. Sold by owner J.R. Singhiser, the property was renovated in 1972 as Ghost Town on the River, then renamed River Glen Park for its unsuccessful last season in 1975. After a series of spectacular fires, the city purchased the site, which since 1981 has been a passive park.

JERRY L. RICE

FOODWAYS. Kentucky's foodways traditions—ideas about what is edible and how to procure it, prepare it, and preserve it—started with Native American foodways, before Europeans settled in the area. Although basically a hunting and gathering society, Native Americans had domesticated corn, pumpkin, squash, beans, and various herbs. The earliest settlers hunted and gathered as well. They integrated many Indian foods into their diet and borrowed Indian methods for preserving and preparing food, most notably drying of corn. Corn became a pioneer staple—milled, roasted, boiled, or baked; served as hominy, mush, or grits; and dried, parched, or pickled. It was a basic ingredient in breads, porridges, cakes, and even whiskey.

Raising a crop was a requirement for a homesteader who wanted to claim land; corn, which yielded well on newly cleared land, was a staple of the pioneer diet. Fresh corn was roasted on the ear, or removed from the cob and stewed in a skillet, but the most prevalent form was meal, finely ground from kernels of dried corn placed in a wooden mortar and pounded with a wooden pestle. According to an old Kentucky adage, "The less you have to eat, the more you know about cooking," and corn meal required of the pioneer cook an exercise in imagination. Depending on how it was cooked, corn meal mixed with water became ash cake, corn pone, mush, griddle cakes, corn bread, or johnny cake (the colloquial version of journey cake, so named because it traveled well). Corn meal served not only as bread in its many forms but—when skillfully fermented and distilled—also as beverage, often used as a nonperishable medium of exchange. As well as being served at the table as grits or hominy, corn was fed to the livestock, making it the ideal pioneer crop.

As cooking utensils, the settlers brought skillets (including the long-legged variety known as spiders), griddles, large iron pots for stews, a few wooden vessels, and perhaps pewter plates. Creekside gristmills for grinding corn, the centers of little settlements, naturally expanded to process wheat into flour, more expensive than corn meal, which went into gravies, biscuits, piecrusts, yeast breads, and the cakes that pioneers baked for special occasions. Compensating for the lack of proper ovens, ingenious stack cakes were assembled from many thin layers, sandwiched with jam or stewed dried fruits.

In the diet of early Kentucky settlers, turnips, cowpeas, and sweet potatoes were the vegetables that turned up most often. Cornbread was the staff of Kentucky life until late in the nineteenth century, when mass marketing brought inexpensive wheat flour. Most herbs grown were used for medicine and home cures rather than in food preparation. Hogs, cattle, and domesticated fowl replaced wild game as major sources of protein. Country hams from Kentucky, preserved through dry salting or sugar curing, became renowned. Fish were a major food source for Kentuckians before indiscriminate fishing practices, such as seining and dynamiting, and pollution of rivers and lakes reduced the take.

Salt from Kentucky's plentiful salt springs was boiled down from brines at the site and then transported in its crystal state. Making salt was a time-consuming process that was also dangerous; there are numerous accounts of Indian ambushes at salt licks. The risk was unavoidable, however, as salt—far more than a seasoning—was essential for the preservation of meats, and indeed for life itself.

As danger lessened and the frontier stabilized, livestock on the family farm diversified, as did the menus. Fed on ever-present corn, hogs were cheap to raise, with little waste. The hams and bacon they yielded were salt- and smoke-cured, lard was rendered (producing cracklings for crackling corn bread), larger pieces of pork were salted away in barrels, and sausage was made of the remainder. Cattle and poultry enriched the diet with butter, cream, eggs, and a wider variety of meats. Kentucky's famous corn pudding, spoon bread, and chess pie came from custardy additions to corn; buttermilk biscuits were a change from beaten ones; and chicken, fried or served with dumplings, was a frequent Sunday treat.

Hocks and fat bacon gave flavor to wild greens and a few home-grown vegetables. By the mid-nineteenth century, the list of cultivated vegetables in Kentucky included tomatoes, green beans, carrots, cabbage, pumpkins, potatoes, turnips, peas, and cucumbers. The most popular fruits were apples, cherries, peaches, pears, plums, and strawberries. Canned, preserved, or dried for winter use, garden produce supplemented wild fruits, nuts, and berries, which—with honey, molasses, and maple syrup—made Kentucky farmers practically self-sufficient. Seasoning came from wild herbs and the carefully tended herb garden, the source also of most medicines.

As a variety of settlers came to Kentucky, bringing their own food heritage, the Anglo-Saxon, Scottish, Irish, and Scotch-Irish joined the Indian as the roots of Kentucky's foodways traditions. The culinary traditions included roasting, stewing, and curing meats; frying foods in lard; and preserving fruits and vegetables as pickles, fruit butter, or marmalades. Immigrants of other ethnic traditions—blacks brought in as slaves, Germans, Dutch, and French—added their foodways traditions to the Kentucky pot.

German immigrants brought sauerkraut to Louisville and Covington, river trade from the South gave barbecue to western Kentucky, and the isolation of the mountains resulted in greater creativity with locally produced foods. Eating habits caused by shortages during wars and the Depression grew into a genuine fondness for soup beans and other simple, nonindigenous, nourishing fare.

The resourceful Kentucky cook, spurred by adversity and a limited number of ingredients, utilized what was available to create a wide variety of appetizing dishes: not just preserved pork, but Kentucky country ham; not raw spirits, but Kentucky bourbon whiskey. Prosperous landholders, particularly in the Bluegrass region, soon emulated their Virginia forebears in the quantity and quality of viands set forth on polished walnut and cherry, but the same basic ingredients, differing only in extent of preparation, were offered on simple homemade tables in hillside cabins.

Women were in charge of gathering, preparing, and preserving food. Female slaves did much of the food production in Kentucky for those able to afford slaves, and after emancipation even the middle class ate meals prepared by black or immigrant women working as domestics. As nineteenth century middle-class white women adopted the cult of domesticity, food preparation, home management, and entertaining took on major importance in their lives, as demonstrated by the proliferation of cookbooks. One of the early American books on food preparation was Lettice Bryan's *The Kentucky Housewife* (1839). Its descendants include Minerva Carr Fox's *The Blue Grass Cook Book* (1904), *The*

Blue Ribbon Cook Book (1904) by Jennie C. Benedict, *Adventures in Good Cooking* (1939) by Duncan Hines, and Marion K. Flexner's *Out of Kentucky Kitchens* (1949). These books contained a variety of recipes covering such distinctive regional Kentucky foods as burgoo, barbecue, country hams, hot brown sandwiches, beaten biscuits, and chess pie.

Industrialization reduced the reliance on local agriculture, and modern technology transformed food production, preparation, and preservation. Canned goods, refrigeration, cookstoves, and staples such as inexpensive wheat flour and white sugar changed food traditions in major ways. Reliance on local, seasonal foods gave way to the variety introduced by mass marketing and distribution through supermarkets. Modern means of transportation and communication brought a wide range of foods to once-isolated areas and swallowed up regional cooking differences in a mass, homogeneous menu that includes Kentucky fried chicken. As the United States became a player in international events, starting with World War I, a distinctive national cuisine has emerged in which barbecue, burgoo, and mint juleps have a place.

See John Egerton, *Southern Food: At Home, On the Road, in History* (New York 1987); Janet Alm Anderson, *A Taste of Kentucky* (Lexington, Ky., 1986).

MARTY GODBEY AND JEANNETTE S. DUKE

FOOTBALL. Ever since Walter Camp began in 1880 to transform rugby into American football, the sport has played a central role in the recreational lives of Kentuckians. Football officially arrived in Kentucky on April 9, 1880, when Kentucky University (now University of Kentucky) played Centre College in what was one of the first organized football games in the state. Kentucky University won the game by 13¾ to 0. Though this may have been the first organized contest in Kentucky, many loosely structured, unofficial football games had been played previously. These nonsanctioned events in many instances met with disapproval from local communities, probably because these games, with twenty-five players per team, more closely resembled a brawl than a sporting event. Indeed, a Maysville ordinance of 1877 prohibited the playing of football in that city. In 1896 the Agricultural and Mechanical College (formerly Kentucky University) tried to abolish football until the faculty agreed to supervise the games more closely.

Rebounding from their initial loss to Kentucky University, Centre College by 1891 had become a football powerhouse. Between 1891 and 1894 the small Danville school recorded three undefeated seasons. The apex of Centre College football came in the early 1920s. After another undefeated season in 1919, Centre had won national recognition and played dominant teams such as Harvard on their 1920 schedule. Although they lost to Harvard that year (31-14), the Centre team was victorious over Harvard in 1921 (6-0). Centre retained its football juggernaut status until 1924, when graduations and the resignation of coach Charles Moran in 1923 cost the Centre squad some of its most important assets.

During this early era, football in Kentucky was tainted by the introduction of ringers (exceptional players who were not students) to play for a team on a given day. To prevent the degradation of the sport, a national rules committee of college officials was formed in 1906. It was the forerunner of the American Intercollegiate Football Rules Committee, which in 1910 became the National Collegiate Athletic Association (NCAA).

Central University (now Eastern Kentucky University) fielded its first team in 1892, and Western Kentucky State Normal School (now Western Kentucky University) played its first football game in 1913. In 1925 Western, along with Kentucky Wesleyan, the University of Louisville, and Transylvania University, became a member of the Kentucky Intercollegiate Athletic Conference (KIAC). This organization soon encompassed nearly every college in the state except the University of Kentucky, which maintained its affiliation with the Southern Intercollegiate Athletic Association (now the Southeastern Conference). Not only did the KIAC enhance the popularity of the sport, but it also led to many exciting intrastate rivalries, such as Morehead State University versus Eastern Kentucky University. As the state regional colleges (Morehead, Eastern, Western, Murray, Kentucky State) grew, however, the smaller private schools such as Union, Centre, and Berea could not successfully compete. With the hope of creating a more equitable structure, Roy Stewart, athletic director at Murray State University, in 1941 proposed the establishment of a new division—the Ohio Valley Conference (OVC). World War II prevented the establishment of the organization until 1948. Made up of Eastern, Western, Morehead, Murray and the University of Louisville, the OVC was, with the exception of Evansville College (Indiana), another all-Kentucky conference. Louisville left the conference in 1949, and Evansville did so in 1952. As the organization evolved, other schools in the region joined. In 1982 Western Kentucky University withdrew, and in 1990 the OVC comprised eight teams from Kentucky and Tennessee.

Throughout the twentieth century, the University of Kentucky (UK) has maintained a moderately successful football program, particularly under the coaching of Paul ("Bear") Bryant (1946-53) and Fran Curci (1973-81). Bryant led the Wildcats to four bowl appearances, winning three. On December 6, 1946, UK defeated Villanova 24-14 in the only Great Lakes Bowl. Two years later Bryant's team compiled nine victories on their way to an Orange Bowl appearance on January 2, 1950. The Wildcats were defeated by Santa Clara College, 21-13. After winning the SEC championship with ten victories in 1950, UK met powerful Oklahoma in the Sugar Bowl on January 1, 1951, defeating the Sooners 13-7. In their final bowl appearance under

Bryant, Kentucky bested Texas Christian 20-7 in the Cotton Bowl, played on January 1, 1952. Twenty-five years later, under coach Fran Curci, UK, led on the field by defensive end Art Still and quarterback Derrick Ramsey, topped North Carolina in the Peach Bowl on December 31, 1976. Despite a 10-1 record in 1977, NCAA sanctions prevented the Wildcats from getting a bowl bid. These problems also led to the departure of Curci after the 1981 season. Jerry Claiborne, who became the head coach in 1982, faced the difficult task of rebuilding the UK program. By the time he retired in 1990, Claiborne had restored credibility in the university's football program. His successor, Bill Curry, faced the task of bringing the Wildcat football team back to national prominence.

Under Coach Howard Schnellenberger the University of Louisville in the 1980s began to rebuild its program as well. Though the team was noted during the 1980s for excellent individual players, such as Ernest Givens, Frank Minnifield, and Mark Clayton, team effort prevailed on January 1, 1991, when the Cardinals trounced the University of Alabama in the Fiesta Bowl, 34-7.

On the high school level, Louisville High School (now Male High School) and Du Pont Manual, also of Louisville, were two of the state's first high schools to play organized football. In the inaugural game between the two on November 18, 1893, Male won, 14-12. The rivalry is the oldest of its kind in Kentucky football. By 1914 football was being played at the majority of larger high schools. Player eligibility was a problem, with numerous schools allowing nonstudents to participate. In 1914 representative from schools in Mt. Sterling, Winchester, Paris, Georgetown, Frankfort, Somerset, and Lexington organized the Central Kentucky High School Athletic Association and established eligibility rules. In April 1916 the association ended when its members helped to create the Kentucky High School Athletic Association.

As football grew, intra- and intercounty rivalries developed throughout the state. Among the rural schools that came to be known as football powerhouses was Somerset High School. In 1916 a transfer student, Bo McMillin, joined the team, after an undefeated season the year before. McMillin, who had played football for four years at a Texas high school, led the 1916 Mountaineers to an undefeated season, including a 51-6 win over Louisville Male High School. Later McMillin played for the 1921 Centre College team that defeated Harvard.

Numerous high school coaches gained near-legendary status for creating successful programs or leading their teams to numerous championships. Coach Joseph Jazzers holds the distinction for having won the most state football championships as a head coach. In 1971 and 1972 he won the class A title while at Trigg County, and in 1983, 1988, and 1990 he won the class AA championship while leading the Fort Knox team. An intense gridiron rivalry began in 1956 between two Louisville schools, St. Xavier and Trinity. By the 1980s their contests drew the largest attendance among all one-night high school sporting events in the state. On September 28, 1990, a record crowd of more than 30,000 fans witnessed Trinity defeat St. Xavier by a score of 13-7. By 1990 St. Xavier led the rivalry in number of games won, 22-20-2.

In 1990, 202 Kentucky high schools had football programs, with 7,195 athletes competing. The schools were divided by size into four classes: A, 2-A, 3-A, and 4-A; the state championship play for all four divisions is held at Cardinal Stadium in Louisville.

See Russell Rice, *The Wildcats: A Story of Kentucky Footfall* (Huntsville, Ala., 1975); Eustace Williams, *That Old Rivalry* (Louisville 1940).

FORD, ARTHUR YOUNGER. Arthur Younger Ford, journalist, banker, and seventh president of the UNIVERSITY OF LOUISVILLE (1914-26), was born November 11, 1861, in Parkville, Missouri. About four years later his parents, Salem Holland and Sarah (Beauchamp) Ford, moved to Owensboro, Kentucky. Ford attended Centre College in Danville for a short time, then Brown University, from which he graduated in 1884. He then returned to his boyhood home and became part owner and editor of the *Owensboro Inquirer*. In 1890 he moved to Louisville and joined the *Louisville Times*. After a few months, he transferred to the *Louisville Courier-Journal*, becoming state editor, then editorial writer, then managing editor. In 1907 he resigned to become treasurer of the Columbia Trust Company. After it became the Fidelity & Columbia Trust Company, Ford served as vice-president. From 1913 until 1922, he was president of Goodwin Preserving Company.

In 1914 Ford succeeded Judge David W. Fairleigh as chairman of the University of Louisville board of trustees and in 1921 he became the university's first full-time president. Ford centralized the university's administrative offices; improved the academic standing of its medical and law schools; acquired use of the Louisville City Hospital as a teaching facility for the medical school; and added a dental school, a school of public health, and the Speed Scientific School. To fund a new campus and to lay the groundwork for postsecondary educational opportunities for blacks, Ford campaigned successfully for a city bond issue in 1925. That year he moved the College of Arts and Sciences from its downtown site to what became the Belknap Campus on South Third Street.

Ford served as president of the Kentucky Commission for the St. Louis World's Fair of 1904, chairman of the local draft board during World War I, and president of the Kentucky Tax League (later the Kentucky Tax Reform Association), from which came the state's 1917 tax law.

In 1887 Ford married Esther Annie Brown, of Cloverport, Kentucky. They had three children: Emmett B., Margaret, and Salem. Ford died June 8, 1926, at his home in Louisville and was buried in Cave Hill Cemetery.   WILLIAM J. MORISON

FORD, LAURA CATHERINE. Laura Catherine Ford, author, was born on February 3, 1844, to Harbin H. Ford and Ann Maria (Brooks) Ford in southern Owen County, Kentucky; her brother was Thomas Benton FORD. Harbin Ford died in 1853, and two years later his widow and the two children moved to Frankfort, Kentucky, where Laura and her brother attended Benjamin B. Sayre's private school. Laura, who at an early age read Ann Ford's scrapbook collection of the works of famous American and British authors, began writing in her teens, encouraged by her mother.

In 1863 the *Frankfort Commonwealth* published Ford's short story "Nellie's Lottery or Love vs. Laziness." During Ford's twenties, George D. Prentice, editor of the *Louisville Journal*, was a source of encouragement and advice. Ford's poetry was published in the *Frankfort Yeoman* and other local newspapers. In 1880 her first novel, *The Lathrop Heritage*, appeared. N.L. Munroe published Ford's *For Honor's Sake* in 1884.

Many of her novels appeared in serial form in magazines such as *Saturday Night* and *The Fireside Companion*, and some of her writing was published in "coat pocket" form. So popular were her short stories and novels that Ford was offered a $2,000 contract, but ill health prevented her from accepting this offer.

Ford was married on January 18, 1888, to Dr. Hugh Gatewood Smith of Owenton, Kentucky; she acted as mother to the youngest of Smith's five children. The family lived in Fort Worth, Texas, until the early 1890s, when they returned to Owenton. Ford continued to write under her maiden name, and some of her novels were published in the *Covington Commonwealth* during the early 1890s, despite decreased demand for her work. She died of tuberculosis on January 18, 1898, and was buried in the Odd Fellows Cemetery in Owenton.

See Willard Rouse Jillson, "Thomas Benton Ford and Laura Catherine Ford," *Register* 41 (Jan. 1943): 11-43.

FORD, THOMAS BENTON. Thomas Benton Ford, lawyer and writer of popular verses, was born on February 11, 1841, to Capt. Harbin H. Ford and Ann Maria (Brooks) Ford in southern Owen County, Kentucky; Laura Catherine FORD was his sister. Their father died in 1853, and in 1855 their mother moved the family from their plantation home to Frankfort. Ford attended Benjamin B. Sayre's private school in south Frankfort, where he read Latin and French. In 1862, after serving as an apprentice in the Frankfort law firm of Judge P.U. Major, Ford was admitted to the bar. He enlisted in the Confederate army late in the war, and became a captain of the commissary. Later in life he was known as "Colonel" Ford.

In 1874 Ford was elected county attorney in Franklin County, a post he held until 1878. During 1873-74 Ford was also the commissioner of fiscal affairs for the Franklin County court. In 1878 he started a four-year term as superintendent of the

Franklin County public schools. In 1878 Ford took on the additional position of deputy clerk of the U.S. district court, remaining in this position for thirteen years. In 1892 Ford was elected on the Democratic ticket to Franklin County circuit court, where he served until ill health forced him to retire on January 8, 1903.

Ford also wrote popular verse. One of his earliest works, around 1860, was "Drowned," published in the *Georgetown Advertiser*. Many of his verses were published in Lexington and Louisville newspapers and in the *Frankfort Yeoman* by a personal friend, Maj. Henry T. Stanton. His rhymes bore such titles as "A Deadly Blow! or a Daughter's Sacrifice" (August 1894), "Norma Norton's Vow, or Overshadowed Life" (June 1885), "A Perilous Plot, or a Proud Woman's Destiny" (June 1886), and "Lucille, The Temptress, or an Evil Thrall" (August 1893). Ford's lecture notes were published in 1889 as *Morton's Manual and Principles of Civil Government in the United States and the State of Kentucky* by John P. Morton and Company. His collection *The Good Old Times of the Long Ago and Other Jingles* was published in 1902.

Ford married Mamie Elliot on March 9, 1878; in 1887 their son Elliot was born. Ford spent his last year in poor health and died on March 13, 1903. He is buried in Frankfort Cemetery.

FORD, WENDELL HAMPTON. Wendell Hampton Ford, governor during 1971-74, was born in Daviess County, Kentucky, on September 8, 1924, to Ernest M. and Irene (Schenk) Ford. After graduating from Daviess County High School, Ford entered the University of Kentucky but left to enter the U.S. Army during World War II. In 1943 he married Jean Neel; they had two children. After his discharge from the army in 1946, Ford graduated from the Maryland School of Insurance and entered the insurance business with his father. During the Bert T. Combs administration (1959-63), he was the governor's chief administrative assistant. Active in civic affairs and Democratic politics, Ford was elected to the state Senate in 1965. Two years later he became lieutenant governor although Henry Ward, the Democratic candidate for governor, lost to Republican Louie B. Nunn. In 1971 Ford challenged his mentor and former chief when Combs sought a second term. Ford beat Combs in the primary, then defeated Republican Tom Emberton, 442,736 to 381,479.

Governor Ford played an active role in national Democratic politics. In the spring of 1974 he announced his candidacy for the U.S. Senate seat held by Republican Marlow Cook. Ford won, 399,406 to 328,982, and resigned as governor on December 28, 1974. He won easy reelections to the Senate, in 1980 over Mary Louise Foust and in 1986 over Jackson M. Andrews. A staunch supporter of coal and tobacco interests, Ford was chairman of the Senate Democratic Campaign Committee. In 1990, he was elected majority whip of the Senate.

Governor Ford worked closely with the legislative leadership, and he enjoyed such tight control of the General Assembly that practically all of his programs were enacted. He obtained additional revenue from a severance tax on coal, a two-cent-per-gallon increase in the gasoline tax, and a higher corporate levy, but he balanced that by removing the sales tax from food. Educational spending increased sharply, and the powers of the Council on Higher Education were expanded. Ford vetoed a bill opposed by school boards that would have provided for collective bargaining for teachers. The merit system for state employees was expanded, although critics protested that politics still played too great a role. Ford sponsored consolidation and reorganization of state agencies for greater efficiency; the most important change was perhaps the creation of several "super cabinets" above departments. More attention was paid to environmental protection. In the 1974 legislative session, during the era of the Arab oil embargo and petroleum shortage, Ford pushed for the creation of a six-year coal research program emphasizing gasification and liquefaction. A large budget surplus from his first biennium allowed him to propose several new state buildings and large increases in the appropriations for higher education, the public schools, and human resources.

See Landis Jones, ed., *The Public Papers of Governor Wendell H. Ford* (Lexington, Ky., 1978).

LOWELL H. HARRISON

FORD MOTOR COMPANY ASSEMBLY PLANTS. In June 1988 Ford Motor Company and Kentucky celebrated the seventy-fifth anniversary of motor vehicle production in Louisville. By that time Ford had made more than 8.5 million passenger vehicles and trucks in Louisville. The first Ford was sold in Kentucky in 1910, and an assembly operation was established in Louisville at 931 South Third Street in 1913. Its seventeen employees (including sales force) produced twelve vehicles a day. Entry-level wages were eight cents per hour. On September 12, 1915, a new factory was completed on a 2⅓-acre site at 2500 South Third Street. Initially the plant employed fifty-three people and produced fifteen vehicles per day. By 1923 the success of Ford's Model T and its variants had resulted in expansion to six hundred employees and a maximum production of two hundred vehicles per day, the limit at that site. World War I interrupted production during 1918-19.

On February 2, 1925, a new plant was completed on a 22½-acre site at 1400 South Western Parkway, with an investment of $1.5 million. The plant was designed for 1,000 employees and production of four hundred vehicles a day. This factory made its last Model T on June 3, 1927, and saw the introduction of the Model A in early 1928 and the V-8 engine in 1934. The plant survived the flood of 1937, which was followed by the disassembly of 325 water-damaged vehicles. It was converted to production of military trucks during World War II. The last vehicle of 1,608,710 manufactured there was produced on April 13, 1955. Five days later, production began at the Fern Valley Road–Grade Lane location, referred to as the Louisville Assembly Plant. This factory, with space of more than 2 million square feet, was located on a 180-acre tract; it built both cars and light trucks. Initial employment was 2,850; by July 1957 employment was 4,700 after the expansion of light-truck operations and the addition of the Edsel, of which the plant made five hundred a day. The same plant began to make heavy trucks in early 1958.

On August 4, 1969, production of heavy trucks began at a new factory that covered sixty-eight of the 415 acres at 11200 Westport Road. The Kentucky Truck Plant represented an investment of $100 million. It was designed to produce three hundred units a day. Through the 1987 model year, 1,482,900 trucks had been made there. By late 1978, Ford facilities in Louisville employed 10,130 people.

Faced with the combination of the energy crisis and globalization of the auto industry, Ford switched production of cars to plants specially designed for the smaller cars of the 1980s. With an investment of $750 million, the Louisville Assembly Plant was converted to make the Ranger (a compact pick-up truck) and the Bronco II (a light sport-utility vehicle). In 1987-89, $263 million was invested and 163,000 square feet were added to the factory in preparation for producing the Explorer line to replace the Bronco II. During the 1980s Ford invested approximately $1 billion in its Louisville factories. As of the end of the 1987 model year, a total of 8,568,396 Ford vehicles had been produced in Louisville.   WILLIAM R. MORLEY

FORESTS, KENTUCKY STATE. The Kentucky State Forest System, made up of six woodland tracts, is 39,388 acres in size. It has grown from the 3,738 acres in Harlan County donated in 1919 by the Kentenia Corporation, a land and coal company. The lands are administered by the Division of Forests of the Department of Natural Resources and Environmental Protection for commercial (timber sales) and recreational use, including hiking, fishing, and hunting in some areas. The majority of acreage—more than 37,247 acres—was deeded to Kentucky by the U.S. government between 1954 and 1956. The remaining land was obtained by U.S. government lease, donation, and purchase.

Dewey Lake State Forest, 7,353 acres, located east of Prestonsburg in Floyd County, is near Jenny Wiley State Resort Park, and is leased to Kentucky by the U.S. Army Corps of Engineers.

Kentenia State Forest, 3,624 acres, is east of Harlan in Harlan County.

Kentucky Ridge State Forest, 11,363 acres, located west of Pineville in Bell County, encircles Pine Mountain State Resort Park.

Olympia State Forest, 780 acres, is in southern Bath County, and lies in the northwest region of the Daniel Boone National Forest.

Pennyrile State Forest, 15,468 acres, lies in northwest Christian County, and borders Pennyrile Forest State Resort Park. Created from a 15,260-acre grant by the U.S. Department of Agriculture, the original tract includes a wildlife refuge.

Tygarts State Forest, 800 acres, is north of Olive Hill in Carter County, and adjoins Carter Caves State Resort Park.

See Arthur B. Lander Jr., *A Guide to Kentucky Outdoors* (Ann Arbor, Mich., 1978).

FORT CAMPBELL. Fort Campbell, Kentucky, a military training base, is located on the Kentucky-Tennessee line, sixteen miles south of Hopkinsville. After the War Department approved the site on January 6, 1942, the government acquired a total of 101,755 acres in Montgomery and Stewart counties of Tennessee and in Christian and Trigg counties of Kentucky, at a cost of $4,064,948, or an average of $39.94 per acre. Residents were required to vacate the area by June 1, 1942.

In the six months from February through July 1942, a military base was constructed to accommodate two armored divisions. Out of the mud and dust came barracks, mess halls, motor pools, streets, an airport, utilities, a hospital, post exchange, movie theaters, and chapels. Over 11,000 laborers worked to construct the base. By the end of 1942, $35 million had been expended. The War Department announced in February 1942 that the camp would be named for Col. William Bowen Campbell, an officer in the Mexican War and a Whig governor of Tennessee (1851-57). Although originally designated Camp Campbell, Tennessee, the base was assigned a Kentucky postal address in March 1942.

The first arrivals at Camp Campbell, on July 1, 1942, were a cadre—one officer and nineteen enlisted men—from Fort Knox. The 12th Armored Division was activated on September 15, 1942, and departed in September 1943 to join the 7th Army in Europe. From January through March 1943, the 8th Armored Division trained at the camp. The 20th Armored Division was activated March 13, 1943, and departed for Europe in December 1944. The IV Armored Corps arrived in April 1943. Known as the Ghost Corps, this group assisted Columbia Pictures in filming *Sahara*, starring Humphrey Bogart. The film premiered at Camp Campbell September 2, 1943. The 14th Armored Division was in training at Fort Campbell from February to October 1944, when it joined the 7th Army. A Women's Army Corps detachment was based at the camp from March 1943 until 1946. The camp held German prisoners of war from 1943 until 1946.

Other milestones in the operation of the base include the establishment in 1948 of Campbell Air Force base, built as an Air Support Command base of the Strategic Air Command; the arrival of the 11th Airborne Division from Japan in the spring of 1949, and its departure in 1956; designation as a permanent fort on April 15, 1950; and the construction of the Clarksville Base, called the Bird Cage, in 1947-48. In the spring of 1956 the 101st Airborne Division was assigned to Fort Campbell. The division went to Vietnam in 1965 and returned in 1972. During the crisis in the Middle East, beginning in the summer of 1990, troops from the camp were sent to Saudi Arabia.

In 1990 Fort Campbell had a troop strength of 21,000; a civilian population of 4,000; and 29,800 military dependents. WILLIAM T. TURNER

FORT HARROD. On June 6, 1774, a company of thirty men under elected leader James HARROD established what became the first permanent white settlement in Kentucky, Fort Harrod. The thirty men were: James Blair, James Brown, John Brown, James Carr, Abraham Chapline, John Clark, John Crawford, Jared Cowan, John Cowan, John Crow, William Crow, Azariah Davis, Patrick Doran, William Fields, William Garrett, Robert Gilbert, James Hamilton, Elijah Harlan, Silas Harlan, Jacob Lewis, James McCulloch, Samuel Moore, Azor Reese, Jacob and James Sadowsky (Sandusky), Thomas Quirk, Martin Shell, James Wiley, David Williams, and John Wilson.

The company had traveled from the Monongahela settlement down the Ohio River to the Kentucky River, up which they traveled for approximately one hundred miles. Landing their canoes at Harrod's Landing, which became Warwick, they proceeded to the Salt River, which they followed to a location in the valley where Harrodsburg now stands. The site for the first settlement was approximately one mile from Salt River, at a large spring. The men laid out the settlement with half-acre in-lots and ten-acre out-lots and began raising eight to ten cabins on the south side of the stream known as Town Branch. They drew lots for the cabins and acreage. On July 8 Shawnee attacked a small party surveying the Fontainbleau Spring area, killing two men. The others escaped to the camp, some three miles distant, and the company left on July 10.

In March 1775, after the Shawnee signed the Treaty of Camp Charlotte with Lord Dunmore, Harrod returned to resettle Harrodstown with almost fifty men, many of them members of his expedition the previous year. After they reentered on March 11, the settlement was continuously occupied. The company built more cabins and made improvements for their land claims. During the summer of 1775, sporadic Indian attacks on the new settlements caused such fear that roughly half the pioneers left Harrodstown for the protection of civilization. But others arrived to take their places, including George Rogers Clark; the Rev. John Lythe, an Episcopal priest and the first minister in Kentucky; and Dr. George Hart, the first physician to settle permanently. The first women and children, the families of Thomas Denton, Richard Hogan, and Hugh McGary, arrived in September.

Construction of a stockade started in the fall of 1775 and was completed the next year, sited on higher ground west of Big Spring and a "pole's distance" from the Town Branch. Its puncheon walls were heavy timbers set on end close together, with twenty cabins forming an irregular square on northeast, southeast, and southwest corners. The cabins were one and a half stories high, with the fort palisades functioning as their back walls. Cabin roofs sloped inward to reduce the damage should they be set on fire during an attack. Blockhouses extended three to four feet above the stockade walls with rifle portholes for protection and observation. The fort enclosed an area of approximately an acre and a half, with a spring and a stream running through for fresh water supply. In the center was a powder magazine.

New settlers who arrived in Kentucky went out from the fort at Harrodstown to build other stations. Among the pioneers who arrived in 1776 were Jane Coomes, who started a school and taught for the next nine years, and a Baptist minister, the Rev. Peter Tinsley. On June 6, 1776, a meeting held in Fort Harrod elected George Rogers Clark and Gabriel John Jones to seek creation of a new county from the Virginia Assembly. On December 31, 1776, the Virginia Assembly created KENTUCKY COUNTY, with Harrodstown the seat of government. In March 1777 a militia was organized at Fort Harrod and on March 7 the first Indian attack on the fort occurred. The year 1777 was to be the most dangerous for pioneers, with continuous attacks on all the settlements. By autumn all Kentucky settlers were living in either Fort Harrod, Fort Boonesborough, Logan's Fort, or Fort McClelland. On September 2, 1777, the first court of quarter sessions was held at Fort Harrod. The elected judges were John Bowman, Richard Callaway, John Floyd, John Todd, and Benjamin Logan, who also served as sheriff; John May was official surveyor and Levi Todd was clerk. Capt. John Cowan took a census while the court was in session: 85 white men, 24 white women, 58 white children under the age of ten, 12 older white children, 12 adult slaves of both sexes, and 7 slave children under the age of ten. Total population of Fort Harrod was 198.

In 1780 the Virginia Assembly divided Kentucky County into Fayette, Jefferson, and Lincoln counties, with Harrodstown the county seat for Lincoln County. In 1785 Mercer County was formed out of Lincoln County, and Harrodstown remained the county seat. At the same time the town's name was officially changed to Harrodsburg.

See George M. Chinn, *Kentucky Settlement and Statehood, 1750-1800* (Frankfort, Ky., 1975); Maria T. Daviess, *History of Mercer and Boyle Counties* (Harrodsburg, Ky., 1924).

FORT HEIMAN. Fort Heiman, in southeastern Calloway County, Kentucky, on a ridge overlooking the Tennessee River, was constructed by the Confederates in January 1862, when it was recognized that Fort Henry across the river would be indefensible during high water. Although Fort Heiman was unfinished, about 1,000 men under Col. Adolphus Heiman, for whom it was named, occupied it when Union forces attacked Fort Henry. Lacking heavy artillery, Heiman withdrew on February 5 without a fight, and the fort was occupied by the 5th Iowa Cavalry until March 1863. In October 1864, Gen. Nathan Bedford Forrest mounted guns at Fort Heiman, dominating the river below. After destroying the steamer *Mazeppa*, he abandoned the fort, using two captured vessels to mount an amphibious attack against the Federal supply base at Johnsonville, Tennessee.

See Benjamin Franklin Cooling, *Forts Henry and Donelson: The Key to the Confederate Heartland* (Knoxville, Tenn., 1987).   KEITH M. HEIM

FORT JEFFERSON. Fort Jefferson was constructed in 1780 under the supervision of Gen. George Rogers Clark. Although the fort was part of Virginia Gov. Patrick Henry's plan for settlement, the executive order to build the fort came from Thomas Jefferson, who succeeded Henry as governor. Fort Jefferson was situated in the valley of Mayfield Creek, near its confluence with the Mississippi River, five miles below the mouth of the Ohio River, in present-day Ballard County.

Construction of the fort began on April 19, 1780, and was completed in June 1780. From May 13, 1780, until they were abandoned on June 8, 1781, the fort and the community of Clarksville were commanded by Capt. Robert George. The fort was about one hundred feet square and had two bastions, in the northeast and southwest corners. The fort served as the major supply link with New Orleans for Clark's Illinois battalion during 1780. In early July 1780, the population numbered about 225 soldiers and 275 civilian men, women, and children. In July and again in August 1780, Fort Jefferson was attacked by the Chickasaw, allies of the British during the Revolutionary War. During the August battle, the Chickasaw were led by Lt. James Whitehead from the British Southern Indian Department (not by James Colbert, who has been mistakenly identified as the leader of the assault).

See Kathryn M. Fraser, "Fort Jefferson," *Register* 81 (Winter 1983): 1-25.

KENNETH C. CARSTENS

FORT KNOX. Fort Knox, a 109,000-acre permanent garrison of the U.S. Army extending over parts of Hardin, Meade, and Bullitt counties, is perhaps best known as the site of the U.S. BULLION DEPOSITORY. It was established by Congress in 1918 as Camp Knox, a field artillery training range for Camp Zachary Taylor in Louisville. It was named for Gen. Henry Knox, chief of artillery in the Revolutionary War and the first U.S. secretary of war. As the branch headquarters of the U.S. Armored Force since 1940, Fort Knox is a center for training officers and enlisted soldiers, developing weapons and tactics, and establishing doctrine.

During the Civil War, Union and Confederate forces were active near the confluence of the Ohio and Salt rivers, just north of what is now Fort Knox. In 1862 the 6th Michigan Infantry built fortifications atop MULDRAUGH HILL, a ridge within the present-day military reservation. In December 1862 Gen. John Hunt Morgan, leading the 2d Kentucky Cavalry, raided the area and captured Union troops. At Brandenburg in Meade County, just west of Fort Knox, Morgan led his troops across the Ohio River to raid Indiana and Ohio.

In 1903 the War Department began seriously considering the Fort Knox area for a permanent military reservation when it established Camp Young as a maneuvers headquarters at West Point, Kentucky. Some 30,000 cavalry, artillery, and infantry troops moved in to stage large-scale maneuvers over land that is now part of Fort Knox. After the United States entered World War I, Congress on June 25, 1918, allocated $1.6 million to purchase 40,000 acres for Camp Knox. Plans called for establishing a firing and training center for field artillery, with barracks and supporting facilities to accommodate six brigades of artillery—60,000 soldiers. Construction of camp facilities began in July 1918 under the direction of Quartermaster W.H. Radcliffe. One of the casualties of Camp Knox development was the small agricultural community of Stithton.

When World War I ended, construction of Camp Knox stopped and the facility was at no point wholly occupied. Some field artillery troops were kept, the Field Artillery Central Officers Training School was established, and a few troops returning from France went to Camp Knox for demobilization.

With the retrenchment of the army in 1921, the artillery activities were transferred to Fort Sill, Oklahoma, while Camp Knox remained as the training center for the 5th Corps. The permanent garrison of one or two companies of infantry was joined in the summer by thousands of troops from the National Guard, Reserve Officers Training Corps, and Citizens Military Training Camps, who trained at Camp Knox. One of the citizen trainees in 1922 was the writer Robert Penn Warren, of Guthrie, Kentucky, whose first published poem, "Prophecy," appeared in the *Camp Knox Mess Kit* in 1922.

In 1925, when Camp Knox National Forest was created, civilian custodians took over the camp. The national forest was abandoned in 1928, however, and the army posted two companies of infantry to the installation as permanent garrison. In 1931, when the army was struggling with the concept of mechanization and motor transport of its weapons and troops, Camp Knox became identified with the form of warfare that has become its hallmark. The army's mechanized force moved from Fort Eustis, Virginia, to form the cadre for a mechanized cavalry regiment at Camp Knox, which was larger and had a varied terrain more suited to training. On January 1, 1932, Congress designated Camp Knox as a permanent garrison and changed its name to Fort Knox.

In 1933 the 1st Cavalry Regiment—the oldest mounted regiment in the U.S. Army—traded its horses and oats for combat cars and fuel and moved to Fort Knox from Marfa, Texas. In 1936 the 13th Cavalry Regiment, also minus its horses, arrived from Fort Riley, Kansas. The cavalry brigade they formed, with its light tanks, combat cars, and motorcycles, soon gained the reputation of being the fastest-moving, hardest-hitting outfit in the U.S.

Army. The pace of activity at Fort Knox during the 1930s was furious. A $2.8 million allotment in 1933 went for construction of much of the brick housing, along with the headquarters building, hospital, storage warehouses, barracks, and ordnance facilities. The U.S. Bullion Depository opened in January 1937 and received its first shipments of gold bullion under the security of the 7th Cavalry Brigade. During the same period, the brigade rushed to aid flood-ravaged Louisville and many other communities along the Ohio River.

As the center for mechanization of the cavalry, Fort Knox developed many of the tactics used by the U.S. Armored Force in World War II. Maneuvers and mock wars, held locally and in remote portions of several northeastern and southeastern states, tested men, equipment, and tactics. Two of the most influential commanders of the 7th Cavalry Brigade (Mechanized) were Lt. Gen. Daniel Van Voorhis and Maj. Gen. Adna R. Chaffee. To counter the devastating blitzkrieg of the German panzer (armored) divisions in World War II, the U.S. Armored Force was created July 10, 1940, at Fort Knox, with Chaffee as commander. Under the Armored Force umbrella, the 7th Cavalry Brigade (Mechanized) became the 1st Armored Division.

The Armored Force played a key role in the Allied forces' final victory. By 1945 it had grown to sixteen armored divisions and more than a hundred separate tank battalions and mechanized cavalry squadrons. The Armored Force School and Armored Force Replacement Training Center were established at Fort Knox in 1940. As the Armored Force expanded, so did Fort Knox itself. In 1940, there were 864 buildings; by 1943 there were 3,820. By 1943 the camp had increased to a total of 106,861 acres.

At Fort Knox, which now stretches fourteen miles north to south and eighteen miles east to west, the daytime population of military and civilian employees has ranged from 35,000 to 40,000 through the years. All armored soldiers of the U.S. Army serve at Fort Knox at least once during their army careers, whether in the permanent garrison or during entry training. The post has its own airfield, school system, and health care and shopping facilities. Fort Knox also sees thousands of visitors annually at the Patton Museum, established in 1949 and named for Gen. George S. Patton, Jr., where vehicles and equipment chronicle the history of armor worldwide.

See Mildred Hanson Gillie, *Forging the Thunderbolt* (Harrisburg, Pa., 1947); H.H.D. Heiberg, "Organize a Mechanized Force," *Armor* 85 (Sept.–Oct. 1976).   DAVID A. HOLT

FORT MASSAC. Fort Massac was located on the Illinois shore of the Ohio, on the long stretch just below the mouth of the Tennessee. This picketed fort, established by the French in 1757, was named for the Marquis de Massiac, French minister of ma-

rines. The fort was only slightly armed. Perhaps its most important historical moment was the landing of George Rogers Clark's little army on June 24, 1778. Between that date and 1794, Fort Massac was what author Zadoc Cramer called "a captain's command." After 1794 the fort ceased to have military significance. The precise location of Fort Massac has troubled historian-cartographers. Perhaps the most accurate cartographic location is that of Zadoc Cramer in 1814. In 1792 Elihu Barker located it generally on his map, and later John Melish copied the Barker map. Five modern historical consultants to the editor of the *Atlas of American History* approved five different locations, one showing the fortress directly opposite the mouth of the Tennessee River.

See Zadoc Cramer, *The Navigator* (Pittsburgh 1814); Mrs. M.T. Scott, "Old Fort Massac," *Transactions of the Illinois Historical Society* (Springfield, Ill., 1903).   THOMAS D. CLARK

FORT MITCHELL. Fort Mitchell is a suburban city in the hills of north-central Kenton County in northern Kentucky. The city is three miles southwest of downtown Covington. The city is the site of one of twenty-seven earthen fortifications that guarded Cincinnati, Covington, and Newport during the Civil War. Fort Mitchell, a star-shaped earthwork on a hill overlooking the Lexington Pike (now U.S. 25) was named for Gen. Ormsby M. Mitchel (*sic*), who was a West Point graduate and a professor of mathematics, astronomy, and philosophy at Cincinnati College. The fort was occupied by Union army soldiers and local Home Guard militia in response to the Confederate invasion of Kentucky in the late summer of 1862. On September 10-11, 1862, advance troops of Gen. Henry Heth's Confederates skirmished with Union forces near the fort before withdrawing south to Lexington.

Even after the war, the area that surrounded the former fort was referred to as Fort Mitchell. By 1870 three cemeteries, St. John's, Highland, and St. Mary's, had acquired 199 acres in Fort Mitchell. The parklike setting of the cemeteries and the commanding view from the hills made the area attractive for suburban development. A town plat was laid out in January 1906, and Fort Mitchell was incorporated as a city on June 21, 1909. Fort Mitchell's location at the end of the streetcar line and the creation of the Fort Mitchell Country Club in 1909 helped the city to develop quickly as a suburb of Cincinnati.

During the planning of I-75 in the 1950s, fears that the interstate would cut through Fort Mitchell and cause the razing of many homes proved to be unfounded, but a sharp S-curve and steep grade resulted, creating the hazard that eventually came to be known as Death Hill. The interstate's completion in the early 1960s brought hotels and other commercial ventures to the city, as well as growth in the number of middle- and upper-middle-class residents. The population of the fourth-class city was 6,982 in 1970; 7,294 in 1980; and 7,438 in 1990.   ROGER C. ADAMS

FORT NELSON. The most impressive fortification in pioneer Kentucky was Fort Nelson in Louisville. Constructed in 1781 by Richard Chenoweth under military contract, it was named for Thomas Nelson, who became Virginia governor in June 1781. It was erected between present-day Sixth and Eighth streets with its north wall on or near Main Street, giving it a commanding position over the Ohio River at the head of the Falls of the Ohio. Its walls encompassed about an acre and were surrounded by a ditch eight feet deep and ten feet wide with a row of sharpened pickets along the bottom. (Parts of the line of pickets were unearthed in 1832 and 1844 on the north side of Main Street.) Gen. George Rogers Clark had a hand in the fort's design and made it his headquarters during the Revolutionary War.

See Blaine A. Guthries, Jr., "Captain Richard Chenoweth—A Founding Father of Louisville," *FCHQ* 46 (April 1972): 147-60.
                                             GEORGE H. YATER

FORT STANWIX, TREATY OF. Much of what is now Kentucky changed hands under the Treaty of Fort Stanwix, which was concluded in New York on November 5, 1768, between representatives of the British government and the Six Nations of Indians—including the Mohawk, Tuscarora, Oneida, Onondaga, Cayuga, and Seneca tribes—as well as the dependent tribes of Shawnee, Delaware, and Mingoe. Acknowledging Indian claims to western land, the treaty defined the boundary between the Indian hunting grounds and the area sold to the British. The treaty deeded to the British Crown the title to the lands south of the Ohio River and east of the Tennessee River, southward to the border of North Carolina, in exchange for 10,000 pounds sterling. The territory purchased by the British included much of present-day Kentucky. The Treaty of Fort Stanwix, combined with the PROCLAMATION OF 1763, which prohibited individuals from purchasing land held by Indian tribes, made it impossible to acquire western land except through British grants.

See John Mason Brown, *The Political Beginnings of Kentucky* (Louisville 1889); Charles C. Royce, *Indian Land Cessions in the United States* (1900).

FORT THOMAS. Fort Thomas is a suburban city in northern Campbell County on the hills overlooking the Ohio River. The area was part of a half-million-acre grant by Virginia to the Ohio Company in 1749, surveyed by Christopher Gist in 1750. The Ohio Company claims were later preempted by the U.S. Congress, which awarded the land to Revolutionary War veterans. As the area lacked good roads, settlement was slow for the next seventy years.

In the Civil War, a series of Union fortifications—the Cincinnati defense perimeter—were built through the present limits of Fort Thomas. During the Confederate invasion of Kentucky in September 1862, Confederate troops commanded by Gen. Henry Heth in northern Kentucky caused hundreds of civilian militia to occupy defensive positions in the trenches. The Confederates retired without an encounter, and a threatened raid by Morgan's cavalry in 1863 likewise failed to materialize.

In 1867 residents of the area joined together to create the District of Highlands. Major roads were built, and in the 1870s two water reservoirs for the cities of Newport and Covington were built on the site of the old Civil War earthworks. In the 1890s the district was selected as the site for a new army post, named in honor of Union Gen. George Thomas. It replaced the Newport barracks, which were prone to flooding by the Ohio and Licking rivers.

The first commander of Fort Thomas, Col. Melville A. Cochran, planted many flowers and trees, creating an environment more like a college campus than a military post. Among the units garrisoned there were the 6th U.S. Infantry, which fought in Cuba in 1898, and the 10th U.S. Infantry, which assisted in flood relief in 1933 and 1937. The small size of the fort and its suburban setting limited military activity, and after World War II it was used for reserve training and as a military induction center. Fort Thomas is now the site of the Brooks-Lawler Army Reserve Center and a Veterans Administration hospital.

Around the turn of the century, a country club, a streetcar connection to Newport, and several resort hotels were built in the District of Highlands. After attempts by Newport to annex the district, the residents of Fort Thomas, Guyville, and Dale incorporated in 1914 as the city of Fort Thomas.

The area has retained its parklike charm, and consists mainly of residential middle- and upper-middle-class neighborhoods. Although the population is large enough to qualify as a third-class city, local officials maintain that as a fourth-class city it has greater powers of self-government. Fort Thomas is the second largest city in Campbell County, with a population of 16,338 in 1970; 16,012 in 1980; and 16,032 in 1990.

FORT WRIGHT. Fort Wright is a middle-class suburb in the hills of northern Kenton County, two miles southeast of COVINGTON and slightly north of the I-75 and KY 1072 interchange. The city was incorporated in 1941, annexed neighboring South Hills in 1960, and merged with the communities of Lookout Heights in 1967 and Lakeview in 1970. Fort Wright takes its name from an earthen fort built as part of the Cincinnati defense perimeter during the Civil War. The Union fort was named for Maj. Gen. Horatio Gouverneur Wright, a Connecticut native and engineer who helped design northern Kentucky's military defenses and who completed the Washington Monument in the nation's capital. The military installations were occupied by hundreds of local militia in response to fears of an imminent Confederate invasion in the late summer of 1862, but the Confederates turned back well short of the forts.

With the exception of businesses located along U.S. 25, the area remained largely rural until well into the twentieth century. In the 1930s Oelsner's Colonial Tavern was a popular dining spot and a favorite of Cincinnati Reds baseball players. Across the street, the Lookout House featured casino gambling and entertainment. In a state police raid at the Lookout on March 6, 1951, eighteen people were arrested and $20,000 worth of gambling equipment was seized, but the club stayed in business until it was destroyed in a fire on August 14, 1973.

Residential development of Fort Wright began around 1940 and continued in the 1950s and 1960s. The city grew rapidly by annexing or merging with adjoining communities, although attempts to annex nearby Park Hills and Kenton Vale were unsuccessful. A twenty-year dispute over annexed land ended in 1980 with Fort Wright owing Covington $250,000 for loss of taxable property.

Fort Wright is a fourth-class city that had a population of 4,819 in 1970; 4,481 in 1980; and 6,570 in 1990.

See Jim Reis, *Pieces of the Past* (Covington, Ky. 1988).

FORWARD IN THE FIFTH. Forward in the Fifth, a nonprofit organization established in October 1986, works to improve the education of adults in Kentucky's 5th Congressional District, in southeastern Kentucky. The organization was formed after the SHAKERTOWN ROUNDTABLE met to discuss the finding that the district had the highest proportion of adults without high school education in the nation. Forward in the Fifth executes its mission through community volunteers in its twenty-seven affiliate county organizations.

RICHARD LA BRECQUE

FOSSILS. From traces of primeval algae to the remains of elephant-like mammoths and mastodons, Kentucky fossils help to unravel the complex story of Kentucky's physical and biological development through time. Fossils are the naturally preserved remains or traces of organisms, and the rocks and sediments of Kentucky contain the remains of an astonishing variety of creatures—both animal and plant—that reflect the conditions in Kentucky during the last 460 million years. Because all organisms are selective about where they live, and change in form as their physical and biological environments change, comparison of modern and fossil organisms has great potential in interpreting ancient environments and the approximate time frames.

Fossils in Kentucky generally can be classified according to the type of organism preserved, its size, and its mode of preservation. As for organism type, both plant and animal fossils are abundant in Kentucky. Animals are also commonly classified according to the presence or absence of a backbone. The ubiquitous shell-like and coral-like fossils in the rocks of Kentucky represent animals that lacked a backbone—invertebrates. On the other hand, fossil fish, amphibians, reptiles, and mammals, all vertebrates, are rarely found in the rocks of Kentucky.

Fossils are grouped into two sizes: microfossils, which can be studied only with the aid of a microscope, and macrofossils, which can be studied with the naked eye. Both types are extremely abundant in Kentucky, but most collectors never see the microfossils. To examine these, rocks must be sliced extremely thin (less than 0.03 millimeters thick) and viewed under a microscope, or disaggregated and broken down with acids or other chemicals that destroy the rock matrix without harming the fossils. The resulting fossil debris is then examined or "picked" under a microscope. Microfossils include both plant and animal remains.

Plants and animals may be preserved either as body fossils or as trace fossils. Body fossils are the preserved remains of plants or animals. Because of the processes involved, body fossils normally form when an organism's hard parts—shells, teeth, or skeletons—are quickly buried. The stone-like quality of most body fossils reflects changes in the mineral composition of the hard part. The unstable organic parts are driven off, and new minerals are added to hard parts, or existing hard-part minerals are reorganized by heat, pressure, and circulating fluids during burial. Trace fossils are another kind of evidence of an organism's existence; they include tracks and trails left by organisms wandering across ancient Kentucky sea floors, reptile tracks on ancient riverbanks, or fossil excrement. No physical remains of the organism are preserved. Both trace fossils and body fossils are widespread in nearly all parts of Kentucky.

The record of fossil life on Earth goes back almost 3.5 billion years, but the oldest exposed fossils in Kentucky are no more than 460 million years old. The type and distribution of these fossils in Kentucky are clearly controlled by the ages of the rocks and their geological disposition. The rocks and fossils of Kentucky were originally deposited on the bottoms of shallow seas and swamps in nearly horizontal layers that accumulated one on top of another. Episodes of continent collision near what is now the East Coast crumpled these layers and lifted them out of the sea, and the process of erosion exposed their fossil content. The single most important result of this crumpling in Kentucky was the formation of the Cincinnati Arch, a large upfolding of rock layers, more than one hundred miles wide, extending from the Cincinnati area to Cumberland County, Kentucky. As erosion stripped the top off this arch, older layers were exposed in the center, and young rocks on its eastern and western flanks. Of course, the ages and distributions of fossils in Kentucky reflect the same pattern.

The oldest fossils exposed in Kentucky occur in the Bluegrass region in the central part of the state. The rocks are Ordovician and Silurian in age (approximately 460 to 408 million years old), and they represent warm, shallow seas, commonly with muddy bottoms. The fossils from the resulting rocks are all marine invertebrates, mostly corals, bryozoans, brachiopods, crinoids, and various mollusks including clams, snails, and the squid-like cephalopods.

Devonian rocks (408 to 362 million years old) crop out in the Knobs region surrounding the Bluegrass. The lower part of the Devonian sequence generally reflects shallow, warm waters; the deposited limestone contains abundant corals, brachiopods, and crinoids. In the Louisville area at the Falls of the Ohio, the large reef-like body of limestone that developed in this period is composed of corals and sponge-like organisms called stromatoporoids. The limestones are overlain by Devonian black shales, which make up most of the Knobs. The shales generally reflect deep, stagnant conditions, and fossils are rare. Most of the fossils represent swimming or floating organisms. The first land-plant fossils in Kentucky, having been washed into seas from swamps and uplands to the east, are found in these shales in the form of stumps, branches, and twigs. The first vertebrate fossils from Kentucky—in the form of fish—are also found in these shales.

The overlying Mississippian rocks (362 to 322 million years old) begin with siltstones and shales that reflect deltas at the mouths of large river systems that emptied into Kentucky seas. Because of all the sediment dumped into the seas, fossils are not generally abundant, but large brachiopods and coiled cephalopods called ammonoids are common locally. On top of these deltaic sediments, pure, nearly white Mississippian limestones were deposited in very warm, shallow-water conditions. These rocks crop out largely in the Pennyroyal Plateau region of south and west-central Kentucky. Fish fossils, as well as many invertebrate fossils from diverse groups like sponges, corals, brachiopods, bryozoans, clams, snails, trilobites, and echinoderms, are common. The limestones are especially well known for their echinoderms, which include crinoids (sea lilies), blastoids, sea urchins, and starfish.

The overlying upper Mississippian and Pennsylvanian rocks (322 to 290 million years old) are restricted to the Appalachian Plateau (Eastern Coal Field) and the Western Coal Field in Kentucky and mark a dramatic change in both sediment type and fossil content. The sandstones, shales, and coals that are typical represent the migration of river systems and extensive swamps into Kentucky.

The swamps were characterized by fast-growing, soft-tissue trees, so plant fossils are especially common in Pennsylvanian rocks. Fossils representing ferns, seed-ferns, sphenopsids (scouring-rushes), and lycopsids (scale trees) are common in Kentucky. Apparently, insects and terrestrial vertebrates also lived in these swampy forests, for rare insect fossils and reptile tracks have been found in Kentucky. However, in similar Pennsylvanian rocks from Ohio, the skeletal remains of amphibians and reptiles have been uncovered. Periodically, shallow seas inundated these swamps, leaving behind thin, muddy limestones and shales containing predominantly fossil brachiopods, clams, and snails.

Although swamps and river sedimentation probably continued in Kentucky after the Pennsylvanian period, most evidence of these rocks and their fossils has been destroyed by later erosion. Erosion continued throughout Kentucky until the late Cretaceous period, about 90 million years ago, when shallow seas moved up the present-day Mississippi River Valley and occupied the extreme western part of Kentucky, called the Jackson Purchase. The shallow sea, along with its beaches, estuaries, swamps, and nearby river floodplains, occupied this area until 35 million years ago, during the Tertiary period, and resulted in the deposition of sands, gravels, clay, and low-quality coal. Cretaceous and Tertiary fossils, locally common in these deposits, represent only clams and snails; some layers contain well-preserved fossils of deciduous leaves, once washed into the sea. Dinosaur fossils have been found in similar Cretaceous rocks from Tennessee, but they are not yet known from Kentucky.

Once again, erosion took place throughout Kentucky until 2 million years ago, during the Quaternary Period, when large glaciers moved southward. Although the glaciers barely entered northernmost Kentucky, meltwater from them transported the bones and tusks of mammoths and mastodons to resting places in sands and gravels along the Ohio River in northern Kentucky. As the glaciers advanced, moreover, many large mammals were forced southward into Kentucky, where they congregated for salt at places like Big Bone Lick and Blue Licks. The fossil mammoths, mastodons, elk, giant ground sloths, giant beavers, and bears found at these licks represent Kentucky's youngest fossil fauna. It was these fossils that were collected by the first European explorers in Kentucky.

See Willard R. Jillson, *The Paleontology of Kentucky* (Frankfort, Ky., 1931); N. Gary Lane, *Life of the Past* (Columbus, Ohio, 1978).

FRANK R. ETTENSOHN

FOSTER, STEPHEN COLLINS. Stephen Collins Foster, who wrote "My Old Kentucky Home, Good-Night!" was born in Lawrenceville, Pennsylvania, a suburb of Pittsburgh, on July 4, 1826. He was the youngest of the nine children of William and Eliza (Tomlinson) Foster. Foster moved to Cincinnati in 1846 to work as a bookkeeper for his brother Dunning. As early as 1848 he began writing songs for minstrel shows, and in 1850 he returned to Pittsburgh to write music full-time. Firth, Pond & Co. published his songs under contract, and in 1851 E.P. Christy, a successful black-face minstrel, bought the rights to perform Foster's songs before publication. This arrangement, which lasted until Christy's retirement in 1854, helped bring popularity to Foster's "plantation" songs, which were not inspired by the music of blacks, but were written to be performed by white minstrel singers.

In January 1853 Foster wrote "My Old Kentucky Home, Good-Night!" which became the commonwealth's state song in 1928. According to folklore, the inspiration for the song was FEDERAL HILL, the estate of his distant Rowan cousins in Bardstown, Kentucky, where he is said to have visited in the spring of 1852 on his way to New Orleans. Foster's trip to New Orleans is well documented, but his trip to Federal Hill, at that time or any other, has not been substantiated, although people were quoted as seeing him there. Foster's only verified trip to Kentucky occurred in 1833, when his mother took him as a child to visit relatives in Augusta and Louisville. His sister Charlotte had visited there in 1828. The inspiration for the Kentucky state song may well have been Harriet Beecher Stowe's novel *Uncle Tom's Cabin* (1851); Foster's first draft in his song workbook, written before the trip to New Orleans, was entitled "Poor Uncle Tom, Good Night."

Foster married Jane Denny McDowell on July 22, 1850; they had one child, Marion. In 1860, after separating from his wife, Foster moved to New York City, where he lived in obscurity. He was injured in a fall and died in Bellevue Hospital there on January 13, 1864. He was buried in Pittsburgh's Allegheny Cemetery.

See Randall Capps, *The Rowan Story* (Bowling Green, Ky., 1976); John Tasker Howard, *Stephen Foster: America's Troubador* (New York 1954).

FOSTER, WILLIAM FORRESTER. W.F. Foster, industrialist, was born in a log house on an eighty-five-acre farm in Graves County, southeast of Mayfield, Kentucky, on August 1, 1895. He was the eldest of three children and the only son of Charles and Ellen (Bennett) Foster. Foster completed high school and graduated from the Mayfield Business College. He began work as a stock boy in the Merit Clothing Company and rose through the ranks to the presidency in 1938. He also operated a 550-acre farm and managed the 1954 campaign of Alben Barkley, who defeated John Sherman Cooper for a seat in the U.S. Senate. Foster was baptized into the Bethel Church of Christ and served as a member of the board of trustees of the Lexington Theological Seminary and the University of Kentucky (1956-67). He was given the Horatio Alger award in 1966—one of only four Kentuckians to have received the "rags to riches" honor.

Foster married Roberta Brizentine in 1930 and was divorced in 1948. He then married Kitty Hawes, to whom a son, Charles, was born. Foster died on February 28, 1967, in a Baltimore hospital and was buried in Mayfield's Highland Park.

ADRON DORAN

FOWLER, JOHN. John Fowler, pioneer political leader, son of John and Judith (Hobson) Fowler, was born in Chesterfield County, Virginia, on April 27, 1756. He joined a Captain Patterson's company as a first lieutenant in the Revolutionary War in 1777 and by 1783 he had become a captain. He studied at William and Mary College in 1780 and was a member of the Williamsburg Lodge Freemasons. Fowler moved to Lexington, Kentucky, in 1783. In October 1786, through an act of the Virginia legislature, he became one of several trustees of the new city of Frankfort, Kentucky. In June 1787 he joined Captain James Brown's company of Kentucky volunteers in battling the Indians. In this same year Fowler was elected to the Virginia legislature, and he represented Fayette County in the third statehood convention, held in Danville, Kentucky. He also served as a Fayette County delegate in the Virginia convention in 1783 that ratified the U.S. Constitution. Fowler was a member of the Kentucky Society for Promoting Useful Knowledge. In 1788, along with Richard Clough Anderson and Green Clay, he established Lexington Freemason Lodge No. 1. From 1787 to 1794, he was an ensign in the Lexington Light Infantry, which fought in Indian campaigns.

Fowler served as Transylvania Seminary's treasurer from 1789 to 1793. He became a gentleman justice for Woodford County on May 5, 1789, retaining this seat until 1794. Between 1792 and 1794, he was a clerk both to the court of oyer and terminer and to the directors of public buildings. In 1797 Fowler was elected to the U.S. House of Representatives, where he served for ten years (1797-1807). He became a member of the board of trustees of Lexington, serving as chairman during 1817-18, and he was Lexington's fourth postmaster (1814-22). Fowler, a large landowner in Virginia and Kentucky, helped create the Kentucky Agricultural Society. Before 1800 he established Fowler's Gardens on three hundred acres near Lexington as a recreational resort. In 1802 he transferred ninety-three acres of land to the Concord Presbyterian Church near Carlisle, Kentucky.

Fowler married Millicent Wills of Virginia at some time before 1789; they had five children. Fowler's wife died in July 1833; he died on August 22, 1840, and is buried in the Episcopal Cemetery in Lexington, Kentucky.

See Mrs. W.T. Fowler, "Captain John Fowler of Kentucky and Virginia," *Register* 37 (July 1939): 263-65.

FOX, FONTAINE TALBOT, JR. Fontaine Talbot Fox, Jr., was the creator of "The Toonerville Trolley that Meets All the Trains," a comic strip that delighted readers of more than 250 newspapers nationwide between 1915 and 1955 with its humorous comments on the social issues of the day. Many of the figures in the comic strip were modeled after people Fox had known when he was growing up in Louisville. He was born there on June 4, 1884, to Fontaine Fox, Sr., a Louisville lawyer, editorial writer, and book reviewer, and Mary Pitkin (Barton) Fox. In 1904 he graduated from Louisville

Male High School, where he had been a staff member of the school newspaper and the artist for the literary journal. While still in high school, he began working for the *Louisville Herald* as a reporter. He became a political cartoonist for the newspaper while he attended Indiana University for two years. He worked briefly for the *Louisville Times*, then joined the staff of the *Chicago Evening Post* as a cartoonist in 1910. Five years later he went to New York City, where his work was syndicated nationwide.

The idea for the "Toonerville Trolley" came to Fox as he was riding a dilapidated old trolley in Pelham, New York, reminding him of the Louisville Brook Street trolley, which ran past Male High School. The trolley, which ceased operating in the 1930s, was often filled with noisy schoolboys who rocked it back and forth until it came off the tracks. Fox later told a reporter about his experience in Pelham: "I thought then to myself, 'Lord, these trolleys are all over the country.' And I drew my first 'Toonerville Trolley' that night." Among the Toonerville Folks were Powerful Katrinka, who put the trolley back on the track; Mickey ("Himself") McGuire, the tough boy smoking a cigar; Tomboy Taylor and the Terrible Tempered Mr. Bang; and Aunt Eppy Hogg, "the fattest woman in three counties."

Three books of Fox's cartoons were published: *Fontaine Fox's Funny Folk* (1917); *Fontaine Fox's Cartoons* (1918); and *Toonerville Trolley and other Cartoons* (1921). When he retired in 1955, the "Toonerville Trolley" was retired as well.

Fox was married to Edith Elizabeth Hinz; they had two daughters. In his later years, he lived in both Vero Beach, Florida, and Greenwich, Connecticut. He died on August 9, 1964, in Greenwich, and was buried in Carmel, New York.

See Kelly Thurman, "Fontaine Fox: Kentucky's Foremost Cartoonist," *Register* 77 (Spring 1979): 112-28.

FOX, FRANCES BARTON. Frances Barton Fox, novelist, was born on January 19, 1887, in Gap-in-the-Knobs, Bullitt County, Kentucky. She was the daughter of Louisville lawyer Fontaine Fox and Mary Pitkin (Barton) Fox. Her brother was Fontaine Fox, Jr., the creator of the "Toonerville Trolley" comic strip. Fox's novels feature strong-willed women and a nostalgic look at Kentucky's agrarian past. *The Heart of Aresthusa* (1918) is a juvenile novel about a young woman of eighteen who travels abroad with her father. *Ridgeways* (1934), published under the pen name Frances Renard, takes a fictitious Kentucky family through five generations.

In 1928 Fox moved to New York City, where she was a member of the New York Society of Kentucky Women and the Pen and Brush Club. She returned to Louisville in 1936. Fox died on February 4, 1967, and was cremated.

FOX, JOHN, JR. John Fox, Jr., a popular writer at the turn of the century who chronicled the folk life of the Cumberland Mountains, was born December 16, 1862, at Stony Point in Bourbon County, Kentucky. He was the first child of John W. Fox, head of Stony Point Academy, and his second wife, Minerva (Carr) Fox, of Mayslick, Kentucky. After attending his father's private boarding school, Fox studied for two years at Transylvania University in Lexington. In September 1880 he entered Harvard as a sophomore and graduated cum laude in June 1883, the youngest member of his class. Following brief periods as a reporter for the *New York Sun* and the *New York Times* and as a student at Columbia University Law School, Fox returned to Kentucky in 1885 because of poor health. For several months he taught in his father's school and did some private tutoring.

Fox had been introduced to mountain people and their folk ways during the summer of 1882, when he lived in Jellico, Tennessee, where his brothers had mining interests. In 1888 he joined his family when they moved their mining and real estate operations to Big Stone Gap, Virginia, near Cumberland Gap. There Fox joined a local vigilante group that succeeded in bringing order to a lawless region. He also began walking tours of the Kentucky-Virginia border country, in particular the Kentucky mountain counties of Letcher, Harlan, Leslie, and Perry, fascinated by the people and their way of life. Encouraged by a former Transylvania professor, the writer James Lane Allen, Fox started writing short sketches of mountain life and in 1892 published his first short story, "A Mountain Europa," in *Century* magazine. At the age of thirty, he became an overnight literary success, publishing stories, articles, and sketches in popular magazines of the day, including *Scribner's Magazine*, *Ladies Home Journal*, *Harper's Weekly*, and *Harper's Monthly*.

Although Fox was retiring, even shy, by nature, he made friends with many prominent men of his day, including President Theodore Roosevelt, who on several occasions invited him to the White House to give readings and to sing mountain songs. Fox was popular in public readings of his stories in the East and South, sometimes teamed with other writer-performers such as James Whitcomb Riley.

In 1895 Fox published his first book, *A Cumberland Vendetta and Other Stories*, followed in 1897 by his first novel, *The Kentuckians*, set principally in the Bluegrass. In 1898 he covered the Spanish-American War in Cuba for *Harper's Weekly*, an experience that gave him the background for his 1900 novel, *Crittenden: A Kentucky Story of Love and War*. In 1901 he published *Bluegrass and Rhododendrum*, a collection of essays on mountain life.

Fox's 1903 novel, *The Little Shepherd of Kingdom Come*, was perhaps the first in the United States to sell a million copies. The novel has all the ingredients of popular fiction at the turn of the century: a masculine but sensitive hero, a dastardly villain, two lovely but contrasting heroines, and an adventure story set against the background of clashing cultures and civilizations, climaxing in war.

Despite a contrived plot and stock characters that frequently melt into sentiment, the book is a well-known American novel. It has been reprinted in numerous editions and reproduced as a successful play and at least four motion pictures.

In 1904 Fox went to Japan and Manchuria to report on the Russo-Japanese War for *Scribner's Magazine*. His six travel articles appeared in *Scribner's* in 1904 and 1905 and were published in 1905 as a book, *Following the Flag: A Vain Pursuit Through Manchuria*.

Fox's 1908 novel, *The Trail of the Lonesome Pine*, is a love story based on Fox's own experiences during the boom-and-bust era at Big Stone Gap. The story is that of a Bluegrass Kentuckian, a mining engineer whose work takes him to the mountains. There he falls in love with an unlettered young woman whom he helps to transform into an educated, cultured lady. After being separated by a series of entanglements, including a feud, they are reunited under the lonesome pine on top of the mountain where they first met. The novel was adapted for the stage in 1912 by Eugene Walter and was filmed three times, in 1916, 1922, and 1936. It was also the basis for a popular song.

Fox's easily accessible writing style blended humor and pathos in the manner popular with local colorists of his time. He probably knew his settings and subjects better than most regional writers, and in his best fiction he painted faithful and moving portraits of life in the southern mountains. None of his subsequent works equaled the success of *The Trail of the Lonesome Pine*.

In December 1908 Fox married Fritzi Scheff, a Viennese opera singer; they were divorced four years later. In 1919, while on a fishing trip near Norton, Virginia, Fox developed pneumonia and died two days later, on July 8, at his home in Big Stone Gap. He was buried in Paris, Kentucky.

See Warren I. Titus, *John Fox, Jr.* (New York 1971); John W. Townsend, *Kentucky in American Letters* (Cedar Rapids, Iowa, 1913).

WADE HALL

FRAKES, HIRAM MILO. Hiram Milo Frakes, founder of the HENDERSON SETTLEMENT SCHOOL in Bell County, Kentucky, was born in Branchville, Indiana, on March 31, 1888, to William and Sarah (Carr) Frakes. One of four brothers raised on the family farm, he received little formal education. After studying telegraphy, he worked for the Southern Railway in southern Indiana. In 1918 he became a Methodist minister, obtaining his deacon's orders through the Indiana Conference. He moved to southeastern Kentucky in 1921 to serve the coal mining town of Benham in Harlan County. Within a year he had received an appointment to the Pineville First Methodist Church. He served Pineville until 1925, when he established the Henderson Settlement School in the Middle Laurel Fork Valley, a remote area of the Appalachian Mountains. Frakes was active at Henderson until his retirement in 1959.

Frakes was married three times, to Leota Walker of Branchville, Indiana; Ruth Wakefield from Ohio; and Rebecca Arend of Spencer, Indiana. Frakes died on December 15, 1975, in Bloomington, Indiana, and was buried in the Walker Cemetery in Branchville.

See Lee Fisher, *Fire in the Hills: The Story of Parson Frakes and the Henderson Settlement* (Nashville 1971).

FRANKFORT. Frankfort, Kentucky's capital and the Franklin County seat, is located astride a double curve in the Kentucky River about sixty miles upstream from the Ohio, at U.S. 60 and U.S. 127. The original townsite is a broad alluvial plain near the geographic center of the county.

The first English explorer to visit the area was Ohio Company surveyor Christopher Gist, who followed an ancient buffalo trace to its junction with the Kentucky River and arrived on March 19, 1751. He was followed by John Finley in 1752; Daniel Boone in 1770; Robert McAfee and Hancock Taylor in 1773; and George Rogers Clark, Nicholas Cresswell, and Hancock Lee in 1775. The event that probably gave Frankfort its name occurred in 1780 when Indians attacked a salt-boiling party from Bryan's Station at a ford on the Kentucky River, killing a pioneer named Stephen Frank. The crossing soon became known as Frank's Ford.

In August 1786, Gen. James Wilkinson, a former Continental army officer, bought a 260-acre tract on the north side of the Kentucky River from Humphrey Marshall. Two months later, the Virginia legislature designated one hundred acres of Wilkinson's land as the town of Frankfort. Wilkinson placed administration of the town in a seven-member board of trustees. Frankfort grew slowly, and in early 1792 Wilkinson sold his property to Andrew Holmes. When Kentucky became a state later the same year, the legislature appointed a commission to select a capital. The commissioners were instructed to choose the town that pledged the largest contribution toward construction of a statehouse. Several towns, including Lexington, made serious proposals. But Holmes's offer of several town lots, rents from a tobacco warehouse, and assorted building materials, in addition to an offer of $3,000 in specie by eight local citizens, overwhelmed all other bids. On December 5, 1792, the commissioners recommended Frankfort as the capital, and three days later the legislature approved the recommendation.

A three-story statehouse was completed in 1794. The 1800 census listed 628 residents, making Frankfort the state's second largest town, after Lexington. During 1799-1800 the commonwealth erected a penitentiary in Frankfort. In 1803 the General Assembly authorized Martin Hawkins to make navigational improvements on the Kentucky River. The following year, Richard Throckmorton began building the town's first public water system, leading to organization of the Frankfort Water Company in 1805.

In November 1813, fire destroyed the statehouse. Local citizens raised $19,600 toward reconstruction, overwhelming second-ranking Woodford County's $550. Completed in 1816, the new capitol stood for only eight years before it burned on November 4, 1824. It was replaced by a magnificent Greek Revival structure, designed by Lexington-born architect Gideon SHRYOCK and completed in 1830. Two years later, Shryock was selected to design the Franklin County court house. Completed in 1835, it still houses major county offices.

Frankfort experienced considerable growth and expansion in the years between the War of 1812 and the Civil War. The population grew from 1,099 in 1810 to 3,702 in 1860. Local factories produced glass, boxes, hemp products, jeans cloth, steamboats, fishing reels, and farm implements. Several internal improvements linked the capital more firmly to surrounding communities. The steamboat era began about 1817 when Capt. John Armstrong's *Sylph* began plying the Kentucky River. By the early 1820s, Frankfort was the hub of river traffic between Louisville and central Kentucky. During the 1830s, Frankfort was connected by turnpikes to Lexington, Louisville, Shelbyville, Georgetown, Versailles, Paris, and other nearby towns.

The most important yet most troubled transportation improvement was the Lexington & Ohio Railroad. For most of the 1840s the line between Lexington and Frankfort was kept solvent by a state-authorized lease to Frankfort businessmen Philip Swigert and William McKee. Reorganized as the Lexington, Frankfort & Louisville Railroad in 1858, the company eventually was absorbed by the Louisville & Nashville Railroad (now CSX Transportation).

Swigert and McKee were part of an antebellum leadership group that included figures such as John H. Hanna, Jacob Swigert, Edmund H. Taylor, Sr., Orlando and Mason Brown, Ambrose W. Dudley, Thomas B. Stephenson, Albert G. Hodges, and Samuel I.M. Major. Although frequently overshadowed by state officials, they were deeply committed to Frankfort's progress. At various times they were instrumental in organizing the Bank of Kentucky, the Farmers Bank, the Capital Hotel, the Frankfort public school system, and numerous turnpike companies, stagecoach and steamboat lines, and churches. Philip Swigert was the capital's first mayor after it became a city in 1849.

As a border state capital, Frankfort felt deeply the sectional tensions that led to the Civil War. Numerous families were divided, notably that of U.S. Sen. John J. Crittenden, whose sons, George B. Crittenden and Thomas L. Crittenden, served as generals in the Confederate and Union armies, respectively. During the Confederate invasion in September 1862, Frankfort was captured and occupied until after the Battle of Perryville on October 8. The governor, the legislature, and other state officials fled to Louisville. Daily civic affairs during this period were directed by Thomas N. Lindsey, a Confederate sympathizer and former legislator

whose son, Daniel W. Lindsey, was inspector general of Kentucky. In June 1864, while commanding a division under Gen. U.S. Grant, Lindsey was recalled by Gov. Thomas Bramlette (1863-67) to organize Frankfort's defense against an expected attack by Gen. John Hunt Morgan's Confederate cavalry. The attack commenced on the evening of June 10, but Lindsey repelled the attackers the following day.

The postwar years were punctuated with incidents of racial and political violence, which culminated in the fatal shooting of William Goebel, the Democratic candidate in the challenged 1899 gubernatorial election, on January 30, 1900. Nevertheless, Frankfort saw considerable growth during this period. The population rose from 3,702 in 1860 to 9,487 in 1900, and dozens of new businesses blossomed in downtown Frankfort, notably the Buhr Hotel and the Deposit Bank in 1869, Selbert's Jewelry in 1872, and State National Bank in 1889. The depressions of 1873 and 1893 caused considerable economic instability, and the hemp industry declined significantly. This was largely offset by expansion in lumber and flour milling, meat packing, barrel making, and distilling. By 1898 a dozen distilleries produced six hundred barrels of bourbon daily. Supporting the city's economic growth was the Frankfort & Cincinnati Railroad. Organized in the early 1880s as the Kentucky Midland, it encountered serious financial reversals before construction began in 1888 and went into receivership in 1894. By the end of the century, however, local leaders touted the reorganized line as one of Franklin County's key transportation assets.

Several important social and governmental landmarks also appeared during the post–Civil War years. The Clinton Street School, opened in 1882, was a major advance in the education of black children. An elaborate U.S. courthouse and post office building was completed in 1887 at the corner of St. Clair and Wapping streets. The new Second Street School, occupied the following year, became the first home of Frankfort High School in 1889. The year 1887 also saw organization of the State Normal School for Colored Persons, forerunner of Kentucky State University.

Frankfort grew dramatically during the twentieth century, largely because of the expansion of state government. The population grew from 9,487 in 1900 to 25,973 in 1980, making Frankfort the commonwealth's sixth largest city. An impressive indicator of governmental expansion was the proliferation of government buildings. After nearly two decades of agitation, an imposing new capitol was constructed in south Frankfort. Designed in the French Renaissance style by Frank Mills Andrews, it was dedicated in June 1910. Two years later, construction began on the nearby executive mansion. Shortly after the 1937 flood, the old Kentucky Reformatory near downtown Frankfort was razed to make room for a new state office building. Construction on the eleven-story structure began in January 1939 and was completed two years later. In

1948 Gov. Earle C. Clements (1947-50) announced plans to build a capitol annex directly behind the capitol. A virtual replica of the capitol, without the dome, the annex was dedicated in October 1952.

A large state office construction project was the Capital Plaza, a massive, multiuse urban renewal development at the northeast corner of Wilkinson and Clinton streets, initiated during the term of Gov. Edward T. Breathitt (1963-67). Its centerpiece, completed in 1972, was a twenty-eight-story state office tower designed by Edward Durrell Stone. The project's final element, the Capital Plaza Hotel, was completed in 1984. The developer was Wallace G. Wilkinson, the Lexington businessman who was elected governor in 1987.

State government remains Frankfort's primary business, but the city has experienced substantial economic diversification since World War II. The population of the second-class city in 1970 was 21,356; 25,973 in 1980; and 25,968 in 1990.

See Carl E. Kramer, *Capital on the Kentucky: A Two Hundred Year History of Frankfort & Franklin County* (Frankfort, Ky., 1986); Willard Rouse Jillson, *Early Frankfort and Franklin County, Kentucky* (Louisville 1936); Stuart Sprague and Elizabeth Perkins, *Frankfort: A Pictorial History* (Virginia Beach, Va., 1980).   CARL E. KRAMER

FRANKFORT CEMETERY. The Frankfort Cemetery, Kentucky's first cemetery of the type known as picturesque, is located on Frankfort's East Main street at the Glenn's Creek Road and is bounded on the south by the Kentucky River. The cemetery was the creation of Judge Mason Brown, Kentucky lawyer and eldest son of Sen. John Brown, after he visited Mt. Auburn at Boston, founded in 1832—the first picturesque cemetery in the country. Brown and other leading citizens of Frankfort—his brother Orlando, E.H. Taylor, A.G. Hodges, Henry Wingate, Jacob Swigert, A.P. Cox, Phillip Swigert, and M.R. Stealy—organized the cemetery in 1843. The state legislature on February 27, 1844, approved the cemetery's incorporation, the second such incorporation in the United States.

Brown hired Robert Carmichael, educated as a landscape gardener in Scotland, to choose the site. On February 16, 1845, the cemetery company purchased thirty-two acres overlooking the Kentucky River, formerly known as Hunter's Garden, for $3,801.00. Brown asked Carmichael for a layout similar to that of Mt. Auburn—irregular curving drives, a circle of vaults, terraces, and lush plantings. Carmichael laid out the central State Mound for burials of notables and a site for the reinterment of Daniel Boone and his wife. Two of the most dramatic features—Cliff Avenue and a river walk below—are now gone.

The picturesque cemetery typically has a great variety of plants and shrubbery. From the mountains of Kentucky, Carmichael collected "splendid pines and young giants, oaks and maples, and splendid shrubs peculiar to that region." Flatboats brought the plants down the river. The plants were meant to be educational as well as beautiful, bringing rare species to those of limited travel. The central feature of the cemetery is the State Mound, which includes a military monument and the grave of U.S. Vice-President Richard M. Johnson. Carmichael suggested employing New York sculptor Robert E. Launitz for the monument, which the legislature had approved in 1848 to commemorate those who had died in defending their country. The monument, finished exactly two months ahead of schedule on July 1, 1850, brought Launitz national attention.

On October 31, 1845, the company offered lots for sale at public auction. Unauctioned lots were offered for sale in the *Frankfort Commonwealth* on November 4, 1845. Additional land was purchased from Thomas S. Page in 1858 and in 1911. The cemetery now covers just over one hundred acres.

See.Elizabeth Alice Trabue, *A Corner in Celebrities* (Louisville 1929); L.F. Johnson, *History of Frankfort Cemetery* (Frankfort, Ky., 1921).
WILLIAM B. SCOTT

FRANKLIN. Franklin, the seat of Simpson County, located at U.S. 31W and KY 100, was established on a sixty-two-acre site that was purchased from William Hudspeth in 1819. The town was incorporated November 2, 1820, and named in honor of Benjamin Franklin, American statesman and inventor.

Franklin has experienced steady growth. The town benefited from its location in a rich agricultural area on the pioneer trace that connected Bowling Green and Nashville; after 1859, being on the main line of the Louisville & Nashville Railroad (now CSX Transportation) was an additional advantage. During the Civil War, however, Franklin was the scene of guerrilla raids that destroyed some property.

After the end of the Civil War, Franklin rapidly recovered its prewar prosperity. In the 1870s, it had six churches, twenty-four stores, three hotels, mills, factories, and a newspaper. The Franklin Female Institute, which operated between 1868 and 1917, was one of several schools. Franklin's annual Mule Day Festival received national recognition before it was discontinued during World War II.

In the early 1950s, Franklin's economy became more diverse. The location of I-65 just east of the town in 1966 promoted industrial growth, and by 1990 there were over 3,000 industrial jobs in and around the city. The largest employers in Franklin are the Kendall Company, which produces adhesive tape, and the Brown Printing Company.

The population of the fourth-class city was 6,553 in 1970; 7,738 in 1980; and 7,607 in 1990.
RON D. BRYANT

FRANKLIN COUNTY. Franklin County, the eighteenth in order of formation, is located in central Kentucky in the Bluegrass region. The county is bordered by Anderson, Henry, Owen, Scott, Shelby, and Woodford counties and has an area of

212 square miles. Franklin County was formed from portions of Mercer, Shelby, and Woodford counties on December 7, 1794, and FRANKFORT, the state capital, is its seat of government. The county was named in honor of Benjamin Franklin, signer of the Declaration of Independence.

The topography of Franklin County is somewhat rolling to hilly. The soil is rich and deep in most portions, and tobacco, corn, hay, and vegetables are raised in abundance. The principal streams are the Kentucky River, the Elkhorn Creek and its north and south branches, and the Big and Little Benson and Flat creeks.

Indians hunted game in the forests of Franklin County and had settlements in the area; many Indian artifacts have been discovered in the Lower Benson and Flat creeks sections. Arrowheads, pottery shards, shell beads, and tomahawks, along with the skeletal remains of Native Americans, were uncovered in the Jett area near Frankfort. One of the Indian trails through Franklin County, the Alanant-O-Wamiowee, was originally an animal trace followed by large herds of buffalo and elk. This trail crossed the Kentucky River at Leestown and in some places was trampled one hundred feet wide by animals traveling toward salt licks.

Among the first explorers in the Franklin County region was Christopher Gist, who in 1751 was employed by the Ohio Land Company of Virginia. In the mid-1770s, explorers and hunters were joined by settlers such as Hancock Lee, who established the first settlement in 1775 in Leestown, on the Kentucky River one mile below the present site of Frankfort.

In 1780 Indians attacked a group of men from Bryan's Station near Lexington on their way to Mann's Salt Lick in Jefferson County. One member of the group, Stephen Frank, was killed at a site that was afterward called Frank's Ford (present-day Frankfort). Near the Kentucky River, Haydon's Station was founded in 1783, followed by Arnold's Station in 1784. Hamilton's Station was founded on trail to the Falls of the Ohio in 1785, and a number of Elkhorn Creek settlements were established, including John Major's Station (1783), Dry Run (ca. 1784), Goar's Station (ca. 1785), Cook's Station (1792), and Harry Innes's Station (1792). In 1788 John Major assembled a group of settlers and founded the Forks of Elkhorn Baptist Church near his settlement. The congregation was the first organized in the county and spurred the growth of the community that came to be known as Forks of Elkhorn. The Marquis de Lafayette visited Frankfort on May 14, 1825, during his triumphal tour of the United States.

During the 1830s and 1840s, steamboats such as the *Argo*, the *Eagle*, the *Frankfort*, and the *John Armstrong* were constructed especially for the Kentucky River trade. Agricultural goods from Franklin County farms and plantations went to market down the Ohio and Mississippi rivers on these vessels.

In the 1830s Franklin County manufacturers produced candles, stovepipes, and coaches. In 1833, E.H. and S. Steadman operated a paper mill about three miles from Frankfort on Elkhorn Creek. A horse-drawn railroad opened in Franklin County on October 23, 1831. By January 1, 1835, the railroad was locomotive-powered and operated between Frankfort and Lexington.

In 1833 an outbreak of Asiatic cholera struck Franklin County, causing the deaths of at least 150 people. Later, a smallpox epidemic was the cause of several deaths.

The location of the state capital made the county a target during the Civil War. Confederate troops commanded by Gen. Edmund Kirby-Smith occupied Frankfort from September 3, 1862, until October 7, 1862, when Union cavalry skirmished with a retreating Confederate rear guard. On June 10, 1864, a portion of Gen. John Hunt Morgan's Confederate cavalry unsuccessfully attacked Frankfort's Fort Hill, which was defended by the Peak's Mill militia. In late August 1864, guerrillas terrorized citizens in the Steadmantown vicinity. In January 1865 a guerrilla band robbed stores in the Bridgeport and Farmdale communities west of Frankfort. After the war, Ku Klux Klan violence focused on a small black community in the Bald Knob area.

The Civil War disrupted the Franklin County economy. Agricultural prices and production levels in 1870 were lower than those of 1850. The emancipation of slaves left Franklin County suffering a severe labor shortage. Between 1870 and 1880, the local economy improved as tobacco replaced hemp as the leading cash crop and the livestock industry prospered. Livestock and the distillery industry were markets for corn. By 1874 farmers organized to further their interests, and the Grange movement was popular.

Between 1900 and 1920, most of Franklin County's rural communities lost population as some moved to Frankfort and others left to seek industrial jobs. In 1919 prohibition effectively shut down the county's largest industry, forced the development of other industries, and resulted in significant gains in retail trade and tourism. The growth of state government helped to reverse the county's population drop. Population grew at established communities such as Forks of Elkhorn and Bridgeport and at newer places such as Swallowfield and Elmville. In other rural precincts, such as Bald Knob and Peaks Mill, population declined.

By 1935, after the repeal of prohibition, five distilleries had reopened or started up in the county: the George Stagg Company in Leestown, Old Crow and Old Taylor in Glen's Creek, Kennebec (later Ezra Brooks) in Benson Valley, and K. Taylor (later Old Grand Dad) at Forks of Elkhorn. In the years following World War II, the continued growth of state government promoted the growth of suburbs in the area surrounding Frankfort. Urbanization and scattered residential development contributed to the loss of nearly 14,000 acres of crop and grazing land between 1940 and 1970 in Franklin County. Although many farmers also had full-time employment in state government, farms in 1987 occupied

72 percent of the county area. Major employers outside Frankfort's city limits in 1990 were Union Underwear Company and National Distillers Products Company.

The population of Franklin County was 34,481 in 1970; 41,830 in 1980; and 43,781 in 1990.

See L. Johnson, *The History of Franklin County, Kentucky* (Frankfort, Ky., 1912); Carl M. Kramer, *Capital on the Kentucky* (Frankfort, Ky., 1986).

RON D. BRYANT

FRAZER, OLIVER. Oliver Frazer, portraitist, was born on February 4, 1808, in Fayette County, Kentucky, to Alexander and Nancy (Oliver) Frazer. In 1825 he left school to study art with Matthew Harris JOUETT. After Jouett died in 1827, Frazer left Kentucky for Philadelphia, becoming a pupil of Thomas Sully. Around 1830 Frazer returned to Lexington to begin work as a portrait painter. Frazer sailed for France in May 1834 to study the Old Masters; he studied painting in Paris under Thomas Couture and Baron Antoine-Jean Gros. During 1835-36 Frazer visited major museums in Germany, Italy, Belgium, Switzerland, and England. Returning to Lexington in 1838, he opened a portrait studio at 12 East Main Street. During the next few years, Frazer painted portraits of Mrs. Henry Clay, Jr. (Julia Prather), Richard H. Menefee, Joel T. Hart, Waller Bullock Redd, Col. William Robertson McKee, and other notable Kentuckians. Four portraits of Henry Clay are known to be the work of Frazer, including the well-known likeness of the aging statesman ca. 1851.

In 1838 Frazer married Martha Bell Mitchell of Lexington, niece of Mrs. Matthew Jouett. They lived in a small house on Georgetown Road in Fayette County for the first few years of their marriage. In the late 1850s they moved into nearby Eothan (now Malvern Hill), built by the Rev. James Moore. Failing eyesight in his later years forced Frazer to cease painting. He died on April 9, 1864, and was buried in the Lexington Cemetery.

See William Barrow Floyd, *Jouett-Bush-Frazer: Early Kentucky Artists* (Lexington, Ky., 1968).

FREE SOUTH. The *Free South*, edited by William Shreve Bailey in Newport, Kentucky, was an antislavery newspaper published in the 1850s. After moving to Newport in 1839, Bailey established a machine shop and wrote articles on abolition for the local newspaper, the *Newport News*. The editor sold the press to Bailey, who began a decade-long attack upon slavery in March 1850. He renamed the paper the *Newport and Covington Daily News*. In the same year he founded the *Kentucky Weekly News*, which he renamed the *Free South* in 1858. Bailey supported immediate emancipation in his appeal to the nonslaveholding "laboring masses" of Kentucky, whose wages were reduced "by forcing them to compete with the unpaid labor of black men and women."

In October 1851, a mob burned the store where Bailey published the newspaper. His friends in Newport raised enough money to get his newspaper

started again. Bailey was often sued for libel and was physically attacked upon occasion. The climax of organized opposition to the abolition-minded editor came following John Brown's raid at Harper's Ferry, Virginia, in October 1859. A mob entered the offices of the *Free South*, above which his family lived, and threw his presses and type into the street.

Not to be intimidated, Bailey reestablished his presses, armed his office, sued his persecutors, and defied the mob to attack again. When he was imprisoned, apparently for issuing an "incendiary" publication, Northern sympathizers bailed him out. Supporters sent him on a lecture tour of England to raise money for the antislavery cause. When he returned, no trial was held because the Civil War had come to Kentucky. Bailey's wartime issues applauded the Lincoln administration's stand. Bailey lived to see the reality of the free South he had so strongly supported in print.

See Will Frank Steely, "William Shreve Bailey, Kentucky Abolitionist," *FCHQ* 31 (July 1957): 274-81.   WILL FRANK STEELY

FREEDMEN'S BUREAU. Established under the War Department by the U.S. Congress on March 3, 1865, the Bureau of Refugees, Freedmen, and Abandoned Lands, more commonly known as the Freedmen's Bureau, was to protect and care for ex-slaves and others set adrift by the war in the former slave states. The Freedmen's Bureau was established in Kentucky by Gen. Oliver O. Howard, commander of the bureau, on December 26, 1865, possibly because of Kentucky's refusal to ratify the Thirteenth Amendment and because of violence against blacks reported by the district military commander, Gen. John Palmer. Howard sent Gen. Clinton Fisk, the bureau's assistant commander in Tennessee, into Kentucky to establish a Freedmen's Bureau there, as part of the Tennessee District.

Kentucky reacted vehemently against the presence of the bureau, claiming that its state rights were violated by applying Reconstruction laws to a state that had remained loyal to the Union. In an apparent attempt to show that the Freedmen's Bureau was unnecessary in Kentucky, the legislature in February 1866 enacted laws to protect black employees, to apply blacks' taxes for their education, to allow blacks to own property, and to allow them to testify in court in all cases not involving whites. The old "master and apprentice" laws were repealed, as were the statutes concerning runaway slaves. These measures failed to offset the effects of reports such as that of General Fisk, who on January 18, 1866, in Lexington, saw thirteen black soldiers publicly whipped and two blinded. In 1867 the Freedmen's Bureau recorded 20 murders, 18 shootings, 11 rapes, and 270 other cases of maltreatment of blacks.

By March 1866 the Freedmen's Bureau had set up three administrative districts in Kentucky with headquarters at Lexington, Louisville, and Paducah. Fisk also established Freedmen's Bureau courts in major cities and towns to secure justice for former slaves. When Gen. Jeff Davis was appointed on June 13, 1866, to take over from Fisk as assistant commissioner for Kentucky, he established four districts, with headquarters at Lexington, Louisville, Paducah, and Bowling Green, and a fifth district, composed of fifteen counties in the center of the state that had no permanent administrative office. On July 16, 1866, Congress extended the life of the Freedmen's Bureau for two years and set up an educational division for Kentucky. By 1869 the schools set up by the bureau numbered 369, with 1,080 teachers and 18,891 pupils. The Education Division established over fifty schools in Kentucky, but hostility to the bureau remained high. In a report to General Howard, Gen. F.D. Sewall, an inspector for the Freedmen's Bureau, noted a "greater degree of hostility" against the bureau in Kentucky than in any other state he inspected. He attributed this to the fact that the bureau had been established in a state that had not seceded.

When the Civil Rights Act was passed in 1866, the situation for blacks improved. Not only did it grant former slaves those rights enjoyed by whites, but the legislation also authorized bureau officials to prosecute violators in federal court, preempting action in state courts. Despite the Civil Rights Act, however, state courts still refused the testimony of blacks in cases involving whites. A Bourbon County court in 1866 even denied the legal existence of the Freedmen's Bureau in Kentucky.

In March 1867 Gen. Sidney Burbank was named assistant commissioner for Kentucky, and after an inspection tour Lt. William H. Merrill, the new bureau inspector, reported that the situation for blacks was much improved. As the need for labor increased, white employers were forced to treat ex-slaves more fairly in order to secure their services. During the first six months of 1869, as a result of the Freedmen's Bureau, former black soldiers maintained a labor agency in Lexington, where 3,000 former slaves found employment.

But depredations against blacks continued, especially in the East. In the counties of Marion, Washington, Boyle, Casey, and Taylor, the so-called REGULATORS were carrying out summary executions of former bondsmen. Because the Freedmen's Bureau was expected to be closed in 1868, General Burbank dispatched Maj. Ben Runkle to the major cities and towns of Kentucky to inform blacks of their rights under the new laws and to encourage their participation in the bureau schools. In July 1868 the Freedmen's Bureau was granted a temporary reprieve when Congress extended its life until January 1869 and reorganized it in the interests of economy and efficiency, closing bureau offices in Covington, Lexington, Central and West Louisville, Mt. Sterling, Owensboro, and Paducah. The extension was seen by Kentuckians as a ploy to secure the votes of blacks in the upcoming November presidential election—an accusation that gained credence when, shortly after the election, all activities of the bureau were ordered to slow down. As of January 1, 1869, all offices were closed except the one in Louisville, which continued to aid blacks

and do educational work. It closed in June 1872. Although the bureau had done constructive work in the state, most white Kentuckians continued to consider its very existence a violation of their state's sovereignty.

See Ross A. Webb, *Kentucky in the Reconstruction Era* (Lexington, Ky., 1979); Ellis Merton Coulter, *The Civil War and Readjustment in Kentucky* (Chapel Hill, N.C., 1926).

FREEDMEN'S SCHOOLS. Established in 1866 under the Bureau of Refugees, Freedmen, and Abandoned Lands, freedmen's schools sought to educate former slaves with the hope of making them productive, contributing citizens. The Freedmen's Bureau Educational Division in Kentucky, under the leadership of army chaplain Thomas K. Noble, was able to establish 219 schools with 10,422 students by 1870. State aid for these schools, however, was quite limited. An act of the Kentucky General Assembly on February 16, 1866, provided for revenues from taxes on blacks to be used for freedmen's schools. On March 9, 1867, the legislature allocated a small per-student payment to black schools from black tax revenue. Because of the impoverished condition of most Kentucky blacks, these measures realized very little for the schools.

White hostility toward blacks found a target in the freedmen's schools. In Paducah, Mt. Sterling, and Glasgow, black school sessions were broken up by whites, and in Crab Orchard the freedmen's school was burned down. Many black schools served as a focal point for the continuing feud between Union and Confederate sympathizers. Despite these adversities, the freedmen's schools prevailed. On February 23, 1874, after the Freedmen's Bureau was dissolved, Kentucky created a uniform school system for blacks and allocated to them all administrative duties except funding, which still came from taxes on blacks and was controlled by the state.

On April 24, 1882, the Kentucky legislature allocated money for black schools to come from the same fund as that for white institutions, on a pro rata basis. This measure ensured the continuation of education for blacks in Kentucky.

See Philip Clyde Kimball, "Freedom's Harvest: Freedmen's Schools in Kentucky after the Civil War," *FCHQ* 54 (July 1980): 272-88; Ross A. Webb, *Kentucky in the Reconstruction Era* (Lexington, Ky., 1979).

FREEMASONRY. Freemasonry, the oldest and largest fraternity in the world, traces its remote origins to the medieval stonemasons of Europe. The members are referred to as Masons. Freemasonry does not solicit members; it requires those who seek membership to express a belief in God and a future state, subjects them to a thorough investigation before admission, and expects a high standard of morality of all members. Discussion of religion and politics is forbidden in the lodges. The ritual, set in the time of King Solomon and using biblical characters, has grown slowly over six centuries. Stonemasons' tools are used symbolically to teach morality.

Freemasonry as now constituted dates from 1717, when four London lodges organized the Grand Lodge of England. After the Revolutionary War, lodges in Virginia organized a grand lodge in 1778. On November 17, 1788, this organization granted a charter to Richard Clough Anderson (master), John Fowler, Green Clay, and others for Lexington (Kentucky) Lodge No. 25. Other lodges were soon chartered in Paris, Georgetown, Frankfort, and Shelbyville. On October 16, 1800, the Grand Lodge of Kentucky was organized, with William Murray as grand master.

The anti-Masonic episodes of the 1820s and 1830s reduced Kentucky membership from 1,800 in fifty-five lodges to about 1,300 in thirty-seven lodges by 1840. Membership reached 100,675 in 470 lodges in 1961. As of June 30, 1989, there were approximately 83,000 members in 457 lodges.

The grand lodge regarded the Civil War as a political issue and took neither side. The lodges, although often disturbed by military and guerilla actions, attempted to continue peaceably. Masons served in both armies. Civilian and military Kentucky Masons of the time included Robert Anderson, Thomas E. Bramlette, John C. Breckinridge, Simon B. Buckner, Cassius M. Clay, the Crittendens, James Guthrie, George W. Johnson, Albert Sydney Johnston, John Hunt Morgan, George D. Prentice, Beriah Magoffin, James F. Robinson, Frank Wolford, and many others. Among other prominent Kentucky Masons: John Bradford, Robert Worth Bingham, A.B. Chandler, George Rogers Clark, Henry Clay (grand master, 1820-21), J. Winston Coleman, Jr., John H. Cowles (sovereign grand commander, Scottish Rite, 1921-52), Joseph Hamilton Daviess (grand master, 1811), and Rob Morris (grand master, 1858-59, and poet laureate of Freemasonry).

The grand lodge sponsors the Masonic Widows' and Orphans' Home, established in 1867, in St. Matthews, and the Old Masons' Home at Shelbyville.

See Charles Snow Guthrie, *Kentucky Freemasonry, 1788-1978: The Grand Lodge and the Men Who Made It* (Louisville 1981); J. Winston Coleman, Jr., *Masonry in the Bluegrass* (Lexington, Ky., 1934).   CHARLES S. GUTHRIE

FRENCH, KATHERINE (JACKSON).

Katherine (Jackson) French, educator and author, was born on January 18, 1875, in Laurel County, Kentucky, to William H. and Mariah (McKee) Jackson. She was educated in the Laurel public school system and attended Laurel Seminary and the Science Hill Academy in Shelbyville, Kentucky. She earned her A.B. and M.A. degrees at Ohio Wesleyan University in Delaware, Ohio, and her Ph.D. at Columbia University; she also studied at Yale. She taught English at Mount Holyoke and Bryn Mawr colleges. She was deeply interested in mountain bal-

lads, often traveling to hear ballad singers and lecturing on the subject. Some of the ballads she discovered date back to the fourteenth century; a manuscript she compiled is kept in the Berea College Library in Berea, Kentucky. She also wrote a history of American Colonial literature. During 1915-16, she held the posts of dean and director of education at the Sue Bennett Memorial School, a coeducational boarding school in London, Kentucky. In 1924 she returned to teaching English, at Centenary College in Shreveport, Louisiana, where she remained until 1948. During her last three years on staff she was head of the English Department.

Katherine Jackson married William Frank French of Richmond, Kentucky, on September 12, 1911. She died in Columbia, South Carolina, on November 10, 1958, and is buried in A.R. Dyche Memorial Cemetery in London, Kentucky.

FRENCHBURG.

Frenchburg, located on U.S. 460 and KY 36, was established in 1869 as the county seat of the newly formed Menifee County. The town was incorporated on March 18, 1871, and named in honor of Richard French, lawyer and judge. Frenchburg is the only incorporated town in the predominantly rural county. The first Menifee County courthouse was erected in 1871-72, and this frame structure was replaced in 1928 with a stone two-story building. The courthouse entrance resembles a castellated Gothic tower and is topped by a colonial cupola.

Frenchburg suffered near destruction on June 27, 1882, when the rain-swollen Beaver Creek overflowed through the town. At least three buildings were swept away and six people were killed.

The lumber industry is a mainstay of the Frenchburg economy. Tourism is also a fast-growing economic factor. Events such as Menifee Mountain Days, held in the month of May, aid the local economy.

The population of the sixth-class city was 467 in 1970; 550 in 1980; and 625 in 1990.   RON D. BRYANT

FRENCH SETTLEMENT.

France's claim to the Ohio Valley rested on the presumed discovery of the valley by René-Robert Cavelier de La Salle in 1669, which historians debate, and his claim in 1682 to the entire Mississippi River watershed. The French attempted no settlement in Kentucky for two reasons: 1) The Iroquois claimed it, having driven out other tribes in the mid-1600s to reserve it for hunting, and the French, having fought them until 1701, tacitly admitted the claim; and 2) Kentucky's furs were much inferior to those from the North.

In 1749, alarmed by growing incursions beyond the Alleghenies by English traders and fearing defection by the region's Indians, Gov.-Gen. Roland-Michel Barrin de la Galissonière dispatched 213 regulars, Canadians, and Indians from Quebec under Maj. Pierre-Joseph Céloron de Blainville. They were to counter English claims to the Ohio, ward off interlopers, and protect the Mississippi corridor.

The expedition, from June 15 to November 10, crossed the Lake Chautauqua portage to the Allegheny, passed down the Ohio to the Great Miami, and at strategic points buried leaden plates stating France's claim. They then returned to Montreal through Detroit.

When this demonstration failed to overawe the English and Indians, the French employed force. Charles-Michel Langlade's Indian irregulars destroyed the English-Indian trading center at Pickawillany on the upper Great Miami on June 21, 1752, and Gov.-Gen. Ange de Menneville de Duquesne in 1754 completed a chain of forts from Presq'Isle to the forks of the Ohio. Among them was Fort Duquesne, which was supplied by annual convoys up the Ohio from the Illinois settlements.

The fort held out until British Gen. John Forbes's expedition and the Pennsylvania Indians' desertion, owing to the Easton Treaty, forced the French to abandon it on November 24, 1758. When France surrendered its American empire in 1763, the English took over.

Gratitude for French aid during the Revolutionary War and sympathy for France's republicanism made Kentucky a hotbed of Francophilia, as evidenced in place names—Versailles, Paris, Bourbon, Fayette, La Grange, and Louisville (which has a statue of Louis XVI). When Spain blocked the free use of the Mississippi and the Washington administration appeared indifferent to the effect on Kentucky's economic future, Edmond-Charles Genêt, the French minister (1793-94), took advantage of Kentucky's Francophilia by trying secretly to enlist Kentuckians under George Rogers Clark to "liberate" New Orleans. Despite reports that thousands would join Clark (only about forty did so), lack of supplies and money, along with stern warnings by Washington against violating America's neutrality policy, ended the French conspiracy.

On May 18-21, 1797, Louis-Philippe of Orleans, who reigned from 1830 to 1848, stopped in Bardstown while traveling through the West.

See Leslie Tihany, "French Legends Die Hard in Kentucky," *FCHQ* 55 (April 1981): 194-201; Huntley Dupre, "The French in Early Kentucky," *FCHQ* 15 (April 1941): 78-104.

DAVID S. NEWHALL

FRIEDMAN, JOSEPH L. Joseph L. Friedman, businessman and philanthropist, was born in Louisville on April 14, 1857, to Leopold and Louisa (Meyers) Friedman, early German-Jewish pioneers in Kentucky. Friedman moved to Paducah, Kentucky, around 1880 to establish a vinegar works, and he eventually made a fortune in the whiskey business together with his partner and brother-in-law, John Keiler. Friedman was an active investor in several of Paducah's major business enterprises. He was president of the Paducah Traction Company and of the Palmer Hotel Company, and vice-president of the City National Bank. Friedman was also a philanthropist of note, contributing, for example, a new wing of Paducah's Home of the Friendless orphanage in memory of his wife, Lizzy Keiler. After Friedman died on July 5, 1913, his family established a settlement house in Paducah in his honor. He was buried in the Temple Israel Cemetery in Paducah.   LEE SHAI WEISSBACH

FRIENDS OF KENTUCKY LIBRARIES. The Friends of Kentucky Libraries, which evolved from a variety of volunteer groups that struggled to bring books to all areas in the commonwealth, held its first meeting in 1952. One outcome of the meeting was a successful drive to establish the bookmobile network. The Friends continue to assist the Department for Libraries and Archives in maintaining the bookmobiles. Other work of the organization includes scholarships for librarians, aid to local libraries and to communities in need of a library, dissemination of information on expanding library services, and assistance in establishing local autonomous chapters of Friends of Kentucky Libraries. In 1990 there were sixty-five volunteer chapters.

See Frances Jane Porter, "Kentucky Bookmobiles Roll," *Library Journal* 80 (Feb. 1955).

JOY BALE BOONE

FROST, WILLIAM GOODELL. William Goodell Frost, educator, was born in Leroy, New York, on July 2, 1854, the eldest child of the Rev. Lewis P. and Maria (Goodell) Frost; he was the grandson of abolitionist William Goodell. Frost received his A.B. from Oberlin College in 1876, where he remained as professor of Greek until 1892, when he accepted the presidency of BEREA COLLEGE.

During his tenure as president (1892-1920), Frost was credited with coping with the DAY LAW litigation and the significant expansion of Berea College as both a regional and a national institution. Changing the original course of Berea's mission from that of the coeducation of blacks and whites to the education of Appalachian Americans, Frost considered himself, and was viewed by his contemporaries as, the discoverer of the southern Appalachian regional culture. In 1911 the college's constitution was amended to make Appalachia Berea's special field. The period 1912-20 saw a significant rise in endowment, from $100,000 to over $2 million, and in enrollment from 350 to 2,400. Plagued by illness for much of his career, Frost retired in 1920. In 1937 Frost wrote *For The Mountains*.

He married Louise Raney on August 9, 1876, and they had three children—Stanley, Wesley, and Norman. After her death he married Eleanor Marsh on July 5, 1891, and they had two children—Edith and Cleveland. Frost died on September 11, 1938, and was buried in Berea.

See Henry Shapiro, *Appalachia On Our Mind: The Southern Mountains and Mountaineers in the American Consciousness, 1870-1920* (Chapel Hill, N.C., 1978).   SHANNON WILSON

FULKS, JOSEPH FRANKLIN. Born on October 26, 1921, the son of Leonard and Mattie (Estes)

Fulks, and raised in the small hamlet of Birmingham, Marshall County, Kentucky, Joseph Franklin ("Jumping Joe") Fulks was one of the leading scorers during his eight years on the professional basketball circuit. Fulks played his first three years of high school basketball at Birmingham and graduated in 1939 from nearby Kuttawa High School, where he was known as the "Kuttawa Clipper." He gave the small school its only trip to the state tournament. He practiced his long arcing jump shots by tossing bricks through outdoor basketball goals in schoolyards. Fulks spent two years at Murray State University on a basketball scholarship before enlisting in the U.S. Marine Corps during World War II. Assigned to a touring military team in the South Pacific, he attracted the attention of the professional basketball scouts. He signed a professional contract in 1946 with Eddie Gottlieb, the owner-coach of the Philadelphia Warriors. Fulks led the league in scoring during his rookie season, averaging 23.2 points per game—very high for the slower-paced game of the 1940s. The Warriors won the world championship in 1947.

The slender six-foot, four-inch Kentuckian scored a record sixty-three points in a game between the Warriors and the Indianapolis Jets on February 10, 1949. The record stood for ten years, until broken by Elgin Baylor. In 1949 Fulks scored thirty or more points in each of nine successive games. He was given credit by many for introducing the jump shot to the game of basketball. *Time* magazine called Fulks the Babe Ruth of professional basketball, the *Sporting News* named him outstanding athlete of the year in America in 1948, and the nation's sports writers selected him as the best professional basketball player. Joe Fulks was inducted into the Helms Foundation's Professional Basketball's Hall of Fame, and in 1971 was one of the ten-man NBA silver anniversary team, which was honored at the All-Star Game that year in San Diego. Fulks retired from professional basketball in 1954, spent twenty years with the GAF Corporation in Calvert City, and at the time of his death was recreation director of the Kentucky State Penitentiary at Eddyville. He died March 24, 1976, in Eddyville and was buried in Briensberg Cemetery in Marshall County.   BILL CUNNINGHAM

FULTON. Fulton, named after its home county of Fulton, is located in the Jackson Purchase region in western Kentucky on the Tennessee state line. The town is situated at the junction of U.S. 45 and KY 307 at the southern end of the Purchase Parkway. Settlers established a post office there in the 1850s known as Pontotoc, an Indian word meaning cattail prairie. With the coming of the Illinois Central Railroad, a station was established there in 1861 and named Fulton. The town was incorporated in 1872 and by the 1920s the city was a major railroad hub with north-south mainlines converging there. Northbound freight trains with refrigerator cars carrying bananas from the Gulf of Mexico were serviced, iced, and reconsigned at Fulton. Eventually,

the city became known as the "Banana Crossroads of the United States." Since 1963 the annual International Banana Festival has celebrated Fulton's transportation history. Tobacco has also been a chief industry; several family-owned warehouses opened in the 1890s, and the American Cigar Company factory opened in the early 1900s. The population of the fourth-class city was 3,250 in 1970; 3,231 in 1980; and 3,078 in 1990.

FULTON COUNTY. Fulton County, the ninety-ninth county in order of formation, is located in the Jackson Purchase region of southwestern Kentucky. It is bordered by the Mississippi River on the west and northwest, by Tennessee to the south, and by Hickman County. The county has an area of 211 square miles and was formed on January 15, 1845, from a section of Hickman County. Its county seat is HICKMAN, on the Mississippi River. The county was named to honor Robert Fulton, who constructed the first commercially successful steamboat in the United States. Fulton's invention had a profound effect upon the communities located along the Mississippi River, a point not lost upon the county fathers in 1845.

The topography of Fulton County varies from broad flat floodplains marked by occasional ponds, sloughs, and marshes to gently rolling uplands located beyond the Mississippi River bluffs. Among the wetlands in the county is the Reelfoot National Wildlife Refuge. Other county waterways are Bayou de Chien, Obion Creek, Mud Creek, and Running Slough.

Settlers may have arrived in the county as early as the 1780s, even though it was then claimed by the Chickasaw Indians. Not even the New Madrid earthquakes (1811-12) kept newcomers away. The largest number came after the Jackson Purchase in 1818, when land became legally available for settlement. The area prospered on agricultural production and the booming Mississippi River trade. The rich bottomlands were ideal for the production of corn, wheat, and soybeans. The Madrid, or Kentucky Bend, section of the far western part of Fulton County, located on a peninsula in the Mississippi River, was once known for growing large amounts of cotton.

Fulton County was strongly pro-Confederate during the Civil War. The county was occupied by the Confederate army from September 1861 to March 1862. The town of Hickman was occupied at different times by both Confederate and Union forces. Although the county was sympathetic to the Southern cause, Confederate forces raided it throughout the war. In 1862 Gen. Nathan Bedford Forrest disrupted the rail line between Columbus, Kentucky, and Jackson, Tennessee. Forrest raided the county again in 1864, followed by raids from William Clarke Quantrill's guerrillas.

On Christmas Day 1875, a tornado struck the county, causing heavy property damage. In 1878 an epidemic of yellow fever caused the deaths of 150 people out of 462 reported cases of the disease.

The efforts of Dr. Luke Pryor Blackburn, later governor of Kentucky (1879-83), alleviated the suffering of many of the fever patients.

One of the most famous residents of the county was the legendary railroad engineer, John Luther ("Casey") JONES. As a youth, Jones lived for a time near Hickman, and at sixteen lived beside the tracks of the Mobile & Ohio Railroad (now abandoned) in the town of Cayce in the central part of Fulton County.

During the twentieth century, Fulton County has remained primarily agricultural (farms occupied 69 percent of the land in 1987), except for Hickman and FULTON, its two largest cities. The majority of citizens who are not farmers work in manufacturing, retail trade, or state and local government. In 1980 35 percent of the labor force was employed in areas outside Fulton County. The population of the rural county was 10,183 in 1970; 8,971 in 1980; and 8,271 in 1990.

See Ouida Jewell, *Backward Glance* (Fulton, Ky., 1977); Fulton County Historical Society, *Fulton County History, Hickman, Kentucky* (Hickman, Ky., 1983).   RON D. BRYANT

FUNKHOUSER, WILLIAM DELBERT. William Delbert Funkhouser, zoologist, son of the Rev. Hugh Clark and Laura (Mobley) Funkhouser, was born on March 13, 1881, at Rockport, Indiana. He was educated in the public schools of Indianapolis and at Wabash College, Crawfordsville, Indiana, where he earned a B.A. in 1905, graduating a member of Phi Beta Kappa. He taught biology and coached at the Brazil, Indiana, high school before entering Cornell University in 1908. While earning an M.A. degree in 1912 and Ph.D. in 1916 in zoology, he taught high school in Ithaca, New York. As a graduate student, Funkhouser published articles on the taxonomy of the Membracidae, or tree hoppers, a family of small leaping insects. At that time he began a lifelong, worldwide correspondence with others in the field. In 1918 he became professor of zoology and department head at the University of Kentucky. In 1925 he was named dean of the graduate school and in 1927 professor of anthropology, having cofounded the Department of Anthropology and Archaeology.

Funkhouser was described in *Entomological News* in 1974 as "the most outstanding student and authority on the family Membracidae" from 1918 to 1948. Of his 327 publications, his major work was *Fascicle I—Membracidae*. Funkhouser was secretary-treasurer of the Southeastern Athletic Conference from its establishment in 1932 until his death. A popular teacher and public speaker, he was a Congregationalist, a Republican, a Rotarian, and a member of numerous professional organizations.

Funkhouser married Josephine H. Kinney, a Cornell student, on June 29, 1910. He died of lung cancer on June 9, 1948, at his home in Lexington, Kentucky, and was buried in the Lexington Cemetery.

See W.R. Allen, "William Delbert Funkhouser 1881-1948," *Anatomical Record* 103 (Feb. 1949): 230-31; Alfred Brauer, "William Delbert Funkhouser 1881-1948," *Science* 108 (Dec. 24, 1948): 726; *Entomological News* 85 (May-June 1974): 131.
                                          CARL B. CONE

FURMAN, LUCY. Lucy Furman, author, was born in Henderson, Kentucky, on June 7, 1869, to William Barnard Furman, a physician, and Jesse (Collins) Furman. Raised in Evansville, Indiana, following her parents' death, Furman graduated in 1885 from the Sayre School in Lexington, Kentucky, lived briefly in Shreveport, Louisiana, and in 1889 returned to Evansville. Drawing on her observations during visits to Henderson, she wrote a series of short stories, published by *Century Magazine* in 1894-96. In 1896 Century published the series in book form as *Stories of a Sanctified Town*. After a ten-year hiatus in Florida and South Texas, Furman returned to Kentucky and visited Hindman, where Katherine Pettit, former Sayre classmate, and May Stone had founded the Hindman Settlement School. Furman stayed at the settlement school for seventeen years, teaching classes, acting as housemother to the male students, gardening, and writing some of her most famous works. Her writings described rural life in southeastern Kentucky in a realistic and positive way. Furman's major works completed at the Hindman Settlement School included "Hard-Hearted Barbary Allen" (*Century Magazine*, 1912), *Mothering on Perilous* (1913), *Sight to the Blind* (1914), and *The Quare Women* (1923). Two of Furman's well-known novels about Appalachia were published after she left the settlement school in 1924: *The Glass Window* (1925) and *The Lonesome Road* (1927).

In 1924 Furman returned to Henderson. Between 1924 and 1934 she experienced bouts of influenza, and spent some time in Florida for recuperation. Furman became vice-president of the Anti-Steel Trap League of Washington, D.C., and lectured throughout Kentucky on the cruelty of steel-jawed traps for animals. In 1934 Furman moved to Frankfort, Kentucky, where she proposed an anti–steel trap bill to the General Assembly. She continued to write, and her editorials appeared in the *Louisville Courier-Journal* and *Louisville Times*. In 1932 she received the George Fort Milton Award for her work as a southern woman writer.

In 1953 Furman moved to Cranford, New Jersey, where she lived with her nephew, Dillard Collins. She died in Cranford on August 25, 1958, and was buried there.

G

GAIN, ROBERT. Winner of football's Outland Trophy for best college lineman in 1950, when he played for the University of Kentucky (UK), Robert Gain was born on June 21, 1929, in Akron, Ohio. He was the son of Zeman and Mary (Maletich) Gain. An All-State lineman at Weir High School in Weirton, West Virginia, Gain entered UK in 1947, playing through the 1950 season. He helped the Wildcats to a four-year record of 33-10-2, including a victory over top-ranked Oklahoma University in the 1951 Sugar Bowl. He was drafted by the Green Bay Packers of the National Football League (NFL) in 1951 but instead played with the Ottawa Roughriders of the Canadian Football League. The next year he played with the Cleveland Browns, then served a year in the U.S. Air Force as a first lieutenant in Korea and Japan. He returned to Cleveland in 1954 and played eleven years, helping the Browns win three NFL Championships (1954, 1955, 1964), and was named to five Pro Bowls. In 1980 he was elected to the College Football Hall of Fame, the first UK player to receive that honor.

Gain married Mary Katherin Bastin in 1952; they have three daughters. After retiring from the NFL, he worked for the Pettiborne Corporation. He lives in Timberlake Village, a suburb of Cleveland.

GAINES, JOHN RYAN. John Ryan Gaines, horseman, philanthropist, and art collector, was born in Sherburne, New York, on November 22, 1928, to Clarence F. and Amelia (Ryan) Gaines. He received a B.A. degree in English from Notre Dame University in 1951; he pursued graduate studies in genetics at the University of Kentucky in 1953. Gaines served as first lieutenant in the U.S. Air Force between 1954 and 1957, attached to the joint chiefs of staff in the Pentagon.

In 1962 Gaines established the Gainesway Farm Thoroughbred Division, which soon became the largest stallion farm in the world. Six Gainesway stallions have led the General Sire List in North America or Europe. With his keen interest in horse racing, Gaines originated the project that became the Kentucky Horse Park in 1974. In 1984 he created the Breeders' Cup racing championship day, a multimillion-dollar annual event that attracts world competition.

Gaines has served on the boards of many institutions of art and education, including the trustees of the National Gallery of Art, the advisers of the Metropolitan Museum of Art, the directors of the Fogg Museum of Art, and the trustees of the University of Kentucky. He assembled a noted personal collection of drawings, ranging from the work of Leonardo to that of Picasso, which was auctioned in 1986. Gaines founded the Gaines Center for Humanities at the University of Kentucky in 1984.

Gaines married Joan Benziger in 1959; they have two children: Gloria Ryan and Thomas Bayley.

RAYMOND F. BETTS

GALLATIN COUNTY. The thirty-first county in order of formation, Gallatin County is located in north-central Kentucky, with the Ohio River as the northern border and Eagle Creek the southern boundary. It is bordered by the counties of Boone, Carroll, Grant, and Owen and has an area of 99 square miles. The county was formed on December 14, 1798, from sections of Franklin and Shelby counties and was named in honor of Albert Gallatin, a Swiss native who was a U.S. representative and was secretary of the treasury under Presidents Thomas Jefferson and James Madison. The county seat of Gallatin County is WARSAW.

The topography of Gallatin County is marked by wide and fertile floodplains. In 1987, 82 percent of the land was used for agriculture. During the first decade of the nineteenth century, Gallatin County became a center of river trade with New Orleans. Produce, furs, salt pork, soap, and hemp, as well as lumber products were shipped to market from Gallatin County. Abundant deposits of sand, gravel, and limestone contribute to the county's economy, although the major industries continue to be agriculturally oriented. Crops of tobacco and corn are raised. The county ranked ninth in agricultural receipts in 1989, of which 73 percent came from crops. Some small industries, such as furniture making, aided the local economy, as did the expansion of tourism.

The proximity to hostile Indians across the Ohio River proved disastrous for some early settlers; several of the first pioneers in the region were killed. In 1791 Charles Scott built a blockhouse at the confluence of the Ohio and Kentucky rivers and constructed a stockade for further protection. This blockhouse and stockade became the first permanent settlement in the Gallatin County area. It was named Port William, the county's first seat, which became the town of Carrollton in 1838. The first court of Gallatin County was held at the home of Richard Matterson on May 14, 1799. The increase in the population led to formation of the counties of Carroll, Owen, and Trimble from Gallatin County. Warsaw, incorporated in 1831, then became the seat of Gallatin County in 1838.

The Civil War disrupted the lives of Gallatin Countians. There were skirmishes in the county and some of its citizens were arrested for treason. In September 1864, George M. Jessee and his Confederate forces reportedly were in control of Gallatin and several other Kentucky counties. The report went on to state that the Confederates forces were rapidly recruiting volunteers in the area.

After the end of the Civil War, the Ohio River near Warsaw was the scene of one of the worst steamboat accidents in history. Two passenger steamers, the *America* and the *United States*, collided. The *United States* carried a cargo of barrels of kerosene, which caught fire, and soon both boats were in flames. The death toll reached 162.

As the twentieth century progressed, the river trade began to decline, and the steamboat era ended. Gallatin County is traversed by the I-71, U.S. 42, and U.S. 127 highways, and is served by CSX Transportation. Construction on the Markland Locks and Dam began in 1956 and was completed in 1964. In 1967 a hydroelectric power plant was built at the dam and provided jobs, but in the 1980s more than 50 percent of the population was employed outside the county. The incorporated towns are Warsaw, Glencoe, and Sparta.

The population of Gallatin County was 4,134 in 1970; 4,842 in 1980; and 5,393 in 1990.

See Gypsy Grey, *History of Gallatin County* (Covington, Ky., 1957).   RON D. BRYANT

GALT HOUSE. Louisville's best-known hostelry in the nineteenth century was the Galt House, built about 1834 on the northeast corner of Second and Main streets. It took its name—which was copied by hotels in Cincinnati and St. Louis—from the residence of early physician Dr. William C. Galt, which had occupied the site. It was in the Galt House that Charles Dickens described himself as being "as handsomely lodged as though we had been in Paris" (*American Notes*, 1842). Enlarged in 1853, the hotel was destroyed by fire on January 11, 1865.

It was succeeded in 1869 by the even larger and grander Galt House designed by architect Henry WHITESTONE, erected on the northeast corner of First and Main. The location near the river proved unfortunate as railroad travel cut into the steamboat trade. By 1910 the hotel was in financial distress; it closed in 1919 and was demolished in 1921. The third Galt House, opened in 1973 at Fourth Street and River Road as part of the Riverfront Urban Renewal Project, borrowed the honored name.

See *The Story of the Galt House* (Louisville 1914; reprinted 1970).   GEORGE H. YATER

GALVIN, MAURICE L. Maurice L. Galvin, businessman and politician, was born in Covington, Kentucky, on July 9, 1872, the son of Maurice and Ellen (Cronin) Galvin. He attended St. Xavier University in Cincinnati, and received a law degree from the University of Cincinnati Law School in 1893. For a brief time he practiced law in Cincinnati while serving as city solicitor. In 1904, after moving back to Covington, Galvin, a Republican, was elected commonwealth's attorney for Kenton County, a heavily Democratic area. Honest and hard-working, Galvin was respected by both Republicans and Democrats; he in turn often lent his influence to Democratic as well as Republican governors. During the 1920s he was one of the chief political bosses in the state bipartisan combine.

In addition to his political interests, Galvin had a long and varied career as a lawyer and businessman. After several years as commonwealth's attorney, he resigned to take the position of internal revenue collector for the 6th Revenue District (Covington) in 1908. He resigned in 1913 and became

director and attorney 'for the Stewart Iron Works in Covington. After that he was director of WCKY radio (Cincinnati); attorney for Union Light, Heat and Power Company; attorney for the Green Line (public transportation company); attorney for the C&O Railroad; director and attorney for the Deerfield Printing Company; president, director, and attorney for the Louisville Gravure Company; and president of the Modern Sales Company (Cincinnati). He was also attorney for the *Kentucky Post* for some years.

Galvin married Grace Wilson of Covington in 1900 and they had three children. She died in 1911 and in 1914 Galvin married Mary C. Powers of Augusta, Kentucky. Galvin died on August 25, 1940, and was buried in St. Mary Cemetery in Covington.

See Jim Reis, "Past VIPs," *Kentucky Post*, Oct. 20, 1986.   H. LEW WALLACE

GARFIELD, JAMES A. James A. Garfield, twentieth president of the United States, was born on November 19, 1831, in Orange, Ohio. On August 21, 1861, he received a commission as lieutenant colonel of the Union army's 42d Ohio Regiment, which he recruited and trained. He was promoted to colonel on November 27. In December Garfield and his regiment were ordered to Louisville. Gen. Don Carlos Buell, commander of the Army of the Ohio, ordered Garfield to take command of the 18th Infantry Brigade in eastern Kentucky and operate against a Confederate force of approximately 2,000 men under Brig. Gen. Humphrey Marshall in the Big Sandy Valley.

Garfield's column, consisting of 3,000 men and some cavalry, confronted the Confederates along Middle Creek between Paintsville and Prestonsburg on January 10, 1862. In a day-long skirmish, referred to as the Battle of Middle Creek, Garfield's force suffered twenty-one casualties, including three killed, while Marshall later reported ten men killed and fourteen wounded. Although tactically indecisive, the battle proved to be a strategic success for the Union as Marshall and his Confederates were compelled to withdraw into Virginia. This battle, coupled with Union Gen. George Thomas's victory over a Confederate force at Logan's Crossroads on January 19, 1862, helped to secure Kentucky for the Union. Publicity for his victory brought Garfield a promotion to brigadier general, with the commission backdated to January 10. After the battle Garfield established his headquarters in Prestonsburg and remained in eastern Kentucky for two months. In March he was transferred to Buell's Army of the Ohio on its march to join Grant at Pittsburg Landing, Tennessee.

Garfield, elected president in 1880, was shot by an assassin on July 2, 1881, and died on September 19.

See John M. Taylor, *Garfield of Ohio: The Available Man* (New York 1970).

GARRARD, JAMES. James Garrard, Kentucky's governor during 1796-1804, was born in Stafford

County, Virginia, on January 14, 1749, the son of Col. William and Mary (Naughty) Garrard. Educated at local common schools and at home, he developed a lifelong fondness for books. In 1765 he married Elizabeth Montjoy. During the Revolution he rose to the rank of colonel in the militia. In 1783 he moved west to what became Bourbon County, Kentucky, where he farmed, opened a lumber mill, made whiskey, and preached in Baptist churches. Garrard held a number of county positions and served in five of the conventions that led to statehood, helping to write Kentucky's first constitution. A Jeffersonian Republican, Garrard opposed slavery, favored domestic reforms, and advocated religious toleration. In the 1796 election, the electors gave Garrard 17 votes, Benjamin Logan 21, Thomas Todd 14, and John Brown 1. Since the constitution did not specify whether a plurality elected, the electors took a second ballot, on which Garrard was the victor. (The 1799 constitution eliminated the electors, providing for a direct popular vote.) Garrard was reelected in 1800 with 8,390 votes to 6,746 for Christopher Greenup, 3,996 for Logan, and 2,166 for Todd. He appointed both Greenup and Todd to judicial positions. Garrard left office on September 4, 1804.

Garrard was a stronger executive than his predecessor, Isaac Shelby. He consulted with and appointed able men to his administration. The General Assembly overrode only one of his vetoes, but it did not always give him the legislation he wanted. Garrard sought to expand the scope of government to reform the organization of the militia, the courts, and the penal system, and to provide for public education. To encourage economic growth, he advocated business subsides. The state's population was growing rapidly, and twenty-six new counties were added during his eight years in office. Garrard arranged for the construction of a governor's mansion (often called the Palace), which is now the official home of the lieutenant governor. He worked for the calling of the second constitutional convention, which he hoped would clarify the electoral process and curb slavery. His antislavery views probably explain why he was not elected a member of the convention, but as a token of esteem he was exempted from the new prohibition against successive terms for governors. As a Jeffersonian Republican, Garrard denounced the 1798 U.S. Alien and Sedition acts, and he approved the Kentucky Resolutions of 1798 and 1799. At the same time the governor urged legislators to reaffirm loyalty to the Union and the federal Constitution. During his second term the legislature overrode his veto of a circuit court bill—the first such defeat for a Kentucky governor. Garrard urged the Jefferson administration to secure rights to unrestricted use of the Mississippi River, and he was delighted by the purchase of the Louisiana Territory. During his last months in office, Garrard and the legislature wrangled over the appointment of a land office registrar. He lived in retirement on his farm until his death on January 19, 1822. The state erected a monument in the family graveyard as testimony to the esteem and respect in which he was held. One of the new counties formed in 1796 was named in his honor.

See H.E. Everman, *Governor James Garrard* (1981); Everman, *History of Bourbon County, 1785-1865* (1977); Lowell H. Harrison, ed. *Kentucky's Governors 1792-1985* (Lexington, Ky., 1985).

LOWELL H. HARRISON

GARRARD, THEOPHILUS TOULMIN. Grandson of Gov. James Garrard (1796-1804) and son of Col. Daniel and Lucinda (Toulmin) Garrard, Theophilus Toulmin Garrard, Union officer, was born in the family home near Manchester, Kentucky, on June 7, 1812. He was long involved in the operation of the Goose Creek salt works in Clay County. In 1843, 1844, 1857, and 1861, Garrard was elected to represent Clay County in the Kentucky legislature. After service as an infantry captain in the Mexican War, he went to California during the 1849 gold rush but soon returned to Kentucky.

When the Civil War broke out, Federal recruiting agent William ("Bull") Nelson authorized Garrard, a staunch Unionist, to raise a regiment. Made up of men from southeastern Kentucky enlisted at Camp Dick Robinson on September 22, 1861, the unit was originally called the 3d Kentucky Infantry, later the 7th Kentucky Infantry. Colonel Garrard first led his men into combat at the battle of Camp Wildcat on October 21, 1861. The next year, he and his unit participated in the Cumberland Gap campaign. At the Battle of Perryville on October 8, 1862, Garrard commanded a detachment of men from his regiment and the 32d Kentucky and 3d Tennessee infantry regiments. In the thick of the fighting on the Union left, Garrard's detachment retreated when inexperienced units around them fled in the face of assaults by veteran Confederate troops. Late in 1862, Garrard was commissioned a brigadier general, and during the 1863 Vicksburg campaign he commanded a brigade in the 13th Corps. Garrard was discharged on April 4, 1864, apparently because of failing eyesight. After leaving the army, Garrard worked the family farm and operated the rebuilt salt works, which had been burned during the war by Union soldiers.

In 1832 Garrard married Nancy Brawner, of Clay County. After her death he married Lucy Barnam Lees in 1849. He died on March 15, 1902, in the house where he was born, and was buried in the small community of Garrard, two miles south of Manchester.

NICKY HUGHES

GARRARD COUNTY. Garrard County, the twenty-fifth in order of formation, is located in the Outer Bluegrass region of central Kentucky. It is bordered by Boyle, Mercer, Jessamine, Madison, Rockcastle, and Lincoln counties and has an area of 232 square miles. The county was created by the legislature on December 17, 1796, and named for Gov. James Garrard (1796-1804). LANCASTER, the county seat of Garrard County and its only incorporated town, was established by the first county court in 1797 on fifty-seven acres of land near Wallace's Crossroads donated by Capt. William Buford, a veteran of the Revolutionary War.

The county is bordered on the east by Paint Lick Creek, on the north by the Kentucky River, and on the west by Dick's (Dix) River and Herrington Lake. The terrain is mostly rolling and includes the Palisades of the Kentucky River on the north and the Knobs and foothills on the southeast.

Garrard County was first settled because of its proximity to the Wilderness Road. Pioneers in the county maintained close ties with Fort Boonesborough and Logan's Station (Stanford) and had somewhat less contact with Lexington and Harrodsburg. The first station in what later became Garrard County was William Miller's, established in 1776 near Paint Lick. It was followed by James Smith's Station in 1779 near Bryantsville; James and John Downing's Station on Sugar Creek in 1779; Humphrey Best's Canebreak Station on Upper Paint Lick Creek in 1779-80; and Zophar Carpenter's Station, was believed to have been near Suck Fork Creek. William Grant established a station in the northern part of the county by 1784 on Hickman Creek. On Gilbert's Creek in the southwestern part of the county, Lewis Craig and his Baptist congregation from Upper Spotsylvania, Virginia, known as the Traveling Church, relocated en masse to Craig's Station in 1780-81.

Cattle, hemp, and tobacco were among the early agricultural products of the county, shipped via the Kentucky River by flatboat to downstream markets. James Hogan established a ferry in 1785 to bring Garrard County products to his warehouse across the river at the mouth of Hickman Creek in what is now Jessamine County. In 1789 Collier's warehouse was built at the mouth of Sugar Creek. Later the town of Quantico developed there, and flour, hemp, tobacco, beef, and pork were inspected and shipped from that point until the 1820s. The county then began a vigorous road-building program so that goods could be taken to market by wagon.

Garrard County provided the commonwealth with a number of distinguished leaders, including Gov. William O. Bradley (1895-99) and George Robertson, who was U.S. congressman (1817-21) and chief justice of the Kentucky court of appeals (1829-43, 1870-71). One of the most prominent families of antebellum Garrard County was the Kennedys. General Thomas Kennedy, a veteran of the Revolutionary War, immigrated from North Carolina in 1776.

In 1840 the Hill-Evans feud started in Lancaster because of a disagreement over the treatment of a slave woman whom Dr. Hezekiah Evans had hired from Dr. O.P. Hill. Members of both families were drawn into the violence, which killed nine people and wounded others. Hill left the county for Mexico after an assassination attempt but returned in 1855 and was murdered in 1862 by a man unrelated to the feud.

In August of 1861, Camp Dick Robinson was established seven miles north of Lancaster as the first Union enlistment station south of the Ohio River. Many Union troops from central and eastern Kentucky as well as eastern Tennessee entered federal service there. During the war, enlistments from Garrard County ran approximately three to one in favor of the Union. After the war, the completion of the Stanford-Richmond line of the Louisville & Nashville Railroad (now CSX Transportation) in 1868 through Lancaster spawned growth in the city. Products grown or raised in the county could be sent rapidly to market. Garrard County produced cattle, sheep, hogs, poultry, and thoroughbred horses, but was most noted for burley tobacco. The railroad helped Lancaster grow into a prosperous market town, but by the 1930s the line suffered from truck and auto competition, which caused the Richmond-Lancaster branch to be abandoned. The Stanford-Lancaster branch lingered until the 1980s, when it too was abandoned.

During the twentieth century, Garrard County has remained primarily an agricultural area with a major emphasis on the production of burley tobacco. In 1989 there were approximately 1,500 tobacco growers in the county, who produced a total of 7 million pounds of burley, for an income of $11,700,000.

The population of Garrard County was 9,457 in 1970; 10,853 in 1980; and 11,579 in 1990.

See Patricia Ballard and Helen Powell, *Historic Sites of Lancaster and Garrard County, Kentucky* (Lancaster, Ky., 1987); J.B. Kinnaird, *Historical Sketches of Lancaster and Garrard County: 1796-1924* (Lancaster, Ky., 1924).

GARTRELL, CHARLES H. Charles H. Gartrell, state and municipal official, was born in Ashland, Kentucky, on July 28, 1914, the son of Ethelbert and Helen (Chadwick) Gartrell. Educated in private schools, Gartrell graduated from Centre College in Danville. He joined the navy in June 1942 and became a test pilot during World War II. A Democrat, he was one of five candidates for the office of lieutenant governor but in 1947 lost to Lawrence Wetherby. As the first commissioner of the state Department of Aeronautics (1948-56), Gartrell often flew the governor and senators around the state. In this capacity, he helped to build many local airports to stimulate both tourism and economic development. Gartrell was mayor of Ashland during 1968-72 and later an administrative supervisor in the state Department of Human Resources.

Gartrell married Nancy Tanner on January 2, 1936; they had three children—Carol, Martha, and Charles Lawrence. Gartrell died on July 3, 1988, and was buried in the Ashland Cemetery.

CHARLES L. GARTRELL

GASPER RIVER. The Gasper River, in southwestern Kentucky, flows in a northeastern direction into the Barren River. About twenty-five miles long and forty to sixty feet wide, it begins in northeastern Logan County, about nine miles east of Russellville. The river's mouth is one-half mile southeast of Rockland in Warren County. The following creeks are tributaries of the Gasper: Belcher, Salt Lick, Brush, Clear Fork, Westbrook, and Rock

House. The only town near the river is Hadley in Warren County.

In 1785 George Washington, Jr., nephew of the first president, surveyed 666 acres on the Gasper, part of a military land grant he had received. The Great Revival began along the Gasper in 1799. In the nineteenth century, Sally's Rock was a river pilot's guide at the confluence of the Gasper and Barren rivers. The rock was named for Sally Beck, who shouted local news to passing riverboats in the late 1880s.

The Gasper is described as one of the most beautiful rivers in western Kentucky. It has a few small rapids, which make it a good canoeing stream.

See Helen B. Crocker, *The Green River of Kentucky* (Lexington, Ky., 1976).

MICHAEL E. WALTERS

GAYLE, CRYSTAL. See Webb, Brenda Gail

GENERAL ASSEMBLY. The General Assembly of Kentucky consists of the Senate, having thirty-eight members, and the House of Representatives, with one hundred members. Senators serve four-year terms, with half elected every two years; representatives serve two-year terms. All legislators are elected from single-member districts. Since the judicial decisions of the early 1960s mandating one person—one vote, the Senate and House districts have been apportioned according to populations.

Members of the Senate and House are elected in even-numbered years; the governor and other state-wide officials are elected in odd-numbered years. This arrangement is unique to Kentucky. The presiding officer of the Senate is the lieutenant governor, while the president pro tem is the top elected leader and wields more power than the lieutenant governor. The Speaker is the presiding officer of the House. Both houses of the General Assembly are organized along party lines, led by majority and minority floor leaders. Throughout the twentieth century, the Democratic party has almost always commanded a majority in both Senate and House.

Kentucky has had a bicameral legislature since the first constitution, adopted in 1792. Although senators were initially chosen by an electoral college, members of both branches have been popularly elected since the 1799 constitution.

The constitution permits the General Assembly to meet in regular session only every second year, in even-numbered years, for sixty days. The sixty-day limit, which originally specified the first sixty days of the year, excluding Sundays and holidays, was imposed by the 1891 constitution. Previously there had been no limit on the length of the session. It was because the legislature had lost public trust that the delegates to the 1890 constitutional convention imposed this limit, as well as specifying many details of legislative organization and procedure, and adopting many provisions that limited the policy-making authority of the General Assembly. The legislature may schedule its meeting days at any time from the beginning of January until mid-April. Only the governor can call special sessions. These limitations on legislative sessions are among the most restrictive in the country. Several times the voters have rejected constitutional amendments to permit annual sessions.

Despite this rigid limit on sessions, since 1968 the General Assembly has taken several steps to increase the amount of time available for work. In 1968 the legislature established an interim committee system, which made it possible for the committees to hold hearings and study issues between regular sessions. The committee system was streamlined so that there were fewer committees and each had specific jurisdictions, with parallel committees in the Senate and House. The joint interim committees operate as subcommittees of the LEGISLATIVE RESEARCH COMMISSION. The commission, created in 1948, is a seventeen-member body consisting of the top Democratic and Republican leadership. It supervises the staff of the legislature, including the staff assigned to committees.

A 1979 amendment to the constitution moved legislative elections from odd- to even-numbered years, permitted a ten-day organizational session in January of odd-numbered years, and permitted the sixty-day session in even-numbered years to be stretched over three and a half months, as noted. A major purpose was to permit interim committees to meet for a year and study issues prior to the regular session. Since the 1968 reform, there have been major changes in the way the legislature operates. In the 1970s the legislature created a number of committees to oversee the operation of the executive branch. They include committees to review administrative regulations and personal services contracts and to oversee capital construction, as well as a general committee on program review and investigations. Rules changes have given the legislative committees greater independence. The committees make much more use of hearings, and they have larger, more experienced staffs. There is also less turnover in the leadership and membership of the committees.

Major changes have also occurred in the budgetary process. Until the 1970s, the legislature usually passed the governor's budget as quickly as its rules permitted, without making any significant changes. The House and Senate Appropriations and Revenue committees now carry out studies between sessions and hold extensive hearings during the session. They usually recommend significant changes in the governor's budget and their proposals are usually adopted.

There have been dramatic changes in the turnover of Senate and House membership since the 1950s. In the legislative elections from 1947 to 1965, every year brought a turnover of about 60 percent of the House membership and about two-thirds of those senators who were up for reelection. At least three-fourths of those leaving retired from the legislature (or ran for another office), rather than risk being defeated. During the 1980s the proportion of members seeking and winning reelection approximately doubled, to about 80 percent in the House and about 70 percent in the Senate. One reason that few incumbent legislators are defeated (only about 10 percent in recent years) is that usually only about half of the races are contested. Democrats are the major beneficiaries, but the Democratic party fails to contest some seats in the traditionally Republican areas of south-central Kentucky. As a result of lower turnover, the proportion of legislators with extensive experience has grown. During the 1980s about a third of the legislators had served more than ten years in the chamber. In 1990 the proportion of women legislators averaged about 6 percent, less than half the national average. There have been only two or three black legislators during the 1980s.

The balance of power between the legislature and the governor has shifted back and forth over the years. The legislature has been seriously handicapped by the brevity of its sessions and—until recently— by the shortage of experienced members and staff. But the legislature has proved willing and able to challenge— sometimes successfully—those governors who were inept and those who were Republicans or factional opponents. The governor's constitutional power is not unusually strong; a veto, for example, can be overridden by an absolute majority of the membership of each house. But the political power of the office, including influence over appointments and budgetary items, is strong if it is used skillfully. In modern times, Earle Clements (1947-50), Bert Combs (1955-59), Wendell Ford (1971-74), and Julian Carroll (1974-79) are examples of governors who have used their power skillfully in dealing with the legislature. But legislative reforms and the reduced turnover of members have made the legislature much more independent of the governor and more willing to challenge his legislative and budgetary initiatives. In 1979, when Gov. John Y. Brown, Jr. (1979-83), abandoned the practice of selecting legislative leaders and Martha Layne Collins (1983-87) did not reinstate it, a new era in legislative-gubernatorial relations began. Antagonistic relations between Wallace Wilkinson (1987-91) and the General Assembly encouraged the legislature to continue to be more independent and to challenge the governor's initiatives.

See Malcolm E. Jewell and Penny M. Miller, *The Kentucky General Assembly* (Lexington, Ky., 1988); Mary Helen Wilson, *A Citizen's Guide to the Kentucky Constitution* (Frankfort, Ky., 1977).

MALCOLM E. JEWELL

GENERAL ELECTRIC'S APPLIANCE PARK.
In 1950, led by newly elected company president Ralph Cordiner, General Electric Corporation decided to consolidate its various major appliance factories in a large complex in a park-like setting in southeastern Louisville. Appliance Park, a leader in technology, in 1953 purchased a UNIVAC computer—the first industrial application. The park flourished until the 1970s, when Japanese and Ko-

rean companies became competitors in the world market. In the early 1980s, GE responded by making major investments in robotic technology for its dishwasher and refrigerator factories.

See Franklin Friday and Ronald F. White, *A Walk Through the Park: The History of GE Appliances and Appliance Park* (Louisville 1987).

RONALD F. WHITE

GEOGRAPHY. With 40,395 square miles of territory, Kentucky ranks thirty-seventh among the fifty states in size. Its major axis is east to west for some 458 linear miles (80°59′ to 89°34′ west longitude) and it is 171 miles wide at its widest point (36°30′ to 39°9′ north latitude). Kentucky is bounded on the north by 664 miles of the meandering Ohio River.

Kentucky is bordered by seven other states: Illinois, Indiana, and Ohio on the north; Virginia and West Virginia on the east; Tennessee to the south; and Missouri to the west. Kentucky's southern boundary with Tennessee is roughly 36°30′ north latitude along the Walker Line, named for the early surveyor Dr. Thomas Walker. Kentucky's two other land boundaries are in the eastern portion of the state. The northeast boundary with West Virginia follows the Big Sandy River and its tributary Tug Fork, while the southeastern boundary trends along the northeast-to-southwest path of Cumberland and Pine mountains. The most unusual boundary is in the west, where the KENTUCKY BEND, or New Madrid Bend, in the Mississippi River has isolated eighteen square miles of land in Fulton County. This "island" of Kentucky can be reached only by ferry or, by land, via Tennessee.

Kentucky has five major physiographic regions: the EASTERN COAL FIELD, the BLUEGRASS, the PENNYROYAL, the WESTERN COAL FIELD, and the JACKSON PURCHASE. Each has a unique combination of landforms. The Eastern Coal Field is dominated by the Appalachian Mountains. It contains all or part of thirty-five of Kentucky's 120 counties. Over one-half of eastern Kentucky is made up of an area known as the Mountain and Creek Bottom subregion. This far eastern area has very little level land and contains the highest point in the state: Black Mountain in Harlan County (4,145 feet above sea level). In the southeast corner of the region is Cumberland Gap, which at 1,648 feet above sea level is still nine hundred feet below the ridge of Cumberland Mountain.

West of the Mountain and Creek Bottom subregion is the Cumberland Plateau subregion. Ranging in elevation up to 2,000 feet above sea level, this plateau has been deeply cut by stream erosion over much of its area. The V-shaped valleys are often several hundred feet below the ridge tops. Travelers moving along roads near the valley bottoms have the impression of traveling through a mountainous area although the region is actually a dissected plateau.

Eastern Kentucky extends as far west as the Eastern Pottsville Escarpment, where part of the Daniel

Boone National Forest lies. A number of waterfalls have been formed as streams leave the escarpment. One of the more famous, Cumberland Falls on the Cumberland River near the border between Whitley and McCreary Counties, drops sixty-eight feet as it flows west. A large number of natural bridges have been carved out of rock by running water. Also found along the escarpment are a series of low hills known as the Knobs. In some classifications, the Knobs is a distinct physiographic region. The conical hills extend from the southwest of Louisville to Marion and Boyle counties, through Berea in southern Madison County, and then northeast to Lewis County on the Ohio River. These hills resemble inverted teacups without handles and are erosional remnants of the escarpment that separates eastern Kentucky from the Bluegrass.

The Bluegrass is perhaps the best-known region of Kentucky, particularly to visitors of the state. With its rolling lush landscape, board fences, and thoroughbred horses, it makes up one-fifth of the state's land area and is home to over half of the population. The Bluegrass is bounded on the west, south, and east by the Knobs and on the north by the Ohio River. The geologic forces that created the rolling physical landscape began as a gradual pushing up or bowing of bedrock along a line running from present-day Cincinnati to Nashville. As this Cincinnati Arch moved upward, erosion cut away at the surface layers, gradually exposing the underlying older rocks. The exposed limestone rocks gradually weathered down to form an exceptionally fertile soil. The first settlers came to this region.

The central subregion of the Bluegrass is the Inner Bluegrass. This area contains nine counties and centers upon Lexington, the second-largest city in Kentucky. The Inner Bluegrass, which some call the Lexington plain, consists of a gently rolling landscape with the greatest relief found along the palisades that have been cut by the Kentucky River. Acre for acre, it is the state's richest agricultural area, as evidenced by the high cost of land. Land use is strictly controlled by ordinance, particularly in Fayette County.

The Outer Bluegrass region is separated from the Inner by a belt of sedimentary rock known as Eden Shale. In some places the Eden Shale has been eroded to a greater degree than in the Inner Bluegrass. The rough topography and poor soils limit agricultural uses. The Outer Bluegrass covers about one-third of the overall Bluegrass region. Limestone bedrock dominates the rolling landscape. Louisville, Kentucky's largest city, is located at the western edge of the Outer Bluegrass, and the Kentucky suburbs south of Cincinnati are located at the northern edge.

The Pennyroyal region, named for a plant of the mint family, is the largest in the state, covering approximately 12,000 square miles. It extends from the Cumberland Plateau on the east to the Tennessee River and from Tennessee north to the Ohio River. The Pennyroyal encircles the Western Coal Field region. Limestone bedrock dominates in the

east. Farther west is a sandstone cliff (Dripping Springs Escarpment) that surrounds the Western Pottsville Escarpment. This upland, in turn, rings the Western Coal Field. In south-central Kentucky near Bowling Green, the limestone rock beneath the surface has been eroded by underground streams, forming numerous caves and circular sinkholes, which occur when the roofs collapse from erosion. In recent years, the movement of wastewater and sewage through the system of underground streams has become a major environmental problem for local residents and the many tourists who visit the area's major natural attraction, Mammoth Cave.

Part of the western Pennyroyal is a complex mixture of rock that has been cracked and then eroded by running water over long periods of geologic time. In the extreme western portion of the region, the construction of dams on the Cumberland and the Tennessee rivers formed Lake Barkley, Kentucky Lake, and Land Between the Lakes. Much of this western portion of the Pennyroyal is a national recreation area operated by the Tennessee Valley Authority. Pennyroyal counties are among the leading producers of many agricultural products.

All or part of twenty Kentucky counties make up the Western Coal Field Region. The region is a part of the larger Interior Coal Field of the United States, which extends through southern Illinois and southern Indiana and contains about 4,700 square miles of land. In several of the region's counties, most employment is in coal mining and reclamation. The Western Coal Field consists of low hills and bottomlands surrounded by an upland area. Much of the soil in the region was brought into the area by wind or by water and deposited in broad bottomlands. These soils are among the best in the state for agricultural production.

The westernmost region of Kentucky, the Jackson Purchase, is made up of the Kentucky portion of lands purchased by Gen. Andrew Jackson from the Chickasaw Indians in October of 1818. The Purchase is Kentucky's smallest region, containing eight counties. It is bounded on three sides by water and on the south by Tennessee. Several of the county boundaries in this region are straight lines, unlike the borders of counties elsewhere in the state. Graves County, in the center of the region, is almost a perfect rectangle.

Most of the region is part of the Gulf Coastal Plain physiographic region and has a surface dominated by sand, gravel, other alluvial deposits, and windblown dust known as loess. Most elevations are less than 350 feet above sea level; Kentucky's lowest elevation, 250 feet, is found where the Mississippi River leaves Fulton County. Much of the Purchase region is made up of bottomlands or river terraces. While these areas are easily worked and quite productive, they often are subject to flooding. Agricultural employment in the Purchase is greater than the overall average for Kentucky counties.

Kentucky's mid-latitude location influences the state's climate. Because the state is located north of the Tropic of Cancer, the sun is never directly overhead anywhere in the state. A second factor is elevation. In general, temperatures are cooler in the highlands of eastern Kentucky than along the Mississippi in the west. A third factor is continental location. Weather systems move generally from west to east, and Kentucky experiences greater seasonal variation in temperature than coastal locations at similar latitudes.

See P.P. Karan and Cotton Mather, eds., *Atlas of Kentucky* (Lexington, Ky., 1977): W.A. Bladen, *Geography of Kentucky: A Topical-Regional Overview* (Dubuque, Iowa, 1984).

DENNIS L. SPETZ

GEOLOGY. The surface geology of Kentucky reflects extensive weathering and erosion of a thick sequence of Paleozoic sedimentary rocks (about 570 to 280 million years old) across three major structural features, the Cincinnati Arch, the Appalachian Basin, and the Illinois Basin. Younger Paleozoic rocks are preserved in the down-warped Appalachian Basin of eastern Kentucky and the Illinois Basin of western Kentucky, but they have been eroded from the uplifted Cincinnati Arch in central Kentucky, a process that has uncovered underlying older Paleozoic strata. This episode of weathering and erosion, which continues today, began around the close of the Paleozoic era (about 250 million years ago).

Ordovician rocks, the oldest strata exposed in the state, (about 460 to 425 million years old) are at the surface on the Cincinnati Arch in the Bluegrass region of central Kentucky and locally in south-central Kentucky. Narrow outcrop belts of progressively younger Silurian and Devonian rocks (about 425 to 365 million years old) border the Ordovician strata along the Outer Bluegrass and in south-central Kentucky. Devonian rocks, in turn, are bordered by younger Mississippian rocks (about 365 to 330 million years old), which form broad plateaus across western and south-central Kentucky and crop out in a northeast-trending belt east of the Cincinnati Arch. The Mississippian strata dip and pass into the subsurface beneath younger Pennsylvania rocks (about 330 to 290 million years old) of the Eastern Coal Field and Western Coal Field, which are preserved in the down-warped Appalachian and Illinois basins, respectively. Devonian and Mississippian strata also crop out along the Pine Mountain Thrust Fault in the southeastern part of the Eastern Coal Field. Permian rocks (about 290 to 280 million years old) are preserved in a small down-faulted block in the Western Coal Field.

The Jackson Purchase region of far western Kentucky is underlain by a fourth major structural feature, the Mississippi Embayment. Instead of Paleozoic bedrock at the surface, the embayment contains late Mesozoic and Cenozoic deposits (about 95 to 30 million years old) consisting of unconsolidated sands, clays, gravels, and silts.

The only igneous rocks occurring at the surface in Kentucky are local igneous intrusions of early Permian age (267 million years old) that have been exposed by erosion. Lamprophyre and peridotite dikes and sills are present in Crittenden, Livingston, and Caldwell counties in the Western Kentucky fluorspar district, and peridotite occurs in Elliott County in eastern Kentucky.

Beneath the surface of Kentucky, at depths ranging from 3,500 feet in central Kentucky to more than 25,000 feet in western Kentucky, lies a basement complex of Precambrian igneous and metamorphic rocks (greater than 570 million years old). Information about the Precambrian basement is sparse and is based on rock samples from a small number of deep exploratory wells and on gravitational, magnetic, and seismic data from geophysical studies. The available information indicates that the basement is cut by numerous faults, including east-west- and north-south-trending, fault-bounded rift systems, which represent major fracturing of the continental lithosphere during late Precambrian and early Cambrian time (about 1.1 billion to 560 million years ago). Major faulting of the basement in Kentucky formed elongate, fault-bounded troughs, or rift valleys, which apparently were partly filled by igneous rocks. Filling of the troughs was completed during the deposition of Paleozoic sediments that overlie the Precambrian basement.

The oldest Paleozoic sedimentary rocks, deposited during Cambrian and early Ordovician time (about 570 to 480 million years ago), are not exposed at the surface in Kentucky. Cambrian sandstones and shales overlie the igneous and metamorphic basement rocks and form deposits thousands of feet thick in several of the troughs. These troughs continued to deepen during Cambrian sedimentation because of recurrent downward movement along faults. The sandstones and shales grade upward into Cambrian and early Ordovician dolomites. Regional uplift interrupted early Ordovician deposition across the state, resulting in widespread exposure and erosion of the carbonate sediments.

In middle Ordovician time, seas spread back across the region, depositing sandstone and shale on the eroded surface and establishing marine environments suitable for the accumulation of middle Ordovician limestones, which now are at the surface in the Inner Bluegrass region of central Kentucky. Thin bentonites, or volcanic ash beds, in the limestone were transported by wind into the state from eruptions occurring east of Kentucky. (Wind-blown volcanic ash also is present in younger Paleozoic and Cenozoic deposits.) Upper Ordovician strata of the Outer Bluegrass region consist of interbedded limestones and shales with lesser amounts of siltstone and dolomite. Succeeding Silurian rocks were deposited mainly as marine limestones and shales; and in the subsurface of eastern Kentucky, they include sandstone and evaporitic deposits of gypsum and anhydrite. The limestone commonly has been replaced by dolomite.

The Cincinnati Arch was a positive structural feature in Silurian and Devonian time. Rock units progressively thicken eastward and westward into the Appalachian and Illinois basins, away from the arch. Increased uplift along the Cincinnati Arch, apparently in early to middle Devonian time, resulted in erosional truncation of Silurian rocks along the flanks of the arch and their removal along its axis, together with part of the underlying upper Ordovician strata. Early Devonian limestones were deposited in the two basins, but seas did not spread back across the uplifted arch until Middle Devonian time. In central Kentucky, middle Devonian carbonate rocks rest unconformably on eroded Ordovician and Silurian strata.

Devonian rocks were deposited in a gradually deepening continental sea. Shallow marine limestone and dolomites are succeeded by a distinctive black shale that is rich in organic matter; the shale accumulated in the anaerobic bottom layer of a deeper, restricted sea. Black shale accumulation continued into early Mississippian time until a wedge of clays and silts representing the submarine front of a westward-advancing delta moved into Kentucky. After the delta stopped its advance and the influx of clay and silt into Kentucky ceased, deposition of carbonate sediments, principally shallow marine limestones, began. It continued, with minor interruptions, into late Mississippian time, forming extensive limestone deposits across the state. Sea-level fluctuations and local uplifts caused short-term interruptions of carbonate deposition in the shallow seas, and environments suitable for the precipitation of evaporitic deposits of gypsum and anhydrite were established temporarily.

In western Kentucky, extensive limestone deposition was succeeded by a sequence of limestones alternating with sandstones and shales. Limestone deposition on a shallow marine shelf was intermittently interrupted by the southward encroachment of lobes of deltaic and coastal sediments, mainly sandstone and shales with local coals, associated with a laterally shifting river system. In eastern Kentucky, the limestones grade upward into a sequence of shales and sandstones representing westward-advancing deltaic and coastal sediments, with relatively few interbedded limestones and dolomites.

Regional uplift in early Pennsylvanian time resulted in widespread exposure and erosion of the Mississippian strata prior to deposition of Pennsylvanian sediments in Kentucky. Rivers crossing eastern and western Kentucky cut valleys, locally as much as 250 to 300 feet deep, in the exposed Mississippian deposits. Pennsylvanian rocks, principally sandstones, siltstones, shales, and coals, were deposited in a variety of environments, including alluvial valleys and plains, coastal plains, swamps, bays, and estuaries. The land was near sea level and was intermittently covered by the sea, which deposited thin but widespread marine shales and limestones. Massive, resistant sandstones, mainly stream deposits, in the lower part of the Pennsylvanian sequence in Kentucky now form scenic cliffs in the Pottsville Escarpment along the western border of the Eastern Coal Field, on Pine and Cumberland mountains in southeastern Kentucky, and

locally along the border of the Western Coal Field. In early Permian time, older sedimentary rocks in eastern and western Kentucky locally were intruded by molten magma, which cooled to form bodies of igneous rock. Shale, siltstone, limestone, and sandstone of Permian age, recently discovered in a small, downfaulted block in the Western Coal Field, are the youngest sedimentary rocks of the Paleozoic era in Kentucky.

The original areal extent of Permian sediments in the state is not known. Pennsylvanian strata apparently originally extended from eastern Kentucky across the central part of the state into western Kentucky. These strata were eroded later from the Cincinnati Arch in central Kentucky, following uplift associated with the Alleghenian Orogeny, which occurred in eastern North America around the close of the Paleozoic era. Forces generated by the orogeny also caused the Pine Mountain Thrust Sheet, composed of Pennsylvanian, Mississippian, and Devonian rocks, to move four to eleven miles to the northwest along the Pine Mountain Thrust Fault in southeastern Kentucky.

The only sedimentary record of the Mesozoic Era in Kentucky is in the Jackson Purchase region and adjacent valleys of the lower Tennessee and Cumberland rivers of far western Kentucky, where sediments of late Cretaceous age (about 95 to 65 million years old) are present. These deposits form the basal part of a sequence of continental and marine sediments deposited during the late Mesozoic and early Cenozoic eras (about 95 to 30 million years ago) in the Mississippi Embayment of the Gulf Coastal Plain. The embayment sediments consist of unconsolidated sands, clays, gravels, and silts, with local lignites.

Younger Cenozoic sediments of Pliocene, Pleistocene, and Holocene (Recent) age (less than 5 million years old), composed of unconsolidated gravels, sands, silts, and clays, are present across the state. They include continental deposits, principally gravels, in the Jackson Purchase region; high-level fluvial deposits above the present entrenched courses of the Kentucky, Ohio, Licking, and Green rivers; alluvial deposits in low terraces and flood plains of streams throughout the state; and glacial drift, outwash, and loess.

Two, possibly three, continental glaciers advanced into north-central Kentucky about 800,000 to 130,000 years ago, during the Pleistone epoch, or Great Ice Age, leaving deposits of glacial drift. Meltwater from the youngest Pleistocene glacier, which stopped just north of Kentucky, transported large quantities of gravel, sand, and clay into the Ohio River Valley, forming thick deposits of glacial outwash. Windblown loess, or rock dust, was carried into Kentucky from glacial deposits west and north of the state.

Bedrock in Kentucky has been broken and displaced by numerous faults. Prominent surface expressions of faulting include the Pine Mountain Thrust Fault of southeastern Kentucky; the highly faulted terrain of the Western Kentucky fluorspar district; and complex linear systems of faults such as the Rough Creek and Pennyrile fault systems of western Kentucky and the Lexington, Kentucky River, and Irvine-Paint Creek fault systems of central and eastern Kentucky. Earthquakes affecting Kentucky during historic time, such as the Sharpsburg earthquake of 1980, have resulted mainly from movement along deep-seated faults. The principal source of seismic activity in the state, including the great earthquakes of 1811 and 1812, has been the New Madrid Fault System, which extends beneath northeastern Arkansas, southeastern Missouri, western Tennessee, and western Kentucky.

Four circular cryptoexplosive structures with diameters of about one to four miles, commonly characterized by concentric faults, occur in Kentucky: Jeptha Knob in Shelby County, Versailles Structure in Woodford County, Middlesboro Basin in Bell County, and Muldraugh Dome in Meade County. The Middlesboro Basin and Jeptha Knob may have been formed by the impact of meteorites.

See Robert C. McDowell, ed., *The Geology of Kentucky—A Text to Accompany the Geologic Map of Kentucky* (Washington, D.C., 1986); Arthur C. McFarlan, *Geology of Kentucky* (Lexington, Ky., 1943). GARLAND R. DEVER, JR.

GEORGETOWN. The seat of Scott County, Georgetown is located in the Bluegrass region on U.S. 25, 62, and 460, just west of I-75. In 1774 a party led by John Floyd were probably the first whites to visit the Georgetown area. On July 9, 1774, while surveying land for soldiers who fought in the French and Indian War, Floyd discovered a spring near the Elkhorn Creek, which he named Royal Spring. Floyd laid claim to 1,000 acres at the site but did not settle on his claim. John McClelland made improvements on the land in April 1775 and moved his family to the station in October 1775. Following an Indian attack on December 29, 1776, the fort was abandoned. The site remained unoccupied until 1782, when Elijah Craig, a Baptist minister, led his congregation to the site and began to plan the town of Lebanon. This town was incorporated by the Virginia legislature in 1784 and in 1790 was renamed George Town, in honor of George Washington. When Scott County was created in 1792, George Town was made the county seat. In 1846 the name of the town was officially changed to Georgetown.

Blessed with fertile land and an excellent water supply, Georgetown was a thriving community before the Civil War. A paper mill, a ropewalk, a fulling mill (for cloth manufacturing), and a distillery were all established before 1808, as was GEORGETOWN COLLEGE, the first Baptist college west of the Alleghenies. Nevertheless, Georgetown remained an agricultural town through the antebellum period.

During the Civil War, Georgetown was visited twice by Gen. John Hunt Morgan and his men. While conducting his first Kentucky raid, Morgan entered the city on July 15, 1862, and, after dispersing the Home Guards and destroying Federal supplies, camped on the courthouse lawn for two days. On July 10, 1864, after pillaging nearby Lexington, Morgan's men returned and looted Georgetown. Shortly thereafter, they retreated to Virginia.

Georgetown rebounded quickly from the effects of the war, spurred by the railroad. By the late 1880s, Georgetown was served by the Cincinnati, New Orleans & Texas Pacific (CNO&TP), the Louisville Southern, and the Frankfort & Cincinnati Railroad. The Louisville Southern line opened in 1889 between Versailles and Georgetown, but was closed in 1900 because it could not compete with the nearby Louisville & Nashville (now CSX Transportation) road. The Frankfort & Cincinnati, traveling the "whiskey route" from Georgetown to Paris, took some of Kentucky's finest bourbon to market. By the mid-1980s the whiskey route was closed. The CNO&TP, which was part of the Southern Railway System, had become part of the reorganized Norfolk Southern Railway.

Early in the twentieth century, economic growth was encouraged by the leadership of James Campbell Cantrill, a Georgetown native who was a leader in regional farm organizations and served in Congress from 1908 to 1923. Until World War II, the economy was based on agriculture. By 1990 Georgetown had become a prosperous industrial town, although about 90 percent of Scott County remained farmland. The construction of I-64 and I-75, between 1960 and 1972, helped the city develop. In 1987 industrialization in Georgetown was greatly accelerated when the Toyota Motor Manufacturing Company opened a plant just north of the city. In 1990 this plant employed nearly 3,000 and plans were then announced to double the operating capacity. County officials in 1990 announced plans to expand Marshall Field, the airstrip near Georgetown, which until then had little more than an 1,800-foot unpaved runway.

The first county courthouse was built in 1792-93. In 1816 a two-story brick building was erected. Though the second courthouse burned on August 9, 1837, the third, a Greek Revival–style building, was not constructed until 1845-46. In 1876, this seat of government was also destroyed by fire. In 1877 the fourth courthouse was completed.

The population of this fourth-class city was 8,629 in 1970; 10,972 in 1980; and 11,414 in 1990.

GEORGETOWN COLLEGE. Georgetown College in Georgetown, Kentucky, was the first Baptist college founded west of the Allegheny Mountains. In 1829 Silas Noel, a Frankfort lawyer and minister, led twenty-four Baptist leaders to charter the Kentucky Baptist Education Society, which considered establishing a college on the Transylvania University campus in Lexington. Instead, the institution became Georgetown College, on the donated campus of the defunct Rittenhouse Academy, established in 1798 under the leadership of Baptist minister Elijah Craig.

Georgetown College today serves fifteen hundred students from all over the United States and from overseas. Twenty-seven major programs cut across the spectrum of academic activity. The school is fully accredited and more than half of its faculty members hold doctorate degrees.

Rockwood Giddings, who became president of Georgetown College in 1839, started the main college building. He brought with him from Maine the first permanent faculty: Danford Thomas and Jonathan Farnam. In 1840 Howard Malcom of Philadelphia succeeded Giddings. He began recruiting students from the length of the Mississippi River Valley and established a modified classical curriculum. Literary societies were also organized, both for entertainment and in preparation for orations at graduation. After Malcom's opposition to slavery forced his resignation, his successor, Duncan Campbell, presided in 1860 over the largest graduating class of the nineteenth century. Georgetown College closed for a few months when the Civil War broke out. At the end of the war, the small faculty struggled to rebuild. In 1877 Basil Manly, Jr., as president led the college to accept an elective curriculum with less emphasis on the classics. After Manly joined the Southern Baptist Theological Seminary in Louisville, his successor as president, Richard M. Dudley, quickly hired new professors with Ph.D.s and raised the endowment to support them. J.J. Rucker led the shift to coeducation in 1889 and the completion of the Rucker Hall for women in 1895. He also supervised the construction of a chapel-library-gymnasium in 1894.

At the turn of the century, the four major buildings on the Georgetown campus served a student body of four hundred. Attention shifted from literary societies to intercollegiate athletics, fraternities and sororities, and trips to Lexington on the new interurban railroad. Arthur Yager became the first lay president in 1908. Intense competition for students came from new state normal colleges and the University of Kentucky. World War I drained the campus of most male students. After the war, under the presidency of Maldon Adams, curricula were enlarged in business, religion, and teacher training. Greek letter organizations were temporarily banned. A new gymnasium was finished in 1926; the chapel burned in 1930. Dean Robert Hinton struggled to keep the college open during the Great Depression. The curriculum was revised to include required courses in the fine arts, literature, modern foreign languages, natural sciences, physical education, social sciences, and world history. A dispute with the Kentucky Baptist Convention cut their contributions, and World War II had brought Georgetown College to a low point when president Sam Hill arrived in 1943. Registration surged in 1946 as veterans returned to school under the G.I. Bill. The newly built John L. Hill Chapel dominated the campus, and it was soon followed by the Cooke Library and the Nunnelley Music Building. Faculty member Orlin Corey brought national attention to Georgetown College with his play *Job*,

which continues to be presented as *The Book of Job* at Pine Mountain State Park in Pineville. Under president Leo Eddleman, enrollment passed fourteen hundred. Proposals to join Georgetown with the new Kentucky Southern College in Louisville were unsuccessful.

Under president Robert Mills in the 1960s, the south campus was developed, with twelve small units housing six hundred students. The basketball team went to the finals of the National Association of Intercollegiate Athletics (NAIA) tournament in 1961; the football team was undefeated in 1965. A major gift was the Cralle Student Center, a science center was dedicated at homecoming in 1968, and Giddings Hall, named in honor of the first president, was renovated with the help of the Brown Foundation. In the late 1970s costs increased sharply, partially offset by new federal and state student aid programs. Hundreds of public school teachers came back to earn master's degrees for certification purposes. President Ben Elrod presided over the Decade of Progress Campaign, which raised the endowment and refurbished the gymnasium. Under president Morgan Patterson in the late 1980s, both Highbaugh Hall and the student center were renovated; the baseball team played in the NAIA world series for the first time.

See Robert Snyder, *A History of Georgetown College* (Georgetown, Ky., 1979).

ROBERT SNYDER

GERMAN SETTLEMENT. Many Kentuckians are probably unaware that Germans and those of German descent were among the early European explorers and settlers in Kentucky. Isaac Hite (Hayd), for example, surveyed in Kentucky in 1773 and returned to Kentucky with James Harrod for the founding of Harrodsburg in 1774. One of Daniel Boone's companions was the German Michael Stoner (Holsteiner), a Pennsylvania Dutchman. Matthias Harmon (Hermann), one of the numerous Harmons of eastern Kentucky, was among the search party that looked for Jenny Wiley in 1789. Both the Kentucky rifle and the Conestoga wagon originated in the German areas of Pennsylvania, and the Appalachian dulcimer is of German origin.

In 1790 German-Americans constituted 14 percent of Kentucky's population of 73,677. They were especially numerous in Jefferson County. Abraham Hite represented Jefferson County at the two convention sessions for statehood in 1788. Two Germans were among the eight men who laid out the town of Lexington in 1781. As the state's population grew, so did the number of Germans, with the majority of them settling along the Ohio River. The unsuccessful German revolution of 1848 brought a new influx to Kentucky. Among them was Karl Heinzen, who came to Louisville to edit the *Herold des Westen* (*Herald of the West*). In 1854 he and other German-Americans published the *Louisville Platform*, which was considered radical for its day. It championed the rights of women and of freedmen, and it called for a minimum wage, the regulation of working hours, and the abolition of the death penalty.

Around 1850 there was a reaction among some native-born Americans to the presence of large numbers of German-American citizens, many of whom were Roman Catholic. The nativist Know-Nothing party in Louisville attempted in 1855 to keep these "foreigners" from voting, setting off riots that killed many. In a further source of friction with those of Anglo-Saxon descent, Germans did not adhere to the austere Sabbath of the Anglo-Saxon tradition, preferring to spend Sundays at family or group gatherings at which the fruit of the brewer's art was well appreciated. At their *Gesangvereine* (choral groups) and *Turnvereine* (gymnastic organizations) they made music and had parades. The Louisville Social Male Chorus is one of the best-known and oldest of these organizations. During the Civil War many Germans supported the Union cause. Germans were recruited into the army and played a significant role in the battles of Mill Springs and Munfordville.

In addition to the Germans and German-speaking immigrants from Austria and Switzerland who settled in the cities, Germans in smaller numbers went to the rural areas. In 1885 the state commissioned Heinrich Lembke to make a tour of German settlements in Kentucky and write a report to be used to attract more German immigrants. He found thirteen German colonies in Kentucky, spread from Lyon County in the west to Laurel County in the east. The heaviest concentrations of Germans were found in Louisville and the northern Kentucky cities of Covington and Newport.

German cultural life flourished in Kentucky in the latter part of the nineteenth and early part of the twentieth century. This is reflected in the number of German-language newspapers, the most prominent of which was the *Louisville Anzeiger* (*Louisville Advertiser*), published by George Doern. Acceptance of Germans into the political life of the state had advanced far enough by 1900 that William Goebel, whose parents were both German immigrants, was elected governor. World War I and World War II struck a telling blow to German-American consciousness. The German presence in Kentucky has been augmented since 1945 by the German spouses of American soldiers, a number of whom settled at Fort Campbell and Fort Knox. Amish and Mennonites have settled in various rural areas of the state, and direct German investment has brought a small but influential group of Germans to Kentucky.

See Albert B. Faust, *The German Element in the United States* (New York 1927); Robert C. Jobson, "German-American Settlers of Early Jefferson County, Kentucky," *FCHQ* 53 (Oct. 1979): 344-57.   THOMAS P. BALDWIN

GETHSEMANI COLLEGE. Gethsemani College was located on a knoll next to the Abbey of Gethsemani, ten miles south of Bardstown, Kentucky. It was founded in 1851 and chartered by an act of the Kentucky General Assembly in 1868. The school closed when on March 1, 1912, the buildings burned; it never reopened. The school was conducted by the Trappist monks of Gethsemani with outside help and its mission was "to impart to boys and young men a thorough Catholic, Christian education, a love of virtue and learning, and to qualify them for the various professions and pursuits in life."

The college was divided into two departments. The preparatory department was for beginners, especially those preparing for first communion and confirmation. It offered courses in catechism, English (reading and grammar), arithmetic, penmanship, U.S. history, and geography. The commercial department was for advanced boys and young men. Those who completed its entire four-year course of studies and passed the examination satisfactorily were entitled to a commercial diploma. During each of the four years, students were required to study catechism, English, arithmetic (including algebra, practical geometry, and land surveying), history, bookkeeping, and penmanship. During the first two years, courses in geography were required; courses in physiology, elocution, and drawing (lineal, free-hand, architectural, and engineering) were required during the last two years. French, German, typing, shorthand, and telegraphy were offered as electives. For those preparing to study for the priesthood, Latin and Greek were available.

The number of students ranged from sixty to 185. Typically, they were ten to eighteen years of age, with a few as young as six or as old as twenty-five. Some were boarders and others day students from the neighborhood. The largest number to graduate with diplomas in any single year was nine.

FELIX DONAHUE

GIBRALTAR OF DEMOCRACY. This phrase signifies the long-standing strength of the Democratic party in the 1st Congressional District of Kentucky, particularly its eight Jackson Purchase counties. Author Irvin Cobb of Paducah wrote: "There was no doubt about our district. Whatever might betide, she was safe and sound—a Democratic Rock of Ages. 'Solid as Gibraltar!' John C. Breckinridge called her once; and taking the name, a Gibraltar she remained forever after, piling up a plurality on which the faithful might mount and stand, even as on a watchtower of the outer battlements, to observe the struggle for those debatable counties to the eastward and northward of us" (*Those Times and These*, 1917). The area remained strongly Democratic into the 1990s, although it occasionally voted Republican, particularly in national elections.   LON CARTER BARTON

GIBSON, WILLIAM H., SR. William H. Gibson, Sr., educator and politician, was born in 1829 in Baltimore, the son of free blacks Philip and Amelia Gibson. Precocious, he studied with Baltimore's best-known black teachers and soon demonstrated talent in instrumental and vocal music. At age eighteen, answering a call from black Methodists to establish a school for their children, Gibson moved to Louisville. His school emphasized the three Rs, music, and vocational training. By the late 1850s Gibson's older students were studying algebra, geometry, and Latin, and on the eve of the Civil War he opened grammar schools in Lexington and Frankfort, only to see them closed because of the conflict. During the Civil War, when harassment of free blacks increased in Louisville, Gibson moved to Indianapolis, where he began recruiting black troops. In 1866 Gibson returned to Louisville, resuming his teaching career.

Gibson was a leader in the post-Civil War black educational conventions, an untiring advocate of public schools for blacks, and eventually a principal in Louisville's black school system. In 1868 he became an assistant to the cashier at the Freedmen's Saving Bank. His status among black Republicans resulted in a number of patronage appointments; in 1870 he was appointed mail agent on the Louisville & Nashville Railroad (now CSX Transportation). Harassment by whites along the line forced Gibson to resign in favor of a position in the U.S. Revenue Department in 1874. He was a delegate to numerous Republican party conventions at the state and national level, but failed in attempts at elective office. With the decline of Republican party support of Kentucky blacks, Gibson was reduced by the turn of the century to accepting a position as night janitor at a Louisville bank.

Gibson was an early member of the Masons and one of the founders of the Louisville-based United Brothers of Friendship. He was a founder or officer of most of Louisville's black cultural organizations, including the Mozart Society and the Colored Music Association, and of social programs such as the black YMCA, the Colored Orphans' Home, and the Louisville Colored Cemetery Company. Gibson died in 1906 and was buried in the Louisville Cemetery.

See W.H. Gibson, Sr., *Historical Sketch of the Progress of the Colored Race, in Louisville, Ky.* (Louisville 1897); William J. Simmons, *Men of Mark: Eminent, Progressive, and Rising* (Cleveland 1887).   MARION B. LUCAS

GILBERT'S CREEK STATION (LEWIS CRAIG'S STATION). Gilbert's Creek Station was founded in December 1781 by the Rev. Lewis Craig, of Spotsylvania County, Virginia, as a haven for his Baptist congregation. Fleeing religious persecution from the Anglican church of colonial Virginia, Craig led his TRAVELING CHURCH of five hundred to six hundred people to their new home in Kentucky. He established a Baptist church on Gilbert's Creek, a tributary of the Dick's (Dix) River, approximately two-and-a-half miles south of what would become Lancaster, in Garrard County. In 1783, probably owing to conflict with Indians and other hardships, Craig and most of the church

members moved to the South Elkhorn area of Fayette County, near Lexington, and founded the South Elkhorn Church, which still operates.

See George W. Ranck, *The Traveling Church* (Louisville 1891).

GILES, JANICE (HOLT). Janice (Holt) Giles, novelist, was born March 28, 1905, in Altus, Arkansas, the daughter of John Albert and Lucy (McGraw) Holt, both schoolteachers. She grew up in Arkansas and Oklahoma, where her parents taught in the old Choctaw Nation. She attended the University of Arkansas and Transylvania University in Lexington, Kentucky. In 1923 she married Otto Jackson Moore, by whom she had a daughter, Elizabeth. She was divorced from Moore in 1939.

In 1941 Janice Holt moved to Kentucky, where she worked for a Frankfort church and the Louisville Presbyterian Seminary. In the summer of 1943, on a bus trip to Texas to visit her aunt, she met Henry Giles, a soldier, when he boarded the bus in Bowling Green, Kentucky. They were married in 1945. In 1949, while she was writing *Miss Willie* (1951), Janice and Henry moved to a small farm near his boyhood home, close to Knifley in Adair County, Kentucky. After publication of her first novel, *The Enduring Hills* (1950), Giles became a free-lance writer and full-time novelist, publishing twenty-four books.

The majority of her published works are novels, which fall into three distinct groups: the Piney Ridge trilogy—*The Enduring Hills*, *Miss Willie* (1951), and *Tara's Healing* (1952); the Kentucky trilogy—*The Kentuckians* (1953), *Hannah Fowler* (1956), and *The Believers* (1957); and the novels of Arkansas and the western frontier, including *Johnny Osage* (1960), *Savanna* (1961), *Voyage to Santa Fe* (1962), and *Six-Horse Hitch* (1969). The novels and nonfiction of the Piney Ridge period reflect the extent of her acclimation to her husband's native area. Her historical novels are well researched, historically accurate, and insightful works about the founding and early settlement of Kentucky. After 1958, her novels about the frontier of her native Arkansas and Oklahoma took the descendants of her Kentucky characters into an even newer land. Giles has been critically overlooked, perhaps because of her prolific output, as well as her appeal to popular tastes.

Giles died on June 1, 1979, and was buried in Caldwell Chapel Cemetery, near her home in Adair County.   BONNIE JEAN COX

GILLESPIE, JAMES HAVEN LAMONT. James Haven Lamont Gillespie, songwriter, was born in Covington, Kentucky, on February 6, 1888, the son of William F. and Anna (Reilly) Gillespie. Haven Gillespie, as he was known, worked as a printer for newspapers including the *Cincinnati Times-Star* and the *New York Times*. Even after he became a successful songwriter, he kept his membership active in the printer's union. Gillespie wrote more than a thousand popular songs including "Violet Blue" (1912), "Drifting and Dreaming" (1925), "Breezin' Along With the Breeze" (1926), "Santa Claus is Coming to Town" (1934), "Lucky Old Sun" (1949), and "I Love to Dream" (1972). His songs have been hits for such stars as Frank Sinatra, Bing Crosby, Rudy Vallee, the Andrews Sisters, Tony Bennett, and George Strait. Gillespie's chief collaborator was composer J. Fred Coots; he also worked with Richard Whiting, Larry Shay, and Beasley Smith. Gillespie received a Freedoms Foundation award in 1950 for "God's Country" (1950) and an ASCAP award for country music in 1985 for "Right or Wrong" (1921). Gillespie, a reformed alcoholic, was a strong supporter of Alcoholics Anonymous.

Gillespie married Corene Parker on March 1, 1909, in Covington; they had one son, Haven Lamont. Corene died in 1958. Gillespie then married Josephine Kruempleman. They were divorced in 1970. Gillespie died in Las Vegas on March 14, 1975, and was buried there.

CHARLES D. KING

GIRTY, SIMON. Simon Girty, the "Great Renegade" who fought with the British and the Indians, was born near Harrisburg, Pennsylvania, in 1741, the son of Simon Girty, an Irish immigrant, and Mary Newton, an Englishwoman. He was ten when his father was killed by an Indian in a brawl. With two of his three brothers, Girty was captured by Indians at Fort Granville in 1756 and lived among the Seneca for three years. After his release, he was an interpreter at Fort Pitt until 1774. Though illiterate, he was commissioned a second lieutenant in the Virginia militia. As a scout, he served with Simon Kenton in Lord Dunmore's War and was hired as an interpreter by the Continental Congress but was discharged for "ill behavior."

In 1778 Girty deserted the American cause and was employed by British governor Sir Henry Hamilton, the "Hair Buyer," as an interpreter and scout, a post he held until a few weeks before his death. Girty was active in arousing the Indians against the white settlers and took part in numerous raids by British and Indians in the Ohio River Valley, including the siege of Bryan's Station and the disastrous defeat of Kentuckians at the Battle of Blue Licks in 1782, the last great Indian battle in Kentucky. That same year he was reported to have been a delighted spectator when Col. William Crawford was burned at the stake in Ohio. Less noted were the occasions when he saved other captives, including Simon Kenton. Granted a British pension at the end of the war, Girty in 1784 married Catharine Malott, another captive, established a Canadian home and started a family near present Amherstburg, Ontario. His scouting activities kept him almost constantly among the Indian tribes of the Ohio country, where he opposed all efforts to make peace with the Americans and took an active part in many battles, including St. Clair's Defeat (1791) and Fallen Timbers (1794).

When the British surrendered Detroit in 1796, Girty returned to his home, where he spent his later years. His wife left him for a time because of his brutal behavior when drinking. Crippled by a fall that broke his ankle and slowly going blind, he died February 18, 1818, and was given a military funeral by the British.

See Consul Willshire Butterfield, *History of the Girtys* (Cincinnati 1890).   RICHARD TAYLOR

GIST, CHRISTOPHER. Christopher Gist, pioneer explorer, was born about 1705 in Baltimore County, Maryland. His records and journals indicate that he had a superior education. Gist married Sarah Howard before 1729. He later worked as surveyor and coroner in Baltimore County. In 1742 he began a mercantile business and dealt extensively in the fur trade.

In 1747 twenty prominent landowners of Virginia and England formed the Ohio Company and petitioned King George II for a land grant west of the Allegheny Mountains. In 1750 the Ohio Company hired Christopher Gist—who was living in the Yadkin Valley of western North Carolina—to explore and survey the immense tract. Gist was instructed also to act as diplomatic envoy to the Indians and to gain intelligence of French intrusion. Gist and a young black companion left Maryland on October 31, 1750. They traveled the Ohio River nearly to the Falls of the Ohio, then through Kentucky and southwestern Virginia, and returned to the Yadkin Valley on May 19, 1751. The Ohio Company again requested Gist's services in November 1751. He represented the company at the Treaty of Logstown, which affirmed the right of the English colonists to settle between the Allegheny Mountains and the Ohio River. That year Gist moved to the Monongahela Valley (now Fayette County, Pennsylvania).

In 1753 Maj. George Washington employed Gist to guide him west to the Ohio River to warn the French troops to leave the disputed territory. During the expedition Gist saved Washington's life, and a deep friendship developed between the two men. That same year Gist and George Croghan were appointed deputies to Maj. John Caryle, commissary for the Ohio expeditions. In 1754 Gist moved to Virginia and later that year his plantation was destroyed by the French. That October he petitioned the Virginia House of Burgesses for restitution, but his plea was rejected. In July 1755 he was the principal guide for Gen. Edward Braddock's ill-fated campaign against Fort Duquesne (near present-day Pittsburgh, Pennsylvania). On October 1, 1755, Gist was commissioned a lieutenant in the Virginia forces and shortly afterward captain of a company of scouts. He was appointed deputy agent of Indian affairs in Virginia in 1757. For the next two years, he employed Indian scouting parties to guard the three hundred-mile Virginia border. On July 25, 1759, he left Williamsburg with a contingent of sixty-two Catawba Indians. En route to Winchester he died of smallpox.

See W.M. Darlington, *Christopher Gist's Journals* (Pittsburgh 1893).   TED FRANKLIN BELUE

GLACIERS. Northern Kentucky marks the southernmost terminus of the great continental ice sheets that first invaded the region 600,000 to 800,000 years ago during the early Pleistocene (Ice Age). These glacial advances profoundly influenced Kentucky geography by destroying the Teays River, a major preglacial river flowing across the Midwest to the Mississippi. Glaciers dammed the Teays's north-flowing tributaries, including the ancestral Kentucky, Licking, and Big Sandy rivers, and transformed them into ice-margin finger lakes. Pebble- to boulder-sized glacial "erratics" derived from the Canadian Shield and found scattered about northeastern Kentucky may have been deposited by icebergs on these lakes. Through a complex sequence of drainage diversions, ice-impounded waters overtopped and breached basin divides so that by the time the last major glacier had retreated from Kentucky 130,000 years ago, the upper Ohio River Valley was established.

Two or possibly three major Pleistocene glaciers left deposits in Kentucky that form a narrow band, one to twenty miles wide, lying between Louisville and Maysville; these ice-contact deposits attain their maximum extent in Boone and Trimble counties. Although the youngest (15,000 to 80,000 years ago) continental glacier stopped several miles to the north of Kentucky, it has had the greatest economic impact on the state. Sediment-laden meltwaters from this glacier deposited vast quantities of sand and gravel and small amounts of clay along the entire length of the Ohio River Valley. Terraces of these deposits form regional aquifers and provide construction materials.

See Louis L. Ray, *Geomorphology and Quaternary Geology of the Glaciated Ohio River Valley—a Reconnaissance Study*, U.S. Geological Survey, Professional Paper 826, 1974; Frank Leverett, *The Pleistocene of Northern Kentucky*, Kentucky Geological Survey, series 6, no. 31, 1929.

EUGENE J. AMARAL

GLASGOW. Glasgow, the county seat, is located in the center of Barren County, near the Cumberland Parkway. When Barren County was organized in 1799 by the Kentucky General Assembly, both its location and the presence nearby of a large spring favored Glasgow as the county seat. John Gorin, the founder of the town, donated fifty acres on which to start building, and the first courthouse was completed in 1800. (Glasgow's present courthouse, the sixth, was completed in 1965.) The town was officially recognized by the Kentucky General Assembly on January 31, 1809. Glasgow was named for the city in Scotland. (Some have main-

tained that the town was named after Glasgow, Virginia, but the latter town was not established until 1890.)

Soon after its establishment, Glasgow quickly grew into an economic, social, and cultural center of activity, not only for Barren County but for the people of neighboring counties as well. The town became a commercial center of gristmills, sawmills, shoemakers, tailors, blacksmiths, wagon makers, distillers, and the like. Until the 1930s Glasgow was a wholesaling center that supplied country stores in a wide area.

Several educational institutions were located in Glasgow, including Urania College (also referred to at times as Glasgow Academy); the Allen Lodge Female Academy, founded in 1853 by the Allen Masonic Lodge; and the Glasgow Normal School, established by state charter in 1874. This school moved to Bowling Green in 1884 and later became Western Kentucky University. In 1853 Glasgow was stricken by cholera, supposedly brought in by a traveling circus. Many Glasgow residents fled the town immediately; the disease killed three-quarters of those who remained. Disaster of another sort threatened when the Louisville & Nashville Railroad bypassed the town shortly before the Civil War, since railroads were vital to commerce and many towns died for lack of access to a railroad. Glasgow solved this problem by building its own railroad, a spur line opened in 1870 that ran from the town to a connection with the Louisville & Nashville at Glasgow Junction, approximately ten miles northwest. Joe Creason wrote in the *Louisville Courier-Journal* in 1951: "Probably no other town in Kentucky owes so much to so little railroad." The town is still one of the commercial centers in the Barren County area.

The population of the third-class city was 11,301 in 1970; 12,958 in 1980; and 12,351 in 1990.

See Cecil E. Goode and Woodford L. Gardner, Jr., eds., *Barren County Heritage: A Pictorial History of Barren County, Kentucky* (Bowling Green, Ky., 1980).

GODMAN ARMY AIRFIELD. Godman Army Airfield at Fort Knox is among the earliest airfields operated in Kentucky. It was named for Lt. Louis K. Godman, a pilot in the aviation section of the U.S. Army Signal Corps, who was killed in an airplane crash in Columbia, South Carolina, on September 28, 1918. Originally built for the U.S. Army 29th Aero Squadron, the field opened on October 26, 1918, and was used by the 31st Balloon Company in 1920-21. The airfield had an unpaved, packed earth runway until 1937, when it was converted to a light-duty surface of rocks sprayed with oil. During the 1930s, the field was not in active use because Fort Knox became a center for army mechanization and motor transport. Construction of the modernized airfield began in 1937 and was completed in 1941.

Godman airfield has only two runways in use, each 150 feet wide. The active runway is 5,200 feet long, and the inactive runway 4,750 feet long. The airfield has served medical evacuation units, has been used as a heliport, and is used now primarily by U.S. Army Reserve and National Guard troops for training.

GOEBEL, WILLIAM. William Goebel, whose brief, contested term as governor of Kentucky ended when he died from an assassin's bullet, was born on January 4, 1856, in Sullivan County, Pennsylvania. His German-born parents, William and Augusta (Greenclay) Goebel, moved the family to Covington, Kentucky, after his father returned from Civil War service in the Union army. After graduating from Cincinnati Law School in 1877, Goebel became at different times a partner of former Gov. John W. Stevenson and of John G. Carlisle. Specializing in corporate and railroad law, often in opposition to those interests, Goebel earned both considerable wealth and determined enemies.

A complex, ambitious person, Goebel was denounced by some as a ruthless, heartless demagogue and hailed by others as a compassionate, dedicated reformer. His northern Kentucky political organization sent him to the state Senate from 1887 to 1900; he was Senate president pro tempore after 1896. Among the reforms he advocated were expanded civil rights for women and blacks, more effective railroad regulation, restriction on toll roads, the abolition of lotteries and pool halls, expansion of workingmen's rights, and an end to the monopoly on state textbook sales. As a member of the 1890-91 constitutional convention, he tried to get such reforms incorporated in the new constitution. Goebel's goals, his methods, and his personality created great controversy. In 1895 he was acquitted after killing John Sanford in a political dispute. After 1898 much of the opposition to him centered on the so-called GOEBEL ELECTION LAW, which gave broad powers to a three-man Board of Elections Commissioners, the first members of which were allied with Goebel.

In 1899 Goebel won the Democratic nomination for governor after a convention fight that caused a party split (see MUSIC HALL CONVENTION). A dissident faction ran ex-Gov. John Y. Brown (1891-95) as its candidate. After the election, the Board of Elections Commissioners certified by a 2-1 vote that Republican William S. Taylor had won, with 193,714 votes to 191,331 for Goebel and 12,040 for Brown. Tension increased after the Democratic majority in the General Assembly decided to investigate the results through a select committee that had only one Republican member. On January 30, 1900, before the committee reached a decision, Goebel was mortally wounded by a rifle shot as he approached the capitol. Governor Taylor declared an emergency, called out the militia, and ordered the legislature to meet in London. Meeting in secret in Frankfort, the Democrats invalidated enough Republican votes to declare Goebel elected. When the Republicans refused to accept that decision, the state had two governments and a civil war seemed

possible. Goebel's only official act in his very brief term as the state's thirty-second governor was to order the militia dissolved. When he died on February 3, 1900, Lt. Gov. J.C.W. BECKHAM (1900-1907) succeeded him. Both sides in the disputed election agreed to seek a court solution, and by May the Democrats had won. Taylor fled to Indianapolis. After a lengthy series of trials and court decisions, three men were convicted of murder or conspiracy to commit murder in Goebel's death (see GOEBEL ASSASSINATION). The three were later pardoned, and the identity of the assassin is still disputed.

See James C. Klotter, *William Goebel: The Politics of Wrath* (Lexington, Ky., 1977); Urey Woodson, *The First New Dealer* (Louisville 1939).

LOWELL H. HARRISON

GOEBEL ASSASSINATION. After a very close canvass, Republican William S. TAYLOR was declared governor of Kentucky over Democrat William GOEBEL and was inaugurated on December 12, 1899. Even after the inauguration, the election results were contested, and in the midst of those deliberations aspirant Goebel was shot and wounded as he approached the state capitol on January 30, 1900. The Democratic majority in the General Assembly declared enough of the ballots fraudulent to make Goebel the victor in the election. He was sworn in as governor on January 31, an action Republicans refused to recognized as legal. On February 3, Goebel died, the only governor in American history to die in office of wounds inflicted by an assassin. Eventual court decisions supported the actions of the Democratic majority, and Governor Taylor fled the commonwealth in May. The state of near-civil war between combatants divided by party finally ended, but questions concerning the assassination persist even to this day.

Eventually, of the sixteen people indicted, three turned state's evidence; of the remaining thirteen, only five went to trial. Two—Garrett Ripley and Berry Howard—were acquitted. Convictions were handed down for the other three: Caleb POWERS, the secretary of state from Knox County; Henry Youtsey, a stenographer from Campbell County; and Jim Howard, a feudist from Clay County. The prosecution presented Powers (absent when the murder occurred) as the mastermind, Youtsey as the intermediary, and Howard as the assassin. According to the scenarios developed over several trials, the shot had been fired from the secretary of state's office on the first floor of the building next to the capitol.

Questions arose, however, about the prosecution's account. Under oath, totally conflicting testimony was given and some of it was later repudiated or shown to be perjured. Moreover, the trial judge's conduct was, in most cases, avowedly partisan, and an exceptionally large percentage of the jurors were Democrats—in one case making up 360 of the 368 in the jury pool. At the appeal level, for much of the time the state's highest court had a Republican majority, which overturned the convictions and remanded the cases for new trials.

Powers's four trials opened in July 1900, October 1901, August 1903, and November 1907. Convictions followed the first three—despite a very skilled appeal by the defendant in the third—but were overturned. His last trial deadlocked. Howard's three trials—starting in September 1900, January 1902, and April 1903—all resulted in guilty findings. He lost his last appeal and was serving a life sentence when, in 1908, he and Powers were pardoned. Former Governor Taylor and several men still under indictment received pardons some months later. Youtsey, who turned state's evidence after his first trial, was not pardoned until 1919, three years after he had been paroled. All of the convicted men continued to their deaths to proclaim their innocence.

The generally accepted facts are that Goebel died from the effects of a rifle bullet fired from, or near, the building next to the capitol. Other than that, what is believed depends on which evidence is accepted. A case can be made for a complicated conspiracy, or for a lone assassin; for a carefully planned plot involving Powers, Howard, and Youtsey, or for the act of an unbalanced mind, such as Youtsey's; for a Republican assassin, or for a Democrat. In a biography of Goebel, this writer concludes: "The evidence is simply too contradictory and the people involved were too partisan to allow any definitive answer. Until new information is uncovered, the answer to the question, 'Who killed William Goebel?' is simply 'We do not know.' Nor may we ever."

See James C. Klotter, *William Goebel: The Politics of Wrath* (Lexington, Ky., 1977); Caleb Powers, *My Own Story* (Indianapolis 1905).

JAMES C. KLOTTER

GOEBEL ELECTION LAW. The so-called Goebel Election Law was introduced on February 1, 1898, in the Kentucky General Assembly by William GOEBEL, a Democratic state senator from Kenton County and the president pro tem of the Senate. The bill created the Board of Elections Commissioners, appointed by the General Assembly every four years to choose the election commissioners for each of the state's counties (who then selected the precinct officials), examine election returns, and rule on the results. Goebel maintained that the new system was needed to replace a partisan method in which the county courts selected election officials. Though introduced as a reform measure, the bill was controversial. Members of both parties viewed it as a self-serving attempt by Goebel to strengthen his political power in the state. The bill, which was enacted by the Assembly, was vetoed on March 10, 1898, by Gov. William O'Connell Bradley, a Republican, but the veto was overridden on March 11 by House and Senate. In the contested 1899 election, the election commissioners surprised almost everyone by voting 2-1 against Goebel's election as governor. Still very

controversial, the board was abolished in a special 1900 session of the legislature.

See Hambleton Tapp and James C. Klotter, *Kentucky: Decades of Discord, 1865-1900* (Frankfort, Ky., 1977).

GOLDEN POND. Now the name of the administrative and information headquarters for Land Between the Lakes recreational area, Golden Pond was once a Trigg County town synonymous with moonshine whiskey. The community was located between the Tennessee and Cumberland rivers from 1848, at least, to 1969. Supposedly, it was named for a pond that looked like molten gold in the afternoon sun. In the early 1900s, especially during prohibition, Golden Pond was known nationally for high-quality moonshine. The town was removed in 1969 to make room for Land Between the Lakes development.

See David W. Maurer, *Kentucky Moonshine* (Lexington, Ky., 1974).   BERRY CRAIG

GOODWIN'S FORT. Goodwin's Fort was located on the north bank of the Rolling Fork of the Salt River, about twelve miles west of Bardstown, in Nelson County, Kentucky. The fort—also known as Goodin's Fort—was founded by Samuel Goodwin in 1780. Goodwin, his brother Isaac, and their families reached the Falls of the Ohio in April 1779 and, after a brief stay, traveled inland. When they came to the Rolling Fork they found an abundance of fresh water, game, and fertile land. They cleared the land and built cabins. Not long after his settlement, Goodwin had an extensive farm, encompassing nearly four thousand acres. By late 1780, however, he was faced with the threat of Indian attack; Goodwin stockaded his cabins and established a small fort. The fort was attacked by Indians only once, in July 1781. Goodwin's Fort occupied a strategic location: Along with Pottenger's and Cox's stations, it protected settlers living in what would become a populated area near Bardstown. Although Indian threats lessened through the 1780s and 1790s, Goodwin continued to live at the fort. In 1799, the Virginia General Assembly issued a land patent for the fort site to Benedict Swope, and because Goodwin had failed to obtain legal title to the property, he was forced off the land. He moved to Larue County, Kentucky, where he died in 1807.

See Evelyn Crady Adams, "Goodwin's Fort (1780) In Nelson County, Kentucky," *FCHQ* 27 (Jan. 1953): 3-15.

GOOSE CREEK SALT WORKS. In 1798 James Collins, a Virginia adventurer and trader, arrived in the area that is now known as Goose Creek in Clay County and began to produce salt there. Salt wells were bored on a complex of saline-bearing creeks known as Collins Fork, Goose, Big Bullskin, Red Bird, and Jack's. By 1846 fifteen SALT MAKERS in the area were producing 200,000 bushels of salt annually, and a decade later the Clay County–Goose Creek salt works was selling salt to a broad area of Kentucky and neighboring states. In 1861 Confederate Gen. Felix Zollicoffer, during his attempted invasion of central Kentucky from Cumberland Gap, sent wagon trains to Manchester to pick up loads of salt for the South.

See John F. Smith, "The Salt-Making Industry of Clay County, Kentucky," *FCHQ* 1 (April 1927): 134-41.   THOMAS D. CLARK

GORDON, CAROLINE. Caroline Gordon, writer, daughter of James Morris and Nancy (Meriwether) Gordon, was born on October 6, 1895, in southern Todd County, Kentucky. Gordon's childhood was spent at Merrymount, her mother's ancestral farm in Todd County, where she was educated by her father. In 1905 she attended her father's classical school for boys in Clarksville, Tennessee. After receiving her B.A. from Bethany College in West Virginia in 1916, Gordon taught school until 1920. She worked as a book reviewer and critic for the *Chattanooga News* during 1920-24. Gordon became acquainted with members of Vanderbilt's Literary Society, which published *The Fugitive* (1922-25) in Nashville. These writers represented the Agrarian movement, which stressed a traditional view of the South and held that industrialization and progress would destroy southern life. In 1924 Gordon married Allen Tate, an Agrarian writer.

Gordon's first published short story, "Summer Dust," appeared in 1929. While she and her husband were abroad in Paris, Gordon worked on her first novel, *Penhally* (1931), which portrays the lives of a Kentucky family over three generations, in the Old South, the Civil War and Reconstruction, and early twentieth century industrialization. Many of Gordon's works chronicled her family's experience at various periods in Kentucky and Tennessee history. In 1932 she received a Guggenheim Fellowship and returned to Paris, where she worked on her most popular book, *Aleck Maury, Sportsman* (1934). The main character, Maury, is based on her father, reflecting values of the Old South. *The Garden of Adonis* (1937) was set during the Depression. Gordon's other early works include *None Shall Look Back* (1937), *Green Centuries* (1941), and *The Women on the Porch* (1944). Collections of short stories are *The Forest of the South* (1945), *Old Red and Other Stories* (1963), and *The Collected Stories of Caroline Gordon* (1981). Gordon's conversion to Catholicism in 1947 influenced her later works and broadened the subject matter of the later novels, *The Strange Children* (1952), *The Malefactors* (1956), and *The Glory of Hera* (1972). Her works of literary criticism are *The House of Fiction: An Anthology of the Short Story* (coedited with Tate, 1950 and 1960), *How to Read a Novel* (1957), and *A Good Soldier: A Key to the Novels of Ford Madox Ford* (1963).

Gordon taught writing at various universities throughout the United States, including the Women's College of the University of North Carolina in 1938, Columbia University in the later 1940s, Emory University in 1966, and the University of Dallas, from which she retired in 1975.

Gordon and Tate had one child, Nancy. They were divorced in 1959. At the end of her teaching career, Gordon, in poor health, moved to San Cristobal, Mexico, to live with her daughter and son-in-law, Percy Wood. Gordon died on April 11, 1981, in San Cristobal and is buried there.

See Radcliffe Squires, *Allen Tate: A Literary Biography* (New York 1971); Rose Ann C. Fraistat, *Caroline Gordon as Novelist and Woman of Letters* (Baton Rouge, La., 1984).

GORDON, JAMES FLEMING. James Fleming Gordon, U.S. district judge for the Western District of Kentucky, was born in Madisonville, Kentucky, on May 18, 1918, to John Fleming and Ruby (James) Gordon. His father sat as a circuit judge and continued a family law practice established in 1807. Gordon earned a law degree from the University of Kentucky in 1941. After serving in the army during World War II and in the military government in post-war Japan, he returned to the family law practice and Democratic state politics.

Gordon's tenure on the federal bench (1965-84) is memorable for two cases. The first, occurring almost as soon as he assumed the job, involved a $2 million libel suit filed by retired army Gen. Edwin Walker against the *Louisville Courier-Journal* and WHAS-TV for their coverage of Walker's participation in a protest against the admission of James Meredith to the University of Mississippi. Gordon dismissed the suit on the grounds that Walker was a public figure who had thrown himself into the "vortex of the news."

Gordon's most controversial action came in 1975, when under orders from a higher court, he drafted the busing plan to desegregate the Louisville and Jefferson County school systems. The original suit, brought against the public schools by a coalition of civil rights groups in 1973, had been dismissed by Gordon, who ruled that segregation in local schools was the result of housing patterns and other factors, rather than the policies of school officials. In the summer of 1975, the U.S. circuit court of appeals reversed the ruling and ordered Gordon to implement a desegregation plan by the start of the fall term. Working with school officials and local leaders, Gordon merged the city and county school systems and imposed a busing plan that integrated the community's public schools. When put into operation, the plan generated enormous resistance, including school boycotts and violent demonstrations. To those opposing the busing plan, Gordon became a target of vilification.

Gordon died on February 9, 1990, six years after retiring from the bench, and was buried in Odd Fellows Cemetery in Madisonville, Kentucky. He and his wife, the former Iola Young, had one daughter, Marianna Dyson, and two sons, Maurice II, and James, Jr.   OLIVIA FREDERICK

GOVERNMENT, LOCAL. Having been part of the Commonwealth of Virginia, Kentucky developed its system of local government on the southern model, which features COUNTIES and incorporated cities as the basic units. Unlike most other states that adopted this model, Kentucky proceeded to develop numerous small counties ranging in size from one hundred to 785 square miles. Indeed, with a total of 120 counties, Kentucky ranks third in the nation, behind Texas and Georgia, in the number of counties; second, behind tiny Rhode Island, in the number of counties per square mile; and very close to the top of the list in terms of the number of county governments per 100,000 people. Kentucky has historically encouraged the incorporation of new municipalities, while making it relatively difficult for cities to annex or otherwise expand their territorial boundaries. This led by 1988 to the creation of 436 incorporated municipalities, over seventy-five percent of which contained fewer than the 2,500 people needed to be classified as an "urban place" by the U.S. Census Bureau. One-third of these incorporated municipalities, many of them not much larger than a small subdivision, are located in three highly urbanized and suburbanized counties: Kenton (21 municipalities) and Campbell (15) in northern Kentucky and Jefferson (95), which also contains the state's largest city, Louisville.

As in most other states, county governments in Kentucky have legal jurisdiction and taxing authority over all residents of the county, including those who live in incorporated municipalities, and as in most other states, incorporated municipalities are classified and granted varying legal powers according to population size. Kentucky's classification scheme designates six categories, from first-class cities (population of at least 100,000) to sixth-class cities (up to 1,000 people). Kentucky law also provides for the creation of urban county governments in counties where the largest city is of the second class or lower. To date the voters of only one county in Kentucky, Fayette, have exercised this option to merge city (Lexington) and county governments into a single, unified system.

With the exception of the Lexington-Fayette Urban County, the basic structure of government is the same in all Kentucky counties. Until the passage of the judicial amendment to the state constitution in 1975, each county was headed by an elected county judge who wielded legislative, judicial, and executive powers. When that amendment stripped the office of its judicial powers, the title was changed to county judge-executive. County judge-executives are voting members of the county fiscal court, the official governing body of county governments. Although fiscal courts vary somewhat in size and composition, members of all are elected on a partisan ballot and serve for four years. In addition to the county executive and members of the fiscal court, voters in all counties, including Lexington-Fayette, are called upon by the state constitution to elect numerous other officers, most of whom are legally and fiscally quite independent of the county executive and fiscal court. Together with constables, justices of the peace, and the county surveyor, these offices include such

posts as the county attorney, county clerk, sheriff, jailer, coroner, and property valuation administrator (or assessor).

There is much more variation in the structure and organization of Kentucky municipalities. Although most of them are listed as having the mayor-council form of government, the size of the council and the scope of the mayor's powers and duties vary considerably. Others operate under the commission form of municipal government, which has been declining in popularity throughout the rest of the nation for several decades. A much smaller number of cities use the council-manager form.

W.E. LYONS

GOVERNOR, OFFICE OF. The governor of Kentucky has, until recently, been considered one of the most powerful political executives in the United States. The sources of that power are many and varied. Formal powers, derived from the Kentucky constitution and statutory law, include the ability to appoint, without legislative approval, a large number of administrative leaders who serve as cabinet heads and commissioners of major departments of state government. It is estimated that the governor makes as many as 2,000 appointments to various boards, commissions, and departments. Other significant formal powers lie in the areas of management, budget, legislative leadership, and quasi-judicial responsibilities. As the state's chief executive, the governor is responsible for the day-to-day management of executive agencies. It is within the governor's authority to reduce the size of state government through reorganization or by cutting the number of state employees. The office of the governor must propose a comprehensive state budget to the General Assembly every other year; until recently, the governor's budget was approved by the legislature with few changes. Powers vis-à-vis the legislature include the veto and, more important, the sole authority to call special sessions of the General Assembly and to determine their agenda. Authority under the Kentucky constitution includes the power to grant pardons and commute sentences of those convicted of crimes. The governor is weakened by the constitutional prohibition against being elected to two consecutive terms.

Many observers consider the governor's informal powers—those derived from tradition, custom, and precedent—as important as the formal powers. Chief among these prerogatives are political patronage and media relations. Although patronage—rewarding political supporters with jobs and other favors—overlaps the governor's formal power of appointment, this tradition in Kentucky politics extends well beyond the appointment of major administrative officials. Kentucky governors have traditionally been able to enhance their political power by awarding major state contracts in such areas as insurance, legal services, and construction. Governors have been able to influence the initiation, as well as the location, of substantial state projects like community colleges, state parks, and public buildings, and they have had a major role in determining when and where state highways are built. Patronage allows the governor to develop and expand his influence over a wide array of Kentucky citizens, particularly state legislators and local party leaders and government officials.

The governor is clearly the one state official who receives the most attention from the state's media, another significant source of power. Governors have used their command of media access to gain support for favored policies and pet projects, to win over wavering allies, and to criticize political opponents.

The state's political culture—that is, Kentuckians' attitudes and feelings toward government offices and the occupants of them—revolves around the governor's office, as political leaders focus primary attention on the governor's every move. Beyond that, many political activists continually speculate on who will be running for governor next time, evaluating many officeholders simply on the basis of the necessary qualities to be elected governor in some future contest. Speculations on the next election often begin even before the current campaign has been completed. In this context, Kentuckians seem willing, even eager, to have their governor exercise substantial power, and they evaluate governors, in part, on how effectively they have exercised their authority. During the 1980s, however, the tradition of strong governors was weakened by a variety of events and circumstances, most notably the development of a more independent, coequal legislative branch. Most observers would rank the governors of the decade—John Y. Brown, Jr. (1979-83), Martha Layne Collins (1983-87), and Wallace Wilkinson (1987-91)—as significantly weaker than their counterparts of earlier decades.

See Joel Goldstein, ed., *Kentucky Government and Politics* (Bloomington, Ind., 1984); Lowell H. Harrison, ed., *Kentucky's Governors 1792-1985* (Lexington, Ky., 1985).   PAUL BLANCHARD

GOVERNOR'S SCHOLARS PROGRAM. The Governor's Scholars Program (GSP) is a five-week, summer academic enrichment program for Kentucky's highest-achieving high school seniors, selected competitively from virtually every school district in the commonwealth. The GSP grew out of a Shakertown conference proposal for a Kentucky honors scholars program. On October 29, 1982, Gov. John Y. Brown, Jr. (1979-83), announced the establishment of the GSP and appointed his counsel, Rush Dozier, Jr., to head a seven-member planning committee; Ashland Oil and Humana were founding sponsors. Robert Sexton and John Stephenson served as initial coordinators. Lillian Press was appointed executive director on January 10, 1983. An independent GSP board of directors was formed in May 1983 with Dozier as chairperson.

The GSP on July 3, 1983, began on the Centre College campus in Danville, with 245 students and James Lee Howard as dean. The program expanded in 1984 to a second campus, Eastern Kentucky University, under the direction of Robert Hemenway. In 1986 Milton Reigelman and Ken Wolf were named as the new deans for the two campuses. During the next year the GSP took the lead in organizing the first National Conference of Governor's Schools, held in Lexington in October 1987; subsequently, a national organization was incorporated in Kentucky. The program has been held on other college campuses.

The program's liberal arts curriculum stresses concepts over facts, discussion over lecture, and collaboration over competition. The small classes, seminars, and colloquiums—in which there are no tests or grades—do not duplicate high school or college courses. The academic courses are complemented by a wide array of cultural and recreational activities. Noted Kentuckians, such as Nobel laureate William Lipscomb, author Bobbie Ann Mason, and astronaut Story Musgrave have spent brief residencies in the program.

The GSP is funded by the Office of the Governor and the private sector. It is housed each summer on two college campuses. On each campus approximately 350 scholars create a "community of learners" with college-age resident counselors and high school and college faculty. The program encourages service in the larger community during and after the session. Newspapers from the *New York Times* to the *Troublesome Creek Times* have lauded the GSP as "a forum for opening ideas" and "an educational utopia."   MILTON REIGELMAN

GOVERNOR'S SCHOOL FOR THE ARTS. The Governor's School for the Arts is a three-week interdisciplinary program for artistically talented high school students entering their junior or senior year. It is held each July at Bellarmine College in Louisville. Students from across the commonwealth are auditioned from among six disciplines: creative writing, dance, drama, instrumental music, visual arts, and vocal music. One hundred twenty to one hundred fifty are selected at a final audition. Talent and regional representation are considered in the selection process. Since its inception in 1987, David X. Thurmond has served as director. The program is cosponsored by the Kentucky General Assembly and the Kentucky Center for the Arts.

LEE BASH

GRAHAM, JOHN. John Graham, pioneer and surveyor, was born January 1, 1765, in Augusta County, Virginia, to David and Jane (Armstrong) Graham. His surveying and writing abilities suggest that he was formally educated, and it is likely that he attended Augusta Seminary (now Liberty Hall), located about sixty miles from his birthplace. He served with the 8th Virginia Regiment during the Revolutionary War and was later a member of the Kentucky militia. In 1787 he first surveyed the Big Sandy River area. He later became the largest landowner in eastern Kentucky. He was a central figure in the formation of Floyd County in 1799 and became the official surveyor in 1805, reappointed by the county court in 1810, 1815, 1820, and 1830. He served two terms as circuit judge of Floyd County (1808-12 and 1814-15). On June 26, 1815, for the price of one dollar, Graham sold to Floyd County the property for the establishment of the streets and courthouse square of Prestonsburg. Graham also was a banker (1800) and a merchant (1815).

Graham married Rebecca Witten on January 29, 1775. They had seven children: Thomas Witten, Eleanor, Rebecca, Dorothy, Sophia, Tabitha, and Elizabeth. Graham died at his home near Prestonsburg on April 20, 1835, and was buried on the old homestead at Dwale in Floyd County.

See Henry P. Scalf, *Kentucky's Last Frontier* (Pikeville, Ky., 1972).

GRAND ARMY OF THE REPUBLIC CONVENTION. Louisville's opportunity to host the twenty-ninth annual convention of the Grand Army of the Republic (GAR) in September 1895 was a coup for the growing city. The organization of Union veterans of the Civil War had not previously convened south of the Mason-Dixon line, and northern cities fought yearly to host the meeting. On October 10, 1893, the Commerce Club of Louisville voted to make an offer to host the GAR convention, a move that received the support of Confederate veterans' organizations in the city. When the offer was approved, a planning committee was formed in Louisville, led by T.H. Sherley, Andrew Cowan, George W. Griffiths, R.M. Kelly, Charles L. Jewett, Isaac F. Whitesides, John H. Leathers, John H. Milkie, and William Cornwall, Jr.

The city of 248,000 prepared well in advance for the meeting of the estimated 150,000 Union veterans. Every business and organization in Louisville was in some way involved in planning the convention. Newspaper advertisers capitalized on the event, selling flags and other patriotic paraphernalia and publicizing their places of business as being directly on the parade route or as standing on historically significant ground. Scrapbooks and GAR plaques were for sale, and the official guidebook of the city featured advertisements by opera houses, theaters, parks, and local madams.

A three-hundred-tent encampment city for visiting veterans was built on fifty acres in Wilder's Woods near Phoenix Hill on Baxter Avenue. Schools were closed to provide extra housing for the September 9-14 convention. All of the hotels were filled, and many conventioneers stayed in private homes. All railroads were readied to supply extra transportation and the Louisville Street Car Company reorganized its entire system to concentrate on the convention's major activity sites. Other communities sent policemen, firemen, and support equipment for public safety, and first aid stations were set up throughout the city.

When the conventioneers began to arrive on September 9, the *Louisville Courier-Journal* greeted them with this headline: "Louisville, the Gateway to War in 1861, is to the Veterans in 1895 the Gateway to a Prosperous South." The agenda of the convention was simple enough—election of officers, discussion of pensions and holidays, and a decision on where to hold the meeting the following year—but what took place within the meeting hall was, for the most part, overshadowed by the events outside the convention. Planned and spontaneous gatherings were everywhere. Concerts were held in the parks, and musicals were performed daily in the theaters. The parks were open at all times, race tracks had full cards, and vaudeville shows and tours of the city competed with personal reunions. The many events, including countless balls, were recounted daily in local newspapers. A tragedy occurred on the morning of Wednesday, September 11, when a cannon mounted on a carriage and filled with sixty pounds of black powder exploded, killing four Louisville veterans and the carriage driver. The cannon was to have been part of the 30,000-person parade through the city. In spite of the accident, the parade proceeded, beginning at Shelby and Broadway and marching down Broadway to Fourth, Jefferson, Eighth, and Market, ending at First Street. A campfire at Phoenix Hill followed the all-day parade, and the convention ended with a picnic at Wilder Park. One hundred head of cattle and three hundred sheep had been slaughtered for the barbecue, and seventy-five gallons of burgoo were prepared to feed the 100,000 picnickers.

See William E. Cummings, "Pomp, Pandemonium, and Paramours: The G.A.R. Convention of 1895," *Register* 81 (Summer 1983): 274-86.

GRANT, TRAVIS. Travis ("The Machine") Grant, born January 1, 1950, in Clayton, Alabama, arrived on the campus of Kentucky State University (KSU) in Frankfort for the 1968-69 basketball season. Under new coach Lucias Mitchell, the team posted a 10-15 record. The next season Grant scored 75 points against Northwood Institute in Michigan and led the nation in scoring, with 35 points per game. He helped KSU win its first National Association of Intercollegiate Athletics (NAIA) championship, which it won again in 1971 and 1972. Grant, a six-foot, eight-inch swingman, led the nation in scoring in 1971-72, averaging nearly 40 points a game and finishing with 4,045 career points, a collegiate record. He was the first choice of the Los Angeles Lakers in the 1972 National Basketball Association draft, but in 1973 he jumped to the San Diego Conquistadors of the American Basketball Association. He played the 1975-76 season with the Kentucky Colonels and Indiana Pacers before a knee injury ended his career. After returning to KSU and earning a B.S. degree in 1979, Grant became the boy's basketball coach at Walker High School near Atlanta, Georgia. In March 1987, the three-time All-American, 1970-72, was named to the NAIA Golden Anniversary All-Star team.

GRANT BROTHERS. The Grant brothers—Samuel, John, and Squire—were early settlers after whom Grant County was named when it was established in 1820. John Grant, born in 1754 in North Carolina, moved to Kentucky in 1779, probably accompanied by his brother Samuel, born around 1762. They erected a fort about five miles from Bryan's Station in Fayette County, but after Indians captured Martin's and Ruddell's stations, John went back to North Carolina and then to Virginia. He returned to Kentucky in 1784 and erected a salt works on the Licking River, then spent some time in Illinois. Samuel was killed by Indians in 1789 or 1794 in Indiana. John died in Kentucky in 1826. Squire Grant, born in 1764, was a surveyor and a large landowner in Campbell County, who served in the state Senate from 1801 to 1806. He lived in Kentucky until his death in 1833.

See Robert Elliston, *History of Grant Co., State of Kentucky* (N.p, n.d.).

GRANT COUNTY. Grant County, the sixty-seventh county established in Kentucky, was created in 1820 from the western part of Pendleton County, which borders it today, along with Boone, Kenton, Gallatin, Owen, and Harrison counties. Covering 259 square miles in the north-central portion of the state, Grant County is almost square in shape and has an average elevation of 1,000 feet above sea level. The land is mostly rolling plains, with few hilly areas. The eastern part of the county is watered and drained by tributaries of the Licking River; the western portion, by tributaries of the Kentucky River. WILLIAMSTOWN is the county seat.

There is some dispute about the origin of the county's name. It was most likely named for Samuel Grant (1762-89), a frontiersman killed fighting Indians, and/or his brothers, Col. John Grant (1754-1826) and Squire Grant (1764-1833). The county was the site of one of the last Indian massacres in Kentucky, when a family was attacked and scalped and their home burned about 1805 on Bullock Pen Creek, west of Crittenden; only the mother survived. In 1824 the Marquis de Lafayette, hero of the Revolutionary War, visited Crittenden as he traveled from Lexington to Cincinnati.

Much of the growth of the county, which is bisected by I-75 and the Norfolk Southern railroad, is attributed to its location, between Lexington and Cincinnati. Major employers in the county include the Kroger Company, the Drisco Company, and Automated Building Components. Many residents commute to work in the Cincinnati and Lexington areas. Agriculture plays a major role in the economy of Grant County, accounting for more than $17.4 million in 1986—$12.1 million in crop receipts and $5.3 million in livestock receipts. Burley tobacco production in 1989 was estimated at 5.63 million pounds, with an estimated value of $8.5 million. The four lakes of Grant County provide numerous recreational activities for residents: Williamstown Lake (300 acres), Bullock Pen Lake (134 acres), Lake Boltz (92 acres), and Corinth Lake (96 acres).

Grant County had a population of 9,999 in 1970; 13,308 in 1980; and 15,737 in 1990.

GRANT'S FORT. Grant's Fort, or Grant's Station, was a Bourbon County settlement on Houston Creek near BRYAN'S STATION and the Fayette County line. It was built in 1779 by John Grant, of North Carolina, and William Ellis, of Virginia, to accommodate twenty to thirty families living in overcrowded Bryan's Station. An Indian war party of approximately sixty men attacked Grant's Fort in June of 1780. The war party was part of the larger British campaign against Kentucky during the Revolutionary War, led by Col. Henry Byrd. Although forty men were dispatched from Bryan's Station to provide relief, Grant's Fort was burned and two men and a woman were killed. The fort was rebuilt in 1784. The Grant family sold their Bourbon County properties, including a two-hundred-acre tract, to George Berry on June 14, 1788. The fort was used as a rest stop for people traveling to and from Lexington. It is considered to be in excellent condition for archeological study.

GRATZ, BENJAMIN. Benjamin Gratz, lawyer and businessman, son of Philadelphia merchant Michael Gratz and Miriam (Simon) Gratz, was born in Philadelphia on September 4, 1792, the youngest of twelve children. He graduated from the University of Pennsylvania in 1811 and earned his master's degree there in 1815. Gratz enlisted in the Pennsylvania Volunteer troops in the War of 1812 and was a second lieutenant in Capt. John Swift's company. He studied law after the war and was admitted to the bar in 1817. His father owned land in Lexington, Kentucky, which may have influenced Gratz's move there in 1819. Shortly after his arrival, he became a trustee of Transylvania University, a position that he held for sixty-three years. At the same time, Gratz, in partnership with Col. James Morrison and John Bruce, began manufacturing hemp. After Morrison's death in 1823, and Bruce's in 1836, he became sole owner of this prominent business, which he ran for the next quarter of a century.

Gratz joined Thomas E. Boswell, Robert Wickliffe, and others in developing the Lexington & Ohio Railway in 1830 and he served as its second president. He was a member of the Lexington Council, which organized the public library. In 1833 Gratz, along with his wife, helped establish the Orphan Asylum of Lexington. He served on the first board of directors of the Bank of Kentucky and the Northern Bank of Kentucky, created in 1834 and 1835, respectively. In 1850 he became the first president of the Kentucky Agricultural and Mechanical Association. When his close friend Henry Clay died in June 1852, Gratz helped make funeral arrangements and in 1857 he served on the Clay Monument Association.

Gratz married Maria Cecil Gist, the daughter of Col. Nathaniel Gist, on November 24, 1819. She was the first secretary of the Orphan Asylum of Lexington and helped manage it until her death on November 4, 1841. They had five children. On July 6, 1843, Gratz married his first wife's widowed niece, Anna Maria (Boswell) Shelby; they had three children. He died on March 17, 1884, and was buried in the Lexington Cemetery. Gratz Park in Lexington is named for him.

See Clay Lancaster, *Ante Bellum Houses of the Bluegrass* (Lexington, Ky., 1961).

GRAVES, BENJAMIN FRANKLIN. Benjamin Franklin Graves, after whom Graves County is named, was the son of Joseph and Frances (Coleman) Graves, born in 1771 in Spotsylvania County, Virginia. Graves settled on a farm in Fayette County, Kentucky, with his widowed mother and siblings in 1791. He was elected to the state legislature as a representative of Fayette County in 1801 and again in 1804. Commissioned in August 1812 to fight in the war against Britain as a major in the 2d Battalion, 5th Regiment of the Kentucky militia, Graves was wounded in a battle at Frenchtown on the River Raisin on January 22, 1813. The following day, after having been left to recuperate at a house in Frenchtown, Graves was captured along with Samuel Ganoe, Timothy Mallory, and John Davenport by Potawatomie Indians. Graves was not seen again.

Graves married Polly Dudley; they had six children. Graves County, Kentucky, was created by an act of the General Assembly in December 1823 in honor of Major Graves.

See Clift G. Glenn, *Remember the Raisin!* (Frankfort, Ky., 1961).

GRAVES COUNTY. Graves County, seventy-fifth in order of formation, is located in the center of the Jackson Purchase on the Tennessee state line and is the largest county in that region. It is bordered by Hickman, Carlisle, McCracken, Marshall, and Calloway counties and has an area of 557 square miles. Graves County was created in 1824 from part of Hickman County, with Mayfield as the county seat. The county was named in honor of Maj. Benjamin F. Graves, a Fayette County soldier killed at the Battle of River Raisin in the War of 1812. MAYFIELD is the county seat.

Mayfield Creek, for which the county seat was named, is a major waterway, as are Clark's River, Bayou de Chien, and Obion creeks. Prior to settlement, the region was a relatively treeless grassland known as the barrens; its level terrain is dotted with rolling hills and a few steep ridges. Fertile land costing one dollar per acre in 1825 attracted the first settlers, who came from Virginia, middle Tennessee, or south-central Kentucky. They brought skills needed to cultivate dark fire-cured tobacco, the cash crop upon which the county's economy was based. Although there was some agricultural diversification by 1860, when substantial amounts of corn, cotton, and rice were produced, tobacco remained the principal crop on virtually every Graves County farm in the nineteenth century. By the 1920s Mayfield's market was the leading exporter of dark fire-cured tobacco in the nation.

The pioneer years 1824 to 1834 saw a steady increase in population and the emergence of churches (Baptist, Methodist, Cumberland Presbyterian) and schools (Mayfield's first opened in 1825). The first courthouse, a log structure, was built in 1824. It was replaced by a brick building in 1834. During the county's first presidential balloting in 1824, most residents voted for Andrew Jackson. In 1830 the federal census reported a population of 2,504 whites and 279 slaves.

Besides Mayfield, other communities included Lynville, Farmington, Lowes, Wingo, Cuba, Pryorsburg, and Feliciana. Fancy Farm, a settlement of Catholics from central Kentucky, grew up around St. Jerome Church, built in 1836. Roads to the Mississippi, Ohio, and Tennessee rivers connected county tobacco farms with New Orleans markets. In 1856 the New Orleans & Ohio Railroad (now the Paducah & Louisville Railroad) connected Paducah with Mayfield and later with Fulton.

The Civil War abruptly ended Graves's progress as personal and property losses in this Confederate stronghold were staggering. When Union forces occupied the area in 1862, Confederates abandoned Camp Beauregard, near Feliciana, which was decimated by disease. Several skirmishes, but no significant battles, were fought in Graves County. In mid-1864 the harsh military rule of Union Gen. E.A. Paine caused much suffering among county residents. To their relief, Paine was removed from command before the war ended. The courthouse was destroyed in 1864 and replaced by a third building in 1866.

After the war an 1860 woolen mill in Mayfield was reorganized, and a second textile mill, Mayfield Pants Company, began operation in 1899. Later both were expanded and as the Curlee Clothing Company and the Merit Clothing Company, respectively, they helped make Mayfield a men's clothing manufacturing center. In 1891 discovery of ball clay used in porcelain, china, and tile generated an important extractive industry and profitable ceramic enterprises, the Kentucky-Tennessee Clay Company and the Old Hickory Clay Company.

As tobacco production rose, Mayfield warehouses did brisk business during the sales seasons. The third county courthouse was destroyed by fire in 1887, and the fourth courthouse, elaborately Victorian in design, was finished in 1888. In Mayfield, water pumping began in 1892 and electrical service in 1893. The county's first telephone system was installed in 1895. By 1900, Mayfield had become urbanized and other county communities such as Folsomdale, Sedalia, Water Valley, and Symsonia had grown into farm trade centers. Feliciana, a thriving trading center until bypassed by the railroad in 1858, was abandoned.

Paved roads and streets, new industries such as Pet Milk Company, and the construction of Mayfield's present post office attested to progress made by the 1920s. Today the two largest businesses are the General Tire Company, in operation since 1960 and owned by the German corporation Continental Tire, and Ingersoll-Rand's Centac Division, built in 1970 to produce air compressors. Two textile firms, the Dillon Manufacturing Company and Mary Nell Industries, manufacture apparel, and a food processing facility, Seaboard Farms of Kentucky, opened in 1990. Agriculture remains a vital economic resource, along with retail stores, banks, and professional and service activities.

Notable citizens of Graves County include former vice-president and senator Alben BARKLEY; six U.S. Congressmen—Lucian Anderson, former Confederate Col. Edward Crossland, A.R. Boone, the brothers Voris and Noble Gregory, and Carroll Hubbard; Confederate Maj. H.S. HALE, who was Kentucky's state treasurer in the 1890s; distinguished artist Ellis Wilson; syndicated columnist and humorist of the 1930s George Bingham; and modern short story writer and novelist Bobbie Ann MASON.

The population of Graves County was 30,939 in 1970; 34,049 in 1980; and 33,550 in 1990.

See D. Trabue Davis, *Story of Mayfield Through a Century* (Paducah, Ky., 1923).

LON CARTER BARTON

GRAYSON. Grayson, the county seat of Carter County in northeastern Kentucky, is located on the Little Sandy River at U.S. 60 and KY 7, just south of I-64. The town was named for the family of Col. William Grayson, upon whose lands the county was founded. Grayson, aide-de-camp to Gen. George Washington during the Revolutionary War, was issued a 70,000-acre patent in 1795 by Gov. Isaac Shelby (1792-96, 1812-16). The area was originally settled around 1801 by salt makers who operated near the Little Sandy River. The community that grew up around the Little Sandy salt works, first called the Crossroads, was renamed Grayson in 1838 when Carter County was established and Grayson was made its seat. A brick courthouse completed in 1842 was replaced in 1907 by one of classical Beaux Arts–influenced design.

The town, officially incorporated on February 6, 1844, grew slowly as a rural trading center dependent on extractive industries in the area. During 1800-50, salt making was the major industry, and from the 1850s until the 1890s iron making, coal mining, and then timber were linchpins of the local economy.

During the Civil War, a number of small skirmishes were fought in the vicinity, most notably on October 1, 1862, when Gen. George Morgan's Union army passed through the city while retreating from Cumberland Gap to the Ohio River. Among the units in Morgan's army were elements of the 22d Kentucky Infantry Regiment, which had been organized in the city in 1861. In September 1863 the 40th Kentucky Infantry Regiment (USA) was mustered in at Grayson and spent the later war years putting down guerrilla activity in the area.

The mining and lumbering activity of the postbellum era prompted the completion of the Eastern Kentucky Railroad (EKR) to Grayson on June 10, 1871, and the EKR maintenance shops were relocated to Grayson from Hunnewell in Greenup County. The line closed in 1928. The residents of Grayson then bought 13.4 miles of the track that ran south to a junction with the Chesapeake & Ohio Railway, but the low-budget operation closed for good in 1932. Improvements of U.S. 60 through the town were made in the late 1920s and the nearby I-64 was completed in 1973.

Grayson is home to KENTUCKY CHRISTIAN COLLEGE. The population of the fourth-class city was 2,184 in 1970; 3,423 in 1980; and 3,510 in 1990.

See George Wolfford, *Carter County: A Pictorial History* (Ashland, Ky., 1985).

GEORGE WOLFFORD

GRAYSON COUNTY. Grayson County, the fifty-fourth county in order of formation, is located in west-central Kentucky and is partly bounded by Rough River on the north and Nolin River on the southeast. It is bordered by Breckinridge, Hardin, Hart, Edmonson, Butler, and Ohio counties and has an area of 493 square miles.

The area was settled in the late 1700s. Among the early landowners was George Washington, who purchased 5,000 acres on the southern shore of Rough River from Henry Lee in 1788. Many others arrived to settle the area, and on January 25, 1810, Grayson County was established from the western part of Hardin and the eastern part of Ohio County. The county was named for Col. William Grayson, an aide to Gen. Washington, and LEITCHFIELD was founded as the county seat.

Millerstown, the county's oldest incorporated city, was formally established in 1826 on the Nolin River; FALLS OF ROUGH grew as a small village around the Green Sawmill, which began operating in 1823; and Grayson Springs, a summer resort community, opened in 1830 and was at the height of its popularity by 1900. The east-west Elizabethtown & Paducah Railroad (now Paducah & Louisville) arrived in the early 1870s and transformed Caneyville, Leitchfield, and eight other towns on the line into agricultural markets and shipping points. Big Clifty operated an asphalt plant and shipped its product nationally, and Clarkson developed several large lumber mills after 1900. Clarkson also became home to the Walter T. Kelley Bee Hive Factory, founded in 1924, which by 1990 had become one of the largest manufacturers of apiary equipment in the country.

By the early 1900s, the railroad and other industries had consumed vast amounts of the region's timber, but much of the county remains forested, and lumber is still an important industry. Mineral resources include natural gas, found near Shrewsbury, and coal, mined in the western part of the county. Tobacco is the leading cash crop, followed by corn, soybeans, hay, and wheat. Hogs, beef, and dairy cattle are also raised.

The county has benefited from its location between two rivers and on the major east-west Western Kentucky Parkway, completed in the mid-1960s. With the impoundments of Rough River Lake in 1959 and Nolin Reservoir in 1963 and the opening of Rough River Dam State Resort Park, Grayson County established a thriving tourism trade and attracted numerous small industries and manufacturing companies to the Leitchfield area. The county had a population of 16,445 in 1970; 20,854 in 1980; and 21,050 in 1990.

See Duvall Morrison, *A History of Grayson County, Kentucky 1810-1958*, (Utica, Ky. 1958).

MARK E. NEVILS

GREAT HOG SWINDLE. The so-called great hog swindle during the Civil War turned even loyal Kentuckians against the administration and pro-Southern. On October 28, 1864, federal commander Stephen G. Burbridge issued a proclamation asking Kentuckians to sell any surplus hogs to the U.S. government. Army agents signed contracts with favored packers, prohibited interstate hog shipments, required permits for citizens to drive swine to market, and then offered a lower price than existing civilian outlets. Farmers, who had to sell to the designated contractors, sustained losses estimated at $300,000 during the month the program was in effect. President Abraham Lincoln soon ordered Burbridge to revoke the order, and the scandal ended. JAMES C. KLOTTER

GREAT REVIVAL. The Great Revival (1800-1805) was a series of religious revivals, beginning in Kentucky, that swept across the southern states in the opening years of the nineteenth century. It is sometimes called the Second Great Awakening in the South; the first one, however, during the period 1739-50, took place primarily north of Maryland. A "great," or general, religious awakening takes place in a network of churches and ministers when a perceived socioeconomic-cultural tension lends itself to interpretation as a religious crisis that can be resolved only by a rebirth or revival of religious faith. These preconditions were not widespread enough in the South before the late 1790s to sustain a significant revival, although brief, one-denominational, localized revivals were scattered across the South in the mid-eighteenth century. Neither the institutions, the leaders, nor the *mentalité* existed for a Great Awakening to occur in the colonial South. Between the 1740s and 1790s, however, these prerequisites were met throughout much of the South.

A catalyst for the Great Revival was a Presbyterian minister from North Carolina, James McGready, who had arrived in Logan County, Kentucky, in late 1796 to preside over the Gasper River, Muddy River, and Red River Presbyterian churches. He had organized his few parishioners into prayer societies to petition God for renewal, and gradually his hard-hitting sermons and captivating presence built up the three small congregations. McGready started holding joint communion services, which began on a Friday with preaching and ended on Sunday afternoon with the sacrament. In June 1800 two visiting ministers, John and William McGee, asked to participate in one of the services at the Red River church. Because McGready had known William McGee in North Carolina and had led him to the ministry, McGready allowed them to join in, even though John McGee was a Methodist and quite passionate in his religion. When the McGees became extremely aroused during the services that evening and began shouting, a spark of excitement leaped from person to person among the normally subdued congregation. With John McGee shouting that the spirit of Jesus was present, a worshiper at the back of the church commenced shouting and crying. Soon many in the crowded church—tired, expectant, feverishly excited—broke out into a religious frenzy. McGready and others present almost instantly interpreted this outbreak of zeal as a clear sign that God in his mysterious way had there in frontier Kentucky begun the long-awaited revival. During the next month, July 1800, an even more emotional outdoor religious service was held at the Gasper River church—the first camp meeting.

Throughout the South, clergy and devout laypeople had been waiting for a sign of deliverance, and the news from Kentucky was heralded as the beginning of a second Pentecost. Quickly, almost like an epidemic, the camp meeting revivals swept across the rural South. Huge crowds, often numbering in the thousands, including blacks as well as whites, came to the revival services, prepared to camp out for several days to hear interdenominational teams of ministers preach. The largest of all the early camp meetings was held, under the sponsorship of Barton W. Stone, at CANE RIDGE, Kentucky, beginning on August 8, 1801, with an attendance that contemporaries estimated at 20,000—a number possibly several times too large. Ministers, caught up in the religious maelstrom, urged listeners to repent and convert. The novelty of these camp meetings, the rather bizarre emotional extremes, and the unusual physical manifestations of conversion (such as falling unconscious or having spasmodic "jerks") seemed to authenticate the ongoing revival as a miraculous act of God. New converts were made, backsliders regained, piety reinforced, church membership augmented. The revival that had begun in Kentucky soon spread across the South and helped transform the region religiously and stamp its character permanently.

Throughout the region, church membership increased significantly over a two-to-five-year period. Presbyterians soon withdrew from the unruly revivals, and to a degree Baptists did likewise, leaving the camp meeting a predominantly Methodist institution. But revivalistic religion—emotionally intense, focused on individual conversion, with little awareness of broader social concerns—remained characteristic of the reinvigorated Protestantism of the South. Numerous evangelical churches were established, ministers were called, and laypeople joined the churches by the thousands. A Baptist-Methodist-Presbyterian trinity of evangelical churches came to dominate the region almost completely. A new sense of religious community resulted, with a system of values and a code of behavior different from those of the eighteenth century Anglican establishment. By the 1830s nearly everyone in the South—the plain folk, wealthy planters, slaves—accepted in broad outline the evangelical tradition that had emerged during the Great Revival. That tradition became one of the essential ingredients of what has been called the mind of the Old South.

See John B. Boles, *The Great Revival, 1787-1805: The Origins of the Southern Evangelical Mind* (Lexington, Ky., 1972); Dickson D. Bruce, Jr., *And They All Sang Hallelujah: Plain-Folk Camp-Meeting Religion, 1800-1845* (Knoxville, Tenn., 1974).   JOHN B. BOLES

GREAT SALTPETER CAVE. One of the best-known caves of southeast Kentucky is Great Saltpeter Cave in Rockcastle County, discovered by John Baker late in the eighteenth century. It was one of the chief sources of SALTPETER for making gunpowder in the early nineteenth century. Mining was intensive during the War of 1812, employing sixty to seventy people from the area in the process of extracting saltpeter. The Mexican and Civil wars later stimulated limited production. Some of the mining vats are still visible, along with trenches and other artifacts. The cave is privately owned.
JAMES R. REBMANN

GREEN COUNTY. Green County, the sixteenth in order of formation, is located in south-central Kentucky, bordered by Adair, Hart, Larue, Metcalfe, and Taylor counties, and has an area of 289 square miles. Green County was formed from portions of Lincoln and Nelson counties on December 20, 1792, with GREENSBURG as its county seat. The county was named in honor of Gen. Nathanael Greene, a hero of the Revolutionary War. Known as the "Quaker general," Greene was an American commander at Boston, Long Island, Trenton, Brandywine, Germantown, Monmouth, and several other engagements. In 1780 he was appointed commander of the southern theater of operations; he and his troops forced the British out of the Carolinas and toward surrender at Yorktown in 1781.

The topography of Green County is hilly. Approximately 80 percent of the county is farmland, about a third of which is forested. There are numerous streams. Green River, which flows through the central portion of Green County, is the largest water source. Several important creeks also flow through the county, among them Brush, Pittman, and Russell creeks and the Little Barren River.

The history of the Green County area before the first pioneer settlements can be traced through the many artifacts from burial mounds and small village sites left by the Indians who lived and hunted there. The first pioneers in Green County were a

group of Long Hunters who explored the region in 1770. The first permanent settlers came from Virginia, North and South Carolina, Maryland, and Pennsylvania. Some of the early settlers were veterans of the Revolutionary War who received land grants as payment for their war service to Virginia. Among the pioneer stations established were Pittman's Station, two miles from Greensburg on Pittman's Creek; Skagg's Station, at the present site of Somersville; and Glover's Station, at the present site of Greensburg. About eight miles east of Greensburg, on the Columbia road, is the site of Gray's Station, erected around 1790.

Green County was the scene of frequent military activity during the Civil War. As the war progressed, guerrilla raids became frequent. In October 1863 a large Confederate guerrilla force occupied Greensburg and terrorized its residents. On November 19, 1864, six Confederates were executed near Osceola in the western part of the county by order of Union Gen. Stephen Burbridge in retaliation for the murder of two Union men. Camp Ward, a Union recruitment station, was established in Greensburg by Gen. William T. Ward, a resident of the town. Also from Green County was Gen. Edward H. Hobson, who formed the 13th Kentucky Infantry for the Union.

In 1958 Green County experienced an extensive oil production boom; in 1959 there were over seven hundred oil wells. By 1969 over 20 million barrels of oil had been produced in the county, but after that year production declined sharply.

In Green County, an agrarian community, tobacco is the leading cash crop, and corn, hay, and vegetables are among the major crops grown. Livestock and poultry are also important to the county's agricultural economy. Many residents are employed in farm-related positions or are employed outside of the county. The industrial base of the county includes the manufacturing of clothing, wood products, and heavy construction machinery.

The population of Green County was 10,350 in 1970; 11,043 in 1980; and 10,371 in 1990.

See Kate Powell Evans, *A Collection of Green County History* (Greensburg, Ky., 1976); Marshall Lowe and Gary Scott, *Green County Historical Fact Book* (Greensburg, Ky., 1970).
RON D. BRYANT

GREEN RIVER. The Green River cuts a wide swath through central and western Kentucky, draining more of the commonwealth than any other Ohio River tributary. The Green River valley covers 9,430 square miles of Kentucky and 377 square miles of northern Tennessee.

Several small streams in the foothills of the Appalachian Mountains join to form the Green River in Lincoln and Casey counties. Flowing west through the Mammoth Cave area, it is fed by many underground streams and by Nolin River and Bear Creek. About halfway to the Green River's mouth at the Ohio River, the Big Barren River joins it from the south. The confluence of the Big Barren and Green rivers near Bowling Green marks the beginning of Green River's lower reaches. Flowing largely north at that point, it is joined by three major tributaries—Mud River, Pond River, and Rough River—before entering the Ohio River between Henderson and Owensboro.

The Green River flows through two major geographical areas: the Pennyroyal and the Western Kentucky Coal Field. The upper river, in the Penny-royal region, crosses the barrens, a once-treeless region characterized by caves and sinkholes. The lower river originally cut through dense forests, and past rich coal seams, which have since been strip-mined.

During the pioneer era, Revolutionary War veterans claimed land in Green River Country, as they called land southwest of the river, as payment for their military service. Nicknamed Rogue's Harbor because of lawbreakers, the valley also attracted revival-minded preachers. By way of flatboats and keelboats, pioneers of all types entered the valley, and the Green River became a major artery of transportation and trade. By the 1820s, however, valley residents realized that snags, overhanging trees, and rocky falls must be eliminated to make the Green River navigable by steamboats, which were already plying the Ohio River. The mania for steamboats, which could go upriver as well as down, inspired the building of the first locks and dams in Kentucky during the 1830s. James Rumsey Skiles, a Bowling Green politician and businessman, led the drive for state funds to improve the Green and Barren rivers. Skiles, who was named for his grandfather, steamboat developer James Rumsey, organized a crew to clear the river. The *United States*, a tiny, single-stacked steamboat, reached the Bowling Green landing in 1828. As a member of the state legislature, Skiles pushed through the first state expenditures for Green River improvements in 1833, to make slack-water navigation possible in dry periods. The river project was declared operable to Bowling Green in 1842.

During the Civil War the state allowed the Green River locks and dams to fall into disrepair. The legislature then sold the system to a group of local rivermen—the Green and Barren River Navigation Company—which collected tolls from all river boats except their own. In 1888 the U.S. Army Corps of Engineers took over the system, making navigation toll-free and promising to extend the locks and dams upriver as far as Mammoth Cave. By 1906 the final locks and dams had been completed. Showboats joined the commercial boats, filling the Green River with activity.

When the *Evansville* burned at the Bowling Green landing in 1931, a century of packet steamboating trade ended. Coal barges began to fill the lower river in the 1950s. When a break occurred in the dam near the confluence of the Barren and Green rivers in 1965, it was not repaired, and only the three lower locks continued to operate. In the 1970s environmentalists attacked the valley strip mines and the high-sulphur coal they produced. As a major commercial artery, the Green River lost importance along with the decline in coal mining.

According to an Ohio River Basin survey, the Green River has great recreational potential. When four flood-control dams were completed in 1969, they brought fishing, camping, and boating enthusiasts to the valley. The Green River's role in Kentucky changes with each generation, but its beauty and significance remain.

See Helen B. Crocker, *The Green River of Kentucky* (Lexington, Ky. 1976).

HELEN B. CROCKER

GREENSBURG. Greensburg, the seat of Green County, is located along U.S. 68 on the Green River. It was established December 4, 1794, on the site of Glover's Station, built in 1780 by John Glover, who owned 193 acres received as part of a military grant. The first Green County courthouse was built in Greensburg in 1796. A second structure was erected in 1802-4, and was used by the county court until 1931, when the present building was completed. The second Green County courthouse is the oldest surviving courthouse in Kentucky and may be the oldest west of the Allegheny Mountains.

Greensburg is the location of several historic structures, including the Jeremiah Abell house, a log structure built in 1796, and the Simpson house, the birthplace of William Herndon, Abraham Lincoln's law partner from 1844 until 1861. Another historic building is Montgomery's Mill, built in 1795.

In October 1863, Greensburg was briefly occupied by a large number of Confederate guerrillas, who looted and terrorized the residents of the town. Greensburg began a slow decline after the war. Nevertheless, by the twentieth century Greensburg began to expand and prosper as a farm trading center. The oil boom of the 1960s was an economic boost to the town and county. The city celebrates its farming heritage with a Cow Days celebration, held each September.

Although the city has remained a rural trading center, some manufacturing firms moved there in the 1960s. By 1988 the largest employers in the city were Fruit of the Loom Company, which produces clothing; Greensburg Manufacturing Company, which makes wood products; and the Edmonton Manufacturing Company, which makes work clothes.

The population of the fifth-class city was 1,990 in 1970; 2,377 in 1980; and 1,990 in 1990.

RON D. BRYANT

GREENUP, CHRISTOPHER. Christopher Greenup, governor during 1804-08, was most likely born in Loudoun County, Virginia, around 1750; his parents are not known. He learned surveying and studied law, then served as a lieutenant in the Continental Line and as a colonel of militia during the Revolutionary War. After moving to Lincoln County, Kentucky, in 1781, Greenup practiced law, did surveying, and speculated in land. Active in numerous community affairs, he represented Fayette County briefly in the Virginia House. During a 1787 trip to Virginia, he married Mary Catherine Pope. He served in two of the Danville conventions that led to statehood in 1792.

Greenup moved to Frankfort in 1792 and was a state elector that year. Appointed to the court of oyer and terminer, he resigned to accept election as a Jeffersonian Republican in the U.S. House of Representatives, where he served from November 9, 1792, to March 3, 1797. He was elected to the Kentucky House the next year and was clerk of the state Senate from 1799 to 1802. He was candidate for governor in 1800, in a four-man race; his 6,746 votes were second to James Garrard's 8,390. Two years later Greenup accepted appointment to the circuit court. Greenup resigned in 1804 to make another race for the governorship. His unopposed election was a tribute to his popularity. During the decade he lived after leaving office, he managed his considerable business interests and played only a minor role in political affairs. He died at his Frankfort home on April 17, 1818, and was buried in the Frankfort Cemetery.

An astute politician, Greenup usually enjoyed a good relationship with the General Assembly, but he was unable to secure many of the reforms that he sought for the militia, the courts, and the revenue system. The perennial problems of land titles and reform of the penal system were other concerns. During his administration the state chartered and bought stock in the Ohio Canal Company (1804) and the Bank of Kentucky (1806). In his last annual message Greenup recommended unsuccessfully that the state provide for public education. During his administrations, two public sensations arose, involving a resurrection of the old Spanish Conspiracy charges and the mysterious activities of Aaron Burr. Greenup testified during a legislative hearing on the conspiracy, defending himself ably there and in print, and emerged with little damage to his reputation. With legislative approval he placed militia along the Ohio River, but by the end of 1807 he reported that Kentucky was safe from any aspect of the Burr Conspiracy. He was concerned about the British violations of American neutral rights, but Kentucky had little direct involvement with that issue. Greenup was perhaps the most active of the early governors in seeking to direct public affairs. He left office on September 1, 1808, with high public esteem.

See Orlando Brown, "The Governors of Kentucky (1792-1825)," *Register* 49 (April 1951): 93-113; Lowell H. Harrison, ed., *Kentucky's Governors, 1792-1985* (Lexington, Ky., 1985).

LOWELL H. HARRISON

GREENUP. The city of Greenup was laid off in 1803-4 as the seat of Greenup County by Robert Johnson, the owner of the land. It was incorporated on February 4, 1818, as Greenupsburg, named after Kentucky's fourth governor, Christopher Greenup

(1749-1818). The name was changed to Greenup in March 1872 to avoid postal confusion with the town of Greenville. The first courthouse was built in 1806. The second, completed in 1816, was damaged in the flood of 1937 and condemned. The existing courthouse was completed in 1940.

Greenup, a fifth-class city, lies 150 miles east of Louisville, at the convergence of the Little Sandy and Ohio rivers. Its economy is based on both agriculture and industry. Greenup's population was 1,284 in 1970; 1,386 in 1980; and 1,158 in 1990.

GREENUP COUNTY. Greenup County, the forty-fifth formed in Kentucky, was established in 1803 from part of Mason County. It lies in the Appalachian region of the state, in the northeast corner, bordered by the Ohio River and by Boyd, Lewis, and Carter counties. GREENUP, the county seat, and the county itself were named for Christopher Greenup (1804-8), Kentucky's fourth governor.

At some time before 1753, French fur traders and Shawnee Indians settled opposite the mouth of the Scioto River. This was believed to be the only white settlement in Kentucky before Fort Harrod, but all traces of the village disappeared before 1800. Indian burial mounds near Siloam and Old Springville are the remains of prehistoric villages where the Adena people lived more than two thousand years before the first white settlers. The Adena, who lived near the major rivers and streams of central and eastern Kentucky, were part of a culture that stretched into Ohio, West Virginia, Indiana, and Pennsylvania.

Parts of Greenup County's original territory were taken in forming other counties: Lawrence in 1821, Carter in 1838, and Boyd in 1860. The first private school in the area was Greenup Academy (1815-35). The county was a Union stronghold during the Civil War. More than nine thousand Federal troops withdrew from Cumberland Gap during the summer of 1862 and retrenched near Greenup. Two covered bridges still stand in the county, one eight miles south of South Shore and the other near Oldtown.

The 350-square-mile area of Greenup County is part of the dissected Cumberland Plateau, with an average elevation of 534 feet above sea level. The terrain is mainly steep, narrow hills. The land is more than two-thirds forested, mostly in hardwoods such as red oak, white oak, and yellow poplar. Mineral deposits include limestone, sandstone, shale, clay, sand, coal, and some iron ore. The ready availability of coal and iron ore made the area a center for smelting iron in the nineteenth century, when river transportation of the smelted iron was an important consideration. The Little Sandy River and Tygart's Creek flow northward into the Ohio River, dividing the county into three almost equal parts. Production of iron in Kentucky began in 1791, and during the 1830s Kentucky ranked third in production in the United States. The remains of old furnaces can still be seen throughout the county, including Buffalo furnace in Greenbo Lake State Resort Park and Argillite, east of Greenbo Lake.

Greenup County's economy is broad-based, depending on both industry and agriculture. Eleven surface coal mines produced 1.05 million tons of coal in 1986. Much of Armco Steel's Ashland plant lies in Greenup County, including two huge blast furnaces—Amanda, once among the world's largest, and Bellefonte. Chesapeake & Ohio Railroad (now CSX Transportation) has a large railyard there and the county is served by the recently completed AA Highway, which connects Greenup with Covington. Combined agriculture receipts in 1986 were $7.2 million, including $4.2 million in crop receipts and $3 million in livestock. Burley tobacco is the main crop, with more than 1.6 million pounds produced in 1988, and the county is one of Kentucky's largest apple producers. The two largest cities in the county are FLATWOODS and RUSSELL, which adjoin one another, directly across the Ohio River from Ironton, Ohio. The county was the home of writer Jesse STUART.

Greenup County's population was 33,192 in 1970; 39,132 in 1980; and 36,742 in 1990.

See Nina M. Biggs and Mabel L. Mackoy, *History of Greenup County, Kentucky* (Evansville, Ind., 1951).

GREEN V. BIDDLE. The U.S. Supreme Court's 1821 and 1823 decisions in the case of *Green v. Biddle* are perhaps the best known of all of its constitutional rulings originating in Kentucky disputes. In two separate *Green* opinions, Associate Justices Joseph Story and Bushrod Washington pronounced Kentucky's 1812 occupying claimants statute a breach of the state's 1789 separation agreement with Virginia, and therefore a violation of the contract clause of the federal constitution. Associate Justice William Johnson spoke for many critics of *Green* when he said that the ruling doomed the state of Kentucky to an "independence beggarly and barren."

Portions of the Kentucky-Virginia agreement forever barred the passage of laws by the Kentucky General Assembly that might prevent Virginians from exercising military land warrants in military reserves, which included part of Kentucky. The 1812 statute, which was part of what Story called a "system" of law, sought to protect Kentuckians who had settled and improved Bluegrass land when others later claimed the land under Virginia laws. The act encouraged Virginians to allow settlers who had tilled land for at least seven years to purchase title in cases where the value of improvements (which Virginians in any case owed to the settlers) exceeded the actual value of the tract.

The hidden target of the Marshall Court probably was a new, unusually stringent occupant law passed by Kentucky in 1820, which virtually eliminated the possibility that absentee land claimants holding what lawyers called "bare title" (the warrant and survey only, without possession of land or a demonstrated right to possess) would be able to use, enjoy, or sell Kentucky land claims. In his 1821 ruling, Story referred indirectly to the 1820 law, implying that such statutes amounted to lawless attempts to deprive citizens of property rights. Technically, he was right, but in Kentucky and elsewhere legislators and journalists vigorously disagreed, contending that a state unable to control land titles within its borders had been deprived of an essential attribute of sovereignty.

The *Green* case began with the curious revival on the Supreme Court docket in 1819-20 of an old dispute involving Bourbon County resident Richard Biddle, a middling planter occupying forty acres of land on a larger tract claimed by the heirs of Virginia's John Green. Biddle thought his dispute with the heirs had been settled much earlier in an out-of-court arrangement in connection with two suits tried in the 7th Circuit Court for the District of Kentucky, *Green v. Gittner et al.* and *Green v. Liter et al.* In these associated equity cases, Biddle had been one of the tenants suing for compensation. Because he had not known of the *Green v. Biddle* revival before the Supreme Court, he had made no provision for a defense attorney. Henry Clay moved for reargument in 1822, but Bushrod Washington's opinion—and even Justice William Johnson's contentious, poignant concurring opinion (which historians have misread as a dissent)—made clear that further courtroom discussion would be futile.

The Green family's Kentucky land claims had been the subject of endless litigation. One of the heirs, John Green of Lincoln County, Kentucky, was the administrator for the Kentucky heirs and a leading anti-RELIEF party figure. When the suit was revived, journalists insisted that Green and another anti-Relief leader, Robert Wickliffe, had been instrumental in the suit's revival. Archival evidence suggests the accuracy of these accusations, and court records reveal that Kentucky's occupant laws were severely hampering the Green family's attempts to secure perfect title to extensive land claims in Bourbon and Fayette counties.

Whatever the origins of the revival, *Green v. Biddle* sparked an uproar in Kentucky. The General Assembly passed more than one resolution condemning the decisions; it also instructed Kentucky congressmen to begin a campaign to limit the Supreme Court's jurisdiction in cases involving the domestic affairs of states. By 1825-26, both the OLD COURT and the New Court of appeals in Kentucky were refusing to follow *Green v. Biddle*. In 1825 the Supreme Court in the case of *Elmendorf v. Taylor* quietly referred a case involving disputed land titles in Kentucky to the decision of state courts, and in 1831 the Marshall court formally reversed *Green* in the case of *Barney v. Hawkins' Lessee*.

SANDRA F. VANBURKLEO

GREENVILLE. The county seat of Muhlenberg County, Greenville is located on U.S. 62, KY 171, and KY 181. Originally settled on land donated by William Campbell, one and a half miles southeast of Caney Station in 1799, Greenville was recognized as an established town by the General Assembly on January 6, 1812. It was incorporated on February 12, 1849. Greenville was named in honor of Gen. Nathanael Greene, a Revolutionary War officer.

It immediately became the county seat. The first Muhlenberg County courthouse was completed in 1800. The log structure was replaced by a brick building in 1814. The third courthouse was completed in 1836; the fourth courthouse was raised in 1907.

Greenville was occupied by both Union and Confederate forces during the Civil War. On November 24, 1861, Confederate Gen. Nathan Bedford Forrest captured a cache of weapons and supplies stored by Union forces in the town. Confederate guerrillas also mounted attacks.

Following the hardships of the war, Greenville began to prosper. The Illinois Central Railroad (now Illinois Central Gulf), completed through Greenville in 1871, opened the region's vast coal reserves. By 1875, the Central Coal & Iron Company, headquartered in nearby Central City, operated ten mines on or near the railroad through Muhlenburg County, which enhanced Greenville's importance as a trading and transportation center. Other mining companies followed into the Greenville area, and by the early twentieth century coal was the most important industry in the region. As elsewhere, the Great Depression slowed the economy of Greenville, but World War II brought a resurgence. Timber and tobacco were and are significant commodities for Greenville.

The population of this fourth-class city was 3,875 in 1970; 4,631 in 1980; and 4,689 in 1990.

RON D. BRYANT

GREENVILLE SPRINGS. Greenville Springs in Mercer County, Kentucky, at the southern limits of Harrodsburg, was a well-known resort in the early nineteenth century. The Rev. Jesse Head, an itinerant Methodist minister, discovered the springs on Lucas Van Arsdal's property in 1806. On Head's advice, Felix Grundy, a jurist from Springfield, bought half interest in the property in the summer of 1806, and along with Van Arsdal began building a travelers' lodge. Daniel Jennings then bought Grundy's share. Greenville Springs was opened by Jennings in June 1808. Tobias Eastland, who purchased the property in 1809, added new buildings and a ballroom. Henry Palmer bought the springs in 1812 and added a gentlemen's bar and bathing houses. In 1819 Greenville Springs became the property of H. Munday and John Hanna, and in the early 1820s it was purchased by Amos Edwards and Dr. Daniel M. Heard. The proprietors claimed that the medicinal value of the springs water would "renovate both mind and body." Since the main ingredient of the water was epsom salt, it was a

somewhat effective treatment for gastritis, constipation, and certain urinary tract disorders and chronic skin ailments. Nevertheless, the operation fell into financial difficulties.

Mercer County foreclosed on the Greenville Springs property in 1826, and Christopher C. Graham, owner of the nearby HARRODSBURG SPRINGS, bought the property at public auction. Graham did not operate a spa there but in May 1830 deeded all the buildings and twenty-four acres of land at Greenville Springs to the Rev. William James for the establishment of a female seminary. The seminary closed in 1834. Another girls' school, the Greenville Institute, was started in 1841 by Samuel Mullins. In 1856, with a new brick building, Daughter's College was founded at the springs. Col. Thomas Smith bought the college in the fall of 1894, and it became known as Beaumont College. Smith operated the college until 1917, when Anne Bell Goddard bought the property and opened the Beaumont Inn there.

See Mai Van Arsdal, "The Springs at Harrodsburg," *Register* 61 (Oct. 1963): 300-328.

GREER-PETRIE, CORDIA. Cordia Greer-Petrie, novelist, was born February 12, 1872, in Merry Oaks, Barren County, Kentucky, the daughter of Newton N. and Sallie Elizabeth (Settle) Greer. The family moved to Louisville, where young Cordia received most of her education in the public schools. For six months she attended Eminence College in Kentucky, and she studied expression privately with Letitia Kempster Barnum of Chicago. Cordia Greer married Dr. Hazel G. Petrie of Fairview, Kentucky, on July 18, 1892. For the next ten years, Greer-Petrie lived in eastern Kentucky and east Tennessee, where she collected material for her books. Her husband served as physician for several coal mining companies there. They returned in 1920 to Louisville, where she lived until her death.

Greer-Petrie began her professional writing career by collaborating on a short story with Leigh Gordon Giltner, "When the Bees Got Busy." It appeared in the August 1904 issue of the *Overland Monthly*. In this story, Greer-Petrie first developed the Angeline Keaton character. In 1921 she attained immediate popularity with *Angeline at the Seelbach*, of which thirteen editions were published in the next two years. She created a series of adventures for Angeline and the other characters in her backwoods family. *Angeline Steppin' Out* and *Angeline Doin' Society*, sequels to her first Angeline book, appeared in 1922 and 1923, respectively. In the next few years, she wrote *Angeline Gets an Eyeful* (1924), *Angeline Hittin' On High* and *Angeline of the Hill Country* (1925), *Angeline Fixin' fur the Queen* (1926), *Angeline Tames her Sheik* (1928), and *Angeline Goes on a Strike* (1928). The stories bring the uneducated, plain-talking Angeline from Bear Holler into confrontation with the modern, urban world. Juxtaposing an unaffected, simple character with pretentious, complicated society,

Greer-Petrie created a style of gently mocking humor.

Greer-Petrie's books sold well through World War II, but few since have read her delightful works. She toured the country, delivering lectures and giving readings from her books, when she often appeared in costume as her heroine, Angeline. Late in life she had plans to transfer her performances to television but never realized this dream. She died July 16, 1964, and was buried at Cave Hill Cemetery, Louisville.   ANDREW VORDER BRUEGGE

GREGG, MARY (PETERSON). "Cissy" Gregg, cookbook author, was born Mary Hanson Peterson, daughter of Hanson Peterson and Mary (Jouett) Peterson, in Cynthiana, Harrison County, Kentucky, on April 26, 1903. Nicknamed Cissy by her sister, she married Edd R. Gregg in 1930. She graduated from Cynthiana High School in 1920 and the University of Kentucky in 1924 with a degree in agriculture and home economics. Her daily food column for the *Louisville Courier-Journal*, "Cissy Gregg's Cookbook and Guide to Gracious Living," first appeared in April 1942 in the newspaper's first magazine section to use color. She tied her love of cooking to the world maps that covered her kitchen walls, saying she could watch the war fronts and cook at the same time. Gregg was much in demand to judge food competitions, and she spoke extensively on the American diet, which she criticized for including too much meat, bread, and potatoes, and not enough green vegetables. She built a collection of more than seven hundred cookbooks and wrote two cookbooks herself. When Gregg retired from the *Courier-Journal* in 1963, she returned to live in Cynthiana. Gregg died on May 10, 1966, and was buried in the Battle Grove Cemetery in Cynthiana.

GREGORY, NOBLE JONES. Noble Jones Gregory, U.S. Representative, was born in Mayfield, Kentucky, on August 30, 1897, to William and Azalee (Boyd) Gregory. He attended public and private schools and graduated from Mayfield High School and Mayfield Business College. Gregory worked as a bookkeeper, cashier, and trust officer of the Mayfield First National Bank and was secretary-treasurer of the Mayfield school board. He represented the 1st District in Congress from January 3, 1937, to January 3, 1959. A Democrat, he succeeded his brother, William Voris GREGORY. Gregory ardently supported President Franklin D. Roosevelt's New Deal and generally favored labor legislation. A supporter of a multipurpose Tennessee Valley Authority dam on the lower Tennessee River, Gregory was on the podium in 1945 when President Harry S. Truman dedicated Kentucky Dam near Gilbertsville.

In 1958, Frank Albert Stubblefield of Murray defeated Gregory in the Democratic primary by a vote of 16,216 to 15,875 and won the general election. Gregory returned to Mayfield, where he engaged in banking and general investments until his

death on September 26, 1971. He was buried in Maplewood Cemetery in Mayfield. Gregory was married to Marion Hale Gregory; the couple had one daughter.   BERRY CRAIG

GREGORY, WILLIAM VORIS. William Voris Gregory, U.S. Representative, was born near Farmington in Graves County, Kentucky, on October 21, 1877, the son of William and Azalee (Boyd) Gregory. He attended public and private schools and in 1896 graduated from West Kentucky College in Mayfield. He taught school and was school superintendent in Mayfield. Gregory studied law at Cumberland University in Lebanon, Tennessee, was admitted to the bar in 1902, and began practicing in Mayfield. He was county surveyor, 1902-10; county judge, 1913-19; and U.S. attorney for the Western District of Kentucky during 1919-23. A Democrat, Gregory represented the 1st District in Congress from March 4, 1927 until his death on October 10, 1936. He was succeeded by his brother, Noble Jones GREGORY.

A member of Mayfield First Presbyterian Church, Gregory was on the board of trustees of the Louisville Presbyterian Theological Seminary from 1920 to 1927 and was its president during 1925-27. He was vice-president of the Jefferson Davis Memorial Commission, which supervised the building of the concrete obelisk at the Confederate president's birthplace in Christian County (now in Todd County).

Gregory was buried in Maplewood Cemetery in Mayfield. He married Marie Miles Gregory; they had a daughter, Elizabeth.   BERRY CRAIG

GRIFFITH, DARRELL ANTHONY. Darrell Anthony Griffith, college basketball's "Dr. Dunkinstein," was born on June 16, 1958, in Louisville, the son of Monroe and Maxine Griffith. As a youngster, he practiced with the Kentucky Colonels of the American Basketball Association. After leading Louisville's Male High School to the 1976 state basketball championship, he was named a high school All-American, and later that year Griffith entered the University of Louisville (U-of-L), the only high school player invited to the 1976 Olympic trials. Following the 1977 World University Games, he was an All-American guard at Louisville in 1979-80. Griffith led the "Doctors of Dunk" to the 1980 National Collegiate Athletic Association national championship and received the John Wooden Award as the nation's top player. He finished as the career leading scorer at U-of-L with 2,333 points. After graduating with a B.A. in mass communications, he was chosen in the first round of the National Basketball Association draft by the Utah Jazz. Following an outstanding first season, Griffith was named the NBA rookie of the year.

See Mike Embry, *Basketball in the Bluegrass State* (New York 1983).

GRIFFITH, DAVID WARK. The motion picture producer D. W. Griffith was born on January 22,

1875, on a 264-acre farm in Oldham County, Kentucky, some twenty miles from Louisville. His mother, the former Mary Oglesby, came from a prosperous Oldham County family. His father, Jacob Wark Griffith, commanded a Confederate cavalry company as part of the Kentucky Brigade throughout the Civil War. Griffith was ten years old when his father died, leaving the family in debt. In 1889 Mary Griffith moved with her children to Louisville, where she took in boarders. Griffith quit school in 1890 and worked as a clerk until 1896, when he signed on as an actor with a touring stock company. For the next ten years, Griffith had only very modest success as an actor. He moved from Louisville in 1899, living first in New York City and then in San Francisco, where he met Linda Arvidson Johnson, an actress whom he married on May 14, 1906.

Griffith and his wife settled in New York City, where he completed writing the play *The Fool and the Girl*, which closed after a brief run. To tide him over while he pursued his career as a playwright, Griffith sought employment in the fledgling motion picture industry. His first role as a film actor was in the Edison Company's *Rescued from the Eagle's Nest* (1908). Soon after, he was hired by the Biograph Company, where acting led to work as a writer of scenarios and then as a director, beginning with *The Adventures of Dolly*, released in July 1908. Griffith's tenure at Biograph from 1908 to 1913 was extraordinary; working with soon-to-be-famous performers like Mary Pickford and Lillian Gish, Griffith directed more than 450 short films, specializing in melodramas, literary adaptations, historical dramas, and films about contemporary social problems. More important, Griffith contributed much to the development of film as a narrative art through his ability to orchestrate actors, sets, camera movement, and lighting in the staging of individual scenes. Through his experiments with editing, he greatly refined the techniques of closeups, for example, and suspenseful cross-cutting. Griffith also made films of unusual length, and the culmination of his career at Biograph was the four-reel *Judith of Bethulia* (1913), a biblical-era spectacle.

The following year Griffith left Biograph and began work on his most famous film, *The Birth of a Nation* (1915). Based on Thomas Dixon's *The Clansman*, a novel glorifying the heroic exploits of the Ku Klux Klan during Reconstruction, the twelve-reel *Birth* cost more than $100,000 to produce. It epitomizes Griffith's technical virtuosity as well as his preoccupation with the melodramatic struggle between good and evil. *Birth* also perpetuates the worst nineteenth century racist stereotypes, and at the time of its initial release was the subject of vigorous protest by the National Association for the Advancement of Colored People (NAACP). This controversy, however, only added to its box office revenues, which are estimated to have been at least $60 million.

Buoyed by the success of *Birth*, Griffith began an even more ambitious epic, *Intolerance* (1916), which combines stories from four historical periods. For all its spectacular sets and lavish attention to detail, *Intolerance* did not fare as well as *Birth*, nor did any of the subsequent twenty-six films Griffith directed between 1917 and 1931, although several of these films are noteworthy, especially *Broken Blossoms* (1919), *Way Down East* (1920), *Orphans of the Storm* (1921), and *America* (1924). In 1919 Griffith formed the United Artists company with the three major stars of American film, Charlie Chaplin, Douglas Fairbanks, and Mary Pickford. He also invested (and lost) much of his personal fortune in building his own studio in Mamaroneck, New York. After the motion picture industry adopted sound in the late 1920s, Griffith produced only two talkies, *Abraham Lincoln* (1930) and *The Struggle* (1931). The failure of *The Struggle* for all purposes ended Griffith's career in the movies, though he continued to write and to plan various projects.

Griffith retained an attachment to his Kentucky roots, and during the later 1930s he spent much of his time in his home state. Griffith died on July 23, 1948, and was buried at Mt. Tabor Christian Church in Oldham County, where he had worshipped as a child.

See Richard Schickel, *D.W. Griffith: An American Life* (New York 1984); Robert M. Henderson, *D.W. Griffith: His Life and Work* (New York 1972).
                                         GREGORY A. WALLER

GRIMES, JOHN C. John C. Grimes, portrait artist, was born in Lexington, Kentucky, in 1799. His mother is thought to have been Mary Sourbray (Sourbright), whose family moved to Lexington from Pennsylvania at some point after 1790. A number of the Grimes families from Maryland, North Carolina, Pennsylvania, and Virginia lived in central Kentucky at that time. Grimes's will mentions aunts named Sowbray in Dayton, Ohio, and a half-brother, Edward Coleman. Grimes was apprenticed as a boy to the oil and paint supply firm of Thomas Grant on Mechanics Alley in Lexington. The boy lived with the Grant family and began to study painting with Matthew Harris JOUETT.

In 1820 Grimes was painting portraits in Huntsville, Alabama. In 1824 he assisted Jouett in painting "The Three Marys," after Carracci, which hangs now at the Cathedral of the Assumption in Louisville. Among the prominent figures whose portraits were painted by Grimes were Chief Justice John Marshall, the Marquis de Lafayette, James Ware Parrish, Gen. and Mrs. Elijah M. Covington, and Judge Abney McLean, a member of Congress from Greenville, Kentucky. His portrait of Mrs. Washington Barrow is owned by the J.B. Speed Art Museum in Louisville.

Grimes lived in Philadelphia during 1825-27, returned briefly to Kentucky in 1828, and in the 1830s worked in Nashville. He died at the home of Mrs. Thomas Grant in Lexington on December 27, 1837, and is buried in the Grant family plot in the old Episcopal Cemetery on Third Street.

See Edna T. Whitley, *Kentucky Ante-Bellum Portraiture* (Paris, Ky., 1956); Samuel Woodson Price, *The Old Masters of the Bluegrass* (Louisville, 1902).

GRUNDY, FELIX. Felix Grundy, lawyer, member of Congress, and U.S. attorney general, was born on Back Creek, Berkeley County, in what is now West Virginia, on September 11, 1777, the son of George and Elizabeth (Beckham) Grundy. Shortly afterward the family moved to Brownstown, Pennsylvania, and in 1780 to Bardstown, Kentucky, where Felix saw Indians kill three of his six older brothers. He attended James Priestley's academy at Bardstown and studied law under George Nicholas. In 1797 he was admitted to the Kentucky bar. In 1799 Grundy was a member of the convention to revise the state constitution, and from 1802 to 1805, he served in the Kentucky General Assembly. He led the battle for circuit court legislation that was a triumph for backwoods democracy, and he waged a fight against the Kentucky Insurance Company that forced it to give up its insurance monopoly. In 1806 Grundy became a judge of the Kentucky Court of Appeals and in 1807 its chief justice. The following year he moved to Davidson County, Tennessee.

In Tennessee, Grundy quickly gained fame as the most skillful criminal lawyer in the Southwest. He was elected to the U.S. House of Representatives in 1811 and 1813 and was conspicuous among the so-called War Hawks, who clamored for the War of 1812 against England. He resigned his seat in 1814. He represented Davidson County from 1819 to 1825 in the Tennessee legislature, which made him a member of a joint commission for establishing the boundary between Tennessee and Kentucky. Grundy ran for Congress again in 1827, with the support of Andrew Jackson, but he lost to John Bell. Two years later he was elected to the U.S. Senate, where he usually supported the policies of President Andrew Jackson, though not always with enthusiasm; he served from October 19, 1829, to July 4, 1838, when he resigned to become attorney general in President Martin Van Buren's cabinet. He resigned his cabinet post on December 14, 1839, and was reelected to the Senate the same day. As a senator, Grundy generally opposed Henry Clay's American System, including the protective tariff and the Bank of the United States.

Grundy and his wife, Ann Phillips Rogers, were the parents of eight children. He died on December 19, 1840, and was buried in Mt. Olivet Cemetery in Nashville, Tennessee.

See Joseph H. Parks, *Felix Grundy, Champion of Democracy* (Baton Rouge, La., 1940); Bernard Mayo, *Henry Clay, Spokesman of the New West* (New York 1937).   OTIS K. RICE

GUERRANT, EDWARD OWINGS. Edward Owings Guerrant, Presbyterian minister, was born in Sharpsburg, Kentucky, on February 28, 1838, to Henry and Marcy (Beaufort) Guerrant, pious Presbyterians of Huguenot heritage. He graduated from Centre College at Danville in 1860, planning to be a minister. When the Civil War intervened, Guerrant joined the Confederacy's Kentucky-based Morgan Raiders, becoming an officer. In 1873, after studying medicine and serving as a physician in Mt. Sterling, Guerrant attended Union Theological Seminary in Virginia and became a Presbyterian minister.

In 1881 Guerrant resigned as pastor of the First Presbyterian Church in Louisville to become the first synod evangelist for eastern Kentucky. He enlisted others, such as "Uncle" Joe Hopper, an elder from Perryville, and began to hold revivals, health clinics, and organizational meetings to establish Presbyterian congregations in the mountains. In 1885 Guerrant left full-time evangelism to serve the Troy and Wilmore churches. In 1908 he founded the Highland Institute in Breathitt County, which included a church, an orphanage, and a hospital. Guerrant wrote *Bloody Breathitt* (1890), *Forty Years Among the Highlanders* (1905), *The Galax Gathering* (1910), and *The Gospel of the Lilies* (1912).

In 1897 Guerrant founded an ecumenical evangelistic effort that encompassed many Presbyterian programs. Guerrant married Mary Jane DeVault of Leesburg, Tennessee, on May 12, 1868. He died on November 27, 1916, and was buried in the Lexington Cemetery.

See J. Gray McAllister and Grace Guerrant, *Edward O. Guerrant: Apostle to the Southern Highlands* (Richmond, Va., 1950).   LOUIS WEEKS

GULLETT, DONALD EDWARD. Donald (Don) Edward Gullett, professional baseball player, was born to Buford and Lettie (Brown) Gullett on January 5, 1951, in Lynn, Kentucky. A basketball, baseball, and football star at McKell High School in South Shore, he scored seventy-two points in one football game. He was the first-round selection of the Cincinnati Reds in the 1969 baseball draft, and after just one minor-league season, he joined the Reds in time to be part of the 1970 team, which won the National League championship. He pitched nine years in the major leagues—1970-76 with the Reds and 1977-78 with the New York Yankees, of the American League. He compiled a 109-50 record and a career earned-run average of 3.11, 266 games, 186 starts, 44 complete games, and 1,390 innings pitched. He allowed 1,205 hits and 501 walks, and he recorded 921 strikeouts and 14 shutouts. He was the best pitcher of the 1975 and 1976 world champion Reds. In 1977 he signed a six-year, $2 million free-agent contract with the Yankees. After an injury to his shoulder, he retired in 1978.

Gullett returned to Lynn and turned his attention to farming until 1990, when the Reds made him pitching coach for the Chattanooga Lookouts, the Reds' AA minor-league team. In 1991 he became the pitching coach for the Cincinnati Reds.

In 1970 Gullett married Kathy Holcomb of Lynn; they have three children, Donald, Jr., Tracey, and Angela.

GUNNING, SARAH (GARLAND) OGAN. The daughter of Elizabeth (Lucas) and Oliver Perry Garland, folk singer Sarah (Garland) Ogan Gunning was born in Bell County, Kentucky, in 1910, one of fifteen children in a singing family including a brother, Jim Garland, and a half-sister, Aunt Molly JACKSON. Sarah Garland married Andrew Ogan, a coal miner, and became involved in labor union organizing in the 1930s. She wrote "Down on the Picket Line" and "Come All Ye Coal Miners" in support of the National Miners Union. After her husband died, Sarah moved to New York City in the late 1930s. There she sang with Woody Guthrie, Pete Seeger, and other folk musicians. She later married Joe Gunning and moved to Michigan. She played a part in the folksong revival of the 1960s by combining powerful lyrics about contemporary issues with traditional Appalachian music and style. She died in Knoxville, Tennessee, on November 14, 1983, and was buried in Hart, Michigan.

See Mimi Pickering, *Dreadful Memories: The Life of Sarah Ogan Gunning* (Appalshop Film, 1988).   JUDI JENNINGS

GUNSMITHS. The product of the gunsmith was vital on the frontier for both food and self-defense. The better-known early American gunsmiths were Pennsylvanians of German or Swiss extraction. Gunsmiths on the Kentucky frontier probably came from Pennsylvania or learned their trade from some of the many craftsmen there. It was these artisans who transformed the German Jäger rifle into the Kentucky rifle, or Pennsylvania rifle, as it is sometimes called.

Gunsmiths, some of early Kentucky's most skilled artisans, worked with at least three different materials—wood, iron, and brass. As the elaborately engraved patch boxes and decorative silver inlays of rifles attest, some gunsmiths' skills rivaled those of the finest silversmith. By 1785, most American arms makers could buy European-made smooth-bore barrels and mass-produced locks, but the artisan's skill was still essential to finish a quality rifle. The smith rifled the barrel, carved the stock, and precisely fit the lock to keep the gun from misfiring.

Kentucky's first gunsmith was probably Squire Boone, who learned the art from his cousin, Samuel Boone, at his gunshop in Maryland from 1759 until 1764. However, it is doubtful that Boone carried gunsmithing tools during his early travels into Kentucky with his brother, Daniel. The first gunsmiths to set up shop in Kentucky probably arrived after the establishment of permanent settlements in the state in the 1770s. Some records indicate that Jacob Hawken, who designed the well-known Plains rifle, or Hawken rifle, was making his guns in Louisville around 1822.

After Eli Whitney perfected his system for mass-producing interchangeable parts for muskets in 1806, large firms such as Winchester (1857) and Marlin (1870) began manufacturing the firearms. Most gunsmiths stopped making unique firearms routinely and turned to maintenance work using factory-made parts. The custom handmade rifle became too expensive for the typical Kentuckian.

See Joe Kindig, Jr., *Thoughts On The Kentucky Rifle in Its Golden Age* (York, Pa., 1960); Henry J. Kauffman, *The Pennsylvania-Kentucky Rifle* (Harrisburg, Pa., 1960).   THOMAS J. KIFFMEYER

GUTHRIE, ALFRED BERTRAM, JR. Alfred Bertram ("Bud") Guthrie, Jr., journalist and novelist, was born January 13, 1901, in Bedford, Indiana, the son of Alfred and June (Thomas) Guthrie. Soon thereafter the family moved to Choteau, Montana, where his father taught school. Guthrie grew up on the Montana frontier, where memories of Indians, the Lewis and Clark expedition, and cowboys were still vivid. He graduated from Choteau High School, attended the University of Washington for one year, then completed work for a bachelor of arts degree from the University of Montana in 1923. After three years in upstate New York, he moved to Kentucky as a reporter for the *Lexington Leader*. He became city editor of the *Leader* (1929-45), then executive editor until 1947. Guthrie was highly respected for his editorial talents, and as a newspaperman he perhaps was a more successful teacher of journalism than most university professors of the subject. As an editorial writer and interpreter of Kentucky public affairs, he exerted real influence.

At heart, Guthrie was from his earliest newspaper years a novelist yearning to write about his beloved West. An opportunity to do so came his way when he was appointed a Nieman Fellow (1947-48) at Harvard University. At the outset he planned a series of five novels to cover the West from the era of the Rocky Mountain fur trappers and scouts to final settlement. The first in the series was *The Big Sky* (1947), followed by *The Way West* (1949), which won the Pulitzer Prize for distinguished fiction; *These Thousand Hills* (1956); *The Last Valley* (1975); and *Fair Land, Fair Land* (1982). His autobiographical work, *The Blue Hen's Chick* (1965), deals with his years in Kentucky.

Guthrie is noted for his influence on Kentucky newspaper and history writing. He was an exceptionally talented reporter, editorial writer, and teacher of creative writing at the University of Kentucky (1947-52). Late in his life, he lived in Montana and was active as an author and crusader for the preservation of western fauna and environment. His books have received almost extravagant critical appraisal, and Guthrie was honored with doctorates by several universities. His awards and public citations include governors' medallions from Kentucky and Montana.

Guthrie married his childhood sweetheart, Harriett Larson, in 1931. She was the daughter of Tom

Larson, a prominent rancher and Montana politician; they had two children, Alfred Bertram III and Helen Larson. After her death, Guthrie married Carol Luthian in 1969. Guthrie died in Bismarck, North Dakota, on April 26, 1991, and was buried in Chateau, Montana.   THOMAS D. CLARK

GUTHRIE, JAMES. James Guthrie, U.S. senator and secretary of the treasury, was born on December 5, 1792, in Nelson County near Bardstown, Kentucky, to Adam and Hannah (Polk) Guthrie. He attended a log schoolhouse and completed the course of study at McAlister's Academy in Bardstown. He spent several years in the river flatboat trade with New Orleans, then read law under Judge John Rowan, a prominent Kentucky attorney. In 1817 Guthrie was admitted to the Kentucky bar, and when Governor John Adair appointed him commonwealth's attorney in 1820, he moved to Louisville. Guthrie, a Jacksonian Democrat, served in the Kentucky House of Representatives from 1827 to 1830 and in the Kentucky Senate from 1831 to 1840. In 1849 he presided over the Kentucky constitutional convention. President Franklin Pierce appointed Guthrie secretary of the Treasury in 1853. When Pierce's term ended in 1857, Guthrie returned to Louisville as vice-president of the Louisville & Nashville Railroad. He served as L&N president from 1860 until 1868.

Guthrie led the National Peace Conference, which met in Washington, D.C., in February 1861, in a last-ditch effort to save the Union. At age 70, he held the conference together and hammered out a viable compromise, although Congress did not enact the proposals. His feelings were strong: "I hate that word secession, because it is a cheat! Call things by their right names! The Southern States have . . . originated a revolution." As president of the L&N, Guthrie encouraged Gen. William T. Sherman's takeover of the railroad. Elected to the U.S. Senate in 1865, Guthrie served from March 4, 1865, until February 7, 1868, when he resigned in ill health and returned to Louisville. Guthrie died on March 13, 1869, in Louisville and was buried in Cave Hill Cemetery there. Guthrie married Elizabeth Prather in 1821; they had three daughters: Mary Elizabeth, Anna Augusta, and Sarah Julia.

CHARLES J. BUSSEY

H

HADLEY, MARY ALICE (HALE). Mary Alice (Hale) Hadley, potter, was born in Terre Haute, Indiana, on May 15, 1911, to Frank R. and Hattie Alice Hale. She attended Indiana public schools and Indiana State University in Terre Haute, and graduated from Depauw College at Greencastle, Indiana, in 1933. At Depauw she met George Hadley, whom she married in 1930. In 1935, when the Hadleys were living in New York City, she took art classes at Columbia University. In 1939, after the Hadleys moved to Louisville, Mary Alice was given a boat, and unable to find dinnerware suitable for boating on the river, she decided to make her own. Friends in New York City and Chicago, impressed by Hadley's work, showed it to others, and orders began to arrive at her home for mugs, plates, and platters. The earthenware pieces were hand painted with cartoons of pigs, chickens, horses, farmers, or sheep, before being glazed, mostly in shades of blue and green. Hadley created a children's pottery series and also did custom designs.

Hadley's first commercial outlet was a gift shop, for which she filled special orders personally. In 1945 Hadley Pottery opened in an old factory on Story Avenue in Louisville. Mary Alice Hadley died on December 26, 1965, in Louisville and was cremated. George Hadley died on January 4, 1991. Hadley Pottery continues to operate.

See Grady Clay, Jr., "Made in Louisville," and Marion Porter, "Charm from Clay," *Louisville Courier-Journal Magazine*, Oct. 8, 1950.

HAGAN, CLIFFORD OLDHAM. Clifford Oldham Hagan, basketball player and athletic administrator, was the son of Wilbur and Mable (Ashley) Hagan, born on December 9, 1931, in Owensboro, Kentucky. The six-foot, four-inch center led the University of Kentucky (UK) to eighty-six wins, five losses during 1950-54. Kentucky's Wildcats won the National Collegiate Athletic Association (NCAA) championship in 1951. Hagan was an All-American in 1952 and again in 1954 (Kentucky, on probabtion, played no basketball games in 1953). He earned a B.S. in physical education. After serving as an officer in the U.S. Air Force during 1954-56, Hagan joined the St. Louis Hawks of the National Basketball Association, where he played during 1956-66 and was named All-Pro six times, 1957-62. He earned an M.S. in education from Washington University in 1958 and joined the Dallas Chapparals in 1967.

When he retired in 1970, Hagan returned to Lexington, Kentucky, where he started a restaurant chain, Cliff Hagan's Ribeye. In 1972 Hagan became assistant athletics director at the University of Kentucky and succeeded Harry Lancaster as director in 1975. During his tenure he upgraded UK's athletic facilities, including a new football stadium, an aquatics center, and an indoor tennis center, and the men's basketball team won the national championship in 1978. Hagan resigned as athletics director on November 15, 1988, in the wake of NCAA investigations into recruiting violations and academic fraud by the basketball program.

Hagan married Martha Milton of Owensboro in 1954; they have four children, Lisa, Laurie, Amy, and Cliff, Jr.

See Bert Nelli, *The Winning Tradition* (Lexington, Ky., 1984).

HAGER, SAMUEL E. Samuel E. Hager, Methodist missionary to Japan, was born October 1, 1869, in Jackson, Kentucky, to James H. and Elmira (Combs) Hager. Hager attended the Jackson public school until the fall of 1882, when the Rev. John Jay Dickey established Jackson Academy, an elementary and high school. Hager graduated in May 1885 and by July had obtained a Kentucky teacher's certificate. From July to November 1885, Hager taught at the Leatherwood School on Lost Creek in Breathitt County. In 1886 Hager entered Central College in Fayette, Missouri, to be near his father, then a Methodist minister in Franklin, Missouri. In February 1887 he registered at Kentucky Wesleyan College in Millersburg.

In January 1888, Hager was ordained as a minister by the Methodist Episcopal Church, South, and that summer he accompanied R.W. Landrum, a mountain circuit rider, on a preaching tour of the state. Hager graduated from Kentucky Wesleyan in 1890 with a B.A. and later received a master's degree there. From 1890 to 1893, he was a theology student at Vanderbilt University in Tennessee. In 1893 Hager went as a missionary to Japan. Hager stayed in Japan for forty-seven years. He helped to establish the Japan Methodist Church and served as principal and member of the board of directors of the Kwansei Gakuin High School and College. Hager retired on September 1, 1940.

Hager married Georgie Anna Dashiell, daughter of William G. Dashiell of Nashville, Tennessee, on June 15, 1893. Hager died in 1950.

See Sam H. Frank, "Samuel E. Hager: Kentucky Missionary to Japan," *Register* 58 (July 1960): 194-223.

HAGGIN, JAMES BEN ALI. James Ben Ali Haggin, horseman, was born in Harrodsburg, Kentucky, on December 9, 1821. He was the eldest of eight children of Terah Temple and Adeline (Ben Ali) Haggin, the daughter of a Turkish army officer. After graduating from Centre College in Danville, he began practicing law. In 1846 he married Eliza Jane Sanders; they had two sons and three daughters. In 1851 he went to practice law in Sacramento, California, making a fortune in the aftermath of the gold rush. Haggin acquired one hundred gold, silver, and copper mines in several states, Mexico, and South America. He was a multi-millionaire by 1880. On his California stud farm, Rancho del Paso, near Fresno, he had nearly 2,000 thoroughbreds, the best of which he had obtained from Kentucky.

In 1897 he married Margaret ("Pearl") Voorhies of Versailles, Kentucky, the beautiful young niece of his deceased wife. In the same year, he bought Elmendorf farm in the Bluegrass horse country and began construction of a palatial mansion for his bride. In later years he added nearly 8,000 acres to the original 544. He sold his California ranch in 1905 to concentrate on his Kentucky farm. Haggin died September 12, 1914, at his Newport, Rhode Island, residence and was buried in Woodlawn Cemetery in New York.

See William H.P. Robertson, *The History of Thoroughbred Racing in America* (New York 1964).

MARY E. WHARTON

HALDEMAN, WALTER NEWMAN. Walter Newman Haldeman, the founder of the *Louisville Courier*, the *Louisville* COURIER-JOURNAL, and the *Louisville Times*, was the son of John and Elizabeth (Newman) Haldeman, born April 27, 1821, in Maysville, Kentucky. He started his career in 1840 as a clerk in the business office of the *Louisville Journal*, one of the leading Whig newspapers in what was then the West. He left after three years to go into business for himself, opening a bookstore with a $300 loan from an aunt. Within months Haldeman took over a fledgling newspaper, the *Daily Dime*, after its owners defaulted on credit for printing supplies and for the out-of-town newspapers and magazines that were their chief sources of news. With Haldeman as publisher, the newspaper prospered to the point that after only four months he invested in new type, increased the paper's physical size and, at advertisers' request, changed its name to the *Louisville Courier*. At first the newspaper was moderately Whig in political orientation, although it attempted to attract readers of all political viewpoints by emphasizing news. The editorial philosophy of the *Courier* shifted wildly, as Haldeman's own views lurched from Whig to nativist to abolitionist and eventually to Southern Democrat and radical pro-slavery spokesman.

When the Civil War started, the *Courier* expressed strong sympathy for the Confederacy, which prompted Union troops to seize the newspaper's office and seek Haldeman's arrest as soon as Kentucky abandoned its neutrality, in September 1861. Fleeing to Nashville, he established a *Courier* in exile that was distributed to Confederate troops and to Confederate-held parts of Kentucky. Publication ceased when Confederate forces withdrew from Nashville in February 1862. Haldeman eventually settled in Madison, Georgia, where he and his family sat out the war as refugees. When the war ended, Haldeman returned with a hero's welcome to a Louisville that had developed Confederate sympathies during four years of Union military occupation. With the help of friends, he reestablished the *Courier*, which quickly eclipsed the other surviving Louisville dailies in circulation.

In 1868 Haldeman bought out the competing *Louisville Journal* and *Louisville Democrat* and merged the staffs of the *Courier* and *Journal* under the *Journal*'s editor, Henry WATTERSON. Watterson, who remained editor of the *Courier-Journal* for fifty years, became a nationally recognized spokesman for the South in his editorial columns. Haldeman concentrated on the business side of the newspaper and on community interests. When baseball's National League was being organized in late 1875, the businessmen behind Louisville's entry into the league gave the Louisville club presidency to Haldeman to lend credibility to the enterprise. The club disbanded after just two seasons, however, when Haldeman's son John discovered that several players had accepted bribes from gamblers.

Haldeman founded the *Louisville Times* in 1884 as an afternoon counterpart to the *Courier-Journal*. In the late 1880s, Haldeman and several associates developed the town of Naples, Florida, as their vacation resort. He was twice a key player in presidential campaigns: in 1876, when he and other publishers facilitated a compromise on the disputed Tilden-Hayes tally, and in 1896, when the *Courier-Journal* first bolted the Democratic party and supported a third-party ticket. Haldeman kept control of his newspaper company until his death at the age of 81. He was struck by a streetcar while on his way to the office on Saturday morning, May 10, 1902, and he died three days later, leaving an estate valued at more than $1 million, most of it in the stock of his newspapers. He was buried in Louisville's Cave Hill Cemetery.

Haldeman married Elizabeth Metcalfe in October 1844, and they had five children.

DENNIS CUSICK

HALE, HENRY STEPHENSON. Henry Stephenson Hale, state senator, was born near Bowling Green, Kentucky, on May 4, 1836, to Nicholas and Rhoda (Crouch) Hale. After his parents' deaths, he moved to Graves County, Kentucky. A Confederate officer during the Civil War, he was made lieutenant colonel in 1865. Elected to the state Senate in 1871, he introduced a model local option law. He was appointed state treasurer in 1890 by Gov. Simon Buckner (1887-91) and was elected to that office for the 1892-96 term. As treasurer, he instituted a requirement, later made law, that banks pay interest on state deposits. He married Virginia Adelaide Gregory on November 8, 1865; they had seven children. He died July 24, 1922, and was buried in Maplewood Cemetery in Mayfield.

LON C. BARTON

HALE V. KENTUCKY. The U.S. Supreme Court decision in the case of *Hale v. Kentucky* (1938) held that blacks had been denied their constitutional rights to representation on a jury. The defendant in the case, Joe Hale, a nineteen-year-old black, was convicted in 1936 of murdering a white who was "stopping colored women and asking them to get in his car." The jury in the case, selected from a pool that contained no blacks, convicted Hale, and he was sentenced to die in the electric chair. When the Kentucky court of appeals in May 1937 denied Hale's request for a reversal, the National Association for the Advancement of Colored People took the case to the U.S. Supreme Court. The appeal showed that no blacks had served on state juries in McCracken County, where Hale was convicted, during 1906-36 although blacks had been represented on federal juries in Paducah in McCracken County during the same period. The Supreme Court held that this violated equal protection under the laws guaranteed under the Fourteenth Amendment to the Constitution and ordered a new trial. Hale appeared in circuit court in Paducah on April 25, 1939, was allowed to plead guilty to a lesser charge, and was sentenced to life imprisonment. He was paroled in 1947.

JOHN E. L. ROBERTSON

HALL, EULA (RILEY). Born on October 29, 1927, in Pike County, Kentucky, to Lee and Nannie (Keen) Riley, Eula (Riley) Hall is a political activist and community action advocate. In the 1960s she put union-style organizing techniques to work to make state welfare administrators and county school boards more responsive to the needs of the people in eastern Kentucky. A member of the Eastern Kentucky Welfare Rights Organization, she picketed the Floyd County school board office to obtain free and reduced-price lunches for deserving children. She founded the Mud Creek Clinic at Grethel, Kentucky, to provide better health care for the indigent, and is a member of numerous eastern Kentucky advocacy groups, including the Floyd County Save Our Kentucky, Big Sandy Community Action, and the Betsy Lane Senior Citizens organizations. A popular speaker, Hall was inducted into the Kentucky Women Hall of Fame in Central City in 1987. Twice married, she has five children: Randy, Troy, Nanetta, Danny, and Dean.

CAROL CROWE-CARRACO

HALL, JOE BEASMAN. Joe Beasman Hall, basketball coach, the son of Charles and Ruth (Harvey) Hall, was born on November 30, 1928, in Cynthiana, Kentucky. He played football and basketball at Cynthiana High School and attended the University of Kentucky (UK), 1947-49, on a basketball scholarship. After his sophomore season, Hall transferred to the University of the South at Sewanee, Tennessee. He earned a B.S. at UK in 1955. He was football, baseball, and basketball coach at Shepherdsville (Kentucky) High School from 1956 to 1958. At Regis College in Denver, Colorado, where he was athletics director and baseball and basketball coach, he posted a basketball record of fifty-seven wins and fifty losses. During 1958-64 he earned an M.A. from Colorado State University in Fort Collins.

After spending 1964 and 1965 as head basketball coach at Central Missouri State University in Warrensburg, Hall returned to UK as an assistant coach in charge of recruiting. In 1972 he succeeded Adolph Rupp as head basketball coach. In his thirteen-

year stint at Kentucky, Hall led the Wildcats to eight Southeastern Conference (SEC) titles, one national championship (1978), and a total of 297 wins and 100 losses. He was named SEC coach of the year in 1973, 1975, 1978, and 1983 and posted a career mark of 373-154.

Hall retired following the 1984-85 season and became vice president of correspondent banking at Central Bank in Lexington, Kentucky. He also worked as a commentator for ABC television and as a public relations representative for Converse Shoe Company, conducting basketball clinics. He enjoys hunting and fishing and owns Tuck A Way, a 160-acre thoroughbred horse farm in Harrison County. Hall married Katharine Dennis on October 27, 1951; they have three children, Judy, Katharine, and Steve.

See Russell Rice, *Joe B. Hall: My Old Kentucky Home* (Huntsville, Ala., 1981).

HALL, TOM T. Tom T. Hall, songwriter and recording artist, was born on May 25, 1936, in Olive Hill, Kentucky, the son of Virgil and Dell Hall. He learned to play the guitar at age four and wrote his first musical composition when he was nine. His early start in radio broadcasting and performing at WMOR in Morehead, Kentucky, was interrupted when Hall joined the U.S. Army. After discharge from the army, he established himself as one of the most successful songwriters in the music industry and began a parallel career in recording and performing. "Harper Valley PTA," which he wrote, sold 6 million records. For his numerous musical hits, Hall received a Grammy and forty-six BMI awards, and he was elected to the Nashville Songwriters Association Hall of Fame in 1978. His best-known country hits include "Old Dogs, Children and Watermelon Wine," "Country Is," "Sneaky Snake," and "The Ballad of Forty Dollars." Successful also as an author, Hall has six books to his credit, including *The Songwriter's Handbook* (1976) and *The Storyteller's Nashville* (1979), an autobiography.   JOHN R. DUNCAN

HALY, WILLIAM PURCELL DENNIS. The preeminent political organizer of his day, William Purcell Dennis ("Percy") Haly was born in Frankfort, Kentucky, in 1874 to Irish immigrant parents, Dennis L. and Jane (Purcell) Haly. In the 1890s he became a close friend and confidant of William Goebel, and was a principal strategist in his quest for the governorship in 1899. Following Goebel's assassination in 1900, Haly allied himself with J.C.W. Beckham, who succeeded Goebel as governor. One of Beckham's first acts as chief executive was to appoint Haly adjutant general. Haly relished using the title "General" throughout his life.

During the first two decades of the twentieth century, Haly built a powerful machine that often dominated state Democratic politics. It was largely through Haly's organizational genius that Beckham won the governorship in 1900, reelection in 1903, and a seat in the U.S. Senate in 1914. Haly also engineered the return of the aging James B.

McCreary to the governorship in 1911. Haly was vilified as a political boss by his opponents, most notably A.O. Stanley, who accused Haly—and Beckham—of using the prohibition issue for partisan gain. Haly drafted campaign platforms and counseled others on how to win and retain office, yet Haly himself did not seek elective office. Some observers believed he held back out of fear that as a Roman Catholic he could not be elected. Others insisted that Haly preferred the art of politics to the reality of governance.

In January 1937, at the request of the mayor, Haly worked around the clock for ten days directing flood relief efforts in Louisville. He developed pneumonia and died in Louisville on February 16, 1937. He was buried in the Frankfort Cemetery.

See Thomas H. Appleton, Jr., " 'Like Banquo's Ghost': The Emergence of the Prohibition Issue in Kentucky Politics," Ph.D. dissertation, University of Kentucky, 1981.

THOMAS H. APPLETON, JR.

HAMILTON, HOLMAN. Holman Hamilton, journalist, historian, and educator, was born in Fort Wayne, Indiana, on May 30, 1910, the son of Allen and Helen (Knight) Hamilton. Educated at Williams College in Massachusetts, he began reporting for the *Fort Wayne Journal-Gazette* in 1932. While still a reporter, he wrote the two-volume *Zachary Taylor* (1941, 1951), a highly acclaimed biography of the president. In World War II he served as an army major. In 1951 Hamilton left journalism and enrolled in graduate study in history at the University of Kentucky. He was awarded a Ph.D. in 1954 and taught at the University of Kentucky until 1975. Hamilton was known for his eloquent lecturing style, and won the outstanding teacher award. He wrote *Prologue to Conflict* (1964) and *Three Kentucky Presidents* (1978). In 1979 Hamilton was president of the Southern Historical Association. He married Suzanne Bowerfind; they had a daughter, Susan. He died June 7, 1980, in Lexington and was buried in the Lexington Cemetery.

See James A. Ramage, "Holman Hamilton: A Transcendent Career in Journalism and History," *FCHQ* 60 (July 1986): 347-72.

JAMES A. RAMAGE

HAMILTON, STEVE ABSHER. The only athlete known to have played in the National Collegiate Athletic Association (NCAA) basketball tournament, the National Basketball Association (NBA) championship, and baseball's World Series, Steve Absher Hamilton was born on November 30, 1934, to James and Ruby (Absher) Hamilton in Columbia, Kentucky. He graduated from Charlestown High School in Indiana in 1952; received a B.A. in 1958 from Kentucky's Morehead State University (MSU), where he lettered in basketball, baseball, and track in all four years; and earned an M.A. there in 1963.

At six feet, seven inches, Hamilton played at the center and forward positions in basketball. At Morehead he set five rebounding records and is the school's fourth top scorer, with 1,829 points. In 1956, after winning the Ohio Valley Conference (OVC) Championship, Hamilton's Morehead basketball team played in the NCAA tournament, reaching the quarter finals. He was All-OVC in 1954-55 and 1957-58, and All-American in 1957. In 1985 he was inducted into the MSU Hall of Fame and was selected the outstanding Kentucky-Indiana senior basketball player by WHAS radio and television in Louisville. Hamilton was the No. 2 draft selection of the Minneapolis Lakers, an NBA basketball team (now the NBA's Los Angeles Lakers), and played for them in 1958-59 and 1959-60. Along with Elgin Baylor, Hamilton was on the 1959-60 Lakers team that lost the NBA Championship series to the Boston Celtics.

Hamilton played a total of twelve years for five professional baseball teams: the American League's Cleveland Indians, 1961; the Washington Senators, 1962-63; the New York Yankees, 1963-70, pitching in the 1963-64 World Series; the Chicago White Sox, 1970; the National League's San Francisco Giants, 1971, pitching in the National League Playoffs. During his professional baseball career, he played in 421 games, won forty and lost thirty-one, and developed the "folly floater," a deceptive slow, high pitch. In 1973 Hamilton was a scout for the Yankees and manager of their Johnson City, Tennessee, team. In 1975 he was pitching coach for the Detroit Tigers. He was player representative for the Senators in 1963, the Yankees in 1965-70, and the American League during 1967-70, acting as treasurer of the Players Representative Association, and a member of the Players Relations Council and the Executive Council.

Hamilton coached baseball at MSU during 1976-89, won two OVC championships, played in the NCAA tournament twice, and was six times the OVC coach of the year. He became the school's athletic director in 1988.

He married Shirley Potter on June 13, 1956, and they have four children: Stephanie, Elizabeth, Robert, and Daniel.

See Studs Turkel, *Working* (New York 1972).

JOHN COLLIS

HAMILTON COLLEGE. Originally established as the Hocker Female College by James Hocker in 1869, the four-story Italianate structure was located on North Broadway, just north of Fourth Street in Lexington, Kentucky. In recognition of William Hamilton, who made a large donation in 1878, the school was renamed Hamilton Female College. In 1889 Kentucky University (now Transylvania University) became a major stockholder of the school and in 1903 assumed complete charge of it. Under the leadership of President Burris Jenkins, Hamilton College was converted into a two-year junior college, the first in Kentucky. Women students who completed their studies at Hamilton frequently transferred to Kentucky University to secure A.B. degrees.

The college offered a high-quality academic program. It also had a policy of strictly supervising the social activities of its students, although this was liberalized when Kentucky University became coeducational in 1889. The school functioned successfully until the 1920s, when diminished financial resources resulted in a large debt. Hamilton College ceased to exist as an independent college after 1932 and the building was converted into a women's dormitory for Transylvania students until 1958. It was razed in 1962.

See John D. Wright, Jr. *Transylvania: Tutor to the West* (Lexington, Ky., 1975).

JOHN D. WRIGHT, JR.

HAMMER, VICTOR KARL. Victor Karl Hammer, painter and typographer, was born in Vienna, on December 9, 1882, the son of Karl and Maria (Fuhrmann) Hammer. After being apprenticed to an architect, he was admitted to the Academy of Fine Arts in Vienna in 1898, where he studied painting and sculpture. In 1939 Hammer and his wife, Rosl (née Rossbach), emigrated to the United States, where he taught art first at Wells College in Aurora, New York. From 1948 to 1952 he taught at Transylvania University in Lexington.

Hammer was active both as an artist and as a hand-press printer. His American Uncial typeface is widely used, and his printing created much interest among private presses. Both his painting and typography are highly formal and traditional in style. Hammer and Rosl had two children, Veronika and Jacob. Hammer married Carolyn Reading in 1955. He died in Lexington on July 10, 1967, and was buried in Pisgah Cemetery in Woodford County, Kentucky.

See Sir John Rothenstein, *Victor Hammer, Artist and Craftsman* (Boston 1978); C.R. Hammer, *Victor Hammer, Artist and Printer* (Lexington, Ky., 1981).

JAMES D. BIRCHFIELD

HAMMON, JOHN. John Hammon, pioneer, was born in Goochland County, Virginia, on January 29, 1760. He was the son of James and Mary (Hargiss) Hammon and great-grandson of Ambrose Hammon, who landed at Old Rappahannock County, Virginia, in 1666. A resident of Wilkes County, North Carolina, John Hammon joined the Revolutionary army at age sixteen and fought at King's Mountain. He was a defender of Bryan's Station in Kentucky in 1782 and also served on Col. Benjamin Logan's expedition against the Ohio Indian towns. Hammon became a charter member of the Mountain Island Baptist Church in Scott County (now Owen County), Kentucky, in 1806. In 1822 he moved to Cincinnati, where he went into the steamboat business. Late in his life he returned to Owen County, where he died in 1868, at age 108. He was buried in the cemetery of the Mussel Shoals Baptist Church. Hammon was married twice, the second time to Mildred Ann Morgan (the identity of his first wife is unknown), and had twenty-two children.

See Stratton Owen Hammon, *The Saga of John Hammon, Revolutionary War Hero and Owen County Kentucky Pioneer* (Louisville 1979).

STRATTON O. HAMMON

HANCOCK, ARTHUR B., JR. Thoroughbred breeder Arthur B. ("Bull") Hancock, Jr., was born on January 24, 1910, to Arthur B. and Nancy (Clay) Hancock, at Marchmont House on the family's Claiborne farm in Bourbon County. Young Hancock grew up working on the thoroughbred farm; his father also owned Ellerslie Stud in Charlottesville, Virginia. Hancock was educated at St. Mark's School, Southboro, Massachusetts, and Woodberry Forest School, Orange, Virginia. In 1933 he graduated from Princeton University, where he studied genetics and eugenics. After serving in the U.S. Air Force in World War II with the rank of major, Hancock joined his father at Claiborne in 1947.

To improve the Claiborne bloodlines, Hancock began importing European horses. In 1949 he bought the temperamental Irish thoroughbred Nasrullah for $340,000—a great bargain, as Nasrullah was the leading sire in 1956-58, 1959-60, and 1962. One of his offspring, Nashua, sold for $1.25 million. Nasrullah's most lasting contribution was Bold Ruler, whose progeny in 1964 were the first to win $2 million in one season and who sired Secretariat. Hancock also imported Ambiorix, the first French horse to be a successful sire in America, and the Irish thoroughbred Princequillo, who sired Somethingroyal, the dam of Secretariat. With his imported stallions and his knowledge of genetics, Hancock changed the pattern of breeding the American thoroughbred.

Hancock was a charter member and vice-president of the Keeneland Association, president of the Thoroughbred Breeders of America, and president of the Thoroughbred Club of America, which honored him as America's outstanding thoroughbred breeder in 1960.

Hancock married Waddell Walker; they were the parents of two sons, Arthur B. III and Seth, and two daughters, Clay and Waddell. Hancock died on April 14, 1972, in Nashville and was buried in the Paris Cemetery in Kentucky.

BETTY B. ELLISON

HANCOCK COUNTY. Hancock County, the eighty-third in order of formation, is located in the Western Coal Field region of the state along the Ohio River. It is bordered by Daviess, Ohio, and Breckinridge counties and has an area of 189 square miles. The county was formed on January 3, 1829, from parts of Ohio, Breckinridge, and Daviess counties and named in honor of John Hancock, president of the Continental Congress and signer of the Declaration of Independence. HAWESVILLE, in the northern part of the county along the Ohio River, has been the county seat since 1829. In 1830 the U.S. Census counted 1,515 people in the county.

Limestone underlies the eastern and southeastern part of the county, with frequent outcroppings such as those at Jefferies Cliffs. Alluvial bottomland covers much of the northern and northwestern part of the county. Several veins of bituminous coal are found in these formations, and in the southeastern part of the county are rich deposits of cannel coal. Other resources include oil, particularly around Pellville and Easton; clay and shale suitable for the manufacture of brick, tile, and sewer pipe; and limestone of commercial quality. Sand and gravel are dredged from the Ohio River. Along the Ohio River and Blackford Creek are found alluvial soils, characterized by low ridges four to five feet high and five hundred feet wide. These soils support production of grains, soybeans, tobacco, and feedlot cattle operations. South and east of Lewisport, the soil is loessial.

Settlement began about 1799, with pioneers arriving by flatboat along the Ohio River or by trails leading from Elizabethtown and Louisville through Breckinridge County and along the ridgelines to Owensboro and beyond. By 1860 the county's population topped 6,000, including some six hundred slaves. During the 1850s, coal mines were opened in Hawesville and cannel coal deposits were developed in Bennetsville. A railroad was built from Bennetsville to haul cannel coal to Cloverport for shipment to New Orleans and from there to England. A rail line also led from the Hawesville mines to the river. Miners from Britain and Germany were attracted to these jobs.

The Civil War brought disruptions in river commerce and raids by guerrilla bands, including one led by Hancock County's William Davison, but the county continued to grow, and by 1890 reached its population peak of 9,214. The building of the Louisville, Henderson, & St. Louis Railroad (now part of CSX Transportation) through the county, completed in 1888, stimulated the coal mining and timbering industries, and furnished additional markets for Hancock County's farmers.

The county's population began to shrink after 1890 because of soil erosion on hill lands, the lure of jobs in the booming cities, and new coal developments in other areas. By 1930 the population had dropped to 6,147. The depression and the outmigration of the World War II years accelerated the decline, and by 1950 the census reported only 6,009 people. Beginning in the 1950s, however, an economic transformation occurred in Hancock County, turning it from a depressed agricultural area into one of the most industrialized rural counties in Kentucky. The process began with the opening of the Murray Tile plant (now American Olean Tile Company) in Lewisport in 1955, followed in 1963 by Lewisport's decision to issue $50 million in industrial bonds to attract the Harvey Aluminum Company (now Commonwealth Aluminum). The state of Indiana began construction of a toll bridge linking Cannelton with Hawesville, which in turn prompted the WesCor Corporation (now Willamette Industries) to locate an integrated pulp and paper mill in the Skillman Bottoms area near Hawesville. Another aluminum plant arrived with the issuance by the Hancock Fiscal Court of $142 million in municipal industrial bonds to finance construction of the National-Southwire smelter and rolling mills. The National Aluminum Corporation (now Alumax Aluminum Corporation) built a rolling mill nearby, and the newly built Kenneth C. Coleman Power Plant provided electricity to meet the needs of these new industries. Between 1960 and 1970, some 1,700 new industrial jobs were created.

In the 1980s these industries were joined by the new plant of World Source Coil and Coating. By 1989 Hancock County citizens had restored a Civil War–era courthouse, built a museum in the old railroad depot, and established an art collection. The population was 7,080 in 1970; 7,742 in 1980; and 7,864 in 1990.

See Charles A. Clinton, *A Social and Educational History of Hancock County, Kentucky* (Cambridge, Mass., 1974); Lee A. Dew, *Shaping Our Society: Transportation and the Development of the Society and Culture of Hancock County* (Hawesville, Ky., 1989); Glenn Hodges, *Fearful Times: A History of the Civil War Years in Hancock County, Kentucky* (Hawesville, Ky., 1986).   LEE A. DEW

HANSON, ROGER WEIGHTMAN. Roger Weightman Hanson, Confederate general, was born to Samuel and Matilda Calloway (Hickman) Hanson on August 27, 1827, in Winchester, Kentucky. At the age of twenty, he volunteered for the Mexican War, serving as a first lieutenant under Gen. John S. Williams. Wounded in a duel after returning to Kentucky, he suffered a permanently shortened leg. Hanson studied law and gained admission to the bar in 1844. He sought his fortune in the California gold rush, but returned to practice law in Winchester just a year later. He served two terms in the Kentucky House, from 1853 until 1857, representing Clark and Fayette counties, successively. Hanson was married to Virginia Peters.

A Know-Nothing candidate for the 1857 U.S. Congress, he lost to James B. Clay. In March 1860 he was appointed a colonel in the Kentucky state guard. In 1860, as the Civil War approached, Hanson supported Constitutional Union candidate John Bell for the presidency. When Abraham Lincoln was elected, Hanson favored state neutrality. At the beginning of the Civil War, Hanson joined the 2d Kentucky Confederate Infantry Brigade, 1st Division (Hardee's), as colonel. He was captured on February 15, 1862, during the battle of Fort Donelson. Exchanged on August 27, 1862, he returned to his brigade. Hanson moved to Gen. John C. Breckinridge's division and on December 13, 1862, was promoted to brigadier general of the 4th Kentucky Brigade. On January 2, 1863, he was mortally wounded in the Battle of Stone's River near Murfreesboro, Tennessee. He died on January 4, 1863, and was buried in Nashville. On November 11, 1866, his remains were reinterred in Lexington, Kentucky.

"HAPPY PAPPIES." The "Happy Pappies" were the beneficiaries of a 1960s federal assistance project in eastern Kentucky, envisioned by President Lyndon B. Johnson and strongly reminiscent of Franklin D. Roosevelt's Civilian Conservation Corps. The public employment program for unemployed fathers, part of the Economic Opportunity Act of 1965, paid a regular salary and provided basic work experience and training. The unemployed Happy Pappies, also known as "Johnson Boys," swept sidewalks and cleaned streets, roads, and streams; in Prestonsburg they built a city park. Often criticized for fostering a "culture of dependency," the program helped to defuse violence in the coal fields. It was dismantled by President Richard M. Nixon in the 1970s.

CAROL CROWE-CARRACO

HARDIN, BENJAMIN, JR. The son of Benjamin Hardin, Sr., and Sarah (Hardin) Hardin, Benjamin Hardin, Jr., jurist and congressman, was born on February 29, 1784, in Westmoreland County, Pennsylvania. The family moved to the area of Springfield, Kentucky, in March 1788. He was educated by tutors and studied law in the office of his cousin, Martin D. Hardin, in Richmond and under Felix Grundy in Bardstown. He commenced practice in 1806 in Elizabethtown and in 1808 moved to Bardstown, where he lived for the rest of his life.

Hardin became one of the foremost trial lawyers of antebellum Kentucky, excelling in criminal law as both prosecutor and defense attorney. In the trial of the Wilkinsons and Murdaugh in Harrodsburg in March 1839 for the alleged murder of two Louisville artisans, friends of the victims paid Hardin a fee of $1,000 to act as special private prosecutor. Defense attorney John Rowan's blistering attack on the tradition of private criminal prosecutors, plus the weight of the evidence, caused Hardin to lose the case despite a brilliant summation to the jury. Hardin's persuasive powers, however, usually enabled him to win such trials, no matter which side of the case he represented. Until Hardin entered the prosecution of one Spencer in 1842 for the murder of his stepson, all, including the commonwealth's attorney, believed Spencer to be innocent. Hardin secured a conviction and heard the condemned confirm the accuracy of the judgment in a confession on the gallows. He also appeared on the winning side in the case of *Green v. Biddle*, in which the U.S. Supreme Court in 1823 declared Kentucky's squatters law unconstitutional.

Hardin served four years in each house of the Kentucky legislature and five terms in the U.S. House of Representatives, at intervals from March 4, 1815, to March 3, 1837. As a state legislator he opposed dueling and the debtor relief laws. In the Congress, Hardin opposed expansion of federal governmental powers, including the recharter of the Bank of the United States. His most significant political influence came as Kentucky's secretary of state (1844-47), in his feud with Gov. William Owsley (1844-48) over the failure to consult him on

matters of patronage. Owsley removed Hardin from office. That feud helped produce a split in the Whig party and put Hardin in the leadership of a movement to convoke a constitutional convention in 1849. Hardin took a leading role at that convention, which helped spell the decline and fall in Kentucky of the once dominant Whig party.

Hardin married Elizabeth Pendleton Barbour on March 31, 1807. They had three daughters (Lucinda, Emily, and Kate) and three sons (James, Rowan, and William). Elizabeth died on August 4, 1852, and Hardin on September 24, 1852. He was buried in the family cemetery near Springfield, Kentucky.

See Lucius P. Little, *Ben Hardin: His Times and Contemporaries, with Selections from His Speeches* (Louisville 1887).   ROBERT M. IRELAND

HARDIN, JOHN. John Hardin, the Revolutionary War officer after whom Hardin County is named, was born to Martin and Lydia Hardin on October 1, 1753, in Fauquier County, Virginia. His early years were spent on the frontiers of Virginia and Pennsylvania, where he became an expert in hunting and rifle shooting. In early 1774 Hardin joined, as an ensign, the militia company organized by Gov. John M. Dunmore. In August of the same year, he volunteered to serve under Capt. Zachariah Morgan and was wounded in battle with the Shawnee. When the Continental Congress sought a military force, Hardin began to recruit; he raised enough men to enable him to enter the Continental army with the rank of second lieutenant. He served Gen. Daniel Morgan's rifle corps until his resignation as a first lieutenant in December 1779. Hardin received land in Kentucky in 1780, and he moved to Nelson County with his family in April 1786. In September 1786 he joined Gen. George Rogers Clark's expedition as quartermaster with the rank of colonel, moving against the Indians up the Wabash River around Vincennes, Indiana. In May 1792 Gen. James Wilkinson sent Hardin to negotiate a peace with the Shawnee in present-day Shelby County, Ohio, but they killed him en route. Hardin was married to Jane Daviess; they had three sons and three daughters, of whom four survived to adulthood—Sarah, Martin, Mark, and Rosanna. In 1792 Hardin County, Kentucky's fifteenth, was carved out of Nelson County to honor John Hardin.

See Faustina Kelly, "The Hardins in the Footsteps of the Boone Trail," *Register* 16 (May 1918): 27-31.

HARDIN, MARTIN D. Martin D. Hardin, legislator and officer in the War of 1812, was born to John and Jane (Davies) Hardin on June 21, 1780, in Pennsylvania. In April 1786 the Hardin family moved to Nelson County, Kentucky. Martin Hardin received his education at Transylvania University in Lexington, studied law under George Nicholas, and was admitted to the bar in 1801. He practiced law in Richmond. From 1805 until 1807, he represented

Madison County in the Kentucky House of Representatives and was reelected in 1812 to represent Franklin County. Gov. Isaac Shelby (1812-16) appointed him secretary of state in August 1812. During the War of 1812, Hardin served as a major under the command of Col. John Allen, fighting in the Tecumseh campaign in Michigan and northern Ohio. On November 13, 1816, he was appointed to the U.S. Senate by Gov. Gabriel Slaughter (1816-20) to fill the vacant seat of William T. Barry, who had resigned; Hardin served until March 3, 1817. Hardin was reelected to the Kentucky House in 1818 and served one term. In December 1820, he lost to John Harvie a bid to become the president of the Bank of Kentucky. In 1821 he served as a presidential elector, voting for James Monroe.

Hardin was married to Elizabeth Logan on January 20, 1809. Their eldest son, John J., served in the U.S. Congress and was killed in the Battle of Buena Vista in Mexico. Hardin died on October 8, 1823, in Frankfort and was buried in the Frankfort Cemetery.

See Faustina Kelly, "The Hardins in the Footsteps of the Boone Trail," *Register* 16 (May 1918) 27-31.

HARDIN, PARKER WATKINS. Parker Watkins Hardin, lawyer and statesman, was born on June 3, 1841, to Parker C. and Carolina (Watkins) Hardin. Educated in Adair County, Kentucky, he studied law with his father, who had served in the Kentucky Senate from 1840 to 1848. In 1865 he was admitted to the bar in Columbia, Kentucky, and in 1865 he served as city attorney of Danville. A Democrat, he was elected Kentucky's attorney general in 1879, 1883, 1887, and 1891. He unsuccessfully sought the nomination for governor in 1891 and 1899, and as the Democratic gubernatorial candidate lost the election in 1895.

Kentuckians admired Hardin's oratory, which the *Louisville Courier-Journal* called "rabble-rousing magic." Between state jobs he practiced law in Harrodsburg. Tall, dark, bearded, and handsome, he was widely respected in legal circles. His friends called him by many variations of his given name and initials, including "P. Wat," "Watt," "P.W.," "Parker," and by the affectionate nickname "Polly Wolly," according to *Kentucky: Decades of Discord*.

In 1864 Hardin married Mary Sallee of Wayne County. Hardin died of pneumonia on July 25, 1920, in Richmond, Virginia, and was buried in the Frankfort Cemetery. His obituary listed three daughters and a son: Dr. Mary Hardin, Mrs. William Harris, a married daughter living in Boston, and the Rev. Martin D. Hardin.

See Hambleton Tapp and James C. Klotter, *Kentucky: Decades of Discord, 1865-1900* (Frankfort, Ky., 1977).   HELEN B. CROCKER

HARDIN COUNTY. Hardin County, the fifteenth county, created in November 1792, was named for Col. John Hardin, the notable pioneer and Indian fighter of Nelson County. Created from a portion of Nelson County, Hardin County was originally 140 miles long and sixty miles wide. Hardin County lies in the west-central part of the state along the Salt River and, at 616 square miles, is Kentucky's fourth largest county. It is bounded on the north by the Ohio River and Bullitt and Meade counties; on the east by Bullitt, Nelson, and Larue counties; on the south by Larue, Hart, and Grayson counties; and on the west by Breckinridge, Grayson, and Meade counties. The county seat is ELIZABETHTOWN.

The terrain is dominated by broad, gentle slopes. The northern and western portions are more hilly and have thin soil, while the southern and eastern portions are rolling and contain rich alluvial soils. In the central part of the county lies a region known as the barrens for its flat, sandy surface. The most prominent land form in the eastern portion of the county is Muldraugh Hill, named for John Muldraugh, captain of the militia in what is now Marion County. Blue Ball Hill, the highest elevation in the county at 1,017 feet above sea level, has been used as a point of reference to locate property claims since the county was first explored.

The first recorded exploration of this region was done in 1766 by Col. John Smith, who was on a hunting trip. Ten years later a group of Virginians known as Shane, Sweeney and Company, led by Samuel Pearman, investigated the area for possible settlement. They returned to Virginia at the onset of winter, after several Indian attacks. Daniel Boone's brother, Squire, explored the area repeatedly in the late 1770s, but no permanent settlements were established until 1780, when Col. Andrew Hynes, Capt. Thomas Helm, and Samuel Haycraft each built a fort, all within a mile of each other, near present-day Elizabethtown. The settlement, named Severn's Valley, was home for at least seventeen families by 1781, when the Severn's Valley Baptist Church was created. At this time Hardin County was still a rich hunting ground for the Indians, who came in the spring to plant corn and returned in the fall, as many as 2,500 strong, to harvest the corn and to hunt. In the last major confrontation, a group of fifteen Indians attacked Severn's Valley in 1792 and killed two women and five children, as well as slaughtering livestock and burning down several cabins. Patrick Brown and fifteen other men pursued the attackers and killed all but one of them. In 1797 the settlement, officially named Elizabethtown, became the county seat.

Hardin County today is crisscrossed by highways, including Interstate 65, the Bluegrass and Western Kentucky parkways, US 31W, and US 62. Commerce across the county began with railroads: the Louisville & Nashville, completed in 1859; the Elizabethtown & Paducah (early 1870s); and the Hodgenville & Elizabethtown (1888).

Abraham Lincoln was born in what was then part of Hardin County on February 12, 1809. He left Kentucky in the fall of 1816. Three years before Lincoln's birth, Hardin Academy, Elizabethtown's first school, was created. Later schools included

Cecilian College, Lynnland College, Hambleton College, and in 1964 the Elizabethtown Community College, part of the University of Kentucky. The first post office in the county was established on March 1, 1819, in the town of West Point. In 1918 one-twelfth of Hardin County was transfered to the U.S. government to establish Camp Knox, named after Henry Knox of the Revolutionary War. The original 10,000-acre tract was later expanded to 100,000 acres, and Camp Knox became FORT KNOX on January 1, 1932. The 3,800 buildings at Fort Knox include the U.S. Bullion Depository, more commonly known as the Gold Vault.

The growth in industry in the county has pushed the total number of businesses above 1,400, and cash receipts for agriculture in 1986 totaled nearly $43 million. The primary agricultural products of the county are hogs, cattle, and hay, followed by corn, wheat, milk, and burley tobacco. The population of the county was 78,421 in 1970; 88,917 in 1980; and 89,240 in 1990.

See Daniel E. McClure, Jr., *Two Centuries in Elizabethtown and Hardin County, Kentucky* (Elizabethtown, Ky., 1979); Mrs. Thomas D. Winstead, *Chronicles of Hardin County, Kentucky* (Elizabethtown, Ky., 1974).

HARDINSBURG. Hardinsburg, the seat of Breckinridge County, is located at the junction of U.S. 60 and KY 261. It is the site of Hardin's Station, erected in 1780 by Capt. William Hardin, a veteran of the Revolutionary War, in whose honor the town was named. The town lots for Hardinsburg were laid off in 1782, and the town was incorporated in 1800. It was officially named Hardinsburg in 1801 and was incorporated on May 3, 1890. The first courthouse was built of logs shortly after the county was formed in 1799. Bricks for the second courthouse, completed in 1869, were made of clay from the site where the high school is now located. The courthouse burned in 1958 and in 1960 was replaced by a three-story brick building.

On October 15, 1864, when a Confederate guerrilla force raided the town, the citizens of Hardinsburg repulsed the attack and forced the raiders to withdraw. On December 28, 1864, a raiding party of about twenty guerrillas entered the town and seized a cache of weapons stored in the courthouse and several other buildings. After citizens overcame the invaders, a Confederate force under the command of Capt. Simeon Hanley, H. Clay Hodges, and Moses Webster restored order. The people of Hardinsburg agreed to accept the protection of the Confederates and were allowed to retain their arms.

The industrial base has remained small, mainly crushed stone, lime, and concrete manufacturers. The population of the fifth-class city was 1,547 in 1970; 2,211 in 1980; and 1,906 in 1990.

RON D. BRYANT

HARD LABOUR, TREATY OF. The Treaty of Hard Labour, guaranteeing to the Cherokee the land that is now Kentucky, was concluded between rep-resentatives of the British government and the Cherokee on October 14, 1768, in South Carolina. The treaty acknowledged the Cherokee claim to western lands, guaranteed the Cherokee peaceful possession, and defined the boundary line between Virginia and the Cherokee nation. The Cherokee were to stay south and west of the boundary and Virginians were not to migrate into the Cherokee hunting ground, thereby closing what is now Kentucky to white settlement. The boundary line agreed upon ran from the North Carolina border northeast to the Kanawha River along a line east of the Holston River and followed the Kanawha to the Ohio River. The area claimed by the Cherokee included some white settlements along the Holston River, and their complaints led to the Treaty of LOCHABER to redefine the boundary lines on October 18, 1770.

HARDWICK, ELIZABETH. Elizabeth Hardwick, writer and critic, was born in Lexington, Kentucky, on July 27, 1916, to Eugene Allen and Mary (Ramsey) Hardwick. After obtaining both her B.A. (1938) and M.A. (1939) from the University of Kentucky, she received a fellowship offer from Louisiana State University, but decided at the last minute to apply to Columbia University in New York, where she did postgraduate work from 1939 to 1941. Deciding not to pursue a Ph.D., Hardwick turned to short story writing. Her first novel, *The Ghostly Lover*, was published in 1945, and a short time later she began writing regularly as a critic for *Partisan Review*.

In July of 1949, Hardwick married American poet Robert Lowell. Their only child, daughter Harriet Winslow, was born on January 4, 1957. Shortly after their marriage, Lowell entered New York's Payne Whitney Clinic, where he underwent three months' treatment for manic depression. Throughout their life together, Lowell's recurrent psychological difficulties put considerable pressure on Hardwick, yet she remained a productive and well-regarded writer. In 1955 she published her second novel, *The Simple Truth*, and in 1960 she edited *The Selected Letters of William James*. In 1962, when her first collection of essays, *A View of My Own*, was published, she was one of the founding editors of the *New York Review of Books*. In 1967 she became the first woman recipient of the George Jean Nathan Award for dramatic criticism.

Hardwick's marriage to Lowell ended in divorce in October 1972. In the decade following, she published two more collections of essays, *Seduction and Betrayal* (1974) and *Bartleby in Manhattan* (1983), and the autobiographical novel *Sleepless Nights* (1979).

In his 1982 biography of Robert Lowell (to which Hardwick contributed many details), Ian Hamilton introduces Elizabeth Hardwick as "a Southerner from Kentucky . . . [who] had left the South in 1940 to do graduate work at Columbia University and had never properly returned." *The Ghostly Lover* and her early short stories led some critics to consider Hardwick a southern writer, but as she herself comments, in a 1984 *Paris Review* interview, "being a southern writer is a decision, not a fate"—and she identifies her selection of Columbia rather than Louisiana State as "a critical, defining moment" in her life. But she goes on to say, "Naturally, I love the best southern writing," and to recall the Lexington of her first twenty-three years as "a very beautiful and interesting place."

See Darryl Pinckney, interview with Elizabeth Hardwick in *Writers at Work: The Interviews, Seventh Series* (New York 1986).

ANTHONY O'KEEFFE

HARGIS, JAMES F. James F. Hargis, a merchant-politician of Breathitt County, Kentucky, was born in Jackson to John S. and Evelyn Brittain (Sewell) Hargis on October 13, 1862. With his brother Alex he operated the largest general store in that section of the mountains. His political skill made him one of the kingmakers during the MUSIC HALL gubernatorial convention of 1899. In November 1901, Hargis was declared to have been elected Breathitt County judge, but disputes about the outcome of the election helped launch what is known as the HARGIS-COCKRILL Feud (1901-12). During that bloody intracounty battle, Hargis was widely considered responsible for arranging several killings. A Baptist, he prided himself on coming from a Democratic family that was politically active. He married Louellen Day in 1880; they had two children, Beach and Evalee. Hargis was shot and killed by his son at Jackson on February 6, 1908, and was buried in the family cemetery near there.

See E.L. Noble, *Bloody Breathitt's Feuds* (Jackson, Ky., 1944).

HENRY MAYER

HARGIS-COCKRILL FEUD. One of the more prominent eastern Kentucky postbellum interfamily wars, the Hargis-Cockrill feud occurred between 1901 and 1912. Prominent participants included James F. Hargis and Edward Callahan, Breathitt County judge and sheriff, respectively; James B. Marcum, mayor of Jackson and University of Kentucky trustee; Gov. J.C.W. Beckham (1900-07); Judge B.F. French; and B.D. Cox, Jr. To some extent, the involvement of Callahan and Marcum grew out of earlier conflicts between members of their families, including the killings of Marcum's uncle, Bill Strong, in 1899.

There had been latent but unspecified conflicts between the Hargises and the Cockrills in earlier years, but it is generally agreed that the immediate cause of the feud was disputes growing out of the local elections of 1901. During the taking of depositions, a breach of the peace occurred. Warrants were sworn out against Hargis and Marcum, and heated charges were made against each other by Callahan and Marcum. When town marshall Jim Cockrill attempted to execute the warrant against Hargis, he resisted arrest, causing another Cockrill, Tom, to draw his gun, which Hargis took as a

threat. The incident precipitated a pistol fight several weeks later between Cockrill and Hargis's brother, Ben, which caused Ben's death.

These shootings and others took place in and around Jackson between early 1902 and mid-1903. B.D. Cox was killed on April 13, 1902; Jim Cockrill on July 21, 1902; and Marcum on May 4, 1903. Several assassins were convicted and served time but three courts were unable to convict Hargis and Callahan of aiding and abetting. The court verdicts virtually ended the war. Callahan, however, died from shots fired on May 4, 1912, and the coincidence of this date with that of Marcum's demise was pointed out by one local historian as evidence that this killing was at least in part revenge for Marcum's murder.

Throughout the conflict, any number of attempts to slay Hargis and Callahan miscarried, and more than thirty men and women lost their lives. As a result of the feud, Hargis was defeated for reelection as county judge in 1905. He was killed with his own gun by his son Beauchamp ("Beech") on February 8, 1908, in an incident that is considered not entirely unrelated to the interfamily conflict.

See E.L. Noble, *Bloody Breathitt's Feuds* (Jackson, Ky., 1944); Thomas D. Clark, *Kentucky: Land of Contrasts* (New York 1968); Harold W. Coates, *Stories of Kentucky Feuds* (Kingsport, Tenn., 1942).

HENRY MAYER

HARLAN, JAMES. James Harlan, U.S. congressman, was born on June 22, 1800, at Harlan Station, Kentucky, the seventh of eight children of James and Sarah (Caldwell) Harlan. His father had accompanied James Harrod in 1774 from Virginia to Harrodsburg. Harlan Station, seven miles south of Harrodsburg and five miles west of Danville, was founded in 1778 by his father and his father's older brother Silas HARLAN, after whom Harlan County was named.

James Harlan studied law, was admitted to the bar in 1823, and established a practice in Harrodsburg. He served as commonwealth's attorney during 1829-35. An early Whig supporter of Henry Clay, Harlan was elected twice to the U.S. House of Representatives (March 4, 1835-March 3, 1839). Upon his return to Kentucky in 1840, he became secretary of state; in 1845 he was elected to the Kentucky House, and in 1851 he was elected attorney general of the commonwealth. Harlan wrote *The Code of Practice in Civil and Criminal Cases* (1854). During the secession crisis of 1860-61, Harlan was a strong Unionist. President Abraham Lincoln appointed him U.S. district attorney of Kentucky in 1861. He served until his death on February 18, 1863, in Frankfort, where he was buried.

Harlan married Eliza Shannon Davenport (1805-70) in Danville on December 23, 1822; they had six sons and three daughters. Their son John Marshall HARLAN became a member of the U.S. Supreme Court.

CHARLES R. LEE, JR.

HARLAN, JOHN MARSHALL. John Marshall Harlan, U.S. Supreme Court justice, was born on June 1, 1833, the fifth son of nine children of James Harlan, Kentucky lawyer-politician, and Elizabeth Shannon (Davenport) Harlan. His birthplace was the Old Stone House at Harlan Station, five miles west of Danville, Kentucky, in what is now Boyle County. James Harlan, ambitious for his young son to become a lawyer, named him after Chief Justice of the United States John Marshall. After living in Harrodsburg for several years while James Harlan served in the U.S. Congress, the family moved to Frankfort when John Marshall Harlan was seven years of age. He was educated at the private school of B.B. Sayre and entered Centre College in Danville in 1848. Harlan was an honor graduate in 1850. After graduating from Transylvania University Law School in Lexington in 1852, Harlan returned to his Frankfort home to study law and was admitted to the bar in 1853.

In 1858 Harlan was elected county judge of Franklin County, his only judicial experience prior to his appointment to the Supreme Court. The next year a convention of Old Whig, Know-Nothing, and American party politicians nominated Harlan to run for the U.S. Congress from Henry Clay's Ashland District against the Democrat Williard E. Simms. In a controversial campaign and election, Harlan lost by fewer than 70 votes. In the even more controversial national presidential election of 1860, Harlan supported and campaigned for the unsuccessful Bell-Everett ticket of the moderate Constitutional Union party. Harlan moved to Louisville in February 1861, established a law firm with William F. Bullock, and resigned as county judge.

Harlan all but abandoned his law practice from May to August 1861 to make speeches with President Abraham Lincoln's attorney general, James Speed, encouraging Kentuckians to stand firm for the Union. That fall, he raised a Union regiment, the 10th Kentucky Infantry, which was part of Gen. George H. Thomas's division. Colonel Harlan served well at the Battle of Mill Springs in January 1862 and in the advance on Corinth, Mississippi, in 1862, but it was Harlan's victory over Confederate cavalry commander John Hunt Morgan at Rolling Fork River Bridge on December 29, 1862, that made his reputation during the war. Before Harlan's promotion to brigadier general could be acted upon, he resigned from the army upon the sudden death of his father. Soon after his return to Kentucky, he was elected attorney general of Kentucky on the Union ticket, replacing his father. He held that office in Frankfort until November 1867, when he resumed his law practice in Louisville.

A nationalist and states' rights, slave-holding Whig follower of Henry Clay before the war, Harlan underwent a political transformation during and after the war. Harlan had opposed the elections of Lincoln and the Thirteenth, Fourteenth, and Fifteenth Amendments, but he accepted the amendments as central to the restoration of the Union when he became a Radical Republican. Harlan campaigned for the first time as a Republican in 1868, when he supported Gen. Ulysses S. Grant for president. Although Harlan was an unsuccessful candidate for governor in 1871 and 1875, his efforts were essential in establishing the Republican party in Kentucky. In 1876 Harlan led the delegation from Kentucky to the Republican National Convention in Cincinnati, which was committed to the nomination of his law partner, Benjamin H. Bristow, for president. When Harlan became convinced that neither Bristow, who had been President Grant's secretary of the Treasury, nor Sen. James G. Blaine could win, he delivered the delegation for Rutherford B. Hayes of Ohio. President Hayes named Harlan to the Supreme Court, and Harlan, at age forty-four, took the oath of office as an associate justice on December 10, 1877.

Justice Harlan was a courteous, thoughtful, eloquent, and independent-minded southern gentleman. During his almost thirty-four years of service on the Court (1877-1911), he authored 745 majority, 100 concurring, and 316 dissenting opinions, for a record 1,161 opinions. He was known as the Great Dissenter, especially in the field of civil rights. His lone dissent in the civil rights cases in 1883 held that the majority had too narrowly interpreted the Fourteenth Amendment; his eloquent lone dissent in *Plessy v. Ferguson* (1896) was against "separate but equal" status for blacks. In *Berea College v. Kentucky* (1908), Harlan wrote the solitary dissent when the majority, including Justice Oliver Wendell Holmes, prohibited schools from admitting both black and white students. His lone dissents in civil rights cases were influential precedents of *Brown v. Board of Education of Topeka* (1954), in which a unanimous Court struck down the separate but equal doctrine. Justice Harlan also filed a strong dissent in *Pollock v. Farmers' Loan and Trust Co.* (1895), when the Court majority held that Congress could not levy an income tax. He believed in the strong enforcement of the Sherman Anti-Trust Act (1890) and dissented in *United States v. E.C. Knight Co.* (1895), but wrote the majority opinion in *Northern Securities Co. v. United States* (1903).

In his support of civil rights and his belief that the Bill of Rights, through its incorporation in the Fourteenth Amendment, protected citizens from the arbitrary power of the states, Justice Harlan was the leading liberal on a conservative Court, and was years ahead of his time. In 1972 sixty-five law school deans and professors of law, history, and political science rated Marshall one of the twelve greatest justices of the Supreme Court.

Harlan married Malvina French Shanklin in Evansville, Indiana, on December 23, 1856; they had six children. Their son John Maynard was the father of the John Marshall Harlan who was appointed to the Supreme Court by President Eisenhower in 1955. Justice Harlan died at his home in

Washington, D.C., on October 14, 1911, and was buried at Rock Creek Cemetery.

See Leon Friedman and Fred L. Israel, eds., *The Justices of the United States Supreme Court 1789-1969* (New York 1969); Frank B. Latham, *The Great Dissenter, John Marshall Harlan, 1833-1911* (New York 1970).   CHARLES R. LEE, JR.

HARLAN, SILAS. Silas Harlan, pioneer, was born on March 17, 1753, on Harlan's Run in present-day Berkeley County, West Virginia, the son of George and Ann (Hurst) Harlan. Journeying to Kentucky with James Harrod in 1774, Harlan served as scout, hunter, and military leader, attaining the rank of major in the militia. He was a member of the Committee for the Defense of West Fincastle and participated in the movement to make Kentucky part of Virginia in 1776 rather than an independent state under the auspices of the TRANSYLVANIA COMPANY. On January 2, 1777, Harlan joined Col. James Harrod's party in Harrodsburg to pick up gunpowder that George Rogers Clark and John Gabriel Jones had previously delivered from Pittsburgh to Three Islands in present-day Lewis County. The powder was then delivered to Kentucky settlers to assist them against the British in the Revolutionary War.

In 1778, with the help of his brother James and his uncle Jacob, Harlan built a log stockade near Danville known as Harlan's Station. He served under Clark in the Illinois campaign of 1778-79 against the British forts, commanded a company in John Bowman's raid on Old Chillicothe in 1779, and assisted Clark in establishing Fort Jefferson at the mouth of the Ohio River in 1780. Harlan was highly regarded by his contemporaries. He died leading the advance party at the Battle of BLUE LICKS on August 19, 1782. At the time of his death, he was engaged to Sarah Caldwell, who later married his brother James and became the grandmother of U.S. Supreme Court Justice John Marshall Harlan. Harlan County was named in Silas Harlan's honor.

See James S. Greene III, *Major Silas Harlan: His Life and Times* (Baxter, Ky., 1963); Alpheus Hibben Harlan, *History and Genealogy of the Harlan Family* (Baltimore 1914).

JAMES S. GREENE III

HARLAN. Harlan, the county seat of Harlan County, in southeastern Kentucky, is located on U.S. 421 and U.S. 119, at the confluence of the Clover and Martins forks of the Cumberland River. Harlan is a commercial center for the southeastern coal fields.

Samuel and Chloe Howard, who arrived in 1796, were the first permanent settlers of what would become Harlan. When the county was formed in 1819, they sold twelve acres of their land for the county seat; the land was divided into lots the next year. The new town was called Mt. Pleasant, after the Indian mound on which the county's first three courthouses would sit. As this name was in use

elsewhere in the state, the post office was designated Harlan Court House. During the Civil War, the town was occupied for a time by Confederate soldiers commanded by Gen. Humphrey Marshall; in October 1863 the courthouse was burned by Confederate guerrillas in reprisal for the burning of the Lee County, Virginia, courthouse.

Incorporated in 1876, the town began to spread east along Clover Fork following the subdivision of the William Turner estate in 1885 and the removal of the courthouse to Central Street in 1886. The fifth courthouse was built in 1922. From 1890 to 1916, the Harlan Presbyterian Academy played an important role in education; in 1911, the Harlan Independent School District, now home of the HARLAN BOYS CHOIR, was organized. The Louisville & Nashville Railroad (now CSX Transportation) arrived the same year, and the period of rapid growth that followed paralleled that of the county. In 1912 the General Assembly changed the city's name to Harlan; George B. Turner became the first mayor.

After World War II development moved south of town, up Martins Fork; in 1980 a three-mile strip was annexed, increasing the city's size and tax base. Shopping centers and fast-food restaurants sprung up and construction of the four-lane U.S. 421 bypass improved traffic flow. Responding to local concern touched off by a 1977 flood, the federal government in 1989 began construction of diversion tunnels to reroute Clover Fork under Ivy Hill, a project that opens opportunities for redevelopment of the older sections of town. The fourth-class city had a population of 3,318 in 1970; 3,024 in 1980; and 2,686 in 1990.

JAMES S. GREENE III

HARLAN BOYS CHOIR. Harlan Boys Choir is a soprano-alto-tenor-bass choir of one hundred boys in grades four through twelve in the Harlan Independent School District, Harlan, Kentucky. Students gain admission to the choir by audition and trial membership. Nicknamed "The Singing Sons of Appalachia," the choir has an eclectic repertoire ranging from J.S. Bach to Barry Manilow. David L. Davies, who taught English, and Marian Maxwell, a music teacher in the district, organized the choir in the summer of 1965. By the following year an adult support group had incorporated itself. Initially an extracurricular activity, the choir became part of the school curriculum in 1972. Marilyn Schraeder started assisting Davies and the choir as associate conductor and accompanist in 1969. In addition to performing extensively in the United States, the group has also made appearances in Canada and Austria. In 1972 the choir achieved top rating in the Graz, Austria, International Youth Music Festival. Perhaps its highest honor, however, was singing "This Is My Country" at the 1989 presidential inauguration of George Bush.

DAVID L. DAVIES

HARLAN COUNTY. Harlan County, the sixtieth county in order of formation, is located in the southeastern corner of the state, on the Virginia border. Bounded by Bell, Leslie, Perry, and Letcher counties, it covers an area of 468 square miles. Harlan County was created in 1819 out of part of Knox County. Later, portions of its territory went to form Letcher, Bell, and Leslie counties. It was named for Silas Harlan, a hero of the Battle of the Blue Licks. HARLAN is the county seat.

Four mountain ranges run across the county—Pine, Black, Little Black, and Stone. A spur of Black Mountain near Lynch is the highest point in the state, at 4,145 feet. Except for its northernmost corner, the county lies in the Cumberland River watershed; Martins Fork, Clover Fork, and Poor Fork converge at the county seat of HARLAN to form the Cumberland. Forests cover much of the county's 305,920 acres, but the coal that lies underneath is the county's most valuable resource.

There are seven incorporated cities in the county—Harlan, CUMBERLAND, Benham, LYNCH, Evarts, Loyall, and Wallins Creek. Principal highways are U.S. 119 and U.S. 421. CSX Transportation provides rail service; Tucker-Guthrie Memorial Airport near Harlan accommodates small planes.

Long Hunters and land speculators explored the county before settlement of the state began: Elisha and Tommy Walden, Joseph and Brice Martin, William Carr, and the McAfee brothers among others. Settlement had begun by 1782; one of the first families, the Catrons, was decimated by an Indian raid. Permanent settlement occurred in the 1790s: Carr Bailey, William Turner, and Samuel Howard were among the first settlers.

During the nineteenth century, residents supported themselves by subsistence farming and by bartering ginseng, produce, and hides. The county's hogs, mules, and cattle went for sale to buyers who drove them to markets outside the mountains.

The Civil War brought disruption to the county; fighting was limited to minor skirmishes, but foraging by both armies and raids by guerrillas occurred.

After the war, the logging industry sent walnut, cherry, poplar, oak, and chestnut logs floating down the Cumberland to mills at Wasioto and Williamsburg. In 1913, Harlan Countians formed the state's first forest fire protective association; in 1919 the county was the site of the first state forest, Kentenia, on Pine Mountain.

After T.J. Asher extended his Wasioto & Black Mountain Railroad into the county from Bell County in 1911, the coal industry grew rapidly. Spurred by World War I, the industry in the 1920s took advantage of nonunion labor and favorable freight differentials. Coal production in the county peaked in 1928, dropped sharply during the early 1930s, then rose to an all-time high of 14.7 million tons in 1942.

The population increased by 556 percent between 1900 and 1930. Though blacks and eastern European immigrants were part of this rise, the majority were mountain whites from nearby counties. Most of the new arrivals were first-generation industrial workers unprepared for living in the close quarters of coal camps and unused to payment in cash. Miners' penchant for whiskey and guns erupted in this volatile environment. The homicide rate in Harlan County in the 1920s was the highest in the nation, but fell sharply as the industry matured. Successful unionization occurred in the 1930s; in the process both sides used violence, giving the county a notoriety that lingers yet.

Since World War II, shifts in markets, technological advances, increases in freight charges, increased state and federal regulation, and environmental concerns have kept the industry in a boom-bust cycle. The 1950s and 1960s were a time of low production and a depressed economy; both coal production and the population of the county were cut in half. The 1970s brought a resurgence; despite occasional setbacks, production climbed to postwar highs in 1980 and 1984. However, a greater degree of mechanization meant that fewer employees were needed, and the need for a diversified economy was the top issue confronting Harlan Countians as they entered the 1990s.

Kingdom Come State Park, Martins Fork and Cranks Creek lakes, the Little Shepherd Trail, and Sand Cave provide outdoor recreational opportunities. Two festivals take place annually—the Poke Sallet Festival and Harlan County Homecoming in June and the Kingdom Come Swappin' Meetin' at Southeast Community College in October.

Floods along the Cumberland River have been a problem in Harlan County, the two most serious being those of March 1963 and April 1977. Martins Fork Dam was built in the 1970s as a flood control measure, and channel diversion and floodwall projects for Harlan and Loyall were under way by 1990.

The county has produced a number of notable journalists, including Don Whitehead, Maxine Cheshire, Cawood LEDFORD, and Jim Hampton, as well children's authors Rebecca CAUDILL and George Ella Lyon. It has been portrayed in literature by John Fox, Jr., Charles Neville Buck, Percy MacKaye, William A. Bradley, John Dos Passos, James Jones, Walter TEVIS, Gurney Norman, and James Sherburne. Its folk songs, dances, and tales have been collected by Cecil J. Sharp, Howard Brockway and Loraine Wyman, Leonard ROBERTS, H.H. Fuson, and Evelyn Wells. Florence Reece, Aunt Molly JACKSON, and Merle TRAVIS have captured the plight of its miners in song; Barbara Kopple did likewise on film. S. McMaster Kerr got the Presbyterian Church, U.S.A. involved in the creation of the Appalachian Regional Hospital chain. Juanita KREPS served as secretary of commerce under President Jimmy Carter. The HARLAN BOYS CHOIR sang at the 1989 inauguration of President George Bush.

The population of Harlan County was 37,370 in 1970; 41,889 in 1980; and 36,574 in 1990.

See Mabel Green Condon, *A History of Harlan County* (Nashville 1962).   JAMES S. GREENE III

HARM, RAY. Ray Harm, wildlife artist and environmentalist, was born on November 9, 1926, in

Randolph County, West Virginia, to Raymond Kline and Lila (Lewis) Deauville. When his mother remarried, the boy adopted the surname of his stepfather, William Harm. At the age of fourteen Ray left home to work on a Nebraska horse ranch and for the next several years he worked at various dude ranches, Wild West shows, and rodeos, as well as for the Ringling Brothers Circus. He served in the U.S. Navy during 1945-47.

Harm attended the Cooper School of Commercial Art in Cleveland and studied portraiture and life drawing at the Cleveland Institute of Art. In 1950 he married Carmella Capretta. In 1961 Wood Hannah, Sr., of Louisville commissioned Harm to paint twenty watercolors of wildlife. Harm moved his family to Pulaski County, Kentucky, in 1962. He established the Frame House Gallery Publishing Company, printers of limited edition reproductions in Louisville. In January 1963 Harm was appointed the first H.L. Donovan artist in residence at the University of Kentucky. He purchased a farm bordering on Bernheim Forest in Nelson County in 1964. That September the *Louisville Times* began featuring the "Ray Harm Sketchbook," a column on Kentucky wildlife that he wrote and illustrated. In 1965 Harm was commissioned to create the centennial painting of a Kentucky wildcat for the University of Kentucky.

In 1967 the World Publishing Company published the *Ray Harm Nature Sketch Book.* The same year Harm received honorary degrees from Centre College and Pikeville College. He helped establish the C.E. Buckley Wildlife Sanctuary in Versailles, and worked to preserve the Red River Gorge from development. He was staff artist at the Kentucky Ornithological Society, and served as artist, naturalist, and lecturer for the Kentucky Department of Parks. In 1969 he married Millie Harm and moved to a five-hundred-acre farm in Bell County. Because of health problems, Harm moved to Arizona in 1976, opening a guest ranch in the Santa Catalina Mountains near Tucson. Harm lives in Arizona with his third wife, Catherine Bertrand. He devotes much time to fund-raising projects and often returns to Kentucky.

HARMAN'S STATION. Harman's Station, near the juncture of John's Creek and the Levisa Fork of the Big Sandy River in Johnson County, is generally believed to have been the oldest permanent settlement in the Big Sandy River valley of eastern Kentucky. The best evidence indicates that the blockhouse at Harman's Station was constructed in the early winter of 1789 by a small party of men from Walker's Creek, Virginia, under the leadership of Mathias ("Tice") Harman. Frontier heroine Jenny WILEY escaped her Indian captors and fled to the safety of this settlement during the early months of 1790.

See Henry P. Scalf, *Kentucky's Last Frontier*, 2d ed. (Pikeville, Ky., 1972).

THOMAS D. MATIJASIC

HARPE BROTHERS. No case matches the heinous record of frontier murders committed by Micaja ("Big") and Wiley ("Little") Harpe, who killed wantonly in Kentucky, Tennessee, and Illinois in the 1790s. They were born in 1768 and 1770, respectively, in North Carolina and migrated to Beaver Creek near Knoxville, Tennessee, in 1795. There they began their bloody trail of murders on their way through Kentucky to Cave-In-Rock, Illinois. They killed young and old, male and female—even babies—and strewed human carnage along their path. On August 20, 1799, the Harpes spent the night, along with Maj. William Love, in the loft of Moses Stegall's cabin, about five miles east of Dixon, Kentucky. During the night they smashed Love's head with an ax. The next morning, they slit the throat of the Stegall baby, killed its mother, and burned the cabin. When Stegall returned, he formed a posse, and they caught Big Harpe in Muhlenberg County at a site later named Harpe's Hill. They cut off his head, brought it back to Hopkins County in a saddlebag, and impaled it on a lance at a location about three miles north of Dixon, now known as Harpe's Head. Little Harpe escaped, only to meet the hangman at Gallows Field, Jefferson County, Mississippi, on February 4, 1804.

See Otho A. Rothert, *The Outlaws of Cave-In-Rock* (Cleveland 1924).   J.T. GOOCH

HARPENDING, ASBURY, JR. Asbury Harpending, Jr., adventurer and entrepreneur, was born in Hopkinsville, Kentucky, in 1839, the son of Asbury and Ann W. (Clark) Harpending. The Harpending family, of Dutch origin, were early settlers of Caldwell County and also owned property in Lyon and Christian counties. Harpending grew up on his father's farm, Millville, in Caldwell County. At fifteen, he ran away from home to join Gen. William Walker on his Nicaraguan expedition. In 1855 his father sent him West, where he accumulated great wealth from gold mining in California and Mexico.

Harpending, with fellow Kentuckian Ridgely Greathouse, organized the Confederate Secret Society in 1862 in San Francisco to halt shipments of California gold to the U.S. Treasury. Harpending, other society members, and the crew were captured aboard the privateer *Chapman* as they attempted to sail from San Francisco. Harpending, sent to Fort Alcatraz to await trial, was found guilty of treason and served four months in San Francisco's Broadway jail. He was pardoned by President Abraham Lincoln under the General Amnesty Act of 1863. By 1865 Harpending had again achieved success in gold mining, and the next year married Ira Ann Thomason, making their home on San Francisco's Rincon Hill. In 1868-76, he developed the Harpending block, between First and Second streets in San Francisco, site of the Harpending Building.

In 1871 Harpending established the *London Stock Exchange Review*. The next year he founded the

San Francisco and New York Mining and Commercial Company, parent company of the New Golconda Diamond Mining Company. The Colorado mines of the latter proved to be fakes, salted with cut diamonds. Harpending returned to Kentucky in 1872 in an effort to escape the scandal, and built a $65,000 mansion on the Millville farm. In 1876 Harpending left Kentucky, dividing his time between his California interests and New York City, where he was successful in the stock market. He died in New York City on January 26, 1923.

See J.T. Gooch, "The Case of Asbury Harpending, Jr.," *Journal of Kentucky Studies* 1 (July 1984): 142-154; Benjamin Franklin Gilbert, "Kentucky Privateers in California," *Register* 38 (July 1940): 256-66.   J.T. GOOCH

HARPER, NATHANIEL R. Nathaniel R. Harper, jurist and politician, son of former slave Hizikie Harper, was born in February 1846 in Indiana. He attended Howard University Law School in Washington, D.C. In 1871 he moved to Louisville and on November 23 of that year became one of the first two blacks to practice law in the Louisville court system. Harper, a conservative Republican, campaigned and took minor posts in the party to supplement his low income. His response to the Federal Civil Rights Act of 1875, which prohibited racial discrimination in restaurants, hotels, public amusement areas, and public transport, was passive. He encouraged blacks to proceed slowly in making demands for equality, stating that "we must educate ourselves to a higher morality than exists at present within the race."

In 1888 Harper was appointed Kentucky's first black judge. He received the support of black Republicans from Louisville's 6th State District (10th Ward) in July 1895 to run on the Republican ticket for the state legislature. Republican officials, fearing that a black on the ticket would hurt their chances of winning, then changed the rules to provide that Republican candidates would be selected not by wards but by a mass vote of delegates. After this controversial rule change was made public, blacks proposed to Harper that they create an independent party. Republican party leaders, wanting to avoid a racial incident, offered to employ Harper to speak to blacks on behalf of Republican candidates, on the condition that he would renounce his candidacy for a seat in the legislature. Harper withdrew, to the outrage of many blacks. The new Republican governor, William O'Connell Bradley (1895–99), appointed Harper commissioner of the Bureau of Agriculture, Labor and Statistics of the Colored People of Kentucky.

Harper died on January 27, 1921, in Louisville and was buried in the Louisville Cemetery.

See George C. Wright, *Life Behind a Veil* (Baton Rouge, La., 1985); Alice Allison Dunnigan, *The Fascinating Story of Black Kentuckians: Their Heritage and Traditions* (Washington, D.C., 1982).

HARRISON, BENJAMIN. Benjamin Harrison, soldier and pioneer, was born most probably in Westmoreland County, Pennsylvania, around 1745, and first came to Kentucky in 1776. With the outbreak of the Revolutionary War, the record seems to indicate, he returned to his home state and served as the colonel of the 4th Battalion of the Westmoreland County militia. Before 1785, probably in 1783, Harrison returned to Kentucky and settled in what is now Harrison County, on a five-hundred-acre land grant about three miles south of present-day Cynthiana.

Harrison became the first sheriff and justice of the peace of Bourbon County on May 16, 1786, and represented that county in the conventions that met in Danville in 1787 and 1788. He also participated in the Danville assembly that created Kentucky's first state constitution, which gathered on April 2, 1792. In 1793 he was elected to the General Assembly as a representative of Bourbon County. He was also a general in the Kentucky militia.

In 1793, while Harrison was a member of the legislature, Kentucky formed its seventeenth county out of parts of Bourbon and Scott counties and named it in his honor. In February 1794 he was sworn in as a justice of the peace in the new county.

In 1800 Harrison migrated to New Madrid, Missouri, and claimed approximately four thousand acres of land. He married Mary Newel around 1784; they had eight children. Harrison died in Missouri in 1808.

See Isabelle Giu Ivezan, *Some Reports of Benjamin Harrison: A Revolutionary War Soldier* (Ashton, Mo., 1973).

HARRISON, CARTER HENRY. Carter Henry Harrison, several times Chicago mayor, was born on February 15, 1825, to Carter Henry and Caroline Evelin (Russell) Harrison on Elk Hill Farm near Lexington, Kentucky. In the fall of 1840, Harrison entered the private academy of Lewis Marshall in Lexington, and he received his B.A. from Yale in 1845. During the summer of 1845, he began studying law at Transylvania University in Lexington, leaving school a year later to live as a gentleman farmer on his family's land. During 1851-53 he traveled extensively throughout Europe, Africa, and Asia, living in Paris for a time.

In the spring of 1855, Harrison earned his law degree at Transylvania and was admitted to the Kentucky bar. He sold his large estate the same year and, after traveling in the Northwest in search of business ventures, settled in Chicago and invested most of his money in real estate. After the devastating Chicago fire in 1871, Harrison turned to campaigning for city offices. A Democrat, he was elected county commissioner in November 1871, a position he held until December 1874. Though he was defeated in his bid for the U.S. Congress in 1872, his popularity as an orator grew, and his success in business overflowed into his political career. Harrison was elected to the U.S. Congress, serving from March 4, 1875, to March 3, 1879. He was then elected mayor of Chicago for the term beginning April 28, 1879, and easily won reelection in 1881, 1883, and 1885. He was unsuccessful, however, in his race for governor of Illinois in 1884.

In 1887-88 Harrison traveled halfway around the world, an experience that was the basis of his book *A Race with the Sun* (1889). In 1891 he published *A Summer Outing and the Old Man's Story*, and in the same year bought the *Chicago Times*. After declining to run for mayor of Chicago in 1889 and being defeated in 1891, Harrison was again elected mayor in 1893. On October 28, 1893, he was assassinated.

Harrison married Sophonisba Preston on April 12, 1855. They had ten children, only four of whom survived early childhood: Lina, William Preston, Sophia, and Carter Henry, who, like his father, served as Chicago's mayor five times. Harrison's first wife died in 1876. He married Marguerite Stearns in London, England, on August 22, 1882. She died in 1887. Harrison is buried in Graceland Cemetery in Chicago.

See John Wilson Townsend, "Carter Henry Harrison, Kentuckian," *Register* 24 (May 1926): 150-62; William John Abbot, *Carter Henry Harrison: A Memoir* (New York 1895).

HARRISON, WILLIAM B. William B. Harrison, who had the longest tenure of all Louisville mayors, from 1927 until 1933, was born in Louisville on July 28, 1889, the son of William and Virginia L. (Trelevant) Harrison. He graduated from Louisville Male High School in 1907 and from the University of Virginia in 1910 with a law degree. He served two years as a captain in the U.S. Army in World War I. He was secretary of the Foundry Products Company until 1925, and from 1922 until 1929 was president of the Kentucky Refrigerating Company.

Harrison, a Republican, was elected to a two-year term as mayor after the U.S. court of appeals threw out the election of Republican Arthur A. Will. The court of appeals also approved Harrison's bid to run for a full term as mayor, succeeding himself. Harrison's administration was responsible for building the Municipal Bridge between Louisville and Jeffersonville, Indiana; the formation of the City Planning and Zoning Commission; the model registration law; civil service for the city's police and fire departments; and the purchase of land creating Seneca Park in Louisville's East End. During Harrison's tenure, the position of mayor was strengthened under the City Government Bill of 1929, which revamped local government by consolidating the Board of Councilmen and Aldermen and the Boards of Public Safety and Public Works into a single legislative body—the Board of Aldermen. The mayor was then given the responsibility for governing and appointing city department directors. Harrison, an articulate and moving speaker,

unsuccessfully ran for governor in 1931. He was defeated by Democrat Ruby Laffoon, by a vote of 446,301 to 374,239 during a time of economic depression.

After his term as mayor, Harrison became president of the Louisville Industrial Foundation, which helps to attract industry to the area. He was also vice president of the Louisville Area Development Association, which worked closely with the foundation on long-range city planning and growth issues. Harrison was a director of several Louisville companies, including the Porcelain Metal Corporation and B.F. Avery & Sons, and he was chairman of the board of the Mengel Company.

Harrison married Margaret W. Allis, of Louisville, in 1912; the couple had five children. Harrison died on July 13, 1948, in Wequetonsing, Michigan, and was buried in Louisville's Cave Hill Cemetery.   JAMES STROHMAIER

HARRISON COUNTY. Harrison County, the seventeenth in order of formation, is located in north-central Kentucky. It is bordered by Bourbon, Grant, Nicholas, Pendleton, Robertson, and Scott counties and has an area of 310 square miles. Harrison was formed on December 21, 1793, out of portions of Bourbon and Scott counties and named in honor of Col. Benjamin Harrison of Pennsylvania, who settled in Bourbon County and wrote part of the constitution of Kentucky. The county seat of Harrison is CYNTHIANA.

Prehistoric Indians hunted and lived in the Harrison County area, as ancient burial mounds attest. The first white settlers arrived in the spring of 1775. Capt. Joseph Hinkston and fifteen men from Pennsylvania established a settlement near the site of Cynthiana. This settlement was quickly abandoned but later rebuilt by Isaac Ruddell in 1779 and named RUDDELL'S STATION. In 1780 a force of British and Indians under the command of Capt. Henry Byrd attacked Ruddell's Station and forced the settlers to surrender. The Indians took the settlers as prisoners and made some of them travel as far as Detroit.

The topography of Harrison County is gently rolling to hilly, with rich productive soils. The major water source is the Licking River. The development of Harrison County in the antebellum period was closely aligned with farming and grazing. Local farms raised the grain for a booming distilling industry, and by the time of the Civil War the county was one of the region's top cattle producers.

During the Civil War, residents of Cynthiana were subjected to occupation by both Union and Confederate armies. The people were deeply divided and large numbers of county citizens took up arms on each side of the struggle.

Harrison County recovered quickly from the war's destruction. Whiskey production, which remained high throughout the nineteenth century, significantly aided this recovery. Cattle continued to be a valuable commodity. Cash crops, mainly tobacco, also gained importance, though the grains continued to predominate. Trade was further enhanced by improved railroads. Financial difficulties forced the small Covington & Lexington Railroad to merge with the Kentucky Central Railroad in 1875. Eventually, in 1891, the Louisville & Nashville Railroad (now CSX Transportation) took over the Kentucky Central, tying Harrison County to an extensive railroad network and opening the county to new trading opportunities in the twentieth century.

During the twentieth century Harrison County has remained an agricultural area. In 1987 farms occupied 92 percent of the county. Though whiskey production has declined, grain remains an important crop. Tobacco and cattle continue to keep the county prosperous, and there is a small industrial base, manufacturing steel products such as tubes, pipes, and valves.

The population of Harrison County was 14,158 in 1970; 15,166 in 1980; and 16,248 in 1990.

See William H. Perrin, ed., *History of Bourbon, Scott, Harrison and Nicholas Counties, Kentucky* (Chicago 1882).   RON D. BRYANT

HARROD, JAMES. James Harrod, a pioneer settler, left behind a number of mysteries, among them his date of birth and the time and manner of his death. As one of "Captain Cochran's Recruits" in June 1760, Harrod listed his age as sixteen. But the fact that his stated height—five feet, two inches— varied so much from his adult height of over six feet suggests that Harrod had inflated his age in order to serve. The dates of birth given for him vary between 1742 and 1746, with the latter possibly correct. It is known that he was born in Pennsylvania, one of a dozen children of John Harrod and his second wife, Sarah (Moore) Harrod. He had little formal education. He was not illiterate, however, as several early sources suggest, for he kept written records. In fact, Harrod proved to be intelligent and apparently was quick to learn several Indian languages, as well as French, when hunting in the Old Northwest.

Much of Harrod's life was shaped by Indians. His father's first wife had been killed by Indians; his brother Sam died by their hand in the 1770s. When Harrod was a child, his mother took the family and fled their home in Great Cove, Pennsylvania, just before Indians attacked. Fleeing, he saw homes burning and heard friends crying out as they died. Yet Harrod never came to hate Indians, nor killed indiscriminately, and one story in fact recounted his kindness to a wounded warrior.

Harrod became an excellent marksman and fine hunter. A slim, tall, erect man with black hair and a black beard, Harrod served as a guard at Fort Littleton and as a ranger as early as 1755. Later he joined Col. Henry Bouquet's British forces as they marched westward in July 1763 to Fort Pitt. After that, he, like others, heard the siren song of the western country, and he began to venture across the mountains in the 1760s. He went first to the Illinois lands, then made forays into present-day Kentucky

and Tennessee, where he encountered Daniel Boone. He visited again in the early 1770s. Attracted by the rich Kentucky land, Harrod set about establishing the first permanent settlement in Kentucky. A small band gathered at old Fort Redstone in Pennsylvania, voted Harrod their leader, took canoes down the Ohio and up the Kentucky River, and then went overland for a short distance to modern-day Mercer County. In June 1774 they established Harrodstown (now Harrodsburg). Town lots were divided, the surrounding land was surveyed, and Harrod claimed a rich tract a few miles away, at Boiling Springs. Others joined the Harrodsburg party, but Lord Dunmore's War soon threatened the little group's existence. After an Indian attack, the exposed settlers left Kentucky, deserting more than thirty cabins. In October 1774, Harrod and many of his men joined other advancing forces, but when they arrived at Point Pleasant close to midnight on October 10, the battle had ended.

Determined to reclaim their settlement, Harrod and some fifty men left Fort Redstone, bound for Harrodsburg by keelboat. They arrived on March 15, 1775, and slowly started to build a fort. In May delegates of the various groups then in Kentucky met at the Transylvania convention in Boonesborough and formulated the first regulations governing the new land. Harrod, who represented his area at the meeting, did not accept dominance by Richard Henderson's feudal TRANSYLVANIA COMPANY and soon led a successful protest against Henderson. When the state of Virginia created Kentucky County, effective December 31, 1776, it made Harrodsburg the county seat. Harrod delved into politics only briefly thereafter. In 1779 he was the new county's representative to the Virginia General Assembly, and in the 1780s he was a trustee of Harrodsburg.

Twice in 1776-77 Harrod led groups eastward to get provisions and gunpowder for protection of the feeble forts in Kentucky. Indians attacked Fort Harrod in March 1777, returned again the next month, and raided the region throughout the summer. As a militia captain and, by 1779, colonel, Harrod led his men in several fights, including difficult expeditions against the Indians in the Northwest Territory in 1780, 1782, and 1786.

In time, relative peace came to Kentucky, and Harrod settled into the comfortable life of a well-to-do farmer. Owner of 1,300 acres at Boiling Springs, with more than 20,000 acres across Kentucky, Harrod had a farm worked by six slaves, who tended scores of cattle, sheep, hogs, and horses. In February 1778, when Harrod was probably in his early to mid-thirties, he married a cultured, attractive twenty-two-year-old widow, Ann (Coburn) McDonald (or McDaniel). Her first husband had been killed by Indians, leaving her with a young son, James. In September 1785, after seven years of marriage, Ann bore a child, the red-headed Margaret, who would marry John Fauntleroy. In November 1787 James, Harrod's stepson, was seized by Indians and burned at the stake.

Distraught, the stepfather went on long surveying and hunting trips.

In the winter of 1792, on one such trip, Harrod disappeared and was not heard from again. He may have been killed, or he may have taken a "wilderness divorce." Ann Harrod married again, but a short time later, in April 1804, her third marriage was annulled—at her request—on the ground that her second husband was still alive. That may have been simply a convenient legal maneuver. Later, in applying for Harrod's pension, she swore that he had died hunting and that his clothes had been found in a river. Another explanation, however, indicated that a man named Bridges had killed Harrod and that Harrod's skeleton and clothes later were found in a cave. Other possibilities are that he was killed by Indians or animals. But there is no known grave site for Harrod. That he never gained the fame of Boone may reflect the lack of an author to tell Harrod's story.

See Kathryn Harrod Mason, *James Harrod of Kentucky* (Baton Rouge, La., 1951); George M. Chinn, *Kentucky: Settlement and Statehood, 1750-1800* (Frankfort, Ky., 1975).

JAMES C. KLOTTER

HARRODSBURG. Harrodsburg, the seat of Mercer County, is located on U.S. 68 and U.S. 127. The town was founded June 16, 1774, by James Harrod and thirty-one other men. Harrodsburg was originally called Harrod's Town, and was often referred to as Oldtown. The town was officially established by the Virginia legislature in 1785 and was incorporated on March 1, 1836. Shortly after the arrival of James Harrod's group, Indian raids became frequent along the Kentucky frontier. The settlers abandoned Harrodsburg for the remainder of 1774, and it was not reoccupied until March 15, 1775. By 1777 the population of the town was reported to be 198.

The town of Harrodsburg was the seat of Kentucky County, which was established in December 1776. By 1777, all settlements in Kentucky except Harrodsburg, Boonesborough, and Logan's Fort had been abandoned, for fear of the Indian wars.

Harrodsburg, during the latter part of the eighteenth and first half of the nineteenth century, was a thriving community. Not only was the town an agricultural market for the surrounding countryside, but it was also a social and educational center. Greenville Springs and Harrodsburg Springs in the area were among the finest spas in the South. Beaumont College, a well-known school for girls, was built on the site of Greenville Springs. Bacon College, founded in 1836 by members of the Christian church, was renamed Kentucky University.

The first Mercer County courthouse was constructed during 1787-89; the second courthouse, completed in 1820, was condemned in 1910; the present edifice was completed in 1913.

This pro-Confederate town was the site of several skirmishes and raids during the Civil War. On October 10, 1862, Lt. John Boyle led the 9th Kentucky Cavalry in a surprise raid on Harrodsburg, where many buildings had been converted into temporary hospitals, and captured 1,600 Confederate soldiers, many of whom were sick and wounded from the recent Battle of Perryville. Some of the captured Confederates were members of a detachment of Gen. Braxton Bragg's rear guard. Harrodsburg was placed under Federal martial law for the remainder of the war.

After the Civil War, Harrodsburg recovered slowly, but again prospered as a commercial center for a wealthy agrarian community. In 1888 the Louisville & Southern Railroad completed a line through the town.

Harrodsburg expanded its industrial base during the twentieth century. Products manufactured in the town included glass, clothing, electrical products, bathroom accessories, and agricultural items. Tourism became an important industry when Pioneer Memorial Park (now Old Fort Harrod State Park) was reconstructed and opened on June 16, 1927. On November 16, 1934, President Franklin D. Roosevelt dedicated a monument to honor the first permanent settlement west of the Allegheny Mountains.

The population of the fourth-class city was 6,741 in 1970; 7,265 in 1980; and 7,335 in 1990.

See George M. Chinn, *The History of Harrodsburg and "The Great Settlement Area" of Kentucky, 1774-1900* (N.p., 1985); Chinn, *Through Two Hundred Years, Pictorial History of Harrodsburg and Mercer County, Kentucky, Bicentennial Edition, 1774-1974* (Harrodsburg, Ky., 1974).

HARRODSBURG SPRINGS. The spa known as Harrodsburg Springs, which had its heyday in the 1830s and 1840s, took advantage of four or five major springs discovered near Harrodsburg, Kentucky, in the late eighteenth century. The spa and its nearby competitor, GREENVILLE SPRINGS, hoped to make Harrodsburg the "Saratoga of the West."

Harrodsburg Springs, owned by Capt. David Sutton, was operating in the early 1820s. Dr. Christopher C. Graham, Sutton's son-in-law, built a four-story hotel; the spa was then capable of accommodating a thousand patrons. In the 1830s and 1840s, the heyday of the spa, visitors came from all parts of the United States and foreign countries.

On June 8, 1853, the property was sold to the U.S. government for use as a veterans' hospital. The main building burned on May 30, 1856, and in 1859 the resident veterans were moved to Washington, D.C. On October 8, 1862, the property served as a hospital for the wounded from the Battle of Perryville. Fire struck again in 1864 and in the early 1880s, leaving little trace of the rich history of Harrodsburg Springs. In 1911 Judge Ben Casey Allin built a mansion on the rear portion of the property. In 1934 it was sold to Mr. and Mrs. William Caudill for the establishment of a sanitarium, and was then sold to the Mercer General Hospital Board.

See C.A. Van Arsdall, "A Medical History of Harrodsburg Springs," *Bulletin of the History of Medicine* (July-August 1949).

HARRODSBURG TANKERS. Company D, 192d Tank Battalion, a Kentucky National Guard unit staffed also by draftees, served in the Pacific during World War II. Organized on June 24, 1932, as the 38th Tank Company in Harrodsburg, the group had served as security forces during coal strikes, at Frankfort and Louisville in the 1937 flood, and at the Kentucky Derby. The Harrodsburg tankers reported to Fort Knox on November 20, 1940, as Company D, 192d Tank Battalion. After training, the battalion sailed on October 27, 1941, for the Philippines. When Japan's attack on the Philippines on December 8, 1941, forced a phased withdrawal to Bataan, the battalion fought as part of the army's rear guard. Harrodsburg tankers took part in the sieges of Bataan and Corregidor and in the Bataan death march. Years of mistreatment and starvation as prisoners of war in the Philippines, Manchuria, and Japan followed. Sixty-six Company D men had left Harrodsburg. Thirty-seven returned.

See James Russell Harris, "The Harrodsburg Tankers: Bataan, Prison, and the Bonds of Community," *Register* 86 (Summer 1988): 230-77.

JAMES RUSSELL HARRIS

HART, JOEL TANNER. Joel Tanner Hart, sculptor, was born near Winchester in Clark County, Kentucky, on February 10, 1810, to Josiah and Judith (Tanner) Hart. Because of his family's limited means, Hart received only three months of schooling. As a young man, he moved to Bourbon County, where he built stone walls and chimneys. At the age of twenty-one he was working in Pruden's marble yard in Lexington, where he carved headstones and monuments. There he met Shobal Vail Clevenger, a young sculptor from Cincinnati, who encouraged Hart to sculpt a marble bust of Cassius Marcellus Clay (now among the collections in the Margaret I. King Library at the University of Kentucky).

In 1838 Hart visited the Hermitage to sculpt Andrew Jackson. On his return to Lexington, Hart made busts of John J. Crittenden, Robert Wickliffe, and the Rev. Alexander Campbell. In 1845 he received a commission from the Ladies' Clay Association in Richmond, Virginia, for a full-length sculpture of Henry Clay to be placed in the Virginia state capitol. Hart traveled to Italy in September 1849 to transfer his plaster molds of the statue into marble, and he lived in Florence for the rest of his life, occasionally visiting the United States, London, and Paris. His invention for modeling the human form by means of measurements was patented in Great Britain and France.

In 1853 Hart submitted a sketch for a monument for the grave of Henry Clay in Lexington. The commission, however, went to architect Julius W. Adams, who used Hart's models for the head of the statue. In the mid-1850s William H. Lowery of New York City ordered a marble replica of Hart's bust of Clay, called *Virginia Mourning Over Her Son*. (Its name was later changed to *Il Penseroso* and it is now in the Margaret I. King Library at the University of Kentucky.) In 1857 Hart obtained a commission from the city of New Orleans for a bronze version of a statue of Clay that the state of Virginia had commissioned. The sculptures in both Richmond and New Orleans were unveiled on April 12, 1860. Hart was in New Orleans for the event. While he was in the United States, Hart was asked by the city of Louisville for another replica of Virginia's statue of Clay, which was placed in the Jefferson County Courthouse.

In 1869 Hart completed *Morning Glory*, another life-size neoclassical ideal sculpture. Of the two versions in marble, one is now in Louisville's Free Public Library and the other is in the collection of the National Museum of American Art in Washington, D.C. Hart's masterpiece, *Woman Triumphant*, was begun in 1875. He died before its completion and George Saul, an English sculptor and former pupil of Hart, finished sculpting the figure. A marble replica of it in the Fayette County Courthouse was destroyed in a fire on May 14, 1897.

During his lifetime Hart was more zealous of his reputation as a poet than as a sculptor. Though not many of his verses were published while he was alive, he provided in his will for compiling and publishing them in book form. Manuscripts of many of his poems, including "Marathon" and "The Old and New Year," are in the collection of the Kentucky Library Archives at Western Kentucky University in Bowling Green.

Hart died on March 2, 1877, in Florence, Italy. Eight years later his remains were brought to Frankfort, Kentucky, for reburial in the Frankfort Cemetery.

See David B. Dearinger, "Joel Tanner Hart: Kentucky's Neo-Classic Sculptor," *Kentucky Review* 8 (Spring 1988): 3-32; Gayle R. Carver, "Joel Tanner Hart: Kentucky's Poet-Sculptor," *Register* 38 (Jan. 1940): 49-53.

HART, NATHANIEL GRAY SMITH. Nathaniel Gray Smith Hart, lawyer and officer in the War of 1812, was born in Hagerstown, Maryland, in about 1784 to Col. Thomas and Susanna (Gray) Hart. His father, a proprietor of the Transylvania Land Company, moved the family in 1794 to Lexington, Kentucky, where he established a rope business. Hart studied law under Henry Clay, the husband of his sister Lucretia, and practiced in Lexington. By 1809, he had entered the hemp business with his father and his older brother, Thomas Hart, Jr.

As captain of the Lexington Light Infantry, Hart organized a company of about one hundred men to fight against the British in the War of 1812. His company was attached to Col. William Lewis's 5th Regiment of the Kentucky Volunteer Militia. In August 1812, the group headed northwest, and in October Hart became deputy inspector of the left wing of the northwestern army. His company fought at the Battle of the River Raisin in Michigan on January 18-22, 1813. On the final day of fighting, Hart was wounded and his men were taken as prisoners to Frenchtown. British Capt. William Elliott, whom Hart had previously known, assured the wounded prisoners that on the next day they would be given safe passage out of Indian territory and conducted to an English prison. Elliott, however, left the prisoners to the Indians, who on January 23 raided the camp, killing many of the men. Hart paid a friendly Pottawattomie to help him escape, but they were overcome by Wyandot Indians and Hart was tomahawked and scalped. His body was buried first in Detroit; in 1834 his remains were transferred to Frankfort Cemetery.

Hart married Anna Edward Gist on April 6, 1809, in Frankfort; they had two sons—Thomas and Henry Clay. On January 28, 1819, Hart County was established in his honor. Some historical accounts of Hart's life reproduce his name as Nathaniel G.T. Hart. According to C. Frank Dunn, the erroneous initial "T." first appeared in Richard Collins's *Historical Sketches of Kentucky* (1874), most likely as a typographical error.

See C. Frank Dunn, "Captain Nathaniel G.S. Hart," *FCHQ* 24 (Jan. 1950): 28-33.

HART COUNTY. Located in the south-central part of the state in the Pennyroyal region, Hart County was the sixty-first in order of formation. Created on January 28, 1819, out of portions of Hardin and Barren counties, Hart County is bordered also by Edmonson, Grayson, Green, Larue, and Metcalfe counties. The 412-square-mile county is named for Capt. Nathaniel G.T. Hart (1784-1813), a Lexington lawyer and brother-in-law of Henry Clay, who was captured and killed by Indians at the Battle of the River Raisin. MUNFORDVILLE is the county seat.

The terrain of Hart County is mainly rolling to hilly. In 1987 about 74 percent of the land was devoted to agriculture, with more than half of this under cultivation. That year Hart County ranked twenty-fifth in agricultural receipts among Kentucky counties. Though burley tobacco is the county's primary cash crop, livestock, poultry, and milk are also important. The Green River follows a serpentine path through the county and the Nolin River forms Hart's border with Grayson County.

Settlers who first entered about 1794 established homesteads in the vicinity of what would become the city of HORSE CAVE. These early residents probably selected the site for its fertile land and abundance of game. As the nineteenth century opened, more and more settlers entered the region and in 1816 the town of Munfordville was established. In the 1840s Horse Cave came into being. Facilitating Hart County's growth, the Louisville & Nashville Railroad (L&N) by August 1859 crossed through Munfordville and Horse Cave on its way from Louisville to Nashville.

During the Civil War, the county's strategic position on the railroad spelled trouble, as both North and South fought for its control. On December 5, 1861, Gen. John Hunt Morgan, to disrupt Federal supply lines, burned the L&N bridge over Bacon Creek, near Bonnieville. During his 1862 Christmas Raid, Morgan destroyed the new bridge. On September 15-17, 1862, in the Battle of Munfordville, Confederates led by Gen. Braxton Bragg captured about 4,000 Union troops and burned the L&N's Green River Bridge.

Hart County remained primarily agricultural well into the 1900s. In the latter half of the twentieth century, however, the county has witnessed great change. Following the establishment in 1941 of Mammoth Cave National Park, part of which lies in Hart County, the county became a major tourist center, with attractions eventually including its own caves such as Horse Cave and Mammoth Onyx Cave, in addition to Nolin River Lake, created in 1963. In the 1960s, when I-65 was built through the county, the tourism industry benefited significantly. In 1988, tourism alone generated over $7 million in revenue for Hart County. In addition to agriculture and tourism, the Hart County economy includes the manufacture of bedding, trailers, motor homes, and lumber products.

The population of Hart County was 13,980 in 1970; 15,402 in 1980; and 14,890 in 1990.

HARTFORD. Hartford, the seat of Ohio County in western Kentucky, is located on the Rough River at U.S. 231 and KY 69, just west of the Green River Parkway. The community was named for a deer crossing, or hart ford, on the Rough River. Hartford was founded on part of a 4,000-acre grant by Virginia to Gabriel Madison. The area was surveyed in 1782 and settled sometime before 1790. The fortified settlement known as Fort Hartford may have been one of the first of its kind in the lower Green River Valley. Early inhabitants may have included William Smothers (or Smithers), John Miller, Michael Riley, William Downs, Thomas Downs, William Sharpe, Phillip Taylor, and Samuel Neal.

The vicinity of the fort was subject to Indian attack, but the community survived and, when the threat passed, was made the seat of newly created Ohio County in 1798. A log courthouse was built in 1800 and in 1808 the town was incorporated. The courthouse collapsed in 1813 and what was left of it was burned later that year in celebration of Commodore Oliver H. Perry's victory on Lake Erie. A brick courthouse built in 1813-15 was destroyed by Confederate soldiers under Gen. Hylan B. Lyon on December 20, 1864, and construction of a third courthouse began in 1865. The two-story brick structure was demolished in 1940 and replaced by a concrete structure built under a grant from the Public Works Administration.

Hartford's population in 1810 was 110, which grew to 242 in 1830 and 309 in 1840. The city's location at the head of navigation on the Rough River was responsible for its early growth. A large grist and flour mill, established around 1830, operated until 1904. Tobacco, timber, and agricultural produce were first shipped from Hartford on small rafts. After improvements were made on the Rough River in 1834, steamboats made regular trips between Hartford and Evansville when water levels allowed. The river traffic declined after railroads came to the county in the 1870s.

During the Civil War, guerrillas masquerading as a detachment of Federal cavalry arrived in Hartford on January 22, 1865, and murdered two Union soldiers some distance from the town before leaving the area. The group may have been led by outlaw William Clarke Quantrill.

Ohio County's post–Civil War economic development, brought on by coal and railroad activity, spurred growth in Hartford. Hartford College for young men and women was opened on September 6, 1880. The college became Hartford High School in 1910. The building was destroyed by fire on June 19, 1912, and was replaced in 1913.

Hartford's hopes for rail transportation were realized when the Madisonville, Hartford & Eastern branch of the Louisville & Nashville (L&N) Railroad entered the city in May 1909. The line provided service until 1942, when the tracks eastward from the city were abandoned. An L&N branch line terminating at Hartford was abandoned in the 1980s.

Manufacturing plants were established in the city during the 1950s. Montpelier Glove Company, Hartford's largest manufacturing firm, was founded in 1954 and was followed by the Hartford Standard Corporation, a producer of metal products, in 1959.

The population of the fifth-class city was 1,868 in 1970; 2,512 in 1980; and 2,532 in 1990.

HASKINS, CLEM. Clem Haskins, basketball player and coach, was born in Campbellsville, Kentucky, on August 11, 1943, the son of Columbus and Lucy (Smith) Haskins. He attended Campbellsville's Durham High School and Taylor County High School, graduating in 1963. He was named to Kentucky's high school All-State team and played in the state's Sweet Sixteen tournament in 1962. Haskins attended Western Kentucky University (WKU) during 1963-67. He was named the Ohio Valley Conference's most valuable player for three years in a row—1965, 1966, 1967—and was named All-American in the 1965-66 and 1966-67 seasons. In 1967 he was the first-round draft choice of the Chicago Bulls and the third draft choice overall. He played during 1967-70 with the Chicago Bulls, during 1970-74 with the Phoenix Suns, and during 1974-76 with the Washington Bullets. In 1977 he joined the coaching staff at Western Kentucky University and became the head coach of the Hilltoppers in 1979. He was named rookie coach of the year in 1979 by NBC. In 1986 he became head coach of the University of Minnesota Golden Gophers.

Haskins married Yevette Penick in 1965. They have three children: Clemette, Lori, and Brent.

STEPHEN V. WISE

HATFIELD-McCOY FEUD. The feud between the McCoy clan of Pike County, Kentucky, and the Hatfield clan of Logan (later Mingo) County, West Virginia, is the most well-known of the FEUDS that racked the mountains of eastern Kentucky in the time between the Civil War and the twentieth century. It was neither the first, the last, the longest, nor the bloodiest of the Kentucky feuds; the violence involving certain members of the two families lasted less than a decade and cost only a dozen lives, but it attracted the attention of the eastern press and consequently a place in history and legend.

The McCoys lived on the Kentucky side and the Hatfields on the West Virginia side of the Tug Fork of the Big Sandy River. Both Anderson ("Devil Anse") Hatfield and Randolph ("Ranell") McCoy headed substantial families and loose confederations of other families in their neighborhoods. There had been some intermarriage of the families (Hatfields referred to Sarah McCoy as "Aunt Sally," and McCoys called Valentine Hatfield, brother of Devil Anse, "Uncle Wall"), and relations between the families at one time were generally amiable. Indeed, when fighting broke out, some McCoys fought on the side of the Hatfields.

Ill feeling arose, however, when Randall McCoy, in the fall of 1878, accused Floyd Hatfield of keeping one of McCoy's hogs in his pigpen. Hatfield denied it, and a trial was held in which a jury of six Hatfields and six McCoys found Hatfield innocent. The McCoys were furious that Selkirk McCoy, one of the jurymen, had agreed in the verdict, and that William Staton, a nephew of McCoy's, had testified that the hog belonged to Hatfield. Shortly afterward Staton was found dead, killed apparently by Sam and Paris McCoy. Sam and Paris were tried for the murder in Logan County, before justice of the peace Wall Hatfield, a brother of Devil Anse, and a Hatfield-picked jury. They were acquitted, an indication that no real feud existed at the time.

Nor did violence erupt at the 1880 spring elections, where eighteen-year-old Johnse Hatfield met Roseanna McCoy and the two were apparently smitten with each other. As the election festivities grew more alcoholic, Johnse and Roseanna slipped away, not returning until after dark, when all the others had gone. Roseanna, fearing her father's wrath, went home with Johnse, and the Hatfields, after their initial surprise, welcomed her. Newspaper reporters later tried to turn the affair into a Romeo-and-Juliet romance, but it was hardly that. Johnse, already a renowned womanizer and a veteran of indictments for fighting, moonshining, and carrying concealed weapons, apparently got Roseanna pregnant, but he refused to marry her, and she returned to her own people. (He later married her cousin Nancy.)

At the fall elections of 1882, Ellison Hatfield was attacked by three McCoy brothers and stabbed and shot. The McCoys were arrested but were seized on their way to jail by Hatfields, who killed them to avenge Ellison's death. The McCoys attempted for months to have the Hatfields arrested and tried, but without success. Perry Cline, an ambitious Pikeville attorney who had lost a dispute with Devil Anse over a valuable piece of timberland, persuaded the governor of Kentucky to ask the governor of West Virginia to extradite the Hatfields to Kentucky for trial. The governor of West Virginia refused, and for a while it seemed that violence between the two states might erupt. In the fall of 1886 Jeff McCoy killed Fred Wolford, a Pike County mail carrier. This apparently was not part of the feud, but a few months later Cap Hatfield, acting as a special constable, killed Jeff McCoy. In the spring of 1887 Tom Wallace, a Hatfield ally, was found dead.

On January 1, 1888, Devil Anse, fearing a trial, determined to remove everyone who had witnessed the capture and killing of the McCoy brothers. Rounding up his followers, he sent them into Kentucky to kill Ranell McCoy and his family. The Hatfield group surrounded the McCoy cabin in the night, set it on fire, and shot the McCoys as they attempted to escape. Alifair, Ranell's daughter, and Calvin, his son, were killed. Ranell's wife, Sarah, was beaten almost to death, but Ranell escaped.

Deputy Sheriff Frank Phillips of Pike County organized a posse and went into West Virginia. In the ensuing months he sent nine Hatfields to the Pike County jail in Pikeville and killed Jim Vance, a leader in the attack on the McCoy cabin, and Bill Dempsey, another Hatfield ally. Phillips's raids precipitated a suit in which the governor of West Virginia charged that Phillips had no constitutional right to invade the state and capture residents without the consent of West Virginia. Kentucky maintained that Phillips had a right, as a lawman, to arrest those under indictment. The U.S. Supreme Court finally ruled that Phillips had arrested the Hatfields illegally, but that jailing them once they were in Kentucky was lawful, and tensions between the states eased.

On February 19, 1890, Ellison Mounts, convicted of the killing of Ranell McCoy's daughter, Alifair, was hanged in Pikeville. Eight other members of the Hatfield clan were sent to prison for assorted murders. Devil Anse was shortly afterward tried for moonshining, released, and returned home, where he reportedly got religion and spent the rest of his life peacefully. Ranell McCoy spent the remainder of his life operating a ferry near Pikeville and brooding, his friends said, over the loss of his family. Though violence lingered, the feud was over.

See Otis K. Rice, *The Hatfields and the McCoys* (Lexington, Ky., 1982); Altina L. Waller, *Feud: Hatfields, McCoys, and Social Change in Appalachia, 1860-1900* (Chapel Hill, N.C., 1988).

JOHN ED PEARCE

HAWES, JAMES MORRISON. James Morrison Hawes, officer in the Confederate army, was born January 7, 1824, in Lexington, Kentucky, to Richard and Hattie (Nicholas) Hawes. His father was to serve as Confederate governor of Kentucky during the Civil War. The young Hawes entered the U.S. Military Academy at West Point on July 1, 1841, and graduated four years later as a second lieutenant of dragoons. His first military service came during the occupation of Texas (1845-46), and he fought in the war with Mexico. He took part in the siege of Vera Cruz and, for his bravery in the battles of San Juan de los Llanos, Contreras, Churubusco, and Molino del Rey, was breveted to first lieutenant. In 1848 Hawes was an assistant instructor of infantry tactics at West Point, where he also taught mathematics and cavalry tactics. In 1850 he left West Point to teach at the Cavalry School of Saumur, France. When he returned to the United States in 1852, Hawes was stationed on the Texas frontier, then served in the Utah expedition in 1857-58 and helped put down disturbances in Kansas.

Commissioned a captain in the Confederate army at the outbreak of the Civil War, Hawes was promoted to major June 16, 1861, and ten days later to colonel of the 2d Kentucky Cavalry. He resigned to accept a position in the regular army. At the request of Gen. Albert Sidney Johnston, he became a brigadier general in the Confederate army, on March 5, 1862, commanding the cavalry in the Western Department. After the Battle of Shiloh, Hawes asked to be relieved of his cavalry command and was assigned to command a brigade in Gen. John C. Breckinridge's division. In October 1862 he was sent to Little Rock, Arkansas, to head the cavalry brigade under Gen. T.H. Holmes, and in 1863 he commanded a brigade in Mississippi and engaged in fighting near the battle of Vicksburg. From 1864 until the war's end, he commanded troops in Galveston, Texas.

Hawes married Marie J. Southgate on February 3, 1857. He spent his years after the Civil War as a hardware merchant in Covington, Kentucky, where he died at his home on November 22, 1889.

HAWES, RICHARD. Richard Hawes, the second of the two governors of Confederate Kentucky, was born to Richard and Clary (Walker) Hawes on February 6, 1797, in Caroline County, Virginia, and moved to Lexington, Kentucky, in 1810. He studied law and was admitted to the bar in 1818. In 1824 he set up a legal practice in Winchester. Hawes served as state representative for Clark County in 1828, 1829, and 1834. During 1837-41 he represented Fayette, Clark, Woodford, and Franklin counties as a Whig in the U.S. House of Representatives. In 1843 he moved to Paris, Kentucky, where he returned to the practice of law. When the Whig party dissolved in the 1850s, Hawes became a Democrat. In April and September of 1861, Hawes, who favored neutrality for Kentucky in the Civil War, attended conventions in Frankfort to decide upon a course of action. Both conventions dissolved inconclusively.

In the fall of 1861 Hawes, a former state militia captain, fled Kentucky to avoid arrest by the Union and enlisted in the Confederate army, where he was posted as a brigade commissary. When the provisional Confederate government of Kentucky was formed, Hawes was appointed state auditor in absentia but declined the position. When Confederate Gov. George Johnson was killed at Shiloh in April 1862, the exiled provisional government appointed Hawes as his successor. On October 4, 1862, Gen. Braxton Bragg escorted Hawes into Frankfort for what was to be a triumphant establishment of Confederate government in Kentucky. Union troops entered the city late that afternoon, however, and drove out the Confederates. Hawes spent the remainder of the war as governor in exile. He was one of the many Confederates who became severe critics of General Bragg.

In 1865 Hawes returned to his law practice and business interests in Paris. He took part in state and local politics, serving several terms as county judge in Bourbon County. In 1866 he became master commissioner of the circuit and common pleas courts in Bourbon County, a position he held until his death. In 1818 Hawes married Hetty Morrison Nicholas; their first child, James Morrison HAWES, served as brigadier general in the army of the Confederacy. Hawes died on May 25, 1877, and is buried in Paris.

See Lowell H. Harrison, "George W. Johnson and Richard Hawes: The Governors of Confederate Kentucky," *Register* 79 (1981): 3-39.

ELIZABETH C. HAWES

HAWESVILLE. Hawesville, county seat of Hancock County and fifth-class city, was named for Richard Hawes, who donated the land for the town when Hancock County was formed in 1829. Hawesville became the major Ohio River port for the county, connected by roads and trails with inland settlements. The city was a convenient ferrying point for westward-moving pioneers. Coal seams in the limestone cliffs behind the town were mined very early, and by the 1850s Hawesville was shipping coal downriver. The Civil War brought guerrilla raids and Union blockades to Hawesville, and the coal mines were destroyed by Confederates to prevent use of the coal by Union gunboats. On July 24, 1864, the gunboat *Springfield* bombarded the town, forcing the inhabitants to seek shelter in caves and churches. Other sporadic shelling occurred, with little damage.

A new courthouse was built in 1867; it has since been restored. The loss of the coal mines in the Civil War caused Hawesville's population to shrink, and it was not until the coming of the Louisville & Nashville railroad in 1888 that prosperity returned. By 1890 Hawesville was flourishing; coal mines were reopened, and the city became the second busiest depot on the line between Louisville and Henderson. In the early years of the twentieth century, Hawesville again declined, especially after the coming of paved roads drew shoppers to bigger cities. With the arrival of industrial development in Hancock County, beginning in the 1950s, Hawesville has developed more stability. It celebrates its past with the annual Steamboat Days festival and is the home of the Hancock County Museum, located in the old depot. The population of the city was 1,262 in 1970; 1,036 in 1980; and 998 in 1990.

LEE A. DEW

HAYNIE, HUGH SMITH. Hugh Smith Haynie, political cartoonist, was born February 6, 1927, in Reedville, Virginia, to Raymond Lee and Margaret Virginia (Smith) Haynie. He served as a lieutenant in the Coast Guard Reserve from 1944 to 1946 and again for a year after his graduation in 1950 from the College of William and Mary with a degree in fine arts. During 1950-53 Haynie was staff artist and cartoonist at the *Richmond Times-Dispatch* in Virginia. He then moved to the *Greensboro Daily News*, with a short stint at the *Atlanta Journal* before becoming a political cartoonist at the *Louisville Courier-Journal* in 1958.

Haynie modeled himself after the cartoonists Herbert Block and Walt Kelly. He uses pen and brush in a distinctive style in open, uncluttered compositions, drawing widely from popular culture, comics, and nursery rhymes for his images. His sardonic cartoons have taken aim at Sen. Joseph McCarthy, the Vietnam War, Watergate, and government censorship. He has contributed to many collections, including *Best Editorial Cartoons of the Year*, edited by Charles Brooks (Gretna, La., 1976). *Hugh Haynie: Perspective*, which documented his work, was published in 1974.

Haynie received the National Headliners Club Award in 1966 and the Freedom Foundation Award in 1966, 1968, 1969, and 1970. He was awarded an honorary doctorate of humane letters from the University of Louisville in 1968 and he received the Alumni Medal from the College of William and Mary in 1977. Haynie became a member of the Kentucky Journalism Hall of Fame in 1987. He has been honored also by Sigma Delta Chi, the U.S. Chamber of Commerce, and the Kentucky Civil Liberties Union for his dedication to liberal, moral, and social causes. He is married to the former Oleta Joanna Stevens.

See Maurice Horn, ed., *Contemporary Graphic Artists*, vol. 3 (Detroit 1988); Charles Press, *The Political Cartoon* (East Brunswick, N.J., 1981).

HAYS, WILLIAM SHAKESPEARE. Born in Louisville on July 19, 1837, the son of Hugh and Martha (Richardson) Hays, William Shakespeare Hays wrote as many as five hundred songs. Sales of sheet music copies of his tunes reached about 20 million—an extraordinary number for his time. Educated at Hanover College in Indiana and Georgetown College in Kentucky, Hays was devoted to the southern way of life and had a lifelong attachment to riverboating, the subject of his regular columns in Louisville newspapers during the last half of the nineteenth century.

Will S. Hays, as he signed his manuscripts, composed patriotic, religious, and sentimental songs. Perhaps his most popular piece was "Mollie Darling," which sold as many as 3 million copies in the 1870s. Other notable tunes included "My Sunny Southern Home," "Evangeline," "We Parted By the River Side," "The Drummer Boy of Shiloh," and "Nora O'Neil." Late in life Hays claimed to have written "Dixie," but credit for this tune must in fact go to Ohio's Daniel Decatur Emmett.

Contemporary writers lavished praise upon Hays and his songs. S.J. Clarke claimed that "in America his songs were more deeply admired and cherished than those of any other composer." Hays was described as "one of the gentlest men in all the Southland" in spite of his "rough ways and his profane language." A music critic credited the success of his music to "charming melodies, easy and effective accompaniments, and a genuine feeling . . . written for the masses and by the masses appreciated." Hays died on July 23, 1907, and was buried in Louisville's Cave Hill Cemetery.

NICKY HUGHES

HAZARD. Hazard, the county seat of Perry County, is located on the North Fork of the Kentucky River at KY 15 and 80, near the eastern terminus of the Daniel Boone Parkway. The town was founded in 1821 by Elijah Combs, Sr., as the seat of newly formed Perry County. Like the county, it was named to honor Oliver Hazard Perry, hero of the Battle of Lake Erie during the War of 1812. Combs, who built the first house in what is now Hazard during the 1790s, was instrumental in the formation of the county, and part of the bottomland he owned was designated the new county seat.

County court was held at the home of Combs until another structure could be built. The first courthouse, probably of logs, served the county until 1836, when a brick structure was completed. A two-story frame structure built in 1866 was the third county courthouse. The fourth courthouse, dating from 1871, burned in 1911. An elaborate Colonial Revival-style building was finished in 1912 and served as the fifth courthouse until 1966, when a sixth building, of modern design, was dedicated.

The post office that served the community, established on April 22, 1834, was called Perry. From the beginning, however, the residents called the town Hazard and the name was officially changed on June 20, 1854. The city of Hazard was incorporated in 1884. Salt making was an early industry and timber was probably cut and floated down the Kentucky River from Hazard as early as the 1830s. During the Civil War, the city was subject to guerrilla depredations and raids by small bands of soldiers. The French-Eversole feud, which peaked in 1889, left many Hazard inhabitants dead.

Hazard's growth was encouraged by the Louisville & Nashville Railroad (now CSX Transportation), which in 1891 reached Jackson, thirty-two miles away. Until the railroad was extended to Hazard, supplies shipped upriver from Jackson on the Kentucky River were often delayed by severe weather or low water. The lumber business boomed in the 1880s, and in 1894 J.L. Johnson used a team of oxen to move a steam mill with circular saw from Paintsville to Hazard. The mill helped to supply lumber for the many new homes in town. In 1912 track was laid to Hazard, and on June 17, the first train entered the city. Coal mining began to surpass logging, and Hazard became a major coal mining center of the southeastern Kentucky coal fields. The population of the city grew from 537 in 1910 to 4,348 in 1920 and to 7,021 in 1930.

By the mid-1920s, KY 15 had been completed through the city. Known as the Red River Trail, the highway connected Hazard with Winchester to the northwest and with Pound Gap, Virginia, to the east. By 1951, KY 80, the Frontier Road, had been completed through the city. Further growth resulted from the early 1970s completion of the Daniel Boone Parkway, which connected to I-75 at London.

Mountain Coal Company is the largest employer in the Hazard area. The city's coal heritage is celebrated with the Black Gold Festival, held each September in downtown Hazard.

The population of the third-class city was 5,459 in 1970; 5,371 in 1980; and 5,416 in 1990.

HAZARD BAPTIST INSTITUTE. Hazard Baptist Institute, an elementary and secondary school, which in 1936 became Hazard College, was established in 1902, with four teachers and 165 students, by A.S. Petrey, a Baptist mission minister in the Three Forks Association of the General Association of Baptists in Kentucky. The institute's first building was completed in 1904. By 1908 the average student attendance at the institute was more than two hundred, and the first high school class graduated. In 1929, the Rev. C.D. Stevens succeeded Petrey and managed, despite the Depression, to keep the institute open. Junior college work began in 1932 in connection with the high school. H.E. Nelson became president of the school in 1936, when the high school course was dropped and only junior college work offered. In 1937 the school had a physical plant valued at $60,000 and debts totaling $2,500, and an estimated $125,000 was required for modernization. Unable to meet the requirements of the Southern Association of Colleges and Secondary Schools, the school closed in 1938, despite Petrey's plea to the Baptist Education Society of Kentucky to keep it open. The property was sold that year to the city schools of Hazard.

HAZEL PATCH. Hazel Patch, a village along U.S. 25 in northern Laurel County, in 1775 was a juncture in the road from Virginia to what is now Kentucky; the east fork (Boone's Trace) led to Fort Boonesborough, and the west fork (Skaggs's Trace) led to Crab Orchard and St. Asaph. Hazel Patch lies on Hazel Patch Creek, a tributary of the Rockcastle River in Laurel County, about a mile above the mouth of Patton Branch. According to an oftentold story, Benjamin Logan, pioneer, and Col. Richard Henderson, owner of the Transylvania Company, disagreed along the way to Kentucky in 1775 and parted company at the Hazel Patch. The story is not true, as Logan was in the company of John Floyd when he came to Kentucky in 1775. In 1793

Wood's blockhouse was constructed at this site, and what is now the town of Hazel Patch was built six miles down the creek from the original site in 1867. Around 1872, during the construction of the Louisville & Nashville Railroad, a small community was built there for the workmen.

See Neal Hammon, "Early Roads into Kentucky," *Register* 68 (April 1970): 92-102.

NEAL O. HAMMON

HEADLEY-WHITNEY MUSEUM. The Headley-Whitney Museum, six miles west of downtown Lexington on Old Frankfort Pike, is a small museum of decorative arts and fine art, with permanent collections and changing exhibitions. Established in 1968 by artist-designer George Headley, the museum features a collection of jeweled bibelots that is ranked as one of the three finest collections of its kind in the world. Programming includes a schedule of changing exhibitions, tours for schoolchildren and tourists, a luncheon lecture series, and a monthly "Music in the Museum" concert series.

HEARON, SHELBY (REED). Shelby (Reed) Hearon, fiction writer, was born of pioneer Kentucky stock on January 18, 1931, in Marion, Kentucky, the daughter of Charles B. and Evelyn (Roberts) Reed. She has lived most of her adult life in Texas, receiving her B.A. from the University of Texas in 1953. She was married to Robert J. Hearon, Jr., an attorney, from 1953 to 1977, and they had two children, Anne Shelby and Robert. In 1981 she married Billy Joe Lucas, a philosopher. Hearon has lectured and taught at the University of California at Irvine, Wichita State University, University of Texas at Austin, Bennington College in Vermont, and the University of Houston. Her awards and honors include fellowships from the Guggenheim Foundation and the National Endowment for the Arts.

Hearon's works include novels and a biography of Barbara Jordan. Her short stories, articles, and reviews have appeared in such periodicals as *Southwest Review*, *Redbook*, *Publishers Weekly*, the *Washington Post*, and *Texas Monthly*. Her fiction, set principally in the Southwest, has been praised for its strong female protagonists. A reviewer for the *New York Times* describes Alma, the narrator of *A Small Town* (1985), as growing "from an abused child with a Huckleberry Finn spunkiness into a high-school Lolita, from a principal's dutiful wife into a trailer-park adulteress, handling each role with an equanimity she never admits to." Her first book was *Armadillo in the Grass* (1968), and her other novels include *Painted Dresses* (1981) and *Owning Jolene* (1989), about a sassy nineteen-year-old heroine.

See Patrick Bennett, *Talking with Texas Writers* (College Station, Texas, 1980).   WADE HALL

HELM, BENJAMIN HARDIN. Benjamin Hardin Helm, Confederate general, was born on June 2, 1831, in Bardstown, Kentucky, to later Gov. John Larue (1850-51, 1867) and Lucinda Barbour (Hardin) Helm. He received his primary education at the Elizabethtown Seminary and the Kentucky Military Institute near Frankfort. On July 1, 1847, he entered the U.S. Military Academy at West Point. He graduated ninth in his class in 1851 and received the rank of second lieutenant in the 2d Regular U.S. Cavalry on July 1 of that year. He served on the Texas frontier at Fort Lincoln for six months, until illness forced him to return to Kentucky. On October 9, 1852, he resigned from the army at his father's request, to study law. He graduated from the school of law at the University of Louisville in the spring of 1853, went to Harvard Law School for a six-month advanced course, then practiced law with his father in Elizabethtown until 1856. In 1855 he was elected to the Kentucky House of Representatives, where he served one term. From 1856 until 1858 he was the commonwealth attorney for the 3d District. At this time, he also practiced law with Judge Martin D. Cofer. In 1858 he moved to Louisville to practice law with his brother-in-law, Harice M. Bruce, until 1861. In 1860 he was appointed assistant inspector general of the Kentucky State Guard.

On the eve of the Civil War, Abraham Lincoln, a brother-in-law of Helm's wife, personally offered Helm the position of paymaster of the Union army with the rank of major. Helm turned it down to recruit for the South and was appointed colonel of the 1st Regiment of the Kentucky Confederate Cavalry in September 1861. After the Battle of Shiloh, he received a promotion to brigadier general of the 3d Brigade of the Reserve Corps, predated to March 14, 1862. On July 8, 1862, he received command of the 2d Brigade of the 1st Division under Gen. John C. Breckinridge and was posted to Vicksburg, Mississippi. He fought in the Louisiana campaigns and on August 5, 1862, was wounded at the battle of Baton Rouge. While recovering in Chattanooga, Tennessee, Helm commanded the eastern district of the Department of the Gulf. On January 31, 1863, he returned to General Breckinridge, to command the Kentucky Brigade of the Army of Tennessee and the Department of the West. He fought in the Mississippi expedition to relieve Vicksburg and later in the Battle of Chickamauga.

Helm was married to Emily Todd, sister of Mary (Todd) Lincoln, on March 20, 1856. He was killed in the battle of Chickamauga on September 20, 1863, and was buried in Citizens' Graveyard in Atlanta. On September 9, 1884, he was reinterred in the Helm Cemetery in Hardin County.

See R. Gerald McMurtry, *Ben Hardin Helm, "Rebel" Brother-in-Law of Abraham Lincoln* (Chicago 1943); Lowell H. Harrison, "Kentucky-Born Generals in the Civil War," *Register* 64 (April 1966): 129-60.

HELM, JOHN LARUE. John Larue Helm, who served two abbreviated terms as governor of Kentucky, in 1850-51 and 1867, was the son of George and Rebecca (Larue) Helm. He was born near Elizabethtown, Kentucky, on July 4, 1802. After a common school education and studies with local attorneys, he was admitted to the bar in 1823. He married Lucinda Barbour in 1830; they had eleven children. Helm was appointed attorney for Meade County in 1824, then went to the Kentucky House of Representatives for the first time in 1826. With only brief interruption, he served in the House until 1844 and was several times elected Speaker. He was the Whig candidate for the U.S. House of Representatives in 1838, but lost. During 1844-48 and 1865-67 Helm was a state senator.

Elected lieutenant governor in 1848 over Democrat John P. Martin by a margin of 64,271 to 56,549, Helm became governor on July 31, 1850, following the resignation of Gov. John J. Crittenden (1848-50) and served until September 2, 1851. From 1854 to 1860 he was president of the expanding Louisville & Nashville Railroad. Helm advocated neutrality for Kentucky in 1861, but he was considered a Southern sympathizer. He resigned from the state Senate in 1867 to accept the Democratic nomination for governor. He won an easy victory, with 90,255 votes to 33,939 for Republican Sidney Barnes and 13,167 for Judge William B. Kinkead, the Union, or Conservative, candidate. Helm, who had become ill during the campaign, died on September 8, 1867, just five days after the oath of office was administered at his bedside. He was buried on the family farm near Elizabethtown.

During his first term Helm unsuccessfully fought a legislative move to balance the school fund by using money from the sinking fund that was to pay off the state's debt. He favored state aid for economic development, election reforms to curb irregularities and violence, higher salaries to attract better judges, and prohibition of the carrying of concealed deadly weapons. He achieved a few minor election reforms. During his 1867 campaign, Helm called for an end to Civil War bitterness and proscriptions against ex-Confederates. Although he promised protection for the rights of blacks, he opposed voting rights. Helm accused the U.S. Congress of interfering in areas that belonged to the states.

See Lowell H. Harrison, ed., *Kentucky's Governors, 1792-1985* (Lexington, Ky., 1985).

LOWELL H. HARRISON

HEMP INDUSTRY. Hemp is the name for the durable fiber extracted from the inner bark of the plant *Cannabis sativa*. Hemp is also a common name for the plant itself.

Cannabis sativa is an annual plant of Asian origin. The species is now widespread throughout the world, having been dispersed by humans since 500 B.C. Hemp was first grown in Kentucky during the mid-1770s, and the period 1775-1800 was the time of the initial hemp boom. The highly fertile soils, especially rich in nitrogen, were well suited to growing the plant. Fibers from the hemp crop were used primarily to make rope and sailcloth, both scarce products that could be sold in New Orleans for a good price. Later, with the construction of machines to process the stems efficiently, Lexington became a hub of the hemp industry, producing large quantities of rope, cloth, sheeting, and floor covering. In the 1860s the hemp industry began to decline. Availability of superior fibers such as Manila fiber and the growing market for tobacco as an alternative crop tended to reduce both demand for and supply of hemp.

A second, brief period of hemp importance in Kentucky occurred during World War II. Because the U.S. supply of Manila fiber, originating in the Philippines, was drastically reduced by the Japanese conquest, an experimental program to grow hemp was developed. Kentucky was chosen as the site for seed production and 36,000 acres were planted in 1942. During 1943 and 1944, Kentucky and a handful of other states produced 60 million pounds of fiber. The project was discontinued in 1945 as other fibers became available. Isolated patches of hemp are still found in the agricultural areas of Kentucky. These plants, now naturalized, likely escaped from early hemp cultivation projects.

The third period of hemp importance in Kentucky began in the mid-1970s. Hemp is grown illegally and sold for its narcotic properties. The leaves or flowering tops are dried and smoked as ganja or marijuana. Law enforcement officials estimate that illegal hemp culture forms a significant part of the economy in the less densely populated parts of Kentucky.

The interest in natural fibers as opposed to synthetic fibers might produce new demand for hemp from selectively bred hemp plants that produce high-quality fibers but no resin. Some see such a potential industry as an alternative to tobacco.

See B. Moore, *Study of the Hemp Industry of Kentucky* (Lexington, Ky., 1905); James F. Hopkins, *A History of the Hemp Industry in Kentucky* (Lexington, Ky., 1951).

JAMES O. LUKEN

HENDERSON, RICHARD. Richard Henderson, who attempted in 1775 to make an independent colony out of part of the area that is now Kentucky, was born to Col. Samuel and Elizabeth (Williams) Henderson on April 20, 1735, in Hanover County, Virginia. In 1742 the family moved to Granville County, North Carolina, where Henderson read law with Judge John Williams and was licensed by the chief justice of the North Carolina colony, Charles Berry. On March 1, 1768, Henderson was appointed by Gov. William Tyron as associate justice of the superior court of North Carolina, where he remained until the court was dissolved in 1773.

On August 27, 1774, Henderson organized the Louisa Company for the purpose of purchasing a "large territory or tract of land on the western waters from the Indian tribes" and establishing a proprietary colony. On January 6, 1775, Henderson reorganized the company, adding new members and forming the TRANSYLVANIA COMPANY, with an agreement outlining the form of government the new colony would take. Henderson commissioned Daniel Boone to begin land purchase negotiations with the Cherokee nation, and despite a February 10, 1775, proclamation by the North Carolina governor prohibiting the purchase, Henderson completed the Treaty of Sycamore Shoals on the Watauga River on March 17. The Transylvania Company claimed present-day western and central Kentucky and north-central Tennessee, establishing the proprietary government of Transylvania.

On March 23 Henderson opened the first general assembly of the proprietary colony at Boonesborough with a speech calling upon the delegates to create a set of laws that would favor the general masses and create incentives for obedience in the new colony. On September 25 the proprietors of Transylvania met in Granville County, North Carolina, and elected James Hogg to represent them in the Continental Congress in seeking recognition as the fourteenth colony. The Continental Congress, however, failed to grant Transylvania its independence, and on November 4 the Virginia legislature, which claimed jurisdiction over Kentucky, annulled the Sycamore Shoals treaty. North Carolina had asserted its jurisdiction over part of the Transylvania colony in a proclamation on March 21, 1775. The Virginia legislature compensated the Transylvania Company with over 200,000 acres of land, and North Carolina also gave the company 200,000 acres, in recognition of the company's improvements in the region.

Henderson served on the North Carolina Council of State in 1778 but on August 14 of that year he declined an offer of his former position of U.S. superior court judge. In 1779 he was one of the commissioners appointed to readjust the western and central boundaries of Virginia and North Carolina. After a dispute with his Virginia counterpart, however, Henderson quit the project to open a land office in Nashville, Tennessee, and sell the holdings of the Transylvania Company. In 1780 he returned to his Hillsborough plantation in North Carolina and was elected to the North Carolina House of Commons in 1781. He was married to Elizabeth Keeling on December 28, 1763. They had four sons. He died on his plantation on January 30, 1785. In 1798 Henderson County, Kentucky's thirty-eighth, was formed from part of Christian County to honor Richard Henderson.

See George W. Ranck, "Boonesborough," *Filson Club Publication* 16 (Louisville 1901); Archibald Henderson, "Richard Henderson and the Occupation of Kentucky, 1775," *Mississippi Valley Historical Review* 1 (December 1914): 341-63.

RONALD B. FRANKUM, JR.

HENDERSON. Henderson, the seat of Henderson County, is located on the Ohio River at the junction of U.S. 60 and 41. The town site was part of the 200,000 acres granted to Col. Richard Henderson's Transylvania Company by the Virginia Assembly in 1778. In the 1790s, the company's heirs established the town at an existing settlement known as Red Banks. Gen. Samuel Hopkins and Col. Thomas Allen arrived to survey the land in

March 1797, laid out the town, and named it for Colonel Henderson.

When Henderson County was formed in 1798, Henderson was named the county seat. A log schoolhouse was used for county government until a permanent structure, a two-story brick building, was completed in 1814. A third courthouse, of Greek Revival style, was completed in 1843 and went through several renovations and additions before it was torn down in 1963. The fourth county courthouse was completed in 1965.

Henderson's location on the Ohio River just below the confluence with the Green River made it an important river port; yet because the city was built on a bluff, it did not suffer flood damage as did many other of Kentucky's Ohio River towns. The rich agricultural region made it a tobacco market, and its proximity to western Kentucky coal mines attracted industry.

In 1810 Henderson was incorporated as a city. Among the 160 town residents at the time was ornithologist John J. Audubon, who operated a general store there. In 1811 the first steamboat on the Ohio River arrived at the city, and by 1814 a tobacco warehouse had been built. German immigration during the 1850s helped to swell the population. The city was divided by the Civil War. A Federal recruiting station was established there in October 1861, while some of those who inclined toward the Confederacy were recruited by Col. Adam R. Johnson, a native of Henderson. Johnson's Confederates captured the town on July 17, 1862, and took away guns and military stores. Federal troops occupied the city for a time in 1863 and used the courthouse as a prison and a garrison in 1864.

Substantial growth took place in the city after the war. In March 1869, the Evansville, Henderson & Nashville Railroad (now part of CSX Transportation) was completed to Madisonville. By 1871 trains were running between Henderson and Nashville, and in 1885 a railroad bridge connected Henderson with Evansville, Indiana. In 1889 a second railroad, the Louisville, St. Louis & Texas (now CSX) reached Henderson from the east. In that same year, a street railway began operation.

The railroads increased Henderson's status as a market city. By the early 1890s, eighteen tobacco factories were located there along with several distilleries and a brewery. The Henderson Wagon Works, the Henderson Cotton Mills, and the Henderson Woolen Mills, which made the well-known Kentucky jeans, were all important industries in the late nineteenth and early twentieth centuries.

From 1916 until 1937, prohibition of alcohol and overseas tobacco tariffs hit the Henderson economy hard, and the wagon works lost out to the rising automobile industry. Ironically, it was the Great Flood of 1937 that started economic recovery. Henderson was the only city between Pittsburgh and Cairo that was not inundated in the deluge, and new industry was attracted to the location.

On July 3, 1932, a bridge for vehicular traffic completed nearby provided access across the

Ohio River. By the 1940s a strip of nightclubs and gambling casinos opened along U.S. 41 to Evansville, and the area became a mecca for criminals. Law enforcement and citizen concern were able to control the night life. Major industries moved to Henderson in increasing numbers during and after World War II. By 1990 the town had a diversified economic base that included farm products, coal, and oil along with the manufacture of chemicals, aluminum, food products, automotive accessories, furniture, and clothing. The city is home to Henderson Community College.

The population of the third-class city was 22,976 in 1970; 22,834 in 1980; and 25,945 in 1990.

BOYNTON MERRILL, JR.

HENDERSON COUNTY. Henderson County, the thirty-eighth county in order of formation, is located in western Kentucky along the Ohio River. It is bordered by Daviess, McLean, Webster, and Union counties and has an area of 438 square miles. A change in the river's course has isolated a small portion of the county on the opposite shore of the Ohio River from the rest of the county. The county was formed in 1798 from a section of Christian County and named to honor Col. Richard Henderson, founder of the Transylvania Company. In 1778 the heirs to Henderson's company were granted 200,000 acres of land in what would become Henderson County by the Virginia House of Delegates. Members of the company were among the area's settlers beginning in 1798.The seat of Henderson County is the city of HENDERSON.

The topography of Henderson County varies from level floodplain to gently rolling land. Mineral resources include oil and coal. The county is a very productive farming area with leading crops of corn, soybeans, wheat, and tobacco. Livestock is also raised there. In addition to the Ohio and Green rivers, numerous small streams that bisect the county include Lick, Canoe, Beaverdam, and Pond creeks.

The first settlement in the county occurred around 1791 at what was then called Red Banks, the future site of the city of Henderson. Settlement of the area was slowed by the threat of Indians and later by outlaws. With the establishment of Henderson County in 1798, and a county court system the next year, the area became generally peaceful. By 1800 the population of the county had increased substantially, and numerous grist and carding mills were built. In 1801 Henderson was designated one of the state's tobacco inspection points, and much of the tobacco exported from the Green River Valley passed through there. A second inspection house was built in 1805 to handle the quantities of beef, pork, flour, and hemp that were shipped out. The 1837 construction of a dirt turnpike through the county, connecting Henderson with Hopkinsville, also helped to stimulate economic growth. The city of Henderson grew rapidly as a trading center, amid scattered agricultural communities and river landings.

In 1851 Henderson Countians were treated to an interesting political dilemma. Two residents of the county, Archibald Dixon, who was a Whig, and Lazarus Powell, a Democrat, faced each other in the gubernatorial race. The two were friends and had been law partners from 1835 until 1839. Powell (1851-55) won the election by a slim margin, while Dixon later went on to fill out the unexpired Senate term (1849-55) of Henry Clay, who died on June 29, 1852. Other Henderson Countians who became governors of Kentucky were John Young Brown (1891-95); A.O. Stanley (1915-19), who had moved there in 1898; and A.B. Chandler (1935-39, 1955-59), a native of the village of Corydon.

During the Civil War, no major battles took place there, although the county was subject to raids by Confederate partisan rangers or lawless guerrilla bands. Union forces occupied the county seat on at least two occasions. After the war, development of the county's resources began in earnest. In 1866 the Henderson and Union Petroleum Company struck oil on the headwaters of Highland Creek. Coal, which had been dug in small amounts since the 1820s, was extracted and barged down the river in ever-increasing quantities.

The promise of economic growth attracted railroads to the county. In 1871 the Evansville, Henderson & Nashville Railroad (now part of CSX Transportation) completed a line through the county, and was followed by the Louisville, St. Louis & Texas Railroad in 1889. The railroads and other industrial activity accounted for rapid growth of some of the small villages in the county. Among the county towns that blossomed in the later part of the 1800s were Corydon, Smith Mills, Zion, and Baskett.

On July 4, 1932, the Audubon Memorial Bridge, also known as the Henderson-Evansville Bridge, was dedicated. Henderson County became a gateway to the south via U.S. 41, which was known as the Dixie B-Line, a main north-south road before the advent of interstate highways. With the increase in tourist traffic, county residents in 1934 began the establishment of what eventually became the John James Audubon State Park. In 1938 a museum was dedicated there to honor the painter and naturalist, who spent time in the area from 1808 to 1819.

The city of Henderson experienced industrial growth during World War II and the years afterward, while the rest of the county was engaged in oil or coal production or remained agricultural. By 1989, bituminous coal and lignite mining was a leading employer in the county. Crude oil production in 1989 was 817,658 barrels.

The population of Henderson County was 36,031 in 1970; 40,849 in 1980; and 43,044 in 1990.

See Writer's Program of the W.P.A., *Henderson, Home of Audubon* (Northport, N.Y., 1941); Maralea Arnett, *The Annals and Scandals of Henderson County, Kentucky, 1775-1975* (Corydon, Ky., 1976).

HENDERSON LINE. The Henderson line along the Kentucky-Tennessee border was the baseline on which William T. Henderson began a survey in 1821. It ran from the Tennessee River to the Green

Timber arm of the Reelfoot, to the Mississippi River at New Madrid Bend 36°30'32'' north latitude. The purpose of Henderson's survey was to establish a boundary from which townships, sections, and ranges could be homesteaded in the 4,600-square-mile Jackson Purchase, obtained by treaty from the Chickasaw Indians in 1818.

Henderson based his survey on the line established in 1819 by surveyors Robert Alexander and Luke Munsell, which settled a boundary dispute between the two states by means of the 1820 Kentucky-Tennessee Boundary Compact.

See Thomas D. Clark, *Historic Maps of Kentucky* (Lexington, Ky., 1979).

THOMAS D. CLARK

HENDERSON SETTLEMENT SCHOOL. Henderson Settlement School, a community development center at Frakes in Bell County, Kentucky, was established in 1925 as an elementary school by Hiram Milo FRAKES, a Methodist minister. He moved to southeastern Kentucky in 1921 to serve coal camps and received an appointment to the Pineville First Methodist Church within a year.

On land donated by the mountaineers and with the aid of Bertha Reil, a graduate of the Chicago Training School, Frakes opened a one-room school in the winter of 1925 in the Middle Laurel Fork valley, an area of Appalachia known as "South America." Established as Partin Settlement School, the institution was renamed Henderson to commemorate Bill Henderson, a mountaineer who had donated his entire farm, and Theodore Henderson, a bishop of the Ohio Methodist Conference who had lent support. A dormitory was erected in 1927 and the next year a high school was added. Tuition and board were financed with the profits of a campus farm. In 1930 the school organized the country's first 4-H Club. With the expansion of public education after World War II, the school became more community-oriented, and a day-care facility and medical clinic were opened. When the settlement's educational operations closed in 1976, the high school became a community center. The Methodist-affiliated, 1,300-acre settlement has expanded into a multifaceted community resource, with agricultural and child care facilities.

See Lee Fisher, *Fire in the Hills: The Story of Parson Frakes and the Henderson Settlement* (New York 1971).

HENRY, PATRICK. Patrick Henry, governor of Virginia, was born in Hanover County, Virginia, on May 29, 1736, to John and Sarah (Winston) Henry. Most of his limited education was obtained at home. After failures at storekeeping and farming, Henry obtained a law license in 1760 and was an immediate success. He became a leader of the Virginia resistance to British colonial policies. He was elected to the House of Burgesses in 1765, and by the early 1770s he favored colonial autonomy. A radical leader in the First Continental Congress (1774), he was denounced for disturbing the peace by the Virginia governor, Lord Dunmore, in 1775.

After serving in the Second Continental Congress and heading the Virginia regular military during the early days of the Revolutionary War, Henry helped draft the state's first constitution and then served three one-year terms as governor, 1776-79. He authorized and supported George Rogers Clark's expedition into the Illinois country. Henry eventually owned several thousand acres in Kentucky, and he signed many of the warrants for other Kentucky claims.

In 1779 he retired to a large tract in Henry County, Virginia, but he served in the House of Delegates during 1780-84. Henry supported forgiveness for the Tories, but he led a bitter fight against the disestablishment of religion.

Governor again in 1784-85, Henry tried to pay Virginia's war debt. After Indians killed his brother-in-law William Christian in Kentucky, Henry urged Congress to protect the frontier. He led the state's successful opposition to the Jay-Gardoqui treaty. Henry refused a seat in the Constitutional Convention, and he unsuccessfully opposed ratification in the 1788 Virginia convention, where most of the delegates from Kentucky supported his position. Henry resumed his successful law practice in 1787. He refused offers to become U.S. secretary of state (1795) and chief justice (1796) and President John Adams's request that he go on a mission to France. As Henry became a Federalist, he lost many of his supporters.

In 1754 he married Sarah Shelton, who died in 1775 after several years of insanity. Henry then married Dorothea Dandridge in 1777. Six children were born to his first wife, eleven to the second. Washington persuaded Henry to run for the Virginia legislature in 1799, but he died on June 6, 1799, before taking his seat, and he was buried at his Red Hill plantation.

See Henry Mayer, *A Son of Thunder: Patrick Henry and the American Republic* (New York, 1986).

LOWELL H. HARRISON

HENRY COUNTY. Henry County, Kentucky's thirty-third, was formed in 1798 from part of Shelby County. Some of its original territory was later carved into Oldham and Trimble counties, which border it, along with Franklin, Carroll, Owen, and Shelby counties. Located in the north-central portion of the state, in the outer Bluegrass region, Henry County covers 289 square miles. NEW CASTLE, the county seat and its highest elevation, is 825 feet above sea level. The eastern portion of the county is mostly hilly terrain, and the rest rolling plains. Mineral resources include limestone, sands, mineral waters, and clays suitable for making bricks. The Kentucky River forms the boundary between Henry and Owen counties, and many small creeks and streams water and drain the area. Lake Jericho Recreation Area, in the southwest part of the county, contains Henry County's largest lake—136 acres—and includes more than four hundred acres for outdoor activities.

Henry County was named for Patrick Henry, Revolutionary War patriot, who in 1785 assigned the first land patent for Drennon Springs, located on Drennon's Lick in the northern portion of the county, between New Castle and the Kentucky River, to George Rogers Clark. The springs, discovered in 1773 by pioneer settlers Jacob Drennon and Matthew Bracken, were a source of salt in the early nineteenth century. In the 1840s and 1850s a spa capitalized on the reputed medicinal qualities of the springs. WESTERN MILITARY Institute operated there in the fall, winter, and spring during the period 1851-61, and during the Civil War Union loyalists used the grounds as a recruiting station. The main hotel and outlying cottages burned March 23, 1865. Among the other private academies that operated in Henry County over the years were EMINENCE COLLEGE in Eminence (1857-95), Henry County Academy in New Castle (1836-85), Smithfield College in Smithfield (1866-ca. 1887), and Home College in Campbellsburg (1883-1927).

Agriculture is the mainstay of Henry County's economy. In 1986 agricultural receipts totaled $34.15 million, including $22.25 million in crop receipts and $11.9 million in livestock receipts. Eminence, the highest point between Louisville and Lexington, is the largest city in the county. This fourth-class city, located at the junction of KY 22 and KY 55, about twelve miles north of Shelbyville, was incorporated in 1851. More than 75 percent of the county's industrial jobs are located in Eminence, including the manufacture of electronic speakers, magnetizers, copper products, strip steel, and sporting goods. I-71 and CSX Transportation Systems run through the western section of the county.

Henry County lays claim to two literary figures. Eminence was the birthplace of Hollis SUMMERS (1916-87), a novelist and poet whose works include City Limit (1948), Brighten the Corner (1952), and The Weather of February (1957). New Castle was the boyhood home of Wendell BERRY, who used the countryside scenery there in Nathan Coulter (1960). The population was 10,910 in 1970; 12,740 in 1980; and 12,823 in 1990.

See Maude Johnston Drane, History of Henry County, Kentucky (n.p., 1948).

HENSLEY SETTLEMENT. Located in eastern Bell County, Kentucky, straddling the Kentucky-Virginia state line, the Hensley Settlement is a living museum of self-sufficient pioneer life. The collection of log cabins is located on a five-hundred-acre plantation atop Brush Mountain. In 1845, Gov. William Owsley (1844-48) granted to two brothers—C. and R.M. Bales—the right to the area at the top of the mountain. The Baleses and their heirs leased the plateau to John Nichols of Union County, Tennessee. Using it mainly for cattle grazing, Nichols cleared most of the plateau, constructed fences, and, along with another lessee, Jim Nelson, built a few small cabins. In May 1903, Barton Hensley, Sr., bought the five hundred acres and redistributed it among his family. The same year,

Sherman Hensley and his family moved into Jim Nelson's old cabin and founded Hensley Settlement. Followed in 1904 by other members of the Hensley clan and their in-laws, the Gibbonses, the settlers built a pioneer community that never had electricity, plumbing, or paved roads.

Maintaining a self-sufficient agricultural lifestyle, the settlers left the mountain only to purchase goods they could not make themselves, to have their corn ground into meal, or to sell their surplus at market. Money to buy manufactured items was earned at the market or by driving stock across the mountains for lowland farmers, and hunting supplemented their meat supply. In 1925 the community had reached its apex, with about one hundred inhabitants, a school, church, and about forty other buildings. With the growth of the coal industry and the coming of World War II, community residents became either miners or soldiers.

After the war, few former settlers returned, and those who had stayed found better opportunities with the coal companies. By 1947 only three families remained, and two years later Sherman Hensley—the settlement's first resident—was the town's only occupant. He left the settlement in 1951. Hensley Settlement, a part of Cumberland Gap National Historical Park since its dedication on July 4, 1959, has become a living museum where park employees perform many of the daily activities once carried out by the townspeople.

See William E. Cox, Hensley Settlement: A Mountain Community (Philadelphia 1978).

HENSON, JOSIAH. Josiah Henson, born on June 15, 1789, in Charles County, Maryland, was a runaway slave from Kentucky who wrote an autobiography said to have influenced Harriet Beecher Stowe's Uncle Tom's Cabin (1852). Indeed, advocates of this view say that Stowe read Henson's book, first published in 1849 and later in half a dozen editions and adaptations, and used him as the model for her "Uncle Tom." Although there is room to debate these claims, Kentucky has placed a historical marker east of Owensboro in Daviess County on U.S. 60 near the spot where Henson, or "Uncle Tom," had a cabin. In 1825 Henson led eighteen slaves from Maryland to relocate on the Amos Riley farm in Daviess County, where he became an overseer. The next five years proved crucial for him. For one thing, he became a preacher, which gave him a sense of mission. For another, in spite of dedicated service to the Rileys, he narrowly avoided being sold, an experience that prompted him in 1830 to escape to Canada with his wife and four children. During his years there, Henson founded a community for runaway slaves. He became a popular abolitionist speaker. Henson died on May 5, 1883, and was buried by the black community of Dresden, Ontario.

See John Lobb, ed., An Autobiography of the Rev. Josiah Henson ("Uncle Tom") From 1789 to 1881 (London, Ontario, 1881).

DAN BRADSHAW

HERMANY, CHARLES. Charles Hermany, the self-educated civil engineer who designed Louisville's water supply system at the turn of the century, was born in Lehigh County, Pennsylvania, on October 9, 1830, to Samuel and Salome (Wannemacher) Hermany. He received his early education in Lehigh County, then attended Minerva Seminary in Easton, Pennsylvania, from 1846 to 1848, when financial difficulties caused him to return to the family farm. For the next three years, he worked on the farm during the summer, taught in the local school in the winter, and studied mathematics and engineering in his spare time, teaching himself the art of land surveying.

In 1853 Hermany took a position in the Engineering Department of the city of Cleveland, and in 1857 he was employed by the Louisville Water Company as first assistant to the chief engineer. Hermany's active role in the construction of the new city water works put him in line for promotion to chief engineer and superintendent on January 1, 1861, just three months after the project was completed. Hermany held that position until his death forty-seven years later.

To keep a continuous supply of water flowing from the Ohio River, where the water level varied by forty feet throughout the year, Hermany designed and built a new main water pump and reservoir on the site of the Louisville Water Tower, at the intersection of River Road and Zorn Avenue just outside the city. Both were completed by 1873. To meet the needs of Louisville's growing population, Hermany designed a new 100-million-gallon reservoir system that was completed in Crescent Hill in 1893. The next year F.W. Dean of the American Society of Engineers praised the Louisville Water Works as one of the finest systems in the country. As his reputation grew, Hermany assisted with the water works in Frankfort and Bowling Green, Kentucky, and consulted on the construction of works in Cincinnati, Chicago, Nashville, St. Louis, and Providence, Rhode Island. In 1904 he was elected president of the American Society of Civil Engineers.

Hermany married Sallie J. Adams on December 19, 1864; they had seven children: Irene, Emily, Madeline, Hetty, Charles, Samuel, and Edward. Hermany died on January 18, 1908, in Louisville and was buried in Cave Hill Cemetery there.

HICKMAN, PASCHAL. Paschal Hickman, soldier in the War of 1812, came to Kentucky in 1784 with his father, the Rev. William Hickman, and his mother, who was a member of the Shackelford family. His military service began in 1794, when he fought alongside Gen. Anthony Wayne at the Battle of Fallen Timbers in Ohio. In 1802 he was an ensign in the 22d Regiment of the Kentucky militia and was promoted to lieutenant on September 24, 1803. Hickman fought at the Battle of the RIVER RAISIN in 1813 during the War of 1812, under the command of Gen. James Winchester. Wounded in the initial skirmish at Frenchtown on January 18,

he was taken to a nearby house for treatment. Hickman was left behind with the other wounded when the U.S. troops were defeated by British and Indian forces led by Col. Harry Proctor on January 22. He was one of approximately sixty-five soldiers who were massacred by Indians the following day.

Hickman married Elizabeth F. Hall on March 11, 1797, and lived in Frankfort; they had three daughters. He was a successful businessman and farmer, and eventually owned almost 6,000 acres in sixteen counties. At his death his property was valued at more than $9,000.

Hickman County in the Jackson Purchase area of Kentucky is one of nine counties named for soldiers killed in the Battle of the River Raisin.

HICKMAN. Hickman, the seat of Fulton County, is located on five bluffs above the Mississippi River at the junction of KY 94 and KY 125. The town was once called Mills Point, in honor of James Mills, who settled on a military grant in 1819. In 1837 the name of the settlement was changed to Hickman, the maiden name of the wife of G.W.L. Marr, who had once owned the town site among his extensive landholdings. The river trade helped make Hickman a thriving town. In 1845 some 2,000 bales of cotton and 3,000 hogsheads of tobacco were shipped from the community.

In 1845, with a population of 350, Hickman was chosen as the county seat of Fulton County. A brick courthouse overlooking the Mississippi River was completed in 1848 at a cost of $4,000. It was replaced in 1903 by an eclectic-style brick courthouse.

Hickman's status as a port lessened because of deposits along the Mississippi River, which made navigation close to the town more difficult. Dredging of the river by the U.S. Army Corps of Engineers helped to ensure that Hickman had a permanent harbor, and by the late 1960s river traffic increased. In the mid-1970s, improvements were made to the city's public cargo handling terminal, which was of major importance to the region.

Major industry came to Hickman with the Mengel Box Company about 1901. By 1929 it was the largest woodworking plant in western Kentucky, covering ninety acres. A fire in October 1942 destroyed the plant, eliminated 850 jobs, and caused the town's only railroad line, the Hickman-Union City branch of the Nashville, Chattanooga & St. Louis Railroad, to abandon the track nine years later.

The city's largest employer in the 1980s was the Sigri Carbon Corporation. Formerly the Carborundum Graphite plant, which moved to Hickman in 1965, Sigri at capacity employed 210 people.

The population of the fourth-class city was 3,048 in 1970; 2,894 in 1980; and 2,689 in 1990.

RON D. BRYANT

HICKMAN COUNTY. Hickman County, the seventy-first county in order of formation, is located in the Jackson Purchase region of Kentucky and is bounded by the Mississippi River, Carlisle, Graves, and Fulton counties, and the Tennessee state line. Because of a change in the main channel of the Mississippi, a small section of the county, known as Wolf Island, lies to the west of the river and borders Missouri. The county now has an area of 245 square miles; at the time of its formation in 1821, it comprised the entire Jackson Purchase, covering 2,300 square miles. By 1886 seven additional counties had been formed from Hickman County—Fulton, Carlisle, Ballard, McCracken, Graves, Marshall, and Calloway.

The county was named for Captain Paschal Hickman, killed in the massacre at the River Raisin in 1813. Columbus, located in the northwestern section of the county on the Mississippi River, was the original county seat; a log structure built in 1823 served as the courthouse. The county seat was moved in 1830 to CLINTON in the central part of the county.

The topography of Hickman County is generally flat, with some bluffs overlooking the Mississippi River. The soil is fertile; no noteworthy mineral resources are known. Some small industries are located in the county but the economy is principally agricultural, the main crops being soybeans, corn, wheat, tobacco, cattle, and hogs. Sweet potatoes were once produced in abundance and in 1936 the county grew 2,625 bales of cotton, now no longer grown locally. The land is drained by the Bayou du Chien and Obion creeks, both having their sources in Graves County and emptying into the Mississippi River from Fulton County.

In the west along Obion Creek are earthen structures or mounds characteristic of the Mississippian culture, a prehistoric people who inhabited the river valleys in the southeastern United States. Many artifacts, such as hunting and fishing tools, farming implements, pottery, and burial goods, have been found on former village sites and burial grounds.

Columbus, first settled in 1804, was called Les Rivages de Fer (Iron Banks) by early French travelers who thought the rust-colored bluffs there might contain iron. Local tradition speculated that Columbus might become the nation's capital, if it were moved from Washington, although research has not confirmed the belief. In support of the tradition is the location of Columbus, which was near the geographical center of the nation after the Louisiana territory was purchased from the French, besides being on a major river that split the country's midsection. There is an indication of ambition in the manner in which the 4,000-acre town tract (six and one-fourth square miles) was laid out, with its streets five poles wide.

The town thrived as a river port, expanding rapidly after becoming the northern terminus of the Mobile & Ohio (M&O) (now the Illinois Central Gulf) Railroad in 1861. The port of Columbus was the transfer point for much of the mid-continent's north- and southbound freight after the St. Louis & Iron Mountain Railway (now part of the Burlington Northern) was constructed into Belmont, Missouri,

directly across the river in 1871. From Union City, Tennessee, the Nashville & Chattanooga ran over the M&O tracks through Columbus to Belmont, where it connected with the Iron Mountain. Train ferries connected the two rail lines, linking St. Louis with Mobile. Daily steamboats transferred freight between Columbus and Cairo, Illinois. In 1874 the Iron Mountain consolidated with the Cairo, Arkansas & Texas Railway, thereby making Columbus a gateway to the West. The town reached its zenith around 1875-80 with a population near 2,000, but declined when the M&O extended its rails northward to connect by ferry with Cairo, Illinois, in 1881. Columbus College, founded in the 1870s, met its end about this time as a result of flood damage. The train ferry was discontinued on January 1, 1912.

During the Civil War the Confederates established Fort de Russey on the strategically located 80- to 120-foot bluffs across the river from Columbus. Gen. Ulysses S. Grant captured the fort in his first battle. The site of the Battle of Columbus-Belmont is now a state park.

Repeated flooding forced removal of the town to the safety of the bluffs in 1927 under the auspices of the American Red Cross. The Columbus ferry closed in 1981, but the town regained port status in the 1980s with river-related industries.

At the turn of the century, Oakton and Moscow were thriving communities south of Columbus on the M&O. About 1915 the Burlington Way, a transcontinental route, was marked along existing roads through Clinton, Croley, and Beelerton. Other rural communities were Fulgham, Spring Hill, Beulah, and Cypress.

Murphy's Pond in northeast Hickman County is a unique cypress swamp owned by Murray State University, which uses it as an outdoor classroom. The population of the county was 6,264 in 1970; 6,065 in 1980; and 5,566 in 1990.

VIRGINIA HONCHELL JEWELL

HIGH BRIDGE. High Bridge, designed by Charles Shaler Smith, spans the Kentucky River downstream from its confluence with Dix River, seven miles southwest of Nicholasville. The original bridge, dedicated by President Rutherford B. Hayes, was opened to traffic of the CINCINNATI SOUTHERN RAILWAY in 1877. The 275-foot-tall bridge had three 375-foot spans resting on two massive piers. At the time it was the highest bridge in North America and the highest railroad bridge in the world, attracting international attention.

Less graceful than a suspension bridge, High Bridge's cantilever design was built outward toward the center span with little support. In 1877 it introduced an era of more scientific bridge engineering. The bridge made no use of the massive stone towers on the Jessamine and Mercer County palisades near the confluence of the Dix and Kentucky rivers, which had been built by John A. Roebling in the 1850s as part of a suspension bridge commissioned by the Lexington & Danville Railroad. The project was abandoned after the failure of the railroad in the financial panic of 1857.

To carry heavy traffic, High Bridge was rebuilt and strengthened in 1911 according to a design by Gustav Lindenthal. The new steel structure was built by the American Bridge Company around the old iron works with no loss of traffic. The new structure could withstand a dead load of seven tons per linear foot. When the bridge was double-tracked in 1929, Roebling's superbly crafted twin towers, never used to support a bridge, were torn down.

Once a center of social life and entertainment on the Jessamine County side, High Bridge in the late twentieth century was a much-neglected historic site. High Bridge has been designated a national historic civil engineering landmark.

See Howard Curry, *High Bridge: A Pictorial History* (Lexington, Ky., 1983).

WILLIAM E. ELLIS

HIGHLAND HEIGHTS. Highland Heights is a suburban city in northern Campbell County in the hills southeast of the I-275 and I-471 interchange. For most of the 1800s the hilly, rugged sector of the county just west of the Ohio River was known simply as the Highlands. The area was incorporated in 1867 as the District of Highlands by Henry Stanbery, a resident who at that time was President Andrew Johnson's attorney general of the United States (1866-68). Fort Thomas was incorporated as a city from the northern part of the district in 1914 but the rest of the district grew more slowly. Highland Heights was incorporated June 25, 1927.

Highland Heights remained largely rural until the 1970s. In 1971 Northern Kentucky State College became a four-year school and was moved from Park Hills in Kenton County to a larger campus in Highland Heights. The institution, now NORTHERN KENTUCKY UNIVERSITY, thrived in its new suburban location, going from an enrollment of 1,784 in 1971 to 10,025 in 1990. The presence of the university attracted numerous small businesses to the city. A symbol of local prosperity was the civic center and city office building completed with a $1.25 million federal grant in 1978.

Highland Heights is a fourth-class city dominated by middle- and upper-class residences and the university campus. The population was 460 in 1970; 4,435 in 1980; and 4,223 in 1990.

HIGHWAY DEVELOPMENT. The earliest roads in Kentucky were buffalo trails, which settlers easily followed on foot and with sure-footed pack animals. They were more difficult for travelers on horseback, and wagon passage was almost impossible. Even for the solitary traveler, detours around gigantic fallen timbers or other natural barriers could be difficult. Nevertheless, before 1800 thousands of hardy souls made the trip to Kentucky over the Boone Trace, or WILDERNESS ROAD.

The Virginia legislature sought to improve the Wilderness Road to handle the growing volume of traffic. Under colonial tradition the government could pay the cost and levy road duty (require all able-bodied men to work on the roads). These resources were not enough in the case of Kentucky. After statehood, the demand for improved roads became so great that the General Assembly in 1795 provided for a heavy wagon road to be built from Crab Orchard to Cumberland Gap. In 1797 a tollgate was built at Cumberland Ford to raise revenue to improve and maintain the road. It was expected that roads would be widened to ten or twelve feet. Trees were to be cut off close to the ground and the stumps rounded. Nothing was added to the soil, however, so of course the "road" became impassable in wet weather. The next step was to lay logs across the road, then cover the logs with a thin layer of soil, creating a corduroy road.

During the early 1800s, the Kentucky state government was actively involved in the development of toll roads, purchasing large blocks of stock in most of the major road companies. The state regulated tolls, even for the small private toll roads. Tollgates and tollhouses were typically erected every five miles. In 1851 the state issued a standard rate chart. Sample rates: a horse or mule and rider, 5 cents; a horse, mule, or jack, led or driven, 3 cents; each head of cattle, 2 cents; each head of hogs, ½ cent; each head of sheep, ¼ cent; each vehicle drawn by one horse or mule, 10 cents; each vehicle drawn by two horses, mules, or oxen, 20 cents; each wagon drawn by six animals, 75 cents; each six-seat stagecoach, 35 cents.

Kentucky was the first state to establish a highway department (the State Board of Internal Improvements in 1835), but abolished it in the 1850s. In doing so the state abdicated any role in highway construction and maintenance until the twentieth century. (The 1891 constitution prohibited the state from establishing highway funds, a restriction lifted by amendment in 1909). After the 1850s, only private toll companies, primarily local in nature, remained.

By the time of the Civil War almost every mile of Kentucky roads was privately controlled. The development of private toll roads in Kentucky was similar to that of southern railroads. Counties subscribed to the stock of private turnpike companies that constructed local roads, but tolls went directly to the turnpike companies themselves. County taxpayers thus provided the funds to build the roads, then paid expensive tolls to private concerns to drive on the very same "public" roads.

Toll roads continued throughout the nineteenth century, although there was growing public indignation over the condition of the toll roads, which were generally impassable for long periods. It was not at all unusual for travelers to pass the hulks of coaches and wagons that had been trapped in the mire and abandoned. Travel was slowed by any sign of bad weather. The wretched conditions led to the "toll-road wars," in which local people raided tollhouses and generally created trouble for tollkeepers. The value of toll-road stock fell drastically.

In 1896 the General Assembly passed a free turn-pike bill signed into law by Gov. William O. Brad-ley (1895-99). The legislation was virtually ignored, however, by county judges and mayors, who adopted the public posture that they had no right to raise taxes for the purposes of buying turnpikes. This stance outraged many, especially in central Kentucky, and soon produced a violent reaction. In forty-four counties throughout the Bluegrass re-gion, vigilantes burned or dynamited more than three hundred tollgates. The public uprising was vividly successful. Before the year was out, turn-pike companies sold all of their holdings to the counties, which operated the turnpikes without charging tolls.

Early in the nineteenth century, Kentucky had sought road construction by the national govern-ment, which began supporting construction in 1802 with net proceeds from the sale of public land. A significant link in the national road system in Ohio was Zane's Trace. Maysville (originally Lime-stone), Kentucky, across the Ohio River from Zane's Trace, was the principal contact point be-tween Lexington and the Ohio River. Lexington by 1815 had become a significant industrial center, but the development of the steamboat put that position in jeopardy; Lexington industries could compete only if a commercially viable road was established between the city and the river. Lexington, led by Henry Clay, sought construction of a branch of the national road from Maysville to Lexington. Veto of the Maysville road bill by President Andrew Jack-son on May 27, 1830, not only affected Kentucky but delayed the establishment of a national road system in the United States until the middle of the twentieth century. In the day of the steamboat and railroad, it was generally felt that highway transpor-tation was obsolete.

The principal roads were macadamized—that is, covered with layers of small crushed stone—by 1850. Macadamized roads included: Maysville to Lexington (64 miles); on to Frankfort and Louis-ville (79 miles); Nashville to Louisville (114 miles from the state line to Louisville); and Covington to Lexington (85 miles). Later additions included the road from Ashland to Lexington and from Lexing-ton to the Tennessee state line; the route from Henderson to the Tennessee border; and the two principal Jackson Purchase area roads, from Wick-liffe and Paducah to the Tennessee border. Other roads constructed in the state were largely local in nature, tying no more than two or three cities to-gether, or were feeders to the principal routes. Ex-cept in the immediate Bluegrass region, local roads were mostly unsurfaced.

The advent of the steamboat brought commercial traffic—except for Louisville's river trade—to the periphery of Kentucky. The advantage to Louisville further complicated the political scene in the state. The advent of the railroad only compounded the problem, because the rails were laid basically north and south and were designed to carry goods through the state, not to unite it. (This trend, in great part, continues in the principal modern inter-state highways.) As river and rail transport devel-oped, the highway system fell into disrepair. This inhibited the development of commerce and the ex-change of ideas between communities and regions of the state and led to further fractionalization.

With the popularization of the automobile, Ken-tucky cities participated in the creation of the Dixie Highway along the two major north-south highways of Kentucky, U.S. 25 East and West and U.S. 31 East and West. Demand for roads led to the creation of a national good roads movement, which lobbied Congress. The secretary of agriculture was charged with the duty of aiding "the States in the construc-tion and maintenance of rural post roads." Each state was required to create a state highway depart-ment and to designate up to 7 percent of its public rural roads as U.S. highways. As a result, Kentucky in 1912 established a state highway commission, which by 1920 had become a centrally organized highway department. By 1927 Kentucky had desig-nated its 3,700 miles of surfaced roads as a part of the U.S. system: U.S. 60 from Ashland to Paducah; U.S. 25 (east and west) from Cincinnati to Cumber-land Gap; U.S. 68 from Maysville across the state to the Tennessee line; U.S. 31 (east and west) from Louisville to the Tennessee line; U.S. 41 from Henderson via Madisonville and Hopkinsville to the Tennessee line; U.S. 51 from Wickliffe to the Ten-nessee line at Fulton; and U.S. 45 from Paducah to Fulton. Connecting routes, U.S. 168 from Louis-ville to Mt. Vernon and U.S. 241 from Hopkinsville to Guthrie, were also included, as was U.S. 23 from Ashland to Pineville, following portions of the old Warrior's Trail.

In 1945 the Interstate System was authorized. Kentucky has five interstate highways: I-65 and I-75 north and south; I-64 from Louisville to Ash-land; I-24 southeast from Paducah; and I-71 connecting Louisville and Covington—a total of 698 miles. I-64, with the Purchase, Western Ken-tucky, and Bluegrass parkways, constructed under provisions of the Kentucky Turnpike Authority (es-tablished 1960), provided the first modern east-west route across the state. This linkage has probably done more to unify Kentucky than any other single event in the state's history.

The modern era of toll roads began with the exis-tence of the Kentucky Turnpike Authority and the construction of the turnpike between Louisville and Elizabethtown in the early 1950s. Toll roads have a great appeal to legislators as a device for establish-ing highway infrastructure. The funding process for toll roads relies on revenue bonds rather than gen-eral revenue funding, with the prospect that the users will pay the costs of the highway. Toll roads allowed Kentucky to open areas of the state not previously accessible. In the late twentieth cen-tury there were seven toll roads (parkways) in Ken-tucky: Purchase, Pennyrile, Western Kentucky, Green River, Cumberland, Mountain, and Daniel

Boone. By the early 1990s the tolls had been removed from nearly all of them.

According to a Federal Highway Administration report, Kentucky in 1990 had 69,629 miles of highways: interstate routes—federal-aid, primary (4,541 miles) and federal-aid, secondary (9,545 miles); state routes (12,350 miles); and local roads (43,193 miles).

See U.S. Department of Transportation, Federal Highway Administration, *America's Highways 1776-1976* (Washington D.C., 1977); Robert L. Kincaid, *The Wilderness Road* (Middlesboro, Ky., 1966).   J. ALLEN SINGLETON

HILL, PATTY SMITH. Patty Smith Hill, educator, was born in Anchorage, Kentucky, on March 27, 1868, to William Wallace and Martha Jane (Smith) Hill. She lived at the Anchorage Female Seminary that her father ran until 1874, when the family moved to Fulton, Missouri. After her father's death in 1878, Hill moved to Louisville, where she attended first the public schools and then the Louisville Collegiate Institute in 1882. Exposure to new theories on the education of preprimary school children inspired her to become an educator. In 1887 she graduated from the first kindergarten training school in Louisville, which opened under Steve Holcombe in 1886. Hill experimented with the idea that children should be placed in settings that stimulated creative thought and openness, and she believed that programs should be adjusted to fit the child. She used music, poetry, stories, and plays to instruct children.

Though criticized, her ideas were of interest to educators all over the world, including John Dewey and G. Stanley Hall, who came to Louisville to study preprimary education. She spoke before the Louisville Education Association in 1900 on "Education Through Play," and by 1900 nine Louisville public schools were offering kindergarten programs. In 1905 Hill left Louisville to study at Columbia University, where she worked at the Speyer School Experimental Playroom (later called the Horace Mann Kindergarten). In 1929 she received an honorary doctor of letters degree for her work as head of the Kindergarten Association. She may be best remembered for a song she wrote with her sister Mildred J. Hill in 1893, entitled "Good Morning to You," the melody of which was later used for the song "Happy Birthday."

Hill died in New York City on May 25, 1946, and was buried in Louisville's Cave Hill Cemetery.

See Frances Farley Gwinn, "Patty Smith Hill: Louisville's Contribution to Education," *FCHQ* 31 (July 1957): 203-24.

HILLERICH AND BRADSBY COMPANY, INC. The manufacturer known for its Louisville Slugger baseball bats dates back to 1884, when John A. ("Bud") Hillerich, the eighteen-year-old son of a Louisville woodworker, painstakingly turned a baseball bat for baseball star Pete Browning. The next day the Louisville Eclipse player collected three hits with his new bat. Soon other players in the American Association, which was a major league in the 1880s, wanted bats similar to Browning's.

At first Hillerich's father, J. Fred Hillerich, wanted nothing to do with his son's venture. The Hillerich woodworking shop, established in 1859, turned out bedposts, posts and balusters for stairways, rolling pins, and bowling balls and pins. At the time, it was having considerable success manufacturing a newly invented swing churn. Soon, however, the bats became the overwhelming choice of most major leaguers. By 1894 Bud Hillerich's bats became known as Louisville Sluggers and in 1897 he became a full-fledged partner in his father's business. As the demand for bats increased, more and more of the shop's space was taken up by the baseball operation, and the company moved in 1901 to new quarters at the intersection of Preston and Finzer streets.

On September 1, 1905, Pittsburgh star Honus Wagner signed a contract with the Hillerich company to allow the use of his signature on Louisville Slugger bats—the first major league player to do so. Before this, players had carved their initials or some other identifying mark on the barrel or knob of their bats. Wagner's contract was soon followed by others, including those of "Home Run" Baker, Ty Cobb, Eddie Collins, Nap Lajoie, Willie Keeler, Hugh Duffy, John McGraw, Hugh Jennings, Cap Anson, and the Delahanty brothers. Ninety percent of all major league players soon signed such contracts with the Hillerich company. In 1911 Frank Bradsby, a former buyer of athletic equipment for Simmons Hardware Company, moved from St. Louis to join the business. It was at this time that the company began to brand its famous oval trademark onto the bats. Five years later, in 1916, the firm's name was changed to Hillerich and Bradsby Company.

The company has made its reputation by selling professional baseball teams bats customized for individual players. Bats are hand-carved to meet a player's exact specifications for length, taper, and weight. Extensive records, stored on microfiche, are kept for more than 20,000 bat specifications. Visits by players who want to pick out their own wood or design their own bats are not uncommon.

Ted Williams often came early in the day to select white ash timbers with a narrow grain. He was so particular that he once returned a bat because it did not "feel right." The taper of the bat was found to be off by 0.005 inch. Williams could also detect variations of as little as a half an ounce in the weight of a bat. Babe Ruth, whose fifty-four-ounce bat was one of the heaviest used in the major leagues, preferred wood that had tiny pin-knots for the area of the barrel where he hit the ball. Ruth, who rarely broke a bat, gave so many of his bats away as gifts to friends and acquaintances that during the 1920s and 1930s he was one of Hillerich and Bradsby's biggest customers.

The player endorsements from such major league stars have popularized the company's mass-produced bats, which are machined on automatic lathes for sale to millions of amateur baseball and softball players and teams. During the wooden bat's heyday, which extended into the early 1970s, the firm was turning out more than 6 million bats a year. With the introduction of aluminum and magnesium bats in amateur baseball, the company now manufactures only 1.5 million wooden bats per year. Of these, 20,000 are turned by master craftsmen at the rate of twenty-five to thirty bats per day.

Louisville Slugger bats are made of choice white ash timbers grown on ridgetops or slopes with northern or eastern exposures. The wood produced there grows more slowly and is harder than wood grown elsewhere. The company draws its timber supply from thousands of acres of forest it owns in New York and Pennsylvania. It has an active reforestation program.

The wood is cut into short dowels, or billets, which are cured outside for several months before being carved or machined into bats. The bats are sanded, roasted over a gas range to bring out their wood grain, branded with trademark and autograph, and dipped into finishing solution.

Hillerich and Bradsby has its own line of aluminum bats, which are produced at its plant in Santa Fe Springs, California. The company diversified long ago into the production of several lines of golf and other athletic equipment, including PowerBilt golf clubs—products that now approximate the sales of its more famous Louisville Slugger Division. The company also produces hockey sticks in a plant in Wallaceburg, Ontario, and manufactures golf club heads made from persimmon wood at a plant in Leitchfield, Kentucky.

During World War II the firm continued making baseball bats but also did its part for the war effort by producing M1 carbine stocks and tank pins. While its corporate headquarters are still in Louisville, the company's main manufacturing center is now located in a 6½-acre factory complex called Slugger Park at 1525 Charleston–New Albany Road in Jeffersonville, Indiana. The complex includes a museum that contains the photographs and bats of many famous baseball players and other memorabilia. Hillerich and Bradsby remains a family-owned operation.

See Kelly Cocanougher, "Babe Ruth's Ghost May Still Watch How 'Sluggers' Are Made." *Louisville Times*, Oct. 10, 1977; George Groh, "Batter's Choice," *MD* (May 1984).

WILLIAM MARSHALL

HILLTOPPERS. Hilltoppers is the name of both WESTERN KENTUCKY UNIVERSITY's athletic teams and a 1950s popular musical group formed by four students from the university. In 1911 Western Kentucky's president, Henry Hardin Cherry (1906-37), moved the institution (then a state normal school) from the bottom of Bowling Green's Vinegar Hill to two new buildings at the top of the hill. In the 1920s the Western athletic teams acquired the nickname Hilltoppers, which became their permanent name in 1928.

Men's baseball ushered in the 1910 arrival of intercollegiate athletics at the hill, renamed College Heights. Football followed in 1913 and basketball in 1914. Posting winning seasons in each of their first years, these teams were called Pedagogues, Diddlemen, then Normalites during the pre-1928 seasons. They only hinted at the success of the post-1928 Hilltoppers. Athletic achievement, best symbolized by the forty-two-year coaching career of Ed Diddle, brought Western national attention. Upon retirement, Diddle had amassed a career 759-302 record, placing him among the coaches with the most wins in basketball history.

The Hilltoppers musical group originated in the 1950s when three Western students, Don McGuire, Jimmy Sacca, and Seymour Speigelman, teamed with a former Westerner, Billy Vaughn. Their first release, "Trying," landed them an October 26, 1952, television appearance on Ed Sullivan's "Toast of the Town." The quartet also appeared on such top-rated shows as "American Bandstand" and those hosted by Milton Berle, Perry Como, and Steve Allen. Ranked as the No. 1 musical group during 1953 and 1954, they consistently remained one of America's Top Ten through 1960.

During its eleven years, the Hilltoppers saw twenty-one recordings reach Billboard's Top Forty. However, the mid-1950s brought a change in the musical current. The Hilltoppers' soft style was replaced by the hard edge of rock and roll. Don McGuire, founder, and Billy Vaughn, chief songwriter, left the group by 1960 and were replaced by Eddie Crowe and Doug Cordoza. By 1963 the quartet had disbanded.

Jimmy Sacca and three new members reorganized the group in 1968 and toured the country through the 1970s singing the original hits. Three of the original Hilltoppers were alive in 1990—McGuire, Sacca, and Vaughn. Speigelman died in 1987.

See Joe Creason, "The Hill Toppers Quartet of Bowling Green is on the Way to Becoming Musical Sensation," *Louisville Courier-Journal*, Oct. 1952.

SHERRY G. SEBASTIAN

HILLVIEW. Hillview is in northern Bullitt County near the Jefferson County line, astride KY 61. Originally a farming area, it experienced rapid growth after the Kentucky Turnpike connected Bullitt County with Louisville in 1954. In the 1960s Bullitt County grew faster than any other in the state. During this rapid expansion, several suburban subdivisions were created, including Maryville, named by developer John A. Walser for his wife and daughter. To provide better services for residents, the Maryville, Overdale, and Lone Acres subdivisions were incorporated in 1974 as a city and named Hillview, either because of the view toward several distant knobs or because there had been a Hill View post office in the county from

1872 to 1874. After its incorporation, the city grew rapidly with an influx of Jefferson Countians. By the 1980s Hillview, a fourth-class city, was Bullitt County's largest town. The population was 7,124 in 1980 and 6,119 in 1990.

HIMLERVILLE. Himlerville, a coal mining town approximately one mile west of the Tug Fork of the Big Sandy River in Martin County, Kentucky, was the site of a short-lived cooperative mining venture undertaken by a group of Hungarian immigrants in the 1920s. Named after Martin Himler, the immigrants' leader and owner of *Magyar Banyaszlap*, a Hungarian-language newspaper, Himlerville was established in 1918. The residents of Himlerville, all of whom owned stock in the Himler Coal Company, formed a cooperative company to bridge the Tug Fork in 1919. On May 21, 1921, the first Norfork & Western train entered Martin County. Himlerville ceased to exist in 1929 when the Himler Coal Company declared bankruptcy. J.H. Mann, the town's new owner, changed its name to Beauty.

DOUG CANTRELL

HINDMAN. Hindman, the county seat of Knott County, is situated in a narrow valley at the fork of Troublesome Creek along KY 80. The city was founded in 1884 as the seat of newly established Knott County and named for James P. Hindman, then lieutenant governor. The land for the city was donated by Peyton M. Duke, who ran the McPherson post office at the site of the city. The first known settler near the fork of Troublesome Creek was Samuel Cornett. Later settlers were the Dukes, of North Carolina, and Capt. Anderson Hays. At the time of the formation of Hindman, a few businessmen and farmers, including F.P. Allen and Robert Bates, lived or owned land there.

When Hindman was established as county seat, it was little more than a few log houses. Wagon roads led out to Whitesburg, Hazard, Jackson, and Prestonsburg, from which most goods arrived via mule-pulled freighters. The first courthouse, a log structure built in 1884, was replaced by a brick structure with a unique arched front in the 1890s. It burned in 1929. The Works Progress Administration built the present courthouse in 1935-36.

Political strife began in Hindman soon after its formation, when Clabe Jones lost a race for jailer to his old Civil War opponent, Anderson Hays. The two and their factions warred for several years and after the feud ended, other men perpetuated the violence in the city. The establishment of Baptist and Methodist churches and George Clarke's school (1888), the predecessor of the HINDMAN SETTLEMENT School, helped to provide outlets other than feuding for the people.

Hindman's location on Troublesome Creek made it susceptible to occasional flooding, and the isolated mountain town grew slowly. The rugged terrain prevented the extension of rail service to the town. The economy of the town is heavily dependent upon coal.

A statue in front of the courthouse honors Hindman's best known native son, Carl D. Perkins, who served eastern Kentucky as a U.S. representative from 1949 until 1984.

The population of the fifth-class city was 808 in 1970; 876 in 1980; and 798 in 1990.

HINDMAN SETTLEMENT SCHOOL. The Hindman Settlement School is located at the forks of Troublesome Creek, in Knott County, Kentucky. Founded in 1902 by May STONE and Katherine PETTIT, Hindman was the first rural social settlement school in the United States. The purposes and goals for which the settlement was founded in 1902 are the same today, namely, to provide educational opportunities for the boys and girls of this region, to keep them mindful of their heritage, and to provide community services. The settlement is a nonprofit, nondenominational institution.

In the early years the settlement provided most of the educational programs in its vicinity. Many of the early instructors came from Smith, Vassar, Mt. Holyoke, Wellesley, and several other prestigious colleges to teach the children of the mountains. The Hindman Settlement School became known for its outstanding academic programs throughout the region. The settlement encouraged the growth of the public school system but continued to supplement educational services. The mission of the school is to provide services not available from other agencies or groups. Students no longer live on campus. With the advent of public school consolidation and the building of better roads in the region, every student is able to travel to school by either bus or private transportation.

The settlement runs the East Kentucky Tutorial Program, which gives remedial education to dyslexic children through after-school programs in several counties and a six-week summer school. The settlement also provides to the community an adult basic education/GED program, a Montessori preschool, scholarship assistance for needy students, facilities for the Knott County Public Library, meeting space for community activities, workshops on Appalachian life and culture, artists-in-residence in the public schools, community education classes, used clothing for the needy, and many other services.

MIKE MULLINS

HINES, DUNCAN. Duncan Hines, a food critic who marketed a line of processed foods under his name, was born to Edward L. and Cornelia (Duncan) Hines at Bowling Green, Kentucky, on March 26, 1880. In 1905 he entered the printing and advertising business. He married Florence Chaffin, and they lived in Chicago. The couple traveled extensively in the United States and at Christmas 1935 mailed a list of "superior eating places" to their friends. The responses to the list prompted the 1936 publication of *Adventures in Good Eating*, a guide to the most highly recommended U.S. restaurants. After a companion work, *Lodging for a Night*, was published in 1938, the sign

"Recommended by Duncan Hines" became a guide for travelers. Hines also published two cookbooks.

In 1949 Hines joined Roy H. Park in establishing the Hines-Park Foods Company, which produced and sold food under the Duncan Hines label. They also founded the Duncan Hines Institute, which conducted food research and granted scholarships to students in hotel and restaurant management. In 1956 Hines-Park Foods was acquired by the Proctor and Gamble Company of Cincinnati.

Hines's wife died in 1939; he married Clara Wright Nahm in 1946. Hines died in Bowling Green on March 15, 1959, and was buried there.

HINES, THOMAS HENRY. Thomas Henry Hines, soldier and jurist, was born October 9, 1838, in Butler County, Kentucky, the son of Warren W. and Sarah (Carson) Hines. He taught at Masonic University in LaGrange from 1859 to 1861. He served in the Confederate army as captain in John Hunt Morgan's command. On March 16, 1864, Confederate Secretary of War James A. Seddon appointed him director of the Northwest conspiracy to free Confederate prisoners and organize a revolt. The plot collapsed on November 7, 1864, in Chicago. In October 1867, Hines began to practice law in Bowling Green. Hines was elected to the court of appeals in 1878 and was chief justice from 1884 to 1886. He and his wife, Nancy Sproule, had two children who lived to adulthood, Alice and William. Hines died January 23, 1898, and was buried in Bowling Green.

JAMES A. RAMAGE

HISTORICAL RECORDS SURVEY (WPA). The Historical Records Survey was a short-lived project of the Works Progress Administration (WPA), and the Federal Writers Project. At the annual meeting of the American Historical Association in Chattanooga, Tennessee, in December 1934, Luther Evans, formerly a professor of political science at Princeton University, recruited state directors for the survey. The Historical Records Survey in Kentucky was organized in 1936 on the basis of the five WPA administrative districts in the state, with Thomas D. Clark as temporary state director. The general objectives of the survey were to inventory, analyze, and perhaps preserve public documents of states and counties. The Historical Records Survey fielded some kind of team in all 120 Kentucky counties, with a subdirector over each of the five districts. Workers varied from almost totally illiterate to the moderately well educated but inexperienced in archival research. Some county officials, especially in eastern Kentucky, were less than enthusiastic about the survey.

Clark, on loan from the University of Kentucky, served as state director until late 1936. He was succeeded briefly by Oren B. Wilder, then by Walter M. Hoepelman (1936-39), Earl D. Hale (1939-40), and Clifford Rader (1940-41). The project dwindled to a close in 1941 in favor of special war services. By that time there were surveys of varying qualities in all the Kentucky counties, and substantial headway had been made in sixty-three counties. Nine reports were published. The records of the survey are held in several depositories, including the Kentucky Department for Libraries and Archives and the Special Collections Division of the Margaret I. King Library, University of Kentucky.

See *Inventory of the Records of the Work Projects Administration in Kentucky* (Frankfort, Ky., 1985). THOMAS D. CLARK

HISTORIC SITES. Nine of Kentucky's state PARKS are classified as historic sites; they are managed by the Kentucky Department of Parks.

Constitution Square State Historic Site, Boyle County. Constitution Square State Historic Site in Danville, Kentucky, became part of the state park system on October 15, 1937. Emma Weisiger deeded it to the state as a memorial to her brother. The three-acre park is a collection of historic buildings, including the Grayson Tavern (ca. 1756), where the DANVILLE POLITICAL CLUB met.

Dr. Thomas Walker State Historic Site, Knox County. WALKER, who arrived in Kentucky in 1750, built a cabin on this site. The American Legion and the people of Barbourville donated the land, which was dedicated as a state shrine on June 20, 1931.

Isaac Shelby State Historic Site, Lincoln County. The site is the burial ground of Isaac Shelby, twice governor (1792-96, 1812-16) of Kentucky. The site was the original Shelby estate, known as Travelers Rest. A monument was built in 1926 by the commonwealth. The site officially became part of the state park system on May 5, 1951.

Jefferson Davis State Historic Site, Todd County. One of the tallest cast concrete obelisks in the world marks the birthplace of Jefferson DAVIS, president of the Confederate States of America. Construction started in 1917. On June 7, 1924, the monument became part of the park system.

Old Mulkey Meeting House State Historic Site, Monroe County. The OLD MULKEY Meeting House and twenty acres of land including an old cemetery became a state shrine on November 8, 1931. The church was built between 1798 and 1804.

Perryville Battlefield State Historic Site, Boyle County. After the Civil War Battle of PERRYVILLE, many of the dead were buried on the farm at this site by local people. A museum and several monuments on seventeen acres honor those who fought in the battle. The site became part of the park system on February 26, 1936.

Waveland State Historic Site, Fayette County. WAVELAND, since 1957 known as the Kentucky Life Museum, was deeded by the University of Kentucky to the Kentucky state park system in 1971. The house and surrounding buildings display hundreds of artifacts of life in central Kentucky. The house was restored in 1985 to its 1847 condition.

William Whitley State Historic Site, Lincoln County. William Whitley, who moved to the Ken tucky frontier in 1775, constructed a brick house between 1787 and 1794 that marked the transition from the era of log cabins to that of more formal homes. The house was built as a fortress against Indian attacks. Whitley Park Association and other local civic clubs restored the house between 1948 and 1955. It became a Kentucky state park on February 25, 1938.

White Hall State Historic Site, Madison County. White Hall, the home of Cassius Marcellus CLAY, and fourteen acres of land were added to the Kentucky state park system on July 5, 1968.

ED HENSON

HOBSON, EDWARD HENRY. Edward Henry Hobson, Civil War general, was born July 11, 1825, in Greensburg, Kentucky, the son of Capt. William and Lucy (Kirtley) Hobson. At eighteen, after attending Danville and Greensburg schools, Hobson went into business with his father, a successful merchant and owner of a Green River steamer. In June 1846 he enlisted in the army, was commissioned a second lieutenant of Company A, 2d Kentucky Infantry, and left for Mexico. He was promoted to first lieutenant for heroism at Buena Vista, mustered out of the army in June 1847, and returned home. He was elected a director of the Greensburg Branch Bank of Kentucky in 1853 and became its president in 1857.

At the outbreak of the Civil War, Hobson enlisted with the Union army and on January 12, 1862, was mustered into service as a colonel commanding the 13th Kentucky Infantry, which he had recruited from counties along the Green River. After the success of his regiment at the battle of Shiloh, President Abraham Lincoln made him brigadier general on November 29, 1862. For most of the rest of his military career, Hobson pursued Gen. John Hunt Morgan and his raiders across Kentucky. In 1864 he fought minor skirmishes with Morgan at Lexington and Mt. Sterling. On June 11, 1864, Hobson engaged Morgan at Cynthiana but was captured with a large number of his troops. Seeking to delay Morgan, Hobson negotiated to exchange himself and other Union officers for Confederates of equal rank held in Ohio. The following day Morgan was defeated by a larger Union force under Gen. Stephen Burbridge. Federal authorities in Cincinnati rejected the prisoner exchange. Hobson remained in Kentucky until the end of the war, stationed at Lexington in command of the 1st Division, Department of Kentucky.

In August 1866 Hobson was the unsuccessful Radical Republican candidate for clerk of the court of appeals. President Ulysses S. Grant appointed him collector of internal revenues for the fourth district in 1869, and he served as vice-president of the 1888 Republican National Convention. For a time he was president of the southern division of the Cumberland & Ohio Railroad, which was later absorbed by the Louisville & Nashville Railroad.

Hobson married Kate Adair, daughter of Alexander and Elizabeth Adair and niece of Gov. John Adair, on October 12, 1847. He died September 14, 1901, while attending a GAR encampment in Cleveland and was buried in the family cemetery in Greensburg.

See Ezra J. Warner, *Generals in Blue—Lives of the Union Commanders* (Baton Rouge, La., 1964).

HODGENVILLE. The seat of Larue County, Hodgenville, on U.S. 31E, was established on land that belonged to Robert Hodgen, an Englishman who moved to Kentucky from Pennsylvania. In 1789 Hodgen constructed a mill on Nolin River on a portion of his 10,000-acre holdings. Hodgen's mill was near Phillips' Fort, built in 1781. The town of Hodgenville was created by the Hardin County Court in 1818, incorporated on February 18, 1839, and became the county seat on March 4, 1843, when Larue County was created out of Hardin County.

During the Civil War, a skirmish occurred at Hodgenville on October 23, 1861. The county courthouse, built in 1844, was burned by Confederate guerrillas on February 21, 1865, because it had been used as barracks for Federal troops. In 1866 a second courthouse was constructed on the foundations of the first. In 1964 a third edifice was built to serve the county court.

The war slowed Hodgenville's economic and physical growth, and farm prices during the period fluctuated wildly. In 1888 the Illinois Central Railroad (now Illinois Central Gulf) built a spur from Hodgenville to Elizabethtown, opening Larue County to markets in the South and West.

The Lincoln Farm Association, formed at the turn of the century, raised more than $350,000 for the creation of the Abraham Lincoln Birthplace National Historic Site about three miles south of Hodgenville. During the twentieth century, Hodgenville has experienced modest growth. The manufacture of clothing and lumber products has aided the local economy, but the town remains largely agricultural.

The population of Hodgenville was 2,562 in 1970; 2,531 in 1980; and 2,721 in 1990.

RON D. BRYANT

HODGES, ALBERT GALLATIN. Albert Gallatin Hodges, newspaper publisher and entrepreneur, was born in Madison County, Virginia, on October 8, 1802, the son of Francis and Mary (Brock) Hodges. The family moved to Fayette County, Kentucky, in 1810, and following his father's death in 1815, Hodges began working as an office boy, then a carrier, for Lexington's *Kentucky Reporter*. At the age of nineteen, he made an unsuccessful attempt at publishing the *Lancaster Kentuckian*, soon afterward returning to the *Reporter*, where he was promoted to foreman. Hodges and D.C. Pinkham bought the *Lexington Semi-Weekly Morning Post* in 1824. William Tanner became Hodges's partner the next year, and their paper followed a slippery path along the middle ground during the raging Old Court–New Court controversy. Hodges sold his interest in the *Post* in 1826 and started Lexington's

Kentucky Whig, with Nelson Nicholas as editor. Nicholas's death ended the venture before the year was out, and Hodges moved to Frankfort as one of the proprietors of the *Frankfort Commentator*. In 1832 he went to Louisville as publisher of *Lights and Shadows*, an anti-Masonic weekly. Ironically, Hodges was to become one of Kentucky's leading Masons later in life.

In 1833 Hodges and editor Orlando Brown founded the *Frankfort Commonwealth* as a joint venture, and the two made their names and fortunes as the newspaper became one of the best in the Ohio Valley. In Brown, Hodges finally found an ideal editor. The paper identified itself with Henry Clay and the Whigs of Kentucky during the 1830s and 1840s to such an extent that the editor of the *Louisville Courier-Journal* stated after Hodges's death that "no political organization was ever served as he served the old Whig party." In 1833 the legislature elected Hodges public printer, a position he held by election for the next twenty-five years. Following the Whig era the *Commonwealth* supported the Know-Nothings. During the Civil War Hodges threw his paper's support behind the Union party in Kentucky, and he became a staunch Republican. He was a friend of President Abraham Lincoln, and he used their friendship often to aid fellow Kentuckians caught up in the problems of citizens living in a border state. In 1872 Hodges turned his printing business over to his son, suspended publication of the *Commonwealth*, and moved to Louisville. He served as treasurer of the Masonic Grand Lodge until his death on March 16, 1881. He was buried in the Frankfort Cemetery.

FRANK F. MATHIAS

HOLIFIELD, MARVIN BERTRIE. Marvin Bertrie Holifield, attorney, son of Dr. John R. and Julia (Dodson) Holifield, was born February 2, 1872, in Graves County, Kentucky. He attended West Kentucky College in Mayfield and Bethel College in McKenzie, Tennessee, and received an LL.B. degree from Cumberland University, Lebanon, Tennessee, in 1896. He was appointed first assistant attorney general of Kentucky in 1928, serving in this capacity—excluding the period of 1932-36—until 1957 and was recognized as an outstanding legal and constitutional scholar. He successfully directed the lengthy struggle in the 1930s to free southern rail shippers from discriminatory freight rates, representing the commonwealth's interests before the U.S. Supreme Court and the Interstate Commerce Commission. He received the first Governor's Award, from Gov. A. B. Chandler (1955-59), in 1957 for "exception-ally meritorious, conspicuous and long-standing public service." A widely recognized authority on Kentucky and Confederate history, Holifield was also a prominent Baptist layman and teacher. Holifield married Lennie Drake of Mayfield on October 31, 1905. He died in Frankfort on April 8, 1957, and was buried at Maplewood Cemetery, Mayfield.

LON CARTER BARTON

HOLLEY, HORACE. Horace Holley, minister and educator, was born in Salisbury, Connecticut, on February 13, 1781, the son of Luther and Sarah (Dakin) Holley. Holley was brought up in a home in which intellectual interests and moral integrity were prized. His evident intellectual ability was encouraged by his parents, who provided him with an education at a Williamstown academy in Massachusetts and at Yale College, then under the domination of Timothy Dwight. Holley studied divinity under Dwight and absorbed his orthodox Calvinist views.

After his marriage to Mary Austin in 1805 and his service as pastor of the Congregational Church in Greenfield Hill, near Fairfield, Connecticut, Holley's views became more liberal. By the time he accepted the pastorate of the Hollis Street Church in Boston he had become a Unitarian, as had a number of the leading ministers of the city, most notably William Ellery Channing. At the Hollis Street Church, Holley's oratorical talents and leadership led to a doubling of the congregation and the construction of a larger church. He also became a member of the Boston School Committee and the Harvard Board of Overseers.

Holley's career and fame were developing rapidly in Boston when he received a request in 1818 from the trustees of TRANSYLVANIA UNIVERSITY in Lexington to become its president. Henry Clay, one of the trustees, was probably influential in persuading Holley to consider the post. After visiting Lexington, Holley accepted the presidency, intending to build Transylvania into a leading western university. Under his leadership the school expanded significantly. Holley recruited the finest faculty to staff his liberal arts school and especially the law and medical departments. The medical school became one of the most outstanding in the country, matching those of Pennsylvania and Harvard. Holley persuaded the Kentucky legislature to appropriate funds for the school. New facilities were constructed, an extraordinary medical library was purchased in Europe, and scientific equipment was acquired. Transylvania's rising reputation drew excellent students from the West and the South, who earlier would have gone to eastern colleges. These young men later became the professional, political, and business leaders of their regions and the nation.

Between 1818 and 1825 Holley's dream of a flourishing university materialized. The promising future of the university dimmed, however, as the Presbyterians, who previously had controlled Transylvania, intensified their attacks on Holley's unorthodox religious views and his sophisticated lifestyle. In addition, Gov. Joseph Desha (1824-28), an ardent Jacksonian who disliked the school because of Henry Clay's association with it and what he perceived as its elitist character, persuaded the Kentucky legislature to halt any further appropriations for the school. Holley, seeing little hope for the school's future under these circumstances, resigned his office in 1825. He left Lexington in 1827 for New Orleans, where he hoped to initiate educational projects. While sailing to Boston to escape the summer's heat, he contracted yellow fever on board ship and died on July 31, 1827. He was buried at sea off the Dry Tortugas.

See Charles Caldwell, *A Discourse on the Genius and Character of the Rev. Horace Holley* (Lexington, Ky., 1828); John D. Wright, Jr., *Transylvania: Tutor to the West* (Lexington, Ky., 1980).

JOHN D. WRIGHT, JR.

HOLLEY, MARY PHELPS (AUSTIN). Born in New Haven, Connecticut, on October 30, 1784, Mary Phelps (Austin) Holley, writer, was the daughter of Elijah and Esther (Phelps) Austin. She received an excellent education in local schools. On January 1, 1805, she married Horace HOLLEY, a graduate of Yale College, and accompanied him to the Connecticut countryside and Boston, where he served as a Unitarian minister. The couple's two children, Horace Austin and Harriet Williams, were born in New England. Although she opposed the move, the couple in 1818 settled in Lexington, Kentucky, where Horace served as president of Transylvania University.

The couple moved to New Orleans in 1827. Their plans to establish a school and to accompany young scholars to Europe were cut short by Horace's untimely death in 1827. Mary assisted Transylvania's Dr. Charles Caldwell in compiling a short biography of her husband, *A Discourse on the Genius and Character of the Rev. Horace Holley* (1828). She became especially interested in Texas because of the activities of her uncle Moses Austin and cousin Stephen Austin, and she visited Texas several times and wrote two books on the area. The first, a series of brief sketches describing her trip, appeared in 1833. The second was a much longer volume, *Mrs. Holley's Texas*, published in 1836. Mary Holley died in New Orleans on August 2, 1846, and was buried in the city's St. Louis Cemetery.

See Rebecca Smith Lee, *Mary Austin Holley* (Austin, Texas, 1962).   JOHN D. WRIGHT, JR.

HOLMES, MARY JANE (HAWES). Mary Jane (Hawes) Holmes, author, was born April 5, 1825, in Brookfield, Massachusetts, to Preston and Fanny (Olds) Hawes. A precocious child who had an impressive early education, she was teaching in a local district school at the age of thirteen and her first short story was published when she was fifteen. On August 9, 1849, she married attorney Daniel Holmes, from New York, and shortly afterward they moved to Versailles in Woodford County, Kentucky, where they lived for about a year while they taught school.

After Holmes's brief stay in Kentucky, the Bluegrass became the scene of her most popular works, including *The Homestead on the Hill, and Other Tales* (1856), *Lena Rivers* (1856), *Marian Grey* (1863), and *Hugh Worthington* (1865). Holmes wrote during the "feminine fifties," a time domi-

nated by the domestic sentimental novel of manners. Of her thirty-nine novels, which sold more than 2 million copies during her lifetime, the first and most successful was *Tempest and Sunshine* (1854), set in Woodford County. Holmes's works are formula novels of virtue rewarded, in which a poor but virtuous young woman is contrasted with a rich, hateful one and marries the perfect husband—rich, brave, and strong—sometimes taking him away from the heiress. In 1859 Holmes began to publish stories serially in the *Weekly*. She rivaled the most prolific and popular story writer of the day, Mrs. E.D.E.N. Southworth, in her appeal to women readers.

In 1852 Holmes and her husband moved to Brockport, New York, where he practiced law and where they spent the rest of their lives. They had no children, but Holmes was very fond of young people and often took them into her home. During the depression of 1893 she organized bread and soup kitchens for the unemployed, and she was a member of many philanthropic and service organizations.

Holmes died on October 7, 1907, and was buried at Brockport, New York.

See Lina Mainiero, ed., *American Women Writers* (New York 1982).   DANNY MILLER

HOLT, FELIX. Felix Holt, author, was born December 20, 1898, in Murray, Kentucky, to Crawford Duncan and Sarah B. (Allen) Holt. His father was a carpenter and his uncle, G.A. Holt, had served briefly as acting lieutenant governor of Kentucky in 1871. As a youth, Felix attended the Stone School in Calloway County and Murray High School. In 1917 he volunteered for military service in World War I and served as a reporter for the army newspaper, *Stars and Stripes*. Following the war, Holt worked as a reporter for several newspapers, beginning with the *Paducah News Democrat* in 1919 and ending with the *Detroit Times* in 1930. Switching to radio in 1931, he accepted a position as news editor for Detroit's WJBK. Three years later Holt became the editorial, news, and publicity director for Detroit station WXYZ, where he built a reputation as a scriptwriter through his work on two radio serials, "Lone Ranger" and "Green Hornet." In 1945 he went to work for CBS in New York as scriptwriter for several television shows, including "Cimarron Tavern," "Studio One," and "Big Town."

Holt left New York in 1946 for Pennsylvania, where he wrote his first novel, *The Gabriel Horn* (1951). The book, which critics credited as one of the significant works of the year, depicts Kentucky frontier life in the Jackson Purchase area during the nineteenth century westward migration. It eventually sold over 1 million copies and in 1954 became a major motion picture, *The Kentuckian*, starring Burt Lancaster. Holt continued the story in his second novel, *Dan'l Boone Kissed Me* (1954).

Holt married Margie Sies of San Diego, California, on September 29, 1920. They had two children. Holt died on June 3, 1954, in Penn's Park, Pennsylvania, and his body was cremated.

See Lawrence S. Thompson, "Felix Holt, Kentucky Historical Novelist," *Register* 53 (July 1955): 247-56.

HOLT, JOSEPH. Joseph Holt, lawyer and political leader, was born near Hardinsburg, in Breckinridge County, on January 6, 1807, to John and Eleanor (Stephens) Holt. He was educated at St. Joseph's College, Bardstown, and Centre College, Danville. Holt practiced law in Elizabethtown from 1828 until 1832, when he moved to Louisville. He became assistant editor of the *Louisville Advertiser* and commonwealth's attorney in 1833. In 1835 Holt moved to Mississippi, where he practiced law in Port Gibson and later in Vicksburg. He built a solid reputation as a brilliant attorney and powerful orator, and he retired with a comfortable fortune at the age of thirty-five. He returned to Louisville in 1842.

In 1856 he worked on behalf of the candidacy of James Buchanan for president and John C. Breckinridge for vice-president. Buchanan appointed Holt commissioner of patents in 1857, postmaster general in 1859, and secretary of war in 1860. In 1861, with the cooperation of Gen. Winfield Scott, Holt prevented hostile demonstrations at the inauguration of Abraham Lincoln, and shortly thereafter reported on plans for a Confederate seizure of the capital. A staunch Unionist, Holt was one of many instrumental in keeping Kentucky loyal to the Union. In 1862 he was appointed to the newly created office of judge advocate general, with the rank of colonel, and in 1864 he was promoted to brigadier general and named to head the new Bureau of Military Justice. He was brevetted major general in 1865. Holt played a conspicuous role in various courts-martial and courts of justice, most notably in the trial of the Lincoln assassins. His popularity peaked during this trial, but increasing opposition to the military tribunal and allegations that he had suppressed evidence during the trial led to his resignation on December 1, 1875.

Holt was married twice: to Mary Harrison in 1838 and, after her death, to Margaret Wickliffe in 1850. Holt lived in semiretirement in Washington, D.C., until his death on August 1, 1894, and was buried in the family cemetery in Holt, Kentucky.

See Robert J. Bartman, "Joseph Holt and Kentucky in the Civil War," *FCHQ* 40 (April 1966): 105-22; James D. Bennett, "Joseph Holt: Retrenchment and Reform in the Post Office Department, 1859-1860," *FCHQ* 49 (Oct. 1975): 309-22.

JAMES D. BENNETT

HOME GUARD. The chaotic situation in Kentucky at the outbreak of the Civil War in 1861 led to the formation of the Home Guard companies across the state. Before the war, the Kentucky legislature had reorganized the state militia and formed a miniature state army of volunteer militiamen

known as the Kentucky State Guard. While most of the rest of the nation went to war during the spring and summer of 1861, Kentucky pursued a policy of neutrality. The majority in the legislature were Union men, displeased to learn that many Kentucky State Guard soldiers were stealing southward to join the Confederate army. The legislature therefore authorized formation of county-based companies of Union men, to be called the Home Guards. In May 1861, the federal government encouraged this development by sending 5,000 weapons, soon dubbed Lincoln guns, into Kentucky for use by known Unionists. Nevertheless, organization of the Home Guard was never uniform throughout the state; in many areas Home Guard organization was very informal.

After the collapse of Kentucky neutrality and the beginning of military operations in the state during the autumn of 1861, many Home Guard units saw action in defense of their communities, although the combat value of most Home Guard companies was slight. Confederate units, especially those led by John Hunt Morgan, who often encountered Home Guardsmen, seldom had much trouble brushing aside even the most persistent of them.

Except for occasional cavalry raids, combat operations by the major armies shifted away from Kentucky after 1862. Still, there was no peace in Kentucky. The secession crisis and the war had divided the citizens. Guerrilla warfare broke out between factions, and bandit gangs with little or no political motivation took advantage of the general disorder to terrorize isolated communities. Although the state reinstituted the Kentucky State Guard as a Unionist force to keep order, in many areas the responsibility for combating guerrillas and brigands fell to the Home Guard. In counties across the state, state military leaders gave Union men authority and weapons but little supervision in the effort to subdue real or imagined Confederate sympathizers. Some Home Guardsmen practiced a brutal style of vigilantism in dealing with their neighbors, often creating a backlash of support for the cause they sought to suppress. The hard feelings engendered endured for generations in the social discord that plagued postwar Kentucky. Well into the twentieth century a Kentuckian might disparage a neighbor by saying, "He's no good; his daddy was in the Home Guard."

While many Home Guardsmen had stood honestly to defend their homes, the misdeeds of others spoiled the reputation of their organization.

See Lowell Harrison, *The Civil War in Kentucky* (Lexington, Ky,. 1975)　　NICKY HUGHES

HOOD, JOHN BELL. John Bell Hood, Confederate general, was born June 1, 1831, in Owingsville, Kentucky, the son of John W. and Theodosia (French) Hood. In 1835 the family moved to Montgomery County, a few miles west of Mt. Sterling, where Hood had a sheltered and comfortable childhood. His imagination was fired by the tales of Indian fighting told by his grandfathers—Lucas Hood, who had fought Indians under Anthony Wayne, and Col. Richard Callaway, one of the founders of Boonesborough. Hood entered the U.S. Military Academy at West Point in 1849. He graduated in July 1853, forty-fourth in a class of fifty-two, and was commissioned a brevet second lieutenant. His first assignment was in northern California; in 1855 he was transferred and spent five years in Texas. In the fall of 1860, Hood was appointed chief of cavalry at West Point, a post he turned down because of his loyalty to the South in the impending Civil War.

He returned to Kentucky in early spring of 1861 in the hope that it would secede from the Union and he could offer his services to his home state. On April 16, 1861, when he had become convinced that Kentucky would remain with the Union, Hood resigned his commission and left for Montgomery, Alabama, where he was commissioned a first lieutenant of Confederate cavalry on April 20. By October 1, he was colonel of the 4th Texas Regiment and rose to brigadier general in command of the Texas brigade on March 7, 1862. His men acquired a reputation for hard fighting and reckless courage during the Peninsula, Second Bull Run, and Antietam campaigns. In recognition of their valor, Stonewall Jackson on September 27, 1862, wrote of Hood as "one of the most promising officers of the army," and Robert E. Lee in the same month wrote that Hood and his men "have fought grandly, nobly and we must have more of them." Both recommended Hood's promotion to major general, which was formally announced on November 6, 1862.

During the battle at Gettysburg on July 2, 1863, where his men led one of the assaults, a shell exploded above Hood, crippling his left arm and hand for life. At the Battle of Chickamauga on September 20, 1863, a bullet struck his right leg and it was amputated at the thigh. On February 11, 1864, he was promoted to lieutenant general. On July 17, 1864, President Jefferson Davis made Hood commander of the Army of Tennessee, replacing Gen. Joseph E. Johnston. At the age of thirty-five Hood was the youngest full general of the Confederacy. He attempted to defend Atlanta but was forced to withdraw on September 1, 1864. Later in the year he was decisively defeated in two battles in Tennessee, at Franklin on November 30 and at Nashville on December 15. On January 17, 1865, Gen. Richard Taylor was placed in command of the Army of Tennessee. Hood never returned to command and surrendered to Union authorities in Natchez, Mississippi, on May 31, 1865.

Hood settled in New Orleans in January 1866, dealing in cotton and insurance; neither enterprise was successful. On April 13, 1868, he married Anna Marie Hennen. They were the parents of eleven children. Hood's remaining years were spent writing *Advance and Retreat*, a bitter and hostile account of his wartime experiences. His wife contracted yellow fever and died on August 22, 1879,

followed by their eldest daughter and by Hood himself on August 31. He was buried in the Metairie Cemetery in New Orleans.

See Thomas R. Hay, *Hood's Tennessee Campaign* (New York 1929); Richard M. McMurry, *John Bell Hood and the War for Southern Independence* (Lexington, Ky., 1982).

SUE McGUIRE'S FOURTH GRADE CLASS,
MT. STERLING ELEMENTARY SCHOOL

HOPKINS, SAMUEL. Samuel Hopkins, political leader, was born April 9, 1753, in Albemarle County, Virginia, to Dr. Samuel and Isabella (Taylor) Hopkins. An officer in the Revolutionary War, Hopkins was wounded at Germantown, Pennsylvania, and taken prisoner at Charleston. In 1797 he settled permanently in Henderson County, Kentucky. Hopkins was state representative four times between 1800 and 1806, presidential elector in 1809, state senator during 1809-13, and U.S. congressman from March 4, 1813 to March 3, 1815. As major general of militia, he led volunteer expeditions against Indians in Illinois in October and November 1812. On January 18, 1783, he married Elizabeth Branch Bugg of Mecklenburg County, Virginia. Hopkins died at his estate, Spring Garden, on September 16, 1819, and was buried there.

See James W. Hammack, Jr., *Kentucky and the Second American Revolution: The War of 1812* (Lexington Ky., 1976); H. Levin, ed., *The Lawyers and Lawmakers of Kentucky* (Chicago 1897).

JAMES W. HAMMACK, JR.

HOPKINS COUNTY. Hopkins County, the forty-ninth in order of formation, is located in western Kentucky. Surrounded by Webster, McLean, Muhlenberg, Christian, and Caldwell counties, it has an area of 552 square miles. The county was created in 1806 from a portion of Henderson County and was named for Gen. Samuel Hopkins, a Revolutionary War veteran and early settler of the region. The county seat is MADISONVILLE.

The topography ranges from flatlands along the broad river valleys of the Pond, Tradewater, and Green rivers, to hilly and rolling land in the southern and central parts of the county. Coal mines operate in the southern part of Hopkins County and agriculture is a mainstay in the northern part. Major crops are soybeans, corn, and tobacco. Along with coal, resources include oil and natural gas.

The earliest inhabitants were prehistoric Native Americans who lived, hunted, and farmed there. One of their settlements was a rough stone structure on Fort Ridge, which has been destroyed by strip mining. Some of the early settlers were veterans of the Revolutionary War who received land grants from Virginia in the area southwest of the Green River. Among these was Friederick Wilhelm, Baron Von Steuben, the Prussian general who had instructed the Revolutionary army at Valley Forge in the winter of 1776-77. According to tradition, the baron was wounded during an Indian attack while on his first visit and subsequently quit-claimed his property. On his grant of several thousand acres in the northwest part of the county, a salt spring came to be known as Steuben's Lick. By the 1880s, the community there was called Manitou.

Roads in the county often followed old animal trails that led to the many salt and mineral springs, the major traces being the ones that connected the county seat of Madisonville with Henderson to the north, Hopkinsville to the south, and Russellville to the southeast. Numerous other trails led to the mills and ferries on the Pond and Tradewater rivers and their tributaries.

On January 3, 1829, Ashbyburg in the northeastern part of the county was incorporated. Located on the Green River, it thrived as a steamboat landing during the nineteenth century. Other antebellum communities included Nebo, northwest of Madisonville, and Charleston, named after "Free Charles," a black freedman who operated a tavern in the southwest part of the county.

Hopkins County was divided by the Civil War. Union supporters joined a regiment recruited locally by James Shackleford; Al Fowler recruited Confederate troops. The courthouse in Madisonville was burned by Confederates led by Gen. Hylan B. Lyon on December 17, 1864, as they passed through western Kentucky. It was the policies imposed by the occupying Union armies, however, that caused most resentment and sparked sympathy for the Confederate cause. Since that time, local politics have been heavily dominated by the Democratic party.

Farming was the major occupation in Hopkins County for most of the 1800s, with tobacco the leading crop. Around 1837 local blacksmith James Woolfolk found an outcropping of coal on his land. John Bayless Earle, for whom the town of Earlington was named, opened the first coal mine in the county in 1869. Mining did not become a major industry until the Louisville & Nashville Railroad pushed its line southward from Henderson through Madisonville and toward Nashville in 1870. Two years later, the Elizabethtown & Paducah Railroad entered the county from the east. Many communities grew quickly as railroad stops, including Mortons Gap, Hanson, Nortonville, and White Plains. Dawson Springs, in the southwestern part of the county, began to thrive in the 1880s as a health resort, but its popularity had faded by the time of the Great Depression.

By 1970 Hopkins County was the second largest producer of coal in the Western Coal Field, after Muhlenberg, and the third-largest coal producer in the entire state after Muhlenberg and Pike counties. In 1971 the county also ranked fifth in Kentucky in oil production. Coal and oil-related businesses were major county employers by 1990. Development of resources was aided by the construction of the north-south Pennyrile Parkway and the east-west Western Kentucky Parkway through the county by the early 1970s. In 1987 farms occupied 41 percent

of the land area, with 72 percent of farmland under cultivation.

The population of the county was 38,167 in 1970; 46,174 in 1980; and 46,126 in 1990.

See Historical Society of Hopkins County, *Original Atlas and Historical Data of Hopkins County, Kentucky* (Madisonville, Ky., 1974).

ANN BROWN

HOPKINSVILLE. Hopkinsville, the county seat of Christian County, is located at U.S. 41 and U.S. 68 in the Pennyroyal Region. The site was settled in 1796 by Bartholomew and Martha Ann Wood, a couple from Jonesborough, Tennessee. The Wood family established a permanent settlement in the vicinity of present-day West Seventh and Bethel Streets, near what would become known as the Old Rock Spring. Wood staked a claim, based on his service in the Revolutionary War, on 1,200 acres of land. He built a second cabin on what is now the northeast corner of Ninth and Virginia streets and a few years later built a home southeast of Fourteenth and Campbell streets, where he died in 1827. Wood's settlement soon attracted other settlers, and a pioneer village emerged.

Wood donated five acres of land and a half interest in his spring for the county seat. The following year a log courthouse, jail, and "stray pen" were built on the public square facing Main Street. The plat for the town, first called Christian Court House, was surveyed by John Campbell and Samuel Means in 1799. In honor of Wood's eldest daughter, the town was renamed Elizabeth that same year. However, a town in Hardin County had the same name, and in April 1804, the General Assembly renamed the settlement Hopkinsville, in honor of Gen. Samuel Hopkins of Henderson County. A colonel in the Revolutionary War, Hopkins had settled in Kentucky in 1797 and was promoted to the rank of general during the War of 1812.

Although Kentucky was tardy in the establishment of a public school system, Hopkinsville was fortunate to have several quality private schools. The first of these was in operation by 1812, preceding the establishment of public schools in the city by almost thirty years. South Kentucky College, established in 1849, and Bethel Female College, organized five years later, provided formal higher education for young women. Circuit riders established a Methodist church in Hopkinsville about 1800, and in 1804 Little River Baptist Church was constituted. Other religious denominations organized in Hopkinsville included: Presbyterian, 1813; Cumberland Presbyterian, 1825; Episcopal, 1831; and Christian Church, 1832.

From the first issue of the *Western Eagle* on January 1, 1813, through 123 years of the *Kentucky New Era*, forty-five newspapers have been printed in Hopkinsville and Christian County. Thirty-eight were weekly publications, one was tri-weekly, five were semiweekly, and four were daily papers. Two papers were morning editions and three were monthly.

Railroad construction and operation in the late 1860s opened markets for agricultural and industrial products. Railroad service was inaugurated in Hopkinsville on April 8, 1868, by the Evansville, Henderson, & Nashville Railroad. This line was later extended north to Henderson and was acquired by the Louisville & Nashville Railroad (now CSX Transportation) in 1879. The Ohio Valley Railroad, purchased by the Illinois Central Railroad (now Illinois Central Gulf) in 1897, was built from Gracey to Hopkinsville in 1892 and abandoned in the 1980s. In 1903, the western division of the Tennessee Central Railway entered Christian County at Edgoten (Edge-of-Tennessee), connecting Clarksville and Hopkinsville. In 1990 the Hopkinsville-Fort Campbell portion was operated by the U.S. Department of Defense.

On December 7, 1907, some 250 masked NIGHT RIDERS captured police and sheriff posts and cut off the town from outside contact. They then pursued city officials and tobacco executives who were buying cheap tobacco from farmers not members of the Dark Tobacco District Planters' Protective Association. Three warehouses were burned during a night of lawlessness.

Jennie Stuart Memorial Hospital was a gift to the community by Dr. Edward S. Stuart of Fairview in 1914. The U.S. government erected a veterans hospital at Outwood in northwestern Christian County in 1922.

The building of the Pennyrile Parkway in 1969 and the city's proximity to I-24, the Land Between the Lakes region, and to Fort Campbell Military Reservation have been important factors in the Hopkinsville's growth. Major employers in 1990 were the Flynn Enterprises, Inc., manufacturers of jeans, and the Elk Brand Manufacturing Company, which produces clothing. The Western State Hospital for the mentally ill, located just outside of town, is one of the oldest such institutions in the country. The population of the third-class city was 21,250 in 1970; 27,318 in 1980; and 29,809 in 1990.

See William T. Turner, *Gateway from the Past: A Pictorial History of Hopkinsville and Christian County, Kentucky Since 1865* (Hopkinsville, Ky., 1974).   WILLIAM T. TURNER

HOPKINSVILLE COLLEGE OF THE BIBLE.

Originally named Male and Female College, later known as the South Western Kentucky Institute, the college was founded at a meeting of the First District Baptist Association at the Green Valley Baptist Church in Clinton, Hickman County, Kentucky, in September 1883. The resolution noted a need for better teachers and preachers for black citizens in the region and recognized the great distance to existing schools. In 1889 the Little River and Cumberland Valley Baptist District associations joined in financing the college. A board of directors appointed in 1890 purchased a tract of land on Vine Street in the northeast section of Hopkinsville. The 1910 catalogue noted that "the college is established for the purpose of training children in the

way they should go; preparing young men and young women for business life, teachers and preachers for better and more effective service in their calling."

In 1895 a board of trustees took the place of the directors. The Rev. A.C. Schoffner was named president of the new institution and was succeeded after one term by the Rev. Patterson T. Frazer on August 23, 1900. Frazer served until 1920.

Early departments included a model or elementary school, a preparatory school, a college department, and a theological department. Music, skills in sewing and dressmaking, and business subjects were taught along with theology. Enrollment ranged from fifty to one hundred students. On May 2, 1935, a severe windstorm swept through Hopkinsville and damaged the building beyond repair. The college building was replaced and reopened for the 1938–39 school year. Despite almost constant financial problems, the college continued serving black citizens through the Depression and war years. To reflect the role of the college as it had developed over the years, it was renamed Hopkinsville College of the Bible on November 4, 1965. The college serves a limited number of evening students, particularly young black men aspiring to the Christian ministry.

See William T. Turner, *History & Hopkinsville M. & F. College* (N.p., 1973).   THOMAS L. RILEY

HORINE, EMMET FIELD.

Emmet Field Horine, physician, was born August 3, 1885, in Brooks, Bullitt County, Kentucky, the son of Dr. George H. and Elizabeth (Barrell) Horine. He graduated from Emory College in Atlanta in 1903, and received his M.D. from the Kentucky School of Medicine in Louisville in 1907. Later he studied cardiology, pathology, and anesthesiology in Europe and Louisville. During World War I Horine was a captain in the Medical Corps, U.S. Army, and chief of the cardiovascular service at Camp Hancock, Georgia.

In private practice, Horine was the first cardiologist in Jefferson County. For nearly fifty years, Horine taught medicine at the University of Louisville School of Medicine and was chief of the section on medical history. He also served as president of the Medico-Chirurgical Society of Louisville and of the Ohio Valley Medical Association. In 1955 he became professor emeritus of medicine. Between 1935 and 1963 he was the historian of the Kentucky State Medical Association. During his long career, Horine accumulated a medical history collection of manuscripts, classic treatises, and other documents, which he bequeathed to the rare books departments of libraries at the University of Louisville, University of Kentucky, and Transylvania University. His most enduring contribution to medical history is *Daniel Drake, M.D. (1785-1852): Pioneer Physician of the Midwest* (1961).

On June 30, 1914, Horine married Helen B. Ruthenburg; they had four children. He died on February 1, 1964, in Brooks, Kentucky.

See E.H. Conner, "Emmet Field Horine, 1885-1964," *Journal of Kentucky State Medical Association* 62 (1964): 216.

ERIC HOWARD CHRISTIANSON

HORNUNG, PAUL. Paul ("Golden Boy") Hornung, football player, was born on December 23, 1935, in Louisville. His parents separated when he was two and he remained with his mother, Loretta, in Louisville. A multisport athlete at Louisville's Flaget High School, he was recruited by Paul Bryant to play football at the University of Kentucky. Hornung chose instead to go to Notre Dame, where he was an All-American quarterback in 1955 and 1956 and won the Heisman Trophy in 1957. He was the first selection of the Green Bay Packers in the 1957 National Football League draft, and after struggling for two years, started under the coaching of Vince Lombardi. Hornung was a great triple-threat back. He led the league in scoring for three years, 1959-61, and was most valuable player in the 1961 title game. His otherwise great career was tarnished when he was suspended for one year on April 17, 1963, along with Alex Karras, for gambling. He played on three NFL championship teams (1961, 1962, and 1965) and in two pro Bowls (1959 and 1960). He was chosen by New Orleans in the 1967 expansion draft, but chose to retire. He was elected to the Professional Football Hall of Fame in 1986.

JAMES C. CLAYPOOL

HORSE CAVE. Horse Cave, the largest city in Hart County, lies at the junction of highways U.S. 31W and KY 218, thirty-six miles northeast of Bowling Green and five miles south of Munfordville. It was established in the 1840s by Maj. Albert Anderson and incorporated as Horse Cave in 1864, named after the local railroad station. Anderson had donated land for the Louisville & Nashville station in 1858, with the stipulation that the station be called Horse Cave, after a nearby cave. The residents of the town voted to change its name to Caverna in 1869, but the new name was confused with that of the rail station, and the town officially became Horse Cave again in 1879. The name may have originated because horse thieves or Indians hid horses in the local cave, because a horse fell into it, or because the slang of the day referred to anything large as "horse." The cave itself is also known as Hidden River Cave.

The fifth-class city of Horse Cave is one of southern Kentucky's largest burley markets. It also has an industrial base, including zinc die casting and corrugated steel pipe manufacturing. Tourism, centering around Horse Cave, Mammoth Onyx Cave, Kentucky Buffalo Park, and other attractions, plays a large role in the local economy. The professional Horse Cave Theatre presents an annual series of contemporary, classic, and new plays. Horse Cave's population was 2,068 in 1970; 2,045 in 1980; and 2,284 in 1990.

HORSE FARMS. The Inner Bluegrass region of Kentucky has the greatest concentration of horse farms in the world. As early as 1800 Kentucky was nationally recognized for the quality of its horses; by 1840 Kentucky had attained the top position in horse breeding in America, a position it still commands.

From the start, the suitable environment in Kentucky attracted those interested in the best of sporting horses. Nature supplied a favorable climate, a topography gently rolling and well-drained, and underlying limestone formations with a remarkably high content of calcium phosphate as well as calcium magnesium carbonate and all the trace elements needed by animals. The mineral richness of the soil and spring water, which promotes strong but light bones and tendons, is made to order for raising strong foals. Since the Bluegrass region has the greatest number of choice broodmares, the nation's best stallions stand there and outstanding equine veterinary services and bloodstock sales agencies do business there. Although thoroughbred horse farms predominate, standardbreds and saddlebreds are very much a part of the Bluegrass picture.

In the antebellum years, farms were diversified, and those famous for horses also produced other livestock and crops. Although the control of racing after the Civil War was in the hands of northeastern interests, Kentucky held undisputed preeminence in breeding. In addition to local horsemen, affluent horse owners from the Northeast began buying Bluegrass farmland on which to breed winners. Breeding emphasized both stamina and distance, since most thoroughbreds in the first three-quarters of the nineteenth century raced in heats—often four-mile heats, sometimes the best three out of five heats to win, sometimes the best two out of three. By 1885 thoroughbred heat racing had died out completely; racegoers wanted longer programs of shorter races to provide more opportunities to bet. Selective breeding then focused on speed and sprinting. Domino, bred by Maj. Barak Thomas of Fayette County, foaled in 1891 and raced by James R. Keene, was the first outstanding American thoroughbred sprinter, and for a half century he and his descendants contributed more to speed than did any other line. Since World War II horsemen from several other nations have bought Bluegrass farms, and during 1960-90 a large number of horse farms were sold to Arabs, South Africans, and New Zealanders.

Other states have adopted incentive programs to attract and expand their horse industries, both thoroughbred and standardbred, such as breeders' prizes, stallion awards, and races restricted to state-bred horses. Kentucky's state government has refused most of the measures used by other states to promote the industry, and as a result has lost some of its margin in the number of thoroughbreds produced, although still ranking first. The Kentucky legislature created incentives for the state's standardbreds starting in 1977, and for thoroughbreds in 1979, by directing 4.25 percent of the pari-mutuel handles into development funds for Kentucky-bred horses, but the amounts are small in comparison with what other states offer.

Despite other states' exclusion of Kentucky-breds in some stakes races (in which Kentucky does not reciprocate), the state still leads in winners of stakes races in North America, and in the highest class, the grade I stakes, Bluegrass-breds consistently demonstrate superior quality. For instance, in the racing period 1979-88, 29 percent of North American stakes winners were Kentucky-bred; next behind Kentucky was Florida, with 13.6 percent. In 1988 Bluegrass-breds won six of the seven prestigious Breeders' Cup races.

British thoroughbred authority Peter Willett writes, "As the thoroughbred entered . . . the fourth century of evolution from the original stock . . . the most productive sources of the Classic racehorse had shifted from the Old World to the North American continent, and predominantly to a tiny portion of that vast land mass called the Kentucky Bluegrass." Today farms such as Airdrie, Ashford, Brookdale, Brookside, Buckram Oaks, Calumet, Claiborne, Clovelly, Darby Dan, Domino Stud, Elmendorf, Gainsborough, Gainesway, Hamburg Place, Lane's End, Mare Haven, Mill Ridge, Jonabell, Spendthrift, Stone Farm, and Three Chimneys are mentioned wherever thoroughbreds are known. Almahurst, Castleton, Stoner Creek, and Walnut Hall farms are famous throughout the standardbred world. Saddlebred farms include Rainbow Farm, Nicholasville; Crabtree Farms and Don Harris Stables in Simpsonville; Belle Reve and Castle Hills farms in Versailles; Foxfire Stud, Lexington; Silver Lining Stables, Danville; and Shawnee Springs and Oak Hill Farms, Harrodsburg.

See Bruce Denbo, Mary Wharton, and Clyde Burke, *The Horse World of the Bluegrass* (Lexington, Ky., 1980); Peter Willett, *The Classic Racehorse* (Lexington, Ky., 1982).

MARY E. WHARTON

HOT BROWN. Louisville's Brown Hotel opened in 1923, and shortly thereafter introduced two sandwiches named for itself. The cold Brown sandwich, an open-faced layering of rye bread, baked chicken or turkey, lettuce, tomato, and hard-boiled egg, topped with thousand island dressing, is rarely served any more; the hot Brown (the word "sandwich" is not used) is consumed all over the country, frequently by people unaware of its Kentucky background. Created by chef Fred K. Schmidt as an alternative to late-night suppers of ham and eggs, the original hot Brown consisted of sliced roast turkey (at that time a rarity) open-faced on white toast, topped with Mornay sauce, sprinkled with Parmesan cheese and broiled. It was garnished with crossed strips of bacon and pimiento.

Immediately successful, the hot Brown soon accounted for ninety-five percent of luncheon entrees at the Brown, and was imitated by home cooks and professional chefs with varying degrees of success. Variations included substitution of cheddar and even American cheese in the sauce, and garnishes of tomato (generally accepted) and canned peaches (not).

The Brown Hotel closed in 1971 but, beautifully restored, reopened in 1985. The hot Brown is once more available—and popular—in its place of origin.

See Kay Gill, *The Brown Hotel and Louisville's Magic Corner* (Louisville 1984); Marion Flexner, *Out of Kentucky Kitchens* (New York 1949).

MARTY GODBEY

HOUSE BILL 44. By any standard of appraisal of Kentucky legislative history, House Bill 44, January 31, 1979, must be considered a piece of legislation with far-reaching importance, if not a stumbling block to the state's progress, by limiting the amount of revenue raised. The law was enacted in an extraordinary session of the General Assembly called by Lt. Gov. Thelma Stovall, who acted in the absence from the state of Gov. Julian Carroll (1974-79). This complex revenue measure bears an extraordinary preface stating thirteen definitions, explanations, and statutory references. The central point of the law is that annual Kentucky property taxes can generate only 4 percent more revenue than in the previous year. Section 6, including numerous subsections, outlines a formula by which school boards may seek to increase local tax rates for educational purposes, if voters approve the increase. Enactment of House Bill 44 reflected a fundamental weakness in the 1890 Kentucky constitution by declaring the governor incapable of action when out of state.   THOMAS D. CLARK

HOWARD, ELHANAN MURPHY. Elhanan Murphy Howard, physician, was born in Harlan, Kentucky, on August 5, 1886, the son of Moses Wilkerson and Nancy (Turner) Howard. A 1908 graduate of the University of Louisville, he served as physician for the Continental Coal Corporation in Bell County until 1914, when he returned to Harlan and entered private practice with Dr. W.P. Cawood. In 1915 the two established Harlan Hospital, the first modern hospital in Harlan County. Howard joined the State Board of Health in 1928 and served as its president from 1929 until 1963. During his tenure, the board established health units in eighty counties and conducted major campaigns against cancer, polio, malaria, tuberculosis, and water pollution. Howard was also active in agricultural and commercial development in Kentucky, Virginia, and Florida as well as in civic organizations, including the Young Men's Christian Association and Kiwanis.

In 1907 Howard married Martha Emily Eager. They had four children: Margaret, Elizabeth, Jacqueline, and Elhanan Murphy, Jr. Following Martha Howard's death, he married Eleanor Boswell in 1968. Howard died at Naples, Florida, on December 23, 1968, and was buried at Resthaven Cemetery in Harlan County.

JAMES S. GREENE III

HOWARD-TURNER FEUD. Starting as a quest for revenge, the Howard-Turner feud in Harlan County, Kentucky, escalated into a crisis of law and order that tagged the county with the epithet "bloody" and cast the state in a backward light. It began on March 7, 1882, with the killing of Bob Turner, son of Democratic county chairman George B. Turner, by Wix Howard a day or so after a dispute over a card game. When Howard was acquitted of murder charges, Turner's brother Will made an unsuccessful attempt on Howard's life. Forced to leave the state, Will returned in 1885 and surrendered to authorities, only to be shot down on the courthouse square. The suspected killer, Wils Howard, was a friend of Wix Howard. While out on bond, Wils and his uncle, Will Jennings, tried twice to ambush the Turners; two innocent bystanders, Alexander and John Bailey, were killed. Wils Howard and Jennings went west, and the Wix Howard faction dropped out of the feud.

In 1888 County Judge Wilson Lewis declared war on the illegal whiskey business; when Howard and Jennings returned to the county the following spring, they aligned themselves with the whiskey interests. Wanted on criminal charges in Missouri, they were tracked to Kentucky by a detective who enlisted the help of George B. Turner, Jr. In August 1889 Howard killed Turner while he was drinking from a spring. Lewis then raided Howard's camp, with the loss of two lives. Howard escaped. Gov. S.B. Buckner (1887-91) sent troops to guard the circuit court; when they left, Lewis's brother-in-law John Cawood and his hired hand were killed by Howard supporters. When Howard and his followers gathered at the mouth of Poor Fork and threatened to storm the county seat, Lewis attacked first, killing one man and routing the rest. Jennings was arrested in Missouri, returned for trial, convicted of killing one of the Baileys, and given a life sentence. Howard was imprisoned in California for robbing a stagecoach, extradited to Missouri, and in 1894 was hanged for killing a deaf-mute.

JAMES S. GREENE III

HUBBARD, HARLAN. Harlan Hubbard, writer and painter, son of Frank Gilbert and Rose Ann (Swingle) Hubbard, was born in Bellevue, Kentucky, on January 4, 1900. His father died in 1907, and in 1915 Harlan and his mother moved to New York City to join his two older brothers, who were working there. Harlan attended Childs High School in the Bronx and later the National Academy of Design in New York and the Cincinnati Art Academy. In 1919 he and his mother returned to Kentucky and settled in Fort Thomas.

Hubbard regarded industrial development as a danger to the earth, and he rejected the consumer culture. By 1929, when he began keeping a journal, his differences with society's dominant assumptions were well established, as were his interests in painting, writing, music, and the landscapes of northern Kentucky and the Ohio River. He married Anna Eikenhout in 1943. The next year, at Brent, Kentucky, upriver from Cincinnati, they built a shanty boat on which they traveled down the Ohio and Mississippi rivers and through the Louisiana bayous, ending the voyage in 1951. From 1952 until their deaths, they lived in a house they built far from the road on the shore of the Ohio River in Trimble County, Kentucky. On the shanty boat and in the house at Payne Hollow, they lived a life that was frugal and abundant, solitary and hospitable, fundamental and elegant. It was a life of homemaking and handmaking. Together, they kept house, gardened, read aloud, made music, welcomed guests. Harlan cut firewood, tended a herd of goats, fished, wrote, and painted.

Shantyboat (1953) is the story of the Hubbards' voyage from Brent to New Orleans, *Shantyboat in the Bayous* (1990) completes the story of their voyage, and *Payne Hollow* (1973) is an account of their life at Payne Hollow. *Journals, 1929-1944* was published in 1987. Together, these books are a detailed account of two landmark lives at odds with our time. Hubbard's first love was painting, but he is better known as a writer. He had few contacts with other artists, and he exhibited his work little and only locally. Nevertheless, he produced hundreds of paintings, watercolors, prints, and drawings, mostly of the landscapes in which he spent his life.

Anna Hubbard died on May 3, 1986. At Harlan Hubbard's death on January 16, 1988, a memorial service was held on the Hanover College campus in Indiana. His body was cremated.

See Don Wallis, *Harlan Hubbard and the River: A Visionary Life* (Yellow Spring, Ohio, 1989); Wendell Berry, *Harlan Hubbard: Life and Work* (Lexington, Ky., 1990).

HUDDLESTON, WALTER D. Walter Darlington ("Dee") Huddleston, U.S. senator, was born in Burkesville, Cumberland County, Kentucky, on April 15, 1926, to the Rev. W.F. and Lottie (Russell) Huddleston. After attending Jeffersontown High School in Jefferson County, he served during World War II as a tank gunner in the 9th Armored Division from 1944 to 1946. Huddleston graduated from the University of Kentucky with a bachelor of arts degree in radio in 1949. He worked as program and sports director at radio station WKCT in Bowling Green (1949-52); as general manager, WIEL, Elizabethtown (1952-72); and as co-owner and director, WLBN, Lebanon (1957-72).

Representing the 10th District, Huddleston served in the state Senate during 1965-72 and was the majority floor leader during 1970-72. He managed Wendell Ford's successful bid for the governorship in 1971. In 1972 Huddleston, the Democratic candidate, defeated Republican Louie B. Nunn for the U.S. Senate by a vote of 529,890 to 495,995. Huddleston was reelected in 1978 but was unsuccessful in seeking a third term in 1984, losing to Addison

Mitchell McConnell. During his time in the Senate, from January 3, 1973, to January 3, 1985, Huddleston served on several prominent committees, including Agriculture and Appropriations, where he supported Kentucky tobacco interests. After leaving the Senate, Huddleston became a consultant for the Tobacco Institute and then senior vice president of Hecht and Associates, a Washington, D.C., consulting firm.

Huddleston married Jean Pearce of Middletown, Kentucky, on December 20, 1947. They live in Elizabethtown, Kentucky, and have two sons, Stephen and Philip.

HUDSON, VIRGINIA CARY. Virginia Cary Hudson, whose girlhood impressions of the Bluegrass were a best-seller when published after her death, was the daughter of Richard N. and Jessie (Gregory) Hudson. She was born on May 28, 1894, in Louisville. Her early childhood was spent in Versailles, Kentucky. At the age of ten, Hudson wrote a series of essays that depicted in a humorous, satirical manner the reality of life as seen through the eyes of a child. The setting of her writing was Versailles and many of her subjects were taken from her experiences there. After graduating from Margaret Hall, an Episcopal school for girls in Versailles, Hudson attended a finishing school for young women in Washington, D.C.

Hudson married Kirtley S. Cleveland of Louisville on May 7, 1914. They lived in Louisville where her husband bred and trained thoroughbred horses. The couple had three children: Richard, Ann Cary, and Virginia, who was responsible for the posthumous publication of her mother's childhood writings. The first volume, *O Ye Jigs and Juleps!* published in 1962, was a best seller. It was followed by *Credos and Quips* (1964) and *Flapdoodle, Trust and Obey* (1966). Hudson died on April 8, 1954, and was buried in the family plot in Cloverport, Kentucky.

See William S. Ward, *A Literary History of Kentucky* (Knoxville, Tenn., 1987).

HUMANA INC. Humana Inc., an investor-owned hospital company, is the largest publicly held corporation headquartered in Louisville and a major international corporation, with more than $2.5 billion in annual revenues. It is also one of the largest patrons of the arts in Louisville and one of the two largest corporate contributors to public education in the commonwealth of Kentucky.

The company was founded by attorneys David A. JONES and Wendell CHERRY, who joined with associates in borrowing funds to finance a nursing home in 1961 on leased land on Bardstown Road in Louisville. They named their new venture Heritage House of America and in 1965 changed the name to Extendicare. In 1968 the company bought the Medical Center Hospital in Huntsville, Alabama. By 1972 Jones and Cherry had acquired a total of forty-five hospitals. The following year they sold off their forty-one nursing homes (which had made

their firm the largest nursing home company in America) to concentrate on hospital acquisition, building, and administration.

In January 1974 the firm changed its name to Humana Inc. Six years later Humana took over American Medicorp, Inc., of Pennsylvania, thereby expanding its number of hospitals from fifty-nine to 114. In 1979 Humana's revenues exceeded $1 billion and the corporation broke into the ranks of America's five hundred largest companies. In 1982 Humana entered into an innovative arrangement with the University of Louisville School of Medicine to lease and operate its $72 million teaching hospital, which also served the community's indigent population. In 1983 the company began to operate Humana Hospital-University of Louisville, one of the few teaching hospitals in America operated by an investor-owned hospital corporation. In the first year of operation, Humana transformed the annual deficits into profits, which it shared with the University of Louisville School of Medicine in accordance with the leasing and operating agreement. In 1983 the company introduced Humana Care Plus, its first health insurance venture. Between 1984 and 1988, Humana Heart Institute International supported William Devries's research on the permanent artificial heart.

Humana has been housed since 1985 in a skyscraper designed by Postmodernist architect Michael Graves, of Princeton, New Jersey. The building is twenty-seven stories high and is made of multicolored granites and marbles from around the world. In 1989 *Business Week* magazine placed Humana in 209th place on its list of the 1,000 most valuable companies in the United States.

ALLEN J. SHARE

HUME, EDGAR ERSKINE. Edgar Erskine Hume, a major general in the U.S. Army medical corps, was born on December 26, 1889, in Frankfort, the son of Enoch Edgar and Mary (South) Hume. He earned bachelor's and master's degrees in 1908 and 1909 from Centre College in Danville and an M.D. degree in 1913 from Johns Hopkins University in Baltimore. Hume began his career in public health as a civilian in Europe before the U.S. entry into World War I. In 1915, at the request of the U.S. ambassador to Italy, he headed U.S. medical relief efforts in the earthquake-stricken province of Abruzzi. In 1916 he entered the U.S. army's medical corps and was given command of all U.S. hospitals in Italy; he transferred to France before the end of the war. Hume later directed the American Red Cross in Serbia during a serious typhus epidemic. During World War II, Hume returned to the Mediterranean as a staff officer with Gen. Mark Clark's 5th Army. Following the invasion of Italy in September 1943, he accepted the surrender of Naples. For the remainder of the war, he commanded the Allied military government in the 5th Army's sector of the Italian theater.

In 1918 Hume married Mary Swigert Hendrick; they had one son. Hume died suddenly on January

25, 1952, just a few weeks after his retirement from the Army. He was buried in Arlington National Cemetery.

See Emmet F. Horine, "Edgar Erskine Hume: Major General, M.C., U.S.A.," *Journal of Kentucky State Medical Association* (May 1952): 212-13.   RICHARD G. STONE

HUMES, HELEN. Helen Humes, jazz singer, was born on June 23, 1913, in Louisville. She made the first of several blues recordings at the age of thirteen. In 1938 she replaced Billie Holiday in the Count Basie band, where her refined ballads were a foil against the blues shouts of Jimmy Rushing. In the 1950s her career was oriented more toward commercial rhythm-and-blues and she made a series of hit recordings in this genre. Her voice was strong and her style was diverse, ranging from jazz ballads, which she handled with sophistication and subtlety, to authentic blues shouts and hollers, presented with control and power. Humes died in Santa Monica, California, in September 1981.

LEE BASH

HUMOR. "Kentucky humor," wrote the late Dr. Eslie Asbury, surgeon, horse breeder, and humorist from Nicholas County, "must not be confused with the so-called humor *about* Kentucky seen in the reports of prejudiced, outside writers and TV crews." Indeed, Kentucky, perceived as a rural state, has been stereotyped in both the literary and vaudeville versions of the city slicker versus the rube. Kentuckians, however, have returned the favor in a whole cycle of stories that depict the visiting outsider as the fool.

Both kinds of humor are discussed perceptively by University of Kentucky folklorist William Hugh Jansen in his piece "The Esoteric-Exoteric Factor in Folklore" (*The Study of Folklore*, 1965). Esoteric humor is about ourselves, he writes, and comes out of our "sense of belonging and serves to defend and strengthen that sense." Exoteric humor is about groups different from ours and is a product of the "same sense of belonging, for it may result from fear of, mystification about, or resentment of the group to which one does not belong." Esoteric humor: Former Gov. Bert T. Combs (1959-63) observed that we do not learn anything from the second kick of a mule. Exoteric humor: The lost tourist stops to ask a Kentucky farmer how far it is to Ashland. The farmer doesn't know. "Well, how far to Morehead?" He doesn't know. "You don't know much, do you?" observes the tourist. "Well, I ain't lost," the farmer says.

Kentucky humor for the most part reflects rural life. It depends on our knowing something of what life is like on the farm, in the coal camp or small town. All humor depends somewhat on an understanding of the culture and values of the humor's setting. Kentucky has a strong folk culture and most natives are steeped in it. Kentuckians, like other southerners, have had a heavy dose of Calvin-

ism, which presents human beings as flawed and teaches that only God (who has already predestined everything) can save us by grace. We are familiar with more optimistic thought about salvation, good works, and perfectibility, and many of us have pursued it, but when we stress good works and perfectibility, we have the haunting fear of pride, false piety, and self-righteousness. Much of Kentucky humor is thus aimed at people who "get above their raising" and serves to level them down to the rest of us ("I'd like to buy him for what he's worth and sell him for what he thinks he's worth"). It also reflects the endless capacity for perversity in human nature ("It's untelling what people will do").

Jokes appear to be frivolous, but as the Berkeley folklorist Alan Dundes has said, all jokes are about serious matters. Jokes and other stories help us to define ourselves and others. Kentuckians have not always come out ahead in dealing with the many outsiders who have come to Kentucky—the industrialists, the missionaries, the social workers, and the like. In their humor, however, Kentuckians come out all right. Example: A well-dressed poverty-fighter in a fancy car stops to ask directions of a mountaineer. He then prepares to drive on but is asked, "What line of work you in?" He replies, "I'm with the war on poverty." The native responds, "Well, it looks like you won."

Many Kentucky storytellers have passed down the Old World folktales about such characters as Jack (of the Beanstalk), who appears to be insignificant and defenseless but who always comes out ahead against giants, witches, and ferocious varmints. Jack is both innocent and sly and gets into many humorous situations, depending on the skill of the teller. There are also "Arshmen" (Irishmen) jokes, the newest settler being the butt, and tall tales, hunting tales, anecdotes about those who settled Kentucky, and quite a few more-or-less-true stories about favorite Kentuckians. Leonard W. Roberts, the leading scholar of Kentucky folktales, has published several collections. Thomas D. Clark's *The Rampaging Frontier* (1939) deals with some of the frontier folk humor, such as sermon parodies. Other collectors of folk humor are John Ed McConnell ("You can't laugh and worry at the same time, and you can't laugh and fight at the same time"), Allan M. Trout, and Joe Creason.

Several Kentucky writers are known for their humorous creations. Leading is Irvin S. Cobb ("I'd rather be an orphan in Kentucky than twins anywhere else"), with the Judge Priest stories being his best-known work. Others are Jesse Stuart, notably in *Foretaste of Glory* (1946) and *Taps For Private Tussie* (1943), as well as James Still, Billy C. Clark, Jim Wayne Miller, Gurney Norman, and Ed McClanahan. Even the Kentucky Jeremiahs Harry Caudill and Wendell Berry have published humorous material and both are superb storytellers.

For the most part, Kentucky literary humor, like the folk humor, is based on the culture of common people, and thus most of it is rural in nature. Nostalgia plays a hand at a time when Kentucky is changing to a more urban way of life. No doubt the humor of the twenty-first century will reflect to a greater degree a cosmopolitan setting.

See Alan Dundee, ed., *The Study of Folklore* (Englewood Cliffs, N.J., 1965); Eslie Asbury, *Horse Sense and Humor in Kentucky* (Lexington, Ky., 1961); John Ed McConnell, *A Compendium of Kentucky Humor* (Frankfort, Ky., 1987).

LOYAL JONES

HUNT, JOHN WESLEY. Among the first millionaires west of the Allegheny Mountains, John Wesley Hunt was born in August 1773 in Trenton, New Jersey, the son of Abraham and Theodosia (Pearson) Hunt. Trained in his father's store, he entered the mercantile trade in 1792 in Richmond, Virginia. In 1795 he opened a general store in Lexington, Kentucky. From 1802 to 1810 he improved the bloodlines of thoroughbreds by transferring English stallions from the East. In 1803 he began making hemp packaging for cotton bales. One of the first in the upriver trade, he began shipping hemp yarn up the Ohio River in 1810. As a commission merchant, he marketed farm products and made Philadelphia credit available in the West.

A leading entrepreneur, he supported economic expansion, yet insisted upon responsibility. He was president of the Farmers and Mechanics Bank of Lexington, which not only stood among the few institutions still solvent after the panic of 1819 struck—it even paid dividends. Hunt was also president of the Lexington Fire, Life & Marine Insurance Company. From December 1798 to May 1802 Hunt was postmaster of Lexington. He led in the establishment of Eastern State Hospital for the mentally ill and was chairman of the board of commissioners (1824-44). He was a member of the board of trustees of Transylvania University, and vestryman and warden of Christ Church Episcopal.

Hunt married Catherine Grosh in September 1797. Their children were Mary, Theodosia, Charlton, Eleanor, Henrietta, John, Abraham, Catherine, Thomas, Francis, Anne, and Robert. Confederate Gen. John Hunt MORGAN was their grandson and the scientist Thomas Hunt MORGAN was a great-grandson. Hunt died on August 21, 1849, in Lexington and was buried in Lexington Cemetery.

See James A. Ramage, *John Wesley Hunt: Pioneer Merchant, Manufacturer and Financier* (Lexington, Ky., 1974).   JAMES A. RAMAGE

HUNT CLUBS. After pursuit of deer with hounds evolved from a necessity into a sport, it was succeeded by the chase of the fox—gray foxes only until 1855, when the first recorded red fox in Kentucky was identified in Estill County. Its origin is not entirely clear. The red fox, known to be indigenous to Canada, had also previously been established on Long Island from English importations. In the South, the first reds, presumably having mi-

grated across frozen rivers, were found in Virginia in 1789. Whether the red fox migrated to Kentucky via a northern route or an eastern route, hunting took on a new dimension when it arrived in Kentucky.

The earliest method of hunting the red fox— night hunting—persists to this day. Night hunters, who take great pride in ownership of a top-quality hound, cast their individual hounds in with a conjoint pack and run the fox after dark. In the traditional English method of fox hunting, by contrast, huntsmen mounted on horseback follow a pack of hounds specifically designed to function as a unit. Master of both methods was Gen. Roger Williams of Lexington, Kentucky, a well-known hound breeder and night hunter who initiated the first foxhound stud book and was a prime mover in organizing the National Foxhunters Association. Williams founded the Iroquois Hunt (Lexington) in 1880 in the English tradition. The Iroquois Hunt is the seventh oldest active hunt in the United States. In 1925 the Camargo Hunt of Cincinnati was founded, hunting country on both sides of the Ohio river. In 1961 the Long Run Hounds of Louisville and in 1981 the Woodford Hounds of Versailles were established. The Licking River Hounds in Bourbon County had only a short existence.

Why hunt the fox? Certainly the quarry has no food value and very little economic importance, either as a pelt or as vermin, although as an active predator it is a meaningful constituent in the balance of nature. It is its talent as a predator that makes it a desirable adversary, understanding well the nature of the hunter and the hunted. The fox is rarely caught, yet stays above ground and does not take to its den until it desires a call to the hounds to retreat. It is this nature, that of a true sportsman, that elevates those who thrill in following the fox.

See Bob Lee Maddux, *A History of the Walker Foxhound* (Cookeville, Tenn., 1962); Alexander Mackay-Smith, *The American Foxhound 1747-1967* (Millwood, Va., 1968).   JOHN W. GARDEN

HUNTER, BUSH A. Bush A. Hunter, physician, was born in Lexington on August 10, 1894, the son of John E. HUNTER, M.D. After attending Hampton Institute in Virginia, he enrolled at the Oberlin Conservatory in Ohio, where he studied voice and played cello. He graduated from Oberlin in 1915 and received a medical degree from Howard University a few years later. Hunter established his medical practice in Lexington in 1926. Health care was then rigidly segregated and black physicians were excluded from hospital staffs. Despite these handicaps, Hunter ministered to patients in Lexington and surrounding communities for more than a half century.

Hunter was the first Afro-American member of the Fayette County Medical Society, and served as vice president of the Fayette County Cancer Society and medical adviser to the Selective Service System. He was honored as Kentucky's Outstanding General Practitioner of the Year. Hunter and his wife, the former Mary W. Royster, had one son, Bush A., Jr. Hunter died in Lexington on November 30, 1983, and was buried at Camp Nelson National Cemetery in Jessamine County, Kentucky.

DORIS WILKINSON

HUNTER, JOHN E. John E. Hunter, physician, was born in 1859 in Mercer County, Virginia (now West Virginia). Raised by a Quaker family who discovered him hidden in a wagon, Hunter graduated from Ohio's Oberlin College in 1887 and received a medical degree from Case Western Reserve University in Cleveland on May 2, 1890. Following graduate work at Cleveland and Boston hospitals and at the Mayo Clinic, he and Perry D. Robinson opened a practice in Lexington, Kentucky. Hunter later became the first Afro-American physician to practice surgery at Lexington's St. Joseph's hospital.

In 1904 Hunter was elected president of the National Medical Association. He also helped to found the Florida A&M College Clinic Association at Tallahassee. Until 1950, when he was ninety years old, he taught clinics annually at the association's hospital. Hunter also played an active role in improving conditions for Kentuckians. He participated in the anti–separate railroad coach movement and was one of the founders of Lexington's Paul Lawrence Dunbar High School. The Hunter Medical Foundation, opened in 1973 and named in honor of his son Bush A. HUNTER, became part of Healthcare of Kentucky in 1982. Hunter died on November 14, 1956, and was buried in Lexington's Cove Haven Cemetery.

DORIS WILKINSON

HURSTBOURNE. Hurstbourne is a fourth-class residential city in eastern Jefferson County. It is bounded by Hurstbourne Lane on the east, the Thomas Bullitt farm on the west, Shelbyville Road (U.S. 60) on the north, and I-64 on the south. The area was part of a French and Indian War land grant to Virginia officer Henry Harrison and was included in the 1774 surveys directed by John Floyd. In 1779 Maj. William Linn, a veteran of George Rogers Clark's Illinois campaign, moved his family to a site on Beargrass Creek and established what would become known as Linn's Station. The pioneer station, one of six on the creek, was located on the road from the Falls of the Ohio to Fort Harrod. In the fall of 1781 the survivors of the Long Run Massacre sought shelter there. As the Indian threat passed in the 1790s, the heirs to Linn's estate discovered that the station was built on land belonging to someone else, and they left. The stockade deteriorated quickly; it was probably located on the east side of what is now Hurstbourne Lane in the Plainview section. Much of Hurstbourne was once the farm of Col. Richard C. Anderson, Sr., who purchased a five-hundred-acre tract in 1789 and named it Soldier's Retreat. Soon

afterward he built a substantial two-story stone house in which he raised a large family.

The Anderson house, which was believed to have suffered structural damage during the earthquake of 1811, was later struck by lightning and was torn down in 1840. By 1842 the property was owned by John I. Jacobs, a wealthy Louisvillian who built a Gothic-style mansion named Lyndon Hall. In 1915 the property was acquired by the Hert family and came to be known as Hurstbourne Farms. Funks Lane, which bordered the property, was widened in 1935 and renamed Hurstbourne Lane. After the death of Mrs. Alvin T. Hert, the property was acquired by L. Leroy Highbaugh, Sr., and his son L. Leroy, Jr., who in 1965 began developing the property as the community of Hurstbourne. When I-64 was built along the southern boundary of the area, it provided quick access to Louisville. In August of 1982, the city of Hurstbourne was incorporated to prevent annexation by Louisville. By 1990 residential building in the subdivision was nearly complete and the city contained several churches, office complexes, and a shopping center.

During the development of Hurstbourne in the late 1970s an archaeological excavation uncovered the foundations of the old Anderson house. Using many of the original stones, L. Leroy Highbaugh, Jr., reconstructed the house to original specifications and moved there with his family in 1983. The rebuilt Soldier's Retreat is the centerpiece of the city, which had a population of 3,530 in 1980 and 4,420 in 1990.

HUTCHINS, FRANCIS STEPHENSON. Francis Stephenson Hutchins, educator, was born on August 17, 1902, in Northfield, Massachusetts, the youngest son of William J. and Anna (Murch) Hutchins. Hutchins earned degrees from Oberlin College in Ohio (B.A. 1923) and Yale University (M.A. 1933). He taught in China as an Oberlin undergraduate and returned to China in 1925 as an instructor and representative of Yale-in-China's educational mission. Hutchins returned to the United States in 1939 to succeed his father as president of Berea College.

During his presidency (1939-67), Hutchins closed the college's secondary schools, strengthened the humanities curriculum, and further enlarged the endowment. Especially noteworthy was the admission once again of black students to Berea College after a 1950 modification of the DAY LAW, which had forced the school to segregate in 1904.

Hutchins married Louise Gilman (HUTCHINS) on February 22, 1934. They had four children: Anne, Francis, William Maynard, and Robert Lawrence. Hutchins died on November 28, 1988, and was buried in Berea.

SHANNON H. WILSON

HUTCHINS, LOUISE FRANCES (GILMAN). Louise Frances (Gilman) Hutchins, physician, was born February 2, 1911, in Changsha, China. Her parents, Alfred and Gertrude (Carter) Gilman, were Episcopal missionaries. The Gilmans returned to the United States in 1926 and moved to Montclair, New Jersey. Louise Gilman graduated from Wellesley College in Massachusetts in 1932 and attended Cornell University. She married Francis Hutchins on February 22, 1934, and completed her education at Yale University Medical School in 1936. After graduation, Louise joined Francis in China, where he was working as a representative of Yale University. She completed her intership in pediatrics at Hunan Hospital in Changsha. When Japan invaded China in 1938, she was trapped with other Americans and Europeans at Mt. Lu Shan. After government negotiations allowed Americans and Europeans to leave, Louise went to Shanghai to work with refugees at a mission. In August 1938, after Berea College offered Francis the presidency, the Hutchinses left China.

In Berea Louise served as the community's only pediatrician from 1939 to 1967. She worked with the Mountain Maternal Health League, established in 1936 to improve the health of rural Appalachian families. The league's services included home visits, parental care, deliveries, instructions in family planning, voluntary sterilization, and supplying contraceptives. At the time, the Kentucky State Department of Health (now the Department of Health Services) did not fund family planning services, and county health officials were not allowed to dispense information or contraceptives. It was not until 1962 that the state sanctioned family planning services.

For forty-seven years Louise was medical director and board president for the Mountain Maternal Health League and was instrumental in establishing the Family Plan Clinic at Berea College Hospital in 1944. Following Francis's retirement from Berea in 1967, the couple moved to Hong Kong for three years, where Louise completed a residency in gynecology and worked with the city's Family Planning Association. When the Hutchinses returned to Berea in 1970, she resumed her duties with the Mountain Maternal Health League. She has worked for the Department of Health Services as family planning clinician, traveling with a staff of four in the mobile family planning unit to twenty-one counties in the Kentucky River and Cumberland Valley districts.

The Hutchinses have four children: Anne, Francis, William, and Robert.

HUTCHINS, WILLIAM JAMES. William James Hutchins, college president and minister, was born in Brooklyn, New York, on July 5, 1871, the eldest son of the Rev. Robert G. and Harriet P. (James) Hutchins. Hutchins received his B.A. degree from Yale in 1892 and additional degrees from Union Theological Seminary (1896), Oberlin in Ohio (1920), and Yale (1921). After serving as a pastor in Brooklyn (1896-1907) and as a professor of homiletics at Oberlin (1907-20), Hutchins became president of Berea College in 1920. President until 1939, Hutchins expanded the college's facilities with a women's gymnasium, a principal classroom

building, and a new science building. He is credited with further development of the college's endowment fund, and with strengthening the collegiate academic program.

He married Anna Laura Murch on August 5, 1896. Their three sons also headed educational institutions: Robert, University of Chicago (1929-51); Francis, Berea College (1939-67); and William, Asheville School for Boys, North Carolina. Hutchins died on February 20, 1958, and was buried in Berea Cemetery.

SHANNON H. WILSON

HYDEN. The county seat of Leslie County, Hyden is located on U.S. 421 and KY 80 along Rockhouse Branch of the Middle Fork of the Kentucky River. The area around Hyden was first settled by the John Sizemore family of North Carolina in about 1817. The town was established on the farm of John Lewis in 1878, incorporated March 18, 1882, and named in honor of John Hyden, who was state senator from Clay County and one of the men responsible for the creation of Leslie County.

The isolation of the region hindered Hyden's early growth. Supplies were brought in by boat up the Kentucky River. The economic base of Hyden has long been the timber trade, but for many years the area lacked any form of transportation for lumber from Hyden or Leslie County. The first road to Hyden was not built until 1880. The Daniel Boone Parkway was constructed about four miles away.

The first Leslie County courthouse was built in Hyden in the early 1880s. A second structure, a glass and stone building, was completed in 1954. To provide health care for infants in the isolation of Leslie County, Mary Breckinridge founded the Frontier Nursing Service in 1925, and the Frontier Graduate School of Midwifery in 1939. The Leslie County Area Vocational Education Center is located at Hyden.

The population of Hyden was 482 in 1970; 488 in 1980; and 375 in 1990.

RON D. BRYANT

HYGEIA. The most elaborate plans for a Kentucky city during the early nineteenth century proposed the town of Hygeia on the Ohio River opposite Cincinnati. Purchasing a tract of land from a wealthy Kentuckian in 1827, English traveler and lecturer William Bullock planned to build a "town of retirement, in the vicinity of a populous manufacturing city." On his return to England, "determined to have it laid out to the best possible advantage, with professional assistance," Bullock engaged John Buonarotti Papworth, self-proclaimed "Architect to the King of Würtemberg," as his town planner. An architect of some repute, Papworth prepared a detailed baroque plan that incorporated most of the forms and building types developed in England during the preceding century. Even though the English traveler Frances Trollope, then living in Cincinnati, praised the "taste and art lavished" on the place, Hygeia soon joined Lystra, Franklinville, and Ohiopiomingo on the growing list of speculative paper towns that never materialized.

See John W. Reps, *The Making of Urban America: A History of City Planning in the United States* (Princeton, N.J., 1965).   ALLEN J. SHARE

I

ILLINOIS CENTRAL GULF RAILROAD. In Kentucky the earliest predecessor of Illinois Central Gulf Railroad was the Elizabethtown & Paducah Railroad, chartered in 1867. In 1878 it connected with the Louisville & Nashville Railroad at Elizabethtown and the Paducah & Memphis Railroad at Paducah. C.P. Huntington in 1881 purchased the E&P and P&M to consolidate with the Chesapeake, Ohio & Southern Railroad (including the South Kentucky Railroad), which ran from Henderson to Princeton to Hopkinsville. Huntington also gained control of the Owensboro, Falls of the Rough & Green River Railroad. These Huntington railroads were purchased by the Illinois Central Railroad in 1896 and were known as the Kentucky Division. H.S. McComb's New Orleans, St. Louis & Chicago Railroad, which had trackage between Fulton and East Cairo, Kentucky, was purchased at auction by the Illinois Central in 1877 and subsequently renamed the Chicago, St. Louis & Northern Railroad, owned and operated by the Illinois Central. The Illinois Central acquired additional lines in western Kentucky as a result of a merger with the Gulf, Mobile & Ohio Railroad in the 1960s to form the Illinois Central Gulf Railroad. It still offers daily passenger service from Fulton, in western Kentucky, to Chicago and New Orleans on the "City of New Orleans," an Amtrak train that retains the name of the famous Illinois Central train.

See Carlton J. Corliss, *Main Line of Mid-America: The Story of the Illinois Central* (New York 1950). LEE A. DEW

IMLAY, GILBERT. Gilbert Imlay wrote the influential 1792 work *A Topographical Description of the Western Territory of North America* and *The Emigrants*, a 1793 novel of frontier adventure set in Kentucky. The former book, printed in London, went through several editions and unabashedly praised the area's promise: "Every thing here assumes a dignity and splendour I have never seen in any other part of the world." How long the author lived in the region about which he wrote is uncertain. Born probably in New Jersey close to 1754, Imlay served as an officer in the Revolutionary War and came to Kentucky as early as 1783. Over the next two years he received land grants of more than 28,000 acres. Although his *Topographical Description* contains letters purportedly written from Kentucky as late as 1791, it is likely that Imlay had left the area by late 1785. Nevertheless, his account proved reasonably sound and certainly stimulated immigration.

By 1793 Imlay began a liaison in Europe with Mary Wollstonecraft, author of *A Vindication of the Rights of Woman* (1792). They had a daughter, Fanny (who committed suicide in 1816). The affair ended with Imlay's virtual abandonment of Wollstonecraft, who attempted suicide. She later married and was the mother of Mary Godwin, who became the wife of Percy Bysshe Shelley. By 1796 Imlay had disappeared from the historical record, although he may have died as late as 1828.

See Ralph L. Rusk, "The Adventures of Gilbert Imlay," *Indiana University Studies* 10 (1923): 3-26; Oliver F. Emerson, "Notes on Gilbert Imlay, Early American Writer," *Publications of Modern Language Association of America* 39 (1924): 406-39. JAMES C. KLOTTER

INDEPENDENCE. Independence, located in the center of Kenton County at the junction of KY 17 and KY 2045, is one of the two county seats, the other being COVINGTON. When Kenton County was created from Campbell County in 1840, the act of establishment required that the county seat be near the geographical center of the new county. Land at a crossroads location was donated by pioneer John McCollum, and the town was incorporated in 1842 and named Independence to celebrate the county's separation from Campbell County. Construction began on a Greek Revival courthouse in 1840. Even before its completion in 1843, residents of the more populous northern part of the county, who found it inconvenient to transact county business in Independence, began using the old Covington city hall as their courthouse. All main county offices were soon located in the Covington courthouse, with the one in Independence maintaining only branch offices. Nevertheless, Independence continued to be the "official" seat of government and a second courthouse was built there in 1912, of classical Beaux Arts design, fronted by a Roman portico.

To prevent annexation by Covington in the 1960s, Independence grew from a small town to one of Kentucky's largest cities in terms of area, by annexing most of the central third of Kenton County, from the Boone County line on the west to the Licking River on the east. In 1984 it annexed the city of Ridgeview Heights. Independence is a fifth-class city surrounded by middle-class suburbs and farmland. The population was 1,784 in 1970; 9,310 in 1980; and 10,444 in 1990.

INDEPENDENT SCHOOL DISTRICTS. In Kentucky any town may establish a school district under its own control—that is, independent of the schools of its county—and receive its share of state public school funds. The landmark school law of February 16, 1838, section 41, permitted Louisville, Lexington, and Maysville to operate independent school districts "so long as they continue to maintain public schools by taxation." No doubt these districts had been formed under the general law of 1830, which was enacted "to encourage the general diffusion of Education in this Commonwealth." The idea of independent districts may hark back to the academy tradition of Kentucky's pioneer days, as it suggests some privilege for students living in a certain area.

The General Assembly in 1845 instructed county commissioners to lay off towns as one or more school districts, as in the cases of Louisville, Lexington, and Maysville, "and by subsequent acts to some other towns and cities." The law was modified on March 1, 1850, to allow parts of county districts to be included in independent districts. These years mark the first legislative action to create independent districts. In 1991 there were fifty-six independent school districts.

See Barksdale Hamlett, *History of Education in Kentucky* (Frankfort, Ky., 1914).

THOMAS D. CLARK

INDIAN FORT. Indian Fort is the name given to a knob, or hill, about three and one-half miles southeast of Berea in Madison County, Kentucky. It rises 620 feet above the surrounding valley. It was first named in print in 1910 and was later the subject of a state Geological Survey report. The name is based on a series of "walls" supposedly erected at strategic points by Hopewell Indians to impede travel to the top of the mountain, where they hoped to control access to the Bluegrass. Study indicates that the walls outlined a ceremonial area.

See Col. Bennett H. Young, *The Prehistoric Men of Kentucky* (Louisville 1910).

Z.L. LIPCHINSKY

INEZ. Inez has been the seat of Martin County since 1873 because of its central location; when the county was formed in 1870, Warfield was the county seat. When it was settled around 1810, the location of the town of Inez was known as Arminta Ward's Bottom, and the name was later changed to Eden in appreciation of its beautiful mountain scenery. That name had been given earlier to another Kentucky town, however, so Inez was the name chosen on June 23, 1874, possibly honoring the daughter of Leo Frank, postmaster of nearby Louisa, Kentucky.

Martin County's first courthouse, built of logs, was used from about 1873 to 1881. The courthouse that replaced it burned in 1892, and the third courthouse stood until 1933. The current courthouse was built in 1938-41. Inez, which lies twenty-four miles east of Paintsville, twenty-one miles south of Louisa, and 165 miles east of Louisville, is one of Kentucky's smallest county seats. The population of the sixth-class city was 469 in 1970; 415 in 1980; and 511 in 1990. The town's economy, like the county's, is dependent upon the coal industry.

INGLES, MARY (DRAPER). Mary (Draper) Ingles, who escaped after months as a captive of Indians in the 1750s, was born in Philadelphia in 1732 to George and Eleanor (Hardin) Draper. Her family moved to Pattonsburg, Virginia, in 1740 and several years later to the headwaters of the Roanoke River, where their land became known as Draper's Meadow. (It is now the site of the Virginia Polytechnic and State University in Blacksburg.) Mary Draper married William Ingles in 1749.

In July 1755 while the men harvested their crops, Shawnee Indians attacked the settlement and captured Ingles, her two young sons, Thomas and George, and her sister-in-law. During the month-long trip on the Kanawha and Ohio rivers to their villages at the mouth of the Scioto River in Ohio, Ingles won the respect of the Indians and was made an adopted daughter by the chief. Her children and sister-in-law, however, were sent to distant villages. Two-year-old George, her younger son, died after several days away from his mother.

In September 1755 the Indians took Ingles and an elderly Dutch prisoner down the Ohio River to Big Bone Lick in what is now Boone County, Kentucky, where the tribe produced salt. Ingles and the Dutch woman escaped and followed the Ohio River, suffering from the weather and near starvation. On the sixth day, in the area of the Indian villages at the mouth of Scioto River, the two turned east and continued to the mouth of the Big Sandy River. They spent the next two days searching for a shallow crossover point south of present-day Louisa, Kentucky. They returned to the Ohio River, following it into West Virginia and the Kanawha River, their guide south toward home.

By the end of November, forty days after her escape and five and a half months after being captured, Ingles arrived at the farm of her old neighbor, Adam Harmon. Harmon took her to the fort at Dunkard's Bottom, where she was reunited with her husband, who had tried earlier to negotiate her release. The Ingles family moved to Bedford in Botetourt County, Virginia, east of the Blue Ridge Mountains. Their son Thomas was returned to his family in 1768. Mary Draper Ingles had four more children after her return to Virginia: John, Mary, Susan, and Rhoda. She died in 1815 at her home in Virginia.

See Roberta Ingles Steele and Andrew Lewis Ingles, eds., *Escape from Indian Captivity: The Story of Mary Draper Ingles and Son Thomas Ingles as told by John Ingles, Sr.* (Radford, Va., 1982).

INNES, HARRY. Harry Innes, the first federal judge for Kentucky, was born in Caroline County, Virginia, on January 4, 1752, to Robert Innes, a Scottish clergyman, and Catherine (Richards) Innes. Educated at Donald Robertson's school and at William and Mary College, he read law under George Wythe and was admitted to the bar in 1773. After practicing law in Bedford County, Innes began his public career in 1776 by administering lead and powder mines in western Virginia for the Virginia Committee of Public Safety. In 1779 Gov. Thomas Jefferson appointed him to adjust and settle land claims in the Montgomery and Washington districts. The following year, he became escheator and later the tax commissioner. In 1782 Innes was appointed assistant judge of the newly established supreme court for the Kentucky District, and he moved to Kentucky in 1783. When Indians killed the court's attorney in 1784, Innes resigned his judgeship to fill the vacancy.

Innes, like many other Kentuckians, speculated in land. He also farmed, practiced law, and in time reared six daughters (four by his first marriage, to Elizabeth Calloway of Bedford County, who died in 1791, and a daughter and a stepdaughter by his second marriage, to the widowed Ann Shields). He became a trustee of Transylvania University, a charter member of the Political Club of Danville, and was involved in a variety of manufacturing ventures. He spearheaded the improvement of the Wilderness Road, and Secretary of War Henry Knox appointed Innes to organize Kentucky's defense against Indian attacks. Innes joined the movement for immediate, unconditional separation from Virginia, and was a member of at least eight of the conventions held before statehood was achieved in 1792, as well as both of the first two constitutional conventions.

Three years before statehood, Innes was appointed first judge of the U.S. Court for the District of Kentucky. The court had jurisdiction over both circuit and district proceedings and during the twenty-seven years of Innes's tenure docketed 2,290 cases, about one-third dealing with land controversies, one-third with other civil cases, and one-third arising from the whiskey tax. Innes demanded strict adherence to the English legal traditions familiar to him, including the rhetoric of classical pleadings. In the few cases that were carried to the U.S. Supreme Court, Innes's decisions were usually upheld—except when litigants or their lawyers were members of the Marshall family.

Until 1795, when the Treaty of Greenville brought relief from Indian warfare and the Treaty of San Lorenzo brought free navigation of the Mississippi, the internal revenue statutes were unenforceable in Innes's court. Grand juries refused to indict and petit juries refused to convict farmer-distillers on criminal charges. It was only when federal attorney Joseph Hamilton Daveiss brought civil charges (for debt) and Jefferson became president, promising to repeal the whiskey tax, that Kentuckians complied fully.

During the era of the Federalist Judiciary Act (1801-2), the district court was abolished and its caseload transferred to the new 6th Circuit Court, whose principal judge was William McClung, with District Judges Innes and John McNairy of Tennessee as subordinates. The Jeffersonian Judiciary Act of 1802 reestablished the district court, and Innes was again the sole judge. In 1807, the court's circuit court caseload was transferred to the 7th Circuit Court. Innes served on that court for its Kentucky cases with Supreme Court Justice Thomas Todd, his younger cousin and protégé, and continued as judge of the district court until his death.

Innes, a Jeffersonian, was often involved in controversies with members and associates of the Marshall family, who were Federalists. Although he worked fairly amicably with Daveiss (who was married to Nancy Marshall) until Daveiss's public frustration in the BURR CONSPIRACY led to his dismissal, it was Innes's quarrels with Humphrey Marshall that enlivened the pages of local newspapers. Marshall believed that Innes participated in the Spanish Conspiracy, and Innes believed that Marshall was guilty of fraud in a land case. Both tried to get the other impeached, but neither was successful. Innes won a libel suit against the Federalist *Western World*, but another libel suit against Marshall resulted in a hung jury.

Mutual friends arranged a truce a few months before Innes's death, which Marshall violated in the second edition of his *History of Kentucky*. Innes died on September 20, 1816, and was buried in the Frankfort Cemetery.

See Harry Innes Papers, Filson Club, Louisville, Ky; Mary K. Bonsteel Tachau, *Federal Courts in the Early Republic: Kentucky 1789-1816* (Princeton, N.J., 1978).   MARY K. BONSTEEL TACHAU

INNES'S STATION. Henry (or Harry) Innes established his station in 1792 on 1,200 acres in Franklin County, about five miles northeast of what is now Frankfort, Kentucky. The sturdily built oak log house, on a stone foundation, was one and a half stories in height and possibly built with a dogtrot or a breezeway; these were usually enclosed to form a central hallway between two rooms. There were portholes in the walls of the second-story loft for shooting at attackers. Innes later added a stone room and basement on the east end and a frame wing on the west. The station was attacked in the same year it was built by a party of Indians who killed one of Innes's male slaves and captured another. Innes lived at his station until his death in 1816.

See George A. Lewis, "A Relic of Indian Days," *Register* 19 (Jan. 1921): 29-31.

NANCY O'MALLEY

INSECTS. In terms of numbers of individuals and numbers of species, insects may be considered the dominant animal in Kentucky and on the planet. Worldwide, over 750,000 species of insects have been identified, but most entomologists agree that thousands of insect species have yet to be discovered. Nearly 100,000 species are found in North America and a large percentage of these are found in Kentucky. The four most common insect groups, familiar to city-dweller and farmer alike, are beetles; flies and mosquitoes; butterflies and moths; and ants, wasps, and bees.

Insects belong to the phylum Arthropoda, a group of animals characterized by jointed appendages and an external skeleton that may be shed many times as the animal grows. Relatives of insects in the phylum Arthropoda include arachnids, such as spiders. Adult arthropod insects differ from their arachnid relatives in certain external features. The insect body is divided into three parts (head, thorax, and abdomen), while the arachnid has only two distinct body regions (a cephalothorax and abdomen); one pair of antennae is attached at the insect's head, while the arachnid has no antennae; and the insect has three pairs of legs attached to the thorax, versus the arachnid's four. One or more pairs of the insect's legs may be adapted for special uses, such as grabbing prey, courtship, burrowing, jumping, or swimming. Many insects have wings, distinguishing them as the only invertebrates able to fly. Besides spiders, common Kentucky arachnids include ticks, pseudoscorpions, daddy longlegs, and mites.

In all parts of Kentucky, the forests, meadows, and fields are home to a multitude of insect types. Some insects are very specialized in their diet and are thus found only in certain types of habitat or during certain times of year. One of these is the monarch butterfly, which makes Kentucky its summer home. The larva of the monarch feeds exclusively on milkweed, a food preference that makes it distasteful and poisonous to birds and other predators. At the end of the summer, Kentuckians may observe groups of monarchs flying south to wintering grounds in Mexico.

Most Kentucky insects are present in some form year round, but it is during the summer that they are most active. Katydids make their presence obvious by the sounds they produce to attract mates and defend their tree-branch territory. Nectar-feeding moths often feed at night, while butterflies and bees are highly visible as daytime visitors of flowers. Resting and feeding in grass during the day, fireflies put on a show after sunset, attracting mates with pulses of light emitted from special cells around the abdomen. Many beetles live their entire lives beneath leaf litter on the forest floor or within decaying logs, and so go unnoticed except to the collector looking for a new specimen, or the hungry skunk looking for a meal. Kentucky's many open lakes and streams provide a breeding ground for the mosquito and the black fly. Hikers and fishermen are bothered by the adult females, which rely on a blood meal to reproduce. Even the caves of south-central Kentucky support small beetles, flies, and crickets. These insects typically make their homes in damp areas and under rocks, and are well adapted to the high humidity and even temperatures of the caves.

As a group, insects have adapted to almost every lifestyle. Even in the largest cities, human dwellings may harbor unwelcome insect guests, such as cockroaches, ants, termites, silverfish, or tiny clothes moths. Fleas and lice are external parasites of birds and mammals, including humans. Some insects have caused significant losses in Kentucky's agricultural production. Tobacco harvests are reduced considerably by the voracious hornworm. This large green caterpillar is the larva of a sphinx moth. Other types of moth larvae, like the tobacco budworm, also eat the leaves or destroy the growing tips of young plants. The Kentucky Agricultural Research Station in Lexington has contributed to the development of farming practices to minimize crop damage by insects. Even other insects have been recruited for this purpose. The praying mantis and the lady beetle have long been known as the gardener's allies because they feed on plant-eating insects.

In fact, most Kentucky insect species are either beneficial or do no harm to humans. Insects play an important role in maintaining a balanced ecosystem by serving as food for fish, birds, and other wildlife; aiding in the production of fruits, vegetables, and seeds through their pollinating activities; recycling nutrients by scavenging decaying plant and animal material; and adding color and interest to the natural beauty of Kentucky.

See R.H. Arnett, *American Insects, A Handbook of the Insects of America North of Mexico* (New York 1985); L. Milne and M. Milne, *The Audubon Society Field Guide to North American Insects and Spiders* (New York 1980).   MARY E. NOSSEK

INTERURBAN LINES. The interurban lines developed in the late nineteenth century as an outgrowth of streetcars and provided a convenient way of moving people between populated centers. They were a major means of public transportation in several urban areas, including Lexington, Louisville, Covington, Paducah, and Henderson. Mule-drawn cars on tracks began to appear in the 1880s; a number of the systems converted to electric cars in the early 1900s. Typical was the Kentucky Traction and Terminal Company's system, extending from Lexington to the Bluegrass towns of Paris, Nicholasville, Versailles, Georgetown, and Frankfort. The first interurban line in Kentucky connected Lexington and Georgetown in 1901. These lines were a powerful influence in binding the central Kentucky communities together within the Inner Bluegrass region.

Similar lines connected Louisville east to Shelbyville and north, through junction with other lines, as far as Indianapolis. Other interstate interurban lines connected Henderson, Kentucky, with Evansville, Indiana; and Covington, Kentucky, with Cincinnati.

When automobiles took over in the 1930s as the major means of public transportation, the interurban lines came quickly to an end. The last car of the Kentucky Traction and Terminal Company left Paris for Lexington on January 13, 1934, as the company entered bankruptcy.   PHILIP ARDERY

IRONCLADS. The first engagement between ironclad warships pitted the *Monitor* against the *Merrimack* off the Virginia coast March 9, 1862, but their first use in the Civil War occurred on the western waters. Realizing that wooden gunboats would be vulnerable to the Confederate guns at Columbus, Kentucky, and other fortifications, the federal government contracted with James B. Eads in August 1861 to build seven ironclad gunboats. The design, modified by naval constructor Samuel M. Pook and Eads, provided for a wide, flat-bottomed hull measuring 175 feet by about 51 feet, displacing 512 tons, and drawing 6 feet of water. The 2½-inch iron plate was backed by 24 inches of oak (thicknesses varying on various parts of the boats). The angle of the surface varied from 35° on the sides to 45° in the bow and stern.

Working at a shipyard near St. Louis and drawing materials from locations throughout the Ohio Valley, including iron plate from Swift and Company of Newport, Kentucky, Eads completed the seven gunboats of the "city series"—the *Cincinnati, Louisville, St. Louis, Carondelet, Cairo, Mound City,* and *Pittsburgh*—also called "Pook's turtles" after the constructor. Each was then outfitted with up to thirteen heavy guns at the navy yard in Mound City, Illinois. Commissioned January 16, 1862, they were assigned to the western flotilla under the command of flag officer Andrew H. Foote and joined by another ironclad, the *Essex,* a remodeled ferryboat.

Coordinating with Gen. Ulysses S. Grant, who commanded two divisions of soldiers, Foote attacked Fort Henry on the Tennessee River on February 6, 1862, with the *Essex* in the lead, the *Cincinnati, Carondelet,* and *St. Louis* following abreast, and the timberclads *Conestoga, Tyler,* and *Lexington* at the rear. When an enemy shell pierced the *Essex's* boiler, it drifted downriver, out of action. Nevertheless, intense fire from the ironclads quickly reduced the number of guns in the already partially abandoned fort to four, and the fleet closed to within three hundred yards, directing telling fire at closer range. As the situation was hopeless, Gen. Lloyd Tilghman surrendered the fort.

Having taken Fort Henry in little more than two hours, the ironclads quickly gained an undeserved reputation for effectiveness. They were believed invulnerable because shells fired horizontally from the Confederate guns, which were mounted at water level, tended to bounce off the angled armor of the ironclads, although the vessels sustained considerable damage and casualties. A few days later at Fort Donelson, where the plunging fire of the defenders' guns was more effective, the ironclads were considerably less successful. Nevertheless, in later battles on the Mississippi—at Island No. 10, for example, when the new *Benton* ironclad joined the flotilla—the Union continued to show unrealistic expectations of the ironclads' capacity to reduce Confederate fortifications.

The earliest use of an ironclad during the war was made by the Confederacy, which employed the ram *Manassas* (or "Turtle") to great advantage on the Mississippi below New Orleans in October 1861. In early December, the ram was positioned near Columbus, Kentucky, but was not used. Later the ram was sunk in action at New Orleans. Although they were no longer vital to Kentucky, ironclads played a part in the fall of Vicksburg, Mississippi, in July 1863 and were used on the Red River in 1863 and 1864.

See Benjamin Franklin Cooling, *Forts Henry and Donelson: The Key to the Confederate Heartland* (Knoxville, Tenn., 1987).   KEITH M. HEIM

IRON INDUSTRY. Not only did early visitors to Kentucky discover an unspoiled wilderness rich with game and natural splendor, but those with a practiced eye also took note of Kentucky's fast-flowing streams, virgin timber, and promising mineral deposits. The combination of power, fuel, and raw materials spawned an early iron-making industry based on Kentucky's plentiful beds of limonite

ore. Iron products crucial to settlers, like rifles, axes, pots, and pans were bulky, heavy, and difficult to transport to the frontier down the Ohio River or across the Cumberland Gap. Large iron kettles were needed for boiling down salt, a staple of which Kentucky had numerous deposits. Cut off from eastern supplies of iron, immigrant iron masters erected simple charcoal-fueled, water-powered blast furnaces to supply local demand.

Jacob Myers constructed the Bourbon iron furnace, thought to be Kentucky's first, in 1791 on Slate Creek, south of Owingsville, in Bath County, where he had claimed 8,000 to 10,000 acres. The charcoal-burning furnace with water-powered bellows produced one ton of iron per day for making kettles, cookware, ax blades, plowshares, and nails. Maryland and Kentucky investors backed Myers, and Col. Thomas Dye Owings from Maryland was the first iron-master. By 1794 the furnace was supplying the Lexington market with iron goods. During the war of 1812 the furnace crews produced large numbers of cannon balls for Andrew Jackson's troops; the ammunition helped bring victory at the Battle of New Orleans, earning the furnace the name "Old Thunder Mill." Recognizing the value of such furnaces, Kentucky's legislature took steps to protect the fledgling enterprises from taxation and to improve the roads and river routes leading to them.

Between 1790 and 1900 about eighty iron furnaces were constructed in Kentucky. The period of greatest furnace construction was the three decades beginning in 1830, when fifty-eight stacks were erected. In the beginning, most of them were fueled with locally made charcoal; toward the end of the nineteenth century, coal and coke were also used in iron making. The early furnaces were constructed near streams to take advantage of water power for bellows operation; later furnaces had steam-operated blast systems. Furnaces were constructed in five regions: the Red River area—Estill, Lee, Powell, Menifee, and Bath counties; Hanging Rock—Greenup, Boyd, Carter, and Lawrence counties; Nolin River—Bullitt, Edmonson, Grayson, Muhlenberg, and Nelson counties; Cumberland—Crittenden, Caldwell, Livingston, Lyon, and Trigg counties; and the Middlesborough region in Bell County. By 1827 eleven furnaces and six forges had been constructed in Greenup County alone.

The iron-making process was simple but extremely labor-intensive. Ore and limestone mined near the furnace were mixed with charcoal prepared on the property and burned together in a stone stack to produce workable iron. Some of this product was further refined under a huge forge hammer to produce wrought iron for blacksmiths. Hollow ware like pots, stoves, and the like was often cast in sand molds in a cast house adjacent to the furnace.

The typical furnace stood thirty to forty-five feet high, was made of cut stone, and produced three to ten tons of iron per day. Each furnace had a unique arrangement of stonework and arches that reflected both the industrial and architectural skills of Kentucky's early entrepreneurs and workmen. Some furnaces, such as the Buena Vista furnace in Boyd County and Laurel furnace in Greenup County were hewn, at least partially, into solid rock cliffs. A classic triangular arch form was found in Greenup County's New Hampshire furnace and the Cottage furnace of Estill County. Furnaces with flat-topped arches, while less attractive, were probably easier to work. Examples of this style were Clear Creek furnace in Bath County and Belmont furnace in Bullitt County. The stepped-arch was another popular form, exemplified by Mt. Savage furnace in Carter County and Mammoth furnace in Lyon County. In the Cumberland-Tennessee rivers region, some structures such as Center furnace were constructed of brick. Fitchburg furnace in Estill County, the largest stone furnace in the state, contained twin furnaces in a single unit sixty feet high and 115 feet long.

On their wilderness "iron plantations," furnace owners came to think of workers black and white as children: ungrateful, lesser beings who needed minding. The seasonal rhythm of iron making imposed a discipline unknown to the mercantile and agrarian communities. The furnace manager scheduled the arrival of materials, the routine of the day, and the distribution and discipline of labor. If the uncertainties of the market stretched beyond his control, the owner adjusted the supplies of men and materials, and the furnace bell rang out the tune. To attract labor, furnace owners constructed homes for workers, stores for supplies, carpenters' and blacksmith shops, boardinghouses and hotels, schools, and even opera houses. They rarely constructed saloons, however, since drinking was a popular way to escape from the grueling, dangerous occupation. Slaves were frequently used as fillers, woodcutters, and general labor. When owned by the furnace master, they frequently were apprenticed to skilled laborers and became skilled themselves in casting and molding. More often, however, slave crews were rented to the furnace on an annual basis.

At Aetna furnace (1816) in Hart County, the "iron plantation" covered more than 10,000 acres and employed hundreds. Its products included kettles, andirons, castings, stoves, and bar iron for foundry work. Some furnaces were the centers of boom-and-bust cycles. One of them was Airdrie furnace (1855), built by Robert S.C.A. Alexander, who bought 17,000 acres considered rich in iron ore. He brought workers from Scotland and built a community near Paradise, Kentucky, for them. The ore was poor and the furnace operated for only two months, but Airdrie remains a legend in Muhlenberg County. Another failure was Alexander Arthur's vision of an iron and coal empire centered at Middlesborough, built around the twin Watts furnaces (1890). The furnaces operated only until 1898. At the same time (1890-91), developers founded Grand Rivers in Livingston County and put up two furnaces sixty feet high. The operation lost millions of dollars before it was dismantled in 1921.

By 1830, on the brink of the American industrial revolution, Kentucky ranked a close third behind Pennsylvania and New York in total pig iron production. The Hanging Rock region in Kentucky and Ohio was the leading iron-producing area in the United States. By 1870, however, Kentucky had dropped to seventh place, producing a mere 2.5 percent of U.S. pig iron output. By 1910 Kentucky had all but ceased iron production.

After the 1830s, demand for iron skyrocketed for construction, for architectural decoration, for consumer goods, and, most important, for the railroads. The demand for finished goods exceeded the capacity of Kentucky's old-fashioned charcoal cold-blast furnaces and forges. Under pressure from British iron makers, Kentuckians adopted mineral fuels, larger hot-blast furnaces, and steam power, but lagged behind their competitors in other states. The investment in a charcoal furnace was well within the reach of a single Kentuckian and a partner, but the larger, more sophisticated furnaces of the 1840s in urban areas like Pittsburgh, close to cheap coal and transportation lines, could operate on a scale unmanageable for a single individual. Corporations began to replace the local owners of Kentucky's small-scale iron industry. Industrial giants like the Boston-owned Red River Iron Manufacturing Company (1866) in Estill County, the family-owned iron empire of John Means in Ashland, and Daniel Hillman in the Cumberland region created massive enterprises out of the disorganized and weakened industry that emerged from the Civil War.

Furnaces in the Hanging Rock iron region in Carter, Boyd, and Greenup counties kept pace with the competition better than those in the central and western iron fields. Iron plants like Hunnewell and Princess began using stone coal in the 1860s, and by the 1880s some of the largest, most modern plants in the nation were located in Ashland. Coke fuel from Pennsylvania and iron ores from Michigan, Missouri, and Canada were mixed with local ores to help these plants compete. Furnaces in western Kentucky were not without their innovators, as the entire industry sought to keep pace with the accelerated pulse of the nation. Airdrie furnace (1856) in Muhlenberg County was the first in Kentucky to attempt using raw coal instead of charcoal, although the experiment failed. William Kelly, working on his Lyon County furnace property in the 1840s and 1850s, discovered the basics of what would become the Bessemer process for making steel.

Despite their advances, Kentucky iron producers slipped further behind their competition. American pig iron output from mineral fuels surpassed charcoal furnace output for the first time in 1855. Mineral fuels did not dominate in Kentucky until 1875. Despite the establishment of a rolling mill and foundry industry in Louisville, Newport, Covington, and Ashland, Kentucky rolling mills produced fewer rails in 1884 than in 1874.

In 1990 the last vestiges of a once-flourishing iron industry were found at only three steel plants, in Owensboro, Newport, and Ashland. The iron industry had failed to keep pace with its competitors for reasons geographic, economic, and social. Kentucky's location near sources of fuel and raw materials had allowed the growth of an industry reliant on the local market and the high price of iron. With the discovery of rich iron deposits in Michigan and Alabama, improvements in transportation, demand for cheap iron, and large-scale technologies, Kentucky's early geographic advantages were negated. Kentucky was handicapped by an inadequate market for iron in the South, where fewer railways were built and there was less manufacturing. Lack of railways increased both the costs of raw materials and the price of Kentucky iron on the market. The institution of slavery discouraged the settlement of skilled immigrants. For a time, the high price of iron and the demand for high-quality charcoal iron for railway wheels and axles kept the industry going. By 1890, however, Kentucky's early iron boom had "blown out" in the wake of cheap Pennsylvania steel.

See J. Winston Coleman Jr., "Old Kentucky Iron Furnaces," *FCHQ* 31 (1957): 227-42; Donald E. Rist, *Kentucky Iron Furnaces of the Hanging Rock Iron Region* (Ashland, Ky., 1974).

MICHEAL HUDSON AND CHARLES D. HOWES

IRVINE. Irvine, the county seat of Estill County, located on the Kentucky River at the junction of KY 52 and KY 89, was built on land once owned by Gen. Green Clay. Established on January 28, 1812, and named in honor of Col. William Irvine, who was wounded during ESTILL'S DEFEAT on March 22, 1782, the town was not incorporated until February 24, 1849.

Though still a small town during the Civil War, Irvine was the scene of two skirmishes. On July 30, 1863, an engagement between a Union Cavalry regiment and a detachment of Confederates under Col. John Scott ultimately resulted in a Confederate retreat. Just over a year later, on October 13, 1864, a group of Confederate guerrillas attacked the town, burning the jail and ransacking the community.

By 1870, Irvine's population was 224, rising to about three hundred by mid-decade. During the coal boom era of the late nineteenth and early twentieth centuries, the area in and around Irvine experienced rapid growth. One mile southeast of Irvine, the town of Ravenna (incorporated on January 18, 1921) became the headquarters of the North Fork Division of the Louisville & Nashville Railroad (L&N) in 1915. Irvine and Ravenna are often referred to as "twin cities."

Railroads facilitated the exploitation of natural resources. Not only did Irvine lie on the L&N line, but it previously served as the southeastern terminus of the Richmond, Nicholasville, Irvine & Beattyville Railroad, more commonly known as the Riney-B, which traveled northwest to Versailles. In 1909 the line was bought by the L&N and closed

after a new line from Winchester to Irvine was constructed in 1916.

Agricultural products such as beef, pork, hay, and tobacco from the surrounding county are shipped through Irvine regularly, and the coal fields to the south and east employ many residents. Clothing manufacture is also an important industrial concern in Irvine.

The first Estill County courthouse was constructed in May 1808, on land in Irvine that belonged to Benjamin Holliday. When this courthouse collapsed in October 1864, it was replaced by a Greek Revival structure in 1867. This building was dismantled in 1939, and the third edifice was completed on May 19, 1941. The fourth-class city had a population of 2,918 in 1970; 2,894 in 1980; and 2,836 in 1990.   RON D. BRYANT

ISSEL, DANIEL PAUL. Daniel Paul Issel, Hall of Fame basketball player, son of Robert and Eleanor (Meyer) Issel, was born on September 25, 1948, in Batavia, Illinois. His family moved to Missouri but returned to Batavia when he was twelve. Issel, a center who enrolled in the University of Kentucky (UK) in 1966, left in 1970 after three years of varsity ball as the men's career scoring leader. He scored 2,138 points (25.7 per game), and he was an All-American in his last two years. He also set the UK scoring record for points in a single game, fifty-three, against the University of Mississippi in 1970. While Issel was at Kentucky the Wildcats won seventy-one games, lost only twelve, and won three Southeastern Conference championships.

In 1970 Issel signed a contract to play professional basketball with the Kentucky Colonels of the American Basketball Association. In 1975 he was traded to the National Basketball Association (NBA) Denver Nuggets. Although he was a short center at six feet, eight inches, when he retired he had scored more than 25,000 points and ranked fourth on the all-time NBA list behind Kareem Abdul Jabbar, Wilt Chamberlain, and Julius Erving.

Issel retired in 1985 to Courtland Farm in Versailles, Kentucky, to breed and train thoroughbreds. He sold the farm in 1988 and returned to Denver to work in the Nuggets' front office, but maintained horses in Kentucky and occasionally returned for the Keeneland sales. Issel married Cheri Hughes of Lexington, who was a UK cheerleader, in 1969. They have two children, Sheridan and Scott.

See Dan Issel with Buddy Martin, *Parting Shots* (Chicago 1985).

IVY MOUNTAIN, BATTLE OF. The Battle of Ivy Mountain, fought on November 8, 1861, was the principal encounter during the Union drive against rebel forces in eastern Kentucky's Big Sandy Valley in the autumn of 1861. Responding to reports of a Confederate troop concentration at Prestonsburg, Kentucky, Gen. William T. Sherman ordered former Navy Lt. William O. NELSON to secure the region. Nelson marched southeastward from Maysville in mid-October 1861 with four undermanned Ohio regiments and an assortment of Kentucky volunteers and militiamen. The Union forces quickly drove Confederate forces from Hazel Green and West Liberty and continued their push toward Prestonsburg.

Confederate forces in the Big Sandy Valley totaled about a thousand men described as being badly clad and badly armed, with not a knapsack, haversack, or canteen. The main body of Confederate troops was stationed at Piketon (Pikeville) under the command of Col. John S. WILLIAMS. A smaller force under Capt. Andrew Jackson MAY abandoned Prestonsburg on November 5 and began to retreat southward toward Piketon. May attempted to delay the advance of the Federals by making a stand at the foot of Ivy Mountain, near the juncture of Ivy Creek and the Levisa Fork of the Big Sandy River. Nelson divided his forces, sending one Ohio regiment with supporting units down John's Creek toward Piketon, while he led the rest of his army down the Levisa Fork from Prestonsburg to Piketon.

On November 8 at 1:00 p.m., the advance units of Nelson's army reached the Confederate defensive works at Ivy Mountain. The initial Confederate volley halted the Union advance, but more Federal troops arrived, outflanking the Confederate position and forcing a retreat. The battle lasted an hour and twenty minutes. Casualty reports vary widely, but the best evidence indicates that six Union soldiers were killed and twenty-four wounded. Confederate casualties were ten killed, fifteen wounded, and forty missing. Union troops captured Piketon the day after the battle, and Nelson's force arrived in the town on November 10. The Confederate forces retreated to Pound Gap on the Kentucky-Virginia border. After capturing Piketon, virtually all of Nelson's Union army was evacuated from the Big Sandy Valley.

See John David Preston, *The Civil War in the Big Sandy Valley of Kentucky* (Baltimore 1984).

THOMAS D. MATIJASIC

J

JACKSON, BELLE (MITCHELL). Belle (Mitchell) Jackson, educator and social activist, was born on December 31, 1848, in Boyle County, Kentucky, to Monroe and Mary E. Mitchell, devout Methodists who had purchased their freedom from slavery. She attended a primary school for free blacks in Danville until age eleven, when her parents moved to Xenia, Ohio. In 1865 Belle Mitchell became the first black teacher at CAMP NELSON, Kentucky. When white teachers refused to associate with her, she moved to Lexington, where she began teaching in a school sponsored by the black First Baptist Church. In 1867 Mitchell enrolled in Berea College.

Over the next three decades, she was one of the most prominent black teachers in the Lexington and Fayette County schools. She was one of the founders of the black Orphan Industrial Home in Lexington and a participant in numerous other programs designed to benefit less fortunate blacks. In 1871 she married Jordan C. Jackson, one of Lexington's most successful black businessmen and a leader among black Republicans, to whom she served as political adviser. They were the parents of a son and a daughter. Belle (Mitchell) Jackson died on October 6, 1942, in Lexington and was buried there in Greenwood Cemetery.

See W.D. Johnson, *Biographical Sketches of Prominent Negro Men and Women of Kentucky* (Lexington, Ky., 1897).   MARION B. LUCAS

JACKSON, MARY MAGDALENE (GARLAND). Mary Magdalene ("Aunt Molly") (Garland) Jackson, union activist and singer, the daughter of Oliver Perry and Deborah (Robinson) Garland, was born in Clay County, Kentucky, in 1880. When Molly was six, her mother died of starvation, and when she was ten she was jailed for her family's unionizing efforts. She married Jim Stewart, a miner, at the age of fourteen, and bore two children. After working as a nurse in a Clay County hospital for a decade she moved to Harlan County, where she was a midwife, delivering 884 babies. In 1917 Jim Stewart died in a mine accident and she married another miner, Bill Jackson. Aunt Molly Jackson, as she was known, became active in unionization efforts on behalf of the United Mine Workers, and she wrote heartfelt, powerful protest songs. Her "I am a Union Woman" (1931), "Kentucky Miner's Wife" (1932), and "Poor Miner's Farewell" (1932) drew attention to conditions in the coal camps. During 1935-36 in New York City, Molly, her half-brother Jim Garland, and her half-sister Sarah Ogan Gunning performed with musicians Pete Seeger and Woody Guthrie, using folk music as a political weapon. Jackson died on August 31, 1960, in Sacramento, California, and was buried there.

See Alan Lomax, Archie Green, and D.K. Wilgus, "Aunt Molly Jackson Memorial Issue" *Kentucky Folklore Record* (Oct.–Dec. 1961): 129-76.   RON PEN

JACKSON. Jackson, the county seat of Breathitt County in eastern Kentucky, is located about seventy-five miles southeast of Lexington at KY 15 and KY 30. When the county was created in 1839, the city, originally named Breathitt Town, was established on the North Fork of the Kentucky River. In 1845 the remote mountain hamlet was renamed Jackson to honor President Andrew Jackson, who died in that year. The first few years of the city's existence saw little growth, and by 1870 Jackson's population had yet to reach one hundred. In that year a gristmill, a log hotel, a few general stores, and houses surrounded the courthouse, a small two-story brick building that was built in 1866 to replace the original log structure.

The whole Cumberland Plateau became a hotbed of feudal revenge for many years after 1865 and Jackson was known throughout America as the capital of Bloody Breathitt County. State troops were sent twice to Jackson during the 1870s and again in 1903 to bring peace to the area. Adding to the city's rough-and-tumble reputation was the 1895 public hanging of "Bad" Tom Smith for murdering the town doctor, and the assassination of U.S. Commissioner J.B. Marcum on May 4, 1903.

A two-story brick Victorian courthouse was completed in 1876, and in 1887 the Jackson Academy (LEES COLLEGE) was established as a Presbyterian institution of learning. The Kentucky Union Railroad arrived in 1891, and as the railroad terminus, Jackson was a major shipping point for the upper Kentucky River region. Large dry goods centers, a lumber company, a brickyard, and other businesses thrived. The city resembled a western boom town, and population by 1910 had reached 2,000. In 1912 the Louisville & Nashville Railroad extended the line to Hazard, and Jackson's importance was diminished. On Halloween night of 1913, a fire destroyed thirty-six buildings, including two churches, a hotel, and the post office.

Jackson's growth for the rest of the twentieth century was slow. With the completion of KY 15 in the 1960s and the establishment of a nearby airport in the 1970s, the city was no longer an isolated mountain town. To provide flood control and a recreational facility, the two-and-three-quarter-mile-long Pan Bowl Lake was created in 1963 by rechanneling the Kentucky River and impounding the former channel. By 1990 most Jackson residents were employed by state or local government, in mining, or in service-related fields. The population of the fourth-class city was 1,887 in 1970; 2,651 in 1980; and 2,466 in 1990.

See Charles Hayes, *Old Scenes of Jackson* (Jackson, Ky., 1973); Work Projects Administration, *In the Land of Breathitt* (Northport, N.Y., 1941).

CHARLES HAYES

JACKSON COUNTY. Jackson County, the 105th county in order of formation, lies in southeastern Kentucky on the western fringe of the Cumberland Plateau. It was established in 1858, and named for President Andrew Jackson. The county was formed out of parts of Madison, Estill, Owsley, Clay, Laurel, and Rockcastle counties, which border it, along with Lee County, and has an area of 346 square miles. The county seat is McKEE.

Much of Jackson County is rugged, hilly, or rolling terrain; more than 50 percent of the area is part of the Daniel Boone National Forest. The county is watered and drained by tributaries of the Kentucky and Cumberland rivers, and the Middle Fork of Rockcastle River is a major water source. Water for consumer use is generally piped from the ninety-acre Tyner Reservoir, which also provides recreational opportunities for residents of the area.

In presettlement days, Native Americans traveled the Warriors' Path, a trail along War Fork Creek southeast of McKee, which connected Shawnee villages in southern Ohio and the Cherokee Nation of eastern Tennessee and Georgia. The trail was later used by pioneer explorers, including Dr. Thomas Walker in 1750, Christopher Gist in 1751, and Daniel Boone and John Finley in 1769. Burial mounds are evidence of prehistoric Native Americans on the South Fork of Station Camp Creek.

Among the first settlers of the area were the Casteel, Fowler, Harrison, McQueen, and Parris families. In 1860, the first census showed a county population of 3,087. For most of its history, the economy of the county has been based on agriculture, lumbering, coal, and milling. Jackson County sent logs, coal, and produce to market on the Kentucky and Rockcastle rivers before the Rockcastle River Railway was built in 1915. The first county oil well was drilled at Sand Spring in 1917. Economic activity was at its height in the county between 1920 and 1940. However, most of the timber had been removed by 1930 and the railroad was abandoned in 1932. Population reached a peak of 16,339 in 1940. After World War II mining in the county declined and many residents moved elsewhere to seek jobs.

David R. Francis, governor of Missouri, U.S. secretary of the interior, and ambassador to Russia, was born in Jackson County on October 1, 1850.

In 1990 agriculture was the mainstay of Jackson County, with burley tobacco, corn, cattle, and hogs the principal products. In 1986 agricultural receipts totaled $9.9 million, made up of $6.3 million for crops and $3.6 million for livestock. Lumber was also a source of income, with more than 70 per cent of the land forested with both hard- and soft-woods. Other natural resources included iron ore and petroleum, most used locally, and coal, of which 256,546 tons were surface-mined in 1987. Industry in the county in 1990 included McKee Manufacturing, Kentucky Woodcrafts in Grey Hawk, and Mid-South Electronics in Annville. The largest county employer was the Jackson County Rural Electric Cooperative Corporation.

Annville in Jackson County, once known as Chinquapin Rough, was home to the Annville Institute, a high school from 1909 to 1978 where students earned the nominal tuition by working for the school. Among the county's small towns are Mummie and Egypt, both in the southeastern part of the county. Mummie was named for the discovery of a mummified human body by early settlers. Egypt was named by the Amyx family, who moved there from Tennessee after the Civil War. Homesick, they felt that they were in the middle of nowhere, miles away from anything—as if they had been "exiled to Egypt." The population of the county was 10,005 in 1970; 11,996 in 1980; and 11,955 in 1990.

JACKSON-DICKINSON DUEL. On May 30, 1806, Andrew Jackson, who would become the seventh president of the United States, killed Charles Dickinson in a duel in Kentucky, protesting Dickinson's remarks about Jackson's wife, Rachel. She had previously been married to Lewis Robards, who had petitioned the legislature of Kentucky for a divorce. When the Jacksons were married, they did not know that the divorce had not yet been granted. Jackson challenged Dickinson in Nashville, where both men were attorneys, but they dueled in Kentucky to avoid legal entanglements in Tennessee.

On May 29 Jackson and Dickinson and their parties rode horseback from Nashville across the state line to Logan County, Kentucky, where they were to meet on the bank of the Red River. Jackson stayed at Miller's Tavern on the river. Dickinson stayed at the home of William Harrison. When they met the next morning, the seconds paced off twenty-four feet, and the call was given to fire. Dickinson fired immediately. When Jackson remained standing, Dickinson cried, "Great God, have I missed him?" Jackson then fired, but the hammer of his pistol stopped at half-cock. This was not considered a shot and Jackson fired again, mortally wounding Dickinson, who died that night at the Harrison home. On the way back across the river to Miller's Tavern, Jackson's party discovered that he too had been wounded.   RENA MILLIKEN

JACKSON PURCHASE. The Jackson Purchase was a historic event before it became a region. The transaction involved prolonged negotiations culminating in a treaty between agents of the United States and those of the Chickasaw Indian Nation. Representing the United States were the aging Isaac Shelby, Revolutionary War hero and twice Kentucky governor (1792-96, 1812-16), and Gen. Andrew Jackson, hero of the Battle of New Orleans and later U.S. president. The Chickasaws were represented by their chiefs, head men, and warriors, including Levi and George Colbert, Chinubby (the Boy King), and Tishomingo. The two sides signed the treaty in northwestern Mississippi on October 19, 1818; it was ratified by the U.S. Senate and confirmed by President James Monroe on January 7, 1819.

In return for the relinquishment of all lands east of the Mississippi River and north of the Mississippi state line, the Chickasaws received $300,000 at the rate of $20,000 annually for fifteen years. The states of Kentucky and Tennessee, neither of which had previously extended beyond the Tennessee River, were enlarged by approximately 2,000 and 6,000 square miles, respectively. The Kentucky addition became known as the Jackson Purchase (or Purchase District), the larger Tennessee portion as West Tennessee. These were the only parts of either state to be surveyed in sections and townships under the Land Ordinance model of 1785.

The Jackson Purchase came into the commonwealth as an extension of Christian County with Old Wadesboro designated as its capital and land office. Over time, the area was divided and further subdivided into eight counties, as follows (with their seats of government): Hickman, 1821 (Columbus, later Clinton); Calloway, 1822 (Wadesboro, later Murray); Graves, 1823 (Mayfield); McCracken, 1824 (Wilmington, later Paducah); Marshall, 1842 (Benton); Ballard, 1842 (Blandville, later Wickliffe); Fulton, 1845 (Hickman); and Carlisle, 1886 (Bardwell).

The Purchase forms a virtual Kentucky peninsula that juts northward from Tennessee and is bounded by the Tennessee, Ohio, and Mississippi rivers to the east, north, and west. Principal streams are Clarks River, Mayfield Creek, Obion Creek, and Bayou de Chien.

The land surface of the Purchase is largely covered by loess, a fine wind-blown soil carried from drying glacial beds and deposited some 10,000 to 20,000 years ago. Such deposits gradually decrease eastward across the Purchase, from maximum depths of one hundred feet or more on the Mississippi River bluffs—the Cane Hills—to a few inches near the Tennessee River. Wetlands (swamps, sloughs, and natural lakes and ponds) are common in the Big Bottoms and the Second Bottoms, low-lying flatlands bordering the Mississippi and lower Ohio Rivers. At the advent of white settlement, much of the central Purchase was prairie (barrens) with tall grasses and scattered shrubby oaks. The largest subdivision of the Purchase is the oak-hickory uplands, which encompasses portions of every county. The Breaks of the Tennessee, a narrow, hilly belt along the western edge of the Tennessee River, is geologically the oldest region of the Purchase, dating from Mississippian times. The other subdivisions are underlain by sands and gravels of Tertiary and Cretaceous age.

A series of massive earthquakes in 1811-12 caused drastic changes to the topography of the western Purchase; the most spectacular resulted in the formation of Reelfoot Lake. A portion of the Reelfoot National Wildlife Refuge extends into Fulton County. Slippage along the New Madrid Fault is still a threat.

The first known human inhabitants of the Purchase were prehistoric mound-building Indians who left the WICKLIFFE MOUNDS, an ancient buried city (approximately A.D. 1000-1300) near the confluence of the Mississippi and Ohio Rivers. Almost four centuries after the unexplained disappearance of this culture, the first white men, French explorers of the Mississippi River, visited the same location: Louis Jolliet and Jacques Marquette, in 1673, and Ren Robert LaSalle, in 1682. A site in the same area was selected in 1780 for the construction of FORT JEFFERSON.

Citizens of the Purchase were predominantly pro-Confederate from the beginning of the Civil War, as reflected by the majorities given to Southern candidate John Breckinridge in the presidential election of 1860, and later by the enlistment of approximately 5,000 Confederate volunteers to a mere six hundred for the Union. A mass meeting held at Mayfield in May 1861 advocated joining with West Tennessee to form a new Confederate state. Much of the region had been settled by people from West Tennessee, so the affinity was natural.

Although no major battles, other than a sizable cavalry raid on Paducah, occurred on Purchase soil, the region was involved in opening and closing phases of the war in the western theater—first, by the breaching of Kentucky's so-called neutrality policy by the sudden occupations of Columbus and Hickman by Confederate forces under Gen. Leonidas K. Polk in September 1861 and, toward the end, by the reoccupation of FORT HEIMAN in October 1864 by Gen. Nathan B. Forrest's cavalry brigades.

The Purchase is a Democratic political stronghold wherein candidates for local office are generally decisively selected by primary well before general elections. Only one native, Julian Carroll, has attained the governorship (1974-79), but many have achieved recognition beyond the Purchase and the state. Among them are Alben W. Barkley, vice-president of the United States (1949-53); Irvin S. Cobb, humorist, author, journalist, and actor; and Nathan B. Stubblefield, inventor of the "wireless telephone," a forerunner of radio.

Murray State University is the region's largest institution of higher learning, having expanded from its founding as Murray State Normal School in 1922 to its present enrollment of approximately 8,000 students in 1990. Next in size is Paducah Community College, which has grown from its beginning as Paducah Junior College in 1932 to its present status within the Community College System of the University of Kentucky, with an enrollment of approximately 2,000 in 1990. Mid-Continent Baptist College, a four-year accredited seminary near Hickory, was founded in Clinton.

Although the Purchase is predominantly agrarian, industries, including those that support agriculture, contribute to its workforce and prosperity: uranium enrichment, railroad yards, and river industries in the Paducah area; tourism and recreation throughout the region; chemical production at Calvert City; clothing and air compressor manufacturing at Mayfield; toy and chemical manufacturing at Murray; and clay mining near Hickory and

Pryorsburg. Paducah, Murray, and Mayfield are the three urban centers; Fulton, smaller, is a rail center. The FANCY FARM picnic in Graves County draws thousands annually to this traditional kick-off of Kentucky's political season.

Because of its distance from the major population and political centers of the state and its location across the Tennessee River, the region was long isolated. Not until the river was spanned with a bridge and better highways built was it tied to the rest of the state. The construction of I-24 and the Purchase Parkway have brought many tourists to the region. Kenlake and Kentucky Dam Village State Resort Parks are both within the Purchase.

See D.H. Davis, *The Geography of the Jackson Purchase* (Frankfort, Ky., 1923).

HUNTER M. HANCOCK

JACOB, RICHARD TAYLOR. Richard Taylor Jacob, political leader, was born in Oldham County March 13, 1825, the son of John and Lucy Donald (Robertson) Jacob. As a young man, Jacob visited South America for his health, returning to Louisville in 1846 to join Edwin Bryant's expedition to California. On the West Coast Jacob raised a company and joined John C. Frémont's fight against Mexican control. Jacob returned to Kentucky by way of the Isthmus of Panama.

Jacob lived in Missouri as a farmer from 1848 to 1853. There he married Sarah Benton, daughter of Thomas Hart Benton, on January 17, 1848. In 1853 he returned to Oldham County and six years later was elected to the Kentucky House; in the presidential election of 1860, he served as a John C. Breckinridge elector. During the period December 1860 to May 1861, Jacob played an active role in keeping the state neutral in the face of the Civil War. In July 1862 Jacob organized a regiment of short-term volunteers to disrupt Gen. John Hunt Morgan's raids into Kentucky. Later, Union Gen. Jeremiah T. Boyle, commander of the District of Kentucky, ordered Jacob to organize a cavalry regiment, and within ten days he had mustered 1,244 men and a greater number of horses at an encampment near Eminence. This unit supported Gen. Don Carlos Buell's army. In a hand-to-hand encounter with Confederates near Lawrenceburg, Jacob was thrice wounded.

Jacob was elected lieutenant governor in November 1863, and in the absence of Gov. Thomas E. Bramlette acted as governor. In the presidential election of 1864, Jacob supported George B. McClellan, to the dismay of his fellow Kentucky Unionists. When he protested federal government violations of citizens' rights, Gen. Stephen Burbridge banished him to Richmond, Virginia, for sedition. Jacob appealed to President Abraham Lincoln, who ordered his release. At the end of the Civil War, Jacob strongly supported the Thirteenth and Fourteenth Amendments and crusaded for substantial improvements in Kentucky's public schools. Later he was appointed interim county judge of Oldham County. In 1879 he was defeated for the

office of clerk of the court of appeals by Confederate veteran T.J. Henry.

Jacob had two children, Richard and Elizabeth, by his first wife, Sarah (Benton) Jacob, who died in 1863. Jacob married Laura Wilson, of Lexington, on June 15, 1865. They had five children, John, William, Donald, Brent, and Laura. Jacob died in Louisville on September 13, 1903.

THOMAS D. CLARK

JAMES, FRANK AND JESSE. The notorious outlaws Jesse James and his brother Frank were the sons of Robert S. James of Logan County, Kentucky, a Georgetown College ministerial student, and Zerelda (Cole) James, who was born in Woodford County, where her grandfather operated a stagecoach inn. The marriage took place in 1841 at the home of Zerelda's uncle and guardian, Judge James Lindsay, near Stamping Ground in Scott County. The couple moved to Missouri, where their four children (including a daughter, Susan, and a son, Robert, who died in infancy) were born. In later years, the James brothers paid frequent visits to family members in Kentucky.

The so-called James gang—largely a postwar band of former Quantrill's Raiders, originally led by Cole Younger—is held responsible for robberies in several states, including holdups of the banks at Russellville and Columbia, Kentucky, and of a pair of stagecoaches near Mammoth Cave. However, neither Frank nor Jesse was ever convicted of any of the crimes. In the 1868 Russellville robbery, there is no convincing proof that the James brothers directly participated. Detective D.G. Bligh, who investigated the case, stated that on the day of the holdup Frank and Jesse were at a hotel in Chaplin, Nelson County, recovering from wounds. Yet Bligh believed that they were involved. George Shepherd, soon imprisoned for the robbery, and his cousin Oliver Shepherd, who was killed resisting arrest for it, were compatriots of the Jameses. The robbery matched the James gang's modus operandi: "genteelly dressed" men arriving in town and posing as cattle buyers, then converging on the bank, with half going inside and the others standing guard with Spencer rifles. The 1872 Columbia bank robbery followed the same pattern, and the robbers fled into Nelson County, a known James sanctuary. As to the stagecoach robberies in 1880, a confessed gang member soon identified Jesse and an accomplice as the perpetrators.

Jesse's cowardly murder by Bob Ford in 1882 helped make him the focus of later legends. Pistols carved with his name proliferated, as did Jesse James impostors (some seventeen by one count). His reputed deeds rivaled those of Robin Hood, becoming so entrenched that, in the words of Will Henry, "the real Jesse James will always remain part man, part myth."

See Will Henry, *Death of a Legend* (New York 1954); William A. Settle, Jr., *Jesse James Was His Name* (Lincoln, Neb., 1966).   JOE NICKELL

JAMES, OLLIE MURRAY. Ollie Murray James, U.S. senator and Democratic party leader, was the son of L.H. and Elizabeth James. He was born on July 27, 1871, near Marion, Crittenden County, Kentucky, where he attended public schools. In 1887 James served as a page for the Kentucky General Assembly and the next year was the Senate's cloakroom keeper. After studying law in his father's office, he was admitted to the Kentucky bar in 1891 and began practicing with his father in Marion.

James, a Democrat and proponent of William Jennings Bryan and free silver, was chosen to head the Kentucky delegation to the Democratic National Convention in Chicago in 1896 and again in 1900 at Kansas City, Missouri. In 1899, he supported William Stone against William Goebel as the Democratic nominee in Kentucky's gubernatorial race. During the Democratic nominating convention held in June 1899 in Louisville, James participated with the anti-Goebel faction in blowing horns, ringing bells, and generally disrupting convention business for a day. After Goebel received the Democratic nomination, James's opposition changed to support. He later used his skill as an attorney to contest the disputed election of Republican William S. Taylor as governor, with the result that Goebel was declared governor. He again held the position of chairman of the state delegation to national conventions of Democrats in 1904 in St. Louis and 1908 in Denver.

James was elected to the U.S. House of Representatives, serving five successive terms from March 4, 1903, until March 3, 1913. As a member of the House Ways and Means Committee, he played an important part in passing the Underwood-Simmons Tariff Act of 1913. He was elected to the U.S. Senate on January 9, 1912, defeating Edwin P. Morrow by a vote of 105 to 28, and served from March 4, 1913, until his death. When newly elected to the Senate, James was appointed to the Senate Finance Committee, a post until that time reserved for senior senators. He gave his support to two progressive constitutional amendments: one to create an income tax and the second to establish the election of senators by popular vote. James was selected to fill the honorary post of permanent chairman for the Democratic National Convention of 1912 in Baltimore and that of 1916 in St. Louis. At the 1912 convention, James, a popular orator, delivered the keynote speech supporting Woodrow Wilson as the party's candidate for the presidency. In 1916 at the nominating convention he gave a brilliant speech praising Wilson's achievements.

James married Ruth Thomas of Marion, Kentucky, on December 2, 1903. He was suffering from bad health when renominated for the Senate on August 3, 1918. He died on August 28, 1918, and was buried in Mapleview Cemetery in Marion.

See Forrest C. Pogue, "The Life and Work of Senator Ollie Murray James," M.A. thesis, University of Kentucky, 1932.

JAMES C. ELLIS PARK. James C. Ellis Park, thoroughbred race course, is north of the Ohio River in Henderson County, Kentucky. It was built in 1922 by the Green River Jockey Club. In 1919 James Cheatham, a Henderson real estate man, had proposed the idea of a local track to another Henderson resident, A.B. Dade, a starter of horse races and later a director and organizer of the Green River Jockey Club. A 204-acre tract of river-bottom land was purchased in 1921, and the Green River Jockey Club was incorporated with $500,000 in March of 1922. The track and buildings were mostly completed by October 12, 1922. The mile-and-an-eighth course was designed after the historic track in Saratoga, New York. A 4,000-seat grandstand at the end of the 1,175-foot home stretch lay almost adjacent to the paddock. Initially named Dade Park, after one of its founders, the track held its first thoroughbred meet on November 8, 1922.

The track had financial difficulties in its first two seasons and was sold for $35,100 at a receivership sale in December 1924 to James C. Ellis, a thoroughbred enthusiast. The track's name was changed in 1954 at the urging of Earl Ruby, then sports editor of the *Louisville Courier-Journal*. Numerous additions were made between 1949 and 1962. A clubhouse built in 1962 has been enlarged to accommodate 1,500 more patrons. The grandstand and its Sky Theatre seat 4,750. Race Inc. of America bought Ellis Park on April 1, 1990. A major event at the track is Gardenia Festival Week, which attracts outstanding fillies and mares in training.

See Frieda J. Dannheiser, ed., *The History of Henderson County, Kentucky* (Evansville, Ind., 1980).

JAMESTOWN. The seat of Russell County, Jamestown is located on U.S. 127. The town, first called Jacksonville, in honor of President Andrew Jackson, was incorporated on December 23, 1827. When the local anti-Jacksonian Party came into power in 1826, the community was renamed Jamestown to honor James Woodridge, donor of the one-hundred-acre town site. Three Russell County courthouses were built between 1826 and 1978. During the Civil War, Jamestown was the site of two recorded skirmishes—one on Christmas Day, 1861, and the second on June 2, 1863. Lake Cumberland, completed by the U.S. Army Corps of Engineers in 1952, is of great economic importance to Jamestown for the recreational fishing and boating along its 1,317 miles of shoreline in the region. Industries in Jamestown include the county's largest manufacturer, Fruit of the Loom, and a food mill.

The population of the fifth-class city was 1,027 in 1970; 1,441 in 1980; and 1,641 in 1990.

RON D. BRYANT

JAY'S TREATIES. In 1786, when John Jay was secretary of foreign affairs under the Articles of Confederation, he and Diego de Gardoqui, the

Spanish minister to the United States, agreed upon the main terms of the treaty designed to settle several problems between the two nations. In return for favorable commercial concessions, Jay proposed that the United States waive for twenty-five or thirty years its claims to the use of the Mississippi River. Kentuckians, who were beginning to produce some surpluses for sale and needed to use the river for shipments, were outraged. Since nine votes were required for ratification, the southern states were able to block the proposed treaty.

In 1794, as chief justice of the United States, Jay went to Great Britain as an envoy extraordinary to resolve serious problems arising from the peace treaty of 1783, which ended the Revolutionary War, and from neutrality issues caused by the European war between France and Britain. The resultant treaty was unpopular in the United States, especially with Jeffersonian Republicans. But it eased tensions for a time, and Kentuckians were pleased by the British promise to evacuate the posts they occupied on American soil in the Old Northwest Territory. The promise was carried out, and the Indian problem in that area subsided for several years.

See Samuel Flagg Bemis, *Jay's Treaty* (New York 1923); Arthur P. Whitaker, *The Spanish-American Frontier* (Boston 1927).

LOWELL H. HARRISON

JAZZ. More than fifty nationally known jazz musicians were born in Kentucky during the last decade of the nineteenth century and the first decade of the twentieth, when jazz was emerging as a new force in American music. Louisville alone produced singer Sara Martin (born in 1884), singer and dancer John Bubbles (1902), vibraphonist Lionel Hampton (1909), trumpeter Jonah Jones (1909), singer Helen HUMES (1913), pianist and composer Don Murray (1925), guitarist Jimmy RANEY (1927), and Don DeMichael (1928), editor of *Down Beat* and *Jazz Record Review*. Among the jazz musicians born elsewhere in Kentucky during this period were pianist Fate Marable (Paducah, 1890), drummer William McKinney (Cynthiana, 1895), banjoist Zach Whyte (Richmond, 1898), saxophonist Jerome Pasquall (Fulton, 1902), trombonist Russell Bowles (Glasgow, 1909), pianist Charlie Queener (Pineville, 1923), singer Rosemary CLOONEY (Maysville, 1928), and bassist Reggie Johnson (Owensboro, 1940).

During the jazz age of the 1920s, jazz bands were regular attractions in nightclubs. The SS *Island Queen* and other excursion boats on the Ohio River carried groups like Sidney Desvigne's Southern Syncopators. By the 1930s the careers of many of Kentucky's jazz musicians were in full swing. After World War II jazz was so prevalent that it had become part of the curriculum in colleges throughout the state. Organizations such as the Louisville Jazz Society sprang up to promote jazz performance, and jazz festivals in the larger cities became commonplace. In 1990 Louisville radio sta-

tion WFPL-FM was airing a wide variety of jazz styles for most of its broadcasting day.

See *Biographical Dictionary of Black Musicians and Music Educators* (Guthrie, Okla., 1978); Gregg Swem, "Louisville Jazz," *Louisville Courier-Journal*, Aug. 24, 1980.

ROBERT BRUCE FRENCH

J.B. SPEED ART MUSEUM. The J.B. Speed Art Museum in Louisville, Kentucky, the state's oldest and largest art museum, was founded in 1925 by Mrs. James Breckinridge Speed as a memorial to her husband, a prominent Louisville businessman and philanthropist. Designed by Arthur Loomis, the museum opened on January 15, 1927. In 1933 it was incorporated as a privately endowed institution and its board of governors was established. The museum is adjacent to, but not a part of, the University of Louisville, and sits on land conveyed by deed from the university.

The Preston Pope Satterwhite wing houses the English Renaissance Room and Satterwhite's collection of medieval and Renaissance European furniture, decorative arts, and sculpture. Another gift is Frederick Weygold's collection of Native American artifacts, paintings, drawings, and photographs. The focus of the museum collection is Western European art from ancient to modern, with particular emphasis on the fine and decorative arts from the Renaissance to the present. It includes paintings, sculptures, drawings, prints, and photographs. Holdings of Netherlandish paintings, French and Italian works, and contemporary art are particularly strong, and sculpture is prominent throughout the collection. The museum has changing exhibitions, programs, films, a museum shop, a library, a cafe, and a 350-seat auditorium. The museum is supported entirely by endowments, special gifts, grants, and memberships.

See William F. Bradbury, *A Brief Chronicle: The Speed Art Museum in Four Decades, 1925-1961* (Louisville 1961).   MARY JANE BENEDICT

JEFFERSON COUNTY. Jefferson County, one of three original counties in what is now the state of Kentucky, is located west of the Outer Bluegrass region along the Ohio River. Bounded by Bullitt, Spencer, Shelby, and Oldham counties, it has an area of 386 square miles. The Virginia General Assembly created Jefferson County in May 1780 by dividing Kentucky County into three parts for better administration. The residents at and near the Falls of the Ohio had petitioned the legislature for a separate county, complaining that they "were near one hundred miles from the Court House" at Harrodsburg. LOUISVILLE was designated the seat of justice of Jefferson County, a territory of more than 7,800 square miles bounded by Green River on the west and south, the Kentucky River and Benson Creek on the east, and the Ohio River on the north. The county was named for Thomas Jefferson, then governor of Virginia.

The county's population in 1780 was concentrated almost exclusively around the Falls of the Ohio and nearby streams that emptied into the Ohio River, notably the Middle and South forks of Beargrass Creek and Goose Creek east of Louisville. This area, liberally endowed with springs and at a higher elevation than the site of Louisville, was especially desirable. In 1780 there were six fortified stations along the Middle Fork: Spring, Hogland's, Floyd's, Low Dutch (or New Holland), A'Sturgus, and Linn's. Sullivan's Station was on the South Fork. Jefferson County, from its exposed position on the river, was particularly vulnerable to Indian raids even some years after the interior of the state was relatively safe. As late as 1789, a raid on the isolated farm of Richard Chenoweth in present-day eastern Jefferson County left five settlers dead.

South of Louisville the early discovery of salt springs (notably Mann's Lick and Bullitt's Lick) prompted the establishment of fortified points in the 1780s along Salt River: Mud Garrison, Dowdall's Station, Fort Nonsense, and Brashear's Station. They offered protection to the salt makers, who began plying their trade in 1779, and salt making became Jefferson County's first industry. As settlers pushed into the farther reaches of Jefferson County, new counties were carved from its original territory, beginning with Nelson in 1784. In all, twenty-eight counties and parts of counties were created from Jefferson, which reached its present size in 1823.

The early settlers in the county represented diverse groups, not only Virginians but also many from North Carolina and the northeastern states, especially Pennsylvania. Mostly of Scotch-Irish and English ancestry, the newcomers also included many of German descent, and a close-knit group of Dutch descent founded the New Holland Station. Slaves brought to frontier Kentucky were a significant part of the population from the earliest days.

Well-to-do Virginians owned the best land, the largest acreages, and the most slaves. They established plantations on the Virginia model. Their ranks included Richard Taylor (father of President Zachary Taylor) of Springfields, Alexander Scott Bullitt of Oxmoor, Richard Clough Anderson of Soldier's Retreat, John Speed of Farmington, William Croghan (brother-in-law of George Rogers Clark) of Locust Grove, and Henry Massie of Ridgeway. The yeoman farmers, by contrast, mostly performed their own labor on smaller and often more rugged acreages. Non-Virginians were hampered in acquiring farms by Virginia's land laws and had few or no slaves. Some of the landless demanded that Kentucky be made a separate state, with different land laws.

Jeffersontown was founded in 1797 by Abraham Bruner, one of the Pennsylvania German immigrants, and was known informally for a number of years as Brunerstown. It was also in 1797 that Philip Buckner founded Middletown. Both settlements were in the eastern section of the county; not until the early years of the nineteenth century did the fertile but low-lying and flood-prone river plains in southwestern Jefferson County see any substantial number of farms.

The most important political entity until the early years of the nineteenth century was the county court, made up of all the justices of the peace (twenty-two in 1815), who exercised legislative, executive, and judicial powers, and selected their own successors. The two most powerful political offices were those of the sheriff (normally the senior justice of the peace) and the county clerk, appointed by the court. The rapid growth of Louisville in the nineteenth century shifted the focus of political power from the courthouse to city hall in the same way that the mercantile interests of the city overshadowed the county's agrarian economy.

While relations between city and county were usually amicable, there were exceptions. In 1835 there was a move to make Louisville a separate county, in part because Whig politicians, who dominated the city, had largely been shut out of membership on the county court. Another factor was a disagreement between city and county over financing the construction of a new courthouse, to be occupied also by city offices—a proposal that originated in the city government. The legislative act to make Louisville a county passed the state House of Representatives, but failed in the Senate. After this, city and county reached agreement on construction, sharing costs, and ownership. Although offers to present the courthouse to the state for a capitol building failed, the General Assembly met there for a month during the 1862 Confederate invasion of Kentucky.

By 1850 there were 5,000 voters in Louisville, more than double the number in the rest of Jefferson County. As Louisville outstripped it in population and political muscle, rural Jefferson County became one of Kentucky's leading agricultural producers. In 1860 it was first among counties in value of animals slaughtered, production of hay, market gardening, and orchards; and second in production of barley and butter. The county both supplied city markets and provisioned steamboats.

Jefferson County also led in the number of slaves in 1860 with 10,304, although only about half this number were in the rural precincts. Small farms predominated. There was only one farm of more than 1,000 acres in 1860, but there were 1,100 of three acres and more, and most were twenty to ninety-nine acres. Many farms were owned by the Germans who came in the wave of immigration in the 1840s and 1850s. A number of agricultural associations were formed, and in 1853 the Southwestern Agricultural and Mechanical Association established a thirty-eight-acre fairground in what is now the Crescent Hill neighborhood in Louisville's East End. Annual agricultural fairs were held there until about 1872. In 1877 the Fern Creek Farmers' and Fruit Growers' Association began a long span of annual fairs at Fern Creek on the Bardstown

Road. This area was noted for strawberry production, just as St. Matthews, east of Louisville, became a potato-growing area. At the turn of the century, an onion farm on the Bardstown Road near Doup's Point was among the world's largest.

The county remained important agriculturally until the post-World War II spread of urbanization consumed much prime farm acreage. In the agricultural setting a number of smaller unincorporated communities developed. They included St. Matthews (originally Gilman's Point) east of Louisville on the Shelbyville Road, Buechel and Fern Creek south of Louisville on the Bardstown Road, Okolona south of Louisville on the Preston Street Road (now Preston Highway), and Valley Station and Pleasure Ridge Park (originally a picnic ground) on the Valley Pike (now Dixie Highway). Typically home to a general store, a blacksmith, a saloon, post office, and perhaps a railroad station, the communities emphasized the rural character of the county. All have since become bedroom suburbs in an urban county.

In the prosperous years after the Civil War, many affluent city residents built impressive country homes, sometimes buying large acreages and becoming gentlemen farmers. Bashford Manor, built in 1871-72 near Buechel, was a typical example. In the 1880s it became a thoroughbred farm, which produced three Kentucky Derby winners. The home was demolished in 1972 and the farm converted to a shopping center as automobile-age strip development engulfed the area.

Most of the exurban development, however, took place in the eastern section of the county along the Louisville-Lexington railroad. Anchorage, a community of fine homes, grew up around the antebellum estate of Edward D. Hobbs. Incorporated as a town in 1879, it was the first municipality to be created since Jeffersontown and Middletown, in 1797. Another prestigious exurban community, Glenview, developed about the same time on the high hills overlooking the Ohio River above Louisville. Glenview, Harrod's Creek, and other exurban centers along the Ohio River were served by a narrow-gauge railroad completed in 1877 to Sand Hill (later Prospect)—the first built primarily to serve commuters from large estates to their Louisville offices. In 1904 it was converted into an electrically operated interurban line, and another interurban was built to Jeffersontown. Soon a network of such lines served the county, and two extended beyond—one to Shelbyville and another to La Grange. The interurban cars dashing through the rural landscape created corridors of urbanization as more city dwellers found their way to the countryside. By 1910 the dim outline of a metropolitan area embracing both city and county was evident. In that year 14.8 percent of the total county population of 263,000 lived outside Louisville, compared with 12 percent in 1900.

Urbanization was beginning to nibble at the county's rural tranquility and the pace increased as the automobile came onto the scene. The fiscal court (known as the court of claims until 1892), made up of ten justices of the peace, one from each precinct, became unequal to the increasing governmental burden of paving roads, building and administering schools, preventing crime, and the like. This, plus the nationwide trend toward shorter ballots, prompted the move toward a commission form of government. With the permission of the General Assembly and the approval of local voters, Jefferson became the first Kentucky county to adopt the commission form of government, replacing the justices with three commissioners on January 1, 1918.

The prosperity of the 1920s brought more urban incursions into county farmland and the creation of the small municipalities of Strathmoor Village (1928) and Strathmoor Manor (1931) near Bowman Field southeast of Louisville. As automobile ownership increased, even during the Great Depression years of the 1930s, the interurban electric lines quietly closed, one by one; the last, to Prospect, quit in 1935. Then in 1938 an act of the General Assembly changed the relationship of Louisville to the smaller municipalities in the county and paved the way to an explosive growth in small incorporated cities in the years after World War II.

With the repeal of prohibition in 1933, distilleries were reopened, many of the new ones choosing an area immediately southwest of Louisville known for many years as St. Helens. The plant built by Joseph Seagram and Son opened in 1937 as the world's largest distillery. Although Louisville had cast annexing eyes at these new enterprises, it had not yet done so when the 1938 General Assembly approved a bill requiring that at least 50 percent of the residents of an incorporated community facing annexation by a Class I city (a category that included only Louisville) must approve the action beforehand. Two months after the bill was passed, the city of Shively was created, including all the distilleries. The law effectively prevented Louisville from annexing the area.

The possibilities inherent in this legislation were not lost on the residents of the spate of new subdivisions that seemed to sprout overnight in the county, beginning in the late 1940s. Nor were they lost on established communities like St. Matthews, which took the precaution of becoming an incorporated city in 1950 to prevent annexation by its larger neighbor. Suburbanization, which began in the 1920s and was held in check for fifteen years by the Great Depression and World War II, burst the dam when the war ended. Between 1950 and 1960, county population outside Louisville nearly doubled, to 220,308, or 36 percent of the combined city-county total. By 1960 the number of incorporated cities, some very small, was about thirty.

A major factor in suburban growth was the expressway system, once seen as a way to discourage commercial growth on the fringes. That was the rationale advanced by the Louisville Area Development Association about 1947 for a belt highway around the city (now the Watterson Expressway) and a connecting spur to the central business district (now I-65). The first sections were opened in the early 1950s, preceding the national interstate highway system that would bisect the county from east to west and north to south. Each interchange became a node of commercial and residential development. By 1972 the county population outside Louisville exceeded the city's. In fact, were it not for signs posted along its perimeter, it would be impossible to identify the Louisville boundaries.

Attempts to merge city and county into a single entity to meet the new circumstances have been consistently rebuffed by the suburban areas in 1956, 1970, 1982, and 1983. The problem of divided governmental authority was partially solved, however, with the approval by the state legislature of a city-county compact effective January 1, 1987, and continuing until the end of 1998. Louisville has agreed not to annex unincorporated county areas, and no new small cities will be created in the county—which counted a total of ninety-three when the agreement took effect. City and county share occupational tax revenues under a complex formula, a single economic development office has replaced the former two competing agencies, and the county has increased its share of funding to joint city-county agencies.

Jefferson County, which in the nineteenth century was one of Kentucky's leading agricultural counties, has become in the twentieth century its most highly urbanized. The population was 695,055 in 1970; 685,004 in 1980; and 664,937 in 1990.

See George H. Yater, *Two Hundred Years at the Falls of the Ohio: A History of Louisville and Jefferson County* (Louisville 1987); Robert C. Jobson, *A History of Early Jeffersontown and Southern Jefferson County* (Baltimore 1977).

GEORGE H. YATER

JEFFERSON COUNTY COURTHOUSE. The Jefferson County courthouse is a monumental Greek Revival structure that originated as a joint venture of Jefferson County and the city of Louisville. Construction began in 1836, but the building was not completed until 1860. An often-repeated legend, not confirmed by any official records, says that leading citizens of Louisville hoped to have the state capital moved from Frankfort to Louisville, and believed that construction of a grand building to house the legislature would advance their cause.

Gideon SHRYOCK, the first Kentucky architect of record, is generally credited with designing the courthouse, although little of his design remains. The financial panic of 1837 and other problems delayed construction, and the building was only partly finished by 1842, when the city and county governments occupied it. By then Shryock had, for unknown reasons, resigned or been fired from the project. The courthouse stood unfinished until 1858, when Albert FINK, a bridge designer and engineer for the Louisville & Nashville Railroad, was appointed architect. He completed the courthouse in 1860 by simplifying Shryock's original plans

while keeping the basic temple form. Most of the architectural details are Fink's work, including the dramatic rotunda and its cast-iron floor and staircase. After a damaging fire in 1905, Louisville architect Brinton B. DAVIS fireproofed the courthouse and added major interior architectural details.

City government moved from the building to the Louisville city hall after its construction in 1871-73. A renovation project completed in 1981 stabilized and refurbished the courthouse, removing many inappropriate alterations while retaining significant architectural elements. The courthouse is listed on the National Register of Historic Places.

See Samuel W. Thomas, "An Enduring Folly: The Jefferson County Courthouse," *FCHQ* 55 (Oct. 1981): 311-43.   MARY JEAN KINSMAN

JEFFERSON SEMINARY. On February 10, 1798, the Jefferson Seminary in Louisville received a charter from the Kentucky General Assembly and became one of the earliest academies in Kentucky not operated by a religious organization. The chartering act granted Jefferson County six thousand acres from Christian County to endow the institution. Title for the public land was vested in the eight-member board of trustees and their successors. On December 7, 1798, the General Assembly passed an act authorizing a lottery to raise $5,000 to build a school with a library and to equip it with teaching materials. In 1813 the board paid Col. Richard C. ANDERSON $700 for a two-acre lot in Louisville on the west side of Eighth Street, between Green (now Liberty) and Walnut (now Muhammad Ali) streets. (In 1817 an adjoining one-half acre was purchased for $100). A one-and-a-half-story brick school building, facing Grayson Street, was completed in 1816. The building had two large classrooms on the first floor and four small rooms above. Classes began in 1816. Mann BUTLER was principal, at a salary of $600 per year, and Reuben Murray and William Tompkins were assistant teachers, at a salary of $500 each. Tuition for the six-month term was $20 for the standard curriculum and $30 for classical language training. When the seminary opened in 1816, between forty-five and fifty pupils attended. As was customary for early academies, Jefferson Seminary was an all-male school.

The seminary organized classes on the high school and college levels and from its beginning had high standards. Although chartered and endowed by the state and owned by the county, Jefferson Seminary had a curriculum more typical of private schools. During an era when the population was embracing democratic principles, there was growing criticism of seminaries that educated only the middle-class clientele for the professions. This criticism of elitism, revealing the growing class consciousness in Louisville, affected enrollment. Although it continued to operate until 1829, the seminary was never widely patronized.

On February 13, 1828, Louisville was incorporated as a city with an act that transferred all property of the Jefferson Seminary to the city of Louisville and established public schools supported through taxation to educate all white children between the ages of six and fourteen. The city took over the building and the lot on September 30, 1830, and opened Louisville College. In 1845 the city sold the property.

See David Post, "From the Jefferson Seminary to the Louisville Free School: Change and Continuity in Western Education, 1813-1840," *Register* 86 (Spring 1988): 103-18.

JEFFERSONTOWN. Jeffersontown, in eastern Jefferson County, is a suburb of Louisville located at the junction of KY 1065 and KY 155. It lies on Chenoweth Run Creek in an area that was surveyed by Thomas Bullitt in 1773 and John Floyd in 1774. Among the families that arrived there before 1790 were the Hites, Tylers, and Oldhams, all recipients of land grants. Settlers who arrived later included families of German descent known as Pennsylvania Dutch. The town was named Jefferson when it was established in 1797 on forty acres of land owned by Abraham Bruner, but residents continued to refer to it as Brunerstown until well into the 1820s. The official name later became Jeffersontown.

By the early 1800s many industries and businesses had developed in the town, including a tannery, wheelwright, tailor, blacksmith, and several taverns. A number of Protestant churches of both German and English backgrounds had been established. In 1848 Peter Funk deeded land for a church "for the African or slave population."

The Civil War largely bypassed Jeffersontown, with one tragic exception. In reprisal for the murder of a Union soldier on Bardstown Pike, Gen. Stephen Burbridge ordered the execution of four men who had been jailed on charges of guerrilla activity. Just outside Jeffersontown Union soldiers shot the men and their bodies were thrown into a ditch. Later they were buried in the old cemetery.

In 1894 Henry Watterson, editor of the *Louisville Courier-Journal*, settled near Jeffersontown on an estate named Mansfield, where he resided until his death in 1921.

Jeffersontown was once just a stop on the Louisville-to-Taylorsville pike. By 1905 an interurban railroad connected it with Louisville. Expansion of Louisville and increased use of the automobile after World War II changed much of the surrounding farmland into suburban neighborhoods. The Bluegrass Research and Industrial Park, built in 1965, stimulated the development of the local economy. Jeffersontown celebrates its heritage with an annual Gaslight Festival. The population of the fourth-class city was 9,701 in 1970; 19,814 in 1980; and 23,221 in 1990.

See Robert C. Jobson, "German-American Settlers of Early Jefferson County, Kentucky," *FCHQ* 53 (July 1979): 344-57; William E. Cummings, *Jeffersontown's Past 175 Years* (Jeffersontown, Ky., 1972).

JENKINS. Jenkins is in eastern Kentucky, on the Elkhorn Creek in Letcher County near Pound Gap. It was constructed in 1911 by the Consolidation Coal Company, which owned 100,000 acres of coal lands in the area. The city was named after George C. Jenkins of Baltimore, one of the company's directors. The four towns of Dunham, Burdine, McRoberts, and Jenkins, all built by the company along a seven-and-a-half-mile section of the Sandy Valley and the Elkhorn Railroad, were incorporated as a single city in the late 1940s, with a total population of almost 10,000 people.

By the 1940s the Jenkins field was Kentucky's largest single coal-mining operation and the town was a typical COMPANY TOWN. Residents quipped that since the hospital and funeral home were owned by Consolidation, the company saw them into this world and escorted them out again. In 1947 the Consolidation Coal Company divested itself of the city of Jenkins and sold its property—waterworks, homes, businesses, stores, hotel, filling stations, hospital, and funeral home—to the residents. Nine years later, Consolidation sold its coal mines to Bethlehem Steel, heralding a period of economic decline for the town. In June of 1982, Mother Teresa of Calcutta visited Jenkins and established the Missionaries of Charity Sisters to work with the area's poor. The population of the fourth-class city was 2,552 in 1970; 3,217 in 1980; and 2,751 in 1990.

See Jenkins Area Jaycees, *The History of Jenkins, Kentucky* (Jenkins, Ky., 1973).

JEPTHA KNOB. Jeptha Knob is a series of hills in eastern Shelby County, seven miles east of Shelbyville, Kentucky. The highest hill in the cluster, easily seen from highways I-64 and U.S. 60, is approximately two miles in diameter and reaches 1,188 feet above sea level—the highest point in the Bluegrass region. The knob is named for Jeptha Layson, who owned the land in the 1880s. The cluster of hills lies more than thirty miles from the Knobs region of Kentucky. Formed during the Ordovician and Silurian periods, with the top layers being Silurian, the cluster was probably created by erosion combined with an upthrust of the central, higher elevations, possibly the result of deep-seated volcanic disturbances. Geologists disagree about the source of the formation, and some suggest a meteoric origin. It consists of alternating layers of shale and limestone. Jeptha Knob lies on a spur of the major divide from which streams flow either into the Salt River on the west or the Kentucky River on the east.

Surrounded by the flat farmland of Shelby County, Jeptha Knob offers excellent views of the countryside and is a prime Kentucky location for geological study.

See Arthur McFarlan *Geology of Kentucky* (Lexington, Ky., 1943).

JERRICO INC. Jerrico Inc. is best known as the parent company of Long John Silver's Seafood

Shoppes, a national quick-service seafood chain. The company started as White Tavern Shoppes—small, six-stool hamburger stands, opened in Shelbyville, Kentucky. The company grew to thirteen units before becoming a casualty of World War II, when shortages of sugar, meat, and manpower closed all but three units. In 1946 company founder Jerome Lederer launched a new restaurant called Jerry's. Warren W. Rosenthal joined Lederer in the company in 1948. In 1957 Jerrico became one of the first restaurant chains to stimulate growth through franchising, which led to the rapid expansion of Jerry's Restaurants. When the Jerry's division was sold in 1990, there were twenty-four franchises and twenty-four company-owned Jerry's operating in Florida, Illinois, Indiana, and Kentucky. The first Long John Silver's Seafood Shoppe opened on August 19, 1969, at 301 Southland Drive in Lexington, Kentucky. By 1989 there were more than 1,500 company- and franchise-operated Long John Silver's in thirty-six states, the District of Columbia, Canada, and Singapore.

Jerrico was a public company from 1969 until 1989, when it was acquired by two private investment firms. Rosenthal retired as Jerrico's chairman of the board in late 1989. The company's headquarters are in Lexington.   O. BRUCE HINTON, JR.

JESSAMINE COUNTY. The thirty-sixth county in order of formation, Jessamine County is located in the Inner Bluegrass region of central Kentucky. Formed on December 19, 1798, from a portion of Fayette, the 174-square-mile county is bordered by Garrard, Madison, Mercer, Woodford, and Fayette counties. The county was named for Jessamine Creek. The county seat, NICHOLASVILLE, was named for George Nicholas, who drew up the first Kentucky constitution.

The topography is gently rolling; the Kentucky River, the county's southern boundary, creates a deeply entrenched valley. In 1987 farms occupied 92 percent of the land area and 74 percent of farmland was in cultivation. The county ranked thirty-ninth in the state in agricultural receipts, from livestock, poultry, hay, corn, vegetables, fruits, tobacco, and nursery and greenhouse crops.

The rich farmland attracted early settlers such as John, Jacob, and Samuel Hunter, who staked out a nine-hundred-acre tract between Hickman Creek and the Kentucky River in the late 1770s. A number of early settlers were of German descent from Pennsylvania and Maryland and others of French Huguenot extraction. Hemp was established as a popular crop around 1796. By 1840 two-thirds of the hemp produced in the state came from Jessamine County, and Nicholasville had a number of rope walks, or hemp factories. As late as 1870, the county was producing 1.8 million pounds of hemp annually.

Whiskey distilling was an early industry. U.S. district court records listed Edmund Singleton, of Jessamine County, as one of the distillers who refused to register his distillery and was fined $250

by Judge Harry Innes on June 30, 1798. In 1801 a Jessamine County farm offered for rent included "a distillery sixty by thirty-four feet with stills and boilers for a house of that size." Around 1875, at Camp Nelson, the E.J. Curley Distillery was established on the Kentucky River in a complex of connected buildings constructed of limestone, known locally as the Great Stone Manor. In 1884, Curley operated two distilleries, one on each side of the river with a total mashing capacity of 1,100 bushels per day and production capacity of one hundred barrels per day. The distillery ceased operation in 1971.

CAMP NELSON, on the Kentucky River, was established in 1863 to recruit Union troops. It was also a haven for black families, some of whom were escaped slaves. A mile and a half above it is Camp Nelson National Cemetery, the burial place of soldiers from the Civil War to Vietnam.

Jessamine County was considered for many years a residential suburb for Lexington's workforce, but by the late twentieth century it had developed its own industrial base. In 1988 twenty-four manufacturing firms employed more than 2,000. In 1957 Faulkner-Fair Company began producing wood fixtures for banks, stores, and hotels. The Hayden Company, established in 1966, builds horse stall equipment and barns. The decade of the 1970s saw a number of industries move into the county: Gulf States Paper's carton division; Donaldson Company; Sargent and Greenleaf, makers of locks; and the automotive trim division of NL Industries. Mainline service is provided by Southern Railway System over the cantilever-designed High Bridge across the Kentucky River, seven miles south of Nicholasville. Highway U.S. 27 is a major north-south route.

Early leaders in education, the county's first schools were private. Bethel Academy was established in 1790; in 1802 Nancy LaFever operated a female academy; in 1859 Neil McDugal Gordon began a boys' school in Keene; and the Jessamine Female Institute was chartered in Nicholasville in 1854 and operated until 1910. ASBURY College and Theological Seminary is located in Wilmore.

Keene, four miles northwest of Nicholasville, grew up around a stone mill in 1794. The Keene Springs Hotel, a Greek Revival-style frame building constructed in 1877, was a popular health spa. Wilmore, three miles west of Nicholasville, the county's second incorporated town, was established by the Cincinnati Southern Railroad in 1876.

The population of Jessamine County was 17,430 in 1970; 26,146 in 1980; and 30,508 in 1990.

See Bennett H. Young, *A History of Jessamine County, Kentucky* (Louisville 1898); S. Duncan, *Jessamine County, Kentucky* (Anchorage, Ky., 1964).   RON D. BRYANT

JESSAMINE FEMALE INSTITUTE. The Jessamine Female Institute, located in Nicholasville, Kentucky, was organized in 1854 by leading citizens of Jessamine County and the Nicholasville Presbyterian Church. On March 5, 1850, the Kentucky General Assembly had approved legislation allowing funds to be raised to start a school to improve female education. In 1866 the General Assembly approved an act of incorporation for the Jessamine Female Institute. Direct affiliation with the Presbyterian church ended at that time.

The school grew from a small institute that served the local population to an institution respected throughout the South. Students from many southern states were housed on the campus and attended classes along with those from the surrounding area. The institute enjoyed its greatest popularity in the late 1800s, under the direction of Mattie Hewitt. Classes were offered on the primary, preparatory, and collegiate levels. A modern three-story school building was constructed in 1888, at the corner of Maple and Third streets in Nicholasville. School records indicate that there were typically ten to fifteen faculty members to teach 125 students. Between 1882 and 1893 five to sixteen students graduated each year. The school began to decline in the early twentieth century as competition from the newly organized public school system increased. In 1909 or 1910 the school was closed and its assets sold at a public auction. The main building burned in 1913. For many years class reunions were held in the homes of local alumni.

JEWS. Kentucky's Jewish history begins with the Gratz brothers, Bernard and Michael, of Philadelphia, who by the 1760s had extended their trading area as far west as the Mammoth Cave region. Michael Gratz and his brother helped outfit George Rogers Clark's expeditions, shipping some of the equipment through the town of Gratz in what is now Owen County. Joseph Simon, Michael's father-in-law, owned much of the site of present-day Louisville in partnership with John Campbell, who advertised in the *Virginia Gazette* on April 7, 1774, four years before Louisville was founded, his intention to lay out a town on the Falls of the Ohio. Benjamin Gratz, youngest son of Michael, settled in Lexington in 1819. He was a trustee of Transylvania University for sixty-three years.

The first charter for a Jewish house of worship in Louisville was obtained largely through the efforts of Abraham Jonas, a native of England who settled in Williamstown in 1827. He was elected to the General Assembly in 1828 and served several terms. Jonas helped to organize the Whig party in Kentucky, and in 1856 tried to nominate his friend Abraham Lincoln as Republican candidate for President. Jones moved to Illinois and worked for Lincoln in that state's legislature. He was in charge of arrangements for the Lincoln-Douglas debates of 1858. Another Lincoln supporter was attorney Lewis N. Dembitz, who moved to Louisville in 1853 and became active in civic and political affairs. Louis BRANDEIS, born in Louisville in 1856, was the first Jew appointed to the U.S. Supreme Court.

Jews took part in defense of their country in every war. Col. Gabriel Netter, who emigrated from France, was a lieutenant colonel in the Union army. Near Owensboro on September 19, 1862, he met a Confederate force that greatly outnumbered his contingent but refused to surrender and was killed in the ensuing skirmish. The county seat of Meade County was named for Col. Solomon Brandenburg, who fought in the War of 1812. Felix Moses, "Old Mose" of John Uri Lloyd's *Stringtown on the Pike* (1927), served with Morgan's Raiders during the Civil War and raised the Confederate flag over the capitol at Frankfort.

In the days of family-owned retail stores, Jewish families settled in many towns across Kentucky. The 1832 Louisville city directory lists the Jewish Benevolent Society. Adath Israel, the city's first congregation, was organized in 1836 and chartered in 1842. This congregation, now the Temple Adath Israel-Brith Sholom, is a bastion of Reform Judaism. After waves of immigration in the 1840s, 1880s, and early 1900s, other congregations were formed. In 1851 an Orthodox group founded Beth Israel, the forerunner of Adath Jeshurun (Conservative). In 1990 Louisville had two Orthodox, one Conservative, and two Reform congregations.

At one time there were Jewish congregations in Ashland, Covington, Henderson, Hopkinsville, Newport, Owensboro, and Paducah, but only those in Louisville, Lexington, Owensboro, and Paducah survive. The 1989 *American Jewish Year Book* lists Kentucky's Jewish population as 11,200, of whom two-thirds lived in Louisville. Louisville's Jewish Hospital is nationally renowned; the city's Jewish Community Federation is an umbrella organization for a broad range of community services and fundraising. Louisville has the third oldest Jewish Community Center in the nation; started in 1862, it celebrated the centennial of its incorporation in 1990. It serves as a recreational and cultural center for a membership of some 5,000, of whom about 25 percent are non-Jewish. A federation in Lexington serves central Kentucky. Both Louisville and Lexington have branches of national Jewish organizations and a network of educational and social services.

Some of the spiritual leaders of Kentucky congregations have earned national reputations through their writings and teachings, among them Rabbi Emil G. Hirsch (1851-1923), Rabbi Hyman G. Enelow (1877-1934), who held pulpits in Paducah and Louisville, and Joseph RAUCH (1879-1957).

Jerry Abramson, the first Jewish mayor of Louisville, was elected in 1985 and reelected in 1989. Circuit Judge Charles M. Leibson was elected to the Kentucky supreme court in 1982. Two decades earlier Samuel Steinfeld served on the court of appeals, then the state's highest court. Arthur KLING, who died in 1981, was known for his efforts on behalf of the aging. Distiller I. W. BERNHEIM, a philanthropist who established the 14,000-acre Bernheim Forest as a nature preserve open to the general public, also donated the Thomas Jefferson statue by Moses Ezekiel that stands near the Jefferson County Courthouse, and statues of Abraham Lincoln at the Louisville Free Public Library and the state capitol. Louisville was the original home of the FLEXNER brothers.

See I. W. Bernheim, *A History of the Settlement of Jews in Paducah and the Lower Ohio Valley* (Louisville 1912); Herman Landau, *Adath Louisville: The Story of a Jewish Community* (Louisville 1981).   HERMAN LANDAU

JILLSON, WILLARD ROUSE. Willard Rouse Jillson, geologist, was born in Syracuse, New York, on May 28, 1890. Beginning in high school, then at Syracuse University, Jillson pursued geology. He received his M.A. in 1915 at the University of Washington, and later studied at the University of Chicago and at Yale University.

In 1917, after working as a petroleum geologist in the South and West, Jillson moved to Kentucky, where he made astute deals in oil, gas, and coal leases and built an estate that allowed him to live comfortably. In 1919 Jillson became state geologist with the Kentucky Department of Geology and Forestry. He was appointed director and state geologist of the reorganized Kentucky Geological Survey in 1920 and held the position until his resignation in 1932. During these years the survey, and Jillson himself, published voluminously and achieved a significant goal by producing at least one map (scale 1:62,500) for every county in Kentucky. These activities contributed to the rapid development of coal and oil resources in the state. Jillson also served as chairman of the Kentucky Park Commission during 1924-28 and was a member of the commission until 1932, aiding in selecting the locations for the parks and writing a book about them.

In 1918 Jillson became assistant professor of geology at the University of Kentucky, and he was curator of the Kentucky State Museum during 1922-24. After his resignation as state geologist in 1932, he wrote extensively and served as a consultant for the coal and oil and gas industries. He served as professor of geology and chairman of the department at Transylvania University during 1947-51. He was first vice-president of the Kentucky Historical Society in 1958-59. Jillson was noted for his prolific writing on paleontology, mining, regional history, biography, bibliography, and the history of Kentucky literature. He produced more than sixty books and more than five hundred articles, brochures, and pamphlets. He and his wife, the former Oriole Marie Gormley, had four children. Jillson died on October 5, 1975, and was buried in the Frankfort Cemetery.

See Willard Rouse Jillson, *The Memoirs of Willard Rouse Jillson* (Frankfort, Ky., 1971).
                                                          IVAN L. ZABILKA

JOCKEY CLUB. The American Jockey Club was incorporated in New York City on February 10, 1894, by a group of prominent horsemen led by August Belmont II and Wall Street financier James R. Keene; they were determined to organize an administrative body for thoroughbred racing. Following the precedent of the English Jockey Club, established nearly 150 years earlier, the American Jockey Club is a nonprofit organization and the nine members of the board of stewards, who direct its affairs, receive no compensation. Membership is by invitation. The nearly one hundred members are distinguished not only by their contributions to thoroughbred breeding and racing, but also by their acknowledged leadership in the fields of politics, law, finance, industry, commerce, and sport.

One of the Jockey Club's first acts was to draw up standard rules of racing. Only thoroughbred racing conducted in accordance with these rules was recognized. As racing spread throughout the developing United States, regulatory authority passed to state racing commissions, but the Jockey Club rules of racing are the foundation on which all individual state racing rules are based.

In 1896 the Jockey Club assumed responsibility for maintenance of the American Stud Book, a register of all thoroughbreds foaled in, or imported into, the United States, Puerto Rico, and Canada. Registration in the Stud Book ensures the correct identification of every thoroughbred and, as such, is essential to the integrity of thoroughbred racing. No horse can run in a pari-mutuel thoroughbred race in North America unless it meets the requirements of the American Stud Book. The first six volumes of the American Stud Book were published by Col. Sanders D. Bruce, of Lexington, Kentucky. When the Jockey Club published its first volume, the foal crop totaled about 3,000. By 1986 the number exceeded 51,000, more than 17 percent of them foaled in Kentucky. Only advanced computer technology can cope with such large numbers.

The Jockey Club has maintained an office in Kentucky for more than thirty years, and in 1988 day-to-day management of the American Stud Book returned to Lexington. Its computer operations are among the most sophisticated in the country. Its data base holds the names of more than 1.6 million horses on a master pedigree file. The mainframe processor handles daily results of every thoroughbred race in North America, as well as processing electronically transmitted pedigree and racing data from England, Ireland, France, and other leading thoroughbred racing countries around the world.

The Jockey Club demonstrates dedication to thoroughbred breeding and racing in many ways, including establishment of the Jockey Club Information Systems, Inc.; support of the Grayson-Jockey Club Research Foundation, the Jockey Club Foundation, and Thoroughbred Racing Communications, Inc.; and the institution of the School for Racing Stewards at the University of Louisville. For almost a century, the Jockey Club has been recognized for its leadership in the funding and support of many education, research, and development programs aimed at the betterment of American thoroughbred breeding and racing.
                                                          JAMES H. PEDEN

JOHN POPE HOUSE. In 1810-11 the architect Benjamin Henry Latrobe designed for John POPE an exceptional suburban villa near Lexington, Kentucky. Trained in England, Latrobe had emigrated in 1795 to the United States and from then on practiced continuously in America as a professional architect. In 1803 President Thomas Jefferson had appointed Latrobe surveyor of public buildings, responsible for the continuing design and construction of the U.S. Capitol and the White House. John and Eliza Pope met Latrobe in Washington during Pope's U.S. Senate term (1807-13).

The most talented designer of the new republic, Latrobe developed an elegantly austere neoclassical style that perfectly suited the tone of Jeffersonian America. Other influential buildings by Latrobe were the Bank of Pennsylvania in Philadelphia (1798-1800) and the Baltimore Cathedral (1804-21).

The Pope house (now 326 Grosvenor Avenue in Lexington) is one of Latrobe's best surviving designs. Its plan is unique in American domestic architecture: a square with a domed, circular rotunda in the center of the second story. Latrobe drew inspiration from sixteenth century Italian architect Andrea Palladio, but unlike Palladio's villas, the severe cubic mass of the Pope house conceals within itself an imaginative sequence of rectilinear and curvilinear rooms splashed with light and shadow. Latrobe called these effects "interior scenery"; they reflect the influence of eighteenth century picturesque landscape planning. This fusion of classical sources and picturesque theory places the Pope house among the most sophisticated buildings of Federal America.

Later owners of the house altered it throughout the nineteenth century; twentieth century owners partitioned it into apartments. Fire damaged it in 1987. In that year, the Blue Grass Trust for Historic Preservation acquired and began a careful restoration of the Pope house.

See Clay Lancaster, *Ante Bellum Houses of the Bluegrass* (Lexington, Ky., 1961).

PATRICK A. SNADON

JOHNSON, ADAM RANKIN. Adam Rankin Johnson, Confederate general, was born February 8, 1834, to Thomas J. and Juliet (Rankin) Johnson in Henderson County, Kentucky. At the age of twenty, he moved to Texas, near Austin, where he was a surveyor. Johnson returned to Kentucky in 1861 to join the Confederate army. En route he volunteered as a scout for Nathan B. Forrest, barely escaping capture at the Battle of Fort Donelson in February 1862. When he arrived in Kentucky, Johnson joined the partisan rangers. On July 18, 1862, Johnson, along with twelve other men and several pieces of stovepipe mounted on a wagon to resemble a cannon, entered the town of Newburgh, Indiana, and captured two hundred Union guns without a fight. The victory earned him the nickname "Stovepipe," and in August he was promoted to colonel of the 10th Kentucky Partisan Rangers

unit. He participated in Gen. John Hunt Morgan's raids into Indiana and Ohio in July 1863, escaping Federal troops on July 19 by swimming across the Ohio River.

On June 1, 1864, Johnson was promoted to brigadier general. In the Battle of Grubb's Crossroads, Kentucky, on August 21, 1864, he was permanently blinded by a bullet accidentally fired by one of his men. Despite his blindness, he was briefly given command of the Department of Western Kentucky on September 6, 1864. He resigned the position on September 26 but stayed with the Confederate army, surrendering to Union forces near Macon, Mississippi, in April 1865. After the war, Johnson returned to Texas and founded the Texas Mining Improvement Company. He also contracted overland mail service and promoted the development of water power on the Colorado River. He founded the city of Marble Falls in 1887. His memoirs of the Civil War were published as *The Partisan Rangers of the Confederate States Army* (1904). He married Josephine Eastland, and they had six children. He died in Burnett, Texas, on October 20, 1922, and was buried in the State Cemetery in Austin.

See Lowell Harrison, "Kentucky-Born Civil War Generals," *Register* 64 (April 1966): 129-60.

JOHNSON, BEN. Born May 20, 1858, near Bardstown, Kentucky, the son of William and Nancy (Crow) Johnson, Ben Johnson, political boss, grew to maturity in the violence-filled era of the Civil War and Readjustment. His father, a state senator and acting lieutenant governor, included among his friends members of Quantrill's raiders. Friendly also with the James brothers, Johnson himself killed a man in an 1880 election-day struggle, exchanged shots with others on at least one other occasion, and engaged in several fights as a congressman. He carried a pistol all his life.

After expulsion for fighting at St. Joseph College in Bardstown, Johnson graduated with a master's degree from St. Mary's College in Lebanon in 1878, and received a law degree four years later from the University of Louisville law school. A shrewd businessman, attorney, and banker, and a generous donor to charity, Johnson gained much wealth and entered politics, first as Bardstown city attorney, then as legislator during 1885-88. At the age of twenty-nine, he was Speaker of the Kentucky House. Johnson was collector of internal revenue for the 5th District during 1893-97, a post that allowed Johnson to distribute hundreds of patronage positions to his Democratic supporters. Throughout his life, he firmly believed in rewarding allies and dealing ruthlessly with enemies.

Johnson sat as state senator in the 1906 session and was then elected to the U.S. Congress, where he served twenty years (1907-27). During that time, he made a strong impression as a generally faithful follower of President Woodrow Wilson's programs (although he moved slowly on the women's suffrage question) and a more controversial impression as the chairman of the District of Columbia Committee, where his frugality long angered Washington residents. In 1911 he sought the nomination for governor, but stepped down before the primary because of opposition to his Catholicism. He then determined to become "Boss Ben," the political power behind the gubernatorial throne. Long opposed to the Democratic faction led by J.C.W. BECKHAM and Percy Haly, Johnson, at age sixty-nine, began a second career on the State Highway Commission in 1927, appointed by Gov. William Fields (1923-27). From that powerful post, he successfully supported a Republican (Flem D. Sampson) over Beckham in the 1927 governor's race, promptly dominated the ensuing administration, and virtually controlled expenditures that made up half the state budget. His faction won the 1931 governor's race, but Johnson soon broke with the state's chief executive, Ruby Laffoon (1931-35), opposing the governor's sales tax. With his son-in-law J. Dan Talbott, Johnson had been A.B. Chandler's strongest ally and with Chandler's gubernatorial victory in 1935 expected continued rewards. But a bitter split again occurred and, after a half-century, Johnson's political power had ended.

Johnson's wife was the former Annie Kouwenbergh, whom he married in 1886. He died, at age ninety-two, on June 4, 1950, and was buried in St. Joseph's Cemetery in Bardstown.

See James C. Klotter and John W. Muir, "Boss Ben Johnson, the Highway Commission, and Kentucky Politics, 1927-1937," *Register* 84 (Winter 1986): 18-50.   JAMES C. KLOTTER

JOHNSON, ELLIS. Ellis Johnson, one of Kentucky's greatest all-around athletes, was born August 8, 1910, in Morehead, Kentucky, to George and Nancy (McGlove) Johnson. He was the star of Ashland High School's 1928 national championship basketball team, a first-team high school All-American, and an All-Kentucky football player in 1929. At the University of Kentucky he was a three-year starter in football (1930-32) and basketball (1931-33). He also played baseball and ran track. An outstanding playmaker in basketball, Johnson was team captain and first-team All-American at guard in 1933. He was named All-American for his defensive skills. He later was a successful college coach at Morehead State University in Kentucky (football, 1936-52; basketball, 1937-53) and then at Marshall University in West Virginia (basketball, 1963-69). Johnson was a charter member of the Kentucky Sports Hall of Fame, and Morehead State named its basketball arena in his honor. When he retired from coaching, he entered the insurance business. Johnson died on August 5, 1990. He is survived by his wife, Myrtle (McCoy) Johnson and their two children, Kenn and Barbara. He was buried at Golden Oaks Cemetery in Ashland.

See Bert Nelli, *The Winning Tradition: A History of Kentucky Wildcat Basketball* (Lexington, Ky., 1984).   JAMES C. CLAYPOOL

JOHNSON, GEORGE W. George W. Johnson, the first governor of Confederate Kentucky, was born near Georgetown in Scott County on May 27, 1811. His parents were William and Betsy (Payne) Johnson. In 1833 Johnson married Ann Viley; they had ten children, seven of whom lived to adulthood. Though he received three degrees from Transylvania University, he made little use of his legal training, choosing instead to become a prosperous and hospitable farmer.

Johnson was not politically ambitious, but he accepted election to the state House of Representatives in 1838, 1839, and 1840. A wealthy slaveholding Democrat, he supported John C. Breckinridge for president in 1860, but denied that Lincoln's election justified secession, for the Republicans controlled neither Congress nor the Supreme Court. When Kentucky's neutrality ended in September 1861, Johnson fled south to avoid arrest. In spite of his age and a crippled arm, he became a volunteer aide to Gen. Simon Bolivar Buckner in Bowling Green. Johnson was a key figure in the two conventions that met in Russellville in late October and November 1861, to declare Kentucky "a free and independent state." It was admitted into the Confederate States of America on December 10, 1861, with Johnson as its governor.

Johnson worked hard to create a viable government, but his jurisdiction extended only as far as the Confederate troops advanced. When the Confederates abandoned Kentucky in early 1862, Johnson and his associates followed the main army. Johnson joined the 4th Kentucky Infantry at Shiloh, and was wounded on April 7, 1862. He died the next day, and friends in the Union army arranged for his body to be returned to Georgetown for burial.

See Lowell H. Harrison, "George W. Johnson and Richard Hawes: The Governors of Confederate Kentucky," *Register* 79 (Winter 1981).
LOWELL H. HARRISON

JOHNSON, JAMES. James Johnson, congressman and soldier, was born January 1, 1774, in Orange County, Virginia, to Robert and Jemima (Suggett) Johnson. His father arrived in Kentucky in 1779, helped build Bryan's Station on the North Elkhorn Creek in Fayette County, and moved the family there in 1781. In the winter of 1783-84, his father built his own station, known as Great Crossing or Johnson's Station, where the Alanantowamiowee Trail intersected the North Elkhorn Creek in present-day Scott County. Johnson grew up there and obtained a preparatory education. The family was influential, and Johnson and his brothers, Richard, John, and Benjamin, were politically prominent.

From 1808 to 1811, Johnson was a representative of Scott County in the state Senate and served under his brother Richard as a lieutenant colonel in the War of 1812. With two of his sons in the company, he led a decisive charge into British lines at the Battle of the Thames on October 5, 1813. Johnson was also present at the Battle of New

Orleans in January 1815, as a major in Gray's regiment, Kentucky Detached Militia. In 1817-18 he promoted the stagecoach industry in the Bluegrass and organized several stagecoach companies, including Johnson, Weisiger and Company, a line that ran from Frankfort to Louisville. Johnson became a provision contractor with the U.S. Army and, although a contract to supply the Yellowstone Expedition (1818-19) hurt him financially, he was reputed to be one of the wealthiest men in Kentucky, with a plantation near Great Crossing in Scott County. He married Nancy Payne in Lexington. Johnson was elected to the U.S. House of Representatives and served from March 4, 1825, until his death in Washington, D.C., on August 13, 1826. He was buried in the family cemetery at Great Crossing.

See Ann Bolton Bevins, *A History of Scott County as Told by Selected Buildings* (Georgetown, Ky., 1981); J. Winston Coleman, Jr., *Stage-Coach Days in the Bluegrass* (Louisville 1935).

JOHNSON, KEEN. Kentucky's governor during 1939-43, Keen Johnson was born on January 12, 1896, at Brandon's Chapel, Lyon County, Kentucky, to Robert and Mattie (Holloway) Johnson. His studies at Central College, Fayette, Missouri, were interrupted by military service in World War I, when he saw overseas duty as an infantry lieutenant. He graduated from the University of Kentucky in 1922 with a journalism major. Johnson edited and published the Lawrenceburg *Anderson News*, then in 1925 moved to the *Richmond Daily Register*. In 1935 he defeated Republican J.J. Kavanaugh by more than 100,000 votes in the race for lieutenant governor. In 1939 he won the Democratic nomination for governor over John Y. Brown, Sr., in the August primary. When U.S. Senator M.M. Logan died in early October, Gov. A.B. Chandler resigned, and Johnson became governor; he appointed Chandler to the vacant Senate seat. In the November general election Johnson won easily over King Swope, 460,834 to 354,704. After his term ended in 1943, Johnson continued his association with the *Richmond Daily Register*. He was U.S. undersecretary of labor during 1946-47, a member of the Democratic National Committee in 1940-48, and he held several positions in the Reynolds Metal Company between 1944 and 1961. In 1960 he was the Democratic nominee for the U.S. Senate, but he lost to John Sherman Cooper in the general election. Johnson died in Richmond on February 7, 1970, and was buried there.

Johnson prided himself upon being "a saving, thrifty, frugal governor." Much of his administration was dominated by World War II, which forced curtailment of many domestic programs, but he was able to continue a number of programs that carried over from the Chandler administration. When he left office the state was out of debt and had a surplus in the general fund. Additional funds went to education, to the mental and penal systems, and to the social service programs. Johnson prodded the General Assembly into passing a bill to allow Kentucky cities to purchase and distribute electric power from the Tennessee Valley Authority. By calling a special session, he pressured reluctant legislators into making the first comprehensive redistricting of the state in nearly fifty years. Johnson said in 1939 that he would not be a spectacular governor, but in his quiet way he was an effective one.

See Willard Rouse Jillson, *Governor Keen Johnson: A Biographical Sketch* (Frankfort, Ky., 1940); Frederic D. Ogden, ed., *The Public Papers of Governor Keen Johnson* (Lexington, Ky., 1982).

LOWELL H. HARRISON

JOHNSON, LYMAN TEFFT. Lyman Tefft Johnson, civil rights leader and educator, was born on June 12, 1906, in Columbia, Tennessee, the eighth of nine children of Robert Graves and Mary (Dew) Johnson. All four of Johnson's grandparents had been slaves in Tennessee. His paternal grandfather, a carpenter, had saved enough money from extra work to buy freedom for himself and his wife.

After completing eleven grades at the local black school where his father was principal, Johnson received his high school diploma in 1926 from the preparatory division of Knoxville College. In 1930 he earned his bachelor's degree in Greek from Virginia Union University in Richmond and in 1931 was awarded a master's degree in history by the University of Michigan. Johnson began his forty-year teaching career in 1933 at Louisville's Central High School, where he spent thirty-three years as an instructor in history, economics, and mathematics. His last seven years as an educator were spent as an assistant principal at Parkland Junior High, Manley Junior High, and Flaget High School—all in Louisville.

While still a young man, Johnson began to fight segregation. During his tenure as president of the Louisville Association of Teachers in Colored Schools between 1939 and 1941, Johnson campaigned successfully for an end to inequalities in salaries paid to black and white teachers in the local schools. In 1949 he was plaintiff in the lawsuit that opened the University of Kentucky to black students. From 1978 to 1982 he served as a member of the Jefferson County Board of Education. From the beginning of his career, Johnson preached the gospel of education to his black students.

Johnson has been active in a number of professional and civil rights organizations, including the Kentucky Civil Liberties Union, the Urban League, and the Louisville chapter of the National Association for the Advancement of Colored People, which he headed for six years. In recognition of his many years of leadership in civil rights and education, he has received numerous plaudits and awards. In 1979 he was awarded an honorary doctor of letters degree by the University of Kentucky. In 1980 the Lyman T. Johnson Middle School was named in his honor by the Jefferson County Board of Education.

In 1936 Johnson married Juanita Morrell, who died in 1977. They were parents of a daughter, Yvonne, and a son, Lyman Morrell.

See Wade Hall, *The Rest of the Dream: The Black Odyssey of Lyman Johnson* (Lexington, Ky., 1988). WADE HALL

JOHNSON, RICHARD MENTOR. Richard Mentor Johnson, vice-president of the United States, was born on October 17, 1781, to Robert and Jemima (Sugett) Johnson at Beargrass, a frontier settlement on the site of what is now Louisville. In the same year the family moved to Bryan's Station, in Fayette County. His mother was considered a heroine of the siege of Bryan's Station in August 1782. Johnson started his formal education when he was fifteen. After attending Transylvania University in Lexington, he studied law under Col. George Nicholas and James Brown. In 1802 he was admitted to the bar and practiced at Great Crossing in Scott County. Johnson represented the county in the General Assembly from 1804 to 1806. He was then elected to the U.S. House of Representatives, serving from March 4, 1807, until March 3, 1819.

Johnson, a Jeffersonian Republican, was a supporter of President Thomas Jefferson and in 1812 cast his vote in Congress in favor of war against Great Britain. He was commissioned colonel in the U.S. Army and in early 1813 headed a regiment of Kentucky volunteers to fight the British in lower Canada. Johnson and his brother, Lt. Col. James Johnson, worked out a strategy for engaging the British forces in the Battle of the Thames on October 5, 1813. Severely wounded, Johnson emerged from the battle as a hero who was said to have killed the Indian chief Tecumseh. The rumor worked to Johnson's political advantage, although the facts of Tecumseh's death remain unknown.

In February 1814 Johnson returned to his seat in Congress, serving until 1819. That year, in the midst of the economic panic, he was reelected to the state legislature and helped enact a law that ended imprisonment for debt in Kentucky. He served out the term of U.S. Senator John J. Crittenden, who had resigned, and was then reelected to the Senate, serving from December 10, 1819 to March 3, 1837. He was loyal to President Andrew Jackson and his policies. Johnson campaigned as Martin Van Buren's vice-presidential running mate. As no candidate received a majority of the electoral votes, he was elected vice-president (1837-41) by the Senate. Defeated for reelection in 1840, Johnson was again chosen to represent Scott County in the Kentucky legislature (1841-43). Johnson then retired from political life for several years but returned to the General Assembly in 1850, serving until his death.

Johnson was interested in education and was a devout Baptist, affiliated with the Great Crossing Baptist Church. In Congress in 1821 he introduced legislation to charter Columbian College in the District of Columbia. With Johnson's guidance and management, the Choctaw Academy was set up on his Blue Spring farm near Great Crossing, under the 1825 Treaty of Dancing Rabbit. Johnson directed the activities and finances of the Indian boys' school.

Johnson had two daughters, Imogene and Adaline, born to Julia Chinn, a mulatto slave given to him as part of his father's estate. His political opponents maligned his character for his relationship with Chinn, who died of cholera in the summer of 1833. Johnson died on November 19, 1850, in Frankfort, and was buried in the Frankfort Cemetery. Johnson County, named for him, was created in 1843 from parts of Floyd, Lawrence, and Morgan Counties.

See Leland Winfield Meyer, *The Life and Times of Colonel Richard M. Johnson of Kentucky* (New York 1932).

JOHNSON, ROBERT. Robert Johnson, pioneer and legislator, son of William and Elizabeth (Cave) Johnson, was born on July 17, 1745, in Orange County, Virginia. In April 1779 Johnson, accompanied by his brother Cave and William Tomlinson, joined the Bryant family in traveling to Kentucky to establish a station on the North Elkhorn River, which became known as BRYAN'S (Bryant's) STATION. Tomlinson and Cave stayed with the Bryants to help build the station and Johnson went on to the Lexington area. He returned to Virginia in June 1779 and prepared his family for the move to Kentucky. In the late fall of 1780, the Johnsons arrived at Bryan's Station. In 1783 Johnson began construction on his own station, Great Crossing, on the North Elkhorn Creek. The 2,000-acre settlement was fifteen miles from Bryan's Station and its eastern border was about two miles west of present-day Georgetown.

Johnson was a community leader and an industrious man. A commissioned officer, he was well known as an Indian fighter and joined Gen. George Rogers Clark's expeditions against the Indians in the summer of 1780 and the fall of 1782. He was elected to Virginia's General Assembly in 1782 and in 1783 became a trustee of Transylvania University. Johnson and his wife became charter members of the Great Crossing Baptist Church in 1785. He participated in both the framing of the first state constitution in Danville in 1792 and the second constitutional convention at Frankfort in 1799. He was Woodford County's first senator and served eight terms, from 1796 to 1813, as representative of Scott County. In 1796 Johnson and Judge John Coburn established the boundary line between Kentucky and Virginia. President John Adams assigned Johnson the task of evaluating slaves and property in Kentucky in 1798. He was also a commissioner of the gentleman justices of Scott County and served as a trustee of Rittenhouse Academy (now the site of Georgetown College) in Georgetown. In 1808 Johnson began construction of a new settlement, Fredricksburg (now Warsaw, Kentucky).

Johnson married Jemima Suggett in 1770. They had eleven children; their four sons, Richard M., James, Benjamin, and John, achieved prominence in their own right. Johnson's wife died in 1814 and he married Fanny Bledsoe in March 1815. Johnson died on October 15, 1815, and was buried at the Great Crossing Baptist Church near Georgetown.

See Mrs. William H. Coffman, "Big Crossing Station, Built by Robert Johnson," *FCHQ* 5 (Jan. 1931): 2-15; Leland Winfield, "Colonel Robert Johnson, A Pioneer Leader in Education and Religion," *Register* 30 (Jan. 1932): 21-23.

JOHNSON COUNTY. Johnson County, the nineteenth county in order of formation, is located in eastern Kentucky and is bordered by Morgan, Lawrence, Martin, Floyd, and Magoffin counties. The county contains 264 square miles in the watershed of the Levisa Fork of the Big Sandy River. Named for Richard M. Johnson, it was created in 1843. Parts of Floyd, Lawrence, and Morgan counties went to make up Johnson; PAINTSVILLE was chosen as the county seat. Other communities are Flat Gap, Staffordsville, Hager Hill, East Point, River, Offut, Thelma, Whitehouse, Oil Springs, Van Lear, and West Van Lear.

Human occupation of present-day Johnson County dates back at least to the Adena culture. In 1938 a Works Progress Administration crew, under the supervision of an archeological team from the Universities of Kentucky and New Mexico, excavated four Adena burial mounds along Paint Creek in Paintsville. According to local legends, by the seventeenth century Johnson County may have been inhabited by a Native American group known as the Totero. Their principal village was at Hager Hill. The Totero were probably related to the Siouian-speaking Tutelo of southwestern Virginia and they may have migrated southward with the Tutelo into western North Carolina. Anglo-Americans from Virginia began to explore the area during the 1750s. Dr. Thomas Walker's party traveled down Paint Creek in 1750 and other whites may have hunted in the area prior to the first permanent settlement, at the site that is now Blackhouse Bottom.

By 1860 the population of the county exceeded 5,000, including twenty-seven slaves and nineteen free blacks. Even though most Johnson Countians remained loyal to the Union during the Civil War, the fiscal court in October of 1861 ordered that anyone publicly raising a Union or Confederate flag would be fined fifty dollars. While both Union and Confederate armies marched through the county during the war, the only substantial skirmish occurred along Jenny's Creek on January 7, 1862.

Coal mining has dominated the economic history of Johnson County. As early as the 1840s, two Johnson County men opened a coal yard in Greentown. In 1888, the Chatterawha Railroad was extended from Ashland to White House to transport the cannel coal being mined there. Largely through the efforts of John C.C. Mayo, the Chesapeake & Ohio extended its line to Paintsville in 1904.

Shortly thereafter, major coal companies began to develop the mineral wealth of the county. The Northeast Coal Company developed mines in the vicinity of Thealka and White House. Consolidation Coal Company purchased the rights to develop the extremely rich Miller's Creek seam. In 1909 Consolidation Coal began to build a model company town on Miller's Creek. The community was named for company director Van Lear Black. Within ten years, Van Lear was the largest town in the county, with a population of more than 4,000.

Unlike Northeast Coal, Consolidation did not rely exclusively on local labor. Van Lear soon had a significant number of immigrants from Eastern Europe and Afro-Americans from the lower South. On Labor Day 1924, thousands of people gathered in Paintsville to witness a parade of two hundred robed members of the Ku Klux Klan.

Coal mining in Johnson County slowly declined after 1946, when Consolidation Coal began to sell off its coal lands to the Farwest Coal Company, which ceased operations in 1955. Even though most of the deep mines were closed by 1960, nineteen strip mines were operating in Johnson County as late as 1973.

In 1970, the state began construction of the Carl D. Perkins Rehabilitation Center in Thelma. In 1980, the U.S. Army Corps of Engineers completed work on a dam at the juncture of Little Paint Creek and Open Fork. Paintsville Lake, four miles west of the city, stretches for eighteen miles and covers more than 11,000 acres. Recreational facilities have been added at various points to make the lake accessible to boaters and swimmers.

Like much of the Big Sandy region, Johnson County has been flooded repeatedly. Major inundations occurred in 1862, 1918, 1929, 1936, 1939, 1955, 1957, 1962, 1963, and 1977. In 1957 the Levisa Fork crested in Paintsville at forty-six feet—fourteen feet above flood stage. The rising waters did more than $4 million worth of property damage. Dams on John's Creek in Floyd County and Little Paint Creek in Johnson County have helped in flood control.

Famous Johnson Countians include entrepreneur John C.C. Mayo, physician Paul B. Hall, poet Rose Wiley Chandler, and country singers Loretta Lynn and Crystal Gayle.

The population of Johnson County was 17,539 in 1970; 24,432 in 1980; and 23,248 in 1990.

See J.K. Wells, *A Short History of Paintsville and Johnson County* (Paintsville, Ky., 1962); C. Mitchell Hall, *Johnson County, Kentucky: A History of the County and Genealogy of Its People Up to the Year 1927* (Louisville 1928).

THOMAS D. MATIJASIC

JOHNSTON, ALBERT SIDNEY. Albert Sidney Johnston, soldier of three republics, was born February 2, 1803, in Washington, Kentucky, the son of John and Abigail (Harris) Johnston. He was educated in private preparatory schools and at Transylvania University. In 1826 Johnston graduated from the U.S. Military Academy, eighth in his class. In 1832 he served in the Black Hawk War as adjutant to the commanding general. Two years later, at the urging of his invalid first wife, he resigned his commission, and two years after that he migrated to the Republic of Texas, where he became the senior general of the Texas army and later the secretary of war. In the Mexican War he served gallantly as a staff officer in the Battle of Monterrey in September 1846. In 1849 he reentered the regular army of the United States as a major and was assigned the duty of paymaster to the frontier posts in Texas.

In 1855 he received command of the newly created, elite 2d Cavalry Regiment, with promotion to the rank of colonel. Among his subordinates were such distinguished officers as Lt. Col. Robert E. Lee and Majs. William J. Hardee and George H. Thomas. Two years later Johnston commanded the expedition dispatched to quell the Mormon rebellion in Utah Territory, and was promoted to the rank of brevet brigadier general. In 1860 he became commander of the Department of the Pacific, with headquarters in San Francisco, where he was located at the time of the secession of the seven states of the lower South.

Johnston disapproved of secession in principle, but he feared and hated abolition and when Texas, his adopted state, separated, he resigned his command. With deep reluctance, he decided to go with the Confederacy. "It looks like fate," he said. "Texas has made me a Rebel twice." In the summer of 1861 he journeyed from California to Richmond, Virginia, where he offered his services to the Confederacy. At that time, he was perhaps the nation's most respected military figure, except for the aged and infirm Gen. Winfield Scott. Johnston also enjoyed the advantage of having been a fellow cadet of Jefferson Davis, who on September 10, 1861, appointed him to command Confederate Department No. 2, the western theater of operations. Johnston received the rank of general, second in seniority only to the elderly Adj. Gen. Samuel Cooper.

In February 1862 Johnston suffered a severe defeat in the loss of Forts Henry and Donelson in Tennessee to a Union army-navy attack led by Brig. Gen. Ulysses S. Grant. With the advanced Confederate line irreparably breached, Johnston withdrew his forces all the way to the rail center of Corinth, Mississippi. On April 6 he attacked Grant's unsuspecting army encamped in the vicinity of Shiloh Methodist Church near Pittsburg Landing on the Tennessee River. The blow came close to destroying the Union force, but in the early afternoon, at the climax of the assault, Johnston was killed and the momentum temporarily lost. Gen. Pierre G.T. Beauregard, second in command, took over and, in the late afternoon, halted the engagement until the following morning. That night Grant received heavy reinforcements, and the next day he counterattacked and drove the Confederates back to Corinth.

Johnston's death so early in the war leaves open the question of his capacity as a general. He was indecisive and ineffectual in the action that lost the Tennessee forts, and he appeared hesitant in comparison with the brilliant and volatile Beauregard. But in the Shiloh operation, Johnston clearly outgeneraled Grant in concentrating his forces for one of the most remarkable strategic surprises in military history. Johnston also demonstrated superiority over Beauregard in poise, judgment, and determination. Late in the afternoon of the day before the battle, at the point that the renowned war philosopher Clausewitz identifies as the "moment of truth" in every military campaign, Johnston ordered the attack to proceed over the vehement objection of his unnerved second in command. It is a fair surmise that Johnston would have been a great asset to the Confederacy if he had lived to develop his capabilities fully.

Johnston was married on January 20, 1829, to Henrietta Preston of Louisville, who bore him three children; she died on August 12, 1835. In October 1843 he married Eliza Griffin of Louisville, who bore him five children and who survived him by thirty-four years. Johnston was buried first in New Orleans and then in the Texas State Cemetery at Austin.

See Charles P. Roland, *Albert Sidney Johnston: Soldier of Three Republics* (Austin, Tex., 1964); William Preston Johnston, *The Life of General Albert Sidney Johnston* (New York 1878).

CHARLES P. ROLAND

JOHNSTON, ANNIE (FELLOWS). Annie (Fellows) Johnston, author of popular children's books, was the daughter of the Rev. Albion and Mary (Erskine) Fellows, born on May 15, 1863, in Evansville, Indiana. She attended Evansville Public School, where she taught for one term before attending the University of Iowa in 1881-82. She returned to her teaching position in Evansville for three years and then worked as a stenographer. On October 11, 1888, she married her second cousin, William L. Johnston, a widower with three children, Mary, Rena, and John. During her marriage Johnston wrote short stories for her stepchildren, which were occasionally published in various children's magazines. After William Johnston died in 1892, she began to write children's novels to support her family. Her first work, *Big Brother*, was published in 1893.

In 1894, on a trip to Pewee Valley, Oldham County, Kentucky, Johnston was inspired to write *The Little Colonel* (1895). The series of eleven novels that followed, most of them set in Pewee Valley, were among the most popular children's literature of the time. For many Little Colonel fans, the community of Pewee Valley nearly became a shrine. Her romanticized children's novels were translated into several foreign languages. In her thirty-six-year career Johnston wrote thirty-eight books, most of them loosely based on actual places and people. Through her vivid imagination, keen observation, and memories of her own childhood, she created charming characters of high integrity who encounter situations where simple virtues and good intentions always triumph. A minor character in the series, Mary Ware, became the protagonist in another series of novels. Johnston's novels idealized attitudes and a way of life that appealed to contemporary sentimental tastes.

Johnston and her stepchildren moved to Pewee Valley in 1898. Rena died in 1901. The family moved to the Southwest in 1901 for John's health, living in Arizona, California, and Texas. John died in 1910, and Johnston and Mary returned to Pewee Valley. She purchased a home, the Beeches, where she lived and worked until her death on October 5, 1931. Johnston was buried in Evansville, Indiana.

See Annie Fellows Johnston, *The Land of the Little Colonel: Reminiscence and Autobiography* (Boston 1929).

JOHNSTON, JOSIAH STODDARD, SR. Josiah Stoddard Johnston, Sr., lawyer, journalist, and political figure, son of John Harris and Eliza Ellen (Davidson) Johnston, was born on February 10, 1833, in New Orleans, Louisiana. After the deaths of his mother in 1833 and his father in 1838, Johnston moved with his brothers to Kentucky to live with relatives, the George Hancocks. He first attended Samuel V. Womack's classical school and then the Western Military Institute in Georgetown. Johnston began studying law at Yale in September 1850 and graduated in 1853. After receiving his law degree in 1854, he moved to Arkansas, where he became a successful cotton farmer. In 1859, he returned to Kentucky, settling in Scott County to farm. He entered the Confederate army in 1862 and became a distinguished staff officer to Gens. Braxton Bragg, Simon Buckner, and John C. Breckinridge. Johnston was promoted to lieutenant colonel and served until May 1865. At war's end he returned to Arkansas and practiced law at Helena.

In 1867 Johnston moved to Frankfort, Kentucky, where he became editor of the *Kentucky Yeoman* until it closed in 1886. He helped establish the KENTUCKY PRESS ASSOCIATION and was its president during 1870-86. He was selected adjutant general of the state in 1871. Johnston was secretary of state of Kentucky during 1875-79. As either chairman or secretary of the Democratic state committee during 1868-88, he wielded much political power in Kentucky. Johnston moved to Louisville in 1889, and from 1903 to 1908 was associate editor of the *Louisville Courier-Journal*. He also wrote *A Memorial History of Louisville* (1896), *First Explorations of Kentucky* (1898), and *Confederate History of Kentucky* (1898). Johnston became president of the Filson Club in 1893, remaining in this position until his death.

Johnston married Eliza Johnson, the daughter of George Johnson, who became Kentucky's provisional Confederate governor, on June 13, 1854; they had five children: Mary, Eliza, George, Harris, and Stoddard, Jr. Johnston died on October 4, 1913, in Clayton, Missouri, and was buried in Cave Hill Cemetery in Louisville.

See George Baber, "J. Stoddard Johnston," *Register* 14 (Jan. 1916): 9-13.

JOHNSTON, WILLIAM PRESTON. William Preston Johnston, lawyer and writer, the eldest son of Henrietta (Preston) and Gen. Albert Sydney Johnston, was born on January 5, 1831, in Louisville. His mother died when he was four years old, and his father soon after left for Texas, leaving Johnston to be raised by his mother's family. He attended public schools and later the academy of S.V. Womack in Shelbyville, Kentucky. He graduated from Yale in 1852 and studied law at the University of Louisville. In the spring of 1853 he opened a practice in Louisville.

At the outbreak of the Civil War, Johnston joined the Confederate Army and was made a major in the 2d Kentucky Regiment, rapidly advancing to lieutenant colonel. After being stricken with pneumonia, Johnston served as aide-de-camp to President Jefferson Davis, with the rank of colonel, starting in May 1862. At the end of the war, Johnston was held captive along with President Davis for several months.

After a year in Canada, Johnston returned to his Louisville law practice. In 1867 he became chairman of the department of history and English literature at Washington University in Lexington, Virginia, a position offered by the university's president, Gen. Robert E. Lee. Johnston was president of Louisiana State University at Baton Rouge in 1880. Two years later, he began to organize the University of Louisiana in New Orleans. It was renamed Tulane University in 1884, and Johnston was its president until his death.

Johnston's biography of his father, *Life of General Albert Sidney Johnston* (1878), contains one of the best accounts of the Battle of Shiloh. His other works include *The Prototype of Hamlet and Other Shakespearian Problems* (1890), as well as three books of poetry: *My Garden Walk* (1894), *Picture of the Patriarchs* (1895), and *Seekers After God: Sonnets* (1898). His family record, *The Johnstons of Salisbury*, was published in 1897.

Johnston married Rosa Elizabeth Duncan of New Orleans on July 6, 1853; they had six children. His first wife died on October 19, 1885, and he married Margaret Henshaw Avery, of Louisiana, on April 25, 1888. Johnston died on July 16, 1899, and was buried in Louisville's Cave Hill Cemetery.

See William Preston Johnston, *The Johnstons of Salisbury* (New Orleans 1897).

JOINER, CHARLES HARVEY. Charles Harvey Joiner, artist, was born on April 8, 1852, to Charles and Elizabeth Joiner in Charlestown, Indiana. In his teens, Joiner worked as a house painter and journeyman sign painter. In the spring of 1874, Joiner became assistant to the German-born portrait painter Hans Hoffman in St. Louis. The following year he worked in Illinois and Utica, Indiana, where he received a substantial commission from the Christian Church. In 1880 he opened a portrait studio in the *Courier-Journal* building in Louisville, where he lived for twenty-seven years. He was a member of the Louisville Artists' League and kept a studio in Louisville, even after he moved to Pittsburgh.

In Pittsburgh Joiner painted several portraits of steel magnates. He also completed a series of portraits of the first five governors of Indiana, which were hung in the first capitol at Corydon. Early in the 1920s Joiner made a tour of Colorado and the West Coast, where he painted landscapes of the Rocky Mountains. He is perhaps best remembered for his numerous landscapes of Kentucky beechwood trees.

Joiner married Helen Annette Cain of Jeffersonville, Indiana. He died on May 30, 1932, and was buried in Walnut Ridge Cemetery in Jeffersonville.

JOLAS, MARIA (McDONALD). Writer and translator Maria (McDonald) Jolas was born in Louisville in January 1893, the daughter of Donald and Betsie (Carr) McDonald. In 1925, while studying voice in France, Maria McDonald met journalist and critic Eugene Jolas (whose brother Jacques Jolas was later the first dean of the University of Louisville's School of Music, 1932-35). McDonald and Jolas were married soon afterward and together the couple founded the influential literary review *transition*, published in Paris from April 1927 to February 1939. Maria served as typist, copy editor, proofreader, translator, and business manager. *Transition* published Gertrude Stein, Ernest Hemingway, Samuel Beckett, and James Joyce, among others. To the Joyces Maria rendered numerous kindnesses, including the postwar rescue of Joyce's papers and possessions from a Paris attic.

Maria Jolas directed a French-English school before World War II, worked for peace in the 1960s and 1970s, and translated into English the novels of Nathalie Sarraute. She died in Paris on March 4, 1987, survived by two daughters, Betsy and Tina, and five grandchildren. She was buried beside her husband in the village of Chérence.

See Shari Benstock, *Women of the Left Bank: Paris, 1900-1940* (Austin, Texas, 1986).

JOHN SPALDING GATTON

JONES, DANIEL J. Daniel J. Jones, state geologist of Kentucky during 1934-58, was born near German, New York, on January 16, 1889. He earned bachelor's and master's degrees in geology from Syracuse University, taught at the University of Texas during 1914-17, then joined the petroleum industry. Shortly thereafter Jones moved to Kentucky, where he has been credited with the discovery of the Big Sinking oil field in eastern Kentucky, the largest known in the state. While state geologist, Jones pioneered in the development of Kentucky's oil, gas, and water resources. He married Matilda Gilcher and they had one daughter, Charlotte. Jones died in Lexington on December 18, 1965, and was buried in Syracuse, New York.

See Preston McGrain "Daniel J. Jones," *Bulletin of the American Association of Petroleum Geologists* 50 (July 1966): 1526. PRESTON MCGRAIN

JONES, DAVID ALLEN. David Allen Jones, chief executive officer and chairman of the board of Humana, Inc., was born on August 7, 1931, in Louisville to Evan L. and Elsie F. (Thurman) Jones. He graduated from the University of Louisville in 1953 with a B.A. in mathematics and accounting and a year later became a certified public accountant. Following three years in the U.S. Navy, Jones entered Yale law school, receiving his degree in 1960. In 1961 he and Wendell CHERRY cofounded Humana, a national investor-owned hospital corporation headquartered in Louisville. In 1987 Jones donated buildings from one of his other enterprises, a gift worth more than $5 million, to the Presbyterian Church (USA), which moved its national headquarters to Louisville. Jones married Betty L. Ashbury on July 24, 1954; they have five children—David, Susan, Daniel, Matthew, and Carol.

ALLEN J. SHARE

JONES, JOHN LUTHER. John Luther ("Casey") Jones, railroad engineer, was born on March 14, 1864, in Fulton County, Kentucky. His nickname came from his hometown, Cayce. At the age of eighteen Jones went to Jackson, Tennessee, to work for the Mobile & Ohio Railroad. In 1888 he became an engineer for the Illinois Central Railroad. As tribute to his skill, Jones was made engineer in January 1900 on the New Orleans Special, popularly known as the "Cannonball," the fastest passenger train between Chicago and New Orleans.

On the foggy evening of April 29, 1900, Jones pulled into the Memphis, Tennessee, station, the end of his run. Because relay engineer Joe Lewis was ill, Jones and his fireman Simeon Wells were asked to take the Cannonball through to Canton, Mississippi. They agreed and their engine, No. 382, was attached. Close to Vaughan, Mississippi, near the end of the run, two freight trains prepared to pull onto the siding to allow the passenger train to pass, but the air hose on train No. 83 broke, freezing the wheels and stalling the caboose and three freight cars on the main track. Jones's attempt to divert was futile, and seeing the impending disaster he told Wells to jump to safety. Jones was able to slow the train sufficiently to save the lives of Wells and all of his passengers. He was the only casualty of the crash, dying on April 30, 1900, at 3:53 a.m. His courage in staying with the train was commemorated in the well-known ballad "Casey Jones," written by Wallace Saunders a few days after the accident. It was recorded in the 1920s by both Fiddlin' John Carson and Furry Lewis. A special U.S. postage stamp in honor of Jones was issued as part of the series Railroad Engineers of America in 1950.

Jones married Janie Brady of Jackson, Tennessee, on November 25, 1886, and they had three children. Jones was buried at Jackson.

See Belden Kittredge, *The Truth About Casey Jones* (Girard, Kans., 1945).

JONES, LOUIS MARSHALL. Country music singer and banjo player Louis Marshall ("Grandpa") Jones was born in Henderson County, Kentucky, on October 20, 1913, to sharecroppers David C. and Arcadia (Wise) Jones. He spent his childhood in Kentucky, Indiana, and Ohio, leaving school in 1928 for an Akron, Ohio, radio show. During the 1930s he had radio programs in Ohio and West Virginia and toured New England with Bradley KINCAID. He was featured on Cincinnati station WLW's "Boone County Jamboree" during 1941-44. He performed on the "Grand Ole Opry" in 1946, left it for other radio programs, then rejoined it in 1959. In 1969 he became a charter member of the cast of the "Hee Haw" television program. In 1978 he was elected to the Country Music Hall of Fame.

See Louis M. Jones and Charles K. Wolfe, *Everybody's Grandpa: Fifty Years Behind the Mike* (Knoxville, Tenn., 1984).   CHARLES F. FABER

JONES, LOYAL. Loyal Jones, scholar and teacher, was born on January 5, 1928, in Cherokee County, North Carolina, the son of George and Cora (Morgan) Jones. Jones served in both the army and the navy after World War II. He received a B.A. from Berea College in 1954 and a master of education degree from the University of North Carolina at Chapel Hill in 1961. In 1958 he joined the staff of the Council of the Southern Mountains and served as executive director from 1967 to 1970. In 1970 he became director of the Appalachian Center at Berea College. An authority on Appalachian music and religion, Jones is the author of numerous articles on mountain life and culture and the books *Radio's "Kentucky Mountain Boy" Bradley Kincaid* (1980) and *Minstrel of the Mountains: The Story of Bascom Lamar Lunsford* (1984). He is also the editor or coeditor of several books on Appalachian humor.

GERALD F. ROBERTS

JONES, ROBERT ELLIOTT. Robert Elliott ("Jonah") Jones, jazz trumpeter, was born in Louisville on December 31, 1909. He began his professional career playing on a Mississippi riverboat and performed with the bands of such greats as Jimmie Lunceford, Fletcher Henderson, Benny Carter, Cab Calloway, and Earl Hines before he began working as a soloist in 1955. At that time, he achieved international success with his recordings of show tunes and jazz standards, which featured him on muted trumpet as the leader of his own quartet. He also appeared frequently on national television. Jones is considered one of the great jazz swing trumpeters and his improvised solos have been cited as models, along with his extensive work with mutes.   LEE BASH

JORRIS, ANN E. (GRIDER). Ann E. (Grider) Jorris, legislator, was born August 26, 1873, in Russell County to Fred W. and Sarah E. Grider. The second of seven children, she was raised on the family farm in the Cumberland River Valley. She attended a local one-room school, St. Theresa's Academy, and the Southern Normal School at Bowling Green, Kentucky. During the 1890s, she taught school and assumed the responsibility of raising her younger brothers and sisters after the early death of both parents. In 1926 she served a term in the Kentucky General Assembly. A Republican known as "The Lady from Russell," she represented Casey and Russell counties. During the late 1920s and early 1930s, she served as a supervisor for the Kentucky houses of reform at Greendale in Fayette County and then retired to a farm in Russell County. She married H.G. Jorris on November 19, 1903. They had four children: Herman, William, Ruth Blair, and James. She died on June 15, 1953, near Orleans, Indiana, and was buried at Fernwood in Henderson, Kentucky.

JOUETT, JAMES E. James E. Jouett, naval officer, was born February 7, 1826, near Lexington, Kentucky, the son of portrait artist Matthew Harris and Margaret Henderson (Allen) JOUETT. Young Jouett, who entered naval service as a midshipman in 1841, had a long and varied career. He saw blockade duty in the Mexican War and was on one of the ships that accompanied Commodore Matthew Perry's expedition to Japan in the 1850s. During the Civil War, his exploits included the capture of several blockade runners and command of the fast gunboat *Metacomet* under David G. Farragut at Mobile Bay. After the war Jouett held several shore assignments; at sea his highest post was command of the North Atlantic Squadron from 1884 to 1886. He was promoted to captain in 1874, commodore in 1883, and rear admiral in 1886. Jouett retired in 1890.

In 1852 Jouett married Galena Stockett and they had one son, James Stockett. Jouett died September 30, 1902, at a country home in Maryland and was buried in Arlington National Cemetery.

See George Baber, "Rear Admiral James E. Jouett," *Register* 12 (May 1914): 11-16.

LLOYD GRAYBAR

JOUETT, JOHN. John ("Jack") Jouett, pioneer legislator, was born in Albemarle County, Virginia, December 7, 1754. At the outbreak of the Revolutionary War, he served as a captain in the Virginia militia. He is best known for his act of courage in June 1781, when he rode from his home on North East Creek, six miles east of the Louisa, Virginia, courthouse to Charlottesville, Virginia, to warn Gov. Thomas Jefferson and the Virginia legislators of an impending attack by Banastre Tarleton's horsemen. Because of Captain Jouett's night ride, Jefferson and most of the legislators escaped capture. For his courageous service the legislature awarded him a sword and a pair of pistols, but did not deliver them until 1803. Jouett emigrated to Kentucky and settled in Mercer County in late

1782. He represented Mercer County in the Virginia Assembly in 1787 and 1790 and was a strong advocate of the separation of Kentucky. He was also a delegate to the separation convention in Danville in 1788. Later, when Kentucky became an independent state, he represented Mercer County in the House of the General Assembly in 1792. In 1795-97 he represented Woodford County. Jouett moved to Bath County, where he gained a fine reputation as a hospitable host, and he imported purebred cattle.

Jouett married Sallie Robards, a member of a well-known Kentucky family, in 1784. They were the parents of the portrait painter Matthew Harris JOUETT. John Jouett died on March 1, 1822.

THOMAS D. CLARK

JOUETT, MATTHEW HARRIS. Matthew Harris Jouett, one of the most significant antebellum portraitists of the South, was born on April 22 in 1787 or 1788 near Harrodsburg in Mercer County, Kentucky. He was one of twelve children born to Capt. John and Sallie (Robards) Jouett. When Jouett was five, his family moved to Woodford County. He enrolled in Transylvania University in Lexington in 1804. After graduating with honors four years later, Jouett began to study law with Judge George M. Bibb of the Kentucky appellate court in Frankfort.

In 1812 Jouett enlisted in the 3d Mounted Regiment of the Kentucky Volunteers. He was appointed first lieutenant and paymaster of the 28th U.S. Infantry and on July 13, 1814, was promoted to a captain. He resigned his position on January 20, 1815. Jouett decided not to practice law but to follow his ambition to become a portrait painter and miniaturist, based in Lexington. After studying with Gilbert Stuart in Boston from July through October 1816, he was able to double his price for portraits.

Jouett was unable to make a living in Kentucky, however, and from 1817 until his death, he spent winters in New Orleans, Natchez, and other southern cities along the Mississippi River, painting portraits of notable citizens. The New Orleans directory of 1824 lists Jouett as a portrait painter with a studio at 49 Canal Street. From 1817 to 1825 Jouett's Lexington studio was in the Kentucky Hotel on Short Street. In June 1817 Jouett arranged an exhibition of his paintings and those of other artists for the benefit of the Fayette Hospital.

A total of 334 portraits and miniatures are attrib-

uted to Jouett between the years 1816 and his death. One of the most celebrated is that of General Lafayette. He painted several portraits of Henry Clay, one of which hangs in Ashland, the Clay estate. Other subjects included Gen. George Rogers Clark, Gov. Isaac Shelby (1792-96, 1812-16), Sen. Isham Talbot, Dr. W.C. Galt, Asa Blanchard, Robert Crittenden, and Dr. Horace Holley. In 1826 Jouett maintained a studio in Louisville as well as Lexington.

As popular as Jouett's portraits were in the South, he did not become known nationally until his paintings of Gen. Charles Scott and John Grimes were shown in the Chicago Exposition in 1893. Jouett's first one-man exhibition was a retrospective held at the J.B. Speed Art Museum in Louisville between February 19 and March 4, 1928. Jouett's paintings are owned by the Filson Club, the Kentucky Historical Society, and the Speed Museum, as well as numerous private collectors.

Jouett married Margaret Henderson Allen of Fayette County on May 25, 1812; they had nine children. Jouett died at his home outside Lexington on August 10, 1827, and was buried in the family burial ground of his father-in-law, William Allen. Around the turn of the century, the bodies of Jouett and his wife were reburied in Louisville's Cave Hill Cemetery.

See Samuel M. Wilson, "Matthew Harris Jouett, Kentucky Portrait Painter," *FCHQ* 13 (1939): 75-97.

JUDD, NAOMI AND WYNONNA. The mother-daughter duo of country music singers known as Naomi and Wynonna Judd were both born in Ashland, Kentucky. Naomi was born on January 11, 1946, to Glen and Polly Judd, who named her Diana. She married Michael Ciminella; their daughter, Christina (who sings as Wynonna Judd) was born on May 30, 1964. In 1968 the family moved to Hollywood. After the Ciminellas' marriage ended, mother and daughter returned briefly to Kentucky. They lived in San Francisco before moving to the Nashville area in 1979, where Naomi worked as a nurse. The father of one of her patients arranged an audition with RCA records for her and her daughter in 1983. Known as the Judds, the two won the Country Music Association's Horizon award in 1984 and Record of the Year in 1985, and they won Grammys in 1985 and 1986. Naomi married Larry Strickland in 1989.

CHARLES F. FABER

K

KAUFMAN, MOSES. Moses Kaufman, businessman and politician, was born in Bavaria on January 15, 1843, the son of Menke and Rela (Strauss) Kaufman. He immigrated to the United States in 1857 and worked in the clothing trade in Cincinnati before settling in Lexington, Kentucky, in 1869. There Kaufman operated a clothing business with a series of partners, and at the same time developed a reputation as an authority on Jewish history, the Bible, and literature in general. In 1879 Kaufman, a Democrat, was elected to the Lexington City Council, where he served for seventeen years. He also served as a member of the Lexington school board, as city treasurer and auditor, and as a state representative. Kaufman was instrumental in securing a modern waterworks and an advanced fire alarm system for the city of Lexington. The University of Kentucky also benefited from his support. Toward the end of his political career, Kaufman served as Lexington's postmaster, retiring shortly before his death. He is credited with establishing door-to-door mail delivery for the city. Kaufman was married to Esther Levy of Cincinnati; they had five children, one of whom died in infancy. Kaufman died in Lexington on October 10, 1924, and was buried in the Lexington Cemetery.

LEE SHAI WEISSBACH

KAVANAUGH ACADEMY. Rhoda (Caldwell) Kavanaugh established the Kavanaugh Academy, "the Annapolis of Kentucky," in Lawrenceburg in 1903, initially to tutor her own daughters. In 1909 the Anderson County board of education incorporated it into the public school system as Anderson County High School. In 1920 it was renamed Kavanaugh High School.

Kavanaugh was a preparatory school for students from all over the United States seeking to enter the Annapolis naval academy and West Point military academy, as well as a high school for day students. Young men who boarded at Rhoda Kavanaugh's home, "the house boys," attended day classes at Kavanaugh with local students. In the evenings Kavanaugh herself coached her students for entrance examinations at Annapolis. By the time she retired in 1946, 150 of her students had entered the naval academy and fifteen had entered the U.S. Military Academy at West Point. Kavanaugh taught for fifty years and served as principal of the school from 1909 until 1946. In 1949 Kavanaugh High School and Lawrenceburg High School were merged to form Anderson High School.

KAZEE, BUELL HILTON. Buell Hilton Kazee, a minister known for his folk music, was born on August 29, 1900, in Magoffin County, Kentucky, to John Franklin and Abigail Jane Kazee. A graduate of the Baptist Magoffin Institute and Georgetown College and an ordained minister for fifty-two years, Kazee served churches in Lexington and-Morehead, Kentucky, and taught at Lexington Baptist College. He collected folk music as a hobby, and at one point during his life made dozens of recordings of folk songs, accompanying himself on the banjo. During 1926-30 he recorded fifty-two songs for Brunswick and Vocalion in New York. In 1928 Kazee first performed for Columbia Records, in Johnson City, Tennessee, and his songs later appeared under the Folkways label.

Kazee was also the author of two books on religion and one on banjo techniques. He married Lucille Jones in 1928; they had two sons, Allen and Philip Ray, both of whom became ministers. He married Jennie Turnmeyer in 1950. Kazee died on August 31, 1976, in Winchester, Kentucky, and was buried in Marsh Fork.

See Charles K. Wolfe, *Kentucky Country* (Lexington, Ky., 1982).   CHARLES F. FABER

KEATS, GEORGE. George Keats, businessman, was born in London, England, on February 28, 1797. Orphaned at an early age, Keats attended a private boarding school along with his two older brothers, Thomas and John, who was to become one of England's great poets. Soon after Keats married Georgiana Wylie in June 1818, they sailed for America. They lived for a few months in Henderson, Kentucky, where Keats lost his money in a boat investment, then moved to Louisville in 1819. Soon after, Keats's brother Thomas died, and with his inheritance, Keats invested in a lumber mill and another boat, this time with success. He became one of Louisville's wealthiest citizens and a great benefactor. In addition to operating lumber and flour mills and dealing in real estate, Keats served on the town council, led a revision of the Louisville schools system, ran several railroads, helped print the first city directory, and promoted the construction of the first bridge at Louisville to cross the Ohio River.

Keats died suddenly on December 24, 1841, survived by his wife and eight children: Georgiana, Rosaline, Emma, Isabel, John, Clarence, Ella, and Alice. Keats is buried in Western Cemetery in Louisville.

See Naomi J. Kirk, "George Keats," *FCHQ* 8 (April 1934): 88-96; Hyder Edward Rollins, ed., *The Keats Circle: Letters and Papers, 1816-1878* (Cambridge, Mass., 1948).

KEELBOATS. The keelboat was used in the late eighteenth and early nineteenth centuries mainly to haul cargo along the Ohio and Mississippi rivers. The carvel-built hull, pointed on both ends, and the keel, usually a four-inch-square beam running the length of the bottom, made the vessel easy to steer, and the keelboat, unlike a flatboat, could travel upstream. Though all keelboats shared the same design, they were built in many different sizes. Most fell into one of three categories. Regular keelboats were about forty feet long and seven to nine feet wide. Larger vessels, called barges, were approximately one hundred feet long and twenty feet wide. On both sizes, a single cabin was constructed on deck for the crew and cargo. A third class of riverboat, the packet, was designed to transport passengers rather than freight; a packet averaged 120 feet long and had separate cabins, as well as toilet facilities, for men and women.

Though keelboats were sometimes outfitted with sails, they might also be rowed or poled, especially when moving against the current. Poling a boat was hard work. Standing on running boards along the sides of the boat, the crew (usually six to eighteen men) set long poles on the bottom of the river and pushed upstream. Despite this laborious, time-consuming method, keelboats delivered goods at a lower cost than wagons traveling overland. After the danger of Indian attack in the Ohio Valley had passed, around the mid-1790s, keelboats became a common sight on the waterways. Carrying goods such as cotton from the Deep South, tobacco, and hemp, these boats made trade profitable between such distant cities as New Orleans and Pittsburgh.

Keelboat shipping began to decline during the 1820s when steamboats assumed primacy on America's main rivers. The larger, faster ships could transport goods and passengers in less time than keelboats. On some of the smaller tributaries of the Ohio and Mississippi rivers, however, keelboats transported freight to the main river ports as late as 1840, when railroads made them obsolete.

See Leland D. Baldwin, *The Keelboat Age* (Pittsburgh 1941).

KEENELAND. The Keeneland Association owns the 1 1/16-mile Keeneland Race Course six miles west of Lexington, Kentucky, where thoroughbred racing began in 1936. As well as three-week race meetings in April and October, Keeneland conducts four of the world's top thoroughbred sales each year. The race course complex, which is a NATIONAL HISTORIC LANDMARK, also houses one of the finest thoroughbred research libraries. The profits of Keeneland, a non-dividend-paying corporation, go for purses to horsemen, capital improvements, and contributions to charitable, educational, and research organizations.

Race-goers at Keeneland are a privileged lot who can park their cars in the shade of long rows of trees before watching the prime products of the Bluegrass race in their natural setting. The horses are saddled around the tall trees of the paddock—sugar maple, dogwood, linden, white pine, crab apple, pin oak, and a huge sycamore. Altogether, Keeneland has thirty-nine varieties of trees on the grounds, as glorious in spring pastels as they are in the blaze of autumn. Unlike other racetracks, which require credentials for entrance to the stable area, Keeneland's forty-six horse barns are open to anyone. The race course is unusual in many respects; it has no public-address system. As well as the main track, there is a 7½-furlong turf course and a ⅝-mile training track. Keeneland's training facilities are open year-round.

Derby fever is in the air at Keeneland's spring meeting, where the Blue Grass Stakes is a major derby prep race. Of the horses that have raced at Keeneland in the spring of their three-year-old seasons, twenty-two have gone on to win the Kentucky Derby. Sixteen of them, including Strike the Gold in 1991, ran in the Blue Grass Stakes.

The Keeneland yearling sales in July attract buyers from all over the world to Lexington. The first two days of the auction are the Selected Yearling Sale; the third day attracts horses with slightly less strict standards for pedigrees. The Keeneland yearling sales in July and September have produced twelve Kentucky Derby winners, starting with Hoop Jr., Derby winner in 1945. Other Derby winners who have graduated from the Keeneland auction ring are Jet Pilot (who triumphed in 1947), Dark Star (1953), Determine (1954), Venetian Way (1960), Majestic Prince (1969), Dust Commander (1970), Canonero II (1971), Spectacular Bid (1979), Alysheba (1987), Winning Colors (1988), and Sunday Silence (1989). Four Epsom Derby winners also have been sold at Keeneland: Sir Ivor (1968), The Minstrel (1977), Golden Fleece (1982), and Secreto (1984).

The world-record price for a horse of any breed sold at public auction was set at Keeneland in 1985 when a son of Nijinsky II and My Charmer was purchased for $13.1 million. The syndicate that bought the colt included European soccer-pool baron Robert Sangster, Irish trainer Vincent O'Brien, and Greek shipping magnate Stavros Niarchos. The colt, Seattle Dancer, was bred in partnership by Warner L. Jones, Jr., William S. Farish III, and William S. Kilroy.

The concept of using Keeneland Race Course for sales as well as racing was expressed in the original prospectus for Keeneland in the mid-1930s. But it was not until the summer of 1943 that a yearling sale was first held on the grounds—and then only because of World War II. Before the war, many Kentucky breeders sent their yearlings to Saratoga, New York, each summer to sell. But a wartime restriction on the types of transport by train changed that. The first sale at Keeneland was conducted by Fasig-Tipton in 1943 under a tent in the Keeneland paddock. At that auction, 312 yearlings sold for a total of $929,850, an average of $2,980. (In 1984 323 yearlings were sold at the two-day selected auction for a record $175,932,000, or an average of $544,681, also a record.)

In 1944 Fasig-Tipton chose not to hold a second sale at Keeneland, and the breeders decided to carry the ball themselves, forming a cooperative known as the Breeders' Sales Company. Through a lease arrangement, Breeders' Sales remained a "partner" with Keeneland until 1962, when the company was dissolved. The Keeneland Association then took over the business of selling thoroughbreds.

Besides the yearling auctions in July and September, Keeneland also sells horses of all ages in

January and breeding stock in November. In the January sale, John Henry—two-time horse of the year—changed hands as both a yearling (1976) and a two-year-old. JAMES BOLUS

KELLEY-KOETT MANUFACTURING COMPANY. The Kelley-Koett Manufacturing Company in Covington, Kentucky, at 210-218 West Fourth Street, was incorporated in 1905 to manufacture the "Grosse Flamme," a pioneer X-ray apparatus invented by the European-trained Albert Koett and later displayed at the Smithsonian Institution. The Virginia-born promoter of the invention, J. Robert Kelley, established a close business relationship with the Mayo Clinic, and in 1917 the U.S. army arranged for the Covington company to manufacture X-ray tables for ambulance services in Europe. After the premature death in 1937 of Covington native Wilbur S. Werner, engineer and president of the company, "Keleket" gradually faded as one of the nationally prominent X-ray manufacturers. The business was transferred out of Covington in 1956. JOHN H. BOH

KELLY, ELEANOR (MERCEIN). Eleanor (Mercein) Kelly, novelist and traveler, was born on August 30, 1880, in Milwaukee, Wisconsin, to Thomas Royce and Lucy (Schley) Mercein. She received her high school education at Georgetown Convent of the Visitation in Washington, D.C., where she was valedictorian of her class in 1898. She moved to Louisville in 1901. Eleanor Mercein married Robert Morrow Kelly, Jr., of Louisville, on June 4, 1901.

Kelly's first novel, *Toya the Unlike*, was published in 1913. Her next three books, set in Kentucky, have strong female characters: *The Kildares of Storm* (1916), which takes place in the foothills of the uplands; *Why Joan?* (1919), which describes the three courtships of a young society woman in Louisville; and *The Mansion House* (1925), which portrays the life of an orphan. Kelly's novel *Basquerie* (1927) chronicles the life and romantic adventures of a wealthy family in the Basque county of Spain. Her last book, *Proud Castle* (1951), is about the Magyars of Hungary, reflecting Kelly's many travels to southern and Eastern Europe. Kelly was the director of the Louisville Arts Club and held memberships in the Louisville Woman's Club, Colonial Dames of America, and the National Arts Club of New York.

She died on October 11, 1968, in Louisville. Her body was cremated and buried in a family lot in Milwaukee, Wisconsin.

KELLY, JOHN SIMMS. He arrived on the University of Kentucky (UK) campus in 1928 driven by a chauffeur, he called a press conference before one of the football games in which he played, to predict a fifty-yard touchdown run, and he refused to warm up until the crowd reached 12,000. He was John Simms ("Shipwreck") Kelly, born in Springfield, Kentucky, on July 10, 1910. Kelly was raised by his grandparents, John and Prudence Simms, after his mother's death. At UK Kelly was known for long runs, including the predicted fifty-seven-yard touchdown against the University of Alabama in 1931. During his varsity career, 1929-31, UK was 16-6-3, and he gained more than 2,000 yards, scoring 126 points. He holds the UK record for most yards gained by a player in a single game—280 vs. Maryville (1930). Kelly was a charter member of the Kentucky Athletic Hall of Fame.

After graduation Kelly played quarterback for the Brooklyn Dodgers of the National Football League, which he bought in 1933. He made national news on June 30, 1941, by marrying the glamorous socialite Brenda Diana Duff Frazier, heiress to $3.5 million. After their 1956 divorce, he married Catherine Manning Hannon on July 10, 1956. He made millions in Florida real estate and he worked as an undercover agent for the Federal Bureau of Investigation during World War II. Kelly lived in Manhasset on Long Island. He died on August 17, 1986, in Pompano Beach, Florida, and was buried on Long Island. He was survived by two children, Victoria and John Kelly.

KELLY, WILLIAM. William Kelly, inventor of the "air-boiling" process of steel production, was born August 11, 1811, in Pittsburgh. The son of Irish immigrants John and Elizabeth (Fitzsimmons) Kelly, he studied metallurgy at Western Pennsylvania University in Pittsburgh. He and his brother, John, joined forces in the Pittsburgh dry-goods firm of McShane and Kelly, for which William served as company agent in Kentucky, Tennessee, Indiana, Ohio, and Pennsylvania. While on a business trip in the summer of 1846, Kelly bought an iron works in Eddyville, Kentucky, and sent for his brother to join him in the iron-making business (see IRON INDUSTRY). Kelly reopened this furnace as the Eddyville Ironworks and began construction of the Suwanee furnace nearby in 1847. In October 1847, at one of these two sites, Kelly made a discovery that would transform the iron industry into the modern steel industry. "After close observation and study," he wrote, "I conceived the idea that, after the metal was melted, the use of fuel would be unnecessary—that the heat generated by the union of the oxygen of the air with the carbon in the metal would be sufficient to accomplish the refining and decarbonizing of the iron."

Kelly constructed a series of small, unsuccessful converters in the forest in an effort to prove his theories. His father-in-law, James N. Gracey, who owned a substantial financial interest in Kelly's operations, questioned the sanity of experimenting with such a controversial process and suggested that the family physician examine Kelly. Dr. George Huggins gave Kelly a clean bill of health. In 1851 one of Kelly's prototype converters produced the first decarbonized iron by the process. The iron worked well in the forge and was used to produce high-quality boilerplate for steam engines.

Meanwhile, in Great Britain, Henry Bessemer, a British iron maker, had designed machinery that closely approximated Kelly's process. In 1856

Bessemer applied for and received a U.S. patent for the technique, which became known as the Bessemer process. Upon hearing of this development, Kelly also applied for a patent. A hearing ensued and Kelly was awarded a patent for his process. Bessemer retained the patent for his converter. Kelly and his brother went bankrupt in 1857, and he sold the patent to his father to keep it from falling into the hands of his creditors. When their father died in 1860, Kelly's sisters transferred the patent back to Kelly in trust for his children. Following the failure of his Kentucky venture, Kelly worked for the Cambria Iron Company in Johnstown, Pennsylvania. The first steel made under his patent was produced in 1864 in Wyandotte, Michigan, by adding a compound patented by the English metallurgist Robert Mushet. The three patents of Kelly, Bessemer, and Mushet were pooled by the Pneumatic Steel Association in 1870. Kelly received more than $450,000 in royalties from steel manufacturers. More a scientist than an entrepreneur, Kelly reaped neither the fame nor the fortune that Bessemer did.

Kelly died in Louisville on February 11, 1888, and is buried in St. Louis Cemetery.

See Corinne Whitehead, "William Kelly and the Air Boiling Process of Steel Making," *Journal of Jackson Purchase Historical Society* 1 (June 1973): 30-35. MICHAEL HUDSON

KENDALL, AMOS. Amos Kendall, journalist, was born in Dunstable, Massachusetts, on August 16, 1789, the son of Zebedee and Molly (Dakin) Kendall. He spent his boyhood working on his father's farm, where he absorbed his family's deep-seated Congregationalism and regard for public morality. Despite a scanty formal education, Kendall entered Dartmouth College at age eighteen, where he became a diligent, occasionally rowdy student and a part-time country schoolteacher. Kendall graduated at the head of his class in 1811 and read law for two years with attorney William Richardson of Groton, Massachusetts.

At age twenty-five, Kendall went to Washington, D.C., where he met Sen. Jesse Bledsoe of Kentucky, who offered him a poorly paid tutoring job and the use of his library. When Kendall arrived in Kentucky, after running out of money and walking the distance from Cincinnati to Lexington, Bledsoe's family had not heard of the tutoring arrangement. After a chance meeting with the wife of Henry Clay, Kendall became tutor to the five Clay children. He then worked briefly at the *Minerva*, a Georgetown newspaper, and in October 1816 he moved to Frankfort to become editor of the *Argus of Western America*.

At the *Argus* Kendall developed a reputation for keen political analysis and elegant writing; he also attracted enemies, among them the editor of the *Louisville Public Advertiser*, who accused him of crass opportunism and partisan treachery when he turned against Henry Clay. During the Kentucky crisis over relief to debtors, Kendall wrote hundreds of impassioned editorials and partisan articles in support of the Relief and New Court parties (see RELIEF CRISIS).

After his final break with Clay in 1826, Kendall put his influential pen to the task of securing a victory for Andrew Jackson in the 1828 presidential election. After the financial collapse of the *Argus*, Kendall moved to Washington, D.C., where he was a powerful member of Jackson's Kitchen Cabinet from 1829 to 1837. For six years, the soft-spoken, prematurely white-haired Kendall was fourth auditor in the U.S. Treasury; he served as postmaster general for five years under Jackson and Martin Van Buren, working to purge the department of corruption. During his final year as postmaster general, Kendall assumed the editorship of a Jackson–Van Buren newspaper, the *Washington Extra Globe*. He also drafted major portions of five of Jackson's annual messages to Congress, the better part of the president's address vetoing the charter of the Second Bank of the United States, and many letters and articles published under Jackson's name.

After leaving government service in 1840, Kendall wrote extensively for the *Globe* (then edited by Francis Preston Blair) and tried repeatedly to start his own newspaper. By the early 1840s, Kendall was hounded by lawsuits originating in controversies with mail contractors during his years as postmaster general. To make ends meet, he reluctantly agreed in 1843 to become an agent for groups which had claims against the federal government, including the Cherokee. Kendall tilled a small farm near Washington; in 1843, his biography of Andrew Jackson was published. On one occasion, Kendall was sentenced to debtors prison and was saved only by a special appropriation by Congress and a favorable Supreme Court decision on the mail contractors' lawsuits.

In 1845 Kendall became the business agent for the inventor of the telegraph, Samuel F.B. Morse; by the 1850s both men were comfortably wealthy, and Kendall could devote time to writing and philanthropy. On the eve of Abraham Lincoln's election as president, Kendall wrote vigorous essays opposing secession; and, while he remained a Democrat, he staunchly resisted disunionism as well as attempts within the Democratic party to ensure white supremacy in the South. After the Civil War, Kendall opposed Radical Republican Reconstruction policies.

In 1823 Kendall's wife, Mary (Woolfolk) died; three years later, he married the very young Jane Kyle, of Georgetown, Kentucky. Kendall died on November 12, 1869.

See William Stickney, ed., *Autobiography of Amos Kendall* (New York 1872); Leonard White, *The Jacksonians: A Study in Administrative History, 1829–1861* (New York 1954).

SANDRA F. VANBURKLEO

KENNEDY, MATTHEW, JR. Matthew Kennedy, Jr., an early architect, was born on August 12, 1781, the son of Matthew and Jane (Buchanan) Kennedy of Augusta County, Virginia. The younger

Kennedy moved to Kentucky, locating in Lexington about 1796. He started building about 1800, but no record survives of his work prior to 1814, when he designed and built the second Kentucky statehouse at Frankfort, a project that must have demanded considerable experience. In 1816 Kennedy returned to Lexington to supervise construction of Transylvania College's main building. His design for the building had been chosen over that of Benjamin Latrobe, the leading architect in the country. By the time the cornerstone was laid for his Grand Masonic Hall in Lexington in 1824, Kennedy had adopted the title architect, the first Kentuckian to do so. The last major public building by Kennedy was Transylvania University's 1827 medical hall, the school's first building designed for that specific use. No public building by Kennedy survives, but a number of his residences do.

Kennedy was the first architect to develop a distinctive residential building type in the Bluegrass region. All the residences are similar in design to that of his own house, constructed shortly after 1816 on Limestone Street: a two-story brick house having a raised basement and covered by a hipped roof. The facades are organized by four brick pilasters rising to a broken cornice, with a pediment containing a lunette placed above. Kennedy built a number of these houses in the Bluegrass region from 1816 until his retirement in the early 1840s, including Grassland in Fayette County. Kennedy's style is also found in houses in Frankfort, Bardstown, and Lebanon.

On September 11, 1811, he married Jane C. Smith of Versailles. The Kennedys and their four sons, Samuel, Thomas, Benjamin, and Matthew, moved to Louisville in 1840. Kennedy died on April 17, 1853, and was buried in Cave Hill Cemetery.

See Clay Lancaster, *Vestiges of the Venerable City* (Lexington, Ky., 1978).

WILLIAM B. SCOTT, JR.

KENNEDY, THOMAS. Thomas Kennedy, son of John Kennedy and his first wife, whose name is unknown, was born on September 11, 1757, probably in North Carolina. In 1775 Kennedy was a captain of dragoons in the North Carolina militia and fought in several Revolutionary War battles. In 1776 the Kennedy family migrated to Kentucky. Between tours of duty, Thomas purchased land in present-day Garrard and Madison counties. In 1780 Kennedy moved permanently to Kentucky. In 1788 and 1791 he served as a Kentucky delegate to the Virginia Assembly. He became a brigadier general of the Kentucky militia in 1792 but resigned his commission in 1793. In 1792 he was a member of the first Kentucky constitutional convention and served on the commission that selected Frankfort as the capital. From 1792 to 1793 Kennedy was senator from Madison County in the Kentucky General Assembly. He also served in the Kentucky House of Representatives from Garrard County from 1799 to 1802, then in 1805, 1807, 1818, and 1824. Kennedy

owned approximately two hundred slaves and a plantation estimated at 7,000 to 10,000 acres four miles west of Paint Lick, making him one of Kentucky's largest landholders and slaveowners. It has been said that it was Kennedy's plantation to which Harriet Beecher Stowe referred in her novel *Uncle Tom's Cabin*, although many places claim to be the setting of the book.

Kennedy married Agnes Ross; they had one daughter. His second wife was Edna Withers; they had four children. At his death on June 18, 1836, Kennedy was survived by his third wife, Elizabeth (Miller) Kavanaugh Kennedy. He was buried at the Paint Lick Cemetery. Legend has it that the family was warned for unknown reasons not to erect a monument on Kennedy's grave. The headstone set up by the family was struck by lightning, as were the two subsequent headstones placed on Kennedy's grave.

See Jonathan T. Dorris and Maud W. Dorris, *Glimpses of Historic Madison County* (Nashville 1955); David G. McDonald, *Kennedy of Kentucky* (Columbia, Mo., 1981).

KEN-RAD COMPANY. The Ken-Rad Company, a manufacturer of vacuum tubes, was founded in 1918 in Owensboro, Kentucky, by Roy Burlew, a native of Emporium, Pennsylvania. Burlew formed Ken-Rad, originally called the Kentucky Radio Company, out of the Kentucky Electrical Lamp Company, which he had purchased. Kentucky Electrical Lamp, founded in 1899, was a major producer of incandescent light bulbs, including the bulbs for the illumination of the Pan American Exposition in Buffalo, New York, in 1901. Burlew turned to the manufacture of vacuum tubes for radio sets in the early 1920s. The vacuum tube business boomed with the popularity of radio, and Ken-Rad began expanding, not pausing even for the Great Depression of the 1930s, as sales of radio sets continued to increase. Ken-Rad was one of the first companies in Kentucky to secure government defense and war contracts, and was so vital to the war effort that, when threatened with a strike in 1944, it was seized by the War Department under direct orders from President Franklin D. Roosevelt. Burlew sold Ken-Rad to the General Electric Company in 1945, and it was sold to MPD Corporation in 1987.

See Leonard Rex, "The Seizure of the Ken-Rad Plant, 1944," *Daviess County Historical Quarterly* 2 (April 1984): 27-31.

LEE A. DEW

KENTENIA CORPORATION. A land company that leased coal and timberland to developers, Kentenia Corporation, incorporated in 1907, took its name from the states of Kentucky, Tennessee, and Virginia, where its landholdings lay. Its holdings came from the 86,000-acre Ledford, Skidmore, and Smith patent issued in 1845 and purchased in 1870 by Edward Mott Davis of Philadelphia. In 1901 his grandson Charles Henry Davis took steps to make the property leasable, arranging for geological surveys and initiating legal action to clear the title. At the height of its prosperity, the company controlled over one hundred square miles of land in Harlan and Bell counties in southeastern Kentucky. In 1919 it donated land for Kentenia State Forest in Harlan County, the first state forest. The company was purchased by the Norfolk & Western Railroad in 1980 for $20 million; at that time it had coal reserves estimated at 118 million tons.

H. FRED HOWARD AND JAMES S. GREENE III

KENTON, SIMON. Simon Kenton, pioneer settler, was born April 3, 1755, in Fauquier County, Virginia, the son of Mark and Mary (Miller) Kenton. Kenton refused to attend school and remained illiterate all his life, learning only to sign his name. At age sixteen, he fought with William Leachman over a girl. He knocked Leachman unconscious and, believing he had killed him, ran away from home. Kenton assumed the name Simon Butler and worked his way to Pittsburgh, where he met adventurers who persuaded him to travel down the Ohio River in search of "cane-lands." After several attempts, he and Thomas Williams entered Limestone Creek (now the site of Maysville) in the spring of 1775 and went into the interior. There they found tall cane, cleared it, made a rough camp, and planted some corn, probably the first cultivated by white men north of the Kentucky River. Kenton and Williams are considered the first permanent settlers of Mason County. In the autumn, Kenton moved to Boonesborough.

For the next few years, Kenton traveled through Kentucky meeting fellow pioneers, including Daniel Boone, Robert Patterson, and George Rogers Clark. In 1777 Clark appointed him spy for defense of the frontier. Kenton is credited with saving the life of Boone during an Indian attack at Boonesborough. In 1784 he built a station on Lawrence Creek in Mason County to which he welcomed incoming settlers. His first guests included the widow Dowden and her four daughters, one of whom, Martha, became his bride on February 15, 1787. They were the first to be married at his station. Four children were born prior to December 1796. As Kenton's family grew, he built a brick house for them near his station. He operated a store in Washington, near Maysville, and hired Israel Donalson, teacher, to keep his books. The new house caught fire, and Martha, who was pregnant with their fifth child, was burned and died of shock. Within fifteen months, Kenton married Elizabeth Jarboe, Martha's first cousin. They had five children. In 1798 he moved to Ohio, where he spent his later years, often in poverty but still a traveler. He made four trips to Missouri, where he bought more land, visited Boone, and considered relocating in the new state.

Kenton managed his finances poorly, lost large acreages of land, and while on a visit to Washington, Kentucky, in 1820, was imprisoned for debt. As he was a popular figure, the jailer, Thomas Williams, allowed him considerable freedom, and the citizenry were incensed by his incarceration. Kenton was released from prison on December 17, 1821, after the Kentucky legislature repealed the Debtor's Law. Kenton died on April 29, 1836, near Zanesville, Ohio, and was buried there. In 1865 his remains were moved to Urbana, Ohio. In 1840 the Kentucky legislature created a new county out of the western half of Campbell County and named it in Kenton's honor.

See Edna Kenton, *Simon Kenton, His Life and Period* (Salem, N.H., 1930); Thomas D. Clark, *Simon Kenton, Kentucky Scout* (New York 1943).

JEAN W. CALVERT

KENTON COUNTY. The nineteenth county in order of formation, Kenton County is located in northern Kentucky along the Ohio River. Bordered by Boone County on the west, Campbell County on the east, and Grant and Pendleton counties on the south, Kenton County occupies 163 square miles. Formed by the legislature on January 29, 1840, from Campbell County, it was named in honor of the pioneer Simon Kenton. Its county seats are COVINGTON and INDEPENDENCE.

In 1751 Christopher Gist, one of the first pioneers in Kenton County, led a party of men sent by the Ohio Land Company to explore the region. As they traveled down the Ohio River, they landed at what is known as the Point. A noted landmark in frontier days, at the confluence of the Ohio and Licking rivers, the Point was used as an encampment by Daniel Boone and Simon Kenton, and Gen. George Rogers Clark in the 1780s mounted his expedition against the Indians from this location. On February 8, 1815, the state legislature established the town of Covington at the Point.

Its advantageous position along the Ohio River brought a steady flow of settlers, particularly German immigrants to the county, and the years before the Civil War were ones of growth and prosperity. Covington emerged as a major riverport. The city's Riverside district, with its many historic buildings, was the heart of Covington during the height of the steamboat era.

With the coming of the Civil War, Kenton County experienced political turmoil. Because of Covington's strategic position on the Ohio River, coupled with its close proximity to Cincinnati, the approaches to the city were fortified. Fort Mitchell and Fort Wright were built in response to the Confederate invasion of Kentucky in 1862. Despite its close association with the North, Kenton's Confederate sympathies were so strong that between July 28 and August 11, 1864, several people were arrested by Gen. Stephen Burbridge on suspicion of disloyalty to the Union.

After the close of the war, Kenton County began rebuilding its disrupted markets with the deep South, as well as maintaining its economic ties with the North. In 1867 these efforts were augmented by the completion of the suspension bridge designed by John Roebling. Though construction had begun in 1856, the war delayed the completion of this link between Covington and Cincinnati. In

1881 the Chesapeake & Ohio Railroad (now CSX Transportation) also became a link via a bridge between Cincinnati and Covington.

In July 1913 Kenton County purchased the section of the Dixie Highway (U.S. 25) inside its borders and in 1916 began paving it with concrete. A collection of fine restaurants, including the White Horse, the Lookout House, and the Town and Country, grew up along the road between Park Hills and FORT MITCHELL. When construction of I-75 was completed in 1963, Dixie Highway was relegated to local road status. Interstate 75 made Kenton County not only a transportation and industrial center, but a population center as well. Towns such as Park Hills, ERLANGER, Fort Wright, and Fort Mitchell grew significantly.

Kenton County's development in the late twentieth century follows closely that of its parent county, Campbell. The industrial base remains along the Ohio River; the highlands, overlooking the river, holds the county's larger residential communities, including Fort Wright, Fort Mitchell, Villa Hills, and Erlanger; and the southern section is mostly rural and agricultural.

The population of Kenton County was 129,440 in 1970; 137,058 in 1980; and 142,031 in 1990.

See Allen Webb Smith, *Beginning At The Point* (Park Hills, Ky., 1977).   RON D. BRYANT

KENTUCKIANS FOR THE COMMONWEALTH. Kentuckians for the Commonwealth (KFTC), founded in 1981, is a statewide citizens' organization whose members are concerned with a variety of local and state issues, including landowners' rights, equitable taxation of mineral property, water quality, disposal of solid and hazardous wastes, education, utility rate reform, and the improvement of community services.

KFTC was instrumental in the passage in 1988 of a constitutional amendment to prevent strip mining of land without the surface owner's permission (see BROAD FORM DEED). The group called for full taxation of unmined mineral property, now mandated by a 1988 Kentucky Supreme Court ruling.

KFTC emphasizes the development of community groups and leaders. It is governed by a steering committee made up of representatives of county chapters. At an annual membership meeting, members approve a platform and elect officers. The group publishes a monthly newsletter, *balancing the scales*.   KRISTIN LAYNE SZAKOS

KENTUCKY, THE NAME. See under PLACE NAMES.

KENTUCKY, U.S.S. Commissioned on May 15, 1900, the 11,520-ton battleship U.S.S. *Kentucky* (BB-6) had electrically powered systems and formidable armament, including controversial stacked turrets. Usually flagship of the Asiatic Fleet, the *Kentucky* patrolled near China, Japan, and the Philippines until March 13, 1904. The battleship was then part of North Atlantic Fleet operations and global circumnavigation with the "Great White Fleet" (December 1907-February 1909). Technological obsolescence led to decommissioning on August 28, 1909, and sale for scrap on January 23, 1924. The Trident missile submarine *Kentucky* (SSBN-737), commissioned in 1991, again took the commonwealth's name to sea.

JAMES RUSSELL HARRIS

KENTUCKY ABOLITION SOCIETY. An association of predominantly Baptist churches that opposed the existence of slavery, the Kentucky Abolition Society was founded in 1808. Seeking a legal end to the "moral evil," the society held its first meeting on September 27, under the leadership of the Revs. Carter Torrant and David BARROW. It adopted a constitution that called on its members to: 1) work toward the constitutional abolition of slavery and the domestic slave trade; 2) speak out publicly against slavery; 3) ameliorate the conditions of slaves; 4) protect the interests of freedmen; and 5) seek justice for any blacks held in bondage contrary to the laws of the state. Religious pressure also was used at an individual level, as member churches refused to commune with slaveholders. The society favored gradual emancipation rather than immediate freedom, and believed the slaveowner should be compensated by the state for the loss of slaves.

In 1815, perhaps its apex in terms of membership, the association asked the Kentucky General Assembly for an act of incorporation; Barrow also petitioned the U.S. House of Representatives to establish a territorial asylum within the United States for all emancipated blacks and to provide financial aid for settlement by freedmen.

Undeterred by its lack of success, the Abolition Society in May 1822 started the monthly newspaper *Abolition Intelligencer and Missionary Magazine*, published at Shelbyville. Lack of support ended the publication after the twelfth issue, in April 1823. The society itself ceased to exist after 1827. Many slaveholders withdrew from churches that became associated with the society, and the most radical members of the organization often moved north, where conditions for helping blacks were more favorable. The removal of blacks to Africa was favored by other groups, such as the American Colonization Society, which had more appeal to southern whites.

See Asa E. Martin, *The Anti-Slavery Movement in Kentucky Prior to 1850* (Louisville 1918); Lowell H. Harrison, *The Antislavery Movement in Kentucky* (Lexington, Ky., 1978).

KENTUCKY ACADEMY. The Kentucky General Assembly on December 12, 1794, granted a charter that created the Kentucky Academy in Pisgah, Woodford County, near the home of Judge Caleb Wallace, a former Presbyterian minister and staunch supporter of the school. Wallace and David Rice (known as the father of Presbyterianism in Kentucky) along with other trustees were distressed by the administration, management, and religious factionalism at Transylvania Seminary in Lexington. They disassociated themselves from Transylvania to establish the academy.

Because of Transylvania's divisive problems, the Kentucky Academy's founders proposed that only one-half of its twenty-one trustees be Presbyterian ministers. While its charter from the state stipulated that the school maintain religious freedom, Kentucky Academy was the first state school to be called denominational. A fund-raising committee toured the East in 1795, acquiring subscriptions of about $10,000. Although many pledges were never paid, in-state contributions assisted in keeping the academy solvent.

Internal changes at Transylvania Seminary, coupled with Kentucky Academy's accomplishments, led to a joint meeting in 1796 to discuss merging the schools. Transylvania University resulted from their consolidation on January 1, 1799.

See Walter Wilson Jennings, *Transylvania: Pioneer University of the West* (New York 1955); John D. Wright, Jr., *Transylvania: Tutor to the West* (Lexington, Ky., 1975).   PATRICIA M. HODGES

KENTUCKY ACADEMY OF SCIENCE. Founded at the University of Kentucky in 1914 to improve scholarly communication among scientists in the commonwealth, the Kentucky Academy of Science holds annual meetings around the state. Its disciplines are the natural, social, and industrial sciences. Its members are students and faculty in public and private schools, colleges, and universities; corporate officers and research personnel; and conservation experts. It publishes the *Transactions*, a forum serving diverse scientific enterprises, and maintains the junior academy for high school programs. Sponsors have been generous, yet without consistent state support or a permanent home, the academy's potential has been minimized. In 1989 the academy returned to its birthplace for its seventy-fifth anniversary meeting, and a plaque commemorating the event was dedicated and placed in front of the chemistry-physics building on the University of Kentucky campus.

ERIC HOWARD CHRISTIANSON

KENTUCKY-AMERICAN WATER COMPANY. For over a century Kentucky-American and its parent agencies have linked the water supplies of six Bluegrass counties to the fluctuating levels of rainfall and water in the Kentucky River. The company was chartered in 1882 as the Lexington Hydraulic and Manufacturing Company. The city council Water Works Ordinance of 1883 endorsed the company's plans to build four reservoirs and a treatment plant. On January 30, 1885, a spectacular fountainlike display of its steam power in Lexington inaugurated service to customers. The last reservoir reached completion in 1906.

In 1922 the company's name became Lexington Water Company, and five years later it became part of the American Water Works System. After the great drought of 1930, the company built the first of four pipelines to the Kentucky River. The American Water Works System's Lexington subsidiary, which became Kentucky-American Water in 1973, could deliver 60 million gallons per day in 1983, a volume that was more than adequate for demands at the time. However, the severe drought of 1988 demonstrated, just as the 1930 event had, the overall vulnerability of Kentucky-American and its customers to climatic changes, and to the volume of water carried by the Kentucky River.

Years before the 1988 drought, the company had reached near-capacity in pumping from the river. The warning signs were clear; even under optimal climatic conditions, demand would soon exceed the available water supply. Kentucky-American worked closely with the Public Service Commission and other state officials to change the Kentucky plumbing code to require water-efficient fixtures in new structures, a change that went into effect in 1988. As a member of the Kentucky River Basin Steering Committee, a group formed after the drought to address water supply problems for the growing region, Kentucky-American is working on future water supply, conservation, and consumer education.   ERIC HOWARD CHRISTIANSON

KENTUCKY ARTS COUNCIL. The Kentucky Arts Council, a division of the Kentucky Department of the Arts, provides financial support for the arts throughout the state. Its major areas of interest are arts education, support of individual artists, community arts development, and development of artistic organizations. It has placed special emphasis on arts education programs. The council was established by the Kentucky General Assembly in 1966 and became a division of the Kentucky Department of the Arts in 1981. It is directed by a nonsalaried board, appointed by the governor.

THOMAS A. GREENFIELD

KENTUCKY BAR ASSOCIATION. A voluntary association of attorneys was formed in 1871 in Louisville following what is believed to have been the first meeting of lawyers held in Kentucky. More stability was added to this organization when, in 1934, the Kentucky General Assembly passed an act creating the Kentucky Bar Association. This act authorized the court of appeals (now the supreme court) to establish rules defining the practice of law and to establish a code of professional responsibility for its members. A board of governors administers these rules. The Kentucky Bar Association is an agency of the supreme court of Kentucky. As such, its members are all lawyers admitted to practice in Kentucky.

One of the bar's programs investigates and processes complaints against attorneys. The bar's Continuing Legal Education Commission oversees the operation of the bar's mandatory continuing education program. The Attorneys Advertising Commission promotes ethical advertising and protects the public from false or deceptive ads. Other programs in which the Kentucky Bar Association participates are the Kentucky IOLTA (Interest on Lawyers Trust Accounts) Fund, Client Security Funds, and Legal Fee and Legal Negligence Arbitration.

There are seventeen bar sections for specific areas of practice, including criminal law, estate law, business law, and young lawyers. The association is housed in the Kentucky Bar Center in the historic district of downtown Frankfort.

VINCENT J. COTTON, JR.

KENTUCKY BEND. The Mississippi River makes a loop in extreme western Kentucky that created a cul-de-sac known as the Kentucky Bend, or New Madrid Bend. It is accessible by land only from Tennessee, as the result of a bitter dispute over the state line between Kentucky and Tennessee. When the line between Virginia and North Carolina was surveyed by Thomas Walker and Richard Henderson in 1780, Walker reached the Tennessee River and then, impeded by hostile Chickasaw, could only estimate the junction with the Mississippi River. Walker's line proved to be ten miles north of the correct 36° 30′ north latitude. When the area in Kentucky and Tennessee west of the Tennessee River was acquired from the Chickasaw in 1819, Kentucky sought to correct the border for its entire length. Tennessee refused. Kentucky appealed to the U.S. Congress, then to the Supreme Court, and even threatened forced occupation. A joint commission finally agreed to abide by Walker's line as far as the Tennessee River and the 36° 30′ boundary west of that point. The result was the creation of the enclave at Kentucky Bend.

JOHN E.L. ROBERTSON

KENTUCKY BROADCASTERS ASSOCIATION. The Kentucky Broadcasters Association (KBA) is a professional organization of radio and television broadcasters. It began in Louisville at the instigation of Hugh Potter of radio station WOMI, Owensboro. The first meeting took place on October 24, 1945, with twenty-two people representing ten radio stations. At that time, only fourteen radio stations had been licensed to operate in Kentucky, and there were no television stations. Potter was elected the first president. J.E. Willis of WLAP in Lexington and Harry McTigue of WINN in Louisville were vice-presidents, and J.H. Callaway of WHAS in Louisville was the first secretary-treasurer.

As the number of radio and television stations increased after the war, KBA membership grew, and the group began to meet regularly in the spring and fall. The KBA is supported by yearly dues from stations and associate members in allied industries. The KBA promotes cooperation among stations, helps establish program interconnects, serves as an educational and political lobbying agency for members; and serves, protects, and unifies broadcast interests in the state. It sponsors statewide meetings, a yearly Washington trip, award presentations, and public-service and promotional campaigns, and it publishes a newsletter.

FRANCIS M. NASH

KENTUCKY CENTER FOR THE ARTS. The Kentucky Center for the Arts, established by the legislature as "the Commonwealth's official performing arts center," opened in Louisville on November 19, 1983, following ten years of planning and development. Kentucky Center, the largest state-built arts facility in the country, was built and funded through a unique partnership of the state, county, city, and private sectors.

The center was designed to be a major cultural focal point to promote the development of the arts, tourism, convention trade, and hotel industry in Kentucky. It showcases regional, national, and international talents in music, theater, dance, and opera. One-half million visitors each year enjoy these talents in the facility's 2,406- and 626-seat theaters, the intimate "black box" theater, rehearsal halls, meeting rooms, and the vaulted lobby. Civic events, business meetings, dinners, and conventions are held there. Kentucky Educational Television broadcasts many statewide performances on its "Kentucky Center Presents" program and some are also nationally distributed. Kentucky Center is one of only four performing arts centers in the United States with a fully staffed, comprehensive education program. The facility serves the students and teachers of Jefferson and surrounding counties with a variety of educational programs and acts as an educational resource for the entire state. Since its opening, Kentucky Center has given Kentucky's 180 school districts at least one learning opportunity, either by bringing students and teachers to Louisville or through outreach programs that take ideas directly into the schools.

Kentucky Center for the Arts is visually striking as well as technically state-of-the-art. A sweeping glass facade reflects the surrounding Victorian architecture, back terraces complement the Belvedere Plaza on the riverfront, and six works of twentieth century sculpture grace the interior and exterior spaces. Caudill, Rowlett & Scott, a Houston architectural firm, designed the building with assistance from the Design and Construction Department of Humana Inc.

MARLOW G. BURT

KENTUCKY CENTRAL RAILWAY. One of the predecessors of the Kentucky Central Railway, the Covington & Lexington Railroad, was chartered by the Kentucky General Assembly on February 27, 1849. Financed by public and private subscriptions to its stock, the railroad company opened to Paris, Kentucky, in September 1854. The route's remaining link, from Paris to Lexington, was constructed by the Maysville & Lexington Railroad Company, and by terms of a lease in December 1854 the two companies shared the Paris-to-Lexington tracks.

The Covington & Lexington Railroad bolstered the export of hogs and wheat from the Bluegrass to Covington and on by ferry to Cincinnati. The sale of Cincinnati merchandise south also expanded. By 1857 an estimated 45 percent of the wheat and nearly 35 percent of the hogs transported to Cincinnati were carried by the Covington & Lexington Railroad.

In March 1850 the Kentucky General Assembly chartered the Lexington & Danville Railroad Company—the other predecessor of the Kentucky Central—expressly to construct a rail line between Lexington and Danville. In December 1851 the charter was amended to extend the road to the Tennessee state line. In March 1856 the Kentucky General Assembly permitted both companies to use the name Kentucky Central Railroad.

Geography proved the greatest obstacle to extension of the Kentucky Central Railroad southward. To span the great gorge of the Kentucky River at Dixville was expensive. In 1853 the Lexington & Danville hired John A. Roebling, one of the great engineering talents of the day, to design a railroad suspension bridge over the Kentucky River at Dixville. Roebling completed the plans, stone piers were erected, and cable wire was delivered to the site, but the company's financial condition prohibited further progress.

In 1858 a director of the Covington & Lexington Railroad, Robert Bonner Bowler, convinced the other directors of the company to defer interest payments on the company's first and second mortgage bonds until $800,000 worth of improvements were made on the line. Subsequently, a major creditor filed suit against the company, and the railroad was ordered sold at public auction. The purchaser was Robert Bowler. In 1865 the original stockholders filed suit against the heirs of Bowler (who had died in 1864), but lost their case on a technicality. The case was appealed to the Kentucky court of appeals, which in 1873 ruled in favor of the original stockholders.

In 1881 Collis P. Huntington of the CHESAPEAKE & OHIO RAILROAD purchased the Kentucky Central Railroad, to be a part of his proposed route from Norfolk to the Mississippi River. The road went into receivership and was reorganized in May 1887. It was then acquired by the LOUISVILLE & NASHVILLE RAILROAD (now CSX Transportation).

See Paul A. Tenkotte, "Rival Cities to Suburbs: Covington and Newport, Kentucky, 1790-1890," Ph.D. dissertation, University of Cincinnati, 1989; Maury Klein, *History of the Louisville and Nashville Railroad* (New York 1972).

PAUL A. TENKOTTE

KENTUCKY CHRISTIAN COLLEGE. Kentucky Christian College was established in 1919 under the name Christian Normal Institute, in Grayson, Carter County. Its mission was to offer "higher education based on a solid foundation of Biblical principles," providing training for religious and for secular vocations. Its founders, J.W. Lusby

and J.O. Snodgrass, proposed that the school serve eastern Kentucky, West Virginia, and Tennessee. The school has had only four presidents in its history: J.W. Lusby (1919-37); J. Lowell Lusby (1937-77); L. Palmer Young (1977-87); and Dr. Keith P. Keeran (1987-). Gradually, the elementary, secondary, and normal school programs were phased out, and the religious and spiritual orientation was strengthened, as reflected in the name adopted in 1944, Kentucky Christian College. Its religious affiliation is the Christian Church/Church of Christ.

Degrees offered are A.B., B.A., B.S. (formerly a B.S.L.), and A.A. The school has been accredited by the American Association of Bible Colleges (1962) and the Southern Association of Colleges and Secondary Schools (1984). The addition of the master of ministry degree in 1982 has attracted students from over thirty states. Courses appeal to older, experienced ministerial students with eight to ten years of pulpit experience. All students major in Biblical studies, with additional majors available in ministry, psychology, social work, teacher education, and business administration. Prominent minors include Christian education, missions, evangelism, youth ministry, pastoral counseling, business, history, secretarial science, and social welfare.

Students and faculty contribute to world missions annually through the college's Matheteuo Society. (the Greek word means "make disciples"). Internships provide on-site experience. Student singing, speaking, and service groups participate at local churches, Christian camps, conferences, and conventions, including the North American Christian Convention. Faculty have authored Greek and other textbooks and contribute regularly to major religious and educational journals. The college's men's and women's teams have been national champions in the National Christian Colleges Athletic Association. Among the alumni are educators, ministers, and evangelists in the United States, many of whom have served in numerous mission fields. (The pioneering work of the Central Africa Mission has often been associated with the college's influence.)

See J. Lowell Lusby and Lela Stone Lusby, *For the Good of the Cause* (Grayson, Ky., 1986).

CHARLES ALLEN PERRY

KENTUCKY COAL ASSOCIATION. The Kentucky Coal Association is a statewide trade association of coal operators organized in Lexington, Kentucky, in 1942 by B.F. Reed, E.R. ("Jack") Price, Harry La Viers, Sr., and probably others. Its constitution and bylaws, adopted on April 28, 1947, were revised on May 23, 1973. Its stated purpose is to promote the best interest of the coal mining industry in Kentucky. The association engages in neither sales nor labor relations but regularly monitors and reports and, when appropriate, responds to actions, proposals, and appraisals by the government or the private sector that affect the Kentucky coal industry.

Throughout its history, the association's leaders have included Reed, La Viers, and William Sturgill.

Day-to-day activities are in the hands of the association president. The association's membership includes both union and nonunion operators. An ongoing relationship is maintained with the University of Kentucky's Department of Mine Engineering and the Kentucky Mining Institute. The association publishes a suppliers' directory and sponsors seminars on topics of interest to members.

HENRY C. MAYER

KENTUCKY COFFEETREE. The Kentucky coffeetree (*Gymnocladus dioica*) is the only tree with Kentucky in its name. Pioneers may have made a coffee substitute from its seeds and used the seed pulp for soap. The tree grows to a height of one hundred feet and has brownish-gray bark, twice-compounded leaves, and brown seedpods up to ten inches long encasing hard brown seeds. The wood, sometimes called Kentucky mahogany, resembles that of ash, oak, and others used in cabinetry. Joe Creason and William C. Johnstone effectively promoted the tree, and early in 1976 Gov. Julian Carroll (1974-79) signed the Senate Bill 150, which made it the official tree of the commonwealth, replacing the tulip tree. The Kentucky coffeetree, which is grown as an ornamental, ranges from southern Minnesota to New York and south to Oklahoma, Arkansas, Tennessee, and West Virginia.

See Mary E. Wharton, *Trees and Shrubs of Kentucky* (Lexington, Ky., 1973).

HELEN PRICE STACY

KENTUCKY COLONEL. The honorary title of Kentucky Colonel is conferred by the governor in recognition of a deed or service that merits recognition. The title originated in Kentucky's early days, when the citizenry maintained a volunteer state militia, and some of its officers were commissioned colonels. Colonels were uniformed members of a governor's staff. Even when the need for a civilian militia waned, governors continued to grant commissions and the military title came to be associated with civil honor and distinction. The Kentucky Colonel has come to represent the daring, glamour, dignity, wit, charm, and attraction of outstanding men who have claimed the title—the stereotype of a southern gentleman. Artistic renderings of the Colonel differ, but generally include a moustache, a goatee, a string-tie and a white frock coat. This image has frequently been used to promote Kentucky, especially as a tourist center.

KENTUCKY COLONELS. The Kentucky Colonels, a charter member of the American Basketball Association (ABA), was a professional basketball team in Louisville. Originally owned by Mamie and Joe Gregory, the Colonels entered the league on March 31, 1967. The Colonels were similar to the other ABA franchises, typified by nickel-and-dime budgets, wacky promotional stunts, and bad players. First coach Johnny Givens lasted only seventeen games before he was replaced by Gene

Rhodes. All of the players except former University of Kentucky (UK) star Louie Dampier left soon after the first season. On October 30, 1969, a group of young Louisville businessmen—Wendell Cherry, Stuart Jay, David Jones, David Grissom, and John Y. Brown, Jr.—who were interested in establishing a viable franchise bought the Colonels. As general manager and president, they hired Mike Storen, who signed former UK All-American Dan Issel and replaced Rhodes, who later became general manager, with former UK and Boston Celtics star Frank Ramsey. Storen then signed center Artis Gilmore and employed Joe Mullaney as head coach, following the resignation of Ramsey.

During the 1972-73 season, Cherry sold the Colonels to a group of Cincinnati-based investors. John Y. Brown, Jr., purchased 51 percent interest almost immediately, however, and introduced his wife Ellie as the majority stockholder. In the 1974-75 season, Brown transformed the Colonels from contenders (they had lost in the playoffs during the previous seasons) to champions. He brought in several new players to augment his core of Gilmore, Issel, and Dampier, and he hired Hubie Brown as head coach. Brown guided the Colonels to the 1974-75 ABA championship. Unfortunately, the league as a whole was in financial trouble, unable to compete with the rival National Basketball Association (NBA). Due to escalating player salaries and the lack of television contracts, most teams were in danger of folding. The six strongest ABA franchises attempted to merge with the competing league, but the NBA owners would allow only four to join. On September 15, 1976, after buying out the Colonels and the St. Louis Spirits for $3.3 million each, the New York Nets, the Indiana Pacers, the Denver Nuggets, and the San Antonio Spurs joined the NBA, marking the end of the ABA. Many of the remaining ABA players were claimed in the NBA's subsequent supplemental draft, including former Colonels center Artis Gilmore.

See David Kindred, *Basketball: The Dream Game In Kentucky* (Louisville 1976).

KENTUCKY COLONIZATION SOCIETY. The Kentucky Colonization Society was founded in 1828 as an affiliate of the American Colonization Society, established in 1817 for the purpose of ending slavery and ridding the country of freed blacks by deporting them to distant colonies. Although it favored emancipation, the Kentucky society, which had five local chapters, placed greater emphasis on removing freedmen from the state than on doing away with slavery. Kentucky's numbers of freed blacks were small (7,317 as late as 1840). Freed blacks were forbidden to associate with either whites or slaves. Transporting them to colonies in Africa or to some distant (but unspecified) location in North America, the society contended, would remove the threat that they might aid runaway slaves, promote abolition, and help foment slave revolts.

Following the lead of the national organization, which had bought land in Africa on December 11,

1821, and founded the colony of Liberia, the state chapter began to raise money to pay for the voyage to Africa. On March 22, 1833, the Kentucky Colonization Society sent approximately one hundred freedmen to New Orleans, where they embarked for Liberia on April 20. Though the organization received some favorable reports from the new colonists, diseases such as cholera resulted in the deaths of many. Among the other setbacks for the society were the high demand for slaves in the cotton states, opposition to the society's antislavery stance, and resistance to migration on the part of blacks born in America. By 1844, eleven years after the initial voyage, fewer than a hundred additional blacks had been sent to Africa.

Nevertheless, the Kentucky chapter persevered. It raised $5,000 in 1845 to buy forty square miles in Liberia. In November of that year, it chartered a ship to carry an estimated two hundred former slaves to the new colony, called Kentucky in Liberia. The capital of this colony was named Clay Ashland in honor of Henry Clay, one of the founders of the American Colonization Society. When the vessel departed in January 1846, it carried only thirty-five former Kentucky slaves. This poor showing, at such a high cost, nearly defeated the organization. With hopes of salvaging the Kentucky society, the legislature passed an act on March 24, 1851, requiring all slaves, when emancipated, to leave the state and prohibiting freedmen of other states from moving to Kentucky. Further, on March 3, 1856, the General Assembly appropriated $5,000 a year to aid the society. The legislative aid made little difference, however, and the last sizable expedition, only forty-two ex-slaves, left Kentucky in May 1857. With the African colony failing because of disease and mismanagement, the society could not pay the high costs of transporting freed blacks to Africa, and it ceased operating in 1859. In its thirty-year history, the Kentucky Colonization Society dispatched an estimated 658 emigrants to Africa.

See J. Winston Coleman, Jr., "The Kentucky Colonization Society," *Register* 39 (January 1941): 1-9; Lowell Harrison, *The Antislavery Movement in Kentucky* (Lexington, Ky., 1978).

KENTUCKY COUNCIL OF CHURCHES. The Kentucky Council of Churches was established in Louisville on December 11, 1947, by representatives of six Protestant denominations. As the successor to the Kentucky Sunday School Union, established in October 1865, it represents more than a century of interchurch cooperation in Kentucky. Formal membership in the Kentucky Council of Churches was held in 1990 by twenty-seven jurisdictional groups (conferences, dioceses, presbyteries, and the like), representing eleven Christian denominations: African Methodist Episcopal, African Methodist Episcopal Zion, Christian Church (Disciples of Christ), Christian Methodist Episcopal, Cumberland Presbyterian, Episcopal, Lutheran, Presbyterian Church USA, Roman Catholic, United

Church of Christ, and United Methodist Church. The Roman Catholic dioceses in Kentucky joined the council in 1984. Two divisions of the Salvation Army hold observer membership and liaisons represent three local ecumenical groups and several Southern Baptist congregations.

The Kentucky Council of Churches serves as a channel for cooperative ministry to identify and meet the social, economic, and spiritual needs of the people of Kentucky. The council's Task Force on Hunger has gained national recognition for its knowledgeable assistance to the hungry and poor in the state. The Commission on Religion and Public Policy keeps churches informed on legislative issues before the Kentucky General Assembly and directs the churches' response. The council has sponsored seminars and publications on the topics of baptism, eucharist, and ministry, as a sequel to the World Council of Churches study of the three topics.   DONALD F. HELLMANN

KENTUCKY COUNCIL ON HIGHER EDUCATION. Kentucky, like about half the other states, divides the responsibility for its system of higher education. Kentucky's coordinating agency, the Council on Higher Education, was created by statute in 1934. In the years since then, the state has shifted controversies over appropriations, unnecessary duplication, establishment of new institutions and facilities, and other matters from legislative floors and committee rooms to this agency. The council, one of the oldest agencies of its kind in the nation, did not gain most of its authority until the period between 1970 and 1990.

Kentucky gives its public universities exclusive jurisdiction over personnel matters, internal budgetary decisions, curriculum development, and student life issues. The institutions operate under a general statement of principles established by the Council on Higher Education in the late 1970s. The council's statutory responsibilities include authority over all new and existing academic programs. No new academic degree program can be initiated without the council's approval. All existing programs from a similar discipline are part of a cycle that brings them up for review at all institutions in the same year. The eight institutions are Eastern Kentucky University, Kentucky State University, Morehead State University, Murray State University, Northern Kentucky University, University of Kentucky, University of Louisville, and Western Kentucky University.

A second major responsibility of the council is to make a unified budget recommendation for higher education. The recommendation covers operating and capital needs and must be delivered to the governor and the General Assembly by November 15 of odd-numbered years. In 1982 the legislature directed the council to use a funding formula to determine the operating needs of the institutions. The formula takes into account the types of education offered at each university or community college and determines the amount of money needed to support the institutions at a level equal to the average for such institutions and programs in selected southern and adjoining states. If the legislature provided this amount, Kentucky's funding for higher education would theoretically be in the middle of the range of the selected states. Kentucky's funding has been below 90 percent of this average since the formula was adopted. Preparing for the 1991-92 fiscal year, the 1990 legislature appropriated 88.2 percent of the target figure produced by the formula. The council also sets tuitions.

Another duty is establishing admission policies. The council requires that, to achieve unconditional admission, students enrolling in baccalaureate programs complete the precollege curriculum the council approved in 1983, take the American College Test, and graduate from high school. The universities may add other requirements. The council's other duties include developing comprehensive plans for higher education and determining the need for new colleges and universities.

The Council on Higher Education is composed of seventeen voting members appointed by the governor, including a student member, and the state superintendent of public instruction, who serves as an ex-officio, nonvoting member. The student member serves a one-year term; the remaining voting members serve six-year terms. The membership must include a recipient of an undergraduate degree from each public university and a member from each congressional district (the same member can fill both requirements). The remaining members are appointed at large.

See Clark Kerr and Marion Gade, *The Guardians* (Washington, D.C., 1989).   GARY S. COX

KENTUCKY COUNTY. The need for creating Kentucky County within Virginia was discussed at a meeting held in Harrodsburg on June 6, 1776. Those present elected George Rogers Clark and John Gabriel Jones as delegates from the western part of Fincastle County to urge the Virginia Assembly to make the region known as Kentucky a new county. They presented this petition on October 8 and, in spite of opposition, the assembly abolished Fincastle County; in its place they created three new counties—Montgomery, Washington, and Kentucky—with the division to take effect December 31, 1776. Kentucky County had essentially the same boundary as the present state.

There were five communities in Kentucky in December 1776: Boonesborough, Harrodsburg, St. Asaph (later called Logan's Station), McClelland's Station, and Leestown. Because of attacks by the northern Indians, only the first three stations were still in existence by the spring of 1777. By then the population of Kentucky had probably declined from over a thousand to fewer than two hundred, as the militia numbered only 145 men.

David Robinson was appointed the county lieutenant of Kentucky County, which at the time was the highest form of civil commission, but since he did not move to Kentucky until many years later,

the office was never filled. Benjamin Logan was the first sheriff and George May the first county surveyor. George Rogers Clark, Isaac Hite, Robert Todd, and several others served as justices of the peace. The militia officers were John Bowman, colonel; George Rogers Clark, major; and John Todd, Benjamin Logan, Daniel Boone, and James Harrod, captains. In April 1777 John Todd and Richard Callaway were elected delegates to the Virginia General Assembly.

In 1779 the Virginia legislature appointed commissioners to determine the validity of the claims for land on the frontier. Between November 1779 and April 1780, these commissioners approved more than 1,300 settlements and preemption claims in Kentucky. Other would-be settlers purchased treasury warrants or made land entries on old military warrants issued for service in the French and Indian War. Before November 1780, over 5,000 claims had been entered at the surveyor's office at Wilson Station, near what is now Henderson.

Kentucky County was abolished on November 1, 1780, and the area was divided into Jefferson, Lincoln, and Fayette counties. (See also DISTRICT OF KENTUCKY.)

See George Morgan Chinn, *Kentucky Settlement and Statehood 1750-1800* (Frankfort, Ky., 1975); Charles Gano Talbert, *Benjamin Logan, Kentucky Frontiersman* (Lexington, Ky., 1962).

NEAL HAMMON

KENTUCKY DEPARTMENT FOR LIBRARIES AND ARCHIVES. The Kentucky Department for Libraries and Archives originated in 1825, when the Kentucky State Library was established by the General Assembly to serve the government in Frankfort. Nine years later, George A. Robertson, a state government clerk, was elected the first state librarian by the General Assembly. In 1839 the legislature passed an act that established a state library in a room of the capitol to serve the state government. In 1910 two events changed the mission to one with a statewide perspective—the Kentucky Library Commission was created by the legislature and the commission was given one hundred traveling libraries by the Kentucky Federation of Women's Clubs. These libraries, 5,000 books packed in a hundred wooden cases, brought reading material to many Kentucky counties for the first time. The year 1910 also brought a survey of Kentucky's archives for the American Historical Association, marking the beginning of formalized, statewide archival activity in local records. A systematic effort was made to salvage and transfer them to the University of Kentucky for safekeeping. In 1936 the General Assembly created a Department of Library and Archives. The Kentucky Library Commission became one of three administrative units within the new department and was renamed the Library Extension Division. In 1938 the State Board for Certification of Libraries was created. In 1950 the Kentucky Records Control Law was passed by the General Assembly to cope with the state's records problems. The State Archives and Records Commission was created in 1958.

In 1952 the state began to award grants-in-aid to local public libraries, and funds were appropriated to purchase and process materials centrally for public libraries. In 1953 the Friends of Kentucky Libraries, Inc., launched the Kentucky bookmobile project and a year later delivered eighty-four bookmobiles to Gov. Lawrence W. Wetherby (1950-55). In 1954 the General Assembly abolished the Department of Library and Archives and made the Library Extension Division an independent state agency. The agency's records holdings were transferred to the University of Kentucky. In 1956 the U.S. Library Services Act was passed to develop rural public libraries. In 1957 multicounty library regions were developed. The following year the Library Extension Division became the Department of Libraries. Legislation also permitted counties to vote for a county or regional district tax.

By 1961 the Records Depository had received its first major group of state agency records and had published the first checklist of state publications. In 1968 the state began an amortization program to appropriate funds for public library construction and renovation, and the department initiated library services to state penal and mental institutions. The Kentucky Regional Library for the Blind and Physically Handicapped was established within the department in 1969. In 1971 the State Advisory Council on Libraries was created.

In January 1974 Gov. Wendell Ford (1971-74) merged the Division of Archives of the Finance Department with the Department of Libraries to form the Department for Libraries and Archives. The same year a micrographics program for filming public records was established and the following year, a documents restoration program. In 1979 the Kentucky Guide Project was initiated. A task force on library network development was appointed in 1981 to plan for greater resources sharing. In 1982 the department's Coffee Tree Road facility in Frankfort was dedicated. During the 1980s, the agency helped establish the Governor's Literacy Commission and began to award literacy and data conversion grants to local libraries. The 1980s also brought the establishment of the Kentucky Library Network, Inc., the Local Records Program, and the state government machine-readable records project.

See Kenneth Noe, "The Vision and the Reality: A History of the KDLA," *Kentucky Libraries* (Winter 1985): 2-7.   MOLLY M. CONE

KENTUCKY DEPARTMENT OF PUBLIC ADVOCACY.

The Kentucky Department of Public Advocacy (DPA) was established in 1972 by the General Assembly to provide the constitutionally required counsel to indigents accused of crimes ranging from driving under the influence of alcohol to capital murder. Citizens are defended in Kentucky's trial and appellate courts and in the federal courts, including the U.S. Supreme Court. The department was founded after the U.S. Supreme Court ruled in *Argersinger v. Hamlin* (1972), *Powell v. Alabama* (1932), and *Gideon v. Wainwright* (1963), that no indigent can have liberty or life taken away without counsel being provided by the state. The Court thus recognized that constitutional protections are not self-enacting and that a person's constitutional right to counsel cannot depend on a person's means.   EDWARD C. MONAHAN

KENTUCKY DERBY. The Kentucky Derby, the most celebrated horse race in America, has been run at Churchill Downs in Louisville since 1875. Known as the Run for the Roses, the derby has attracted a crowd in excess of 100,000 every year since 1969.

The derby is a 1¼-mile race for three-year-old thoroughbreds. With the exception of the 1945 race, the derby has been held on the first Saturday in May each year since 1938. A wartime ban on racing in 1945 was not lifted until May 9, and the derby was run on June 9 that year.

For Louisville, the derby is a civic celebration: a two-week extravaganza known as the Kentucky Derby Festival. The festival includes a minimarathon, a balloon race, and the Great Steamboat Race. The derby also is a social affair, with high society entertaining guests at lavish parties. It is one big party for thousands of spectators who converge on the infield for a day of fun, while other fans, including celebrities, politicians, and business leaders, watch from the stands.

Country philosopher Irvin S. Cobb of Paducah, Kentucky, a man gifted with words, was asked to explain the derby's magic. "If I could do that, I'd have a larynx of spun silver and the tongue of an anointed angel," he said. Cobb added: "Until you go to Kentucky and with your own eyes behold the derby, you ain't never been nowheres and you ain't never seen nothin'!"

Eleven horses that won the derby have won the Preakness and the Belmont Stakes races as well, capturing the Triple Crown: Sir Barton (1919), Gallant Fox (1930), Omaha (1935), War Admiral (1937), Whirlaway (1941), Count Fleet (1943), Assault (1946), Citation (1948), Secretariat (1973), Seattle Slew (1977), and Affirmed (1978). Among the other outstanding derby winners are Hindoo (1881), Old Rosebud (1914), Exterminator (1918), Twenty Grand (1931), Swaps (1955), Carry Back (1961), Northern Dancer (1964), Spectacular Bid (1979), Alysheba (1987), and Sunday Silence (1989). Three fillies have captured the derby: Regret (1915), Genuine Risk (1980), and Winning Colors (1988).

Calumet farm, near Lexington, has won more derbies (eight) than any other stable. Ben A. Jones trained a record six derby victors, all but one for Calumet. Eddie ARCARO and Bill Hartack each rode five winners of the derby, a record. SECRETARIAT ran the fastest derby of all time—1:59 2/5.

Two men are responsible for making the derby one of America's leading sports spectacles: Col. M. Lewis Clark, Jr., founder of Churchill Downs, and

Col. Matt J. WINN. In 1872, a group of discouraged Kentucky breeders met with Clark, a Louisville socialite, to discuss a solution to racing's plight in Kentucky. Racing was being conducted at the Kentucky Association track in Lexington, but the breeders were distressed because Louisville, the biggest city in the state, was without a track. Racing had been held previously in Louisville, as early as 1783 on a downtown street, but the last venture had resulted in the bankruptcy of the Woodlawn Course in 1870. The breeders, some on the verge of abandoning racing, asked Clark if he could do anything to rejuvenate the sport in Louisville. Clark agreed to help. He had no racing experience, having worked in the banking and tobacco businesses, and he decided to go to Europe to study racing on a higher level than in the United States. Clark, a grandson of William Clark of the Lewis and Clark expedition, thus set out for Europe on a scouting mission of his own.

In England, Clark was deeply impressed with the interest generated by a series of tradition-rich stakes races—the Epsom Derby, the Epsom Oaks, the St. Leger Stakes, and the Ascot Gold Cup. In France Clark studied the operation of the wagering system. After investigating European racing practices, Clark returned to Louisville and summoned the breeders for a meeting. Telling them of a plan he had for establishing a track in Louisville, he outlined the formation of permanent stakes races patterned after the English classics. He envisioned a race called the Kentucky Derby, which would be modeled after the Epsom Derby. He wagered that in a decade the winner of the Kentucky Derby would be worth more than the farm on which the horse was bred.

In 1874 Clark formed a corporation formally known as the Louisville Jockey Club and Driving Park Association. With Clark overseeing proceedings as track president and presiding judge, the first Kentucky Derby was run at CHURCHILL DOWNS on May 17, 1875. The winner was ARISTIDES, a little red colt bred and owned by Lexington horseman H. Price McGrath. The young black jockey, Oliver Lewis, piloted Aristides to victory before a crowd generally estimated at 10,000 to 12,000.

The first derby was a grand success, and the race continued to pull in excellent fields in its early years. Indeed, eight of its first eleven winners were considered the best in their age group. The derby then went into a slump, however, and the track suffered financial problems. During the 1894 spring meeting, the Downs lost some $8,000, money for which Clark assumed the responsibility. Clark himself had not drawn his salary as track president for more than two years. After the 1894 spring meeting, the Clark regime ended, and the track was sold.

The Downs was still in financial difficulty early in the twentieth century, and following the 1902 derby, it appeared that the track would be permanently closed. Enter Matt Winn. Winn, a Louisville tailor who had no previous experience in racetrack operations, helped form a syndicate of Louisvillians to put up $40,000 to purchase the track. Winn, a master promoter, would, in time, lure eastern horses and the eastern press to the derby, but it did not happen overnight. A three-year period of newsmaking finishes helped put the derby over the hump, starting in 1913 when Donerail won at a whopping $184.90 payoff—a record for the derby—and set a track record of 2:04 4/5. The very next year Old Rosebud broke that record with a blazing 2:03 2/5. Given the combination of Donerail's long shot victory and Old Rosebud's record-shattering triumph, Winn got widespread publicity for the derby.

In 1915, for the first time in years, leading eastern stables came to the derby in full force. Regret, owned by New York turfman Harry Payne Whitney, won the derby, the first filly to do so, and Pebbles and Sharpshooter ran second and third, respectively, in an eastern-dominated finish. In his book *Down the Stretch* (1945), Winn, who would see the first seventy-five runnings of the derby, commented on the significance of the 1915 derby: "It needed only a victory by Regret to create for us some coast-to-coast publicity, and Regret did not fail us. The derby thus was 'made' as an American institution."

See Jim Bolus, *Run for the Roses: 100 Years at the Kentucky Derby* (New York 1974); Joe Hirsch and Jim Bolus, *Kentucky Derby: The Chance of a Lifetime* (New York 1988).   JIM BOLUS

KENTUCKY EDUCATIONAL TELEVISION. Kentucky Authority for Educational Television, a state agency, was created by the Kentucky General Assembly in 1962. By 1990 KET operated fifteen television transmitters and nine translators. The full-power, full-service manned transmitter sites are located in Ashland, Bowling Green, Covington, Elizabethtown, Hazard, Lexington, Louisville, Madisonville, Morehead, Murray, Owensboro, Owenton, Paducah, Pikeville, and Somerset. The unmanned translator sites are located in Augusta, Hopkinsville, Cowan Creek, Falmouth, Hawesville, Letcher, Louisa, Whitesburg, and Tompkinsville. The central staff is housed in a network production and operations center in Lexington.

Since 1988, KET has also operated two channels that transmit programs of instruction to every public school in Kentucky via satellite receiving dishes provided to the schools by the state. The original network concept included state matching funds for studios at the state universities. All eight state universities are so equipped; they are connected to the KET Network Center by microwave so that programs or program segments originating from any of them can be broadcast over the network.

KET's programming includes instructional enhancement for teachers in the classroom; direct instruction in subjects that may not be available in many schools; college-credit courses; cultural and performing arts; commentary on the news; call-in participation programs; and programs acquired from the Public Broadcasting System and from other educational and public broadcasting sources. KET is one of the largest educational and public television networks in the nation and is particularly noted for its nationally distributed educational productions, such as "GED-TV."

KET began when the 1960 General Assembly passed a resolution calling for a study of educational television. The legislation that established the television authority was passed in 1962. Gov. Bert T. Combs (1959–63), who appointed five of its nine members, called for the establishment of a statewide KET advisory committee that, with more than 150 members, was an important auxiliary to the network, as are outgrowth groups of influential Kentuckians such as the Study Commissions of 1975, 1985 and 1987, the Futures Conference of 1989, and the Friends of KET, established in 1971.

In 1990 KET received approximately two-thirds of its budget from the state. The other third was raised from private sources by the KET Foundation, whose eleven-member board includes the nine members of the Kentucky Authority for Educational Television plus KET's executive director and a representative from the board of directors of the Friends of KET, a public relations and fund raising section of the network. The KET budget for fiscal year 1990 was approximately $10 million in state funds and $6 million in foundation funds.

O. LEONARD PRESS

KENTUCKY EDUCATION ASSOCIATION. The Kentucky Education Association (KEA) is a voluntary membership organization for school employees, the vast majority of whom are public school teachers. It also has members among school administrators and support personnel. KEA advocates education and teachers' employment rights by lobbying for higher education funding, better materials, smaller class sizes, and school restructuring. The Kentucky Education Association is affiliated with the National Education Association and has local affiliates in every school district.

The group that became KEA organized in Louisville in 1857. Throughout its early years, the Kentucky Education Association was dominated by the state superintendent of public instruction and the board of education. Controversy over self-governance surfaced at several early conventions, most notably in 1884. In the same year the organization called for higher salaries and federal aid for education. In 1936 the organization adopted as its legislative objective the establishment of a teachers' retirement system, a goal achieved in 1938.

In 1950 teachers, demanding higher salaries, marched on Frankfort during the legislative session. In the same year, KEA's Commission on Teacher Education and Professional Standards was established. In 1952 Marvin Dodson was selected as executive secretary, a position he held until 1975. The year 1957 marked the merger of KEA with the Kentucky Teachers Association, an organi-

zation of black teachers, which had 1,400 members at the time of merger.

In 1966, after KEA lobbying and a one-day strike, the General Assembly increased teacher salaries according to rank and experience. In the late 1960s the association began aggressively pursuing professional negotiation rights for teachers, and in 1970 more than 25,000 teachers struck Kentucky's schools in a dispute over school funding, salaries, and equity concerns.

The late 1960s and early 1970s saw conflicts in the association over independence from the state superintendent and board of education, a controversy that echoed the disputes of nearly one hundred years earlier. The objective of the more recent struggle was to wrest control of the organization from local school superintendents who had dominated the organization. The last quarter of the twentieth century saw unprecedented growth of the organization. KEA moved its headquarters to Frankfort in 1985 to become a stronger legislative force.

KEA is organized into twelve district associations, whose members elect the KEA board of directors, the organization's governing body, and the annual delegate assembly, the policymaking body.

MARY ANN BLANKENSHIP

KENTUCKY EQUAL RIGHTS ASSOCIATION (KERA). Founded in November 1888 by suffragists from Fayette and Kenton counties, the KERA was the first permanent women's rights organization in Kentucky. The Kentucky Woman Suffrage Association (KWSA), organized at Louisville in 1881, was the first state suffrage society in the South, but it failed to grow and was incorporated into the KERA in 1888. Laura CLAY, the leading figure in founding the KERA and its president until 1912, attributed the failure of the KWSA to its narrow purpose—the winning of the franchise, an objective that she believed was too radical for Kentuckians at that time. She was careful to include the winning of legal, educational, and industrial rights, as well as the ballot, in the goals of the new organization.

Starting with fewer than one hundred members drawn almost exclusively from Lexington, Covington, Newport, Richmond, and Louisville, the KERA began a vigorous campaign of lecturing, writing pamphlets, organizing new chapters, circulating petitions, and lobbying at Frankfort in the interest of women's rights. During the 1890s the KERA won a number of significant victories for women. These included state laws making a wife's wages payable only to her, giving a married woman the right to make a will and control her real estate, and equalizing the rights of courtesy and dower. In 1894 the General Assembly granted the women of Lexington, Newport, and Covington the right to vote in all school board elections. The KERA also successfully petitioned several colleges, including Transylvania, Georgetown, Wesleyan at Winchester, and

Central University in Richmond, to admit women as students. Concerned about conditions for children as well, the KERA in 1896 secured legislation to establish reform schools for both female and male juveniles and two years later a law mandating the appointment of a woman physician in every state asylum with female inmates.

Joined by the Women's Christian Temperance Union and the Kentucky Federation of Women's Clubs at the turn of the century, the KERA made new gains for women and children. Responding to the groups' pressure, the legislature appropriated money for a women's dormitory at the University of Kentucky, created juvenile courts, passed a child labor law, and raised the age of consent from twelve to sixteen years of age. By 1910 the KERA and its women's club allies were concentrating on women's suffrage, believing that this reform would make all others possible. Led by Madeline McDowell BRECKINRIDGE, who served two terms as its president (1912-15, 1919-20), the KERA won legislative enactment of school suffrage for all literate women in 1912. With a membership approaching 20,000, it spearheaded the campaign for the commonwealth's ratification of the Nineteenth Amendment to the Constitution, which came on January 6, 1920, making Kentucky the twenty-third state to support political equality for American women.

In addition to Clay and Breckinridge, Elizabeth Bennett Smith (1915-16) and Christine Bradley South (1916-19) served as KERA presidents. Following the final suffrage victory in 1920, the association voted to become the LEAGUE OF WOMEN VOTERS OF KENTUCKY.

See Paul E. Fuller, *Laura Clay and the Woman's Rights Movement* (Lexington, Ky., 1975); Susan B. Anthony, Elizabeth Cady Stanton, and Ida Husted Harper, eds., *The History of Woman Suffrage*, 6 vols. (Rochester, N.Y., 1922).   PAUL E. FULLER

KENTUCKY FEDERATION OF MUSIC CLUBS. The Kentucky Federation of Music Clubs was organized in Richmond, Kentucky, in 1921 to promote American music. Its founders were Mrs. Harvey Chenault, Mrs. G. W. Pickles, Mrs. B. L. Middleton, and Sallie Ashbrook, and its first president was Mrs. D. E. Fogle, of Georgetown. In 1990 members of the federation were the Ladies Matinee Musical Club, Glasgow; Junior Music Club, Glasgow; Aeolian Club, Central City; Cynthiana Musicale, Owensboro; MacDowell Club, Lexington; and Federation of Music Clubs, Richmond (Cecilian, Mary Pattie, Apollo, Chromatic, and Piano). The Kentucky Federation is affiliated with the National Federation of Music Clubs.

KENTUCKY FEDERATION OF WOMEN'S CLUBS. The Kentucky Federation of Women's Clubs (KFWC), founded in 1894, was the fourth state federation to affiliate with its parent organization, the General Federation of Women's Clubs, which began in 1890. Kentucky women, largely from middle- and upper-class backgrounds, joined the ranks of other females throughout the nation who were providing leadership for cultural activities and social reforms in their local communities. In fact, the women's club movement became an important part of the national Progressive reform movement in the early years of the twentieth century.

Beginning with a project to support traveling libraries for remote communities in eastern Kentucky, the federation launched a crusade to reform Kentucky's state school system. This campaign culminated in the 1908 General Assembly's passage of several laws revamping Kentucky's school system. To ensure enforcement of the laws and support for the state superintendent of education, women's clubs organized local school improvement associations. Federation members showed a special interest in educational issues, including endorsement of funding for public kindergartens and continuing support for the General Education Development (GED) program and other literacy projects. The GED is the equivalent of a high school diploma, earned through testing instead of coursework. In 1930, the federation established a student loan fund to assist deserving young people. In the 1980s the federation began a project, Dollars for Scholars, giving substantial financial assistance to qualified students. The members endorsed other progressive reform measures, including: women's suffrage, public libraries, support for Mammoth Cave as a national park, good roads, tuberculosis hospitals, prison reform, enforcement of child labor laws and pure food and drugs legislation, efforts to eradicate illiteracy, and the appointment of women to state boards and commissions. When World War I began, they wholeheartedly championed the war effort.

The Kentucky Federation of Women's Clubs has continued to work for improvement of local communities and the commonwealth. Its programmatic structure, divided into departments and divisions, has included projects related to conservation, education, the arts, home life, international affairs, and public affairs and health issues. Some of the noteworthy projects of the federation have included: financial assistance to the Kentucky Bicentennial Bookshelf series, funding for a Historymobile, continuing support for Kentucky Education Television, providing kidney dialysis machines, and a wide variety of programs supporting health awareness.

In 1956, the KFWC established permanent headquarters at 1228 Cherokee Road in Louisville.

See Nancy Forderhase, " 'The Clear Call of Thoroughbred Women': The Kentucky Federation of Women's Clubs and the Crusade for Educational Reform, 1903-1909," *Register* 83 (Winter 1985): 19-35.   NANCY FORDERHASE

KENTUCKY FISHING REEL. The Kentucky fishing reel was a bait casting reel manufactured in Kentucky during the nineteenth century, invented between 1805 and 1810 by George Synder of Paris, Kentucky, a watchmaker and president of the Bourbon County Angling Club. The Kentucky fishing reel was the first multiplying reel. In such reels, every turn of the handle results in two to four revolutions of the spool. Using Synder's design, jewelers Jonathan and Benjamin Meek of Frankfort, Kentucky, began making reels under the name Meek and Meek in 1835. The firm became Meek and Milam in 1853, after Jonathan Meek left the company and his apprentice, Benjamin Milam, became a partner. Reels made by this firm until 1878 were of such high quality that they set the standard for the reel-making industry.

Because the design of the reels allowed the angler to cast bait a great distance, multiplying reels were also known as bait casting reels. (In fly fishing, by contrast, the line, rather than the bait, is cast.) As sport fishing gained in popularity in the nineteenth and twentieth centuries, they became the reel of choice for most bass fishermen. After the Horton Manufacturing Company of Bristol, Connecticut, bought the Meek name in 1916, the products became known simply as bait casting reels rather than Kentucky fishing reels. Despite some modifications, such as antibacklash devices, all bait casting reels are still based on Synder's original design.

See Albert J. Munger, *Those Old Fishing Reels* (Philadelphia 1982).

KENTUCKY FUTURITY. The Kentucky Futurity is the oldest classic stakes race for harness horses and the first trotting futurity; the competitors in a futurity are nominated at birth or before. The Kentucky Futurity has been trotted since October 9, 1893, with the exception of four years in the early 1940s. The first race was won by Oro Wilkes. The race is held at Lexington's RED MILE each fall and has been associated with the Grand Circuit since 1912, when the track joined that series. It is the climax of the season for the country's best three-year-old trotters, the final jewel in the Triple Crown for trotters, along with the Hambletonian and the Yonkers Futurity. The leading sires of Kentucky Futurity winners (in order) are Star's Pride, Peter Volo, Peter the Great, and Guy Axworthy. The top breeders (in order) are Walnut Hall farm, Hanover Shoe farm, and Castleton farm. Thirty-five fillies have won the race.

In 1898 Peter the Great won in straight heats, the first heat by twenty lengths. His get won many more Kentucky Futurities: daughter Sadie Mac in 1903, son Peter Volo in 1914, daughter Volga in 1916, and daughter Ethelinda in 1923; grandsons and granddaughters Bertha in 1930, Protector in 1931, The Marchioness in 1932, and Peter Astra in 1939; and great-grandsons and great-granddaughters Twilight Song in 1937, Victory Song in 1946, and Kimberly Kid in 1953.

See Biff Lowry, Terry Todd, and Tom White, *A Century of Speed: the Red Mile, 1875-1975* (Lexington, Ky., 1975).   MARY E. WHARTON

KENTUCKY GAZETTE. The *Gazette* was the first newspaper published west of the Alleghenies. Delegates to the second statehood convention, meeting at Danville in 1785, saw a distinct need for a print medium to help unify public opinion; they adopted a resolution stating: "To assure unanimity in the opinion of the people respecting the propriety of separating the District of Kentucky from Virginia and forming a separate state government, and to give publicity to the proceedings of the convention it is deemed essential to the interests of the country to have a printing press."

As no printer had so far crossed the mountains to settle in Kentucky, a special committee of John Coburn, Christopher Greenup, and James Wilkinson was appointed to entice a printer to move west. They sought to persuade John Dunlap of Philadelphia, but were unsuccessful. They had no better luck with Miles Hunter of Richmond, Virginia, who turned the committee down because of his fear of Indians and unhealthful conditions on the frontier. In the meantime, John Bradford, a land surveyor who had moved to Cane Run in Fayette County in 1785 from Fauquier County, Virginia, applied for the assignment of public printer.

It is doubtful that the thirty-eight-year-old John Bradford had ever seen a stick of type or a printing press. Once he was named printer-editor of the *Kentucky Gazette*-to–be, he was joined by his brother Fielding, who was sent to Pittsburgh during three months in the spring and summer of 1787 to learn the printing trade from John Scull, editor of the newly established *Pittsburgh Gazette*. He was also charged with procuring type, a press, and other printing supplies. The type was almost certainly cut in Philadelphia and the press came from that city, but the paper and ink may have come from Pittsburgh.

The printing materials were brought down the Ohio River by flatboat to Limestone (now Maysville) and from there overland by packhorse to Lexington. The type for the first issue of the *Gazette* may have been set in the office of John Scull, on the flatboat, or at Limestone. In any case, as the galleys of typeset text were being carried overland, the type became scrambled and had to be reset in Lexington. There has been a rather heated argument in recent years as to whether the first printing was done by the Bradfords or by Thomas Parvin, an immigrant schoolteacher living in Fayette County. Parvin had some printing experience and certainly helped with the printing of the first issues of the *Gazette*.

The first issue, published August 11, 1787, contained an apology from John Bradford for the delay in publication. Bradford's apology and a single advertisement were the only material of local origin in the paper. It may have been the original intent of the delegates to the second Kentucky separation convention that the *Gazette* would be published in Danville because that town was the site of the separation conventions and later the location of the first U.S. post office in Kentucky. The trustees of

Lexington, however, offered free use of a lot and a cabin near the corner of West Main and Main Cross (now Broadway) streets. In time, the *Gazette* office occupied various locations in that general neighborhood.

No copy of the first issue of the *Kentucke Gazette* is known to have survived. There is, however, a surviving copy of the second issue, August 18, 1787, and evidence indicates that the second issue was largely a rerun of the first. The first issues of the paper were printed in small folio form, measuring approximately eight by ten inches. The sheets were pulled from the press at the rate of fifty to sixty per hour. The type was inked with "dog skin" balls (animal skins tied in small bundles), and the freshly printed sheets had to be dried to keep them from smearing.

Many of the earlier issues of the *Gazette* contained almost no news of local consequence. The contents were mainly letters pertaining to various public issues, advertisements of stallion services, and requests that parties returning east assemble at Crab Orchard or Hazel Patch. Some merchants listed goods just received. In time the paper published verbatim many of the U.S. congressional debates and the proceedings of the Kentucky General Assembly. In the issue of March 7, 1789, the "e" was dropped in favor of the "y" in "Kentucky," after the General Assembly of Virginia officially decreed the name of its western district to be Kentucky.

As time passed, more paper, ink, and news became available in the western country. The *Gazette* from the start was a chronicler of public affairs. It first appeared weekly, then as a bi- and a triweekly. It was first delivered to Danville, Boonesborough, and Louisville by post rider, but after the U.S. post office opened in Danville the paper was distributed by mail.

John Bradford remained owner and editor of the *Gazette* until 1802, when he transferred ownership to his son Daniel. In turn Daniel sold the newspaper to Thomas Smith in 1809, and in 1814 Smith sold it to Fielding Bradford, Jr. The *Gazette* was published from August 11, 1787, to December 29, 1848. The name was revived in another Lexington newspaper that was published from 1866 to 1910.

In 1788 John Bradford began a twenty-year period of publishing the *Kentucky Almanac*. He also published the earlier volumes of the *Acts* of the Kentucky General Assembly. The *Gazette* print shop published a relatively large number of pamphlets, broadsides, and books. Many of these have disappeared, but are known to have existed from notices published in the *Gazette*. Among the most important publications of the *Gazette* are John Bradford's "Notes on Kentucky," sixty-six articles published in the *Gazette* from August 25, 1826, to January 1829. John Bradford returned to the editorship of the *Gazette* from May 1825 to June 1827. He was then succeeded by Albert G. Merriwether.

See Charles R. Staples, "John Bradford and the 'Kentucke' Gazette . . . First Newspaper," *Kentucky Press* 8 (February 1937): 2-3; Charles R. Staples, *The History of Pioneer Lexington (Kentucky) 1779-1806* (Lexington, Ky., 1939); William H. Perrin, *The Pioneer Press of Kentucky* (Louisville 1888).　　　　　　Thomas D. Clark

KENTUCKY GEOLOGICAL SURVEY. The Kentucky Geological Survey, one of the country's oldest state geological organizations, is a research and service department of the University of Kentucky. It conducts basic and applied research on Kentucky's geology and mineral resources and compiles and disseminates the resulting data. William W. Mather, the first designated state geologist, recognized Kentucky's mineral districts and in 1838 delimited the state's eastern and western coal fields and central and southern limestone areas.

The first Kentucky Geological Survey was organized in 1854, twenty-five years before the U.S. Geological Survey was established. David Dale Owen was appointed state geologist that year. Owen, an Indiana resident popularly regarded as the premier scientist of the Midwest, remained state geologist until 1860, although he did little field work in Kentucky after 1857, when he was also appointed state geologist of Arkansas. Four volumes of geological information, totaling 2,000 pages, were published describing the coal, iron ore, building stone, and other mineral resources of Kentucky. Some maps and plates of fossils with related text were included. In the work, Robert Peter, a Transylvania University chemist, drew attention to the soil composition of the state. This first survey lasted until 1860, when it was terminated upon the death of Owen.

The second Kentucky Geological Survey was established in 1873. Nathaniel Southgate Shaler, a Newport native and a Harvard professor, was appointed director. With only $10,000 budgeted, the staff that Shaler put together was relatively inexperienced, but over the next eight years it produced the first map that accurately located the main geological features of the state on a scale of one inch to one mile. While Shaler himself was interested in paleontology and caves, circumstances dictated that he devote attention to economic geology. The county reports produced by the Shaler survey and the following Procter survey were devoted mainly to matters of coal, oil, gas, building stone, road materials, and other useful minerals. The survey contributed to the expansion of the railroads and to a sixfold increase in coal mining during Shaler's years with the survey.

Shaler remained state geologist until 1880, when he was succeeded by John R. Procter, who was appointed commissioner of immigration as well as state geologist and director of the Kentucky Geological Survey. Procter, an efficient administrator but an amateur geologist, contributed little to the understanding of the geology of the state. Reports begun under Shaler were published, but without Shaler's editorial and theoretical skill. The publications, while impressive in size, were of little long-range worth. In 1893 Procter moved to the Civil Service Commission in Washington, D.C., and the survey quietly disappeared.

In 1904 Charles J. Norwood, dean of the University of Kentucky College of Mining and Metallurgy, was named to head the third survey. In 1912, however, the General Assembly specified that the state geologist not be connected with any school, so that he could devote full time to the survey, and Joseph B. Hoeing replaced Norwood that year. Hoeing's professionally run survey produced over 4,300 pages of original work. Hoeing resigned as state geologist in 1918, when the legislature combined the state Board of Forestry with the Kentucky Geological Survey. John E. Barton, the former state forester, was appointed commissioner of geology and forestry. Barton hired Willard R. JILLSON as an assistant geologist late in 1918, and the following year appointed him state geologist and deputy commissioner. The two organizations were then separated again, and Jillson was appointed state geologist and director of the sixth Kentucky Geological Survey in 1920. Jillson, a petroleum geologist with broad education and experience, concentrated on economic geology, as the earlier surveys had done. The most comprehensive mapping, both geologically and topographically, was completed during his thirteen years with the survey. He sought the best geologists for summer field work, without concern for year-round availability. Jillson wrote prolifically, as well as publishing the work of his subordinates, resulting in an outpouring of material. It was followed by another sixfold increase in the amount of coal mined in the state.

The sixth survey was abruptly terminated in 1932 because of political conflicts. The Kentucky Geological Survey was renamed the Bureau of Mineral and Topographic Survey of the University of Kentucky, and Arthur C. McFarlan was named state geologist and director of the bureau. This version of the Kentucky Geological Survey lasted only until 1934, when the survey was made a division of the Kentucky Department of Mines and Minerals. Daniel J. Jones was named to head the new division.

In 1948 the Kentucky Geological Survey was transferred from the state Department of Mines and Minerals to the University of Kentucky, where it became a research bureau attached to the Department of Geology in the College of Arts and Sciences. Jones continued as state geologist, and McFarlan was reappointed director of the survey. The survey was made a separate bureau of the university in 1958, and upon the retirement of Jones later that year, Wallace W. Hagan was named state geologist and director of the tenth Kentucky Geological Survey. Hagan retired in 1978 and was succeeded by Donald C. Haney. In 1988 the survey celebrated its sesquicentennial and moved into a new building on the campus.

Since coal is a major part of the state's economy, much of the survey's research is devoted to it. A project during 1974-83 assessed Kentucky's remaining coal resources at 95.5 billion tons. A new project was undertaken to determine how much of this can actually be mined. Other research includes a study of the limestone resources in eastern Kentucky; subsurface investigations of structure and stratigraphy related to oil and gas occurrence; an experiment to construct an artificial aquifer in coal mine spoils; a hydrogeologic study of the quantity and quality of ground and surface water in the Kentucky River drainage basin; and stratigraphic studies in the eastern and western Kentucky coal fields.

The Kentucky Geological Survey has a long history of joint programs with the U.S. Geological Survey. The first was begun in 1904 to map parts of Kentucky topographically at a scale of 1:62,500. A joint program during 1949-56 made Kentucky the first state in the nation to be completely mapped topographically at a scale of 1:24,000. Those 7.5-minute quadrangle maps were used as bases for an even more ambitious project during 1960-78: the complete geologic mapping of Kentucky at a scale of 1:24,000. The $21 million program was at that time the largest geologic mapping project that had been undertaken in the United States, and represented about 660 man-years of work.

The survey, the official repository for oil and gas drilling records, has on file the records for an estimated 225,000 wells. The survey's well sample and core repository is one of the largest in the country; it should ultimately have at least one set of well cuttings or core samples for every square mile in the state.

See Willard R. Jillson, "A History of the Kentucky Geological Survey (1838-1921)," *Register* 19 (1921): 89-112; L. C. Robinson, "The Kentucky Geological Survey," *Register* 25 (1927): 1-10.

MARGARET LUTHER SMATH

KENTUCKY GOVERNMENT COUNCIL. The Kentucky Government Council was a nonpartisan advocacy group founded in August 1961 to improve state government on behalf of the whole citizenry. The council's strength was its independence of any particular administration, clique, person, or economic persuasion. Its method of influencing change was to analyze state problems, bring findings to the attention of the public, and recommend significant reforms.

The council's achievements during its fifteen years of existence were impressive. It backed the move that raised the rate of investment return on idle surplus state funds from 0.56 percent to 4 percent. It organized a forty-person committee representing various civic and political interests that provided key support to the General Assembly's efforts to reform itself and to end its dominance by the executive branch. At the council's urging, legislation was passed to end unrealistic limits on campaign contributions and expenditures and to require disclosure of both the amounts of contributions and the nature of expenditures.

The council was also responsible for a fundamental reconstruction of the Council on Public Higher Education (now Council on Higher Education). Reforms placed control of comprehensive fiscal and educational planning for institutions of higher education under a single board of regents, with an executive director as chief administrative officer. The role of the university presidents was reduced to service as ex-officio advisers. Among its other significant contributions, the council contracted for and published the only definitive study of the history and administration of the Merit System Law, compiled strict standards to govern the incurring of bonded indebtedness, and recommended guidelines to improve the old, disorganized systems of highway construction.

The council was dissolved in January 1976.

W.S. BOWMER

KENTUCKY GUILD OF ARTISTS AND CRAFTSMEN. Joining the interests of the Department of Economic Development and those of artists and craftspersons, the Kentucky Guild of Artists and Craftsmen was incorporated in 1960. In creating the guild, the department sought to encourage and market crafts to help local economies, and the artists/craftspersons sought a way to ensure high standards of design and production. Under a state grant, the guild established a program of education, design development, and marketing. In 1961 two Louisville & Nashville railroad cars were converted into a gallery and a demonstration-workshop, and the "Guild Train" traveled for six years, bringing art exhibitions and production assistance to communities throughout the state.

Although membership in the guild is open, those who exhibit and sell through its facilities meet exacting quality standards. Craft centers, workshops, galleries, and fairs are the major means of education and marketing. The guild is financed primarily by sales at the biennial Crafts Fair in Berea, Kentucky. It is managed by an elected board of directors and a salaried executive. LESTER F. PROSS

KENTUCKY HIGHLANDS MUSEUM. When Eliza Gartrell built her home at 1516 Bath Avenue, Ashland, Kentucky, in 1864, she most likely had no idea that it would one day become the repository of the history and heritage of the Kentucky Highlands. The three-story house, now known as the Mayo Manor, was extensively remodeled in 1917 by Alice Mayo Fetter, widow of John C.C. Mayo, and it became the home of the Kentucky Highlands Museum in 1984, when the Kentucky Highlands Museum Society was incorporated. The society's purpose is "to enhance public awareness of area history through preservation, investigation, display and interpretation of artifacts, collections and information concerning the history of the Kentucky Highlands region of Appalachia . . . and to establish educational programs for the public good and maintain the Mayo Manor as a museum for that purpose." A board of trustees, paid staff, and volunteers carry out that mission, financed by grants, memberships, and private contributions.

Among the museum's permanent collections are the $400,000 antique clothing collection of thousands of articles of apparel and accessories, and the home furnishings and memorabilia of folklorist Jean Thomas, "The Traipsin' Woman," who promoted Appalachian culture. Indians, industry, aviation, World War II, and coal mining are represented, and traveling exhibits add variety.

C. RICHARD LOVEGROVE

KENTUCKY HISTORICAL SOCIETY. On April 22, 1836, in the secretary of state's office in Frankfort, Sen. John Brown presided over the meeting that voted to organize a historical society to collect and preserve items related to Kentucky history. John Rowan was elected the first president of the Kentucky State Historical Society. The society was incorporated and a constitution was adopted in 1838, when the headquarters of the organization moved to Louisville. In 1841 the Kentucky legislature directed that copies of all public printed documents be deposited with the society.

The death of Rowan in July 1843 left the society without strong leadership, and interest in the organization declined. In 1852 Louisville historian Ben Casseday stated that the group was no longer in existence. The historical society remained dormant until October 1878, when George W. Ranck of Lexington and the members of the Frankfort Lyceum arranged a meeting to revive the organization. In 1880 the society was incorporated anew and rooms for its collection of books and relics were provided in the Old State House in Frankfort. The state stood guardian over the society's collection but provided no outright funds for its maintenance. Lack of support by the legislature and various governors probably contributed to the second lapse in the operation of the society in the spring of 1889, when the Historical Rooms in the Old State House were closed and the state became the keeper of the historical society's collection. Not content to let the society languish, however, Jennie C. Morton and the Frankfort Colonial Daughters held a public meeting on October 6, 1896, and in June 1897 the historical society was legally reorganized.

By 1902 the state had agreed to provide for the printing of the society's publications and in January 1903 the first issue of the *Register of the Kentucky State Historical Society*, a quarterly history journal, was published. It was edited by Morton, the first secretary-treasurer of the society. In 1906 the commonwealth appropriated $5,000 annually for operating the society; it has received state support ever since. In 1909 the society moved into rooms in the new capitol building and remained there until 1920, when its headquarters was transferred back to a renovated Old State House. Since Morton's death in 1920, the following have served as directors of the society: Jouett Taylor Cannon (1920-47), Bayless E. Hardin (1947-56), Charles F. Hinds (1956-59), George M. Chinn (1959-73), William R.

Buster (1973-83), Robert B. Kinnaird (1983-90), and James C. Klotter (1990-).

The name was changed in 1947 to the Kentucky Historical Society. In 1954 the society became an independent agency of state government, while retaining its status as a nonprofit membership organization. The 1960s saw increased membership growth, aided greatly by expanding programs and services. In 1965, *Kentucky Ancestors*, a genealogical quarterly, was born; soon afterward, the newsletter *Communique* (started in 1947) became the bimonthly *Bulletin*. In 1962 the Kentucky Young Historians Association (now the Kentucky Junior Historical Society) was formed to sponsor school projects and competitions dealing with Kentucky history. Such activities as workshops for teachers, mobile museum exhibits, a cemetery records project, a highway markers program, and a local history program all reach large numbers of Kentuckians across the entire state.

The society's Kentucky History Museum in the Old State House Annex interprets the state's cultural history. The Kentucky Military History Museum opened in 1974 in the old State Arsenal building. The Kentucky Historical Society's research library contains 80,000 volumes, 50,000 photographs, and more than 1,000 cubic feet of manuscripts and maps. The preservation services section of the library provides conservation, encapsulation, and microfilming of historical and genealogical documents.

See Willard Rouse Jillson, "A Sketch and Bibliography of the Kentucky State Historical Society 1836-1943," *Register* 41 (July 1943): 179-230.

GRETCHEN M. HANEY

KENTUCKY HORSE PARK. On September 7, 1978, the Commonwealth of Kentucky opened the $35 million Kentucky Horse Park. The 1,032-acre complex was conceived by noted Lexington horseman John R. GAINES, and championed in Frankfort by Rep. William R. Kenton, Jr. Designed as an equestrian theme park and located at the junction of I-75 and Iron Works Pike in northern Fayette County, the park immediately became a major tourism magnet for the Lexington area.

The park has the following attractions: a 28,000-square-foot visitors' center with twin 35mm theaters; the 52,000-square-foot International Museum of the Horse; a model farm, featuring a farrier's and a harnessmaker's shop; the Breeds Barn, housing many of the park's thirty-two breed representatives and the daily Parade of Breeds educational presentations; the Kentucky Equine Institute, an equestrian vocational school; the Hall of Champions, home to racing and show-ring greats; and the draft horse and carriage horse barns, which support the park's tours by horse-drawn carriage. A 261-site resort campground has swimming, tennis, volleyball, and basketball facilities.

During the Kentucky Horse Park's first decade, development centered on expanding facilities for horse shows and competitions, of which many are held each year. The keystone is the 3,500-seat Frederick L. Van Lennep Arena. The annual Rolex Three Day Event draws international riders to compete over the prestigious cross-country course.

BILL COOKE

KENTUCKY HUMANITIES COUNCIL. The Kentucky Humanities Council, headquartered in Lexington, sponsors presentations about literature, history, philosophy, anthropology, and folklore for public, adult audiences. Its programs include speeches by scholars, humanities festivals, films and other media projects, adult reading and study groups, and elderhostels. Founded in 1972 by the act of Congress that created the state humanities programs under the National Endowment for the Humanities, the Humanities Council funds approximately 150 programs a year in all Kentucky congressional districts. The council has received recognition for several of its projects, including New Books for New Readers (books for adults learning to read) and the Humanities Institute for School Administrators (a seminar for superintendents and principals). THOMAS A. GREENFIELD

KENTUCKY INSURANCE COMPANY. The Kentucky Insurance Company (KIC) was organized in Lexington in January 1802 by merchants who hoped to profit by insuring boats engaged in the burgeoning Ohio and Mississippi river trade. In December 1802 the company acquired a charter from the state legislature that included a clause authorizing banking, and in the spring of 1803 the KIC abandoned insurance for banking. It was soon the target of a bitter political campaign to revoke its charter for engaging in the "unrepublican" activity of banking. The KIC issue agitated Kentucky politics for the next two years and launched the political careers of Felix Grundy, who led the attack on the company, and Henry Clay, who was the bank's chief spokesman. The controversy was settled in 1806 when the legislature chartered the Bank of Kentucky, modeled on the Bank of the United States, with branches in Frankfort, Lexington, and Bardstown. The KIC retained its charter and prospered until 1818, when James Prentiss, a Rhode Island entrepreneur, drained its assets in a vain attempt to save his failing manufacturing enterprise.

See Dale Royalty, "James Prentiss and the Failure of the Kentucky Insurance Company, 1813-1818," *Register* 73 (Jan. 1975): 1-16.

DALE ROYALTY

KENTUCKY INTERCOLLEGIATE ATHLETIC CONFERENCE. The Kentucky Intercollegiate Athletic Conference was formed in 1923. Charter members included five private colleges—Kentucky Wesleyan, Berea, Georgetown, Transylvania, and Centre—and three public institutions: Eastern Kentucky and Western Kentucky State Teachers Colleges, and the University of Louisville. Other schools joined in the 1940s, including Morehead and Murray State Teachers Colleges, while others left for other conferences. In 1991 the members, a mix of two- and four-year colleges, were Lindsey Wilson, Berea, Campellsville, Cumberland, Georgetown, Pikeville, and Union. While the conference administers championship competition in track, baseball, tennis, and golf, basketball remains the primary sport. The first basketball tournament was held in 1926. Early tournaments were held at Kentucky Wesleyan in Winchester; more recently they have been hosted by the college with the better record of the two participating teams. In 1982 a women's program was added. The conference has had two commissioners: Jack Thompson, Louisville (1966-75), and Jack Wise, Georgetown (1975-).

JAMES C. CLAYPOOL

KENTUCKY IRISH AMERICAN. The first weekly edition of the *Kentucky Irish American* newspaper was published on July 4, 1898, by its founder and editor, William M. Higgins, for Louisville's more than 19,000 citizens of Irish descent. Like most major U.S. cities in the late nineteenth century, Louisville was divided into ethnic neighborhoods where cultural heritage and traditions were preserved. By the 1890s, however, these areas were becoming less defined along ethnic lines, and Higgins saw a need for a publication that would hold the Irish-American community together.

The *Irish American*'s offices at 319 West Liberty Street in Louisville shared space with a German-language publication, the *Louisville Anzeiger*. The early articles, almost all written by Higgins, emphasized cultural pride and Irish nationalism. The 1798 Irish uprising against the British was celebrated in centennial articles, and Higgins also took on current issues in Ireland, including famine and home rule. While the first few editions of the *Irish American* were not written along religious or political lines, Higgins's stands on issues soon began to favor the Democratic party and the Roman Catholic church. As journalistic objectivity became less important, he gave wide publicity to Irish-American organizations and published front-page editorials of scathing commentary with an ethnic slant. Beginning in 1900, the paper printed below the masthead the motto "Devoted to the Social and Moral Advancement of Irish-Americans and Catholics." Although not an official Catholic paper, the *Irish American* engaged many Baptist newspapers in journalistic warfare, attacking prohibition and racism.

In 1925 John J. Barry, Higgins's business associate, took over the *Irish American* and ran it until his death in 1950, publishing editorials that criticized all who crossed him. Republicans were his main targets, but Barry also took on Kentucky Democrat A.B. CHANDLER, charging him with bigotry, and he referred to the Louisville Police Department as "the Keystone Coppers." By 1930, when Ireland had achieved its independence and interest in Irish nationalism had begun to wane, Barry began to feature articles from other journals that reflected his political opinions.

After Barry died in 1950, his sons Michael and Joseph took over. Joseph was the paper's business manager, and Michael, who had written a sports column for the paper since 1934, was the editor and chief writer, turning out at least 7,000 words of copy each week. He preserved the hard-hitting journalism that was the *Irish American*'s trademark, but circulation rarely exceeded 4,000, even though subscriptions came from forty-three states. Barry could not make a living from the *Irish American* alone, and also worked as a track handicapper and as a radio sportscaster for Louisville's WKLO. Barry continued his assault on the "anti-Semitic, anti-Negro, and anti-moderate" Republicans, including 4th District Congressman Gene SNYDER. Ethnic papers were no longer popular, however, and the last issue of the *Kentucky Irish American* was published on November 30, 1968.

See Stanley Ousley, "The Kentucky Irish American," *FCHQ* 53 (April 1979): 178-95.

KENTUCKY LIBRARY AND MUSEUM. The Kentucky Building at Western Kentucky University houses a special collections library and a museum where historical materials document life in Kentucky. The collection began in the 1920s as an aid for the school's history classes. It expanded rapidly when several innovative teachers acquainted their students with the variety of items that could serve as primary resources and challenged them to locate and donate additional pieces. The collection outgrew the professors' office space and then the allotted library area. In 1929 school president Henry Hardin Cherry announced a drive to raise money for a structure that would house the collection. Students, faculty, alumni, and even grade school children contributed money for the Kentucky Building.

Louisville architect Brinton B. DAVIS designed the colonial-style edifice. Construction began in 1931, but the Great Depression delayed completion until state and federal funds became available. The 40,000-square-foot structure opened to the public in 1939. Forty years later the overcrowded building was enlarged and remodeled to double its space and provide modern care for the collections.

The library's noncirculating materials include more than 35,000 published books; 3 million manuscript pages; folklore/folklife archives of 2,300 projects and 3,700 audiotapes; 12,000 photographs; and hundreds of maps, broadsides, newspapers, and ephemera. The museum houses 100,000 Native American artifacts and 70,000 pieces of nineteenth and twentieth century household items, textiles, glassware, and art works. In 1980 a log house built in Logan County in 1820 was moved to the grounds.

NANCY D. BAIRD

KENTUCKY MANUFACTURING COMPANY. The Kentucky Manufacturing Company was an early attempt to bring manufacturing to the western region of Virginia. It was established in the fall of 1789 to make cotton cloth and stockings at

Danville. Members of the company included early political leaders, among them Harry Innes, Thomas Barbee, Christopher Greenup, George Nicholas, and Samuel McDowell. Local residents purchased stock in small blocks, and machinery was transported from Philadelphia in 1790; production began that fall. There are no records of the success or termination of the company.

KENTUCKY MEDICAL ASSOCIATION. Responding to a petition by thirty-five physicians, the General Assembly in 1851 incorporated the Kentucky State Medical Society, the predecessor of the Kentucky Medical Association. The association, headquartered in Louisville, plays a vital role in advancing medical education and enhancing the delivery of medical care throughout the state. Its major publication is the *Journal of the Kentucky Medical Association*.   ERIC HOWARD CHRISTIANSON

KENTUCKY MILITARY INSTITUTE. The Kentucky Military Institute (KMI) was a prestigious military preparatory school that attracted boys from the South interested in a military career. While many KMI graduates rose to prominence in the military, thousands of others provided leadership in the professions and in business. KMI was founded by Robert Thomas Pitcairn Allen, a graduate of the U.S. Military Academy at West Point with both military and educational experience. Allen purchased the Scanlan Springs resort in 1845, opened his academy that year, and in 1847 received a charter from the state of Kentucky. The school's original home was six miles from Frankfort, on the road from Farmdale to Lawrenceburg. The trip from the capital to the school took an hour by carriage, and nineteenth century promotional literature claimed that "an advantage possessed by this Institute, of the greatest importance, is the distance of its location from the tempting and corrupting influences of the city."

The school's excellent instructors, demanding course of study, and strict discipline attracted students from across the South, and a few from northern states as well. During the 1850s, beginning students studied Virgil, Latin composition, English grammar and synonyms, and American history. Graduating seniors had completed a semester each in architecture, political economy, physiology, international and constitutional law, history and statistics of the United States, and the lives of the founding fathers.

School operations continued during the Civil War, when many KMI students and graduates served in each army. By the 1870s, the curriculum was designed to prepare students for industrial and professional occupations. Throughout the school's history, study of the classics, science, mathematics, history, and literature was accompanied by training in tactics and vigorous physical exercise.

In 1887 the school went bankrupt and closed. It reopened the next year. During his term as superintendent around the turn of the century, Charles

Wesley Fowler introduced many changes at KMI. In 1896 he moved the school from Mt. Sterling to a campus near Lyndon, Jefferson County, that could house three hundred cadets. In 1906 Fowler began a policy of moving the students and faculty to a winter campus in Florida between Christmas and Easter of each year. The school closed again in 1924 but opened the next year and entered prosperous years under superintendent Charles B. Richmond (1925-65).

By the late 1960s, Vietnam War era disaffection with the military and inflationary costs had made attraction of students difficult for KMI and for most other military schools. Financial difficulties closed KMI in 1971.   NICKY HUGHES

KENTUCKY MILITIA. The Kentucky militia was both the organized and the unorganized citizen soldiery of Kentucky from the American Revolution until the 1850s. From colonial Virginia the original settlers brought west with them a militia system, over which the royal governors had presided as commanders in chief. For each county in Virginia, the chief executives selected county lieutenants, each holding the rank of colonel. A militia colonel enlisted and drilled all able-bodied males from eighteen to forty-five years of age. To defend and retaliate against Indian attacks, the Kentucky pioneers copied the Virginia system in the western counties they began organizing.

In training, discipline, and endurance, the original Kentucky militiamen did not match the effectiveness of army regulars. Nevertheless, Kentucky militia volunteers under Col. George Rogers Clark undertook with varying success several punitive raids north of the Ohio River. Clark's followers established a preference in Kentucky for service as mounted riflemen. From the mid-1780s, militia officers advocated statehood for Kentucky. In the early 1790s, Kentucky militiamen supplemented the regulars in the successive northwestern campaigns of Gens. Josiah Harmar, Arthur Saint Clair, and Anthony Wayne. They served well at the August 1794 Battle of Fallen Timbers, which helped Ohio achieve statehood nine years later. In the War of 1812, the Kentucky militia served mostly on the northwestern frontier. Following several setbacks, a force of 3,500 men under the personal command of Gov. Isaac Shelby (1792-1796, 1812-1816) played a pivotal role in Gen. William Henry Harrison's climactic October 1813 victory over the British and Indians in the Battle of the Thames.

Once the Indian wars of the Old Northwest ceased, the Kentucky militia had outlived its usefulness. Its national and state appropriations declined and muster days became mostly social occasions. The Kentuckians who went off to the Mexican War did so as state volunteers mustered into federal service. In 1854, by stipulating that each county was to conduct only one muster every six years, the General Assembly effectively abolished the militia system.

See Richard G. Stone, Jr., *A Brittle Sword: The Kentucky Militia, 1776-1912* (Lexington, Ky., 1977).
RICHARD G. STONE

KENTUCKY NEGRO EDUCATION ASSOCIATION. The Colored Teachers State Association was organized in 1877 in Frankfort, at a black teachers' convention called by the state superintendent of public instruction, H.A.M. Henderson. During this meeting the association launched the movement to establish what became Kentucky State College. Corporal punishment and industrial training were major concerns of the association during the late nineteenth century. In 1913 the association was reorganized and incorporated under a new state charter as the Kentucky Negro Education Association (KNEA). The organization sponsored annual essay-writing and spelling contests for students, as well as industrial and fine arts exhibits of students' work.

As the twentieth century progressed, the KNEA contributed funds toward the struggle to equalize teacher salaries and facilities in black schools. It encouraged the admission of black students to the University of Kentucky's graduate schools and sought repeal of the Day Law, which prohibited enrollment of black and white students in the same institution. In 1954 the members of the KNEA voted to change the name to Kentucky Teachers Association. In 1957 the Kentucky Teachers Association was dissolved in merging with the formerly all-white Kentucky Education Association.

See Alice A. Dunnigan, *The Fascinating Story of Black Kentuckians: Their Heritage and Tradition* (Washington, D.C., 1982).　　GERALD L. SMITH

KENTUCKY OPERA. The Kentucky Opera was founded in 1952 in Louisville by Moritz von Bomhard. A native of Germany who had become a U.S. citizen, Bomhard served as conductor, and in the early days he also designed the sets, trained the singers and chorus, directed the staging, and, until 1970, even designed the brochures for the opera company. The company presented works in the Columbia Auditorium on Fourth Street, which lacked an orchestra pit, until the 1963-64 season, when performances were moved to the Brown Theatre on Broadway near Fourth. After a major restoration, it was renamed Macauley's Theatre.

In the 1950s five operas were commissioned by the Kentucky Opera and given their world premieres. In addition to the standard opera repertoire, Bomhard presented one opera each year that was new to his audience. Stravinsky's *Oedipus Rex*, Britten's *Peter Grimes*, and Janacek's *Jenufa* were most successful, as was *The Flying Dutchman*, the company's first presentation of a Wagnerian opera. Each season the company performed four operas, one of them by Mozart. Bomhard did not present any opera more than once in five years.

Bomhard retired in 1982 at the age of seventy-four and Thomson Smillie became general director. A native of Glasgow, Scotland, Smillie had worked for the Scottish Opera for twelve years, in addition to being the artistic director of the Wexford Festival of Ireland. Before replacing Bomhard, Smillie had been general manager at the Opera Company of Boston. Mary Ann Krebs joined Smillie at the Kentucky Opera as executive director in 1983. The opening of the Kentucky Center for the Arts in the 1983-84 season presented a real challenge to Smillie. The new center's Whitney Hall seated 2,400, or 1,000 more than Macauley's. Smillie met the challenge by presenting grand operas such as *Aida* at the center, medium-size works such as *The Barber of Seville* at Macauley's, and chamber operas such as Britten's *Albert Herring* in the arts center's Bomhard Theater, which seats fewer than seven hundred. This three-theater concept worked well.

The board that oversees the Kentucky Opera had fifty-four members in 1990. The Kentucky Opera Guild consists of two chapters, Outreach and Development. The Kentucky Opera is financed by ticket sales, corporate and individual sponsors, the National Endowment for the Arts, the National Endowment for the Humanities, the Kentucky Arts Council, the Greater Louisville Fund for the Arts, and local fund raisers, such as a book sale and the Hard Scuffle Steeplechase, using 1,000 volunteers.

The Kentucky Opera's budget was less than $10,000 the first year; in the late 1980s, the annual budget exceeded $2 million.　　JANET GRAFF

KENTUCKY POST. The *Kentucky Post* was founded as a daily newspaper in Covington on September 15, 1890, by Edward Willis Scripps, who ranked with Joseph Pulitzer and William Randolph Hearst among the leading turn-of-the-century American newspaper publishers. The paper was small and inexpensive: four pages for two cents a copy. It found a ready niche and grew, pursuing Scripps's policy of fighting for the working classes. Scripps founded forty-five such "penny papers" from coast to coast.

In 1899 and 1900, the *Kentucky Post* published many extra editions in covering the turbulent campaign, election, and assassination of Gov. William Goebel (1900) of Covington. It waged successful campaigns for the charter and city-manager forms of government in Covington and nearby Newport in the early 1920s; was responsible for passage of a uniform small-loan law; unearthed facts in the 1938 WPA scandal; and helped establish the Greater Cincinnati–Northern Kentucky Airport in Boone County, as well as Northern Kentucky University.

Initially printed on presses of the *Cincinnati Post*, the *Kentucky Post* had its own shop for a few years, then went to a printing plant jointly controlled by the *Cincinnati Post* and the *Cincinnati Enquirer*. The *Kentucky Post*'s editorial offices are in its own building, erected in 1902 at 421 Madison Avenue, Covington. The paper increased to eight pages in the 1890s and in time became the leading newspaper in the twelve counties of northern Kentucky, regularly publishing 24- to 48-page editions. In 1914 the newspaper began a Sunday edition, which was discontinued on December 18, 1932, because of the Depression.

The first editor of the newspaper was William P. Campbell. He was succeeded in 1904 by Harry W. Brown; in 1906 by Milton Bronner; in 1915 by Frank Crippen; in 1916 by Charles W. Larsh; in 1918 by Albert W. Buhrman and Edward P. Mills; in 1919 by Max B. Cook; in 1921 by Bruce Susong; in 1931 by Donald E. Weaver; in 1936 by Carl A. Saunders; in 1963 by Vance H. Trimble, who had just won the Pulitzer Prize in Washington, D.C., for national reporting; in 1979 by Paul F. Knue, who moved on to edit the *Cincinnati Post*; and in 1983 by Judith Clabes, former editor of the *Evansville Sunday Courier & Press* in Indiana.

See Vance H. Trimble, ed., *Scripps Howard Handbook*, 3d ed. (Cincinnati 1981).

VANCE H. TRIMBLE

KENTUCKY PRESS ASSOCIATION. The Kentucky Press Association (KPA) was organized in January 1869 in Frankfort. The leading proponents of the association were two rival Frankfort publishers, J. Stoddard Johnston and S.R. Smith. There is no record of any specific goals being stated but the expectations were that the press would help reunite Kentuckians after the schisms of the Civil War. The early meeting records reflect concerns that were to preoccupy the association for the next one hundred years: the need to be truthful and unbiased in the news columns, to be responsible on the editorial pages, and to generate more revenue while avoiding the suspicion of being beholden to special interests. Since association officers were expected to secure for their conventions as much free lodging, transportation, food, and drink as they could extract from host towns, newspaper suppliers, railroads, distillers, and brewers, there were periodic discussions about the propriety of accepting gifts. As early as 1874, the *Louisville Courier-Journal* was scolding members for traveling by train without paying the fare.

A century later, the KPA successfully campaigned for sunshine laws—laws requiring that records and meetings be open to the public—which went on the books in the 1970s. The liquor industry no longer donated convention beverages, and panels on all phases of the newspaper business, including ethics, were a regular feature of meetings. Nevertheless, the KPA did not admit the black press to membership until a decade after the Supreme Court integrated the schools in 1954 and did so only after some larger newspapers threatened to resign. Since that fight, a more professionalized KPA, representing about 150 newspapers (twenty-five of them dailies), has supported scholarships and provided visiting oversight for journalism schools.

The association's membership roster includes the nation's biggest chains, among them the *New York Times*, Gannett, Knight-Ridder, Scripps Howard, Dow Jones, Park Communications, Thomson, Don-

rey, and others. Newspapers not owned by national media companies are the independent, Kentucky-based dailies in Bowling Green, Hopkinsville, Owensboro, Henderson, and Paducah.

See Herndon J. Evans, *The Newspaper Press in Kentucky* (Lexington, Ky., 1976).

ALBERT SMITH

KENTUCKY RAILROAD COMMISSION. The creation of the Kentucky Railroad Commission on April 19, 1880—seven years earlier than the federal Interstate Commerce Commission—reflected the sharp conflict between the agrarian-populist forces and those representing the railroads. The legislation gave the commission authority over railway companies' extensions of total mileage, tariffs, complimentary passes, movement of freight cars, and details of management. In 1890 delegates to the constitutional convention gave even greater authority to the Railroad Commission in sections 209-18 of the 1891 constitution. When the federal Interstate Commerce Commission assumed most matters of railway regulation, the Kentucky Railroad Commission became a superfluous official body with no significant responsibilities.   THOMAS D. CLARK

KENTUCKY RESOLUTIONS. The indignation of the Jeffersonian Republicans over the Alien and Sedition acts passed by the Federalist-dominated Congress in June and July of 1798 found its most lasting expression in a series of resolutions adopted by the Kentucky legislature later that year. The acts, directed against supposedly subversive influences in the United States, gave the president sweeping powers to deport "dangerous" aliens (such as the French émigré editors who had come to America after the revolution) and—far more important in Kentucky, where there were few resident aliens—to punish speech and writing critical of the U.S. government. Protest meetings were held in Kentucky, giving the young Henry Clay, recently come from Virginia, the chance to deliver a blistering oration against the federal laws.

Thomas Jefferson was the principal author of the resolutions. His friend John BRECKINRIDGE brought them from Virginia and introduced them in the Kentucky House of Representatives on November 9. The authorship of Jefferson, then vice-president of the United States, was kept from the public, and the resolutions were long thought to be Breckinridge's work. (Jefferson confirmed his authorship in a letter to Joseph Cabell Breckinridge in 1821; Breckinridge is known to have modified only the last two of the nine resolutions.)

The House approved the resolutions with only one dissenting vote, the Senate adopted them unanimously, and Gov. James Garrard (1796-1804) signed them on November 13, 1798. The Alien and Sedition acts were condemned primarily on the grounds that they violated the Tenth Amendment, which states that powers not delegated to the federal government, nor prohibited to the states, are reserved to the states. The Kentucky Resolutions stated that:

1) The federal government is made up of free and independent states that have delegated "certain and definite powers" to the national government. Whenever the federal government assumes undelegated powers, its acts are "void, and of no force."

2) Because the Constitution provides for federal prosecution of specific crimes—sedition not among them—and no other crimes, the Sedition Act is "void and of no force."

3) The power to regulate licentious speech is not delegated to the federal government; thus the states are the only entities enabled to regulate the freedoms of speech and press.

4) Power over aliens is not delegated to the national government, and aliens are under the jurisdiction of the states in which they reside. Thus the Alien Act "is not law, but is altogether void and of no force."

5) The Constitution expressly states "that the migration or importation of such persons as any of the States now existing shall think proper to admit, shall not be prohibited by Congress prior to the year 1808"; because deportation, in effect, prevents migration, the Alien Act is unconstitutional, and void.

6) Deportation of any individual by order of the president only, violates the provision that "no person shall be deprived of liberty without due process of law" (Fifth Amendment) and violates the right of trial by jury (Sixth Amendment); the Alien Act grants the president judicial power, which again violates the Constitution.

7) These acts give the national government unlimited powers that are not "necessary and proper" for carrying out its delegated powers and thus the acts violate the Constitution.

8) The senators and representatives in Congress from Kentucky should introduce these resolutions in Congress, and work fervently for the repeal of the acts.

9) These resolutions should be submitted to other state legislatures to gain their support in rebuking the Alien and Sedition acts.

The Kentucky Resolutions met with support from no other state except Virginia, which adopted a similar statement in December 1798. A further resolution (authorship uncertain) was introduced by Breckinridge and adopted by the Kentucky legislature in 1799. It asserted the right of a state to resist infractions of the Constitution on the part of the U.S. government by "nullification" of the offending act—a prophetic first use of that term.

With the election of Jefferson to the presidency in 1800 and the subsequent repeal of the Alien and Sedition Acts, the immediate object of the Kentucky Resolutions passed from the scene. But their historical significance reverberates in some decisions of the U.S. Supreme Court in the John Marshall era; in Georgia's resistance to the Court in its conflict with the Cherokee nation (1831); and in South Carolina's nullification argument of 1832.

See Ethelbert Warfield, *The Kentucky Resolutions of 1798* (New York 1887); Lowell Harrison, *John Breckinridge* (Louisville 1969).

KENTUCKY RIFLE. The weapon that helped open the western frontier had its origins in European firearms—notably the old German *jäger* (hunter) flintlock rifle. Eighteenth century Pennsylvania gunsmiths of German and Swiss ancestry, who developed the Kentucky rifle, made a number of refinements to fit the needs of the frontiersman. They lightened the stock to make it easier to handle and lengthened the thirty- .to forty-inch octagonal barrel to forty to forty-five inches or more. The longer barrel not only increased the rifle's accuracy but also allowed the slow-burning powder then used more time to ignite. A third modification of the *jäger* rifle was the reduction of the .60 to .70 caliber bore size to approximately .38 to .45 caliber. Not only did the smaller bore require less lead and powder, saving money, but the rifleman could also carry significantly more of the smaller, lighter ammunition when embarking on a long hunt. The bullets used in the guns were slightly smaller than the bore diameter, with the difference made up by a greased patch. Wrapped around the bullet, the patch cleaned the barrel and speeded reloading.

Although the country's expansion brought regional variations, certain features were common. The typical rifle had a streamlined stock of curly maple, more elaborately engraved and inlaid as years passed. The wooden cover on the patchbox, located on the stock near the butt, was replaced with a hinged brass plate—a distinctive American or "Pennsylvania" feature. The metal plate was easier to handle and not as readily lost or broken; it also added to the beauty of the piece.

Despite its Pennsylvania roots, the rifle became associated with Kentucky through the exploits of Long Hunters such as Simon Kenton, John Findley, and Daniel Boone. Kentucky rifles were celebrated in Samuel Woodworth's ballad "Hunters of Kentucky," one of the most popular songs of the 1820s, written in honor of the role that Kentuckians played in the Battle of New Orleans (1815). Touring singers performed the song with bravado, dressed in frontier garb: "But Jackson he was wide awake, / and wasn't scar'd at trifles, / For well he knew what aim we take / with our Kentucky rifles." In fact Kentucky Rifle was the commercial name for a flintlock model produced by James Brown and Sons in Pittsburgh beginning in 1848, though by that time most flintlocks had been replaced by guns with the caplock (percussion) system.

Over the years, Pennsylvanians and Kentuckians engaged in friendly wrangling over proprietary rights to the rifle's name. Following a good-natured challenge in 1963 by Pennsylvania's governor, the two states met for a shoot-off. After the smoke had cleared, Kentucky's team, which featured such expert marksmen as Rex Maxey, had won. The name Kentucky Rifle remained secure.

See John G.W. Dillin, *The Kentucky Rifle* (York, Pa., 1967); Henry J. Kauffman, *The Pennsylvania-Kentucky Rifle* (Harrisburg, Pa., 1960).

JOE NICKELL AND NICKY HUGHES

KENTUCKY RIVER. Nearly 255 miles in length, the Kentucky River flows from the confluence of the North and South forks at Beattyville on a generally northwesterly course to the Ohio River at Carrollton. The headwaters of the Three Forks—the North, Middle, and South—rise in the mountains of eastern Kentucky near Pine Mountain. The river drains an area of nearly 7,000 square miles and drops 226 feet as it flows from Beattyville to Carrollton. In the river basin, the Cincinnati Arch, which crests at Camp Nelson, caused the land to rise during the Pliocene and the Pleistocene epochs. At one time the Kentucky flowed into the Ohio River far north of present-day Carrollton, but glaciation and constant weathering have changed the river's course.

The river flows through four subregions: the Cumberland Plateau, the Knobs, the Lexington Plain, and the Outer Bluegrass (see GEOGRAPHY). The oldest of the state's rock formations, the Ordovician, is found in the Bluegrass area, where the meandering river has cut deeply, exposing rugged limestone cliffs known as the Palisades. Old river channels in several areas have long since been isolated by flooding and the shifting of the earth. There are major faults along the river, two particularly large ones in the Clay's Ferry area.

Woolly mammoths and other ancient animals roamed the region during the successive ice ages and warming periods. Early humans were drawn to the region. In more recent prehistoric times, Native Americans lived on or near the river and used its resources. Early white settlers also used the river for transportation and livelihood. Fort Boonesborough, built in 1775, was dependent on the river.

The Kentucky River became a major transportation route early in state history. Flatboats built on its banks transported tobacco, whiskey, and other early agricultural products. James Wilkinson's trip with a flatboat flotilla down the Mississippi River to New Orleans in 1787 revealed the potential of the Kentucky River and the region for commercial development. Some of the first industries to use the river included the salt works on Goose Creek in Clay County and the Red River area iron smelters. Steamboats made their appearance on the river beginning in 1816, when Lexington investors built a small vessel according to an original design of Edward West. The Shaker community at Pleasant Hill in Mercer County was among the first to use the river regularly to ship products out of state.

Being a relatively narrow and meandering river, the Kentucky in its natural state was subject to periods of flood and low water. Pools of deep water, impounded by sand and gravel bars or rocky shoals, existed every few miles throughout the length of the river. As flatboats, keelboats, and steamboats became increasingly important to the state's economy, plans were made for a system of locks and dams to be constructed by the federal government. When no federal funds were forthcoming, the state built five locks between 1836 and 1842, regularizing transportation for less than one hundred miles of the river's length. Well-known steamboats such as the *Blue Wing*, the *Argo*, and the *Ocean* used the Kentucky River before the Civil War.

Railroads pushed into the region, superseding much of the river transportation of freight. In 1880 the federal government took over the old system of lock and dams, which were dilapidated and unusable, and began rebuilding Nos. 1 through 5. By 1917 fourteen locks and dams had been completed from a point four miles above Carrollton to just below Beattyville, creating a channel six feet deep. Plans to build similar projects up the Three Forks failed to win congressional approval. Obsolete when completed in 1917, the locks were too narrow and short for the rapid lockages necessary for competing with railroads. The original intent of the project had been to open up the coal mining region, but railroads soon took over that function.

At the turn of the century, such steamboats as the *Falls City II*, *Royal*, and *Richard Roe* were the last of their kind to navigate the Kentucky. As late as the 1920s, gas-powered packet boats such as the *Hanover*, *White Dove*, and *Revonah* (Hanover spelled backward) worked the lower river. The showboat *Princess*, operated by Capt. Billy Bryant, brought entertainment to communities during the summertime until the Great Depression.

Kentucky River navigation in the twentieth century has not lived up to the expectations of its boosters. The logging industry has benefited most, but construction of the dams meant that logs had to be rafted rather than drifting downstream from the eastern Kentucky forests. Before World War II, river sawmills had disappeared at such places as Beattyville, Irvine, Ford, High Bridge, Valley View, and Frankfort.

Transportation on the Kentucky probably had little overall effect on the cost of internal transportation in the state except for a short while near the end of the nineteenth century. Nevertheless, for many places along the river from Carrollton to Frankfort the river offered the most convenient contact with the outside world. Until the construction of highways in the 1930s, small towns such as Lockport, Gratz, and Monterey prospered because of their river links.

Improvements in rail and highway transportation ended any possible importance of the Kentucky River for transportation after World War II. The U.S. Army Corps of Engineers continued upkeep of the fourteen locks and dams but continually looked for ways to trim expenses in the postwar period. When all commercial transport ceased on the river above Frankfort, the corps turned over the responsibility for maintaining locks and dams Nos. 5 through 14 to the state. In the 1980s the state and federal governments fought a prolonged legal battle over the responsibility of maintaining the locks and dams above No. 4. In 1990 the Corps of Engineers still operated the lower four locks; the upper ten were welded shut.

Draining a large portion of the eastern and central portions of the state, the Kentucky is vital to many communities as a source of water. For its growing population, Lexington, in particular, has sought a more reliable source of water. The drought of 1988 brought near-disaster to many towns that draw water from the river. An effort to build a reservoir on the Red River failed in the 1970s. Dams built at Buckhorn and at Carr Fork provide some flood protection for the Kentucky River basin, but flooding continues to cause problems in the floodplain. In 1978, for example, Frankfort was devastated by a sudden rise of water.

Sewage, salt water from oil and gas wells, and runoff from coal mines are only a few of the environmental problems that strain the river's ability to regenerate itself. The nondegradable waste floating in the river during the spring floods or left hanging from trees along the river bank is only the more visible sign of the pollution of the Kentucky River.

Portions of the river provide fishing and boating recreation. The Middle Fork in Perry County is stocked with trout. Boating is extensive along the river from Boonesborough to Frankfort and at various points from there to Carrollton. A stern-wheel excursion boat operates from Shaker Landing in Mercer County.

Commissions have studied the future of the Kentucky River for more than a decade. The 1990 General Assembly passed a law creating the Kentucky River Authority, which is empowered to develop comprehensive long-range water reservoir management and drought response plans; to maintain locks and dams; to issue administrative regulations for clean water; to develop recreation areas; and to conceive methods of protecting groundwater within the river's basin.

Natural wonders still abound along the river, and each locale has its favorite rock formation or picturesque bend. Many of these were painted by Frankfort artist Paul Sawyier around the turn of the century. Gone is the famous Camp Nelson covered bridge but the Singing Bridge in Frankfort is still in use. The railroad bridges at High Bridge and Tyrone are outstanding examples of early cantilever-style construction, and some of the stonework on the old locks matches the quality found in buildings in Frankfort.

See Thomas D. Clark, *The Kentucky* (New York 1942); J. Winston Coleman, *Steamboats on the Kentucky* (Lexington, Ky., 1960).

WILLIAM E. ELLIS

KENTUCKY SCHOOL FOR THE BLIND. The Kentucky School for the Blind (KSB) educates visually impaired children in kindergarten through twelfth grade. The tax-supported public school in Louisville operates as part of the Kentucky Department of Education. The school offers courses in career development, home economics, independent living, orientation and mobility, industrial arts, arts and crafts, and computer skills. Special equipment and materials, such as braille books, braille writers, large-print books, recorded materials, abacuses, computers, and low-vision aids, enhance the teaching process. Field trips and instruction in recreational skills are available. Some students travel to the school each day, while others live in supervised housing, with meals and routine health services provided. They learn independent living skills.

The school's outreach services provide professional consultants and materials to blind and visually impaired preschool and school-age children enrolled in local public or private schools.

KSB was established by an act of the state legislature in 1842, after Samuel Gridley Howe, founder and director of the Perkins School for the Blind in Massachusetts, came to Kentucky with four students to demonstrate the effectiveness of teaching blind students. Kentucky School for the Blind was the sixth school of its type in the United States. After several moves, the KSB permanently located at a site on Frankfort Avenue in east Louisville, on October 8, 1855. Bryce M. Patten was the school's first superintendent. In 1884 a separate school on the KSB campus was established for visually impaired black students, and in 1954 KSB classes were racially integrated. In 1911 the first Boy Scout troop in America for the blind was founded at KSB—one year after American scouting began. In 1945 KSB formed the first wrestling team in the commonwealth and in 1961 won the first Kentucky Invitational Wrestling Tournament.

ADAM RUSCHIVAL

KENTUCKY SCHOOL FOR THE DEAF. The Kentucky Asylum for the Tuition of the Deaf and Dumb, later called the Kentucky School for the Deaf (KSD), was established in Danville on April 10, 1823. It was the first state-supported school of its kind in the nation and the first school for the deaf west of the Alleghenies. The deaf were a special concern of Gen. Elias Barbee, a Kentucky state senator, whose daughter, Lucy, was deaf. In 1822 Barbee collaborated with Judge John Rowan in writing the legislation authorizing the creation of the school. On December 7 of that year the legislation was signed into law by Gov. John Adair (1820-24). In the first two years the school rented quarters on Main Street, then moved to its present location on South Second Street in Danville.

Until 1870 the Centre College board of trustees operated the school, which grew from the first three pupils in 1823 to more than three hundred a century later. From 1870 to 1960 it was governed by its own board of commissioners, who were appointed by the governor to serve six-year terms (later reduced to four years). Legislation in 1960 placed the jurisdiction of the school with the state Board of Education and Department of Education.

With the help of Henry Clay and others, the school received two federal land grants, in 1826 and 1836. These tracts of land in Florida and Arkansas were eventually sold to finance the construction of school facilities. The school remained open during the Civil War. It charged tuition for deaf persons from outside the commonwealth. In the early years it was thought that the Kentucky school might be able to meet the educational needs of all deaf persons in the South and the West. Pupils from all the southern states except Florida, and from as far away as Montana, attended KSD. Eventually, other states established their own schools. At first, students could attend the school for only three terms. As the ineffectiveness of only three years of schooling became apparent, the school's leadership expanded the maximum length of attendance. State and federal laws now permit KSD to teach deaf students from preschool through high school. Graduates of the school go on to attend college or technical schools or enter the workforce. Many become professionals, and some return to their alma mater to carry on the mission of the school.

Many of the officers and teachers at KSD have had long tenures. George M. McClure was associated with the school for eighty years as both pupil and teacher. The school has had thirteen superintendents since its inception. The Rev. John Rice Kerr, the first superintendent, and John Adamson Jacobs, the third superintendent, are credited with nurturing the school from its infancy. Jacobs began his work in 1825, became superintendent in 1835, and held that office until his death in 1869.

See James B. Beauchamp, *The Kentucky School for the Deaf Established 1823* (Danville, Ky., 1973).   JOHN W. HUDSON, JR.

KENTUCKY SOCIETY FOR THE ENCOURAGEMENT OF DOMESTIC MANUFACTURE.

The Kentucky Society for the Encouragement of Domestic Manufacture was organized in 1817 to promote local production of manufactured goods and to combat the influx of foreign products believed to be competing unfairly with domestic manufacturing. The society held quarterly meetings in Lexington under the leadership of Robert Wickliffe, president. Branches of the society were soon established throughout the state, but the organization failed to achieve either of its goals.

KENTUCKY STATE BOARD OF HEALTH.

The Kentucky Board of Health was established in 1878 to protect Kentuckians from epidemics of cholera and smallpox. The General Assembly approved the establishment of local boards of health in 1882 and city boards of health in 1886. The State Board of Health in 1888 began to regulate the practice of medicine in Kentucky, first by requiring lists of certified physicians from county clerks, then by certification of medical practitioners and revocation of the right to practice medicine. The board's powers also included declaring and enforcing quarantines, inspecting baggage and other items in transit, and

building hospitals. Other areas that came under its jurisdiction included housing, sanitary engineering, pure food and drugs, bacteriology, and school inspections. Much of this work was accomplished with little funding. The annual appropriation for the board was $2,500 from 1878 to 1900, $5,000 in 1900, and $30,000 in 1910.

By the late 1890s state health reports began to indicate that more people died from diseases such as tuberculosis and typhoid fever than from epidemic diseases. The need for more accurate record keeping led to a revision of the ineffective 1874 vital statistics legislation. The revised law adopted in 1910 established a State Bureau of Vital Statistics, responsible for registering births and deaths, and Kentucky joined the national registration system for births in 1911 and for deaths in 1918.

The first president of the board was Dr. Pickney Thompson. Joseph N. McCORMACK became the leading force on the board after 1883 and served as secretary and executive officer until his retirement. His son, Dr. Arthur T. McCormack, replaced him. The McCormack home in Bowling Green served as the board's headquarters from 1883 until 1919, when the board moved to Louisville. The state abolished the board in 1974 and transferred its duties to the State Department of Human Resources.

See John H. Ellis, *Medicine in Kentucky* (Lexington, Ky., 1977).   JUDY CORNETT

KENTUCKY STATE FAIR. No fair is more American than the Kentucky State Fair, an annual celebration of economic progress and cultural activity, emergent from the agricultural fair tradition. The legislature initiated the Kentucky State Fair in 1902 and provided for financing it. The Livestock Breeders' Association was the driving force behind the establishment of the fair. Some 75,000 visitors appeared during the fair's inauguration on September 22-27, 1902, at Churchill Downs in Louisville.

Owensboro served as the site in 1903 and Lexington in 1905; in 1907 the Board of Agriculture decided on Louisville as the permanent site. One hundred fifty acres of land in the southwestern corner of the city were purchased on December 6, 1907. The 1908 fair opened dramatically in the shadow of a newly constructed livestock pavilion, at that time the largest in the state. More impressive, however, was the Merchants and Manufacturers' Building, which opened in 1921 accompanied by the proud announcement that it was larger than Madison Square Garden in New York City.

The 1946 legislature authorized the sale of bonds to construct the Fair and Exposition Center on 357 acres of land south of Louisville, adjacent to Standiford Field Airport. The new facility, opened in 1956, was designed to be used around the year for exhibitions and sporting events. In 1990 the new South Exposition Hall added some 129,000 square feet of space, bringing the total under roof to 830,000 square feet, or nearly twenty acres.

Rivaled by other forms of mass entertainment, the Kentucky State Fair nevertheless retains its popular appeal as a late-summer, multidimensional festivity. It hosts horse shows, cooking contests, amusements, educational programs, and nationally known entertainers, with many of these activities appearing along a traditionally defined midway. An official part of state government, this sprawling piece of popular American culture has not only endured but has grown in content and in appeal. On the occasion of its fiftieth anniversary in 1953, the Kentucky State Fair counted 305,000 visitors. By 1990, that number had increased to 637,500.

See Kentucky Writer's Project, *Kentucky State Fair*, vol. 2 of *Fairs and Fair Makers of Kentucky* (Frankfort, Ky., 1942); H. Clyde Reeves and Lawrence A. Cassidy, "Fairs in Kentucky," *FCHQ* 34 (1960): 335-57.

KENTUCKY STATE GUARD. The Kentucky State Guard was the commonwealth's organized volunteer militia in 1860-61 and again from 1878 to 1912. It succeeded the state's universal militia system, which became moribund in the early 1850s. Legislation to create the first State Guard passed after Gov. Beriah Magoffin (1859-62) urged the creation of a volunteer militia in response to John Brown's "widespread and hellish conspiracy against the slave states." Under its inspector general, Simon Bolivar Buckner, the State Guard numbered perhaps 4,000 men, largely pro-Southern and pro-slavery in outlook. The guard was widely perceived as working toward Kentucky's secession from the Union. During the state's uneasy period of neutrality, from April to September 1861, Unionists formed rival Home Guard companies. Both groups sought to attract recruits and obtain weapons but stopped short of fighting each other. Once Northern and Southern forces entered the state in September, Buckner and numerous other State Guardsmen moved from the organized militia to the Confederate army.

The General Assembly reestablished the State Guard in April 1878, after strikes and rioting in Louisville had caused widespread alarm. The guard, supervised by the state's adjutant general, was poorly funded and initially numbered fewer than 1,000 men. Its three regiments were headquartered in Louisville, Lexington, and Bowling Green. For more than three decades its members contended with lynchings, night riders, mountain feuds, and unrest in the coal fields. In 1912 the guard became the Kentucky National Guard. As such it came under close federal supervision and received significant War Department financial support.

See Richard G. Stone, Jr., *A Brittle Sword: The Kentucky Militia, 1776-1912* (Lexington, Ky., 1977).   RICHARD G. STONE, JR.

KENTUCKY STATE PENITENTIARY. Kentucky State Penitentiary, often called the Eddyville penitentiary, is Kentucky's only maximum-security prison, located on the banks of Barkley Lake in Eddyville, county seat of Lyon County. It was originally a branch penitentiary designed to relieve overcrowding at the principal penitentiary in Frankfort, which closed in 1937. The construction of the medieval-looking stone structure began in 1884 and was officially completed in 1886, at a cost of $275,000. Substantial additions and renovations have taken place. When the Cumberland River was impounded, creating Lake Barkley in 1966, the structure was left high on a peninsula overlooking the lake. It is thus often referred to as "The Castle on the Cumberland." In 1911 an electric chair was installed at the penitentiary. James Buckner of Marion County, the first prisoner to die, was executed on July 8 of that year. The last to be put to death at the prison was Kelly Moss, in 1962. According to the decree of federal courts, the number of inmates incarcerated at Eddyville is not to exceed nine hundred. A major cell house was added in 1986, and for security reasons most of the older buildings on the prison yard have been razed. (See also PRISONS.)   BILL CUNNINGHAM

KENTUCKY STATE POLICE. The General Assembly established the Kentucky State Police, effective July 1, 1948. The police force was an outgrowth of the Kentucky Highway Patrol, which in 1936 had been organized as a division of the Department of Highways. Guthrie F. Crowe served as the first commissioner of the state police (1948-52).

The state police are charged with the detection and prevention of crime, the apprehension of criminals, and the maintenance of law and order throughout the commonwealth. They also are responsible for the collection, classification, and maintenance of information for the detection of crime; identification, apprehension, and conviction of criminals; and enforcement of criminal and motor vehicle and traffic laws of the commonwealth. The state police collect criminal record information from other law enforcement agencies throughout the commonwealth and supply this information to appropriate federal agencies at their request.

The state police became a division of the Department of Public Safety on March 31, 1966; a bureau in the Department of Justice on March 18, 1974; and a department in the Justice Cabinet on April 1, 1982. The 1990 authorized personnel for the department included 901 sworn officers, 53 cadets, 154 dispatchers, and 564 civilian employees. The headquarters, training academy, and principal laboratory for the department are located in Frankfort; sixteen district posts are located strategically in various parts of the commonwealth. With the approval of the commissioner, officers from other law enforcement agencies in the commonwealth may attend programs offered at the academy. On request, criminalists in the laboratory assist investigators in other law enforcement agencies with the analysis of specimens. State police officers operate a juvenile community relations and crime prevention program at Trooper Island Boys' Camp on Dale Hollow Lake State Park near Burkesville.

See Kentucky Public Affairs Branch, Research and Development Section, *Kentucky State Police: A*

History 1948-1988 (Frankfort, Ky., 1988); Department of Law, "State Police," *Kentucky Law Journal* 52 (1963-64): 125-47.

B. EDWARD CAMPBELL

KENTUCKY STATE REFORMATORY. Establishment of the Kentucky State Reformatory, near La Grange in Oldham County, was authorized by Gov. A. B. Chandler in his first term (1935-39). By the fall of 1937, construction of the new reformatory was well underway and 2,660 inmates were living at the site. Most inmates were housed in open-wing dormitories rather than in small cells. In eleven separate housing units, inmates were classified, treated according to their needs, and prepared for release. A large farm provided employment and food for inmates. Although academic, vocational, recreational, and religious programs were planned, personnel to carry out these rehabilitation programs were not hired until 1961. The number of security personnel was often inadequate to manage an institution that was frequently overpopulated.

In the beginning, inmates ate in silence and mail was censored. Misbehavior was punished by work in the stone quarry or solitary confinement on bread and water. Inmates marched to work in uniform and produced goods for state use such as printed forms, metal furniture, road signs, license plates, and soap, but providing adequate employment was a continuing problem. Investigations in 1963 and 1973 deplored the brutal and abusive conditions and prompted funding for additional treatment, custodial personnel, and programs to prepare inmates for release. The 1980 settlement of a class action lawsuit filed by inmates limited the prison population to 1,500. (See also PRISONS.)

T. KYLE ELLISON

KENTUCKY STATE UNIVERSITY. At the urging of the Colored Teachers State Association, the Kentucky legislature on May 18, 1886, voted to establish a normal school to train black teachers, which became Kentucky State University in the 1970s. The General Assembly in 1886 appropriated $7,000 to erect a recitation building and voted an annual appropriation of $3,000 to pay the salaries of teachers. The City of Frankfort donated the grounds for constructing the school, forty acres on a hill on the east side of town. On October 11, 1887, the school officially opened as the State Normal School for Colored Persons. Under the direction of the president, John Jackson, subjects were divided between the literary department (spelling, reading, penmanship, arithmetic, history, geography, and vocal music) and the industrial department (agriculture, horticulture, mechanics, manual training, and industrial arts).

After the federal government in 1890 provided for the development of land grant colleges for blacks, the State Normal School for Colored Persons set up departments for instruction in agriculture and mechanics to qualify for federal funds. In 1902 the school's name was changed to Kentucky Normal and Industrial Institute to reflect the im-

proved offerings in industrial education. Federal and state funds did not meet the school's financial needs, however.

Because the school was located in the state capital, it was difficult for it to be aloof from political intrigues. The governor reserved the right to appoint the school's board of trustees, which in turn appointed the president of the institution, and the board gained a reputation for choosing a president who had supported the governor's election to office. The presidency of the school thus became a matter of political influence, and the frequent changes in administration denied the school a consistent form of leadership: John H. Jackson, 1887-98; James E. Ginens, 1898-1910; James S. Hathaway, 1910-12; G.P. Russell, 1912-23, 1924-29; and F.M. Wood, 1923-24. Rufus ATWOOD, the school's sixth president, 1929-62, refused to involve himself in partisan politics and thereafter the office gained professional legitimacy.

Throughout the late nineteenth and early twentieth centuries, the institution was slow to develop into a fully accredited college. Although the school's name was changed again in 1926, to Kentucky State Industrial College for Negroes, the institution was a college only in name. It did not offer a college curriculum. In 1929 when Atwood was appointed as the school's sixth president, Kentucky State was $18,000 in debt, the faculty was not well trained, and the library had been closed to students. Campus facilities were in a state of neglect and the girls' dormitory was the only building not in need of repair. Atwood set standards for developing Kentucky State as an accredited institution. With a grant from the New Deal's Public Works Administration and monetary gifts from the General Board of Education and the Julius Rosenwald Fund, substantial improvements were made on the campus during Atwood's first decade as chief administrator. Equipment and supplies were purchased for chemistry, physics, mathematics, and biology. By 1939, the library of 12,000 books was appraised at $54,000.

During the 1930s the college was reorganized into the Division of Applied Sciences; Division of Arts and Sciences; and Division of Education. The number of student organizations, which stood at seven in 1929, tripled by the end of the next decade. Fraternities, sororities, dormitory clubs, and a debating society were added. As student services, organizations, and facilities improved so did the school's athletic teams. In football, Kentucky State won the national championship for black colleges in 1934 and 1937. On July 1, 1938, the name of the school was changed to Kentucky State College for Negroes, and in 1939 it was recognized as a class A college by the Southern Association Committee on Approval of Negro Schools.

Between 1940 and 1962, when Atwood retired, the college became Kentucky's foremost black institution of higher learning. Although it remained a small liberal arts college, Kentucky State provided a professional curriculum that met the entrance requirements for law, medicine, dental, and veterinary schools. Two-year curricula were offered in engineering and medical technology.

In 1952, the state legislature voted to remove the phrase "for Negroes" from the official school name, and transferred administrative control of the institution from the State Board of Education to an independent board of regents. In 1957, the board approved a $410,000 program to construct a library, an alumni guest house, and a student union building. During the same year, Atwood and University of Kentucky president Frank Dickey announced joint sponsorship of a new program of evening courses at Kentucky State. The program was designed to meet the educational needs of state government employees as well as business, industrial, and professional groups. This program was expanded by President Atwood's successors.

By the mid-1960s more than a thousand students were enrolled in the college and the campus consisted of 220 acres. An auditorium, athletic complex, and an industrial arts and technology building were among the construction projects completed in the late sixties and early seventies. During this period the college began offering programs in computer science, electronics, drafting, and public administration.

In 1972, the Kentucky General Assembly passed legislation that created Kentucky State University. The university has undergone several physical changes, and academic and administrative programs have been revised to meet student needs. The Whitney M. Young, Jr., College of Leadership Studies attracts outstanding high school seniors to the university. Since 1962 enrollment has approximately tripled and the campus has expanded to 344 acres.

See Alice Dunnigan, *The Fascinating Story of Black Kentuckians: Their Heritage and Tradition* (Washington, D.C., 1982); John Hardin, *Onward and Upward: A Centennial History of Kentucky State University 1886-1986* (Frankfort, Ky., 1987).

KENTUCKY TURNPIKE. The Kentucky Turnpike, which connected Louisville with Elizabethtown, was to be the first section of a north-south road from the Great Lakes to the Gulf of Mexico. Ground was broken in Bullitt County on July 25, 1954, and the turnpike was officially opened to traffic on August 1, 1956. Built at a cost of $39 million, the road ran a distance of thirty-nine miles. Eight roads gave access to the turnpike. An extension was later authorized in Louisville from the Watterson Expressway to Eastern Parkway. The terrain over which the turnpike was built was considered difficult; it included portions of the Kentucky knobs, several rivers, and steep hills. Advanced engineering design produced concrete-paved lanes twenty-four feet wide, blacktopped outside shoulders ten feet wide, and no grade steeper than 3 percent. In the 1955 gubernatorial election, A.B. Chandler questioned the need for the road, saying it started nowhere and went nowhere. The issue helped him to defeat his primary opponent, Bert T. Combs.

The road was financed with bonds, and tolls were established to pay off the bonds within forty years. Tolls were collected at two toll plazas, one at Elizabethtown, the other at Shepherdsville. There were two service areas, one at Shepherdsville, where the Glass House Restaurant was located, the another with a snack bar just south of the Rolling Fork of the Salt River. On June 30, 1975, the toll was removed, nineteen years ahead of schedule. An estimated 90 million vehicles, excluding local traffic in Louisville, traveled the road before the toll was lifted. In 1975 the turnpike was officially made a part of Interstate 65, which connected with it on both the north and south ends. The road has since been widened to ten lanes south of the Watterson Expressway, and it is at least six lanes wide for its total length.

See "Future Superhighway," *Louisville Courier-Journal Magazine*, July 25, 1954; "Kentucky Turnpike Is in Business," *Louisville Magazine* 7 (Aug. 20, 1956): 18-19.   KATHERINE L. HOUSE

KENTUCKY UNIVERSITY. Kentucky University was founded by John B. BOWMAN, and chartered by the General Assembly on January 15, 1858. Classes began on September 19, 1859, in the building of the former BACON COLLEGE in Harrodsburg, Mercer County (from which Bowman had graduated in 1842). Despite a promising beginning, Kentucky University soon felt the effects of the Civil War. Enrollment dropped from 194 students during the first session of 1860 to sixty-four in the fourth session. During the Battle of Perryville (October 8, 1862), the college building was used as a hospital, most probably by the Confederates. (Sources conflict over which side actually occupied the structure.) Most devastating, however, was the fire on February 16, 1864, which destroyed the university's facilities. Believing that sufficient funds for rebuilding the school could not be raised in Mercer County, Bowman began searching for another location for his university. Lexington, a thriving community, seemed to be the best choice. TRANSYLVANIA UNIVERSITY in Lexington had been seeking a merger with Kentucky University since 1860.

Pursuant to his goal of creating "a first-class university," Bowman convinced the Kentucky legislature in February of 1865 to merge the two institutions and to establish the AGRICULTURAL AND MECHANICAL COLLEGE as part of the new school, under the Morrill Act, which provided lands in each state for agricultural and mechanical schools. Although it was located on Transylvania University's land, the new school retained the name of Kentucky University. In 1908 the school assumed the name of Transylvania University, as approved by the state legislature, to avoid confusion between Kentucky University and the new State University, formerly the Agricultural and Mechanical College.

See John D. Wright, Jr. *Transylvania: Tutor to the West* (Lexington, Ky., 1975); James T. Hopkins, *The University of Kentucky: Origins and Early Years* (Lexington, Ky., 1951).

KENTUCKY WESLEYAN COLLEGE. Kentucky Wesleyan College was chartered by the General Assembly in 1860, under the sponsorship of the Kentucky Conference of the Methodist Episcopal Church, South. A building was constructed in Millersburg, Bourbon County, but the Civil War delayed the opening of the institution until the fall of 1866. The college offered a liberal arts curriculum with strong emphasis on classics, mathematics, and science, and soon courses in bookkeeping and pedagogy were added to prepare students for positions in business and teaching. The first degree was awarded in 1868. In 1890 the college moved to Winchester, Clark County, which had much better rail facilities, and shortly thereafter it became coeducational.

After a major dispute over the role of athletics and the departure of some faculty members, intercollegiate athletics programs were developed. The main building was destroyed by fire in 1905 but was quickly rebuilt, and the college entered a period of relative prosperity. In 1926 the Louisville Conference of Methodists joined in the sponsorship of the college, thus broadening its base of support. The Depression of the 1930s brought substantially diminished enrollment and financial hardships, exacerbated in the war years of the early 1940s, but the college survived, largely through the leadership of president Paul Shell Powell, a Louisville Conference minister. In 1947 it became fully accredited by the Southern Association of Colleges and Secondary Schools.

In 1950 the church proposed that the college relocate from Winchester to Owensboro because of increased competition for students from the many other institutions in the Bluegrass region. The city of Owensboro raised $1 million to build a new campus, and in 1951 the college began conducting classes in a number of buildings near downtown Owensboro. The new campus, located on South Frederica Street, opened in the fall of 1954.

The college was racially integrated in the late 1950s and reached its peak enrollment in 1966. Additional dormitories were constructed. The college achieved national recognition with the National Collegiate Athletic Association (NCAA) division II basketball championship in 1966, 1968, and 1969. A faculty governance plan was enacted in 1967, giving faculty a voice in policy-making at all levels. Later a similar plan was put into effect for students. The 1970s saw fluctuations in enrollment and increased financial problems. The college introduced a number of programs, such as computer science, nursing, and criminal justice, to attract vocationally oriented students. Student union facilities and a new library were completed during this period, and the old library was remodeled to serve as a chapel. Another championship basketball team in 1973 added to the college's reputation for excellence in athletics. In the 1980s the college built a modern health and physical education building and expanded the operations of radio station WKWC, which featured a variety of programs from classics to jazz and public service features. Football, eliminated at the beginning of the Depression, was reintroduced, and in 1987 Kentucky Wesleyan won a fifth NCAA division II basketball title.

Paul Hartman of Texas Christian University was named president in 1988 and immediately began a study on the future of the college. Enrollments were to be limited and a balanced budget, achieved in the early 1980s, maintained. The college substantially raised the average ACT scores of incoming students during the 1980s.

See Susie Dickens, "The Coming of KWC to Owensboro," *Daviess County Historical Quarterly* (Jan. 1, 1986): 15-19.   LEE A. DEW

KIDD, ROY L. Roy L. Kidd, football coach, was born on December 4, 1931, in Corbin, Kentucky, to Edward and Pearl (Brafford) Kidd. A graduate of Corbin High School, he received both his bachelor's and master's degrees at Eastern Kentucky University in Richmond. He played football there and earned All-American status as a quarterback. His coaching career began at Madison High School in Richmond in 1956. In six seasons, his teams won fifty-four games, losing only ten. After two years as a college assistant—in 1962 at Morehead State University in Morehead and in 1963 at Eastern—he became the head football coach at his alma mater. In 1990, at the end of his twenty-seventh year as head coach of the Colonels, he had compiled a record of 218 wins, 79 losses, and 8 ties, placing him sixth on the list of all-time winning coaches. Among active National Collegiate Athletic Association (NCAA) division I and I-AA coaches, only Eddie Robinson of Grambling College in Louisiana, Bo Schembechler of Michigan, and Joe Paterno of Penn State had recorded more victories. Kidd's Eastern teams played in the NCAA Division I-AA championship playoffs in ten of the playoffs' first twelve years. His team won the national championship in 1979 and 1982, and was runner-up in 1980 and 1981. On two other occasions, Eastern reached the semifinal round. His 1967 team won the Grantland Rice Bowl. In 1991 Kidd became Eastern's director of athletics.

Kidd married Susan Purcell of Richmond; they have three children: Mark, Keith, and Kathy.

CHARLES WHITLOCK

KILGORE, BENJAMIN WESLEY. Benjamin Wesley Kilgore, politician and editor, was born in Raleigh, North Carolina, on February 24, 1901, son of Benjamin and Elizabeth Carrington (Dinwiddie) Kilgore. He was educated in the Raleigh public schools, attended North Carolina State College, and graduated from Iowa State College of Agriculture in 1922. He joined the staff of the *Progressive Farmer*, a national publication managed by his father. In 1928 he moved to Louisville, where he became the paper's associate editor for the Kentucky-Tennessee edition. In April 1933 Kilgore became executive secretary of the Kentucky Farm Bureau. He was instrumental in the passage of the 1937 Rural Electric Cooperative Corporation Act which made electricity available to the inhabitants of rural areas of the commonwealth at minimal cost. Kilgore resigned to seek the Democratic gubernatorial nomination in 1943. After a hard-fought campaign, he lost to J. Lyter Donaldson by a vote of 135,576 to 81,127. In 1944 Kilgore moved to Franklin, Kentucky, and became assistant general manager of the Eastern Dark Fired Tobacco Growers Association. He managed the unsuccessful 1947 gubernatorial primary of Harry Lee Waterfield. Four years later Kilgore withdrew from consideration for nomination as governor because of failing health.

Kilgore married Violet Wright of Raleigh, North Carolina; they had two children, Ben and Betty. He died in Frankfort, Kentucky, on May 29, 1951, and was buried at Raleigh.

KIMMEL, HUSBAND EDWARD. Husband Edward Kimmel, naval commander, was the son of Marius Kimmel, a former U.S. and Confederate army officer and mining executive, and Sibbella (Lambert) Kimmel. He was born in Henderson, Kentucky, on February 26, 1882, and educated in Henderson schools and at Central University in Richmond. Kimmel received an appointment to the U.S. Naval Academy in 1900. He graduated in 1904, thirteenth in a class of sixty-one, and after two years of required sea duty he received his ensign's commission in 1906. Kimmel soon developed expertise in gunnery and ordnance and spent much of his early sea duty on battleships. During World War I, he served as a liaison officer in gunnery with the Royal Navy and as gunnery officer on the staff of Rear Adm. Hugh Rodman, then commanding a group of U.S. battleships attached to the British Grand Fleet.

In the years after the war, Kimmel served as executive officer of the battleship *Arkansas*, commanded destroyers on two occasions, and attended the Naval War College in 1925-26, when he was promoted to captain. He was promoted to rear admiral in 1937 while serving as budget officer in the Navy's Washington, D.C., headquarters. Kimmel then returned to sea and held two assignments in the Pacific before being named to command the Pacific fleet itself in February 1941. In the months of peace that remained, Kimmel prepared the Pacific fleet for war with demanding training exercises and defenses on island bases such as Midway and Wake Island. The aircraft carriers, cruisers, destroyers, and submarines that remained after the Japanese onslaught of December 7, 1941, were certainly better prepared to fight than when Kimmel had taken command some nine months before, but Kimmel had no chance to demonstrate whether he had the ability to lead the fleet in wartime: On December 17, 1941, when a major operation (subsequently canceled) was in progress, he was relieved of command by an interim appointee and then by Adm. Chester Nimitz. Kimmel then testified at the first of several Pearl Harbor investigations and requested retirement in early 1942.

Kimmel believed there had been a carefully plotted effort by President Franklin D. Roosevelt and other senior civilian and military leaders to make him the scapegoat for the navy's vulnerablity at Pearl Harbor, covering up their own more serious culpability. He related his own version of events in *Admiral Kimmel's Story* (1955). The consensus among historians seems to be that while Kimmel was by no means the only high-ranking American military or civilian official, including President Roosevelt himself, to be surprised by the audacious Japanese attack on the Pacific Fleet and nearby air bases, he had had enough information by the start of December 1941 to indicate that war between the United States and Japan was imminent. In this light, he should have ordered more thorough reconnaissance measures based on the limited data made available to him, rather than the measures he thought adequate given his widely shared opinion that the U.S. bases most likely to bear the brunt of any Japanese attack were the ones near Manila in the Philippine Islands. Kimmel remained bitter about Roosevelt's treatment of him until his death on May 14, 1968, in Groton, Connecticut. He was buried in the U.S. Naval Cemetery at Annapolis. He was survived by his wife, Dorothy (Kinkaid) Kimmel, and two sons, Edward and Thomas, both veterans of World War II. A third son, Marius, died in combat in the Pacific.

See Samuel Eliot Morison, *History of United States Naval Operations in World War II* (Boston 1948); Martin V. Melosi, *The Shadow of Pearl Harbor: Political Controversy over the Surprise Attack, 1941-1946* (College Station, Tex., 1977).

LLOYD J. GRAYBAR

KINCAID, BRADLEY. Bradley Kincaid, one of the country's first and most popular radio singers, was born on July 13, 1895, in Garrard County, Kentucky, to William and Elizabeth (Hurt) Kincaid, singers who taught him folk songs. Kincaid entered the Berea College Academy at the age of nineteen and graduated at twenty-six after service in World War I. He then moved to Chicago to attend the YMCA College (later George Williams College). After singing with a YMCA quartet at newly formed radio station WLS in Chicago, Kincaid agreed to sing mountain ballads on the WLS "National Barn Dance." Delighted listeners made him a star performer. On his first road trip, Kincaid was astonished that queues of people in Peoria, Illinois, his first stop, were actually there to see him. The demand for copies of his songs was so great that he published a series of songbooks, *Mountain Ballads and Old Time Songs*, which sold hundreds of thousands of copies.

To increase his repertoire, Kincaid spent several summers collecting songs from traditional singers in the mountains. He moved from radio station to radio station beginning in 1930: from Cincinnati's WLW to Pittsburgh's KDKA, Schenectady's WGY, New York City's WEAF and NBC Red Network, Boston's WBZ, Hartford's WTIC in Connecticut,

Rochester's WHAM in New York, and thence to Nashville's WSM and the "Grand Ole Opry." During his career Kincaid recorded for such labels as Gennett, Champion, Challenge, Silvertone, Supertone, Brunswick, Conqueror, Vocalion, Decca, Bluebird, RCA Victor, Capitol, and Bluebonnet. When he left the "Grand Ole Opry." in 1950, he bought and managed a radio station and later a music store in Springfield, Ohio. Kincaid married his music teacher from Berea, Irma Foreman; they had four children: Barbara, Alene, William B., and James E. Kincaid died on September 23, 1989, and was buried in Springfield, Ohio.

See Loyal Jones, *Radio's 'Kentucky Mountain Boy': Bradley Kincaid* (Berea, Ky., 1980); Charles K. Wolfe, *Kentucky Country* (Lexington, Ky., 1982).   LOYAL JONES

KINCAID, GARVICE DELMAR. Garvice Delmar Kincaid, real estate developer, was born on August 9, 1912, in Tallego, Lee County, Kentucky, to Douglas and Minnie (Johnson) Kincaid. In 1916 his family moved to Richmond, Kentucky, where he graduated from Madison High School in 1930. He attended Eastern Kentucky University in Richmond for three years and supported himself by delivering the local newspaper, the *Richmond Register*. Kincaid transferred to the University of Kentucky in 1933 and received his B.A. in political science in 1934 and his law degree in 1937.

After graduation Kincaid began a private law practice in Richmond. As his main interest, however, was real estate investment, he soon returned to Lexington and began to buy and sell properties. In 1940 he purchased the Lexington Finance Company, which became the Kentucky Finance Company. In 1945 he was part of a group that purchased Lexington's Central Exchange Bank, renamed Central Bank. Kincaid became its president at age thirty-two, the youngest bank president in Kentucky at that time. In 1959 he bought controlling interest in Kentucky Central Life Insurance Company. Kincaid owned radio stations WVLK-AM and FM, WKYT-TV, the Campbell House hotel, the Phoenix and Lafayette hotels, and Joyland Park, all in Lexington. He also owned Cardinal Life Insurance Company in Louisville, the Fincastle Building and WINN-AM in Louisville, WFKY-AM in Frankfort, the Bank of Richmond, People's Bank in Berea, and the First National Bank of Georgetown.

Kincaid was one of the central figures in the economic transformation of Lexington through the urban renewal programs of the late 1960s and early 1970s. He served as chairman of the Lexington Downtown Development Commission and promoted the renovation of Main Street and Broadway. Many central Kentucky charities received major donations of both time and money from Kincaid. He won the Horatio Alger Award of the American Association of Schools and Colleges in 1960. He was a University of Kentucky trustee during 1972-74 and was named to the UK Hall of Distinguished Alumni in 1974.

Kincaid married Nelle Wilson on October 14, 1940; they had twin daughters, Jane and Joan. Kincaid died while on a business trip to Elizabethtown, Kentucky, on November 21, 1975, and was buried in the Lexington Cemetery.

See Richard Crowe, ed., *Eastern Kentucky Entrepreneurs* (Hazard, Ky., 1987).

KING, JOHN EDWARD. John Edward King, army officer and political figure, was born to William and Elizabeth (Edwards) King in Stafford County, Virginia, on December 21, 1757. He was the eleventh of twelve children; his brother William was a member of the 1792 Kentucky constitutional convention. At age nineteen, King fought in the Revolutionary War as a private in the Stafford County militia, 3d Virginia Regiment, with his brothers Jack, William, Valentine, and Nimrod. He was discharged at Valley Forge on February 16, 1776, and returned to Stafford County. In 1780, after his father's death, King moved to present-day Bracken County, Kentucky. King rejoined the army and at the age of twenty-three fought under the command of Col. Issac Shelby in the Battle of King's Mountain in North Carolina on October 7, 1780. After the war, he returned to Kentucky and built a large estate near Burksville, which he named Melmont. In 1798 Burksville became the Cumberland County seat, and King served as clerk for both the county and circuit courts.

In the War of 1812, King was commissioned general and led the only brigade in the 5th Regiment, under the command of William Rennick. He fought under Gen. William Harrison in the Battle of the Thames on October 5, 1813, and after the war retuned to Burksville. In 1821 and 1825, he was a presidential elector for Kentucky, voting for James Monroe and John Quincy Adams, respectively.

King was married twice, first to Sarah Clifton, who died in 1815 after bearing seven children: Edward, Valentine, William, Milton, Sophia, Elizabeth, and Alfred. King's second wife was Ellen Jefferson. He died at his estate on May 13, 1828, and was buried there.

See Goode King Feldhauser, "General John Edward King, of Kentucky," *Register* 27 (May 1929): 548-51.

KING, MARGARET ISADORA. Margaret Isadora King, after whom the University of Kentucky (UK) library is named, was born in Lexington, Kentucky, on September 1, 1879, to Gilbert and Elizabeth K. King. She graduated from UK in 1898. From 1899 to 1905 King did clerical work in the Lexington law firm of Allen and Bronston. Between 1905 and 1912 she served as secretary to James K. Patterson, president of UK. In 1909 she took over management of the university's small book collection, housed in a new library built in 1908 with a gift from Andrew Carnegie. King was named UK librarian in 1912 and for the remainder of her career she oversaw the development of the modern university library.

King received a B.S. degree in librarianship from Columbia University in 1929. She was president of the Kentucky Library Association (1926-27) and served as a member of the board of trustees of the Lexington Public Library. King was a part-time instructor in both library science and English at UK. In June 1948, the UK Library was named in her honor. She retired as librarian on September 1, 1949. King died on April 13, 1966, and was buried in the Lexington Cemetery.

TERRY BIRDWHISTELL

KING, PEE WEE. Songwriter and musician Pee Wee King, the son of John and Helen (Mielczarek) Kuczynski, was born in Milwaukee, Wisconsin, on February 18, 1914. He joined the "Badger State Barn Dance" on Milwaukee's WJRN radio in 1933. The next year he was discovered by J.L. Frank and went to Louisville with a group called the Log Cabin Boys. In 1936 he went to WNOX in Knoxville and in 1937 to Nashville and the "Grand Ole Opry," where he stayed ten years. In 1942 he and his Golden West Cowboys were featured on the "Camel Caravan," which presented 175 shows in sixty-eight service-related establishments. In 1947 he returned to Louisville to appear on WAVE and other radio/television stations. He appeared in dozens of movies. The song *Tennessee Waltz*, which King wrote in collaboration with Redd Stewart, is country music's most-recorded (500 times), most-sold (70 million records) song of all time. Patti Page's version was one of the biggest hits in modern popular music history. King is a member of the Country Music Hall of Fame and the Nashville Songwriters Association Hall of Fame. In 1936 he married Lydia Frank.   CHARLES F. FABER

KINGDOM COME CREEK. Kingdom Come Creek in Letcher County is approximately three miles long, having two main forks near its headwaters and emptying into the North Fork of the Kentucky River, eight miles below Whitesburg in Letcher County. A post office a short distance from the mouth of the creek has been given the Indian name Oscaloosa. The land along Kingdom Come was first permanently settled around 1815 by families such as the Fraziers, Isons, Joneses, and Kings. The creek's unusual name is generally believed to have been taken from the words of the Lord's Prayer by an early religious-minded settler. Kingdom Come may also be a corruption of "King done come," the response often given in pre–Civil War days to the question of later settlers: "Who came here first?" Descendants of the original settlers still make up the majority of the residents.

The creek is cited in the title of John Fox, Jr.'s best-selling novel *The Little Shepherd of Kingdom Come* (1903).   WILLIAM TERRELL CORNETT

KINGSOLVER, BARBARA. Barbara Kingsolver, fiction writer and poet, was born April 8, 1955, to Wendell R. and Virginia Lee (Henry) Kingsolver in Annapolis, Maryland. The family moved to Car-

lisle, Kentucky, when she was two years old. She attended Nicholas County High School and graduated magna cum laude in 1977 from Depauw University, in Greencastle, Indiana, with degrees in biology and English. In 1981 she received a master's degree from the Department of Ecology and Evolutionary Biology at the University of Arizona. She has lived in Europe in Athens (1976) and Paris (1976-77), and since 1977 has made her home in Tucson, Arizona.

Her writings include technical articles and poetry and have been published in such periodicals as *Mademoiselle*, *Progressive*, *New York Times*, *Redbook*, *Virginia Quarterly Review*, and *New Mexico Humanities Review*. Her first novel, *The Bean Trees* (1988), was highly acclaimed. She wrote *Homeland and Other Stories*, published in 1989, and the nonfiction *Holding the Line: Women in the Great Arizona Mine Strike of 1983* (1989). *The Bean Trees* is the story of a young Kentucky woman, Taylor Greer, who moves west to Tucson and acquires an unusual family that includes an orphaned baby girl she names Turtle, a Guatemalan refugee couple, a single mother, and several elderly neighbors. She becomes involved in the sanctuary movement for illegal aliens. A reviewer for the *New York Times* (April 10, 1988) called it "a remarkable, enjoyable book, one that contains more good writing than most successful careers." The novel won an American Library Association Award and was selected by the *New York Times* as one of "the notable books of 1988." In 1989 she received a citation of accomplishment from the United Nations National Council of Women of the United States.

In 1985 Kingsolver married Joseph Hoffmann, a chemist. They are the parents of Camille.

WADE HALL

KIRK, ANDREW DEWEY. Andrew Dewey Kirk, jazz musician, was born in Newport, Kentucky, on May 28, 1898. He is known for his performances as a jazz bass/baritone saxophonist, tubaist, and orchestra leader. Kirk's band, the Clouds of Joy, was based primarily in Kansas City during 1929-48, although they performed several successful coast-to-coast tours. Kirk was partially credited with the "Kansas City sound" in jazz. The band had numerous outstanding soloists, including Mary Lou Williams (who also served as composer and arranger), Shorty Baker, Don Byas, Kenny Kersey, Howard McGhee, Fats Navarro, and, for a short time, the great Charlie Parker. The band was primarily a dance band, but recorded numerous works, including the popular *Until the Real Thing Comes Along*.

See Andy Kirk, *Twenty Years on Wheels* (Ann Arbor, Mich., 1989).   LEE BASH

KIRKPATRICK, LEE H. Lee H. Kirkpatrick, educator and author, was born on July 22, 1886, in Nicholasville, Jessamine County. He was awarded a B.A. at Georgetown College in Kentucky, an M.A. at Columbia University, and an honorary doctorate at Harvard University. Kirkpatrick supervised the Lawrenceburg-Nicholasville schools before becoming superintendent of the Paris, Kentucky, city schools (1918-53). During his tenure as superintendent, he published the pragmatic, philosophical work *Teaching School Day by Day* (1941).

Kirkpatrick earned a reputation as a superb administrator, strong disciplinarian, and astute judge of character. He insisted that his faculty members sharpen their skills by traveling, attending enrichment programs, and taking graduate courses. He created a stimulating atmosphere for students and faculty by inviting guest speakers; by organizing debates, music competitions, and scholastic tests; and by encouraging the formation of honor societies and the first Latin club in the state. Paris High School was the first secondary school evaluated by the Southern Association of Colleges and Secondary Schools in 1922 and earned its highest rating (AA) for years. Kirkpatrick's model system offered night classes, home economics, and vocational training by 1920. All his teachers had degrees by the 1920s, and 70 percent held master's degrees a decade later. His policies had the support of businessmen and parents, and his era came to be known as the golden age of education in Paris. That era ended with his retirement in 1953. Kirkpatrick died on February 28, 1958, and was buried in the Paris Cemetery.   H.E. EVERMAN

KIRWAN, ALBERT DENNIS. Albert Dennis Kirwan, athlete, educator, and historian, was born on December 22, 1904, in Louisville, the sixth of eight children of Martin John and Margaret (Sullivan) Kirwan. Kirwan starred in football at Louisville's Male High School and at the University of Kentucky, where he graduated in 1926. Between 1929 and 1944 he coached football in high school and at the University of Kentucky. He earned a law degree at Louisville's Jefferson School of Law while coaching. In 1938 he became UK's head football coach.

After Kirwan received a Ph.D. in history from Duke University in 1947, he became dean of men at the University of Kentucky and then dean of students. He presented the university's case to the National Collegiate Athletic Association council concerning the 1948-49 basketball gambling scandals. He also helped move the university through its first tense period of integration. In 1954 Kirwan entered the history department, becoming a popular teacher and productive scholar. His six books include his pathbreaking *Revolt of the Rednecks* (1951); his prize-winning biography *John J. Crittenden* (1962); and *The South Since Appomattox* (1967), coauthored with Thomas D. Clark. He played a major role in the organization of the University Press of Kentucky in 1968. Kirwan was dean of the graduate school from 1960 until 1968, when he became the seventh president of the university, leading the school out of a time of student unrest. A year later he presented a more peaceful campus to the new president, Otis A. Singletary.

Kirwan married Elizabeth Heil, of Louisville, on August 4, 1931, and they had two sons, Albert Dennis, Jr., and William English II. After he retired from the presidency, Kirwan returned to teaching and writing until his death on November 30, 1971. He is buried in the Lexington Cemetery.

See Frank Furlong Mathias, *Albert D. Kirwan* (Lexington, Ky., 1975).   FRANK F. MATHIAS

KITTY LEAGUE. The Kitty League, a professional minor league baseball organization, was started in 1903 by six teams representing towns in western Kentucky ("K"), southern Illinois ("I"), and west Tennessee ("T"). The KIT, later called Kitty, lasted for fifty-one nonconsecutive years of what some feel was high-caliber baseball performance. The circuit did not operate in 1907-9, 1915, 1917-21, and 1925-45. In 1922 it qualified for class D rating. At various times league cities included Paducah, Mayfield, Hopkinsville, Fulton, Owensboro, Madisonville, Princeton, Dawson Springs, and Bowling Green in Kentucky; Union City, Clarksville, Lexington, Paris, Dyersburg, Jackson, and Springfield in Tennessee; Cairo and McLeansboro in Illinois; and Vincennes, Indiana. Many major league careers began in the Kitty, which ended operations permanently in 1955.

LON CARTER BARTON

KLAIR, WILLIAM FREDERICK. William Frederick ("Billy") Klair, a political leader in Kentucky from the early 1900s through the 1930s, was born in Lexington on December 14, 1874, to Henry M. and Barbara (Voltz) Klair. He was educated at St. Paul's parochial school. In 1899 Klair was chosen to represent the 61st Representative District in the General Assembly. He served five consecutive terms until 1911, when he was elected to the state railroad commission. After losing his bid for a second term on the railroad commission in 1914, Klair was reelected to the legislature in 1917 and served one more term before retiring from public office.

Klair was of German parentage, and his marriage to Mary Slavin, of Irish descent, on November 15, 1900, proved politically advantageous, as did his business ventures. Klair owned the Navare saloon in downtown Lexington and the Leland Hotel, and was a member of the boards of several Lexington banking firms. He formed Klair-Scott Insurance Agency in partnership with Thomas Scott in 1912. Klair did not hesitate to use private funds in his political activities. In 1916 he was elected chairman of the joint city and county Democratic committee, and was also named to the party's state central and executive committee. Serving continuously on the state committee until 1936, Klair extended his power and influence beyond Lexington. A Democrat, he advocated several reform causes in his early legislative career. He was also involved, however, in the bipartisan combine, an organization of urban Democratic and Republican politicians from around the state who worked to protect the state's railroad, coal mining, liquor, and racetrack interests.

In 1936 Klair was appointed postmaster of Lexington, but poor health forced him to resign only a few days before his death on October 29, 1937. He was buried in Calvary Cemetery in Lexington.

JAMES DUANE BOLIN

KLING, ARTHUR SOMMERFIELD. Arthur Sommerfield Kling, businessman and humanitarian, was born in Louisville on December 10, 1895, son of Benjamin and Anna (Sommerfield) Kling. He helped to establish the Kentucky Combined Committee on Aging and the Kentucky Association for Older Persons, both of which he served as chairman.

Kling attended the University of Cincinnati and Hebrew Union College in Cincinnati. He left rabbinical training for Chicago, where he drove a cab. When World War I broke out, he became a morale officer for the National Jewish Welfare Board, first at Fort Ogelthorpe, Georgia, and later at Camp Taylor, on the outskirts of Louisville, during the 1918 flu epidemic. After the war he founded Kling Co., wholesaler of merchandise for variety stores in Louisville. He helped organize the Kentucky chapter of the American Civil Liberties Union and was the first white board member of the Urban League in Louisville. He founded the Jewish Vocational Service (now Jewish Family and Vocational Service), was president of the Jewish Community Center, and was a life board member of the Jewish Community Federation of Louisville. He ran as a Socialist candidate for mayor in the 1930s. In 1959 he was chosen man of the year by the Louisville lodge of B'nai B'rith and in 1969 received the Blanche B. Ottenheimer Award for outstanding civic service. In 1978 he and his brother, Morris, were jointly chosen for the B'nai B'rith National Humanitarian Award.

Kling married Selma Marcus in 1920, and they had one child, David. Kling died on October 7, 1981 and his body was cremated. During his lifetime, the Kling Center for senior citizens in Louisville was named in his honor.

See Herman Landau, *Adath Louisville: The Story of a Jewish Community* (Louisville 1981).

HERMAN LANDAU

KLING, SIMCHA. Simcha Kling, rabbi and scholar, was born in Dayton, Kentucky, on January 27, 1922, the son of Eli and Ann (Niman) Kling. After attending high school in Tel Aviv, he received a B.A. at the University of Cincinnati, and an M.A. at Columbia University, and in 1948 was ordained at Jewish Theological Seminary in New York City, where he also received a doctorate. He served as an assistant rabbi in St. Louis during 1948-51, rabbi of Beth David in Greensboro, North Carolina, during 1951-65, then came to Adath Jeshurun in Louisville. He was president of the North Carolina Association of Rabbis and of Louisville's Board of Rabbis. For twenty-five years he was president of Louisville's Hebrew Speaking Circle. He taught sociology of religion for five years at the University of Louisville and lectured at Bellarmine College in

Louisville and elsewhere. Kling wrote *Embracing Judaism* (1970) and five other books, among them biographies of Zionist leaders and a historical account of Israel. He also wrote seventeen articles for *Hadoar*, an American Jewish weekly, translated essays, and wrote study guides, besides serving as editor of *Mercaz Newsletter*. He married Edith Leeman June 15, 1947. They had three daughters, Elana, Adina, and Reena. Kling died on February 26, 1991, and was buried in Louisville's Adath Jeshurun Cemetery.

HERMAN LANDAU

KNOBS. The Knobs is the irregular 230-mile-long arc of hills, ten to twenty miles in width, that extends around the eastern, southern, and western fringes of the Bluegrass region of east-central Kentucky. The Knobs area stretches across twenty counties, from the Ohio River in Lewis County on the northeast to near the Ohio River in Jefferson and Bullitt counties in the west. The southernmost segment of the Knobs arc crosses Marion, Boyle, Casey, Lincoln, and Madison counties. The zone covers between 2,200 and 2,500 square miles, with a 1980 population of about 240,000.

The Knobs is underlain by rock layers of the Devonian and Silurian periods of the Paleozoic Era, penetrated by Mississippian limestones. On the east the Knobs merges into the Pottsville Escarpment at the western edge of the Cumberland Plateau, and it grades into Mississippian limestone of the Mississippian Plateau on the east, south, and west.

The distinctive hills of the Knobs zone are conical when composed of sandstone and shale, and flat-topped when capped by Mississippian limestone or Pottsville conglomerate. Oil in Devonian and Silurian shale is a potential natural resource, but no economically viable means of recovering shale oil has been developed. While the distinctive conical shape of flat-topped hills is the source of the region's name, a considerable part of the Knobs is relatively level, fertile river plains, the site of farmland, routes of transportation, and settlements. Morehead in the east, Berea in the south, and Lebanon in the southwest are the three largest cities in or bordering on the Knobs zone. Parts of Louisville border the region on the west.

The Knobs area is drained by many small streams and several of Kentucky's larger rivers. The Ohio River forms the northern boundary of the Knobs. The Licking River flows through the Knobs northwestward and serves as the boundary that separates Bath County from both Rowan and Fleming counties. The Kentucky River and its Red River and Dix River tributaries flow through the Knobs on the east and the south. Farther west the Rolling Fork and Salt rivers penetrate segments of the Knobs.

On the east, the individual knobs or knob clusters are outliers of eastern Kentucky's Cumberland Plateau. On the south and west, the escarpment known as MULDRAUGH HILL is the most striking topographic feature, rising as much as five hundred feet above nearby stream lowlands. In Lincoln County and eastward, maximum elevations in the Knobs zone are fifteen hundred feet or higher. Farther west, peak elevations of individual knobs range from less than eight hundred feet in Jefferson County in the Louisville area to eleven hundred feet in other areas.

Historically, the Knobs zone has been a gateway to the east, near Morehead in Rowan County and near Berea in southern Madison County, and to the south at Hall's Gap south of Stanford in Lincoln County. Since the 1960s, I-64 has cut across the Knobs near Morehead; I-75 crosses the Knobs near Berea. These routes and the Mountain Parkway east of Winchester serve as modern gateways; somewhat older is the U.S. 27 route southward through Hall's Gap.

The Knobs region has been the site of many of Kentucky's best-known bourbon whiskey distilleries and it has a history of hemp production.

See Wilbur Greeley Burroughs, *The Geography of the Kentucky Knobs* (Frankfort, Ky., 1926).

WILLIAM A. WITHINGTON

KNOTT, JAMES PROCTOR. James Proctor Knott, governor during 1883-87, was born to Joseph Percy and Maria (Irvine) Knott on August 29, 1830, in Marion County, Kentucky. He received a common school education before moving in 1850 to Missouri, where he became a lawyer in 1851. Knott served in the Missouri legislature and in the offices of the circuit and county clerks. After his first wife, Mary E. Forman, died in childbirth, he married a Kentucky cousin, Sarah R. McElroy, in 1858. Appointed in 1858 to an unexpired term as Missouri's attorney general, Knott was elected to a full term in 1860. A moderate secessionist, he resigned in 1862 rather than swear allegiance to the United States. He returned to Kentucky, where he opened a legal practice in Lebanon.

A Democrat, Knott was elected to six terms in the U.S. House of Representatives, serving from March 4, 1867, to March 3, 1871, and from March 4, 1875, to March 3, 1883. Knott opposed Radical Reconstruction and a high tariff. He won recognition for his 1871 "DULUTH" speech, in which he ridiculed federal aid for a proposed railroad. Knott was rejected for the Democratic gubernatorial nomination in 1871, but won endorsement in a party convention filled with controversy in 1883. He then won an easy victory over Republican Thomas Z. Morrow, 133,615 to 89,181. After he left office in 1887, Knott practiced law in Frankfort for five years. In 1887-88 he served as a special assistant to the Kentucky attorney general and in 1890 was elected to the state's constitutional convention. In 1894, after teaching civics and economics at Centre College in Danville, he became professor and dean of the school's new law department. Ill health forced his retirement in 1902, and he lived in Lebanon until his death on June 18, 1911. He was buried there.

Governor Knott asked for a thorough reform of the state's tax system, but the legislature gave him little more than a Board of Equalization that was charged with making equitable assessments. The legislature also refused to give the Railroad Commission all of the powers requested by the governor. The General Assembly finally approved construction of a new penitentiary at Eddyville, a project for which Gov. Luke Pryor Blackburn (1879-83) was largely responsible. Aided by the recommendations of a blue-ribbon commission of prominent citizens, Knott secured a comprehensive overhaul of the state's system of public education. Duties and responsibilities were spelled out, often for the first time, and a state teachers' association was authorized. A deficit of nearly $500,000 led Knott to renew his request for the transfer of a number of functions from the state to the county governments and for an end to the tax immunities that had been granted to corporations. Despite the violence in the form of feuds that was making Kentucky notorious, Knott refused to admit that crime was a serious issue, even when he failed to end a war fought for several years in Rowan County. He became known for the number of pardons he granted.

See Hambleton Tapp, "James Proctor Knott and the Duluth Speech," *Register* 70 (April 1972): 77-93.

LOWELL H. HARRISON

KNOTT, SARAH GERTRUDE. Sarah Gertrude Knott, founder of the National Folk Festival, was born in Kevil, Ballard County, Kentucky, in 1895, to Clinton and Ella (Wren) Knott. She attended McCracken County High School, Georgetown (Kentucky) Preparatory School (1919-20), the University of North Carolina, Washington University in St. Louis (1928-29), and several drama schools.

She served as national director of the National Folk Festival from its start in St. Louis in 1934 through 1971. It was the first multiethnic festival, a model followed by hundreds of other festivals and events. It presented blacks and Asians on stage with whites when this was a radical innovation. Subsequent festivals were held in Chattanooga, Tennessee; Dallas, Texas; Chicago; Philadelphia; Cleveland; and other cities. The festival visited Constitution Hall in Washington, D.C., in 1938, with Eleanor Roosevelt as honorary chairman. The 1963 festival was held at Devou Park in Covington, Kentucky, and the 1964 event at the Latonia Race Course (now Turfway) at nearby Florence, Kentucky. During 1971-82 the event was held at Wolf Trap Farm near Washington, D.C. In 1989 the festival was held in New York City as part of the Statue of Liberty centennial. The event is held annually as a program of the National Council for the Traditional Arts at various national parks.

Knott received many awards during her tenure as national director, including the Laurel Wreath of Victory (North Carolina, 1941), the Burl Ives Award (1971), and the Kentucky Folk Heritage Award (1973). She returned to Princeton, Kentucky, after her retirement and died there on November 20, 1984. She was buried in the Bayou Baptist Church Cemetery in McCracken County.

JOHN M. RAMSAY

KNOTT COUNTY. Knott County, the 118th county in order of formation, is located in the heart of the rugged mountains of eastern Kentucky. The county is bounded by Perry, Breathitt, Magoffin, Floyd, Pike, and Letcher counties, and covers an area of 352 square miles. It was formed from portions of Perry, Letcher, Floyd, and Breathitt counties in 1884. The county was named for Gov. James Proctor Knott (1883-87). The county seat is HINDMAN. Letcher County legislator Robert Bates helped to oversee the creation of the new county, which is the site of the headwaters of several major creeks that flow into either the Big Sandy or Kentucky rivers. Knott is the only Kentucky county that does not have a river within its boundaries or bordering it.

No known Native American groups inhabited Knott County in the early historic era, but it is likely that Shawnee, Cherokee, and others hunted in the area. Among the first settlers were the Johnsons, who built cabins near Cody in 1786, when the area was still a part of Virginia. Families who settled by 1825 in what would become Knott County included the Breedings, Amburgeys, Everages, Adamses, Dukes, Francises, Mullinses, Slones, Draughns, Newlands, Combses, Pigmans, Hayeses, Joneses, Halls, Gibsons, and Martins. The area remained isolated and substantial settlement occurred only in the early 1880s.

As in most of eastern Kentucky, mineral and timber speculators purchased the rights to the county's valuable natural resources for relatively insignificant sums from the 1880s through the early 1900s. The county had no railroad system until the 1960s, with the exception of a few spur lines to the mines near the county borders. Knott County's coal reserves were among the state's largest, and by the mid-1920s coal was being produced on Yellow Creek in the western part of the county both by local companies such as the Perkins-Bowling Coal Company and by out-of-state firms that included the Wisconsin Coal Company. Many families left their farms to live in the coal camps at Yellow Creek, Garrett, Wayland, and other locations.

The county is known for the beginnings of the movement demanding stricter control over surface mining. To protest the abuses in the Lotts Creek and Clear Creek area, Ollie Combs lay down in front of a bulldozer to stop mining and Uncle Dan Gibson scared off miners with his rifle in the 1960s. A mine explosion in Topmost on December 7, 1981, killed eight men.

The county is the home of ALICE LLOYD College, a four-year college that has educated many of the region's educators and leaders. At the urging of resident Sol Everidge, May Stone and Katherine Petit came to Hindman to start the HINDMAN Settlement School in 1902. The school became a major cultural center, attracting talented artists, scholars, and writers. George Clarke established a school in Hindman in 1887 that served many county residents. Alice Slone, a graduate of Alice Lloyd College, established the Lotts Creek Settlement School and Community Center in 1928 at Cordia.

Knott County was the political base of Carl D. PERKINS, a U.S. representative from 1949 until his death in 1984. Knott County's Grady Stumbo ran for governor in 1983 and 1987.

The population of the rural county was 14,698 in 1970; 17,940 in 1980; and 17,906 in 1990.

See "Knott County Comes Into Being" *Appalachian Heritage* 2-3 (Fall 1974–Winter 1975): 3-13.

RONALD DALEY

KNOW-NOTHING PARTY. The Know-Nothing party in Kentucky was an unusually strong outgrowth of the nativist political movement in the United States during the 1850s. Nativism, which dates back to the early days of the Republic, is an attitude or policy favoring native-born citizens over immigrants. Unfamiliar habits, speech, and religion (primarily Roman Catholicism) became targets of Kentuckians in the 1850s, although the census of 1850 revealed that only 31,420 Kentuckians, or 4.1 percent of the population, were foreign-born, and there were perhaps 35,000 Catholics.

Apart from Protestant antipathy toward Catholicism, nativism in Kentucky and the nation was an outgrowth of the flux in political parties in the mid-nineteenth century. Texas annexation, the Mexican War, and the bitterly debated slavery issue threatened the parties with dissolution. When the Kansas-Nebraska Act of 1854 repealed the Missouri Compromise limit on the expansion of slavery, the end of the Whig party was at hand. The Democrats managed a feeble unity until 1860 only because they controlled national patronage. Southern Whigs temporarily joined the Democrats on a slavery expansion program, but many northern Whigs joined the new Republican party. Kentuckians, however, as border-state people sensed that both parties were too radical on the slavery question to govern a united country. Kentuckians were therefore more susceptible than most to a new party—and one was waiting in the wings.

By 1854 a national nativist organization had entered the political arena. Although such parties had been formed before, the so-called American party was the first to win much success. It sought to use government power to impose Anglo-Saxon Protestant values. The party demanded that immigration be limited, that native Americans be favored for public office, that stringent naturalization legislation be enacted, and above all else, that the alleged influence of the Roman Catholic Church be strictly curbed. The party was popularly designated "Know-Nothing" because its secretive members nearly always answered questions with "I know nothing."

By 1855 the Know-Nothings could count 50,000 voters in Kentucky. Men of two types joined the party. First, there were those who viewed the vast influx of foreigners as likely to upset the peace won in the compromise of 1850, thereby turning Kentucky into a battleground; they viewed the

American party as the last chance to push the slavery issue off the stage and thereby delay civil war. Also lurking in their minds was a belief that Henry Clay's defeat in 1844 was owing to illegal immigrant voting in several key states. In short, these were respectable men, such as John J. Crittenden, and they were intent on saving the Union, not on harassing Catholics or immigrants as such. The second type was the roughneck and bigot who gave the Know-Nothings a bad name.

Prominent among party leaders in Kentucky were three former Whigs: Garrett Davis, a Bourbon County politician who had helped establish the party in the state; Robert J. Breckinridge, a powerful educator and Protestant leader; and George D. Prentice, the editor and publisher of the *Louisville Journal*. The party easily carried the spring municipal elections in Louisville, Lexington, and Covington in 1855, and entered gubernatorial candidate Charles S. Morehead against Democrat Beverly L. Clarke. Morehead, a former Whig congressman, joined the party because it was more "Union" than the Democrats. He won the governorship by 4,403 votes; his party carried both houses of the legislature and chose six of the ten congressmen. This election, inflamed with hatred for foreigners and Catholics, resulted in the Louisville riots of August 6, 1855—"BLOODY MONDAY." At least nineteen men were killed, most of them Irish or German Catholic immigrants.

Know-Nothings hoped to gain the presidency in 1856. They nominated Millard Fillmore, but his case was rendered hopeless by party factionalism over slavery. Kentucky Know-Nothings, fearing that a division in anti-Republican votes might elect John C. Frémont, crossed over in great numbers to vote for James Buchanan, thereby giving a Democratic presidential candidate victory in Kentucky for the first time since 1828. Nationally the Know-Nothings were defeated, and their decline was stunning in its speed. The name was soon being used as a scornful epithet. By 1858 the Kentucky legislature was in Democratic hands and Know-Nothing power was at an end.

See Wallace B. Turner, "The Know-Nothing Movement in Kentucky," *FCHQ* 28 (July 1954): 266-83; Agnes G. McGann, *Nativism in Kentucky to 1860* (Washington, D.C., 1944).

FRANK F. MATHIAS

KNOX COUNTY. Knox County, the forty-first in order of formation, is in southeastern Kentucky; bounded by Clay, Laurel, Whitley, and Bell counties, it has an area of 388 square miles. It was created on December 19, 1799, from Lincoln County and was named after Gen. Henry Knox of Massachusetts, the nation's first secretary of war. BARBOURVILLE is the county seat. Knox County originally embraced all the upper Cumberland Valley and several counties were later created from its territory—Clay (1806), Rockcastle (1810),

Whitley (1818), Harlan (1819), Laurel (1825), and Bell (1867).

Knox County's topography is hilly and mountainous, and it is on the watershed of the Cumberland River. Highest elevations are in the southern and eastern sections, which reach about 2,000 feet above sea level. Lowest elevations are along the Cumberland River, which runs from east to west through the south-central portion of the county. Soil conditions are generally well adapted to agriculture in the valleys. Tobacco is the main cash crop; beef cattle are the principal livestock. Approximately three-fourths of the county is forested. Coal and timber are the county's most profitable natural resources, followed by natural gas.

The primary manufactured products in 1990 were steel wire and fiber products, food service equipment, brassieres and girdles, industrial sealants, lumber, roofing materials, machine parts, and fishing and pleasure boats. Other industries included railroad car repair and coal processing.

Rail transportation through the county is provided by CSX Transportation. The Cumberland Gap Parkway (U.S. 25E) is the county's main highway and connects with I-75 near Knox County's northwestern border, not far from the Tri-County Industrial Park.

The population of Knox County has remained stable since 1940, with natural increase and immigration offset by emigration to industrial sites, a trend that had slowed by 1990. A major city is CORBIN, located partially in Knox County but extending into Laurel and Whitley counties. Other communities include Artemus, Bimble, Bryant's Store, Cannon, Dewitt, Flat Lick, Girdler, Gray, Green Road, Heidrick, Hinkle, Mills, Scalf, Trosper, Walker, and Woolum.

A large number of residents trace their ancestry to English, Scotch-Irish, and German settlers. The main religious denomination is Southern Baptist, followed by Pentecostal congregations and other Baptist groups.

Primary and secondary public education is provided by the Knox County Schools and the Barbourville Independent School District. Union College, founded in 1879 in Barbourville, is a four-year school affiliated with the United Methodist church.

The area known as Knox County was the home of prehistoric Native Americans, and remains of villages and mounds have been located. The first English explorers who came to the region were Dr. Thomas WALKER and companions.

In the 1760s parties of the Long Hunters roamed the region for months at a time and often followed the Warriors' Path to the Flat Lick-Stinking Creek area. In 1775 Daniel Boone blazed the trail later known as the Wilderness Road through Knox County. The county's frontier heritage is celebrated each October with the Daniel Boone Festival, established in 1948. Daniel Boone Trail Memorial Park is located at Flat Lick, and the Knox Historical Museum in Barbourville contains many items relating to the frontier era.

Knox County's population grew steadily after the Civil War, reaching 10,587 in 1880. In 1888 the Louisville & Nashville Railroad (now CSX Transportation) completed lines through the county, generating a land boom. Another boom occurred around 1900 with the discovery of oil. A large mining community flourished in the Artemus–Kay Jay area from 1900 to the late 1940s.

Knox County's notable citizens include Joseph Eve, the nation's only chargé d'affaires to the Republic of Texas; Caleb Powers, involved in the assassination of Gov. William Goebel (1900); and U.S. congressmen James Love, Green Adams, George M. Adams, John H. Wilson, and John M. Robison. Knox County has provided the state with two Kentucky governors, James Black (1919) and Flem Sampson (1927-31).

The completion of I-75 in the early 1970s brought business growth near Corbin. The four-laning of U.S. 25E in the early 1990s brought similar growth to the Barbourville area. The population of Knox County was 23,689 in 1970; 30,239 in 1980; and 29,676 in 1990.

See K.S. Sol Warren, *A History of Knox County, Kentucky* (Barbourville, Ky., 1976).

DAVID H. COLE

KOREAN WAR. From the time that the United States and other members of the United Nations went to South Korea's aid in the Korean War until the end of hostilities on July 27, 1953, 868 men from Kentucky were classified as dead from hostile action in that war. One hundred seventy of those men were missing in action (presumed dead) and forty died while prisoners of war.

At the very first battle fought by Americans, near Osan, on July 5, 1950, five Kentuckians were killed in action. As follow-up units of the army's 24th Division were hastily thrown into combat during July to stem the enemy tide, Col. Robert Martin, the highest-ranking Kentuckian to die in Korea, was killed in action against a tank. Seventy-four men from Kentucky were killed in combat in July. With the immediate need for replacements, reservists in all branches across the state were recalled to active duty. Many World War II veterans had to leave their civilian pursuits and return to the hazards of war. About 15 percent of the Korean War troops were World War II veterans. From September 3, 1950, to January 23, 1951, ten National Guard units located across the state from Middlesborough to Owensboro were ordered into federal service. A total of 1,860 citizen soldiers reported to active duty with their units: one Air National Guard group, three field artillery battalions, one engineer battalion, and five separate companies.

When the war appeared to be over in November 1950, hidden Chinese armies in the North Korean mountains struck and sent the U.N. forces reeling backward. It was at the initiation of the Chinese action that Capt. William E. Barber of West Liberty, Kentucky, won the Medal of Honor. Against a Chinese regiment, he and his company of Marines held a mountain pass open for six days. His actions enabled the 1st Marine Division to escape encirclement in the Chosin Reservoir sector. During the war, four other Kentuckians were awarded the Medal of Honor: Cpl. John W. Collier, honored posthumously, and Pfc. Ernest E. West (both of Boyd County); 2d Lt. Carl H. Dodd (Harlan County); and Pfc. David M. Smith (Rockcastle County), honored posthumously.

By July 1951 the battle lines had stabilized generally just north of the 38th Parallel (the boundary between North and South Korea). For the last two years of the war, while bitter negotiations continued at Kaesong and Panmunjom, the front lines became bunkered in. Interest in the war dropped and the war news moved off the front pages. On December 23, 1951, the 623d Field Artillery Battalion arrived in Korea. Headquarters, A, B, C, and Service batteries were from Glasgow, Tompkinsville, Campbellsville, Monticello, and Springfield, respectively. The battalion was awarded the Navy Unit Commendation Medal and the Republic of Korea Unit Citation Medal. No other Kentucky National Guard units on active duty served in Korea. Kentucky units did, however, provide individual replacements. The 123d Fighter Bomber Group from Louisville went to England, but some of its pilots went to Korea. Maj. Meade Brown, Capt. John W. Shewmaker, 1st Lt. Lawrence B. Kelly, and 1st Lt. Eugene L. Ruiz, of the group's 165th Fighter Bomber Squadron, were killed in action.

The Korean War moved back to the front pages on January 3, 1952, when the Communists violently objected to the U.N. Command's proposal of voluntary repatriation of prisoners of war. Just over two-thirds of the 20,879 Chinese POWs refused to go home. The war dragged out for a year and half over the issue—time that cost Kentucky 199 young lives. Kentuckians learned about the mistreatment of American POWs when they began returning home. Forty of about 190 Kentuckians captured did not survive the inhumane treatment and the many death marches.

Both at the beginning and at the ending of the war, Kentucky suffered a disproportionate number of casualties. Six of the forty-three marines killed in the 1st Marine Division's final battle (July 24-27, 1953) were Kentuckians. Of the 868 battle deaths, the counties with the highest losses were Jefferson (102), Harlan (43), Perry (28), Pike (27), Kenton (22), Floyd (21), Fayette (19), Whitley (18), Daviess (18), Campbell (17), Boyd (17), Letcher (15), and Bell (15). Seventy-four counties lost five or fewer; fifteen counties lost one; and Carlisle, Hickman, Spencer, Jackson, and Green counties did not lose any. Harlan County suffered the highest loss rate per capita. The Kentucky losses by branch of service were: army (750), Marine Corps (94), air force (16), and navy (8).

By nationality, the military deaths were: United States, 54,246; South Korea, 415,004; other U.N. members, 3,094. Of the 5.72 million U.S. troops that served in the Korean War, 123,000 were from Kentucky, according to the Department of Defense progress reports and a Statistics Office report (April 20, 1955), although that figure appears high. Kentucky paid 73,854 war bonus claims and 18,220 multiple war bonus claims in 1962. In addition to the 868 killed in hostilities, 157 Kentuckians died of other causes and 2,545 received nonfatal wounds.

COL. ARTHUR L. KELLY, U.S. ARMY, RET.

KREPS, JUANITA (MORRIS). Juanita (Morris) Kreps, U.S. secretary of commerce, was born on January 11, 1921, in Lynch, Harlan County, Kentucky, to Elmer M. and Larcenia (Blair) Morris. She graduated from Berea College in 1942 with a B.A. degree and earned her Ph.D. in economics in 1948 at Duke University. Morris married Clifton H. Kreps, Jr., on August 11, 1944; they have three children, Sarah, Laura, and Clifton III. Juanita Kreps taught economics at Duke from 1955 to 1977 and served as the university's vice-president from 1973 to 1977.

On January 23, 1977, Kreps became U.S. secretary of commerce under President Jimmy Carter. She sought to expand the Commerce Department's focus from business enterprises alone to include the consumer public and employees. Kreps was considered Carter's chief economic diplomat, traveling all over the world to negotiate economic policies. She served as secretary of commerce until the end of the Carter administration in 1981.

Kreps has written and edited a variety of books and articles on economics, many focusing on women and the elderly in the marketplace and workplace. She has served on the boards of directors of the New York Stock Exchange, J.C. Penney Co., Eastman Kodak, and Citicorp and on the board of trustees of Berea College. In 1975 the University of Kentucky awarded her an honorary doctorate of law, and she received the Outstanding Alumni of Kentucky Award from Kentucky Advocates for Higher Education in 1987.

KROCK, ARTHUR. Arthur Krock, journalist, was born in Glasgow, Kentucky, on November 16, 1886, the son of Joseph and Caroline (Morris) Krock. Winner of four Pulitzer prizes, he was considered the outstanding conservative political commentator of his era for his column "In the Nation," which ran in the *New York Times* for thirty-three years. Krock attended Lewis Institute in Chicago and Princeton University. He received honorary degrees from the University of Louisville in 1939, Centre College in 1940, and the University of Kentucky in 1956.

Krock began his journalistic career in 1906 on the *Louisville Herald*, was editor in chief of the *Louisville Times* during 1919-23, and left Louisville in 1923 to become Washington correspondent of the *Courier-Journal* and the *Louisville Times*. He acted as intermediary in the purchase of the *Courier-Journal* and the *Louisville Times* by Robert W. Bingham in 1918, but left the Louisville newspapers because of a policy disagreement. He left journalism to be assistant to the chairman of the Democratic National Committee during the 1920 presidential campaign and also worked for Will Hays, who headed the Motion Picture Producers and Distributors of America. As a reporter at the Versailles Peace Conference, he was one of three American members of a press committee that urged open sessions for the World War I settlement talks. France honored him with the Legion d'Honneur and Norway with the Order of St. Olaf. Krock joined the *New York Times* on May 1, 1927, and became its Washington, D.C., bureau chief in 1932. His coverage of the New Deal won a Pulitzer prize in 1935. Three years later he received a second Pulitzer for an interview with President Franklin D. Roosevelt. An interview with President Harry Truman produced a third Pulitzer in 1950, and he was honored again in 1955 for distinguished Washington coverage. Krock wrote two autobiographical works, *Memoirs: 60 Years on the Firing Line* (1968), and *Myself When Young: Growing Up in the 1890s* (1973). He compiled *The Editorials of Henry Watterson* (1923).

Krock married Marguerite Pelleys on April 22, 1911, and they had a son, Thomas Pelleys. She died in 1938 and the following year Krock married Martha Granger Blair, bringing into the family two stepsons, William Granger and Robert H. Blair. He died in Washington on April 12, 1974.

HERMAN LANDAU

L

LABOR ORGANIZATIONS. The development of Kentucky labor organizations closely paralleled union growth in the rest of the nation. Unionism began in the 1830s among skilled workers in the state's major urban areas. Several craft groups in Louisville formed locals and then established a loose coordinating body. Other northern Kentucky craftsmen who formed local unions joined Cincinnati locals to form a central organization. Workers' organizations among at least seven crafts in Lexington were functioning before the Civil War. Unionism in Louisville and northern Kentucky was spurred in the 1840s by the influx of German immigrants, many of whom were craftsmen.

Many of the trade unionists in Kentucky helped form national unions of their respective crafts, and a few became leaders of these organizations. Two Louisville trade unionists—George Greene and James L. Gibbons—became officers of the International Typographical Union during the 1850s. Others focused on securing legal rights for trade unions by lobbying for special statutes. The Kentucky Association of Teachers, organized in Louisville in 1857, was incorporated by an act of the General Assembly in 1858. Kentucky trade unionists lobbied and secured a mechanics' lien law. During the pre–Civil War period they joined in antislavery activities and they opposed secession. Interest among Kentucky unionists in workers' cooperatives culminated in legislation in 1867 sponsored by the molders' union, which incorporated a cooperative foundry. The union had been successful in the pre–Civil War period in organizing foundries in Louisville and northern Kentucky.

The Knights of Labor were active in the state during the 1870s and 1880s. Although there are no records indicating when the first locals were established, there were thirty-six in the state by 1880. Nationally, the Knights' membership peaked in 1886; at that time there were 177 local assemblies in Kentucky, primarily in Louisville and Covington. The Knights sponsored several strikes and founded a state labor party in 1887. In one action, more than eight hundred workers in woolen mills in Louisville, mainly women, struck in July 1887 but were unsuccessful despite the local labor movement's active assistance. By the end of the decade, membership in the Knights had declined significantly, both nationwide and in Kentucky. In 1889 there were only three local assemblies left in Louisville.

The formation of the American Federation of Labor (AFL) in 1886 made personnel available to assist the organization of workers. Efforts to establish a state federation of labor were begun in 1899 by James McGill of Louisville. The federation's charter was revoked in 1904 but reissued in 1908. With the demise of the Knights by this time, the AFL emerged in Kentucky, as it did elsewhere, as the dominant American labor organization. The Kentucky State Federation of Labor (KSFL) thus became the voice of organized labor.

Kentucky labor presented proposals to the 1890 constitutional convention, where William Goebel of Covington was labor's spokesman. The new constitution provided for the payment of wages in legal tender and set a minimum age at which children could be employed at dangerous work. Because other labor proposals were rejected, the entire labor movement failed to endorse the new constitution. In subsequent years, however, the legislature became more receptive to the proposals labor had made at the 1890 convention. In 1902, for example, the legislature passed a general child-labor law, established Labor Day as a holiday, and created a factory inspector system. In 1904 the legislature passed a compulsory education law for children of ages seven through fourteen.

When large-scale coal mining developed after the Civil War, unionism soon followed. Coal mining developed in three regions of the state—the western, southeastern, and northeastern counties. Local organizations of miners were formed throughout the state during the 1870s and 1880s, with varying success (see MINERS' UNIONS). The UNITED MINE WORKERS (UMW) of America, founded in 1890, quickly gained the Kentucky miners' allegiance. The union was more successful in securing and maintaining membership in the western than in the two eastern coal fields. During World War I the union was greatly helped by an order from the federal fuel authority mandating union recognition. In 1919, when mine owners wanted to return to prewar labor conditions, the UMW called a nationwide strike in an attempt to maintain wartime benefits. Twenty-two thousand coal miners in Kentucky joined the strike, but it was not successful. The drop in demand for coal led to price cuts, which in turn compelled wage cuts. When the UMW called a second national strike in 1922, the number of Kentuckians who participated was less than half the number in 1919. Unionism continued to decline during the 1920s, and, as a result, wages were reduced and safety conditions deteriorated.

Unionism among railroad workers in Kentucky developed soon after the Civil War but was not so visible as among the coal miners. The operating employees (engineers, firemen, switchmen, conductors, and trainmen) developed independent railroad brotherhoods, rarely cooperating with other unions. The nonoperating employees joined AFL unions, but their craft unions often included nonrailroad employees. Nevertheless, the railroad workers' unions were important in Louisville because the Louisville & Nashville Railroad had its headquarters and central offices there. In 1877, during the nation's first great railroad strike, the city became a battleground, and federal troops were eventually dispatched to maintain order.

In the 1920s and early 1930s, union membership in Kentucky was sharply reduced. Under the friendly federal government of President Franklin D. Roosevelt, organizational efforts became common. Perhaps the most spectacular achievement in Kentucky was that of Samuel Hubert Caddy, who in 1933 organized 15,000 members in the northeastern coal fields in five weeks. Unionism proceeded more slowly in the southeastern fields, particularly in Harlan County, which became a battleground between the UMW and the coal mine owners and was quickly labeled "Bloody Harlan." Distillery workers were unionized in the late 1930s in Louisville and Cynthiana, and a local was formed at the Louisville Ford plant in 1940. Among public employees in Louisville, a teachers' union and firefighters' local were chartered in 1941.

The formation of the Congress of Industrial Organizations (CIO) as an alternative federation led inevitably to the formation of the Kentucky Industrial Union in 1938. Over three-quarters of KSFL affiliates left for the new federation, but organizing successes by AFL unions enabled the KSFL to recover. When the UMW left the CIO in the mid-1940s, the KSFL again became the dominant Kentucky labor federation. In 1944 it took over the Louisville central body's *Kentucky Labor News* and published it as the official statewide labor voice. Following World War II, the KSFL developed an educational program for local union leaders.

Labor organizations were active in the legislature during the 1930s and 1940s. The Kentucky Education Association was successful in obtaining a statewide teacher tenure act in 1942 and legislation to fund a teachers' retirement system it had established. Gov. Simeon Willis (1943-47) promulgated the state's first minimum wage order in 1940. A few years later the Kentucky old-age pension law was passed. At the end of World War II, the Louisville community established the Louisville Labor-Management Committee to promote industrial peace. The UMW negotiated a health-welfare fund with the Bituminous Coal Operators Association in 1946. In addition to providing retirement, disability, and medical care benefits, the program led to the construction of a network of hospitals in Kentucky's coal-producing counties. Financed by employer contributions, the program encountered difficulties and was forced to curtail benefits. The hospitals eventually became independent of the UMW.

The merger of the AFL and CIO in 1955 necessitated that all statewide organizations be merged. Kentucky merged its labor federations in August 1958, one of the last states to do so. Henry Siebert of the Clothing Workers was elected president, John E. McKiernan of the Distillery Workers was elected executive vice-president, and Sam Ezelle of the Iron Workers was elected executive secretary. In the late 1960s and 1970s the state federation developed several retirement housing projects for aged workers.

Although the merger was intended to facilitate union development and expansion, unionism did not grow. In Kentucky, unions represented about 25 percent of the nonagricultural employees until the early 1980s, when the figure declined to about 20 percent. Nevertheless, Kentucky is one of the better organized states, ranking twentieth in 1982. In that year, seven unions—the Automobile Workers, the Electronic Workers, the Food and Commercial Workers, the Machinists, the Mine Workers, the Steelworkers, and the Teamsters—accounted for about half of the state's membership. Unionization in the public sector is lower in Kentucky than in the nation as a whole. In the late 1980s, despite the decline in union membership, Kentucky unions continued to have some political influence. In 1986 the legislature raised the state's minimum wage to the federal level. Given the decline of unionism nationwide, the prospects for unionism in Kentucky are doubtful.

See Kentucky Department of Education, *Labor History in Kentucky* (Frankfort, Ky., 1986); Herbert Finch, "Organized Labor in Louisville, Kentucky, 1880-1914," Ph.D. diss., University of Kentucky, 1965; Virgil Christian, "Kentucky Labor Since the Wagner Act," M.A. thesis, University of Kentucky, 1949.

JOSEPH KRISLOV

LADY POLK CANNON. Mounted 180 feet above the Mississippi River on an iron carriage at Columbus, Kentucky, the Lady Polk cannon threw 128-pound, cone-shaped shot (nicknamed lampposts) three miles during the Battle of Belmont on November 7, 1861. The cannon was an experimental 15,000-pound, 6.4-inch iron Anderson rifle named in honor of the wife of Confederate Maj. Gen. Leonidas Polk, an Episcopal bishop. During a test firing on November 11, 1861, the Lady Polk exploded and killed eleven men. In 1869 the shell of the cannon was used as an armchair inside the navy yard in Mound City, Illinois.

See Bromfield L. Ridley, *Battles and Sketches of the Army of the Tennessee* (Mexico, Mo., 1906); Warren Ripley, *Artillery and Ammunition of the Civil War* (New York 1970).

JOHN KELLY ROSS, JR.

LAFAYETTE'S VISIT. The visit of the Marquis de Lafayette to Kentucky in 1825 was an occasion for grand celebration in the commonwealth. Lafayette had long been accorded the status of a hero for his role in the American Revolution. Born in France in 1757, he joined the French Royal Army in 1771. He came to America in 1777 to aid the cause of American independence against the British, a commander under the leadership of Gen. George Washington. Lafayette returned to France in December 1781 and was caught up in the French Revolution. He fled the country in 1792, returning in 1800, after Napoleon came to power. He took no further part in politics until 1818, when he entered the Chamber of Deputies, serving until 1824. He took part in the July Revolution of 1830, which failed to convert France into a republic.

When President James Monroe invited Lafayette to visit the United States, his journey became symbolic of the struggle for independence, and wherever he went he was accorded a hero's welcome. The marquis arrived at Staten Island, New York, on August 15, 1824. In March of 1825 he began a tour of the southern states. He boarded the steamboat *Natchez* at Natchez, Mississippi, on April 18, 1825, and traveled up the Mississippi River to St. Louis, passing along the shores of western Kentucky. He then returned downriver, entering the Ohio River on April 30, thus passing into the territory of the commonwealth of Kentucky. Lafayette and his party transferred to the steamboat *Mechanic* on May 2, and entered the waters of the Cumberland River. His itinerary from then on:

May 3 and 4—passed through Lyon, Livingston, and Trigg counties on the way up the Cumberland toward Nashville, where he arrived on May 4.

May 5 and 6—steamed back down the Cumberland.

May 7 and 8—entered the Ohio River, and steamed upriver toward Louisville. The steamboat *Mechanic* struck an obstacle and sank on the evening of May 8, and Lafayette and his party spent that night on the shore.

May 9—picked up in the morning by the steamboat *Paragon*, which delivered the group upriver to Louisville on May 11. They remained in Louisville until May 13. Lafayette then began a tour of central Kentucky.

May 13—journeyed down the Old State Pike to Shelbyville, where he spent the night.

May 14—attended a dinner and a ball in Frankfort.

May 15—passed through Versailles, and then spent the night at the home of Maj. John Keene, five miles outside of Lexington.

May 16—arrived in Lexington, where he was greeted with a military parade and speeches at Transylvania University and the Lexington Female Academy.

May 18—journeyed to Georgetown, where he stayed the night.

May 19 and 20—visited Cincinnati and at midnight on May 20 boarded a steamer that traveled up the Ohio River toward West Virginia.

May 21—visited Maysville for several hours in the afternoon.

May 22—passed out of Kentucky territorial waters.

During his trip through Kentucky, Lafayette was frequently honored with spontaneous celebrations, formal ceremonies, dinners, and dances, to which he responded with speeches extolling the virtues of Kentucky and its citizens. During much of the trip, however, he was in poor health, and inclement weather made road travel difficult. Lafayette was accompanied on his tour by his son, George Washington Lafayette, his secretary, Au-

guste Levasseur, and his servant Sebastien. Lafayette left the United States on September 7, 1825. He died in 1834.

See Ida Earle Fowler, "Log of Lafayette's Journey through Kentucky," *Register* 27 (Sept. 1929): 651-53; Edgar Erskine Hume, *Lafayette in Kentucky* (Frankfort, Ky., 1937).

LAFFOON, RUBY. Ruby Laffoon, governor during 1931-35, was born in Madisonville, Kentucky, to John Bledsoe and Martha (Earle) Laffoon on January 15, 1869. He opened a law practice in Madisonville after graduating from Washington and Lee University in 1890. In January 1894 he married Mary Nisfer; they had three daughters. A lifelong Democrat, Laffoon lost races for state treasurer in 1907 and state auditor in 1911, but he was appointed chairman of the first Insurance Rating Board in 1912, and he was elected Hopkins County circuit judge in 1921 and reelected in 1927. In 1931 the Democrats selected their state-wide candidates in convention instead of in an open primary. Although he was not a party leader, Laffoon secured the nomination for governor with the aid of such party stalwarts as Ben Johnson, Allie W. Young, and Thomas Rhea. The Republicans selected William B. Harrison, a former Louisville mayor. Laffoon's margin of victory (446,301 to 374,239) was the largest any Kentucky governor had won. When he left office in 1935, Laffoon returned to his law practice in Madisonville, where he died on March 1, 1941. He was buried there.

Governor Laffoon was confronted by a failing economy and declining revenues. While he talked of making improvements in the usual areas, money was not available from existing sources. When Laffoon proposed a sales tax in the 1932 legislative session, it was blocked by Ben Johnson, whom Laffoon had made highway commissioner, and by Lt. Gov. A.B. Chandler. The governor vetoed a proposed reduction in the state property tax, along with several appropriations bills. In efforts to deal with the economic crisis, he closed both the banks and the burley tobacco markets in 1933. New Deal programs held some promise of badly needed assistance, but Kentucky was often unable to raise the required matching funds. Laffoon's continued effort to get a sales tax split the Democratic party, with Chandler and Johnson leading the opposition. In the 1934 session the governor won a reorganization bill that curtailed much of the power of Chandler and of the state auditor, J. Dan Talbott. By cutting state property and automobile taxes, Laffoon hoped to force acceptance of the sales tax. After a lengthy struggle, the legislature approved a three-cent sales tax in a 1934 special session. In an effort to keep Chandler out of the 1935 gubernatorial race, Laffoon and Thomas Rhea kept the party from requiring a direct primary. But when they went to Washington to explain this omission to President Franklin D. Roosevelt, acting Governor Chandler called a special legislative session to consider a primary election bill. Laffoon was forced to accept a primary in which a run-off was to be held if no candidate had a majority in the first balloting. In the 1935 primary, Rhea got a plurality but not a majority, Chandler beat him in the runoff, and Laffoon and Rhea bolted the party. Before leaving office, Laffoon set new records for the number of pardons granted and the number of Kentucky Colonels commissioned. Party factionalism and a sick economy left Laffoon with a meager record as governor.

See Vernon Gipson, *Ruby Laffoon, Governor of Kentucky, 1931-1935* (Earlington, Ky., 1978).

LOWELL H. HARRISON

LA GRANGE. La Grange, the seat of Oldham County, is located at the junction of KY 53 and KY 146, just northwest of I-71. The site of the city, where the Shelbyville-Westport Road crossed the Louisville–New Castle Road, was originally owned by Maj. William Berry Taylor. In 1827 Taylor offered the crossroads site to the county in a successful attempt to move the seat of government from the Ohio River town of Westport to a more central location. The new town was created and named by Taylor for the French country estate of the Marquis de Lafayette, hero of the Revolutionary War.

While a courthouse was being constructed in La Grange, the General Assembly in 1828 moved the county seat back to Westport; it was permanently returned to La Grange in 1838. La Grange was officially incorporated in 1840. The city expanded in 1851 when the Louisville & Frankfort Railroad Company—later part of the Louisville & Nashville (L&N)—constructed a connecting line through La Grange. In 1869 La Grange became a junction city when the L&N's Louisville-Cincinnati line was completed.

On December 27, 1864, Federal soldiers shot a Confederate guerrilla in La Grange for his part in partisan raids in the area during the Civil War. After the war, the thriving city became home for two black neighborhoods. By the 1870s several stores, the Masonic College, and a small woolen mill were located there. The courthouse was destroyed by fire in 1873 and replaced in 1875 by a brick structure of classical design.

Among those who lived in La Grange were D.W. Griffith and Dr. Rob Morris. Griffith, a pioneer in film production, was born in 1875 near La Grange and spent his boyhood there. Morris, founder of the Order of the Eastern Star and "poet laureate of Freemasonry," resided in the city for twenty-eight years and was president of the town's Masonic University from 1861 to 1865.

In the early 1900s, two disastrous fires destroyed most of the business section of La Grange, which was rebuilt. In 1907 an interurban rail line, the Louisville & Eastern, was extended from Louisville to La Grange, making the latter a suburban city with hourly train service to the larger metropolis. Although progress virtually ceased during the Great Depression, La Grange grew steadily as a residential city in the years before and after. Near the city

are several correctional facilities, including the Kentucky State Reformatory, Luther Luckett Correctional Complex, and the Roederer Farm Center. The completion of I-71 just south of the city during the 1970s brought a wave of rapid expansion and commercial development, and many residents work in the metropolitan Louisville area.

The population of the fourth-class city was 1,713 in 1970; 2,971 in 1980; and 3,853 in 1990.

RON D. BRYANT

LAINE, JOSEPH. Joseph Laine, physician, was born on April 9, 1881, in Clark County, Kentucky, and received his undergraduate training at Berea College. He completed his medical education at Nashville's Meharry Medical College, founded in 1876 to educate Americans of African ancestry, and did postgraduate training at Tuskegee Institute, Talladega College, and Meharry. Surgeon John E. Hunter invited Laine to establish his medical practice in Lexington. Laine had an office in Lexington for eighteen years and then moved to Louisville, where he practiced medicine for twenty-two years. In 1924 he founded the Laine Medical Clinic and was instrumental in recruiting other Afro-American physicians to practice in Kentucky. Laine died on August 18, 1967, and was buried in the Louisville Cemetery.

DORIS WILKINSON

LAIR, JOHN LEE. Country music entrepreneur and folklorist John Lee Lair was born July 1, 1894, in Renfro Valley, Kentucky, to Thomas Burke and Isabelle (Coffey) Lair. He attended the Redbud School in Renfro Valley and was in the first graduating class of Mt. Vernon High School in 1914. Lair was in the first group of U.S. Army enlistees from Rockcastle County for World War I. He was assigned to produce musical shows for servicemen. Portions of the Washington, D.C., production of *Atta Boy*, which Lair wrote, were included in a Ziegfield Follies show.

After the war, Lair returned to Renfro Valley. He taught at Livingston, Pine Hill, and Mt. Vernon schools before taking a job with the *Corbin Tribune* in the early 1920s. In 1922 Lair began to work as a claims adjuster for the Liberty Mutual Insurance Company in Louisville and Chicago. In 1927 he joined the staff of Chicago radio station WLS as program director, music librarian, and producer of the station's "National Barn Dance." He also wrote a column for the station's publication, *Stand By*, and continued to collect folk music. By 1936 WLS referred to Lair as the outstanding authority on American folk music.

Many of the performers that Lair presented at WLS came from the Renfro Valley area and other regions of Kentucky. Two such groups were the Cumberland Ridge Runners—Slim Miller, Karl David, Harty Taylor, Doc Hopkins, Linda Parker, and Red Foley—and the Coon Creek Girls, Lair's most famous group, which included Daisy Lang, Violet Koehler, Rosie Ledford, and Lily May LEDFORD. *Country Music, U.S.A.* credits Lair with "a major role in encouraging women entertainers in country music."

Lair was concerned with the impact of cowboy songs and western swing on country music during the 1930s. Seeing that "National Barn Dance" drew crowds from outside Chicago, he theorized that country music in an authentic setting would attract audiences. In 1937 Lair, Red Foley and his brother, Cotton Foley, and Whitey Ford, also known as the "Duke of Paducah," purchased land in Renfro Valley along U.S. 25, to develop a barn dance complex. At the same time WLW (Cincinnati) became a 50,000-watt clear channel radio station and persuaded Lair to join the station. With Lair came the musical stars he originally brought out of Kentucky. The "Renfro Valley Barn Dance" made its radio debut October 9, 1937, over WLW from the Cincinnati Music Hall. Within months, Lair was sending touring groups from the show to play theaters across the South. He was the first country music promoter to book his own road troupes. In 1938 Lair moved the "Renfro Valley Barn Dance" to Memorial Auditorium in Dayton, Ohio.

On November 4, 1939, Lair announced over the microphone: "This is the Renfro Valley Barn Dance coming to you directly from a big barn in Renfro Valley, Kentucky, the first and only barn dance on the air presented by actual residents of an actual community." Through a Columbia Broadcasting System network, radio station WHAS (Louisville) was soon carrying the "Saturday Night Barn Dance" to a national audience. Lair extended the Renfro Valley complex to include a 1,000-seat theater; a museum, restaurant, horse show ring, and grandstand; the Little Red School House; offices of the *Renfro Valley Bugle* newspaper; radio station WRVK; and the Great Salt Peter Cave. The "Sunday Morning Gatherin', " a religious and folk music program carried by CBS, originated from the Little Red School House.

Because of his devotion to the authentic traditions in country music, which made his productions such a success, Lair refused to produce his shows on television, calling the production methods fakes. His Renfro Valley barn dance played to smaller, regional audiences. In the 1970s Lair wrote a column, "Recollections of Rockcastle County," for the *Mt. Vernon Signal*, a local newspaper, drawing on his vast collection of folklore. In 1975 Rockcastle County honored him with the first of the annual John Lair Days at Renfro Valley. Lair was also a songwriter; his composition "Take Me Back to Renfro Valley" followed his weekly radio program.

In 1924 Lair married Virginia Crawford in Renfro Valley; they were the parents of four daughters: Ann, Virginia Lee, Nancy, and Barbara. Lair died November 12, 1985, in Lexington and was buried in Elmwood Cemetery in Mt. Vernon.

See Bill C. Malone, *Country Music, U.S.A.* (Austin, Texas, 1968); Charles K. Wolfe, *Kentucky Country* (Lexington, Ky., 1982).

BETTY B. ELLISON

LAKES. The majority of Kentucky's lakes are manmade and are under the jurisdiction of the U.S. ARMY CORPS OF ENGINEERS and the Kentucky Department of Fish and Wildlife Resources. They were designed principally for flood control, recreation, and hydroelectric power generation. Seventeen of the state's major impoundments were built by the Corps of Engineers under the Flood Control Act of 1938. The period of greatest expansion was the 1960s and early 1970s, when seven major lakes were completed. Fishing is a popular pastime in the state, and the lakes in conjunction with the state parks system are the basis of a successful tourist industry. The lakes listed here are at least one hundred acres in size; all except Shelby, Swan, and Reelfoot lakes are artificial.

Barren River Lake. Located in Allen, Barren, and Monroe counties; impounded in 1964 from Barren River by the Louisville District of the Corps of Engineers; seasonal pool is 10,000 acres; bordered by the 2,187-acre Barren River Lake State Resort Park.

Beaver Lake. Anderson County; built in 1963; owned by the Kentucky Department of Fish and Wildlife Resources; 158-acre seasonal pool.

Buckhorn Lake. Leslie and Perry counties; impounded from the Kentucky River by the Louisville District of the Corps of Engineers in 1967; 1,230-acre seasonal pool; located in Buckhorn Lake State Resort Park, an 856-acre park in the northern region of the Redbird Purchase Unit of the Daniel Boone National Forest.

Bullock Pen Lake. Anderson County; built in 1963; owned by the Kentucky Department of Fish and Wildlife Resources; 134-acre seasonal pool.

Cannon Creek Lake. Bell County; built in 1972; 243-acre seasonal pool.

Carr Fork Lake. Knott County; impounded from Carr Fork, a tributary of the Kentucky River; completed in 1976 by the Louisville District of the Corps of Engineers; 710-acre seasonal pool.

Cave Run Lake. Bath, Menifee, Morgan, and Rowan counties, in the northern region of the Daniel Boone National Forest; impounded from the Licking River by the Louisville District of the Corps of Engineers in 1974; 8,270-acre seasonal pool.

Cranks Creek Lake. Harlan County; built in 1963; 219-acre seasonal pool.

Dale Hollow Lake. Clinton and Cumberland counties, Kentucky, and Overton and Pickett counties, Tennessee; Kentucky's oldest artificial lake, impounded in 1943 from the Obey River, and one of the earliest lakes built by the Corps of Engineers under the 1938 Flood Control Act; 27,700-acre seasonal pool; bordered by the 3,398-acre Dale Hollow Lake State Park. The world's record smallmouth bass—eleven pounds, fifteen ounces—was caught on the Kentucky side of the lake on July 9, 1955.

Dewey Lake. Floyd County; impounded from John's Creek by the Huntington, West Virginia, District of the Corps of Engineers in 1949; 1,100-acre seasonal pool; adjacent to the 1,651-acre Jenny

Wiley State Resort Park. The lake was named after a local post office, which was named for either Adm. George Dewey, the hero of Manila Bay, or Dewey Wells, a resident of the area.

Elmer Davis Lake. Owen County; built in 1958; owned by the Kentucky Department of Fish and Wildlife Resources; 149-acre seasonal pool. It is named for Elmer Davis, a former Fish and Wildlife commissioner.

Fishtrap Lake. Pike County; impounded from the Levisa Fork of the Big Sandy River by the Huntington, West Virginia, District of the Corps of Engineers in 1968; 1,130-acre seasonal pool. The lake was dedicated by President Lyndon B. Johnson on October 29, 1968, and named for the fishtraps used on the stream by Indians.

Grayson Lake. Carter and Elliott counties; impounded from the Little Sandy River by the Huntington, West Virginia, District of the Corps of Engineers in 1968; 1,500-acre seasonal pool; adjacent to the 1,512-acre Grayson Lake State Park. The lake shares the name of the Carter County seat, which was probably named for Col. William Grayson, a military aide to George Washington.

Green River Lake. Adair, Casey, and Taylor counties; impounded from the Green River by the Louisville District of the Corps of Engineers in 1969; 8,200-acre seasonal pool; bordered by the 1,331-acre Green River Lake State Park.

Greenbo Lake. Greenup County; built in 1955 by the Greenbo Lake Association and the Kentucky Department of Fish and Wildlife Resources; 181-acre seasonal pool; adjacent to the 3,008-acre Greenbo Lake State Resort Park.

Guist Creek Lake. Shelby County; impounded from Guist Creek in 1961; 317-acre seasonal pool; owned by the Kentucky Department of Fish and Wildlife Resources.

Herrington Lake. Boyle, Mercer and Garrard counties; built in 1925 by the Kentucky Utilities Company for hydroelectric power generation; 2,335-acre seasonal pool. At the time of completion, it was the largest rock-filled dam in existence.

Kentucky Lake. Calloway, Lyon, Marshall, and Trigg counties, extending into Tennessee; impounded in 1944 from the Tennessee River by the Tennessee Valley Authority; bordered by Kentucky Dam Village State Resort Park (1,351 acres) on its northern shore and Kenlake State Resort Park (1,795 acres) on its western shore. When built, it was the largest manmade lake in the world; it is now the state's second largest lake, with 49,511 acres of its seasonal pool of 160,309 acres lying in Kentucky. Part of the Western Waterlands, Kentucky Lake parallels Lake Barkley for over forty miles. They encircle Land Between the Lakes, the 170,000-acre isthmus and national recreational facility.

Kincaid Lake. Pendleton County; impounded in 1961 from Kincaid Creek, a branch of the Licking River; 183-acre seasonal pool. Owned by the Kentucky Department of Fish and Wildlife Resources and bordered by the 850-acre Kincaid Lake State Park.

Lake Barkley. Caldwell, Livingston, Lyndon, and Trigg counties; impounded in 1966 from the Cumberland River by the Nashville District of the Corps of Engineers; bordered on its eastern shore by the 3,600-acre Lake Barkley State Resort Park. Named for Alben W. Barkley, Kentucky senator and U.S. vice-president, it is the state's third largest lake, having a seasonal pool of about 58,000 acres, of which 42,020 acres are in Kentucky.

Lake Beshear. Caldwell and Christian counties; built in 1962; 760-acre seasonal pool. Located in the 863-acre Pennyrile Forest State Resort Park and owned by the Kentucky Department of Fish and Wildlife Resources.

Lake Carnico. Nicholas County; built in 1962; 114-acre seasonal pool.

Lake Cumberland. Clinton, Laurel, Pulaski, Russell, and Wayne counties; impounded from the Cumberland River by the Nashville, Tennessee, District of the Corps of Engineers in 1952; largest lake in Kentucky, with a 50,250-acre seasonal pool. Bordered by the 3,117-acre Lake Cumberland State Resort Park, and site of Kentucky's only island park—the 430-acre General Burnside State Park, named for Union Gen. Ambrose E. Burnside.

Lake Linville. Rockcastle County; built in 1968; 274-acre seasonal pool.

Lake Malone. Logan, Muhlenberg, and Todd counties. Impounded from Rocky Creek in 1961; owned by the Kentucky Department of Fish and Wildlife Resources; 826-acre seasonal pool; located in the 325-acre Lake Malone State Park.

Laurel River Lake. Laurel and Whitley counties; impounded from the Laurel River by the Nashville District of the Corps of Engineers in 1977; 5,600-acre seasonal pool; located in the southeastern region of the Daniel Boone National Forest.

Martins Fork. Harlan County; impounded in 1979 from Martins Fork, a branch of the Cumberland River, by the Nashville, Tennessee, District of the Corps of Engineers; 340-acre seasonal pool. The lake is named for James Martin, an early pioneer and land owner.

Nolin River Lake. Edmonson, Grayson, and Hart counties, near Mammoth Cave National Park; impounded from the the Nolin River by the Louisville District of the Corps of Engineers in 1963; 5,800-acre seasonal pool. The river and lake are believed to be named for Col. Benjamin Lynn, a companion of James Harrod's who became lost in 1779 on a hunting expedition. Though he was later found, scouting parties for several nights reported: "No Lynn."

Paintsville Lake. Johnson and Morgan counties; impounded from Paint Creek by the Huntington, West Virginia, District of the Corps of Engineers in 1983; 1,139-acre seasonal pool; bordered by 242-acre Paintsville Lake State Park.

Reelfoot Lake. See separate entry.

Rough River Lake. Breckinridge, Grayson, and Hardin counties; impounded from Rough River by the Louisville District of the Corps of Engineers in 1959; 5,100-acre seasonal pool; bordered by 637-acre Rough River Dam State Resort Park.

Shanty Hollow Lake. Warren County; built in 1951; owned by the Kentucky Department of Fish and Wildlife Resources; 135-acre seasonal pool.

Shelby Lake. Ballard County; part of the Ballard County Wildlife Management Area; owned by the Kentucky Department of Fish and Wildlife Resources; a natural lake with one hundred surface acres.

Swan Lake. Swan Lake, Kentucky's largest natural lake (three hundred acres), is in Ballard County and is part of the Cummins Tract Lakes, a twelve-lake confederation.

Taylorsville Lake. Anderson, Nelson, and Spencer counties; impounded from the Salt River by the Louisville District of the Corps of Engineers in 1982; 3,050-acre seasonal pool; surrounded by the 2,650-acre Taylorsville Lake State Park.

Wilgreen Lake. Madison County; built in 1966; 169-acre seasonal pool.

Williamstown Lake. Grant County; impounded in 1955 from Grassy Creek; three-hundred-acre seasonal pool.

Willisburg Lake. Washington County; built in 1969; 126-acre seasonal pool.

Wood Creek Lake. Laurel County; impounded from Wood Creek in 1969; 672-acre seasonal pool; located in the mid-region of the Daniel Boone National Forest.

See Bonny Dale Laflin and Peter W. Pfeiffer, *A Guide to Public Fishing Lakes In Kentucky,* 1989.

LAKESIDE PARK. Lakeside Park is a suburban city in north-central Kenton County north of I-275, southeast of I-71, and straddling U.S. 127. Along with Crestview Hills, the Lakeside Park area is part of a 999-acre land grant to the family of Col. John Leathers and was first settled around 1785. The area remained rural farmland until suburban development began in the early twentieth century. At that time Lakeside Park consisted of forty acres developed by landowner Paul Hesser, a Kenton County water commissioner. In an attempt to block annexation by South Fort Mitchell, which bordered Lakeside Park on the east, Hesser led a drive that ended in Lakeside Park's successful incorporation as a city on May 12, 1930. By 1990 the city had grown to cover almost 530 acres and included fourteen subdivisions.

One of Lakeside Park's best-known historical landmarks is the restaurant Barleycorn's Five Mile House. Located on Dixie Highway (U.S. 127) five miles from Covington, the building was once a toll house on the old Lexington pike. When the Dixie Highway was dedicated in 1921, the building, by then a restaurant, was named the Dixie Inn in celebration of the new road. In 1943 the inn was bought by Carl Retschulte, who operated it as a popular gambling spot until 1962, when the era of illegal gambling came to an end in northern Kentucky. The restored restaurant was reopened in 1983 as Barleycorn's Five Mile House.

Lakeside Park is a residential city of middle- and upper-middle-class houses, many of which date to the 1930s. The population of the fifth-class city was 2,511 in 1970; 3,062 in 1980; and 3,131 in 1990.

LANCASTER, CLAY. Clay Lancaster, architectural historian, a native of Lexington, Kentucky, was born on March 30, 1917, to Della (Pigg) and J.W. Lancaster, Jr. In 1936, he spent a half year at the Art Students' League of New York City. He then earned an A.B. (1938) and an M.A. (1939) from the University of Kentucky. In 1943 Lancaster returned to New York to become the Ware librarian of the Avery Library at Columbia University, where he studied Asian cultures. He taught at Columbia, Vassar College, New York City's Cooper Union, the Metropolitan Museum of Art, and New York University.

Lancaster received two Guggenheim Fellowships—the first, in 1954-55, for research for the book *The Japanese Influence in America* (1963), and the second, in 1963-64, for research on Kentucky architecture, the basis of numerous publications. In 1971 Lancaster moved to Nantucket, Massachusetts, where he devoted himself exclusively to writing. Books of this period include *The Architecture of Historic Nantucket* (1972), *The Far Out Island Railroad* (1972), and *Nantucket in the Nineteenth Century* (1979). In 1978 Lancaster returned to Kentucky to live at Warwick, on the Kentucky River, in Mercer County. He soon completed *Vestiges of the Venerable City* (1978) and *Eutaw—The Builders and Architecture of an Ante-Bellum Southern Town* (1979). He taught at Transylvania University and the University of Kentucky and was the Morgan professor at the University of Louisville in 1983.

Lancaster has written several children's books, including *The Periwinkle Steamboat* (1961), *Michiko, or Mrs. Belmont's Brownstone on Brooklyn Heights* (1965), *The Flight of the Periwinkle* (1987), *The Toy Room* (1988), and *The Runaway Prince* (1990). His scholarly publications include *Architectural Follies in America* (1960), *Old Brooklyn Heights, New York's First Suburb* (1961), *Ante Bellum Houses of the Bluegrass* (1961), *Victorian Houses: A Treasury of Lesser Known Examples* (1973), *The American Bungalow, 1880-1930* (1985), and more than a hundred articles.

WILLIAM B. SCOTT, JR.

LANCASTER. Lancaster, the county seat of Garrard County, is located at U.S. 27 and KY 52. Lancaster was founded in 1797 on land donated by Capt. William Buford. Joseph Bledsoe, Jr., surveyed the site and drew up the plans for the town. Since a number of the residents in the area were from Lancaster, Pennsylvania, the new community was named for their former home. Buford gave fifty acres for the public square and for town lots in Lancaster. The first trustees for Lancaster were Richard Ballinger, William Bryant, Joseph Bledsoe, William Jennings, and Samuel Gill. In 1800 the population of Lancaster was 102.

In 1833 Lancaster was struck by a severe outbreak of cholera; between June 14 and July 8, 116 people died of the disease. In some instances entire families perished. In 1834 a fever (perhaps typhoid) epidemic occurred. Several residents of the town died during this particular outbreak. Cholera broke out again in 1873, and thirty-two people died. As the epidemic worsened, townspeople fled their homes. One report stated that the town was nearly deserted.

The Civil War era was one of extreme tension. Camp Dick Robinson, north of Lancaster, was the first Union recruiting center south of the Ohio River. On October 13-14, 1862, skirmishes took place between rearguard Confederate cavalry, under the command of Gen. Joseph Wheeler, and the advance units of Gen. Don Carlos Buell's Federal troops in the vicinity of Lancaster, following the Battle of Perryville. More violence occurred in 1873, when a riot broke out over a disputed election for circuit court clerk. Two people were killed and several were wounded. The riot ended when a company of state guards from Louisville entered Lancaster and placed the town under martial law.

The first courthouse for Garrard County was built by Stephen Giles Letcher and Benjamin Letcher, who completed the stone and brick work in February 1799. In 1868 this structure was demolished and a new building erected. Lancaster was the home of Govs. Robert P. Letcher (1840-44), William Owsley (1844-48), and William O. Bradley (1895-99). Also in the town is the home of author and editor Eugenia Dunlap Potts, who wrote nine novels, including *Idle Hour Stories* (1909), and was the editor of the magazine *Illustrated Kentuckian*.

During the middle of the twentieth century, Lancaster ceased being primarily a farm trading center and turned to a more diversified economy with new industry that promoted the growth of residential subdivisions and new retail establishments. In 1987 the largest employer in the city was the Cowden-Lancaster Company, which produces work clothing.

The population of the fifth-class city was 3,320 in 1970; 3,365 in 1980; and 3,421 in 1990.

RON D. BRYANT

LAND BETWEEN THE LAKES. Land Between the Lakes is a national recreation and environmental education area managed by the Tennessee Valley Authority (TVA). This wooded peninsula is bordered by Kentucky Lake and Lake Barkley in western Kentucky and Tennessee. In 1944 TVA impounded the Tennessee River to create Kentucky Lake. Lake Barkley was formed by the Army Corps of Engineers' Cumberland River impoundment in 1965. Together the two lakes form one of the largest man-made bodies of water in North America. A free-flowing canal constructed during the Barkley project joins the lakes and forms the northern boundary of Land Between the Lakes.

Land Between the Lakes is forty miles long and ranges from six to eight miles wide. It covers 170,000 acres (106,458 acres in Kentucky). Over 300 miles of roads and 200 miles of trails provide access to the area. Its mission is to provide outdoor recreation and environmental education. The area is neither wilderness nor a national park. TVA manages it for a variety of outdoor activities, from bird watching and backpacking to use by off-road vehicles.

On June 14, 1963, President John F. Kennedy announced that TVA would develop the area between Kentucky Lake and Lake Barkley as a demonstration in resource development. When TVA opened its office at Golden Pond, Kentucky, on January 28, 1964, about 2,500 people lived in the area. Unlike most national parks and national forests, Land Between the Lakes includes no private holdings. The last resident moved from the Kentucky portion in the fall of 1970.

Settlers from Virginia and the Carolinas first came to the area in the late 1700s and early 1800s. For over 150 years it was called Land Between the Rivers, and former residents still refer to it in that way. By the 1840s this land was no longer on the frontier. The availability of iron ore, limestone, and wood for charcoal helped make Kentucky the third largest iron producing state in the nation. During the region's period of peak productivity, seventeen iron furnaces blazed between the rivers. In 1851 the Kelly process of producing steel was developed by William ("Crazy") Kelly in nearby Eddyville, Kentucky.

In February 1862 a battle on the southern boundary of Land Between the Lakes, near Dover, Tennessee, helped change the course of the Civil War. Gen. Ulysses S. Grant accepted the unconditional surrender of the Confederate garrison at Fort Donelson. This significant Union victory gained control of the Tennessee and Cumberland Rivers and access to Nashville.

During prohibition (1920-33) the town of Golden Pond, Kentucky, became nationally known for producing high-quality moonshine whiskey. Much of this moonshine was sold in the speakeasies of midwestern cities such as Chicago, Detroit, and St. Louis. Although only a small percentage of those living between the rivers were actually involved in moonshining, the legend and lore live on.

Over 90 percent of Land Between the Lakes is forested, and the remaining land is narrow hollows and scattered fields left after the flooding of Kentucky Lake and Lake Barkley. About 85 percent of the forest is mixed oak-hickory woodland. Over 250 species of birds have been observed in the Land Between the Lakes area since 1963, making it one of the most popular inland birding areas in the eastern United States. Wildlife species include white-tailed deer, European fallow deer, eastern wild turkey, fox, coyote, bobcat, skunk, raccoon, opossum, beaver, rabbit, squirrel, and river otter.

In 1989 visitors from all fifty states and over thirty foreign countries visited Land Between the Lakes. About two-thirds of Land Between the Lakes lies in Trigg and Lyon counties in Kentucky and the rest in Stewart County, Tennessee.

See Frank E. Smith, *Land Between the Lakes* (Lexington, Ky., 1971).   SCOTT A. SEIBER

LAND CLAIMS, EARLY. The complicated Virginia land law of 1779 was reenacted in Kentucky in 1792, with only slight modification. The statutes prescribed four steps to be completed in sequence: 1) obtaining a warrant; 2) making an entry; 3) SURVEYING the land; and 4) returning the survey and entry to the land office. Afterward the land office issued a patent which, according to the statute, carried "absolute verity." Each step had its own complications, and the result was an extraordinary volume of litigation that continued for more than a century.

Royal and, later, state governors issued warrants with such extravagance that the total acreage in the grants was probably greater than the entire land area of Kentucky and certainly exceeded the amount of desirable land. Several categories of people were eligible for free warrants. Veterans of the Virginia and Continental armies could apply for military warrants of one hundred to 5,000 acres, depending on rank; settlers who brought immigrants to the frontier could apply for warrants based upon "importation rights"; settlers who erected buildings and cleared land could apply for "preemption" warrants; and poor settlers could obtain warrants on credit. Others could purchase treasury warrants costing forty pounds sterling for a one-hundred-acre area.

Warrant holders filed an entry with the county surveyor, specifying the number of acres allotted in the warrant and describing the location of the tract by referring to existing buildings or natural landmarks that, under the doctrine of notoriety, were to be recognized by other people in the vicinity. Such people were sometimes sought to give evidence years later regarding the validity of the reference points.

The county surveyor was then required to survey the entry according to the true meridian rather than the magnetic meridian. Since the only available instruments registered the magnetic meridian, however, a surveyor needed either training in astronomy or fairly sophisticated mathematics to translate information about the degree of variation from the true meridian. Frequently surveyors had neither—especially in Kentucky, which unlike Virginia, did not require surveyors to have educational qualifications or to pass examinations. (One observer wrote that the Kentucky surveyors were never correct, except by accident.)

Finally, the statute required that surveys be marked upon the ground, and the plat and notes returned to the land office within twelve months after entry, except when the warrant holder was a person under disability (infants, captives, married women, and the insane). The land office then issued a patent. Because there were no comprehensive or accurate maps on which the entries could be marked, the land office at various times issued multiple patents on a single tract to different people. As generations of commentators noted, much of the land was "shingled over" with successive layers of patents, providing still further grounds for litigation. It was entirely possible for a person with a patent to clear the land, erect cabins and outbuildings, and plant crops and orchards—only to discover that there had been some defect in one of the four patenting steps or that someone else had an earlier patent to the same land.

The only redress under those circumstances was to sue, under Kentucky's occupying claimant statutes of 1797 and 1812. The General Assembly of Virginia created the first land court of Kentucky in its May-June session, 1779. The intent of the law was to bring about adjudication of the woefully confused situation of land claims in Virginia's Fincastle County. Four commissioners, William Fleming, James Barbour, Samuel Lyne, and James Steptoe, were appointed and were instructed to go to the western country to organize the land court. The commissioners held their first meeting at Logan's Station (St. Asaph) on October 13, 1779. The court remained in session until April 1780. It settled 1,328 claims covering 1,354,050 acres of land. Sittings of the court, held at St. Asaph, Harrodstown, the Falls of the Ohio, Boonesborough, and Bryan's Station, were seriously handicapped by the severity of the winter of 1779-80.

Land suits took years to reach judgment and often left everyone concerned dissatisfied. The example of Kentucky led the federal government to require that six-mile-square surveys be made before settlement was permitted in the national domain under terms of the Northwest Land Ordinance.

See Lewis N. Dembitz, *Kentucky Jurisprudence* (Louisville 1890); Mary K. Bonsteel Tachau, *Federal Courts in the Early Republic: Kentucky 1789-1816* (Princeton, N.J., 1978); Samuel M. Wilson, "The Proceedings of the Land Court," *Register* 21 (Jan., May, Sept. 1923): 3-323.

MARY K. BONSTEEL TACHAU

LANGLEY, KATHERINE (GUDGER). Katherine (Gudger) Langley, member of the U.S. Congress, was born on February 14, 1888, near Marshall in Madison County, North Carolina, the daughter of James Madison and Katherine (Hawkins) Gudger, Jr. She graduated from Woman's College in Richmond, Virginia, did graduate work at Emerson College of Oratory in Boston, and taught expression in Bristol, Tennessee, at the Virginia Institute. Katherine Gudger married John Wesley Langley, from Floyd County, in 1903; they had three children: John Wesley, Katherine, and Susanna. Her husband was elected to the U.S. Congress in March 1907, and Langley served as his secretary. She was clerk of the House Committee on Public Buildings and Grounds between 1919 and 1925, while her husband was chairman. In 1920 Langley became the first chair of the Woman's Republican State Committee and vice-chair of the Republican State Central Committee of Kentucky. She also served as an alternate delegate to the Republican National Convention. In 1924 she was a delegate to the presidential nominating convention. When her husband resigned from Congress on

January 11, 1926, after having been convicted of a liquor law violation, Langley was elected to replace him. She served two terms, from March 4, 1927, to March 3, 1931, but was defeated in her second bid for reelection.

From 1939 to 1942 she was railroad commissioner in Kentucky's 3d District. Langley served as Pikeville's postmaster, and during World War II she chaired Pike County's Red Cross. She died in Pikeville on August 15, 1948, and was buried there in the Johnson Memorial Cemetery.

LARUE, JOHN P. John P. LaRue, a prominent landowner in what is now Kentucky, was born in Frederick County, Virginia, on January 24, 1746, to Isaac and Phebe (Carman) LaRue. He owned land in Spottsylvania County, Virginia, and he took part in the Revolutionary War.

In 1779 he and his brother Samuel built a cabin on Guist Creek, a branch of Brashers Creek, a fork of the Salt River, about five or six miles from Squire Boone's Station in present-day Shelby County. In 1783 John married Mary Brooks in Virginia and returned to Kentucky with his wife the following year. They settled at Nolin Station, at the mouth of Beech Fork, a tributary of Rolling Fork of the Salt River, about fifty miles from the Falls of the Ohio. Through his acquaintance with Squire Boone, a prominent surveyor in Kentucky, LaRue gained title to large tracts of land in Shelby County and throughout the region, eventually laying claim to 40,000 acres. He died January 4, 1792, at his home on a branch of the Nolin River above Hodgenville.

In 1843 the state legislature established Larue County, the name chosen by John LaRue Helm, Speaker of the House and later governor (1850-51, 1867), in honor of his maternal grandfather.

See Otis M. Mather, *Six Generations of LaRues and Allied Families* (Hodgenville, Ky., 1921).

LARUE COUNTY. The ninety-eighth county in order of formation, Larue County is located in central Kentucky. The county is bordered by Green, Hardin, Hart, Nelson, and Taylor counties and has an area of 263 square miles. Larue County was formed on March 4, 1843, from a portion of Hardin County and was named in honor of John LaRue, an early settler. The seat of Larue County is HODGENVILLE.

The topography of Larue County is rolling to hilly. The MULDRAUGH Escarpment is the most dominant geographical feature of the county. The principal streams in Larue County are the Nolin River and the Rolling Fork of the Salt River. Among the numerous creeks, Otter Creek is one of the largest. The land is also marked by a number of large sinkholes formed by the collapse of underlying caves.

Burial mounds in Larue County attest to the occupation of prehistoric Native American tribes. The first white settlers came into the region in the early 1780s. Originally surveyed by Benjamin Lynn in 1778, the first permanent white settlement was established by Phillip Phillips in 1781. Called Phillips' Fort, this site was located 1¼ miles from what is now Hodgenville.

One of the pioneer families of Larue County was that of Thomas Lincoln, who settled on the Sinking Springs farm in Larue County. It was there that Abraham Lincoln was born on February 12, 1809. During the Civil War, the Confederate army under the command of Gen. Braxton Bragg marched through Larue County in 1862 on its way north to Louisville.

Larue County, largely agrarian, had a small industrial base by the twentieth century, manufacturing lumber products, clothing, and concrete. Tobacco, wheat, corn, and vegetables such as sweet peppers are staple crops. Cattle and hogs are also raised. The industrial potential of the county was enhanced in 1938 with the creation of the Nolin Rural Electric Cooperative Corporation, which supplied electricity to all reaches of Larue County. A significant industrial competitor is the city of Elizabethtown in adjacent Hardin County, at the junction of I-65, the Bluegrass Parkway, and the Western Kentucky Parkway. Larue is served only by U.S. 31E.

The population of Larue County was 10,672 in 1970; 11,922 in 1980; and 11,679 in 1990.

See Bessie Miller Elliott, *History of Larue County* (Hodgenville, Ky., 1967).

RON D. BRYANT

LAUREL COUNTY. Laurel County, the eightieth county in order of formation, is located in southeastern Kentucky and is bounded by Rockcastle, Jackson, Clay, Knox, Whitley, McCreary, and Pulaski counties. The county has an area of 434 square miles and was created on December 21, 1825, from sections of Rockcastle, Clay, Knox, and Whitley counties. The prescribed boundaries of the new county were the Rockcastle River on the north, and metes and bounds on the other three sides. The latter were poorly defined, and frequent changes were made in the boundary. LONDON is the county seat.

The county is named for the flowering shrub of the local forest. When it was formed, Laurel County was heavily wooded and penetrated by only a few trails. In February-March 1775 Daniel Boone and his trail-blazing party opened a narrow path across the area from the Laurel River crossing on the south to that of the Rockcastle on the north. Later the Wilderness Road crossed the county. Natural resources in Laurel County are timber and coal. Three major streams, the Laurel, Rockcastle, and South Rockcastle rivers, drain the land. Possibly the most important resource has been the Wilderness Road and its successor highways, U.S. 25, I-75, and KY 80. From its opening the Wilderness Road (not identical to Boone's Trace) was an artery of emigration, official travel, and commerce.

Laurel County has been predominantly rural. Until 1880 its population depended almost wholly upon subsistence farming and logging. After 1880 a profitable coal mining industry developed, made possible by the extension of the Knoxville branch of the Louisville & Nashville Railroad (now CSX Transportation) across the county.

Although Laurel County suffered only minimal physical destruction in the Civil War, its economy and politics underwent major changes. Development of the coal field in the northern and eastern sections of the county after 1880 had substantial bearings on both economy and demography. In this coal field, organized labor gained a substantial foothold in the state. Between 1880 and 1894 approximately 120 Swiss families arrived. They settled around two major centers, Bernstadt and East Bernstadt. They erected Protestant churches and two schools, a new, seminal cultural force in the Appalachian county.

Following World War I, the building of U.S. 25 and KY 80 quickly lowered the ancient isolative barriers. World War II brought even greater changes. In the postwar era, a major tourist trade developed, and new businesses and industries moved to the county. The construction of I-75 in the 1960s helped to make London an economic, social, and political hub of the region.

By 1975 Laurel County had a fertilizer factory, a church furniture plant, wood-using industries, and several burley tobacco sales floors. London became a wholesale grocery and drugstore center and APPALACHIAN COMPUTER Services catered to a growing national clientele. More than a third of the area of Laurel County was consolidated in the Daniel Boone National Forest. In the 1940s and during the era of the New Deal, the county was a center of Civilian Conservation Corps activities.

The population of the county was 27,386 in 1970; 38,982 in 1980; and 43,438 in 1990.

See Russell Dyche, *History of Laurel County* (London, Ky., 1954).   THOMAS D. CLARK

LAWRENCEBURG. Lawrenceburg, the county seat of Anderson County, is located on U.S. 127 at KY 44. The town was incorporated in 1820 as Lawrence, named for a local tavern owner, William Lawrence, who was instrumental in its founding. When it became the county seat in 1827, the name was changed to Lawrenceburg.

A pioneer station was established by Jacob Kaufman (or Coffman) at the future site of Lawrenceburg in 1780. After Kaufman's death in 1792, some of his land passed to Samuel Arbuckle, who along with Lawrence was an early town builder. The community grew as a small collection of homes, taverns, and businesses on the Frankfort-to-Harrodsburg road.

The first courthouse, a two-story brick structure completed on July 12, 1830, burned on October 26, 1859. A second, of stone construction, was completed in 1861 but almost completely destroyed by fire on April 13, 1915. A third courthouse, of Beaux-Arts design with an imposing dome, was begun soon afterwards and retained the original outer walls of the second one.

Cholera was responsible for many deaths in Lawrenceburg in 1833 and 1855. The Civil War disrupted life in the city, particularly during early October 1862, when numerous skirmishes took place in the vicinity. On October 6, 1862, Col. Scott's Confederate cavalry engaged Col. R.T. Jacob's 9th Kentucky Cavalry (USA) in and around the city, just before to the battle of Perryville. Later in the war, a Home Guard unit was stationed at Lawrenceburg in an attempt to quell guerrilla activity.

By 1870 Lawrenceburg had a population of 393 and contained numerous small factories, tanyards, ropewalks, and manufacturers. The city benefited from a growing distilling industry in surrounding Anderson County. With the arrival of the Southern Railroad (now Norfolk Southern) in 1888 and the construction of Young's High Bridge over the Kentucky River in 1889, rail connection to Lexington permitted distilleries to increase their output. Lawrenceburg became a shipping center for grain, livestock, whiskey, and other products. Expensive residences were built by bankers, distillers, and merchants as the city prospered. A water works was installed in 1904 and electric lights the following year. KAVANAUGH Academy was organized in 1903 by Rhoda C. Kavanaugh and operated for forty-one years; many of its graduates were accepted by the U.S. military academies at West Point and Annapolis.

By 1990 other industries besides distilling had located in the city, which had a diverse manufacturing economy. Among the larger employers were the Florida Tile Co. and Textron Inc., a producer of metal buttons and rivets.

The population of the fourth class city was 3,579 in 1970; 5,167 in 1980; and 5,911 in 1990.

LAWRENCE COUNTY. Located in eastern Kentucky along the West Virginia border, Lawrence County was formed on December 14, 1821, out of parts of Greenup and Floyd counties. The Big Sandy River and its Tug Fork form its eastern border and it is also bounded by Johnson, Martin, Carter, Elliot, Morgan, and Boyd counties. It covers an area of 420 square miles. Lawrence County was named in honor of Capt. James Lawrence, commander of the U.S.S. *Chesapeake* during the War of 1812. LOUISA is the county seat.

Lawrence County is primarily a rural, nonfarm area. With farms occupying only about 23 percent of the land, Lawrence County in 1987 ranked ninety-sixth among Kentucky counties in agricultural receipts, mainly from livestock and tobacco. The county lies within the Eastern Coal Field region, and many residents work in coal-related industries. Most farmers also augment their incomes by working in the mines.

In 1789 Charles Vancouver established a settlement at the fork of the Big Sandy River, but Indians soon forced him away. Migrating from Philadelphia in 1815, Frederick Moore began a second settlement at the confluence of the Tug and Levisa forks, which in 1822 became the town of Louisa. Subsistence farming, along with hunting and limited timber harvesting, was the principal occupation of most county residents during the nineteenth century. But because the Big Sandy River supplies water power and easy access to the Ohio River, industry developed in Lawrence County before it did in most other mountain counties. By the 1840s, timber was floated down the river and barges, laden with tanbark and hoop-poles, made regular trips down the Big Sandy. River transportation also facilitated the development of the coal industry, and, during the 1850s, one of eastern Kentucky's first coal camps was established at Peach Orchard. Boat traffic was enhanced by 1897 with the construction of three locks on the Big Sandy and one on each of the forks. In 1881 the Chattaroi Railroad (now the CSX Transportation) reached Louisa as it edged southward into the coal fields. From 1873 until 1933, the county was also served by the Eastern Kentucky Railroad.

Oil and gas drilling in the Blaine-Martha region began in earnest in 1920 but fell victim to the Great Depression; by the 1980s most of the oil wells were sealed. In 1963 the Kentucky Power Company built a 1,060,000-kilowatt coal-fired plant at Potters. The Mayo Trail (U.S. 23) by 1991 had been converted into a four-lane highway.

The population of Lawrence County was 10,726 in 1970; 14,121 in 1980; and 13,998 in 1990.

See George Wolfford, *Lawrence County: A Pictorial History* (Ashland, Ky., 1972); Henry P. Scalf, *Kentucky's Last Frontier* (Prestonsburg, Ky., 1966).

GEORGE WOLFFORD

LAW SCHOOLS. Kentucky's three law schools are at the University of Louisville, Northern Kentucky University, and the University of Kentucky. At the University of Louisville, chartered in 1846, the Law Department was created and operated independently of the university board of trustees. In the earliest days, the fee was $20 per course, paid directly to the school's professors. By 1909 the school had adopted the case method of teaching law. In 1923 the Law Department became the School of Law, which moved from downtown Louisville to the Belknap campus in 1939. In 1974 a library was added to the original building and in 1982 a new office wing and classroom wing were completed.

The Salmon P. Chase College of Law, which merged with Northern Kentucky University in 1972, was founded in 1893 as an educational program of the Cincinnati and Hamilton County (Ohio) YMCA. The first YMCA night law school and only the second night law school in the United States, it originally offered only part-time legal education. In 1943 the school received its present name in honor of the former chief justice of the United States. It became a private educational institution in 1968. Since the Chase College of Law merger with Northern Kentucky University, full-time programs are offered.

Legal training at the University of Kentucky, created by the legislature in 1908, was originally a two-year program, but in 1909 it was expanded to the current three years. Attempts to merge with the law schools of Transylvania and Centre College (which closed in 1912) were unsuccessful. Classes began in the Education Building, known now as Frazee Hall, and after a period in the Agricultural Experiment Station, classes in 1937 moved to newly constructed Lafferty Hall, named after the school's first dean. In 1965 a modern law building opened, and additions to it were made in 1977. In 1983 a Mineral Law Institute was created.

VINCENT J. COTTON, JR.

LEAGUE OF WOMEN VOTERS OF KENTUCKY. When the Nineteenth Amendment to the Constitution was ratified in 1920, giving women the right to vote, many long-term suffragists refocused their efforts on educating voters and training women to take part in the political process. The National American Woman Suffrage Association, which had led the fight for the amendment, dissolved officially in 1920 and immediately reorganized as the National League of Women Voters, to operate on national, state, and local levels. Kentucky's League of Women Voters (previously the KENTUCKY EQUAL RIGHTS ASSOCIATION) and local leagues in Louisville and Lexington were also organized in 1920, among the earliest state and local leagues. Membership in the league, originally limited to women, has been open to men since 1974.

The league has two parallel purposes: to inform and educate voters and to promote public action on issues where the league has taken a stand after study and formal consensus of the membership. It does not support parties or candidates for office, although it does support ballot issues such as constitutional amendments or tax referenda. In its educational role, the league has been prominent in sponsoring candidate debates and forums, including television debates for the presidential elections in 1976, 1980, and 1984. In October 1984 Louisville was the site of a debate between Ronald Reagan and Walter Mondale. The league has also traditionally been active in voter registration. In its advocacy role, the Kentucky league has supported constitutional revision, juvenile justice reform, universal access to health care, strict enforcement of natural resource laws, land use planning, reform of the state income tax system, taxes on unmined minerals, a uniform statewide minimum property tax, repeal of rollbacks or limitations on property tax, bail bond reform, open meetings and open records laws, land and water conservation, a ban on electioneering at the polls, and statewide kindergartens.

The Kentucky league's first major lobbying success was passage of the 1926 city government bill, which gave Louisville a strong mayoral form of government. The league was one of the major supporters of the 1975 Judicial Amendment to the state constitution, which reformed the state's court system, and the 1988 amendment on the broad form deed.

There are fourteen local leagues in Kentucky: Bell County, Berea and Madison County, Boone-

Campbell-Kenton counties, Clark County, Hardin County, Henderson, Hopkinsville and Christian County, Louisville and Jefferson County, Lexington and Fayette County, Murray and Calloway County, Owensboro, Paris and Bourbon County, Richmond, and Taylor County.

See Louise M. Young, *In the Public Interest: The League of Women Voters, 1920-1970* (New York 1989).   KATHLEEN LOOMIS

LEBANON. Lebanon, the county seat of Marion County, is located at the junction of U.S. 68 and KY 55. The town was settled around the Hardin's Creek Meeting House, which was constructed about 1798 by Presbyterians from Virginia. Benedict Spalding and John Handley were responsible for establishing the town in 1814. Lebanon was incorporated January 31, 1815, and named for the Biblical Lebanon because many cedars grew there. The first courthouse was built in Lebanon in 1835; in 1838 a clerk's office was built to hold county records. Judge T. Scott Mayes held court on the lawn to protest the poor conditions of the courthouse. The building was condemned in January 1935 and a new one built.

Lebanon grew steadily in the years before the Civil War. In 1857 the Louisville & Nashville (L&N) Railroad (now CSX Transportation) built a branch through Lebanon, from the main line on the Rolling Fork River, at a cost of $1,007,736. Marion Countians subscribed $200,000 of that amount. In 1859 eight southbound and seven northbound trains passed through daily.

The Civil War was a severe blow to Lebanon. Its location on the railroad made the community vulnerable to attack. During the war Lebanon was the site of three battles fought in 1861, 1862, and 1863. On September 18, 1861, Confederate Gen. Simon B. Buckner seized the thirty-seven-mile Lebanon branch with twenty-two locomotives, eleven passenger cars, eighty-three freight cars, and five baggage cars. On September 8, 1862, the town was occupied by Confederate forces, who remained until early October. On July 5, 1863, Gen. John Hunt Morgan's cavalry clashed with Col. Charles S. Hanson's three-hundred-man Federal force. Hanson and his troops fought for seven hours against Morgan's men, burning the railroad roundhouse and commissioned stores with $100,000 of supplies. Nevertheless, the Confederates set fire to the railroad depot, the Lebanon Hotel, Harris House, and several residences, and at last defeated the Union troops. Orders were then given to burn the county court clerk's office and county records, to destroy indictments of treason recorded against several of Morgan's men.

Lebanon recovered rapidly from the Civil War, with the L&N making it an important trade center. As a result, when rail traffic decreased so did the town's economy. In 1950 Lebanon began building an industrial base, and in 1990 nineteen manufacturing firms produced products ranging from plastics to furniture. Lebanon's location, three miles southeast of the geographic center of the state, attracts satellite plants.

The population of the fourth-class city was 5,528 in 1970; 6,590 in 1980; and 5,695 in 1990.
         RON D. BRYANT

LEDFORD, CAWOOD. Cawood Ledford, "the Voice of the Wildcats" at University of Kentucky (UK) sports events, is the son of James Washington and Susie Cawood Ledford, born in Cawood, Harlan County, Kentucky, in 1926. After graduating from Hall High School in Harlan and attending Centre College in Danville for one year, Ledford enlisted in the Marine Corps in 1944 and served in the Pacific theater. After the Battle of Okinawa, he was transferred to northern China, where he spent the final months of the war. In 1949 he earned a B.A. degree from Centre College. By 1951 he was conducting a sports call-in program at radio station WHLN in Harlan and announcing high school football and basketball games. In 1953 the newly established WLEX-TV in Lexington hired him as a sports commentator, and on September 19 of that year he worked his first UK sports event—a football game against Texas A&M. By his fourth game, Ledford was promoted to the play-by-play announcer. In 1956 he joined the sports team at Louisville's WHAS, where he served as sports director, did play-by-play for UK football and basketball, and announced horse racing. The University of Kentucky, which had sold its broadcast rights to WHAS, hired Ledford as the school's sports broadcaster in 1968. After twenty-two years with WHAS, Ledford, in conjunction with Jim Host of Host Communications, formed Cawood Ledford Productions, based in Lexington, which covers UK athletics. In 1987 he was elected to the Kentucky Athletic Hall of Fame. He has announced four NCAA championship basketball games for national radio networks.

Ledford married Frances Johnson, a co-worker at WHAS, in December 1974.

LEDFORD, HOMER. Homer Ledford, dulcimer maker and musician, the son of Abraham and Ova Lee (McDonald) Ledford, was born in Ivytown, Tennessee, on September 26, 1927. At the age of eighteen, Ledford left home to attend the John C. Campbell Folk School in Brasstown, North Carolina, where he saw his first dulcimer. Interested in industrial arts, Homer entered Kentucky's Berea College in 1949 and graduated from Eastern Kentucky University with a B.S. degree in 1954. The next year he took an industrial arts teaching position in the Clark County school system, remaining there until he resigned in 1963 to become a full-time instrument maker.

Homer constructed his first musical instrument, a fiddle in 1942, and his first dulcimer in July 1946. He has completed an estimated 5,320 dulcimers and 395 banjos, as well as 23 guitars, 12 mandolins, 3 fiddles, and 1 autoharp. He has also designed and built 23 dulcibros (combining aspects of a dulcimer and a dobro), and 13 patented dulcitars (combining features of a guitar and a dulcimer). Homer's craft is represented in the Smithsonian Institution by a dulcitar, a fretless banjo with a seven-and-a-half-inch goatskin head, and a dulcimer. Ledford is also a fine bluegrass musician who has performed regularly with his group, the Cabin Creek Band, since 1976. He married Colista Spradlin. They have four children: Mark L., Cindy Yvonne, Julia Ann, and Mattie Lee.

See R. Gerald Alvey, *Dulcimer Maker: The Craft of Homer Ledford* (Lexington, Ky., 1984).

RON PEN

LEDFORD, LILY MAY. Lily May Ledford, musician, was born in Pilot, Kentucky, in the Red River Gorge area of Powell County on March 17, 1917. The seventh of fourteen children of Daw White and Stella May Ledford, Lily May grew up on a tenant farm. The Ledfords were musically gifted, and by the time Lily May was a teenager she was playing fiddle and banjo in a family band called the Red River Ramblers. In 1936 Ledford auditioned and was chosen to perform in Chicago on the WLS "National Barn Dance." The next year John Lair, Ledford's manager, assembled an all-female string band that featured her clawhammer banjo sound. The group, known as the Coon Creek Girls, included Ledford's sister Rose (guitar), "Daisy" Lange (bass), and "Violet" Koehler (mandolin). In 1939 Daisy and Violet left the band and were replaced by a third Ledford sister, Minnie, known as "Black-eyed Susie." The band was featured regularly for the next eighteen years on the "Renfro Valley Barn Dance" radio program; it disbanded in 1957. Following World War II Ledford married Glenn Pennington; they had three children: Barbara, James, and Robert. She died on July 14, 1985, in Lexington and was buried in the Berea Cemetery in Berea, Kentucky.

See Lily May Ledford, *Coon Creek Girl* (Berea, Ky., 1980); Kenneth C. Hull, *Lily May: A Legend in Our Time* (New York 1975). RON PEN

LEE, HENRY. Henry Lee, political leader, son of Henry and Lucy (Grymes) Lee, was born on January 29, 1756, at Leesylvania, Prince William County, Virginia. He graduated from the College of New Jersey (now Princeton) in 1773. In 1776 he joined the Revolutionary army as a cavalry officer. Noted for his exploits in that role, he came to be known as "Light-Horse Harry" and rose to the rank of lieutenant colonel.

In the years after the war, Lee became a large-scale investor and speculator in land, including tracts in Kentucky. In 1785 the Virginia legislature chose him to be one of that state's representatives to Congress under the Articles of Confederation. Lee held this office, with one brief interruption, until 1788. In Congress, Lee personally supported John Jay's proposal that the American claim to free navigation of the Mississippi River be abandoned for a time in return for trade concessions from Spain—an idea that was anathema to most Kentuckians who looked to the river for exporting commodities. Obeying instructions from the Virginia legislature, Lee voted against Jay's proposal when it came before Congress in 1786.

A strong proponent of the U.S. Constitution, Lee was a prominent member of the Virginia convention of 1788, which voted that state's crucial ratification of the federal document. Elected governor of Virginia in 1791, Lee held that office for three consecutive one-year terms. Though Lee had little to do with Kentucky statehood, it was during his tenure as governor that Kentucky separated from Virginia and became the nation's fifteenth state in 1792. He was thus the last Virginia governor who was, by virtue of that office, also governor of Kentucky.

During Lee's time as Virginia governor, the American West simmered with opposition to the unpopular federal excise tax on whiskey. There was extensive resistance to it in Kentucky, but the most conspicuous and disorderly opposition—the Whiskey Rebellion—erupted in western Pennsylvania. President George Washington appointed Lee to command the 13,000-man militia army, drawn from four states, that was sent into western Pennsylvania in 1794 to uphold federal authority. Lee later served a single term in the U.S. Congress (March 4, 1799-March 3, 1801) as a Federalist.

In April 1782, Lee married his second cousin Matilda Lee, heiress of the Stratford estate on the Potomac River in Westmoreland County, Virginia. They had five children, only two of whom lived to maturity. Matilda Lee died in August 1790. Lee married Ann Hill Carter of Shirley plantation, Virginia, on June 18, 1793. Robert E. Lee, the Civil War general, was the fifth of six children born of that marriage.

Henry Lee's land speculations and other business endeavors ended in failure, and he was imprisoned for debt in 1809-10. While in custody, he wrote much of his *Memoirs of the War in the Southern Department of the United States* (1812). Also during that year, Lee was seriously and permanently injured in a political riot in Baltimore. In 1813 he departed for the West Indies, hoping to find relief from his injuries in a warmer climate.

After spending five years there, he decided to return to the United States. He became ill during the return voyage and died on March 25, 1818, at Cumberland Island, Georgia, where he was buried. In 1913 his body was returned to Virginia and placed with that of his son Robert E. Lee and other family members in the crypt of the Lee Chapel at Washington and Lee University in Lexington, Virginia.

See Charles Royster, *Light-Horse Harry Lee and the Legacy of the American Revolution* (New York 1981). THOMAS E. TEMPLIN

LEE, WILLIS AUGUSTUS, JR. Willis Augustus Lee, Jr., naval officer in World War II, was the son of Willis Augustus Lee, a lawyer and judge, and Susan Ireland (Arnold) Lee. He was born May 11,

1888, in Natlee, Owen County, Kentucky, and raised in Owenton. Lee, nicknamed "Ching" by his fellow midshipmen, graduated from the U.S. Naval Academy in 1908. Over the next few years, he became an expert in gunnery and ordnance and served tours on gunboats of the navy's Yangtze and South China Sea patrols. From the end of 1915 until November 1918, Lee was inspector at a naval ordnance plant in Rock Island, Illinois, then served aboard destroyers based in Ireland and in Brest, France. Lee was a gold medalist on the 1920 U.S. Olympic rifle team. He commanded destroyers on two occasions, served as navigator and then as executive officer of the battleship U.S.S. *Pennsylvania* and as commanding officer of the cruiser U.S.S. *Concord*. He studied at the Naval War College. Lee also had several assignments with the Division of Fleet Training in Washington, D.C., ending as director.

Promoted to captain in 1936 and rear admiral in 1942, Lee spent the first several months of World War II as an assistant chief of staff to the commander in chief of the U.S. fleet, in Washington. He then departed for the Pacific in mid-1942 to command the new fast battleships that were just beginning to enter combat. On the night of November 14-15, 1942, Lee led Task Force 64, made up of the new battleships U.S.S. *Washington* and U.S.S. *South Dakota* and four destroyers, into combat with a larger Japanese force near Guadalcanal. It was the first of only two occasions in the entire war when U.S. and Japanese battleships met in combat. Although the U.S.S. *South Dakota* was quickly disabled and Lee's other ships sustained heavy damage, the Japanese retired after losing a battleship. Lee's victory in this second phase of the naval Battle of Guadalcanal ended the last major Japanese effort to force Americans to yield this strategic island.

Lee subsequently commanded fast battleships in the Gilberts, Marshalls, Marianas, Leyte, Iwo Jima, and Okinawa campaigns. He was promoted to vice-admiral in 1944 and in May 1945 was assigned to develop antikamikaze tactics with a special naval force operating out of Casco Bay, Maine. Lee died of a heart attack on August 25, 1945, while taking a launch out to his flagship. He was buried at Arlington National Cemetery. Lee was survived by his wife Mabelle (Allen) Lee.

See Clark G. Reynolds, *Famous American Admirals* (New York 1978); Samuel Eliot Morison, *History of U.S. Naval Operations in World War II* (Boston 1947-62). LLOYD J. GRAYBAR

LEE COUNTY. The 115th county in order of formation, Lee County is located in eastern Kentucky. Bordered by Breathitt, Estill, Owsley, Powell, and Wolfe counties, it has an area of 211 square miles. Lee County was formed on March 1, 1870, from portions of Breathitt, Estill, Owsley, and Wolfe counties, and in 1872 BEATTYVILLE was established as the county seat. Most sources say the county was named after Robert E. Lee, but others cite Lee County, Virginia, to which many of the county's inhabitants trace their roots. The latter is a more likely explanation, given the strong Union sentiment exhibited by the residents of this area during the Civil War.

The topography of Lee County is hilly to mountainous. The valleys are fertile and productive farmland. Tobacco and corn are staples of the agricultural economy. Apple orchards also provide a significant income for the county's farmers. Livestock, mostly beef cattle and chickens, is raised on a small scale, principally for home consumption. Much of Lee County is heavily forested with large stands of commercial hardwood timber. Oak, beech, black walnut, buckeye, yellow poplar, and pine are found abundantly within the woodlands of the area. Daniel Boone National Forest includes more than 7,000 acres of the western portion of the county. The Kentucky River rises in the county and flows through the middle. There are some sixty creeks in the county. Lee County also has substantial deposits of coal, iron ore, and oil.

The first explorer in the area was Dr. Thomas Walker, who traveled through Kentucky in 1750. Among the first settlers in the early 1800s were Josiah (or Jacob) Miller and his family and John and Michael Stufflebean. Some of the early settlers came into the area to mine SALTPETER, which was used to make gunpowder.

The Civil War badly divided the sympathies of the people of the Lee County area. Union sympathizers formed a Home Guard, headquartered at Rocky Gap, eight miles north of Beattyville. On November 7, 1864, a Confederate force under the command of Lt. Jerry South fought the 20th Kentucky Militia at the Middle Fork of the Kentucky River in Lee County.

Steamboats and railroads made Lee County and Beattyville a regional transportation center during the mid- and late 1800s. At the confluence of the three forks of the Kentucky River, Beattyville was the eastern terminus for steamboats on the river, and state and federal governments constructed locks and dams to improve the river. The railroads that supplanted riverboat shipping benefited Beattyville and Lee County. In November 1902, the Louisville & Atlantic Railroad (L&A) extended its Versailles-to-Irvine line to include Beattyville, and after the Louisville & Nashville (now CSX Transportation) acquired the L&A in 1909, it constructed a second road from Beattyville, by way of Irvine, to Winchester. Despite the fact that the route to Versailles was closed in 1932, the county remained a regional shipping center.

In the 1950s and 1960s, Lee County experienced a degree of exceptional prosperity from the production of oil and coal, but the industries declined steadily during the 1970s and 1980s. Other types of industrial development in Lee County included the production of lumber, concrete, agricultural lime, shoes, and glass-fiber boats.

The population was 6,587 in 1970; 7,754 in 1980; and 7,422 in 1990.

See Bernice Calmes Caudill, *Remembering Lee County* (Danville, Ky., n.d.); Dennis L. Brewer, *The Land of Lee* (Beattyville, Ky., 1983).

RON D. BRYANT

LEES COLLEGE. Lees College in Jackson, Kentucky, is a private two-year liberal arts college with an average enrollment of three hundred students from eastern Kentucky and surrounding areas. The coeducational college serves the people of Appalachia through traditional academic transfer programs as well as career programs such as nursing, computer information science, and applied business. The school is fully accredited by the Southern Association of Colleges and Secondary Schools and confers two degrees: the associate of arts and the associate of science. There are more than 4,000 Lees College alumni.

Lees College originated as Jackson Academy, a Presbyterian-affiliated elementary and secondary school founded by the Rev. J.J. Dickey, who was traveling through eastern Kentucky in 1883 when his horse fell lame in Jackson. In 1891 the school was vested in the Transylvania Synod of the Presbyterian church. In 1897 it was renamed the S.P. Lees Collegiate Institute, in honor of Susan P. Lees, who had donated $25,000 to the institution. In that year, Dickey finished hand-bricking what is now the administration building—declared an official Kentucky landmark in 1975.

In October 1927, Lees Collegiate Institute became Lees Junior College and offered two years of college coursework. In the same year, Jackson Hall was completed and named after the city of Jackson, whose residents had made many donations. The Meter Building, which contains a gymnasium and a recreation center, was built in 1957 and named after J.O. Meter, president of Lees College from 1928 to 1948. Meteer Hall, a dormitory for men, was completed in 1966 and named after trustee Robert Meteer. The library/science building was completed in 1970 with donations from the E.O. Robinson Mountain Foundation Fund and others. Lees College presidents since J.O. Meter have been Robert H. Landolt (1948-58), J. Phil Smith (1958-59), Lawrence H. Hollander (1959-60), the Rev. Troy R. Eslinger (1961-88), and the Rev. William B. Bradshaw (1988-).

ELLA MACLEAN

LEESTOWN. A settlement that once existed in Franklin County, Leestown was founded and named by surveyor Capt. Hancock Lee and his brother, Willis Lee of Virginia in June 1775. It was located on the Kentucky River one mile below Frankfort along what is now U.S. 421 (Wilkinson Boulevard). Before its establishment, the site was visited by hunters and explorers, who camped on the sandy beach where a buffalo trace forded the river. After Boonesborough, founded in the spring of 1775, Leestown was the second pioneer settlement on the Kentucky River. In April 1776, Willis Lee was killed by Indians and by 1777 sporadic attacks against Leestown forced residents to abandon the town for a time. When the Indian threat subsided, Hancock Lee conducted a public sale of lots in March 1789, and in 1792 offered the city as a site for Kentucky's state capital. Frankfort was chosen as the site for the capital city, but the stone for the third state capitol, which was completed in 1830, was quarried in Leestown from along the Kentucky River by Harrison Blanton.

Although Leestown eventually was absorbed by Frankfort, it remained a commercial and shipping center in the 1800s. Corn, tobacco, hemp, and whiskey were shipped from there to New Orleans, and during the War of 1812 it served as a supply base for operations against the British and the Indians. After the war, Leestown boasted a large tobacco warehouse and after 1877 was the site of Kentucky River Mills, a major producer of binder's twine. Distilleries at Leestown produced bourbon, including the Carlisle and the O.F.C. (old-fire copper-distilled) brands established by Edmund H. Taylor, Jr., in the 1860s and later owned by the George T. Stagg Company and Schenley Distillers. In 1990 the distilling facilities were operated by Ancient Age Distilling Company.

See Samuel M. Wilson, "Leestown—Its Founders and Its History," *Register of Kentucky State Historical Society* 29 (Oct. 1931): 385-96.

CARL E. KRAMER

LEGISLATIVE RESEARCH COMMISSION. The Legislative Research Commission (LRC), a sixteen-member panel consisting of the General Assembly's majority and minority leadership, is the administrative arm of the General Assembly, providing support services and overseeing legislative business during the interim period between sessions. The highest elected officers of each chamber—the president pro tem of the Senate and the Speaker of the House—serve as co-chairs of the LRC. Policy decisions are made at the commission's monthly meetings.

The commission employs a full-time director, who oversees a staff of researchers, budget analysts, attorneys, computer operators, librarians, secretaries, and other professional and clerical staff. They provide such essential services as statute revision (incorporation of new laws within existing laws), research, bill drafting, and clerical support for committees and special panels and the 138 members of the legislature. The agency has its own print shop for publication of the *Acts of the General Assembly*, administrative regulations, research reports, and informational pamphlets. Legislative documents, reference works, periodicals, and other materials are copied and maintained in the LRC library.

The modern LRC evolved from the Legislative Council, which was created as part of the Governmental Reorganization Act of 1936. The council, which lacked adequate financial and staff support, was replaced in 1948 by the LRC. Originally, the LRC was chaired by the governor, although the chief executive was empowered to designate the lieutenant governor to fill that role.

In 1956 legislation removed the governor as chair and stipulated that the lieutenant governor preside over LRC meetings as ex-officio chair. The lieutenant governor would also serve as director of the agency staff. That arrangement continued until 1960, when an independent staff director, appointed by the House and Senate leadership, replaced the lieutenant governor. In 1975 the Speaker of the House and president pro tem of the Senate became co-chairs of the LRC proper, and the commission assumed its current configuration as an independent agency of the legislative branch.

The functions of statute revision, bill drafting, compilation of administrative regulations, publication of the *Legislative Record* and custody of legislative equipment, papers, and other vital items were added to the commission's duties in 1954. Two years later that list was expanded to include editing and publication of the Senate and House *Journals*, the *Acts* and the *Administrative Register*.

The LRC eventually assumed responsibility for the biennial presession conferences of the General Assembly, first held in 1951, in which new members were advised of legislative procedures and leadership was elected. Those conferences ended following the adoption of a constitutional amendment in 1979 allowing the General Assembly to meet in an organizational session in odd-numbered years, when no regular legislative session is held.

Since the late 1960s there has been great growth in the legislature's independence and its participation in and oversight of state government activities. This is evidenced by the increase in committee work and the growth of the LRC's interim committee system.

The House's and Senate's standing committees began meeting as joint panels during the interim. Then the LRC charted new waters when subcommittees such as Administrative Regulations Review, Personal Service Contract Review, Program Review and Investigations, and Capital Construction and Equipment Purchase Oversight (changed to Capital Projects and Bond Oversight in 1988) were created. In addition, a number of task forces on specific topics such as tobacco, waste management, and veterans are established by resolution of the General Assembly or action of the LRC to conduct studies during each interim. In addition, the LRC is directed by statute to study and examine the expenditures of state agencies. Staff budget analysts sift through the programs and budgets, conduct fiscal studies, and provide data required for effective review of proposals. During a General Assembly session, the budget review staff prepares fiscal notes on the budget implications of pending legislation and works with the Appropriations and Revenue committees in reviewing the executive budget.

To enhance accountability, the LRC, during the 1970s, pushed to open up the legislative process to the public. A public information office was established and toll-free telephone lines installed. Since 1978 daily highlights of General Assembly sessions have been televised by the Kentucky Educational Television network. A sophisticated computer system was installed in the 1980s to upgrade the agency's research and communication capabilities.

Work space for staff, leadership offices, and committee rooms were added during a 1954-55 renovation of the third floor of the capitol. Later the fourth floor was occupied by committee staff, and by 1978 space was acquired in the capitol annex, where legislators for the first time had desks (other than those in the House and Senate chambers) and phones for their own use.

The growth and maturation of both the LRC and its support staff reflect the changes that have occurred within the General Assembly and in the balance of power between branches of government. The evolution of the legislature's independence, and with it the power and responsibilities of the LRC, has not been without controversy and setbacks. In *LRC v. Brown* in 1984, the Kentucky supreme court held unconstitutional statutes passed by the legislature in 1982 that empowered the LRC to veto administrative regulations, to advise and consent to gubernatorial appointments to certain administrative boards, to appoint or nominate members of certain boards, and to veto the governor's temporary reorganization of the executive department. In 1990, voters overwhelmingly rejected proposed constitutional amendments that would have empowered the legislature to call itself into special session and would have authorized the LRC to veto administrative regulations.

JULIE HAVILAND

LEITCHFIELD. Leitchfield, the seat of Grayson County, is located in the west-central part of the state, at the intersection of U.S. 62 and KY 259 just north of the Western Kentucky Parkway and thirty miles southwest of Elizabethtown. It was first settled around 1786, when the first frame house in the area was built by Benjamin Ogden; a 1795 map refers to a Shaw's Station at that location. The city was organized at the time of the county's establishment in 1810 and was named in honor of Maj. David Leitch (1753-94) of Campbell County, whose widow donated the site for the new county seat on condition that it be named for her late husband. A log courthouse was erected by Richard May on a corner of the public square in 1810, and about the same year the first brick residence in the county was built by Jack Thomas, the first county and circuit court clerk. The Thomas house, altered twice between 1870 and 1890, was acquired by the Grayson County Historical Society in 1981 and restored.

The log courthouse was burned on December 24, 1864, by a contingent of Confederate Gen. Hylan B. Lyon's retreating force in an attempt to delay pursuing Union troops. All county records were destroyed. A second courthouse, built in 1870, was victim to a fire of unknown origin on June 16, 1896, also destroying public records. A third courthouse, built in 1898, burned on April 3, 1936, and was replaced by a Beaux Arts structure built with a grant from the Public Works Administration in January 1938.

Leitchfield was incorporated on February 5, 1866, and six years later the Elizabethtown & Paducah (now the Paducah & Louisville) Railroad was completed through the city, giving it a connection to coalfields in the western part of the state and to Louisville markets. The railroad's arrival on September 6, 1872, sparked a boom in the growth of business and industry, which by 1903 included the Leitchfield Clothing Company, employing over 200 people, the Leitchfield Ice and Laundry Company, a branch of the Armour Packing Company of Chicago, and R. Dinwiddie and Company, which manufactured staves, headings, and lumber and annually shipped over 1,000 boxcar loads of products.

In the mid-1960s, completion of the Western Kentucky Parkway improved access to newly created recreation areas at nearby Rough River Dam State Resort Park and Nolin River Reservoir. Leitchfield's location between the two lakes has made tourism an important industry. Light industry was attracted to the city because of its proximity to the parkway and railroad lines. Among the companies attracted to Leitchfield was the Phar-Shar Manufacturing Company, makers of clothing. Established in 1979, the company was the leading employer in the city by 1990.

Population of the fourth-class city was 2,983 in 1970; 4,533 in 1980; and 4,965 in 1990.

MARK E. NEVILS

LEONARD, JAMES FRANCIS. James Francis Leonard, master telegrapher, was born to John and Harriet (McQuiddy) Leonard on September 8, 1834, in Frankfort, Kentucky. He completed his grammar school and secondary education there. Leonard began work as a messenger in Frankfort's first telegraph office in 1848 and soon became a telegraph operator skilled in reading Morse code. Leonard was transferred to the Louisville telegraph office in July 1849. In the spring of 1851 he transmitted a message from circus owner P.T. Barnum, who was so amazed at the young operator's speed that he offered Leonard a well-paying job traveling with the circus. Leonard turned down the offer. In 1853 he left Louisville to work as a bookkeeper in Edmund H. Taylor's private bank in Lexington.

By 1855 Leonard had returned to his post in the Louisville telegraph office, where he came to the attention of the inventor of the telegraph, Samuel F.B. Morse. Morse was testing the speed of telegraph operators throughout the United States, and he was present in the Louisville office in the spring of 1855 when Leonard, unknowingly, was timed in receiving messages. From the Nashville telegraph office, Joseph W. Fisher sent a steady stream of messages for five minutes to Leonard, who received fifty words a minute with no mistakes, mak-

ing him the fastest telegrapher at this time. Morse exhibited Leonard's winning message at the International Fair in Paris in May 1855. In the autumn of 1861 Leonard took a position as a telegrapher in Memphis, Tennessee. In April 1862 he joined Gen. P.G.T. Beauregard's staff as a military telegrapher in Corinth, Mississippi, for a brief period. After leaving the military in June 1862, he worked for Southwestern Telegraph Company in Columbus, Mississippi.

Leonard married Ruth Marion Brown, of Cleveland, Ohio, on December 21, 1860, in Louisville; they had a daughter, Carlotta. Leonard died of typhoid fever on July 29, 1862, and is buried in the Frankfort Cemetery. A monument over his grave commemorates the telegrapher's achievements.

See John Wilson Townsend, "The Life of James Francis Leonard," *Filson Club Publication* 24 (1909): 4-85.

LESLIE, PRESTON HOPKINS. Preston Hopkins Leslie, Kentucky's governor during 1871-75, was born in Wayne (now Clinton) County, Kentucky, on March 8, 1819, to Vachel and Sally (Hopkins) Leslie. He had a limited education and worked at several jobs before reading law with Judge Rice Maxey. Admitted to the bar in 1840, he practiced law and farmed in Monroe County. After service as deputy clerk of the Clinton County courts and as Monroe County attorney, Leslie was elected to the state House in 1844 as a Henry Clay Whig. In 1846, in his first campaign for the state Senate, he was defeated by one vote, but he was then elected to serve as senator from 1850 to 1855. Leslie became a Democrat in the 1850s as the Whig party died out. His 1841 marriage to Louisa Black resulted in seven children; his 1859 marriage to Mrs. Mary Kuykendall produced three more. By 1861 he was prosperous enough to add a Texas estate to his Kentucky property. With divided views on the Civil War, Leslie refused military service and kept a low political profile. In 1867 he was again elected to the state Senate, where he served as president.

Leslie became Kentucky's governor on February 13, 1871, when Gov. John W. Stevenson took a U.S. Senate seat. Later that year he was nominated by the Democrats on a vague, reactionary platform, despite the opposition of editor Henry Watterson of the *Louisville Courier-Journal*. When the Republican candidate, John M. Harlan, and a more progressive platform seemed to be gaining votes, Leslie moved closer to the views of the more liberal New Departure faction of his party. In the first Kentucky gubernatorial election in which blacks voted, Leslie beat Harlan, 126,089 to 89,083, for the 1871-75 term.

In 1875 Leslie resumed law practice in Glasgow, Kentucky. From 1881 to 1887 he was a circuit court judge; he then accepted President Grover Cleveland's appointment as territorial governor of Montana. Confronted by a hostile press and strong machine politics, he was removed by President Benjamin Harrison in 1889. Leslie opened a legal practice in Helena, Montana, and in 1894 President Cleveland appointed him U.S. district attorney for Montana, a post he held for four years. He died on February 7, 1907, and was buried in the Forestvale Cemetery in Helena.

Governor Leslie asked for increased support for public education and internal improvements, for the admission of blacks' testimony in the courts, for an end to violence in the state, and for a more efficient revenue system. He got some of his requests, but the legislature seemed more interested in the struggle between the proposed Southern Railroad from Cincinnati and the Louisville & Nashville Railroad for control of the central Kentucky market. Leslie also secured some improvements in the treatment of the insane, as well as another geological survey of the state's resources. A temperance advocate, Leslie secured laws to regulate the sale of liquor, and the legislature made some provision for the education of black children. Leslie's administration was more progressive than most Kentuckians had anticipated.

See Lowell H. Harrison, ed., *Kentucky's Governors 1792-1985* (Lexington, Ky., 1985).

LOWELL H. HARRISON

LESLIE COUNTY. The 117th county in order of formation, Leslie County is located in southeastern Kentucky in the Eastern Coal Field region. It is bordered by Bell, Clay, Harlan, and Perry counties and has an area of 412 square miles. Leslie County was formed by an act of the General Assembly on March 29, 1878, from sections of Clay, Harlan, and Perry counties and named for Preston H. Leslie, governor of Kentucky (1871-75). The county seat is HYDEN, named in honor of state Sen. John Hyden, one of those responsible for establishing the county.

The topography of Leslie County is mountainous. The land is not suitable for agriculture and less than 2 percent of the county is used for farming. Leslie County, contained by the Daniel Boone National Forest, is heavily forested with large stands of ash, beech, hemlock, oak, maple, yellow poplar, and black walnut. The major water sources are Buckhorn Lake to the north and the Middle Fork of the Kentucky River. The two principal creeks in the county are Cut-Shin and Hell-Fer-Sartin. These streams supposedly received their colorful names from a disillusioned pioneer who endeavored to ford the swollen creeks after heavy rains.

Not until the 1880s did a passable road connect the Leslie County with the rest of Kentucky. Travel by land was so difficult that supplies to the area were brought up the Middle Fork of the Kentucky River by canoe and other small boats. For many years the river remained vital to the county's commerce. The principal supply point for the county was Clay's Ferry, located between Lexington and Richmond. Among the communities, towns, and villages established in Leslie County are Hyden, Cinda, Confluence, Cutshin, Sizerock, Smilex, Thousand Sticks, Toulouse, and Wendover.

Among the historic sites in Leslie County are the homes of John Shell and Will SANDLIN. Shell lived on the Laurel Fork of Creasey Creek in a log house constructed in 1830, now the oldest house in the county. He was believed to be more than a hundred years old at the time of his death. Owl's Nest is the home of Sandlin, a World War I hero who was awarded the Congressional Medal of Honor for capturing three German machine gun nests. The Kentucky legislature voted $10,000 to build a house for Sandlin.

Leslie County industry includes lumber mills and coal and lignite mines. On December 30, 1970, an explosion in the Finley Mine in the county killed thirty-eight people.

The population of Leslie County was 11,623 in 1970; 14,882 in 1980; and 13,642 in 1990.

See Sadie W. Stidham, *Trails Into Cutshin Country: A History of Leslie County, Kentucky* (Viper, Ky., 1978); Mary T. Brewer, *Rugged Trail To Appalachia* (Viper, Ky., 1978). RON D. BRYANT

LETCHER, ROBERT PERKINS. Robert Perkins Letcher, governor during 1840-44, was born in Goochland County, Virginia, on February 10, 1788. His parents, Stephen Giles and Betsey (Perkins) Letcher, moved the family to Garrard County, Kentucky, about 1800. Educated at Joshua Fry's private school near Danville, Letcher studied law and entered practice in Garrard County. He was married twice, to Susan Oden Epps and Charlotte Robertson. He was elected to the state House of Representatives in 1813, 1814, 1815, and 1817, then served in the U.S. House from March 4, 1823, to March 3, 1833. A heated 1833 campaign against Democrat Thomas P. Moore was so close that the U.S. House ordered another election, which Letcher won by 258 votes, serving from August 6, 1834, to March 3, 1835. A National Republican-Whig who supported Henry Clay, Letcher went back to the state House in 1836, 1837, and 1838, and in his last two years was Speaker of the House. In August 1839 the Whig state convention selected Letcher to run for governor. Noted for his ready wit, his stump speaking, and his fiddling, Black Bob, as he was called, swamped his Democratic rival, Judge Richard French. When the votes were recorded, Letcher had a majority of 15,720 in a total poll of 95,020. The Whigs also captured a comfortable majority in both houses of the General Assembly.

The first years of Letcher's gubernatorial administration were dominated by the aftermath of the panic of 1837. As a Henry Clay Whig, he blamed the depression upon the federal government's failure to recharter the Second Bank of the United States. To maintain the state's credit, he curbed spending on such projects as turnpike construction and the improvement of navigation on the Green, Kentucky, and Licking rivers. While Letcher opposed any major legislative relief for debtors, he accepted several minor measures that provided some assistance to those in danger of losing their property. As a result of his economic measures and the beginning of economic recovery, Letcher was able to report a small but growing budget surplus each full year of his term. In 1842 Kentucky banks resumed specie payments, but the state's good credit was maintained at the expense of a number of much-needed programs.

After his term ended in 1844, Letcher practiced law in Frankfort and remained active in politics. In 1847 he made a strong bid for a seat in the U.S. Senate but was defeated by Joseph R. Underwood of Bowling Green. From 1850 to 1852 Letcher was the U.S. minister to Mexico, where the treaties he negotiated to protect American interests in the Isthmus of Tehuantepec were rejected by the Mexican government. In 1853 the aging Letcher waged a stirring but losing battle against Democrat John C. Breckinridge for a seat in the U.S. House. When the Whig party dissolved in the 1850s, Letcher supported Know-Nothing candidates, and in 1860 he backed John Bell, the Constitutional Union presidential candidate, who seemed to offer the best prospects for a peaceful solution to the sectional crisis. Letcher died in Frankfort on January 24, 1861, and was buried in the Frankfort Cemetery.

See Will D. Gilliam, Jr., "Robert Perkins Letcher, Whig Governor of Kentucky," *FCHQ* 24 (Jan. 1950).   LOWELL H. HARRISON

LETCHER COUNTY. Letcher County, the ninety-fifth county in order of formation, is located in southeastern Kentucky. It is bounded by Harlan, Perry, Knott, and Pike counties in Kentucky and by Wise County, Virginia, and contains 339 square miles. The county was formed in 1842 from portions of Perry and Harlan counties, and was named for Gov. Robert P. Letcher (1840-44). The county seat is WHITESBURG.

The terrain of Letcher County is rugged and mountainous, with narrow but fertile valleys along the streams. Three of the state's major rivers—the Cumberland, the North Fork of the Kentucky, and the Levisa Fork of the Big Sandy—all have headwaters in the county. Resources are coal, oil, and timber. In 1987 farms occupied only 2 percent of the land, with poultry and corn being the major crops.

The Pound Gap of Pine Mountain on the county's eastern border with Virginia placed it on a pioneer trail into the state, but most of the first pioneers only passed through, settling elsewhere. In 1795 Peter Whitaker built a cabin on what is now Whitaker's Branch. Nine years later George Ison II and his family settled on Line Fork. Other early settlers were Benjamin Webb of Maryland, James Caudill of Virginia, and William Stamper of North Carolina. By 1806 nearly every main creek area had been settled by one or more families. By 1810 there were over one hundred different families living there.

Between 1810 and 1840 the population grew rapidly. Most people settled in the vicinity of Mayking, but the county seat went to Whitesburg, two

miles to the southwest. The new county was visited by Confederate and Union armies that passed through the strategic Pound Gap during the Civil War. At Pound Gap, on March 16, 1862, Brig. Gen. James A. Garfield and seven hundred Union troops defeated a Confederate force of five hundred under the command of Gen. Humphrey Marshall. Other skirmishes took place in late 1863 near Whitesburg, and on June 1, 1864, John Hunt Morgan's Confederate cavalry dislodged a Union force from Pound Gap.

The Civil War violence was only a prelude to greater bloodletting in the forty or so years after the Civil War in many of the counties surrounding Letcher; Letcher County was less tumultuous, but some FEUDS reached it as well. The Wright-Jones feud, which began in Knott County in 1886, carried over to Letcher County, and continued until both clans called a lasting truce around 1895. Violence resurfaced in 1897 between the Wrights and the Reynolds families, but by 1900 feuding was on the wane.

In 1885, coal speculation by big business began in Letcher County. From 1903 to 1905 a great deal of the county's mineral rights were deeded by residents to buyers that included Consolidation, Elkhorn, and South-East coal companies. The companies established the towns of JENKINS, Fleming, McRoberts, and Seco (South-East Coal Co.) and by November of 1912 had completed the Lexington & Eastern Railroad (now CSX Transportation) from Breathitt County to McRoberts. Eastern European immigrants and Afro-Americans from the Deep South worked the mines and built the railroads. Some of the newcomers were highly skilled Italian artisans who constructed fine stone bridges and houses.

Around 1898, John Fox, Jr., first visited Letcher County, the setting of two of his best-sellers, *The Little Shepherd of Kingdom Come* (1903) and *The Trail of the Lonesome Pine* (1908). The latter characterized "Bad" John Wright and his feud. To honor the contribution of Fox to the mountain people, Kingdom Come State Park was founded in 1962 in the southwestern part of the county.

With the coming of industry, the county surrendered some of its isolation. But residents had become dependent upon mining and suffered greatly during the Great Depression years. A flood that swept the area on May 30, 1927, heightened the misery. The Works Progress Administration (WPA) created some employment, and World War II's industrial boom and the demand for coal stimulated mining. During the war, 174 county men were killed in military action. Outmigration from Letcher County was heavy; between 1940 and 1950, the population declined by 1,007. The trend continued during the 1950s (9,420 fewer people) and in the 1960s (6,837 fewer). With the decline in the production of coal, the companies had sold off their towns by the 1960s. National attention focused on the county's economic depression and the substandard living conditions portrayed by Harry CAU-

DILL's *Night Comes to the Cumberlands* (1963). Caudill, a Whitesburg lawyer, helped to inspire President Lyndon B. Johnson's WAR ON POVERTY.

In 1990 coal mining continued to be a mainstay of the local economy. Most jobs in the county are in mining and quarrying, wholesale and retail trade, services, or the county school system. There are relatively few manufacturing positions.

The population of the rural county was 23,165 in 1970; 30,687 in 1980; and 27,000 in 1990.

See William T. Cornett, *Letcher County, Kentucky: A Brief History* (Prestonsburg, Ky., 1967); I.A. Bowles, *History of Letcher County, Kentucky* (Hazard, Ky., 1949).

LEVISA FORK. The Levisa Fork of the Big Sandy River, 189 miles in length, flows north from its headwaters in southwestern Virginia. Its major tributaries are Russell Fork and the Shelby, Island, Mud, Elkhorn, Beaver, and Johns creeks. The Levisa joins the Tug Fork at Louisa in Lawrence County, and together they form the Big Sandy River, which flows northwest and empties into the Ohio River at Catlettsburg. At one time it was an avenue of slack-water navigation with a lock and dam and steamboat travel to Pikeville. It is still subject to flooding. The Levisa Fork gives rise to Dewey, Fishtrap, and Paintsville lakes and offers recreational fishing to area residents.

See Carol Crowe-Carraco, *The Big Sandy* (Lexington, Ky., 1979).   CAROL CROWE-CARRACO

LEWINSKI, THOMAS. Thomas Lewinski, architect, was born to a Polish father and English mother in London, England, probably in 1800. He trained as a Roman Catholic priest, then joined the military and took part in conflicts in Spain and South America. Lewinski received an excellent architectural education in England. He first appeared in Kentucky in 1838 as a modern languages instructor at the University of Louisville. In 1842 Lewinski moved to Lexington.

Lewinski's earliest designs reflect the classical style of the English Regency, which relies on subtle planar gradations to establish design. One such building was Lewinski's earliest known commission, the Gen. Leslie Combs house of 1842 on Main Street in Lexington, known as Babel. The building is no longer standing. Of the same style was the house on North Limestone that Lewinski designed in 1845-46 for Edward P. Johnson; this building has been remodeled and is now Sayre School.

The reception of Lewinski's English Regency style in Lexington prompted him to develop a grander tetrastyle portico formula, which he popularized through numerous designs for the Bluegrass aristocracy. He developed a standard grid of horizontal and vertical elements (based on a traditional grid system developed by the Greeks) that he could expand and contract as the situation dictated. Henry Clay commissioned the first known house of this type for his son Thomas. Known as Mansfield and built on East Main Street, Lexington, this 1845-46 cottage was only one and a half stories. Months later, Lewinski expanded the grid to a two-story version for Henry Bell, a wealthy merchant; the Bell house still stands in Lexington. Lewinski received several other well-known commissions during this period, including one for the Madison County courthouse in 1848.

Lewinski left the Bluegrass in 1850. Henry Clay, one of his major patrons, found Lewinski a position in the Department of the Treasury as an on-site supervisor of Marine hospitals, including hospitals in Paducah, Kentucky; Napoleon, Arkansas; and Natchez, Mississippi.

After Lewinski returned to Lexington in 1853, his buildings became increasingly ornate. Although he did not abandon the Greek Revival style, he began also to use the then-popular Italianate style. His best-known Italianate designs include the Alexander Brand house, known first as Cane Run and later as Glengarry, which was located on Newtown Pike; and Jacobs Hall at the Kentucky School for the Deaf in Danville. Both were designed in 1853. During the same period, he may have designed his finest Greek Revival residential work, WARD HALL in Scott County. In 1854 Lewinski became secretary of the Lexington Gas Works, a secure and lucrative position he occupied until 1872. After the start of the Civil War in 1861, his architectural practice declined to the point of disappearing.

On October 29, 1840, Lewinski married Hannah Carey of Louisville, who bore him a daughter, Mary. Hannah died on June 2, 1845. On May 29, 1856, Lewinski married Mary Watkins. Their only child, Carrie, was born on August 20, 1856. Lewinski died on September 18, 1882, and was buried in the Lexington Cemetery. His wife Mary died on September 25, 1895, and was buried at his side.

See Clay Lancaster, *Ante Bellum Houses of the Bluegrass* (Lexington, Ky., 1961) and "Major Thomas Lewinski: Emigré Architect in Kentucky," *Journal of Society of Architectural Historians* (Dec. 1952): 13-20.   WILLIAM B. SCOTT, JR.

LEWIS, ISHAM AND LILBURNE. In 1811 in the frontier county of Livingston in western Kentucky, a boy slave was the victim of one of the most horrifying crimes in Kentucky history. On the night of December 16, plantation owner Lilburne Lewis and his younger brother Isham assembled their slaves in a meat house, where in an insane rage of drunken anger, they used an ax to hack to death Lilburne's young slave, George, and then tried to burn his body. They accused George of trying to run away after breaking their mother's water pitcher. During the slaughter, the first shocks of the great New Madrid earthquake struck, collapsing the chimney of the meat house. That night a dog carried off the head of the corpse. The head was found by a neighbor a few months later, and indictment of the brothers resulted. They were never tried. Lilburne shot and killed himself while released on bail shortly before his trial was scheduled. Isham was then jailed but escaped to Louisiana, where he died three years later in the Battle of New Orleans (1815).

Before moving to western Kentucky in 1808, the Lewis family had been part of the Virginia landed gentry. Lucy (Jefferson) Lewis, the mother of Isham and Lilburne, was the sister of President Thomas Jefferson, whose home, Monticello, was close to the extensive Lewis plantations. The Lewis and Jefferson families had intermarried for at least three generations. After the Lewises lost their property in Virginia, most of the family moved to the wild new land on the Ohio River near the mouth of the Cumberland. They took their old aristocratic pretensions with them, and their indebtedness as well. Amid the crude independent democracy of the frontier, they did not flourish.

After the murder of George, several of the Lewis adults left the area, Lilburne Lewis's children were let out to guardians by the court, and the family died out.

See Boynton Merrill, Jr., *Jefferson's Nephews: A Frontier Tragedy* (Lexington, Ky., 1987).

BOYNTON MERRILL, JR.

LEWIS, JOHN LEWELLYN. John L. Lewis, president of the United Mine Workers of America (UMW), was born on February 12, 1880, in Lucas, Iowa, to Thomas and Louisa (Watkins) Lewis. He left school in the seventh grade to work in the coal mines, where he joined the UMW. In 1920 he became president of the UMW, leading it in the 1920 and 1922 strikes, which left the union weaker in eastern Kentucky. Western Kentucky miners split over his strike call in 1924, when he made his first known visit to the state.

Lewis replaced locally chosen district presidents in both Kentucky coal fields, beginning with Ed Morgan in District 23 in 1930. In the wake of the National Industrial Recovery Act of 1933, which guaranteed the right to collective bargaining, Lewis gradually organized all of Kentucky's miners. The victory in Harlan and adjoining counties came only after a protracted conflict. In 1936 Lewis was one of the founders of the Congress of Industrial Organizations (CIO). Lewis's strong personality and aggressive conduct of union affairs brought him into collision with the courts, and a 1946 court case cost the union $3.5 million and Lewis himself $10,000 in fines.

Lewis became a folk hero in his day and his influence on younger labor leaders, such as western Kentucky's Le Roy Patterson, who sought to become president of the UMW, has endured. He won the respect of some Kentucky coal operators, among them B.F. Reed and Bryan Whitfield, Jr. Loss of the domestic and railroad fuel markets crippled the union, however, and led to the sale of six Kentucky hospitals that the union had built in the 1950s. The last strike that Lewis led in Kentucky, beginning in March 1959, was at best a partial success, with operators in eastern Kentucky settling individually that fall. Lewis retired in 1960.

Lewis married Myrta Bell in 1907; they had three children. Lewis died in Washington, D.C., on June 11, 1969, and was buried in Springfield, Illinois.

See John Hevener, *Whose Side Are You On?* (Champaign, Ill., 1978); F. Ray Marshall, *Labor in the South* (Cambridge, Mass., 1967).

HENRY MAYER

LEWIS, JOSEPH HORACE. Joseph Horace Lewis, Civil War general and jurist, was born to John and Eliza Martz (Reed) Lewis on October 29, 1824, in Glasgow, Kentucky. He was educated at Centre College in Danville, graduating in 1843, and was admitted to the bar in 1845 after reading law under Judge C.C. Tompkins. Lewis served in the Kentucky House of Representatives as a Whig from 1851 to 1855, ran unsuccessfully as a secessionist Democrat for the U.S. Congress in 1857 and 1861, and strongly supported the presidential campaign of John C. Breckinridge.

With the outbreak of the Civil War, Lewis began to recruit for the Confederate 6th Kentucky Infantry regiment, for which he received the commission of colonel in September 1861. He was made brigadier general of the 1st Kentucky Brigade (Orphan Brigade) on September 30, 1863, after its commander, Gen. Benjamin Hardin Helm, was mortally wounded at the battle of Chickamauga. During the war, Lewis led regiments in the battles of Shiloh, Murfreesboro, the Tullahoma campaign, Chattanooga, the Atlanta campaign, and Savannah. At war's end, Lewis and his men became a part of President Jefferson Davis's escort as he fled south from Richmond, Virginia. Lewis surrendered his forces on May 6, 1865, at Washington Court House, Georgia, four days before the capture of Davis.

Lewis was paroled and returned to Kentucky to practice law. In 1869 he reentered the Kentucky House. He was then elected to the U.S. House of Representatives as a Democrat, serving two terms (May 10, 1870, to March 3, 1873). In 1880 he was elected a circuit court judge. He served on the Kentucky court of appeals from 1882 until 1899, and was elected chief justice in 1882, 1888, and 1897. Lewis was married twice, to Sarah H. Rogers on November 29, 1845, and to Cassandra (Flournay) Johnson on March 29, 1883. He died on his farm in Scott County on July 6, 1904, and was buried in the Glasgow Cemetery.

LEWIS COUNTY. Lewis County, the forty-eighth county in order of formation, is located in northeastern Kentucky along the Ohio River. It is bordered by Carter, Fleming, Greenup, Mason, and Rowan counties and has an area of 484 square miles. Lewis County was formed from a portion of Mason County on December 2, 1806, and named in honor of explorer Merriweather Lewis, who accompanied William Clark to the Pacific Northwest in 1803-6. The county seat is VANCEBURG.

The topography of Lewis County is a highly dissected upland area with hilly to mountainous terrain. A large stone quarry near Vanceburg, which operated early in the county's history, supplied the white limestone used to construct the present courthouse. Esculapia Springs, a major resort during the nineteenth century, was destroyed by fire in 1860. Current recreation and travel attractions include park and boating facilities on the Ohio River, the July Jubilee, the Sorghum Festival in September, and one of Kentucky's thirteen remaining COVERED BRIDGES. The Cabin Creek Bridge, built in 1873, was constructed with a single-span Burr tress without arches. In the southern section of the county is the Mead Forest Wildlife Area.

In the 1700s, the mouths of Cabin and Sycamore creeks were two of the Ohio River crossings used by the Indian war parties to enter Kentucky from Ohio, where they traveled the Upper Blue Licks prongs to the interior. Frequent Indian attacks during the Revolutionary War caused George Rogers Clark to appeal to the Virginia legislature to send gunpowder to the settlers. Five hundred pounds of powder was brought down the Ohio to the mouth of the Cabin Creek and hidden at Three Islands until an escort could be raised to convey it to FORT HARROD.

The earliest settlers in Lewis County entered the region in the 1770s. By 1840 the county's population was 5,873. In 1870 the county's farmers produced 369,855 bushels of corn and 48,450 pounds of tobacco. In 1987 farms occupied 54 percent of the land area, with 35 percent of farmland in production. The county ranked sixty-sixth in agricultural income from livestock, tobacco, hay, corn, and vegetables in 1988.

Lewis Countians were intensely devoted to the Union cause during the Civil War. The county lost 107 men who served in the Union army. In 1884 a monument was erected to the memory of those who had died for the Union cause. Following the Civil War, Lewis County became a stronghold of the Republican party. The dedication of many Lewis Countians to the Grand Old Party continued into the twentieth century.

U.S. Shoe Corporation established a plant in Vanceburg in 1957 and in 1967 built a component plant. Other industrial sites include four wood products plants and a drainage pipe plant. Although many people commute to jobs outside the county, particularly to Maysville, Kentucky, and Portsmouth, Ohio, the county remains largely agricultural. The county is served by CSX Transportation.

In 1970 the population of Lewis County, of which Vanceburg is the only incorporated town, was 12,355. The population was 14,545 in 1980 and 13,029 in 1990.

See O.G. Ragan, *History of Lewis County, Kentucky* (Cincinnati 1912).　　　　RON D. BRYANT

LEXINGTON. Lexington, the county seat of Fayette County and the second largest city in Kentucky, lies in the Bluegrass region. It is noted for the breeding and sale of thoroughbred and standardbred horses, a major burley tobacco market, and diversified manufacturing. The University of Kentucky and Transylvania University are located in Lexington.

Pennsylvania frontiersmen, camping in the area in 1775, named the prospective town Lexington, for the historic Massachusetts battle. Permanent settlement began in 1779, when Col. Robert Patterson led a group of Harrodsburg settlers to the location. They built Fort Lexington to defend themselves against British and Indian attacks during the last year of the Revolutionary War.

Once peace came, the town leaders laid out the streets and lots. As major roads in the frontier area intersected at Lexington, the town became the fastest growing settlement in Kentucky. Between 1790 and 1800 the town was transformed from a rude frontier post into an attractive community of fine homes, landed estates, and diverse manufacturing and mercantile enterprises. One of the most profitable businesses was the manufacture of rope and bagging for cotton bales, made from the hemp that was widely cultivated in the area. In the early 1800s, Lexington had a growing university, Transylvania, bookstores, a theater, musical ensembles, a subscription library, and a talented portrait painter, Matthew Jouett. Skillful silversmiths like Asa Blanchard crafted pieces for the emerging social elite. John Wesley Hunt, who made a fortune out of trade, rope manufacturing, and horse breeding, built a splendid townhouse to display his success. Noted lawyers and physicians settled in the city, including Dr. Samuel Brown, who introduced vaccination into the region. John Bradford founded the Kentucky Gazette, the state's first newspaper.

Numerous taverns and inns were built, the most famous being Postlethwait's, which became the Phoenix Hotel. In the environs of Lexington emerged a growing number of large estates where fine thoroughbreds, cattle, and sheep were bred and large quantities of agricultural products were raised. Horse racing early became a familiar feature of Lexington and an excellent race track was built in 1828 in northeast Lexington.

By the 1820s Lexington could claim to be the "Athens of the West," although it rapidly lost its commercial predominance to the river towns of Louisville and Cincinnati after the invention of the steamboat. Lexington's most prominent citizen was Henry Clay, who had risen quickly to political leadership after his arrival as a young lawyer from Virginia in 1797. His estate, Ashland, became the best-known home in town. Under the administration of Horace Holley, Transylvania University in the 1818-26 period developed exceptionally fine law and medical departments and became one of the preeminent universities in the country.

In 1831, the state legislature incorporated the city of Lexington, to be governed by a mayor and twelve councilmen. The new government moved to improve living conditions in the city by passing ordinances to raise the standards of building construction, improve sanitary conditions, organize fire companies, and create a police force. The city also had one of the first mental hospitals in the nation, Eastern Lunatic Asylum, which opened in 1824. Action on public education lagged, however, and not until the 1830s were the first public schools opened in the city; they were also the county's first. By the 1850s a sizable number of schools were furnishing a basic education to Lexington children.

In 1833 Lexington suffered an epidemic of cholera, which then plagued many U.S. cities. Within less than three months, the town lost nearly 10 percent of its 6,000 population. William ("King") Solomon, an indentured servant, became a legendary hero during this scourge by risking his life in burying the numerous dead.

To improve transportation to and from Lexington in these early decades, private turnpike companies constructed numerous toll roads with macadamized crushed rock surfaces. Lexington also tried to offset the riverside advantage of Louisville by beginning in 1831 to construct the first railroad connection with Frankfort, and later with Louisville.

In Lexington and Fayette County, slaves made up about one-half the population. By the late 1830s and through the 1850s, Lexington became a major market for slaves from Kentucky and those transported from Virginia down the Ohio and the Mississippi rivers to the cotton states. Lexingtonian Cassius Marcellus Clay, one of the region's most ardent emancipationists, started an antislavery newspaper in Lexington called the True American, which was soon shut down by a mob.

Once the Civil War started, Lexington, like the rest of the badly divided state, saw hundreds of citizens joining the armies of both sides. Lexington's most significant military figures were the Confederates John C. Breckinridge and John Hunt Morgan, the dashing cavalry raider. For most of the war, Lexington was occupied by Union troops, who commandeered Transylvania's buildings to use as hospitals.

Following the Civil War, Lexington had to adjust to changed race relations and an influx of free blacks. Segregated housing areas were constructed to provide shelter for the blacks. Most found employment in some eighty different occupations. The public school system was improved. Private schools such as the Sayre Female Institute and the Hocker Female College were founded. In 1865, with the federal land grant available under the Morrill Act, the state founded the Agricultural and Mechanical College of Kentucky, which in 1878 was placed on its own campus in southern Lexington under the presidency of James Patterson. It would develop into the University of Kentucky. Transylvania University was combined with Kentucky University of Harrodsburg, whose buildings had been destroyed during the war. Under regent John Bowman, Kentucky University brought money and resources to the Transylvania campus, and the combined schools were known as Kentucky University from 1865 until 1908. The College of the Bible, a seminary for Disciples of Christ ministers, was located on the campus until 1949. Not until the 1880s did Lexing-

ton begin to modernize significantly, as telephones, electricity, a city waterworks, and a street railway system were introduced. A new opera house was erected in 1886 to house a variety of theatrical and musical events. Andrew Carnegie donated funds for the construction of an impressive public library in Gratz Park in 1905. Lexington's native son James Lane Allen became a national bestselling novelist in the late nineteenth and early twentieth centuries.

The main addition to Lexington's prosperity in the late nineteenth century was the establishment of a large burley tobacco marketing center. While maintaining much of its traditional character, Lexington grew in population and its businesses expanded. In 1907 Union Station was erected on Main Street to serve various railroads such as the Chesapeake & Ohio and the Louisville & Nashville. Main Street's traditional skyline was abruptly changed with the erection of the fifteen-story Fayette National Bank in 1913-14. In 1921, the luxurious ten-story Lafayette Hotel was constructed.

Lexington also fostered some progressive movements and individual reformers such as Laura Clay, daughter of Cassius Clay, who became a national leader in the women's rights movement, especially in the campaign for women's suffrage. Sophonisba Breckinridge became the first woman to pass the Kentucky bar exam and to receive a Ph.D. at the University of Chicago. Madeline McDowell Breckinridge was not only a leader in the women's suffrage movement but was also instrumental in founding Lincoln School to serve the needs of Lexington's poor immigrants. She started the Bluegrass Sanitarium for victims of tuberculosis.

The remarkably cohesive black community produced such notables as the sculptor Scott Hathaway, the jockey Isaac Murphy, and doctors T.T. Wendell and John E. Hunter. Yet blacks were kept tightly segregated and subordinated in Kentucky's white-dominated society. The Ku Klux Klan operated freely for the most part, and lynching of blacks was not uncommon. In 1920 a mob in Lexington attempted to storm the Fayette County courthouse to seize and lynch a black named Will Lockett being tried for the murder of a young white girl. State troops sent by Gov. Edwin Morrow (1919-23) fired on the crowd, killing six and wounding many others, causing a national sensation.

Because of Lexington's diverse economic activities, the city did not suffer as badly from the Great Depression of the 1930s as many other parts of the country did. In fact, it was during this decade that a fine new racecourse was built at Keeneland to replace the antiquated one on Race Street. The city bought land opposite the Keeneland Race Course to build the Blue Grass Airport, which went into operation in 1942.

Lexington's major expansion occurred in the post-World War II period. Business leaders persuaded such major firms as Square D, Dixie Cup, and Mengel Company, a subsidiary of the Container Corporation of America, to establish plants in Lexington in the early 1950s. The giant IBM Corporation moved its electric typewriter division to Lexington, starting production in 1956. Between 1954 and 1963 employment rose 260 percent. The population of the greater Lexington area, including Fayette County, rose from 100,746 in 1950 to 204,165 in 1980. Construction of new houses and shopping malls proceeded at a rapid pace. The school system was hard pressed to meet the needs of a sharply increased enrollment and to comply with the Supreme Court's ruling on desegregation of schools.

In higher education, both the University of Kentucky and Transylvania University shared the national trend of sharp increases in student enrollment and in federal and state aid, which enabled them to greatly expand their facilities. The University of Kentucky became Lexington's largest employer and was further expanded with the addition of the Chandler Medical Center in 1962.

The civil rights movement of the late 1950s and 1960s was relatively peaceful in Lexington despite sit-ins and boycotts that persuaded most businesses to abandon their segregation policies. A black was elected as a city commissioner and another to the school board.

Urban renewal funds from the government enabled Lexington to remove the railroad tracks running through downtown and to raze a number of decaying structures. A major achievement in city government was the merger of the city and county governments under a new charter, approved by the voters, which went into effect in 1974. The merged government consists of a mayor and a fifteen-member Urban County Council.

The physical character of downtown Lexington was substantially changed in the late 1970s with the construction of the Civic Center, Rupp Arena, new high-rise hotels and office buildings, and shopping malls. The 1886 opera house was restored and became a major entertainment center. A large new public library was opened on Main Street in 1989 to replace the aging building in Gratz Park.

The Blue Grass Trust and the Historic Commission are evidence that many Lexingtonians want to preserve the community's most treasured landmarks while cooperating with those agencies planning for Lexington's continued growth. The population of the second-class city was 108,137 in 1970; 204,165 in 1980, six years after the merger of city and county governments; and 225,366 in 1990.

See John D. Wright, Jr., *Lexington: Heart of the Bluegrass* (Lexington, Ky., 1982).

JOHN D. WRIGHT

LEXINGTON. The thoroughbred stallion Lexington (1850-75), brilliant in racing, led the sire list for sixteen years, longer than any other stallion. Of his 238 winning offspring, eighty-four were "top class" (now called stakes winners), and eleven were champions. If not for the fact that many of his sons and daughters did cavalry duty in the Civil War, the numbers would be even greater.

By Boston out of Alice Carneal, Lexington was bred by Dr. Elisha Warfield, Jr., of Lexington, Kentucky, who named him Darley. He was purchased as a three-year-old by Richard Ten Broeck of New Orleans, who changed his name. He raced often in four-mile heats, setting a record for four miles in 7:19 ¾. He won six of his seven races, defeated only by a half-brother. His racing career was shortened by the onset of blindness, and he was retired to stud at age five. In 1856 he was sold to R.A. Alexander of Woodburn farm in Woodford County, Kentucky, where he spent his remaining years at stud.

See William H.P. Robertson, *The History of Thoroughbred Racing in America* (New York 1964).

MARY E. WHARTON

LEXINGTON & OHIO RAILROAD. The Lexington & Ohio (L&O) Railroad Company was chartered on January 27, 1830. The legislative act named twenty of Lexington's most prominent citizens among its incorporators, with Elisha Winters and Gen. Leslie Combs as the leading organizers. The charter allowed the L&O to build a railroad west from Lexington to one or more points on the Ohio River.

The L&O Company was authorized to begin operating trains as soon as fifteen miles of track were constructed. A horse-drawn car began operating over the first mile and a half of track on August 15, 1832. Stone sills, cut in the Water Street quarry in Lexington, were covered with flat strap iron rails imported from Liverpool by way of New Orleans and Louisville. The railroad was not completed into Frankfort until January 31, 1834. At first the cars were lowered on an incline into the town, using a stationary engine and cable suspensions. The L&O's first locomotive was completed in March 1833 by Barlow and Bruen, of Lexington. The engine was more of a curiosity than a practical machine. In 1835 two small steam locomotives, the *Nottoway* and *Logan*, were purchased in the East.

Between 1831 and 1857 the railroad company experienced almost constant financial crises and underwent at least three changes of name, ending as the Lexington & Frankfort Company. On January 16, 1858, the Louisville & Frankfort Railway Company, chartered in 1844 and completed by 1851, merged with the Lexington & Frankfort Company. There was genuine irony in this, for the stated original purpose of chartering the Lexington & Ohio Railroad Company was to bypass Louisville and give Lexington direct rail and river access to the New Orleans market.

See Thomas D. Clark, "The Lexington and Ohio Railroad—A Pioneer Venture," *Register* 31 (Jan. 1933): 9-28.

THOMAS D. CLARK

LEXINGTON CEMETERY. Lexington Cemetery, chartered in 1848 and dedicated on June 25, 1850, is considered one of the outstanding examples of the rural cemetery type. Located on West Main Street in Lexington, Kentucky, the 173-acre cemetery is listed on the National Register of Historic Places. The original land purchase was forty acres of woodland on the west end of Lexington.

The cemetery has earned a national reputation as an arboretum, with more than two hundred varieties of trees. Many of the original forest trees survive, including the second-largest known American linden in the world. These trees display a range of color throughout the year, starting with the weeping cherries, crabapples, and dogwoods in the spring, succeeded by a rich display of fall foliage. Winter is adorned with berried hollies and many other varieties of evergreens. More than 15,000 tulips bloom in the landscaped gardens each year, followed by summer annuals. Lakes and lily ponds are home to ducks and geese. The local chapter of the Audubon Society has identified 179 species of birds on the grounds. More than sixty pieces of statuary adorn family lots, as well as many unusual memorials.

Lexington Cemetery is operated by a nonprofit corporation governed by a self-perpetuating board of nine directors. Four men have held the position of superintendent: Charles S. Bell and James H. Nicol, both Scottish gardeners, and Richard F. Allison and Robert F. Wachs, graduates of the University of Kentucky who majored in ornamental horticulture. A Victorian-style office, built in 1890, is listed with the Blue Grass Trust for Historic Preservation. A garden mausoleum was constructed in 1974, a columbarium and crematory in 1978, and a chapel mausoleum in 1982.

Among the notable figures buried in the cemetery are Henry Clay, John C. Breckinridge, James Lane Allen, John Hunt Morgan, W.C.P. Breckinridge, James Morrison, Mary Desha, Mary Breckinridge, and Adolph Rupp.

See Burton Milward, *A History of the Lexington Cemetery* (Lexington, Ky., 1989).

ROBERT F. WACHS

LEXINGTON HERALD-LEADER. The *Lexington Herald-Leader* traces its origins to October 1870, when the *Lexington Daily Press* was begun by Col. Hart Foster and Maj. Henry T. Duncan. Disputes over Reconstruction in the defeated South were still raging; the newspaper's sympathies were with the South. In January 1895 the *Press* was consolidated with the *Lexington Transcript*, and the combined paper was later called the *Morning Herald*. In 1905 it became the *Lexington Herald*. In 1897 the newspaper came under the editorship of Desha BRECKINRIDGE, who served until his death in 1935. Breckinridge was a progressive who pushed for good roads, rural free delivery, women's suffrage, better prisons, better education, and repeal of the Eighteenth Amendment. He also joined a long fight that prevented Cumberland Falls from becoming the property of an electric power company.

The *Kentucky Leader* was started in May 1888 by a group of prominent Fayette County Republicans, and within two years had a Lexington circulation larger than that of all the other daily newspapers

combined. The newspaper's first editor was Samuel Judson Roberts. The name was changed to the *Daily Leader* in 1895 and to the *Lexington Leader* in 1901.

In August 1937, John G. Stoll, editor and publisher of the *Leader*, bought the *Herald*. Both were then printed at the same plant and had a combined Sunday edition. Their editorial policies were unchanged, as the *Leader* remained Republican, the *Herald* staunchly Democratic.

Thomas UNDERWOOD, who succeeded Breckinridge as editor of the *Herald*, served for twenty-one years. During that time, he was chairman of the Democratic state central executive committee, served twice in the U.S. House of Representatives, and was appointed to the U.S. Senate. He also was chairman of the state Racing Commission for fourteen years. For many years, the paper had a standing offer to give away an entire edition on any day that no Bluegrass-bred horse won a race at any major track. That offer was never tested. Herndon J. EVANS, who became editor in 1956, began expanded coverage of eastern Kentucky.

Knight Newspapers, Inc. (now Knight-Ridder) purchased the Herald-Leader Co. in 1973. In 1980 the newspaper company moved to Main Street and Midland Avenue. Three years later the afternoon *Leader* was merged with the morning *Herald*. John Carroll, the *Herald*'s editor, became editor of the combined newspaper. At the combined paper, editorial resources were greatly increased, more bureaus were established, and investigative and public service reporting was expanded. In 1985 the *Herald-Leader*'s coverage of improper payoffs to University of Kentucky basketball players won the Pulitzer Prize for investigative reporting. The *Herald-Leader* in 1990 was the state's second largest newspaper, with a daily circulation of more than 120,000 and Sunday circulation of more than 150,000. The *Herald-Leader* is the dominant newspaper in much of central and eastern Kentucky and is the only paper linking all the state's Appalachian counties.

See John D. Wright, Jr., *Lexington: Heart of the Bluegrass* (Lexington, Ky., 1982).   ANDY MEAD

LEXINGTON LIGHT INFANTRY. In 1789 the Lexington Light Infantry became the first organized military company in Kentucky, then a part of Virginia. The company was formed to defend against the frequent Indian raids and was first led by Gen. James WILKINSON, a veteran of the Revolutionary War. Nicknamed "Old Infantry," the company under Wilkinson's leadership participated in successful expeditions against the Indians in the Northwest Territory during the years 1789-94. It shared in the defeats of Gens. Josiah Harmar and Arthur St. Clair, and played a part in the campaign of Gen. Anthony Wayne against the Scioto and other Indian tribes.

At the time of statehood, the company was the honor guard at the first inauguration of Gov. Isaac Shelby (1792-96). During peacetime the company was a ceremonial drill unit. The uniform adopted at that time by the company was a blue cloth coat, with cuffs, breast, and collar faced in red and ornamented with bell buttons. The pantaloons were of blue cloth, and the hat was black with a red plume.

The Lexington Light Infantry was one of the first companies to volunteer in the War of 1812 and met with disaster in January 1813 at the Battle of RIVER RAISIN, where half of its members were killed, wounded, or taken prisoner. During the Mexican War (1846-48), the Light Infantry fought bravely at the Battle of Buena Vista. The Lexington Light Infantry was actively engaged in every call for troops in the commonwealth until the Civil War, at which time its members divided according to their beliefs, and the Lexington Light Infantry ceased to exist.

JOHN M. TROWBRIDGE

LEXINGTON THEOLOGICAL SEMINARY.

Known during its first century as the College of the Bible, Lexington Theological Seminary in Kentucky is the oldest ministerial school of the Christian Church (Disciples of Christ). The seminary was founded in 1865 as one of several colleges of KENTUCKY UNIVERSITY. It shared facilities, students, and—from 1912 to 1938—presidents with Transylvania University. During 1865-73 and 1875-1911 Hopkinsville native JOHN W. MCGARVEY dominated the faculty, serving as president from 1895. Educated at Bethany College in West Virginia, McGarvey stressed a detailed knowledge of the Bible. The faculty changed dramatically when theological liberals A.W. Fortune, W.C. Bower, and E.E. Snoddy were hired (1912 to 1914). Opposed by conservative students, alumni, and faculty—especially by McGarvey's heir-apparent, Hall Laurie Calhoun—the liberals emerged the victors from a heresy trial in 1917.

In the 1930s Charles Lynn Pyatt led the seminary toward independence, and in 1936 it began requiring an undergraduate degree for admission. In 1938 it elected its own president, Stephen J. Corey, and was listed as an accredited charter member of the Association of Theological Schools. Under the leadership of presidents Kenneth Blount Bowen (1945-48) and Riley B. Montgomery (1949-64), the school moved to its own campus on South Limestone Street in 1950.

On its 1965 centennial the College of the Bible changed its name to Lexington Theological Seminary. In 1990 the seminary offered master of divinity, master of arts, and doctor of ministry degrees. Still Disciples-related, it draws about a third of its students from other churches and offers an M.A. in religious education for Roman Catholics. The seminary belongs to the ecumenical Theological Education Association of Mid-America and the Applachian Ministries Educational Resources Center. It offers a joint divinity/social work program with the University of Kentucky. The seminary has been international since its beginning and coeducational since 1904. It awarded its first B.D. degree to an African-American student (William Henry White) in 1955.

See Richard M. Pope, *Lexington Theological Seminary: A Brief Narrative* (Lexington, Ky., 1973).   ANTHONY L. DUNNAVANT

LIBERTY. The seat of Casey County, Liberty is located in the eastern section of the Pennyroyal region and on the southern edge of the Knobs. Revolutionary War veterans who received land grants for their military service selected the town name out of patriotic sentiment. For its central location, the town was selected as the county seat on January 1, 1808, and was incorporated in 1830, with a population of 250. At that time, the town included the courthouse and public offices, four churches, eight stores, three taverns, eleven mechanic shops, six lawyers, and four doctors.

The first courthouse, a log structure, was built in 1808. The second courthouse, a brick building, was begun in 1837 and finished in 1844. The present courthouse, an elaborate Victorian-style structure of stone and brick, was completed in 1889. The "Doughboy" statue on the courthouse square was dedicated on November 11, 1935, to commemorate the death of thirty-two Casey Countians in World War I.

On June 1, 1929, Liberty first received continuous electrical service. Since 1945, when Tarter Gate Company was established, there has been a gradual increase in manufacturing. A number of lumber firms, producing handles, furniture squares, and dowels, opened plants in Liberty in the 1960s. Eight manufacturers of farm gates employed more than 350 in 1989. The children's apparel firm Oshkosh B'Gosh came to Liberty in 1985 and in 1989 expanded its facilities to include a screen printing and embroidery division.

The Casey County Apple Festival, held each September, brings thousands of visitors to Liberty. Hunting and fishing contribute to the more than $1 million a year that travelers spend in Liberty and Casey County. Waterfowl and geese, deer, turkey, and quail attract hunters, and the Green River and Goose Creek trout are popular with fishermen. Lake Liberty, an eighty-eight-acre reservoir, also offers fishing.

In 1990 the "world's largest yard sale," held at points on the roadside of U.S. 127 in Kentucky, Tennessee, and Alabama, drew travelers to numerous booths that lined the road through Liberty and the rest of Casey county.

Both Gov. Wallace G. Wilkinson (1987-91) and his wife Martha (Stafford) Wilkinson are natives of Liberty.

A fifth-class city, Liberty had a population of 1,765 in 1970; 2,206 in 1980; and 1,937 in 1990.

See Gladys C. Thomas, *Casey County, Kentucky, A Folk History 1803-1977* (n.p., 1977).

GLADYS C. THOMAS

LIBRARIES. The first major library in Kentucky came about when the board of the newly created Transylvania Seminary near Danville decided on March 4, 1784, to raise money through subscription to bring a donated collection of books across the Alleghenies. They raised the twenty-one pounds thirteen shillings necessary, but within ten years it became clear that more books were needed, and in 1795 the Lexington Library Company was formed. In November 1800, library companies in Danville and Georgetown were combined with that of Lexington by an act of the General Assembly. This trend of consolidation continued and in 1841 a state collection was initiated by the State Historical Society. By 1875 there were seventy-two libraries in Kentucky. Andrew Carnegie gave $85,000 to Covington in 1881 for a public library building, and by 1935 there were twenty-seven Carnegie buildings, including some on university campuses. In 1896 the Kentucky Federation of Women's Clubs began a traveling library project with Berea College that reached into the mountains in the late 1890s.

In 1898 a legislative act allowed first- and second-class cities to establish public libraries. The Kentucky Library Association was established in June 1907 and in 1910 the Kentucky Library Commission was created by the legislature at the request of the Federation of Women's Clubs. Between 1930 and 1935 new libraries opened at several universities; library science courses were offered at the University of Kentucky, three of the state teachers' colleges, the University of Louisville, and Berea and Nazareth colleges; and a full-time school library supervisor was appointed at the Department of Education. A substantial contribution from the Julius Rosenwald Fund established collections for blacks in Kentucky. By 1933 every high school in Kentucky had some type of book service. Packhorse libraries started by the Works Progress Administration in 1937 employed ninety-six women and eleven men. Regionalized service, including public and university libraries, grew in the early 1940s, as did availability of library education courses.

In 1953 the FRIENDS OF KENTUCKY LIBRARIES bought bookmobiles to increase service to rural Kentucky. In 1954 the Library Extension Division became an independent agency, and in 1957 the Library Services Act made the first federal appropriation. This legislation was championed by Congressman Carl Perkins from Knott County. The 1964 renewal of the act set aside construction funds for public libraries, and in 1968 it included funds for cooperative programs among all types of libraries. The Kentucky Library Network was initiated in 1980. Today, automation connects many libraries in the state. During the 1980s libraries became very involved in literacy programs; the KENTUCKY DEPARTMENT FOR LIBRARIES AND ARCHIVES initiated the state Literacy Commission, which became an independent agency in 1987.

JAMES A. NELSON

LICKING RIVER. The Licking River, 320 miles long, rises in Magoffin County, Kentucky, and flows northwest through Morgan, Bath, and Rowan counties and into Menifee County, where it enters the northern part of the Daniel Boone National Forest and forms Cave Run Lake. It continues through Fleming and Nicholas counties, where the Upper Blue Licks and Blue Lick Springs are located, and forms the boundary between Robertson County and Nicholas and Harrison counties. The river flows northwest and divides at Pendleton County into the North and South forks. North Fork flows southeast into Bracken, Robertson, Mason, Lewis, and Fleming counties. The South Fork flows south into Harrison county and in Bourbon County splits to form Hinkston and Stoner creeks. The main branch continues north through Pendleton and flows between Kenton and Campbell counties. It empties into the Ohio River at Covington and Newport.

The origin of the river's name is unclear. Charles Kerr's *History of Kentucky* (1922) states that Licking means "land with springs and meadows." An earlier name, Great Salt Lick Creek, made reference to salt licks along the river. Thomas Walker discovered the river in June of 1750 and named it Frederick's River. Indians called it Nepernine and used it to transport goods for trade and to reach the buffalo and deer on the grasslands of central Kentucky. Early explorers, including Christopher Gist (1751), Simon Kenton (1771), and Thomas Bullitt (1773), used the Licking to explore Kentucky's cane lands and to mount expeditions against the Indians.

The first official survey of the Licking was authorized in 1835 after the establishment of the state Board of Internal Improvements. The board authorized $375,000 to be spent on improvement of the river for navigation because of its importance to the eastern Appalachian and central Bluegrass regions. In the nineteenth century the Licking's principal commercial use was floating timber downstream to Covington and Cincinnati. The Licking is considered navigable for only a short distance above its confluence with the Ohio River. In 1936 Congress approved construction of Falmouth Dam in Pendleton County, which would have enhanced the region's agricultural and mining potential by controlling floods and improving navigation. Although Cave Run Lake was formed by impoundment in 1974 by the U.S. Army Corps of Engineers, Falmouth Dam was placed in the corps's inactive file in 1981 for lack of funding.

See Willard Rouse Jillson, *Filson's Kentucke* (Louisville 1930).

LIEUTENANT GOVERNOR, OFFICE OF. The lieutenant governor of Kentucky, who must have the same qualifications as the governor, is elected for a term of four years. Successive terms are not permitted. The chief constitutional function is to preside over the Senate while the General Assembly is in session and, in the event of a tie, to cast the deciding vote. The office was created in the second constitution (1799), to be filled at the same time that the governor was elected. The first lieutenant governor, Alexander Scott Bullitt, took office in 1800.

Under statutory mandate from the General Assembly, the lieutenant governor also serves on numerous boards and commissions, including the State Property and Buildings Commission, the Commission on Women, the Kentucky Turnpike Authority, the Council on Agriculture, the County Debt Commission, the Port and River Development Authority, the Kentucky Housing Corporation, the Appalachian Development Council, the Southern Growth Policies Board, and the Kentucky Mining Advisory Council.

The lieutenant governor may also act as governor when the governor leaves the state, dies, or cannot serve. Exercising this right in 1935, Lt. Gov. A.B. Chandler waited until Gov. Ruby Laffoon (1931-35) had crossed the state line, then called the legislature into special session to enact a compulsory primary law for election of party candidates. After it did so, Chandler in 1935 was elected the Democratic party nominee. Lt. Gov. Thelma Stovall called a special session in 1978 to reduce taxes.

Since 1956 the Old Governor's Mansion in Frankfort has been the official residence of the lieutenant governor. Under the 1890 constitution, the governor and lieutenant governor are not elected as a team and may be members of different parties. On occasion, there has been discussion of abolishing the position, which has been used as a steppingstone to the governorship.

See Frederick A. Wallis and Hambleton Tapp, *A Sesqui-Centennial History of Kentucky* (Hopkinsville, Ky., 1945).   JOHN S. GILLIG

LILLEY CORNETT WOODS. Lilley Cornett Woods, the largest protected tract of old-growth forest in eastern Kentucky, is located in Letcher County, southeast of Hazard and southwest of Whitesburg, about twenty-five miles from each town. Lilley Cornett Woods is one of the few remaining old-growth forests in the entire Appalachian Plateau region. The total area is 554 acres; the old-growth portion is 252 acres. The woods is nationally recognized as a unique representative of presettlement forests of the southern Appalachians, having significant biological diversity, large old trees, and an absence of human disturbance. It is a registered national natural landmark (U.S. Department of Interior), a registered natural area (Society of American Foresters), and a state wildlife refuge.

Lilley Cornett owned the entire tract by the time of his death in 1958. In 1969 his heirs sold the property to the state. Kentucky River Coal Company and Virginia Iron, Coal and Coke Company ceded their surface mining rights within the boundaries of the forest. From 1969 to 1977 Lilley Cornett Woods was managed by the Kentucky Division of Forestry. In 1977 it was transferred to Eastern Kentucky University in Richmond; the university's Division of Natural Areas has stewardship responsibilities.

Lilley Cornett Woods is open to the public and educational groups only by guided tours. Long-term

scientific investigations are being conducted to monitor the environment and to study native plants, animals, and the old-growth forest.

See William H. Martin, "The Lilley Cornett Woods: A Stable Mixed Mesophytic Forest in Kentucky," *Botanical Gazette* 136 (1975): 171-83.
                                            WILLIAM H. MARTIN

LINCOLN, ABRAHAM. Abraham Lincoln, the sixteenth president of the United States, was born to Thomas and Nancy (Hanks) Lincoln on February 12, 1809, near Hodgenville, Kentucky, on the south fork of the Nolin River. His earliest recollections were of the nearby Knob Creek farm where his family moved in 1811. Like several generations of Lincolns and Hankses before them, young Abe and his parents and his older sister, Sarah, kept moving west, first to Indiana and then to Illinois. The Lincolns left Kentucky for Indiana in 1816 when Abe was seven years old. He later recalled that his father decided to cross the Ohio River partly because Kentuckians were slaveholders and partly as a result of his difficulty in securing land titles in Kentucky.

Kentucky continued to play an important role in Lincoln's life, however. His wife, his law partners, and his closest friend, Joshua SPEED, were all from Kentucky, and his political mentor was Henry Clay. As president (1861-65), Lincoln often noted how essential Kentucky and her Ohio River border were to Union victory during the Civil War. On occasion he visited the state to spend time with his inlaws in Lexington and at the Speed estate, Farmington, outside Louisville.

In 1837 Lincoln settled in Springfield, Illinois, to practice law. There he met Mary Todd from Lexington, and they married in 1842. Their four sons—Robert, Edward, William, and Thomas—were born in Springfield between 1843 and 1853. Only Robert survived to maturity.

Even while Lincoln was alive, it was difficult to uncover details about his past, and after he was assassinated his image became distorted by myths. There is little doubt, however, that he stood six feet, four inches tall and weighed about 180 pounds. There is ample evidence that he possessed a rare western style of humor. Although his formal schooling lasted only a year, he gained—mostly by reading—an unusual facility in the English language. An introspective, moody man, he often used his skill as a storyteller to advantage. As he traveled the Illinois legal circuit, he also developed a political ability that later confounded his opponents.

A loyal Whig, Lincoln gained a statewide reputation as an Illinois legislator. In 1846 he was elected to a term in the U.S. House of Representatives, serving from March 4, 1847, to March 3, 1849, but his opposition to the Mexican War proved so unpopular that he was not nominated for a second term. Believing that he had no political future, he returned to full-time law practice and became, for the first time, financially independent. When

Lincoln denounced the Kansas-Nebraska Act (1854) and the possibility of slavery's extension into the territories, his stand drew him into the national arena again. He reluctantly left the dying Whig party to join the new Republican party in 1856. When he ran for the U.S. Senate in 1858 against Stephen A. Douglas, their debates on slavery catapulted Lincoln to national recognition. He lost the Senate election, but the Republicans nominated him for the presidency in 1860.

Lincoln defeated Douglas as well as two other candidates and was inaugurated as president of the United States on March 4, 1861. Seven southern states had already seceded and four others soon followed. The Civil War began the following month, and Lincoln's struggle to save the Union dominated his entire presidency. As the conflict deepened, Lincoln resorted to martial law, conscription, emancipation, and a scorched-earth policy. He turned his hard-won political skills to handling his cabinet and generals and winning reelection in 1864. His second inaugural address and his Gettysburg address are his most notable speeches.

As a war president, Lincoln overcame many obstacles. He was an outsider who offended professional politicians with his informal western manners. Union setbacks early in the war convinced many Republicans in Congress that Lincoln was a poor leader. The Radical Republicans, especially critical, pressured Lincoln to make emancipation of slaves a war goal long before he was ready to do so. They charged Lincoln with favoring the conservative wing of the party, whereas conservatives complained that Lincoln was too much influenced by the Radicals. In fact, Lincoln skillfully kept lines of communication open with both wings of the party. He wisely picked some of his most vocal critics, like Salmon P. Chase, to serve in his cabinet. Lincoln is most often remembered for his humanitarianism, but many historians contend that his political shrewdness was more impressive.

Although he had little military experience, Lincoln also distinguished himself as commander in chief of the army and navy. He made plenty of mistakes, but he nevertheless developed a keen insight into strategy, urging his generals to put constant pressure on the Confederacy's defensive line until they could find a weak spot. He recognized early that he had numbers and resources on his side, and took full advantage of them. He had trouble dealing with some of his generals, but eventually he found Ulysses S. Grant to attack the Confederate forces with relentless determination until Confederate Gen. Robert E. Lee surrendered at Appomattox, Virginia, on April 9, 1865.

Lincoln's plan for Reconstruction favored the prompt restoration of Southern states to the Union, but he lived only a short time after Lee's surrender. He was shot while attending Ford's Theatre in Washington and died the following day, Good Friday, April 15, 1865. A funeral railroad car carried his body slowly back by the same route he had followed on his way to Washington four years earlier. He is buried in the Oak Ridge Cemetery in Springfield, Illinois.

See David Donald, *Lincoln Reconsidered* (New York 1956); Mark E. Neely, Jr., *The Abraham Lincoln Encyclopedia* (New York 1982).

HELEN B. CROCKER

LINCOLN, MARY (TODD). Born in Lexington, Kentucky, on December 13, 1818, Mary (Todd) Lincoln, first lady of the United States, was descended from two of central Kentucky's best-known families—the Todds and the Parkers. Her grandfather, Levi Todd, had been instrumental in the establishment of Lexington. Her father, Robert Smith Todd, was a prosperous cotton merchant, businessman, and Whig politician. Her mother, Eliza (Parker) Todd, died in childbirth when Mary Todd was six. Shortly thereafter her father married Elizabeth Humphreys, of Frankfort, Kentucky. Mary lived with them and their children in a brick house on West Main Street in Lexington. As a girl Mary attended John Ward's school in Lexington and then Charlotte Mentelle's boarding school, across from Henry Clay's estate, Ashland. Her twelve years in school made her one of the best-educated women of her era.

In 1839 Mary Todd followed her older sisters to Springfield, Illinois, where she lived in her sister Elizabeth Edwards's home. In November 1842 she married Abraham Lincoln, then a lawyer who had three times won election to the state legislature. They had four sons, Robert Todd, Edward, William, and Thomas (Tad). Mary Lincoln lived the typical domestic life of a nineteenth century middle-class woman, though she maintained an unusual interest in politics and in her husband's career as a politician. Her great expectations for her husband were realized when, after two unsuccessful campaigns for the U.S. Senate, he was elected president of the United States in November 1860.

During Mary Lincoln's four years in the White House (1861-65) she worked hard to turn it into a fashionable mansion worthy of her husband, herself, and the nation. But the Civil War made these efforts seem frivolous. Throughout the war she was often attacked in the newspapers for her extravagance and for her supposed Confederate allegiance, especially after it was reported that three of her Kentucky half-brothers were fighting with the Confederate army. In 1863 she took in her beloved half-sister, Emilie (Todd) Helm, widow of Confederate Gen. Benjamin Hardin Helm, who had been killed at Chickamauga. At the White House, Emilie's presence reinforced the suspicion that Mary Lincoln was a Confederate sympathizer. In fact the first lady (she was the first to be called that) was a staunch Unionist who, like many other women during the war, visited hospitals to comfort the wounded and raised money for the war effort. After the death of her son Willie in 1862, a distraught

Mary Lincoln often sought comfort among spiritualists, who she believed could return her two dead sons to her in seances.

On April 14, 1865, five days after Lee surrendered, President Lincoln was assassinated. As a widow Mary Lincoln struggled financially. Though she eventually received $36,000 from her husband's estate, she fought for a pension. Increasingly restless, she traveled with Tad to Europe. In 1871 she received another devastating blow when Tad died of pleurisy. In 1875 her only surviving son, Robert, committed her to a private asylum for the insane, but she struggled for freedom and after three months was released. Fearing that Robert would continue to threaten her for behavior that was bizarre but not deranged, Mary Lincoln lived in Pau, France, from 1878 to 1882. Only when her health made it necessary did she return to her sister's home in Springfield, Illinois. There she died on July 16, 1882, and was buried in the Oak Ridge Cemetery in Springfield.

See Jean H. Baker, *Mary Todd Lincoln: A Biography* (New York 1987); Ruth Painter Randall, *Mary Lincoln: Biography of a Marriage* (Boston 1953).   JEAN H. BAKER

LINCOLN COUNTY. Lincoln County is one of three counties created by Virginia in 1780. As settlements in Kentucky County of Virginia became increasingly numerous during the late 1770s, the need for seats of government within the vast territory led to the formation of Jefferson, Lincoln, and Fayette counties to replace Kentucky County. The law creating these counties was enacted by the Virginia General Assembly on June 30, 1780, and became effective November 1, 1780. Lincoln County was named for Gen. Benjamin Lincoln, a military commander in the Revolutionary War who was a prisoner of war in British hands when the county was formed.

Two more counties, Mercer and Madison, were formed by Virginia in 1786 from parts of Lincoln County. After Kentucky became a state in 1792, the Kentucky legislature continued to subdivide Lincoln County into smaller counties. Lincoln County assumed its present boundary in February 1843. The county is bordered by Boyle, Garrard, and Rockcastle counties, and has an area of 337 square miles. The first county court session for Lincoln County was held at Fort Harrod (now Harrodsburg) in January 1781. The county seat was moved to Fort Logan (now STANFORD) in 1787.

Lincoln County is divided into three distinct topographical areas. The northern half of the county, lying within the southern edge of the Bluegrass region, is known for its excellent farmland and is drained by the Dix River and its smaller tributaries. This area was a prime hunting territory for prehistoric Native Americans, as witnessed by a few scattered Indian mounds and the small artifacts that occasionally turn up in the soil. Stretched from west to east across Lincoln County is the Knobs region of Kentucky; its hills range from one to two hundred feet in height and are mostly covered in woodland, which supported a lumbering industry throughout the middle to late 1800s. The rest of the county lies in the Pennyroyal region, dominated by broad plateau-like areas and ridges separated by deep fertile valleys and streams.

Throughout its history, Lincoln County's economy has been primarily agricultural. Gristmills and steam mills were common in the middle to late 1800s for grinding meal and producing woolens. The fertile land in the Dick's (now Dix) River valley drew the earliest pioneers. Among the first settlements established within the county's present boundary were Isaac Shelby's Knob Lick Station, Logan's Fort (Stanford), Montgomery's Station, Pettit's Station, Spear's Station, McCormack's Station, McKinney's Station, Whitley's Station, Owsley's Station, Barnett's Station, Briggs Station, and Helm's Station. Through the nineteenth century, towns and villages emerged at the major crossroads in the county. The towns included Stanford, Hustonville, Crab Orchard, and Waynesburg. The smaller villages included McKinney, Kings Mountain, Preachersville, Walnut Flat, Milledgeville, Turnersville, Hubble, Turkeytown, Broughtontown, and Dog Walk.

The first railroad built through Lincoln County was the Louisville & Nashville (now CSX Transportation), which entered the county near Knob Lick Creek and passed through Stanford and Crab Orchard. Between 1860 and 1920, thousands of visitors to the Crab Orchard Springs resort patronized this railroad. Passenger service ended in the 1940s. The Cincinnati & Southern Railroad (now Norfolk Southern) was built through Lincoln County in the late 1870s; this railroad became the major north-south line through central Kentucky.

During the Civil War, sympathies in Lincoln County were fairly evenly split between the Union and the Confederacy. The northern half of the county, having many slaveholders, was sympathetic to the Confederates; the south end of the county was strongly Unionist. Three black communities in Lincoln County developed in the post–Civil War era: Bonneyville, Chicken Bristle, and Logantown. During the 1880s and 1890s, the Lincoln Land Company, a private enterprise, encouraged the development of a German-Swiss community, Ottenheim, in south-central Lincoln County. The German, Austrian, and Swiss immigrants were sold rough knobs land, which they quickly turned into some of the best farmland in the county.

In the 1820s, the Restoration movement of Barton STONE and Alexander CAMPBELL was a strong influence in Lincoln County. McCormack's Meetinghouse, initially a mixed congregation of Baptists and Presbyterians, became a member of the Disciples of Christ denomination in 1829 and later a member of the Christian Church denomination. McCormack's Meetinghouse, a brick structure built in 1819-20, is the oldest church building standing in

Lincoln County. Catholicism had no major impact in Lincoln County until the 1880s, when the German and Swiss settlements at Ottenheim and Blue Lick were developed.

The county's best secondary education facility was the Christian Church College at Hustonville, established in the 1850s by a joint effort of the Hanging Fork Presbyterian Church and the Hustonville Christian Church. It was a college preparatory institution and like the old Hanging Fork Presbyterian Parochial School it replaced, it had close ties with CENTRE College at Danville.

The streams of Lincoln County and the Indian and buffalo trails were the first pathways into central Kentucky. A western extension of the Wilderness Road passed from the Hazel Patch to Fort Logan (Stanford) and on to Harrodsburg. (U.S. 150 roughly follows the original Wilderness Road through the county.) Another old trail left Fort Logan and went southwest to near Turnersville, where one fork went south to the Green River settlements and the other went west to the Carpenter's Station area. (KY 78 parallels this trace.) By the late 1860s most of the major county roads were maintained as private turnpikes that travelers paid a fee to use. A few tollgate houses still stand in the county.

Among the influential residents of Lincoln County, Isaac Shelby, Kentucky's first governor (1792-96, 1812-16), settled on Knob Lick Creek in 1779 and called his home Travelers Rest (now a state shrine). It became the center of a vast farming enterprise. Benjamin LOGAN'S FORT, established in 1775, was one of few in Kentucky that did not fall to the Indian attacks of 1777. William Whitley located in the county and built Sportsman's Hill, one of the first brick houses in Kentucky. His home is preserved as a state shrine on U.S. 150 near Crab Orchard and is an excellent example of Kentucky frontier architecture.

The county's population was 16,663 in 1970; 19,053 in 1980; and 20,045 in 1990.

See Sylvia Wrobel and George Grider, *Isaac Shelby: Kentucky's First Governor and Hero Of Three Wars* (Danville, Ky., 1974); Mrs. M.H. Dunn, *Early Lincoln County History 1780-1975* (Stanford, Ky., 1975).   ALLAN R. LEACH

LINCOLN INSTITUTE. The Lincoln Institute, an educational facility for blacks, opened on October 1, 1912. Its founding was a direct result of the 1904 DAY LAW, which prohibited the instruction of black and white students together and was aimed specifically at Berea College, which had been integrated since 1866. Forced to segregate and dependent on funds designated for educating black students, the Berea board of trustees began a fund drive to establish an institution for black men and women. A total of $400,000 was raised in state and national pledges, including a donation from industrialist Andrew Carnegie.

Located twenty-one miles east of Louisville on 444 acres in Shelby County, Lincoln Institute offered a teachers' training program past the eighth

grade, as well as vocational education. In 1922 all graduates of the six-year normal courses were automatically certified as high school teachers. In the Great Depression of the 1930s, the school was able to remain open, thanks in part to the financial assistance of William Henry Hughes, a wealthy Lexington black who bequeathed the institute a $10,000 grant and a trust fund of $100,000 for yearly scholarships. Lincoln Institute received no state funding until the 1940s. In 1947 the grounds and buildings were deeded to Kentucky and the institute became a public high school. The 1954 decision of the U.S. Supreme Court in *Brown v. Board of Education* reduced the school's enrollment, and the last class graduated in 1966.

Lincoln Institute was served by five presidents: the Rev. A. Eugene Thomas, 1911-27; the Rev. B.E. Robinson, 1927-31; Randy B. Truett, 1931-34; William Benhower, 1934-35; and Whitney M. YOUNG, Sr., 1935-66.

See George C. Wright, "The Founding of Lincoln Institute," *FCHQ* 49 (Jan. 1975): 57-70.

LINDSAY, WILLIAM. William Lindsay, legislator and jurist, was born in Rockbridge County, Virginia, on September 4, 1835, to Andrew and Sallie Gilmore (Davidson) Lindsay. He attended school in Lexington, Virginia. In 1854 he moved to Clinton, Kentucky, to teach school and to read law with Judge Edward Crossland. Lindsay was admitted to the Kentucky bar in 1860 and set up a private practice in Clinton. In May 1861 Lindsay enlisted as a private in the Confederate army, rising to captain of Company B, 22d Tennessee Infantry, on February 23, 1862. Lindsay was subsequently transferred to the 7th Kentucky Infantry, where he became assistant quartermaster. After being paroled as a prisoner of war on May 16, 1865, at Columbus, Mississippi, Lindsay returned to Clinton and resumed practicing law.

He served as a Democrat in the state Senate for one term, beginning in 1867. He was judge of the Kentucky court of appeals from 1870 until 1878 and was chief justice between 1876 and 1878. Lindsay retired from the bench in 1878 and moved to Frankfort to set up a law practice. Between 1889 and 1893 he again served in the state Senate. When John G. Carlisle resigned from the U.S. Senate, the General Assembly elected Lindsay to fill the vacancy by a count of 79 to 17 over Augustus E. Willson, and Lindsay took office on February 15, 1893. Lindsay was reelected on January 17, 1894.

During the presidential campaign of 1896, Lindsay aligned with the so-called sound-money Democrats, thereby alienating himself from the majority of the Democratic party, and on January 27, 1898, the Kentucky legislature passed a resolution requesting Lindsay's resignation from the Senate. Lindsay served until the end of his term on March 3, 1901, but was not a candidate for reelection in 1900. He moved to New York City to join the law firm of Lindsay, Kremer, Kalish and Palmer, where he practiced until 1907, when he returned to Frankfort. Lindsay also served as a U.S. commissioner-at-large to the World's Columbian Exposition in Chicago in 1893, as regent of the Smithsonian Institution, and as trustee of the Carnegie Institution.

Lindsay was married to Swann Semple in 1864. She died in June 1867, leaving one daughter, Marion Semple. In October 1868 Lindsay married Harriet Semple, his sister-in-law, who died in 1879. He married Eleanor Holmes of Union County in 1883. After a long illness, Lindsay died at his home in Frankfort on October 15, 1909, and was buried in the Frankfort Cemetery.

See Leonard Schlup, "William Lindsay and the 1896 Party Crisis," *Register* 76 (Jan. 1978): 22-33.

LINDSEY WILSON COLLEGE. Lindsey Wilson College was established in Columbia, Kentucky, in 1903 by the Louisville Conference of the United Methodist Episcopal Church, South. Its name, originally Lindsey Wilson Training School, commemorated the deceased nephew and stepson of Mrs. Catherine Wilson of Louisville, who donated $6,000 to help found the school. Its original purpose was to prepare the young people of south-central Kentucky for Vanderbilt University in Nashville, while also offering a primary school program and a normal course curriculum for state teacher certification. The first principal was F.E. Lewis, who served from January to June of 1903. In 1923 the curriculum was expanded to meet more stringent state teacher certification standards, a two-year liberal arts program was added, and the school was renamed Lindsey Wilson College. R.V. Bennett, the training school's principal from 1918 to 1923, assumed the new office of president. In 1951 Lindsey Wilson College was accredited by the Southern Association of Colleges and Secondary Schools, and on December 16, 1986, the association gave it the right to grant the baccalaureate degree.

LINNEY, WILLIAM MARCUS. William Marcus Linney, geologist, was born on January 1, 1835, in Lawrenceburg, Kentucky, to William Henderson and Jane (Verbryke) Linney. He was a self-educated cobbler when he married Elizabeth Marrs on December 11, 1856, in Campbellsville, where he was employed by her father. They had eight children. Linney independently studied geology and botany, and by 1871 he was teaching at Harmonia College in Perryville. In 1875 he attended Harvard's summer school in geology, the first in the nation, held at Cumberland Gap under the direction of Nathaniel S. Shaler. In 1878 Linney moved to Harrodsburg and taught science at Daughters College. During 1880-87, the Kentucky Geological Survey published several of his county geological and botanical reports. Linney was the last amateur geologist to make a significant contribution to the state geological survey. His experience as a geologist was extensive. During his second trip to the Colorado mining field, he became ill, and he died on Sep-

tember 22, 1887. He was buried in Springhill Cemetery in Harrodsburg.

See Grace Linney Hutton, "William Marcus Linney," *Register* 19 (Jan. 1921): 25-28.

IVAN L. ZABILKA

LIPSCOMB, WILLIAM NUNN, JR. William Nunn Lipscomb, Jr., physical chemist, was born December 9, 1919, in Cleveland to William N. and Edna Patterson (Porter) Lipscomb. In the early 1920s the family moved to Lexington, where his father was a faculty member at the University of Kentucky (1922-26), serving as resident physician, head of the department of physical education, and associate professor of hygiene and public health. Lipscomb attended Sayre Elementary and Picadome High School, both in Lexington. In 1937 he entered the University of Kentucky, where he received a bachelor of science degree in 1941. In 1946 he received a Ph.D. in chemistry from the California Institute of Technology, Pasadena, and then joined the department of chemistry at the University of Minnesota (1946-59). He was professor of chemistry at Harvard University during 1959-71, was chairman of that department during 1962-65, and became Abott and James Professor there in 1971.

In 1976 Lipscomb won the Nobel prize in chemistry for his work with the element boron. He had provided the majority of experimental data on boron compounds, including the study of the molecular structure of the combined gases boron and hydrogen. He wrote *The Boron Hydrides* (1963). In 1976 Lipscomb's work received practical application in Japan as doctors used irradiated boron in the experimental treatment of brain tumors. His honors include the Harrison Howe Award in chemistry in 1958 and the Distinguished Alumni Centennial Award of the University of Kentucky in 1965.

Lipscomb married Mary Adele Sargent on May 20, 1944. They have two children: Dorothy Jean and James Sargent.

LITERACY PROGRAMS. Encouraged by her success with the moonlight schools in Rowan County, Cora Wilson STEWART in 1913 asked Kentucky Gov. James B. McCreary to create a state commission to free illiterate men and women "from this bondage" and place Kentucky "in a better light before the world." Governor McCreary responded by return mail with a thorough endorsement of her plan.

The governor subsequently secured the unanimous vote of both branches of the General Assembly in favor of a bill creating the Kentucky Illiteracy Commission (KIC). Besides Stewart, the first members were J.G. Crabbe, president of Eastern Kentucky State Normal School; H.H. Cherry, president of Western Kentucky State Normal School; and Ella Lewis, superintendent of Grayson County schools. The state superintendent of public instruction served in an ex-officio capacity. No money was appropriated for the commission's work and cynics uniformly predicted that it would fail miserably. The commission's first task was to secure financial support for its program, along with volunteers to teach the state's estimated 208,804 illiterates.

Soon KIC representatives were teaching 30,000 illiterate Kentuckians who were preparing to serve in World War I. Letters and literacy took on an urgent new meaning for young men who would soon be sent overseas. In spite of a vigorous statewide effort to teach Kentucky's soon-to-be soldiers, as late as 1917 some of the men arrested for failure to register for the draft claimed that they did not even know that America was at war. During the war years, the KIC conducted moonlight schools for the wives, sisters, mothers, and sweethearts of Kentucky's fighting men.

When the war was over, many returning soldiers enthusiastically supported the work of the KIC. Sgt. Willie Sadlin, an eastern Kentuckian whose courageous exploits were second only to those of fellow mountaineer Alvin York, aided Cora Stewart's promotional efforts. The KIC helped many soldiers readjust to civilian life. For example, on September 30, 1919, Ira Cundiff of Elizabethtown wrote that during his sixteen months in France, he "could not write home," but that on his return he had learned to read and write in a local moonlight school taught by Mildred Smith.

Gov. James D. Black (1919) publicly praised the KIC's efforts to promote literacy and to help former soldiers adjust to civilian life. In the postwar years, the state appropriated a modest amount of money ($75,000 in 1918) to cover travel expenses to educate the state's adults within the context of the major social, political, and economic issues of the day. In a week-long institute held annually in Frankfort, county agents gathered at the state's expense to discuss specific methodologies for teaching adult illiterates.

A new dimension to the crusade against illiteracy in Kentucky extended the program to the state penal institutions. In 1919 literacy became a condition of parole, an additional incentive to the learning efforts of state prisoners. According to the warden's report in 1919, 2,700 prisoners had been "redeemed from illiteracy" during 1912-19. The commission also expanded its efforts by taking a census of the remaining illiterates in the state, thus charting a course for future action.

As Americans moved into the 1920s, they adopted new heroes and embraced new ideologies. Many states launched adult education programs patterned after the programs of the Kentucky Illiteracy Commission. As Kentucky's literacy movement grew, it received support and encouragement from the National Education Association and other national organizations. By 1920 the campaign against illiteracy had blossomed into a national crusade. After 1920, the social and political climate of Kentucky changed, however, and the General Assembly did not fund the Kentucky Illiteracy Commission again.

The launching of Sputnik by the Soviet Union in 1957 focused American attention on education and the workforce. Federal initiatives for education were enacted, and funds for literacy training and adult education flowed. Kentucky used federal funds to establish its General Educational Development (GED) program in 1960. Locally, voluntary literacy activities multiplied to the point of confusion. To tie local activities together, superintendent of public instruction Raymond Barber and Kentucky Library and Archives director James Nelson organized the Kentucky Coalition for Literacy in 1983. A $70,000 federal library grant funded its operation for one year.

In 1985 Gov. Martha Layne Collins (1983-87) created the Kentucky Literacy Commission and directed it to develop a statewide effort against illiteracy. In 1985 the commission received its first state funds, with which it awarded grants to local literacy commissions being formed to educate adults. The General Assembly made the commission permanent in 1988.

Stung by its position as the least-educated state in the nation, Kentucky began actively promoting adult education and literacy training. In 1979 the Jefferson County adult reading program developed literacy training models now in use throughout the country. Sharon Darling, who developed and directed that program, also helped develop Kentucky's award-winning parent and child education program, in which undereducated adults attend school along with their preschool children. The Kenan Trust funded the literacy campaign in Kentucky and other southern states. With the support of Martha Wilkinson, wife of Gov. Wallace Wilkinson, Kentucky has the most active GED program in the nation. Approximately 125,000 GED certificates were awarded to formerly illiterate or undereducated adults during the 1980s.

See Wilson Somerville, ed., *Appalachia/America* (Johnson City, Tenn., 1981).

JAMES M. GIFFORD AND
ANNE ARMSTRONG THOMPSON

LITERATURE. The first acknowledged Kentucky literary work, *The Kentucky Miscellany* by Thomas Johnson, Jr., appeared in print in 1789. From that year to the present, Kentucky's literary figures have produced hundreds of novels, plays, and collections of poems, essays, and literary criticism.

The landmark work of the frontier period is Gilbert IMLAY's *The Emigrants, or the History of an Expatriated Family* (1793), a novel in the epistolary form common to that era and of historical interest not for its literary quality but also for its advocacy of women's rights well before women had a significant voice in American society. As in coastal areas of the new nation, postfrontier literature in Kentucky began with poetry. William Orlando Butler, born in Nicholasville and a veteran of the War of 1812, gave the state its first popular poem, "The Boatman's Horn," in 1821. Theodore

O'Hara, a veteran of the Mexican War, wrote "Bivouac of the Dead" to commemorate fellow Kentuckians killed in that war; it is fixed in stone at the portal to Arlington National Cemetery.

Kentucky writers produced works of historical fiction in the antebellum period. Noteworthy is Robert Montgomery BIRD's *Nick of the Woods: or, the Jibbenainosey: A Tale of Kentucky* (1837), which depicts Indian warfare in the late eighteenth century. It was the life of the pre–Civil War era, especially in the Bluegrass region, however, that attracted most writers. Antebellum author Mary Jane HOLMES focused on this subject, most popularly in *Tempest and Sunshine; or, Life in Kentucky* (1854), the story of two sisters in Woodford County. Born near Lexington, William Wells BROWN, America's first black novelist, focused on the darker side of that society. His best-known work is *Clotel; or, the President's Daughter: A Narrative of Slave Life in the United States* (1853).

The life of the Bluegrass gentry later became the province of James Lane ALLEN and other Kentucky authors whom literary critics include in a national school known as the genteel tradition. Allen, born in 1849 near Lexington, was an outstanding Kentucky writer in this tradition, although his themes range wider than the classification suggests. Although no longer widely read, Allen was in his lifetime regarded by some critics as America's greatest novelist. Another school that Allen is associated with, the local colorists, made a major contribution to Kentucky literature in the thirty years leading up to World War I. Allen's regional focus is the Bluegrass. John Fox, Jr., probably the best known of the Kentucky local colorists, set his novels in the southeastern mountain region. He contrasts the people of this region with those of the Bluegrass. Alice Hegan RICE, known for *Mrs. Wiggs of the Cabbage Patch* (1901), set her stories in Louisville. Irvin S. COBB's "Judge Priest" stories concern Paducah and the Jackson Purchase, and John Uri LLOYD wrote of northern Kentucky in his "Stringtown" stories.

Contemporaneous with the local color movement was a renaissance of POETRY by Kentuckians, some of whom won significant critical acclaim. Most prominent nationally of these was Madison CAWEIN. His work, mostly nature poems containing numerous allusions to classical mythology, won high praise both in the United States and in England, but Cawein subsequently fell into obscurity. The same fate befell Robert Burns WILSON, who also had a national reputation at the time. Joseph Seamon COTTER, born in Nelson County, was Kentucky's first black poet of consequence. Israel Jacob SCHWARTZ, originally from Lithuania, lived in Lexington and produced the epic poem *Kentucky*, one of the the nation's first works of Yiddish literature. James T. Cotton NOE also achieved some fame as the commonwealth's first poet laureate by virtue of his "Tip Sams" poems. In the same time period, Kentuckians made their first successful venture into theater with plays such as Charles T. Dazey's *In Old Kentucky* (1892) and Ann Crawford Flexner's adaptation of *Mrs. Wiggs of the Cabbage Patch*.

The late nineteenth century Kentucky authors made numerous contributions to juvenile fiction. Most memorable of these children's authors was Annie Fellows JOHNSTON. A native Hoosier, she set her best-selling "Little Colonel" stories in Pewee Valley, Oldham County. Other contributions to the children's literature of the period came from Mrs. George Madden Martin, Joseph ALTSHELER, and Maria Thompson Daviess. These writers and numerous others helped to pave the way for Kentucky authors who have made outstanding contributions to American fiction, poetry, drama, and criticism, beginning in the 1920s. One of the first important fiction writers was Elizabeth Madox Roberts. Though she began her literary career as a poet, it was when she turned to the novel that she found her medium. Her classic novels, *The Time of Man* (1926) and *The Great Meadow* (1930), both focus on Kentucky—the former on tenant farming and its hardships, the latter, a major work of historical fiction, on the frontier in the Revolutionary War era.

Fiction written by Kentuckians in the modern era attained international significance in the works of Robert Penn WARREN, a giant among the state's authors, who achieved major stature not only in fiction but also in criticism and especially in poetry. Two of Warren's near contemporaries also attained renown in more than one genre. Novelist, short story writer, and critic Caroline GORDON set her most popular work of fiction, *Aleck Maury, Sportsman* (1934), in her home area of Todd County. Gordon's husband, Allen TATE, became, like Warren, a member of the Agrarian movement, which he touted in his works of criticism and his novel *The Fathers* (1938). Tate also gained recognition as a poet. Warren, Gordon, and Tate, along with Cleanth BROOKS helped to foster New Criticism, the major school of literary criticism of their time, which was initiated by John Crowe Ransom, who taught both Warren and Tate at Vanderbilt University in Nashville.

Among authors of the modern era who focus on the life of eastern Kentuckians, the most prominent nationally is Harriette (Simpson) ARNOW. Her major work, *The Dollmaker* (1954), adds a new dimension to the portrait of eastern Kentuckians, seen when cut off from their roots in a Detroit ghetto. By contrast, in the works of James STILL, not as well known as Arnow, eastern Kentuckians persist in their native setting, as in Still's best known novel, *River of Earth* (1940), which focuses on the life of a coal-mining family.

Probably the most popular Kentucky writer of this generation was the prolific Jesse STUART. His works, though nearly always set in his birthplace of W-Hollow, go well beyond the limited intent of his local color predecessors. He wrote a few classic short stories; several popular novels, including *Taps* for Private Tussie (1943); and a large body of poems reminiscent of Walt Whitman. The tradition of historical fiction was well maintained in the modern period by numerous writers, probably most successfully by a team of collaborators—Isabel McMeekin and Dorothy Park Clark—who adopted the pen name Clark McMEEKIN. Thoroughbred racing was a frequent theme in their works. Their success in historical fiction was complemented by that of Janice Holt GILES, who, like Clark, was a transplant from another state.

Three natives of Louisville have made a notable Kentucky contribution to American theater. John Mason BROWN became one of the best-known drama critics in the nation. John Patrick attained an international reputation with his *Teahouse of the August Moon* (1953), winner of the Pulitzer Prize. Marsha NORMAN repeated Patrick's achievement when her *'night Mother* won the Pulitzer Prize in 1983. The works of these two dramatists surpass those of their Kentucky predecessors.

The earlier strength in children's literature continues through several award-winning writers. Rebecca CAUDILL's *House of the Fifers* (1954) won the Nancy Bloch Award, and her *Tree of Freedom* (1949) was a runner-up for the Newbery Medal. *John Henry McCoy* (1971) by Lillie D. Chaffin won the Award of the Child Study Association, and two of her earlier books won first prize from the National League of American Pen Women.

Perhaps the dean of Kentucky's contemporary authors, Wendell BERRY follows Warren in three genres—poetry, fiction, and essay. Berry, a legatee of the Agrarians, consistently touts the virtues of traditional farming in such novels as *Nathan Coulter* (1960) and *The Memory of Old Jack* (1974). Three of Berry's contemporaries—James Baker HALL, Gurney NORMAN, and Ed McCLANAHAN—have also garnered acclaim, McClanahan in particular with his well-received *The Natural Man* (1983). Promising writers of a still more recent generation include Gayle Jones and Bobbie Ann MASON, as well as Marsha Norman. Jones's novels have won numerous awards, including the Breadloaf Writers Conference Award. Mason's *Shiloh and Other Stories* (1982) won the Ernest Hemingway Foundation Award and the PEN/Faulkner Award.

Throughout most of its history, Kentucky literature has evoked certain themes native to the area besides those of the Bluegrass gentry and eastern Kentucky. One of these themes is life on the river—most often the Ohio River, as in the books of Ben Lucien Burman.

In *A Literary History of Kentucky* (1988), the definitive study of the state's literature, William S. Ward singles out other prevalent themes he terms "three delectable Kentucky vices"—thoroughbred racing, bourbon whiskey, and tobacco. The single most popular work to use the racing theme is the play *In Old Kentucky* by Charles T. Dazey, an Illinois native. Whiskey plays a role in books by such writers as Irvin Cobb, Buck, and Burman. Perhaps

the most frequently used theme, tobacco, appears in works by Fox, Roberts, Gordon, Stuart, and Warren, whose *Night Rider* (1939) is probably the best fictional treatment of the tobacco wars in Kentucky.

The divergent paths that Kentucky literature has followed run through the works of three modern writers notable for their distinctive voices. Three of the novels of Walter TEVIS, who came to live in Kentucky at the age of ten—*The Hustler* (1959), *The Man Who Fell to Earth* (1963), and *The Color of Money* (1984)—have been made into films. Another adopted Kentuckian, Thomas MERTON, who entered the Trappist monastery at Gethsemani in 1941, produced worthy contributions in autobiography, poetry, and philosophy. From his spiritual autobiography, *The Seven Storey Mountain* (1948), to his last volume of poems, *The Geography of Lograire* (1969), he commanded a national and international audience. Totally different from either of these writers, Hunter S. THOMPSON of Louisville created "gonzo journalism," as exemplified by *Fear and Loathing in Las Vegas: A Savage Journey to the Heart of the American Dream* (1972). Three such disparate authors who share a connection with Kentucky suggest that the state's writers follow a tradition of diversity—and of prolific output.

See Lawrence Thompson and Algernon D. Thompson, *The Kentucky Novel* (Lexington, Ky., 1953); Dorothy Edwards Townsend, *Kentucky in American Letters, 1913-1975* (Georgetown, Ky., 1976); William S. Ward, *A Literary History of Kentucky* (Knoxville, Tenn., 1988). DAVID BURG

LITSEY, EDWIN CARLISLE. Edwin Carlisle Litsey, novelist and poet, was born at Beechland, Kentucky, in Washington County, on June 3, 1874, the son of William Henry and Sarah Elizabeth (Johnston) Litsey. He was educated in the local public and private schools but did not attend college. He was a lifelong employee of the Marion National Bank in Lebanon, Kentucky; he began at age seventeen emptying waste baskets, worked his way up to first teller and was offered the bank's presidency, which he declined. He continued to work at the bank into his nineties.

In 1898, at age twenty-four, Litsey made his debut as an author with a fantasy novel, *The Princess of Gramfalon*. He soon found subjects and settings in his native south-central Kentucky, particularly the counties of Marion, Washington, and Nelson. *The Love Story of Abner Stone* (1902), the tragic tale of a middle-aged bachelor's doomed love for a girl who dies of typhoid fever, won popular acclaim and went into three editions. In 1904 his story, "In the Court of God," won first place over 10,000 other entries in *The Black Cat* short story contest. In 1905 he published *The Race of the Swift*, a series of seven animal stories similar in style to those of Jack London. In *The Man from Jericho* (1911), he made use of local subjects such as horse racing, fox hunting, and chicken fighting. *Grist* (1927) has a setting similar to the Trappist monastery at Gethsemani, Kentucky. Perhaps Litsey's most successful novel is *Stones for Bread* (1940), a story of two lonely brothers.

Most of his poems and stories, with their large doses of sentimentality and didacticism, are no longer popular. His reputation rests instead on his realistic fiction and a few lyrical poems. Much of his poetry, like these lines from "Song for Spring," reads like a pale echo of Wordsworth or Shelley: "Pixy and sprite hold gay carouse / In the dell where a brooklet flows, / While elf and fay hold open house / At the sign of the Lily and Rose." Litsey's volumes of poetry include *Spindrift* (1915), *Shadow Shapes* (1929), and *The Filled Cup* (1935). His more realistic poetry and fiction remain powerful and accurate records of rural Kentucky life. In 1954 Litsey and Jesse Stuart were appointed joint poets laureate of Kentucky.

Litsey married Carrie Rachel Selecman on June 5, 1900, and they had one daughter, the writer Sarah Selecman LITSEY. He died on February 3, 1970.

See William S. Ward, *A Literary History of Kentucky* (Knoxville, Tenn., 1988); John Wilson Townsend, *Kentucky in American Letters* (Cedar Rapids, Iowa, 1913).   WADE HALL

LITSEY, SARAH SELECMAN. Sarah Selecman Litsey, poet, was born on June 23, 1901, in Springfield, Kentucky, the home of her father, Kentucky poet laureate Edwin Carlile LITSEY. Her mother, Carrie Rachel (Selecman) Litsey, was from nearby Lebanon. Sarah Litsey's first poem appeared in print in the *Springfield Kentucky Sun* when she was nine years old. She graduated from the Louisville Collegiate School in 1920. After studying at the Sargent School for Physical Education in Cambridge, Massachusetts, Litsey returned to Louisville to teach at Atherton High School. After her marriage in 1933 to Frank Wilson Nye, son of humorist Bill Nye, they lived in Connecticut, where she raised their son, Christopher. She has written three novels, *There Was a Lady* (1945), *The Intimate Illusion* (1956), and *A Path to the Water* (1962), and five books of poetry: *Legend* (1936), *For the Lonely* (1937), *The Oldest April* (1957), *Toward Mystery* (1974), and *Reading the Sky* (1989). Her short stories, novellas, and poems have been published in such magazines as the *Saturday Evening Post*, *McCall's*, *Poetry*, *Cosmopolitan*, and *Kentucky Poetry Review*.

For many years Litsey was an instructor at the Famous Writers School in Westport, Connecticut, and conducted workshops in poetry and fiction. Her articles on writing techniques appeared in *Writer* magazine. She has won many prizes for her poetry, including a first prize in 1940 from the Poetry Society of America. Two of her novels, *There Was a Lady* and *The Intimate Illusion*, are set in small Kentucky towns. Many of her poems, such as "Words for Kentucky" from *The Oldest April*, tap memories of her native state. After the death of her husband in 1963, she traveled widely in Europe and

the Orient and in 1979 married retired Brig. Gen. William Wallace Ford.

See William S. Ward, *A Literary History of Kentucky* (Knoxville, Tenn., 1988).   WADE HALL

LITTELL, WILLIAM. William Littell, legal historian, was born in New Jersey in 1768 and spent his early childhood in Pennsylvania. He studied theology and physics at an early age. In 1801 Littell moved to Kentucky, where he briefly practiced medicine in Mt. Sterling. Two of his works were published in 1806: *A Narrative of the Settlement of Kentucky* and *Political Transactions in and Concerning Kentucky*. In 1810 he received his LL.D. degree from Transylvania University. After moving to Frankfort, Littell spent most of his career writing about Kentucky law. Littell had signed a contract with the state of Kentucky in 1805 to edit and compile the *Statute Law of Kentucky*, which appeared in five volumes from 1809 to 1819. In the 1820s he compiled similar works on Kentucky law and court cases. Littell also wrote a collection of satirical works, *Epistles of William, Surnamed Littell, to the People of the Realm of Kentucky* (1806), and *Festoons of Fancy: Consisting of Compositions Amatory, Sentimental, and Humorous in Verse and Prose* (1814). Littell married Martha Irwin McCracken in 1816; after her death, he married Eliza P. Hickman in 1823. Littell died in Frankfort on September 26, 1824.

LIVERMORE LYNCHING. The victim of the lynching at Livermore in McLean County, Kentucky, on April 20, 1911, was Will Porter (or Potter), a black man who shot and wounded Frank Mitchell, a white man, after a barroom quarrel. Porter was then arrested by the sheriff, V.P. Stabler. The incident received national and international news coverage; except for the shooting and the arrest, the accounts vary. The *New York Times* said that Stabler, concerned for Porter's safety, hid him in the opera house basement and locked the doors; however, a mob of fifty men reached Porter, tied his hands and feet, brought him to center stage, and shot him standing there. A second version, reported in several Kentucky newspapers, maintained that the mob took Porter from jail to the opera house, where they charged admission to his hanging. Those who purchased orchestra seats were allowed to empty their guns into the hanging figure, while those in the gallery had only one shot.

On May 2 the National Association for the Advancement of Colored People (NAACP) adopted a resolution condemning the lynching and sent letters to President William Howard Taft, Congress, and Kentucky Gov. A.E. Willson (1907-11), requesting that they do the same. After Willson and other whites demanded the arrest of the lynchers, warrants were issued for eighteen of the men involved. Frank Mitchell's brother, Lawrence, and two other men identified as the leaders of the lynch mob were separately indicted and tried on the charge of murder. All the defendants were quickly acquitted.

LIVINGSTON COUNTY. The twenty-sixth county in order of formation, Livingston County is located in the "big rivers" section of western Kentucky. The county is bordered on the north and west by the Ohio River, on the south by the Tennessee River, Kentucky Lake, and Lake Barkley. Adjacent counties are Crittenden, Lyon, Marshall, and McCracken. Livingston County, which has an area of 312 square miles, was created on December 13, 1798, from a section of Christian County. It was named for Robert R. Livingston, who helped to draft the Declaration of Independence and was minister to France, where he assisted in arranging the Louisiana Purchase. SMITHLAND is the county seat.

The topography is divided between flood plains and hilly terrain. South of the Cumberland River are low rolling hills; north of the river the terrain is more rugged. Farms in 1987 occupied 55 percent of the land area, and 67 percent of farmland was in cultivation. Livingston ranked eighty-first among counties in agricultural receipts from livestock, poultry, soybeans, corn, and hay. There are deposits of limestone, dolomite, sand, and gravel. The iron furnace industry thrived in the county from 1832 to the late 1850s. The Eddyville furnace was built in 1832 in what was then Livingston County. It was was purchased in 1846 by William KELLY. In 1847 Kelly built Suwanee Furnace, near Kuttawa (then part of Livingston) where he perfected his "air boiling process" of manufacturing steel.

The flatboats, packets, and riverboats on the streams provided the flavor of a riverside area. In the nineteenth century, many southern planters brought their families to Smithland in the summer to escape the heat of the deep South. Edward Zane Carroll Judson, who wrote western adventure novels as Ned Buntline, came to Smithland to live in 1845. In 1961 Metro-Goldwyn-Mayer used Smithland to film the Albany, New York, setting of the movie *How The West Was Won*. Cherokees passed through the county in 1838, when the federal government removed them from their homeland in the southeast to Oklahoma. The Trail of Tears they traveled entered the county at Salem and roughly followed what is now KY 135 to Jay, where they crossed the Ohio River to Galcouda, Illinois.

Civil War activity in the county was heavy because of its strategic location. Federal gunboats were supplied at Smithland and other points along the Ohio.

Livingston's industrial plants include producers of hardwood lumber, asphalt, limestone products, and custom slaughtering and processing. Incorporated towns include Caversville, Gravel Rivers, Salem, and Smithland. The population of Livingston County was 7,596 in 1970; 9,219 in 1980; and 9,062 in 1990.

See Leslie McDonald, *Echoes of Yesterday* (Smithland, Ky., 1972).   RON D. BRYANT

LLOYD, ALICE SPENCER (GEDDES). Alice Spencer (Geddes) Lloyd, social reformer, was born in Athol, Massachusetts, on November 13, 1876, the daughter of William E. and Ella (Ainsworth) Geddes. Educated at Chauncey Hall and Radcliffe College, she worked at the *Boston Transcript* as a feature writer and developed a passion for social reform. Along with her husband, Arthur Lloyd, and her mother, she hoped to start a model community in Appalachia. In 1916 a landowner on Caney Creek in Knott County offered her his land if she would educate his children. Alice Lloyd's husband returned to New England, but she and her mother plunged into the task of organizing the community. Believing that reformers and native Appalachians could live and work together, Lloyd established the Caney Creek Community Center in Knott County. In 1919, with volunteer help and donated money, she founded Caney High School. That same year fellow-reformer June BUCHANAN arrived from Wellesley College and became Lloyd's assistant.

Although the many community-based projects flourished at Caney Creek, Lloyd and Buchanan realized that one model community would not ease the overwhelming problems of Appalachia. Shifting their focus to training the region's future leaders, they founded Caney Junior College (later Alice Lloyd Junior College) in 1923. Accredited in the 1950s, the institution became a four-year school in 1981. By 1955 when Lloyd appeared on the television program "This Is Your Life," the national print and broadcast media had acknowledged her work, which included founding more than a hundred public schools in the region. She died on September 4, 1962, and was buried on a hillside overlooking the college.

See William Dutton, *Stay on Stranger!* (New York 1954).   STEPHEN DOUGLAS WILSON

LLOYD, ARTHUR YOUNG. Arthur Young Lloyd, political scientist and state official, son of Arthur Lee and Susan Mabel (Young) Lloyd, was born January 12, 1908, in Lisman, Webster County, Kentucky. He completed high school in Providence, Kentucky, in 1923, and in 1926 received a bachelor's degree in history from Western Kentucky University. He joined the U.S. Army Reserve in 1927. He was principal of Webster County High School in Wheatcraft, Kentucky, during 1926-28. Lloyd then attended graduate school at Vanderbilt University in Nashville, where he received a master's degree (1929) and a Ph.D. (1934) in political science. From 1931 to 1936 Lloyd taught political science at Morehead State University, serving as head of the history and political science department during 1934-36. In 1936 Lloyd became director of the Kentucky Department of Welfare, where he served until 1942. Lloyd joined the U.S. Army as lieutenant and by 1944 was made a colonel. In 1946 he left active duty service but remained in the Army Reserve.

Lloyd served as commissioner of the Kentucky Welfare Department in 1947-48, then as first director of the LEGISLATIVE RESEARCH COMMISSION until 1956. From 1957 until 1959 he was vice president of the Burley and Dark Leaf Tobacco Export Association and executive director of the National Cigar Leaf Association in Washington, D.C. Lloyd returned to Kentucky in 1959 to become adjutant general of the Kentucky National Guard, where he served until 1967. He was promoted to major general in 1960 and was elected president of the national Adjutant General Association. Lloyd was a lecturer on public welfare administration at the University of Kentucky from 1968 to 1970. From 1973 to 1978 he was a lecturer on political science at Eastern Kentucky University, serving in 1974–75 as acting chairman of the political science department. He was vice-president of the Kentucky Historical Society from 1976 to 1982, then president during 1982–84. Lloyd wrote numerous articles and two books, *The Slavery Controversy* (1939) and *Kentucky Government* (1980).

Throughout his active career, Lloyd simultaneously managed Airdrie in Woodford County, a livestock and tobacco farm owned, since its establishment in the mid-1800s, by his wife's family. Lloyd married Lucy B. Simms on November 27, 1941; they had one daughter, Elizabeth. He died on October 17, 1986, and was buried in the Frankfort Cemetery.

LLOYD, CURTIS GATES. Curtis Gates Lloyd, botanist, was born on July 17, 1859, in Florence, Kentucky, the third son of Nelson Marvin and Sophia (Webster) Lloyd. Although he had little formal training, Lloyd's early study of botany and later interest in mycology (the study of fungi) developed into lifelong pursuits that earned this self-taught scientist international renown. He and his older brothers, Nelson Ashley and John Uri LLOYD, devoted themselves to the collections that would become the LLOYD LIBRARY AND MUSEUM. In this pursuit Lloyd traveled extensively abroad and shared his findings with the scientific community through the *Bulletin* of the Lloyd Scientific Library. His correspondence with colleagues from around the world helped build his mycological collection, now housed in the Smithsonian Institution in Washington, D.C.

Lloyd died on November 11, 1926; he bequeathed his entire estate to the Lloyd Scientific Library. His body was cremated and the ashes scattered in the C.G. Lloyd Wildlife Area in Grant County, Kentucky.   MICHAEL FLANNERY

LLOYD, JOHN URI. John Uri Lloyd, chemist and novelist, was born on April 19, 1849, in West Bloomfield Township, New York, the eldest son of Nelson Marvin and Sophia (Webster) Lloyd. His mother was a descendant of Gov. John Webster of Connecticut. When he was four years old, his family moved to Petersburg in Boone County, Kentucky, where his father worked as a surveyor and both parents were teachers. Lloyd was educated at local private schools in Petersburg, Burlington, and Florence. At the age of fourteen, he was apprenticed in Cincinnati to William J.M. Gordon, a pharmacist, and at sixteen he was employed by George

Eger, beginning his lifelong career as a scientist and pharmacist. In 1871 he became manager of the laboratory of H.M. Merrell and Company, which he and his brothers, Curtis and Nelson, took over in 1885 as Lloyd Brothers Pharmacists, Inc. He and Curtis donated to the city of Cincinnati the Lloyd Scientific Library, containing 35,000 volumes on chemistry, pharmacy, and medicine. Lloyd promoted eclectic medicine (the use of plant extracts in treating patients) and he has been called the father of colloidal chemistry. In collaboration with his brother, he was the author of eight scientific books, including *Chemistry of Medicine* (1881) and *Drugs and Medicines of North America* (1884).

Although most famous as a plant scientist and chemist, Lloyd was also well-known as a novelist. His most famous novel is perhaps *Stringtown on the Pike* (1900), which immortalizes Florence, Kentucky (known earlier as Stringtown), and reveals Lloyd's interest in the folklore, superstitions, and dialect of northern Kentucky and the feuds of eastern Kentucky. He wrote eight novels, among them *Etidorpha: or The End of the Earth* (1893); *Warwick of the Knobs* (1901); *Red Head* (1903), a sequel to *Stringtown on the Pike*; and *Felix Moses: The Beloved Jew of Stringtown* (1930).

In 1876 Lloyd married Adelaide Meader, who died ten days after their marriage. In 1880 he married Emma Rouse of Crittenden, Kentucky, the mother of his three children: Annie, John Thomas, and Dorothy. Lloyd died in Van Nuys, California, on April 9, 1936; his ashes were buried at the Hopeful Cemetery near Florence, Kentucky.

See Corinne Miller Simons, *John Uri Lloyd: His Life and His Works, 1849-1936, With a History of the Lloyd Library* (Cincinnati 1972); "John Uri Lloyd Memorial Issue," *Eclectic Medical Journal* 92 (May 1936).   DANNY MILLER

LLOYD LIBRARY AND MUSEUM. The Lloyd Library and Museum in Cincinnati is a source for specialized research in the history of Kentucky and the surrounding region, as well as an internationally recognized research library in the areas of pharmacy, botany, and materia medica. Its holdings on the botany of Kentucky and the entire Ohio River region are notable.

The library began in 1864 as the personal collection of John Uri LLOYD, then a pharmacy student. In the 1870s he began manufacturing drugs for eclectic physicians and with his brother Nelson established Lloyd Bros. Pharmacists. To research and formulate new medicines, John Uri systematically purchased works on pharmacy and medical botany. As the success of the business grew, so did his personal library. In 1886 John Uri's other brother, Curtis LLOYD, joined the firm, bringing his own collection of works on botany and mycology. In the 1890s, John Uri and Curtis began collecting books for the library on a major scale. Curtis made frequent research trips to Europe to make major purchases of rare volumes in the botanical, pharmaceutical, and mycological fields. The collection outgrew the original building, purchased in 1891, and a new building was erected in 1907. In 1942 the library and archives of the Eclectic Medical College of Cincinnati were placed in the Lloyd Library. The library moved to Plum Street in 1971.

The major archival holdings are the personal papers and research files of the Lloyd brothers, especially of John Uri, whose fiction writings depicted the everyday life of northern Kentuckians. The Jeuttner Papers on Daniel DRAKE, a prominent physician in frontier Kentucky, are included, as well as miscellaneous collections from the northern Kentucky area, including papers of Drs. John Scudder and John King. The Lloyd also houses several herbaria of Kentucky assembled prior to 1900.

See Caswell A. Mayo, *The Lloyd Library and Its Makers* (Cincinnati 1928).   WILLIAM C. BLACK

LOCHABER, TREATY OF. The Treaty of Lochaber, governing territorial rights, was negotiated in South Carolina between British representative John Stuart and 1,000 Cherokee, and concluded on October 18, 1770. Lochaber was a renegotiation of the 1768 Treaty of Hard Labour, which set the boundary line between Virginia and the Cherokee nation. The British government paid 2,500 pounds sterling for its newly acquired territory. A survey in 1771 altered the terms agreed to at Lochaber: a boundary line from six miles east of Big or Long Island in the Holston River to the mouth of the Kanawha River. The leader of the survey, John Donaldson (Donelson), and the accompanying Cherokee representatives decided to follow the Holston River to the Louisa (Kentucky River) and up the Louisa to its mouth, then up the Ohio River to the mouth of the Kanawha. This course opened a greater amount of present-day Kentucky territory for white settlement than had been intended, because Donaldson mistook the Louisa for a branch of the Big Sandy River, located much farther east.

See Charles C. Royce, *Indian Land Cessions in the United States* (Washington, D.C., 1899).

LOCKETT, WILL. Will Lockett, whose birth date is unknown, was the self-confessed killer of Geneva Hardman, a ten-year-old white girl, in the Lexington, Kentucky, area on February 4, 1920. Lockett, a black World War I veteran, had pleaded guilty without benefit of counsel at the time of his arrest. His trial at the Fayette County courthouse in Lexington on February 9, 1920, lasted barely thirty minutes, and the judge sentenced him to death. A large lynch mob attempted to seize Lockett that day but was repulsed by gunfire from state troops called out by Gov. Edwin Morrow (1919-23). Six of the mob were killed and scores injured. Regular U.S. Army troops were sent in to preserve order. Because this was the first time troops had been called out to disperse a lynch mob south of the Mason-Dixon line, it was widely publicized in the national press. The day after the trial, Lockett was escorted by four hundred troops to Union Station in Lexington. From there he was transported by train to the State Penitentiary, where he was electrocuted on March 11, 1920.

See John D. Wright, Jr., "Lexington's Suppression of the 1920 Will Lockett Lynch Mob," *Register* 84 (Summer 1986): 263-79.

JOHN D. WRIGHT, JR.

LOCUST GROVE. Locust Grove was the estate of Maj. William Croghan, who in April 1790 purchased 387 acres on a bluff overlooking the Ohio River near Louisville. The estate eventually grew to 693 acres. The twelve-room Georgian house Croghan built there became home to his wife, Lucy Clark, and their eight children. Locust Grove was one of the finest houses built along Beargrass Creek in the late eighteenth century. Timber came from the black walnut, poplar, cherry, and white ash trees found in the area. The bricks were fired on the site.

Among the many guests at Locust Grove were Presidents Monroe, Jackson, and Taylor, Vice-President Aaron Burr, John James Audubon, Cassius Marcellus Clay, Meriwether Lewis, and Lucy's brothers, Revolutionary War hero George Rogers Clark and explorer William Clark. George Rogers Clark moved to Locust Grove to live in 1809 and died there in 1818.

Locust Grove was purchased by Jefferson County in 1961 and opened as a museum in 1964. The restored house and seven dependencies are furnished with period pieces dating between 1761 and 1830. On the fifty-five acres remaining of the original tract, a four-square garden and cutting garden contain plants known to grow in Kentucky around 1800. Locust Grove was designated a NATIONAL HISTORIC LANDMARK in 1986.

GWYNNE BRYANT

LOGAN, BENJAMIN. Benjamin Logan, frontiersman and legislator, was born in Orange County, Virginia, in 1743 to David and Jane (McKinley) Logan. He enrolled in the county militia when he was sixteen, and participated in Col. Henry Bouquet's Indian campaign in 1764 as a sergeant. In 1774 he served as a captain in an expedition to northwestern Ohio led by Lord Dunmore (John Murray), governor of Virginia. In the spring of 1775 Logan helped start a settlement called St. Asaph in what is now Kentucky, and in March 1776 he moved his family and four slaves to that location. When Kentucky County was established on December 31, 1776, Logan became its first sheriff and one of its four militia captains, and in the winter of 1776-77 he led the way in building a fort at St. Asaph, often referred to as Logan's Fort. In the spring of 1779 he was one of three captains in a volunteer expedition into the Shawnee country north of the Ohio River led by Col. John Bowman. As colonel in the Kentucky County militia in 1780, Logan took part in another Shawnee campaign as second in command to Col. George Rogers Clark.

In the spring of 1781 Logan was elected to the Virginia Assembly as a delegate from Lincoln County, which had been formed from part of Kentucky

County, and in July of that year he was appointed by Gov. Thomas Jefferson to the post of county lieutenant (militia commander) of Lincoln. In November 1782 he was again second in command to George Rogers Clark in leading 1,050 Virginia regulars and Kentucky militiamen in a successful campaign against Shawnee villages in the valley of the Miami River. In November 1784, Logan called a meeting at Danville to discuss a suspected Indian invasion. Under Virginia law, no militia officer had the authority to lead his men beyond the borders of Virginia except in immediate pursuit of Indians.

Logan was a member of eight of the ten conventions called to pursue statehood for Kentucky, including the tenth convention, which wrote a constitution for Kentucky. During the same period Logan served two more terms in the Virginia Assembly. In 1786 he led a successful campaign against the Shawnee villages on the upper reaches of the Miami River in what is now Logan County, Ohio. Kentucky's first governor, Isaac Shelby (1792-96, 1812-16), gave Logan a commission as a major general in the state militia and placed him in command of a full division. Logan also served in the first, second, third, fourth, sixth, and seventh Kentucky General Assemblies. In 1792 Logan County, carved from part of Lincoln County, was named for him.

Under Kentucky's first constitution, the governor was chosen not by popular vote but by a board of electors. In 1796, Logan, who had become a resident of Shelby County, was one of three candidates for governor, receiving twenty-one electoral votes to sixteen for James Garrard and fourteen for Thomas Todd. The constitution did not require a majority vote, but the electors believed that this was its intent. They eliminated Todd and took a second ballot. This time Garrard received a majority vote and was declared the winner. In 1799 Logan was a member of the convention that wrote Kentucky's second constitution, which provided for a popular vote in choosing a governor. Logan was one of four gubernatorial candidates in 1800 but ran third, behind James Garrard and Christopher Greenup.

Logan married Ann Montgomery in 1772; they had nine children: David, William, Jane, Mary, Elizabeth, John, Benjamin, Robert, and Ann. Logan died on December 11, 1802.

See Charles Gano Talbert, *Benjamin Logan: Kentucky Frontiersman* (Lexington, Ky., 1962).

CHARLES G. TALBERT

LOGAN, JOHN. John Logan, army officer and first state treasurer, was born to David and Jane (McKinley) Logan in the spring of 1747. The Logan family lived in Virginia along the North River, a tributary of the South Fork of the Shenandoah River. In the years that followed David Logan's death in 1757, the family moved several times. John Logan and his brother Benjamin (LOGAN) participated in Lord Dunmore's War in 1774. In 1776 John, Benjamin, and other members of the Logan family settled in Kentucky in the region of Dick's

(now Dix) River, a tributary of the Kentucky River. The Logan brothers took part in a number of campaigns against the Indians, who at that time often raided frontier outposts and settlements. John Logan was made a captain of the militia in the fall of 1779 and was promoted to lieutenant colonel in 1781. While pursuing a party of Chickamauga raiders into present-day Tennessee, Logan and his seventy men mistakenly attacked a group of friendly Cherokee and killed seven of them. The Cherokee protested this action to the Virginia government, which threatened to take legal action against Logan for making an unauthorized foray into another state. Logan escaped prosecution when it became evident that the Indians he had attacked had themselves been guilty of criminal acts.

Logan represented Lincoln County in the Virginia legislature in 1784 and from 1789 to 1791. During the 1780s he participated in the first, fourth, fifth, and seventh Danville STATEHOOD conventions. In June of 1788, Logan was one of two delegates sent from Lincoln County to Virginia to attend the convention that considered adoption of the federal Constitution. Although Logan and nine of the other thirteen delegates from Kentucky voted against it, the Constitution was approved by a narrow margin. When Kentucky became a state in 1792, Logan served for a brief time in the state Senate. He resigned after the houses of the legislature together elected him Kentucky's first state treasurer on June 18, 1792. Logan was reelected to this position every year until his death.

Logan married Jane McClure during the early 1770s; they had six daughters and a son. He died in July 1807 in Frankfort.

See Charles Gano Talbert, "John Logan, 1747-1807," *FCHQ* 36 (Apr. 1962): 128-151.

LOGAN, MARVEL MILLS. Marvel Mills Logan, jurist and U.S. senator, was born on January 7, 1874, to Gillis Franklin and Georgia Ann (Houchin) Logan in Brownsville, Edmonson County, Kentucky. Logan received his early education at public and private schools in Edmonson County and studied law under the tutelage of A.A. Sturgeon; he passed the Kentucky bar examination in 1896. He began to practice law at Brownsville and was elected chairman of the town's board of trustees in 1897. Four years later he became the Edmonson County attorney and in 1910 was elected county judge. Logan became attorney general of Kentucky in 1915, after serving as the office's assistant during 1912-14. After successfully defending the state in several tax collection cases against the railroads, he resigned as attorney general in 1917 to become chairman of the first Kentucky State Tax Commission. He resigned from the commission in 1918 and returned to private practice, first in Louisville, and in 1922 in Bowling Green, Kentucky. In 1926 he was elected to the Kentucky state court of appeals, where he served until March 1931 and for several months was chief justice.

In 1930, Logan ran for the U.S. Senate on the Democratic ticket, defeating the Republican nominee, John M. Robsion, by 336,748 to 309,180. He was reelected in 1936 after a hard-fought primary that featured a controversial three-way race with John Y. Brown, Sr., and J.C.W. Beckham. Brown was considered a favorite because of an agreement made for A.B. Chandler to back Brown in 1936 in exchange for Brown's support in Chandler's 1935 gubernatorial campaign. But the newly elected governor chose to endorse J.C.W. Beckham instead, and Logan won the primary. He had a less strenuous test against the state's Republican candidate, Robert M. Lucas, defeating him by a 174,118 plurality. At the end of his congressional career, Logan was the ranking member of the Senate Military Affairs Committee, chairman of the Claims Committee, and a member of the Judiciary Committee. Logan served in the Senate from March 4, 1931, until his death on October 3, 1939.

Logan was married to Della Haydon of Glasgow Junction, Kentucky, on September 25, 1896. They had four children: Victor Hubert, Agnes, Leland Hallowell, and Ralph Hunter. Logan died in Washington, D.C., while in office and was buried in the Logan family cemetery near Brownsville.

See John Ed Pearce, *Divide and Dissent: Kentucky Politics 1930-1963* (Lexington, Ky., 1987).

LOGAN, WILLIAM. William Logan, U.S. senator and judge, was born on December 8, 1776, in the fort at what is now Harrodsburg, Kentucky, to Gen. Benjamin and Ann (Montgomery) Logan. He was one of the first white children born in the state. He was educated by tutors at St. Asaph, a fort established in 1775 near present-day Stanford, Kentucky. About 1798 the family settled in Shelby County, where Logan studied law.

Logan was frequently a member of the state legislature from Lincoln and Shelby counties. He represented Lincoln County at Kentucky's second constitutional convention, from July 22 to August 17, 1799. He was appointed judge of the court of appeals on January 11, 1808, but resigned nineteen days later. He was reappointed on January 20, 1810, and served until 1812. In 1809, 1813, and 1817 Logan was a Democratic presidential elector. In 1818 he was elected to the U.S. Senate, defeating Richard M. Johnson by a vote of 67 to 55. He served from March 4, 1819, to May 28, 1820, when he resigned to make a bid for governor. He ran second in a four-way race. John Adair was elected with a vote of 20,493 to Logan's 19,947, Joseph Desha's 12,418, and Anthony Butler's 9,567.

Logan married Priscilla Wallace, daughter of Judge Caleb Wallace of the court of appeals, in 1801. They had three children; Caleb, Anna, and Rosa. Logan died at his home in Shelby County on August 8, 1822, and was buried in the family plot near Shelbyville, Kentucky.

LOGAN COUNTY. Logan County, the thirteenth county in order of formation, is located in the Pennyroyal region of western Kentucky. The county is bounded by Todd, Muhlenberg, Butler, Warren, and Simpson counties, and the Tennessee state line, and contains 556 square miles. At its formation from Lincoln County on September 1, 1792, it ran from the Little Barren River on the east to the Mississippi River on the west and from the Ohio and Green rivers on the north to Tennessee on the south. Twenty-eight additional counties were formed wholly or in part from Logan. It was named after Gen. Benjamin Logan, a Virginian who came to the Kentucky frontier in 1774 and participated in several campaigns against the Indians. The county seat is RUSSELLVILLE. Other incorporated cities are Adairville, Auburn, and Lewisburg; unincorporated communities include Olmstead and Chandlers Chapel.

The northern part of the county is somewhat hilly. The southern part is level to gently rolling and contains fertile soil. Leading crops in the county are burley and dark air-cured tobacco, along with corn, soybeans, wheat, barley, and forage. Principal streams are the Red River, which runs west across the county and flows into the Cumberland River, and the Mud and Gasper rivers, which flow northward into the Green. Major lakes in Logan County are Lake Malone, Spa Lake, and Lake Herndon, which supplies Russellville with water.

Prehistoric occupation of Logan County is evidenced by Lost City, also known as the Page Site, in the northeastern part of the county. Excavated in 1929 by a team from the University of Kentucky, the site, which included sixty-seven mounds, yielded many artifacts. It provided a wealth of information about people of the Mississippian culture, who inhabited the area from A.D. 900 until some time before the pioneer era.

The first settlement was Maulding's Station on the north fork of the Red River in 1780; the Maulding family became prominent county residents. A diverse mixture of people immigrated to Logan County. Peter Cartwright, a noted Methodist minister who lived near Adairville from 1793 to 1802, damned the area as "Rogue's Harbor" because it was the home of the lawless from almost all parts of the Union—murderers, horse thieves, highway robbers, and counterfeiters. In this setting, the GREAT REVIVAL of 1800, led by the Rev. James McGready, a Presbyterian minister, started at Red River Meeting House. In 1807 many members of the Gasper Presbyterian Church, including John Rankin, the minister, joined with three Shaker missionaries to form the Shaker settlement at South Union (twelve miles east of Russellville).

On May 30, 1806, Andrew Jackson and Charles Dickinson fought a duel in southern Logan County at what was then Harrison's Mill on the bank of the Red River.

By the 1830s, Logan County experienced a time of prosperity and progress. Many leading families from the East relocated in the county, and a number of men who either had spent their boyhood there or practiced law there rose to prominence.

The Civil War divided families in Logan County, where the short-lived provisional Confederate government was formed in November 1861. Logan County furnished 1,000 men to Confederate units, including Company A of the 9th Kentucky infantry, known as the Logan Grays; various Union regiments also recruited about five hundred soldiers. No major battles took place in Logan, although the Louisville & Nashville Railroad (now CSX Transportation) was a focal point for damage by raiders and for minor skirmishes.

A Logan County family that wielded influence for some 120 years was the Rheas. Around 1810 Charles Rhea began publication of the town newspaper. His son, Albert G. Rhea, continued publishing the paper, which was variously known as the *Mirror, Messenger, Herald, Herald-Ledger, Democrat,* and *News-Democrat.* One of his sons, Thomas RHEA, used the paper to produce a Democratic political organization that exerted strong county and statewide influence.

Among the noteworthy county residents was Alice Allison DUNNIGAN, who during the Harry S. Truman and Dwight D. Eisenhower administrations was chief of the Washington Bureau of the Associated Negro Press, and who became the first black female to serve as capitol, State Department, and White House correspondent.

For many years, Logan County was mainly agricultural, but industrial development accelerated in the 1950s, and by 1970 manufacturing had replaced agriculture as the dominant source of income. Nevertheless, Logan remains second among the counties in the commonwealth in cash receipts from agriculture. Leading manufacturers in the county are Logan Aluminum, Emerson Electric, Red Kap, E.R. Carpenter Company, Illinois Tool Works, Shakeproof Division, Auburn Hosiery Mills, BTR Die Casting, and Odom Tennessee Pride. Russellville is one of the state's leading tobacco markets.

The R.J. Corman Railroad Corporation provides branch line rail services to the county by connecting with the CSX mainline at Bowling Green.

The population was 21,793 in 1970; 24,138 in 1980; and 24,416 in 1990.

See Edward Coffman, *The Story of Logan County* (Nashville 1962).

EVELYN B. RICHARDSON

LOGAN FEMALE COLLEGE. Logan Female College, located in Russellville, Kentucky, developed from the Russellville Academy, a coeducational school in southern Kentucky founded in 1846. In 1860 it received a charter under the name Russellville Collegiate Institute. Ministers of the Louisville Conference of the Methodist Episcopal Church, South, served as principals, and the school was formally affiliated with the conference in 1860. Under the direction of David Morton, the institution was reorganized and rechartered in 1867 as Logan Female College. The school for girls then enlarged its curriculum and its governing board. In 1868 the conference appointed the Rev. R.H. Rivers to be the first president of Logan Female College. During the next sixty-eight years the college en-joyed variable success. It conferred bachelor's degrees in arts, science, and law, with special certificates in music and art; it also offered elementary and secondary school education. At the annual meeting in 1931 the Louisville Conference voted to close Logan Female College because of financial problems.

CONNIE MILLS

LOGAN'S STATION (ST. ASAPH). Located at Buffalo Spring, west of Stanford in Lincoln County, Benjamin LOGAN's station (also known as St. Asaph) was established in 1775, with the aid of John FLOYD, after a surveying trip by Logan in 1774. Logan quickly assumed a major leadership role on the developing Kentucky frontier and his station was one of the most important pioneer settlements. According to various records, three blockhouses and a conventional cabin were constructed at the corners of a rectangle measuring 150 by ninety feet, with a total of seven cabins along the sides, gates at each end, and stockading between the structures. Logan's Station was unusual because the settlers reportedly dug a ditch to the spring that was their source of fresh water. The ditch was covered with puncheon logs and dirt, forming a protective tunnel through which they obtained water in times of danger.

Like other large stations and forts, Logan's Station provided shelter for many families moving to Kentucky. Much of its population was transient, making a complete list of occupants and visitors difficult to compile. Among the more notable occupants, in addition to Logan, were Ben Pettit, William Whitley, William Menifee, George Clark, James Mason, Samuel Coburn, and their families. John Martin, John Kennedy, James Craig, William Hudson, John King, Azariah Davis, Burr Harrison, and William May, as well as many women, children, slaves, and other unidentified visitors who also visited or lived at the station temporarily.

Logan's Station was the subject of many Indian raids. A hair-raising siege that began May 20, 1777, continued for thirteen days. To reach dairy cattle for milking, the wives of Benjamin Logan and William Whitley, accompanied by a slave woman, left the stockade under heavy guard. The party was attacked by Indians and Burr Harrison, one of the guards, was wounded. Logan rescued Harrison while protecting himself with a feather bed. Logan, one of the captains of the county militia, was also sheriff and justice of the peace. He led one of the military divisions on the raids of the Indian settlements at Chillicothe, Ohio, in 1779 and 1780. In 1786 he deeded ten acres, including Buffalo Spring, for a courthouse and public buildings. Logan died in 1802.

Logan's Station was one of the sites for the land courts of 1779-80 and was one of the few stations that did not close in 1777, when Indian raids became so intense that the Kentucky territory was nearly abandoned altogether. Like many other pioneer sites, it faded from importance as other locations were chosen for urban development.

See Charles Talbert, *Benjamin Logan* (Lexington, Ky., 1962). NANCY O'MALLEY

LONDON. London, the seat of Laurel County, is located on U.S. 25 and KY 80, east of I-75 and at the western terminus of the Daniel Boone Parkway. The town, named for London, England, began as a small pioneer settlement at the midpoint of the Wilderness Road, between the Cumberland Gap and Lexington. There was no waterway nearby, but the relatively high ground protected London from the flood waters that periodically devastated other mountain towns. When Laurel County was established in 1825, London was named the county seat. The first Laurel County courthouse was built in 1826-27. The two-story brick structure was replaced by a second courthouse in 1886. It was destroyed by fire on December 9, 1958, and replaced by a third courthouse, of colonial Georgian style, in 1961.

Although many immigrants passed through the city on the Wilderness Road, its growth was slow from 1825 to 1860. The lure of more fertile lands to the west discouraged many from staying. In 1860 London was little more than a courthouse town with a few stores and the Laurel Seminary. There was no industry, but there were several taverns for travelers.

London's location on the Wilderness Road caused it to be occupied several times during the Civil War. The Battle of London took place on August 17, 1862, when Confederate cavalry under Col. J.S. Scott defeated Union troops led by Col. L.C. Houk and forced them to retreat. Scattered fighting continued around London until about October 19, 1862, when Gen. Braxton Bragg's Confederate army retreated southward. Afterward, London experienced nearly a constant procession of Union troops to and from the South.

London was incorporated as a city in 1866, but remained a tiny roadside village. With the arrival of the Louisville & Nashville Railroad (now CSX Transportation) on July 17, 1882, the town grew as a trading, agricultural, and livestock center. Coal and timber resources made the city a point of trade, but lack of public services inhibited industrial growth. In 1925 U.S. 25 was completed through London. Known as the Dixie Highway, the north-south road brought the tourist trade, and a variety of industries located in the city. By 1954 there were twenty-six manufacturing concerns. With the opening of I-75 on December 4, 1969, many of the smaller tourist businesses ceased to exist. Among the largest employers in the city are Kern's Bakery; Griffin Pie Company; and the Caron Spinning Company, which produces yarns.

The population of the fourth-class city was 4,337 in 1970; 4,002 in 1980; and 5,757 in 1990.

See Thomas D. Clark, *A History of Laurel County* (London, Ky., 1989).

LONG, FRANK WEATHERS. Frank Weathers Long, artist and craftsman, was born in Knoxville, Tennessee, on May 7, 1906, to Clifton J. and Leora May (Weathers) Long. After graduating from high school in 1925, Long entered the Art Institute of Chicago. In 1927 he enrolled in advanced figure painting and composition classes at the Pennsylvania Academy of Fine Art in Philadelphia, and in 1928-29 he studied at the Acadmie Julien in Paris. He then established a studio in Chicago. A portfolio of his wood engravings, *Heracles, the Twelve Labors*, was published in 1932.

On a visit to Lexington, Kentucky, in the summer of 1934, Long was commissioned to paint two murals in the library building at the University of Kentucky, and later that year he opened a studio in Berea, Kentucky. In an open competition sponsored by the Treasury Department Art Projects during the Depression, Long was selected to design ten murals in Louisville's new Federal Building and Post Office. In 1939 he completed *Rural Free Delivery*, a mural in the post office in Morehead, Kentucky, and *Old Time Commencement at Berea College* in the post office in Berea.

In August 1942 Long joined the army. In the fall of 1946, he enrolled in the crafts department of New Mexico's State Teachers College (now New Mexico State University). After a year, Long returned to Kentucky, where he built a house and workshop near Berea and established a handmade-jewelry business with outlets in Berea, Louisville, and Lexington. From 1951 to 1957 Long directed a program for the development of native crafts in Alaska, sponsored by the Indian Arts and Crafts Board. In 1958 he returned to Kentucky and reopened his jewelry business.

In 1962 Long moved to Albuquerque, New Mexico, where he worked at the Southwest headquarters of the Indian Arts and Crafts Board until 1969, when he became self-employed as a jeweler and sculptor. In 1977 Long's book *The Creative Lapidary* was published. He closed his jewelry shop at the end of 1987 to devote his time to painting and writing. Long, who married Laura May Whitis in 1942, lives in Albuquerque.

See Sue B. Beckham, "A Kentucky Artist and a Federal Program: Frank Long and the Treasurer Section of Fine Arts," *Kentucky Review* (Spring 1988): 35-36.

LONG HUNTERS. Early hunters in the West who traveled long distances and were gone for extended periods were called Long Hunters, a term specifically applied to a party of twenty Virginia and North Carolina hunters who entered the western wilderness in June 1769. They crossed through Cumberland Gap and traveled into the Cumberland River Valley as far as present-day Wayne County, Kentucky, and as far north as the Dick's (now Dix) and Laurel rivers. Prominent in this party were Gasper Mansker, James Knox, Abraham Bledsoe, Joseph Drake, and Uriah Stone. Bledsoe recorded the party's presence when he carved on a poplar tree in Wayne County "2300 deer skins lost. Ruination by God." The party's fur and skin cache had been raided and destroyed by Indians and animals. Daniel Boone, John Finley, and their party in 1769 were also Long Hunters, as were the McAfee Brothers, James Harrod, and many others.

See Otis Rice, *Frontier Kentucky* (Lexington, Ky., 1975).   THOMAS D. CLARK

LONG RUN MASSACRE. The Long Run massacre was a major incident in the series of battles in which early settlers in Kentucky fought Indians and their British allies on the western frontier during the Revolutionary War. Long Run is located near Eastwood in Jefferson County, Kentucky. In September 1781 Maj. Bland Ballard discovered Indian signs near Squire Boone's Painted Stone Station, near what is now Shelbyville. He warned the settlers there and at Beargrass Station to move to Lynn Station, which was a more secure area. For unknown reasons, Boone's and several other families delayed moving for two days. When they finally left the station on September 14, 1781, they were surrounded at Long Run Creek by a large party of Indians reinforced by British soldiers under the command of Capt. Alexander McKee. An estimated sixty people were killed by the Indians; only a handful, including Squire Boone, escaped.

See Lou Catherine Clore, "Long Run Massacre," *Register* 10 (Jan. 1912): 75-6.

LÓPEZ'S EXPEDITIONS. Kentucky volunteers were numerous in the attempts led by Narciso López between 1848 and 1851 to wrest control of Cuba from Spain. López, a Venezuelan born in either 1798 or 1799, had been a general in the Spanish army; he was one of a small group in Cuba who were clandestinely conspiring with U.S. interests to oust the Spanish and annex Cuba. Of López's five attempts to invade the island with expeditionary armies, two reached Cuban soil and engaged Spanish regulars.

López's expeditions openly defied three U.S. presidents—James K. Polk, Zachary Taylor, and Millard Fillmore—and Washington used military, diplomatic, and judicial measures against López. Massive publicity, however, aided his cause. López enjoyed moral, and occasionally public, support from such luminaries as Jefferson Davis, Robert E. Lee, and John C. Calhoun. Lured like others by promises of land and money in a liberated Cuba, Kentucky volunteers flocked to his army. Kentucky's Theodore O'HARA, Mexican war hero and a principal recruiter for López, served as a colonel on one of the invasion attempts from U.S. soil. On May 18, 1850, while O'Hara was leading a contingent of Kentuckians against the Spanish garrison at the port of Cárdenas, Cuba, his leg was wounded and he had to be carried back to the conspirators' steamer, the *Creole*. The ship hastily proceeded to Key West, Florida, barely escaping a pursuing Spanish man-of-war.

Another Mexican War hero from Kentucky, William Logan Crittenden, a nephew of former Kentucky Gov. John J. Crittenden (1848-50), resigned his U.S. Army commission in 1850 and joined López. He led a Kentucky regiment in the López conspiracy's final invasion attempt, during August of 1850. Crittenden and his battle-weary comrades were captured by the Spanish army as they sought to escape to Key West in four small boats. In an episode that entered the folklore of martyrs, Crittenden and his men were executed by firing squad the next morning on a slope in front of Havana's Castle Atares. Crittenden was executed first, alone. According to legend, Crittenden refused to be blindfolded or to prostrate himself before his executioners, saying, "A Kentuckian kneels to none except his God, and always dies facing his enemy."

See Anderson C. Quisenberry, *López's Expeditions to Cuba 1850 and 1851* (Louisville 1906).
                                                 TOM CHAFFIN

LORD DUNMORE'S WAR. Lord Dunmore's War in 1774 began a twenty-year struggle between whites and Indians for mastery of the Ohio Valley and was instrumental in opening for settlement the future state of Kentucky. The conflict began when Lord Dunmore, Virginia's last royal governor and—like the colony's other leading planters—an avaricious land speculator, called out the provincial militia against the Northwest Indians. In three separate columns the Virginians invaded the upper valley of the Ohio. On October 10, 1774, at Point Pleasant at the confluence of the Ohio and Kanawha rivers, a large war party led by Shawnee Chief Cornstalk ambushed one of the commands under Gen. Andrew Lewis. Only after hours of desperate, costly fighting did the Indians abandon the battlefield. Their undocumented but severe losses may well have discouraged the Indians from waging a large-scale war against Kentucky's new settlements during their formative and most vulnerable years, from 1775 to 1777. In the Treaty of Camp Charlotte soon after the battle, Dunmore managed to extract a tentative Indian promise to remain north of the Ohio River. Among the prominent future Kentucky leaders who participated in various aspects of Lord Dunmore's War were Isaac Shelby, John Floyd, Benjamin Logan, William Christian, and James Harrod.

See Randolph C. Downes, "Dunmore's War: An Interpretation," *Mississippi Valley Historical Review* 32 (Dec. 1934): 311-30.
                                                 RICHARD G. STONE

LORETTO ACADEMY. Loretto Academy began in 1812 as a small school on Hardins Creek, Marion County, Kentucky, operated by the Sisters of Loretto, a religious order for the moral and intellectual training of the young. On December 29, 1829, the Kentucky legislature granted a charter to the Loretto Literary and Benevolent Institution. The Loretto Academy building was erected in 1834 and superseded in 1886 by larger quarters. Like most academies for women in the nineteenth century, it offered a broad curriculum that included history, science, literature, languages, philosophy, religion, art, music, and plain and fancy sewing. Financial difficulties closed Loretto Academy in 1918.

CONNIE MILLS

LOST CITY. Lost City (sometimes called the Page site) is one of the largest prehistoric Native American mound groups in Kentucky. It is located two and a half miles east of Lewisburg, Logan County, on the western bank of the Mud River. The site was excavated in 1929 by a University of Kentucky archaeology team led by William Webb. They found sixty-seven mounds, used for ceremonies and burials, and ossuary and crematory pits. A rockshelter and earthworks are further proof of Native American habitation. From the artifacts found at the site, Webb concluded that three distinct cultures inhabited the area during the Mississippian period (A.D. 900-1650).

See W.S. Webb and W.D. Funkhouser, *The Page Site* (Lexington, Ky., 1930).

LOTTERIES. The lottery in early Kentucky was simply an extension of that in Virginia, where the first lotteries were organized to finance the construction of churches, to improve town streets and other facilities, to build paper mills and repair bleaching mills, and to finance academies, including Transylvania University in Virginia's Kentucky District. In both Virginia and the new state of Kentucky, the use of lotteries to finance public projects was indicative, first of all, of the failure to devise adequate means of generating revenue, as well as public resistance to taxes.

In its December 1792 session, the newly organized Kentucky General Assembly enacted legislation permitting the Dutch Presbyterian Society to hold a lottery to raise funds for financing construction of a meetinghouse. Three years later, a law permitted the Masonic Order to hold a lottery to raise funds for building a Grand Lodge Hall. Throughout the first century of the Commonwealth of Kentucky, the General Assembly received numerous requests to charter lotteries to raise funds for a wide variety of purposes. The most popular objectives were the founding and operation of colleges and academies; building and maintenance of roads; improvement of stream channels; construction of bridges, factories, and Masonic lodges; and improvements in town streets. Few or none of the lotteries prior to the Civil War offered prizes large enough to create sudden wealth for lucky ticketholders, and local prize offerings were generally rather modest. There is little available information about the winners of lottery prizes or the success of lotteries in achieving their claimed objectives. The records of failures include the 1814-15 attempt by the Masons of Kentucky to raise $30,000 in construction money. In the end they lost their proposed building to Dr. Lewis Marshall of Woodford County, who demanded payment of his prize in sound specie instead of Bank of Kentucky notes.

From the outset there was a real potential for fraud and corruption, not to mention mismanagement, in the conduct of lotteries, especially those that were privately conducted for personal gain. In 1779 the Virginia General Assembly outlawed private lotteries, and in 1816 the Kentucky legislators enacted a similar law. That law was upheld by the Kentucky court of appeals in *Morton v. Fletcher* (1819), on the condition that all prior contracts were to be "impeached by special plea." In 1823 the General Assembly outlawed the sale of lottery tickets "contrived or drawn outside the state." These laws, however, did not truly control either private lotteries or sales in Kentucky of tickets from other states.

In 1842 the U.S. Congress barred lotteries in the District of Columbia, and in 1852 the Kentucky General Assembly undertook to bar all lottery privileges within three years. Under the state law, the promotion, management, or advertising of a lottery was a criminal offense, and it was unlawful to print tickets or maintain a house where they could be sold and the lottery operated. The 1852 law duplicated many of the elements of the 1779 Virginia law barring the operation of private lotteries. In 1859 the Kentucky court of appeals, in *Gregory's Executrix v. Trustees of Shelby College*, overturned the 1852 law on the grounds that it violated the rights of William T. Waller, who held a mortgage and a lien on the lottery charter and privileges of the trustees of Shelby College. Since the mortgage and lien had been executed prior to the law's enactment in 1852, the court upheld Waller's claim and essentially validated his right to conduct a private lottery. The case became an important precedent in Kentucky lottery history.

After the Civil War, lotteries in general came under fire because of abuse and corruption, particularly in privately operated lotteries like Louisiana's. At the time, Kentucky was one of the few states in which private lottery operators could function with minimal legislative interference. Private companies such as Fletcher and Company of New York City, the Kentucky State Lottery, the Commonwealth Distributing Company, the Havana Lottery of Kentucky, S.T. Dickinson of New York, and Morris Richmond of Covington operated in the state, but their management offices were elsewhere, despite the quasi-Kentucky implications of their names. In 1890 seven external lotteries were still operating in Kentucky under state franchises.

The U.S. Congress in 1890 enacted a law that prohibited the distribution of lottery tickets and the advertising of games by mail. In *Champion v. Ames* (1903), the U.S. Supreme Court upheld the law on the grounds that it protected the people of the nation against the pestilence of lotteries. In Kentucky the legal history of lotteries from 1792 to 1890 is a jagged one. The General Assembly in 1878 repealed the laws permitting the granting of charters and franchises. Two years later, in 1880, it partially rescinded its previous action by permitting tickets to be sold and lotteries held under legislative oversight and specific rules. Violators of the law were to be fined $100 a day, and indigent offenders unable to pay the fines were to work them out at the rate of seventy-five cents a day. To end corruption and fraud, repeal of lottery laws was a ready-made issue for the reformers of the day, both in and out of the General Assembly, during the 1880s. There was no doubt that the operation of private lotteries in Kentucky in those years was out of hand, and the state was in an untenable position before the nation when the 1890 constitutional convention met.

Despite the contradictions in Kentucky lottery history, the constitutional convention of 1849 did not discuss the subject. No doubt the omission reflects the pressing importance of other issues; the convention was hotly involved in discussions of slavery, state finances, and internal improvements, and lotteries in Kentucky were mostly of a public nature. By 1890, however, lotteries had become predominantly private, and the issue of repressing gambling was a rising one. With good reason, the public lacked faith in the General Assembly's capability or will to deal effectively with the issue. In the 1890 constitutional convention, delegates responded to the rising antigambling public sentiments by seeking to abolish lotteries. The Committee of the Whole proposed a prohibitory clause in the Bill of Rights in the new constitution.

Thompson Funk, a delegate from Jefferson County, offered an amendment to the proposed lottery prohibition that would have abolished all forms of gambling in Kentucky, including betting on horse races and the dealing in commodities futures. The amendment was defeated. The lottery prohibition was then moved from the Bill of Rights to section 226, under "General Provisions" of the constitution, as it had been discovered that a section for the confiscation of tickets and other lottery paraphernalia conflicted with the Bill of Rights section guaranteeing the sanctity of property. Unequivocally, section 226 declared lotteries in any form to be unconstitutional. The General Assembly was charged with the enforcement of the law, and all lottery privileges and charters formerly granted were revoked.

The blunt revocation of lottery charters in Kentucky in 1890 followed a national precedent. Kentucky was among the last of the states to take such action. Despite the positive constitutional mandate against this form of gambling, there lingered on in Kentucky an urge to gain quick wealth by chance. In time there crept into quasi-legal status a subtle form of gaming—"bank nights" and raffles operated by merchants, banks, and motion picture theaters. The somewhat vague piece of legislation permitting such activities was recorded in the published *Acts* as being "Neither approved nor disapproved." There was in the law ominous warning against the use of the word "lottery." No special fee could be charged.

Setting off the recent wave of revivals of lotteries as a means of raising state revenue, New Hampshire in 1964 flew in the face of history and revived the institution. In every legislative session in Kentucky after 1980, lottery proponents introduced a bill to nullify section 226 of the constitution. They argued that funds generated by a state lottery would provide bonuses for veterans, support for the elderly, and aid for education.

In 1987 Wallace Wilkinson advocated the legalization of the lottery in his campaign for governor, on the grounds that it would raise money for the veterans of the Vietnam War, supply funds for aid to the elderly, and would go far toward improving Kentucky's educational support. In April 1988 the General Assembly approved submission of an amendment of section 226, and in the general election that year the electorate voted in the majority to revive the lottery. In 1989 the Kentucky state lottery began operation amidst much publicity. Though legal documentation of the history of the lottery in the state is abundant, there is no appreciable amount of information about either the effectiveness of the lotteries, public or private, or of the personal experience of those holding winning tickets.

See James C. Klotter, "Two Centuries of the Lottery in Kentucky," *Register* 87 (Autumn 1989): 405-21; Thomas D. Clark, "Lotteries," *Rural Kentuckian* (Jan. 1988): 12-15.　　THOMAS D. CLARK

LOTTS CREEK COMMUNITY SCHOOL. Lotts Creek Community School in Cordia, Knott County, was one of the last settlement schools established in eastern Kentucky. Founded in 1933 by Alice H. Slone, the school provided educational opportunity in the isolated area. Slone, a native of Caney Creek, Kentucky, received a bachelor of science in education from Ohio State University in 1932. She returned to Kentucky to teach for one year at Caney Creek Settlement School (now Alice Lloyd College). In 1933 Slone started what became Lotts Creek Community School. She served as the first teacher, then as principal, and was director until she retired in 1986. The community built the log cabin that served as the schoolhouse for the first nineteen students. Funding for the school came from donations of materials, supplies, and volunteer help. Contributions received from outside Appalachia helped the school grow.

In 1937 Lotts Creek Community School was selected as a radio listening center for the University of Kentucky, and equipment was placed in the school to bring radio broadcasts to residents of the community who met there. This project made the school known beyond the region. The construction of a graded road and the introduction of electricity into the valley in 1948 made access easier. Dormitory facilities were built in 1951 and 1960 for students from surrounding areas. In 1953 a three-story classroom building was completed, and in 1990 construction of new school facilities began.

Lotts Creek Community School became incorporated in 1957 and received a standard school rating in 1988. It successfully resisted consolidation into the state educational system. With continued community support, the school operated as a joint effort of the private sector through donations, with some assistance from the county for teachers' salaries.

See Diane K. Gentry, *An Appalachian Community Views Its School: Lotts Creek Community School* (N.p., 1978).

LOUISA. The county seat of Lawrence County, Louisa is located on U.S. 23, where the Tug and Levisa forks meet to form the Big Sandy River. Some believe the town was named by settlers from Louisa County, Virginia. A second theory is that the source of the name was the Louisa Fork River, with the spelling corrupted to "Levisa." Still others say that the name honored Louisa Swetnam, one of the first white children born at the forks. In February 1789, Charles Vancouver attempted to found a settlement at the point between the two forks of the Big Sandy River. Indians raided the nascent settlement the following March, driving away most of its residents, and the remaining three or four settlers left in April 1790. A second station, called Balclutha, was built just west of the first sometime between 1790 and 1795. It, too, disappeared. In 1815 Frederick Moore, of Philadelphia, planned a town at the forks. By 1818 a substantial community was thriving along the river. On December 11, 1822, the town became the county seat of Lawrence County.

Built in 1823, the first Lawrence County courthouse was a wooden structure. The second, a two-story brick building in Italianate style, built in the 1870s, lasted nearly ninety years. Lawrence County's third courthouse, a modern stone and glass structure, was completed in 1964.

Its favorable location, on a major river near rich timber and coal reserves, made Louisa a major regional trading center by mid-nineteenth century. Vast amounts of raw timber floated down the river from Louisa, and barges carrying timber products such as tanbark made regular journeys on the Big Sandy.

During the Civil War, both sides sought to control the strategic Big Sandy River valley. Under the leadership of Col. James A. Garfield, Federal troops occupied Louisa in December 1861. On March 12 and again on March 25-26, 1863, Confederates unsuccessfully attempted to wrest control of the valley from the Union. In September 1864 Northern forces began the construction of Fort Bishop, near Louisa, which was only partly completed, but the Union presence in Louisa was not contested again.

With the growing importance of coal in the late nineteenth and early twentieth centuries, Louisa continued to grow as a regional trading center. In 1881 the Chattaroi Railroad (CSX Transportation), reached Louisa on its way to the Appalachian coal fields. Locks built on the Big Sandy River in the late 1890s eased river navigation.

During the early twentieth century, Louisa prospered. The coal industry was booming and the increasing popularity of the automobile in the 1920s led to exploration for oil in the river valley. The

Great Depression ended the good times, and in the 1930s New Deal programs provided most of the jobs to be had in the area. In 1963 the Kentucky Power Company opened a large plant in Potters, just north of Louisa, to supply electricity throughout the Big Sandy River valley. Soon afterward Louisa Carpet Mills arrived.

The population of the fifth-class city was 1,781 in 1970; 1,832 in 1980; and 1,990 in 1990.

GEORGE WOLFFORD

LOUIS-PHILIPPE. The son of Louis Philippe Joseph and Louise Marie Adelaide, Louis-Philippe, Duc d'Orleans and future king of France, visited Kentucky in the spring of 1797. Refugees from the French Revolution, he, his two brothers, and a servant left Philadelphia in March 1797 to explore the American frontier. Following an itinerary prepared by President George Washington they rode horseback through Virginia, North Carolina, Tennessee, and Kentucky.

The entries in their travel diary note their arrival at "Mr. Hodgins place" (now in Larue County) on the morning of May 18, 1797. After dark on the same day they arrived at "Captain Been's" in "Beardstown," of which they said: "Good people and a good inn." The "Captain Been" was actually Capt. Joseph Bane, whose tavern was on Lot No. 54 on East Arch Street in Bardstown. During the two-day visit, Louis-Philippe commented "How little these local folk know of the world." These were the last diary entries, though the party continued on to Louisville and Lexington.

Born in Paris on October 6, 1773, Louis-Philippe occupied the throne of France from 1830 to 1848. Deposed in 1848, he fled to England, where he died on August 26, 1850.

See Louis-Philippe, *Diary of My Travels in America* (New York 1977).   DIXIE HIBBS

LOUISVILLE. Louisville, Kentucky's largest metropolitan area, was founded in 1778 during George Rogers Clark's expedition on behalf of Virginia to wrest the territory northwest of the Ohio River from British control. Clark's small band of militia, accompanied by a group of settlers bound for Kentucky, journeyed down the Ohio River from the Pittsburgh area and stopped at the Falls of the Ohio on May 27. On a small island there, Clark trained his 175 or so militiamen, awaited reinforcements, and revealed that the expedition was not to defend Kentucky but to take the offensive in the Illinois country.

When the troops started on their daring mission on June 24, the civilian settlers were left on Corn Island, named for the crop planted that first year. The settlers late in 1778 moved to the Kentucky shore, built a stockade and cabins, and laid the foundation for the city of Louisville. Its name, bestowed in 1779, honors French King Louis XVI and his decision to aid the American colonies in their struggle with England. The news of the French alliance had reached the Falls of the Ohio within a month of Clark's arrival there. In 1780 the settlement was granted a town charter by the state of Virginia.

Louisville's growth was slow at first, lagging behind that of Lexington and other inland communities. Even as late as 1800 it was smaller than the area's Frankfort, Washington, or Paris. Its exposed position as the farthest west of American settlements led to frequent Indian raids and deterred settlers in the earlier years. The site, dotted with mosquito-breeding ponds, also was reputed to be unhealthy. The town was not able to capitalize on its greatest asset, the commercial potential of the Ohio River, as long as the Spanish controlled the lower Mississippi River and New Orleans—the natural outlet for the agricultural produce of Kentucky. These early barriers to growth were gradually eliminated. Gen. Anthony Wayne's defeat of the Indians at Fallen Timbers in Ohio in 1794 practically ended the threat from the original possessors of the Ohio Valley. Filling and draining the ponds ended the malarial illnesses that plagued the early inhabitants. The Louisiana Purchase of 1803, which put New Orleans in American hands the following year, cleared the way for free navigation to the sea.

The coming of the steamboat was the greatest contributor to the growth of Louisville and other river towns. The small settlement, huddled close to the river, was roused from sleep on the night of October 28, 1811, by unaccustomed hissing and roaring sounds from the riverfront. The *New Orleans*, first steam vessel on the Ohio and Mississippi rivers, had arrived on a moonlit midnight on its pioneer journey from Pittsburgh to New Orleans. Louisville had by then already begun to assume the rudiments of its later commercial character. In 1807 some 2,000 keelboats arrived from upriver bound for New Orleans. Most had to unload their cargo to be carried by wagon around the falls. This carrying trade led naturally to warehousing, wholesaling, and the proliferation of commission merchants and freight forwarders. Yet the traffic was predominantly one-way. It took a keelboat, propelled by manpower, three to four months to reach the falls from New Orleans. The result was that while downriver traffic averaged 60,000 tons a year in presteamboat days, upriver it was only 6,500. With the advent of mechanical propulsion, boats could navigate more easily upstream and the time from New Orleans to Louisville was eventually reduced to a week. The steamboat, along with the break in navigation at the falls, was the key to the city's sudden spurt of growth. Between 1810 and 1820 the population tripled to 4,012, and by 1830 Louisville was the largest city in the state with a population of 11,345, including the satellite communities of Portland and Shippingport at the lower end of the falls.

In 1835 Charles Fenno Hoffman wrote in *A Winter in the West* that "the shops, which are large and airy, offer a very showy display of goods; and the spacious and substantial warehouses, with the numerous drays continually passing to and fro, the concourse of well-dressed people in the streets and the quantity of river-craft in front of the town, give Louisville the appearance of being the greatest place of business upon the western waters." In 1828 Louisville was granted city status by the General Assembly, the first community in Kentucky to obtain the greater measure of home rule that accompanied this status.

But with accelerated growth came numerous civic problems. Louisville had early gained a reputation as a rowdy town. Many boats terminated trips above or below the Falls of the Ohio, discharging crews while repairs were under way or a cargo was assembled. Waterfront taverns, brothels, and gambling dens catered to these free-spirited, often brawling, boatmen, and any others of like mind. In 1820 a grand jury was appalled by the many "nurseries of vice and immorality" and "the great and unusual increase of tippling houses and houses of ill-fame," reported the *Louisville Public Advertiser* on April 26. This seamy side of town life was one of the compelling reasons for seeking city status. The monthly meetings of the county court could not mete quick justice to petty offenders. But a city court, with the mayor presiding, could dispose of cases quickly—even daily. As a city, Louisville had greater taxing power and began an overdue program of grading and paving the principal streets, using stone quarried at low water from the ledge that created the Falls of the Ohio.

The rapid change from sleepy village in 1800 to bustling city in 1830 was accompanied by new elements in local leadership and a change in political coloration. The town trustees had been predominantly of the merchant class, but in the 1820s nonmercantile professionals, especially attorneys, began sharing leadership roles. The most notable was attorney James Guthrie, principal mover toward incorporation as a city. He later served as chairman of the new city council's finance committee, using the post to push a series of projects, including the new courthouse, the University of Louisville, public schools, aid to a private company to install gas street lighting (seen as a deterrent to crime), and homes. He even entertained hopes of making Louisville the state capital. The Greek Revival-style courthouse, begun in 1837 after the design of Gideon Shryock, was offered to the state as the capitol building in 1843, but was refused. Louisville began to learn that largely rural Kentucky had no particular love for its largest city.

During these years the political leanings of the city switched from strongly Democratic to strongly Whig, symbolized by the demise in the 1840s of the Democratic *Louisville Public Advertiser* and the ascendancy of Whig editor George D. Prentice and his *Louisville Daily Journal*, founded in 1830. The shift was probably due in part to Kentuckian Henry Clay's national leadership of the Whigs, but it also reflected mercantile Louisville's desire that the federal government provide stable currency and credit through the Bank of the United States.

Despite unfulfilled hopes for a national bank and the fear (unfounded) that the 1830 Louisville &

Portland Canal around the falls would undermine the city's middleman economy, Louisville weathered the financial storm of the panic of 1837. One factor was the emergence of manufacturing enterprises, particularly shipyards, steam-engine builders, and iron foundries, plus tobacco processing and meat packing. Manufacturing was still overshadowed by the mercantile trade, however.

One reason for slow industrial growth was the institution of slavery, which discouraged able white mechanics from a market where even skilled handwork was regarded as a servile occupation. In an urban setting most owners rented out their slaves or encouraged them to hire themselves out (although this was illegal), and many slaves performed menial labor in the city's nascent factories. Statistics suggest that slavery was a fading institution in Louisville and Jefferson County by the late 1840s. From 1850 to 1860, the number of slaves in the city decreased by 10 percent, to 4,903, totaling a mere 7.5 percent of the city's population. Much of the decline in numbers reflected the sale of slaves southward to meet the voracious demand of the cotton states, but the main reason for the percentage decline was the huge increase in the white population because of the influx of foreign immigrants, especially German and Irish. The city's white population showed an impressive increase of nearly 42 percent between 1850 and 1860, reaching 61,213. This new population pool also was instrumental in the acceleration of manufacturing during the 1850s. The sudden tide of newcomers (most of whom were also Roman Catholic) produced severe tensions, culminating in the BLOODY MONDAY riots of August 6, 1855, but the immigrants and their progeny became some of the community's most successful and patriotic citizens.

While the population mix was changing, Louisville faced other problems. The advent of railroads began a slow shift of the nation's major transportation routes from water to land, threatening the city's position as a transshipment point. Louisville gained a rail connection to Frankfort and Lexington in 1851, but the city needed a rail route south to maintain its mercantile economy. Thus was born the Louisville & Nashville Railroad (now CSX Transportation), financed by the city and private capital, completed to Nashville in 1859 and connecting there with railroads to the deep South.

Ironically, less than two years after the L&N was completed, the long-impending storm of the Civil War cut off the southern trade by both river and rail. As a border city in a slave state with strong commercial ties to both North and South, Louisville was divided in sentiment and first attempted a neutral stance, even naming a municipal brigadier general to command local armed forces in repelling invaders from north or south. But, like Kentucky as a whole, Louisville wanted an essentially impossible status quo: union and slavery. Local recruits for the Union army outnumbered those for Confederate forces three to one.

The city became an important Union base of operations, a major military supply center, and home to nineteen military hospitals. The new L&N Railroad, the only direct rail route into the Confederacy west of the Alleghenies, was pushed to the limit carrying Union troops and supplies southward. Gen. William T. Sherman wrote after the war that "the Atlanta campaign would simply have been impossible without the use of railroads from Louisville . . . to Atlanta."

At the end of the war in 1865, Louisville was not only unscathed but even prosperous, on the basis of military purchases and its role as a military headquarters. Its fledgling industries, especially iron foundries, had gained a firmer economic footing. The L&N Railroad, its coffers comfortably filled from military traffic, embarked on an ambitious expansion program that would take it to the Gulf of Mexico. As railroads proliferated and river trade declined, the city shifted toward a manufacturing economy, building on the rudimentary prewar industrial operations. The merchant princes were now joined by the manufacturers as shapers of Louisville's prosperity. Other changes also marked the postwar era. The end of slavery brought hundreds of rural Kentucky blacks to the city seeking jobs. Most found only disappointment and segregated neighborhoods. (In slavery days the black population was fairly evenly distributed across the city.) The Democratic party again dominated until the early years of the twentieth century, leading to machine politics orchestrated by brothers John and James Whallen, sons of Irish immigrants. These political bosses built their machine on the loyalty of the blue-collar industrial workers. Lastly, the city cultivated a regional identity with the South (in earlier days it considered itself western) as an adjunct to its competition with northern cities for southern trade.

In 1870 Louisville's population passed the 100,000 mark and its burgeoning smokestacks symbolized the near-doubling of industrial output during the following decade—primarily steam engines and boilers, agricultural implements, furniture, cement, and iron pipe. Tobacco processing and distilling, although important, were small in comparison. The last thirty years of the nineteenth century were a period of steady growth and consolidation of earlier gains, including extension of city boundaries, a system of public parks, electric streetlights and electric streetcars, railroad bridges across the Ohio River, and the Southern Exposition in 1883, in which Louisville displayed its industrial products and commercial advantages. The most pervasive issue throughout the period, however, was political reform, which succeeded now and then against long odds. Perhaps the most notable victory was the introduction of the secret ballot in 1888, its first use in the United States. This did not end vote buying but sharply reduced its effectiveness. As the century ended, Louisville doubled its 1870 population, reaching 204,000.

In the new century the city experienced a slowing of growth, as shown by the 1910 census, attributable partly to the demise of many small local manufacturers unable to compete with the large national corporations that were emerging, and partly to the growth of new suburban areas outside the city limits. These were made possible by the electric streetcar and its push into the countryside. The answer to the suburban growth was again to expand the borders, although the annexation was not completed until 1922 because of court challenges.

The industrial decline was a more difficult problem, but in 1916 the Board of Trade launched the Million Dollar Factory Fund, raising private funds to make loans to promising enterprises that might have difficulty in securing bank credit. When the United States entered World War I, the Board of Trade was instrumental in securing a military training base, Camp Zachary Taylor, for Louisville.

The national prosperity of the 1920s seemed to erase any economic deficit that the city had experienced earlier, even though national prohibition, outlawing production and sale of alcoholic beverages, caused a loss of 6,000 to 8,000 jobs. New manufacturing plants (more than 150 during the decade), plus the 1922 expansion of city boundaries, increased population by 21 percent, for a total of nearly 308,000 by 1930. Automobile ownership paved the way for extensive suburban development beyond the reach of public transportation. Once stable and prestigious neighborhoods, such as Old Louisville, immediately south of the central business district, began to lose their luster. The automobile and the helter-skelter growth it generated were also factors in the beginning of planning and zoning in 1927. Louisville was the first Kentucky city to adopt such measures. During the decade the city also finally put the University of Louisville on a firm footing with a new home on Belknap Campus, constructed the first bridge exclusively for motor vehicles across the Ohio River, and gained its first art museum, built to memorialize James B. Speed, businessman and philanthropist.

The situation changed radically during the Depression years of the 1930s. Unemployment climbed to unprecedented levels of more than 25 percent in 1932. The only bright spots were in cigarette production, where one plant even built an addition to keep up with demand, and in the repeal of prohibition, which put distilleries and breweries back in business. The greatest local catastrophe was the failure of the venerable National Bank of Kentucky in 1930, precipitating a wave of mortgage foreclosures and personal bankruptcies. The great Ohio Valley flood of 1937 increased the suffering of the Great Depression as most of the city was inundated by flood waters.

World War II, however, turned the economic gloom of the 1930s into an industrial bonanza. Even before the United States entered the conflict, plans were announced for a huge powder plant in cross-river Clark County, Indiana; a naval gun plant; an aircraft plant; and a series of chemical plants that would make Louisville the world's largest producer of synthetic rubber. Other war-related plants quickly followed, and after the nation entered the war in December 1941 practically all of the city's industrial resources were turned to military production. Louisville became "the biggest, busiest industrial community" it had ever been, said the *Louisville Courier-Journal* (January 1, 1942).

After the war the defense plants were converted to peacetime production and the influx of new industries kept Louisville and Jefferson County the leading industrial center in the Southeast. The largest new employer was the General Electric Company, which moved its entire home-appliance operation to the area in 1953 and by 1958 employed more than 16,000 persons at the 1,000-acre Appliance Park. Blue- and white-collar jobs in manufacturing were 45 percent of city and county employment in 1974, when the peak of 107,000 such jobs was reached. A new airport, Standiford Field, was another legacy of the war. Built to serve the aircraft plant, it became the commercial field in 1947, replacing Bowman Field, which had handled commercial flights from their beginning in 1928.

Meanwhile, Louisville began to create a name for itself in the arts, especially the performing arts. The Louisville Orchestra, founded in 1937, began a program of commissioning works by contemporary composers. An opera company and ballet company were formed and Actors Theatre of Louisville became one of the nation's foremost regional theatre groups. To accommodate growing audiences, the Kentucky Center for the Arts, with two performance halls, was completed on downtown Main Street in 1983 as part of the renewal of the central business district.

That renewal was a response to the challenge posed by the automobile. After reaching a peak of 390,000 in 1961, Louisville's population began to decline; over 100,000 residents were lost between 1960 and 1980. The population was 269,063 in 1990. The departures to suburban areas beyond the city and even beyond Jefferson County were made possible by the personal mobility of the automobile on the developing expressway system (begun in 1949). The suburban surge included not only housing but also shopping centers, motels, office buildings, and even hospitals. Downtown Louisville, the traditional commercial heart of the region, began showing the effects in the 1960s. New downtown construction virtually ceased. Empty stores, vacant hotels, and closed movie palaces peppered the central business district.

Renewal began modestly in 1957 with the development of the Medical Center east of downtown and was expanded through the years with federal urban-renewal funds and large infusions of state, city, and private funds. By 1970 new office towers were rising and the historic riverfront was being redeveloped. Since then the heart of the city has been largely transformed with new shopping facilities, housing, hotels, parking garages, rehabilitation of historic structures, and a near-doubling of office space. The emphasis on office space is an indicator of the continuing shift of the city's economy from blue- to white-collar. In 1970 manufacturing was still an important part of the economy (especially motor trucks, home appliances, paints, and plastics and other chemical products), but manufacturing in 1980 accounted for only 24.8 percent of the workforce, a steep decline from the mid-1970s. The office category now accounts for most of the workforce and is growing; the single category of finance, real estate, and insurance rose from 20 percent of jobs in 1960 to 32 percent in 1980. The city is also an important regional medical center. This shift to the knowledge/information/services sector was foreshadowed in 1954 when General Electric's Appliance Park saw the first application of computer technology by private business.

The emerging economic base includes such firms as Humana, Inc., operating hospitals across the nation; Capital Holding, with a nationwide insurance empire; Mercer-Meidinger, nationwide employee-benefits consulting firm; Kentucky Fried Chicken and its chain of fast-food outlets; and BATUS, holding company for the properties of the British-American Tobacco Company. Louisville became the headquarters of the Presbyterian Church (U.S.A.) in 1987. The city's early role as a warehousing and distribution center continues in the air age, underscored by United Parcel Service's choice of Standiford Field as its principal distribution hub in 1983. By 1989 it was the area's second largest employer, after General Electric, and Louisville's largest taxpayer.

Since its founding, Louisville has been home to a number of notable residents, among them artist-ornithologist John James Audubon; William Clark of the 1803-06 Lewis and Clark Expedition to the Pacific Coast; Supreme Court justices Louis D. Brandeis and John Marshall Harlan; Henry Watterson, long-time editor of the *Louisville Courier Journal*; Augustus E. Willson, governor of Kentucky during 1907-11; Thomas Coleman du Pont, who transformed the Du Pont Company from a powder manufacturer to a chemical giant; Fontaine Fox, Jr., creator of the *Toonerville Trolley* cartoon; Robert Worth Bingham, publisher of the *Louisville Courier-Journal* and the *Louisville Times* after 1918; John S. Crowell, founder of the Crowell Publishing Company (the *Saturday Evening Post*); author Alice Hegan Rice, best known for *Mrs. Wiggs of the Cabbage Patch*; Mrs. Potter Palmer, wife of the Chicago hotelier; trumpeter Jonah Jones; and Roland Hayes, the first black American to carve out a career as a concert singer.

See George H. Yater, *Two Hundred Years at the Falls of the Ohio: A History of Louisville and Jefferson County*, 2d ed. (Louisville 1987); Samuel W. Thomas, *Views of Louisville Since 1766* (Louisville 1971); George C. Wright, *Life Behind a Veil: Blacks in Louisville, Kentucky, 1865-1930* (Baton Rouge, La. 1985).   GEORGE H. YATER

LOUISVILLE, U.S.S. The U.S.S. *Louisville*, a Northhampton-class heavy cruiser constructed at Puget Sound Navy Yard near Seattle, Washington, was the third and most famous of the navy ships named for the city. Christened by Jane Brown Kennedy of Louisville on September 1, 1930, the

Louisville was commissioned January 15, 1931. The ship displaced 9,050 tons and was 600 feet long. The *Louisville* carried a main battery of nine 8-inch guns in three turrets and a wartime crew of 1,200.

The "Lady Lou" saw extensive prewar service in both Atlantic and Pacific, and was at sea and heading toward Pearl Harbor when the Japanese attacked on December 7, 1941. During World War II she fought throughout the Pacific, winning thirteen battle stars. As the United States pushed toward Japan, the battleship took part in many naval engagements and island bombardments, including Guadalcanal, Eniwetok, and Guam, and served as flagship of the U.S. forces in the victory at Surigao Strait, the Philippines, October 25, 1944—the largest naval surface battle of the war. Kamikazes struck the ship in the Philippines on January 5-6, 1945, killing thirty-two and wounding fifty-six. Another kamikaze caught *Louisville* off Okinawa in June 1945. After the war the Lady Lou served briefly in the occupation, then was decommissioned on June 17, 1946, and placed in reserve. The ship was sold for scrap on September 14, 1959, after efforts in Louisville failed to raise funds to buy the ship.

The first *Louisville* was a 468-ton ironclad river gunboat built for the Union navy during the Civil War; the second was a passenger liner converted into a troop ship during World War I. The fourth *Louisville* (SSN-724), a Los Angeles-class attack submarine displacing 6,900 tons and 360 feet long was commissioned November 8, 1986.

See Larry A. Pearson, "Remembering the Lady Lou," *Kentucky Monthly* 3 (Jan./Feb. 1982).

JOHN S. GILLIG

LOUISVILLE & NASHVILLE RAILROAD. The Louisville & Nashville (L&N), chartered by the Kentucky General Assembly in 1850, became Kentucky's dominant rail carrier in the decades after the Civil War. By 1920 it operated more than 1,800 miles of line in the commonwealth. During much of its history, the L&N provided essential passenger, freight, and mail transportation services to more than half the counties in the state. It moved products of Kentucky's farms and industries to regional, national, and export markets, and it played an important role in the growth of the Harlan and Hazard coal fields. Especially during the presidency of Milton H. Smith, L&N's influence as an industry leader and political force was far reaching. Principal routes ran southward from Cincinnati, Chicago, and St. Louis, bisecting the state to serve Memphis, Tennessee; Atlanta; Birmingham, Alabama; and the Gulf Coast. Intrastate routes linked Hazard and Harlan with Lexington, Louisville, Owensboro, Henderson, and Madisonville. Long under stock control, L&N ceased to exist at the end of 1982 and became part of the Seaboard System.

It was Louisville's need for better transportation and its economic struggle with Cincinnati and

Nashville for southern markets that set the stage for L&N's chartering in March 1850. A total of $3.8 million was raised by on-line communities and counties to capitalize the road; Louisville alone subscribed more than $1 million. In the field by 1851, surveyors selected a route south via Elizabethtown, Bowling Green, and Franklin and through an agriculturally productive corridor. According to historian Thomas D. Clark, "The building of the L&N was the most significant internal improvement undertaken in Kentucky [before 1860]. . . . It connected the commonwealth with the expanding South and immediately became economically profitable. With its branches, [it] added significantly to the economic dimensions of Kentucky."

The mainline to Nashville opened on November 1, 1859. Passenger trains ran the 185 miles in ten hours, three times faster than stagecoaches; although somewhat slower, freight trains beat the several-day transit by wagon road or water. Branches to Lebanon and Bardstown, finished in 1858 and 1860, fed additional traffic to the main stem, as did a direct Louisville-Memphis route, completed in April 1861 by way of Russellville, Clarksville, and Paris, Tennessee, over two connecting roads south of Guthrie.

With lines squarely in the paths of opposing armies, L&N suffered considerable damage during the Civil War. In 1861, its trains moved food and material into Tennessee for the Confederate cause, but after 1862, L&N became a part of a vital supply route supporting Federal armies advancing deeper into the South. Periodically, Gen. John Hunt Morgan and other Confederate raiders damaged tracks, bridges and stations, but after each raid, work crews—often under military guard—rebuilt the line to restore service.

L&N remained in private ownership during the war and emerged in 1865 in reasonably good condition, both physically and financially. Its wartime profits permitted the road to expand into the South, rebuild other damaged railroads (including the two west Tennessee lines that connected Memphis) and bring improved transportation to an almost prostrate region. The push southward continued in the 1870s, first when L&N acquired the Nashville & Decatur and then completed the projected South & North Alabama to Montgomery in 1872. Later acquisitions brought L&N tracks to the ports of New Orleans; Mobile, Alabama; and Pensacola, Florida by 1880-81, greatly expanding the road's territory and offering new markets for Kentucky products. In 1881, L&N entered Evansville and St. Louis when it acquired the St. Louis & Southeastern properties in Illinois, Indiana, and Kentucky. The adjacent western Kentucky coal fields had been reached in 1871 by Southeastern's Henderson-Nashville main stem. In July 1885 a time-consuming river transfer between Henderson and Evansville was eliminated when the new Ohio River bridge opened, giving L&N an all-rail route to and from the Midwest.

Meanwhile, L&N pushed its Lebanon branch to the Tennessee state line by 1883. That work created a new trade route to Knoxville, Tennessee, and Atlanta and brought rail service to coal mines already active in southern Kentucky. During the decade, routes to Cincinnati and Lexington were acquired, and in 1893 L&N purchased the Kentucky Central's Covington-Paris-Livingston mainline, which was to provide an artery for coal moving north from Harlan and Hazard district mines. Such expansion transformed L&N from a small local road into a major southern carrier having more than 2,000 miles of track.

Rapid growth also shifted control from Kentucky to the East, where far greater capital was available to sustain such expansion. Control was forever removed from Kentucky in 1902, when the Atlantic Coast Line secured a controlling interest through purchase of a majority of L&N stock. Either through direct interchange or by "family" connections in Atlanta and Montgomery, L&N and Coast Line began to exchange growing volumes of traffic, leading to formation of a single system by the 1980s.

Much of L&N's expansion was achieved under the inspired and controversial leadership of Milton H. Smith, who as president during 1884-86 and 1891-1921 served longer than any other president. From geological surveys Smith knew of eastern Kentucky's extensive coal reserves, and he directed construction of a branch from Corbin to Pineville and Middlesborough in 1886-89 and on to southwest Virginia in 1891. Real penetration of the Harlan and Bell counties fields came in 1909-11 when Smith built a sixty-mile line from Pineville to Benham. The first car of coal from a Harlan County mine was shipped in August 1911. From Benham, tracks were extended in 1917-18 to reach U.S. Steel's huge development. In 1929-30, L&N built a more direct route (via Chevrolet, Kentucky, and Hagans, Virginia) over which coal moved from the Cumberland Valley to Virginia and the Carolinas.

L&N, meanwhile, reached coal deposits in Breathitt, Perry, and Letcher counties when it purchased two shorter roads, then built track from Jackson through Hazard to Whitesburg in 1911-12. Dozens of tributary branches followed, to tap new mining opportunities in the Hazard and Harlan fields. What began as a mere trickle before 1900 grew into a flood of coal tonnage after 1920, flowing over L&N from eastern and western Kentucky origins. Both in tonnage and revenues, coal became the top commodity for the road, and in the decades since it has invested millions in new locomotives, cars, track improvements, and facilities to better serve the coal industry.

L&N continued to grow after 1945, although passenger service declined after World War II and eventually ceased. In 1957 L&N acquired the Nashville, Chattanooga & St. Louis, which it had controlled since 1880. This 1,200-mile system connected Paducah and Memphis with Chattanooga, Tennessee, and Atlanta. A decade later, L&N purchased part of the Chicago & Eastern Illinois, acquiring direct entry into Chicago. A second Chicago access was secured in 1971 when L&N merged the 573-mile Monon Railroad into its system. By 1972, L&N operated 6,500 miles of lines in thirteen states. System car and locomotive shops remained in Louisville until the 1980s. Other terminals were at Covington (DeCoursey Yard), Bowling Green, Hazard, Harlan, Madisonville, and Ravenna. Over 7,000 persons were employed by L&N in the state that year.

In 1972 L&N became a wholly owned subsidiary of Seaboard Coast Line Industries, parent of Seaboard Coast Line (SCL) Railroad (successor to the former Atlantic Coast Line and Seaboard Air Line). Under the "Family Lines System" banner, L&N, SCL, and three small affiliates were operated as a combined system. Although L&N's identity was preserved and its headquarters remained in Louisville, most departments were consolidated with those of SCL in Jacksonville, Florida, leading to the creation in January 1983 of Seaboard System Railroad.

In 1986, CSX, a Richmond, Virginia, transportation holding company, melded the Chessie System (representing the former Baltimore & Ohio and Chesapeake & Ohio) and Seaboard System (including L&N) into a single rail system, CSX Transportation, serving the eastern third of the nation.

See Thomas D. Clark, *Beginning of the L & N* (Lexington, Ky., 1933); Maury Klein, *History of the Louisville & Nashville Railroad* (New York 1972);   CHARLES B. CASTNER

LOUISVILLE AND NASHVILLE TURNPIKE.
The Louisville and Nashville Turnpike was the common name for the toll road that extended in the mid-1800s from Louisville through Elizabethtown, Munfordville, Glasgow Junction, Bowling Green, and Franklin to the Tennessee line. In a message to the General Assembly in 1825, Gov. Joseph Desha (1824-28) promoted construction of two turnpike roads, one being a Louisville-Nashville route by way of the Green River. In 1829 the legislature chartered the Louisville, West Point and Elizabethtown Turnpike Road Company to build a road from Louisville by way of West Point to Elizabethtown. The road had not been built after the stipulated three-year limit, and in 1833 a new charter was issued to build a road from Louisville to Bowling Green. In a series of amendments (1837, 1838, 1847), the legislature approved division of the road into five sections, managed by five companies. The projected road was extended to the state line, a total of 143 miles, and was to be constructed of macadamized materials. Toll gates were to be installed every five miles. Work actually began in 1837. In 1849 the Board of Internal Improvements reported nearly 106 miles completed, with much of the remaining route graded.

Travel accounts of the day report heavy traffic in both directions throughout the 1850s. After the Louisville & Nashville Railroad (now CSX Transportation) was completed in 1859 to serve much of the same area, the turnpike declined in popularity. Much of the road fell into disrepair and maintenance of various sections was taken over by local county authorities. In 1901 Jefferson County bought part of the turnpike, by then called the Valley Turnpike, that lay within the county.

The legislature used various names for the company it chartered to build the turnpike, among them the Louisville Turnpike Road Company, the Louisville and Nashville Turnpike Road Company, and the Louisville and Elizabethtown Company, the name that occurs most often. The turnpike itself was not given an official name. The road from Louisville to Nashville through Bardstown, New Haven, Buffalo, Uno, Bear Wallow, Glasgow, Scottsville, and Gallatin, Tennessee, was sometimes referred to as the Louisville and Nashville Turnpike, but the name was more commonly applied to the lower route through Elizabethtown.

By 1924, portions of the turnpike had become part of the western route of U.S. 31W, which ran from Sault Ste. Marie, Michigan, south through Louisville and Nashville to Fort Myers, Florida.

See S.G. Boyd, "The Louisville and Nashville Turnpike," *Register* 24 (May 1926): 163-74; Frank Dunn, "The Official Opening of the Eastern Dixie Highway," *Kentucky Outlook* 1 (Oct. 17, 1925): 38-41.   KATHERINE L. HOUSE

LOUISVILLE AND PORTLAND CANAL.
When the trustees of the new town of Louisville met for the first time on February 7, 1781, they petitioned the Virginia General Assembly for the right to construct a canal around the Falls of the Ohio, a serious impediment to Ohio River traffic. During the next half-century, both Kentucky and Indiana made numerous failed attempts to build a canal. It was not until 1830 that the falls were bypassed with a man-made channel, the Louisville and Portland Canal.

Upriver cities, especially arch-rival Cincinnati, blamed Louisville for hampering construction of a canal, as the forced break in the river journey because of the falls was the basis of the warehousing, commission, and forwarding businesses, drayage, hotels and inns, and steamboat provisioning on which Louisville prospered. There was opposition to a canal among some Louisvillians, but others espoused it. The *Louisville Public Advertiser* (February 7, 1824) stated that with canal construction, "the storage and forwarding business would be diminished—and there might be less use for hacks and drays," but that a canal would provide "the necessary power for manufacturing." The overriding obstacle to a canal was the cost; the Ohio Valley itself did not have the resources. When outside aid, both public and private, became available, the Louisville and Portland Canal Company was chartered in 1825. Most private investment came from Philadelphia, which had close commercial ties with the Ohio Valley. The U.S. Congress was convinced by statistics of boats lost on the falls to authorize government purchases of canal company stock.

Construction began in 1826 and the Louisville and Portland Canal opened in December 1830.

Some segments of Louisville business lost trade, and attempts were made to sabotage the lock gates. Within a few years, however, Louisville's "carrying trade" reached probably a greater volume than ever before as the spread of cotton plantations to Alabama and Mississippi in the 1830s immensely increased the demand for farm produce and manufactured goods from the Ohio Valley. The increase in size of steamboats made it apparent as early as 1840 that the fifty-foot-wide "ditch" around the falls was inadequate, and by the early 1850s nearly 40 percent of vessels on the Ohio were too large to pass through the canal. They kept Louisville's wharf busy, and the drayage, warehousing, and forwarding business reaped the benefit. To enlarge the canal, construction of ninety-foot-wide locks began in 1860, but the Civil War and inflation brought construction to a halt at the end of 1866. The federal government, which after 1855 held the majority of stock in the Louisville and Portland Canal Company, agreed to fund completion of the work. After the canal became fully federal property in 1874, tolls were gradually reduced and were abolished in 1880.

In 1910 Congress authorized a plan for "canalization" of the Ohio River through a series of locks and dams that would provide a nine-foot minimum depth of water. To meet the requirement that all locks be one hundred feet wide, a new lock at Louisville was completed in 1921. By the 1950s the increase in barge tonnage required a radical reconstruction of the Portland Canal. The work, completed in 1962, widened the canal to five hundred feet and added a new lock of the same width and 1,200 feet long.

See Leland R. Johnson, *The Falls City Engineers: A History of the Louisville District, Corps of Engineers, United States Army* (Louisville 1975); Louis C. Hunter, *Steamboats on the Western Rivers: An Economic and Technological History* (Cambridge, Mass., 1949).   GEORGE H. YATER

LOUISVILLE BRIDGE. Attempts to bridge the Ohio River at Louisville began in 1829, when city resident James Guthrie obtained a charter for a bridge company. That and other attempts failed until Guthrie received the backing of the LOUISVILLE & NASHVILLE (L&N) RAILROAD in the 1860s. The Louisville Bridge was designed by Albert Fink, a noted structural engineer and railroad executive. Work on the railroad bridge began August 1, 1867; it was opened to traffic in February 1870. At 5,280 feet, it was the longest iron bridge of its time. It began at the foot of Fourteenth Street in Louisville, crossed to Corn Island and then to Clarksville, Indiana. The twenty-seven spans rested on stone cut from a quarry in Utica, Indiana, and were up to four hundred feet wide to allow river traffic to pass easily.

The link formed by the bridge between the L&N and the Jefferson & Indianapolis Railroad provided a significant connection between northern and southern commerce. The bridge was viewed with hostility by business leaders in Cincinnati, who feared that their city might be bypassed, and by merchants in Louisville who feared they would become "simply a way station." The power structure of Louisville indeed changed as the city made the transition from commercial center to manufacturing center in the 1870s.

The Louisville Bridge, sometimes known as the Fourteenth Street Bridge, was replaced by the Pennsylvania Bridge in 1918-19. The upper structure was removed and the new bridge was built upon the original stone bases.

See George H. Yater, *Two Hundred Years at the Falls of the Ohio: A History of Louisville and Jefferson County* (Louisville 1987); Leonard P. Curry, *Rail Routes South: Louisville's Fight for the Southern Market, 1865-1872* (Lexington, Ky., 1969).

LOUISVILLE COLONELS. In its ninety years, the professional BASEBALL club known as the Louisville Colonels won numerous pennants and Junior World Series titles, as well as the affection of four generations of fans. On July 19, 1865, Louisville hosted the first baseball game west of the Alleghenies played under standard rules, defeating the Nashville Cumberlands. When Louisville businessman Walter Haldeman and others formed the National League in 1876, the Louisville club was a charter member. The team, then known as the Louisville Grays, finished fifth in 1876 and the next year led the league in the final weeks of the season but finished second. It was later discovered that gamblers had paid Grays pitcher Jim Devlin and three other Louisville players to lose games in 1877 so that Boston would win the championship. Baseball's first scandal led to the demise of the Grays, and the four team members were banned from playing professional baseball for life. Louisville was ousted from the National League and muddled through four dismal years at the amateur level.

In 1882 the Louisville baseball club became a charter member of the American Association, another major league. Initially the Louisville team was made up primarily of players of a local semi-professional squad, the Eclipses. Louisville native Pete Browning, the most popular Louisville player of the nineteenth century, played for the Eclipses. Browning finished his thirteen-year, hard-drinking career with a .343 batting average, tenth highest in the history of baseball. The Eclipses were briefly renamed the Cyclones (1890), the Night Riders (1890s), and the Wanderers (1899), then became known as the Louisville Colonels. They introduced paid umpires in 1882. In 1884, when Louisville hosted Toledo in the season opener, the Toledo catcher, Moses Fleetwood Walker, was the first black to play in a major league game. In 1890 Louisville won the city's only major league pennant and met the Brooklyn Bridegrooms in the World Series. The series ended in a tie at three games apiece, as the final game was snowed out.

After the American Association was merged into the National League in 1892, Louisville was one of four teams absorbed into the expanded league. When the National League was reduced to eight teams in 1899, Louisville traded some players with the Pittsburgh Pirates, giving up two future members of the Baseball Hall of Fame—outfielder-manager Fred Clarke and shortstop Honus Wagner. Louisville later sold its franchise back to the National League.

The Louisville teams included many local players, including Fred Pfeffer, a second baseman who edited a popular book of the period, *Scientific Ball* (1889); outfielder William ("Chicken") Wolf, who led the team to its only championship, in 1890, after it had lost 111 games in 1889; and infielder-outfielder Pete Browning, who compiled a .343 career batting average. In 1884 Browning first used the customized bat called the Louisville Slugger.

In 1902 Louisville became a charter member of the American Association, which had been reorganized as a minor league. The city's team won fourteen pennants or playoffs in the next sixty years. From 1919 to 1925 the team's manager was Joe McCarthy, who in his twenty-four-year career as a major league manager recorded the highest winning percentage. The Colonels won the 1939 Junior World Series, led by local favorite Harold ("Pee Wee") Reese. In 1962 the American Association suspended operations and Louisville moved to the International League. The Colonels won the 1972 International League pennant.

By the early 1970s the Louisville club was in trouble because of declining attendance—a problem throughout the league—and in 1972 it left the city without a professional baseball team. The club now plays out of Pawtuckett, Rhode Island, as the Red Sox. In 1982 the Redbirds professional baseball team moved to Louisville from Illinois and revived in eres in the game, playing at the city's refurbished Cardinal Stadium. In 1984 Louisville was the first minor league franchise to draw more than 1 million fans. As part of the American Association, which resumed operations in 1969, the Redbirds have won two championships under the leadership of owner A. Ray Smith and manager Jim Fregosi.

See A.H. Tarvin, *Seventy-five Years on Louisville Diamonds* (Louisville 1940); Bob Bailey, "The Ballparks of Louisville," *Ballpark* 27 (1988): 77-83.   Bob Bailey and David Williams

LOUISVILLE DEFENDER. The *Louisville Defender* was founded in 1933 after Alvin H. Bowman of Louisville approached John H. Sengstacke of the *Chicago Defender* about starting another newspaper for blacks with the assistance of the Robert S. Abbott Publishing Company of Chicago. The *Defender* joined the *Louisville News* (established in 1912) and the *Louisville Leader* (established in 1917) as the major newspapers for blacks. The first officers of the board of directors of the newspaper, which operated first on Walnut Street in Louisville, were Sengstacke, chairman; William Craighead, president; Frank H. Gray, secretary; and Theodore Samuels, vice president. Frank L. Stanley, Sr., was named editor of the *Defender*, a position he held for thirty-seven years.

In the lean first years of the *Defender*, the staff was part-time or wrote on commission. Articles concerned segregation and racial inequality, and the *Defender* came to serve as the voice of Louisville's black community. Editor Stanley achieved his hope of a circulation of about 15,000 by 1942, and as circulation grew during World War II, the *Defender*'s voice against segregation grew louder. The newspaper advocated the "Double V": victory against the enemy in Europe and Japan, and victory against segregation in the United States. Stanley traveled to Europe to inspect black troops, a trip that was highly publicized. The *Defender* also ran a photo-story on the segregated conditions in Fort Knox in 1942, showing the tents used by many blacks when there was insufficient room in dormitories.

The newspaper was in debt for the first half of its existence. Offices were moved several times, to Fifth Street in 1944, Second Street in 1954, and Chestnut Street in 1955. Stanley became chief stockholder of the paper in 1950, and printing debts caused it to sever all ties with the Abbott Publishing Company in 1950. The newspaper purchased the first printing press of its own in 1956, and by the next year the *Defender* was making a profit. In the 1960s the *Defender* championed the fight for integration in Louisville. In 1961 Stanley led a group of students in protest when they were denied admission to a Louisville movie theatre. As a result the *Defender* received a great deal of hate mail, and many businesses stopped advertising in the paper. The 1963 Defender Home Service Exposition in Louisville was attended by huge crowds, boosting the profits and the circulation of the paper. In 1964 offices were moved to West Broadway, and a print shop was opened on Sixteenth Street. Stanley joined several white newspapermen in forming the Greater Kentucky Publishers, Inc., with its own printing operation, in 1967.

In 1968 the *Defender* moved its offices to 1720 Dixie Highway in Louisville. Six years later Stanley died suddenly. His family has continued to run the newspaper that has won countless awards from both state and national associations for its work as the voice of Louisville's black community.

LOUISVILLE JOURNAL. The *Louisville Journal* was first issued as a daily newspaper on November 24, 1830, and soon began publishing both a triweekly and a weekly edition that circulated throughout Kentucky, the South, and the Midwest. The newspaper, founded to promote Henry Clay's candidacy for the presidency, was financed and published by A.J. Buxton, with Clay's biographer, George D. Prentice, as the editor. On January 31,

1832, the *Journal* merged with the *Focus*, another Louisville daily established in 1826. Within two years Buxton sold out to George W. Weissinger, who continued to manage the *Journal's* business affairs until his death in 1850.

The *Journal* prospered and soon became one of the most widely circulated newspapers west of the Appalachian Mountains, primarily because of Prentice's sparkling writing. The western farmer, logger, trapper, and riverman all enjoyed reading the *Journal*. Prentice made the *Journal* a great supporter of the Whig party. The *Journal* also encouraged public education, municipal reform, and the commercial and economic development of the city of Louisville. In 1836 the *Journal* began publishing the *Literary News-Letter*, edited by Edmund Flagg, and the *Western Journal of Education*, edited by B.O. Peers, but both were short-lived.

Following the Whig party's demise, the *Journal* endorsed the Native American (or KNOW-NOTHING) party. In the presidential election of 1860, Prentice favored John Bell as the only candidate who could save the Union. Once Abraham Lincoln was elected, Prentice appealed to the southern states to remain loyal to the Union; after Lincoln called for troops, Prentice urged Kentucky to remain neutral.

In 1868 the *Journal* merged with the *Courier*, Louisville's Democratic newspaper, becoming the *Courier-Journal*.

See Betty Carolyn Congleton, "The Louisville Journal: Its Origin and Early Years," *Register* 62 (April 1964): 87-103.

BETTY CAROLYN CONGLETON

LOUISVILLE LEADER. The *Louisville Leader* was a weekly newspaper that covered issues important to the black community in the city during the first half of the twentieth century. Edited by its founder, I. Willis Cole, the *Leader* was first issued in November 1917. The LOUISVILLE DEFENDER (March 18, 1954) wrote that "beginning with $50.00," Cole had made the *Leader* "one of the largest Negro newspaper organizations" in Louisville. By the 1930s the I. Willis Cole Publishing Company, located at 930 West Walnut Street, employed twenty people and the paper's circulation approached 20,000.

The *Leader* announced births and deaths, named those suffering from illness, listed Louisville churches and their schedules of services, and printed news items from black correspondents elsewhere in the state. It advertised black businesses and professionals and sponsored contests. A voice for civil rights, the *Leader* styled itself "your newspaper—militant but stable." It implored blacks to vote; opposed Jim Crow laws, segregation, and black allegiance to the Republican party; and deplored lynchings as late as the 1940s. At the opening of Chickasaw Park in the West End in 1922, the newspaper labeled it an attempt by segregationists to mollify Louisville's black community.

Cole died in February 1950. His family, led by his widow, Rosa, published the newspaper until September, when it ceased operation.

See Alice Allison Dunnigan, ed., *The Fascinating Story of Black Kentuckians: Their Heritage and Traditions* (Washington, D.C., 1982).

WILLIAM J. MORISON

LOUISVILLE LEGION. Since 1836 a succession of volunteer military organizations from Kentucky's largest city have been called the Louisville Legion. The title remains the oldest continuously used unit designation in the Kentucky National Guard. The Kentucky STATE GUARD's 1st Regiment of Infantry was known as the Louisville Legion through most of the nineteenth century. It participated in the Mexican and Spanish-American wars. During the Civil War, the 5th Kentucky Volunteer Infantry Regiment, made up largely of Union men from the Louisville area, received the designation. It was one of the outstanding combat units in the Union army, and Gen. William T. Sherman said of it, "No single body of men can claim more honor for the grand result than the officers and men of the Louisville Legion of 1861." The Louisville Legion has served as the Kentucky National Guard's 138th Artillery in most of the nation's wars and as a peacekeeping force in domestic disturbances.

See Thomas Speed, *The Union Regiments of Kentucky* (Louisville 1897).   NICKY HUGHES

LOUISVILLE MUNICIPAL COLLEGE. The Louisville Municipal College, a liberal arts college for blacks, enrolled its first students on February 9, 1931. Raymond A. Kent, then president of the University of Louisville, selected Rufus Early Clement as dean of the new institution, which was a division of the university. The school was located at Seventh and Kentucky streets on property previously occupied by SIMMONS UNIVERSITY, which closed in 1930. Louisville Municipal was the result of a demand by leading black taxpayers that the city make provisions for higher education for blacks. A bond issue was passed in 1925 and $100,000 was set aside for black education. The school was one of three such liberal arts colleges for blacks established in the United States at the time, and assumed the role that Simmons University had played as the principal institution for blacks in the city. The college operated until June 1951, when the University of Louisville opened all divisions to black students.

See George D. Wilson, *A Century of Negro Education in Louisville* (Louisville 1986); Lawrence H. Williams, *Black Higher Education in Kentucky 1879-1930* (New York 1987).   NETTIE OLIVER

LOUISVILLE NATIONAL MEDICAL COLLEGE. The General Assembly incorporated the Louisville National Medical College on April 24, 1888, to grant diplomas to practice medicine and perform surgery. The college, which operated until

the early twentieth century, was affiliated with SIM-
MONS UNIVERSITY, the only black institution in
Kentucky then offering a degree in theology, medicine, or law. Henry FITZBUTLER, Rufus Conrad,
and W.A. Burney were appointed trustees of the
medical college, and the first classes met in October 1888 in the United Brothers of Friendship Hall
at Ninth and Magazine streets. In 1889 the college
purchased the former home of the Louisville College of Pharmacy at 122 Green Street (now Liberty). In 1898, to meet the new standards of the
state Board of Health, the course of study was
expanded to four years. After it graduated more
than 150 physicians, a lack of funds and the rising
standards in the medical profession forced the college to close on April 29, 1912.

DOROTHY C. RUSH

LOUISVILLE ORCHESTRA. Founded in 1937,
the Louisville Orchestra earned an international
reputation in the 1950s for its innovative program
of commissioning, performing, and recording contemporary classical music. Early in 1948 Charles P.
Farnsley, president of the Louisville Philharmonic
Society and later mayor of Louisville, proposed an
ingenious plan to strengthen the orchestra: commission new pieces of music that would premiere at
Louisville Orchestra performances and be recorded
on the then-new long-playing records.

The orchestra's founding conductor, Robert S.
Whitney, set about putting Farnsley's ideas into
practice during the 1948-49 concert season. On
April 7, 1953, Farnsley announced that the Rockefeller Foundation had awarded the Louisville
Orchestra $400,000 for commissioning and record-
ing new music. By the late 1980s the Louisville
Orchestra had issued more than 150 recordings featuring over 350 compositions by almost 250 composers. In 1965 the music critic of the *Washington
Post* called the Louisville Orchestra's First Edition
Records "the most distinguished series of phonograph records yet issued." A number of the Louisville Orchestra commissions—including works by
Aaron Copland, Juaquin Rodrigo, William Schu-
man, Elliott Carter, and Walter Piston—have become part of the established repertoire of the
modern symphony orchestra.

See Carole C. Birkhead, "The History of the Orchestra in Louisville," M.A. thesis, University of
Louisville, 1977.   ALLEN J. SHARE

LOUISVILLE PRESBYTERIAN SEMINARY.
The Louisville Presbyterian Seminary was founded
in 1901 by merging the Danville Theological Seminary of the Presbyterian Church U.S.A. and the
Louisville Theological Seminary of the Presbyterian
Church U.S. (or Southern Presbyterian Church). By
1990 the seminary had grown to 250 students and a
faculty of sixteen, with a budget of $4.2 million
and an endowment of $35 million. The Danville,
Kentucky, seminary had resulted from a collaboration between John C. YOUNG, the president of
Centre College in Danville, and Robert J. BRECKIN-

RIDGE, the influential pastor of the First Presbyterian Church of Lexington. The Danville seminary
flourished briefly before the Civil War began.

During and after the Civil War, Breckinridge and
other pro-Union Presbyterians managed to keep
control of Centre College and the Danville Theological Seminary. Most Kentucky Presbyterians, however, followed Stuart Robinson into the Presbyterian
Church U.S., formed by Confederate sympathizers.
The Southern Prebyterians started Central University in Richmond, Kentucky, to compete with
Centre College, and established a seminary in Louisville, along with their medical and dental schools.
Competing seminaries in Danville and Louisville
made little sense, however, and Kentucky Presbyterians voted to merge the institutions in 1901.

A neo-Gothic building for the Louisville Presbyterian Seminary was constructed at First and Broadway, and joint support assured good instruction in
the training of ministers. Plans for an interstate
highway caused the seminary to relocate in 1963 on
Alta Vista Road, near the campus of the Southern
Baptist Theological Seminary. The president of
Louisville Seminary, Frank H. Caldwell, led a
successful drive to build the new campus free of
long-term debt. In 1987 the seminary purchased
Gardencourt, an adjacent estate, giving the campus
a total of fifty-two acres.

Louisville Seminary presidents include Charles
R. Hemphill, 1910-20; John M. Vander Meulen,
1920-30; John R. Cunningham, 1930-36; Frank H.
Caldwell, 1936-64; Albert C. Winn, 1965-73; C.
Ellis Nelson, 1974-81; and John M. Mulder, 1981- .

See Robert S. Saunders, *History of Louisville
Presbyterian Theological Seminary, 1853–1953*,
(Louisville 1953); Louis Weeks, *Kentucky Presbyte-
rians* (Atlanta 1983).   LOUIS WEEKS

LOW DUTCH COLONY. Founded in 1786, the
Low Dutch Colony was the dream of over fifty
Dutch families who had migrated to Kentucky from
settlements in New Jersey and Pennsylvania in
1780. Thirty-four families living in various stockades in Mercer County united in 1784 to form the
Low Dutch Company with the purpose of settling a
colony, building a church for the Low Dutch Reformed Church Society, cultivating the land, and
perpetuating their culture. In 1784 the company
purchased approximately 3,000 acres from Richard
Beard in what is now Henry and Shelby counties.
Indian attacks forced the members to abandon the
first settlement in 1785.

In the spring of 1786 the company purchased six
thousand acres adjacent to their original holdings
from Squire Boone, selling off approximately 1,350
acres to help finance the investment. On March 4,
1786, the Low Dutch Company formally signed the
articles of agreement governing the colony. All land
was held in common, with all profits or losses to be
shared equally. The land, totaling more than 7,600
acres, was divided into thirty-four lots of varying
sizes and allocated to members. In 1790, when the
Indian threat had been reduced, the permanent set-

tlement of Bantatown (now Pleasureville) was established. Other Dutch families who moved to the area and purchased land adjacent to the colony strengthened the ethnic homogeneity of the settlement, although they did not join the Low Dutch Company.

Several families left the colony in 1805 to join the SHAKER community at Pleasant Hill, and in 1817 the migration of Dutch families to Indiana began, further reducing the population. Litigation over the purchase of Boone's land began when it was discovered that prior claims existed, and lawsuits were taken through Shelby and Henry County circuit courts to the Kentucky supreme court. In 1813 a claim on more than a thousand acres was decided against the company, forcing the members to repurchase the land, and in 1820 the company lost more property, including the land on which Bantatown was situated, in a decision of the Henry County circuit court. Other suits sought to retrieve land for the company from the heirs of original company members who were holding tracts in private ownership.

On March 9, 1831, at the last Low Dutch Company meeting, the trustees were instructed to settle the company's affairs, and the company was dissolved.

See Vincent Akers, *The Low Dutch Company: A History of the Holland Dutch Settlements of the Kentucky Frontier* (Bargersville, Ind., 1982); Richard Shuck, "Low Dutch Colony," *Register* 20 (Sept. 1922) 301-3.

LOYAL LAND COMPANY. In 1749 a group of prominent Virginians organized the Loyal Land Company in Charlottesville, with John Lewis as the first director, to take advantage of British offers of land to settle in the West. In the same year, with the King of England's approval, the governor of Virginia granted the company 800,000 acres in southwest Virginia and what is now southeast Kentucky for settlements. The Loyal Land Company hired physician and land surveyor Dr. Thomas WALKER, who had previously explored southwest Virginia, to lead an exploratory expedition that set off March 6, 1750. Walker, accompanied by Ambrose Powell, William Tomlinson, John Hughes, Colby Chew, and Henry Lawless, headed westward across southwestern Virginia and through what was called the Cave Gap (Cumberland Gap) in search of unsettled lands to fill the company's grant. They came across a large river that Walker named the Cumberland after the Duke of Cumberland. The party built a cabin near present-day Barbourville that was to serve as the company's base for operations. After exploring the mountainous region of southeastern Kentucky, the party traveled east to the Big Sandy River. Walker's party made a mistake in continuing eastward into the mountain region instead of heading west into central Kentucky's rich, fertile meadows, and the group returned to Virginia unsatisfied by their search.

Walker succeeded Lewis as director of the company in 1753, and the company named Walker agent. He remained in this position until his death on November 9, 1794. The company did not settle any lands in Kentucky; its settlements were all east of the Alleghenies. After the death of the company's original members, the company's business was handled by heirs. Francis Walker took over his father's position in 1794. The Loyal Land Company's last recorded legal suit was settled in 1872.

See Archibald Henderson, *Dr. Thomas Walker and the Loyal Land Company of Virginia* (Worcester, Mass. 1931); Henry P. Scalf, *Kentucky's Last Frontier* (Prestonsburg, Ky., 1966); J. Stoddard Johnston, *First Explorations of Kentucky* (Louisville 1898).

LUCAS, MILDRED (SUMMERS). Mildred (Summers) Lucas, who because of her sex was removed from the office of county jailer by Kentucky courts, was born on June 8, 1846. In July 1884 her husband, Daviess County jailer W.J. Lucas, was killed in Owensboro by a mob while defending a black prisoner, and the Daviess County court appointed her to succeed him until an election could be held. Although Mildred Lucas won the election, the attesting board denied certification of the election and named her male opponent as jailer. She refused to vacate the office, appealed the board's decision, and served as jailer for sixteen months. The Kentucky court of appeals in *Atchison v. Lucas* ruled that she could not serve as jailer because she was not eligible to vote. Lucas died on March 13, 1898, and was buried in Elmwood Cemetery in Owensboro.

See Lee A. Dew and Aloma W. Dew, *Owensboro: The City on the Yellow Banks* (Bowling Green, Ky., 1988).   ALOMA WILLIAMS DEW

LUCAS, ROBERT HENRY. Robert Henry Lucas, politician, was born in Louisville on August 8, 1888, to Robert and Hattie (Galey) Lucas. He attended Male High School and received both his B.A. (1908) and his LL.B. (1909) from the University of Louisville. Lucas began his legal practice in Louisville in 1909, and in 1917 he became the prosecuting attorney, a position he held until 1921. He served as commissioner of the Internal Revenue Service during 1921-29. In 1927 he lost the Republican primary for governor of Kentucky to Flem Sampson. From 1930 to 1932 Lucas was the executive director of the Republican National Committee. During that time in Washington, D.C., he caused a scandal by his tactics in opposing Sen. George Norris of Nebraska, an independent Republican who had not supported either of the two Republican presidents, Calvin Coolidge and Herbert Hoover, under whom he had served. In an attempt to undermine Norris's reelection bid in 1930, Lucas anonymously distributed slanderous material about him. Lucas admitted to the charges, defending his actions by saying simply, "[Norris] is not a Republican."

After Lucas's stint in Washington, he reopened his legal practice, working in both Washington and

Louisville. In 1936 he was unsuccessful in an attempt to unseat Marvel Mills Logan as U.S. senator, losing the election by a vote of 539,968 to 365,850. Lucas remained active in public affairs on both the national and state level.

Lucas married Gertrude Losch on October 19, 1910; they had one daughter, Martha. Lucas died in Washington, D.C., on October 13, 1947, and is buried in Louisville's Cave Hill Cemetery.

LUDLOW. Ludlow is an Ohio River port city in northern Kenton County on KY 8 and is situated just west of the COVINGTON city limits, northeast of Bromley and north of Fort Wright. The area was settled by Col. Israel Ludlow, who had helped found Cincinnati, and others around 1790. One of the first substantial homes was Elmwood Hall, which was completed in 1821 by Thomas Corneal. Many dignitaries were guests there, including the Marquis de LAFAYETTE during his 1825 travels through Kentucky.

By 1836, most of the town site had been acquired by Israel Ludlow, son of the original settler, who developed the area, sold parcels of land, and gave the village his name. The city was chartered in 1864 primarily as an attempt to regulate ferry service to and from Cincinnati. Among those who were active in civic affairs was Alexander Bonner Latta, first president of the city council and builder of an early steam-powered fire engine.

During the Civil War, John Hunt Morgan and Thomas Henry Hines crossed the Ohio River on a skiff and reentered Kentucky at Ludlow on November 28, 1863. They had escaped Union imprisonment at the Ohio Penitentiary and were aided by a local resident, a Mrs. Ludlow, who assisted them in returning to Tennessee.

The city grew quickly with the coming of the Southern (now Norfolk Southern) Railway and the building of a bridge across the Ohio River in 1873. A railroad yard and maintenance shop were built in Ludlow and numerous other industries, including a Pullman car repair shop and a resin refinery, located there. The refinery was destroyed in a fire that burned from July 26 to August 13, 1892, but the railroad and other new businesses continued to attract newcomers, many of whom were Irish and German immigrants.

A former landmark in Ludlow was the Lagoon Park, where a manmade lake was completed in 1894. The amusement park featured many rides, game booths, and other attractions. A series of mishaps included a fatal motorcycle accident in 1914 and tornado damage in 1915, and the park could not recover from the loss of business under prohibition in 1919. It closed shortly afterward.

Ludlow experienced rapid residential growth in the 1920s in the southern portion of the city, and the heart of the city moved from the older section to the new suburbs in the hills overlooking the river. The fourth-class city had a population of 5,815 in 1970; 4,959 in 1980; and 4,736 in 1990.

See Ludlow Centennial Celebration, Inc., *Centennial Celebration, Ludlow, Kentucky: Commemorating 100 Years of Progress, 1864-1964* (Ludlow, Ky., 1964).   JOHN E. BURNS

LYNCH. In 1917 the U.S. Coal & Coke Company, a subsidiary of the United States Steel Company, built Lynch, then the largest coal camp in the world, on part of the 19,000 acres it had purchased in the southeastern tip of Harlan County in Kentucky, near the Virginia border. The camp's population peaked at about 10,000 but the reported figures vary because of the fluidity of its migrant population. One thousand structures provided housing for people of more than thirty-eight nationalities. Among the most prominent were Italian, Spanish, Czechoslovakian, Polish, Yugoslavian, Russian, English, Welsh, Irish, and Scottish. By the 1940s this massive mining complex employed over 4,000 people. Among the many notables who worked here was Ken Maynard, who learned to ride the company mine mules before leaving his surveying job to star with Buck Jones and Tom Mix in the cowboy movies of the 1930s.

The public buildings were constructed with Italian cut sandstone and included a company commissary, post office, theater, hotel, car showroom, hospital, churches, and schools. The industrial complex included the largest coal tipple in the world, with a capacity of 15,000 tons. On February 12, 1923, the world record for coal production in a single nine-hour shift was set here when 12,820 tons were mined by men operating forty shortwall cutting machines and loading it into 256 cars in six-unit trains.

Although Lynch was considered one of the model coal camps in Appalachia because of its quality health care, education, housing, social services, wages and benefits, and recreation, it was a closed community with a corporate owner who dictated political and economic policies for years. It was sold to the residents and incorporated in the late 1950s, when it came under democratic rule with an elected mayor and city council. The population of this fifth-class city was 1,517 in 1970; 1,614 in 1980; and 1,166 in 1990.

JAMES B. GOODE

LYNDON. Lyndon, a suburb of Louisville, is located in eastern Jefferson County in an area that is bounded by the Watterson Expressway on the west, Westport Road on the north, Whipps Mill Road on the east, and Shelbyville Road on the south. Lyndon began its existence in 1871 as a depot on the Louisville, Cincinnati & Lexington Railroad (now CSX Transportation.) Alvin Wood, local landowner, donated the land for a railroad station and built the structure. Wood named the station Lyndon, probably for Linn's Station, a pioneer fort on nearby Beargrass Creek built by William Linn in 1779.

In 1896 one of America's oldest military schools, the KENTUCKY MILITARY INSTITUTE, moved its campus to Lyndon. The school's junior high school and high school divisions prepared cadets for college or military service. In 1973 KMI closed and the school grounds were eventually occupied by Ten Broeck Hospital, which specializes in drug and alcohol treatment.

By the early 1900s an interurban electric train made regular stops in Lyndon on the route linking Louisville and La Grange. The area grew as a commuter suburb. In 1912 the old Hamilton Ormsby estate was sold and became Ormsby Village, a home for needy and troubled youth. The complex was closed by county government in 1979, but the old mansion was restored in 1987 as the centerpiece for a commercial office park called Hurstbourne Greene.

Lyndon was incorporated as a fourth-class city in 1965 to avoid annexation by nearby St. Matthews. The population was 460 in 1970; 4,267 in 1980; and 8,037 in 1990.

LYNN, LORETTA (WEBB). Loretta (Webb) Lynn, the country music singer known as "The Coal Miner's Daughter," was born April 14, 1935, at Butcher Holler, Johnson County, Kentucky, to Melvin and Clara (Butcher) Webb. Named after Loretta Young, her mother's favorite actress, she walked several miles daily to attend the one-room Miller's Creek School in nearby Van Lear, where she completed the eighth grade. At age thirteen she met Oliver Lynn, an ex-soldier seven years her senior, and one month later she married him. They moved soon after their marriage to Custer, Washington. Mother of four by age eighteen, Loretta Lynn learned to play a twenty-dollar guitar while singing lullabies. A five-minute appearance in 1960 on radio station KPUG in Bellingham, Washington, propelled Lynn into a professional career as a regular on Nashville's "Grand Ole Opry" and eventual recognition as country music's first lady. She has recorded over sixty singles and fifty albums for Decca and MCA, many of the songs her own compositions. Her honors include a Grammy, twelve nominations and three awards from the Country Music Association as top female artist, two awards from *Record World*, three from *Billboard*, and four from *Cash Box*.

In 1972 Lynn was the first woman selected Country Music Association entertainer of the year; in 1980 she was named entertainer of the decade. Her best-known songs include "I'm a Honky Tonk Girl" (1960), "Blue Kentucky Girl" (1965), "You Ain't Woman Enough" (1966), and "You're Looking at Country" (1971). The 1980 movie *Coal Miner's Daughter* was based upon her autobiography. Typically, Lynn's songs are lyrical and send strong but simple messages. Her siblings Crystal Gayle, Tracey Lee, and Jay Lee also became successful country singers. JAMES C. CLAYPOOL

LYON, CHITTENDEN. Chittenden Lyon, congressman, was born on February 22, 1787, in Fair Haven, Vermont, the son of Democrat-Republican U.S. Rep. Matthew Lyon and Beulah (Chittenden) Galusha Lyon. In 1801 the family moved to Caldwell County, Kentucky, where they engaged in extensive farming. Lyon represented Caldwell County in the Kentucky House of Representatives during 1822-24, and as a Jacksonian Democrat was elected to the U.S. House of Representatives, serving from March 4, 1827, to March 3, 1835. He died in Eddyville on November 23, 1842, and was buried in the Eddyville Cemetery. In 1854 a new county formed from Caldwell County was named in his honor. DAVID W. KRUEGER

LYON, HYLAN BENTON. Hylan Benton Lyon, Confederate general, a grandson of Matthew LYON, was born on February 22, 1836, in Caldwell (now Lyon) County, Kentucky. Lyon was orphaned as a child. He was educated in the common schools of Eddyville, where he moved at the age of eight to live with F.H. Skinner. At fourteen, he entered Masonic University in LaGrange, Kentucky. In 1852 he received an appointment to the U.S. Military Academy at West Point, graduating nineteenth in his class in 1856. He was brevetted a second lieutenant in the 3d Artillery, serving in Florida. In 1857 he was made second lieutenant and stationed in California and in the Washington Territory.

On April 30, 1861, Lyon resigned his commission to join the Confederate army and served as a first lieutenant in Capt. Robert Cobb's battery. He was made lieutenant colonel in the 8th Kentucky Infantry, Army of the Tennessee. During the Battle of Fort Donelson, in February 1862, Lyon was captured by the Union army and imprisoned on Johnson's Island, Ohio. He was released in September 1862.

On June 14, 1864, Lyon was made brigadier general, serving under Gen. Abraham Buford. From September 26, 1864, until the spring of 1865, Lyon commanded the Department of Western Kentucky. He fought in several battles during the Civil War, including the siege of Vicksburg in July 1863. He also took part in the Battle of Chattanooga on October 28, 1863; the Battle of Brice's Crossroads on June 10, 1864; and the Franklin and Nashville campaign from November 29 to December 27, 1864. Lyon was responsible for burning several western Kentucky courthouses.

After the war, Lyon spent a year in Mexico, then returned to Lyon County to farm. The state penitentiary was built on his land and he served on the State Penitentiary Commission. He served in the Kentucky House of Representatives from 1899 to 1901.

On August 29, 1869, Lyon married Grace Machen. They had six children—Frank, Grace, Hugh, Ernest, Maybelle, and Lorraine. Lyon died on April 25, 1907, on his farm in Eddyville and was buried in the Eddyville Cemetery.

LYON, MATTHEW. Matthew Lyon, U.S. representative and soldier, was born in Wicklow County, Ireland, probably on July 14, 1749. He attended school in Dublin and began learning the printing trade in 1763. Immigrating to the United States in 1764, Lyon was first a farm worker in Litchfield, Connecticut, and in 1774 purchased land in what is now Vermont. He fought in the Revolutionary War, was a member of the Vermont House of Representatives from 1779 to 1796, and published two newspapers in the 1790s. Lyon represented Vermont in the U.S. Congress from 1797 to 1801.

Lyon moved to Kentucky in 1801 and settled in Caldwell (now Lyon) County, which he represented in the state House in 1802. He was elected from Kentucky to four successive U.S. Congresses, serving from March 4, 1803, to March 3, 1811. In 1820 President James Monroe appointed him U.S. factor to the Cherokee Nation in the Arkansas Territory. When he ran again for Congress, he was defeated. Lyon married Mary Horsford, daughter of Samuel Horsford, on June 23, 1773. She died on April 29, 1784, and Lyon soon after married Beulah Galusha Chittenden, daughter of Vermont's first governor, Thomas Chittenden. The couple were the parents of Chittenden LYON, the man for whom Lyon County was named. Matthew Lyon died August 1, 1822, in Spadra Bluff, Arkansas, and was buried there. His remains were removed to the Eddyville Cemetery in Kentucky in 1833.

See Aleine Austin, *Matthew Lyon: "New Man" of the Democratic Revolution, 1749-1822* (University Park, Md., 1981).

LYON COUNTY. The 102d county in order of formation, Lyon is located in the western Kentucky waterlands and is bordered by Caldwell, Crittenden, Livingston, Marshall, and Trigg counties. Lyon County has an area of 209 square miles. It was formed from Caldwell County on January 14, 1854, and named for Chittenden Lyon, a U.S. representative whose family settled in the area in 1801. The seat is EDDYVILLE, which previously served in that capacity for Livington and Caldwell counties.

The topography is level to hilly. Thirty-four percent of Lyon county is in the Land Between the Lakes National Recreation Area. Farms occupy 33 percent of the land area, and 66 percent of farmland is in cultivation. The county in 1987 ranked ninety-third in agricultural receipts from livestock, poultry, tobacco, corn, and hay. There are deposits of limestone and dolomite in the county.

Early settlers included David Walker, who in 1790 acquired a land patent where Eddyville is now located, and Matthew Lyon, who brought his family from Vermont in 1801 and established a shipyard there on the Cumberland River. Lyon constructed hulls of several ships for the U.S. Navy during the War of 1812. The county's extensive iron ore deposits contributed to the county's economy in the nineteenth century. Some of the ore was exported but a number of local furnaces to process the ore were built, one being the Suwanee furnace. It was there that William Kelly perfected his air-drying process of steel making. Illegal whiskey distilling was a large-scale industry in the Golden Pond section for many years, especially during prohibition (1920-33). Golden Pond, separated from the remainder of the county by the Cumberland River and accessible only by a ferry, was ideally isolated from the distillers' point of view.

Lyon County's major industry is tourism, which in 1988 brought in $21.4 million. Shawnee Plastics employs 250 in Kuttawa. An asphalt company in Kuttawa and a barge construction and repair firm in Eddyville are the county's other industries.

Lyon County is the western terminus of the 137-mile Western Kentucky Parkway and is intersected by I-24. Mainline rail service is provided by the Paducah & Louisville Railway. Lyon County has its own port authority at the Lick Creek embayment on Lake Barkley. The port, which has a three hundred-foot-wide entry channel and is navigable by barge traffic all year, is called the Gateway to the North for users of the Tennessee-Tombigbee Waterway.

Kuttawa and Eddyville are the county's only incorporated towns. The population of Lyon County was 5,562 in 1970; 6,490 in 1980; and 6,624 in 1990.

See Lyon County 1964 High School Seniors, *One Century of Lyon County History* (Eddyville, Ky., 1964).   RON D. BRYANT

LYSTRA. In 1795 a group of speculators began promoting sales of lots in the projected Kentucky towns of Lystra and Franklinville, described in glowing terms and depicted on elaborate maps as having churches, town halls, aqueducts, piers, colleges, markets, granaries, and "places of amusement." Lystra was to be located on the south creek of the Rolling Fork of the Salt River in Nelson County. Both towns were laid out on "very eligible" plans "combining everything necessary for utility and ornament," so that "no doubt can be entertained but that a rapid progress will be made in settling them." Like so many of the promotional towns in the early West, the towns never got much beyond the stage of a gleam in the speculator's eye.

See Mariam S. Houchins, "Three Kentucky Towns That Never Were," *FCHQ* 40 (Jan. 1966): 17-21.   ALLEN J. SHARE

M

McAFEE, GEORGE ANDERSON. One of the fastest players in the National Football League (NFL), George Anderson ("One Play") McAfee was born on March 13, 1918, in Corbin, Kentucky, the son of Clarence and Mary (Lydia) McAfee. His family moved to Ironton, Ohio, where he was a track, baseball, and football star. He entered Duke University in 1936 and was named All-American in his senior year, after the team posted nine straight victories. McAfee was drafted by the NFL's Chicago Bears in 1940, and was named All-Professional the next year, after leading the NFL with a 7.3-yards-per-carry average. He served in the Navy during 1942-45. A football injury sidelined him in 1946, but he returned to the Bears in full strength in 1947 and played until 1950 as the Bears' safety. He intercepted twenty-one passes in that time. Long touchdown runs, especially punt returns, in which he usually led the league, gave McAfee his nickname. In 1961 he became a head linesman, an NFL official. In 1966, after retiring, he was elected to the Pro Football Hall of Fame. He established the McAfee Oil Company in Durham, North Carolina.

McAfee married Jeane Mencke on June 15, 1945; they have three children.

McAFEE, ROBERT. Robert McAfee, pioneer, was born near Port Deposit, Pennsylvania, on July 10, 1745. He was the sixth child of James, Sr., and Jane McAfee, of Scottish descent, who had emigrated to the United States from Ireland. The family settled in Augusta County, Virginia, in 1748. On May 10, 1773, McAfee left Virginia on his first trip to explore what is now Kentucky, accompanied by his brothers, James, Jr., and George; his brother-in-law James McCoun, Jr.; and Samuel Adams. They spent almost four months along the stream they called Crooked Creek—the present-day Salt River in Mercer County, Kentucky—and along the Kentucky River in Franklin County where Frankfort now stands. In 1775 Indian threats cut short their second exploratory trip.

The McAfee brothers and McCoun moved their families to Kentucky in 1779. They built McAfee Station at James McAfee's Spring during October 1779, near what is now Talmage in Mercer County. Robert McAfee and his family built a cabin at nearby Wilson's Station. At both the McAfee and Wilson stations, the McAfee and McCoun families suffered occasional casualties from Indian attacks, which were common until Gen. Anthony Wayne's victory over the Indians at Fallen Timbers on August 20, 1794.

McAfee married Anne McCoun, a distant cousin, on December 10, 1766; they had six surviving children: Margaret, Sallie, Samuel, Mary, Robert Breckinridge, and Annie. McAfee, sometimes called "First Commodore of Western Rivers," operated the first flatboats from the Salt River to the Ohio River and from there to New Orleans via the Ohio and Mississippi rivers. McAfee was murdered in New Orleans during one of these expeditions in 1795. He died on May 10 and was buried in New Orleans.

See Robert B. McAfee, "The Life and Times of Robert B. McAfee," *Register* 25 (Jan. 1927, May 1927, and Sept. 1927).

McAFEE, ROBERT BRECKINRIDGE. Robert Breckinridge McAfee, legislator and statesman, was born near the Salt River in Mercer County, Kentucky, on February 18, 1784. He was the sixth child of Robert McAfee, an early Kentucky pioneer, and his wife Anne (McCoun). In 1795, after his parents' deaths, his guardians were John Breckinridge, who became attorney general of the United States in the cabinet of President Thomas Jefferson, and James McCoun. McAfee attended Transylvania University 1795-97, and after studying law with Breckinridge was admitted to the bar in 1801. He opened a private practice in Franklin County later that year.

In 1800 McAfee was elected to represent Mercer County in the state legislature. He served there until the outbreak of the War of 1812, when he volunteered for service. By war's end he had been promoted to captain. In 1819 he was reelected to the legislature and in 1821 was chosen to serve in the state Senate. He resigned his Senate seat in 1824 to run for lieutenant governor, a post he held until 1828, when he returned to the legislature. McAfee was very active in the Democratic party. He attended the 1832 Baltimore national convention and voted for the nomination of Gen. Andrew Jackson for president and Martin Van Buren for vice president. He left the Kentucky legislature in 1832 and was named chargé d'affaires to the Republic of Colombia in 1833, a post he held until 1837. McAfee returned to Kentucky in 1837 and was reelected to the Kentucky Senate in 1841. In 1842 he was appointed to the Board of Visitors at West Point and elected its president. He retired from active public service in 1845 and spent his remaining years in private law practice on his farm in Mercer County.

McAfee married Mary Cardwell in October 1807. He was an honorary member of the Kentucky Historical Society and a member of the Royal Antiquarian Society of Denmark. He was also author of *History of the War of 1812* in 1816. McAfee died March 12, 1849, and is buried in New Providence Churchyard in Harrodsburg, Kentucky.

See Robert B. McAfee, "The Life and Times of Robert B. McAfee," *Register* 25 (Jan. 1927, May 1927, and Sept. 1927).

MACAULEY'S THEATRE. Macauley's Theatre opened in Louisville on October 13, 1873. It was the dream of Bernard Macauley, who first worked at a theater in Buffalo, New York, then went to Memphis in 1859 at the age of twenty-two. In 1861, while managing an Indianapolis theater, Macauley started acting for the Louisville Theatre and the Louisville Opera House, where he was a favorite of theatergoers. He also performed at the Lexington Opera House and elsewhere in the South. In 1866 he settled in Louisville, where he managed the Weisinger Hall Theatre.

After the Civil War, when Louisville reemerged as a major center of trade, Macauley saw a need for a first-class theater and bought a lot on Walnut Street (now Muhammad Ali) near Fourth Street, in a residential area called Old Prather Square. The first brick of his theater was laid on July 1, 1873, and construction was completed in ninety days, at a cost of $200,000. The opening night play was *Extremes* by J. Austin Sperry, which received very good reviews. Newspapers across the country marveled at the theater itself. The building, four stories high, had a richly detailed French Renaissance facade, and the interior was equally ornate. Macauley's Theatre was praised as the first great theater of the West, and performances there continued to receive good reviews. Public interest, however, began to wane, the theater lost money, and Macauley's debts continued to mount. In 1880 he turned the management of the theater over to his younger brother, Col. John T. Macauley, with whom he had briefly managed a theater in Indianapolis almost twenty years earlier.

Colonel Macauley, first and foremost a businessman, saved the theater from closing. In 1882 he attracted the world's attention by running the first American production of Henrik Ibsen's *A Doll's House*. He worked with other theaters in the touring network to keep fresh performers appearing on stage at Macauley's. This strategy began the commercialization of theater in Louisville and also its resurgence in popularity. In 1893 Macauley joined the syndicate that established theater circuits around the country for the finest stage actors. Some criticized Macauley for moving away from traditional acting companies, but his success could not be questioned. Among the actors to grace the stage of Macauley's Theatre were Maude Adams, Otis Skinner, Billie Burke, Helen Hayes, Al Jolson, and Ethel Barrymore.

Colonel Macauley died unexpectedly in 1915. The theater came under the management of Arthur Bigelow (1915-19) and then Harry J. Martin and Augustus Pitou (1919-25). They were unable to compete with movie houses and with the other theaters that new forms of transportation made accessible. On August 29, 1925, Macauley's Theatre held its final performance, before a packed house. On December 14, 1925, Macauley's Theatre, once a symbol of the performing arts in Kentucky, was demolished. Bernard Macauley, its founder, died in New York City. The date of his death is unknown.

The present Macauley's Theatre opened in October 5, 1972, in the remodeled building of the former Brown Theater. The Louisville Orchestra and the Kentucky Opera perform part of their seasons there. The Theater Workshop of Louisville stages productions at Macauley's and other theatrical groups rent the facility for performances.

See West T. Hill, Jr., "Opening of Macauley's Theatre, Louisville, Kentucky, October 4, 1873," *FCHQ* 32 (April 1958): 151-66; John Jacob Weisert, *Last Night at Macauley's: A Checklist, 1873-1925* (Louisville 1950).

McBRAYER, PAUL S. Paul S. McBrayer, basketball coach, son of H.J. and Louria (Sullivan) McBrayer, was born on October 12, 1909, in Lawrenceburg, Kentucky. He played baseball and basketball at Kavanaugh High School in Lawrenceburg, and basketball at the University of Kentucky (UK) (1928-30), where he was named an All-American in 1930. McBrayer began his coaching career at Morton Junior High School in Lexington, Kentucky, after graduation from UK. After a year there, he coached at Kavanaugh High School. In 1934 he became an assistant to Adolph Rupp at UK. During the nine years he coached UK's freshman teams, they had only eight losses. He was drafted into the army in 1943 and became a drill instructor at Fort McClellan, Alabama, with the rank of staff sergeant. McBrayer was head coach at Eastern Kentucky University at Richmond from 1946 to 1962, when he retired. At EKU he compiled a record of 214 wins and 141 losses, won three league championships, and took teams to the National Collegiate Athletic Association tournament in 1953 and 1959. He was inducted into the Naismith Memorial Basketball Hall of Fame in 1961, and he became a member of the Dawahares' Kentucky Sports Hall of Fame. Eastern Kentucky University named its basketball arena after McBrayer and established a scholarship in his honor.

McBrayer married Kathrine McNult in 1962; they live in Lexington.

See Dave Kindred, *Basketball: The Dream Game in Kentucky* (Louisville 1976).

McCALL, JACK. It was Jack McCall who killed Wild Bill Hickock in 1876, shooting him from behind while Hickock was playing poker, at about 4:00 in the afternoon at Saloon Number 10 in Deadwood, South Dakota. The night before the attack, Hickock is said to have "broke" McCall at the poker table. On August 3, 1876, McCall was found innocent of murder in an unofficial "miner's trial" by peers at a mining camp. At his official trial on December 4 in Yankton, South Dakota, McCall was found guilty of the murder of Hickock. He was hanged on March 1, 1877, when apparently twenty-six years of age. The day before McCall's execution, U.S. Marshal Burdick received a letter from Mary McCall of Louisville that, along with Louisville city directories, is the main source of evidence that McCall grew up in Louisville and left for the western frontier about 1871. McCall's mother, on this basis, was a housekeeper at the

Merchants hotel, his father possibly a worker on Ohio riverboats.

See Joseph G. Rosa, *Alias Jack McCall* (Kansas City, Mo., 1967). ALAN NASLUND

McCLANAHAN, EDWARD POAGE. Edward Poage McClanahan, author, the son of Edward Leroy and Jesse (Poage) McClanahan, was born in Brooksville, Kentucky, on October 5, 1932. He attended school there and in Maysville, where the family moved in 1948. He received a bachelor of arts in English from Miami University in Ohio in 1955 and a master of arts in English from the University of Kentucky in 1958. He taught at Oregon State University from 1958 to 1962, when he received a Wallace E. Stegner Fellowship in Creative Writing from Stanford University in California. He stayed on at Stanford as E.H. Jones Lecturer in Creative Writing until 1972. He taught at the University of Montana from 1973 to 1976. He also taught at the University of Kentucky and at Northern Kentucky University. In 1976 he moved to Port Royal, Kentucky.

From the late 1950s on, McClanahan published stories, essays, and reviews in numerous magazines, including *Esquire*, *Rolling Stone*, and *Playboy*. He received *Playboy* magazine's award for nonfiction in 1972 and 1974. *The Natural Man*, a novel that had been in the making since 1961, was published in 1983 to the delight of both reviewers and readers who appreciated its humor and its language, which is at once raunchy and elegant. The *Chicago Tribune*'s reviewer said that this book "is written perfectly." *The Natural Man* was followed, in 1985, by *Famous People I Have Known*, autobiographical essays.

McClanahan married Katherine Andrews in 1957; they had three children: Kristin, Caitlin, and Jess. In 1975 he married Cia White; the children of this marriage are Annie June and William White.

See Lee Sigelman, "Solitary, Poor, Nasty, Brutish—and Tall? Man and Society in *The Natural Man*," *Journal of Kentucky Studies* (Sept. 1985): 198-212.

McCLELLAND'S STATION. McClelland's Station, one of the first stockaded stations north of the Kentucky River, was founded by John McClelland in October 1775. Situated at Royal Spring, which flows north into North Elkhorn Creek, in what is now downtown Georgetown, Kentucky, this station was built on land originally claimed by John FLOYD in 1774. McClelland, from Westmoreland County, Pennsylvania, received permission from Floyd to settle at the springs and began to make improvements on the property in April 1775. He returned to Pennsylvania in June to prepare his family for resettlement. His wife, Sarah, his brothers, William and Alexander, and others including Robert Patterson arrived in Kentucky with McClelland in October 1775 and began to build his station. At that time McClelland, probably to retain the rights to his station, surveyed another parcel of land adjacent to Floyd's claim, just north of the spring, which he exchanged for Floyd's property in 1776.

In April 1776, an Indian attack on Leestown (now part of Frankfort) greatly alarmed the settlers at the station. With the help of Simon Kenton and John Todd, the inhabitants fortified their settlements. An Indian attack on December 29 killed McClelland and in effect ended the settlement. The inhabitants, who at the time numbered about thirty families, fled the station for the greater security of Harrodsburg. Though an occasional traveler temporarily used the facilities remaining at Royal Spring, the location was uninhabited until Elijah Craig, in 1782, began to plan the town of Lebanon, which was incorporated by the Virginia legislature in 1784. In 1790 Lebanon was renamed Georgetown, in honor of Gen. George Washington.

See Nancy O'Malley, *Stockading Up* (Lexington, Ky., 1987); Ann B. Bevins, *The Royal Spring of Georgetown, Kentucky* (Georgetown, Ky., 1970); Samuel Wilson, *McClelland and His Men* (Lexington, Ky., 1956).

McCLUNG, JOHN ALEXANDER. John Alexander McClung, Presbyterian minister, was born on September 25, 1804, in Washington, Kentucky, the son of Judge William and Susan T. (Marshall) McClung. He was educated at his uncle Louis Marshall's academy near Versailles, Kentucky, and in 1823 entered the Princeton Theological Seminary in New Jersey. He was ordained as a Presbyterian minister in 1828 and returned to Kentucky. After preaching for several years, McClung became disillusioned with religion and moved south of Maysville to a large farm, where he wrote. His *Camden* (1830), about the Revolutionary War in the South, was highly acclaimed but criticized by some for its profane characters. *Sketches of Western Adventure* (1832) employed the use of both fiction and facts to depict history. McClung also wrote the "Outline History" in the first edition of Collins's *Historical Sketches of Kentucky* (1847).

McClung studied law independently and in 1835 moved to Washington, Kentucky, where he practiced for several years. McClung was elected to the Kentucky House and served two terms, beginning December 4, 1837. In 1848 he moved to Maysville, Kentucky, and returned to the ministry. McClung was ordained a second time and preached for several months at the First Presbyterian Church in Louisville and then at the Seventh Presbyterian Church in Cincinnati. Afterward he spent four years in Indianapolis as pastor of the First Presbyterian Church. In 1857 he returned to Kentucky and served as minister of the Presbyterian Church in Maysville.

McClung married Eliza Johnson of Mason County on November 24, 1825; they had several children. He drowned while swimming on August 6, 1859, in Niagara, New York, and was buried in the Maysville Cemetery.

See W.M. Paxton, *The Marshall Family* (Cincinnati 1885).

McCONNELL, ADDISON MITCHELL. Born in Louisville, on February 20, 1942, Addison Mitchell ("Mitch") McConnell, U.S. Senator, is the son of A.M. and Dean McConnell of Shelbyville, Kentucky. He attended Louisville's Manual High School, received his B.A. from the University of Louisville in 1964, and graduated from the University of Kentucky law school in 1967. McConnell was chief legislative assistant to U.S. Senator Marlowe Cook and was named deputy assistant attorney general in President Gerald Ford's administration (1974-77). After serving two terms as the elected judge executive in Jefferson County, McConnell, a Republican, was elected to the U.S. Senate in 1984, defeating incumbent Walter Huddleston. He was reelected in 1990, defeating Dr. Harvey Sloane of Louisville. McConnell has served on the Senate Agriculture, Foreign Relations, Energy and Natural Resources, and Rules committees. Among McConnell's interests is the national effort on behalf of missing and exploited children; President Ronald Reagan appointed him to serve on the National Partnership on Child Safety. McConnell and his former wife, Sherrill Redmon, are the parents of three children—Elly, Claire, and Porter.

JANE C. BRYANT

McCONNELL'S STATIONS. The city of Lexington, in Fayette County, grew out of stations established by Francis and William McConnell. The two brothers surveyed and staked claims to numerous land tracts in Fayette and Scott counties on the waters of Elkhorn Creek in 1775-76. Both men established small stations and gave the name Lexington to the town that they planned around the stations in 1775. Of the two stations, Francis McConnell's became the better known, after several families settled there around 1780, including those headed by the McConnells and by Robert Edmiston, David Campbell, John Brookey, John Nutt, Matthew Harper, and John Stevenson. That station reportedly broke up around 1784. Francis McConnell did not survive the pioneer era, but William became a prominent citizen and trustee of the city of Lexington.

See Carolyn Murray Wooley, *The Founding of Lexington, 1775-76* (Lexington, Ky., 1975); Bettye Lee Mastin, *Lexington, 1779: Pioneer Kentucky as Described by Early Settlers* (Lexington, Ky., 1979).

NANCY O'MALLEY

McCORMACK, ARTHUR THOMAS. Arthur Thomas McCormack, physician and director of the Kentucky State Board of Health, was born in Nelson County, Kentucky, on August 21, 1872, the son of Joseph Nathaniel McCORMACK and Corine (Crenshaw) McCormack. After graduating in 1892 from Ogden College in Bowling Green, McCormack earned an M.D. from Columbia University in 1896. He began his medical practice in Bowling Green the following year. From that base, he advanced through the ranks of public health work in Kentucky, serving as health officer for Warren County from 1897 to 1900, as assistant state health officer from 1898 to 1912, and as state health officer from 1912 until his death. McCormack served as the surgeon general of the Kentucky National Guard from 1900 to 1908. He was active in the Medical Reserve Corps and organized Base Hospital No. 59 for service in World War I. Before completing this hospital, he succeeded Gen. William Crawford Gorgas as chief medical officer in the Panama Canal Zone.

McCormack and his father, whom he replaced as state health officer, are credited with establishing a health administration plan for Kentucky that provides full-time health care through county, bicounty and tricounty administrative units. Their design served as a model for many counties throughout the United States. McCormack founded and edited the *Kentucky State Medical Journal*. He organized and served as dean of the School of Public Health of the Kentucky State Board of Health.

McMormack and his first wife, Mary Moore (Tyler), were the parents of a daughter, Mary, and two sons who died in infancy. He and his second wife, Jane Teare (Dahlman), had no children. McCormack died in Louisville on August 7, 1943, was cremated, and his ashes were buried in Bowling Green's Fairview Cemetery.

See John W. Kelly, "Kentucky's Contributions to Medicine," *Bulletin of Commonwealth of Kentucky Department of Health* 15 (Oct. 1942): 553-59.

JUDY CORNETT

McCORMACK, JOSEPH NATHANIEL. Joseph Nathaniel McCormack, physician and public health official, was born in Nelson County, Kentucky, on November 9, 1847, the son of Thomas and Elizabeth (Brown) McCormack. He earned M.D. degrees from Miami Medical College of Cincinnati in 1870 and the Medical Department of the University of Louisville in 1873. He practiced medicine in Bowling Green from 1875 until he moved to Louisville in 1914.

McCormack was appointed to the Kentucky State Board of Health in 1879 and became its secretary from 1883 to 1912; he served as the state's chief health officer until his death. Soon after his appointment, McCormack secured passage of much of the state's public health legislation, including the enactment of Kentucky's medical practice act in 1888 and its revision four years later. In later years he perfected the Kentucky Sanitary Privy, a "fly-proof, self-cleaning" privy connected to a concrete septic tank that was widely accepted in the United States and abroad. He organized and was the first president of the Conference of State and Provincial Health Authorities of North America. In 1900 McCormack became the chairman of the American Medical Association (AMA) Committee on Reorganizations. In a crusade that lasted until 1913 and that took him into every state, he brought thousands of physicians into the membership of their local societies and the AMA. He reduced much hostility to physicians and brought considerable power to a politically impotent profession, giving it a clearer sense of direction and of public responsibility. In 1912 he was elected to the Kentucky General Assembly.

In 1871 McCormack married Corrine Crenshaw of Glasgow, Kentucky. In 1872 she gave birth to Arthur Thomas (McCORMACK), who also became prominent in the public health movement. McCormack died in Louisville on May 4, 1922. His body was cremated and buried in Bowling Green.

See James G. Burrow, *AMA: Voice of American Medicine* (Baltimore 1963).   JAMES G. BURROW

McCRACKEN, VIRGIL. During the War of 1812, Virgil McCracken was one of the Kentucky soldiers massacred by Indians following the Battle of the RIVER RAISIN in 1813. He was the son of Cyrus and Elizabeth McCracken, two early settlers of the state who came with Hancock Lee in 1776 to build a settlement one mile south of Frankfort, Kentucky. His father was killed while fighting under the command of Gen. George Rogers Clark in Ohio in 1782. McCracken represented Woodford County in the General Assembly of 1810-11 and raised a company of soldiers when the War of 1812 began. He was commissioned a captain in the 1st Rifle Regiment and marched north with the troops from Kentucky who were sent to reinforce Gen. William Hull at Detroit. He was wounded in the Battle of the River Raisin and was one of forty to sixty-five soldiers too ill to move who were left behind by the other defeated Kentuckians and massacred by Indians on January 23, 1813.

McCracken was married on December 31, 1800, to Sally Caldwell of Woodford County; they had five children. McCracken County, formed in the Jackson Purchase area of the state in 1825, is one of nine counties named for Kentucky soldiers who died at the battle of the River Raisin.

See G. Glenn Clift, *Remember the Raisin!* (Frankfort, Ky., 1961).

McCRACKEN COUNTY. McCracken County, the seventy-eighth county in order of formation, is located in the Jackson Purchase region of the state on the Ohio and Tennessee rivers and is bordered by Ballard, Graves, Livingston, and Marshall counties. The county was originally part of Hickman County, on land purchased from the Chickasaw in 1818. As soon as population warranted, the territory was divided into Hickman, Graves, Calloway, and McCracken counties. McCracken County was formed on January 15, 1825, and was named for Captain Virgil McCracken, killed at the Battle of the River Raisin, January 22, 1813, during the War of 1812. The county seat is PADUCAH. The county covers an area of 251 square miles.

In addition to the Ohio and the Tennessee rivers, the county has numerous small streams. Clark's River and Island Creek empty into the Tennessee River; Mayfield Creek flows into the Mississippi in Ballard County; Massac, Willow, Newton's, and Perkin's creeks empty into the Ohio River. Mc-

Cracken County has two incorporated communities: Paducah and Lone Oak, a fast-growing middle-class suburb of Paducah, incorporated in 1970 and located at the junction of U.S. 45 and I-24.

The first meeting of the county court was held in the house of Isaac Lovelace, followed by meetings at Luke Swetman's (total costs $2 per session) until the town of Wilmington was laid out in January, 1827; frame courthouse and jail were completed there by Frederick Harper and James Martin. Paducah became the county seat in late 1831, and Braxton Small, who served as county clerk for thirty-three years, transferred the county records to Paducah by skiff during a flood in 1832. In 1842 Ballard County was created from McCracken and Hickman counties.

As the hub of river traffic on the Ohio, Tennessee, and Cumberland rivers, Paducah became a center of wholesale merchandising for the region. Tobacco was an important export, with much of the leaf going to New Orleans. Because the profitability of tobacco depended on slave labor, the area was linked economically and socially with the South.

During the Civil War, Paducah was occupied by the Union army in retaliation for the Confederate seizure of Hickman and Columbus on September 3, 1861. Many young men had followed native son Gen. Lloyd Tilghman into Confederate service during the early part of the war, and the "D" Company of the 3d Kentucky was heavily populated by Paducahans. They accompanied Gen. Nathan Bedford Forrest on his two raids into Paducah. Other McCracken Countians opposed secession and joined the Union cause during the war.

Politically, McCracken was split, with Paducah espousing the Whigs, Know-Nothings, and later the Republicans, while the remainder of the county was staunchly in the camp of the Democrats.

One of the oldest educational institutions in McCracken is St. Mary's. Originally an academy run by the Catholic Sisters of Charity, the school served as a hospital during the Civil War, when Paducah was flooded with wounded from the Battle of Shiloh. Later, student enrollment reached five hundred. In 1990, the school was a private high school with some parish assistance. Public high schools include Reidland, Lone Oak, Heath, and Tilghman. Various proprietary schools have served McCracken over the years, such as Draughon's Practical Business College, which opened about 1900 and claimed to be the largest of its kind in the world, with thirty colleges in seventeen states. The name changed in 1986 to Careercom Junior College of Business and later to Franklin.

Well-known residents of McCracken County include Vice Adm. Joe Clifton, a hero of World War II and earlier an all-American football player at the Naval Academy; Clarence ("Big House") Gains, of Winston-Salem State University in North Carolina, the "winningest" coach in college basketball and a member of the Hall of Fame of that sport; and John Thomas Scopes, whose "monkey trial" in Dayton, Tennessee, generated a storm of concern over evolution and freedom of thought. An enduring local curiosity is the body of Henry ("Speedie") Atkins, who died in 1928 and was embalmed using an experimental technique that has left his body in a remarkable state of preservation. The body survived the 1937 flood and a 1980 national television appearance and remains at a Paducah funeral home.

The population of the county was 58,281 in 1970; 61,310 in 1980; and 62,879 in 1990.

See John E.L. Roberston, *Paducah: A Pictorial History* (St. Louis 1988).

JOHN E.L. ROBERSTON

McCREARY, JAMES BENNETT. James Bennett McCreary, governor of Kentucky (1875-79, 1911-15), was born in Madison County on July 8, 1838, to Dr. Edmund R. and Sabrina (Bennett) McCreary. He graduated from Centre College in Danville, then earned a law degree from Cumberland University in Tennessee. During the Civil War he rose to the rank of Confederate lieutenant colonel in the 11th Kentucky Cavalry. After the war he resumed his legal practice. His 1867 marriage to Katherine Hughes produced one son. McCreary, a Democrat, was elected to three successive terms (1869-75) in the Kentucky House; during the last two terms he was Speaker.

In 1875 he won the Democratic party's nomination for governor and defeated Republican John M. Harlan, 130,026 to 94,236, by stressing the abuses of the Ulysses S. Grant administration and its Reconstruction policy. After his first term as the state's governor, McCreary resumed his legal practice. From March 4, 1885, to March 3, 1897, he was a member of the U.S. House, and from March 4, 1903, to March 3, 1909, he served in the U.S. Senate, where he tried to advance the state's agricultural interests and to secure the free coinage of silver. In 1891 McCreary was a member of the U.S. delegation to an international monetary conference. Despite his age, he won the party's nomination for governor again in 1911. Running on a progressive platform, McCreary defeated Republican Judge Edward C. O'Rear, who advocated similar views, 226,771 to 195,436. After his second term ended, McCreary failed to get his party's nomination for the U.S. Senate. He was practicing law in Richmond when he died on October 8, 1918, and was buried there.

In his first term McCreary won approval for only a few of his modest proposals: reductions in the property tax and the legal rate of interest, establishment of a state Board of Health, a higher assessment of railroad property for tax purposes, and some minor improvements in educational institutions. During his second term, McCreary provided more active leadership for a more progressive program, and Kentuckians benefited from his successes. He won passage of a mandatory primary election law, some restrictions on lobbyists' access to the legislative chambers, and a tax commission to study the revenue system. Departments were created for state banking and highways, and the Board

of Assessments and Valuation made a more realistic appraisal of corporate property. Women were again made eligible to vote in school elections, and counties were allowed local option in dealing with the sensitive liquor issue. The public schools benefited from a Compulsory Attendance Act, a 25 percent increase in the per-pupil expenditure, and an optional system of textbook selection. McCreary failed to win passage of a comprehensive workmen's compensation act or a requirement for full disclosure of campaign contributions and expenditures.

See Nicholas C. Burckel, "From Beckham to McCreary, The Progressive Record of Kentucky Governors," *Register* 76 (Oct. 1978): 285-307.

LOWELL H. HARRISON

McCREARY COUNTY. McCreary County, the 120th and last county in order of formation, is located in south-central Kentucky between the Big South Fork and the main body of the Cumberland River. It was created in 1912 from parts of Pulaski, Wayne, and Whitley counties and is bordered by those counties, by Laurel County, and by the Tennessee state line. The county contains 427 square miles. Although intensely loyal to the Union in the Civil War and overwhelmingly Republican, the county was named for a Confederate army veteran and two-time Democratic governor, James B. McCreary (1875-79, 1911-15). WHITLEY CITY is the county seat.

For the most part, the county is less than 1,500 feet above sea level. Sandstone, which underlies the surface, has led to a terrain of narrow ridges and deep ravines, numerous waterfalls and sandstone arches. Coal production began early in the nineteenth century, and the area led the state in the production of coal from 1836 until 1865. Shipments of coal by barges, which could move only when the Cumberland River was almost at flood stage, were too erratic to withstand competition from railroad shipments, and it was not until the completion of the Cincinnati & Southern Railroad (now the Norfolk & Southern Railway) in 1880 that extensive exploitation of the coal and timber resources could begin. By 1900 seven mines were operating and two spur railway lines were in service. Approximately 1,000 miners were employed. Efforts to organize the miners were largely unsuccessful until miners near Greenwood were laid off to put convicts to work. The resulting strike was violent, troops were ordered into the area, and the resulting publicity helped eradicate the convict leasing system.

In 1902 a new group of entrepreneurs arrived, headed by Justus S. Stearns. Well educated and well financed, they built within thirteen months of their arrival a new town named Stearns, an electrical generating plant, America's first all-electric saw-mill, five miles of railroad through rugged terrain, and the first of many mines.

The industrial activity in an area inaccessible to county seats led to the creation of McCreary County, under a resolution by state Sen. William B.

Creekmore of Pine Knot. After two elections bitterly contested between the northern and southern parts of the new county, Whitley City was chosen as the county seat.

McCreary County was probably first seen by Zachary Green's party, who discovered Cumberland Falls in 1770. The first mention of the area in a newspaper probably occurred in 1819 when the *Frankfort Argus of Western America* reported the discovery of oil on the Big South Fork of the Cumberland River by congressman Martin Beatty. The oil well was Kentucky's first and according to the late newspaper writer Joe Creason, America's oldest commercial well. Barrels were hauled by oxen to Nashville for sale as a medicinal liniment.

The mining and lumber industries grew rapidly after the turn of the century, and the county was quite prosperous until after World War II. The purchase by the federal government of over seventy percent of the land area of McCreary to form part of the Daniel Boone National Forest and the BIG SOUTH FORK RIVER AND RECREATION AREA slowed lumber production in a county that once boasted the state's largest lumberyard. With the demise of the coal and timber industries, McCreary's unemployment figures have been among the worst in Kentucky. The textile manufacturing plants employ fewer than six hundred people, and other citizens either move from the county or commute to adjacent areas to find work.

Sen. John Sherman Cooper fathered legislation that led to the creation of the Big South Fork River and Recreation Area in 1974. The restoration of the Blue Heron Mining Community and the Big South Scenic Railway, on tracks that once served mines, have brought many visitors to the county. The business section of old Stearns has been placed on the National Registry of Historic Places, and the large office building built in 1907 to house the offices of the Stearns Coal & Lumber Company is now occupied by the Stearns Museum. Cumberland Falls, Yahoo Falls, and Natural Arch are scenic areas that are popular tourist sites.

Highways in the county were formerly poor; rebuilding of U.S. 27 and KY 90 and KY 92 have improved access to wilderness areas. McCreary County has staked its economic future on the tourism industry. The population was 12,548 in 1970; 15,634 in 1980; and 15,603 in 1990.

See L.E. Perry, *McCreary Conquest: A Narrative History* (Whitley City, Ky., 1979).

FRANK C. THOMAS

McCREERY, THOMAS CLAY. Thomas C. McCreery, U.S. senator, was born on December 12, 1816, near Owensboro, Kentucky. McCreery matriculated at Centre College and graduated from St. Joseph's College, Bardstown, Kentucky, in 1837. During the next two years he studied law with future Gov. Thomas Morehead (1834-36) in Frankfort and then practiced in that city until 1840, when he returned to Owensboro to pursue literary interests and to farm. McCreery was an unsuccessful Democratic party candidate for the U.S. Congress

in 1842 and 1844 in a district that was described as being "hopelessly Whig." During the mid-1850s, at the height of the Know-Nothing party's ascendancy, McCreery was an outspoken critic of the party's discriminatory activities and statements against Catholics and foreigners. In 1868 he was chosen by the General Assembly to fill the unexpired U.S. Senate term of James B. Guthrie and served from February 19, 1868, to March 3, 1871. He was elected to a full Senate term over John Marshall Harlan (March 4, 1873, to March 4, 1879).

McCreery was not particularly active in the Senate, but he had a well-deserved reputation as an orator. His keen sense of humor and distinctive voice and mannerisms engendered almost immediate sympathy from his listeners. An opponent of protectionism, McCreery believed in the political maxim "Those who are least governed are governed best." McCreery died at Owensboro, Kentucky, on July 10, 1890, and was buried there in the Elmwood Cemetery. WILLIAM J. MARSHALL

McDOWELL, EPHRAIM. Ephraim McDowell, physician and surgeon who introduced pioneering techniques in abdominal surgery, was born on November 11, 1771, in Augusta (later Rockbridge) County, Virginia. He was the ninth of eleven children of Samuel and Mary (McClung) McDowell. His family moved to Danville, Kentucky, in 1784. Schooled in Georgetown and Bardstown, McDowell studied medicine with Alexander Humphreys of Staunton, Virginia, attended a course of lectures at the University of Edinburgh School of Medicine, and studied anatomy and surgery with John Bell.

McDowell returned to Danville in 1795 and built a busy practice, earning a regional reputation as a skillful anatomist and surgeon, widely consulted by other practitioners. McDowell did not keep notes on his cases, however, and published only two articles, both of them in an obscure journal, the *Eclectic Repertory and Analytical Review*. Recognition of the significance of his work came slowly and only decades after he performed the first successful ovariotomy, on Christmas Day 1809. The forty-seven-year-old patient, Jane (Todd) CRAWFORD, who had been thought to be pregnant with twins, was in fact suffering from a large cystic ovarian tumor that weighed more than twenty pounds.

In a letter describing the surgical procedure that would subsequently bring him international fame, McDowell said he had warned Crawford that four of the "most eminent Surgeons in England and Scotland had uniformly declared in their Lectures that such was the danger of Peritoneal Inflammation, that opening the abdomen to extract the tumor was inevitable death. But notwithstanding this, if she thought herself prepared to die, I would take the lump from her if she could come to Danville." The surgery went well and Crawford was "perfectly well in twenty-five days." McDowell performed the operation well before the discovery of the importance of aseptic techniques or the introduction of anaesthetics.

McDowell performed the procedure at least eleven additional times, with but one death. He was one of the first surgical pathologists, carefully preserving and studying specimens removed during surgical procedures. Dr. Samuel D. Gross, a professor of surgery in the school of medicine of the University of Louisville during the 1840s and 1850s, publicized McDowell's accomplishments and secured for McDowell his proper place in the annals of abdominal and gynecological surgery. McDowell was one of the founders of Centre College in Danville, and between 1819 and 1829 served on the college's board of trustees.

On December 29, 1802, McDowell married Sarah Hart Shelby, the daughter of the first governor of Kentucky, Isaac Shelby (1792-96 and 1812-16). The couple had six children, five of whom survived: Susan, Mary, Adaline, Catherine, and William Wallace. McDowell died on June 25, 1830, and is buried in Danville.

. See Laman A. Gray, Sr., "Ephraim McDowell: Father of Abdominal Surgery, Biographical Data," *FCHQ* 43 (July 1969): 216-29; Josephine Rich, *Pioneer Surgeon* (New York 1959).

ALLEN J. SHARE

McDOWELL, ROBERT EMMETT, SR. Robert Emmett McDowell, Sr., writer, son of Robert Chester and Alice Lucile (Furnas) McDowell, was born in Sentinel, Oklahoma, on April 5, 1914. He attended the University of Louisville and began his writing career while serving in the merchant marine in World War II. After first writing science fiction, he became a successful author of detective novels, many set in Kentucky. McDowell was of pioneer Kentucky ancestry and had a keen interest in history. His fondness for history is evident in his work: *Tidewater Sprig* (1964), a novel set at the Bullitt salt springs; *City of Conflict* (1962), a history of Louisville in the Civil War; and his outdoor drama *Home is the Hunter*, performed in Harrodsburg 1963-65. He wrote many articles on historical topics for the *Louisville Courier-Journal Magazine*, *Louisville Magazine*, and the *Filson Club History Quarterly*. McDowell wrote *Rediscovering Kentucky*, a tour guide, for the Kentucky Department of Parks in 1971. He was editor of publications for the Filson Club from 1971 until his death in 1975 and was active in several civic, environmental, and historical organizations throughout Kentucky.

McDowell married Audrea Adams in Louisville on August 31, 1940. They had one son, Robert Emmett McDowell III. McDowell died in Louisville on March 29, 1975, and was buried in Cave Hill Cemetery, Louisville.   JAMES R. BENTLEY

McFARLAN, ARTHUR CRANE. Arthur Crane McFarlan, educator and geologist, was born in Mansfield, Ohio, on May 7, 1897, the son of Frank and Mary Ella (Henninger) McFarlan. He graduated from the University of Cincinnati in 1919 with a B.A. and in 1924 received a Ph.D. from the University of Chicago. In 1922-23 he worked as an oil geologist in Kentucky and Texas. McFarlan joined the University of Kentucky faculty as associate professor of geology in 1923. He became a professor in 1926 and was chairman of the department from 1927 until his retirement in 1966. McFarlan was state geologist and director of the Bureau of Mineral and Topographic Survey during 1932-34 and director of Geological Survey of Kentucky during 1948-58. McFarlan, who was named distinguished professor of the year, published many professional writings, probably the most well-known being *Geology of Kentucky* (1943), an expanded version of the book written in 1919 by A.M. Miller, his predecessor. McFarlan was an active member of several local, statewide, and national geological societies.

McFarlan married Gail Parker on September 19, 1921. They had two children: Mary Beth Graves and Arthur, Jr., who died in 1947. McFarlan died on April 9, 1985, and was buried in the Lexington Cemetery.   THOMAS G. ROBERTS

McFARLAND, LESTER. Lester McFarland, musician, was born February 2, 1902, in Grays, Kentucky. He shared musical interests with Robert Gardner in 1915 at the Kentucky School for the Blind, where both were students. As Mac and Bob, they became the first popular male duet in country music recordings. They toured on the Keith vaudeville circuit, performed on WNOX radio in Knoxville, Tennessee (1925-31), and joined the "National Barn Dance" on WLS in Chicago in 1931, where they were a long-time staple. Their sound had an old-fashioned, cultivated flavor, suggestive of music hall or barbershop singing. McFarland usually sang tenor and picked instrumental leads on his mandolin.

See Bill C. Malone, *Country Music, U.S.A.* (Austin, Texas, 1985).   CHARLES F. FABER

McGARVEY, JOHN WILLIAM. John William McGarvey, minister, was born on March 1, 1829, near Hopkinsville, Kentucky, the son of Sarah Ann (Thomson) and John McGarvey. He was raised by his mother and his stepfather, Gurdon F. Saltonstall. In 1839 the family moved to Tremont, Illinois, where he attended a school directed by James K. Kellogg. McGarvey entered Bethany College in Bethany, Virginia (now part of West Virginia), in April 1847, and graduated in 1850. While at Bethany, McGarvey was greatly influenced by Alexander Campbell, a leader of the Christian Church (Disciples of Christ). From the fall of 1850 to January 1853, McGarvey taught at a boys' school he had founded in Fayette, Missouri, and in his spare time prepared himself for the ministry. In September 1852 he began preaching at the Dover Church in La Fayette County, Missouri. He moved to Lexington, Kentucky, in 1862 to be the minister of the Main Street Christian Church.

McGarvey influenced the founding in 1865 of the College of the Bible (LEXINGTON THEOLOGICAL SEMINARY), and he wrote *A Commentary on the*

Acts of the Apostles (1866). McGarvey married Otwayana Frances Hix of Fayette, Missouri, on March 23, 1853; they had eight children. He died on October 6, 1911, and was buried in the Lexington Cemetery.

See W.C. Morro, *Brother McGarvey* (St. Louis 1940); Dwight Stevenson, *Lexington Theological Seminary* (St. Louis 1964).

JOHN D. WRIGHT, JR.

McGARY, HUGH. Hugh McGary, pioneer, migrated to Kentucky from the Yadkin settlement in North Carolina in the fall of 1775 with his wife, Mary (Buntin) Ray McGary; their sons, Robert and Daniel; and Mary's three sons from a previous marriage—William, James, and John Ray. They were among the twenty to thirty families that Daniel Boone led through the Cumberland Gap. The McGarys and a few other families separated from Boone's party and continued to Fort Harrod, arriving in mid-September.

In March 1777 McGary was elected captain of the militia at Fort Harrod. He was also appointed a justice in Kentucky's first court, held in the same year. In 1778 McGary participated in Gen. George Rogers Clark's expedition to capture Vincennes and Kaskaskia. By 1782 McGary held the rank of major in the militia. On August 17, 1782, when the militia assembled at Bryan's Station to pursue the Indians who had attacked the settlement, McGary protested and suggested waiting for reinforcements under Benjamin Logan. The other officers would not be deterred. On August 19, the Kentuckians rode into an ambush set by the British and Indians at the Lower Blue Licks crossing of the Licking River. McGary was blamed by many for the disaster of the Battle of BLUE LICKS because he led the company across the river. He remained in the militia and by 1787 held the rank of colonel.

In 1779 McGary established a stockade at Shawnee Springs in Mercer County. In 1780 Mary McGary died and Hugh married Caty Yocum. They had several children. In 1787, after the death of his second wife, McGary moved to Harrodsburg, then to Shawneetown, Illinois, where he died in 1808.

See R.S. Cotterill, *History of Pioneer Kentucky* (Cincinnati 1917); George M. Chinn, *Kentucky: Settlement and Statehood* (Frankfort, Ky., 1975); Nancy O'Malley, *Stockading Up* (Frankfort, Ky., 1987).

McGREADY, JAMES. James McGready, a Presbyterian minister in the GREAT REVIVAL of the early 1800s, was born to Scotch-Irish parents in Pennsylvania in 1758, and moved at an early age to North Carolina. He returned to Pennsylvania in 1785 to attend Joseph Smith's Academy at Upper Buffalo and then to study under John McMillan at Canonsburg. On August 13, 1788, he was licensed as a minister by the Redstone Presbytery. On his way back to North Carolina, McGready was impressed by a revival he witnessed at Hampden Sydney College in Virginia, led by John Blair Smith.

At his church in Orange County, North Carolina, McGready soon gained attention as a fiery preacher who filled his congregation with fear of eternal damnation unless they experienced a spiritual rebirth. This style won a number of converts, but his exhortations against the materialism and immorality of society, and his attacks on the sins of the wealthy offended many important families in the area. After repeated threats of violence and damage to his church, McGready migrated west with part of his congregation and settled in Logan County, Kentucky, in 1796.

In Kentucky he became pastor of the three Presbyterian meetinghouses at the Red, Muddy, and Gasper rivers. His first few years in Kentucky brought about only a small number of conversions, but the revival spirit then began to grow. McGready was joined by William McGee, William Hodge, Samuel McAdow, and John Rankin—Presbyterian ministers whom he had converted in North Carolina—and they began holding revivals at the three meetinghouses and in the surrounding countryside. In July 1800 they invited settlers to a camp meeting revival, where worshippers set up camp in a clearing in the woods for several days and listened to sermons delivered from a pavilion constructed for the purpose. Many participants shook and danced or fell to the ground during the emotional proceedings.

The Kentucky Presbytery viewed the revival as an attack against church doctrine. When the Cumberland Presbytery separated from the Synod of Kentucky, McGready first sided with the new group, but his Calvinist background and commitment to a theological understanding of the scripture brought him back to the Presbyterian church. In later years McGready moved to Henderson, Kentucky, and served as a missionary to the Indiana Territory. He died in Henderson in February 1817.

See Thomas Whitaker, "The Gasper River Meeting House," *FCHQ* 56 (Jan. 1982): 30-61.

McGUFFEY, WILLIAM HOLMES. William Holmes McGuffey, teacher and compiler of the *McGuffey Reader*s, was born on September 23, 1800, near Claysville, Pennsylvania, the son of Alexander and Anna (Holmes) McGuffey. In 1803 the family moved near Youngstown, Ohio, where he was educated by his mother and in rural schools. In 1826 he graduated from Washington College in Pennsylvania, where he studied Latin, Greek, Hebrew, and philosophy. While attending college, McGuffey taught elementary school in Paris, Kentucky, during breaks. He set up a school there in 1823 in the dining room of the Rev. John McFarland's home, with seven children as pupils. In 1826, McGuffey became professor of languages at Miami University in Oxford, Ohio.

In 1833, at the proposal of Cincinnati book publisher Truman and Smith, McGuffey began to create the "eclectic" reading texts for schoolchildren for which he is known. Texts then in use had been written by northeasterners who had little idea of what growing up in the West was like. McGuffey set out to create "Western books for Western people" by compiling poems, stories, speeches, and essays by various authors, including classic works as well as pieces on rural life and nature. McGuffey's first- and second-grade readers were published in 1836. The increasingly difficult series through sixth grade, as well as a primer and speller, was completed in 1857. The McGuffey readers embodied "a complete code of ethics and behavior," as well as instruction in reading and in speaking correctly. This series was edited and reprinted many times, and by 1845 McGuffey had little say on the new revisions.

McGuffey was president of Cincinnati College from 1836 to 1839, and of Ohio University in Athens from 1839 to 1843. He was professor of moral philosophy at the University of Virginia, Charlottesville, from 1845 until his death there on May 4, 1873.

See Herman B. Feustel, "William Holmes McGuffey 1800-1873," *Daughters of the American Revolution Magazine* 92 (April 1958): 348-52.

MACHEN, WILLIS BENSON. Willis Benson Machen, iron manufacturer, soldier, and politician, was born to Henry and Nancy (Tarratt) Machen on April 10, 1810, in Caldwell (now Lyon) County, Kentucky. He received his education through the common schools in the county and later at Cumberland College in Princeton, Kentucky. Machen divided his time in his earlier years between working on his farm in Eddyville, Kentucky, and at the Livingston iron forge. In 1844 he was admitted to the bar and began a successful law practice, which he abandoned in 1851 to return to his farm. In 1849 he was elected a delegate to the Kentucky constitutional convention. He served in the state Senate in 1854 and was elected to the state House of Representatives for the period 1856-60. An anti-Union Democrat and a strong supporter of Confederate President Jefferson Davis, Machen served as one of the members of council in the provisional government of Kentucky, which sought admission into the Confederacy. He was elected to two terms in the Confederate Congress, serving from February 22, 1862, until its dissolution in April 1865. When the first regular Confederate Congress met in Richmond, Virginia, on January 19, 1863, he represented the 1st Kentucky District, serving on the Accounts and the Ways and Means committees. He worked in the quartermaster and commissary departments during the second Confederate Congress.

On September 22, 1872, Machen was appointed to fill the U.S. Senate seat vacated when Garrett Davis died. On January 21, 1873, Machen defeated Republican Tarvin Baker, 104-18, in a joint ballot by the legislature to fill the senatorial position until the end of its term on March 3, 1873. In 1880 Machen was appointed one of the three Kentucky railroad commissioners. He spent the remainder of the 1880s operating iron furnaces in Lyon County and working on his farm.

Machen was married three times, to Margaret A. Lyon, Eliza W. Dobbins, and Theresa Mims. He died in the Western Asylum in Hopkinsville, Kentucky, on September 29, 1893, and is buried in Riverview Cemetery at Eddyville.

McKEE. McKee, the seat of Jackson County, is located on Indian Creek, a tributary of the Rockcastle River, between Richmond and Manchester on U.S. 421. The city is one of Kentucky's smallest county seats. McKee was founded in 1858, when the county was established, and was probably named for Judge George R. McKee, a county judge and legislator from the area. The first county courthouse, a log structure built around 1858, was replaced by a frame building in 1872. Jackson County's third courthouse, built in 1923-24, was destroyed by fire in 1949. The courthouse built in 1950 incorporates the brick walls from the old structure.

Timber was an important natural resource but rugged terrain prevented extensive logging operations in the area until the coming of the railroad in 1915. Logs were hauled to the Bond-Foley Company sawmill at Bond, ten miles south of McKee, and were shipped on the Rockcastle River Railway to the Louisville & Nashville Railroad connection at East Bernstadt.

McKee is located in the DANIEL BOONE NATIONAL FOREST. Several local scenic areas are administered by the U.S. Forest Service, including the "S" Tree Lookout and Turkeyfoot recreation areas, and Flat Lick Falls. McKee is also home to the McKee Manufacturing plant, the *Jackson County Sun* newspaper, Kentucky Woodcrafts, and several sawmills and rock quarries.

McKee is a fifth-class city that was incorporated in 1882. The population in 1970 was 250; 759 in 1980; and 870 in 1990.

McLAUGHLIN, LENNIE LEE (WALLS). Lennie Lee (Walls) McLaughlin, a leader of the Louisvillle Democratic party from 1933 to 1965, was born on June 1, 1900, in Sample, Breckinridge County, Kentucky, the daughter of Lee and Mary (Dorcas) Walls. She was educated in Breckinridge County and moved to Louisville to attend business school. She married William Lester McLaughlin in 1921. They were divorced in 1930. Lennie McLaughlin began working for the Democratic party organization in the early 1920s, and in 1923 she became a grassroots organizer and the right-hand woman to Michael ("Mickey") Brennan, who held the official title of organization chairman of the local party. McLaughlin served as party secretary, a position at the center of organization activity.

The Democrats regained both the Jefferson County courthouse and Louisville city hall in 1933. McLaughlin resigned the party secretary post in 1939 as a result of a power struggle with the faction headed by Mayor Joseph Scholtz. The next year she was appointed clerk of the Jefferson County fiscal court, the only public office she held. In 1947 McLaughlin was again elected Democratic party secretary. Her political prominence continued during the 1950s, when the Democratic party maintained supremacy in Louisville and Jefferson County politics.

A woman who wielded political power was unusual in the annals of Louisville history, but McLaughlin survived as a political leader by drawing on precinct workers, political patronage, legislative influence, primary and general election victories, organizational expertise, and experience. Her power diminished after Republicans were elected Jefferson County judge-executive and mayor of Louisville in 1961, and reform Democrats called for her ouster. McLaughlin retired from her position in 1965, marking the end of an era in Louisville politics.

McLaughlin died on May 21, 1988, in Louisville, and was buried in Ivy Hills Cemetery, Hardinsburg.

See Paul Bulleit, "Miss Lennie Recalls Power and Presidents," *Louisville Courier-Journal*, Jan. 23, 1976; Carolyn L. Denning, "The Louisville (Kentucky) Democratic Party: 'Miss Lennie' McLaughlin," M.A. thesis, University of Louisville, 1981.   CAROLYN LUCKETT DENNING

McLEAN, ALNEY. Alney McLean, active in the political and social life of Muhlenberg County, Kentucky, in the early 1800s, was born in Burke County, North Carolina, on June 10, 1779, to Ephraim and Eliza (Davidson) McLean. At the age of twenty he came to Kentucky and was appointed surveyor of Muhlenberg County. In that capacity he laid out Greenville and became a trustee of that town when it was formed in 1799. McLean studied law and was admitted to the bar in 1805. During the War of 1812 he was a captain and fought in the Battle of New Orleans. McLean represented Muhlenberg County in the General Assembly during 1812-13, and served in the U.S. House of Representatives from March 4, 1815, to March 3, 1817, and from March 4, 1819, to March 3, 1821. In 1821 he was appointed circuit judge and held that position until his death. He was chosen a presidential elector in 1824 and again in 1832, both times casting his vote for Henry Clay. McLean was married to Tabitha Campbell and was the father of ten children. He died on December 30, 1841, and was buried at Old Caney Station cemetery near Greenville. When McLean County was formed from Muhlenberg and other counties in 1854, it was named in his honor.

McLEAN COUNTY. McLean County, the 103d in order of formation, is located in the Western Coal Field region traversed by U.S. 431 and KY 136. The county is bordered by Daviess, Henderson, Hopkins, Muhlenberg, Ohio, and Webster counties and has an area of 256 square miles. McLean County was formed from portions of Daviess, Muhlenberg, and Ohio counties on January 28, 1854, and named in honor of Alney McLean, veteran of the War of 1812, state representative, and congressman (1835-39). The county seat is CAL-

HOUN. The Green River forms a portion of its eastern border and dissects the county. The topography of McLean County is level to rolling, with wide bottomlands along the Green River and its tributaries, including Pond River. Less than 25 percent of the land remains forested.

The first white settlers in the McLean County area were in conflict with the Indians and some dug caves in the hillside near Calhoun for protection. Fort Vienna, the present site of Calhoun, was established in 1785 by Solomon and Henry Rhoads. Other communities include the incorporated towns of Island, Livermore, and Sacramento.

The Green River provided a deep channel for steamboat traffic in the nineteenth century. The first steamboat built on the Green River was completed at Rumsey in 1846 by the Jones Brothers. The river channel was improved greatly in the late 1830s, when a series of locks and dams was constructed. The river permitted farmers to trade with markets in the Ohio and Mississippi river valleys.

During the Civil War the county was divided in its loyalties. Several skirmishes took place between 1861 and 1864. A Confederate force under the command of Gen. Nathan Bedford Forrest defeated a Union force at Sacramento in December 1861. On August 9, 1862, a guerrilla force captured the towns of Calhoun and Rumsey. Federal forces, however, soon defeated the Confederates and drove them from the county.

Following the war in 1865, McLean County returned to a more stable existence. Its economy remained agrarian into the twentieth century. During the first half of the twentieth century, dark-cured and fired-cured tobaccos were the main crops. By 1987 soybeans and corn were primary crops. Over three-fourths of the county is farmland, and in 1987 it ranked fortieth in the state in agricultural receipts. During the twentieth century, the county's economic base expanded to include the manufacture of such products as furniture, metal products, cabinets, and food stuffs, as well as kerosene and lumber.

McLean County was the home of James Bethel Gresham, reputed to be have been the first United States soldier killed in World War I. Gresham died in the Battle of Sommerville, November 3, 1917.

The population of McLean County was 9,062 in 1970; 10,090 in 1980; and was 9,628 in 1990.

See Edith L. Bennett, *Lest We Forget* (Hartford, Ky., 1977).   RON D. BRYANT

McMEEKIN, CLARK. Clark McMeekin was the name under which Isabel (McLennan) McMeekin and Dorothy (Park) Clark collaborated in writing thirteen historical novels about Kentucky, two plays, and several local histories during a twenty-year period beginning in 1940. Isabel was born on November 19, 1895, to Alexander and Rosa (Harbison) McLennan in Louisville, Kentucky. Dorothy was born on September 14, 1899, to William and Eugenia (Dowden) Park in Osceola, Iowa. Their collaborative novels under the name Clark McMeekin include *Show Me a Land* (1940), *Reckon* the River (1941), *Welcome Soldier* (1942), *Red Raskall* (1943), *Black Moon* (1945), *Gaudy's Ladies* (1948), *City of the Flags* (1950), *Room at the Inn* (1953), *Tyrone of Kentucky* (1954), *October Fox* (1956), *Old Kentucky Country* (1957), and *The Fairbrothers* (1961). The books that they cooperated in writing are among the most successful historical novels set in Kentucky.

The books of the joint authors typically mix action and adventure with romance, as in *Show Me a Land* and *Gaudy's Ladies*. Clark and McMeekin, who lived their adult lives in Louisville, wrote about the places and periods that were familiar to them: nineteenth century Louisville, the Bluegrass country, and the Ohio River. Historical figures such as Henry Clay, Abraham Lincoln, Aaron Burr, and Mike Fink and legendary characters such as Johnny Appleseed enhance the historical flavor of such novels as *Tyrone of Kentucky* and *City of the Flags*, which are set in Kentucky during the Civil War and Reconstruction eras. The turmoil and hardships of those times provide dramatic incidents in the plots. The historical novels offer a fairly accurate view of morals, manners, fashion, and attitudes of the nineteenth century. The coauthors supplied the reader generously with realistic details about thoroughbred racing, life on the river, and the social tensions in the divided state of Kentucky during the Civil War.

Both Clark and McMeekin individually enjoyed successful careers as writers, each producing children's literature, short stories, historical novels, mysteries, and operettas. Isabel McLennan married Samuel H. McMeekin in 1921; they had three children: Isabel, Sandy, and Rosalind. Dorothy Park married Edward Clark of Louisville in 1923; they had two daughters: Cristy and Martha. Isabel McMeekin died September 4, 1973, and Dorothy Clark on June 23, 1983. Both were buried in Cave Hill Cemetery in Louisville.

ANDREW VORDER BRUEGGE

McNITT'S DEFEAT. In McNitt's Defeat, Indians massacred pioneer families on October 3, 1786, on the bank of the Little Laurel River, one mile east of the present-day village of Fariston in Laurel County. The McNitt party of fourteen families had come from Virginia by way of Cumberland Gap without incident. On the night of the massacre they camped alongside the Little Laurel and danced and celebrated until quite late. The leaders had grown careless about setting a night guard. Cherokee warriors fell upon the party, butchering and mutilating some twenty of them. Legend has it that a woman in an advanced state of pregnancy hid in a hollow tree, where she gave birth. The bodies of the victims were buried in two large pits, and survivors took refuge at Crab Orchard Station. The goods of the victims were transported to Logan's Fort, where they were sold at auction for the support of the survivors. The site of the defeated camp lies within Levi Jackson Wilderness Road State Park.

THOMAS D. CLARK

McREYNOLDS, JAMES CLARK. James Clark McReynolds, U.S. attorney general and Supreme Court justice, the second child of physician John Oliver and Ellen (Reeves) McReynolds, was born on February 3, 1862, in Elkton, Kentucky. He was valedictorian of his graduating class at Vanderbilt University in 1882, and received his law degree from the University of Virginia two years later. McReynolds served as secretary to Tennessee Sen. Howell E. Jackson (U.S. Supreme Court justice, 1893-95) for two years and practiced law in Nashville from 1884 until 1903. He was on the faculty of Vanderbilt Law School for several years and ran unsuccessfully for Congress in 1896. Republican President Theodore Roosevelt appointed Democrat McReynolds assistant attorney general (1903-7), and in 1913 President Woodrow Wilson appointed him attorney general of the United States. In both positions McReynolds was an antitrust reformer and prosecutor. In 1914 Wilson appointed him to the Supreme Court.

Justice McReynolds served on the Court for twenty-seven years (1914-41), during which he wrote 503 majority opinions; however, he was most famous for his many (310) dissents. While he was considered liberal early in his career, he was very conservative during his last ten years on the Court. Many of McReynolds's dissents were directed at President Franklin D. Roosevelt and his New Deal. McReynolds retired on February 1, 1941.

McReynolds, a bachelor, during his retirement adopted thirty-three children who were refugees of the war in Europe. He died in Washington, D.C., on August 24, 1946, and was buried in Elkton, Kentucky.   CHARLES R. LEE, JR.

McVEY, FRANK LEROND. Frank LeRond McVey, third president of the UNIVERSITY OF KENTUCKY, was born to Alfred Henry and Anna (Holmes) McVey on November 10, 1869, in Wilmington, Ohio. McVey served during 1891-92 as principal of the high school in Orient, Iowa. He graduated from Ohio Wesleyan University in 1893. Two years later he received a Ph.D. in economics from Yale University. In 1895-96 McVey taught history at Teachers College, Columbia University, and also was an editorial writer for the *New York Times*. In the fall of 1896 he joined the economics faculty at the University of Minnesota, and he served as president of the Minneapolis Associated Charities from 1898 to 1907. In 1907 McVey was appointed to the Minnesota Tax Commission. Two years later he was named president of the University of North Dakota, and in 1917 he became president of the University of Kentucky.

McVey presided over a period of growth in both the university's academic programs and the physical plant. He took a firm stand in the antievolution controversy against legislation to restrict academic freedom at the university and throughout the commonwealth. During his tenure, McVey also served as president of organizations such as the Southern Association of Colleges and Secondary Schools, the National Association of Land-Grant Colleges and Universities, the National Association of State Universities, and the Southeastern (athletic) Conference. He was a respected scholar and the author of several monographs on history, economics, government, and education, as well as being an accomplished amateur painter.

McVey married Mabel Sawyer on September 21, 1898. They had three children: Janet, Virginia, and Frank, Jr. Mabel McVey was active in the Lexington and university communities, serving as president of the Fayette County League of Women Voters. She died on April 19, 1922, and was buried in the Lexington Cemetery. On November 24, 1924, McVey married Frances Jewell, then dean of women at the University of Kentucky. They made Maxwell Place, the president's home, a center of social and cultural activity on the campus. Frances McVey died June 13, 1945. Frank McVey died January 4, 1953. They were buried in the Lexington Cemetery.

See William E. Ellis, "Frank LeRond McVey: His Defense of Academic Freedom," *Register* 67 (Jan. 1969): 37-54.   TERRY BIRDWHISTELL

McVEY, MARY FRANCES (JEWELL). Mary Frances (Jewell) McVey, educator, was born December 23, 1889, in Berry, Harrison County, Kentucky, to Asa Hickman and Elizabeth (Berry) Jewell. She attended Sayre School in Lexington and graduated from Baldwin School in Bryn Mawr, Pennsylvania, in 1909. She received an English degree from Vassar College in 1913. Jewell began teaching English at the University of Kentucky in 1915. During 1917-18 she lived in New York City and attended Columbia University, where she received an M.A. in English literature in 1918.

In 1921 Jewell became dean of women at the University of Kentucky. In November 1923 she married University of Kentucky president Frank LeRond McVey and gave up her official positions at the university but did not abandon public life. During the 1920s and 1930s she served as an ambassador of goodwill for the University of Kentucky. She worked on literacy projects in Kentucky, served as an elected member of the Lexington school board, and was a member of the board of directors of the Frontier Nursing Service. She was a leader in the International Club, the YWCA, the University of Kentucky Women's Club, and the Lexington chapter of the American Association of University Women, and was a charter member of the Lexington Junior League. She also served for several years as the alumna member on the Vassar College Board of Trustees.

After a long battle with cancer, McVey died on June 13, 1945, and was buried in the Lexington Cemetery.

See Frances McVey, ed., *A University is a Place . . . a Spirit: Addresses and Articles by Frank LeRond McVey, President, University of Kentucky, 1917-1940* (Lexington, Ky., 1944); Robert Berry Jewell and Frances Jewell McVey, *Uncle Will*

of Wildwood: Nineteenth Century Life in the Bluegrass (Lexington, Ky., 1974).

                                                      TERRY BIRDWHISTELL

MADDEN, JOHN EDWARD. John Edward Madden, horse breeder and trainer, was born on December 28, 1856, in Bethlehem, Pennsylvania, to Patrick and Catherine (McKee) Madden. His father died in 1860, and as a teenager, Madden worked for four years in Bethlehem steel mills. He excelled as an athlete in broadjumping, running, boxing, and baseball, and by age sixteen, Madden was racing his own trotters. Class Leader set a record of 2:22 1/4 at the 1887 Cleveland Grand Circuit Race. In 1889 Madden moved to Lexington, Kentucky, and in June 1890 he bought nineteen-year-old Robert McGregor, a sire of champion trotting horses, for $35,000, a significant price at the time. Silko, a trotter he bought in 1905 as a two-year-old, won the 1906 Kentucky Futurity.

Although Madden continued to breed, race, and sell top trotters, by the early 1890s he had entered the business world of thoroughbreds. One of the first champion thoroughbreds he produced was Hamburg, winner of numerous stakes. He sold Hamburg to Marcus Daly for $41,001 in 1897. Several months later, Madden bought 235 acres east of Lexington on Winchester Pike; he named the farm Hamburg Place and bred most of his successful racers there. The farm later grew to 2,000 acres. Statistics on breeders were not kept until 1917, two decades after Madden's entry into the thoroughbred business, but from 1917 to 1927 he was the chief American breeder of winning horses. He owned and trained Plaudit, winner of the 1898 Kentucky Derby, and he bred five Derby winners: Old Rosebud (1914), Sir Barton (1919), Paul Jones (1920), Zev (1923), and Flying Ebony (1925). Sir Barton was the first Triple Crown winner, and Zev ($313,639) and the filly Princess Doreen ($174,745) were top money winners.

Madden married Anna Louise Megrue of Cincinnati in June 1890; they had two sons, John Edward, Jr., and Joseph M. Madden. The Maddens divorced in 1906. Throughout his career, Madden owned stables in New York as well as in Kentucky. He died in New York City on November 3, 1929, at the Pennsylvania Hotel and he was buried in Calvary Cemetery in Lexington. His grandsons, Patrick and Preston Madden, began reestablishing Hamburg Place as a prize horse farm in the mid-1950s. The 1987 Kentucky Derby winner, Alysheba, was bred there.

See Kent Hollingsworth, *The Wizard of the Turf* (Lexington, Ky., 1965).

MADISON, GEORGE. George Madison, governor for only weeks in 1816, was born in Rockingham County, Virginia, in June 1763 to John and Agatha (Strother) Madison. His brother James Madison became the Episcopal bishop of Virginia and president of William and Mary College. U.S. President James Madison was a second cousin. Little is known of Madison's early years. He served in the militia during the Revolutionary War, and by the mid-1780s he was in Kentucky. He was twice wounded in the Indian campaigns of 1791 and 1792, and served as a major in the Kentucky Volunteers during the War of 1812. He was captured soon after the Battle of Frenchtown (January 18, 1813) and was held prisoner until 1814.

A public-minded citizen, Madison served as auditor of Kentucky public accounts for twenty years and was a trustee of the Kentucky Seminary and a director of the Bank of Kentucky. Despite failing health, which prompted him to resign as auditor, he acceded to public demand that he run for governor in 1816. James Johnson, the other Jeffersonian Republican in the race, withdrew, and Madison was elected without opposition. Too ill to return to Frankfort, he was administered the oath of office by a justice of the peace in Bourbon County on September 5, 1816. He died on October 14, 1816, the first Kentucky governor to die in office. His wife, Jane Smith Madison, had died five years earlier. Madison was buried in the Frankfort Cemetery.

See Lowell H. Harrison, ed., *Kentucky's Governors 1792-1985* (Lexington, Ky., 1985).

LOWELL H. HARRISON

MADISON COUNTY. Madison County, the sixth county in order of formation, is located in central Kentucky, where the Bluegrass meets the foothills of the Appalachians. The 443-square-mile area is bounded by Fayette, Clark, Estill, Jackson, Rockcastle, Garrard, and Jessamine counties. Paint Lick Creek is the western boundary, and the Kentucky River, a major means of transportation and communication since settlement times, forms the north and northeast boundaries. Madison County was created on December 15, 1785, and was named for the Virginia statesman James Madison, who became the fourth president of the United States. The county court first met on August 22, 1786, at George Adams's house near the site that would become the town of Milford. Milford served as the county seat until 1798, when court was moved to land owned by Col. John Miller, one of the county's first state representatives. The new county seat was named RICHMOND after Miller's birthplace of Richmond, Virginia.

Early explorers, including Daniel Boone in 1769, entered from the southern part of the county along creeks that flow northward to the Kentucky River. As employees of the Transylvania Company, Boone and other pioneers traveled into the area in 1775 through the Cumberland Gap. They blazed Boone's Trace to establish Fort Boonesborough on the south bank of the Kentucky River in the northern part of the county. In 1779 Boonesborough was the first town in what was then Kentucky County to be chartered by Virginia. The earliest recorded religious service (Anglican) in Kentucky took place in Boonesborough in May 1775. The Tates Creek Baptist Church, organized in 1783-85, was the first founded by any religious denomination.

The county's early history was dominated by Gen. Green Clay, a member of the county court for nearly forty years. Clay used his political power to develop a vast economic empire that included large estates, ferries, taverns, and toll roads. His son, Cassius Marcellus Clay, served as ambassador to Russia during the Civil War and was an outspoken antislavery advocate. The western pioneer Christopher ("Kit") Carson was a native of Madison County.

Madison County produced corn, hemp, and tobacco very early in its history. By 1783 distilleries were processing corn; water-powered gristmills were constructed as early as 1787 along small creeks; and three tobacco warehouses operated by 1798. The oldest continuous industry in the county, pottery making, was established around 1809. Burley tobacco and cattle raising remain a major portion of the county's economic base.

The first ferry rights in Kentucky were granted in 1779 to Boonesborough settler Col. Richard Callaway, who offered transportation across the Kentucky River. This and other ferries at various locations operated until the 1950s, when Valley View ferry on the Tates Creek Road was the only one left in the county. Bridges gradually replaced ferries; one was built across Paint Lick Creek in 1857. A wood and steel bridge, built in 1870 at Green Clay's ferry landing, was replaced in 1946 by a reinforced concrete bridge that later became the northbound lane of I-75. During the last quarter of the nineteenth century, several railroad lines were built through the county. The first of them, the Louisville & Nashville Railroad (now CSX Transportation), still operates north-south freight service.

The first private school in the county, Madison Male Seminary, was chartered in 1798. Even after public education was established in 1830, private academies flourished, patronized by wealthy families who scorned the "pauper" schools.

In the southern portion of the county, Berea School was founded in 1855 and became BEREA COLLEGE in 1858 through the efforts of Cassius Clay and the Rev. John G. FEE. The small community of BEREA, led by Fee, John A.R. Rogers, and his wife Elizabeth, was staunchly opposed to slavery, at odds with the rest of the county. In 1859 pro-slavery proponents attacked Berea supporters, forcing the college to close and the leaders to flee Kentucky until after the Civil War.

Some of the small communities developed along creeks, such as Paint Lick, were settled in the 1770s. Many early communities, such as Union City, Crooksville, Kingston, and Kirksville, grew up at road intersections. Other communities developed around industrial concerns. Bybee village had its genesis in pottery making around 1843 and grew as a Louisville & Atlantic Railroad depot around 1900. The Red House, Valley View, and Baldwin communities also thrived as railroad stops. The Bluegrass Ordnance Depot, now the Bluegrass Army Depot, was established in 1941. Located in the central portion of the county, its 14,650 acres of land are used for storage of materials and ammunitions. Since World War II, both Richmond and Berea have attracted light manufacturing businesses, which, along with Eastern Kentucky University and Berea College, were in 1990 the major employers in the county.

The population of the county was 42,730 in 1970; 53,352 in 1980; and 57,508 in 1990.

See William Ellis, H.E. Everman, and Richard Sears, *Madison County: 200 Years in Retrospect* (Richmond, Ky., 1985).   LAVINIA H. KUBIAK

MADISONVILLE. Madisonville, the county seat of Hopkins County, is located at the junction of U.S. 41 and KY 70 just west of the Pennyrile Parkway. It was named for James Madison, who was U.S. Secretary of State in 1807, when the city was established and made county seat. In 1807 Solomon Silkwood and Daniel McGary each donated twenty acres for the town site. Silkwood built the first courthouse of logs in that year. The second courthouse, a frame structure built in 1820, was razed in 1840 for the county's first brick courthouse. On December 17, 1864, it was burned by soldiers during a raid led by Confederate Gen. Hylan B. Lyon, who first ordered all county records to be removed. The fourth courthouse, built soon afterward, was replaced by a Victorian structure in 1892. It was razed in 1936 to make way for the sixth courthouse, a three-story brick building fronted by a stone portico.

Madisonville grew in string-town fashion as its original forty acres straddled the north-south Henderson-to-Hopkinsville road. In 1810 its population stood at 37; by 1830 it had risen to 112, but a cholera epidemic in 1835 and the national financial panic in 1837 reduced the town's population to 57 in 1840. By the time of the Civil War, Madisonville had 602 people. Although the war divided the town, postwar hostilities were reduced by the economic activity that resulted from the coming of the railroads and increased coal mining in the county during the 1870s. In 1870 the Louisville & Nashville Railroad (now CSX Transportation) entered the city from Henderson and was followed by the Illinois Central (now Paducah & Louisville) and the Madisonville, Hartford & Eastern (now CSX) in 1910.

By 1900 Madisonville had a population of 2,075 and by 1910 had become a coal center and a major railroad junction, with twenty-five passenger trains departing daily. In 1925 a local paper dubbed Madisonville the "Queen City of the Coalfields and the Best Town on Earth." Kentucky Gov. Ruby Laffoon (1931-35) was born in a log cabin on the outskirts of the city.

After World War II Madisonville began to change from a coal town to a prosperous city with a diversity of industries. Credit for some of the growth is due to David ("Pee Wee") Parish, elected mayor in 1946. The popular and somewhat eccentric Parish served in that capacity for twenty-eight years. Among other accomplishments, he helped to attract a Goodyear tire plant to the city in

1966. In 1979 the Regional Medical Center opened and became Madisonville's largest employer. Madisonville Community College opened in 1968.

The population of the fourth-class city was 15,332 in 1970; 16,979 in 1980; and 16,200 in 1990.

See Wallace M. Wadlington and David M. Sullivan, *Our Town* (Madisonville, Ky., 1962).

ANN BROWN

MAGOFFIN, BERIAH. Beriah Magoffin, governor during 1859-62, was born in Harrodsburg, Kentucky, on April 18, 1815, to Beriah and Jane (McAfee) Magoffin. After graduating from Centre College at Danville in 1835, he studied law at Transylvania University. He started practicing law in Mississippi but returned to Harrodsburg in 1839. In 1840 he married Anna Nelson Shelby, a granddaughter of Isaac Shelby; ten of their children survived infancy.

Magoffin was appointed Harrodsburg's police judge in 1840. A Democrat, he was elected to the state Senate in 1850 and was a delegate to four national party conventions, but in 1851 he refused a nomination for the U.S. House of Representatives. Magoffin was the Democratic nominee for lieutenant governor in 1855, but lost the race to a Know-Nothing candidate. In 1859 he defeated Joshua Bell in the gubernatorial election by 76,187 to 67,283 and served from August 30, 1859, to August 18, 1862. Magoffin accepted slavery and states' rights; he believed in the right of secession but hoped to prevent it by collective action of the slave states in reaching an agreement with the North.

At the onset of the Civil War, Magoffin rejected both Union and Confederate requests for troops and after the legislature voted a neutrality resolution, he proclaimed the policy on May 20, 1861. Unionists distrusted him, and after they gained more than a two-thirds majority in both houses of the General Assembly in the summer of 1861, his vetoes were routinely overridden. In August 1862 Magoffin indicated that he would resign if replaced by a "conservative, just man," but Lt. Gov. Linn Boyd had died in 1859, and Magoffin would not accept Speaker of the Senate John F. Fisk, the next in succession. Fisk resigned as Speaker, and was replaced by James F. Robinson; Magoffin then resigned. Robinson assumed the governorship and Fisk was reelected as Speaker. Magoffin returned to his legal practice and farming at Harrodsburg. Postwar real estate speculation in the Chicago area made him wealthy. Elected to the Kentucky House in 1867, he urged Kentuckians to accept the results of the Civil War, to ratify the Thirteenth Amendment, and to grant civil rights to blacks. Magoffin died at home on February 28, 1885, and was buried at Harrodsburg.

Magoffin's administration was dominated by the secession crisis, the Civil War, and the Unionists' distrust. They blocked his effort to hold a state convention to determine what position Kentucky should take, and his numerous vetoes were ineffective after the legislative elections of 1861. Despite his southern sympathies, Magoffin denounced the "self-constituted" Russellville convention of November 1861, which created a provisional government that was admitted into the Confederacy in December. The governor and the legislators could agree only upon the most innocuous of matters; ultimately, resignation was the best option.

See Michael T. Dues, "Governor Beriah Magoffin of Kentucky," *FCHQ* 40 (Jan. 1966): 22-29.

LOWELL H. HARRISON

MAGOFFIN COUNTY. Magoffin County, the 108th county in order of formation, is in eastern Kentucky, surrounded by Breathitt, Floyd, Johnson, Knott, Morgan, and Wolfe counties. It has an area of 310 square miles. The county was formed on February 22, 1860, from portions of Floyd, Johnson, and Morgan counties and named for Gov. Beriah Magoffin (1859-62). SALYERSVILLE is the county seat.

Magoffin's topography is quite mountainous, with ridgetops reaching an elevation of 1,100 to 1,400 feet. This rugged landscape precludes substantial farming operations. In 1987 approximately 26 percent of the land was devoted to agriculture, and, of this, about 20 percent was under cultivation. Crops such as tobacco and corn, as well as small-scale livestock production, placed Magoffin County 106th in the state in agricultural receipts in 1987.

Although Dr. Thomas Walker in 1750 was the first explorer known to enter the area that would become Magoffin County, the first attempt at settlement was not made until 1794. In that year, a small group of pioneers from South Carolina started a station along the Licking River, near the present town of Salyersville. Soon after their cabins were erected, however, Indians forced the settlers to flee. In 1800, they returned and founded Licking Station, which survived and began to thrive. As more people migrated to the region, a new settlement, Adamsville, was established just north of Licking Station. In 1849 the post office was removed from Licking Station to the new town, which had become the population center. In 1860, when Magoffin County was formed, Adamsville was renamed Salyersville and made the county seat.

During the antebellum period, most of Magoffin County was sparsely populated and survived mostly on subsistence agriculture and limited trade. The Civil War brought violence and turmoil to the region. Two minor engagements occurred at Salyersville in the fall of 1863. In a third engagement, near present-day Royalton on April 14, 1864, Union soldiers under Col. George Gallup attacked and defeated Confederates retreating from a defeat in Paintsville the day before.

After the war, the county experienced massive industrialization. Around 1890 northern timber companies began purchasing huge tracts of land throughout Magoffin County and eastern Kentucky. Many residents sought employment in the new industry, and lumber camps began to dot the landscape. A Canadian firm, the Dawkins Log and Mill

Co., built the town of Royalton around their sawmill before World War I. Close on the heels of the lumber companies came the coal barons. After they bought up mineral rights, which had the effect of removing people from their homes, coal companies dominated the economy, making the people dependent on them for jobs. During periods of high demand, such as the two world wars, Magoffin and other coal counties prospered, but during the Great Depression and the post-World War II era, when demand for coal was low, Magoffin suffered greatly.

In the late twentieth century, Magoffin County was able to ease its dependence on coal. With the completion of the Mountain Parkway during the administration of Gov. Bert Combs (1959-63), the county became more attractive to industry. In 1971 the Continental Conveyor and Equipment Company was founded in Salyersville. America's growing dependence on foreign energy sources, especially since the early 1970s, led to the exploration for and production of natural gas and oil in the county. Nevertheless, coal in the 1990s continued to dominate the economy.

The population of Magoffin County was 10,443 in 1970; 13,515 in 1980; and 13,077 in 1990.

See *Magoffin's First Century: 1860-1960* (Salyersville, Ky., 1960).

MAMMALS. Mammals that occur naturally in Kentucky range in size from deer and bear down to shrews that weigh about as much as a dime, with a body less than half the size of your little finger. Of the 4,000 species of mammals in the world, sixty-eight occur as wild animals in Kentucky. Only three of them are not native to Kentucky; the Norway rat and the house mouse were introduced from the Old World, as was the fallow deer, which is established in the Land Between the Lakes.

The northern element of Kentucky's mammalian fauna includes the red-backed vole, cloudland deer mouse, and New England cottontail, found only at the higher elevations of the mountains along the Virginia border. The southern element is found in western Kentucky, where cotton rats, cotton mice, rice rats, swamp rabbits, and the southeastern bat range up the Mississippi River to the state's westernmost region, known as the Jackson Purchase. The prairie contingent consists of the prairie vole and the prairie deer mouse, which now occupy most of the state, and the badger, a most surprising recent addition that apparently crossed the Ohio River and now ranges nearly from Paducah to Covington and increasingly inland. Appalachian species include the hairy-tailed mole, woodland jumping mouse, and smoky shrew, which range throughout the eastern woodlands, and the gray long-tailed shrew, which was recently found in Letcher County.

Many mammals have adapted well to human activities, and some have invaded even the largest cities. Most city dwellers are familiar with the eastern cottontail rabbit, the gray squirrel, and the chipmunk, conspicuous creatures active in daylight. The flying squirrel, on the other hand, is strictly nocturnal and is thus rarely seen, although it is not uncommon in city parks and urban woodlots. Opossums and muskrats also occur in the cities but are rarely seen there except as casualties of the automobile. Other urban dwellers include the short-tailed shrew, the white-footed mouse, the big brown bat, and the red bat. The shrew is a black creature with pointed snout and small feet, without noticeable eyes and ears. Although rarely seen except when the cat leaves one on the doorstep, this shrew occurs wherever leaves, weeds, or other material provides concealment for the runways it makes on the surface of the ground.

The white-footed mouse, which rivals the short-tailed shrew as the most abundant mammal in Kentucky, occurs wherever rocks, trees, brush, or other objects protect it from predators. It likes buildings; this is the mouse that chews up the toilet paper in your summer camp. Friendly and attractive, the strictly nocturnal animal makes a delightful pet. The big brown is by far the most common of the bats that enter buildings in Kentucky. Although the wingspread is more than a foot, the body is little bigger than your thumb, enabling the creature to enter a crevice half an inch wide. The red bat, also abundant throughout Kentucky, roosts by day among green leaves. In June a female with nearly grown young attached to her nipples may lose her grip and fall to the lawn, an occasion when red bats and people sometimes meet.

Some former mammalian fauna is gone forever. Many extinct mammals, such as the mammoth, the dire wolf, and the peccary, once roamed the state. The fossil record also shows several northern species that were pushed southward by the glaciers and became extinct with the retreat of the ice. Early European settlers eliminated some of the large mammals such as the elk, bison, panther, and wolf. These creatures remain part of the state's heritage only in the names of natural features such as streams, hollows, and ridges. Other species that were once eliminated from Kentucky have since been restored; the white-tailed deer is probably more abundant now than ever before, and the beaver has returned throughout the state. The black bear and river otter are beginning to come back, helped by Kentuckians' new appreciation for the aesthetic values of our natural heritage.

Kentucky is host to three mammals on the federal list of endangered species: the Indiana bat, gray bat, and Virginia big-eared bat, which find refuge in Kentucky's magnificent caves. These bats are intolerant of human disturbance; in efforts to save them, entry to certain caves is restricted during the season when the bats are present.

See Roger W. Barbour and Wayne H. Davis, *Mammals of Kentucky* (Lexington, Ky., 1974).

WAYNE H. DAVIS

MAMMOTH CAVE NATIONAL PARK. Mammoth Cave National Park, about thirty miles northeast of Bowling Green, Kentucky, just west of Interstate Highway I-65, has attracted millions of visitors to the world's longest known cave system, with more than 340 miles of underground passages. In 1991 it celebrated its fiftieth anniversary as a national park. Mammoth Cave was designated by the United Nations as a World Heritage Site in 1981 for its significance as both a natural and a cultural site. In 1989 more than 1.8 million people visited the park.

The eighty-square-mile surface area of the park, a terrain of rugged hills, deep sinkholes, and valleys, is bisected by the scenic Green River. Hikers enjoy more than sixty miles of surface trails, including the Heritage Trail for the disabled in a scenic, wooded area of the park. The geological features of Mammoth Cave are explored by walking tours of various lengths, including one for the disabled. The Green River is accessible by canoe, fishing boat, or a concession-operated scenic boat tour.

Mammoth Cave was discovered in the late 1700s, according to a local legend handed down for many years, by a Kentucky hunter who chased a wounded bear into the gaping mouth of the cave, now known as the Historic Entrance. (The validity of the story, however, is sometimes questioned by historians.) The first recording of the Mammoth Cave property dates from 1798, when a land certificate was issued to Valentine Simmons (or Simons). The certificate refers to two saltpeter caves, along with two hundred acres of land. Simmons had the property surveyed in 1799 and later sold the cave and surrounding land to John Flatt, who after a few years sold the tract to the McClean (or McLean) brothers of Virginia—George, John, and Leonard. In January 1810 a 156-acre tract containing Mammoth Cave was sold by the McCleans to Fleming Gatewood and Charles Wilkins, a prominent Lexington saltpeter dealer. In 1812 Gatewood sold his half-interest to Hyman Gratz, a Philadelphia merchant and saltpeter dealer.

Commercial mining of SALTPETER from the cave probably began with the McClean brothers, although John Flatt may have mined saltpeter on a very small scale. During the War of 1812 the partnership of Wilkins and Gratz mined significant quantities of saltpeter from Mammoth Cave and others in the area, including Dixon Cave. E.I. du Pont de Nemours and Company bought the mine production for manufacturing gunpowder, known as black powder, which was made up of about 80 percent saltpeter and 20 percent sulfur-charcoal mixture. According to early sources, Mammoth Cave saltpeter was very high in quality and in quantity per bushel of cave dirt. Records indicate that Dupont sold at least 750,000 pounds of black powder to the U.S. government during the War of 1812, which would have accounted for 570,000 pounds of saltpeter, according to one historian. Even considering that approximately 275,000 pounds of saltpeter were on hand prior to the start of hostilities, Dupont bought a significant quantity of saltpeter from Wilkins and others during the war, giving

Mammoth Cave a significant role in the U.S. prosecution of the war against Great Britain.

Mining at Mammoth Cave ended about 1815 or 1816, but articles written by visitors to the mining operations made it an attraction for sightseers. In 1837 or 1838 Mammoth Cave and some 2,000 acres of surrounding land were sold to Franklin Gorin, of Glasgow, Kentucky. After making improvements in the log "hotel" and the road to the property to accommodate the growing number of curious visitors, Gorin sold the cave in 1839 to Dr. John Croghan, a Louisville physician. Under the deed, Croghan received the ownership of the slave Stephen Bishop, who became the most popular guide to Mammoth Cave during the 1840s and 1850s, when the tourist attraction blossomed. Visitors who had read published travel logs requested tours led by Bishop, who was said to be quite personable and adept at showing off the cave features. Bishop was also adept at exploration. In 1838, with the aid of a visitor, he is reported to have been the first to cross the deep chasm known as the Bottomless Pit and to reach the Echo River on the cave's lowest level, with its unique eyeless fish and crayfish. Bishop continued to delight visitors until his death in 1857.

In the mid-1800s a medical experiment seeking a cure for consumption (tuberculosis) was conducted inside the cave, where the air was thought by some physicians at the time to have regenerative powers. Several patients lived for a time in nine huts constructed within the cave during 1842, but all ultimately succumbed to the illness while in the cave or shortly after leaving. No positive effects could be observed, and the experiment was abandoned in the spring of 1843. Dr. Croghan himself later died of consumption, and having no children of his own, willed the Mammoth Cave estate to his nieces and nephews. Through legal trustees, the absentee heirs leased the property, and resident managers supervised operations at Mammoth Cave until the death of the last Croghan heir, Serena (Croghan) Rogers, in August 1926.

Fearing that the estate might be put up for public sale, several Kentucky businessmen, with the support of the Louisville & Nashville Railroad, formed the Mammoth Cave National Park Association in 1924. Congressional sentiment at this time was growing for establishment of national parks east of the Mississippi River, where most of the nation's population lived, to match the great recreation areas in the West. In 1926 the U.S. Congress passed legislation authorizing the creation of the park as a natural recreation area, with the land to be acquired by private donation or by purchase with state or private funds.

The Mammoth Cave Association took on fund raising to purchase the proposed 70,618 acres from roughly six hundred property holders, most of them the owners of small farms that had been handed down from generation to generation. In 1928 the Commonwealth of Kentucky established the Kentucky National Park Commission, which provided for condemnation of land in state courts, expediting the land acquisition process. In July 1941, when 48,000 acres had been acquired, Congress formally established Mammoth Cave as the nation's twenty-sixth national park. It was dedicated in September 1946, after the end of World War II. In 1961 the park was enlarged by two additional caves, Great Onyx and Floyd Collins Crystal, purchased by the National Park Service.

See Roger W. Brucker and Richard A. Watson, *The Longest Cave* (New York 1978); Cecil E. Goode, *World Wonder Saved* (Mammoth Cave, Ky., 1986).   NATIONAL PARK SERVICE

MANCHESTER. Manchester, the seat of Clay County in southeastern Kentucky, is located on U.S. 421 north of the Daniel Boone Parkway. Established in 1807, Manchester was known first as Greenville in recognition of Green Clay, a leader during Kentucky's formative period, for whom the county also was named. Local history relates that the community was renamed for the British manufacturing city, in hopes that its economic vibrance would transfer. Nevertheless, owing primarily to inadequate transportation, Manchester and Clay County remained rural. The town grew slowly, reaching only about 150 persons by the 1880s. One hundred years later the population was 1,634.

Located in the Appalachian foothills, Manchester lies near the center of Clay County on the west bank of Goose Creek, a remote tributary of the Kentucky River. The town's specific location is credited to a salt spring, which was purchased for commercial development shortly after the Revolutionary War by James and Daugherty White of Abingdon, Virginia. A descendant, John D. White, served in the 1970s and 1980s on the commonwealth's court of appeals and supreme court. After James Garrard, the second governor of Kentucky (1796-1804), received a land grant in 1798, his son opened a salt works in competition with that of the Whites. The Garrard works operated until 1908. The White and Garrard families were also involved in one of Kentucky's feuds, extending from the 1850s to 1904.

In conjunction with the burgeoning coal industry, the Louisville & Nashville Railroad reached Manchester in 1914. Road development was slow until 1971, when the Daniel Boone Parkway linked Manchester with Hazard to the east and London to the west. Manchester retained its village atmosphere well into the twentieth century; the town served primarily as a community center, offering churches, schools, government offices, and shops to support the outlying areas. Little independent industry was established. It was not until 1905 that the town's first bank, the First National, was incorporated. By the early 1920s, it competed with a second facility, the State Bank. In 1990 the area had two weekly newspapers, the *Manchester Enterprise* and *Clay County News*. Manchester Municipal Hospital, a primary care facility, is administered by the Seventh Day Adventist church. The population of the fourth-class city was 1,664 in 1970; 1,838 in 1980; and 1,634 in 1990.

See Mr. and Mrs. Kelly Morgan, *History of Clay County, Kentucky, 1767-1976* (Manchester, Ky., 1976).   MARY LATTA LEE

MANN'S LICK. The town that is now Fairdale in Jefferson County grew out of a salt works founded at Mann's Lick by Joseph Brooks in 1787. The origin of the name is unknown. The land was part of a military grant made in 1780 to John TODD, who died in the Battle of Blue Licks on August 19, 1782. Five years later, Brooks leased the land from Todd's widow and built the salt works. Because of the threat of Indian attack, Brooks constructed fortifications around the works in 1788. Shortly after its establishment, Mann's Lick became well known for its high-quality salt, and it expanded its production to twenty-four hours a day. Newtown was incorporated in 1794 at the site. Around 1830 the salt supply was exhausted and the salt works closed. Opportunities in agriculture and the town's location along transportation routes kept it alive. It was renamed Fairdale in 1910.

See Thomas D. Clark, "Salt: A Factor in the Settlement of Kentucky," *FCHQ* 12 (Jan. 1938): 42-52.

MAN O' WAR. "Almost from the beginning, Man O' War touched the imagination of men and they saw different things in him. But one thing they will all remember is that he brought an exaltation into their hearts"—Master of ceremonies at the burial of "Big Red."

The chestnut thoroughbred known as Big Red, who was the odds-on favorite in every race he ran and who twice went to the post at odds of 1 to 100, was foaled at the Nursery Stud, near Lexington, Kentucky, on March 29, 1917. He was sired by Fair Play, out of Mahubah, by Rock Sand. The owner and breeder was New York horseman August Belmont II, president of the American Jockey Club. It was Mrs. Belmont who gave the yearling the name Man O' War, in honor of her husband, then absent in Europe during World War I.

When Belmont sent his entire crop of yearlings to the Saratoga, New York, sales in 1918, trainer Louis Feustel bought the colt Man O' War for Samuel Riddle, owner of Faraway Farm, a small racing stable near Lexington. Riddle paid only $5,000 for what would turn out to be a piece of history (the top colt at the sale, Golden Broom, went for $15,000). Big Red won his first race at Belmont Park in New York on June 19, 1919, by six lengths. He went on to win his next five races with ease, even though the handicappers assigned him to carry 130 pounds—an onerous weight for a two-year-old, unthinkable today. The only defeat in Man O' War's career occurred in his seventh race, the six-furlong Sanford Memorial at Saratoga, on August 13, 1919, when he lost to the colt Upset. Man O' War beat Upset decisively, however, in each of the remaining six races in which the two were entered.

Big Red ran all of his twenty-one races in Canada and in New York, where he won the Belmont Stakes by twenty lengths on June 12, 1920. His time of 2:14 1/5 in the Belmont set a world record for the 1⅜-mile distance. At his peak at that time, Man O' War stood 16.2 hands and weighed 1,150 pounds. From his first race at Belmont, Man O' War ran away with the hearts of race-goers, and he captivated the American public. He was the hero not just of the sports pages, but of the editorial writers at major daily newspapers, who turned from world events and politics to celebrate his victories. He won one race by one hundred lengths. He set five world records. Jockeys held him back and crossed the finish line pulling him up. How fast Man O' War could have run was not established; as Riddle explained it, the chestnut was never allowed to run flat-out, for fear that in his intense speed, he might injure himself.

Big Red's last run was a match race against Sir Barton, the first Triple Crown Winner, at Kenilworth Park in Toronto on October 12, 1920. The $80,000 purse raised Man O' War's total earnings to $249,465, a world record at the time. At that point Riddle decided to retire the horse rather than let him carry the excess weight that the handicappers laid on him. In his twentieth race, Man O' War had been assigned 138 pounds. When asked how much Big Red would probably carry if he ran as a four-year-old, a Jockey Club handicapper said the weight would be the heaviest ever assigned to a thoroughbred. Although Riddle had been offered $1 million for the chestnut stallion, he sent Man O' War back to Kentucky in January 1921 to stand at stud at Faraway Farm. Man O' War's success as a sire is not generally as well known as his dominance of the track, yet his 379 offspring included two Kentucky Derby Winners, Clyde Van Dusen (1929) and War Admiral (1937), and his progeny were among the ten leading broodmare sires for twenty-two years.

For all his mighty achievements, Man O' War was a good-natured horse who gave every evidence of enjoying the spotlight with Will Harbut, his caretaker in retirement. The pair delighted the more than 1 million visitors who signed the guestbook at Faraway Farm. Harbut escorted visitors around the barns, filling in the histories of the farm's winners and ending at Man O' War's stall. There he recounted the accomplishments of "the mostest hoss what ever was," while Big Red preened and nodded.

Man O' War died on November 1, 1947, a month after Harbut's death. The stallion's body was embalmed and buried in an oak casket lined with his black and yellow racing silks. Close to 1,000 people were present at the burial ceremony, and thousands more listened to the radio broadcast of the eulogies. Among those who paid their last respects to Big Red were 3,000 crack troopers of the U.S.

Army's 1st Cavalry Division in Tokyo, who snapped to attention as the ceremony began. Man O' War in his lifetime had been made honorary colonel in the 1st Cavalry. He was buried on Faraway Farm beneath a life-size statue of him by Herbert Hesseltine. In 1977 the remains and the statue were transferred to the Kentucky Horse Park in Fayette County.

See Jack Clowes, "The Mostest Hoss," *Kentucky Burgoo*, Kentucky Department of Public Information Bulletin, December 11, 1969; Page Cooper and Roger L. Treat, *Man O' War* (New York 1950).

SHARON IHNEN

MAPS, EARLY. No detailed maps of the area now known as Kentucky appeared before 1784, when John FILSON's work was published in Wilmington, Delaware. Filson's work provided much useful information on the approximate locations of streams, salt licks, roads, forts, settlements, and the lands available to newcomers. Because of extensive interest abroad in the "new country," this map, with Filson's short descriptive text, was also published in England, Germany, and France.

A number of printers produced maps of Kentucky during its early years. Most of them attempted only to show towns, counties, streams, and roads. Difficulties in communicating information, complicated by Kentuckians' penchant for county-making, resulted in many inaccuracies. (In 1792 Kentucky was made up of the nine counties created by Virginia. Fifty-nine counties were created during the years between statehood and 1820, and thirty-two of the others by 1850. See also MUNSELL MAP.)

River travel was so important to the legions of adventurers and families seeking to locate somewhere in the West that descriptive detail on river navigation was published early. *The Navigator*, the first book of Ohio River charts, was prepared by Zadok Cramer and printed in Pittsburgh in 1801. A number of later works served the growing river traffic of flatboats and steamboats.

MARTIN F. SCHMIDT

MARCUM, JULIA ANN. Julia Ann Marcum, schoolteacher, was recognized by the U.S. government in 1885 as a combatant in the Civil War, entitling her to a military pension in her own right. She is believed to be the only woman so honored. She was born on November 7, 1844, the daughter of Hiram C. and Permelia (Huff) Marcum, who farmed in Scott County, Tennessee. Because Marcum's family were Union sympathizers, their home was attacked by Confederates in September 1861. In the ensuing battle, Marcum fought a soldier with an ax, inflicting several wounds before her father shot the man dead. She lost an eye and a finger in the assault. The Marcums successfully staved off the Confederate force on that occasion, but later attacks drove the family to Casey County, Kentucky.

Julia Marcum returned to Tennessee after the war and taught school. When her war wounds eventu-

ally disabled her, she made a plea to Congress for a pension, which was originally granted at $30 a month. (In 1922 the amount was raised to $40.) After retiring, she moved to Williamsburg, Kentucky, where she died on May 9, 1936. Marcum was the only woman admitted as a full member of the Grand Army of the Republic, and the chapter in Williamsburg accorded her military honors at her funeral.

MARY MARGARET BELL

MARION. Marion, the fourth-class city that is county seat of Crittenden County, is located near the center of the county, at the junction of U.S. 641 and U.S. 60 on the Tradewater Railroad, a ninety-two-mile line from Princeton to Morganfield. Marion is also intersected by KY 91 and KY 120. Founded in 1842, Marion was named after Francis Marion, the "Swamp Fox" of the American Revolution. The first county seat was a few miles north of Marion, at a location that is disputed between Cross Keys and the Crooked Creek community; Marion became the seat in 1844. The post office was established in 1846. Marion was a busy agricultural center, but the FLUORSPAR industry overshadowed agriculture in the 1840s, as the largest fluorspar mine in the country sent the economy booming. The industry peaked in 1947 and has declined rapidly since then because of competition from imports.

The first court in Crittenden County was held at the home of Samuel Ashley, and the first courthouse in Marion, built on land donated by John S. Gilliam, housed its first session on June 10, 1842. The courthouse was burned by Confederate Gen. Hylan B. Lyons on January 25, 1865, during the Civil War. A fire that swept through Marion on March 28, 1905, consumed at least forty buildings, including the courthouse. In 1870 the third courthouse was also destroyed by fire. The present courthouse was dedicated in December 1961.

In 1849 the private Crittenden Academy opened in Marion, the first school in the county. The first public school was the Marion Academy and Normal School, which opened in 1886 on land donated to Marion on August 8, 1868, by Nancy Gilliam. Marion was the home of U.S. Sens. William Joseph Deboe and Ollie M. James, who were neighbors and friends.

Manufacturers in Marion include producers of lumber, modular homes, agricultural lime, electromagnetic relays, paving materials, and roofbolts and plates for the mining industry. Marion's population was 3,008 in 1970; 3,392 in 1980; and 3,320 in 1990. Marion was designated by the Kentucky Chamber of Commerce an All-Kentucky City in 1969, 1970, and 1971 and is one of the thirteen original members of the Hall of Fame of Kentucky Chambers of Commerce.

MARION COUNTY. The eighty-fourth county in order of formation, Marion County is located in central Kentucky. Bordered by Boyle, Casey, Larue, Mercer, Nelson, Taylor, and Washington counties, it contains an area of 347 square miles. Marion was formed from Washington County on January 25, 1834, and was named in honor of Gen. Francis Marion, the "Swamp Fox" of the Revolutionary War who won fame for his military tactics against the British forces in the southern theater of operations. The county seat of Marion County is LEBANON.

The county is located within the Knobs geographic region of Kentucky, and the topography is undulating to hilly. Farms occupy 82 percent of the land area with 66 percent of those in cultivation of tobacco, livestock, poultry, fruits, hay, soybeans, and vegetables. In 1987 the county ranked twenty-first in Kentucky in agricultural receipts. It has deposits of dolomite and limestone. The major stream is the Rolling Fork of the Salt River.

The area was first explored by the surveyors James and Jacob Sandusky and was settled in 1779, along Hardin's Creek, by Charles and Edward Beavin. Marion County became a settlement for Roman Catholics from Charles, Prince George, and St. Mary's counties, Maryland. By 1785 Basil Hayden, Sr., had settled twenty-five Catholic families on the headwaters of Pottinger's Creek. The first Roman Catholic church in Kentucky was built on this site in 1792, where the town of Holy Cross is now located. Several of the Catholic churches were formed by the missionary priest, Charles Nerinckx, of Belgium. The Catholic influence was further demonstrated in 1821, when St. Mary's College was established at Loretto. The motherhouse of the Sisters of Loretto is located in the county.

The communities developed in Marion County include the incorporated towns of Lebanon, Bradfordsville, Loretto, and Rayswick. The county is served by CSX Transportation and U.S. 68. The largest industries are Jane & Linda Sportswear Company, established in 1952, producing women's sportswear, and the Independent Stave Company, manufacturer of whiskey barrels. Both plants are in Lebanon. Loretto is the site of the county's most famous industry, Star Hill Distillery, which produces one of Kentucky's premiere bourbon whiskeys, Maker's Mark. In 1988 tourism spending was $3.3 million. Each October, Country Ham Days draw a large number of visitors.

The population of Marion County was 16,714 in 1970; 17,910 in 1980; and 16,499 in 1990.

See William T. Knott, *History of Marion County, Kentucky* (Frankfort, Ky., 1952).

RON D. BRYANT

MARRS, ELIJAH P. Elijah P. Marrs, educator and an early advocate of civil rights through the Baptist ministry and the Republican party, was born in January 1840 in Shelby County, Kentucky. He was the son of Andrew Marrs, a freedman, and his wife, Frances, a slave. He was converted to the Baptist faith at age eleven and was taught to read and write by a local black man and several white children. At the outbreak of the Civil War, Marrs informed blacks of events by reading to them from newspapers and in September 1864 he led a band of twenty-seven slaves to Louisville to join the Union army. He trained at Camp Nelson, Kentucky, and took part in minor engagements at Glasgow and Big Springs. Marrs rose to the rank of sergeant. After his discharge on April 24, 1866, he taught school in Simpsonville, LaGrange, New Castle, and Louisville.

Marrs spent the fall term of 1874 at Roger Williams University in Nashville. In 1879, he and his brother, Henry C. Marrs, founded Baptist Normal and Theological Institute in Louisville, which was renamed State University in 1883 and later Simmons Bible College. He was a strong advocate of public education for blacks throughout his life. Marrs began preaching in the Baptist church in the early 1870s and was ordained on August 22, 1875. He founded the Beargrass Colored Baptist Church at Crescent Hill in Louisville, where he was pastor from 1880 until his death. During much of that period, he was treasurer in the General Association of Colored Baptists.

Marrs was a delegate to every major statewide political convention Kentucky blacks held in the postwar era. Convinced that blacks could prosper only if they acquired political and civil rights, he began speaking in behalf of the Republican party in the late 1860s, and played a prominent role in the election of 1870, the first in which Kentucky blacks voted. Marrs sat on the state central committee of the anti–separate coach movement.

On August 3, 1871, Marrs married Julia Gray, daughter of Harriet Gray of Shelbyville. His wife died in 1876. Marrs died on August 30, 1910.

See Elijah P. Marrs, *Life and History of the Reverend Elijah P. Marrs, First Pastor of Beargrass Baptist Church, and Author* (Louisville 1885).

MARION B. LUCAS

MARSHALL, HUMPHREY. Humphrey Marshall, one of the most controversial and colorful citizens of early Kentucky, was born in Fauquier County, Virginia, in 1760, the son of John and Mary (Quisenberry) Marshall. As a young man, he was educated with his first cousins at the home of his uncle Thomas Marshall and later studied law. Humphrey Marshall's close relationships with that family were reinforced in 1784 by his marriage to Mary Marshall, by whom he had a daughter and two sons. The marriage made him also a brother-in-law of the chief justice of the United States, John Marshall.

After service in the Virginia forces from 1778 to 1782 during the Revolutionary War, Humphrey Marshall moved to what is now Fayette County, Kentucky. He was deputy surveyor under Thomas Marshall until 1790, when he was made deputy surveyor of present-day Woodford County. The land he claimed, when added to the 4,000 acres granted him as a veteran, in time made him one of the wealthiest citizens in the region. (It was said that he measured his money by the peck.) Although initially blackballed from membership in the Danville

Political Club, whose members were leading political and economic figures, Marshall later became one of its most vocal members. He was vehemently antireligious, and his convictions so embarrassed his nineteenth century descendants that they burned his papers.

Marshall was deeply suspicious of James WIL-KINSON's plans to negotiate with Spain to gain free navigation of the Mississippi River and possibly to secede from the Union, and from 1786 to the end of his life he carried on a vigorous campaign against everyone whom he suspected of membership in the SPANISH CONSPIRACY. Unlike most Kentuckians, he opposed immediate separation from Virginia, and in the Virginia ratifying convention of 1788, when ten delegates from what is now Kentucky voted against ratification of the federal Constitution and one abstained, Humphrey Marshall cast one of the area's three votes for the Constitution.

Marshall was an ardent and partisan Federalist. After serving in the Kentucky legislature in 1793 and 1794, he was chosen as U.S. senator (March 4, 1795, to March 3, 1801) over Jeffersonian John BRECKINRIDGE. His support for the unpopular Jay Treaty with Great Britain led to mob violence after his return to Kentucky. Not only was he defeated for reelection, but he was also stoned in Frankfort and narrowly escaped being thrown into the Kentucky River. He was elected to the lower house of the General Assembly in 1807 and 1808.

In 1806 Marshall resumed his attack on the players in the Spanish Conspiracy through the pages of the *Frankfort Western World*. This time his charges elicited action and a select committee of the Kentucky House of Representatives found that Court of Appeals Judge Benjamin Sebastian had received a pension from Spain. Among the witnesses acknowledging the Spanish overtures (but not his own complicity) was Harry INNES, judge of the U.S. District Court for Kentucky, who had long been the principal object of Marshall's suspicion. Marshall's brother-in-law, federal attorney Joseph Hamilton Daveiss, was unable to persuade federal grand jurors to indict Aaron Burr after his 1805 and 1806 trips to enlist Kentuckians and gather supplies for his dubious ventures. Marshall's attacks on Innes then intensified. Innes sued Marshall for libel and, with his political allies, hired William LITTELL to write a book giving their version of the negotiations with Spain. Marshall in turn wrote *History of Kentucky* (1812), which became the most popular and widely read early history of the commonwealth.

An advisory jury in the U.S. district court found that evidence of fraud by Marshall in a land case was inconclusive, and Innes dismissed this suit. Marshall then began a campaign in the U.S. House of Representatives through John ROWAN to impeach Innes, and Innes's son-in-law Thomas Bodley began one in the Kentucky House of Representatives to censure Marshall. Rowan failed, but Bodley succeeded. In 1808 Marshall was expelled—but won reelection the following year.

The libel suit dragged on until 1815, when a truce was arranged between Marshall and Innes, and each signed an agreement promising not to write or publish anything disrespectful of the other. Innes kept his pledge, but Marshall did not: The 1824 edition of his *History* is even more virulent than the earlier one in accusations about the Spanish Conspiracy. The charges and countercharges of these remarkable antagonists echoed for generations among their descendants and partisans and are a principal theme in Kentucky historiography.

Marshall died on July 3, 1841, and was buried on his farm, Glen Willis, in Frankfort.

See John Mason Brown, *The Political Beginnings of Kentucky* (Louisville 1889); William McClung Paxton, *The Marshall Family* (Cincinnati 1885).

MARY K. BONSTEEL TACHAU

MARSHALL, HUMPHREY. Humphrey Marshall, politician and Confederate general, was born to John Jay and Anna Reed (Birney) Marshall on January 13, 1812, in Frankfort, Kentucky. He was the nephew of antislavery leader James Birney and grandson of Humphrey MARSHALL. Graduating from the U.S. Military Academy at West Point in 1832, Marshall soon resigned his commission for a career in law and Whig politics. After serving as colonel of the 1st Kentucky Cavalry in the Mexican War, he was minister to China (1852-54) and spent two terms in the U.S. House of Representatives (March 4, 1855, through March 3, 1859). Marshall supported John C. Breckinridge in the 1860 presidential campaign but then lobbied for Kentucky's neutrality during the secession crisis. With the onset of the Civil War, he accepted a commission as brigadier general in the Confederate army effective October 30, 1861, and was assigned to eastern Kentucky.

Standing five feet eleven inches and weighing over three hundred pounds, Marshall was physically unfit for active duty in the rugged mountains, but he was obsessed with an independent command for his army of 2,000. At Middle Creek in Floyd County on January 10, 1862, lesser numbers of Union troops under Col. James Garfield forced Marshall to withdraw. After playing a minor role in Confederate Gen. Braxton Bragg's invasion of Kentucky, Marshall resigned his commission on June 17, 1863. He then served in the Second Confederate Congress until the end of the war, when he fled to Mexico. Marshall returned to Louisville in 1866, where he practiced law until his death on March 28, 1872. He was buried in the Frankfort Cemetery.

See Lowell H. Harrison, *The Civil War in Kentucky* (Lexington, Ky., 1975); C. David Dalton, "Confederate Operations in Eastern Kentucky, 1861-1862," M.A. thesis, Western Kentucky University, 1982.   C. DAVID DALTON

MARSHALL, THOMAS ALEXANDER. Thomas Alexander Marshall, congressman and jurist, was born near Versailles in Woodford County, Kentucky, on January 15, 1794, to Humphrey and Mary Marshall. Marshall received his B.A. from Yale in 1815, was admitted to the bar, and began practice in Frankfort in 1816. He moved to Paris in Bourbon County in 1819. Marshall served two terms in the state House of Representatives, in 1827 and 1828, and was a member of the U.S. House of Representatives from March 4, 1831, to March 3, 1835. He was an advocate of the Whig party and supported high protective tariff rates and the Bank of the United States. Marshall was appointed to the Kentucky court of appeals by Gov. James T. Morehead (1834-36) in March 1835 and when the position became elective in 1850, he won election to a further six-year term. He served as chief justice from 1847 to 1851 and from 1854 to 1856. Marshall was also a professor in the Transylvania University law department from 1836 to 1849. He served in the Kentucky House from 1863 to 1865. He was appointed to the court of appeals by Gov. Thomas Bramlette (1863-67) on February 12, 1866, to fill a vacant term, but because of pro-Union sympathies was defeated for election in August 1866.

Marshall married Eliza Price on November 26, 1816. He died in Louisville on April 17, 1871 and was buried in the Lexington Cemetery.

MARSHALL COUNTY. Marshall County, the ninety-second county in order of formation, located in the extreme western region of Kentucky, is bounded by Livingston, Lyon, Trigg, Calloway, Graves, and McCracken counties, and contains 304 square miles. The county was once part of the Chickasaw Indian lands acquired in the Jackson Purchase of October 19, 1818. From 1818 to 1822 the area that is now Marshall County was part of Hickman County; from 1822 to 1842 it was the northern part of Calloway County. On June 1, 1842, Marshall County was created and named for John Marshall, chief justice of the United States. BENTON was established at a central location as the county seat.

The terrain of the county varies from gently rolling hills to level wooded areas and bottomlands. Much of the bottomland on the eastern border of the county along the Tennessee River was flooded by waters from Kentucky Lake, created by building Kentucky Dam. Within the county the principal stream is Clark's River with its three branches, the East, Middle, and West forks. Most of the surface area of the county was originally covered with hardwood timber.

The first settlers of the area included Banister Wade, John Irvan, James Stewart and the Rev. Henry Clay Darnall, all of whom may have entered the Chickasaw lands before the Jackson Purchase. In 1819 Darnall, a Baptist, founded the first church west of the Tennessee River, on Soldier Creek in Kentucky.

Early roads in the area included one from Egner's Ferry on the Tennessee River, which ran east to Wadesboro and then on to Mayfield and finally to Columbus. It is the approximate route of KY 80.

Roads that connected Benton with Paducah to the northwest and Wadesboro and Murray to the south eventually came to be part of U.S. 641.

Shortly after the Civil War the rail line was completed from Paducah to Louisville; it became the Illinois Central Railroad (now Paducah & Louisville). Calvert City and Gilbertsville in the northern part of the county were both established on this line around 1871. The county's other railroad, built in 1890, was the Paducah, Tennessee & Alabama Railroad, with stops at Benton and Hardin. Hardin was founded by Hardin Davenport Irvan, who moved his store from Wadesboro to the new rail line in 1890. Soon after the turn of the century the town had five stores, three blacksmith shops, a mill, drugstore, livery stable, phone office, theater, and three churches. Electric power arrived in 1915. The railroad later became part of the Nashville, Chattanooga & St. Louis Railroad, and then the Louisville & Nashville (now CSX Transportation). When the line from Hardin to Paducah was abandoned and the ties and rails removed in the 1970s, a local grain elevator bought the track lying between Hardin and Murray and called it the J&J Railroad.

Until the period after World War II, Marshall County was almost totally agricultural. It was considered a poor county because the soil was thin. Crops included corn, tobacco, and soybeans, as well as beef and dairy cattle and hogs. During the 1930s it was a major strawberry-producing area and Benton became a loading point for crates of Dixie Aroma brand berries. With the completion of Kentucky Dam in 1945, chemical plants and other industries arrived in Calvert City. Some towns, such as Birmingham, were covered by the lake. Others, such as Aurora and Gilbertsville, grew as tourist centers.

By 1988, 26 percent of the county's employed labor force worked in some aspect of manufacturing. In 1990 Marshall County's largest employers, all manufacturing plants in Calvert City, were the GAF Corporation, Air Products and Chemicals, Inc., and Atochem North American.

The population of the rural county was 20,381 in 1970; 25,637 in 1980; and 27,205 in 1990.

See Edward C. Olds, *The History of Marshall County* (Benton, Ky., 1933).

RAYMOND MOFIELD

MARTIN, GEORGE BROWN. George Brown Martin, U.S. senator, was born on August 18, 1876, in Prestonsburg, Kentucky, to Alexander L. and Nannie Frances (Brown) Martin. His father, a Confederate soldier and successful lawyer, served in both houses of the Kentucky legislature and for a period was president pro tempore of the state Senate. Martin County was named for George's grandfather, John P. Martin. The family moved to Catlettsburg, Kentucky, in 1877, where Martin attended the public schools and graduated from the Catlettsburg high school in 1889. After receiving an A.B. from Central University in Richmond,

Kentucky, in 1895, he studied law. In 1900 he was admitted to the bar and entered with his uncle, Thomas R. Brown, into the firm of Brown and Martin.

In 1904 Gov. J.C.W. Beckham (1900-1907) appointed Martin to serve the remainder of William Poage's term as Boyd County judge. Gov. A.O. Stanley (1915-1919) appointed Martin to the U.S. Senate on September 7, 1918, to fill the term of Ollie M. James, which expired March 4, 1919. Martin chose not to run for a full term but instead resumed his law practice at Catlettsburg. He was a member-at-large for the state Democratic executive committee from 1916 to 1924 and was a delegate to the majority of Democratic state conventions after 1900. He was a delegate-at-large at the Democratic National Convention in Houston, Texas, in 1928 and was a Democratic elector in 1932 and 1936. In 1932 he unsuccessfully sought the Democratic nomination for U.S. senator, losing to Alben W. Barkley by 124,775 to 55,556. Martin served as the general counsel and director of the Big Sandy & Kentucky River Railway Company, vice president of the Ohio Valley Electric Railway Company, director of the Kentucky Farmers Bank of Catlettsburg, and vice-president of the American Bar Association in 1934. Martin died on November 12, 1945, and was buried in the Catlettsburg Cemetery.

MARTIN, JOHN P. John Preston Martin, politician, was born in Lee County, Virginia, on October 11, 1811. He was educated as a lawyer, and in 1828 he moved to Harlan County, Kentucky. He ran for the state House of Representatives in 1830, losing to John Bates, but was elected to the General Assembly in 1841 and 1843 as a representative of Floyd County. On March 4, 1845, Martin, a Democrat, was elected to the 29th Congress of the United States, serving in the House of Representatives until March 3, 1847. In 1849 Martin lost the race for another term to Daniel Breck. In 1848 he was the Democrats' candidate for lieutenant governor of Kentucky but was defeated by John L. Helm. In 1855 Martin was elected to the state Senate, where he served until 1859, representing the counties of Floyd, Morgan, Johnson, and Pike. He was a Kentucky delegate to the Democratic National Convention in Cincinnati in 1856, and he supported his close friend Linn Boyd for the presidency against James Buchanan. Martin was popular in the Kentucky mountains as an outspoken opponent of Know-Nothingism. Martin County, established in 1870, was named for him.

Martin married Elizabeth Lackey on May 24, 1835. They had at least one son, Alexander Martin, who represented Floyd County in the legislature from 1867 to 1869 and who also served as a state senator. John P. Martin died in Prestonsburg, Kentucky, on December 23, 1862 and is buried in May Cemetery there.

MARTIN, JOSEPH. Joseph Martin, frontiersman, son of Joseph and Susannah (Childs) Martin, was born near Charlottesville, Virginia, in 1740.

While on a hunting trip in 1761 he first saw Powell Valley, Virginia, and in 1768 Dr. Thomas Walker asked him to head a settlement party there. Martin's Station, in present-day Lee County, Virginia, was at first the only station on the Wilderness Road between Blockhouse, Virginia, and Crab Orchard, Kentucky, a distance of nearly two hundred miles. Nothing more than a stockade consisting of five or six cabins, it was an important stopping point during the initial migration into Kentucky. Martin abandoned the station in the fall of 1769, but it remained a refuge for travelers. In 1775 Martin returned with eighteen men to resettle the station, but in 1776 he again abandoned it. He subsequently became an agent for the Transylvania Company in exchange for preferential rights to his land claim in Powell Valley. He was commissioned agent and superintendent of Indian affairs for Virginia in 1777, a position he held until 1786. Between 1783 and 1789, Martin held a similar position in North Carolina.

Martin made a third effort at settling Martin's Station in 1783, but sold his interest in the settlement in 1788. In 1789 he established a fort in Georgia, where he lived briefly. By 1791 Martin had returned to his home in Virginia and served in the Virginia legislature from that year until 1799. On December 11, 1793, he was commissioned a brigadier general in the Virginia militia by Gov. Henry Lee. While a member of the legislature, Martin was on the 1799 commission to settle the boundary dispute between Kentucky and Virginia. In 1803 he moved from Pittsylvania County to Henry County, Virginia, where he died on December 18, 1808.

See Robert L. Kincaid, *The Wilderness Road* (Indianapolis 1947); William A. Pusey, "General Joseph Martin, an Unsung Hero of the Virginia Frontier," *FCHQ* 10 (April 1936): 57-82.

MARTIN, ROBERT RICHARD. Robert Richard Martin, educator and politician, was born on December 27, 1910, near McKinney, in Lincoln County, Kentucky. Martin, reared on a farm, was one of eight children born to Frank and Annie Frances (Peek) Martin. He received his early education in the Lincoln County schools and graduated from Stanford High School in 1930. He attended Eastern Kentucky State Normal School and Teachers College (now Eastern Kentucky University), where in 1934 he received a bachelor's degree. Martin received a master's degree from the University of Kentucky in 1940 and in 1951 earned a doctorate in education from Teachers College, Columbia University.

In 1937 Martin became the principal of Sardis High School, and from 1938 to 1942 he served as principal at Orangeburg, both schools in Mason County. After serving in the army from 1942 to 1945, he became principal of Woodleigh Junior High School and in 1947 the principal of Lee County High School. Martin joined the state Department of Education in 1948, where he was an auditor, director of finance, then head of the Bureau of Administration and Finance from 1948 to 1955.

He worked for enactment of the MINIMUM FOUN-
DATION PROGRAM for education during the 1954
session of the General Assembly.

In 1955 Martin was elected state superintendent
of public instruction. In December 1959 he was appointed by Gov. Bert T. Combs (1959-63) as commissioner of finance for Kentucky. In 1960 he was
named the sixth president of Eastern Kentucky
State College, which under his leadership became
Eastern Kentucky University in 1966. He retired
from the presidency in 1976. In 1977 Martin was
elected to the Kentucky State Senate, where he represented the 22d District for two terms. While in
the Senate, he served as chairman of the Committee on Health and Welfare, was a member of the
Committee on Appropriations and Revenue, and
was vice-chairman of the Committee on Education.
Martin was the recipient of the Civilian Service
Award in 1971 from the U.S. Army. In 1964 he
received the Kentucky Press Association's Kentuckian of the Year Award. He has served on the
board of directors of the YMCA and as a member
of the board of managers of the Presbyterian Child
Welfare Agency, Synod of Kentucky.

Martin married Anne French Hoge on May 31,
1952.   DONNA M. MASTERS

MARTIN COUNTY. Martin County lies in the
Appalachian Mountains, in the easternmost reaches
of the commonwealth. The 116th county formed, it
was made from portions of Floyd, Johnson, Pike
and Lawrence counties, which, with the Tug Fork
of the Big Sandy River on the east, form its boundaries. The land is very mountainous, with high elevations and narrow valleys cut by streams. The
original land surface has changed dramatically with
the advent of strip mining. Places in the 231-
square-mile area rise to elevations of fifteen hundred feet above sea level.

Martin County, formed September 1, 1870, was
named for Col. John P. Martin, a state senator and
U.S. congressman from Prestonsburg. The county
seat was moved from Warfield to a more central
location at INEZ in 1873.

Coal was first mined in Martin County in the late
nineteenth century at Warfield. One of the first major mining operations was at Himmlerville, where
in 1918 Hungarian immigrant Martin Himmler began mining a seam of good coal. Himmler's company was sold in 1929 and the town was renamed
Beauty in an effort at improvement.

President Lyndon Johnson visited the Thomas
Fletcher family in Martin County on April 24,
1964, to initiate his war on poverty, but not until
the infusion of coal company wages began did the
standard of living improve. In 1986 about one hundred mines were in operation, producing more than
7 million tons of coal underground and 5.5 million
tons by surface mining. It is estimated that at this
rate the known coal reserves will last forty to fifty
years.

During the 1940s and 1950s the Norfolk & Western Railroad (later the Norfolk & Southern) acquired four large tracts of land in Martin County,
and control of nearly 100,000 acres of mineral
rights. With the energy crisis foreshadowed in the
early 1970s, Norfolk & Western built a twenty-four-
mile spur from its main line in West Virginia across
the Tug Fork of the Big Sandy River and into the
heart of Martin County's coal wealth. In 1981 Norfolk & Southern, through its subsidiary Pocahontas
Corporation, owned nearly 48,000 thousand acres
of surface land and more than 81,000 acres of mineral rights. Other major landowners in Martin
County include the Martiki Coal Corporation, Mt.
Sterling Land Company, and Harvard University.
Fully 75 percent of the owned mineral rights are
held by out-of-state corporations and individuals.
Artificially low tax rates allow for major profits for
the owners and operating coal companies, while
limiting benefits to local citizens. In 1980, for example, the largest owner of mineral rights—more
than 81,000 acres valued at more than $7 million—
paid Martin County only $76 in taxes.

In addition to coal, the county's chief resources
are oil, natural gas, and hardwood timber. In 1971
a total of 10,735 barrels of oil were pumped; in
1982, nine oil and gas extraction establishments
were in operation. In 1982 only 1.7 percent of the
land was in farms, with less than $500,000 in com-
bined livestock and crop receipts.

Most of the employment depends either directly
or indirectly on the coal industry, with the most numerous employers being the twenty-four in mining,
twenty-four in transportation and public utilities,
forty-nine in retail trade, and twenty-eight in services. The population of Martin County was 9,377
in 1970; 13,925 in 1980; 12,526 in 1990.

See Concerned Citizens of Martin County, Inc.,
Readings of Martin County, Kentucky (Inez, Ky.,
1983).

MARTIN'S STATION. John Martin, an early
Kentucky pioneer who spent time at Fort Boonesborough, established his station on Stoner Creek in
Bourbon County in the spring of 1779, after first
improving the property in 1775 or 1776 with
William Whitsett. Located along a well-used aboriginal path, the Alantowamiowee Trail, the station provided homes for numerous families, many
of Pennsylvania German origin. In the spring of
1780, Capt. Henry Byrd and his British soldiers
and Indians captured the station. Although the station was reportedly stockaded, the presence of two
pieces of field artillery brought by Byrd and the absence of Martin, who was on a hunting trip, persuaded the inhabitants to surrender without a fight.
Most of them were marched to Detroit as captives,
and many waited out the remainder of the war in
detention. The property later became part of Fairfield farm, owned by James Garrard, Jr., who built
a stone house and family cemetery near the site of
the old station.

See Nancy O'Malley, *Stockading Up* (Archaeo-
logical Report 127, Department of Archaeology,
University of Kentucky, Lexington, Ky., 1987);
Willard Rouse Jillson, *Pioneer Kentucky* (Frankfort,
Ky., 1934).   NANCY O'MALLEY

MARVIN COLLEGE. Marvin College, established in 1885 at Clinton in Hickman County, Kentucky, provided the youth of the region with an affordable education until the 1920s. Although founded and operated under the auspices of the Methodist Episcopal Church, South, it was open to students of all denominations. The school offered a basic college curriculum, awarding both the bachelor of arts and bachelor of science degrees. Between 1900 and 1910 the campus expanded from one to three buildings, adding a president's house and a dormitory. One distinguished alumnus was Alben W. Barkley, U.S. senator and vice-president. In 1908 the board of curators decided Marvin College was best equipped for preparatory-level instruction and it was renamed Marvin University School. With the advancement of free public education, the school was closed in 1922.

See Alben W. Barkley, *That Reminds Me —* (New York 1954).

MASON, BOBBIE ANN. Bobbie Ann Mason, author of short stories and novels, was born May 1, 1940, in Mayfield, Kentucky, the daughter of Wilburn and Bernice Christie (Lee) Mason, and grew up on the family's fifty-four-acre dairy farm. She received an A.B. in English from the University of Kentucky in 1962, an M.A. from the State University of New York at Binghamton in 1966, and a Ph.D. from the University of Connecticut in 1972.

While still in college, Mason wrote for the *Mayfield Messenger*, and after college she contributed to popular magazines such as *Movie Stars*, *Movie Life*, and *T.V. Star Parade* in New York City. She taught English at Mansfield State College in Pennsylvania from 1972 to 1979. Her first books were nonfiction: *Nabokov's Garden: A Nature Guide to Ada* (1974), and *The Girl Sleuth: A Feminist Guide to the Bobbsey Twins, Nancy Drew, and Their Sisters* (1975). Mason's first published short story appeared in the *New Yorker* in 1980, and her work soon began appearing in other national magazines. *Shiloh and Other Stories* (1982) and *Love Life* (1989) are collections of short stories. Her stories have appeared regularly in the *New Yorker*, *Paris Review*, *North American Review*, *Redbook*, *Atlantic*, *Mother Jones*, *Southern Magazine*, and *Harper's*, and in the annual volumes of Houghton Mifflin's *Best American Short Stories*.

Mason's first novel, *In Country* (1985), is about teenager Samantha Hughes's obsessive search to know her father, killed in Vietnam before she was born. The characters in her next novel, *Spence + Lila* (1988), are a farm couple who, after more than forty years of married life, cope with the problems of old age and death.

The scene of most of Mason's fiction is her native western Kentucky. She underscored the importance of her Kentucky background and its influence on her fiction in an interview with Mervyn Rothstein: "I think it's a matter of temperament and heredity and region. I think the style very much grows out of the place I come from." In 1988, when *In Country* was made into a motion picture by Warner Brothers, much of the filming was done near Paducah. A writer for the *New York Review of Books* (December 16, 1982) called Mason "one of those rare writers who, by concentrating their attention on a few square miles of native turf, are able to open up new and surprisingly wide worlds for the delighted reader."

In 1969 Mason married Roger B. Rawlings, a writer and magazine editor; they live in Anderson County.

See Mervyn Rothstein, "Homegrown Fiction," *New York Times Magazine*, May 15, 1988.

WADE HALL

MASON COUNTY. Mason County, the eighth county in order of formation, is located in the Outer Bluegrass region of northeastern Kentucky. The county is bounded by Bracken, Robertson, Fleming, and Lewis counties and by the Ohio River on the north; it covers 241 square miles. Named for statesman George Mason of Virginia, whose writings influenced Thomas Jefferson, the county was established by the Virginia legislature in 1788. Nineteen Kentucky counties were later formed from the original Mason County. Hemp and tobacco were the earliest crops of the rich, productive soil. The limestone base gave the name to the original landing place on the Ohio River, Limestone (now MAYSVILLE), which is the county seat.

In prehistoric eras large mammals roamed the hills and valleys in great numbers and Native Americans lived and hunted in the area. Explorers and early travelers noted the herds of bison that remained in the area until soon after settlement and were impressed by the large buffalo path, or trace, that extended from the Ohio River to the Inner Bluegrass region. This path was extensively used by both Indians and pioneers.

Christopher Gist in 1751 was among the first white explorers to enter this area. Simon Kenton and Thomas Williams are credited with being the first permanent settlers, having staked out land in a canebrake where they made camp and planted corn in 1775. Because Indian raids were frequent, Kenton built a station for the protection of the many families who were coming into Mason County. Kenton's haven was responsible for the growth of the town of WASHINGTON, established in 1786 on land purchased from Kenton. When the citizens won the right to separate from Bourbon County, they set about making Washington a town and county seat. With a population of 462 in 1790, it was the second largest town in the state after Lexington. By the 1840s, however, Maysville became an important river port and eclipsed Washington.

Mayslick was settled by New Jersey families that included Daniel Drake, who became a well-known doctor. The town was named for William May, brother of John, from whom Maysville got its name. Lewisburg and Germantown were settled in 1795, then Orangeburg (first called Williamsburg), Rectorville, Minerva, Dover, Sardis, and Murphysville.

In 1931 a bridge named for Simon Kenton was opened across the Ohio River to connect Maysville with Aberdeen, Ohio. The old buffalo trace, once the pioneer thoroughfare into the interior of Kentucky, gradually was improved and developed into U.S. 68. The AA Highway, running east-west through the county, gives access to the Ashland and Covington areas. Although floods, tornadoes in 1860, 1968, and 1974, and earthquakes in 1830 and 1980 hit Mason County, many historic houses survive. Two covered bridges also remain.

The county's population was 17,273 in 1970; 17,765 in 1980; 16,666 in 1990.

See G. Glenn Clift, *History of Maysville and Mason County, Kentucky* (Lexington, Ky., 1936).

JEAN W. CALVERT

MASON & HANGER–SILAS MASON CO. A section of railroad constructed in Virginia in 1827 by Claiborne Mason was the start of Mason & Hanger–Silas Mason Co., the engineering and construction firm based in Lexington, Kentucky, that is the nation's second-oldest contractor. The firm has contributed to missile development, water purification technology, oil spill and hazardous waste management, precision measuring, and robotics. The original company was Mason & Hanger; the Mason family has roots in Kentucky dating back to coal mining operations during the late nineteenth century. In 1935, from his Duntreath farm, Silas Mason was one of the founders of the Keeneland Association.

The Mason & Hanger Company merged with the Silas Mason Company in 1955. Their construction projects have included expansion of the New York City sewer system, the Lincoln Tunnel, Grand Coulee Dam, the layout of the Nevada Test Site for the development of nuclear weapons, and the construction and management of the nation's first nuclear weapons assembly plant. Since 1956, the corporation has managed the only nuclear weapons assembly facility in the nation—the Pantex plant, near Amarillo, Texas.

See Ann Arnold Lemert, *First You Take a Pick & Shovel: The Story of the Mason Companies* (Lexington, Ky., 1979).

ERIC HOWARD CHRISTIANSON

MASONIC UNIVERSITY. Masonic University, closed since 1911, was established as Funk Seminary in 1841 at La Grange in Oldham County, Kentucky, through a $10,000 donation from William M. Funk, a native of the county. The school, which began operating in 1842 upon the completion of a two-story brick building, was renamed Masonic College in 1844, when the Masons' Grand Lodge of Kentucky obtained control of it. The school was divided into an upper college, which offered a four-year program and awarded A.B. and B.S. degrees, and a lower college. The lower college was subdivided into upper and lower

sections, with English, classical, and mathematical preparatory work required. Enrollment was around two hundred, with the majority of the students coming from the South. A medical department in Louisville was added to the college in 1850. In 1852 the school assumed the name Masonic University of Kentucky, and it enjoyed its greatest success during the next two decades. A cholera outbreak in 1849-50 and the advent of the Civil War severely curtailed enrollment, and the university reverted to high school status on May 1, 1873. The school closed after fire destroyed the main building on September 24, 1911. Prominent leaders who served Masonic University included the Rev. J.R. Findley, Robert Morris, the Rev. John Trimble, Jr., Henry B. Parsons, Robert A. Logan, T.H. HINES, H.H. DeGarms, and the Rev. D.M. Graves.

See R.F. Johnson, "The History of Education in Oldham County, Kentucky," M.A. thesis, University of Kentucky, 1938.

MATHER, WILLIAM WILLIAMS. William Williams Mather, geologist, was born May 24, 1804, in Brooklyn, Connecticut, to Eleazar and Fanny (Williams) Mather. A descendant of Cotton Mather, he was educated at West Point, New York (1828); Wesleyan University in Middletown, Connecticut (1833); and Brown University in Providence, Rhode Island (1836). While engaged in geological investigations in New York during 1837-40, he was also state geologist of Ohio (1837-40) and of Kentucky (1838). As Kentucky's first state geologist, Mather recognized Kentucky's mineral districts, delimited its coal and limestone areas, and noted Kentucky's abundant surface water resources. He was married to Emily Maria Baker; they had six children. Mather's second wife was Mary Curtis, with whom he had one child. He died in Columbus, Ohio, on February 25, 1859.

See Preston McGrain, "The History of the Kentucky Geological Survey," Open file report, Kentucky Geological Survey, 1987; L.C. Robinson, "The Kentucky Geological Survey," *Register* 25 (Jan. 1927): 86-93. MARGARET LUTHER SMATH

MATTHEWS, JOSEPH BROWN. Joseph Brown Matthews was born in Hopkinsville, Kentucky, on June 28, 1894, the third child of Burrel Jones Matthews and Fanny Wellborn (Brown) Matthews. He embraced the Methodism of his childhood, graduated from Asbury College in 1915, and served as a missionary. In 1921 he began to be attracted by the political left, moving from the Social Gospel through pacifism to a pro-Soviet, revolutionary socialism. By 1935, however, his political orientation was moving back to the right, and from 1938 to 1945 he worked as director of research for the U.S. House of Representatives Committee to Investigate Un-American Activities. Matthews and his third wife, Ruth, whom he married in 1949, moved in influential conservative circles until his death on July 16, 1966. He is buried in the Lexington Cemetery.

See J.B. Matthews, *Odyssey of a Fellow Traveler* (New York 1938); Nelson L. Dawson, "From Fellow Traveler to Anticommunist: The Odyssey of J.B. Matthews," *Register* 84 (1986): 280-306.

NELSON L. DAWSON

MATTHEWS, KATE SESTON. Kate Seston Matthews, photographer, was born August 13, 1870, in New Albany, Indiana, to Lucien and Charlotte Ann (Clark) Matthews. She was one of eight children. When she was very young, the family moved to Pewee Valley, Kentucky, where they lived in a fourteen-room residence known as Clovercroft. Because of a childhood illness, Matthews was educated at home.

While she was sixteen years old, she spent time in Vermont visiting her sister and brother-in-law, Lillian and Charles Barrows Fletcher, who introduced Matthews to photography. Upon her return home, her father bought her a camera and she taught herself the art of photography.

In an era when few women ventured into photography, Matthews made a name for herself when her photos were published in *Youth's Companion*, *Illustrated American*, *Cosmopolitan*, and *Good Housekeeping*. In 1895 *Southern Magazine* included her in an article on women artists. Her photographs were used in advertisements of the Old Flour Mill Company and the J.B. Williams Company. Matthews chose as her subjects the people, architecture, and landscape of Pewee Valley. She is perhaps best known for her illustrations in Annie Fellows Johnston's books *The Little Colonel* (1895) and *The Land of the Little Colonel* (1929). Matthews herself was portrayed as the character Miss Katharine Marks in another series by Johnston.

Matthews won several prizes for her photographs at the Kentucky State Fair and in Chicago and Pittsburgh. Her technique remained the same even after innovations in the art of photography. She disdained color photography and continued to make all her own prints.

Late in her career, Matthews began painting in oils. At the age of eighty-three, she won a prize for a painting in an exhibition sponsored by the Kentucky Federation of Women's Clubs. In May 1956 an exhibition of Matthews' photographs was held at the University of Louisville. Today the Photographic Archives of the university's Ekstrom Library has the largest collection of her prints in order to control the light and shading.

Matthews died July 5, 1956, and was buried in the Pewee Valley Cemetery. Her family home, Clovercroft, was destroyed by fire shortly after her death.

See Norma Prendergast, "Kate Matthews, Photographer," *Kentucky Review* 1 (Spring 1980): 11-28.

MATURE, VICTOR. Victor Mature, actor, was born in Louisville, on January 29, 1915, to George and Clara (Ackley) Mature. He grew up in the Germantown neighborhood and attended Roman Catholic schools, including St. Xavier High School, be-fore completing his education at the Kentucky Military Institute in Lyndon (1928-31). Mature, who planned to open a business locally, attended the Spencerian Commercial College during 1933. He sold candy and operated a restaurant until 1935, when he headed for Hollywood, where he became a successful actor.

Mature was spotted by Hollywood talent scouts at the Pasadena Community Playhouse. Soon after, he made his debut in the film *One Million B.C.* (1941). He went on to star in over fifty films, including *No, No, Nanette*, *The Robe*, *Samson and Delilah*, and *Chief Crazy Horse*. Mature also performed on stage, most notably in the play *Lady in the Dark* (1941). He often played the role of the tough leading man. Some of Mature's films had world premieres in the Louisville Palace Theatre, and he returned to Louisville to visit old friends and relatives. Mature has appeared at a variety of charity events in Louisville, especially the Foster Brooks Pro-Am Golf Tournament for Kosair children's hospital.

Divorce ended Mature's first four marriages, to Frances Charles (1938-41), Martha Stephenson Kemp (1941-43), Dorothy Stanford (1948-55), and Adrienne Joy Urwick (1959-69). Mature married Lorey Sabina in 1972; they have a daughter, Victoria.

MAULDING'S STATION. James Maulding and his family made their first settlement attempt in the fall of 1780 on the Red River, southeast of what is now Adairville, Kentucky, in present-day Tennessee. This settlement, called Maulding's or Red River Old Station, was abandoned in 1782. The family made a second attempt in 1783 or 1784 at a different location on the Red River in what is now Logan County, Kentucky. Maulding's Station was reportedly visited by George Rogers Clark on one of his trips from Fort Jefferson to Harrodsburg. James Maulding died in 1796 or 1797, leaving his wife, Caty, and four grown sons, Ambrose, Richard, Morton, and Wesley. Three sons left the county by 1812 but Wesley stayed, serving as sheriff in 1792 and as a magistrate.

See Edward Coffman, *The Story of Logan County* (Russellville, Ky., 1962).

NANCY O'MALLEY

MAURY, MASON. Mason Maury, architect, was born in Louisville in 1846, one of the four children of Matthew and Sallie (Mason) Maury. He attended Male High School there and studied engineering at the University of Louisville. In the mid-1870s, Maury spent two years studying architecture in Boston, where the most noted architect of the period, H.H. Richardson, was then building Trinity Church, a major landmark of his Romanesque Revival style. Maury adopted Richardson's ideas and those of his contemporaries, known as the Chicago school.

After returning to Louisville in 1877, Maury worked under local architect William Redin. In 1883 Maury opened his own office. Two of the main advances of the Chicago school were the sky-scraper of iron skeleton construction and the Richardsonian Romanesque, known for its semicircular arches. Maury introduced both of these concepts to Kentucky in 1886, through the Kenyon Building and the Judge Russell Houston residence. During his forty-year career, Maury was the most progressive designer in Kentucky. By 1902 he had more than seven hundred buildings to his credit. Among his well-known designs were the 1892 Nelson County courthouse, the 1899 Ferguson house (now housing the Filson Club), the 1902 Kaufman-Straus Building, and the 1905 Louisville Woman's Club building. Maury worked with Oscar Haupt for the year 1887; with William J. Dodd from 1889 until 1896; and with E. Walter Hillerich, his last partner, from 1905 until 1909.

In November 1885, Maury married Gertrude Vaughn. She died four years later. He was married again on August 22, 1895, to Sarah Webb. Maury practiced architecture until his death on January 1, 1919. He was buried in Louisville's Cave Hill Cemetery.

See C. Julian Oberwarth and William B. Scott, Jr., *A History of the Profession of Architecture in Kentucky* (Lexington, Ky., 1987).

WILLIAM B. SCOTT, JR.

MAXEY FLATS NUCLEAR WASTE FACILITY. In 1962 the Commonwealth of Kentucky received permission from the U.S. Atomic Energy Commission to create a low-level radioactive waste disposal facility. After tests, state and federal agencies recommended a site in Fleming County about ten miles northwest of Morehead. In January 1963 the Kentucky Department of Health granted a license to the Nuclear Engineering Company of California to operate the commercial facility at Maxey Flats.

Burial operations began in May 1963 and were terminated fourteen years later. During these years the three-hundred-acre site became the repository of some 4.95 million cubic feet of radioactive materials, making it the largest commercial nuclear waste disposal facility in the nation. Approximately 85 percent of the waste buried in the trenches at Maxey Flats was classified as low level; the remainder was high-level wastes such as uranium, thorium, plutonium, and tritium-augmented compounds. About 99 percent of all these radioactive wastes from medical, industrial, and nuclear weapons plants were generated outside the commonwealth.

While conducting routine monitoring in 1972, field workers from the Radiation Control Branch of the Kentucky Department of Health discovered significant off-site migration of plutonium and other radioactive substances. These preliminary findings were later confirmed by studies conducted by the U.S. Environmental Protection Agency, the U.S. Nuclear Regulatory Agency, and the U.S. Geological Survey. The operator's disposal techniques had allowed the infiltration of rainwater into the trenches, thus contaminating groundwater and run-

off into the Licking River system. In December 1977 the site was closed. The following year the state assumed in perpetuity the responsibility for care and maintenance of the facility.

State and federal agencies financed intensive studies at Maxey Flats between 1978 and 1990. They explored various techniques to prevent infiltration of surface water (including forty-three acres of plastic cover over the trenches), and to reduce groundwater contamination by injecting grout-like materials into the soil to create impenetrable barriers. Mechanical evaporation of accumulated liquids was halted in 1986 because of the tritium present in the steam produced. The Environmental Protection Agency and the U.S. Department of Energy have worked together to limit the damage from what may be the most enduring environmental disaster in the state's history (plutonium is radiologically toxic for more than 25,000 years).

MICHAEL J. DONAHUE

MAXWELL, JOHN. John Maxwell, pioneer settler, was born in Scotland in 1747 and was brought to America in 1751 by his parents, George and Jane Maxwell. In 1774 he settled in Kentucky with a group of pioneers organized by James Harrod. Tradition has it that Maxwell was one of the party of hunters camped along a branch of Elkhorn Creek who in 1775 named the site Lexington. Maxwell was among the earliest settlers in the blockhouse constructed there in 1779. There he married Sarah, whose last name is unknown, that spring, probably the first such ceremony performed in the area. They chose a site for their cabin south of the blockhouse, near a large spring. Maxwell's land, now the part of Lexington lying east of Broadway and south of High Street, was estimated at 1,000 acres. Maxwell's signature was on a petition, sent to the Virginia Assembly in April 1782, requesting official establishment of the town of Lexington.

Maxwell was a man of generosity and civic responsibility. All citizens had free access to the spring that bore his name. He was Fayette County's first coroner and one of the original members of the Presbyterian church organized in 1792. He lent a cabin to a slave congregation, from which grew the Pleasant Green Baptist Church. He was one of the two town assessors in 1793 and 1796. In 1798 Maxwell chaired a meeting of local Scots to organize the St. Andrew's Society. He was also responsible for the annual Fourth of July celebration held at Maxwell Springs in Lexington, on what is now the University of Kentucky campus. He died on July 13, 1819, and was buried in the Maxwell cemetery on Bolivar Street, which later gave way to factories and tobacco warehouses.

See George W. Ranck, *History of Lexington, Kentucky: Its Early Annals and Recent Progress* (Cincinnati 1872).

MAXWELL SPRINGS. The residence of the president of the University of Kentucky, Maxwell Place, is located on the site once known as Maxwell Springs. The source of the three springs was

Elkhorn Creek. On April 13, 1778, John and Sarah Maxwell were married in Lexington and built a house near the largest of these three springs. The Maxwells lived there for forty years.

In 1820 a portion of Maxwell Springs was sold to the son-in-law of John and Sarah Maxwell, William Robards, husband of Dorcas Maxwell, to satisfy a debt of $150. It was then purchased by John Love. Another part of Maxwell Springs was bequeathed to John Maxwell's daughter Sarah, wife of Hallet M. Winslow. A major portion of this area was used as a park and gathering place for the city of Lexington. Fourth of July celebrations, political gatherings, picnics, barbecues, and fairs were held there. The state militia gathered in formation and departed from there. It became so well known that Henry Clay said of it, "No man can call himself a true Kentuckian who has not watered his horse at Maxwell Springs."

The water from the springs on the Winslows' property was in such great demand that the Winslows bottled it for public sale. In 1850 Willa Viley, of Woodford County, purchased the property that had been owned by John Love, and presented it to his daughter Elizabeth and her husband Thomas W. Bullock, Fayette County superintendent of public schools. On June 3 of that year the section of land that had belonged to the Winslows was sold to the Maxwell Springs Company for $5,000. Benjamin Gratz, president of the Kentucky Agricultural and Mechanical Association, held the deed in trust; the association held agricultural and mechanical fairs on the site. Before the Civil War, most of the lands that now constitute the campus of the University of Kentucky were owned by the Maxwell Springs Company and Robert Frazier. The Maxwell Springs Company purchased the Frazier lands and united them with their own. Fairs continued to be held there until the Civil War, when the grounds and buildings were occupied by federal troops and used as quarters and a storage area for wagons and artillery. All the original trees were felled to provide heating fuel for the troops, and most of the buildings were demolished. The only building left in good condition was the commandant's, formerly the custodian's, which had also served as a hospital for the wounded. The Maxwell Springs Company had borrowed heavily from the Lexington Cemetery Company to purchase the Frazier lands and had been unable to keep up payments during the war. The entire parcel was put up for sale in 1870 by the commissioner of the Fayette County Circuit Court.

Thomas Bullock's Maxwell Springs property was purchased in 1870 by Dennis Mulligan, an Irish immigrant who had become a local Democratic party leader and member of the city council. He presented it and a newly built home to his son and daughter-in-law, James H. and Mary H. (Jackson) Mulligan, and their son Louis. The elder Mulligan urged the Lexington City Council to purchase the adjacent historic Maxwell Springs Company land for use as a public park. He was concerned that the area would be subdivided among freed slaves and recently discharged soldiers. The city council agreed and purchased the property for about $17,000. The grounds were laid out as a park and planted with trees and shrubs for about $1,700. The city then ran short on funds and the area was enclosed by a high fence for several years. When the Agricultural and Mechanical College separated from Kentucky University (now Transylvania University) in 1878, the city of Lexington offered the A&M College (now the University of Kentucky), the old Maxwell Springs Company land and $30,000, and Fayette County contributed $20,000. The offer was accepted and the campus was established.

Judge James H. Mulligan's home at Maxwell Springs became famous as the center of many Lexington social activities. Among those entertained there were William Jennings Bryan, Julia Marlowe, Robert Taber, and Thomas Hunt Morgan. It was at Maxwell Springs in 1902 that Mulligan wrote perhaps the most famous poem about the commonwealth, "In Kentucky," for presentation at a banquet of the Kentucky state legislature at the Phoenix Hotel in Lexington. After Mulligan's death on July 2, 1915, his heirs sold the property. The University of Kentucky bought it on June 19, 1917, for $40,000. When the board of trustees selected Frank L. McVey as president of the university on August 15, 1917, his contract required him to live on campus in the Mulligan home. Since that time it has been the official residence of the president.

The house and its grounds are known as Maxwell Place. The house was designed in the style of the Italian villa and is built of locally made brick. Its grounds include a crescent pool and informal gardens, and the house is covered with ivy brought from the Blarney Castle in Ireland. It was placed in the *National Register of Historic Places* in 1982.

See James F. Hopkins, *The University of Kentucky: Origin and Early Years* (Lexington, Ky., 1951); Charles G. Talbert, *The University of Kentucky: The Maturing Years* (Lexington, Ky., 1965).

MAY, ANDREW JACKSON. Andrew Jackson May, Confederate colonel, was born January 28, 1829, in Prestonsburg, Kentucky. Before the Civil War, he was an attorney in Prestonsburg and was among the leaders of the Democratic party in Floyd County. On May 26, 1861, May was commissioned captain by the Confederate States of America. Working with Hiram Hawkins and G.W. Connors, he helped to form the 5th Infantry Regiment of Kentucky Volunteers, under the command of Col. John S. Williams. May, who was placed in charge of Company A, was promoted to lieutenant colonel on November 17, 1861, and to colonel on April 18, 1862.

May commanded a detachment of Confederate troops in an unsuccessful attempt to defend West Liberty, Kentucky, against an advancing Union army led by William O. Nelson on October 22, 1861. They managed to delay the Federals' advance on Piketon (now Pikeville) by engaging a larger

Union force at Ivy Mountain on November 8. Later in the month the 5th Kentucky was attached to Gen. Humphrey Marshall's brigade, and it participated in the Confederate reoccupation of the Big Sandy Valley in December and January. Following the Confederate defeat at Middle Creek on January 10, 1862, Colonel May led a raid into Floyd County and on February 23 defeated a band of Union partisans at the head of Mud Creek. He also commanded two companies in Marshall's victory over General Cox's Union army at Priceton, Virginia, on May 16. Later in the year, May led a dramatic cavalry attack to rescue Capt. Joel E. Stallings from his Union captors. May left active service in September and resigned his commission on November 14, 1862.

After the war, May opened a law practice in Tazewell, Virginia. He was married to Matilda Davidson and later to Nell Davidson. He died in Tazewell County on May 3, 1903, and was buried there.

See John David Preston, *The Civil War in the Big Sandy Valley of Kentucky* (Baltimore 1984); Henry P. Scalf, *Historic Floyd, 1800-1950* (Prestonsburg, Ky., 1950).   THOMAS D. MATIJASIC

MAY, WILLIAM H. William H. May, contractor and politician, was born on May 6, 1908, in Prestonsburg, Kentucky, to William and Mary Leona (Butler) May. His father, a circuit court judge, died when William was eleven. May attended high school in Prestonsburg and then went to Randolph-Macon Academy in Front Royal, Virginia. He attended Eastern Kentucky University in Richmond and the University of Kentucky, and at the outset of the Great Depression found work in the Kentucky Highway Department. In the early 1930s, he traveled as a land appraiser in the right-of-way department of the Southern Railway System. May moved to Louisville in 1934 to work as a land appraiser for the Federal Land Bank, a New Deal agency designed to help farmers refinance their land.

In 1939 May ran as a Democrat for state agriculture commissioner and defeated Van B. Alexander for the term 1940-44. He was defeated for lieutenant governor in 1943 on a ticket with J. Lyter Donaldson. After service in World War II, May began manufacturing store fixtures in Frankfort, Kentucky, and established May-Bilt, Inc., general contractors, which he sold at a loss in the early 1950s. In 1947 May lost in the Democratic primary for lieutenant governor by 9,062 votes to Lawrence Wetherby, who ran on a ticket with Earle Clements. May then backed the ticket and supported Wetherby for governor in 1950. May joined Clements, Wetherby, Frankfort attorney Louis Cox, Lexington legislator Richard Moloney, and future governor Bert T. Combs (1959-63) in forming a powerful political faction, known as the Kingmakers, which largely controlled the state legislature, the election of governors, and the distribution of patronage for nearly twenty years. May established Brighton Engineering in 1952, which served as consultants or designers for state turnpikes and other major roads. In 1959 Combs appointed May state racing commissioner, a position to which he was reappointed by Govs. Edward T. Breathitt (1963-67), Wendell H. Ford (1971-74), and Julian M. Carroll (1974-79). May supervised the transition of thoroughbred racing from a Kentucky pastime to a leading state industry. He retired as commissioner in 1978 and resigned as chairman of Brighton in 1980. He raised thoroughbreds at his Frankfort horse farm, Glenary, and took part in real estate development.

May married Betsy Lynn Simpson of Madisonville on June 12, 1931. They had three children: Margaret, Elissa, and William. May died at his residence on October 16, 1986, and was buried in the Frankfort Cemetery.

MAYFIELD. Mayfield, the county seat of Graves County in the Jackson Purchase region, is located at the junction of U.S. 45 and KY 80, just south of the Purchase Parkway in the center of the county.

Mayfield presumably was settled in 1819 by John and Nancy (Davenport) Anderson, who migrated to far western Kentucky from South Carolina. Anderson evidently started a post office at Mayfield in 1823, the same year the legislature created Graves County and established Mayfield as its county seat. The town was named for nearby Mayfield Creek, which possibly was named for George Mayfield, who had been kidnapped and murdered along the creek.

In 1854, the New Orleans & Ohio Railroad (now part of the Paducah & Louisville) entered Mayfield, boosting the town's growth. In 1830, Mayfield numbered forty-four inhabitants; its population was 556 in 1860.

During the Civil War, Mayfield, like the rest of the Jackson Purchase, was strongly pro-Confederate. In 1861, at a meeting in Mayfield attended by politicians and other leaders from the region, the secession of western Kentucky and the forming of a Confederate state with western Tennessee were discussed. Although nothing came of the plan, Confederate volunteers from Mayfield far outnumbered Union recruits from the city. In 1864, a small Union force occupied the town and ordered citizens to help build an earthen fort around the courthouse. Confederate sympathizers accused the Union commander, Gen. E.A. Paine, of a reign of terror; it was said that he executed more than sixty-one people in the region.

After the war, Mayfield's population grew steadily; by 1870, it was 779. It also was the center of one of the largest tobacco-producing areas in the state; Graves County grew more than 4.6 million pounds in 1870. In the 1990s the city is a tobacco marketing town with large sale barns.

In the early twentieth century, Mayfield became synonymous with clothing that was made and shipped nationwide. The town's minor league baseball team was the Clothiers. In 1990, Mayfield's and the region's largest employer was the General Tire and Rubber Co. plant, with a payroll of more than 2,000 union and management employees. Other local industries produce clothing, air compressors, and processed poultry.

In 1988, much of the Warner Brothers movie *In Country* was filmed in Mayfield. Starring Bruce Willis and Emily Lloyd, the Norman Jewison-directed film was based on a novel by Mayfield native Bobbie Ann Mason about a Vietnam veteran and his niece.

The population of the third-class city was 10,724 in 1970; 10,705 in 1980; and 9,935 in 1990.

BERRY CRAIG

MAYO, ALICE JANE ALKA (MEEK). Alice Jane Alka (Meek) Mayo, philanthropist, daughter of Greenville and Hulda (Price) Meek, was born on Buffalo Creek in Johnson County, Kentucky, on March 27, 1877. She attended school in Johnson County and worked as a postal employee and telegraph operator in Paintsville. She married future coal baron John Caldwell Calhoun MAYO on February 21, 1897. They had two children, John, Jr., and Margaret. Wearing a specially designed riding skirt with hidden pockets for carrying gold coins, she frequently accompanied Mayo on his trips to buy mineral rights.

Alice Mayo supervised the construction of the Mayos' three-story residence in Paintsville and of the Mayo Memorial Methodist Episcopal Church. After her husband's death in 1914, Alice became a director of the Mayo Companies. She married Dr. Samuel P. Fetter of Portsmouth, Ohio, in 1916. Before the marriage, she formed the Mrs. John C.C. Mayo Company, transferred all the property of the estate to this corporation, and divided the stock between her children. She donated the Mayo home and land to Sandy Valley Seminary, which became the John C.C. Mayo College and is now Our Lady of the Mountains parochial school. After Dr. Fetter's death, Alice legally changed her name back to Mayo. She died in Ashland on September 5, 1961, and was buried behind the Mayo mansion in Paintsville.

See Carolyn Turner and Carolyn Traum, *John C.C. Mayo: Cumberland Capitalist* (Pikeville, Ky., 1983).   CAROLYN C. TURNER

MAYO, JOHN CALDWELL CALHOUN. John Caldwell Calhoun Mayo, self-made entrepreneur and coal baron, was born on September 16, 1864, in a log cabin on a worn-out mountain farm in Pike County, Kentucky, and died, at the age of forty-nine, the state's wealthiest citizen. The son of Thomas Jefferson and Elizabeth (Leslie) Mayo, Mayo as a toddler was clothed in a medieval weaning dress called a wamus. Boyhood school was another log cabin. Mayo read every book available to him and at sixteen became a schoolteacher. He enrolled in Kentucky Wesleyan College in Millersburg and later returned to Johnson County to teach at Paintsville for forty dollars per month. At college he heard geology lectures by visiting professor A.C. Sherwood and learned about east Kentucky's vast mineral resources. He read the geological sur-

veys made by William Mather, David Owen, Nathaniel Shaler, and John Proctor and filled notebooks with mineral data.

In time, Mayo saved $150 and with partners he formed the trading firm of Castle, Turner & Mayo, capitalized at $450. He abstracted titles and paid a few dollars each for options to buy minerals underlying tracts of land. He pledged fifty cents to five dollars per acre if the option was later exercised. Mayo continued to teach and bought out his partners. At twenty-six he engineered changes in the state's land law. He read law and was admitted to the bar. When the constitutional convention met in 1890, Mayo knew many of the delegates, whom he lobbied to drop from the new constitution the VIRGINIA COMPACT provision that "shadowed" the title to hundreds of thousands of acres of eastern Kentucky land. (A 1911 U.S. Supreme Court decision upheld the Kentucky land titles.)

Mayo hired Floyd County attorney F.A. Hopkins and his firm of Hyde and Hopkins to draft the broad form deed, which may have been used earlier by Richard Broas. Mayo used this form in mineral buying to sever title to minerals from the remainder of the land title, making mineral rights dominant and residuary rights subservient "forever." With money advanced by the Merritt brothers of Duluth, Minnesota, Mayo then began to operate on a grand scale. He acquired 29,000 acres, which he sold to the Merritt brothers for $100,000 and a promissory note for the same sum. Mayo acquired options on an additional 100,000 acres, for which he paid by attaching the mineral lands previously deeded by him to the Merritts. He borrowed $20,000 from W.S. Dudley of Carlisle, Kentucky, and three of Dudley's neighbors. In the process Mayo became land-poor, possessing many thousands of acres of coal but little money. He took his problem to Peter L. Kimberley, president of Sharon Steel Company in Chicago, paying his way with money borrowed from his friend John Buckingham. Mayo conveyed his mineral rights to Kimberley for five dollars per acre, retaining a 25 percent interest.

When Mayo returned to Paintsville, he had $10,000 in cash, new suits and shoes, and new furniture for his office. He paid his debts to Buckingham and others, and headed into the eastern Kentucky backlands for renewed coal buying. He took with him Alice Meek Mayo, whom he had married in 1897. By 1900 Mayo was a wealthy man by Kentucky standards, with a net worth of more than $250,000.

When Mayo learned of immense coal developments in West Virginia, he went to Fairmont and introduced himself to Johnson Newlon Camden, Jr., Aretus Brooks Fleming, and Clarence Wayland Watson, the most prominent men in the coal industry. Mayo persuaded them to invest in his operations and they and their associates (including the Delano and Roosevelt families) developed landholdings in Pike, Floyd, Letcher, and Knott counties. Mayo's Northern Coal & Coke Company bought the coal, which was then conveyed to such companies as Consolidation Coal Company and Elk Horn

Coal Corporation, in return for stocks. Mayo also became a major figure in the region's railroad corporations. The Chesapeake & Ohio, the Baltimore & Ohio, and the Louisville & Nashville lines were extended to the 265,000 acres Mayo acquired for Northern Coal & Coke Company.

The upheaval wrought by Mayo transformed the Big Sandy and Kentucky River valleys. Simultaneously, Mayo operated a timber company in West Virginia and Collins & Mayo Collieries. He had much political influence in Kentucky, Maryland, Virginia, and West Virginia.

Mayo died May 11, 1914, at the Waldorf Astoria hotel in New York City. He was buried on a hilltop above the Levisa Fork near Paintsville.

See Carolyn C. Turner and Carolyn H. Traum, *John C.C. Mayo* (Pikeville, Ky., 1983).

HARRY M. CAUDILL

MAYO, JOHN C. CALHOUN, JR. John C. Calhoun Mayo, Jr., businessman, son of John C.C. and Alice (Meek) MAYO, was born in Paintsville, Kentucky, on December 18, 1900. He was educated at Millersburg Military Institute and Tennessee Military Institute and attended Amherst College in Massachusetts in 1919-20. Mayo grew up amid the wealth accumulated by his father from coal assets. Mayo served as executive officer of Mayo Oil Service Company, Mayo Equipment, Mayo Arcade Company, Midland and Atlantic Bridge Corporation, and Mason Coal and Coke. He was chairman of the board of the Second National Bank in Ashland, Kentucky, vice-president of the Kentucky River Coal Corporation of Lexington, and director of the Kentucky Unemployment Compensation Commission during 1937-43 and 1948-60. At the time of his death Mayo was the executive officer of Collins and Mayo Collieries, Thealka and Jefferson Coal Companies, William Coal and Coke, and the Mrs. John C.C. Mayo Company, which had been created by his mother after his father's death to keep the family assets intact after her remarriage.

On June 17, 1938, Mayo married Mary Nancy McClure of Man, West Virginia; they had five children: Thomas Jefferson, John C.C. III, Andrew Jackson, Nancy McClure, and Alice Margaret. Mayo died on February 17, 1980, and was buried in the Ashland Cemetery.

CAROLYN C. TURNER

MAYO TRAIL. The Mayo Trail, completed in the 1920s, was eastern Kentucky's first extensive public road-building project. Named for John Caldwell Calhoun MAYO, Paintsville coal baron, the winding highway stretches approximately 250 miles, from Ashland on the Ohio River, through the Big Sandy watershed, across Pine Mountain to Pineville on the Cumberland River, where it connects with U.S. 25E. Routes U.S. 23 and U.S. 119 follow the original roadbed. The Mayo Trail was the principal thoroughfare into the interior of the mountains until the Bert T. Combs Mountain Parkway and I-64 superseded it in the 1960s.

The Kentucky General Assembly authorized the Mayo Trail in 1920. The road was to be "all-weather and hard-surfaced," which meant graveled. Much blasting was needed to traverse the rugged terrain. The highway opened for its entire length in early 1928.

In later years the Mayo Trail became a major farm-to-market and coal-hauling road. In spite of the relatively primitive road-building technology of the 1920s, it remains one of Kentucky's most impressive engineering achievements. Appalachian Regional Commission funding during the 1960s and 1970s widened the highway to three and four lanes in several sections.

WILLIAM TERRELL CORNETT

MAYSVILLE. Maysville, the county seat of Mason County, is located in the northeastern part of the Outer Bluegrass region at the junction of U.S. 68 and KY 8. The city is at the confluence of Limestone Creek and the Ohio River, and was formerly known as Limestone. Maysville was named for John May, a Virginia surveyor and clerk of the Land Commission sent out by Virginia in 1779 to settle claims. May and Simon Kenton owned the land lying along the Ohio River on the lower side of Limestone Creek. When it was established as a town on December 11, 1787, the area was part of Bourbon County. Among its first trustees were Daniel Boone and his cousin Jacob.

The city's early growth was slow because pioneers sought safety from Indian raids by settling at Washington on the hill above Maysville, away from the river. A boon to the city's growth was the Limestone Warehouse established in 1787 by the Virginia legislature for the inspection of tobacco that was to be shipped by river to distant markets.

The defeat of the Indians at the Battle of Fallen Timbers in 1794 made the area safe for settlement. Brick houses were erected, and Maysville enjoyed a nationwide reputation as a harbor town and port. Maysville in its early history was the entrance to the Inner Bluegrass region from the Ohio River. A road connecting Maysville with Lexington to the southwest became one of the most heavily traveled routes in Kentucky. Ferries were in operation and a militia was appointed to supplement Kenton's scouts. Good taverns developed, and Maysville welcomed famous visitors. Henry Clay stopped on his way home from signing the Treaty of Ghent in 1815, and several English travelers complimented their hosts in the town. In 1825, Maysville entertained General Lafayette with great splendor at the Eagle Tavern. The Bank of Limestone opened in 1818. A jail was built next to Jacob Boone's tavern.

When the steamboat was invented, Maysville's future was assured, and the population increased with trade on the river. The city was incorporated on January 31, 1833, and in 1848 became the county seat, replacing Washington. A Greek Revival–style building was completed in 1846 in hopes of making it the courthouse. The *Maysville Eagle*, the town's first newspaper, reported that Charles Wolfe, son of Pennsylvania's governor, was the first mayor. A cholera epidemic in 1833 took the lives of several citizens, including the new mayor. The new fire department was tested by a major fire on April 4, 1833, which destroyed five businesses and one residence.

Its proximity to the free state of Ohio created economic ties to the North, and the institution of slavery tied it to the South, dividing Maysville during the Civil War. Confederate sympathizers went to Tennessee, where many joined the 4th Kentucky Infantry Regiment (CSA); Union men were recruited at Camp Kenton and Camp Lee, both near Maysville, to join the federal 16th Kentucky Infantry or the 10th Kentucky Calvary Regiment. Maysville was the Union center of operations during the Battle of AUGUSTA in September 1862, and was occupied by Confederate cavalry on June 14, 1864.

After the war Maysville grew by annexing surrounding areas. The city was progressive and maintained its economic stability. The Simon Kenton Memorial Bridge, which was completed in 1931, created an important link to southern Ohio. Maysville Community College, a part of the University of Kentucky system, was opened in 1968, and in 1975 the Mason County Museum opened in the former county library building. The city retains a great number of antebellum homes that give a good idea of how a nineteenth century river town looked.

Maysville became and remains one of the three largest burley tobacco markets in the world and at one time was among the largest hemp markets. In 1990 the oldest family-owned business was a cotton factory, dating from the 1840s. The Ohio Valley Pulley Works was by then the Browning Division of Emerson Electric. Wald Manufacturing Company produced bicycle parts. In 1989 the city's largest employers were the Browning Manufacturing Division, Emerson Electric Company, which manufactured pulleys and ballbearings, and TechnoTrim, which produced auto trim covers. The population of the third-class city in 1970 was 7,111; 7,983 in 1980; and 7,169 in 1990.

See G. Glenn Cliff, *History of Maysville and Mason County, Kentucky* (Lexington, Ky., 1936).

JEAN W. CALVERT

MAYSVILLE ROAD BILL. The Maysville-to-Lexington road followed an ancient buffalo trace. It took early settlers to inland settlements and later businessmen and politicians back and forth from the East. In 1830 one of the frequent travelers on the road, Henry Clay, proposed that the national government subscribe $150,000 to the Maysville, Washington, Paris, and Lexington Turnpike Road Company. The project would extend the Cumberland National Road from Zanesville, Ohio, to Lexington, Kentucky, and in the future to points south; thus it would advance his American System, part of which called for building up America's economy through internal improvements.

Acquiring federal funds for the road had been attempted before. On February 13, 1828, the Kentucky General Assembly had asked Congress to extend the National Road to Lexington. The effort failed by one vote in the Senate; had Congress approved the extension, it would have likely proceeded, as John Quincy Adams was president at the time. The 1830 proposal was made when Clay's long-time political rival, Andrew Jackson, was president. In the debate before the House, Kentuckian Richard M. Johnson put the case for the road, saying that there was no road in the Union "(except those between the great seaports) more traveled, and none of the same extent by which you can [so substantially] promote the common good" (*Maysville Eagle*, June 8, 1830). On a close vote, the bill passed, but Jackson vetoed it, on the basis of what he saw as a constitutional prohibition of federal funding of projects entirely within the confines of a single state. It also gave Jackson an opportunity to strike at his political enemy Clay.

The veto established a precedent, particularly in the case of roads, that made federal support for internal improvements difficult to obtain. It also continued to define the differences between the Whigs and Democrats on policy matters. JOHN KLEE

MEADE, JAMES M. James M. Meade, a native of Woodford County, was killed at the Battle of the RIVER RAISIN in 1813, during the War of 1812. Very little is known about his early life. He enlisted in the 17th U.S. Infantry when the War of 1812 began and fought under Joseph Hamilton Daveiss at the Battle of Tippecanoe Creek, Indiana Territory, on November 7, 1811. Following that battle, he was promoted to captain and marched north with hundreds of other soldiers from Kentucky to reinforce Gen. William Hull's forces at Detroit. He was killed January 22, 1813, during the second phase of the Battle of the River Raisin near Frenchtown (present-day Monroe, Michigan). Meade was one of nine soldiers from Kentucky whose deaths in the battle were honored by naming Kentucky counties after them. Meade County, which was formed out of parts of Hardin and Breckinridge counties in 1823, lies along the Ohio River in the northwest-central part of the state.

MEADE COUNTY. The seventy-sixth county in order of formation, Meade County is located in the northwestern section of Kentucky along the Ohio River. Bordered by Breckinridge and Hardin counties, from which it was formed on December 17, 1823, it has an area of 305 square miles. The county was named in honor of Capt. James Meade of Woodford County, who fought in the Battle of Tippecanoe and was killed at the Battle of the River Raisin in 1813. The county seat is BRANDENBURG.

The topography of Meade County is level to undulating. Rich river bottomlands extend to rolling hills covered with woods and pasture. Sixty percent of the land is in farms, of which 66 percent are cultivated with tobacco, corn, and vegetables and which raise livestock, poultry, and hogs.

Before settlement, herds of wild game, such as buffalo, deer, and elk, abounded in the area, which attracted pioneers who were seeking homes in the Kentucky wilderness as well as Indian tribes who hunted there. Among the early settlers were Squire Boone and his son Enoch. In 1780 Boone claimed 1,000 acres at the head of Doe Run for Joseph Helm. That same year, John Essery and others claimed land in Buck Grove. Boone claimed 6,000 acres below Doe Run for himself in 1783. Wolf Creek was the first permanent settlement in the county. Periodically, the Indians from across the Ohio River would raid the Meade County area. Lookouts were placed on the hills above the river to detect the approach of hostile Indians.

The county owes much of its early development to churches. Local historian George Ridenour placed the first Baptist church gathering between the forts of Thomas Helm, Andrew Hynes, and Samuel Haycraft in Severn's Valley on June 18, 1781. Four churches met on October 29, 1785, to form what later became the Salem Association of Baptists.

During the early years of the nineteenth century, John James Audubon came through Meade County making sketches of the birds for which later he became famous. During the Civil War, Meade County was the site of a daring raid by Confederate Gen. John Hunt Morgan's troops on July 7, 1863. The Confederates captured two steamboats, the *John T. Combs* and the *Alice Dean*, and Morgan stopped briefly in Brandenburg before invading Indiana and Ohio. During the war, Confederate guerrilla Marcellus Jerome Clarke ("Sue Mundy") was captured near the community of Guston.

The FORT KNOX Military Reservation, established in 1918, occupies 15,000 acres in Meade County. The Meade County economy is aided by the proximity of the fort, which employs 21 percent of the county's work force. The Olin Corporation located in the county in 1952 and produces chemicals. The county is served by CSX Transportation, U.S. 60, and U.S. 31W. Tourism expenditures in 1988 were $5.9 million, a 26 percent increase over the previous year. Recreation facilities are available at the 3,000-acre Otter Creek Park. Each September, the Down by the Riverside Festival is held.

The population of Meade County was 18,796 in 1970; 22,854 in 1980; and 24,170 in 1990.

See George L. Ridenour, *Early Times in Meade County, Kentucky* (Louisville 1929); Alice Scott Bondurant, *The Doe Run Settlement* (Vine Grove, Ky., 1976).   RON D. BRYANT

MEAGHER, MARY TERSTEGGE. Mary Terstegge Meagher, Olympic swimmer, was born on October 27, 1965, in Louisville to James L. and Floy (Terstegge) Meagher. She graduated from Sacred Heart Academy in Louisville in 1982 and received her B.A. in child development from the University of California at Berkeley in 1987. At the 1979 Pan American Games in San Juan, she swam the women's 200-meter butterfly in 2:09.77, setting a world record. During January–August 1980 she trained with Dennis Pursley in Cincinnati. In March 1980 at the U.S. Indoor Nationals (the Olympic trials) in Austin, Texas, Meagher set a world record of 59.46 in the 100-meter butterfly. At the U.S. Longcourse Swimming Championship in Irvine, California, in August 1980, Meagher bettered her own world record, swimming the 200-meter butterfly in 2:06.37 and qualifying for the U.S. Olympic team.

After the U.S. boycotted the 1980 Olympics in Moscow, Meagher returned to Kentucky to train with Bill Peak, her longtime Louisville coach. In August 1981 she won the national championships at Brown Peer, Wisconsin, establishing two world records: 100-meter butterfly (57.9) and 200-meter butterfly (2:05.9). In 1983 she trained with Mark Schubert in Mission Viejo, California, for the 1984 Olympics in Los Angeles. Meagher won three gold medals in the 1984 Olympics: the 100- and 200-meter butterfly and the 4 x 100 medley relay. She qualified for the Olympic team in August 1988, at Austin, Texas, winning the 100- and 200-meter women's butterfly. At the 1988 Olympics in Seoul, Meagher won a bronze medal and announced her retirement from swimming. In 1989 she began work as a public relations specialist for the First National Bank in Louisville.

MEDICINE. Practitioners of the healing arts were among the eighteenth century pioneers who settled the Kentucky wilderness. They faced numerous ailments and diseases that afflicted Kentuckians from the late eighteenth through the nineteenth century: measles, mumps, whooping cough, scarlet fever, diphtheria, smallpox, dysentery (bloody flux), influenza, typhoid fever, yellow fever, cholera, and diarrheal diseases. Healers employed a variety of therapies and concoctions to combat these maladies, including home remedies. Alcoholism, milksickness (trembles), pneumonia, pleurisy, and venereal diseases further challenged the skills of early physicians. Illness was thought to be an imbalance in body fluids (the humors), calling for depletive therapies (such as induced sweating, purging, and bleeding). Surgery included the treatment of various wounds and fractures, and frequent amputations. As historian John H. Ellis noted, the "principal elements of medical practice in colonial times and on the Kentucky frontier were traditional therapy and limited surgery."

One of the most notable achievements of early Kentucky medicine was medical education. Lexington's Transylvania University in 1799 opened the first facility for educating physicians west of the Allegheny Mountains. Its medical department hosted such prominent educators as Drs. Benjamin W. DUDLEY, James Overton, William H. Richardson, Samuel Brown, Frederick Ridgely, Daniel DRAKE, Charles CALDWELL, and Lunsford P. YANDELL. Personality conflicts fanned internal strife at Transylvania almost from the beginning. Perhaps the most dramatic example is the 1818 pistol duel fought between colleagues Dudley and Richardson, in which the latter was seriously wounded. Despite this episode, Transylvania's faculty until 1837 remained relatively stable. By then, however, challenges from more competitive medical schools in nearby Louisville and Cincinnati combined with the declining economic fortunes of Lexington to erode Transylvania's faculty. In 1859 it graduated its last class of physicians.

The Louisville Medical Institute, which opened in 1837 as the city's first school for physicians, became in 1846 the Medical Department of the University of Louisville. Through the 1840s, the Louisville school, Transylvania, and the University of Pennsylvania were the nation's three largest medical schools. Competition for medical students within Louisville intensified with the organization of other institutions in that city: the Kentucky School of Medicine (1850); the Louisville Medical College (1869); the Hospital College of Medicine (1874); the Louisville National Medical College (1879) for blacks; the Southwestern Homeopathic Medical College (1892); and the Kentucky University Medical Department (1898).

Medicine joined the spirit of progressive reform pervading the United States in the early twentieth century. Two Kentuckians, Dr. Joseph N. McCormack and educator Abraham FLEXNER, were advocates of medical reform. For many years, McCormack served as director of the Kentucky State Board of Health. Public health education and practices improved considerably under his able leadership. Aid from the Rockefeller Foundation International Health Division and the U.S. Public Health Service from 1913 to 1933 helped to eradicate trachoma (a chronic contagious form of conjunctivitis sometimes resulting in blindness) and hookworm (an intestinal parasite). As chairman of the American Medical Association (AMA) Committee on Organizations, McCormack emphasized professionalization of medicine and greater status for physicians at a time when medical practitioners were not highly regarded. Flexner studied U.S. medical education facilities under the auspices of the Carnegie Foundation for the Advancement of Teaching. His *Medical Education in the United States and Canada* (1910) recommended closing most U.S. medical schools and reforming the remainder using Johns Hopkins University's medical school as the model.

By 1911 reform pressures had closed all Kentucky medical schools except the municipally supported University of Louisville School of Medicine. In the next five decades, the supply of physicians in Kentucky decreased. Calls to establish a state-supported medical school went unheeded, largely due to the Great Depression and World War II. After 1945 the federal government's willingness to fund modern, university-based health sciences centers led to a push for a state-sponsored facility in Kentucky. Urban rivals Louisville and Lexington vied for the funding. In 1956 the Kentucky General Assembly approved the establishment of the state medical school at the University of Kentucky in Lexington. Named for the governor, the Albert B.

Chandler Medical Center first matriculated students in medicine and nursing in 1960.

Growth of Kentucky's medical complexes accelerated in the 1960s and 1970s. In 1970 the University of Louisville joined the state-supported higher education network, giving Kentucky two state-funded medical schools. Private hospitals and clinics opened or grew in urban and rural districts. The physician supply increased. Nevertheless, distribution of physicians in rural areas was still a problem in 1990, especially for the delivery of primary health care to rural Appalachia. The enormous societal and individual costs of medical care could not escape notice.

Among the advances of the late twentieth century, Dr. William R. Willard, first dean of medicine at the University of Kentucky, led national efforts to establish family practice as a distinct medical specialization. Dr. Harold E. Kleinert, founder of the Louisville Hand Surgery Clinic, gained an international reputation in his area of research. In 1983 the University of Louisville's University Hospital formed Humana Hospital University in a public-funding venture with HUMANA Inc., a private health care company, headquartered in Louisville.

See Nancy Disher Baird, *David Wendel Yandell: Physician of Old Louisville* (Lexington, Ky., 1978); John H. Ellis, *Medicine in Kentucky* (Lexington, Ky., 1977).   RICHARD C. SMOOT

MENEFEE, RICHARD HICKMAN. Richard Hickman Menefee, lawyer and politician, was born in Owingsville, Kentucky on December 4, 1809. He was the third of five sons of Richard Menefee, a state legislator and one of Owingsville's founders, and Mary (Longsdale) Menefee. His father, of Irish descent, emigrated from Virginia in the 1790s; his mother was from Maryland. Menefee's father died in 1815; four years later his mother married Col. George Lansdowne, proprietor of Olympian Springs, a spa in Bath County. Richard attended Walker Bourne's preparatory school in Bath County, but family troubles forced Menefee to find work at age fourteen. He worked as an Owingsville bartender, then taught school. He attended Transylvania University in Lexington in 1826-28, studied law with Mt. Sterling's Judge James Trimble, and opened a practice in 1831. He received a law degree from Transylvania on March 3, 1832. Menefee was appointed commonwealth's attorney for the 11th Judicial District in 1831 and 1833. On August 14, 1832, he married Sarah Bell Jouett, the daughter of Matthew Harris Jouett, Kentucky painter. The marriage produced three children: Alexander, who died in infancy, Richard, and Mary.

Menefee resigned as commonwealth's attorney in 1836 and, campaigning as a Whig, won Montgomery County's legislative seat. The next year, after a bitterly fought campaign, he was elected to the 25th U.S. Congress over Judge Richard French, a powerful Montgomery County Democrat, serving from March 4, 1837, to March 3, 1839. On January 8, 1838, he orated on the attack on the ship *Car-*

oline, an issue involving British and American rights on the Great Lakes. A month later he and Sen. John J. Crittenden allowed themselves to be drawn in as seconds for Congressman William J. Graves in a duel in which Graves, a Kentuckian, killed Jonathan Cilley. Graves was censured by the House for the killing, and Menefee's and Crittenden's reputations were tarnished by this affair.

Menefee returned to Kentucky in 1839, moved his family to Lexington, and opened law practice there. Although dying of tuberculosis, he argued the noted 1840 Rogers will case against Henry Clay and Robert C. Wickliffe, Sr., losing this, his last case. Kentucky's Whigs honored their dying colleague on February 15, 1841, by electing him as U.S. senator to succeed John J. Crittenden, who had recently resigned. Menefee died five days later, on February 21, and was buried in Louisville's Cave Hill cemetery. In 1869 the Kentucky legislature created a new county in eastern Kentucky and named it in his honor, inadvertently misspelling his name as "Menifee."

See John A. Richards, *A History of Bath County, Kentucky* (Yuma, Ariz., 1961); John W. Townsend, *Richard Hickman Menefee* (New York 1907).

FRANK F. MATHIAS

MENIFEE COUNTY. Menifee County, the 114th in order of formation, is located in eastern Kentucky in the foothills of the Cumberland Plateau. It is bordered by the counties of Bath, Morgan, Montgomery, Powell, Rowan, and Wolfe and has an area of 203 square miles. Menifee County was formed on May 29, 1869, from portions of Bath, Montgomery, Morgan, Powell, and Wolfe counties and named in honor of Congressman Richard H. Menefee (with a variation in spelling). The county seat is FRENCHBURG.

The topography of Menifee County is mountainous and heavily forested. The northern and western portions have cliff-lined ridges, and the southeastern part has cliffs along the lower elevations. The Red River forms a portion of the county's southern boundary. Most of the county is within the Daniel Boone National Forest; only 35 percent of the land is in farms, of which 35 percent are in cultivation. The county ranks 102nd among Kentucky counties in agricultural receipts from tobacco, livestock, hay, and vegetables. William Suiters discovered and nurtured a strange new grass on the farms he purchased in 1887. The grass changed farm practices in Kentucky and other states after it was officially recognized in 1931. What Menifee Countians had called Suiters' Grass became known as Kentucky 31 Fescue. For many years, fine sorghum molasses was produced in the county, but by 1968 only one hundred acres were planted with sorghum cane.

Menifee's early history was marked by violent confrontations between Indians and settlers. The proximity of the region to the Warriors' Path, which connected the Shawnee and Cherokee territories, was one of the reasons for the numerous conflicts. In April 1793, nineteen women and children were captured by Indians at Morgan's Station, ten miles east of Frenchburg. A group of settlers overtook the Indians and their captives, although some of the captives were killed before they could be rescued.

During the early nineteenth century, Menifee County was the location of some of the first iron furnaces in Kentucky. Robert Crockett built a factory that used locally produced iron to make kettles, nails, and plowshares. Lumber mills flourished around Scranton in the nineteenth and early twentieth centuries. Significant deposits of oil and natural gas were found in the early 1900s, and today a major gas pipeline runs through the county from Oil Springs in Johnson County to Louisville. The county is bisected by U.S. 460. Broke Leg Falls, ten miles east of Frenchburg, is a popular attraction for residents and visitors. Other recreation areas include Koomer Ridge and the Pioneer Weapons Area, a 7,480-acre preserve in the Daniel Boone National Forest where only primitive weapons may be used for hunting. Cave Run Lake, which forms part of the county's northern border, attracts fishermen and boaters.

The population of Menifee County was 4,050 in 1970; 5,117 in 1980; and 5,092 in 1990.

See *The History of Menifee County* (n.p., 1986).

RON D. BRYANT

MENNONITES. The Mennonite church began its work in Kentucky in the 1940s. There was a Mennonite mission in Relief, Kentucky, as early as 1943. In July 1946 the Conservative Mennonite Conference began a drive to evangelize Kentucky's Appalachian region by sponsoring its first Bible school, at Turner's Creek in Breathitt County. Under the leadership of Alvin and Eula Swartz, the converts dedicated their first meetinghouse in November 1948. Subsequent churches were established at Bowling Creek in 1947 and Gay's Creek in 1950.

Most Mennonites are pacifists who refuse to bear arms or swear oaths. They believe in the divine inspiration of Scripture and in a new life in Christ, accessible through faith. Mennonites are also evangelical and believe it is their duty to bear witness of Christ to the world. The Mennonites sponsor a variety of socially benevolent enterprises, especially relief coordinated by the Mennonite Disaster Service, which aids tornado and flood victims. The Mennonite Central Committee has also supplied medical volunteers to several Appalachian regional hospitals.

See Frank S. Mead, *Handbook of Denominations in the United States* (Nashville 1975).

KEITH HARPER

MENTAL HEALTH. As early as 1793 the Kentucky General Assembly provided funds for boarding "the insane poor" in private institutions. The first mental hospital, the Fayette Asylum, was established by a group of Lexington's citizens. Taken over by the state in 1824 as the Kentucky Asylum (now EASTERN STATE HOSPITAL), it was patterned after the Colonial Mental Hospital in Williamsburg, Virginia. Western State Hospital in Hopkinsville was established in 1848 and Central State Hospital near Louisville in 1873, and Kentucky State Hospital opened after World War II. A home and school for the mentally retarded was established in Frankfort in 1861.

In 1938 the mental hygiene division of the Department of Welfare took over the hospitals, and the era of modern improvements began. In 1952, with the encouragement of the newly formed Kentucky Association for Mental Health, the General Assembly created an autonomous Department of Mental Health; by 1962 the department operated state institutions and facilities for the mentally retarded as well. When the new antipsychotic drugs became available, the number of patients began to decrease.

During the early 1960s, the U.S. Congress passed a series of laws to create, construct, and staff community mental health centers to be operated by local nonprofit boards. Kentucky was the first state to establish a statewide system of community mental health clinics. By 1970 there were twenty-four community mental health–mental retardation centers in Kentucky, serving all 120 counties. In 1973 the state created the Cabinet of Human Resources, and the mental health functions and institutions were amalgamated into the Department of Health within the new cabinet. In 1983 the Department of Mental Health and Mental Retardation started operating as an independent agency, with emphasis on community care of the long-term mentally ill and services by the community mental health centers.

The Kentucky Mental Health Association held its organizational meeting on June 20, 1951, and elected Barry Bingham, Sr., the first president. The purpose of the association was to educate the public about mental illness, to promote care and treatment, and to serve as an advocate for the mentally ill. As a part of the National Association for Mental Health, the Kentucky association has lobbied for state and national legislation to improve the lot of the mentally ill in the areas of commitment laws, confidentiality of physician-patient information, special education for emotionally disturbed children, and guardianship laws. The group has published a number of surveys of mental health needs in Kentucky.

Separate services for children began in Louisville in 1913 with the formation of the Psychological Laboratory (now the Bingham Child Guidance Clinic), one of only four in the country. In 1932 Dr. Spafford Ackerly, the first full-time professor of psychiatry at the University of Louisville, was named to head the Louisville clinic and to introduce changes in the care of the mentally ill in Kentucky. He also initiated the state's first four-year program in psychiatry for medical students, established the first postgraduate residency program to train physicians in psychiatry, and improved the care of adults and children in the Louisville General Hospital Psy-

chiatric Ward. He stimulated the formation of new training programs for psychiatric nurses, psychiatric social workers, and special programs for seminarians.

With the creation of a medical school at the University of Kentucky in Lexington in the 1950s, increasing numbers of psychiatrists, psychologists, social workers, and nurses were available for hospital and outpatient care. The veterans hospitals in Louisville and Lexington established strong psychiatry units; the U.S. Public Health Hospital in Lexington developed treatment and research services for drug addicts; and a number of private psychiatric hospitals have been built throughout the state. Mental health professionals in private practice add to the services previously available only in state hospitals and community mental health centers. The Kentucky Alliance for the Mentally Ill, a support group of families and friends of the mentally ill, has chapters across the state and is affiliated with a national organization. The Coalition for Mental Health represents professional groups who work together for the mentally ill in areas such as health insurance coverage and housing. New facilities have been opened across the state for the care of alcoholism and substance abuse, including hospitals for children and adolescents who are mentally ill or substance abusers. A critical need is housing for the chronically mentally ill and case managers to help with independent living after hospitalization. One-third or more of the homeless fall into this group.

FRANK M. GAINES

MENTELLE'S FOR YOUNG LADIES. Mentelle's female academy opened in Lexington late in the eighteenth century. Its founders, Charlotte Victorie (Leclere) Mentelle and her husband, Augustus Waldemarde Mentelle, fled their native Paris during the French Revolution. The Mentelles, who lived in Gallipolis, Ohio, for several years, moved to Lexington in 1798 and opened a French school at Transylvania Seminary. Madame Mentelle directed the school while her husband was occupied with other business ventures. In 1805 Mary Owen Russell, wealthy widow of Col. James Russell and the great-aunt of Mary (Todd) Lincoln, gave the Mentelles lifelong use of Rose Hill and five acres of land near Ashland, Henry Clay's estate. The Mentelles moved their school to Rose Hill around 1820.

Mentelle's for Young Ladies taught social etiquette, literature, dancing, and French, which was spoken both at the school and in the Mentelle household. At the family school, the enrollment in 1830 included boarders and day students. Mary (Todd) Lincoln, who attended from 1832 to 1836, boarded with the Mentelles during the week. The cost of room, board, and tuition in 1838 was $120 per year; the school year included three holidays: a week at Christmas, one day at Easter, and another day for Whitsuntide. Augustus Mentelle died on June 26, 1846. After Charlotte Mentelle's death on September 8, 1860, the land at Rose Hill reverted to Gen. William Preston, an in-law of the Mentelles' benefactor.

See William H. Townsend, *The Boarding School of Mary Todd Lincoln* (Lexington, Ky., 1941).

MERCER COUNTY. Mercer County, the sixth county in order of formation, is located in central Kentucky. Bordered by Anderson, Boyle, Garrard, Jessamine, Washington, and Woodford counties, it has an area of 250 square miles. Mercer County was formed on December 15, 1785, from a portion of Lincoln County and was named in honor of Gen. Hugh Mercer, a Scotsman who was killed at the Battle of Princeton in the Revolutionary War. HARRODSBURG, the first permanent pioneer settlement in Kentucky, is the county seat.

The topography of Mercer County is rolling to hilly. There are steep hillsides near the Kentucky and Dix rivers. The deep soils are excellent for crops such as tobacco, corn, and hay; large numbers of livestock are also raised. The major water courses of Mercer County are the Kentucky, Dix, and Salt rivers and Chapline's, Jennings, Lyon's, McCoun's, Thompson's, Rocky, and Shawnee Run creeks.

Mercer County was the site of several unique communities and institutions during the nineteenth century. Shakers built a large and prosperous community at Pleasant Hill and lived and worshipped there from 1805 to 1910. They were excellent farmers and craftsmen and for most of the nineteenth century their community was a self-supporting enterprise. Also located in Mercer County was the first meetinghouse of the Dutch Reformed church west of the Allegheny Mountains. Erected in 1800, it was called the Old Mud Meeting House for the extensive mud daubing used in its construction.

One of the early settlements in Mercer County was McAfee Station, established in 1779 by the McAfee, Curry, McGee, and McCoun families. Other communities in the county include the incorporated town of Burgin.

During the Civil War, several skirmishes took place in the county, and some citizens were arrested on suspicion of disloyalty to the Union. When the war ended, the county remained a large livestock and grain-producing region, where other crops included hay, corn, tobacco, and strawberries. Industrial development began on a modest scale with the products of the Shakers. Although distilleries, a coal oil refinery, and a calcite mine opened, the economy remained agricultural. By the twentieth century, the industrial base expanded to production of clothing, metal, glass, and heating and refrigeration items. Construction of the Dix River Dam and electric generating plant was completed in 1925 and created Herrington Lake.

Tourism increased in 1927 with the reconstruction of Fort Harrod. During the 1940s, rail excursions to the Roebling Suspension Bridge and the Dix River Dam were popular. In 1962 Shakertown at Pleasant Hill was incorporated as a nonprofit organization and opened the restored community as a historic area.

The population of Mercer County was 15,960 in 1970; 19,011 in 1980; and 19,148 in 1990.

See George M. Chinn, *Through Two Hundred Years: Pictorial Highlights of Harrodsburg and Mercer County, Kentucky, Bicentennial Edition, 1774-1974* (Harrodsburg, Ky., 1974); Maria T. Daviess, *History of Mercer and Boyle Counties* (Harrodsburg, Ky., 1924).   RON D. BRYANT

MERCHANDISING. The period after the Civil War witnessed the growth of more formal institutions among the forms of merchandising in the South. Kentucky—as part of an essentially rural southern society—shared in the increasing importance of the first of these innovations, country (general) stores. The country store was both an economic and a social institution, selling a bit of every kind of goods and providing a meeting place and source of news for an often isolated country community. As a part of the popular culture, it contributed much to the character of rural life. Because it provided credit to the rural poor when many banks would not, the country store was essential to the financial and physical well-being of its customers. Mail-order houses such as Sears, Roebuck and Montgomery Ward caused socio-economic rumblings, and in one sense were country stores by mail, but often it was the country storekeeper who processed mail orders for the community.

Although department stores provided new merchandising forms in urban areas, the next merchandising revolution was the advent of specialty stores—which sold one type of goods (such as shoes) rather than a variety of products—and their combination under common ownership into multi-unit chains. Such stores grew in number during the early twentieth century until by the 1920s they held a sufficiently large share of the market to offer the standardized goods and lower prices made possible by economies of scale. If there was the prospect of a higher standard of living, however, there was also the threat—or so it seemed to some—of the destruction of local proprietorships and community involvement, in the service of absentee owners from the North. The issue was regional versus national culture; the forum was Populist rhetoric in the context of an urban-industrial Progressivism. It was in urban areas that chain stores made their initial impact, although they soon expanded their influence into rural areas. Kentucky shared in this trend. In 1925 Danville enacted one of the first laws in the nation to regulate chain stores. The license fee required by this act varied according to the size of the store involved and its policy on providing credit. The Kentucky court of appeals, at the time the highest court in the state, ruled against the measure.

During the late 1920s, the Federal Trade Commission selected Louisville for extensive market analysis through the so-called Louisville Grocery

Survey, which pointed to the rise of chain stores at the expense of small merchants as one retail trend. This study emphasized the growing concern of merchants and others that new marketing tactics threatened economic and social redistribution of power.

In 1929 the neighboring state of Indiana enacted what was to become a model for chain store taxation, a graduated tax on the number of units under common ownership operated within the state. When the 1930 Kentucky legislature met, the Indiana measure was in litigation. The Kentucky assembly, hoping to avoid a similar legal challenge, enacted a method of taxation based on gross sales rather than on the number of chain store units owned. Kentucky's tax began at one-twentieth of 1 percent on the first $400,000 of gross sales and culminated in a tax of 1 percent on all sales above $1 million. The measure was contested in the courts and struck down by the U.S. Supreme Court (*Stewart Dry Goods Co. v. Lewis*, 1935).

Even in the face of such opposition, chain stores prospered as the South's urban areas joined in the creation of innovative merchandising. The growth of national and regional chains within the South reflected its increasing urbanization and transformation from a region characterized by Franklin D. Roosevelt as "the nation's No. 1 economic problem" to a part of the developing Sunbelt. As it changed from exploited to exploiter, the South altered its characteristic forms of marketing. In a nation where merchandising is a key to culture, the results have been startling. Kentucky has shared in the national distribution of chain stores, supermarkets, and other large-scale discounters without the hindrance of any unusual legislative opposition. Kentucky itself, in fact, became the corporate home of national chains as diverse as Humana in the medical field and Kentucky Fried Chicken in the fast-food market. The most interesting development, both in Kentucky and elsewhere, may be the rebirth of smaller shops, under the guise of convenience stores (often part of chains) to complement the role of larger merchandisers.

In response to the great changes in retailing during the twentieth century—particularly the dramatic growth of chain stores during the 1920s and the development of the supermarket during the 1930s—many retailers organized. At times they opposed such developments and at other times defended them. In Kentucky there were a number of merchants' organizations, such as the Louisville Retail Merchants' Association (dating from about 1905). By the 1930s there was a state Retail Merchants' Association. Although such groups promoted community activities for public relations purposes, they concentrated on lobbying against laws at any level that seemed to threaten merchants, such as special taxes based upon gross sales or the number of stores operated. In 1939 the Kentucky Chain Stores Council was founded, reorganized as the Kentucky Retail Federation in 1963.

See Thomas D. Clark, *Pills, Petticoats and Plows* (Indianapolis 1944); Godfrey M. Lebhar,

Chain Stores in America (New York 1963); Carl G. Ryant, "The South and the Movement Against Chain Stores," *Journal of Southern History* 39 (May 1973): 207-22.   CARL RYANT

MERIWETHER, DAVID. David Meriwether, political leader, was born in Louisa County, Virginia, on October 30, 1800; his family moved to Jefferson County, Kentucky, in 1803. Meriwether received a common school education and later engaged in fur trading in Iowa and agricultural pursuits in Kentucky. He was admitted to the bar and practiced law. Meriwether served in the state House of Representatives from 1832 to 1845. He failed to gain election to the U.S. Congress in 1846. He was a delegate to the 1849 state constitutional convention, and served as Kentucky's secretary of state in 1851. On July 6, 1852, Meriwether entered the U.S. Senate as a Democrat to fill the vacancy caused by the death of Henry Clay, holding this position until August 31, 1852. He did not run for reelection to the Senate. In 1853 President Franklin Pierce appointed Meriwether governor of the New Mexico Territory, a position he held from May 6, 1853, to October 31, 1857. He was elected a member of the Kentucky House from 1858 to 1885 and was the Speaker in 1859. In Meriwether's honor, S. P. Douthitt of Henry County, Kentucky, introduced a bill in the House on January 24, 1880, to create a county named Meriwether from portions of Laurel, Whitley, and Knox counties. The bill was defeated by 54 to 28.

In the later years of his life Meriwether lived on a plantation near Louisville. He died on April 4, 1893, and was buried in Cave Hill Cemetery.

MERRILL, BOYNTON, JR. Boynton Merrill, Jr., writer, son of Boynton and Virginia (Worsham) Merrill, was born on October 21, 1925, in Boston. After graduation from high school, he served as an electronic technician in the aviation sector of the U.S. Navy from 1944 to 1946. Merrill received his B.A. from Dartmouth College in 1950.

Merrill moved after college to Henderson, Kentucky, where he managed his mother's family farm. In 1960 he became involved in real estate development in addition to farming. In the early 1970s, Merrill turned to writing. His first work was a volume of poetry, *A Bestiary* (1976). Merrill's *Jefferson's Nephews: A Frontier Tragedy* (1976) is a historical work characterizing the lives of Thomas Jefferson's nephews Lilburne and Isham Lewis and their gruesome murder of a family slave, George. Highly praised for its scholarship and style, this history of the Lewis family is an accurate description of the difficult life in western Kentucky during the early 1800s. Merrill was editor of *Old Henderson Homes and Buildings* (1985), an architectural study of surviving buildings in Henderson that were at least eighty-five years old.

Merrill married Marian Royster on November 12, 1952; they have two children: Clark Addison and Frances Boynton.

MERTON, THOMAS. Thomas Merton, Trappist monk and writer, was born in Prades, France, on January 31, 1915. He was the son of Owen Heathcoate Grierson Merton, a painter born in New Zealand, and Ruth Calvert (Jenkins) Merton, an artist-designer born in the United States. After his mother's death when he was six, Merton spent his childhood in several places, sometimes in the company of his father, sometimes with his maternal grandparents on Long Island, and sometimes with friends of his father. The younger Merton was exposed early to a literary and artistic milieu best described as bohemian. He received his elementary education in the United States, Bermuda, France, and England, where he graduated from Oakham School in 1933. He attended Clare College, Cambridge University (1933-34), then returned to the United States. He attended Columbia University, receiving a B.A. in 1937 and an M.A. in English in 1938.

By that time, with both his grandparents dead, his "journey" (as he often described his life) led him from conventionality to the margins of society. Merton dabbled with communism and the peace movement and apparently followed a bohemian lifestyle, perhaps because his childhood had left him comfortable only with a way of life perceived as marginal (and questionable) by the rest of society. In the late 1930s, he and his friends stood in the vanguard of what was later dubbed the Beat movement. Merton converted to Roman Catholicism in 1938 and attempted to join the Franciscan order but was rejected. In 1939-40, he taught English at Saint Bonaventure University in Olean, New York. On December 10, 1941, he joined the Order of Cistercians of the Strict Observance (Trappists), and entered the Abbey of Our Lady of Gethsemani, south of Bardstown, Kentucky. The order followed a basically medieval lifestyle, based on prayer, silence, and work. Merton, known in religious life as Louis, was ordained a priest on May 26, 1949. He became a United States citizen in 1951. From 1951 to 1955, he was master of scholastics (students preparing for the priesthood), and from 1955 to 1965 he served as master of novices at Gethsemani.

Merton had written several novels, mostly autobiographical, before he entered Gethsemani. His search for himself and for God caused him to abandon these early aspirations for a time, although he continued to write poetry. His own inclinations and the requirements of his order, however, led him back to writing as part of his monastic vocation. His first published book was *Thirty Poems* (1944). His early work consisted, aside from his poetry, of short books on contemplation, pamphlets about the Trappist order, collections of notes on Cistercian saints, and two lengthier biographies of Cistercians (*Exile Ends in Glory* and *What Are These Wounds?*). In 1948 his autobiography *The Seven Storey Mountain*—the story of his conversion and entrance into Gethsemani—was an immediate best seller and brought him international recognition.

Speaking from the margins of society, Merton touched a nerve in the postwar world. During the next twenty years, he produced a large number of books and articles. His major works after *The Seven Storey Mountain* included *Seeds of Contemplation* (1949), *The Ascent to Truth* (1951), *The Sign of Jonas* (1953), *No Man Is an Island* (1955), *Thoughts in Solitude* (1958), *Disputed Questions* (1960), *Seeds of Destruction* (1964), *Seasons of Celebration* (1965), *Conjectures of a Guilty Bystander* (1966), and *Faith and Violence* (1968). Since his death, more of his writings have been collected and edited, including *Thomas Merton on Peace* (1971), *The Asian Journal* (1973), *The Collected Poems* (1977), *The Literary Essays* (1981), *The Hidden Ground of Love: Letters on Religious Experience and Social Concerns* (1985), *The Alaskan Journal* (1988), and *The Road to Joy: Letters to New and Old Friends* (1989).

His concern for cultural integrity and social justice led Merton in the 1960s to write on such issues as ecumenism and religious renewal, racial conflict, genocide, nuclear armament, the Vietnam War, ecology, and the Third World. His writings on the non-Christian traditions of Taoism and Zen Buddhism helped to introduce them to American readers. He corresponded widely with scholars and leaders of Hinduism, Islam, Judaism, and other religious traditions. In literature his translations of little-known Latin American poets helped to introduce Latin American literature to the United States. Merton was not a systematic writer or thinker, however, and he cannot be considered a theologian in the usual sense of the word.

In 1965 Merton was given permission to withdraw from the routine of community life and to live in solitude on the abbey grounds in a small concrete block cabin. In 1968 he made two extended trips to survey possible sites in New Mexico, Alaska, and California for a more isolated hermitage. After the second trip to California, he left on a pilgrimage to Asia, and in India he had an audience with the Dalai Lama, in exile at Dharamsala from the Communist Chinese government. After visiting Sri Lanka and Singapore, Merton attended a Buddhist-Christian conference on monasticism outside Bangkok, Thailand. He died in his quarters there on December 10, 1968, apparently having touched a fan with faulty wiring while still wet from bathing. He was buried at the Abbey of Gethsemani.

See David D. Cooper, *Thomas Merton's Art of Denial: The Evolution of a Radical Humanist* (Athens, Ga., 1989); Monica Furlong, *Merton: A Biography* (San Francisco 1980); Michael Mott, *The Seven Mountains of Thomas Merton* (Boston 1984).

ROBERT E. DAGGY

METCALFE, THOMAS. Thomas Metcalfe, governor during 1828-32, was born in Fauquier County, Virginia, on March 10, 1780, to John and Sarah Dent (Chinn) Metcalfe. The family moved to Fayette County, Kentucky, about 1804, then settled in Nicholas County. The future governor had a limited education in the common schools. His skill as a stonemason prompted the nickname "Stonehammer." Metcalfe married Nancy Mason about 1806; they had four children.

Metcalfe served in the Kentucky House from 1812 to 1816, and was a captain of volunteers during the War of 1812. From March 4, 1819, to June 1, 1828, he was a U.S. representative; he advocated easier sale of public lands, internal improvements, and protective tariffs. He opposed banks and any restriction of slavery in the Louisiana Purchase. As the Democratic Republican party dissolved, Metcalfe joined the John Quincy Adams-Henry Clay faction, which became known as the National Republicans. In December 1827 he became the first Kentucky candidate for governor nominated by party convention. A month later the Democrats' convention nominated William T. Barry, the chief justice of the late New Court. After a spirited campaign, Metcalfe won a narrow victory, with 38,930 votes to Barry's 38,231. The Democrats' candidate for lieutenant governor, John Breathitt, however, defeated Metcalfe's running mate, Joseph Underwood, by a 1,087-vote margin.

Metcalfe served from August 26, 1828, to September 4, 1832. After leaving the governorship he was a state senator (1834-38) and in 1839 a delegate to the Whig national convention. From 1840 to 1848 he presided over the Kentucky Board of Internal Improvements. As a U.S. senator for a few months (June 23, 1848, to March 3, 1849), he denounced secession. Thereafter he lived quietly at Forest Retreat, his Nicholas County farm, until his death of cholera on August 18, 1855. He was buried in the family graveyard.

Metcalfe was one of the state's most progressive governors in the pre–Civil War era. Believing that internal improvements were "essential to the welfare of the state," he pushed such projects as a canal at the Falls of the Ohio, the Lexington & Ohio Railroad, the Green River Navigation Company, and the Shelbyville-Louisville Road. Federal aid for the Maysville-Lexington road, part of a proposed interstate road, was blocked by President Andrew Jackson's famous veto in 1830, but Metcalfe continued to build it with state funds. He denounced South Carolina's nullification of the tariff as a danger to the Union; Kentucky would not take such a course, he said. Despite his genuine concern for improved education, Metcalfe did not give effective leadership in that area. An education act of 1830 was neutralized when county participation was made optional. "Stonehammer," however, did secure some reform in the penal system, he won reorganization of the courts, and the state provided some aid for the American Colonization Society. When the branches of the Bank of the Commonwealth were closed, Metcalfe obtained some protection for claimants who were actually occupying Kentucky lands.

See Leonard Curry, "Election Year—Kentucky, 1828," *Register* 55 (July 1957): 196-213.

LOWELL H. HARRISON

METCALFE COUNTY. Metcalfe County, the 106th county in order of formation, is located in south-central Kentucky in the eastern Pennyroyal region. It is bordered by Green, Hart, Barren, Monroe, Cumberland, and Adair counties, and has an area of 291 square miles. The Little Barren River and its tributaries, including the South and East forks, drain the northern and central part of the county. Southeastern Metcalfe is drained by the headwaters of Marrowbone Creek.

Metcalfe County was formed May 1, 1860, primarily from the county of Barren, with small sections coming from Hart, Green, Adair, Cumberland, and Monroe counties. The county was named in honor of Kentucky's tenth governor, Thomas Metcalfe (1828-32). EDMONTON, close to the geographic center of the county, was chosen as county seat. It was named for Edmund Rogers, who owned the land and laid out the town in 1818.

Shortly after Metcalfe County was established, the county courthouse was built. In March 1865 a band of Confederate guerrillas looted the town and burned the courthouse. A temporary replacement burned in July 1868. The present courthouse, of Italianate design, was completed in 1869.

Metcalfe has no large cities, only small villages and rural communities. Center, located at the county's north end and equidistant from four county seats, was founded by Joseph Philpot in the early 1800s; it was earlier named Frederick and later Lafayette. On KY 70, ten miles north of Edmonton, is the village of Sulphur Well, where in 1845 Ezekiel Neal, while drilling for salt water, discovered an artesian well. People began to travel to Sulphur Well to take the water and C.W. Thompson built the Beula Villa Hotel, which opened in 1903. It became one of the watering holes of southern Kentucky until it closed in 1969.

Summer Shade is located on KY 90 in southwestern Metcalfe County. Originally the area was known as Sartain Precinct and later as Glover's Creek; W.M. Riggs, the postmaster, changed the name to Summer Shade in 1872.

John Filson located Big Blue Spring on his 1784 map of Kentucky as being between the Little and Big Barren rivers in northwestern Metcalfe County. Two Indian trails crossed at Big Blue Spring. The Warriors' Trail, which extended from the Cherokee settlements near Chattanooga to the Falls of the Ohio, intersected a trail that reached from the Lexington–Dix River area to the Indian villages near Nashville. Stephen McKinney, granted a military warrant on the South Fork of the Little Barren, built a station there and was killed by Indians in 1792.

Center was the birthplace in 1834 of Ed Porter Thompson, who served as Kentucky's superintendent of public instruction in the 1890s; he wrote *History of the First Kentucky Brigade* (1868) and the *History of the Orphan Brigade* (1898). Center was also the birthplace in 1845 of Eugene Newman, who edited various newspapers before going to Washington, D.C., where he wrote a syndicated column. In 1911 he wrote and published *The Pennyrile of Old Kentucky* under the pen name Savoyard. William H. Newman, who grew up in Metcalfe County in the 1850-60s, merged fourteen rail lines to form the New York Central system and became president of all Vanderbilt lines in 1901.

One of the foremost doctors in southcentral Kentucky and the state during the twentieth century was Dr. C.C. Howard, who was born in Summer Shade. He worked to establish tuberculosis hospitals throughout Kentucky and to improve medical care in the rural areas of the state.

Metcalfe County is primarily rural. Burley tobacco is the main cash crop; farmers also grow corn and hay and raise dairy and beef cattle.

Metcalfe County has no railroads or navigable waterways. Several highways, including KY 90, KY 80, U.S. 68, KY 163, and the Cumberland Parkway, cross the county.

Natural resources include timber, oil, natural gas, and limestone that is quarried for road construction and as lime for farms.

The population of Metcalfe County was 8,177 in 1970; 9,484 in 1980; and to 8,963 in 1990.

KAY HARBISON

METEORITES. At least twenty-three meteorites have been found in Kentucky, according to written records. Six of them were observed as they fell to Earth, including the most recent, which fell on January 31, 1977, in Louisville. The other five observed falls of meteorites occurred in the counties of Christian (1868), Harrison (1877), Bath (1902), Whitley (1919), and Calloway (1950). The 7,000-meter-diameter circular depression at Middlesborough in Bell County may be a meteorite impact crater, as may be the case with the 3,200-meter-diameter raised circle of terrain at Jeptha Knob in Shelby County, and a 1,500-meter slightly raised circular feature on the Big Sink Road in Woodford County. Firm evidence of a meteoritic origin, such as meteoritic residue at the sites, is lacking, however.

Meteorites are extraterrestrial solid objects large enough to survive passage through the atmosphere and fall to Earth's surface. Most meteorites are believed to originate in the asteroid belt between Mars and Jupiter, although some may have been ejected from Mars and Earth's moon by impact events. They differ from meteors, which are luminous streaks in the sky made primarily by the burnup of cometary remnants too small to survive atmospheric passage. Meteorites can be grouped into three classes:

(1) Aerolites—stony meteorites that consist largely of silicate minerals, but may also contain small bits of metal. Stony meteorites containing small spheroidal or pebble-like mineral aggregates are known as chondrites.

(2) Siderites—metallic meteorites made up largely of an iron-nickel-cobalt alloy.

(3) Siderolites—stony-iron meteorites with about equal amounts of metal and silicate phases.

At least 5,000 meteorites have been identified, approximately half of them being recent finds in Antarctica. Nearly 1,000 of the meteorites collected were observed falling to Earth. Stony meteorites make up more than 80 percent of the identified specimens, and most of them are chondrites—the kind that fell in Louisville in 1977. High levels of the elements nickel and iridium in meteorites as compared with terrestrial rocks, and the presence of a smooth glassy fusion crust on stony meteorites (caused by friction with Earth's atmosphere), are helpful in identification.

See A.L. Graham, A.W.R. Bevan, and R. Hutchison, *Catalogue of Meteorites* (Tucson, Ariz., 1985).   WILLIAM D. EHMANN

METES AND BOUNDS. The English who settled at Jamestown transported to Virginia an ancient system of land survey based on natural landmarks, a practice that dated back to Roman times. As applied in Virginia and Kentucky, the metes and bounds system designated land boundaries from one marked tree to another, along stream courses, around cliff lines and rock outcroppings, or along trails and roadways. A characteristic Kentucky land deed description often constitutes no more than a cursory botanical inventory of the area. The casual system of SURVEYING of land boundaries has from the outset been the source of endless litigation. Particularly troublemaking has been the so-called boundary deed, which lacks any precise description of the area to which it applies.

See Samuel M. Wilson, *The First Land Court of Kentucky, 1779-80* (Lexington, Ky., 1923).

THOMAS D. CLARK

METHODIST CHURCH. Methodism in Kentucky is represented primarily by four Christian denominations: the African Methodist Episcopal; African Methodist Episcopal, Zion; Christian Methodist Episcopal; and United Methodist. All of these churches are governed through conferences from the local to the world level; they are administered by bishops elected to life tenure by either a general or regional conference, and they engage in denominational programs and ministries through general boards and agencies. Ordained ministers in all four episcopal Methodisms are appointed to their work by the bishop. In addition to the four main Methodist denominations in Kentucky, three congregations in the Louisville-Shelbyville area are known as the Congregational Methodist Church, and the Free Methodist Church (1860) has twelve congregations in Kentucky. This article discusses only the four episcopal Methodisms.

Francis CLARK, a lay preacher, not an ordained minister, is considered the father of Methodism in Kentucky. He moved from Mecklenburg County in southern Virginia and settled on the Salt River, six miles west of Danville, where he organized several Methodist societies as early as 1783. At that time, Methodism had not yet formally separated from the Church of England. (The Methodist Episcopal

Church was organized in Baltimore in 1784). Clark formed his first Methodist society in the home of the John Durham family, also pioneers from Mecklenburg County. In 1784 another Virginian, Richard Masterson, built a log house five miles northwest of Lexington, off the Leestown Pike, where a Methodist class was organized. A log structure he built in 1788 has traditionally been recognized as the first Methodist meetinghouse in Kentucky.

Bishop Francis ASBURY appointed James Haw and Benjamin Ogden as missionaries to the Kentucky District in 1786. Asbury himself made the first of fifteen journeys into Kentucky in 1790. At Masterson's Station he presided over the first Methodist conference in Kentucky.

The GREAT REVIVAL movement, which erupted in Kentucky in July 1800 at a camp meeting in Logan County on the Mud River, gave the Methodist movement new life. John McGee, a Methodist lay preacher, was one of the leading preachers at that meeting. Methodist itinerant William Burke won a name for his denomination at Barton Stone's great Cane Ridge revival in Bourbon County in August 1801. Between 1800 and 1812 Methodist membership in the western sector increased tenfold, and the Methodist Episcopal Church surged to the front rank of Kentucky's denominations.

In 1830 reformers who had long demanded a more democratic polity in American Methodism broke off to form the Methodist Protestant (MP) Church. The largest single break in Methodist Episcopal Church unity came at the troubled General Conference of 1844, over disagreement as to whether a bishop should exercise the episcopal office while he owned slaves. The Kentucky Conference of the church voted to side with the South and establish a separate denomination. In May 1845 the Methodist Episcopal Church, South, was inaugurated in Louisville.

The African Methodist Episcopal (AME) Church became an autonomous denomination in 1816 in Philadelphia, under the leadership of Richard Allen, in response to indignities suffered by the black members of St. George's Methodist Episcopal Church. William Paul Quinn, later a bishop, brought AME work to Kentucky about 1838, and the church formed a Kentucky Conference in 1868. QUINN CHAPEL, Louisville, is the mother church of the AME movement in Kentucky and the largest AME congregation in the state.

The African Methodist Episcopal Zion (AMEZ) Church was established in 1820 in New York City, separating from the Methodist Episcopal Church over local church property control issues. The Kentucky Conference was organized in 1866. Broadway Temple Church in Louisville is the oldest and numerically strongest AMEZ church in the commonwealth.

Both of the predominantly white episcopal Methodisms retained many black members, for whom there was a separate conference in the Methodist Episcopal Church. To preserve a black Methodism with a native southern identity after the Civil War,

leaders from both races opted for autonomous church government for the blacks, and in 1870 the remaining blacks of the Methodist Episcopal Church, South, were established as the Colored Methodist Episcopal (CME) Church (since 1956, Christian Methodist Episcopal). William H. Miles, the first CME bishop, was a native of Springfield, Kentucky. Brown Memorial Church in Louisville is the mother church and the largest CME congregation in Kentucky.

In 1939 the Methodist Episcopal, Methodist Episcopal, South, and Methodist Protestant churches united under the name Methodist Church. This denomination maintained separate congregations and conferences for blacks and whites until 1968, when it merged with the Evangelical United Brethen Church, a German-heritage denomination that was Methodistic in doctrine and polity. The merger of 1968 created today's United Methodist Church, committed to full racial inclusiveness.

With the exception of ASBURY COLLEGE and Asbury Theological Seminary in Wilmore, all Methodist social service institutions in Kentucky are related to the United Methodist Church. They are: Kentucky Wesleyan College, Owensboro (1866); Union College, Barbourville (1879); Sue Bennett College, London (1896); Lindsey Wilson College, Columbia (1903); Methodist Home of Kentucky, Versailles; Mary Kendall Home, Owensboro; Lewis Memorial Home, Franklin; Wesley Manor Retirement Community, Louisville; Methodist Evangelical Hospital, Louisville (in cooperation with the United Church of Christ); Community Methodist Hospital, Henderson; Good Samaritan Hospital, Lexington; Methodist Hospital, Pikeville; Wesley Community House, Louisville; Camp Loucon, Leitchfield; Aldersgate Camp, Ravenna; Camp O'-Cumberland, Loyal; Kavanaugh Life Enrichment Center, Crestwood; Henderson Settlement, Frakes; United Methodist Mountain Mission, Jackson; and Wesley Foundations at all eight state universities. Asbury College (1890) and Asbury Theological Seminary (1923) were established as part of the revival of the late 1800s, by Methodists who intended them to be independent of any denomination.

Ruptures in Methodism have generally not focused on theological points but on issues of polity such as episcopal authority and local church property rights, and on issues of human rights and dignity. Of course, in a religious body, matters of authority, property, and human relationships are ultimately theological issues. Nevertheless, Methodism in America has not couched its disagreements in theological idiom as much as some other movements. Theologically and socially, Methodism in Kentucky is conservative without being given to extreme expressions. In 1990 the four episcopal Methodisms had a total of 195,327 members in 1,178 organized congregations in Kentucky.

See William E. Arnold, *A History of Methodism in Kentucky* (Louisville 1935-36).

CHARLES W. BROCKWELL, JR.

MEXICAN WAR. On May 13, 1846, in response to battles in disputed territory on the Rio Grande, the United States declared war on Mexico. Four days later, before the federal government requested troops from the states, Kentucky Gov. William Owsley (1844-48) called for volunteer units. The commonwealth's response included journalistic evocations of the state's martial past, individual vows to sustain national and personal honor, and an excess of would-be soldiers. Ignoring Washington's guidelines on company size in the two infantry and one mounted regiments sought, Owsley accepted units unwisely, apparently heedless of Kentucky's regional jealousies.

Mustered the day of Owsley's proclamation, the Louisville Legion, a prewar militia organization, soon journeyed south as the 1st Regiment, Kentucky Foot Volunteers (led by Col. Stephen Ormsby, 781 personnel). In the following weeks 105 companies from seventy-nine of Kentucky's ninety-nine counties vied for the thirty positions authorized. Owsley chose the company quota from fourteen counties, mostly in the Bluegrass region. He then appointed majors, lieutenant colonels, and colonels from his own Whig party. Democratic President James K. Polk's appointed Democrats William O. Butler, Owsley's defeated 1844 rival for governor, and Thomas F. Marshall as Kentucky's generals, appointments that surely rankled Owsley.

Other unpleasant realities awaited the governor. State arms stores proved inadequate and so, in June, a cache of muskets and accoutrements was purchased and sent to troops already in the field. Nevertheless, equipment shortages continually plagued the commonwealth's units, and Owsley's volunteers soon met other hard facts of military service. For example, 19 percent of the 1st Foot were discharged (Kentuckians typically were thus turned out, sometimes far from home, for "physical disability," disobedience, sickness, injury, or for procuring a substitute). Many volunteers who were ill were left behind en route, with orders to rejoin the regiment later. Unknown numbers of men in this situation died or deserted.

The 1st Foot found adversity in combat as well. At the Battle of Monterrey, September 19-24, 1846, the regiment guarded a mortar battery. The Kentuckians stood under orders not to return enemy fire, but the press unfairly criticized them for not honorably engaging their foe. Garrison duty thereafter prevented the regiment from clearing its record of this supposed blot. About the same time questions of honor also nettled those at home. In the fading enthusiasm for war, Whigs questioned the conflict's legitimacy; Democrats questioned Whig patriotism.

Regiments raised after the 1st Foot also found war less than the grand adventure many civilians expected. Entering service on June 9, 1846, the 1st Regiment, Kentucky Mounted Volunteers (Col. Humphrey Marshall, 820 personnel, 27 percent discharged), briefly occupied Louisville's Camp Owsley. When these rowdy horsemen, some of whom

had fired on a regimental officer (without hitting him) left town, the city reportedly viewed their departure with relief. Less ludicrous but equally reprehensible was the routine exploitation of all volunteers by sutlers, who gouged the seldom-paid soldiers. Included in such abuse was the 2d Regiment, Kentucky Foot Volunteers (Col. William McKee, 892 personnel, 20 percent discharged), which mustered at the same time and place as the 1st Regiment. Bureaucratic bungling long delayed the southward progress of John S. Williams's Independent Company, Kentucky Volunteers (66 personnel, 11 percent discharged).

After finally reaching the theatre of conflict in northern Mexico, the 1st Mounted and the 2d Foot endured months of drill, boredom, and disease. In late January 1847, two parties of Kentucky cavalry were taken prisoner at Encarnacion. A few weeks later in Buena Vista, on February 22-23, came the opportunity for Kentucky soldiers to affirm the romantic sense of honor so many had invoked in the rush to volunteer. Greatly reduced in numbers by discharges and sickness (and outnumbered by the enemy), the Kentuckians and other Americans nevertheless fought well. The 1st Mounted suffered twenty-nine killed and thirty-four wounded. The 2d Foot sustained forty-four killed and fifty-seven wounded. Months later, some dead were buried ceremoniously in Frankfort Cemetery. For years afterward all the Kentuckians at Buena Vista were lionized as heroes, as was their commander, Gen. Zachary TAYLOR, who also had a Kentucky background.

Williams's company, so long detained in Kentucky, reached central Mexico in time to fight in the decisive Battle of Cerro Gordo, April 17-18, 1847, where four of them were killed. But fervor for the war had declined so much in Kentucky in the wake of U.S. victories that only thirty-two volunteer companies answered the federal call for two more infantry regiments (twenty company openings). Bluegrass counties did not predominate as they had in 1846. Owsley, stung by criticism of his earlier performance, selected many companies from eastern and western parts of the state. Early October saw the formation of the 3d Regiment, Kentucky Foot Volunteers (Col. Manlius V. Thompson, 1,058 personnel, 9.3 percent discharged, 17 percent died) and the 4th regiment, Kentucky Foot Volunteers (Col. John S. Williams, 1,100 personnel, 7.3 percent discharged, 13.5 percent died). A detachment of regulars (Col. John W. Tibbats, 396 personnel, 4 companies, 13.6 percent discharged) had been recruited in Kentucky earlier that year. All the units mustered in 1847 did garrison duty.

Of the 5,113 Kentuckians entering service, 77 (1.5 percent) were killed in action, 509 (9.9 percent) died of disease or accident, 792 (15.5 percent) were discharged, and 161 (3.2 percent) deserted. At the expiration of their one-year enlistments, the volunteer regiments disbanded. Correspondingly, the militia institution had faded into oblivion by the mid-1850s.

The Mexican War's social effect boded ill for Kentucky. The sentimental haze which in 1846 had obscured war's grim potential revived in the glow of national triumph. A record of duty in a volunteer regiment advanced countless political careers and social ambitions. Kentuckians, like other Americans, entered the 1850s with a questionable concept, the glory of war, dangerously intact. (All preceding statistics on mustered units are approximations derived from the *Report of the Adjutant General . . . Mexican War Veterans* [1889], the best available source.)

See John Eisenhower, *So Far From God* (New York 1989).   JAMES RUSSELL HARRIS

MEYZEEK, ALBERT ERNEST. Albert Ernest Meyzeek, educator, was born in Toledo, Ohio, on November 5, 1862, the son of a white Canadian father and a black mother and the grandson of John Lott, a member of the underground railroad. Soon after his birth his family moved to Toronto in Canada, where he began his education. In 1875 his family moved to Terre Haute, Indiana, where he attended Terre Haute Classical High School. He was valedictorian at his graduation. Meyzeek completed his education at Indiana University in Bloomington in 1884.

He first taught school in Terre Haute. He went to Louisville in 1890, to begin more than fifty years of service to public education. In Louisville he first served as principal of the Maiden Lane School. After a year there, he went on to work as principal of the Eastern School (1891-93) and of Central High School (1893-96). In just three years at Central, he lengthened the curriculum from three to four years and established a school library, which led to the opening of a public library branch for blacks on Chestnut Street. In 1896 Meyzeek was asked to run the new Colored Normal School while at the same time serving as principal of the Jackson Junior High School. Increased attendance forced him to concentrate all of his energy on Jackson, where he retired in 1943.

Meyzeek, for whom Meyzeek Middle School in Louisville was named, was a leader in the field of civil rights. He helped to open the first YMCA, secure adequate libraries for blacks, and open the University of Louisville to blacks. He helped found the Louisville Urban League, and he campaigned for two black local junior high schools. As a member of the State Education Association (1948-56), he urged the desegregation of the state public school system, which occurred in Louisville in the fall of 1956.

Meyzeek was active in the Louisville community until his death at the age of 101, on December 19, 1963. He was buried in Eastern Cemetery in Louisville.

See George D. Wilson, *A Century of Negro Education* (Louisville 1986).

MIDDLESBOROUGH (MIDDLESBORO). Middlesborough, the largest city in Bell County in southeastern Kentucky, is located in the southeastern part of the county just northwest of the Cumberland Gap at the junction of U.S. 25E and KY 74. The city is situated in the valley of Yellow Creek, a large bowl-like depression. A popular but unlikely theory holds that the cause of the depression was the impact of a colliding meteorite 30 million to 300 million years ago.

Located at the base of the Cumberland Gap, the site that became Middlesborough witnessed Indians on the Warriors' Path, explorations of early pioneers, and the movement of thousands of settlers into Kentucky via the Wilderness Road. At or near the city site, the pioneer Yellow Creek settlement was made around 1810 by John Turner of Virginia. Other early settlers of the area included the Partin, Colson, and Marsee families. The area consisted of scattered homesteads and remained rural until well after the Civil War.

A few industrious farmers mined coal from the creek banks as early as the 1850s. Relatively small amounts of coal and timber were hauled out by oxen and floated to downstream markets. Surface and mineral rights were sold to wealthy businessmen in the East beginning around 1870, but large-scale mining and logging operations did not go into full swing until the 1890s. Alexander Alan Arthur of Scotland, who arrived on Yellow Creek in the 1880s, had been involved in iron, coal, and steel enterprises in Great Britain and timbering in Sweden, and he saw great economic potential in the mineral and natural resources of the Yellow Creek Valley. He convinced European backers of easily obtainable wealth in the Kentucky hills and formed the American Association Limited. The company purchased 100,000 acres in Kentucky and nearby Tennessee and Virginia, and in 1889 Arthur began planning for a new city to be named after the industrial and manufacturing center of Middlesborough, England. Arthur hired skilled and unskilled workers from the region and even brought in craftsmen from Europe. The Yellow Creek Valley was cleared of trees and surveyed, streets were laid out, and whole blocks of buildings were constructed. A tunnel through Cumberland Mountain connected the Louisville & Nashville Railroad with Pineville, thirteen miles to the north. A beltline railroad that would encircle the valley and provide access to deposits of iron and coal was also begun.

The city of Middlesborough was incorporated in 1890 and was a town of 5,000 with long, wide avenues, an iron furnace, tannery, city hall, opera house, hospital, two schools, four banks, five churches, sixteen hotels, and numerous homes and businesses of English-style architecture. By the end of the year, a number of the English backers went bankrupt and Arthur's grandiose plans were scaled down. When it was discovered that local iron deposits were not as rich as originally thought, new investment in the town virtually ceased. The financial panic of 1893 almost completely dried up American and British investment capital and much of Middlesborough went bankrupt, resembling a ghost town. Most of the property of the American

Association was auctioned off or sold at a fraction of the original cost.

Although the iron industry never came to fruition in Middlesborough, coal mining was the backbone of the local economy for most of the twentieth century. The economy boomed during World War I, suffered during the postwar recession of 1920-22, rose during the latter part of the 1920s, and fell again with the Great Depression that began in 1929. A flood the same year did half a million dollars damage to the town.

During the 1930s, the federal government decided to proceed with plans to create the Cumberland Gap National Historical Park in the depressed area. Other than major improvements to U.S. 25E, little was done until after World War II toward the development of the park, which was not dedicated until July 4, 1959.

In the late 1960s shopping centers, stores, restaurants, and motels were constructed along U.S. 25E, separate from the old downtown business district. The Middlesborough Mall, a large retail complex that fronts U.S. 25E, attracts shoppers from throughout the mountain region. Plans to revitalize the old business district were upset when a tornado struck the downtown area on May 9, 1988. Several brick buildings were destroyed and many others were damaged beyond repair. One person was killed, and damage was estimated in millions of dollars.

Middlesborough's status as a regional commercial and tourism hub was enhanced by the construction of the Cumberland Gap Tunnel. The tunnel bypassed a steep grade on U.S. 25E through the Cumberland Gap and provided better access between I-75 at Corbin, Kentucky, and I-81 at White Pine, Tennessee.

The city sponsors an annual Cumberland Mountain Festival in mid-October. The largest city employers are Cowden Manufacturing Company, a maker of jeans; Cumberland Gap Provision Company meat processors; and Middlesboro Tanning Company of Delaware. The tanning company and the city were at the center of a heated debate and a long-running legal action that began in the 1970s. Pitted against them were environmentalists and a local citizens' group who feared the effects of what they alleged was dangerous waste released into Yellow Creek. Residents living beside the creek that runs through the city from southwest to the northeast feared possible health hazards.

Although the name is commonly spelled Middlesboro, the city was incorporated as Middlesborough, which continues to be the official spelling. The population of the third-class city was 11,844 in 1970; 12,251 in 1980; and 11,328 in 1990.

See Lou DeRossett, *Middlesborough: The First Century* (Jacksboro, Tenn., 1988).

DAVID F. WITHERS

MIDDLETON OFFSET. On July 6, 1859, a team of surveyors, Austin P. Cox representing Kentucky and Benjamin Peebles from Tennessee, turned their compasses three-fourths of a mile north from the Black Jack Corner in Simpson County, creating a one-hundred-one acre indentation, called the Middleton Offset, in the Kentucky-Tennessee border. The Middleton Offset was within the Simpson Triangle irregularity on the border. There is no hint in the official survey log or the legislative records as to why they did this. Possibly Samuel Middleton of Sumner County, Tennessee, preferred that his entire farm remain in that county and state and used political pressure to influence the state BOUNDARY.

See Thomas D. Clark, *Historic Maps of Kentucky* (Lexington, Ky., 1979).

THOMAS D. CLARK

MIDDLETOWN. Middletown is in eastern Jefferson County on the headwaters of Beargrass Creek at U.S. 60 and KY 1065. The hills around Middletown were the scene of several Indian attacks in the 1780s. On Long Run Creek, east of Middletown, Abraham Lincoln, grandfather of the sixteenth president, was killed in an ambush on September 16, 1781. The next day, John Floyd was killed four miles east of Middletown. In 1789 Indians attacked the Chenoweth homestead, killing three children and leaving their parents wounded.

The town was officially established in 1797 by landowner Philip Buckner. The name Middletown was apparently chosen because the town was midway between Louisville and Shelbyville. A popular stagecoach stop was the Middletown Inn, built around 1800, where a stairway of fifteen steps commemorated Kentucky as the fifteenth state. From 1800 to around 1820, Middletown rivaled Louisville as a bustling center of commercial activity. Products for trade, arriving down the Ohio River at the mouth of Harrod's Creek, were reloaded and transported to Middletown's wholesale and retail establishments. After 1820, the growth of Louisville as a major port city overshadowed Middletown, which developed into a quiet farming community.

During the Civil War, the town was the site of two skirmishes between Union and Confederates that were preludes to the Battle of PERRYVILLE. Although Middletown was spared the destruction of battle, violence was common in the area. Outlaws hid in the woods along the Louisville road and frequently robbed and killed.

The arrival of an interurban railroad in 1910 made the city a commuter community of Louisville, but growth remained slow until the automobile became widespread. When U.S. 60 was built around Middletown rather than through it in the early 1930s, a major controversy erupted. Residents feared that the town would die if the highway bypassed Main Street. The bypassing, however, is credited with saving the city's historic district from destruction.

Middletown was incorporated in 1979 as a fourth-class city. The population was 4,262 in 1980; and 5,016 in 1990.

See Edith Wood, *Middletown's Days and Deeds* (Louisville, Ky., 1946).

MIDWAY COLLEGE. Midway College, Kentucky's only college for women, was founded in 1847. The independent, residential college emphasizes career preparation based on a liberal arts background. The campus is located in Midway, Woodford County. The institution was established to prepare financially disadvantaged young women for teaching careers. Formerly the Kentucky Female Orphan School, the college was the brainchild of Lewis Letig Pinkerton, a young physician and minister of the Christian Church (Disciples of Christ). He and James Ware Parrish, the church elder who raised the funds necessary to open the school, joined with other progressive thinkers to launch a revolutionary educational experiment: a formal education for female orphans, who at that time were rarely offered even a meager amount of schooling. Enrollment in 1990 reached a record 535 traditional residential, commuter, and nontraditional students.

Midway encourages the enrollment of students representing varied cultural, geographical, racial, religious, and socioeconomic backgrounds with diverse talents in academic and creative areas. Students benefit from the small class sizes, individual faculty attention, and a variety of extracurricular programs. The college calendar includes a fall and spring semester, evening coeducational classes, and a summer school program. Discussion and study groups, arts and lecture series, seminars, films, and chapel services enrich the academic program. Midway's 105-acre campus includes classrooms, a library, student center and gymnasium, dining hall, early childhood education center, residence halls, administrative buildings, an amphitheater, tennis courts, the Keeneland Equine Education Center, and outdoor riding facilities with fifty acres for cross-country riding.

The college is accredited by the Southern Association of Colleges and Secondary Schools. It offers associate degrees in computer information systems, business administration, early childhood education, equine management, equine office administration, fashion merchandising, general studies, nursing, office administration, paralegal studies, and teacher education.

In fall 1989 the college began offering four-year programs leading to the degrees of B.S. in nursing and B.A. in business administration. In 1991 additional programs were being developed to offer the B.A. in accounting, paralegal studies, equine management, and liberal studies.

MARSHA TANNER STREIN

MIGRATION PATTERNS. Since the first white settlers moved into Kentucky in the late eighteenth century, migration has been primarily responsible for the distribution of the state's residents and has shaped the age-sex composition and social characteristics of the population. Migration patterns are indicators of economic conditions of the state and its regions.

The movement of settlers into Kentucky began in the 1770s, when it was still a part of the state of Virginia. To settle the territory, Virginia initially issued land warrants to veterans of the French-Indian and Revolutionary wars but soon opened the territory to the general public. The general westward movement into Kentucky continued for the next several years. Most migrants came overland by way of the Wilderness Road, but increasing numbers traveled down the Ohio River. After 1820, when the Kentucky population exceeded half a million, the growth rate dropped well below that of the nation, indicating a loss of residents to other states.

In 1850 the federal census began to collect data on places of birth of the population. A comparison of place of birth with place of current residence data reveals a rather slow change in the origin of Kentucky migrants, although in all decades most came from neighboring states. In 1860 Virginia was the origin of most migrants to Kentucky, followed in order by Tennessee, Ohio, North Carolina, and Pennsylvania. By 1870 most migrants to Kentucky came from Tennessee. By 1970 most came from Ohio. Migrants from Indiana, Illinois, and West Virginia came to Kentucky in greater numbers during the twentieth century, while the numbers from North Carolina and Pennsylvania declined.

The movements of Kentucky natives to other states show a significant shift from a movement west in the nineteenth century to a movement north by the mid-twentieth century. In 1850 Missouri, followed by Texas, was the leading destination of Kentucky migrants and remained so until 1910. Gradually the migrant streams shifted to the north and northwest; Ohio, Illinois, Indiana, and Michigan became major destinations of migrating Kentuckians. The availability of land had been the major attraction for nineteenth century migrants, but the lure of industrial jobs was a stronger moving force in the twentieth century.

Economic factors have exerted the greatest influence on the movements of people both into and out of Kentucky. Within sixty years after the first settlers moved in, the availability of good farmland farther west caused a net loss in population. The failure of Kentucky to develop major manufacturing industries to supplement agriculture and mining made it even more difficult for the state to retain its population in the years following World War II. The energy crisis of the 1970s produced simultaneously an industrial recession and a coal boom that temporarily reversed the direction of migration, creating Kentucky's first gain in recent history. Since 1980, though, deteriorating economic conditions have sent migrants south and to the far West rather than to the industrial North.

Compared with more urbanized states of the region, Kentucky has attracted relatively few foreign immigrants. In 1850 the first count of the foreign-born tallied 31,400 immigrants, or 4 percent of the state's population. The highest percentage (6.4) of foreign-born persons in Kentucky was recorded in 1869 and the greatest number (63,400) in 1870. From 1860 until 1950 both numbers and percentages of the foreign-born decreased. Since 1950 there has been a slight increase, but the 34,562 foreign-born counted in 1980 constituted less than 1 percent of the total population. Many of these foreign nationals were university students rather than true immigrants, while others were refugees or spouses of service personnel who had been stationed abroad.

See Howard W. Beers, *Growth of Population in Kentucky 1860-1940* (Lexington, Ky., 1942); George A. Hillery, Jr., *Population Growth in Kentucky, 1820-1960* (Lexington, Ky., 1966); Simon S. Kuznets, ed., *Population Redistribution and Economic Growth: United States, 1870-1950* (Philadelphia 1957).   THOMAS R. FORD

MILK-SICKNESS. Dr. Thomas Barbee, a Bourbon County physician, first described milk-sickness in 1809. Known also as "the trembles" and "the slows," this mysterious malady, "under which man turns sick and his domestic animals tremble," afflicted nineteenth century settlers in various parts of Indiana, Ohio, Kentucky, Tennessee, and Illinois. It was transmitted to humans through milk, butter, or flesh from cattle that had eaten the wild, flowering white snakeroot, *Eupatorium urticaefolium*, containing the deadly poison tremetol. The disease hit the sparsely settled pioneer communities hard. Even the few who survived the torment of retching, vomiting, and aching legs were often incapacitated for months or years. Remedies prescribed included bleeding, purging, and cold effusions. The problem was overcome only when grazing was limited to cultivated pastures and milk was pasteurized. The cause of milk-sickness was not proven until 1928.

See Daniel Drake, "A memoir on milk-sickness," *Western Journal of Medicine and Surgery* 3 (1841): 161-226.   PORTER MAYO

MILLER, ARTHUR McQUISTON. Arthur McQuiston Miller, geologist and educator, was born in Eaton, Ohio, on August 6, 1861, to Robert and Margaret Ann (McQuiston) Miller. After his early education in Eaton public schools, he studied at the University of Wooster in Ohio during 1880-82. In 1883 he transferred to Princeton University, where he graduated in 1884. After serving as short-term principal at two Ohio high schools, he returned to Princeton to earn a master's degree in 1887, and stayed on under a fellowship through 1889. After a year as professor of natural history at Wilson College in Pennsylvania and a year studying at the University of Munich, he joined the University of Kentucky faculty as professor of geology in 1892. Miller served as dean of arts and sciences at the University of Kentucky during 1908-17. During World War I he was a consulting field geologist and, on leave of absence from the university, he wrote many scientific studies. He retired as professor emeritus of geology at the university on June 30, 1925. Miller spent his retirement years in Asheville, North Carolina, where he died suddenly from a heart attack on October 28, 1929. He was buried in Eaton, Ohio.   T.G. ROBERTS

MILLER, HENRY M. Henry M. Miller, a pioneering Kentucky physician, was born in Glasgow, Kentucky, November 1, 1800, the son of Henry Miller, a Maryland native and one of Barren County's first settlers. At age seventeen Miller studied with two Glasgow physicians, and he received his medical degree from Transylvania's medical school in 1822. He served as an anatomy instructor at Transylvania until 1823, then took up private practice in Glasgow. In 1826 Miller moved to Harrodsburg, where he was in private practice for five years with Dr. Christopher Graham, owner of the Harrodsburg Springs resort.

In 1837 Miller became professor of obstetrics and diseases of women and children at the Louisville Medical Institute, which became the Medical Department of the University of Louisville in 1846. In 1869 he was made professor of obstetrics at the Louisville Medical College. In Miller's private practice, he pioneered in the use of anesthesia, particularly ether, during labor and childbirth. Miller co-edited the *Louisville Journal of Medicine and Surgery* in 1838, and his extensive writings include *Principles and Practice of Obstetrics* (1858), one of the foremost texts on the subject. He served as president of the American Medical Association in 1859.

Miller married Clarissa Robertson on June 24, 1824. They had four children: George R., Edward, Caroline M., and Mary E. Miller died in Louisville on February 8, 1874, and is buried in Cave Hill Cemetery.

See Franklin Gorrin, *The Times of Long Ago* (Louisville 1929).

MILLER, JIM WAYNE. Jim Wayne Miller, poet, was born October 21, 1936, in Leicester, North Carolina, son of James Woodrow and Edith (Smith) Miller. He attended Leicester public schools and graduated from Kentucky's Berea College in 1958 with a B.A. degree in English literature. He served two years as a German instructor at Fort Knox, Kentucky, and did graduate studies in German and English literature at Vanderbilt University in Nashville, where he was awarded a Ph.D. degree in 1965. Miller became a professor of German at Western Kentucky University in Bowling Green, taught folklore and creative writing courses, and served as consultant to Appalachian studies programs in neighboring states. A major southern poet and fiction writer popular at poetry readings and workshops, he is known throughout Kentucky. Miller has been a featured poet on several television programs. His first collection of poems was *Copperhead Cane* (1964), followed by *The More Things Change, the More They Stay the Same* (1971); *Dialogue with a Dead Man* (1974); *The Mountains Have Come Closer* (1980), winner of the Thomas Wolfe Award; and *Vein of Words* (1985). Miller's translations include *The Figure of Fulfillment* and *The Salzach Sibyl* by the Austrian poet Emil Lerperber. His work appears in the anthologies *Contemporary Southern Poetry*, *A Geography of Poets*, and *Going Over to Your Place*. His first novel, *Newfound* (1989), is set in Appalachia.

Miller married Mary Ellen Yates of Carter County, Kentucky, in 1958; they have three children: James, Frederic, and Ruth Ratcliff.

JOY BALE BOONE

MILLER, MARY MILLICENT (GARRETSON). Mary Millicent (Garretson) Miller, steamboat captain, the daughter of Andrew J. and Luanna Garretson, was born in Louisville in 1846. She married George ("Old Natural") Miller on August 3, 1865, and raised his three young children with their own four: Lula Ann, George, Emma, and Norman. She and her husband built steamboats in their Portland front yard, and she worked as a steamboat captain from 1884 to 1892. The Millers transported freight from New Orleans on the Red River in the 179-ton sternwheeler, the *Saline*, he as a pilot, she as captain, until railroad expansion made business unprofitable. They then built the *Swan*, a deep-water sailboat for oyster dredging. Miller died on October 30, 1894, and was buried in Louisville in the Portland Cemetery.

JANICE THERIOT

MILLER, SAMUEL FREEMAN. Samuel Freeman Miller, U.S. Supreme Court justice, was born to Frederick and Patsy (Freeman) Miller on April 5, 1816, in Richmond, Kentucky. With no previous formal education, Miller entered the medical department of Transylvania University in 1836 and received his M.D. degree on March 9, 1838. During the next twelve years he practiced medicine in the eastern Kentucky community of Barbourville. He became interested in politics, studied law, and was admitted to the bar in Knox County on March 22, 1847. Miller, a Whig, favored the gradual abolition of slavery. In 1850 he moved his family and his law practice to Keokuk, Iowa, where he was a founder of the Iowa Republican party. On July 16, 1862, President Abraham Lincoln appointed Miller, then forty-six years old, to the Supreme Court. Justice Miller's twenty-eight productive years on the Court (1862-90) spanned a significant period of history and constitutional interpretation. He wrote the majority opinion in more than six hundred of the 5,000 cases in which he participated. Miller married Lucy Ballinger in Barbourville, Kentucky, and they had three children. After Lucy's death, he married Elizabeth Winter Reeves in 1857; they had two children. Justice Miller died in Washington, D.C., on October 13, 1890, and was buried in Keokuk.

See Charles Fairman, *Mr. Justice Miller and the Supreme Court, 1862-1890* (Cambridge, Mass., 1939). CHARLES R. LEE, JR.

MILLERSBURG COLLEGE. Millersburg College for young women at Millersburg in Bourbon County was chartered by the Kentucky legislature on February 20, 1860, as Millersburg Female College, repealing the charter of the Millersburg Male and Female Collegiate Institute granted on March 5, 1856. George S. Savage, one of the incorpora-

tors, became the first president. In June 1867 Millersburg Female College awarded four diplomas to the first graduating class. Fire destroyed the building housing the school during Christmas holidays in 1878, and the structure that replaced it burned on October 9, 1907. In October 1908 the college president, the Rev. Charles Crockett Fisher, enlisted the assistance of alumni and Bourbon County citizens to erect a four-story replacement, with steam and electricity, equipped for over one hundred students. A basic junior college curriculum offered an associate of arts degree with the option to work in specialized departments. Ownership of the institution largely fell upon Millersburg residents, and in the fall of 1915 the school was renamed Millersburg College. In 1931 Millersburg Military Institute purchased the college and established there an elementary school for its junior students.

MILLERSBURG MILITARY INSTITUTE. The Millersburg Military Institute (MMI), the only remaining military school in Kentucky, is a coeducational boarding school at Millersburg in Bourbon County, Kentucky. It was established by Col. C.M. Best in 1893. Until 1898 the institute occupied the buildings of the former KENTUCKY WESLEYAN COLLEGE and was known as the Millersburg Training School. Kentucky Wesleyan had been the male department of the Millersburg Male and Female Collegiate Institute, a Methodist college. When Best purchased the facilities in 1898 the school was renamed Millersburg Military Institute. Male boarders were accepted and a military regime was introduced. Although primarily intended for Kentucky youth, it also drew students from several other states.

In the spring of 1920, community concern arose over the closing of the school when the Bourbon County board of education bought the property. Seven residents formed a corporation and purchased the eighteen-acre Sanfor Allen homestead, and classes began on the new site in 1921. That year Col. Walton R. Nelson became superintendent. The institute purchased the grounds of the old Millersburg Female College in 1931 and established a junior school for elementary school students there; it was the only southern military academy with a separate elementary school. In 1944 MMI was organized as a nonprofit institution with a perpetual charter under a board of trustees. The junior school closed in 1975 and the senior campus expanded its curriculum to accommodate grades six through twelve.

See James R. Welch, *The History of Education of Bourbon County* (Lexington, Ky., 1933); Walter E. Langsam and William G. Johnson, *Historic Architecture of Bourbon County, Kentucky* (Paris, Ky., 1985).

MILL SPRINGS, BATTLE OF. The Union victory in the Battle of Mill Springs in 1862 was the first in a series that destroyed the Confederate line of defense across southern Kentucky. In late November 1861 Confederate Brig. Gen. Felix Zollicoffer and 4,000 men traveled from Knoxville, Tennessee, through Cumberland Gap to Mill Springs, Kentucky, a small community on the southern bank of the Cumberland River. The area had an abundance of crops and forage and offered a strong defensive position, on the bluffs high above the Cumberland. Within two weeks, however, Zollicoffer divided his forces, placing some of his men north of the river at Beech Grove, presumably to threaten Union forces in central Kentucky. This strategy was opposed by Maj. Gen. George Crittenden, who arrived at Beech Grove on January 3, 1862, to assume command of the operation, though Zollicoffer remained with the troops.

The opportunity to strike a divided Confederate force was a great temptation, and by mid-January 4,000 Union troops under Brig. Gen. George Thomas were encamped at Logan's Cross Roads, ten miles north of Beech Grove. Crittenden, incorrectly assuming that his men could not withdraw across the river to Mill Springs, ordered an advance early on January 19. A constant rain and muddy roads prevented the Confederates from preparing for attack before dawn, but they had the best of the early fighting. Their repeated attempts to breach the loosely constructed Union lines failed, however. Rain and fog limited the visibility, and during the battle Zollicoffer mistakenly rode into the enemy lines and was killed.

News of Zollicoffer's death circulated quickly through the Southern ranks, and Crittenden tried to rally his stunned men. But Thomas ordered a timely bayonet charge, spreading confusion and panic among the Confederates, who fell back to Beech Grove, arriving late in the afternoon. Believing the Confederates were trapped by the river, Thomas did not press the advantage of victory. The Confederates escaped capture by crossing the Cumberland at night.

Union casualties were given as 39 killed and 207 wounded. The Confederates suffered 125 killed, 309 wounded, and 99 missing.

See Lowell H. Harrison, "Mill Springs, the Brilliant Victory," *Civil War Times Illustrated* 10 (Jan. 1972): 4-9, 44-49; C. David Dalton, "Zollicoffer, Crittenden, and the Mill Springs Campaign: Some Persistent Questions," *FCHQ* 60 (Oct. 1986): 463-71.   C. DAVID DALTON

MINERAL RESOURCES. Kentucky has an abundance of mineral resources—coal, oil, natural gas, limestone, dolomite, sand, gravel, and clay. Bituminous COAL accounted for about 90 percent of the total value of minerals produced in the commonwealth in 1982. That year Kentucky also ranked second among the states in production of ball CLAY and fourth in production of lime.

In 1972 the General Assembly established the Department for Natural Resources and the Environment, pulling together various programs. The department focused on coordinating the monitoring of air, water, and land resources in Kentucky. It also

formed a citizens' panel, the Environmental Quality Commission, as an adviser.

Of all the mineral production in Kentucky, coal mining is responsible for more jobs and more tax revenue than any other industry. From 1973 through 1987, Kentucky led the nation in production of coal, most of it originating in the Appalachian region, where reserves are still ample. In 1990 Kentucky ranked second in coal production in the nation and fifth in the world market. Kentucky has produced more than 6.3 billion tons of coal since the middle 1850s, when coal became a significant component of the state's economy. Although resources are dwindling, advanced technology and effective management practices have maintained a high level of production and profits. According to the Kentucky Geological Survey, about 54 million tons of coal greater than 14 inches in thickness remain in the ground in eastern Kentucky and about 37 million tons remain in western Kentucky, but not all of this will be mineable. The Kentucky Geological Survey recently undertook a study to estimate the amount of coal resources available for mining and the obstacles that will limit mining in the future. The Coal Availability Project, done in cooperation with the U.S. Geological Survey, should provide valuable information about the future for coal production in Kentucky.

According to the Kentucky Department of Economic Development, Kentucky's Eastern Coal Field region produces low- and medium-sulfur bituminous coal used primarily by electric utilities, with lesser amounts used in coke and gas making and for other industrial uses and export. The Western Coal Field produces mainly high-sulfur coal consumed by the electric utility industry, with lesser amounts employed in coke production, industrial uses, and export. Underground mining methods have accounted for about two-thirds of the total production in Kentucky, and surface mining for the remainder.

OIL AND GAS, next to coal the state's most important mineral resources, are found in eastern, central, and western Kentucky. Western Kentucky is the leading oil-producing region, with about 50 percent of the statewide total. Eastern Kentucky ranks second in oil production and first in natural gas production, with minor amounts produced in Kentucky's central region. In 1990 Kentucky ranked twenty-first in the nation in oil production and eighteenth in gas production.

The state's most important industrial mineral in tonnage and value is crushed stone, produced in sixty-seven of Kentucky's 120 counties. (See also BUILDING STONE.) Since 1960 demand for Kentucky's crushed stone has almost tripled because of increased development in the state and the construction of federally funded interstate highways as well as state-funded parkways and toll roads. Limestone is by far the most abundant of the stones quarried. Although Kentucky has many limestone deposits, not all formations meet today's specifications for commercial use. Limestone, lime, and dolomite are currently being used by utilities and industrial plants to remove sulfur dioxide from their stacks to meet federal Clean Air laws. Industrial use of the state's high-calcium limestone resources, mainly deposits in western and north-central Kentucky, has increased in recent years.

The second most important mineral construction material in Kentucky is sand and gravel. In 1990 at least two-thirds of Kentucky's annual output came either from floating dredge operations in the Ohio River channel or from glacial outwash along the river valley. Most of this production was used by communities bordering the Ohio River.

More than three-fourths of the FLUORSPAR produced in the United States has come from the Illinois-Kentucky fluorspar district. In 1979 the production of fluorspar ceased in Kentucky for the first time in a century but resumed on a small scale in the late 1980s. The loss of production is due to several factors, including increased import of foreign ore and changes in the steel and aluminum industries.

CLAYS occur widely in Kentucky and are used for the manufacture of brick, tile, stoneware, ceramics, and refractories. Kentucky is second in the nation in the production of ball clay, which is mined in the Purchase region and used for whiteware and ceramics. IRON furnaces in Kentucky were among the first iron producers west of the Alleghenies, but the industry died in Kentucky with the discovery of iron ores in the Lake Superior region.

See Kentucky Department of Economic Development, "Energy and Natural Resources in Kentucky," 1984; Kentucky Department for Environmental Protection, "Land, Air and Water," Fall, 1989.

JACKIE SWIGART

MINERS' SAFETY AND HEALTH. Coal mining was somewhat more than a century old when Pennsylvania enacted the first mine safety statute in 1869 to cover its anthracite mines. Kentucky in 1884 became the fourteenth state to follow suit; federal action did not begin until 1910.

Provisions of the earliest statutes were modest; the initial law in Kentucky focused on ventilation, drainage, roof support, and adequate exits. Kentucky's first inspector was a geologist, Charles Norwood, who was to serve under nine governors and may be considered the pioneer of mine safety in the commonwealth. Singularly indefatigable, conscientious, and outspoken in a courteous way, he lobbied unsuccessfully in 1880 for a bill opposed by many lawmakers from coal counties. When the 1884 law took effect, 4,500 Kentuckians were producing approximately 2 million tons of coal annually.

By 1914, when the legislature enacted a comprehensive mine safety and health measure, employment had risen to 25,000 and tonnage had soared to 20 million. Electrification had become a fact of work, and, with the greater degree of mechanization, mining generated great amounts of coal dust. Inadequate treatment of dust resulted in numerous explosions between 1895 and 1914. The 1914 act was probably precipitated by the largest disaster in Kentucky mining to that date, an explosion at Browder in Muhlenberg County that took thirty-four lives. It was the first mine safety act in Kentucky brought to passage by labor-management collaboration. The 1884 act totaled several printed pages; that of 1914 required more than forty.

When Norwood retired in 1920, the state had eight inspectors and the tonnage had almost doubled from that of 1914. The 1920s were the era of the most mine fatalities in the state's history. The Workers Compensation Act of 1916 was an incentive to safety though it was not specifically a safety measure. The next major change came with legislation that covered wagon and truck mines. Individual inspectors were given the power to shut down mines in 1952, educational and training requirements for working in mines were spelled out in 1972, and a 1976 law authorized the department to hire mine safety analysts to complement the work of inspectors.

In 1969, following a West Virginia disaster that took almost 380 lives, U.S. Rep. Carl Perkins piloted to passage the Coal Miners Health and Safety Act. Union contracts paid increasing attention to safety, and under certain conditions, miners could leave a situation they considered life-threatening. Increased efficiency and mechanization plus demands for expanded production often have preceded development of relevant safety technology.

HENRY MAYER

MINERS' UNIONS, EARLY. The earliest indications of labor organizational activity among Kentucky miners took place at Peach Orchard in Lawrence County around 1853-54. A strike occurred in Hancock County in 1855-56. Following Daniel Weaver's formation of the American Miners Association in 1861, his collaborator, John Hinchcliffe, published the *Weekly Miner* and mentioned having subscribers in both eastern and western Kentucky coal fields. Legislative annals reveal two collective actions, one by miners in eastern Kentucky about 1854 and the other by Union County miners in 1867, but it is not clear that in either case a union was formed. The size of operations in Union and the propinquity of its workforce to the scene of Weaver's activities around that time suggest that at least some of the miners in that county were or had been members of his first organization.

The earliest definite indication of organizing activity among miners is the 1873 legislature's enactment of a bill incorporating the Miners Union of Boyd and Carter County. John Siney's National Miners Association invited Kentucky miners to participate in its opening convention at Youngstown, Ohio, in October 1873. Around the same time, William Webb arrived at Pine Hill in Rockcastle County, then the largest mine in eastern Kentucky; the miners in Union County contributed to a fund for striking Indiana miners; the St. Bernard Coal Company had its first victory in frustrating attempted unionization; and John Siney himself accompanied Andrew Roy to inspect both Kentucky coal fields.

By 1878 the Knights of Labor were replacing Siney's organization as the miners' union in Kentucky. Webb and others reorganized the miners in Boyd, Carter, and Greenup counties in 1878-79, along with chartering a district assembly. In 1880 grand master workman Terence Powderly, president of the Knights, sent the miners at Spottsville in Henderson County a local assembly charter. The earliest known leaders of that era include Webb, Dan Wallace, W.H. Smith, William Fultz, Hamilton Risinger, and Sampson Platt. Union activities in western Kentucky were related to those in Indiana; activities in southeastern Kentucky and northeastern Tennessee were put together in what became known as subdistrict 9 of the Knights, now District 19 of the United Mine Workers of America.

The 1880s witnessed the most extensive unionization up to that time, with organization taking place in fifteen counties and Webb being named to the Knights' national honor roll in 1889 by Powderly. In late 1885 and early 1886, W.H. Smith and others gathered in St. Louis to form the National Trade Assembly 135, which became the Knights' national umbrella for miners' unions. The more significant achievements of that era include the complete organization of all the miners in Laurel County by mid-1883 under a common contract; the peaceable removal of convict labor from the eastern Kentucky coal fields in an unprecedented exhibition of union-citizen collaboration; the opening of miner cooperatives, notably at Powderly in western Kentucky; and the beginnings of semiannual wage conferences between miners and operators in the Laurel and Jellico coal fields. Kentucky also sent five of the 350 delegates, including Webb, to the January 25, 1890, convention, which brought into being the UNITED MINE WORKERS OF AMERICA. Webb was elected to positions of regional and national leadership.

See Andrew Roy, *History of the Coal Miners of the United States* (Columbus, Ohio, 1907); George McNeill, *The Labor Movement* (Boston 1887).

                                      HENRY MAYER

MINIMUM FOUNDATION PROGRAM. The Minimum Foundation Program was an educational reform measure enacted by the Kentucky General Assembly in 1954. Section 186 of the 1890 constitution required that all state educational funds be allocated to school districts strictly according to the number of school-age children living in each district. Many state officials and educators considered this system to be wasteful and unfair. Particularly harmful was the provision in section 186 that all state funds must be used for teachers' salaries; student services such as transportation, school maintenance, and textbook materials suffered for lack of funds. A 1941 amendment to the constitution allowed 10 percent of total education funds to be placed in an equalization fund for allocation to the needier districts. In 1949 the equalization fund was increased to 25 percent of the money available for education.

In 1952 Wendell BUTLER, the state superintendent of public instruction, initiated a campaign to amend section 186 of the constitution so that the legislature could distribute educational funds on any basis it deemed fair and efficient. Butler convinced the General Assembly to submit the amendment to a popular referendum, and the voters of the state approved the amendment on November 3, 1953. As a result the General Assembly established the Minimum Foundation Program in 1954. The program sought to equalize the public school system by distributing funds statewide according to need.

Two accounts were created to administer the program: a per capita account and an equalization fund. Each school district received money from the per capita account according to the number of pupils enrolled in school. Districts in need could qualify for extra funds from the equalization account.

The Minimum Foundation Program was superseded by the EDUCATION REFORM ACT of 1990.

See John E. Kleber, ed., *The Public Papers of Governor Lawrence W. Wetherby 1950-1955* (Lexington, Ky., 1983).

MINT JULEP. In 1792, the year Kentucky became a state, the average American (counting women and children) consumed two and a half gallons of spirits a year, much of it before breakfast. A "julap," taken upon arising, was considered a healthful way to combat fevers arising from night air and hot climates.

The word julap, or julep, originated in Arabic or Persian words meaning rosewater, and has transliterations in most western European languages. Its earliest English use (ca. 1400) described a nonalcoholic medicinal syrup, but by mid-eighteenth century a julep was a beverage made of spirits, and, in America, frequently containing mint. Nineteenth century juleps, consumed at any hour, often contained claret or Madeira rather than spirits, which were usually rye or brandy; impoverished postbellum southerners turned to bourbon whiskey, which has remained the ingredient of choice—at least in Kentucky—ever since.

Mint juleps are generally conceded to be made of bourbon whiskey, sugar, water, fresh mint, and crushed ice; whether the mint is to be crushed, the sugar and water to be boiled to a syrup or merely blended, and the bourbon to be stirred or quiescent are the subjects of controversies that rage annually. Ideally, mint juleps are served in frosted silver julep cups, with straws, garnished with sprigs of mint.

Florid verse and rapturous prose have been written about the mint julep, no longer a popular social drink but a tradition primarily associated with the Kentucky Derby. Requiring leisure in its preparation and contemplation in its degustation, it is a luxury in fast-paced modern life.

See Richard Barksdale Harwell, *The Mint Julep* (Charlottesville, Va., 1985).   MARTY GODBEY

MODREL'S STATION. To protect emigrant parties moving westward from attacks by Cherokee warring parties, Modrel's Station and three others—Langford's, Middleton's, and Daveisses's stations—were established as defense posts along the Wilderness Road, authorized by the Virginia General Assembly in a law enacted November 27, 1790. Modrel's station was located south of Crab Orchard and north of Cumberland Gap, at or near the Wilderness Road crossing of the Laurel River in present-day Laurel County, Kentucky. The station apparently existed only a year or so, until the Indian menace was ended. Robert Modrel, for whom the station was named, was later active in the laying out and settlement of Somerset, Kentucky, in 1801, and in 1806 he represented Pulaski County in the Kentucky House.

See Russell Dyche, *Laurel County, Kentucky* (London, Ky., 1954).   THOMAS D. CLARK

MOLONEY, RICHARD PATRICK. Richard Patrick Moloney, politician, was born on April 27, 1902, in Lexington, Kentucky, to Richard and Mary Catherine (Ready) Moloney. He received his early education at Lexington parochial schools and in 1918 left school to join the U.S. Navy. After his two-year enlistment, Moloney worked briefly in the merchant marine. In 1921 he entered the University of Kentucky and in 1924 passed the state pharmaceutical examination. Moloney worked as a pharmacist while attending law school in Lexington and became involved in politics as a Democrat. In 1934-35, he served as Fayette County probate commissioner. He was elected to the Kentucky Senate in 1944 and became a member of the three-person Senate Committee on Committees. Moloney left the Senate in 1956. Elected to Kentucky's House of Representatives in 1960, he served as House majority leader in 1962-63, after which he left office. Moloney influenced state politics both as an elected official and behind the scenes. His political influence was strongest during the administrations of Govs. Lawrence W. Wetherby (1950-55) and Bert T. Combs (1959-63). He was especially instrumental in the advancement of mental health programs and served as director of the Kentucky Association for Mental Health in 1954.

Moloney was married to Mary Cecilia Daugherty; they had Richard, Jr., and Mary. After his first wife's death, Moloney married Mildred Rabe on January 27, 1937; they had Rose and Michael. Moloney died on December 23, 1963, and was buried in Lexington's Calvary Cemetery.

See John E. Kleber, ed., *The Public Papers of Governor Lawrence W. Wetherby 1950-1955* (Lexington, Ky., 1983).

MONKEY'S EYEBROW. Monkey's Eyebrow is an elevation in northern Ballard County on the otherwise level floodplain of the Ohio River. A small community once existed there. At the turn of the century, John and Dodge Ray operated a general store and a blacksmith's shop at the base of this hill. WPSD-TV of Paducah now uses the land for a 1,638-foot transmission tower. Robert Rennick says of the origin of the name: "The most plausible [explanation] refers to the crescent-shaped elevation called Beeler Hill behind Ray's store, the tall grass growing from which seemed to resemble in someone's imagination the eyebrow of a monkey." Monkey's Eyebrow plays a unique role in the affairs of the commonwealth, as the cartographic department uses it as a hallmark, and all official state maps include the location.

See Robert M. Rennick, *Kentucky Place Names* (Lexington, Ky., 1984).   JOHN E.L. ROBERTSON

MONROE, WILLIAM SMITH. William Smith ("Bill") Monroe, known as "the father of BLUE-GRASS MUSIC," was born September 13, 1911, near Rosine, Kentucky. He was the youngest of eight children born to James Buchanan and Malissa (Vandiver) Monroe. His Ohio County birthplace lies in western Kentucky, miles from the Bluegrass area and even farther from the eastern Kentucky mountains traditionally associated with bluegrass music.

Monroe came from a musical family. His mother sang and played the fiddle for local dances, his brother Birch played the fiddle, and his brother Charlie played the guitar. Bill Monroe, so the story goes, chose the mandolin so that he would have a better chance to perform with his brothers. After his parents died and his brothers left home for work in the factories of Detroit in 1921, Monroe lived with his uncle, Pendleton ("Pen") Vandiver, whom he credits with teaching him to play the mandolin. By the time Monroe left Rosine to join his brothers, he had already absorbed what would be the primary influences in bluegrass music: the timing of his fiddle-playing Uncle Pen, the high-pitched, emotional singing he had heard in the country churches and singing schools, the mandolin playing of Walter Taylor (Ohio County's "Mandolin King"), and—perhaps most important for the development of bluegrass music as opposed to mountain string band or western swing—the blues-style guitar playing of Arnold Shultz, a black who let Monroe play alongside him at dances. Monroe's distinctive chordal "chop" on the mandolin emphasized the second and fourth beat, which gave bluegrass its drive. In the early 1950s this style was first referred to as "bluegrass."

Bill and Charlie Monroe, working as the Monroe Brothers, performed on North Carolina radio shows beginning in 1927. It was in the Carolina mountains, not those of Kentucky, that Bill was influenced by mountain ballads and mountain-style string bands. In 1938 Charlie and Bill split up, Charlie forming the Kentucky Partners, and Bill the Blue Grass Boys. Bill Monroe and the Blue Grass Boys band, which later included Lester Flatt, Earl Scruggs, and Chubby Wise, joined Nashville's WSM radio in 1939. Monroe then moved to Goodletsville, Tennessee. During the 1940s Monroe combined baseball with bluegrass in traveling throughout the South. He made certain his backup performers could play baseball and often he could field two teams. At its peak the Monroe road show traveled in seven trucks and a stretched-out bus, carrying 1,000 folding seats and a 7,000-capacity tent, a generator-run light plant, a complete kitchen, and the baseball paraphernalia.

Although Monroe has recorded for over fifty years and sold more than 25 million records (under the RCA Victor label during 1936-41, Columbia 1941-49, and Decca/MCA 1950), he considers himself an in-person performer. His performances invariably include ballad-style tunes that he calls "true songs." Monroe is especially well known for his high-pitched, fast-moving renditions of "Blue Moon of Kentucky," "Molly and Tenbrook," "My Rose of Old Kentucky," and "Muleskinner Blues." He has performed in all the states except Alaska, as well as in Canada, Germany, Italy, Japan, and England. He was inducted into the Country Music Hall of Fame in 1970.

Bill and Caroline Monroe, his first wife, had two children, Melissa and James, before their divorce. His second marriage ended in separation.

See Neil V. Rosenberg, *Bluegrass, A History* (Urbana, Ill., 1985), and *Bill Monroe and his Blue Grass Boys: An Illustrated Discography* (Nashville, Tenn., 1974).   GAIL KING

MONROE COUNTY. Monroe County, the sixty-fifth county in order of formation, is located in south-central Kentucky along the Tennessee state line. It is bordered by Allen, Barren, Metcalfe and Cumberland counties and has an area of 331 square miles. In was formed on January 19, 1820, from portions of Barren and Cumberland counties, and named in honor of James Monroe of Virginia, who was then president of the United States. The county seat of Monroe County is TOMPKINSVILLE, named in honor of James Monroe's vice-president, Daniel Tompkins of New York.

The topography of Monroe County is varied. Level and extremely fertile lands near the Cumberland River extend to undulating and then to very hilly lands in the central portion of the county. The fertile river bottomlands produce an abundance of grain crops. The more rolling lands are devoted to pasture and woods. Approximately half of the county is forested by a variety of second-and third-growth timber consisting of oak, yellow poplar, black walnut, ash, hickory, beech, cedar, and some pine. The major water source is the Cumberland River, which makes a large loop in the southeastern section of the county. The Big Barren River also courses through the county.

Before the first pioneers entered the area, prehistoric peoples hunted and lived near the streams and in the caves throughout the region. Numerous Native American artifacts document these camp and village sites. By the time of European settlement, however, the inhabitants had left the region.

Within the present borders of Monroe County, the first European settlers migrated in the late 1780s and early 1790s mainly from Virginia and North Carolina, with some from Pennsylvania and Maryland. These families settled along the banks of the Cumberland River and had spread throughout the area by the end of the eighteenth century. Among the earliest settlements in Monroe County were Watson's Store and Jim-Town (later Fountain Run). Watson's Store, located on the bluffs of Mill Creek, became Tompkinsville in 1819 and the county seat of Monroe County in 1820. Another prominent community is the town of Gamaliel, established about 1840.

The county was vulnerable to invasion from both Union and Confederate armies, and the war was devastating to its growth and development. The area had few Southern sympathizers in 1861, and fewer than 5 percent of the population owned slaves. Monroe County was strongly pro-Union. Shortly after the outbreak of hostilities, John M. Fraim established a Union recruiting station on his farm. The 9th Kentucky Infantry was recruited at Camp Anderson and was mustered into service at Columbia, Kentucky. In October 1861, Camp Anderson was seized and destroyed by Confederate forces under the command of Col. S.S. Stanton. By the end of the war in 1865, 801 Monroe Countians had joined the Union army; about thirty men had officially joined the Confederacy.

Monroe County was invaded on several occasions by both sides. The Confederate Army, under Gen. Braxton Bragg, invaded Kentucky through Monroe County in 1862. Gen. John Hunt Morgan passed through the county on raids into the state. The most intense clash between Union and Confederate forces in Monroe County occurred on July 9, 1862, when a Confederate force, under the command of Maj. R.M. Gano, attacked the 9th Pennsylvania Cavalry, commanded by Maj. Thomas J. Jordan. In the ensuing battle, the Union force was turned back, but soon retook the area. On April 22, 1863, a Confederate force under the command of Col. Ollie Hamilton captured Tompkinsville and burned a portion of the town, including the courthouse. In the process, the early court records of Monroe County were destroyed.

During the Civil War, the county lost a great deal of its livestock. Crop production was severely limited, markets disrupted, and the county was subjected to a virtual reign of terror by bands of toughs who had been soldiers. Monroe County was so devastated by the Civil War that full economic recovery did not occur until the twentieth century.

After the Civil War, Monroe County became a bastion of the Republican Party. From 1868 until the 1980s, very few Democrats won county-wide office. Before the Civil War, Monroe County shunned the Republican party. For example, the county gave Republican candidate Abraham Lincoln only three votes out of 963 votes cast in the 1860 election and less than 25 percent of its vote in the 1864 election. Many Monroe Countians blamed the Democratic party for the destruction caused by the Civil War.

During the first decade of the twentieth century, a relatively obscure Monroe County family laid the foundations for one of the most successful political dynasties in Kentucky history. The Carter family of

Tompkinsville virtually controlled Monroe County politics for the next seventy years. Members of the family served in nearly every elective and appointive office in the county. Tim Lee CARTER, a Tompkinsville physician, was elected to the U.S. House of Representatives in the 1960s, but in the early 1980s the virtual monopoly of the Carter family in Monroe County politics came to an end with his death.

Throughout the county's history, tobacco has been the staple crop. During the nineteenth century, however, Monroe County experimented with such crops as cotton and rice. Industrial growth has been steady since the 1950s. There is no heavy industry in the county; several small to moderate-sized factories employ several hundred people.

The Baptist, Church of Christ, and Methodist denominations are the dominant faiths, but there are numerous other Protestant denominations and one Roman Catholic congregation in Monroe County. One of the oldest church buildings in Kentucky is the Old Mulkey Meeting House, built in the late eighteenth century by Baptists.

Several newspapers have served Monroe County. The county's first newspaper was established in Tompkinsville in 1885 by Bert Rogers. The *Enterprise* was published in the late 1880s, followed by the *Monroe County News* (later called the *Southern Recorder*). In 1903, John E. Leslie established the *Tompkinsville News*, which is still in operation. From 1974 to 1976 Monroe County was served by the *Monroe County Messenger*.

The population of Monroe County was 11,642 in 1970; 12,353 in 1980; and 11,401 in 1990.

See Lynwood Montell, *Monroe County History, 1820-1970* (Tompkinsville, Ky., 1970) and *The Saga of Coe Ridge* (Knoxville, Tenn., 1970).

RON D. BRYANT

MONTGOMERY COUNTY. Montgomery County, the twenty-second county in order of formation, was created on December 14, 1796. It is located east of Lexington in the outer Bluegrass region and is bounded by Clark, Bourbon, Bath, Menifee, and Powell counties. It has an area of 199 square miles. The county was named for Gen. Richard Montgomery, who was killed at the Revolutionary War battle of Quebec. Montgomery County once stretched to the Virginia border but with the formation of Floyd, Bath, Powell, and Menifee counties, it assumed its present size in 1869. The northern two-thirds of the county has the rolling landscape typical of the Outer Bluegrass; the southern portion is much more hilly, with the thin soils and more abundant forests of the foothills region.

The major town in the county is MT. STERLING, the county seat. Founded in 1792, the community has been the economic and social focal point of the county. During the nineteenth century a number of crossroads villages—such as Grassy Lick, Levee, and Spencer—also emerged to serve rural needs in an era of difficult transportation. Camargo and Jeffersonville (long known as Ticktown) became economic centers of the southern portion of the county and, in the twentieth century, grew to over 1,000 citizens.

During the pre-Civil War era the county developed a prosperous, slave-based economy with hemp, livestock, and wheat as staples. The population grew rapidly until the 1820s and then levelled off with out-migration to Missouri, Texas, and other western areas. During this period the county became the political center of a congressional district that included more backward mountain areas. Mt. Sterling lawyers represented the district in Congress for twenty-six of the thirty-two years, from 1817 to 1849.

With slaves making up 36 percent of the population, the county was deeply split by the Civil War. Located at the junction of routes from central Kentucky to the Big Sandy River Valley in the east, Mt. Sterling had considerable strategic importance. There were substantial clashes in 1862 and 1864 and smaller skirmishes as possession of the county seat changed hands several times. Considerable damage was done by guerrillas to business buildings, and Confederate cavalry burned the courthouse in 1863. The more isolated regions of the county were infested with outlaw bands of deserters and thieves. In October 1863, Jeffersonville was burned and a guerrilla leader killed. The war inflicted substantial crop losses and disrupted the slave-labor force.

After the war, many of the former slaves forsook the rural areas for the county seat and drained the agricultural economy of labor. Hemp production virtually ceased, with cattle becoming the focus of the economy until the commencement of the burley tobacco boom in the 1870s.

As railroads and better roads began to penetrate the mountain counties, Montgomery County's trade declined. Its economy became based on the local tobacco-livestock agricultural system. In the 1960s the combination of several new factories and the completion of I-64 led to rapid growth.

Notable residents of the community have included a number of congressmen in the 1800s, including Garrett DAVIS, Richard MENEFEE and Richard French, and several justices on the state court of appeals, among them B.J. Peters, James Hazelrigg, and E.C. O'Rear. Prominent military figures from the county included Gen. Samuel Williams, a veteran of the War of 1812; his son, Confederate Gen. John "Cerro Gordo" Williams; and Confederate Gen. John Bell Hood. Among notable religious leaders were John ("Raccoon") Smith and David Barrow.

The population of Montgomery County was 15,364 in 1970; 20,046 in 1980; and 19,561 in 1990.

See Richard Reid, *Historical Sketches of Montgomery County* (Lexington, Ky., 1926).

CARL B. BOYD, JR.

MONTICELLO. Monticello, the county seat of Wayne County in southeastern Kentucky, is located near the center of the county at the intersection of KY 90 and KY 92. The city is situated on Elk Creek, a tributary of Beaver Creek, which flows westward into Lake Cumberland.

Monticello was established as the county seat when Wayne County was formed in 1800. The city was incorporated in 1810. It was named for the home of Thomas Jefferson by Col. Micah Taul, the first Wayne County clerk, later U.S. congressman (1815-17) and colonel of Wayne County Volunteers in the War of 1812. The town was laid out by surveyor Joshua Jones, a Revolutionary War veteran, on thirteen acres owned by William Beard. Only four families resided in Monticello at the time. By 1810, the population had grown to twenty-seven people.

In the late 1800s, an oil boom in Wayne County temporarily created a great deal of business activity in Monticello. In 1905 an electric system was installed and in 1929 city water was made available. Tennessee Valley Authority power was made available to the city. The Wayne County Industrial Foundation, Inc., was created in 1964. Since the mid-1960s, several manufacturing plants have located in the city, including the Belden Corporation (wire and cable), Monticello Manufacturing Company (women's blouses), Gamble Brothers Inc. (wood products), and WPM Manufacturing Company, Inc. (jeans). By 1990 manufacturing led the economy in Monticello.

The population of the fourth-class city was 3,618 in 1970; 5,677 in 1980; and 5,357 in 1990.

GALE EDWARDS

MONUMENTS. The most famous monument in Kentucky may be the Abraham Lincoln Memorial, three miles south of Hodgenville on U.S. 31E in Larue County. Financed by contributions to the Lincoln Farm Association, the monument was designed by John Russell Pope, a noted New York architect, who designed the National Archives, the National Gallery of Art, and the Jefferson Memorial in Washington, D.C. The temple-shaped Lincoln monument is built of Connecticut pink granite and Tennessee marble. The building is fronted by fifty-six steps, one for each year in Lincoln's life. The interior contains the cabin where Lincoln is believed to have been born. President Theodore Roosevelt laid the cornerstone on February 12, 1909, the centenary of Lincoln's birth. The memorial was dedicated by President William Howard Taft on November 9, 1911. In September 1916, President Woodrow Wilson accepted the property as a gift to the federal government, making it a national historic site.

The Frankfort Cemetery, established in 1845, is the location of most of the major memorials in Kentucky. The central feature of the cemetery is the State Mound. The military monument, which dominates the State Mound, was the subject of a $15,000 appropriation by the Kentucky legislature on February 25, 1848. New York sculptor Robert E. Launitz designed and executed the square sixty-

two-foot white Italian marble column, where the goddess of war holds in her outstretched hands the wreaths of victory. Names of those who fell in the Indian, 1812, and Mexican wars are inscribed on the sides of the column. The monument was completed on June 25, 1850.

At the back of the State Mound in the Frankfort Cemetery is the monument to Richard Mentor Johnson, vice-president of the United States (1837-41). On March 15, 1851, the legislature appropriated $900 to pay for the monument, also Launitz-designed. One of the two carved panels depicts Johnson killing the noted Indian warrior Tecumseh at the Battle of the Thames; the other is a bust of Johnson. At the front of the State Mound is the Philip Norbourne Barbour monument, a small obelisk that honors the Kentucky native who died a major in the Mexican War, while leading a charge in Monterrey. The legislature voted to move Barbour's remains to Frankfort in 1847.

Monuments over the graves of Kentucky governors at the Frankfort Cemetery honor Charles Scott (1808-12), James Clark (1836-39), John J. Crittenden (1848-50), Robert P. Letcher (1840-44), William Owsley (1844-48), Charles S. Morehead (1855-59), John Adair (1820-24), Christopher Greenup (1804-8), and George Madison (1816). At other cemeteries state monuments honor Governors Isaac Shelby (1792-96, 1812-16), buried in the family graveyard near Shelby City in Lincoln County; John Breathitt (1832-34), Russellville Cemetery; Joseph Desha (1824-28), Georgetown Cemetery; John L. Helm (1867), Elizabethtown Cemetery; and Gabriel Slaughter (1816-20), Mercer County.

The Henry Clay Monument is the centerpiece of the Lexington Cemetery. Julius W. Adams won the design competition, and the 120-foot Corinthian column was built by John Haly of Frankfort, under the supervision of architect Thomas Lewinski. The whole is topped by a statue of Clay designed by Joel T. Hart. The legislature appropriated $10,000 for the monument, but most of the funds to build the $58,000 memorial were raised by private subscription from contributors across the United States. The cornerstone was laid on July 4, 1857, and the monument completed in the summer of 1861. During a thunderstorm on July 22, 1903, lightning or perhaps wind destroyed the head and shoulders of the statue, and on September 21, 1910, lightning damaged the right hand and leg. In each case the legislature appropriated $10,000 for repairs. By the early 1970s the statue had badly deteriorated. The money for restoration came from the Lexington-Fayette County government ($35,000), the State Parks Commission ($50,000), and the cemetery company ($2,000). The monument was rededicated on July 29, 1976.

The Daniel Boone Monument in the Frankfort Cemetery marks the grave where the remains of Daniel Boone and his wife, Rebecca, were reburied in 1845, twenty-five years after his death. The legislature in 1860 appropriated $2,000 to build the monument, and the remainder was raised by private subscription. The monument was built by Frankfort builder John Haly. The panels depicting events in Boone's life were made by the sculptor Launitz. The monument was restored in 1906-7, at a cost of $2,000, after souvenir hunters defaced the panels; a second restoration took place in the mid-1940s after a sycamore tree fell on the monument.

Two monuments in Frankfort honor the memory of William Goebel, the only state governor to be assassinated. Charles H. Niehaus, a New York sculptor, designed and executed both. The monument in the Frankfort Cemetery was paid for by private subscription collected by the Goebel Monument Commission. Known as "The Orator," the monument was dedicated on February 3, 1910. The legislature appropriated $20,000 for a monument at the capitol, dedicated on March 11, 1914. Originally located in a traffic circle in front of capitol, the monument was moved to the grounds of the old state capitol, where Goebel was assassinated.

A monument to Jefferson Davis is located at Fairview, Kentucky, his birthplace. The 351-foot-tall obelisk is one of the highest cast-concrete structures in the United States. Construction started in 1917, but work was stopped by a shortage of materials. The monument was finished in May 1924, at a cost of $200,000. The legislature provided $22,500 toward the cost, and subscriptions, mainly from Confederate veterans and the Daughters of the Confederacy, paid the rest.

WILLIAM B. SCOTT, JR.

MOONLIGHT SCHOOLS. Cora Wilson Stewart, an educator who led the crusade against illiteracy in Kentucky, started an experimental education program in 1911 to teach adults in Rowan County, Kentucky, to read and write. Since most people were employed during the day, classes were held at night—specifically on moonlit nights, when students could more easily find their way to the schools. The term "moonlight schools" differentiated this program from the urban night schools of the northern United States.

Stewart first recruited volunteer teachers who were willing to teach at night and to canvass their own school districts to attract adult students to the program. As a text, she established a newspaper, the *Rowan County Messenger*, which combined local news with lessons in mathematics, literature, and history. By learning to read the newspaper, adult students could avoid the embarrassment of using an elementary primer.

Although only 150 students were expected in the first session, 1,500 adults between the ages of eighteen and eighty-six enrolled on September 5, 1911. The first session lasted eight weeks and was held in Rowan County's fifty school buildings. By the second year, enrollment had grown to 1,600, of whom 350 persons learned to read and write. In 1912 Stewart directed a moonlight school institute in Morehead, Kentucky, where teachers discussed the task of attracting new students and methods of teaching illiterate adults. A home department was developed in 1912 to provide instruction at home to persons too old or sick to attend school. By 1913 moonlight schools had been opened in Boyle, Johnson, Garrard, Mercer, Carter, Martin, and Lawrence counties. Stewart's philosophy was to open schools wherever there were illiterate persons, including prisons and reformatories. Stewart's work led to the development in Kentucky of state-supported LITERACY PROGRAMS and served as a model for programs in other states.

See Cora Wilson Stewart, *Moonlight Schools* (New York 1922); Florence Estes, "Cora Wilson Stewart and the Moonlight Schools of Kentucky, 1911-1920: A Case Study in the Rhetorical Uses of Literacy," Ed.D. diss., University of Kentucky, 1988.

MOONSHINE. Emerging from the Whiskey Rebellion of 1791, when Kentucky distillers refused to pay the newly imposed federal excise tax, the moonshiner became a folk hero in escaping from revenue agents. Urban criminals exploited the illegal distiller during Prohibition and afterward the legal DISTILLING industry accused the moonshiner of being a criminal himself. Unable to withstand intense law enforcement efforts, the moonshiner after two hundred years gradually faded from the scene.

From 1817, when the second excise tax was lifted, until 1862, when the excise tax became a permanent fixture, the moonshiner was nothing more than an unlicensed distiller. Small distillers were something of a frontier cottage industry, accepted, for the most part, by the community. Refusal to pay the 1862 excise tax, however, made such distillers illegal. The moonshiner's exploits became the subject of mountain folk songs. The community often protected him from revenue agents.

In 1878 the federal government offered moonshiners a blanket pardon if they pledged to halt illegal distilling. They crowded into courthouses and signed the document, but continued to make their untaxed whiskey. In 1881 revenue agents seized 102 illegal stills in Kentucky and made 153 arrests. From 1895 to 1900, six revenue agents were wounded in battles with moonshiners. In 1914 seizures of illegal stills totaled 214. During World War I the moonshiner could easily make $300 a month, while revenue agents each year seized an average of a hundred stills and 20,000 gallons of distilled spirits, costing the moonshiner an estimated $231,500 in sales.

The prohibition years (1920-33) brought the Kentucky moonshiner out of his family operation into a world of greedy racketeers and crooked operators who profited from his distilling knowledge and left him with an image forever tainted. For the most part, the moonshiner prided himself on producing high-quality whiskey, since he counted on repeat customers from his community; the racketeers not only reaped most of the whiskey's profits but even used lethal ingredients to increase the volume. Al Capone bought whiskey from eastern Kentucky as well as Golden Pond whiskey from western Kentucky. Records of still seizures during Prohibition indicate the volume of moonshining activity in the state: An annual average of 675 stills were seized, 2,799 arrests made, 21,681 gallons of distilled spirits and 424,564 gallons of mash confiscated, and 217 vehicles seized.

When prohibition was repealed, the moonshiner's business declined from its peak. During World War II sugar was rationed, copper difficult to obtain, and the Selective Service succeeded where revenue agents had failed, by inducting the moonshiner into the armed services. After the war, the volume of moonshine increased but was far short of the production during prohibition. From 1945 to 1953, still seizures averaged 379 a year; arrests, 489; seized distilled spirits, 2,987 gallons; and confiscated property, $54,540. During 1960-69, an annual average of 316 stills were seized in Kentucky, while the national average was 6,290 per year.

In 1957 the federal government designed law enforcement procedures targeted at the illegal distiller and courts began to hand down harsher sentences. The price of legal whiskey became too competitive for the moonshiner's business to survive. The legal distilling industry in 1960 began a concentrated campaign to portray the moonshiner as a part of a $600 million tax fraud and informed the public of potentially lethal additives in such whiskey. From 1972 to 1979, moonshine seizures in the state averaged sixteen stills per year, while the national average was 1,845.

By 1984 seizures of illegal distilleries and arrests in the state were no longer listed on federal law enforcement charts. With the exception of a few isolated areas, moonshine whiskey has disappeared in Kentucky. The moonshiner is active in another line of work, however, according to law enforcement officials who charge his breed with growing marijuana. In 1986 the marijuana seized in Kentucky had a street sale value of $900 million. Making moonshine whiskey was hard work; it required a considerable investment, as well as wholesale and retail outlets. Plastic bags of marijuana are more easily concealed and transported than gallon jugs of moonshine. In 1989 an Organized Crime Drug Enforcement Task Force found the largest domestic marijuana production in Marion County, calling the operators the "Cornbread Mafia." The past practice of moonshining has no doubt created a favorable context for such a multimillion-dollar operation.

The Kentucky moonshiner had a long life, almost two hundred years. His pride was the estimated 700,000,000,000 gallons of moonshine that he and his fellow illegal distillers in the South produced.

BETTY B. ELLISON

MOORE, CHARLES CHILTON. Charles Chilton Moore, founder and editor of a liberal newspaper at the turn of the century, was born December 20, 1837, at his father's farm, Quaker Acre, eight miles outside Lexington, Kentucky, on Huffman Pike. Moore was the only son of the four children of Charles Chilton and Maryann (Stone) Moore, a daughter of the Rev. Barton Warren Stone, a founder of the Christian Church (Disciples of Christ). Moore attended Transylvania University and graduated from Bethany College in West Virginia in 1858. He was ordained a minister of the Christian Church in 1864 and traveled the mountains of eastern Kentucky as an itinerant preacher, then became pastor of the Versailles Christian Church.

Moore resigned his pastorate in Versailles, worked for a short time as a banker and a farmer, then turned to reporting for the *Lexington Observer and Reporter*, the *Lexington Press*, and the *Lexington Transcript*. In 1884 he began sporadic publication of his own paper, the BLUEGRASS BLADE. In 1890, after three false starts, the paper began weekly publication. In it Moore espoused women's suffrage, prohibition, an international league of nations, publication of scientific information about human sexuality, and agnosticism. He used the personal pronoun "I" instead of the editorial "we" when presenting his views and was accused of personal attacks in the paper.

The fiery nature of the *Bluegrass Blade* led to more than one physical attack on Moore, including an assassination attempt. In February 1899 in Cincinnati, Moore was convicted of sending obscene material through the mail and sentenced to two years' imprisonment in the Ohio penitentiary. His publisher, James Edward Hughes, was found innocent. While in prison Moore wrote his autobiography, *Behind the Bars; 31498* (1899). President William McKinley commuted his sentence to six months; he was released July 7, 1899, for good behavior. He returned to Quaker Acre and the *Bluegrass Blade*, which he toned down in character. Moore wrote *Tamam*, a mixture of autobiography and fiction that was not published until 1908, two years after his death. In 1903 he traveled to the Mediterranean and Middle East and wrote of his experiences in *Dog Fennel in the Orient* (1903).

Moore married Lucy G. Peake of Georgetown on February 14, 1867; they had four children: Charles, Leland, Brent, and Lucille. After a long illness, Moore died on February 7, 1906, and was buried in the Lexington Cemetery. According to news accounts, more than 1,000 people attended his funeral. Moore's epitaph is "Write me as one who loves his fellow man."

See Charles C. Moore, *Behind the Bars; 31498* (Lexington, Ky., 1899).

MORAN, CHARLES B. Charles B. Moran, college football coach and professional baseball umpire, was born in Nashville on February 22, 1879. He coached football at Texas A&M during 1908-13 (38-8-4) and at Carlisle Indian School in 1914-15, then went on to train the Praying Colonels of Centre College in Kentucky during 1917-23 (53-6-1).

"Uncle Charlie" was an inspiring coach, a strict disciplinarian, and an imaginative football strategist. He coached the Praying Colonels in their 1921 victory, 6-0, over Harvard University (see CENTRE-HARVARD). Moran left Centre in 1923 to coach football at Bucknell College in Pennsylvania, then at Catawba College in North Carolina until 1939. Moran, also a National League baseball umpire during 1917-39, officiated in four World Series, in 1927, 1929, 1933, and 1939. Moran considered Horse Cave, Kentucky, his home from 1904 until his death there on June 14, 1949. He was buried there.

See John Y. Brown, *Legend of the Praying Colonels* (Louisville 1970).   CHARLES R. LEE, JR.

MOREHEAD, CHARLES SLAUGHTER. Charles Slaughter Morehead, governor during 1855-59, was born in Nelson County, on July 7, 1802, the son of Charles and Margaret (Slaughter) Morehead. After graduating from Transylvania University he practiced law, first in Christian and then in Franklin County. Morehead married Amanda Leavy on July 10, 1823; after her death, he married her sister Margaret, on September 6, 1831, and fathered four children.

First elected to the Kentucky House in 1828 as a Whig, he was the state attorney general from 1830 to 1835. In 1834 Morehead and Mason Brown published the *Digest of the Statute Laws of Kentucky*. Morehead was again a state representative in 1838-42 and 1844; three times he was elected Speaker. In 1847 he won election to the U.S. House of Representatives, serving from March 4, 1847, to March 3, 1851, and in the 1850s he joined the American, or Know-Nothing, party. He was elected Kentucky's governor in 1855 over Democrat Beverly L. Clarke in a campaign that played upon antiforeign and anti-Catholic prejudices; the final vote was 69,816 to 65,413. In 1859, when his term ended, Morehead resumed his legal practice. In 1861 he favored a pro-Southern neutrality policy for the state. Critical of the Lincoln administration, Morehead was imprisoned for four months during the Civil War, then lived outside the country for the duration of the war. Upon his return he moved to his plantation near Greenville, Mississippi, where he died on December 21, 1868. He was buried in the Frankfort Cemetery.

Morehead's gubernatorial administration was active. In 1856 Transylvania University was reorganized as a state school that included a teachers' college, although the legislature terminated this promising arrangement two years later. The comprehensive geological survey undertaken earlier was completed, private investment in roads and railroads was encouraged, the Kentucky State Agricultural Society was chartered in 1856, a state fair was initiated to encourage improvements in agriculture, the penitentiary was enlarged and improved, and changes were made in the convict leasing system. Additionally, Morehead used his veto to curb the establishment of unnecessary banks. The economic panic of 1857 hindered progress during the latter part of his administration.

See Lowell H. Harrison, ed., *Kentucky's Governors 1792-1985* (Lexington, Ky., 1985).

LOWELL H. HARRISON

MOREHEAD, JAMES TURNER. James Turner Morehead was the first native-born Kentuckian to become governor (1834-36). Born on May 24, 1797, near Shepherdsville in Bullitt County, he was the son of Armistead and Lucy (Latham) Morehead. The family soon moved to Russellville, and James was educated there and at Transylvania University. After studying law with Judge H.P. Broadnax and John J. Crittenden, he was admitted to the bar in 1818 and opened an office in Bowling Green. On May 1, 1823, he married Susan A. Roberts, with whom he had two children. A supporter of the OLD COURT, Morehead was a member of the state House of Representatives, where he promoted internal improvements, during 1828-31. A National Republican, he was elected lieutenant governor in 1832 over Benjamin Taylor, although Democrat John Breathitt won the race for governor. He was sworn in as Kentucky's eleventh governor on February 22, 1834, the day after Breathitt's death. Denied his party's nomination for governor in 1836, Morehead left office on August 31, 1836, and served again in the state House in 1837-38. Appointed and then elected to the U.S. Senate, he served from February 20, 1841, to March 3, 1847. A staunch Henry Clay supporter, Morehead defended a federal bank bill and opposed the annexation of Texas, although he supported the Mexican War once it began. He practiced law in Covington until his death on December 28, 1854. He was buried in the Frankfort Cemetery.

Governors of his era had limited power, and Morehead was essentially a caretaker executive who had no definite program of his own. As ex officio president of the Kentucky Board of Internal Improvements, he helped formulate plans, most of which were blocked by the economic panic of 1837. Morehead provided little leadership for the cause of education, although the formation of the Kentucky Association of Professional Teachers (1833) and the Kentucky Common School Society (1834) indicated a growing interest in the topic across the state. The governor helped complete the transition of his party from National Republican to Whig; the great Whig convention in Frankfort on July 4, 1834, marked the change. He favored judicial reform without doing much about it, and he denounced abolitionism, a safe stand in a slaveholding state. Overall, Morehead did no more than an adequate job as governor.

See Willard Rouse Jillson, "Early Political Papers of Governor James Turner Morehead," *Register* 23 (January 1925): 36-61.

LOWELL H. HARRISON

MOREHEAD. Morehead, the county seat of Rowan County, is situated on Triplett Creek at U.S. 60 and KY 32, south of I-64. The town was named for Gov. James T. Morehead (1834-36) and established at the time of the creation of Rowan County in 1856, during the administration of Gov. Charles S. Morehead (1855-59). Richard Hawkins donated the land for the public square to the city. The town was incorporated on January 26, 1869.

The first settlers on Triplett Creek were probably Virginians who arrived to claim land granted in exchange for their military service during the Revolutionary War. An early trail through what would become Morehead provided access to the Little Sandy salt works at the site of Grayson.

During the Civil War, guerrilla bands terrified the citizenry of the small town. On November 10, 1863, they captured the town for a short time, and on March 21, 1864, they burned the courthouse. The courthouse built about 1865 burned in the 1890s. A third courthouse, of Victorian style, was built in 1899. It was replaced in 1981 by a modern structure. With the coming of the Elizabethtown, Lexington & Big Sandy Railroad (later the Chesapeake & Ohio and finally abandoned) in the early 1880s, Morehead grew rapidly. Virgin timber was hauled into the city, where sawmills, spoke factories, and stave mills operated at capacity. A variety of stores and other businesses were established. The Gault House hotel, built in 1887 by Judge and Mrs. James M. Carey, was a local landmark until it was torn down in 1919.

The workers who migrated to Morehead as a result of the boom-town economy had a disrupting effect on local politics. A shooting during the 1884 election sparked a feud that came to be known as the ROWAN COUNTY WAR. The feud ended in a gun battle in front of the Gault House and focused national attention on the town. William T. Withers, a former Confederate soldier from Lexington, felt that education was the only answer to the problem and contributed $500 to found the Morehead Normal School and Teacher's College, the predecessor of Morehead State University.

The lumber business helped Morehead to become the largest trading center between Ashland and Lexington. When timber was exhausted in the 1920s, clay mining became a major industry, and various clay products were shipped from the refractories and kilns in the county via the Morehead & North Fork Railroad (later abandoned) to the Chesapeake & Ohio Railroad connection at Morehead. In 1929 the old east-west road known as the Midland Trail was concreted through Morehead and made part of U.S. 60.

As the logging and extractive industries gradually slowed down in the area, Morehead's growth became more dependent upon Morehead State University. The college and the town grew rapidly during the presidency of Adron Doran, who oversaw the campus from 1954 to 1977. The growth of St. Claire's Medical Center as a regional hospital in the early 1960s and the completion of I-64 just north of the city in 1969 also helped the city to grow. Morehead's location in the Daniel Boone National Forest made it an attractive residential city as well as an educational center. In addition to the university and the medical center, local industries include a clothing factory and a ball bearing plant.

The population of the fourth-class city was 7,191 in 1970; 7,789 in 1980; and 8,357 in 1990.

MOREHEAD STATE UNIVERSITY. Morehead State University in Morehead, Rowan County, was founded as Morehead Normal School by Phoebe Button, of Midway Junior College, and her son Frank Button. The school, operated by the Kentucky Christian Missionary Society, was intended to have an educational, religious, and stabilizing influence on the county after the ROWAN COUNTY WAR, one of the state's bloodiest feuds.

The school opened on October 3, 1887. The first student was Anna Page, an orphan girl, who lived with the Buttons. After thirteen years, control of the school passed from the Kentucky Christian Missionary Convention to the Christian Women's Board of Missions. Following the death of Phoebe Button, her son Frank operated the school until 1911. He was followed by principals J.M. Robinson, Wesley Hatcher, and W.O. Lappin. The school closed in 1922, when only three persons received diplomas. In 1922 a state commission recommended that two state normal schools be established—one in eastern Kentucky and one in western Kentucky. In March 1922 Gov. Edwin Morrow (1919-23) appointed a commission to determine locations for the two new schools. The commission recommended Morehead and Murray.

On September 23, 1923, Morehead State Normal School (the mission of which was to train "white elementary school teachers" for the eastern section of Kentucky) registered its first students. Button became the first president. Eight faculty members were employed and seventy-three students were enrolled. Five buildings were built during Button's administration. In 1926 the name of the school was changed to the Morehead State Normal School and Teachers College. Button resigned the presidency in 1929 and was succeeded by John Howard Payne, a school superintendent from Maysville. Under Payne, the college became Morehead State Teachers College. During the Depression in the 1930s, the college grew from twenty-two faculty members and 256 students to a faculty of fifty-eight with 585 students and four new buildings were constructed. Payne left the presidency in 1935 and was succeeded by Harvey Babb. In 1940, William Vaughn became the school's fourth president.

After the United States entered World War II, enrollment dropped to 144 students in the fall of 1944. During the war six hundred U.S. Navy personnel were trained on the campus. William Jessie Baird was named the school's fifth president in 1946. The number of students grew to a record of 614 immediately after the war.

In December 1946 the Southern Association of Colleges and Secondary Schools removed Morehead from its list of accredited colleges, alleging political interference by the governor in the school's operation. Over 25 percent of the enrolled students immediately withdrew. A new board of regents was appointed to correct the alleged political problems identified by the accrediting body and the college was reaccredited in 1948. That year, the name of the school was changed to Morehead State College. By the end of the decade, enrollment equaled its previous record number. Following the death of Baird in 1951, Charles Spain became the sixth president of the college. After Spain's three-year term of office, the board of regents in 1954 appointed Adron DORAN as the seventh president. Doran served the institution for twenty-three years.

Between the mid-1950s and the mid-1960s enrollment grew tenfold. Numerous new buildings were erected, and the faculty increased to 160 members. In February 1966 the Kentucky General Assembly granted the college university status and the university was reorganized into five academic schools and a graduate division. The 1960s and the 1970s were characterized by further growth in student enrollment, development of diversified programs, building and renovation of the facilities, and increases in faculty and staff. The enrollment reached 7,829 during the 1970s.

Morris Norfleet was appointed as Morehead's eighth president in 1977. Morehead was given a mission statement by the Kentucky Council on Higher Education to "enhance the economic growth of Appalachian Kentucky." During Norfleet's seven-year presidency, both academic standards and private funding for the university rose.

In 1984 Herb Reinhard became the ninth president of Morehead. Reinhard instituted great changes in the academic structure and administrative organization of the university, arousing controversy that polarized the campus. The media focus upon the division was intense, and Gov. Martha Layne Collins (1983-87) asked for the resignation of the members of the board of regents. Seven regents were replaced and the new board did not renew Reinhard's contract. The board appointed A.D. ALBRIGHT as tenth president of the university. Albright's one-year term (1986-87) successfully rallied public opinion in favor of the institution; he often paid personal visits to educators and civic leaders in the twenty-two counties of the university's service region. Although enrollment had been projected to decline by 9 percent, it increased 3.5 percent during his tenure. Private gifts exceeded $1 million for the first time in the history of the institution.

In the fall of 1987, with the enrollment growing at an annual rate of 10 percent, the board of regents appointed C. Nelson Grote as Morehead State University's eleventh president. Grote, a dean in the Doran administration, had also served as president of Schoolcraft College in Michigan and as chief executive officer of the community colleges of Spokane, Washington. In the fall of 1989, the enrollment grew to 7,962 students.   JOHN R. DUNCAN

MORGAN, GARRETT AUGUSTUS. Garrett Augustus Morgan, black inventor, was born to Sidney and Elizabeth (Reed) Morgan on March 4, 1877, in Paris, Kentucky, the seventh of eleven children. After six years of education in the common schools of Kentucky, he went to Cincinnati to work as a handyman for a wealthy landowner. He moved to Cleveland in 1895 to work in a clothing factory, which he left in 1907 to open his own business. In 1914 Morgan received a patent for a "breathing device"—the gas mask used during World War I. This invention won a gold medal at the New York City meeting of the Second International Exposition of Sanitation and Safety in 1914. The city of Cleveland gave him a gold medal after the mask was used successfully to rescue men trapped in a tunnel of the Cleveland waterworks on July 25, 1916. On November 20, 1923, Morgan received a patent for the electric-light traffic signal with different colors for Stop, Caution, and Go.

Morgan developed glaucoma in 1943, which left him nearly blind for the remainder of his life. He was married twice: to Madge Nelson in 1896, and to Mary Anne Hasek in 1908. He died in Cleveland on July 27, 1963, and was buried there in Lake View Cemetery.

See Alice A. Dunnigan, *The Fascinating Story of Black Kentuckians: Their Heritage and Traditions* (Washington, D.C., 1982).

MORGAN, JOHN HUNT. John Hunt Morgan, Confederate guerrilla and regular officer, was born in Huntsville, Alabama, on June 1, 1825, the eldest son of Calvin and Henrietta (Hunt) Morgan. In 1831 the family moved to Lexington, Kentucky, and in 1842 he enrolled in Transylvania University. During his second year, in July 1844, he was suspended for dueling with a fellow student. In the Mexican War (1846-48), he served as a first lieutenant in the Kentucky Mounted Volunteers from June 9, 1846, to June 7, 1847, and fought in the Battle of Buena Vista on February 23, 1847. Back in Lexington, he became a respected manufacturer and captain of the Union Volunteer Fire Company. He was a Mason and served on the town council and school board. In 1852 he organized a state militia artillery company and was its captain until the state deactivated the militia in 1854. Three years later he organized the Lexington Rifles volunteer infantry company.

In the Civil War, Morgan supported Kentucky neutrality and joined the Confederacy only after the state declared itself for the Union. On September 20, 1861, he led the Lexington Rifles into Confederate lines on Green River, where he conducted guerrilla warfare for twenty-seven days. He formally enlisted in the Confederate army on October 27, 1861. As captain of a cavalry company he continued raiding behind enemy lines, achieving small victories that earned him promotion to colonel on April 4, 1862, and won him the tag "Francis Marion of the War." He was the primary model for the Confederacy's Partisan Ranger Act of April 21, 1862, which authorized the president to commission units of Partisan Rangers for detached guerrilla operations.

Having fought in the Battle of Shiloh on April 6-7, 1862, Morgan's men were organized as the 2d

Kentucky Cavalry, and Morgan began a series of raids from Tennessee into Kentucky. In addition to disrupting communications and causing other damage, he sought to inspire support for the Confederates. On the first Kentucky raid, July 4 to 28, 1862, the raiders marched from Knoxville to Cynthiana and circled back into Tennessee, having recruited three hundred volunteers. Abraham Lincoln was impelled to wire: "They are having a stampede in Kentucky. Please look to it!" Morgan's reports exaggerated southern sentiment in Kentucky and convinced the Confederate high command that an invasion would inspire a secessionist uprising.

On August 12, 1862, Morgan conducted the most strategic raid of his career, burning the twin Louisville & Nashville Railroad tunnels north of Gallatin, Tennessee. The damage disrupted the main artery of supply for the Army of the Ohio, and Gen. Don Carlos Buell suspended the Union advance on Chattanooga for ninety-eight days. The raid gave Gen. Braxton Bragg the initiative to move into Kentucky. Morgan participated in the Confederate invasion of Kentucky during September and October of 1862. At Hartsville, Tennessee, on December 7, 1862, Morgan's force captured 1,834 Union troops. Six days later he was promoted to brigadier general. In the long term, Morgan's greatest strategic role was diverting Union forces from the battlelines. By the time of the Christmas Raid, December 22, 1862 to January 1, 1863, he and other cavalrymen had forced the Union to deploy 20,357 men in the rear in the West. With fewer than 4,000 men on the Christmas Raid, he diverted 7,300 soldiers from Gen. William S. Rosecrans's army at the Battle of Stone River.

Early in 1863 Morgan suffered a series of defeats and decided to restore morale with a raid across the Ohio, which came to be called in the Morgan legend the Great Raid (July 1-26, 1863). The division crossed the Ohio River (without the permission or knowledge of Morgan's superiors) at Brandenburg and advanced through Indiana and Ohio, living on the land. At Buffington Island the Union cavalry in pursuit captured several hundred of the command. Morgan and most of the men fled, and he was captured a week later near West Point, Ohio. In spite of the losses, the raid restored his status as a hero in the South. On November 27, 1863, he escaped from the Ohio State Penitentiary in Columbus. Although Confederate authorities were not pleased with Morgan's freewheeling, he was restored to command. He requested assignment to southwestern Virginia, and from there he launched the last Kentucky raid in June 1864. On June 12, 1864, a Union force attacked at Cynthiana and drove Morgan's men from the state in retreat.

On June 22, 1864, Morgan was appointed commander of the Department of Western Virginia and East Tennessee. On August 22 he was relieved of the departmental command, and on August 30 suspended from command of his men. A court of inquiry was scheduled for September 10 to consider reports of robbery and looting by some of Morgan's men on the last Kentucky raid.

On September 4, 1864, he was surprised in Greeneville, Tennessee, and killed attempting to escape. He was buried first in Richmond, Virginia, then in the Lexington Cemetery on April 17, 1868.

Morgan married Rebecca Bruce on November 21, 1848. In 1853 she had a stillborn son and was an invalid until her death on July 21, 1861. Morgan's second wife was Martha Ready, of Murfreesboro, Tennessee; their daughter, Johnnie, was born after Morgan died. The equestrian statue unveiled in Lexington in 1911 exemplifies his appeal as a symbol of the Confederate cause.

See James A. Ramage, *Rebel Raider: The Life of General John Hunt Morgan* (Lexington, Ky., 1986); Basil W. Duke, *History of Morgan's Cavalry* (Cincinnati 1867).   JAMES A. RAMAGE

MORGAN, LOUIS. Louis Morgan, self-taught portrait painter, was born in Westmoreland County, Pennsylvania, on November 21, 1814. His parentage is unknown. When Morgan was fifteen or sixteen, his family moved to Pittsburgh, where he began work as an apprentice to a chair painter in a cabinet shop. By early 1835 Morgan had a painting studio on St. Clair Street in Frankfort, Kentucky, which he advertised in the January 2 edition of the *Frankfort Commentator*. Simon Kenton in the last years of his life sat for a portrait by Morgan, which was exhibited at the Pennsylvania Academy and later sold to the Ohio State Museum in Columbus. In the winter of 1838 or 1839 Morgan had a studio on Market Street in Louisville, where he painted portraits of the Joyes and Bullock families and of Sidney S. Lyon, a fellow artist.

From 1848 to 1850 Morgan lived at Winton, the home of Dr. Robert PETER in Fayette County, where he painted portraits of the physician-chemist and his family and of Maj. William Smith Dallam and his wife. An unfortunate infatuation with one of the daughters of the Winton household caused Morgan to move to Montgomery County, Tennessee, the home of his brother, John L. Morgan, where the artist died in 1852. Other portraits of Kentuckians attributed to Morgan but unsigned include those of Bardstown architect Col. James Marshall Browne, the family of David Castleman of Frankfort, the Rev. William L. Breckinridge, and Orlando Brown, noted Frankfort editor.

See Edna T. Whitley, *Kentucky Ante-Bellum Portraiture* (Paris, Ky., 1956); Samuel Woodson Price, *The Old Masters of the Bluegrass* (Louisville 1902).

MORGAN, THOMAS HUNT. Thomas Hunt Morgan, born on September 25, 1866, in Lexington, Kentucky, influenced more than any other the direction of biological science in this country. Internationally, he ranks as the most important contributor to the knowledge of genetics following Gregor Mendel. Thomas was the first of three children of Charlton Hunt and Ellen Key (Howard) Morgan. Morgan's distinguished family included his great-grandfather, Francis Scott Key, who wrote the "Star-Spangled Banner"; a governor of Maryland; his uncle, Confederate Gen. John Hunt Morgan; and the renowned financier J. Pierpont Morgan. His father had been the American consul to Messina, Sicily.

Morgan was educated in the preparatory school of the State College (University of Kentucky) and in 1882 enrolled in the college proper. An outstanding student, he graduated at the top of his class in 1886 with a B.S. in zoology. Two years later, with his M.S. completed, Morgan went to Johns Hopkins University, where in 1890 he earned a Ph.D. He began teaching at Bryn Mawr College in 1891, then moved to Columbia University as professor in 1904. In 1928 Morgan became director of the new Kerckhoff Laboratories of Biological Science at the California Institute of Technology. He spent the rest of his professional life at Cal Tech, where he devoted much of his energy to fostering research and graduate programs in biology. That department was a forerunner in the integration of biology and chemistry.

Around 1900 Morgan began exploring the mechanisms of heredity, testing experimentally some of the findings of Mendel and Darwin. By 1908 he was raising fruit flies (*Drosophila melanogaster*), which proved to be ideal subjects for studying the role of mutations in heredity. Early in 1910 Morgan concluded that the eye-color gene is located on one of the so-called sex chromosomes, thus establishing the chromosomal theory of inheritance. The discovery that the genes are on the chromosomes of all organisms was a major advance in understanding the physical basis of heredity and led to many other advances.

In 1933 Morgan became the first American nonphysician to win the Nobel prize in physiology or medicine. His numerous other awards and honors included election to the National Academy of Sciences; the presidency of the American Association for the Advancement of Science and several other societies; and the Darwin and Copley medals from England's Royal Society. He characteristically attributed much of the credit for most honors to those with whom he worked. Morgan was active in research until his death. In 1904 Morgan married Lilian Vaughn Sampson; they had four children— Howard Key, Edith Sampson, Lilian Vaughn, and Isabel Merrick. Morgan died in Pasadena, California, on December 4, 1945, and was buried there.

At the University of Kentucky, both the School of Biological Sciences and the building in which it is housed are named after Morgan. The Blue Grass Trust for Historic Preservation lists as a historical site the house on North Broadway where he grew up.

See Garland E. Allen, *Thomas Hunt Morgan* (Princeton, N.J., 1978); Ian Shine and Sylvia Wrobel, *Thomas Hunt Morgan, Pioneer of Genetics* (Lexington, Ky., 1976).

MORGAN COUNTY. Morgan County, the seventy-third in order of formation, is located in east-central Kentucky. Covering 382 square miles, it is bounded by Rowan, Elliott, Menifee, Wolfe, Magoffin, Johnson, and Lawrence counties. It was created from Bath and Floyd counties in 1822, and during 1843-69 parts of Morgan County were used to form six of the surrounding counties. The county was named for Gen. Daniel Morgan, a veteran of the Revolutionary War, and WEST LIBERTY was established as the county seat in 1824.

The county's major waterway is the Licking River, and Cave Run Lake forms a portion of its northwest boundary. The northwest corner of the county is also a part of the Daniel Boone National Forest. The major highways are KY 7, U.S. 460, and the Mountain Parkway. Morgan County's principal towns are West Liberty and the farming villages of Ezel, Wrigley, Cannel City, and Crockett. Cattle and burley tobacco are the main agricultural pursuits and timber production is a major industry. Because of its fertile valleys, Morgan has long been called "the Bluegrass county of the mountains." Morgan County also has one newspaper, *The Licking Valley Courier*, published weekly.

As early as 1787, when it was still part of Virginia, surveying parties saw the wilderness area that later became Morgan County. Settlement in the mountainous eastern region of the state lagged behind that in central Kentucky, but by 1800 the area had some population. Pioneers were drawn there by cheap but fertile land, forested with virgin timber and teeming with game. Among the earliest settlers were Daniel Williams, who, tradition says, came to Kentucky from North Carolina with Daniel Boone in the 1770s and was a veteran of the Battle of Blue Licks; Thomas Lewis, who had served with Gen. George Rogers Clark in Kentucky; Gardner (or Garner) Hopkins, a Revolutionary War veteran from New York; and others, including Thomas Caskey, who had married Hopkins's daughter Lydia.

In 1822 residents of the area, which by then was part of Floyd and Bath counties, sought to form a new county and an act for that purpose was approved by the General Assembly on December 7. The following year, on March 10, twelve justices of the peace met at Edmund Wells's tavern on the Licking River and presented their commissions signed by Gov. John Adair (1820-24). In addition to Wells, they were William Biddle, Joseph Carroll, John Hammans, Fielding Hanks (brother of Abraham Lincoln's mother), William Lewis, Isaac Lykins, Thomas Nickell, John S. Oakley, Holloway Power, John Williams (son of Daniel), and Mason Williams. At this first court, the county was divided into seven districts, and officials were installed, including sheriff James Kash, clerk James G. Hazelrigg, jailor Edmund Vest, tax commissioner Francis Lewis, and commonwealth's attorney William Triplett. Chosen by the next term were coroner Sanders Montgomery and county surveyor Peter Amyx. In 1823 the General Assembly established the county seat, a town to be called West Liberty and created from land provided by Edmund Wells. Wells, a millwright, was subsequently awarded the contracts to erect the civic buildings. These consisted of a log jail, completed in 1825, and a two-story frame courthouse that was finished in 1828.

A second courthouse was among some twenty-nine buildings destroyed by fire during the Civil War, along with the offices of the circuit and county clerks, and many irreplaceable county records. Although some influential families were pro-Union during the war, most Morgan County residents had Confederate sympathies. Confederate leaders from Morgan included Capt. John T. Williams and Maj. William Mynheir (who, as sheriff in 1853, carried out the county's only hanging). Although no major battles occurred in the county, there were a few skirmishes, including three at West Liberty and one at McClannahan Hill.

At the beginning of the twentieth century, railroads entered the county, drawn by the rich resources of timber and cannel coal. The Morehead & North Fork Railroad (abandoned in the 1920s) extended to Blairs Mills, Wrigley, Redwine, and Lenox, and the Ohio & Kentucky Railroad (abandoned in 1933) ran through Adele, Cannel City, Caney, Stacy Fork, Malone, Index, Liberty Road, and Licking River.

By 1930, Morgan's common-school system— which had seen forty school districts established by 1850—reached a peak of ninety-two districts, with as many schools. Subsequently, consolidated school centers replaced the one- and two-room rural schools. The last one, at Peddler Gap, was destroyed by fire in 1967. A county high school was created at West Liberty in 1910 and a new stone building, built by the Works Progress Administration, was dedicated in 1937 by Eleanor Roosevelt. Later came a separate elementary school (1957), a new high school (1974), and a modern middle school building (1989). In 1990 plans were under way to restore the old WPA building to house county offices. The population of the rural county was 10,019 in 1970; 12,103 in 1980; and 11,648 in 1990.

See Arthur C. Johnson, *Early Morgan County* (West Liberty, Ky., 1974); Helen Price Stacy and William Lynn Nickell, *Selections from Morgan County History* (West Liberty, Ky., 1973); Joe Nickell, *Morgan County: The Earliest Years* (West Liberty, Ky., 1986).   JOE NICKELL

MORGANFIELD. The county seat of Union County, Morganfield is located on U.S. 60 and KY 56. The town was established on January 6, 1812, on land that Presley O'Bannon acquired from the heirs of Gen. Daniel Morgan, a Revolutionary War officer. The town was built around Morgan Springs, the major water source for early residents. On March 16, 1870, Morganfield was incorporated by act of the General Assembly. The Morganfield & Atlanta Railroad (later Louisville & Nashville) was built in the late nineteenth century, and passenger and freight trains passed through the town several times a day.

The first courthouse for Union County was erected in Morganfield in 1811-12, the second in 1819-20, and the third in 1871-72. A fire in the spring of 1910 that began in a department store and rapidly spread to surrounding buildings destroyed nearly an entire city block, including the opera house, the masonic hall, and Baptist church and parsonage.

The town's industries in 1989 were Sheller-Globe, manufacturer of automotive trim and lamps; Rayloc, maker of auto parts; and Western Kentucky Rubber Company, producer of auto ball joint seals.

The population of Morganfield, a fourth-class city, was 3,563 in 1970; 3,781 in 1980; and 3,776 in 1990.   RON D. BRYANT

MORGANTOWN. Morgantown, the county seat of Butler County in western Kentucky, is located on U.S. 231 in the center of the county two miles northeast of the Green River Parkway and on the south bank of the Green River. The city was chosen as the county seat by eleven justices of the peace commissioned by Gov. Charles Scott (1808-12). In June 1811 they authorized the building of a brick courthouse there. The building faced Butler Street. The three other streets that bounded the courthouse square were named Ohio, Warren, and Logan, for three of the surrounding counties. The courthouse, which doubled as a house of worship, burned in 1872; all county records were saved. It was replaced in 1873 by a brick structure of Italianate design, which was replaced by a third courthouse, a colonial-style building, in 1975.

The city at one time may have been known as Funkhouser Hill after Christopher Funkhouser, who donated part of his land to be used for the proposed county seat in 1810. Funkhouser may have named the town, possibly after a hunter named Morgan, or for the first child born there, Daniel Morgan Smith, on December 14, 1811.

Morgantown grew slowly and by 1830 had seventy-six inhabitants. The Green River was a lifeline to the city, and citizens received their mail and goods by packet boats, which were common on the river. Although Morgantown was a port city, it was not such a thriving river center as Rochester, downstream, or Woodbury, upstream. After the Civil War Morgantown emerged as a center of culture as well as the seat of county government. Sometime prior to 1885 a normal school and seminary for the training of teachers was established.

William Sylvester TAYLOR, elected Butler County judge in 1886, was born near Morgantown on October 10, 1853. In December 1899 he was elected governor of Kentucky but was removed from office in January 1900 by the General Assembly, which awarded the election to William Goebel. Goebel died from an assassin's bullet days afterward.

By 1900 Morgantown had a population of 587 and had surpassed Rochester as the largest town in the county. In 1917 the Green River froze over and for two months Morgantown was unable to get supplies. Perhaps as a result of this, the 1920s was a decade of road building, with the first hard-surface road built in 1926. In 1930 the road from Morgantown to Bowling Green was built and provided an important economic connection. Since there were no railroads, packet boats continued to transport passengers and freight to and from Morgantown, but increased competition from roads began to take a toll on the river traffic in the 1930s.

Downtown Morgantown was the victim of a major fire that in 1946 destroyed five businesses and another in 1971 that destroyed nine businesses and severely damaged six others. Local citizens formed a development corporation and built a shopping center to replace buildings lost in the 1971 fire.

A municipal park, developed in the 1970s, provides recreational facilities for the citizens of Morgantown and Butler County. The park is the site of the Green River Catfish Festival, held annually during the week of July 4.

Seven manufacturing firms have moved to Morgantown since 1953: Kane Industries, Kellwood Company, Morgantown Manufacturing Company, Morgantown Plastics Company, Sumitomo Electric Wiring Systems, Inc., American Rubber Products Corporation, and IMCO Recycling Inc.

The population of the fifth-class city was 1,394 in 1970; 2,000 in 1980; and 2,284 in 1990.

LOIS RUSS

MORMONISM. The Church of Jesus Christ of Latter-Day Saints, or Mormon denomination, began proselytizing in Kentucky in 1834. Levi Hancock and Wilford Woodruff established the first congregation in Kentucky in Calloway County, and Woodruff became church president in 1889. About a year and a half later, the church members migrated to far-west Missouri. One member of the group, Charles C. Rich, later became a member of the Quorum of the Twelve Apostles, one of the most responsible positions in the church administrative hierarchy. In the following years, many western Kentuckians embraced the new faith, but most moved west with the main body of the denomination.

The aftermath of the Civil War, family feuding, actions of the Ku Klux Klan, and other acts of lawlessness kept Mormon missionaries out of the state. It was not until the 1880s that missionaries again tried to organize branches of the church in central and western Kentucky. However, most Mormon converts found themselves targets of persecution, falsehoods, and physical attacks, mainly because of the Mormon practice of polygamy. Many fled west to the relative security of the Mormons' main body.

In the 1890s numerous branches of the church were established among local converts. The Mormons founded the Sulphur Wells branch in Metcalfe County on August 8, 1897. Ison Creek branch, the first in eastern Kentucky, was organized in Elliott County on September 20, 1896, with elder Richmond Ison as president. After flourishing for several years, the branch dispersed when persecution intensified and most of the members fled to Arizona in the early 1900s. During the late 1890s fourteen branches were organized in eastern Kentucky and most built chapels, but virtually all were destroyed by fire in mob violence. Persecution of the Mormons in Kentucky continued into the first half of the twentieth century.

It was not until 1902, when a branch was organized at Owingsville in Bath County with elder John W. Shrout, a prosperous farmer, as president, that the Church of Jesus Christ of Latter-Day Saints finally gained a permanent home in Kentucky. Over the next twenty years Owingsville became the largest congregation in the southern region, and Owingsville also established additional branches in the state.

In 1990, the church in Kentucky was organized into three stakes, bodies similar to Roman Catholic dioceses, totaling forty-four local organizations with a total membership of about 16,000.

See Daniel Rolph, *Kentuckians and Mormonism: An Overview* (Lexington, Ky., 1985).

DONALD R. CURTIS AND ROBERT A. BYLUND

MORRIS, HORACE. Horace Morris, civic leader and newspaper editor, was born a freedman in Louisville in the first half of the 1800s. He received his education in Ohio, where he was active in the underground railroad, helping slaves escape to the freedom of Canada. Returning to Louisville after the Civil War, he quickly demonstrated leadership. Basically conservative, Morris urged blacks to seek civil and political rights, but he moderated demands for political and social equality with the idea that blacks must earn the rights. An excellent speaker, he impressed whites as "responsible" with his go-slow approach to equality, and was highly visible on both Republican party committees and local black advisory boards.

During the 1870s Morris edited the *Kentuckian* in the 1880s the *Bulletin*, both highly political newspapers with moderate black views, and he was particularly adept in getting patronage from Republican administrations. The only black cashier in the Louisville Freedman's Savings and Trust Bank, he was appointed to the Treasury Department in 1881 and was the first black to serve as steward at Louisville's Marine Hospital. His attempts to acquire elective office failed. An early advocate of public support for black education, he provided leadership at postwar educational conventions and was a member of the black-created State Educational Board. In 1873 city officials appointed Morris to the board of visitors for Louisville's black schools. As secretary of that board, he played a prominent role in Louisville's black public schools for years. The date of his death, like that of his birth, is unknown.

See George C. Wright, *Life Behind a Veil: Blacks in Louisville, Kentucky 1865-1930* (Baton Rouge, La., 1985). MARION B. LUCAS

MORROW, EDWIN PORCH. Edwin Porch Morrow, governor during 1919-23, was born at Somerset, Kentucky, to Thomas Zanzinger and Catherine

Virginia (Bradley) Morrow on November 28, 1877. His father, a founder of the Republican party in Kentucky, had been an unsuccessful candidate for governor in 1883 and Gov. William O. Bradley (1895-99) was his mother's brother. Morrow was educated at St. Mary's College near Lebanon, Cumberland College in Williamsburg, and the law school of the University of Cincinnati, where he graduated in 1902 after noncombat service in the Spanish-American War. Soon after opening a law practice in Lexington, Kentucky, he won acquittal for a black man accused of murder.

Morrow moved to Somerset in 1903 and married Katherine H. Waddle; they had two children. He was Somerset city attorney (1904-08), and the U.S. district attorney for eastern Kentucky (1910-13). As Republican candidate for the U.S. Senate, he lost to Ollie M. James in 1912. Morrow refused to run for governor in 1911 but became the party's candidate in 1915. He and his friend (and opponent) A.O. Stanley gave the state a spectacular campaign, although both men ran on progressive platforms. Morrow lost by only 471 votes (219,991 to 219,520) but refused to contest the result. Four years later he was nominated by acclamation at the Republican convention. The Democratic candidate was Gov. James D. Black (1919), who had served the last months of A. O. Stanley's term (1915-19) when Stanley resigned to go to the U.S. Senate.

Morrow again ran on a progressive platform, attacking the alleged corruption and mismanagement of the Stanley-Black administration. He gave strong support to the women's suffrage amendment and milder support to the prohibition amendment, and he promised to clean house and to make better appointments. Just before the election the Republicans revealed an excessive cloth contract that the Board of Control had given to a nonexistent company. Black's refusal to replace the members of the board probably sealed his defeat. Morrow won 254,490 to 214,114 and entered office on December 9, 1919. After he left office on December 11, 1923, Morrow worked actively with the Watchmen of the Republic, an organization devoted to the eradication of prejudice and the creation of harmony and tolerance. In 1924-26 he was on the U.S. Railroad Labor Board and in 1926-34 on its successor, the U.S. Board of Mediation. He continued to be active in politics, but failed to get his party's nomination for the U.S. House in 1934. He died in Frankfort on June 15, 1935, and was buried in the Frankfort Cemetery.

In 1920 the Republicans controlled the House and trailed in the Senate by only two votes; Morrow was able to get most of his program enacted. He achieved considerable reorganization of state government, including the centralization of highway work, improvement of both the public schools and the state colleges, better roads, creation of the Board of Charities and Corrections, revised property tax laws, and better textbook selection. His efforts to remove charitable and penal institutions from politics and to create a nonpartisan judiciary

were less successful than he had hoped. Morrow urged strict enforcement of the laws, including the seldom-invoked prohibition against carrying concealed weapons, and he restricted pardons. He strongly opposed the Ku Klux Klan. In February 1920 he sent the National Guard in Lexington to protect Will Lockett, a black on trial for murder, and in 1921 he removed the Woodford County jailer who had allowed Richard James, a black, to be lynched. In 1922 the governor used the National Guard to curb violence at a mill strike in Newport.

In his 1922 message to the legislature Morrow called for more adequate funding and other improvements throughout the state government. Legislators were asked to approve large bond issues, including $50 million for a highway system, to finance the programs, and he urged repeal of all laws that denied equal legal rights to women. But the Democrats by then had majorities in both houses, and they rejected practically all of his proposals. Morrow vetoed a number of Democratic bills. Two new normal schools were created, at Morehead and Murray.

See Willard Rouse Jillson, *Edwin P. Morrow—Kentuckian* (Louisville, Ky., 1921).

LOWELL H. HARRISON

MORTON, DAVID. David Morton, journalist and poet, was born February 21, 1886, in Elkton, Kentucky, the son of Thomas B. and Mattie (Petrie) Morton. His boyhood was divided between Louisville and Elkton. His initial education came in Louisville public schools, and he graduated from Vanderbilt University in Nashville in 1909. He later married Elizabeth Merrick. Morton, a reporter for the *Louisville Evening Post*, the Associated Press, and the *Louisville Courier-Journal*, was also a poet and critic, winning the Borestone Prize and others for poetry, as well as recognition for two books of criticism. His best-known work is *Poems, 1920-1945* (1945). Morton taught English at Louisville Boys' High School, Morristown High School in New Jersey, and Amherst College. He contributed editorials to the *New York Sun* and the *New York Evening Post*. He died on June 13, 1957, and was buried in Morristown, New Jersey. Western Kentucky University at Bowling Green is the repository for a collection of Morton works.

See Marion Williams, *The Story of Todd County, Kentucky 1820-1970* (Nashville 1972).

JOY BALE BOONE

MORTON, JENNIE CHINN. Jennie Chinn Morton, who helped revitalize the Kentucky Historical Society and who founded its *Register*, was born on January 10, 1838, in Franklin County, Kentucky. She was the daughter of Judge Franklin Bryan and Annie (Bell) Chinn and received her education at private female academies in Frankfort and Shelbyville. In 1860 Jennie Chinn married John Calhoun Morton of Hartford, Kentucky; she was widowed within a year. In the 1870s, after her parents died, Morton became a published poet. She moved to Frankfort to live with her girlhood friend Sally Jackson. Having long had an interest in history, Morton worked to revive the Kentucky Historical Society.

The society, established in 1836, had been recreated in the late 1870s, with a legislative charter in 1880, but had been overcome by financial difficulties. In 1896, with support from the Lyceum, a Frankfort literary society to which Morton belonged, and the Frankfort Society of Colonial Daughters, former members of the Kentucky Historical Society met to resuscitate it. Morton and Jackson operated the society from their home with personal funds until Morton persuaded Gov. J.C.W. Beckham (1900-1907) to provide room in the state capitol. With Beckham's assistance, the society obtained annual state appropriations.

Morton founded, edited, and wrote for the *Register* and served as both society secretary-treasurer and regent until her death. Her efforts to collect artifacts and books relating to Kentucky history led to the establishment of the society's museum and library. Morton was also active in the Presbyterian Church and was at one time editor of a regional temperance periodical, *The Riverside Weekly*. She died on January 9, 1920, and was buried in the Frankfort Cemetery.

See Henry T. Stanton, "Sketch in the Life of Mrs. Jennie C. Morton," *Register* 4 (May 1906): 37-39.   MARY MARGARET BELL

MORTON, THRUSTON BALLARD. Thruston Ballard Morton, U.S. senator, was born on August 19, 1907, in Louisville to David Cummings and Mary Harris (Ballard) Morton. Morton was the seventh Kentucky generation of the Ballard family, which had grain and milling interests in Louisville. Morton's grandfather, Samuel Thruston Ballard (1855-1926), served as lieutenant governor of Kentucky from 1919 to 1923. Morton attended public schools and the Woodbury Forest School in Orange, Virginia, and graduated from Yale University in 1929. He served as a lieutenant commander in the U.S. Naval Reserve from 1941 to 1946. In 1946 Morton was elected to represent Kentucky's 3rd Congressional District, defeating incumbent Emmet O'Neal by a vote of 61,899 to 44,599. He served three terms in the U.S. House of Representatives, from January 3, 1947, to January 3, 1953. Morton was appointed assistant secretary of state for congressional relations 1953-56 by President Dwight D. Eisenhower. He defeated Democratic incumbent Earle C. Clements in the 1956 election for the U.S. Senate by 506,903 to 499,922. Morton served in the Senate for two terms, from January 3, 1957, to January 3, 1969. He was chairman of the Republican National Committee from 1959 to 1961. He later became one of the first conservatives to withdraw his support for President Lyndon Johnson's Vietnam War policies. Morton declined to run for reelection in 1968.

Morton married Belle Clay Lyons of Louisville in 1962; they had two children, Thruston, Jr., and Clay Lyons. Morton served at various periods of his life as president of Ballard and Ballard, the grain and flour-milling business; vice-chairman of the board and director of the Liberty National Bank; director of the Louisville Board of Trade; and chairman of the board and director of Churchill Downs. Morton lived in Louisville until his death on August 14, 1982. He was buried at Cave Hill cemetery in Louisville.

MOTHER OF GOD CHURCH. The Mother of God Roman Catholic Church, located on West Sixth Street in Covington, Kentucky, is an outstanding example of Italian Renaissance Revival architecture. It dates from 1870-71. Designed by the noted Cincinnati architectural firm Walter and Stewart, the church features two massive, two-hundred-foot bell towers and a dome rising 150 feet above the crossing of the church. Stained-glass windows, most of them executed by the studio of Mayer and Company in Munich, enrich the interior.

In 1890-91, in anticipation of the golden jubilee of the parish, the church commissioned noted artisans to embellish the interior. Johann Schmitt, a local artist who was the first teacher of Frank DUVENECK, painted the five large canvas murals in the sanctuary, which depict the "Five Joyful Mysteries" of the Catholic Rosary. The hand-carved oak altars were the handiwork of Schroeder Brothers of Cincinnati; the ceiling frescoes were executed by Wencelaus Thien. The dome is supported by slender columns decorated in gold leaf. The fourteen stations of the cross were painted by Paul Deschwanden in 1872, the large crucifix above the main altar is the work of Covington sculptor Ferdinand Muer, and the hand-carved wooden statue group surmounting the main altar is by Mayer and Company. The sanctuary floor is English mosaic tile, installed in 1903, and the aisle floors are German Mettlach tile, laid in 1921. The rear gallery houses the pipe organ, installed in 1876 by the Cincinnati firm Koehnken and Grimm.

The exterior of Mother of God Church includes a finely sculpted facade. On September 25, 1986, the church suffered a major fire that badly damaged the dome and caused extensive smoke and water damage to the interior. A $1.2 million restoration of the church followed.

See Paul A. Tenkotte, *A Heritage of Art and Faith: Downtown Covington Churches* (Covington, Ky., 1986).   PAUL A. TENKOTTE

MOTTO, STATE. "United We Stand, Divided We Fall" was approved by the Kentucky General Assembly and Gov. Isaac Shelby (1792-96) as the motto for the state seal on December 20, 1792. The motto is taken from "Liberty Song," a popular composition that was written in 1768 by John Dickinson of Pennsylvania. One of the verses of "Liberty Song" states: "Then join hand in hand, / Brave Americans all, / By uniting we stand, / By dividing we fall." The song was popular during the Revolutionary War.   RON D. BRYANT

MOUNTAIN EAGLE. The *Mountain Eagle*, Letcher County's oldest continuously published newspaper, has been a Whitesburg weekly since August 1907. Its founder was Nehemiah M. Webb, pioneer eastern Kentucky journalist. W. Pearl Nolan bought it during the Great Depression. In 1956 he sold both the newspaper and a related job-printing business to Tom and Pat Gish, husband and wife, who have served as both editors and publishers. The *Mountain Eagle* has become increasingly viewed as a promoter of liberal (often controversial) causes, such as ecological opposition to strip mining and advocacy of greater health benefits for miners with black-lung disease. Its wide-ranging and hard-hitting reporting (as well as its down-home flavor) have made it controversial; an arsonist once burned the offices. Its influence lies in its investigative reporting on politics, education, and the environment. Its masthead says, "It Screams!"

WILLIAM TERRELL CORNETT

MOUNTAIN LAUREL FESTIVAL. The highlight of the Mountain Laurel Festival, held each spring in Pineville, Kentucky, since 1931, is the coronation of the festival queen. The event is a gala of parades, folk singing and dancing, receptions and banquets, and tours through the mountains. Kentucky Gov. Flem D. Sampson (1927-31) originated the festival with the suggestion that the state promote tourism by taking advantage of the beauty of the mountain laurel, while at the same time commemorating the discovery and exploration of southeastern Kentucky by Dr. Thomas Walker.

Approximately 5,000 people participated at the first event, called the Rhododendron and Mountain Laurel Festival, on June 5-6, 1931. The festival's first president was Dr. H.L. Donovan, president of Eastern Kentucky University in Richmond. Thirteen candidates from Kentucky's schools and colleges vied for queen of the festival, who is traditionally crowned by the governor of Kentucky. Only World War II has stopped the Mountain Laurel Festival, which was not celebrated from 1942 to 1947.

MT. OLIVET. Mt. Olivet, the county seat of Robertson County, is located at the center of the county at the junction of U.S. 62 and KY 165. The town was established about 1820 and according to local folklore was once called Hell's Half Acre. The town was officially incorporated December 27, 1851, and named for the Mt. Olivet of biblical origin.

During the 1870s, the town had two hotels, a high school, four churches, and several businesses. The courthouse was constructed in the city in 1872 on land donated by John and Mary Riggs, and bricks for the Italianate-style structure were made at the site. The courthouse, with various additions, has been in use since January 1873 and was placed on the National Register of Historic Places in 1978. The twenty-three-room Louisiana Hotel, a local landmark, was built by a man from New Orleans in 1869.

Mt. Olivet is a small community with an agrarian economy and no industry. Most of the town's labor force is employed in other counties or in the few retail establishments in the residential city. The population of the fifth-class city was 442 in 1970; 346 in 1980; and 384 in 1990.

See T. Ross Moore, *Echoes From the Century* (N.p., 1967).   RON D. BRYANT

MOUNT ST. JOSEPH ACADEMY. Mount St. Joseph Academy, founded in 1874 as a boarding school, educated young women of high school age for 109 years. Located in Daviess County, seventeen miles southwest of Owensboro, Kentucky, on 750 acres, it consisted of a campus, farmland, and grazing pastures.

Father Paul Joseph Volk was instrumental in founding the academy. Born in Hunfeld, Germany, he came to St. Joseph, Kentucky, in 1870 as the third pastor of St. Alphonsus Church. In 1862 two Sisters of Loretto had helped the first pastor, Father Schacht, establish the Panther Creek school in the wilderness. The nuns lived and taught in a one-room log cabin that burned in December 1869, forcing their return to the motherhouse in Nerinx, Kentucky. In 1873, with the aid of parishioners, Volk fired and laid bricks at the same site, establishing Mount St. Joseph. The next year a small number of Ursuline nuns came from Louisville to assist Volk in founding the academy, which became known as Maple Mount, for the groves of maple trees he planted. A novitiate opened in 1895 and it was granted autonomy in 1912. In 1925 Mount St. Joseph Junior College was added. In 1950 it was transferred to Owensboro and renamed BRESCIA COLLEGE in honor of the Italian city where the Ursulines were founded in 1535.

Structures erected at Maple Mount from 1882 to 1980 are dominated by the North Wing, added in 1904 to the original 1874 building. The setting of the four-story brick edifice includes elaborate terraces, formal gardens, a sweeping tree-framed valley to the east, and woodlands to the west. Rolling farmland lies south and southeast. The academy closed in 1983; Mount St. Joseph continues as a convent and center for retreats and workshops.

See Norbert Russwurm, O.S.B., *Reverend Paul Joseph Volk, a Pioneer Missionary in Two Continents* (St. Bernard, Ala., 1935).

ALICIA M. HOERTER

MT. STERLING. Mt. Sterling, the county seat of Montgomery County in the outer Bluegrass region of Kentucky, is located thirty-five miles east of Lexington at the junction of U.S. 60 and U.S. 460, adjacent to I-64. The settlement, founded in 1792 on Enoch Smith's farm, may originally have been called Little Mountain Town, for a large Indian mound in the area. The name was changed by Hugh

Forbes, one of the town proprietors, to honor his hometown of Stirling, Scotland. (The original spelling was corrupted to the present version.)

By 1860 the town had a population of 754. As the center of a prosperous farming region, Mt. Sterling developed into a retail center, aided by its location at the junction of roads leading from Lexington to Olympian Springs in Bath County and to Virginia via Pound Gap. The community was also a political center for its congressional district, which included the isolated and thinly populated eastern mountains. As a gateway to the eastern Kentucky mountains, the town frequently changed hands between Union and Confederate forces in the Civil War. Several businesses were destroyed in a March 22, 1863, raid by Col. Roy Cluke's Confederate cavalry, and later that year the courthouse was burned by another unit of Confederates. On June 8, 1864, Confederate Gen. John Hunt Morgan raided homes and businesses, and his men took $72,000 from the Farmer's Bank.

After emancipation there was a marked influx of rural blacks into the town. Prosperity followed the war and ushered in a period of rapid growth, pushing the population to 3,624 by 1890. In 1872 the arrival of the Elizabethtown, Lexington, & Big Sandy Railroad (later the Chesapeake & Ohio Railroad, abandoned in the mid-1980s by CSX Transportation) connected Mt. Sterling with markets in Lexington and Cincinnati. In 1881 the route was completed to Ashland and helped Mt. Sterling to build up a substantial wholesale trade with the mountain counties and become a major livestock market in the last years of the nineteenth century. Although better roads to eastern Kentucky led to a decline of the livestock market in the early 1900s, the biggest of the market days, October Court Day, continues as a major festival, which annually brings tens of thousands of people to the community.

Mt. Sterling's growth was slow for most of the twentieth century until I-64 was completed through the area during the 1960s. The opening of the interstate led to the establishment of several electrical manufacturing companies as major local employers by 1990, including the A.O. Smith Corporation, Kitchen Aid, Inc. (Division of Whirlpool), and Trojan Manufacturing Company. The population of the fourth-class city was 5,083 in 1970; 5,820 in 1980; and 5,362 in 1990.

See Carl B. Boyd, Jr. and Hazel M. Boyd, *History of Mt. Sterling, Kentucky, 1792-1918* (Mt. Sterling, Ky., 1984).   CARL B. BOYD, JR.

MT. STERLING–POUND GAP ROAD. The Mt. Sterling–Pound Gap road was the longest road built and maintained by the commonwealth in the eastern mountains before the Civil War. As early as 1817 the General Assembly authorized the surveying of a route from Mt. Sterling, Kentucky, to Virginia via Pound Gap. Livestock were driven to the Virginia market over the road, which extended for ninety-four miles, from Mt. Sterling to a point five miles beyond Prestonsburg. The state appropriated $2,700 in 1824 and $23,000 between 1836 and 1845, but the difficulties of maintaining a road across the rugged terrain were great. In 1838 the road was given over to the counties to maintain, and it began to fall into disrepair. It continued to be a main road into the mountains, but in time its poor condition limited trade. During the Civil War the road was a main thoroughfare for troops moving between central Kentucky and Virginia. Today U.S. 460 roughly parallels the old road.

CARL B. BOYD, JR.

MT. VERNON. Mt. Vernon, the county seat of Rockcastle County in eastern Kentucky, is located at the junction of U.S. 25 and U.S. 150, two miles west of I-75. The city originated before 1790, when settlers congregated around Spout Springs. Tradition has it that the founder was Stephen Langford, who named the settlement in honor of George Washington's Mt. Vernon. The Wilderness Road was rerouted through Mt. Vernon in 1792. By 1810, when Rockcastle County was created, Mt. Vernon was the principal settlement of the county although its population did not exceed 750 before 1900. Much of what is present-day Mt. Vernon and the area west of it was swampland during the early history of the town.

The first business in Mt. Vernon, other than the inn for travelers at Stephen Langford's station, was the Rev. James McCall's tanyard near Spout Springs. James Maret established the *Mountain Signal*, the county's first newspaper, in 1887; its files are the source for much of Mt. Vernon's history. The county's first bank was established in the city in 1900 and the first railroad through the town was the Louisville & Nashville's Lebanon Branch from Lebanon Junction to Knoxville, Tennessee. The track reached Mt. Vernon in 1868, and the first through train, from Louisville to Knoxville, passed on July 14, 1883. Before the coming of the railroad, the round trip to Louisville was usually a six-day undertaking for merchants. In 1990 CSX Transportation maintained service into Mt. Vernon from its main line to the east of the city.

Before the city of Mt. Vernon established a graded school district, a number of private schools and academies served the area, including Langdon Memorial School, which functioned from 1899 to 1927. The associated Mt. Vernon College Institute held classes for local white students during the day and black students at night. Langdon itself was a boarding school for girls run by the Presbyterian church. It was a mixture of grade school, high school, and junior college and included a "kept house" for practical training in home economics. Scholarships were awarded and students came from throughout the central part of the state. All students dressed alike and marched in groups to church or to the downtown business district. In 1927 the school became a shelter for girls and provided some training; it functioned until 1938.

Mt. Vernon and Rockcastle County remain rural areas. In the early 1970s the completion of I-75 east of the city helped to attract industry to Mt. Vernon. The Mt. Vernon Plastics Corporation, which opened in the city in 1980, is one of the county's largest employers. The population of the fifth-class city was 1,639 in 1970; 2,334 in 1980; and 2,654 in 1990.

See Cepha Davis Kincer, *Mt. Vernon, Kentucky* (Covington, Ky., 1983).   J. ALLEN SINGLETON

MT. WASHINGTON. Mt. Washington, in northeastern Bullitt County, grew up at the junction of stagecoach roads connecting Louisville with Bardstown and Taylorsville with Sheperdsville; by 1822 enough people had settled at the crossroads to incorporate a town that was named Mt. Vernon, after George Washington's Virginia home. In 1833 the name was changed to Mt. Washington to avoid confusion with a similarly named town in Rockcastle County. By the 1850s the local economy was thriving and the city was the county's largest, with a population of 700. Businesses included a rifle factory, a coffin shop, two taverns, a tannery, and manufacturers of pianos, furniture, and hats. The Buck Mill was available for grinding flour and meal as well as turning wood on a lathe.

In the fall of 1862, with the Confederate army occupying Bardstown, the area around Mt. Washington was held by elements of John Wharton's Confederate cavalry. On October 1, 1862, Union infantry under Maj. Gen. Thomas L. Crittenden moved out of Louisville and skirmished with Wharton's men north of Mt. Washington along Floyd's Fork; on October 2, twenty-five Union soldiers were killed along the Bardstown Pike. By October 3, fighting had moved south of the city to the Salt River as the Confederates retreated toward Bardstown.

By the 1930s the town had relinquished its primary role in the county and contained only a few of its original industries. A disastrous fire swept through the business district on November 18, 1940, and destroyed the four-story Maccabee Hall and several adjacent buildings. The town was reincorporated in 1955 and experienced rapid growth in the 1960s, especially after the opening of General Electric's Appliance Park in nearby Jefferson County.

The population of the fourth-class city was 2,020 in 1970; 3,997 in 1980; and 5,226 in 1990.

MUD RIVER. The Mud River, a thirty-five-mile-long tributary of the Green River, flows through southwestern Kentucky, beginning in Logan County about three miles east-northeast of Russellville. The river travels north through Butler County and empties into the Green River one mile west of Rochester, Muhlenberg County. Three tributaries of the Mud River are Wolf Lick Creek, Rocky Mud Creek, and Elk Lake Creek. Lake Herndon is on Elk Lick Creek and Lake Malone is located on the Rocky Mud tributary. Before the 1860s, this river was more frequently referred to as Muddy River or Big Muddy River.

In the early nineteenth century the region was the site of notable religious revivals. After 1850, coal from the Mud River Mile mine was barged down the Mud River, up the Green River, and south to Bowling Green. In 1862, when Confederate Gen. John Hunt Morgan's troops crossed the Mud River, they are said to have built a bridge of sunken flatboats in two hours on their way from Gum Springs to Hopkinsville on a guerrilla raid.

See Agnes S. Harralson, *Steamboats on the Green and the Colorful Men Who Operated Them* (Berea, Ky., 1981).   MICHAEL E. WALTERS

MUHLENBERG COUNTY. The thirty-second county in order of formation, Muhlenberg County is located in west-central Kentucky. It is bordered by Butler, Christian, Hopkins, Logan, McLean, Ohio, and Todd counties and has an area of 478 square miles. Muhlenberg County was formed from portions of Christian and Logan counties and was named in honor of Gen. John Peter Muhlenberg, a hero of the Revolutionary War and congressman from Pennsylvania. The county seat is GREENVILLE.

The topography of Muhlenberg County is varied. The southern section of the county is somewhat rugged; the central portion of the county, extending toward its northern boundary, is more level. Over 40 percent of the county is still covered by hardwood forests, mostly of oak and hickory. The principal streams are the Green, Mud, and Pond rivers.

Several Native American burial mounds have been discovered in the county. White settlers came into the Muhlenberg County area in the 1780s and 1790s, many of them soldiers in General Muhlenberg's regiment. It was soon discovered that the region was rich in coal and iron deposits. One of the first coal mines in the county was established in 1820 on a farm on the Green River. Initially this coal was sold to local blacksmiths to fire their forges. As more deposits were found near the Green River, which provided easy access to other markets such as Owensboro and Evansville, Indiana, Muhlenberg's coal industry grew. During the antebellum period, Muhlenberg County was a center of the Kentucky iron industry. In 1855 Sir Robert Alexander built the Airdrie Iron Furnace with the assistance of imported Scottish labor. Tobacco farming, especially in the county's northwest section, predominated during the 1850s. Grains and hogs were also raised.

During the Civil War, Greenville was occupied by both Confederate and Union armies. On November 24, 1861, Gen. Nathan Bedford Forrest and a Confederate force captured a store of Union guns and equipment in Greenville. Muhlenberg County sent 836 men to fight for the Union; the exact number of Confederate recruits from the county was not determined.

Following the hardships of the war, railroads made mining and agriculture more profitable. When the Owensboro & Russellville Railroad (O&R), part of the Louisville & Nashville (now CSX Transportation) system, which transversed the county, was completed in 1882, many towns such as Bevier and Cleaton sprang up along its routes. These villages were built to accommodate people searching for jobs in the coal fields. CENTRAL CITY is at the intersection of the O&R and the Elizabethtown & Paducah. As technology advanced and mining became more profitable, the coal industry grew. The Peabody Coal Company owned and operated one of the world's largest earth-moving shovels in Muhlenberg County.

About 39 percent of the land is occupied by farms, on which dark and light tobaccos, corn, and soybeans are grown; livestock and poultry are raised also.

The Tennessee Valley Authority's power plant on the Green River at Paradise enhances the county's industrial potential. Lake Malone State Park provides recreational facilities as well as helping to attract tourist dollars.

The population of the county was 27,537 in 1970; 32,238 in 1980; and 31,318 in 1990.

See Paul Camplin, *A New History of Muhlenberg County* (Nashville 1984); Arthur Otto Rothert, *A History of Muhlenberg County* (Louisville 1913); Leslie Shively Smith, *Around Muhlenberg County, Kentucky: A Black History* (Evansville, Ind., 1979).

RON D. BRYANT

MULDOON, MICHAEL McDONALD. Michael McDonald Muldoon, a stone cutter, was born in Ireland on August 16, 1836, to Michael M. and Margaret (McDaniel) Muldoon. When he emigrated to the United States, he worked briefly in Steubenville, Ohio, then moved to Louisville about 1860. He formed a firm with Charles Bullett, who supervised their studios in Carrara, Italy. By age thirty-five Muldoon had several hundred employees and operated marble yards in St. Louis, Memphis, and New Orleans. He made Louisville into a regional center for burial monuments, and his firm built the Louisville city hall, the board of trade building, and the old Second Presbyterian Church.

In 1865 Muldoon married the daughter of Louisville Mayor James Smith Lithgow. They had four daughters; Anita, Margaret, Aleen, and Hannah. Muldoon died on April 26, 1911, and was buried in Cave Hill Cemetery, where his monumental art is on view.

See Samuel W. Thomas, *Cave Hill Cemetery: A Pictorial Guide and Its History* (Louisville 1985).

SAMUEL W. THOMAS

MULDRAUGH HILL. Muldraugh Hill is a long steep ridge that roughly follows the Rolling Fork River and rises about five hundred feet above it. The ridge extends approximately seventy-five miles from West Point, Hardin County, to Calvary, Marion County. Muldraugh Hill was named for John Muldraugh, who settled near its eastern extreme in Marion County in about 1776. Though the name originally applied only to that part of the ridge where Muldraugh lived, it is used now for the entire expanse. (Another explanation of the name traces it to Mule Draw Station, a stable at the foot of the ridge that rented mule teams to settlers to draw their wagons over the hill.)

When the Louisville & Nashville (L&N) Railroad's main line to the south was under construction in the 1850s, the first obstacle encountered was Muldraugh Hill. A series of trestles and a tunnel, 1,986 feet long and 135 feet below the summit, were built five miles north of Elizabethtown in 1860. During the Civil War, Muldraugh Hill and the L&N became strategically significant. By 1862 the railroad was being used to supply Federal armies advancing into Tennessee. During his Christmas Raid on December 28, 1862, Confederate Gen. John Hunt Morgan defeated the Federal forces at Muldraugh Hill and burned the railroad trestles. Though Morgan succeeded in closing the L&N for five weeks, Union logistics were little affected as Union Gen. William Rosecrans had already sent supplies to Nashville. The raid nevertheless slowed the Union advance, as more than 7,000 men from Rosecrans's army worked to repair the trestles. Union forces were able to hold the railroad for the remainder of the war, minimizing any further damage to the lines by the Confederates, and the L&N emerged from the war in relatively sound financial and physical condition.

The town of Muldraugh, a fifth-class city that takes its name from the hill to its east, lies about ten miles southeast of Brandenburg, Meade County. The Muldraugh post office was established in 1874. The town was incorporated in 1952 and is now surrounded by the Fort Knox military reservation. In 1986 its population was 2,050. See Otis Mather, "Explorers and Early Settlers South of Muldraugh Hill," *Register* 22 (Jan. 1924): 21-39; James Ramage, *Rebel Raider* (Lexington, Ky., 1986).

MULLIGAN, JAMES HILLARY. James Hillary Mulligan, poet, was born in Lexington, Kentucky, on November 21, 1844, the son of Dennis and Ellen Alice (McCoy) Mulligan. In 1870, with the help of his father, a prominent businessman, Mulligan built Maxwell Place in Lexington and moved into the residence with his wife of one year, the former Mary Huston Jackson. Mulligan, an attorney, was judge of the recorder's court during 1870-76. He also served in the Kentucky House (1881-89) and Senate (1889-93). In 1890 Mulligan, regarded as one of the greatest Kentucky orators of his time, made the nominating speech for John G. Carlisle, to fill the vacancy created by the death of U.S. Senator James B. Beck. In a speech before a legislative group at Lexington's Phoenix Hotel in 1902, Mulligan first delivered his poem "In Kentucky," which characterizes Kentucky's politics as "the damndest." President Grover Cleveland named Mulligan consul-general to Samoa in June 1894. He resigned in 1896 and returned to Lexington to practice law.

Mulligan and Mary (Jackson) Mulligan had four children: James, Lewis, Alice, and Mollie. Mary died on April 10, 1876. In 1881 Mulligan married Genevieve Morgan Williams of Nashville, a cousin of Gen. John Hunt Morgan, President John Tyler, and Mrs. Stonewall Jackson. They had six children:

Samuel and Henrietta, who died in infancy, and Dennis, Marion, Kathleen, and Willoughby. Mulligan died on July 1, 1915, and was buried in Lexington's Calvary Cemetery. The family sold Maxwell Place with thirteen acres of land to the University of Kentucky, and it became the residence for the presidents of the university.

E.I. (BUDDY) THOMPSON

MULLINS, EDGAR YOUNG. Edgar Young Mullins, Baptist minister and educator, the fourth of eleven children of Seth Granberry and Sarah Cornelia Barnes (Tillman) Mullins, was born January 5, 1860, in Franklin County, Mississippi. He grew up in Baptist parsonages in Mississippi and Texas. He was educated at the public school of Corsicana, Texas; the Agricultural and Mechanical College of Texas (1876-80); and Southern Baptist Theological Seminary in Louisville (1881-85). Pastorates in Harrodsburg, Kentucky; Baltimore; and Newton Center, Massachusetts, prepared Mullins for his position as president of SOUTHERN BAPTIST THEOLOGICAL SEMINARY in 1899. The school was in the throes of a theological controversy, ending the presidency of William H. Whitsitt. Mullins served as president of the institution until his death.

Tall, thin, bearded, and somewhat courtly, Mullins combined scholarship and denominational leadership with his administration of one of the world's largest non-Catholic seminaries. He wrote ten major books, dozens of pamphlets, and over one hundred articles and book reviews. During his administration the seminary moved to new facilities on Lexington Road in Louisville. As president of the Southern Baptist Convention in the mid-1920s, Mullins opposed the passage of antievolution laws in the South. A moderate among Southern Baptists, he eschewed the growing fundamentalism of many of his co-denominationalists while criticizing the liberalism or modernism of many of his northern Baptist colleagues.

Mullins married Isla May Hawley in 1886; one son died in infancy and another at the age of seven. Mullins died in November 1928, and was buried in Louisville's Cave Hill Cemetery.

See William E. Ellis, *E.Y. Mullins and the Crisis of Moderate Southern Baptist Leadership* (Macon, Ga., 1985); Isla May Mullins, *Edgar Young Mullins: An Intimate Biography* (Nashville 1929).

WILLIAM E. ELLIS

MULLINS, JEFFERY VINCENT. One of the best Kentucky high school basketball players who did not play college ball in the state, Jeffery Vincent Mullins was born in Astoria, New York, on March 19, 1942, the son of Vincent and Mary (Eustice) Mullins. Growing up in Lexington, Mullins played basketball at Lafayette High, where he was Kentucky's 1960 "Mr. Basketball." Mullins, a six-foot, four-inch swingman, won a scholarship to play at Duke University in Durham, North Carolina. He was named All-American in 1963-64 and was the 1964 Atlantic Coast Conference player of the year. In 1964 the St. Louis (now Atlanta) Hawks selected Mullins in the first round of the National Basketball Association (NBA) draft, and he was a member of the U.S. Olympic basketball team that won the gold medal at the Tokyo Games. During 1966-76 he played with the Golden State Warriors, then retired from playing, a five-time All Star (1967-71). Mullins served as associate athletic director at Duke and as a television analyst for basketball and in 1985 became basketball coach and athletic director at the University of North Carolina at Charlotte. Mullins married Carolyn Lee Johnson on October 8, 1966; they have two daughters—Kelly and Kristen.

MUNDY, JAMES AHYLN. James Ahyln Mundy, choral director and music arranger, was born in Maysville, Kentucky, on July 9, 1886. Mundy was educated in Maysville and became choir director and organist for the Bethel Baptist Church there. Sponsored by the church Sunday school, Mundy won a statewide competition that gave him further musical training, first in Louisville (Simmons University, Normal Department) and then Chicago (Cosmopolitan School of Music). His arrangements and conducting of large choirs in Orchestra Hall, Chicago, are credited with reviving black spirituals in the Chicago area in the early 1900s. He also presented singers and choirs in musical festivals, operas, and other special programs, helping to celebrate black history through a pageant in Orchestra Hall with three hundred singers in 1917 and the rededication of Lincoln's Tomb in 1932. He gave acclaimed performances at the Chicago World's Fair (1933-34), and at Carnegie Hall in 1946. He was named to the Chicago Senior Citizens' Hall of Fame in 1972. Mundy died in Chicago on December 25, 1978.

JOHN KLEE

MUNDY, SUE. See Clarke, Marcellus Jerome.

MUNFORDVILLE. Munfordville, the seat of Hart County, was originally known as Big Buffalo Crossing. The city is named for Richard J. Munford, an early pioneer and landowner who donated 100 acres of land for the establishment of the town in 1816. It became the county seat in 1819 and was incorporated in 1858. Hart County's first courthouse was completed in 1821 and was replaced in 1893 by a structure that burned in 1928. The current Hart County courthouse, built in 1928, was placed on the National Register of Historic Places in 1980.

The Battle of Munfordville was one of the more important Civil War engagements in Kentucky. Many unsuccessful attempts had been made by Confederate raiders to disrupt the Louisville & Nashville Railroad, the Union supply line that crossed the Green River at Munfordville. On September 13, 1862, Col. John T. Wilder, commander of the 4,000 Union troops in Munfordville, received a demand to surrender from Confederate Col. John Scott. Wilder refused and his position was attacked the next morning, after he had been reinforced and after a senior officer, Col. Cyrus L. Dunham, had taken command. The Union troops repulsed the Confederates and held Munfordville until the arrival of the main Confederate army from Glasgow, under the command of Gen. Braxton Bragg. At the request of Confederate Gen. Simon B. Buckner, a resident of the Munfordville area, Bragg surrounded the city and prepared for a siege instead of a direct assault. When confronted with the overwhelming size of their opposition, Dunham and Wilder surrendered the Union force. There were 357 casualties, Union and Confederate, during the Battle of Munfordville. Although Munfordville was captured by Confederate forces, it was not the fatal blow to Union supplies that had been hoped. Bragg and his troops were expected to march on Louisville, Cincinnati, or Lexington next. He became involved with other matters, however, and his army saw little action until the Battle of Perryville on October 8, 1862.

Munfordville, a fifth-class city, lies sixty-three miles south of Louisville. The industry located there produces millwork, pallets, lumber, and the like, but as in the rest of the county, tourism and agriculture are the economy's foundations. Munfordville is a station on the CSX Transportation System. The population was 1,233 in 1970; 1,783 in 1980; and 1,556 in 1990.

MUNSELL MAP. Luke Munsell, a Frankfort, Kentucky, surveyor, in 1818 prepared a map of Kentucky that approximated the present state boundaries. The boundaries are those of the Jackson-Shelby treaty with the Chickasaw Indians on October 19, 1818, for the western areas of Kentucky and Tennessee. The large wall map, drafted on a scale of five miles to the inch, was engraved by Hugh Anderson, a prominent Philadelphia artist and illustrator. The elegant vignettes decorating the corners of the map were drawn by Thomas Sully. A copy of the Munsell map is owned by the Kentucky Historical Society; there are two copies in the Library of Congress. The commonwealth lent Munsell $6,000 in 1820 to complete the map, and agreed to purchase two hundred copies at six dollars each.

See Thomas D. Clark, *Historical Maps of Kentucky* (Lexington, Ky., 1979).

THOMAS D. CLARK

MURALS. Kentucky enjoys a rich and varied history of mural paintings throughout much of the state. Some of the earliest examples are no doubt lost, but the works that survive include paintings at the Old Talbott Tavern in Bardstown and in several Woodford County private homes. The Bardstown works, which include scenes of Don Quixote, a volcano, and tropical trees, are painted in a second-floor room of the tavern, a part of the building that was added in the 1790s to the original structure. According to local legend, the murals were painted by LOUIS-PHILIPPE, later king of France, who vis-

ited Bardstown in late 1797 while in exile in America. Although a European authorship may well be disputed, these primitive scenes may be among the most unusual extant murals in the midwestern United States.

The Woodford County murals, at Airy Mount, the Gen. James McConnell house, and at Pleasant Lawn, are all attributed to a French émigré, Alfred Cohen, who settled in Midway in the early nineteenth century. Painted in oil directly on the plaster walls of these homes, the murals combine a mix of trompe l'oeil architectural devices with a whimsical disregard of perspective and consistent horizon lines. The original murals at Pleasant Lawn were lost in a fire in 1964; the present works are reproductions.

More recent academic murals are found in Covington and Frankfort. The murals in Covington, painted by Frank DUVENECK, one of the Midwest's leading artists in the late nineteenth century, represent the Crucifixion, the giving of the old law and the new law, and the supper at Emmaus. Duveneck designed the four oversize oil-on-canvas panels, which are meant to be seen as a unit, for the Basilica of the Assumption in Covington, as a memorial to the artist's mother. The Frankfort murals, painted by T. Gilbert White in 1909, are in the state capitol. In these paintings, Daniel Boone explores the Bluegrass region and Richard Henderson negotiates the Treaty of Sycamore Shoals.

Most of Kentucky's finest mural paintings took place under the auspices of President Franklin Delano Roosevelt's New Deal art programs. The Public Works of Art Project sponsored the University of Kentucky's Memorial Hall mural by Ann Rice (O'Hanlon), a Lexington native who learned the technique of fresco from a student of the Mexican muralist Diego Rivera. The Memorial Hall work, a pictorial history of Kentucky from pioneer days to the twentieth century, was painted in 1934. Because true fresco, an ancient method of wall painting that achieved its greatest expression in the Italian Renaissance, bonds pigment with the plaster-covered walls as the wet plaster dries, the Lexington work's brilliant colors have retained their glowing tones for over fifty years. Other 1930s federally sponsored murals, mainly works in oil on canvas, survive throughout the state, including a Federal Art Project commission in Covington by Kentucky artist Harlan Hubbard. In keeping with other federally sponsored murals throughout the country, these Kentucky works show episodes in the history of a city or region.

When federal art programs ended as the United States entered World War II in 1941, mural painting declined in this country, at least on any kind of systematic, professional scale. As Americans tried to forget the Great Depression, the art projects of the 1930s took on a dated, overly self-conscious look. The administrators of public buildings, contemplating expansion, renovation, or even replacement of their properties, occasionally decided to sacrifice a mural in the interest of progress. Fortunately for Kentucky, a region that has cherished its history, the state's major murals have been preserved.

See Marlene Park and Gerald E. Markowitz, *Democratic Vistas: Post Offices and Public Art in the New Deal* (Philadelphia 1984); Clay Lancaster, "Primitive Mural Painter of Kentucky: Alfred Cohen," *American Collector* 17 (Dec. 1948): 6-8.

HARRIET W. FOWLER

MURPHY, ISAAC BURNS. Isaac Burns Murphy, record-setting jockey, born in 1861 on the Fayette County farm of David Tanner, was the child of freedman James Burns. In the fall of 1876 he took Murphy, his mother's maiden name, as his last name. Murphy worked as an exercise boy at Lexington stables, where blacks typically performed many of the jobs, including those of trainer and jockey. Indeed, blacks rode fourteen of the fifteen horses in the first Kentucky Derby, and one, Oliver Lewis, won aboard Aristides. Over the next twenty-eight years, black jockeys won the Kentucky Derby more than half the time.

The superabundance of talented black jockeys made it difficult for Murphy to acquire his first mount, but in 1875 at the age of fourteen he won his first race as a replacement rider. Murphy soon dominated the sport. He won the St. Leger Stakes at Louisville's Churchill Downs in 1877 and a record thirty-five of seventy-five races entered in 1879, including the Travers Stakes in Saratoga, New York. In 1882 he won forty-nine of fifty-one starts at Saratoga, and on several cards he rode winners in every race, feats that acquired him the best mounts of the era. Murphy won the Latonia Derby in northern Kentucky five times, the Clark Stakes in Louisville four times, and four of the first five runnings of the American Derby at Washington Park in Chicago. In 1884, at a time when black patrons were segregated and often harassed in the grandstands at Kentucky racetracks, Murphy won his first Kentucky Derby aboard Buchanan, a horse prepared by black trainer William Bird. Murphy became the first back-to-back and three-time Derby winner by riding Riley to victory in 1890 and Kingman in 1891, and he finished in the money on three other occasions.

After 1885 Murphy rode under a $4,000 annual retainer that gave first choice of his services to Edward Corrigan, a Kansas City turfman who owned Alpine Stock Farm on Bowman's Mill Pike in Fayette County. In addition to his regular pay per race, Murphy received bonuses for winning certain races. On several occasions he made $1,000 in a single day, and he estimated his 1885 earnings at about $10,000.

At season's end, Murphy's weight soared, and he found it harder each year to achieve his riding weight of 110 pounds. He retired to become a trainer in 1892, with a record of 628 wins in 1,412 races during the fifteen seasons he rode. He died on February 12, 1896, survived by his wife, Lucy. In 1955 Murphy was belatedly inducted into the Jockey's Hall of Fame at Saratoga, and in 1977 his body was reinterred at the Kentucky Horse Park in Fayette County.

See Betty E. Borries, *Isaac Murphy: Kentucky's Record Jockey* (Berea, Ky., 1988).

MARION B. LUCAS

MURPHY, LOUISE (NATCHER). Louise (Natcher) Murphy, novelist, was born on March 12, 1943, in Bowling Green, Kentucky, the daughter of Rep. William H. and Virginia (Reardon) Natcher. After graduation from the University of Kentucky, she taught in a junior high school in Delaware, married her second husband, Michael Murphy, and moved to California, where she earned her M.A. degree in creative writing at San Francisco State University. Her first novel was *The Sea Within* (1985). A reviewer for the *New York Times* (April 21, 1985) described the novel as "a lovely, brave piece of work by a first novelist of shining promise," and a reviewer in the *Louisville Courier-Journal* (May 5, 1985) called it "a wise book that deserves careful, deliberate reading and reflection."

WADE HALL

MURPHY TOLL BRIDGE ACT. Until 1928, numerous privately owned toll bridges in Kentucky stood in the way of a unified highway system. That year, Gov. Flem D. Sampson (1927-31) signed the Murphy Toll Bridge Act (also known as the State Highway Bridge Act), giving the state power to condemn or purchase privately owned toll bridges and to issue bonds for construction of new facilities as part of the state primary system of highways. The state could charge tolls on these bridges until the cost of their construction and maintenance was paid. The bill was sponsored in the House by L.P. Murphy, of Georgetown, and was ushered through the legislature by Ben Johnson, head of the State Highway Commission. The act was the center of much controversy, but it withstood several lawsuits and attempts to amend or repeal it. State ownership of bridges paved the way for the construction of a modern road system in Kentucky.

MURRAY. Murray, the county seat of Calloway County, is located on U.S. 641 and KY 94. A post office and trading center was established in the 1820s and named Williston, for James Willis, an early settler. Later, the community was called Pooltown, in honor of Robert Pool, a local merchant. The name was again changed to Pleasant Hill. Murray was incorporated January 17, 1844, and named for John L. Murray, who represented the area in the U.S. Congress (1837-39).

The first courthouse was constructed in Wadesboro in 1823, and was a one-room log structure. The second Wadesboro courthouse, a two-story brick structure, was completed in 1831. The first courthouse in Murray was a two-story brick building constructed in 1843. The present courthouse, a three-story brick edifice in the Beaux Arts style, was built in 1913. Portions of the business district were burned in the Civil War by Union soldiers. By the 1870s, the town had recovered and was a prosperous community that had several mills and factories. Murray Seminary was established in 1858, the Murray Male and Female Institute in 1871, and Murray Normal School in 1922, which later became MURRAY STATE UNIVERSITY. The proximity of Murray to Kentucky Lake and the Land Between the Lakes has aided the economic growth of the town. It is the home of the national Boy Scouts museum.

Perhaps the best-known resident of Murray was Nathan B. STUBBLEFIELD, who in 1888 created a wireless telephone and in 1892 made a wireless voice transmission. The population of the third-class city was 13,537 in 1970; 14,248 in 1980; and 14,439 in 1990.

See E.A. Johnston, *History of Calloway County, Kentucky* (Murray, Ky., 1931).

RON D. BRYANT

MURRAY STATE UNIVERSITY. Murray State University was authorized as a teacher training institution on March 8, 1922, when Gov. Edwin P. Morrow (1919-23) signed legislation to establish two such normal schools in the commonwealth. On September 17 of that year the State Normal School Commission selected Murray, county seat of Calloway County, as the location of the school to be built in the western portion of the state. Citizens of Murray and Calloway County raised a total of $117,000 toward the purchase of land and construction of the first building. Murray was chosen over eight other western Kentucky contenders. The school opened with no campus, no building, and no library but with a faculty of eight and a student body of eighty-seven, who had a choice of approximately sixty college-level courses. The operating budget for 1923-24 was $32,000. The first classes at Murray State Normal School were held on September 24, 1923, in the newly completed facilities of the Murray High School at the corner of Main and Eighth Street. Total enrollment was 202, including the eighty-seven of college rank.

In 1926 the name of the institution was changed to Murray State Normal School and Teachers College and in 1930 to Murray State Teachers College. Murray State College was the name adopted in 1948, and on February 26, 1966, Gov. Edward T. Breathitt (1963-67) signed legislation changing the name to Murray State University. The first baccalaureate degrees were conferred on twelve graduates in May 1926. Liberal arts and preprofessional degree programs were accredited in 1930, and graduate-level work was first approved by the school's board of regents in 1935. The next year the first graduate degrees were awarded, in conjunction with the University of Kentucky. From its founding to 1990, Murray State University awarded 43,478 degrees to more than 36,000 graduates.

Lying on the western outskirts of Murray, the original campus consisted of thirty-five acres. The main campus in 1989 totaled 234 acres and was the site of seventy-eight major buildings, valued at $148 million. The campus includes two demonstration farms, the Hancock Biological Station, and the Frances Miller Memorial Golf Course, all in Calloway County. The university also owns Murphy's Pond wildlife area in Hickman County, Savage Cave in Logan County, and the Breathitt Veterinary Center in Christian County. The Harry Lee Waterfield Library and the Forrest C. Pogue Special Collections Library house approximately 800,000 volumes insured for more than $13 million. Notable research collections housed in Pogue include the Forrest C. Pogue collection of twentieth century war and diplomacy, the nation's largest Jesse Stuart collection, and major collections in southern history, Civil War, Kentucky history, Tennessee history, and genealogy. Murray State University is also the site of the National Boy Scout Museum, the world's largest collection of memorabilia relating to the history of scouting, including a number of Norman Rockwell paintings.

Murray was first accredited by the Southern Association of Colleges and Secondary Schools in 1928 and by the National Council for the Accreditation of Teacher Education in 1963. Since the 1920s Murray has offered extension courses at numerous locations in Kentucky, in 1989 at Paducah, Madisonville, Henderson, and Hopkinsville. Three master's level programs were offered at Fort Campbell, and an M.B.A. program was offered at Owensboro, in cooperation with Western Kentucky University. Associate degree programs were offered at the Kentucky State Penitentiary at Eddyville, real estate courses at Fulton and Princeton, and both high school and college-level courses at the Breckinridge Job Corps Center at Morganfield.

John Wesley Carr was the first president of Murray State University, serving from August 1, 1923, to May 1, 1926. Rainey T. Wells was president from May 1, 1926, until January 1, 1933. He was succeeded by Carr, whose second term ended on January 6, 1936, and who served the school as dean between his terms as president. James H. Richmond was appointed president on January 6, 1936, and served until his untimely death on July 24, 1945. A friend of President Franklin D. Roosevelt, Richmond brought a number of New Deal and wartime naval training programs to the Murray campus, credited with keeping the school open during the war years. During World War II Murray was one of twenty nationwide training sites for the Navy Flight Preparation School and one of only eight sites for the Naval Academic Refresher Unit. Over four thousand men received training at Murray from January 1943 to December 1945.

Ralph H. WOODS began his twenty-three year tenure as Murray's president on November 1, 1945, presiding over the greatest building and expansion boom in the school's history. At his retirement on January 8, 1968, Woods was succeeded by Harry

M. Sparks, a former Kentucky superintendent of public instruction. Sparks retired on August 4, 1973. Constantine William Curris assumed the office of president on that date and served until June 10, 1983. Kala Mays Stroup became the school's and the state's first woman university president on July 1, 1983. She served until July 31, 1989. In 1990, Ronald J. Kurth became Murray's eighth president.

Marvin Otis Wrather served Murray as interim president on three occasions, and James L. Booth served twice in this capacity.

See Ralph H. Woods, *Fifty Years of Progress: A History of Murray State University, 1922-1972* (Murray, Ky., 1973).   ERNIE R. BAILEY

MUSGRAVE, FRANKLIN STORY. Franklin Story Musgrave, astronaut, was born on August 19, 1935, in Stockbridge, Massachusetts. He graduated from Southborough (Massachusetts) High School in 1953 and joined the U.S. Marine Corps, where he received training as an electrician. He received a B.S. in mathematics from Syracuse University in 1958 and an M.A. in business administration and computer programming from the University of California at Los Angeles in 1959. He went on to receive a B.A. in chemistry from Marietta College in Ohio (1960), an M.D. from Columbia University (1964), and an M.S. in physiology and biophysics from the University of Kentucky (1966). He remained at UK as a postdoctoral fellow in aerospace medicine and physiology. The University of Kentucky made him an honorary doctor of science in 1984. While living in Fayette County, Musgrave learned to fly and eventually flew more than 120 different types of military and civilian aircraft.

In 1967, when the National Aeronautics and Space Administration (NASA) selected Musgrave to be a scientist/astronaut, he moved to Houston, Texas, but maintained his residency in Kentucky. After completing the astronautic academic program and flight training, he worked on the design and development of the Skylab program. From 1979 to 1982 Musgrave worked in NASA's Space Shuttle Avionics Integration Laboratory. As mission specialist on the Challenger's second mission with a shuttle deployment on April 4-9, 1983, he was one of the two astronauts who walked in space. He served as systems engineer on the Spacelab-2 mission from July 29 to August 6, 1985, and went on the secret military mission by Discovery that lifted off August 10, 1989. Musgrave returned often to Kentucky to speak with groups, particularly students enrolled in the Governor's Scholars Program.

Musgrave married Marguerite Van Kirk on September 1, 1960; they have five children; Lorelei, Bradley Scott, Holly Kay, Christopher Todd, and Jeffrey Paul. After their divorce, he married astronaut Carol Peterson, on April 18, 1986, in Clark County, Kentucky.

MUSIC. As early as 1792, Lexington had a vocal teacher, followed soon by a music academy (1795) and a singing school (1797). In 1805 Joseph Green advertised in Lexington that he was available to build pianos that would hold up in Kentucky's erratic climate. In 1817 Anthony Philip Heinrich, a German-Bohemian, arrived in Lexington, gathered a group of musicians, and presented a varied program that included the *Symphony No. 1* by Beethoven. The Liederkranz, a German male singing society formed in 1848, became an influential musical organization in Louisville. Stephen Collins Foster's "My Old Kentucky Home, Good Night!" was first heard in 1853 and became the official state song in 1928. Music was introduced into the public school curriculum in Louisville in 1853. The one-day event called the Big Singing, which began in Benton in 1884, has been held annually since then on the fourth Sunday in May (see Southern Harmony singing).

In 1887 the Lexington Opera House opened. In 1916 the Jewish Community Center Orchestra, the oldest orchestral ensemble in the state and the predecessor of the Louisville Orchestra, was founded by Louisville businessman Morris Simon. Josephine McGill, pianist and composer, sparked interest in Appalachian music when she published *Folk-Songs of the Kentucky Mountains* (1917). The Foster Music Camp, founded by James E. Van Peursen, opened at Eastern Kentucky University in Richmond in 1936. Mayor Charles Farnsley initiated the Louisville Orchestra Commissioning Project in 1948 to pay composers for new works. The orchestra's label, First Edition Records, issued about a hundred of the commissioned works. In 1949 the Greater Louisville Fund for the Arts was established to raise money for performing arts groups. The Kentucky Opera was founded in Louisville in 1952 under the direction of Moritz von Bomhard, who conducted the organization for the next thirty years. In 1959 the *Stephen Foster Story*, an outdoor musical, opened in Bardstown, featuring more than fifty of the composer's songs. The Harlan Boys Choir, an internationally recognized group, was organized by Harlan-born David L. Davies in 1966. The Kentucky Arts Commission, formed by the legislature in 1966, was reorganized in 1981 by Gov. John Young Brown, Jr. (1979-83), as the Kentucky Arts Council under the Department of the Arts. In 1978 the Youth Performing Arts School, a public school, opened in Louisville at a cost of $5 million. In 1984 philanthropist and retired industrialist H. Charles Grawemeyer established a first prize of $150,000 in music awards at the University of Louisville. The first award went to Polish composer Witold Lutoslawski in 1985.

A wide variety of native Kentucky musicians have achieved national and international repute. Robert Todd Duncan, baritone, created the role of Porgy in Gershwin's *Porgy and Bess* in 1935. Edwin Franko Goldman, bandmaster and composer, wrote over one hundred marches, including "Kentucky March," and formed a band that performed under his name from 1918 until 1979. Lionel Hampton, vibraphonist and Kentucky's best-known

JAZZ musician, recorded extensively and toured worldwide. "You've Been a Good Old Wagon but You've Done Broke Down," one of the earliest ragtime songs, was published in Louisville in 1895, the work of Benjamin Robertson Harney, ragtime pianist and composer. William Shakespeare HAYS, composer and river editor of the *Louisville Courier-Journal*, wrote 322 songs, which sold an estimated twenty million copies. The tune of "Happy Birthday to You" came from a songbook by Kentuckians Mildred J. Hill and Patty S. HILL, published in 1893.

Lee Luvisi, concert pianist, the only student to win the Louisville Orchestra Young Artist Competition three times, joined the faculty of the Curtis Institute of Music in Philadelphia as the youngest member in its history. Loretta LYNN, the COUNTRY MUSIC singer and songwriter, is internationally known through her recordings and the film *Coal Miner's Daughter*, based on her autobiography. Hugh Whitfield Martin, tenor, who performed as Riccardo Martin, was a member of New York City's Metropolitan Opera, where he sang from 1907 to 1915 under the baton of Arturo Toscanini. William Smith ("Bill") MONROE played on the "Grand Ole Opry" for many years and was an originator of BLUEGRASS music. Jean RITCHIE, folksinger, composer, and author, wrote many songs and was the author of *Singing Family of the Cumberlands* (1955) and *Celebration of Life* (1971).

In 1990 there were four professional orchestras and three YOUTH ORCHESTRAS in the state. The oldest, the Louisville Orchestra, in 1981 became professional, with a full-time rehearsal and performance schedule. The Lexington Philharmonic Orchestra, incorporated in 1965, is the outgrowth of the Central Kentucky Philharmonic Orchestra, a community group founded by Robert King in 1961. The Owensboro Symphony Orchestra is the result of a merger in 1966 of a chamber orchestra at Kentucky Wesleyan College and the Brescia (College)-Owensboro Orchestra. The Paducah Symphony Orchestra is the youngest organization, formed in 1979 when musicians were recruited to perform at the city's annual Summer Festival.

Since 1970 a number of major arts centers have been built. The oldest, the Norton Center for the Arts on the campus of Centre College in Danville, opened in 1973, when it was called the Regional Arts Center. In 1979 the Otis A. Singletary Center for the Arts was built on the campus of the University of Kentucky. Bowling Green solved its performing arts problems by buying the Capitol Theatre and renovating it at a cost of $1.2 million. Renamed the Capitol Arts Center, it opened in 1981. Two years later the KENTUCKY CENTER FOR THE ARTS opened in Louisville at a cost of $33.75 million. In 1989 the Madisonville Community College Fine Arts Center opened. Owensboro built RiverPark Center on the banks of the Ohio River at a cost of $11 million. The center houses the International Bluegrass Association.

Kentucky counts among its musicians many composers: Clifford Shaw, Carl Bricken, Karl Kroeger, Patrick O'Sullivan, Roy Nolte, Donald Murray, Robert French, Granville English, James Furman, Christopher Gallaher, David Livingston, John Jacob Niles, Karl Schmidt, William Reddick, Edward Redding, and Mary Tunstall Ijames (known as Marion Sunshine).

The diversity of Kentucky music is shown in the many festivals presented throughout the year. They include the Festival of the Bluegrass in Lexington, the Shaker Festival in South Union, the Official Kentucky State Championship Old Time Fiddlers Contest in Falls of Rough, the Kentucky Music Weekend in Louisville, the All-Night Gospel Sing in Renfro Valley, the Kentucky Highlands Folk Festival in Prestonsburg, the Great American Dulcimer Convention in Pineville, the Celebration of Traditional Music in Berea, and the Classics in Context in Louisville.

See Joy Carden, *Music in Lexington Before 1840* (Lexington, Ky., 1980); Nora Dixon McGee, *Kentucky Composers and Compilers of Folk Music: Native and Adopted* (Frankfort, Ky., 1950).

ROBERT BRUCE FRENCH

MUSIC HALL CONVENTION. One of the most tumultuous of Kentucky's Democratic nominating conventions for governor took place in Louisville's Music Hall on Market Street in June 1899 and is thus known as the Music Hall convention. The candidates were P. Wat Hardin, William J. Stone, and William Goebel. Hardin, a former state attorney general from Mercer County, had the support of business interests, the *Louisville Dispatch*, and, perhaps most important, the Louisville & Nashville (L&N) Railroad. Stone, an ex-Confederate soldier from Lyon County, had the backing of agricultural interests. Goebel, a lawyer and state senator from Kenton County, had support from urban areas. Goebel entered the convention in third place because of the unpopularity of the recently enacted Goebel Election Law, giving the full legislature (which was overwhelmingly Democratic) the power to select an election board to handle statewide election returns. The day before the convention, Goebel and Stone combined forces against Hardin, the leading candidate. Both signed a pact in which Goebel agreed to give Stone half of his Louisville delegate support and to support Stone in the event that Goebel withdrew or was defeated, and Stone agreed to do the same for Goebel.

The convention started on June 21, 1899, with Goebel and Stone forces electing a Goebelite, Judge David Redwine, as temporary chairman of the convention, over Hardin's man. The crucial task of deciding on contested delegates was left to the committee on credentials, which had been selected by Redwine and was made up of a majority of Goebel-Stone backers. The delay in the committee's decision increased the excitement and tension in the hall. Hundreds of people, mainly nondelegates, entered the hall in hope of disrupting the convention. The *Dispatch* and the *Louisville Courier-Journal* differed in identifying these troublemakers. Redwine had requested the presence of city police to keep order, which further angered Hardin supporters, who accused Redwine of intimidation tactics. When the credentials committee report was released on June 23, it gave twenty-six of the twenty-eight contested cases to Goebel or Stone supporters. Hardin and his backers had lost nearly 160 votes through a procedural manipulation by Stone and Goebel backers.

The nominating process for governor began on June 24. Disgusted by the turn of events, Hardin dropped out of the race briefly. John S. Rhea nominated Stone for governor. Stone's managers thought he and Goebel had an understanding that with Hardin's withdrawal, Goebel would drop out of the race, while retaining dominance of the Democratic party. When Goebel was nominated, any understanding, perceived or real, vanished. When balloting reached the Louisville delegates, all roll call votes were recorded for Goebel, rather than being divided. Many Stone supporters then began to back Hardin as revenge on Goebel. At the end of the night of June 24, the convention was deadlocked.

Redwine filled the hall with police on Monday, June 26. When Rhea requested that the police be removed to prevent intimidation, the chairman ruled the motion out of order. Stone and Hardin forces then joined in disrupting the business of the convention, standing on chairs, yelling, blowing tin horns, and singing. The *Courier-Journal* blamed agents of the L&N Railroad as instigators of the disorder. Voting took place amidst the confusion, but many abstained because of the difficulty in hearing over the uproar. The day's proceedings for the most part halted and the convention adjourned.

The crowded hall was calm the following day, June 27, when voting proceeded. Stone and Hardin were unsuccessful in joining forces against Goebel, but both were ahead of him on the twentieth and twenty-first ballots. By the twenty-fourth ballot, Goebel led by three votes. On the next ballot, a resolution to drop the third-place candidate from the race put Stone out of the running. On the last ballot, Goebel won Union County's sixteen votes, putting him ahead of Hardin.

Goebel's political maneuverings throughout the convention had brought him new enemies as well as the nomination for governor.

See James C. Klotter, *William Goebel* (Lexington, Ky., 1977).

MUSTER DAYS. Early in the nineteenth century, U.S. and Kentucky laws required nearly every ablebodied male citizen to enroll in the militia, which would be called up to defend the state in emergencies. The laws mandated periodic muster days, when the part-time soldiers were to assemble for military training. Few Kentuckians took militia musters very seriously. Musters became little more than social gatherings and occasions for hard drinking. By the 1820s, most Kentuckians preferred tending their own affairs to attending musters. Few judges collected the fines levied on absentees. James Weir, Sr., in *Lonz Powers: or, the Regulators* (1850), expressed the ridicule with which most came to view the militia system when he termed the muster "a great, grand, sometimes laughable but always silly farce, . . . legalized and even commanded by our laws. Yet do we suffer . . . three times annually leaving our labor and business to undergo this most absurd of all absurdities." After adoption of the 1850 Kentucky constitution, the legislature tried without success to reform the musters. When the Civil War began in 1861, musters were no longer being held with any regularity.

NICKY HUGHES

MYERLE, DAVID. David Myerle was a hemp manufacturer who attempted to introduce the waterretting method of hemp production to Kentucky farmers. Myerle, who operated cordage factories in Philadelphia and Pittsburgh, purchased a patent from Robert Graves for steam-generated rope manufacturing that wound the rope tighter and faster than conventional horse-powered methods. He moved to Kentucky from Pennsylvania in 1838 and established a modern steam-generated ropewalk in Louisville that employed sixteen slaves and ten free laborers. As early as 1823, Myerle had contracted to supply cordage to the U.S. Navy and in 1838 began negotiating to sell the navy his steam patent. Although unsuccessful, he convinced Secretary of the Navy James Paulding to issue a contract to him in 1841, to supply the navy with two hundred tons of water-retted hemp.

Most of the cordage used on navy ships came from Russian snow-retted hemp, which was stronger than the dew-retted hemp produced in the United States. In dew retting, hemp was cut and left to dry in the field for a week and then gathered into sheaves until November. When the cold weather came, the stalks of hemp were then spread on the ground again for approximately six weeks, or until the strands of fiber began to separate from the wood pulp of the plant. Hemp "brakes" were then used to complete the removal of the fiber. The water-retting method of separation called for the hemp to be placed in streams, ponds, or vats of water immediately after being cut. After soaking for about ten days, the fibers were separated from the wood pulp by hemp brakes. This process was much quicker than dew retting and also produced a stronger fiber, but it was a messy, stinky job that was thought to be unhealthy for humans. It also required great amounts of water, and it killed the inhabitants of streams or ponds. It was met with skepticism by Kentucky hemp farmers and never adopted on a large scale.

Opposed by some of the more powerful families in Kentucky, Myerle was unable to gather enough water-retted hemp to meet the navy contract and what he did produce was unsatisfactory, even though it was stronger than the Russian-grown hemp. Henry Clay feared that hemp purchases by the navy would raise the price of hemp for bagging used by the cotton growers of the Deep South. Nathaniel Hart, a prominent hemp grower from Woodford County, used his considerable influence in an attempt to gain the water-retted market for himself. Myerle, a successful manufacturer, was a failure in the agricultural and promotional aspects of his business and lost his factory and fortune in what he viewed as a patriotic endeavor to free the country from dependency on foreign hemp.

Myerle went to Missouri in 1842, where he was no more successful in convincing farmers there to employ the water-retting method. He then began a project of teaching the Indians in that state to grow hemp as a step toward self-sufficiency. He received a $30,000 payment from the government in 1860 for losses incurred in the water-retting project.

Hemp farmers in Kentucky and elsewhere in the United States continued to use the traditional dew-retting method, and the navy remained tied to the use of Russian hemp. As domestic hemp was used primarily for cotton bagging, its profitability depended upon the cotton market.

See Ralph M. Aderman, "David Myerle and Kentucky Hemp," *FCHQ* 35 (Jan. 1961): 11-25; James Franklin Hopkins, *A History of the Hemp Industry in Kentucky* (Lexington, Ky., 1951).

MYERS, RODES KIRBY. Rodes Kirby Myers, lawyer and politician, was born in Bowling Green, Kentucky, on June 29, 1900, to W.H. and Helen (Kirby) Myers. He attended Ogden College in Bowling Green, the University of Cincinnati Law School, and the University of Kentucky Law School, where he received his LL.B. degree in 1925. Myers had taught at Ogden College in 1920 and Morganfield High School in 1921. He began practicing law in Bowling Green in 1925. Myers's father was active in Warren County politics for more than twenty-nine years, and his son followed in his footsteps, serving as commonwealth attorney for the 6th Judicial District in 1933, state representative from 1934 to 1939 and in 1945, and state senator from 1948 to 1950. He also served as lieutenant governor under Gov. Keen Johnson from 1939 to 1943. In 1941, while Johnson attended the inauguration of President Franklin D. Roosevelt, Myers used his powers as acting governor to pardon two men and commute the sentences of two others who had been convicted for their parts in the 1931 Battle of Evarts, one of the bloodiest encounters during the time when the United Mine Workers were organizing the eastern Kentucky coalfields. Myers sought the Democratic nomination for governor in 1943, losing to Lyter Donaldson.

Myers was married first to Beulah Gardner of Bowling Green, then to Mary Lou Hubbard of Hodgenville, both marriages ending in divorce. On June 29, 1942, he married Neill Mohead; they had three children. Myers died on March 10, 1960, and is buried in Fairview Cemetery in Bowling Green.

See Frederick D. Ogden, ed., *The Public Papers of Governor Keen Johnson* (Lexington, Ky., 1982).

N

NANCY HANKS. Nancy Hanks, a trotter, was queen of the national harness track in the 1890s. She lost no races and failed to win only one heat. On September 28, 1892, she set a trotting record of 2:04 for a mile. Sired by Happy Medium out of a dam by Dictator, she was bred and owned by Hart Boswell of Fayette County, Kentucky. When very young, she showed a tendency to pace, a gait not desired in her day. Boswell hired Ben Kenney to train her to trot, which he did principally by laying wooden rails on the training track in such a way that she had to adopt a diagonal gait—a trot—to avoid stepping on the poles.

Nancy Hanks, retired from racing at the age of seven, became a distinguished broodmare whose descendants were outstanding performers. For the last eight of her twenty-nine years, she was owned by John E. Madden of Hamburg Place near Lexington. She died in 1915 and was given the place of honor in the Hamburg cemetery.

See Bruce Denbo, Mary Wharton, and Clyde Burke, *The Horse World of the Bluegrass* (Lexington, Ky., 1980). MARY E. WHARTON

NASH, CHARLES FRANCIS. Charles Francis ("Cotton") Nash, basketball player, was born on July 24, 1942, in Jersey City, New Jersey, to Frank and Nell (Isganatis) Nash. The family moved frequently. At Jeffersonville High School in Indiana, Nash was coached by former Kentucky basketball player Cliff Barker for two years. In Louisiana, at Lake Charles High School, he won All-State honors in baseball, basketball, and football and was the state discus champion. In 1960 the Louisiana Sports Writers Association named Nash the top athlete in the state. Offered numerous scholarships to play both basketball and football, as well as professional baseball contracts, Nash chose to play basketball at the University of Kentucky (UK). In each of his varsity years, the 1961-62 through 1963-64 seasons, Nash was named All-Southeastern Conference and All-American and was UK's leading scorer and rebounder. He finished his career at 1,770 points, an average of 22.7 a game, and was at that time the Wildcats' career scoring leader. Nash also played varsity baseball at the university (1962-64) and was on the track team in 1962.

Nash signed a professional baseball contract with the California Angels in 1964, reached the major leagues at the end of the 1967 season with the Chicago White Sox, and signed with the Minnesota Twins in 1969 and 1970, playing in a total of thirteen career major league games. Twice during his baseball career, Nash played professional basketball during the winter months, in 1964-65 for Los Angeles, of the National Basketball Association, and in 1967-68 for the Kentucky Colonels, of the American Basketball Association. In 1972 he returned to Lexington, where he is an investment and management counselor; his business interests include a small manufacturing company and real estate.

Nash married Julie Rachey; they have three children: Patrick, Richie, and Audry.

See Russell Rice, *Big Blue Machine* (Huntsville, Ala., 1978); Bert Nelli, *The Winning Tradition* (Lexington, Ky., 1984).

NATCHER, WILLIAM HUSTON. William Huston Natcher, U.S. congressman, was born in Bowling Green, Kentucky, on September 11, 1909, to J.M. and Blanche (Hays) Natcher. He received a public school education and attended high school at Ogden Preparatory Department of Ogden College in Bowling Green. Natcher earned his B.A. from Western Kentucky State College (Western Kentucky University) in 1930 and his law degree from Ohio State University in 1933. He was admitted to the bar in 1934 and began to practice law in Bowling Green. Natcher served as a Federal conciliation commissioner for Kentucky's western district in 1936 and 1937, and as the county attorney for Warren County from 1938 to 1950. He was a delegate to the Democratic National Convention in 1940, president of the Young Democratic Clubs of Kentucky from 1941 to 1946, served in the navy from 1942 to 1945, and was the commonwealth attorney for the 8th Judicial District of Kentucky from 1951 to 1953.

Natcher was elected on August 1, 1953, to fill the vacancy in the U.S. House of Representatives caused by the death of Garrett L. Withers. Natcher became a member of the House Appropriations Subcommittee for the District of Columbia in 1955 and assumed the chairmanship of the subcommittee in January 1962. During his career he also served on the Veterans Affairs Committee and the Foreign Aid and Agricultural subcommittees of the Appropriations Committee. In February of 1979 he became the chairman of the House Appropriations Subcommittee for the Departments of Labor and Health, Education and Welfare (HEW), one of the most powerful positions in the House. A private man, Natcher makes a point of opening his own mail and refuses to accept campaign contributions. As of January 1991, he held the record for consecutive votes cast in the legislature: 4,191 quorum calls and 12,644 roll-call votes.

Natcher married Virginia Reardon on June 17, 1937; they had two children, Celeste and Louise. Virginia died on January 6, 1991.

NATION, CARRY AMELIA (MOORE). Carry Amelia (Moore) Nation, temperance crusader, was born on November 25, 1846, in Garrard County, Kentucky, to George and Mary (Campbell) Moore. Her father was a planter and livestock dealer. Her mother, who was mentally ill, was often under the delusion that she was Queen Victoria. Between 1851 and 1865 the family lived in Boyle and Woodford counties, Kentucky; Grayson County, Texas; and Belton, Missouri. Ill health curtailed Carry's formal education.

Carry Moore married Dr. Charles Gloyd, a Missouri physician, in 1867. She left Gloyd, an alcoholic, several months later and returned to her parents' home, where she gave birth to a daughter, Charlien. Gloyd died within six months of her departure. Having earned a teaching certificate from the Normal Institute in Warrensburg, Missouri, Carry taught school. In 1877, after losing her teaching position, she married David Nation, lawyer, journalist, and minister. In the early 1890s the Nations moved to Medicine Lodge, Kansas, where he practiced law and she campaigned with a religious fervor against drinking. After her second marriage ended in divorce, Carry Nation developed a branch of the Women's Christian Temperance Union to rid Kansas of saloons. Kansas had outlawed alcohol, but liquor was sold by many establishments there. In June 1900 Nation used bricks to wreck a saloon in Kiowa, Kansas, and a hatchet later became her weapon in traveling throughout the United States to destroy drinking places. She was often imprisoned for "hatchetation" (her own term).

Nation lectured extensively in the United States and abroad. She was concerned with equal rights for women, the plight of the homeless, sex education, and the evils of tobacco. In July 1904 she was attacked by an irate bar owner in Elizabethtown, Kentucky, after a temperance lecture she had delivered. The police who saw the incident failed to arrest her assailant. Nation last wrecked a bar, Mrs. Maloy's Dance Hall and Cafe, in Butte, Montana, on January 26, 1910. She retired to a farm in Boone County, Arkansas, and died in Leavenworth, Kansas, on June 9, 1911. She was buried in a family cemetery in Belton, Missouri.

See Robert Day, "Carry from Kansas Became a Nation All Unto Herself," *Smithsonian Magazine*, April 1989.　　　　　　LISE SMITH-PETERS

NATIONAL GUARD. The Kentucky National Guard, if viewed as the successor to earlier Kentucky-based military forces, is one of the oldest military organizations in the United States. On October 10, 1774, when Kentucky was a county of colonial Virginia, James Harrod, the founder of Harrodsburg, led a group of frontiersmen against an Indian coalition led by the Shawnee. The Battle of Point Pleasant took place in what is now West Virginia. In 1775 Virginia formally recognized Harrod's men, naming the group the KENTUCKY MILITIA and appointing him its captain. The militia was active in the defense of Kentucky settlements throughout the Revolutionary War.

After the war, a militia force led by Simon Kenton patrolled northern Kentucky to repulse Indian raiding parties coming from north of the Ohio. The Kentucky militia took part in several unsuccessful campaigns to destroy Indian base camps in the Northwest. At the Battles of Fallen Timbers in 1794 and Tippecanoe in 1811, the Kentucky militia helped end hostilities in the Northwest.

During the WAR OF 1812, Kentuckians joined the militia by the thousands, hoping for American expansion into Canada and an end to Indian raids on Kentucky. During the MEXICAN WAR, 1846-48, Kentuckians who volunteered for militia duty served under Gen. Zachary Taylor at Buena Vista and Monterrey and Gen. Winfield Scott at Cerro Gordo and Chapultepec. Many Kentuckians who fought in the Civil War received their first military experience in Mexico.

The outbreak of the Civil War split the new National Guard organized in 1860; many guardsmen who joined the Confederacy became members of the 1st Kentucky "Orphan Brigade." Some served with John Hunt Morgan. Many volunteers in both Union and Confederate armies came from the Louisville Legion. Unionists formed loyalist Home Guard units, under Federal control, and were kept busy in Kentucky protecting Federal supply lines and local communities during the war.

In 1878, the State Guard was reestablished with regiments in Louisville, Lexington, and Bowling Green. It served principally as a domestic peacekeeping force, but was augmented to serve briefly in the Spanish-American War, 1998-99.

In 1903 Congress passed the Dick Law, which promised the states an annual appropriation in return for meeting federal military standards. It was not until 1912 that Kentucky conformed to this law and became a part of the National Guard system. This system was first tested on the Mexican border in October 1916, when violence from that country's revolution spilled across the border. In April 1917, the Kentucky units returning from the Mexican border were immediately mobilized for service in World War I, where they provided replacements to combat units in the American sector.

In 1941, before U.S. entry into World War II, guardsmen from Harrodsburg were part of the Provisional Tank Group in the Philippines. They participated in the defense of Bataan, and when U.S. forces surrendered to the Japanese they endured the Bataan Death March. Kentucky Guard units returned to the Philippines in 1944, and during weeks of hard-fought combat in the ZigZag Pass of Luzon Island earned the name "Avengers of Bataan." Other Kentucky Guard units fought from Sicily to Czechoslovakia in the European theater.

The conflicts of the Cold War presented new challenges to the Guard. The 623d Field Artillery was called up to provide artillery support to the X Corps during the Korean War, a war that seemed to lack the urgency that had rallied Kentuckians to military service in the past.

During the Berlin crisis the 413th Ordnance Company and the 2d Battalion of the 123rd Armor were assigned to Fort Stewart, Georgia; the 3d Battalion was assigned to Fort Knox, Kentucky. During the Pueblo incident members of the Kentucky

Air National Guard were called into overseas duty in Alaska, Panama, Japan, and Korea.

The Vietnam War found the 2d Battalion of the 138th Field Artillery supporting the 101st Airborne Division. "C" Battery of the 138th sustained heavy casualties repulsing a North Vietnamese assault on Firebase Tomahawk on June 19, 1969.

The Kentucky Guard assisted during the truckers' strike in 1974 and in the wake of the tornadoes of 1974, as in all major natural disasters. Guard units were called to help check race riots in Louisville in May 1968 and the antiwar demonstrations of 1970 at the University of Kentucky.

During the Persian Gulf War of 1990-91 the Kentucky National Guard supplied forces whose missions included water purification, transportation, field artillery support, and duty in field hospital and prisoner of war camps.

See Kentucky National Guard, *The Story of the Kentucky National Guard* (Frankfort, Ky., 1988); Richard Stone, *A Brittle Sword* (Lexington, Ky., 1977).　　　JOHN M. TROWBRIDGE
AND THOMAS W. FUGATE

NATIONAL HISTORIC LANDMARKS. National historic landmarks are designated sites, buildings, or objects judged to have exceptional value in identifying, illustrating, interpreting, or commemorating the heritage of U.S. history and prehistory, architecture, archaeology, science, and culture. Historic Sites and Buildings, a branch of the National Park Service, was established in July 1935 to identify properties of national historical significance. The Historic Sites Act of August 21, 1935, set the national policy and established the National Historic Landmarks Program to preserve and rehabilitate historic sites. The program began in 1936 with a national survey to identify landmarks. After a halt during World War II, the U.S. government reactivated the program and in 1960 designated the first national historic landmarks.

By 1990 the National Historic Landmarks Program had made twenty-two designations of places of national significance in Kentucky.

(1) Ashland estate (see separate entry).

(2) *Belle of Louisville* (see separate entry).

(3) Churchill Downs (see separate entry).

(4) Covington-Cincinnati suspension bridge (see ROEBLING BRIDGE).

(5) Daniel Carter BEARD House, 322 East Third Street, Covington. The boyhood home of Daniel C. Beard, one of the founders of the Boy Scouts of America, was built ca. 1850. The brick residence has a two-story main section with a two-and-a-half story ell wing.

(6) Dr. Ephraim MCDOWELL House, 125 South Second Street, Danville. The two-story frame and brick house with brick apothecary shop and office is a landmark in the progress of American medicine. The brick ell was built ca. 1786 and the clapboard block was constructed ca. 1800. McDowell purchased the house in 1802, built the one-story addition to house an apothecary shop and office, converted a room in the ell to serve as an operating room, and added the rear porch. On December 25, 1809, McDowell performed the first ovariotomy on Jane Todd Crawford in the upstairs operating room. The Kentucky Medical Association purchased the house in the early 1930s and restored it in 1936. It was dedicated as a state shrine on May 20, 1939.

(7) Indian Knoll, Archaeological Site No. 15-OH-2, near Paradise. Indian Knoll is an aboriginal habitation site, dating between 5000 and 2000 B.C. It consists of an Archaic Native American shell midden and evidence of Woodland and Mississippian Native American occupation (see PREHISTORIC PEOPLES). C.B. Moore conducted excavations in 1916 and published the first report on a prepotter culture in the area. In 1939 William S. Webb conducted more extensive excavations of the site. His report, completed in 1946, resulted in a list of various characteristics of southeastern Archaic shell middens, and it has contributed significant information on the temporal and cultural society known as the Archaic. The excavations yielded 1,200 burial sites and over 55,000 artifacts. The privately owned property is accessible only to qualified researchers.

(8) Jacobs Hall, KENTUCKY SCHOOL FOR THE DEAF, South Second Street, Danville. Jacobs Hall is the oldest surviving building on the campus of the first publicly supported institution for the education of the deaf in the United States. Named after school superintendent J.A. Jacobs, it was designed by Thomas LEWINSKI and built in 1855-57. The four-story brick building, with full basement, is of Italianate design with a two-story octagonal wooden cupola, a one-story portico in front, and one-story porch at the rear. The main hall, with a curving staircase, opens to the skylight in the cupola. Jacobs Hall served as the main building on campus until 1882, then as administrative offices, auditorium, and school post office.

(9) KEENELAND Race Course, Versailles Road, Lexington. The Keeneland landmark was laid out in 1916 as a private 1 1/16-mile track by John Oliver Keene on his Keeneland stud farm in 1916, where he built a three-story limestone clubhouse and training complex. In the mid-1930s Keene sold the unfinished training-racing complex on a 146-acre tract to the Keeneland Association, which held the first race meet in October 1936. Architect Robert W. McMeekin completed and renovated the multipurpose limestone clubhouse, erected a stone and wood 2,500-seat grandstand, and converted an incomplete quarter-mile training track to a paddock, using the colors "Keeneland green" and cream throughout the complex. Periodic additions have increased the grandstand capacity to approximately 7,000 seats and the landholdings to 441 acres. The gap between the clubhouse and grandstand was closed in 1963 and in 1974 a new clubhouse dining room and an officials' building were erected. Keeneland's grandstand faces west, and the clubhouse is at the head of the stretch—at variance with the layout at most tracks.

(10) Liberty Hall, 218 Wilkinson Street, Frankfort. This example of late Georgian architecture was built as a home for Margaretta and John Brown. Construction began in 1796 and was completed in 1800, using bricks and nails made on the Brown estate and timber harvested from their land. The Flemish bond brick structure stands two-and-a-half stories with an ell wing. On each floor are two rooms on either side of the central hall staircase. The two symmetrically placed interior brick chimneys have Adam-style mantels. The house remained in the Brown family until 1937, when it was sold to Liberty Hall, Inc. It operates as a museum.

(11) Life-Saving Station No. 10, 4th Stand River Road, Louisville. The lifeboat *Mayor Andrew Broaddus* is a historic landmark that was once an inland floating U.S. Coast Guard station. Another lifeboat served as Station No. 10 when the station was established at the Falls of the Ohio River in Louisville at the foot of Second Street on October 22, 1881. No. 10 was the first life-saving station on western rivers and the Broaddus is now one of the few remaining former stations of the Life-Saving Service, which was established in 1878 to aid shipwrecked mariners.

The *Broaddus*, the third lifeboat to serve as Station No. 10, was built in Dubuque, Iowa, and brought to Louisville in 1928. It was originally named the *Louisville*. It is a standard lifeboat station in design, placed on a movable floating foundation. The two-deck steel superstructure, with a lookout tower, sits atop a rectangular steel scow-form hull, measuring ninety-eight feet long and thirty-eight feet in the beam. Construction of the George Rogers Clark Memorial Bridge in 1936 forced relocation of the *Louisville* downriver on October 1, 1972. At that point, the Coast Guard transferred the boat to the City of Louisville. Renamed the *Mayor Andrew Broaddus*, it was converted into shops and offices for the *Belle of Louisville*.

(12) Lincoln Hall, BEREA COLLEGE, Berea. Lincoln Hall exemplifies the identity of Berea College, established for the specific purpose of integrated education. Lincoln Hall, a brick three-story T-shaped Georgian Revival structure, was built in 1885-87 with a donation from Roswell C. Smith, who requested that the building be named after President Abraham Lincoln. The architectural firm of Babb, Cook, and Willard of New York designed the building. Originally a multipurpose structure containing classrooms, library, meeting rooms and offices, Lincoln Hall now houses administrative offices.

(13) Locust Grove (see separate entry).

(14) Louisville Water Company Pumping Station No. 1, River Road and Zorn Avenue, Louisville. Designed by Theodore R. Scowden, engineer, and built during 1857-60, the station consisted of engine and boiler room and a 169-foot standpipe tower in Classical Revival style, imitating a Roman temple and column. The engine-boiler room was a two-story brick building with portico and one-story wings. The standpipe tower was designed as a Corinthian colonnade with statuary of nine classical Greek figures and an American Indian around the brick columned base, topped with a cupola. The shaft of the standpipe tower was constructed of riveted plates of steel and sheet metal. Blown over in the March 27, 1890, tornado, the tower was immediately reerected, with damage to a few of the statuaries. The Louisville Water Company retired the pumping station in 1909. In 1979-80 renovations were made to preserve the unique industrial architecture. In 1980 the Art Center Association, now the Louisville Art Association, leased the building for a museum and offices.

(15) Maker's Mark Distillery on Star Hill Farm, Rural Route 1, Loretto. In September 1805 Charles Burks built a water-powered gristmill on Hardin Creek in Happy Hollow Valley and began a distilling operation. The gristmill operated until 1906 but the distillery shut down at Burks's death in 1831. His great grandson, George R. Burks, restarted distillery operations in 1889. Early in the twentieth century the plant was expanded and modernized, and the gristmill was converted to a steam boiler in 1906. Burks sold the property in 1919 at the onset of prohibition, and the plant was closed until 1937, when Frank Bickett revived distilling operations. He sold the plant to Glenmore Distilleries, which then sold it to David Karp. Taylor William Samuels IV purchased it in 1953 and expanded and improved the production of sour mash whiskey under the name Maker's Mark Distillery.

Most of the structures in the distilling complex date from the early twentieth century. In location and arrangement, the buildings preserve the earlier sequence of stages in the production of whiskey: toll house (ca. 1890), visitors' house (1910), quart house (1905), still house (1935), cistern room (1935), bottling house (1910), two bonded warehouses (1890), former Burks residence (1901), and contemporary office building, warehouse, boiler room and maintenance shop.

(16) Old Bank of Louisville, 320 West Main Street, Louisville. The Louisville Bank of Kentucky was chartered on February 2, 1833, and its Greek Revival building was completed during 1836-37. James H. Dakin was architect and Gideon SHRYOCK supervised construction of the monumental example of small-scale commercial architecture. The one-story brick and native limestone has a recessed entrance behind a portico of Ionic columns with palmette motifs. The interior is a long, rectangular room with smaller vault rooms. Four Corinthian columns support the domed ceiling, which functions as a central skylight. Throughout its varied history, the building has maintained its architectural integrity. It now houses the Actors Theatre of Louisville.

(17) Old Morrison, West Third Street, Lexington. Old Morrison, the oldest existing building on the Transylvania University campus, is an excellent example of Greek Revival architecture, designed by Gideon Shryock. Named after benefactor Col.

James Morrison, it is a stuccoed brick three-story building with basement and two-story portico with six Doric columns flanked by two wings. Begun in 1830, it was dedicated on November 4, 1833, although not completed until May 1834. It was the central college building for the campus. During the Civil War the college closed and the buildings were commandeered at different times by both Union and Confederate troops, who used Morrison as an army hospital. After the Civil War, Old Morrison returned to its role as administration building. It was remodeled during the early 1880s but restored to its original plans in 1962. On January 27, 1969, a fire swept through the building, leaving only the exterior walls intact. Reconstruction was completed in 1970-71 and the building was rededicated on May 9, 1971. It serves as administrative center for the university.

(18) Old State House (see CAPITOL BUILDINGS).

(19) Perryville Battlefield, Perryville. The Battle of Perryville, fought northwest of the town on October 7 and 8, 1862, ended a major Confederate invasion of Kentucky. The battle was the bloodiest fought in Kentucky and among the most severe engagements of the Civil War in terms of the sizes of the armies. A one-hundred-acre tract near the northern end of the battlefield, the area of the heaviest fighting, is operated by the Commonwealth of Kentucky as the Perryville Battlefield State Park. At the center of the park are the Confederate cemetery, a museum built in 1967, and numerous commemorative markers. The remainder of the battlefield site is privately owned.

(20) Shakertown at Pleasant Hill Historic District (see SHAKER COMMUNITIES).

(21) Whitney M. Young, Jr., Memorial House, Lincoln Ridge. The birthplace of Whitney M. YOUNG, Jr., director of the National Urban League, is located on what was once the campus of Lincoln Institute. The two-story white wood house, with one-story porch at the rear and a one-story wing built in 1972, was originally the home of the president of Lincoln Institute. Young was born there in 1921 during the presidency of Whitney M. Young, Sr., and lived at Lincoln Ridge for the first twenty years of his life.

(22) Springfield, Zachary Taylor house (see separate entry).

NATURAL BRIDGE. Natural arches, developed mainly in resistant sandstones of Pennsylvanian age (about 320 million years old), are present along the Pottsville Escarpment in eastern Kentucky, on Pine Mountain in southeastern Kentucky, and locally in western Kentucky. The state's most famous arch is Natural Bridge in Powell County. It has been a tourist attraction for many years and is the focus of the Natural Bridge State Resort Park. Natural Bridge, a ridge-top arch, was formed in a narrow sandstone ridge along a drainage divide in the intricately dissected topography of the Pottsville Escarpment. Development of the narrow ridge and arch resulted from the processes of erosion, mass

wasting, and differential weathering, including the action of water, ice, and roots that penetrated along joints and bedding planes in the sandstone.

See Thornton L. Neathery, ed., *Centennial Field Guide—Southeastern Section of the Geological Society of America* (Boulder, Colo., 1986); Arthur C. McFarlan, *Geology of the Natural Bridge State Park Area* (Lexington, Ky., 1954).

GARLAND R. DEVER, JR.

NATURE PRESERVES. Nature preserves are areas of unusual natural significance that are valuable for scientific research; as habitats for plant and animal species and biotic communities; as living museums; as places of historic and natural interest and beauty; and as reminders of the vital human dependence upon fresh air, clean water, and unspoiled land. When dedicated into the Kentucky Nature Preserves System, such areas receive the highest level of land protection. Kentucky has a rich diversity of plants, animals, and natural features, but the demands of an expanding human population and ever-increasing development are having irreversible impacts on the natural world. The Kentucky State Nature Preserves Commission is saving the best of what is left.

The author of the Nature Preserves Act, passed by the Kentucky General Assembly in 1976, was Jon Rickert of Elizabethtown, the first chairman of the Nature Preserves Commission. The act was considered progressive at the time, with the most obvious compromise being that three of the five citizens who serve on the commission must represent farm groups. In 1988 the commission's name became the Kentucky State Nature Preserves Commission, and the permission of mineral owners was first required for areas to be dedicated as nature preserves.

The commission's first director was Donald F. Harker, Jr., who served during 1977-82. He was succeeded by Richard Hannan, formerly the commission's botanist and ecologist.

In identifying natural areas to be preserved, the commission uses the natural-heritage method of mapping endangered plants and animals and other natural features, developed by the Nature Conservancy, a private, nonprofit organization. The commission monitors those elements of natural diversity in the state that are considered threatened if no action is taken on their behalf: plant and animal species, biological communities, recognizable ecosystems, and geologic structures such as cave systems. The areas that harbor the most critical or rarest components of Kentucky's natural heritage become the target of preservation. The commission's computerized data base is also useful to developers and decision-makers in other state and federal agencies.

Land that is purchased by or given to the commission is dedicated to protection against development. Owners of natural areas may elect to retain land ownership but relinquish their right to develop an area. The first area dedicated into the system was Blackacre Nature Preserve in Jefferson County, donated to the commission by Macauley and Emile Smith. It is operated by the Jefferson County school system, and thousands of students use it each year for environmental education. Second to be dedicated was the Jesse Stuart State Nature Preserve, more than seven hundred acres, known as W-Hollow, in Greenup County. It was donated by Kentucky poet laureate Jesse Stuart and his wife, Naomi. By the end of 1989, sixteen other nature preserves had been dedicated.

A landowner who wants to protect a natural area without relinquishing any interest in the property may do so by making a commitment to the Natural Areas Registry. These areas, however, do not receive the legal protection afforded dedicated nature preserves. There were forty-four registered natural areas at the end of 1989.

In 1980 Kentuckians were given the opportunity to mark their Kentucky tax forms to donate all or part of their tax refund to nature preservation. The money supports the nongame wildlife programs of the Department of Fish and Wildlife Resources, as well as buying and maintaining natural areas for the Nature Preserves Commission.

The eighteen state nature preserves encompass a total of 5,812 acres.

Bad Branch. Dedicated December 26, 1985, Bad Branch State Nature Preserve is a 435-acre area in Letcher County containing Bad Branch Gorge, a forested gorge on the south face of Pine Mountain. This preserve protects the scenic beauty of the gorge and one of the largest concentrations of rare and unusual species known in the state. The stream Bad Branch has been designated a Kentucky wild river.

Bat Cave and Cascade Caverns. Dedicated December 16, 1981, Bat Cave and Cascade Caverns State Nature Preserves are two tracts totaling 126 acres in Carter County, within Carter Caves State Resort Park. Bat Cave was dedicated to the nature preserve system for the protection of the Indiana bat, which is on the federal endangered species list. Its wintering numbers in Bat Cave are estimated at 38,000. The Cascade Caverns portion of the preserve was dedicated to protect two plant species rare in Kentucky, the mountain maple and the Canadian yew.

Beargrass Creek. Dedicated February 17, 1982, Beargrass Creek State Nature Preserve is a forty-one-acre, second-growth woodland near Joe Creason Park and the Louisville Zoological Gardens in Jefferson County. This urban green space, popular among birdwatchers, offers passive recreation and nature education near downtown Louisville.

Blackacre. Dedicated on March 19, 1979, Blackacre State Nature Preserve is a tract of approximately 170 acres in Jefferson County near Jeffersontown that is used as an environmental education center by the Jefferson County public schools and the University of Louisville. In the outdoor laboratory, children have a unique opportunity for environmental education. The area is managed by the

county school system and the Blackacre Foundation through an agreement with the commission. Visits are scheduled by contacting the director at Blackacre or the school system.

Blue Licks Battlefield. Dedicated December 16, 1981, Blue Licks Battlefield State Park Nature Preserve is a fifteen-acre tract in Robertson County within Blue Licks State Park. It protects Short's goldenrod, a species of plant found nowhere else in the world and protected under the Federal Endangered Species Act.

Boone County Cliffs. Dedicated November 5, 1987, Boone County Cliffs State Nature Preserve is a forty-six-acre area along a tributary to Middle Creek. The preserve protects the twenty- to forty-foot conglomerate cliffs that outcrop on the valley slopes. The conglomerate is composed of gravel deposited as glacial outwash about 700,000 years ago. In addition, the preserve protects four major forest community types. The preserve is owned by the Kentucky Chapter of the Nature Conservancy.

Brigadoon. Dedicated March 14, 1987, Brigadoon State Nature Preserve is ninety-two acres of mostly mature forest in Barren County adjacent to the Barren River Reservoir. The rich woodlands contain an impressive array of spring wildflowers, including several species rare or uncommon in Kentucky. The preserve also provides habitat for a large number of resident and migratory birds.

Cumberland Falls. Dedicated September 26, 1983, Cumberland Falls State Park Nature Preserve encompasses approximately 1,294 acres in Cumberland Falls State Resort Park in McCreary County. This preserve protects six species of rare plants and ten rare animals, including the Cumberland bean mussel, which is classified as an endangered species. In addition, the preserve includes a number of waterfalls, among them Cumberland Falls, which plummets sixty-seven feet into a rocky gorge. The Cumberland River, designated a Kentucky wild river, flows through the preserve.

Cypress Creek. Dedicated December 5, 1985, Cypress Creek State Nature Preserve is a ninety-seven-acre portion of bottomlands adjacent to Cypress Creek in Muhlenberg County. The preserve contains a mosaic of natural communities, including a bald cypress swamp and a bottomland hardwood complex. The preserve and adjacent areas contain numerous rare species typically associated with wetlands. Access is by written permission only.

Jesse Stuart. Dedicated December 7, 1979, Jesse Stuart State Nature Preserve, 733 acres in Greenup County, was acquired through a gift-purchase arrangement with the internationally known author whose name it bears. The area is used for passive recreation and environmental education. Natural, cultural, and historical research on the preserve is coordinated with the Jesse Stuart Foundation, a public foundation that oversees Stuart's literary estate.

Jim Scudder. Dedicated on September 2, 1987, Jim Scudder State Nature Preserve is a fifty-eight-acre glade and prairie complex in Hardin County. The dry, rocky glade openings provide habitat for several rare plant species, including the small white lady's-slipper, silky aster, and small skullcap. The preserve, owned by Hardin County, is managed by the commission to protect one of the best remaining examples of a limestone glade in Kentucky. Access is by written permission only.

John James Audubon. Dedicated on September 19, 1979, John James Audubon State Park Nature Preserve consists of approximately 325 acres within Audubon State Park, in Henderson County. This area is a rich mixed-hardwood forest originally set aside as a bird sanctuary and memorial to the distinguished naturalist for whom it was named. The preserve protects an excellent example of the forested loess bluffs along the Ohio River.

Metropolis Lake. Dedicated on August 10, 1984, Metropolis Lake State Nature Preserve is a 123-acre tract in McCracken County that contains the fifty-acre Metropolis Lake, one of the few remaining natural lakes in the Ohio River floodplain. The lake is ringed with bald cypress and swamp tupelo and provides habitat for a water snake and four species of fish that are rare or uncommon in Kentucky. This area is also inhabited by beaver and is visited by bald eagles during the winter.

Natural Bridge. Dedicated December 16, 1981, Natural Bridge State Park Nature Preserve consists of approximately 994 acres in Powell County within Natural Bridge State Resort Park. This area was dedicated to protect a significant geological system and habitat of rare species. The Virginia big-eared bat, which is on the federal list of endangered species, has been found in the preserve.

Pilot Knob. Dedicated September 26, 1985, Pilot Knob State Nature Preserve is a 308-acre area in Powell County considered to be the elevation on which Daniel Boone first stood and looked out over the Bluegrass region of Kentucky. A sandstone outcrop at the southeast end of the 730-foot-high knob is known as Boone's Overlook. This preserve is managed by Eastern Kentucky University through an agreement with the commission.

Pine Mountain. Dedicated September 26, 1983, Pine Mountain State Park Nature Preserve consists of two tracts, totaling 868 acres, within Pine Mountain State Resort Park in Bell County. This area contains an old-growth forest of hemlock, tulip poplar, and white oak, many of which are two hundred to three hundred years old, as well as a large sandstone shelter known as the Rock Hotel, which was inhabited by prehistoric Native Americans. The preserve is part of the Pine Mountain Fault block, one of the most prominent geological structures in the eastern United States.

Six Mile Island. Dedicated on June 24, 1979, Six Mile Island State Nature Preserve is an eighty-one-acre island in the Ohio River in Jefferson County near Louisville that is noted for its variety of water birds. Protection of this island will allow it to return to its natural state, a unique opportunity to study the ecology of riverine island systems.

See R.R. Hannan, C.A. Justis, and B.D. Anderson, *Evaluation and Protection Methodologies for Kentucky's Natural Areas* (Frankfort, Ky., 1982); D.F. Harker, Jr., et al., *Kentucky Natural Areas Plan* (Frankfort, Ky., 1980).

DONALD F. HARKER, JR.

NAZARETH COLLEGE OF KENTUCKY. Nazareth College of Kentucky, located in Nelson County, originated as Nazareth Academy, the first convent school west of the Appalachian Mountains, opened by the SISTERS OF CHARITY OF NAZARETH on August 23, 1814.

The first school of the sisters, housed in a log cabin located on St. Thomas Farm five miles southeast of Bardstown, met a need for educating the daughters of farmers of the area. By the end of the first year the names of nine girls were on the student roster; soon pupils came from Nelson, Washington, and Gallatin counties. In 1822 the school was transferred to a new location, Nazareth, on 237 acres of farm property two miles north of Bardstown, and it became known as Nazareth Academy.

In July 1825 the first public examination in the presence of parents and guardians was held; Henry Clay, a friend of bishop Benedict Joseph Flaget, presided and presented the honors. Margaret Carroll (later known as Sister Columba) was the school's first graduate (1825) and served as its director for thirty years (1832-62).

Nazareth Academy obtained a charter from the General Assembly on December 29, 1829. The charter was amended in 1920. During the tenure of Sister Mary Ignatius Fox, director of Nazareth Academy (1913-37), the upper classes of the academy and an added second year were combined in 1922 to establish Nazareth Junior College, of which Fox was director until 1937. In January 1924 the Kentucky State Board of Education approved the granting of state teaching certificates. Nazareth College of Kentucky was a junior college from 1922 to 1940; then it was a corporate senior college with the separate Nazareth College of Louisville (now SPALDING UNIVERSITY) from 1940 to 1960; and it became an independent liberal arts college in 1960. In 1971 the college merged with Spalding University in Louisville, and all classes were transferred to that campus.

As early as the 1820s, the school attracted students from several states, including Louisiana, Mississippi, Tennessee, Arkansas, and Alabama. A century later it began educating foreign students and since then has enrolled students from forty nations.

Most of the educational facilities on campus are housed in a group of historic buildings, dating from 1854 onward. Notable among the buildings stands O'Connell Hall (1855), named in honor of Sister Ellen O'Connell, the first director of Nazareth Academy (1816-32).

See Agnes Geraldine McGann, *SCNs Serving Since 1812* (Nazareth, Ky., 1985); Anna Blanche

McGill, *Sisters of Charity of Nazareth* (New York 1917). MARY MICHAEL CREAMER

NEAL, PATRICIA. Patricia Neal, actress, was born January 20, 1926, in Packard, Whitley County, Kentucky, to William and Eura (Petry) Neal. After studying drama at Northwestern University and working as a model, Neal made her Broadway debut in *The Voice of the Turtle* in 1946. In 1949 *John Loves Mary*, her first film, was released. Neal's marriage to Roald Dahl, a British screenwriter and novelist, in 1953 led to her prolonged absence from the screen. Neal's return in *A Face in the Crowd* (1957) established her as one of Hollywood's top actresses. In 1963 the deep-voiced actress received an Academy Award for her performance in *Hud*, a modern western.

In 1965 Neal suffered a series of strokes that left her partially paralyzed and confined to a wheelchair. She recovered and returned to acting, starring in the 1968 production of *The Subject Was Roses*, which brought her another Oscar nomination. Her most recent film is *An Unremarkable Life* (1989).

Neal and Dahl divorced in 1983; they have five children, Olivia Twenty, Tessa Sophia, Theo Matthew, Ophelia Magdaline, and Lucy.

NELSON, WILLIAM. William Nelson, a Civil War major general, was born September 27, 1824, in Maysville, Kentucky, the son of Dr. Thomas W. and Frances (Doniphan) Nelson. His uncle, Gen. Alexander Doniphan, was a hero of the Mexican War. Nelson was educated at Maysville Boys Academy and the U.S. Naval Academy. He served in the Mexican War and was a naval officer at the outbreak of the Civil War. When Nelson offered his services to President Abraham Lincoln, he was sent to Kentucky to win support for the Union cause. CAMP DICK ROBINSON, which he established in Garrard County, became a major recruiting location. On September 16, 1861, he was commissioned a brigadier general of volunteers. He fought at the Battles of Shiloh, Corinth, and Chattanooga. When Kentucky was invaded, Nelson was sent back to the state to organize troops. He was wounded at the battle of Richmond on August 30, 1862. On September 29, 1862, Nelson, by then a major general, was shot and killed at the Galt House in Louisville in a personal disagreement with a fellow soldier, Jefferson Davis. In 1863, CAMP NELSON, named in his honor, was established in Jessamine County; it became the principal Union recruiting and training location for black soldiers in Kentucky. Nelson was buried first in Louisville, then at Camp Nelson, and finally at Maysville.

JEAN W. CALVERT

NELSON, WILLIAM STUART. William Stuart Nelson, educator and theologian, was born on October 15, 1895, in Paris, Kentucky, to William Henry and Emma (Kersands) Nelson. The family later moved to Paducah, where Nelson graduated from Lincoln High School. Stuart Nelson Park in Paducah was built and named for him in the 1940s, when the town's Bob Noble Park was restricted to whites.

Nelson joined the army in World War I and became a combat officer in the Second Army's 92d Division, whose members were awarded twenty-one Distinguished Service crosses. He earned a bachelor of arts degree from Howard University in Washington, D.C., in 1920, and a bachelor of divinity degree from Yale in 1924. He also studied in France at the Sorbonne and the Protestant Theological Seminary, both in Paris.

Nelson began teaching philosophy at Howard University in 1924, and became an assistant to the president there. He left to become president of Shaw University in Raleigh, North Carolina, and then served as president at Dillard University in New Orleans. Nelson returned to Howard in 1940 as dean of the School of Religion. He became dean of Howard in 1948 and vice president in 1961. He established the *Journal of Religious Thought* at Howard, where he also taught. Nelson retired in 1968. He died in Washington, D.C., on March 26, 1977, and was buried there in Lincoln Memorial Cemetery. He was married to Blanche Louise (Wright) Nelson, who also taught at Howard.

BERRY CRAIG

NELSON COUNTY. The fourth county in order of formation, Nelson County was created on November 29, 1784, from part of Jefferson County and named for Thomas Nelson, Virginia governor and signer of the Declaration of Independence. The county covers 437 square miles and is bordered by Marion, Washington, Anderson, Spencer, Bullitt, Hardin, and Larue counties. BARDSTOWN, the county seat, was settled in 1780 and named for David Baird, one of the original settlers.

The topography is varied and extends from the flatlands around Bardstown to rolling hills in the east and knobs in the west. The Rolling Fork River forms the southwest border, and the Beech Fork River runs along the eastern county line. In 1987, 75 percent of the land was in farms, and 65 percent of farmland was in cultivation. Nelson ranked thirteenth among counties in agricultural receipts from tobacco, livestock, nursery and greenhouse crops, hay, vegetables, and fruit. Natural resources include limestone and dolomite.

Mounds, earthworks, and relics indicate prehistoric Native Americans inhabited the area before the first settlers arrived in 1775. Cols. Isaac Cox and James Rogers built their stations in the area in 1780, and Samuel Pottinger built his station in 1781. By 1783 land warrants had been issued for 20,000 acres. The county became an important early settlement for Roman Catholics. In 1808 Bishop Benedict J. FLAGET established the first inland diocese in the nation at Bardstown. In 1812 Catherine Spalding became the first superior of the SISTERS OF CHARITY of Nazareth at St. Thomas Farm. In 1819 St. Joseph's Seminary and St. Joseph's College were opened in Bardstown. In 1848 the Abbey of Our Lady of Gethsemani was founded.

Two small Civil War skirmishes occurred in Nelson County. On October 4, 1862, detachments of Gen. Don Carlos Buell's troops were defeated by soldiers from the command of Confederate Gen. Braxton Bragg, and the Union's 78th Indiana Regiment was captured at Bardstown. On July 5, 1863, Gen. John Hunt Morgan led his troops through the county and engaged Union cavalry. The county was raided by Marcellus Jerome Clarke ("Sue Mundy") and William Quantrill for the Confederates, and by Edward Terrell for the Union.

In 1844 T.W. Samuels began commercially distilling whiskey at Deatsville. In 1896 more than twenty-six Nelson County distilleries were producing whiskey for national distribution. Many did not survive prohibition, but after repeal in 1933, several new plants were built on the old sites. The Churchill Distilling Company built a plant near Boston in 1934, and nineteen years later it was purchased by the James B. Beam Distillery, makers of Jim Beam bourbon. Old Heaven Hill Distillery, which produces a bourbon of the same name, was built two miles from Bardstown in 1934. Tom Moore Distillery (1889) was sold in the 1940s to Barton Brands, Ltd., which produces Tom Moore, Very Early Barton, and Kentucky Gentlemen.

Other industries include American Greetings Corporation; Owens-Illinois, plastic bottle and carrier producer; and Nu-Hote International, which came in 1972 and employs 382 in production of business machine ribbons. Rail service is provided by R.J. Corman Railroad Transportation. The Bluegrass Parkway traverses the county, which is also served by U.S. 31E and U.S. 150. In 1990 tourism brought in more than $43.6 million. Among the tourist attractions are My Old Kentucky Home State Park; the outdoor drama *The Stephen Foster Story*; St. Joseph Proto-Cathedral; Old Talbott Tavern, an inn since the late 1700s; the Oscar Getz Museum of Whiskey History; Knobs State Forest; and Old Bardstown Village.

There are four incorporated towns in Nelson County: Bardstown, Bloomfield, Fairfield, and New Haven.

Nelson County had a population of 23,477 in 1970; 27,584 in 1980; and 29,710 in 1990.

See Dixie Hibbs, *Nelson County Kentucky: A Pictorial History* (Norfolk, Va., 1989); Sarah Smith, *Historic Nelson County* (Bardstown, Ky., 1983).   DIXIE HIBBS

NERINCKX, CHARLES. An early Catholic missionary priest, Charles Nerinckx was born in Belgium on October 2, 1761. After studies at Louvain, he was ordained a priest in 1785. First forced into hiding by the French Revolution, and later into exile, he arrived in Baltimore in November 1804, offering his services to Bishop John Carroll. The bishop sent him to Georgetown College in Washington, D.C., to study English, and then to join

Stephen BADIN in Kentucky. Morally stern but personally affable, the Belgian served in the Kentucky ministry from 1805 to 1824, building fourteen churches during that time. For many years he shared Badin's residence, Priestland, eventually moving to live among the Hardin's Creek congregation in Marion County, to which he gave the name of his patron saint, St. Charles.

The rugged Nerinckx was well-matched to his pioneer environment. Bishop M.J. Spalding later wrote of him: "He feared no difficulties and was appalled by no dangers." He was a founding force in 1812 in establishing the SISTERS OF LORETTO. An attempt to found an order of black sisters was unsuccessful. His special concern as priest was the pastoral care of children. He was noted as well for separating his congregations during worship, male from female, and for constructing churches in the shape of a cross.

Because of disputes with the bishop, including one concerning the rules of the Sisters of Loretto, Nerinckx in 1824 left Kentucky for Missouri, where he died on August 12 of the same year. He was buried at the Loretto Motherhouse in Marion County, where one of his early chapels was preserved.

See W.J. Howlett, *Life of Rev. Charles Nerinckx* (Techny, Ill., 1915).   CLYDE F. CREWS

NEVILLE, LINDA. Linda Neville, Appalachian health crusader, was born in Lexington on April 23, 1873, the daughter of University of Kentucky professor John H. Neville and Mary Payne Neville. As a child she was educated at home by her father and she subsequently graduated from Bryn Mawr College. While visiting Katherine Pettit, who had recently helped establish the HINDMAN SETTLEMENT SCHOOL, Neville learned of the disease trachoma which, untreated, results in blindness, and which affected 33,000 residents of the remote areas of eastern Kentucky. The treatment is simple, and upon her return to Lexington Neville began to recruit medical assistance and funds to fight the disease. Through her efforts eleven permanent clinics and several traveling medical units were established; the culmination of Neville's efforts came in 1952, when the disease was eradicated and the last permanent clinic at Richmond was closed. In later years Neville successfully pressured the state legislature to enact laws mandating preventive treatment of the eyes of newborns, as well as the medical examination of marrying adults, and was largely responsible for the establishment of the Kentucky Society to Prevent Blindness. She died in a Lexington nursing home on June 2, 1961, and is buried in the Lexington Cemetery.   VAUGHN McBRIDE

NEW CASTLE. New Castle, the seat of Henry County, is located on U.S. 421 thirty miles northeast of Louisville, toward the center of the county. It was founded as the seat of the new county in 1798 and incorporated in 1817. The origin of its name is unknown. The first courthouse to serve Henry County was built in New Castle in 1799. It was replaced in 1804. The third courthouse was completed in 1875 and placed on the National Register of Historic Places in 1977.

This sixth-class city has little industry. The population was 755 in 1970; 832 in 1980; and 893 in 1990.

NEW DEAL. President Franklin D. Roosevelt's New Deal was designed to combat the Great Depression, which began in 1929. Its emergency measures began in March 1933 and lasted until the early days of World War II. Many reform measures, however, became permanent and the "alphabet soup" agencies continue to affect Kentuckians.

To assist approximately 15 million unemployed Americans, the New Deal experimented with several relief and work programs. The Federal Emergency Relief Administration (FERA) distributed money and surplus food to the needy, dispensing $35 million to more than 500,000 Kentuckians. The Works Progress Administration (WPA) created jobs for thousands of Kentuckians, spent $162 million in the state, and left a legacy that included 14,000 miles of improved highways, 9,000 public buildings, and packhorse libraries. The WPA also employed artists and writers who produced murals and such books as *Kentucky, A Guide to the Bluegrass State* (1939). An autonomous WPA organization, the National Youth Administration (NYA), found part-time jobs for high school and college students, thousands of whom could not otherwise have finished their education. The Public Works Administration (PWA) completed six hundred projects, including the Student Union building at the University of Kentucky, a new prison at LaGrange, and the gold depository at Fort Knox.

Probably the most popular New Deal program was the Civilian Conservation Corps (CCC), created to improve the national domain and provide relief jobs. Thousands of work camps were established on national, state, and private lands, and more than 3 million young men learned skills of reforestation, fire-fighting, and construction. More than 80,000 Kentuckians enrolled in the CCC. In the peak year of 1935, the state had fifty-nine camps. The camps developed Mammoth Cave, excavated an amphitheater at Pine Mountain, built Dupont Lodge at Cumberland Falls, planted trees at the Kentucky Dam site, demonstrated forestry techniques for farmers, and provided emergency crews during the 1937 floods.

Of the approximately 5,000 banks that failed in the United States after the 1929 financial panic, more than one hundred were in the commonwealth. Roosevelt's Banking Holiday in March 1933 closed all banks to stem this crisis; federal inspection then determined which banks could reopen. Subsequent reforms such as the Federal Deposit Insurance Corporation (FDIC) stabilized financial institutions and restored depositors' confidence.

Several New Deal measures rescued distressed homeowners and those living in substandard housing. To prevent mortgage foreclosures, the Home Owners Loan Corporation (HOLC) arranged refinancing, and more than 9,000 Kentuckians benefited. A similar measure, the Farm Credit Administration (FCA), assisted 18,000 rural Kentuckians in refinancing their farm properties. An additional 38,000 property owners got loans from the Federal Housing Administration (FHA) for construction or repair work. These three agencies provided more than $100 million during the 1930s to secure households when other options had vanished. The U.S. Housing Authority (USHA) pioneered slum clearance and low-cost housing complexes. Six Kentucky cities—Louisville, Lexington, Covington, Paducah, Frankfort, and Newport—received a total of $19 million to participate in this new urban initiative.

Predominantly rural Kentucky benefited greatly from New Deal agricultural programs. To reduce surpluses and raise farm prices in 1933, the Agricultural Adjustment Administration (AAA) paid farmers to destroy crops and animals. Hundreds of Kentuckians plowed up crops and took their pigs to an early slaughter in this controversial experiment. Later AAA programs paid farmers to remove part of their acreage from production and institute conservation practices. By 1941 more than 250,000 participating state farmers were receiving federal subsidies that averaged $10 million per year. The Resettlement Administration (RA) and its successor, the Farm Security Administration (FSA), helped farmers to rehabilitate their facilities, purchased marginal land and relocated four hundred Kentucky families to new sites, and constructed two experimental rural communities in Laurel, Christian, and Trigg counties. The Rural Electrification Administration (REA) brought power and light to remote farms through government-assisted cooperatives, quadrupling the percentage of electrified farms in five years.

Located in the Jackson Purchase, Kentucky Dam was a massive enterprise that affected the entire state. Begun in 1938, this Tennessee Valley Authority (TVA) project was part of a seven-state network of dams and reservoirs to bring flood control to the region. Ancillary benefits from the TVA were inexpensive electricity, fertilizers, and recreation opportunities. Frequently criticized as socialistic, the TVA in Kentucky relocated 3,500 families and 2,000 graves from the reservoir area, submerged the town of Birmingham, and spent $100 million prior to dedication of the dam in 1945.

New Deal labor reforms generated much controversy in Kentucky and brought many permanent changes. The National Recovery Administration (NRA) raised hopes of better working conditions and union rights, but its demise in 1935 reflected one of Roosevelt's major failures. Later legislation replaced the NRA experiments. The National Labor Relations Act encouraged growth of labor unions, and several years of strikes and violence followed, especially in Harlan County coal mines, before conditions stabilized. Federally mandated minimum wage, maximum hour, and child labor regulations came with the Fair Labor Standards Act. The national Social Security Act revolutionized Kentucky welfare activities. Federal-state matching programs for pensions, workmen's compensation, and other required benefits restructured state agencies and tax schedules to follow national guidelines.

Immediate and enduring effects of the New Deal were obvious. The roughly $1 billion in federal spending in Kentucky during a single decade helped revive the economy. Stronger federal regulations forced state government and private enterprise to alter traditional practices. Although several New Deal agencies expired, many programs affecting labor, agriculture, welfare, and banking became permanent federal responsibilities. The New Deal accelerated several trends in Kentucky: urbanization, larger farms, unionization, and a heavy dependence on national revenues.

Many Kentucky politicians were active New Dealers, while others remained aloof. Marvin McIntyre, Alben W. Barkley, Fred M. Vinson, Virgil Chapman, and William and Noble Gregory were all Roosevelt allies, and Solicitor General Stanley Reed defended several New Deal programs before the Supreme Court. Kentucky governors adapted to the New Deal with varying success. Ruby Laffoon (1931-35) resisted and usually lost; A.B. Chandler (1935-39) was ambivalent but generally acclimated. Keen Johnson (1939-43) accepted the New Deal with more enthusiasm than his two predecessors and enjoyed a smoother relationship with Washington.

See George T. Blakey, *Hard Times and New Deal in Kentucky, 1929-39* (Lexington, Ky., 1986); James T. Patterson, *The New Deal and the States: Federalism in Transition* (Princeton, N.J., 1969).

GEORGE T. BLAKEY

NEW DEPARTURE DEMOCRATS. Favoring industrialization, natural resource development, improved transportation networks, and public education, New Departure Democrats broke with the traditions of the Kentucky Democratic party during the era of Readjustment (1866-77). Led by Henry Watterson, editor of the *Louisville Courier-Journal*, the New Departure Democrats believed the state would serve its own best interests by aligning itself with the national Democratic party; accepting the Thirteenth, Fourteenth, and Fifteenth amendments; and following the example of the industrialized North.

From their stronghold in Louisville, the New Departures challenged the Bourbon Democrats, who advocated the traditional southern plantation lifestyle. The Bourbon Democrats, who represented the aristocratic Bluegrass region, continued to dominate politics in Kentucky throughout the late nineteenth century. Nevertheless, the political influence of Watterson and his faction resulted in improved railroads and greater industrial development, especially during Gov. Preston Leslie's term (1871-75).

Despite their differing points of view, the two factions of the Democratic party formed a coalition that proved strong enough to withstand all Republican challenges until the gubernatorial election of 1895. Badly divided over the free silver policy, which called for the minting of silver coins and an end to the gold standard, the Democrats failed to close ranks in 1895 and the state's first Republican governor, William O'Connell Bradley (1895-99), was elected. By the late 1890s, however, the era of Bourbon domination of the organization had passed as Populism gained control of the state's Democratic party.

See Hambleton Tapp and James Klotter, *Kentucky: Decades of Discord, 1865-1900* (Frankfort, Ky., 1977).

NEW MADRID EARTHQUAKES. The earthquake sequence that began on December 16, 1811, and continued for at least a year thereafter, in what is now northeastern Arkansas, southeastern Missouri, and northwestern Tennessee, is the greatest recorded sequence of earthquakes in the history of North America. The four major earthquakes of the sequence—two in the early-morning hours of December 16, 1811, one on the morning of January 23, 1812, and the largest one at 3:00 a.m. on February 7, 1812—were felt as far away as Hartford, Connecticut, to the northeast; Charleston, South Carolina, to the east; and New Orleans to the south. Closer to the epicenters of the events, in an area extending from Cairo, Illinois, to the north and Memphis, Tennessee, to the south, the land was severely disrupted by subsidence, uplifting, sand blows, landslides, and fissuring. Large tracts of forest were submerged as a result of the subsidence. The quake destroyed the settlements of New Madrid, Missouri; Little Prairie (now Caruthersville), Missouri; and Big Prairie, near the mouth of the St. Francis River, in what is now Arkansas.

Although the number of people killed or injured by the earthquakes is not known, the number was not large. The area of major devastation was very sparsely populated, and the manmade structures were log structures, which are very resilient to earthquake damage. In Kentucky the earthquake caused severe damage to homes and other structures in Henderson and Mortons Gap, and minor damage to structures in the central Kentucky communities of Louisville, Lexington, Frankfort, and Maysville. The lack of newspapers at the time of the events makes it difficult to document the effects throughout the remainder of sparsely populated Kentucky. However, recent geological investigations indicate that landslides occurred in the Hickman area.

In addition to the four major upheavals, at least six other quakes were felt as far east as Charleston, South Carolina, and 197 were felt as far east as Louisville.

See James Penick, Jr., *The New Madrid Earthquakes of 1811-1812* (Columbia, Mo., 1976).

R.L. STREET

NEW ORLEANS (STEAMBOAT). The *New Orleans* was the first steamboat on the western rivers. She was built by Robert Fulton and Robert Livingston's Mississippi Steamboat Navigation Company at Pittsburgh under the direct supervision of Nicholas Roosevelt. Designed to steam between Natchez and New Orleans, she was 148.5 feet long, 32.5 feet wide, had a 12-foot depth of hold, and drew 4 feet of water. She left Pittsburgh on October 20, 1811, and reached New Orleans in January of 1812, having survived the massive New Madrid earthquake. In her first year of operations, she cleared $20,000 in profits, having cost about $40,000 to build. The *New Orleans* struck a snag and sank in 1814.

See Mary Helen Dohan, *Mr. Roosevelt's Steamboat* (New York 1981). JOHN B. BRILEY

NEWPORT. Newport is one of the two county seats of Campbell County, the other being ALEXANDRIA. Newport is located in the northwestern part of the county, across the Licking River from COVINGTON to the west, and across the Ohio River from Cincinnati to the north. The city is the oldest river settlement on the south shore of the Ohio River in the Cincinnati area. It was laid out in the early 1790s by Hubbard Taylor, a young Virginia Revolutionary War veteran, who named it for Christopher Newport, commander of the first ship to reach Jamestown, Virginia, in 1607. James Taylor, Jr., a cousin of James Madison, brought the first settlers to Newport and was influential in having Kentucky create Campbell County in 1794. He also convinced Madison, who had become President Thomas Jefferson's secretary of state, to establish a military barracks in Newport, which had been incorporated as a village in 1795. The Newport barracks was the mustering center for U.S. troops in the West when they marched on Canada in the War of 1812.

In 1830 Newport had only 715 inhabitants, but was elevated to the status of a city by 1835. The first large influx of population came in the 1840s with Irish and German immigrants. By the 1850 census Newport boasted almost 6,000 people. There were no bridges across the Ohio River before the Civil War, and the Licking River was not bridged until 1854. The initial structure collapsed in two weeks but was quickly rebuilt, reopening travel to Covington. Lack of bridges led to more autonomous growth of the river-separated communities in their early decades. William Shreve Bailey, a self-styled "poor mechanic," edited an abolitionist newspaper, the FREE SOUTH in Newport in the 1850s.

The large German immigration in the 1880s and 1890s and the completion of bridges from northern Kentucky to Cincinnati promoted the development of Newport as a residential suburb of the Ohio metropolis. One of the largest steel mills in the South and the largest brewery in the United States south of the Ohio River, Wiedemann, were industrial bases for Newport's development in the early twentieth century.

In the 1920s, national prohibition gave birth to organized syndicate crime, which was a dominant force in Newport and throughout northern Kentucky until the early 1960s. In the 1930s, 1940s, and 1950s, the city was a major headquarters for big-time gambling, especially lay-off betting, in which one bookmaker, inundated with a large sum of money bet on a single horse, would move a portion of the bets to another bookmaker; if the horse won, the payoff was split. State government in Kentucky did not undertake to stamp out this illicit activity until the local Protestant Ministerial Association and later the Committee of 500 (led by local businessmen) gave support to a reform movement. Assistance from the U.S. attorney general's office helped to banish syndicate criminals to other points in the early 1960s.

The Northern Kentucky Chamber of Commerce and NORTHERN KENTUCKY UNIVERSITY were factors in the growth of Newport in the early 1970s. The university, located in suburban Highland Heights, helped to raise the percentage of local high school graduates who attended college and went on to become leaders of Newport and the other northern Kentucky communities. The population of the second-class city was 25,998 in 1970; 21,587 in 1980; and 18,871 in 1990.

WILL FRANK STEELY

NEWPORT BARRACKS. Established in 1803 as an arsenal, the Newport barracks was erected at the confluence of the Licking and Ohio rivers on about five acres of land, most of which was donated by James Taylor, who supervised the construction of the facility. Between 1811 and 1815, the barracks supplied both men and material for William Henry Harrison's military campaigns. In 1814 more than four hundred enemy soldiers were incarcerated at the barracks. In the early 1820s the Newport post was converted to a recruiting depot. Under commandant Nathaniel Macrae (1841-52), the physical plant was improved and enlarged, and thousands of men were processed for Mexican War service. Philip Sheridan and Earl Van Dorn served at Newport in the early 1850s. During the Civil War, the barracks doubled as a base hospital and a political prison for Confederate sympathizers. Following the war, it fell into disrepair and was virtually abandoned between 1875 and 1877. Reinvigorated in 1878 as headquarters of the Department of the South, the barracks enjoyed a short-lived prosperity until successive floods between 1882 and 1884 so badly damaged the grounds and buildings that the government relocated the post on the higher ground of Fort Thomas in 1890. The barracks facility was deeded to the city of Newport in 1894.

LOUIS R. THOMAS

NICHOLAS, GEORGE. A prominent lawyer and political thinker, George Nicholas was born in Williamsburg, Virginia, around 1743 to Robert Carter and Anne (Cary) Nicholas. His father was a noted Virginia lawyer and president of that state's Revolutionary convention in 1775. After serving as an officer in the Revolutionary War and as a member of the Virginia legislature and the convention in 1788 to ratify the federal Constitution, Nicholas migrated to Kentucky, settling in Danville.

Nicholas, with his wealth of experience in the Virginia government, soon became a leader in the cause of Kentucky statehood. Nicholas was a member of the select committee that drafted the first constitution of Kentucky at the convention in Danville in 1792. Nicholas served as the state's first attorney general. He resigned on December 7, 1792, to practice law and manage his estate, which by then included holdings in Fayette, Montgomery, Clark, Campbell, Pendleton, and Bath counties. Nicholas in 1799 became Transylvania University's first law professor.

Nicholas died on July 25, 1799, in Lexington and was buried in the Third Street Cemetery there. When a new county was created in 1799 out of parts of Bourbon and Mason, it was named in his honor, as was Nicholasville in Jessamine County.

See Huntley Dupree, "The Political Ideas of George Nicholas," *Register* 39 (July 1941): 201-23; J.W. Crawford, *The Kentucky Constitutions of 1792 and 1799* (Evanston, Ill., 1971).

NICHOLAS, SAMUEL. Samuel Nicholas, first president of the University of Louisville, was born in Lexington, Kentucky, in 1796 to Mary (Smith) and George NICHOLAS. His father was a lawyer and influential in framing Kentucky's first constitution. Nicholas's parents died while he was a child and by the age of twelve he was working for an uncle in Baltimore. After a brief time operating a mercantile business in New Orleans, Nicholas moved to Frankfort, Kentucky, and studied law under George Mortimer BIBB. He was admitted to the bar in 1823 and two years later opened a law office in Louisville. During his career as an attorney, Nicholas was a member of the court of appeals (1831-36), chancellor of the Louisville chancery court (1844-50), and a member of the Kentucky constitutional convention in 1849. In 1850 Gov. John J. Crittenden (1848-50) appointed Nicholas, Charles Wickliffe, and Squire Turner to revise the Code of Practice. Nicholas, a slaveowner who argued for gradual emancipation, remained a Union supporter during the Civil War and published several tracts on constitutional topics at the time.

Nicholas served as the first president of the newly chartered UNIVERSITY OF LOUISVILLE in 1846-47. At that time, the university consisted of the recently merged Louisville College and the Louisville Medical Institute. A law department was established, and Nicholas granted degrees to the first graduating class. Nicholas also worked for the formation of the public school system in Louisville.

Nicholas married Matilda Prather in 1829; they had seven children. She died in 1844, and in 1848 Nicholas married his cousin Mary Smith, with whom he had three children. She survived Nicholas, who died on November 27, 1869, and was buried in Cave Hill Cemetery in Louisville.

MARGARET L. MERRICK

NICHOLAS COUNTY. Nicholas County, the forty-second county in order of formation, is located in north-central Kentucky in the Outer Bluegrass region. The county is bounded by Bourbon, Fleming, Bath, Robertson, and Harrison counties and contains an area of 197 square miles, most of which is hilly. The county was formed in 1799 from Mason and Bourbon counties and was named for Col. George Nicholas of Fayette County, a Revolutionary War veteran and a popular lawyer in early Kentucky. CARLISLE has been the county seat since 1816. Robertson County, the smallest county in the state, was formed from Nicholas County in 1867.

Large prehistoric mammals that inhabited Kentucky after the last Ice Age were drawn to the salt licks at what is now Blue Licks Battlefield State Park on the Nicholas-Robertson county line. In the early historic era, buffalo created trails through the area to the licks. These trails were used by Indians on hunting trips and by pioneers such as Daniel Boone and Simon Kenton, who came to the licks to make salt. The Buffalo Trace, later known as Smith's Wagon Road, became an important connection between the Ohio River at Limestone (now Maysville) and Lexington. The existence of the road, sixty feet wide in places, was the prime reason for the settlement of the county. The Limestone Road was the first macadamized road in the state and is now part of U.S. 68.

The first settlement in Nicholas County was made at Blue Licks around 1784 by David Tanner. Blue Licks, which has been known as Salt Springs, Lower Blue Lick Springs, and Blue Lick Springs, received its name from the blue-gray deposit left by mineral water between the original spring and the Licking River. The water in the spring drained toward the river, creating a quagmire that trapped thirsty animals attracted to the salt.

In 1800 the first session of the county court was held at the home of Martin Baker, Jr., at Lower Blue Licks. In August 1800 the court began meeting in the new courthouse at Blue Licks. Typical court matters during the early years included issuing orders for surveying roads, appointing overseers for construction crews, issuing licenses to tavernkeepers, inventorying estates of deceased persons, and granting permission for construction of gristmills and routes for the transportation of salt water from Blue Licks. A new county seat named Ellisville was established in 1805 on the James Ellis farm along the Lexington-Maysville Road. A log courthouse was built there the same year. The county seat was moved to Carlisle in 1816.

During the mid-1800s, Blue Lick Springs in Nicholas County became a spa, where wealthy travelers flocked to enjoy the rejuvenating effects of mineral water, which was bottled and shipped all over the world. Two cooper shops were kept busy making staves and assembling kegs and barrels to ship the water in bulk. At one time the Arlington Hotel at Blue Licks had three hundred rooms. There was also a military school at Blue Licks around 1848, where James G. Blaine, an 1884 presidential candidate, taught prior to becoming a politician.

The Lexington & Maysville Railroad (later a part of the Louisville & Nashville and in 1990 part of TTI Systems, a local short line) was completed to Carlisle by 1871. It brought many visitors through Carlisle to Deering Camp, a Methodist religious camp at Parks Hill with fifty-two cabins, which closed in 1912. As many as 10,000 people were said to have attended a Sunday service at Deering Camp. The August 17, 1910, *Carlisle Mercury* reported, "A train out of Lexington passed Carlisle going to Parks Hill with eleven coaches filled and overflowing. Both trains out of Maysville were crowded. Three thousand tickets sold by L&N Railroad (700 here)."

Nicholas County resident Leason T. Barlow is credited by some with having invented the Barlow knife, and R.C. King of Carlisle obtained a patent for a bluegrass seed stripper around 1870. The county has produced several authors, including Barbara Kingsolver, who wrote *The Bean Trees* (1988); Frank Mathias, who wrote *G.I. Jive* (1982); and Eslie Asbury, who wrote *Horse Sense and Humor in Kentucky* (1981). Walter Tevis, who wrote *The Hustler* (1959), taught for one year at Carlisle High School.

Within the county's boundaries is the five-hundred-acre Lake Carnico Development District, which includes a 150-acre lake. The county is also the site of the 4,000-acre Clay Wildlife Management Preserve.

The population of the rural county was 6,508 in 1970; 7,157 in 1980; and 6,725 in 1990.

See Joan W. Conley, *History of Nicholas County* (Carlisle, Ky., 1976); Rev. Albert W. Sweazy, "Deering Camp Ground a Light From the Past," *Carlisle Mercury* (July 18, 1985).

JOAN W. CONLEY

NICHOLASVILLE. Nicholasville, the seat of Jessamine County, is located on U.S. 279 and KY 169. The town was planned by the Rev. John Metcalfe. He chose the name to honor Col. George Nicholas, a prominent attorney who played a vital role in drafting the Kentucky constitution. Nicholasville received its charter February 8, 1812, and was incorporated on February 13, 1837. It grew rapidly, being located on a much-traveled north-south route, and many passed through it on the way to and from Lexington. The first Jessamine County courthouse was built in the town in 1823. The first Jessamine County court, however, was held at the tavern of Fisher Rice. The present courthouse was completed in 1878. Two railroads passed through Nicholasville in the nineteenth century: the Louisville & Nashville (now CSX Transportation) and the Southern Railway.

During the Civil War, Nicholasville was occupied at various times by both Union and Confederate forces. The nearby Camp Nelson was a Federal recruiting center. On September 3, 1862, Gen. John Hunt Morgan's cavalry entered Nicholasville and in a few days recruited nearly 1,000 men for the Con-federate cause. After the close of the Civil War, Nicholasville returned to being a prosperous agrarian center, and in the 1870s, it was a bustling community with a population of over a thousand. It has become a thriving industrial center, home to many who commute to work in Lexington.

The population of the third-class city was 5,829 in 1970; 10,400 in 1980; and 13,603 in 1990.

RON D. BRYANT

NICHOLS, ROBERT HERMAN. Robert Herman Nichols, golf's long-hitting "Louisville Slugger," was born April 14, 1936, in Louisville to Owen and Artie Nichols. He attended Louisville's Saint Xavier High School, where he was a starting player in football, basketball, and golf. In 1952, while he was still in high school, a car accident left him in a thirteen-day coma. Nichols entered Texas A&M on a football scholarship but instead played golf. He graduated in 1958 and turned professional in 1959. Nichols won his only major championship, the Professional Golfers Association tournament title, in 1964. In 1975 he survived another life-threatening accident when he, Lee Trevino, and Jerry Heard were all struck by lightning at the Western Open in Oak Brook, Illinois. In the top sixty money earners every year from 1960 through 1975, Nichols made the top twenty a total of eight times (1962-74) and was fifth in 1964. He has played for many years on the senior pro golf circuit.

JAMES C. CLAYPOOL

NIGHT RIDERS. Night riding was a form of vigilantism that erupted in Kentucky from 1905 to 1909, when chronically poor farmers resorted to violence in desperation over low tobacco prices. Democratically formed organizations of tobacco planters had proved ineffective against the American Tobacco Company, which monopolized tobacco buying. The original violence by the hooded men on horseback occurred within the dark-tobacco area of western Kentucky and western Tennessee known as the BLACK PATCH. Led by a physician, Dr. David Amoss, the night riders attacked agents and warehouses of the tobacco monopoly, as well as planters who would not cooperate with other growers in pooling their crops and withholding them from the market in an attempt to force prices up. In central Kentucky, the so-called Silent Brigade was formed in 1908 by farmers who destroyed young tobacco plants, wrecked machinery, and burned barns to increase the effectiveness of the tobacco pools. The outbreaks of violence by night riders included threats, whippings, and sometimes killings. Gov. A.E. Willson (1907-11) dispatched troops to various areas, but they were unable to quell what was essentially guerilla warfare. By 1909 the cooperative tobacco organizations within the state had disintegrated and the riders quickly disappeared.

See James O. Nall, *The Tobacco Night Riders of Kentucky and Tennessee, 1904-1909* (Louisville 1939); Christopher R. Waldrep, "Augustus E. Willson and the Night Riders," *FCHQ* 58 (April 1984): 237-52.   TRACY A. CAMPBELL

NILES, JOHN JACOB. John Jacob Niles, ballad writer and collector, eldest son of John Thomas and Lula (Sarah) Niles, was born on April 28, 1892, in Louisville into a musical family. His great-grandfather was a composer, organist, and cello manufacturer, and his father had a local following as a folksinger and square dance caller. From his mother he learned music theory and the piano. Niles first sang publicly at the age of seven, and in 1907, at fifteen, he composed "Go 'Way from My Window." He was encouraged to continue his musical career by Henry Watterson, editor of the *Louisville Courier-Journal*. He later studied music at the Universite de Lyon in France, the Schola Cantorum in Paris, and the Cincinnati Conservatory of Music.

In 1909 Niles graduated from Du Pont Manual Training High School in Louisville and began work as a mechanic at Burroughs Machine Company. In 1917 he enlisted as a private in the aviation section of the Army Signal Corps and was a pilot in France during World War I. When a plane crash left him partially paralyzed, he was discharged in 1918. He moved to New York City and in 1921 became master of ceremonies at the Silver Slipper nightclub there. He teamed with contralto Marion Kerby, and they toured both Europe and the United States giving performances. Niles also sang briefly for the Chicago Lyric Opera Company. He was described as a flamboyant, charismatic performer, and his performances did much to make folk music popular and were often imitated. His last concert was at Swannanoa, North Carolina, in September 1978.

Although he preferred performing, Niles is best remembered as a collector and popularizer of folk music. At the age of fifteen he began to record in a notebook the music of the Ohio Valley region. During the periods 1909-17 and 1928-34, he gathered and recorded songs of eastern Kentucky and the southern Appalachian area, a pioneer in collecting the songs of the common people. Niles arranged or composed more than 1,000 ballads, folk songs, carols, and wartime songs. Among his best known works are "I Wonder as I Wander," "Black is the Color of My True Love's Hair," "Jesus, Jesus, Rest Your Head," "Lamentation," "Mary the Rose," and "The Hangman." In 1961 many of his songs were published in the *Ballad Book of John Jacob Niles*. His friendship with Trappist monk Thomas Merton resulted in the publication of Niles's last major work in 1972, when he set twenty-two of Merton's poems to music. He lectured and performed extensively, particularly on college campuses.

Niles also carved wood, made furniture, invented, and gardened. He married Rena Lipetz in 1936; they had two sons, Thomas Michael Tolliver and John Edward. Niles died at his Boot Hill Farm near Lexington on March 1, 1980, and was buried at St. Hubert's Cemetery in Clark County.

See David F. Burg, "John Jacob Niles," *Kentucky Review* 2 (1980): 3-10.

NOBLE, THOMAS SATTERWHITE. Thomas Satterwhite Noble, artist and educator, was born in Lexington, Kentucky, on May 29, 1835, the son of Thomas Hart and Rosamond (Johnson) Noble. Noble studied painting with Samuel Woodson Price in Louisville in 1852, and in 1856 he went to Paris to study for three years under the French painter Thomas Couture.

Noble, who served in the Confederate army, gained his artistic reputation through the sympathetic portrayal of black subjects. His painting *The American Slave Mart* (1865) proved a popular sensation and was exhibited in the Capitol rotunda in Washington, D.C. *John Brown's Blessing*, *The Price of Blood*, and *Margaret Garner*, all interpretations of racism and oppression, heightened the artist's popularity. He was elected an associate of the National Academy of Design and a member of the Chicago Academy of Fine Arts.

In 1869 Noble won appointment as first principal of the McMicken School of Design, which in 1887 became the Art Academy of Cincinnati. His pupils included Kentucky water colorist Paul Sawyier. During a two-year leave (1881-83) in Bavaria, he studied at the Munich Academy. Noble retired in 1904 and died in New York City on April 27, 1907. He was buried in Spring Grove Cemetery in Cincinnati.

See James D. Birchfield et al., *Thomas Satterwhite Noble: 1835-1907* (Lexington, Ky., 1988).

JAMES D. BIRCHFIELD

NOE, JAMES THOMAS COTTON. James Thomas Cotton Noe, poet and educator, was born in Thompsonville (later Fenwick), Washington County, Kentucky, on May 2, 1864. He was educated in Springfield and Perryville, Kentucky, public schools and attended Franklin College in Indiana, Cornell University, and the University of Chicago. He was nicknamed Cotton as a youth because of his light-colored hair, and in adulthood legally added the word to his name. Noe practiced law in Springfield, Kentucky, for four years and then turned to teaching, serving on the faculties of Cumberland College in Williamsburg, Kentucky, and Lincoln Memorial University in Harrogate, Tennessee. In 1908 he joined the faculty at the University of Kentucky and remained there until his retirement in 1934.

Noe was named Kentucky's first poet laureate by the Kentucky General Assembly in 1926. His best-known poem is "Tip Sams"; his works include *The Blood Of Rachel* (1916), *Tip Sams of Kentucky and Other Poems* (1926), *The Valley of Parnassus* (1953), and *Tip Sams Again* (1947). He was married to Sidney Stanfill; they had two sons and one daughter. He moved to Beverly Hills, California, for his health in 1934 and died there November 9, 1953. He was buried in the Lexington Cemetery.

See Dorothy Edwards Townsend, *Kentucky in American Letters* (Georgetown, Ky., 1976).

JOY BALE BOONE

NOLIN RIVER. The Nolin River is a major tributary of the Green River of west-central Kentucky. Beginning in Larue and Hardin counties, the Nolin River joins the Green River in Edmonson County about two hundred miles from the Green's mouth, which is near Evansville, Indiana. The Nolin River flows through the western section of Mammoth Cave National Park. The river was used by flatboats long before the U.S. Army Corps of Engineers built locks and dams on the Green River, which deepened the Nolin enough for larger boats. In 1811 the Kentucky General Assembly initiated the first Nolin River improvements, and the stream was declared navigable in high water by 1818.

In 1890 Congress funded Lock and Dam Nos. 5 and 6 on the Green River, largely to allow development of the outstanding mineral deposits near the Nolin River, particularly asphalt. Slackwater navigation began in 1906. In 1925 about 246,000 tons of asphalt, half of Green River's tonnage, came from the Nolin River. Later the locks and dams were enlarged, and they continued in operation until 1951, when they were closed because of the lack of traffic. The Kyrock Company on the Nolin River could no longer compete with asphalt from foreign producers.

In the 1960s the building of Nolin River Lake brought both flood control and recreational opportunities to the valley.

See Helen Bartter, *The Green River of Kentucky* (Lexington, Ky., 1976); Leland R. Johnson, *The Falls City Engineers: A History of the Louisville District Corps of Engineers, U.S. Army* (Louisville 1974).

HELEN B. CROCKER

NORMAN, MARSHA (WILLIAMS). Marsha (Williams) Norman, playwright, daughter of Billie and Bertha Williams, was born on September 21, 1947, in Louisville. She attended Durrett High School in Louisville, where she excelled as a musician, and graduated from Agnes Scott College in Decatur, Georgia, in 1969 with a B.A. in philosophy. Since her first marriage in 1969 she has been known professionally by the name of Norman. She received an M.A. in theater at the University of Louisville in 1971. Norman worked with mentally disturbed children from 1969 to 1971 at Central State Hospital in Louisville. She later credited this experience and her own strict religious upbringing with some of the subject matter and emotional context of her plays. Norman taught in the Jefferson County public schools from 1970 to 1972 and at the Brown School for gifted children in 1973. She was project director for the Kentucky Arts Commission from 1972 until 1976, working with children in managing arts programs and classes in film making. She edited the children's supplement of the

Louisville Times, the "Jelly Bean Journal," from 1974 until 1979.

By 1976 Norman had turned to full-time playwriting and was associated with Actors Theatre of Louisville. Her first play, the award winning drama, *Getting Out*, produced in 1977, was published in *The Best Plays of 1977-78* (1980), the first non-New York production to be included in this annual collection. Set in Louisville, the play portrays weak, sensitive Arlene, who in adapting to life outside of prison must fight the temptation to return to what she knows as security—her pimp. At the same time, Arlene battles her own violent, rebellious inner self, Arlie, played by a second actress. Norman later said that she had based the character of Arlie on a difficult young ward at Central State Hospital.

Most of Norman's plays have been produced first in Louisville, where she refined them for the New York stage. *'night, Mother*, produced in 1982, won the 1983 Pulitzer Prize for drama. It is the story of two women: a daughter who feels she has failed in marriage, parenthood, and life, and who decides to take control of her life by ending it, and her mother, who after much anguish comes to accept the decision. It was made into a movie in 1986, starring Sissy Spacek and Anne Bancroft.

Norman's works inquire into moral and philosophical questions. She wrote two plays for television, *It's the Willingness* (1978) and *I'm Trouble at Fifteen* (1980). Norman's other works include the plays *Traveler in the Dark* (1985) and *Sarah and Abraham* (1987), and a novel, *The Fortune Teller* (1987).

Norman was married to Michael Norman from 1969 to 1974 and to Dann Byck in 1978. She married Tim Dykman in 1987; they have a son, Angus.

NORTHERN KENTUCKY UNIVERSITY. Northern Kentucky University is a state institution of higher education in Highland Heights, in the Greater Cincinnati metropolitan area. The university confers baccalaureate and master's degrees and one professional degree, the juris doctor. Northern Kentucky University's predecessor was Northern Kentucky State College, created in 1968 by the General Assembly. The college took over the Northern Community College of the University of Kentucky (in Covington) in 1970 and built a senior college program on the student-faculty nucleus already in place. It became Northern Kentucky University in 1976.

Before 1968, the need for a four-year state college in the second largest metropolitan area in the commonwealth had been dramatized by studies indicating that only about one-third of the high school graduates in the counties of Boone, Kenton, and Campbell went on to college, in contrast to 50 percent nationally. Under the 1968 law that created Northern Kentucky State College, independent consultants planned the campus and selected the Highland Heights site from among the three nominated by the area counties. In 1970 Will Frank Steely, a dean in the University of Virginia system and a native Kentuckian, became Northern's first president, faced with the dual tasks of recruiting a senior college faculty and building a new campus. Three hundred and twenty-five acres were purchased at a site that was to become the junction of I-275 and I-471.

On March 31, 1971, the college broke ground for the first building. In contrast to Kentucky's older state institutions of higher education, Northern's architecture is starkly modern and functional. The buildings are of textured concrete and glass in a style popularized by the French architect Corbusier. The architecture was disagreeable to some in the early years but gained more acceptance later. In autumn 1971, the college added the third year of academic work at the old community college campus, which had 1,200 students when it was taken over by Northern on July 1, 1970; that autumn enrollment topped 1,600. In the fall of 1971, more than 3,000 students crowded onto the little campus. Prefabricated classroom facilities were erected to relieve overcrowding. In the fall semester of 1972, more than 4,000 students registered for the first four-year college matriculation. In the spring of 1973, Northern conferred over six hundred degrees in its first baccalaureate commencement. By 1975 enrollment at the new school topped 6,000.

The state had arranged for funding of the first seven major buildings on the campus: Nunn Hall, Regents Hall, the Natural Science Center, the W. Frank Steely Library, the Fine Arts Center, the Landrum Academic Center, and the University Center. The 1974 legislature approved what was then the largest appropriation for construction at any one time for strictly academic facilities. Land was leased for the construction of the Campbell County Vocational School, and a large maintenance facility was funded.

Most of the full-time faculty at the community college, thirty-three in all, stayed with the new senior college. Northern was founded at a time when instructors in most disciplines were plentiful and it recruited many outstanding young faculty. By 1975, the end of Steely's administration, there were two hundred full-time faculty, 70 percent of whom had terminal degrees. The annual budget had climbed from $1.5 million in 1970-71 to $10 million by 1975-76.

In addition to twenty associate and thirty-three baccalaureate degree programs, by 1975 Northern had added a master of arts in education program and had merged with the private Salmon P. Chase College of Law, bringing the juris doctor degree to the campus. Chase had been established as a private law college in Cincinnati in 1893. The college's extended services to Northern Kentucky include paralegal, legal aid, and continuing legal education programs. Cooperative Reserve Officer Training Corps (ROTC) programs were established with Xavier University and with the University of Cincinnati. Taking advantage of the cultural facilities of a major metropolis, Northern has created a consortium with universities in Greater Cincin-

nati. From its early years, Northern shared library and curricular programs with other consortium universities.

During the interim years of 1975-76, Ralph Tesseneer was acting president. A business-education-psychology building and administration building were funded. In 1976 A.D. Albright became president of Northern Kentucky University and served until 1983. During his administration, a four-year nursing program was started, and an honors program was instituted in 1981. Under the 1978 postmaster's program in education, teachers can achieve rank 1, the highest degree level mandated by the Kentucky Department of Education. At the same time, a cooperative graduate center created a master's degree program in social work and one in library science on the Northern campus, each supported by the University of Kentucky. In the 1981-82 academic year, Chase College of Law moved to the new Highland Heights campus.

Leon E. Boothe became president in 1983. During his tenure, the American Association of Law Schools accredited Chase, a master's program in public administration was established, business programs were consolidated into the College of Business, and the technical science center was built. Radio station WNKU, Northern's first broadcast medium, came on the air in 1984. The university began to offer master's degrees in public affairs from Kentucky State University and in community nutrition from Eastern Kentucky University. In 1987 the National Academy of Criminal Justice Sciences was located at Northern. By the late 1980s, 40 percent of the institutional budget came from nonstate sources. In autumn of 1989, enrollment exceeded 10,000.   WILL FRANK STEELY

NUNN, LOUIE BROADY. Louie Broady Nunn, Kentucky governor during 1967-71, was born on March 8, 1924, in Park, Barren County, to Waller H. and Mary (Roberts) Nunn. He attended the Bowling Green Business University after graduating from Hiseville High School. When he returned from infantry service (1943-45) in World War II, Nunn attended the University of Cincinnati, then the University of Louisville, where he received his law degree in 1950. The same year he opened a law practice in Glasgow and married Beula Cornelius Aspley; they have two children. Active in civic affairs, Nunn was elected Barren County judge in 1953 although he was a Republican. An able political organizer, he ran campaigns within the state for John Sherman Cooper, Thruston Morton, Dwight D. Eisenhower, and Richard M. Nixon.

In his first attempt at statewide office, Nunn lost the close 1963 governor's race to Democrat Edward T. Breathitt, 338,479 to 325,876. Four years later he defeated Jefferson County judge Marlow Cook in the Republican primary, then beat Democrat Henry Ward in the general election, 454,123 to 425,674. Nunn played upon the divisions within the Democratic party and charged his opponents with seeking higher taxes to pay for administrative inefficiency. Nunn was inaugurated on December 12, 1967, and left office on December 7, 1971. He then opened a law practice in Lexington. He lost a 1974 race for the U.S. Senate to Walter Huddleston, 528,550 to 494,337. In 1979, when he tried to regain the governorship, he lost to John Y. Brown, Jr., 558,008 to 381,278. Nunn has stayed active as an attorney and is a prominent figure in state and national Republican politics. As a member of the boards of regents in the 1980s, he played an active role in dealing with problems at Morehead State University and Kentucky State University.

When the outgoing Breathitt administration projected a budget deficit of over $24 million, Nunn decided that the motor vehicle license fee would have to be increased and the sales tax raised from 3 percent to 5 percent. His budget emphasized increases for mental health, education on all levels, and economic development, and he persuaded a Democratic-controlled legislature to enact nearly everything he wanted. The University of Louisville was made a state school, and a community college became Northern Kentucky University, actions that diluted state support to the existing institutions of higher education. Nunn continued the emphasis that had been placed on Kentucky Educational Tele-vision (KET) and the state park system. In the 1970 legislative session he secured elimination of the sales tax on prescription drugs and the use tax on automobiles transferred within a family; his recommendations to reduce the personal income tax for low-income families and to increase tax credits for the blind and the elderly were rejected. During the unrest stirred up by racial issues and the war in Vietnam, Nunn was a law-and-order supporter of President Richard M. Nixon. He sent National Guard units into Louisville in 1968 to stop riots that followed civil rights marches, and in May 1970 he ordered guard units into Lexington after antiwar demonstrations on the University of Kentucky campus climaxed in the burning of a classroom building used by the Reserve Officers Training Corps. Blunt, outspoken, and a practitioner of tough politics, Nunn restored fiscal solvency, made significant advances in several areas, and avoided major scandals.

See Robert F. Sexton, ed., *The Public Papers of Governor Louie B. Nunn* (Lexington, Ky. 1975); Lowell H. Harrison, ed. *Kentucky's Governors 1792-1985* (Lexington, Ky., 1985).

LOWELL H. HARRISON

O

OAKDALE. Incorporated as a sixth-class city in 1904 and growing to a fifth-class city by 1908, Oakdale was annexed by the City of Louisville in 1922, after a four-year court battle that went to the U.S. Supreme Court. Oakdale, in south-central Jefferson County, had a tax base that included Churchill Downs and the Louisville & Nashville Railroad's Central Avenue yards. Oakdale was the first Louisville suburb directly attributed to the development of Grand Boulevard (Southern Parkway) and Jacob's Park (Iroquois Park) by Mayor Charles D. Jacob. BARBARA N. BISHOP

OAK GROVE. Oak Grove is a town in Christian County near the Tennessee state line, twelve miles south of Hopkinsville on U.S. 41A. Because much of the southeastern corner of the county was prairie, or barrens, pioneers valued such groves of trees as a source of fuel and building materials. The Oak Grove post office was established in 1828 in the store of Samuel Gordon on what became the road from Hopkinsville, Kentucky, to Clarksville, Tennessee. In 1907 Gordon's store burned and it and the post office, which kept the name Oak Grove, were relocated to nearby Thompsonville on the Tennessee Central Railroad. In 1965 the post office moved into a new building on U.S. 41A.

During the Civil War, the Oak Grove Rangers, a unit representing southern Christian County, became part of the 1st Kentucky Cavalry Regiment. They served under Confederate Gen. Simon Bolivar Buckner and took part in the campaign leading up to the Battle of Fort Donelson.

The Oak Grove area was a quiet farming community until 1942, when Oak Grove became a satellite community of Fort Campbell, home of the 101st Airborne Division. The city was incorporated in 1974 and became a fifth-class city in 1976. Its population was 2,088 in 1980 and 2,863 in 1990.

See Charles Mayfield Meacham, *A History of Christian County, Kentucky* (Nashville 1930).

OAKLAND RACE COURSE. Oakland Race Course, the first Louisville track to gain national attention, was opened in October 1832 on the west side of Seventh Street, south of present-day Magnolia Avenue, in what was then open countryside dotted with oak trees. Although he disapproved of horse races, Samuel Osgood, a New England cleric who visited Louisville in the 1830s, nevertheless found himself intrigued by "the furor that prevailed . . . the whole city in commotion," while "the august head of Henry Clay towered up among the sporting magnates on the stand erected for the judges."

Oakland had its days of glory in the late 1830s, when it was operated by Louisiana racing entrepreneur Yelverton Oliver, who put up liberal purses—especially for match races. The most famous of these pitted the Lexington horse Grey Eagle against Louisiana's Wagner on September 30, 1839. The winner of three grueling four-mile heats would carry off the then-unheard-of purse of $20,000. The match brought hundreds of racing enthusiasts to Louisville: "The Bench, the Bar, the Senate and the Press, the Army and Navy, and all the et cetera that pleasure and curiosity attracted were here," in the words of a magazine of the day. Wagner won the first heat by two lengths; in the second Grey Eagle took the lead for part of the way, but Wagner won by a neck, in 7:44—"best time ever, south of the Potomac," according to the *Louisville Daily Journal*.

Despite good attendance at such widely publicized races, Oakland Race Course suffered financial reverses in the early 1840s. It remained an influential track until it closed in the mid-1850s. Oakland served as a rendezvous point for Kentucky troops during the Mexican War and as a cavalry remount station during the Civil War. Later, the haphazard proliferation of shabby housing at the site led to the name CABBAGE PATCH.

See Samuel Osgood, "Eighteen Years: A Reminiscence of Kentucky," in *Knickerbocker Gallery* (New York 1855); "The Running Turf in America," *Harper's New Monthly Magazine* 41 (July 1870): 245-55. GEORGE H. YATER

O'BANNON, PRESLEY NEVILLE. Presley Neville O'Bannon, soldier and legislator, son of William and Anne (Neville) O'Bannon, was born in 1776 in Faquier County, Virginia. He entered the U.S. Marine Corps on January 18, 1801, as a second lieutenant and in March 1802 was promoted to first lieutenant. He served two tours of duty in the Mediterranean. In 1805, when President Thomas Jefferson ordered an attack on the Bay of Tripoli to release Americans held prisoner, O'Bannon, under Gen. William Eaton, led the expedition, consisting of seven marines and approximately four hundred Arabs. O'Bannon marched the army across five hundred miles of the North African desert from Alexandria to the fortified city of Derne and took the city on April 27, 1805. O'Bannon then held the city against attacks from the army of Tripoli until a peace treaty was signed on June 4, 1805. O'Bannon became known as "The Hero of Derne," and Congress awarded him a sword.

In 1807 O'Bannon retired from the marines and joined the U.S. Army as a captain. His regiment was disbanded in March 1809. O'Bannon moved to Logan County, Kentucky, and served in the Kentucky House in 1812, 1817, 1820, and 1821, and in the state Senate from 1824 to 1826.

O'Bannon married Matilda Heard on January 24, 1809. They were divorced in 1826. O'Bannon died on September 12, 1850.

See "Brief Sketch of Services of Lieutenant P.N. O'Bannon, A Kentucky Soldier in the War With Tripoli," *Register* 18 (Jan. 1920): 73-76.

OBENCHAIN, ELIZA CAROLINE (CALVERT). Eliza Caroline (Calvert) Obenchain, suffragist and author who wrote under the pen name Eliza Calvert Hall, was born in Bowling Green, Kentucky, on February 11, 1856. She was the eldest child of Thomas Chalmers and Margaret (Younglove) Calvert, and her paternal grandparents, Samuel Wilson and Elizabeth Caroline (Hall) Calvert, were early settlers of Bowling Green. She was educated at private schools there and attended Western College, Cincinnati, for one year. She taught in Bowling Green until her marriage on July 8, 1885, to William Alexander Obenchain.

Eliza Obenchain was the author of poems, essays, and stories about western Kentucky, which appeared in magazines such as *Scribner's*, *Cosmopolitan*, *Ladies' Home Journal*, and the women's page of the *New York Times*. She was a suffragist who worked for women's rights to property and divorce. Her most popular short story, "Sally Ann's Experience," combined her concern for women's rights with western Kentucky local color. "Sally Ann's Experience" appeared in Obenchain's *Aunt Jane of Kentucky* (1907), a popular collection of short stories. Obenchain wrote a sequel, *The Land of Long Ago* (1909), as well as *Clover and Bluegrass* (1916) and *To Love, To Cherish* (1911), but none achieved the same popularity. Obenchain also wrote *A Book of Hand-Woven Coverlets* (1912), a nonfiction examination of the folk craft that is considered a classic of its type.

William and Eliza Obenchain had four children—Margery Winston, Cecilia Reams, William Alexander, and Thomas Hall. After her husband's death in 1916, Obenchain moved to Dallas, Texas, where she died on December 20, 1935.

DANNY MILLER

OBERWARTH, CLARENCE JULIAN. Clarence Julian Oberwarth, architect, was born on March 1, 1900, in Frankfort, Kentucky, to Leo L. and Ruth Oberwarth. After serving in the navy in World War I, he attended Massachusetts Institute of Technology in Boston, where he received a B.S. degree in architecture in 1924. He then returned to Frankfort and became a partner with his father in the architecture firm Leo Oberwarth & Son.

During the 1930 session of the General Assembly, Oberwarth represented the Kentucky chapter of the American Institute of Architects as a lobbyist, succeeding in passage of the Architectural Registration Law. Under the law, persons using the title of "architect" must be sufficiently trained to protect the public safety. Oberwarth was assigned the first registration in the state—No. 1.

Oberwarth designed a number of Frankfort landmarks, including the Second Street School for the Works Progress Administration; several buildings at Georgetown College, Kentucky State University, and the Kentucky School for the Deaf; the Frankfort Municipal Building; and the State Police Barracks and Training Center. He restored the state capitol and the Dr. Ephraim McDowell house in

Danville. After retiring in 1965, Oberwarth became the first executive director of the Kentucky Board of Examiners and Registration of Architects. He left this post in 1974, spending the next four years preparing a history of the registration law and its effect on the profession. He died in 1983.

See C. Julian Oberwarth and William B. Scott, Jr., *A History of the Profession of Architecture in Kentucky* (Lexington, Ky., 1987).

WILLIAM B. SCOTT, JR.

OGDEN COLLEGE. Ogden College, founded in 1877 in Bowling Green, Kentucky, to educate young men, has operated as a part of Western Kentucky University since 1928. The school was the creation of Robert W. Ogden, a Warren County businessman, who died in 1873 and bequeathed $50,000 for the establishment of a local college and a similar sum for scholarships for Warren County and Kentucky boys. Under Hector Loving, who served as regent and trustee until his death in 1913, two buildings and seven or eight acres of land overlooking Bowling Green were rented in 1877 and then purchased in 1880 from the Methodist Episcopal Church, South. The church had operated Warren College, a preparatory school, on the grounds from 1872 to 1876 but closed it when plans to offer tuition-free education at Ogden College were announced.

The foundation's modest endowment limited Ogden's enrollment to one hundred students. Preparatory and college curriculums were instituted although 80 percent of the first class was beneath the collegiate level. The college curriculum leading to a B.A. degree required four years of Latin, Greek, and natural science; three years of English and mathematics; and two years of political and mental science. In 1880 the college program was restructured into the schools of philosophy, mathematics, ancient languages, natural science, civil engineering, grammar, English literature, modern languages, and commercial science.

Although a higher percentage of students were doing college-level work from 1883 to 1900 and an athletic program was initiated in the 1890s, low enrollment and inadequate finances were continual problems. In 1895 financial difficulties forced the school to change its traditional policy of free tuition for in-state students. The number of scholarships was limited to forty. Enrollment fell so low that in July 1900 the college division was closed. The four-year preparatory program continued. Ogden partially reinstated the college program in 1906, and under William M. Pearce, who became president in 1912, four-year status resumed.

Enrollment increased, but the annual operating budget was $10,000 and the endowment only $6,000. The financial problems were compounded when the Kentucky Association of Colleges and the Southern Association of Colleges and Universities failed to grant accreditation, and enrollment fell. On January 1, 1928, the nearby Western State Normal School and Teachers College (now Western

Kentucky University) took over operation of Ogden. Under an agreement signed on November 19, 1927, Ogden's property was leased to Western at no cost for twenty years, a scholarship fund was established for Western students, and the school's name was retained as the Ogden Department of Science. The lease was extended in 1947 and 1956 with only minor revisions. A ninety-nine year lease started on June 1, 1960.

See Jesse B. Johnson and Lowell H. Harrison, "Ogden College: A Brief History," *Register* 68 (July 1970): 189-220.

O'HARA, THEODORE. Theodore O'Hara, journalist and soldier, son of Kean O'Hara, was born in Danville, Kentucky, on February 11, 1820. He graduated in 1839 from St. Joseph College in Bardstown, then studied law with Judge William Owsley and was admitted to the bar in 1842. In 1845 he worked at the Treasury Department in Washington, D.C. On June 26, 1846, O'Hara secured an appointment as captain and assistant quartermaster of the Kentucky volunteers serving in the Mexican War. He attained the rank of brevet major on August 20, 1847, and was discharged on October 15, 1848. He is remembered as the author of the poem "The Bivouac of the Dead," written for the interment at the Frankfort Cemetery in 1847 of Kentuckians killed at the Battle of Buena Vista. Several versions of the poem exist. The second quatrain of the first stanza has often been inscribed on the tombstones of soldiers and it appears at the gateway to Arlington National Cemetery: "On Fame's eternal camping-ground / Their silent tents are spread, / And Glory guards with solemn round / The bivouac of the dead."

In the winter of 1849 O'Hara joined Narciso LOPEZ'S EXPEDITION to Cuba, where he was wounded at Cardenas in 1850. O'Hara worked as a reporter for the *Yeoman* in Frankfort, Kentucky, and in 1852 for the *Louisville Daily Times*. While residing in Louisville, he vehemently opposed the actions of the Know-Nothing party. During the Civil War O'Hara fought for the Confederacy as lieutenant colonel of the Alabama 12th Infantry. He served on the staffs of Gens. Albert Sidney Johnston and John C. Breckinridge. After the war he lived in Columbus, Georgia, and Guerrytown, Alabama. He was editor of the *Mobile Register* in Alabama.

O'Hara died in Guerrytown on June 6, 1867, and was buried at Columbus, Georgia. On September 15, 1874, his body was reinterred in the Frankfort Cemetery, where his grave is marked by a large monument.

See Jennie C. Morton, "Theodore O'Hara," *Register* 1 (Sept. 1903): 49-62; J. Stoddard Johnston, "Sketch of Theodore O'Hara," *Register* 11 (Sept. 1913): 67-72.

OHIO COMPANY. The Ohio Company was formed in 1748 by a group of prominent colonials, most of them Virginians, for the purpose of western exploration, trade with the Indians, and land acquisition. In 1751 Christopher Gist, acting for the company, traveled westward along the north side of the Ohio River and crossed into Kentucky when he reached the Scioto River. He had been directed to go as far as the Falls of the Ohio, but having been warned by friendly Indians that a party of Indians allied with the French were there, he turned back. Traveling eastward to the Kentucky River, he followed it upstream and crossed into present-day Virginia at Pound Gap.

The Ohio Company did not make a land claim in Kentucky until 1775, when Hancock Lee was appointed as its surveyor. The company met only disappointment in its claim to a tract of land believed to total 200,000 acres in the valley of the South Fork of the Licking River. The company had been established under the British Crown, and the Commonwealth of Virginia was not friendly to its claims. The formation of the Commonwealth of Kentucky on June 1, 1792, and the death of the company's leading member, George Mason, on October 7, 1792, were fatal blows to the company.

See Kenneth P. Bailey, *The Ohio Company of Virginia and the Westward Movement, 1748-1792* (Glendale, Calif., 1939). CHARLES G. TALBERT

OHIO COUNTY. Ohio County, the thirty-fifth county in order of formation, is in the Western Coal Field region of Kentucky. It is bordered by Breckinridge, Butler, Daviess, Grayson, Hancock, McLean, and Muhlenberg counties and has an area of 596 square miles. The county was established from part of Hardin County on December 17, 1798, and was named for the Ohio River, which formed its northern boundary until Daviess County (1815) and Hancock County (1829) were created from it. HARTFORD is the county seat.

The topography of Ohio County is undulating and well suited for agriculture. County farms produce light and dark air-cured tobacco, soybeans, corn, cattle, and hogs. An attempt was made at cultivating silkworms there during 1842-48. The principal waterways are Green River, Rough River, and various creeks.

Large burial mounds found along the Green River in the southern part of the county indicate that the area was once extensively occupied by prehistoric people. Excavations there in the late 1930s by the University of Kentucky and the Works Progress Administration uncovered more than 1,200 skeletons at Indian Knoll. The first pioneers in Ohio County experienced several bloody encounters with the Indians, starting in the 1780s. In 1790 Barnett's Station (now Calhoun) was attacked and two children were killed. Attacks continued into August of the same year. After 1797, the raids ceased to be a danger.

Daniel Boone and Joseph Barnett were among the first surveyors in the region. A Maryland Methodist minister, Ignatius Pigman, was a land speculator credited with bringing in a large number of settlers. One of the first physicians in the county, Dr. Charles McCreery, arrived around 1807.

River traffic down the Green and Rough rivers promoted the county's growth. Hartford became a riverport and mill town on Rough River. On Green River the major towns were Smallhous, Ceralvo, Rockport, and Cromwell. The river traffic was disrupted during the Civil War and dealt a serious blow by the advent of railroads to the county in the 1870s.

During the Civil War, Ohio County was the scene of intense guerrilla activity. On July 21, 1864, a partisan force, commanded by Capt. Dick Yates, ambushed a detachment of Daviess County Home Guards at Rough River Creek, killing four of the Guard. On February 20, 1865, a group of Grayson County Home Guards attacked an encampment of guerrillas near Hartford. Six of the guerrilla force were killed and four wounded. The most damaging event of the war in Ohio County occurred December 20, 1864, when Confederate Gen. Hylan B. Lyon's troops captured the county seat of Hartford and burned the courthouse.

Extensive coal mining took place in Ohio County after the Elizabethtown & Paducah Railroad (now the Paducah & Louisville) came through the county in 1871. A second railroad, the Louisville, St. Louis & Texas, crossed through Fordsville and Hartford in 1890 but was abandoned in 1942 except for a line from Muhlenberg County to Centertown in western Ohio County (operated in 1990 by CSX Transportation). The Illinois Central (now Illinois Central Gulf) completed a third line through the eastern part of the county in 1893, but it had been abandoned by the 1980s. In 1912 oil was discovered four miles east of Hartford, and since then Ohio County has consistently been one of western Kentucky's leading oil producing counties.

By 1986 the county economy was a mixture of coal mining, agriculture, and oil. The county's incorporated cities in order of size were BEAVER DAM, Hartford, Fordsville, McHenry, Rockport, and Centertown. The unincorporated village of Rosine, which was established in 1872 eight miles east of Hartford, is best known as the birthplace of Bill Monroe, the "Father of Bluegrass Music."

The population of the rural county was 18,790 in 1970; 21,765 in 1980; and 21,105 in 1990.

See McDowell A. Fogle, *Fogle's Papers: A History of Ohio County, Kentucky* (Evansville, Ind., 1970); Harrison D. Taylor, *Ohio County, Kentucky in the Olden Days* (Louisville 1926).

RON D. BRYANT

OHIOPIOMINGO. Ohiopiomingo was an eighteenth century promotional scheme of Pennsylvania financier, entrepreneur, and land speculator John Nicholson. Although its promoters claimed that Ohiopiomingo "will be a most capital township and town," the place never materialized. It was to be built thirty miles south of Louisville in Nelson County and was to have upward of a thousand houses, located on forty-three streets. Nicholson died in debtors' prison, leaving a wife and eight children, an army of creditors, and debts amounting to $12 million. William Winterbotham advertised the projected towns of LYSTRA, Franklinville, and Ohiopiomingo in his four-volume work entitled *An Historical, Geographical, Commercial, and Philosophical View of the United States of America, and of the European Settlements in America and the West-Indies*, published in 1796.

See Robert D. Arbuckle, "Ohiopiomingo: The 'Mythical' Kentucky Settlement that Was Not a Myth," *Register* 70 (Oct. 1972): 318-24.

ALLEN J. SHARE

OHIO RIVER. The Ohio River Basin is a vast area of 204,000 square miles draining a region the size of France and serving a population larger than that of Canada. It reaches northeast into New York, west to the flat land of Illinois, and south through the drainage area of the Tennessee River, extending into Georgia, Alabama, and Mississippi. Through the heart of this vast geographical parcel of the United States, the 981-mile-long Ohio River carries the largest volume of water of the major tributaries of the Mississippi River. Formed by the juncture of the Allegheny and Monongahela rivers at Pittsburgh, the Ohio borders Kentucky for 665 miles from Catlettsburg to its mouth, where it empties into the Mississippi.

Native Americans drank from the waters of the Ohio River, floated on its currents in dugouts and canoes, and ate its fish and shellfish. The Ohio River was the principal route of transport during the great migration to the trans-Appalachian West in the late eighteenth and early nineteenth centuries. Goods were carried first by canoe, then by flatboat and keelboat, and later by steamboat. In its natural, unimproved state, the Ohio was littered with snags (fallen trees and brush rafts) and strewn with boulders. Its flow was broken by sand and gravel bars, rocks, rapids, and the Falls of the Ohio at Louisville, where in a distance of two and a half miles the level of the river drops twenty-six feet. The unaltered river fluctuated widely from a series of shallow, stagnant pools in drought season to a raging torrent rising eighty to one hundred feet in flood times. As cities grew and as riverine vessels evolved, authorities sought ways to overcome these impediments to safe, dependable navigation.

Prior to the Civil War, the U.S. Congress debated the constitutionality of federally funded internal improvements such as roads and navigation projects. Many believed that such federal public works were undue extensions of federal powers. Before 1824 federal navigation improvements were largely limited to the construction of lighthouses, harbors, and projects considered essential to coastal defense. Two surveys of the Ohio River were performed, the first completed in 1819 by a joint state commission and covering the river from Pittsburgh to Louisville, the second completed in 1821 and extending downriver to the mouth and then via the Mississippi to New Orleans. The surveys identified the worst obstructions to navigation; recommended the removal of rocks, snags, and other obstacles;

and proposed a canal route around the falls at Louisville. The reports from these surveys formed the basis for the federal program of navigation improvements on the Ohio.

The Rivers and Harbors Act of 1824, the first inland river navigation bill enacted at the federal level, appropriated $75,000 for improving the Ohio and Mississippi rivers. The responsibility went to the U.S. Army Corps of Engineers, its first official engineering assignment on the Ohio. The engineers' Maj. Stephen H. Long in 1824-25 built a dam on the Ohio near Henderson, Kentucky, to improve channel conditions. Known as a wing dam, or spur dike, it consisted of parallel rows of wooden piling driven into the riverbed at a downstream angle from one bank out into the channel. The space between rows was filled with stones, increasing the current velocity at low flow stages to erode an obstructive gravel bar and deepen the channel. The 1824 act also included a directive to clear the river of snags, and the chief of engineers offered a $1,000 prize for the best-designed machine for removing obstacles that threatened wooden-hulled craft. The winning design was submitted by Capt. John W. Bruce of Vanceburg, Kentucky. He and Capt. John ("Roarin' Jack") Russell of Frankfort, together with Capt. Henry M. Shreve, removed snags and made other channel improvements through the 1840s, when the work was halted on constitutional grounds. Work did not resume until the Rivers and Harbors Act of 1852 was passed. The federal role in Ohio River work during the Civil War was minimal. As a result, many steamboats were lost to snags and other obstructions, and the earlier navigation improvements deteriorated.

The main barrier to navigation on the Ohio River was the falls at Louisville, six hundred miles downstream from Pittsburgh and the only place on the river with exposure to bedrock. The falls, formed nearly 400 million years ago by geologic processes, contained the fossilized remains of marine life. They were navigable for only a brief period each year during high-water season. Pilots could then "shoot the falls," navigating through narrow, boulder-strewn passages that often caused the loss of cargo, craft, and life. The hydrographic studies and mapping of the area in 1766 by Thomas Hutchins publicized the nature and extent of this barrier, and as early as 1781 Thomas Jefferson speculated on possible improvements at the falls. After the first settlement of the area on both sides of the river in the late eighteenth century it became apparent that some sort of improvements at the falls would have to be made to fulfill the region's potential for growth. After years of debate, petitions, and politicking, the Kentucky Legislature in 1825 chartered the LOUISVILLE AND PORTLAND CANAL Company, a stock venture, to construct a canal with locks around the falls. The project was completed in 1830.

The U.S. government purchased stock in the state-chartered canal company over the years, and by 1870 it was the principal shareholder. Navigation interests pushed for federal takeover of canal operation and maintenance. In the 1860s army engineers aided in a major project at the canal in which the noted hydraulics engineer Theodore Scowden designed improvements that were not completed until 1872. This project widened the canal and built a two-flight lock—the largest in the world at the time. This greatly relieved the operation of the original locks. The federal government finally took over operation and maintenance of the canal in June 1874. The Corps of Engineers undertook to improve navigation over the falls at high water by removing rocks and widening the navigable chutes. By 1880 the corps had completed the first dam across the river at Louisville.

After the Civil War, army engineers resumed open channel improvements on the Ohio in the form of wing dam construction and dredging. But these methods failed to achieve the ultimate goal: a year-round dependable navigation depth adequate for the growing coal trade and shipping by barge and towboat. After an international investigation of navigation projects, engineer officers W. Milnor Roberts and William E. Merrill concluded that the Ohio could best be improved by constructing a series of locks and dams to create slack-water pools. The experimental works were constructed at Davis Island, below Pittsburgh, and were opened to navigation in 1885. The project proved its worth, and Congress passed the Rivers and Harbors Act of 1910, which authorized construction of the slackwater system with a depth of nine feet. At its completion in 1929, the canalization project consisted of fifty-one movable dams with wooden wickets and a lock chamber 600 feet long and 110 feet wide. At low-water stage, the dams were raised to pool water requiring lockage, and at high stage the wickets were lowered, allowing open river navigation.

Further improvements at Louisville were carried out at the time, and the project there was designated Lock and Dam No. 41. Twenty-five of the fifty-one dams bordered Kentucky, some with locks located within the commonwealth's boundaries, and others located on the north side of the river. Even before completion of the canalization project, work was underway to replace the oldest locks and dams on the upper river with fixed (nonnavigable) concrete dams with steel gates, together with lock chambers measuring 600 feet by 110 feet. Built in the 1920s and 1930s, four constructions of this type replaced nine of the old wooden wicket dams on the upper Ohio.

Commercial traffic on the Ohio declined during the Great Depression and continued to diminish during the next decades as new industrial and electric generating plants were constructed elsewhere to take advantage of more economical river transport and abundant water supply. The length of barge tows increased as diesel-powered boats replaced steam towboats, and the 600-foot locks required double lockage; the long tows of barges had to be locked through in two maneuvers. The army engineers in the 1950s undertook the Ohio River Navigation Modernization Project to replace the obsolete navigation system. Each of the high-lift concrete and steel dams completed by 1990 replaced at least two of the old structures. Each consists of two locks, one the standard 600 by 110-foot chamber, the other measuring 1,200 by 110 feet. Smithland Locks and Dams on the lower river has two 1,200-foot locks. Bordering the commonwealth are eight of these massive projects. Lock and Dam No. 41 at Louisville was modified in the 1960s by widening the canal, adding the 1,200-foot lock, and making other improvements. It was renamed McAlpine Locks and Dam in honor of William H. McAlpine, the only civilian to serve as district engineer at Louisville. Locks and Dams No. 52 and 53, on the lower river between Paducah and the mouth, are the last of the old wooden wicket dams, but temporary improvements have been made to provide a 1,200-foot lock to augment the old 600-foot chamber. These two antiquated structures are slated for replacement by a single modern navigation structure, to be built by the year 2005. The Ohio River structures serve navigation purposes only, not flood control.

Nearly two-thirds of the freight traffic on the Ohio River now consists of bulk forms of energy-related commodities such as coal, crude oil, and petroleum products, along with sand and gravel, iron and steel, chemicals, and grain. More commerce moves through the Ohio River navigation system annually than through the Panama Canal. In addition, the Ohio supplies water and provides recreational boating and harbor facilities to the nation's heartland.

See Michael C. Robinson, *History of Navigation in the Ohio River Basin* (Washington, D.C., 1983); George A. Baer, Jr., *Ohio River Basin Navigation System: 1986 Report* (Cincinnati 1986); Leland R. Johnson, *The Falls City Engineers: A History of the Louisville District Corps of Engineers* (Louisville 1984).   CHARLES E. PARRISH

OIL AND GAS INDUSTRY. In 1819 a well drilled for producing salt water in the valley of South Fork of the Cumberland River in Kentucky encountered oil at a depth of several hundred feet. The well, drilled by Martin Beatty of Abingdon, Virginia, is the first recorded discovery of hydrocarbons in the commonwealth. Ten years later a salt-seeking well drilled in Cumberland County became what may be considered the first commercial well in Kentucky. The oil encountered was bottled and sold as medicine to be used both internally and externally for a variety of ills, in both humans and animals.

The discovery in the late 1850s that paraffin oil could be obtained more economically from oil than from either cannel coal or bituminous shales set off drilling that was cut short by the Civil War. Renewed drilling in the late 1860s was encouraged by oil and gas seepages that had been observed by soldiers on both sides of the conflict. During this time discoveries were recorded in Meade, Allen, Barren, Wayne, Russell, Cumberland, and Clinton counties.

Growing demand for kerosene and the byproducts of oil refining kept exploration for and production of oil and gas active for the rest of the century. The first year of recorded oil production was 1883, when 4,755 barrels were reported. After 1900 exploration and production increased significantly. The more important discoveries included the Ragland pool in Bath County, Warfield Fork gas pool in Martin County, Campton pool in Wolfe County, Big Sinking pool in Lee County, Sunnybrook pool in Wayne County, Bowling Green pool in Warren County, and the Big Sandy gas field in Floyd County.

Exploration for oil and gas resources in western Kentucky began in earnest in the late 1930s and expanded considerably during World War II. Notable discoveries were made in northern Ohio County and Henderson, Daviess, and Union counties. During this time Henderson County first led the state in oil production and it stayed No. 1 for a long period. In the late 1950s the Greensburg pool in Green County was discovered, pushing oil production in Kentucky to 27,271,998 barrels during 1959.

To curb excessive drilling and disregard for environmental matters by the oil industry, the 1960 General Assembly passed the first statewide law regulating permits for oil and gas wells and created the Water Pollution Control Commission. Permitting was housed in the Department of Mines and Minerals. The Water Pollution Control Commission evolved into a department of the Cabinet for Natural Resources and Environmental Protection.

Many wells were drilled before record keeping began, so the number of drilling operations cannot be verified. The Kentucky Geological Survey estimates that the number of wells covered by records of one sort or another is approximately 200,000, drilled either for production or to support production. The deepest well, a dry hole in Webster County, is 15,200 feet. Production depths range from 60 feet to 10,430 feet, with the average close to 2,000 feet. Initial production of oil wells ranges up to 3,500 barrels per day, and the open flows of gas wells may reach 52 million cubic feet per day. These figures are the maximums, however, and the average production and open flow are considerably less. In 1989 there were approximately 23,000 oil wells, producing 5 million barrels a year, and 11,000 gas wells producing 70 billion cubic feet of gas per year. Crude oil production has been declining while natural gas production inches upward.

The main deposits of oil and gas are found in three of the five geographic provinces of the state. There has been little drilling and little production in the Jackson Purchase and the Bluegrass. The major gas producing area is the Eastern Coal Field, the major oil producer is the Western Coal Field, and lesser amounts are found in the Pennyroyal.

Drilling has encountered producible oil and gas in seventy-five of the 120 counties in Kentucky. As of 1990 the more significant producing counties were Henderson, Union, Ohio, and Daviess in the west; Warren in the central part; and Magoffin and Lee in the east. The major counties for natural gas production were Pike, Martin, Floyd, and Knott in the east.

To produce more oil from known reservoirs, the industry started using enhanced recovery procedures in the early 1930s. The technique injects a fluid (water, air, gas) into the producing formation to replace the original pressure. The oil yield in barrels per day is nearly as much as produced originally. Fields in Lawrence, Magoffin, Lee, Ohio, Daviess, Henderson, and McLean counties have been found to be the most responsive to the enhanced recovery.

Severance taxes on oil and gas in Kentucky amounted to $14,960,000 in 1988. In dollar value, natural gas is ranked third among the state's natural resources, and crude oil is ranked fourth. Nationally, Kentucky ranks eighteenth in the production of natural gas and seventeenth in the amount of proved natural gas reserves. The state ranks twenty-first in crude oil production and twentieth in reserves. In 1988 5,813 Kentuckians were employed in the extraction and transportation phases of the industry.

See Arthur C. McFarlan, *Geology of Kentucky* (Lexington, Ky., 1943); W.R. Jillson, *The Oil and Gas Resources of Kentucky* (Frankfort, Ky., 1919).

FRANK H. WALKER

OLD COURT–NEW COURT CONTROVERSY.

Between 1819 and 1823, Kentuckians became embroiled in one of the most notorious struggles in the state's history—the RELIEF CRISIS, in which proponents of debtor relief and of a public bank (the Bank of the Commonwealth) did battle with advocates of good-faith contract performance and sound banking. In the fall of 1823, at the peak of this controversy, the Kentucky court of appeals struck down the laws inspired by the Relief party. Relief partisans then moved to reorganize the court of appeals.

In October 1823, Chief Justice John Boyle and Associate Justices William Owsley and Benjamin Mills of the Kentucky court of appeals, in *Blair v. Williams* and *Lapsley v. Brashear*, invalidated the General Assembly's 1820 stay law (sometimes called the replevy law), and condemned all related attempts to alter or postpone contract performance. Chief Justice Boyle's opinion in *Blair* (October 8) followed several months of argument by the Relief party's George Bibb and anti-Relief activist Robert Wickliffe. In *Lapsley* (October 11), Judge Owsley wrote the majority opinion after a vicious battle between Relief partisans John Rowan and William T. Barry and their anti-Relief opponents, Ben Hardin, George Robertson, and Wickliffe. In both cases, the anti-Relief position prevailed. Although Boyle and Owsley offered very different reasons for their decisions, they agreed that the Assembly's remedial powers did not extend to alteration of contract terms. The citizen's "obligation to perform the duties of justice," especially the "duty of fulfilling our contracts," wrote Boyle, was a "*perfect* obliga-

tion"; creditors had ample ground to "demand . . . performance, and to use force [to extract] it."

Relief party supporters were outraged. Editor Amos Kendall of the ARGUS OF WESTERN AMERICA was "astonished" that Kentucky's own judiciary would adopt principles "repugnant to the vast majority of the people, as well as to the practice of every state and to the laws of every government, despotic or free." Gov. John Adair (1820-24) urged resistance, asserting that the real issue was the people's right to govern themselves.

Anti-Relief partisans disagreed; indeed, the minority party offered a legislative resolution on November 6, 1823, condemning Adair's excessive "patriotism and energy." But Wickliffe's party was no match for the Relief party. A few days later, Sen. John Rowan read a long document, "Preamble and Resolutions," which pronounced the court of appeals decisions "ruinous . . . to the good people of this Commonwealth, and subversive of their dearest and most invaluable rights." By late 1823, Rowan and others had come to believe that the legislature was the supreme branch of government and that judges served at the legislators' pleasure; with *Blair* and *Lapsley* in hand, Rowan's colleagues were prepared to act on their convictions.

The Relief party first tried to secure the judges' removal by Adair's address to the legislature; when that effort failed, they decided to abolish and reorganize the court. On December 24, 1824, the General Assembly passed a statute "to Repeal the Law Organizing the Court of Appeals, and to Reorganize the Court of Appeals." The law disestablished the court, erected the New Court, to be staffed by William T. Barry as chief judge and three associate judges, listed judicial duties in painstaking detail, introduced a new oath of office, and ordered Achilles Sneed, the Old Court clerk, to deliver his books to the New Court clerk by January 1825.

The 34th General Assembly opened in November 1825, with an explosive speech by Gov. Joseph Desha (1824-28), in which he accused the Old Court party of plotting to strip the assembly of rightful powers. Almost at once, however, the New Court party encountered ferocious opposition. Voters had returned an Old Court majority to the General Assembly; the group immediately formed a committee to make recommendations as to the future organization of the court of appeals. On November 23, the Old Court party introduced a bill to repeal the reorganization act. A month later, the investigative committee submitted a report pronouncing the Old Court's justices "constitutional judges," whose positions could not be abolished by the legislature.

During the 1825 session, the Old Court contingent secured only a nonbinding resolution condemning the reorganizing act, but the 1826 general elections confirmed and augmented the party's majority in both houses. On December 29, 1826, Gov. Desha's objections notwithstanding, the Old Court party approved a revised version of the 1825 bill removing the "unconstitutional obstructions . . .

thrown in the way of the Court of Appeals." Desha vetoed the restoration act; within hours of his incendiary veto message, both houses had overridden it.

With passage of the restoration act and the containment of Governor Desha, Kentucky's court struggle came to an end. New Court partisan George Bibb, who insisted for the rest of his life that the reorganizing act had been well within the General Assembly's authority, agreed to speed the conciliation process by serving as chief judge of the reconstituted Kentucky court of appeals. By 1826, prosperity had returned; with an almost audible sigh of relief, Kentuckians turned their attention to the great work of economic development and internal improvement.

See Arndt Stickles, *Critical Court Struggle in Kentucky, 1819-1929* (Bloomington, Ind., 1929).

SANDRA F. VANBURKLEO

OLDHAM, WILLIAM. William Oldham, soldier in the American Revolution, was born in Berkeley County, Virginia, on June 17, 1753, to John and Ann (Conway) Oldham. He fought in the early part of the Revolutionary War, rose to the rank of captain in 1775, and resigned in 1779. At that time he emigrated to the Falls of the Ohio, probably with his wife, Penelope (Pope) Oldham. He took part in some of the engagements against the Indians in the Northwest Territory and was in command of a regiment of the Kentucky militia in the ill-fated and poorly conducted expedition led by Gen. Arthur St. Clair, governor of the territory northwest of the Ohio River. On November 4, 1791, troops were attacked by Indians near the Wabash River and the border between Ohio and Indiana. William Oldham was killed, one of the hundreds killed or wounded. Two years later Capt. Alexander Gibson's men built Fort Recovery at the site of the battle. In 1823 Oldham was honored by the Kentucky legislature in naming a newly formed county for him.

OLDHAM COUNTY. Oldham County, the seventy-fourth county in order of formation, is located in north-central Kentucky along the Ohio River. The county is bordered by Henry, Jefferson, Shelby, and Trimble counties and has an area of 190 square miles. Oldham County was created from sections of Henry, Jefferson, and Shelby counties on December 15, 1823, and was named for Col. William Oldham of Jefferson County, a Revolutionary War officer and a native of Virginia. Oldham was killed in 1794 while leading a regiment of Kentucky militia against the Indians during the St. Clair campaign on the Wabash River. The seat of Oldham County is LAGRANGE.

The western portion of the county is gently undulating land, while the eastern section is broken and hilly. The economy is agricultural, and the predominant crops are tobacco, corn, and hay. Farms also produce beef and dairy cattle, hogs, and poultry. The principal waterways are the Ohio River, Harrod's Creek, Eighteen Mile Creek, Curry's Fork, and Floyd's Fork.

The Oldham County region was explored by Col. John Floyd in 1774 and, being close to the Ohio River, it was settled rapidly. One of the earliest established communities was Westport, founded in 1800. Located on the river, Westport became a thriving trade center and was the first seat of Oldham County, from 1823 to 1827; the county seat was briefly moved to LaGrange, back to Westport from 1828 to 1838, then to LaGrange permanently. Other communities in Oldham County that grew during the 1820s and 1830s include Ballardsville, Brownsboro, and Goshen. The coming of the Louisville & Frankfort Railroad Company (later part of the Louisville & Nashville) in 1851 prompted the growth of communities such as Pewee Valley, Buckner, and Crestwood in the late antebellum era. Annie Fellows Johnston, the author of the "Little Colonel" series of children's books, lived in Pewee Valley. La Grange was the home of pioneer film maker D.W. Griffith, who produced *Birth of a Nation*. Oldham County was also the site of the Kentucky Confederate Veterans Home, founded in 1902 in Pewee Valley.

Oldham County remains an agrarian area with numerous scattered small towns. Industrial growth in eastern Jefferson County and the completion of I-71 in the 1970s led to rapid residential growth in western Oldham County. During the 1970s many people moved there to avoid busing for the purpose of racial desegregation in Jefferson County and Louisville. In 1980, 64 percent of the employed labor force had jobs elsewhere, mostly in Jefferson County. The county is home to the Kentucky State Reformatory, Luther Luckett Correctional Complex, and the Roederer Farm Center, all near LaGrange, and the Kentucky Correctional Institute for Women and the Lonnie Watson Center, both near Pewee Valley.

The population of Oldham County was 14,687 in 1970; 27,795 in 1980; and 33,263 in 1990.

See Ruben Thornton Taylor, *A Pageant to Celebrate the Founding of LaGrange, Oldham County, Kentucky* (LaGrange, Ky., 1927).

RON D. BRYANT

OLD MUD MEETING HOUSE. The Old Mud Meeting House in Harrodsburg, Kentucky, was built in 1800 of oak, straw, and stick-filled mud on a fieldstone foundation by agents of the Dutch Reformed Church. Later it served Presbyterian and Baptist congregations. The meetinghouse is situated on a three-and-a-half-acre site that includes a cemetery. It is in the possession of the Mercer County Historical Society and has been placed on the National Register of Historic Places.

See Helen C. Powell, *Historic Sites of Harrodsburg and Mercer County* (Harrodsburg, Ky., 1988).

OLD MULKEY MEETING HOUSE. The Old Mulkey Meeting House, located near Tompkinsville in Monroe County, Kentucky, appears to have been established in either 1797 or 1798 by a group of Baptists who followed Phillip and Ann Mulkey into the region from east Tennessee. In 1804 a new meetinghouse was completed. Its unique twelve-corner design was dictated by the building materials; the logs were of insufficient length and thickness for conventional design. Originally called Mill Creek Church, it suffered a schism, and some members joined the Campbellite movement. The building was seldom used after 1856 and was abandoned about 1910. In 1925 a local fund drive restored the meetinghouse, and in 1931 it became a state park and is now a state historic site.

See William Lynwood Montell, *Monroe County History, 1820-1970* (Tompkinsville, Ky., 1970).

OLD STATE ARSENAL. The Old State Arsenal, in Frankfort, Kentucky, was the third storage place for the state's munitions. The first two buildings were located on the northeast corner of Capitol Square, now known as the Old Capitol grounds. The first "gun-house" was built in the 1820s. To replace this building, the legislature on February 22, 1834, authorized the first official arsenal. The new building was consumed by fire in March 1836, but was not replaced immediately, as no state of war or civil unrest existed at the time. In March 1850 the legislature authorized construction of a new arsenal within a half mile of the capitol. The site is the intersection of East Main Street and Capitol Avenue.

The building committee of Ambrose Dudley, E.H. Taylor, and Philip Swigert selected Nathanial C. Cook to design the building and supervise construction. Cook was probably trained under James Dakin, the leading architect of New Orleans. Cook's design in the castellated Gothic style is quite similar to Dakin's 1847 Louisiana state capitol. Cook also designed the 1849 Good Shepherd Church in Frankfort and the 1857-58 Owen County courthouse.

The $8,000 arsenal was used to store and distribute the arms and equipment of the Kentucky state militia, which became the Kentucky National Guard in 1903. During the night of June 30, 1933, the arsenal was gutted by fire after an explosion on the second floor. Approximately $150,000 in federal and state property was destroyed and damage to the building amounted to $30,000. Local architect Leo Oberwarth directed the renovation of the building. The Old State Arsenal is now operated by the Kentucky Historical Society as the Kentucky Military History Museum. The Boone National Guard Center, in Frankfort, operates as the statewide headquarters of the National Guard, and local armories house state munitions. WILLIAM B. SCOTT, JR.

OLIVE HILL. Olive Hill is in western Carter County in northeastern Kentucky, situated along Tygart's Creek and U.S. 60. The first settlement in the area was made by Robert Henderson in 1792. The village of Olive Hill grew as a trading center on an east-west road built in 1804 to connect the salt works on the Little Sandy River with established towns in central Kentucky. The road became a stagecoach turnpike to Washington, D.C., and was known as the Midland Trail. The first post of-

fice was established in 1838, and the town of Olive Hill was incorporated in 1861 by the state legislature. The origin of the name is unknown.

The Civil War came to Olive Hill in early October 1862, when elements of John Hunt Morgan's Confederate cavalry passed through the city after harassing George W. Morgan's Federal army for several days as it retreated from the Cumberland Gap to the Ohio River. The Civil War brought an increasing demand for iron produced in Carter County and plans were made for a railroad that would parallel the Midland Trail. The Elizabethtown, Lexington & Big Sandy Railroad (later the Chesapeake & Ohio) reached Olive Hill from the west in January 1882. Logging became a major industry and sawmills kept the railroad supplied with timber for cross-ties. In 1893, as the timber industry was declining, it was discovered that the mountains near Olive Hill contained an abundance of high-grade fire clay. Two major brick plants were built in the city, and the brick companies sponsored a baseball team, the Olive Hill Brickies, during the 1920s. By 1942 the two plants employed more than 1,700 people.

Citing the distance to the county seat at Grayson, citizens of the western end of Carter County persuaded the 1904 Kentucky General Assembly to create a new county, BECKHAM, from adjoining sections of Carter, Rowan, and Elliott counties, with Olive Hill as the seat. However, the Kentucky court of appeals struck down the creation of Beckham County on constitutional grounds.

A legacy of division from the Civil War, combined with an influx of industrial workers from other states caused Olive Hill, traditionally Republican, to lean toward the Democrats. In 1910 William Jason Fields, running as "Honest Bill from Olive Hill," became the first Democrat elected to the 9th District U.S. congressional seat in two decades. He was elected governor in 1923.

After World War II, technological changes in the railroad and steel industries greatly reduced the need for firebrick to line steam boilers and furnaces. The economy of Olive Hill went into a slow decline as employment was reduced at the brick plants. The Harbinson-Walker Works closed in 1964 and the General Refractories Company shut down on Christmas Day in 1972.

The population of the fourth-class city was 1,197 in 1970; 2,539 in 1980; and 1,809 in 1990.

See George Wolfford, *Carter County: A Pictorial History* (Ashland, Ky., 1985); Carter County Bicentennial Committee, *Carter County History 1838-1976* (Grayson, Ky., 1976).

OLYMPIAN SPRINGS. Olympian Springs was located in what was originally Montgomery County (now Bath County), Kentucky, thirty-six miles east of Lexington. It was identified as Mud Lick in a land grant given to Jacob Meyers by Virginia's governor in 1784. The springs, which consisted of a salt well, a salt-sulphur well, a black sulphur well, two chalybeate springs, and an alkaline-saline well and spring, changed hands many times. William

Ramsey, around 1796, was the first owner to make any improvements on the property; he was mainly interested in extracting salt from the spring's water, a venture that proved unprofitable.

The springs were purchased by Col. Thomas Hart, father-in-law of Henry Clay, around the turn of the century, and renamed Olympian Springs. It was during Hart's ownership that the first hotel was built, with a dining room that would seat one hundred. The medicinal value of the springs' water was praised by physicians, who recommended the waters for ailments from skin to digestive disorders. The social life at Olympian Springs included music, dancing, bathing, hiking, horseback riding, and hunting. It was often said that the social offerings of the springs were more popular than the medicinal use of the waters. The resort proved so popular that it was the destination of Kentucky's first stagecoach line, which originated in 1803 in Lexington. In 1807 Cuthbert Banks, formerly proprietor of Henry Clay's hotel in Lexington, purchased the 625-acre site. He expanded the hotel and its reputation for fine food, including the best venison in the western country. He purchased the land with money borrowed from Hart, guaranteed by a mortgage on the property; upon Hart's death in 1812, Henry Clay as executor of his estate sold the mortgage to Col. Thomas Dye Owings. This episode may have given rise to the legend that at one time Clay owned the springs and lost it in a poker game.

The property was purchased by George Lansdowne in 1830. His son-in-law, Harrison Gill, then became proprietor and owner. In 1833 many residents of central Kentucky summered at Olympian Springs to escape the cholera epidemic that swept Kentucky. This helped to solidify the resort's reputation. In October 1863 a portion of the 1st Kentucky Federal Cavalry fought about 250 Confederate cavalrymen there. Both sides claimed victory in the skirmish, during which many of the outlying buildings were burned, but the hotel remained and flourished again after the war.

In 1903 a syndicate purchased the springs and added a new four-story hotel with steam heat, electric lights, and a sewer system. Other improvements included a thirty-five-acre fishing lake and a golf course. The hotel's popularity diminished with the availability of better transportation to other vacation sites. Judge James P. Lewis purchased the property for use as a farm, and the buildings housed a Baptist school. On September 30, 1946, the site was broken into parcels and sold.

See J. Winston Coleman, Jr., *The Springs of Kentucky* (Lexington, Ky., 1955); J.A. Richards, *An Illustrated History of Bath County, Kentucky* (Yuma, Ariz., 1961).

ONEIDA BAPTIST INSTITUTE. Located near the South Fork of the Kentucky River in northern Clay County, Oneida Baptist Institute was opened in 1900 by James Anderson Burns, a Baptist minister and chatauqua circuit lecturer. He was determined to substitute the opportunities of education

for the violence of local feuding. Recognized for its adherence to Christian values and quality education, Oneida operates year-round as a boarding school, offering instruction for grades six through twelve on a work-study plan to students from twenty states and twelve countries. Among the school's past students is Gov. Bert T. Combs (1959-63), whose grandfather took part in its founding.

MARY LATTA LEE

ONE-ROOM SCHOOLS. One of the greatest engines for change in Kentucky was one of the state's smallest institutions—the one-room school. The tiny schools that dotted the hills and valleys were, collectively, a salvation to a state recovering from the Civil War and, later, the Great Depression.

In the nineteenth century, these early schools were located within walking distance of a few families who could pay the teacher. By the early twentieth century little had changed except that the teacher was paid by the county. During the 1918-19 school year, Kentucky had 7,067 one-room schools in operation. By 1968-69 the number had dwindled to 146, all in eastern Kentucky. In the 1980s several one-room schools still operated in southeastern Kentucky. Tim Salisbury, the teacher of the Daniels Creek School in Floyd County observed: "If I don't die, they'll have to pry me out of that place. What I teach the most is reading. If you can read, you can learn." Kentucky's last one-room school, in Perry County, closed in 1989.

What these schools lacked in modern conveniences, they overcame with students motivated enough to endure hardships in order to learn, and teachers willing to work under difficult circumstances to achieve progress. These forgotten heroes and heroines, whom Jesse Stuart termed "immortal teachers," did not, according to one former teacher, "give poverty a chance to impede their love of learning." One-room schoolteachers received little recognition and few tangible rewards. Some became certified teachers by taking a qualifying examination that was developed annually by the state Department of Education and administered by the county superintendent. The one-room schoolteacher was also nurse, counselor, janitor, playground director, and lunchroom supervisor. In spite of the hard work and long hours, the pay was very low. Some became teachers because economic and social conditions blocked other professional opportunities. "I don't think I chose to be a teacher," one former teacher reflected. "My grandmother said many of us became teachers because we liked to 'be boss.' Economic conditions really made me become a teacher. The Great Depression was four years old—there was no money anyplace. I had wanted to be a lawyer or an interpreter in the diplomatic corps."

The one-room schoolteachers usually boarded with families in their school districts. A return trip to the teacher's family home was often more difficult than the daily walk to and from school.

To maintain appropriate school conduct, some teachers had a lengthy catalog of rules, which specified a punishment for each infraction. Gradually, this approach to discipline improved as teachers became better trained. Many teachers did not control their classes by punitive measures. Instead they induced their students to like them and to behave well to please them. In most schools, a teacher had to maintain credibility as a disciplinarian. If students knew they would be punished they rarely misbehaved, and if parents knew their children were fairly punished, they were almost always supportive of the teacher.

The routine of school life was occasionally interrupted by special social activities. Daytime events were student celebrations of holidays or scholastic competitions. Evening activities such as pie suppers were community socials that also provided operating funds for the school.

Transportation to and from school, by today's standards, ranked somewhere between inconvenient and impossible. Both students and teachers usually walked. It was not uncommon for children to face a three-mile walk each way. Some teachers rode a horse or pony. Others came in a horse-drawn buggy. By the 1930s some were driving cars to school. The automobile, however, did not greatly facilitate travel because of the poor roads and the isolation of the schools. There were no "snow days" in the one-room schools; the teacher and the students dressed warmly and walked through the snow. For the most part, transportation difficulties were accepted as part of the rugged way of life in early twentieth century Kentucky. The hike to school often provided a time for unsupervised recreation for young people. The adventures they experienced became an exciting part of the history and folklore of one-room school life.

The school building was of wooden frame construction. It typically had a front door that faced the road or path, three windows on each side of the building, and a painted blackboard across the back. Two long recitation benches faced the teacher's desk and blackboard. Rows of desks or benches, a "warm-morning" stove, and a water bucket completed the list of basic equipment. Teachers were often quite ingenious in equipping their school buildings. For example, a teacher from Letcher County who had no timepiece in her classroom cut notches in the doorstep on the east side of the building. When the sun hit the first notch, it was time to begin school. The second mark signaled recess, and the third indicated lunch time; notches on a west window marked the afternoon hours. Another cut up a calendar to help first graders learn to put the numbers in order. In many instances, the teachers spent much of their meager earnings on their school and students. "By the time I got through dressing those children and buying my materials, I never had anything left," said one former teacher. "I just might as well have been staying at home. All I was getting was experience." Successful one-room teachers usually made good use of the skills and interests of older students. The older boys and girls often helped younger students with their lessons. Advanced students also conducted drills for lower-grade classes and supervised play activities. Many former one-room school students remember these responsibilities as good learning experiences.

Almost without exception, former one-room schoolteachers report happy memories of their teaching days and personal pride in their accomplishments. Although teaching eight different grades each day was hard, the teacher did not feel that the students learned less. Some of these former teachers even say that the old ways were preferable, claiming that one-room school education produced students with more creativity, self-reliance, and independence.

See Ellis Ford Hartford, *The Little White Schoolhouse* (Lexington, Ky., 1977); Jesse Stuart, *To Teach, To Love* (Ashland, Ky., 1987).

JAMES M. GIFFORD

ORAL HISTORY. Oral history may be defined as recorded interviews that preserve historically significant memories for future use. For centuries historians and others have used oral history methods to gather information. The tape recorder has made the preservation of verbatim interviews an essential characteristic of oral history as practiced today.

The establishment of Columbia University's oral history program in 1948 is frequently cited as its beginning as an organized activity in the United States. Other institutions across the country then began collecting interviews to supplement their archival holdings. From late 1960s through the 1970s, the ability of oral history to document the lives of those generally neglected by traditional sources attracted large numbers of practitioners from a variety of backgrounds, and hundreds of oral history programs concentrating on grassroots history were established.

In Kentucky, Alice Lloyd College and Lees Junior College started the Appalachian Oral History Project in 1970 to record interviews on the history and folklore of the central Appalachian region. Murray State University established the Forrest C. Pogue Oral History Institute in 1973, which was closely followed by programs at the University of Kentucky, University of Louisville, and Eastern Kentucky University. Western Kentucky University furthered the preservation of western and southern Kentucky's folk life and culture by having folklore students collect interviews. Public libraries and heritage organizations also began oral history projects in the 1970s, and many independent researchers conducted interviews and deposited them in appropriate repositories.

Efforts to preserve Kentucky's past through oral history were significantly enhanced when Gov. Julian Carroll (1974-79) created the Kentucky Bicentennial Oral History Commission in 1976. Under the leadership of journalists Albert Smith (chairman, 1976-80) and John Ed Pearce (chairman, 1981-88), the commission established a grant program to support oral history research projects and a local history program to provide training and equipment to volunteer interviewers in each county. In 1981 Gov. John Y. Brown, Jr. (1979-83), created the Kentucky Oral History Commission through executive order, and in 1982 the legislature clarified the status of the commission as an independent state agency, the only such agency in the United States. The commission is administered by a twelve-member board, ten appointed by the governor and two ex-officio members—the director of the Kentucky Historical Society and the commissioner of the Kentucky Department for Libraries and Archives.

As of 1990, the Oral History Commission had awarded grants to more than 130 projects covering a broad range of subjects, including: ethnic and women's history, the coal and tobacco industries, authors Robert Penn Warren and Harriette Arnow, Vietnam and World War II veterans, political leaders, and folk musicians. Efforts to collect local history through volunteer interviewers have resulted in a collection of over 3,500 interviews, which are maintained by the commission in Frankfort. Throughout the state, approximately 20,000 interviews are available to researchers, adding immeasurably to the record of Kentucky life in the twentieth century.

See John Ed Pearce, "The Genesis of Kentucky's Oral History Commission," *Kentucky Review* 10 (Summer 1990): 5-11.   KIM LADY SMITH

ORGANIZED CRIME (NORTHERN KENTUCKY).

Although gambling and crime can be found in all regions of Kentucky, northern Kentucky for a long time represented the most obvious examples in the state. The region played a prominent role in the illegal liquor trade, becoming one of the major supply and distribution centers for Cincinnati during the prohibition era. Sometime toward the end of prohibition (1933) the national crime syndicate switched from liquor to gambling, allotting specific areas to various syndicates. The Cleveland syndicate was given territory that included northern Kentucky. In the 1930s the area manager, Sam Tucker, began to organize and consolidate the region. Local gambling operators were given the choice of joining the syndicate or leaving the business. Most joined; those who did not were squeezed out. One of the syndicate's primary aims was to keep down petty crime and public violence, both of which called attention to organized crime. The job of "peacekeeper" was given to Red ("The Enforcer") Masterson, a local who joined the syndicate. The Eastern syndicate, allowed a limited interest in the area, was represented by Michael ("Trigger Mike") Cappola, whose interests were in turn represented by another erstwhile independent, Frank ("Screw") Andrews.

By the early 1940s the Newport, Kentucky, area was well-organized, and night spots such as the Beverly Hills, the Lookout House, and the Latin Quarter provided a plush setting for organized crime. In Newport, the less glamorous but more lucrative business of lay-off betting flourished, adding untold amounts of money to the coffers of organized crime and making Newport the national center of lay-off betting. In this illegal practice, a bookie, inundated with bets on one horse, moved part of the money to another bookie in case the horse won, and the pay-off was then split.

Not all efforts went smoothly for organized crime. Groups such as the Kenton County Protestant Association and Newport Ministerial Association tried to raise public and political awareness of corruption. In 1952 state police raided the Lookout House, made several arrests, and permanently closed the club's casino. Such activities were viewed by the syndicate more as annoyance than threat. More seriously viewed were investigations on a national level in the 1950s when the committees of Sen. Estes Kefauver (Tennessee) and Sen. John McClellan (Arkansas) focused attention on northern Kentucky, though neither committee seemed to grasp the extent of organized crime.

At the same time, local reform gained momentum. Campbell County businessmen formed the "Committee of 500" to add support to ministerial groups. George Ratterman, of Ft. Thomas, Kentucky, a former Notre Dame and professional football player, agreed in 1960 to run for sheriff of Campbell County on a reform ticket. Ratterman secured the support of the Catholic bishop of Covington, thus uniting religious support. Reform efforts were also ably abetted by a series of articles by the *Louisville Courier-Journal*'s investigative reporter, Hank Messick. The syndicate struck back by drugging Ratterman and arranging for him to be arrested in bed with an exotic dancer by the Newport police. The frame backfired and Ratterman was elected with the full support of his backers. Aware of a now-national focus, the Cleveland syndicate pulled out. In April 1961, Cappola was indicted for income tax evasion. The era of the Newport area's prominence in the national scheme of organized crime had ended.

See Howard Abadinsky, *Organized Crime* (Boston 1981); Hank Messick, *The Silent Syndicate* (New York 1967).   H. LEW WALLACE

ORPHAN BRIGADE.

The 1st Kentucky Brigade of the Confederate army came to be known as the Orphan Brigade after the Union capture of Fort Donelson, Tennessee, on February 16, 1862, and Confederate evacuation of Kentucky and western Tennessee. The 1st Kentucky Brigade, cut off from its native state for the duration of the Civil War, distinguished itself on and off the battlefield by exhibiting discipline, high morale, and effective military tactics. Only about five hundred of the original 4,000 men survived to the war's end. The brigade was initially commanded by Maj. Gen. John Cabell BRECKINRIDGE, from November 2, 1861, to March 29, 1862. The Orphan Brigade lost two of its brigadier generals in battle: Roger Weightman HANSON at Stone's River and Benjamin Hardin HELM at Chickamauga. Regiments from the Orphan Brigade fought with distinction in the Battles of Shiloh, Corinth, Baton Rouge, Vicksburg, Stone's River, Chickamauga, and Missionary Ridge and throughout the Atlanta campaign. During the final months of the war, the brigade was mounted as cavalry. Its last commander was Col. Joseph H. LEWIS, who led the Orphan Brigade until it surrendered at Washington Court House, Georgia, during the first week of May 1865. It was one of the last Confederate groups east of the Mississippi River to lay down its arms.

See Edwin Porter Thompson, *History of the First Kentucky Brigade* (Cincinnati 1868); William C. Davis, *The Orphan Brigade* (New York 1980).

OSBORNE BROTHERS. The country music singers Robert, Jr. ("Bobby"), and Sonny Osborne, sons of Robert and Daisy (Dixon) Osborne, were born in Hyden, Kentucky—Bobby on December 7, 1931, and Sonny on October 29, 1937. The family left Kentucky in 1941, and the boys were raised in Dayton, Ohio. Both began performing professionally as teenagers. After appearing separately with groups such as the Lonesome Pine Fiddlers, the Stanley Brothers, Jimmy Martin, and Bill Monroe, the two began appearing as a team in 1953. The Osborne Brothers' concert at Antioch College in 1960 sparked the spread of bluegrass music on college campuses. They appeared on the WWVA "Jamboree" in Wheeling, West Virginia, during 1956-63 and joined the "Grand Ole Opry" radio program in Nashville in 1964. They fused bluegrass with country music and enjoyed wider exposure than any other bluegrass ensemble. In 1971 the Osborne Brothers were named vocal group of the year by the Country Music Association, the first bluegrass group to be so honored.

See Neil Rosenberg, "The Osborne Brothers," *Bluegrass Unlimited* 6 (Sept. 1971): 5-10, and (Feb. 1972): 5-8; Peter Kuykendall, "The Osborne Brothers—From Rocky Top to Muddy Bottom," *Bluegrass Unlimited* 12 (Dec. 1977): 10-16.

CHARLES F. FABER

OTTENHEIM. The settlement that became Ottenheim, Kentucky, began as a project of the State Commission of Immigration, an office that the legislature created in 1880 as an additional responsibility of the state geologist, then John Robert Procter. The theory was that the state was being deprived of growth by receiving a disproportionately small number of the immigrants who were pouring into the United States. Procter, head of geological surveys that were taking place in the southern parts of the state, was to promote Kentucky as an area of settlement.

In 1883 Procter's campaign interested Jacob Ottenheimer of New York, who made several trips to the state and began to purchase tracts of land in Lincoln County in south-central Kentucky. He planned a settlement, mainly for immigrants, but also to draw Americans from other areas. By the end of the year, Ottenheimer had purchased 18,585.85 acres between the communities of Stanford and Crab Orchard, which he hoped to clear and sell as farmland. His advertising campaign in New York and other major port cities attracted settlers to Lincoln County. By the end of 1884, one hundred families, mainly German and Swiss, lived in the settlement, which was built around a Lutheran church and was first named Lutherheim. The immigrants and migrants who arrived in Lutherheim were culturally diverse. To many, the name of the town represented a narrow point of view, and in 1886 the name was changed to Ottenheim, in honor of its founder.

The settlement remains a small farming community in a rural part of the state, relatively self-sufficient. Ottenheim is known for cheese-making.

See A.E. Bigge, "Ottenheim, Kentucky: A Planned Settlement," *FCHQ* 30 (Oct. 1956): 299-314.

OWEN, ABRAHAM. Col. Abraham Owen, for whom Owen County and the city of Owensboro were named, was a native of Prince Edward County, Virginia, who moved to Kentucky in 1785, settling in what is now Shelby County. He served in the summer of 1791 in the campaigns on the White and Wabash rivers in Indiana and was twice wounded. Elected to the legislature in 1799, he was also a member of the state's constitutional convention in that year. In 1811 he volunteered to serve with Gen. William Henry Harrison in his campaign against the Indians in Indiana, and was killed at the battle of Tippecanoe on November 7, 1811, at almost the same time that Col. Joseph Hamilton Daveiss was mortally wounded. On February 3, 1817, the General Assembly provided that the town formerly called Rossboro "shall hereafter be called and known by the name of Owensborough."

See Lee A. Dew and Aloma W. Dew, *Owensboro: The City on the Yellow Banks* (Bowling Green, Ky. 1988).   LEE A. DEW

OWEN, DAVID DALE. David Dale Owen, geologist, born in Scotland on June 24, 1807, was the second of four children of Robert Owen, the industrialist and social reformer, and Ann (Dale) Owen. Initially educated in North Lanark, England, Owen studied chemistry and geology in Switzerland. In 1823 he arrived in the United States to study medicine at the Ohio Medical College in Cincinnati. He practiced medicine for a short while, served as an assistant to the Tennessee geologist Gerard Troost, and traveled to Europe for further study. When he returned to the United States in 1833, he became the director of the Indiana Geological Survey in 1837, and produced brief reports in 1838 and 1839. On August 17, 1839, Owen was appointed to survey the lead regions of Illinois, Wisconsin, and Iowa. He organized 139 agents, who surveyed 11,000 square miles by November 24, locating numerous mineral deposits.

The first efforts in Indiana and Illinois provided Owen with experience that led to more fruitful work in Kentucky and Arkansas. Owen was an excellent organizer, but not a great theoretician. In 1854 he was appointed state geologist of Kentucky, a post he held until his death on November 13, 1860, although he did little work in Kentucky after 1857, when he was also appointed director of the Arkansas survey. By that time Owen was considered the preeminent midwestern scientist, which was one of the reasons Kentucky was willing to share his services with Arkansas. The result for Kentucky was the publication of four large volumes devoted to economic geology, with attention to coal, iron ore, building stone, and other useful minerals. Robert Peter of Transylvania University completed the publication of the survey results after Owen's death. While only a fragmentary survey, it was the most comprehensive geological information about Kentucky until the mid-1870s.

Owen married Caroline Neef in 1837; they had four children. He was buried at New Harmony, Indiana.

See Walter Brookfield Hendrickson, *David Dale Owen: Pioneer Geologist of the Middle West* (Indianapolis 1943).   IVAN L. ZABILKA

OWEN COUNTY. Owen County, the sixty-third county in order of formation, is located in north-central Kentucky. The county is bordered by Carroll, Franklin, Gallatin, Grant, and Henry counties and has an area of 354 square miles. Owen County was formed from sections of Franklin, Gallatin, and Scott counties on February 6, 1819, and was named in honor of Col. Abraham Owen, Indian fighter and Kentucky legislator, who was killed at the Battle of Tippecanoe. The county seat is OWENTON.

The topography is rolling to hilly, with deep productive soil. Tobacco, corn, and livestock are produced on the farms of the county. Deciduous forests, mostly of oak, ash, elm, and black walnut, cover about 36 percent of the land, with extensive growths of cedars on the hills of the area. The major waterways include the Kentucky River and Eagle, Big Twin, Cedar, and Severn creeks.

Evidence of prehistoric Native American inhabitants was discovered when settlers after the Revolutionary War found the remains of numerous Native American burial mounds. Many of the pioneers made their homes on land grants along the many streams which flow through the county. Colonel Owen surveyed and mapped the region that became Owen County.

The development of Owen County was steady during the nineteenth century. In 1844, after the state began to construct locks and dams on the Kentucky River, packet boats on regular trips between Frankfort and Louisville made stops in Owen County at Moxley, Gratz, Monterey, and other towns. The community of New Liberty was founded before 1800 and was the site of one of the first churches. Other communities include the incorporated towns of Gratz, Monterey, and Sparta.

From the summer of 1862 to March 1865, the county was subjected to skirmishes and guerrilla warfare during the Civil War. Many Owen Countians were sympathetic to the Confederate cause and joined the armies of the South. During the course of the war, Federal troops had to fend off frequent attacks from Confederate forces at Lusby's Mill and Vanlandingham's farm, two very active recruiting camps. On March 28, 1864, a portion of New Liberty was destroyed by fire at an estimated loss of $120,000. Confederate Col. George M. Jessee gained control of most of the county by September 1864. After the war, the Democratic party maintained control of the county for many years. "Sweet Owen" was the nickname given to the county in the early 1850s by Democrat John C. Breckinridge, U.S. congressman, senator, and vice-president. In the 1851 and 1853 U.S. congressional elections, Owen County gave Democratic candidate Breckinridge a margin of victory in the 8th U.S. Congressional District, traditionally dominated by the Whig party.

As Owen County entered the twentieth century, it developed a cash crop economy centered on tobacco. Given the low tobacco prices between 1890 and 1914, some county residents migrated to the urban areas of the north, mostly Cincinnati and northern Kentucky and, after the establishment of the automobile industry, to Detroit. Though the Great Depression brought hard times back to the county, federal programs, such as the Works Progress Administration, gave Owen County a refurbished courthouse and improved roads.

Owen County remains an agricultural area, in which tobacco, hay, and corn are the predominant crops. In 1987, 79 percent of the land was occupied by farms, with 52 percent of farmland under cultivation. A limited industrial base has developed. The population of Owen County was 7,470 in 1970; 8,924 in 1980; and 9,035 in 1990.

See Mariam S. Houchens, *History of Owen County, Kentucky* (Owenton, Ky., 1977).
                    RON D. BRYANT

OWENSBORO. Owensboro, the county seat of Daviess County, is located on the Ohio River at U.S. 60 and U.S. 231, on the edge of the Western Coal Field region of the state. The site was called YELLOW BANKS by travelers as early as 1776. William Smeathers (Smothers) made the first permanent settlement there around 1798. In 1816 the town was surveyed and platted; the Kentucky legislature named it in honor of Col. Abraham Owen, who was killed at the Battle of Tippecanoe.

Located in a rich agricultural region, Owensboro, a port city, became a commercial center and enjoyed steady growth in the years before the Civil War. The city's strategic location on the Ohio River made it the object of Union occupation early in the war. On January 4, 1865, Confederate guerrillas commanded by Capt. William Davison burned the courthouse in retribution for billeting black Union troops there. After the war, Owensboro was well positioned to become a major tobacco processing and shipping center for Green River tobacco, and the distillery boom in the 1880s made it known for the quality of its bourbon whiskey. By the 1890s it was a major industrial town, with flourishing wagon and buggy companies, foundries, brick and clay plants, and tobacco factories. Three railroads linked it to markets, and numerous packet lines offered connections by water. The towing industry opened opportunities for shipping grain and coal to markets throughout the Ohio and Mississippi systems.

By 1900 Owensboro was the site of an electric light bulb manufacturing plant, which later, as KEN-RAD, expanded into vacuum tubes for radios and television sets. By the 1960s the Ken-Rad plant, then owned by General Electric, employed more than 6,000 people and was the keystone of an industrial boom that made Owensboro the third largest city in the commonwealth. Other industries, including meat packing, grain shipping and processing, distilling, tobacco products, steel, chemicals, plastics, and electronics, employed not only county residents but also citizens of surrounding counties.

By the 1970s, following a national trend, manufacturing jobs began to decline as a percentage of total employment, and Owensboro developed a broader economic base of service industries to complement the traditional "smokestack" jobs. The city became a regional banking, medical, cultural, commercial, and retail center for a growing trade area. Its two hospitals attracted patients from many counties. The building of the Audubon and Green River parkways made it much easier to do business by truck. Although rail service declined, the development of the Owensboro Riverport enabled many industrial shippers to operate their own barge-loading facilities, capitalizing on the city's primary transportation resource, the Ohio River. By the late 1980s, Owensboro's economy was a mix of manufacturing and service industries, of traditional and high-technology activities.

Agriculture remains a major source of wealth. Owensboro is a major tobacco market for both burley and dark air-cured varieties, and is the home of the Pinkerton Tobacco Company, manufacturer of a variety of consumer tobacco products. The Field Packing Company markets meat products over a wide area, and grain companies process and ship corn and soybeans by rail and barge to customers throughout the nation. The distilling industry has declined, but the Glenmore Distillery Company still operates a major bottling and shipping facility in Owensboro.

By the late 1980s tourism brought an estimated $50 million per year to the city. Conventions were attracted to Owensboro by the Executive Inn Rivermont and other motels. The Owensboro Area Museum contains historical exhibits, Indian and archaeological relics, and a variety of other displays. The Owensboro Museum of Fine Art features a permanent collection of both European and American art as well as traveling exhibits and special programs. In the 1980s the Owensboro Symphony Orchestra appeared on Kentucky Educational Television and gained a statewide audience. The River Park Center, planned for completion in late 1992,

gives the orchestra a permanent concert hall, as well as a smaller auditorium for chamber concerts and other performances. The center is the home of the Bluegrass Music Association and features performances designed to appeal to a great variety of musical tastes.

The self-proclaimed "Barbecue Capital of the World," Owensboro holds the International Barbecue Festival each year in May.

BRESCIA College was founded in Owensboro in 1950, and KENTUCKY WESLEYAN College moved from Winchester to Owensboro in 1951. Owensboro Community College was founded in 1985.

The population of the second-class city was 50,329 in 1970; 54,450 in 1980; and 53,549 in 1990.

See Lee A. Dew and Aloma W. Dew, *Owensboro: The City on the Yellow Banks* (Bowling Green, Ky., 1988).

LEE A. DEW

OWENSBORO & RUSSELLVILLE RAILROAD. The Owensboro & Russellville Railroad was chartered by the General Assembly in 1867 and construction started in 1869. It was completed to Owensboro Junction (now Central City) in 1872. Rechartered as the Evansville, Owensboro & Nashville Railroad in 1873, it went bankrupt in 1875, was bought by a group of Owensboro investors in 1877, and was renamed the Owensboro & Nashville Railroad. In 1879 Edwin W. ("King") Cole, of the Nashville, Chattanooga & St. Louis Railroad, obtained control of the line and construction was resumed. In 1880 the LOUISVILLE & NASHVILLE took control of the NC&StL. The line was completed to Russellville in 1883 and to Adairville in 1884. Passenger service ended in 1941, and the Owensboro-Livermore section was abandoned in 1984.

LEE A. DEW

OWENSBORO CATTLE CASES. The Interstate Commerce Commission during 1912 and 1913 heard a series of cases dealing with freight rates on cattle shipped to and from Owensboro. The question at issue was the long haul–short haul differential, which meant shippers in small cities on branch lines had to pay higher rates than those shipping from major rail centers. The Owensboro shippers received some relief in these decisions, which served as precedents in a growing body of case decisions that helped build the power of the Interstate Commerce Commission as a regulatory agency, especially after the Mann-Elkins Act of 1910. They also illustrate some of the problems faced by companies seeking to do business in smaller cities and towns in Kentucky in the early years of the twentieth century.

See Lee A. Dew, "The Owensboro Cattle Cases: A Study in Commerce Regulation," *FCHQ* 49 (April 1975): 195-203. LEE A. DEW

OWENSBORO WAGON COMPANY. The Owensboro Wagon Company, founded in 1884, became one of the largest wagon manufacturers in the nation, with nearly eighty styles or sizes of wagons available by 1900. It had a peak capacity of 10,000 wagons per year; in 1899 it bought the Blunt Wagon Company of Evansville, Indiana. The Owensboro wagon was the standard of quality throughout much of the South and West, and many wagons were exported to Cuba and elsewhere. During World War II the company made "coolie carts" for shipment to China. It was a leader in the mechanization of woodworking equipment, operated its own electric plant, fired its boilers with its own waste materials, and installed one of the first timeclocks in Kentucky. The company closed in 1957.

See Lee A. Dew and Aloma W. Dew, *Owensboro: The City on the Yellow Banks* (Bowling Green, Ky., 1988). LEE A. DEW

OWENTON. The county seat of Owen County, Owenton is located on U.S. 127 and KY 22. Established on a fifty-acre tract surveyed in 1822, the town was named for Col. Abraham Owen, pioneer, legislator, and soldier, killed at the Battle of Tippecanoe. When Owen County was created in 1819, county officials first met in the home of Jacob Hesler, in the town of Hesler, five miles southeast of Owenton. Owenton became the seat of government in 1822, and was incorporated on December 18, 1828. The first county courthouse, a log structure, was completed in 1823. A second edifice, in the Greek Revival style, was built in 1857-58. In 1868 one-story wings were added to the building, and in 1977 the Owen County courthouse was listed on the National Register of Historic Places.

During the Civil War, Union soldiers were encamped at nearby Lusby's Mill and the Vanlandingham farm, but Owenton was spared destruction. In the late nineteenth century, Owenton was a small but thriving community. Owenton served as a trading center for the county's tobacco farmers despite the lack of rail service; the Short Line Railroad, part of the Louisville & Nashville system running from Louisville along the Carroll-Owen County line to Covington, was the closest road.

Owenton is now an agricultural community with a small industrial base, including a sandal factory and meter device factory. The population of the fifth-class city was 1,280 in 1970; 1,341 in 1980; and 1,306 in 1990. RON D. BRYANT

OWINGSVILLE. Owingsville, the seat of Bath County, is located roughly in the center of the county, about fourteen miles east of Mt. Sterling and twenty-one miles west of Morehead at the junction of U.S. 60 and KY 36.

The town was laid out on land donated by two local men: Richard Menefee, who served in the state legislature and the U.S. Senate; and Col. Thomas Dye Owings, owner of a nearby iron foundry. Both men wanted the honor of naming the town, so a contest was devised to see who could build the finest home in the shortest time. Owings was the victor, hence the town's name. Owingsville was incorporated in 1829 and was the birthplace of

John Bell Hood, a Confederate Civil War general; two governors of Indiana, Henry S. Lane, who also served as a U.S. Senator, and Claude Matthews; and a governor of Tennessee, Alvin Hawkins. Bath County's first courthouse was completed in Owingsville in 1813 and was replaced in 1831. Union troops used this building as barracks during the Civil War. When Confederate troops drove them from the area, an overlooked stove started a fire that destroyed the building. The federal government compensated Bath County for the accident and the present courthouse was completed in 1868.

Owingsville's industrial mainstay has been a men's shoe factory, with retail trade and service establishments providing the bulk of local employment. The population of the fourth-class city was 1,381 in 1970; 1,419 in 1980; and 1,491 in 1990.

OWSLEY, WILLIAM. William Owsley, governor during 1844-48, was the son of William and Catherine (Bolin) Owsley, born in Virginia on March 24, 1782. The following year the family moved to Lincoln County, Kentucky, near Crab Orchard. William was educated in the common schools and was a teacher, a deputy surveyor, and a deputy sheriff before studying law. In 1803 he married Elizabeth Gill, one of his pupils; they had six children.

Owsley was elected to the Kentucky House in 1809. Though appointed to the state's court of appeals in 1810, he lost his seat when the court's membership was reduced. Elected to the House once more in 1811, he accepted another appointment to the court of appeals in 1813 and remained there until 1828. Owsley resigned from the OLD COURT to resume his legal practice; he was elected to the Kentucky House in 1831 and to the state Senate in 1832. He was Gov. James T. Morehead's secretary of state during 1834-36, and in 1844 he was nominated by the Whigs to oppose the Democratic candidate, Gen. William O. Butler, a hero of the War of 1812, in the campaign for governor. Owsley won the close race, 59,680 to 55,056. When he left office in 1848, he retired to private life in Boyle County.

Owsley was a fiscal conservative who was able to reduce the state's debt slightly. On the other hand, he urged the legislature to fund public education: "Nothing but money will do it, and it is left to the appropriate department—the legislature—to determine on the expediency or inexpediency of raising it." The legislature did little, but Owsley's superintendent of public instruction, Robert J. Breckinridge, made notable progress during his time in office (1847-53). By contrast, Owsley was reluctant to spend money on rebuilding the state penitentiary, which had been severely damaged by fire. Though he deplored the Mexican War, Owsley responded promptly to the call for volunteers, and he reported proudly that 13,700 Kentuckians had volunteered for 2,400 requested enlistments. The governor attracted criticism when he pardoned Delia A. Webster, convicted of abetting the escape of slaves. He engaged in a bitter controversy with Ben Hardin, his secretary of state, who was denied the patronage that he believed was promised him. Owsley removed Hardin in 1846, but the Senate voted that no vacancy existed, and the court of appeals ruled in Hardin's favor. Thus vindicated, Hardin resigned, but his charges of nepotism damaged the governor's reputation. Such dissatisfaction with Owsley's administration may have increased the demands for constitutional revision. Owsley defended his actions, but he told the General Assembly that the end of his term "excites in my breast no emotions of regret." Owsley died on December 9, 1862, and was buried in the Belleview Cemetery in Danville. When a new county was created in 1843 from parts of Clay, Estill, and Breathitt counties, it was named in his honor.

See Lucius P. Litte, *Ben Hardin: His Times and Contemporaries* (Louisville 1887); Jennie Chinn Morton, "William Owsley," *Register* 3 (Jan. 1905): 25-29.

OWSLEY COUNTY. Owsley County, the ninety-sixth county in order of formation, is located in eastern Kentucky on the Cumberland Plateau. Bordered by Breathitt, Clay, Jackson, Lee, and Perry counties, Owsley has an area of 198 square miles. It was created from parts of Breathitt, Clay, and Estill counties in 1843 and was named for Gov. William Owsley (1844-48). The county seat is BOONEVILLE. The South Fork of the Kentucky River roughly bisects the county, flowing south to north. Despite the rugged terrain, much of the county's acreage is farmland.

A large boulder near the mouth of Sexton Creek in the southern part of the county is known locally as Boone's Rock because it was noted as a landmark by Daniel Boone on a 1784 survey of land for James Moore and Col. John Donelson. Early permanent settlers of the area included James Moore and his family, who established Moore's Station, also known as Boone's Station, at Boone's old campsite. John Renty Baker and John Abner arrived by boat in the 1790s and settled near Cortland in the southeastern part of the county. The population of the area grew steadily. Parts of Owsley County went to form Jackson County in 1858 and Wolfe County in 1860.

During the Civil War, most Owsley Countians were pro-Union, although there were 112 slaves in the county in 1860. Owsley County led all Kentucky counties in the percentage of 1860 voters who enrolled in the Union army: slightly over 13 percent. Many men from the county enlisted in Company A of the 7th Kentucky Infantry Regiment, which was organized by Elisha B. Treadway at Congleton Springs (now in Lee County). Several times during the conflict, armies passed through the county, among them the Union command of Gen. George W. Morgan as it retreated from the Cumberland Gap to Greenup, Kentucky, in the late summer of 1862. Bands of lawless men rode into the county and in reprisal Owsley County men led

similar raids into Wolfe and Breathitt counties. After the war, the county became identified with Republican politics, and because the Democratic party controlled state government during Readjustment, Owsley County reaped few benefits. Part of the county was split off in 1870 to form Lee County.

As it had scant mineral reserves, the county did not attract significant railroad transportation. A narrow-gauge line, the K&P Lumber Company Railroad, was built from Tallega in Lee County to a lumber mill at Lerose in the northeastern part of Owsley County in 1905. By 1909 most of the large timber near the line had been hauled out and the line was abandoned. The iron rails were taken up for scrap in World War I. A standard-gauge line, the Kentucky, Rockcastle, & Cumberland Railroad, which crossed the northwestern corner of the county along Wild Dog Creek, was abandoned by 1930.

By 1930 most of the timber had been removed and with it the economic lifeblood of the county. Mills closed, and after 1940 migration started to depopulate the county. Unrestricted clearing of steep slopes led to erosion of farmland. Extensive federal and state aid helped to maintain the standard of living in the county. Often unemployed county youth joined the military, and the rural county furnished large numbers of men to the Korean and Vietnam wars.

By 1989 Owsley County had the lowest per capita income in the state; 53 percent of the population were below the poverty line. In 1989 most employed residents worked in service occupations, government positions, or agriculture. The population of the rural mountain county was 5,023 in 1970; 5,709 in 1980; and 5,036 in 1990.

See Joyce Wilson, *This Was Yesterday* (Ashland, Ky., 1977). MORRIS M. GARRETT

OXMOOR. The Oxmoor farm, owned by the Bullitt family of Louisville, was built by Alexander Scott Bullitt shortly after he settled in Louisville in 1785. He purchased the original thousand acres of land (which sprawled along Beargrass Creek near the juncture of Shelbyville Road, Taylorsville Road, and the Watterson Expressway) to be near the farm of William Christian, whose daughter Bullitt was to marry in the fall of 1785. Bullitt built a small log cabin in which to live until the main farmhouse was completed, in 1787. His land was the site of one of the final battles between settlers and Indians in Louisville, when a band of marauding Indians attacked Christian's farm, killing Bullitt's father-in-law.

Bullitt named his farm Oxmoor for the Oxmoor of Laurence Sterne's novel *Tristram Shandy*. He made it one of the finest farms in Kentucky, with housing for 120 slaves. When Bullitt died, he left the land to his son, William C. Bullitt, who gave two hundred acres to his brother Cuthbert. That gift became known as Winchester Place. William C. Bullitt eventually bought a tract of land called Evinger field to restore the farm to its original size.

The Bullitts lived at Oxmoor year-round until 1863, when they closed the residence because of the Civil War. When the war ended, tenant farmers worked the land, and the main house was used for storage. In 1909 William Marshall Bullitt restored and refurnished the house so that his father, Thomas Bullitt, could live his final years at Oxmoor, where he grew up. Ownership of the house passed to William Bullitt's son Thomas W., who is now the fifth-generation Bullitt to reside there.

During the twentieth century, the Oxmoor farm and the surrounding land have been part of the east- ward development of Louisville. In 1968 plans were drawn up for the Oxmoor Woods real estate development, and in 1971 the Oxmoor Shopping Center was built on what was once the finest farm in the state. The Oxmoor Steeplechase is held annually to benefit charity on a steeplechase course built in 1945. The Bullitts have retained ownership of the land beneath all of the developments, thereby retaining a say in its future.

See Ella Hutchison Ellwanger, "Oxmoor—Its Builder and Its Historian," *Register* 17 (Jan. 1919): 9-21.

P

PACE, PEARL (CARTER). Pearl (Carter) Pace, first female county sheriff in Kentucky, was born in Tompkinsville, Kentucky, on January 25, 1896, to James Clark and Idru Illinois (Tucker) Carter. Her father was a Republican Kentucky circuit court judge. She grew up in Cumberland County and attended Western Kentucky University in Bowling Green. Beginning in 1917, she taught for three years in secondary schools in Monroe and Cumberland counties. On December 24, 1917, she married Stanley Dan Pace, a Democrat, who later became sheriff of Cumberland County. When his term ended in 1937, she was elected as the Republican candidate to succeed him, since the incumbent sheriff was prohibited by state law from succeeding himself. Pace was sheriff until 1941, and was active in politics throughout her life, serving as district chairman on the Republican executive committee and later as the Republican National Committeewoman for Kentucky (1948-53). She retired from public life in 1962.

Pace and her husband had three children: Patty Nell, Stanley Carter, and Mary Elizabeth. She died on January 14, 1970 and was buried in the Allen-Pace Cemetery in Cumberland County.

See J.W. Wells, *History of Cumberland County* (Louisville 1947).

PADUCAH. Paducah, the county seat of McCracken County and the largest city in the Jackson Purchase region, is located on the Ohio River at U.S. 60 and U.S. 45. The city may have been named for a legendary Chickasaw leader, Chief Paduke. The site was selected by George Rogers Clark during the Revolutionary War. His brother William, of Lewis and Clark fame, established the settlement and selected the name. The location was also claimed by another family and the dispute eventually went to the Kentucky Supreme Court in *Porterfield v. Clark*, in 1844.

Paducah was the last town to develop in Kentucky west of the Tennessee River, yet it quickly became the largest community. Its location at the junction of the Ohio and Tennessee rivers made trade and commerce prosper. As a break-in-bulk point on the inland waterway, Paducah became a center of wholesale trade for southern Illinois and western Kentucky. In 1831, when the original seat of McCracken County, Wilmington, proved unsuitable, Paducah was chosen, even though Paducah was not centrally located but was on the northern edge of the county.

A board of trustees controlled Paducah as a village. Beginning in 1856, the third-class city had a mayor and a board of councilmen. After a special census in 1901 confirmed the requisite 20,000 residents, the second-class city elected a mayor, four aldermen-at-large, and one from each of the six wards. In 1990 the city had a mayor, city manager, and commissioner form of government.

Before the Civil War, the river and timber industries were vital to Paducah. James Langstaff established a sawmill and brickyard in 1847 to help build a federal marine hospital in Paducah. A marine way established in 1843, of eight rail sections 350 feet in length, was capable of handling the largest barges and boats. Craft could be retrieved by means of a cradle on the tracks. In 1990 drydocks continued this pioneer industry.

In 1853 Lloyd Tilghman, a graduate of West Point and an experienced civil engineer, supervised construction of the New Orleans & Ohio Railroad, which reached Troy, Tennessee, in 1860. After the Civil War, Paducah became the midpoint in a system linking Louisville and Memphis. Other lines connected Paducah to Nashville and to points north. A railroad bridge over the Ohio opened in 1917 and the next year was used by the Illinois Central. In 1927 the Illinois Central built one of the largest locomotive repair and maintenance shops of that time in Paducah. In 1942-43 large steam locomotives of the 2600 class known as "mountain" types were manufactured in Paducah. In 1990 VMV Enterprises operated the shops, and the Paducah & Louisville Railroad operated the former Illinois Central tracks in the city.

Being a commercial center, Paducah was more cosmopolitan than the rest of the county or the surrounding region. German immigrants arriving in Paducah in the 1840s soon acquired leadership positions, including the third mayor of the city, John G. Fisher, and Meyer Weil, a German Jew, who served as mayor during the economic depression of 1873 and helped the city through financial crisis. Only a few Germans settled outside the town, among them the group that founded St. Johns, a Roman Catholic church that celebrated its 150th year in 1989. An active Jewish population immigrated at about the same time. Among them was Isaac BERNHEIM, who resided in Paducah before moving to Louisville and founding the distillery bearing his name. Temple Israel is one of the oldest Reform congregations in the United States. The diverse population in Paducah voted Whig, Know-Nothing, and Republican, whereas the county and the Purchase region were staunchly Democratic.

When the Confederates on September 3, 1861, occupied Columbus, Kentucky, Gen. Ulysses S. Grant moved from Cairo and occupied Paducah to protect the northern terminus of the NO&O railroad. The residents often viewed the Federal troops as oppressors rather than defenders. Nathan Bedford Forrest and his Confederate cavalry raided Paducah twice in 1864 and the population gave him active support. Union Gen. Eleazor A. Paine set out to punish those sympathetic to the Confederate-cause, in what many called a reign of terror. Investigation indicated corruption and Paine was court-martialed but exonerated.

Paducah was flooded in 1884, 1913, and 1937, when thousands of refugees fled the city, and many went as far as Nashville to find shelter. A flood wall was completed in 1946. Dams on the Cumberland, Tennessee, and Ohio helped alleviate the threat of floods.

Paducah is a pioneer in two-year college education. In 1909 D.H. Anderson opened WEST KENTUCKY INDUSTRIAL COLLEGE to train blacks. In 1938 the college-level courses were moved to Kentucky State College in Frankfort, leaving a postsecondary vocational school in Paducah that moved to the present campus in 1979. In 1932 Paducah Junior College came into being; it was converted into a public institution in 1936 and in 1968 merged into the University of Kentucky system of community colleges. Paducah Community College is a pioneer in the use of cable television to serve community needs.

The construction of the U.S. Atomic Energy Commission's gaseous diffusion plant, the Tennessee Valley Authority's Shawnee steam plant, and the power plant of Electric Energy Inc. at Joppa, Illinois, caused an influx of more than 20,000 people into the Paducah area in 1951. Retailing started shifting from the downtown area to malls in the 1960s, and the growth of suburbs such as Lone Oak south of the city along I-24 caused Paducah's population to decline.

Annual events include the Dogwood Festival, the Paducah Summer Festival, and the National Quilt Show.

Paducah's most well-known citizens include Alben Barkley, vice-president under President Harry Truman; Irvin S. Cobb, a noted correspondent, writer, humorist, and actor; Linn Boyd, twice Speaker of the U.S. House of Representatives; and Gov. Julian Carroll (1974-79). The population of the second-class city was 31,627 in 1970; 29,315 in 1980; and 27,256 in 1990.

See John E.L. Robertson, *Paducah, 1830-1980: A Sesquicentennial History* (Paducah, Ky., 1980).

JOHN E.L. ROBERTSON

PADUCAH, BATTLE OF. In the spring of 1864 Confederate Gen. Nathan B. Forrest headed north from western Tennessee into Kentucky on a raid. His intent was to disrupt Union supply lines running through Kentucky and to secure supplies and mounts, as well as to discourage enlistment of blacks in the Union army. The Confederates attacked Paducah on March 25. Gen. Abraham Buford's Kentuckians led 1,800 Confederate troops, which drove Union pickets from Eden's Hill into Paducah, dismounted in the town, and moved against Fort Anderson on the Ohio. Union Col. Stephen Hicks commanded this post, with the 122d Illinois Infantry, 16th Kentucky Cavalry, 1st Kentucky Artillery, and 8th U.S. Heavy Artillery (Colored) supported by the gunboats *Peosta* and *PawPaw* on the Ohio River. Hicks refused the demand for unconditional surrender.

Col. Albert P. Thompson of Paducah led an assault on the fort, only to be driven back. Thompson was killed near his own home by a cannonball. Some of the attackers withdrew into buildings nearby and kept up a galling fire on the fort, while others destroyed Union headquarters, quartermaster and commissary buildings, and military stores and rounded up two hundred horses and mules. Ten hours after the raid started, Forrest withdrew to Mayfield for the night. Union losses were fourteen killed, forty-six wounded, and forty captured. Confederate losses were estimated at some three hundred. Sixty homes in Paducah were destroyed, warehouses and the railroad depot were demolished, and the steamboat *Dacotah* burned.

After the attack, Forrest gave the Kentuckians in his command furlough; all returned on time, with new mounts and clothing. Buford was sent north to direct attention away from Fort Pillow, Tennessee, Forrest's next objective. Forrest took Fort Pillow and was accused of giving no quarter to the blacks in the garrison. Had the Paducah garrison surrendered, the 8th U.S. Heavy Artillery (Colored) might have suffered a similar fate.

See John E.L. Robertson, *Paducah 1830-1980: A Sesquicentennial History* (Paducah, Ky., 1980).

JOHN E.L. ROBERTSON

PADUCAH JUNIOR COLLEGE. Paducah Junior College began as a private school on September 12, 1932, in the Young Men's Christian Association building at 707 Broadway in Paducah, McCracken County, with sixty-eight students and seven instructors. In 1936 it became a public institution when the city agreed to impose a tax to support it, and the tax base was expanded in 1963 to include the entire county. It received accreditation from the Southern Association of Colleges and Secondary Schools in 1954. When Paducah Junior College joined the University of Kentucky's COMMUNITY COLLEGE SYSTEM in 1968, the college was financially solvent, occupied a new campus, and had been reaccredited by the Southern Association.

U.R. Bell was the first president of Paducah Junior College. R.G. Matheson, who served as dean from 1936 until the merger in 1968, was responsible for many innovations at the college, including flexible class scheduling and coeducational intercollegiate athletics. With a strong program in sports, particularly basketball and baseball, the college has won many state championships and has participated in national tournaments, winning the national junior basketball tournament in 1969. Graduates of the college include Kentucky Gov. Julian Carroll (1974-79) and Warren Rosenthal, chief executive officer of JERRICO INC. Alice H. ("Dolly") McNutt, a member of the first graduating class, served as mayor of Paducah (1971-76) before taking a seat in the Kentucky General Assembly.

See John E.L. Robertson, *Paducah 1830-1980: A Sesquicentennial History* (Paducah, Ky., 1980).

JOHN E.L. ROBERTSON

PADUCAH SUN. The *Paducah Sun*, far-western Kentucky's largest newspaper, was founded in 1896 as the *Paducah Evening Sun*. Started by Frank M. Fisher, W.F. Paxton, and others, the *Evening Sun* was a Republican paper. In 1900 Paxton's son, Edwin, became editor and publisher. In 1929, he bought the *Paducah News-Democrat* from George H. Goodman and merged it with the *Sun*, producing the *Sun-Democrat*, which became widely read in the region. Paxton died in 1961, and was succeeded as editor by his son, Edwin, Jr., who had been a Nieman Fellow at Harvard University. When he retired in 1977, his son Jack, a veteran NBC-TV network correspondent, was named editor. Upon Jack Paxton's death in a 1985 airplane crash, he was succeeded by Jim Paxton, his cousin.

In 1978 the newspaper's name was once more changed, this time to the *Paducah Sun*. It was a Monday-through-Friday afternoon paper, with a Sunday morning edition, until March 1990, when it switched to seven days and became a morning paper. Monday-Saturday daily circulation in 1990 was about 32,000; Sunday circulation was about 35,000. Generally, the *Sun* has not endorsed political candidates or parties, but editorially it is conservative. The paper's parent company, Paducah Newspapers Inc., also owns WPSD-TV, the local NBC affiliate.

See Herndon J. Evans, *The Newspaper Press in Kentucky* (Lexington, Ky., 1974); John E.L. Robertson, *Paducah 1830-1980: A Sesquicentennial History* (Paducah, Ky., 1980).   BERRY CRAIG

PAGE, THOMAS SCUDDER. Thomas Scudder Page, Kentucky's first elected auditor of public accounts (1851-59) and the first elected state executive officer tried for corruption, was born in New York City on April 19, 1800. Page came to Frankfort, Kentucky, via Richmond, Virginia, in 1817. He obtained a position as clerk in the Land Office and in 1839 was appointed auditor of the state by Gov. James Clark (1836-39). By 1852 he had worked alternately in state government and in private enterprise, married into two prominent families, and developed influential friends and substantial investments.

After the position of auditor became an elected office under the third state constitution, Page was elected to two terms as state auditor, in 1851 and 1855, on the Whig and Know-Nothing tickets, respectively. During these terms he embezzled $88,927 by directing local officials to deposit their revenue collections with him rather than with the state treasurer as required by law. When Page's defalcation was discovered, the state began proceedings to sue for embezzlement (not a criminal offense at that time), and Page filed for bankruptcy in 1863. The case was settled in 1867 by a special act of the legislature that ordered Page to pay half the judgment ($88,000), interest, and court costs.

Page was married in March 1820 to Sophia Woolfolk, who died ca. 1828; they had one daughter. He married Jane Julian in 1828; they had eleven children. Page and his second wife lived their later years in destitution in Frankfort. He died on April 17, 1877, and was buried in the Frankfort Cemetery.   GLEN EDWARD TAUL

PAINE'S PUBLIC GOOD. Thomas Paine's forty-one-page pamphlet *Public Good* (1780) challenged Virginia's authority over the western country, in an extension of the argument he used against the Crown in *Common Sense*. Paine wrote *Public Good* in response to protests raised by the smaller states during ratification of the Articles of Confederation. He argued that the British government originally applied the name Virginia to all of North America and not to a specific colony. Later the Colony of Virginia was founded with prescribed boundaries on all but its western end, which was left open to expansion. The Proclamation of 1763 fixed the western boundary at the watershed of the Appalachian Mountains. Paine further contended that it was the stated intention of the Crown to organize a new colony "in back of Virginia" when a sufficient number of settlers had moved into the region, and further, that once the Confederation was organized in 1781, the central government would have the power to create a new state. He noted that the western country was well beyond Virginia's capacity to manage. Moreover, "she cannot," he said, "make a good title to the purchasers, and consequently can get but little for the lands."

Just as *Common Sense* had supplied an argument for American independence from Great Britain, *Public Good* supplied Kentuckians with material to argue for the creation of a new state. Paine's comment on the validity of land titles, however, became the source of disturbing rumors that Virginia deeds were invalid, angering claimants to large landholdings under Virginia cessions.

In one such incident, two Pennsylvanians, George Pomeroy and a man named Galloway, arrived in Kentucky in 1784 as disciples of Paine. So persuasive were these men that they set people to clearing and settling on the lands of their neighbors, with the contention that only the Continental Congress could grant legal titles to western lands.

On May 7, 1784, in Louisville, George Pomeroy was brought before a magistrate on a charge of spreading false rumors, or as "propagator of civil, and political, heresy." Search of the Virginia statutes revealed an ancient law that imposed a fine in tobacco at the discretion of the court "upon the propagators of false news, to the disturbance of the good people of the colony." Pomeroy was fined 2,000 pounds of tobacco and made to give security in the amount of 3,000 pounds to assure his good behavior. He was also assessed court costs. In Lexington Galloway was brought to trial under the same statute, charged with having created "a great hubbub." He was fined 1,000 pounds of tobacco, and threatened with having to spend time in the public stock, but was let off on the promise that he would leave the state.   THOMAS D. CLARK

PAINTSVILLE. Paintsville, the seat of Johnson County, is located at the confluence of Paint Creek and the Levisa Fork of the Big Sandy River at the junction of KY 40 and U.S. 23/460. The names of the town and of Paint Creek derived from the Indian drawings that settlers found on tree trunks along the banks of the creek. In 1789 a party from southwestern Virginia led by Mathias Harman pursued the Indian captors of Jenny Wiley into present-day Johnson County, where severe weather halted their expedition. Early in the nineteenth century, the Rev. Henry Dickson (or Dixon) of North Carolina gained possession of the land at the mouth of Paint Creek and named the growing settlement Paintsville. Paintsville was established as a town by an act of the Kentucky General Assembly in 1834. When Johnson County was created, Paintsville was chosen as the county seat (1843).

Paintsville was occupied by Confederate troops several times during the Civil War. In December 1861 Gen. Humphrey Marshall led a large force into the area. Col. James A. Garfield's Union army soon outmaneuvered Marshall on January 5-7, 1862, and forced the Confederates to retreat southward. Marshall's troops returned for a short time in September 1862. In April 1864 a Confederate cavalry unit made a raid on Union troops camped at Paintsville, but it was easily repulsed. Paintsville suffered little physical damage from the war and the town's population increased from 200 to 270 during the 1860s.

Paintsville's real period of growth began in the early twentieth century, when the town became the center of a vast coal-mining region. Paintsville resident John C.C. MAYO amassed a fortune by accumulating mineral rights to valuable coal lands throughout eastern Kentucky and attracting national mining companies to the area. In the late 1930s, oilman E.J. Evans began a movement to create "a practical college" in Paintsville. His efforts were rewarded in 1938 when the legislature approved $56,000 for the creation of Mayo State Vocational School for secondary and adult education. On April 24, 1964, President Lyndon Johnson visited Paintsville as part of his publicity tour of Appalachia in his War on Poverty. In June 1969 American Standard opened a plant five miles south of Paintsville. Its several hundred employees produce faucets, showerheads, and drains.

In October 1962 Paintsville hosted the first Kentucky Apple Festival to celebrate the county's apple production. The festival grew into a five-day fair that included a number of beauty pageants, a parade, dances, and craft displays. Paintsville's population was 3,868 in 1970; 3,815 in 1980; and 4,354 in 1990.   THOMAS D. MATIJASIC

PALISADES. Following regional uplifts during the late Tertiary and Quaternary periods (less than 5 million years ago), the meandering Kentucky River entrenched its course below the Lexington Plain. The river cut downward into resistant limestone and dolomite of the High Bridge Group, forming palisades, the picturesque rock cliffs along most of the river's course between Boonesborough and Frankfort. The Middle Ordovician-age High Bridge limestone and dolomite (about 460 million years old) in the Kentucky River gorge are the oldest rocks exposed at the surface in the state.

See Arthur C. McFarlan, *Geology of Kentucky* (Lexington, Ky., 1943); William D. Thornbury, *Regional Geomorphology of the United States* (New York 1965).   GARLAND R. DEVER, JR.

PALMER, JOHN McCAULEY. John McCauley Palmer, lawyer and politician, was born near Eagle Creek in Scott County, Kentucky, on September 13, 1817, to Louis D. and Ann Hansford (Tutt) Palmer. In 1819 the family moved to Christian County near Hopkinsville. In April 1831 Palmer's father, an antislavery Democrat, moved the family to Alton, Illinois, where Palmer attended Shurtleff College, studied law, and was admitted to the bar in December 1839. He became a state senator in 1851 and helped form the Republican party in Illinois. In 1859 Palmer was defeated in his bid for a seat in Congress.

In May 1861 Palmer entered the Federal army as colonel of the 14th Illinois Infantry. He was made brigadier general on December 20, 1861, and given command of the 1st Division of the Army of the Mississippi. As major general after March 16, 1863, he was involved in the campaigns of Island No. 10, Murfreesboro, Chattanooga, and Atlanta. In February 1865, he was given command of the Department of Kentucky. Although he was initially popular among Kentucky residents, his later decisions encouraging black emancipation caused severe tensions. Palmer resigned from the army on April 1, 1866. An indictment was brought against him on November 20, 1866, by the Louisville grand jury, for aiding in the escape of slaves, a violation of the state's slave code. The indictment was later voided.

Palmer was elected governor of Illinois on the Republican ticket in 1868, defeating John R. Eden. In 1872 he joined the Liberal Republicans and then the Democratic party. Palmer was defeated as the Democratic candidate for governor in 1888, but in 1891 he won a Senate seat on the Democratic ticket, serving from March 4, 1891, to March 3, 1897. He was a presidential candidate of the Gold Democrats with Simon B. Buckner as his running mate in 1896. After his defeat, he returned to his law practice and began writing. He edited the two-volume work *The Bench and Bar of Illinois* (1899) and wrote his memoirs in *Personal Recollection of John M. Palmer: The Story of an Earnest Life* (1901).

Palmer married Malinda Ann Neely of Carlinville on December 20, 1842; they had ten children. In 1888 he married Hannah (Lamb) Kimball. He died in Springfield, Illinois, on September 25,

1900, and is buried at Carlinville with his first wife and four of their children.

See George Thomas Palmer, *A Conscientious Turncoat: The Story of John M. Palmer 1817-1900* (New Haven, Conn., 1941); Lowell H. Harrison, "Kentucky-Born Generals in the Civil War," *Register* 64 (April 1966): 129-60.

PANIC OF 1819. The panic of 1819 was the culmination of general economic depression that had begun for manufacturing and commerce as early as 1816, when reopening of foreign trade after the War of 1812 restored foreign competition, amidst declining demand for war materials. For two years beyond the setback for manufacturing, agriculture was highly profitable, because of crop failures in Europe. Farmers of the middle states and the Ohio Valley, in particular, profited from provisioning West Indies plantations. By 1818, however, resumption of European trade restrictions and enactment of countervailing legislation by the United States began to curtail foreign commerce. Crop prices fell abruptly.

The contraction in economic activity revealed weaknesses in American banking. In 1816 a second Bank of the United States had been chartered, with provision for branches throughout the nation and the expectation that through their acceptances they could command accountability in local issues. As depositories for public funds, the bank and its branch offices were required to redeem their notes in specie on demand. Politically, however, the institutions were under strong pressure for leniency in accepting remittances in notes of local banks, which in the back country generally were insolvent. Widespread corruption in the capital development and management of the branch banks further weakened the system. As the flow of foreign trade became unfavorable and heavy payments fell due on government debt abroad, the parent bank in July 1818 called on its branches to curtail their discounts and the following month discontinued its policy of interchangeability of notes among the offices. Since the balance of payments tilted heavily eastward from public land revenues and mercantile exchange, the pressure to accumulate specie reserves was especially severe on the banks of the West and South.

In the ensuing liquidation, many business houses failed, unemployment rose in cities, and property values declined precipitately. Demand for legislative action developed in both the U.S. Congress and the state legislatures. In many states, notably those of the West and South, laws were enacted authorizing stays in debt collection, reduction in contracts through reassessment of mortgaged property, taxation of the national bank, and state funding of local banks empowered to issue additional paper currency. Kentucky adopted all these measures. The resulting political upheaval is known as the OLD COURT-NEW COURT controversy. The economic effects of the panic of 1819 were not ameliorated until the mid-1820s.

See Murray N. Rothbard, *The Panic of 1819: Reactions and Policies* (New York 1962); Samuel Rezneck, "The Depression of 1819-1822, A Social History," *American Historical Review* 39 (Oct. 1933): 28-47.   MARY W.M. HARGREAVES

PARAMOUNT ARTS CENTER. The Paramount Arts Center in Ashland, Kentucky, housed in what was formerly the Paramount movie theater, was established as a nonprofit performing and visual arts center in 1972. The theater presents an annual concert series and performing arts series for schools, and an annual family concert series. The arts center houses an art gallery and gift shop. The purchase of the movie house and the establishment of the arts center were the first project of the Greater Ashland Area Cultural and Economic Development Foundation (now the Foundation for the Tri-State Community). The arts center became an independent nonprofit organization on July 1, 1990. The Paramount theater, which opened on September 5, 1931, was based on a design from Paramount Publix Corporation, the construction division of Hollywood's Paramount Studios, and was one of the first movie theaters in the Ohio Valley constructed for "talkies." The first film shown at the art deco movie palace was the Paramount picture *Silence*, starring Clive Brook and Marjorie Rambeau. The building was designated a Kentucky landmark and placed on the National Register of Historic Places in 1975.   TAMI A. JONES

PARILLI, VITO. Vito ("Sweet Kentucky Babe") Parilli, football player, was born May 7, 1929, in Rochester, Pennsylvania, to August Parilli and his wife. A single-wing fullback in high school, he was converted to a T-formation quarterback by University of Kentucky football coach Paul Bryant. In three seasons (1949-51), Parilli led Kentucky to a 28-8 record and to victories in the 1951 Sugar Bowl and 1952 Cotton Bowl. He set numerous school records, including most career touchdown passes (fifty). Parilli was the most valuable college player in the 1952 Chicago College-Professional All-Star Game and a first-round draft pick of Green Bay. He played with five professional American teams—Green Bay and Cleveland of the National Football League (NFL); Boston, Oakland, and New York of the American Football League; and the Ottawa Rough Riders of the Canadian Football League. In his final season (1969-70), he was Joe Namath's backup in Super Bowl III, when the New York Jets upset the Baltimore Colts. He has coached at both the college and professional levels: at Virginia Polytechnic Institute and Texas A&M, and for the Chicago Winds of the World Football League and the Pittsburgh Steelers, NFL.

See Russell Rice, *The Wildcats: A Story of Kentucky Football* (Huntsville, Ala., 1975).
                                          JAMES C. CLAYPOOL

PARIS. Paris, the seat of Bourbon County, is located in the center of the county approximately fifteen miles northeast of Lexington. Pioneers lived in the area as early as 1776. In 1786 Lawrence Protzman bought land near the present site of Paris and offered 250 acres of it for the establishment of the county seat. In 1789 the Virginia legislature officially established the town, naming it Hopewell after Protzman's New Jersey hometown. A year later the town was renamed Paris, to correspond with the naming of the county after the French royal house. The post office was established in 1795 and was referred to as Bourbontown; contrary to a widely held belief, however, there is no evidence that the town itself ever went by that name. The first courthouse was completed in 1787; fire destroyed the second and third courthouses in 1872 and 1901, respectively. Paris's fourth and present courthouse was constructed during the period 1902-5 and was listed on the National Register of Historic Places in 1974.

The Bourbon Academy was established in Paris in 1798 by the Kentucky legislature on 6,000 acres of land and opened for classes in 1800. Lyle's Female Academy opened in 1806. William H. McGuffey, the author of the famous *McGuffey Reader*, taught in Paris from 1823 to 1826, between his periods of attendance at Washington College.

Paris was an agricultural center boasting market houses, warehouses, taverns, and hotels as well as mills, carding factories, distilleries, stockyards, and groceries. The Lexington & Covington Railroad was completed as far as Paris in 1853. This railroad, which later became the Kentucky Central, helped make Paris the urban and commercial center of Bourbon County. Paris boomed during Reconstruction as freedmen and railroad workers tripled the population to 5,000 by 1875.

At the close of the century, Paris converted from gas to electric lights and enjoyed telephones, streetcars, city sewers, a fire fighting company, and public mail service. New public schools and a Paris High Alumni Association (1892) supported the expanding community consciousness. The Commercial Club (1908) underlined Paris's economic development in the early 1900s. Many new city services were established, including a sewer system, a water company, a lighting plant, hospitals, a YMCA Center, and a power plant. Parisians built magnificent churches and converted hundreds in well-known religious revivals.

Today Paris is a major tobacco market and the site of industrial interests as well. John Fox, Jr., is buried in the Paris Cemetery. Paris is also the location of the DUNCAN TAVERN, built by Maj. Joseph Duncan in 1788.

The population of Paris was 7,823 in 1970; 7,935 in 1980; and 8,730 in 1990.

See G.R. Keller and J.M. McCann, *Sketches of Paris* (Paris, Ky., 1876).   H.E. EVERMAN

PARK HILLS. Park Hills, a suburban city in the hills of northern Kenton County along U.S. 25, is situated west of COVINGTON, north of I-75, east of Fort Wright, and south of Devou Park, from which the name of the city is derived. With the exception of a few homes and businesses along the Covington-Lexington Pike (now U.S. 25), the Park Hills area was sparsely populated in the nineteenth century because it was too hilly for farming and too inaccessible for housing. A landmark on the pike was the Stonewall House, a restaurant-tavern that dated to the mid-1800s as a stopover point for stock drovers on the way to market at Covington or Cincinnati. During the 1930s it was remodeled and named the Hotel Hahn. The Hahn and the White Horse Restaurant were popular night spots on the "Gourmet Strip," a group of restaurants and taverns on the Dixie Highway (U.S. 25). The Hotel Hahn has since been torn down and the White Horse was destroyed by fire on January 26, 1972.

Development of Park Hills into a residential suburb began in the 1920s, decades after other northern Kentucky cities such as ERLANGER, Elsmere, and Crescent Springs were taking shape. Investors D. Collins Lee and Robert Simmons developed the land, and enough residents had moved there by 1927 to enable Park Hills to incorporate as a city. Three of the city's best-known landmarks are Roman Catholic institutions: St. Joseph Heights, opened in 1927, a provincial convent for the Sisters of Notre Dame; Covington Catholic, a boys' high school, built in 1954; and Notre Dame Academy, a girls' high school, built in 1959.

Park Hills is a fourth-class city with a population of 3,999 in 1970; 3,500 in 1980; and 3,321 in 1990.

PARKS, STATE. Kentucky has forty-four state parks, of which nine are classified as HISTORIC SITES. Most of the rest of the state parks have facilities for picnicking, hiking, swimming, fishing, and tennis, and the state resort parks also have lodges for overnight guests. The Department of Parks in Kentucky is part of the Tourism Cabinet, reflecting the importance of parks to the tourist industry. The department concentrates on resort parks in areas of Kentucky that will benefit from tourism, providing lodges, camping areas, marinas, golf courses, restaurants, gift shops, and museums.

In the early 1900s various civic organizations backed the creation of a state park system, and in 1924 the General Assembly created the Kentucky State Park Commission, which recommended seven sites for parks. To create the first park, Pineville donated a large tract of land on Pine Mountain. The Louisville & Nashville Railroad, which had developed a park at Natural Bridge, offered it to the commonwealth. To add to the parks given outright to the state, the 1936 General Assembly empowered the State Park Commission to acquire land by purchase, lease, rental, or other agreements. The sale of bonds raised the money for land acquisitions and for construction of park facilities. Between 1948 and 1955, the state significantly increased appropriations for state parks and advertised the parks widely as tourist attractions. Tourist expenditures increased from $84 million to $146 million during this period, making the parks generally sound business investments. In the 1960s additional bond issues financed the creation of new parks and improvements of existing facilities. General fund appropriations for 1988-90 were $37.37 million.

Barren River Lake State Resort Park, 2,187 acres, is located in Barren County, twenty miles north of the Tennessee state line. The lake itself, which maintains a seasonal pool of approximately 10,000 acres, extends into Allen and Monroe counties.

Ben Hawes State Park, 297 acres, four miles west of Owensboro, was named for a former Owensboro mayor.

Big Bone Lick State Park, 525 acres, is in Boone County. The museum in the park displays the fossils of large prehistoric animals that came to the site for salt.

Blue Licks Battlefield State Park, 148 acres, is located near Mt. Olivet in Robertson County. A monument commemorates the battle fought there on August 19, 1782.

Breaks Interstate Park (see separate entry).

Buckhorn Lake State Resort Park, 856 acres, lies in the northwestern corner of Perry County, at the northern edge of the Redbird Purchase Unit of the Daniel Boone National Forest. The park is adjacent to a 1,230-acre mountain lake reservoir.

Carter Caves State Resort Park, 1,350 acres, is located near Olive Hill in Carter County. There are more than twenty of the Carter Caves, discovered in the 1780s, some explored and others uncharted.

Columbus-Belmont Battlefield State Park, 156 acres, is located at Columbus in Hickman County. The museum in the park commemorates the Civil War battle there.

Cumberland Falls State Resort Park, 1,794 acres, lies in Daniel Boone National Forest, fifteen miles southwest of Corbin. It is known mainly for the falls from which its name is taken. At full moon, the mist of the falls creates a moonbow, one of only two such phenomena in the world.

Dale Hollow Lake State Park, 3,398 acres, lies in Clinton and Cumberland counties. The 27,700-acre lake straddles the Kentucky-Tennessee border.

E.P. "Tom" Sawyer State Park, 377 acres, eight miles northeast of Louisville, was named for a former Jefferson County judge.

Fort Boonesborough State Park, 153 acres, is located on the Kentucky River in northern Madison County. The park contains the reconstructed fort for which it is named. A museum tells the story of Daniel Boone and of the fort, the second settlement in Kentucky.

General Burnside State Park, 430 acres, is eight miles south of Somerset. Surrounded by the waters of Lake Cumberland, it is Kentucky's only island park. It bears the name of Gen. Ambrose E. Burnside, whose Union detachment was stationed here during the Civil War.

General Butler State Resort Park, 791 acres, is located near Carrollton. The park features year-round recreation with a twenty-acre winter skiing facility. The park was named for Gen. William O. Butler, a hero of both the War of 1812 and the Mexican War.

Grayson Lake State Park, 1,512 acres, lies in Carter and Elliott counties.

Green River Lake State Park, 1,331 acres, is located near Campbellsville in Taylor County. The 8,200-acre lake offers a variety of water sports.

Greenbo Lake State Resort Park, 3,300 acres, is thirty-seven miles west of Ashland in Greenup County. Its terrain is rugged woodland typical of the Appalachian region.

Jenny Wiley State Resort Park, 1,651 acres, is three miles east of Prestonsburg. The park is adjacent to the 1,100-acre Dewey Lake and features summer performances at an outdoor amphitheater. Jenny Wiley, a Kentucky pioneer, was kidnaped by Indians but escaped and made her way back over a great distance.

John James Audubon State Park, 692 acres, is located in Henderson County. The park carries the name of the artist who painted in the area during 1810-19. The museum contains more than 125 original prints from his *Birds of America,* published in 1827-38.

Kenlake State Resort Park, 1,795 acres, is forty miles southeast of Paducah in Calloway County. The park lies on the western shore of Kentucky Lake. An indoor tennis center offers climate-controlled courts.

Kentucky Dam Village State Resort Park, 1,351 acres, is located in Marshall County on the northern shore of Kentucky Lake. Excellent accommodations make this one of the state's most popular resorts.

Kincaid Lake State Park, 850 acres, is in Pendleton County near Falmouth.

Kingdom Come State Park, 1,283 acres, straddles the border between Harlan and Letcher counties. The park takes its name from the novel *The Little Shepherd of Kingdom Come,* by the Appalachian writer John Fox, Jr. Nearby is Lilley Cornett Woods, a virgin forest.

Lake Barkley State Resort Park, 3,600 acres, is seven miles west of Cadiz, on the eastern shore of Lake Barkley. The park is one of three on the Land Between the Lakes, the 170,000-acre isthmus that separates Barkley and Kentucky lakes. The resort features a trapshooting range.

Lake Cumberland State Resort Park, 3,117 acres, is located near Jamestown. The park lies on the northern edge of the 50,250-acre lake, which offers excellent fishing.

Lake Malone State Park, 325 acres, lies west of the town of Dunmor in Muhlenberg County, with extensions into Logan and Todd counties. The 826-acre lake is surrounded by high sandstone bluffs.

Levi Jackson State Park, 896 acres, is located two miles south of London in Laurel County. It is named for a Kentucky pioneer. Winding through the park is part of the Wilderness Road. The Mountain Life Museum includes a restored pioneer village.

Lincoln Homestead State Park, 120 acres, is five miles north of Springfield in Washington County. The park features historic and reproduced homes of Abraham Lincoln's family.

My Old Kentucky Home State Park, 235 acres, is located at Bardstown. The heart of the park is the house known as Federal Hill, in popular legend the subject of Stephen Foster's song "My Old Kentucky Home, Good-Night!" The park features an outdoor drama, *The Stephen Foster Story*.

Natural Bridge State Resort Park, 1,900 acres, lies within the Daniel Boone National Forest, in Powell County near the Red River Gorge Geological Area. The stone bridge for which the park is named is seventy-eight feet long and sixty-five feet high.

Old Fort Harrod State Park, 15 acres, is located in Harrodsburg. A reconstruction of the fort commemorates the first permanent settlement in Kentucky. Also featured are a museum and the cabin where Abraham Lincoln's parents were married.

Paintsville Lake State Park, 242 acres, is located four miles west of Paintsville. The 1,139-acre lake extends into Johnson and Morgan counties.

Pennyrile Forest State Resort Park, 863 acres, is eight miles south of Dawson Springs. Its name is a colloquial form of pennyroyal, the name of a tiny plant found in the area. It is one of the state's most beautiful natural forest lands.

Pine Mountain State Resort Park, 1,519 acres, is located in Bell County. It was Kentucky's first state park, and each spring since 1935 it has hosted the Mountain Laurel Festival.

Rough River Dam State Resort Park, 637 acres in Breckinridge, Hardin, and Grayson Counties, is located six miles upstream from the Falls of the Rough River. The dam is 1,590 feet long, 310 feet high, and impounds a summer recreational lake of 5,100 acres.

Taylorsville Lake State Park, 1,625 acres, is located in Spencer County. The lake extends into Anderson and Nelson counties.

See J.W. Wells, *Kentucky Parks* (Nashville 1966); Robert E. McDowell and J. Seaton Huff, eds., *Rediscovering Kentucky* (Louisville 1971).

PAROQUET SPRINGS. Paroquet Springs, a well-known mineral water spa, was located at Shepherdsville in Bullitt County. In 1838 John D. Colmesnil purchased one hundred acres of land, setting aside twenty acres to develop. Colmesnil constructed bathhouses, cabins, and other buildings to accommodate approximately 250 guests. Advertisements boasted warm showers and vapor baths to be enjoyed at any hour of the day. In 1844 the rate was one dollar per day or six dollars per week, with a discount for those staying four or more weeks. Children and servants could stay for half-price.

Visitors to the springs came from the eastern and southern states; it was also very popular with peo-

ple from Louisville and Jefferson County. Some visitors came to Paroquet to stay the season, from the first of June until the middle of October. The spa closed during the Civil War and was reopened by a group of investors from Louisville. In 1871 they erected a larger hotel, 410 feet long, 80 feet wide, and two stories high, with 12-foot porches extending all the way around both floors. The facilities could then accommodate eight hundred guests. In March 1879 a fire destroyed the hotel building. Afterward the spa gradually declined, never regaining its popularity. TOM PACK

PARRISH, CHARLES HENRY, SR. Charles Henry Parrish, Sr., educator, was born into slavery in Lexington, Kentucky, on April 18, 1859. He was freed at the age of six, when the Civil War ended, and attended the special public school for freedmen in Lexington. He was a member of the first graduating class of the Louisville Normal and Theological Institute (later SIMMONS UNIVERSITY), receiving his degree in theology in 1886. In the front ranks of Louisville's black leadership in the 1890s, Parrish worked as an activist even before his graduation. He was a delegate to the National Convention of Colored Men in 1883, and he served as a delegate to both the Republican state convention and the Colored Education Convention in 1884. He was pastor of Calvary Baptist Church in Louisville from 1886 until 1931.

In 1890 Parrish succeeded William J. Simmons, the founder and first president of Eckstein Norton College in Cane Spring, Kentucky, which trained young black men to become teachers. Parrish stayed there until the college closed in 1912. In 1908 he founded the Kentucky Home Society for Colored Children, and he served as secretary of the board of trustees of the Lincoln Institute High School in 1918. He was president of Simmons University from 1918 until his death. Parrish served as a delegate to the Baptist World Alliance meeting in Stockholm in 1923 and in Toronto in 1928.

Parrish married Mary V. Cook on January 26, 1898; they had one son, Charles, Jr. He died on April 8, 1931, and was buried in Louisville Cemetery.

See George C. Wright, *Life Behind a Veil* (Baton Rouge, La., 1985).

PATRONS OF HUSBANDRY. The Patrons of Husbandry, more commonly known as the Grange, was a national farmers' organization founded in 1867 by Oliver Hudson Kelley, a clerk in the U.S. Agricultural Bureau. The order had local, state, and national units. The first Kentucky Grange was established at Allensville in Todd County by W.S. Reeves on August 10, 1871. Growth was rapid, with more than 52,000 members in 1,540 local Granges by 1875. The organization was particularly strong in parts of western Kentucky, such as Christian County, where the Church Hill Grange was a model. Among the organization's objectives were maintaining the laws, reducing farmers' expenses, avoiding litigation, and discountenancing the credit system. The rapid growth of the Grange during the 1870s was based on its success in securing cheaper transportation of agricultural goods and developing marketing cooperatives to avoid the middleman and increase profits.

The Grange was of considerable importance in improving the economic, social, and intellectual life of farmers, in pioneering equal rights for women, and in paving the way for federal railroad regulation. Its inability to operate its many cooperatives effectively, and the rise of competing organizations (Farmers' Alliance, the Agricultural Wheel, the Farmers' Union, the Populist Party), contributed to the rapid decline of the Grange in most areas of the country before the end of the century.

See James D. Bennett, "Some Notes on Christian County, Kentucky, Grange Activities," *Register* 64 (July 1966): 266-34.   JAMES D. BENNETT

PATTERSON, JAMES KENNEDY. James Kennedy Patterson, the first president of the UNIVERSITY OF KENTUCKY, was born to Andrew and Janet (Kennedy) Patterson in Glasgow, Scotland, on March 26, 1833. In 1842 his family immigrated to Bartholomew County, Indiana, where Patterson received a B.A. in 1856 from Hanover College and an M.A. three years later. Patterson taught at the Presbyterian Academy in Greenville, Kentucky, from 1856 to 1859. He married Lucelia W. Wing there on December 29, 1859. The couple relocated to Clarksville, Tennessee, where he served as principal of the preparatory department and later as professor of Latin and Greek at Stewart College. At the outbreak of the Civil War, Patterson moved to Lexington, Kentucky, to become principal of TRANSYLVANIA UNIVERSITY, which functioned as a high school during the war.

The merger of Transylvania with Kentucky University in 1865 included the newly created AGRICULTURAL AND MECHANICAL COLLEGE (A&M), where Patterson taught and subsequently served as presiding officer. The A&M College separated from KENTUCKY UNIVERSITY in 1878, and Patterson became the college's first president. He oversaw the early development of the new institution and the erection of its first buildings. His greatest achievement, by his own assessment, was his fight for a state property tax to support the new public institution. The tax became law in 1880. When opponents attempted to repeal the tax during the 1882 legislative session, Patterson, appearing before the General Assembly, gave what some have described as the greatest speech ever delivered by a University of Kentucky president. The attempt to repeal the tax failed. Patterson retired from the presidency in 1910. He died on August 15, 1922, and was buried in the Lexington Cemetery.

See Mabel Hardy Pollitt, *A Biography of James Kennedy Patterson: President of the University of Kentucky from 1869 to 1910* (Louisville 1925).
                                              TERRY BIRDWHISTELL

PATTERSON, ROBERT. Robert Patterson, who laid out the town of Lexington, Kentucky, and served in the first state government, was born on May 15, 1753, in Bedford County, Pennsylvania, to Francis and Jane Patterson. In October 1775 Patterson and six other men left Fort Pitt and canoed down the Ohio and Kentucky rivers to settle in Kentucky. After assisting in building John McClelland's station at Royal Springs (now Georgetown), Patterson went on to Harrodsburg. In October 1776, when BRYAN'S STATION was under siege, Patterson led a small contingent to Fort Pitt for ammunition to rescue the station.

Patterson commanded an expedition of twenty-five men in April 1779 to build a garrison north of the Kentucky River. The blockhouse was the first permanent settlement in LEXINGTON, where Patterson built the first house. He was elected a city trustee for seven terms between 1781 and 1791 and every year from 1796 to 1803. In 1788 he formed a partnership with Mathias Denmar and John Filson to settle Cincinnati and received one-third ownership in the town site. Patterson was a delegate to the third Kentucky convention, which met at Danville in August 1785 to discuss the issue of statehood. In 1792 he was elected to the Kentucky House of Representatives from Fayette County and served a total of eight years.

Patterson's illustrious career as a soldier spanned his entire life. In Pennsylvania, he joined the Lancaster Rangers as a scout in 1772 and was discharged in January 1775. After migrating to Kentucky, Patterson was a sergeant in Gen. George Rogers Clark's campaign against the British in Illinois in 1778. In May 1779 he participated in John Bowman's campaign against the Indians in Chillicothe and afterward received a promotion to captain. He again served under Clark in 1780 in the Little Miami Battle in southwest Ohio. In 1782 he was promoted to colonel and was second in command in the Battle of BLUE LICKS on August 19, 1782. He served in the 1783 campaign against the Miami under Clark and in the 1786 campaign against the Shawnee with Benjamin Logan. During the War of 1812, Patterson was commissioned forage master.

Patterson married Elizabeth Lindsey, of Pennsylvania, on March 29, 1780. They had eleven children. Patterson died November 9, 1827, and was buried in Dayton, Ohio, where he had moved in 1803, after selling his Kentucky landholdings.

See Charles R. Staples, *The History of Pioneer Lexington, 1779-1806* (Lexington, Ky., 1939).

PAULINE'S. Pauline's was the name of each of a series of brothels in Bowling Green, Kentucky, operated by Pauline Tabor. The best known of her houses, at 627 Clay Street, was in business from April 1944 to 1969. Tabor opened her first enterprise on November 12, 1933, in a rented house on the outskirts of town. Pauline's clientele included wealthy businessmen, political figures, GIs from nearby Fort Knox and Fort Campbell, and the region's students. Married three times and the mother of two sons, Tabor retired in 1969 and moved out of state in the 1980s. Urban renewal took her house on Clay Street, and entrepreneurs sold the bricks as mementos.

See Pauline Tabor, *Pauline's* (Greenwich, Conn., 1971).   JAMES G. SALTER

PAYNTER, THOMAS H. Thomas H. Paynter, U.S. senator, was born on December 9, 1851, in Lewis County, Kentucky, the son of Elisha and Sarah Paynter. After a brief time at Centre College, Danville, he read law and was admitted to the bar in 1872. He served six years (1876-82) as prosecuting attorney in Greenup County. A Democrat, he was elected in 1888 to the first of three successive terms in the U.S. House of Representatives (March 4, 1889, to January 5, 1895). Declining renomination in 1894, he sought instead a seat on the Kentucky court of appeals, where he served from 1895 to 1906, when he was elected to the U.S. Senate (March 4, 1907, to March 3, 1913). He retired to Frankfort and resumed the practice of law. Paynter married Elizabeth Pollock in 1876; they had a son, Pollock, and a daughter, Winifred. Paynter died on March 8, 1921, and was buried in the Frankfort Cemetery.   THOMAS H. APPLETON, JR.

PEARCE, JOHN ED. One of the most widely read writers in Kentucky in 1990, John Ed Pearce was born on September 25, 1919, in Norton, Virginia, to John Edward and Susan (Leslie) Pearce. He spent part of his boyhood in Kentucky and graduated from the University of Kentucky. Pearce served as a navy officer in World War II and in the reserve until 1977, retiring as a commander. He worked as editor of the *Somerset Journal* before joining the *Louisville Courier-Journal* in 1946. An editorial writer for twenty-five years, he is known to his fans as John Ed.

Admired as a newspaper columnist and an author, appreciated as a raconteur and historian, Pearce has attracted respect as a political pundit who wields a witty but caustic pen. He is a fixture at the *Courier-Journal*, where even after his retirement in 1986 he has continued to write his Sunday column. His column also appears regularly in the *Lexington Herald-Leader*.

Pearce has won a Nieman Fellowship to Harvard, a Governor's Medallion for Public Service, a share in a Pulitzer Prize, and Headliner, Meeman, and American Bar Association awards. He was named outstanding Kentucky journalist by Sigma Delta Chi, and is a member of the University of Kentucky Journalism Hall of Fame. He is the author of *Nothing Better on the Market* (1970), *The Colonel* (1982), *Seasons* (1983), *Divide and Dissent* (1987), and *The Ohio River* (1989). He has served on the boards of the Kentucky state park system and the Filson Club, as chairman of the Kentucky Oral History Commission, and as an instructor for the National War College. Pearce has been married twice,

to Jean McIntire and Virginia Rutledge, and has five daughters, Susan, Martha, Virginia, Elizabeth, and Alida.   JAMES S. POPE, JR.

PENDENNIS CLUB. The Pendennis Club is a social club established in Louisville in 1881. The name was taken from Thackeray's *The History of Pendennis* and may have been derived from the Cornish words *Pen Dinas*, meaning "high place." The first permanent clubhouse was the Belknap home on the south side of Walnut Street (now Muhammad Ali) at Second Street. The present clubhouse, a Georgian building inspired by great English houses, was constructed in 1928 in the same block. The third floor ballroom has been the scene of the introduction of debutantes at the Bachelors' Club Ball since 1930. Originally a men's club, it first admitted women members in 1984.   JO M. FERGUSON

PENDLETON COUNTY. Pendleton County, the twenty-eighth county in order of formation, is located in north-central Kentucky in the Outer Bluegrass region. The 281-square-mile county is bordered by Grant, Kenton, Campbell, Bracken, and Harrison counties. The Ohio River borders Pendleton County for five miles along its northeastern border, and the South Fork and the main stream of the Licking River join at Falmouth and flow northward out of the county. The terrain consists of fertile river valleys surrounded by undulating hills. Most of the farm production is burley tobacco and beef and dairy cattle.

The county was created on December 13, 1798, from portions of Campbell and Bracken counties and was named after Edmund Pendleton (1721-1803), a longtime member of the Virginia House of Burgesses (1752-74) and the Continental Congress. FALMOUTH is the county seat. The other incorporated city in the county is Butler, located on the Licking River seven miles north of Falmouth. In 1820, 250 square miles of the county were taken to establish Grant County.

The Licking River was an important avenue for the early exploration of Kentucky. Along with an overland route through the county, English Capt. Henry Bird took the river in leading six hundred Indians and Canadians in the June 1780 attack on Ruddell's and Martin's stations in central Kentucky. The first settlement in the county is believed to have been the one at the fork of the Licking at some time around 1780. The settlement, which became Falmouth, was established by James Cordy, Gabriel Mullins, James Tilton, Peter DeMoss, and Samuel Jones of Virginia.

With the exception of the county seat, Pendleton County remained rural during the nineteenth century. The farm economy was based on tobacco, and legend has it that the first crop was raised in the southwestern part of the county with seed brought from Virginia. In the 1830s Oliver Browning floated one-hundred-pound hoop-pole packages of the crop from McKinneysburg on flatboats down the Licking River to Cincinnati and points beyond. The coming of the Kentucky Central Railroad (later part of the Louisville & Nashville) through the county in 1852 gave sellers a connection to markets at Cincinnati and Louisville.

By the 1890s, intensive tobacco production had depleted much of the soil in Pendleton County. Sweet clover brought from Alabama in 1895 was planted in worn-out tobacco fields, restoring profitability to tobacco cultivation, as well as to apiary and dairy industries. Pendleton, "the county that came back," nevertheless lost one-third of its residents at the height of the economic crisis. Another forage crop that succeeded in the county was alfalfa, probably introduced between 1900 and 1910 by traveling Mormon preachers. By 1925 local farmers produced hundreds of tons and were exporting alfalfa to other areas.

In the late 1850s, a company of Pendleton County soldiers was organized to perform peacekeeping duties among the Mormons in Utah. During the Civil War, the county sent men to both armies. A Union recruiting camp was established in Falmouth in September 1861. Two Confederate recruiters were captured and executed in the Peach Grove area of northern Pendleton County. In July 1862 a number of county citizens were rounded up by Union troops during a crackdown against suspected Confederate sympathizers. In June 1863 a number of women were arrested at Demossville because they were believed to be potential spies "dangerous to the federal government." Falmouth was the site of a small skirmish on September 18, 1862, between twenty-eight Confederates and eleven Home Guardsmen.

The city of Butler was established around 1852 when the Kentucky Central Railroad was built through the area. Originally called Clayton, for reasons unknown, the city was named for William O. Butler, U.S. congressman from the area (1839-43), when it was incorporated on February 1, 1868. Like Falmouth, Butler in the 1870s and 1880s was a major tobacco market and its other businesses included lumber and sawmills, flour and gristmills, churches, schools, railroad depot, blacksmith shop, and various stores. In 1871 what was billed as the largest covered bridge in the world was built across the Licking River at Butler. The bridge was used until the 1937 flood weakened its supports. The structure was later torn down and replaced with a steel bridge.

Major floods of the Licking River in 1937, 1948, and 1964 made flood control a major concern of residents. The creation of Falmouth Lake (now Lake Kincaid) State Park near Falmouth, a 200-acre impoundment, failed to prevent the 1964 flood. Initial planning for a 12,000-acre impoundment of the Licking River nine miles south of Falmouth got underway in the mid-1970s, but because of the magnitude of the project, the time of completion has not been projected.

The largest employers in Pendleton County are the county school system; Dravo Lime Co.; Black River Division, producers of hydrated limestone and quicklime; and the Fuller Manufacturing and Supply Company, which rebuilds automobile engines and parts. Most of the county residents not engaged in farming are employed outside of the county. The population was 9,949 in 1970; 10,989 in 1980; and 12,036 in 1990.

WARREN J. SHONERT

PENNYROYAL REGION. The Pennyroyal, largest of Kentucky's geographical divisions, abuts all the others: the Eastern Coal Field; the Bluegrass, along its girdling fringe of the Knobs; the Western Coal Field; and the Jackson Purchase—as well as northern Tennessee and southern Indiana and Illinois. Within Kentucky, the Pennyroyal extends across thirty-five of the state's 120 counties, westward from the margin of the eastern mountains to the Tennessee and lower Cumberland rivers (now the Kentucky and Barkley Lakes) and northward from Tennessee's border to the Ohio River facing Illinois on the west, Indiana farther east. Two broad north-reaching arms of the western Pennyroyal encircle the Western Coal Field region. The Pennyroyal covers about 11,500 square miles and had an estimated population of 620,000 in 1985. The region takes its name from the pennyroyal plant, a member of the mint family (*Hedeoma puligiodes*).

The Pennyroyal's physiographic identification as the Mississippian Plateau is based on its soils and underlying rock layers of largely Mississippian geologic era limestone. The Pennyroyal has three principal subregions: an eastern, somewhat more hilly area surrounding Lake Cumberland; a middle segment of rich karstic rocks having a distinctive sinkhole landscape, extending both east and west of highway I-65; and a western segment from Logan County west to the Land Between the Lakes and northwest to the Ohio River.

Physical characteristics of the Pennyroyal vary from those of the higher limestone elevations—the Mississippian Plateau—in the east, to gently rolling plains in the central section, to the sandstone formations of the cave country and the flatter lands of the lake region. The western Pennyroyal lies south of the western Pottsville Escarpment, the southern edge of the Western Kentucky Coal Field. A fringing formation in the Pennyroyal south of the western Pottsville Escarpment is the Dripping Springs Escarpment, separating the sandstone to the north from the Mississippian limestone to the south. The plateaus are relatively low in elevation, with generally fertile soils underlain by limestone rocks of Mississippian geological age. The extensive cave systems of Mammoth Cave and many other caves near I-65 are subsurface karst or limestone solution features, with the pockmarking of sinkhole topography as surface indicators of the limestone solution processes. Along the fringes of the Western Coal Field are sandstone rocks, part of the Dripping

Springs Escarpment. Because of its position and extent, the Pennyroyal is a region of transit, with both north-south and east-west routes. Among these are I-65, southwest from Louisville toward Nashville; the north-south routes of the CSX Transportation rail network and the Green River and Pennyroyal parkways; and the east-west routes of highway KY 80 (much of it also a segment of U.S. 68), the Cumberland Parkway, parts of the Western Kentucky Parkway, and I-24.

The westernmost segment of the Pennyroyal region since 1964 has become a somewhat separate entity, the LAND BETWEEN THE LAKES, between Barkley Lake on the east and Kentucky Lake to the west, setting this area off more than when it was the Land Between the Rivers (lower Cumberland River and lower Tennessee River). As the Land Between the Lakes, it is administered from a headquarters at Golden Pond by the Tennessee Valley Authority.

No one city is truly the core or center of the region, but Bowling Green is the largest and most nearly central. Among the region's other urban centers are Hopkinsville at the fringe of Fort Campbell, Elizabethtown, a highway focus near Fort Knox, and Glasgow. The Pennyroyal region is the site of Kentucky's two principal U.S. Army encampments—Fort Knox and Fort Campbell.

Higher education facilities within the Pennyroyal region are Western Kentucky University at Bowling Green; Lindsey-Wilson College at Columbia in Adair County; Campbellsville College in Taylor County; and three of the state's public two-year community colleges, at Somerset, Hopkinsville, and Elizabethtown.

Commercial and industrial activities in the Pennyroyal are concentrated in the county seats, shifting to the outlying lands fringing the county seat. Beyond these are the more rural agricultural and recreational activities. The apple production is celebrated by the fall Apple Festival in West Liberty, Casey County, in the eastern Pennyroyal. Elsewhere burley and dark tobacco, soybeans, dairy products, and beef cattle are major agricultural commodities.

The Pennyroyal has a diversity of recreational activities, from Fort Knox's Armored Museum and U.S. Gold Repository, to the limestone caves. The monument at Fairview honoring Jefferson Davis is one of several historic sites. Several of Kentucky's major lakes lie entirely or partially within the Pennyroyal and several lakes are part of state resort parks—Cumberland, Green River, Barren River, and Rough River lakes.

See Carl O. Sauer, *The Geography of the Pennyroyal* (Frankfort, Ky., 1927).   J.T. GOOCH

PERKINS, CARL DEXTER. Among the last of the New Deal liberals, Carl Dexter Perkins, who served eastern Kentucky in the U.S. House of Representatives, was born October 15, 1912, in Hindman, Kentucky. He was the son of James Elbert Perkins, a lawyer, and Dora (Calhoun) Perkins, a teacher. Following his education in the Knott County

Schools, at Caney Junior College (now Alice Lloyd), and at Lees College, he taught in a remote Knott County school. In 1935 he graduated from the University of Louisville law school. He entered private practice for the next three years, during which he married Verna Johnson, a teacher. They had one child, Carl Christopher. Perkins completed an unexpired term as commonwealth attorney in 1939 and the following year was elected to the Kentucky General Assembly. He was elected Knott County attorney in 1941, and again in 1945, his tenure interrupted by combat service in the European theater during World War II.

A Democrat from Kentucky's mountainous 7th District, Perkins was first elected to Congress in 1948 and began to serve on January 3, 1949. He was appointed to the House Education and Labor Committee, arena for many of the ideological struggles over the social agenda of the federal government. A conservative coalition on the committee frustrated many liberal initiatives supported by Perkins, but the landslide election of 1964 produced a liberal majority sufficient to enact legislation fundamental to President Lyndon Johnson's program. Perkins became chairman of the committee in 1967, as it prepared to consider major antipoverty legislation. Many doubted whether the unsophisticated country lawyer was equal to the demands of his new position, but Perkins's diligence, persistent commitment to liberal principles, mastery of congressional procedures, and skills of personal persuasion soon gained him a reputation as one of the most influential men in Washington.

Perkins became a champion of the rights of labor, one of the nation's foremost advocates of federal social welfare programs for the disadvantaged, and, in the words of the former president of the National Education Association, Mary Hatwood Futrell, "the father of virtually every postwar federal education program." Perkins's bill supporting vocational education became law in 1963. The following year his committee produced landmark legislation to provide financial aid to disadvantaged college students, and, for the first time, extend general federal aid to elementary and secondary education. Perkins helped formulate the Economic Opportunity Act, centerpiece of Johnson's War on Poverty, and was one of its strongest advocates. He was a champion of the Head Start program, the school lunch program, adult education, federal assistance to libraries, and federal aid for the construction of highways and hospitals in the depressed Appalachian region. An early supporter of civil rights, Perkins backed President Harry S. Truman's attempt to establish a permanent Fair Employment Practices Commission, and was one of eleven Southern Democrats to vote for the 1964 Civil Rights Act. He also wrote federal legislation to improve safety standards in coal mines and to extend compensation to victims of black lung disease.

In his final years, Perkins fought vigorously to protect federal education and social welfare programs from budget cuts, and he emerged as a leading Democratic spokesman in opposition to the Reagan administration. Perkins died of a massive heart attack on August 3, 1984, en route from Washington to his home in Hindman and was buried in Perkins Cemetery, Leburn, Kentucky.

See Bill Peterson, "Carl Perkins: Kentucky's most powerful Congressman," *Louisville Courier-Journal Magazine*, February 2, 1975; Bob Johnson, "Perkins, advocate for Appalachia and education, dies," *Louisville Courier-Journal*, August 4, 1984; Robert T. Garrett, "Congressman's influence extended beyond district," *Louisville Courier-Journal*, August 4, 1984.   DANIEL G. STROUP

PERRY COUNTY. Perry County, the sixty-eighth county in order of formation, lies in the southeastern section of Kentucky, at the headwaters of the Kentucky River, and is bordered by Breathitt, Owsley, Leslie, Harlan, Letcher, Knott, and Clay counties. It covers 341 square miles of the Appalachian region and is drained by the north and middle forks of the Kentucky River and their tributaries. The land surface is hilly and mountainous and abounds in coal and natural gas.

Christopher Gist was the first to leave a written record of his travels through the valley where HAZARD, the seat of Perry County, now stands; in his journal on March 27, 1751, he noted the presence of large coal deposits. John and Nicholas Combs and their sons traveled over the mountains from Virginia in the early 1790s. The Combs brothers spread out along the river valley, some settling along Carrs Fork, others in what is now Lothair, and still others in parts of Breathitt County. Elijah Combs built the first home on the site that is Hazard. His cabin stood in the upper end of old Hazard, fronting Main Street.

In the years following the War of 1812, the population of eastern Kentucky grew slowly but steadily, and in 1819 the citizens of two counties, Floyd and Clay, petitioned the state for the creation of a new county, with a less-distant county seat. Perry County, named to honor Oliver Hazard Perry, hero of the War of 1812, was thus created on November 2, 1820. Five other counties were later carved from the territory of Perry County.

The Civil War brought to the region an era of suffering and misery that lasted over a generation. A Confederate veteran, quoted in a county history, recalled the condition of Hazard when he returned from war: "the neglected farms, the roads and paths overgrown with weeds, and almost no business of any kind being carried on." During the late eighteenth and early nineteenth century there had been some coal mining and timbering in the mountains, but for the most part the inhabitants had mined only enough coal to heat their homes and had used logs for building houses and making tools. Any coal or timber for sale had to be floated down the Kentucky River on flatboats.

It was the railroad that opened Perry County to development. In 1911, at a time when the population of Hazard had increased to five hundred, the

Louisville & Nashville Railroad (now CSX Transportation) extended its tracks into Perry County. By 1912 the railroad was completed and coal was being hauled out in trainloads of about thirty cars. During the 1940s the number of truck mines in Perry County increased rapidly, to a total of 259 in 1947.

During the 1960s, improvement of KY 15 connected eastern Kentucky with the Mountain Parkway and reduced travel time to central Kentucky by half. Perry County became a commercial center of eastern Kentucky when KY 15, the Daniel Boone Parkway, and new KY 80 intersected just north of Hazard. The East Kentucky Regional Airport, dedicated on October 19, 1983, is located fifteen miles north of Hazard. Built on a reclaimed mining site, it replaced the Hazard Airport in use since 1945.

Hazard Community College, founded in 1968, serves college students from the surrounding counties. Buckhorn Lake State Resort Park and Carr Fork Lake provide opportunities for recreation.

The population of Perry County was 25,714 in 1970; 33,763 in 1980; and 30,283 in 1990.

See Hazard Chapter, Daughters of the American Revolution, *History of the Perry County, Kentucky* (Hazard, Ky., 1953).   MARTHA HALL QUIGLEY

PERRYVILLE, BATTLE OF. The Battle of Perryville, sometimes called the Battle of Chaplin Hills, was fought on October 8, 1862, around the small town of Perryville in Boyle County, Kentucky. It was by far the largest military engagement to take place within the commonwealth during the Civil War, pitting 16,000 Confederate troops against 58,000 Federals on the battlefield. The battle was a tactical victory for the South but a strategic defeat, breaking the back of the Confederacy's Kentucky campaign.

The Confederates began the counteroffensive later known as the Kentucky campaign in August 1862. By the summer of 1862, the Civil War had entered its second year and Confederate fortunes were waning, especially west of the Appalachian Mountains. With defeats at Forts Henry and Donelson and at Shiloh, the Confederates had been forced out of Kentucky and driven almost out of Tennessee. The Confederates' plan in the Kentucky campaign was to sweep around the eastern flank of the Federal army under Maj. Gen. Don Carlos Buell in middle Tennessee and to invade Kentucky. With popular support and fresh Kentucky recruits, the Confederates believed they could defeat the Federal armies that would move north out of Tennessee in pursuit. Then, with Kentucky securely in their hands, they foresaw a quick and favorable conclusion to the war.

From Knoxville, Tennessee, Maj. Gen. Edmund Kirby-Smith led a force of 20,000 Confederates into southeastern Kentucky. After destroying a small Federal force at Richmond on August 30, 1862, they marched north and took Lexington, Frankfort, and the surrounding Bluegrass area. In the other half of the offensive, Gen. Braxton Bragg led his 32,000-man Army of the Mississippi out of

Chattanooga, Tennessee, on August 28. By September 17 Bragg's forces reached Munfordville, Kentucky, where they captured a Federal garrison force of over 3,000 men.

In the reaction anticipated by the Confederates, Buell and his 50,000-strong Army of the Ohio evacuated middle Tennessee and headed back north into Kentucky. As they approached from Bowling Green, Bragg was forced to move northeast to Bardstown. Unimpeded, Buell reached Louisville, where he incorporated into his army 25,000 reinforcements, and on October 1 set out to crush the Confederates. Buell sent a force of 20,000 to the east on the Shelbyville Road as a feint to occupy Kirby-Smith while he himself led 58,000 troops south toward Bragg's army at Bardstown.

Bragg, meanwhile, had left his army at Bardstown under the command of Maj. Gen. Leonidas Polk, and had gone to Lexington to confer with Kirby-Smith and to install Richard Hawes as the Confederate governor in Frankfort, in hopes of rallying support from Kentuckians. As Buell neared Bardstown, Polk and the Army of the Mississippi fell back through Springfield and Perryville. When Bragg heard of this move and of the Federal advance from Shelbyville toward Frankfort, he ordered both the Confederate armies to concentrate at Harrodsburg, expecting to meet Buell in battle near Salvisa, just south of Lawrenceburg.

Buell pushed on through Bardstown after Polk, and by the evening of October 7 his three corps were approaching Perryville. Buell himself, with Maj. Gen. Charles Gilbert's III Corps, was three miles west of Perryville, on the Springfield Road. Maj. Gen. Alexander McCook's I Corps was seven miles to his left, at Mackville, and Maj. Gen. Thomas Crittenden's II Corps was on his right, within ten miles of Perryville along the Lebanon Road. Thinking that both Confederate armies had now concentrated in his front at Perryville, Buell ordered both flank corps to march at dawn on October 8, planning to attack when all 58,000 of his men were up.

Bragg, having been informed of a large Federal column approaching Perryville on October 7, ordered Maj. Gen. William Hardee to halt his two divisions at Perryville. Later that day Bragg sent Polk with one division back to Perryville with orders to attack the Federal force at once, destroy it, and then return toward Harrodsburg. The three Confederate divisions, when assembled, would together total approximately 16,000 men. Polk reached Perryville during the night of October 7-8, but word of other Federal columns moving toward Perryville persuaded him not to attack in the morning as ordered by Bragg, but instead to form a strong defensive line. When Bragg arrived at Perryville from Harrodsburg around 10 a.m. on October 8, he was irritated by Polk's decision and ordered his men across the Chaplin River west of Perryville, with orders to attack at 1:00 p.m. Bragg's battle plan was to concentrate his strength north of the Springfield Road and open his attack against the Union's exposed left flank. He would then follow up in echelon, driving the Federals back upon themselves along the Springfield Road and destroying them there. Hardee would command the left and center of Bragg's line, made up of Brig. Gen. James Patton Anderson's and Maj. Gen. Simon Bolivar Buckner's divisions. Polk would command the right with Maj. Gen. Benjamin Cheatham's division.

On the Union side, McCook's I Corps had arrived and formed into line on the left of Gilbert's Corps. A delay in arrival of Crittenden's II Corps, however, caused Buell to hold off on the attack planned for dawn of October 8. By noon on that day, Bragg had his troops in position and opened fire with his artillery. Polk, however, was unable to open the attack until 2:00 because McCook's developing line had forced him further to the right, behind a bend in the Chaplin River. Polk then sent Cheatham's three veteran brigades charging across the shallow river bed and up the steep bluff on the western bank. Catching the Federals by surprise, the Confederates, after a desperate and bloody fight, drove in the Union left. Hardee followed up on Polk's move, driving McCook's right back about a mile, after heavy losses by both sides.

While McCook's I Corps was being shattered, Gilbert's III Corps along the Springfield Road was busy repulsing a spirited attack by Col. Samuel Powell's brigade, which formed the extreme left of Bragg's line. This suicidal attack revealed that Bragg still believed he was facing only a single Federal corps. On the Lebanon Road, Crittenden's II Corps was engaged by Col. Joseph Wheeler's cavalry.

Late in the afternoon, when Buell learned of McCook's plight, he immediately sent two brigades of the III Corps as reinforcements, and they were able to halt the Confederate onslaught. With the enveloping darkness, the guns on both sides fell silent. The full moon that lit the battlefield revealed a ghastly sight of carnage and destruction. The dead and dying of both sides lay everywhere. A Federal soldier wrote home to his father, "The moon shone full upon the scene, it is utterly useless to try to describe. Oh, may you never see such a sight."

After meeting with his officers and realizing that he was facing Buell's main army, Bragg decided to fall back to Harrodsburg and unite with Kirby-Smith's army. The Battle of Perryville left Bragg with 510 dead and 2,635 wounded; on the Union side, 845 were killed and 2,851 wounded.

From Harrodsburg the Confederates moved east across the Dick's (now Dix) River to Bryantsville. On October 13 Bragg put his army on the road back to Tennessee by way of the Cumberland Gap, ending the Kentucky campaign.

See Kenneth A. Hafendorfer, *Perryville, Battle for Kentucky* (Owensboro, Ky., 1981).

KENNETH A. HAFENDORFER

PETER, ROBERT. Robert Peter, physician and geologist, was born in Launceton, Cornwall, England, on January 21, 1805. He came to the United

States in 1817 with his parents, Robert and Johanna (Dawe) Peter, who first settled in Baltimore. Later the family moved to Pittsburgh, where Peter served an apprenticeship with a local druggist. In 1828, the year he became a naturalized citizen, he attended lectures at the Rensselaer Institute Scientific School in Troy, New York. In 1832 Peter moved to Lexington, joined the faculty at Dr. Benjamin O. Peers's Eclectic Institute, and served as demonstrator for chemistry classes in the medical department of Transylvania University. He received his M.D. in 1834. Peter served Transylvania in the academic department (1833-57) as professor of geology, mineralogy, and chemistry, and in the medical department as librarian (1833-35), professor of chemistry and pharmacy (1838-59), dean of the faculty (1841-57), and editor of the *Transylvania Journal of Medicine and Associate Sciences* (1837-38).

Between 1850 and 1853, Peter was professor of chemistry at the Kentucky School of Medicine in Louisville. In 1854 Peter was appointed chief chemical assistant to the KENTUCKY GEOLOGICAL SURVEY. During the Civil War, he was senior surgeon of the U.S. military in Lexington. He was professor of chemistry and experimental philosophy at Kentucky University (1865-78) and professor of chemistry (1878-87) at the Agricultural & Mechanical College (University of Kentucky). An ardent proponent of education and public health, Peter was among the first to observe that the phosphates so abundant in the limestone of the Bluegrass plateau might contribute not only to the production of superior thoroughbreds, but also, through drinking water and corn products, to the formation of urinary calculi in humans.

Peter married Francis Paca Dallam at the Lexington Episcopal Church on October 6, 1835. They had eleven children. He died April 26, 1894, and was buried in the Lexington Cemetery.

See Robert Peter and Johanna Peter, *The History of the Medical Department of Transylvania University* (Louisville 1905); Eric H. Christianson, "The Conditions for Science in the Academic Department of Transylvania University, 1799-1857," *Register* 79 (Autumn 1981): 305-25.

ERIC HOWARD CHRISTIANSON

PETTIT, KATHERINE. Katherine Pettit, founder of Hindman and Pine Mountain settlement schools, was born in Fayette County, Kentucky, on February 23, 1868, the daughter of Benjamin F. and Clara Mason Pettit. She attended Lexington's Sayre School from 1885 to 1887. Between 1899 and 1901, Pettit and her co-worker May STONE conducted summer schools near Hazard and Hindman, Kentucky. In 1902 Pettit and Stone opened Hindman Settlement School in Knott County. Pettit left Hindman School and founded Pine Mountain Settlement School in Harlan County in 1913. A strong, energetic person, Pettit supervised the outdoor work at Pine Mountain, including construction projects and management of farming activities, while her co-worker, Ethel (de Long) Zande, managed academic

and fund-raising activities. Pine Mountain School sponsored county fairs, health clinics, and community centers and gave support and encouragement to rural schools and farming institutes. Appreciative of mountain culture, Pettit and her associates encouraged the collection and preservation of crafts, ballads, and mountain customs.

After Pettit retired from Pine Mountain School in 1930, she promoted conservation projects and encouraged local farmers to adopt modern farming techniques in eastern Kentucky. She died of cancer in Lexington, Kentucky, on September 3, 1936, and was buried in the Lexington Cemetery.

See David E. Whisnant, *All That Is Native and Fine* (Chapel Hill, N.C., 1983).

NANCY FORDERHASE

PETTIT, THOMAS STEVENSON. Thomas Stevenson Pettit, journalist and reformer, was born on December 21, 1843, in Frankfort, Kentucky, the son of Franklin Duane and Elizabeth (Zook) Pettit. He became editor of the *Owensboro Monitor*, where his ardently pro-Union, pro-slavery, anti-Lincoln editorials resulted in his arrest in November 1864 and banishment to the Confederacy for being disloyal. He was pardoned by President Abraham Lincoln and in 1868 was elected assistant reading clerk of the Kentucky House of Representatives. He then served as private secretary to Gov. James B. McCreary (1875-79), resigning to become reading clerk to the U.S. House of Representatives. He was elected Daviess County's senior delegate to the 1890-91 Kentucky constitutional convention and assumed a leadership position there, advocating such reforms as the secret ballot, taxing of corporations as individuals, and two-thirds agreement on juries for civil cases. He was also an early supporter of women's suffrage and Populist programs. In 1891 he was elected as the People's party representative to the Kentucky General Assembly from Daviess County, where he fought against Jim Crow laws. He was later expelled from the Democratic party and became the unsuccessful People's party candidate for governor in 1895. His candidacy caused enough division among Democrats that a Republican, William O. Bradley (1895-99), was elected. Pettit died on November 30, 1931, and was buried in Elmwood Cemetery in Owensboro.

ALOMA WILLIAMS DEW

PHOENIX HOTEL. The Phoenix Hotel, a Lexington landmark, was located at the corner of Main and Limestone streets. The Phoenix Hotel was a popular hostelry for stagecoach travelers to and from Louisville, Cincinnati, Nashville, and lesser townships in the 1830s and 1840s. Early visitors included Aaron Burr, James Monroe, Andrew Jackson, William Henry Harrison, Ulysses S. Grant, Chester E. Arthur, and Mexican Gen. Santa Anna. The restaurant and meeting rooms were favorite gathering places for local residents as well. Postlethwait's Tavern opened in 1797 on the site, and the first hotel that operated there was a two-story, thirty-six-room structure, to which a third story was added later. Fire destroyed the hotel in 1820, and when it was rebuilt it was named the Phoenix; the phoenix is a mythical bird that is consumed by fire every five hundred years and is resurrected from its own ashes.

A fire in 1879 destroyed the hotel again. In 1914 an eight-story building with ninety rooms was erected and a new main entrance was added. The Phoenix Hotel closed in 1974 and was leveled in 1982 for urban development purposes. The main branch of the Lexington Public Library was built on the site and opened in 1989.

See J. Winston Coleman, Jr., *The Squire's Sketches of Lexington* (Lexington, Ky., 1972).

PHOTOGRAPHY. While on a trip to Europe to buy medical equipment for Transylvania University in the summer of 1839, Robert PETER recorded in his diary the formula for producing "photogenic drawings" by a photographic process invented earlier that year by Englishman William Henry Fox Talbot. If Peter carried out his stated intention to make photographs on his return to Lexington, he was probably the first photographer in Kentucky.

The daguerreotype, a rival process announced almost simultaneously in France, was a great commercial success as a portrait medium, and itinerant daguerreotypists visited Kentucky as early as 1841. The first permanent studio in the state was probably the one established in Louisville in about 1842 by John Hewitt. The surviving examples of Hewitt's daguerreotypes include portraits, now in the collections of the Filson Club, that were found in the cornerstone of a Masonic temple built in 1851.

Photographs on paper displaced daguerreotypes after the 1850s, and this era saw the rise of many prosperous studios, which employed multiple camera operators and large numbers of finishers, who prepared the prints. Successful studios included those of Edward Klauber, J. Henry Doerr, and Frank Wybrant in Louisville and James Mullen in Lexington. Mullen made numerous souvenir views and stereo cards of Bluegrass and eastern Kentucky scenery. Klauber's and Wybrant's large photographs of Ohio River locks, dams, bridges, and water works were published as albums. Studios operated by women included those of Carolyn Bergman, Ella M. Crosby, and Sallie Garrity, all of Louisville. Afro-Americans Harvey C. Husbands and Jesse R. Neighbors operated studios that served Louisville's black community.

The end of the nineteenth century, when great improvements were made in photographic materials, was perhaps the time of Kentucky's greatest contribution to the field. William G. Stuber, while working in his father's Louisville studio, experimented with improvements in plate emulsions in the 1880s. His work so impressed George Eastman that he hired Stuber to direct the Eastman Kodak Company's sensitive-material laboratories in 1894. Eastman then hand-picked Stuber to succeed him

as president of the company in 1924. When he retired from the presidency, Stuber served as chairman of the board of directors of Eastman Kodak. During Stuber's directorship, significant developments by Eastman's sensitive-materials division included both motion picture film and color photographic materials.

During the 1920s, Will Bowers of Louisville was a prize-winning contributor to pictorialist salons. Members of the Lexington Camera Club, founded in 1936, include Ralph Eugene Meatyard, who has been the subject of numerous books, articles, and exhibitions. His mysterious, often surreal works are sought after by museums and collectors. Robert May and Guy Mendes are club members whose works are exhibited widely, as are those of Van Deren Coke. Coke has been curator at the San Francisco Museum of Modern Art, and was director of the International Museum of Photography (IMP) at the George Eastman House during 1970-72. Coke was succeeded as director of the IMP by Robert J. Doherty, an art professor at the University of Louisville at the time of his appointment. More recently, the works of Louisvillian Stern Bramson have been collected by museums and have been exhibited in major galleries.

Significant collections of both historical and fine art photographs are housed at the Kentucky Historical Society in Frankfort, Alice Lloyd and Berea colleges, the University of Louisville, University of Kentucky, and the Filson Club.

See Robert C. May, *The Lexington Camera Club, 1936-1972* (Lexington, Ky., 1989); Gerald J. Munoff, "Dr. Robert Peter and the Legacy of Photography in Kentucky," *Register* 78 (Summer 1980): 208-18.   JAMES C. ANDERSON

PIATT, SARAH MORGAN (BRYAN). Sarah Morgan (Bryan) Piatt, poet, was born on August 11, 1836, to Talbot Nelson and Mary (Spiers) Bryan. Her grandfather Morgan Bryan, the brother-in-law of Daniel Boone, helped settle the area of Bryan's Station, Kentucky. In 1839 Sarah's family moved to Versailles, Kentucky, where her mother died in 1844. She and her sister lived first with their maternal grandmother in Woodford County, near Versailles, and then with an aunt, a Mrs. Boone, in New Castle, Kentucky. Sarah earned a degree from Henry Female College in New Castle. After reading the works of Shelley, Byron, Coleridge, and Scott, Sarah tried her own hand at verse, and her earliest works were printed in the *Galveston News* in Texas. The editor of the *Louisville Journal*, George D. Prentice, published some of her poems and also provided encouragement and advice.

Sarah married an Ohio poet, John James Piatt, on June 18, 1861. They lived in Washington, D.C., until 1867, when they moved to North Bend, Ohio. In 1871 the collection *A Woman's Poems* was published anonymously. This work is considered one of Sarah Piatt's best, and it gained recognition when Barnard Taylor included it in his book, *The Echo*

Club. She and her husband worked jointly on *The Nests at Washington and Other Poems* (1864) and *The Children Out-of-Doors, a Book of Verses, by Two in One House* (1885). In 1882 John Piatt took the post of U.S. consul in Cork, Ireland, and the family lived there for thirteen years. Many of Sarah Piatt's books of poetry were published while she was in Ireland. Some of the better-known ones are *Selected Poems* (1886), *Child's World Ballads* (1887), *An Irish Wild-Flower* (1891), *An Enchanted Castle, and Other Poems: Pictures, Portraits and People in Ireland* (1893), and *Complete Poems* (1894). In 1895 the Piatts returned to North Bend. After her husband's death in 1917, Piatt moved to Caldwell, New Jersey. She lived there with her son, Cecil Piatt, until her death on December 22, 1919. She is buried in Spring Grove Cemetery in Cincinnati.

See John Wilson Townsend, *Kentucky in American Letters, 1784-1912* (Cedar Rapids, Iowa, 1913).

PICKETT, ALICE N. Born in 1888 in Shelby County, Kentucky, Alice N. Pickett earned a medical degree in 1909 from the Women's Medical College in Philadelphia. During World War I she served overseas with the Red Cross; for part of her tour she was the only physician for a French city of 40,000. On her return to Kentucky, Pickett joined the medical faculty of the University of Louisville and for twenty-five years headed the school's obstetrics department. She also served on the U.S. Children's Bureau and on the board of directors of the Louisville Red Cross. In the 1960s when the *Louisville Courier-Journal* and *Louisville Times* Foundation made a large contribution to the local Red Cross, it did so in Pickett's name, to honor her years of service. In 1957 the University of Kentucky bestowed on Pickett the Sullivan Medallion for Service. Pickett died on November 17, 1971.

NANCY D. BAIRD

PICKETT, JAMES CHAMBERLAYNE. James Chamberlayne Pickett, diplomat and soldier, was born to Col. John and Elizabeth (Chamberlayne) Pickett on February 6, 1793, in Faquier County, Virginia. His family moved three years later to Mason County, Kentucky, where he received a classical education. On August 14, 1813, Pickett entered the U.S. Army 2d Artillery from Ohio with the rank of third lieutenant. When the war with Great Britain ended, he left the army and moved to Maysville, Kentucky, where he was editor of the *Eagle* newspaper from May 3, 1816, until August 9, 1816, and read law. From 1818 to 1821, he served in the army with the rank of captain, then returned to Mason County to practice law. In 1822 he was elected to the Kentucky House, serving one term. He succeeded William Barry as the Kentucky secretary of state in 1824, serving until the end of Gov. Joseph Desha's term (1824-28).

On June 9, 1829, Pickett became secretary of legation in Colombia. In 1835 he served briefly as superintendent of the U.S. Patent Office. In January 1836 he became the fourth auditor of the Treasury Department and in June 1838 he assumed the positions of U.S. chargé d'affaires to Ecuador and special agent to the Peru-Bolivia Confederation. From 1848 until 1853, Pickett edited the "Congressional Globe," an insert in the *Washington Globe* concerning congressional affairs.

On October 6, 1818, he married Ellen Desha, daughter of Governor Desha; they had two sons, Joseph and John. Pickett died on July 10, 1872, in Washington, D.C.

See James A. Padgett, "Letters of James Chamberlayne Pickett," *Register* 37 (April 1939): 151-70.

PIKE COUNTY. Pike County, the seventieth county in order of formation, is the easternmost county in Kentucky. It is bordered by Martin, Floyd, Knott, and Letcher counties; by Virginia on the southeast; and by West Virginia on the northeast. The county is separated from West Virginia by the Tug Fork of the Big Sandy River, while Pine Mountain forms the border with Virginia. The county seat is PIKEVILLE.

Topographically, the county is a part of the Central Appalachian Highlands, a well-dissected plateau with alternating steep, narrow ridges and narrow stream-made valleys extending in all directions. The county's highest elevation is Pine Mountain (also known locally as Cumberland Mountain), part of the one-hundred-mile-long ridge that is Kentucky's southeast border. Settlements and transportation lines are largely restricted to the valleys. Pike County is drained exclusively by the two forks of the Big Sandy River. Over two-thirds of its area is drained by the larger of these, the Levisa and its main Pike County tributaries (the Johns, Island, Shelby, Grapevine, and Feds creeks and Russell Fork). Tug Fork and its principal branches (Big, Pond, Blackberry, Peter, and Knox creeks) drain over two hundred square miles of the county's northeast and eastern sections.

The first white explorers known to have visited Pike County were the members of Maj. Andrew Lewis's ill-fated Big Sandy expedition of 1756, who camped on the Kentucky side of the Tug Fork. Daniel Boone and a companion are believed to have descended Shelby Creek in their 1767 search for the Bluegrass region. In 1773 Enoch Smith and party may have built a horse pen on upper Johns Creek. The first known permanent settlement in Pike County was made in 1790 at the mouth of Sycamore Creek, on lower Johns Creek by the family of William Robert Lesley. By 1800 other settlements were being made on the Levisa in the vicinity of present-day Pikeville.

Before Pike County was formed on December 19, 1821, it had been, in succession, a part of Fayette, Bourbon, Mason, and Floyd counties. The county was named for Gen. Zebulon M. Pike, the U.S. Army officer and explorer who discovered Pike's Peak. The first session of the county court met on March 4, 1822, at the home of Spencer Adkins on the Levisa Fork near the mouth of Russell Fork. On March 25 a permanent county seat was selected at a site to be called Liberty, about a mile and a half below the mouth of Russell Fork. Opposition by settlers north of the Levisa led to a decision the following year to relocate the seat on Elijah Adkins's land on Peach Orchard Bottom, across the Levisa from the mouth of Lower Chloe Creek. After the site was surveyed by James Honaker, a town was laid out in the early spring of 1824 and named Pikeville after the county. Pikeville, the county's largest city, is on the Levisa Fork, seven and a half stream miles from the Floyd County line and 145 road miles east-southeast of downtown Lexington. Elkhorn City, on Russell Fork, two stream miles from the Virginia line, is the county's second largest town. Other major communities include Belfry, Phelps, Virgie, Coal Run, Hellier, Huddy, and McCarr-Buskirk.

Pike County, located in the heart of the Appalachian coal fields, has been one of the principal coal producing counties in the nation since 1910. Though exploitable coal deposits in nearly every section of the county were known to geologists and others before the Civil War, their large-scale commercial development awaited the coming of the railroads in the first two decades of the twentieth century. In 1986 Pike County had 319 underground coal mines and 148 surface mines, more than any other Kentucky county. In 1987 some 31.4 million tons were mined (18 percent of the state's total) with a gross value in excess of $697 million.

Until rail shipping made coal production practical, Pike County's hardwood forests were its major economic resource. In the late nineteenth century, millions of board feet of timber were shipped down nearly every major stream to the Big Sandy River and ultimately to the Ohio River markets at Catlettsburg and Cincinnati. Excessive exploitation depleted this valuable resource, and today the resurgence of the timber industry is still years away. Extensive gas deposits in the northern section of the county have also contributed substantially to Pike County's economic development.

Many Pike Countians have been subsistence farmers, but because of irregular terrain and the limited amount of available land, commercial agriculture was never an important source of income. Mining and quarrying continue to employ the highest proportion of the county's work force (28 percent in 1986). Economic planners see tourism and light industry as Pike County's hope for the future. Today there are several small manufacturing plants on Johns Creek and in the greater Pikeville area.

Since the 1910s, Pike County has been served by two major railroads: the Chesapeake & Ohio Railway (now part of CSX Transportation) and the Norfolk & Western Railroad (now part of the Norfolk-Southern Corporation). An improved system of state and federal highways, which includes U.S. 23/119, U.S. 460, and KY 80, links the county with the rest of the state and the eastern states. A county airport for small private craft is six miles north of Pikeville.

The county's most notable landmarks include the Fish Trap Dam and its 1,331-acre impoundment of the Levisa Fork, ten stream miles southeast of Pikeville. Authorized by the Federal Flood Control Act of 1938, the 1,100-foot-long, 195-foot-high dam was built by the U.S. Army Corps of Engineers and dedicated in 1968.

The Breaks of the Big Sandy, often called the Grand Canyon of the South, is a five-mile-long, 100-foot-deep channel formed by the Russell Fork on the Kentucky-Virginia border just above Elkhorn City. Since 1945 the two states have jointly maintained the 4,600-acre Breaks Interstate Park.

During the decade of the 1970s, Pike County was one of the fastest growing counties in eastern Kentucky and experienced a 33 percent increase in population. The population of the county was 61,059 in 1970; 81,123 in 1980; and 72,583 in 1990.

See Henry P. Scalf, *Kentucky's Last Frontier* (Prestonsburg, Ky., 1966); Robert Rennick, *Pike County Place Names* (Lake Grove, Ore., 1991).

ROBERT M. RENNICK

PIKEVILLE. Pikeville, the county seat of Pike County in eastern Kentucky, is located on U.S. 23/460 and U.S. 119 on the Levisa Fork of the Big Sandy River. It is the county's largest city and has become the major trade and service center for the upper Big Sandy Valley. In 1990 it was served by the Chesapeake & Ohio Railroad (CSX Transportation), three banks (making it the state's third largest financial center), a regional hospital, a triweekly newspaper, an independent school district, and a four-year college. It was also the headquarters for several major coal companies.

The first proposed location of the new Pike County seat—the present Garden Village—was rejected because of public opposition. On December 24, 1823, a commission selected a site owned by Elijah Adkins on Peach Orchard Bottom, on the west side of the Levisa Fork across from the mouth of Lower Chloe Creek. From the outset the town was called Pikeville in honor of the western explorer and U.S. Army officer Zebulon Montgomery Pike, for whom the county and Pikeville's northeast suburb of Zebulon were also named. The site was surveyed and a town was laid out by James Honaker in the spring of 1824. The county court first convened there in May 1824. No court buildings were erected at the first proposed site, originally called Liberty; court proceedings were held instead at the home of Spencer Adkins, near the mouth of Russell Fork.

When the post office was established on August 5, 1825, with William Smith as the first postmaster, it was called simply Pike. In 1829 the post office was renamed Piketon, the name given to the town when it was incorporated in 1848. The town became Pikeville in 1850 but this name was not adopted by the post office until 1881. Pikeville was officially chartered as a city in 1893.

In October 1987 Pikeville completed one of the most ambitious engineering efforts east of the Mississippi River: a $77.6 million federally funded cut-through project designed to eliminate frequent flooding, relieve traffic congestion, and alleviate the critical shortage of level land in the downtown area. The Levisa Fork was diverted from its looping course through the city into a half-mile-long cut through Peach Orchard Mountain. Railroad tracks and streets were rerouted from the area and bridges were removed. The former river channel was filled in with dirt and rock from the cut-through, the end result giving the city nearly four hundred acres of new level land for commercial and institutional development.

Pikeville College, established in 1889 by the Presbyterian Church (USA) as a preparatory school for mountain youth, is a four-year liberal arts college with an enrollment of more than nine hundred. The population of the third-class city was 4,576 in 1970; 5,583 in 1980; and 6,324 in 1990.

ROBERT M. RENNICK

PIKEVILLE COLLEGE.

Pikeville College is an independent four-year liberal arts school founded to make quality education accessible in the mountains of Pike County. Most Pikeville College students are from eastern Kentucky and the neighboring counties in Virginia and West Virginia. Many of the students are the first in their families to attend college, and more than half are adults who have returned to school after spending time in working or rearing families. Most remain in the area after graduating.

The school was established in 1889 by Presbyterian missionaries from Ashland, Kentucky, as the Pikeville Collegiate Institute and offered elementary and high school level courses to the young people of the region. It was the first such school in the Big Sandy Valley. The early years were hard for the school; roads and railroads did not yet reach into eastern Kentucky, and shortages of money and supplies plagued the early teachers. A typhoid epidemic closed the school for a year in 1891, and an early distrust of the school's Presbyterian affiliation led to at least one attempt to bomb the main school building. Despite these setbacks, the school graduated its first high school class in 1894 and was soon drawing students from throughout the area. Teacher training courses were instituted in 1901, and college courses were added in 1918. The school graduated its first junior college class in 1923. The last high school freshman class was admitted in 1953, and the high school curriculum was dropped four years later. In 1957 Pikeville College awarded its first four-year degrees.

The original Pikeville Collegiate Institute building stands on the south side of Pikeville, beside what is now the college gymnasium. The main campus lies on a hill overlooking the town and consists of almost a dozen buildings, including a women's dormitory erected in 1908, an administration building erected in 1925, the Record Memorial Fine Arts Building, a student center, and dormitories and apartments for students and faculty. In 1989 the college purchased a former hospital building adjacent to the upper campus and began renovations to create a new Pikeville College library and learning center there.

In 1990, Pikeville College offered baccalaureate degrees in seventeen fields of study. Associate degrees were offered in five areas. For students whose academic preparation in reading, writing, or mathematics is inadequate for college, developmental studies are offered. Graduate level courses are available on campus through the Appalachian graduate consortium with Morehead State University.

See Alice J. Kinder, *Pikeville College Looks to the Hills: 1889-1989* (Pikeville, Ky., 1989).

KRISTIN LAYNG SZAKOS

PILOT KNOB.

Of seven Kentucky hills called Pilot Knob, the one in northwestern Powell County is a steeply rising, flat-topped prominence with a peak of 1,440 feet, the highest elevation in the county. It is probably the "eminence" from which on June 7, 1769, Daniel Boone, John Finley, and their companions first viewed the rolling upland of the Bluegrass region. The knob lies north of the Red River valley near Boone's Oil Springs camp, three miles northwest of Clay City. Pilot Knob State Nature Preserve surrounds the elevation, which rises more than seven hundred feet above the nearby river plains.

A second Pilot Knob, elevation 1,411 feet, is located four miles east of Berea and north of Bighill in southeastern Madison County, within sight of early travelers on the Wilderness Road.

WILLIAM A. WITHINGTON

PINE MOUNTAIN.

Pine Mountain is a 125-mile-long ridge in the southeastern part of Kentucky. It extends from a point near Jellico, Tennessee, to a location near Elkhorn City, Kentucky, and traverses Bell, Harlan, and Letcher counties. The elevation of the crest increases gradually from southwest to northeast; the highest point is just east of Whitesburg, at an altitude of 3,273 feet above sea level. The crest of Pine Mountain rises 1,000 to 2,000 feet above the streams that parallel the northwest side of the ridge. For a distance of nearly ninety miles no stream has cut through the mountain, making it an effective barrier to transportation and migration of population. The only water gaps are those at either end of the ridge and at Pineville, where the Cumberland River has breached it.

Pine Mountain forms the northwest boundary of the Cumberland Overthrust block. The block is a trough-shaped segment of the earth's crust that is approximately 125 miles long and twenty-five miles wide and has been moved laterally a distance of six to ten miles from the southeast by mountain-building forces. Pine Mountain is the upturned edge of the block where rock strata have been brought to the surface by displacement along the Pine Mountain Overthrust Fault. Displacement has caused the rocks to be tilted at steep angles and has exposed strata that would normally occur approximately 2,000 feet below the surface of the earth. This movement took place about 270 million years ago in the Permian period, when the Appalachian Mountains were being formed. The mountain's rugged topography is due in large part to resistant sandstones in the Pennington and Lee formations that cap the crest of the ridge. These sandstones and conglomerates were originally deposited as sands and gravels during the Carboniferous period, approximately 315 to 325 million years ago. Erosion of softer strata on either side of the resistant, steeply dipping rocks has resulted in the sandstone beds' projection above the surrounding areas.

Pine Mountain, with its wooded coves and towering rock formations, is one of the most scenic places in the eastern United States. The outstanding natural beauty is preserved in Pine Mountain and Kingdom Come state parks, Breaks Interstate Park, Kiwanis Raven Rock Park, and the Little Shepherd Trail.   DONALD C. HANEY

PINE MOUNTAIN SETTLEMENT SCHOOL. Pine Mountain Settlement School is a nonprofit educational institution located at the head of Greasy Creek in Harlan County. Founded in 1913 by Katherine PETTIT and Ethel de Long Zande on land donated by William Creech, Pine Mountain began as a combination of social settlement and boarding school for mountain youth. In the 1930s, under Glyn Morris, the school developed a distinctive secondary curriculum built on student interests and community service. In 1949 the school became an elementary day school operated jointly with the Harlan County public schools and Berea College. The school began to operate as an environmental education center in 1972 and in the late 1980s became involved in preventing teenagers from dropping out of school. Community service has been a tradition at Pine Mountain, which supports health and recreational programs, economic development, and the preservation of mountain folkways.

See Mary Rogers, *The Pine Mountain Story 1913-1980* (Pine Mountain, Ky., 1980).
JAMES S. GREENE III

PINEVILLE. Pineville, the seat of Bell County, is located sixteen miles east of Barbourville and thirteen miles north of Middlesborough on the west bank of the Cumberland River. It sits on a very narrow strip of land where the river cuts through Pine Mountain.

In pioneer days, Pineville was known as Cumberland Ford and was first settled in 1781, making it one of the oldest settlements in what is now Kentucky. Isaac Shelby, Kentucky's first governor (1792-96), is said to have originally owned Cumberland Ford. It was sold to J.J. Gibson and family before the Civil War. When Bell County was formed in 1867, Cumberland Ford was named the best site for the county seat, but the Gibsons refused and instead donated a one-acre site on Pine Mountain for this purpose. A large frame court-

house was built on the site in 1869, but was refused by the court because of its inferior construction. A new courthouse in the center of town was completed in 1871 and occupied in 1889, the same year Pineville was incorporated as a city. The courthouse burned in 1914; the third courthouse suffered the same fate in 1918. The fourth Bell County courthouse was built in 1919-20. It was renovated after being gutted by fire in 1944.

Pineville's location has made it susceptible to flooding. Major damage occurred on April 4, 1977, when fourteen inches of rain fell upstream, swelling the Cumberland River out of its banks. The floodwall built by the U.S. Army Corps of Engineers in 1952 could not contain the swollen river. More than one hundred houses were moved off their foundations and the downtown area was caked with two feet of mud. An extension of the floodwall was completed in 1988 by the Army Corps of Engineers.

Pineville's economy depends heavily on the coal mining industry and its manufactured goods, mainly acetylene, explosives, and oxygen products. CSX Transportation Systems (formerly the Louisville & Nashville Railroad) is the railroad operator. The beautiful scenery in the area is the basis of an active tourism industry. Kentucky Ridge State Forest, located just south of Pineville, is an 11,916-acre site maintained by the Kentucky Division of Forestry. It contains Pine Mountain State Resort Park and Pine Mountain State Park Nature Preserve, where trees are estimated to be more than two hundred years old and rare wildflowers grow among the prevalent mountain laurel. The MOUNTAIN LAUREL Festival is held annually in Pineville. Clear Creek Baptist Bible College, a seminary, is located in Pineville.

The population of the fourth class city was 2,817 in 1970, 2,599 in 1980, and 2,198 in 1990.
RON D. BRYANT

PIRTLE, JAMES SPEED. James Speed Pirtle, attorney and university president, was born in Louisville, on November 8, 1840, to William and Jane Ann (Rogers) Pirtle. After his graduation from Male High School in 1859, Pirtle studied law. He received his degree from the law department of the University of Louisville in 1861 and entered into a partnership with John Speed. In 1873 Pirtle became a professor in the university's law department. He was made a trustee of the University of Louisville in 1880, sat on the board of trustees until 1915, and was its secretary for twelve years. From 1886 to 1905 Pirtle served as president of the University of Louisville. During his tenure, there was greater attention to academic concerns, especially in the School of Medicine. New facilities were added and admissions requirements were made more rigorous.

Pirtle, a partner in Pirtle, Trabue, Doolan & Cox and Pirtle & Caruth, sat as a special judge on the chancery court and acted as attorney for the Illinois Central Railroad (now Illinois Central Gulf). He served as president of the Louisville Bar Association. He was a founder in 1878 and charter member of the American Bar Association, and a founder in 1884 and charter member of the Filson Club.

Pirtle married Emily Bartley on May 22, 1878; they had four children—Robert, William, Jane, and Emily. Pirtle died on September 25, 1917, after a short illness, and was buried in Cave Hill Cemetery in Louisville.

See James S. Pirtle biographical files, University of Louisville.   MARGARET L. MERRICK

PISGAH CHURCH. Among the first group of Presbyterian congregations organized in Kentucky in 1784 was one at Shannon's Run, three-and-a-half miles east of Versailles in what is now Woodford County, Kentucky. Presbyterian families, including the Scotts, Evanses, Gays, and Dunlaps, called Adam Rankin as their first pastor. He probably named the church Mt. Pisgah as a companion to his other charge, Mt. Zion, in Lexington. After Rankin was deposed from the ministry in a controversy concerning presbytery authority and hymnody, James Blythe was called to serve Pisgah in 1793.

In 1794, the Kentucky Academy was opened nearby by Presbyterians discontented with the administration of Harry Toulmin at Transylvania University. The academy merged with Transylvania in 1798, and the school building next to the Pisgah church was used for other church functions. A stone church building from 1812 was renovated in the Gothic style in 1868. Pisgah is one of the minority of rural Presbyterian congregations that have flourished. In 1988 the pastor was Michael Ward and the membership was 204.

See William O. Shewmaker, *Pisgah and Her People* (N.p., 1934).   LOUIS WEEKS

PLACE NAMES. The more colorful of Kentucky's place names have especially intrigued those who have sought their explanations in humorous accounts of eccentric persons or unusual events. Kentucky's place names—and personal names too—have their share of the amusing and bizarre, it is true, but most were given merely to locate and identify places as conveniently as possible, and to describe the people who lived there. In short, most Kentucky place names have fairly mundane and obvious origins.

From the outset, names were given to natural features, settlements, and countless man-made works to identify them and distinguish them from one another. These names can reveal much of Kentucky's history and culture, being a fairly accurate record of the persons and events that contributed to the state's development.

Natural features, especially waterways, were the first in Kentucky to be named, and only later were names given to the settlements that were established in their vicinity. Later still were the post offices, railroad stations, and mines named. At first, names were given of necessity, without much thought, and then evolved through long local usage until they were affixed to a map or officially recorded on some public document. This lengthy evolution may account for the difficulty in tracing their derivations. Some names, usually those of post offices, railroad stations, and planned communities, were bestowed by deliberate act, a method of naming that makes their origins readily accessible. There are precise records, for example, of dates when post offices and railroad stations were established and when cities were incorporated. Most of Kentucky's estimated 110,000 known place names, however, have never appeared on published maps. References to their origin may be found only at the sites themselves, among the people who live there, or in obscure records.

At least half of all Kentucky place names are simply the personal names of founders, discoverers, first settlers, or early landowners. Many describe the natural setting at the time the names were given—such apt labels as Brush Creek, Long Fork, Bearwallow, Bald Knob, Cold Spring, and Pleasant View. Other names, though—like those brought by the first settlers from their former homes, or those that honored famous persons or commemorated historic events elsewhere, or those inspired by religious and patriotic sentiments—have no intrinsic association with the Kentucky places or features they came to identify, but reveal much about the settlers themselves. Less often, a local incident or the typical activities or behavior patterns of local people gave rise to a name. Of course, a few names—Hardscrabble, Skullbuster, Poverty, Pinchem—simply reflect the settler's characteristic sense of humor.

A place name may be either a single word, usually applied to a settlement, or two or more words that combine (1) the *generic* type of place, such as creek, knob, mine, road, or school, and (2) the *specific* identifier that makes the place unique. Few Kentucky places are uniquely named, however. In fact, over 95 per cent of Kentucky's specific names are duplicated, either within the state or elsewhere. The sheer number of places needing to be named tested the limits of human experience, imagination, and vocabulary—leading inevitably to repetitions in the names bestowed on Kentucky places. Among the handful of place names that are uniquely Kentucky are Monkey's Eyebrow, Helechawa, Whoopflarea, Thousandsticks, Mousie, Black Gnat, Eighty Eight, Fancy Farm, and Thealka.

Despite Kentucky's colorful history of conflicts between Indians and settlers, only one place name may in fact have been bestowed by Indians: the name Kentucky itself. Yet the precise meaning of the state's name is unknown. There has been no confirmation of several possible explanations: a Wyandot name meaning "land of tomorrow"; a generalized Algonquian term referring to a river bottom (*kin/athiki*); a Shawnee word signifying the head of a river; an Iroquoian name meaning "place of meadows." The folk etymology that sees the name Kentucky as the combination of "cane" and "turkey" has no credence. The one thing that historians and linguists agree on is that the state's name does not denote a "dark and bloody ground" in any known Indian language.

The only authentic Indian name applied to a Kentucky place about whose derivation we can be fairly certain is *Eskippakithiki* (place of blue licks) in Clark County. No other relatively permanent settlements of Indians are known to have been made in Kentucky in historic times. The Indians who used Kentucky as their hunting grounds made no ownership claims to any of the territory. Nor did they share the European custom of affixing permanent names to anything, but merely identified a site or feature for a particular purpose at a particular time. Most of the Indian-sounding names borne by Kentucky places were given to them by the white man for a variety of reasons. *Helechawa* (in Wolfe County) has often appeared on lists of Kentucky's alleged "Indian names" but it is in fact an acronym—a not uncommon form of naming—for the name of *Hele*n *Cha*se *Wa*lbridge, the daughter of the man who brought one of the first railroads to eastern Kentucky.

Place names are seldom permanent. Though the names of natural features tend to survive for many years, those given to settlements and other man-made features (schools, churches, mills, roads, bridges, mines) have often changed with successive occupancy or ownership. Even stream and hill names have changed in recent decades, and of course new Kentucky features such as housing subdivisions, roads, and malls call for new names.

In 1970 several Kentucky scholars initiated the Kentucky phase of a fledgling national effort to systematically survey all of the place names in the United States. Most of Kentucky's named places and features have since been identified, located, and supplied with significant data on their history and name derivations. This information will be made readily available to future generations of Kentucky scholars.

See Robert M. Rennick, *Kentucky Place Names* (Lexington, Ky., 1984); Lawrence Thompson, "The Naming of Kentucky," *American Notes and Queries* 7 (Jan. 1969): 68-71.   ROBERT M. RENNICK

PLATO, SAMUEL M. Samuel M. Plato, one of the first black building contractors and architectural designers, was born in Waugh, Montgomery County, Alabama, in 1882, the son of James and Katie (Hendricks) Plato. His father, who passed on his carpentry skills to his son, was a farmer who had apprenticed in carpentry under black artisan Samuel Carter, for whom the younger Plato was named. Plato as a youngster attended Mt. Meigs Training School near Waugh. He spent a year of study in Winston-Salem, North Carolina, then enrolled at Simmons University in Louisville in 1898. Plato enrolled in a teachers' training course and liberal arts courses, with plans to study law. While attending Simmons he took correspondence courses in architecture and carpentry from the International Correspondence School in Scranton, Pennsylvania.

In 1902 Plato moved to Marion, Indiana, where he lived until sometime between 1919 and 1921. While in Marion, Plato formed a partnership with black building contractor Jasper Burden, which lasted about ten years. Plato then moved to Louisville, where he practiced building design both independently and for a time with William L. Evans. At a time when few blacks were practicing the architectural profession, Plato's contract to build a U.S. post office in Decatur, Alabama, was the first received by a black. He built more than thirty-nine post offices at various locations throughout the United States. During the era of World War II, he was one of the few blacks to be awarded contracts to build defense housing. He designed and built numerous residences, apartment houses, office buildings, and several banks as well as schools and churches in Louisville and in Marion. He served as contractor for Westover, a subdivision developed between 1925 and 1947 in Louisville's West End.

Plato was twice married, first to a Marion native, Nettie (maiden name unknown). After her death, he married Elnora Davis Lucas. Plato died in Louisville on May 13, 1957, and was buried in the Louisville Cemetery.

See Kathrine Jourdan, "The Architecture of Samuel M. Plato," *Black History News and Notes* 37 (August 1989): 4-7.   JOANNE WEETER

POETRY. In Kentucky, where there is poetry in grass that is sometimes blue and in such names as Pippa Passes, Bonnieville, Rosine, and Uz, the earliest published poet was Thomas Johnson, Jr., an ex-Virginian known for his "raucous rhymes." In *The Kentucky Miscellany* (1789), for example, Johnson wrote "Epigram on William Hudson Who Murdered His Wife": "Strange things of Orpheus poets tell, / How for a wife he went to Hell; / Hudson, a wiser man no doubt, / Would go to Hell to be without."

Probably the most widely quoted lines of poetry from the state are "And politics—the damndest / in Kentucky," from the seven-stanza poem *In Kentucky* (1902). Its author, James Hilary Mulligan, wrote other poems of local color and many parodies. Among other nineteenth century Kentucky poets was Theodore O'Hara, whose *Bivouac of the Dead* (1847) is a martial elegy honoring Kentuckians who fell in the Mexican War. The first elegy written by O'Hara (1845) honored Daniel and Rebecca Boone.

Joseph Seamon COTTER was Kentucky's first recognized black poet. Self-taught in literature, he became a teacher and wrote poetry, fiction, and drama. His *Links of Friendship* was published in 1898. The poetry of his son Joseph Seamon Cotter, Jr., was cut off by his death at age twenty-three, leaving only one published collection, *The Band of Gideon and Other Lyrics* (1918).

The first Kentucky poet to gain national and international recognition was Madison CAWEIN, a traditionalist whom Joyce Kilmer called "the greatest nature poet of his time." A prolific writer, Cawein complained of financial hardship, claiming that in Louisville, where he lived, "Nobody reads poetry nor wants to read it." The city, nevertheless, recognized him in 1913 with a bronze bust in the Louisville Free Public Library. James Thomas Cotton NOE was Kentucky's first official poet laureate (1926-53), less of a dubious honor than in later times, when such a designation has been indiscriminately bestowed by hyperbolic legislators. With a happy sense of rhyme and rhythm, Noe has been called Kentucky's James Whitcomb Riley.

Elizabeth Maddox ROBERTS, known primarily as a novelist, published three books of poetry, and her poems appeared in prestigious magazines in the early 1900s. Roberts was the last Kentuckian born in the nineteenth century who made an appreciable contribution to poetry. Kentucky was fairly undistinguished in poetry during her time, as was the South in general.

Robert Penn WARREN brought maturity to poetry in Kentucky, becoming not only Kentucky's most outstanding poet but one of the world's finest. A true man of letters, he wrote in many genres, but his stature as a poet overshadowed his achievements in other literary forms. The winner of two Pulitzer prizes and countless other awards honoring poetry, Warren once said modestly that winning an award is like winning a raffle. Appointed poetry consultant to the Library of Congress for 1944-45, he became in 1986 the first poet laureate of the United States. In his poetry as well as his fiction, many of Warren's settings are in Kentucky. The Center for Robert Penn Warren Studies was established at Western Kentucky University at Bowling Green in 1987. Kentuckian Cleanth BROOKS, a literary critic, coauthored with Warren the influential textbook *Understanding Poetry* (1938). Lifelong friends, Brooks and Warren founded and coedited *The Southern Review*, which was published during 1935-42.

Though all Kentucky poets dim beside Warren, Allen TATE also gathered national and international laurels. His *Ode to the Confederate Dead* has been called a masterpiece. A leader in literary and philosophical movements at Vanderbilt University in Nashville, Tate moved widely among academic locales. At one time he edited the *Sewanee Review*. Other poets of Kentucky whose reputations are worldwide include Thomas MERTON, a Trappist monk at Gethsemani, Kentucky, and Jesse STUART, author of the collections *Man with a Bull-Tongue Plow* (1934) and *Hold April* (1962). Wendell BERRY, novelist, environmentalist, essayist, and poet, has a firm national reputation. James STILL and Jim Wayne MILLER are well-known far beyond Appalachia, a frequent subject for them.

Among Kentucky's other poets of note are Ann Jonas, Charles Semones, Lillie Chaffin, Roberta Bunnell, Wade Hall, George Ella Lyon, Prentice Baker, and Albert Stewart. Some of them were brought together in the early 1960s, when the anthology *Contemporary Kentucky Poetry* (1964) and the poetry quarterly *Approaches* were published for the purpose of discovering Kentucky's unknown poets. There were more than had been thought, the largest group being in eastern Kentucky. When the first issue of *Approaches* appeared in 1964, there were no other publications confined to poetry in Kentucky. In time, there was a proliferation, and the Poetry Society of Kentucky was founded. After twelve years, *Approaches* became the *kentucky poetry review*, accepting poems from outside Kentucky.

See Dorothy Edwards Townsend, *Kentucky in American Letters* (Georgetown, Ky., 1976); Thomas D. Clark, *Kentucky: Land of Contrasts* (New York 1968).

JOY BALE BOONE

POGUE, FORREST CARLISLE. Forrest Carlisle Pogue, a historian best known as the biographer of Gen. George C. Marshall, was born September 17, 1912, in Eddyville, Kentucky, the son of Forrest Carlisle and Frances (Carter) Pogue. He earned degrees at Murray State University (A.B., 1931), University of Kentucky (M.A., 1932), and Clark University in Massachusetts (Ph.D., 1939) and was American Exchange Fellow in Paris (1937-38). He taught at Western Kentucky University (1933) and Murray State University (1933-42, 1954-56), and served in the U.S. Army (1942-45).

As a World War II combat historian, Pogue recorded interviews with front-line fighting men from Omaha Beach to Czechoslovakia, and won the Bronze Star and the Croix de Guerre. Selected to write the official history of Gen. Dwight D. Eisenhower's command, he became a civilian war department historian (1946-52) and wrote *The Supreme Command* (1954). He was one of the authors of *The Meaning of Yalta* (1956) and he contributed between 1960 and 1983 to a number of other military and foreign relations histories.

In 1956 Pogue was recruited by the George C. Marshall Foundation to write Marshall's biography. While completing the task, he served as director of the Marshall Library and Foundation (1956-74) and of the Smithsonian Institution's Dwight D. Eisenhower Institute for Historical Research. Pogue's research included interviews with Marshall and over four hundred other wartime leaders and associates. His first volume on Marshall, *Education of a General: 1880-1939* (1963), was succeeded by *Ordeal and Hope, 1939-1942* (1966), *Organizer of Victory, 1943-45* (1973), and *Statesman, 1945-59* (1987). Pogue's writings on Marshall have won international acclaim for their historical and literary quality. Murray State University's oral history program was named in honor of Pogue, who is a pioneer in the field.

He married Christine Brown, of Fulton, Kentucky, in 1954.

See H. Lew Wallace, "Forrest C. Pogue: A Biographical Sketch," *FCHQ* 60 (July 1986): 373-402.

JAMES W. HAMMACK, JR.

POINT. The Point is a tract of two hundred acres at the confluence of the Licking and Ohio rivers in northern Kentucky in what is now Covington. Christopher Gist, an agent of the Ohio Land Company, arrived in the area in March 1751 and may have been the first white man there. A British agent, Col. George Croghan, explored the area in May 1765. A year later the Western Department's chief engineer, Capt. Harry Gordon, traveled through the region to complete his land survey. In the fall of 1771 Simon Kenton, John Strader, and George Yeager explored the Point for cane.

Military maneuvers against local Indians were often staged from this area. Col. John Bowman, of the Kentucky Company of Virginia, led a group of men from the point against the Shawnee in Ohio in April 1779. George Rogers Clark gathered two regiments here under the direction of Cols. Benjamin Logan and William Linn in July 1780. They built a blockhouse across the river where Cincinnati now stands. The party attacked and destroyed the Shawnee towns of Chillicothe, Pickaway (Piqua), and Loramie's Store. In November 1782 Clark called two more regiments, under the command of Cols. John Floyd and Benjamin Logan, to the Point to participate in another campaign, in revenge for the Battle of Blue Licks. Simon Kenton led a contingent and William B. Allen, in *A History of Kentucky* (1872), claimed that Daniel Boone also took part in this campaign. The regiment's attack wiped out five Indian towns along the Miami and Scioto rivers. Gen. Charles Scott and his troops returned to Kentucky through the Point after completing their campaign against the Eel Indians in 1792. Gov. Isaac Shelby (1812-16) assembled 4,000 Kentucky volunteers there in 1813. After joining Gen. William Henry Harrison in the northwest, the party went on to defeat the British at the Battle of the Thames.

The present-day city of Covington was established on this military vantage point.

See Charles B. Eilerman, *Historic Covington* (Covington, Ky., 1973).

POPE, JOHN. One of Kentucky's earliest nationally prominent leaders, John Pope, congressman and senator, was born in Prince William County, Virginia, in 1770 to William and Penelope (Edwards) Pope. Pope moved to Kentucky with his family in 1779, was educated at James Priestly's school at Bardstown, and later read law with George Nicholas in Lexington. His political career began in 1800 in Kentucky's electoral college, where he voted for Thomas Jefferson. Two years later, Pope was elected to the Kentucky legislature. In 1807 he was elected as a Democratic Republican to the U.S. Senate (March 4, 1807, to March 3, 1813) and in 1810 was selected president pro tempore. Pope's vote against the War of 1812 hurt him politically, both nationally and at home, and he did not seek reelection in 1813.

Pope served as secretary of state during 1816-19 and in the Kentucky Senate during 1825-29. Pope supported John Quincy Adams, his brother-in-law, for president in 1824 over fellow-Kentuckian Henry Clay. Four years later, he supported Andrew Jackson, who named Pope territorial governor of Arkansas in 1829, a post he held for six years. After a falling-out with Jackson, Pope returned to Kentucky and aligned himself with the Whig party, winning election to the U.S. House of Representatives three times (March 4, 1837, to March 3, 1843). Twice a widower, Pope was married to Anne Christian, Elizabeth Johnson, and Frances Walton. Defeated for reelection, Pope retired to his home in Springfield, where he died on July 12, 1845. He was buried in the Springfield Cemetery.

See Orval W. Baylor, *John Pope, Kentuckian: His Life and Times, 1770-1845* (Cynthiana, Ky., 1943); Orval W. Baylor, "The Life and Times of John Pope, 1770-1845," *FCHQ* 15 (April 1941): 59-77.   TODD ESTES

POPULATION OF KENTUCKY. At the time of the first U.S. Census in 1790, 74,000 people lived in the area that would in 1792 become the state of Kentucky. In the two centuries since then, Kentucky's population has grown in every decade, increasing almost fifty-fold to 3,685,296 at the time of the 1990 census.

In terms of interstate migration, Kentucky has more often been a place of origin than a place of destination. In the century after the Civil War (1870-1970), approximately 1.7 million more people left the state than moved into it. Out-migration peaked in the 1940s and 1950s, when there was a net population loss of more than 700,000. The pattern reversed during the 1970s, when those moving into Kentucky exceeded out-migrants by more than 200,000. The trend was short-lived, however, as out-migrants during 1980-90 exceeded the number of in-migrants by an estimated 179,000.

In the 1980-90 period, Kentucky had 555,000 births and 351,000 deaths. This gain in population, combined with the net migration loss, gave Kentucky an increase of about 25,000 people after the 1990 census. In other words, Kentucky's population has grown because the number of births to residents has been large enough to compensate not only for out-migration, but also for the population loss due to deaths.

In spite of having many more births than deaths in recent years, Kentucky had a birth rate in 1989 of only 14.3 per 1,000 population, one of the lowest in the United States, where the national rate is 16.2 per 1,000 population. Kentucky's death rate, 9.4 per 1,000 population, is higher than the national average of 8.7. The mortality rate of infants (under one year of age) is 9.1 deaths per 1,000 births, lower than the national rate of 9.7. In the decade of the 1980s, growth was under 1 percent, compared with the national rate of growth of just under 10 percent.

Life expectancy in Kentucky is, on average, about 73 years, just below the U.S. average of 74 years. Women in Kentucky live an average of eight more years than men; life expectancy for the former is 77 years, for the latter, 69 years.

The 1990 U.S. Census enumerated slightly more females than males in the state, for a sex ratio of 94 males per 100 females. The median age of the state's population was 33.0 in 1990. At that time, about 26 percent of Kentucky's population was under 18 years of age; about 61 percent was between the ages of 15 and 64; and 13 percent was age 65 and over. In 1990 Rowan County, home of Morehead State University, had the state's youngest median population: 26 years. Christian County, home to Fort Campbell, and both Hardin County and Meade County, home to Fort Knox, were next, at 28 years. The counties with the oldest median ages tend to be rural counties with small total populations, most of them located in the far western part of the state: Trigg (median age 40 years); Hickman (39); and Ballard, Caldwell, Carlisle, Lyon, and Marshall (all at 38).

A small majority of Kentucky's population lives in urban areas (communities of more than 2,500); nationally, three-fourths of the population is urban. Until the late 1960s, a majority of Kentuckians lived in rural areas. In general, the urban proportion has been steadily increasing since the late 1700s, when all of the state's population was classified as rural.

Kentucky is the location of all or part of seven metropolitan areas:

1) Cincinnati, Ohio, which extends into Kentucky and Indiana (including Boone, Campbell, and Kenton counties in Kentucky).

2) Clarksville-Hopkinsville, Tennessee-Kentucky (Christian County).

3) Evansville, Indiana-Kentucky (Henderson County).

4) Huntington-Ashland, West Virginia-Kentucky-Ohio (Boyd, Carter, and Greenup counties).

5) Lexington-Fayette, Kentucky (Bourbon, Clark, Fayette, Jessamine, Scott, and Woodford counties).

6) Louisville, Kentucky-Indiana (Bullitt, Jefferson, Oldham, and Shelby counties).

7) Owensboro, Kentucky (Daviess County).

The four counties that comprise the Kentucky portion of the Louisville metropolitan area contain 770,591 people, just under 45 percent of the entire metropolitan population in the state and about one-fifth of the total state population. Overall, 47 percent of Kentucky's population lives in metropolitan areas, compared with 77 percent nationally.

Louisville has the largest population among cities in Kentucky, 269,063 in 1990. Lexington was second largest, with 225,366. Only one other city in the state, Owensboro, has as many as 50,000 residents (53,549). The counties with the largest populations are Jefferson (estimated at 664,937 in 1990), Fayette (225,366), and Kenton (142,031). The least-populated county, Robertson, had 2,124 residents in 1988. No other county had fewer than 5,000 population.

The proportion of Kentucky's population that was born in another state is about 20 percent, one of the lowest proportions in the nation. Less than 1 percent of the state's population was born in another country, with the largest proportions of the foreign-born coming from Germany (18 percent), the United Kingdom (7 percent), and Canada (6 percent).

Kentucky's population is predominantly white; more than 92 percent so report their race. Most of the remainder are black (7 percent). Of the 1 percent belonging to other races, there are at least 1,000 inhabitants in each of the categories of American Indian, Asian Indian, Chinese, Filipino, Korean, Japanese, and Vietnamese. Persons of Spanish origin (of any race) make up less than 1 percent of the state's population. Kentucky's white population traces its ancestry largely to northern and western Europe, the region that dominated settlement of the United States in the colonial period and the first century of independence. Almost 1 million Kentuckians list English as their sole ancestry; 245,000 list only German; 230,000, only Irish. Several hundred thousand others list multiple ancestry groups, including English, German, Irish, and Scottish. That immigrants to the United States since the Civil War have bypassed Kentucky is highlighted by the small number of state residents who trace their ancestry to southern and Eastern Europe, areas that dominated nationally as the origin for immigrants in the four decades before World War I. Only 14,000 Kentuckians list Italian as their sole ancestry group, and only 7,000 list Polish as their sole ancestry group.

Kentucky's households averaged 2.82 people in 1980. By 1988, this average had declined to 2.60, almost identical to the national figure of 2.63. Given Kentucky's long history of almost uninterrupted net out-migration, as well as a relatively low birth rate, slow growth seems the most likely prospect for the near future. If the state's population continues to grow at the rate of less than 1 percent in the next decade, by the year 2000 Kentucky will have about 3,710,000 inhabitants.

JOHN P. MARCUM

POPULIST PARTY. The Populist, or People's, party, founded in Cincinnati in 1891, drew its support and its platform largely from the FARMERS' ALLIANCE. Emerging from agrarian economic discontent, the third-party movement ran candidates on national and local ballots between 1891 and 1896. The party backed direct election of U.S. senators, government regulation of railroads, and free coinage of silver at a ratio of sixteen to one with gold.

The Kentucky Farmers' Alliance had supported independent candidates in 1890; the first official Populist ticket was nominated at Covington in 1891. S. Brewer Erwin, former president of the Alliance, headed a slate of nominees for state office, and the party ran more than twenty legislative candidates. Only a handful of them were elected and Erwin's showing in the governor's race was disappointing. Since the national leadership had hoped this election would prove that southern members of the Alliance would be willing to desert the Democratic party, the results were disheartening to Populists everywhere. Populist support was limited largely to the dark-tobacco belt of western Kentucky. Efforts to increase support by cooperation with the Republicans only hurt the cause, and eventually the Democratic party adopted the most popular Populist demands. The new party faded away, but the Populist revolt in Kentucky left its mark by fostering some pro-farmer reform and a more representative nominating procedure within the Democratic party.

See Gaye Keller Bland, "Populism in Kentucky, 1887-1896," Ph.D. diss., University of Kentucky, 1979. GAYE KELLER BLAND

PORTER, JAMES D. James D. Porter, "the Kentucky Giant," was born in Portsmouth, Ohio, in 1810, the son of Sarah Porter. The next year they moved to Shippingport, Kentucky. As a child, Porter was described as undersized, and he in fact trained to be a jockey. Those plans ended around Porter's seventeenth birthday, when his amazing growth began. Porter claimed that neighbors came to his house nightly to measure him, and said he had usually grown detectably in just twenty-four hours. By the time he was twenty-one, Porter stood six feet, nine inches tall. Over the next nine years, he grew a foot taller and was said to be the tallest man in the world at the time, earning the nickname of Kentucky Giant.

Porter opened a tavern near the Portland Canal locks in 1836, which attracted travelers from Cincinnati, New Orleans, and Pittsburgh. He spent a year traveling across the country, performing with two dwarfs (as Lilliputians) in a play based on *Gulliver's Travels*. Charles Dickens, during his brief stay in Louisville in 1842, visited Porter in his tavern, and referred to the giant as a "lighthouse among lamp posts" in *American Notes* (1842). The description impressed P.T. Barnum, who asked Porter to join his famous circus, an offer that Porter turned down.

In 1848 Porter used the earnings from his tavern to build a bigger one on Front Street in Shippingport. Jim Porter's Tavern became famous around the state and along the Ohio. The business began to falter, however, as rail transport cut into river traffic. Porter, never in good health, died of a heart attack on April 24, 1859. He was buried in Cave Hill Cemetery in Louisville. No undertaker stocked coffins big enough, so a nine-foot-long coffin was custom-made. Among Porter's personal effects that were preserved are his custom-made, ninety-five-inch-long shotgun, and a bedroom slipper fourteen inches long and five inches wide.

PORTER, JOHN WILLIAM. John William Porter, Baptist minister, was born August 8, 1863, in Fayette County, Tennessee, the son of John and Martha (Tharp) Porter. He received an LL.B. from Cumberland University in 1882, a Th.G. from South-

ern Baptist Theological Seminary (Louisville) in 1893, and two honorary doctorates. From 1908 to 1922 he was pastor of Lexington's First Baptist Church, then moved to Lexington's Immanual Baptist Church, where he was pastor from 1924 until his death. Between 1909 and 1921 he edited the Baptist *Western Recorder*. Porter is known for promoting state legislation to prohibit the teaching of Darwinian evolution in the public schools. His books included *The Menace of Evolution* (1921), *Dangers of the Dance* (1922), and *Feminism* (1923). He married Lillian E. Thomas on July 19, 1892. They had five children: Martha Frances, Mary, Blanche Elizabeth, John William, and Russell Thomas. Porter died in Lexington on September 7, 1937, and was buried in the Lexington Cemetery.

See Frank L. McVey, *The Gates Open Slowly: A History of Education in Kentucky* (Lexington, Ky., 1949). DOUGLAS E. HERMAN

PORTLAND. Now a neighborhood of Louisville, two miles west of center along the Ohio River, Portland developed in the early nineteenth century along with Louisville and Shippingport to the east. Gen. William Lytle of Cincinnati, surveyor general of the Northwest Territory, sent his agent, Joshua G. Barclay, and a surveyor, Alexander Ralston, to lay out the town of Portland in 1811 on part of 3,000 acres of land Lytle had bought from Henry Clay and Fortunatus Cosby. The first commercial buildings in the town were built in 1812 and soon included a wharf and a seven-story warehouse at the river's edge. Capt. Henry M. Shreve bought one of the five-acre lots, called country seats, and took over Lytle's ferry from Portland to New Albany, Indiana.

In 1817 Lytle sold lots in an "enlargement," as mapmakers referred to the expansion, extending the boundaries of Portland to Thirteenth Street on the east and Fortieth Street on the west, a division that still defines the town. Lytle expected to use the proceeds to further his ambitious dream of building a canal to take river traffic around the Falls of the Ohio, but economic conditions in 1819 forced him to abandon his plans, selling out to Judge John Rowan of Bardstown and the Bank of the United States. Starting in 1820, Portland real estate was divided into smaller and smaller lots, making it possible for working-class families to buy homesites.

Many early settlers came to Portland from France after the fall of Napoleon in 1815. Charles Maquaire arrived in Shippingport and later moved to Portland, where he and Paul Villier established the St. Charles Hotel. Father Stephen T. Badin, the first Roman Catholic priest ordained in America, often stayed at the Maquaire home and celebrated mass there. Portland's most famous personality, Jim Porter, moved to the town from Shippingport, like Maquaire and others. Porter, known as the Kentucky Giant, ran coffeehouses in both locations and later served as Portland's councilman. Squire Jacob Earick was the town's first magistrate.

In 1834 the Kentucky legislature chartered Portland. Lexington businessmen, eager for access to a river port below the Falls of the Ohio, planned to lay track for the Lexington & Ohio (L&O) Railroad from Lexington to Portland's wharf. The financially strapped L&O arranged for financing from Louisvillians to cross the Kentucky River at Frankfort. Louisville Mayor Frederick A. Kaye, however, wanted the railroad to terminate at the Louisville wharf and threatened to block the deal. In a compromise, Louisville annexed Portland on February 23, 1837, and Portland was promised the railroad terminus. Track was laid between Louisville and Portland but was never linked to the Bluegrass. In 1842, angered when Louisville businessmen reneged on the deal, Portlanders demanded and won independence. Ten years later, however, the citizens voted to become part of Louisville once again.

Landmarks include Cedar Grove Academy, founded in 1842 by the Sisters of Loretto as a finishing school for young women, and the U.S. Marine Hospital, opened in 1852. The hospital was designed in the office of federal architect Robert Mills. The 1937 flood drove many families from the Portland neighborhood, and construction of a floodwall, which displaced more than 140 homes in the 1960s, and later the I-64 interstate highway pushed Portland away from the riverbanks. In 1967 Portland lost its political identity when it was divided into three aldermanic wards. Nevertheless, Portland retains much of its nineteenth century river town heritage.

See Judy Munro-Leighton, et al., *Changes at the Falls: Witnesses and Workers* (Louisville 1982).

NATHALIE TAFT ANDREWS

POTTENGER'S STATION. Capt. Samuel Pottenger of Prince Georges County, Maryland, established a station in 1781, about a half a mile north of the present Gethsemani (Nelson County) post office and half a mile south of Gethsemani Abbey. Pottenger, born April 29, 1754, to Robert and Elizabeth (Willett) Pottenger, first visited Kentucky in 1776. He served as a Revolutionary War soldier in Maryland in 1777, with James Harrod in 1778, and with William Harrod in 1780. Numerous families settled with Pottenger at his station before moving to their own land nearby. Among the settlers were Samuel Pottenger's siblings (Elizabeth, Jemima, Susannah, William, Robert, John, Dennis, Anne, and Eunice) and their uncle Samuel Pottenger with his wife and their children. A contingent of Pennsylvanians representing the Masterson family added to the station's population. Charles, John, John, Jr., Thomas, William, William, Jr., Hugh, Hugh, Jr., Jerry, and Zachariah Masterson as well as their wives and children (whose names are not compiled) lived at Pottenger's Station.

During the winter of 1782-83, the station's population swelled to include thirty-seven people from Samuel Cartwright's station, eighteen miles east. Captain Pottenger and his company had joined Gen. George Rogers Clark in the fall of 1782 to invade Indian territory in the Upper Miami River drainage in retaliation for Indian raids into Kentucky earlier that year. Upon their return, they discovered that the settlers at Cartwright's Station were starving and took them to Pottenger's Station. As the country settled and the Indian threat abated, the families of Pottenger's Station moved to their own lands, and many eventually resettled in the Great Miami Valley in Butler and Preble counties, Ohio. Captain Pottenger built a house in 1788 about two miles east of his station, where he died on January 20, 1831. He was buried in the Cox Creek Baptist Cemetery.

See Sarah B. Smith, *Historic Nelson County, Its Towns and People* (Bardstown, Ky., 1983).

NANCY O'MALLEY

POTTER COLLEGE. Potter College in Bowling Green, Kentucky, was a private, nondenominational women's college incorporated by the General Assembly on May 12, 1890. The Rev. B.F. Cabell, its first president, and Pleasant J. Potter, a local banker, raised $21,160 for the construction of a three-story building to provide living and academic facilities. Located on Vinegar Hill, the college opened on September 9, 1889, with eleven faculty members and approximately two hundred students. The curriculum was a mixture of commercial classes and liberal arts courses. During the 1890s the college enjoyed moderate success, although enrollment never rose much above its initial number. The college closed in 1909 as a result of the growth of public education and the ill health of President Cabell. Over the protest of local residents, the property and buildings were sold to the Western Kentucky State Normal School (now Western Kentucky University).

See Lowell H. Harrison, *Western Kentucky University* (Lexington, Ky., 1987).

POWELL, LAZARUS WHITEHEAD. Lazarus Whitehead Powell, Kentucky's governor during 1851-55, was born in Henderson County, on October 6, 1812, to Lazarus and Ann (McMahon) Powell. After graduating from St. Joseph's College in Bardstown, he studied law with John Rowan and at Transylvania University and was admitted to the bar in 1835. He married Harriet Ann Jennings in 1837, and they had three sons before her death in 1846.

A Democrat in a Whig stronghold, Powell won election to the Kentucky House in 1836. He was defeated for reelection in 1838, and in 1848 lost a bid for the governorship to John J. Crittenden, 65,860 to 57,397. Whig strength was on the wane, and in 1851 Powell became governor by defeating his close friend and former law partner Archibald Dixon, 54,613 to 53,763. In that election emancipationist Cassius M. Clay received only 3,621 votes. Powell served from September 2, 1851, until September 4, 1855.

Powell was elected to the U.S. Senate in 1858 and President James Buchanan appointed him to the two-man commission that was to settle the troublesome Mormon question. Powell favored Kentucky's neutrality in 1861, and he opposed many acts of the Lincoln administration. The General Assembly demanded his resignation, and some of his colleagues tried to expel him from the Senate. He completed his term on March 3, 1865, then resumed his legal practice in Henderson. Garrett Davis defeated him in the Senate race in 1867. Powell died on July 3, 1867, and was buried at Henderson. Powell County was named in his honor.

Governor Powell encouraged private investments for internal improvements, and he persuaded the Whig majority in the legislature to undertake a comprehensive geological survey that he believed would stimulate economic development. He vetoed several bills that he thought would create an overabundance of banks. Despite his veto, the Whigs were able to gerrymander congressional districts to give their party control of the state delegation. Firmly committed to the need for a better public school system, Powell supported the reforms of Superintendent of Public Instruction Robert J. Breckinridge, which included an increase in the school tax from two to five cents per $100 of taxable property. Kentucky and North Carolina had the best public schools among the slave states before the Civil War. Powell suffered from severe rheumatism, but he did not allow it to interfere with the discharge of his duties.

See John E. Wright, "Robert Peter and the First Kentucky Geological Survey," *Register* 52 (July 1954): 201-13.   LOWELL H. HARRISON

POWELL COUNTY. The 101st county in order of formation, Powell County is located in eastern Kentucky and is bordered by Lee, Menifee, and Wolfe counties; it has an area of 180 square miles. The county was formed on January 7, 1852, out of portions of Clark, Estill, and Montgomery counties. It was named in honor of Gov. Lazarus Whitehead Powell (1851-55). STANTON is the county seat.

With rich, fertile bottomlands giving way to steep mountainous terrain, the topography of Powell County is quite varied. The eastern and southern sections of the county are covered by the Daniel Boone National Forest, with its vast stands of hardwoods. This section of the county, which also includes Natural Bridge State Resort Park and the Red River Gorge, is the heart of the natural bridge region of the state. Within the park and gorge region are numerous natural stone arches, or bridges, as well as sandstone-capped ridges, steep valley walls, and rocky pinnacles. In contrast, the western portion contains the county's principal flatlands. It is here that the majority of the county's farms, which in 1987 made up about 35 percent of the land, are located. Hay, corn (for grain and seed), and tobacco, as well as hogs and cattle, are raised on these farms.

Before white settlement, Powell County was a prime hunting ground for both the Shawnee and Cherokee because of its abundance of wildlife. Agricultural potential also drew Indians to settle in this area. One of the last Indian villages in Kentucky was located in the northeastern section of the county. In 1769, Daniel Boone and John F. Finley were among the earliest pioneers to explore the Powell County region. Camping at Oil Springs, Boone climbed nearby Pilot Knob (the highest point in Powell County) and viewed the great expanse of Kentucky.

During the early years of the nineteenth century, the county was the scene of early Kentucky iron works. In 1786 iron pyrite was discovered near the present town of Clay City; shortly thereafter, one of the first forges west of the Alleghenies was built there. By 1805, a furnace was established on the site. Borrowing its name from the nearby Red River, the iron furnace operation soon became known as the Red River Iron Works. Producing domestic items such as pots and nails, as well as cannonballs used in the War of 1812, the Red River Iron Works manufactured items of superior quality. The logging industry was also significant to the development of Powell County in the 1800s, when Red River turned many lumber mills.

Powell County, especially Stanton, received its share of hardships during the Civil War. Most of the depredations came at the hands of Confederate guerrilla forces. In the spring of 1863, Stanton was raided by a guerrilla force that burned the courthouse. About a year later, on June 1, 1864, the county seat was invaded for a second time and the jail was destroyed.

Powell County rebounded quickly from the adverse effects of the war. Though by 1870 the lumber industry was operating on a large scale, the Kentucky Union Railway (in 1894 the Lexington & Eastern), which came to the county in 1886, brought even greater trading opportunities. By 1889, one of the largest sawmills in the county was operating at Clay City. Tourism also gained importance at this time. The Louisville & Nashville Railroad (L&N; now CSX Transportation) bought the land that is now Natural Bridge State Park, built a hotel, and after buying out the Lexington & Eastern line in 1909, began to offer excursions to the natural wonder. When the Great Depression hit, the county's economic progress ground to a halt. As the timber industry declined, the railroads were abandoned. In 1941, the L&N disassembled its road, ending all railroad activity in the county.

In the 1960s, Powell County witnessed a resurgence. With the construction of the four-lane Mountain Parkway under the administration of Gov. Bert Combs (1959-63), the county recouped some of the losses it had suffered when the railroad left. The easier access provided by the highway also revived logging. Controversy as well as prosperity surfaced during this period. Following the 1962 flood of Clay City by the Red River, many Powell Countians advocated the construction of a dam to guard against floods, attract industry, and make a large recreational lake. Opponents of the project contended that damming the river and filling the gorge would destroy the delicate ecosystem of the area. After a legal battle that lasted well into the 1970s, the dam proposal was defeated.

In the late twentieth century, Powell County has developed along three lines—agricultural, industrial, and residential. Agriculture remains important, and industry has grown around Clay City and Stanton. Metal fabrication and uniform shirt manufacturing were the largest industries in 1990. Most significant, however, was the development of the county as a residential community. In 1987 46 percent of the labor force worked outside Powell County, in communities such as Winchester and Lexington.

The population of Powell County was 7,704 in 1970; 11,101 in 1980; and 11,686 in 1990.

RON D. BRYANT

POWERS, CALEB. Born February 1, 1869, in Whitley County, political leader Caleb Powers was the son of Amos Powers, a farmer, and Elizabeth (Perkins) Powers. He was educated in local Knox County schools, then Union College, the Agricultural and Mechanical College (now the University of Kentucky), and the U.S. Military Academy. Leaving West Point because of eyesight problems, according to his fine autobiography, *My Own Story*, Powers taught for a time, then graduated in 1894 from the law department of Northern Indiana Normal School at Valparaiso. He took a postgraduate course in law at Centre College in Danville.

Powers was elected school superintendent of Knox County as a Republican in 1893, was admitted to the bar the next year, and was reelected superintendent in 1897. His educational reforms helped bring him, at age thirty, his party's nomination and subsequent victory in 1899 as Kentucky secretary of state. The entire election was contested, however, and Powers brought in a "mountain army" to support his cause. At the end of January 1900, in the midst of the General Assembly's deliberations over the election of Republican William Sylvester Taylor as governor, Democratic gubernatorial candidate William GOEBEL was shot. Goebel, certified by the legislature as the winner of the election, died only days later. The assassin's shot was said to have been fired from Powers's office. Powers, who had been in another county at the time of the shooting, was arrested and indicted as an accessory to the murder. In a series of trials marked by partisan judicial rulings, packed juries, and some perjured testimony, he was convicted three times. In each case, however, the state's highest court reversed the decision. A fourth trial, which concluded in January 1908, ended in a deadlocked jury; six months later the Republican governor, Augustus Willson, pardoned Powers. After spending eight years in jail, Powers then spent as many in Congress, serving from March 4, 1911, to March 3, 1919. Declining renomination, he became assistant counsel for the U.S. Shipping Board in 1921.

In January 1896, Powers married Kentuckian Laura Rawlings; six months later she died of spinal meningitis. Powers died July 25, 1932, and was buried in Barbourville, Kentucky. He was survived by his second wife, Dorothy.

See Caleb Powers, *My Own Story* (Indianapolis 1905); James C. Klotter, *William Goebel: The Politics of Wrath* (Lexington, Ky., 1977).

JAMES C. KLOTTER

POWERS,   GEORGIA   (MONTGOMERY) DAVIS. Georgia (Montgomery) Davis Powers, civil rights leader and state senator, was born October 29, 1923, in Springfield, Washington County, Kentucky. She was the only daughter of the nine children of Ben and Frances (Walker) Montgomery. In Louisville she attended Virginia Avenue Elementary School (1929-34), Madison Junior High School (1934-37), Central High School (1937-40), and Louisville Municipal College (1940-42).

From 1962 to 1967 Powers (as she has been known since her second marriage) served as campaign chairperson for candidates running for a variety of offices, including mayor of Louisville, governor of Kentucky, and the U.S. Congress. She was Kentucky chairperson for the Jesse L. Jackson presidential campaigns in 1984 and 1988, and the first black woman to serve on the Jefferson County Democratic executive committee, beginning in 1964. Powers was one of the organizers of the Allied Organization for Civil Rights, which worked for passage of the statewide Public Accommodations and Fair Employment Law in 1964.

Powers was the first woman and the first black to be elected to the Kentucky Senate, serving from January 1968 to January 1989 as a Democrat. As senator, she chaired two legislative committees: Health and Welfare (1970-76) and Labor and Industry (1978-88). Powers was also a member of the Cities Committee, Elections and Constitutional Amendments Committee, and Rules Committee, as well as secretary of the Democratic caucus (1968-88). Throughout her Senate tenure, Powers championed blacks, women, children, the poor, and the handicapped. She sponsored or cosponsored an open housing law; a low-cost housing bill; a law to eliminate the identification of race from Kentucky operator's licenses; an amendment to the Kentucky Civil Rights Act to eliminate discrimination based on race, gender, or age; an equal opportunity law; the Equal Rights Amendment resolution; Displaced Homemaker's Law; and a law to increase the minimum wage in Kentucky.

Powers served on the University of Louisville board of overseers, the board of directors of the Kentucky Indiana Planning and Development Agency (KIPDA), and the governor's Desegregation of Higher Education Implementation Committee. In 1981 she helped lead the efforts to retain Kentucky State University as a four-year institution of higher learning, and in 1982-83 was a leader in the successful opposition in a referendum to merge Louisville and Jefferson County. In 1989 Powers received an honorary doctor of laws degree from the University of Kentucky and an honorary doctorate of humane letters from the University of Louisville.

Powers was married to Norman F. Davis from 1943 to 1968; they have one son. She married James L. Powers in 1973.

PREHISTORIC PEOPLES. Kentucky ARCHAE-OLOGY embraces the material remains of at least 12,000 years of human occupation: the sites of domestic camps and dwellings, earthworks, burial mounds and cemeteries, and the artifacts and other materials associated with them. Archaeologists divide Kentucky's past into five periods: Paleo-Indian (ca. 10,500 B.C. to 8000 B.C.), Archaic (8000 B.C. to 1000 B.C.), Woodland (1000 B.C. to A.D. 1000) Late Prehistoric (A.D. 1000 to A.D. 1750), and Historic (post–A.D. 1750). The first four periods, all prehistoric, are marked by evolutionary continuity during the growth and adaptation of Native American populations to the state. This development ended with the coming of Old World settlers from the Atlantic seaboard. After about 1750, Kentucky archaeology reflects events and patterns of growth characteristic of developing America.

The Paleo-Indian is the time of the earliest known human occupation, during the end of the Pleistocene and the earliest Holocene. Humans were never in contact with a retreating glacier in Kentucky but lived in an environment that was ameliorating toward the modern climate with the onset of the Holocene. A characteristic forest developed rapidly, supporting abundant wildlife. The Paleo-Indian first became a hunter and gatherer in these forests. The best indicators of Paleo-Indian peoples are their chert or flint tools, particularly large, beautiful spear tips used for hunting large mammals. At various locations in Kentucky, such as the present-day Big Bone Lick State Park, extinct Pleistocene animals, mastodon, and buffalo, and the more prosaic animals of the post-Pleistocene, gathered in great numbers to lick salt. Humans came to hunt them, and they were a mainstay of human diet.

During the 7,000 years of the Archaic period, humans became established throughout the state, adapting to its varied landscape. Population growth was gradual but the changes in human culture were dramatic. In the Archaic occurred the first settlement pattern, in which the native people moved around in the forest, living from its resources. In isolated areas of the Cumberland Plateau, for example, are found chipping stations where chert was mined from exposed geological strata and made into tools. In other upland areas with dominant oak-hickory forest are gathering stations where nut crops were harvested, and hunting camps that were used in the autumn when deer were attracted by acorn mast.

During the Archaic period, trees, other plants, animals, and humans were closely interrelated. Life could hardly have been easy, and no one stayed alive in Archaic Kentucky by standing still. A lifestyle was established that left its stamp on later Native American life. Agriculture began during the Archaic period. Viewed over a thousand years, these first attempts look less like purposeful experiments than trends of change in the elemental relationship between humans and nature. By 2000 B.C., a primitive species of squash may have been cultivated; it may have been a plant native to the Midwest, or one imported from elsewhere. Even after the much later introduction of corn agriculture, prehistoric peoples in Kentucky looked first to environmental resources, an economic reserve that could be tapped no matter how crowded the land became or how badly the crops fared.

One of the best known Kentucky Archaic sites is Indian Knoll, on the Green River in Ohio County. Excavation reveals an intensively occupied Archaic base camp. People gathered seasonally, repeatedly returning to this river bank. Deer were hunted, but most noticeable among the refuse are quantities of freshwater mussel shells. The dead were buried within the camp, tightly flexed in round graves. With them were placed their domestic tools, spears, distinctive spear throwers called *atlatls*, tools for the preparation of game and fiber, and ornaments of Gulf Coast marine shell and Great Lakes hammered copper. Life was hard but neither isolated nor devoid of artistic embellishment. Marking the earliest occurrence of a pattern that survives among the Iroquois, dogs were specially regarded and were buried either by themselves or in the graves of their masters.

At the eastern end of the state in Rowan County, a site called Bluestone, reoccupied several times, was home to a much smaller group. Bluestone is the remains of a number of pits for heating and cooking, a type of site that is widespread in the Knobs and on the Cumberland Plateau. At Bluestone, shellfish were not important but game was. Small camps were the rule, with frequent movement between them as the people sought seasonal resources. Perhaps in this rugged area large groups could not congregate for long in one spot because the natural resources were insufficient.

Characteristic of the Archaic period is the diversity of stone tools, which changed over a long time span and varied from group to group. Projectile points (inaccurately called arrowheads, for the bow and arrow did not appear until later) serve to distinguish different social groups or tribes.

During the Woodland period, the increase in cultural diversity can be measured not only in stone tools but in ceramics (appearing as early as ca. 600 B.C.), types of burial, earthworks, and settlements. The Woodland is best known from the culture called Adena, in the Ohio Valley above Louisville, in the Bluegrass, and in northeastern Kentucky. For their dead the Adena people built burial mounds, first appearing about 450 B.C., which grew in size and complexity. They also built earthworks enclosing ceremonial areas in which communal rituals were performed. They even explored caves seeking minerals for ritual purposes. The new emphasis on burial indicates a growing concern with mortuary ritual and the afterlife. It is probably not true, however, that mound burials were limited to high-status persons.

What we know of Adena economy suggests that hunting and gathering remained its basis. The food experimentation begun in the Archaic period continued and the people practiced horticulture. The burial mounds and earthworks represent the results of cooperation rather than labor directed by chiefs. These groups exchanged marriage partners and shared the ritual that accompanied the deaths of relatives. Into Adena graves with the dead went personal artifacts of animal bone, copper, mica, galena, and marine shell. The artifacts were made locally of materials obtained in long-distance trade, continuing an Archaic practice. Pottery, made locally, was first used in mortuary feasts. Stone tools were used for hunting and deer remained a principal food.

Other cultural groups in the Woodland period built few burial mounds and earthworks and are known by their pottery. The earliest is crude, in some areas imitating bowls carved from soapstone and sandstone, sometimes adopting technological innovations from elsewhere. Along the lower Cumberland River the earliest pottery may have been imported from southern Tennessee and northern Alabama. Shortly thereafter local styles developed; in western Kentucky we identify the Baumer culture by their distinctive ceramics.

The economy of Woodland peoples intensified the horticulture started in the Archaic. In addition to squash and gourd, native weed plants were also cultivated—marsh elder, sunflower, and chenopodium. The types of settlements built did not differ greatly from those of the Archaic period. Domestic sites may have been more ephemeral than earlier, suggesting that groups in the Woodland period were smaller than before, more dispersed, and—despite the fact that they built some mounds and earthworks—more on the move.

Throughout Kentucky the Late Prehistoric period marked dramatic changes in human life, perhaps linked to the widespread introduction of corn agriculture around A.D. 1000. The origin of corn is not certain, although the earliest examples seem to occur in Central and South America. However corn came to Kentucky, it rapidly made agriculture much more important, as dramatically reflected in human settlement. Houses became ubiquitous, indicating permanent occupation at chosen sites. They were grouped together into hamlets and villages, often fortified with a stockade. Local groups were larger and intervillage competition often led to warfare. In parts of Kentucky settlements began to differ, from small homesteads to stockaded towns with temple mounds, suggesting chiefdoms with leaders and subjects.

Agriculture made suitable land a critical commodity. The houses and villages of the Late Prehistoric, particularly in the great river valleys of western Kentucky—the Mississippi, Ohio, Cumberland, Tennessee, and Green—occurred near the most fertile bottoms, enriched by yearly floods. Stockades around larger settlements suggest competition for control of river bottoms. Temple mounds within the villages, distinctive houses, and elaborate grave offerings indicate differences in social status and wealth. Beans were added to corn, both originating in Meso-America, providing a diet in which domesticated plants were central for the first time. Game remained an important adjunct of Late Prehistoric diet, perhaps fortuitously increasing in importance as crop fields attracted raccoon, deer, and migratory waterfowl. The dual economic emphases are reflected for the first time in tools. Among Late Prehistoric tools are chert hoes for gardening and, finally appearing, an efficient bow and arrow tipped with a small triangular chert point.

Variability continued in the Late Prehistoric. With its large floodplains, western Kentucky became the focus of a culture called Mississippian. In eastern Kentucky quite a different agricultural adaptation developed, called Fort Ancient. Temple mounds and chiefs' houses occurred in Mississippian but were lacking in Fort Ancient. The structure of local power was different, probably reflecting the differing environments. Agriculture was important throughout, but varied in importance.

The origins of modern Native Americans lie in the Late Prehistoric. It is a feature of Kentucky prehistory, however, that the links between the Native American tribes and prehistory were disrupted during the last century of the Late Prehistoric. The disjunction resulted in part from the contact with the Old World invaders (post–ca. A.D. 1600), in part from the continued evolution of native cultures themselves.

The first indications of Old World contact lie in artifacts made of Old World materials: tools of metal, brass and iron, beads of glass, and French and English flints from flintlock muskets. They have been found in Fort Ancient sites in Greenup County and in Mississipian sites in Henderson and Daviess counties. Such sites are few, however. It is clear that massive contractions in local populations occurred before 1750. It is fairly certain that ancestors of the Shawnee inhabited northern Kentucky, perhaps as one of the varieties of Fort Ancient, and ancestors of the Cherokee inhabited the southeastern mountains, where they may be related to the Late Prehistoric Mississippian variant called Pisgah. The tribal identities of most archaeological groups, notably those of Mississippian culture in the West, are unknown.

What might have become of native cultural evolution in the state had European culture not arrived is a fascinating question. Certainly native cultures would have developed beyond the complexity and variety of the Late Prehistoric. The impermanence of Late Prehistoric settlements, which in part explains the lack of settlements encountered by the first European arrivals, would have been superseded. Certainly agriculture, with increasingly sophisticated varieties of corn, would have remained central, but 12,000 years of prehistory indicate that hunting, too, would have been important. Some suggest that native groups' ability to live off the land may have worked against the development of more permanent political forms. Faced with crop failure, or coercion, or a number of other factors, the native inhabitants could always escape to Kentucky woods and live as people lived long ago in the Archaic.

See Douglas W. Schwartz, *Conceptions of Kentucky Prehistory* (Lexington, Ky., 1967); Noel D. Justice, *Stone Age Spear and Arrow Points* (Bloomington, Ind., 1987). R. BERLE CLAY

PRENTICE, GEORGE DENNISON. George Dennison Prentice, one of Kentucky's best-known journalists, was born December 18, 1802, in a cottage near the village of Pachaug in New London County, Connecticut, the second of two sons of Rufus and Sarah (Stanton) Prentice. He was a precocious child who learned to read at age three and a half, and he had mastered both Latin and Greek at age fourteen. He graduated at the head of his class from Brown University in Rhode Island in 1823. Prentice began his journalistic career in Hartford, Connecticut, first as acting editor of the *Connecticut Mirror*, in 1827, and later as editor of the *New England Weekly*. Early in 1830 he traveled to Kentucky to write *The Biography of Henry Clay* and remained to become editor of the LOUISVILLE JOURNAL, founded to promote Clay's candidacy for the presidency.

Louisville was one of the most desirable locations in America for the establishment of a daily newspaper when the *Journal* was first distributed on November 24, 1830. But Prentice faced overt opposition from his Democratic rival, Shadrach Penn. Prentice's pen quickly prevailed because he was blessed with a vivid imagination, an exceptional memory, and a superb command of the English language, which he used to appeal to the taste of the westerner of his day. His talent for writing short paragraphs that sparkled with wit, humor, and sarcasm soon made the *Journal* a household word throughout the Ohio and Mississippi river valleys. During the next four decades it was the most widely circulated newspaper in western America. Prentice, who was widely acclaimed throughout the United States and in Europe as one of America's most brilliant editors, was also a poet. His best-known poem, "The Closing Year," composed on New Year's Eve 1836, was published in William McGuffey's *New Sixth Eclectic Reader*.

Prentice not only made the *Journal* a great newspaper of the Whig party, but he also soon became a party leader. He attended numerous party conventions and frequently visited the national capital and other cities in the East on behalf of the Whig party. In April 1855, following the demise of the Whig party, Prentice endorsed the Native American, or KNOW-NOTHING, party. Because he continued to print the same militant paragraphs he had used prior to every election for twenty-five years, Prentice was falsely accused of responsibility for Louisville's bloody election riots on Monday, August 6, 1855.

In 1860 Prentice favored the Constitutional Union party and its candidate, John Bell. Following the news of Abraham Lincoln's election, Prentice pleaded for the southern states to remain loyal to the Union, and once Lincoln called for troops, he urged Kentucky to remain neutral. Despite Prentice's strong Union sympathies, both of his sons joined the Confederate army.

On August 18, 1835, Prentice was married to Harriet Benham, daughter of attorney Joseph Benham; they had four children: Mary Louise and George Benham, both of whom died in infancy, and William Courtland and Clarence Joseph, who grew to manhood. Harriet (Benham) Prentice, a former student at Nazareth College in Bardstown, Kentucky, was an accomplished musician who served for twenty years as choir director of Louisville's Christ Church Episcopal. She died at age fifty on April 26, 1868. Prentice died on January 22, 1870, and was buried in Louisville's Cave Hill Cemetery.

See Betty Carolyn Congleton, "George D. Prentice: Nineteenth Century Southern Editor," *Register* 65 (April 1967): 94-119.

BETTY CAROLYN CONGLETON

PRESBYTERIAN CHURCH. James, George, and Robert MCAFEE, who brought a Presbyterian heritage with them when they settled in 1775 at McAfee Station, formed the New Providence Church in what is now Mercer County, Kentucky. They named it for what they saw as a work of providence in delivering them from a perilous time. Many of the Bluegrass settlers in the 1770s and early 1780s came from Presbyterian congregations in Virginia, North Carolina, and Pennsylvania, where distinctive, American Presbyterian tradition had arisen from a melding of British Puritanism and Scotch-Irish confessionalism. Dutch Calvinists, Welsh Reformed, and French Huguenots, as well as slaves and free African-Americans, contributed to the evolving Presbyterianism as the denomination moved into Kentucky.

Their heritage included heavy reliance on the reading of Scripture and expository preaching; belief in the sovereignty of God and human propensity for sin, as outlined in the *Westminister Standards*; and inclinations to separate institutions of church and state. Though some Presbyterians came to Kentucky with some wealth, most did not.

The first Presbyterian minister in Kentucky was Terah Templin. David RICE, who settled in Danville in 1783, organized the first formal congregations. During the next eighteen months, Rice with Templin and others helped found seven churches—Concord, in Danville; New Providence, at McAfee Station; Cane Run, at Trigg's Station; the Fork of Dick's (now Dix) River church; Paint Lick, on Jessamine Creek; Pisgah, in what is now Woodford County; and Mt. Zion, in Lexington, which called Adam Rankin as its minister.

Presbyterians, committed to universal literacy, started schools almost immediately. Several of the churches had academies soon after their founding, and Presbyterians in Virginia collaborated with western migrants to fund Transylvania University.

Presbyterian government featured shared leadership by ordained laypersons, or elders, meeting in sessions with their ministers. Sessions elected elder representatives to a presbytery, which also included all ministers serving in the area. In 1785 Kentucky Presbyterians formed the Transylvania Presbytery from the parent presbytery in Virginia. In 1799 the Transylvania Presbytery was divided into three presbyteries, which formed the Synod of Kentucky, the governing body within the commonwealth.

Although some division of the Presbyterians occurred with Adam Rankin's opposition to "Christian songs" in worship and with the discipline of some slaveowners for "un-Christian behavior" during the 1790s, real strife came with the GREAT REVIVAL. Presbyterians, remembering such occasions of religious celebration before their moves to the frontier, flocked to the revival sites, where they fell into semiconscious trances in response to the preaching of some ministers, notably at Cane Ridge in Bourbon County in 1801. Presbyterians on the frontier generally approved of the revival meetings, as did some of their ministers. Rice and others, however, led the Synod of Kentucky to discipline revival-oriented leaders for impropriety in worship and theology. Out of this conflict came the CUMBERLAND PRESBYTERIAN denomination.

A greatly reduced Presbyterian church struggled in antebellum Kentucky to accommodate Christianity and slavery, to foster new congregations, and to support educational enterprises. The controversy over slavery led to a national division of the Presbyterians during 1836-38. Almost all Kentucky Presbyterians remained with the Old School, more tolerant of slavery and more conservative theologically than the New School.

New congregations came with the growth of cities and the movement of Presbyterians into new regions. Frankfort's First Presbyterian started in 1816. In Lexington, where the Mt. Zion Church followed John Rankin into the Associate Reformed Presbyterian Church, Presbyterians virtually started over in 1790 with a congregation that became First Presbyterian. Louisville Presbyterians organized a Presbyterian society in 1816 that became the First Presbyterian Church, with the Second Presbyterian following in 1830.

Rural churches predominated in Kentucky Presbyterianism through the years before the Civil War. Bethesda Presbyterian Church became First Presbyterian, Ashland, when the city was laid out in 1854. First Presbyterian, Owensboro, began in 1844. Large congregations existed in rural areas of Jefferson County—Penns Run, Middletown—and elsewhere in the center of the state. In 1853 the Presbyterian minister Robert J. Breckinridge collaborated with John C. Young, the president of Centre College and the moderator of the Old School Assembly that year, to establish a theological seminary at Danville. Other Presbyterian schools appeared in the state. Sunday school, which became very popular among the churches in the 1820s, served both the children of the congregation and poor children in the vicinity.

The Civil War brought deep division among Presbyterians in the border state, with Breckinridge leading a pro-Union faction and Stuart Robinson heading a pro-Southern party. Robinson fled into exile, but upon his return in 1866 he led most Presbyterians into the Presbyterian Church, U.S. (PCUS), or the Southern Presbyterian denomination. Support from Kentucky Presbyterians helped greatly in rebuilding churches and social structures in the deeper South. When Old and New School denominations reunited in the Presbyterian Church, USA (PCUSA), the Northern denomination, they redoubled efforts to assist freed slaves in the deep South. Southern Presbyterians sought to compete with the PCUSA institutions of CENTRE COLLEGE and DANVILLE THEOLOGICAL SEMINARY by establishing CENTRAL UNIVERSITY in Richmond, Kentucky, in 1874, fed by a system of preparatory schools. Partially successful, they also opened a law department and began a medical school in Louisville. The LOUISVILLE PRESBYTERIAN SEMINARY was founded in 1893 as a part of their system.

Meanwhile Presbyterian interest in missions increased, and the synods of Kentucky sent missionaries into the rest of the state, especially into Appalachian regions. E.O. Guerrant, W.D. Morton, Joseph M. Evans, ruling elder "Uncle" Joe Hopper, and others held revivals and clinics and organized congregations in eastern and western Kentucky.

Presbyterian revivals also augmented membership in existing congregations. In 1888 Dwight L. Moody conducted a crusade in Louisville from a tabernacle built beside the Warren Memorial Presbyterian Church. Presbyterians and other Protestants flocked to the revival. For several years afterward, followup revivals took place in many churches, and the so-called special services became a fixture among Presbyterians until well into the twentieth century.

At the turn of the century, cooperative efforts replaced competition between the PCUS and PCUSA. In 1901 Central University merged with Centre College and Danville Seminary with Louisville Seminary, producing the first college and the first theological seminary jointly owned by the PCUSA and the PCUS. Several orphanages, community centers, and other service institutions were started, as well as congregations for Afro-American Presbyterians in Taylor County, Bowling Green, and Louisville. Presbyterians founded congregations and chapels for the poor, middle-class, and wealthy, with differing programs and missions.

Cumberland Presbyterian Church (CPC) congregations flourished, especially in western Kentucky. In 1904 majorities in both the PCUSA and CPC assemblies voted to merge. About half the Cumberland congregations in Kentucky held themselves apart from the merger. Cumberland Presbyterians in western Kentucky had ordained Louisa Woosley to the gospel ministry in 1889, probably the first

Presbyterian woman to serve as a regular pastor anywhere. Other CPC women were ordained to the ministry during 1910-1920, long before the practice was permitted in the PCUSA (1955) or the PCUS (1967).

Distinctive Presbyterian cultures became submerged in the general mainline Protestantism that evolved during the twentieth century. With the development of cooperative social ministeries, suburban congregations, ecumenical campus ministries, shared curricula in Sunday schools, and prevalent denominational switching, Kentucky Presbyterianism changed enormously in the 1970s and 1980s.

In 1983 the PCUSA and the PCUS merged to form the Presbyterian Church (USA), consolidating church offices. Kentucky Presbyterian leaders, especially elder David Jones of the Highland Presbyterian Church (Louisville), and John Mulder, president of the Louisville Presbyterian Seminary, in 1987 convinced the assembly to move its offices to Louisville.

See Ernest T. Thompson, *Presbyterians in the South* (Atlanta 1972); Louis Weeks, *Kentucky Presbyterians* (Atlanta 1983).   LOUIS WEEKS

PRESETTLEMENT VEGETATION.

The presettlement vegetation of Kentucky was complex and floristically diverse. Although deciduous hardwood forests covered more than 90 percent of the state, the barrens (prairies), wetlands (swamps), and evergreen communities created a vegetational mosaic on the landscape. The vegetational patterns were influenced by geologic substrate, soils, topography, and fire.

Mixed forests, growing under medium conditions of moisture, blanketed the rugged eastern Kentucky terrain with beech, yellow buckeye, white basswood, yellow poplar, and hemlock in coves; oaks and pines on ridges; and mixed hardwoods, especially white oak, on slopes. American chestnut flourished in the Knobs and in the Pennyroyal (Mississippi Plateau).

Open savanna-woodlands growth, dominated by blue ash and bur, chinquapin, and Shumard oaks, with an understory of cane and wild ryes, occupied the rolling Bluegrass uplands. Red cedar was confined mostly to limestone outcrops of the Kentucky River Gorge area. Mixed hardwood communities of sugar maple, northern red and chinquapin oaks, white and blue ashes, and American basswood sorted out on the steep slopes. Oak-hickory forests (white and northern red oaks, shagbark and pignut hickories) predominated in the Eden Shale belt.

The Knobs supported forests of chestnut, scarlet, black, and white oaks, especially on ridges and upper slopes. Lower slopes and coves supported mixed mesophytic communities.

Forests of the Pennyroyal were a blend of oaks (white, black, northern, red, and southern red), some hickory, yellow poplar, beech, and sugar maple. Diversity came from barrens (tall grass prairies of big and little bluestems and Indian grass); scattered herb-dominated cedar glades; and hemlock-mixed mesophytic associations of deep ravines.

Upland plant communities of the Western Coal Field were similar to those of the Mississippi Plateau. Southern bottomland hardwoods were quite prominent along streams and on floodplains.

Oaks (post, black, blackjack, white, and southern red) and various hickories characterized the Jackson Purchase, variegated by scattered to extensive barrens, swamps of bald cypress and tupelo, and bottomland hardwood forests along the major rivers and their tributaries.

See E.L. Braun, *Deciduous Forests of Eastern North America* (New York 1950).

    W.S. BRYANT

PRESTON, WILLIAM.

William Preston, politician and soldier, was born near Louisville on October 16, 1816, to Maj. William Preston, a Revolutionary War veteran who acquired choice land at the Falls of the Ohio, and Caroline (Hancock) Preston. He received a classical education in several preparatory schools of Kentucky and obtained a degree in literary studies from Yale College in 1835 and an LL.B. at Harvard in 1838. After establishing a successful law practice in Louisville, he launched a political career as a Whig.

Preston participated in the Mexican War (1846-48), achieving the rank of lieutenant colonel in the 4th Kentucky Volunteers. He was a delegate to the 1849 Kentucky constitutional convention and served in the Kentucky House in 1851 and the state Senate in 1852. In September 1852 he was elected to fill the vacant U.S. congressional seat of Democrat Humphrey Marshall. Preston advocated a proslavery position in the House, where he served until he was defeated by Marshall in the 1855 election. By 1856 he had switched allegiance to the Democratic party. He participated as a delegate to the 1856 Democratic convention, where he supported James Buchanan and successfully nominated fellow Kentuckian John C. Breckinridge for the vice-presidency. In late 1858 Preston received an appointment as U.S. minister to Spain. He successfully negotiated the long-standing Amistad claims with Spain, but the U.S. Senate on a sectional vote rejected it. He tried to purchase Cuba from Spain for $30 million and, using principles from the Monroe Doctrine, protested Spanish intervention in Santo Domingo.

Preston resigned the ambassadorship and joined the Confederate States of America, formed in February 1861. He rose to the rank of major general and engaged in numerous battles, including those at Fort Donelson, Nashville, Shiloh, Vicksburg, and Chickamauga. At Shiloh his brother-in-law, Gen. Albert Sidney Johnston, died in his arms. In January 1864 he was selected Confederate minister to Mexico. Frustrated by the lack of recognition from the Mexican government, Preston resigned and joined Gen. Edmund Kirby-Smith's Trans-Mississippi Department in Texas in December 1864, where he served until the war ended. At war's end he spent several months in exile in England and Canada before obtaining a federal pardon in 1866 and returning to Lexington.

Preston served a single term in the state legislature in 1868 and was a delegate to the 1880 Democratic convention. He devoted most of his time to overseeing the large estate he had inherited from his father-in-law.

In 1840 Preston married Lexingtonian Margaret Wickliffe, daughter of Robert Wickliffe, Kentucky's largest slaveholder. They had five daughters; Mary Owen, Caroline Hannah, Margaret, Susan C., and Jesse Freemont, and a son, Robert Wickliffe. Preston died in Lexington on September 21, 1887, and was buried in Louisville's Cave Hill Cemetery.

See J. Frederick Dorman, "General William Preston," *FCHQ* 43 (Oct.1969): 301-308; J. Frederick Dorman, *The Prestons of Smithfield and Greenfield in Virginia* (Louisville 1982).

CHARLES C. HAY III

PRESTONSBURG. Prestonsburg, the seat of Floyd County in eastern Kentucky, is situated on the floodplain of a broad meander of the Levisa Fork of the Big Sandy River. Located in the northern part of the county, the town is 120 miles southeast of Lexington at the junction of U.S. 23/460, KY 114, and the tracks of CSX Transportation. The area was part of a 100,000-acre grant from Virginia to Col. John Preston in 1787. It was first settled in 1791 by John Spurlock of Montgomery County, Virginia, and founded as a town site on May 3, 1797, with the name of Preston's Station. The town was surveyed by John Graham, under the direction of Maj. Andrew Hood, Mathias Harman, and Solomon Stratton, and was renamed Prestonsburg when it was established as the seat of Floyd County in 1799. It was incorporated on January 2, 1818.

Having been the seat of a county that originally covered all of the eastern portion of the state, Prestonsburg was for several decades the center of political activity in eastern Kentucky. The first courthouse, a log structure, was built in 1806 but burned in 1808. Another log structure served the county as a courthouse from 1808 until a brick building was completed in 1821. A fourth courthouse, also of brick, was finished in 1891 and was the seat of county government until it was demolished in 1963 and replaced with a modern structure in 1964.

In 1810 the town consisted of only six families: those of James Cumming, Thomas Evans, Christian Jost, Benjamin Morris, Martin Simms, and John Turman. Prestonsburg was slowly growing as a trading center on the Big Sandy River. One early entrepreneur was Solomon DeRosset, who established a fur-collecting headquarters at Prestonsburg and from there shipped skins and pelts via the river to eastern markets. Among the furs were bearskins that were favored by Napoleon's army for use as grenadiers' hats. Soon large shipments of beaver fur, corn, livestock, and tobacco moved out in small boats from the city; returning boats brought goods in from Catlettsburg on the Ohio River. The river was an important contact to the outside world because roads in the area remained poor until after 1865.

The presence of steamboats on the river in 1837 prompted the start of coal mining in the area. Coal was either used as steamboat fuel or carried to downstream markets. Logs were also floated down from Prestonsburg to the mouth of the Big Sandy River. Numerous investors and businessmen were attracted to Prestonsburg until the Civil War put a temporary halt to operations.

Coal mining and logging were renewed in earnest after the Civil War. Coal boats drifted in increasing numbers from Prestonsburg, down the Big Sandy to the Ohio River and beyond. The method of movement, however, was slow, costly, and hazardous. Not until 1903 did the Chesapeake & Ohio Railway (now CSX Transportation) enter Floyd County, and on November 15, 1904, the first passenger train came to Prestonsburg. The city was the center of a booming region from 1900 to 1920. Population between those years increased from 409 to 1,667.

By the 1930s, the price of coal had fallen, many local mines had shut down, most of the timber was gone, and the soil had worn out. World War II drew men to the armed forces and to northern industrial cities. In the 1950s, mechanization and suspended operations took a heavy toll on the number of employed miners.

Movements toward improvement began in the 1950s. Dewey Lake State Park, renamed Jenny Wiley State Resort Park, was established near Prestonsburg in 1954. Dr. George P. Archer III, a surgeon and three-time mayor, brought a thirty-member health team to Prestonsburg in 1954 in order to study the area's special health problems. The KY 114 extension of the Bert T. Combs Mountain Parkway was completed to the city in 1962, giving the city easier access to Lexington. In 1964 Prestonsburg opened a University of Kentucky community college.

The economy of the city is based on mining and quarrying operations, wholesale and retail trade, service operations, and state and local government jobs. Prestonsburg expresses an awareness of the region's historical heritage by hosting Floyd County Sesquicentennial Celebration and since 1982, a Jenny Wiley Festival. The population of the fourth-class city was 3,422 in 1970; 4,011 in 1980; and 3,558 in 1990.

TRISHA A. MORRIS

PRICE, SAMUEL WOODSON. Samuel Woodson Price, portrait artist, was born August 5, 1828, near Nicholasville, Kentucky, to Daniel Branch and Elizabeth (Crockett) Price. At an early age he began to draw in pencil and charcoal and had set up a studio in Brown's Hotel by the age of fourteen. He attended the Nicholasville Academy and in 1846 entered the Kentucky Military Institute near Frankfort, where he was soon teaching drawing. After studying under William Reading, a portrait painter from Louisville, and under Lexington's Oliver FRAZER, he left for New York City in the winter of 1848 to enroll in the School of Design, where he remained five months. By the spring of 1849, Price had reopened his painting studio in Lexington and at the request of A.L. Shotwell, a prominent Louisvillian, Price moved to that city in 1851. For the next several years, he traveled through Tennessee and other states painting portraits. In 1859 Price bought a house at 100 Constitution Street (now 233 East Second) in Lexington.

During the Civil War, Price led Federal troops. On February 26, 1862, Captain Price was made colonel of the 21st Infantry of the Kentucky Volunteers. He was wounded at the Battle of Kennesaw Mountain on June 27, 1864, and was then assigned as post commander of Lexington until the end of the war. On March 13, 1865, by a special act of Congress, the title brevet brigadier general was bestowed on Price for meritorious service. Following the war, Price went to Washington, D.C., to paint portraits, including those of Gens. George H. Thomas and William S. Rosecrans. On April 5, 1869, Price was appointed twelfth postmaster in Lexington, and he painted in a studio on the upper floor of the post office. He was removed as postmaster by President Ulysses S. Grant in April 1876.

In 1878, facing financial difficulties, Price moved to Louisville, where he lived on Breckinridge Street. The Louisville city directory of 1879 lists him as occupying a studio in the *Courier-Journal* office building. In 1880, as a result of his war wound and subsequent ill health, Price lost his sight in one eye, and a year later was completely blind. In 1882, Price dictated a history of the 21st Infantry, which was later published in Speed's *The Union Regiments of Kentucky* (1897). He wrote about Kentucky painters in *The Old Masters of the Bluegrass*, published by the Filson Club in 1902.

Price married Mary Frances Thompson on May 26, 1853; they had a son and two daughters. Following the death of his wife in 1892, Price lived with his son, Robert Coleman Price, in Louisville and later in St. Louis. Price died on January 22, 1918, in St. Louis and was buried in Arlington National Cemetery.

See J. Winston Coleman, Jr., "Samuel Woodson Price: Kentucky Portrait Painter," *FCHQ* 23 (Jan. 1949): 5-24.

PRICE, SARAH FRANCES. Sarah Frances ("Sadie") Price, botanist and educator, was born in Evansville, Indiana, in 1849, to Maria F. and Alexander Price. She attended St. Agnes Hall, an Episcopal church school for girls in Terre Haute, Indiana. The family moved to Bowling Green, Kentucky, in the decade before the Civil War. In the late 1880s Price began her career as an amateur botanist and teacher of nature classes. She discovered and named new species of aster, clema-

tis, dogwood, groundnut, sour grass, and violets. She acquired an herbarium collection of almost 3,000 specimens, and in 1894 her water color paintings of Kentucky plants won first prize in the Herbarium Sketch Work Exhibit at the Chicago Columbian Exposition. Price's observations and discoveries were published in three books: *Flora of Warren County, Kentucky* (1893), *Fern Collectors Handbook and Herbarium* (1896), and *The Trees and Shrubs of Kentucky* (1898). She also wrote articles in popular botanical journals and farm periodicals. She died on July 3, 1903, in Bowling Green and was buried in Fairview Cemetery.

CAROL CROWE-CARRACO

PRICHARD, EDWARD FRETWELL, JR. Edward Fretwell Prichard, Jr., attorney and noted political adviser, was born on January 21, 1915, in Paris, Kentucky, the son of Edward and Allene (Power) Prichard. Prichard attended public schools and entered Princeton University at the age of fifteen. Graduating from college at the top of his class, he entered Harvard law school and, upon graduation, became research assistant to professor Felix Frankfurter. When President Franklin D. Roosevelt appointed Frankfurter to the U.S. Supreme court, Prichard joined him in Washington, D.C., as his law clerk. After a year Prichard moved to the Immigration Service in the Justice Department and then served as assistant to the U.S. attorney general and on the War Production Board. In 1942, at the age of twenty-seven, he became legal counsel and adviser to President Roosevelt. In Washington he impressed political observers such as Katherine Graham, later publisher of the *Washington Post*.

In 1945 Prichard returned to Kentucky to practice law. Raised in a highly political Bourbon County family and touted in the press as a "boy wonder," Prichard at thirty made it clear that his eye was on the governorship of Kentucky, and he was considered a prime choice to succeed Earle Clements. It was shocking, therefore, when Prichard was convicted of vote fraud conspiracy in the 1948 Bourbon County election and sentenced to two years in federal prison. He had served five months when President Harry S. Truman pardoned him in 1950.

Prichard returned to his law practice, and by the late 1950s had begun his slow and difficult political rebirth as a campaign strategist for Bert Combs. In the ensuing years, he advised Govs. Clements, Wetherby, Combs, and Breathitt and, to a lesser degree, Carroll and Brown. Nicknamed "the Philosopher" by Combs, Prichard came to be considered by many to be Kentucky's greatest intellect and sharpest legal mind. His voracious appetite for all forms of intellectual stimulation was legendary, as were his gifts of wit and repartee. The stigma of his conviction remained, however, and he never sought political office himself.

Prichard emerged as Kentucky's most visible political sage through the late 1960s and 1970s. In political philosophy he was a strong advocate of civil rights, strip mine regulation, constitutional reform, improved health care, and public education. In 1966 Gov. Edward Breathitt (1963-67) appointed Prichard to the Council on Higher Education, beginning the period of his full return to public life. Serving often as the council's vice chairman, he became a powerful advocate for Kentucky's universities. In 1980, the council appointed a citizens' committee to recommend improvements in Kentucky's universities, and Prichard led the committee in preparing its 1981 report on higher education, *In Pursuit of Excellence*. The committee afterward became an independent organization, the Prichard Committee for Academic Excellence.

In 1947 Prichard married Lucy Elliot of Lexington. He died on December 23, 1984, and was buried in the Paris Cemetery.   ROBERT F. SEXTON

PRICHARD COMMITTEE FOR ACADEMIC EXCELLENCE. The Prichard Committee for Academic Excellence began as the Committee on Higher Education in Kentucky's Future in 1980, when the KENTUCKY COUNCIL ON HIGHER EDUCATION appointed thirty citizens to recommend future directions for public universities. Edward F. Prichard, Jr., a well-known Frankfort attorney, was appointed chairman. Upon completion of the committee's 1981 report, the members renamed the group the Prichard Committee.

The committee's 1981 report, *In Pursuit of Excellence*, stressed the dangers of declining financial support for higher education and the lack of planning across the Kentucky system. The committee called for adequate funding, admission standards at public universities, faculty improvement programs, creation of a Fund for Academic Excellence, creation of a nationally competitive research university, and a reduction of duplication in professional schools, with specific reference to law. The report was hailed by university presidents and leaders in Kentucky and across the nation. In the years following, the committee's recommendations for Centers of Excellence, scholarships for gifted students, and a required precollege curriculum and admission standards, especially at the University of Kentucky, were implemented.

In the fall of 1983 committee members, frustrated by the limited governmental response to their recommendations, formed a new organization, the Prichard Committee for Academic Excellence, an independent, privately funded citizen group. Their purpose was to focus public attention on the need for improved education at all levels and to build a credible public force to accomplish that aim. Prichard was the first chairman of the new organization, and Robert F. Sexton, who organized the original group for the Council on Higher Education, became the committee's executive director.

The new group's concentrated study of Kentucky elementary and secondary education produced the report *The Path to a Larger Life* (1985). The committee argued that Kentucky education was woefully inadequate and needed major financial investments and radical reform. The report stressed expanded early childhood education, a vastly improved teaching profession, restructured schools, the elimination of patronage politics from school management, and adequate funding.

In November 1984 the committee organized a statewide Town Forum that attracted 20,000 concerned citizens to simultaneous meetings in each of Kentucky's 177 school districts. Observers credited the Town Forum with creating the political momentum to support the special legislative session called by Gov. Martha Layne Collins (1983-87) in 1985 to deal with education.

The committee campaigned to stimulate public interest in improved schools through support and training for local citizen groups and public forums and hearings. The committee also filed legal briefs, conducted research, and testified before the state supreme court in the historic case, *Council for Better Education vs. Martha Layne Collins, et al.* (1989), which led to a decision mandating legislative reform of the school system. The result was the 1990 Kentucky EDUCATION REFORM ACT, for which the Prichard Committee helped to develop the grass-roots consensus and made far-reaching recommendations.

In 1990 the committee began a multiyear program of monitoring results and stirring public support to ensure implementation of the Education Reform Act.

PRINCETON. Princeton, the county seat of Caldwell County in western Kentucky, is located at the junction of U.S. 62 and KY 91, just south of the Western Kentucky Parkway. The site was first called Eddy Grove, because of its location at the head of Eddy Creek. In 1817 it was renamed Princetown to honor William Prince, an early settler, and the spelling later changed.

The area was made attractive to settlement by a spring. The first settlers of the spring area were William Prince, who had been awarded a military land grant from Virginia, and Thomas Frazier, who arrived sometime around 1797. Frazier built a home, a brick kiln, and an inn at the spring. The settlement grew as a crossroads community, at the junction of a major trace that led from Hopkinsville to an Ohio River ferry crossing in Crittenden County, and a road that ran from the Big Spring southwest to the Cumberland River.

Eddyville became the seat when Caldwell County was formed in 1809; in 1817 the seat was permanently transferred to Princeton. The first courthouse in Princeton was a two-story log structure that was completed in 1820. It was replaced by a second courthouse in 1840. The third courthouse, of Italianate design, was completed in 1866 and razed in September 1938. The Works Progress Administration completed a new building on February 15, 1941.

In 1830 Princeton was a town of 366 inhabitants. For six months in 1838, the residents of the city witnessed the forced march of much of the Cherokee Indian Nation from its ancestral home to reservations in Oklahoma, along the Trail of Tears through Princeton. At that time, Princeton was something of an educational center with the Princeton Academy, which had been founded in 1821 as the Caledonia Academy, and Cumberland College, which operated from 1826 until 1860. Princeton College was established in 1860, but its construction was delayed by the Civil War. In 1866 it was sold to the Presbyterians, who operated it until its closure in 1907.

During the Civil War, Princeton was subject to raiding and foraging parties of both Confederate and Union armies. A Confederate regiment camped on the grounds of Princeton College, and one of the buildings was used as a hospital. On October 15, 1864, Gen. Hylan B. LYON's Confederates burned the courthouse, on the ground that it had been used by the Union army for other than civilian purposes.

In 1872 the Elizabethtown & Paducah Railroad (now part of the Paducah & Louisville) was completed through Princeton, and a junction was formed in 1887 with the north-south Ohio Valley Railroad (now the Tradewater Railroad), which connected Evansville, Indiana, and Hopkinsville. The town grew and thrived as a business, educational, religious, transportation, and agricultural center.

Princeton was a center for fire-cured tobacco, and violence during the BLACK PATCH WAR destroyed two tobacco stemmeries and caused damages of more than $75,000. (Princeton now celebrates an annual Black Patch Festival.) Violence returned to Princeton during the 1920s in the form of Ku Klux Klan activity. In 1924 dynamite damaged the courthouse and the home of the county attorney. On July 4, 1924, the Klan held a large parade in the city.

Industry came with the establishment of the Princeton Hosiery Mills in 1918. By 1990 the company was known as Le Roi Princeton and was the city's largest employer. With the completion of the Western Kentucky Parkway in the mid-1960s, the city was able to attract other industries. Products manufactured in Princeton include hosiery, jeans, metals, trophies, pallets, and limestone products.

The population of the fourth-class city was 6,292 in 1970; 7,073 in 1980; and 6,940 in 1990.

PRISONS. Before the establishment of a prison system, the penalty for all felonies in Kentucky was death. In 1799 the Kentucky State Penitentiary, the first penitentiary west of the Allegheny Mountains, was established in Frankfort. The prison held thirty prisoners, under a keeper appointed by the governor; inmates cut stone and made nails, shoes, chain, chairs, and tinware. By 1817 the penitentiary was overcrowded and expansion funds were requested. In 1825 entrepreneur Joel Scott offered to run the penitentiary as a business, to pay for itself and return a profit to the state. The General Assembly accepted his offer, instituting the lease system.

In return for running the penitentiary and paying the state a percentage of the profits from inmate labor, the lessee had control of both the institution and the inmate labor. Under the lease system, which continued for fifty-five years, Scott and some of his successors made huge profits by selling inmate-made products, including processed hemp. Lessees used their profits to influence legislators who allowed them to avoid paying rent. Not even the governor could remove the powerful lessees from office. Under this system, inmate living conditions deteriorated and scores of inmates died of scurvy and pneumonia.

Faced with huge increases in the inmate population after the Civil War, the legislature expanded the penitentiary, raised the grand larceny threshold from four dollars to eight dollars, and reduced sentences for good behavior. Even so, the inmate population increased fivefold between 1865 and 1878. The contract system, which replaced the lease system in 1880, allowed private contractors to bid for the right to use convict labor outside the penitentiary. Contractors paid the state a per diem rate for each inmate laborer and were to provide housing, food, and clothing. This had the effect of reducing the prison population. Hundreds of inmates were used to build rail lines and tunnels. At least one such tunnel, located under the lodge at Natural Bridge State Resort Park, still exists. Use of inmate labor in coal fields near Central City was stopped by striking miners. In Lexington over six hundred convicts were used to dig a reservoir for the city water supply.

When Luke Blackburn became governor (1879-83), he pardoned 850 inmates, requested funds for a four-hundred-cell branch penitentiary, and instituted parole. Contractors used inmates to help construct the branch penitentiary at Eddyville, which opened in 1890. (In 1912 the Kentucky State Penitentiary at Frankfort was renamed KENTUCKY STATE REFORMATORY and the branch penitentiary at Eddyville was renamed KENTUCKY STATE PENITENTIARY.)

Inmates working in remote areas were completely dependent on contractors, who were seldom held accountable for living and working conditions. Over four hundred inmates were reported to have escaped from contractors' worksites between 1884 and 1889. They were probably victims of maltreatment and unsafe working conditions. Although investigative hearings were held, those responsible for inmate deaths were seldom punished. When renegotiating per diem rates, contractors secured favorable terms by threatening to return hundreds of inmates to an overcrowded penitentiary. As competition among contractors declined, the state again found it difficult to profit from its prison system. In 1887 the only contractor to submit a bid was the holder of the expired contract.

The new state constitution of 1891 prohibited leasing convict labor outside the penitentiary walls. Contractors responded by expanding operations inside the prisons at Frankfort and Eddyville, concentrating on labor-intensive, assembly-line production of shoes, shirts, chairs, brooms, and leather goods, which were sold throughout the United States. So many goods were produced in prison factories that companies that employed free laborers at standard wages were unable to compete. In response to pressure from organized labor, the U.S. Congress in 1929 adopted the Hawes-Cooper Act, which allowed states to prohibit interstate shipment of prison-made products. Faced with loss of their market, private contractors withdrew from prison factories at Frankfort and Eddyville, leaving almost 3,000 inmates without jobs. Increased production of goods for state use provided some jobs, but many factories were converted to house inmates.

When the prison population increased from 1,649 in 1928 to 4,300 in 1935, Kentucky officials told large counties to stop sending prisoners to the reformatory at Frankfort until provision could be made to house them. At Eddyville, inmates slept on bunk beds in cellhouse corridors. Inmates who were once profitably employed now marched in military drills, crushed stone, or lounged in factories converted to dayrooms. On his last day in office in 1931, Gov. Flem Sampson (1927-31) pardoned 187 inmates, and his successor, Gov. Ruby Laffoon (1931-35), pardoned five hundred. The number of inmates paroled increased rapidly, and laws permitting probation were passed. These efforts to reduce prison population failed. By 1937 almost 3,000 inmates were jammed into the four-acre, 137-year-old reformatory at Frankfort. Newspapers reported that the floors could not be swept because there was no space for inmates to stand out of the way. The Great Flood of 1937 hastened replacement of the outdated reformatory with a new $3 million reformatory and prison farm near La Grange and a separate women's prison near Pewee Valley.

During the 1940s and 1950s, the three prisons were understaffed and political patronage controlled hiring. Without adequate personnel, escape rates were high, punishments were severe, and exploitation of weak or mentally incompetent inmates was common. Since no money was appropriated until the early 1960s to hire any vocational or academic teachers, rehabilitation was done on an informal basis by concerned guards or the chaplain. Investigations in the mid-1960s called attention to the deplorable conditions. Additional treatment, educational, and security personnel were hired. Three minimum-security prisons were opened by 1970. These improvements were made possible, in part, by the reduction in the inmate population from 4,000 inmates in 1960 to 3,300 in 1970.

During the 1970s emphasis was placed on community-based programs. Population pressures were moderated by expanding the number of offenders on probation or parole, which doubled to 7,200 by 1979, while the prison population increased by only 12.5 percent. In addition, five minimum-security prisons were opened and programs to prepare inmates for release were emphasized. Other improvements included more staff

training, hiring women as guards, racial desegregation of inmate living areas, and hiring black personnel for treatment jobs.

By 1980 population pressures resurfaced. Corrections officials settled a class action suit filed in federal court by inmates from the reformatory and the penitentiary. The settlement put population ceilings on these two prisons and mandated extensive construction and renovation, improvements in education opportunities and medical care, and staff increases. Inmate living conditions improved at the two prisons, but overpopulation problems shifted to other prisons. From 1980 to 1987 the inmate population increased 78 percent, partly because of legislation that lengthened sentences. Two new medium-security prisons were opened and other prisons expanded, but the inmate population increased so fast that over a thousand inmates backed up in county jails awaiting bed space. In 1986 the state contracted with a private prison corporation to house selected minimum-security inmates at a privately owned facility in Marion County. A new prison costing $73 million opened in Morgan County in 1990.

See Robert G. Crawford, "A History of the Kentucky Penitentiary System 1865-1937," Ph.D. diss., University of Kentucky, 1955.

T. KYLE ELLISON

PROCLAMATION OF 1763. After the defeat of the French by the British in the French and Indian War (1755-63), the Treaty of Paris, signed February 10, 1763, ceded the French possessions of Canada and the land east of the Mississippi River, excluding New Orleans, to the British. The Indians, who had aligned with the French, felt betrayed by the grants of land to the British. As many as seven Indian tribes banded together in 1763 under Ottawa chief Pontiac to defend their lands. The Indians attacked soldiers, traders, and the settlers of the newly acquired areas west of the Appalachian Mountains.

In response, King George III on October 7, 1763, issued a proclamation, prepared in part by Lord Shelburne, president of the Board of Trade, that prohibited land grants in the area south of the Hudson's Bay Company, west of the Appalachian Mountains, and north of the thirty-first parallel. Specifically, it affected the area beyond the heads or sources of any of the rivers that fell into the Atlantic Ocean from the West and Northwest. Private purchases of land from the Indians were also made illegal and settlers already living in the large territory were to leave. Free trade with the Indians was permitted under license and regulation.

The colonies, especially Virginia (which then included Kentucky), resisted the proclamation on the grounds that the land between the mountains and the Mississippi River had been given to them by King George's predecessors. Some argued that the French had had no legal right to cede the land to the British. As for the motives of the proclamation, some viewed it as an attempt to prevent another Indian war; others thought England wanted the new territory as a royal domain or was seeking to protect the fur trade for London business. Whatever the reasons for the Proclamation of 1763, it did little to stop the settlers from encroaching on Indian land in exploring and settling Kentucky.

See Charles Alvord, *The Mississippi Valley in British Politics* (Cleveland 1917).

PROCTER, JOHN ROBERT. John Robert Procter was born in Mason County, Kentucky, on March 16, 1844, to George Morton and Anna Maria (Young) Procter. He attended the University of Pennsylvania (1863) and Harvard University (1875). He became Kentucky state geologist and commissioner of immigration in 1880. Proctor was not a geologist and the volumes published during his term hold little original material. Of value was the publication of county surveys. Lacking adequate funding and burdened with the responsibilities of being director of the state Immigration Bureau as well, Procter had a term of small achievement. In 1892 Gov. John Young Brown (1891-95) dismissed Procter because he refused to hire Brown's son. In December 1893 President Grover Cleveland appointed Procter to head the U.S. Civil Service Commission, where he served until his death. He married Julia Leslie Dobyns in 1869 and they had three children. Procter died on December 12, 1903, in Washington, D.C.

See L.C. Robinson, "The Kentucky Geological Survey," *Register* 25 (Jan. 1927): 86-93.

MARGARET LUTHER SMATH

PROVIDENCE. Providence, the largest city in Webster County, is located in the southwestern part of the county, east of the Tradewater River, at the intersection of KY 293, KY 120, and KY 109. The town was founded by Richard B. Savage, who arrived in the vicinity from Virginia in 1820 with his eldest sister, Mary (Savage) Settler.

Between 1820 and 1830, Savage laid out twenty-four town lots on land purchased from William Jenkins and built a trading post and residence. The settlement post office was established at Providence on October 16, 1828. The town name may have been copied from the city in Rhode Island; other accounts credit an old trader who thanked Providence for the Good Samaritans among local farmers. On February 18, 1840, when the town of Providence was officially sanctioned, it had a population of 150, including three physicians, as well as five stores, two hotels, a school, a Baptist church, a Masonic hall, and three tobacco stemmeries. In the heart of the state's Black Patch tobacco-growing region, Providence eventually became the third largest stemming market in America.

Providence was incorporated as a city on March 1, 1860. The onset of the Civil War slowed economic growth in the city, although no major battles took place there. A Confederate reconnaissance and foraging force commanded by Gen. Nathan Bedford Forrest passed through Providence between November 24 and December 5, 1861.

By 1890 the town's population had reached only 522. Population growth accelerated with the coal boom in the 1890s, reaching 1,286 by the turn of the century. Commercial coal mining began in 1888, and by 1930 Providence residents numbered 4,742. In the 1930s depressed conditions in the coal fields resulted in a loss of population that continued through the 1960s. The town's economy remains tied to coal and agriculture. Providence accounts for 30 percent of the population of Webster County.

The population of the fourth-class city was 4,270 in 1970; 4,434 in 1980; and 4,123 in 1990.

JAMES DUANE BOLIN

PUBLIC EDUCATION. Common schools in Kentucky have a long and complex history, reflecting the deterrent forces of economics, religion, politics, and human resistance. Kentucky has lacked a central educational philosophy and objectives, and running through the entire fabric of its history is a thread of casualness about educational values and objectives.

As early as 1775, children attended a dame school (if it could be dignified with such a title) taught briefly by Mrs. William Coomes in Fort Harrod. But Kentucky common school history had its origin earlier, in the academy movement in Virginia. There were three basic justifications for the public support of schools: the necessity of keeping public records; the expectations of some religious bodies that the clergy be literate enough to read the Scriptures; and the textbook knowledge required in the professions of law and land surveying. The organizers of private academies attempted to give an elementary education to a more or less select group of students to serve the professions, unsupported by taxes. For the great mass of the population, education was a luxury. The pioneering agrarian society demanded physical, not intellectual, energies.

The early Kentucky legislation pertaining to education centered on the creation of academies. In December 1794 the newly organized Kentucky General Assembly chartered the Kentucky Academy at Pisgah in Woodford County, setting an educational precedent. As new counties were established, the legislature chartered academies in them, although the academies chartered on paper were not always created. Because Kentucky's political system was formed before the education clause in the Northwest Ordinance became applicable, it did not receive the benefits of a federal land reserve. Running through the acts of the Kentucky General Assembly from 1794 to 1850 is a considerable volume of legislation pertaining to the land grant academies. The act of 1798 set the standard grant of 6,000 acres for each county, and by 1860 approximately 450,000 acres of public lands had been appropriated.

A challenge even greater than that of financing schools was the one of finding suitably prepared teachers. As late as the second decade of the twentieth century, Kentucky failed to deal with the problems of teacher training, certification, and compensation. For more than a century there were no formal teacher training institutions and no set standards of qualifications or objectives. Early Kentucky educational history bears the imprint of such academy masters as John Filson, John McKinney, James Moore, and Jacob Lehre. Academy masters were of several types: ministers of the Gospel who taught as a sideline, itinerant teachers (many of them New Englanders), lawyers, and land surveyors.

Textbooks were no easier to find than teachers, and the texts available as late as the second decade of the nineteenth century were limited to the Bible and miscellaneous bound books that the teachers were able to obtain. Teachers copied by hand from various sources the rules of mathematics and geometry. Arithmetic lessons dealt with the subject through "the rule of three," and geometry lessons used theorems and diagrams. Students also learned the rules of grammar. The scarcity of instructional materials, including books, blackboards, and chalk, is reflected in the "blab school," a method and a term probably brought over the mountains from Virginia. It required pupils to recite assignments aloud in singsong voices. In reciting spelling, for instance, they had to pronounce letters, syllables, and words. Other pupils were expected to learn from the speaker.

Most of the older settled communities generated their own chapters of provincial educational history, but none had any overall significance. Kentucky made only a minimal response to the national movement for establishing and sustaining public school systems after the War of 1812. On December 18, 1821, the General Assembly established a literary fund from a portion of the profits of the Bank of the Commonwealth. There was, however, no provision for a central administration or an established course of study, and no schedule for distributing the funds. Most Kentuckians probably were unaware of the fund.

When Lt. Gov. Gabriel Slaughter was elevated to the office of governor after the death of the aged George Madison (1816), he advocated without success the establishment of a state common school system. The General Assembly in 1821 authorized the appointment of a commission of six members, with Lt. Gov. William T. Barry as chairman, to make a state and national survey. The Barry committee made its report to the General Assembly on December 11, 1822 (see BARRY REPORT). The General Assembly, embroiled in an explosive partisan debate, simply filed the report away—one of the most egregious blunders in American educational history.

As though it believed that gathering the facts would meet Kentucky's educational needs, the General Assembly in 1829 authorized a second survey, to be made by Thomas Alva Wood, president of Transylvania University, and Benjamin O. Peers, a professor there. Their report was in fact a competent blueprint for creating a public school system, but it too was ignored.

Framers of Kentucky's first two constitutions had ignored the subject of education, leaving the matter squarely up to the General Assembly. That body on February 16, 1838, enacted Kentucky's first major bit of serious educational legislation. The law was in fact a formal blueprint of public educational organization. It undertook to cover every aspect of creating a system of universal free public schools: school taxes, teacher qualifications, a board of elected local trustees, and ownership of school property.

A critical need was the establishment of a central school administration. As a result of private crusading, the office of SUPERINTENDENT OF PUBLIC INSTRUCTION was created as a quasiofficial one. Joseph J. Bullock was appointed to a one-year term as the first superintendent in 1838. He tried to generate sentiment for public education, and he gathered information about the rate of illiteracy in the commonwealth. A sample survey in Rockcastle County revealed that 2,676 children of school age were growing up there in abject illiteracy. This appalling deficiency was assumed to prevail throughout most of the state. Bullock quickly learned that there was still opposition to public education.

In 1836 the Jackson administration and the U.S. Congress had acted to distribute surplus federal funds to the states; Kentucky's share was $1,433,757. The Kentucky General Assembly mandated in 1845 that approximately $1 million be placed in a separate fund for the support of public schools, with the earnings from school bonds to be distributed pro rata to the counties. The General Assembly and the governor, however, could not keep their partisan hands off the fund. The legislators ordered the governor, treasurer, and auditor to destroy the school bonds—one of Kentucky's public scandals.

On February 10, 1845, the General Assembly made the office of superintendent of public instruction a state post, created a state board of education, and encouraged the organization of common schools in the counties. The law reiterated most of the provisions of the law of 1838, prefatory to the consideration of public education in the constitutional convention of 1849. Perhaps there is no clearer revelation of Kentuckians' attitudes toward public education than in the reports of the debates in this convention. The resulting article 11 of the new constitution, however, reflected little or none of the philosophy expressed in the debates. It concerned itself with the management of education funds, and it provided for a public school system and the election of a state superintendent of public instruction as a constitutional officer.

Adoption of the education article in the new constitution marked the beginning of a new era in Kentucky's public school history. Educational authority, which previously had been a matter of legislative fiat, now had a constitutional basis. In this era the strong-willed Presbyterian minister Robert Jefferson BRECKINRIDGE, as superintendent of public instruction, was able to stand off grasping state officials who would have dissipated the public school funds. He reorganized school districts, stabilized the school programs, compiled fairly reliable school statistics, and assured the levying of a two-cent property tax for school support. Breckinridge also effected a compilation and redrafting of school laws, and he convened a meeting of the Friends of Public Education in Kentucky in 1851 to consider eight specific recommendations. Among the latter were a set curriculum, standard textbooks, the length of school terms, the status of the Bible in the schools, and SCHOOL ARCHITECTURE.

The Civil War disrupted the momentum of Kentucky educational progress in the decade 1850-60. The postwar era was characterized by the struggle to get legislators, governors, and county officials to levy and collect sufficient taxes to improve the primitive school system. Immediate demands were adequate housing, regularization of textbook adoption, teacher training and certification, teachers' pay, length of school terms, and the conduct of a biracial system of schools, in which blacks had historically been shamefully, if not criminally, discriminated against.

Perhaps the biggest of the postwar problems was the difficulty in securing public support for and patronage of schools. In an intensely rural agrarian society, education was of remote interest. School terms were synchronized with crop seasons. Most of the few teachers available were poorly educated, some no doubt little better prepared than their pupils. County normal schools, conducted annually during 1870-1910 to prepare teachers for the new school terms, did little more than give elementary instruction on classroom procedures, record-keeping, and student discipline.

The black beast of Kentucky educational history from 1838 to 1920 was the local district trustee. No doubt a majority of the thousands of trustees were thoroughgoing political animals. Most of them may have been only semiliterate at best, and many were in fact corrupt. Accounts of trustee interference and misconduct run like a dark thread through the county superintendents' reports to the superintendent of public instruction.

Perhaps the most distinguished superintendent of public instruction before 1907 was H.A.M. Henderson (1871-79). He made progress in the areas of taxation, textbook adoption, schools for blacks, teacher training and certification, graded schools, and schoolhouse architecture. For the most part, however, Kentucky common school education during 1865-1910 might well be classified as being of shabby, backwoods, log-cabin-era quality.

At the fourth constitutional revision convention in 1890, where there was a superfluity of orating, debating, and legalistic pawing of the constitutional air, the delegates finally adopted an educational article. In the process some delegates delivered philosophical discourses on the subject of public education that were full of high purpose and wishful thinking. One delegate in particular, William

Beckner of Clark County, had a decisive influence as the author of this mandate in the educational article: "The General Assembly shall, by appropriate legislation, provide for an efficient system of schools throughout the state." The word "efficient" was to haunt school districts, the courts, and the General Assembly with a mighty challenge a century later.

Measured by almost any criteria, progress in education in Kentucky during 1865-1910 occurred at a snail's pace. A sizable amount of school legislation, the programs of the state superintendents, the constitutional mandate, and some increase in the rate of tax levies reflected minimal progress. An achievement of far-reaching consequence during this time was the enactment of the law of 1906 requiring the counties to organize high schools. At that date, there were fewer than fifty high schools in Kentucky, where fewer than 5,000 students were enrolled. Again in 1914 the General Assembly enacted a mandate that each county organize a public high school. On the eve of World War I, however, only 15,474 Kentuckians were enrolled in high school classes, compared with 144,477 in 1941.

John Grant Crabbe, who became superintendent of public instruction in 1907, brought to the office a far-reaching vision of what public education should be and the energy to achieve that goal. In his four-year term, he secured the passage of legislation that created the two teacher normals—Eastern and Western—regulated child labor, created a textbook commission, and made school attendance compulsory.

The so-called "Education Legislature" of 1908 enacted a fresh blueprint for Kentucky public education in the SULLIVAN LAW, as well as other landmark legislation. Following this session of the General Assembly, two public "whirlwind" campaigns attempted to arouse interest in and support for public schools. The campaigns involved a wide diversity of organized groups, the Kentucky press, and school representatives. Simultaneously with the enactment of compulsory school attendance laws and the movement for consolidation, the General Assembly enacted the basic highway improvement law of 1912. There was a close parallel between consolidation and compulsory school attendance, on the one hand, and the condition of Kentucky's roads on the other.

After World War I the Kentucky General Assembly made a timid gesture at reforming the state's system of public education. The law of 1920 effected two major changes: the appointment of county superintendents of schools and a reduction in the number of school districts. Throughout the next decade, political interests attempted to revoke the law relating to superintendents, but were finally defeated by a Kentucky court of appeals decision in 1932.

The issue of black education became a thorny problem after 1865. Several of the superintendents of public instruction undertook to deal with the issue within the context of public opinion and the times; although the law provided for the establishment of separate schools for blacks, the counties made only minimal financial appropriations to support the schools. The issue was further complicated in 1904 by the enactment of the DAY LAW, which forbade coracial education, a ban that prevailed until 1954, when the U.S. Supreme Court required desegregation in *Brown vs. Board of Education.* This decision rendered section 187 of the Kentucky constitution unconstitutional, and Gov. Lawrence Wetherby (1950-55) took the positive stand that Kentucky would observe the law. Except for instances of resistance at Slaughters and Clay in Webster County, and a later upheaval in Louisville over bussing of students, Kentucky's public schools were integrated racially with minimal resistance as compared with schools in the lower South.

In 1954 a more pressing problem than racial integration was the low statistical ratings for Kentucky's educational progress. Kentucky battled almost hopelessly against the humiliation of low ratings during the decades 1920-90. So critical was the state's educational plight considered in 1932 that a special commission was appointed to do some fact-finding and make recommendations for improvements. In its disturbing report, published in 1933, the commission underscored this section: "Measured by generally accepted standards, however, Kentucky's progress simply parallels (though on a much lower plane) the progress made in education throughout the United States. Kentucky's educational rank, relative to other states, has not advanced during the past twenty years. Kentucky still ranks fortieth among the states."

Voters approved a 1941 amendment to section 186 of the constitution to equalize educational opportunities for all the state's children through more equitable appropriation of funds. In 1949 Kentuckians voted for an amendment to permit distribution of 25 percent of the school funds to poorer districts, and in 1953 a third amendment nullified distribution of funds on a per capita basis. The General Assembly enacted an equalization law in 1954 in accord with the latter amendment, preparing the way for the MINIMUM FOUNDATION PROGRAM.

Since 1838 the bulk of Kentucky's school legislation has dealt with financing, teacher preparation and certification, curricula for all grades, the makeup of school districts and boards, and changing educational objectives. While the commonwealth has suffered from unfavorable comparative statistics on progress in education, governors and legislators have further aggravated the problem by the enactment of three unfortunate pieces of legislation: the repeal of the sales tax in 1937 and the enactment of the Rollback Bill and House Bill 44. These bills stymied the educational effort by striking at the very foundations of basic public school support in a rural-agrarian state.

The burden of adverse statistical comparison, the low level of educational achievement, the gross inequities of support in at least sixty-six school districts, and demands of an advancing technological age produced a state of crisis in the Kentucky public school system. In a lawsuit filed in November 1985 in the Franklin County circuit court, sixty-six public school districts, seven boards of trustees, and twenty-two public school students protested the inequities of support. Circuit Court Judge Ray Corns ruled in 1988 that the Kentucky General Assembly was in violation of sections 183 and 186 of the constitution. On appeal, the Kentucky supreme court ruled in June 1989 that the entire system of elementary and secondary public schools was unconstitutional, on the ground that the General Assembly had failed to provide an efficient system of common schools.

In response to the supreme court's all-embracing decision, the Kentucky General Assembly in its 1990 session created a task force of legislators, educational specialists, and administrative officials to devise a new system of public education for the commonwealth. The result of this body's investigations was the enactment of the omnibus law known as the EDUCATION REFORM ACT OF 1990. For at least the fourth time in Kentucky's educational history, the General Assembly restructured and set a new course for the operation of an efficient system of public schools. None of the previous attempts, however, were so all-inclusive of reform as the Reform Act of 1990.

See C.W. Hackensmith, *Out of Time and Tide: The Evolution of Education in Kentucky* (Lexington, Ky., 1970); Frank L. McVey, *The Gates Open Slowly* (Lexington, Ky., 1949).

THOMAS D. CLARK

PULASKI COUNTY. Pulaski County, the twenty-seventh county in order of formation, is located in south-central Kentucky. The county is bounded by Casey, Lincoln, Rockcastle, Laurel, McCreary, Wayne, and Russell counties and contains an area of 660 square miles. It is roughly diamond shaped and contains a wide variety of terrains, including rugged hills to the east and south and rolling farmland to the west. The dominant geographical feature is the Cumberland River, which meanders across the southern part of the county. The river is impounded by the Tennessee Valley Authority's Wolf Creek Dam, which created Lake Cumberland in 1952 and helped to make tourism an important local industry. Despite the rapid growth of Somerset in the 1970s and 1980s, the county is mostly rural and has little fertile soil. SOMERSET is the county seat.

Permanent settlement of the area north of the Cumberland River and west of the Rockcastle River occurred after the end of the Revolutionary War, when around 3,000 people located in the area between 1782 and 1798. Led by several Revolutionary War veterans, these citizens petitioned for the creation of a county to serve their needs. Kentucky's legislature responded favorably to the request and proposed to divide Green and Lincoln counties to form the new county. Gov. James Garrard (1796-1804) signed the act into law on December 10, 1798.

Since many of the early settlers were veterans, they chose to name the county after a famous Revolutionary War figure. Nicholas Jasper suggested that the county bear the name of the Polish-American patriot Casimir Pulaski, who was killed at Savannah in 1779. On June 24, 1801, the commissioners directed that the county seat be called Somerset, located on forty acres donated by William Dodson for that purpose.

Because of the lack of good roads, Pulaski County was isolated and grew slowly. In spite of slow population growth—from 3,000 in 1800 to just over 17,000 in 1860—numerous businesses and industries developed in the antebellum period. Pioneer merchant Cyrenius Wait moved to Pulaski County from New England and developed a salt-works, operated a wharf on the river at Waitsboro, and planted mulberry trees in hopes of creating a silk industry. Along with Tunstall Quarles, a local politician and U.S. congressman (1817-20), he helped pioneer both the banking and insurance industries in the county.

By the mid-nineteenth century, the county's economic mainstays included farming, cattle, and coal. In 1870 Pulaski ranked sixth among livestock-producing counties in the state. During the years before and after the Civil War, twelve mines in eastern Pulaski County produced coal that was transported to Nashville by barge. In 1878 eighteen of these barges carrying 100,000 bushels of coal sank in the treacherous waters of Smith's Shoals above Burnside. The industry never fully recovered.

At the beginning of the Civil War, fewer than 10 percent of Pulaski County's population consisted of black slaves. Many county residents were Southern sympathizers, but the majority of the population supported the Union. Two important Civil War battles, Mill Springs and Dutton's Hill, took place within the county's boundaries. Neither was especially destructive to life or property. Somerset was occupied by a Union garrison for a portion of the war and was raided by Confederate Gen. John Hunt Morgan and his cavalry. Toward the end of the war, engineers and surveyors from the Union army visited Pulaski to map out a roadbed for a military railroad, and their survey reached as far as Point Isabel on the Cumberland River. Point Isabel was renamed Burnside in honor of the Union general. In 1866 the U.S. War Department established a permanent national cemetery in western Pulaski County near the site of the Civil War engagement of Mill Springs, where over six hundred Union dead were buried. Less than a mile to the south is a Confederate cemetery, near where Confederate Gen. Felix Zollicoffer fell during the Battle of Mill Springs.

In the years after the Civil War, Pulaski County became a political bastion of the Republican party. Thomas Z. Morrow, of Somerset, was one of the founders of Kentucky's Grand Old Party. In its history, only three Democrats—Andrew Jackson, James Buchanan, and Woodrow Wilson—have carried Pulaski County in a presidential contest. From Lincoln's second election in 1864, the Republican majority for president has exceeded 60 percent in almost every election. County residents in the twentieth century have also voted Republican in state and local elections.

In 1877 the Cincinnati & Southern (now Norfolk Southern) Railway came to Pulaski County, which led to rapid growth in Somerset, Ferguson, Burnside, and other towns along the right-of-way, and to virtual abandonment of many of the county's smaller hamlets. Afterward came large logging and sawmill operations. The period of industrial activity peaked when the Cincinnati & Southern ("Queen and Crescent") opened its Ferguson repair yard. For over a generation, the railroad and the shops were an economic mainstay. A sleepy county seat with only 587 people in 1870, Somerset swelled to be a regional metropolis by 1900 with almost 6,000 people.

At the turn of the century, Pulaski County's Edwin Porch Morrow, future governor (1919-23), began his political rise. A familiar figure at numerous Republican national conventions, Morrow was a formidable orator, and after losing by only 471 votes in the 1915 governor's race, Morrow returned to the political wars in 1919 to upset the incumbent governor, James D. Black (1919). After his election, an estimated 10,000 people gathered around the Pulaski County Courthouse to congratulate the only governor the county has produced.

Pulaski County's population reached its peak in 1920 and thereafter began a slow decline which was not reversed until the 1960s. Despite a relatively high county birth rate, young residents of Pulaski and other rural counties emigrated for jobs offered by Cincinnati's Procter & Gamble and Detroit's booming automobile industry.

John Sherman Cooper began his long career of service to the county, state, and nation as the Great Depression worsened. In the 1930s, Cooper served as county judge and watched as Pulaski tax receipts fell from $95,000 in 1930 to $57,000 by 1936. In the depression's bleakest days, 2,000 county families received federal food commodities. In 1933 the Pulaski County sheriff sold 460 farms for nonpayment of taxes. Before the Great Depression ended, Franklin D. Roosevelt's New Deal poured $800,000 in aid into the county.

After World War II, the Southern Railroad closed the Ferguson shops, but the completion of Wolf Creek Dam and the creation of the vast Lake Cumberland opened new possibilities for fishing, recreation, and tourism. By the 1960s the county's economy became more diversified with several small industries producing clothing, charcoal, houseboats, and automobile parts. In the 1980s, Pulaski County evolved into a regional business, medical, and educational center. Most of the county, however, remained rural and as of 1985 contained 2,400 farms which produced large quantities of pork, beef, poultry, milk, corn, soybeans, and tobacco. Many Pulaski Countians who have city jobs live in rural areas. Ever since 1798, most residents have been Baptist and the Flat Lick congregation in eastern Pulaski County is as old as the county itself. In 1990 about ninety of the county's 140 churches were Baptist.

Burnside's Harriette Simpson Arnow dealt in her novels with Kentuckians confronting the early twentieth century. *The Dollmaker* (1954), her most famous work, examined the human cost of the migration of Kentuckians to the factories of the north. Her novels and historical works, *Seedtime on the Cumberland* (1960) and *Flowering of the Cumberland* (1963), gave Pulaski County a place in American literature.

The population of Pulaski County was 35,234 in 1970; 45,803 in 1980; and 49,489 in 1990.

See Kentucky Heritage Council, *Pulaski County: Architectural and Historical Sites* (Lexington, Ky., 1985); Alma Owens Tibbals, *A History of Pulaski County* (Louisville 1952); George Tuggle, *Pulaski Revisited* (Lexington, Ky,. 1982).

ROGER D. TATE, JR.

PURSELL, ION. Ion Pursell, naval officer, was born in rural Ohio County on April 1, 1896, to John Williams and Frances Pursell. He graduated from the U.S. Naval Academy in 1917. He served in World War I, the Nicaraguan Campaign in the 1920s, and in Guam, where he was chairman of the board of the Bank of Guam. For several years he taught at the naval academy. Pursell participated in the invasions of North Africa in 1942 and Sicily in 1943, and was awarded the Legion of Merit with Star for these services. He served as chief of the U.S. Naval Mission to Ecuador from 1943 to 1946, then as commander of the naval base at Subic Bay in the Philippines. He also served at the Great Lakes Naval District, and from 1949 until his retirement in 1950 was attached to the office of the chief of naval operations in Washington, D.C.

Pursell took an early interest in the problem of illiteracy. When he was a young officer aboard the U.S.S. *Tennessee*, he discovered that many of the crew members were illiterate and set up an educational program for them. Later in Guam he established a similar program for station personnel. While in Ecuador, he was active in a literacy campaign among the sailors of that country's navy, for which he was awarded a decoration by the Ecuadorean government. Pursell moved to Frankfort, Kentucky, and began a financial consulting service, but his main interest continued to be adult literacy. Gov. Lawrence Wetherby (1950-55) appointed Pursell chairman of the Governor's Commission on Adult Education. He was known as the "Good Samaritan for the Three Rs." He was published widely in the area of adult education.

Pursell married Karola Froesick Frick of Berlin, Germany, on May 5, 1923. He died in Lexington on July 23, 1983, and was buried in Annapolis, Maryland.

See Tim Young, "Admiral Ion Pursell," *Daviess County Historical Quarterly* 6 (Jan. 1988): 17-20.

LEE A. DEW

Q

QUILTING. Immigrants to Kentucky brought their sewing skills, patterns, and techniques for quilt-making with them. As the state was settled, the craft was shared with or picked up by later immigrants. Quilts were made by both free women and slaves, rich and poor, for utility and decoration. While most utility quilts are gone, some are treasured heirlooms. The provenance of many of Kentucky's quilts has been lost because they were ignored for generations, perhaps sold or given away, before the importance of creator and date was recognized.

Quilts were made of natural fibers—cotton, wool, linen, and silk—before the introduction of synthetic fibers made possible rayon, nylon, and polyester fabrics, and blends as well. The top sides of quilts were pieced in simple or complex designs, or were appliqued. The primary sources of pieced patterns were existing quilts, traced to make a template. Pieced patterns were worked in blocks, then joined. Appliqued patterns were worked on a bed-sized piece of fabric or on blocks that were then sewn together. Whole-cloth quilts on which elaborate stuffed work was done are found in western Kentucky. The familiar patterns and genres of quilts, such as log cabin, crazy, album, friendship, and commemorative, were made at one time or another in some part of Kentucky.

From the mid- and later 1800s through the early years of the twentieth century, women's magazines and farm journals reproduced patterns, frequently with light and dark value given in addition to line, and they often carried suggestions for fabric, print, and color. Women could order patterns cheaply from the *Ladies Art Catalog*, first issued in 1898, and the ingenious enlarged the one-and-a-quarter-inch sketches from its pages. In the 1930s the explosion of demand for patterns such as flower garden, double wedding ring, and Dresden plate quilts can be traced to the magazine and newspaper columns of the time. They published patterns for mail order and department store outlets. Paralleling the general history of the craft, Kentucky's quilt-making has reflected society's changes: the decrease in materials and sewing time during the Civil War, an observable neglect of handcraft in urban centers following World War I, the persistence of the craft in the rural areas, the spurt of renewed interest during the Depression, the reduction of interest when employment of women increased during World War II, and the resurgence in the early 1970s, which continued throughout the 1980s.

A major stimulus to quiltmaking was county fairs, culminating in the Kentucky State Fair, which began in 1902. The work of Kentucky women was prominent among the more than 24,000 entries in Sears, Roebuck, and Co.'s "Sears Century of Progress Quilt Contest" in 1933. Interest in Kentucky's quilts heightened when it became known that six of the twenty-nine finalists were from the state. Margaret Rogers Caden of Lexington won the grand prize of $1,000, and her quilt was presented to Eleanor Roosevelt.

Kentucky was one of the thirty-six states for which folk arts and crafts were recorded in the Index of American Design, a Works Progress Administration arts program during 1935-42. For this project, Kentucky artists, under the direction of Adele Brandeis, created replicas in pencil, ink, watercolor, and colored pencil of at least thirty-six quilts, parts of quilts, or blocks. The items came from Louisville, Elizabethtown, Harrodsburg, and Glasgow.

The statewide Kentucky Heritage Quilt Society was incorporated in 1981 by women from Frankfort, Lexington, Louisville, Madisonville, and Whitesburg. It sponsors seminars and quilt shows throughout the state, and initiates and supports the development of local guilds. The society's Quilters-on-File and Kentucky Quilt Registry help collect and preserve information on the craft. Kentucky Quilt Registry volunteers have documented quilts from Kentucky both within and outside the state. These files are lodged in the archives at Western Kentucky University in Bowling Green.

The Kentucky Quilt Project, Inc. was launched in 1981 to identify quilts made in the state prior to 1900 and to link their development with Kentucky history. During 1981 and 1982, forty-four quilts were selected from roughly a thousand for exhibition and inclusion in "Kentucky Quilts 1800-1900," an exhibit put together by John Finley and Jonathan Holstein. A portion of this show traveled throughout the United States during 1982-83 under the auspices of the Smithsonian Institution and was also sent to Ireland. By 1989, similar projects had been completed or were under way in thirty-five other states and the District of Columbia.

In 1984 the newly formed American Quilter's Society, an organization dedicated to promoting the accomplishment of American quilters, held its first annual show and contest in Paducah. This show features some of the finest quilts being made and offers dozens of workshops and lectures on quilting. In recent years, as many as 30,000 people have attended the annual four-day event. Paducah is also home to AQS's main offices and extensive publishing business, and in April 1991 the Museum of the American Quilter's Society opened its doors. In addition to its permanent collection, the museum features three exhibition galleries, a library, and workshops that are held throughout the year.

See Mary Washington Clarke, *Kentucky Quilts and Their Makers* (Lexington, Ky., 1976); John Finley and Jonathan Holstein, *Kentucky Quilts 1800-1900* (Louisville 1982). KATY CHRISTOPHERSON

QUINN CHAPEL. The Quinn Chapel, which during the civil rights movement of the 1950s and 1960s served as the central meeting place for demonstrators who supported integration of public facilities, was the first African Methodist Episcopal (AME) church in Louisville. The AME denomination was established in Philadelphia in 1787 to protest discrimination against blacks; Quinn Chapel was founded in 1838. It was named for the Rev. Paul Quinn, a black minister who preached equality and abolition on the Indiana bank of the Ohio River. His preaching made him one of the most highly respected bishops of the denomination. The first congregation, under the leadership of the Rev. George W. Johnson, met in a room above a stable across from the Galt House at Second and Main streets. The name Upper Room Church was changed to Bethel Church before it became Quinn Chapel.

The congregation met at several locations—Fourth and Green (now Liberty) streets, Ninth and Green streets, and Ninth and Walnut (now Muhammad Ali)—before settling at its present location at 912 West Chestnut Street in 1910.

Quinn Chapel stood in the forefront of the civil rights movement from its founding during the slave era through the 1960s. The first school for blacks in Louisville opened in the basement of the church at Fourth and Green streets. In 1870 the congregation sponsored a march in Louisville to protest segregated seating on streetcars. In 1914 the church sponsored a rally against a proposed housing segregation law.

R

RADCLIFF. Radcliff is a city in northern Hardin County located on U.S. 31W six miles northwest of Elizabethtown and adjacent to the western boundary of FORT KNOX Military Reservation. The city was founded in 1919 when Col. Horace McCullum, one of Kentucky's well-known auctioneers, purchased land on Dixie Highway and sold building lots to military personnel stationed at nearby Fort Knox. McCullum named his town Radcliff as a token of his friendship with a Major Radcliff, one of the U.S. Army Corps of Engineers supervisors in charge of building the federal military establishment, then known as Camp Knox, in 1918 and 1919. Radcliff was incorporated as a sixth-class city on March 6, 1956. At that time its population was estimated to number 2,000. In 1962 it became a fifth-class city. Radcliff's first mayor was Elmer Hargan.

Economically, Radcliff is dependent on Fort Knox. Many residents are employed on the base and many retired military personnel have chosen to live in Radcliff after leaving the service. Radcliff regards Fort Knox as its largest industry. With a payroll of millions of dollars, Fort Knox guarantees a huge cash flow. Radcliff recognizes the importance of the military base to the city's economy by holding an annual weeklong Golden Armor Festival on the military base.

During the 1970s and 1980s Radcliff was one of the fastest growing cities in the state. Its population was 7,881 in 1970; 14,656 in 1980; and 19,772 in 1990.   DOUGLAS CANTRELL

RAFINESQUE, CONSTANTINE SAMUEL. Constantine Samuel Rafinesque, naturalist and philologist, was born on October 22, 1783, in Galata, a suburb of Constantinople, to Francois G.A. and Madeleine (Schmaltz) Rafinesque. His father was a French merchant and his mother the daughter of a German merchant family long resident in the Levant. Rafinesque's family moved to France the year following his birth; during the turmoil of the French Revolution, the boy was sent to live with relatives in Tuscany. He was taught by tutors; his hopes of a university education in Switzerland were thwarted by the family's reduced income after his father died in Philadelphia in 1793, of yellow fever contracted during a commercial voyage to China.

At age nineteen Rafinesque became an apprentice in the mercantile house of the Clifford Brothers in Philadelphia. During the next two years, he roamed the woods and fields from Pennsylvania to Virginia, making plant and animal collections and developing a wide correspondence with fellow naturalists. He returned to Europe in 1805 and spent the next decade in Sicily, where he was secretary to the U.S. consul. He carried on a lucrative international trade in commodities while exploring the island for plants and identifying fishes in the Palermo market that were scientifically unrecorded. During this time his first scientific books were published.

Rafinesque fathered two children in Sicily but could not legally marry their mother, Josephine Vacarro, because he was a Protestant and she a Roman Catholic. On his return to the United States in 1815, he was shipwrecked on Long Island Sound, losing all his collections and unpublished manuscripts. He remained in America the rest of his life, becoming a naturalized citizen in 1832, and did not see his family again.

Assisted by friends, he lived in New York until 1818, when he set off on a collecting trip down the Ohio River as far as Shawneetown, Illinois. During the trip he began the first comprehensive survey of the river's fish population (*Ichthyologia Ohiensis*, 1820). He stayed eight days with John James Audubon in Henderson, Kentucky, and on his return to Philadelphia passed through Lexington, where his former employer, the merchant John D. Clifford, had settled. Clifford, a trustee of Transylvania University, arranged for Rafinesque to become professor of botany and natural science there.

Rafinesque's years at Transylvania, 1819-26, though often troubled by quarrels with colleagues, were among his most productive. He published scientific names, both locally and in Europe, for thousands of plants and hundreds of animals. He became interested also in prehistoric Indian sites—identifying 148 of them in Kentucky alone—and in Indian languages, leading to his preservation of the *Walam Olum*, the epic of the migration of the Delaware Indians. At Transylvania he taught botany through the innovation of examining physical specimens and he tried, unsuccessfully, to found a botanical garden in conjunction with the university. When he returned to Philadelphia in the spring of 1826, he shipped ahead forty crates of specimens, which were the basis of his studies for the rest of his life.

Rafinesque's remaining years in Philadelphia were sustained by a variety of means. He traded in specimens and books; he gave public lectures; he organized a workingmen's bank; he invented and marketed a nostrum for tuberculosis. With the patronage of the wealthy Charles Wetherill, he issued an astonishing array of books—not only natural history works but also philosophical poetry and a linguistic study of Hebrew—although they found few buyers. By Rafinesque's own count, he published 220 "works, pamphlets, essays, and tracts," yet he left as great a bulk in manuscript, most of which was sold as junk after his death. Best known for remarkable fecundity in devising scientific names—6,700 in botany alone—Rafinesque also had some insight into a number of theoretical issues in biology that became important later: the impermanence of species, the significance of fossils in dating sedimentary geological strata, and such ecological considerations as plant geography and plant succession.

Rafinesque died in Philadelphia in 1840, probably on September 19, and was buried in Ronaldson's Cemetery. Eighty-four years later, friends of Transylvania excavated the gravesite and reinterred at Transylvania the bones thought to be his. (Because of a misunderstanding about the succession of six burials that had taken place in the same Philadelphia gravesite over time, the stone at Transylvania that today bears the name Rafinesque in fact covers the remains of a woman named Mary Passimore.)

See Huntley Dupre, *Rafinesque in Lexington, 1819-1826* (Lexington, Ky., 1945). Charles Boewe, *Fitzpatrick's Rafinesque: A Sketch of His Life with Bibliography* (Weston, Mass., 1982).

CHARLES BOEWE

RAILROADS. Kentucky's first railroad was the result of Lexington's need for an efficient transportation system to compete with the Ohio River cities of Louisville and Cincinnati. The LEXINGTON & OHIO (L&O) was chartered in 1830. In 1836, a crude tramline, the Barren River Railroad, was built in Warren County, giving Bowling Green elementary freight service to a wharf about a mile and a half away on the Barren River; the LOUISVILLE & NASHVILLE (L&N) acquired the spur in the 1850s.

Various schemes to build railroads through the state abounded during the 1830s and 1840s. Foremost was a projected road from Charleston, South Carolina, to Cincinnati via Cumberland Gap and Paris. From 1850 until the Civil War, more than 450 miles of new railroads were constructed in the state. The L&N completed its mainline through Bowling Green to Nashville. Covington, Paris, and Lexington were joined in 1856 by predecessors of the KENTUCKY CENTRAL Railway, and the Mobile & Ohio (M&O), running north from the gulf, reached Columbus in the Jackson Purchase in early 1861. Paducah interests built a branch through Mayfield to meet the M&O. Several roads were projected from Lexington, but only thirteen miles of a line toward Danville were built.

The Civil War interrupted state rail development, but the war years demonstrated the worth of railroads as vital support systems for the military. From 1865 to 1880, much of Kentucky's trunk and primary network was built and rebuilt, and state rail mileage swelled from 567 to 1,536. A Louisville-Cincinnati link opened in 1869; the L&N sent its Lebanon branch toward Knoxville; an Evansville-Nashville trunk that passed through Madisonville and Hopkinsville was finished in 1871; a year later, the Elizabethtown & Paducah connected the Jackson Purchase with north-central Kentucky; in 1873, an Illinois Central (IC) affiliate finished a through route from East Cairo to Fulton; and new bridges across the Ohio at Louisville and Newport assured connections to the Northeast and Midwest early in the decade.

Central Kentucky got the CINCINNATI SOUTHERN by 1877, and segments of the Lexington & Big Sandy began from the Bluegrass and Ashland. Secondary and feeder lines were built during the period to tap natural resources and connect rural communities with population centers. Railroad construction accelerated in the 1880s and early 1890s. The Chesapeake & Ohio's (C&O's) main line from Ashland to Covington and its newly acquired Lexington & Big Sandy were completed, as was a Louisville-Owensboro-Henderson line. The Kentucky Union reached Jackson from Lexington, while other coal-gathering lines entered Bell, Knox, Lawrence and Johnson counties. Through passenger trains took travelers from Kentucky to New York City; Washington, D.C.; New Orleans; Jacksonville, Florida; Atlanta; Chicago; and Memphis, Tennessee. New steel bridges across the Ohio replaced ferry operations at Henderson, Louisville, and Covington. Rail mileages doubled, from 1,536 miles in 1880 to more than 3,000 miles by 1900.

Various forms of aid encouraged railroad construction during the second half of the nineteenth century. Most prevalent were stock subscriptions taken by towns and counties to support specific lines; other forms of aid were loans or donations of property for facilities or rights of way. The state, which was prohibited from directly aiding railroads, nonetheless granted liberal charters for many projects and offered tax exemptions to several roads. A few were required to guarantee lower rates on some commodities. Only the Mobile & Ohio in western Kentucky received federal aid, in the form of land grants. In recent decades, some federal funds came to Kentucky and other states to rehabilitate lightly used branch lines.

Primary and feeder routes to the Elkhorn, Hazard, and Harlan coal-producing districts were built by C&O, L&N, and N&W from 1900 to 1920; IC and L&N extended lines to coal sources in Webster and Ohio counties; and a dozen or more short lines were constructed in the same period, mainly to reach coal and timber. Some 250 miles of electric INTERURBAN railroads also were introduced, principally as commuter carriers to serve growing metropolitan areas in Louisville, Lexington, Covington, and Henderson.

Kentucky rail mileage reached its maximum by 1930; over forty companies (including the interurbans) operated 5,005 miles of line, scheduling hundreds of passenger trains. From rural counties flowed raw materials, agricultural products, minerals, and livestock to urban markets and manufacturing centers. The urban centers shipped back tools, furniture, housewares, and other staples needed by a rural populace. After 1870 minerals accounted for a large segment of freight traffic, and with development of the coal fields, coal became the principal commodity originating in Kentucky.

Routes operated by Kentucky railroads included trunk lines; primary and secondary intrastate routes; and shortlines, branches, and feeder lines.

The intercity trunk routes traversed Kentucky from north to south. The primary and secondary routes—some of which were also acquired by the larger carriers—joined all regions of the state, including the eastern and western coal fields. Shortlines, branches, and feeders reached all but twelve county seats, feeding traffic to the secondary, primary and trunk routes. No new mainline routes were built after 1930, although some new trackage was constructed during and after World War II, even as late as 1989, to serve coal and industrial developments.

Close proximity of the eastern and western coal fields to industrial centers in the Ohio Valley stimulated industrial growth, and completion of trunk and primary rail routes greatly expanded markets for Kentucky coals. Until they adopted diesels in the 1950s, Kentucky railroads were major consumers of coal mined in the state. Later, manufactured products—automobiles and trucks, automotive parts, chemicals, and plastics—as well as grains, tobacco, and beverages became volume commodities in the Kentucky railroad traffic.

Technical improvements developed by railroads nationally benefited lines in the state. Over the decades, great strides were made in upgrading track; heavy steel rails and continuously welded rail lengths were installed in many miles of trunk and primary routes. Similarly, freight equipment evolved from small tub-shaped units of a few tons of capacity to large, high-volume cars capable of carrying up to 125 tons each. Locomotives developed from the diminutive "teakettles" of the 1850s to large-boilered, multidriver machines with great tractive power. Kentucky's first diesel locomotives, a pair of yard switchers, went into service in L&N's Louisville terminals in 1939. Southern introduced the state's first diesel road freight locomotives on its Cincinnati, New Orleans & Texas Pacific through Somerset in 1941. By 1960, all Kentucky lines had replaced steam power with the cleaner and more efficient diesels.

Railroad growth years in the state were not without tensions between carriers, the public, and governmental bodies. Shippers contended with uneven and illogical rates and lawmakers agonized over fair taxation of rail properties. The legislature in 1880 created the KENTUCKY RAILROAD COMMISSION, an agency empowered to investigate railroad operations and adequacy of service across the state. The commission's role was strengthened in 1882 by a bill giving it a clearer definition of duties, and it could then levy penalties for "violations of unjust passenger and freight rates and discrimination in charges." It could also hear and determine the disposition of complaints.

Greater federal regulation over intercity rail operations came later in the decade with passage of the Interstate Commerce Act (1887) and creation of the Interstate Commerce Commission. William Goebel, a legislator from Covington, became Kentucky's champion for transport reform upon election to the legislature in 1887. It was Goebel who led the fight to make the Railroad Commission permanent in sections of the 1891 constitution, and during the decade he continued to address transport abuses and inequities. Almost a century later, passage of the Staggers Act gave roads, including Kentucky's, more contractual and rate-making freedoms with shippers. The act allowed railroads to discontinue lightly patronized services, and branch lines were greatly streamlined.

After 1920 Kentucky railroads faced growing competition from the primary system of paved roads that linked county seats, and from the U.S. highways in the 1930s and interstates after 1960. Branch lines were the first to lose traffic, although some feeders had been cut before 1900 when depletion of minerals and natural resources occurred in certain counties. Mergers also eliminated duplicate routes, and from 1930 to 1989, almost 2,000 miles of secondary, branch, and shortlines in the state were abandoned. Some were sold to shortline operators, industries, or communities—Trans-Kentucky Terminal, for one, along with Tradewater, R.J. Corman, TennKen, and several other operating shortlines. Longer regional railroads like the Paducah & Louisville (P&L) acquired more substantial track segments—in P&L's case the Illinois Central Gulf's principal western Kentucky route.

Rail passenger service in the state also suffered sharp declines as a result of highway competition. Lightweight streamlined trains and self-propelled railcars, introduced in the 1940s on trunk and secondary routes, failed to attract the patronage anticipated by the carriers, and in 1971 the remaining passenger train services in the state were integrated into Amtrak, the national system formed jointly by the carriers and the federal government. After 1980, only two Amtrak trains served the state. Several tourist railroads offered seasonal excursions over branch lines spun off by the larger systems.

By 1990, the railroads in Kentucky had become heavy freight haulers, with coal the dominant cargo. Two trunk carriers, CSX Transportation and Norfolk Southern, diversified services to include highway and river transport. Overall, the state was served by six trunkline railroads and seven regional, shortline, and terminal switching companies. Route miles operated by all railroads totaled just under 3,000 miles near the end of the decade. These companies employed approximately 8,000 men and women.

See *Rail Transportation in Kentucky*, Kentucky Transportation Cabinet, Frankfort, 1983.

CHARLES B. CASTNER

RAMSEY, FRANK VERNON, JR. Frank Vernon Ramsey, Jr., Hall of Fame basketball player, was the son of Frank Vernon, Sr., and Sarah (Muncaster) Ramsey, born on July 13, 1931, in Corydon, Kentucky. Growing up in Madisonville, Kentucky, he was a high school opponent of Cliff Hagan, with whom he attended the University of Kentucky (UK). Ramsey played varsity basketball in 1951-52, 1952-53, and 1953-54; along with Hagan, he led

UK to an undefeated season. They were denied a chance at a national championship when Ramsey, Hagan, and Lou Tsioropoulos were ruled ineligible for tournament play because of their status as graduate students. Ramsey was a three-time All-Southeastern Conference selection (1951, 1952, and 1954), and was twice an All-American, in 1952 and 1954, the year he received his B.A. degree. Although he played mainly guard, Ramsey ranked second in career rebounds at UK (1,038), and he scored 1,344 points.

Selected in the first round of the 1953 National Basketball Association (NBA) draft by the Boston Celtics, he played with the Celtics in 1955, then reported to Fort Knox, Kentucky, for army reserve duty. He returned to the Celtics in 1957 and played until 1964. He was known as Boston's "sixth starter," contributing mightily to the team's NBA championships. Coaxed out of retirement in 1971, he coached the Kentucky Colonels of the American Basketball Association for a year. Ramsey was elected to basketball's Hall of Fame in Springfield, Massachusetts, in 1981. In 1972 he became president of Dixon Bank in Webster County, and he served as a UK trustee from 1974 to 1988. Ramsey married Martha Hardwick on April 21, 1954; they have three children.

See Bert Nelli, *The Winning Tradition* (Lexington, Ky., 1984).

RANCK, GEORGE W. George W. Ranck, Kentucky historian, editor, and educator, was born in Louisville on February 13, 1841, the son of Solomon Ranck. He was raised in Shelbyville, where he attended Shelby College. He continued his studies at Kentucky University in Harrodsburg, and in 1865 became principal of its academy when the university moved to Lexington. During 1868-71 Ranck was editor of the *Lexington Observer and Reporter*. His *History of Lexington* (1872) is a 482-page book based on popular oral accounts of the early days of the city. Other works include *O'Hara and His Elegies* (1875) and *History of Fayette County* (1882).

In 1868 Ranck married Helen Carty, granddaughter of one of Lexington's founding fathers. The couple had two daughters and a son, Edwin C., a reporter for the *Kentucky Post* in Covington. Ranck was struck by a train and killed on August 2, 1901, while walking on the Louisville & Nashville Railroad tracks west of Lexington. He was buried in the Lexington Cemetery.   DAG RYEN

RANEY, JAMES ELBERT. James Elbert Raney, jazz guitarist, was born in Louisville on August 20, 1927. He was influenced by the innovative musician Charlie Christian in developing his own style, which coincided with the emergence of bebop. With his internationally acclaimed performances with jazz saxophonist Stan Getz and his reputation as the first musician to translate the bebop style to the guitar, Raney is widely considered to have had profound influence among guitarists of the day. He

has received numerous international awards, twice being a winner of the *Downbeat* international critics' poll.

See Jamey Aebersold, *Play Duets with Jimmy Raney* (New Albany, Ind., 1983).   LEE BASH

RATTERMAN, GEORGE W. George W. Ratterman, a former football player who was elected sheriff of Campbell County, Kentucky (1962-66), was born to Leander F. and Claribell (Cahill) Ratterman on November 12, 1926. Following his graduation in 1946 from Notre Dame, he played ten years of professional football, first with the Buffalo Bills of the old All American Football Conference, then with the New York Yankees, and finally with the Cleveland Browns. During his football career, he performed a piano solo with the Buffalo Symphony and he later wrote the book *Confessions of a Gypsy Quarterback* (1962). After injuries ended his football career in 1956, Ratterman studied law while working as an investment counselor in Cincinnati and doing sports commentary for network television broadcasts. Ratterman assisted in forming the National Football League Players Association and was the legal counsel for the American Football League.

In 1961 an alliance of ministers from various churches joined a Campbell County citizens group, the Committee of 500, in attempting to rid the county of gambling and prostitution run by organized crime. The group decided to run its own slate of candidates for county office, and in April 1961, Ratterman agreed to run for sheriff as a high-profile candidate. On the night of May 9, Ratterman went to a meeting set up by a business associate with a reputed syndicate member, to talk about moving casino operations out of Campbell County. At the meeting Ratterman lost consciousness after he was served a drink, apparently because of chloral hydrate—"knockout drops"— in the drink. He regained consciousness in the company of a nightclub dancer in a hotel bedroom, where the local police arrested him for prostitution and disturbing the peace. In the sensational police court trial in Newport, it became apparent that the gambling interests were working with law enforcement officials to discredit Ratterman and the reform movement. A photographer testified that he had been contacted weeks earlier and asked to photograph such a scene. Charges against Ratterman were dropped, and the reform movement, which had stood behind Ratterman throughout the ordeal, gained momentum. Gov. Bert T. Combs (1959-63) responded to the public outcry, ordering prosecution of four officials, including the sheriff and police chief of Campbell County and the police chief of Newport. After an investigation by the U.S. Department of Justice, six other persons, among them police officers and an attorney, were brought to trial for violating the civil rights of Ratterman.

In November 1961, Ratterman and the other reform ticket candidates were swept into office and the operators of the casinos and nightclubs left town. Ratterman lost the election for county judge in 1965. In 1966 he was defeated by Gene Snyder in a bid for election to the U.S. Congress. In 1967 he moved to Denver, Colorado. Ratterman was married to Anne Henglebrook of Newport on December 12, 1947, and is the father of ten children.

See John Ed Pearce, *Divide and Dissert: Kentucky Politics, 1930-1963* (Lexington, Ky., 1987).

MICHAEL W. FRENCH

RAUCH, JOSEPH. Joseph Rauch, Louisville rabbi and internationally known civic leader, was born on December 25, 1880, in Podhajoe, Austria. He immigrated to the United States at age twelve to join his parents, who had traveled separately to Galveston, Texas. Rauch attended the University of Cincinnati and was ordained at Hebrew Union College in Cincinnati. From 1905 to 1912 he was rabbi at Sioux City, Iowa. On April 12, 1912, he arrived in Louisville to become rabbi of Temple Adath Israel (now Temple Adath Israel-Brith Sholom). An outstanding orator, he was rabbi there for forty-five years; in 1942 he was elected rabbi for life.

For seventeen years Rauch was president of the board of the Louisville Free Public Library, ending segregation there during his tenure. In 1953 he headed a citizens' committee for a six-year school building program; he also served as a University of Louisville trustee for twelve years, and was chairman of the Louisville Red Cross for four years. He became the first chairman of the International Center at the University of Louisville, was one of the original panelists on WHAS radio's "Moral Side of the News," and, with two others, organized Louisville's first Community Chest campaign.

After World War I, Herbert Hoover, then head of the American Relief Program, sent Rauch on an investigatory mission to Europe; he made a fact-finding visit to Israel after World War II. Rauch founded the World Union of Liberal Judaism in 1955 and was a member of the International Prison Congress, Southern Council on International Affairs, Central Conference of American Rabbis, National Conference of Christians and Jews, Young Men's Hebrew Association (now the Jewish Community Center), and National Jewish Welfare Board. In 1952 Rauch was named CBS's "Man of the Week." He also studied at the University of Chicago, Columbia University in New York, and Cambridge University in England, and he received a Th.D. from Southern Baptist Theological Seminary in Louisville. Hebrew Union College, where he served as a trustee, awarded him an honorary Ph.D. in 1944.

Rauch married Etta Rosenfelder on June 17, 1913. Rauch died on February 17, 1957, and was buried in Adath Israel Cemetery in Louisville. He is memorialized by the Rauch Planetarium at the University of Louisville and by a school for retarded children in New Albany, Indiana, that bears his name.

See Herman Landau, *Adath Louisville, The Story of a Jewish Community* (Louisville 1981).

HERMAN LANDAU

RAY, JAMES. James Ray, political leader, was born in North Carolina in 1760 or 1761. When he and his two brothers were young, his father, given name unknown, died and his mother, Mary (Buntin) Ray, then married Hugh McGary. The family migrated to Kentucky in 1775. They were among the twenty to thirty families led by Daniel Boone through the Cumberland Gap. McGary decided to go on to Fort Harrod with a few other families and arrived in mid-September. On March 6, 1777, Ray and his older brother William, Thomas Shores, and William Coomes were clearing land near Shawnee Run in Mercer County when Indians attacked. William Ray and Shores were killed, Coomes saved himself by hiding under a log, and James Ray outran the Indians back to the fort to warn of the danger. The next day, March 7, the Shawnee began their first siege of the fort. Ray enlisted in the militia at Fort Harrod as a scout. In 1778 he was a lieutenant in Gen. George Rogers Clark's expedition to capture Vincennes and Kaskaskia. In May 1779, Ray was a captain in Col. John Bowman's attack on the Indian village of Old Chillicothe. Ray survived the defeat of the Battle of Blue Licks in 1782 and participated in the retaliatory campaign into Ohio in November of that year under Clark.

In 1779 McGary built a stockade on his Shawnee Run property and Ray aided his stepfather in settling McGary's Station. In 1787 Ray settled in Mercer County along Shawnee Run. He remained active in the militia, receiving the rank of major in 1789 and colonel in 1797. In 1808 Ray was major general in the Kentucky militia and during the War of 1812 became a brigadier general. He served twelve terms in the Kentucky House of Representatives: in 1801-03, 1807-1812, 1814, 1815, and 1818. On July 5, 1781, Ray married Millie Yocum. She died on December 1, 1783, leaving two infant sons, William and Jesse. On February 7, 1787, Ray married Elizabeth Talbot. They had eleven children who survived into adulthood. Ray died at his Mercer County home on May 9, 1835. He was buried in his orchard on a knoll overlooking Shawnee Springs, as he had requested.

See Kathryn H. Mason, "The Career of General James Ray, Kentucky Pioneer," *FCHQ* 19 (April 1945): 86-114; Kathryn H. Mason, "The Family and Fortune of General James Ray, Pioneer of Ft. Harrod," *Register* 43 (Jan. 1945): 59-68.

READJUSTMENT. Although it had remained within the Union during the Civil War, Kentucky, as a slave state, was subjected to brief military occupation in the Reconstruction period. It felt the impact of the FREEDMEN'S BUREAU, suffered the ignominy of a congressional investigation into the qualifications of its elected representatives in 1867, and for years was terrorized by lawless and violent guerrilla bands who wandered the countryside after the war's end.

As the war came to an end, new issues arose to rankle Kentuckians. The promulgation of the Thirteenth Amendment to abolish slavery in January 1865, the Civil Rights Act of 1866, and the extension of the Freedmen's Bureau to Kentucky in December 1865 increased antagonism toward the federal government. Democrats insisted that "reconstruction" was "base usurpation" of the rights of the people, and thereby won the backing of conservatives. In the August 1866 election, ratification of the Thirteenth Amendment was the primary issue, together with Union Gen. John M. Palmer's supervision of elections during the period of occupation. The Democrats gained a majority in the General Assembly and five of the nine U.S. congressional seats. When the newly elected legislators repealed the Expatriation Act of March 11, 1862, which had denied citizenship to Confederates, Republicans charged that the Democratic party was infested with "Rebels." Hostility toward the federal government increased when rumors circulated that Congress was intervening in Kentucky elections. In the end, Kentucky rejected ratification of the Thirteenth Amendment, as it did with the Fourteenth and Fifteenth.

When President Andrew Johnson attempted to create a moderate wing of his party, Kentucky Republicans hoped to entice into their ranks the large political faction in the state known as conservatives, but the conservatives were politically more sympathetic to the Democrats. In the senatorial election of 1867, Democrat Garrett DAVIS's victory over Republican Benjamin H. BRISTOW indicated that most conservatives had supported the Democrats. A united Democratic party elected John L. HELM (who died a few days after assuming office) as governor, on a platform that condemned congressional Reconstruction, the high protective tariff, and the corruption of public offices. Those conservatives unable to accept the Democratic party line, like John M. HARLAN, joined the Republican party.

In Kentucky, the major issue in the elections of 1867 was the Fourteenth Amendment, which threw the cloak of federal protection around the freedman. Whereas Republicans supported the amendment, Democrats attacked it as a further invasion of the rights of the state. In the May congressional elections, the Democrats elected nine congressmen and in August they won not only the governorship but also majorities in both houses of the legislature. The charge by Sen. Charles Sumner of Massachusetts that Kentucky was disloyal and needed reconstruction had much to do with the Democratic landslide. Kentucky Republicans claimed that the "lost cause" had captured the state, but in reality the Democrats were not pro-Confederate but anticongressional, as a result of longstanding controversies with the federal government.

During the spring of 1868 the Fifteenth Amendment, which enfranchised blacks, further increased Kentucky's hostility toward the government. Democrats regarded this as a move by the Republicans to regain their political strength and insisted that the amendment was an unconstitutional violation of the "inherent sovereignty" of the state. In an effort to counter Democratic criticism, the Republicans founded the *Louisville Daily Commercial*. But the consolidated COURIER-JOURNAL, of which Henry WATTERSON emerged as editor, established an even stronger advocate for the Democrats. Calling for a "new departure," Watterson urged Kentuckians to put aside their prejudices and to accept the results of the war, the Fourteenth and Fifteenth amendments, industrial development, and railroad expansion.

Kentucky Democrats criticized the impeachment proceedings against President Andrew Johnson, but Republicans remained silent, waiting for the presidential election of 1868. Despite Republican support for Gen. Ulysses S. Grant, the Democrats not only carried the state for Horatio Seymour but also captured the governorship and elected a full delegation to Congress.

The Freedmen's Bureau closed its offices at the end of 1868. Despite Kentucky's hostility toward the bureau, it had done creditable work for the freedmen. It helped to stabilize labor conditions for former slaves, organized its own bank, set up its own Freedmen's court to ensure justice for former slaves who were denied due process in Kentucky courts, and attempted to protect them against violence.

In the postwar years Kentucky was plagued by white racist groups known as Regulators or Ku Klux Klan (KKK), who created a reign of terror in Marion, Boyle, Jessamine, Lincoln, Mercer, Nelson, Nicholas, Franklin, and other counties. The *Frankfort Weekly Commonwealth* newspaper on March 31, 1871, cited 115 instances of shooting, hanging, and whipping of blacks between 1867 and 1871 by roaming bands of terrorists. During January 1868 the Freedmen's Bureau recorded fifty-three crimes committed against blacks. Gangs took black prisoners out of jails to hang or shoot them; in October 1866 the black section of Lebanon was destroyed; in 1869 in Frankfort a band of assassins set fire to a neighborhood of black homes, shot blacks as they ran from their homes, and threw the bodies back into the flames. As late as 1871-73, George Armstrong Custer was stationed at Elizabethtown with the 7th Cavalry to break up the KKK and ferret out illegal distillers.

With the adoption of the Fifteenth Amendment in 1870, Republicans believed that the newly enfranchised blacks would vote Republican. At the first black convention—"First Republican Convention of Colored Citizens of the State of Kentucky"— held in Frankfort, the freedmen asked for equal patronage with whites. But Republicans, fearing this would alienate their white supporters, rejected their request.

Education received a boost during this period. In 1862 Congress had passed the Morrill Act, which granted public lands to states for the establishment of agricultural and mechanical colleges, and in 1865 the General Assembly created a state university at Lexington. Superintendent Zach F. Smith also secured increased support for the public schools, and to ensure segregation of the races, a separate school fund and increased appropriations for blacks were provided in 1875. Berea College opened its doors to blacks and whites in 1866.

The movement for women's rights spread in Kentucky during the postwar period, with suffrage groups springing up in various parts of the state and out-of-state leaders visiting to speak and recruit volunteers. Laura Clay and her sisters were early leaders in Kentucky. Although the movement was roundly rejected in the local press, it laid the groundwork for the successful movement of the twentieth century.

The issues in the gubernatorial contest of August 1871 were competition between the LOUISVILLE & NASHVILLE Railroad and the CINCINNATI SOUTHERN Railroad for an Ohio-Tennessee line through central Kentucky, the right of blacks to testify in courts, the suppression of Klan activity, and increased support for public education. Despite Republican courtship of the black vote, a well-organized Democratic party elected Preston H. Leslie (1871-75) governor. In the ensuing legislative session the Cincinnati Southern Railroad Bill was passed. Black testimony was admitted in state courts for the first time in 1871 in the famous Crittenden case.

Kentucky Republicans backed Grant for a second term in 1872. The faction that called itself Straight-Out Democrats bolted their party, refusing to support party nominee Horace Greeley, and nominated the Bourbon Democrat Charles O'Connor for the presidency. However, the Democrat-Liberal-Republican ticket headed by Greeley carried Kentucky.

With the resumption of specie payment in 1875, debt-ridden Kentuckians, suffering in the western counties from the depression of 1873 and the collapse of tobacco prices, left the Democratic party and joined the Grange movement. The Republicans were thus able to elect John D. WHITE, their first representative to Congress since 1866. Democrats now courted the black vote. When J.B. McCREARY (1875-79) won the governorship, he proclaimed in his inaugural address the demise of Reconstruction and urged Kentuckians to look "to the Constitution" as "the safeguard of every citizen." The election of Rutherford B. Hayes as president in 1877 confirmed McCreary's beliefs about the end of Reconstruction.

See Ross A. Webb, *Kentucky in the Reconstruction Era* (Lexington, Ky. 1979); E. Merton Coulter, *The Civil War and Readjustment in Kentucky* (Chapel Hill, N.C. 1926); Hambleton Tapp & James C. Klotter, *Kentucky: Decades of Discord 1865-1900* (Frankfort, Ky. 1977).

ROSS A. WEBB

RECEVEUR, BETTY (LAYMAN). Betty (Layman) Receveur, novelist, was born October 25, 1930, in Louisville, the daughter of Russell and Georgia (Heyser) Layman. She was reared by her paternal grandparents, Frank Fuller and Addie (Shelton) Layman. She attended local public and parochial schools and credits the Dominican nuns with her respect for language and her love for literature. In 1945 she married Donald William Re-

ceveur; she is the mother of three sons—Donald, Jr., Richard, and Brett. Receveur has written three historical romances set in New Orleans and San Francisco: *Sable Flanagan* (1979); *Molly Gallagher* (1982); and *Carrie Kingston* (1984). Her *Oh, Kentucky!* (1990), is a historical novel that deals with the settlement of the Bluegrass section of Kentucky.

WADE HALL

RECONSTRUCTION. See Readjustment.

RECORDS SURVEY (STATE). In 1950 the Commonwealth of Kentucky began to turn its attention to proper maintenance of its public records. A budget request by the Kentucky Historical Society to establish a microfilm unit for the preservation of some of the records in the society's care inspired Gov. Earle Clements (1947-50) to authorize a survey of all state records. A Committee on Records, appointed by the governor, hired James C. Boyd of Lexington, a records management consultant, to conduct the survey. Boyd's report, dated February 28, 1950, detailed in text and photographs the parlous state of records storage in many state offices at that time. Improper record storage created a fire hazard in many offices.

As a result of the survey, the General Assembly established the Records Control Board on March 24, 1950. Declaring an emergency, the legislature named the commissioner of finance, the attorney general, the auditor of public accounts, the clerk of the court of appeals, and the secretary-treasurer of the Kentucky Historical Society (the last serving as chairman) to the board. Its duties were to promulgate regulations for the disposal of public records. Drawing on an emergency fund, Gov. Clements made available the initial money to establish microfilming at the Historical Society and to pay $5,000 for the records survey. No further money, however, was provided, so no records management officer was hired under the plan and no further action was taken.

Most of Kentucky's public records languished in neglect for another eight years, until legislation in 1958 established the Archives and Records Commission and the Archives and Records Service (now the Public Records Division, Kentucky Department for Libraries and Archives). The survey and related activity sparked the eventual addition of a permanent microfilming laboratory to the Kentucky Historical Society.

See Charles F. Hinds, "The Editor's Desk, Public Records Management in Kentucky," *Register* 55 (July 1957): 291-92.   MARY MARGARET BELL

RED MILE. The 175-acre Red Mile complex for standardbred horse racing is operated by the Lexington Trots Breeders Association. Racing began on September 28, 1875, at the inaugural meeting of the Kentucky Trotting Horse Breeders Association (KTHBA). A small crowd saw a bay colt named Odd Fellow win the first race, the Lexington Stakes. The Agricultural and Mechanical Fair

Association then owned the track and grandstand at South Broadway in Lexington, Kentucky. The grandstand was an elaborate Victorian structure stretching from the finish line to the first turn. After some lean years, the KTHBA in 1893 was stable enough to purchase half interest in the Fair Association grounds, and help construct a new $25,000, double-decked grandstand that seated 5,000. Lumber from the original grandstand, which had collapsed in 1892, was used to build track barns. During construction, the one-mile track was moved to its present location and a half-mile track was added to the infield. In 1896 the KTHBA bought out the remaining interest in the track at auction for $32,000. Fire destroyed the second stands in 1931, and the third grandstand was completed in 1934.

The three-story octagonal building, topped by a large cupola, that stands at the track entrance was designed by Lexington architect John McMurty in 1879 and constructed in 1880. It was originally used to house floral exhibits. The structure was partially financed by a $25,000 appropriation from the U.S. Congress for damages done to the old fair grounds, between Limestone and Rose streets, by federal troops during the Civil War. At the turn of the century, it was known as the Round Barn, as it had been converted to stables on the first and second floors, while grooms used the third story. When a city ordinance in the late 1800s prohibited gambling within the city limits, sale of auction pools (wagering) was moved from the PHOENIX HOTEL to the Round Barn, which was then located outside the city limits of Lexington. Parimutuel wagering began at the Red Mile in 1942. The KTHBA had serious financial difficulties in the early 1940s, and the Trotting Horse Clubs of America stepped in to save the 1942 season. In 1945 the Lexington Trots Breeders Association was organized specifically to operate Red Mile complex.

The Red Mile instituted the Kentucky Futurity in 1893 with a purse of $11,800 for three-year-old colts and fillies. Oro Wilkes won the first meet in five heats; his best time was 2:14.5. In 1990 the Futurity purse of $180,000 was won by Star Mystic, in three heats, with a top time of 1:54.2. Since 1955, the Kentucky Futurity, the Hambletonian, and the Yonkers Trots have formed trotting's Triple Crown. In 1912 the Red Mile first hosted the Grand Circuit, a series of standardbred races from May to November that began in 1893 at other tracks across the nation. Now the oldest stop on the circuit, the Red Mile hosts the event for eight days in September and October. The Red Mile handle for the Grand Circuit was $1.1 million in 1980; in 1990, including intertrack betting, it grew to $1.6 million. For the entire season, the Red Mile's handle was $8 million in 1980, $11.5 million in 1988, and $8.8 million in 1990.

Since 1892, standardbred auctions have been part of the Red Mile's operations. The current Tattersalls sales began in 1934, when eighty-one standardbreds sold for $62,937. In 1990, the 527 horses sold brought a total of $12,238,900. In 1983 a filly

pacer, Laugh A Day, brought a record $650,000 for the annual September yearling sale; Winky's Gill, also a pacer, holds the record for the October mixed sale at $800,000, set in 1986.

See Tom White, *A Century Of Speed: The Red Mile, 1875-1975* (Lexington, Ky., 1975).

TOM WHITE

RED RIVER. The ninety-six-mile-long Red River rises in Wolfe County, Kentucky, and flows almost due west to drain into the Kentucky River. For a long distance it travels through a wide flat valley. The headwaters, at an elevation of 1,200 feet above sea level, deeply dissect the Cumberland Plateau, and its mouth, at 567 feet above sea level, is opposite College Hill in Madison County. The Red River also passes through Menifee, Powell, Clark, and Estill counties. It takes its name from the iron pyrite, a reddish mineral, found along its banks. Towns along the Red River include Palmer, Clay City, Stanton, Hazel Green, Campton, Slade, Rosslyn, Lee City, Bowen, and Malaga. Its tributaries are the Peck and Osborne branches, and the Stillwater, Gladie, Chimney Top, Swift Camp, Cane, Hardwick, and Cat creeks.

In 1962 the Red River received wide publicity during the successful national effort to preserve the RED RIVER GORGE—an area of towering cliffs, rock houses, chimney rocks, and natural arches—from inundation by an impoundment. The U.S. Army Corps of Engineers had studied possible improvements to the river for flood control, navigation, and the generation of hydroelectric power and had recommended that a dam be built in this region. This plan was deferred and placed in the inactive file in 1976.

The Red River of central Kentucky and its gorge are located within two and a half hours' driving time for more than 3 million people. About nine miles of this river, between KY 715 and KY 746, is classified as a Kentucky wild river. This scenic area has many natural arches, white-water canoeing, wildflowers, and more than fifty species of fish.

In June 1769 Daniel Boone, John Findley, John Stewart, and others reached the Red River from the Yadkin River in North Carolina. Landowner deeds date back to 1793, when a land grant was made by Patrick Henry to an early Kentucky settler in the Red River area. In 1786 Stephen Collins and his brother discovered deposits of iron ore near Clay City and built an iron forge. In the 1800s the Red River iron works produced bar iron and nails.

A lesser-known river in southwestern Kentucky is also named Red River. It flows through Logan and Simpson counties and is part of the Cumberland River drainage system.

See Wilford A. Bladen, *A Geography of Kentucky: A Topical-Regional Overview* (Dubuque., Iowa, 1984).   MICHAEL E. WALTERS

RED RIVER GORGE. The Red River Gorge is a scenic area that extends for approximately twenty-five miles along the middle and upper sections of the RED RIVER, a tributary of the Kentucky River. The gorge lies within the Daniel Boone National Forest in Powell, Wolfe, and Menifee counties, about forty miles east of Lexington near Slade, Kentucky, and just north of the Bert T. Combs Mountain Parkway.

The area is noted for its dramatic natural features and a diversity of flora and fauna. Cliffs, rockshelters, rock arches known as natural bridges, and other features are composed largely of sandstone and sandstone conglomerates that date to the Mississippian period, more than 300 million years ago. Stream erosion and weathering processes formed the gorge along the serpentine path of the Red River and its tributary creeks.

Prehistoric Native Americans lived on the numerous rock ledges in the gorge as early as 8000 B.C. Daniel Boone is believed to have explored the area, and he may have spent the winter of 1769-70 in the Red River Gorge. Permanent settlement took place after 1787, when iron was discovered and a furnace was built on the Red River. Saltpeter was also mined from the sandstone formations. Both industrial operations peaked during the War of 1812.

In 1886 the Kentucky Union Railroad (later the Louisville & Nashville) laid tracks through the vicinity, and logging was extensive until the 1920s. Several narrow-gauge railroads were constructed into the gorge for the purpose of hauling timber to the mainline railroad, but all were abandoned by 1930. A permanent landmark of the logging railroads is a tunnel constructed near the town of Nada in 1912 by the Dana Lumber Company. After the railroad was abandoned, the tunnel was converted for one-lane automobile traffic and is part of KY 77.

The Red River Gorge was not well known until a controversy in the late 1960s and early 1970s, when environmentalists fought a proposal by the U.S. Army Corps of Engineers for a $34 million, 5,000-acre impoundment of the North Fork of the Red River. Opponents of the proposed dam were encouraged by Supreme Court Justice William O. Douglas, whose well-publicized hike in the gorge helped to rally support. In October 1975 the dam proposal was stopped by Gov. Julian Carroll (1974-79) and in 1976, 25,630 acres of the unique area were given federal protective status as a national geological area.

See Robert H. Ruchhoft, *Kentucky's Land of the Arches* (Cincinnati 1976); Sara Alexander, "Conflict, Environmental Protection, and Social Well-Being: The Exercise of Power in Red River Gorge," Ph. D. diss., University of Kentucky, 1987.

WILLIAM A. WITHINGTON

REED, BOYD F. Boyd F. Reed, eastern Kentucky coal operator and community leader, was born on September 3, 1897, in Shamokin, Pennsylvania, to Daniel and Katherine (Reitz) Reed. After working for coal companies in Pennsylvania and Ohio for thirteen years, Reed moved to Floyd County, Kentucky, where he and his brother, C.D., started a number of coal companies. Reed also helped found

the Big Sandy Elkhorn Coal Operators, later serving as its president. He helped bring about the Kentucky Coal Association, and was later elected its president. He was named by acting Gov. Harry Lee Waterfield (1955-59, 1963-67) as chairman of the Eastern Kentucky Regional Planning Commission, 1957-62. The commission's Program 60 led the way to the enactment of the Federal Appalachian Planning Act and Commission in 1964. Reed was also active in many civic and philanthropic causes and a leader in national coal circles. He was named to the board of regents at Morehead State University, where an industrial science building carries his name.

Reed married Ruth Mauer in 1920; they had five children: Alvin, Helen, David, Marianna, and Phyllis. Reed died on July 13, 1989, in Lexington, Kentucky, and was buried in Davidson Memorial Gardens in Floyd County.

See B.F. Reed, *My Life in Coal* (Lexington, Ky., 1985).   HENRY C. MAYER

REED, STANLEY FORMAN. Stanley Forman Reed, U.S. Supreme Court justice, was born on December 31, 1884, in Minerva, Kentucky, into an old-line, prominent family of Mason County. His mother, of colonial ancestry, was the former Frances Forman, and his father, John Anderson Reed, was a medical doctor, bank president, and landowner. This combination of business and agricultural interests profoundly influenced the young Reed, particularly the organizing work that his father did with the first tobacco cooperative soon after the turn of the century. Reed earned an A.B. degree from Kentucky Wesleyan at Winchester in 1902 and a second A.B. from Yale in 1906. He studied law at the University of Virginia, Columbia University, and the Sorbonne.

Reed returned to Maysville to read law, and began practicing after Judge Charles Newell admitted him to the Kentucky bar in 1910. In 1912, as soon as his age allowed, he was elected to the Kentucky General Assembly and was reelected in 1914. He worked on legislation on child labor and workmen's compensation. As president of the Kentucky Young Democrats, Reed campaigned for the election of Woodrow Wilson in 1916. He served as an army first lieutenant in World War I.

In 1920 Reed was one of the central figures in the restoration of the Burley Tobacco Growers Cooperative Association and became its lawyer. Partly through intercession of James Stone, past president of the co-op, Reed was appointed by the Hoover administration as counsel for the Federal Farm Board. In 1933, during the last months of the Hoover administration, Reed became counsel for the Reconstruction Finance Corporation. President Franklin Roosevelt kept Reed in that position, and he argued successfully before the Supreme Court the government's right to reduce the gold backing of the dollar.

Reed became solicitor general in 1935 and went about the task of defending New Deal legislation to the Supreme Court with mixed results. He successfully argued the legality of the Wagner Act and the Tennessee Valley Authority, but the Court did not accept his arguments concerning the constitutionality of the National Recovery Act and Agricultural Adjustment Act. Those defeats stimulated Roosevelt's "court-packing" scheme, in which Reed wisely played no meaningful role. In 1938 Roosevelt nominated Reed to the Supreme Court. He was confirmed by the Senate as the sixty-ninth associate justice on January 25, 1938, and served until his retirement on February 25, 1957, the last Supreme Court justice who had no law degree.

Reed's New Deal background proved to be a poor predictor of his actions as a justice. Reed illustrated in his more than three hundred opinions an independence that quickly made him a swing vote on the court. He was not an ideologue, but rather decided each case on its basis in law and what he felt objectively to be the best possible outcome for all concerned. Not an activist judge in the sense of enlarging the powers of the court, Reed deferred to the legislative and executive branches of government.

The most celebrated lawsuit during Reed's term, the desegregation case *Brown v. Board of Education* (1954), may have been the one to cause the justice the most personal anguish. Reed had voted several times for the rights of blacks and had written the opinion that struck down the South's "white primary" (*Smith v. Allwright*, 1944). On the other hand, the deeds for Reed's own housing development in Maysville contained racially restrictive clauses, and he probably believed the schools in question in *Brown v. Board of Education* were not unconstitutional. George V. Mickum, his law clerk, explained Reed's vote, which completed the unanimous decision in favor of desegregation in this way: "Because he was a Southerner, even a lone dissent by him would give a lot of grist for making trouble. For the good of the country, he put aside his own basis for dissent."

Reed continued to hear cases for the U.S. court of appeals after his retirement, making his home at the Mayflower Hotel in Washington, D.C. Throughout his career Reed traveled back to Mason County, where he kept a residence and farm and maintained business interests. He helped dedicate the Albert Sidney Johnston House in 1955 and was honored in 1957 by Maysville with a special day of celebration, a bronze plaque on the courthouse, and the renaming of Court Street as Stanley Reed Court. Reed married Winifred Elgin on May 11, 1908. He died in Huntington, New York, on April 2, 1980, and was buried in the Maysville Cemetery.

See Leon and Fred Israel, eds., *The Justices of the United States Supreme Court, 1789-1969, Their Lives and Opinions* (New York 1969); William Obrien, *Justice Reed and the First Amendment: The Religion Clauses* (Washington, D.C., 1958).

JOHN KLEE

REELFOOT LAKE. Reelfoot Lake is located in Fulton County, Kentucky, and in Lake County, Tennessee. It covers an area of 27,000 acres in a cres-

cent shape fourteen miles long and three to four miles wide. Beneath the lake lie former channels of the Mississippi River and of the Bayou de Chien and the Reelfoot River, for which the lake is named. The lake was formed by the NEW MADRID earthquake on December 16, 1811, and two aftershocks on January 23 and February 7. The immense sunken area left by the quake slowly filled with water, forming Reelfoot Lake. The lake surface is dotted with yankapins, lotus pads with yellow and cream-colored flowers. Moss seed and duckweed form green films in and around the stunted cypress groves. Sawgrass, mulefoot, smartweed, and wild rice grow along the borders of the lake.   WILLIAM B. SCOTT, JR.

REESE, HAROLD HENRY. Harold Henry ("Pee Wee") Reese, baseball player, son of Carl and Emma Reese, was born on a small farm in Meade County, Kentucky, between Ekron and Brandenburg, on July 23, 1918. When he was a child, the family moved to Louisville, where he got his nickname not because of his size but because of his prowess at marbles. One year he was the runner-up to the national champion in the *Louisville Courier-Journal* marble tournament. He graduated from DuPont Manual High School in 1936.

As a professional baseball player, Reese was first signed by the Louisville Colonels of the American Association in 1937. His fielding skill at shortstop attracted the notice of major league scouts, and in 1939 a group that included Boston Red Sox owner Tom Yawkey purchased the Louisville Colonels baseball club for $195,000, largely because they wanted Reese's contract. Later that year the club sold Reese to the Brooklyn Dodgers for the equivalent of $75,000 ($35,000 in cash and four players). At the time, Larry MacPhail, president of the Dodgers, described Reese as the most instinctive base runner he had ever seen.

During his rookie year (1940), the Kentuckian displaced Dodger regular Leo Durocher and thus began a sixteen-year tenure at shortstop that was interrupted only by a three-year stint in the Navy (1943-45). During the seasons that Reese played full-time with the Dodgers (1941-42 and 1946-57), his team finished first in the league seven times, second four times, and third twice. He played in seven World Series. Reese was known for his clutch hitting and for big plays in the field. He also led the National League in stolen bases (thirty in 1952), in double plays four times (1942 and 1946-48), in runs scored (132 in 1947), and in fielding average (.977 in 1949). He was named to the All-Star Team eight times (1947-54). Reese was such a dominant shortstop that the well-stocked Dodger farm system was unable to produce a player capable of dislodging him. Players who tried (Tommy Brown, Mike Sandlock, Stan Rojek, Eddie Miksis, Chico Carrasquel, Bobby Morgan, Billy Hunter, Don Zimmer, and Chico Fernandez) all ended up playing for other teams. Reese's offensive career totals (126 home runs, 885 runs batted in, and a .269 batting average) do not begin to measure his value to the team. He was the team's captain, and Dodger sportscaster Red Barber described him as the glue that kept his team together. Reese, instrumental in smoothing Jackie Robinson's entrance into baseball, was called "the catalyst of baseball integration," by author Roger Kahn.

After his baseball career, Reese worked as a broadcaster with CBS, NBC, and the Cincinnati Reds. He was elected to Baseball's Hall of Fame in Cooperstown, New York, on August 12, 1984. He is director of the college and professional baseball staff at Hillerich and Bradsby, maker of the Louisville Slugger bat. Reese married Dorothy Walton on March 29, 1942; they have two children, Barbara and Mark.

See Roger Kahn, *The Boys of Summer* (New York 1972); Gary Luhr, "Dizzy, Jackie and the 'Boys of Summer': Pee Wee Reese Talks About Baseball Then and Now," *Rural Kentuckian* (July 1981): 7-10.   WILLIAM MARSHALL

REGISTER OF THE KENTUCKY HISTORICAL SOCIETY. The principal publication of the state historical society, the *Register* has appeared continuously since 1903. Articles in the quarterly focus primarily on Kentucky history; an extensive book review section features critiques of current works in Kentucky and U.S. history. A sampling of the scholars who have contributed to the journal reads like a who's who in Kentucky studies: Harry M. Caudill, Thomas D. Clark, J. Winston Coleman, Jr., Lowell Harrison, Willard Rouse Jillson, Otto A. Rothert, Jesse Stuart, and Edna Talbott Whitley. Eight people have served as editor of the journal: Jennie Chinn Morton, H.V. McChesney, Bayless E. Hardin, Charles F. Hinds, George M. Chinn, G. Glenn Clift, Hambleton Tapp, James C. Klotter, and Thomas H. Appleton, Jr.

THOMAS H. APPLETON, JR.

REGULATOR UPRISING. The lawlessness that plagued Kentucky after the Civil War led to frequent outbreaks of vigilantism throughout the state. The majority of these organizations described themselves as "Regulators"—a term popularized by vigilantes on the southern frontier before the Revolutionary War. Although generally local and sporadic in nature, postwar vigilantism sparked a popular uprising that swept through northeastern Kentucky in 1879-81.

The uprising began in Elliott County, where outlaws in 1877 had burned a portion of Sandy Hook, the county seat. In September 1879, following a wave of crime marked by violence against women, the citizens of Elliott banded together and took it into their own hands to enforce the laws. In a proclamation to the people, "Judge Lynch" warned that lawlessness would no longer be tolerated. On the night of October 20, 1879, two hundred armed Regulators dragged two alleged outlaws from the Elliott County jail and hanged them on the courthouse grounds. The lynchings inaugurated a reign of terror against all suspected lawbreakers and un-

desirables in the region. Masked horseback riders whipped many victims and drove them out of the area. The vigilantes also punished many men and women accused of violating the moral standards of the community.

By the spring of 1880, the movement had spread to the neighboring counties of Morgan, Rowan, Carter, Boyd, and Lawrence. On the night of March 17, 1880, the Elliott County organization claimed two more victims during a raid in Carter County. Openly defying the authorities, the Lawrence County Regulators forcibly rescued several jailed members in Louisa and Catlettsburg.

Despite frequent death threats, Judge James E. Stewart of the 16th judicial district vowed to uphold the law against the Regulators and called on Gov. Luke P. Blackburn (1879-83) for state troops. Stewart's firm stand, the threat of military force, and the promise of executive clemency for Regulators who voluntarily surrendered broke the back of the movement. On May 28, 1880, over two hundred Lawrence and Carter County Regulators surrendered to Judge Stewart at Louisa. The voluntary disbanding of the Elliott and Morgan County organizations in July marked the end of the uprising, although outbreaks of terrorism in the region continued until 1881. Governor Blackburn subsequently pardoned hundreds of former Regulators throughout the region. Nevertheless, isolated acts of vigilantism continued to occur in the area until the early twentieth century.

Remarkable for the numbers involved, the Regulator uprising was defended by many as a necessary evil when the legal system failed to curb lawlessness. But the extreme violence that characterized the movement succeeded only in reinforcing the perception of late nineteenth century Kentucky as a lawless, violent society.

JAMES M. PRICHARD

RELIEF CRISIS. In mid-1818, after the collapse of the Ohio River trade, Kentucky plunged headlong into financial panic and economic depression. The panic of 1819 hit the American West and South—especially Kentucky—with particular severity. After the War of 1812, traders and speculators had ridden the crest of an unprecedented expansion of the American economy; the Kentucky General Assembly, faced with burgeoning demands for credit and currency, had in 1818 licensed over forty undercapitalized private banks (later dubbed the "Forty Thieves"). A year later, the instability of these fly-by-night banks was laid bare: As relatively stable financial institutions such as the Bank of Kentucky and Second Bank of the United States (which had opened branch offices in Louisville and Lexington in 1817-18) began to call in notes and to exert pressure upon individual debtors and weaker banks, the "Forty Thieves" locked their doors.

The depression's effects were cataclysmic. In Kentucky and elsewhere, money disappeared from circulation; farmers and artisans resorted to barter. Bank credit was unattainable, even for propertied, established families; tenant farmers and day-workers were unable to buy seed and tools. As mercantile houses and factories closed, citizens' committees organized county meetings to drum up popular support both for legislative intervention in relations between creditors and debtors and for state-led currency enhancement. The meetings were sometimes rigged by the organizers. But the resulting petitions—notably the starkly worded, fourteen-part Frankfort Resolutions of 1819, which demanded passage of a three-year debt postponement law and an expanded money supply—pushed reluctant legislators toward intervention in economic life.

In Kentucky, Ohio, Missouri, Tennessee, and other hard-pressed states, Relief parties formed within state legislatures; not surprisingly, there was opposition, in the form of anti-Relief parties. In Kentucky, as elsewhere, an anti-Relief party arose less to oppose the idea of relief for debtors than to challenge the Relief party's conception of how "the best relief," as one partisan put it, might be achieved.

Kentucky's earliest Relief party, led by the charismatic Sen. Jesse Bledsoe, was a relatively limited vanguard within the legislature devoted to bank charter revocation and revival of Jeffersonian republicanism in state government. After the difficult summer of 1820, however, the party mutated into a potent coalition of law reformers and political activists determined to revamp the law of contract and property and to bring the full weight of government to bear upon economic revitalization. Kentucky's "Relief men" thought that the General Assembly ought to adopt a stop law (a moratorium on bank calls) and stay laws (postponements of debt repayment for twelve months whenever creditors refused the banknotes offered by debtors); they argued, too, that the best relief would be energetic, state-supported domestic improvements to avoid financial collapse in Kentucky in future decades.

By 1820, assemblyman James Davis and others, inspired by parallel developments in Missouri and Tennessee, came to advocate the creation of a public bank, to be called the Bank of the Commonwealth, backed by the value of unsold land reserves and Bank of Kentucky stock. Such a bank, these men argued, would augment the currency and facilitate debt repayment by means of relatively inexpensive banknotes; banking profits could be channeled into improvement projects. Critics called Davis's project a chimera, predicting that a bank "bottomed upon no capital whatever," as one writer put it, "but upon the slipry [sic] faith of the state" could only sink.

By 1821-22, the Relief party claimed solid majorities in both houses of the legislature; with the election of Gov. John Adair (1820-24) and Lt. Gov. William T. Barry in 1820, they controlled the statehouse. Between 1821 and 1823, Relief men and allied journalists—Francis Preston Blair, Sr., and Amos Kendall, for example—rallied support for a temporary stop law, a twelve-month stay (or replevy) law, a one-year stay law extension, a revised valuation law (which disallowed execution of judgments against debtors if auction bids fell below three-quarters of the property's predepression value), the abolition of imprisonment for debt, the treasury-backed Commonwealth Bank (which opened its doors in May 1821), and numerous minor relief measures.

Almost at once, the Kentucky court of appeals and the 7th Circuit Court for the District of Kentucky pronounced the great bulk of Kentucky's debtor relief system unconstitutional; only the abolition of debtor's prison passed muster. To make matters worse, the value of Bank of the Commonwealth currency steadily sank. Still, Relief partisans insisted that they hoped not simply to relieve debtors, but to refashion state government to reflect better the "moral justice" at the heart of the American experiment in self-rule—to replace old habits of mind with new ones, to allow the people to help themselves through their legislature. Why, asked one Relief writer, should the community not be allowed to "bring its property in aid of the scanty circulating medium" by means of a "Faith Bank"? If the sovereign people believed "Rag Money" to be valuable, it would have value: In the end, faith underlay all banks—and, for that matter, all governments.

Conflicts escalated. Disagreements over the merits of key relief laws, and the Relief leadership's frantic pursuit of "moral justice," led directly to the party's decision in 1824 to erect the "New Court" of appeals and to abolish the OLD COURT by means of an ordinary statute. The electorate's adverse reaction to these developments, combined with the return of prosperity and the disintegration of the Bank of the Commonwealth, ended Kentucky's crisis. During the elections of 1824-25, the Relief party (by then called the New Court party) unceremoniously collapsed, marooning the pro-Relief Gov. Joseph Desha (1824-28) in the statehouse. By then, early members of the Relief party, like Robert McAfee and Samuel Daviess, had come to sound like anti-Relief cautionaries.

See Arndt Stickles, *The Critical Court Struggle in Kentucky* (Bloomington, Ind., 1929).

SANDRA F. VANBURKLEO

RELIGION. Of the religious beliefs of Native Americans who lived for thousands of years in what is now Kentucky, little is known. According to the interpretations of archaeological remains, they did, however, believe in supernatural powers and an afterlife. When settlers of European stock began to enter Kentucky in the last quarter of the eighteenth century, they brought traditional religious forms with them. Religion helped to transform and civilize the frontier, and the frontier brought transformations in traditional religious life as well. The first known Christian worship service in Kentucky took place in Boonesborough on Sunday, May 28, 1775, led by Anglican minister John Lyth. Beneath an old elm tree, the colonial residents prayed for

England's "most gracious sovereign Lord King George."

After the Revolutionary War, vast migration began into the western outpost of Virginia, bringing into the Bluegrass area the earliest leaders of the three largest traditions in the frontier era: BAPTISTS, METHODISTS, and PRESBYTERIANS. EPISCOPALIANS also settled in the region, as well as ROMAN CATHOLICS, who predominated in the area around Bardstown. From there, under the leadership of Stephen Badin and Benedict Flaget, they established the institutional base of Catholicism for the American Midwest and upper South.

The largest early migration of Baptists occurred in 1781 with the arrival of the TRAVELING CHURCH from Spotsylvania, Virginia. This hardy group of some five hundred was led by the Rev. Lewis Craig, who saw his flock's trek across the mountains as parallel to that of the Israelites leaving Egypt for Canaan. Although Terah Templin conducted Kentucky's first Presbyterian services in 1780, Princeton-educated David Rice was the outstanding clergyman of that denomination on the frontier. Reflecting a Presbyterian emphasis on education, Rice was instrumental in establishing Transylvania University as the state's earliest center of learning. Francis Clark became the area's first Methodist preacher in 1783. Kentucky Methodists were visited periodically by their national leader, Francis Asbury, in pioneer days.

Early Kentucky was not unduly pious by any standards. In 1800 less than 10 percent of the population of 200,000 claimed allegiance to any church. Denominational squabbling had soured some, while minor evidences of deism in the Bluegrass had kept others from a traditional Christian congregational commitment. The early settlers were not a godless folk, but most joined their own biblical piety with a brand of stubborn individualism. In addition to danger, privation, and punishingly hard work, a crushing loneliness was often their lot. The frontier took an emotional as well as physical toll.

When they gathered for services, frequently in cabins or in the open air, congregations were often seated in a way that separated male and female. Nor was decorum always maintained. One early minister, quoted by James Robertson, Jr., in "Revelry and Religion in Frontier Kentucky" (*Register* 79, 1981), lamented a congregation consisting of "forty-five babies and seventy-five dogs with only sixty adults to police the mob." Across denominational lines, the Sunday sermon was typically at least ninety minutes long. Early Protestant congregations were called to account on a regular basis for unbecoming conduct. One historian's statistical accounting revealed the leading causes of admonition (in ranked order) to be drunkenness, dancing, fornication, church nonattendance, adultery, and swearing.

With the turn of the century, a new chemistry bubbled in the Kentucky religious crucible. In Logan County in 1800, Presbyterian minister James

McGready began a series of emotional revival meetings that resulted in dozens of his hearers collapsing on the floor, newly convinced of their sinful condition. Another Presbyterian divine, Barton Warren Stone, observed first-hand the new intensity of religious life in Logan County, and declared that it "baffled description," and was, indeed, "passing strange" (*Religion in Antebellum Kentucky*, 1976). In 1801 Stone arranged for an August revival in Bourbon County, and thousands appeared for the religious exercises at Cane Ridge. As years of pent-up emotions were unleashed, vast numbers of worshippers were visited with "the jerks" and with uncontrollable laughing and singing, barking, swoons, and dashing about the woods. Such transitory and extraordinary manifestations did not, however, mask the fact that many religious conversions occurred at Cane Ridge.

The Kentucky revivals, considered by historians to be the beginning of a national "Second Great Awakening," did much more than add a few new believers to the religious rolls. The GREAT REVIVAL proved to be epochal in its long-term effects as well. The revival multiplied church memberships in Kentucky; both Baptists and Methodists tripled in their numbers within a three-year period. After the New Madrid earthquakes of 1811-12, another surge of revivals and conversions occurred. Beyond the numbers, the Great Revival set a pattern for southern religious revivalism in the U.S.—a cast of mind that historian John Boles has described as highly individualistic, localist, and conversion-oriented. At the same time, it created new division and diversity within Kentucky religion. From this era sprang the CUMBERLAND PRESBYTERIANS, the CHRISTIAN CHURCH, and the DISCIPLES OF CHRIST. The religious excitement also led to establishment of SHAKER COMMUNITIES.

The greatest institutional growth in the antebellum era occurred among Roman Catholics. The first inland diocese in the United States was established at Bardstown in 1808, soon followed in the region by three colleges, academies, motherhouses of sisters, a seminary, and the Trappist Abbey of Gethsemani. As immigrants flooded into America in the nineteenth century, Kentucky religious life became more diverse. By mid-century, Jewish temples had been established in both Louisville and Lexington, while German and Irish Catholics and German Lutherans and evangelicals had swelled the population of such river ports as Covington and Louisville. Some of the newcomers were periodically harassed by opponents, most notably in the anti-Catholic Bloody Monday riot in Louisville in 1855. In the same period, Unitarians, early arrivals in Kentucky, were seeing congregational growth in the cities.

Moral concerns in the antebellum era included the U.S. entry into the War of 1812, subject to some minor clerical opposition, and the abuse of alcohol. The first temperance society in Kentucky was formed in Lexington in 1830, under religious auspices. The primary social concern for all religious groups was clearly education. Presbyterians took the early lead in the establishment of Transylvania, envisioned as the major college for all male Kentuckians. With the presidency (1818-27) of the brilliant and resourceful Unitarian Horace Holley, however, fears rose that students were being exposed to an excessively liberal curriculum and ethos. From the time of Holley's departure, in the judgment of historian Niels Sonne, Protestant orthodoxy was triumphant in Kentucky. The church-related colleges chartered in the commonwealth included Centre (Presbyterian), Georgetown (Baptist), and St. Joseph and St. Mary (Catholic). At the other end of the educational spectrum, Kentucky's first Sunday School, the work of Margaretta Brown, began at Frankfort in 1815.

No issue before the Civil War so exercised religious emotions in the commonwealth as the question of slavery. Kentucky blacks, both free and slave, found great strength in Christian faith. As early as 1829, Louisville's premier black congregation, First African Baptist, opened; in 1838 the first African Methodist Episcopal church—later known as Quinn Chapel—began functioning in the city. By mid-century, one of the largest congregations in Kentucky was the First African Baptist in Lexington, where the eminent London Ferrill was minister; Louisville had nine black congregations.

Among the early ministers of Kentucky who spoke out against slavery were the Baptist David Barrow, Catholic John Thayer, Methodist Peter Cartwright, and Presbyterian David Rice. In the 1840s and 1850s, Delia Webster of Lexington and the Methodist minister Calvin Fairbanks were charged with freeing slaves through the underground railroad, and both served time in the Frankfort penitentiary. Presbyterian John Fee, who had a role in the beginnings of Berea College, an integrated institution, was subjected to mob action twenty-two times for his abolitionist energies.

While such groups as the Shakers and many of the small Lutheran congregations tended to be antislavery, Kentucky believers generally were either pro-slavery or thought the question best left to the state. Many of the major Kentucky denominations found themselves divided by the issue into northern and southern allegiances, as the Presbyterians were in 1836-38 and Baptists and Methodists during 1845. Kentucky lost its last chance to rid itself of slavery in 1849, when a new constitution was drafted. While leading political figures chose sides, an abolition party of 150 met at Frankfort, twenty-one of their number being clergy. So outspoken were these and other religious leaders that the newly written constitution, in reaction, contained a prohibition against any "minister of the Gospel" serving in the Kentucky legislature.

At the onset of the Civil War in 1861, all major religious groups in the commonwealth saw many of their members march off to battle in opposing armies. Just before the war began, James Craik,

rector of Louisville's Episcopal Christ Church, addressed the state legislature urging adhesion to the Union. Lexington minister Robert J. Breckinridge sought to lead Kentucky's Presbyterians to support the North, while Louisville pastor Stuart Robinson urged them toward neutrality. At Our Lady's Catholic Church in Louisville, an organist caused a minor sensation by weaving "Dixie" into the recessional one Sunday morning.

Episcopal Bishop Benjamin Bosworth Smith, himself antislavery and pro-Union, was publicly moderate throughout the hostilities, offering special wartime prayers for his congregations. Catholic Bishop Martin John Spalding, himself a slave owner, also adopted a public posture of neutrality, holding memorial masses at the Louisville Cathedral for the fallen of both sides. Confederate Gen. Leonidas Polk, an Episcopal bishop, offered a famous prayer after the Battle of Perryville in October, 1862, beseeching blessings "on friend and foe alike."

The war played havoc with religious institutions and publications. The Baptist *Western Recorder* and the Catholic *Guardian* both ceased publication for a time because of wartime turmoil. Churches and colleges were commandeered as hospitals, while St. Joseph's College in Bardstown had to close entirely for several years.

After the war women played bigger roles in the life of the churches and of their communities. Catholic sisters by the hundreds had long been active in works of education, health care, and benevolence. In the short space of the 1830s, Sister of Charity Catherine Spalding at Louisville founded an academy, a hospital, and an orphanage. Over the years the sisters created a veritable network of such institutions across Kentucky. Methodist women were instrumental in forming Deaconess Hospital in Louisville in 1898. Both the Baptist Women's Missionary Union and the Women's Christian Temperance Union were formed in the 1880s. Temperance sentiment swept Kentucky in those years. At Bowling Green in 1893, while church bells rang all day, the city voted to go "dry" by a margin of twenty-eight votes.

As the century neared its end, revivals began to take on a more urban cast. The noted evangelist Dwight Moody arrived in Louisville in January 1888 to preach more than sixty sermons before huge assemblies; city churches gained more than 4,000 new members as a result. Theological agitation, though diminished from the first half of the century, did not disappear. At Southern Baptist Theological Seminary in Louisville, Crawford Toy and William Whitsitt were forced to resign their faculty positions for espousing liberal theological views. As late as 1894 a Lexington grand jury indicted a man for blasphemy, although the charge was disallowed by a Kentucky civil court.

Especially with the arrival of Eastern European immigrants near the turn of the century, Judaism grew apace in urban areas of the commonwealth. In the isolated mountainous regions of eastern Kentucky, alongside the traditional Christian denominations, Holiness and Pentecostal churches of a nondenominational and fundamentalist cast flourished. Here, as in other areas of Kentucky, snake handling was not unknown in worship services.

Many of the moral energies of the early twentieth century in Kentucky focused on such concerns as evolution, prohibition, and gambling. The 1915 Kentucky gubernatorial campaign was waged largely over the issue of prohibition. The "wet" candidate, A.O. Stanley, won by nearly five hundred votes, but the Kentucky legislature in 1919 approved the Eighteenth Amendment, enforcing prohibition by a huge majority. On January 19, 1922, William Jennings Bryan appeared before the legislature to urge a ban on teaching evolution in schools, and the Anti-Evolution League of America established its national headquarters in Louisville with strong religious leadership. Even so, the legislative ban introduced on January 23, 1922—ultimately defeated—met with significant opposition by Christian religious educators of the commonwealth, fearful of any state dictation in matters of education.

Spurred on by the Louisville Churchmen's Federation, and with the support of such politicians and civic leaders as Alben Barkley from western Kentucky and Robert Worth Bingham, owner of the *Louisville Courier-Journal*, a movement emerged in the mid-1920s seeking to end pari-mutuel gambling in Kentucky. Once again a gubernatorial race became the arena of the battle. Despite heavy ministerial opposition in some quarters to track betting, the results of the 1927 election made it clear that no new legislation on the matter would be forthcoming. The national election of 1928, in which Roman Catholic Alfred E. Smith was the Democratic candidate, brought latent anti-Catholicism to the surface in Kentucky. Herbert Hoover won the the state's vote handily, though the commonwealth may well have been more interested in prohibition than in religious allegiance.

Church-state conflicts in the 1940s arose over the right of Catholic schoolchildren to public transportation, and in the 1950s over the appropriateness of Catholic sisters as teachers in selected public schools. In both cases the Kentucky court of appeals judged that the principle of separation of church and state was not violated by the existing arrangements.

In the wake of World War II and its nuclear devastation, the establishment of the World Council of Churches (1948) and the convocation of the Second Vatican Council (1962) helped bring religious leaders in Kentucky together in interfaith and ecumenical dialogues. The Kentucky Council of Churches, established in 1947, welcomed Roman Catholics into full membership, while the Kentuckiana Interfaith Community became one of the first such organizations in the nation to include both Jewish and Christian members. Religious diversity was on the increase in Kentucky as Jehovah's Witnesses,

Christian Scientists, and Mormons became more numerous; in the cities, such faiths as Bahai, Buddhism, and Islam, relatively new to the American scene, began to appear.

Religious leaders, both black and white, were much in evidence in the March 1964 march on Frankfort for civil rights legislation, where the Rev. Martin Luther King, Jr., was a featured speaker. During the same period, Quinn Chapel in Louisville served as one of the gathering centers for opponents of restrictive racial policies, continuing a tradition begun in 1870 with protests against segregated streetcars. Kentucky's Bishop C. Eubank Tucker, the Rev. A.D. King of the Southern Christian Leadership Conference, and the Rev. W.J. Hodge of the National Association for the Advancement of Colored People were leaders in the struggle for racial justice.

On a wide range of social issues—from systemic poverty to abortion, from U.S. military involvement to gun control, from environmental pollution to drug control—religious voices, usually reasoned, sometimes intense, were to be heard debating the questions. Father Thomas Merton of Gethsemani Abbey in Nelson County became nationally and internationally known for his extensive writing on social issues, ecumenism, and spiritualities of both the Orient and the West.

In the 1980s the Kentucky Council of Churches reported that 1.98 million Kentuckians, or about 55 percent of the population, adhered to specific religious traditions. They worshipped in some 6,700 churches, synagogues, and temples. Reports at the decade's end indicated that, in line with national trends, mainline Protestant churches in Kentucky, including Episcopal and Presbyterian, were experiencing decline in memberships, while more conservative groups such as Assemblies of God and the Church of the Nazarene were increasing in numbers.

A *Courier-Journal* state-wide poll in 1989 reported that 91 percent of Kentucky adults prayed occasionally, while 53 percent did so daily. Some 60 percent of those surveyed "feel a sense of closeness to God daily." The current Kentucky constitution, adopted in 1891, affirms in the preamble that the people of the state are "grateful to Almighty God," while article 1 grants the right of worshiping God according to conscience.

According to figures from the Kentucky Council of Churches, the three largest religious traditions in Kentucky in the 1980s were: Baptist (888,000), Catholic (365,000), and Methodist (236,000). In the 1990 Kentucky General Assembly, all 138 members claimed allegiance to the Christian faith. The legislature paralleled the general religious population in allegiance: Baptists, 43; Catholics, 40; Methodists, 18.

See Ira V. Birdwhistell, *Gathered at the River: A Narrative History of the Long Run Baptist Association* (Louisville 1978); John Boles, *Religion in Antebellum Kentucky* (Lexington, Ky., 1976); George Moore, *Interchurch Cooperation in Kentucky 1865-*

1965 (Lexington, Ky., 1965); Herman Landau, *Adath Louisville: The Story of a Jewish Community* (Louisville 1981).   CLYDE F. CREWS

RENFRO VALLEY BARN DANCE. John LAIR envisioned the "Renfro Valley Barn Dance," a traditional COUNTRY MUSIC show broadcast from Renfro Valley, Kentucky, while he was program director for WLS radio in Chicago during the 1930s. Concerned that country music was following the western influence of Gene Autry and Bob Wills, Lair looked for a method to preserve the music's traditional sound. In 1937 Lair, together with partners Whitey ("Duke of Paducah") Ford, Red Foley, and Red's brother, Cotton, purchased a tract of land in the Rockcastle County valley along Renfro Creek as the setting for a country music entertainment complex.

The first "Renfro Valley Barn Dance" program was broadcast over WLW radio on October 9, 1937, from the Cincinnati Music Hall. "Barn Dance" touring groups went on the road and the show moved to Memorial Auditorium in Dayton, Ohio, in 1938. In the meantime the Big Barn, a 1,000-seat theater, was completed in Renfro Valley, and on November 4, 1939, the first show there was presented to a full house and to thousands of listeners over the NBC radio network. Many of country music's finest traditional performers, some of whom had started with Lair at WLS, appeared on the barn's stage, including Clyde ("Red") FOLEY, Homer ("Slim") Miller, Whitey Ford, the comedy team of Homer and Jethro, Ernie Lee, Jerry Byrd, the Coon Creek girls (see Lily May LEDFORD), and gospel singer Martha Carson. "The Sunday Morning Gatherin'," a radio program of gospel music, was broadcast from Renfro Valley's Little Red Schoolhouse.

A radio broadcasting station, a newspaper, and a museum were soon added to the Renfro Valley complex. The "Renfro Valley Barn Dance" was a popular show, both live and over national radio networks, but Lair rejected the medium of television. In 1968, when attendance at Renfro Valley had become much smaller, Lair sold the development to Tennessee interests headed by Hal Smith, who was not successful with the complex. Lair resumed ownership of the Renfro Valley complex in 1976, but could not restore it to its earlier heights.

Lair died in 1985, and five years later his four daughters—Ann Henderson, Virginia King, Nancy Griffin, and Barbara Smith—and the owners of the Renfro Valley motel and restaurant sold the complex to a group of local businessmen. The new owners, incorporated as Renfro Valley Folks, began construction of a $1.8 million auditorium with 1,530 red cushioned seats, a block of turn-of-the-century shops, a country music museum, and festival grounds. They signed a contract for a thirteen-week television run on Country Music Television, and planned a thirty-acre amusement park. The Renfro Valley Folks took John Lair's traditional country music complex into the corporate world, twentieth century commercialization, and television.

See Charles K. Wolfe, *Kentucky Country* (Lexington, Ky., 1982).   BETTY B. ELLISON

REPUBLICAN PARTY. The Republican party of Kentucky, as much as any state party organization in America, can lay claim to the title "The Party of Lincoln." Its origin and development were closely tied to the personality of the Kentucky-born sixteenth President; his personal friends were its founders; his view that Kentucky was important to the Northern war strategy led him to take a major interest in the state's politics.

The Republican Party of Kentucky resulted from the bitter divisions created by the Civil War. Martial law, which began during the war, continued for many months after the Confederate surrender. The uncompensated economic loss was deeply resented, particularly in western Kentucky, and partisanship in the administration of military justice created resentment. The writ of habeas corpus was suspended in 1864, and Kentuckians were often imprisoned arbitrarily. These events alienated many Kentuckians who had been sympathetic to the Union cause, and in the 1864 election Lincoln won only 30 percent of the vote. Returning veterans brought back with them to Kentucky politics a bitterness and viciousness that had not existed before.

The strongest resistance to slavery and the greatest pro-Union sentiment were voiced in the eastern and southeastern mountains, where the terrain made slave-based agriculture less feasible. With the exception of Floyd, Magoffin, and Breathitt counties, most of far eastern Kentucky was strongly Union. That area became a Republican stronghold and part of it remains so. Western Kentucky was the direct opposite.

Republican party members, dubbed Radicals during the war, included adherents of the prewar Whig, Know-Nothing, and Opposition parties. The Radicals exercised the wartime patronage of the federal government and enjoyed a strength and influence in the state disproportionate to their small numbers. But because of their association with the policies of the national Republican party, Kentucky was dominated by the Democrats for three decades after the war. The state Republican party did not become a small federally oriented cell, however, as it did throughout most of the South; the party's base was consistently around 40 percent of the electorate. Although Kentucky was generally carried by the Democrats in presidential elections, the median Democratic percentage was only slightly over 50 percent.

In wartime and thereafter, the Democratic party retained political dominance in Kentucky, although it split into Union Democrats and Southern Rights Democrats, the former being far more numerous. The wartime and postwar Reconstruction policies of the national Republican party drove most of the Union Democrats back into alliance with the pro-Southern Democrats, creating a political majority that remains. Had the Republican leaders compromised to form an alliance of pro-Union forces, both likely would have benefited. As it turned out, Southern sympathizers, though a distinct minority, united throughout the state and were successful for years in electing their adherents to office because of their solidarity, in contrast to the lack of unity among pro-Unionists.

Kentucky's first postwar Republican gubernatorial candidate, Col. Sidney M. Barnes of Irvine, was resoundingly defeated in 1867 by Democrat John Larue Helm. Early leaders of the state party were John Marshall Harlan of Louisville, later a U.S. Supreme Court justice; Judge Bland Ballard and Lincoln's friends James and Joshua Speed, all of Louisville; and Thomas Morrow of Somerset.

Kentucky Republicans' first serious campaign for governor took place in 1871, when Harlan, a Louisville lawyer and former Whig, led a ticket with a full slate of candidates for constitutional office. Defeat followed, with a total of 126,000 votes for former Gov. Preston H. Leslie to 89,000 for Harlan. In the race, Harlan attempted to distance himself from the Radical Reconstruction policies of the national regime and condemned the Republicans for waving the "bloody shirt" of Civil War loyalties. Harlan called for a healing of war wounds, but he endorsed the unpopular Thirteenth, Fourteenth, and Fifteenth amendments to the Constitution.

Defeats by margins similar to Harlan's in 1871 continued for the party until William O'Connell Bradley of Lancaster was elected governor in 1895 with the help of conservative Democrats on a sound money platform. Bradley, like many other early Republican candidates, had suffered numerous defeats before emerging victorious. A short, stocky man, Bradley was a powerful orator with a remarkable command of the language. Love of politics, wit, and persistence were his hallmarks. In his second attempt at the governorship in 1895, Bradley defeated the Democrat, former Kentucky Attorney General P. Wat Hardin, and the Populist, Thomas S. Pettit. Pettit's candidacy aided Bradley by drawing a substantial Democratic vote in western Kentucky.

Under Bradley, the father of Kentucky's modern Republican party, the party grew in strength, winning five of the ten gubernatorial elections between 1895 and 1927. During that time, Republicans also elected four U.S. senators: W.J. Deboe in 1897, Bradley in 1908, Richard Ernst in 1914, and Frederick Sackett in 1924.

Bradley's term as governor was marked by dissension and political division. During the first General Assembly of his term, his party narrowly controlled the House, but not the Senate. His hands were thus tied on major legislation, notably the GOEBEL ELECTION LAW, which Republicans saw as a dangerous attempt to control elections. Bradley's veto of that measure was overridden in 1898. Shortly thereafter, the Goebel Law gave rise to Kentucky's most vicious and deadly partisan era.

Although Bradley initially opposed Republican William S. Taylor of Morgantown, his former attorney general, in the gubernatorial election of 1899, Bradley later became the principal adviser. Taylor's campaign was successful and he was by any objective measure elected governor. He served but fifty days as chief executive, however, before being removed from office by an order of the Kentucky court of appeals that upheld certain actions of the Democratically controlled General Assembly. Democrat William GOEBEL was sworn in after he was mortally wounded by an assassin and after a protracted and unprecedented struggle for power. Taylor was later indicted for the murder of Goebel.

In 1907 Kentuckians elected John Marshall Harlan's protégé, Republican Augustus E. ("Gus") Willson, a Harvard-educated Louisville lawyer, as governor. In a campaign marked by charges of Democratic duplicity on the temperance issue, Willson defeated his opponent, Democrat Samuel W. Hager, a vociferous "dry," by a large majority. Urban conservative Democrats joined him on the prohibition question. Willson was bright and widely thought to be a man of integrity. He, too, was unable to work with the Democratic-controlled General Assembly to advance his program.

In 1919 Edwin P. Morrow of Somerset became the fourth Republican elected governor. Four years earlier Morrow had been defeated by A.O. Stanley in one of Kentucky's most colorful campaigns. Morrow and Stanley denounced one another during the day, then supped together at night. Governor Morrow's party controlled the House, while the Democrats controlled the Senate by only two votes, and the Morrow administration was thus successful in passing most of an aggressive and vigorous program. To his credit, Morrow was anti-Klan and antilynching at a time when Kentucky and neighboring states went through an era of lawlessness directed at blacks.

In 1927, Republican Flem D. Sampson of Barbourville was elected governor by a sizable majority. Every other member of his ticket lost. In office, he was plagued by opposition from the Democratic-dominated General Assembly. Many of his patronage powers, particularly at the Highway Commission, were stripped from him by statute. Many of the executive powers were vested in a three-member commission on which he was the lone Republican. The Depression, which hit Kentucky hard shortly after his election, further weakened Sampson's position and decimated the Kentucky Republicans for over a decade. The effects of the Depression, coupled with New Deal patronage, directed particularly at the Kentucky mountains, eliminated the partisan balance of power for a time.

It was not until 1943, when Simeon Willis of Ashland was elected governor, that the Republicans made a recovery; Willis carried into office with him Lt. Gov. Kenneth Tuggle of Barbourville and several other constitutional officers. Although

Willis, a legal scholar and former judge, did not suffer the major ripper legislation inflicted upon Sampson by the Democrats, he was hamstrung by the General Assembly. To Willis's good fortune, the Democrats in the General Assembly were divided into factions over the major candidates to succeed him, Harry Lee Waterfield and Earle C. Clements. Willis was thus able to maintain most of his powers.

The second heyday of Kentucky Republicans began during the mid-1950s when, in federal elections, the party consistently carried Kentucky, electing three U.S. senators: John Sherman Cooper of Somerset, Thruston B. Morton of Louisville, and Marlow Cook of Louisville. Cooper, unquestionably the leader, was one of the most outstanding men produced by the Kentucky party. Morton served ably as the Republican national chairman and was seriously considered for vice-president in 1960 by Richard Nixon. In the eight presidential elections from 1956 to 1988, Kentucky went Democratic only twice—in 1964 for Lyndon Johnson over Barry Goldwater and in 1976 for Southerner Jimmy Carter over incumbent Gerald Ford.

At the state level, success was more limited, but in 1967 Republicans elected Louie B. Nunn of Glasgow governor. Nunn, a former Barren County judge and party activist, carried with him four of the seven other constitutional officers and a substantial Republican component in each house. Nunn's political success, as well as that of both Senators Morton and Cooper, was made possible in part by the backing of the Democratic two-time governor, A.B. Chandler, who made a practice of supporting Republicans in the general election rather than his factional opponents in the Democratic party. In 1956 Chandler covertly supported both Cooper and Morton and in 1967 he openly campaigned for Nunn. He had similarly been of help to Cooper, his friend, in the 1946 and 1948 elections.

Nunn, a strong leader confronted by a severe financial emergency, forced a major tax increase through the General Assembly in its first session during his term. The backlash, exacerbated by virulent opposition from General Assembly Democrats led by Lt. Gov. Wendell H. Ford and House Speaker Julian Carroll, practically eliminated the party from competition in state races for years. After sixteen years between statewide victories for Republicans, Jefferson County Judge Addison Mitchell McConnell was narrowly elected to the U.S. Senate in the Ronald Reagan presidential landslide of 1984; he was reelected in 1990.

The Republican party of Kentucky has generally been a moderate, conservative organization. The bulk of its strength still derives from Louisville and the formerly pro-Union Appalachian areas of eastern and southeastern Kentucky and Louisville. However, as the national political scene turned more liberal during the New Deal and again in the Great Society of the 1960s, Republican strength in far eastern Kentucky eroded. Various welfare and benefit programs sponsored by the national Democrats were extremely popular with less affluent eastern Kentuckians, and many switched their party allegiance to support the programs. Later on, the more conservative national scene of the Nixon and Reagan eras benefited the Republicans in other areas of the state. Republicans hold newfound strength around Lexington and the cities of Owensboro and Bowling Green.

While the national trends have helped Kentucky Republicans in some respects, an unusual phenomenon has partially obstructed success. Most southern and midsouthern states have seen their major cities turn toward Republicans with the advent of urban sprawl and suburbia, but Louisville, a labor-dominated city with over 20 percent of the state vote, has consistently remained in Democratic hands except for a period in the 1960s. Factors in their success are the strength of organized labor, weak Republican leadership, the personalities of Democratic leaders who developed politically in the early 1970s, and the *Courier-Journal*, the city's Democratic daily newspaper.

In the 1980s the Kentucky Republican party was plagued by factionalism between the elected congressional Republican leaders and those active at the state level. The congressionals and their organizations, with one exception, seldom became involved in state elections for fear of Democratic retaliation against them. As the saying goes, Kentucky is Republican nationally, but Democratic in state elections.

In organization, the Kentucky Republican party is a corporate body governed by the State Central Committee, made up of local and regional members. It is administered by a state Republican chairman elected by the Central Committee. State headquarters are located in Frankfort. It is represented on the Republican National Committee in Washington by national committee members elected by the Central Committee. Each county has a Republican committee, although many are not active.

LAWRENCE E. FORGY, JR.

RHEA, THOMAS STOCKDALE. Thomas Stockdale Rhea, a power in Kentucky Democratic politics for forty years, was born in Russellville, Kentucky, on December 29, 1871. He was the son of Albert Gallatin and Jane (Stockdale) Rhea and grandson of Charles Rhea, owner and editor of the first newspaper in Logan County. Thomas Rhea was instrumental in the election of several governors and U.S. senators, but was unsuccessful in his one attempt to obtain the governor's office himself.

Rhea began his career as Logan County sheriff in 1906. He was elected state treasurer in 1911 and during World War I served on the U.S. Munitions Board. He was chairman of the Workmen's Compensation Board under Gov. W.J. Fields (1923-27), and a member of the Kentucky Highway Commission under Gov. Ruby Laffoon (1931-35). While serving a second term as Logan County sheriff (1941-45), he was president of the state sheriffs' association. Throughout most of his adult life he was chairman of the Logan Democratic Committee, and from 1912 until his death he was a delegate at every national Democratic convention. As one of five floor leaders for Franklin D. Roosevelt at the 1932 convention in Chicago, Rhea helped line up the conservative South for the New York liberal.

Thirty years of factional strife in the Kentucky Democratic party resulted from Rhea's alliance with Governor Laffoon and his efforts to succeed Laffoon. Although Rhea was at the peak of his power in 1935, he and Laffoon were outmaneuvered by A.B. Chandler, then lieutenant governor, into accepting the double primary as a substitute for a nominating convention, which was their preference. When Rhea lost the popular primary race, he bolted to Chandler's Republican opponent, King Swope, setting a precedent often invoked by Chandler to excuse his own support of Republicans. In the years that followed, Rhea's protégé and 1935 gubernatorial campaign manager, Earle Clements of Morganfield, and Chandler led opposing wings of the Democratic party. The Clements group tended to be moderates or liberals more linked with New Deal philosophy than their rivals.

Rhea's ability to deliver lopsided Democratic margins in Logan County elections grew out of his deep roots there. Rhea was married in January 1916 to Lillian Clark of Russellville, who died on January 21, 1951. Their children were Lillian Rhea Noe, Thomas Jr., Albert III, and Roland. When Rhea died in Russellville on April 16, 1946, the *Louisville Courier-Journal* called him "the sage of Russellville" and editorialized that "he was a figure whose like will not be seen again in Kentucky politics. Rhea's close friends delivered a deep attachment and loyalty to him, while many men who fought him bitterly . . . ended by giving him the tribute of friendship and respect." He was buried in the Maple Grove Cemetery, Russellville.

See Edward Coffman, *The Story of Logan County* (Nashville 1962).   AL SMITH

RICE, ALICE CALDWELL (HEGAN). Alice Caldwell (Hegan) Rice, author, was born in Shelbyville, Kentucky, on January 11, 1870, to Samuel Watson and Sallie P. (Caldwell) Hegan. She attended a private school in Shelbyville and Miss Hampton's College in Louisville, where she began writing. During that time she wrote a parody of *Reveries of a Bachelor* by Ik Marvel, which the *Louisville Courier-Journal* published. She and several other women in Louisville organized an authors' club, where they discussed writing and read their works aloud.

At a time when reformers and settlement house workers were calling attention to the living conditions of the urban poor, Hegan began volunteer social work in a truck-farming area south of Oak Street and west of Sixth Street known as the Cabbage Patch. There she taught a boys' Sunday school class at a city mission of the First Christian Church. Inspired by a resident of the desperately poor area, Mary Bass, Hegan transformed her into the fictional Mrs. Wiggs, a widow with five children who lived in dire poverty and had many misfortunes, but who faced life with steadfastness, cheerfulness, and hope. Mrs. Wiggs took in washing and her children—Jimmy, Billy, Asia, Australia, and Europena—sold kindling to try to forestall the landlord from foreclosing on the family home.

In 1901 Hegan introduced her novel *Mrs. Wiggs of the Cabbage Patch* to the authors' club. She submitted her manuscript to a publisher, and within six months of publication, 10,000 copies a month were being printed—later 40,000 copies per month. The novel was a best-seller for two years. It was translated into French, Spanish, Norwegian, Danish, German, Japanese, and braille. *Mrs. Wiggs* was such an international success that Louisvillian Anne Crawford Flexner helped adapt the novel for a stage play presented at Macauley's Theatre in 1903. The *Courier-Journal* proclaimed the play "a distinct success," and it ran for seven years in the United States and for two in England. *Mrs. Wiggs* also spawned four movies. The first two (1919 and 1926) were silent movies. The 1934 film, featuring W.C. Fields and Zasu Pitts, had its world premiere at the Rialto Theatre on Fourth Street in Louisville. It was proclaimed "the literary event of the season." A fourth film adaptation premiered in December 1942 at the Strand Theater in Louisville, and Louisville actress Fay Bainter won an Oscar for her portrayal of Mrs. Wiggs in this version.

On December 18, 1902, Hegan married Cale Young RICE, a poet, playwright, and philosopher from Louisville. Samuel McClure, publisher of *McClure's Magazine*, bought Cale Rice's first book soon after the wedding and invited the Rices to accompany him on a vacation trip to Europe. Alice Rice's novel *Sandy* (1905) was a fictional portrayal of McClure and his career. On the trip, she met and formed a friendship with social reformer and muckraker Ida Tarbell.

Alice Rice wrote twenty books, including several sequels to *Mrs. Wiggs*, most notably *Lovey Mary* (1903). Her personal favorite was *Mr. Opp* (1909), in which the title character to all outsiders appeared a failure, yet saw himself as a success in the world, one who refused to recognize defeat. Mrs. Wiggs's observation at the end of the novel expressed this kind of optimism: "Looks like ever'thing in the world comes right, if we jes' wait long enough!" Rice wrote in her autobiography *The Inky Way* (1940) that she did not want to record life's tragedy. Rather she wanted her autobiography "to follow, through a long life, the course of an inky way that happened to follow a flowery path." Her posthumously published work *Happiness Road* was described by the *New York Herald Tribune* as "an exercise in the discipline of happiness."

The Rices built a house in 1910 at 1444 St. James Court, where for thirty years she played the role of gracious hostess. Throughout her life, Rice was involved in philanthropic work. In 1910 Louise Marshall founded the Cabbage Patch Settlement on Sixth Street, a settlement house to reach out to the poor families in the urban neighborhood. Rice was a member of its first board. During World War I, she served as a hospital volunteer at Camp Zachary Taylor. She used that experience as a source for her 1921 novel *Quin*. Rice supported prohibition and served on the Kentucky State Committee of Law Enforcement.

During the 1920s, Rice collaborated with her husband on two books of short stories. In the 1930s the Rices suffered illness and financial reversals, and her works from that time were written under the burden of financial necessity: *Mr. Pete & Co.* (1933), a picaresque tale of the Louisville waterfront; *Passionate Follies* (1936), written with her husband; *My Pillow Book* (1937), a book of devotions and comments on life. In 1937 she received an honorary doctor of literature degree from the University of Louisville. Rice died on February 10, 1942, and was buried in Cave Hill Cemetery in Louisville.

See Mary Boewe, "Back to the Cabbage Patch: The Character of Mrs. Wiggs," *FCHQ* 59 (April 1985): 179-205.   GAIL HENSON

RICE, CALE YOUNG. Cale Young Rice, poet, dramatist, and novelist, was born in Dixon, Kentucky, on December 7, 1872, the son of Laban M. and Martha (Lacy) Rice. He received a bachelor of arts degree from Cumberland University, Lebanon, Tennessee (1893), and a master's degree from Harvard (1896), where he studied under philosophers William James and George Santayana. After teaching English literature at Cumberland for a year (1896-97), Rice settled in Louisville. His first book, *From Dusk to Dusk*, appeared in 1898. Some three dozen volumes of poetry, verse drama, and prose, including two novels, followed during a four-decade career that earned him recognition in America and abroad, particularly in England. His autobiography, *Bridging the Years*, was published in 1939. Critical response to Rice's work varied widely. The *Bookman*, of London, England, described him in 1920 as "the most distinguished master of lyric utterance in the New World" (*Louisville Evening Post*, May 18, 1920). The *New York Times* termed him a poet without inspiration (November 20, 1921).

On December 18, 1902, Rice married Alice Caldwell Hegan, the Louisville author of *Mrs. Wiggs of the Cabbage Patch* (1901) (see Alice RICE).

The couple were active in local literary circles, traveled extensively, and collaborated on three collections of short stories. Rice helped found and was the first president of Louisville's Arts Club, served on the governing board of the city's J.B. Speed Art Museum, and belonged to the Society of American Dramatists and Composers and the Poetry Society of America.

Shortly after the death of his wife in February 1942, Rice sold their home in St. James Court,

Louisville, and moved into the nearby Mayflower Apartments. He continued to write, but despondent over the loss of his wife, he died of a self-inflicted gunshot wound during the night of January 23-24, 1943. He was buried in Cave Hill Cemetery, Louisville.   JOHN SPALDING GATTON

RICE, DAVID. David Rice, Presbyterian minister, was born in Hancock County, Virginia, on December 29, 1733, one of twelve children. He was named for his father, who was of Welsh descent. Though raised as an Anglican, Rice converted to Presbyterianism as a young man. After he had studied with older ministers and had attended the College of New Jersey, the Presbytery of Hanover in 1762 licensed him to preach.

In October 1783 Rice and his family left his congregation at Peaks of Otter, Virginia, in response to a petition signed by three hundred religion-seeking Kentucky pioneers. The next spring he organized three Presbyterian congregations, including one at Danville, with which he was most closely associated. Although small in stature and lacking in outward charm, Rice impressed people with his sincerity, learning, and organizing skill. In Kentucky he helped to organize Transylvania Presbytery, the Synod of Kentucky, and Transylvania Seminary, which became Transylvania University. Rice expressed his opposition to slavery in sermons and in writing. Nevertheless he failed as an elected delegate to the Danville convention of 1792 in his attempt to insert into Kentucky's first constitution a clause that would have ended slavery in the state.

Rice married Mary Blair, daughter of Presbyterian minister Samuel Blair. Together they had twelve children. Later in life, Rice and his wife moved to Green County, where he died, after his wife, on June 18, 1816. Rice and his wife were reburied by order of the Synod of Kentucky in the old cemetery beside the Presbyterian church of Danville.

See Vernon F. Martin, "Father Rice, the Preacher Who Followed the Frontier," *FCHQ* 29 (Oct. 1955): 324-30; Robert H. Bishop, *An Outline of the History of the Church in the State of Kentucky: Containing the Memoirs of the Reverend David Rice* (Lexington, Ky., 1824).
                                       RICHARD C. BROWN

RICHESON, WILLIAM WEST. William West Richeson, educator, was born on March 13, 1809, in King William County, Virginia, the son of John Bret and Mildred (Ragsdale) Richeson. He was educated at the University of Virginia. In 1831 he came to Maysville, Kentucky, and founded the Maysville Academy, of which he was principal for nearly forty years. Among his pupils was Ulysses S. Grant. He married Mary Hodge Triplett; they had two daughters. He died in Maysville some time before 1881.   JEAN W. CALVERT

RICHMOND. Richmond, the county seat of Madison County, is located near the center of the county at the junction of U.S. 25/421 and KY 52 just east of I-75. The area was settled in 1785 by Col. John Miller, a Virginia-born Revolutionary War veteran who donated fifty acres on Town Fork of Dreaming Creek for the transfer of the county seat from Milford, located four and a half miles to the southwest. Richmond was created by legislative act on July 4, 1798, and became the county seat that year. It was named for Miller's birthplace in Virginia.

The city was organized by Miller, Archibald Woods, John Campbell, and Asa Searcy. Green Clay, James French, John Patrick, William Irvine, William Goodloe, Christopher Irvine, and Archibald Curle were selected as trustees. In 1799 a courthouse was erected, which served the county until a Greek Revival-style structure was built between 1849 and 1852.

Miller built the first house in the city, and in 1809 Richmond was incorporated. Its first newspaper was the *Globe-Register*. In 1810 the town had 110 citizens, which made it the fifteenth largest town in the state. By 1812 a hotel had been constructed, and in 1817 a bank opened.

Although a private school had been established in 1799 by Israel Donaldson, not until 1821 was there a city-sponsored school, the Madison Seminary. In 1858 the Madison Female Institute opened and provided a classical preparatory education for young women until 1919. Following the Civil War Battle of RICHMOND on August 30, 1862, it was used as a hospital for several months, with teachers and students caring for the wounded. In 1863 the trustees of the institute filed a claim against the United States for damages incurred but did not receive payment until 1915.

Among the participants in the Battle of Richmond was Maj. James B. McCreary, who afterward organized the Confederate 11th Kentucky Cavalry in the city. McCreary, who was born in Madison County, later became a two-term Kentucky governor (1875-79, 1911-15). Other governors who resided in Richmond were Keen Johnson (1939-43); Green Clay Smith, of the Montana Territory; and William J. Stone and David R. Frances, both of Missouri. Supreme Court Justice Samuel Freeman Miller also resided in Richmond.

After the Civil War, Richmond grew both in population and in size as it expanded the city limits four times between 1866 and 1890. Fires did substantial damage to the town in 1854, 1871, 1874, 1884, 1887, 1891, and 1892. Smallpox epidemics struck Richmond in 1864 and again in 1872 when fourteen people died. The disease returned in 1898, and frightened residents of nearby Berea quarantined their town and turned away travelers who came from Richmond.

Numerous industries and institutions grew in Richmond after 1865. A baseball club was organized in 1868, and a cheese factory was started in 1869. Three railroad lines entered the city in the 1870s and 1880s. In 1871 the Stanford-Richmond branch of the Louisville & Nashville (L&N, now CSX Transportation) entered the city and carried

trains until it ceased operations in 1930. In 1883 the Central Kentucky Railroad (later part of the L&N) extended its line southward from Winchester to Richmond, and the Richmond-Irvine Three Forks Railroad was built to Irvine in Estill County. As a city, Richmond secured modern public utilities relatively early. Gas mains and street lamps were turned on in 1874, and in 1879 the town had the only telephone system in the state outside of Louisville. A water plant opened in 1891, and public electricity was produced in 1899.

Politics between 1850 and 1900 was dominated by Curtis Field Burnam. Staunchly Republican and a friend of Abraham Lincoln, Burnam and his law partner James W. Caperton supported religious, educational, and social institutions in the area. Burnam was a strong advocate of the movement to locate Central University, a predecessor of Eastern Kentucky University (EKU), in Richmond during the mid-1870s. Eastern Kentucky University was formally founded in 1906 as Eastern Kentucky State Normal School.

Prominent city residents at the turn of the twentieth century were Belle Bennett and Henry Allen Laine. Laine, a poet and educator, has been called by some the black poet laureate of Kentucky. Bennett broke new ground for women in education and religion. In 1916 Bennett and Laine initiated a black chautauqua, an institution offering religious and social gatherings.

During World War II, the Blue Grass Ordnance Depot was constructed just south of Richmond and provided a major boost in the area's employment. In 1948 the Westinghouse Electric Corporation opened a large light bulb manufacturing plant in Richmond, but in the early 1980s the plant was sold to the North American Phillips Company.

In 1963 I-75 was completed from Richmond to Athens, in Fayette County. The interstate highway helped to spur commercial and residential development in the county. Some of the growth can be attributed to spillover from Lexington, where higher property costs and taxes prompted many to reside in Richmond and commute to jobs in Fayette County. Richmond's largest employers are EKU and college-related service businesses.

The population of the second-class city was 16,861 in 1970; 21,705 in 1980; and 21,155 in 1990.   FRED ALLEN ENGLE

RICHMOND, BATTLE OF. In midsummer 1862, the Confederates undertook an offensive aimed at central Tennessee and Kentucky. Gen. Braxton Bragg moved with about 30,000 men from Chattanooga and Maj. Gen. Edmund Kirby-Smith with 19,000 from Knoxville toward Cumberland Gap. Bypassing a Federal garrison there, Kirby-Smith with two of his four divisions quickly marched toward the Bluegrass. His cavalry, under Col. John S. Scott, routed a small Federal force near Big Hill in Madison County on August 23. At Richmond, 6,500 untrained Federal troops in two brigades, under Brig. Gens. Mahlon D. Manson and Charles Cruft, were ordered by their commander in Lexington, Maj. Gen. William NELSON, to move toward Lancaster. But Manson, in temporary command, did not receive the message and advanced his brigade south toward Rogersville as Kirby-Smith's lead division, under Brig. Gen. Patrick Cleburne, neared it on August 29. After limited fighting in the afternoon, Cleburne fell back to wait for Kirby-Smith's other division, under Brig. Gen. James Churchill, to arrive.

At dawn on August 30, the main battle began near Mt. Zion Church, with Cleburne east of the Old State Road, facing Manson's brigade, which was heavily concentrated on the Federal left flank. Kirby-Smith ordered Cleburne to hold his attack until Churchill, still on the way, could form against the weaker Federal right flank. After two hours of skirmishing and counter-battery artillery fire east of the road, Manson's overextended left flank was overwhelmed. At that time, Cruft's troops arrived, marched toward the sound of the guns, and began to reinforce the Federal right flank. Cleburne, guessing that Manson was now weakest at the center, was moving one of his brigades there when he was wounded and a subordinate took over his command. The entire Confederate army then advanced, with Scott's cavalry on either flank.

The Federal troops were routed and they reformed at White's farm, some four miles from Richmond. As Nelson arrived on the field, Federal troops fell back in disorder to the edge of Richmond. Nelson rallied 2,200 men just south of the town, but three volleys from a wide Confederate advance broke this defense. Scott's cavalry rode west to cut off their retreat, and virtually all of Nelson's army was captured. The official records show Nelson's loss as 206 killed, 844 wounded, and 4,303 missing, for a total of 5,353. Kirby-Smith's loss was 98 killed, 492 wounded, and at least 10 missing, for a total of 600. Tactically, the Confederates' victory was one of the most complete of the entire war but it was negated by failure to coordinate their forces in the campaign that ended at PERRYVILLE.   D. WARREN LAMBERT

RIDGEWAY. The Ridgeway estate, located on a plot of five acres at 4095 Massie Avenue in St. Matthews, Kentucky, in eastern Jefferson County, was built during 1804-5. Col. Henry Massie built the home for his bride, Helen Scott Bullitt, daughter of Alexander Scott BULLITT. The house originally rested in the middle of a five-hundred-acre plantation purchased by Bullitt from John Draper, who had received the land as a gift from King George II of England when the area was still a part of Fincastle County, Virginia. The western boundary of the plantation was a small lane that connected what are now Shelbyville and Westport roads. The southern boundary is known as Ridgeway Corner in St. Matthews. Ridgeway was separated from the OXMOOR plantation of the Bullitt family by farms and woodland.

The house, which was added to the National Register of Historic Places in 1973, has been described as the best example of Federal domestic architecture in the state of Kentucky. The one-story, red brick house with white trim is designed in typical Federal style: a triple massing, with the central section of the house adjoined by symmetrical wings on either side. Helen (Bullitt) Massie survived three husbands, including Marshall Key, brother of Francis Scott Key.

RITCHIE, JEAN RUTH. Jean Ruth Ritchie, folksinger, the youngest of Balis W. and Abigail (Hall) Ritchie's fourteen children, was born December 8, 1922, in Viper, Perry County, Kentucky. The Ritchies had a reputation as a singing family interested in collecting and preserving mountain ballads and play-party songs. The family was visited by various folk music collectors, including Cecil Sharp in 1917. All of the Ritchie children—May, Ollie, Mallie, Una, Raymond, Kitty, Truman, Patty, Edna, Jewel, Opal, Pauline, Balis Wilmer, and Jean— were musical, and both Edna and Jean became professional musicians. By the age of five, Jean had learned to play the mountain dulcimer from her father.

Ritchie children, residing halfway between Pine Mountain Settlement School and Hindman Settlement School, attended both. All of them graduated from high school and nine attended college. Jean Ritchie graduated from Perry County High School in 1940 and attended Cumberland College in Williamsburg for two years. She taught school in Perry County for a year in 1943, then transferred to the University of Kentucky, graduating in 1946 a member of Phi Beta Kappa with a degree in social work. Ritchie returned to Perry County as supervisor of elementary education for a year. She moved to New York City in 1947 to work at the Henry Street Settlement House. While there, she became known for singing ballads and playing the mountain dulcimer. Alan Lomax, a folk song collector, recorded Ritchie in 1949 for the Library of Congress Folk Song Archives and she became a regular performer on his radio program in New York City.

Ritchie began her recording career in 1952 when she signed a contract with Elektra Records. She has recorded more than thirty-five albums with various recording companies. Emphasizing traditional ballads in their original form, Ritchie is considered a major contributor to the folk music boom of the 1950s and 1960s. She popularized the mountain dulcimer, which she played mainly as an accompaniment to her vocals. Besides singing ballads such as "Go Tell Aunt Rhodie," "Shady Grove," and "Pretty Betty Martin," Ritchie wrote songs, including "Sorrow in the Wind." In 1977 her album *None But One* won the *Rolling Stone* critics award.

In 1952 Ritchie wrote *The Swapping Song Book*, a collection of twenty-one ballads for children, with photographs by George Pickow. Ritchie has since written and edited ten books of music and a family biography, *Singing Family of the Cumberland* (1955).

Ritchie has performed internationally, as well as touring the United States in concerts and music festivals, often alternating mountain ballads with European or contemporary folk songs to show similarities and differences. She has appeared on radio and television and in motion pictures. In 1963 Ritchie was one of the seven original board members of the Newport Folk Festival.

Ritchie received a Fulbright fellowship to study songs of Ireland and England from September 1952 to October 1953. In 1980 she was scholar in residence at California State College, at Fresno. She was awarded an honorary doctoral degree from the University of Kentucky in 1982.

Ritchie married George Pickow on September 29, 1950. They have two sons, Peter and Jonathan. Ritchie maintains residences at Port Washington, New York, and Viper, Kentucky.

See Kristin Baggelaar and Donald Milton, *Folk Music: More Than a Song* (New York 1976); Loyal Jones, "Jean Ritchie, Twenty-Five Years After," *Appalachian Journal* 8 (Spring 1981): 224-29.

RIVER RAISIN, BATTLE OF. On January 22, 1813, River Raisin in what is now Michigan was the site of a major defeat for Kentuckians in the War of 1812. Soon after Detroit's surrender in August 1812, a hastily organized Northwest Army under Gen. William Henry Harrison marched by three distinct routes through Ohio and Indiana with orders to reunite on the Maumee River in northern Ohio to attack Detroit. Slowed from October into January by heavy snows, the 1,300 Kentuckians who made up the left column, under Gen. James Winchester, were first to reach the rendezvous. As his troops were half-frozen and near starvation, Winchester, without awaiting Harrison's arrival, decided to capture a lightly guarded store of enemy provisions at Frenchtown (now Monroe, Michigan) on the River Raisin, only eighteen miles from British Fort Malden. After a sharp skirmish on January 18, 650 Kentucky militia under Lt. Cols. William Lewis and John Allen occupied the tiny settlement. Colonel Samuel Wells and 250 regulars, all Kentuckians, reinforced them on January 20, camping in an open field beyond the low pickets partially encircling the overcrowded hamlet. Gen. Henry Proctor struck there at dawn on January 22 with 1,200 to 1,400 Britons and Indians. The Kentuckians were completely exposed to devastating artillery fire, and both they and the militia companies led out by Lewis and Allen to rally them were quickly routed. Hunted through the woods by Indians, few survived.

Winchester, galloping belatedly from lodging upriver, was captured. Maj. George Madison was thus left to command the remaining militia in Frenchtown. Despite unanswerable artillery bombardment, Madison held out until midday, when dwindling ammunition forced his surrender. About eighty wounded were left in Frenchtown when the prisoners were marched away. That night, roistering Indians burned the houses and killed forty to sixty-five of the wounded. Altogether, more than four hundred Kentuckians died at Frenchtown, and in every

engagement thereafter, Kentucky troops rallied to the battle cry "Remember the Raisin!"

Nine counties in Kentucky are named for Kentuckians who died in the Battle of the River Raisin: Allen, Ballard, Edmonson, Graves, Hart, Hickman, McCracken, Meade, and Simpson.

See Alec R. Gilpin, *The War of 1812 in the Old Northwest* (East Lansing, Mich., 1958); G. Glenn Clift, *Remember the Raisin!* (Frankfort, Ky., 1961).

JAMES W. HAMMACK, JR.

RIVERS. Kentucky is the only state that is entirely bounded by rivers in three directions—west, north, and east. Its western boundary is the Mississippi River, which has a number of relatively small tributaries draining the northwestern two-thirds of the Jackson Purchase, west of the Tennessee River and Kentucky Lake. Its eastern boundary is formed by the Big Sandy River and the Tug Fork. On the north, Kentucky is bounded by the northern low-water mark of the Ohio River.

The state has 13,000 miles of streams. When the more than fifty man-made reservoirs now in existence are added, there are 1,500 square miles of water surface. There are more than 1,500 miles of navigable waterways, more than in any other of the contiguous states. Dams with locks permit cargo to be barged into and out of the state. Even such interior cities as Beattyville and BOWLING GREEN have had direct commercial access to the Gulf of Mexico, though access is becoming severely limited.

Early in Kentucky's history, its rivers were used mainly for transportation. Later, as river travel gave way to other means of transport, rivers assumed greater importance as sources of water for private and industrial use and as places of recreation. Waterways have also been convenient sites for sewage discharge, which has polluted them. Kentucky's rivers have been modified in the past two centuries to facilitate transportation and to control flooding. Waterways have been deepened by damming or rerouted by flood control projects. Thousands of acres that at one time were cultivated have become reservoirs, including Barkley, Kentucky, Cumberland, Fishtrap, and Buckhorn lakes.

Fifty-one of the state's 120 county seats are located on rivers, and more than one-fourth of Kentucky's population lives along its waterways. Wherever a river was shallow enough to be forded, as at Pineville, people and goods tended to funnel to that crossing point. At salt licks along the streams, such as Flat Lick, Blue Licks, Shepherdsville, and Manchester, pioneers came to collect salt and hunt the game drawn to these salt deposits. Where smaller streams merged with major river arteries, cities like Ashland, Newport, Covington, Carrollton, and Paducah arose as crossroads centers of commerce. Rapids that interrupted navigable streams made natural break-in-bulk points, most notably the Falls of the Ohio at Louisville. At such points, raw materials were unloaded, some were used in manufacturing, and both unprocessed raw materials and finished products were reloaded below or above the barrier. To bypass the falls at Louisville, the Portland Canal (1830) and later the McAlpine Dam and Locks were built.

Even though most rivers have been tamed by flood control dams and projects, Kentucky streams each year pour about 30 billion gallons of water into the Ohio. There are still some stretches of water where we can see Kentucky through the eyes of the Indians and pioneers. Rafting down the Upper Cumberland River from Red Bird Bridge to the falls or canoeing the Little South Fork or the Rockcastle River, the adventurous spirit can grasp the thrill of the wild river, and the yearning soul can envision an earlier day. The names of some streams celebrate people (Cumberland, Dick's [now Dix], Levisa, Martin's), while others describe the surrounding land (Licking, Laurel, Rockcastle, Barren) or the river itself (Rough, Green, Big Sandy, Ohio—the "beautiful river").

During the Pleistocene epoch, or Ice Age (from about 1.5 million to about 10,000 years ago), at least four major advances and retreats of continental glaciers affected the courses of Kentucky's rivers, in particular the ancient Ohio and the Teays rivers. Kentucky's rivers at first flowed northwest into the Teays, which crossed north-central Ohio, Indiana, and Illinois. As the glaciers advanced, Kentucky's rivers were impounded by the ice, and deep linear lakes were formed, beginning in the west and advancing to the east. When the glaciers melted, the waters were diverted west toward the Mississippi through the gradually developing Ohio River. When the last (Wisconsin) glacier melted, about 10,000 years ago, the northern sections of the Kentucky and the Licking rivers turned west and formed part of the present-day Ohio River.

The river valleys of Kentucky contain the remains and artifacts of successive ancient Native American occupations. Valley walls vividly portray Kentucky's geologic stages, and river terraces indicate varying levels of water in Kentucky's river valleys. Floodplain sediments are stark reminders of the relentless power of erosion, of high places brought low, the ghosts of mountains past. When earth forces intervene to raise or lower the land, the rivers carve a new face and leave the void filled with rich soils brought from other places. If you would know the soul of Kentucky, visit its rivers.

See Joseph R. Schwendeman, *Geography of Kentucky* (Lexington, Ky., 1987); William D. Thornbury, *Regional Geomorphology of the United States* (New York 1965); P.P. Karan and Cotton Mather, *Atlas of Kentucky* (Lexington, Ky., 1977).

C.M. DUPIER, JR.

ROARK, RURIC NEVEL. Ruric Nevel Roark, educator, was born in Greenville, Kentucky, on May 19, 1859, the son of Martin Jefferson and Nancy (Davis) Roark. After receiving a B.S. from National Normal School in Lebanon, Ohio, in 1881, he married one of his teachers, Mary Creegan. Immediately he began teaching there and obtained a master's degree in 1885. He became principal of Glasgow Normal School in Glasgow, Kentucky, in 1885, and served there until 1889, when he was appointed dean of the normal, or teacher training, department of the State Agricultural and Mechanical College (now University of Kentucky) in Lexington. A philosophical disagreement with President James K. PATTERSON over the role of the normal department led to his departure in 1905. Roark advocated the establishment of separate teacher training institutions in Kentucky, which resulted in 1906 in the creation of two state normal schools, in Richmond and Bowling Green. He was the first president of Eastern Kentucky State Normal School (now EASTERN KENTUCKY UNIVERSITY) in Richmond, serving from 1906 until his death on April 14, 1909. He is buried in the Richmond Cemetery.

See James F. Hopkins, *The University of Kentucky: Origins and Early Years* (Lexington, Ky., 1951). CHARLES C. HAY III

ROBERTS, LEONARD W. Leonard W. Roberts, a pioneer folklorist, teacher, and publisher, was born in Floyd County, Kentucky, on January 28, 1912, to Lewis Jackson and Rhoda Jane (Osborn) Roberts. He graduated from Berea College, studied creative writing at the University of Iowa, earned a doctorate in English at the University of Kentucky, and after collecting folktales, mostly from his students and their families, studied folklore at Indiana University. He wrote numerous articles and books dealing with folklore, including *South from Hellfer-Sartin* (1964), *Old Greasybeard: Tales From the Cumberland Gap* (1969), *Sang Branch Settlers* (1974), and *In the Pine* (1978). While teaching at Pikeville College, he founded a college press where he published the literary journal *Twigs* (later *Cumberlands*) and a number of books on poetry and regional history by Kentucky writers. He also taught at the Berea Foundation School, Union College in Barbourville, Morehead State University, and West Virginia Wesleyan College. He was killed in a traffic accident on April 29, 1983, and was buried at Ivel in Floyd County. He and his wife Edith (Reynolds) had four daughters: Sue Carolyn, Margaret Anne, Rita Helen, and Lynneda Jane.

LOYAL JONES

ROBERTS, PHILIPINE. Philipine ("Fiddlin' Doc") Roberts, musician, son of William and Rosa Roberts, was born in Madison County, Kentucky, on April 26, 1897. Considered Kentucky's outstanding fiddler, he performed with various other Kentuckians, including Edgar Boaz, Ted Chestnut, Dick Parman, Marion Underwood, Green Bailey, and Welby Toomey. In 1927 he teamed up with Asa Martin, who played the guitar, saw, and jug. He appeared on Nashville's "Grand Ole Opry" and on several other radio stations, including WLAP Lexington. Martin and Roberts recorded more than two hundred sides, under a dozen stage names, on eleven labels. They made up the Doc Roberts Trio along with Doc's son James Roberts, who later married Irene Amburgey and formed with her the gospel duo James and Martha Carson. Roberts died on August 4, 1978, and was buried in the Richmond Cemetery.

See Charles K. Wolfe, *Kentucky Country* (Lexington 1982); Ivan M. Tribe, "James (Carson) Roberts: Thirty-three Years in Old-Time, Gospel, and Bluegrass Music," *Bluegrass Unlimited* 14 (May 1980): 66-72.   CHARLES F. FABER

ROBERTSON, GEORGE. George Robertson, jurist and congressman, was born November 18, 1790, in Mercer County, Kentucky, the son of Alexander and Margaret (Robinson) Robertson. He was educated in Mercer County and at Transylvania University, and he studied law under Martin D. Hardin in Frankfort (1808) and Samuel McKee in Lancaster (1809). He was admitted to the bar in September 1809 and set up practice in Lancaster. From 1817 to 1821, he served in the U.S. House of Representatives, where he supported the 1820 Missouri Compromise and cheap public land. He served in the Kentucky House from 1822 to 1827, being elected Speaker in 1823, 1825, 1826, and 1827. In 1824 he rallied the OLD COURT party with a stirring written protest against the constitutionality of the statute that had abolished the court of appeals and established a new one. For three years he was a leader of the party, which succeeded in 1826 in abolishing the New Court.

In 1828, after serving briefly as Kentucky's secretary of state, Robertson accepted an appointment to the Kentucky court of appeals, where he served until 1843, most of the time as chief justice. He resigned from the court in 1843 and practiced law in Lexington. He was defense lawyer for Abner BAKER, who was tried and convicted for the murder of Daniel Bates in Manchester in July 1845. Robertson described Baker's conviction as "judicial murder," but failed to secure a pardon for his client from Gov. William Owsley (1844-48).

Robertson was elected again to the Kentucky House in 1848 and 1851-53, serving as Speaker during the latter period. He also was an instructor of law at Transylvania from 1834 to 1857. In 1864, when Robertson was seventy-four, the voters elected him to the Kentucky court of appeals, where he served until a stroke forced his resignation in 1871. During his last tenure on the court, he was the author of some very radical opinions on criminal law. In *Carico v. Commonwealth* (1870), Robertson, in writing for the majority, argued that it was lawful under the doctrine of self-defense for a person previously threatened by a man of "violent passions" to kill such a man upon their next encounter by shooting him in the back. A leading authority on American criminal law called this opinion a "new and startling doctrine, calculated to arrest attention, and apparently dangerous to the peace of society." In *Smith v. Commonwealth* (1864), Robertson wrote an opinion that, contrary to recognized law, accepted drunkenness as a defense against a murder charge and delineated a very permissive standard of legal insanity. Experts likewise criticized this opinion, which, when coupled with *Carico*, detracted from Robertson's reputation as one of the more able state jurists of his era.

Robertson married Eleanor Bainbridge in November 1809. She died on January 13, 1865, and he on May 16, 1874. Only three of his ten children survived him. He was buried in the Lexington Cemetery. The county created in 1867 out of parts of Nicholas, Harrison, Bracken, and Mason counties was named in his honor.

See George Robertson, *Outline of the Life of George Robertson, Written by Himself, with an Introduction by His Son* (Lexington, Ky., 1876); Robertson, *Scrap Book on Law and Politics, Men and Times* (Lexington, Ky., 1855).

ROBERT M. IRELAND

ROBERTSON COUNTY. Robertson County, the 111th county in order of formation, located in northeastern Kentucky, is bordered by Bracken, Fleming, Harrison, Mason, and Nicholas counties. It has an area of 100 square miles. Robertson County was formed August 1, 1867, from portions of Bracken, Harrison, Mason, and Nicholas counties and was named in honor of George Robertson, a chief justice of the court of appeals. The county seat is MT. OLIVET.

The topography of Robertson County is hilly, with about 25 percent of the county covered in forests of hardwood and cedar. The principal streams in the county are the Licking River and its North Fork, and the Cedar, Johnson, Panther, and West creeks.

The first explorers in the area were Daniel Boone and Simon Kenton in 1767. Robertson County was the site of one of the bloodiest defeats of the settlers at the hands of the Indians. On August 19, 1782, at the Blue Licks, about ten miles south of Mt. Olivet, a force of 176 Kentuckians were ambushed by about one hundred Indians led by British officers and the renegade Simon Girty. Some historians state that Blue Licks was the last battle of the American Revolution. In 1882 Gov. Luke P. Blackburn (1879-83) dedicated the cornerstone of the Blue Licks Monument. The Blue Licks State Park was established in the 1930s.

Duncan Harding of Kentontown, a state representative from Harrison County, worked for the passage of the bill to create the county. Among the communities in Robertson County are Mt. Olivet, Abigail, Kentonville, Piqua, Sardis, and Bratton's Mill, also called Pinhook. Pinhook, according to local folklore, is the origin of the tobacco "pinhooker," a speculator who buys a tobacco crop for resale.

Robertson County remains an agrarian community of small family farms. Approximately 82 percent of the land is in farms, of which tobacco and livestock are the major products. In 1980, 50 percent of the local labor force was employed in other counties.

The population of Robertson County was 2,163 in 1970; 2,265 in 1980; and 2,124 in 1990.

See John Ed Pearce, "Robertson County," *Louisville Courier-Journal Magazine*, January 11, 1981.
RON D. BRYANT

ROBINSON, JAMES FISHER. The son of Jonathan and Jane (Black) Robinson, James Fisher Robinson, governor during 1862-63, was born on October 4, 1800, in Scott County. An 1818 graduate of Transylvania University, Robinson became a successful farmer-lawyer in Georgetown. In 1851 he won election to the state Senate as a Henry Clay Whig; in 1861 he was elected to the state Senate as a Democrat. Robinson supported the CRITTENDEN COMPROMISE proposals and opposed war, but he realized that Kentucky's neutrality could not last. In the political deal that called for Gov. Beriah Magoffin's (1859-62) resignation, Robinson was elected Speaker of the Senate on August 16, 1862. Magoffin then resigned, and Robinson was sworn in as governor on August 18. After his term ended on September 1, 1863, Robinson became increasingly critical of the national administration. He supported George B. McClellan for president in 1864. Robinson practiced law, farmed in Scott County, headed the Farmers' Bank of Georgetown and chaired the Georgetown College Board of Trustees. He died on October 31, 1882, and was buried in the Georgetown Cemetery.

Robinson's short term was dominated by the Civil War, and the major Confederate invasion of Kentucky occurred soon after he took office. He sought higher taxes to revive the state militia and to preserve the educational progress that had been made, but he could do little in either area. Robinson boasted of the number of Kentuckians in Union service, but he complained that Federal authorities treated the state as if it were disloyal. He adamantly opposed the Union army's policy of sheltering runaway slaves, enlistment of blacks, and President Abraham Lincoln's Emancipation Proclamation, although the latter did not apply to Kentucky. His fellow citizens, Robinson contended, should oppose both secession and abolition.

See "Notes Concerning the Life and Death of Governor James F. Robinson," *Register* 5 (Jan. 1907): 14-22.
LOWELL H. HARRISON

ROBINSON, STUART. Presbyterian minister and theologian, Stuart Robinson was born in Strabane, Ireland, on November 14, 1814. He grew up in Virginia, sometimes in the care of foster parents. Educated at Amherst College in Massachusetts, Union Seminary in Virginia, and Princeton Seminary, Robinson undertook ministry for congregations in western Virginia and Maryland. In Kentucky, he served Frankfort Presbyterian (1846-53) and Second Presbyterian in Louisville (1858-81), where he came to be called the "evangelical pastor to the city." He also served during 1856-58 as a professor at the Danville Seminary.

Robinson, who had deep convictions that church and state should be separate, fled into exile in Canada during the Civil War. He served in Toronto as a pastor to a sizable exile community. After the war, he returned to Kentucky, where he led most Kentucky Presbyterians into the Presbyterian Church, U.S. (or Southern Presbyterian Church), which he served as moderator in 1869.

Robinson developed the doctrine of the spirituality of the church, which held that denominations ought not meddle in political affairs. His more radical formulation of this belief caught the imagination of many, especially southern Protestants. Though he did not own slaves, Robinson argued that the Bible justified the institution. His books, *The Church of God* (1858) and *Discourses of Redemption* (1868), were respected for decades in Southern evangelical circles. A person of business acumen, Robinson helped direct financial and real estate markets in Louisville during his years in Kentucky. He also helped instigate mission efforts in Appalachia and elsewhere in the state. His contributions launched a pension fund for Presbyterian ministers.

In September 1841 he married Mary Elizabeth Brigham of Massachusetts. Five of their eight children died in infancy. Robinson died October 5, 1881, and is buried in Louisville's Cave Hill Cemetery. See Louis Weeks, "Stuart Robinson: Kentucky Presbyterian Leader," *FCHQ* 54 (Oct. 1980): 360-77.
LOUIS WEEKS

ROBSION, JOHN MARSHALL. John Marshall Robsion, U.S. congressman and senator, son of John A. and Mary (Hyland) Robsion, was born in Bracken County, Kentucky, on January 2, 1873. Both his parents died while he was young, but he managed to put himself through school. He attended National Northern University in Ada, Ohio, and Holbrook College in Knoxville, Tennessee, and graduated from National Normal University in Lebanon, Ohio. In 1898 he received a law degree from Centre College in Danville, Kentucky.

Robsion moved to Barbourville, Kentucky, where he taught both in the public schools and at Union College while establishing a legal practice. In 1911 he became president of the First National Bank of Barbourville. He was elected on the Republican ticket to the U.S. House of Representatives from the 11th District, serving from March 4, 1919, to January 10, 1930. On January 11, 1930, Gov. Flem D. Sampson (1927-31) appointed Robsion to complete the unexpired U.S. Senate term of Frederic M. Sackett. In November of that year Robsion ran for both the remainder of Sackett's term and for a full Senate term; he lost the former to Ben Williamson by 326,723 to 297,510 and the latter to M.M. Logan by 336,748 to 309,180. He left the Senate on November 30, 1930. He returned to Congress as representative from the 9th District, serving from January 3, 1935, until his death on February 17, 1948. He was chairman of the House Committee on Mines and Mining and was the ranking Republican member of the Committees on Roads, Education, Pensions, Judiciary, and Revision of Law.

Robsion married Lida Stansbury of Grays, Kentucky, on January 25, 1902. They had three children, Daisy, Edmonds, and John Jr. Robsion died in

Barbourville on February 17, 1948, and was buried in the Barbourville Cemetery.

ROCKCASTLE COUNTY. Rockcastle County was formed in 1810 from portions of Lincoln, Madison, Knox, and Pulaski. The fifty-second county established in Kentucky, it has an area of 318 square miles. The county shares the name of the Rockcastle River, named by explorer Isaac Lindsey in 1767 for the towering rock formations along the stream, which resemble castles. The eastern portion of the county went into the formation of Laurel County in 1825, making the river a boundary. Legislative action in 1972 included the Rockcastle in the Wild Rivers System of Kentucky. Other waterways include the Dix River and Boone's Fork. The county seat is MT. VERNON.

About one-fourth of the county is a part of the DANIEL BOONE NATIONAL FOREST. The western edge of the Knobs region, a transitional area surrounding the Outer Bluegrass, covers about two-thirds of the county and the terrain is quite rugged. Narrow valleys, huge boulders, steep hillsides, and swift winding creeks make the county difficult to traverse; indeed, in the 1820 census, enumerators were unable to reach some sections of the county. The official census report included a note by Sheriff William Grisham, who explained that the "Mountainous and rugged county" made the census enumeration "as hard a task and perhaps more so than any county in the state." Confederate Gen. Felix Zollicoffer, in an October 1861 report to the adjutant general's office, referred to the Union's position on Rockcastle Hills as an "intrenched camp, a natural fortification, almost inaccessible."

Settlers from the east passed through what is now Rockcastle County along Boone's Trace, Skaggs's Trace or the Wilderness Road. Tradition holds that Stephen Langford led the first settlers into the county and founded Mt. Vernon, the county seat, in 1790. The original log courthouse burned in 1873, destroying official records. The other incorporated towns are Broadhead, since 1885 the site of the "Little World's Fair," in the western part of the county, and Livingston, on the Rockcastle River. Between Mt. Vernon and Livingston is Pine Hill, which in 1873, during its height as a coal and lumber town, had a population of six hundred, but the community now numbers only a handful of residents.

The earliest industry was the extraction of SALT-PETER from Great Saltpeter Cave for manufacturing gunpowder. The cave lies in the southeastern section of the county, north of Livingston, and is most easily reached via KY 1004. The cave was a shelter for both Confederate and Union troops during the Civil War. The Battle of Camp Wildcat, or Battle of Rockcastle Hills, was fought in October 1861 across the Rockcastle River, in Laurel County.

Settlers in the county were sparse until the advent of the railroad in the latter part of the nineteenth century. The Louisville & Nashville Railroad reached Broadhead and Mt. Vernon in 1868. In 1870 Livingston became the terminus of the railroad and remained so until 1882, when the rails were extended to London, in Laurel County. The Kentucky Central Railroad reached Livingston two years later (1884). Coal in Livingston and Pine Hill was of exportable quality. Lime, building stone, barrel staves, and tannin bark were also shipped by rail. These developments pushed the population from 5,343 in 1860 to a peak of 17,165 in 1940.

The county's first newspaper, the *Mountain Signal*, was published in 1887. It later became the *Mountain Eagle* and is now published as the *Mount Vernon Signal*. The earliest compiler of historical notes about the county was Col. James Maret, founder and editor of the *Mountain Signal*; his material was published only in the newspaper. An engineer by training, Maret pushed for paved roads in the state to "open the mountains to civilization." Maret wrote his "Notes and Clips" column until his death in 1936.

Renfro Valley, probably the best-known area of Rockcastle County, was the home of John Lair, who started national radio broadcasts of the "Renfro Valley Barn Dance," a country music program, in November 1939. The county's only radio station is located in Renfro Valley. Lair also chronicled the county in his *Mount Vernon Signal* column, "Rockcastle Recollections," from 1972 to 1974.

From 1835 to the early 1900s, the Rockcastle Springs Hotel on the Rockcastle River, about five miles from its mouth, was a popular summer resort. Rockcastle County is the site of a large number of summer homes, including the community of Lake Linville, formed in the early 1970s along I-75 near Renfro Valley. Rafting along the Rockcastle and through the narrows, a mile and a half of white water, is popular. While tourism has been increasing, agriculture is the economic backbone of the county. There are some isolated industries in the county's three incorporated towns. Transportation routes include U.S. 25 and U.S. 150, and I-75 is the major traffic artery. The population of the county was 12,305 in 1970; 13,973 in 1980; and 14,803 in 1990.

See E.E. Norton, "History of Education in Rockcastle County," M.A. thesis, University of Kentucky, 1932.   J. ALLEN SINGLETON

ROCKCASTLE RIVER. The Rockcastle River was named the Lawless River by Dr. Thomas Walker, for a member of his exploring party who came to Kentucky in 1750. It was renamed the Rockcastle River by Long Hunter Isaac Lindsey for the huge rock formations, resembling castles, along its banks. The river is about seventy-five miles long and varies from 200 to 250 feet wide. The Rockcastle has two main branches. The Middle Fork rises in southern Jackson County, at the confluence of Laurel Fork and Indian Creek. The South Fork, which forms most of the border between Laurel and Clay counties, originates just west of the Laurel County line. Martin and Mill creeks join the South Fork in Laurel County. The Middle and the South forks meet on the Jackson County line near the confluence of Horse Lick Creek, forming the Rockcastle River. The river flows south and forms the southeast boundary of Rockcastle County. It is joined by Roundstone Creek at Livingston and, further downstream, by Skeggs Creek. At its southern end, the Rockcastle forms the border between Pulaski and Laurel counties. It becomes a tributary of the Cumberland River at the intersection of Pulaski, Laurel, and McCreary counties.

See Thomas D. Clark, *A History of Laurel County* (London, Ky., 1989).

ROCK FENCES. Only about 10 percent of the rock fences built in Kentucky still stand. The most extensive rock fence network was built in the Bluegrass region, especially those areas known as the Inner Bluegrass and the Eden Shale hills. Rock fences also stand in some of Kentucky's Appalachian counties and in the Pennyroyal area. A few rock fences date from the late eighteenth century, constructed by Scots and Ulster settlers at mill sites, springs, farm yards, and cemeteries. The heaviest period of construction, however, began in the 1820s and peaked during the 1840s and 1850s. Faced with a scarcity of wood for constructing fences, builders turned to the limestone that underlies the Bluegrass counties, which they quarried or picked up in pieces from the surface of the more steeply sloped fields.

Migrants from Ireland arrived in increasing numbers during this time, and it was Irish stonemasons, bringing with them a heritage of rock-building techniques, who built or directed fence building during this era. Two contrasting forms of construction were used: on rolling land, horizontally coursed dry-laid fences (without mortar); on the rougher lands of the Eden Shale hills, steeply angled "edge" fences. Slaves may have been called into use in quarrying, hauling rock, or assisting with the construction itself. After the Civil War, freedmen who had learned the craft often continued to build rock fences, some as contractors.

See Frederick Rainsford-Hannay, *Dry Stone Walling* (London 1957); Carolyn Murray-Wooley and Karl Raitz, *Rock Fences of the Bluegrass* (Lexington, Ky., 1992).

KARL RAITZ AND CAROLYN
MURRAY-WOOLEY

RODMAN, HUGH. Hugh Rodman, naval officer, was the son of Dr. Hugh and Susan Ann (Barbour) Rodman. Rodman was born in Frankfort, Kentucky, on January 6, 1859. In 1875 he was appointed to the U.S. Naval Academy and began his sea duty five years later, just as steel ships began to replace wooden vessels. Much of his early sea duty was in the Pacific, with the U.S. Coast and Geodetic Survey. During the Spanish-American War (1898), he was commended for his conduct in commanding the forward gun batteries of the cruiser *Raleigh* under George Dewey at Manila Bay. Promoted to lieutenant in 1897 and captain in 1911, he

served in Asia after the war and attended the Naval War College. Rodman also commanded the Cavite Naval Yard in the Philippine Islands and served as the first superintendent of operations when the Panama Canal was opened to traffic in 1914.

Rodman was captain of two battleships before the United States entered World War I and was promoted to rear admiral in May 1917. He commanded Battleship Division 3 and then Battleship Division 9 of the U.S. Atlantic Fleet. Under Rodman, Division 9 was ordered to the British naval base at Scapa Flow for duty with the British Grand Fleet. After the war, Rodman commanded the newly established U.S. Pacific Fleet and then the 5th Naval District before his retirement in 1923. In 1937 he was invited to attend the coronation of King George VI and for the occasion was returned to active duty with the rank of admiral. Rodman married Elizabeth Ruffin Sayre, of Frankfort, Kentucky, in 1889. Rodman died on June 7, 1940, and was buried in the Arlington National Cemetery.

See Hugh Rodman, *Yarns of a Kentucky Admiral* (Indianapolis 1928).   LLOYD J. GRAYBAR

ROEBLING SUSPENSION BRIDGE. When the Covington and Cincinnati suspension bridge opened to traffic on January 1, 1867, its span of 1,057 feet made it the longest suspension bridge in the world. Total cost of construction was nearly $1.8 million. Later in 1867, the Covington Street Railway Company laid rails for its horsecars across the bridge, further contributing to the accessibility of Covington. By July 1868, the streetcars carried 2,600 passengers per day over the bridge.

The guiding light of the Covington and Cincinnati Bridge Company was Amos Shinkle, a Covington banker and philanthropist, who invested in the enterprise and was a member of the board of directors. In August 1856 the board chose as architect John August Roebling, a German émigré engineer who later designed the Brooklyn Bridge in New York City. Construction began in September 1856 but was interrupted by the bridge company's financial problems in the nationwide economic panic of 1857 and by the outbreak of the Civil War.

Proposals to link Cincinnati and northern Kentucky by a bridge had been made as far back as 1815; ferries generally closed in the early evening, and flooding or the formation of ice caused them to cease operation altogether. The Kentucky General Assembly chartered the Kentucky and Ohio Bridge Company in 1829. There was opposition from steamboat operators, who feared that a bridge would impede river navigation, particularly during times of high water, and from some Cincinnati business interests, who feared that a bridge would advance the economic interests of their rivals in Covington and Newport. The company ceased to exist after the Ohio General Assembly failed to enact a comparable charter. In 1846 the Kentucky General Assembly passed a new bridge charter, which the Ohio legislature finally approved in March 1849, after adding controversial amendments dealing with the passage of runaway slaves and the Ohio River boundary dispute.

By 1895 nearly 1.4 million people crossed the bridge annually, and six hundred streetcars made the trip daily. In 1895-96 the bridge was reconstructed to accommodate the increased traffic and the transition to heavier electric streetcars. The addition of two new steel cables to the original two wrought iron ones more than doubled the original strength of the bridge. By 1918 the company had completed a new Cincinnati approach to the bridge, placed well above the normal floodplain. During the great Ohio River flood of 1937, it remained the only span open to traffic between Steubenville, Ohio, and Cairo, Illinois.

In 1953 the bridge company sold the structure to the state of Kentucky, which operated it as a toll bridge until 1963. In 1975 the bridge was listed on the National Register of Historic Places and became a NATIONAL HISTORIC LANDMARK. In 1983 the American Society of Civil Engineers designated the span a national historic civil engineering landmark. In 1983 the bridge was renamed the John A. Roebling Bridge, in recognition of its designer. The nonprofit Covington-Cincinnati Suspension Bridge Committee, Inc. raised the funds to illuminate the bridge with seventy-six necklace lights on its upper cables, and a complete floodlighting system for its piers. The system was installed and officially dedicated in 1984 in memory of Julia E. Langsam of the committee.

See D.B. Steinman, *The Builders of the Bridge: The Story of John Roebling and His Son* (New York 1945); Joseph S. Stern, Jr., "The Suspension Bridge: They Said It Couldn't Be Built," *Bulletin of the Cincinnati Historical Society* (Oct. 1965).

PAUL A. TENKOTTE

ROGERS, JOHN. Architect-designer John Rogers was born in Ireland in 1785. Orphaned, he was raised by his uncle, Sir Arthur Rogers. In 1804 he came to America and located in Baltimore. There he became associated with Roman Catholic institutions, including St. Mary's Seminary and College, where the architect lay-teacher, Maximillian Godefroy, taught design. Whether by apprenticeship or instruction, Rogers acquired both formal and practical training in building practices.

By 1814 Rogers had been summoned to Nelson County, Kentucky, to assist in the building plans of Bardstown's first Roman Catholic bishop, Benedict Joseph Flaget. Rogers first directed the seminarians in building St. Thomas Church a few miles south of Bardstown. Finished by 1815, it was a small version of St. Mary's Chapel in Baltimore, designed by Godefroy, and it was the first design of gothic influence erected west of the Alleghenies.

Rogers was chief supervisor of all construction when building began in 1816 on ST. JOSEPH Cathedral in Bardstown, the first Catholic cathedral in the new West. It was Rogers who provided the classically detailed plans for the columned portico, steeple, and interior decoration when the hoped-for gothic design by Godefroy did not materialize. The church was in use by 1819, but not fully finished before 1825. In the interim, Rogers embarked on residential designs in and near Bardstown, including those for Shadow Lawn, Roseland, and EDGEWOOD, his own home, still standing. Most famous of his domestic designs is WICKLAND, built about 1828 for Gov. Charles A. Wickliffe just east of Bardstown. Also his is Spalding Hall, the main building of St. Joseph College, erected by 1825 just north of the cathedral in Bardstown.

Rogers was married to Sarah Rosensteel of Philadelphia on February 2, 1812; their children were James, Elizabeth J., Susan M., John D., Ann R., William F., Charles A., and Mary Josephine. Despite his talents and successful designs, financial success eluded Rogers. He died suddenly on January 27, 1836, while supervising construction of the Bank of Louisville building.

See J. Herman Schauinger, *Cathedrals in the Wilderness* (Milwaukee, Wis., 1952).

DAVID H. HALL

ROMAN CATHOLIC CHURCH. With some 350,000 members in Kentucky at the end of the 1980s, Roman Catholics constituted about 10 percent of the commonwealth's population. In Roman Catholic administrative terms, Kentucky and Tennessee constitute a province headed by the archdiocese of Louisville, with suffragan dioceses (or sees) at Covington, Owensboro, and Lexington in Kentucky; and at Nashville, Memphis, and Knoxville in Tennessee. A bishop (or ordinary) presides over each diocese, with an archbishop at Louisville.

In 1775 a few Catholics came to the western part of Virginia that is now Kentucky. Among those settling at Fort Harrod were Jane Coomes and Dr. George Hart, probably the first schoolteacher and physician, respectively, in the state, according to Richard Collins's *Historical Sketches of Kentucky* (1874). Significant Catholic settlement began in 1785, when families from Maryland came to the rich farmland of modern-day Marion, Nelson, and Washington counties. The first of twenty families, led by the Haydens and Lancasters, established themselves near Pottinger's Creek in Marion County, their parish eventually becoming known as Holy Cross. Other eighteenth century settlements included those at Hardin's Creek (St. Charles); Poplar Neck (St. Thomas); Cartwright's Creek (St. Ann/St. Rose); Rolling Fork (Holy Mary); Scott County (St. Francis); Cox's Creek (St. Michael); and Bardstown (St. Joseph). The pioneer colonies were initially led by laymen, including Robert Abell, the only Catholic to serve in the 1799 Kentucky constitutional convention; John Lancaster, a state representative and senator; and Grace Newton Simpson, noted for her intellect.

Bishop John Carroll of Baltimore sent the first priests—Maurice Whelan and William de Rohan—who served briefly in Kentucky. The arrival of Stephen BADIN, the first priest ordained in the United States, brought a lasting clerical leader. Badin estimated that there were three hundred Catholic families in Kentucky at the time of his arrival in 1793. From St. Stephen's farm in Marion County, Badin made his horseback rounds as a circuit rider from Michigan to Tennessee. In 1805 Belgian priest Charles NERINCKX began nineteen years of pastoral service to the "iron race" of Kentucky pioneers. Also in 1805, Dominican priests established their first American foundation at St. Rose near Springfield. Within three years, this religious order founded ST. THOMAS COLLEGE there.

On April 8, 1808, Pope Pius VII subdivided the single American diocese of Baltimore into the dioceses of Bardstown, Boston, New York, and Philadelphia. The jurisdiction of the original Bardstown see, headed by Benedict Joseph FLAGET, the "First Bishop of the West," extended from the Great Lakes to the Deep South, and from the Alleghenies to the Mississippi. More than thirty other dioceses were later carved out of this expanse, including those of Chicago and Detroit. Flaget, like Badin an émigré from the French Revolution, and his colleagues made Bardstown the center from which Catholicism developed in the Midwest and the South.

Among Bishop Flaget's most notable colleagues were Bishop Guy Chabrat; Bishop John Baptist David; scholar Francis P. Kenrick, later archbishop of Baltimore; Mother Catherine SPALDING; and Bishop Martin John SPALDING, who succeeded Flaget. After spending the years 1812-19 at St. Thomas farm in Nelson County, Flaget moved to Bardstown in 1819 upon completion of St. Joseph Proto-Cathedral there.

Under Flaget's leadership, the institutions founded included St. Thomas Seminary (1811-69); St. Joseph's College, Bardstown (1820-62; 1869-89); St. Mary's College (1821-1976); the *Catholic Advocate*, one of the first Catholic newspapers in the West; and the Kentucky parishes of St. Peter at Lexington (1818) and Holy Name at Henderson (1824). In the same period, some of the earliest communities of Catholic religious women in the United States were established in Kentucky—the Sisters of Loretto (1812); the Sisters of Charity of Nazareth (1812); and the Dominican Sisters at Springfield (1822). Early religious communities of men included the Society of Jesus (Jesuits) and Trappist monks from France, who founded the Abbey of Gethsemani in Nelson County.

By the 1840s, partly due to the inflow of German and Irish immigrants, port cities such as Louisville and Covington were growing rapidly. In 1841 Flaget transferred the seat of his diocese to Louisville where there were three congregations: St. Louis, the Cathedral parish (1806), for English-speaking; St. Boniface (1837) for Germans; and Notre Dame du Port—Our Lady's—(1839) for the French. Construction on the Cathedral of the Assumption began in 1849. In Covington, the first parish to be formed was St. Mary's (1837), followed by the German congregation Mutter Gottes (Mother of God) in 1842. Although Covington and Newport were for a brief time (1847-53) under the

jurisdiction of Cincinnati, Rome created Kentucky's second diocese at Covington in 1853, with George Carrell as its first bishop. The new diocese was responsible for the Appalachian counties. Catholic families from the early settlements migrated to such western Kentucky counties as Breckinridge, Grayson, and Union, the latter served by Elisha Durbin. Early notable establishments included St. Vincent's Academy (1820) in Union County, the parish of St. Stephen at Owensboro (1833), St. Francis de Sales at Paducah (1848), and St. Joseph at Bowling Green (1859).

Flaget died in 1850. His successor in Louisville was the Kentucky-born Martin John Spalding, whose pacific response to the anti-Catholic Bloody Monday riot of August 6, 1855, helped to prevent additional loss of life. With its heavily German population, Covington, too, was subject to distress from the Know-Nothing element, who feared the increasing number and influence of foreign-born Catholics. Spalding was responsible for the arrival in the diocese of the fourth motherhouse, that of the German Ursuline Sisters at Louisville in 1858, and of the Xaverian Brothers, a teaching order from Belgium (1854). The Sisters of St. Benedict came to the Covington diocese in 1859. Many Kentucky sisters served as nurses in the Civil War.

Lay leaders after the Civil War included Patrick Henry Callahan; Edward McDermott, lieutenant-governor of the commonwealth (1911-15); and Benedict Webb, historian and political leader. In the Covington diocese, religious communities were founded by the Sisters of Notre Dame (1874) and the Sisters of Divine Providence (1889). As the century turned, Covington's Bishop Camillus Maes was overseeing the construction there of St. Mary's Cathedral, while Louisville's Bishop William George McCloskey quarreled often, sometimes openly, with his priests and religious. In western Kentucky, the Ursuline Sisters at Maple Mount, originally a foundation from Louisville, established an independent motherhouse in 1912.

Kentucky's Catholic social service organizations were severely strained during the Great Depression of the 1930s and by the Ohio River flood of 1937. Pope Pius XI raised Louisville to the status of an archdiocese in 1937 and established the state's third diocese, in Owensboro. The Second Vatican Council (1962-65) brought extensive changes to the church. Among Kentuckians taking part in the assembly in Rome were J.L. Garrett of the Southern Baptist Seminary, and Mary Luke Tobin of Loretto, the only official woman auditor from the United States. A new array of agencies and commissions emerged to promote spirituality, lay leadership, involvement in social justice, and ecumenical relationships.

Since 1950 Catholic politicians have become a regular part of the Kentucky scene, even though no Catholic has served as full-term governor. Earlier, Catholics were occasionally the power behind the throne, as in the case of the Whallen Democratic machine in Louisville before World War I. As late as the 1930s, according to historians James Klotter and John Muir, such powers in the state as Michael Brennan, Percy Haly, Billy ("King") Klair, and Ben Johnson, as Catholics, realized that any office requiring statewide election stood out of their reach.

By 1990 Kentucky had 340 Catholic parishes and mission churches, 485 diocesan priests, 100 deacons, nearly 2,400 religious women (representing over 80 communities), and 175 religious men. Kentucky also had 14 Catholic hospitals, 26 Catholic high schools, and a total of some 48,000 students in all Catholic schools. The Catholic institutions of higher learning in the commonwealth were Bellarmine (Louisville), Brescia (Owensboro), St. Catharine (Springfield), St. Thomas More (Covington), and Spalding (Louisville). By diocese, the membership was: Louisville (archdiocese), 193,000 Catholics in 24 central Kentucky counties; Covington, 78,000 members in 14 northeastern counties; Owensboro, 50,000 Catholics in 32 western counties; and Lexington (established 1988), 40,000 members in 50 eastern counties.

See Clyde F. Crews, *An American Holy Land: A History of the Archdiocese of Louisville* (Wilmington, Del., 1987); Judy Hayden, *This Far By Faith: The Story of Catholicity in Western Kentucky* (Owensboro, Ky., 1987); James Klotter and John Muir, "Boss Ben Johnson, the Highway Commission and Kentucky Politics 1917-1937," *Register* 82 (Winter 1984): 18-50.   CLYDE F. CREWS

ROOSTER RUN. Rooster Run, one of the best-known general stores in the country and one of Kentucky's best-known unincorporated businesses, is located seven miles outside of Bardstown on KY 245 in Nelson County, Kentucky. In 1967 Joe Evans's store, then called Evans' Beverage Depot, was located on the former route of KY 245. The small store and service station were a popular place of congregation for the men of the community. Now and then when a wife arrived looking for her husband or a state trooper was spotted down the road, the men would scatter and take flight down a little hill to escape detection. "Look at that rooster run!" one regular was heard to exclaim, giving the spot a new name. Evans had a new sign made: "Evans' Beverage Depot, Rooster Run, Kentucky."

When the highway relocated, Evans moved his business and changed the name to Rooster Run General Store. Evans began selling caps with embroidered patches of roosters, which became a hit with customers. On January 28, 1986, Rooster Run received U.S. Trademark Registration for both the general logo for the store and the specialized logo for the caps, which shows a rooster kicking up dust as he races across the words "Rooster Run, Kentucky." By 1990 more than a million of the official caps had been sold throughout the world. Even a Kentucky Highway Department sign marks the nonexistent town for visitors.   HETTIE DELONG

ROSINE. Rosine, a small rural town in eastern Ohio County, is located eight miles east of Beaver Dam and fourteen miles west of Caneyville on both U.S 62 and the Paducah & Louisville (P&L) Railroad. The area was originally known as Pigeon Roost, after a local branch of Muddy Creek, where in pioneer days huge flocks of pigeons came to roost in the large cedar trees. With the coming of the Elizabethtown & Paducah Railroad (now the P&L) in 1872, the town was founded as Rosine by Col. Henry D. McHenry (1826-90), a local lawyer, coal entrepreneur, and U.S. congressman. His wife, Jenny (Taylor) McHenry, in 1867 had used the pen name Rosine for a book of poetry, *Forget Me Not*. The post office, established on January 16, 1872, as Pigeon Roost, changed its name to Rosine in 1873. The town was officially incorporated on March 16, 1878, and grew quickly, with lumber as a major industry until a fire destroyed the business district in 1900.

By 1990, Rosine was no longer a thriving city and was unincorporated. The city is known as the home of Bill Monroe, the "Father of Bluegrass Music," who was born three miles to the south.

WENDELL C. ALLEN

ROTHERT, OTTO ARTHUR. Otto Arthur Rothert, historian, was born in Huntingburg, Indiana, on June 21, 1871. He was the youngest of the five children of Herman Rothert, who came to the United States from Germany in 1844, and Franziska (Weber) Rothert, also born in Germany. The family moved to Louisville in 1889, where his father had a tobacco exporting business. Rothert graduated from the University of Notre Dame in 1892 with a science major; he had written several articles published in the *Notre Dame Scholastic*. After graduation, Rothert worked for his father and later for his brother John at the Falls City Tobacco Works, then became a clerk at the Galt House, where his genial nature served well. In 1904 and 1905 he made an extended tour of the western states, Hawaii, and Mexico, sending back descriptive articles to the *Huntingburg Independent*. When he returned he wrote articles for the *Muhlenberg Sentinel* and the *Greenville Record* on the history of Muhlenberg County, where his family owned 2,600 acres of land. The result of that work was his classic *History of Muhlenberg County* (1913).

In 1908 Rothert became a member of the Filson Club, where he read several of his papers on historical topics. In 1917 he was elected secretary of the club, serving in that role until his retirement on November 1, 1945. As secretary Rothert edited books in the Filson Club Publication series, arranged the annual lecture series, and, beginning in 1928, edited the *Filson Club History Quarterly*. He set high editorial standards and earned scholarly respect for the journal. His devoted service helped establish the Filson Club as a leader among local history societies in the United States. He gave the club his large library of books and manuscripts.

Rothert's many publications included *The Outlaws of Cave-In-Rock* (1924), *The Story of a Poet: Madison Cawein* (1921), and *The Filson Club and Its Activities, 1884-1922* (1922). He was known as

"Uncle Otto" to the emerging historians of Kentucky who profited by his tutelage, among them Holman Hamilton, Hambleton Tapp, Thomas D. Clark, and J. Winston Coleman. Otto A. Rothert died on March 28, 1956, in Greenville, Kentucky, and was buried in Huntingburg, Indiana.

See Hambleton Tapp, "Otto Arthur Rothert, 1871-1956," *FCHQ* 61 (Jan. 1987): 54-67.

JAMES R. BENTLEY

ROUGH RIVER. The Rough River, which rises in Hardin County in north-central Kentucky and forms the boundary between Breckinridge and Grayson counties, is a tributary of the Green River. The Rough River enters the Green at Livermore, Kentucky, in McLean County. After the Barren River, the Rough is the largest tributary of the Green River. As early as 1810 the Kentucky legislature declared the Rough River navigable and later approved the first bridge over the river at Hartford in Ohio County. Hartford became the center of Rough River navigation after passage of the River and Harbor Act of 1890, which provided for the concrete lock that was completed in 1896. Rough River shipping, mainly of timber products, peaked in about 1900. The Rough River Lake, part of the state resort park, was created in the 1960s for flood control and recreation.   HELEN B. CROCKER

ROUSSEAU, LOVELL HARRISON. Lovell Harrison Rousseau, soldier and congressman, was born in Stanford, Lincoln County, Kentucky, on August 4, 1818, of unknown parentage. He attended local schools until his father died of cholera in 1833. To earn a living, he joined a construction crew that was building a turnpike from Lexington to Lancaster. Rousseau studied law in Louisville for a period and in 1840 moved to Bloomfield, Indiana, where the following February he was admitted to the bar. He served as a captain in the Mexican War and participated in the Battle of Buena Vista. Rousseau returned to Louisville in 1849, was successful as a criminal lawyer, and was elected to the Kentucky House of Representatives (1860-61). At the outbreak of the Civil War, he raised troops for the Union and was made a colonel of the 3d Kentucky Infantry on September 9, 1861. On October 1, 1861, Rousseau was promoted to brigadier general of volunteers and later major general for his gallantry at the Battles of Shiloh and Perryville. Later he fought at Chickamauga and Nashville and in minor battles in Alabama, Mississippi, and western Tennessee.

Returning to Kentucky in 1865, he resigned his commission after being elected to the U.S. House of Representatives. Rousseau served from March 4, 1865, to July 21, 1866, when he was forced to resign for striking Josiah Grinnell, a representative from Iowa. Rousseau was subsequently reelected and remained in Congress from December 3, 1866, to March 3, 1867. In 1867 he returned to the army and that year formally received the transfer of Alaska from Russia. Rousseau took command of the District of Louisiana during Reconstruction in 1868, and he died in New Orleans on January 7, 1869. He was buried in the Arlington National Cemetery.   JACK DEBERRY

ROWAN, JOHN. Jurist and congressman, John Rowan was born to William and Eliza (Cooper) Rowan, in York, Pennsylvania, on July 12, 1773. The family moved to Louisville in 1783. Rowan settled in 1790 in Bardstown, where he began his education at nearby Salem Academy, headed by James Priestly. Completing his studies in 1793, Rowan moved to Lexington to study law under George Nicholas, Kentucky's first attorney general. He was admitted to the bar in 1795 and set up private practice. Espousing Jeffersonian republicanism, Rowan, as one of Kentucky's leading defense attorneys, fought for individual liberty and limited government. He represented Nelson County in the second constitutional convention, which met in Frankfort on July 22, 1799. Rowan was a strong advocate of legislative supremacy over executive and judicial branches and of a greater role for the people; the constitution adopted by the convention on August 17, 1799, called for the direct election of the governor and state senators. On February 3, 1801, Rowan killed Dr. James Chambers in a duel near Bardstown. Brought to trial, he was released on grounds of insufficient evidence. The case was widely reported but did not hamper Rowan's political rise.

Rowan was appointed secretary of state in 1804 by Gov. Christopher Greenup (1804-8). In 1806 he was elected to represent Nelson County in Congress (March 4, 1807, to March 3, 1809). Rowan was elected to the Kentucky House by Nelson County (1813-17) and by Jefferson County in 1822 and 1824. Between 1819 and 1821 Rowan also served on the Kentucky court of appeals. In 1824, he was elected to the U.S. Senate (March 4, 1825, to March 3, 1831). Rowan then returned to Kentucky, dividing his time between Bardstown and Louisville. In 1838 he became president of the Kentucky Historical Society, a position he held until his death.

Rowan married Anne Lytle on October 29, 1794, and in 1795 began to build FEDERAL HILL on property given to him as a wedding present by his father-in-law. Rowan died on July 13, 1843, and was buried in the family plot at Federal Hill. When the General Assembly created Kentucky's 104th county, in 1856, out of parts of Fleming and Morgan, it was named in Rowan's honor.

See Stephen Fackler, "John Rowan and the Demise of Jeffersonian Republicanism in Kentucky, 1819-1831," *Register* 78 (Winter 1980): 1-26; Randall Capps, *The Rowan Story: From Federal Hill to My Old Kentucky Home* (Bowling Green, Ky., 1976).

ROWAN COUNTY. Rowan County, the 104th county in order of formation, is located in the mountains of northeastern Kentucky. It is bounded by Fleming, Lewis, Carter, Elliott, Morgan, Menifee, and Bath counties and has an area of 282

square miles. Rowan County was formed from sections of Fleming and Morgan counties in 1856. The county was named for John ROWAN, who represented Kentucky in the U.S. House of Representatives (1807-09) and the U.S. Senate (1825-31). The county seat is MOREHEAD, the largest city in the county.

The topography of the county is hilly to mountainous. Most of the county is part of the Daniel Boone National Forest and has extensive hardwood forests. Only 32 percent of the county land is farmland; 35 percent is government-owned. Natural resources include timber, limestone, clay, and some coal. The principal water source is the Licking River and its impoundment, Cave Run Lake, which together form the county's southwestern border. Triplett Creek is the major tributary in the county.

It is believed that a party of surveyors from Pennsylvania, led by George William Thompson, first explored the area around Triplett Creek in the summer of 1773. The first settlers of the area came mostly from Virginia to claim land grants for service in the Revolutionary War. Many of these people settled in fertile valleys along the Licking River and Triplett Creek. One of the first communities to develop was Farmers, located in the western part of the county on the Licking River. It was settled by Maj. Jim Brain, who established a hotel at the junction of two roads. Clearfield, located just south of Morehead, was settled by Dixon Clack in the early nineteenth century and grew around his water-powered sawmill and store. Morehead was probably the third community to be established in the county and likewise grew around a sawmill, which was operated by Jake Wilson. It became the county seat when Rowan County was founded in 1856.

By the 1860s Rowan County was made up of a scattering of small communities. Corn was the dominant crop and timbering the major industry, with logs floated down Triplett Creek and the Licking River. During the Civil War, the residents of the county were often threatened with attack by guerrillas who, on March 21, 1864, burned the new county courthouse. On June 12, 1864, Gen. John Hunt Morgan's Confederate cavalry camped near Farmers.

Although stone, coal, and timber were the county's main resources, they were not exploited in great quantities until the Elizabethtown, Lexington & Big Sandy Railroad arrived in the county in the early 1880s. The town of Farmers expanded quickly and was the largest city in the county until most of the timber was depleted around 1900. Rodburn, Eadston, and Brady also grew as lumber towns situated on the railroad. Rockville and Bluestone developed as rock quarry centers.

To serve the mining and logging operations, several small railroads were built in Rowan County. The largest was the Morehead & North Fork Railroad (later abandoned), which by 1908 connected the Chesapeake & Ohio Railroad at Morehead with Redwine in Morgan County. Numerous tributary spur lines extending from it moved products of the mills and mines to Morehead. Two other short lines in the county were the Kentucky Northern Railroad, which hauled logs from 1896 until its abandonment in 1900, and the Christy Creek Railroad, built by the General Refractories Company to haul clay from 1920 until 1948, when it was abandoned.

The Martin-Tolliver feud, known as the ROWAN COUNTY WAR, focused national attention on the county. After three years it ended in a bloody gun battle in Morehead on June 22, 1887. In an unsuccessful attempt to stop the fighting, the General Assembly took the unusual measure of proposing to dissolve Rowan County unless the feud stopped.

Prompted by donations from a former Confederate soldier, Morehead Normal School was founded in 1887 by Phoebe Button. In 1922 the school gained state support and in 1966 became known as Morehead State University. MOONLIGHT SCHOOLS were first established in Rowan County in 1911 to give night instruction to pupils of all ages. The founder, Cora Wilson Stewart, was credited with making great strides in the fight against illiteracy in the area.

As the timber resources in the county were exhausted, clay deposits were mined on a large scale. The town of Haldeman was founded five miles northeast of Morehead by L.P. Haldeman to accommodate workers of his Kentucky Firebrick Co., which opened before 1907. The plant closed during the Great Depression. Lee Clay Products, which purchased the assets of the Clearfield Lumber Company in 1925, produced clay sewer and chimney pipe until the 1970s.

By the 1950s, tobacco had replaced corn as the county's leading farm crop. Corn, hay, poultry, and cattle are also raised. When I-64 was completed through the somewhat isolated area in 1969, some industrial growth was experienced. In 1990 the leading employer in the county was Morehead State University. A boost to tourism was the 1974 impoundment of Cave Run Lake. The 8,200-acre lake is the largest in eastern Kentucky.

The population of Rowan County was 17,010 in 1970; 19,049 in 1980; and 20,353 in 1990.

See Stuart Sprague, *A Pictorial History of Eastern Kentucky* (Norfolk, Va., 1986).

ROWAN COUNTY WAR. Also known as the Martin-Tolliver Feud, the Rowan County War was Kentucky's bloodiest feud, surpassing the Hatfield-McCoy vendetta in the number of people killed: twenty men dead and sixteen wounded during 1883-87.

The seeds of the Rowan troubles were sown in 1874 in a circuit judge's race between Thomas F. Hargis of Carlisle, a former Confederate officer and Democrat, and George Thomas, a prominent Republican from Vanceburg. Opponents of Hargis argued that he did not have the requisite legal experience and did not meet the age requirements for circuit judge. When Hargis attempted to provide evidence to the contrary, he found the entry concerning his admission to the bar torn from the courthouse record books, and proof of his birth missing from the family Bible. The campaign grew increasingly acrimonious after that, as charges and countercharges flew back and forth between the two camps. Hargis's eventual loss by twelve votes only aggravated the antagonism.

Rowan County was deeply scarred by the 1874 election. In each succeeding political campaign, old wounds were reopened and new ones inflicted. Tensions finally erupted into open warfare in August 1884, during a race for Rowan County sheriff between Cook Humphrey, the Republican (and eventual winner), and Sam Goodin, the Democrat. The secret ballot had not yet been instituted in Kentucky and liquor was legally sold on election day. Vote buying was rampant, and violent brawls, fueled by whiskey, were tolerated as a necessary evil of democracy. Several days before election day, a dance was held at a Morehead hotel. As the evening wore on, William Trumbo's wife, Lucy, grew tired, went upstairs, and mistakenly fell asleep in a room rented to H.G. Price. When Price returned to his room, he awoke the intruder and allegedly made indecent remarks to her. Lucy Trumbo excused herself and told her husband of the incident.

On election day, Trumbo confronted Price. A fight broke out, and friends of both men joined the fray. When the incumbent sheriff attempted to quell the disturbance, he was met with a shower of rocks. At this point, the truth is held hostage by conflicting testimony. Apparently Floyd Tolliver, a Democrat and small landowner from the Farmers community in Rowan County, took a swing at John Martin, member of a leading Republican family. Enraged, Martin drew his pistol, and others responded in kind. In the ensuing battle, an innocent bystander, Solomon Bradley, father of seven and a friend of Martin's, was killed and another man injured. Martin blamed Tolliver for the killing, but Tolliver dismissed his claims. A grand jury, unable to sift through conflicting stories, indicted both men and the sheriff. A court date was set for December.

Shortly before Tolliver and Martin were due in court to explain their part in the August 1884 ruckus, they ran into each other at the Galt House saloon in Morehead. Drinking, the two men began to argue. Both reached for their pockets, and as Tolliver raised his gun, Martin took aim from his pants pocket and sent Tolliver reeling to the barroom floor. "Remember what you swore to do," Tolliver told his friends with his last breath, "you said you would kill him, and you must keep your word."

Martin was arrested and sent, for his own protection, to the Winchester jail. A week later, five members of the Tolliver faction, using forged legal documents, traveled to Winchester and persuaded the jailer to release Martin into their custody for transport back to Morehead. As their train approached Farmers, several masked men boarded the

coach and left Martin's body riddled with bullets. He died the next morning in Morehead.

Craig Tolliver assumed control of the clan and instituted a reign of terror in Rowan County against the Martin faction. Ambush was common, and the streets of Morehead, like the Wild West of that era, were an open battleground. Within four months only one elected county official, the county clerk, was still at his post. Sheriff Humphrey, a Tolliver adversary, walked the streets at his own risk. Stewart Bungardner, a deputy sheriff, was killed from ambush six miles from Morehead in March 1885. The next month county attorney Taylor Young was ambushed and seriously wounded. By June 1885 the Tolliver faction controlled not only county government, but also the liquor trade. Craig Tolliver, now town marshall, began to consolidate his power. Learning that Sheriff Humphrey was staying at the Ben Martin house on the outskirts of town, Tolliver obtained a warrant for his arrest on bogus charges. Tolliver led a posse to the house and demanded the sheriff's surrender. Humphrey refused, and a fierce gun battle ensued. Eventually—in a scenario that would often be repeated—the house was set afire and its occupants forced to flee. Humphrey, having survived the fire, abandoned the office, leaving the town and county to the Tollivers.

State officials made some attempts to restore order to Rowan County. Gov. Proctor Knott (1883-87), at the urging of several local citizens, sent in the state militia, and a few offenders were put on trial. Peace descended briefly, but little was accomplished. At the end of the summer of 1885, believing the troubles to be over, the state withdrew its forces, and new fighting broke out.

Early in 1887, Tolliver charged John B. Logan of Bratton Branch, near Morehead, with killing a judge. In any other county, the charge would have been dismissed, but not in the Rowan County of that day. Law-abiding and amiable, John Logan had the misfortune of being related to Boone Logan, an attorney who did not fear to oppose the Tolliver clan openly. To undercut Boone Logan, Tolliver began eliminating his kinsmen.

Tolliver knew that John Logan's two sons—Billy, ill with tuberculosis, and Jack, who was preparing for the ministry—would be the chief witnesses in their father's behalf at the upcoming trial. Armed with warrants charging the two boys with "kukluxing" (conspiring and banding together), the Tolliver gang rode out to arrest them. After shooting out all the windows and setting fire to the porch, the Tollivers persuaded the boys to surrender peaceably, with assurances that they would not be harmed. Barely forty yards away, at a nearby spring, the two were gunned down and trampled into the mud by the Tollivers' horses.

Boone Logan traveled to Frankfort to seek Governor Knott's help. But the state had already spent $100,000 to bring peace to Rowan County, and the governor would do no more. Logan and Hiram Pigman, a Morehead merchant, then turned to several prominent citizens of Rowan County, who met in secret to plan strategy. Logan bought sixty Winchester rifles in Cincinnati and smuggled them into the county in packing crates marked "Hardware." Warrants were obtained and an early morning plan of attack solidified, and 113 men from Rowan and surrounding counties surreptitiously gathered.

On June 22, 1887, Logan's posse surrounded Morehead and demanded Tolliver's surrender. A final gun battle, lasting for more than two hours, raged through the streets of Morehead, with probably more than 1,500 shots fired. Tolliver, who appeared in the street in his stockinged feet, guns blazing, was killed, as were many of his faction. Several were shot in the head at close range.

After the battle, Logan and Pigman called a mass meeting at the courthouse in Morehead, where the Law and Order League, a citizens' protective association, was formed. It kept the peace until the state sent troops to restore order on August 1, 1887, under Col. W.L. McKee, 2d Regiment, Kentucky State Guard. The guard supervised the function of the Rowan County courts. Pigman and Apperson Perry were indicted for the murder of Craig Tolliver. After a seven-day trial, the jury members, Fleming countians, were instructed by Judge Allaniah E. Cole to render a guilty verdict, but the jury acquitted the two men. Gen. Sam E. Hill, in his report to Gov. S.B. Buckner (1887-91) on November 22, 1887, recommended that the act establishing Rowan County be repealed, that the county be transferred to another judicial district, that Circuit Judge Cole's conduct be made the subject of a legislative review, that he be replaced by a circuit judge from an adjacent court district, and that pardons be granted to all persons indicted for violence at Morehead on June 22, 1887.

See Juanita Blair and Fred Brown, Jr., *Days of Anger, Days of Tears: Rowan County, Kentucky, 1884-1887* (Morehead, Ky., 1984); Harold Wilson Coates, *Stories of Kentucky Feuds* (Knoxville, Tenn., 1942).   DAVID WILLIAMS

"RUBBER DOLLAR" COURT DECISION. In *Robert E. Matthews v. Charles W. Allen, et al.*, the Kentucky court of appeals on July 17, 1962, issued a concurring opinion that approved an increase in salaries of the judges of that court to $12,000 annually, circuit judges to $8,500, and all other officers of the state to $7,000. Kentucky voters in the general election in 1949 had approved amending section 246 of the 1890 constitution to raise the $5,000 limitation on salaries paid public officials. The judges of the Kentucky court of appeals based their 1962 "rubber dollar" decision on a reinterpretation of sections 133 and 246 of the constitution and the 1949 amendment, saying, "The sections can be truthfully harmonized only through equating 'dollars' with what they will do in the market place." The relative value of the dollar was determined by comparing the Consumer Price Index for March 1962 with that of 1949. The appeals court judges stated that the framers of the 1890 constitution "did not intend to forbid a common-sense application of its provisions."   THOMAS D. CLARK

RUBY, EARL. Earl Ruby, sports editor for the *Louisville Courier-Journal* for thirty years, was born in Louisville on November 3, 1903, to William and Sarah Waterman (Sweetser) Ruby. He graduated from Manual High School in 1922, where he was captain of the football team. He attended the University of Louisville, leaving it in 1926, his second year, to marry his childhood sweetheart, Mary Evelyn Reiling. The couple have three children—Paul Hart Ruby II, Margaret Smock, and Joan Perry.

Ruby started as an office boy at the *Courier-Journal* in 1921, and by 1936 he was writing a daily column, "Ruby's Report." In his career, he wrote more than 10,000 columns, and he was outdoor editor for more than twenty years. Ruby has had more stories published in *Best Sports Stories*, an annual anthology of sports reporting and photography, than any other sports reporter. He won the National Headliner Award in 1945 and was Kentucky's goodwill ambassador to the London, Rome, and Mexico City Olympics. He was a cofounder of the Kentucky Derby Festival in 1954 and founder of the Kentucky Athletic Hall of Fame in 1969, into which he himself was inducted in 1975. He was named sportsman of the year in 1969 by the League of Kentucky Sportsman and was elected to the Kentucky Journalism Hall of Fame by the University of Kentucky Journalism Alumni Association in 1988.

Ruby is the author of *Hunting & Fishing in Kentucky* (1978), a guide to the state's streams and preserves; *The Golden Goose* (1974), the story of the 1913 Kentucky Derby long-shot winner Donerail; and *Red Towel Territory: A History of Athletics at Western Kentucky University* (1972).

Ruby retired as sports editor of the *Courier-Journal* in 1968 and continued as outdoor editor until 1989.   JAMES STROHMAIER

RUDDELL'S (HINKSTON'S) STATION. In 1775 John Hinkston and other settlers built fifteen crude cabins on a broad flat ridge above the South Fork of the Licking River, along an old game trail from MCCLELLAND'S STATION (Scott County) to Lower Blue Licks. The site is now in Harrison County. Simon Kenton and Thomas Williams helped build a blockhouse at the station in the winter of 1776-77. Indian threats then caused its abandonment. Isaac Ruddell enlarged and fortified the station in 1779; after that, the site was interchangeably referred to as Ruddell's or Hinkston's. A large number of Pennsylvania German families lived there and at MARTIN'S STATION, only a few miles away. Ruddell's Station was attacked by Capt. Henry Byrd and his British and Indian troops in 1780. About twenty inhabitants were killed at the site. The survivors were subjected to a forced march to Detroit, where they remained prisoners for the remainder of the Revolutionary War. The bones of the victims were later gathered and buried in a mass grave covered with stones. The site was included in Hinkston's 1,400-acre settlement and preemption grant, filed in 1784, and is marked by a stone monument.

See *Destruction of Ruddle's and Martin's Forts in the Revolutionary War* (Frankfort, Ky., 1957).

NANCY O'MALLEY

RUPP, ADOLPH FREDERICK. Adolph Frederick Rupp of the University of Kentucky (UK) was one of the most successful coaches in college basketball history. In a forty-two-season career as coach of the UK Wildcats (1930-72), Rupp garnered 880 victories and 190 defeats, for a winning percentage of .822. He led the Wildcats to twenty-eight Southeastern Conference championships, five Sugar Bowl Tournament championships, one National Invitational Tournament (NIT) championship, twenty-one appearances in the National Collegiate Athletic Association (NCAA) Tournament, and four NCAA championships. In 1948 the Wildcats participated along with the Phillips Oilers in London as the U.S. basketball entry in the Olympic Games, and defeated France for the gold medal.

Rupp was born on September 2, 1901, on a farm in Halstead, Kansas, the fourth of six children of Heinrich Rupp, a native of Einsiedel, Austria, and Anna (Lichti) Rupp of Kisselhof, Germany. They had immigrated with their families to Halstead. Rupp played on school basketball teams in both elementary school and high school and graduated from Halstead High School in 1919. In the fall of 1919, Rupp enrolled at the University of Kansas, where he majored in economics and played on the Jayhawk basketball team, coached by Forrest C. ("Phog") Allen. During Rupp's three years of varsity competition, (1921-23), he did not score a single point. During the summer of 1924, while pursuing a graduate degree, Rupp taught and coached football and basketball at Burr Oak High School in Kansas, backed by a strong recommendation from Allen. After a year, he went to Iowa's Marshalltown High School to coach football, track, wrestling, and basketball. Rupp, who had never seen a wrestling match, bought a book on wrestling for pointers, then led his team to the state championship.

In 1926 Rupp moved to Freeport High School in Illinois, where he compiled a record of 66-17, won eighteen games in 1929, and took third place in the Illinois state tournament. It was during the four years at Freeport that Rupp completed an M.A. degree in education, spending four summers at Columbia University Teachers College in New York. He married Esther Smith, of Freeport, on August 29, 1931. The couple had one son, Adolph, Jr.

In 1930, when John Mauer resigned as coach at the University of Kentucky, Rupp was among seventy-one applicants for the job. He received a strong recommendation from Craig Ruby, athletic director at the University of Illinois, whose support was crucial since most of Kentucky's basketball and football coaches during the 1920s had been University of Illinois products. The UK board of trustees on May 31, 1930, appointed Rupp instructor in physical education, in charge of varsity basketball. He assisted in football and track. His two-year contract paid $2,300 for 1930-31 and $3,000 for 1931-32.

Rupp's dynamic personality and his genius for public relations made an immediate impact at the university. He was even then described as portly in appearance, but his personality made a still greater impression. Mauer had experienced success during his three years as coach of the Wildcats (a record of 40-14), and Rupp adopted Mauer's offensive system, including specific plays and practice routines. Unlike Mauer, however, Rupp freed his players to run when the opportunity presented itself, and unlike the former coach, he delighted the press with quotable statements and witty anecdotes.

Rupp's first Wildcat team, including veterans Louis McGinnis, George Yates, and All-American Carey Spicer, sported a record of 15-3. Although the 1930-31 team won one fewer game than Mauer's team of the previous year, Rupp's continued success dimmed Wildcat fans' memories of the former coach. During Rupp's first five seasons, UK compiled a record of eighty-five victories and only eleven defeats, for a winning percentage of .885. The team won its first Southeastern Conference (SEC) Tournament in 1933.

Rupp's success held through the 1940s and 1950s. His team won the prestigious National Invitational Tournament in the 1945-46 season, as well as four national championships (1947-48, 1948-49, 1950-51, and 1957-58). In the 1965-66 season, the Wildcats came within one victory of winning still another national championship. Rupp's unparalleled success was not without controversy, however. A point-shaving scandal resulted in the suspension of the team for the 1952-53 season, and only on the edge of retirement did Rupp recruit a black player, Tom Payne. Rupp's retirement itself was controversial. When the UK Athletics Board agreed that the university policy of mandatory retirement age would apply to Rupp, forcing the seventy-year-old coach to bow out, he told a newspaper reporter that he might as well be taken to the Lexington Cemetery.

After five years in retirement, Rupp died on December 10, 1977. He had lived to see the dedication in 1976 of the 23,000-seat Rupp Arena for basketball. One of the most successful and colorful coaches in the history of college basketball was buried in the Lexington Cemetery not far from the arena that bears his name.

See Bert Nelli, *The Winning Tradition: A History of Kentucky Wildcat Basketball* (Lexington, Ky., 1984); Tev Laudeman, *The Rupp Years: The University of Kentucky's Golden Era of Basketball* (Louisville 1972); Russell Rice, *Kentucky Basketball's Big Blue Machine* (Huntsville, Ala., 1976).

JAMES DUANE BOLIN AND HUMBERT S. NELLI

RURAL ELECTRIFICATION. In 1935 President Franklin D. Roosevelt signed into law an act creating the Rural Electrification Administration, a federal lending agency to finance local cooperatives that would distribute electricity. Two Kentuckians played a role in securing the passage of legislation in 1937 that made rural electrification possible: Gov. A.B. Chandler (1935-39) and Ben Kilgore, executive secretary of the Kentucky Farm Bureau. A state highway marker on U.S. 41A just outside Henderson commemorates the occasion when Frank T. Street, a local peach grower, became the first Kentuckian to receive electricity from a rural cooperative. While the city of Henderson itself had electric lights in 1886—less than a decade after Edison's perfection of the incandescent lamp—rural electricity remained a novelty until the 1930s.

In 1934 J.B. Kelley at the University of Kentucky directed Kentucky's first rural electrification survey. In 1936, under the supervision of Earl Welch, the Extension Division at the university adopted the first plan aimed at aiding development of rural electric projects and furnishing information on use of electricity. The University of Kentucky survey found that barely 3 percent of farms in the state received electricity from a central source, because private utilities had found it uneconomical to extend their service outside the urban areas. The cooperatives financed by the Rural Electrification Administration created distribution networks, erected poles and ran lines, then purchased electrical power wholesale from the private utilities.

By 1941 twenty-six cooperatives had been formed, which served 19,000 families with 7,500 miles of line. Private utilities supplied 2,300 miles of line and an additional 17,000 rural customers. In 1942, 17 percent of Kentucky farms were electrified, or half the national average. In 1990 electrification was virtually 100 percent complete. It is by choice, not necessity, that a farm today has no electrical power. The last cooperative was formed in 1951, bringing the number to a total of twenty-seven. The greatest growth of rural electrification came in the 1950s, followed soon by a shortage of wholesale power from private utilities. To solve this problem, Kentucky created its first co-op generation and transmission system, the East Kentucky Power Cooperative, headquartered at Winchester, which began delivering power to central and eastern Kentucky in 1954. To serve western Kentucky, Big Rivers Electric Corporation, headquartered at Henderson, was organized in 1961. Eighteen of the twenty-seven Kentucky co-ops get their power from East Kentucky Power, four from Big Rivers Electric, and the rest from the Tennessee Valley Authority. With the inauguration of its own generation and transmission facilities, rural electrification became an independent, self-supporting member of the utility industry. In 1948 the Kentucky Association of Electric Cooperatives was formed to serve the twenty-seven distribution co-ops and the two generation and transmission organizations.

See Richard A. Pence, *The Next Greatest Thing* (Washington, D.C., 1984).   JOHN JACKSON

RUSCH, PAUL. Paul Rusch, a national hero in Japan for his social development programs there, was born on November 25, 1897, the eldest of seven children of Andrew and Anna Dora (Paul) Rusch. His father was a grocer in Louisville's Portland area, but he was born in Fairmont, Indiana,

while his father was temporarily assigned there. Rusch left school in the eighth grade, and later graduated from Louisville's Spencerian Business School (1916). He was later awarded several honorary degrees.

Rusch arrived in Tokyo in 1925 to help rebuild YMCAs destroyed by the great Kanto earthquake of 1923. He remained in Japan to teach at St. Paul's University, where, among other accomplishments, he introduced American football. In 1938 he established a summer retreat for his students near the isolated village of Kiyosato in Takane Province. Rusch suspended his activities during World War II, but returned in 1945 as a member of Gen. Douglas A. MacArthur's staff, and soon organized the Kiyosato Education Experiment Project (KEEP). Through KEEP he pioneered comprehensive rural development and successfully introduced new agricultural enterprises, on-the-job training camps, environmental protection projects, a health clinic, and child care. His achievements had wide influence in Japan and became a model for programs in other countries. He died December 12, 1979, and his ashes are buried under the altar of St. Andrew's Church in Kiyosato, Japan. His statue faces Mt. Fuji, across the valley in which he inspired thousands of Japanese with his motto, "Do your best and it must be first class."

JOHN M. RAMSAY

RUSSELL, WILLIAM. William Russell, soldier and statesman, was born March 6, 1758, to Gen. William and Tabitha (Adams) Russell in Culpeper County, Virginia. In 1774 he joined one of Daniel Boone's expeditions into Powell's Valley against the Shawnee. He served in the Revolutionary War as an aide to Col. William Campbell, fighting at King's Mountain, Whitsell's Mills, and Guilford Court House. In 1783 Russell moved to Fayette County, Kentucky, and settled on land his father had received for military service. He participated in several expeditions under Gens. James Wilkinson, Charles Scott, and Anthony Wayne against the Indians in 1791 and 1794 on the Wabash and Maumee rivers in the Northwest Territory.

Russell was a member of the Virginia legislature that passed the act separating Kentucky from the Commonwealth of Virginia. He served in the Kentucky House in 1792, 1796-1800, 1802-7, and 1823. In 1808 President James Madison appointed Russell colonel of the 7th Infantry Regiment in the regular army. He fought in the November 7, 1811, Battle of Tippecanoe against the Shawnee. After Gen. William Harrison was appointed to supreme command of the Army of the Northwest on September 17, 1812, Russell replaced him as commander on the Indiana, Illinois, and Missouri frontiers. In October 1812 Russell and Illinois Gov. Ninian Edwards executed a successful expedition against the Kickapoo and Peoria Indians. Russell held command of the 7th Regiment until the end of the War of 1812, when it was partially disbanded and reorganized. He returned to Fayette County, retiring to his farm.

In 1824 he ran for governor but Joseph Desha defeated him, 38,278 to only 3,900.

Russell married Nancy Price on December 25, 1786. They had sixteen children. He died at his home on July 3, 1825, where he was buried. In 1825 Russell County, Kentucky's eighty-first, was named in his honor.

See Anna Russell Des Cognets, *William Russell and His Descendants* (Lexington, Ky., 1884).

RUSSELL. Russell is an industrial city on the Ohio River in eastern Greenup County, along U.S. 23 and the railroad tracks of CSX Transportation. It is bounded by Ashland, Bellefonte, and Raceland and is directly across the Ohio River from Ironton, Ohio. The city was founded by John Russell and his colleagues of the Means and Russell Iron Co. in 1869. The city was originally known as Riverview, but property owners renamed it in 1872. It was incorporated on February 23, 1874.

Residential property sold quickly after the town was laid off in 1869. In 1870 Anthony W. Carner established a ferry service to Ohio. Most residents worked either at the Means and Russell iron works or across the river at Ironton. When the Chesapeake & Ohio (C&O) Railroad arrived in 1889 and built a major railroad roundhouse, shops, and yards there, the town grew quickly and by 1905 Russell had become the largest city in the county. By 1910, when the town's population was 1,058, the city had good schools, fine homes, and several hotels, including the landmark Russell YMCA (Young Men's Christian Association), which served the railroad workers.

Numerous disasters befell the city, including a smallpox epidemic in 1901 and a fire that burned the city hall in 1903. Before 1950, when a floodwall was built, the city was hit by Ohio River floods in 1884, 1913, and 1937. In the 1937 flood only thirty homes escaped water damage and over five hundred homeless people sought refuge in C&O railroad cabooses and boxcars.

A highway bridge that connected the city with Ironton was completed in 1922 and economic growth continued to be steady, although by the 1950s Russell was no longer the most populous city in Greenup County. In the 1960s Russell increased its size by annexing surrounding land, and its tax base grew with the building of the Ashland Oil, Inc., headquarters there in 1974. Improvements to U.S. 23 in 1967 eased traffic problems but the new shopping centers built along it shifted the shopping district from the old downtown area to the east. The city celebrates its heritage with "Russell Railroad Days" each August.

The population of the fourth class city was 1,982 in 1970; 3,824 in 1980; and 4,014 in 1990.

RUSSELL COUNTY. The eighty-first county in order of formation, Russell is located in south-central Kentucky and is bordered by Adair, Casey, Clinton, Cumberland, and Wayne counties. Russell County, which has an area of 250 square miles, was formed December 14, 1825, from portions of Adair, Wayne, and Cumberland counties. It was named in honor of Col. William Russell, a Revolutionary War officer who fought in the Battle of Kings Mountain. The county seat is JAMESTOWN.

The topography is hilly, with fertile, level bottomland along the Cumberland River and along Alligator, Carrey, Goose, and Greasy creeks. Farms occupy 62 percent of the land area. The county ranks forty-seventh in the state in agricultural receipts, 70 percent of them from poultry and livestock. Crops include hay, corn, tobacco, peppers, and tomatoes.

Settled in the late eighteenth and early nineteenth centuries, Russell County had the resources to be an early manufacturing center. In the 1780s, the region south of Jamestown was a center for local manufacturers. By the 1840s, cotton and woolen mills were in production. By the 1890s, the county had a number of resorts, including the Big Boiling Springs health spa, established by Sam Patterson around 1850. A large frame hotel and twelve log cabins accommodated guests who came to take the mineral water and escape the summer heat. Creelsboro was the center of an oil boom in the 1920s. While oil production has declined, the county's wells produced 17,219 barrels of crude in 1989.

The county's industrial growth began in the 1950s, when wood products—furniture, pallets, and railroad ties—were first manufactured. In the 1960s, Russell Sports Company, which produces women's sportswear, and Medaria Marine, a houseboat manufacturer, came to the county. In the 1970s, new operations included Stephen Pipe and Steel, manufacturers of farm and chain link gates, hay feeders, and dog kennels, and Sutton Shirt Corporation, makers of men's clothing. In the 1980s, Fruit of the Loom began manufacturing women's apparel and men's and boys' underwear.

In 1990 nineteen of the county's twenty-four manufacturing plants were located in Russell Springs, where U.S. 127 intersects the Cumberland Parkway. Fifty-nine percent of the workforce is employed in manufacturing. In 1988 tourism expenditures of $30.6 million generated 1,060 jobs in the county. The $15 million Jamestown Resort and Marina opened in 1990 with 750 boat slips, a dinner boat, houseboat rentals, and a forty-unit motel.

The county has three incorporated towns: Jamestown, Russell Springs, and Rayville. The population of Russell County was 10,542 in 1970; 13,708 in 1980; and 14,716 in 1990.   RON D. BRYANT

RUSSELL'S CAVE. Russell's Cave on Russell Cave Pike, approximately seven miles north of Lexington, is one of many caves in the Inner Bluegrass region. The cave bears the name of Col. William Russell, Revolutionary War soldier, Indian fighter, and longtime Kentucky legislator. In 1820 Transylvania University scientist Constantine Rafinesque explored the cavern and described the large chamber near its mouth. The bones of prehistoric Native Americans and animals were found around the mouth of the cave. The land around Russell's Cave was at one time a popular gathering place for politicians at barbecues and picnics. In 1843 Russell's Cave gained historical notoriety as the site of the fight between Cassius M. Clay and Samuel M. Brown. Clay mortally wounded Brown with his bowie knife and threw the body into the water of the cave.   THOMAS D. CLARK

RUSSELLVILLE. Russellville, the county seat of Logan County in the Pennyroyal region of western Kentucky, is located at the junction of U.S. 431, U.S. 79, and U.S. 68. In 1790 William Cook, his wife, and eighteen-year old William Stewart built the first permanent residence at the site of Russellville, known as Logan Court House. The name was changed to Russellville on March 13, 1798, in honor of Gen. William Russell, a Revolutionary War soldier who owned a 2,000-acre military grant at the townsite.

Russellville was laid off in 1795. It was four blocks long and two blocks wide. By act of the legislature, Russellville was incorporated as a town on January 13, 1810, and became the county seat of Logan County.

Four men whose homes are still standing in Russellville became governors of Kentucky: John Breathitt (1832-34), James T. Morehead (1834-36), John J. Crittenden (1848-50), and Charles S. Morehead (1855-59). Crittenden also served in the U.S. Senate and was the U.S. attorney general under three presidents. George M. Bibb, son of Maj. Richard Bibb, whose home is now a museum, was secretary of treasury under President John Tyler.

The Civil War divided families in Russellville. On November 18-20, 1861, 116 delegates from forty-three Kentucky counties met in what is now the Clark building on West Fourth Street to form the provisional Confederate Government of Kentucky. It functioned throughout the war, from various locations.

In 1868 Jesse James, son of a native Logan Countian, and his gang are said to have robbed the Nimrod Long Bank on South Main Street of $9,000.

Bethel College began as a Baptist high school in 1854 and continued as a men's college in 1856. It later became coeducational and operated until 1933. Logan College for women was formed in Russellville by the Methodist Church in 1856; it later became a four-year college that operated until 1916, then a junior college until it closed in 1931. Cottage Home College (1857-82) was located five miles south of Russellville. The United Methodist Temple, founded in 1808, is the oldest organized

church in Russellville. Other long-established downtown churches are Baptist, Episcopal, Presbyterian, Christian, and Roman Catholic.

The third courthouse, first occupied in 1904, was remodeled in 1974 and a new jail was built. The old jail was restored in 1979-80 and now houses county records. A new post office was opened for business on November 18, 1984. Logan Memorial Hospital was completed in 1985.

Russellville was once a railroad center for the Louisville & Nashville Railroad (now CSX Transportation); in 1987 the R.J. Corman Railroad Co. bought a private line that served some of the industrial plants and grain elevators. Two newspapers are published in Russellville each week, the *New Democrat* and *The Logan Leader*.

The population of the fourth-class city was 6,456 in 1970; 7,858 in 1980; and 7,454 in 1990.

RENA MILLIKEN

RUTLEDGE, WILEY BLOUT. Wiley Blout Rutledge, U.S. Supreme Court justice, was born to Wiley Blout and Mary Lou (Wigginton) Rutledge on July 20, 1894, near Cloverport, Kentucky. He received his basic education in Pikesville, Tennessee. In 1914 he received an A.B. degree from the University of Wisconsin. Rutledge moved to Albuquerque, New Mexico, in 1917 and served as the assistant superintendent of the public schools in that city until 1920. He received his LL.B. in 1922 from the University of Colorado at Boulder, then practiced law in Boulder.

Rutledge taught as an associate professor at the University of Colorado from 1924 until 1926, when he moved to St. Louis to teach law at Washington University. He served as dean of the law school from 1931 until 1935. From 1935 until 1939 he served as professor of law and dean of the law school at the University of Iowa. He was a member of the National Conference of Commissioners on Uniform State Laws, representing Missouri from 1931 until 1935 and Iowa from 1937 until 1943.

In 1939 Rutledge was appointed associate justice of the U.S. circuit court of appeals for Washington, D.C. On February 11, 1943, the Senate confirmed him as U.S. Supreme Court justice after President Franklin Roosevelt nominated him to replace the retiring James F. Byrnes. During his six-year tenure, Rutledge became one of the foremost proponents of civil liberties in the Court's history and a staunch supporter of labor.

Rutledge married Annabel Person on August 27, 1917. They had three children: Mary Lou, Jean Ann, and Neal. Rutledge died on September 10, 1949, in York, Maine.

SACKETT, FREDERIC MOSLEY. Frederic Mosley Sackett, U.S. senator and ambassador to Germany, was born on December 17, 1868, in Providence, Rhode Island, the son of Frederick M. and Louisa (Paine) Sackett. Educated at Brown University and Harvard Law School, Sackett moved to Louisville in 1898. As well as practicing law, he served as president of Louisville Gas Company, Louisville Lighting Company, Louisville Board of Trade, and Louisville Cement Company, and as a director of the Federal Reserve Bank. President Woodrow Wilson appointed Sackett federal food administrator for Kentucky during World War I. Sackett, a Republican, was his party's choice in 1924 to challenge Democrat Augustus A.O. Stanley, the incumbent in the U.S. Senate race. After an acrimonious Democratic primary, in which the Anti-Saloon League and other prohibitionists lambasted Stanley for his opposition to prohibition and his personal habits, Sackett defeated Stanley in the general election. In the Senate, Sackett served on the Committee on Expenditures in Executive Departments. He was senator from March 4, 1925, to January 9, 1930, when he resigned to become ambassador to Germany; he initiated talks leading to a moratorium on international war debts from World War I. With Hitler's rise to power in 1933, Sackett resigned his position and returned to Louisville. Sackett married Olive Speed, the daughter of J.B. Speed, the founder of Louisville Cement and Speed Realty. Sackett died on May 18, 1941, and was buried in Cave Hill Cemetery.   ROBERT F. SEXTON

SADDLEBRED INDUSTRY. The American saddlebred is the only breed of horse that Kentucky claims to have originated in the commonwealth. The breeding and training of American saddlebreds have been a major industry since Kentucky's early years. Thoroughbred stallions were used liberally in the development of the saddlebred, crossed with easy-gaited mares descended from Galloways and hobbies brought to North America by English colonists. The resulting horses, selected for endurance, intelligence, beauty, and style, were often referred to as Kentucky saddle horses. They were in great demand for their smooth gaits in the days when nearly all traveling was done on horseback. Saddle horses became a major farm product. In 1824 more than 4,000 horses and mules passed through the Cumberland Gap headed for the eastern market. The first horse show on record for saddlebreds was held near Lexington in 1816. Denmark, a thoroughbred foaled near Lexington in 1839, was declared the foundation sire of the saddlebred breed. Kentucky has been the home of the AMERICAN SADDLEBRED HORSE ASSOCIATION since its founding in 1891.

The economic impact of the saddlebred industry on the commonwealth is substantial. Starting with a prominent training stable in the small Shelby County town of Simpsonville in 1958, much of the area has become devoted to saddlebred farms and training operations, with millions of dollars invested in land and buildings, horses, supplies and labor. Lexington is home to Tattersalls Sales Company, which three times a year holds the major public saddlebred auction in the nation. There are also several private annual saddlebred auctions in Lexington. While the prices of saddlebreds vary greatly and the average at Tattersalls is in the neighborhood of $2,500, finished show winners have sold for up to $1 million.

Although American saddlebred horses find a variety of uses, the heart of the industry is the show horse. The first national saddlebred horse show was held at the St. Louis Fair in 1856, and from the beginning Kentucky horses were prominent. After the Civil War, a fierce rivalry between Kentucky and Missouri show horses led to the emergence of the professional trainer. The World's Championship Horse Show for the breed is held indoors in Louisville. Most Kentucky county fairs have a horse show; the oldest continuous horse show in America is at the Mercer County Fair in Harrodsburg, dating back to 1827. The Lexington Junior League Horse Show is the largest outdoor saddlebred show in the country. Since 1937 the show has raised hundreds of thousands of dollars for Junior League charitable projects. The saddlebred industry cannot compare in scope with the thoroughbred or standardbred industry, but one breeder who also has a major thoroughbred operation called the saddlebred "Kentucky's little jewel of a breed."

See Jack Harrison, *Famous Saddle Horses and Distinguished Horsemen* (Columbia, Mo., 1933); Emily Ellen Scharf, *Susanne's Famous Saddle Horses* (Louisville 1946).

LYNN P. WEATHERMAN

ST. CATHARINE COLLEGE. St. Catharine College is a two-year liberal arts college in Washington County, northwest of Springfield, founded by the Dominican Sisters. In 1920 a normal training school with the right to issue state teachers' certificates was established. In 1931 it became a junior college, granting associate degrees in arts. The college was accredited in 1958 by the Southern Association of Colleges and Secondary Schools. The college constructed Lourdes Hall in the 1960s, which provided additional classrooms, an athletic facility, and administrative offices. St. Catherine offers programs in agriculture, business, computer information systems, and vocational technology along with its liberal arts tradition.

The college is marked by its student and faculty diversity. Although it was originally a women's college, men were permitted to enroll as special students until 1951, when St. Catharine formally became coeducational. Enrollment is almost evenly divided between men and women, Catholics and Protestants. In addition to Kentucky Dominicans, the faculty and administration are nuns from several other religious communities and include many lay faculty of different faiths.

A board of directors was formed in 1969 to assist the Dominican congregation in shaping major policies and institutional management. The college was separately incorporated in 1978, and legal and financial responsibilities were transferred to a board of trustees. In 1990 former governor Martha Layne Collins (1983-87) became the college's president.

VERONA WEIDIG

ST. CATHARINE DOMINICAN SISTERS. Father Samuel Wilson, a Dominican priest and prior of St. Rose Church, Springfield, Kentucky, appealed to the young women of his parish in February 1822 to dedicate their lives to Christian education. Maria Sansbury and eight companions responded to his appeal. Sansbury, who became Mother Angela, and Wilson are considered the cofounders of the St. Catharine Dominican Sisters, the first foundation of Dominican Sisters in the United States. After a year of training as religious women and educators, the sisters, who had converted an old building on the banks of Cartwright Creek into a school, opened St. Mary Magdalen Academy with fifteen students on the first Monday of July 1823. Eventually moving to a larger school, the sisters continued teaching and engaged professors to instruct them in French, music, and art so that they could expand the curriculum.

By 1891 a need for more space arose, and after three years of struggle an elaborate three-story building, the new St. Catharine Academy, was completed in Siena Vale. After a fire completely destroyed the new building in early January 1904, the sisters lost no time in building a new motherhouse and an academy on a more accessible site, known as Siena Heights. By the fall of 1905 students were again enrolled in a partially completed academy. Decreasing enrollments and shortage of personnel brought about the decision to close the academy in 1971, ending 148 years of elementary and secondary Christian education of Kentucky youths at that site. The sisters continue to operate the St. Catharine College, a two-year college founded in 1931.

Throughout the decades, the sisters responded to contemporary needs. As far back as 1832 and again in 1851, the sisters cared for cholera victims. During the Civil War, the dormitories housed the wounded from the Battle of Perryville. The sisters operated Mary Immaculate Hospital in Lebanon from 1944 to 1980 and Rosary Hospital in Campbellsville from 1948 to 1969.

See Anne C. Minogue, *Pages from a Hundred Years of Dominican History* (New York 1921).

VERONA WEIDIG

ST. JOSEPH PROTO-CATHEDRAL. St. Joseph Proto-Cathedral in Bardstown, Kentucky, is the first Roman Catholic cathedral erected in the United States west of the Allegheny Mountains. Planned by Bishop B. J. FLAGET soon after his 1811 arrival in Kentucky, construction was delayed until July 16, 1816, when the cornerstone was blessed. As many Protestants as Catholics pledged money, materials, and labor to the building subscription, insisting on a "good, large substantial church—with the ornament which Bardstown is to derive from so magnificent a building," in Flaget's words.

John Rogers, an architect-builder from Baltimore, designed and supervised construction of the church. Rogers mixed various neoclassical elements inside and out, including a colossal order portico and frontispiece with steeple-capped belfry. Native limestone was quarried nearby and nearly 1 million handmade bricks were formed and fired near the site. The forests nearby supplied massive beams and planks, including interior columns fashioned from individual trees, lathed and plastered to look like polished marble pillars. Rogers himself is credited with fashioning and installing extensive decorative plasterwork in ceiling medallions, acanthus leaf arch surrounds, and column caps. He was skilled in wood carving, intricate carpentry, and joinery techniques. A large crowd surrounded the cathedral at its consecration on August 8, 1819. More than six years passed before the portico and steeple were completed and a great bell made in Alost, Belgium, began signaling the hours and summoning the faithful to services.

Flaget moved the episcopal see to Louisville in 1841 under papal authorization. The diocese of Bardstown became simply a parish and Flaget's "Cathedral in the Wilderness" a parish church. For many years after the move, many priests and prelates chose the Proto-Cathedral of St. Joseph as the site for their ordinations. Interior decorations in the church include gold candlesticks and tabernacle presented to Bishop Flaget by Louis-Philippe, the king of France, plus a major painting by Van Bree (*The Crucifixion*) and another painting generally credited to Van Eyck.

DAVID H. HALL

ST. MATTHEWS. St. Matthews, five and one-half miles east of downtown Louisville, is a fourth-class city incorporated in 1950. The crossroads community lies at the junction of Shelbyville Road (US 60) and Westport Road (KY 1447). It dates back to the Beargrass stations of 1779, six pioneer settlements along Beargrass Creek that were developed into large plantation tracts. The area became known as "the garden of the state" for the produce that it grew and for which it served as a distribution point. The community was originally called Sale's Precinct (1800) and then Gilman's Point (1840), after local tavern owners Edmund Sale and Daniel Gilman. It was later given the name of St. Matthews, for the Episcopal church that was established there in 1839.

The construction of the Shelbyville Turnpike (1820) and of railroad lines (1851) linked St. Matthews to Louisville and Shelbyville, bringing German and Swiss immigrant farmers to the area. Commercial greenhouses and Irish potato production made St. Matthews the leading U.S. point for rail distribution of produce in the early twentieth century. The sale of farms for middle-class subdivisions began in the late 1920s, and development was accelerated by the exodus of Louisville's west end after the 1937 flood. The economic base of St. Matthews is retail trade and health, educational, and service industries. The population was 13,152 in 1970; 14,409 in 1980; and 15,800 in 1990.

ST. THOMAS FARM. The four-hundred-acre St. Thomas farm in Nelson County near Bardstown, Kentucky, was bequeathed by Edward and Ann (Gough) Howard to the Roman Catholic church in 1810. A brick church was built between 1812 and 1816. The earliest Kentucky candidates for the priesthood moved from the residence of Bishop Benedict J. Flaget at St. Stephen's in November 1811 and became the first residents of St. Thomas Seminary. The seminary closed in 1869. To care for and educate the orphaned children of the area, the SISTERS OF CHARITY OF NAZARETH was formed at St. Thomas in 1812. The school and orphanage at St. Thomas moved to another site in Nelson County in 1922.   EMMA C. BROWN

ST. THOMAS OF AQUIN COLLEGE. St. Thomas of Aquin College was the first Roman Catholic college in Kentucky, founded by the Dominican priests who were sent to the state in 1805 by Edward D. Fenwick to establish a priory and a college. Classes first took place in 1806 in a farmhouse near Springfield, Washington County, and moved to the college building, completed in 1812, that had been erected nearby as part of St. Rose Priory. The college provided not only a classical education for boys but also preparatory studies for those who wished to enter the Dominican order. Under the presidency of Samuel Thomas Wilson, its curriculum and discipline were modeled on the practices of the Dominican College of Holy Cross in Bornheim, Belgium, over which Wilson had presided.

Few records of St. Thomas College remain, but it is known that it was attended by both Catholics and Protestants and had a peak enrollment of two hundred students. Jefferson Davis came to the school from Mississippi in 1816 and devoted several pages in his memoirs to his two-year stay there. St. Thomas College declined after the opening of St. Joseph's College in Bardstown in 1820 and St. Mary's College near Lebanon in 1821, and as a result of the increasing interest of the Dominicans in Ohio. When it closed, probably in 1828, it was little more than a country school.

See V.F. O'Daniel, *A Light of the Church in Kentucky: Very Reverend Samuel Thomas Wilson* (New York 1932); Reginald M. Coffey, *The American Dominicans* (New York 1970).

THOMAS W. SPALDING

SALE, FOREST. Basketball star at the University of Kentucky and coach Adolph Rupp's first All-American, Forest ("Aggie") Sale was born on June 25, 1911, in Lawrenceburg, Kentucky, son of Foster and Mary (Mothershead) Sale. After graduating from Kavanaugh High School in Lawrenceburg, Sale entered UK in 1930 and the following year began to display the basketball skills that made him All-American in 1931–32 and again in 1932-33. A six-foot, five-inch center, he was a ferocious rebounder and a dominant offensive force. He was the Helms Foundation player of the year in 1933, when he graduated. Sale returned to Kavanaugh as boys' basketball coach, compiling a 74-18 record. He became basketball coach and a history teacher at Harrodsburg High School in 1937. His coaching career was interrupted by service in the navy for four years during World War II, with eighteen months on Midway Island. Sale retired from coaching in 1960 but retained his faculty position at Harrodsburg until 1964. In 1964 he established a retail business, Sale's Sporting Goods, in Lexington. He served five terms (1972-82) in the Kentucky House of Representatives. He was elected to the Kentucky Sports Hall of Fame in 1957 and the National Basketball Hall of Fame in 1963.

Sale died on December 4, 1985, survived by his wife Elizabeth (VanArsdall) Sale and a daughter, Betsy. He was buried at the Spring Hill Cemetery in Harrodsburg.

See Bert Nelli, *The Winning Tradition* (Lexington, Ky., 1984).

SALT MAKING. Underlying much of Kentucky's sandstone formation, especially in coal-bearing areas, are salt-bearing veins. In 1859 David Dale Owen noted in the *Fourth Report* of the Kentucky Geological Survey that some salt veins produced brine strong enough to evaporate twenty-five to fifty pounds of the mineral per 1,000 gallons. In many areas of Kentucky, well-drillers seeking other resources have struck salt veins.

Long Hunters and other early visitors to the western country noted the existence of salt licks, perhaps one of the most attractive features of the land to future settlers, as salt was essential for preserving meat, but they could bring little salt with them. A lick was a large area of salt-impregnated soil that resulted when salt was deposited from the water of several springs. Wild game, including deer and buffalo, cut wide paths to this area to lick the salt from the ground, and Indians frequented the area to hunt the game. These landmarks became a prominent part of the Kentucky nomenclature; many Kentucky landmarks and settlements carry the word "Lick" in their names.

So vital was salt to the settlers that they risked their lives in the process of salt making. On February 15, 1778, Indians captured Daniel Boone and a party of Boonesborough salt makers at work at the Upper Blue Licks. The Kentucky General Assembly made generous grants of public land to early settlers with the provision that they produce specified amounts of salt annually, and between 1792 and 1850 the General Assembly enacted numerous laws to encourage and protect salt making. The most important salt-producing licks in early Kentucky were BULLITT'S, Mann's, Upper Blue Licks, and BIG BONE. In later years the most productive source of salt in Kentucky was the lick on GOOSE CREEK in Clay County, where the Whites, Bakers, Garrards, and others developed major evaporative works.

The first wells that pioneers sank to tap the saltwater were dug by hand, and later ones were bored with an auger. The pioneers then dug a narrow trench into a bank and lined it with slate, forming a "furnace," ending in a chimney. Kettles weighing as much as a hundred pounds and holding twenty-two gallons of saltwater were placed on top of the trench or furnace, sometimes in a string of up to fifty. The settlers then filled the kettles with saltwater and fired them to boil the water until the salt formed grains. Salt was stored until sold to settlers, who bought it by the pound, bushel, or barrel. In time all the timber close to the salt works had been cut to fuel the furnaces. The furnaces then were moved closer to the source of wood, and water was transported through hollowed logs fitted together to make a crude string of pipes. One such array of pipes extended from Bullitt's Lick to Shepherdsville, a distance of about three miles, where it crossed the Salt River and ran from there to the furnace.

Kentucky salt makers, however, could not compete with those of Virginia and Ohio. In 1850 Kentuckians produced 246,500 bushels of salt, compared with 3,749,890 in Virginia, and 550,350 in Ohio. That year the salt industry returned to Kentucky $57,825, compared with $700,466 in Virginia. A decade later salt production in Kentucky had shrunk to 69,665 bushels.

See Thomas D. Clark, "Salt, a Factor in the Settlement of Kentucky," *FCHQ* 12 (Jan. 1938): 42-52; Robert E. McDowell, "Bullitt's Lick: The Related Saltworks and Settlements," *FCHQ* 30 (July 1956): 241-69.

THOMAS D. CLARK AND TOM PACK

SALTPETER INDUSTRY. Saltpeter, as potassium nitrate was commonly known to the settlers of Kentucky, was—like common salt (sodium chloride)—a chemical vital for their survival. Just as the preservation of food depended on common salt, production of gunpowder required saltpeter, derived from calcium nitrate found in dry caves and rockshelters. Since both chemicals were difficult to transport, pioneers made good use of Kentucky's natural sources of both.

Monk Estill, a slave, was one of Kentucky's first manufacturers of saltpeter, which he supplied to Fort Boonesborough and Estill Station for gunpowder as early as 1780. By 1805, twenty-eight saltpeter caves and rockshelters were being mined in Kentucky. The first scientific description of Kentucky saltpeter production was a paper read in Philadelphia in 1806 by Samuel Brown, M.D., professor of chemistry, anatomy, and surgery at Transylvania University. His subject was GREAT SALTPETER CAVE in Rockcastle County, where saltpeter was produced by leaching calcium nitrate, or niter, from dry soil.

Saltpeter production reached its peak during the War of 1812, when a blockade of U.S. ports under the British embargo of 1807 cut off imports of saltpeter from India. The resulting inflation in the price of saltpeter encouraged the exploration of many caves and rock shelters. MAMMOTH CAVE was among the most important sources of saltpeter in Kentucky. After Mammoth Cave and the adjacent Dixon Cave were identified as saltpeter sources in 1799, ownership changed frequently as the value of saltpeter increased.

By 1808 saltpeter was being produced using wooden V-vats at the entrance to Mammoth Cave. Large square vats were later constructed at Booth's Amphitheater and the Rotunda of the cave. Log pipes carried water into the cave to leach calcium nitrate from the soil, and the "mother liquor" leachate was pumped to the surface, treated with wood ashes, and boiled in large iron kettles near the cave entrance to cause the saltpeter to crystallize. Production declined after 1811, when the soil containing niter was depleted, and the works were damaged by the New Madrid earthquakes of 1811-12. Statewide, Kentucky production topped 300,000 pounds of saltpeter in 1812.

Imports of saltpeter resumed after the end of the war and the price fell from a high of one dollar per pound to fifteen cents per pound. Saltpeter works in the caves were abandoned, and further production in Kentucky went for local consumption. Today, 133 Kentucky caves and six rockshelters have been identified as former saltpeter mines. Tours at both Mammoth Cave and Saltpeter Cave in Carter Caves State Resort Park allow visitors to study the remains of saltpeter works preserved for close to two hundred years.

See Burton Faust, "The History of Saltpetre Mining in Mammoth Cave, Kentucky," *FCHQ* 41 (1967): 5-20, 127-40, 227-62, 323-52; Carol A. Hill and Duane DePaepe, "Saltpeter Mining in Kentucky Caves," *Register* 77 (Fall 1979): 247-62.

STANLEY D. SIDES

SALT RIVER. The Salt River, located in north-central Kentucky, has a drainage area of more than 2,920 square miles and forms the fifth largest watershed in the state. The river starts about three miles east-southeast of Danville in Boyle County, flows about fifty miles north toward Lawrenceburg, then turns west toward Shepherdsville and flows for about ninety miles to the point where it empties into the Ohio River, one mile north of West Point. The river is about eight yards wide at its mouth and flows through Boyle, Mercer, Anderson, Spencer, Hardin, and Bullitt counties. Its tributaries include the Rolling and Beech forks, and Clear, Guist, Plum, Cox, and Brashears creeks.

The Salt River travels through some of the most fertile agricultural land in the state: the Inner Bluegrass physiographic region, the Eden Shale Belt in Spencer County, and the Knobs region in Bullitt County. It is one of the finest wade-fishing and rock bass streams in the state. Cities along the river include Shepherdsville, Bondville, West Point, Taylorsville, Glensboro, and Vanarsdell.

The river takes its name from the salt-producing operations that Henry Crist established in 1779 near Bullitts Lick and present-day Shepherdsville. In a typical salt pan operation, four hundred gallons of water were evaporated, leaving fifty pounds of salt. The water was drawn from wells sunk about thirty feet deep. In 1808 Quarry and Tyler established a water mill on the Salt River in Bullitt County to power an iron and steel plant. They built a dam of hewn timber across the river, fastened to the bedrock of the stream by iron bolts. Surveys in 1837 and 1873 to determine whether the river could be improved for navigation by building locks and dams yielded unfavorable reports. A century later a dam was constructed near Taylorsville and completed in 1983, forming Taylorsville Lake in Spencer County, approximately sixty miles above the confluence of the Salt and Ohio rivers.

In 1832, when Henry Clay was campaigning for the presidency against Andrew Jackson, he boarded a riverboat on Salt River at Pitts Point in Bullitt County for a campaign speech in Louisville. A Jackson supporter is said to have bribed the boat's captain to take Clay inland, up Salt River, instead of downriver to the Ohio and on to Louisville. Clay missed the speaking date and lost the national election. The expression "up Salt River" thus refers to political defeat.

See James P. Henley, *The Inventory and Classification of Streams in the Salt River Drainage* (Frankfort, Ky., 1983); Warren Raymond King, *The Surface Waters of Kentucky* (Frankfort, Ky., 1924).   MICHAEL E. WALTERS

SALYERSVILLE. Salyersville, the county seat of Magoffin County, is located at U.S. 460 and KY 40 at the eastern terminus of the Bert T. Combs Mountain Parkway. The town was named in 1861 for Samuel Salyer (1813-90), a local representative who was instrumental in the 1860 creation of the county.

Situated on the upper part of the Licking River, Salyersville was the site of a pioneer station known as Prater's Fort or Licking Station. An attempt at settlement was made there in 1794, but the pioneers were driven off by Indians. Many of the same group of early settlers returned around 1800 to remain permanently. Among these were John Williams, Archibald Prather, Clayton Cook, Ebenezer Hannah and a few others, most of whom had come from South Carolina.

By 1849, the small community of Licking Station was renamed Adamsville for William "Uncle Billy" Adams, a prominent local farmer, merchant, manufacturer, and hotel keeper. His energy helped to stimulate the town's growth as a small regional manufacturing center. Although Adams donated

land for the establishment of the county seat in 1860, the town was renamed Salyersville.

The first county courthouse was built in 1862 and used until 1893. A second courthouse, of Victorian style, was completed in 1893 and used local sandstone for its trim. It was destroyed by fire on February 22, 1957, and replaced in 1959 by a three-story steel, concrete, and glass structure of modern design.

For most of the Civil War, Salyersville was in Union territory held by elements of the 14th Kentucky Infantry (USA). On October 30, 1863, a company of Union soldiers of the 19th Kentucky led by Lt. Col. Orlando Brown, Jr., won a minor battle and took about fifty Confederate prisoners, and on November 30, 1863, Confederates led by Capt. Peter Everett surprised a Union force and captured twenty-five men and forty horses.

By 1870, Salyersville was a courthouse town of 106 people with one jail, four stores, three churches, two blacksmiths, and a steam-powered saw-, grist-, carding-, and flour mill. The town's growth was slow in the nineteenth century because it was never able to attract a railroad. Logging was the only major industry and as late as 1984 the town's second largest employer was a lumber mill. A county oil boom sparked rapid city growth from 1900 to 1930. In 1916, the first car arrived in town and in 1924 the Salyersville-Paintsville road was blacktopped. Three years later the road to West Liberty (later U.S. 460) was gravelled.

The Great Depression years, annual flooding of the Licking River, and the decline of the county's timber industry adversely affected the city during the late 1920s and the 1930s. Salyersville maintained itself as an agricultural and coal center. With the coming of the Mountain Parkway in 1962, the city's relative isolation was eased. The town's largest employer, Continental Conveyors and Equipment Company, moved there in 1971. Numerous retail and service establishments grew along U.S. 460 during the 1980s.

The population of the fourth-class city was 1,196 in 1970; 1,352 in 1980; and 1,917 in 1990.

SAMPSON, FLEM D. Flem D. Sampson, governor during 1927-31, was born near London, Kentucky, on January 25, 1875, to Joseph and Emoline (Kellum) Sampson. He attended, then taught in, local schools before entering Union College in Barbourville. After receiving a law degree in 1894 from Valparaiso University in Indiana, he opened a practice in Barbourville. Three years later he married Susie Steele, with whom he had three daughters. Sampson was city attorney, then a youthful president of the town's First National Bank. He built a firm base in the local Republican party and in 1906 was elected county judge of Knox County. In 1911 and 1916 he won election as circuit judge of the 34th Judicial District. His reputation for strict law enforcement helped send him to the Kentucky court of appeals in 1916 and got him reelected in 1924. He was chief justice in 1923-24.

He and Kentucky Congressman John M. Robsion forged a powerful Republican faction in the eastern part of the state that gained him the party's nomination for governor in 1927. The Democrats were badly divided over such issues as parimutuel gambling on horse races, the liquor industry, and a severance tax on coal. When the antigambling faction of the Democrats managed to nominate former governor J.C.W. Beckham for governor in 1927, many supporters of the racing and liquor industries bolted the party and supported Sampson instead. After an unusually bitter campaign in which his opponents fastened the label "Flem-Flam" on Sampson, he defeated Beckham, 382,306 to 350,796, although all other Republicans on the state ticket lost. When he left office in 1931, Sampson returned to Barbourville and his legal practice. He died at Pewee Valley near Louisville on May 25, 1967, and was buried at Barbourville.

During his term in office the Democratic-controlled General Assembly killed most of Sampson's proposals. It passed his free textbook plan but refused to fund it. A Kentucky Progress Commission was established under Sampson, and some improvements were made to the state park system. Sampson rejected an offer from the duPont family to purchase Cumberland Falls and turn it into a park; instead, he favored a proposal for a hydro-electric project. The legislature rejected his plan and passed, over his veto, a bill accepting the du-Pont offer. The governor was indicted by a grand jury for accepting gifts from textbook companies, but the indictment was dismissed. "Ripper" bills stripped Sampson of many of his statutory powers and gave them to a three-man commission, on which he was outvoted by the Democratic lieutenant governor and attorney general. The advent of the Great Depression hit Kentucky with devastating effect and made Sampson's administration appear even worse than it was.

LOWELL H. HARRISON

SANDERS, HARLAND DAVID. Harland David Sanders, the creator of the Kentucky Fried Chicken franchise, was born to Wilbert and Margaret Ann (Dunlevy) Sanders in Henryville, Indiana, on September 9, 1890. When he was six years old, his father died; his mother later married William Broaddus. Sanders quit school after the sixth grade and went to work at a variety of jobs—as farmhand, streetcar conductor, steamboat ferry operator, railroad fireman, secretary, insurance salesman, tire salesman, and furniture store owner.

In 1930 Sanders moved to Corbin, Kentucky, where he opened a service station. Behind the station, he operated a lunchroom that seated six around the single table. The business expanded rapidly, and by 1937 Sanders' Cafe seated 142 customers, who made fried chicken the most popular item on the menu. Sanders often told of his experimentation with a variety of recipes until he hit upon the unique combination of eleven herbs and spices that "stand on everybody's shelf." He also refined the frying process by using the pressure cooker. After a fire destroyed the cafe in 1939, Sanders rebuilt the business as a restaurant and motel. Business was good until the construction of Interstate 75, which bypassed Corbin.

Sanders auctioned the restaurant and motel, and at the age of sixty-six began to sell franchises based on his fried chicken recipe. The first franchise went to Pete Harman of Salt Lake City. Sanders was a pioneer in the new business of franchising, and initial sales were slow. By 1959, however, more than two hundred Kentucky Fried Chicken outlets in the United States and Canada sold food under the Colonel Sanders trademark. Sanders was first commissioned a Kentucky Colonel, an honorary title, in 1934 by Gov. Ruby Laffoon (1931-35), and was recommissioned in 1950 by Gov. Lawrence Wetherby (1950-55). After 1950 he began to look the part, growing a mustache and a goatee and wearing a white suit and a string tie. Sanders's oldest daughter, Margaret, suggested selling fried chicken as a take-home item—an innovation at that time—and the first carry-out Kentucky Fried Chicken was built in Jacksonville, Florida. In 1960 Sanders moved the growing company to Shelbyville, Kentucky.

On February 18, 1964, Sanders sold his franchising business to John Y. Brown, Jr., Kentucky governor during 1979-83, and Jack Massey for $2 million. He kept the foreign franchises, however, and rewarded Pete Harman by giving him those in Utah and Montana. Sanders was retained on salary as spokesman for Kentucky Fried Chicken, often appearing in television commercials. Heublein, Inc. of Connecticut bought Kentucky Fried Chicken in 1971 for $275 million. In 1978 Heublein sold the business to R.J. Reynolds Company, which in turn sold it to Pepsico, Inc. for $840 million in 1986. Displeased with the operation of the company after 1971, Sanders brought suit against Heublein over the alleged misuse of his image in the sale of products with which he had no connection. In 1975 an unsuccessful libel suit was brought against Sanders after he publicly referred to Kentucky Fried Chicken gravy as "sludge" and claimed it had a "wallpaper taste."

Sanders contributed money to religious charities, hospitals, medical research, education, the Boy Scouts, Junior Achievement, and the March of Dimes. A highly visible figure, he was immediately recognizable. At the age of eighty-seven, he testified against mandatory retirement before the U.S. House of Representatives Select Subcommittee on Aging.

Sanders was married to Josephine King in 1908; they had three children: Margaret, Harland Jr., and Mildred. They were divorced in 1947. Sanders married Claudia (Leddington) Price in 1949. Sanders died on December 16, 1980, and lay in state at the Capitol rotunda in Frankfort. He was buried in Louisville's Cave Hill Cemetery.

See Harland Sanders, *Life as I Have Known It Has Been "Finger-Lickin" Good* (Carol Stream,

Ill., 1974); John Ed Pearce, *The Colonel: The Captivating Biography of the Dynamic Founder of a Fast-Food Empire* (Garden City, N.J., 1982).

SANDERS, LEWIS. Lewis Sanders, entrepreneur and livestock breeder, was born August 9, 1781, the son of John and Jane (Craig) Sanders, in Spottsylvania County, Virginia. He arrived in Kentucky as a baby with the Traveling Church congregation of the Rev. Lewis Craig, the child's uncle and namesake. In Kentucky John Sanders settled two farms in Fayette County. He apprenticed Lewis to the Lexington merchant Patrick McCullough. In time John Sanders deeded two hundred acres of land to each of his children except Lewis, who received the cash equivalent. He used the money to form a partnership to operate a cotton factory and to invest in real estate. The partners built houses in Lexington on Merino Street, which they had opened. In 1807 Sanders married Ann Nicholas, daughter of George Nicholas. Sanders bought five hundred acres of land on the Georgetown Pike in 1812 and began to construct an elaborate home, but in 1815 he sold the unfinished structure for lack of money. On July 11, 1817, he sold his household goods and moved to Carroll County. Regaining his fortune, he built the estate Grass Hills on a 750-acre tract near Ghent.

Sanders bred and raced horses and he imported and improved the shorthorn breed of cattle, which he showed at Sanders' Garden in 1816 and 1817. Sanders was also known for the peaches he grew. He was active in both state and national politics, taking part in the nomination of James K. Polk for the presidency and in the annexation of Texas. In his later years he strongly advocated adding new states in the West as a means of strengthening the Union. Sanders died at Grass Hills on April 15, 1861, perhaps the last survivor of the Traveling Church congregation's move to Kentucky.

See Ann Virginia Parker, *The Sanders Family of Grass Hills* (Madison, Ind., 1966).

THOMAS D. CLARK

SANDLIN, WILLIE. Willie Sandlin, awarded the congressional Medal of Honor for service in World War I, was born near Buckhorn, Perry County, Kentucky, on January 1, 1890. He enlisted in the army in 1914, and served on the Mexican border. In 1917 he was sent to France with the 132d Infantry. Promoted to sergeant, Sandlin single-handedly destroyed three German machine gun emplacements and killed twenty-four of the enemy on September 26, 1918, at Bois de Forges. For that action, he was awarded the congressional Medal of Honor on July 9, 1919. After the war, Sandlin returned to Kentucky and bought a farm on Owls Nest Creek near Hyden, Kentucky. He and his wife, the former Belvia Roberts, were active in the Frontier Nursing Service. They had one son and four daughters. Sandlin died on May 29, 1949, of a lingering lung infection resulting from a poison gas attack on his company in the Battle of the Argonne. He was buried in Hurricane Cemetery near Hyden; in September 1990 his remains were reburied in Zachary Taylor National Cemetery in Louisville.

See Fred P. Caldwell, "Above and Beyond the Call of Duty," *Register* 18 (May 1920): 9-12.

JACK W. THACKER

SANDY HOOK. Sandy Hook, the seat of Elliott County, Kentucky, lies 27 miles southeast of Morehead. It was originally settled in the 1820s. Lying on the Little Sandy River, it derives its name from a "fish-hook" curve in the stream. It was chosen as the seat for Elliott County on April 5, 1869, as a result of James K. Hunter's donation of a one-acre tract upon which the courthouse and public square were laid out. In 1872 Sandy Hook was reincorporated as Martinsburg to honor John P. Martin (1811-62) of Floyd County, a U.S. congressman and state legislator. The post office, however, was established as Sandy Hook in 1874, and that name survives. The first courthouse was built in 1869; it was replaced by a new building in 1937. That structure burned December 19, 1957, and the third courthouse was dedicated in February 1968.

The population of Sandy Hook was about 200 in 1970; 627 in 1980; and 548 in 1990, making it one of Kentucky's smallest county seats. Industrial production includes Formica sink tops, kitchen cabinets, and cotton and rayon yarn.

SAUFLEY, RICHARD CASWELL. Richard Caswell Saufley, a naval aviation pioneer, was born September 1, 1885, in Stanford, Kentucky, the son of Judge M.C. and Sallie (Rowan) Saufley. He attended Centre College in Danville and in 1908 graduated from the U.S. Naval Academy. In April 1911 he married Helen O'Rear Scruggs. Saufley flew as a naval aviator in the 1914 Mexican Campaign and later served in the Office of Naval Aeronautics, Naval Aeronautical Station, Pensacola, Florida, where he set altitude and endurance records for hydroplanes. On June 9, 1916, while attempting to set another record, he crashed and was killed. Saufley is buried in Buffalo Spring Cemetery, Lincoln County. A World War II destroyer and Saufley Field at Pensacola Naval Air Station were named for him.

JAMES RUSSELL HARRIS

SAWITZKY, SUSAN CLAY. Susan Clay Sawitzky, poet and art historian, was born in Frankfort, Kentucky, on July 21, 1897, to Col. Charles and Mariah (Pepper) Clay. Great-granddaughter of Henry Clay, she was raised in her grandmothers' Victorian homes and on her father's horse farm. She attended Miss Ella Williams's School, then briefly Sayre School, Transylvania University, and the University of Kentucky.

Her early poems and stories appeared in *Town and Country Magazine* and the *New York Times* and in local publications, and in 1923 the book *Poems by Susan Clay* was published in Chicago. On May 5, 1927, fleeing family interference, she eloped with Russian-born New York art dealer William Sawitzky. Only one poem was published after her marriage, appearing in *Poetry: A Magazine of Verse* in 1941. From 1927 to 1947 she helped Sawitzky conduct pioneering research on early American art, research she continued after his death in 1947. Sponsored by the New York Historical Society, she published articles on Reuben Moultrop, Ralph Earl, and Abraham DeLanoy.

Susan Sawitzky wrote poetry for over sixty years and a short collection was published posthumously by the *Kentucky Poetry Review* in 1984. Her collected poetry speaks poignantly of her struggle against family and community for the right of self-expression and of the tenacity of traditional Southern values well into the twentieth century. Sawitzky died on July 11, 1981. Her ashes were scattered near a millpond at Stamford, Connecticut.

See Woodridge Spears, ed., "The Circling Thread: Poems by Susan Clay Sawitzky," *Kentucky Poetry Review* (Jan. 1984).   LINDSEY APPLE

SAWYER, DIANE. Diane Sawyer, journalist and television correspondent, was born on December 22, 1945, in Glasgow, Kentucky, the second daughter of E.P. and Jean W. (Dunagan) Sawyer. The family moved to Louisville soon after Sawyer was born, and she received her early education in the public school system. She graduated from Seneca High School in 1963. Sawyer received her B.A. in English from Wellesley College in Massachusetts in 1967.

Upon graduation, Sawyer went to work as a part-time reporter at Louisville's WLKY-TV, an ABC affiliate, where she did weather reports. Sawyer left Kentucky in 1970 and moved to Washington, D.C., in search of a broadcasting position. She became an assistant to Jerry Warren, the White House deputy press secretary. Her initial task was writing press releases, but she was soon asked to make drafts of some of President Richard Nixon's public statements. After several months, Sawyer was made administrative assistant to the White House press secretary, Ron Ziegler. Her next position was staff assistant to the president. During the Watergate scandal, her job was to monitor media coverage. After Nixon's resignation on August 9, 1974, Sawyer accompanied him to San Clemente, California, to help research his memoirs. In mid-1978 she returned to Washington, D.C., where she became a general assignment reporter for CBS News. Sawyer was promoted to correspondent in February 1980 on the basis of her coverage of the nuclear power accident at Three Mile Island in Pennsylvania on March 28, 1979. In May 1981 she became a co-anchor on CBS's "Morning with Charles Kuralt and Diane Sawyer." Despite an increase in ratings, CBS overhauled the morning show in mid-1984, and Sawyer in August 1984 became the first female reporter on "60 Minutes." She went to ABC in February 1989 to co-anchor "Prime Time Live" with Sam Donaldson. Sawyer married director Mike Nichols in 1988.

SAWYIER, PAUL. Paul Sawyier, painter, son of Nathaniel J. and Ellen (Wingate) Sawyier, was born on March 23, 1865, at Table Rock Farm in Madison County, Ohio. His father and other family members were amateur artists; his sister Natalie became a professional painter. In 1870 the family moved to Frankfort, Kentucky, the childhood home of both Sawyier's parents. There Sawyier attended Second Street Elementary School and the Dudley Institute, an Episcopal school. His father employed Elizabeth Hutchins, a Cincinnati artist, to give art lessons to his children.

In 1884-85 Sawyier attended the Cincinnati Art Academy, where he studied under Kentucky artist Thomas S. Noble. During 1885-86 Sawyier supported himself with his portraits in crayon. In August 1886, at the request of his father, he returned to Frankfort to work as a hemp salesman for the Kentucky River Mill. By the spring of 1887, Sawyier had left this job to paint river scenes and landscapes around the capital. During 1887-88 he made six copperplate etchings of a Frankfort landmark, the *Old Covered Bridge* series. The prints became very popular when the old bridge was closed in December 1893.

In the fall of 1889, Sawyier moved to New York City, where he lived with his sister Lillian and her family. He enrolled in the Arts Students League under the tutelage of William Merritt Chase, studying watercolor. In 1890 he returned to Cincinnati to study under Kentucky artist Frank Duveneck, a well-known portrait painter in oils. The next year Sawyier moved to Frankfort, where he concentrated on landscape painting, including views of the Kentucky River and its tributaries Benson and Elkhorn creeks, in a variety of media—pastels, oil, copperplate etchings, and his favorite, watercolor. Sawyier relied heavily on the use of photographs as models, and he shared a studio with the photographer Henry G. Mattern.

In 1908 Sawyier bought a houseboat on the Kentucky River, which served as both his studio and his home while he traveled the river, stopping along the way to work at various places, including Highbridge and Camp Nelson in Jessamine County. He visited Frankfort, Lexington, Danville, and Cincinnati to sell his works. In the fall of 1913, Sawyier moved to Brooklyn, New York, where he again lived with his sister. In 1914 he was commissioned to paint for New York art dealer Edward Jackson. He moved to High Mount, New York, in the Catskill Mountains in 1915 and in 1916 to neighboring Fleischmann, New York.

Sawyier's work are best known in the state of Kentucky. Most of his paintings and etchings are not dated, and because he kept no diary it has been almost impossible to date them. Some of his most popular prints are *Wapping Street Fountain*, *The Old Capitol*, *Winter in Kentucky*, *A Rainy Day in Frankfort*, *Kentucky River Scene*, *Kentucky Arsenal*, and *Old Covered Bridge*. Sawyier died on November 5, 1917, and was buried in Fleischmann, New York. His remains were moved to Frankfort Cemetery in June 1923.

See Arthur F. Jones, *The Art of Paul Sawyier* (Lexington, Ky., 1976); Mary Michele Hainel, *A*

Kentucky Artist: Paul Sawyier 1865-1917 (Richmond, Ky., 1975).

SAYRE SCHOOL. Sayre School has long been recognized as one of the premier private schools in the South. The school, located in Lexington, Kentucky, was founded in November 1854 by David Austin Sayre, a noted banker, philanthropist, and devoted advocate of high-quality female education. The school was known originally as the Transylvania Female Institute and in 1885 was renamed the Sayre Female Institute. It has remained in continuous operation since its inception.

Initially, the school educated female day students and boarding students through a rigorous liberal arts curriculum. It flourished throughout the late nineteenth century, attracting young women from across Kentucky and the entire South. Boys were admitted to the primary grades in 1876. The name Sayre School was adopted in 1942. Enrollment declined in the 1940s and in 1947 the high school was discontinued and the boarding of students ended. Until 1961 Sayre remained a coeducational day school serving prekindergarten through junior high school. In 1961 its high school program was reestablished.

Sayre School remains on its original site in the historic district of downtown Lexington. The main administration building (Old Sayre) predates the school's founding; its renovation was completed in 1986. All other buildings on the five-acre campus have been erected since World War II. Numbered among Sayre's many outstanding graduates are the noted suffragist Laura Clay and the Nobel laureate David Lipscomb. Preeminent among Sayre's headmasters is Maj. Henry B. McClellan, J.E.B. Stuart's adjutant during the Civil War and author of an acclaimed biography of his commander. Headmaster from 1870 to 1904, McClellan was recognized as one of the leading educators in the South. Distinguished Sayre trustees include: David Sayre, Ephraim Sayre, John C. BRECKINRIDGE, W.C.P. BRECKINRIDGE, and Otis SINGLETARY. The school remains committed to David Sayre's ideal of "education of the widest range and highest order."

See J. Winston Coleman, Jr., *A Centennial History of Sayre School* (Lexington, Ky., 1954).

F. KEVIN SIMON

SCHNELLENBERGER, HOWARD LESLIE. Howard Leslie Schnellenberger, football coach, was born on March 16, 1934, in St. Meinrad, Indiana, to Leslie and Rosena (Hoffman) Schnellenberger. The family moved to Louisville in 1936, where he became an All-State basketball and football player at Flaget High School. Schnellenberger enrolled at the University of Kentucky (UK) in 1952 on a football scholarship, playing end for both Paul Bryant and Blanton Collier, and became an All-American in 1955. After earning a B.S. degree at UK in 1956, he played briefly in the Canadian Football League, then returned to UK as an assistant coach in 1959. He was then assistant coach at the University of Alabama (1961-65), the Los Angeles Rams

(1966-69), and the Miami Dolphins (1970-72 and 1975-79), and, head coach of the Baltimore Colts (1973-74). In 1979 he took over the coaching reins at the University of Miami and led Miami to the national championship in 1983. Schnellenberger in December 1984 moved to the University of Louisville, where he was determined to build a national football power. By 1990 he had compiled a 32-33-2 record, with his best year (1990) culminating in a Fiesta Bowl victory over the University of Alabama.

Schnellenberger married Beverlee Donnelly of Montreal, Canada, on May 3, 1959. They have three sons: Stephen, Stuart, and Timothy.

SCHOOL ARCHITECTURE. In 1798 Kentucky chose the academy as the model for public schooling. The academies were generally substantial brick or stone buildings. The private academies chartered later were owned and operated primarily by religious denominations, and the early schools were often held in the community church. Log cabin schools that were first built were ramshackle structures, "inadequate for school purposes . . . too small, built without taste, almost without form . . . of indifferent materials on ineligible sites," according to Moses Edward Ligon's history of education. By 1867 the ravages of the Civil War and the lack of funds had further devastated Kentucky schoolhouses. To encourage well-designed, efficient places of learning, state Superintendent of Schools H.A.M. Henderson in 1876 published the first manual on schoolhouse construction, which was to help local school boards design comfortable buildings, with seats and desks built to meet physiological needs.

In 1909 plans were authorized for one-, two-, three-, and four-room buildings, complete with specifications for heat, light, ventilation, equipment, and beautification of the grounds. By 1912 the School Improvement League had organized groups in several school districts to establish and maintain efficiency in the schools. School buildings were cleaned, conditioned, and supplied with pure drinking water, cups, organs, pianos, libraries, pictures, and equipment. Even so, by 1923 the small rural school and its low grade of efficiency had become intolerable. In 1924 local school boards were required to submit plans for improvement to the state Department of Education. By the next year, improvements were noted in plans and specifications for health, comfort, and efficiency.

Through the 1930s and 1940s, however, adequate school buildings were one of the outstanding problems facing public education in Kentucky. During the 1940s, modern buildings and shops were constructed, including administrative offices, electric installations, and fire alarms in civil defense areas to accommodate the war effort. Throughout the state, however, rising enrollments and the damage done by fires demanded new buildings, additions, and repairs. Many schools were overcrowded, forcing some to schedule double sessions and to use temporary classrooms and portable buildings, which were poorly heated, illuminated, and ventilated, and highly combustible. By the mid-1950s, due to increased construction costs, multipurpose rooms were erected to accommodate physical education and lunchroom space for students as well as community program activities. By the end of the 1950s, school construction projects had leveled off, but school buildings remained Kentucky's second major problem, next to teachers' salaries.

The 1960s and 1970s were periods of diversity and experimentation in school architecture. New construction dominated the 1960s, but by the 1970s the need for new buildings declined and the need for renovation increased. As a result of changes in technology and learning theory, schools incorporated open spaces, carpeting, air conditioning, and movable walls. Changing enrollments required new spaces and new uses for old spaces. Spatial improvements addressed the needs for energy conservation, career education, special and handicapped students, and new community uses. Other influences on school architecture continued into the 1980s, including preschool care, school consolidation, mainstreaming of atypical children, adult and vocational education, and technological improvements in construction materials and equipment. The decade ended with the closure of the last public one-room school building in Kentucky: Little Leatherwood School in Perry County, which closed on August 22, 1989.

In 1990 the State Board of Education used a formula for determining a local school district's need and unmet need (total cost, less available revenue) for new construction or major renovation, and the priority of needs. Such long-range planning is designed to use public construction dollars in the most rational manner.

See John W. Brooker, "Planning and Financing School Buildings and Grounds," *Educational Bulletin* 11 (June 1983): 204-23; Moses Edward Ligon, "A History of Public Education in Kentucky," *Bulletin of the Bureau of School Service* 14 (June 1942): 50-366.   JOANNE KURZ GUILFOIL

SCHOOL BOARDS AND TRUSTEES. Kentucky's first system of free public education, created in 1838 by the General Assembly, provided for the first SUPERINTENDENT OF PUBLIC INSTRUCTION, appointed by the governor; the first state board of education made up of constitutional officers; and the first county boards of education, each consisting of five commissioners appointed by the state board. County school boards in turn appointed five trustees to run each school district in the county. The act charged the county courts, not the county school boards, with the task of dividing the counties into a convenient number of districts and voting school systems into existence in those districts. The county courts moved so slowly on these tasks, however, that in 1842 the General Assembly transferred the power to district the counties from the county courts to the county commissioners of education. In subsequent sessions, the legislature cut the number

of district trustees from five to three. The number of county commissioners was also reduced from five to three and then, in 1856, from three to one.

The Civil War devastated education in Kentucky. Systems of accountability that had been established by State Superintendent Robert J. BRECKINRIDGE (1847-53) crumbled. Teachers went to war and did not return. Schoolhouses fell into disrepair. Where schools operated at all, they were controlled by the trustees.

After another period of unsuccessful county court involvement in education, the General Assembly in 1884 enacted the Common School Law. The law established a plan of organization for state, county, and school district levels and defined the duties of state and county school boards and the district trustees. It converted the county commissioner of education into a county superintendent and stipulated that the post was to be filled by election. Trustees, however, retained effective control of the schools. To achieve quality in local school administration, an 1888 statute imposed the first job requirements for trustees, defining them as persons of good moral character and, where possible, able to read and write. Local residents were authorized to establish independent graded schools upon petition of ten voters. Each school so established was to have six trustees of its own.

The "Education Legislature" of 1908 made the first inroads into the power of the state's 25,000 district trustees. It did so by establishing county boards of education and giving them the authority to run the schools. Each district in the county would continue to elect trustees, but only the district chairpersons would sit on the county board. The 1908 act also decreed the establishment of a high school in every county by 1910.

In 1912 county boards were further strengthened. The General Assembly authorized them to combine state and county school funds and to distribute them to the schools according to their needs. This measure abolished the old procedure of apportioning state funds directly to local school districts. County boards were also authorized to consolidate or realign their school districts and were directed to set single salary scales for their county's teachers. Trustees, as previously, were to employ the teachers.

George COLVIN, a Republican, superintendent of public instruction during 1920-24, attacked the dishonesty and immorality prevalent in the state's school systems by taking steps to deal with the trustees. He enforced all the school laws on the books, prosecuted violators, established a uniform system of accounting, and required local school boards to file regular financial reports. At Colvin's urging, the General Assembly passed the County School Administration Law of 1920, which ended the practice of electing county school superintendents. It stipulated that five-member county boards of education be elected by the people, and it gave the boards the power to appoint the county superintendent, the district trustees, and the teachers. The

Department of Education took over the tasks of certifying teachers and promoting the consolidation of rural schools. However, these sweeping measures had little effect on the trustees, isolated as they were in their rural subdistricts.

In 1934 the legislature enacted another landmark bill, based on extensive study and careful preparation. The new school code brought order into the chaos of school district organization and rid Kentucky of trustees forever. It did so by reducing the six categories of local school districts (each with its own rules and layers of trustees) into two—the county district and the independent district—each to be governed by an elected school board of five members. The EDUCATION REFORM ACT of 1990 reauthorized this structure, while reducing somewhat the power of the county boards.

The concept that local citizens should care for the local schoolhouse was simple. The trustee in the local district built and maintained the schools; levied and collected taxes to operate them; and hired, housed, and paid the teachers. The trustee, who received no pay, set the school term, rounded up the students, and assisted the teacher with youngsters who were unruly. When the trustee was honest and conscientious, the arrangement was practical. When venality of trustees combined with dishonesty, ignorance, and downright meanness, however, the results were disastrous for teachers and pupils alike. In such cases, teachers were tyrannized, abuses were legion, and accountability was nonexistent. The result was local control, local politics, local nepotism/cronyism, and favoritism—all rolled into a school system that Jesse Stuart, in his book *The Thread That Runs So True* (1949), described as "worthy of the Dark Ages."

See Edwina Ann Doyle, Ruby Layson, and Anne Armstrong Thompson, *From the Fort to the Future: Educating the Children of Kentucky* (Lexington, Ky., 1987); The Efficiency Commission of Kentucky, *The Educational System of Kentucky* (Frankfort, Ky., 1923).   LYMAN V. GINGER

SCHOOL CONSOLIDATION. A truly statewide system of common schools supported at public expense was established in Kentucky only with the Common School Law of 1884. A law enacted in 1838 had required counties to lay out school districts and to create both county and district school governance structures, but many of the school districts within each county were able to avoid establishing adequate district schools, as county courts rarely imposed taxes to fund the costs of hiring a teacher and setting up a school.

The size of school districts in terms of enrollment appears to have been an issue throughout the nineteenth century, as it continues to be today. The school law of 1838 stipulated that a district could have as many as one hundred students, but no fewer than thirty. Trustees of each school district were charged with conducting many district affairs, including a census of school-age children that the state then provided money to educate. Some early

school leaders encouraged small school districts within Kentucky's counties, hoping they would stimulate parent involvement and support for formal education. Yet fraud by district trustees in reporting the number of students eligible for state funds, mismanagement of school resources, nepotism, and lack of coherent curricular initiatives led later school reformers to challenge the district system of public education. There was growing criticism of the autonomy of Kentucky counties in administering state funds and setting county tax rates related to public education. Many Kentucky counties refused to levy any local school taxes until late in the nineteenth century.

Over the years, the trustee system was gradually abandoned by reassigning many of the trustees' duties to the county school board. The School Act of 1922 also mandated that no new independent graded school district could be created in the state. At that time, Kentucky had approximately 120 county school systems and 388 independent (or city) districts. Later, the dependence of twentieth century county school systems upon the larger county governance and tax structure was relieved by channeling state money directly through county school boards and empowering the school boards themselves to set county school tax rates.

Meanwhile, accountability efforts in the state Department of Education began to mandate higher requirements for curricula, buildings, and teacher certification. The net effect was to increase educational costs for county and independent school systems, and to encourage the consolidation of districts and of schools within districts, particularly in poorer counties. School mergers became popular options for independent and county school leaders and taxpayers throughout the mid-twentieth century. Typically, impoverished independent districts merged with larger adjacent county districts as local economies declined, and the state legislature continually increased the minimum enrollment that entitled school districts and schools to state support. As a result, the total of 508 school districts in the state as recently as 1920 had declined to only 176 by 1990. The closure of nongraded elementary schools and small rural high schools increased dramatically after 1945 as state highways improved, as illustrated by the demise of the one-teacher school in Kentucky. In the early 1930s there were over 5,000 such schools; in 1990 there were none. Nevertheless, school closings in the commonwealth still set off heated battles on the part of parents, communities, and school leaders.   ALAN DEYOUNG

SCHWARTZ, ISRAEL JACOB. Israel Jacob Schwartz was born in 1885 on the Jewish holiday of Sukkot in the province of Kovno in Lithuania, and emigrated to New York in 1906. A poet and journalist, he also translated the works of Hebrew and English poets into Yiddish. In 1918 Schwartz moved to Lexington, Kentucky, where he lived with his wife and daughter and operated a millinery shop until 1929. Between the years 1918 and 1922,

Schwartz composed his epic Yiddish poem cycle, *Kentucky*, which speaks of the natural beauty of the Bluegrass region, the growth of urban Lexington, and Jewish life in the South. The central poem of this work tells the story of a Jewish peddler who rises from poverty to affluence and becomes a respected member of central Kentucky society. Largely because of the work he did in Lexington, Schwartz has been called the first Yiddish poet to deal with fundamentally American themes. He translated *Kentucky* into Hebrew in 1962. After leaving Lexington, Schwartz returned to New York and continued to write and translate poetry. In 1952, he published his autobiographic poem, *Yunge Yorn* (Young Years). Schwartz died in New York City on September 19, 1971.

See Joseph R. Jones, "I.J. Schwartz in Lexington," *Kentucky Review* 3 (1981): 23-40.

LEE SHAI WEISSBACH

SCIENCE AND TECHNOLOGY. The history of science and technology in Kentucky has been one of barriers rather than frontiers, of indifference rather than support. The state has made many individual and institutional contributions to advancements in science and technology, but it has not sustained a tradition of such endeavors.

The scientists, engineers, and inventors that Kentucky attracted and produced during its first century were the products of a nation in which the self-taught dominated. Efforts to civilize the frontier and to harness its resources were evident everywhere in what was then the West. In Kentucky, private academies, colleges, and the first university in the West, Transylvania University, were created to inspire leadership and a creative citizenry. During most of the antebellum period, Lexington possessed the credentials to be known as the "Athens of the West."

There were early signs, however, that the state's scientific and technical talent, both native and recruited, would, like some of its natural resources, find employment elsewhere. In a rural society, politicians and constituents alike generally believed that the study of nature would have to pay its own way; Kentucky produced many short-lived institutions of learning. One of the first in the West, the Lexington Botanical Garden, was established in 1824, but without financial support it soon withered away. A few years later, its founder, the well-known naturalist and professor at Transylvania, Constantine RAFINESQUE, left the state. When the American Association for the Advancement of Science was created in 1848, no Kentucky resident was invited to join. A decade later, the school most adequately equipped to teach contemporary science in the state, Transylvania, was declining in all departments for lack of financial support and closed its famous medical school in 1859. In a state only recently settled, the brain drain had begun.

From mid- to late-nineteenth century, the geological surveys of the state were the most extensive scientific activity and the location of anthracite coal deposits their most important product. These surveys brought to the state talented scientists, including David Dale OWEN, Covington native Nathaniel S. SHALER, and Dr. Robert PETER. Shaler, like many others, went east to study; as a graduate of Harvard, he returned to Kentucky only temporarily. Kentucky fell behind national trends as new knowledge began flowing from the colleges, universities, and technical institutes of other states. Simon FLEXNER and Thomas Hunt MORGAN were part of the exodus of talent. A Lexington native, Morgan graduated with honors in zoology from the Agricultural and Mechanical College of Kentucky (University of Kentucky) in 1886, but he went to the Johns Hopkins University in Baltimore for his Ph.D., and he spent most of his professional life in California. In 1933 he won the Nobel Prize for his pioneering work in genetics. Louisville native Simon Flexner, a graduate of the local college of pharmacy and medical school, made his name as director of laboratories at the Rockefeller Institute for Medical Research, where he demonstrated that poliomyelitis was caused by a virus.

Their native state had few incentives for Shaler, Morgan, and Flexner to make their homes there. Indeed, there was no state university until 1908, and no statewide academy of science until 1914. A later example of the pattern is that of William N. Lipscomb. After receiving his B.S. from the University of Kentucky in 1941, he, too, went east to graduate school; as a professor of chemistry at Harvard, in 1976 he, too, became a Nobel laureate. To Kentucky's credit, Lipscomb now serves on the board of directors of the Kentucky Science and Technology Council, Inc.

When Kentucky entered the 1980s at the low end of the nation's educational profile, proposals emerged from all quarters to shape the future of scientific and technical activity in the state and to stem the outflow of talent. But as late as 1989 Kentucky ranked forty-sixth nationally in the number of scientists and engineers employed in its workforce. On the other hand, recent gains for the state in this area are well-established enterprises dependent upon robotics and automation, such as the G.E. Appliance Park and the Ford plant in Louisville, and Toyota in Georgetown. Native Kentuckians have created others, such as Appalachian Computer Services, Thiel Loudspeakers, and the Projectron and DataBeam corporations of Lee T. Todd, Jr. To educate and retain talent, and to attract talent and high-tech employers, the state in 1986 initiated a multimillion-dollar bond sale to upgrade equipment at the state's universities. The same year Kentucky became a participant-recipient in the National Science Foundation's experimental program to stimulate competitive research. Such funds provided facilities and startup money to apply for major research grants from federal sources. The results of these initial investments have been impressive; in 1988-89, grants from federal agencies to University of Kentucky faculty topped $34 million. In 1988 Robert Shepherd became the state's first faculty member elected to the National Academy of Sciences, the nation's most prestigious advisory organization for scientific and technological activity. Shepard has been a professor of plant pathology at the University of Kentucky since 1984. By the end of the decade, the state had become home to nationally recognized supercomputer and robotics centers and the Coldstream Industrial Park for high-technology research and development.

Most far-reaching in its consequences was the 1989 court decision that the state's system of public schools was inequitable and unconstitutional. Poor school systems do not produce scientists and engineers, nor do communities with poor schools attract the businesses that would employ such talent. The educational reform measures enacted by the 1990 General Assembly became the object of national interest. As the 1990s began, the stage had been set for intense discussions of the priorities for the state's public schools and universities and the question of educational and employment opportunities for Kentucky students.

See Charles E. Rosenberg, *No Other Gods: On Science and American Social Thought* (London 1976); Alan I. Marcus and Howard P. Segal, *Technology In America: A Brief History* (New York 1989). ERIC HOWARD CHRISTIANSON

SCIENCE HILL FEMALE ACADEMY. Science Hill Female Academy in Shelbyville, Kentucky, opened March 25, 1825, and operated continuously for 114 years. Julia Ann (Hieronymous) Tevis founded the school for white female students aged six to twenty-one. Both day-school and boarding students were admitted to the school in Tevis's home. Enrollment increased as prejudice against education for women was overcome. In time the school became renowned, drawing students from nearly every state, especially from the South, although the depressed economy after the Civil War cut into southern patronage.

From 1829 until 1906, Science Hill was affiliated with the Methodist Episcopal Church, but in terms of management Tevis was the guiding force until 1880. Tevis's administration focused on education as moral training for women as future wives and mothers. But instruction at Science Hill went beyond the superficial female education typical of most academies; it included reading, writing, arithmetic, grammar, history, rhetoric, astronomy, conversational French, music, and painting. Science Hill had both male and female teachers, but Tevis preferred female instructors. The building was enlarged to meet the growing enrollment, which reached two hundred to 350 pupils in the 1850s. By the end of Tevis's administration, more than 3,000 students had matriculated at Science Hill.

W.T. Poynter purchased the school on March 25, 1879, and remained principal until his death on July 30, 1896. He changed the curriculum to that of a secondary school with a college-trained staff and made Science Hill one of the foremost college preparatory schools for women. Of the five hundred women who graduated from Science Hill between 1888 and 1934, more than 150 went on to graduate from Wellesley and Vassar. After Poynter's death,

his wife, Clara M. Poynter, served as principal until 1937. Their daughter, Juliet Jameson Poynter, was president from 1937 until the school closed in June 1939. Juliet and her sister Harriet sold the building to Mark Scearce, who opened the Wakefield-Scearce Antique Gallery on the premises in 1940.

See Jo Della Alband, "History of the Education of Women in Kentucky," M.A. thesis, University of Kentucky, 1934; Julia A. Tevis, *Sixty Years in a School-Room* (Cincinnati 1878).

SCOPES, JOHN THOMAS. John Thomas Scopes, educator known for his defense of Darwinism in the classroom, was born in Paducah, Kentucky, on August 3, 1900, to Thomas and Mary Scopes. In 1911 he moved with his parents to Salem, Illinois, and he later attended the University of Illinois. He transferred to the University of Kentucky as a sophomore in 1921, graduating with an A.B. in 1924. Scopes taught general science for one year at Rhea County Central High School in Dayton, Tennessee. While substituting for a biology teacher there, he tested the state's Butler Act by expanding upon Charles Darwin's theory of evolution in the classroom. For this he was arrested and tried.

The eleven-day trial, which began on July 10, 1925, in the Rhea County courthouse, became famous as the Monkey Trial. Clarence Darrow was hired by the American Civil Liberties Union to defend Scopes against the prosecuting attorney, William Jennings Bryan. The trial bore upon the issues of academic freedom, separation of church and state, and the power and influence of fundamental Christianity. Scopes was found guilty and fined $100. In 1955 a successful Broadway play and subsequent movie, *Inherit the Wind*, revived interest in the trial. Scopes described the experience in *Center of the Storm* (1967).

After the trial, Scopes studied geology at the University of Chicago, then worked briefly for Gulf Oil of South America. In 1932 he returned to Paducah. He was defeated when he ran for a seat in the U.S. House of Representatives on the Socialist ticket. He began work for the United Gas Company in Texas and Louisiana in 1933, retiring in 1964. On February 13, 1970, Scopes returned to the University of Kentucky to address the Societus Pro Legibus.

Scopes married Margaret Walker; they had two sons, William C. and John, Jr. Scopes died of cancer in Shreveport, Louisiana, on October 21, 1970, and was buried in the Oak Grove Cemetery in Paducah.

See Sheldon N. Grebstein, ed., *Monkey Trial: The State of Tennessee vs. John Thomas Scopes* (Boston 1960); John T. Scopes and James Presley, *Center of the Storm* (New York 1967).

SCOTT, CHARLES. Charles Scott, Kentucky's governor during 1808-12, was born in present-day Powhatan County, Virginia, in 1739, probably in April, the son of Charles Scott. He saw extensive military service during the French and Indian War and achieved the rank of captain. He married

Frances Sweeney in February 1762, and was a successful farmer and miller before the Revolutionary War. In February 1776 he was commissioned lieutenant colonel of the 2nd Virginia Regiment of the Continental Line, and in April 1777 became a brigadier general. Scott fought in the majority of George Washington's campaigns in the middle Atlantic states in 1776-78, serving as Washington's chief of intelligence toward the end of this period. After leading the state militia in 1779, Scott joined the southern army and was captured at Charleston in May 1780. He was paroled in March 1781 and exchanged in July 1782.

Scott visited Kentucky in 1785 and two years later moved to a tract on the Kentucky River nine miles from present-day Versailles. Two of his sons were killed in Indian warfare. He served a term (1789-90) in the Virginia House of Delegates and was twice a presidential elector. Scott's military reputation was enhanced by participation in several Indian expeditions, including the Battle of Fallen Timbers on August 20, 1794. In 1807, three years after his first wife died, Scott married a widow, Judith Cary (Bell) Gist, and moved to the Gist plantation in Bourbon and Clark counties. As a military hero and a sound Jeffersonian Republican, he was overwhelmingly elected governor in 1808, with 22,050 votes to 8,430 for John Allen and 5,516 for Green Clay. Jesse Bledsoe, a Transylvania law professor who had been Scott's campaign manager, was Scott's choice as secretary of state and proved an able second-in-command. After his retirement in 1812, Scott lived at his estate, Canewood, until his death on October 22, 1813. He was buried at Canewood, and his remains were later removed to the Frankfort Cemetery.

Injured in a fall during his first year in office, the handicapped governor relied heavily upon Bledsoe. A firm believer in the public interest, Scott sometimes clashed with the legislature when he believed it acted unwisely. In the time of controversy preceding the War of 1812, for instance, Scott pointed out in England's favor that France as well as England had violated American rights, but when conditions deteriorated he advocated raising volunteer troops to fill the army. He appointed William Henry Harrison as brevet major general of Kentucky's militia. Without success, Scott during his term pursued sound finances with low taxes, reform of the militia system, increased pay for public officials, economic development of the state, and heavy punishments for persistent criminals. He won General Assembly enactment of a replevy law that allowed debtors to stave off creditors for one year if they offered bond and security. Most Kentuckians did not seem overly concerned with the rumors of the governor's heavy drinking and profanity; on the contrary, he was well-liked for his modesty and sense of public duty.

See Harry M. Ward, *Charles Scott and the "Spirit of Seventy-Six"* (Charlottesville, Va., 1988); Lowell H. Harrison, ed., *Kentucky's Governors 1792-1985* (Lexington, Ky. 1985).

LOWELL H. HARRISON

SCOTT, ROBERT WILMOT. Robert Wilmot Scott, agriculturalist, was born on November 2, 1808, on his grandfather Robert Wilmot Scott's farm in Bourbon County, Kentucky, the son of Joel and Sarah (Ridgely) Scott. He graduated from Transylvania University in 1824 and became an apprentice lawyer in the office of Haggin and Loughborough in Frankfort. On September 17, 1829, he left Frankfort on horseback for a *wanderjahr*, during which he visited the major cities on the eastern seaboard. He arrived in Richmond, Virginia, just as delegates were assembling for the Virginia constitutional convention of 1830. He became acquainted with most of that state's great men, whom he described in precise physiognomic detail. From Richmond, Scott went to New York City; New Haven and Hartford, Connecticut; Providence, Rhode Island; Boston; Albany, New York; Princeton, New Jersey; and Philadelphia, Baltimore, and Washington, D.C. His journal entries and his detailed physical descriptions of men and women of the Jacksonian period in the nation's capital are unparalleled. In February 1831 Scott returned to Kentucky by way of Baltimore; Philadelphia, Harrisburg, and Pittsburgh, Pennsylvania; and Wheeling, West Virginia.

In the 1830s Scott abandoned his law practice to become a farmer. In 1835 he purchased the first 205 acres of what was to become Locust Hill Plantation in Franklin and Woodford counties, a mile east of Jett, where he became one of Kentucky's most progressive farmers and livestock breeders. He stabilized the breed known as Improved Kentucky sheep and he crossbred hogs to produce a new type. On several visits to the Lower South with herds of purebred farm animals, Scott was credited with helping to improve herds and flocks in the growing cotton belt. His letters to his wife are revealing as to the state of livestock production and social conditions in that region. In the quarter of a century before the outbreak of the Civil War, Scott was active in promoting scientific farming and in advocating the establishment of an agricultural college, the enactment of much agrarian legislation, and the creation of a public school system. In the years immediately after the Civil War, Scott became an active Democrat.

Scott married Elizabeth Watts Brown on October 28, 1831; they had three sons and four daughters. Scott's health failed after 1870, and on the morning of November 8, 1884, he died in the home of his son-in-law, S.I.M. Major, in Frankfort, and was buried in the Frankfort Cemetery. The Scott family papers, in the archives of the National Society of Colonial Dames in the Commonwealth of Kentucky, are important sources of Kentucky agricultural and social history.

See Thomas D. Clark, *Footloose in Jacksonian America: Robert W. Scott and His Agrarian World* (Frankfort, Ky., 1989).   THOMAS D. CLARK

SCOTT, WALTER E. Walter E. ("Death Valley Scotty") Scott, an adventurer and promoter, was born in Cynthiana, Kentucky, on September 20, 1872. The youngest of six children, he followed his elder brothers, Bill and Warner, to Nevada at the age of fourteen. He joined Buffalo Bill's Wild West Show in the 1890s after working as a ranch hand for John Sparks (governor of Nevada in 1903-8). Scott stayed with the show for nearly a decade, riding bucking broncs and fighting off staged Indian attacks, and he dabbled in gold mining during the off-season. He became a national celebrity in 1905 by setting a record for the rail trip from Los Angeles to Chicago. He rented the Sante Fe Railroad's Coyote Special from July 9 to 11, and the train's engineer made the journey in forty-four hours and fifty-four minutes. The record stood until 1934.

Scott received the attention of the press throughout most of his life for his ability to attract investment in a fictitious Death Valley gold mine. He benefited from the financial support of Albert M. Johnson of Chicago, president of the National Life Insurance Company of America, whom Scott lured into the mining scheme in 1904. Scott was declared a fake in 1912, but Johnson later resumed his financial support. Although Scott was prosecuted for his schemes, he never served a lengthy jail term.

Scott reemerged as a national figure in the 1920s. In 1922, amid rumors of a lost gold mine, Scott, with Johnson's financial assistance, began building an estimated $3 million mansion in Death Valley known as Scotty's Castle. Work halted in 1931 after a survey revealed the castle was on government land. On February 11, 1933, President Herbert Hoover signed a bill declaring Death Valley a national monument. Though special legislation was drawn up to allow Johnson to purchase the land around the castle for $1.25 an acre, work on the castle never resumed. The Great Depression had hurt Johnson financially, and he and Scott opened what had been built of the castle to tourists.

Scott married Ella Josephine McCarthy in November 1900. They had one child, Walter, Jr. Scott died January 5, 1954, en route to a hospital in Las Vegas, Nevada. He was buried at the castle in Death Valley.

See C.B. Glasscock, *Here's Death Valley* (Indianapolis 1940).   JOHN ERNST

SCOTT-COLSON BATTLE. The bloody Scott-Colson gun battle between two eastern Kentucky Republicans grew out of a grudge over a breach of military protocol during the Spanish-American War. In 1898 Ethelbert D. Scott, a Somerset attorney and nephew of Gov. William O. Bradley (1895-99), reported for duty as a newly commissioned subaltern with the 4th Kentucky Volunteers, then stationed in Anniston, Alabama. On his arrival in camp he asked for Col. D.G. Colson of Bell County, the commanding officer and a former congressman, to present a letter of introduction. When Colonel Colson came into the room where Scott was seated reading a newspaper, the lieutenant failed to arise and salute. Angered by this affront, Colson left the

room. In many other incidents Scott proved a recalcitrant soldier and was recommended for dismissal from the army but used political influence to stay in place. Such bad blood developed between the two men that after the 4th Kentucky was retired from service and Colson and Scott later met accidentally in an Anniston restaurant, they engaged in gunfire and Colson was wounded in the groin.

On January 16, 1900, two weeks after the assassination of Gov. William Goebel (1900), Scott and Colson had a second chance meeting, this time in the lobby of the Capitol Hotel in Frankfort. Both were armed, Colson with a .44 service revolver and a .38 caliber pistol. Coming face-to-face, the two men fired simultaneously. Eighteen shots were fired. Scott, wounded three times, was attempting to escape when Colson shot him dead. The gunfire also killed four bystanders and wounded at least two other men. Colson was arrested, jailed, tried, and cleared. In fact, the court returned his pistols to him. His life, however, was afterward made miserable by ill health and, it was said, by alcohol.

See Harold Wilson Coates, *Stories of Kentucky Feuds* (Knoxville, Tenn., 1923); L.F. Johnson, *Famous Kentucky Tragedies and Trials* (Louisville 1916).   THOMAS D. CLARK

SCOTT COUNTY. Scott County, the eleventh county in order of formation, is located in north-central Kentucky. It is bounded by Owen, Grant, Harrison, Bourbon, Fayette, Woodford, and Franklin counties and contains 286 square miles. Southern Scott County is part of the Inner Bluegrass region and has rich phosphatic loam soils, watered by Elkhorn Creek. The northern portion is located in the Eden Shale belt in the Eagle Creek watershed. GEORGETOWN, the county seat, is seven miles north of Lexington. Highway and rail connections with Lexington, Louisville, and Cincinnati have given Scott trade advantages.

Scott County was explored in June and July of 1774 by Virginians locating land warrants for soldiers of the French and Indian War. The party's journal commented eloquently on the natural wealth and beauty of the "Elkhorn country." In July 1774 the Royal Spring tract, including the site of Georgetown, was plotted for John Floyd. In late 1775, John McClelland, of Pennsylvania, and his family built a cabin near the spring. In July 1776, soldiers and explorers, including Simon Kenton, constructed McClelland's Fort on the spring bluff. The fort, attacked by Indians on December 29, 1776, was abandoned in 1777.

In late 1783, Robert and Jemima Suggett Johnson established Johnson Station, Scott County's first permanent settlement, near a buffalo crossing on North Elkhorn Creek. Later known as Great Crossing, it became the county's first commercial center. By 1785 settlers were clearing forests and canelands and establishing farmsteads. Baptists were the dominant religious group, followed by Presbyterians. Around 1786, Catholics from Maryland settled in western Scott County and in 1793-94 organized St. Francis Church, an early center of Catholic missions and the second Catholic parish in Kentucky.

Scott County was one of two counties established by the first Kentucky legislature on June 1, 1792, and was named in honor of Gen. Charles Scott, governor during 1808-1812. Created from Woodford County, Scott County was reduced to its present boundaries in 1819.

Agriculture was Scott County's leading source of income until 1960. Farmers produced cattle, hogs, sheep, horses, and mules, as well as corn, hemp, flax, orchard products, and tobacco. Local industry processed agricultural products into whiskey, flour, meal, linen and woolen cloth, coarse bagging, hempen rope, paper, and lumber.

Georgetown was settled in late 1785 or early 1786 by the Rev. Elijah Craig and Virginia Baptists and was incorporated on December 16, 1790. Craig's mills on Royal Spring Branch were among the first west of the Appalachians to full and card cloth (1789) and the first to manufacture paper (1793). Craig also established an early ropewalk (1789) and a whiskey still. Craig's 1788 classical school became Rittenhouse Academy in 1799. In 1829 Georgetown College was organized with the assets of the Craig/Rittenhouse schools.

Stamping Ground, incorporated in 1834, grew up around a buffalo spring and wallowing ground and was laid out as a village in 1818. Stamping Ground had several taverns for Frankfort-to-Cincinnati travelers. Antebellum industries included a tanyard and woolen mill. Other important crossroads commercial centers were Patterson's Crossroads (present-day Oxford), Newtown, and Turkeyfoot.

On November 18, 1861, Scott County native George W. Johnson was elected provisional Confederate governor of Kentucky. On August 8, 1862, James Fisher Robinson, also a Scott County native and a Union Democrat, became governor. Scott County furnished the Union army with 118 white soldiers and the Confederacy with approximately 1,000. After the Civil War, former slaves who remained in the county occupied tenant houses or built dwellings in hamlets such as New Zion, Zion Hill, and Watkinsville; on the edges of villages and towns; and in neighborhoods encircling downtown Georgetown and extending northeast into the all-black village of Boston.

Between 1870 and 1900, burley tobacco replaced hemp as the major cash crop, and air-curing tobacco barns were built. Georgetown's James Campbell Cantrill, congressman from 1908 to 1923, led growers' struggles for market equity.

Railroads brought economic vitality to Scott County, including Lexington-Portland (1835), Cincinnati Southern (now the Norfolk Southern), established in 1876, Kentucky Midland (1888), Louisville Southern (1888), Georgetown Street Railroad (1888, 1895), and Lexington-Georgetown Interurban (1902). Grist and lumber milling, carriage manufacturing, and distilling were leading postbellum industries. Sadieville, on the Cincinnati Southern Railroad, was established as northern

Scott County's shipping and commercial center in 1877. Industries that developed along railroads included Stamping Ground's Buffalo Springs Distillery and Georgetown's Blue Grass Cordage (1890), Model Mills (1897), and Indian Oil Refinery (1905-15). Popular use of the automobile brought about improvement of Dixie Highway (U.S. 25) after 1916.

Beginning in 1910, Anne Payne Coffman and the Georgetown Civic League/Woman's Club organized public improvement projects, including the library, health department, and school reform.

Post–World War II industrialization began in 1944-45 with Mallard Pencil Company's plant on Bourbon Street. In 1957 Electric Parts Corporation began manufacturing electric blankets. Construction of I-75 and I-64 between 1960 and 1972 brought more development, which climaxed in 1985 with the establishment of a Toyota Motor Manufacturing plant north of Georgetown. The population of Scott County was 17,948 in 1970; 21,813 in 1980; and 23,867 in 1990.

See Ann Bolton Bevins, *A History of Scott County as Told by Selected Buildings* (Georgetown, Ky., 1981); B.O. Gaines, *History of Scott County* (Georgetown, Ky., 1906; reprinted 1961).

ANN BOLTON BEVINS

SCOTTSVILLE. The seat of Allen County, Scottsville is located on U.S. 31 and U.S. 231, on the West Bays Fork of the Barren River. It was settled in 1797 and was the site of an early stagecoach stop and relay station. The town was laid out in 1816 and named for Kentucky's fourth governor, Gen. Charles Scott (1808-12). The site was selected as the county seat for its water supply and central location. In 1830, Scottsville had a population of 180, which more than doubled to 400 in 1850, but declined to 217 in 1870.

The first courthouse, an unusual structure built in 1816, was a two-story octagonal building with a shuttered cupola. The second courthouse, finished in 1903, was in the eclectic style typical of the Victorian period; the two-story brick building was topped with a large cupola containing a clock and bell tower. When the building was demolished in 1967 to streamline traffic flow around the square, the bell was placed atop the City-County Building. The third courthouse, completed in 1969, is a modern two-story building of brick and concrete.

Scottsville experienced some Civil War action. On December 8, 1863, Col. John M. Hughs, with two hundred troops of the Confederate 25th Tennessee Infantry, captured the town and eighty-six men of the 52d Kentucky Regiment along with quartermaster and commissary supplies, five hundred small arms, and several hundred saddles and bridles. One Confederate soldier was killed. Colonel Hughs paroled the prisoners.

Located in an agricultural county, Scottsville has a strong industrial economy that began in 1939, when the entrepreneurial father-son team of J.L. and Cal Turner established the Dollar General Stores. In 1991 the firm, with headquarters and warehouses at 427 Beech Street, operated 1,460 retail stores in twenty-three states. Manufacturing plants in the town include General Electric's large plant for production of Hemetic motor parts, and Clifty Farms, which cures country hams. Tourism adds to the economy, with Barren River Lake forming part of the northeast boundary of Allen County. Visitors also attend the Allen County Fair in July and the Fiddlers and Bluegrass Festival in September.

A fourth-class city, Scottsville had a population of 3,584 in 1970; 4,278 in 1980; and 4,278 in 1990.

SEARCY, CHESLEY HUNTER. Chesley Hunter Searcy, Republican party official, was born in Louisville, Kentucky, on December 14, 1881, to John and Rosa (Colter) Searcy. He attended the Louisville public grade and high schools and studied at Vanderbilt University (1901-3) in Nashville. He received his law degree from the University of Louisville in 1904 and set up a law practice in Louisville. He was named assistant county attorney for Jefferson County during 1908-10. In 1911 Searcy was the Republican nominee for the state Senate but was defeated. At this point, Searcy put his charm and quick wit to use in the behind-the-scenes organization of the Republican party. He started off as a campaign manager for the gubernatorial candidates in 1911 (Edward C. O'Rear) and 1915 (Edwin P. Morrow). Both were defeated. By 1916 Searcy had brought together the nucleus of the Republican League in Louisville, which controlled the party well into the 1920s. He held every major leadership position within the party, serving as the Louisville Republican Committee chairman (1917-18), the Republican State Committee chairman (1919-20), and as a member of the Republican National Committee (1921-24).

Searcy and two other party leaders, Robert H. Lucas and J. Matt Chilton, came to be known as the "Triumvirate" for orchestrating major Republican victories in local and state elections, particularly in 1920 and 1921. Searcy's influence began to wane when he and Chilton refused to support Lucas's bid for the 1927 Republican gubernatorial nomination. Four years later the Democratic party, under the leadership of Mickey Brennan, won back the Louisville mayor's office; the Democrats dominated local politics for thirty years afterward. With the Republicans' defeat in 1931, Searcy returned to his law practice.

Searcy married Mary Lillian Black on February 16, 1906; they had four children, Chilton, Alvin Hert, Lillian Lucas, and Frances Rose. Searcy died on May 9, 1935, and was buried in Cave Hill Cemetery in Louisville.

SECRETARIAT. Secretariat, the chestnut thoroughbred that in 1973 was the first winner of the Triple Crown since Citation in 1948, was sired by Bold Ruler out of Somethingroyal. He was foaled on March 29, 1970, at the Meadow Stud in Doswell, Virginia. The foal was won by Penney (Chenery) Tweedy in a coin toss for Bold Ruler's

stud fee, and Secretariat raced for Tweedy's Meadow Stud; his trainer was Lucien Laurin and his jockey, Ron Turcotte. Like Man O' War in earlier years, Secretariat was nicknamed Big Red.

Secretariat finished fourth in his first race, six furlongs, on July 4, 1972, at Aqueduct in New York. Bumped into the rail at the start, he came from tenth place at the head of the stretch. Eleven days later at the same track he finished first, and he went on to win his next seven races. In 1973 he was named horse of the year. On May 5, 1973, Secretariat won the ninety-ninth Kentucky Derby in 1:59 2/5, setting the current derby record for the distance of 1¼ miles. Two weeks later he won the Preakness, and on June 9, 1973, he won the third race of the Triple Crown, the Belmont, by thirty-one lengths, setting a world record of 2:24 for a mile and a half—a record that stands today. Secretariat went on to finish first in four of his next six starts.

Tweedy retired Secretariat to stud at Claiborne Farm near Paris, Kentucky, in 1974. He sired more than three hundred sons and daughters, including Risen Star, winner of both the Preakness and the Belmont in 1988, and Lady's Secret, horse of the year in 1986. In the fall of 1989, Secretariat developed laminitis, a painful disease of the inner tissue of the hoof. He was humanely destroyed on October 4, 1989. An autopsy found that his heart was twice the average size, which may help to explain his speed. He was buried near his sire and his grandsire, Nasrullah, on Claiborne Farm.

See William Nack, "Pure Heart," *Sports Illustrated*, June 4, 1990.

SECRETARY OF STATE, OFFICE OF. Under the first, second, and third Kentucky constitutions, the secretary of state was appointed by the governor. The present constitution (1891) requires election by the people; the first elected secretary of state took office in 1896. The Office of Secretary of State is the official registry of foreign and domestic corporations in the commonwealth. Specified corporate documents must be filed with the office, and the secretary of state is agent for service of court papers against out-of-state corporations. As head of the State Board of Elections, the secretary of state is responsible for the smooth functioning of the election process. Candidates for statewide office must file candidacy papers with the office, which maintains lists of qualified voters in each precinct and certifies election returns. The State Land Office, part of the Office of the Secretary of State, houses the official records for all land grants, warrants, and surveys. The secretary of state is also the keeper of the seal of the Commonwealth of Kentucky. The seal is used to attest to official acts of the governor or to certify documents to be used in court.   JOHN S. GILLIG

SEGREGATION. The Civil War and the Thirteenth Amendment to the U.S. Constitution resulted in citizenship for former slaves. Many southern whites, with their racist notions and frustrations brought on by military defeat, were determined to identify the ex-slaves as the enemy and to resist them by every means available. Although Kentucky had not left the Union, slavery had been a major feature of its society, and the enfranchisement of blacks caused widespread resentment. By 1900 most of the civil rights gained earlier by blacks had for all practical purposes ceased to exist throughout the South, including Kentucky. The Civil Rights Act of 1875 banned discrimination in public accommodation and in jury selection, but in 1883 the U.S. Supreme Court ruled the public accommodations section of this law unconstitutional. The Court again reacted strongly against blacks in 1896 in the "separate but equal" ruling in the case of *Plessy v. Ferguson* (Justice John Harlan, from Kentucky, wrote a strong dissent).

Jim Crow laws had been passed in Kentucky as early as 1892, when the SEPARATE COACH LAW was adopted requiring separate coaches for blacks and whites on interstate railroads. Blacks challenged the constitutionality of the law, and a United States district court ruled it unconstitutional because the Kentucky law interfered with interstate commerce. But another case involving the law was appealed to the U.S. Supreme Court, which ruled in 1900 that the law was valid.

The Kentucky legislature in 1904 enacted the DAY LAW, which required segregation in education. Carl Day, a state representative from Breathitt County, had visited BEREA COLLEGE (an interracial school) and expressed shock at blacks and whites "living together." He successfully sponsored a bill forbidding the teaching of blacks and whites together in public or private schools. The trustees of Berea College challenged the Day Law, but the U.S. Supreme Court ruled it constitutional on November 12, 1908.

In 1914 the Louisville Board of Aldermen passed an ordinance designed to promote residential segregation. This law stated that if the majority of a given community was of one race, then only members of that race could occupy homes in that community. The U.S. Supreme Court in *Buchanan v. Warley* overturned this law in 1917, principally because the law limited property rights. Despite this decision residential segregation was a fact of life in most Kentucky communities until the period of the late 1960s.

The rigid walls of legal segregation in Kentucky began to crumble in the late 1940s. The University of Kentucky was ordered by a federal court to admit blacks to its law, engineering, pharmacy, and graduate schools in 1949. A bill calling for repeal of the Day Law was defeated in the General Assembly in 1954, but the landmark U.S. Supreme Court decision *Brown v. Board of Education* on May 17 of the same year made the vote moot. Most Kentucky school districts complied with the ruling; those that did not faced more federal suits, and all were eventually integrated.

Unwritten discrimination practices continued to affect Kentucky blacks as they searched for ade-quate housing. During the 1960s, marches, demonstrations, and boycotts were effective tools used by blacks in their pursuit of equal rights in housing. In march 1968 Kentucky became the first state in the South to enact a statewide housing law. By the middle 1970s, however, changing housing patterns resulted in much resegregation.

In the 1990s Kentucky faces some of the same problems it struggled against in past years. De jure segregation has been effectively abolished, but much de facto segregation remains, especially in the area of housing. As long as most Afro-Americans remain outside the economic mainstream of American life, segregation will continue to be a serious problem not only in Kentucky but throughout the nation.

See George C. Wright, *Life Behind a Veil: Blacks in Louisville, Kentucky 1865-1930* (Baton Rouge, La., 1985); C. Vann Woodward, *The Strange Career of Jim Crow* (New York 1974).

THOMAS LLEWELLYN

SELDEN, DIXIE. Dixie Selden, painter, daughter of John and Martha Selden, was born in 1868 in Covington, Kentucky. She attended Bartholomew's Girls' School in Cincinnati and studied under Frank DUVENECK at the Cincinnati Academy. She also studied in Venice under William Merritt Chase; in St. Ives, England, with Henry B. Snell; and in Paris and Vienna under other artists.

Selden's impressionistic style of painting has been described as "fresh, vigorous and dexterous." She created colorful landscapes and genre paintings of her travels in Europe, and her oil portraits include *Frank Duveneck*, *Mrs. Mary Emery*, and that of Judge A.M. Cochrane of Maysville, Kentucky. Her most popular landscapes were *Cathedral Towers*, *Taxco*, *The Alhambra*, *The Garden of Washington Irving*, and small paintings of Normandy. Selden's works were exhibited throughout the United States. She died on November 15, 1935, in Cincinnati and was buried in the Highland Cemetery in Covington.

See Mrs. H.V. McChesney, "Dixie Selden," *Register* 35 (July 1937): 273-76.

SELLERS, MATTHEW BACON. Matthew Bacon Sellers, aeronautics pioneer, was born in Baltimore, Maryland, on March 29, 1869, to Matthew and Annie Leathers (Lewis) Sellers. He received his early education at private schools and studied in Göttingen, Germany, and Evreux, France. He received a doctor of law degree from Harvard in 1892, then studied at Harvard's Lawrence Scientific School and at Drexel Institute in Philadelphia. In 1888 his mother purchased property previously owned by her family in Carter County near Grahn. The family lived part of the year at the farm, where Sellers built a laboratory to experiment with aerodynamics. In 1897 he set up a miniature wind tunnel and in 1903 built a fully equipped wind tunnel to measure the lift and drift of the arched surfaces of various wing designs. He also experimented with designs of propellers and glider-style airplanes. Seller's experiments were independent of the research being done by the Wright brothers. On December 28, 1908, five years after the Wright brothers' first flight at Kitty Hawk, North Carolina, Sellers successfully flew a quadroplane—a four-winged, motorized glider powered by a two-cylinder engine—for a short distance in Carter County. Sellers patented his design in July 1911. His assistant, Lincoln Binion, died on October 25, 1911, in an accident when a propeller blade struck him, and Sellers left Kentucky and moved to New York soon after.

In 1912, in recognition of his achievements in experimenting with aerodynamics, Sellers became a member of the Aerodynamic Laboratory Commission. He served from 1915 to 1918 on the National Advisory Commission for Aeronautics, which was reorganized in 1958 to become the National Aeronautics and Space Administration. Sellers was technical editor of *Aeronautics* magazine.

Sellers married Ethel Clark on June 18, 1918; they had two sons—Matthew III and John. Sellers died on April 5, 1932, at Ardsley-on-Hudson, a year after his last visit to Kentucky.

SEMPLE, ELLEN CHURCHILL. Ellen Churchill Semple, geographer, was born on January 8, 1863, in Louisville, to Alexander Bonner and Emerine (Price) Semple. She attended private schools in Louisville and entered Vassar College in Poughkeepsie, New York, at age fifteen. In 1882 she received her B.A. in history with highest honors from Vassar and began graduate work there in economics and social science, for which she received her M.A. degree in 1891. Semple studied under Friedrich Ratzel at the University of Leipzig from 1891 to 1892 and again in 1895. It was Ratzel who influenced Semple to pursue the study of geography.

Semple was a member of a group of scholars who advised President Woodrow Wilson for the Peace Conference of Versailles in 1919. She urged the president to consider the ethnic characteristics of Europe when redrawing its territorial borders. In 1921 Semple joined the staff at Clark University's school of geography in Worcester, Massachusetts. Semple was influential in the development of modern geographic thought. She lectured extensively in the U.S. and Europe, and traveled to remote regions of Asia.

One of Semple's first publications was "The Influence of the Appalachian Barrier upon Colonial History" (1897), an article in the *Journal of School Geography*. Other works include *American History and Its Geographic Conditions* (1903), *Influences of Geographic Environment* (1911), and *The Geography of the Mediterranean* (1931). Semple's writing talent lay in her clear presentation of facts and ideas in a manner of interest to both scholars and the general public.

Semple received many awards, including alumna membership in Phi Beta Kappa at Vassar in 1899, the American Geographical Society's Cullum Geographical Medal in 1914, and the Geographical Society of Chicago's Helen Culver Medal in 1931 for distinguished leadership and eminent achievement in geography. In 1923 she became the first woman to receive an honorary degree from the University of Kentucky. Semple was also a charter member of the Association of American Geographers of which she was president in 1921. A grade school in Louisville was named after her.

Semple died on May 8, 1932, in West Palm Beach, Florida, while on special leave from Clark University for prolonged illness. She was buried in Louisville's Cave Hill Cemetery. She has been honored annually since 1973 at the University of Kentucky by Ellen Churchill Semple Day, a symposium on geography sponsored by the Department of Geography.

See Wilford A. Bladen and Pradyumna P. Karan, eds., *The Evolution of Geographic Thought in America: A Kentucky Root* (Dubuque, Iowa, 1983).

MATTHEW J. BRANDON

SEPARATE COACH LAW. Racial segregation of railroad passenger traffic was legalized in Kentucky when the General Assembly on March 15, 1892, enacted the Separate Coach Law, which stipulated that all passenger trains operating in the state must provide clearly labeled individual coaches for "colored" and "white" passengers. The law was similar to those of other states throughout the South. The act was challenged by a black minister, W.H. Anderson, who boarded a train in Evansville, Indiana, and remained in a coach marked for whites when the train entered Kentucky. In the ensuing lawsuit, federal district Judge John W. Barr ruled on June 4, 1894, that the Kentucky statute was unconstitutional because it interfered with interstate commerce, an area of law reserved to the U.S. Congress (*Anderson v. Louisville & Nashville Railroad Co.*).

Two years later, in a case originating in Louisiana, the U.S. Supreme Court ruled that separate intrastate railroad coaches for the races were legal (*Plessy v. Ferguson*, 1896), and in 1900 the Court upheld Kentucky's Separate Coach Law as it applied to intrastate commerce (*Chesapeake & Ohio Railway v. Kentucky*). In 1920 the court upheld the law as it applied to interstate commerce (*South Covington & Cincinnati Street Railway v. Kentucky*), thus in effect overruling *Anderson v. Louisville & Nashville*.

Reflecting an increased sympathy for civil rights, the U.S. Supreme Court in 1946 placed in jeopardy Kentucky's Separate Coach Law when it invalidated a Virginia statute requiring segregated interstate bus travel (*Morgan v. Virginia*). In 1955 the Interstate Commerce Commission banned racial discrimination in interstate railroad passenger traffic, thus rendering invalid Kentucky's law as it applied to train traffic to and from other states. The Kentucky statute's validity as to intrastate traffic came into question in light of *Brown v. Board of*

Education (1954), which held that state-mandated public school segregation violated the Constitution. In 1966 the Kentucky General Assembly repealed the Separate Coach Law.

See Catherine A. Barnes, *Journal from Jim Crow: The Desegregation of Southern Transit* (New York 1983).

SETTLEMENT SCHOOLS. As late as the early twentieth century, the Appalachian region of eastern Kentucky was still physically isolated from the mainstream of American life. Few roads penetrated the area, and the people living in the remote hollows and narrow valleys had limited access to public schools and health care. Reformers from outside the region began to establish settlement schools in remote locations. Some of the earliest schools in the mountains were church-affiliated, but the settlement schools that began in the early twentieth century followed the principles of the urban settlement house movement. Although teachers included religious ideals in the curriculum, the settlement schools of eastern Kentucky were nondenominational and sought children of all religious faiths.

Although the primary function of the settlement schools in eastern Kentucky was to provide a quality education to mountain children, the settlement workers viewed their role as one of service to the community. Settlement schools assisted public authorities in providing services for rural schools; held teachers' and farmers' institutes, county fairs, and health clinics; and established community centers in tiny hamlets. Traveling nurses and doctors visited homes in isolated areas to deliver babies and gave medical assistance to the sick and disabled. Settlement workers also helped needy young students to attend institutions such as Berea College and the University of Kentucky.

Two outstanding examples of settlement schools patterned after the urban model were HINDMAN SETTLEMENT SCHOOL (1902) and PINE MOUNTAIN SCHOOL (1913). Katherine Pettit and May Stone founded the Hindman School in Knott County; when it was well established, Pettit, assisted by Ethel de Long, a teacher and graduate of Smith College, opened the Pine Mountain sister institution in a remote location in Harlan County. Other schools that followed the urban example included Caney Creek School (1916) in Knott County, founded by Alice LLOYD of Boston; Redbird Mission School (1921) and HENDERSON SETTLEMENT SCHOOL (1925), both in Bell County; the Letcher County institutions Stuart Robinson School (1913) and Kingdom Come School (1924); and LOTTS CREEK COMMUNITY SCHOOL (1933) in Knott County.

By the 1920s and 1930s the early functions of these institutions began to decline with the arrival of better roads, public schools, and public health services. Financial pressures made it difficult for the private settlement schools to continue to operate. Over time, some of the schools became part of the public school systems, while others remained open to students. In 1990 the two most notable examples of the urban settlement school were still operating: Hindman School, serving children with learning disabilities, and Pine Mountain School, an environmental center. Caney Creek School, renamed ALICE LLOYD COLLEGE, is now a private, four-year college.

See David Whisant, *All that is Native and Fine* (Chapel Hill, N.C., 1983); Nancy K. Forderhase, "Eve Returns to the Garden: Women Reformers in Appalachian Kentucky in the Early Twentieth Century," *Register* 85 (Summer 1987): 337-61.

NANCY FORDERHASE

SETTLES, MARY (CARMICHAEL). Mary (Carmichael) Settles, the last survivor of the Pleasant Hill Shakers, was born to Daniel and Mary Ann (McKing) Carmichael on October 31, 1835, in Louisville. She attended public school there. In 1854 she married Franklin Settles and in 1858 was widowed, left with a three-year-old son, Edward C., and a one-year-old daughter, Fannie. She moved to Pleasant Hill with her children on January 31, 1859, and joined the United Society of Believers in Christ's Second Appearance. Mary Settles lived in the Center Family House and worked in the community as a schoolteacher and later as secretary of the society. On September 18, 1910, Settles and the other eleven surviving Shaker members deeded Pleasant Hill to George Bohon, who agreed to care for them until the end of their lives. Settles, the last Pleasant Hill Shaker, died in the Center Family House on March 29, 1923. She was buried in the cemetery at Pleasant Hill.

See Ella Hutchison Ellwanger, "Shakertown, Its Present and Its Past," *Register* 17 (Sept. 1919): 31-43; Thomas D. Clark and F. Gerald Ham, *Pleasant Hill and Its Shakers* (Pleasant Hill, Ky., 1968).

SHAKERAG. Shakerag is a residential area west of Hanson and northeast of Madisonville in Hopkins County, Kentucky, at the convergence of Shakerag Road, Tucker's Schoolhouse Road, and Fridy Schoolhouse Road. The name Shakerag may have originated with settlers from Shakerag, North Carolina. In early times Shakerag residents were a rough lot, but by the 1990s north-central Hopkins Countians clamored for their properties to be included in definitions of the neighborhood, which is characterized by large houses. Native Shakerag residents delineate Shakerag as a restricted area surrounded by other neighborhoods such as Tuckers, Olive Branch Church, Wolf Hollow, and Buntin. Newer residents expand Shakerag to include all areas the others see as separate neighborhoods, and most of north-central Hopkins County as well.

See J.T. Gooch, *The Story of Shakerag* (Madisonville, Ky., 1984).   J.T. GOOCH

SHAKER COMMUNITIES. The Shakers, or Society of Believers, lived in two communities in Kentucky: Pleasant Hill near Harrodsburg and South Union near Bowling Green, founded in 1806

and 1807, respectively, when Shakers "gathered" on lands belonging to local converts.

American Shakerism had originated with a group of eighteenth century English Quakers, religious dissidents whose ecstatic manner of worship earned them the name Shaking Quakers, or Shakers. Their leader, a charismatic woman named Ann Lee, claimed to be in personal contact with the Divine. Her visions and teachings became the fundamental doctrines of the Shaker faith. At the core of the Shaker faith was a belief in the possibility of direct communication between Christ and his followers. The revelations that Lee claimed to have received inspired the Shaker doctrines of celibacy, perfectibility, and communal living.

The doctrine of celibacy was closely related to the Shaker belief in human perfectibility. Rejecting Calvinist notions of predestination and election, the Believers maintained that the confession of sin and the adoption of celibacy would allow participation in "the resurrection of life." According to the Shakers, the Millennium had already begun with the infusion of the Holy Spirit in Lee and her followers. To many of them, Lee appeared to represent the second coming of Christ, this time in female form.

Persecuted in England for their commitment to celibacy and pacifism and their liberal approach to Biblical interpretation, Lee and her small band of followers emigrated to America in 1774. By the 1830s the Shakers were flourishing in nineteen communities ranging from New England and New York to Ohio, Indiana, and Kentucky.

Like the early Christians, the Believers saw common ownership of property, shared labor, and common worship as the purest expression of their faith. Set apart from the world, Shaker communities were efforts to live the "resurrected" life here on earth. Each family in the community consisted of fifty to one hundred and fifty men and women who lived together as brothers and sisters. Most of the nineteen societies in the United States were each made up of three or more families, which functioned relatively independently, much like a congregation. Each family had its own dwelling, workshops, barns, handicrafts, and industries.

Leadership of the family was entrusted to two elders and two eldresses, spiritual parents who guided and disciplined the younger members in the performance of shared obligations. These spiritual counsellors were assisted by family deacons and deaconesses, who managed the temporal activities of Believers, such as assigning Sisters and Brothers to their occupations and directing work in the various shops and industries. The economic affairs of each community were in the care of village trustees, who carried on commerce with the "world's people," and received all visitors and travelers. A central ministry watched over the affairs of the entire society, consulting as necessary with the elders and eldresses of the separate families and ensuring consistency in their policies and practices. The Millenial Laws, drawn up by the central ministry at Mount Lebanon, New York, codified the Shaker way of life in minute detail and resulted in a remarkable degree of uniformity in societies separated by long distances.

Visitors to Shaker communities were impressed by their orderliness, serenity, and simplicity. A typical Shaker day began early, at four o'clock on summer mornings and five in the winter. After kneeling for a moment of silent prayer, the Brothers went about their morning chores while the Sisters moved through the dwelling closing windows, making beds, and putting the rooms in order. After the cows had been milked, the cattle fed, and the fires lit in the workshops, all assembled for breakfast, Brothers and Sisters sitting at separate tables. After a meal taken in monastic silence, Believers knelt again before departing for their labors.

As the Shakers returned to the tasks of the day, each member had his or her own lot, or calling. The Sisters prepared meals; did the washing, ironing, sewing, and weaving; tended to the poultry; and produced goods for sale, including cloth, canned fruits and vegetables, and medicinal herbs and seed packets. The Brethren worked about the farm, in the shops and mills. Strict rules and the watchful eye of community elders and eldresses enforced the separation of the sexes. Following the evening meal, the Shakers returned to their labors until they were called for evening worship, which often included dancing and singing. At the conclusion of such meetings, the family returned quietly to rest.

The main religious service began at one o'clock on Sunday afternoon, when all families in the village gathered at the meetinghouse. Marching in pairs, the Sisters behind the Brothers, they entered the church through separate doors. Once inside, the members were seated on long benches, with the two sexes facing each other. The presiding elder usually directed the worship service, which included singing and vigorous marching, dancing, and whirling. Occasionally, the worship service was opened to the public in the hope of converting new members. Rarely were such efforts successful, although it is recorded that many visitors witnessed these public displays of Shaker religious rituals.

As in early monastic communities, the work of the Believers was part of their worship, inseparable from their religious beliefs. The Shakers believed that God dwelt in the details of their work and the quality of their craftsmanship, and their devotion to excellence resulted in countless inventions and some of the greatest architecture in America. The Shakers won renown for their cloaks, oval boxes, and furniture. Shaker improvements in farming and industry were legion—from the introduction of new kinds of seeds to the invention of the common clothespin and circular saw.

A curve plotting the growth and decline of the Shakers would be almost symmetrical. The Society of Believers had about a thousand adherents in the year 1800. Fifty years later, in the decade before the Civil War, the Shakers reached their zenith with some 5,000 members. By the turn of the century, however, their ranks had dwindled to about a thousand again, as one society after another closed its doors, sold its lands. The causes of the decline of the Shakers are many. The waning of religious enthusiasm in the years after the Civil War, the growth of a more rational and scientific outlook among the general population, the industrial revolution, which made the artisan traditions of Shaker craftsmen obsolete—all contributed to the gradual extinction of the Shaker church.

Pleasant Hill. On January 1, 1805, Shaker missionaries Issachar Bates, Benjamin S. Youngs, and John Meacham left New York for Kentucky to spread the utopian doctrine of the United Society of Believers in Christ's Second Appearing. Pleasant Hill was founded in December 1806, when forty-four converts signed the first covenant on the land of Elisha Thomas, a Mercer County farmer. They called their settlement Shawnee Run, for a small tributary of the Kentucky River. The Shakers lived there until 1808, when they purchased adjoining lands on an attractive knoll, which they named Pleasant Hill.

The Thomas property was the location of the Shakers' early water-powered mills. A sawmill, gristmill, oil mill, and fulling mill made up the first industry that supplemented the economy of the Shakers, who were primarily farmers. The earliest buildings were log with stone underpinning and masonry chimneys. A stone meetinghouse was built in 1810 along the north road, supplanted in 1820 by a more commodious frame structure on the east-west road.

The Shakers on the Thomas property were known as the Mill family. The senior order at Pleasant Hill was composed of three families. Each Shaker family occupied a large dwellinghouse at the center of the village. East family was for the young, enterprising members. The Centre family, which occupied the massive forty-room stone structure built between 1824 and 1834, were the spiritually mature of the community. An 1821 brick dwelling housed the West family, the elderly brothers and sisters whose physical tasks were not demanding. The North Lot and West Lot "gathering" orders were for novices, who were instructed by older Believers.

The Pleasant Hill Shakers flourished in the first half of the nineteenth century. Blessed with fertile land and temperate climate, they proved to be the best farmers not only in Kentucky, but in all of the upper South, producing abundant crops of wheat, rye, corn, flax, tobacco, and hemp. Tobacco was grown and was smoked in clay pipes by Brothers and Sisters alike as early as 1811. Hemp was an important cash crop for the Shakers in the nineteenth century. Extensive fruit orchards and vegetable gardens, which made the Shakers virtually self-sufficient, bore ample fruit for sale to the "world's people." Experts in the art of preserving fruits and vegetables, the Pleasant Hill Shakers processed 55,115 jars of fruit in the period 1858-60, much of it for market. Located on the Kentucky River, a ma-

jor artery of the Ohio River, the Shakers were able to ship their goods as far away as New Orleans. They sent a variety of products to market, from garden seeds and brooms to bonnets, pincushions, willow baskets, and cloth. Herb, or "physic," gardens provided pure medicinal herbs, augmenting those gathered in the wild, for their own health needs and for sale to the "world."

Well-watered bluegrass pastures supported superior livestock development at Pleasant Hill. In 1811, together with the Shaker Union Village in Ohio, Pleasant Hill bought a purebred English shorthorn bull they named Shaker, which did much to improve the quality of livestock in Kentucky. By the 1830s livestock production had become a major source of income. In addition to beef cattle, the Pleasant Hill Shakers built a good herd of milking shorthorns, the source of the butter and cheese they shipped downriver, and they raised herds of hogs and sheep.

The name Shaker became the hallmark for quality across the land. Around 1830, the population of Pleasant Hill reached its zenith of five hundred, making the village the third largest of the nineteen Shaker communities in the United States. The only deficiency on the village's horizon was a scarcity of wood caused by harvesting the prime hardwoods used in the buildings and furnishings. The Believers at Pleasant Hill prospered on more than 4,000 acres of land, enclosed by forty miles of rock fence on the farmlands, and by picket and plank fences in the village. In the mid-nineteenth century, hundreds of agricultural and dependency buildings were part of the busy community. By 1860 all the major structures had been built. The more than 250 buildings included dwellings, barns, shops, a laundry, a tannery, a water pumping and supply station, and a gristmill. The meetinghouse, the Centre family dwelling, and the Trustee's Office stand as lasting memorials to the skill and ingenuity of the community's resident architect, Micajah BURNETT, and a host of Shaker builders. The Trustees' Office, an elaborate brick building with Federal-style details, was built as an outer court for housing visitors from the "world" and for visiting Shaker dignitaries.

The village at Pleasant Hill began to deteriorate in the two decades preceding the Civil War. The community received almost no dependable new adult members after 1845. Of the orphans adopted and educated in the Shaker faith, most left the society by the age of twenty-one. The onset of the Civil War hastened the decline of the Pleasant Hill Shakers. Their principal market, New Orleans, made accessible by floating flatboats down the Kentucky, Ohio, and Mississippi rivers, was blockaded. The bloodiest battle of the Civil War in Kentucky was fought in the town of Perryville, just seventeen miles away. The armies of both sides advanced and retreated through the village, and hungry soldiers camped on Pleasant Hill property. Thousands of meals were served daily, without charge, to Yankees and Rebels alike, and the Shakers were helpless as the armies appropriated their wagons and horses. Even after the war, guerrilla bands roamed the county, harassing and robbing the peaceful Shakers again.

Both village stores and Shaker morale were depleted by the events of the Civil War. Internal dissension and the inability of the society to attract and hold younger and more imaginative leaders contributed to the decline. An expensive endeavor to attract Swedish converts ended disappointingly. In 1878 the West family, followed shortly by the East, seceded from the church order, leaving the population at 168 members. By 1896 there were fewer than sixty Shakers left, most of them elderly. Village unity was disrupted by dissenting groups; poor business supervision brought unmanageable debt and the resulting sale of property.

By 1910 there were only a dozen Shakers left in the once thriving community. Col. George Bohon, a businessman from Harrodsburg, offered the remaining members perpetual care in exchange for the 1,800 acres of remaining property. The last Shaker to live at Pleasant Hill, Sister Mary Settles, a revered teacher of the community, died in 1923.

During the following years, many attempts were made to adapt or restore the site, which had become a sleepy agricultural community. In 1961 a not-for-profit private organization was formed to restore, protect, and interpret the rich heritage of the Pleasant Hill Shakers. Under the leadership of Earl D. WALLACE, the group raised money to purchase the lands and refurbish the buildings. James L. Cogar, first president of the Pleasant Hill organization, was engaged to create a concept for sensitive adaptation of the structures for modern use. In 1968 eight buildings at Shakertown opened to the public and Pleasant Hill once again became a destination for visitors.

Shakertown draws an average of 280,000 visitors a year to Pleasant Hill to experience the way that Shakers lived and worked. Artisans use Shaker tools and methods to demonstrate such crafts as weaving, broom-making, candle-dipping, and quilting. In addition to overnight accommodations, the community is the host to many conferences, including the SHAKERTOWN ROUNDTABLE. Thirty original buildings have been restored, on more than 2,700 acres of land. Shakertown is the largest restored Shaker village in the United States, a monument to the Believers who created for a short time a heaven on earth.

South Union. The Shaker Village at South Union, Kentucky, about twelve miles southwest of Bowling Green in Logan County, "gathered" in 1807.

The village of South Union was the smaller of the two Kentucky communities, with about 350 members at its peak in the 1840s and 1850s, when South Union's communal landholdings grew to about 6,000 acres. More than two hundred buildings were constructed during the village's 115-year history. The magnificent forty-room Georgian-style Centre family dwelling house served as the administrative center for the four communal Shaker fam-

ilies in the immediate area. Other structures included the meetinghouse, barns, shops, mills, and the Victorian-style Shaker Tavern, constructed in 1869. The tavern, located on the rail line that passed near South Union, served as a hotel and restaurant for the "world's people." The Shaker Tavern did a thriving business for more than 30 years.

Like the other Shaker communities, the Believers at South Union were versatile and exacting artisans. Their goods enjoyed a well-deserved reputation for excellence and were marketed across a wide territory. In addition to brooms and bonnets, the Shakers also sold garden seeds and award-winning preserves. From the sisters' looms came cheesecloth, wool, carpets, and chair tapes. Between 1825 and 1875 the society's row of mulberry trees produced silk for the kerchiefs and men's handkerchiefs that the women made. Goods brought by wagon to flatboats on the Barren River near Bowling Green made their way downriver to sites as far away as New Orleans. The South Union Shakers were also livestock breeders and by 1822 had purchased their first fine Durham bull, named Comet. Their merino sheep and Berkshire hogs were in great demand by neighboring farmers.

In other Shaker villages, blacks lived alongside whites in the various family houses, but at South Union the black family who were members lived separately, in a number of cabins at the west side of the community. Although complete equality between the races was a central tenet of the Shaker faith, the separate living quarters at South Union were probably deemed necessary in light of the pro-slavery views in the surrounding area.

Like the Shakers at Pleasant Hill, the South Union community was greatly affected by the events of the Civil War. They held onto their communal way of life until 1922, when the communal land, buildings, livestock, and farm equipment was sold. The few remaining members of the South Union community took up lives in mainstream America. Several of the original buildings have been restored by a nonprofit organization, Shakertown at South Union, devoted to the preservation and interpretation of this remarkable chapter in Kentucky history. Part of the property is owned by the Benedictine fathers.

See Thomas D. Clark and Gerald F. Ham, *Pleasant Hill and Its Shakers* (Pleasant Hill, Ky., 1968); Julia Neal, *The Kentucky Shakers* (Lexington, Ky., 1977); Edward Demming Andrews, *The People Called Shakers* (New York 1953).

SUSAN MATARESE AND JAMES C. THOMAS

SHAKERTOWN ROUNDTABLE. The Shakertown Roundtable is an annual conference to inform Kentucky's leaders, especially those in the business community, on issues of specific importance to Kentucky. Held at the Shakertown conference center in the restored SHAKER COMMUNITY at Pleasant Hill, it was organized by Earl D. Wallace and has been chaired since Wallace's death in 1990 by publisher Albert Smith. The Kentucky Center for Public Issues coordinates the yearly conferences.

SHALER, NATHANIEL SOUTHGATE. Nathaniel Southgate Shaler, geologist, was born on February 20, 1841, near Newport, Kentucky, to Nathaniel Burger Shaler, a Harvard-educated physician, and Ann Hinde (Southgate) Shaler. Shaler was educated, primarily by tutors, in the classics and mathematics. In 1858, he entered Harvard, where he studied botany and zoology under Louis Agassiz, the noted naturalist. In 1862 Shaler graduated from Harvard summa cum laude with a B.S. He was made captain of the 5th Kentucky Volunteer Battery, in which he served during 1862-64. In 1864 he returned to Harvard to teach and then spent two years in Europe. In 1868 he lectured on paleontology at Harvard.

In 1873 Shaler was appointed Kentucky state geologist and began work in late August. While he was most interested in scientific geology, political realities led him to focus upon economic geology. The reports of the KENTUCKY GEOLOGICAL SURVEY during Shaler's directorship emphasized coal, iron ore, lead, and petroleum. A sixfold increase in coal production occurred during his years with the survey. Shaler published several articles on the paleontological finds and the caves of Kentucky. He was succeeded as state geologist by John R. Procter in 1880. Shaler's history of the state, *Kentucky: A Pioneer Commonwealth*, written for the American Commonwealth Series, was published in 1884.

Shaler became a professor of geology at Harvard in 1884. His introductory geology became the most popular course at the university, and at one time Shaler was believed to have trained more geologists than all the other teachers in the country. At Harvard he was a pioneer in the concept of summer school, and in 1875-76 he directed the first summer school for geology at Cumberland Gap, in conjunction with the Kentucky Geological Survey. In 1891 Shaler became the dean of Harvard's Lawrence Scientific School, a position he held for the rest of his life. His professional work became focused on the Atlantic Coast for the U.S. Geological Survey.

Shaler was a writer not only of geological studies but also of material for a wider audience, ranging from essays and Elizabethan verse plays to works on natural history and transportation.

Shaler married Sophia Penn Page in 1862; they had two daughters. Shaler died on April 10, 1906, on Martha's Vineyard in Massachusetts.

See David N. Livingstone, *Nathaniel Southgate Shaler and the Culture of American Science* (Tuscaloosa, Ala., 1987).   IVAN L. ZABILKA

SHANKS FAMILY MASSACRE. In 1787 or 1788 a small party of Indians posing as settlers attacked the cabin of Catherine Shanks, a widow, and her family at Cooper's Run, four miles west of Paris in Bourbon County. (The family name is sometimes given as Scraggs, Skaggs, or Skeggs.) The widow, two daughters, and a son were killed on the night of the incident; one daughter was kidnaped. The eldest son and two daughters, one carrying a baby, escaped into the woods during the attack. An Indian was killed on the site. The cabin was burned to the ground, causing neighbors to investigate in the morning. A party of thirty men led by Col. John Edwards, one of Kentucky's first two U.S. senators, pursued the Indians. They killed one and wounded another, but not before the Indians had slain their captive.

SHARP, SOLOMON P. Solomon P. Sharp, a politician of tragic fate, was born in Virginia on August 22, 1787, and moved to Kentucky about 1800. He read law briefly, was admitted to the bar, and set up a practice in Russellville in 1806. He was elected to the state legislature from Warren County, 1809-11, was twice elected to Congress, where he served from March 4, 1813 to March 3, 1817, and then returned to the Kentucky legislature (1817-18). Sharp, a War of 1812 veteran, married Eliza T. Scott of Frankfort on December 17, 1818; the marriage produced three children. Gov. John Adair (1820-24) appointed Sharp attorney general in 1820, and he moved his family to Frankfort from Bowling Green. He resigned this post to win a Franklin County legislative seat for the New Court party in August 1825.

Sharp was stabbed to death at his Frankfort home by Jereboam O. BEAUCHAMP on November 7, 1825, after public allegations had been made about Beauchamp's wife. Beauchamp's actions were probably related in part to the hatreds generated by Kentucky's Old Court–New Court struggle. Stunned by the tragedy, the legislature moved on December 9 to create Sharp County from Muhlenberg but did not follow through on the proposal, probably because of the tumultuous politics of the 1825 session.

See J. Winston Coleman, Jr., *The Beauchamp-Sharp Tragedy* (Frankfort, Ky., 1950).

FRANK F. MATHIAS

SHAWNEE INDIANS. For the Shawnee Indians, Kentucky's broad valleys, lush meadows, and forested hills were an ideal home and hunting territory. Archaeological evidence indicates that the Algonquian-speaking ancestors of the Shawnee lived in Kentucky. Artifacts found at sites such as Hardin Village in Greenup County link the earlier Fort Ancient peoples with the Shawnee (see PREHISTORIC PEOPLES). The Hardin Village locale is said to have been a Shawnee village during the period from 1500 to 1675.

The Shawnee preferred village locations near the river banks, where the fertile soil yielded crops of corn, beans, and squash, and where the Shawnee had immediate access via the Ohio River and its tributaries to all the important trade and communication networks. Shawnee travelers could easily reach the Great Lakes, the Atlantic, or the gulf by following canoe routes and well-established trails. Game that came to the streams and to Kentucky's salt licks assured the Shawnee of food in abundance. Consequently, they were reluctant to abandon Kentucky in response to either seventeenth century Iroquois expansionism or eighteenth century European settlement.

A Shawnee town might have from forty to one hundred bark-covered houses similar in construction to Iroquois longhouses. Each village usually had a meeting house or council house, perhaps sixty to ninety feet long, where public deliberations took place. A child born into a Shawnee lodge automatically became a member of one of five patrilineal divisions: *calaka* (Chillicothe), *kispoko* (Kispokotha), *mekoce* (Mequachake), *pekowi* (Piqua; sometimes Pickaway), and *oawikila* (Hathawekela). Within Shawnee society, these groups assumed different responsibilities; traditionally, political leaders came from the Chillicothe and Hathawekela groups, ritual leaders from the Piqua, healers from the Mequachake, and war chiefs from Kispokotha. Often the members of such a division lived in a town named after their group.

Before the arrival of the Europeans, the Shawnee subsisted in an economy that combined farming, gathering, and hunting, but they soon became dependent on the fur trade as the flow of manufactured goods reached them after 1650. Driven from Kentucky in the 1670s, apparently by the Iroquois fur wars, the Shawnee began a migration to eastern Pennsylvania, western Pennsylvania, and back to Kentucky by the middle of the eighteenth century. Denied their claims to Kentucky both by the Iroquois in the 1768 Treaty of Fort Stanwix and by the Cherokee negotiations with North Carolina land speculators in the 1770s, the Shawnee nevertheless tried to stand their ground. In 1774 they began a struggle for survival in a frontier conflict known as LORD DUNMORE'S WAR.

The cabins rising south of the Ohio River foreshadowed the end of Shawnee residence in their beloved valley. Kentucky settlements denied access to hunting lands, cut off communication to the south, and raised the threat of settlers crossing the Ohio boundary. The Shawnee fought in Lord Dunmore's War to stop westward expansion; they were fighting for their lives and their livelihood. Only after they were twice abandoned by their British allies, once in 1783 at the Peace of Paris and again during the War of 1812, did the Shawnee discard their dreams of the Kentucky homeland. Soon almost all traces of Shawnee residence disappeared. In Kentucky today only Piqua in Robertson County and a few other place names commemorate the proud Shawnee peoples.

See Randolph C. Downes, *Council Fires on the Upper Ohio: A Narrative of Indian Affairs in the Upper Ohio Valley until 1795* (Pittsburgh 1968); James B. Griffin, *The Fort Ancient Aspect: Its Cultural and Chronological Position in Mississippi Valley Archaeology* (Ann Arbor, Mich., 1943).

JAMES H. O'DONNELL

SHELBY, ISAAC. Isaac Shelby, Kentucky's first governor, was born near Hagerstown, Maryland, on December 11, 1750, to Evan and Letitia (Cox) Shelby. The family moved to western Virginia in 1772. Young Shelby gained military experience in Lord Dunmore's War and the Revolutionary War. He emerged from the latter as one of the heroes of the Battle of King's Mountain, South Carolina, on October 7, 1780, when Great Britain's Maj. Patrick Ferguson was killed and his command was eliminated. In late 1783 Shelby and his bride, Susannah (Hart) Shelby, moved to his preemption holding near Knob Lick in Lincoln County, and his reputation made him a leader in Kentucky politics. He participated in several of the conventions that preceded Kentucky's statehood in 1792, and on May 17 of that year the state's electors unanimously chose him as the first governor. He served from June 4, 1792, to June 1, 1796.

After leaving office, Shelby spent sixteen years developing his properties and increasing his fortune. In 1812, as war with Great Britain became imminent, the public persuaded him to run for governor again. The electoral college had been discarded by then, and Shelby defeated Gabriel Slaughter easily, 29,285 to 11,936, on the strength of his military experience. He held office from August 24, 1812, to September 5, 1816. Shelby insisted that Gen. William Henry Harrison be given top command in the western theater, and he pushed for a statewide preparedness program. In 1813 Shelby raised 3,500 troops, double the number requested. With the permission of the General Assembly, he personally led the troops to join Harrison's army. The doughty sixty-two-year-old governor was active at the Battle of the Thames on October 5, 1813, when the British and the Indians were decisively defeated. After his second retirement, his last public service of consequence occurred in 1818, when he and Andrew Jackson negotiated with the Chickasaw Indians the purchase for Kentucky of the area west of the Tennessee River that became known as the Jackson Purchase.

In his first administration, Shelby provided sound, reliable leadership in the implementation of the new constitution. His role was much like that of George Washington on the national scene three years earlier. Shelby was a Jeffersonian Republican as that party emerged, and he sought federal assistance in curbing the Indians in the Northwest and in securing the vital use of the Mississippi River. His refusal to take action against pro-French groups upset the federal administration, but Shelby proved correct in his belief that the Genêt affair would collapse of its own accord when Genêt failed to win support for France in the United States. The economy proved stable, as adequate finances were found for a relatively passive government.

Shelby's second administration was dominated by the War of 1812, and he paid little attention to domestic concerns. The militia laws were revised in an effort to create a more effective organization, and women were urged to sew and knit for the cause. But the Kentuckians who fought in the Battle of New Orleans were poorly equipped. When Shelby left office, honored by most Kentuckians for his service, he returned once more to his farm,

Travelers Rest, south of Danville, where he died on July 18, 1826. He was buried in the family cemetery.

See Sylvia Wrobel and George Grider, *Isaac Shelby: Kentucky's First Governor and Hero of Three Wars* (Danville, Ky., 1974); Patricia Watlington, *The Partisan Spirit: Kentucky Politics, 1779-1792* (New York 1972).   LOWELL H. HARRISON

SHELBY, SUSANNAH (HART). Susannah (Hart) Shelby, wife of Kentucky's first governor, was born in Caswell County, North Carolina, on February 18, 1764, the daughter of Capt. Nathaniel Hart and Sarah (Simpson) Hart. She met Isaac Shelby at Fort Boonesborough, and they married there two years later, on April 19, 1783. The couple lived at Travelers Rest in Lincoln County, where they raised ten children. Susannah Shelby died June 19, 1833, and was buried at Travelers Rest beside her husband.

See Samuel M. Wilson, *Susan Hart Shelby: A Memoir* (Lexington, Ky., 1923).

FRANCES KELLER BARR

SHELBY COLLEGE. Shelby College was chartered by the Kentucky General Assembly on December 22, 1798, as the Shelbyville Academy, with a grant of 6,000 acres of land south of the Green River. In 1836 it was reorganized and rechartered, and the name was changed to Shelby College. It came under the auspices of the Protestant Episcopal Church in 1841, when the campus consisted of eighteen acres with a brick building and the president's home. The college had a preparatory department for ages ten to sixteen and a college that offered a liberal arts curriculum and military instruction. In the late 1840s and 1850s the college expanded to include an astronomical observatory and a scientific school for surveyors, civil engineers, astronomers, pharmacists, and physicians. Disputes over the use of a lottery to provide funding hurt the college, and it closed in 1868. Leaders of the institution included the Rev. R.B. Drane, William J. Waller, and A. Guentz.

See Edward D. Shinnick, *Some Old Time History of Shelbyville and Shelby County* (Frankfort, Ky., 1974).

SHELBY COUNTY. Shelby County, the twelfth in order of formation, is located in north-central Kentucky, bordered by Anderson, Franklin, Henry, Jefferson, Oldham, and Spencer counties. It has an area of 385 square miles. The county was formed from a portion of Jefferson County on June 23, 1792, and was named in honor of Kentucky's first governor, Isaac Shelby (1792-96, 1812-16). The county seat is SHELBYVILLE.

The topography of Shelby County is rolling and some sections are hilly. Corn, hemp, and wheat were the primary crops before the Civil War. Shelby County was a major hemp-growing county, producing 308,200 pounds in 1870. In 1870 the county produced 239,450 pounds of tobacco and 2,626 head of mules, many of which were sold elsewhere. Tobacco, corn, hay, beef, and dairy cattle are now the principal farm products. Shelby County is well known for its alfalfa hay, grown in deep, limestone-shale-embedded soil. Farms in 1987 occupied 91 percent of the land area, and 71 percent of farmland was in cultivation. In 1987 the county ranked fifth in the state in agricultural receipts, 60 percent of which were derived from livestock and poultry.

The first settlers arrived in the Shelby County area in 1779. Squire Boone founded Painted Stone Station, located between present-day Shelbyville and Eminence. Other early settlers were Alexander Bryan, John Buckles, and Richard Cates. Squire Boone's Station was abandoned in September 1781, because of Indian attacks. In October 1788, at Tyler's Station on Tick Creek, Bland Ballard and his family were killed by Indians. Among the early settlements were Shelbyville, Pleasureville, and Simpsonville.

From September 1862 to January 1865, several Civil War skirmishes were fought in Shelby County. On August 26, 1864, a band of Confederate guerrillas, commanded by Capt. David Martin, attacked Shelbyville.

Tourism expenditures in the county totaled $2.6 million in 1988, a 14 percent increase over the previous year. Attractions include the Old Stone Inn, once a stagecoach tavern near Simpsonville, Science Hill Inn, and Claudia Sanders Dinner House, established by Col. Harlan Sanders, creator of Kentucky Fried Chicken. Thousands each June attend the Shelby County Fair and Horse Show, whose gaited event is one of the largest in the state. Lake Shelby is a one-hundred-acre fishing lake, and fishing, water-skiing, and camping are available on the 325-acre Guist Creek Lake. The birthplace of Whitney M. Young, Jr., director of the National Urban League, is in Lincoln Ridge; it is listed on the National Register of Historic Places.

The majority of the county's industry is located in Shelbyville, where twenty-seven manufacturing firms employed 2,464 in 1990. Shelby County's largest employer is Leggett and Platt, manufacturers of swivel chairs, sofa beds, and reclining chair mechanisms in Simpsonville. Also located in Simpsonville is the F.B. Purnell Sausage Company. The Bagdad Roller Mills, which produce livestock feed, are located in Bagdad.

The population of Shelby County was 18,999 in 1970; 23,328 in 1980; and 24,824 in 1990.

See George L. Willis, *History of Shelby County, Kentucky* (Hartford, Ky., 1929); Edward D. Shinnick, *Some Old Time History of Shelbyville and Shelby County* (Frankfort, Ky., 1974).

RON D. BRYANT

SHELBYVILLE. Shelbyville has been the seat of Shelby County since William Shannon donated the land for the courthouse on December 20, 1792. The selection of the Shannon site ended an argument by those who favored Squire Boone's Station, on Clear Creek, as the county seat. Shelbyville, incorporated

February 21, 1846, was named in honor of Isaac Shelby (1792-96, 1812-16), Kentucky's first governor. In 1793 Shannon built the first Shelby County courthouse of logs at a cost of fifteen pounds. Succeeding courthouses were built in 1796, 1841, and 1847. The present courthouse, built in the classical Beaux-Arts style in 1912, is listed on the National Register of Historic Places.

Shelby College was founded in 1836 and became affiliated with the Episcopal church in 1841. There were three nineteenth century female schools: Kentucky Female College, Shelbyville Female College, and Science Hill Female Seminary, founded in 1825 by Julia A. Tevis, who was principal for forty-four years.

During the Civil War Shelbyville was the site of a skirmish on September 9, 1862, and of a guerrilla raid by Capt. David Martin on August 26, 1864, seeking a cache of weapons stored in the courthouse. Martin and his men were forced to retreat. A guerrilla leader, Ed Terrill, was killed in Shelbyville in 1864.

After the Civil War, Shelbyville became one of the most prosperous towns in Kentucky. By the mid-1870s, the town had eleven churches, colleges for men and women, two newspapers, four hotels, and more than sixty stores and shops, as well as a depot for the Louisville, Cincinnati & Lexington Railroad.

Shelbyville is now balanced between being a suburban and an industrial town. Located midway between Louisville and Frankfort and within a short distance of Lexington, Shelbyville is a commuter town. Twenty-seven manufacturing firms, each employing more than fifteen people, produced a variety of goods and services in Shelbyville in 1989. In 1990 Reynolds Aluminum Company moved its regional headquarters to Shelbyville. Another major employer is Lee-McClain Company, which produces men's clothing; its outlet store draws customers from the central Kentucky area. Tourist attractions include historic homes, the Kentucky Renaissance Festival held each May, and Wakefield-Scearce Galleries, housed in the Science Hill Seminary buildings, the state's largest collection of English antiques, Georgian silver, and porcelain. Science Hill Inn is a popular dining place that serves traditional Kentucky dishes.

Shelbyville has mainline service from CSX Transportation and Southern Railway System and is intersected by U.S. 60 and U.S. 420. It is three miles from I-64 via KY 53.

The population of the fourth-class city was 4,182 in 1970; 5,329 in 1980; and 6,238 in 1990.

RON D. BRYANT

SHELL, JOHN. John Shell, a resident of Leslie County, Kentucky, attracted many visitors during public appearances in 1919, when he was said to be 131 years old, having been born in 1788. The press dubbed him "The Oldest Man in the World." In the time of readjustment following World War I, Shell came to symbolize the continuity of the nation and the endurance of traditional values such as hard work and self-reliance. He was also a curiosity: an old man newly acquainted with automobiles, trains, and indoor plumbing, whose youngest child was only four years old, who could still bag a squirrel with a rifle. While in Lexington, he made his first speech (to the Board of Trade) and in Louisville flew over the city in a plane piloted by a World War I ace.

Despite debunkers, Shell became a Kentucky legend. Behind the legend stands a man who, lacking written records, lost track of his birthday and gradually stretched his age. Census and tax records suggest 1822 as a likely true birth year. Shell was born on the Hiwassee River in Tennessee, the son of Samuel and Mary Ann (Frye) Shell. The family moved to Kentucky around 1830, settling on Poor Fork in Harlan County. As an adult, Shell moved to Greasy Creek in Clay (now Leslie) County where he became a farmer, storekeeper, and blacksmith. He married twice: in youth, Elizabeth Nantz, by whom he had eleven children; and in old age, Betty Chappell, by whom he had a son born in 1915. He died at his home on July 5, 1922, reportedly of injuries incurred while breaking a horse.

See Sadie Stidham, *Pioneer Families of Leslie County* (Berea, Ky., 1986).

JAMES S. GREENE III

SHEPHERD, ROBERT J. Robert Shepherd, educator and scientist, was born on June 5, 1930, in Clinton, Oklahoma, to Lee and Ruby (Gilleland) Shepherd and received his primary and secondary schooling in Clinton schools. After high school he served two years in the army, including fifteen months in Korea and Japan. Upon his discharge Shepherd entered Oklahoma State University, receiving his B.S. in 1954 and M.S. in 1955. From 1955 to 1956, Shepherd, a Fulbright scholar, worked in the laboratory of Scottish botanist Kenneth Smith in Cambridge, England. Shepherd received a Ph.D. in 1958 from the University of Wisconsin in Madison, and served as an assistant professor of plant pathology at the university from 1959 to 1961. From Wisconsin Shepherd went to the University of California at Davis, where he remained for twenty-three years. In 1984 he became professor of plant pathology at the University of Kentucky's Tobacco and Health Institute.

In 1988 Shepherd was elected to the National Academy of Sciences; he is the first member from Kentucky. He was honored for his ongoing work with a group of approximately twelve viruses unique to plants, particularly the cauliflower mosaic virus, figwort mosaic virus, and peanut chlorotic streak virus. Shepherd's group tries to enhance plants' ability to resist a spectrum of viral infections by applying chemicals to plant surfaces. Some of the viruses may also be used to model gene expression in higher plants. DAVID COHEN

SHEPHERDSVILLE. Shepherdsville, the seat of Bullitt County in west-central Kentucky, is located eighteen miles south of Louisville at the intersection of KY 44 and KY 61, just west of I-65. It was established on December 11, 1793. The town was laid out on fifty acres of land on the north bank of the Salt River set aside by Adam Shepherd, for whom the town was named.

Shepherdsville became the seat of the county's government when Bullitt County was formed in 1797. The first meeting of the court was held in the home of Benjamin Summers. In the census of 1800, the town was the eighteenth largest in Kentucky, with a population of ninety-six. Six years later, the first post office was opened with Thomas T. Grayson as postmaster. John W. Beckwith started construction of a combination gristmill and iron forge at the city in 1819. Power for the mill and forge came from a dam built across Salt River. The forge in 1837 became the Shepherdsville Iron Manufacturing Company.

Paroquet Springs, a popular mineral water spa, was opened in 1837 by John D. Colmesnil. Except for an interruption during the Civil War, the combination health and vacation spot operated until 1879, when the large hotel burned. The water continued to be sold and used until the 1920s.

Shepherdsville became a stop on the Louisville & Nashville Railroad (now CSX Transportation) when the railroad was constructed in 1855. On September 28, 1862, Confederate forces occupied Shepherdsville and destroyed the railroad bridge that spanned Salt River. Federal forces retook the town on October 2, 1862.

One of the worst rail disasters in Louisville & Nashville Railroad history occurred on December 20, 1917, in Shepherdsville. The Cincinnati-New Orleans Flyer, No. 7, had been due to leave Louisville, headed south, at 3:00 p.m., but was delayed until 4:53 p.m. The engineer was instructed to make up twenty-three minutes between Louisville and Bowling Green. On the same track was the Bardstown Accommodation, No. 41, a local filled with Christmas shoppers that had left Louisville at 4:35 p.m., stopping on schedule at the smaller stations and flag stops. In 1917 the main line was double-tracked to Shepherdsville, with sidings for all the scheduled stops. Through trains had priority, and locals were to remain on the sidings as through trains passed. The Flyer had a green light when it passed Brooks station, about five miles from Shepherdsville. The No. 41 engineer, who had just stopped at Shepherdsville, pulled past the siding, intending to back into it. Before No. 41 could do so, the fast train plowed into the rear of No. 41, splintering the wood coaches. Fifty-one people died and forty-eight were injured in the wreck.

Construction of the Kentucky Turnpike (now I-65) from Louisville to Elizabethtown during the 1950s gave Shepherdsville access to a modern highway and opened the way for a new period of growth and prosperity. Inclusion of the turnpike in the federal highway system ensured the city's growth. Fast-food restaurants and shopping centers grew near the interstate exchange and the city's business

district extended from KY 61 west to I-65. During the 1970s many Louisvillians relocated to Shepherdsville and commuted to work in Jefferson County.

The town is subject to frequent flooding by the Salt River. During the 1937 flood, every business in town experienced some damage.

The city's largest employers are Publishers Printing Company; Interlake, which manufactures conveyors; and Monarch Hardware Manufacturing Company, which makes door and exit hardware. The population of the fourth-class city was 2,769 in 1970; 4,454 in 1980; and 4,805 in 1990.

TOM PACK

SHERBURNE, JAMES ROBERT. James Robert Sherburne, novelist, was born on May 22, 1925, in East Lansing, Michigan, to Thomas L. and Ida May (Mead) Sherburne. His father was in the armed forces and Sherburne lived in many places as a child. In 1941 his family moved to Lexington, Kentucky. From 1943 to 1946, Sherburne served in the U.S. Navy in the Pacific Command. In 1947 he received his A.B. in English from the University of Kentucky. Sherburne worked at several Chicago advertising agencies as a copywriter and creative director until 1970. After the acceptance for publication of his first novel, *Hacey Miller* (1970), Sherburne moved to Kentucky and made his home near Midway in Woodford County. *Hacey Miller* and his second novel, *The Way to Fort Pillow* (1972), are set primarily in Kentucky. Sherburne's writings are known for their historical accounts and action-packed adventures. His novels are: *Stand Like Men* (1973), *Rivers Run Together* (1974), *Death's Pale Horse: A Novel of Murder in Saratoga in the 1880s* (1980), *Death's Gray Angel* (1981), *Death's Clenched Fist* (1982), *Poor Boy and a Long Way From Home* (1984), *Death's White City* (1988), and *Death's Bright Arrow* (1989).

Sherburne married Nancy Garner of Des Moines, Iowa, on April 19, 1952. They have four children. The Sherburnes moved to Lawrenceburg, Kentucky, in May 1988, and both are active in the Kentucky Arts Council as artists in residence.

SHERLEY, JOSEPH SWAGER. Lawyer and U.S. congressman Joseph Swager Sherley was born in Louisville on November 28, 1871, to Thomas Huffman and Ella (Swager) Sherley. A graduate of Male High School in 1889 and the University of Virginia Law School in 1891, Sherley practiced law in Louisville until 1903, first with the firm of Judge L.H. Noble, then with O'Neal and O'Neal.

Sherley was elected to the U.S. House of Representatives from Kentucky's 5th District, including Jefferson County (March 4, 1903, to March 3, 1919). He was a member of the Appropriations Committee and advisor to President Woodrow Wilson. Offered a judgeship in the U.S. Court of Appeals, Sherley declined and instead served as director of the Division of Finance of the U.S. Railroad Administration (1919-20). He then formed a

Washington, D.C., law firm with Frederick De Courcy Faust and Charles Frederick Wilson. As an adviser to President-elect Franklin D. Roosevelt, Sherley reorganized the government finance system, and he was appointed director of the Bureau of the Budget in 1941.

Sherley married Mignon Critten of Staten Island, on April 21, 1906; they had five children—Olive, Mignon, Swager, Thomas, and Marjorie. Sherley died on February 13, 1941, and was buried in Cave Hill Cemetery.   JANICE THERIOT

SHIPPINGPORT. Located on a manmade island at the Lower Falls of the Ohio River at Louisville, Shippingport is the site of the McAlpine Locks and Dam. Where once a town thrived, a grassy plain now surrounds a surge basin that serves as a fleeting area for the U.S. Army Corps of Engineers' repair fleet. Three Frenchmen and their Philadelphia backers selected the forty-five-acre site in 1803 as a deep harbor for their shipbuilding and mercantile ventures. Louis and Jean Antoine Tarascon and James Berthoud, the Marquis de Saint Pierre, having fled the French Revolution, settled first in Philadelphia, then in Pittsburgh. When their interest in building ocean-going vessels dictated a site below the Falls of the Ohio, the Tarascon brothers sent Berthoud ahead, first to reconnoiter and then to purchase the site; a French surveyor named Valcour laid out lots. Confident of a strategic location, the developers built a large wharf, shipyard, and a 1,200-foot rope-walk. Settlers, many of them French immigrants, started arriving in 1806.

In the decade 1810-20, the new town's population climbed to five hundred, and as many as thirty steamboats at a time docked at the wharf. The Salt River Turnpike (now Louisville's 18th Street) connected the salt works of Bullitt County with river transportation at Shippingport. In 1815 the Tarascon brothers began construction of a six-story commercial mill for flour, meal, and lumber. Nicholas Berthoud, Anthony and William Maquille, Fortunatus Cosby, and Thomas Prather served as directors when the mill opened for business in 1819. Considered a technological wonder because of its size, the beauty of its machinery, and its use of automated production lines, the great mill was nevertheless soon outstripped by steam-powered mills. The discovery of natural cement during the digging of the Louisville & Portland Canal (1828) pressed the mill into service; later it became the Louisville Cement Company.

Shippingport was doomed as a commercial effort by creation of the canal, which separated it from the Louisville shoreline, and by changing economic conditions and the disastrous flood of 1832. The once-elegant brick houses washed away with the floods, and residents moved to Louisville and Portland, a small town to its west. Cement making continued in the postbellum years but most production eventually moved across the river to Clark County, Indiana. In 1927 the Louisville Gas and Electric Company completed a large dam and hydroelectric plant on the Ohio River at Shippingport, which generates electricity near the site of the Tarascon Mill. During the 1950s a few residents, including fishermen and shanty boat dwellers, lived on the island, but with the widening of the canal in 1958 by the U.S. Army Corps of Engineers, the little that was left of the town was demolished.

See George H. Yater, *The Tarascon Mill: Shippingport's Great Mill Reconstructed in Words, Pictures and a Model* (Louisville 1981).

NATHALIE TAFT ANDREWS

SHIVELY. Shively is a suburb of Louisville, located in western Jefferson County near the intersection of U.S. 31W and I-264. Settlers of the area in the 1780s included Col. William Pope, Maj. Abner Field, and Christian and Jacob Shively. Christian Shively established a mill and tavern that by 1810 became the focal point for a growing community on the road from Louisville to the Salt River. This road became part of the Louisville and Nashville Turnpike and by 1831 regular stagecoach travel was available to residents of Shively. The stagecoaches were a favored means of travel until the arrival of the Elizabethtown & Paducah Railroad in the 1870s.

Beginning before the Civil War and continuing into the latter part of the nineteenth century, many German immigrants settled the farmland around Shively. They founded St. Helen's Catholic Church in 1897 and some residents referred to the community as St. Helens. When the post office was opened in 1902, the name Shively was adopted because a city in Lee County had been named St. Helens.

On May 20, 1938, Shively was incorporated as a sixth-class city and immediately annexed a section of Louisville that included eight distilleries with a property value of over $20 million. A rich tax base combined with a post-World War II building boom helped Shively become one of Kentucky's fastest growing cities in the 1950s. By the 1970s, most of the distilleries had moved away; the city government tried to recoup its tax base in 1984 by annexing nearby Pleasure Ridge Park. The attempt was unsuccessful, and echoes of the controversy persist in Shively politics.

The population of the third-class city was 19,223 in 1970; 16,645 in 1980; and 15,535 in 1990.

See L.A. Williams and Co., *History of the Ohio Falls Cities* (Cleveland 1882).

SHORT, CHARLES WILKINS. Charles Wilkins Short, botanist, was born to Peyton and Maria (Symmes) Short on October 6, 1793, in Woodford County, Kentucky. He attended the Joshua Fry School and Transylvania University, where he earned a bachelor's degree in 1811. In 1815 he obtained an M.D. degree from the University of Pennsylvania, where he cultivated what became a lifelong interest in botany through studies with the medical professor and botanist Benjamin Smith Barton. From 1817 until 1825 Short practiced medicine in Christian County, Kentucky, where he continued his botanical studies through the identification and collection of that region's flora. In 1825 he was called to Transylvania University as professor of materia medica and medical botany in the Medical Department. He served as dean of the faculty and co-founded the *Transylvania Journal of Medicine and the Associate Sciences*, where he published articles on botany. In 1838 he joined the faculty and later was the dean of the Louisville Medical Institute, which in 1846 became the Medical Department of the University of Louisville. He retired from teaching in 1849 and lived at his estate, Hayfield, outside Louisville.

Through publications, correspondence, and plant exchanges, Short promoted the study of botany, especially the flora of his native region. Botanists still refer to Short's catalogue of Kentucky flora, which appeared in the *Transylvania Journal* and the *Western Journal of Medicine and Surgery*, a publication of the Louisville Medical Institute. In 1840 the eminent American botanist Asa Gray dedicated the plant genus *Shortia* in his honor; Gray praised Short's "eminent services in North American botany," which were "well known and appreciated at home and abroad."

Short died on March 9, 1863, and was survived by his wife, Mary Henry Churchill, one son, and five daughters. He was buried at Louisville's Cave Hill Cemetery.

See Deborah Susan Skaggs, "Charles Wilkins Short: Kentucky Botanist and Physician, 1794-1863," M.A. thesis, University of Louisville, 1982.

DEBORAH SKAGGS

SHORTHORN CATTLE. The cattle of the earliest Kentucky pioneers had no element of Tidewater Virginia-English stock. Purebred stock arrived in 1785, when three of Matthew Patton's sons moved to Kentucky from the Potomac Valley, bringing with them a bull and several heifers from their father's herd. Later Matthew Patton himself moved with his herd, including the bull Mars and the cow Venus, to Clark County. The Patton stock was the first English-grade cattle to reach Kentucky. The body type was somewhat coarse and rangy.

The War of 1812 disrupted the importing of livestock from England to America. In 1817 Lewis Sanders and Henry Clay imported a Durham bull and ten cows, introducing into Kentucky a more refined type. Other imports of Durham stock, also known as shorthorns, arrived in several shipments between 1836 and 1875.

Among the other Kentucky shorthorn cattle breeders were Joel and Robert Wilmot Scott, Brutus Clay, James Haggin, Elisha Warfield, Robert Aitcheson Alexander, and Brother Rufus Bryant of Pleasant Hill. During the last three-quarters of the nineteenth century, the names of such Kentucky shorthorns as Mrs. Motte, Tecumseh, Lady Munday, Hetty Haggin, Prince Frederick, Duchess of Athol, Fair Maid of Frankfort, Stonehammer, and

Sally Jackson became familiar in somewhat the same way as those of racehorses. Many of the prize-winning shorthorns of the era enjoyed as much prestige as some of the governors—and perhaps contributed as much or more to the national recognition of the commonwealth. Into the early decades of the twentieth century, Kentucky shorthorn cattle were known as superior beef animals. In time the imported white-faced Herefords, Aberdeen Angus, and other beef types, as well as dairy breeds, supplanted the historic shorthorns. (See CATTLE INDUSTRY.)

See Lewis F. Allen, *History of the Short-Horn Cattle and Their Origin, Progress, and Present Condition* (Buffalo, N.Y., 1874).

THOMAS D. CLARK

SHRYOCK, GIDEON. Gideon Shryock, architect, was born in Lexington, Kentucky, on November 15, 1802, the eldest of three sons of Mathias and Mary Elizabeth (Gaugh) Shryock. The couple and her brother, Michael Gaugh, had moved to Lexington from Frederick County, Virginia, in the late 1780s. The two men were partners in the carpentry business.

Gideon Shryock received his primary education at Mr. Aldrige's Lancastrian School in Lexington and apprenticed as a builder under his father's guidance. In October 1823 he was apprenticed to architect William Strickland of Philadelphia, who had been a student of Benjamin Latrobe. After a year with Strickland, Shryock returned to Kentucky, the state's first native-born, professionally trained architect.

In 1824, just before Shryock's return, the Kentucky statehouse burned. In 1827, when the legislature had raised the funds for rebuilding, they chose Shryock's design, modeled on the temple of Minerva Polias at Priene. The building, completed in 1830, was the first Greek Revival statehouse in the United States. It is centered on the curved freestanding stair in a drum under the dome; the plaster is highly ornamental for that period in Kentucky.

The commission made a name for Shryock, who was the state's most prominent architect for the next ten years. After finishing the capitol he returned to Lexington to build Morrison Hall for Transylvania University, completed in 1833 after considerable delay. The portico of the building is based on the Greek Temple of Theseus. In 1832 Shryock returned to Frankfort to build the Franklin County courthouse, a Doric-style building topped by a drum-shaped cupola based on the choragic monument of Lysicrates. In early 1835, as the courthouse was being finished, local lawyer Orlando Brown hired Shryock to design a home for him. Based on a plan of a country house in England, this house, now a museum, is the only residence known to have been designed by Shryock.

In 1835 Shryock moved to the rapidly growing city of Louisville, where his design was chosen for the new Jefferson County courthouse. Shryock's most ambitious design, this project was the downfall of his career. After numerous early mishaps—including the shearing off of a large amount of faulty stone—and delays, he worked on the court house until 1842, when he quit in frustration. The building was finished by others just before the Civil War.

Shryock's last completed Greek Revival project was for the medical department of the University of Louisville, during 1837-38. Shryock did not recover from the courthouse debacle and died penniless on June 19, 1880. He was buried in Louisville's Cave Hill Cemetery.

Shryock married Elizabeth Pendleton Bacon on June 30, 1829; they had ten children—Althea, Mary, Lucy, William, Charles, James, Theodore, Elizabeth, Laura, and A. Lee.

See Clay Lancaster, *Vestiges of the Venerable City* (Lexington, Ky., 1978).

WILLIAM B. SCOTT, JR.

SILVERSMITHS. After the Revolutionary War, the silversmith's craft spread from New England in two waves: southward through Virginia and the Carolinas, then through the Cumberland Gap to Kentucky; and westward through Pennsylvania and Ohio, down the Ohio River to the Bluegrass. Spoons, ladles, and U-shaped spring-form sugar tongs were the primary forms of flatware produced in Kentucky during the Federal period (1785-1800). Handle shanks were narrow and tapered; the tips of handles, clipped at angles that resembled those of an eighteenth century coffin, were known as "coffin ends." The bowls of spoons were deep and elongated; those of ladles were deep and round. Bright-cut surface decoration was minimal. The primary silversmiths of Kentucky's Federal period were Samuel Ayres (Lexington), Alexander Frazer and his brother Robert (Paris), and Edward WEST (Lexington), who was also a gunsmith and inventor.

New silver forms appeared in Kentucky in the Empire period (1810-40)—tea sets en suite (matching teapot, sugar, and creamer on platform base with ball feet), beakers, spectacles, and pitchers. Flatware handle tips became more rounded and turned down. The right-angle flange on handle shanks appeared around 1820. By 1830 handles were spatula-shaped and known as fiddlebacks; coin silver forks appeared in Kentucky about 1830. After 1835 naturalistic motifs of flowers, leaves, wreaths, and trees appeared as surface decoration. The leading silversmiths of the Empire period were Asa BLANCHARD, Lexington; Antoine Dumesnil, Lexington; T.J. Shepard, Georgetown; Elias Ayers, Louisville; and the Louisville partnership of Lemon & Kendrick, forced into bankruptcy by the financial panic of 1838-42.

Naturalistic scenes and chinoiserie designs were combined with the curvilinear, pear-shaped bodies of ewers and pitchers in an exaggerated redefinition of mid-eighteenth century European Rococo style (1840-50). Flanged, fiddleback flatware handles remained in vogue into the 1870s; tongs retained the springform U-shape; beading appeared on beaker rims. The Lexington firms of Garner & Winchester and George W. Stewart produced many monumental racing trophies that combined naturalistic surface decoration with regional racing scenes.

European exhibitions inspired new designs on both the Continent and America's eastern seaboard between 1850 and 1870. Pitchers and ewers became elongated, mounted on pedestal feet. Straight architectural lines appeared in conjunction with earlier curvilinear shapes. Borders were molded, gadrooned, beaded, or edged with guilloche. Designs were given depth by the juxtaposition of opposing surface textures, such as flat chasing and a pebbled filler. Garner & Winchester, Hudson & Dolfinger (Louisville), and William Kendrick (recovered from bankruptcy) produced some of the major pieces of this era of Renaissance Revival.

The Civil War and mass production sounded the death knell of the individual silversmith in Kentucky. The pieces of Kentucky coin silver that are the heritage of the old families are an irresistible lure to today's collector, bearing witness to the skill and artistry of the silversmiths of the commonwealth.

See Marquis E. Boultinghouse, *The Silversmiths, Jewelers, Clock and Watch Makers of Kentucky, 1785-1900* (Chicago 1980).

MARQUIS BOULTINGHOUSE

SIMMONS, WILLIAM J. William J. Simmons, minister and educator, was born into slavery in Charleston, South Carolina, on June 29, 1849, to Edward and Esther Simmons. In September 1864 he joined the Union army and fought with the 41st U.S. Colored Troops. After the war, Simmons moved to Bordentown, New Jersey, where he lived until 1867. In 1868 Simmons began his education at Madison University in New York; in 1871 he transferred to Howard University in Washington, D.C., where he received his A.B. degree in 1873, and his A.M. degree (honorary) in 1881.

Simmons moved to Kentucky to become pastor of the First Baptist Church of Lexington in 1880. That year he replaced Elijah P. MARRS as president of the Kentucky Normal and Theological Institute, founded November 25, 1879. He remained in that position until the summer of 1890. The school offered both high school and college-level courses to blacks, and later added postgraduate classes in law, medicine, music, and theology. It became State University in 1885, and in 1918 it was renamed SIMMONS UNIVERSITY in his honor. Simmons organized many groups and presided over many conventions to help improve education. In 1882 he became the editor of the *American Baptist*, which he turned from a regional magazine into one with a national scope. In 1883 he organized the Baptist Woman's Educational Convention, and he was the first president of the American National Baptist Convention, held in St. Louis in 1886. In 1890 Simmons, along with C.H. PARRISH, founded the Eckstein Norton

Institute in Cane Spring, Kentucky, to train blacks as teachers.

Simmons married Josephine Silence in August of 1874; they had three children: Josephine, William, and Effie. Simmons died on October 30, 1890, and was buried in Eastern Cemetery in Louisville.

See William J. Simmons, *Men of Mark: Eminent, Progressive and Rising* (Cleveland 1887); George C. Wright, *Life Behind a Veil: Blacks in Louisville, Kentucky, 1865-1930* (Baton Rouge, La., 1985).

SIMMONS UNIVERSITY. In August 1865 the General Association of Colored Baptists of Kentucky voted to establish a college for blacks. After years of planning and fund raising, the Kentucky Normal and Theological Institute opened on November 25, 1879, at Seventh and Kentucky streets in Louisville.

William J. SIMMONS was president of the institute from 1880 to 1890. Under his leadership, the school developed preparatory (elementary), academic (secondary), and normal (teacher training) departments, as well as religious education programs. It also began offering professional training in nursing, medicine, and law. After a college department was created in 1882, the institute was renamed State University. By 1893, thirty students had graduated from the college department and 159 from the normal school. State University was the only Kentucky institution of higher learning established and controlled by blacks. Lacking public funds or support from white philanthropic organizations, it was constantly beset by financial problems.

In 1918 the Rev. Charles H. PARRISH, Sr., a State University graduate, was appointed its president. Parrish renamed the school in honor of William J. Simmons and worked diligently to revitalize the curriculum and improve facilities. Fund-raising campaigns in 1922 and 1925 were unsuccessful, and with the onset of the Great Depression, Simmons became insolvent. On August 31, 1930, the University of Louisville purchased Simmons University as the site of Louisville Municipal College for Negroes, which assumed some of the nontheological courses taught by Simmons. Simmons retained the use of one building and limited its offerings to religious education. In 1934 the University of Louisville exercised its option on the remaining property, and Simmons, as Simmons Bible College, moved to a location at Eighteenth and Dumesnil streets in Louisville, its present location.

See Lawrence H. Williams, *Black Higher Education in Kentucky 1897-1930: The History of Simmons University* (Lewiston, N.Y., 1987); George C. Wright, *Life Behind a Veil: Blacks in Louisville, Kentucky, 1865-1930* (Baton Rouge, La., 1985).

J. BLAINE HUDSON

SIMMS, PHIL. Phil Simms, football player, was born November 3, 1956, in Louisville. His parents were Barbara (McConnell) and William Simms, an employee of Brown and Williamson Tobacco Company. A good yet relatively unheralded quarterback at Louisville's Southern High School, Simms entered Morehead State University in 1975. In four seasons (1975-78), he established four Morehead passing records and was named Ohio Valley Conference offensive player of the year in 1977. Drafted into the National Football League in 1978, he was an immediate starter for the New York Giants. His career as a quarterback has been brilliant but marred by injury. In 1986 a mature, healthy Simms led the Giants to a National Conference Eastern Division title and to playoff victories culminating in a 39-20 win over the Denver Broncos in Super Bowl XXI. He established a Super Bowl and play-off record in a game in which he completed twenty-two of twenty-five passes, and he was named most valuable player in the Super Bowl. Simms and his wife, Diana, have three children: Christopher, Matthew, and Deidre.

See David Sloan, ed., *Pro Football Guide* (St. Louis 1988).   JAMES C. CLAYPOOL

SIMMS, WILLIAM ELLIOTT. William Elliott Simms, Confederate legislator, was born on January 2, 1822, near Cynthiana in Harrison County, Kentucky, to William Marmaduke and Julia (Shropshire) Simms. In 1828 his family moved to Bourbon County, where he and his brother, Edward, received their education in the county schools. After his father's death in 1844, Simms read law in the Lexington office of Judge Aaron K. Wooley. In 1845 he entered the law department of Transylvania University in Lexington, completing his studies with distinction in 1846. He was admitted to the bar that year and began his practice in Paris, Kentucky. In 1847, during the Mexican War, Simms recruited ninety-one men to form the 4th Company of the 3d Kentucky Regiment and became its captain. He served in Mexico under Gen. Winfield Scott.

In 1849 Simms was elected as a Democrat to the Kentucky House of Representatives, serving one term. In 1851 he returned to his law practice in Paris. In 1857 he began editing the *Kentucky State Flag*, a weekly Democratic newspaper published in Paris, using his position to help in the election of James B. Clay to the U.S. House of Representatives (1857-59). On March 4, 1859, Simms succeeded Clay, having defeated John Marshall HARLAN, 6,932 to 6,865. On December 25, 1860, he urged Kentucky to join the Confederacy if coercion was used in an attempt to keep it in the Union. After losing his seat in Congress to John J. CRITTENDEN, 8,272 to 5,706, Simms joined the Confederate forces as a temporary colonel on September 21, 1861. In November the provisional CONFEDERATE STATE GOVERNMENT of Kentucky selected him as one of three commissioners whose purpose was to gain admission to the Confederacy. On December 24, 1861, Simms was commissioned a lieutenant colonel of the 1st Battalion, Kentucky Cavalry, under the command of Gen. Humphrey Marshall. He resigned from the army on February 17, 1862, to represent Kentucky in the Senate of the Confederate States Congress in Richmond, Virginia, where he stayed until the end of the war.

As the Confederate armies began to disband, Simms moved briefly to Charlottesville, Virginia, then to Canada. He returned to Kentucky in January 1866, and spent the rest of his life as a farmer. On September 27, 1866, he married Lucy Ann Blythe. They lived on his estate, Mt. Airy, in Paris with their son and two daughters until his death there on June 25, 1898. Simms was buried in the Paris Cemetery.

SIMPSON, JOHN. John Simpson, lawyer, congressman, and soldier, was born in Virginia and moved to Lincoln County, Kentucky, at an early age. In 1794 he was one of the many men from Kentucky who fought under Gen. Anthony Wayne against the Shawnee at the Battle of Fallen Timbers in Ohio. Simpson represented Shelby County in the Kentucky House in 1806 and again between 1808 and 1811. He was elected Speaker of the House in 1810 and 1811 and then defeated Stephen Ormsby in the U.S. congressional election of 1812. Before he could take his place in Congress, the War of 1812 began and Simpson joined the 1st Rifle Regiment under the command of Col. John Allen. He participated in the Battle of RIVER RAISIN and was killed in the early stages of the second battle at Frenchtown, when the British troops under Gen. Henry Proctor counterattacked on January 22, 1813. His burial site is unknown. He was one of nine Kentuckians killed in the Battle of River Raisin who were honored in the names of Kentucky counties. Simpson County was formed in 1819. The town of Simpsonville, on the Midland Trail in Shelby County, is also named for this fallen hero.

SIMPSON COUNTY. Simpson County, the sixty-second in order of formation, is located in southern Kentucky along the Tennessee state line. It is bordered by Allen, Logan, and Warren counties and was created from sections of those counties on January 28, 1819. It has an area of 236 square miles. The county was named in honor of Capt. John Simpson, killed during the War of 1812 in the Battle of the River Raisin. The county seat is FRANKLIN, established in 1819. One of the earliest settlements was Bracken's Ford, eight miles northwest of Franklin, near salt deposits. Settlers in the late 1780s and 1790s found Native American artifacts throughout the region.

The topography of Simpson County is level to gently rolling. The major water sources are the Red River, the Licking Creek, and the West Fork of Drakes Creek. The level land and rich soil of the county produce large crops of tobacco, corn, and hay, as well as cattle and hogs.

Along the county's southern border with Tennessee is a jag in the otherwise straight line, for unknown reasons. One explanation for this surveying mystery credits the hospitality of a local landowner who persuaded the surveyors to allow his land to remain north of the border.

In its early years, Simpson County was known as a dueling ground. The farm of Sanford Duncan, near the state line, was the site of several "affairs of honor." Duncan built an inn where duelists gathered before meeting each other in battle. Among those who dueled in Simpson County was Sam Houston, who in September 1826 severely wounded his opponent, Gen. William White. Dueling in the county ended in 1827.

The Civil War bitterly divided the citizens, who sent young men to both the Confederate and Union armies. In 1862 Confederate Gen. Nathan Bedford Forrest fought a skirmish with federal troops there. In 1863 two trains on the Louisville & Nashville Railroad (now CSX Transportation) line through Simpson County were attacked by Confederate forces. The residents were subjected to looting and destruction of property by guerrillas. Among the more notorious of these was Marcellus Jerome CLARKE, a county native better known as "Sue Mundy." In 1865 Mundy was captured and imprisoned in Louisville, where he was eventually hanged for his guerrilla activities. Simpson County recovered slowly from the effects of the Civil War. Bands of marauders roamed the area until federal troops were called in to restore order.

For many years, Simpson County was recognized as one of the largest mule markets in the world. The superior stock of mules commanded high prices in most of the southern markets. In the early 1950s, Simpson County attempted to diversify its economy. With the completion of interstate highway I-65 in 1966, some industry located in the vicinity of Franklin, but the county remained primarily agricultural, 81 percent being farmland in 1987. In 1980, 56 percent of the employed labor force in the county had jobs in other counties.

The population of Simpson County was 13,054 in 1970; 14,673 in 1980; and 15,145 in 1990.

See J. Denning, *Brief History of Franklin and Simpson County, Kentucky* (Bowling Green, Ky., 1921); Margaret Beach, *Franklin and Simpson County, Kentucky, a Picture of Progress, 1819-1975* (Tompkinsville, Ky., 1976). RON D. BRYANT

SINGLETARY, OTIS ARNOLD, JR. Otis Arnold Singletary, Jr., historian and educator, was born October 31, 1921, in Gulfport, Mississippi, the son of Arnold and May Charlotte (Walker) Singletary. He was educated in the Gulfport public schools, at Millsaps College (B.A. 1947) in Jackson, Mississippi, and at Louisiana State University (M.A. 1949, Ph.D. 1954). He served as an officer in the U.S. Navy during both World War II and the Korean War.

In 1954 Singletary joined the history department of the University of Texas, where he taught and served in a number of administrative capacities. In 1961 he accepted the position of chancellor of the University of North Carolina at Greensboro. During 1964-65, on leave from the university, he directed the Job Corps of the federal government's Office of Economic Opportunity. The following year he resigned from the university to become vice-president of the American Council on Education. In 1968 he left this post to become vice-chancellor for academic affairs of the University of Texas system. In 1969 he became president of the UNIVERSITY OF KENTUCKY.

Singletary assumed his presidential responsibilities during the turmoil kindled by the Vietnam War. His entire tenure was beset by ruinous inflation in the national economy, crippling stringency in the education budget, and unsettling vicissitudes in state politics. Yet he was able, through vision, purpose, and personality, to achieve impressive gains in both the physical and financial resources and the academic quality of the university. He retired from the presidency in 1987.

He was married on June 6, 1944, to Gloria Walton; they have three children: Bonnie, Scot, and Kendall Ann.   CHARLES P. ROLAND

SISTERS OF CHARITY OF NAZARETH. In
December 1812 the community of the Sisters of Charity of Nazareth (SCN) was founded in Nelson County by Catherine Spalding, the first mother superior, and John B.M. David, a French émigrè priest and seminary professor who had arrived in America on March 25, 1792. David trained the first three members (Spalding, Teresa Carrico, and Elizabeth Wells), gave the group its name, and adapted for Kentucky conditions the rules of the Daughters of Charity in France. On June 1, 1813, Spalding was elected mother superior of the six-member group, who pronounced vows of poverty, chastity, and obedience on February 2, 1816. The principal works of the community were teaching, health care, and social service.

The sisters opened a one-room school for girls on St. Thomas farm in Nelson County on August 23, 1814, and five years later they were also caring for orphans, the poor, and the sick of newly formed parishes. In 1822 the motherhouse and the boarding school moved to a new site of 237 acres, three miles north of Bardstown. The Kentucky legislature incorporated the community on December 29, 1829, as the Nazareth Literary and Benevolent Institution. At Spalding's death on March 20, 1858, 145 Sisters of Charity were in service throughout Kentucky in thirteen schools, two orphanages, and St. Joseph Infirmary in Louisville.

During the Civil War thirty-seven Sisters of Charity of Nazareth served as nurses for both the Blue and the Gray in military hospitals in Kentucky. After the Civil War, colonies of sisters opened foundations in the mining districts of Ohio, the Deep South, Massachusetts, Maryland, and Virginia. The opening of St. Augustine School in Louisville (1871-1967) was followed by one hundred years of service in ten schools for black youth throughout the South.

Nazareth's second century opened in 1912 with nine hundred sisters. Its foundations then included three hospital schools of nursing—St. Mary and Elizabeth in Louisville (1915), St. Joseph in Lex-ington (1918), and St. Joseph Infirmary in Louisville (1919); a liberal arts college, Nazareth College, Louisville (1920); and the mental hospitals Mount St. Agnes (1913) and Our Lady of Peace (1951), both in Louisville. In 1947 the first six SCN volunteers for a mission in Mokama Junction, Patna District, India, included four Kentuckians.

In 1990 the Sisters of Charity of Nazareth were engaged in a variety of services in United States, India, Nepal, and Belize.

See Agnes Geraldine McGann, *SCNs Serving Since 1812* (Nazareth, Ky., 1985).

MARY MICHAEL CREAMER

SISTERS OF LORETTO. The Sisters of Loretto,
one of the first native American communities of religious women, was founded on the Kentucky frontier in 1812. One of the founders was Maryland-born Mary Rhodes, who had arrived in 1811 to visit relatives near St. Charles Mission Station on Hardin's Creek, near present-day Bardstown. She began teaching their children to read and write, and soon neighboring parents were asking her to instruct their children. A primitive school was organized in an abandoned log cabin, and two other women, Christian Stuart and Ann Havern, came to assist in the project. To help them form a community of religious women, the trio appealed to their pastor, Charles NERINCKX, a Belgian priest exiled by the French Revolution who had been working in the early Kentucky missions since 1805. Under his guidance they established the Sisters of Loretto at the Foot of the Cross on April 25, 1812. Twelve years later the three moved ten miles north to St. Stephen's farm, now Nerinx, Kentucky, where the first priest ordained in the United States, Stephen Badin, had made his headquarters. At the Loretto Motherhouse there, which has operated since 1824, more than 3,000 young women have been trained as Sisters of Loretto. They have established educational institutions and social works across the United States and in foreign countries.

In Kentucky more than forty schools were established by the order in the 1800s, west to Daviess County and east to Maysville, with clusters around the Motherhouse and Louisville. Many of these schools were short-lived, but others continued into the twentieth century. The most noted schools were Holy Mary's at Calvary, 1816-99; Gethsemani, 1818-48; Bethlehem Academy at St. John's, 1823-1958; Loretto Academy at Loretto, 1834-1918; Cedar Grove at Louisville, 1842-1925; and its successor, Loretto High School, 1925-73. These academies, according to old newspaper advertisements, taught a broad liberal arts curriculum, with emphasis on history, science, language, philosophy, religion, art, and music, plus plain and fancy sewing. The establishment of branch schools paralleled the westward movement of the American frontier. In 1823, shortly after the Missouri Compromise, the Sisters of Loretto opened a school in the southeast corner of Missouri. In 1847 they made a foundation in Kansas at Osage Mission. They advanced to

Santa Fe, New Mexico, in 1852, four years after the treaty of Hidalgo-Guadalupe. From there they pushed on to Colorado in 1864 and to Texas in 1879. Loretto schools were opened in California in 1866, in China in 1923, and in South America in 1953.

The Loretto Motherhouse today is not only an administrative headquarters and training center, but also serves as an ecumenical retreat and a licensed nursing home facility.

See Anna C. Minogue, *Loretto Annals of the Century* (New York 1912).   FLORENCE WOLFF

SKAGGS, RICKY. Ricky Skaggs, musician, the son of Hobert and Dorothy (Thompson) Skaggs, was born on July 18, 1954, in Cordell, Kentucky. He was a child star, performing country music with the family band at age six and appearing one year later on the "Flatt and Scruggs" radio program. When fifteen years old, Skaggs left high school and took his first professional job, playing mandolin with Ralph Stanley's Clinch Mountain Boys, then joined the Kentucky Gentlemen as a fiddler. In 1974 Skaggs moved to Lexington, where he played mandolin and fiddle for J.D. Crowe and the New South before forming his own band, Boone Creek, in 1975. From 1977 to 1980 Skaggs played in Emmylou Harris's Hot Band and wrote arrangements for the critically acclaimed album *Roses in the Snow*. In 1980 he began a solo career.

Skaggs's unique blend of bluegrass, country, jazz, and "new traditional" styles has been recognized by various awards from the Country Music Association, the Academy of Country Music, and the National Academy of Recording Arts and Sciences (Grammy Award). His albums include *Kentucky Thunder* (1989), *Love's Gonna Get Ya!* (1986), and *Don't Cheat in Our Hometown* (1984). On August 4, 1981, he married Sharon White; they have four children: Mandy, Andrew, Molly, and Lucas.

See Charles Wolfe, *Kentucky Country* (Lexington, Ky., 1982); Neil Rosenberg, *Bluegrass: A History* (Urbana, Ill., 1985).   RON PEN

SKAGGS'S TRACE. Skaggs's Trace was a hunters' trail leading from Flat Lick to the Dick's (now Dix) River in Lincoln County. It was named for Henry or Richard Skaggs, who hunted in Kentucky as early as 1769. Skaggs's Trace left the WARRIORS' PATH at Flat Lick in Knox County, crossed Stinking Creek, and headed northwest along the west branch of Turkey Creek, almost as U.S. 25E does today. It passed north of present-day Barbourville, westward along Poplar Branch of Richland Creek, then northward across several western branches of the Middle Fork. It crossed Robinson Creek, passed Raccoon Spring, and reached the Laurel River at Happy Hollow Branch. The old trace went through what is now the Levi Jackson State Park and followed the Little Laurel River northward, passing what is now London to the east. From the headwaters of the Little Laurel River, it went to the headwaters of Hazel Patch Creek, down the creek

to the Rockcastle River, down that river to Skeggs Creek, and up Skeggs Creek to the headwaters. From there it crossed over to the Little Negro Creek, a branch of Dick's River, and went down Dick's River to Crab Orchard and Stanford. This road was extended through Harrodsburg to Louisville by 1779. It is believed that more pioneer families used Skaggs's Trace than Boone's Trace when journeying to Kentucky.

See Robert L. Kincaid, *The Wilderness Road* (Middlesborough, Ky., 1966); Neal Hammon, "Early Roads into Kentucky," *Register* 68 (April 1970): 118-23.   NEAL O. HAMMON

SKILES, JAMES RUMSEY. James Rumsey Skiles, entrepreneur, was born in Virginia in 1800 to Jacob, a merchant, and Susan (Fraley) Skiles. The family moved to Warren County, Kentucky, where Skiles grew up. He attended Cumberland College in Nashville, read law with a Nashville attorney, and served as a representative from Warren County in the Kentucky legislature during 1825-28. Skiles and a number of other businessmen formed a company to improve the narrow, winding, snag-filled Green and Barren rivers to bring steamboats to south-central Kentucky. Skiles lobbied the state legislature for funds to erect locks and dams, which were completed in the early 1840s. To develop Bowling Green's potential as a commercial center, he urged area residents to macadamize the town's streets, improve county roads, and develop a public transportation system that would carry passengers and goods from the center of town to the wharf and warehouses on the river. The resulting "portage railroad" of horse-drawn carriages that traveled along wooden rails, built around 1832, may have been the state's first railroad. Skiles's heavy investments in these and other projects, including a mill, warehouse, and hotel, overextended his financial resources and taxed his health. He moved to Texas in the early 1850s.

Five of the children born to Skiles and his wife, the former Eliza Bell of Nashville, survived to adulthood—James Rumsey, George, William Russell, Charles, and Frances. Skiles died in 1886 near San Antonio.

See Helen B. Crocker, "Steamboats for Bowling Green: The River Politics of James Rumsey Skiles," *FCHQ* 46 (Jan. 1972): 9-24.

NANCY D. BAIRD

SLAUGHTER, GABRIEL. Gabriel Slaughter, Kentucky's governor during 1816-20, was the son of Robert and Susannah (Harrison) Slaughter. Born in Culpeper County, Virginia, on December 12, 1767, he received a sound education in local schools. He married a cousin, Sarah Slaughter, in 1786; they had two children before her death. In 1797 he married Sara Hord; they had three children. In 1811, after his second wife's death, he married a widow, Elizabeth (Thomson) Rodes.

After moving to Mercer County, Kentucky, in the early 1790s, Slaughter served in both the state

House of Representatives (1797-1800) and the Senate (1801-08). By 1803 he was a colonel in the militia. A Jeffersonian Republican, he was elected lieutenant governor in 1808. Four years later he ran for governor against a formidable opponent, former Gov. Isaac Shelby (1792-96), who was drawn into the race by the impending war with Great Britain. Slaughter refused to withdraw, and Shelby easily defeated him, 29,285 to 11,936. Slaughter regained his popularity by leading a regiment at the Battle of New Orleans, and in 1816 he was again elected lieutenant governor. Slaughter took the oath of office as governor on October 19, 1816, five days after Gov. George Madison's death. After leaving office on September 7, 1820, Slaughter lost an 1821 bid for the state Senate; he was elected to the state House in 1823. Upon completion of his term, he retired to his farm, where he was active as a Baptist lay preacher and as a trustee of Georgetown College in Scott County. Slaughter died on September 19, 1830, and was buried in the family cemetery in Mercer County.

During his administration, Slaughter was usually referred to as the "acting governor." He outraged many supporters when he replaced Secretary of State Charles S. Todd, Shelby's son-in-law, with the unpopular John Pope. A House attempt to elect a governor to replace Slaughter failed in 1817. A savagely fought legislative election, in which Slaughter and Pope were denounced as Federalists, resulted in a largely hostile General Assembly. The House passed a bill calling for the election of replacements for both the sitting governor and the lieutenant governor, but it died in the Senate. The legislature censured Slaughter and Pope for failing to require the proper security and oath of office for the state treasurer. Most of Slaughter's recommendations were ignored by the legislature, and his vetoes were often overridden.

The legislature's opposition was unfortunate in the case of Slaughter's proposal for a comprehensive system of public schools, including—unlike the plans of some of his successors—a means of financing. Over his vetoes, the legislature passed several acts that let individual schools use lotteries for their support. Slaughter also proposed reform of the penal system, creation of a state library, and increased aid for internal improvements. All were rejected. When the state was hit by the panic of 1819, Slaughter and the legislature clashed over various proposals to provide relief for debtors while protecting the rights of creditors, the beginning of a controversy that would dominate state politics in the coming decade. Slaughter adopted a strong states' rights platform and challenged the constitutionality of the Bank of the United States, as well as a Supreme Court decision that a state could not tax its branches. His stormy administration had few accomplishments.

See John Frederick Dorman, "Gabriel Slaughter, 1767-1830, Governor of Kentucky, 1816-1820," *FCHQ* 40 (Oct. 1966): 338-56; Lowell H. Harri-

son, ed., *Kentucky's Governors 1792-1985* (Lexington, Ky., 1985).   LOWELL H. HARRISON

SLAUGHTER, HENRY PROCTOR. Born in Louisville to Charles Henry and Sarah (Smith) Slaughter on September 17, 1875, Henry Proctor Slaughter was one of the leading black journalists of his day. After graduating as salutatorian of his class from Louisville Central High School, he accepted a journalistic apprenticeship with the *Louisville Champion*. Slaughter became associate editor of the *Lexington Standard* in 1894. He was appointed compositor at the U.S. Government Printing Office in Washington, D.C., in 1896 and occupied that position until 1937. Committed to education, Slaughter did not allow his responsibilities at the printing office to interfere with his learning. Although not a practicing attorney, he received a bachelor of law degree (1899) and a master of law (1900) from Howard University in Washington. Slaughter's collection of books and papers, mostly concerning the Civil War and slavery, went to Atlanta University in 1976. Although he lived outside Kentucky for most of his life, Slaughter remained in contact with his home state as a correspondent for Louisville's *Kentucky Standard*. He also served as secretary of the Kentucky Republican Club in Washington, D.C.

Slaughter married Ella Russell on April 27, 1904; she died on November 2, 1914. On November 24, 1925, he married Alma Level, whom he later divorced. Slaughter died in Washington, D.C., on February 14, 1958, and was cremated.

SLAVE NONIMPORTATION LAW. In 1833 a coalition of diverse elements of Kentucky's population—humanitarians, abolitionists, slaveowners, and others—was successful in pressuring the General Assembly to prohibit the importation of slaves into the commonwealth. Under the nonimportation legislation of 1933, only immigrants to Kentucky who swore within sixty days of their arrival their intention to become residents could bring slaves into Kentucky. All others who purchased, sold, or hired illegally imported slaves were subject to heavy fines.

The 1833 law proved to be virtually unenforceable and its effect is difficult to assess. The percentage of blacks in the population declined thereafter, but maturing economic forces and the exportation of slaves to the Southwest may have been more important factors. Furthermore, interpretations that the 1833 law was evidence of an increasing determination of Kentuckians to end slavery were overly optimistic. The anticipated constitutional convention that was to provide for gradual emancipation never materialized, and opponents of the 1833 law soon weakened its force by allowing newcomers to Kentucky to avoid fines by pleading ignorance of the law. Meanwhile, the threatened clash between the North and the South over slavery so strengthened opponents of the 1833 law that they achieved its repeal, including exculpation of all who had violated the measure, in 1849. In the 1850s Kentucky increasingly became a clearinghouse for the sale of slaves southward.

See Lowell H. Harrison, *The Antislavery Movement in Kentucky* (Lexington, Ky., 1978); J. Winston Coleman, Jr., *Slavery Times in Kentucky* (Chapel Hill, N.C., 1940).   MARION B. LUCAS

SLAVERY. In the 1750s and 1760s, black slaves accompanied white explorers into what is now Kentucky, and by 1775 slaves were among the permanent residents of Kentucky. Slavery eventually grew into an important institution in Kentucky, although in comparison with the states of the lower South, Kentucky's slaves made up only a small proportion of the state's total population. From 1790 to 1860 Kentucky's slave population at no time exceeded 24 percent of the total population—less than half the comparable figure for the lower South—and the percentage declined after 1830. Slaves were most numerous in the Bluegrass region of north-central Kentucky, where they made up 40.3 percent of the population in 1850. Significant numbers of slaves were also found in southwestern Kentucky, along the Tennessee border and in some counties on the Ohio River. In the mountain counties of eastern Kentucky, slaves accounted for only 5.6 percent of the population in 1850, the smallest figure in the southern Appalachian region.

Kentucky slaves were primarily agricultural workers. In the nineteenth century the Bluegrass region developed a diversified economy based on the production of hemp, grains, livestock, and small manufactures. Of these, hemp cultivation made the greatest use of slave labor. Slaves also worked in the tobacco fields of southwestern Kentucky. Because the total demand for labor was greater on tobacco farms than on hemp farms, farmers in southwestern Kentucky were more likely to view slavery as an economic necessity than farmers of the Bluegrass, who often complained that their region had an oversupply of slaves. Neither hemp nor tobacco, however, was as labor-intensive as cotton, sugar, and rice, the staple crops of the lower South, where farms averaged 11.7 slaves in 1850; the comparable figure for Kentucky farms was 5.5 slaves. Most white Kentuckians were not slaveholders; in 1850 only 23 percent of Kentucky's white males owned slaves. Slaves were also used in several mining and manufacturing operations in Kentucky. Slave laborers mined iron, saltpeter, and coal, they processed salt, and they manufactured iron products, cotton textiles, paper, and hemp bagging and rope.

For most Kentucky blacks, slave labor meant a lifetime of racial oppression, dawn-to-dusk work, monotonous food, inadequate clothing, primitive housing, and harsh punishments. Nevertheless, both white and black Kentuckians voiced the opinion that the labor of slaves was easier in Kentucky than in the states of the lower South. Because most Kentucky farms grew a variety of crops rather than a single cash crop, the growing season was spread throughout the year, thus making harvest-time labor less grueling. On the other hand, the long growing season also meant that Kentucky slaves worked throughout the year, with few slack periods.

Recent historical research has demonstrated that American slave families were remarkably stable, given the many pressures that worked against them. Although Kentucky slaves worked hard to maintain strong families, the families may have been less stable in Kentucky than in the states of the lower South. Because of the small size of Kentucky farms, a Kentucky slave often had to look outside the home farm to find a spouse. Dual ownership of a slave couple made it more likely that the family would be split up by actions of the owners. In comparison with the states of the lower South, Kentucky sent large numbers of slaves out of the state through sale and migration, exporting as much as 16 percent of its slave population from 1850 to 1860. The stability of Kentucky slave families suffered also from miscegenation and the sexual abuse of slave women by whites. Some historical studies suggest that miscegenation occurred more frequently on small farms in border states like Kentucky, where whites and blacks lived closer to one another than on the large plantations of the lower South.

Like slaves in other states, Kentucky bondsmen tried to improve their living conditions through acts of resistance, which might take the form of petty vandalism, stealing, work slowdowns, or lying. Occasionally, Kentucky slaves killed masters and overseers. Because of the proximity of Kentucky to the free states, Kentucky had a larger number of fugitive slaves than the states of the lower South. Among the most famous of Kentucky's fugitive slaves were Henry Bibb, Lewis Clarke, Lewis Hayden, and Josiah Henson. A mass slave escape occurred in August 1848, when fifty-five to seventy-five armed slaves from several Bluegrass counties tried to escape across the Ohio River to freedom. After several days and a gun battle between slaves and the state militia, most of the slaves were recaptured. This little-known episode was one of the largest slave escapes in American history.

Virtually every variety of pro-slavery and antislavery thought existed in Kentucky. Until the 1850s most white Kentuckians thought of slavery as a necessary economic and social evil, to be tolerated because no satisfactory plan of emancipation existed. For most Kentuckians, this served as a rationalization for doing nothing about the problem of slavery. Even so, Kentucky had the largest and most enduring antislavery movement among the slave states. In the 1790s reformers tried to drive slaveholders out of churches and to abolish slavery in Kentucky's first two state constitutions (1792 and 1799). A notable leader in both of these movements was David RICE, a Presbyterian minister who wrote the influential pamphlet *Slavery Inconsistent with*

Justice and Good Policy (1792). Baptist ministers David BARROW and Carter Tarrant helped form an antislavery religious association, the Baptized Licking-Locust Association, Friends of Humanity, in 1807. The next year, members of the Friends of Humanity helped form the Kentucky Abolition Society. In 1822-23 this society published the *Abolition Intelligencer and Missionary Magazine*, edited by John Finley Crowe; at that time the only other full-time antislavery periodical in the United States was the *Genius of Universal Emancipation*, published in Greeneville, Tennessee, by Benjamin Lundy.

From the late 1820s to the late 1840s, opposition to slavery grew. Most opponents of slavery during this period were conservative emancipationists who favored plans of gradual emancipation and the colonization of freed slaves in Africa. The rise of conservative antislavery was reflected in the formation of the KENTUCKY COLONIZATION SOCIETY in 1829. Leaders of the conservative emancipationists included Robert Jefferson BRECKINRIDGE, John Clarke YOUNG, Joseph Rogers UNDERWOOD, James Madison Pendleton, Samuel Smith NICHOLAS, and Henry CLAY. The most outspoken of the conservatives was Cassius Marcellus CLAY, whose efforts to establish an antislavery newspaper, the TRUE AMERICAN, in Lexington were suppressed by mob action in 1845. From 1847 to 1849, however, emancipationists successfully published an antislavery newspaper, the *Louisville Examiner*.

Given the diversity of opinion in Kentucky concerning slavery, political conflicts were inevitable. One of the most controversial issues was whether the state legislature should limit the commercial importation of slaves into Kentucky. Supporters of such a ban argued that nonimportation would retard the growth of slavery, increase the monetary value of existing slaves, and keep out of the state those rebellious slaves often sold to slave traders. The Kentucky General Assembly took several actions to limit slave importation, most notably in laws of 1815 and 1833. Eleven of the fifteen slave states passed nonimportation laws, but Kentucky's laws were especially notable for their longevity and strictness. The Nonimportation Act of 1833, usually known as the Law of 1833, not only banned commercial importation of slaves, but also prohibited Kentucky citizens from importing slaves for their own personal use. No other southern state enacted such a restriction on slave importation. This restriction immediately created controversy in the state. Many slaveholders, especially those living in southwestern Kentucky along the Tennessee border, bitterly resented a law that restricted their access to cheap slave labor. The Law of 1833 was widely violated, and proposals to repeal it were debated in every session of the General Assembly from 1834 to 1849. It was finally repealed in 1849, when proslavery forces gained strength in writing Kentucky's third constitution.

The second major political question was whether Kentucky should amend its state constitution to outlaw slavery. The abolition of slavery was debated at Kentucky's first constitutional convention in 1792, and slavery was the principal issue in the campaign for delegates to Kentucky's second constitutional convention in 1799. Because of the prominence of the slavery issue in these early constitutional debates, constitutional reform became associated with abolition, and before the 1840s many Kentuckians opposed any movement to reform the state constitution for fear that such an effort would result in emancipation. In 1838 an effort to call a constitutional convention was defeated in a referendum by a three-to-one margin, largely because of the voters' fear of emancipation.

In the 1840s attitudes toward constitutional reform began to change as many Kentuckians became concerned about certain undemocratic features of the second constitution and as pro-slavery forces became confident they could control a constitutional convention. The voters of the state approved the calling of a constitutional convention to be held in 1849. In the campaign for election of delegates to the convention, slavery became the principal issue of debate. Pro-slavery forces organized themselves at a meeting of the Friends of Constitutional Reform in February 1849; antislavery forces organized at the Frankfort Emancipation Convention in April 1849. In the election, antislavery forces suffered a disastrous loss, winning only 10 percent of the statewide vote. The constitutional convention itself was packed with pro-slavery delegates who wrote into the third constitution such strong provisions to protect slavery that some historians consider Kentucky's third constitution the most strongly pro-slavery state constitution produced in the United States. The effect of the slavery debate of 1849 was to make slavery stronger than ever in Kentucky. The emancipationists' disastrous loss eliminated them as an important political force, and the new pro-slavery constitution convinced Kentuckians that slavery was to be a permanent institution in the state.

In the 1850s conservative emancipationists largely withdrew from the antislavery movement, which became dominated by radicals and abolitionists. In Newport, William Shreve Bailey produced a free-soil paper, the FREE SOUTH, from 1850 to 1865. In Louisville, refugees from the abortive German Revolution of 1848 issued the radical Louisville Platform of 1854, which called for gradual abolition and the political equality of the races. Most important of all was the work of John Gregg FEE and the American Missionary Association in establishing a network of abolitionist churches, communities, and schools in eastern Kentucky. A mob drove Fee and at least ninety-four of his followers from Kentucky after John Brown's 1859 raid.

Slavery in Kentucky collapsed during the Civil War, as thousands of Kentucky slaves took advantage of wartime disruptions to flee from their masters. By the end of the war, perhaps three-quarters of the state's slaves had been freed or had escaped servitude. The border slave states of Maryland and Missouri abolished slavery by state law before the end of the war. But Kentucky refused to acknowledge wartime realities; slavery in Kentucky was outlawed after the war by the federal government with the ratification of the Thirteenth Amendment in 1865.

See J. Winston Coleman, *Slavery Times in Kentucky* (Chapel Hill, N.C., 1940); Lowell H. Harrison, *The Antislavery Movement in Kentucky* (Lexington, Ky., 1978) and "Memories of Slavery Days in Kentucky," *FCHQ* 47 (July 1973): 242-57.

HAROLD D. TALLANT, JR.

SMITH, ADRIAN. Basketball player Adrian ("Odie") Smith was born on October 5, 1936, in Farmington, Kentucky, the son of Oury and Ruth (Penner) Smith. Although he was an outstanding basketball player at Farmington High School, the five-foot, ten-inch 135-pound guard was not recruited by college coaches because of his height. In 1954 he entered North East Mississippi Junior College in Booneville, where he grew taller and his twenty-six-point-per-game scoring average caught the attention of University of Kentucky (UK) coach Adolph Rupp. Subbing for injured guard Vernon Hatton, Smith established himself at UK, and he teamed with Hatton, John Crigler, Ed Beck, and Johnny Cox to win the 1958 national championship. In *The Winning Tradition* (1984), Humbert Nelli writes that the team was called the "Fiddlin' Five" after Rupp said, "We've got fiddlers, that's all. But I'll tell you, you need violinists to play in Carnegie Hall." Smith played on the 1959 Pan American team, which won a gold medal, and was a starting guard on the gold medal U.S. Olympic team in 1960. In 1962 Smith began a professional basketball career that lasted eleven years. He played first with the Cincinnati Royals of the National Basketball Association, then was traded to the San Francisco Warriors. In 1971 he moved to the American Basketball Association, playing for the Virginia Squires for one year.

Smith married Paula Jones of Mayfield, Kentucky, on September 9, 1962; they have one son.

SMITH, BENJAMIN BOSWORTH. Clergyman, educator, and first Episcopal bishop of Kentucky, Benjamin Bosworth Smith was born on June 13, 1784, in Bristol, Rhode Island, the son of Stephen and Ruth (Bosworth) Smith. Although his parents were Congregationalists, he studied for the ministry in the Protestant Episcopal church after graduating from Providence College (Brown University). He was ordained deacon in 1817 and priest in 1818. After serving churches in Massachusetts, Virginia, Vermont, and Pennsylvania, he became rector of Christ Church, Lexington, Kentucky, in 1830. He was consecrated the first Episcopal bishop of Kentucky at St. Paul's Chapel in New York City on October 31, 1832. His diocese consisted of six parishes: Lexington, Louisville, Danville, Henderson, Paris, and Hopkinsville. As he was in need of clergy, he founded the Theological Seminary of the Protestant Episcopal church in 1834 in Lexington.

In 1837 Smith stood accused of "illegal and arbitrary conduct" in office and was tried by an ecclesiastical court. The court reinstated him in office, declaring that there was "human infirmity" on both sides. He served as the third superintendent of public instruction for Kentucky (1840-42) and as a result of his efforts the number of schools increased from 2,160 to 3,384 and enrollment rose from 4,950 to 10,221. In 1868 as the senior bishop, he became the ninth presiding bishop of the Episcopal church. In ill health, he moved to Hoboken, New Jersey.

Smith edited *Episcopal Register* (1826-28) and *Episcopal Recorder* (1828-30), and published a number of scholarly works. He married Elizabeth Bosworth in 1818. He died in New York City on May 31, 1884, and was buried in the Frankfort Cemetery.

See Robert Insko, "Benjamin Bosworth Smith: Kentucky Pioneer Clergyman and Educator," *Register* 69 (Jan. 1941): 37-87; Insko, "Benjamin Bosworth Smith, a Pioneer Kentucky Bishop," *FCHQ* 39 (April 1965): 135-146.

ROSS A. WEBB

SMITH, EFFIE (WALLER). Effie (Waller) Smith, poet, was born in Pike County, Kentucky, on January 6, 1879, the daughter of former slaves. Her father, Frank Waller, was from near Fredericksburg in eastern Virginia and her mother, Sibbie (Ratliff) Waller, was a native of eastern Kentucky. She took up writing at age sixteen, preferring traditional poetry in the manner of Tennyson and Longfellow. Effie Waller's older brother and sister, Alfred and Rosa, had attended Kentucky Normal School for Colored Persons in Frankfort (now Kentucky State University) and almost certainly were her initial mentors. She also attended Kentucky Normal in 1900-1901.

She wrote three books of poetry: *Songs of the Months* (1904), *Rhymes from the Cumberland* (1909), and *Rosemary and Pansies* (1909). Seven of her works were published in major American literary magazines between 1908 and 1917. She stopped writing after "Autumn Winds" was published in *Harper's Monthly* in September 1917.

Effie Waller married Charles Smith in February 1909; they had one child, who died shortly after birth. Her husband died in 1911 from a gunshot wound received in the line of duty as a deputy sheriff attempting to arrest a moonshiner. She moved to Wisconsin in April 1918 and died there on January 2, 1960. She was buried in Neenah, Wisconsin.

See David Deskins, "Effie Waller Smith: An Echo Within the Hills," *Kentucky Review* 8 (Autumn 1988): 26-46.

DAVID DESKINS

SMITH, GREEN CLAY. Green Clay Smith, Civil War general, was born to John Speed and Elizabeth Lewis (Clay) Smith on July 4, 1826, in Richmond, Kentucky. He received his basic education from the common schools in Richmond and spent two years at a preparatory school in Danville. On June 9, 1846, he was commissioned a second lieutenant in the 1st Cavalry; he served under Col. Humphrey Marshall during the Mexican War. After graduating from Transylvania University in Lexington in 1849, Smith studied at the Lexington Law School and was admitted to the bar in 1852. During 1853-57 he was school commissioner of Madison County. In 1858 he moved to Covington, where he practiced law until the outbreak of the Civil War in 1861. Smith was elected to the Kentucky House of Representatives in 1861; he resigned on August 29, 1862.

There has been some confusion about Smith's military record in the Union army during the Civil War, but he appears to have volunteered as a private in 1861. He was promoted to major of the 3d Kentucky Cavalry, assigned to recruiting. On March 15, 1862, he was appointed colonel of the 4th Kentucky Cavalry, and he played an important role in the defeat of Gen. John Hunt Morgan at the battle of Lebanon, Tennessee, on May 5, 1862. Smith was promoted to brigadier general in the U.S. Volunteers on June 11, 1862, and assigned to the 2d Division of the Army of Kentucky, Department of the Ohio, on August 25, 1862. On October 14, 1862, he received the command of the 1st Brigade in the 2d Division, which he resigned on December 1, 1863. On March 13, 1865, he was brevetted a major general of volunteers.

Elected to the 38th U.S. Congress, then reelected, Smith served from March 4, 1863, until July 13, 1866, when he resigned to accept President Andrew Johnson's appointment as governor of the Montana Territory. He resigned that position on April 9, 1869, and entered the Baptist ministry. In 1876 he ran for president of the United States on the National Prohibition party ticket, receiving 9,522 votes. In 1890 he became pastor of the Metropolitan Baptist Church in Washington, D.C., and remained there until his death.

Smith was married to Lena Duke in 1856; they had two sons and three daughters. He died in Washington, D.C., on June 29, 1895, and was buried in Arlington National Cemetery.

See Thomas Speed, *The Union Regiments of Kentucky* (Louisville 1897); Lowell H. Harrison, "Kentucky-Born Generals of the Civil War," *Register* 64 (April 1966): 129-60.

SMITH, JOHN. John Smith, a minister known as "Raccoon" John, was born October 15, 1784, in Sullivan County, Tennessee, to George and Rebecca (Bowen) Smith. His father, a Revolutionary War soldier, moved the family from Tennessee to Kentucky in 1796 and settled in the Cumberland River Valley in what became Clinton County.

Smith obtained most of his education from Robert F. Ferrell, a wheelwright who owned a farm in nearby Stockton's Valley where Smith lived and worked. Baptized by Isaac Denton in 1804, Smith joined the Baptist church at Clear Fork, Kentucky, and soon began preaching. He purchased two hundred acres of farmland in Wayne County, Kentucky, and married Anna Townsend, a neighbor, on De-

cember 9, 1806. In May 1808 Smith was ordained a minister by the Presbyterians of the Stockton's Valley Association and was encouraged to organize a congregation.

Smith sold his Kentucky holdings in 1814 and moved to Huntsville, Alabama, to establish a cotton plantation. In January 1815, before he bought land there, fire destroyed the cabin Smith had been renting and with it perished two of his children and the majority of his savings. Smith's wife died soon after. Smith's health failed in April 1815, and neighbors attended him for several months.

Returning to Kentucky, Smith preached at the August 1815 meeting of the Tates Creek Association at Crab Orchard in Lincoln County. There he was nicknamed Raccoon after introducing himself as having lived on the frontier in Wayne County, where raccoons made their homes. On December 25, 1815, Smith married Nancy Hurt of Wayne County, and they settled in Montgomery County, Kentucky, in 1817, after Smith had been appointed minister of several churches near Mt. Sterling. In 1824 Smith met Alexander CAMPBELL, an evangelical Christian minister whose followers became the Christian Church (Disciples of Christ). Smith supported Campbell's ideas and broke with the Baptist church in 1829. He made extended preaching tours in Kentucky, Tennessee, and Indiana.

Smith returned to Mt. Sterling in 1849 to preach there and at Somerset in Pulaski County. He moved to Georgetown, Kentucky, in 1851, and served as the elder of the church. His wife died there on November 4, 1861. After her death, Smith lived much of his remaining years with one of his daughters, Emma S. Ringo, in Mexico, Missouri. He died there on February 28, 1868, and was buried with his wife in the Lexington Cemetery.

See John Augustus Williams, *Life of Elder John Smith: With Some Account of the Rise and Progress of the Current Reformation* (Cincinnati 1870).

SMITH, JOHN HAMMOND. John Hammond Smith, musician, was born in Louisville on December 16, 1933. He studied piano as a child and later played professionally. He switched to the organ in the late 1950s and led his own ensembles, recording primarily as a soul artist. During the 1960s, he gained prominence as a jazz musician for his use of the Hammond organ, and he helped popularize the instrument. Smith continued to experiment with electronic keyboards and in the 1970s began performing on synthesizers. His range of styles is extensive, from organ jazz to soul music.

LEE BASH

SMITH, LUCIUS ERNEST. Lucius Ernest Smith, physician, was born on October 6, 1878, in Sacramento, McLean County, Kentucky, where his father, Willis Smith, was a Presbyterian minister. Smith attended the University of Kentucky and in 1915 received an M.D. from Johns Hopkins University. In 1920 Smith married Beulah Grace Lipps of

Lexington. For more than a decade he served in Africa as a physician with the Presbyterian Board of Foreign Missions. When his wife's poor health forced their return to the United States, the Smiths settled in Breathitt County, where he battled tuberculosis, the state's No. 1 killer among preventable diseases.

In 1930 Smith moved to Louisville, accepted a position as executive secretary of the Kentucky Tuberculosis Association, and dedicated the remainder of his career to eradicating the disease. Knowing that the malady could be prevented and treated in its early stages, he launched a statewide educational crusade. Showing films, slides, and charts, Smith encouraged Kentuckians to have physical checkups and chest X-rays, and he urged schools to teach courses on personal and public hygiene. He raised hundreds of thousands of dollars through the Christmas Seal program, and he lobbied the legislature for money to build and staff sanitariums. His efforts paid off. When he commenced his work in 1930, Kentucky's death rate from the "white plague" was 94 per 100,000 deaths; twenty years later, the rate had been reduced to 33 per 100,000.

Smith retired in 1951. A stroke and heart disease marred his last few years. He died on August 31, 1955, and was buried in Louisville's Cave Hill Cemetery.   NANCY D. BAIRD

SMITH, MILTON HANNIBAL. Milton Hannibal Smith, railroad magnate, was born in Greene County, New York, on September 12, 1836, to Irulus and Almira (Blakeslee) Smith. He grew up near Chautauqua, New York, and the family moved to Shaumberg, Illinois, in 1850. He received his education in a one-room school, where he went on to teach his own brothers and sisters and other town children. Smith left home when he was twenty to work as a clerk in western Tennessee.

In 1858 Smith began his long career in the railroads as a clerk and telegraph operator for the Mississippi Central Railroad in Holly Springs, Mississippi, working there until the Civil War. In 1862 he took a position with military rail transport in Alabama. In 1865 Smith moved to Louisville to work as the freight manager for the Eclipse Fast Freight Service of the Adams Express Company. He began his long and sometimes controversial career with the LOUISVILLE & NASHVILLE RAILROAD (L&N) in 1866, working as the local agent until 1869, when he was promoted to general agent. It was in this position that Smith began to guide the L&N in its expansion, turning it into a national system.

Smith set out to buy coal and iron mines in Alabama as suppliers during the early 1870s, and the L&N then began to buy up other railroads. Major expansions into Alabama benefited Louisville's business interests at the expense of such cities as St. Louis, Cincinnati, and Nashville and Chattanooga in Tennessee. Smith's plans for further expansion of the railroad, heedless of many government regulations, brought him into conflict with the

board of directors of the L&N, and he resigned in 1878. He became general freight agent for the Baltimore & Ohio Railroad during 1878-81 and for the Pennsylvania Railroad during 1881-82.

After Smith left, the L&N had financial difficulties. It had continued to buy up smaller railroads (for example, the Nashville, Chattanooga, & St. Louis Railroad in 1879) and it had doubled its miles of track in just one year. Despite its control of all railways along the Gulf of Mexico except in Brunswick, Georgia, it did not prosper. The L&N, under four different presidents in four years, had won rate wars in the South but had lost them in the North, and it was bordering on bankruptcy. The railroad's efficiency was dragged down by the proportion of its rails that not been converted from iron to steel, as other railroads had done. To reverse its fortunes, the L&N brought Smith back in 1882 as third vice-president and traffic manager and soon made him vice-president. In 1884 Smith was elected president. He saved the L&N from bankruptcy. By the time he died in 1921, the majority of the rails had been replaced with steel, and efficiency had risen rapidly. Continuing to buy up its competitors, the L&N was soon the most powerful railroad in the South.

Smith remained a controversial figure. A firm believer in social Darwinism, he is quoted as saying, "All legislative bodies are a menace." When L&N rates were accused of discriminating against the individual shipper, he replied: "He could walk. He can do as he did before he had the railroad, as thousands do who have not railroads."

Smith and his first wife, Eva Jones, had two children: Stanton, who died in infancy, and Nettie Belle. After his first wife's death, he married her sister, Annette M. Jones, with whom he had three children: Milton, Sidney, and Eva Lee. Smith died on February 22, 1921, and was buried in Cave Hill Cemetery in Louisville.

See Mary K. Bonsteel Tachau, "The Making of a Railroad President: Milton Hannibal Smith and the L & N," *FCHQ* 43 (April 1969): 125-43.

SMITH, ZACHARY F. Zachary F. Smith, historian and educator, was born on January 7, 1827, in Henry County, Kentucky. He was the only child of Zachariah and Mildred (Dupuy) Smith; his father died before his birth. Smith was educated in the Henry County schools and at Bacon College in Harrodsburg. He then farmed and raised livestock. Before the Civil War he became president of Henry College in New Castle, where he served until 1866. In 1867 Smith was elected Kentucky's superintendent of public instruction. He is credited with designing Kentucky's postbellum school system, significantly improving schools. Smith founded the Cumberland & Ohio Railroad Company in 1869 and served as its president until severing ties with the company in June 1873. He was also involved with railroads in Texas and the Southwest. In 1884 Smith settled in Louisville. He was a member of the board of curators of Transylvania University (1858-1909); a founder and president of the Kentucky Christian Education Society (1857-ca. 1870); and author of numerous works, among them *The History of Kentucky* (1886, 1892, 1901), *A School History of Kentucky* (1891), *The Mother of Henry Clay* (1899), and *The Battle of New Orleans* (1904).

Smith married Susan Helm in 1852. They had eight children: Mildred, Zachary, Joseph, Winthrop, Austin, William, Susan, and Virgil. In 1890 he married Anna Asa Pittman. Smith died on July 4, 1911, and was buried in Eminence, Kentucky.

JAMES J. HOLMBERG

SMITHLAND. The county seat of Livingston County, Smithland is located at the junction of the Ohio and Cumberland rivers. The original town, founded by Zachariah Cox in 1780, was about three miles from the present location. It was built on 175 acres, part of a land grant belonging to Maj. William Croghan, and was incorporated November 4, 1805. The town was later reincorporated on March 8, 1843. Smithland was named in honor of James Smith of Pennsylvania, who explored the Cumberland and Tennessee rivers.

Eddyville, located in what is now Lyon County, became the first seat of Livingston County in 1799, and the courthouse there was completed in 1801. In 1804 the county court ordered the seat moved to Centerville, near what is now Crayne in Crittenden County. No courthouse was built in Centerville. Salem, near the Crittenden County line, became the seat of Livingston County in 1809 and had a log courthouse. Smithland became the seat in 1841, and the courthouse there was completed in 1845.

The town of Smithland grew rapidly in the days of the river trade. Trade from the interior of Kentucky and the northern states poured into the area for shipment south. Riverboats plied the Cumberland and Ohio rivers. Southern planters came to Smithland's river hotels to escape the sweltering heat of their homes. One of the most well-known, the St. Felix Hotel, was completed in 1810 and used during the Civil War as a Union base of operation. The Gower House, built around 1780, hosted many nineteenth century celebrities, among them the Marquis de Lafayette, Aaron Burr, Henry Clay, James K. Polk, Zachary Taylor, Charles Dickens, Clara Barton, and the Union's Gen. Lew Wallace, who wrote *Ben Hur* (1880). The Union army occupied the town during the Civil War, but the townspeople were mainly Confederate sympathizers.

When railroads replaced river transport, Smithland faded to a small agricultural community. Many old homes remain along its riverfront. The population of Smithland, a sixth-class city, was 514 in 1970; 512 in 1980; and 384 in 1990.

See Leslie McDonald, *Echoes of Yesterday* (Smithland, Ky., 1972). RON D. BRYANT

SNYDER, MARION GENE. Marion Gene Snyder, U.S. congressman, was born on January 26, 1928, in Louisville. He attended the University of Louisville (1945-47) and received an LL.B. from the Jefferson School of Law in 1950. He pursued careers in farming, real estate, law, and beginning in 1954, politics. After serving as Jeffersontown city attorney (1954-58) and Jefferson County magistrate (1951-61), he was elected to the U.S. House of Representatives (1963-65). He was defeated in 1964 but reelected in 1966 and thereafter, serving from January 3, 1967, to January 3, 1987, when he declined to run. He served on the Merchant Marine Committee and the Public Works Committee. A tough-minded, aggressive Republican legislator, often acerbic in debate, Snyder had the respect of many of his colleagues. He married Louise Hodges March 23, 1951; they have a son, Mark. He married Patricia Creighton Robertson on April 10, 1973. H. LEW WALLACE

SOLDIERS' RETREAT. Soldiers' Retreat was the nine-hundred-acre farm and home of Col. Richard Clough Anderson, a Virginia native and Revolutionary War veteran who came to Louisville in 1784. Soon after buying land on Beargrass Creek in Jefferson County, Anderson built a large, Georgian-style stone house with surrounding stone dependencies. According to family accounts, the mansion was partly destroyed by lightning in 1840 and razed several years later. Four of the original stone outbuildings still exist. A replica of the main house has been built on the original site using descriptions in family records to guide the reconstruction. The Anderson family cemetery is on adjacent land; both sites are privately owned.

See Kitty Anderson, "Soldiers' Retreat, a Historical House and its Famous People," *Register* 17 (Sept. 1919): 67-77. MARY JEAN KINSMAN

SOLOMON, WILLIAM. William ("King") Solomon, an odd-job man regarded as the "hero of the cholera plague" in the 1830s in Lexington, Kentucky, was born in Virginia around 1775. In the late 1790s Solomon arrived in Lexington, where he supported himself by digging cellars, cisterns, and graves. In June 1833, Solomon, an alcoholic, was adjudged a vagrant, without visible means of support, and his labor as an indentured servant for a twelve-month period was sold at public auction. Aunt Charlotte, a black who was well-known as a pie maker and seller, had been an acquaintance of Solomon's since his boyhood days in Virginia and she outbid two Transylvania University students for his services. Asiatic cholera struck Lexington the day after the auction, and many inhabitants fled the town. Solomon heard of the dead being left unburied and he dug the victims' graves, winning the gratitude of the citizens of Lexington. When he died at the poorhouse on November 22, 1854, the community paid for a casket, and his remains were buried in the Lexington Cemetery. On September 18, 1908, a monument was erected to honor "King" Solomon, with the inscription "For Had He Not a Royal Heart."

See James Lane Allen, *Flute and Violin and Other Kentucky Tales* (New York & London 1899).

ROBERT F. WACHS

SOMERSET. Somerset, the seat of Pulaski County in southeastern Kentucky, is located in the center of the county at U.S. 27, the Cumberland Parkway, and KY 80. Established June 24, 1801, the town was named by a group of settlers from Somerset County, New Jersey. The original log courthouse cost $23.00 to construct and was first used in September 1801. A second and more substantial brick courthouse was completed in 1808. A jail and post office were also built at about the same time.

Somerset was isolated and grew slowly in the first half of the nineteenth century. The population numbered under five hundred until the 1850s. The original town plan called for forty acres. Additional land was added in 1819 and again in 1849. There was a vigorous and varied religious life. Early settlers brought in different denominational beliefs and established churches quickly. The Baptists arrived in 1799, the Presbyterians in 1828, the Methodists in 1830, and the Christians (Disciples of Christ) in 1841. Somerset Academy, a private school, began in 1802. In these early years, roads were built toward the surrounding towns. Regular stagecoach runs were made to Stanford, Crab Orchard, Mt. Vernon, and Columbia. Much of the city's trade was tied to the nearby Cumberland River, where products could be shipped to Nashville and New Orleans.

In 1871 the courthouse and much of the downtown were destroyed by fire. A third courthouse was completed in 1874. With the coming of the Cincinnati & Southern Railroad (now Norfolk Southern) in the 1870s, Somerset became a division headquarters for the rail line, with a large shop area and a terminal. The southern end of the city grew in size and activity. Railroad construction brought many Irish immigrants to Somerset and a Catholic church was established there in 1878. A street railway system was built to connect the public square and the railroad station. The railroad continued to be a vital part of Somerset and its business community until the 1950s, when diesel locomotives replaced those driven by steam. This made the Somerset train shops obsolete. Passenger service also declined and the railroad played a less important role than before.

As late as 1880, Somerset continued to have fewer than 1,000 people, but ten years later the population increased to 2,625. With population growth, Somerset was incorporated in 1888 and changed its government from the trustee system to the mayor-council plan. Abraham Wolfe, a butcher, was elected mayor. Educational needs for the post–Civil War period were fulfilled by the Masonic College, a private high school housed in the Masonic Hall. The Somerset Public School System began in 1889.

The beginning of the twentieth century brought many modern-day conveniences such as electric lights, telephones, and natural gas. A city fire department was established in 1898. An electric street railway was completed in 1907 and served the city until the automobile became common in the 1920s. North-south route U.S. 27 was paved in 1930, and east-west KY 80 was paved in 1939. The same year, a two-story addition was built onto the 1874 courthouse.

Following World War II, Somerset continued steady growth and developed a balanced economy based on industry, farming, coal, oil, and tourism. A fire in 1950 again destroyed a large downtown area. A fourth courthouse was completed in 1975. The Cumberland River became Lake Cumberland with the completion of Wolf Creek Dam in 1951. A new emphasis on tourism filled much of the business void left by the railroad's decline.

Two state institutions were established in Somerset. Somerset Community College, a branch of the University of Kentucky, was established in 1965, and the Oakwood Training Center for the mentally retarded opened in the early 1970s. In 1966 the Republican *Somerset Commonwealth* and the Democratic *Somerset Journal* were combined into the *Somerset Commonwealth Journal* and became the town's first daily newspaper. In the late twentieth century, Somerset has become a medical center for south-central Kentucky. The city is served by Humana: Lake Cumberland Hospital. Among Somerset's more outstanding citizens were Cyrenius Wait, who produced the first raw silk in Kentucky in the 1840s, and Tunstall Quarles, who was Somerset's first member of the U.S. Congress (1817-20). Gov. Edwin P. Morrow (1919-23) and Sen. John Sherman Cooper (1946-49, 1952-55, 1956-73) were born in Somerset. The population of the third-class city was 10,436 in 1970; 10,649 in 1980; and 10,733 in 1990.

J.H. DEBERRY

SOUSLEY, FRANKLIN RUNYON. Franklin Runyon Sousley, a marine private first-class who helped raise the American flag on Iwo Jima in World War II, was born September 19, 1925, at Hilltop, Fleming County, Kentucky, to Duke and Goldie (Mitchell) Sousley. He graduated in 1943 from Flemingsburg High School. The famous photograph of the raising of a large American flag on Mt. Suribachi, Iwo Jima, on February 23, 1945, was later represented in cast bronze in the Marine Corps War Memorial, in Washington, D.C. The second figure from the left, the Marine with a rifle, represents Sousley. Sousley was killed in action on March 21, 1945, and is buried in Elizaville Cemetery near Hilltop.

See U.S. Marine Corps, *The Iwo Jima Flag Raising: The Event and Its People* (Washington, D.C., 1960).

JAMES RUSSELL HARRIS

SOUTH, LILLIAN H. Lillian H. South, physician, was born on January 31, 1879, to Dr. John F. and Martha (Moore) South of Bowling Green, Kentucky. South earned a nursing degree from a New Jersey hospital and an M.D. degree in 1904 from the Women's Medical College of Pennsylvania. Six years later she accepted a position with the Kentucky State Board of Health. During her forty years as the board's bacteriologist, she helped bring under control many of the debilitating and fatal diseases that plagued the commonwealth. South once estimated that she had prepared enough vaccine to inoculate more than 12 million Kentucky schoolchildren. A popular lecturer and author on public health matters, South belonged to numerous professional organizations, including the American Medical Association (vice-president, 1913) and American Public Health Association. She was named a member of England's Royal Society of Health in 1963.

South married Judge H.H. Tyre of Williamsburg, Kentucky in 1925. She died on September 13, 1966, and was buried in Williamsburg.

NANCY D. BAIRD

SOUTHERN BAPTIST THEOLOGICAL SEMINARY. Located in Louisville on Lexington Road, the Southern Baptist Theological Seminary is controlled by a board of trustees nominated by a committee of the Southern Baptist Convention. Full accreditation has been granted by the American Association of Theological Schools and the American Association of Schools of Religious Education.

The slavery controversy caused a schism among American Baptists in the pre–Civil War era. Baptists in the South, desiring their own separate institutions, founded Southern Baptist Theological Seminary in 1859 at Greenville, South Carolina. During the Civil War the institution suspended operations and then struggled through the next two decades to develop an educational program and establish an endowment. James Petigru Boyce, as chairman of the faculty, led the seminary to an enrollment of sixty-five in 1876-77, the last year in Greenville. Because of the depressed economy of the Deep South, the seminary then moved to the more prosperous city of Louisville. Despite a healthier endowment, the institution used only rented facilities until 1888, when the trustees purchased property on the southeast corner of Fifth and Broadway. Soon New York Hall, named for the significant contributions from that state, became the first permanent structure on the new campus.

Boyce died in 1888, not long after being designated president. During his last year, the enrollment grew to more than 150 students. During the presidency of his successor, John A. Broadus, Memorial Library and Norton Hall were completed, and the seminary conferred its first doctorate of theology, in 1894. During the presidency of William H. Whitsitt, following the death of Broadus in 1895, the student body grew steadily and a gymnasium was erected. However, Whitsitt aroused controversy over the origins of Baptists and the role of baptism by immersion, and he resigned in 1899.

Edgar Young MULLINS, who held a pastorate outside Southern Baptist territory at the time, succeeded Whitsitt. During his nearly twenty-nine years as president, enrollment topped four hundred, the faculty increased from seven to twelve mem-

bers, and annual guest lectureships were added. In 1904 the seminary started publishing the quarterly *Review and Expositor*. The Woman's Missionary Union Training School, established near the seminary in 1907, educated single women and the wives of students for denominational service. Mullins pushed hard for a new physical plant, and in 1926 the seminary moved into its first buildings on the new campus on Lexington Road, known as the Beeches. At the time of his death more than $2 million had been expended on buildings.

Despite financial struggles during the Great Depression, John R. Sampey as president (1928-42) was able to reduce the school's debt, while enrollment exceeded five hundred. The Woman's Missionary Training School moved from its Broadway properties to the Beeches in 1941. Enrollment nearly doubled during the administration of President Ellis A. Fuller (1942-51), and the beneficence of the Norton family and other donors added substantially to the seminary's endowment and revenues.

In 1951 Duke K. McCall, past president of New Orleans Baptist Theological Seminary and executive secretary of the Southern Baptist executive committee, became the seventh president of the Louisville seminary. He once described himself as a "standard-brand conservative evangelical." Reorganization into schools of theology, church music, and religious education modernized the curriculum during McCall's early years. During his thirty-year tenure, the longest in seminary history, conservatives often attacked the Louisville institution for liberalism. The presidency of Roy L. Honeycutt (1981-) has likewise been beset by controversy. With a reputation as the most liberal of the six Southern Baptist theological seminaries, the school became the focal point of the fundamentalist-moderate controversy that grew in the late 1970s and continued into the 1990s.

Fundamentalists, or fundamental-conservatives, profess allegiance to a literal interpretation of the Bible, a belief that separates them from the moderate-conservatives. Both declare their belief in the evangelical tenet of Baptist doctrine, yet for over a decade they have fought for control of the Southern Baptist Convention. Since 1979 the fundamentalists have controlled the office of the president, who nominates members of a committee that indirectly nominates members of official Southern Baptist boards and institutions. In 1989 fundamentalists gained a majority of the board of trustees of the seminary, the last major Southern Baptist institution that remained outside their hands.

See William A. Mueller, *A History of Southern Baptist Theological Seminary* (Nashville 1958); John R. Sampey, *Southern Baptist Theological Seminary: The First Thirty Years, 1859-1889* (Baltimore 1890).   WILLIAM E. ELLIS

SOUTHERN EXPOSITION. The Southern Exposition in Louisville was a major cultural event in the history of nineteenth century Kentucky and one of the nation's most significant regional fairs. It opened on August 3, 1883, when the attendance was 20,000. The exposition was illuminated that evening by 4,600 "Edison lights," the first such fair to be so electrified.

The headline of the *Louisville Courier-Journal* for August 2, 1883, proclaimed: "The Great Southern Exposition Throws Its Doors Open to the World." The physical scale of the exposition was indeed great. The principal structure was a large rectangular building with interior sections divided by courtyards, creating a cruciform. A frame structure two stories high, the building measured six hundred feet by four hundred feet; the central cross measured four hundred by one hundred. It was exceeded in size only by the Crystal Palace of the Great London Exposition of 1851 and by the Machinery Hall at the Centennial Exhibition in Philadelphia in 1876. The structure was arranged in the rational manner of all such exposition halls, an expression of nineteenth century scientific confidence and the spirit of progress. There were five "departments," individual sections reserved for exhibits in five areas of human endeavor: natural products, machinery, manufactured products, transportation, and the arts. All told, 1,500 exhibits were on view within the building.

The main structure was located on forty acres of land, which today make up the areas of Central Park and St. James Court in Louisville between Fourth and Fifth Streets. Streetcars and a spur of the Louisville & Nashville Railroad provided easy transportation for visitors to the grounds, which at the time of the exposition were two miles from the center of the city. On the grounds, fair-goers could enjoy a horticultural garden, a miniature southern plantation, and an art gallery that housed some of the finest paintings in this country, on loan from major collectors. Band concerts and scientific lectures were diversions from the formal exhibits.

When President Chester A. Arthur spoke at the opening ceremonies on the morning of August 3, he praised "the splendid triumph of American genius, activity, and skill which are arranged within these walls." The moment was a triumphant one for the exposition—a boost for the city of Louisville, national recognition for both the city and the state, and a display of human industry that was not matched in this country until the Columbian Exposition of 1893 in Chicago.

Although eclipsed by the St. Louis Exposition of 1904, the Southern Exposition was one of the most successful elaborate regional fairs in national history. After eighty-eight days, the exposition finished its first year with a total attendance of 770,048, one of the most proudly hailed cultural events in the history of Kentucky. It ended in 1887. The Southern Exposition was, as the *Courier-Journal* stated in its August 2, 1883, edition, "A Dream Realized."   RAYMOND F. BETTS

SOUTHERN HARMONY SINGING. Southern Harmony singing by informal groups was once heard across most of the United States and it blanketed the South. The name is taken from William Walker's best-selling tunebook of 1835 and 1854, *Southern Harmony,* of which 600,000 copies were printed before the Civil War. (The book has been kept alive by reprints in 1939, 1966, and 1987.) The late George Pullen Jackson of Vanderbilt University in Nashville argued for the folk origins of much of the music in the book, although the music is also indebted to Ananaias Davidson's *Kentucky Harmony* (1815). The four-shape note system of Southern Harmony singing first came into use in the British Isles about the same time as the King James Bible—1611. *Fa* was a note with a triangular head, *sol* was round, *la* was square, and *mi* had a diamond shape. The scale was sung as *fa sol la fa sol la mi fa.* The note system was first used in America by John Connelley, a Philadelphia printer. It appears in many popular tunebooks, including the famous *Sacred Harp* (1844), which has given its name to the singing traditions of many communities.

Southern Harmony singing is celebrated at an annual festival called Benton's Big Singing Day, begun by James R. Lemon, publisher of the Benton, Kentucky, *Tribune-Democrat.* The event has been held since 1884 on the fourth Sunday in May at the Marshall County courthouse. During the 1930s and 1940s an estimated 10,000 people attended the festival each year. Later crowds were much smaller. The traditional singing began with fifteen to twenty leaders, each sounding out the notes first and then the words line by line, all a capella.

In 1973 the Society for the Preservation of Southern Harmony Singing was incorporated to perform concerts and make recordings. In 1976 the National Music Council chose Benton's Big Singing Day as one of eighty-eight events in the United States to be designated a landmark of American music.

See Lon Carter Barton, ed., *Jackson Purchase: 150 Years, 1819-1969* (Mayfield, Ky., 1969); George P. Jackson, *White Spirituals in the Southern Uplands: The Story of the Fasola Folk* (New York 1965).   WILLIAM RAY MOFIELD

SOUTHERN RAILWAY SYSTEM. The Southern Railway network was formed in Virginia in 1894 and subsequently covered much of the South from Washington, D.C., to the Gulf Coast and Florida. In Kentucky, it operated 190 miles of a 336-mile trunk route from Cincinnati to Chattanooga, Tennessee, that was owned by the city of Cincinnati and leased through a subsidiary, the Cincinnati, New Orleans & Texas Pacific Railway. Southern also owned a 92-mile line from Danville to Louisville.

As far back as the 1830s, proposals were considered to link Cincinnati with the Southeast and the Atlantic Ocean, but not until the late 1860s did such a project unfold. Cincinnati had long sought to break neighboring Louisville's monopoly on trade with the South (enhanced after 1859 with the completion of the Louisville & Nashville's main line to Nashville). An 1869 Ohio law authorized Cincinnati to build a railroad through central Kentucky to Chattanooga. The Tennessee legislature approved the project in 1870 but bitter battles in Frankfort in 1870-71 kept Kentucky from approving the line until February 1872. Construction of the CINCINNATI SOUTHERN, as the road was called, began in December 1873 near Kings Mountain in Lincoln County, Kentucky. Rough terrain south of Danville slowed progress, and the track did not reach Somerset, Kentucky, until summer 1877. The entire route to Chattanooga opened in early 1880.

As originally constructed, the Cincinnati Southern main line passed through twenty-seven tunnels and crossed 105 bridges and viaducts, including four lengthy spans over the Ohio, Cumberland, Tennessee, and Kentucky rivers. High Bridge, which crossed the Kentucky River at Wilmore, was completed in 1877, and for many years ranked as one of the world's highest railroad bridges over a navigable stream. It was extensively rebuilt and double-tracked in 1911. While remaining the property of the City of Cincinnati, after 1881 the Cincinnati Southern was leased to the Cincinnati, New Orleans & Texas Pacific Railway (CNO&TP), which at a later time was acquired by the Southern System.

The CNO&TP connected with lines of the Southern at several points, including Danville. Rental fees and operating revenues went to Cincinnati; the road was upgraded periodically, as in 1961-63, when thirteen small-bore tunnels (seven in Kentucky) were eliminated. Three other tunnels were enlarged, and numerous curves and grades were reduced. As a north-south bridge route, the Cincinnati Southern carried one of the heaviest volumes of freight traffic among main lines in Kentucky for many years.

The origins of the Southern System's Louisville-Danville line can be traced to a proposed railroad linking the Ohio Valley to southwest Virginia, chartered in 1868 as the Louisville, Harrodsburg & Virginia. No track was ever laid, and in 1884 the company was reorganized as the Louisville Southern, which built a line between Louisville and Harrodsburg in 1887. From there a connection to the Cincinnati Southern was made at Burgin via the tiny, four-mile-long Southwestern.

Louisville Southern properties were leased to the Monon (Louisville, New Albany & Chicago) in 1889-90 in an aborted attempt to extend rail service to the eastern Kentucky coal fields; in 1890 the Louisville Southern was acquired by the East Tennessee, Virginia & Georgia, which in 1894 became one of the two railroads forming the Southern System. Louisville Southern branches were built between 1885 and 1890 from Lawrenceburg to Georgetown and Lexington, and at Tyrone tracks crossed the Kentucky River on the 1,665-foot-long structure that is known as High Bridge.

In 1982 the Southern System was acquired by Norfolk Southern, headquartered in Norfolk, Virginia. It also acquired the Kentucky & Indiana Terminal Railroad Company of Louisville in 1982. The other major component of the Norfolk Southern is the Norfolk & Western Railway, a Virginia-Midwest carrier, which in Kentucky operates about

65 miles of track, mostly coal-gathering lines, in Martin and Pike counties.

See Fairfax Harrison, *History of the Legal Development of Southern Railway Company* (Washington, D.C., 1901); Michael Iczkowski, *Trains* (Milwaukee, Wis., 1976).

CHARLES B. CASTNER

SOUTHGATE. Southgate, a suburban city in the hills of northeastern Campbell County, is situated one mile southeast of Newport on U.S. 27. It was incorporated in 1907 and named by Albert S. Berry, a prominent local politician, for pioneer landowner Richard Southgate, who settled in the area around 1795. Berry wanted to draw significance to the place as the southern entrance to Newport on the principal route between northern Kentucky and Lexington. Southgate shared in the gambling and dinner club business for which Newport was renowned from the 1930s until the 1960s. On February 3, 1936, Peter Schmidt, a convicted moonshiner, opened the BEVERLY HILLS supper club, a casino reputed to have been taken over by organized crime during the 1940s. The Beverly Hills Club was the scene of a disastrous fire that killed 161 patrons in 1977.

The population of the fourth-class city was 3,212 in 1970; 2,833 in 1980; 3,266 in 1990.

SOUTH KENTUCKY INSTITUTE. South Kentucky Institute was a day finishing school for girls, organized by the Christian Church in Hopkinsville in 1849. It operated on the lower floor of the church for its first ten years. The trustees purchased an eight-acre campus on the crest of Belmont Hill, east of town, in the fall of 1858. There a three-story brick Greek Revival building, containing classrooms, dormitory, parlor, library, chapel, and dining room, was constructed at a cost of $30,000. The name South Kentucky Female College was then adopted.

The school was closed in 1861-62, when it was used as a hospital for Confederate soldiers. School charter amendments in 1880 brought coeducation, and the name was changed to South Kentucky College. The school burned on February 24, 1884, but was rebuilt and reopened that fall. As the curriculum expanded, bachelor's and master's degrees were granted during the 1890s and early 1900s. In 1903 a football team called the Maroons and a girls' basketball team were organized. Fire destroyed the main building on November 2, 1905, but an endowed gift of $10,000 revived the school.

In 1908 the trustees voted to rename the school McLean College in honor of Archibald McLean, president of the Foreign Christian Missionary Society. A third fire destroyed the school on February 1, 1912, but arrangements were made for the school term to be completed. Boarding students numbered 160 that fall. The rebuilding exhausted the resources and credit of both the college and its Christian Church supporters. In October 1913 the McLean trustees proposed to transfer all property to

Transylvania University in Lexington, and the contract was signed January 21, 1914.

WILLIAM T. TURNER

SPALDING, CATHERINE. Catherine Spalding, cofounder of the SISTERS OF CHARITY OF NAZARETH, was born December 23, 1793, in Charles County, Maryland, to Edward and Juliet (Boarman) Spalding. The Spaldings moved from Maryland to Nelson County, Kentucky, about 1795. After the death of her parents, Catherine was raised first by Mrs. Thomas Elder, her aunt, and then by Richard and Clementine (Elder) Clark. In January 1813 she joined two other women invited by the Rev. John David to ST. THOMAS FARM, near Bardstown, Kentucky, to begin the Roman Catholic Sisters of Charity of Nazareth. Spalding was chosen general superior and whenever eligible was returned to the office by vote, serving a total of twenty-five years.

As "a constructive genius with a natural gift for administration," Spalding made most of the policy decisions affecting the community. In 1814 the first school was opened at St. Thomas; in 1822 it was moved to the site of the present motherhouse near Bardstown. Spalding founded St. Vincent's Academy in Union County (1821), St. Catherine's Academy in Lexington (1823), and Presentation Academy in Louisville (1831).

Spalding opened St. Vincent's Orphanage in 1832 in Louisville. In 1836, in a wing of the orphanage, she started St. Joseph's Infirmary, which became the largest private hospital in the state; it closed in 1979. She inaugurated the causes for which the Sisters of Charity of Nazareth became noted: education, the care of orphans, and health care. Spalding was among the outstanding businesswomen of the nineteenth century. In her leadership she deferred to no man, on one occasion scolding the mayor of Louisville. She had consummate tact, however, along with great compassion for the disadvantaged and concern for the members of her order. Spalding University in Louisville is named for her.

In her last term as general superior, Spalding raised buildings at the motherhouse, including a magnificent chapel. She died in Louisville on March 20, 1858, after having contracted bronchitis on an errand of mercy. She is buried in the Nazareth Community Cemetery near Bardstown.

See Anna Blanche McGill, *The Sisters of Charity of Nazareth, Kentucky* (New York 1917); Agnes Geraldine McGann, *SCNs Serving Since 1812* (Nazareth, Ky., 1985); Mary Michael Creamer, "Mother Catherine Spalding—St. Catherine Street, Louisville, Kentucky," *FCHQ* 63 (April 1989): 191-223.

THOMAS W. SPALDING

SPALDING, JOHN LANCASTER. Identified with the cause of Roman Catholic higher education, the cleric John Lancaster Spalding was born in Lebanon, Kentucky, on June 2, 1840, the son of Richard Martin and Mary Jane (Lancaster) Spalding. He was educated at St. Mary's College near Lebanon. The nephew of Martin John SPALDING,

bishop of Louisville during 1850-64, Spalding completed his clerical studies at Mount St. Mary's Seminary in Cincinnati and the American College at Louvain, Belgium. He was ordained a priest at Mechelen, Belgium, in 1863.

Returning to his home diocese of Louisville, Spalding served as assistant at the Cathedral of the Assumption, editor of the diocesan newspaper, chancellor of the diocese, and founding pastor of St. Augustine's, the first black parish in the city. Partly because of disputes with William G. McCloskey, bishop of Louisville, Spalding in 1872 moved to New York City, where he wrote a biography of his uncle, *The Life of the Most Rev. M.J. Spalding* (1873), and a collection titled *Essays and Reviews* (1876). Spalding was named first bishop of Peoria, Illinois, in 1877, serving until 1908.

Spalding was a driving force in the establishment of the Catholic University of America in Washington, D.C, in 1889. Among the bishop's writings on education are *Education and the Higher Life* (1890), *Things of the Mind* (1894), *Means and End of Education* (1895), and *Religion, Agnosticism and Education* (1902). Called the Roman Catholic Emerson, he produced *Aphorisms and Reflections* (1901), *Socialism and Labor* (1902), *Glimpses of Truth* (1903), and *Religion, Art and Other Essays* (1905). A champion of academic freedom and higher education for women, Spalding received honorary degrees from Columbia University and Western Reserve.

In the later nineteenth century, Spalding was largely identified with a group of more liberal Catholic clerics known as the Americanists for their stress on the separation of church and state, freedom, diversity, ecumenism, and the superiority of American institutions. The bishop could be critical of the nation as well. In "A National Calamity," a major address after the assassination of President William McKinley, Spalding insisted that Americans were "too ready to persuade ourselves that all is well as long as wealth and population increase. We seek facile solutions to the great problems." Still, he credited his nation in the same oration for being "dedicated to the securing of the largest freedom, the fullest opportunity, the completest justice to all, to men and women, to the strong and the week, to the rich and the poor." Putting his concern for social justice into action, Spalding served on the arbitration panel during a major coal strike in 1902, at the request of the workers and by appointment of President Theodore Roosevelt.

Spalding retired as bishop of Peoria in 1908. In that year he was given the honorary title of archbishop by Pope Pius X. Spalding died in Peoria on August 25, 1916, and was buried there.

See J.T. Ellis, *John Lancaster Spalding* (Milwaukee, Wis., 1962); D.F. Sweeney, *The Life of John Lancaster Spalding* (New York 1965).

CLYDE F. CREWS

SPALDING, MARTIN JOHN. Martin John Spalding, Catholic bishop and writer, was born on May

23, 1810, on the Rolling Fork in Marion County, Kentucky, to Richard and Henrietta (Hamilton) Spalding. He was educated at St. Mary's College near Lebanon, St. Joseph's College in Bardstown, and the Urban College of the Propaganda in Rome. He received his doctorate in divinity and was ordained a priest in Rome on August 13, 1834. He served as pastor of St. Joseph's Church, Bardstown, and president of St. Joseph's College, then as pastor of St. Peter's Church, Lexington. He returned to St. Joseph's Church before the aging Bishop Benedict FLAGET called him to Louisville in 1844 to be his vicar general. On September 10, 1848, he was raised to episcopal rank as coadjutor to Flaget, whom he succeeded as bishop of Louisville on February 11, 1850.

The years of Spalding's episcopacy in Louisville (1850-64) coincided with its golden age. The Catholic population doubled (from 35,000 to 70,000) during his tenure, and the number of churches, schools, priests, religious orders, and parish societies kept pace. Spalding created the parochial school system and in 1857 was a founder of the American College of Louvain, which provided the diocese with several outstanding priests.

On May 6, 1864, Spalding was appointed archbishop of Baltimore, where he became the leader of the Roman Catholic church in the United States. At Vatican Council I (1869-70) he attempted, unsuccessfully, to create a compromise party on the question of papal infallibility.

Spalding's historical and apologetic works include *Sketches of the Early Catholic Missions of Kentucky* (1844), *Life of Bishop Flaget* (1852), *Miscellanea* (1855), *Evidences of Catholicity* (1857), and *History of the Protestant Reformation* (1860). He died on February 7, 1872, and was buried in the cathedral of Baltimore.

See Thomas W. Spalding, *Martin John Spalding: American Churchman* (Washington, D.C., 1973); Clyde F. Crews, *An American Holy Land: A History of the Archdiocese of Louisville* (Wilmington, Del., 1987).   THOMAS W. SPALDING

SPALDING UNIVERSITY. Spalding University was established in Louisville in 1920 and given the name Nazareth College by the SISTERS OF CHARITY OF NAZARETH under a state charter issued in 1829. It was the first four-year Roman Catholic liberal arts college for women in Kentucky. The Sisters of Charity of Nazareth, a Roman Catholic order founded in Nelson County, was among the educational pioneers of the state in primary and secondary schools as well as on the college level. In 1963 the name of Louisville's Nazareth College was changed to Catherine Spalding College, in honor of Catherine SPALDING, a cofounder of the Sisters of Charity of Nazareth, recognized for her contributions to education, health care, and social service. The name was shortened to Spalding College in 1969. In 1973 Spalding College was separately incorporated as a coeducational institution in the Catholic tradition, and in 1984 it became Spalding University.

The college opened its doors to the first students in a twenty-five-room residence on South Fourth Street, which had been erected in 1871 by Henry WHITESTONE, the well-known Louisville architect, for Joseph T. Tompkins, a merchant and importer; the house was redecorated in 1880 for the second owner, George C. Buchanan. On October 31, 1918, the Sisters of Charity bought the house and the grounds from the widow of the third owner, Rhodes B. Rankin, and Nazareth College opened there on October 4, 1920. Since that date the educational institution has occupied the historic house as the core of its campus.

The program first offered was a broad liberal education with majors and minors in standard academic disciplines. One professional program, teacher preparation, was offered in the earliest curricula, and a library science major was added in 1929. In 1925 Nazareth College was recognized by the Kentucky Department of Education; in 1938 the institution was accredited by the Southern Association of Colleges and Secondary Schools. In 1933 Nazareth College was a pioneer in responding to the need for college-trained registered nurses, offering a supplemental program leading to the B.S. in nursing education.

In 1949 the first generic baccalaureate nursing program in Kentucky was established at the college; the program was accredited by the National League for Nursing in 1963. During 1935-68, the college cooperated with six local hospitals by providing academic courses for the hospitals' three-year diploma schools, whose graduates could become registered nurses.

In 1960 the Louisville college became associated with NAZARETH COLLEGE of Kentucky, which had been founded as a junior college by the Sisters of Charity in 1922 in Nelson County. Nelson County's Nazareth College was merged with Louisville's Spalding College in 1971.

In 1962 the Louisville college inaugurated master's degree programs in education, library science, and theology. Other graduate-level programs, all professional, followed: the master of arts in teaching (1968), and master's degree programs in religious studies (1971), psychometry (1971), and nursing (1985). In doctoral programs, it added doctor of psychology in 1982 and doctor of education in 1989. Spalding University's weekend college opened in 1980.

See Agnes Geraldine McGann, *SCNs Serving Since 1812* (Nazareth, Ky., 1985).

MARY MICHAEL CREAMER

SPANISH-AMERICAN WAR. During the Spanish-American War, 6,065 Kentuckians served in the military between April 24, 1898, and December 10, 1898; eighty-nine Kentuckians were killed or missing in action. Three state-mandated regiments of volunteer infantry from guardsmen of the state militia eventually traveled to Cuba, but the war ended before these men saw combat action. The 1st Regiment, under Col. John B. Castlemen, was the Louisville Legion. The 2d Regiment, under

Col. E.H. Gaither, became known as Lexington's Regiment. The Pennyroyal and Jackson Purchase regions supplied the 3d Regiment, under Col. T.J. Smith. Even after the quota of men per company was reduced, Kentucky was unable to equip the number of men mandated.

Perhaps the greatest commitment to the war made by a Kentuckian was that of Henry Watterson, editor of the *Louisville Courier-Journal*, who interpreted the war with Spain as an expression of higher law proclaiming the American system superior to all other forms of government.

LEE BUTTON

SPANISH CONSPIRACY. The Spanish Conspiracy is the name given to secret negotiations during the period 1787-92 between early Kentuckians and Spain on the issues of statehood for Kentucky and freedom of navigation of the Mississippi River. In the last years of the Revolutionary War, Spain refused to recognize American independence until the United States yielded the rights to navigation of the Mississippi River. Anxious to form a buffer zone between the Americans and the valuable Spanish colonies in Mexico, the Spanish court intended to control access to the Mississippi to discourage settlers from spilling over the Appalachian Mountains into the area that is now Kentucky and Tennessee. When Spain closed the river to Americans at New Orleans, it denied the settlers access to markets for crops and merchandise that could not be marketed on the eastern seaboard because of distance and the natural barrier of the Appalachian Mountains.

At the same time, western settlers were frustrated by being subject to the Virginia Assembly. The physical distance of Richmond not only made judicial appeals prohibitively expensive, for example, but even worse, it left the settlers vulnerable to the scattered but persistent Indian attacks. The federal government, under the Articles of Confederation, was of little help because it could not raise enough troops or money for defense. In 1784 the settlers in Kentucky began to petition the Virginia Assembly for legislation to make Kentucky an independent state within the Confederation. James WILKINSON was one of those who advocated immediate, unconditional separation from Virginia.

In 1786 Wilkinson and his allies received word that John Jay of New York, secretary of foreign affairs in the Continental Congress, intended to give in to Spanish demands that Americans waive access to the Mississippi River for twenty-five years. The proposed Jay-Gardoqui Treaty would have strangled the western territory economically; leaders like Wilkinson held that the western settlers owed no further allegiance to the Confederation and could separate not only from Virginia but even from the United States. They argued that Kentucky could then form alliances of its own choosing. Wilkinson's allies included the early Kentuckians John Brown, Benjamin Sebastian, Harry Innes, and Caleb Wallace.

In 1787 Wilkinson reached an agreement with the Spanish governor of New Orleans, Esteban Miro,

who agreed to allow the settlers to use the Mississippi River in exchange for Wilkinson's aid in securing Kentucky's independence, not only from Virginia but also from the Confederation. Wilkinson would then guide the independent sovereign state of Kentucky into an alliance with Spain that would benefit Kentucky commercially while protecting Spain's valuable colony in Mexico.

Many Kentuckians, including Brown, Sebastian, Innes, and Wallace, saw the value of the Spanish connection, and during the various STATEHOOD CONVENTIONS held between 1788 and 1791, they endorsed an immediate separation from Virginia and the United States. For their support in this plan, Wilkinson, Brown, Innes, and Sebastian received Spanish pensions. Wilkinson and his supporters were opposed by Thomas Marshall, Humphrey Marshall, John Allen, and Ebenezer Brooks, among others. Support for a sovereign state and a Spanish alliance quickly faded when news arrived that the Jay-Gardoqui Treaty had been defeated.

See Thomas Marshall Green, *The Spanish Conspiracy: A Review of Early Spanish Movements in the South-West* (Cincinnati 1891); Arthur Preston Whitaker, *The Spanish-American Frontier* (Boston, New York 1927).

JEFFREY SCOTT SUCHANEK

SPARKS, HARRY MAGEE. Harry Magee Sparks, educator, was born in Livingston, Rockcastle County, Kentucky, on July 27, 1907, the son of Robert A. and Lena (Bentley) Sparks. He completed his elementary and secondary education locally before attending Bethany College in West Virginia, later transferring to Transylvania University, in Lexington, Kentucky, where he earned an A.B. in 1930. The same year Sparks began his teaching career at Breckinridge County High School, remaining there until 1934. He then moved to Irvington, Kentucky, where he was principal, coach, and superintendent of the city schools; from 1938 to 1941 he was principal of Livingston High School. Sparks earned an M.A. from the University of Kentucky in 1941, and received his doctorate there in 1954.

Between 1941 and 1944 he was principal of the senior high school in Russell, Kentucky, leaving to enlist in the U.S. Navy. Sparks served until 1946 and achieved the rank of lieutenant commander. Upon his return Sparks became principal at Mayfield High School, where he remained until 1948, when he became associate professor of education at Murray State University. He later became chairman of the education department and served there until 1964, when he was elected state superintendent of public instruction, a post he held until 1968. He was also president of the Kentucky Education Association in 1959-60. In 1968 Sparks became the fifth president of MURRAY STATE UNIVERSITY. During his five-year tenure the university underwent considerable growth.

He married Lois Stiles of Maceo, Kentucky, on June 5, 1934. They have three children: Harry Magee, Jr., Phillip Stiles, and Susan Nunnelley.

WILLIAM RAY MOFIELD

SPAS. In the early nineteenth century, when Kentuckians began to find time for leisure, many, especially the wealthy, visited the numerous health resorts, or spas. Modeled after the spas of Europe, Kentucky spas, located on or near mineral springs, offered a luxurious atmosphere. Springs containing minerals such as salt, alum, copper, and white, black, or red sulfur were believed to benefit the stomach, liver, and kidneys and to cure a wide range of illnesses, including gout, asthma, and rheumatism. During the cholera epidemics in Kentucky in 1833 and 1849, the vaunted curative properties of the waters drew people hoping to be either saved from, or cured of, the dreaded disease.

At the springs, resort owners built large, elaborate hotels, as well as private cabins, bathhouses, steam rooms, and pools. Kentucky had no fewer than fifty spas; among the most renowned were GREENVILLE and HARRODSBURG Springs in Mercer County; OLYMPIAN Springs in Bath County; CRAB ORCHARD Springs in Lincoln County; PAROQUET SPRINGS in Bullitt County; Esculapia Springs in Lewis County; DRENNON SPRINGS in Henry County; BLUE LICK Springs in Nicholas County; ESTILL Springs in Estill County; Grayson Springs in Grayson County; and White Sulphur Springs in Scott County.

During the summer months—the watering season—spas drew visitors seeking relief from the intense heat of the Deep South or the grime of cities such as New Orleans, Nashville, Cincinnati, and Lexington. For their vacationing clientele, resort owners built riding stables, ballrooms, and saloons (for gentlemen only) and advertised music and dancing, gambling, billiards, fishing, and hunting. In many instances, such activities became a bigger draw than the springs themselves. At such spas as Blue Lick, Crab Orchard, and Estill Springs, the masquerade and fancy dress balls every three weeks were the star attractions. In 1828 Dr. Christopher Columbus Graham, owner of Harrodsburg and Greenville Springs (at times known collectively as Graham's Springs) built what became the most fashionable spa in Kentucky.

The vastly improving transportation network in Kentucky swelled the numbers of the spas' clientele. In 1807, four years after a stagecoach line was opened between Lexington and Olympian Springs, that resort became so easily accessible that the lodgings had to be significantly expanded. Steamboats brought wealthy plantation owners from Mississippi, Louisiana, and Alabama up the Mississippi and Ohio rivers to Louisville, where they boarded a stagecoach to their chosen resort. Drennon Springs was accessible by boat up the Kentucky River to Drennon's Creek Landing, only a two-mile carriage ride from the springs.

The spas, most popular during the 1840s, began to decline in the 1850s. In 1853 the federal government bought the Harrodsburg Springs property and converted the hotel into the Western Military Asylum, a home for retired soldiers. On May 30, 1856, fire destroyed the building at Harrodsburg Springs, as fires destroyed the Esculapia Springs hotel in 1860, the Drennon Springs hotel in 1865, and the Crab Orchard hotel in 1871. But the Civil War did more damage to Kentucky's spas than any fire. Not only did patronage suffer in the wartime economy, but many spas were also the scenes of skirmishes, as at Olympian Springs on October 19, 1864, or were requisitioned for military use, like Estill Springs, which became the headquarters for the 8th Kentucky Federal Infantry.

After the Civil War, many of Kentucky's spas recovered to a remarkable degree. Crab Orchard Springs, Blue Lick Springs, and Olympian Springs were all doing a thriving business by the late 1880s. The revival was short-lived, however, as scientific advance produced medicines much more effective than mineral water, and improved means of transportation made vacation spots accessible in other areas, such as Niagara Falls, Atlantic City, and the American West. Faced with steadily declining patronage, spas soon fell into disrepair and were closed. Crab Orchard survived until the Great Depression.

See J. Winston Coleman, "Old Kentucky Watering Places," *FCHQ* 16 (Jan. 1942): 1-26; J. Winston Coleman, *Springs of Kentucky* (Lexington, Ky., 1955).

SPEED, JAMES. James Speed, U.S. attorney general, was born on March 11, 1812, at Farmington, the family estate near Louisville. He was the son of John Speed and his second wife, the former Lucy Gilmer Fry. Speed was educated in local schools and graduated from St. Joseph's College in Bardstown, Kentucky, in 1828. After working in the Jefferson County clerk's office in Louisville for two years, he entered the law department of Transylvania University, graduating in 1833. He set up a Louisville law practice, which he continued with some interruptions until shortly before his death. Speed served in the Kentucky House of Representatives (1847-48), on the Louisville Board of Alderman (1851-54), and in the state Senate (1861-63). In 1861 Speed was appointed mustering officer for Kentucky Union volunteers and commander of the Louisville Home Guard. From 1856 to 1858 and 1872 to 1879 he served as a law professor at the University of Louisville Law School.

Speed long opposed slavery, a belief that limited his political career in Kentucky before the Civil War. After the war his status as a Radical Republican worked against him. Speed's leading role in keeping Kentucky in the Union, his long association with the Whig Party, and his documented stance against slavery stood him in good stead with Abraham Lincoln, however. Although Speed was not Lincoln's first choice to replace Edward Bates as U.S. attorney general, Lincoln was determined to name a Kentuckian and for both political and personal reasons offered the position to Speed in December 1864. As attorney general, Speed was increasingly drawn into the radical faction of the Republican party. Political differences with President

Andrew Johnson led to Speed's resignation on July 16, 1866.

Speed returned to his Louisville law practice and worked to further the interests of the Republican party at both the state and national levels. In September 1866 he became permanent chairman of the Southern Loyalist Convention in Philadelphia, which opposed Johnson and his policies. The state House and Senate nominated Speed for the U.S. Senate in 1867 but he was defeated in three votes. At the 1868 Republican National Convention, Speed was an unsuccessful candidate for nomination as vice-president. He ran unsuccessfully for the Kentucky House of Representatives in 1870.

Speed married Jane L. Cochran on April 23, 1840. Their children were John, Henry, Charles, Breckinridge, James, Jr., Joshua F., and Edward. Speed died on June 25, 1887, and was buried at Cave Hill Cemetery, Louisville.

See James Speed, *James Speed, a Personality* (Louisville 1914).   JAMES J. HOLMBERG

SPEED, JOSHUA FRY. Joshua Fry Speed, businessman and confidant of Abraham Lincoln, was born in Louisville on November 14, 1814, the son of Judge James and Lucy (Fry) Speed. He was educated first at a private school and then at St. Joseph's Academy in Bardstown, Kentucky (1832-33). Speed left Louisville in 1835 for Springfield, Illinois, where he worked in merchandising and assisted in editing a local newspaper. In Springfield Speed befriended Lincoln and became his confidant. In 1841 Lincoln was a guest at the family home, Farmington, where he stayed for six weeks. During the Civil War Speed served as President Lincoln's adviser on western affairs, and Lincoln on several occasions offered Speed the position of secretary of the treasury, but each time he declined.

In 1842 Speed returned to Louisville to marry Fannie Henning. He was an active member of the Louisville community for the rest of his life. In 1851 he went into a real estate partnership with his wife's brother, William Henning, which lasted until Speed's death. He was president of the Louisville, Cincinnati & Lexington Railroad during 1853-55. In 1867 Speed built a new home on a tract of land that was part of the Farmington plantation where he grew up, naming it Cold Spring. Speed died on May 29, 1882, and was buried in Cave Hill Cemetery in Louisville.

See Robert L. Kincaid, "Joshua Fry Speed: Lincoln's Confidential Agent in Kentucky," *Register* 52 (April 1954): 99-110; Kincaid, "Joshua Fry Speed—Abraham Lincoln's Most Intimate Friend," *FCHQ* 17 (April 1943): 63-121.

SPENCE, BRENT. Brent Spence, U.S. congressman, was born in Newport, Kentucky, on December 24, 1874, the son of Philip and Virginia (Berry) Spence. He received a law degree from the University of Cincinnati in 1894 and was admitted to the bar the same year. Active in local and state politics, Spence served in the state Senate during 1904-08. In 1930 he was elected on the Democratic ticket to the U.S. House of Representatives from the 6th District, serving from March 4, 1931, until January 3, 1963, when failing health forced him to retire. At that time he was one of the oldest members to serve in the House. Often underestimated, Spence was chairman of the powerful House Banking and Currency Committee from 1943 to 1964, except for four years when Republicans controlled Congress.

A quiet, gentle man, he was a strong supporter of the New Deal and the Fair Deal and voted for legislation such as the Agricultural Adjustment Act, the National Industrial Recovery Act, the Social Security Act, and authorization of the Reconstruction Finance Corporation. In 1944 he was selected to attend the Bretton Woods conference, which established the International Monetary Fund and the International Bank for Reconstruction and Development. Spence sponsored and successfully led the fight that established the Bretton Woods proposals. Although suffering from poor hearing and bad eyesight, he provided strong but impartial leadership on the Banking and Currency Committee. A poor speaker, he let others do the debating, but he provided the skills to get crucial legislation passed, especially in the realm of financial legislation. A former banker, Spence sponsored legislation that charted the Export-Import Federal Deposit Insurance Act, which doubled insured savings from $5,000 to $10,000.

Spence married Ida Bitterman on September 6, 1919. After leaving Congress, he lived in Fort Thomas until his death on September 18, 1967, and was buried in the Evergreen Cemetery at Southgate, Kentucky.

See Richard Hedlund, "Brent Spence and the Bretton Woods Legislation," *Register* 79 (Winter 1981).   RICHARD HEDLUND

SPENCER COUNTY. Spencer County, the seventy-seventh in order of formation, is located in western central Kentucky. It is bordered by Bullitt, Jefferson, Nelson, Shelby, and Anderson counties and contains 193 square miles. The county was formed on January 7, 1824, from parts of Nelson, Shelby, and Bullitt counties and named for Capt. Spears Spencer. A member of Kentucky's "Corn Stalk Militia" from 1792 to 1801, Spencer formed the Yellow Jackets rifle company in 1809 and joined Gen. William Henry Harrison's command in the Tippecanoe campaign, where he was killed on November 7, 1811. The county seat is TAYLORSVILLE.

In 1776, a boatload of explorers went up the Salt River to the present site of Taylorsville. Two years later Indians attacked there, and in 1782 Indians massacred an entire settlement near the present Spencer-Nelson county line.

The topography is rolling and hilly, with the Salt River cutting valleys 200 to 250 feet deep. Primarily an agricultural county from the arrival of the first settlers in 1776, Spencer had a slave-based economy. In 1840 there were 1,911 slaves and 4,650 whites; by 1860 the ratio was 2,205 to 3,974.

The number of slaves in the county undoubtedly inclined the populace to support the Confederacy in the Civil War. In 1870 the county produced 458,109 bushels of corn, 13,404 head of livestock, and 1,274 tons of hay, along with wheat and barley. In 1988 farms occupied 81 percent of the land area with 62 percent of farmland in cultivation. The county ranks fifty-first among Kentucky counties in agricultural receipts from tobacco, livestock, hay, and vegetables.

Edward Massie, a Spencer Countian who was a Unionist, cast one of the votes in the 1861 legislature to keep Kentucky in the Union. After Massie returned to his home in Spencer County, he was murdered. In early 1865 a force of Confederate guerrillas, including William C. Quantrill and Marcellus Jerome Clarke ("Sue Mundy") were chased back and forth across Spencer County. Capt. Edwin Terrill, referred to as a scout but more likely a guerrilla working for both sides, was commissioned by federal authorities to locate Quantrill and his band. Terrill found Quantrill at the farm of James Wakefield in the south-central section of the county on May 10, 1865, and fatally wounded him. Quantrill, who died in a military prison hospital in Louisville on June 6, 1865, had been a house guest of Spencer County Judge Jonathan Davis when President Abraham Lincoln was shot, and proposed a toast to his death.

With the loss of slave labor, some farms failed after the war, but others flourished. Shipping goods down the Salt River to the Ohio ended when the Louisville, Cincinnati & Lexington Railroad completed a line from Bloomfield, in Nelson County, through Taylorsville to a main line at Shelbyville in 1881. The railroad was later operated by Louisville & Nashville Railroad (now CSX Transportation); the track was abandoned in 1952. A large number of Spencer Countians are employed outside the county, many in Louisville and Jefferson County. Tourism expenditures brought $4.4 million into the economy in 1988. Taylorsville Lake, impounded on the Salt River in 1982, covers 3,050 acres and offers fishing and boating activities. The Louisville District U.S. Army Corps of Engineers operates a visitors' center at the dam, boat ramps, and a marina. Over 10,000 acres surrounding the lake are devoted to wildlife preservation and recreation. Spencer County is served by KY 44 and 55 and U.S. 31E-150.

The population of Spencer County was 5,488 in 1970; 5,929 in 1980; and 6,801 in 1990.

SPERTI, GEORGE SPERI. George Speri Sperti, scientist and inventor, was born on January 17, 1900, in Covington, Kentucky, the son of George Anthony and Caroline (Speri) Sperti, immigrants from Italy. He attended public schools in Covington and graduated from the School of Engineering of the University of Cincinnati in 1923. In 1925 he founded the Basic Science Research Laboratory of the university and became research professor and director. After a close friend died of cancer, he con-centrated on cancer research and in 1935 founded St. Thomas Institute, a graduate school of scientific research, in Cincinnati. Sperti, who invented the Sperti radiation lamp to treat rheumatism, developed products and processes for the food and drug industries, electronic and radiation devices, gaseous discharge and illumination products, cosmetics, and other products. He was appointed to the Pontifical Academy of Sciences by Pope Pius XI in 1936. The institute he founded stopped teaching and granting degrees in 1987 but research continued. Sperti died on April 29, 1991, and was buried in St. Mary Cemetery, Fort Mitchell, Kentucky.

MARY PHILIP TRAUTH

SPORTS. Kentuckians have always loved sports, whether organized or unorganized. From the fishing, hunting, frontier-style wrestling, target shoots, footraces, and matched horse races of pioneer days to the showdowns between rival basketball teams of the University of Kentucky and University of Louisville, sports have been an integral part of life in the Bluegrass State.

Most identify Kentucky sports with basketball and horse racing, and in a sense this is proper. The nationwide reputation of the commonwealth's collegiate basketball teams is built upon National Collegiate Athletic Association (NCAA) records that designate the University of Kentucky (UK) the top collegiate basketball program of the 1940s and 1950s (85 percent winning percentage in 1940-49, 87 percent in 1950-59, and four of five NCAA Championships in 1948, 1949, 1951, 1958, and 1978). The University of Louisville (U-of-L), with a 72 percent winning percentage in 1980-89 and two NCAA championships in 1980 and 1986, joined UK (73 percent in 1980-89) among basketball's elite during the 1980s. In seven seasons (1930-37), Western Kentucky University's basketball team posted a winning percentage of 80.6.

Kentucky horse racing, conducted in the streets of Lexington before 1780, is paced by the annual May running of the Kentucky Derby, America's premier race for three-year-olds, and by the Kentucky Futurity, a Grand Circuit three-year-old championship trot run in October at Lexington's Red Mile. The oldest continuous organized sport in Kentucky, horse racing, is perpetuated by annual thoroughbred racing at Louisville's Churchill Downs, Henderson's Ellis Park, Lexington's Keeneland, and Florence's Turfway Park; trotting at Lexington's Red Mile and Louisville Downs; quarter horse racing and trotting at Henderson's Riverside Downs; and quarter horse and Arabian racing at Paducah's Bluegrass Downs.

Baseball and football both predate basketball as team sports in Kentucky. The origins of organized baseball in Kentucky date back to the American Civil War, when veterans brought back the game they had learned from contacts with Union soldiers. A club of baseball enthusiasts was formed in Louisville on April 10, 1865. Within two years, other clubs existed in Lexington, Frankfort, Maysville,

Dayton, Newport, and Covington. On October 22, 1869, the Louisville club lost to the undefeated professional Cincinnati Red Stockings, 59 to 8. When the National League was formed in 1876 in Louisville, it included the city's team. The Louisville Grays left the league after four players were implicated in a fix scandal in 1877. After a stint in the rival American Association (1882-91), Louisville reentered the National League in 1892, remaining until 1899 (see LOUISVILLE COLONELS). Thirty cities in Kentucky have had minor league teams, most of them class D. The Bluegrass League (1909-12, 1922-24), with ten Kentucky teams, and the Kitty League, with nine Kentucky teams (1903-05, 1906, 1901-14, 1916, 1922-24, 1935, 1936-42) were most prominent. There are also numerous youth, social, fraternal, club, business, collegiate, prep, church, and semiprofessional and federations and congresses that play baseball throughout Kentucky.

The first intercollegiate football game in Kentucky was played on April 10, 1880, at the old City Park (Stoll Field) in Lexington. In the game, Kentucky University defeated Centre 13 3/4 to 0. Played by rules established during the first American football game, the Princeton-Rutgers game of 1869, the Centre-Transylvania match was organized by an inventive Kentucky University student named Thurgood, from Australia. Five hundred attended the game. Football in Kentucky is played at youth, prep, collegiate, and semipro levels. In 1921 Centre College won national recognition when it upset Harvard, the nation's top team, 6 to 0. Other highlights include thirteen major-bowl appearances and a cumulative 8-4-1 winning record by teams from Kentucky (UK 5-2; U-of-L 2-1-1; Centre 2-1) and two division 1-AA national championships for Eastern Kentucky University (1979 and 1982).

Golf, tennis, and track and field (called "pedestrianism" in earlier days) have century-long histories in Kentucky. The first golf course in the South was the nine-hole course constructed at the English settlement in Middlesborough, Kentucky, in 1889. Men's and women's golf is played by professionals and amateurs statewide. In 1926, Jeff Sweetser of Cobb, Kentucky, became the first native-born American to win the British amateur title. Kentucky golfers have also become members of the men's and women's pro tours and the men's senior tour. Lawn tennis appeared regularly in Kentucky just after the Civil War. Private courts dated to the 1870s; among the first public park courts were two built in Louisville at Cherokee and Shawnee in 1897. Both men and women from Kentucky have competed on the pro tennis tours. One of the earliest feats in pedestrianism occurred in Lexington on July 17, 1880, when a Transylvania professor walked 390 miles around the courthouse square in 390 hours. Track and field remains a popular prep and collegiate sport. Of note are NCAA division II championships in cross-country (1964) and outdoor track (1971) by Kentucky State University (1988).

Men's basketball, which along with volleyball originated in the 1890s as a YMCA sport, clearly remains Kentucky's most popular competitive sport. It is played statewide at almost every level by seemingly limitless age groups. Kentucky basketball has produced legends: Coaches Adolph Rupp (Kentucky), Ed Diddle (Western Kentucky University), S.T. Roach (Lexington Dunbar High School), Willy Lee Kean (Louisville Central High School); high school phenomena like Owensboro's Cliff Hagen, and Wayland's "King" Kelly Coleman; memorable state tournament teams like Ashland and Carr Creek (a four-overtime championship game in 1928); tiny Cuba, the classic underdog (1951 and 1952); the whistling ballhawks from Breckenridge County (1964 and 1965); and collegiate performers such as Kentucky's Fabulous Five and Fiddling Five (1948 and 1958), Louisville's magical 1980 national champions, and Western's heartbreak NCAA team of 1966. Kentucky teams have made multiple appearances in national basketball tournaments, producing National Association of Intercollegiate Athletics champions (Louisville, 1948; Kentucky State (1971, 1972, and 1973); division II NCAA champion Kentucky Wesleyan (1966, 1968, 1969, 1973, 1987, and 1989); small college champions (Sullivan Business College, 1967, 1968, 1969, and 1980; Lindsey Wilson College, 1972); and Christian college champion Kentucky Christian (1988 and 1989).

High school athletics in Kentucky are regulated by the Kentucky High School Athletics Association (KHSAA). Begun in 1917 with nineteen schools, the KHSAA has conducted the boys' state basketball tournament since 1918—first at Centre College in Danville and later at locations in either Lexington or Louisville. Held in March, and known as the Sweet Sixteen because it features champions from sixteen state regions, this tournament is the premier high school sporting event in Kentucky. The girls' basketball tournament, begun in 1921, but abandoned in 1932, was reinstituted in 1975. A class-A small school state tournament was established for boys in 1990 and for girls in 1991.

Kentuckians participate in a wide variety of seasonal and year-round competitive and leisure sports, from badminton, billiards, and bowling to skydiving, steeplechases, and tractor pulls. Kentucky has sent out four world champion boxers: heavyweights Marvin Hart (1905-06), Muhammad Ali (1964-67, 1974-78), Jimmy Ellis (1968-70), and featherweight Davey Moore, (1959-63); a fast-pitch softball world champion (Covington Carr's, 1939); and an NCAA national pocketpool champion (Leroy Kinman, Eastern Kentucky University, 1949). Several sports, such as those involving distance races, competitive shooting, and equestrian skills are part of annual festivals, fairs, and special shows, of which there are more than one hundred statewide.

Kentucky also hosts three structured statewide amateur sports competitions: the Governor's Bluegrass State Games, the Kentucky Senior Games, and the Kentucky Special Olympics of Sport. The Governor's Games are scheduled the last weekend in July at sports sites throughout the city of Lexington. Begun in 1986 and limited to Kentucky residents, some of whom must qualify, the twenty sport competitions in 1989 involved more than 14,000 individuals ranging in age from four to eighty-six. The Kentucky Senior Games were first held in Lexington in July 1987. Sponsored by recreation agencies and those for the aging, these year-round competitions, which include forty separate sporting events, are held at regional sites around Kentucky. They lead to state competitions, which have been held at Lexington, Bowling Green, Henderson, and Owensboro. Competitors, some 6,000 annually, are divided into men's and women's bracketed age groups, beginning at ages fifty-five to fifty-nine. The oldest competitor, a male bowler from the Owensboro area with a 183 average in 1989, was ninety-six years old. The Kentucky Special Olympics of Sport began in 1970. Statewide competition among 12,000 participants in twenty-two sports leads to state championships, and every fourth year qualifiers become eligible to represent Kentucky at the International Special Olympics.

Kentucky's history is interspersed with sports imagery. Kentucky's streams brought fishermen, its wild game brought hunters, its competitive way of life spawned fisticuffs and frontier-style wrestling. Wrestlers now have cushioned mats and gymnasiums, and boxers wear gloves, but 500,000 Kentuckians still hunt, and a similar number fish; atop rugged hills, men still sit listening to their hunting dogs chase a fox—a part of their Anglo-Saxon heritage. Louisville-born Ralph Waldo Rose captured the essence of the Kentucky sportsman. One of the seven native-born Kentuckians who have won Olympic medals, Rose—a shot putter, discus and hammer thrower—was chosen to carry the American flag at the 1908 Olympic parade in London. As Rose passed King Edward VII, this proud Kentuckian established an Olympic tradition by walking straight by without dipping his nation's flag to a foreign ruler. In such ways, and by many of those earlier mentioned, Kentucky's sports history remains uniquely rich.

See John McGill, *Kentucky Sports* (Lexington, Ky., 1978); Mike Embry, *Basketball In The Bluegrass State* (New York 1983).

JAMES C. CLAYPOOL

SPRINGFIELD. Springfield, the seat of Washington County in the southwestern part of central Kentucky, is located at the junction of U.S. 150, KY 555, and KY 55. The town was established December 7, 1793, on fifty acres of land donated by Gen. Matthew Walton, one of pioneer Kentucky's largest landowners, and was named for the area's many springs. The town grew as a result of its location on the trace that connected Bardstown and Danville.

The first county courthouse, a log structure built by Hugh McElroy, was completed in January 1794 and burned eleven months later. The brick building that replaced it was occupied from July 1797, until destroyed by fire in 1814. The third courthouse, a two-story brick building of Georgian style with a peaked roof, built for $2,500, was completed in 1816. In 1990 the building was the oldest Kentucky courthouse still in use as such.

By 1800 Springfield's population of 163 made it the tenth largest city in the state. Among the early inhabitants was the Rev. Jesse Head, who as justice of the peace officiated at the June 12, 1806, wedding of Thomas Lincoln and Nancy Hanks, the parents of Abraham Lincoln. Other early prominent citizens included Felix Grundy, a celebrated criminal lawyer and political leader.

During the Confederate invasion of Kentucky in the late summer of 1862, Gen. Braxton Bragg's Confederate army passed through the city, preceding Union Gen. Don Carlos Buell. Buell made his headquarters at Elmwood, the Springfield home of Hugh McElroy, just prior to the battle at nearby Perryville on October 8, 1862. Gen. John Hunt Morgan's Confederate cavalry entered Springfield on three occasions during the war, in July 1862, in December 1862, and on July 5, 1863. In the latter years of the war, the city was threatened by guerrilla attacks led by Dick Mitchell, a local man who had been one of Morgan's soldiers. A Home Guard unit was organized at Springfield to maintain the peace.

After the war, economic growth was greatly enhanced when the Bardstown branch of the Louisville & Nashville Railroad (now CSX Transportation) was extended to Springfield in January 1888. In 1908 Springfield was one of only five loose-leaf tobacco markets in the state. By the fall of 1910, it had four tobacco companies and warehouses. A renowned writer who spent most of her life in Springfield during that era was Elizabeth Madox Roberts, author of *Time of Man* (1926).

Springfield remains an agricultural center. The Springfield Redrying tobacco processing plant is one of the town's largest employers. Armour Food Company, which makes dairy products and provides the area's dairy farmers with a market, is also a leading employer. Industrial products made in Springfield include plastic pipe, insulation, jeans, and golf bags. The population of the fourth-class city was 2,961 in 1970; 3,179 in 1980; and 2,875 in 1990.

SPRINGFIELD. The Springfield estate, in Jefferson County, Kentucky, was the boyhood home of Zachary Taylor, twelfth president of the United States. Taylor was an infant when his father, Col. Richard Taylor, moved the family from Orange County, Virginia to Jefferson County in 1785. In the late 1780s Colonel Taylor built the brick, Georgianstyle house. A two-story wing was added ca. 1810-20.

Zachary Taylor lived at Springfield until he joined the army in 1808. In later years he visited the farm and some of his children were born there. Several years after his death in 1850, Taylor's remains were removed from Washington, D.C., and reinterred in the Taylor family graveyard on the farm. The graveyard is now part of the Zachary Taylor National Cemetery, just southeast of Springfield.

The Taylor farm was sold by the family in 1868, and the land was subdivided in the 1950s. Springfield, a private residence, has been designated a national historic landmark.

See Holman Hamilton, *Zachary Taylor, Soldier of the Republic* (New York 1941).

MARY JEAN KINSMAN

SQUIRE BOONE'S STATION. In 1779, when Daniel Boone's younger brother, Squire BOONE, left Boonesborough, he settled in what is now Shelby County, Kentucky, and founded a station that bore his name; it was also known as Painted Stone Station. Located in the vicinity of present-day Shelbyville, for nearly two years it was the only station between Harrodsburg and the Falls of the Ohio. Indian threats in September 1781 resulted in the abandonment of the station, but it was reoccupied around Christmas of that year. After being elected to the Virginia legislature about 1783, Squire Boone sold his interest in the station to a Colonel Lynch, and it was thereafter known as Lynch Station.

See George L. Willis, Sr., *History of Shelby County, Kentucky* (Louisville 1929).

STAHR, ELVIS, JR. Lawyer, educator, and conservationist, Elvis Stahr, Jr., was born to Elvis J. and Mary Anne (McDaniel) Stahr in Hickman, Fulton County, Kentucky, on March 9, 1916. Stahr served as president of his senior class in 1936 at the University of Kentucky, where he earned a B.A. in English literature and a Rhodes Scholarship to Oxford University. While at Oxford (1936-39), Stahr earned a B.A. in jurisprudence in 1938 and a bachelor of civil law degree in 1939. After practicing law in New York City (1939-47), he returned to Kentucky, becoming an associate professor of law at the University of Kentucky in 1947. With his acceptance by the Kentucky bar in 1948, Stahr became a full professor and dean of the College of Law. He held both positions until 1956. Stahr also served as university provost (1954-56) and as a member of the Constitutional Review Committee of Kentucky (1952-56).

In 1956 Stahr was appointed to President Dwight D. Eisenhower's Committee on Education beyond High School, which examined the university system in the United States. He resigned from the committee in 1957 and became vice-chancellor of the University of Pittsburgh, then president of the University of West Virginia (Morgantown) in 1958. In 1961 Stahr left West Virginia to become President John F. Kennedy's secretary of the army. After a brief tenure (1961-62), he left government service to succeed Herman B. Wells as president of Indiana University on July 1, 1962. Stahr left Indiana in 1968 to become president of the National Audubon Society in New York City. He held this position until 1979, when he became the society's senior counselor (1979-81). He joined the Washington, D.C., office of the San Francisco law firm of Chickering and Gregory in 1982.

Stahr married Dorothy Howland Berkfield on June 28, 1946; they have three children: Stephanie, Stuart, and Bradford.

STANDARDBRED INDUSTRY. Descended from the thoroughbred, the Morgan, and draft horses, the standardbred horse races not at a gallop but at a trot or by pacing—a gait in which the hooves strike the ground in lateral pairs (right front and right hind together, then left front and left hind), rather than in the diagonal pairs of the trot. A standardbred trotter or pacer is expected to cover a mile within a fixed time. Messenger is the standardbred foundation sire.

Early standardbreds both raced and worked as farm animals. As early as 1804, Cabell's Dale, now Castleton farm, advertised standardbred sire service. Throughout the nineteenth and well into the twentieth century, Kentucky was a standardbred breeding center. The Virginia stallion Hiatoga was brought to Kentucky in 1822. Standardbreds were sometimes named for popular public figures, such as Andrew Jackson, Davey Crockett, or Henry Clay, and three horses in the 1800s were named Cassius M. Clay.

Except for local fairs and match races, standardbred races were seldom organized events until 1850, when a number of races were held in Lexington. Nine years later, the Kentucky Trotting Association (KTA) was organized, with Robert A. Alexander as president. Owner of WOODBURN FARM in Woodford County, Alexander, like many other breeders, owned both standardbreds and thoroughbreds. The KTA started racing in 1859. After the Civil War, private cup races were offered by stallion owners. A four-day meet in Lexington in 1872 brought hundreds into the town. The KTA was reorganized into the Kentucky Trotting Horse Breeder's Association, which in 1875 opened the RED MILE track on South Broadway in Lexington.

Other standardbred race meets were held across the state as the breed's popularity increased. In 1887 Somerset held races on July 4. In August 1887 Harrodsburg had a five-day meet; Columbia, five days; Bowling Green, four days; Covington, four days; Sharpsburg, four days; and Maysville, four days, including the Mason County Stakes. Paris had a five-day meet in September 1887, as did Owensboro in October. In 1900, standardbred races were held in Winchester, Guthrie, Bowling Green, and Richmond, as well as Lexington. By 1919 races were held in Louisville, Erlanger, and Uniontown.

While standardbreds performed across the state, farms were concentrated in the Lexington area. Castleton farm on Iron Works Pike, still breeding and racing standardbreds, is said to have produced more great trotters and pacers than any other thoroughbred-standardbred farm. Almahurst on Harrodsburg Road, which dispersed its Kentucky thoroughbred and standardbred operations in 1990, produced the world champion trotter Claude. It was at

Poplar Hill, on Russell Cave Pike outside of Lexington, that NANCY HANKS was foaled. Walnut Hall, on Newtown Pike, and Calumet, on Versailles Road, were premier standardbred breeding and racing establishments in the 1930s.

Standardbreds attained great popularity in the 1960s and 1970s as the horses shattered the two-minute mile. In 1966 Bret Hanover covered the distance in 1:53.3. Steady Star completed the mile in 1:52 in 1971. Matt Scooter's top time of 1:44.2 was recorded in 1986 at the Red Mile. Standardbreds race at a number of other tracks in Kentucky, including Riverside Downs (formerly Audubon Raceway) in Henderson.

See James C. Harrison, *Care and Training of the Trotter and Pacer* (Columbus, Ohio, 1968).

STANFORD. Stanford, the seat of Lincoln County, is located in the northern part of the county on St. Asaph Creek at U.S. 27 and U.S. 150. Stanford traces its origin to a camp made by Benjamin Logan in 1775 at Buffalo Spring, a large spring at the western edge of the town. A short distance north of the spring, Logan erected his settlement and fort, which he called St. Asaph. Later the site became known as Logan's Fort. The small branch that has its source at Buffalo Spring is still known as St. Asaph Creek.

The original site of Logan's Fort is about one mile west of the courthouse in Stanford, at the end of Water Street. Part of an old buffalo trail to the salt lick at Buffalo Spring became what is now Main Street in Stanford. Logan's Fort became known as the Standing Fort because it withstood many Indian attacks during the late 1770s. Although it was one of the smaller forts in Kentucky in both size and population, it never fell to the Indians.

Benjamin Logan donated some of the land along St. Asaph Creek in 1781 for the Lincoln County courthouse. The county court initially met at Fort Harrod (now Harrodsburg). After several years of delays, the Virginia General Assembly finally accepted Logan's offer. The new county seat was issued its charter in October 1786, making Stanford one of the first chartered towns in the Kentucky territory of Virginia. The origin of the town's name is unknown; it may have been a derivation of Standing Fort.

The town's first trustees were Benjamin Logan, John Logan, William Montgomery, Henry Pawling, Isaac Shelby, Walker Baylor, and Alexander Blain. John Logan, brother of Benjamin Logan, later became the first state treasurer of Kentucky. The first courthouse was built of logs in 1787; the fourth courthouse was built on the same site in 1909. Unlike many other Kentucky courthouses, none of the old courthouse buildings that stood in Stanford was lost to fire. All the original records of the county's history are intact. The earliest court records date to November 1779. Many old land records name pioneers such as Daniel Boone and Simon Kenton. A few original land deeds are recorded on sheepskin.

Stanford developed slowly during the antebellum period. The earliest church was Presbyterian, established about 1790 in a log house, which is now a part of the Harvey Helm Memorial Historic Library and Museum on West Main Street. The Baptist, Methodist, and Christian churches were not organized until the 1830s and 1840s. The Logan family, staunch Presbyterians, were influential in organizing the Presbyterian Meetinghouse, which stood during the early 1800s in what is now the Buffalo Spring Cemetery. The Presbyterian church has been located on the site on East Main Street since about 1850.

Stanford's earliest known educational institutions were located in the old Female Academy building on West Main Street (later Fox Funeral Home) and the Male Academy building on Somerset Street. The Male Academy was established in the 1850s, and the Female Academy in the 1870s. Since 1900 the town's school has occupied its present site on Danville Street. A subscription library was located in Stanford in the 1830s.

Stanford experienced a period of economic expansion in the 1870s and 1880s, after the construction of the Louisville & Nashville Railroad (now CSX Transportation) through the town. The railroad opened Stanford's long-isolated economy to the state's larger region. The town's first newspaper, the *Stanford Banner* (now the *Interior Journal*), began publication in the late 1860s. The lack of an industrial base slowed Stanford's growth by the early 1960s. The town lost its railroad service to Lebanon, Kentucky, in 1988, but a spur line remained open to Mt. Vernon, Kentucky.

One of Kentucky's native sons who was associated with Stanford for many years was U.S. Rep. Harvey Helm, born in Danville, Kentucky, in 1867 to parents who were natives of Lincoln County. The Helm family established Helm's Station near Milledgeville about 1780, and another branch of the family settled in the northern section of the county near Hubble in the late 1780s. Harvey Helm attended the Stanford Male Academy and Central University in Richmond, and studied law under Col. T.P. Hill, of Stanford. He was admitted to the bar in 1890 and was elected to the state legislature in 1894. Helm, a Democrat, then served as the Lincoln County attorney for two terms between 1897 and 1905 and in the U.S. Congress for twelve consecutive years (1907-19). The county public library was named in Helm's honor in 1966. In 1970 a new library building was built behind the courthouse. The Helm home is now known as the Harvey Helm Memorial Historic Library and Museum.

The population of the fifth-class city was 2,474 in 1970; 2,764 in 1980; and 2,686 in 1990.

See Mrs. M.H. Dunn, *Early Lincoln County History* (Stanford, Ky., 1975).   ALLAN R. LEACH

STANLEY, AUGUSTUS OWSLEY. Augustus Owsley Stanley, governor during 1915-19, was born in Shelbyville, Kentucky, on May 21, 1867, to William and Amanda (Owsley) Stanley. He attended the Kentucky Agricultural and Mechanical College in Lexington, and graduated from Centre College in Danville in 1889. After teaching at several schools, he read law and was admitted to the bar in 1894. In his first try for public office, Stanley, a Democrat, was defeated for Fleming County attorney in 1897.

The next year he moved to Henderson, and in 1902 he was elected to the first of six terms (March 4, 1903-March 3, 1915) in the U.S. House of Representatives, where he was known for his defense of the tobacco farmer and his attacks on corporate trusts. In 1914 Stanley pursued a seat in the U.S. Senate, but lost in the Democratic primary to former Gov. J.C.W. Beckham (1900-1907); the pivotal issue was Stanley's defense of the liquor industry. Beckham won, 72,677 votes to Stanley's 65,871, with incumbent James B. McCreary polling 20,257.

In January 1915 Stanley announced his candidacy for the Democratic nomination for governor. He pledged better roads, an end to convict and contract labor, and enforcement of the county option law instead of statewide prohibition of alcohol. He won the nomination over Henry V. McChesney, 107,585 to 69,722. His Republican opponent was Edwin P. Morrow. Stanley and Morrow were close friends, and they provided the state with one of the most colorful campaigns in its history. The dog tax of 1886, which placed a one-dollar tax on all dogs, was an issue. Morrow held that every person should be allowed to have one dog tax-free. Stanley labeled the proposal "Free Old Dog Ring" and ridiculed the idea in his speeches, sometimes by howling like a hound dog. Stanley won the governorship by a narrow margin, 219,991 to 219,520.

Stanley's true ambition was to sit in the U.S. Senate, and when Sen. Ollie M. James died in August 1918, Governor Stanley announced his candidacy for the vacant office. He won in November, defeating Republican Ben L. Bruner by a 5,600-vote margin and resigned the governorship in May 1919. He served in the Senate from May 19, 1919, to March 3, 1925, losing his bid for reelection to Frederic M. Sackett in a Republican landslide. Stanley then opened a law practice in Washington, D.C. In 1930 President Herbert Hoover appointed him to the International Joint Commission, which mediates U.S.-Canadian border disputes. He resigned under party pressure in 1954.

Stanley married Sue Soaper in 1903; they had three sons. He died in Washington, D.C., on August 12, 1958, and was buried in the Frankfort Cemetery.

During Stanley's governorship the question of prohibition was dominant. A prohibition amendment to the state constitution failed in both houses in 1916, but passed the General Assembly in 1918. In 1919 Kentucky was the first "wet" state to ratify the Eighteenth Amendment to the U.S. Constitution, which made prohibition the law of the land. Stanley secured a corrupt practices act, a convict labor bill, an antitrust measure, and a worker's compensation act. He called a special session in February 1917 to reform Kentucky's "grossly inadequate" tax system. He was not completely successful, but a three-member tax commission was established to supervise the administration of the tax system. The General Assembly later passed a redistricting bill and provided for the state's budget system. During World War I Stanley vetoed a bill that would have banned the teaching of German in the public schools. When he resigned, Stanley had seen most of his programs enacted.

See Thomas W. Ramage, "Augustus Owsley Stanley: Early Twentieth Century Kentucky Democrat," Ph.D. diss., University of Kentucky, 1968; Nicholas C. Burckel, "A.O. Stanley and Progressive Reform, 1902-1919," *Register* 79 (Spring 1981): 136-62.   LOWELL H. HARRISON

STANLEY, FRANK, SR. Frank Stanley, Sr., editor and publisher of the LOUISVILLE DEFENDER and champion of civil rights, was born in Chicago on April 6, 1906, to John and Helen (Cole) Stanley. When he was six, his family moved to Louisville, where he graduated from Central High School. He graduated from Atlanta University in 1929, majoring in English and minoring in journalism.

In 1933 Stanley went to work for the *Louisville Defender* as a reporter. Three years later he became one of the newspaper's three owners, its general manager, and editor. During his tenure as publisher, the newspaper received more than thirty-five awards in journalism, including one for Stanley's syndicated column "People, Places and Problems." He helped to found the Negro Newspaper Publishers' Association (now National Newspaper Publishers' Association) and served as juror for the Pulitzer Prize award in 1969 and 1972.

Stanley's involvement in civil rights included participation in federally sponsored trips in 1946 and 1948 to study the segregation of American troops after World War II in occupied Europe. His report helped pave the way for desegregation of the armed forces. At the state level, Stanley drafted Senate Resolution No. 53 in 1950, which led to the integration of higher education in Kentucky. Ten years later, at the behest of Gov. Bert Combs (1959-63), Stanley proposed the organizational structure for Kentucky's Human Rights Commission and subsequently served as its vice-president.

Stanley was married to Vivian Clark; they had two sons, Frank, Jr., and Kenneth. He died on October 19, 1974, and was buried in Louisville's Cave Hill Cemetery.   OLIVIA FREDERICK

STANTON, HARRY DEAN. Harry Dean Stanton, actor, was born to Sheridan and Ersel (McKnight) Stanton on July 14, 1926, in West Irvine, Kentucky. His family soon moved to Lexington, where he graduated from Lafayette High School in 1944. He served in the U.S. Navy during World War II. After the war Stanton attended the University of Kentucky from the fall of 1946 until the spring of 1949. While there he began acting, playing such characters as Alfred Doolittle in *Pygmalion*.

Stanton moved to New York City and then to California in the early 1950s. After working at the Pasadena Playhouse for four years, he made his film debut in 1957 in *Revolt at Fort Laramie*. He played supporting roles in *Cool Hand Luke* (1967), *Kelly's Heroes* (1970), *Pat Garrett and Billy the Kid* (1971), *Farewell, My Lovely* (1975), *The Missouri Breaks* (1976), *Alien* (1979), *Private Benjamin* (1980), *Repo Man* (1984), *Pretty in Pink* (1986), and *The Last Temptation of Christ* (1988). Stanton had his first starring role in *Paris, Texas* (1984) as a man who after several years of alienation hopes to rebuild his life with his family. The film won the Palme D'Or grand prize at the Cannes Film Festival, and the London Film Critics Circle selected Stanton as best actor. He has worked also in television.

STANTON. The seat of Powell County, Stanton is located at the junction of KY 15 and 213, just north of the Mountain Parkway. Once called Beaver Pond for a small lake that was the result of a beaver dam near the town, it was renamed Stanton in honor of Richard M. Stanton, of Maysville, who was a member of the U.S. House of Representatives (1849-55). Though it was designated the seat of government for the newly created Powell County in 1852, Stanton was not incorporated until March 9, 1854.

Stanton grew slowly during the nineteenth century. In the spring of 1863 a band of guerrillas raided and burned the courthouse in support of the Southern cause. Later, on June 1, 1864, the town again was ransacked and the jail was destroyed by fire. A second courthouse was constructed after the war and served the county until 1890, when it was replaced by a two-story brick Victorian style building. This courthouse was razed in 1977 to make room for the fourth courthouse. When the Kentucky Union Railway—later the Lexington & Eastern (L&E) Railway—reached Stanford in 1886 the town reaped the benefits of an improved lumber and coal trade. After 1909, when the Louisville & Nashville Railroad (now CSX Transportation) bought out the L&E, Stanton became an important stop on the route, bringing coal and lumber out of the Appalachian Mountains.

In 1941 the railroad through Stanton and Powell County was dismantled for scrap. Stanton experienced hard times throughout much of the 1940s and 1950s. When the Mountain Parkway was built through the county during Gov. Bert Combs's administration (1959-63), the town experienced rebirth. Easy access to Stanton encouraged industrial development in the town. Industries such as lumber, stone, and metal fabrication provide employment for many people who work in nearby Winchester and Lexington and settle in Stanton. The population of this fourth-class city was 2,037 in 1970; 2,691 in 1980; and 2,795 in 1990.

See John Ed Pearce, "Powell County," *Louisville Courier-Journal Magazine*, July 16, 1978.

RON D. BRYANT

STANTON ACADEMY. The Stanton Academy, affiliated with the United Presbyterian Church of North America, was an elementary and secondary school that opened in the fall of 1908 in Stanton, Kentucky. At an organizational meeting in 1907, subscriptions totaled $2,300, and James C. Patrick donated ten acres of land. When the school opened, the principal was R.A. McConagha, and there were five teachers for the 133 pupils. The first building was constructed in 1908 by A.B. Hamilton at a cost of $20,000. The academy closed in 1931 and the Powell County board of education used the building for a high school until 1937. Later, the building was used for the Head Start Program. It burned in 1984.

DAVID EUGENE RULE

STAR ROUTES. When the U.S. Postal Service was formed by congressional act on September 29, 1789, it delivered mail over star routes to areas not located on stagecoach lines or, later, on railroad lines. Star route carriers rode horses and mules carrying bags of mail to and from the tiny outlying post offices. In Kentucky, star mail routes were concentrated in the eastern part of the state, which was served by small fourth class rural post offices. London in Laurel County, a central point from which mail riders delivered mail to Barbourville, Manchester, Corbin, Williamsburg, and points in between, was also an important center of star route contracting. During the latter quarter of the nineteenth century, more than 10,000 bids for star routes were submitted from London, and in 1893 local contractors had gained contracts on 2,500 routes, half of those awarded nationwide. During 1870-90, contracting of star routes became a profitable business.

THOMAS D. CLARK

STATEHOOD CONVENTIONS. The creation of the first trans-Appalachian political community admitted to the Union may be traced to a May 15, 1780, petition to the Continental Congress requesting admission as a separate state. Serious statehood efforts did not begin until Indian troubles, in which Virginia had little interest, prompted Col. Benjamin Logan to call a public meeting in Danville, Kentucky, in November 1784. This meeting discussed Kentucky's lack of legal authority to organize and support a militia, and it explored solutions, including separation from Virginia, but committed that issue to a more representative body of men chosen from each militia company.

The first statehood convention began on December 27, 1784. Like the nine that followed, it was held in Danville. After debating the problems of the frontier, delegates, who were militia officers, decided that statehood was the best solution, and then passed a resolution to separate from Virginia and unite with the Confederation government. Since the delegates did not believe they had been elected for the express purpose of requesting separation, they called for a second convention, for which delegates would be chosen at the spring 1785 election of Virginia legislative delegates.

The second convention, which assembled on May 23, 1785, prepared a petition (never sent) to the Virginia legislature requesting separation and promising to join the Confederation as soon as possible. Believing further public discussion was warranted, it issued a call for the election of delegates to a third convention, which met on August 8, 1785, and took final action. In response, Virginia passed an act of separation (ENABLING ACT), the first of four, which required a fourth convention to meet in September 1786 and which depended on the assent of Congress by June 1, 1787, for Kentucky's admission to the Confederation.

The fourth convention did not meet until January 1787 because a majority of the delegates were engaged in two volunteer armies organized by Gen. George Rogers Clark and Logan to fight the Wabash and Shawnee Indians. In the interim, the remaining delegates suggested that Virginia make several changes in the act of separation. In response, the Virginia legislature revised the act, required a fifth convention to be called, and set July 4, 1788, as the deadline for congressional assent. At its January 1787 meeting, the fourth convention, unaware of Virginia's action, decided upon separation, but adjourned when informed about the second act of separation.

When the fifth convention assembled on September 17, 1787, the delegates unanimously agreed to separation, adopted a petition to Congress for admission to the Confederation, and then authorized a sixth convention to write a state constitution. On the same day in Philadelphia, however, the federal convention had adopted a new Constitution. The ensuing campaign to secure its ratification caused another delay for Kentucky's statehood efforts. When the petition for admission was finally considered on July 3, 1788, Congress, aware that ten states had already adopted the new Constitution, refused to act on Kentucky's request and referred the petition to the new government.

When the sixth convention met on July 28, Kentucky's growing Mississippi River trade and Spain's control over New Orleans had acquired considerable importance in the statehood debate. In the so-called SPANISH CONSPIRACY, several Kentuckians had taken the first steps toward the establishment of an independent state. John Brown had discussed Kentucky's future with the Spanish minister to the Confederation. At the convention, Brown—along with George Muter, Harry Innes, and other members of the group (the Court party) who favored separation without applying for admission to the Union—called for a convention to form a constitution for an independent government. A large majority of delegates voted down the proposal and agreed to another statehood convention.

The Spanish Conspiracy had progressed further when the seventh convention began on November 4, 1788. James Wilkinson, a delegate to the convention and a member of the Court party, had returned from New Orleans, where the Spanish governor-general had agreed to accept Wilkinson's shipment of goods if Wilkinson would represent Spain's interests in Kentucky. In his convention address, Wilkinson stressed the importance of the Mississippi River to Kentucky's economic development and then proposed immediate independence and the organization of a separate state. When Brown failed to support him, the leaders of the Country party—Thomas Marshall, Gen. Robert Breckinridge, and Humphrey Marshall—were able to gain the adoption of petitions to both Virginia and Congress, requesting separation from Virginia and admission to the Union. The Virginia legislature, however, notified of the refusal of the Confederation Congress to act on Kentucky's petition for admission, passed a third enabling act that required another statehood convention. The delegates to the eighth convention, which assembled on July 20, 1789, objected to two new conditions in the act of separation: that Kentucky pay a portion of Virginia's domestic debt and that it secure bounty lands set aside for its soldiers. The Virginia legislature subsequently removed the two conditions and then, in its fourth act of separation (which included the VIRGINIA COMPACT), provided for the ninth statehood convention and congressional assent by November 1, 1791.

The ninth convention met on July 26, 1790, accepted the fourth act of separation, submitted a petition to Congress requesting admission, and issued a call for a constitutional convention. At President George Washington's initiative, the first Congress accepted Kentucky's statehood petition and passed an act on February 4, 1791, admitting Kentucky to the Union. Vermont was admitted fourteen days later, but Vermont formally preceded Kentucky as the fourteenth state, because the ninth convention had fixed June 1, 1792, as the date for Kentucky's admission. In the interim, a tenth convention assembled in April 1792 and wrote the state's first constitution. Kentucky's lengthy statehood movement had been shaped by the major political events of the new American nation: Indian hostilities, foreign intrigues, and creation of a new national government. In these times, Kentucky's political leaders had moved cautiously to assure public support for statehood, rejected appeals for an independent government, and worked patiently with Virginia to achieve a legal separation and admission to the Union.

See Temple Bodley, *Littell's Political Transactions in and Concerning Kentucky* (Louisville 1926); George M. Chinn, *Kentucky: Settlement and Statehood, 1750-1800* (Frankfort, Ky., 1975).

WILLIAM GREEN

STATES' RIGHTS PARTY. The genesis of the States' Rights (Dixiecrat) party of 1948 was the intention of President Harry S. Truman and the liberal wing of the Democratic party to make the issue of civil rights a significant part of the 1948 presidential campaign. In February 1948 Truman proposed such legislation in a message to Congress. The proposal coincided with the Southern Governors' Conference held in Wakulla, Florida, where the governors discussed ways to persuade Truman to abandon his civil rights stand. Various stratagems failed to move Truman. At that point, States' Rights Democrats held a conference in Jackson, Mississippi, on May 10, 1948, where the southern leaders decided to try to block Truman's nomination at the Democratic National Convention and, if that failed, to reconvene in Birmingham, Alabama, immediately afterward. Gov. Ben T. Laney of Arkansas was chosen permanent chairman of the States' Rights Democrats.

At the Democratic convention in Philadelphia in July, the southern wing was unsuccessful in blocking Truman's nomination but denied him a unanimous vote by nominating and supporting Sen. Richard B. Russell of Georgia. After the party adopted a strong civil rights plank, half of the Alabama delegation walked out of the convention.

On July 17 States' Rights Democrats met in Birmingham. The Dixiecrat delegates were divided over procedure and purpose but ultimately adopted a platform and selected candidates: Gov. Strom Thurmond (South Carolina) and Gov. Fielding Wright (Mississippi). (The convention only "endorsed" its nominees. After Alabama, Mississippi, and South Carolina later officially chose them as candidates, Thurmond and Wright "accepted" nomination in Houston, Texas, in August 1948.)

The States' Rights party was listed on the ballot in several states, including Kentucky, and Thurmond took himself seriously as a presidential candidate. The party, however, failed to draw into its ranks many prominent southern leaders and some, such as Laney, defected. By late October, it seemed obvious to nearly all political observers that the Dixiecrat party (like the other notable breakaway, Henry A. Wallace's Progressive party) was floundering badly. Thurmond campaigned in Kentucky in mid-October, delivering major speeches in Lexington (October 12), Louisville (October 13), and Covington (October 15) and making brief stops in Shelbyville, Frankfort, Bedford, and Carrollton. He drew his largest audience, 1,000 or so, in Louisville, where he was introduced by the Kentucky States' Rights party chairman, Orval Baylor of Versailles.

In his addresses Thurmond attacked both major parties for their "unconstitutional, totalitarian" platforms. "Our racial minorities," he said in Covington, "are supporting programs under which they will be the first to suffer," thus adding an unusual twist to the issue of civil rights. He made frequent reference to the national support his party had received in California, Illinois, New York, and Colorado.

Republicans hoped for a Dixiecrat surge in Kentucky, believing that a split in Democratic ranks might translate into a crossover vote (as had hap-

pened in 1928, when Kentucky Democrats supported Herbert Hoover). This possibility would at least ensure the reelection of Republican Sen. John Sherman Cooper. All hopes pinned to the Dixiecrats were dashed, however. The Kentucky vote for Truman and Barkley exceeded that for Roosevelt in 1944. Although Cooper led his Democratic rival until late in the race, the heavily Democratic vote carried the Senate seat for Virgil Chapman. Kentucky Dixiecrats drew only 10,000 votes.

Dixiecrats contributed color, drama, and uncertainty to the 1948 campaign, but played a surprisingly insignificant role in the election, carrying but four states (Alabama, Louisiana, Mississippi, and South Carolina), winning but thirty-nine electoral votes, and receiving only a smattering of votes in states such as Kentucky. In Kentucky the vote was: Truman 466,756 (56.7%); Dewey 341,210 (41.5%); Thurmond 10,411 (1.3%); Wallace 1,567 (0.2%); other 2,715 (0.3%).

See V.O. Key, Jr., *Politics, Parties and Pressure Groups* (New York 1964); Samuel Lubell, *Revolt of the Moderates* (New York 1956).

H. LEW WALLACE

STATE UNIVERSITY SYSTEM. The Kentucky state university system is composed of eight schools—UNIVERSITY OF KENTUCKY, EASTERN KENTUCKY UNIVERSITY, KENTUCKY STATE UNIVERSITY, UNIVERSITY OF LOUISVILLE, MOREHEAD STATE UNIVERSITY, MURRAY STATE UNIVERSITY, NORTHERN KENTUCKY UNIVERSITY, and WESTERN KENTUCKY UNIVERSITY. The system is designed to provide public higher education within the economic range of most Kentucky families, and to enhance educational opportunity within all regions of the commonwealth by providing appropriate facilities at locations accessible to various regional populations. The KENTUCKY COUNCIL ON HIGHER EDUCATION is a coordinating agency that oversees the development of academic programs at all eight institutions and recommends a unified biennial budget proposal for the entire system to the General Assembly.

In 1901, Kentucky Agricultural and Mechanical College (later to become the University of Kentucky) graduated only thirty-three students at the baccalaureate and four on the graduate level. In 1990, the state's four-year universities awarded 14,787 undergraduate and graduate degrees. A critical need for trained teachers in the public elementary and secondary schools led to the establishment in 1906 of two state normal schools, Eastern and Western; additional state normal schools at Morehead and Murray were established in 1922. As the number of public high schools increased, more advanced TEACHER TRAINING was needed, and during the 1920s all four normal schools evolved, with expanded curricula, into state teachers' colleges, which offered four-year degrees as well as normal school programs. In 1930, Western was by far the largest of these colleges. All four became state universities in 1966.

As the concept of statewide planning for higher education gained acceptance, the Council on Public Higher Education was created by the legislature in 1934 (the word "public" was dropped in 1977). Three more institutions were subsequently added to the state university system: in 1972, Kentucky State University, which had evolved from a normal school established in 1886 for the training of black teachers; in 1970, Northern Kentucky University, which had begun as a UK community college and was expanded to a state college in 1968; also in 1970, the University of Louisville, which evolved from a municipal college established in the nineteenth century.

The so-called regional universities, while maintaining undergraduate and graduate programs, have developed special areas of expertise. Among these are Western Kentucky University's folklife and history programs; Eastern Kentucky University's College of Law Enforcement; Murray State University's equine studies, including the Breathitt Veterinary Center in Christian County; Morehead State University's outstanding music department; and the Chase Law School and National Academy of Criminal Justice Sciences at Northern Kentucky University. Kentucky State University, located in the state capital, provides specialized courses for state government employees. The University of Louisville continues to be nationally recognized for its medical school. Most of the universities operate community colleges serving their regions.

The University of Kentucky administers the COM-MUNITY COLLEGE SYSTEM, which includes fourteen institutions in widely scattered locations that both confer two-year associate degrees and prepare students for transfer to the state universities. In 1990, 25 percent of the students enrolled in college-level courses were in the community college system.

As the demand increased for public higher education in the 1980s, the universities developed extension centers reaching into small towns and isolated areas of the state; Western Kentucky University opened an extension center in Glasgow, Eastern Kentucky University in Corbin, Murray in Henderson, and Morehead at the Eastern Kentucky Correctional Facility at West Liberty. College level courses are also offered through the facilities of Kentucky Educational Television.

The Council on Higher Education created the Committee on Higher Education in Kentucky's Future (see PRICHARD COMMITTEE) to make recommendations for the future directions of the state university system.

STATIONS. The station, a type of defensible residential site, was common during Kentucky's early settlement, in the last quarter of the eighteenth century. Similar sites were built on other frontiers where defense against Indian attack was paramount. The emergence and development of the station were grounded in the political and legal characteristics of the frontier settlement movement. The layout and individual physical characteristics of the stations owed much to explicit legal requirements for land claims (most of which were based on military service) and to the hostile relationship between the Euroamerican settlers and the Indians as well as to the physical environment.

Groups of men traveled to Kentucky to survey land tracts in particularly desirable areas such as the Bluegrass, which was surveyed as early as 1773-75, in some cases by those interested only in speculation. Virginia law required that a land tract conform to certain surveying rules, that an improvement in the form of a crude house be built, and that a crop of corn be grown as part of the residence requirement. The acreage that could be claimed depended on the military rank of the individual settler if all other requirements were met. Many veterans sold their rights to a land speculator, or "land jobber," who filed large numbers of tracts in his name and privately sold the tracts to individuals who did not qualify for a military grant or who had already exercised their service claims.

The improvements built on the surveyed land tracts numbered in the thousands in Kentucky, but only a small proportion were further developed into stations where settlers resided. The number of stations built in Kentucky is not known, but a 1987 study of stations in the Inner Bluegrass documented more than 150 in a twelve-county area, probably a minimum figure since some sites that fulfilled the characteristics of stations may not have been reported in available documents from the early settlement period. There were also concentrations of stations in the Louisville area and in the western section of Christian, Todd, and Logan counties, as well as many scattered stations along the Ohio River, in the eastern mountains, and in other regions.

Stations varied in size, number, and distribution of residential cabins, presence of stockading, and other respects. All were located at or near freshwater springs and most made use of the abundant timber on the Kentucky frontier for building material. Stations are distinguishable from forts by their generally smaller size and their use as private residential sites rather than public facilities. Each station was identified with an individual man, who usually owned the land on which it was built and served as leader of the settlement. A station usually housed more than one family, although the occupants were often related by blood or marriage. Visitors were generally given shelter. Many stations were stockaded for defense, as the settlers relied on being able to barricade themselves within their cabins to hold off minor Indian attacks; otherwise, they took refuge at larger forts nearby. The better-known stations were usually located on frequently used trails, where their visitors' experiences were recorded in interviews, court depositions, and other records. Many of the smaller, more remote stations that were undoubtedly built were simply not recorded in written documents.

Most of the stations, particularly those built before the end of the Revolutionary War, were only temporary residences, and their occupants put relatively little effort into solid construction designed to last. Cabin logs were frequently green, with the bark left on, which caused warping and invited insects; structural walls were not always chinked or were filled in only with mud; chimneys were usually built of stick and mud daub, without a stone base. Settlers might live at a site for as little as a year or even less, or as long as seven or eight years, depending on the situation when they moved in. Although a few sites were built in a much more permanent fashion after 1785, when the Indian threat had abated, most stations were abandoned within a few years, when conditions allowed the construction of more permanent homes.

See Nancy O'Malley, *Stockading Up*, Department of Anthropology, Archaeological Report 127, University of Kentucky, 1987; Willard Rouse Jillson, *Pioneer Kentucky* (Frankfort, Ky., 1934).

NANCY O'MALLEY

STEAMBOATS. More than any other single factor, the steamboat was responsible for the rapid expansion and economic progress of the trans-Appalachian United States during the first half of the nineteenth century. For livestock, produce, raw materials, manufactured goods, people, and news, the steamboat was a faster way of getting to distant destinations. For the first time commerce could travel upstream with ease on the broad superhighways of the day—the rivers.

This hissing, fire-breathing phenomenon roared onto the western rivers in 1811 at the time of the great comet and the New Madrid earthquake. The steamer NEW ORLEANS was built in Pittsburgh by the Robert Fulton and Robert Livingston interests for trade between Natchez and New Orleans. Fulton and Livingston had persuaded Louisiana to give their company a monopoly on the steamboat business in the territory, much to the dismay of many others who saw the potential of steam on the rivers. The two were unsuccessful, however, in maintaining their monopoly in spite of court battles, and by 1818 the door was open to all.

The early steamboats were strongly framed, deep-hulled vessels powered by heavy low-pressure engines that could not penetrate very far up the tributary streams, and even the mighty Ohio presented numerous navigation hazards at low water. The effective range of steamboat operation was greatly extended by two developments: the deepening of river channels and the reduction of steamboat drafts.

In the second and third quarters of the nineteenth century, private corporations, with state, county, and city financial assistance, undertook the building of dams and locks on the Licking, Kentucky, Green, and Barren rivers. By the mid-1840s, when construction was largely suspended because of financial stringencies, the navigability of all of these rivers had been significantly improved.

Far more important in extending the river transport network, however, was the modification of the western steamboat. The newer hulls, lightly framed, were much longer, slightly wider, and far less deep; hull bottoms were made flat and keels shrank (surviving only as slender strips of wood), further diminishing the depth of water required for navigation. Enormous superstructures rose above the waterline, and almost all machinery and cargo were moved out of the rapidly shrinking hold. High-pressure engines replaced the heavier, more complex, less powerful low-pressure machinery. The new equipment was wasteful of fuel, frequently poorly constructed, and explosion-prone. It nevertheless provided a relatively light power plant to drive the boats at high speeds against strong currents.

In all these modifications, the primary considerations were speed, cargo capacity, and, above all, shallow draft. Great strides were made in achieving the desired ends, but the final product was a rather flimsy craft. By 1853 the record New Orleans-to-Louisville time had been cut below four and one-half days. Cargoes had increased enormously, and average depth of hull had been reduced by about 40 percent in all tonnage categories. Draft reduction was most dramatic in vessels designed for service on the tributary streams. In 1856 the 120-ton *Isaac Shelby* steamed up the Kentucky River drawing (light) eleven inches of water; three years later a vessel was put into service on the Green River that carried ten tons of freight on only eight inches of water. At times of low water, captains were known to wade ahead of their boats to pick out the channel. Indeed, as summed up by a quote from George Fitch in *Steamboats on the Western Rivers* (1949), such vessels "must be so built that when the river is low and the sandbars come out for air, the first mate can tap a keg of beer and run the boat four miles on the suds."

Boilers and engines were put on the main deck instead of in the hold. Cargo, too, went on the main deck. The wealthier passengers were in the cabin on the second, or boiler, deck. A smaller cabin, called the Texas, sat atop that cabin roof, and perched high atop the Texas was the pilothouse, from which lofty height the pilot directed the course of the vessel beneath him.

The boilers were unique to the river steamboats using their high-pressure steam. The smokestacks were tall to create more draft and help keep the sparks off the cabin roof. Both wood and coal were burned, depending on which was more plentiful and cheaper, to power the engines that turned the large paddlewheels. Pre–Civil War steamboats were almost all side-wheelers, but stern-wheelers predominated in the late nineteenth century, as barge towing increased in importance. One or two barges had occasionally been tied alongside in the 1830s and 1840s, but not until the 1850s did the demands of the coal and grain trades produce well-lashed tows of up to a dozen barges, pushed by boats especially designed for the purpose.

Steamboats called packets engaged in regular trade between specific ports with stops between. Occasionally, several packets cooperated to provide better service to the same ports. The Cincinnati and

Louisville U.S. Mail Line was one of the most prominent and long-lasting lines. Steamboat owners and captains were independent breeds, however, and many lines found it difficult to hang together for long. They frequently did not offer the same service during periods of low water, either, as the boats went elsewhere to find cargo. Many steamboats engaged in a kind of tramp trade, going wherever cargo took them or wherever cargo could be obtained. When a boat was sold, the new owners might change its name and move it to a different location and trade.

Rivers had always been a significant means of transportation in Kentucky for shipping goods downstream. The steamboat made it possible to go upstream even more quickly than was formerly possible for downstream travel. Between Louisville and Cincinnati, the steamboat reduced the upstream trip to only twelve hours in the 1850s, from about forty-eight hours in 1819. Along with the quicker trip came cheaper freight rates.

The steamboat was also the comfortable, even luxurious, way to travel throughout most of the nineteenth century. Steamboats were veritable moving hotels, speeding along over the placid river waters, in stark contrast to the jostling, dusty, cramped accommodations on stagecoaches or the early railroad trains. Rather plain and straightforward at first, the main cabins of the larger boats had become quite ornate toward the end of the century. Passengers who could afford the cabin fare were much more fortunate than deck passengers, who slept anywhere they could find a space among the cargo on the main deck, were provided no food or other amenities, and might even be reduced to helping the roustabouts load firewood or cargo to pay their way. On these often crowded decks, disease was frequently an unexpected, dangerous cargo delivered to towns just as rapidly and efficiently as passengers or freight.

Because of the steamboat, villages along the Ohio River grew quickly into towns and some— Paducah, Covington, Newport, Henderson, Owensboro, and Louisville—into cities. Steamboats not only improved supply and demand for the goods they carried, but they even created their own industry, to build, outfit, repair, and operate them.

The only major navigational hazard on the river—the Falls of the Ohio—made Louisville grow quickly as the natural transshipment point or stopover while boats waited for the river to rise or for a pilot to take them through. The Portland Canal, built around the falls in 1830, helped only the smaller packets, which could fit through its small locks.

Steamboats were relatively cheap to build, unlike railroads, which needed vast amounts of capital to purchase right of way and lay track. As few as three or four persons could easily afford a boat. Not only that, but in the early days, before there was much competition, profits were amazingly high. Henry Shreve's *Washington*, in but two round trips from New Orleans to Louisville, was said to have paid not only its operating costs, but its construction costs as well, leaving a $1,700 profit to divide among the owners. As more and more boats were built, however, there was greater competition for freight, and lower freight rates cut into the profit.

Steamboats reached their zenith in the 1850s. Even then, the railroad was beginning to chip away at the steamboat's supremacy. River levels were usually very low in the summer and many boats just tied up. In winter, massive ice floes impeded or stopped steamboats altogether. The railroads were not affected by such problems. A train departed on schedule, or reasonably close to it, whereas a steamboat might wait for days or weeks for a full cargo. In handling freight, a steamboat whistled, offloaded freight at its destination on the riverbank or levee, and went its way—no matter that the river was rising, imperiling the shipment, or that no one had heard the whistle. Then, too, the steamboat was more susceptible to disaster. Packets had a life expectancy of only five or six years. Many of the wrecked vessels had run into snags, or had been grounded, or crushed by ice, but a goodly number suffered boiler explosions or fires, which made headlines—and uneasy shippers and passengers. There was thus little doubt that the railroad would take over from the steamboat. The advent of the automobile, paved highways, and trucks only hastened the steamboat's demise.

See Louis C. Hunter, *Steamboats on the Western Rivers* (Cambridge, Mass., 1949); Norbury L. Wayman, *Life on the River* (New York 1971); John Hartford, *Steamboat in a Cornfield* (New York 1986).

JOHN B. BRILEY AND LEONARD P. CURRY

STEELE, MARTHA (McKAMIE). Martha (McKamie) Steele, pioneer, daughter of Robert and Martha (Breckinridge) McKamie, was born near Mercersburg, Pennsylvania, ca. 1748. She married Richard Steele in 1769; they had thirteen children. In the spring of 1780 the family migrated to Kentucky, where Richard Steele had been granted land for military service. The Steele family and relatives traveled down the Ohio River on flatboats to Corn Island at the Falls of the Ohio. They settled along Beargrass Creek in eastern Jefferson County and erected Spring Station stockade.

Family tradition tells of Martha Steele's bravery during an Indian attack on Spring Station, after she and all the other women and children had gone for safety to the larger and better fortified Floyd Station. During the attack Richard Steele was badly wounded in the shoulder. On learning of his injury, Martha left Floyd Station against the protests of others at the stockade. Traveling at night and carrying her small child, she rode back to Spring Station, past the Indian encampment, to nurse her husband back to health.

The Steele family moved to Fayette County in 1784 and settled on a 1,000-acre farm near Lexington. After the death of her husband in 1808, Martha Steele moved to the home of her eldest son in Shelbyville. She died there on September 22, 1822.

See William Baxter, "Mrs. Martha McKamie Steele," *Register* 3 (Jan. 1905): 69-74.

STEPHENS, WOODFORD CEFIS. Woodford ("Woody") Cefis Stephens, Hall of Fame horse trainer, was born on September 1, 1913, in Stanton, Kentucky, to Lewis and Helen (Welch) Stephens. When his family moved to Midway, Stephens became acquainted with the thoroughbred farms of the Bluegrass. In 1929, at age sixteen, he quit school to become an exercise boy. Two years later he became a jockey and raced for nine years, then became a professional trainer. During his fifty years as a trainer, Stephens has both worked for private owners and operated a public stable. He has trained more than three hundred stakes winners, including two Kentucky Derby winners, Cannonade in 1974 and Swale in 1984, and one Preakness winner, Blue Man, in 1952. He holds the record for training consecutive winners (six) of the Eclipse Award, given by three groups representing the thoroughbred racing industry for the year's best horse: Sensational (1978), Smart Angle, Heaven Cause, De La Rosa, Conquistador Cielo, and Devil's Bag. He sent off the winners of four consecutive Belmont Stakes, 1982-85: Conquistador Cielo, Caveat, Swale, and Creme Fraiche. Stephens was named outstanding trainer by the New York Turf Writers Association in 1982 and again in 1983, and he was elected to the Thoroughbred Racing Hall of Fame at Saratoga, New York, in 1976.

Stephens married Lucille Elizabeth Easley of Lexington on September 11, 1937. Since 1952 they have lived in Elmont, New York.

See Woody Stephens and James Brough, *Guess I'm Lucky* (New York, 1987).

STEVENSON, ADLAI EWING. Born in Christian County, Kentucky, on October 23, 1835, Adlai Ewing Stevenson, vice-president of the United States, was the son of John Turner and Maria (Ewing) Stevenson. He spent his youth on his family's tobacco farm in the Pennyroyal region of the state. As a boy he attended a local school and the Presbyterian church near Hopkinsville. In 1853 his family moved to McLean County, Illinois, where Kentucky relatives had previously settled. Stevenson returned to Kentucky in the late 1850s to attend Centre College at Danville. Stevenson's father's death in 1857 interrupted his education and he returned to Illinois to read law. By 1858 he was a practicing attorney in Metamora, Illinois.

Stevenson was twice elected to the U.S. House of Representatives (March 4, 1875-March 3, 1877, and March 4, 1879-March 3, 1881). He served as first assistant postmaster in Grover Cleveland's first administration (1885-89). An ardent Democrat, Stevenson in 1892 was elected vice-president in Cleveland's second administration, after campaigning in Kentucky on the platform of lower tariffs and no federal regulation of elections. Stevenson ran unsuccessfully for vice-president on William Jennings Bryan's ticket in 1900 and, at seventy-three

years of age, for governor of Illinois in 1908. He married Letitia Green, daughter of Lewis Warner Green, president of Centre College, on December 20, 1866. Their four children were Lewis Green, Mary, Julia, and Letitia. Stevenson died in Chicago, Illinois, on June 14, 1914, and was buried in the Bloomington Cemetery.

See Adlai Ewing Stevenson, *Something of Men I Have Known* (Chicago 1909).   JEAN H. BAKER

STEVENSON, JOHN WHITE. John White Stevenson, governor during 1867-71, was born to Andrew and Mary (White) Stevenson of Richmond, Virginia, on May 4, 1812. Educated by private tutors, he later attended the University of Virginia and subsequently read law. After a short period in Vicksburg, Mississippi, he moved to Covington, Kentucky, in 1841. Two years later he married Sibella Winston, and they had five children. Stevenson, a Democrat, was in 1845 elected to the state House of Representatives for the first of two successive terms. He attended the state's constitutional convention in 1849 and was a delegate to three national party conventions. After serving two terms in the U.S. House (March 4, 1857-March 3, 1861), he was defeated for reelection. In 1860 he supported John C. Breckinridge for president, and in 1866 was a delegate to the National Union party convention.

Stevenson was elected lieutenant governor in 1867 by a vote of 88,222 to R. Tarvin Baker's 32,505 and H. Taylor's 11,473. He became governor when John L. Helm died five days after taking office. In the August 1868 special election for the remaining three years of the term, Stevenson defeated Republican Baker, 115,560 to 26,605. Elected to the U.S. Senate by the state legislature in 1871, he resigned the governorship on February 13, 1871. He served in the Senate from March 4, 1871, until March 3, 1877, then returned to his Covington legal practice. Stevenson taught in the Cincinnati Law School, chaired the Democratic National Convention of 1880, and was elected president of the American Bar Association in 1884. He died in Covington on August 10, 1886, and was buried in Cincinnati.

Governor Stevenson used the militia several times to curb mob violence, some of which was directed against blacks who attempted to vote. He opposed federal interference in areas that he believed belonged to the states. He also supported the early restoration of rights to ex-Confederates, and he insisted that blacks were entitled to their state-conferred legal rights. His term saw considerable improvement in the public schools, including the 1870 creation of the Bureau of Education. A fiscal conservative, Stevenson ordered a careful study of the state's financial system. Some improvements were made in the state prisons and asylums. The governor's well-publicized criticism of the wartime conduct of Gen. Stephen G. BURBRIDGE may have been calculated to help Stevenson's bid for the U.S. Senate in 1871.

See Jennie C. Morton, "Governor John W. Stevenson," *Register* 5 (May 1907): 13-15.

LOWELL H. HARRISON

STEWARD, WILLIAM HENRY. William Henry Steward, civic leader, was born July 26, 1847, in Brandenburg, Kentucky. A freedman, he moved to Louisville about 1860 to attend the Rev. Henry Adam's school at the First African Baptist Church. Through his ties to the white community, Adams found Steward a teaching position in 1872 at Louisville's Eastern Colored School. In 1875 Steward was hired by the Louisville & Nashville Railroad, first as a messenger and then as purchasing agent. In 1876 he became Louisville's first black postman. The postal route, located in an affluent district, allowed Steward to develop and maintain ties with influential whites.

A member of the Baptist Church since 1867, Steward was a founder of the *American Baptist* newspaper (1879), the official organ of black Baptists of Kentucky, and served as its editor for fifty-six years. Steward became president of the National Afro-American Press Association in the 1890s. As president he was active in Republican politics at the national level. In 1896 he met with presidential candidate William McKinley and urged him to speak out against lynching. In the early 1900s, Steward fought segregation in Louisville and formed a local chapter of the National Association for the Advancement of Colored People (NAACP). In litigation backed by the NAACP, Steward, and other local black leaders, the U.S. Supreme Court overturned Louisville's Residential Segregation Ordinance in November 1917. Although active in the NAACP, Steward was a moderate on racial issues, and his position in the black community was predominantly based on his close association with white business and political leaders.

Steward served as the Republican party's patronage dispenser in the black community and approved applicants for police and firemen when the city began hiring blacks in the 1920s. He was a member of the Colored School Board of Visitors, a supervisory adjunct to the city board of education, where he helped to obtain teaching positions for blacks. Steward was also chairman of the board of trustees for State University, a black Baptist College in Louisville. Steward died on January 3, 1935.

See Alice A. Dunnigan, *The Fascinating Story of Black Kentuckians: Their Heritage and Traditions* (Washington, D.C., 1982).

STEWART, CORA (WILSON). Cora (Wilson) Stewart, pioneer in adult education, was born to Dr. Jeremiah and Annie Eliza (Hally) Wilson on January 17, 1875, and reared in Farmers, Rowan County, Kentucky. She attended Morehead Normal School and the National Normal University in Lebanon, Ohio, and then began a teaching career in her home county in 1895. She quickly earned a reputation as an outstanding educator, and in 1901 she was elected Rowan County school superintendent.

In 1904 she married Alexander T. Stewart, a Rowan County school teacher. Cora Stewart was reelected school superintendent in 1909 and two years later became the first woman president of the Kentucky Educational Association.

In 1911 Stewart launched an experimental adult education program, the MOONLIGHT SCHOOL, to combat illiteracy in her home county. In 1923 Stewart was elected to the executive committee of the National Education Association. Six years later President Herbert Hoover named her to chair the executive committee of the National Advisory Committee on Illiteracy. She also presided over the illiteracy section of the World Conference on Education. Success and recognition brought prizes and honors. In 1924, for example, she received *Pictorial Review*'s $5,000 achievement prize for her contribution to human welfare, and in 1930 she accepted the Ella Flagg Young medal for distinguished service in the field of education.

She moved to Pine Bluff, Arkansas, in 1936 and subsequently to various rest homes in North Carolina. She died on December 2, 1958, and was buried in Tryon, North Carolina.

See Wilson Somerville, ed., *Appalachian America* (Johnson City, Tenn., 1981).

JAMES M. GIFFORD

STICKLES, ARNDT MATHIAS. Historian Arndt Mathias Stickles was born on January 4, 1872, in Owen County, Indiana, to Mathias and Elizabeth (Kiefaber) Stickles. After attending local schools he received an A.B. (1897), an M.A. (1904), and a Ph.D. (1923) from Indiana University. He earned a second M.A. (1910) from Harvard University, and he also attended the universities of Illinois and Chicago. After several years of teaching in Indiana high schools, Stickles joined the staff of Western Kentucky University in January 1908. He retired in 1954 after forty-six years as head of the Department of History.

His major publications were *The Critical Court Struggle in Kentucky* (1929) and *Simon Bolivar Buckner, Borderland Knight* (1940). He also wrote two successful textbooks: *Elements of Government* (1914) and, with Thomas Crittenden Cherry, *The Story of Kentucky* (1940). His monograph "Our Government in Kentucky" was added to Sheldon E. Davis and Clarence H. McClure's book *Our Government* (1929).

In 1911 Stickles married Laura Gordon Chambers; they had three children. Stickles died in Bowling Green on October 13, 1968, and was buried there.

See Lowell H. Harrison, "Two Kentucky Historians: A Personal Appreciation," *Register* 69 (Jan. 1971): 30-36.   LOWELL H. HARRISON

STILL, JAMES. James Still, author, was born on July 16, 1906, in Lafayette, Alabama, the son of J. Alex and Lonie (Lindsey) Still. He graduated from Lincoln Memorial University in Harrogate, Tennessee, in 1929, earned an M.A. degree from

Vanderbilt University in 1930, and later received a degree in library science from the University of Illinois. For the next six years he served as librarian of the HINDMAN Settlement School at the forks of Troublesome Creek in Knott County, Kentucky, where, among other duties, he conducted a library-on-foot, delivering books in a carton on his shoulder to one-room schools.

His first poem appeared in the *Virginia Quarterly Review* in 1935 and his first short story in *Atlantic Monthly* a year later. In 1939 he moved into a two-story log house on Dead Mare Branch of Little Carr Creek in Knott County, where he expected to stay only long enough to complete the novel *River of Earth*. With time out for military service in World War II, fellowships at writers and artists colonies, and parts of fourteen winters spent in the Yucatan, Guatemala, and Honduras, Still has lived in his log house for over half a century.

Still draws on everyday experiences and observations, especially the speech of the area, for his poems, stories, and novels. Even when writing stories and novels, Still is primarily a poet. Themes and images of his early poems, such as the "river of earth," his metaphor for the human condition, are elaborated in the novels and stories. His novel *River of Earth* (1940) is considered an American classic. Still's works include: *Hounds on the Mountain* (poems, 1937); *On Troublesome Creek* (stories, 1941); *Way Down Yonder on Troublesome Creek* (juvenile, 1974); *The Wolfpen Rusties* (juvenile, 1975); *Pattern of a Man* (stories, 1976); *Sporty Creek* (novel, 1977); *Jack and the Wonder Beans* (juvenile, 1977); *The Run for the Elbertas* (stories, 1980); *The Wolfpen Poems* (collected poems, 1986); and *The Wolfpen Notebooks: Appalachian Life* (1991).

Still's work is part of the literary flowering in the American South during the late 1920s and early 1930s, which included Thomas Wolfe, William Faulkner, and Kentuckians Elizabeth Madox Roberts, Jesse Stuart, Harriette Simpson Arnow, Caroline Gordon, Allen Tate, Cleanth Brooks, and Robert Penn Warren.

See Terry Cornett, "A James Still Bibliography," *Iron Mountain Review* 2 (Summer 1984): 29-33; Jim Wayne Miller, "Jim Dandy: James Still at Eighty," *Appalachian Heritage* 14 (Fall 1986): 8-20.   JIM WAYNE MILLER

STINKING CREEK. Stinking Creek originates in the northeast corner of Knox County and flows through the county to the Cumberland River. It was named by a group of Long Hunters, who are said to have killed a bear and thrown its carcass into the creek, where it rotted. Another account is that it was so named because of the odor of the corpses of game animals that hunters indiscriminately slaughtered when they came to the Flat Lick salt licks at the creek's mouth. The name also refers to the area drained by the creek, comprising a large portion of northeastern Knox County. The Warriors' Path followed the creek after it left the Wilderness Road; the creek attracted early settlers with its rich land and abundant game. The land gradually deterio-

rated, and in wet weather the roads along the creek beds were impassable. Stinking Creek gained notoriety after the publication of John Fetterman's *Stinking Creek* (1967), a social commentary on the lives of certain residents along the creek. The depressed conditions had improved by the 1990s.
                    SUSAN ARTHUR

STONE, BARTON WARREN. Barton Warren Stone, Presbyterian minister and advocate of Christian unity, was born on December 24, 1772, in Port Tobacco, Maryland, to John and Mary Warren (Musgrave) Stone. In 1779 his widowed mother moved her family to Pittsylvania County, Virginia. In 1790 Stone entered David Caldwell's Academy in Greensboro, North Carolina. By the time of his graduation in 1793, he had decided to pursue a career in the Presbyterian ministry, rather than practice law as he had originally intended. At his ordination examination, he was asked if he accepted the Westminister Confession. His equivocal reply, "I do, as far as I see it consistent with the Word of God," reflected the liberalizing influences of many of his associations in the preceding years. In contrast to the Calvinist emphasis upon human depravity and the wrath of God, Stone stressed God's love and decried the divisions among Christians caused by excessive concentration on doctrinal exactness.

After teaching in Georgia and North Carolina, Stone received his first pastorates at Cane Ridge and Concord, Kentucky, in 1798. In 1801 he traveled to Logan County, Kentucky, to witness an outbreak of the religious excitement developing in Tennessee and southwestern Kentucky. What most impressed Stone was the way in which a variety of denominations cooperated in a practical demonstration of church unity. While dismayed by some of the emotional manifestations, he concluded that the good outweighed the bad and encouraged similar gatherings in his section of Kentucky. The climax came at a series of camp meetings at CANE RIDGE on August 7-12, 1801—part of the Great Revival.

Stone withdrew from the Kentucky Presbytery and organized the Springfield Presbytery on September 19, 1803. On June 28, 1804, Stone and five others signed *The Last Will and Testament of the Springfield Presbytery*, dissolving the presbytery. They expressed the desire for union with the body of Christ, singled out the Bible as the only standard of Christian faith and practice, and referred to themselves simply as Christians. The movement they founded continued to grow. Stone cannot be considered its initiator, but his steadfastness and his publication of the journal *Christian Messenger*, which was a unifying element in a movement with no central organization, made him its leader and foremost spokesman.

After spending the years 1812-14 in Tennessee, Stone returned to Kentucky, living in Lexington during 1814-19, then becoming principal of the Rittenhouse Academy in Georgetown in 1819.

In 1824 Stone first met Alexander Campbell, leader of a movement also seeking unity among

Christians on the basis of a rejection of creeds and a restoration of the New Testament church. Although never close personal friends, the two recognized their essential similarities. On January 1, 1832, at the Hill Street Church in Lexington, Stone for the group known specifically as Christians and John Smith for the Disciples of Christ, as Campbell preferred to designate the members of his movement, shook hands, beginning a process of unifying the two movements. Out of that handshake grew the CHRISTIAN CHURCH (DISCIPLES OF CHRIST), the CHRISTIAN CHURCH, and the CHURCH OF CHRIST.

Stone married Eliza Campbell in 1784; they had four daughters—Amanda, Tabitha, Mary Anne, and Eliza—and a son, Barton, who died at birth in 1809. Stone's wife Eliza died in 1810. He married Celia Wilson Bowen in 1811; they had four sons—William, John, Barton, Jr., and Samuel—and two daughters, Mary and Catherine. In 1834 Stone moved to Jacksonville, Illinois, where he remained until his death on November 9, 1844. He was buried at Cane Ridge.

See William Garrett West, *Barton Warren Stone: Early American Advocate of Christian Unity* (Nashville 1954).   FREDERICK I. MURPHY

STONE, MAY. May Stone, educator and cofounder of HINDMAN SETTLEMENT School, was born in Owingsville, Kentucky, on May 1, 1867, the daughter of Henry L. and Pamela (Bourne) Stone. She attended private secondary schools in Owingsville and Mt. Sterling and Wellesley College (1884-87). Stone became interested in education in eastern Kentucky when she and Katherine PETTIT conducted a series of summer schools near Hazard and Hindman, between 1899 and 1901. Encouraged by those experiences, Stone and Pettit founded Hindman Settlement School in 1902. It was firmly established by 1912, when Pettit left to found Pine Mountain Settlement School.

Under Stone's leadership, Hindman School followed the tradition of the urban settlement movement. The curriculum included courses in traditional academic subjects and in industrial arts. Hindman teachers worked to improve other rural schools in Knott County and offered medical clinics for the people in the region. Stone and other staff members encouraged production and sale of handicraft items and supported preservation of mountain ballads and customs.

In 1936 May Stone retired as principal of Hindman Settlement School but remained on the board of directors at the school until her death in Louisville on January 29, 1946. She was buried in the Lexington Cemetery.

See David E. Whisnant, *All That is Native and Fine* (Chapel Hill, N.C. 1983).

NANCY FORDERHASE

STOVALL, THELMA LOYACE (HAWKINS). Thelma Loyace (Hawkins) Stovall, lieutenant governor, was born on April 1, 1919, in Munfordville, Kentucky, to Addie Mae and Samuel Dewey Hawkins. She received her early education at Louisville Girls High School and Halleck Hall, studied law at LaSalle Extension University in Chicago, and took summer courses at the University of Kentucky and Eastern Kentucky University in Richmond. After completing secretarial school, she became secretary for the Tobacco Workers International Union Local 185, remaining in this position for eleven years. She married Lonnie Raymon Stovall in 1936.

Thelma Stovall, an ardent supporter of unions, represented the 38th District in the Kentucky House of Representatives in 1950, and was reelected until 1955. She was a national committee member for the Young Democrats of Kentucky from 1952 to 1956 and served as its president from 1956 to 1958. Stovall was elected Kentucky's secretary of state for three terms: 1956-60, 1964-68, and 1972-75. She also served as state treasurer for two terms: 1960-64 and 1968-72. In December 1975 she became lieutenant governor in Julian Carroll's administration (1974-79).

On November 13, 1978, Stovall, as acting governor in Carroll's absence, signed a proclamation calling for a special session of the General Assembly to cut taxes. Floods in Frankfort postponed the extraordinary session until January 8, 1979. The majority of Stovall's proposed legislation was enacted on February 10, 1979, including the elimination of a 5 percent sales tax on home utilities, and a 4 percent ceiling on yearly increases in revenue created from taxes on existing property. As lieutenant governor, she vetoed the General Assembly's rescission of its ratification of the Equal Rights Amendment to the federal Constitution. Stovall announced her bid for governor in the fall of 1978, but lost the primary to John Y. Brown, Jr., in May 1979. She left the lieutenant governorship in December 1979 and returned to her home in Louisville.

STRIP MINING. In the strip mining process, the soil and rock overlying a coal seam, called overburden, are removed to reach the coal. Strip miners in Kentucky use different techniques—area mining, contour mining, and auger mining—to deal with the various kinds of terrain found in the state's coal-bearing regions. In area mining, practiced on the relatively flat land that is common in western Kentucky, a cut is first made to expose the coal seam. Miners then make parallel cuts, and deposit the overburden from each in the previous cut. The second method, contour strip mining, is often used in the mountainous terrain of eastern Kentucky. It creates a bench, or shelf, on the hillside, bordered by a high wall. Current law requires that the hillside be returned to its approximate original profile after contour strip mining. Auger mining, the third technique, recovers additional coal from old underground mines and from beneath the high wall of strip mines. A large machine bores holes as much as seven feet in diameter to reach remnants of the coal seam.

Kentucky's first attempts to regulate the coal industry in 1954 required strip mine operators to secure permits, post reclamation bonds, and grade the disturbed area "where practicable." Changes in the law over the next ten years strengthened reclamation requirements but did not satisfy the public's growing concerns about environmental damage caused by strip mining.

In 1966 the legislature adopted the most stringent reclamation law in the nation, according to *Coal Age*, an industry publication. It restricted the amount of overburden that could be removed and prohibited strip mining on slopes steeper than thirty-three degrees. It required catch basins to protect drainage. The new law specified certain reclamation before bonds could be released and set both permit fees and fines for violators.

At the federal level, the Surface Mining Control and Reclamation Act of 1977 adopted many of Kentucky's provisions and allowed the individual states to control their own programs as long as they met certain requirements.

In 1981, under Gov. John Y. Brown, Jr. (1979-83), Kentucky was the first state to participate in the federal program to enforce the strip mining legislation. Many public meetings were held to explain the program, inspectors were trained, and the industry had to adjust to more stringent environmental standards. The National Wildlife Federation and the state of Kentucky have set guidelines to measure the success of the state regulatory program, which is monitored by the U.S. Department of Interior.   JACKIE SWIGART

STRODE'S STATION. Strode's Station, an early settlement about two miles west of Winchester in present Clark County, Kentucky, was built by John Strode in 1779. A gunsmith, Strode came from Berkeley County, Virginia, to Kentucky in April 1776, and erected a half-face cabin on a thousand-acre tract to which he claimed preemption on December 24, 1779, when the Virginia Land Commission court convened at Fort Boonesborough. Returning to his land, Strode and several other settlers began constructing a stockade station. Strode promised land to those who cleared it and by 1780, with the bulk of the station completed, about thirty families were residing there. Strode's Creek on the station's east side provided water, and a wet-weather stream was channeled through the settlement's northern section. Each man was allowed a garden in a nearby common field and a corn crop was raised.

Strode reportedly left the station in 1780 and was away for three or four years, during which Indian confrontations and horse-stealing raids were common. In a major incident on March 1, 1781, two men, Patrick Donnalson (Donaldson) and Jacob Spahr, died. Indian attacks were a threat for several years and Strode's, being the largest fortified settlement in the area, was occupied most of the time until 1790. Settlers moving into the territory stayed there first and the station became a center of early county activity. Strode's was considered as a site for the county seat when Clark County was formed in 1792, but nearby Winchester was selected.

See A. Goff Bedford, *Land of Our Fathers: History of Clark County, Kentucky* (Mt. Sterling, Ky., 1958); Nancy O'Malley, *Stockading Up*, Archaelogical Report 127, Department of Anthropology, University of Kentucky, 1987.

STUART, JESSE HILTON. Jesse Hilton Stuart, writer, was born on August 8, 1906, in northeastern Kentucky's Greenup County, where his parents, Mitchell and Martha (Hilton) Stuart, were tenant farmers. Stuart grew up with a strong appreciation for the life lived close to the soil and with a keen awareness of the hardships of rural poverty. Mitchell Stuart could neither read nor write, and Martha had only a second-grade education, but they taught their two sons and three daughters to value education. All the children became college graduates and schoolteachers, with Jesse leading the way. He graduated from Greenup High School in 1926 and from Lincoln Memorial University in Harrogate, Tennessee, in 1929. He then returned to Greenup County to teach.

By the end of the 1930s, Stuart had served as a teacher in Greenup County's one-room schools and as high school principal and county school superintendent. These experiences served as the basis for his autobiographical book, *The Thread That Runs So True* (1949), called by the president of the National Education Association "the best book on education written in the last fifty years." The book helped to dramatize the need for educational reform in Kentucky. By the time it appeared, Stuart had long since left the classroom to devote his time to lecturing and writing. He returned as a high school principal in 1956-57, taught at the University of Nevada in Reno in the 1958 summer term, and served on the faculty of the American University of Cairo in 1960-61.

Stuart began writing stories and poems about the hill people of his section of Kentucky while still a college student. During a year of graduate study at Vanderbilt University in Nashville in 1931-32, Donald Davidson, a poet who was one of his professors, encouraged him to continue writing. Following the private publication of Stuart's *Harvest of Youth* (poems) in 1930, *Man with a Bull-Tongue Plow*, poems that celebrate his people and the natural world, appeared in 1934 and was widely praised. Mark Van Doren, for instance, called Stuart an "American Robert Burns."

His autobiography, *Beyond Dark Hills*, was published in 1938 and his first novel, *Trees of Heaven*, in 1940. His first short story collection was *Head o' W-Hollow* (1936), followed by *Men of the Mountains* (1941) and by more than a dozen other collections in Stuart's lifetime. His published stories—in magazines and in book form—number more than five hundred. Stuart also published more than a dozen novels and autobiographical works. *Taps for Private Tussie* (1943) is an award-winning satirical look at New Deal relief and its effect on the hill man's self-reliance, and *God's Oddling* (1960) is a biography of Stuart's father. Stuart's books of poetry also include *Album of Destiny* (1944) and *Kentucky Is My Land* (1952). He was designated poet laureate of Kentucky in 1954 and was made a fellow of the Academy of American Poets in 1961. *Hold April: New Poems* was published in 1962. Stuart also lectured widely for many years, particularly on the subject of education and its value, and wrote a number of highly regarded books for children and youth. Prominent among the latter are *The Beatinest Boy* (1953) and *A Penny's Worth of Character* (1954). *Hie to the Hunters*, a novel published in 1950, is a celebration of rural life that has been popular with high school readers.

Stuart suffered a major heart attack on the lecture circuit in 1954. During his convalescence, he produced daily journals that were the basis for *The Year of My Rebirth* (1956), a book recording his rediscovery of the joy of life.

Stuart married Naomi Deane Norris on October 14, 1939; they had one child, Jessica Jane. Stuart placed many of his manuscripts, letters, and other memorabilia at Murray State University in 1960, and he authorized the establishment of the Jesse Stuart Foundation in 1979. The foundation, headquartered in Ashland, Kentucky, controls the rights to Stuart's literary works and is charged with oversight of W-Hollow, which Stuart and his wife, Naomi, donated to Kentucky as a nature preserve in 1980. Stuart had acquired over seven hundred acres in his native valley over the years, in fulfillment of the dream of someday owning all the farms that his parents had worked on shares in his youth. W-Hollow shows evidence of Stuart's lifelong devotion to conservation in the luxuriance of its fields and timber.

Stuart died on February 17, 1984, and was buried in Plum Grove Cemetery in Greenup County.

See Harold E. Richardson, *Jesse: The Biography of an American Writer, Jesse Hilton Stuart* (New York 1984); Ruel E. Foster, *Jesse Stuart* (New York 1968).   JERRY A. HERNDON

STUBBLEFIELD, NATHAN BEVERLY. Nathan Beverly Stubblefield, inventor, was born to William Jefferson and Victoria Frances (Bowman) Stubblefield on December 27, 1860, in Murray, Kentucky. He attended the public schools of Calloway County beginning in the fall of 1866, but he did poorly and dropped out by age fifteen. Stubblefield educated himself in science by reading books and periodicals. By 1887 he had made various improvements in the relatively new invention of the telephone. He patented these improvements, as well as a lamp lighter, an electric battery, and a mobile radio transmitter-receiver. In a demonstration of the radio transmitter-receiver in Murray on January 1, 1902, before a crowd of about 1,000, Stubblefield transmitted his son's voice from the family home to a shed and then to a receiver approximately one mile distant. A description of the demonstration by a reporter from the *St. Louis Post-Dispatch* aroused national interest in the invention. Stubblefield was asked to demonstrate his discovery to a group of

congressmen and public officials in Washington, D.C., on March 20, 1902.

Stubblefield refused large sums of money for the invention and instead attempted to develop it through the Wireless Telephone Company of America, incorporated on May 22, 1902, in which he held stock. The company failed, and only one Stubblefield wireless telephone system was sold. Though he was the first to transmit and receive radio airwaves, many argue that Stubblefield did not invent radio because his system had a range of only eight miles.

At age twenty-one, Stubblefield married Ada May Buchanan; they had ten children, six of whom lived past adolescence: Victoria, Patty, Nathan, Helen, Oliver, and Bernard. When their youngest child left home, he and his wife separated. Stubblefield died on March 28, 1928, and was buried near Murray.   WILLIAM RAY MOFIELD

SUBLIMITY SPRINGS. Sublimity Springs is a dramatically beautiful wild natural place, now part of the Daniel Boone National Forest. In the mid-1800s, a resort was located there approximately ten miles above the confluence of the Rockcastle and Cumberland rivers on the Rockcastle in Pulaski County. In 1853 Dr. Christopher Columbus Graham, the proprietor of the Harrodsburg Springs resort, recorded a deed to 1,500 acres of wild lands around the Sublimity Springs and Bee Rock, along the narrows of the Rockcastle River. On the north bank of the river he established a gristmill and sawmill, then a resort hotel. In 1858 J. Campbell and C.S. Kromp advertised that they were operating the hotel, at rates of five dollars a week for lodging and meals and three dollars a week for stabling and caring for horses. The Sublimity Springs hotel in time lost out to competition from the older Rockcastle Springs resort nearby, which operated a steamboat to enhance its accessibility.

See J. Winston Coleman, *The Springs of Kentucky* (Lexington, Ky., 1955).

       THOMAS D. CLARK

SUE BENNETT COLLEGE. Sue Bennett College, a private junior college, originated as the Sue Bennett Memorial School. It was opened in London, Kentucky, on January 1, 1897, by the Woman's Parsonage Missionary Society of the Methodist Episcopal Church, South. Among the founders were Lucinda B. Helm, Belle and Sue Bennett, John J. Dickey, and Sarah Harding Sawyer. This group made an extensive survey of eastern Kentucky in search of a location that would best serve that educationally barren region. Their report is eloquently descriptive of social conditions in Appalachia in the 1890s. London was chosen because of its accessibility (it was located on two major highways and on the Knoxville branch of the Louisville & Nashville Railroad), on the condition that the citizens of the town would match contributions already made.

London businessmen, including E.H. Hackney, W.D. Catchings, Charles R. Brock, Vincent Boreing, and H.K. Taylor, either subscribed to or enlisted support for the school. Ground was broken for the main building on May 8, 1896, and classes began January 5, 1897. J.C. Lewis was elected principal and two other instructors were hired. The curriculum included a surprising number of basic courses, exceeding in sophistication the curriculum of the Kentucky public schools. Early in the school's history, students came from Clay, Knox, Bell, Jackson, Letcher, and Laurel counties. To enable very poor students to attend, cottages were erected as living quarters where the occupants could prepare their own meals and rent rooms for very modest fees.

The school began offering junior college courses in 1922. In 1932 the school received accreditation from the Southern Association of Colleges and Secondary Schools; in the following year high school instruction ended. In 1939 the school came under control of the Woman's Division of Christian Service in the Methodist church. The college is affiliated with the Board of Global Ministries of the United Methodist church.

See Thomas D. Clark, *A History of Laurel County* (London, Ky., 1989).   THOMAS D. CLARK

SULLIVAN LAW. The landmark education law titled Government and Regulation of the Common Schools of the State, enacted March 24, 1908, mandated an almost complete reform of the Kentucky public school system. It is commonly known as the Sullivan Law in honor of its sponsor, Sen. Jere A. Sullivan of Madison County. It was the result of a campaign conducted during 1907-9, when John Grant Crabbe was state superintendent of schools. The Sullivan Law's blueprint for restructuring the school system marked a distinct end to the era of the one-room district school, burdened by the infamous three-trustee system.

Each county was made a school district, organized into subdistricts, each of which was to contain no fewer than fifty white children, except under extraordinary conditions, and the absolute minimum was forty children. District lines could be changed from time to time by popular vote. One trustee chosen from each subdistrict would sit as a member of the county board of education. Trustees were to supervise school affairs in their districts, make annual reports of the eligible child census, see to the hiring of teachers, and be responsible for school buildings. The law required each county to organize by March 1910 a public high school in one of three classes: first-class high schools, to offer the full curriculum devised by the state Department of Education over a four-year period; second-class schools, to offer only three years of the curriculum; and third-class schools, two years. Teachers' salaries were to be fixed at the local level.

One of the most important elements of the Sullivan Law was the mandate that the counties levy a school tax at the rate of at least twenty cents, but no more than twenty-five cents, on each $100 of assessed property value, with the proceeds to be set aside for education. Much of the body of the new law pertained to the election, administration, and conduct of officials and the operation of schools. Its cardinal provision: "All laws and parts of laws in conflict with this act are hereby repealed."

The enactment of the Sullivan Law set the stage for two "whirlwind campaigns" to gain public support for school reform. In November and December of 1908, State Superintendent Crabbe initiated a public campaign to garner support among Kentucky's local communities for the recent education reform. For nine days twenty-nine speakers traveled throughout the state promoting public education. They visited every Kentucky county, delivering a total of three hundred speeches to about 60,000 people. The state's newspapers gave support to the campaign through news coverage and editorials. The apparent success of the initial effort led to a second whirlwind campaign in June and July of 1909. For eight days one hundred speakers held large public rallies in each of Kentucky's counties in support of public education.

See "The Clear Call of Thoroughbred Women: The Kentucky Federation of Women's Clubs and the Crusade for Educational Reform, 1903-1909," *Register* 83 (Winter 1985): 19-35; Barksdale Hamlett, *History of Education in Kentucky* (Frankfort, Ky., 1914); Frank L. McVey, *The Gates Open Slowly* (Lexington, Ky., 1949).

THOMAS D. CLARK AND TERRY BIRDWHISTELL

SUMMERS, HOLLIS SPURGEON, JR. Novelist, poet, and educator, Hollis Spurgeon Summers, Jr., was born on June 21, 1916, in Eminence, Kentucky, to Hollis Spurgeon, Sr., and Hazel (Holmes) Summers. He grew up in Madisonville and graduated from the local high school. He received a B.A. from Georgetown College in Kentucky in 1937, an M.A. in 1943 from the Bread Loaf School of English of Middlebury College in Vermont, and a Ph.D. in 1949 from the University of Iowa in Iowa City.

Summers began his teaching career at Holmes High School in Covington, Kentucky, in 1937. He left in 1944 to teach at Georgetown College, then taught at the University of Kentucky during 1949-59. After that, he taught English at Ohio University in Athens until his retirement in 1986. His first book of poetry was *The Walks Near Athens* (1959), and other poems and collections followed: *Someone Else* (1962), *The Peddler and Other Domestic Matters* (1967), *Occupant Please Forward* (1976), and *Dinosaurs* (1977). Summers's novels include *City Limit (1948), Brighten the Corner* (1952), *The Weather of February* (1957), *The Garden* (1972), *How They Chose the Dead* (1973), and (with James Rourke, under the pseudonym Jim Hollis) *Teach You a Lesson* (1956). He edited the anthology *Kentucky Story* (1954). He was recognized many times for his contributions in both teaching and writing; he received a grant from the Fund for Advancement of Education in 1951-52; a *Saturday Review* poetry award in 1957; distinguished professor awards from the University of Kentucky and Ohio University in 1958 and 1964, respectively; an honorary doctor of literature award from Georgetown College in 1965. He was also a Fulbright lecturer in New Zealand in 1978.

Summers married Laura Vermont Clarke on June 30, 1943; they had two children, Hollis Spurgeon III and David Clarke. Summers died on November 14, 1987, in Athens, and is buried in Millersburg Cemetery in Bourbon County, Kentucky.

WILLIAM HENDRICKS

SUPERINTENDENT OF PUBLIC INSTRUCTION, OFFICE OF. The Office of Superintendent of Public Instruction was established in an 1821 amendment to the second constitution of Kentucky. The superintendent was to be appointed by the governor and confirmed by the state Senate for a two-year term with a $1,000 annual salary. The primary function of the office was to equitably distribute a permanent school fund as stipulated by the legislature on February 23, 1837. The first person to hold the office was Fayette County native Joseph James BULLOCK, who was appointed in February 1837 and resigned in February 1838. Bullock's January 3, 1839, report on analysis of the legislative act of 1821, which allotted $1 million and its annual interest to be distributed to school districts, concluded that one-third of Kentucky's children could not read and had no opportunity for common school education. The report recommended that school funding be increased. Tax increases were approved in 1849 by a vote of 74,628 to 37,746, and again in 1870.

The early appointees to the office were often ministers with no teaching experience and, like Bullock, they often combined the responsibilities of preaching with those of being superintendent. In 1850 the third constitution of Kentucky provided that the superintendent of public instruction be elected by the qualified voters of the commonwealth at the same time the governor is elected. The only qualifications were that the officer be at least thirty years of age and at least a two-year resident of the state at the time of election. Robert J. BRECKINRIDGE was both the last superintendent to be appointed and the first to be elected. In 1985 the PRICHARD COMMITTEE FOR ACADEMIC EXCELLENCE recommended a constitutional amendment providing for an appointed, not elected, state superintendent.

In 1990 the Education Reform Act was the response to the state supreme court decision that Kentucky's schools were unconstitutional in failing to meet the requirement for an efficient system of common schools throughout the state. The reform package calls for a major shift in decision-making away from the state and local boards to individual schools. The General Assembly stripped the superintendent of virtually all power beginning in 1991 and replaced the elected superintendent with an appointed commissioner of education as the chief state school officer, with a mission to provide tech-

nical assistance to local school districts. The new law abolished the state Department of Education as of June 30, 1991, and required the governor to appoint a new state board with eleven members, seven to be appointed from the state supreme court districts and the other four from the state at large. The function of the commissioner is to conduct studies, analyze information, and make appropriate recommendations to the Education Professional Standards Board. All Department of Education positions were abolished on June 30, 1991, and reorganized on July 1. The first commissioner under the new act was Thomas C. Boysen.

See Frank L. McVey, *The Gates Open Slowly: A History of Education in Kentucky* (Lexington, Ky., 1949); Prichard Committee Report, *The Path to a Larger Life* (Lexington, Ky., 1985).

JANE C. BRYANT

SUPREME COURT, STATE. In the winter of 1776 Virginia granted county status to Kentucky, providing it with a limited court system that included no appellate jurisdiction. Judgments by lower Kentucky courts were reviewed in the Virginia court of appeals. No detailed state COURT SYSTEM was established with the ratification of Kentucky's first constitution in 1792. However, the legislature did establish the Kentucky court of appeals as the highest court. This court had original and final jurisdiction in all cases involving titles to land and also had appellate jurisdiction, including that of reviewing certain judgments of the court of quarter-sessions. The three judges of the court were appointed for life by the governor, with no qualifications specified, subject to impeachment. Each court of appeals judge received an annual salary of $667.

Harry Innes was appointed the first chief justice of the appellate court on June 28, 1792. Soon thereafter he was appointed judge for the U.S. District of Kentucky. He was replaced on the state court by George Muter on December 7, 1792.

Many changes have been made to the Kentucky court system. The constitution of 1850 increased the court membership to four and provided that each judge be elected by voters from different districts. The court was limited to appellate jurisdiction. In 1894 the legislature increased the membership of the court to seven.

Major reforms in the court system were instituted on November 4, 1975, with the ratification of the Judicial Article, a constitutional amendment. As part of the amendment, the court of appeals was renamed the Kentucky supreme court. The supreme court is Kentucky's final interpreter of state law and hears appeals from lower state courts. Under very rare circumstances, the U.S. Supreme Court hears an appeal from a decision of the Kentucky supreme court. Cases involving the death penalty or imprisonment for twenty or more years go directly from the circuit court level to the supreme court for review. Cases are presented by way of written briefs and oral arguments.

One justice from each of Kentucky's seven appellate districts is chosen in a nonpartisan election. The minimum requirements are that a candidate has been licensed to practice law for at least eight years and has lived in the district for at least two years before the election. The terms of each justice are staggered among the seven districts, according to statute. A majority constitutes a quorum. The chief justice is chosen by his or her colleagues for a four-year term.   VINCENT J. COTTON, JR.

SURVEYING. After the Revolutionary War the rapid inflow of immigrants into Virginia's Kentucky District created hopeless confusion in land surveys and LAND CLAIMS and in the recording of valid deeds. Aggravating questions of overlapping claims, carelessly marked boundaries, and the lack of an effective central land-granting policy turned Kentucky into a region of defective surveys, bitter land disputes, and endless litigation. Far too many early Kentucky land claims were described as being delineated only by shallow "tomahawk" markings, or by what Henry Clay called "fireside surveys."

Because of the rugged topography of much of Kentucky, surveying land was an arduous physical undertaking, requiring a more sophisticated skill in the use of plane geometry than many surveyors were able to master. Doubtless the calling of surveyor is Kentucky's oldest profession. Administration of this office was transferred directly from Virginia, where originally the masters of William and Mary College set the standards and guidelines for surveying lands. The Kentucky land court, 1779-80, was created to deal with a host of early and conflicting claims and surveys, but it directed little if any attention to actual surveying of tracts.

Virginia survey laws prevailed in Kentucky until 1794. On December 20, 1794, during its second session, the Kentucky General Assembly enacted a law "to ascertain the boundaries of land and for other purposes," largely for establishing internal land boundaries and properly recording and determining the validity of warrants and deeds. Five years later, delegates to the second constitutional convention provided in section 8 of the Judicial Article the procedure for appointing county surveyors. Each county court was to submit the names of two "proper persons" to the governor, who in turn, with the consent of the Senate, was to appoint one of them surveyor. If no names were submitted, the governor was authorized, with the consent of the Senate, to appoint surveyors. In January 1814, the Kentucky General Assembly outlined more specifically the duties of county surveyors.

One of the most important chapters in the history of surveying in Kentucky is that pertaining to the BOUNDARIES of the commonwealth itself. These boundaries were surveyed piecemeal between 1799 and 1860, with at least nine surveys along the southern Kentucky-Tennessee boundary alone. In 1856 the *Revised Statutes of Kentucky*, volume 1, compiled by Richard H. Stanton, described the boundaries of the commonwealth and their evolution. The history of county boundaries is similar; there is a considerable volume of legislation relating to the establishment and revision of county boundaries. As late as 1990, boundaries were labeled "indefinite" on the topographical maps of the U.S. Geological Survey.

In many instances early surveyors established baselines from which to begin their internal surveys, especially when large tracts were involved. For instance, Matthew Walton of Springfield established such a line in Estill and Madison counties. Ancient baselines are frequently the subject of litigation today, as they were apparently never indicated on a map or made the subjects of legislation.

The most dependable historical documentation of individual Kentucky land surveys is found in the county deed books and in the reports of cases before the court of appeals. The depositions filed in circuit clerks' offices are also enlightening. The first volume of the court of appeals, popularly known as "Hughes No. 1," is made up largely of land cases and accompanying plats. County surveyors were almost always called upon to give expert testimony in land cases. One reason that Kentucky has been a hospitable home to so many lawyers is the long history of confusing land claims, overlapping of boundaries, poor marking of land lines, and the haphazardness of the old METES AND BOUNDS system of platting landholds.

Neither the Kentucky statutes nor the state constitution stipulates educational requirements for public surveyors. There is, however, a superabundance of documentation of their educational attainments—or lack of attainments—in the thousands of deed descriptions they have written. Some descriptions are clear and precise, but far too many are confused, poorly written, and too vague to be of much help in actually locating land boundaries. Under the metes and bounds system of survey in heavily wooded country, surveyors had to be reasonably well versed in botany and silviculture, and in all cases conversant with local nomenclature of landmarks and directional terms.

All of Kentucky's early surveyors used an instrument known as a Jacob's staff, the same kind George Washington used as an apprentice surveyor. On the one-legged staff was mounted an open-face brass compass that could be tilted to balance the directional needle. It could be quickly set in place, and sightings could be made through twin forks centered by hair-thin wires. Surveyors' handbooks supplied relevant astronomical and geometrical information, but how well the earlier surveyors read declinations and took astronomical sightings may well be questioned. Measurements of land lines were stated in terms of sixteen-and-a-half-foot poles. Old-style flexible looped-wire chains were made up of sixteen-inch segments, the entire chain being four poles in length. The accuracy of the "chaining" of boundaries has often been called into question; dragging the old-style looped chain over gritty ground caused the joints to wear and become inaccurate. In rugged topography, chaining was carelessly done, in some instances not at all.

Land in much of early Kentucky, especially the Appalachian highlands, was too cheap to expend much time surveying it. It would be a rare occurrence indeed if a tract of rough, hilly land described by magnetic calls and stated distances could now be duplicated with anything approaching precision by means of modern instruments, solid steel tapes, and stadia. The time spent in surveying was entirely too brief to produce accurate results. Early county surveyors sometimes established boundaries around as much as four or five hundred acres in a day's time, hence the use of the protective term "more or less" following statements of acreage. Historically, it has not been at all unusual for tracts of land to survey out at more acreage than stated in original deeds.

The introduction of the transit and other sophisticated equipment lifted the art of surveying in Kentucky onto a new and more scientific plane, and the college-trained engineer has almost completely replaced the old-time practical surveyor. If any of the latter still practice their profession, they are a small minority. In more recent years, few if any candidates for the office of surveyor have appeared on electoral ballots. Many old established surveyors became walking encyclopedias of land lore and practical information, as most of them had become acquainted with the location and boundaries of almost all the landholdings in their counties. As the value of land increased, however, owners had more incentive to establish exact acreages for their holdings, especially in areas underlain by minerals, oil, and gas. An excellent example is the ten massive volumes of precise plats and descriptions prepared by Rogers Clark Ballard Thruston concerning timber and mineral lands in the Black Mountain area of Kentucky and Virginia. Kentucky timber, coal, and oil and gas companies consider their land survey records to be among their most important documentary holdings. The art of surveying in 1990 is no less important in Kentucky than it was in 1790.

The term surveying is a broad one, obviously implying more than the location of land, state, or county boundaries. In the broad sweep of Kentucky history, the surveyor has been deeply involved in the laying out of towns, public squares, roads, canals, railroads, military bases, public utility lines, rivers and navigable channels, industrial areas, and public parks. Development of Kentucky's modern highway system since 1914 has involved a phenomenal chore of surveying. Both the airplane and the helicopter are now used as survey vehicles. In the Kentucky coal fields, the surveyor has been a vital functionary. No agency, however, has produced more dramatic survey results than the U.S. Geological Survey in topographically mapping the entire area of the commonwealth.

See Samuel M. Wilson, *The First Land Court in Virginia* (Lexington, Ky., 1923); James W. Sames III, *Four Steps West* (Frankfort, Ky., 1971); Thomas D. Clark, *Historic Maps of Kentucky* (Lexington, Ky., 1979).   THOMAS D. CLARK

SUTTON, WILLIAM LOFTUS. Born May 21, 1797, William Loftus Sutton, a public health advocate, received his medical education at Transylvania University and the Maryland Medical College. In 1833, after living for a number of years in Catlettsburg and Morganfield, Kentucky, he returned to his native Scott County, where he practiced medicine for the remainder of his life. Long interested in the causes of the epidemics that ravaged Kentucky, Sutton believed that a statewide medical organization might raise the commonwealth's health consciousness and the medical profession's standards. In 1851 he and a number of his colleagues founded the State Medical Society (now the Kentucky Medical Association), which Sutton served as the first president and as chairman of the committee on epidemics.

Sutton and other members of the society lobbied the Kentucky legislature to establish a state registry of diseases in the commonwealth. When it did so on January 9, 1852, Sutton became the registrar of vital statistics and seven years later he finished a monograph on the commonwealth's major diseases. The report also called attention to Kentucky's lack of health legislation and the need for state and county boards of health. Although twenty years passed before the legislature created the State Board of Health, Sutton's recommendations for such a board and for uniform registration laws won immediate recognition at the 1858 meeting of the American Medical Association. Applauding the resolutions he introduced at the meeting, the AMA elected him vice-president.

Sutton was married three times. His first wife, Mary Belle Catlett, bore him four children: George Catlett, John, and William (all of whom became physicians), and Mary Belle. He and his second wife, Nancy Cooper, had a son, William Henry. Sutton and his third wife, Ann Tibbs Webb, had three children: Annie Temperance, Caroline, and Henry Craig. Sutton died July 20, 1862, in Georgetown, Kentucky, and was buried in Georgetown Cemetery.

See Carrie T. Goldsborough and Anna G. Fisher, *William Loftus Sutton, M.D., 1797-1862* (Lexington, Ky., 1948).   NANCY D. BAIRD

SWIFT'S SILVER MINES. According to a two-centuries-old legend, the "lost" silver mines of one "Jonathan Swift" (whose name recalls the satiric author of *Gulliver's Travels*) await discovery somewhere in the "clifty and rough" terrain of eastern Kentucky. Countless hopefuls have pursued the treasure—some to the detriment of their health, families, and fortunes.

According to J.H. Kidwell's *Silver Fleece:* "Men, hoary with age and . . . half insane on the subject of the Swift mines ranged the mountains and the likely places, and died in the belief that they were very near the source of the mines as outlined in the Swift *Journal.*" In the purported *Journal,* the legendary Swift relates how he and a company of men preceded Daniel Boone into the state on mining expeditions beginning in 1760.

Swift claimed that he—as well as Frenchmen working nearby—had several productive mines. The *Journal* relates how a wounded bear led Swift to a cave with "a very rich vein of silver ore." On annual excursions over the next nine years, Swift and his crew allegedly "carried in supplies and took out silver bars and minted coins." However, after suffering harassment by Indians, a mutiny of his men, and other troubles, Swift walled up his treasure trove and discontinued his operation. When he returned fifteen years later, he had gone blind and was unable to relocate his fabulous hoard.

Unfortunately for Kentucky treasure hunters, the *Journal* exists in various versions, most of which are incapable of being reconciled with others and all of which are highly questionable. The best-known and most detailed copy contains portions plagiarized from a Kentucky history written after the purported time frame of the *Journal*. It is also replete with Masonic symbolism. In this version, for instance, Swift states that he marked a tree with "the symbol of a compass, trowel and square." (A combination of compass and square is the emblem of Freemasonry, and the trowel is the symbol of the mason's craft.) Swift adds that when he left the "richest mine" for the last time, he "walled it up with masonry form." Such wording, along with the contrived plot of the tale, invites an interpretation of the *Journal* as an allegory. Its moral clearly stresses the futility of "laying up treasures."

There is, in fact, no proof of the existence of a John or Jonathan Swift who mined silver in frontier Kentucky. Investigation has shown that one real-life person of that name, reputed to be the Swift of silver-mine legend, in fact lived many years after the latter's supposed death. (In any case—given the birth date for Swift recorded in the *Journal*—the man would have to have lived to the remarkable age of 112 years.) The geological evidence would seem to preclude the existence of such a treasure as Swift describes, and two centuries of mining, road construction, and other excavations have failed to unearth even one vein of silver in the area.

The Swift tale was making the rounds at least as early as 1788, when John FILSON—Kentucky's first mapmaker and an inveterate schemer—laid claim to a tract supposed "to include a silver mine" once worked by "a certain man named Swift" (according to the text of Filson's claim). However, the location is vague, and Filson's actions belie his belief in the fabled mines; he failed to mention it in a subsequent letter to his brother, and he even proceeded in the opposite direction on other business. Along the way, he wrote a poem telling how he had been spurned in love and threatening suicide. He soon disappeared, and his body was never found. Whatever he might have known about the truth or falsity of "Swift's mines" was lost with him.

See Michael Paul Henson, *John Swift's Lost Silver Mines* (Louisville 1975); Joe Nickell, "Uncovered—the Fabulous Silver Mines of Swift and Filson," *FCHQ* 54 (Oct. 1980), 324-45.

JOE NICKELL

SWINEBROAD, GEORGE. George Swinebroad, auctioneer and director of racing sales, was born on July 21, 1901, in Lancaster, Kentucky, to Greenberry Bright and Nell (Marrs) Swinebroad. In 1923 he graduated from Centre College in Danville. He auctioned tobacco in Kentucky and Carolina markets for twenty years. Tattersalls, a horse sales company in Lexington, Kentucky, hired Swinebroad for his clear, loud, rapid chant in 1936; he held this sales position until his death. Swinebroad was director of sales for Standardbred Horse Sales Company in Harrisburg, Pennsylvania, starting in 1939. During 1943-58 Swinebroad also auctioned thoroughbreds for New York's Fasig-Tipton Company and in 1944 he became associated with Lexington's Breeder's Sales Company (now Keeneland Sales). In 1947 Swinebroad and partner J.T. Denton established Swinebroad-Denton Auctioneers, which sold farms and horses. Swinebroad was made director of sales for Keeneland in 1957 and presided over sales until his death. Nine Kentucky Derby winners went under his gavel.

Swinebroad married Minerva Gordon; they had one daughter, Mary Marrs. His second wife was Elizabeth West. He died in Houston, Texas, on May 10, 1975, and was buried in Lancaster Cemetery.

SWOPE, KING. A prominent jurist and politician, King Swope was born in Danville, Kentucky, to James H. and Jesse (King) Swope, on August 10, 1893. After graduating from Centre College in Danville in 1914, he attended the University of Kentucky Law School. In 1917, Swope set up private practice in Lexington. At the age of twenty-six, he was elected to fill the U.S. House seat vacated by the death of Harvey Helm. Though he served only one term, August 2, 1919, to March 3, 1921, Swope developed a lifelong interest in Kentucky politics. In 1931 Gov. Flem Sampson (1927-31) appointed Swope judge of the circuit court of the 22nd Judicial District of Kentucky after the resignation of Judge R.C. Stoll. He served in this capacity for twenty years.

Claiming that the Democrats and the New Deal had "doubled the state debt, multiplied the number of state employees and neglected state institutions," Swope became one of Kentucky's leading Republican spokesmen. He was his party's choice for governor in 1935 and 1939, but was defeated first by A.B. Chandler, 556,262 to 461,104, then by Keen Johnson, 460,834 to 354,704. In 1938 there was a move to impeach him as judge, growing out of a dispute with the Scott County sheriff, who had refused to carry out a court order. Swope was charged with ridiculing public officers and attorneys in court and with exceeding his jurisdiction in dealing with state institutions. The state House committee that investigated these charges dismissed them as being "without foundation."

Swope married Mary Margaret Richards in 1918. They had one child, William. Swope died on April 23, 1961, and was buried in the Lexington Cemetery.

SYCAMORE SHOALS, TREATY OF. As the basis for the TRANSYLVANIA COMPANY's claims to territory in western Virginia, the Treaty of Sycamore Shoals (sometimes called the Treaty of Watauga) had an indirect influence on the political development of Kentucky. When Richard Henderson formed the Transylvania Company in 1774, he abandoned his judicial position in North Carolina for western land speculation. Accompanied by several members of his land company, he journeyed west with hopes of securing land from the Indians. On March 17, 1775, Henderson met with the Cherokee chiefs Okonistoto, Attakullakulla, and Savonooko at Sycamore Shoals on the Watauga River, in far eastern Tennessee, and negotiated an agreement to buy all land (17 to 20 million acres) lying between the Ohio, Kentucky, and Cumberland rivers in exchange for goods worth 10,000 pounds sterling.

The treaty was the downfall of the Transylvania Company. Lord Dunmore, governor of Virginia, declared that Henderson's purchase violated Virginia's territorial boundaries. Moreover, Henderson had breached the Proclamation of 1763, which prohibited colonial expansion in Virginia's western lands; he had violated the Treaty of Fort Stanwix (November 5, 1768), between the British and the Six Nations of Indians, which granted the land in question to the King of England; and he had broken the Virginia statute of 1705 that prohibited private citizens from purchasing Indian land. In December 1776, Virginia consolidated its control over the territory by dividing Fincastle County into Kentucky, Montgomery, and Washington counties. By granting Kentucky County representation in its General Assembly, Virginia placed the land under the direct control of the colonial government and repudiated the Treaty of Sycamore Shoals.

T

TACHAU, JEAN (BRANDEIS). Jean (Brandeis) Tachau, social reformer, was the daughter of Alfred and Jennie (Taussig) Brandeis, born on August 22, 1894, in Louisville. She was the niece of Louis Brandeis, justice of the U.S. Supreme Court; the family had a tradition of community service. After graduating from the Kentucky Home School in Louisville, Jean Brandeis spent a year at Bryn Mawr College in Pennsylvania. She married Charles G. Tachau on May 11, 1921, in Louisville.

During the 1920s Jean Tachau was a social worker for the Children's Protection Association in Louisville. In 1933, despite the prevalent social attitude opposing contraceptives, Tachau and a small group of volunteers established the Kentucky Birth Control League and a clinic, the forerunner of Planned Parenthood, in Louisville. Concerned also with child welfare, Tachau worked on the advisory committee that outlined the Kentucky child welfare laws of 1954; helped produce the legislation that set up the Kentucky Department of Child Welfare in 1960; and served as president of the Kentucky Citizens for Child Welfare in 1956. In 1963 she retired as executive director of the Kentucky Birth Control League.

Tachau also served as chairman of the Health and Welfare Council of Louisville Community Chest (now United Way), president of the Family and Children's Agency, member of the Governor's Advisory Council on Child Welfare, member of Save the Children Foundation, and chairman of the Louisville Juvenile Court Advisory Committee. In 1966 the Kentucky Children's Home in Lyndon, Kentucky, honored her with a certificate for her work on child welfare, and in 1967 she received an award from the Western Kentucky Chapter of the National Association of Social Workers.

Tachau and her husband had three children: Charles, Eric, and Jean. Tachau died on July 3, 1978, in Louisville; her ashes were buried in Cave Hill Cemetery.

TALBOT, ISHAM. Isham Talbot, U.S. Senator, was born near Talbot, Bedford County, Virginia, in 1773 to James and Elizabeth Talbot. His father, a Revolutionary War veteran, moved the family to Harrodsburg, Kentucky, in Mercer County. Talbot read law with Col. George Nicholas and was admitted to the bar on May 12, 1796. He opened a practice in Versailles, Kentucky, then moved to Frankfort. Talbot was elected to the state Senate from Franklin County in 1812 and served until 1815. In that year he was elected to the U.S. Senate to fill the vacancy caused by the resignation of Jesse Bledsoe. He defeated Benjamin Mills by a vote of 56 to 50 and served from January 3, 1815, to March 3, 1819. In 1820 Talbot defeated John Rowan by 69 to 67 for the U.S. Senate seat resigned by William Logan. Talbot served from October 19, 1820, to March 3, 1825, then returned to his law practice in Frankfort.

Talbot married Margaret Garrard, daughter of James Garrard, Kentucky's second governor (1796-1804), on January 24, 1804; she died on March 22, 1815. Talbot married Adelaide Thomason on March 29, 1817. He died on September 25, 1837, at his home, Melrose, near Frankfort and was buried in the Frankfort Cemetery.

TALBOTT, JOHN DANIEL. John Daniel Talbott, Democratic politician, was born February 10, 1883, near Bardstown, Kentucky, the son of Mary Ann (Roney) and John C. Talbott, Jr. After elementary education at home, Talbott entered Bethany Academy in Bardstown; he then worked in a local drugstore, and attended Valparaiso University in Indiana from 1903 to 1905. He reentered the pharmacy business in early 1906; three years later, in October 1909, he married Rebecca Cox Johnson, the daughter of Rep. Ben Johnson. Talbott's father-in-law had earlier helped him obtain an education and the two worked together in the political arena. Facing election obstacles at the state level because of their Catholicism, Johnson and Talbott became powers behind the political thrones of the 1920s and 1930s. In 1931 the younger man won election as state auditor, but soon broke with the new administration and became part of a Democratic faction that opposed Gov. Ruby Laffoon (1931-35). In 1935 that group engineered the gubernatorial nomination and election of A.B. Chandler (1935-39).

Gov. Chandler made Talbott his chief adviser and named him insurance commissioner and later commissioner of finance, positions from which Talbott approved and distributed patronage. Honest and capable, "the Old Bear" (as Talbott was called) was credited with much of the planning of the of the first Chandler administration. During that time, disagreements involving both political decisions and family matters caused a bitter break between Talbott and Johnson, a rift that never healed. Talbott subsequently ran for Congress in a special election in 1943. His defeat by Republican Chester O. Carrier by a wide margin (29,855 to 17,218) marked the end of his political career. Talbott died May 17, 1950, and was buried in Bardstown.

See Orval W. Baylor, *J. Dan Talbott: Champion of Good Government* (Louisville, 1943); John Ed Pearce, *Divide and Dissent: Kentucky Politics, 1930-1963* (Lexington, Ky., 1987).

JAMES C. KLOTTER

TALT HALL WAR. The so-called Talt Hall War in Letcher County, Kentucky, and Wise County, Virginia, in the 1880s and early 1890s was a series of murders from ambush, most associated in some way with liquor-making and bootlegging. This area of Appalachia had its crop of rural criminals, among them "Devil" John Wright, Talton ("Bad Talt") Hall, the "Red Fox" (Dr. M.B. Taylor), and "Big Ed" Hall, a manhunter. Among them were law officers, moonshiners, feudists, and plain lowdown ornery fellows. The arrival of a group of college bred engineers and entrepreneurs in the Pound Gap–Big Stone Gap area in the 1880s brought a distinct change to the region. The "outsiders" organized a private constabulary to bring peace.

The notorious Talton Hall was said to have killed twenty persons. He was arrested in March 1893 in Memphis, Tennessee, by Wise County Sheriff Wilson Holbrook on the charge of having killed Enos B. Helton, the Norton, Virginia, town marshall. Hall was confined in the primitive jail in Wise under heavy guard by the mountain constabulary, and was tried, convicted, and hanged on September 3, 1893. "Devil" John Wright hauled Hall's body back to the mouth of Wright's Fork of the Kentucky River to be buried. The "Red Fox" was captured and charged as the leader in a Pound Gap ambush and massacre on May 14, 1892. In that incident, five members of "Old Man" Ira Mullins's family and two horses were killed. On October 27, 1893, "Red Fox" was hanged from the same gallows as Talt Hall. John Fox, Jr., wrote a dramatic sketch of the hanging in *Blue Grass and Rhododendron* (1901).

See Amy Paine and Brian Boyd, "Big Ed Hall: Mountain Manhunter," *Mantrip* (Wheelwright, Ky., 1987).   THOMAS D. CLARK

TATE, ALLEN. Allen Tate was born in Winchester, Kentucky, on November 10, 1899, the son of John Orley and Eleanor (Varnell) Tate. His parents moved to Ashland, Kentucky, when he was three years old. He attended Cross School for Boys in Louisville, Ashland High School, and Georgetown University Preparatory School in Washington, D.C. He entered Vanderbilt University in Nashville in 1918 and quickly became associated with such well-known literary figures as John Crowe Ransom, Robert Penn Warren, Merrill Moore, Andrew Lytle, and Donald Davidson.

In 1924 Tate moved to New York City, where he gained recognition as a poet, literary critic, and biographer, for whom the Civil War was a central theme. He won a Guggenheim Fellowship in 1928 and spent most of that year and the next in England and France. While in Europe his associates were among the most widely known authors and poets of the day, including T.S. Eliot, e.e. cummings, and Gertrude Stein. In February 1930 he returned to Tennessee, where his home on the Cumberland River, Benfolly, became a fashionable haven for many writers.

Tate was writer in residence at Princeton University in New Jersey during 1939-42 and lectured at Oxford University in England in 1953. He held many teaching positions at the university level, including appointments at Southwestern College in Memphis; University of the South in Sewanee, Tennessee, where he edited the *Sewanee Review* during 1944-46; University of North Carolina at Greensboro; and the University of Minnesota. He was poetry consultant to the Library of Congress in 1943-44. Among Tate's best-known works are the poems "Ode to the Confederate Dead" (1927) and "The Swimmers" (1952); the novel *The Fathers* (1938); and the biographies *Stonewall Jackson, The Good Soldier* (1928) and *Jefferson Davis: His Rise and Fall* (1929).

Tate married Caroline Gordon of Todd County, Kentucky, in November 1924; they had one daughter, Nancy Meriwether. In 1958, following a divorce, he married Isabella Gardner McCormick. After their marriage ended, Tate married Helen Heinze in 1966; they had three sons: John Allan, Michael (who died in childhood), and Ben. Tate died in Nashville on February 9, 1979.

See Ann Waldron, *Close Connections* (New York 1987).   JOY BALE BOONE

TATE, JAMES W. James W. Tate, who absconded as treasurer of Kentucky in 1888, was born January 2, 1831, in Franklin County, the only child of Nancy (Taylor) Tate, the daughter of a prominent minister, and her second husband, Thomas L. Tate, a farmer. At the age of seventeen, James Tate served as a clerk in the Frankfort post office. He was appointed assistant secretary of state for the terms 1854-55 and 1859-63 and assistant clerk of the Kentucky House of Representatives during 1865-67. A Democrat, he was elected treasurer in 1867 and was reelected every two years thereafter, through 1887. Friendly and outgoing, Tate was described by the *Biographical Encyclopedia of Kentucky* (1878) as one whose "judgement is held in high esteem and his integrity, prudence, and foresight are regarded of the highest order."

When he disappeared from the treasurer's office on March 14, 1888, Tate took with him two sacks of gold and silver coin, along with a four-inch roll of bills. Gov. Simon B. Buckner (1887-91) soon announced that Tate had embezzled $247,128.50. An investigation revealed extremely slipshod practices in the treasurer's office; state officials had been given illegal advances on their salaries and even loans (often not repaid). Tate's scattered records were almost impossible to decipher, but Tate had apparently used state funds to invest in real estate and mines.

Impeached by the House, tried and found guilty on four counts by the Senate, Tate was removed from office. A criminal indictment followed. "Tate-ism" became equated with political corruption, for accommodating officials had consistently neglected to check Tate's accounts. Moreover, his wealthy bondsmen were freed from all judgments to repay the state, in a case decided in 1895 and marked "Not to be officially reported." Distrust of leaders grew so pervasive that in 1890-91 delegates who drafted the state's present constitution (its fourth) repeatedly cited the example of "Honest Dick"

Tate as one reason for limiting state officials to one term in office.

What became of Tate? Secret letters from "Honest Dick" to family and friends placed him in Canada, Japan, China, California, and, finally, Brazil. Then the letters stopped; his fate is still unknown. Tate was married in 1856 to Lucy J. Hawkins and was father of a son, who died at age three, and a daughter, Edmoina.

See Emmet V. Mittlebeeler, "The Great Kentucky Absconsion," *FCHQ* 27 (1953): 336-51; Hambleton Tapp and James C. Klotter, *Kentucky: Decades of Discord, 1865-1900* (Frankfort, Ky., 1977).   JAMES C. KLOTTER

TAULBEE, WILLIAM PRESTON. William Preston Taulbee, U.S. congressman, was born October 22, 1851, in Morgan County, one of twelve children of Mary Ann (Wilson) and William H. Taulbee, farmer and later state senator. He attended local schools, married Lou Emma Oney in 1871, entered the Methodist ministry, and in 1881 was admitted to the bar. Taulbee was twice Magoffin County court clerk. A Democrat, he was elected to two terms in the U.S. House of Representatives, serving from March 4, 1885, to March 3, 1889. Taulbee's political career ended in scandal when newspaperman Charles E. Kincaid reported the married congressman's relationship with a young Washington, D.C., woman. Months later, on February 28, 1890, Taulbee threatened Kincaid; in the Capitol a few hours later, Kincaid shot the unarmed Taulbee. He died on March 11 and was buried in Mt. Sterling. Kincaid, who was charged with murder, was acquitted despite two eyewitnesses to the shooting.

See James C. Klotter, "Sex, Scandal, and Suffrage in the Gilded Age," *Historian* 42 (Feb. 1980): 225-43.   JAMES C. KLOTTER

TAXATION. Kentuckians have struggled with the politics of taxation and spending for two hundred years. The public historically has leaned toward low taxation, even if the result is reduced—sometimes minimal—services. Taxation in Kentucky has been an emotional event as much as an economic reality. When the passage of a tax on liquor by the federal government brought on the Whiskey Rebellion in 1794 in Pennsylvania, many Kentuckians believed the violent reaction to be a natural and proper response. In Kentucky, states' rights were popular and federal involvement unpopular.

The Kentucky tax system has changed many times. In the beginning, Kentucky, like other states, was relatively self-financing. However, in modern times Kentucky has increased its dependence on the federal government. During the 1980s, federal aid made up 25 to 30 percent of the state's total revenue. Kentucky is far above the national average in federal dependence. In 1985 the average Kentuckian paid $953 in state taxes, the sixth lowest of the fifty states, or $101 per $1,000 of income. Kentucky's low tax revenue can be explained partly by its low tax capacity. Kentucky had an aggregate

taxable capacity of 80 to 85 percent of the fifty states' average during the 1980s, and the state used only about 90 percent of that capacity. As a result, the state collected taxes of less than $75 when the average state collected $100. Nevertheless, opinion polls on state and local taxation during the 1980s indicated that about half of Kentuckians believed their tax burden was excessive. The other half believed their tax burden was approximately correct. An insignificant number of Kentucky residents, approximately 2 percent, thought their tax liability was too low.

Beyond taxation by the General Assembly, each of Kentucky's 120 counties may raise tax revenues independently, within the limits of state law. Local school districts and municipal governments can also tax independently of the commonwealth, but under its control.

The state derives its tax revenue from a variety of sources, including general and selective sales taxes, individual and corporate income taxes, property taxes, excise taxes, license taxes, and, most recently, the state lottery. These tax revenues go chiefly to fund highways, education, and public welfare services. In the modern era, Kentucky has shown an above-average reliance (based on tax capacity) on the use of the individual income tax. Kentucky's individual income tax, adopted in 1936, produces 25 to 30 percent of the state's total revenue. Kentucky's corporate income tax, also adopted in 1936, brings in less than 10 percent of the state's revenue. Kentucky's emphasis on corporate income tax, when compared with tax capacity, is low.

The 1934 General Assembly enacted an intensely unpopular 3 percent sales tax that was virtually inoperable. In 1936 the Kentucky tax system was significantly altered, and the 3 percent sales tax was replaced with individual and corporate income taxes. Effective July 1, 1960, a 3 percent retail sales tax was applied to a wide range of tangible items. The 1960 sales tax was better received than the one in 1934 and significantly boosted the general fund. Originally, there were few exemptions from the tax, but the list grew steadily over the years. The tax was increased in 1968 from 3 percent to 5 percent. The tax of five cents per dollar was known as "Nunn's nickel," after Republican Gov. Louie Nunn (1967-71). The sales tax was raised to 6 percent in 1990. Contemporary Kentucky receives slightly less than 30 percent of its revenue from the general sales tax.

Taxation of property in Kentucky has always been controversial. Among Kentuckians, evasion or avoidance of property taxation has not been unusual. In 1884 the state had a budget deficit of $491,375, and reform-minded Gov. James Proctor Knott (1883-87) blamed what he called gross deficiencies in both the system of assessment and the way the system was administered. Knott told the General Assembly that the most recent assessment of property value in Kentucky, $374.5 million, was estimated to be no more than half the actual value. The aggregate assessed property values in Indiana for 1884 were 53 percent greater than Kentucky's. Based on assessments in 1884, the average Indiana resident's wealth was $406, while the average was $222 in Kentucky. The cause of the disparity was that Indiana assessed values much more efficiently than Kentucky did. Much of the property in Kentucky had been granted exemptions, was delinquent, and/or had been underassessed. Knott and the 1885-86 legislature produced the most comprehensive tax revision to that time, raising tax revenues from $1,630,000 in 1886 to $3,693,000 in 1888.

The tradition of low assessments persisted, however. In 1966 the courts ordered full valuation of property in *Russman v. Luckett*. Average assessments for tax purposes had been as low as 26 percent of fair market value across the state. The 100 percent market valuation would thus have quadrupled tax revenue. However, a special legislative session in 1965 had rolled back property tax rates to avoid large revenue increases. Although full assessment is still a state requirement, it has a weak record of implementation. In 1979 a special legislative session passed HOUSE BILL 44, which restricted property tax revenue from increasing more than 4 percent per year, regardless of net assessment growth. House Bill 44 was criticized for restricting revenue growth, especially in view of the inflation rate, which typically exceeded 4 percent per year throughout the 1980s.

In the late 1980s and in 1990, there were significant efforts to boost tax revenue. The new tax revenues of the 1990s will go primarily to improve education. Such efforts are in direct conflict with the Kentucky tradition of low taxes and minimum public services.

See Joel Goldstein, ed., *Kentucky Government and Politics* (Bloomington, Ind., 1984); Kentucky Department of Economic Development, *Kentucky Economic Statistics 1979-1989*, Frankfort, Ky.; Kentucky Revenue Cabinet, *Annual Report 1979-89*, Frankfort, Ky.; Don M. Soule, *Annual Economic Report, 1985, Commonwealth of Kentucky*, Lexington, Ky.　　　　PHILIP K. FLYNN

TAYLOR, CAROLINE (BURNAM). Caroline ("Carrie") (Burnam) Taylor, fashion designer and dressmaker, was born on April 1, 1855, in Bowling Green, Kentucky, to Thomas L. and Sarah (Hampton) Burnam. She was the granddaughter of John Burnam, Kentucky's Confederate government treasurer. She received her education in the Warren County schools. In the mid-1870s she began a small dressmaking business in her home, planning to become a fashion designer. In 1879 she married Aaron H. Taylor, who joined her work force. In time, Caroline Taylor's name was synonymous with that of fine clothing; her operation in Bowling Green employed about three hundred women, and her mail order business reportedly had 24,000 customers. She advertised on engraved cards bearing poetic messages and in a short-lived fashion magazine, *Styles and the Gist of It*. Not content with re-

gional fabrics and trims, Taylor made annual buying trips to New York and Europe. In April 1912, when she stayed in Europe to attend an extra fashion show, she missed her passage on the maiden voyage of the *Titanic*.

Carrie and Aaron Taylor had two children: William (1880) and Louise (1882). Carrie Taylor died on November 24, 1917, in Bowling Green, leaving a successful business and an estate valued at more than $250,000. She was buried in the Fairview Cemetery in Bowling Green.

CAROL CROWE-CARRACO

TAYLOR, JAMES. James Taylor, early landholder, was born April 19, 1769, the fifth child of Col. James and Anne (Hubbard) Taylor of Caroline County, Virginia. He was educated privately and at the Rappahannock Academy. In 1793 he came to Kentucky to supervise the sale of his father's land at the mouth of the Licking River, and to help establish the town of Newport, where he lived for the remainder of his life. On November 15, 1795, Taylor married Keturah (Moss) Leitch, widow of Maj. David Leitch, and added her extensive landholdings to his own. Of the Taylors' eleven children, only four survived infancy: James, Keturah, Ann Wilkinson, and Jane Maria. As a result of his kinship with Secretary of State James Madison, Taylor obtained in 1803 an army facility, Newport Barracks, for the small village, and he was later appointed an army paymaster. In 1812, as quartermaster general, he joined Gen. William Hull's ill-fated campaign against British forces at Detroit. Following the war, General Taylor, as he was then called, acquired a considerable fortune through banking, manufacturing, and land speculation. He died on November 7, 1848, just hours after voting for his cousin, Zachary Taylor, and was buried in Evergreen Cemetery, Southgate, Kentucky.

See Robert C. Vitz, "General James Taylor and the Beginnings of Newport, Kentucky," *FCHQ* 50 (Oct. 1976): 353-68; Robert C. Vitz, "James Taylor, the War Department, and the War of 1812," *Old Northwest* 2 (June 1976): 107-30.

TAYLOR, WILLIAM SYLVESTER. William Sylvester Taylor, governor during 1899-1900, was born on October 10, 1853, to Sylvester and Mary G. (Moore) Taylor in Butler County, Kentucky. He had no formal education until he was fifteen, but he later taught school (1874-82) and became a successful attorney. In 1878 he married Sarah Belle Tanner, and they had nine children. His second marriage, to Nora A. Myers in 1912, produced one son. Taylor was elected Butler County clerk in 1882, then to two terms as county judge (1886-94). He joined the Republican party in 1884 and soon began to serve on state committees and to attend national conventions. He was elected state attorney general in 1895 when William O. Bradley won the governorship.

Four years later Taylor took the party's nomination for governor and opposed William Goebel

(1900) in a campaign bitter even by Kentucky's standards. Taylor had a clean record, but he was attacked for the Republicans' ties to big business, for their support by black voters, and for the disarray of the Bradley administration. Taylor assailed the Democrats for bossism, for the GOEBEL ELECTION LAW, and for the obvious factionalism within the party. The Board of Election Commissioners, in a 2-1 split, certified that 193,714 had voted for Taylor, 191,331 for Goebel, and some 15,000 for minor candidates. Taylor was inaugurated as the state's governor on December 12, 1899.

He served only until January 31, 1900, however, because the Democratic-dominated General Assembly challenged Taylor's victory. An eleven-man committee that had only one Republican member was established to hear testimony and make recommendations. Armed men, many of them Republicans from eastern Kentucky, traveled to Frankfort to prevent what they perceived as the stealing of the governorship by Democrats. Goebel was critically wounded by a rifle bullet at the capitol on January 30, 1900, and Governor Taylor declared a state of insurrection, called out the militia, and ordered the General Assembly to meet in the Republican city of London. In a secret meeting in Frankfort, the Democrats in the legislature invalidated enough Republican votes to declare Goebel the winner. On January 31 Goebel was sworn into office as governor. Suddenly Kentucky had two governments, and open warfare seemed probable. But when Goebel died on February 3, 1900 (see GOEBEL ASSASSINATION), each side agreed to consult the courts.

The Democrats won a circuit court decision in March that was upheld by the state court of appeals in April, and the Kentucky supreme court agreed. Taylor had done little as governor except to make several appointments and grant a few pardons. Upon his indictment as an accessory to murder in the shooting of Goebel, Taylor fled to Indianapolis, and the governor of Indiana refused to extradite him. In 1909 he was pardoned by Republican Gov. Augustus E. Willson (1907–11). Even so, Taylor rarely returned to Kentucky. He became a successful insurance executive before his death on August 2, 1928. He was buried at Indianapolis.

See James C. Klotter, *William Goebel* (Lexington, Ky., 1977). LOWELL H. HARRISON

TAYLOR, ZACHARY. Zachary Taylor, twelfth president of the United States, was born on November 24, 1784, at Montebello in Orange County, Virginia. In the spring of 1785, Taylor's parents, Richard and Mary (Strother) Taylor, moved the family to a plantation in Jefferson County, Kentucky. At SPRINGFIELD, as the Taylor residence was known, Zachary Taylor helped with farm work and was educated by a tutor. In 1808 he was commissioned a first lieutenant in the 7th Infantry. Taylor saw active service in the War of 1812, distinguishing himself in particular in the defense of Fort Harrison against an Indian assault in September of 1812.

After the war Taylor returned briefly to civilian life, working for a year (1815-16) on the 324-acre farm given to him by his father near Louisville. He then rejoined the military and in succeeding years was stationed at various outposts along the American frontier. He participated in the Black Hawk War in 1832 and commanded American forces in a successful campaign against the Seminole Indians in Florida in 1837. During the Mexican War (1845-47) he earned popular acclaim as the victorious commander of the Army of the Rio Grande. After the war he won election to the presidency as a Whig candidate and was inaugurated on March 5, 1849.

Taylor maintained Kentucky as his official residence during most of his adult life. He lived in Louisville while on furlough, from the late summer of 1818 until February of 1820. On June 30, 1819, during President James Monroe's tour through the southern states, Taylor dined with the president and Gen. Andrew Jackson at ex-senator John Brown's Frankfort residence. During his period of service in the army, Taylor often visited his father's home at Springfield. He owned stock in two Kentucky banks and purchased warehouses and town lots in Louisville. Taylor eventually sold his Kentucky farm and made various land purchases in Louisiana and Mississippi during the 1820s, 1830s, and 1840s. On February 14, 1849, during his last visit to Kentucky on the way to his inauguration in Washington, Taylor visited Frankfort and was honored there by the local population.

Taylor married Margaret Mackall Smith of Calvert County, Maryland, on June 18, 1810, and had six children by her, two of whom died in childhood. Taylor died in office on July 9, 1850. He was buried in Washington, D.C.; later his remains were moved to the family graveyard at Springfield. This graveyard became a part of the Zachary Taylor National Cemetery.

See Holman Hamilton, *Zachary Taylor, Soldier of the Republic* (New York 1941); Hamilton, *Zachary Taylor, Soldier in the White House* (New York 1951). JOHN FORGY

TAYLOR COUNTY. Taylor County, the 100th county in order of formation, is located in south-central Kentucky. The county is bordered by Green, Larue, Marion, Casey, and Adair counties and contains 270 square miles. It was named for Mexican War hero Gen. Zachary Taylor, who later became the twelfth president of the United States. Taylor County was formed by the Kentucky legislature from the northeast half of Green County on March 1, 1848. CAMPBELLSVILLE is the county seat.

The terrain is made up of gently rolling and hilly land. The crest of the Muldraugh Hill (also called the Mississippi Escarpment) serves as the boundary between Taylor and Marion counties. The county is drained by three major water systems: on the northwest by Pitman Creek, on the northeast by Robinson Creek, and on the south by the Green River.

The county had no early stations but was frequented by Long Hunters and pioneers from other stations. Thomas Denton and William Stewart built cabins on Sinking Creek, now called Pitman Creek, in 1780. The Cumberland Trace traversed the county by 1779. Scores of Indians, hunters, and settlers used it, after trails leading from the Wilderness Road and Skaggs's Trace, to get to central and western Kentucky, the Cumberland settlements, and the Natchez Trace. The Cumberland Trace was replaced by the Lexington and Nashville Road, which was used by stagecoaches on the federal mail route between Zanesville, Ohio, and Florence, Alabama. Sanders Tavern, operated by Thomas Sanders in 1797 and later by Henry Sanders, Jr., served as an inn and stagecoach stop for travelers on this route.

Most of the early settlers of Taylor County came from Virginia, North Carolina, Maryland, and Pennsylvania, including Elias Barbee, who attained the rank of general during the War of 1812 and later served in the state legislature.

Campbellsville Baptist Church is the oldest congregation in Taylor County, dating back to 1791, when a church was established at Pitman Creek. Robinson Creek Church merged with it, and in 1852 the congregation moved to the new county seat. The second oldest church is Good Hope Baptist, formed in 1796, and the third oldest is Bethel Presbyterian, formed in 1799. In about 1802, a school was established in the Bengal area by Elias Barbee and Revolutionary War soldiers James and Jonathan Cowherd. The Irish Seminary, Science Hill Academy, and Mt. Clifton School followed.

During the Civil War, two Union camps were set up in Taylor County: Camp Hobson at the Green River Bridge and Camp Andy Johnson, which moved between Greensburg and Campbellsville. Many men from the county served the Union in the 13th and 27th Kentucky infantries and the 6th Kentucky Cavalry. Others served in Gen. John Hunt Morgan's 3d Confederate Cavalry. General Morgan campaigned extensively in Taylor County. After his capture in Ohio and his escape from prison in 1863, Morgan returned to Taylor County, where he took refuge on his way to Tennessee.

After years of negotiations and the floating of several bond issues, the Cumberland & Ohio branch of the Louisville & Nashville Railroad (now CSX Transportation) opened in 1879. The stagecoach continued its run between Campbellsville and Columbia until 1914.

A fair association was formed in 1867, and county fairs, with horse and cattle shows, operated almost continuously until the 1970s. Two resorts, Griffin Springs and Lorain Wells, were in operation by 1910 and were known for their sulphur water, fine accommodations, generous tables, and recreation. Both resorts closed in the 1930s.

The U.S. Army Corps of Engineers impounded the Green River in 1969 to control flooding in the basins of the Green and the Ohio rivers. Part of the towns of Elkhorn and Yuma were moved to make way for the reservoir, and the Green River Lake State Park was created. The reservoir and park area cover 34,000 acres—16,687 acres in Taylor and the rest in Adair County.

Taylor County's black population provided two of the county's most noted citizens—Clem Haskins, basketball player and college coach, and Margaret (Buckner) Young, author of children's books and wife of Whitney Young, Jr., executive director of the National Urban League. Another native was Union Democrat Aaron Harding, a member of the U.S. House of Representatives from 1861 to 1867. The county is the location of CAMPBELLS-VILLE COLLEGE.

The population of Taylor County was 17,138 in 1970; 21,178 in 1980; and 21,146 in 1990.

See Garnett Graves, *Taylor County: Its Public Buildings, Officers and Principal Murder Trials* (Campbellsville, Ky., 1898); Robert Lee Nesbitt, *Early Taylor County History* (Campbellsville, Ky., 1941).   BETTY MITCHELL GORIN

TAYLOR MILL. Taylor Mill is a residential suburb in northeastern Kenton County on KY 16, five miles south of Covington. The area was part of a 5,000-acre patent issued in 1790 to Raleigh Colston by Virginia's Gov. Beverly Randolph. It was first settled in 1795, when Jacob Foster began operating a sawmill and gristmill on Banklick Creek. In 1810 James Taylor, founder of Newport, purchased the property, and the road leading from the mill to what is now Covington became known as Taylor's Mill Road. The mill ceased operation sometime between 1853 and 1864.

The old mill road was developed as a route connecting Covington with Pendleton County to the south by the Covington and Taylor Mill Turnpike Road Company, incorporated in 1848. The road was later macadamized. Growth along the turnpike was slow until 1902, when a subdivision near Banklick Creek was developed and named Forest Hills. By 1928 it included Forest Hills School, St. Anthony Catholic Church, and an eight-acre park. Other communities sprang up in the area, including Winston Park in 1929, Sunny Acres in 1953, and Taylor Mill in 1957. Sunny Acres was merged into Taylor Mill in 1959, Winston Park annexed Forest Hills in 1962, and Winston Park was merged with Taylor Mill in 1972. The fourth-class city of Taylor Mill in 1988 annexed land extending to the Licking River.

The building of I-275 in the 1970s cut east-west through a section of Taylor Mill; it increased the area's accessibility and stimulated residential development. Middle-and upper-middle-class homes replaced much of the original surrounding farmland. The population of Taylor Mill was 3,253 in 1970; after annexation, it was 4,509 in 1980 and 5,530 in 1990.

See Michael J. Hammons, *History of Taylor Mill, Kentucky* (N.P., 1988).

TAYLOR MINES. Taylor Mines in the 1920s was a thriving coal town. It grew up where Milton Taylor, with a few laborers and little capital, in the 1870s began operating a shaft coal mine on family land in southwestern Ohio County, Kentucky, two miles from the Illinois Central Railroad. Though the coal mined was primarily intended for home use, company stock was sold, and around 1910 Ignatius P. Barnard of Beaver Dam, Kentucky, began to purchase the shares. In 1915 he and J. P. Speed of Louisville, president of the Ohio County Land and Mining Company, formed the Beaver Dam Coal Company to mine coal where Milton Taylor had started. By special contract with the United Mine Workers of America (UMW), the company expanded until it employed over nine hundred men. Daily production climbed to 270 tons and miners' average wages were seven dollars per day. Taylor Mines became a town of approximately 1,500, including a company store, a doctor's office, drugstore, grade school, meeting hall, and hotel. A power plant furnished electricity for the mine machinery and the community.

On April 4, 1924, the UMW contract lapsed and the miners walked out. When they returned after eighteen months, wages had dropped to four dollars per day, and the Depression further reduced wages, to twenty cents an hour; despite such hardship, few miners left. On October 27, 1937, Speed announced the closing of the mines effective October 30, and within two years most of the town's population had left. The reasons for the mine closings were unclear but there were rumors of labor unrest in adjacent fields. There are few reminders of the once thriving community.

See Corinne Taylor Gregory, *Once There Was a Town* (Beaver Dam, Ky., 1983).

CORINNE T. GREGORY

TAYLORSVILLE. Taylorsville, the county seat of Spencer County, is located at the junction of KY 44 and KY 155. By 1790 the town had several brick homes. Nine years later it was laid out and named for Richard Taylor, the owner of a gristmill and a large tract of land at the confluence of the Salt River and Brashears Creek. The town was incorporated on January 22, 1829. As early as 1794 Taylorsville had a Baptist church, and in 1808 a Catholic church opened. The Spencer Institute, a private school, started classes in 1846. Four years later the first public school opened in a log building.

In 1833, a covered bridge joined Taylorsville with counties to the south. In 1837 a stagecoach route ran from Louisville through Taylorsville to Chaplin in Nelson County. The forty-five-mile trip took nine hours and cost nine dollars. In 1869 the legislature approved the charter of a railroad from Shelbyville through Taylorsville to Bloomfield in Nelson County. The road was completed in 1881, at a cost of $395,524 for the 26.7-mile line.

The first courthouse was established in an existing building in 1825. The second courthouse was burned by Confederate guerrillas in 1865. The county's records were saved and Union troops apprehended the guerrillas at Mt. Eden, ten miles from Taylorsville, where one was killed. The next courthouse, an Italianate structure built in 1866, burned in 1914. The present courthouse, of classic Beaux Arts design, was completed in 1915.

Taylorsville's economy is geared to the county's agricultural products. The 1982 impoundment of the Salt River, creating the 3,050-acre Taylorsville Lake, brought additional revenue to local merchants.

The population of the sixth-class city was 897 in 1970; 801 in 1980; and 774 in 1990.

TEACHER TRAINING. In Kentucky, interest in programs for the training of teachers began in the 1820s, although it took a half-century to achieve solid progress. In 1827 the trustees of Transylvania University developed a plan to teach pedagogy along with liberal arts courses. The plan was never implemented because of a costly fire in 1829 and because the trustees could not obtain state funding to cover the tuition costs of teacher trainees.

One of the first contributors to pedagogy in Kentucky was Benjamin Peers, who in 1832 established the Eclectic Institute, a school for boys in Lexington, and who was president of Transylvania (1833-36). Through scholarship, writing, and practical application, Peers brought his own ideas and those of leading educators to Kentucky. Peers introduced the work of the renowned Swiss educator Johann Pestalozzi, who emphasized child study and active, rather than passive, learning. Peers also encouraged the Rensselaerean method in science instruction, which stressed laboratory work and student demonstration of experiments. Peers and a number of nineteenth century state superintendents of public instruction strongly urged state involvement in teacher training. Requests regularly went to the legislature to fund professorships in leading private colleges, such as Transylvania, and to establish state-funded normal schools.

The 1838 law that established Kentucky's first public school system included no provision for training teachers. For more than fifty years the preparation of teachers for the developing public school system was a piecemeal matter. During that time teaching certificates were awarded on the basis of examination. Initially county officials controlled this testing, but by the 1870s it was centralized under the State Department of Education. Since many teaching candidates found the certification testing difficult, several privately operated normal institutions appeared throughout the state to help prepare students for the examinations. The sessions of the institutes were short, lasting one to five months, and their programs heavily emphasized drills on questions from previous examinations. Despite their shortcomings, these institutes became the first organized efforts to assist in the training of teachers in Kentucky.

Gradually, Kentucky placed more emphasis on teacher training. From 1870 until 1890 the state chartered eighteen privately owned normal schools and granted five-year teaching certificates to graduates. At least ten more private normal schools operated without charters. In 1871 the City of Louisville established its own normal school and started a pedagogical trend when it introduced a program of internship in the city's public schools. Direct state involvement with pedagogical instruction came in the 1870s when the commonwealth began to fund programs to update teachers' skills. Initially, annual six-day institutes were developed to update all current teachers. In 1878-79 state education officials operated ten-week normal schools with free tuition for three students per county. In 1880 the first continuously state-funded pedagogical instruction began with the establishment of a normal department at the state Agricultural and Mechanical College (now the University of Kentucky). This was followed in 1886 by the creation of the State Normal School for Colored Persons in Frankfort. In 1906 the legislature established two major normal schools, Western Kentucky State Normal School in Bowling Green and Eastern Kentucky State Normal School in Richmond. Before these two institutions opened, Kentucky was the only state in the southeast region of the United States that did not fund and operate normal schools.

Although Kentucky's normal schools were established later than many in the nation, they had comparable programs. Most admitted students with little more than an elementary school education and the academic work was never at college level. Pedagogical programs varied. Some did little more than review school subjects to be taught in public schools. Others, especially the state schools, offered required courses in methods and practice of teaching and optional study in the history of education. Late in the normal-school era, practice teaching became more common. In the twentieth century, normal schools were forced to raise their standards or close. The number of high schools and the need for high school teachers began to increase. Normal-school graduates, most of whom were not high school graduates themselves, were not viable candidates for high school teaching positions.

Accelerated demands ended the existence of most private normal schools, although a number of private liberal arts colleges with legitimate collegiate programs continued to train teachers. Kentucky's two state normal schools, although forced to struggle with insufficient financing, increased the scope of their curricular offerings and in 1922 became teachers' colleges as well as normal schools. In the same year the legislature created the State Normal School Commission to manage and control two new normal schools, at Morehead and Murray, where degrees could be conferred.

The normal-school era had ended in Kentucky by 1930. As with similar institutions across the country, Kentucky's state normals evolved into state teachers' colleges, then into state colleges with expanded programs, and eventually into state universities that prepare students for a wide variety of careers, including the teaching profession.

See Travis Edwin Smith, *The Rise of Teacher Training in Kentucky* (Nashville 1932).

GEORGE A. DILLINGHAM

TELEPHONE SERVICE. After James B. Speed observed a demonstration of the new technology of telephones at the Centennial Exposition in Philadelphia in 1877, he immediately ordered a set of two telephones to connect the downtown office of his Louisville Cement Company with the plant office in the Portland area of Louisville. By 1879, just three years after Bell patented his new invention, Speed had organized Louisville's first telephone company, the American District Telephone Company, with two hundred subscribers.

At about the same time, telephone service came into the northern Kentucky area across the river from Cincinnati. In January 1879 the City and Suburban Telegraph Association of Cincinnati, which offered free local telephone service, ran lines across the suspension bridge into Covington, Kentucky. The annual fee for this service in Kentucky was seventy-two dollars. Telephone service was so popular that within three months an independent telephone exchange was founded in Covington, serving nearly sixty customers. By 1882 the number of subscribers had more than doubled, to 132. In 1884 Louisville became the first city in Kentucky where a building was constructed solely for housing a telephone company office and exchange.

Rapid growth and change in telephone service followed in the northern Kentucky area. In 1880 the first pay telephone came to Covington. In 1884 the company created telephone numbers for its 2,500 customers. Also in that year, northern Kentuckians heard their first female telephone operators, who completely took over the day shift duties. The City and Suburban Telegraph and Telephone Company of Cincinnati incorporated telephone services in Covington, Kentucky, in 1884, and at about the same time a rival—Citizens Telephone Company—established services in nearby Newport, Kentucky. By 1885 these companies were competing to extend service into the outlying areas of northern Kentucky. In 1892 the northern Kentucky area saw several upgrades in service. Cables began to go underground, and new telephones that automatically signaled the operator were installed, thereby eliminating the need for cranking the instrument. Nevertheless, hand-cranked telephones remained in service until 1968 in some parts of Kentucky.

Intercity and interstate telephone service came rapidly in Kentucky. The first underwater telephone cable in the Midwest connected Petersburg, Kentucky, with Lawrenceburg, Indiana, across the Ohio River in September 1886. The first major long-distance lines in Kentucky were begun in 1895, when American Telephone and Telegraph linked Kenton County, Kentucky, with Lexington, Frankfort, and eventually Louisville. A more extensive long-distance network emerged in the early decades of the twentieth century, connecting those cities with Bowling Green, Richmond, Owensboro, and Paducah as telephone service became available in these communities.

From the earliest days, the popular and lucrative telephone industry attracted many entrepreneurs to establish service operations in Kentucky. In urban areas, several companies served the same communities. Louisville, for example, had two independent telephone companies until 1926. Customers had to subscribe to both services if they wanted to be able to talk to everyone who had a telephone in the city. Ultimately, these separate companies merged their networks or were bought by large companies such as Southern Bell.

The Southern Bell System, reorganized in Kentucky and four other southern states as South Central Bell in 1968, by no means established a monopoly on service in Kentucky. As late as 1969, Kentucky had twenty-five small, independent telephone companies in business, mostly in rural areas, accounting for over one-third of all the state's telephone service. Business boomed for all telephone companies after World War II. Southern Bell, for example, enjoyed threefold growth in rural service between 1945 and 1949. By the time of the breakup of the Bell System in 1984, South Central Bell served well over 500,000 customers in Kentucky. General Telephone and Electric, the second largest company in Kentucky, served approximately 300,000 customers.

Advances in technology after World War II brought better service to keep pace with rapid growth. In the late 1940s, rotary dial telephones began to appear in the urban areas of Kentucky, reducing—if not all but eliminating—the need for operators to connect local calls. In the 1960s, satellite transmission of telephone service began, and by that time video telephones had been developed for commercial and residential service. This technology, however, did not attract the public, and it disappeared. In 1966 push-button equipment entered the system in Kentucky, broadening direct-dial service for customers. This technology, along with fiber-optical wiring, has created a boom in automated information services for telephone companies in the 1980s and 1990s. Indeed, in the same way that the primary market for telephone companies shifted from commercial to residential service in the early part of the twentieth century, advanced technology has led telephone companies in new directions. The 1984 introduction of cellular telephone service to Kentucky, made possible by new developments in microwave transmission of signals and computer control of networks, exemplifies this trend. Some companies have identified computerized information management as the service field they will enter, leaving traditional telephone service altogether. Late twentieth century technology is bringing changes and opportunities for telephone service almost faster than the companies, the public, and the ever-present government regulators can accommodate them.   ANDREW VORDER BRUEGGE

TELLICO LAND CESSIONS. On October 25, 1805, the third Treaty of Tellico was concluded at Tellico Block House in Tennessee between thirty-three chiefs of the Cherokee Indian Nation and the United States. Representing the U.S. government were Return J. Meigs, federal Cherokee agent, and Daniel Smith, treaty commissioner. The treaty ceded from the Cherokee to the United States possession of 7,032 square miles of land in Tennessee and 1,086 square miles of land south of the Cumberland River in what is now Bell, Whitley, and McCreary counties in Kentucky. For this, the Cherokee received $14,000 in cash and goods, and an annuity of $3,000. Some Kentuckians had already settled in the area before the treaty was concluded and had no legal claim to their land for at least six months. They obtained possession by having the land surveyed and by paying the state treasurer at the rate of forty dollars per hundred acres. Known as "Tellico claims," 572 grants had been issued in the area by 1853.

See Thomas D. Clark, *Historic Maps of Kentucky* (Lexington, Ky., 1979); William Littel, *The Statute Law of Kentucky* (Frankfort, Ky., 1814).

THOMAS D. CLARK

TENNESSEE RIVER. The Tennessee, a 652-mile-long navigable river, is formed by the confluence of the Holston and French Broad rivers near Knoxville, Tennessee. It flows southwest into northern Alabama, then northwest across western Tennessee into western Kentucky's Jackson Purchase, where it forms Kentucky Lake. It flows north into the Ohio river near Paducah. Called Cherokee River (Riviere des Cheraquis) by explorers, after the powerful Indian tribe on its banks, it once led to the tribal capital of Tanasee, from which its modern name evolved. The river drains 40,569 square miles in parts of seven states and is the Ohio's largest tributary. Before its impoundment in 1944 by the Tennessee Valley Authority (TVA), the river was a principal boundary line between Calloway, Marshall, and McCracken counties to the west and Trigg, Lyon, and Livingston counties to the east.

Serving as the eastern boundary of the Jackson Purchase, the Tennessee and the nearby Cumberland River at one time isolated the area from the rest of the state. The advent of the steamboat established the river as a primary commercial carrier. Although the falls called Muscle Shoals obstructed passage in northern Alabama, the Tennessee became a route of pioneer migration and commerce. Steamboats first ascended it in 1819, and the U.S. Congress funded clearance of its channel to provide market access for the lumber and agricultural produce of western Kentucky and other states. The river carried Union forces on gunboats and steamboats to the South during the Civil War.

Although the expansion of the railroad in the 1870s slowed the Tennessee's economic development, its potential was realized when the TVA completed Kentucky Dam in 1944. A multipurpose waterway project, Kentucky Dam lured new industry into the region. The dam limited the Tennessee's potential for flooding, produced inexpensive hydroelectric power, and established a system of navigational locks. During the 1960s, the U.S. Army Corps of Engineers built Barkley Dam and Lake on the Cumberland River, which flows parallel with the Tennessee River northward through western Kentucky. In 1964 the TVA established the Land Between the Lakes, a wilderness recreation area between Barkley and Kentucky lakes. In 1966 the army engineers completed a 1.5-mile canal integrating Barkley and Kentucky lakes for purposes of power production and flood control. The canal created the Loop, which allows circumnavigation, from the Tennessee up the Ohio, up the Cumberland, and via the canal back to the Tennessee. During repairs, boats may use either Kentucky or Barkley Lock.

Kentucky counties bordering the Tennessee and its tributary, Clark's River, benefit from the industrial and recreational development, and industries find the inexpensive hydroelectric power, water supply, and transportation on the Tennessee attractive. Barges carry Kentucky coal via the Tennessee to TVA steam power plants and farther upriver to utility systems in the deep South. The 1985 completion of the Tennessee-Tombigbee Waterway, linking the Tennessee with the Gulf of Mexico at Mobile, opened additional markets for Kentucky commodities. Commercial traffic had so congested the Tennessee River by 1990 that a larger lock at Kentucky Dam was planned.

See P.P. Karan, ed., *Kentucky: A Regional Geography* (Dubuque, Iowa, 1973); Wilmon H. Droze, *High Dams and Slack Waters: TVA Rebuilds a River* (Baton Rouge, La., 1965).

LELAND R. JOHNSON

TENNESSEE-TOMBIGBEE WATERWAY. The Tennessee-Tombigbee Waterway is a 234-mile canal stretching from the Tennessee River to the Gulf of Mexico via the Tombigbee River. Its feasibility was evaluated in the nineteenth century. It was approved by Congress in 1946 and constructed during 1972-85 by the U.S. Army Corps of Engineers. With ten 100-by-600-foot navigation locks, the waterway lowers boats 341 feet to pass them through Mississippi and Alabama to Mobile. The governors of Kentucky and other states headed the Tennessee-Tombigbee Waterway Development Authority, an interstate compact promoting the project. Kentucky's governors expected it to contribute economically to the counties bordering the Tennessee River. Opposition to the canal was voiced by railroad and environmental lobbies, which argued before the U.S. Congress and in the courts on the basis of expected economic and environmental damages.

Construction, managed by Euclid Moore and Richard Russell of the Nashville Engineer District, excavated 150 million cubic yards of soil to depths of 175 feet, making the project the largest in the

Corps of Engineers' history. It was completed ahead of schedule, but initial use of the canal and the related economic development was disappointing. When drought closed the Mississippi River in 1988, however, traffic shifted to the waterway and the predicted economic growth began.

See Leland R. Johnson, *Engineers on the Twin Rivers* (Nashville 1978).   LELAND R. JOHNSON

TENNESSEE VALLEY AUTHORITY. When the U.S. Congress passed the Tennessee Valley Authority Act, on May 18, 1933, it charged the agency with "planning for the use, development and conservation of the natural resources of the Tennessee River drainage basin and its adjoining territory." Its responsibilities included flood control, soil conservation, family resettlement, recreation, and cheaper electricity. In general, western Kentuckians favored the authority's work because they directly benefited. Until his death in 1936, Rep. William Gregory from Mayfield, Kentucky, staunchly supported the Tennessee Valley Authority; his brother Noble, who succeeded him in office, was also a supporter of the agency. Sen. Alben Barkley of Paducah supported the act. On the part of eastern Kentucky, Rep. Andrew May saw it as an adversary of the coal industry and feared that it was a trend toward socialization.

The Tennessee Valley Authority launched three major projects in Kentucky: the construction of the Kentucky Dam and of the Paradise steam plant and the development of the Land Between the Lakes. The Kentucky Dam was authorized on December 20, 1937. Constructed near the small town of Gilbertsville, about twenty-two miles upstream from Paducah, the dam was dedicated in 1945 by President Harry Truman. It represented the completion of a 640-mile river channel from Paducah to Knoxville. Its reservoir, one of the largest manmade lakes in the world, is 184 miles long with a shoreline of 2,200 miles. In 1944 the Tennessee Valley Authority reported sales of over 51 million kilowatts of electricity to Kentucky municipalities and cooperatives.

In 1959 the Tennessee Valley Authority began constructing the steam plant at Paradise, in Muhlenberg County on the Green River, in the midst of the west Kentucky coal fields. By the close of 1963, two 650,000 kilowatt generating units were in operation and that year burned more than 23 million tons of coal, 64 percent of it purchased from Kentucky mines. In 1965 the agency began construction of an additional unit at Paradise, completed in 1969, with a capacity of over 1 million kilowatts. In 1971 nearly 27 million tons of Kentucky coal were delivered to Tennessee Valley Authority steam plants.

The Land Between the Lakes project, planned by the Tennessee Valley Authority in 1959, was submitted for review to President John F. Kennedy in 1961. Its purpose was to develop an exemplary outdoor recreation area that included educational programs. Funds for the project were provided in

December 1963. The project included about 170,000 acres of land lying between the Kentucky Dam reservoir and the reservoir formed by the Barkley Dam on the Cumberland River, an area forty miles long and six to twelve miles wide. To complete the Land Between the Lakes project, the Tennessee Valley Authority had to relocate 865 families who lived in the area—a source of controversy for any who saw relocation as too great a price for development of a recreational area. The completed project includes campsites, lake access areas, overlooks, and educational centers. When Land Between the Lakes started taking attendance in 1964, it had 12,000 visitors; by 1969 more than 1 million tourists had visited there; in 1989 visitors totaled 128,993.

See Arthur Morgan, *The Making of TVA* (Buffalo, N.Y., 1974): N. Callahan, *TVA* (South Brunswick, N.J., 1880). JOHN D. MINTON

TENNIS. Newspapers credit Thomas Kennedy with establishing Louisville's first tennis court: the one he built at his home in Crescent Hill in the late 1870s. In the late nineteenth century, tennis was played at several Louisville locations; the city's first public park courts were built at Cherokee and Shawnee in 1897. In the early 1900s courts were constructed at three private clubs that became prominent in local tennis: Audubon Country Club, Louisville Country Club, and the Louisville Boat Club.

In 1905 the Estill Springs resort hotel near Irvine was the site of the first Kentucky State Championships. In 1910 the Kentucky Lawn Tennis Association was founded in connection with the Ohio Tennis District. In 1911, representing the association, Thomas Tuley brought Louisville its first major tournament, the Bi-State (Kentucky and Ohio). Tennis grew in popularity through the 1920s and 1930s, with state and southern championships being held at Audubon and the Louisville Boat Club. After World War II, Robert Piatt and O.K. Kelsall were instrumental in bringing such prominent events as the Davis Cup to Louisville, and in 1952 they founded the Kentucky Junior Invitational. The Kentucky Tennis Patrons Foundation was also founded in 1952, and in 1955 Kentucky became a district of the Southern Lawn Tennis Association. Outside Louisville, the Weldon Invitational in Glasgow and the Lexington Country Club Event were the most prominent tournaments in the 1950s. In 1970 Louisville held the state's first professional tournament; prize money totaled $25,000. National television coverage of the event became an annual occurrence. After 1979, however, poor sponsorship forced the termination of the event.

Several prominent Kentucky players emerged in the 1980s. Mel Purcell of Murray was ranked tenth nationally in 1981. Caroline Kuhlman of Lakeside Park near Fort Mitchell and Lexington's Susan Sloane won major U.S. junior titles. Kuhlman won the girls' doubles at Wimbledon in 1984 and Sloane won her first professional singles title in 1988. The University of Kentucky men's and women's teams have consistently been ranked in the nation's top ten and twenty. A Kentucky Tennis Hall of Fame was founded at the university in 1985.

SAM ENGLISH, JR., AND STEVE IMHOFF

TEVIS, WALTER STONE, JR. Walter Stone Tevis, Jr., author of popular novels that made award-winning films, was born in San Francisco, on February 28, 1928, to Walter Stone and Anna Elizabeth (Bacon) Tevis. The Tevis family moved to Lexington, Kentucky, in 1938. After graduating from Model High School in Richmond, Kentucky, Tevis served in the U.S. Naval Reserve in the Pacific theater (1945-46). He received his A.B. in English at the University of Kentucky in 1949, then taught high school English in several Kentucky cities between 1950 and 1956: Science Hill, Hawesville, Carlisle, and Irvine. He was a part-time English instructor at the University of Kentucky from 1955 to 1956. In 1957 Tevis worked as an editor for the Kentucky Department of Highways. That same year he received his M.A. in English from the University of Kentucky. In September 1958, Tevis joined the faculty at the University of Kentucky's Northern Kentucky Center (now Northern Kentucky University) in Covington.

By 1958 many of Tevis's short stories had been published in popular magazines. His first novel, *The Hustler* (1959), was made into a movie starring Paul Newman and Jackie Gleason. In 1961 he received a master of fine arts degree from the University of Iowa. Tevis spent the next year in Mexico, where he worked on his second novel, *The Man Who Fell to Earth* (1963). In 1976 it was made into a movie starring David Bowie. Between 1965 and 1978, Tevis taught creative writing at Ohio University. Throughout his teaching career, he wrote short stories and articles about playing pool and chess. In 1978 Tevis resigned from teaching and moved to New York City, where he completed the following novels: *Mockingbird* (1980), *Far From Home* (1981), *The Queen's Gambit* (1983), *The Steps of the Sun* (1983), and *The Color of Money* (1984). The last novel in 1986 became a movie starring Paul Newman and Tom Cruise.

Tevis and his first wife, Jamie Lewis (Griggs) Tevis, had two children: William Thomas and Julie Ann McGory. Shortly before his death, Tevis married Eleanora Walker. He died in New York on August 9, 1984, and was buried in Richmond, Kentucky.

TEXAS EMIGRATING SOCIETY. The Texas Emigrating Society was formed in Lexington, Kentucky, during the mid-1820s to encourage colonization in Texas, then a state of Mexico. The Mexican government's policy to promote settlement there was to give away public domain lands through an empresario or colonizing agent. Three agents, Stephen F. Austin, Felix Robertson, Nashville native, and Green C. DeWitt, born in Lincoln County, Kentucky, operated colonies with settlers mostly from Kentucky, Tennessee, and Missouri. These colonization ventures were promoted by Lexingtonian Littleberry Hawkins, who had attended Transylvania University with Austin. His brother, Joseph Hawkins, who served as U.S. representative (1810-15) from Kentucky, spent approximately $30,000 on the initial expenses of Austin's colony before his death in 1823. When the Mexican government in 1830 stopped colonization of Texas by American settlers, Austin used a loophole law to exempt his colony; the law was repealed on May 1, 1834. Organized colonization continued until the Texas War for Independence was declared on March 2, 1836. According to Samuel Wilson's *History of Kentucky* (1928), "there were few families in Blue Grass Kentucky that did not have relatives or friends in Texas" at the beginning of the Texas revolution.

THAMES, BATTLE OF. The Battle of the Thames on October 5, 1813, climaxed attempts by Gen. William Henry Harrison's Northwest Army to recover territories lost to Gen. Henry Proctor's British and Indian forces after the surrender of Detroit in August 1812. British command of Lake Erie largely defeated Harrison's efforts until Oliver Hazard Perry's naval victory there on September 10, 1813.

Following Perry's victory, Harrison quickly assembled a small body of regulars, about 1,000 mounted Kentuckians under congressman Richard M. Johnson and 3,500 Kentucky volunteers commanded by Gov. Isaac Shelby (1812-16). They moved against Detroit by land and against Canada by water. Fearing entrapment, Proctor abandoned Detroit and Amherstburg and, with 1,000 regulars and many of Tecumseh's Indians, retreated inland. Harrison pursued rapidly with 120 regulars, Johnson's mounted regiment, and about 2,000 of Shelby's volunteers. On October 5, the hard-pressed British made a final stand in a wooded area near Thamesville in Ontario. The regulars formed a double line between the Thames River on their left and a dense swamp that paralleled the river on their right. From the swamp, Tecumseh's hidden warriors could fire into the advancing Kentuckians' right flank. Holding his infantry in reserve, Harrison ordered an attack by Johnson's mounted Kentuckians.

The Kentucky horsemen swept through the British lines, routing the regulars but drawing heavy fire from Tecumseh's well-protected Indians. To lessen casualties in an assault on the swamp, twenty men volunteered to draw the first fire and enable the main body to close before the Indians reloaded. Nineteen were killed or wounded, and Johnson, riding with them, was shot twice. In the ensuing struggle, the Indians were slowly routed and Tecumseh was killed, allegedly by Johnson. The battle demolished both Proctor's army and

Tecumseh's Indian Confederation. More than six hundred British soldiers were killed or captured, and Indian hopes of holding back settlement of the Northwest died with Tecumseh.

See Bennett H. Young, *The Battle of the Thames* (Louisville 1903); James W. Hammack, Jr., *Kentucky and the Second American Revolution* (Lexington, Ky., 1976).   JAMES W. HAMMACK, JR.

THATCHER, MAURICE HUDSON. Maurice Hudson Thatcher, U.S. congressman, was born August 15, 1870, in Chicago to John and Mary (Graves) Thatcher. The family moved to Butler County, Kentucky, near Morgantown in 1874, and he attended public and private schools, including the Bryant and Stratton Business College in Louisville. In 1892 Thatcher was elected clerk of the circuit court of Butler County and served from 1893 to 1896. He studied law in Frankfort, was admitted to the bar in 1898, and began a practice there. From 1898 to 1900 he served as assistant attorney general of Kentucky. In 1900 Thatcher moved to Louisville, and from 1901 to 1906 was the assistant U.S. attorney for the Western District of Kentucky. From 1908 to 1910 he was state inspector and examiner for Kentucky and was appointed by President William Howard Taft in 1910 to the Isthmian Canal Commission. He served as civil governor of the Panama Canal Zone from 1910 to 1913 and afterward resumed his law practice in Louisville, where he was a member of the Board of Public Safety from 1917 to 1919 and was department counsel for the city from 1919 to 1923.

In 1922 Thatcher, the Republican candidate, defeated Democrat Kendrick R. Lewis by 38,806 to 35,124 to represent the 5th Congressional District in the U.S. Congress. He was elected to five consecutive terms, serving from March 4, 1923, to March 3, 1933. Thatcher, a member of the Appropriations Committee, was author of several bills providing for the establishment of public parks, among them Mammoth Cave National Park and Zachary Taylor National Cemetery. He also was instrumental in the construction of the Clark Memorial Bridge at Louisville and the Veterans Hospital in Lexington. Thatcher declined to run for reelection in 1932 and sought a U.S. Senate seat. He lost to the Democratic candidate, Alben Barkley, 575,077 to 393,865. He stayed in Washington, D.C., to practice law and served from 1939 to 1969 as vice-president and general counsel for the Gorgas Memorial Institute of Tropical and Preventive Medicine, an organization he helped establish. From 1969 to 1972 he was the institute's honorary president and general counsel.

Thatcher married Anne Bell Chinn, daughter of Frank Chinn of Frankfort, on May 4, 1910. Thatcher died in Washington on January 6, 1973, and was buried in the Frankfort Cemetery.

THEATER. Two years before Kentucky achieved statehood, Lexington's *Kentucky Gazette* mentioned the April 10, 1790, performance of two unnamed plays by the students of Transylvania University and the presence of a "respectable audience." This is the first notice of a dramatic production in what became the commonwealth of Kentucky.

Between 1790 and 1820, Kentuckians attended almost six hundred productions of plays. In 1806 Luke Usher, who was apparently the first professional theater manager in the state, reached Kentucky, perhaps from Philadelphia. On October 12, 1808, Luke Usher's New Theatre opened in Lexington. By 1810, Usher appears to have controlled theaters in Louisville, Lexington, and Frankfort. In 1814 Usher's nephew, Noble Luke Usher, recruited Samuel Drake, a theater manager in Albany, New York, to operate the Kentucky theater circuit established by his uncle. After a successful run at Usher's Frankfort theater, Drake's company opened in Louisville at the City Theatre on February 28, 1816. Drake's company performed in Kentucky until 1835.

Another actor-manager of the early nineteenth century was James Douglas. He was the son of David Douglas, first theater builder in the United States and an associate of Lewis Hallam, organizer of America's first theatrical circuit. On January 12, 1811, James Douglas opened the first recorded theatrical season in Frankfort. Earlier productions there had been sporadic performances by the Usher companies. After Samuel Drake opened in Frankfort in 1815, Douglas joined Drake's troupe. During his first Kentucky season, Drake performed between seventy-five and one hundred plays in Lexington, Frankfort, and Louisville.

In the 1820s Drake settled in Louisville, concentrating on productions in the City Theatre. Between 1814 and 1843, when the building burned, 1,024 plays were performed. The Louisville Theatre, built in 1846, housed dramatic productions until 1869, when it became the Louisville Opera House. The Macauley Theatre opened in 1873 and soon ranked among the major American playhouses. Among the stars who appeared at these three Louisville theaters were Louisa Lane Drew, Charles Kean, Edwin Forrest, Charlotte Cushman, Edwin Booth, Laura Keene, and Mary Anderson.

After the Macauley Theatre closed in 1925, professional dramatic productions became available in Louisville only when traveling companies played at the Memorial Auditorium on South Fourth Street. Kentucky's colleges, universities, and civic groups, however, shared in the amateur theater movement, beginning in 1911. Later, groups such as C. Douglas Ramey's Carriage House Players provided dramatic entertainment in Louisville during the 1950s. In 1962 Ramey inaugurated Shakespeare in Central Park, an open-air theater that provided free summer entertainment in Louisville. In 1835 Owensboro began enjoying amateur theatricals at Philip Thompson's theater, which closed in 1846. The three largest subsequent theaters in Owensboro were Hill's Grand, which opened in 1880, the Temple (1888), and the Grand (1905). Performers such as

Mary Anderson and Helen D'Este appeared in these playhouses. In 1886 Lexington acquired an opera house on North Broadway that played host to Shakespearean companies and musical plays presented by both European and American performers. Victor Herbert often directed orchestras there. In the 1970s it was restored, and theater returned in the form of road companies performing Broadway plays.

Many summer theaters offer a wide variety of dramatic fare across Kentucky. In 1989 the Kentucky Department of Travel Development listed the following: Pine Knob Theatre, Caneyville; Iroquois Park Players, Louisville; Jenny Wiley Theatre, Prestonsburg; *The Stephen Foster Story*, Bardstown; Hilltopper Dinner Theatre, Bowling Green; *The Legend of Daniel Boone*, Harrodsburg; Pioneer Playhouse, Danville; Kincaid Regional Theatre, Falmouth; Midway Summer Dinner Theatre, Midway; Horse Cave Theatre, Horse Cave; and the Shakespeare Festival in Woodland Park, Lexington.

By the 1990s the theater for which Kentucky was best-known was Actors Theatre of Louisville (ATL), a professional company that was named the state theater of Kentucky in 1974. Kentuckians' contributions to theater include the work of John Mason Brown, drama critic for *Theatre Arts* magazine and for two major New York newspapers. Distinguished performers with Kentucky ties include Mary Anderson, Patricia Neal, Florence Henderson, Susan Kingsley, Leo Burmester, and Daniel Jenkins. A number of plays that had their premieres at Actors Theatre have brought international recognition to the playwrights: *Agnes of God* by John Pielmeier, *Crimes of the Heart* by Beth Henley, *Getting Out* and *Third and Oak: the Laundromat* by Marsha Norman, and *The Gin Game* by D.L. Coburn. Louisville native Marsha Norman received the Pulitzer Prize for drama in 1983 for *'night, Mother*.

Orlin Corey's well-known dramatization *The Book of Job* has long been a favorite outdoor production at Pine Mountain State Resort Park. This play was first produced at Georgetown College of Kentucky in 1957. Irene Corey's unique "stained-glass" makeup and costume design helped make *Job* an acclaimed event in American theater history.

See George D. Ford, *These Were Actors* (New York 1955); West T. Hill, *The Theatre in Early Kentucky: 1790-1820* (Lexington, Ky., 1971).

MIRIAM CORCORAN

THIEL AUDIO PRODUCTS. The high-quality Thiel loudspeakers are manufactured in an inconspicuous building on the north side of Lexington, Kentucky. Company founder James Thiel was born in Covington, Kentucky, on September 29, 1947. He attended Thomas More College in Crestview Hills, Kentucky, and in 1976 founded Thiel Audio. It offered products for sale the next year, the creations of Thiel and his brother, Tom, who attended the University of Kentucky and the University of Dayton in Ohio. Even with innovative in-house robotics and a large number of employees who fabricate and assemble parts, production of a pair of top-of-the-line speakers takes days. Thiel's registered trademark "Coherent Source" loudspeakers receive critical acclaim from the leading audiophile publications, and the new CS5 received the *Audio-Video International* Hi-Fi Grand Prix Award in the 1989 product of the year category.

ERIC HOWARD CHRISTIANSON

THOMAS, CLINTON. Clinton Thomas, baseball player, was born on November 25, 1896, in Greenup, Kentucky, the son of James and Lutie Thomas. Instead of attending high school, he moved to Columbus, Ohio, in 1910 to play amateur baseball, and he worked in a restaurant and grocery store. Thomas served in the army during World War I. He began his professional career in 1920 as a second baseman with the Brooklyn Royal Giants, then played for the Columbus Buckeyes in 1921 and the Detroit Stars in 1922. Joining the Philadelphia Hilldale Giants, a black major league team, in 1923, he became an outfielder who combined speed, power, and defense. He appeared in two Negro World Series and earned the nickname "Hawk" for his defensive prowess. He played with the Atlantic City Bacharach Giants in 1928-30. He closed out his career with the New York Black Yankees, with a lifetime .333 batting average. He then moved to Charleston, West Virginia, where he worked for the West Virginia Department of Mines. He retired as staff supervisor of the state Senate at eighty years of age. Thomas married Ellen Odell (Smith) Bland in 1963.

THOMAS, JAMES EDWARD. James Edward Thomas, a dulcimer maker known as Uncle Eddy, was born in Letcher County, Kentucky, in 1850. He lived near the village of Bath in a home described by Appalachian writer James Still as being "on Big Doubles under the Bell Coney Knob at the border between Knott and Letcher counties." Thomas was the earliest known dulcimer builder on the Cumberland Plateau. He may also be the creator of what has become the standard dulcimer design: an hourglass-shaped body, three strings, and four heart-shaped sound holes. Thomas, who built his first instrument in 1871, created approximately 1,500 dulcimers before he died in 1933. His dulcimer design was later disseminated and popularized through the performances of JEAN RITCHIE.

See Ralph Lee Smith, *The Story of the Dulcimer* (Cosby, Tenn., 1986).   RON PEN

THOMAS, JEAN (BELL). Folk festival promoter and author Jean (Bell) Thomas was born Jeanette Mary Francis de Assisi Aloysius Marcissum Garfield Bell on November 14, 1881, in Ashland, Kentucky, to W. William George and Kate (Smith) Bell. One of five children, she attended Holy Family School and graduated on June 3, 1899, from Ashland High School. As a young girl, she became interested in the mountain music she heard in the Ashland area. Later, as a court stenographer, following the circuit in eastern Kentucky, she had an opportunity to gather original mountain folklore and was called "The Traipsin' Woman." She spent thirteen years writing in Greenwich Village and she became involved in New York City's social and entertainment world.

In 1913 she married Albert Hart Thomas, a New York accountant, and they moved to Logan, West Virginia, where he worked for his family's coal interests. The marriage lasted for a year and there were no children. Jean Thomas held a variety of positions following her divorce. She was secretary in 1917 to Joe Tinker, manager of the Columbus Senators, a National League baseball team. In 1923 she was a script girl for Cecil B. de Mille's production *The Ten Commandments*. While working for socialite Gloria Gould Bishop in New York City, she met Ruby ("Texas") Guinan, nightclub entertainer and owner. She worked for Guinan until 1928.

Thomas heard James William Day, a blind fiddler, playing and singing in front of the Rowan County courthouse in Morehead, Kentucky, in 1926. Having a background in promotion and entertainment, Thomas signed him to a management contract; changed his name to Jilson Settles; and staged his concerts with the singer clothed in homespun attire and with only a ladderback chair and an egg basket for props. She booked him in appearances in Kentucky, at Loew's Theater in New York, and at London's Royal Albert Hall as the "Singin' Fiddler from Lost Hope Hollow." She obtained the first recording contracts for Day in 1928 from RCA Victor. Before embarking on the concert tour, Day had cataracts removed from his eyes and regained his sight. His encounter, as a mountain man from Rowan County, with the modern world of New York and London was the subject of Thomas's first book, *Devil's Ditties* (1931). Folklorists have criticized Thomas's books as being more fictional than documentary, overdramatizing both people and their culture. Thomas wrote seven other books, including *The Traipsin' Woman* (1933).

While working as a consultant for the National Broadcasting Company's Dorothy Gordon, moderator of "Youth Forum," in 1930, Thomas staged a folk festival in the backyard of her Tudor-style cottage in Ashland, Kentucky. The next year Thomas incorporated the American Folk Song Society and began planning a folk song festival to be held in Ashland. On the society's advisory board were national figures such as Carl Sandburg, Erskine Caldwell, and Stephen Vincent Benet, who Thomas hoped would bring her endeavor national publicity. Her failure to include local residents in festival plans, however, proved detrimental in later years, when she needed assistance. On June 12, 1932, Thomas staged the first American Folk Song Festival, with eighteen acts, on the Mayo Trail, fifteen miles south of Ashland. By 1938 the festival had grown to forty-two acts, playing to 20,000 people. Except for the period 1943-48, Thomas produced the yearly festival until 1972, when ill health forced her to retire. Many of the same performers appeared in the Kentucky Folk Song Festival the next year in Grayson, Kentucky, and the event continues there.

Thomas died in Ashland on December 7, 1982, and was buried in Rose Hill Mausoleum. She had made arrangements for her extensive collection of folklore to be preserved in her home, where the Jean Thomas Museum opened in 1979. After her death, there was little local support for preserving her home, and the collection was moved to the Highlands Museum in Ashland in the 1980s. By 1990, her collection had found a permanent home in the Dwight Anderson Memorial Music Library at the University of Louisville.

See Charles K. Wolfe, *Kentucky Country, Folk and Country Music of Kentucky* (Lexington, Ky., 1982); D.K. Wilgus, *Anglo-American Folksong Scholarship since 1898* (Trenton, N.J., 1959).

BETTY B. ELLISON

THOMAS MORE COLLEGE. Thomas More College is a Catholic coeducational college operating under the diocese of Covington, Kentucky. Established in 1921 as Villa Madonna College, the institution was originally a part of the educational program of the Benedictine Sisters of Covington. Although it was established primarily for the education of young women entering the Order of St. Benedict, it accepted lay women as students from the beginning. It first shared grounds with Villa Madonna Academy and St. Walburg Convent, the motherhouse of the Benedictine Sisters.

Villa Madonna, the first four-year college in the Greater Cincinnati area of northern Kentucky, was chartered by the Kentucky General Assembly as a degree-granting institution on August 14, 1923. In 1928 it became a central diocesan college under the bishop of Covington, Francis W. Howard. It was then housed in what had been St. Walburg Academy on Twelfth Street in Covington. In 1929 the Sisters of Notre Dame of Covington and the Congregation of Divine Providence of Melbourne, Kentucky, joined the Benedictine Sisters in teaching at the college, as did a few priests of the diocese of Covington, and they composed almost the entire faculty until 1945. When William T. Mulloy became bishop of Covington that year, Villa Madonna became a coeducational diocesan college. Boys who graduated from neighboring Covington Latin School between 1934 and 1941 had attended classes in a nonaccredited college known as the St. Thomas More College project, and boys had been admitted to certain courses at Villa Madonna College between 1941 and 1945. In 1945 the St. Thomas More College project became an integral part of Villa Madonna.

New college facilities on the 223-acre campus in Fort Mitchell–Crestview Hills were completed in 1968 under Bishop Richard Ackerman. The name of the institution was changed to Thomas More College, after Thomas More, lord chancellor of England, who was martyred for his faith under Henry VIII. The new campus was dedicated in September 1968 by President Lyndon B. Johnson. Marian Howard Hall and Ackerman Hall were opened for residence in 1968 and 1970, respectively. The science center was added in 1972, and an athletic-convocation center opened in 1988. The college began a major land development process in 1977 with the erection of a doctor's office building. Law offices and other enterprises followed.

The college was accredited by the Southern Association of Colleges and Secondary Schools in 1959. Later it was accredited also by the National League of Nursing, the American Chemical Society, the Council on Social Work Education, the Kentucky State Department of Education, and the Kentucky State Board of Nursing; it is affiliated with the universities of Dayton, Cincinnati, Detroit, Kentucky, and Notre Dame in a liberal arts engineering program, and with various medical facilities in a medical technology program. In 1967 the college acquired the former U.S. Lock and Dam No. 35 on the Ohio River and established a biological station at that site. The biology department conducts a successful summer project, commissioned by local industries, to test the river for pollution. In 1982 the nursing department graduated its first senior class. In August of that year, Bishop William A. Hughes closed the college at the diocesan St. Pius X Seminary and began sending seminarians to Thomas More College, but in 1988 the entire seminary program was discontinued. Summer, evening, Saturday, and extension courses, however, have been offered since 1923. In the 1980s the college's average annual enrollment was about 1,500 students.

MARY PHILIP TRAUTH

THOMPSON, HUNTER STOCKTON. Hunter S. Thompson, journalist, son of Jack R. and Virginia (Ray) Thompson, was born on July 18, 1939, in Louisville. He began his journalistic career as a sportswriter while in the U.S. Air Force from 1956 to 1958. From 1961 to 1963, he traveled in South America, sending back dispatches to various publications, including the *National Observer*. In the mid-1960s, Thompson's occasional free-lance writing assignments included a *Nation* piece on the Hell's Angels Motorcycle Club that led to many book offers. Thompson's *Hell's Angels: A Strange and Terrible Saga* (1966) was based on conversations with members of the gang, with whom Hunter had ridden. This kind of involvement marks Thompson's own style "Gonzo journalism," in the genre of New Journalism, which combines nonfiction with the emotional impact of a novel or short story. In his *Fear and Loathing in Las Vegas: A Savage Journey to the Heart of the American Dream* (1972), Thompson's alter ego Raoul Duke goes to "the city that never sleeps" to cover both an annual motorcycle race in the desert and a national seminar on narcotics and dangerous drugs.

Thompson began writing for *Rolling Stone* in 1970 and covered the 1972 presidential campaign for the magazine. Thompson's *Fear and Loathing on the Campaign Trail '72* (1973) "recorded the nuts and bolts of a presidential campaign with all the contempt and incredulity that other reporters feel but censor out," in the words of Anne Janette Johnson (*Contemporary Authors*, 1988).

In 1963 Thompson married Sandra Dawn; they have a son, Juan. Thompson lives as a hermit in Woody Creek, Colorado.

See "Interview: Hunter Thompson," *Playboy*, Nov. 1974; Sam Allis, "An Evening (Gasp!) with Hunter Thompson," *Time*, January 22, 1990.

BRUCE SMITH-PETERS

THOMPSON, JOHN BURTON. John Burton Thompson, political leader, son of John B. and Nancy Porter (Robards) Thompson, was born on December 14, 1810, near Harrodsburg. Thompson was educated by tutors and later studied law under his father. In 1831 he was admitted to the Harrodsburg bar and took over his father's prominent law practice there. Thompson was elected to represent Mercer County in the state Senate from 1829 to 1833. In 1835, he served in the Kentucky legislature and was reelected to a second term in 1837. After the death of Rep. Simeon Anderson, Thompson, as a Whig, filled his seat in the 26th Congress. He was reelected to the next term in the U.S. House of Representatives (December 7, 1840, to March 3, 1843) and again for the 1847-51 term. Thompson became lieutenant governor of Kentucky in 1852, winning the position over Robert N. Wickliffe. He was then elected to the U.S. Senate (March 4, 1853, to March 3, 1859).

Thompson married Mary Hardin Bowman in 1869. He was a respected and well-liked public servant. Thompson died on January 7, 1874, in Harrodsburg and was buried in Spring Hill Cemetery.

THOMPSON, JOHN TALIAFERRO. John Taliaferro Thompson, designer of the tommygun—the first submachine gun—was born December 31, 1860, in Newport, Kentucky, the son of Lt. Col. James and Julia Maria (Taliaferro) Thompson. Thompson attended the U.S. Military Academy at West Point and graduated in 1882 with a commission as second lieutenant of artillery. He served in the Spanish-American War as a lieutenant colonel of volunteers, first at Tampa, Florida, and then in Cuba. As chief of the Small Arms Division of the Ordnance Department, he supervised the development of the Springfield rifle. In 1913 Thompson became the army's youngest colonel. He resigned from the army a year later to become chief engineer of the Remington Arms Corporation. When the United States entered World War I in 1917, Thompson returned to the army and served as the director of arsenals, in charge of all small arms production. In 1919 Congress awarded him the Distinguished Service Medal for "exceptionally meritorious and conspicuous service." Thompson retired from the army in 1919 as a brigadier general. The following year his private company developed the submachine gun.

Thompson married Juliet Estelle Hagans in 1882. They had one son, Marcellus Hagans. Thompson died on June 21, 1940, and was buried at West Point.

See William J. Helmer, *The Gun That Made the Twenties Roar* (New York 1970).

JAMES RUSSELL HARRIS

THOMPSON, KELLY. Kelly Thompson, president of WESTERN KENTUCKY UNIVERSITY (1955-69) in Bowling Green, was born January 28, 1909, in Lebanon, Marion County, Kentucky, to Charles B. and Josephine (Clark) Thompson. Thompson entered Western Kentucky College in the fall of 1928 on a football scholarship, but a preseason shoulder injury ended his athletic career. Coach E.A. Diddle secured a loan for him to continue his education, and the next year Thompson became a field representative for the college. In 1935 he received a B.A. and became director of public relations at the college. Thompson obtained his master of arts from the college in 1943 and left in 1944 to serve as a naval lieutenant during World War II. Returning in 1946, he became assistant to President Paul L. Garrett, a position created for Thompson by the college's board of regents. When Garrett died in February 1955, Thompson became acting president. He was appointed by the board to a full term on October 17, 1955, after controversy subsided over his Catholicism and his lack of a doctorate.

Thompson guided Western Kentucky College during its years of most rapid growth. The college experienced a significant increase in its enrollment and development of its physical plant. It became desegregated in 1956, and on June 16, 1966, assumed university status. Departmental changes were made during Thompson's presidency, including the creation of elementary and secondary divisions in the College of Education and the addition of majors in speech, drama, German, and Spanish. Greek organizations were approved in 1961 and a student government was instituted in the 1966-67 school year. Thompson resigned on May 21, 1969, for health reasons but remained active through his work as president and then chairman of the board of the College Heights Foundation, an organization created in 1923 to provide financial assistance to students and make structural improvements in the school.

Thompson married Sarah Pearce, of Bowling Green, on June 23, 1931. They have three children: Patricia, Kelly, Jr., and Hardin.

See Lowell H. Harrison, *Western Kentucky University* (Lexington, Ky., 1987).

THOMPSON-DAVIS CASE. U.S. Congressman Philip Burton ("Little Phil") Thompson's killing of Walter Davis near Harrodsburg Junction on April

27, 1883, represented Kentucky's most sensational example of the unwritten law of the nineteenth century that a husband could justifiably assassinate his wife's paramour. Thompson believed that Davis, his best friend, had the previous November seduced Thompson's wife, Mary, in a hotel room in Cincinnati, where "Little Phil," en route to Congress, had left his wife to shop.

Tried for murder only eleven days after the killing, Thompson received the volunteer services of several eminent trial attorneys, including Indiana Sen. Daniel W. Voorhees, who made something of a specialty of such cases. Henry W. Watterson likewise aided his cause with several powerful editorials in the *Louisville Courier-Journal* defending both the unwritten law and Thompson's invocation of it.

Thompson easily won acquittal despite the fact that his witnesses testified only that Davis had gotten Thompson's wife drunk and spent an hour alone with her in his hotel room. Throughout the case Mary Thompson steadfastly maintained her innocence, as supported by an undelivered letter from Davis to Thompson that was found in Davis's pocket after his killing. Thompson divorced his wife, who continued to live in Harrodsburg until her death in 1929 and during that time commanded a respected social standing. Thompson, who failed to secure reelection to Congress, died in 1909 after a lucrative career in Washington, D.C., as a government claims lawyer.

See Robert M. Ireland, "The Thompson-Davis Case and the Unwritten Law," *FCHQ* 62 (Oct. 1988): 417-41.   ROBERT M. IRELAND

THOMPSON EXPEDITION. The Thompson expedition was a 1773 survey of lands in Virginia (now Kentucky) near the Ohio River by Pennsylvania militia officers who had served in the French and Indian War. The intent was to locate lands promised them for their military service in the war. Designating Capt. William Thompson as their leader, the expedition of over sixty men departed Pittsburgh in either late June or early July. They traveled down the Ohio River by flatboat to the mouth of the Scioto River, where they camped on the Kentucky side and waited for the arrival of their horses and of Thomas BULLITT, an official Virginia surveyor (Thompson's party was not legally authorized to make surveys). By July 10 Thompson learned that Bullitt had left on his way downriver and would not be meeting them. A few days later he learned that the expedition's horses had been stolen by Indians.

Hoping they could later convince the Virginia authorities to accept their claims, the expedition continued down the Ohio in canoes to Cabin Creek, where Thompson divided the group into three parties. They surveyed the North Fork of the Licking River, Salt Lick Creek, and Upper Blue Licks. Fear of Indian attack prevented them from reaching the Kentucky River area. They surveyed approximately 200,000 acres and divided the land into claims. The entire expedition reassembled at Cabin Creek and

departed for Pennsylvania, where a lottery was held to dispense the claims in August or September of 1773.

The expedition however, had no authority to make the surveys. Thompson had applied for a surveyor's license when he realized that Bullitt would not be joining them, but it was not validated until May 1774. Through their agent, Dr. John Morgan, the expedition formally applied in 1774 for permission to make land claims in Virginia. The application was approved and land warrants were issued by Lord Dunmore, governor of Virginia, but the claims made in 1773 were not validated. The Revolutionary War ended the matter until 1783. Two further attempts were made at validation, in 1783 and 1807, but both were denied. None of the expedition's members received title to Kentucky land on the basis of the Thompson surveys, but the publicity they received attracted settlers to the Kentucky area.

See R.S. Cotterill, "The Thompson Expedition of 1773," *FCHQ* 20 (July 1946): 179-84.

THOROUGHBRED INDUSTRY. Kentucky, which annually produces more thoroughbreds than any other state, has many of the finest horse farms in the world and its yearling sales attract buyers from all parts of the globe. As the center of the international breeding industry, Lexington is the hub of much of the industry's business activity. It is the headquarters for the Association of Racing Commissioners International (formerly the National Association of State Racing Commissioners), the Kentucky State Racing Commission, Breeders' Cup Ltd., the Kentucky Thoroughbred Association, the Jockey Club, the Grayson–Jockey Club Research Foundation, the Jockeys' Guild, and the Thoroughbred Owners and Breeders Association. Such publications as the *Blood-Horse* and the *Thoroughbred Times* are based in Lexington. The Maxwell H. Gluck Equine Research Center opened on the University of Kentucky campus in 1987.

The thoroughbred industry provides thousands of jobs in Kentucky, and the racing business generates millions of dollars in revenue for the state. Moreover, thoroughbred racing is a major attraction on the Kentucky sports calendar, with millions of fans attending races at the state's four thoroughbred tracks: Churchill Downs in Louisville, home of the Kentucky Derby; Keeneland Race Course, Lexington, which holds two of the highest-quality meetings of the year; Turfway Park, near Florence; and Ellis Park, near Henderson. Both of the latter have made significant improvements in their facilities in recent years.

In a tradition inherited from colonial Virginia, Kentuckians take great pride in their thoroughbreds—and rightly so. Consider the numbers:

• Kentucky-breds won eighty-nine of the first 117 runnings of the Kentucky Derby.

• Eight of the eleven horses to win the Triple Crown (the combination of Kentucky Derby, Preakness, and Belmont Stakes) were born in Kentucky.

• Twenty-six of the first forty-nine winners on the Breeders' Cup Championship Day cards were foaled in Kentucky, including the first six victors in the $3 million Breeders' Cup Classic—Wild Again (1984), Proud Truth (1985), Skywalker (1986), Ferdinand (1987), Alysheba (1988), and Sunday Silence (1989).

Kentucky boasts many of the most well-known, most beautiful, and most tradition-rich farms to be found in the world: Calumet, with its gleaming white fences and green, lush pastures, and Claiborne, with its natural beauty and its blue-blooded stallion roster; Darby Dan, with its long line of classically bred horses; Hamburg Place, with a great heritage stemming back to John E. Madden, "the wizard of the turf"; Lane's End, where Queen Elizabeth II has stayed during her visits to Kentucky; and Gainesway, with its stud barns fit for royalty.

Indeed, the thoroughbred itself is treated like royalty in Kentucky, occupying a prominent place in the state's economic, social, and sports worlds. How did Kentucky become so closely identified with the thoroughbred? Why did this state develop into the best place in the world to breed thoroughbreds? Joe Estes, the late editor of the *Blood-Horse* magazine, addressed himself to that question in 1936: "The settlers of central Kentucky were in the main from Virginia and the Carolinas, a people of cavalier associations, among whom horse racing had long been accepted as the king of sports. When they brought blooded horses with them from beyond the Alleghenies, it was as much a matter of course as when they brought their rifles and powder horns."

The geology of the state played a major role: The soil in Kentucky "was obviously fertile," Estes wrote; "it was that characteristic which made the section such a magnet for pioneers. And, as it was a rare outcropping of the deep Ordovician limestone, at the apex of what geologists call the Cincinnati anticline, it was rich in calcium and phosphorous. This legacy of phosphatic limestone, inherited from millions of shells and skeletons, deposited millions of years earlier when central Kentucky was an ocean bed, was now to be used to build the skeletons of horses. It was essential that the racehorse have a framework strong enough to withstand the enormous strains put upon it by his prodigious musculature and his desperate courage. At the same time the framework must be so light that it would require a minimum amount of energy for its locomotion. In accomplishing this ideal of maximum strength and minimum weight the phosphatic limestone which forms the basis of central Kentucky's soil has proved its efficacy."

Geography played a part, too: "Another advantage possessed by central Kentucky as a breeding ground for horses was its rolling topography and the porous nature of its subsoil, assuring adequate drainage at all times—for hard feet and bone cannot be developed by horses raised on marshy, soggy or ill-drained land," Estes wrote.

Estes added another key factor to this equation: "It was to be found neither in the nature of the country nor in the heritage of thoroughbred blood, but in the character of the people who came to be called Kentuckians. Such was their heritage, from the colonies to the east and from their ancestral background in England, that they needed action, adventure, creation, conquest—the Alpine heights of life. When there were no Indians to be chased, there were arguments to be settled, and in Kentucky it usually takes a horse race to settle an argument."

See Dan White, *Kentucky Bred: A Celebration of Thoroughbred Breeding* (Dallas, Tex., 1986); Jocelyn De Moubray, *The Thoroughbred Business* (London 1987); Kent Hollingsworth, *The Kentucky Thoroughbred* (Lexington, Ky., 1985).

JIM BOLUS

THRUSTON, BUCKNER. Buckner Thruston, political leader and jurist, was born on February 9, 1763 (or 1764), to Col. Charles Minn and Mary (Buckner) Thruston in Gloucester County, Virginia. He graduated from William and Mary College and went on to study law. In 1788 Thruston moved to Lexington, Kentucky, (then part of Virginia), where he was admitted to the bar and practiced law. The next year, he became a member of the Virginia Assembly. After Kentucky gained its statehood in 1792, Thruston was elected as the state's first senate clerk. In 1791-92, Thruston was a district judge of Kentucky and in 1802-3 a circuit court judge. He was a Fayette County delegate to the second constitutional convention in Frankfort in 1799. When Louisiana was purchased from France in 1803 he declined a position as U.S. judge of the Orleans territory, instead becoming a U.S. senator (March 4, 1805, to December 18, 1809, when he resigned). A Democrat, Thruston was selected by President James Monroe to be U.S. circuit court judge for the District of Columbia, serving until his death.

Thruston married Janette January in March 1795 and they had eight children. Thruston died in Washington, D.C., on August 30, 1845, and was buried in the Congressional Cemetery.

THRUSTON, ROGERS CLARK BALLARD. Rogers Clark Ballard Thruston, historian, engineer, and photographer, was born November 6, 1858, in Louisville. A son of Andrew Jackson Ballard and Frances Ann (Thruston) Ballard, he adopted his mother's maiden name in 1884. Thruston graduated from Yale University's Sheffield Scientific School in 1880, and in 1882 began work with the Kentucky Geological Survey. He resigned in 1887, founded the Inter-State Investment Company with his brothers, and for two decades was active in surveying, platting, and buying timber and mineral lands in Kentucky and Virginia. In 1909 he retired to devote his life to historical and genealogical research; to charitable and patriotic organizations; and to the Filson Club, a historical research institution. He was instrumental in guiding the club through a critical period after the death of its founder, Col.

Reuben T. Durrett. Serving as president from 1923 to 1946, Thruston provided the impetus for acquiring the club's first headquarters, established an endowment fund, and contributed his research materials, photograph collection, and personal library.

Thruston was an expert on the evolution of the the American flag; the genealogies of the signers of the Declaration of Independence; and George Rogers Clark, a collateral ancestor. His photographs record nineteenth century mountain life in Kentucky, as well as people, places, and events in other states and in foreign countries from 1900 through the 1930s. His meticulous research, his respect for historical accuracy, and his dedication to the preservation of historical materials were his legacy to Kentucky history. He died on December 30, 1946, and was buried in Cave Hill Cemetery in Louisville.

See Thomas D. Clark, "Rogers Clark Ballard Thruston, Engineer, Historian, and Benevolent Kentuckian," *FCHQ* 58 (Oct. 1984): 408-35.

MARY JEAN KINSMAN

THUM, PATTY PRATHER. Patty Prather Thum, artist, was born in Louisville on October 1, 1853, to Mandeville and Louisiana (Miller) Thum. As a child she was taught by her mother to draw, and she studied art at Vassar College under Henry Van Ingen and at the Art Students' League in New York City with William Merritt Chase. In the mid-1870s Thum returned to Louisville, where she painted landscapes, still lifes, and portraits. For more than thirty-five years she maintained an art studio there.

She was a member of the Louisville Art Association and the Art Club of Louisville, and was art critic for the *Louisville Herald*. Thum also studied briefly with Thomas Eakins at the Students' Guild of the Brooklyn Art Association in New York City in the mid-1880s. She illustrated the book *Robbie and Annie: A Child's Story*, and in 1893 she received honorable mention for book illustrations at the Chicago Columbian Exposition. Her work was exhibited at the New York State Fair in 1898 and the St. Louis Exposition of 1904. In 1921 she served as art director of the Kentucky State Fair. Thum died at her home on September 28, 1926, after an illness of several months, and was buried in Louisville's Cave Hill Cemetery.

TILGHMAN, LLOYD. Lloyd Tilghman, Confederate general, was born in Baltimore, Maryland, on January 26, 1818, one of four children of James and Ann Caroline (Shoemaker) Tilghman. He graduated from the U.S. Military Academy at West Point but resigned his commission shortly after graduation to work on railroads. He served in the Mexican War in 1846, achieving the rank of captain. He moved to Paducah in 1852 to supervise the construction of the New Orleans & Ohio Railroad, which linked Paducah to Troy, Tennessee, and the Gulf of Mexico. Tilghman commanded the western State Guard in the abortive attempt to keep Kentucky neutral in 1861. He then decided to join the Confederacy and moved his family to Clarksville, Tennessee, where he organized the 3d Kentucky Regiment. Shortly thereafter he was promoted to brigadier general and took command at Fort Henry, just in time to surrender to U.S. Gen. Ulysses Grant early in 1862, after token resistance. Tilghman was released by prisoner exchange and commanded the 1st Brigade in Loring's Division. On May 16, 1863, Tilghman fought gallantly in defending Champion's Hill near Vicksburg, where he was struck in the hip by artillery fire and died. Tilghman was buried at Vicksburg; his remains were moved to New York City in 1901.

Tilghman married Augusta Murray Boyd; they had eight children. The family gave funds in 1921 to purchase land for Tilghman High School.

JOHN E.L. ROBERTSON

TIMBERLAKE, CLARENCE L. Clarence L. Timberlake, who worked to expand educational opportunities for black Kentuckians, was born in Fleming County, Kentucky, in 1885. Timberlake was a graduate of the agriculture program of Kentucky Normal and Industrial Institute in 1904. Upon graduation he accepted a position as a messenger in Kentucky's Department of Education. In 1914 he wrote a pamphlet, "Politics and the Schools," to protest politicians' interference in the development of schools. He was one of the supporters of the law passed by the General Assembly requiring regents who governed state schools to be selected from the state at large, rather than from the community in which they served.

Timberlake organized a four-year high school in Madisonville and teacher training schools in Pembroke and Greenville, Kentucky. In 1948 he became the fourth president of West Kentucky Vocational School in Paducah, a position he held until his retirement in July 1957. He died in 1979.

See Osceola A. Dawson, *The Timberlake Story* (Carbondale, Ill., 1959). GERALD L. SMITH

TOBACCO CULTIVATION. Tobacco has influenced the economic, cultural, and political history of Kentucky more than any other agricultural product. The entire process from seed to cigarette takes place in the commonwealth—a source of some controversy.

Clay pipes found in the fields and excavations of the state attest to tobacco's long connection with the area. The Shawnee were using tobacco when the first white settlers came onto the scene. The white settlers, however, needed no introduction to the crop, for in many cases they had moved West specifically to grow tobacco. The custom of tilling new soil for tobacco, growing tobacco on virgin land, necessitated westward movement, and many regions of Kentucky were particularly well suited for the crop. As early as 1787 Virginia, of which Kentucky was then a part, licensed inspection warehouses to ensure the quality of tobacco.

One of the first obstacles for Kentucky farmers was marketing the product. The market of the time was New Orleans, but the Spanish controlled the Mississippi River and resisted American encroachment. Gen. James WILKINSON was successful in negotiating with the Spanish in 1787 to open the river for a time. The purchase of Louisiana in 1803 solved the transport problem permanently. Even so, the profitability of tobacco fluctuated and farmers had to adjust accordingly. While the War of 1812 cut off foreign trade almost completely, Kentucky farmers supplied domestic manufacturing. Some of the manufacturing in the pre–Civil War era was centered in Kentucky. Tobacco was grown largely in the western regions of the state; manufacturing of snuff, chewing tobacco, cigars, and pipe tobaccos took place in the cities.

Tobacco in the 1800s was not as important as it has become in the twentieth century. During the Civil War Kentucky topped Virginia as the country's leading producer, a position it held until surpassed by North Carolina in the late 1920s. It was also during the war that Bracken County seed was planted in Ohio to grow the first white burley tobacco. The bitter tobacco soon won acclaim for holding the sweeteners popular in plug tobacco at the time. Plug was the most popular product until World War I, when blended cigarettes took its place. Fortunately for Kentucky tobacco farmers, white burley was an important ingredient in both products.

Another advantage in growing white burley was that it could be air-cured rather than being flue- or fire-cured. It was harvested by the stalk instead of pulling off leaves as they cured. For all these reasons, the 1864 fluke called white burley (also golden burley or just plain burley) swept the state and was grown in all regions. Some fire-cured and dark air-cured tobaccos are still grown in the western part of the state, recalling the times when chewing tobacco and snuff were the tobacco products of choice.

During the transition from dark to light tobacco, the American Tobacco Company monopolized the tobacco business, and farmers responded by organizing into associations and cooperatives to raise prices. Much of the anger that arose over pricing was centered in western Kentucky, where low prices combined with declining demand for the dark leaf. At the height of the BLACK PATCH WAR, vigilante-style night riders took over the town of Princeton on December 1, 1906. Less dramatic incidents of violence occurred in central and eastern Kentucky, where warehouses were burned in Bath and Fleming counties. The tobacco wars came to an end after successful lawsuits against farmers' associations in western Kentucky, and after the government's 1911 break-up of the monopolistic American Tobacco Company. Membership in the associations declined and tobacco companies competed as buyers. The offspring of the breakup of the monopoly became the tobacco companies of today.

Another monopoly of sorts was broken up at the turn of the century. From the early days tobacco had been packed in hogsheads weighing up to five hundred pounds for shipment to market. Louisville and Cincinnati dominated the hogshead auctions. In the last decades of the nineteenth century, some farmers tried selling directly from the barn. However, it was the loose-leaf auction system started in 1904 in Lexington that became the marketing method of choice for the farmer. Under this system, several buyers competed for the crop, and the warehouseman was interested in obtaining the highest price for clients—the farmers.

More tobacco was planted during World War I as the blended cigarette caught on in popularity. High prices in 1919 were followed by a bust in the 1920s. The response was the formation of the BURLEY TOBACCO GROWERS COOPERATIVE ASSOCIATION, a revived farmers' cooperative that had mixed results during the decade. Cigarette consumption dropped with the onset of the Great Depression, but the association found new life when the New Deal came to the tobacco fields with the Agricultural Adjustment Act of 1933. In its various reincarnations, this legislation for controlling production and price is commonly known as the "tobacco program."

Many methods in growing tobacco are traditional. However, a farmer from the early part of the century would be totally lost in growing the crop as practiced today. In a sort of poor man's breeding program, farmers traditionally allowed a few of their best plants to go to seed instead of topping them. After the blooms fully matured, they were hung in the barn to dry and the seed was used the next season. Seed might also be borrowed, as was the case with the first white burley grown. Because the seed is so small—more than 300,000 seeds to an ounce—early farmers planted tobacco first in a bed to produce seedlings large enough for transplanting, as is done today. Farmers gather wood and brush in the fall in cleaning up around the farm to burn on the surface of beds to prepare them for the tobacco seed. The beds are planted in mid-March; they were covered with cotton canvas in earlier times. Near the end of May or the first of June, workers pull the plants ready for transplanting. Farmers formerly prepared the fields for planting using horses or mules. When farmers planted fields by hand, the ground had to be wet enough for a worker to punch a hole easily, yet dry enough to support growth. When the first mechanical setters were used, the weather requirements were reversed; the ground had to be dry if the machinery was to function and if the animals pulling the machinery were not to bog down.

Worms, weeds, weather, and disease were the biggest problems in the tobacco fields of old. Despite an early pesticide called paris green, the tobacco worm was largely controlled by pulling individual insects off the leaves and destroying them by whatever method, usually pressure between the fingers. The weeds were controlled by frequent plowing and hoeing, a process that kept the farm-boys busy (which some saw as its main purpose). Because the suckers that grew on nearly every leaf of tobacco would cut down the size and quality of the leaf, workers walked through the field several times to remove suckers by hand. In the case of disease, farmers in the past could only rotate their fields and beds from season to season and try different varieties of tobacco. The effects of the weather were out of the farmer's control. Despite the hardiness of the plant, many crops were destroyed by hail, floods, high winds, or other weather extremes.

Today, as in the past, workers break the bloom and top leaves off the plants sometime in late July or early August. This causes the lower leaves to grow larger and to cure, turning the tobacco its distinctive golden color. This is the time when suckers cause the most problems. Around Labor Day the harvest crew goes to work. In days past a worker split the stalk with a knife before cutting it off at the base and draping the harvested plant over one of the sticks that had been dropped between the rows of tobacco. Splitting the stalk is largely gone, replaced by the tomahawk-style knife and spear. The tobacco sticks, containing about five plants each, are stacked on wagon beds. The wagons, which used to be wooden, today are often made of metal; the sticks stay on the wagon without overheating. The configurations of stacking may vary from farmer to farmer, each having a favorite method for effectiveness.

The wagons then go to the tobacco barn, an architectural feature unique to burley regions. The barn usually has a stripping room attached, central doors, and various devices to control the flow of air to the tobacco. The tobacco sticks are lifted from the wagon up to a worker who hangs them from parallel poles running the length of the barn, taking the utmost care with each stick. Hanging sticks was formerly the job of a single person; today all workers hang sticks as well as handing up to the person above. The best curing weather is a variety of conditions. Too much heat soon after harvesting can bring on curing too quickly, resulting in so-called houseburn—low weight and bad color. Around the first of November, the cured tobacco becomes moist, called having a "season" or being "in case," and it can then be handled. The tobacco is taken down from the poles in the barn and off the sticks so that the leaves can be stripped from the stalk. The tobacco is often stacked to be stripped within the next few days. It may be covered to keep it "in case."

Stripping was a skill viewed with pride by traditional farmers. The stripped leaves were sorted into bundles according to the position in which they grew on the stalk—called, from the bottom up, the flyings, trash, leaf, and tip. The leaves might also be sorted according to size, quality, and color. When a farmer had a handful of the same type of leaf, a single leaf was used to tie up the bundle, thus creating a "hand" of tobacco. Farmers until recent years took many grades of tobacco to market, where each type was stacked on baskets to be bid on separately. The stripping process, much abbreviated today, lasted until the late spring.

Between the era when farmers packed their tobacco and shipped it to market and the 1930s, when the auction system became entrenched, some farmers sold directly to tobacco companies, as they still do in some of the dark-tobacco regions of Kentucky. Speculators of that time who bought from the farmer with the intention of resale for a profit were called pinhookers. Under the loose-leaf warehouse auction system, there is little for the farmer to influence once the crop gets to market. The farmer chooses the warehouse on the basis of friendships, service, and price. Not seen much today is some farmers' custom of seating their children on the baskets of tobacco leaves in hopes of eliciting a higher price. Farmers themselves are usually present when the crop is sold, sometimes talking to the warehouseman and buyers.

Since the 1930s the market has guaranteed a price to the farmer. The tobacco at the warehouse is assessed by a government grader, and the Department of Agriculture sets a support price for the one hundred different grades, based on such considerations as color, leaf position, moisture content, and quality. If the buyers at the auction do not bid at least one cent above the support price assigned by the government for the grade, the government takes the tobacco under loan. It goes to the "pool" of the Growers Cooperative, which handles, stores, and sells it at a later date. The system worked without a loss until rising foreign competition created a glut at the co-op in 1983. Since that time, the farmer absorbs any losses.

Much has changed in the tobacco growing process since World War II. Many tobacco growers were forced off the farm by the Great Depression, and some who served in the war did not return to the farm. The number of farmers has thus declined and the age of the average farmer has increased. The size of farms has gradually increased and the rate of tenancy has declined drastically. Many farmers and/or their wives have taken urban jobs to earn enough money to keep their farms, reducing the relative importance of their farm work.

The age of technology has come to the tobacco farm. Very few farmers know the proper signs of a poor time for planting. Seed is now certified by the University of Kentucky, hybrids have been developed, and disease problems are reduced. Seed beds are now gassed to kill weeds and covered with a synthetic cloth. Mechanical setters pulled by tractors do in a short time what took days before. Herbicides and pesticides have made the tobacco worm, weeds, and most diseases a subject of nostalgia. Chemical control gets rid of the suckers and also yellows up the plant more quickly. Even the weather is partially taken into account when farmers purchase crop insurance, as many do. Stripping is more efficient. Fewer grades are grown, and critics claim the entire crop is handled with less care.

Since the early 1980s hand-tied bundles have given way to baling, a labor saver for the farmer, warehouse, and processors.

Health concerns about cigarettes and tobacco use in general have been expressed since colonial times. The U.S. Surgeon General's report in 1965 was the watershed in the modern health argument over cigarettes. Since that time, the growing evidence indicting tobacco use and its relationship to health has changed what was once a popular social behavior, seen as glamorous, into a social taboo. A corresponding decline in demand has put new strains on the tobacco producer. Many other crops can be grown in Kentucky soil, but at this point nothing legal seems able to replace the golden burley. Until such a replacement takes over, or until the drop in consumption wipes out the market for the product, the relationship of the Kentucky farmer and tobacco will continue.

See W.F. Axton, *Tobacco and Kentucky* (Lexington, Ky., 1975); James Nall, *The Tobacco Night Riders of Kentucky and Tennessee, 1905-1909* (Louisville 1939); Tobacco Institute, *Kentucky and Tobacco*, 5th ed. (Washington, D.C., 1976).

JOHN KLEE

TODD, GEORGE D. George D. Todd, the first Republican mayor of Louisville, was born in Frankfort, Kentucky, on April 19, 1856, to Harry and Jane (Davidson) Todd. Owner of the Todd-Donigan Iron Company, he was appointed mayor of Louisville by the Republican-dominated Board of Aldermen on January 31, 1896, after the death of Henry Tyler, a Democrat. The Republican party was rife with factionalism during Todd's administration. Moderate Republicans criticized his attempts to compromise with the conservative faction of the party, and black members of the party were disappointed with the few appointments of blacks to city or political jobs. When Todd attempted to appoint Republicans to the city's Boards of Public Safety and Public Works, the city divided into warring factions, and his well-intentioned fiscal reforms were never enacted.

In 1897 Todd ran for reelection against Charles Weaver, who was supported by the Democratic machine. Along with dissension among Republicans, rainy weather and election fraud contributed to Todd's defeat. Todd returned to his iron company after the election and in the 1920s moved to New Albany, Indiana, to live with his two sisters.

Todd was married to Laura (Durkee) and they had three children—Laura, George, and Helen. He died in Indiana on November 23, 1929, and was buried in the Frankfort Cemetery.

See George H. Yater, *Two Hundred Years at the Falls of the Ohio: A History of Louisville and Jefferson County* (Louisville 1979).

DAVID WILLIAMS

TODD, JOHN. John Todd, pioneer, was born in Montgomery County, Pennsylvania, on March 27, 1750, to David and Hannah (Owen) Todd. His family sent him at an early age to Parson John Todd's school in Louisa County, Virginia, to study the classics. He studied law under Gen. Andrew Lewis, a prominent Botetourt County, Virginia, attorney, was admitted to the bar on May 14, 1771, and practiced law in Fincastle County, Virginia. Todd served as General Lewis's aide at the Battle of Point Pleasant, often referred to as the first battle of the Revolutionary War, in the fall of 1774.

Todd came to Kentucky early in 1775 and joined Col. Benjamin Logan and John Floyd at Logan's Station (St. Asaph). From St. Asaph he explored and surveyed areas west along the Barren River to where Bowling Green is now located, and south into middle Tennessee, along the Cumberland River. In 1777 Todd settled in Lexington, where he was later joined by his younger brothers, Robert and Levi TODD, with whom he founded a dynasty with land and political influence in Kentucky. Todd was one of the first two burgesses sent to the Virginia legislature by Kentucky County in 1777. He introduced bills to emancipate slaves and to set aside land grants for educational institutions.

Todd owned more than 20,000 acres of land in central Kentucky along Elkhorn Creek and the Ohio River, as well as vast acreage in Tennessee. Some of the land he had purchased and some he obtained as payment for military service. Todd participated in the conquest of Illinois with Gen. George Rogers Clark in 1778 and was appointed the first civil governor of Illinois by Virginia Gov. Patrick Henry. He arrived in Kaskasea in May 1779. After the 1780 term of the Virginia legislature, Todd made one or two more trips to Illinois, but delegated most of his duties to deuties. Todd was the first colonel of the Fayette County militia, second in rank on the frontier only to General Clark. Upon learning that the Canadians and Indians had attacked Bryan's Station in August 1782, Colonel Todd gathered the 182 available men at Lexington, Boonesborough, and Harrodsburg and began pursuit, without waiting for General Logan and his men from Lincoln County, locating the attacking force at BLUE LICKS on August 19. Todd died in the disastrous ensuing battle.

Todd was married in 1780 in Virginia to Jane Hawkins. They had a daughter, Mary Owen, who upon her father's death became one of the wealthiest people in Kentucky. In 1819 the Kentucky General Assembly named a new county in Todd's honor. He is buried in a common grave with others killed at Blue Licks.

See Thomas M. Green, *Historic Families of Kentucky* (Cincinnati 1889).   BETTY B. ELLISON

TODD, LEE T., JR. Lee T. Todd, Jr., electrical engineer, was born in Easlington, Hopkins County, Kentucky, on May 6, 1946, to Lee and Barbara (Edwards) Todd. He graduated from the University of Kentucky in 1968. He received his M.S. (1970) and Ph.D. (1973) in electrical engineering from the Massachusetts Institute of Technology (MIT), where he held an IBM postdoctoral fellowship in 1973. In 1974 Todd joined the University of Kentucky

College of Engineering faculty as assistant professor of electrical engineering. Todd took a leave of absence from UK to start two advanced-technology companies in Lexington to manufacture devices he had patented while at MIT. Databeam, chartered in 1976, achieved operational funding to produce teleconferencing systems in 1983. The other company, Projectron, founded in 1981, manufactures projection cathode-ray tubes for military and civilian avionics applications. In 1990 Hughes Aircraft joined Projectron in the venture that will become the first proprietor in the Science Park of the Coldstream Farm development project in northern Lexington. Todd married Patricia Brantley; they have two children—Kathryn and Lee III.

ERIC HOWARD CHRISTIANSON

TODD, LEVI. Born in 1756, the son of David and Hannah (Owen) Todd, Levi Todd was one of the founders of Lexington, Kentucky. He moved to Kentucky from Virginia in 1775 or 1776 and settled at Harrodsburg, where he became the first clerk of Kentucky County in the spring of 1777. In 1779 Todd established a station in present-day Fayette County a short distance from Lexington, on the northern bank of the South Elkhorn Creek, along the road to the mouth of the Dick's [now Dix] River. (Some sources, including Collins's *Historical Sketches of Kentucky* [1874] and Jillson's *Pioneer Kentucky* [1934], say that another station was founded by Todd in present-day Jessamine County, near Keene. The existence of the Fayette County station, however, is better established.)

Todd's station was short-lived. By the summer of 1780, Indian threats caused Todd to abandon the settlement and move to the site of present-day Lexington. According to legend, while camped there in 1775, Todd and his party, led by Maj. John Morrison, received word of a skirmish between the British and the Minutemen in Lexington, Massachusetts. In commemoration of the event, they named their camp Lexington. A member of the party, William McConnell, built a cabin on the spot, which was known as MCCONNELL'S STATION. Todd settled permanently in Lexington, where his older brother, John TODD, was already established. Levi was one of the original property holders within the city limits when the plan for the city was adopted, according to Collins, on December 26, 1781. He was one of the original town trustees and also among the first trustees of Transylvania Seminary (now Transylvania University). Todd was a delegate to the Kentucky statehood conventions that met in Danville on May 23, 1785; on August 8, 1785; and September 17, 1787.

In 1779, Todd married Jane Briggs; they had four children, one of whom, Robert S. Todd, was the father of Mary Todd, wife of Abraham Lincoln. Todd died in 1807.

See George W. Ranck, *History of Lexington, Kentucky* (Cincinnati 1872); Charles Staples, *The History of Pioneer Lexington, 1779-1806* (Lexington, Ky., 1939).

TODD, THOMAS. Thomas Todd, jurist, was the youngest son of Richard and Elizabeth (Richards) Todd, born on January 23, 1765, in King and Queen County, Virginia. After serving in the army for six months during the latter part of the Revolutionary War, he attended Liberty Hall (now Washington and Lee University) in Lexington, Virginia, and graduated in 1783. He then made his home and studied law in Virginia with Judge Harry Innes, his mother's cousin and Kentucky's first federal district judge. By 1784 Todd had moved to Danville, Kentucky, where he was secretary-clerk at most of the conventions seeking separation from Virginia. (The original of the Kentucky constitution of 1792, in Todd's handwriting, is in the hands of the Kentucky Historical Society.) He rode the circuit as a lawyer, was a clerk to Judge Innes until 1792, and served as clerk of the Kentucky House of Representatives. In 1801 Gov. James Garrard (1796-1804) appointed him to the Kentucky court of appeals, where he served for six years and became chief justice. On March 3, 1807, President Thomas Jefferson appointed him to the U.S. Supreme Court.

Politically, Justice Todd was a Jeffersonian, but he followed the constitutional lead of Chief Justice John Marshall, a former Federalist, during his nineteen years on the court. He wrote only fourteen opinions and dissented but once; much of his time and energy were spent in arduous travel to circuit court in Nashville; Frankfort, Kentucky; and Chillicothe, Ohio.

Todd married Elizabeth Harris in 1788. One of their children, Col. Charles Stewart Todd, was an aide to Gen. William Harrison during the War of 1812 and later was minister to Russia. A year after Elizabeth's death in 1801, Todd married Lucy Payne, a sister of Dolly Madison; they had three children. Todd died on February 7, 1826, and was buried in the Frankfort Cemetery.

See Edward C. O'Rear, "Justice Thomas Todd," *Register* 38 (Apr. 1940): 112-19.

CHARLES R. LEE, JR.

TODD COUNTY. Sixty-fourth in order of formation, Todd County in southwestern Kentucky was formed on December 30, 1819, from parts of Logan and Christian counties. The rectangular county has 376 square miles and is bordered by Christian, Muhlenberg, and Logan counties and the Kentucky-Tennessee line. The county was named in honor of Col. John Todd, who was killed at the Battle of Blue Licks on August 19, 1782. Todd and his brothers Robert and Levi were instrumental in founding Lexington. ELKTON, the county seat, was incorporated on May 18, 1820.

The topography is divided into two distinct areas. The southern half of the county is a sinkhole plain with gently rolling terrain; the more rugged area to the north contains higher elevations. The county was and is predominantly agricultural. Some early settlers brought slaves with them. By 1840 the slave population was 3,879 and the nonslave population 6,070; in 1850 the totals were 4,810 and 7,361; in

1860, 4,849 and 6,681. Tobacco, corn, and live-stock were the early cash crops. Cattle were first imported into the county in 1845. Todd County to-bacco farmers on September 24, 1904, met with 5,000 other growers at Guthrie to form the Dark Tobacco Productive Association to pool their crops in opposition to the price-fixing policies of the American Tobacco Company and other purchasers. The association, later renamed Planters' Protective Association of Kentucky, Tennessee, and Virginia, wanted to set prices for their own crops. Indepen-dent growers opposed the association, and the BLACK PATCH WAR's night riders, with their black masks and white scarves, caused destruction in Todd and adjoining counties. In 1870, farmers pro-duced 2.3 million pounds of tobacco, 415,555 bushels of corn, and 153,475 bushels of wheat. In 1988, farms occupied 72 percent of the land area, with 76 percent of farmland in cultivation. The county ranks twelfth among Kentucky counties in agricultural receipts, with income from tobacco, soybeans, corn, and livestock. The average farm size is 255 acres.

Among the early settlers were Franklin M. Chestnut, John Montgomery, and James Davis, who built a fort in 1783 on the West Fork of the Red River. By 1812, Joseph Robertson constructed a horse-powered mill on the Trenton Road. The first brick house is said to be one completed by John Gray in 1821; its first floor served as the county court. On June 3, 1808, Jefferson Davis, who later became president of the Confederate States of America, was born to Samuel and Jane (Cook) Davis at Fairview, seven miles west of Elkton. His birthplace is commemorated by a 351-foot concrete obelisk, completed in 1929. Davis returned to the county in 1875 and was a guest in his parents' former home. He again returned in 1886 to dedi-cate the Bethel Baptist Church on the site of his birthplace.

In November of 1838, when the Cherokee were moved westward, the "Trail of Tears" brought them through Todd County. The Trail entered the county near Guthrie on the state line, continued through Hopkinsville, and crossed the Ohio River below Carrsville in Livingston County.

There is no record of a Civil War skirmish in Todd County, though troop movements probably crossed the county. The inhabitants certainly leaned toward the Confederacy. In 1860, Abraham Lincoln received four votes in the county, but four years later received 104 votes there.

The Elkton-Guthrie Railroad was incorporated in 1870, and the line was completed on February 1, 1885. In 1927, the Elkton & Guthrie made three round trips daily. The eleven-mile line was aban-doned in 1957. Current transportation facilities in-clude CSX Transportation and U.S. 79, 41, and 68.

Robert Penn Warren, distinguished poet, novel-ist, and scholar, was born in Guthrie in 1905.

Twenty-two percent of the labor force works in manufacturing. The oldest manufacturing firm, Koppers Company, Inc., was established in Guthrie

in 1914. The Elkton Apparel Company, which came to Elkton in 1941, is the largest manufacturing em-ployer. Thirty-two percent of the labor force is em-ployed outside the county. Tourism expenditures added nearly a million dollars to the local economy in 1988; a part of Lake Malone is in the northeast corner of the county. Incorporated towns include Allensville, Elkton, Guthrie, and Trenton. Popula-tion of the county was 10,823 in 1970; 11,874 in 1980; and 10,940 in 1990.

See J.H. Battle, *Counties of Todd and Christian* (Chicago 1884).

TOMPKINSVILLE. Tompkinsville, the seat and the largest town of Monroe County, is located at the junction of KY 100 and KY 163. Its predecessor, a settlement known as Watson's Store, was founded in 1809 by J.C. Watson of Virginia, who built a store on the grounds of the present Monroe County jail. In January 1819, the village was incorporated as Tompkinsville in honor of the vice-president of the United States, Daniel Tompkins of New York. With a population of about one hundred people, Tompkinsville won an election over the villages of Martinsburg and Pikeville by four votes to become the county seat of the newly formed Monroe County in 1820.

The land for the town of Tompkinsville was ob-tained from Thomas B. Monroe, who had pur-chased the land from Samuel Marrs. Abijah Marrs in 1817 laid out the plan for the town, the major portion located on the west bluff of Mill Creek.

The population of Tompkinsville in 1830 was 220. By 1900 it had increased only to 366. Brick buildings were uncommon in Tompkinsville until the late nineteenth century.

On April 22, 1863, the courthouse, built in 1822-23, and several other buildings were burned on the orders of Col. Ollie Hamilton of the Confederate army in reprisal for the Union's burning of Celina, Tennessee. The second courthouse, built in 1864-65 on the site of the first, was destroyed by a fire that broke out on November 16, 1887, after thieves had used explosives to break open a safe in the Nelson Brothers store on the town square. The courthouse and the post office were among the twenty-one buildings lost. A fire that started in the Pitcock Brothers drygoods store destroyed several busi-nesses on January 2, 1913. On May 9, 1933, a tor-nado struck the southern edge of town, killing fourteen people.

From the late 1950s through the 1980s, Tomp-kinsville experienced both industrial and residential growth, but remains a small agrarian community. Population of the fifth-class city was 2,207 in 1970; 3,077 in 1980; and 2,861 in 1990.

RON D. BRYANT

TOURISM. Tourism in Kentucky, coordinated by a cabinet-level agency of state government, gener-ated $4.9 billion in 1990 for the state's economy. The Kentucky tourism industry is the second-largest private employer in the state.

It was not until after World War I, however, that tourism began to get organized in Kentucky. As early as 1919, the citizens of Bell County secured a 2,000-acre tract of land in the Cumberland Gap area and offered it to the state for development as a recreation and conservation area. More than a hundred men gathered at the first meeting for tourism promotion in Kentucky, where Willard Rouse Jillson, state geologist and chairman of the Kentucky State Parks Commission, spoke to the Pineville Kiwanis Club at an intercity meeting with Middlesborough about his views on the potential development of the Cumberland Gap area. Some present at the meeting called for the Cumberland Gap to be the site of a national park, but many others favored a state park. Enough private land was pledged at that late-night meeting for the state park that was Kentucky's first—Pine Mountain State Resort Park.

Acreage around the Cumberland Falls was the subject of a raging dispute in 1930 between the Commonwealth of Kentucky, which stood to gain a state park, and the Cumberland River Power Company, which wanted to build an electricity-generating dam above the falls. T. Coleman du Pont had offered to buy the property for the state and present it for a state park. In the dispute on the state Senate floor, the young senator from Woodford County, A.B. Chandler, ended his discourse with: "If we allow this, they [the power company] will have a dam site and we won't have a damn thing." On March 10, 1930, the General Assembly voted to accept du Pont's offer. He had died in the meantime, but his widow completed the purchase according to his wishes. Cumberland Falls State Park was formally dedicated on August 21, 1931.

Kentucky was beginning to learn how to receive visitors in a professional manner, and the tourism industry was born. Since that time, parks have been developed across the state from the Big Sandy to the Pennyrile. In 1990 there were forty-four state parks (including historic sites), fifteen of them resort parks, which offer full vacation amenities. Fifteen more state parks could probably be filled in the summer months if developed.

The Kentucky Progress Commission, created by the 1928 legislature to advertise Kentucky to the world, was empowered to "promote the development of the Commonwealth of Kentucky, making a general study of its resources, facilities, and advantages for agricultural, commercial, and industrial development and for the attraction of tourists to the Commonwealth." The first budget for promotion was $50,000 for the biennium. In 1956 the Department of Public Relations was created to produce and distribute maps, brochures, news stories for the media, and photos for promotion. Over the years, it has been known variously as the Department of Public Information, the Department of Tourism, and the Department of Travel Development.

As the tourism industry in the United States has grown and flourished, so it has in Kentucky. The Department of Travel Development and the private sector tourism industry in Kentucky share personnel and expenses for many sales efforts, advertising initiatives, and promotions. Booths are shared at sport, boat, and vacation shows, and cooperative marketing with tour operators and bus line owners at major marketplaces is an annual event. The Department of Travel Development's toll-free telephone number responds immediately to requests for travel information, and packets of brochures, maps, calendars of events, and state park rates are mailed on request. Festivals celebrate items of local pride—tobacco, sorghum, oil, pioneers, even green peppers—all over the state.

Among the independent initiatives in the Kentucky tourism industry, the Middlesborough Tourist Commission and local promoters had the idea of "seceding" from Kentucky and calling themselves the State of Cumberland. Bell County joined Knox and Harlan and several counties in Tennessee and Virginia in declaring their own "state," complete with governor, state flag, constitution, and legislature. This innovative idea received national publicity and had the desired effect of attracting travelers.

Kentucky is within a day's drive of two-thirds of the population of the United States. The climate is mild and moderate; the interstate highway system is excellent; Kentucky even has more miles of running water than any other state in the union except Alaska—all inviting to tourists.   MIMI C. LEWIS

TOWNSEND, JOHN WILSON. John Wilson Townsend, historian and book dealer, was born in Lexington, Kentucky, on November 2, 1885, to Charles Wesley and Jeannie (Dillon) Townsend. He received his early education in local schools, graduated from Transylvania University in 1906, and studied for a year at Harvard. Townsend held several positions during his career, most of them in writing, editing, and collecting books. He was especially knowledgeable about Kentucky literature, and his major work was the two-volume *Kentucky in American Letters* (1913), an expanded version of *Kentuckians in History and Literature* (1907). His third wife, Dorothy, added a third volume in 1976 to cover the years 1913-1975. Other important works were *Richard Hickman Menefee* (1907), *James Lane Allen* (1928), and *John Bradford's Notes on Kentucky* (1932), which he edited. Townsend wrote several articles, some of which were published as pamphlets, on little-known Kentucky personalities.

After a brief marriage to Clara Offutt (1911-12), Townsend married Grace Cole in 1915; they had four daughters before divorcing in 1936. In 1943 he married Dorothy Louise Edwards.

In 1930 Eastern Kentucky University bought his Kentucky collection of some 1,500 items, and in 1966, when ill health forced him to dispose of his bookstores, he donated some 6,000 volumes to Transylvania University. Townsend died on January 12, 1968, and was buried in the Lexington Cemetery.

See Dorothy Edwards Townsend, *The Life and Works of John Wilson Townsend* (Lexington, Ky., 1972).   LOWELL H. HARRISON

TOWNSEND, WILLIAM HENRY. William Henry Townsend, Lincoln scholar and collector, was born on May 31, 1890, in Glensboro, Anderson County, Kentucky. He was the only child of Dr. Oliver L. and Susan Mary (Brown) Townsend. After attending public schools in Anderson County, he received his law degree from the University of Kentucky in 1912 and was admitted to the bar in Lexington. Townsend was a founder of the law firm of Stoll, Townsend and Park, specializing in corporate law. He served as corporation counsel for the city of Lexington from 1920 to 1932.

Outside of Lexington, Townsend was best known as a biographer of Abraham Lincoln and a collector of Lincoln materials. After World War I, Townsend formed a friendship with Dr. William E. Barton, the Lincoln biographer, accompanying him on several research trips into Illinois and Indiana. Beginning about 1919, Townsend acquired some 2,500 items and built one of the finest collections in the country. Among his most prized possessions were Lincoln's pocket watch, his first law book, and a five-dollar check the president made out to his son Tad when the child was sick. Most of the collection of manuscripts and books are now in the New York Public Library. The artifacts are in the possession of his daughter in Lexington. Townsend published numerous works on Lincoln and his Kentucky associates, often in pamphlet form. His earlier books, *Abraham Lincoln Litigant* (1923) and *Lincoln Defendant* (1925), related Lincoln to the Bluegrass in law as well as by marriage. He completed and revised Dr. Barton's *President Lincoln* (1932). Townsend's *Lincoln and His Wife's Home Town* (1929) was reprinted in an enlarged version as *Lincoln and the Bluegrass: Slavery and Civil War in Kentucky* (1955), which was his most important work.

A noted raconteur, Townsend combined the lawyer's exhaustive research with a quick wit and humor. His recording of his 1952 speech on Cassius Marcellus Clay to the Chicago Civil War Round Table has become a classic bit of Kentuckiana. *Hundred Proof* (1964), his last book, was a collection of some of his favorite tales. Townsend was the founder and longtime president of the Lexington Civil War Round Table, a member of Lexington's Cakes and Ale Club, and one of the book lovers known as the BOOK THIEVES. Acclaimed as a Lincoln scholar, Townsend served on numerous commissions and similar bodies.

Townsend married Genevieve Johnson on June 16, 1915; they had one child, Mary Genevieve. He died on July 25, 1964, and was buried in the Lexington Cemetery.

See J. Winston Coleman, *Scholar, Raconteur, Lawyer* (Lexington, Ky., 1980).

LOWELL H. HARRISON AND
HELEN B. CROCKER

TOYOTA. The Toyota Motor Company of Japan announced in December of 1985 that it would build an $800 million plant to employ 3,000 workers on a 1,472-acre site near Georgetown, Kentucky. Later, with the addition of an engine assembly plant, these figures were raised by $300 million and five hundred workers. The production goal would be 200,000 vehicles a year. At least two hundred firms would be needed to supply the facilities. The Georgetown site was attractive because of the intersection of two interstate highways (I-64 and I-75) and a major railroad (Southern) nearby. Toyota officials, considering the need to build a plant within the United States in the face of protectionist pressures in the U.S. Congress, visited twenty-two states before deciding on the site in Kentucky, which was ringed by other auto plants in Ohio, Tennessee, Illinois, and Michigan.

An important factor in the location decision was the financial incentive package offered by Kentucky officials, led by Gov. Martha Layne Collins (1983-87). The $125 million package included industrial development bonds that would pay for land acquisition, site preparation, a training school, and a portion of the costs of road improvements, in addition to training programs. Other benefits included a Saturday school for Japanese adults and children plus a robotics institute at the University of Kentucky. The actual bond program was finally set at $92 million, but the final costs over a twenty-year period may exceed $300 million. Offsetting these figures, a study suggested that tax collections would increase by more than $600 million in the same time frame. Governmental approval of the package proved to be an intense process in 1986. The General Assembly approved it over objections that too many benefits would go to central Kentucky. A counterargument suggested that Toyota would become one of the heaviest users of electricity produced from the burning of coal mined in eastern Kentucky. A few letters to the editor showed some lingering bitterness from World War II.

The coming of Toyota to Kentucky raised questions about how deeply state government should get involved in economic development. The tough, competitive automobile business is worldwide in character and subject to the effects of oil prices set in the Middle East. The inducement package compared favorably with those of the northern states but was high when compared with that of Tennessee. However, the prime motivation in the deal was the chance of 5,000 to 10,000 new jobs to be generated by the original plant and any new plants at the same site, in combination with supplier firms and/or service businesses across the state. The hope was that Toyota, with its top management team and high-tech operation, would supplement other industries already in Kentucky in stabilizing a job base threatened by uncertainty in both the coal industry and in tobacco.

Toyota Motor Manufacturing USA, Inc. opened its Georgetown plant in December 1987, and the first car came off the assembly line in May 1988. Toyota's annual production in 1990 was 218,000 vehicles. An expansion at the plant announced in 1990 represented an additional investment of $800 million as well as 1,500 more jobs and a production increase of as many as 200,000 vehicles.

See Theodore C. Koebel et al., "Socioeconomic Impacts of Toyota on Scott County," *Review and Perspective* 10 (Spring 1987).   ROBERT SNYDER

TRADEWATER RIVER. The sixty-seven-mile-long Tradewater River flows north-northwest from Christian County through the Western Coal Field physiographic region. By 1990, the river was no longer navigable because heavy mining activity in this region had filled it with silt. It no longer supported aquatic life. The Tradewater empties into the Ohio River one and a half miles south of Caseyville, and its basin occupies the region between the Green River and the Cumberland River basins. Starting a little south of Kelly in Christian County, the river travels through Caldwell, Hopkins, Crittenden, and Union counties. The cities of Dawson Springs, Blackford, Sturgis, and Grangertown are located on the river. It has an average width of one hundred feet and during low-water periods people can walk across the stream bed. Lick Creek, Donaldson Creek, Slover Creek, and the Cyprus River flow into the Tradewater.

As early as 1812, saltpeter was mined in caves along the Tradewater. Nicholas Casey, a Kentucky state legislator, began shipping coal down the river in 1836. A steam sawmill and the Bell Steam Coal Company near Sturgis were started in 1842 by John Bell, of Tennessee. Coal was sold to power Ohio River steamboats. Tobacco was also shipped by barge down this river. When Confederate Col. Nathan Bedford Forrest and three hundred cavalry invaded Kentucky in 1861, they found a large supply of hogs and whiskey in the Tradewater region near Caseyville.

See Wilford Bladen, *A Geography of Kentucky: A Topical-Regional Overview* (Dubuque, Iowa, 1984); George B. Simpson, *Early Coal Mining on the Tradewater River* (Sturgis, Ky., 1987).

MICHAEL E. WALTERS

TRAIL DRIVES. Early Kentucky settlers' livestock herds thrived in their new surroundings, and when production exceeded local demand, the settlers drove animals overland to eastern markets. Trail drives in Kentucky began even before 1800. Hogs were the first animals to be driven to market on the Wilderness Road. Cattle, then horses and mules followed; later, turkey drives occurred. Herds fed on acorns and beech nuts along the way. In later years, drovers favored the overland route because they were able to keep weight on the livestock being taken to market. The early Kentuckians drove mixed herds of cattle and hogs and sometimes sheep; the hogs and sheep fed on the cattle droppings. During the 1815-20 period, 10,000 head each year were driven to market.

Many drives started at Winchester or Mt. Sterling and moved through Cumberland Gap or Pound Gap. Bourbon County in 1838 shipped 10,000 cattle, 40,000 hogs, 3,000 horses and mules, and $70,000 worth of bourbon whiskey. Often the only way to market the corn crop was to sell livestock fattened with it or bourbon made from it.

Drovers bought the animals at farms or local markets, then drove them to be sold in Baltimore, Philadelphia, and Charleston. Drovers hired younger men along the way to work the herds for whatever distances parents would allow their sons to follow—usually only a day or two. Stock losses in the drives were light. Lame animals could be traded to pay daily bills. Unfortunately, the few records of this colorful segment of Kentucky history have been lost.

See Paul C. Henlein, *Cattle Kingdom in the Ohio Valley, 1783-1860* (Lexington, Ky., 1959).

J. ALLEN SINGLETON

TRANSPORTATION. Kentuckians have been continuously and sometimes desperately concerned with transportation facilities. Indeed, the earliest settlements in the region owed their existence to the proximity of two lines of communication that pierced the Appalachian barrier—one by land, through Cumberland Gap, and one by water, along the Ohio River. The first of these—the WILDERNESS ROAD—was initially a buffalo trace followed successively by Indian war and hunting parties and by the white Long Hunters. For many years the path was improved only to the extent that it became better marked by virtue of its continued use. Other trails in the area developed in the same manner, and the pack horse was long the prime instrument of land transport. In the 1780s pioneers began to convert some of these trails into wagon roads by felling trees and removing stumps (or some of them). They sometimes corduroyed the roads by laying logs at right angles to the track and covering them with a thin layer of earth, which rapidly washed away.

Such roads were far from satisfactory, and Kentuckians desiring further improvement obtained turnpike charters as early as 1817. It was not until the early 1830s, however, that construction of graded and macadamized toll roads began. Cities, counties, and the state purchased stock in construction companies, and in 1835 the commonwealth created a Board of Internal Improvements to coordinate state aid for road and river improvements. By the mid-1840s almost nine hundred miles of surfaced turnpikes stretched from Maysville in the east to Franklin in the west. Stagecoach lines, established in the first quarter of the century, extended their activity as the road network grew. (See HIGHWAY DEVELOPMENT.)

It was rivers, however, more than roads, that were essential to Kentucky's early growth and prosperity, and with these the region was bountifully supplied—the Big Sandy, the Licking, the Kentucky, the Green, the Cumberland, the Tennessee, and, above all, the Ohio. Along these riparian arteries moved the expanding produce of Kentucky, at first in canoes and pirogues, then on rafts, FLAT-BOATS, barges, and KEELBOATS, guided by a hardy and violent breed of men. Of these craft, only keelboats and barges could transport any significant amount of material upstream, and then only by dint of great exertion.

Although flatboats served as downstream carriers until the middle of the nineteenth century, the rivers of the commonwealth could not be viewed as truly effective transportation routes until the introduction of steam navigation. The downstream voyage of the *New Orleans* in 1811 and the arrival of the *Enterprise* in Louisville in 1814, only twenty-five days out of New Orleans, marked the beginning of the STEAMBOAT era for Kentucky.

Except for the canal around the Falls of the Ohio at Louisville, completed in 1833, the canal era left little imprint upon Kentucky. The 1837 proposal to connect the headwaters of the Kentucky and the Cumberland promised little advantage, and the ambitious scheme for joining the Kentucky with the Savannah, via the Tennessee, must have been recognized as visionary by even its most ardent proponents.

RAILROADS promised greater rewards. The legislature chartered the Lexington & Ohio Railroad in 1830, and the line between Lexington and Frankfort was completed in 1835. At this point, railroad construction virtually ceased for some fifteen years; then the 1850s saw the opening of lines connecting Louisville with Frankfort, and Covington with Lexington, and, most important, the completion of the main stem, Memphis branch, and Lebanon branch of the Louisville & Nashville Railroad. Moreover, by the end of the decade the Mobile & Ohio, the Mississippi Central, and the New Orleans & Ohio had reached the Ohio River in the Jackson Purchase. The greatest development of rail facilities in Kentucky, however, followed the Civil War. This was, of course, the era of the emergence of the major rail systems; in the commonwealth the Louisville & Nashville expanded its holdings, and the Chesapeake & Ohio, the Illinois Central, and the Southern purchased existing lines and constructed new ones. Other, smaller lines were built or survived, but most were eventually leased or purchased by the larger corporations. By the 1920s, trains moved over almost 4,000 miles of rails in the state.

By that time, the railroads, which had dominated transportation in the last half of the nineteenth century, were already being challenged by an emerging road system that each year opened greater areas of the state to automobiles, buses, and trucks. By the late 1920s the number of miles of roads under state maintenance roughly equaled railroad mileage in the state, and thereafter rapidly surpassed it. The first four-lane highway in the commonwealth was built between Versailles and Lexington in the 1930s.

In the meantime, Kentucky had been but slightly touched by a form of transportation popular in the northeastern quarter of the United States: the electric INTERURBAN. The Henderson-Evansville, Indiana, interurban, built in 1912, suspended service in 1928, and financial difficulties and increasing competition from buses and automobiles forced the abandonment of the remaining interurbans in the 1930s.

When aviation arrived on the transportation scene, the first recognized airport in the state was BOWMAN FIELD in 1919, then a pasture on the outskirts of Louisville. By the outbreak of World War II, there were ten municipal airports and nine other fields in the state. The postwar decades saw the construction of new and larger airports—notably Standiford Field in Louisville, Blue Grass Field in Lexington, and the Greater Cincinnati–Northern Kentucky Airport in Boone County—to accommodate the jet-powered aircraft whose higher landing speeds demanded longer runways. New generations of jetliners and increasing air traffic led to further expansion of a number of Kentucky's airports, and the hope of attracting still more flights sparked more terminal construction.

Doubtless the most notable transportation development in the post–World War II era has been the proliferation of automobile, bus, and truck traffic over a vastly expanded and improved highway system. Not unrelated to the innovations in the highway system was the dramatic change in rail transportation in the postwar era. Beginning shortly after World War II, passenger traffic declined significantly, then precipitously, as the combination of increasing automobile production, more widespread affluence, and the enhancement of highways privatized more and more travel. Some of the same influences made it increasingly difficult for railroads to compete as freight carriers in areas of low traffic density. The railroads first reduced, then totally eliminated passenger service within the state, and they suspended freight service on many branch lines. The trunk lines, however, still carried enormous amounts of freight throughout the 1980s.

Unlike the railroads, river traffic benefited from postwar developments. Extensive federal expenditures on locks and dams, in part for purposes of flood control, made it possible to move more freight in the larger barges at almost all periods of the year, and traffic rose significantly, at least on the Ohio, the Tennessee, and the Cumberland. On some of the smaller rivers, however, commercial traffic declined to the vanishing point in the 1970s and especially in the 1980s, and governmental agencies were unwilling to man the locks for the sole benefit of pleasure boaters.

In air traffic, the federal deregulation of the 1980s brought some disarray in the state. Scheduled air service was reduced for many smaller cities and terminated for some. Bus lines were permitted to eliminate unprofitable routes. By the end of the 1980s, Kentucky transportation thus presented a mixed picture. Private automobiles and motor freight carriers had easier access to more of the state than ever before; tremendous volumes of freight flowed along the major rail lines and the major rivers; and air traffic was on the upswing at the largest airports. In many of the commonwealth's smaller communities, however, the residents and businesses alike found themselves not with less access to the outside world, but with fewer transportation alternatives than a half-century before.   LEONARD P. CURRY

TRANSYLVANIA COMPANY. After the Proclamation of 1763, Richard Henderson, a prominent lawyer originally from Virginia, organized a land company to settle the area bounded by the Cumberland, Ohio, and Kentucky rivers. Richard Henderson and Company, seeking opportunities for land settlements, hired notable explorers such as Daniel Boone, Henry Skaggs, and Richard Callaway to scout the wilderness. Boone, who reached the Red River in Kentucky in 1769, has been linked as a secret agent to Henderson's scouting projects, although there is no proof that Boone worked for Henderson before 1773.

Henderson devoted more time to his land company after his term on the North Carolina supreme court expired. On August 27, 1774, along with Thomas Hart, William Johnston, John Williams, John Luttrell, and Nathaniel Hart, Henderson established the Louisa Company from its predecessor, Henderson and Company. The new company was to secure the Cherokee Indians' land titles to the area south of the Ohio and west of the Kanawha River. Henderson and Nathaniel Hart met with the Cherokee in the fall of 1774 and entered into preliminary agreements for the purchase of the land. The organizers of the land company felt so certain that they would obtain the land that they placed advertisements to attract settlers in Virginia and North Carolina newspapers in December 1774. On January 6, 1775, the company was once again reorganized, as the Transylvania Company, and on March 17, 1775, it signed a treaty with the Cherokee at SYCAMORE SHOALS on the Watauga River in present-day Tennessee.

Henderson's plans sent Boone and a party of about thirty axmen in March 1775 to open up the Wilderness Road through Kentucky. On April 1, 1775, they established a fort and settlement named Boonesborough. Henderson arrived at the settlement several weeks later, and the first Transylvania Convention opened on May 23, 1775. Four elected representatives each from Harrodsburg, Boiling Springs, and St. Asaph and six from Boonesborough met from May 23 to 27 at Boonesborough, which was to be the capital of the colony. In only four days the convention not only formed a system of stockholders but also passed nine laws, which addressed acceptable behavior for the citizens and the government of a court system; punishment of criminals; regulation of a militia; prohibition of swearing and Sabbath-breaking; writs of attachment for the payment of debts; clerk's and sheriff's fees; preservation of the range; improvement of horse breeding; and game preservation. The fairly progressive provisions reflected the dependence of the settlers on game for food and on good horses and an ever-ready militia for defense against Indians.

The Transylvania government was to be short-lived. Calling them land pirates, both Governor Dunmore of Virginia and Governor Martin of North Carolina immediately denounced the Transylvania Company's excursions in the West. Other settlers, such as James Harrod, opposed the convention because it would force them to relinquish their earlier land claims to the proprietors. In September 1775, hoping to gain recognition for their colony, the Transylvania Company sent a petition to the Continental Congress asserting the legality of its claim and requesting acceptance as the fourteenth member of the united colonies. Because the proposed Transylvania colony was located within the boundaries of the original Virginia charter, the Continental Congress refused to acknowledge the new colony until sanctioned by Virginia. In March 1776, the Transylvania colony again petitioned the Virginia convention for recognition. While debating this issue in October 1776, the Virginia convention considered a request from George Rogers Clark, representing Harrodsburg, asking the legislature to assume responsibility for the western territory and to make it a political subdivision of Virginia. Such an action would repudiate Henderson's claims. With the support of Virginia Gov. Patrick Henry's petition, Clark's petition succeeded. On December 7, 1776, the legislature created Kentucky County, Virginia, effective December 31, 1776. It compensated Henderson with 200,000 acres in the region of what is now Henderson County, Kentucky, but his dream of creating an independent colony ended.

See John Mason Brown, *The Political Beginnings of Kentucky* (Louisville 1889); William Stewart Lester, *The Transylvania Colony* (Spencer, Ind., 1935).

TRANSYLVANIA UNIVERSITY. Transylvania University is a small liberal arts college in Lexington, Kentucky. In 1780 the Virginia Assembly, in an attempt to foster learning on its Kentucky frontier, chartered a "public school or Seminary of Learning," to which it granted 8,000 acres of land confiscated from British Loyalists as an endowment to be administered by thirteen trustees. Three years later the assembly amended the charter to enlarge the number of trustees to twenty-five, added 12,000 acres to the endowment, and named the school Transylvania Seminary.

The Revolutionary War, conflicts with Indians, and harsh frontier conditions made the establishment of any school difficult. Nevertheless, the trustees authorized a grammar school to be started in the cabin of the Rev. David RICE near Danville, Kentucky, where the first small classes were held in February 1785. This arrangement lasted barely a year when the trustees decided to move the school to Lexington, a rapidly growing community. In 1789 classes were started in a cabin on the outskirts of Lexington, and a year later moved to the home of the Rev. James Moore, who was not only a schoolmaster but also rector of Christ Church, Lexington's first Episcopal church. In 1793 a group of public-spirited citizens purchased a lot, now Gratz Park, built a brick house on it, and offered both to Transylvania if the trustees would agree to locate permanently in Lexington, which they agreed to do. In 1799 Transylvania was combined with nearby Kentucky Academy, a competing Presbyterian school, to form Transylvania University. Law and medical departments, the first in the West, were added to the small liberal arts department, and James Moore was appointed the university's first president. The curriculum was typical of colleges elsewhere, with a strong classical emphasis. Local doctors and lawyers, some of them prominent, such as Dr. Samuel BROWN and Henry Clay, served as faculty in these departments.

In 1802 Moore resigned and the Rev. James Blythe, a staunch Presbyterian, was appointed acting president by the Presbyterian-dominated board of trustees. The school struggled along for fourteen years under his leadership until a successful revolt by liberal trustees against Presbyterian control led to the appointment of the Rev. Horace HOLLEY, a noted Unitarian minister and educational leader in Boston, to the presidency. Holley, a Yale graduate, was a gifted orator and administrator who saw the possibility of creating a notable state university at Transylvania. In 1818 Holley, his wife, Mary Austin, and their two children moved to Lexington.

From 1818 to 1825 Holley worked to bring outstanding faculty to Transylvania, including the eccentric but brilliant naturalist Constantine RAFINESQUE. In addition to the noted surgeon Benjamin DUDLEY, Holley recruited Daniel DRAKE, Charles CALDWELL, and William Short to join the medical department. Holley also recruited two notable lawyers, Jesse BLEDSOE and William T. BARRY, to teach in the law department. Enrollment grew rapidly as word of Transylvania's remarkable improvement spread. A new building had been erected in 1818 to accommodate students as well as classrooms.

During its first two decades of existence, the medical department was little known, but between 1819 and 1859 it achieved eminence nationwide. During those years virtually every state in the expanding nation sent students to Transylvania, some 4,300 in all, of whom 1,800 received M.D. degrees. More than 40 percent of the students were Kentuckians, and over 80 percent came from the slaveholding South and trans-Mississippi West.

Transylvania's medical department had an outstanding faculty, library, scientific apparatus, and natural history collection. In 1829 and again in 1839, faculty members traveled to the Continent and England to purchase books and medical and scientific displays and apparatus for the medical department. On his 1839 purchasing trip to Paris and London, Robert Peter, professor of chemistry, confidently wrote to his wife in Lexington that Transylvania would now be the "best equipped to teach modern medicine." Without effective state or na-

tional regulation, however, medical schools as local enterprises proliferated. In 1820 there were ten schools of MEDICINE in the nation. By 1859 there were nineteen in the South alone, three of them in Kentucky. In 1837, after nearly twenty years at Transylvania, Caldwell persuaded half of the medical faculty to move west and create the Louisville Medical Institute. Transylvania granted its last medical degree in 1859.

Gifted young men, mostly from the southern and western states, who enrolled at Transylvania became professional, political, and business leaders of their regions and of the nation. Among them were Jefferson DAVIS, Albert Sidney JOHNSTON, and David Rice ATCHISON. Many became U.S. senators, two became associate justices of the U.S. Supreme Court, and two became vice-presidents of the United States. This golden era under Holley's leadership was short-lived as he became the target for Presbyterian attacks on his religious liberalism. In addition, Gov. Joseph Desha (1824-28) and the General Assembly withdrew state support, accusing Holley of allowing Transylvania to become an elitist institution. With no substantial financial resources available, Holley despaired of future growth and resigned in 1825.

The main college building burned down in 1829, and the school's academic department barely survived. The medical and the law departments, however, continued to prosper until the 1850s. A gift from Col. James Morrison enabled the trustees to engage Gideon SHRYOCK, a talented Kentucky architect, to design and construct the impressive neoclassical structure, completed in 1833, that dominated the campus and became known as Morrison Hall. The medical department built a separate facility in 1839 to house its activities, library, and apparatus. This building was destroyed by fire in 1863.

Transylvania was substantially revived when the trustees gave effective, if not legal, control of the university to the Kentucky Conference of the Methodist church. The Rev. Henry Bidleman Bascom, a Methodist of great oratorical and administrative ability, was appointed president, and under his leadership in the period of 1842-49 the school's enrollment greatly increased and new faculty members were hired. This period of revival ended in 1850 when a split in the Methodist church over the slavery issue led to the formation of the Methodist Episcopal Church, South, which severed its ties with Transylvania when it realized it did not have complete legal control.

Transylvania declined in all departments during the 1850s despite an attempt to convert it into the state's first normal school. The famed medical department closed its doors in 1859 after having trained more then 6,000 students. During the Civil War, Transylvania operated only as a high school, and its buildings were taken over by the Union army for use as hospitals.

John Bryan BOWMAN, a Mercer County farmer and educational crusader and fund-raiser, had been instrumental in the creation of KENTUCKY UNIVERSITY, a Disciples of Christ institution in Harrodsburg, whose buildings were destroyed during the Civil War. In 1865 he proposed to the trustees of Transylvania that the financial resources of Kentucky University and the physical campus and facilities of Transylvania be combined into one institution, to be called Kentucky University. The Transylvania trustees agreed and the state legislature legalized the fusion. Under Bowman as regent, Kentucky University flourished for a few years, reviving the law department and establishing the College of the Bible (now LEXINGTON THEOLOGICAL SEMINARY), a seminary for training Disciples of Christ ministers. The state even placed its new AGRICULTURAL AND MECHANICAL COLLEGE under the administration of Kentucky University. Sectarian controversy led to Bowman's resignation in 1878. The College of the Bible became a separate legal entity, though it remained on the campus until 1949. The Agricultural and Mechanical College was removed by state action to a new campus on the south end of Lexington. In 1889 Kentucky University became coeducational. Intercollegiate athletics, and fraternities and sororities were added to its activities. It functioned as a small liberal arts college with strong Disciples control until 1908, when it resumed its historic name of Transylvania and the growing A&M College became State University (now University of Kentucky).

Throughout the 1900-40 period Transylvania went through recurring financial crises, and World War II brought it to the brink of collapse. A strong postwar revival was due to the influx of veterans under the G.I. Bill and an innovative general education program under President Raymond McLain. The renaissance of Transylvania continued as Frank Rose became president in 1952. He rescued the college financially and constructed a new library and gymnasium. His administration was followed by the remarkable period of prosperity and physical rebuilding and expansion of the institution under Irvin Lunger from 1957 to 1976, a longer term than that of any other president. Following William Kelly and David Brown, the presidency of Charles Shearer oversaw an unprecedented growth in enrollment, physical facilities, and financial endowment. The prime mover was William T. Young, a Lexington businessman, whose ability to raise funds—including money to improve the quality of the faculty from the Mary and Barry Bingham, Sr. Fund —has greatly increased the university's endowment and provided money for an innovative scholarship program that has brought significant numbers of exceptionally gifted students to Transylvania.

See John D. Wright, Jr., *Transylvania: Tutor to the West* (Lexington, Ky., 1980); Walter Wilson Jennings, *Transylvania: Pioneer University of the West* (New York 1955); Johanna Peter and Robert Peter, *The History of the Medical Department of Transylvania University* (Louisville 1905).

JOHN D. WRIGHT, JR.,
AND ERIC H. CHRISTIANSON

TRAPPISTS. The Trappists are monks of a Roman Catholic order; their name is derived from la Trappe, the site of a French monastery that led a seventeenth century monastic reform movement. The formal name is Order of Cistercians of the Strict Observance. The first group of Trappists came to Kentucky in September 1805, driven out of France by Napoleon and the Revolution. They leased land just south of the Holy Cross churchyard in Marion County, and purchased property in Clementsville on Casey Creek. As they were unable to meet the payments, they left Kentucky in 1809, and they returned to France after Napoleon's fall. During their stay, they had conducted one of the earliest schools in Kentucky.

On December 21, 1848, forty-four Trappists arrived from the monastery of Melleray in western France and founded the abbey of Our Lady of Gethsemani, located ten miles south of Bardstown and four-and-a-half miles west of the earlier cloister at Holy Cross. From 1851 to 1912, the monastery sponsored a boys' school. The founding of a sisterhood, the Franciscan Sisters of Clinton, Iowa, grew out of efforts to establish a school for girls. Two members of the Gethsemani community are noteworthy for their literary work: Raymond Flanagan, who has written at least eighteen books, and Thomas Merton, whose sixty books on spirituality include his highly acclaimed autobiography, *The Seven Storey Mountain*.

Trappists live in silent community and gain the benefits of solitude by locating their monasteries away from population centers. The silence and partial withdrawal from the world are intended to engender communion with God. In addition to daily mass, the monks participate in the seven canonical hours of common prayer, beginning with matins, and spend several hours each day in meditative reading and solitary prayer. Five or six hours each day are devoted to work. The main sources of income at Gethsemani are the sale of cheese and fruitcakes by mail order and of beef cattle from the farm. The monks also maintain and administer the abbey, initiate newcomers into the monastic life, care for the sick and the elderly of the community, and attend to the needs of guests at the retreat house, which can accommodate thirty.

Five monasteries have been founded from Gethsemani (in Georgia, Utah, South Carolina, New York, and California) and it adopted another monastery in Chile. There are twelve houses of Trappists and five of Trappistines (women) in the United States.

See Clyde F. Crews, *An American Holy Land: A History of the Archdiocese of Louisville* (Wilmington, Del., 1987); Eutropius Proust, *Gethsemani Abbey: A Narrative of the Foundation With an Account of Its Present State by Edmund Obrecht* (Gethsemani, Ky., 1899).   FELIX DONAHUE

TRAVEL AND TOURISM, EARLY. Travel in early nineteenth century Kentucky was arduous, and the inns and taverns at frequent intervals along primitive roads were a welcome source of rest, nourishment, and entertainment for weary travelers. Accommodations were limited at the early taverns, where strangers often shared the same room and occasionally the same bed. Meals were served at a common table, and the few inns offering a bathhouse were a welcome relief from the dusty road. By the 1830s, Kentucky had several taverns of national reputation, such as the Galt House in Louisville, Cross-Keys Tavern near Shelbyville, and the Phoenix Hotel in Lexington.

The first stagecoach line in the state started operating in 1803. The stage ran forty-seven miles, from Lexington through Winchester and Mt. Sterling to Olympian Springs, a popular resort in what is now Bath County. The stagecoach soon became the dominant means of travel, with an average speed of seven or eight miles an hour. Stage travel reached its heyday during 1835-52 and was gradually replaced by the railroad during the last half of the century. Like Olympian Springs, most of Kentucky's SPAS closed between 1905 and 1910, with the advent of the automobile.

Actively promoted to paying customers by 1816, Mammoth Cave became Kentucky's first major tourist attraction and the second oldest in the United States, preceded only by Niagara Falls. A stagecoach stop was established in 1827 at Bell's Tavern in Glasgow Junction (now Park City), nine miles from the cave, with visitors completing the journey on foot or horseback. By 1842 a tourist map of Kentucky had been published, with Mammoth Cave prominently noted. Stagecoaches by then arrived directly at the cave, as did steamboats if conditions on Green River were favorable. A large hotel was constructed to accommodate guests, and in 1886 the Mammoth Cave Railroad was established, connecting the cave with the Louisville & Nashville line in Glasgow Junction. Visitors toured the cave by kerosene lantern (one allotted to every fifth hiker), and guides threw torches into the large chambers to illuminate the dark recesses.

Cumberland Falls was the destination for many tourists and fishermen as early as 1850, when the first crude "hotel" was built—a log cabin with two lean-to rooms and an enclosure for horses and mules. By 1875 Socrates Owens had purchased the property and constructed the Cumberland Falls Hotel. In 1888 the proprietors of the facility— Owens and Boswell—advertised their hotel as "Kentucky's Popular Resort." Visitors traveled twelve miles from Cumberland Falls Station at Parker's Lake in joltwagons pulled by mules, a four-hour journey. When parties reached the falls, they crossed the river by wading, rafting, or fording in the wagons. The Cumberland River teemed with all types of fish, and there are accounts of a catfish catch below the falls weighing ninety pounds. The primary method of reaching the falls was wagon transport from Parker's Lake until 1927, when a road was completed from Corbin.

By the 1880s, railroad excursions to popular attractions such as Mammoth Cave were common.

Excursion trains usually originated from the major metropolitan areas of Louisville, Lexington, and Cincinnati, carrying passengers for a day or weekend outing. Excursions to High Bridge, the first cantilevered bridge in North America, were popular by 1881, when a nearby resident, Lucy Lowe, observed in her diary: "There is an excursion to the bridge to day of Cincinnatians & Southern people. I would like to see the many strange faces." At High Bridge Park, visitors enjoyed picnic grounds, riding stables, and a restaurant.

In 1894 Natural Bridge and the spectacularly beautiful Red River Gorge became accessible to the public when the Lexington & Eastern Railway began twice-daily passenger service. In the special excursions on Sundays, ten or more cars arrived from Cincinnati alone. By 1899 over 25,000 people visited Natural Bridge each year, enjoying amenities such as hiking paths, picnic grounds, dining facilities, a dance pavilion, bowling alleys, and a pond for swimming and boating. Those staying overnight were welcome to use tents set on platforms and furnished with cots and cooking utensils. Others chose to travel five miles farther to the L. Park Hotel in Torrent, where one hundred guests could be accommodated, with orchestras from Cincinnati for entertainment.

See John Winston Coleman, Jr., *Stage-Coach Days in the Bluegrass* (Berea, Ky., 1976); Jeannie McConnell Rogers, *The History of Cumberland Falls* (1982).   BETH EVANS COOKE

TRAVELING CHURCH. The Traveling Church was a congregation of perhaps five or six hundred independent Baptists who immigrated to Kentucky from Orange and Spottsylvania counties in Virginia. Leaving behind the discrimination against them by the established church in colonial Virginia, they sought fertile soil. Leaders of the movement were Lewis and Elijah CRAIG and Capt. William Ellis.

In the harvest season of 1781, with some crops still in the fields, the Baptists prepared for the arduous journey to Kentucky. They assembled in their church on the Old Catharpin Road, twenty-two miles below Fredericksburg, where the Rev. Lewis Craig preached to them on the morning of September 29. Ellis sounded the tocsin, and the congregation headed its wagons and herds westward.

The initial destination of the Traveling Church was Gilbert's Creek, at the head of Dick's (now Dix) River near Lancaster, Kentucky. The congregation was on the road from September 29 to early December in 1781. At Fort Chiswell the travelers were forced to abandon their wagons and travel on horseback and on foot. On the second Sunday in December, Lewis Craig placed the church's Bible on a crude stand in the log church at Gilbert's Creek and held the first Kentucky meeting of the congregation.

In time, Traveling Church members founded the South Elkhorn and Providence churches in Fayette and Madison counties, and the Minerva church in Mason County. Lewis Craig, perhaps relinquishing some of his strict Baptist commitments, became a millmaster and distiller in Bourbon (Scott) County. Elijah Craig had a long career as a Baptist minister. Members of the Traveling Church scattered throughout the Kentucky settlements as farmers and landowners, or as ministers.

See Thomas D. Clark, *Kentucky: Land of Contrast* (New York 1968). THOMAS D. CLARK

TRAVIS, MERLE ROBERT. Merle Robert Travis, guitarist, was the son of William Robert and Laura Etta (Latham) Travis, born in Muhlenberg County, Kentucky, on November 29, 1917. He began his career on radio station WGBF-Evansville in Indiana in 1935 and joined Clayton McMichen's Georgia Wildcats band in 1937. About 1940 he went to WLW-Cincinnati. In 1944 Travis moved to California, where he performed on radio and television, led a band that toured the Southwest, and appeared in some forty movies. He originated the "Travis picking style," a three-fingered style of playing melody and rhythm simultaneously on the guitar, using the thumb to maintain a bass rhythm while the forefinger played a syncopated melody on the treble strings. He is credited with designing the first solid-body (flat top) electric guitar, known as the Fender guitar. He and Chet Atkins won the Grammy for the best country instrumental in 1974. Travis was inducted into the Country Music Hall of Fame and the Nashville Songwriters Hall of Fame. He died October 20, 1983, and is buried in Greenville, Kentucky.

See Bob Baxter, "Merle Travis: The Man, the Music," *Guitar Player* 10 (Sept. 1976): 20-21.
CHARLES F. FABER

TREES. Each Kentucky tree species is either a softwood (gymnosperm) or a hardwood (angiosperm). The softwoods (bald cypress, eastern red cedar, hemlock, northern white cedar, pines) bear needle-like or scale-like leaves; they have no flowers or fruits but produce their seeds in cones (in eastern red cedar, the cones are fleshy and berry-like). The hardwoods (ashes, elms, hickories, maples, oaks) bear broad, flat, usually stalked leaves; they have flowers and produce their seeds in fruits. Differences in the "hardness" of wood of commercial softwoods and hardwoods are well known, as in the case of white pine vs. white oak. The hardness of the wood does not necessarily determine the category, however, as in the case of the bald cypress, a softwood, which produces lumber that is "harder" than that of the tulip tree, classified as a hardwood.

About 175 species of native and introduced trees grow wild in Kentucky; of these, some 155 are natives, including the eight softwoods. A "tree" is arbitrarily defined as a woody plant having one well-defined stem no less than three inches in diameter, a definite crown, and a height of at least fifteen feet. There is no clear dividing line in size between trees and shrubs. The exact number of native trees is not known because of uncertainty in at least four areas: (1) the status of some kinds of trees, such as

the number of species of hawthorns in Kentucky; (2) the actual occurrence of some trees reported from Kentucky, such as the trembling aspen; (3) naturalization or persistence and reproduction in the wild of a few kinds of introduced trees, such as the Norway maple; and (4) the size reached by certain woody plants in Kentucky compared with the tree size they reach in other parts of their range.

The native groups with the most species are oaks, seventeen; hawthorns, perhaps fifteen; maples, eight; hickories, six; elms, five; and pines, four. In numbers of individual trees, oaks rank first, maples second, and pines probably third. About eighteen of Kentucky's wild-growing trees were introduced from elsewhere. These include mimosa, Osage orange, paper mulberry, princess tree, tree-of-heaven, white mulberry, and white willow, all well established and often weedy.

In 1990 forest industries involved more than 1,000 firms and 24,000 employees, who every year earn at least $325 million. The annual timber harvest yields more than $900 million. The most valuable trees are hardwoods; among them, white and red oaks, the tulip tree, ashes, and black walnut rank high. Uses for the wood include lumber (flooring, furniture, millwork), railroad ties, pallets, and mine timbers. Various kinds of wildlife depend on trees and forests for food, shelter, and nesting sites. Buds, leaves, twigs, flowers, fruits, seeds, and roots—all are valuable. Especially significant as food for birds and mammals are American holly, black cherry, eastern red cedar, maples, mulberries, oaks, and pines. Under a forest canopy, soil erosion is almost nil and stream quality is protected. When the canopy is removed, erosion is accelerated. Native trees, invading the site, help stabilize it. The planting of trees, too, can help reclaim damaged land, as in surface-mined areas, and may in time create a productive forest.

Kentucky native trees in parks, streets, and yards include American basswood, ashes, birches, black walnut, flowering dogwood, honeylocust, maples, oaks, redbud, sweet gum, and tulip tree. Such trees not only are ornamental but provide shade and protection from wind as well. Many Kentucky trees have long been used in folk medicine. Well known are sassafras, the root bark of which is brewed into a spring tonic, and slippery elm, the inner bark of which is used to brew a tea to treat sore throats, coughs, and digestive troubles. Trees are important as sources of fuel. Christmas trees are grown in plantations (pines, firs, Douglas fir) or collected from the wild (red cedar, pines). Choice wild foods for humans are the fruits of pawpaw and persimmon and the nuts of black walnut, some hickories, and pecan. In western Kentucky "orchards" of wild pecan trees were spared during land clearing.

A few Kentucky trees can poison people and livestock. Some that are dangerous after ingestion are buckeyes (leaves, seeds), mountain laurel and rosebay rhododendron (leaves), Kentucky coffeetree (leaves), black cherry (leaves, fruit pits), and black locust (bark, leaves, seeds).

Kentucky's trees—and forests—have great aesthetic value. As an element of landscape, they may be more valuable for recreation than when cut for lumber or cleared for pasture or cropland. Some Kentucky trees are weedy, invading waste places, fallow fields, and fencerows. Prime examples are ashes, eastern red cedar, persimmon, and sassafras.

A few Kentucky trees are listed in the American Forestry Association's 1988 *National Register of Big Trees*. Kentucky's champions (largest known individuals of their species) are a blue ash at Danville, an Ohio buckeye at Liberty, and a sassafras at Owensboro. The co-champions are a bigtooth aspen in Estill County, a sweet birch in Dewey Lake State Forest, a Kentucky coffeetree at West Liberty, and two chinquapin oaks, one in Montgomery County and one in Breckinridge County.

Tree species rare in the state are the mountain maple and yellow-wood, classified as threatened, and the endangered species Allegheny chinkapin, Carolina silverbell, and American smoketree. Other rare trees are waterlocust and water hickory. There are no trees unique to Kentucky. The state tree is Kentucky coffeetree, a species widely distributed in northeastern United States.

In the mild, humid climate of the Pennsylvanian period, ca. 310 million to 280 million years ago, the wild growing trees of Kentucky were strikingly different from those of today. Huge, spore-bearing trees—giant clubmosses and horsetails—dominated the great coal forests; there were no seed-bearing trees. Beneath the trees were ferns and seed-ferns, both often tree-like and the latter among the first softwoods. The compressed remains of all these, especially clubmosses and horsetails, are the coal that is now so important to the Kentucky economy.

See Mary E. Wharton and Roger W. Barbour, *Trees and Shrubs of Kentucky* (Lexington, Ky., 1973); Kentucky Division of Forestry, *Kentucky's Big Trees* (Frankfort, Ky., 1985).

JOHN W. THIERET

TRIGG, STEPHEN. Stephen Trigg, one of Kentucky's earliest political and military leaders, was born in Bedford County, Virginia, in 1742 to Abraham and Dosia (Johns) Trigg. Trigg helped organize Botetourt County, Virginia, established on February 15, 1770, and was appointed one of the county's first justices. In 1775 he represented Fincastle County—which was formed from Botetourt in 1772 and included southwest Virginia and all of present-day Kentucky—in the Virginia General Assembly. In 1779 Trigg was assigned to the land court, which was designed to settle the many conflicting land claims on Virginia's frontier. As a member of this court, Trigg relocated permanently in Kentucky. According to some accounts, he established a station four miles northeast of Harrodsburg in 1780. Because Trigg traveled freely throughout Kentucky, his station was probably nothing more than a single cabin used on occasion by other settlers in his absence.

After KENTUCKY COUNTY was formed from Fincastle in 1776, Trigg represented the county in the Virginia legislature in 1780 and served as a trustee of the newly created Transylvania University. On January 16, 1781, Trigg was appointed colonel of the militia for Lincoln County, formed from Kentucky County in 1780. On August 19, 1782, Trigg, Col. John Todd, leader of the Fayette County militia, and Daniel Boone led about 180 men into the Battle of BLUE LICKS, one of the worst defeats in frontier history. Trigg and about seventy others perished during the fighting. They were buried in a mass grave on the battlefield.

In 1820 Trigg County was formed out of Christian and Caldwell counties and named in his honor.

TRIGG COUNTY. Trigg County, the sixty-sixth county in order of formation, is located on the southwestern edge of the Pennyroyal region. It is bounded by the Tennessee state line to the south and by Kentucky Lake to the west and contains 421 square miles. Trigg County is surrounded by Calloway, Marshall, Lyon, Caldwell, and Christian counties. It was created on January 27, 1820, and was formed principally from Christian County and a small portion of Caldwell. The county was named for Col. Stephen Trigg, a native of Virginia, who came to Kentucky in the fall of 1779 as a land commissioner. He was fatally wounded on August 19, 1782, in the disastrous Battle of Blue Licks. The first census of 1820 listed Trigg County's population at 3,874 inhabitants. The first government was organized on May 15, 1820, at the house of Samuel Orr in the town of Warrington. The county seat is CADIZ.

The land in Trigg County is comparatively level in the east, with ranges of broken hills in the south and west. Tributaries of the Cumberland and Tennessee rivers that cross the western portion of the county include the Little River. The soil is limestone with a red clay foundation, and farmland in the river and creek valleys is rich and productive. From the time the first settlers arrived, the area has been largely agricultural. Tobacco became the cash crop, and corn and other grains are also grown, as are beef and dairy cattle. Settlement of the county began in the late 1700s.

The politician Linn Boyd probably attained more prominence than any other native Trigg Countian.

During its early years the county's major contact with the outside world was by steamboat on the waters of the Tennessee and Cumberland rivers. Landings at Linton, Canton, and Rock Castle were major shipping points. The coming of a railroad in adjoining Christian County and construction in 1901 of the Cadiz Railroad (abandoned in the late 1980s) to connect with a major line at Gracey was the beginning of the end for local river traffic. Improved highways, particularly the east-west U.S. 68, helped to move Trigg County into Kentucky's mainstream.

In the early 1930s the U.S. government acquired land for military and civilian projects, among them the construction of large dams on the Tennessee and Cumberland rivers, which formed Kentucky and Barkley lakes. The nucleus of the area's water playground, which attracts over a million visitors each year, is Lake Barkley State Resort Park. With the completion of I-24 through the northeastern section of the county, the lake's area became accessible to urban centers to the south, including Nashville.

The center of the county's commerce is Cadiz, the county seat, established in 1820. Other principal areas, none of which is now incorporated, are Canton, Linton, Cerulean, and Montgomery. The population of Trigg County was 8,620 in 1970; 9,384 in 1980; and 10,361 in 1990.

See Trigg County Historical and Preservation Society, *Trigg County, Kentucky: The Past 100 Years, 1885-1985* (Cadiz, Ky., 1987).

VIRGINIA T. ALEXANDER

TRIMBLE, ROBERT. Robert Trimble, U.S. Supreme Court justice, was born in 1777, probably in Augusta County, Virginia. When Trimble was a boy, his father, William, procured a patent to seven hundred acres of unimproved Kentucky land and the family moved to Clark County. Robert and his four brothers spent their boyhoods clearing, tilling, and defending a frontier farmstead. Robert's education was haphazard, but he devoured books given to the family by friends, and was a self-motivated, self-disciplined, uncommonly serious student. In 1795 he entered Bourbon Academy, but illness forced his withdrawal after one year. Following a brief stint as a schoolteacher, he completed the course of study at Kentucky Academy in Woodford County, and read law with George Nicholas and James Brown. In 1800 Trimble was admitted to the Bourbon County bar in Paris, where he lived for the rest of his life.

A staunch Jeffersonian Republican, Trimble intensely disliked the hurly-burly of politics. In 1802 he served in the Kentucky Assembly; five years later, he accepted a post as judge of the Kentucky court of appeals. He resigned the judgeship after only two years, complaining about the low salary and disruptions of family life. Meanwhile, his Paris law practice flourished. Between 1813 and 1817, Trimble served as a district attorney, and developed a reputation for dogged legal research and energetic prosecution. In 1817, when President James Madison commissioned Trimble to serve alongside his friend, Thomas Todd, as judge of the federal district court of Kentucky, he quit his law practice. In 1826 President John Quincy Adams elevated Trimble to the U.S. Supreme Court to replace Todd.

Trimble's tenure on the federal circuit court coincided with a period of economic distress and political turmoil. After 1819, Kentucky's Relief party enacted a system of debt postponement laws, abolished imprisonment for debt, and revised the state's execution statutes; when Todd and Trimble refused to apply Relief party–inspired legislation in federal debt cases, Relief men denounced them as traitors and judicial Federalists. After 1822-23, Todd and Trimble paved the way for several well-known Supreme Court decisions that invalidated the better part of Kentucky's debtor relief system, as in the Marshall court's 1825 rulings, on appeal from the circuit court for the District of Kentucky, in *Bank of the United States v. January* and *Wayman v. Southard*. In such disputes, Trimble refused to question the Supreme Court's hard line against contract abridgement.

On the other hand, Judge Trimble eloquently defended his home state's system of occupying claimant statutes in his 1826 circuit court opinion in the case of *Kincannon v. Owings*; well before the Supreme Court's formal overrule of *Green v. Biddle* in 1831, Trimble was prepared to ignore the terms of the 1789 separation agreement (Virginia Compact) between Kentucky and Virginia in land cases. As associate justice of the Supreme Court, Trimble argued brilliantly (contrary to John Marshall's opinion) in the landmark case of *Ogden v. Saunders* (1827), that, while insolvency laws plainly were invalid when applied retrospectively, they passed constitutional muster when applied to future contracts.

Trimble's tenure on the Supreme Court ended abruptly with his death on August 25, 1828, at home. He was buried in the Paris Cemetery. Kentuckians named Trimble County in his honor.

See Woodford Gardner, "Kentucky Justices on the United States Supreme Court," *Register* 70 (April 1972): 121-42; John Goff, "Mr. Justice Trimble of the United States Supreme Court," *Register* 58 (Jan. 1960): 6-28.

SANDRA F. VANBURKLEO

TRIMBLE COUNTY. Trimble County, the eighty-sixth county in order of formation, is located in northern Kentucky, and the Ohio River forms the county's northern and western boundaries. Bordered by Carroll, Henry, and Oldham counties, Trimble has an area of 146 square miles. The county was formed from sections of Gallatin, Henry, and Oldham counties on February 9, 1837, and named in honor of Robert Trimble, an associate justice of the U.S. Supreme Court. The county seat is BEDFORD.

The topography near the Ohio River is level and highly productive. The remainder of the county is hilly, with steep inclines in some places. Principal streams are the Ohio and Little Kentucky rivers. In 1987 farms occupied 73 percent of the land area, with half of the farmland under cultivation. Trimble County ranked seventy-ninth in the state in 1987 agricultural receipts, of which 70 percent came from crops, including tobacco, corn, hay, sweet pepper, strawberries, and cabbage. The county also produces dairy cattle and hogs.

The first settlers arrived in the late eighteenth century. Around 1805 Richard Ball constructed a cabin on land that later became the county seat of Bedford. By 1800 settlers were coming down the Ohio River on flatboats, and Trimble County was soon settled. Several communities were built during the course of the nineteenth and twentieth centuries. The county seat of Bedford and the town of Milton are the only two incorporated communities.

The proximity of the Ohio River, however, made Trimble County one of the primary destinations of slaves who attempted to escape from their servitude in Kentucky. Delia Webster, the "petticoat abolitionist," was a New England school teacher who used the Preston farm in Trimble County as a refuge for runaway slaves endeavoring to cross the river to freedom.

The Civil War brought division and unrest to Trimble Countians. In the 1860 election, Stephen A. Douglas, Democrat, received 581 votes in Trimble County; the Independent Democrats, led by John C. Breckinridge, polled 84 votes; and the Constitutional Union Party, led by John Bell of Tennessee, received 258 votes. The Republican Party candidate, Abraham Lincoln, received only one vote. During the course of the Civil War, many soldiers from the Trimble County area used a large rock as a repository for letters to their friends and families when passing through the county, and the site became known as the Rock Post Office.

Industrial development came slowly to Trimble County, as it was 1927 before the construction of U.S. 42 and U.S. 421 ended the overland isolation of the county. In the 1870s, the town of Bedford had a wool-carding factory as well as a steam-powered gristmill. In 1957 Fold-Away Basket Company, which manufactures stamped and precoated metal parts, was established. Martin Marietta Aggregates operates a sand and gravel plant at Milton. The county is served by the Seaboard Systems Railway. Recreation brings in revenue for Milton, which is across the Ohio River from Madison, Indiana, where the annual Madison Regatta attracts thousands of hydroplane-racing enthusiasts. The county has twenty-one miles of Ohio River shoreline.

The population of Trimble County in 1970 was 5,349; 6,253 in 1980; and 6,090 in 1990.

See Donna Stark Thompson, *Trimble County Heritage* (N.p., 1989).   RON D. BRYANT

TROUBLESOME CREEK TIMES. The *Troublesome Creek Times* is a colorful weekly newspaper that serves Knott County and is published in Hindman, Kentucky. By 1990 the *Times* had won 220 state and national press awards for excellence since its formation on June 5, 1980. The National Newspaper Foundation named it a national blue ribbon newspaper. The *Times*'s aggressive and investigative news reporting has won several awards, and the layout has been featured in a college textbook on journalism. Noted for its sense of humor, the *Times* publishes an annual April Fool's news edition on its front page. The newspaper was the first charter member of the Associated Press Newsfinder service in Kentucky.   RON DALEY

TROUT, ALLAN M. Allan M. Trout, journalist, was born August 8, 1903, near Churchton, Tennessee. He attended local public schools. After graduating from Dyersburg High School in Dyersburg,

Tennessee, in 1922, he enrolled in Georgetown College in Kentucky. While there, he was a reporter for the *Georgetown Times*, the *Lexington Herald*, and the *Lexington Leader*. After Trout received his A.B. in 1926, he purchased the *Kentucky Times* of Jackson, but the paper failed in early 1929. He joined the *Louisville Courier-Journal* as a reporter on February 15, 1929, and remained with the paper for thirty-eight years.

In 1932 he received an honorable mention for the Pulitzer Prize. He was also awarded the Governor's Medallion twice, in 1959 and 1966, for distinguished public service through journalism. Trout was best known, however, for his daily column, "Greetings!," a collection of musings on both ordinary events and the outstanding happenings of the day. "Greetings!" ran 8,998 times, for a total of nearly 5 million words. Trout also served as the *Courier-Journal*'s senior news reporter for fifteen consecutive regular sessions of the Kentucky General Assembly beginning in 1940. His "Greetings!" columns were compiled and published as *Greetings from Old Kentucky* (1960); he also wrote *Your Kentucky Constitution* (1966). Trout retired in 1967, and that year was awarded an honorary doctor of laws degree by the University of Kentucky. He also served as director of company relations for Investor's Heritage Life Insurance Company of Frankfort, Kentucky.

Trout married Martha Collier in 1934; she died in 1962. He then married Edith Cooper Taylor. Trout died in Frankfort on December 8, 1972, and was buried in the Frankfort Cemetery.

See Mary C. Browning, *Kentucky Authors* (Evansville, Ind., 1968); Kenneth E. Harrell, ed., *The Public Papers of Governor Edward T. Breathitt, 1963-1967* (Lexington, Ky., 1984).

TROYE, EDWARD. Edward Troye, one of the foremost American painters of horses in the nineteenth century, was born Edouard de Troye near Lausanne, Switzerland, on July 12, 1808, of French parents. His father, Jean Baptiste de Troye, was an eminent artist who encouraged his son in the fine arts. Following the death of his mother while Troye was an infant, his father moved the family to England, where Troye studied art. Windsor Castle was the subject of many of his paintings between the ages of ten and fourteen. When he was twenty, Troye settled in Jamaica, then left for the United States, landing in Philadelphia on October 5, 1831. He studied at the Pennsylvania Academy of Fine Arts and worked with the artist John Sartain, reproducing portraits and animal paintings in the form of mezzotint engravings.

Beginning in 1832 Troye traveled throughout the southern states painting blooded horses on plantations and farms. He first visited Kentucky in 1834. In the summer of 1837, he began a series of paintings of purebred livestock for the *Kentucky Stock Book*. His depictions of horses, shorthorn cattle, and jacks for this project survive in the form of thirty-one lithographs. On one of his visits to

Kentucky, Troye became acquainted with Robert Aitcheson Alexander of Woodburn Farm in Woodford County. There he met Cornelia Ann Van de Graaf of Scott County, whom he married on July 16, 1839. The couple lived on her father's farm until 1844, when they sold it to buy a large farm near Paducah in McCracken County. Four children were born to the couple, but only the third, Anna Van de Graaf, survived past infancy.

In the fall of 1849, Troye moved his family to Mobile, Alabama, to become a professor of French and art at Spring Hill College. During the six years he taught there, he continued his travels and painted some of his most notable works, among them *Self Portrait* (1852), now owned by Yale University Library, and the horse painting *Lexington* (1854) for the stable of Frank Harper of Woodford County. Troye left his family in Mobile in 1855 for a two-year trip to Syria, the Holy Land, and Europe with his friend and patron A. Keene Richards of Woodford County. Upon his return to the States, Troye agreed to write the text and paint small oil portraits of stallions with their full pedigrees for a series entitled *The Race Horses of America*. The first issue of twelve pages, published in March 1867, featured the horses Boston and Lexington. It was the only issue published. In the winter of 1869-70, Troye moved to a 750-acre cotton farm in Madison County, Alabama, given to him by his friend Richards. Troye's love for Kentucky made him a frequent visitor at Blue Grass Park, Richards's farm near Georgetown, where he continued to paint despite failing eyesight in his final years.

Troye died on July 25, 1874, of pneumonia. He is buried in Georgetown Cemetery, where his grave is marked with an eight-foot marble muse designed by Richards.

See J. Winston Coleman, Jr., "Edward Troye: Kentucky Animal Painter," *FCHQ* 33 (Jan. 1959); Alexander Mackay-Smith, *The Race Horses of America, 1832-1872: Portraits and Other Paintings by Edward Troye* (Saratoga Springs, N.Y., 1981).

TRUE AMERICAN. On February 19, 1845, Cassius M. Clay, who supported gradual constitutional emancipation of slaves, announced the future publication of his antislavery newspaper, the *True American*, in Lexington. In the heated debate over slavery, other Lexington newspapers had stopped publication of Clay's antislavery articles. He secured a three-story red brick building on North Mill in Lexington for an office. Expecting militant opposition, he fortified the building with muskets, Mexican lances, two brass cannons, and a keg of gunpowder, and he created an escape route through trap doors. The first edition of the *True American* was published on June 3, 1845, and by mid-August it had seven hundred Kentucky subscribers and 2,700 in other states.

Clay became ill with typhoid fever in mid-July, and several of his friends ran the newspaper while he directed from his bed. The newspaper was open to a wide variety of opinions, and on August 12,

1845, a guest article advocated equality for freed blacks, a position different from Clay's. Two days later, Clay faced a group of approximately thirty men outside the courthouse, who had assembled to propose the closing down of the *True American*. He received no hearing from the mob. Later a letter was delivered to his home from a citizens' committee, stating the committee's aim to close down the newspaper for disrupting the peace of the community. The letter hinted that the editor's own safety was in jeopardy. Clay dismissed the letter.

On the morning of August 18, 1845, city Judge George R. Trotter served Clay with an injunction against the newspaper, and the editor handed over the keys to the office. Later that morning, lawyer Thomas F. Marshall addressed more than 1,000 people outside the courthouse in Lexington about what he called the evil doings of Clay and his newspaper. Another citizens' committee was formed, and it resolved to seize the press and send it to Cincinnati. When the group arrived at the *True American* office, Mayor James Logan was on hand. Unable to stop them, Logan warned the group that they were committing a crime and then surrendered the keys. The group stored the press and then moved it to Ohio. Clay later sued the group and received $2,500 in damages.

By October 1845, Clay was again editing the *True American* in Lexington; it was printed in Cincinnati. He stopped editing the newspaper after May 27, 1846, when he joined U.S. forces in the Mexican War. John C. Vaughan took over as editor with Clay's brother, Brutus, as financial adviser and supervisor. The newspaper ceased publication after Northern sponsors refused to support it because of Clay's involvement in the war. Vaughan used Clay's subscriber list and materials to start the *Louisville Examiner*, a small, temperate emancipation paper that lasted until late 1849.

See Lowell Harrison, "Cassius Marcellus Clay and *The True American*," *FCHQ* 22 (Jan. 1948): 30-49.

TUBMAN, EMILY HARVIE (THOMAS). Emily Harvie (Thomas) Tubman, an emancipationist, was born on March 21, 1794, in Ashland, Virginia, to Edmund and Anne Thomas. Her father became registrar of the Kentucky Land Office, and the family moved to Kentucky, settling between Lexington and Paris, when Emily was a child. Her father died when she was ten, and Henry Clay, a close friend of the family, became her legal guardian. She was probably educated in private schools in the Frankfort area.

In 1818 Emily moved to Augusta, Georgia, to live with Col. Nicholas Ware's family for the winter. She married Richard Tubman, an Englishman from Maryland, in 1818. Her husband died in 1836 and left her with a vast estate in Georgia, which she managed with expertise. In addition to running several large plantations, Emily Tubman also operated a textile mill. She was generous with her fortune, contributing to Kentucky schools, including

Midway's Orphan School, Kentucky University, and Millersburg College, and she donated nearly $30,000 in 1872 to rebuild the Frankfort Christian Church after it had been destroyed by fire.

In 1842 Tubman gave her slaves the choice of remaining in her household or being freed to join a colony that emancipationists had established in Liberia on the west coast of Africa. Of her 144 slaves, seventy-five chose to stay and the remainder opted for the freedom of the Liberia colony. She made their transportation arrangements to Liberia via Baltimore. They settled at Harper, a city in Maryland County, Liberia. A town was named after the Tubman family in Maryland County, Liberia, and William V.S. Tubman, the grandson of two of her former slaves, became the eighteenth president of Liberia, serving during 1944-71.

Tubman died on June 9, 1885, in Augusta, Georgia, and was buried next to her husband in the Frankfort Cemetery in Kentucky.

See Nettie Henry Glenn, *Early Frankfort Kentucky, 1786-1861* (Frankfort, Ky., 1986).

TUCKER, CHARLES EUBANK. Charles Eubank Tucker, minister and civil rights leader, was born in the British West Indies in 1896. He received his elementary and intermediate education in the West Indies, completing his schooling there at Beckford-Smith College in Spanishtown, Jamaica, in 1915. He continued his education in the United States, at Lincoln and Temple universities in Pennsylvania, during 1917-19. Tucker was ordained into the ministry of the African Methodist Episcopal (AME) Zion Church in 1918 at the Philadelphia-Baltimore AME Conference. Livingston College awarded him an honorary D.V.R. of divinity in 1956. Tucker was an active leader in the AME church, serving as pastor of congregations in several states, including Pennsylvania, Alabama, Mississippi, Georgia, Florida, Indiana, and the Stoner Memorial Church in Louisville. He was a presiding elder of the AME Zion Church for years and in 1956 was elevated to the bishopric, the first presiding elder to hold that position.

Tucker was also a noted leader in the struggle for civil rights in the United States. He was the leader of numerous demonstrations in Louisville during the 1940s, 1950s, and 1960s. He began sit-ins in the Louisville bus station and other segregated facilities ten years before the Student Nonviolent Coordinating Committee popularized the tactic throughout the country. A staunch Republican, he was one of the few prominent blacks to support the election of Richard M. Nixon in 1968, and he delivered the benediction at Nixon's 1969 inauguration. He died December 25, 1976.

See George C. Wright, *Life Behind a Veil: Blacks in Louisville, Kentucky, 1865-1930* (Baton Rouge, La., 1985).

TUG FORK. The Tug Fork of the Big Sandy River is 140 miles in length. From its headwaters in extreme southwestern West Virginia, it flows north-west, forming the boundary between Kentucky and West Virginia for ninety-four miles. Tug Fork's major Kentucky tributaries are the Pond, Big, Wolf, and Rockcastle creeks. The Tug joins the Levisa Fork at Louisa in Lawrence County, forming the Big Sandy River, which flows north and empties into the Ohio River at Catlettsburg. At one time the Tug was an avenue of slack-water navigation, with a lock and dam and steamboat travel. Now it provides recreational fishing for area residents.

CAROL CROWE-CARRACO

TUGGLE, KENNETH HERNDON. Kenneth Herndon Tuggle, politician, was born June 12, 1904, to Jesse D. and Sue Gregory (Root) Tuggle at Barbourville in Knox County. Tuggle graduated from the Union College Academy in 1920 and received a law degree from the University of Kentucky in 1926. He later received an honorary LL.D. from Union College. Tuggle was admitted to the Kentucky bar in 1926 and practiced law from 1927 until 1943 in Barbourville. In 1934 he helped organize the Union National Bank of Barbourville and was its chairman until 1953. He was the Republican candidate for attorney general in 1939 but was defeated. In 1943 he was elected lieutenant governor over Democrat candidate William H. May by a vote of 265,833 to 264,793. From 1950 to 1952 Tuggle was a member of the state Council on Resources and Functions. In 1953 President Dwight D. Eisenhower appointed Tuggle to the Interstate Commerce Commission, a position he held until retirement in 1975. He served as chairman of the agency in 1959, and as head of the motor carrier division from 1968 to 1975. Tuggle was considered one of the government's leading experts on the railroad industry.

Tuggle was active in community affairs and served forty-two years on Union College's board of trustees. He married Vivian Shifley of Barbourville on August 20, 1938, and they had two children, Sarah and Kenneth. Tuggle died February 17, 1978, and was buried in the Barbourville Cemetery.

WILLIAM SHERMAN OXENDINE

TURFWAY PARK. Turfway Park is a thoroughbred racetrack on a 241-acre tract of land in Florence, Kentucky, that Nashville developer Jerry L. Carroll purchased on April 9, 1986. Growth was assured with the start of intertrack wagering throughout the commonwealth. Before 1986 the track was known as Latonia. The "Old Latonia" track, which opened for business in 1883 in Latonia, a suburb of Covington, offered some of the finest racing in the Midwest. The Latonia Derby ranked in stature with the Kentucky Derby at its zenith. Fifteen Kentucky Derby winners either won or placed in the Latonia Derby. Competition from other, more populous racing centers in the Midwest closed Old Latonia in August 1939. Twenty years later, the "New Latonia" track was built, drawing a crowd of 11,117 on August 27, 1959, to welcome the thoroughbred sport back to northern Kentucky. Latonia introduced night thoroughbred racing on March 29,

1969, and was the first track in Kentucky to offer Sunday racing, on December 7, 1980.

Turfway Park's showcase event is the Grade II Jim Beam Stakes. The 1⅛-mile test for three-year-olds is a major preparatory race leading to the Kentucky Derby, Preakness, and Belmont Stakes, thoroughbred racing's Triple Crown.

CHARLES SCARAVILLI

TURNER, MARIE (ROBERTS). Political leader and educational reformer, Marie (Roberts) Turner was the daughter of John and Louraine (Watts) Roberts, born in Hindman, Knott County, Kentucky, in 1900. She moved with her family to Breathitt County, and at age seventeen became a teacher at Leatherwood Creek. In the winter of 1919, she married Ervine Turner, and together they created a political machine that dominated Breathitt County for nearly forty years.

Marie Turner succeeded her husband as county school superintendent in 1931 and she began work to modernize Breathitt's educational system by abolishing one-room schools. Turner used the patronage that came with her position, and her husband used his influence as state senator. Through their efforts, the county secured desperately needed school funding. In the 1940s and 1950s Marie Turner testified several times before the U.S. Congress on the need for aid to education. During President Lyndon Johnson's War On Poverty, she obtained funds to build the Lyndon B. Johnson Elementary School on the North Fork of the Kentucky River, then one of the most modern educational facilities in the country.

After she resigned from the superintendent's office on June 22, 1969, Turner's administration was accused of conflict of interest and mismanagement of funds. It was alleged that Turner had rented the superintendent's office space in a building her family owned and had obtained federal funds to enhance her political power. These charges, however, were not substantiated. Some county residents criticized her school consolidation plan, claiming it was not the answer to Breathitt's education problems. Nevertheless, many believe that Turner did much to bring better quality education to her county.

Turner died on March 26, 1984, and was buried in the Jackson Cemetery.

TYLER SETTLEMENT. The 600-acre Tyler Settlement, a rural historic district, is the first such area that has been fully documented in Kentucky. Located in eastern Jefferson County, it is made up of three surviving farms established by Edward Tyler and his family in the 1780s. These properties retain many of the structures of the farm units. The settlement was a family community complete with its own system of interconnecting roads and a centrally located cemetery. The Tylers were surveyors whose advanced road system offered access not only to their own farms but to the surrounding community as well. The old Moses Tyler farm, Blackacre, has been restored almost to its original condition. It contains an Appalachian style double-crib log barn, a loom house, a springhouse, a smokehouse, a quarry, and a nineteenth century brick farm home. Blackacre and 170 acres of surrounding property were established as a nature preserve in 1979. The preserve is owned by the Commonwealth of Kentucky and managed as an environmental education site by the Jefferson County public schools.

JOELLEN TYLER JOHNSTON

TYRA, CHARLES EDWARD. Charles Edward Tyra, basketball player, was born in Louisville on August 16, 1935, to William and Margaret (Hagan) Tyra. After graduating from Louisville's Atherton High School, Tyra played basketball for the University of Louisville (1953-57). During his university career, the six-foot, eight-inch center averaged 18.2 points and 17 rebounds a game. Tyra was a Helms Foundation All-American player during both his junior and senior years. He led the University of Louisville basketball team to its first National Invitational Tournament (NIT) victory, playing against the University of Dayton on March 24, 1956, in New York City. Tyra was named most valuable player of the 1956 NIT. During his career at Louisville, the basketball team accumulated an 88-23 record and played in the NIT in three consecutive years. Tyra amassed 1,617 rebounds in his career, one of the school's all-time highs. He holds the school's career record for free throws, 448 points. In one game against Notre Dame, Tyra scored 40 points. His No. 8 jersey was retired after his playing career ended at the university.

Following graduation, Tyra played for two professional basketball teams—the New York Knickerbockers during 1957-61 and the Chicago Bulls during the 1961-62 season. In 1990 Tyra was associated with the St. Joe Paper Company in Anchorage, Kentucky. Tyra married Sylvia Saunders on March 4, 1957; they have five children: Charles Edward, Jr., Terry Thomas, Robin Marie, Vincent John, and Kelly Sue.

See Dave Kindred, *Basketball, the Dream Game in Kentucky* (Louisville 1976).

MARGARET L. MERRICK

U

UNCLE TOM'S CABIN. Harriet (Beecher) Stowe's fiery antislavery novel, published in 1852, is believed to have been influenced by what she had seen and heard of slavery in Kentucky. The Connecticut-born author had visited Kentucky while living in Cincinnati, where her father was president of Lane Theological Seminary; she married Calvin Stowe, then a professor at Lane, during her residence there.

Harriet Stowe explained in *A Key to Uncle Tom's Cabin* (1853) that many of her characters—slaves and others—were composites of people she had heard about or met. She noted that the slave Josiah HENSON, who once lived on the Amos Riley plantation near Blackford Creek in northeastern Daviess County, Kentucky, and who later became a clergyman in Canada, was one of the inspirations for the character she called Uncle Tom. She is believed to have obtained most of her information about Henson from his 1849 autobiography. In 1833 Stowe visited the family of Col. Marshall Key in the town of Washington, in Mason County, where she is believed to have seen slaves being sold in front of the Maysville courthouse and to have observed slave life at a nearby plantation.

Another Kentucky site from which Stowe may have drawn impressions for her novel is the Garrard County community of Paint Lick, where Revolutionary War veteran Gen. Thomas Kennedy and his son owned a large plantation and many slaves. Lewis Clark, an escaped slave from Kentucky who was acquainted with Stowe and who was born near Paint Lick, implied in an 1846 narrative of his life that he had once belonged to the Kennedys. His description of people and events during his years as a Kentucky slave closely parallel those of Stowe's fictional character, George Harris.

See Johanna Johnston, *Runaway to Heaven: The Story of Harriet Beecher Stowe* (Garden City, N.J., 1963).   BYRON CRAWFORD

UNDERGROUND RAILROAD. Kentucky counties with the largest slave populations were all within 125 miles of the Ohio River, the seven-hundred-mile border that separated commonwealth bondsmen from free soil. The nearness of the river made running away the best option for many slaves who hoped to attain freedom. Not even the restrictions placed upon Kentucky slaves, including the 1798 slave code, a series of ever-tightening fugitive slave laws, and a system of patrols organized at the county level, could prevent some fugitives from escaping across the Ohio.

Deciding to flee to free soil north of the Ohio River was a difficult choice for Kentucky slaves. Love of family constrained parents to take their children, but secretly uniting the family when the members lived on separate farms was difficult and dangerous. Roads were poor and difficult to follow, yet asking directions aroused suspicion and sometimes led to arrest. The Ohio River, the most formidable barrier, thwarted many escapes, resulting in capture or death. Northern whites frequently proved to be as hostile as slaveowners, betraying or capturing fugitives for rewards. Such obstacles explain why in 1850 the U.S. census reported only ninety-six fugitives from Kentucky's 210,981 slaves and in 1860 just 119 escapes, or one for each 1,900 bondsmen.

Assistance from the underground railroad became a part of the antislavery legend. Traditional accounts of the underground railroad tell of a network of "conductors," mostly whites, who led runaways from one safe house to another, until fugitives reached Canada and freedom. There were, of course, a few notable whites, such as Calvin Fairbanks and Delia A. Webster, and a few less-well-known blacks, including Horace Morris and Elijah Anderson, who risked their lives to rescue Kentucky slaves. But very few whites or blacks in fact entered Kentucky to lead slaves to free soil. Kentucky slaves who fled their homes because they feared being sold south typically traversed the commonwealth without the aid of abolitionists. Most had no contacts in the North and, upon crossing the Ohio River they sought aid in the nearest black community, commonly at a black church. A friendly first contact frequently put the runaways in touch with abolitionists associated with the underground railroad and resulted in assistance, from station to station, to Canada. Some of Kentucky's most well-known successful fugitives include Josiah HENSON, who fled a Mason County owner; Henry BIBB, who ran away from a Trimble County farm; and Lewis Clarke, who escaped from Madison County.

See Larry Gara, *The Liberty Line: The Legend of the Underground Railroad* (Lexington, Ky., 1961).
MARION B. LUCAS

UNDERWOOD, JOHN COX. John Cox Underwood, lieutenant governor of Kentucky, was born on September 12, 1840, in Georgetown, Kentucky, to Joseph Rogers and Elizabeth (Cox) Underwood. His father served in the U.S. Congress. Underwood spent most of his childhood in Bowling Green. Shortly after receiving a degree in 1862 from Rensselaer Polytechnic Institute in New York City, Underwood joined the Confederate army and served as a military engineer in Virginia and Tennessee. After the Civil War, Underwood returned to Bowling Green, pursued a career as an engineer and architect, served as city mayor (1870-71), and edited a newspaper for a few years. He was elected lieutenant governor of Kentucky in 1875, but his 1879 bid for the governorship failed when the Democratic nomination went to Luke P. Blackburn of Louisville. During the 1880s Underwood edited a newspaper in Cincinnati.

In the early 1890s Underwood agreed to raise money for a Confederate monument and museum at

Richmond, Virginia, but lawsuits and countersuits over the project consumed Underwood's fortune and ruined his health. During the legal battle, eleven portraits of Confederate leaders commissioned by Underwood and completed by artist E.F. Andrews were abandoned in a Covington, Kentucky, warehouse. Auctioned in 1910 to pay the storage bill, most of the life-sized canvases were taken to Virginia. Portraits of Gen. John C. Breckinridge, Tennessee Gov. Isham Harris, and Adm. Raphael Semmes belong to the Kentucky Museum at Western Kentucky University.

Underwood and his wife, the former Drucilla Duncan, had two children, Drucilla and Helen. He died on October 26, 1913, in New York City and was buried in Bowling Green.

NANCY D. BAIRD

UNDERWOOD, JOSEPH ROGERS. Joseph Rogers Underwood, congressman and Unionist, was born on October 24, 1791, in Goochland County, Virginia. As a child, Underwood went to live with his uncle, Edmund Rogers, in Barren County, Kentucky. After graduating from Transylvania University in Lexington, he studied law with Robert Wickliffe, saw action during the War of 1812, established a law office in Glasgow, Kentucky, and served in the state legislature (1816-20). In 1823 Underwood moved to Bowling Green. He ran unsuccessfully for lieutenant governor in 1828 and sat on the bench of the Kentucky court of appeals during 1828-35. An anti-Jackson man turned Whig, Underwood served in the U.S. House of Representatives (March 4, 1835, to March 3, 1843) and the U.S. Senate (March 4, 1847, to March 3, 1853). During his congressional career he opposed the distribution of surplus revenues, the "gag rule" prohibiting debate on the question of slavery, the Mexican War, and acquisition of western territory. He applauded Henry Clay's compromise of 1850.

An outspoken emancipationist, Underwood sent his own able-bodied slaves to a colony in Liberia and urged that other owners do likewise. When the slavery and states' rights issues climaxed in 1860, Underwood campaigned in Kentucky for the Constitutional Union party and the following year returned to the state legislature as a Democrat to fight the secession movement. (Two of his sons, however, supported the Confederacy.) Underwood spent two terms in the wartime legislature, attended the Democratic National Convention in Chicago in 1864, and aided in reorganizing the party in Kentucky.

Underwood and his first wife, Eliza Trotter, had four children who survived infancy—Eugene, Julia, Eliza, and Jane; Sen. Oscar W. Underwood of Alabama was one of their grandchildren. Underwood and his second wife, Elizabeth Cox of Georgetown in the District of Columbia, also had four children who grew to adulthood—John Cox, Robert, Elizabeth, and Josephine. John Cox Underwood served

as mayor of Bowling Green (1870-71), and lieutenant governor of Kentucky (1875-79).

Underwood died August 23, 1876, and was buried in Bowling Green's Fairview Cemetery.

See Jean E. Keith, "Joseph Rogers Underwood: Friend of African Colonization," *FCHQ* 22 (April 1948): 117-33.   NANCY D. BAIRD

UNDERWOOD, THOMAS RUST. Thomas Rust Underwood, journalist and U.S. congressman, was born to Thomas Cuthbert and Frances Pettris (Rust) Underwood on March 3, 1898, in Hopkinsville, Kentucky. He was educated in the public schools in Hopkinsville and graduated in 1917 from the University of Kentucky. While at the university, Underwood began reporting for the *Lexington Herald*. He served as sports editor, state editor, managing editor, and general manager (1931-35) before succeeding Desha Breckinridge as editor in chief (1935-56). He served as a member of the state planning board (1931-35), secretary of the state racing commission (1931-43, 1947-48), secretary of the National Association of State Racing Commissioners (1934-48), and assistant to the director of the Office of Economic Stabilization (1943). Underwood represented the 6th Congressional District in the U.S. House of Representatives from January 3, 1949, to March 17, 1951; he resigned after Gov. Lawrence W. Wetherby (1950-55) appointed him to a vacant seat in the U.S. Senate at the death of Virgil M. Chapman. Underwood served from March 19, 1951, to November 4, 1952. Underwood was unsuccessful in his bid for reelection, losing to Republican John Sherman Cooper, and he returned to his editorial duties at the *Herald*.

He was married to Eliza McLean on June 20, 1925; they had two children, Thomas and Walter. Underwood died on June 29, 1956, in Lexington, and was buried in the Lexington Cemetery.

UNDERWOOD, WARNER LEWIS. Born August 7, 1808, in Goochland County, Virginia, Warner Lewis Underwood, state and U.S. legislator, was the brother of Joseph R. UNDERWOOD. He studied law at the University of Virginia, briefly practiced law in Bowling Green, Kentucky, and in 1833 moved to Texas, where he served as attorney general for the republic's eastern district. Returning to Bowling Green in 1840, he represented Warren County in the state legislature, 1848-53, and the 3d District in the U.S. Congress, March 4, 1855, to March 3, 1859.

On the eve of the Civil War, slaveowner Underwood shared the anti–Abraham Lincoln, pro-Union sentiments of many residents of the state and in 1860 campaigned for Constitutional Union presidential candidate John Bell. His outspoken sentiments placed his family and property in jeopardy when several thousand Confederate troops camped on Underwood's farm during their occupation of south-central Kentucky. Before the army retreated southward, the troops destroyed Underwood's home.

Shortly thereafter, President Lincoln appointed Underwood consul to Glasgow.

One of the Kentuckian's major duties in Scotland was keeping the president apprised of Confederate shipbuilding operations, a distasteful assignment to Underwood, who in the early autumn of 1864 resigned his position. He practiced law for two years in San Francisco and then returned to Bowling Green.

Underwood and his wife, the former Lucy Craig Henry, were the parents of a large family—Henry L., Frances R., Juliet B., Lucy, Johanna L., John, and Mary. Underwood died March 12, 1872, and was buried in Fairview Cemetery, Bowling Green.

NANCY D. BAIRD

UNDERWOOD-HOLBROOK FEUD. One of postbellum Kentucky's first mountain feuds, the Underwood-Holbrook violence occurred in western Carter County during 1877-79. During the course of sporadic fighting that claimed at least a dozen lives, the followers of Squire V. Holbrook and George Stamper waged a war of extermination against the clan of George Underwood. Led by Capt. Alfred Underwood, the many sons of "Old George" formed the nucleus of a pro-Union guerrilla band that earned a reputation for horse stealing during the Civil War. By war's end the Underwoods, who were described in the *New York Times* as the "James-Younger Gang" of Kentucky, were regarded by many as outlaws.

The organization of a vigilance committee by Squire Holbrook in 1873 led to death threats from the Underwoods and sowed the seeds of the feud. When Old George offered sanctuary to alleged outlaws in June 1877, the Holbrook-Stamper factions banded together to eliminate what they termed a nest of criminals. In the fighting that followed, the Underwoods were supported by John P. Martin, a key figure in the notorious Martin-Tolliver Feud in adjacent Rowan County, and James C. ("Clabe") Jones, a Knott County feudist of the 1880s. Gov. James McCreary (1875-79) sent the militia to the area on July 7 and an uneasy truce was maintained for over a year.

The assassination of Elverton Underwood on May 22, 1879, bred further violence. On September 5, 1879, following the death of an Underwood, Squire Holbrook was shot from ambush. His death was quickly followed by the killings of William and Jesse Underwood, and the brutal murder of Old George by masked REGULATORS on October 12. The extermination of all the adult members of the Underwood clan in Kentucky brought the feud to a close. Although overshadowed by other mountain feuds, the Underwood war contributed to the climate of violence that sparked the Regulator movement and the Martin-Tolliver feud. The vendetta also contributed to the image of lawlessness that plagued Kentucky in the late nineteenth century.

See Harold Wilson Coates, *Stories of Kentucky Feuds* (Cincinnati 1942). JAMES M. PRICHARD

UNION COLLEGE. Union College in Barbourville, Kentucky, was founded in 1879 by a group of progressive citizens of the town. The first building was formally opened the next year. The college was purchased by the Kentucky Conference of the Methodist Episcopal Church in 1886; Daniel Stevenson served as the first president (1888-97). A major bequest from Fanny (Henning) Speed of Louisville led to the construction of Speed Hall, Stevenson Hall, and Centennial Hall.

After the college curriculum was discontinued in 1908, Union was maintained as a junior college, an academy, and an elementary school. In 1922, during the presidency of Ezra T. Franklin (1915-28), Union became a four-year college again and was recognized as such by the University of Kentucky in 1927. During the 1920s, the Memorial Gymnasium and a president's home were built.

President John Owen Gross (1929-38) emphasized improvement of the curriculum. In 1932 Union College received full accreditation when it became a member of the Southern Association of Colleges and Secondary Schools. In 1937 it was placed on the accredited list of the board of regents of the University of the State of New York. During Conway Boatman's presidency (1938-59), the curriculum was expanded, the endowment increased, and seven new buildings were completed. After Mahlon A. Miller was elected president in 1959, the college introduced the master of arts in education degree; developed College Park, a faculty residential area; and constructed additional student housing, a physical education building, the student center, and the science center. Under Jack C. Phillips, who became president in 1983, enrollment has increased significantly and the physical plant has expanded to include a $1.5 million library addition and a $2.1 million cafeteria.

Union College draws most of its students from central Appalachia, and its commitment to the area is manifested in unique academic programs based on regional characteristics, student financial aid, and community service projects for students. Classes are small, and the basic liberal arts curriculum is supplemented by developmental and remedial programs and by new career-oriented studies. A number of courses are taught off-campus in various communities surrounding Union, and the college offers credit and noncredit continuing-education courses and programs geared to the educationally disadvantaged.

In addition to training students for service-oriented professions in the Appalachian region, including teaching and the ministry, Union College serves as a cultural center for all of southeastern Kentucky.

See W.G. Marigold, ed., *Union College 1879-1979* (Barbourville, Ky., 1979).

MILTON H. TOWNSEND

UNION COUNTY. The fifty-sixth county in order of formation, Union is located in western Kentucky. Bordered by the Ohio and Tradewater rivers, and Crittenden, Henderson, and Webster counties, Union has an area of 343 square miles. It was formed from part of Henderson County on January 15, 1811, and was probably named for the unanimous agreement of its citizens to create a new county. MORGANFIELD is the county seat.

Union County's topography is level to hilly. Ninety-four percent of the land is farmland, of which 83 percent is in cultivation. The county since the Civil War has been a top producer of livestock and grain. In 1870 livestock numbered 31,000, and 801,745 bushels of grain were produced. In 1987 Union ranked ninth among counties in agricultural receipts from soybeans, corn, cattle, and hogs.

There are many Native American burial and ceremonial mounds in Union County. In 1987 more than 1,000 of the graves were desecrated by relic collectors, and in 1988 the General Assembly made such an act a class D felony. That year, more than two hundred Native Americans held a reburial ceremony of the recovered remains taken from Union County graves.

Union County was settled during the westward migration following the Revolutionary War. The river towns of Caseyville and Unionville were incorporated, along with the towns of Sturgis, Morgantown, and Waverly. Marshes near Slim Island, Dennis O'Man, and Goose Pond ditches and the wildlife areas of Higginson, Henry, and Jenny Hole-Timber Slough are managed to provide a haven for ducks and geese, as well as game in controlled hunting situations.

In July 1862 Union troops from a Federal gunboat on the Ohio River arrived in Caseyville and took all the town's residents prisoner, charging them with treason. All but nineteen were released. With a slave population of over 2,000 in 1860, many Union Countians supported the Confederacy. Confederate Col. Nathan Bedford Forrest and his command entered the county in late 1861. On September 1, 1862, a Union detachment was defeated in a skirmish at Morganfield.

After the Civil War, the Louisville & Nashville Railroad (now CSX Transportation) brought freight and passenger service to Union County. In 1905 a three-story opera house was built in Morganfield. During World War II, CAMP BRECKINRIDGE Training Center was established near Morganfield, and between 1942 and 1946 more than 30,000 infantry recruits were trained there, and more than 1,300 captured German and Italian prisoners of war were interned there. In 1965 the Breckinridge Job Corps Center, which teaches vocational courses, was established on eight hundred acres of the original camp land. The Job Corps Center provided a labor pool for Union County industries. In 1989 twenty manufacturers employed 1,010 in industries such as furniture and automotive parts production and the rebuilding of coal-mining equipment. Transportation needs are met by U.S. 60, Tradewater Railway Company, a feeder line to the Paducah & Louisville Railroad, and CSX Transportation, as well as a nine-foot navigation channel on the Ohio River. In 1989 crude oil production reached 560,919 barrels.

Recreational facilities include Uniontown's boat dock on the Ohio River, the 5,420-acre Higginson-Henry Wildlife Area, Moffit Lake, the Corn Festival at Morganfield, and the Union County Fair Horse Show at Sturgis.

The population of Union County was 15,882 in 1970; 17,821 in 1980; and 16,557 in 1990.

See *History of Union County, Kentucky* (Evansville, Ind., 1886); *Union County: Past and Present* (Louisville 1941). RON D. BRYANT

UNITAS, JOHN CONSTANTINE. John Constantine Unitas, Hall of Fame football quarterback, was born to Leonard and Helen (Superfiski) Unitas on May 7, 1933, in Pittsburgh. He quarterbacked at St. Justin's High School in Pittsburgh. University of Louisville offered him a scholarship, and Unitas played there for four years (1951-54). The Cardinals rarely won, but Unitas threw twenty-seven touchdown passes during his career and set a school record with four in one game in 1951. Unitas was selected by the Pittsburgh Steelers in the ninth round of the 1955 National Football League (NFL) draft, was subsequently released, and was playing sandlot football for $6 a game when a Baltimore Colts scout discovered him. He played most of his career with the Colts (1956-72), and finished with the San Diego Chargers (1973-74). He led the Colts to the Super Bowl in 1969 and 1970; was the NFL's most valuable player in 1957, 1964, and 1967; made Pro Bowl appearances in 1957-59, 1964-65, and 1967; was voted player of the decade in 1970; and was elected to the Pro Football Hall of Fame at Canton, Ohio, in 1979.

After leaving football, Unitas was a broadcaster with CBS Sports and a restaurateur in Baltimore; he then became a marketing representative for Atlantic Electric Corporation. His first wife was Dorothy Jean Hoelle; they have five children. He then married Sandra Lemon; they have three children.

UNITED MINE WORKERS OF AMERICA. Unions among U.S. coal miners had existed for about forty years when 350 delegates from the Knights of Labor and the Miners and Mine Laborers met in Columbus, Ohio, on January 25-28, 1890, to form the United Mine Workers of America (UMW). Five Kentuckians participated, including William Webb of Laurel County, who was elected to the national executive board.

The union has had a checkered history in Kentucky. Its original membership, including Webb, largely derived from the Knights of Labor. The new union's first district was No. 19 in southeastern Kentucky, with Webb as leader. He organized District 23 (western Kentucky) in 1892 but it failed to survive. Internal dissension and economic troubles broke up District 19 in 1895. By 1897 both districts had been reorganized.

In the early 1900s the coal industry in eastern Kentucky expanded, with the mines growing in size and largely in the hands of absentee owners who successfully resisted unionization. By 1910 the operators in the old District 19 refused to renew their contract, and the district office was reduced to a skeleton staff with a handful of locals. Western Kentucky remained split approximately 50-50 between union and nonunion miners until 1924-25. Eastern Kentucky remained nonunion until 1933 except for the World War I years, when the national administration required some measure of union recognition. After the war ended and Republicans took over the White House, nonunion status returned.

John L. Lewis, who became the international president in 1920, concentrated power into his hands. District presidents were his men and often not from Kentucky. His ironclad decisions regarding the 1924 strike led to a split in District 23 and the union did not return until the mid-1930s. Lewis took advantage of pro-union laws under the Franklin D. Roosevelt administration (1933-45) and organized eastern Kentucky completely, although Harlan County did not come into his fold until 1940-41. Western Kentucky continued split until Lewis intervened with the Riggs National Bank in Washington, D.C., to grant Cleveland industrialist Cyrus Eaton a loan so that he could buy control of the largest producers in western Kentucky. In return, Eaton recognized the union, around the time of the outbreak of the Korean War in 1950.

After 1945 rail mines declined as the dominant operation in the mountains, and the industry lost its domestic and railroad markets. For the most part, this made only truck mines profitable, and they were of such a size that they refused to sign a union contract. In eastern Kentucky, as a result, there was a decline in union miners, with only a few locals continuing. The size of the organization in 1933 had split the mountains into Districts 19 and 30, with some Kentucky locals going into District 28. The districts had only a fraction of the former members, but many retirees kept their union cards. The gains in western Kentucky proved temporary, as the coal miners there have been split 50-50 between union and nonunion since the early 1960s. Western Kentucky unionists have largely been strong for Lewis and those who carried his colors in the search for union office. When Arnold Miller won the international presidency in 1972, they in the main opposed Miller and never worked fully with him.

In western Kentucky, the UMW suffered a defeat in 1990 when it sought for the second time to organize the workers at Pyro Mines, one of the largest employers. On the other hand, in eastern Kentucky the dominance of truck mines or smaller units has prevailed and in only a few counties are there rail mines of significant size. Moreover, except for several counties around Harlan, strip mines are in the majority. Since 1960 the union's only major victory in eastern Kentucky came at the Duke Power Company's mine at Eastover in Harlan County, but it was also short-lived. The union was turned back at two mines owned by Blue Diamond Coal Company, at Leatherwood in 1964 and at Stearns in 1976-79. In the 1980s, it lost other elections in Perry and Breathitt counties.

As the UMW entered its centenary year, it faced an uncertain future in both Kentucky coal fields. The factors making for miner solidarity and the need to organize were either absent or not widely perceived by miners, and in the last decade of the twentieth century a number of owner/operators have convinced workers that they can better what the union has to offer.

See Joseph Finley, *Corrupt Kingdom* (New York 1972); John Hevener, *Whose Side Are You On?* (Champaign-Urbana, Ill., 1978); Homer L. Morris, *Plight of the Bituminous Coal Miner* (Philadelphia 1934). HENRY C. MAYER

U.S. ARMY CORPS OF ENGINEERS. The U.S. Army Corps of Engineers is the country's oldest and largest water management agency. When the corps was established by Congress early in the nineteenth century, its primary mission was to support the nation's military in the engineering and construction of defense-related facilities. Since 1824 it has been the principal manager and developer of America's water resources.

In Kentucky, two Corps of Engineers divisions and four districts are responsible for water resource development and other activities. The Ohio River Division, headquartered at Cincinnati, oversees the programs of the Huntington, Louisville, and Nashville districts, while the Lower Mississippi Valley Division performs the same task for the Memphis District, which has a small area of jurisdiction in the Jackson Purchase in western Kentucky. District and division engineers are corps officers, usually with rank of colonel and general, respectively, commanding forces of civilian engineers, scientists, technicians, and others.

The two major river drainage basins in Kentucky under the jurisdiction of the corps are the Ohio River Basin and the Mississippi River Basin. The Kentucky portion of the Ohio River Basin consists of the watersheds of those left-bank tributaries (as seen when facing downstream) between the confluence of the Big Sandy River with the Ohio River and the confluence of the Ohio River with the Mississippi River. Within that reach of the Ohio River, the major tributary drainages are Big Sandy River Basin, Licking River Basin, Kentucky River Basin, Salt River Basin, Green River Basin, Tradewater River Basin, Upper Cumberland River Basin, Lower Cumberland River Basin, and Tennessee River Basin. The Mississippi River Basin in Kentucky includes the left bank tributaries of the Mississippi from its confluence with the Ohio to the Kentucky-Tennessee line. The Ohio and Mississippi rivers border Kentucky for more than seven hundred miles, and the Ohio and its tributaries provide Kentucky more miles of major navigable streams than found in any other of the contiguous states.

The corps operates locks and dams for navigation on the Ohio River, the Kentucky River, and the

Green River. The Ohio River structures bordering Kentucky consist of eight high-lift dams. Each of those has two lock chambers, one measuring 1,200 feet by 600 feet, and one 600 by 110 feet—except at Smithland Locks and Dams, which has twin 1,200-foot locks. In addition, two movable wooden wicket dams, part of the Ohio River navigation system completed by the corps in 1929, remain in place on the river below Paducah and are scheduled for replacement by a single lock and dam structure. Throughout the state numerous local flood protection projects (levees and floodwalls) have been constructed; upon completion, they are turned over to local governments for maintenance. The corps has built seventeen multipurpose lakes in Kentucky for flood control, water supply, wildlife enhancement, hydropower, and recreation. At many of these large projects, land surrounding the lakes is often leased to state agencies for development and management of recreation facilities. In the southeastern part of the state, the corps's Nashville District is developing facilities in the Big South Fork National River and Recreation Area in McCreary County, which will be managed by the National Park Service. The Louisville District is responsible for managing the Falls of the Ohio National Wildlife Conservation Area, established to protect the historic and natural features there.

The Louisville District's military mission is design and construction of facilities at numerous installations in Kentucky, Illinois, Indiana, Ohio, and Michigan. Support of the military entails engineering and construction assistance and real estate services for the army and air force.

See *Water Resources Development by the U.S. Army Corps of Engineers in Kentucky* (Louisville 1987); *The Falls City Engineers: A History of the Louisville District Corps of Engineers, United States Army*, 2 vols. (Louisville 1974 and 1984).

CHARLES E. PARRISH

U.S. BULLION DEPOSITORY. In a quiet corner of FORT KNOX between the Lindsey Golf Course and one of the housing areas is the U.S. Bullion Depository, better known as the gold vault. Since its construction in 1936 at a cost of $560,000, it has been a major landmark for sightseers and certainly one of the most photographed structures in Kentucky.

In the mid-1930s, federal authorities determined that U.S. gold storage sites, located along the nation's coasts, might be vulnerable to enemy action. Less vulnerable sites well inland with access roads and railroads and security forces were considered vital. Fort Knox, thirty miles southwest of Louisville, met these requirements. It was a long way from any coast, and the recently formed 7th Cavalry Brigade (Mechanized), the forerunner of the U.S. Army Armored Force, provided an ideal security force.

The land on which the gold vault stands was purchased by the federal government in 1918, when Camp Knox was founded as an artillery training center during World War I. The depository, 105 feet by 121 feet with a height of 42 feet, is constructed of granite, concrete, and steel. The outer walls are granite lined with concrete. The gold vault is in fact two buildings under one roof. The compartmented security vault, a combination of steel plates, T-beams, and reinforced concrete with a roof, forms an altogether separate structure within the outer wall. In the corridor between the outer wall and the vault is administrative and storage space.

The Bullion Depository was constructed under the supervision of the U.S. Treasury Department. A total of 16,500 cubic feet of granite, 4,200 cubic yards of concrete, 750 tons of reinforcing steel, and 670 tons of structural steel went into construction. Each vault door weighs thirty tons and can be opened only by select members of the staff, each with a distinct combination known only to that person. The gold vault was completed in December 1936, and the first gold shipments arrived from Philadelphia and New York in January 1937. This series, completed in June 1937, was shipped by rail, with security provided by the mechanized forces at Fort Knox.

The gold stored at Fort Knox is a major part of the U.S. depository system, under the Treasury Department's director of the mint. Other storage areas are the Philadelphia and Denver mints, the U.S. Bullion Depository at West Point, New York, and the Assay Office in San Francisco.

The bullion in the depository is in the form of almost pure refined gold bars or bars resulting from the melting of gold coins. The bars measure 7 inches by 3⅝ inches by 1¼ inches, and are approximately the size of ordinary building bricks. Each bar weighs twenty-seven and one-half pounds, or 400 troy ounces. The bars are stored without wrappings in the vaults.

Throughout its history, the gold vault has stored more than gold bars. On December 27, 1941, the U.S. Bullion Depository at Fort Knox received through the Library of Congress the following historic documents for safekeeping:

• The Lincoln Cathedral copy of the British Magna Carta of 1215, one of the remaining four original copies signed by King John, sent to the United States for safekeeping at the outbreak of World War II.

• The St. Blasius–St. Paul copy of the Gutenberg Bible from 1450–55, also sent from England.

• The original U.S. Declaration of Independence of 1776.

• The original U.S. Articles of Confederation of 1778.

• The original and signed copy of the Constitution of the United States of America of 1787.

• The original, autographed manuscript of President Abraham Lincoln's Gettysburg address of 1863.

• The original, autographed manuscript of Lincoln's second inaugural address of 1865.

All of the documents were returned to the Library of Congress in September 1944, near the end of World War II, just about the time a royal group of treasures—the ceremonial crown jewels of Hungary—was beginning its tortuous journey to the security of the gold vault. A group of loyal citizens secretly removed the ceremonial crown, orb, scepter, sword, and robe along an escape route through Austria and Germany. It was not until 1953 that the crown jewels arrived at the Bullion Depository, accompanied by an impressive honor guard from the U.S. Army, Marines, and Air Force. President Jimmy Carter returned the jewels to Hungary in 1978.

The U.S. Bullion Depository at Fort Knox was added to the National Register of Historic Places in 1988.

See U.S. Treasury Department, "The Fort Knox Gold Depository," memorandum prepared for the National Convention of the American Institute of Banking at Louisville, June 6-10, 1938.

JOHN A. CAMPBELL

U.S. MARINE HOSPITAL. The U.S. Marine Hospital on Portland Avenue in Louisville was one of seven Marine hospitals built on the Mississippi and Ohio rivers and Lake Erie in the mid-1800s. A congressional act of March 3, 1837, authorized the secretary of war to appoint a board of medical officers of the army to select and purchase sites for marine hospitals. Louisville was selected as one of seven sites. The design was adapted from a standard plan commissioned in 1837 from Robert Mills, a student of architect Benjamin Latrobe. In 1841 a Louisville site on high ground above the Ohio River was purchased for $6,000. Excavation began in 1845. The U.S. Army Corp of Engineers, supervised by Stephen H. Long, erected the hospital, which was to be for civilian use. The Mexican War curtailed government building projects but progress resumed in the winter of 1848. The $62,000 hospital opened in the fall of 1851 and assumed care of rivermen previously treated at the city's expense at the Louisville Marine Hospital, on Chestnut near Preston.   WILLIAM B. SCOTT, JR.

UNIVERSITY OF KENTUCKY. The University of Kentucky in Lexington is a land grant institution founded in 1865. In 1989 it had an enrollment of 23,742 in the twenty colleges on the Lexington campus and about 35,000 in its statewide Community College System.

The faculty in Lexington, including the medical center, numbers about 1,900. In 1988 the university awarded about 4,000 earned degrees, of which some 70 percent were undergraduate degrees, 7 percent professional, and 23 percent graduate. The operating budget for the 1988-89 fiscal year was $671 million, with 40 percent being state appropriations. The campus covers seven hundred contiguous acres in Lexington. The Agricultural Experiment Station operates 1,600 acres on the northern limits of Lexington and substations and experimental farms throughout the state.

The university evolved through three stages before becoming the University of Kentucky in 1916: the Agricultural and Mechanical (A&M) College of Kentucky University, 1865-78, a private, denominational institution in Lexington created by an act of the legislature on February 22, 1865; the Agricultural and Mechanical College of Kentucky, 1878-1908; and State University, Lexington, 1908-1916. The presidents of these successive institutions were James Kennedy Patterson (1869-1910), Henry Stites Barker (1910-17), Frank Le Rond McVey (1917-40), Herman Lee Donovan (1941-56), Frank Graves Dickey (1956-63), John W. Oswald (1963-68), Albert Dennis Kirwan (1968-69), Otis A. Singletary (1969-87), David P. Roselle (1987-90), and Charles T. Wethington (1990-).

The A&M College was located at Woodlands-Ashland farms, purchased by Kentucky University. The only classroom building was the residence on Woodlands. A mechanical building was constructed at Ashland in 1868. Classes began in 1867 with an enrollment of 190 and a faculty of ten. The agricultural program was largely farm work, and the mechanical course was conducted at the forge and in the shops. Until a state property tax was imposed in 1880, the annual income was $9,900 from the endowment created by the federal Morrill Land Grant Act in 1862.

A denominational split in the university governing board prompted the legislature to separate the college from the university in 1878. The A&M College relocated in 1882 to South Limestone Street on fifty acres given by the city of Lexington; the city and Fayette County donated a total of $50,000 toward construction of three buildings. President Patterson persuaded the legislature to continue the property tax. The annual income was $30,000, but a revenue increase was anticipated. Enrollment had declined in the mid-1870s but on the new campus increased to 319, with a faculty of seventeen. The Morrill Act did not restrict the curriculum to agriculture and mechanical arts, and Patterson, a historian, promoted the liberal arts. In 1885 the board authorized the establishment of an agricultural experiment station, two years before the federal government began sponsoring such stations. The normal school, established before the move from Woodlands, admitted women, and soon they entered degree programs. In 1876 the college granted an earned master's degree. In 1908 it conferred thirteen master's degrees and eighty-five undergraduate degrees, fifty-two of them in engineering. The faculty numbered eighty-two, and the college income was $189,000. The experiment station farm occupied 240 acres adjacent to the campus.

Acting on Patterson's request, the legislature in 1908 conferred by statute the title State University, implying a collegiate and departmental structure. Colleges of agriculture, law, arts and sciences, and three engineering colleges were established. His dream realized, Patterson retired. The board chose as the next president a judge, Henry Stites Barker, though his only previous academic experience was as a trustee. Internal discontent and external criticism grew after Barker proposed consolidating the three engineering colleges. An investigating committee in 1917 recommended Barker's early resignation, and he resigned at once. Frank Le Rond McVey, president of the University of North Dakota, then took office.

A statute in 1916 changed the name to University of Kentucky. The new president took up the investigating committee's recommendation to write a constitution, which provided for a faculty-administration university senate. New departments and new faculty were added. A graduate school was established in 1924. Among the new buildings was a central library. Enrollment doubled the first year after World War I and doubled again in the 1920s, totaling 4,992 in 1932, when the impact of the Depression was greatest. By World War II not only had the university recovered, but enrollment was a record 6,242, with a faculty of nearly five hundred. Income recovered more slowly, reaching $3,370,405. During his presidency McVey successfully fought the enactment of antievolution laws in the 1920s.

Herman Lee Donovan assumed the presidency as the United States was entering World War II. Donovan anticipated a postwar expansion, which became a certainty after enactment of the G.I. Bill. The expansion was greater than expected and the campus experienced much stopgap improvization before permanent facilities could be provided. The establishment of the University Press and of the Kentucky Research Foundation, to manage research grants and contracts, were other preparations for the future. In March 1949 a federal district court in the Lyman Johnson case required the university to admit blacks to graduate and professional programs. Integration proceeded with exemplary smoothness. In 1954 a landmark decision established a medical center. The legislature in 1956 voted money to begin construction, and Donovan retired so that a younger man could assume the burden of building the center.

Donovan was succeeded by Frank G. Dickey, dean of the College of Education. He and Donovan jointly recommended William R. Willard of Syracuse University as vice-president of the medical school, with immediate responsibility for creating a medical center. The first class entered in 1960, and the hospital was ready in 1962. The medical center conferred a sense of maturity and professionalism that had not existed previously. Graduate programs were stimulated, and the university acquired a new character. No longer, as before 1960, could it be considered an undergraduate institution in which research, graduate, and professional studies were of secondary importance.

Dickey's successor, John W. Oswald, brought an aggressive conviction that the vision of greatness was attainable. Revenue increases from the 1960 sales tax made it possible to enlarge the faculty in all areas of the university, promote research, and fund graduate studies more generously. An unprecedented research ethos developed at the University. Not since McVey's early years had the president's office initiated so much change or enlisted faculty support so widely in the common effort. The 1962 statute creating the statewide Community College System took effect, and in 1964 the new Donovan Fellowship Program started admitting people of sixty-five or older to classes or degree programs free of tuition charges.

At the university's centennial in 1965, the spirit of demonstrative activism and protest, infused with anti–Vietnam War sentiments, was growing. In 1968 Oswald resigned, leaving friends who had welcomed change and critics who opposed it. The state government faced revenue problems and the brief abnormal period of financial prosperity ended. The interim president, Albert Dennis Kirwan, a professor of history and former graduate school dean, attempted to bring calm to the campus and helped the search committee select his successor.

In May 1969 Otis A. Singletary accepted the presidency, coming from the vice-chancellorship for academic affairs at the University of Texas, Austin. He was, like Kirwan, a specialist in Southern history. As Singletary assumed the presidency, the General Assembly was bringing the University of Louisville into the state system and creating an eighth institution, Northern Kentucky State College, without increasing the appropriation for state higher education. The effect was to reduce the state contribution to the University of Kentucky budget from 60 to 40 percent, and the university's share of the state higher education appropriation also dropped from 60 to 40 percent. Singletary's difficult first year ended at the time of the Kent State University shootings, against which there was vehement student protest. The end of the military draft helped restore calm on the campus and, through established channels for bringing about change, there has been greater student participation in university affairs.

The remainder of Singletary's eighteen-year tenure was beset by financial stringencies, alleviated in part by increasing amounts of private funding, research grants, and contracts. Research and graduate programs assumed greater importance to the university for generating external funding. Developmental grants and gifts supported expansion of facilities. In 1970 the Council on Higher Education identified the university with a statewide research mission, emphasizing its distinctive place in the state system of public higher education.

When David P. Roselle, a mathematician, succeeded Singletary, an emphasis on research and graduate training seemed a certainty. Roselle continued to support the graduate programs while striving to make clear the obligation to undergraduates, who made up three-fourths of the enrollment. Emphasis upon nonstate funding continued. In 1988-89 $60 million in research grants and contracts and $22 million in developmental gifts were awarded. But financial problems remained acute, in spite of an expanding enrollment.

Roselle's brief administration was marked by controversy over the administration of athletics, leading to an investigation by the National Collegiate Athletic Association, which imposed disciplinary measures. The apparent lack of state financial support led to Roselle's quick departure. Charles T. Wethington, Jr., succeeded him as president in 1990.

See Carl B. Cone, *The University of Kentucky: A Pictorial History* (Lexington, Ky., 1989); James Franklin Hopkins, *The University of Kentucky: Origins and Early Years* (Lexington, Ky., 1951); Charles Talbert, *The University of Kentucky: The Maturing Years* (Lexington, Ky., 1965).

CARL B. CONE

UNIVERSITY OF LOUISVILLE. The University of Louisville originated in 1837, when the city council created the Louisville Medical Institute and the Louisville Collegiate Institute. No official connection existed between the two, but friends of the less prosperous Collegiate Institute advocated their consolidation, as did local physicians envious of the Medical Institute faculty. In 1846 the General Assembly combined the two schools and added a law department to form the University of Louisville. Each division remained financially autonomous. This disappointed friends of the former Collegiate Institute, which became the academic department. In 1851 a new city charter ordered financial integration of all university units, but three years later a court decision overturned this provision. The academic department remained dormant until the twentieth century.

In 1850, meanwhile, opponents of the medical department established a second medical school in the city, the Kentucky School of Medicine. This was the first of several local rivals of the medical department of the University of Louisville. Competition became most intense during the two decades following the Civil War. In 1907 the University of Louisville absorbed several of these rival schools. Except for the University of Louisville's, the remaining medical schools closed shortly after the appearance of Abraham FLEXNER'S 1910 report on medical education in the United States, which pointed out problems at Kentucky schools.

The medical school mergers coincided with other developments that brought the University of Louisville closer to the twentieth century model of a university. In 1907 the academic department reopened as the College of Arts and Sciences. President A.Y. FORD (1914-26) directed successful municipal bond issues and increased private donations to the university. In 1923 he oversaw purchase of what became the Belknap Campus on South Third Street at Eastern Parkway. President George COLVIN (1926-28) sought to continue the consolidation of central authority initiated under Ford, but the changes he made came at the cost of faculty and community support. President Raymond A. Kent (1929-43)

stressed conformity with academic standards as defined by accrediting agencies.

In 1925 local black leaders traded their endorsement of a university bond issue for a promise that some of the new revenue would support black higher education. This pledge was fulfilled in 1931 with the opening of the Louisville Municipal College, the black undergraduate division of the University of Louisville. Legal pressure from blacks, the financial strain of operating a separate black school, and the support of some influential whites led to the desegregation of the University of Louisville in 1950-51. One professor from the Municipal College joined the faculty of the College of Arts and Sciences, while others lost their positions as a result of the school's closing.

With the inauguration of President Philip G. Davidson (1951-68) a period of administrative stability began at the University of Louisville. Davidson struggled to increase municipal support for the university at a time when the tax base of many U.S. cities, including Louisville, was shrinking. In 1966, meanwhile, the General Assembly created a committee to recommend alternatives under which the University of Louisville might enter the state system of higher education. State affiliation posed numerous political hurdles, but in 1970 the University of Louisville entered the state system of higher education with all its programs intact. President Woodrow M. Strickler (1968-72) followed Davidson in leading the university into the state system. The first decade as a state-supported institution tested the University of Louisville's endurance, as allocation of the state's resources for higher education became a persistent political dispute. Within the system the University of Louisville's material resources increased, and the school's physical plant and enrollment grew, but this rapid evolution also produced internal strains. President James G. Miller (1973-80) clarified and solidified the university's position in the state system of higher education, but harmony evaded his administration. In 1981 he was followed by Donald C. Swain.

See Dwayne Cox, "The Louisville Medical Institute: A Case History in American Medical Education," *FCHQ* 62 (April 1988): 197-219.

DWAYNE COX

UNIVERSITY PRESS OF KENTUCKY. The University Press (UPK) is a scholarly publishing house organized in 1969 as successor to the University of Kentucky Press. The university had sponsored scholarly publication since 1943; in 1949 the press was established as a separate academic agency under the university president, and the following year Bruce F. Denbo, then of Louisiana State University press, was appointed as the first full-time professional director. Denbo served as director of UPK until his retirement in 1978, building a small but distinguished list of scholarly books with emphasis on American history and literary criticism. Since 1969, UPK has represented a consortium that now includes all of Kentucky's state universities, five of its private colleges, and two historical societies (a list of consortium members appears on the copyright page of this book). Each constituent institution is represented on a statewide editorial board, which determines editorial policy. UPK has its offices at the University of Kentucky, which is responsible for the overhead cost of the publishing operation. Denbo was succeeded as director of UPK by Kenneth H. Cherry, who came to Kentucky from the University of Tennessee Press.

UPK's editorial program emphasizes history, literature, and the social sciences, with regional interests in Kentucky, Appalachia, the Ohio Valley, and the South. Since the formation of the consortium in 1969, UPK, while expanding its traditional scholarly publication programs, has broadened its appeal to readers in Kentucky and surrounding states with publications of special regional interest. In the 1970s it produced the Kentucky Nature Series and the forty-seven-volume Kentucky Bicentennial Bookshelf. More recent publications in this area are *Kentucky Place Names* (1984), *The Ohio River* (1989), and *Antebellum Architecture of Kentucky* (1991). UPK also republishes from time to time classics by Kentucky authors; many works by Harriette Arnow, Janice Holt Giles, John Fox, Jr., and Jesse Stuart are available in UPK editions.

UPK has more than five hundred titles in print and an annual income of more than $1 million.

UNSELD, WESLEY. Wesley Unseld, Hall of Fame basketball player, was born on March 14, 1946, in Louisville to Charles and Cornelia Unseld. An All-State player, he led Louisville's Seneca High School to two state championships, 1963 and 1964. He attended the University of Louisville during 1965-68, was named All-Conference three times, All-American twice, and ranked among the national leaders in rebounding. He was selected in the first round of the 1968 National Basketball Association (NBA) draft by the Washington Bullets and was named the NBA's rookie of the year and most valuable player for the 1968-69 season. Unseld played until 1981 with the Bullets, was named to the NBA All-Star team five times, and was the most valuable player of the 1978 NBA Championship Series. He retired as the Bullets' career leader in games, rebounds, minutes played, and assists.

Moving directly from the court to the front office, Unseld became the vice president of the Bullets and also served as a television broadcaster for Bullets' games. He returned to the bench in 1988 as an assistant coach and later that year became head coach. In 1988 he was elected to the Basketball Hall of Fame in Springfield, Massachusetts. Unseld served on the board of trustees at St. Mary's College in Baltimore and as the head of Capital Center Charities in Washington.

He married Connie Martin; they have two children, Kimberly and Wesley.

See J. McCallum, "Blast From the Past," *Sports Illustrated*, March 28, 1988.

URBAN LIFE. From the earliest days of settlement in Kentucky, as elsewhere in the Ohio River Valley, the planting of cities at strategic military and commercial sites along the banks of major waterways and in the hearts of fertile farming districts was a vital economic and social activity. As historian Richard C. Wade demonstrated in his classic study *The Urban Frontier: The Rise of Western Cities, 1790-1830* (1959), these young communities functioned as "spearheads of the frontier" and rose long before the intensive settlement of the agricultural hinterland. Pioneer urbanites established the town of Louisville in 1778 and founded Lexington in 1779. Daniel Drake, a prominent physician and one of the foremost citizens of early nineteenth-century Cincinnati, Louisville, and Lexington, referred to what he termed the prevalent tendency to "rear up" towns in advance of the country.

During the last decade of the eighteenth century and the first two decades of the nineteenth, Kentucky and the rest of the Ohio Valley were caught up in what one newspaper editor termed a "city-making mania," in which pioneer settlers envisioned flourishing cities at the mouth of every creek and bayou. During this era the number of urban failures probably exceeded the number of successful townsite promotions. Pioneer Kentuckians brought with them across the mountains the Puritan conception of cities as bulwarks against the savagery of raw wilderness and as instruments to bring civilization to a vast new land. The urban frontiersmen and women shared a confident belief in the power of cities, industry, and technology to speed the transformation of the Ohio Valley from a gloomy wilderness to a flourishing region. Although small by twentieth century standards, the early cities exerted a disproportionately large influence in the life of the commonwealth, performing functions and providing services that were historically urban in nature. Even the tiny stockaded outposts that formed the nuclei of infant Louisville and Lexington served as havens for new migrants, shelters in time of attack, centers for religious worship and social gatherings, clearinghouses for economic and commercial activities, and seats of administrative and governmental affairs. As crucibles of culture, nurseries of enterprise, and focal points of scientific and intellectual activity, the towns fulfilled the classical role of cities as the agencies of civilization.

During the early decades of the nineteenth century, the rise of the steamboat on the western waters dramatically speeded up the development of Louisville even as it spelled the decline of inland Lexington, a major urban center known as the "Athens of the West." By 1860 Louisville was a thriving commercial emporium with a population of 68,033, the eleventh largest city in the United States. In 1857 traveler Frederick Law Olmsted reported in *A Journey through Texas* that Louisville "has grown withall at a Western rapidity," representing "a good specimen of a brisk and well-furnished city." Lexington, by contrast, had but

9,321 residents in 1860 and had fallen behind Covington and Newport, which in 1860 registered populations of 16,471 and 10,046, respectively.

By the eve of the Civil War, urban ambitions in Kentucky—and the urban imperialism and rivalries that reflected those ambitions—had given rise to a haphazard but vital transportation matrix of turnpikes, canals, and railroads. The outlines of an urban network were emerging in the commonwealth. By 1860 more than 120,000 people, or slightly more than 10 percent of Kentucky's total population, lived in the eight urban places of 2,500 or more inhabitants. In 1840 towns and cities were still concentrated in the Inner Bluegrass region, along the Ohio River, and between the Inner Bluegrass and Louisville. Only two decades later urbanization had begun to transform all but the southeastern and south-central portions of the commonwealth. Although the Bluegrass centers still predominated, cities were rising, from Ashland and Catlettsburg in the East, where the Big Sandy joins the Ohio River, to Columbus and Hickman in the far West on the Mississippi River. In between, places like Maysville, Newport, Covington, Carrollton, Owensboro, Henderson, and Paducah thrived on the trade carried along the Ohio River, while other communities emerged along Kentucky's principal tributary rivers. In the west-central portion of the state, Russellville, Hopkinsville, Bowling Green, Franklin, and Madisonville had begun to grow. Paducah had attained a population of 4,590, Frankfort had reached 3,702, and Owensboro and Hopkinsville had climbed to 2,308 and 2,289, respectively.

The fate of youthful communities in Kentucky often hinged on timely action and aggressive entrepreneurial leadership. When the Louisville & Nashville (L&N) Railroad (now CSX Transportation) was chartered in 1850, for example, every hamlet between the two terminal cities viewed the project as a potential vehicle for its own urban ambitions. There ensued a mad scramble among these places to persuade the new company to run its tracks through their respective towns. Two alternate routes through Kentucky were proposed, the lower route to pass through Elizabethtown, Bowling Green, and Franklin, and the upper or "air-line" route to pass through Bardstown, Glasgow, Scottsville, and New Haven. In September 1851 the L&N board passed a resolution stating that it had no preference as to route and that local subscription pledges should decide the matter. Proponents of both routes began a bidding war, and the dispute crystallized around the conflicting ambitions of Bowling Green on the lower route and Glasgow on the upper. Glasgow moved slowly and eventually offered $300,000, but Bowling Green took decisive action. Recognizing that a railroad would be the key to their city's aspirations, Bowling Green entrepreneurs refused to play the L&N's waiting game. They procured a charter similar to the L&N's from the Tennessee legislature in February 1852 and announced their intention of building their own railroad from Bowling Green to Nashville. The company promptly put surveyors in the field and opened subscription books, while the citizens of the city approved a subscription of $1 million to the company's stock. The board of the L&N could no longer ignore the threat of a competing line, and in May 1852 it authorized a consolidation of the two companies. The lower route indeed offered fewer serious engineering problems, passed through some large coal beds, and could easily be linked to Memphis, but it was Bowling Green's bold and independent action that played a major role in the ultimate decision to follow the lower route. The different responses of Bowling Green and Glasgow to the same challenge helped shape the destinies of both places.

During the last decades of the nineteenth century and the opening three decades of the twentieth, thousands of Kentuckians joined what had become a nationwide migration to cities. By 1930, 800,000 Kentuckians, almost one-third of the state's entire population, lived in the fifty-three urban places of 2,500 people or more, and thirteen cities in the commonwealth registered populations in excess of 10,000. A number of new cities developed as satellites of such established centers as Louisville in Jefferson County and Covington and Newport in northern Kentucky. From 1870 to 1930, cities rose in portions of the state previously untouched by urbanization. During the late nineteenth century, Princeton, Providence, and Morganfield began to develop in west-central Kentucky, and Mayfield, Fulton, and Murray sprang up in the far western section of the commonwealth. In the southeastern corner of the state, Middlesborough, Somerset, Pineville, Corbin, and Williamsburg were planted before 1900, while during the opening decades of the new century the eastern and southeastern sections witnessed the beginnings of Jenkins, Hazard, Harlan, Lynch, Barbourville, Wayland, Elkhorn City, Pikeville, Prestonsburg, Van Lear, and Paintsville. Between 1900 and 1930 Dawson Springs, Greenville, and Sturgis began to grow in west-central Kentucky. Some of the mountain towns were overgrown mining camps dominated by a single large mining company—Jenkins, Lynch, Benham, and Stearns, for example. Other mountain communities, although primarily dependent upon coal mining, developed independently of a single mining company and built up manufacturing establishments such as lumber mills, canning factories, and clay-working plants, which relied heavily upon local resources.

Throughout the twentieth century, the proportion of Kentucky's inhabitants living in cities has continued to grow, and the state's network of cities has become more extensive and complex. The Bluegrass region and its fringes have experienced substantial urban development, with the rise of new suburbs outside Lexington and with the growth of places like Berea, Lancaster, and Wilmore to the south, Morehead to the east, and Lawrenceburg to the west. Older centers such as Lexington and Bardstown have come to life again. Lexington's dynamic growth from the 1960s through the 1980s was stimulated by the arrival of large manufacturing firms such as IBM Corporation, by the expansion of the University of Kentucky, by the development of a large-scale health-care industry, and by the decision in 1972 of the residents of Lexington and Fayette County to consolidate their city and county governments. The population of Lexington jumped from less than 63,000 in 1960 to more than 220,000 in 1990 as the rejuvenated "Athens of the West" threatened to challenge Louisville (which had twice defeated proposals for city-county consolidation) for urban supremacy within the commonwealth. According to preliminary statistics from the 1990 census, Louisville's population declined 11 percent during the 1980s, from 298,451 to 265,660, while Lexington-Fayette County registered a 10 percent increase during the same period.

During the twentieth century, upstart towns and cities vied with economic rivals for primacy and power. Radcliff boomed after World War II as "the Post Town of Fort Knox," its population soaring from a few hundred to almost 20,000 in 1990 as the fort developed into a permanent major military installation. In Hardin County, Radcliff's rapid expansion gave rise to a spirited urban rivalry with neighboring Elizabethtown (where the population exceeded 18,000 in 1990), resembling the urban rivalries characteristic of the age of city building in the nineteenth century.

Radcliff and Elizabethtown, along with dozens of other communities, benefited from the construction of a network of roadways throughout Kentucky and from the increasing use of automobiles and trucks. The building of the Purchase, Western, and Blue Grass parkways stimulated the development of towns and cities along their routes. The almost universal adoption of the automobile after 1945 sparked a suburban explosion on the "crabgrass frontiers" of the state's larger and older urban centers. Satellite cities developed in northern Kentucky—the Greater Cincinnati area around Covington and Newport and the Louisville–Jefferson County area—and to the south, in the vicinity of Ashland and Paducah. Nationally, the suburban trend had become so pronounced that in 1970, for the first time in American history, more residents of metropolitan areas lived outside the central cities than within them. Kentucky's metropolitan population conformed to the national pattern, as slightly more than half of the state's metropolitan residents lived in suburban communities outside the political boundaries of their central cities.

The growth of sprawling metropolitan regions has been one of the most significant developments in the urban history of the twentieth century. By 1980, 45 percent of Kentucky's total population had come to reside within the seven Standard Metropolitan Statistical Areas (SMSAs). (The Census Bureau defines an SMSA as consisting of at least one entire county that contains a central city of 50,000 or more inhabitants, plus adjacent counties considered economically and socially integrated with the central city according to an elaborate set of crite-

ria.) Census officials ignored the somewhat arbitrary political boundaries of the states in charting the contours of metropolitan regions, and five of the seven SMSAs in Kentucky thus included portions of one or more neighboring states. The Huntington-Ashland SMSA spread over portions of West Virginia, Kentucky, and Ohio, while the Greater Cincinnati–Covington–Newport complex took in parts of Ohio, Kentucky, and Indiana. Both the Greater Louisville and the Evansville-Henderson areas straddled the Ohio River and included portions of Kentucky and Indiana, while the Clarksville-Hopkinsville region took in parts of Kentucky and Tennessee. Only the Owensboro and Lexington SMSAs lay entirely within the borders of the commonwealth in 1980.

The process of urbanization in Kentucky has conformed to the urban pattern typical of the South as a region. Throughout most of American history, the South lagged behind the rest of the nation in the degree of urbanization by roughly fifty years at any given decennial census. Kentucky similarly trailed the national level of urbanization by approximately fifty years. Whereas 25.7 percent of all Americans lived in cities by 1870, not until 1920 did the urban population climb to 26.2 percent for Kentuckians and 25.4 percent for all southerners. Similarly, the urban population first topped 50 percent for the entire country in 1920, and for Kentucky in 1970. Of the state's total population of slightly over 3.2 million in 1970, 52.3 percent lived in the 102 cities of 2,500 people or more. Most Kentuckians had moved to town, and although they might entertain a somewhat wistful nostalgia for the good old days, they had no intention of returning to the land.

At the beginning of the 1990s there was little agreement among urban affairs experts and scholars concerning the state of the cities or their future prospects. What did seem clear was that the cities in the commonwealth of Kentucky, like cities elsewhere in the United States, had weathered a series of so-called crises. They had served as dynamic agents of modernization, spearheading advances in economic, social, and cultural life. They had provided a vital safety valve for economically distressed agricultural areas and small towns. They had made a high standard of living possible for an increasing proportion of the population. And they had continued to represent, as municipal reformer Frederic C. Howe observed in 1906, "the hope of democracy."

See Allen J. Share, *Cities in the Commonwealth: Two Centuries of Urban Life in Kentucky* (Lexington, Ky., 1982); George H. Yater, *Two Hundred Years at the Falls of the Ohio: A History of Louisville and Jefferson County* (Louisville 1979); John D. Wright, Jr., *Lexington: Heart of the Bluegrass* (Lexington, Ky., 1982).   ALLEN J. SHARE

URSULINES. Ursulines are members of the Company of St. Ursula, an order of religious women founded by St. Angela Merici in Brescia, Italy, in 1535. It is known for promoting education. From

Italy the Ursulines spread to France, and then to Germany. In 1858, in response to a request by Bishop Martin John SPALDING of Louisville, Mother Salesia Reitmeier, Mother Pia Schoenhofer, and Sister Maximilian Zwinger came from Straubing, Bavaria, to Louisville to take charge of St. Martin's Parochial School. During the first ten years, Reitmeier established a novitiate and a boarding school (Ursuline Academy), procured the legal charter for the Ursuline Society and Academy of Education, and opened five additional elementary schools in Kentucky. The next years saw steady growth in membership. At the requests of pastors, the Ursulines taught in the parochial schools in Louisville.

MOUNT ST. JOSEPH ACADEMY in Daviess County was founded as a mission from Louisville in 1874 by five Ursulines, with Schoenhofer as superior. The school flourished and other mission schools were opened. Often the Ursulines pioneered in isolated areas, teaching in one- or two-room schoolhouses. In 1895 an English-speaking novitiate was opened. In 1912 the Holy See granted Mount St. Joseph permission to become an autonomous motherhouse with Aloysius Willett as its first mother superior. A junior college was opened in the fall of 1925 at Mount St. Joseph; in 1950 it was relocated in Owensboro and is now BRESCIA COLLEGE. In the fall of 1983 Mount St. Joseph Center opened. The center offers various educational, religious, social, and cultural programs.

Since its foundation the Congregation of Ursulines has served in three hundred schools and ministries in Kentucky and twenty-five other states and countries. In Louisville it operates the following schools and programs: Sacred Heart Academy, Sacred Heart Model School, Ursuline Montessori School, Ursuline Speech Clinic, Ursuline School of Music and Drama, Ursuline Child Development Center, and Ursuline Tutoring Center. Other schools that were once owned and operated by the Ursulines in Louisville: Ursuline College, which merged with BELLARMINE COLLEGE in 1968; Ursuline Academy, which closed in 1972 after 114 years of service; and Angela Merici High School, which merged with Bishop David High School to form Holy Cross High School in 1984. Ursuline Sisters teach at Bellarmine College and Holy Cross High School.

See Eugenia Scherm, *Born to Lead* (Maple Mount, Ky., 1970); Helen M. Schweri, *Under His Mighty Power* (Louisville 1983).

M. CONCETTA WALLER AND
EMMA CECILIA BUSAM

V

VALLEY VIEW FERRY. Kentucky's oldest recorded commercial business, the Valley View ferry, crosses the Kentucky River to connect Fayette and Madison counties on KY 169. The Virginia legislature in 1785 granted Revolutionary War hero John Craig, who owned land along the Kentucky River, a "perpetual and irrevocable franchise" to establish the Valley View ferry and it has been in operation since that time. For seventy years, workhorses pulled the ferry across the river; later it was modernized by stretching two steel guiding cables across the river and adding a motor for the ferry's 100-year-old paddle wheel. The ferryboat in use in 1990 could carry up to three cars in a crossing time of two and a half minutes and it operated seven days a week. Over its history, the Valley View ferry has been owned by seven families.

VANCEBURG. Vanceburg, the seat of Lewis County, is located on the Ohio River on KY 8, KY 10, and KY 59. It was named for Joseph C. Vance, who with Moses Baird bought fifty-five acres on June 30, 1797, from Alexander K. Marshall, a brother of John Marshall, chief justice of the United States. The settlement founded there took advantage of the proximity of the Ohio River and the availability of salt about a mile from the town, on Salt Lick Creek. The city charter for Vanceburg was granted by the General Assembly on January 24, 1827. Roland Parker, Ben Holton, and Joseph Ralston were among the first trustees of the town. Vanceburg became a major landing on the Ohio for flatboats and, later, steamboats. Because of its location on higher ground, the city experienced less damage than other river cities during the periodic floods, even the devastating one of 1937.

The first seat of Lewis County was Poplar Flat, where a courthouse was built in 1806. The second courthouse, a log structure, was built in 1810 in Clarksburg. Not until December 1863 was Vanceburg approved as the county seat. In 1864-65 the third courthouse was built of brick in Vanceburg. The present three-story courthouse, constructed from limestone quarried four miles away, was completed in 1940. Located on the courthouse lawn is one of the few Civil War monuments to the Union cause in Kentucky. The monument, built by public subscription, is dedicated to the memory of the 107 Lewis County soldiers who died for the Union.

Although Vanceburg experienced some light industrial development during the mid-twentieth century, and womens' shoes and some wood products are manufactured there, the region is basically agrarian. The completion of the AA Highway tied the city to the metropolitan area of Cincinnati.

The population of the fourth-class city was 1,773 in 1970; 1,939 in 1980; and 1,713 in 1990.

See O.G. Ragan, *History of Lewis County, Kentucky* (Cincinnati 1912).   RON D. BRYANT

VARNEY, JAMES. James Varney, comedian and actor, is a native of Lexington, Kentucky, born there probably in 1949, the son of James A. and Nancy Elizabeth (Howard) Varney. Varney became a performer at Lexington Children's Theatre at the age of eight. He made his professional debut at age sixteen as Puck in a University of Kentucky summer theater production of *A Midsummer Night's Dream.* Varney also performed in several productions by Studio Players of Lexington. While attending Lexington's Lafayette High School, he won the best actor award twice in the state high school drama festival. He left high school two weeks before graduation for an acting apprenticeship with the Barter Theatre in Abingdon, Virginia, but later earned a high school equivalency certificate. He worked in comedy clubs and dinner theaters and had roles in the television series "Operation Petticoat," "Pink Lady and Jeff," and "The Rousters."

In 1980 Varney filmed his first commercial as Ernest P. Worrell, a character known for his one-sided conversations with his unseen, long-suffering pal Vern. His "Hey Vern! Know what I mean?" became a familiar phrase. Over much of the next decade, Varney filmed more than 2,500 commercials for a variety of products and companies. He played the role of Ernest in feature films, including *Dr. Otto and the Riddle of the Gloom Beam*, *Ernest Goes To Camp*, and *Ernest Saves Christmas*, and in a live-action Saturday morning show for children. "Ernest's" popularity created an international fan club of 22,000 members by 1988, an Ernest newsletter, and Ernest merchandise. *The Ernest P. Worrell Book of Knowledge* was published in 1985 by Carden & Cherry Advertising Agency, Inc. of Nashville, the agency that originated the Worrell character in collaboration with Varney. Varney married his second wife, Janie Hale, in June 1988.

MARY MARGARET BELL

VEECH, ANNIE. Annie Veech, physician, was born in 1871 in Jefferson County, Kentucky, the youngest child of Richard Snowden and Mary (Nichols) Veech. She graduated from Miss Hampton's School for Girls in Louisville in 1890 and traveled extensively throughout the world for the next fifteen years. Veech entered the Women's Medical College of Pennsylvania in 1905 and received an M.D. degree in 1909. She worked at the Women's Hospital in Philadelphia from 1909 until 1911. The following year she became a staff member of the Student Hospital at State Normal College (now Longwood College) in Farmville, Virginia. Veech returned to Louisville in 1913 and entered private practice. During World War I she served with the Red Cross as a civilian physician in Blois, France.

Veech then served as public health inspector in the Louisville public schools and helped organize the state Bureau of Child Hygiene in 1921. In 1922

918

she became the director of the bureau in Frankfort. Veech returned to Louisville in 1937 to direct the Louisville Department of Health (later City-County Health Department). In 1948 the department reorganized and Veech became director of the child hygiene program. At her request, the next year she became associate director and consultant, serving until her retirement in 1950. Even after retirement, she continued the weekly lectures and workshops for mothers that she had begun in 1943. Veech died July 10, 1957, and was buried in Cave Hill Cemetery in Louisville.

VERSAILLES. The seat of Woodford County, Versailles is located on U.S. 60 and U.S. 62. The town was established on June 23, 1792, on eighty acres belonging to Hezekiah Briscoe, a child whose guardians included the Marquis Calmes. Calmes named the town in honor of Versailles, the birthplace of General Lafayette, on whose staff he served in the Revolutionary War. Versailles, incorporated on February 13, 1837, was located on the site of an earlier community called Falling Springs.

The rich farmlands that surrounded the town made it a vital agricultural trading center. Many of the residents built impressive homes early in the nineteenth century, making Versailles one of the most architecturally interesting communities in Kentucky.

The first Woodford County courthouse was constructed in 1790 of buckeye logs, at a cost of $22.50. The second courthouse was built in 1793, and the third in 1809. The third courthouse was extensively remodeled and stood until October 11, 1965, when it was destroyed by fire. A fourth courthouse, a brick structure in the Georgian style, was completed in 1970 at a cost of $1.1 million.

During the Civil War, Versailles was occupied by both Confederate and Union troops. On September 2, 1862, Confederate forces briefly took control of the town. However, Federal occupation was soon established, and black soldiers were ordered into the town. Many citizens angrily protested the occupation and threats of violence were made. The black troops were then ordered to occupy every street corner, and an assembly of more than two people was forbidden.

By 1880, the town was a thriving agricultural community, with ten stores, five churches, a national bank, two schools (male and female), eight lawyers, and six doctors. Industrial development in the twentieth century has included printing of books and maps and production of electrical transformers, thermostats, and fluorescent lights.

John J. Crittenden, governor of Kentucky (1848-50), was born near Versailles. The town was also the home of Albert B. Chandler, twice governor of Kentucky (1935-39, 1955-59), and of Lt. Gen. Field Harris, commander of the Marine Corps in World War II and the Korean War.

The population of the fourth-class city was 5,679 in 1970; 6,427 in 1980; and 7,269 in 1990.

RON D. BRYANT

VEST, GEORGE GRAHAM. George Graham Vest, Kentucky newspaper editor and U.S. senator from Missouri, was born in Frankfort, Kentucky, on December 6, 1830, the son of John Jay and Harriet (Graham) Vest. He graduated from Centre College in Danville in 1848 and from the law department of Transylvania University in 1853. He became a partner with his brother-in-law, Capt. R.S. Triplett, in the *Bulletin*, established April 10, 1852, as the second newspaper in Owensboro, Kentucky. Vest, who served as editor, is known for the essay "Tribute to a Dog," which he made use of in testifying in a lawsuit seeking damages for the death of a favorite dog. Vest sold his interest in the *Bulletin* in a few months' time and moved to Missouri, where he began practicing law.

Vest was a Democratic presidential elector from Missouri in 1860, served in the Missouri legislature during 1860-61, and was a member of the Confederate Congress in Richmond, Virginia, during 1862-65. He returned to Missouri in 1865 and was elected as a Democrat to the U.S. Senate in 1879, serving from March 4, 1879, to March 3, 1903. He died on August 9, 1904, and was buried in Bellefontaine Cemetery in St. Louis.   LEE A. DEW

VIETNAM WAR. An estimated 125,000 Kentuckians served in the military in Vietnam from 1961 to 1975, and 1,066 Kentuckians were killed or missing in action. The first Kentuckian to die in Vietnam was Fergus Coleman Groves II, of Jefferson County, on February 2, 1962; the last was Tommy R. Nealis, of Montgomery County, on May 13, 1975.

The 101st Airborne Division, stationed at Fort Campbell, Kentucky, the "Screaming Eagles" of World War II fame, played a key role in the war. The 1st Brigade was one of the first American units to be sent to Vietnam in 1965 and participated in numerous operations. The remainder of the division was ordered to Vietnam in August 1967, scattered from Bien Hoa to Cu Chi, and took part in fighting around Hue during the Tet Offensive, in the A Shau Valley in 1968 and 1969, and as a support unit in the South Vietnamese incursion into Laos in 1971.

By a quirk of circumstances, Bardstown, Kentucky, suffered perhaps greater losses per capita than any other community in the United States. In a reserve callup following the Tet offensive of February 1968, the nearly six hundred men of the 138th Artillery Battalion, Kentucky National Guard (the Louisville Legion), were ordered into combat. Around one hundred of the men challenged the constitutionality of their activation for an undeclared war, but the U.S. Supreme Court ultimately ruled against them and they were sent to Vietnam. Battery C of the 138th Battalion, mostly men from Bardstown, was attacked on the night of June 19, 1969, by North Vietnamese sapper units at a firing position called Tomahawk Hill. Five guardsmen from Bardstown and four army men died that night; nineteen guardsmen and twenty other army men were wounded. In all, the attack on Tomahawk claimed forty-eight casualties, roughly 50 percent of the soldiers there. The losses left Bardstown in a state of shock.

Although the vast majority of Kentuckians probably supported the war until very late, the commonwealth was the scene of various kinds of individual and group protest. Some Kentuckians went to jail rather than be inducted into military service. Numerous other Kentuckians participated in the local and national protest marches that began on a small scale in 1965 and grew to major proportions between 1970 and 1973.

Two Kentucky senators gained national prominence for questioning the prosecution of the war. The national media and the White House saw moderate Republican Thurston B. Morton's conversion from hawk to critic of the war in late 1967 as a barometer of the national shift from support for, to questioning of, the Lyndon Johnson administration's policies. Liberal Republican John Sherman Cooper was among the earliest and most consistent congressional critics of the war, and in the Nixon years (1969-74) Cooper gave his name to a series of amendments that would have cut off funds for military operations in Indochina.

In the spring of 1968, amid much controversy, the national council of the radical organization Students for a Democratic Society (SDS) met in Lexington. Several local clergymen and veterans' organizations appealed to Gov. Louie Nunn (1967-71) to prevent the meeting of what they believed to be a Communist-front organization. The University of Kentucky eventually permitted the meeting, provided it was closed to the public, and during March 28-31, 102 delegates gathered at the university to plan the spring's protest activities. Internal controversy prevented any agreement, and the council left to local organizations whether to participate in antiwar demonstrations planned for April by another antiwar organization, the Student Mobilization Committee. The University of Kentucky chapter of SDS was subsequently investigated by a Fayette grand jury for alleged subversive activities and for disseminating "indecent literature."

In the aftermath of the incursion into Cambodia ordered by President Richard Nixon on April 30, 1970, and the subsequent killing of four students at Kent State University by National Guardsmen, campus protest flared up across Kentucky. On most campuses, the protest was limited to peaceful marches, the cancellation of classes to urge a moratorium on the war, and the filing of petitions. At the University of Kentucky the burning of a building housing Reserve Officer Training Corps offices prompted Governor Nunn to dispatch National Guardsmen to the campus. Continued protest sparked occasional outbreaks of violence and led to the arrest of thirty-three protesters, including two faculty members. At the end of the semester, the campus quieted and the National Guard was withdrawn. Protests were undertaken on many other campuses throughout the state.

After the war, Kentucky veterans joined those of other states in deploring their treatment by a seemingly ungrateful nation. They complained that they had been denied the recognition accorded veterans of other wars and had been discriminated against in hiring and in other areas. Eventually, the veterans themselves took the lead in building a uniquely impressive memorial on the State Library and Archives grounds in Frankfort. In 1988 the General Assembly mandated a bonus for Vietnam-era veterans; Kentucky was among the last states in the nation to so honor those who had served.

See George Herring, *America's Longest War* (Philadelphia 1986); Mitchell Hall, "A Crack in Time," *Register* 85 (Winter 1985): 33-63.

GEORGE HERRING AND
ANTHONY A. MCINTIRE

VILLA HILLS. Villa Hills is a residential city in northeastern Kenton County on the hills above the Ohio River, eight miles north of INDEPENDENCE and three miles west of Bromley. The name of the city is derived from the Villa Madonna Academy, a Catholic convent and girls' boarding school that located in the area in 1903 and was operated by the Benedictine Sisters. Villa Madonna College, the forerunner of Thomas More College, originated at the academy in 1921 and operated there until 1929, when it moved to COVINGTON. By 1990 Villa Madonna Academy had become a coeducational institution serving grades one through twelve.

With the exception of the academy, the area remained wooded hills and farmland until the nearby construction of I-75 in the late 1950s brought rapid suburban development. The city of Villa Hills was incorporated on June 8, 1962, and included the Madonna and Woodlawn subdivisions. A major employer of many residents is Delta Air Lines, which opened a $46 million terminal in 1987 at the nearby Greater Cincinnati International Airport, making it a regional hub.

Villa Hills is a fourth-class city with many upper-middle-class homes. The population was 1,647 in 1970; 5,598 in 1980; and 7,739 in 1990.

VINE GROVE. Vine Grove is located in northern Hardin County at the intersection of KY 144 and the Paducah & Louisville Railroad (P&L). The city is approximately twelve miles northwest of ELIZABETHTOWN and contiguous to RADCLIFF on the east.

The first permanent settlers arrived in the area in 1850 and named the settlement Vine Grove for the numerous wild grapevines there. Originally, Vine Grove was constructed on Otter Creek, approximately one mile west of its present location. Town inhabitants decided to relocate to take advantage of commercial opportunities when the Illinois Central Railroad (now the P&L) was built through northern Hardin County in the 1860s. The original town consisted of two blacksmith shops operated by William Settle and Mike Flaherty, a gristmill run by Josh

Stith, and two mercantile stores run by Van B. Nelson and Alex Schwabenton. E.R. Graham, president of the Farmers Bank, built the first road through Vine Grove, which is now KY 144. William T. Sheets was the town's first postmaster and Dr. Frank G. Pusey was the first physician. The Rev. Ben F. Hagan, pastor of the Baptist church, served as teacher in Vine Grove's first school.

Although Vine Grove was destroyed twice by fire in 1905 and 1908, it continued to grow and prosper. Until it was surpassed by Radcliff, Vine Grove was the second largest city in Hardin County, after Elizabethtown. The town owes much of its prosperity to the federal military reservation at nearby FORT KNOX, where many residents are employed in the civilian work-force.

The population of the fourth-class city was 2,987 in 1970; 3,648 in 1980; and 3,586 in 1990.

DOUGLAS CANTRELL

VINSON, FREDERICK MOORE. Frederick Moore Vinson, U.S. secretary of the Treasury and thirteenth chief justice of the United States, was born to James and Virginia (Ferguson) Vinson near Louisa, Kentucky, on January 22, 1890. He attended Kentucky Normal School in Louisa, graduated from Centre College law school in 1911, and was admitted to the bar the same year. While attending law school, Vinson edited the *Basilisk* law journal, taught mathematics at the local prep school, and played baseball. He briefly considered playing professional baseball. In 1913 he was elected city attorney, a post he held until he entered the army in 1918. He was elected commonwealth's attorney in 1921 and, on the Democratic ticket, to the U.S. House of Representatives in 1923. He served from January 12, 1924, to March 3, 1929, and again from March 4, 1931, to May 12, 1938.

In Congress, Vinson developed close friendships with John Nance Garner, Sam Rayburn, and John McCormack. "The Judge," as Vinson was often called, was a serious student of government and a cagey politician. On economic matters he adopted a middle-of-the-road approach between liberalism and conservatism, and he developed a strong local organization among both parties. Pragmatic and flexible, Vinson proved an able behind-the-scenes negotiator whose forte was compromise. On the powerful House Ways and Means Committee, Vinson developed the concept of pay-as-you-go taxes and helped draft the complex tax system that funds Social Security.

A strong supporter of New Deal programs, he cosponsored seven revenue acts of the 1930s. He was also coauthor of the Guffey-Vinson Coal Act of 1935 and 1937, designed to aid the bituminous coal industry. He favored President Franklin D. Roosevelt's "court-packing" scheme and was prepared to lead the fight in the House to win its approval. In 1937 Roosevelt appointed Vinson a judge on the U.S. circuit court for the District of Columbia, and in 1943 Roosevelt named him director of

economic stabilization. Vinson held a series of posts in 1945, including federal loan director and director of war mobilization and reconversion. In June 1945 President Harry S. Truman appointed him secretary of the Treasury, where he served from July 23, 1945, to June 23, 1946. Vinson developed a close personal and professional relationship with Presidents Roosevelt and Truman. He played an important role in setting up the International Monetary Fund and the International Bank for Reconstruction.

To help resolve the bitter personal rivalries that dominated the U.S. Supreme Court, Truman appointed Vinson chief justice on June 24, 1946. Vinson's harmonizing skills helped heal the deep personal wounds on the court, but the number of dissenting opinions increased. Writing fewer opinions than most justices, Vinson reflected the mid-American point of view. He rarely tried to overrule precedents. If there was a choice between the individual and the state, he usually ruled in favor of the state. In his dissent in the steel seizure case (*Youngstown Sheet and Tube v. Sawyer*) in 1952, he bitterly protested that the courts and Congress should uphold the executive in times of crisis.

Vinson was often accused of turning back the clock by allowing the police broad power to maintain law and order. The case that shaped his reputation in this area was *Dennis v. United States* (1951), in which he used the "clear and present danger" theory to uphold the convictions under the Smith Act of Eugene Dennis and ten other Communist leaders. In civil rights, the Vinson court chipped away at state and federal statutes that were discriminatory and it laid the basis for overturning the 1896 *Plessy v. Ferguson* decision for separate but equal facilities. Racial discrimination, Vinson said, had no place in public education. The case of *Brown v. Board of Education* (1954) appeared before his court, but the final decision was postponed and Vinson did not live to rule on it. Justice Tom Clark, who served with Vinson on the Supreme Court, was convinced Vinson would have voted to overturn the Plessy decision.

In 1951 President Truman offered to support Vinson if he sought the Democratic nomination for president in 1952, but Vinson declined.

Vinson married Roberta Dixon in 1923; they had two children, Frederick and James. Vinson died of a massive heart attack on September 8, 1953, and was buried in Pinehill Cemetery in Louisa.

See C. Herman Pritchett, *Civil Liberties and the Vinson Court* (Chicago 1954); James Bolner, "Fred Vinson: 1890-1938, Years of Obscurity," *Register* 63 (Jan. 1965): 3-16; James Bolner, "Mr. Chief Justice Fred Vinson and Racial Discrimination," *Register* 64 (Jan. 1966): 29-43.

RICHARD P. HEDLUND

VIOLENCE. Nineteenth century Kentucky was one of the most violent states in the Union. Although reliable statistical data is scarce, the little that is available suggests that in 1880 Kentuckians killed at a rate twice that of 1980 and were likely as bloodthirsty in earlier years, when even fewer records were kept. Anecdotal information portrays a rather steady stream of homicide throughout the century.

Several reasons account for this carnage. The code of honor that placed high value on a man's reputation and that of his loved ones and demanded deadly retribution for its violation found reverence and application among all classes of Kentuckians. The widespread use of alcohol by Kentucky's menfolk and their habit of carrying concealed weapons led to frequent invocation of the code of honor and its often fatal consequences. The isolation of Appalachian Kentuckians contributed to their tendency to apply the code to entire families and their allies, a tradition that led to bloody longstanding feuds that sometimes enveloped entire counties. The Civil War, divisive to Kentuckians, produced hostilities that did not end at Appomatox. Slavery tended to reduce the worth of human life, making it easier to kill rather than compromise. The excessive number of counties served to aggravate differences.

As in many other states of the nineteenth century, Kentucky's generally defective criminal justice system served as both cause and symptom of violence. The constabulary suffered from mediocrity and poor training. The sheriff, the most important law enforcement officer of most counties, usually spent too little time in crime detection, preferring more profitable and less dangerous responsibilities. In poorer counties, in fact, sheriffs sometimes assumed leadership positions among feuding factions. The few urban police forces that existed suffered from too much political interference and too little professional training.

Because of the realities of the marketplace, the best lawyers usually found themselves defending rather than prosecuting accused killers. The position of commonwealth's attorney paid poorly and demanded strenuous work, a combination that in most counties produced prosecutors either young and inexperienced or old and mediocre. Indeed, the calibre of public prosecution, as in many other states, ranked so low that the survivors of murder victims typically hired private lawyers to assist the commonwealth's attorney in the prosecution of the alleged killer. Despite these efforts, the balance of lawyering normally tilted decisively in favor of the defendant. The tradition of defense attorneys serving in the legislature and creating a code of criminal procedure that favored criminal defendants tilted those scales even further in favor of crime.

Nor did Kentucky's jury system, also part of an American tradition, assure the conviction of killers. During the early part of the nineteenth century, the sheriff formed a jury simply by rounding up the most available white male adults, a process that too often filled the jury box with "courthouse bums." Even the more sophisticated jury commissioner system did not produce more balanced demographics among homicide juries; since the rules emphasized little previous knowledge of the case on the part of potential veniremen, "the best men" found it relatively easy to evade jury service altogether. This left for the jury box too many individuals who were easily swayed by legally irrelevant but strongly emotional rhetoric of forceful defense attorneys, or by the bribes of corrupt wealthy defendants.

Trial judges suffered from somewhat the same strictures as public prosecutors: low pay for too much work. As a result less-than-able men too often served as circuit court judges. Provisions in the Code of Criminal Procedure made it easy for defendants to swear hard-nosed judges off the bench, and the rampant lawlessness in some counties frightened some of the most courageous away from the courthouse altogether. Starting in 1854, a convicted felon could turn to the Kentucky court of appeals as another avenue of possible escape. Kentucky's appeals court issued some of the nation's most permissive rulings on self-defense, legal insanity, and drunkenness as a defense in the acquittals of accused murderers.

Kentucky's governors had a significant role in the criminal justice system of the nineteenth century, acting in ways, critics charged, that further undermined law and order. For most of the century Kentucky had no parole system; instead, the governor, with his very broad pardoning power, served as a one-man review board of most convictions. Observers argued that too often governors pardoned convicts without a thorough examination of the record and a full opportunity for the opponents of pardoning to state their case.

Feuds burned as Kentucky's most celebrated form of violence in the nineteenth century. No other state suffered through as many such episodes. Although the Hatfield-McCoy feud is the most familiar today, the Rowan County feud, which lasted three years (1884-87), involved the most bloodshed and turmoil. Modern roads and other conveniences that connected Appalachian Kentucky to the outside world helped end the feuds in the early part of the twentieth century. Improved law enforcement, the sexual revolution, the decline of the code of honor, and laws against drinking on election day helped reduce Kentucky's homicide rate to a level in line with that of the American mainstream (a reduction somewhat marred by the Harlan County coal war of the 1930s and 1940s). Yet for much of the nineteenth century, her violent tradition comported with the Indians' description of Kentucky as the "dark and bloody ground."

See Robert M. Ireland, "Homicide in Nineteenth-Century Kentucky," *Register* 81 (Spring 1983): 134-53; James C. Klotter, "Feuds in Appalachia: An Overview," *FCHQ* 56 (July 1982): 290-317.

ROBERT M. IRELAND

VIRGINIA COMPACT OF 1789. The Virginia Compact of 1789, part of the Virginia General Assembly's fourth enabling act (December 1789), made it possible for Virginia's western district to achieve independent statehood. The series of enabling acts more or less tracked the ten Kentucky conventions that met from 1784 to 1792.

The principal obstacles to separation involved Virginia land grants and the shared responsibilities for Virginia's debt from the Revolutionary War. The fourth enabling act followed Kentucky's eighth convention and the earlier disclosure by some Kentucky leaders of negotiations with Spain to gain trading rights on the Mississippi, which had led to widespread suspicion that there were also plans to separate from the confederation. Virginia's willingness to compromise on critical issues to forestall the SPANISH CONSPIRACY, and the complexity of the land laws, are reflected in the compact's terms:

1) Kentucky's boundaries as a state to remain as they had been while it was a district.

2) Kentucky to assume "a just proportion" of the war debt and to pay all certificates granted for Kentucky expeditions against the Indians since January 1, 1785.

3) All land titles derived from Virginia to remain valid and secure.

4) The lands of nonresidents not to be taxed by either state at a higher rate than that for residents; and failure to cultivate or improve the land not to be grounds for forfeiture in either state for six years after Kentucky's statehood.

5) Kentucky land warrants not to interfere with any Virginia warrants located on or before September 1, 1791.

6) Kentucky not to interfere with land appropriated, but not yet located, for military grants until May 1, 1792.

7) The Ohio River to be free for the people of the United States.

8) Six commissioners (two appointed by each state, and two appointed jointly) to have authority to settle any disputes arising from the conditions of the compact.

Kentucky accepted these terms, and Congress voted to admit Kentucky as the fifteenth state. The terms of the compact itself were litigated in *Wilson v. Mason*, a land case that the U.S. Supreme Court decided in 1801. Chief Justice John Marshall wrote the Court's opinion upholding the plaintiff, by declaring that the constitutional grant of power over cases involving lands granted by different states in article 3 superseded agreements by states. The decision had the effect of awarding 30,000 acres in the Green River area to Joseph Hamilton Daveiss, a brother-in-law of Marshall, and overruled a decision by Judge Harry Innes of the Kentucky District federal court, which supported George Mason's claim under the Virginia land law of 1779.

MARY K. BONSTEEL TACHAU

VOCATIONAL EDUCATION. Vocational education, which prepares students for careers that do not require college degrees, uses hands-on teaching methods, including equipment-intensive training in such areas as agriculture, construction, health services, home economics, manufacturing, business and office work, and retail sales. It is similar to technology education—which has also been called industrial education, industrial arts, manual arts, and manual training—but technology education provides an overview of careers and does not prepare students for specific careers, as does vocational education. Kentucky's vocational education programs are delivered by five types of institutions: (1) local high schools; (2) high schools supported jointly by the district and the state; (3) vocational technical schools, which are state-controlled and offer programs for adults; (4) community colleges and universities, which offer teacher training; and (5) private schools, such as business colleges. Vocational schools provide instruction for entry-level careers and for upgrading and retraining currently employed persons.

Until the middle of the nineteenth century, when state colleges began to teach farming and manufacturing, apprenticeship was the main form of vocational education. The first formal recognition of vocational education occurred with the Morrill Act of 1862, which granted each state land to establish and maintain one college for "agriculture and the mechanic arts." Kentucky's 33,000-acre share was used to establish the AGRICULTURAL AND MECHANICAL COLLEGE of Kentucky University on October 2, 1865. Known as a land grant college, it became the University of Kentucky in 1916 and was the first Kentucky university to offer courses in vocational education.

Vocational education in Kentucky's secondary schools began with the establishment in 1893 of the Du Pont Manual High School in Louisville. The Louisville board of education's first report, for the period 1911-12, set forth goals to establish a vocational school and to cooperate with the city's manufacturers. The result was the Prevocational School, which opened in September 1913 with thirty-two students. Ethel Martha Lovell was the first principal and one of the first two teachers. It became the Louisville Vocational School in January 1918 and was dedicated the Theodore Ahrens Trade School on December 1, 1926, naming it to honor a local manufacturer who donated $650,000 to the board of education. Lovell started the Kentucky Vocational Association in 1926, the same year the American Vocational Association (AVA) was established; the AVA conducted its first national convention in Louisville December 2-4, 1926.

Another important piece of federal legislation was the Smith-Hughes Act of 1917, which allowed long-term state planning by providing continuing funding for high school vocational education in agriculture, trades and industry, home economics, and teacher training. The Vocational Education Act of 1963 and an amendment known as the Carl D. PERKINS Act of 1984 helped Kentucky fund new programs and new state-operated vocational technical schools and fostered a reevaluation of the importance of proper training in skill-oriented careers. (Perkins was the eighteen-term Kentucky representative from the 7th Congressional District who sponsored the bill and was chairman of the House Committee on Education and Labor from 1967 until his death in 1984.)

Kentucky has 173 school districts operating high school vocational programs. Twenty-two of those districts have area centers or vocational departments with five or more programs. The instructional goals focus on the development of leadership skills, job readiness skills, work attitudes, and occupational skills for high school students. The Kentucky Department of Education has established fifteen vocational education regions, each with a minimum population of 100,000 and, over a period of several years, has built seventeen postsecondary, state-operated vocational technical schools, each of which offers a minimum of twelve programs to at least five hundred adult students. The programs link academics with skill training and vary from one to two years in length. In addition there are fifty-four vocational education centers, five health occupation centers, and one advanced technology center. The annual enrollments in the programs are approximately 192,000 high school students, 17,000 adult students, and 91,000 part-time adult students in short-term classes.

Community colleges and universities have agreements with the state vocational technical schools that allow the transfer of credits toward an associate degree. Many students go on in higher education to earn bachelor's and master's degrees. Most Kentucky universities offer some vocational education. Vocational teachers and administrators can receive state certification based on their education and work experience.

See Edwin K. Binford, *Ethel M. Lovell, Pioneer in Vocational Education in Kentucky* (Louisville 1952); Moses Ligon, "A History of Public Education in Kentucky," *Bulletin of the Bureau of School Service* 14 (1942): 1-369.   DENNIS KARWATKA

W

WALKER, GEORGE. George Walker, U.S. senator, was born in Culpeper County, Virginia, in 1763. The brother of David Walker, a U.S. representative, George attended local common schools. He served in the Revolutionary War under Gens. Nathanael Greene and David Morgan and was at the Battle of Cowpens (January 17, 1781), Guilford Court House (March 15, 1781), and the surrender at Yorktown on October 19, 1781. He moved to Jessamine County, Kentucky, in 1794. After studying law, he was admitted to the bar there and established a practice in Nicholasville in 1799. In 1801 he was a commissioner of the Kentucky River Company and from 1810 to 1814 represented Jessamine County in the state Senate. Gov. Isaac Shelby (1792-96) appointed him to the U.S. Senate to fill the opening caused by the resignation of George M. Bibb. Walker served from August 30 to December 16, 1814. He died in Nicholasville on August 19, 1819, and was buried on his estate near there.

See Bennett H. Young, *A History of Jessamine County, Kentucky from its Earliest Settlement to 1898* (Louisville 1898).

WALKER, THOMAS. Thomas Walker, physician and explorer, was born on January 25, 1715, in King and Queen County, Virginia, to Thomas and Susanna (Peachy) Walker. Presumably educated at the College of William and Mary in Williamsburg, he practiced medicine in Fredericksburg and engaged in business. As a member of the LOYAL LAND COMPANY, Walker engaged in land speculation and led the first organized English expedition on record through Cumberland Gap into Kentucky on April 13, 1750, naming the gap and the Cumberland River. His party erected a crude cabin near Barbourville. After wandering in the mountains for several weeks, they returned to Walker's Virginia plantation, Castle Hill in Albemarle County, on July 13. Beginning in 1752, Walker served several terms in the Virginia House of Burgesses. He continued as agent of the Loyal Land Company through 1775. In 1765 he built a home on the Castle Hill estate. Walker was associated with the Lee, Madison, and Washington families and in Albemarle County was a neighbor of Peter Jefferson, father of Thomas Jefferson; for a time he was Thomas Jefferson's guardian. In 1768 Walker served as a commissioner to a congress of the Six Nations of the Iroquois. During the winter of 1779-80 Walker surveyed the boundary line between Virginia and North Carolina west to the Tennessee River.

He married Mildred (Thornton) Meriwether in 1741; they had twelve children. Mildred died on November 16, 1778, and Walker later married her cousin, Elizabeth Thornton. He died on November 9, 1794, and was buried at Castle Hill.

See J. Stoddard Johnston, ed., *First Explorations of Kentucky* (Louisville 1898); Keith Ryan Nyland,

"Doctor Thomas Walker (1715-1794), Explorer, Physician, Statesman, Surveyor and Planter of Virginia and Kentucky," Ph.D. diss., Ohio State University, 1971. CHARLES S. GUTHRIE

WALLACE, CALEB. Caleb Wallace, minister and early political leader, was born at Cub Creek in Lunenburg (now Charlotte) County, Virginia, in 1742 to Samuel and Esther (Baker) Wallace. At age twenty-five he entered the Elizabethtown Grammar School in New Jersey to prepare for admittance to the nearby College of New Jersey (now Princeton). He entered the college as a junior, studied for the ministry, and graduated in either 1770 or 1771. He was licensed to preach on May 28, 1772. Wallace worked as an itinerant minister in the southern colonies until October 1774, when he was ordained in Virginia by the Hanover Presbytery to serve the Cub Creek and Falling River churches. In the same year, he helped the Hanover Presbytery in founding Washington University and Hampden-Sidney College, both in Virginia.

Wallace left the ministry and moved in 1782 to Kentucky, where he settled in what is now Woodford County and practiced law. In 1783 he represented Lincoln County in the Virginia legislature and introduced the bill to found Transylvania University. Wallace was appointed to the Kentucky district of the Virginia supreme court on July 2, 1783, and was involved in the movement to separate Kentucky from Virginia. He was a member of the first and second constitutional conventions (1792 and 1799) and from 1792 to 1813 served on the Kentucky court of appeals. He was an elector in the 1796 presidential election.

Wallace was married three times: first in 1774 to his cousin Sarah McDowell, of Virginia, who died after one or two years, then to Rosanna Christian, also of Virginia, whom he married on May 11, 1779. She died on December 4, 1804. He then married Mary Brown, of Frankfort. Wallace died in 1814 in Woodford County and was buried at his residence there.

See William Whitsitt, *Life and Times of Judge Caleb Wallace* (Louisville 1888).

WALLACE, EARL DICKENS. Earl Dickens Wallace, an oil industry executive who initiated the restoration of Shakertown at Pleasant Hill, was born on October 19, 1898, in Gray, Knox County, Kentucky. He attended Sue Bennett College in London, Kentucky, and graduated from the University of Kentucky in 1921 with a degree in engineering. He worked first as a petroleum geologist in Lee County. In 1932 he was appointed president of the People's Gas Company of Kentucky, and served as a director of the Petroleum Exploration Company and the Wiser Oil Company. He was president of the Kentucky Oil and Gas Association from 1934 to 1939, and for three years was director of the

Independent Petroleum Association of America. Wallace was vice-president and director of the Standard Oil Company of Kentucky from 1942 to 1953; he was also president of a Standard Oil subsidiary, the Sohio Petroleum Company. In 1953 Wallace left Standard Oil and joined Dillon, Read, and Company, a Wall Street investment banking firm. He retired from the firm in the mid-1960s. Wallace served as a director of Lexington's Second National Bank and Trust Company in the 1960s and was appointed to the Transylvania University board of curators in 1964. The Kentucky Press Association recognized Wallace as Kentuckian of the year in 1965, and in 1982 he was awarded the Governor's Distinguished Service Medallion. He also received President Ronald Reagan's Volunteer Action Award in 1984.

Wallace was best known in Kentucky for his efforts to restore Shakertown, the nineteenth century SHAKER settlement at Pleasant Hill in Mercer County. Wallace initiated the restoration project in 1961, and persuaded Gov. Bert T. Combs (1959-63) to provide $50,000 of state money for the project. Wallace ultimately raised $12 million for Shakertown, which opened to tourists in 1968. Wallace served as Shakertown's board chairman and chief executive officer until his death.

Wallace and his wife, the former Mary F. Wilson, had two children, Earl D., Jr., and Betty Tenney. After his wife's death in 1946, he married Jane Gregory, who died in 1983. Wallace died on April 3, 1990, and was buried in the Lexington Cemetery.

WALLER, JOHN LIGHTFOOT. John Lightfoot Waller, Baptist theologian, was born on November 23, 1809, to Edmund and Elizabeth (Lightfoot) Waller in Woodford County, Kentucky. He was educated by his older brothers and subsequently attended the Nicholasville Academy, where he studied the classics. Though admitted to Transylvania University, Waller did not matriculate, but rather purchased the required texts and studied independently. He later taught at Greenhill Academy in Madison County.

Waller was a devoted Baptist and wrote a variety of essays on religion, including "Church Without a Creed" (1827). A division in Baptist doctrine prompted his 1835 work *Letters to a Reformer, Alias Campbellite*, which was an analysis of the "Current Reformation." It was well-received, and Waller was encouraged to become editor of the *Baptist Banner*, published in Shelbyville, Kentucky. Under Waller's direction, the *Baptist Banner* bought and consolidated with the *Illinois Pioneer* and the *Tennessee Baptist* under the name *Baptist Banner and Western Pioneer*, and its publication site was moved to Louisville. In 1840 Waller was ordained, and he replaced his father as pastor of Glen's Creed Church in Woodford County in 1843, remaining there for nine years. He retired as editor of the *Banner* in 1841 and became a general agent and the first secretary of the board for the General

Association of Kentucky Baptists, a position he held until 1843.

Waller participated in several public debates with such religious figures as Nathan L. Rice, John Brown, Robert C. Grundy, John T. Hendric, and E.M. Pingree. In 1845 Waller created the *Baptist Review*, later called the *Christian Repository*, and he wrote "The History of Kentucky Baptists" in Lewis Collins's *Historical Sketches of Kentucky* (1847). In 1849 he was elected to represent Woodford County at Kentucky's constitutional convention, defeating Thomas P. Marshall by 219 votes. Waller returned to edit the *Baptist Banner and Western Pioneer* in 1850, and was elected president of the Bible Revision Association in 1852, a position he held until his death.

Waller married Amanda M. Beatty in August 1834; they had three daughters. He died on October 10, 1854, in Louisville and was buried in the Frankfort Cemetery. A collection of his writings, *Open Communion Shown to be Unscripted and Deleterious*, was published in 1859.

WALLERSTEIN, HERMAN L. Herman L. Wallerstein, businessman, was born August 3, 1839, in Frankfurt, Germany, the son of Mose and Sophia Wallerstein. He came to the United States around 1856, and served four years with a Georgia regiment during the Civil War. After the war, Wallerstein opened a clothing store in Griffin, Georgia, and in 1868 he moved to Paducah, Kentucky, where he opened another store. For over fifty years, Wallerstein was Paducah's foremost clothier and an active participant in the city's civic life. He was a lifelong Mason and president of Paducah's Temple Israel. He married Fannie Uri of Paducah in 1877; they had three children. Wallerstein died in Paducah on December 15, 1922, and was buried in the Temple Israel cemetery there. He was the model for the fictional character Mr. Felsburg in several short stories by Irvin S. COBB.

See Camille Wells, *Architecture of Paducah and McCracken County* (Paducah, Ky., 1981).

LEE SHAI WEISSBACH

WALLIS, FREDERICK A. Frederick A. Wallis, politician, son of Allan Morgan and Albertine (Roos) Wallis, was born on March 13, 1869, in Hopkinsville, Kentucky. In 1896 Wallis moved to Louisville where he became an agent for the Northwest Life Insurance Company. He worked in the company's Lexington office from 1899 to 1901, then moved to New York City. Wallis became independently wealthy through his insurance career. He served as police commissioner of New York City in 1915. In 1918 President Woodrow Wilson appointed Wallis commissioner of immigration at Ellis Island, a post he held until 1922. He then served as New York's commissioner of corrections for the next four years. In 1929 Wallis returned to Bourbon County, Kentucky, where he owned a 2,400-acre farm known as Walliston. Wallis served as chairman of both the state campaign committee in 1931 and the Kentucky Democratic Finance Committee during 1932-35. A.B. Chandler and Thomas Rhea both defeated him in the 1935 Democratic primary. Wallis then turned his support to Chandler, who appointed him commissioner of welfare. He also served as a trustee of Centre College in Danville. Wallis devoted much of his time to conservation and served as both chairman of the Kentucky State Parks Advisory Board and executive chairman of the Cumberland Falls Preservation Committee. He was supervising editor of the four-volume series, *A Sesqui-Centennial History of Kentucky* (1945).

Wallis married Nannine Williams Clay of Paris, Kentucky, on April 10, 1901; they had one daughter, Frances Clay. He died on December 21, 1951, in Paris and was buried in the Paris Cemetery.

WARD, CHARLES. Charles Ward, who wrote songs in tribute to the Confederacy, was born in Wheeling, West Virginia, on February 27, 1838. His father, William Ward, a dentist, was a highly talented musician, and Charles showed musical talent at an early age. The Ward family moved to Pittsburgh in 1840, and when Charles was seven he joined the choir of the Presbyterian Church of Pittsburgh, under the direction of the Stone family. When the Stones decided to move to Louisville in the 1840s, they asked that Charles, who had a beautiful alto voice, be allowed to join them. The boy's parents at first refused, but when they sent their son to visit the Stones in 1850, he stayed on, singing in the choir and working for the music establishment of Brainerd and Stone. It was there that Ward wrote the first of his nearly two hundred songs, "The Old Play Ground" (1855).

When the Civil War began, Ward joined the Confederate army and played the A-flat alto saxhorn in the band of Gen. Simon Bolivar Buckner's troops. During the war, Ward wrote one of his most well-known songs, "Old Town Pump" (1861). At war's end, he wrote a series of songs for the South, which included "Conquered Flag," "The Faded Gray Jacket," and "We Know that We Are Rebels." It was said about Ward that had his ambition equaled his natural talent, he would have been a world-famous songwriter. Ward married Kate Miller in 1865. They had two daughters, Margaret and Ermine. Ward died on April 21, 1874, after a long illness and was buried in Eastern Cemetery in Louisville.

WARD, HENRY THOMAS. Henry Thomas Ward, state congressman and senator, was born June 20, 1909, in New Hope, Kentucky, the youngest child of Gustavus Adolphus and Beulah (Jernigan) Ward. He attended public schools and graduated with honors from Tilgman High School in Paducah in 1928. Ward joined the staff of the *Paducah Sun-Democrat* (now *Paducah Sun*) after graduation and became city editor and editorial columnist. Ward served five consecutive terms (1934-43) from McCracken County in the state House of Representatives and was majority leader in 1942. He cam-

paigned for the Democratic party's nomination for lieutenant governor in 1943 but lost the primary to William May. In 1945 he was elected to the Kentucky Senate and served until 1948, when he became commissioner of conservation. He held that office until 1956 and was instrumental in expanding the modern state park system, as well as in implementing new forestry programs.

In 1956 Ward became top aide to U.S. Senator Earle Clements and in January 1957 began working as a lobbyist for the National Real Estate Association. In mid-1957 he became general manager of the Louisville Chamber of Commerce. In 1960 he returned to state government as commissioner of the Highway Department under Govs. Bert T. Combs (1959-63) and Edward T. Breathitt (1963-67). Ward ran for governor on the Democratic ticket against Louie B. Nunn in the 1967 election, receiving 425,674 votes to Nunn's 454,123. After his defeat, Ward returned to the *Paducah Sun-Democrat* as publisher.

Ward retired from public life in 1974 and moved to Howey-in-the-Fields, Florida; he returned to Lexington, Kentucky, in 1987. Ward married Gladys Lindsey of Water Valley, Mississippi, on September 21, 1934. They have one daughter, Patricia.

WARD, SALLIE. Sallie Ward, socialite, was born in Scott County near Georgetown on September 29, 1827, to Robert J. and Emily (Flournoy) Ward. She grew to maturity in her wealthy family's mansion at the corner of Second and Walnut streets in Louisville. Ward attended a French finishing school in Philadelphia and completed her education there in 1844. Pretty, quick-witted, unconventional, and spoiled, she enjoyed widespread popularity. The center of attention at social gatherings, she sponsored perhaps the first fancy dress ball in Kentucky, set a trend in using cosmetics to enhance her beauty, and introduced opera glasses to the commonwealth. Her frequent benefit balls for the poor contributed to her status as one of Louisville's best-loved residents.

Ward's social prominence extended beyond the local area. During her many trips abroad she was presented to European courts and became a favorite of Napoleon III, emperor of France. Commercial products bore her name, and steamboats, racehorses, and babies were christened in her honor.

Ward married four times. Her 1848 marriage to Bigelow Lawrence ended in a highly publicized divorce a year later. In 1851 she married Robert P. Hunt and moved to New Orleans. The couple had three children: Robert, Jr. (who died in infancy), Emily (who died at age nine), and John Wesley. A supporter of President Abraham Lincoln, Ward returned to Louisville when the Civil War started, but her husband joined the Confederate Army. Hunt died in 1865; in 1876 Ward married Vene Armstrong. After Armstrong's death in 1885, she married George F. Downs. The couple lived at the Galt House until Ward's death on July 8, 1896. She was buried in Cave Hill Cemetery in Louisville.

See Ella Hutchison Ellwanger, "Sallie Ward: The Celebrated Kentucky Beauty," *Register* 16 (January 1918): 9-14.

WARD, MATTHEWS, TRIAL. The trial of Matthews Flournoy Ward for the murder of William H.G. Butler in April 1854 represented one of the classic cases to result from the code of honor. On November 2, 1853, Ward demanded that Butler, principal of the Louisville High School, apologize for punishing one of Ward's younger brothers. Butler's refusal provoked a scuffle and Ward shot Butler point-blank. Ward's father, Robert J. Ward, Sr., politically powerful as well as wealthy, retained a host of defense lawyers, including the prominent John J. Crittenden. The lawyers secured a change of venue to Hardin County, where Matt Ward's trial in Elizabethtown attracted national attention. Despite testimony that Ward had been the aggressor and was never seriously threatened by Butler, Ward's lawyers secured an acquittal on the grounds of self-defense in the name of manly honor. Crittenden's summation to the jury ranks as one of the most effective ever given in an American trial.

After Ward's acquittal, thousands of protesters in Louisville and its environs demanded that the Wards move from the state and Crittenden resign from the U.S. Senate. Several of the nation's leading newspapers and at least one prestigious law journal also denounced the acquittal. Ward sought refuge in Arkansas. Despite public distress over the verdict, nineteenth century Kentuckians continued to revere the code of honor with its deadly consequences.

See Robert M. Ireland, "Acquitted Yet Scorned: The Ward Trial and the Traditions of Antebellum Kentucky Criminal Justice," *Register* 84 (Spring 1986): 107-45.   ROBERT M. IRELAND

WARD HALL. Ward Hall in Scott County, one mile west of Georgetown on the Frankfort Road, is the largest and most ornate Greek Revival–style residence in Kentucky and is the epitome of southern grandeur. It was built by Scott County native Junius Ward in the mid-1850s. In the 1830s, Ward lived in Mississippi, where he owned thousands of acres of cotton plantations, but returned each summer to Scott County. He employed regional architect Thomas LEWINSKI, who, given an unlimited budget, made Ward Hall his finest residential design. The house was built for only one purpose— entertaining. Its Italian marble mantles, chandeliers, woodwork, and plasterwork were meant to impress the viewer with their opulence.

Ward Hall was completed in 1859. Ward, a Southern sympathizer, lost his fortune in the Civil War and had scarcely used the house when it was sold to pay his debts in 1867. The house has remained in private hands.

WILLIAM B. SCOTT, JR.

WARE, ORIE S. Orie S. Ware, U.S. congressman, was born on May 11, 1882, at Peach Grove, Pendleton County, Kentucky, to Sol and Ida (Petty) Ware. He attended the Covington public schools and graduated from George W. Dunlop's private academy in Independence, Kentucky, in 1889. In 1903 he received his law degree from the University of Cincinnati and was admitted to the bar. Ware was a member of the Covington law firm of Shaw and Ware from 1910 to 1914. He was director of the First National Bank and Trust Company in Covington, a member of the city's Chamber of Commerce, and a delegate to all Democratic state conventions from 1910 to 1939. He was grand master of the Masons of Kentucky (1913-14). Ware served as postmaster of Covington from 1914 to 1921, resigning to become commonwealth's attorney (1922-27). In 1926 he ran for the U.S. Congress as the Democratic candidate from the 6th District, defeating Republican E.H. Daugherty by a vote of 26,063 to 19,487. He declined to run for reelection and returned to his Covington law practice. Ware was a Kenton County circuit judge in 1957-58.

Ware married Louise Culbertson of Covington on September 19, 1906. They had three children— William, Louise, and James. Ware died on December 16, 1974, and was buried at Highland Cemetery in Fort Mitchell, Kentucky.

WAR OF 1812. The War of 1812 had its origins in Anglo-American controversies over neutral rights during the wars between Britain and France and their allies in 1793-1801 and 1803-15. Resumption of the war in 1803 opened enormous trade opportunities for neutral American shippers. On the other hand, the United States had a rising toll of confiscated ships and cargoes and impressed seamen as a consequence of blockade policies adopted by both warring nations in 1804-6 and Britain's insistence on seizing men of British birth from American merchantmen.

Kentuckians showed little interest in these distant events until June 1807, when the British warship H.M.S. *Leopard* attacked the U.S.S. *Chesapeake* and forcibly removed four alleged British deserters. The *Chesapeake* affair transformed British blockades and impressment policies in Kentuckians' minds from problems for private shippers into intolerable infringements of U.S. national rights and prompted from them a near-universal demand for war. When Congress adopted instead the December 1807 Embargo Act prohibiting American ships from engaging in foreign trade, Kentuckians embraced the measure both as an effective form of retaliation and as a policy that would free American agrarians from dependence on foreign markets by diverting investment capital from shipping to domestic manufacturing. No subsequent policy so fully satisfied Kentucky interests. As Congress moved from partial to full restoration of trade in the Non-Intercourse Act (1809) and Macon's Bill No. 2 (1810), charges of congressional submission to British dictates mounted in the state. Disgruntled Kentuckians loudly proclaimed either embargo or war preferable to submission.

Britain's refusal in August 1811 to modify its maritime policies left compliance with British regulations or war as the only alternatives. Kentucky impatience for immediate war escalated after the November 7 Battle of Tippecanoe between Indian followers of Tecumseh and a force under Indiana Territory Gov. William Henry Harrison. Kentuckians charged that, through its Indian allies, Britain had already commenced hostilities on the frontier.

Impatience turned to frustration in Kentucky as Congress debated for nearly three weeks before finally deciding upon war in June 1812. Among Kentucky's delegates, only Sen. John POPE failed to vote for war, and all but Pope and Speaker of the House Henry Clay promptly sought service in the field. Across Kentucky, news of war occasioned jubilant celebrations. That many New England Federalists bitterly opposed war, that the navy had only twenty ships and the army's ten existing regular regiments were only half-filled, and that Congress adjourned without voting new taxes to support the war did little to diminish military ardor in the state. Enthusiastic Kentuckians quickly filled two and one-half of thirteen newly authorized regular regiments, and by September Gov. Isaac Shelby (1812-16) was turning away eager militia volunteers for lack of arms and equipment.

Relying primarily upon militia, U.S. strategy was to conquer Canada and use it to negotiate concessions from Great Britain. Invasions along Lake Champlain, across the Niagara River, and from Detroit were planned. From the outset Kentuckians assumed that as the leader in the region, their state would bear primary responsibility for military operations in the Northwest. Kentucky volunteers expected a single swift, victorious campaign against Upper Canada. In August 1812, however, U.S. Gen. William Hull surrendered Detroit, leaving much of the northwestern frontier exposed to British and Indian attack.

To retrieve the advantage, Governor Shelby acted in close concert with Gen. William Henry Harrison in Ohio. Urging Harrison to drive straight for Detroit with his Northwest Army, largely Kentucky militia, Shelby sent 2,000 mounted volunteers under Major Gen. Samuel HOPKINS into Indiana and Illinois in an unsuccessful attempt to draw British-allied Indians away from Harrison's advance. Meanwhile, Harrison's advance northward along three separate routes was slowed by the early onset of winter. It was mid-January 1813 before the first column of 1,300 Kentuckians under Gen. James WINCHESTER arrived at the designated rendezvous on the frozen Maumee River.

Without awaiting the remainder of Harrison's army, Winchester on January 18 attacked a small British force guarding badly needed stores at Frenchtown, thirty-five miles away on the RIVER RAISIN. Nearly 1,000 Kentuckians occupied the tiny settlement. When Gen. Henry Proctor counterattacked on January 22 with British and Indians from Fort Malden, over five hundred Kentuckians were captured, more than one hundred killed, and many others wounded or missing. The calamity worsened that night when Indians massacred forty to sixty-five badly wounded Kentuckians left at Frenchtown after the British withdrawal.

The River Raisin debacle completely dispelled early illusions of a swift, victorious dash into upper Canada, crippled Harrison's advance on Detroit, and convincingly demonstrated that American control of Lake Erie was essential to successful land campaigns in the upper Northwest. So dampened was war spirit in Kentucky that few responded to Governor Shelby's call for 3,000 reinforcements for Harrison's weakened army. By the time Shelby was able in April 1813 to send forward 1,200 men under Green CLAY, Harrison's main body, further reduced by expiring enlistments to about 1,000, was besieged at Fort Meigs on the Maumee River by 2,400 British and Indians. Clay, hastening down-river by boat, hoped to surprise the British batteries bombarding the fort from the opposite riverbank. He ordered Lt. Col. William Dudley with 796 men to spike the enemy cannon and immediately withdraw across the river to the fort before superior British forces could counterattack. Instead of withdrawing after overrunning the guns, Dudley's overexcited militiamen pursued the fleeing artillerymen into the main British camp, where 634 Americans were either killed or captured. As the surviving Kentuckians were marched toward a temporary prison compound, Indians overwhelmed the guards and slaughtered an additional forty.

"Dudley's Defeat" was a second stunning disaster for Kentucky arms. Though the British soon abandoned their unsuccessful siege of Fort Meigs, Harrison's position was little improved. On July 31 Shelby again appealed for a large force of Kentucky volunteers, promising to lead them personally to Canada. A month later, Shelby left Newport with 3,500 mounted volunteers. On September 10, two days before he joined Harrison, Oliver Hazard Perry's naval victory on Lake Erie opened the way to Canada. Perry's ships transported a large part of Harrison's army to Canada near Fort Malden; the remainder marched against Detroit. Threatened by encirclement, Proctor abandoned both posts and with nearly 1,000 regulars and more than 3,000 Indians under Tecumseh retreated eastward along the Thames River. Harrison pursued with slightly more than 3,000 men, including Kentucky Sen. Richard M. Johnson's cavalry regiment, Shelby's volunteers, and about 120 regulars. On October 5 in the Battle of the THAMES, most of the British regulars were captured, the Indians were routed, and Tecumseh was slain.

The defeat of the British army in upper Canada fulfilled Kentucky's principal goal in the war, but British victory in Europe soon doomed further American offensives against Canada. During 1814 a British expedition harried the Virginia coast and burned Washington before being repulsed at Baltimore; a second British invasion threatened New England until checked by an American naval victory at Plattsburg Bay on Lake Champlain

(September 1814); and Andrew Jackson hastily assembled a makeshift army to oppose a third attack at New Orleans. Yet the Kentucky legislature did nothing to replenish the state's exhausted military stores or prepare its militia for further service. When in October the War Department directed Shelby to provide 2,500 reinforcements for Jackson, he not only had to draft men for service but was unable to arm them. Arriving in New Orleans on January 4, 1815, only about 1,200 were able to secure weapons before the British assault on January 8. Of these, 1,000 under Gen. John ADAIR were positioned at the main point of attack and effectively aided in inflicting on the British the bloodiest defeat of the war.

Unknown to the combatants, the Treaty of Ghent had been signed on December 24, 1814, though it provided for little more than a return to the antebellum status quo. During the course of the war, Kentucky furnished 25,705 regulars, militia, and volunteers (the estimated equivalent of four of every six eligible males in the state) and was frequently pointed to as a model of patriotism. Moreover, unlike states that required large numbers of troops to garrison coastal or other fortresses, nearly all Kentucky troops campaigned actively against the enemy, suffering in consequence more deaths in battle than all other states combined. Their efforts and sacrifices made possible the expulsion of the British from the upper Northwest and aided in the defense of New Orleans.

See James W. Hammack, Jr., *Kentucky & the Second American Revolution: The War of 1812* (Lexington, Ky., 1976).

JAMES W. HAMMACK, JR.

WAR ON POVERTY. In April 1964 President Lyndon B. Johnson dramatized his intention to wage war on poverty in America by visiting the family of an unemployed coal miner in Inez, Kentucky. Johnson's destination was appropriate. Kentucky, especially those counties located in the eastern, or Appalachian, portion of the state, was not only the site where the War on Poverty began, but also a major focal point in the nationwide effort to end the paradox of poverty in the midst of plenty. Lasting roughly a decade, the antipoverty campaign brought to Kentucky millions of dollars in federal aid, supported dozens of antipoverty projects, energized reform groups and hundreds of antipoverty warriors, and influenced governors, legislatures, agency officials, local politicians, and citizens in every single county in the state. It has led to a reappraisal of the history and culture of Appalachian Kentucky, and it continues to exert an impact on state and regional economic policymaking.

National concern about the poor had slowly grown during the late 1950s and early 1960s. John F. Kennedy deplored the conditions he had seen during the 1960 presidential primary campaign in West Virginia, and although Congress often stymied his proposals as president to expand social welfare programs, publications like Michael Harrington's *The Other America* (1962) and Whitesburg attorney Harry M. Caudill's *Night Comes to the Cumberlands* (1963) increased public awareness of poverty. In the fall of 1963, Kennedy, reportedly moved by Homer Bigart's *New York Times* article on poverty in eastern Kentucky, ordered the initiation of a comprehensive crash program of emergency aid for the area and agreed to push for a broader attack on poverty in his 1964 legislative program. Following Kennedy's assassination in 1963, Lyndon Johnson immediately embraced what he called "my kind of program," declared an unconditional War on Poverty in his State of the Union message in January 1964, and in August signed the Economic Opportunity Act, which created the Office of Economic Opportunity (OEO) to administer the antipoverty initiative.

Within a few months after OEO Director Sargent Shriver announced the first antipoverty grants in November 1964, well over a dozen state and local programs had begun in Kentucky. Generally the bulk of the federal funds flowed into the Appalachian portion of the state. But by November 1965 Kentucky's overall allocation of funds totaled over $54 million—an amount exceeded only by California and New York—and counties across the state were operating at least one of several antipoverty projects. The centerpiece of each local effort, and the most innovative component of the War on Poverty, was the Community Action Program, which was to mobilize all available community resources to address local poverty. Through the equally novel concept of "maximum feasible participation," Community Action agencies were to involve representatives of local government, key public and private agencies, and the poor themselves in the creation and management of broad-based attacks on poverty.

Kentucky's War on Poverty also included more than five hundred Head Start preschool education centers, Neighborhood Youth Corps jobs programs, work experience and training projects for unemployed fathers (popularly known as the "HAPPY PAPPIES" program), a work study program involving twenty-one colleges, adult basic educational programs, rural and small business loans, Job Corps vocational training centers for teenaged school dropouts, and Volunteers in Service to America (VISTA), the domestic equivalent of the Peace Corps. The Council of the Southern Mountains, headquartered in Berea, Kentucky, also received OEO grants for several projects. The most publicized was the APPALACHIAN VOLUNTEERS (AVs), college students whose energies initially went into refurbishing eastern Kentucky's numerous one- and two-room schoolhouses and aiding curriculum, recreation, and library expansion efforts.

In design, the antipoverty campaign, Community Action in particular, was to be an all-purpose, all-inclusive effort. It sought to build community consensus at a time when it seemed not only possible but entirely reasonable that poor people could work as equals with others to eradicate poverty. It offered something to almost anyone affected by poverty, rural or urban, and it proposed to improve their conditions by creating opportunities for people to escape poverty through their own efforts. No one at the policymaking level of OEO envisioned the possibility of irreconcilable, or even significant, conflicts between the organized poor and locally powerful political and economic interests.

In operation, the War on Poverty in Kentucky proved to be complex and controversial. Certainly there was plenty of activity: comprehensive surveys of local conditions, education and employment programs enrolling thousands of youths and adults, neighborhood action councils meeting regularly to discuss needs and plans, community centers providing numerous services, hot school lunch programs, road and home improvement projects, and small business enterprises. Yet for both critics and supporters, the vital issue was whether the poor were really involved in the Community Action programs, and whether the War on Poverty was leading to meaningful social and economic change.

What had become clear by early 1966, as one activist wrote, was that while the problems of poverty appeared sharper than ever before, "the solutions seem[ed] much further away." Uncertainty about the full meaning of maximum feasible participation abounded. Community Action agencies showed little interest in serving the poor, in seating representatives of the poor on their boards of directors, or in forming community organizations. Some agencies contended with a welter of old battles between school superintendents, health officials, and welfare workers. Complex internal conflicts and friction with local VISTAs and Appalachian Volunteers tormented others. Communication among local agencies, the Kentucky Office of Economic Opportunity, and the federal OEO was sometimes muddled. There were debates over the relative merits of multicounty versus single-county Community Action units, as well as ongoing complaints about bureaucratic red tape, administrative salaries, and the wages paid program participants. Agencies faced charges of nepotism and political favoritism; indeed, powerful county machines frustrated OEO's insistence on political neutrality and rejected programs contrary to their interests. Partisanship assured Republican charges of alleged Democratic waste and inefficiency. Too many Head Start and Job Corps enrollees came from middle- and upper-income families; too many jobless fathers did menial work instead of upgrading their skills. OEO's Community Action strategy and focus on the poor made coordination difficult with the APPALACHIAN REGIONAL COMMISSION and its trickle-down, bricks-and-mortar approach to economic development. In short, despite signs of progress, the War on Poverty was resulting in compromise, confusion, and a perpetuation of the status quo.

As the shortcomings of the reform-by-consensus assumptions of Community Action became increasingly evident, restive activists and members of the target population decided that the poor should organize under their own leaders and challenge the authority of established institutions and groups. For a time this confrontational strategy dramatically altered the tenor and thrust of the antipoverty campaign. Frustrated by what they saw as the conservatism of the Council of the Southern Mountains, the Appalachian Volunteers became an independent organization in May 1966 and proceeded to spearhead a number of aggressive, controversial, and highly successful community organizing efforts in several eastern Kentucky counties. Meanwhile, in the Cumberland Valley, in the Big Sandy River area, in Harlan and Knox counties, and to a lesser extent in Louisville and western Kentucky, poor people contested the policies and power of both Community Action agency boards and state and federal OEO officials.

Politicians, businessmen, and Community Action directors, faced with increasingly sophisticated demands from previously quiescent people, moved decisively to halt the insurgency. Congress imposed more restrictive spending and operating procedures and in 1967 passed an amendment sponsored by Oregon Rep. Edith Green, which in effect permitted local governments to assume control of Community Action agencies. The AVs, even those who were native Kentuckians, were especially vulnerable to charges of outside agitation. The resulting furor led to the demise of the Appalachian Volunteers in 1971, widened rifts between the OEO and local Community Action agencies, made Gov. Edward Breathitt (1963-67) and his successor, Gov. Louie Nunn (1967-71), wary of approving further antipoverty funding, solidified opposition to the War on Poverty, and ultimately disillusioned Kentucky's poor.

In the four years following the election of Richard M. Nixon in 1968, the War on Poverty slowed to a standstill. OEO appropriations shrank steadily, forcing several Community Action agencies to cut back activities or to cease operations entirely. Those that survived worked under the close scrutiny of the Nunn administration. OEO itself was dismembered, with components like Job Corps and Head Start placed under old-line federal departments, while the Nunn administration organized Area Development Districts that minimized the involvement of the poor in economic projects. Unwilling to concede that the War on Poverty had been lost, eastern Kentucky Rep. Carl D. Perkins led the congressional fight to extend the life of OEO. New, independent grass-roots organizations also refused to concede defeat: the Kentucky Poor People's Coalition presented a mule to Governor Nunn at the 1969 Republican Governor's Conference to dramatize the contrast between the plight of the poor and the affluence surrounding the meeting, and in 1970-71 the Eastern Kentucky Welfare Rights Organization forced the restructuring of a Floyd County health project that had not adequately served the poor. Despite such efforts, the deterioration of the War on Poverty continued. After a brief reprieve in 1973-74 under OEO Director Alvin Arnett, a Salyersville, Kentucky, native, federal antagonism, political controversies, internal battles, and a lack of commitment to eradicating poverty brought an end to OEO and the antipoverty campaign in 1974.

See John M. Glen, "The War on Poverty in Appalachia—a Preliminary Report," *Register* 87 (Winter 1989): 40-57; David E. Whisnant, *Modernizing the Mountaineer: People, Power, and Planning in Appalachia* (Boone, N.C., 1980).

JOHN M. GLEN

WARREN, ROBERT PENN. Robert Penn Warren, one of the most distinguished scholar-writers America has produced, was born in Guthrie, Todd County, Kentucky, on April 24, 1905. He was one of three children of Robert Franklin and Ann Ruth (Penn) Warren. Warren attended public schools in Guthrie and graduated summa cum laude from Vanderbilt University in 1925. (An eye injury had forced the cancellation of his appointment to the U.S. Naval Academy.) He had intended to major in chemistry, but under the influence of John Crowe Ransom, he switched to English. While at Vanderbilt, he joined the group known as the Fugitives, participating in literary discussions and in founding the journal called *The Fugitive*, published during 1922-25. He later belonged to the Agrarians, a social-political group that included other such literary lights as Ransom, Donald Davidson, and Allen Tate. Warren (known to his friends as "Red") continued his studies at the University of California, Berkeley, earning his M.A. in English there in 1927. He subsequently studied at Yale and, for two years, at Oxford as a Rhodes scholar. He earned the B.Litt. degree at Oxford in 1930.

Warren's long and distinguished teaching career began at Louisiana State University in 1934. While there, he cofounded (along with Cleanth BROOKS, another Kentuckian, and Charles W. Pipkin) *The Southern Review*, a literary journal that lasted from 1935 until 1942. Warren taught at the University of Minnesota during 1942-51, then returned to Yale as a professor of playwriting and retained that post until 1956. He was named professor of English at Yale in 1961 and retired in 1973.

As well as teaching and lecturing, Warren achieved both critical and popular acclaim as a poet, novelist, essayist, dramatist, literary critic, and editor. Among his better-known works are *Night Rider* (1939), *All the King's Men* (1946), *Audubon: A Vision* (1969), *Now and Then: Poems 1976-1978* (1979). The nation's first Poet Laureate and a three-time winner of the Pulitzer prize (the only writer to win for both fiction and poetry), Warren also received a National Book Award, the Copernicus Award for Poetry, the Bollingen Prize for Poetry, the National Medal for Literature, and a MacArthur Foundation award. He was awarded the Gold Medal for Poetry from the American Academy and Institute of Arts and Letters.

Practically all of Warren's critics have commented on how his poetic powers improved as he grew older. (Friends said he was writing until the last few months of his life.) In *A Literary History of Kentucky* (1988), William S. Ward expresses the widespread critical view: "Nothing has distinguished Warren's career so much as the late flowering of his poetic powers, during which he became both a more prolific and steadily better poet. His *New and Selected Poems, 1923-1985*, presumably well-represents the poetry he is willing to trust his reputation to; and indeed it reflects well the informal, personal and meditative poem that has become the trademark of the work that traces back to *Promises* and even to 'The Ballad of Billy Potts.' "

Western Kentucky University in 1987 established the Center for Warren Studies, and a committee in Guthrie completed restoration of Warren's birthplace in 1989. In 1988 Warren received the Milner Award of the Governor's Awards for the Arts in Kentucky.

Warren married Emma Brescia in 1930; they were divorced in 1951. He married the writer Eleanor Clark in 1952; they had two children: Rosanna Warren Sculley, a poet, and Gabriel, a sculptor. Warren died on September 15, 1989, and was buried in the Stratton, Vermont, cemetery.

See James H. Justus, *The Achievement of Robert Penn Warren* (Baton Rouge, La., 1981); James A. Grimshaw, Jr., *Robert Penn Warren, A Descriptive Bibliography* (Charlottesville, Va., 1981).

MARY ELLEN MILLER

WARREN COLLEGE. Warren College, an institution of higher education founded in the nineteenth century, was located in Bowling Green, Kentucky. In 1859 the Louisville Conference of the Methodist Episcopal Church, South, appointed a committee to consider the establishment of a school for young men in the community. Within a year it secured the transfer of the charter of an unsuccessful state school, the Southern College of Kentucky. A new charter, under the name of Warren College, was obtained in 1866, but only the preparatory school, under S.G. Scott and G.B. Doggett, flourished. On September 5, 1872, the college division opened under President J.G. Wilson with an enrollment of eighty. Warren College continued for four years with faculty members Wilson, Doggett, Wilbur Barclay, H.A. Scomp, C.F. Dillard, and Benjamin F. Cabell, principal of the preparatory school. The founding in 1877 of the privately endowed OGDEN COLLEGE in Bowling Green and the growing interest of the Louisville Conference in Vanderbilt University led to the closing of Warren College. In 1878 all property was sold to Ogden College.

CONNIE MILLS

WARREN COUNTY. Warren County, the twenty-fourth in order of formation, is located in southern Kentucky. It is bordered by Allen, Barren, Butler, Edmonson, Logan, and Simpson counties and has an area of 546 square miles. Warren County was formed from a section of Logan County on December 19, 1796, and was named in honor of Gen. Joseph Warren, who dispatched William Dawes and Paul Revere on their midnight ride to warn the countryside of the British approach and who was a hero of the Battle of Bunker Hill during the Revolutionary War. The county seat is BOWLING GREEN.

The topography of Warren County is undulating, with some expanses of level land. The soil is fertile and produces tobacco, corn, and hay. Warren County ranks high in the production of beef and dairy cattle and hogs. The principal streams in Warren County include the Green River, which forms the northern boundary of the county, and its tributaries, the Barren and Gasper rivers, Drake's Creek, Bay's Fork, and Jennings Creek.

Remains of Native American villages and burial mounds have been discovered in some sections of the county. The first pioneers in the area were Long Hunters who came in the 1770s. Gen. Elijah Covington and George and Robert Moore were among the early landowners. One of the earliest settlements was McFadden's Station, established on the north bank of the Barren River at the Cumberland Trace by Andrew McFadden in 1785. The trace, an important artery for development of the region, connected the Barren River settlements with the Cumberland River settlement of Nashville to the south, and the Green River settlements to the northeast. Communities were established in rapid succession in the county. Among incorporated communities are Bowling Green, Oakland, Plum Springs, Smith's Grove, and Woodburn.

The rich farmland of Warren County attracted settlers in the closing years of the eighteenth century and the first part of the nineteenth. By the 1830s, the county was well populated and growing steadily, and the river transported goods to market. In the 1830s, a portage railroad was constructed from the Barren River to the site of the present Warren County courthouse in Bowling Green, perhaps the first of its kind built in Kentucky. Warren County thrived on the flourishing riverboat trade in the nineteenth century. By 1859 the Louisville & Nashville Railroad (now CSX Transportation) was constructed through Warren County.

The Civil War deeply divided many Warren County families, although most residents favored the preservation of the Union. Because of its strategic position, Bowling Green was a prime target of both Confederate and Union armies. In September 1861, Gen. Simon Bolivar Buckner's Confederate forces occupied the county, evacuating it on February 14, 1862. Before leaving Bowling Green, the Confederate forces destroyed the bridges over the Barren River, the railroad depot, and other buildings and stores of supplies. Warren County was subjected to numerous raids and disruptions during the remainder of the war. In the summer of 1864, Union Gen. Stephen Burbridge ordered the arrest of twenty-two men from Warren County on suspicion

of treason. Subject to harsh treatment from Federal authorities, during the latter part of the war, many residents began to be more sympathetic to the Southern cause. This pro-Confederate bias continued into the twentieth century.

By the 1870s, Warren County was one of the wealthiest in the commonwealth. It had one of the finest courthouses in the state and many business and agricultural enterprises. During the latter half of the nineteenth century, Bowling Green became the site of various educational institutions, including the predecessors of Western Kentucky University.

Except for Bowling Green, Warren County was primarily agricultural until the completion of I-65 through the central and eastern part of the county during the late 1960s and the Green River Parkway through the western part in the late 1970s. The county then underwent an industrial boom that changed its nature. By 1979, 64 percent of the county population was urban, 23 percent was rural nonfarm, and only 13 percent lived on farms. There was an increase in the number of farms in the county but a decrease in their size, as many rural residents were part-time farmers who worked full-time jobs in Bowling Green. The population of Warren County was 57,432 in 1970; 71,828 in 1980; and 76,673 in 1990.

See Irene Moss Sumpter, *An Album of Early Warren County, Kentucky Landmarks* (Clarksville, Tenn., 1976).   RON D. BRYANT

WARRIORS' PATH. Warriors' Path, shown on the 1784 map of John Filson, was one of several Indian roads that crossed Kentucky from north to south. Called *Athiamiowee*, "path of the armed ones," by the Indians, it was used by war parties traveling between the Shawnee in Ohio and the Cherokee in Tennessee. According to the pioneer Simon Kenton, war roads were distinctive in leading from one Indian community to another and in the marks and blazes upon them; buffalo roads, wider than war roads, were much more worn down and lacked the identifying marks.

The *Athiamiowee* went northward through the Cumberland and Pine Mountain gaps and forded the Cumberland River at Cumberland Ford (now Pineville, Kentucky). It followed the east side of the Cumberland River to Flat Lick, then went along Stinking Creek to its headwaters, where it passed over the ridge to Goose Creek, which flows into the South Fork of the Kentucky River. Continuing northward, it followed Station Camp Creek, crossed the Red River near the mouth of Lulbegrud Creek in Clark and Powell counties, and passed near the old Shawnee village of Eskippakithiki. In northern Kentucky, Warriors' Path crossed the Licking River at the Upper Blue Licks, reaching the Ohio River near Cabin Creek in Mason County.

See Neal Hammon, "Early Roads into Kentucky," *Register* 68 (April 1970): 91-131.

NEAL HAMMON

WARSAW. The seat of Gallatin County, Warsaw is located on U.S. 42 on the Ohio River in an area settled between 1800 and 1803 by pioneers from Pennsylvania and Virginia. The town, first called Ohio River Landing, was established around 1814. The villagers named it Fredericksburg in honor of Adolphus Frederick, of Pennsylvania, who constructed a dockyard in the area and built his first boat in 1809. Plans for a town were drawn by Robert Johnson and Henry Yates, and on December 7, 1831, the town was incorporated as Fredericksburg, but soon changed to Warsaw, since a Washington County town was named Fredericksburg. The name of Warsaw was recommended by John B. Summons and Benjamin F. Beall, who were impressed with Jane Porter's work, *Thaddeus of Warsaw* (1803), four volumes of fiction relating to Poland.

The county's first two courthouses were built in the old county seat of Port William. The third courthouse, a Greek Revival-style structure built in 1838, has been extensively renovated, including the removal of a dome-topped cupola added in 1868. County government continues to use the building. In 1869 Short Line Railroad was built through the towns of Glencoe and Sparta, which lessened the importance of Warsaw as a commercial center. As river traffic gave way to railroads, Warsaw began a slow decline.

In December 1932, a fire broke out in the Masonic building and several buildings in the business district of Warsaw were heavily damaged, at an estimated loss of $100,000. On November 30, 1939, a fire that started in the projection room of the movie theater caused damages of about $40,000. In 1987 Warsaw Furniture Company, manufacturer of wooden furniture, and Sugar Creek, which produces precast concrete products, were established.

The population of this fifth-class city was 1,232 in 1970; 1,328 in 1980; and 1,202 in 1990.

RON D. BRYANT

WASHINGTON. Washington is located in northern Mason County, three miles south of Maysville, at the junction of U.S. 68 and U.S. 62. The community, now part of the city of MAYSVILLE, lies near Lawrence Creek, next to the path of an ancient buffalo trace from the Bluegrass region to the Ohio River. Many early explorers passed through the area, including Christopher Gist, James McBride, and Simon Kenton. Kenton and Thomas Williams in 1775 cleared about an acre of land and planted corn at the headwaters of Lawrence Creek, thus establishing a claim there. Kenton built a station in 1784 along what was then known as Smith's Wagon Road. The area was removed from the Ohio River and offered more protection from Indians attacking from the North. In 1785 he sold 700 acres of land to two Virginians, Arthur Fox, a surveyor, and William Wood, a Baptist preacher. Fox and Wood laid out a town site and named it for Gen. George Washington. By 1786 more than fifty families were living there and the Virginia legislature officially established Washington as a city.

When Mason County was formed from Bourbon County in what was then Virginia, Washington was named as the county seat in May 1789. Master stonemason and Baptist preacher Lewis Craig, who migrated to Kentucky from Virginia with his entire congregation, built the limestone courthouse in 1794. Washington, the federal post office mail distribution center for the entire Northwest Territory, was by 1795 an educational, political, and religious center. Commercial activity flourished and by 1800 the city was the third largest in Kentucky, after Lexington and Frankfort.

Washington's growth continued until the advent of the steamboat shifted commercial activity to the nearby landing at Maysville on the Ohio River. In 1848 Mason County residents successfully persuaded the state of Kentucky to move the county seat to Maysville. Although Washington lost its political prominence, it remained an agricultural and educational center. The former courthouse was put to use as a school until it was struck by lightning and burned on August 13, 1909. Although some of the other town buildings were lost to fire during the 1800s, many of the original structures remained. When U.S. 68 bypassed the town in the 1960s, many of Washington's historic buildings were restored and opened to the public. Among the more significant were the childhood home of Confederate Gen. Albert Sidney Johnston (ca. 1795), the Washington Hall hotel (ca. 1840), and numerous other log, clapboard, and early brick houses.

Residents of the city of Washington voted to merge their city with their larger neighbor Maysville, on August 13, 1990. The population of the former fifth-class city was 439 in 1970; 624 in 1980; and 795 in 1990.

See Edna Hunter Best, *The Historic Past of Washington, Mason County, Kentucky* (Cynthiana, Ky., 1944).

JEAN W. CALVERT

WASHINGTON COUNTY. Washington County, the tenth in order of formation, is located in central Kentucky in the Outer Bluegrass region. It is bordered by Nelson, Spencer, Anderson, Mercer, Boyle, and Marion counties and has an area of 301 square miles. The county is entirely within the watershed of Salt River, and fertile farms and pastures lie between the numerous hills, or knobs. The county seat is SPRINGFIELD.

The first settlers came to what is now Washington County in 1775 from the fort at Harrodsburg, drawn by the area's abundance of game, water, and salt. They traveled along the numerous animal traces. The first settlements were made by James Sandusky on Pleasant Run in 1776 and by Samuel Cartwright, who in 1779 built a house on the creek that now bears his name. The influx of settlers increased dramatically after the Revolutionary War. Many came to claim land owed to them for military service, and by 1800 there were 9,050 people in Washington County. This first generation was a mobile and ambitious lot who staked their claims, planted corn, built cabins, and often moved on. The

1810 census for Washington County counted 13,248 people. By 1820 the number had grown to 15,956, including 12,159 whites, 3,752 slaves, and 52 free people of color.

The area was originally a part of Kentucky County, Virginia, and then part of Jefferson County. Washington County totaled nearly 450,000 acres when it was formed by the new state of Kentucky on June 2, 1792. It was named for President George Washington and was created through the intercession of Gen. Matthew Walton, a landowner and resident of the area. The first court met at the home of Col. John Hardin. Springfield became the county seat in 1793.

In 1827 Washington County was split up to form Anderson County. The population continued to grow and reached a maximum of 19,144 in 1830. Washington County lost its southern area to form Marion County in 1833, a move that reduced the county's population to 10,596 by 1840. In 1833 a cholera epidemic killed eighty people in Springfield alone. Washington County acquired its first covered bridge, across the Little Beach River on the Harrodsburg Road in 1834, and its first turnpike, from Springfield to Bardstown with a connection to Louisville, in 1837. In the 1850s, Washington County joined the state school system and opened the first county fair, staged by the Springfield Union Agricultural and Mechanical Society.

During the Civil War, most men from the county fought for the Union, but some joined the Confederate army. Confederate Gen. Braxton Bragg's army passed through Springfield on October 6 and 7, 1862, followed by Union Gen. Don Carlos Buell's army, both en route to the Battle of Perryville. There was a brief skirmish between Buell's vanguard and Bragg's rear guard west of town. According to a local legend, Union soldiers looted a distillery warehouse west of Springfield, became very drunk, and made off with great quantities of whiskey.

In the era between the War of 1812 and the Civil War, Washington County produced corn, hogs, and whiskey, but only negligible amounts of tobacco. After the Civil War, the prewar levels of trade were not reestablished for twenty-five years. The recovery was prompted by the advent of white burley tobacco into the region, the arrival of the railroad, and the subsequent connection to the Louisville market. The black population of the county declined by nearly 50 percent after the war. Vigilantes known as "Skagg's men," who harassed and attacked the new freedmen in adjacent Marion, Boyle, and Mercer counties, were one factor in the exodus.

After the war, the county voted to sell $400,000 in railroad bonds and to levy a 1 percent tax to finance the proposed Cumberland & Ohio Railroad link between Nashville and Cincinnati. Resentment arose over the routing through Springfield instead of the northerly towns, and vigilantes destroyed a railroad camp. After the line went bankrupt, the county seized what assets it could and persuaded

the Louisville & Nashville Railroad (now CSX Transportation) to build a line to Springfield, completed on January 1, 1888. The line gave Washington County vital access to Louisville markets for livestock, milk, grain, and tobacco. It was abandoned by CSX in 1984. In June 1890 the county got its first modern public utility when the Springfield Electric Light and Water Company won a franchise. By November 1901, a power plant was in operation. Just after the turn of the century, the BLACK PATCH WAR over the tobacco prices paid to farmers brought a period of lawlessness to the county.

The farm depression of the mid-1920s and the Great Depression of the 1930s cost the county its two daily passenger trains to Louisville. Washington County's first park, the Lincoln Homestead State Park, was dedicated June 12, 1934, on the site where President Abraham Lincoln's grandfather had settled in 1782. After World War II, the railroad-era relationship between Louisville as consumer and the down-state counties as suppliers began to disintegrate. Persistent high unemployment caused the population to diminish and the commodity markets to fade. Nevertheless, the county acquired a new state golf course in the 1950s, and a new airport and consolidated high schools were built in the 1960s. The Bluegrass Parkway connecting Lexington and Elizabethtown was completed across the northern part of the county in 1965 and a substantial rural water system was created in the 1980s.

In 1990 the county remained rural, with many residents engaged in tobacco farming or cattle production. Most of the county's industrial jobs were located in Springfield; the largest employers were the Springfield Redrying Corporation (tobacco), Armour Food Company (milk products), H&W Industries (construction materials), and Shelburne Industries (clothing). The population of the county was 10,728 in 1970; 10,764 in 1980; and 10,411 in 1990.

See Michael L. Cook and Bettie Ann Cook, *Pioneer History of Washington County, Kentucky* (Owensboro, Ky., 1980); Orval Walker Baylor, *Early Times in Washington County, Kentucky* (Cynthiana, Ky., 1942).   DANIEL C. KELLY

WATERFIELD, HARRY LEE. Harry Lee Waterfield, politician, publisher, and farmer, was born January 19, 1911, in Tobacco (now Midway), Calloway County, Kentucky. His parents, Grover B. and Lois (Burton) Waterfield, divorced shortly after his birth and he was raised by his mother and her parents. He lived most of his life in the Purchase region of western Kentucky. He graduated from Murray State University in 1932 and embarked on a career in journalism. In 1934, he bought the *Hickman County Gazette* and eventually published five newspapers in far western Kentucky. He published the *Gazette* for over thirty-eight years. In 1941, he served as president of the Kentucky Press Association. On his Hickmandale Farm, near Clinton,

Waterfield was a noted shorthorn cattle breeder and well known for practicing modern conservation methods in his farming operation.

Waterfield entered politics in 1937, winning election to the Kentucky House. He served during 1938-46 and again in 1950. He was Speaker of the House in 1944 and 1946. He sponsored a successful bill that exempted farmers from paying tax on gasoline used exclusively for farming. He won funds to build farm-to-market roads throughout the state. He led the drive to create the Legislative Research Commission to serve as monitor of government activities between General Assembly sessions.

In 1947 Waterfield made the first of three unsuccessful attempts to become governor of Kentucky. He lost to Earle Clements by 32,000 votes in the primary. Waterfield lost a bid for the state Senate in 1951. In 1955 he ran for lieutenant governor on the ticket of long-time political adversary A.B. Chandler. They won the general election by a record margin. In 1959 Waterfield entered the gubernatorial primary, with Chandler's support, but lost to Bert T. Combs by 33,000 votes. In 1963 Waterfield accomplished a first in Kentucky history—becoming lieutenant governor for a second term, this time with Edward T. Breathitt. Waterfield made a final attempt to become governor in 1967, when Henry Ward won the primary.

In 1960 Waterfield became president of National Investors Life Insurance Company of Kentucky. In 1964, the company was renamed Investors Heritage, with Waterfield as chairman of the board, a position he held until his death. Waterfield died on August 4, 1988, after a brief illness and was buried in the Frankfort Cemetery. He was survived by his wife, Laura (Ferguson) Waterfield, a son, Harry Lee II, and two daughters, Rose Gayle Hardy and Nancy Walton.   WILLIAM G. DUNCAN V

WATKINS, HAYS T. Hays T. Watkins, railroad executive, was born to Hays T., Sr., and Minnie C. (Whitely) Watkins in Fern Creek, Kentucky, on January 26, 1926. The family later moved to Henry County. A 1947 accounting graduate of Western Kentucky University, Watkins earned an M.B.A. from Northwestern University. In 1949 he joined the accounting department of the CHESAPEAKE & OHIO (C&O) Railway in Cleveland, where he became treasurer in 1961; he became vice-president of finance in 1964 for the combined C&O and Baltimore & Ohio Railroad (B&O), which had merged the previous year. In 1971 Watkins was elected president and chief executive officer of C&O-B&O, and then chairman and chief executive officer of the roads' parent company, Chessie System Inc.

Together with Prime F. Osborn III, chairman of Seaboard Coast Line Industries, Watkins in 1980 organized CSX, which brought together the Chessie and Seaboard system railroads as CSX Transportation Inc. The Seaboard holdings included the LOUISVILLE & NASHVILLE. Upon Osborn's retirement in 1982, Watkins became chairman and chief executive officer of CSX, expanding it into truck, river,

pipeline, and international container shipping, as well as real estate, energy, and technology.

Watkins, now retired, holds many business and professional affiliations; he is the recipient of several honorary degrees and many awards. He married Betty J. Wright on April 15, 1950; they have one son, Hays T. Watkins III.

CHARLES B. CASTNER

WATTERSON, HENRY. The noted editor of the Louisville COURIER-JOURNAL and a major figure in the Democratic party, Henry Watterson was born in Washington, D.C., on February 16, 1840. He was the only child of Rep. Harvey and Talitha (Black) Watterson of Tennessee. Initially through his father's contacts and later through his own active role in politics, Watterson knew personally every president of the United States from John Quincy Adams through Franklin Delano Roosevelt, with the single exception of William Henry Harrison.

A sickly child who had very little sight, and that in only one eye, young Watterson was tutored by his mother until the age of twelve, when he was sent to the Academy of the Protestant Episcopal Church in Philadelphia for four years, his only formal education. His father after 1843 edited the *Washington Union*, the main organ of the Democratic party in the nation's capital. There Watterson received his first instruction in the making of a newspaper and a love for the printed word that was to determine his future.

With the outbreak of the Civil War, Watterson joined his parents in Tennessee, intending to sit out the conflict. Peer pressure proved too strong, however, and Watterson enlisted in the Confederate army. His military career was at best intermittent. At various times he served on the staffs of Gens. Leonidas Polk, Joseph Johnston, John Hood, and Nathan B. Forrest. Watterson's major contribution to the war was by the way of the pen, not the sword, through his editorship of *Rebel*, the most widely read newspaper of the Confederate army. While the paper was based in Chattanooga, Tennessee, Watterson met Walter N. HALDEMAN, editor of the *Louisville Courier*, who was later to become his partner.

Before the war ended, Watterson abandoned all hope for Southern victory and headed north to Cincinnati, where he served as editor-in-chief of the *Evening Times*. With the conclusion of the war, he returned to Nashville to help revive the defunct *Republican Banner*. There he first enunciated his "New Departure" program for the South: accept the three postwar amendments to the Constitution as the North's peace terms, forget the past, and work for an industrialized South.

So successful had been Watterson's newspaper career in Nashville that in 1868 he was invited by the owners of the *Louisville Journal* to take over from its distinguished but then aged editor, George D. Prentice. As editor, Watterson waged a spirited six-month competition with the *Courier*, and Walter Haldeman, publisher of the *Courier*, then accepted Watterson's proposal to consolidate the two papers. On November 8, 1868, the *Louisville Courier-Journal* made its appearance under the combined ownership of Haldeman and Watterson. Although poles apart in temperament, the two men were ideally suited partners in journalism. Haldeman had the business acumen that Watterson lacked, and Watterson had the showmanship, the enthusiasm, and the talent for writing that would quickly make their paper the best known regional paper in the country.

Watterson over the years attracted to the paper a distinguished group of young journalists, among them Harrison Robertson, Ballard Smith, Tom Wallace, and Arthur KROCK. His willingness to delegate editorial responsibilities gave Watterson the freedom for the next fifty years to play an active role in national politics; to make frequent trips to New York, Florida, and Europe; and to engage in lecture tours, which won him national acclaim. The editorial page of the *Courier-Journal*, however, remained his greatest love and his most influential platform. Watterson's gift for vivid language made him the most widely quoted editor since Horace Greeley. Such phrases as "bridging the bloody chasm" to describe the reconciliation of North and South, "the star-eyed Goddess of reform" to exalt the free trade movement, "through a slaughterhouse to an open grave" to decry the renomination of Grover Cleveland in 1892, "no compromise with dishonor" to oppose the candidacy of William Jennings Bryan in 1896, and "To Hell with the Hohenzollerns and the Hapsburgs" became part of the nation's political vocabulary in the years from 1868 to 1918.

Watterson made his first significant appearance in national politics at the Liberal Republican convention of 1872. Watterson went to Cincinnati committed to Charles Francis Adams as the candidate for a combined Liberal Republican–Democratic ticket. Disappointed by Horace Greeley's nomination, Watterson nevertheless dutifully worked for the New York editor's election and believed that, even in defeat, Greeley had "bridged the bloody chasm." Watterson's most conspicuous political role was backer and chief confidant of Gov. Samuel J. Tilden of New York in the campaign of 1876. Having achieved what he considered a victory for Tilden, Watterson went to the U.S. Congress in December 1876 to fill out the unexpired term of a Kentuckian who had died. Watterson was thus on the scene to witness and try to block Tilden's victory from being turned into defeat by the electoral commission established to settle the disputed election of 1876. His brief tenure in Congress (August 12, 1876, to March 3, 1877) was the only political office Watterson held, although he was frequently mentioned as a possible presidential candidate.

Often at odds with his party's chosen leaders—Cleveland, Bryan, and Woodrow Wilson—Watterson was accused of being the only Democratic editor who was happy when in opposition to his own party. To this charge, Watterson had a sharp rejoinder: "Things have come to a hell of a pass / When a man can't whip his own jackass."

Although his readers often had difficulty in following his erratic changes in party favorites, Watterson claimed that he was consistent in his political philosophy. On domestic issues he was a true Jeffersonian Democrat, believing in individual liberty, free trade, and an honest accountability in public office. In foreign policy, he stood for nationalism, isolationism, and pacifism. If the latter tenets came into conflict with one another, as they frequently did, then nationalism had to prevail. Basically a conservative, Watterson nevertheless supported much of the Progressive program of the early twentieth century, breaking with the Progressives only on the issues of prohibition, women's suffrage, and the League of Nations. No matter how often he might be out of step with his party, however, he remained the epitome of the great "personal editor." In 1917 he won the Pulitzer Prize for his pro-war editorials.

Walter Haldeman died in 1910 and was succeeded by his son Bruce as president and publisher of the *Courier-Journal*. Watterson broke with the younger Haldeman in a dispute over Watterson's strong anti-German stand in 1915. In league with Haldeman's older brother, William, Watterson took over the paper in 1917; one year later he sold out to Robert Worth BINGHAM. Watterson continued as editor emeritus for another year, but with the *Courier-Journal*'s support of the League of Nations at the same time that Watterson was writing daily editorials in angry opposition to "Wilson's folly," his position became untenable. On April 2, 1919, at his own request, Watterson's name was removed from the masthead of the paper he had served for over fifty years.

On December 20, 1865, Watterson married Rebecca Ewing, the daughter of a former Tennessee congressman, Andrew Ewing. They had five children: Ewing, Henry, Harvey, Milbrey, and Ethel. Watterson died on December 22, 1921, in Jacksonville, en route to his winter home in Florida and was buried in Louisville's Cave Hill Cemetery.

See Joseph F. Wall, *Henry Watterson: Reconstructed Rebel* (New York 1956); Henry Watterson, *Marse Henry: An Autobiography* (New York 1919).

JOSEPH FRAZIER WALL

WATTS, JOHN CLARENCE. John Clarence Watts, U.S. congressman, was born on July 9, 1902, in Nicholasville, Jessamine County, Kentucky, to William Montague and Frances Elizabeth (Wilson) Watts. He attended local public schools and graduated from the University of Kentucky with a B.A. in 1925 and an LL.B. in 1927, when he was admitted to the bar. He served as Nicholasville police court judge during 1929-33, and from 1933 to 1945 he was Jessamine County attorney. Elected to the Kentucky General Assembly as a democrat in 1947, Watts served as House majority leader until his appointment in 1948 as commissioner for motor transportation. He resigned this position in 1951 to seek the seat in the U.S. House of Representatives vacated by the resignation of Thomas R. Underwood from the 6th Congressional District. Watts, the Democratic nominee, defeated the Republican candidate, Otis C. Thomas, by a vote of 28,599 to 23,108 in a special election held on April 14, 1951. Watts was reelected for ten consecutive terms, serving on the Public Works Committee and the House Agricultural Committe, and at the time of his death was the ranking Democrat on the House Ways and Means Committee, as well as a member of the Joint Committee on Internal Revenue Taxation. Reflecting his ties to the Bluegrass region, he supported legislation favoring the state's distilling, tobacco, and thoroughbred industries.

Watts married Nora Mae Wilburn on March 27, 1945; they had one daughter, Lillian. Watts died on September 24, 1971, in Lexington, and was buried in Maple Grove Cemetery in Nicholasville.

WATTS, WILLIAM COURTNEY. William Courtney Watts, entrepreneur and author, was born on February 7, 1830, in Salem, Livingston County, Kentucky, to Joseph and Lucinda (Haynes) Watts. As a child he lived there and in Smithland, Kentucky. In the late 1850s Watts moved to New Orleans, where he worked as a clerk in the cotton brokerage firm Givens, Watts and Company. After a short time, Watts became a partner in the firm's New York branch, Watts, Crowe and Company. When the company expanded overseas, Watts moved to Liverpool, England, where he set up W.C. Watts and Company. After the decline of the cotton brokerage business, he started a business venture in New York City. Later in life, Watts returned to live in Smithland. In 1893, despite crippling rheumatism, he began writing *Chronicles of a Kentucky Settlement*, which was published in 1897. This historical account of Kentucky's pioneer settlers was Watts's single literary accomplishment. Watts married Nannie Ferguson; they had six children. He died in Smithland, Kentucky, on December 27, 1897 and is buried in Smithland Cemetery.

See William S. Ward, *A Literary History of Kentucky* (Knoxville, Tenn., 1988).

WAVELAND. Waveland, once the estate of Daniel Boone Bryan, a nephew of Daniel Boone, is a state HISTORIC SITE in Fayette County, off Nicholasville Road. Bryan was the original settler there, establishing a large farm that produced primarily tobacco and hemp. When Bryan died in 1845, the land passed to his son, Joseph, who built the Greek Revival house in 1847. Of the many outbuildings that made up the farm, only the slave quarters, smokehouse, and ice house remain. After the Civil War, the Bryans raised standardbred horses for racing, and a public racetrack was built across the road from the house. The property left the Bryan family in the 1890s, but remained privately owned until 1956, when the University of Kentucky bought it. In 1971 the university transferred Waveland to the Kentucky Department of Parks.

SARA L. FARLEY

WAYNE COUNTY. Wayne County, the forty-third county in order of formation, is located in the south-central section of Kentucky along the state border with Tennessee. Created in 1800 from parts of Pulaski and Cumberland counties, it was named in honor of Gen. Anthony Wayne, a Revolutionary War hero. The 446-square-mile county is bordered by Clinton, Russell, Pulaski, and McCreary counties. The county seat is MONTICELLO.

The county is divided into three distinct physical regions: the Cumberland Plateau, the level plain in the southeastern part of the county; the Knobs, rolling plains that run through the center of the county; and the Pennyroyal or Mississippi Plateau, the northwestern part of the county.

Pioneer Long Hunters visited what was to become Wayne County in 1770 and established a camp near Mill Springs, a few miles north of Monticello. In 1775 Benjamin Price built a cabin and established a camp near Mill Springs. Price's Station was one of Kentucky's first permanent settlements. Many settlers in the county had participated in the Revolutionary War. Joshua Jones, one of the most prominent early settlers, came in 1794; Jonathan and James Ingram in 1796; Cornelius Phillips in 1798; and Isaac West, James Simpson, Nicholas Lloyd, and Henry Garner in 1799. Between 1800 and 1810 a large number of families arrived.

The first means of transportation was the Cumberland River. In 1880 a turnpike was built from Monticello to Burnside. In 1881 toll roads were first used in Wayne County; the last of them, the Shearer Valley Pike, closed in 1927. The last stagecoach to operate in Kentucky connected Monticello and Burnside until 1915. Highways KY 90 and KY 92 now run through the county. The Monticello Wayne County Airport, completed in 1974, has 4,000 feet of paved runway. Since the nearest rail service is twenty miles northeast of Monticello, trucks transport all goods to and from the county.

At the onset of the Civil War, Gen. Felix Zollicoffer's Confederate army headquarters were located in the Lanier House at Mill Springs. Zollicoffer was killed and the Confederates defeated on January 19, 1862, at Mill Springs. The mill there, built in 1840, has one of the largest overshot water wheels of its kind and in 1990 was still grinding cornmeal.

Agriculture and forest products were the basis of the economy until the mid-1950s. In 1955, a manufacturing plant was built, and beginning in the mid-1960s Wayne County's economy began to diversify. In 1982 employment totaled 6,905, with nonagricultural jobs accounting for 5,960. The economic base of the county includes tourism.

The author Harriette Simpson Arnow was born near Pueblo in Wayne County. John Catron, who lived in the Beech Hollow community, migrated to Tennessee and served in several capacities as a public official before President Andrew Jackson appointed him associate justice of the U.S. Supreme Court. William Armstrong Cooper, a prominent minister, is credited with great influence upon public thinking in Wayne County during the 1800s. He baptized six persons who later became governors of states.

Monticello, the only incorporated town, is the retail trade center for Wayne County. The population of the county was 14,268 in 1970; 17,022 in 1980; and 17,468 in 1990.

See Bobby Gale Edwards, *Glimpses of Historical Wayne County, Kentucky* (Lexington, Ky., 1970).

GALE EDWARDS

WEBB, BRENDA GAIL (CRYSTAL GAYLE). The country singer known as Crystal Gayle was born Brenda Gail Webb, daughter of Melvin ("Ted") and Clara (Ramey) Webb, in Paintsville, Kentucky, on January 9, 1951. She grew up in Wabash, Indiana, after her family left the eastern Kentucky coal fields. Gayle sings both country and pop songs with a contemporary pop sound—a style of clear, modulated, and slightly affected phrasing that bears no resemblance to the sound of her sister, Loretta LYNN. Lynn wrote the first song that Gayle recorded and also gave her the stage name Crystal, after a hamburger chain. Gayle was Country Music Association female vocalist of the year in 1977 and 1978 and has won four Academy of Country Music Awards and three Grammies. Gayle married Vassalios ("Bill") Gatzimos on June 3, 1971; they have two children.

See Andrew David, *Country Music Stars* (New York 1980).   CHARLES F. FABER

WEBB, WILLIAM CLARKE. William Clarke Webb, miner and mine union organizer, about whose early life little is known, was born in September 1855 in Jacksboro, Tennessee. Webb was a member of the Knights of Labor (1885-90) and a delegate to the founding convention of the United Mine Workers of America (UMW). He served as UMW national executive board member (1890-1906) and the president of District 90 (1890-1902). In 1873 Webb moved to Pine Hill, Kentucky, then to Pittsburgh, Kentucky, in 1878 and later to Drakesboro. Webb organized and served more than twenty local unions in Kentucky and Tennessee in addition to locals in Ohio, Virginia, West Virginia, and Indiana. He was an exponent of arbitration, and a major achievement was the removal of convict labor from southeastern Kentucky without violence. Webb married Lauretta Onkst on October 3, 1878; their children were Luther, William C., Jr., James, and Stella. Webb was killed in a boiler explosion on July 4, 1920, and was buried in the Haden Cemetery, Drakesboro.   HENRY MAYER

WEBSTER, DELIA ANN. Delia Ann Webster, abolitionist, was born on December 17, 1817, in Vergennes, Vermont, the daughter of Benejah Webster. Educated at Vergennes Classical School, she became a teacher in the spring of 1835. In early 1843 Webster traveled with friends to Lexington, Kentucky, where they remained to teach art. Prompted by several prominent Kentuckians, the three established the Lexington Female Academy.

On September 28, 1844, Webster accompanied abolitionist Calvin Fairbanks to northern Kentucky. When they returned to Lexington two days later, they were arrested and charged with assisting three slaves to escape to Ohio. At her trial Webster pleaded not guilty. The jury, many of whom were slaveholders, found Webster guilty, and she was sentenced to two years in the state penitentiary. Later, in the autobiographical *History of the Trial of Delia Webster* (1845), Webster wrote that Fairbanks had left her in Millersburg, Kentucky, while he continued to Ohio. She did not mention slaves or say what business Fairbanks had in Ohio. Pardoned on February 24, 1845, despite the protests of many citizens, Webster returned to the Northeast and taught for several years in New York.

In 1854, with the financial help of northern abolitionists, Webster purchased a six-hundred-acre farm in Trimble County, Kentucky, on the Ohio River. Her farm used the labor of freed blacks and operated as an underground railroad station for slaves seeking freedom in the North. After the disappearance of some slaves in the area in the spring of 1854, she fled to Madison, Indiana, to escape a warrant for her arrest. In her absence the property was looted. In the fall of 1857, slaveholders successfully blocked Webster's attempts to secure a credit extension on her farm loan. The following year Bostonians created the Webster Kentucky Farm Association, which helped to save her property.

In August 1866 Webster, who remained unpopular after the war, was ordered to leave Kentucky, and in early November she lost $8,000 worth of property, including building materials for a school, in fires set by her opponents. Over time arsonists destroyed seventeen dwellings, four barns, and finally Webster's residence. Unable to pay her debts, and with the Webster Association defunct, she lost her farm in October 1869. Webster later taught school in Madison, Indiana. She died in 1876 in Jeffersonville, Indiana.

WEBSTER COUNTY. Webster County, the 109th county in order of formation, is located in the Western Coal Field region of Kentucky. It is bounded by Union, Henderson, Hopkins, McLean, and Crittenden counties and has an area of 336 square miles. The Tradewater River forms its western border and the Green River its eastern border. A ridge that runs through the middle of the county divides the watersheds of the two rivers. The county was created on July 1, 1860, from portions of Henderson, Hopkins, and Union counties and was named for Daniel Webster, U.S. congressman, senator, and secretary of state. The county seat is DIXON.

William Jenkins, a Revolutionary War veteran, was probably the first settler in the area. Jenkins came to the Tradewater country in 1794 and built a stagecoach inn known as the Halfway House on the old Indian trail between Nashville and St. Louis. Halfway House, five miles north of present-day Dixon, included among its guests Meriwether

Lewis, governor of the Louisiana Territory. Following his capture and escape from a band of Indians in the early 1800s, Jenkins served as a constable (1808-10) of what was then Hopkins County, and he fought in the War of 1812. He returned to the area in 1816, enlarged Halfway House, and built a cotton gin and the first frame house in the vicinity. Jenkins remained in the area, observed its settlement and growth, witnessed the formation of Webster County, and noted the divided loyalties of the Civil War years. According to Richard Collins's *Historical Sketches of Kentucky* (1874), Jenkins, "aged 103, was, in Nov., 1871, still living in Webster County."

The Civil War divided Webster County residents along with the rest of the state. Skirmishes took place at Slaughtersville (Slaughters), a Confederate stronghold, and on Deer Creek at Burnt Mill, near Vandersburg and east of Providence. The skirmish on Deer Creek on September 15, 1861, became known as the Battle of Burnt Mill, "the first battle of the Civil War fought in Kentucky," although only twenty-five Union soldiers were taken captive by the local Confederate contingent, led by Capt. Al Fowler of Hopkins County.

Webster County is characterized by rolling hills and fertile creek bottoms. Since the end of the Civil War, the county's prosperity has been tied to its fertile soil and mineral resources. While 90 percent of the county's farm income is derived from corn and soybean production, wheat and fruit are also grown. Beef and hogs and both dark and burley tobacco provide supplementary income. Almost 30 percent of the county's acreage is commercial forest land.

Oil production in Webster County peaked in the late 1960s and early 1970s. In 1971 Webster ranked sixth among the oil-producing counties of the state. Alfred Townes, who became a surveyor for the Louisville & Nashville Railroad (now CSX Transportation), and others mined coal in the area on a small scale even before the Civil War, but commercial production in the county began only in 1888, with the organization of the Providence Coal Mining Company. The Louisville & Nashville Railroad (CSX Transportation) and the Illinois Central Railroad (now the Tradewater Railway) established lines in the county to transport coal. Surface mining is an important local industry.

Dixon, located in the center of the county, has served as the county seat since its incorporation on February 6, 1861. The county's largest community is Providence, founded by Richard B. Savage and established on February 18, 1840. It has almost a third of the county's population. Sebree, incorporated in 1871, was the location of Sebree Springs, a summer resort and park operated by G.L. Dial. Other Webster County communities include Clay, Slaughters, Poole, Tilden, Onton, Wheatcroft, and Blackford.

The population of Webster County was 13,282 in 1970; 14,832 in 1980; and 13,955 in 1990.

JAMES DUANE BOLIN

WEIL, MEYER. Meyer Weil, mayor of Paducah, Kentucky, was born to a German-Jewish family in Hohenzollern, Prussia, on June 29, 1830. Weil immigrated to America in 1847 in search of business opportunities. After several years in Smithland, Wadesboro, and Mayfield, Kentucky, he settled in Paducah in 1863. First a Paducah merchant, he then became a successful whiskey and tobacco trader and opened a prosperous brokerage business. In 1870 Weil was elected to the city council. A Democrat, he was elected mayor of Paducah in 1871, serving in that capacity until 1881. During Weil's first term, Paducah's first city hospital was built. He is credited with restoring the financial soundness of Paducah after the Civil War. Weil was elected in 1887 and again in 1889 to the state House of Representatives, where he was known as an opponent of high taxes and as a sharp-witted speaker. In 1853 Weil married a Miss Wilson of Wadesboro, who died a year later. In 1860 he married Rose Funk in Mayfield; the couple had three sons and two daughters. Weil died on April 13, 1891, and was buried in Paducah's Oak Grove Cemetery.

See Fred G. Neuman, *Paducahans in History* (Paducah, Ky., 1922).

LEE SHAI WEISSBACH AND BERRY CRAIG

WEIR, JAMES. James Weir, novelist and attorney, was born in Greenville, Kentucky, on June 16, 1821, the son of James and Anna Cowman (Rumsey) Weir. His early education was in Greenville. Weir earned a literary degree and a master of arts degree at Centre College in Danville in 1840 and 1844, respectively. In 1841 he earned a law degree at Transylvania University in Lexington and the next year began practicing chancery law in Owensboro. Weir's first novel, *Lonz Powers: or, the Regulators* (1850), described the relations between outlaws and vigilantes on Kentucky's western frontier; the rest of his Kentucky trilogy is *Simon Kenton: or, the Scout's Revenge* (1852) and *The Winter Lodge: or, Vow Fulfilled* (1854). Weir was elected president of the Owensboro Deposit Bank on February 17, 1864, and held this position until his death. He ended his practice of law after 1865 but remained an adviser of the firm Weir, Weir, and Walker. Weir was president of the Evansville, Owensboro & Nashville Railroad from 1869 until the line's absorption in 1878 by the Louisville & Nashville Railroad. Weir was also associated with the Owensboro Wheel Company and is credited with bringing the first telegraph lines to Owensboro.

Weir married Susan C. Green of Danville on March 1, 1842, and they had ten children, eight of whom lived to adulthood. He died on January 31, 1906, in Owensboro and is buried in the city's Elmwood Cemetery.

WEISSINGER ACT. Gov. John Young Brown (1891-95) signed the Married Women's Property Act on March 15, 1894, after a campaign led by suffragists and equal rights activists Josephine K. Henry and Laura Clay. Named for its legislative sponsor, George Weissinger, the statute superseded the English common law of coverture, under which married women were without legal rights because the independent legal existence of a woman was suspended during marriage and incorporated into that of her husband. The 1894 law gave married women the right to make wills and a limited right to hold and dispose of real (immovable) property. However, not until 1942 could a married woman in Kentucky sell, convey, or mortgage property without her husband's signature, and other legal disabilities remained in effect until passage of a series of statutes by successive legislatures in the 1970s.

See Paul E. Fuller, *Laura Clay and the Women's Rights Movement* (Lexington, Ky., 1977); Martha Carson, "The Kentucky Married Women's Property Act: An Early Appeal for Justice," *Border States: Journal of Kentucky-Tennessee American Studies Association* 5 (1985): 20-28.

MARY K. BONSTEEL TACHAU

WELBY, AMELIA B. (COPPUCK). Amelia B. (Coppuck) Welby, poet, daughter of William and Mary Coppuck, was born in St. Michael's, Maryland, on February 3, 1819. She went to school in Baltimore, where her family had moved shortly after her birth. In 1833 they moved to Lexington, Kentucky, and in 1834 to Louisville. Her poetry was published in the *Louisville Journal* in 1837, and under the tutelage of the paper's editor, George D. Prentice, her popularity grew. In 1845 *Poems by Amelia* was published, and by 1860 it had reached its seventeenth edition. This collection touched on a variety of topics: love, death, children, nature, religion, and brides. Her best-known poem was "The Rainbow." In June 1838 Amelia Coppuck married George Welby, a Louisville businessman, and in March 1852 she gave birth to a son. She died on May 3, 1852, and was buried in Louisville's Cave Hill Cemetery.

See William Ward, *A Literary History of Kentucky* (Knoxville, Tenn., 1988).

WENDELL, THOMAS W. Thomas W. Wendell, an Afro-American physician who concentrated on the treatment of the mentally ill, was born in 1877 in Lexington, Kentucky. He earned degrees in pharmacy and in medicine and served as a physician in Lexington from 1900 until his death. Wendell was especially concerned with the application of practical new techniques such as occupational therapy in the control of mental illness. For many years, he served as a resident psychiatrist at the Eastern State Hospital in Lexington. Wendell died in 1953, two years before Eastern State Hospital offered occupational therapy for Afro-American patients. At the time of his death, he had served the Lexington community and surrounding towns for more than half a century. A building at Eastern State Hospital is named in his honor. Wendell is buried in Lexington's Cove Haven Cemetery.   DORIS WILKINSON

WERNWAG, LOUIS. Louis Wernwag, born in Württemberg, Germany, December 4, 1769, built covered bridges in Kentucky. Wernwag came to Philadelphia about 1787 and served apprenticeships to wheelwrights and builders. In 1810 he built his first bridge, on a road between Philadelphia and Briston, Pennsylvania. Wernwag's designs for longer and more enduring structures established his reputation on the eastern seaboard. His successful innovations in long-span design led him to purchase a wood-shaping factory at Harper's Ferry, Virginia (now West Virginia), in 1824, from which he fabricated waterworks, churches, houses, and covered bridges on what was then the western frontier.

Improvements to the Maysville-Lexington Pike brought Wernwag to Kentucky in the 1830s. He received several contracts for bridges on that road and others in the Bluegrass region. The massive timbered structure that he built over the Kentucky River south of Nicholasville bridged a 241-foot span when completed in 1838. Accounts suggest that Wernwag did not enjoy good health in later life, and so may have undertaken the Kentucky projects as an architect in the modern sense, providing drawings for a field assistant who supervised construction. Wernwag erected a brick house in Mays Lick (Mason County), Kentucky, in 1835.

Wernwag died at Harper's Ferry, on April 12, 1843, and was buried near there.

See Allen Sanders, *Covered Bridges of the South* (New York 1927).   L. MARTIN PERRY

WEST, EDWARD. Edward West, craftsman and inventor, was born in Stafford County, Virginia, to Edward and Elizabeth (Mills) West in 1757. He moved to Lexington, Kentucky, in 1785 and announced the opening of a clock and watch shop on High Street in the August 9, 1788, *Kentucky Gazette*. In 1793 he successfully demonstrated a model steamboat on the Town Fork of Elkhorn Creek in Fayette County. West received a patent on July 6, 1802, for his steamboat invention. Robert Fulton's better-known work with a larger model was done in 1803. West also received patents for a nail-cutting and -heading machine and a gun lock. He sold the patent on the nail-cutting machine for $10,000; his work in other areas produced a pistol, wire-bound cannon, and a hemp-breaking machine. In 1800 the *Gazette* listed Edward West as a silversmith. He was elected in December 1805 to the Lexington Board of Trustees and was commissioned to make the first county seal.

West married Sarah Brown, daughter of Samuel and Maria (Creed) Brown. They had one son, William Edward West, an artist known for his portrait of Lord Byron. Edward West died on August 23, 1827, and was buried in the grounds of the family home on High Street. His remains were later removed to the Lexington Presbyterian Cemetery.

See Margaret M. Bridwell, "Edward West—Silversmith and Inventor," *FCHQ* 21 (Oct. 1947): 301-8.

WESTERN BAPTIST THEOLOGICAL INSTITUTE. This short-lived institution, a victim of the intersectional tensions preceding the Civil War, originated in 1833 at a meeting of the Western Baptist Convention in Cincinnati. This group of 108, concerned about the lack of Baptist theological education west of the Alleghenies, in 1834 formed the Western Baptist Education Society, led by an executive committee of twelve that included two members from Kentucky. After months of planning and fund raising, the society purchased three tracts of land south of Covington, Kentucky, for $33,250. The society sold building lots from the original property to raise money, saving land for three major buildings: a professors' residence, a president's home, and the classroom building.

Chartered by the Kentucky legislature in 1840, the Western Baptist Theological Institute opened its doors for classes in 1845. By 1847 the institute had become embroiled in a controversy between the northern-minded (Ohio) trustees and the southern-minded (Kentucky) trustees. The Kentuckians and their supporters farther south felt that attitudes at the institute were tilted against slavery. Opposition was especially strong against Robert Everett Pattison, president and professor of theology. Appeals to the Kentucky legislature led to the resignation of two of the three professors, including Pattison. By 1852 the student body numbered twenty-five.

After several legal actions on the part of the Ohio trustees, both sides agreed to let Justice John McLean of the U.S. Supreme Court serve as arbitrator. McLean's decision in 1853 divided the property of the institute between the two parties. The school's library went to Granville College (now Dennison) in Ohio. With cash proceeds, the northern trustees began a new seminary in Cincinnati, which survived only five years. The Kentucky trustees established the Western Baptist Theological Institute at Georgetown College, where it nominally existed until 1879. The institute's charter was finally dissolved in June 1891, and its meager resources were transferred to the Kentucky Baptist Education Society.

See W.C. James, "Western Baptist Theological Seminary," *Publications of Kentucky Baptist Historical Society* 1 (1910).

IRA ("JACK") BIRDWHISTELL

WESTERN COAL FIELD. The Western Coal Field region of Kentucky forms a compact, almost circular area south of the Ohio River in western Kentucky. The region's western, southern, and eastern margins are marked by the Western Pottsville Escarpment, which overlooks the encircling Pennyroyal region. The Western Kentucky Coal Field, stretching across all of nine counties and segments of at least eight others, is a relatively small region of about 4,200 square miles with a 1985 population of about 320,000. The region's surface extent is coincident with the western Kentucky lands underlain by carboniferous rocks mainly of the Pennsylvanian period. From these rocks comes the coal that is the source of the region's name. This area is also the southward extension of the larger Eastern Interior Basin, which stretches across southern and central Illinois and southwestern Indiana.

The surface of this area is gently rolling to considerably hilly, particularly in the south, where the Western Pottsville Escarpment marks the edge of the Western Coal Field region. The land is most nearly level in the northern areas facing the Ohio River. There the soil is alluvial or glacially derived and is generally fertile. The Ohio, Green, and Tradewater river systems have left extensive surface areas of alluvium. Along with a mantle of wind-deposited loess, it is the basis for the diversified agriculture of the region.

About one-fourth of Kentucky's annual production of bituminous coal is mined within this region. The coal is generally higher in sulfur and ash content than the coal mined in eastern Kentucky and somewhat less attractive since power plants using the coal require costly scrubber equipment to remove the sulfur from plant emissions. In addition to coal, there are pockets of natural gas and petroleum from Mississippian rock layers of the Carboniferous period.

The region's largest cities, Owensboro in Daviess County and Henderson in Henderson County, are Ohio River ports. The third principal city, Madisonville in Hopkins County, is located within the region's southern tier of coal-producing counties. The Green River, flowing northwestward across the region, is navigable for vessels of up to six-foot draft as far upstream as Central City in Muhlenberg County. Nearby is Kentucky's largest coal-burning electric generating plant, at Paradise. Highway routes form a close-knit transportation network for the Western Coal Field region. East-west routes include the Western Kentucky Parkway across the south-central part of the region; the older, parallel route, U.S. 62; and the Audubon Parkway between Owensboro and Henderson, just south of the Ohio River. Route U.S. 60 is an older highway roughly parallel to the south side of the Ohio River. North-south routes are the Green River Parkway, between Owensboro and Bowling Green in the Pennyroyal region outside the Western Coal Field, and the Pennyrile Parkway, from Henderson south to Madisonville and beyond to Hopkinsville. Older north-south routes include U.S. 231 and U.S. 431, both extending southward from Owensboro, and U.S. 41 and 41A, which extend southward from Henderson.

Only the Owensboro–Daviess County Airport has regularly scheduled daily flights within the region. The Henderson and Madisonville airports have a considerable volume of business in unscheduled flights. Both CSX Transportation and the Paducah & Louisville railroads provide east-west lines into the south-central coal field areas and limited north-south connections as well.

Agriculture in the Western Coal Field region has a diversity similar to that of the midwestern Corn Belt, north of the Ohio River. The principal agricultural products are corn, soybeans, wheat, hay, burley and other tobaccos, hogs, and beef cattle.

The region's recreational facilities include John James Audubon State Park, Ellis Raceway, Lake Beshear, Pennyrile Forest State Resort Park, Rough River Dam State Resort Park, Nolin River Lake, and Mammoth Cave National Park, which straddles the region's border with the central Pennyroyal region.

See Wilford A. Bladen, *A Geography of Kentucky* (Dubuque, Iowa, 1984); Preston McGrain, *The Geologic Story of Kentucky* (Lexington, Ky., 1983).   WILLIAM A. WITHINGTON

WESTERN KENTUCKY UNIVERSITY. Western Kentucky University traces its history to the Glasgow Normal School, opened by A.W. Mell in 1875 in Glasgow, Kentucky. When it outgrew local facilities, Mell and his partner, J. Tom Williams, founded the Southern Normal School and Business College in Bowling Green in 1884 and took many of the students along. After several changes in ownership, the school had only twenty-eight students in 1892, when it was purchased by brothers Thomas Crittenden and Henry Hardin CHERRY. H.H. Cherry was a promotional genius, and by 1899, when he became the sole owner, enrollment had grown to nearly seven hundred students.

Concerned over Kentucky's urgent need for better-trained teachers, Cherry had an active role in persuading the 1906 legislature to create two state normal schools. When the regents of the newly formed Western Kentucky State Normal School elected him president (1906-37), Cherry sold the Business College to private investors, and Southern Normal School was absorbed into Western Kentucky State. Cherry put every available dollar into an ambitious building program on the hilltop location to which the school moved in February 1911. The adjacent OGDEN COLLEGE for men merged with Western in 1928, and by 1937 fourteen major buildings had been added at Western. The Kentucky Building with its library and museum in time housed one of the finest collections of Kentuckiana in the state.

When classes at Western Kentucky State Normal School started in 1907, few students had a high school education, and most teaching was done at that level. Student preparation gradually improved, and the addition of "and Teachers College" to the name in 1922 meant that Western could award bachelor's degrees. The number of students who elected to become teachers diminished, and the "Normal School" designation was dropped in 1930. Despite low salaries, Cherry built a strong faculty, and by 1930-31 Western was one of the largest teachers' colleges in the country, with an enrollment of 4,253. Cherry was philosophically opposed to intercollegiate athletics, but he entered that field to meet competition from other schools. In the 1930s coach Ed DIDDLE's basketball teams began to gain national recognition.

In the 1920s a student newspaper, the *College Heights Herald*, and a yearbook, *The Talisman*, were established. The curriculum expanded as more nonteaching students enrolled; the premedicine program was outstanding. Western began graduate work in education in 1931 but was forced to discontinue it in 1936 when the University of Kentucky protested. The Great Depression devastated Western. State funding declined from $775,344.44 in 1930-31 to $253,433.97 in 1933-34. Salaries were slashed 16 percent for the faculty who were retained. Student enrollment did not decline as drastically, and Cherry kept as many as possible in school by dividing campus jobs and by granting small loans from the College Heights Foundation, which he had established.

Cherry ran the institution with a firm, paternalistic hand, and most students and faculty accepted that approach. Since he believed that any Greek letter society was undemocratic, both honor and social societies were banned. The daily chapel was the pulpit from which Cherry inspired generations of students with "a burning zeal to do and to be something." The school's motto, "The spirit makes the master," was a favorite theme.

When Cherry died in 1937, Gov. A.B. Chandler (1935-39) engineered the election of his friend Paul L. Garrett as president (1937-55). Garrett was an unpretentious man who loved reading more than administration. His tenure was dominated by World War II. Enrollment fell to 403, with 75 percent of the students female, but the arrival of Air Force trainees kept the college open. The flood of postwar students under the G.I. Bill made it necessary to hire more teachers and find more housing. Western expanded its curriculum, and in 1948 "Teachers" was eliminated from its name; education continued to be important, but it did not dominate the curriculum as it once had. Graduate work in education was resumed in 1941.

The greatest boom in Western's history started in the late 1950s, during the administration of Kelly THOMPSON (1955-69). Between 1955 and 1969, fall enrollment soared from 1,975 to 11,069 and a score of new buildings were constructed to house and educate the ever-increasing student body. Obtaining and retaining a well-qualified faculty was a constant problem. The curriculum expanded rapidly, and after the private Bowling Green Business College closed, Western began offering course work in that area. Six colleges were created in 1965-66, and Western achieved university status.

The boom era was ending when Thompson retired in 1969, succeeded by another long-time Western administrator, Dero G. Downing (1969-79). Downing experienced one of the most difficult tenures among Western presidents. The university did not suffer the violence that swept many campuses, but some students were radical by local standards. Black students staged a sit-in in the administration building. For the first time, regents sometimes took issue with presidential recommendations, and the new faculty senate sometimes clashed with the administration. Yet the institution made progress in many areas, and Downing's success in finding a way through a difficult transitional period made their tasks easier for all of his successors.

Presidential terms became much shorter after Downing's retirement in 1979. John D. Minton served during the search that ended with the election of Donald Zacharias (1979-85). When Zacharias resigned, he was followed by Kern Alexander (1986-88), who was replaced by Thomas Meredith (1988-). All of the later presidents faced financial crises as state funding became less and less adequate. Some programs were dropped or curtailed, essential maintenance was delayed, and an excellent fine arts series was canceled. Zacharias fought the KENTUCKY COUNCIL ON HIGHER EDUCATION's "Bluegrass Plan" of 1981, which would have redefined the roles of the state schools and reallocated inadequate state funds to the benefit of the Universities of Kentucky and Louisville. The Council on Higher Education became more powerful, and state and national regulations became more numerous and irksome. Enrollment declined from 13,533 in the fall of 1979 to 11,259 in the fall of 1985, and major construction almost ceased.

An upswing that began in the fall of 1986 pushed student enrollment to a record 15,240 in 1990. Freshman test scores also improved. A campus was established in Glasgow, and classes were taught at several off-campus centers. Some overdue maintenance was done, and funds were allocated for the construction of more dormitories and an activities building, but adequate funding remains the institution's greatest problem.

Today Western is a comprehensive university organized into five colleges and a community college. Undergraduates have a choice among eighty-nine academic majors and sixty-four minors, a number of professional and preprofessional curricula, twenty-one associate degrees, and three certificate programs. The Graduate College offers six master's degrees, the specialist degree, and Rank 1 and 2 programs. Some joint doctoral programs are available in association with the Universities of Kentucky and Louisville.

See Lowell H. Harrison, *Western Kentucky University* (Lexington, Ky., 1987); James P. Cornette, *A History of the Western Kentucky State Teachers College* (Bowling Green, Ky., 1938).

LOWELL H. HARRISON

WESTERN MILITARY INSTITUTE. Western Military Institute was founded by Col. Thornton F. Johnson in 1847 in Georgetown, Kentucky. It was modeled after the U.S. Military Academy at West Point and the Virginia Military Institute. The curriculum emphasized engineering, mathematics, and military science leading to an A.B. or M.A. degree. One of the notable early instructors was James G. Blaine, later senator from Maine, who taught Greek, Latin, and algebra from 1848 until 1851. In 1850 the institute relocated to Blue Lick Springs in Nicholas County and in 1851 to Drennon Springs, Henry County. The institute allocated $80,000 for new buildings there, to accommodate

three hundred cadets and ten instructors. The school drew students from eighteen states. Col. Bushrod Rust Johnson became president of Western Military Institute in 1851. Outbreaks of disease on the property forced the school to relocate again, to Tyree Springs, Tennessee, in 1854, and to Nashville in 1855, where it became associated with the University of Nashville. The Civil War closed the school in 1862; it is estimated that more than 1,000 of its graduates served in the Confederate army.

See Mabel Altstetter and Gladys Watson, "Western Military Institute, 1847-1861," *FCHQ* 10 (April 1936): 100-115.

WESTERN RECORDER. The *Western Recorder*, the official denominational weekly of the Kentucky Baptist Convention, began as the *Baptist Register*, a paper published in Bardstown in 1825. It was followed by a series of similar weeklies, published under various names by a series of Baptist leaders, in several places: the *Baptist Chronicle and Literary Register*, Georgetown, 1830-32; the *Baptist Banner*, Shelbyville, 1834-36; the *Baptist Banner and Western Pioneer*, Louisville, 1836-48; the *Baptist Banner*, Louisville, 1848-51. Known as *Western Recorder* since 1851, the paper was purchased in 1919 by the General Association of Baptists in Kentucky (now the Kentucky Baptist Convention) as part of the process of centralization and consolidation of denominational resources. Published in Louisville during 1919-57, the paper then followed the convention's offices to Middletown, Kentucky. The publication has been edited by a series of able men: Thomas Treadwell Eaton, 1887-1907; John William Porter, 1909-21; Victor Irvine Masters, 1921-42; John D. Freeman, 1942-45; Reuel Tipton Skinner, 1946-57; Chauncey Rakestraw Daley, 1957-84; Jack D. Sanford, 1984- . Circulation figures for representative years: 1957, 65,000; 1970, 60,000; 1980, 65,000; 1989, 49,000.

See Leo T. Crismon, ed., *Baptists in Kentucky, 1776-1976* (Middletown, Ky., 1975).

IRA ("JACK") BIRDWHISTELL

WESTERN STATE HOSPITAL. Western State Hospital, the second state-supported mental facility in Kentucky, was established in Hopkinsville by an act of the Kentucky General Assembly on February 28, 1848. The citizens of Hopkinsville raised $4,000 to help establish the institution. Cincinnati architect Maj. N.B. Kelley designed the Greek Revival building, and master builders Samuel L. Salter and John Orr directed the construction. The new asylum opened with twenty-nine patients on September 18, 1854. Cost of construction was $202,000. On November 30, 1860, chimney sparks ignited the wood shingle roof and the entire structure burned. Patients were housed in the courthouse, a hotel, and private homes until twenty-three temporary log cabins, twenty feet square, were constructed on the grounds. Reconstruction started in 1861 and was completed in 1867 at a cost of $258,900.

Antiquated methods of medical and mechanical restraint were discarded by 1913. As part of the treatment of patients, they worked in a dairy barn constructed in 1911, a form of treatment used into the 1950s. Breakthroughs in the treatment of mental illness came in the early 1950s with psychological counseling and the development of psychiatric medications. The hospital had more than 2,000 patients when it observed its centennial in September 1954. In 1990 the hospital's expanded facilities housed a resident population of 534, supported by a staff of approximately 610.   WILLIAM T. TURNER

WEST KENTUCKY INDUSTRIAL COLLEGE.

D.H. and Artelia (Harris) Anderson built the two-year West Kentucky Industrial College in Paducah virtually with their own hands. On December 9, 1909, Anderson turned the first shovel of dirt for the school; in fact, he dug the entire basement, on a lot donated by Armour Gardner. In 1913 the Paducah *Sun-Democrat* reported that "an industrial school has been hewn by hand out of logs and faith." Donations consisted of $3,551.05 by 1913. (The nickel in that figure symbolized many of the individual contributions.) The city gave $350 in 1911 and $250 in 1912. When the walls were up, the city of Paducah donated the roof. Artelia Anderson donated her salary of $55 per month from teaching at White Oak, about two miles from Paducah. With half of the first building completed, her husband approached Frankfort for state support. An appropriation was passed by the legislature in 1912 only to be vetoed by Gov. James McCreary (1911-15), who "thought the founding of a school at Paducah an impossibility."

In 1914 Anderson again appeared in Frankfort to lobby for funding for his school, which was approved in the Senate, but not in the House. The same sequence was repeated in 1916. In 1918 legislation finally reached Gov. A.O. Stanley (1915-19), who signed a bill providing "for the mental, moral and physical development of the colored people after the manner of the Booker Washington School of Alabama" by operating a "training school for colored teachers, boys and girls." The bill added that "there is no normal school in the west end of our State, and the Kentucky Normal and Industrial Institute at Frankfort is too remote to afford opportunity for attendance from the west section without great expense." The West Kentucky Industrial College charged no fees. On completion of the college courses, it awarded a certificate that qualified a person to teach in the black common schools. The state provided $3,000 for operations and $5,000 for improvements. Funding increased to $15,000 in 1920; in 1928, $107,000 was approved to build a girls' dormitory. In 1938, the legislature provided a four-year college for blacks by merging the Paducah school with the one in Frankfort to form Kentucky State College for Negroes (now Kentucky State University).

During the twenty years of its existence, West Kentucky Industrial College had two presidents, Anderson (1909-37) and H.C. Russell (1937-38). More than five hundred students graduated from the junior college.   JOHN E.L. ROBERTSON

WEST LIBERTY.

West Liberty, the county seat of Morgan County, is located in the center of the county and lies on the Licking River at the junction of KY 7 and U.S. 460.

Around 1805, Baptist preacher Daniel Williams (1763-1820) may have built the first log cabin at the future town site in what was then part of Floyd County. Others followed, and with the installation of a gristmill, completed about 1816 by Edmund Wells, the settlement became known as Wells Mill. After Morgan County was organized on March 10, 1823, the settlement was chosen as the site of the county seat, which was laid out on thirty-nine acres of land provided by Wells.

Despite its name, West Liberty lies some one hundred miles northeast of Liberty, which is in Casey County. According to tradition the name came about when the Wells Mill settlement was to be officially converted into Morgan's county seat. Pike County, to the east, was in the process of creating its own seat of government (eventually Pikeville), which at the time was to be named Liberty. Thus Morgan chose the name West Liberty. It was incorporated in 1840.

During the Civil War, West Liberty was the site of three skirmishes. The earliest, on October 23, 1861, was one of the first important battles that occurred in eastern Kentucky. In the war twenty-nine town buildings burned, including the 1840s-era courthouse. It was replaced soon after the war and in 1907 the fourth courthouse was completed; the latter was renovated in 1980 and listed on the National Register of Historic Places. Since 1971, West Liberty has been the home of the annual Morgan County Sorghum Festival, held during the last full weekend in September. The city is the site of a small airport, an Appalachian Regional Hospital, the John F. Kennedy Memorial Library; and a medium-security prison, the Eastern Kentucky Correctional Complex.

The population of the fourth class city was 1,387 in 1970; 1,381 in 1980; and 1,887 in 1990.

JOE NICKELL

WETHERBY, LAWRENCE WINCHESTER.

Lawrence Winchester Wetherby, governor of Kentucky during 1950-55, was born on January 2, 1908, at Middletown, Kentucky, the son of Samuel David and Fanny (Yenowine) Wetherby. He received his law degree from the University of Louisville in 1929. On April 24, 1930, he married Helen Dwyer of Louisville; they had three children. From 1933 to 1937 and again in 1942 he was part-time attorney for the Jefferson County juvenile court. In March 1943 he was appointed the first trial commissioner of Jefferson County juvenile court. He resigned in 1947 after being elected lieutenant governor over Republican Orville M. Howard, with a vote of 367,836 to 271,893. When Gov. Earl C. Clements was elected to the U.S. Senate in 1950, he resigned as governor, and Wetherby took his place on November 27. In 1951 Wetherby was elected to a full term as governor, defeating Republican Eugene Siler 346,345 to 288,014. After leaving office on December 13, 1955, Wetherby went into private law practice. In 1956 he ran for the U.S. Senate but Republican John Sherman Cooper defeated him, 538,505 to 473,140. In 1964-66 he was a member of a state assembly to revise the 1890 constitution. He served in the state Senate in 1966 and 1968 and was its president pro tempore during the first term. In retirement, Wetherby served as a consultant to Brighton Engineering. He lives in Frankfort.

Wetherby called a special session of the General Assembly in 1951 to increase both teachers' salaries and benefits to the needy and to government employees. Later, he created a separate Department of Mental Health, supported enactment of the first state law to regulate strip mining, and began construction of toll roads and a new state fairgrounds. Improvements in education came with a constitutional amendment known as the Minimum Foundation Program, permitting the allocation of educational funds to school districts on the basis of need rather than the number of pupils. In 1954 and 1955, as chairman of the Southern Governors' Conference, Wetherby supported the Supreme Court's school desegregation order and urged its peaceful implementation as the law of the land.

See John E. Kleber, ed., *The Public Papers of Governor Lawrence W. Wetherby 1950-1955* (Lexington, Ky., 1983).   LOWELL H. HARRISON

WHALLEN, JOHN HENRY AND JAMES PATRICK. John Henry Whallen, Democratic boss in Louisville, was born in May 1850 in New Orleans to Irish immigrants Patrick and Bridget (Burke) Whallen. The family settled in Maysville, Kentucky, and later in Cincinnati. In 1862 Whallen joined Schoolfield's Battery in the Confederate army, serving as powder monkey and scout and later as courier for Gen. John Hunt Morgan. In the late 1870s, Whallen moved to Louisville. In 1880 he and his brother, James Patrick, born on December 4, 1857, opened the Buckingham Theater on West Jefferson between Third and Fourth streets. In addition to the "Buck," Whallen and his brother owned the Grand Opera (later the New Buckingham; later still, the Savoy) at 211 West Jefferson in Louisville and the Empire and Casino theaters in Brooklyn, New York. In 1897 the Whallen brothers were founders of the Empire Circuit, a burlesque theater syndicate. The Whallens' theater interests meshed with political ones, and by the mid-1880s the Buckingham Theater's "green room" became the reputed hub of local Democratic politics, with John Whallen the "Buckingham Boss." Whallen was widely known for his charities, and he amalgamated into a political base the working-class Catholic and Irish immigrants.

John Whallen was married three times, first to Marian Hickey; their children were Ella, Nora, and Orri. There were no children of his second marriage, to a woman known only as Sarah Jane. He later married Grace Edwards Goodrich and adopted her daughter, Gracie. Following John Whallen's death on December 3, 1913, his Spring Bank Park estate became Chickasaw Park, and James assumed control of all his brother's assets, including the political organization. However, James lacked the charisma of his older brother and did not hold the public's favor as John had. James Whallen married Susannah McDermott in 1875. Following his death on March 15, 1930, his home at 4420 River Park Drive was sold to the archdiocese of Louisville and became Flaget High School. Both John and James Whallen were buried in St. Louis Cemetery, Louisville.

See Karen R. Gray and Sarah R. Yates, "Boss John Whallen: The Early Louisville Years (1876-1883)," *Journal of Kentucky Studies* 1 (July 1984): 171-86.   KAREN R. GRAY AND SARAH R. YATES

WHAS RADIO. WHAS, the first licensed commercial radio station in Kentucky, began broadcasting from Louisville on the evening of July 18, 1922. The station was owned and operated as a broadcast service of the *Louisville Courier-Journal* and the *Louisville Times*. Robert Worth BINGHAM, who owned the newspapers, took a personal interest in the station's creation and hired Credo Harris as its first manager. Until WHAS was founded, Kentucky was one of only seven states without a radio station. Throughout the commonwealth and from many distant states, listeners responded favorably, and WHAS quickly became a national leader in radio broadcasting. During its first year of operation, WHAS broadcast no commercials, but it succumbed to the inevitability of radio advertising in 1923. Still, the station operated at a deficit until the early 1930s.

Initially, all WHAS programming was live performances from the station's studios. In 1926 WHAS helped establish the Southern Network of the National Broadcasting Company's Red Chain of stations, and network programming came to fill the station's schedule. In 1928 WHAS was granted clear-channel status and was permitted to increase power from 500 to 5,000 watts. The clear-channel status is still coveted by competitor stations. In 1929 WHAS began a long association with the University of Kentucky. Each day, Monday through Friday, the university broadcast musical and educational programming from its campus studios over WHAS. WHAS and UK also worked together to establish radio "listening centers" throughout eastern Kentucky where donations of battery-powered radios gave the residents public access to educational programming.

In 1932 WHAS joined the Columbia Broadcasting System, ending its five-year association with NBC. The 1937 flood brought WHAS into national prominence. As water from the Ohio River began to cover downtown Louisville and the surrounding area, WHAS first switched to auxiliary power and then began broadcasting via phone lines over WSM Radio in Nashville. WHAS's messages of flood relief were relayed to a worldwide audience as both national radio networks picked up the broadcasting.

Coverage of the 1937 flood and news reports during World War II demonstrated the importance of radio to an increasingly information-conscious society. By the late 1940s, however, WHAS and its many competitors had begun playing recorded music and the very nature of radio changed. WHAS is still important as a radio station for Kentuckians, but it has never regained the distinction of its first two decades of operation.

In 1986 the entire Bingham communications empire was divided and sold. WHAS-AM and its affiliate station, WAMZ-FM, were sold to Clear Channel Communications of San Antonio, Texas, for $20 million.

See Terry L. Birdwhistell, "WHAS Radio and the Development of Broadcasting in Kentucky, 1922-1942," *Register* 79 (Autumn 1981): 333-53; Credo Fitch Harris, *Microphone Memoirs of the Horse and Buggy Days of Radio* (Indianapolis 1937).   TERRY BIRDWHISTELL

WHEELER, MARY. Mary Wheeler, educator and musicologist, was born in 1892 in Paducah, Kentucky, to Charles K. and Mary Kirkpatrick (Gutherie) Wheeler. After graduating from Paducah High School in 1908, she began serious voice study at the Gardner School in New York and with private coaches there and in Chicago. In 1925 she enrolled at the Cincinnati Conservatory of Music, her mother's alma mater; she studied there for twelve years, attending classes mainly in the summers, while continuing to give recitals and to teach privately and in schools in Kentucky, Georgia, Ohio, and Virginia. She earned a bachelor's degree in voice (1933) and a master's degree in musicology (1937). Her master's thesis on folk songs received the conservatory's Chalmers Clifton Award for musicological research.

In 1926 Wheeler taught music at the HINDMAN SETTLEMENT SCHOOL in Hindman, Kentucky. During her year-long stay, the school's director, May Stone, assisted Wheeler in compiling folk songs collected during her visits with local residents. While living in Hindman, Wheeler learned to play the dulcimer, which she used for years after to perform mountain songs. Wheeler's first collection of folk songs, with Clara Gregory Bridge's musical accompaniment, appeared as *Kentucky's Mountain Songs* (1937). Her next compilation, *Roustabout Songs: A Collection of Ohio River Valley Songs* (1939), depicted riverboat life on the Ohio. Many of these songs may have been collected around 1935, when she taught music at Paducah Junior College. By June 1937 she had compiled the music and words to sixty-eight songs. Wheeler's final work, *Steamboatin' Days: Folksongs of the River Packet Era* (1944), was a history of the steamboat era on the Ohio, Tennessee, and Mississippi rivers.

Wheeler died on July 26, 1979, in Paducah, Kentucky, and was buried in Oakgrove Cemetery.

See Bonnie Cave Bradley, "Mary Wheeler: A Collector of Kentucky Folksongs," *Kentucky Review* 3 (1982): 55-67.

WHITAKER, FESS. Fess Whitaker, a colorful Letcher County politician who has become almost a legendary folk figure, was born on June 17, 1880, to Isaac D. and Matilda (Hogg) Whitaker. He served in the military and worked as a coal miner and railroader before running for the office of Letcher County jailer during World War I. Winning the election on the Republican ticket, he spent his victory night in the county jail on a charge of public drunkenness, thus becoming Letcher County's only "jailed jailer." His 1918 campaign autobiography, *History of Corporal Fess Whitaker*, begins with the straightforward notion that "among the people of Letcher County no other man has so remarkable history as Fess Whitaker." Elected judge of Letcher County during the 1920s, Whitaker was planning to run for a U.S. congressional seat at the time of his death in a car crash on September 17, 1927. He was buried in the Rockhouse community.

WILLIAM TERRELL CORNETT

WHITE, JOHN. John White, political leader, son of Hugh and Ann (Lowrie) White, was born on February 14, 1802, in Carter County, Tennessee. His father owned the Goose Creek salt works in Clay County, Kentucky. White was educated at Greeneville College in Tennessee and studied law in Lancaster, Kentucky, with William F. Owsley. He was admitted to the bar in 1823 and began his practice in Richmond, Kentucky. In 1832 White was elected to the Kentucky General Assembly as a representative of Madison County. He was then elected as a Whig to the U.S. House of Representatives (March 4, 1835, to March 3, 1845). White was Speaker of the House from 1843 to 1845. On his return to Richmond he was made judge of the 19th Judicial District and served in this post until his death. White married Mary Hume of Knoxville, Tennessee; they had seven children: William L., Hugh L., Margaret R., Katherine, Anne L., John, and Mary. White committed suicide on September 22, 1845, in Richmond. He was buried in the Frankfort Cemetery in Frankfort, Kentucky.

See William E. Ellis, H.E. Everman, Richard D. Sears, *Madison County: 200 Years in Retrospect* (Richmond, Ky., 1985).

WHITE HALL. White Hall, former home of antislavery activist Cassius Marcellus CLAY, is located in Madison County about seven miles northwest of Richmond, Kentucky, and approximately one mile south of the Kentucky River. In its time, the imposing residence sat amid 2,000 acres of gently rolling Bluegrass terrain and rustic landscape.

The house was built in two parts, each having a distinct appearance and style. The original house, known as Clermont, was built in 1798-99 for Revolutionary War veteran Gen. Green Clay of Virginia. The second portion was completed in the 1860s for Cassius Clay, who renamed the house White Hall. Italianate in design, the addition is attributed to two noted figures in Bluegrass design, architect Thomas LEWINSKI and builder John

McMurtry. The house remained in family ownership until the state of Kentucky purchased it and thirteen acres surrounding it in 1967 to ensure its preservation. In 1968 it became a state historic site. L. MARTIN PERRY

WHITEHAVEN. Whitehaven is a two-story brick house built about 1866 by Edward L. Anderson in McCracken County, Kentucky, near Paducah. On April 7, 1903, Anderson's heirs sold the house to Edward L. Atkins, cashier of the American German Bank, for $4,000. Atkins remodeled the house in the Colonial Revival style and named it Whitehaven. Local architect A.L. Lassiter designed extensive interior and exterior features, including the semicircular Corinthian portico. Atkins, who moved to Oklahoma on May 21, 1908, sold the house and attached fifty-seven acres for $7,000 to James P. Smith, who further remodeled the interior, using the services of Marshall Field of Chicago.

In 1981 the house was sold to Paducah Community College. With the support of Gov. John Y. Brown, Jr. (1979-83), the state allocated funds to restore the house. The very elaborate Colonial Revival house is now the tourist welcome center in Paducah. WILLIAM B. SCOTT, JR.

WHITESBURG. Whitesburg, the county seat of Letcher County in eastern Kentucky, is located on KY 15 along the headwaters of the North Fork of the Kentucky River, about twelve miles from the Virginia state line. Until the coming of the railroads in 1911-12 and the building of coal camps, Whitesburg was Letcher County's only true town. It was designated the county seat when Letcher County was created in 1842, and was surveyed in early 1843. The town was named in honor of Clay County politician John Daugherty White. An apocryphal story relates that the town received its name as a joke when some plats were surveyed on a snowy day late in 1842. What is now the central area of Whitesburg was owned in 1842 by Stephen Hiram Hogg, who donated a courthouse site as an inducement to move the seat of government from nearby Pert Creek, where the first court had been held.

A roomy log-and-frame courthouse was erected in 1843-44. It and an adjacent jail were destroyed by fire in a guerrilla raid in 1864 during the Civil War. The brick courthouse that replaced it in 1867 was torn down and replaced by a more spacious brick structure in 1898. The present courthouse was erected in 1964-65.

Whitesburg experienced a slow but steady growth up to the Civil War, but was nearly depopulated for a time during the 1860s. The city was incorporated in 1876 and grew quickly between 1910 and 1930, when it became the major shipping point for goods of the county and the principal trading center. Although not a coal town itself, it was ringed by small mining communities, several of which later disappeared. The Great Depression in the 1930s slowed Whitesburg's growth, which accelerated in World War II. The 1950s saw the coming of the modern Miners' Memorial Hospital, which later became an Appalachian Regional Hospital, and the advent of a widespread truck-mining industry. The 1960s brought national attention to the town through the writings of Whitesburg attorney Harry M. CAUDILL; the crusading spirit of the local newspaper, *The Mountain Eagle*; and the creation of Appalshop, a regional media and activist center.

A typical mountain town on level land along the Kentucky River, Whitesburg has three public schools and a branch of Southeast Community College. The population of the fifth-class city was 1,137 in 1970; 1,525 in 1980; and 1,636 in 1990. WILLIAM TERRELL CORNETT

WHITESTONE, HENRY. Henry Whitestone, architect, was born in County Clare, Ireland, in July 1819, the son of Thomas and Catherine (Fitzgerald) Whitestone. Henry is said to have attended the University of Dublin. He probably apprenticed under Dublin architect J.B. Keane; both are credited with the design of the County Clare courthouse, built 1840-50. In January 1852 Whitestone emigrated to the United States with his wife, the former Henrietta Sautelle Baker. In Cincinnati, Whitestone became an associate of Isaiah Rogers, known as "the father of the American hotel." In 1852, Rogers and Whitestone moved to Frankfort to build the Capital Hotel. After the Louisville Hotel burned to the ground in 1853, Rogers was asked to rebuild it, and he and Whitestone soon formed a partnership in Louisville. The physical character of Louisville rapidly changed as Rogers and Whitestone raised the skyline from three to five stories and introduced the Italianate style to the city. The partners' best-known designs include the Louisville Hotel, the 1854 Newcomb and Alexander buildings on Main Street, and the public school building still at the corner of Fifth and York (1855). Whitestone took over the business in 1857 and became the city's major practitioner until the 1880s.

Whitestone is best known for his 1869 design of the second GALT HOUSE, and the 1877 offices of the Louisville & Nashville Railroad (now CSX Transportation). He also designed James C. Ford's residence (1858-59) and the Ronald-Brennan house (1870). On November 16, 1887, Whitestone was elected an honorary member of the Western Association of Architects.

Whitestone in 1865 turned down the office of supervising architect of the U.S. Treasury, which designs and oversees construction of most federal buildings. In the same year Whitestone's wife died, leaving him to care for two young daughters, Austine Ford and Henrietta. When Whitestone retired about 1881, his firm was taken over by D.X. Murphy, his head draftsman. The firm became Luckett and Farley in 1962. Whitestone died on July 6, 1893, and was buried in Cave Hill Cemetery.

See C. Julian Oberwarth and William B. Scott, Jr., *A History of the Profession of Architecture in Kentucky* (Lexington, Ky., 1987); Elizabeth H.

Jones, "Henry Whitestone: Nineteenth-Century Architect," master's thesis, University of Louisville, 1974.   WILLIAM B. SCOTT, JR.

WHITLEY, WILLIAM. Pioneer, Indian fighter, and horseman, William Whitley was born on August 14, 1749, to Solomon and Elizabeth (Barnett) Whitley in Augusta County, Virginia. In the spring of 1775, Whitley and his brother-in-law, George Clack, explored Kentucky, selected a settlement location on Cedar Creek, a branch of Dick's (now Dix) River, and returned to Virginia for their families. They began their journey west in November of 1775. After planting ten acres of corn at his station, Whitley moved his family to the safety of St. Asaph, which Indians attacked in May 1777. He volunteered for three months as a member of Capt. John Montgomery's company to accompany George Rogers Clark on his invasion of the Northwest. In 1779 Whitley moved his family back to his station.

In 1792 Gov. Isaac Shelby (1792-96) appointed him a major in the 6th Regiment, Kentucky militia. The next year he became a lieutenant colonel. In 1794 Whitley, aggravated by continued Indian raids, led two hundred men against a Chickamauga village in Tennessee. After resoundingly defeating the Indians, Whitley gave a barbecue at his newly completed home, Sportsman Hill. Having an aversion to anything English, he used clay instead of turf for the surface of the racetrack that he laid out in 1788, and he raced the horses in a counterclockwise direction. To this day, all American sports using oval tracks race counterclockwise.

In 1797, Whitley was elected to the state House of Representatives and served one term. He was one of the Lincoln County commissioners of the Kentucky River Company in 1801. Although he was sixty-four years old and a veteran of more than twenty Indian engagements, Whitley volunteered in the Kentucky Mounted Infantry of the War of 1812. In the main engagement of the Battle of the Thames, on October 5, 1813, Whitley led the charge against the Indians led by Tecumseh. Both Whitley and Tecumseh fell in the battle.

In 1771 Whitley married Esther Fullen; they had eight daughters and three sons. The commonwealth in 1818 named a county in Whitley's honor. He was buried near the battle site of Chatham, Ontario, Canada.

See Charles G. Talbert, *A History of Colonel William Whitley* (Louisville 1977).

BETTY B. ELLISON

WHITLEY CITY. Whitley City, in McCreary County in southeastern Kentucky, is one of two unincorporated towns in the state that serve as county seats. The city is located in the central part of the county in the Daniel Boone National Forest, at the junction of U.S. 27 and KY 1651 and along the Norfolk Southern Railway (NSR). Built at an undetermined date around springs on Jenny's Creek that were reputed to have medicinal value, the settlement was originally called Coolidge. The name was

changed after the Cincinnati & Southern Railway (now the NSR) established a depot there soon after 1880 and named it Whitley. The depot may have been named for Col. William Whitley, a Kentucky pioneer, or after Whitley County.

After the Civil War, Union Capt. John Geary bought substantial acreage in the area that was to become Whitley City and promoted the founding of a town. It was on his tract of land that the third McCreary County courthouse was built in 1953; the first two burned in 1927 and 1951.

Whitley City had been incorporated before 1902, when outside capital began the development of the area and prompted the formation of McCreary County in 1912. Much of the available land was controlled by a group interested in building a new town to serve as the county seat. Incorporation meant higher taxes, so the corporate charter of Whitley City was dropped. A fierce battle ensued between residents of the southern portion of the county, who favored Pine Knot as the seat of government, and the northern portion, who favored Whitley City. After two referendums, Whitley City was chosen, but the battle between the two factions left long-lasting political divisions in the county.

Plans to promote Whitley City as a health resort failed and for many years the town languished, but after World War II many of the county's businesses moved to Whitley City. Local, state, and federal governments are the major employers of Whitley City residents. A few are employed in the textile industry or by the *McCreary County Record* newspaper; others commute to Stearns to work for the McCreary Manufacturing Company, the county's largest employer. The population of the unincorporated city was 1,060 in 1970; 1,683 in 1980. (Estimates for 1990 are unavailable.)

FRANK C. THOMAS

WHITLEY COUNTY. The fifty-ninth county in order of formation, Whitley County is located in southeastern Kentucky, along the Tennessee state line. It is bordered by Bell, Knox, Laurel, and McCreary counties and has an area of 443 square miles. The county was formed January 17, 1818, from a section of Knox County and was named in honor of Col. William Whitley, a Kentucky pioneer and Indian fighter. The county seat, WILLIAMSBURG, was originally called Whitley Courthouse.

The topography of Whitley County is hilly to mountainous, a steep and rugged landscape. Three-fourths of the county is forested with oak, black walnut, yellow poplar, hickory, and pine. The Daniel Boone National Forest covers 38,000 acres of the county, including Jellico Mountain, with an elevation of 2,124 feet. The major water sources are the Cumberland and Laurel rivers.

In April 1759 explorer Dr. Thomas Walker and his party entered the Whitley County area at Blake's Fork Creek. Raiding parties of Indians frequently attacked and killed hunters and trappers. Among those killed, probably by Cherokee, were Joseph Johnson at Lynn Camp and the son of Joe

Tye on Big Poplar Creek. In 1786 Indians attacked the large group of settlers known as McNitt's company and killed twenty-one of them in the area between the Big and Little Laurel rivers.

Williamsburg and CORBIN are the two incorporated towns in the county. Corbin is the county's largest town. The county's largest employers, located in Corbin, are American Greetings Corporation; NCR Systems Media, which makes business forms; National Standard Company, which manufactures industrial wire, cloth, and fibers; Tri-County Manufacturing and Assemblies, which produces typewriter components; and CSX Transportation. CSX completed a $41 million expansion of its railroad service facilities at Corbin in 1988.

Although the rugged terrain limits agriculture in Whitley County, some tobacco, corn, and livestock are raised. Lumber and coal have been the mainstays of the county's economy. Among the mineral resources of the area are coal, oil, iron, and minute traces of silver.

CUMBERLAND FALLS, the "Niagara of the South," is located in Whitley County. Cumberland Falls State Resort Park offers a lodge, cottages, camping, swimming, hiking, horseback riding, and convention facilities. Laurel River Lake covers 5,600 acres in Whitley County. These attractions, along with the Nibroc (Corbin spelled backwards) Festival and the scenic trails of the Daniel Boone National Forest, make Whitley County a major recreation area.

The population of Whitley County was 24,145 in 1970; 33,396 in 1980; and 33,326 in 1990.

See Eugene Lovett, *The History of Williamsburg, Kentucky, 1818-1978* (Williamsburg, Ky., 1981).

RON D. BRYANT

WHITNEY, ROBERT SUTTON. Robert Sutton Whitney, composer and orchestra conductor, was born in Newcastle-upon-Tyne, England, on July 9, 1904. The son of Robert P. and Edith Ogilvie (Stewart) Whitney, he grew up in Chicago and attended the American Conservatory of Music and later the Berkshire Music Center. In 1937 he founded the Louisville Orchestra and in 1948 he started commissioning, performing, and recording symphonic music of living composers worldwide. Whitney conducted the Louisville Orchestra in Carnegie Hall, New York City, in 1950, and at the White House Festival of the Arts in 1965. Whitney appeared as conductor with the orchestra in many Kentucky cities and towns during 1947-67. He was dean of the School of Music, University of Louisville (1956-71), and music consultant for the Louisville Board of Education (1971-75). Whitney received honorary doctoral degrees from the University of Louisville in 1952; Hanover College, 1956; and University of Kentucky, 1967. The 2,400-seat auditorium at the Kentucky Center for the Arts bears his name, and in 1986 he received posthumously from Gov. Martha Layne Collins (1983-87) Kentucky's award for outstanding contributions to the arts.

In 1936 Whitney married Margaret Gilbert, who died in 1965; they had two children, Martha and Margaret. He married Clarita Baumgarten in 1966. He died in Louisville on November 22, 1986, and his body was donated to the University of Louisville Medical School.   CLARITA B. WHITNEY

WICKLAND. The landmark Wickland mansion, east of Bardstown, Kentucky, was erected about 1825-28 as the residence of Charles Anderson Wickliffe; it is considered one of the best Federalstyle houses in Kentucky. It is called the "Home of Three Governors" in honor of the original owner, Kentucky's governor during 1839-40; his son Robert C. Wickliffe, who was governor of Louisiana during 1856-60; and his grandson J.C.W. Beckham, Kentucky's governor from 1900 to 1907.

The Baltimore trained architect-builder John ROGERS designed the spacious fourteen-room mansion, and the design was executed by his associate, James Marshall Browne, a master mason also credited with work on St. Joseph Cathedral, another Rogers design. Wickland's design features an unusual T-hallway with garden-side carriage entrance matching the larger main front entry. The perfectly proportioned front facade is complemented by the garden-side gable, and Georgian balance in fenestration is achieved by using false windows with closed shutters. Left of the main front entry are double parlors divided by large folding doors, becoming a single large room for entertaining. Paired mantels with Adamesque swags and elegantly reeded window surrounds enhance the formal effect. The staircase sweeps up to the third level, as in Federal Hill and Edgewood; all three staircases are probably the work of master woodwright Alexander Moore, an associate of both Rogers and Browne in many other Bardstown area homes and buildings.

In 1919 Wickland was sold by the children and heirs of Julia Beckham, youngest daughter of Gov. C.A. Wickliffe, finally passing from family hands. The house is open to the public year-round.

DAVID H. HALL

WICKLIFFE, CHARLES ANDERSON. Charles Anderson Wickliffe, governor in 1839-40, was born in a log cabin near Springfield, Kentucky, on June 8, 1788, four years after his parents, Charles and Lydia (Hardin) Wickliffe, moved there from Virginia. He read law in Bardstown with his cousin Martin D. Hardin and in 1809 he was admitted to the bar. Wickliffe married Margaret Cripps and they built WICKLAND ("Home of Three Governors") in Bardstown. The couple had eight children. After service as a commonwealth's attorney, Wickliffe supported the War of 1812 in the state House (1812-14) and in active duty on the western Canadian front. Elected to the state House again in 1820 and 1821, he then spent a decade (March 4, 1823-March 3, 1833) in the U.S. House of Representatives.

Politically independent, Wickliffe was a Whig who disagreed with several of Henry Clay's positions. Despite such differences, the Whigs selected him to be James Clark's gubernatorial running mate in 1836. Clark and Wickliffe were elected. Clark died in 1839, and Wickliffe served the last year of the term (September 27, 1839, to September 2, 1840). A friend of President John Tyler, Wickliffe was appointed U.S. postmaster general during 1841-45. His support for the annexation of Texas and a secret mission to Texas that he undertook for President James K. Polk undermined Whig confidence in Wickliffe. He served in Kentucky's 1849 constitutional convention, and during the sectional crisis that led to the Civil War he was active in various unsuccessful peace conferences. Elected to the U.S. House in 1861 as a Unionist, Wickliffe was crippled in a carriage accident the next year, and his service was cut short. Kentucky's Peace Democrats ran him for governor in 1863, but he was considered subversive by military authorities, who helped ensure his defeat by regular Democrat Thomas Elliot Bramlette, 68,422 votes to 17,503. Wickliffe died on October 31, 1869, and was buried in Bardstown.

Much of Wickliffe's year in office was dominated by the panic of 1837, which had swept the nation. The state had been operating at a deficit that reached $42,000 in 1839, and Wickliffe called for higher property taxes and economy in government to restore fiscal soundness. He asked for increased expenditures in only three areas: improvement of river navigation, preservation of state archives, and public education. The legislative response was to borrow money to meet current expenses, but Wickliffe was able to maintain the state's credit rating by paying all the interest due on state securities. Much of his time was spent on the endless requests for pardons, patronage positions, and special exemptions that have plagued all governors.

See Jennie C. Morton, "Governor Charles A. Wickliffe," *Register* 2 (Sept. 1904): 17-21.

LOWELL H. HARRISON

WICKLIFFE, ROBERT. Attorney and legislator Robert Wickliffe was born at Redstone, Pennsylvania, on January 16, 1775, one of nine children of Charles and Lydia (Hardin) Wickliffe. They soon settled near Bardstown, Kentucky. Privately educated, Wickliffe read law with George Nicholas in Lexington, where he opened a law practice. In 1805 Wickliffe was appointed U.S. attorney for Kentucky. Around 1809, he turned to real estate and was widely known for the litigious manner in which he acquired vast acreages. Wickliffe served three terms in the Kentucky House (1818, 1823, and 1824), and one in the Senate (1825). He was often an adviser to his brother Charles A. Wickliffe when Charles was governor of Kentucky (1839-40). Robert Wickliffe was a staunch advocate of the OLD COURT in the controversy over relief to debtors and one of the most consistent pro-slavery spokesmen of the Democratic party. In 1840 he held more than two hundred slaves, one of the largest slaveholdings in the state.

Wickliffe's handling of Breckinridge family legal affairs in the early 1800s had brought him into conflict with antislavery spokesman Robert Jefferson Breckinridge. In the 1840s Wickliffe and Breckinridge expounded their views in newspapers and pamphlets, some of them thirty to seventy pages long. The verbose titles ranged from *A Further Reply of Robert Wickliffe to the Billingsgate Abuse of Robert Judas Breckinridge, Otherwise Called Robert Jefferson Breckinridge* (an 1843 publication of seventy pages), to *The Second Defense of Robert J. Breckinridge Against the Calumnies of Robert Wickliffe; Being a Reply to His Printed Speech of Nov. 9, 1840* (a thirty-nine-page publication commercially printed in 1841).

In 1805 Wickliffe married Margaret Howard Preston; they were the parents of seven children: Sally, Charles, John, Benjamin, Robert, Mary, and Margaret. In 1825, Margaret, his wife, died, and in 1826 Wickliffe married the widow Mary (Todd) Russell, the only daughter of Col. John Todd, whose fortune in land and slaves was estimated to exceed $250,000. Wickliffe and his second wife had no children. Wickliffe obtained ownership of his second wife's property in 1828 through a tripartite deed in which Mary (Todd) Wickliffe transferred all of her property, and Wickliffe transferred part of his, to Richard H. Chinn, who in turn deeded all the property involved back to Wickliffe on the same day. In the 1820s there was no legislation to protect married women's property rights in Kentucky. In 1849, the Todd family filed suit for the return of the vast properties of Colonel Todd, claiming that his will (lost in an 1803 fire that consumed the Fayette County clerk's office) ordered that his property be divided among the rest of his family if his daughter Mary had no heirs; the only child of her first marriage had died before she married Wickliffe. *Todd Heirs v. Wickliffe* continued through lengthy trials until an 1857 court of appeals decision allowed the property and slaves to remain in the Wickliffe family, since Colonel Todd's will could not be produced.

Robert Wickliffe died in Lexington on September 1, 1859, and was buried at his home, Howard's Grove. His will emancipated his personal slave, William Box, and gave a three-day holiday to his other slaves upon his death.   BETTY B. ELLISON

WICKLIFFE. Wickliffe, the seat of Ballard County, is located in the southwestern corner of the county on the Mississippi River. The town was laid out in 1880 and incorporated two years later. It was named after Col. Charles A. Wickliffe, who served variously as a Kentucky legislator, a Confederate officer, and an attorney. He was the nephew of Kentucky's fifteenth governor, also named Charles Wickliffe (1839-40).

Blandville was the seat of Ballard County until the courthouse there burned in February 1880. Judge Samuel H. Jenkins offered to donate the land and funds to build a new courthouse in Wickliffe. A referendum in May 1880 to determine whether to move the county seat to Wickliffe was approved, and although the supporters of Blandville declared the voting unfair, the court of appeals in 1882 upheld the legitimacy of the results. The county records were moved to Wickliffe and another public election was held in 1884, again resulting in the selection of Wickliffe. The town grew rapidly from that point on. Its location on the Mississippi River gave the town access to commerce. It also benefited from the presence of the Illinois Central and the Mobile & Ohio railroads (now the Illinois Central Gulf), which were extended into the town during the 1860s and 1870s. These water and rail transportation and communication routes linked Wickliffe with commercial centers to the north and south.

The population of Wickliffe was 1,211 in 1970; 1,034 in 1980; and 851 in 1990.

WICKLIFFE MOUNDS. The Wickliffe Mounds in Ballard County, Kentucky, mark the site of a village or small town that Mississippian Native Americans inhabited from A.D. 1000 to 1300. The mounds lie on the bluffs of the Mississippi River, about three miles below its confluence with the Ohio. Typical of Mississippian period sites in western Kentucky, the town at Wickliffe Mounds was both a ceremonial and an administrative center. Two platform (temple) mounds dominate the site, and several smaller mounds are scattered around the village area. Archaeological excavation in the mounds and village has provided evidence of a late prehistoric society characterized by staple corn agriculture; trade contacts as far away as North Carolina, Wisconsin, and the Gulf of Mexico; and a social system organized under hereditary chiefs.

Fain W. King, a Paducah businessman, excavated privately at the Wickliffe Mounds site during the 1930s. With his wife, Blanche Busey King, he operated the site as a tourist attraction under the misnomer "Ancient Buried City." The Kings' commercial venture was controversial because of their sensational advertising and unsophisticated interpretation, putting them at odds with professional archaeologists. In 1946 the Kings deeded the site to Western Baptist Hospital of Paducah, which maintained the tourism business until it donated the property to Murray State University in 1983. Since 1983 the Wickliffe Mounds Research Center has established a comprehensive program of public education, research, and preservation at the Wickliffe Mounds. The site has been listed on the National Register of Historic Places (1984), and was the first entry in the Kentucky Archaeological Registry (1987).

See David Pollack and Mary Lucas Powell, eds., *New Deal Era Archaeology and Current Research in Kentucky* (Frankfort, Ky., 1988).

KIT W. WESLER

WILDCAT MOUNTAIN, BATTLE OF. During the Civil War, Union forces under the command of Brig. Gen. Albin F. Schoepf fortified themselves on Wildcat Mountain in Laurel County, Kentucky, in mid-October 1861 against attack by the Confederate army, led by Brig. Gen. Felix K. Zollicoffer. During four days of skirmishes, charging attacks, and heavy gunfire, the Union forces maintained their position as the Confederates retreated. At the major battle on October 21, Confederate forces charged up the hill but retreated in the face of Union reinforcements. Union losses were given as four killed, while General Zollicoffer reported eleven killed and missing.

The Battle of Wildcat Mountain was one of the first Civil War engagements in Kentucky and the first Union victory. It was critical for each side. The Confederacy needed the position in the Rockcastle Hills to prevent Union forces from moving into Virginia, where Gen. Robert E. Lee was preparing to march north. The Union's initial concern was to protect Louisville, Lexington, and Union camps by preventing Confederate forces from moving west, and to protect Union supply lines. The skirmish at Wildcat Mountain was the prelude to the Battles of MILL SPRINGS and PERRYVILLE.

See Eastham Tarrant, *The Wild Riders of the First Kentucky Cavalry* (Lexington, Ky., 1969).

MARK MCFERRON

WILDERNESS ROAD. The first written record of the Wilderness Road is an announcement in the *Kentucky Gazette* on October 15, 1796: "The Wilderness Road from Cumberland Gap to the settlements in Kentucky is now compleated. Waggons loaded with a ton weight, may pass with ease, with four good horses." Before that time, most people called the route either Kentucky Road or the road to the Holston settlements, depending upon the direction of travel. On John Filson's map, the old trail is called "The Road from the Old settle[ments] thro' the great Wilderness."

The Wilderness Road more or less followed the old Warriors' Path through the Cumberland Gap to Flat Lick, then parts of Skaggs's Trace from Flat Lick to Crab Orchard, Kentucky. Old trails and county roads that extended from Crab Orchard to Harrodsburg and Louisville are also frequently called the Wilderness Road by historians. To follow the Wilderness Road today, the traveler starts from Gate City, Virginia, and takes U.S. 58 to Jonesville. At this point the old road went northward to the base of the Cumberland Mountains and followed the mountains southwest to the Cumberland Gap after rejoining U.S. 58 east of today's Rose Hill, Virginia. Martin's Station was located on the road near Rose Hill and Davis Station was on the Kentucky side of the gap, in what is now national park land. From Cumberland Gap to present-day Baughman, Kentucky, the Wilderness Road was nearly the same as U.S. 25E, except that it followed the west side of Yellow Creek north of Middlesboro and the east side of the Cumberland River north of Pineville.

The original route ran north of the present Barbourville, then joined and followed KY 229 to present-day London. Modrel's Station was built along the road on the west side of the Little Laurel River in 1795; twenty-two militia were stationed there. North of London the road was approximately the same as U.S. 25 to Wood Creek, where it turned north and led to the top of Wildcat Mountain, where there was a trench battle during the Civil War. Farther north, the road ran along the ridge inside the bend in Rockcastle River, ascended on the northwest side, and crossed the river at Ford Creek below Livingston. The road then went up the south fork of Ford Hollow Creek to Sand Hill and followed the former Chestnut Ridge road into present-day Mt. Vernon. Part of the old road was destroyed during the construction of interstate highway I-75.

West of Mt. Vernon the original Wilderness Road is still visible, crossing Little Renfro Creek about 1.5 miles below U.S. 150, and following Boone's Fork of the Dick's (now Dix) River to Brodhead. The road followed the north side of the river for about two miles to a salt lick, then crossed to the south side, and followed for the most part U.S. 150 into Crab Orchard. From this point, travelers took county roads to their destinations. One of the most frequently used routes northward from Crab Orchard led to Danville and Harrodsburg, then to the salt works at Bullitt's Lick, and finally to Louisville. Another road to Louisville from Harrodsburg ran north along the town fork of Salt River past McAfee's Station to Hammons Creek, then across Big Benson Creek to Squire Boone's Station, and westward past Lynn's Station, Asturgus's Station, the Dutch Station, Floyd's Station, and the Spring Station.

The original Wilderness Road was not paved, but logs were added later in some sections as a surface material; one such section of corduroy road near Wildcat Mountain could still be seen as late as 1970. The log surfaces were probably installed by the Union army during the Civil War to support artillery and heavily loaded army wagons. On the north side of Wildcat Mountain, two parallel roads led up the hill, about sixty feet apart. One lane was used by double-teamed wagons going up the hill, the other by the spare horses going back down the hill to be double-teamed to another wagon.

See Robert L. Kincaid, *The Wilderness Road* (Middlesborough, Ky., 1966); Neal Hammon, "Early Roads into Kentucky," *Register* 68 (April 1970): 91-131.   NEAL HAMMON

WILDLIFE PRESERVATION. Wildlife management areas and wildlife refuges are state-owned tracts of land administered by the Kentucky Department of Fish and Wildlife Resources. They provide food, cover, and water for a wide variety of wildlife species in their natural habitat, such as deer, fox, groundhog, rabbit, raccoon, squirrel, dove, grouse, quail, turkey, woodcock, and waterfowl. The areas restrict the use of vehicles, and very few of them have developed recreational facilities. Wildlife management areas are open for hunting during regular statewide hunting seasons; wildlife refuges are

closed to the public from mid-October to mid-March. There are twenty-five wildlife refuges:

Ballard 300-Acre Tract—northwest Ballard County four miles south of Oscar; sloughs and bottomlands; some stands of hardwood.

Ballard Wildlife Refuge—northwest Ballard County west of Monkey's Eyebrow and bordering the Ohio River; 8,373 acres; sloughs and bottomlands; eleven lakes.

Beech Creek—Clay County five miles east of Manchester; 1,260 acres; sloping hills with narrow valleys; 34-acre Bert Combs Lake.

Central Kentucky—Madison County six miles east of Berea; 1,635 acres; flat to rolling hills with stands of timber; bridle and hiking paths.

Clay—Nicholas County eight miles northwest of Carlisle, bordering the Licking River; 4,901 acres; rolling to steep hills; more than 3,000 acres in woodland.

Cranks Creek—Harlan County fifteen miles southeast of Harlan; 1,288 acres; bordered by Cranks Creek on the northwest and Virginia on the south; mountainous terrain, with heavily forested hollows and steep slopes.

Curtis Gates Lloyd—northern Grant County one mile southeast of Crittenden; 1,179 acres; level to rolling and steep hills, with woods interspersed by clearings.

Fleming County—east of Flemingsburg in central Fleming county; 1,650 acres; hilly and heavily wooded, with sporadic clearings.

Grayson Lake—seven miles south of Grayson in Carter and Elliot counties; 4,763 acres; steep and hilly; 1,500-acre Grayson Lake.

Higginson-Henry—Union County two miles south of Morganfield; 5,424 acres; wooded rolling hills interspersed with clearings; ten miles of hiking trails, eighteen miles of roads, and Cap Mauzy Lake.

John A. Kleber—Owen County ten miles south of Owenton; 2,228 acres; steep hills with narrow ridge tops; numerous hiking trails. The Frankfort Audubon Society and Frankfort Bird Club conduct a Christmas bird count in this area.

Jones-Keeney—six miles east of Princeton in Caldwell County; 1,604 acres; wooded, hilly terrain with clearings along the ridges and in the valley bottoms.

Kaler Bottoms—northeastern Graves County at the West Fork of Clark's River; 1,587 acres; low-lying bald cypress swamps with limited access when the bottoms are wet.

L.B. Davidson—eastern Ohio County fifteen miles northeast of Hartford; 150 acres; Rough River forms its southern border; hilly with some cliffs, forested in virgin hardwood.

Mullins—southwest corner of Kenton County one mile north of Crittenden; 266 acres; some steep, wooded hills with hiking trails and bridle paths.

Peal—western Ballard County; 2,019 acres split into two tracts about five miles apart; river bottomland with cypress swamps and marshland. Mitchell

Tract is located one mile northwest of Wickliffe and just below the convergence of the Ohio and Mississippi rivers. Upper Blenderman Tract, the larger of the two areas, is located four miles west of Barlow and contains three oxbow lakes.

Pine Mountain—southern Letcher County five miles south of Whitesburg; 5,018 acres; extremely mountainous, with hollows and narrow ridges. A portion of the Little Shepherd Trail runs the entire length of the area.

Sloughs—Henderson and Union counties; 10,000 acres, split into four tracts. Sauerheber Refuge for waterfowl consists of 1,775 acres in western Henderson County, bordered on the north by the Ohio River. Jenny Hole-Highland Creek is located two miles north of Uniontown in western Henderson County, with a portion in Union County. Ash Flats is located in eastern Henderson County, three miles east of Hebbardsville. Grassy Pond-Powell's Lake is located in western Henderson County, and the Ohio River forms its western boundary. The entire terrain is swampland, which alternates between sloughs and ridges with open fields and woodlands.

Swan Lake Wildlife Refuge—Ballard County six miles northwest of Wickliffe; 2,536 acres; bottomland and floodplain of the Ohio and Mississippi rivers; 300-acre Swan Lake.

Tradewater—southwest Hopkins County, 724 acres; adjacent to Pennyrile Forest, with its southern border formed by Tradewater River; wooded, hilly terrain with numerous bluffs and rock overhangs.

Twin Eagle—northeast Owen County four miles from Perry Park; 166 acres; bordered on the west by the Kentucky River. The terrain is a steep Kentucky River terrace with hiking and climbing trails.

West Kentucky State—McCracken County, twelve miles west of Paducah; 6,969 acres. The flat terrain is nonforested, with five hundred acres in woods.

White City—Hopkins County thirteen miles southeast of Madisonville; 5,472 acres; level to rolling hills and abandoned strip mines. Muhlenberg County forms its eastern border.

Winford—Carlisle County six miles northwest of Bardwell; 237 acres; flat creek bottomland with several small lakes.

Yellowbank Wildlife Refuge—northern Breckinridge County twenty miles north of Hardinsburg, between the Ohio River and Meade County; 4,500 acres; moderate to steep wooded hills, with the flat riverbottoms of Yellowbank Creek.

The Kentucky Division of Forestry administers five wildlife areas:

Kentenia State Forest—northern Harlan County adjacent to Daniel Boone National Forest; 3,624 acres; rugged mountainous terrain with narrow ridge tops, heavily forested with hardwoods.

Kentucky Ridge State Forest—five miles southwest of Pineville in Bell County, adjacent to Pine Mountain State Resort Park; 11,363 acres; forested, rugged mountains.

Olympia State Forest—southeastern Bath County, within the Daniel Boone National Forest; 780 acres; steep mountains completely forested.

Pennyrile Forest—ten miles south of Dawson Springs in Christian County; 15,468 acres; forested hills; paved roads and hiking trails.

Tygarts State Forest—Carter County adjacent to Carter Caves State Resort Park; 800 acres; forested hilly to gently sloping ridge tops.

Several wildlife areas are federal property, administered by the U.S. Forest Service:

Beaver Creek—McCreary and Pulaski counties, within the Daniel Boone National Forest; 17,347 acres; steep, mountainous, and heavily wooded terrain interspersed with about 150 acres of open fields.

Cane Creek—Laurel County fifteen miles west of London, within the Daniel Boone National Forest; 6,672 acres; heavily forested steep hills with few clearings.

Jefferson National Forest—two tracts: 845 acres in Letcher County and 116 acres in Pike County, along the border between Virginia and Kentucky; mountainous, steep, and heavily forested.

Mill Creek—Jackson County two miles south of McKee, within the Daniel Boone National Forests; 13,558 acres; steep hills with long, narrow, forested ridge tops and few clearings.

Pioneer Weapons Hunting Area—southern Bath County, five miles south of Salt Lick, and northeastern Menifee County, along Cave Run Lake; 7,610 acres; heavily forested hills varying from steep to gently sloping with ridge tops; creek valleys with marked hiking trails; the only area in Kentucky where crossbow hunting is allowed.

Redbird—Leslie and Clay counties; 25,529 acres within the Daniel Boone National Forest; hilly terrain, steep to gentle slopes, heavily forested; about twenty-five miles of hiking trails.

WILEY, VIRGINIA (SELLARDS). Virginia ("Jenny") (Sellards) Wiley, a pioneer captured by Indians, was the daughter of Hezekiah Sellards, born around 1760 in Pennsylvania. She married Thomas Wiley in 1779 and they lived on Walker's Creek in what is now Bland County, Virginia. On October 1, 1789, Indians attacked their cabin while Thomas was away. The warriors killed Jenny's brother and three of her children and captured pregnant Jenny and her baby son. The Indians murdered this child and a baby boy that Jenny delivered in captivity. She was a prisoner of the Indians for nine months. Her captors took her north into the Big Sandy Valley of Kentucky, but they were unable to cross the flood-swollen Ohio River. Retreating southward, they wintered in camps in present-day Carter, Lawrence, and Johnson counties. She escaped from a camp at the falls of Little Mudlick Creek (now Johnson County), found her way to Harman's Station on John's Creek, and returned home with a hunting party.

After her return, Jenny and Thomas had five more children; they emigrated to the Big Sandy

Valley in 1800 and settled in Johnson County. Widowed in 1810, Jenny died in 1831 at the age of seventy-one and was buried in Johnson County. Her memory has been kept alive by two highway markers, a state park named for her, and a yearly outdoor drama depicting her ordeal. Her story has become legendary; the most pertinent dates have been substantiated by official records in the *Calendar of Virginia State Papers.*

See Henry P. Scalf, *Jenny Wiley* (Prestonsburg, Ky., 1964).   TRISHA MORRIS

WILKINSON, JAMES. James Wilkinson, soldier, political opportunist, and entrepreneur, was born in Calvert County, Maryland, in 1757, the son of Joseph, a prominent merchant-planter, and Betty (Heighe) Wilkinson. Wilkinson was sent to Philadelphia at age seventeen to study medicine and graduated in 1775. During the Revolutionary War, he served as a staff officer for Gens. Nathanael Greene, Benedict Arnold, Arthur St. Clair, and Horatio Gates. Wilkinson participated in battles at Quebec, Trenton, Princeton, Ticonderoga, Freeman's Farm, and Saratoga. Gates entrusted to Wilkinson the delicate task of negotiating Gen. John Burgoyne's surrender at Saratoga, New York, in 1777.

The "Conway cabal," infighting about leadership of the Continental army, resulted from Wilkinson's indiscretion regarding a private letter from a member of Gen. George Washington's staff, Gen. Thomas Conway, to General Gates. The letter criticized Washington's weaknesses as commander in chief and suggested that Gates replace him. Washington parried efforts by some congressional delegates to remove him as commander of the Continental army, and Gates was appointed instead as president of the Board of War. On Gates's recommendation, Congress also promoted Wilkinson to brigadier general and secretary of the Board of War, although he was only twenty years old. Lingering controversy over Wilkinson's role in the affair forced his resignation from the Board of War. Wilkinson accepted Congress's appointment as clothier-general to the Continental army in the summer of 1779, but he resigned amidst some controversy in the spring of 1781. As a member of the Radical party in Pennsylvania politics, he was elected a representative from Bucks County, where his farm, Trevose, was located, to the Pennsylvania General Assembly in October of 1781, and re-elected in 1782. In late 1783, his personal finances in tatters, the influence of the Radical party waning, and the war drawing to a close, Wilkinson divested himself of his Pennsylvania interests and moved west to the Kentucky country, where his influential brothers-in-law, Owen and Clement Biddle and Dr. James Hutchinson, held a number of land grants.

Wilkinson's war record, intellect, and magnetic personality quickly established him as a leader on the frontier. He involved himself in land speculation, salt mining, milling, shopkeeping, medicine,

and politicking. He laid out the town of Frankfort, incorporated by the Virginia legislature in 1791, from which he hoped to build a commercial empire. In 1787 he reached an agreement with the Spanish governor of New Orleans, Esteban Miró, to represent Spanish interests in Kentucky; Miró agreed to accept Wilkinson's future shipments of products. Wilkinson's overt and covert involvement in the Kentucky statehood movement and his relationship with Governor Miró came to be called the SPANISH CONSPIRACY. Wilkinson advocated in the various STATEHOOD CONVENTIONS that Kentucky separate from Virginia and from the Union of states under the Articles of Confederation. He circulated the notion of a possible Kentucky-Spanish alliance. But once the Jay-Gardoqui treaty, which would have closed the Mississippi River to American trade for a number of years, had been rejected and the new federal Constitution was ratified, Wilkinson lost interest in the separation movement. Although rumors persisted for many years regarding his continued employment by the Spanish government, conclusive proof was never gathered to convict him of any crime.

His finances in ruin once again, Wilkinson sought and was given a commission in the U.S. Army by President Washington in 1791. Controversy continued to dog his military career as he became embroiled in disputes with his superior, Gen. Anthony Wayne, until Wayne's death in 1796. Later, as governor of the Louisiana Territory and military commander of the Southern Department during 1805-06, he was forced to defend his actions regarding land deals and government contracts. In the period 1804 to 1806, he became involved with Vice-President Aaron Burr in a nebulous western enterprise involving a possible invasion of Mexico (see BURR CONSPIRACY). Wilkinson exposed the plan to President Thomas Jefferson, either to protect himself from discovery or because he suspected that Burr planned to sack New Orleans before sailing to Mexico. Wilkinson faced a battery of inquiries, including several conducted by Congress, as well as an army court martial regarding his role in the Spanish and Burr conspiracies. He was acquitted of all charges.

During the War of 1812, Wilkinson was promoted to the rank of major general and commanded the army for the invasion of Canada. He was relieved of command by President James Madison, an old political enemy, after the failure of the Montreal campaign in the fall of 1813. He spent the next several years in Philadelphia writing his *Memoirs of My Own Times* (1816), a defense of his career and an attack on Madison and the Federalists, who he believed were usurping the Constitution for their own aggrandizement. In 1817 he moved back to his plantation just outside of New Orleans and in 1820 ventured to Mexico, where he was later an adviser to Emperor Agustin de Iturbide.

In November 1778, Wilkinson married Ann Biddle, of a prominent Philadelphia family. He died on December 28, 1825, and was buried in Mexico City.

See Royal Ornan Shreve, *The Finished Scoundrel* (Indianapolis 1933); Gen. James Wilkinson, *Memoirs of My Own Times* (Philadelphia 1816).

JEFFREY SCOTT SUCHANEK

WILKINSON, WALLACE GLENN. Wallace Glenn Wilkinson, governor during 1987-91, was born on December 12, 1941, in Casey County, Kentucky, to Herschel and Cleo (Lay) Wilkinson. When he was a youth, the family moved to the county seat of Liberty, where Wilkinson helped his father run a grocery store. In 1960 he married Martha Stafford. They ended their studies at the University of Kentucky to start a paperback store in Lexington, which evolved into a used-textbook company and one of the nation's largest book firms. They have two sons, Wallace and Andrew.

Wilkinson engaged in real estate, banking, and farming and invested in coal, lumber, and other ventures. In 1983 he was finance chairman for Louisville Mayor Harvey Sloane's second unsuccessful campaign for the Democratic gubernatorial nomination, and in 1984 he managed the brief, aborted U.S. Senate campaign of former Governor John Y. Brown, Jr. (1979-83). Wilkinson won the 1987 nomination for governor with 35 percent of the vote, after putting much of his own money into the campaign and advocating a lottery as an alternative to higher taxes. In the general election, Wilkinson carried 115 counties and defeated Republican state Rep. John Harper by a record margin, 504,674 to 273,141.

After taking office, Wilkinson pushed for a constitutional amendment that would allow statewide elected officials, including those then serving, two successive terms. The succession battle damaged his relations with legislative leaders. The amendment passed the House but died in the Senate. Except for a plan to reward improved schools, the rest of his legislative program passed, and voters amended the constitution to allow a lottery.

In 1989 the state supreme court declared Kentucky's school system unconstitutional, effectively mandating a tax increase. Wilkinson reversed his antitax stand, and his second two-year budget included a $1.1 billion tax boost, with new money for almost every program, not only education. He proposed extending the 5 percent sales tax to certain services, but the legislature favored raising the rate to 6 percent instead. Wilkinson agreed in exchange for approval of a bond issue that gave a quick start to road projects he had promised during his campaign. Educators hailed the final school reform plan as the nation's best.

Early in the second session (1990), Wilkinson abandoned a television advertising campaign that criticized the legislature. His wife, Martha Wilkinson, campaigned for the Democratic gubernatorial nomination in 1991 but withdrew shortly before the primary election.

AL CROSS

WILLIAMS, CRATIS D. Cratis D. Williams, a leading scholar of the literary and cultural history of the southern Appalachian region and a pioneer in the development of Appalachian studies, was born on April 5, 1911, in Lawrence County, Kentucky, the son of Curtis and Mona (Whitt) Williams. He grew up on a farm in the Big Sandy Valley. At the age of twelve he left his mountain home to attend high school in Louisa, Kentucky. He was a student at Cumberland College in Williamsburg and received a B.A. in 1933 from the University of Kentucky and an M.A. in 1937. In 1961 he was granted a Ph.D. in English from New York University. His doctoral dissertation, "The Southern Mountaineer in Fact and Fiction," won a special citation for distinguished scholarship from the board of regents of that institution.

Williams's teaching career began in one-room schools in the mountains of eastern Kentucky. In 1942 he joined the English department of Appalachian State University in Boone, North Carolina. In his teaching and research, Williams especially emphasized the oral tradition of Appalachia, and his many articles on mountain balladry, speech, folklore, and cultural history contributed significantly to the development of Appalachian studies. Known as a great teacher and a meticulous scholar, Williams also won praise as an administrator at Appalachian State, serving as dean of the graduate school and acting chancellor. In 1973 he received the prestigious O. Max Gardner Award from the University of North Carolina. He also received several honorary degrees from Kentucky's Cumberland College, Berea College, and Morehead State University. He died on May 12, 1985, in North Carolina and was buried at Caines Creek in Lawrence County, Kentucky.

GERALD F. ROBERTS

WILLIAMS, JOHN STUART. John Stuart Williams, Confederate general and political leader, was born in Montgomery County, Kentucky, on June 29, 1818. His father was Gen. Samuel Williams, a veteran of the War of 1812. Williams attended the Houston Seminary in Bourbon County, Kentucky, and graduated from Miami University in Oxford, Ohio, in 1838. After studying law with Maj. Thomas Elliott in Paris, Kentucky, Williams was admitted to the bar in 1840 and practiced law in Paris until 1845. At the beginning of the Mexican War, Williams raised an independent company of one hundred men, the Clark Independent Rifles, attached to the 6th Infantry, and was their captain. He served with distinction at the Battle of Cerro Gordo, for which he was nicknamed "Cerro Gordo" Williams. He was promoted to colonel by Gov. William Owsley (1844-48). Williams served one term in the General Assembly (1851-53). When the Crimean War began in 1853, he was commissioned to serve as an observer and to report to the U.S. government on the military conditions he saw in Europe.

Although he personally opposed secession, Williams joined the Confederate army as a colonel in 1861, and was made brigadier general in April 1862. After the war, Williams returned to Kentucky. He ran for commonwealth's attorney from the 10th Judicial District but was defeated. In 1873-75 he was returned to the General Assembly. In 1875 he lost the Democratic nomination for governor by a small margin to James B. McCreary. In 1876 he ran unsuccessfully for the U.S. Senate, losing to James B. Beck. In 1878 he campaigned for the vacant Senate seat of William McCreery, defeating Robert Boyd by 126 to 11 electoral votes and serving from March 4, 1879, to March 3, 1885. He failed to win reelection in 1884.

Williams married Ann Harrison of Clark County on April 19, 1842. They had one daughter, Mary. Ann (Harrison) Williams died in 1844, and Williams married Henrietta (Lindsey) Hamilton in 1871. He died in Mt. Sterling, Kentucky, on July 17, 1898, and is buried in the Winchester, Kentucky, cemetery.

WILLIAMSBURG. Williamsburg, the seat of Whitley County, is located on the Cumberland River at U.S. 25W and I-75. The community was established on February 5, 1819, and incorporated on March 3, 1851. The town was originally called Whitley Courthouse in honor of William Whitley, a pioneer. The name was changed to Williamsburgh in 1882 and modified to Williamsburg in 1890. The first Whitley County courthouse was built about 1818. The second courthouse was constructed in the 1880s and the third in 1931. A fourth structure, of brick and stone, was erected in the 1970s.

In 1889 Cumberland College, a four-year liberal arts institution, was established in Williamsburg. It includes the Appalachian Center and Museum, where the area's arts and crafts are sold, and a restaurant that trains students in hotel management.

A 1933 fire destroyed a large section of the Williamsburg business district, and another major fire occurred in 1945 in the downtown area. The worst recorded floods of the Cumberland River at Williamsburg occurred in January 1946, January 1947, March 1975, and April 1977.

In 1989 Firestone Tire and Rubber opened a $29 million plant to produce air springs for the automobile industry, slated to employ three hundred people by 1992. The population of the fourth-class city was 3,687 in 1970; 5,560 in 1980; and 5,493 in 1990.

See Eugene Lovett, *The History of Williamsburg, Kentucky, 1818-1978* (Williamsburg, Ky., 1981).

RON D. BRYANT

WILLIAMSON, BEN MITCHELL. Ben Mitchell Williamson, businessman and U.S. senator, was born in White Post, Pike County, Kentucky, on October 16, 1864, the son of Wallace J. and America (Slater) Williamson. He attended local schools and entered Bethany College in West Virginia. In 1886 he co-founded Ben Williamson and Company, a wholesale hardware business in Catlettsburg, Kentucky. In 1924 he moved the company to Ashland and it became one of the biggest stores of its type in eastern Kentucky. Williamson remained its pres-

ident until his death. He presided as well over a mining and manufacturing company and was chairman of the board of the First National Bank of Williamson, West Virginia. He founded the Kentucky Crippled Children's Commission and served as its president from 1924 until 1941. He was later a director of the International Society for Crippled Children and in 1929-30 a member of the Kentucky Board of Charities and Correction.

In November 1930 Williamson ran on the Democratic ticket to fill a vacancy in the U.S. Senate caused by the resignation of Frederic M. Sackett. He defeated Republican John M. Robsion by a vote of 326,723 to 297,510 and served in the Senate from December 1, 1930, until March 3, 1931. He declined to seek a full term. Williamson married Ceres Wellman of Catlettsburg on January 19, 1887; they had three children—Wallace, Geraldine, and Ben. Williamson died in Cincinnati on June 23, 1941, and was buried in the Ashland Cemetery.

See Joseph W. Alley, *Alden Williamson Genealogy* (Huntington, W. Va., 1962).

WILLIAMSTOWN. Williamstown, the seat of Grant County, is located in the center of the county at the junction of U.S. 25, KY 22, and KY 467, just east of I-75. At the time Grant County was established in 1820, the county commissioners accepted William Arnold's offer of land at the site of Littell's Station for the new county seat. Although the name Philadelphia was proposed, the town was named for Arnold, a New Jersey native and veteran of the Revolutionary War and Indian campaigns of the 1790s, who had brought his family there in 1795. The town was incorporated in 1825.

In 1821 Arnold built the first county courthouse, a two-story brick structure that was replaced in 1856. A third courthouse was built during 1937-39 under a grant provided by the Works Progress Administration. On November 1, 1864, a Confederate force of thirty-two commanded by Col. R.J. Breckinridge, Jr., raided the town in an unsuccessful attempt to capture government money, which had been removed. On August 15, 1864, three Confederate prisoners of war were removed from a Lexington prison and hanged in Williamstown in retaliation for the alleged murder of two Union men.

The city grew slowly and by 1870 the population was only 281. The coming of the Cincinnati Southern Railroad (now Norfolk Southern) about 1877 helped to provide better access, but the town remained primarily rural. North of the city, Williamstown Lake was created in 1957 to provide water and recreation. The biggest change came in the 1960s with the construction of I-75 just west of town, which gave commuters access to work in the Greater Cincinnati metropolitan area to the north and the Lexington-Georgetown area to the south. The population of the fifth-class city was 2,063 in 1970; 2,502 in 1980; and 3,023 in 1990.

WILLIS, MARGARET FRISTOE. Margaret Fristoe Willis, library administrator, was born April

7, 1906, in St. Louis, Missouri, the daughter of Prior Fristoe and Elva (Moss) Willis. She received a bachelor of arts degree from Washington University and a master of library science degree from the St. Louis Library School. During the early 1930s she worked for the St. Louis Public Library. From 1935 until 1940 she reviewed books for the American Library Association in Chicago. She spent the following three years as a U.S. Army librarian at Jefferson Barracks, Missouri, where she developed and directed a library for the army hospital.

From 1943 to 1954 Willis was director of the Louisville Free Public Library's circulation department. While in that post she became actively involved in the Kentucky bookmobile project, a private citizens' effort that raised $300,000 to buy converted postal trucks. The project made library services available to many counties for the first time. She also played a principal role in a statewide library expansion, when donations totaled more than 600,000 books for use in areas where reading materials were scarce. In January 1955 Willis was named coordinator of the state's Library Extension Division. The following year she was named acting director, and in 1957 she became the division's director. In 1962 the division was given departmental status by the General Assembly and Willis's title was changed to that of state librarian. Altogether, she headed the state's library program during five administrations—from 1956 through 1973.

Willis supervised an unparalleled expansion of public library systems, bringing free public library service for the first time to the majority of Kentucky's 120 counties. Under her leadership the state's bookmobile fleet grew to 110 vehicles—the largest in the nation. She supervised more than one hundred library construction projects in Kentucky counties. She had a part in establishing the Library for the Blind and Physically Handicapped, the Regional Library System, and centralized book processing for public libraries that lacked the funds or expertise to process their own materials. Willis was a council member of the American Library Association and served on the executive board of the Southeast Library Association. She was president of the Kentucky Library Association. She received Catherine Spalding College's Sister Mary Canisius Award for excellence in library science. Following her retirement as state librarian, Willis became active in the downtown revitalization of Frankfort, the city she made her home. She died September 9, 1987, and was buried in St. Louis.

MOLLY M. CONE

WILLIS, SIMEON. Simeon Willis, Kentucky's governor during 1943-47, was born in Lawrence County, Ohio, on December 1, 1879. His parents, John H. and Abigail (Slavens) Willis, moved the family to Greenup County, Kentucky, about 1889. After attending a private normal school, Willis taught in the county schools. He read law with private tutors, was admitted to the bar in 1901, and opened a practice in Ashland. A Republican, he lost the race for city attorney in 1905 and for the court of appeals in 1916; he was elected city solicitor for 1918-22. In 1920 he married Idah Lee Millis; they had one daughter.

Gov. Flem D. Sampson (1927-31) appointed Willis to the court of appeals on December 31, 1927. Elected to a four-year term in 1928, he served with distinction and was acclaimed for revising the six-volume standard authority, *Thornton on the Law of Oil and Gas*. Defeated for reelection in 1932, Willis returned to private practice. Nominated without opposition for governor in 1943, he defeated a weak Democratic nominee, J. Lyter Donaldson, 279,144 to 270,525, and served from December 7, 1943, to December 9, 1947. In 1947 Willis resumed his law practice and the quiet home life, with much reading and fishing, that he loved. He lost a bid for a seat on the court of appeals to Bert T. Combs in 1952. Willis served on the Public Service Commission during 1956-60 and the parole board during 1961-65 and was active in several public organizations. He died in Frankfort on April 2, 1965, and was buried in the Frankfort Cemetery.

Willis's refusal to make wholesale dismissals of Democratic officeholders cost Willis some Republican support but gained Democratic votes for parts of his program. State revenue increased rapidly and much of it went to long-needed improvements in education; teachers' salaries and per-pupil expenditures nearly doubled, the school year was lengthened from seven to eight months, and counties were allowed to double their maximum tax rate for schools. In the neglected area of civil rights, Willis created a Commission on Negro Affairs, appointed the first black to the state Board of Education, and increased assistance to blacks who attended out-of-state professional schools because they had been denied access to the Kentucky schools. The old-age and dependent children programs were expanded, tolls were eliminated on twelve of thirteen bridges, and much more attention was paid to the treatment of tuberculosis patients. One of Willis's campaign promises had been repeal of the income tax, but he did not propose it until 1946 and the legislature refused to eliminate it at that time, at least in part because it had passed a considerably larger budget than Willis had recommended.

See James C. Klotter, ed., *The Public Papers of Governor Simeon Willis 1943-1947* (Lexington, Ky., 1988).   LOWELL H. HARRISON

WILLSON, AUGUSTUS EVERETT. Augustus Everett Willson, governor during 1907-11, was born in Maysville, Kentucky, on October 13, 1846, to Hiram and Ann Colvin (Ennis) Willson. Orphaned at age twelve, Willson lived for some years with relatives in New York and Massachusetts. After graduating from Harvard University in 1869, he read law there. Returning to Kentucky, Willson entered the Louisville law firm of John Marshall Harlan, who became a lifelong friend. In 1877 Willson married Mary Elizabeth Ekins; their only child died in infancy.

A Republican in a predominantly Democratic state, Willson lost bids for the state Senate (1879) and the U.S. House (1884, 1886, 1888, 1892). As the party's nominee for governor in 1907, he took part in a bitterly contested campaign that focused on alleged Republican scandals during the William O. Bradley administration (1895-99) and the temperance question. Willson and Democratic candidate Samuel Wilber Hager both favored enactment of a uniform local option law on alcoholic liquor on a county basis. With strong support from Louisville and Jefferson County, Willson beat Hager, 214,481 to 196,428, and became governor on December 10, 1907. When he left office on December 12, 1911, Willson resumed his Louisville legal practice. He lost the 1914 race for a U.S. Senate seat to former Gov. J.C.W. Beckham (1900-1907). Willson died on August 24, 1931, and was buried in Louisville's Cave Hill Cemetery.

When his administration failed to mediate the tobacco Black Patch War, Willson declared martial law in western Kentucky and sent in National Guard troops. The continuing fight over the temperance issue, in the form of the so-called county unit law, split the Democratic party and almost halted other legislative activity; a bill passed the House in 1908 but was blocked in the Senate. Pressing issues such as tax reform and redistricting remained unresolved, and almost all of Willson's suggestions were ignored.

See Christopher R. Waldrep, "Augustus E. Willson and the Night Riders," *FCHQ* 58 (Apr. 1984): 237-53.
LOWELL H. HARRISON

WILSON, L.B. L.B. Wilson, businessman, was born in Covington, Kentucky, on May 20, 1891, the son of Lyda (Miles) and Wesley Berry Wilson. In his youth he and his brother Hansford toured Europe as vaudeville dancers. Wilson then began his career as a cigar store operator and he later operated a chain of movie theaters with Kentucky Sen. Richard Ernst's realty company. In 1929 Wilson built Covington's first radio station, WCKY. He became the president of People's National Bank and was involved with other business ventures such as the Covington-Cincinnati Bridge Company and Churchill Downs. Wilson married Constance Freshwater (stage name Jean Oliver) on October 7, 1929. They were separated on June 28, 1948. Wilson died in Cincinnati on October 28, 1954, and was buried in Miami, Florida.
CHARLES D. KING

WILSON, ROBERT BURNS. Robert Burns Wilson, artist and poet, was born to Thomas M. and Elizabeth Anne (McLean) Wilson on October 30, 1850, near Parker, Pennsylvania. An orphan at the age of ten, Wilson lived with his grandparents in Wheeling, West Virginia. In 1871 he moved to Pittsburgh, where he studied art and shared a studio with John W. Alexander. After a year, Wilson moved to Louisville, where his drawings included a crayon portrait of Henry Watterson, editor of the

Courier-Journal. In 1875 Wilson moved to Frankfort, Kentucky, where local residents were the subjects of most of his portraits, in oil, crayon, and charcoal. He reserved watercolor for Kentucky landscapes, many depicting the Kentucky River and Elkhorn Creek, among them *The Land of the Sky*, *The Cedars of Culmer's Hill*, and *The Quiet Fields*. Several of his Kentucky landscapes were well-received at both the 1883 Louisville and 1884 New Orleans exhibitions.

One of Wilson's poems, "When Evening Cometh On," was published in *Harper's Magazine* in 1885. He published three books of poetry: *Life and Love* (1887), *Chant of a Woodland Spirit* (1894), and *The Shadows of the Trees* (1898). Wilson wrote "Remember the Maine" shortly after the sinking of the battleship U.S.S. *Maine* in Havana Harbor. The poem, set to music, brought instant acclaim to the author and became the U.S. battle song in the Spanish-American War.

Wilson married Anne Hendricks of Frankfort on March 4, 1901. They had one daughter, Elizabeth. The family moved to Brooklyn, New York, in 1904, where Wilson believed his painting would have a wider audience. He died on March 31, 1916, in Brooklyn and was buried in the Frankfort Cemetery.

See J. Winston Coleman, Jr., *Robert Burns Wilson: Kentucky Painter, Novelist and Poet* (Lexington, Ky., 1956).

WILSON, SAMUEL MacKAY. Samuel MacKay Wilson, lawyer and historian, was born October 15, 1871, in Louisville to Samuel Ramsay and Mary Catherine (Bell) Wilson. He was educated at Centre College, Danville, and at Williams College, Williamstown, Massachusetts. He studied law both at Centre and in the office of Judge Jere Morton of Lexington and was admitted to the Fayette County bar on October 15, 1895. In September 1916 Wilson enlisted in the Citizens Military Training Program and was stationed at Plattsburg, New York. He was commissioned a judge advocate in the military on October 2, 1917, served throughout World War I in France with the American Military Expedition, and was discharged as a lieutenant colonel on May 2, 1919.

During his career, Wilson developed an extensive law practice and distinguished himself as a keen lawyer, a bulldog debater, and a spirited public citizen. Wilson's monuments are his sixty-five books and articles. He wrote with the precision and clarity of the legal scholar, not in a popular style, and was a perceptive and pungent critic. A meticulous scholar, he collected voluminous notes and biographical materials. In time he assembled a major collection of books, pamphlets, manuscripts, newspapers, and public documents relating to the westward movement in American history, especially in the Ohio Valley and Kentucky. Wilson's writings and collections must be classed with those of Lyman Copeland Draper and Reuben T. Durrett. He bequeathed his literary properties to the University of Kentucky's Margaret I. King Library, where they form a foundation of rare books and manuscripts.

Wilson was active in many historical and cultural organizations, and he punctuated his life with the annual meeting of the Cakes and Ale Club, which he had organized in 1936. He died on October 10, 1946, in St. Louis and was buried in the Lexington Cemetery.

See G. Glenn Clift, "Samuel MacKay Wilson, 1871-1946," *Register* 45 (Jan. 1947) 27-38; Samuel M. Wilson, *Samuel M. Wilson and the Cakes and Ale Club* (Lexington, Ky., 1948).

THOMAS D. CLARK

WINCHESTER, JAMES. James Winchester, commander of U.S. forces at the Battle of RIVER RAISIN during the War of 1812, was born in Carroll County, Maryland, to William and Lydia (Richards) Winchester on February 6, 1752. He joined the military in 1776, saw action in several Revolutionary War battles, and was commissioned a captain before the war ended. In 1785 he and his brother, George, moved to Tennessee, settling in present-day Sumner County. When Tennessee became a state in 1796, Winchester was elected to the state senate, where he served as speaker.

At the beginning of the War of 1812, Winchester was commissioned a general and sent to Kentucky to take command of the Army of the Northwest. When William Henry Harrison was later appointed to that position, Winchester was assigned command of the left wing and sent to reinforce the troops of Gen. William Hull in Detroit. Winchester's forces, primarily troops from Kentucky, took the town of Frenchtown, near present-day Monroe, Michigan, on January 18, 1813. On January 23, the British and their Indian allies counterattacked, killing or capturing Winchester's entire force in the Battle of River Raisin. After parole by the British, Winchester took command of the U.S. forces in the Mobile (Alabama) District until the war ended, when he retired from miltary service. Winchester spent the next several years defending himself against accusations of neglect and military incompetency at River Raisin, as charged by Robert B. McAfee of Kentucky in *History of the Late War in the Western Country* (1816).

In 1802 Winchester married Susan Black; the Tennessee legislature legitimatized their four children in 1803. They had a total of fourteen children. Winchester died on July 26, 1826, and was buried at Cragton, his home in Tennessee.

See John H. DeWitt, "General James Winchester," *Tennessee Historical Magazine* 1 (June 1915): 79-105.

WINCHESTER. Winchester, the seat of Clark County in central Kentucky since the county was created in 1792, is located at the intersection of U.S. 60 and KY 627, south of I-64. The town was established in 1792 on sixty-six acres of John Baker's farm and named for his hometown in Virginia. Strode's Station was founded in 1779 just northwest of present-day Winchester. When the Indian threat ceased, the station fell into disuse and the village of Winchester was established at a crossroads on the Lexington Pike. A two-room log courthouse was completed in 1794 and replaced by a brick courthouse in 1818. A third courthouse served from 1819 to 1852. A fourth courthouse was completed in 1855 and remodeled by the Works Progress Administration in 1938-40.

By the early 1800s, the city had become an agricultural trading center. Numerous small industries began operations, and a few substantial homes were built.

During the Civil War the town was occupied twice by Gen. John Hunt Morgan's Confederate cavalry. On July 19, 1862, the Confederates destroyed weapons there before withdrawing, and in June 1864 Morgan's men passed through the town after a battle at Mt. Sterling.

In the postbellum years, profound changes occurred with the coming of the Elizabethtown, Lexington & Big Sandy Railroad (now CSX Transportation) in 1873. In 1881 a second railroad line, the Kentucky Central (now CSX) was constructed eastward into adjacent Powell County in 1883. The railroads helped to generate new business and industry. Educational establishments, banks, hotels, and residential neighborhoods were built. Winchester was incorporated in 1877, and in 1888 KENTUCKY WESLEYAN College relocated there from Millersburg. The town had a sizable professional class, many of whom built handsome residences. Many of the commercial buildings built around the turn of the century were also of sophisticated design.

The population of Winchester increased steadily during the twentieth century. In the automobile era, it found itself in economic competition with both Mt. Sterling and Lexington. In 1952 Kentucky Wesleyan College moved to Owensboro and its campus was occupied by Kentucky Christian Bible College, which closed in the 1970s. By the mid-1960s, Winchester's location near the intersection of two recently constructed highways, I-64 and the Mountain Parkway, brought a new wave of economic growth and residential activity. By 1984 the largest manufacturing firms in or near the city were Rockwell International, which manufactures truck axles; Leggett & Platt, which makes beds and bed parts; and Winchester Clothing, which produces men's suits.

The population of the third-class city was 13,402 in 1970; 15,216 in 1980; and 15,799 in 1990.

A. GOFF BEDFORD

WING COMMANDER. Wing Commander, five-gaited American saddlebred show stallion, was world grand champion from 1948 through 1953. Earl Teater, manager-trainer of Dodge Stables at Castleton farm in Lexington, Kentucky, was the only person to show Wing Commander. The saddlebred was foaled April 23, 1943, at Meadowbrook Farm in Rochester, Michigan; his sire was Anacacho Shamrock and his dam was Flirtation Walk, by King's Genius. Wing Commander was dark chestnut with four white stockings and a blaze; solidly built, he stood 15.2 hands and weighed 1,100 pounds. His exceptional traits included extremely high natural action, power, speed, and endurance. It was estimated that he could trot a mile in 2:10. At the Illinois State Fair in 1949, he won a contest in one hour and forty-five minutes of competition in heat that reached 100° Fahrenheit.

Wing Commander stayed sound and healthy after showing in eleven states over nine years. Between 1946 and 1954, he competed 123 times and placed first 121 of those. The only horse to defeat him was Easter Parade, beating him in championships at the Kentucky State Fair and the New York National, when Wing Commander was a four-year-old showing against older horses. Wing Commander retired to stud in 1955 and was first in *Saddle & Bridle*'s sire rating from 1963 through 1968. He died January 19, 1969, and was buried at Castleton farm. He headed the list of deceased sires from 1969 through 1973. His get included two five-gaited world grand champions, Valerie Emerald and Yorktown. A daughter, Tashi Ling, was *Fine Harness World*'s grand champion. Eleven world grand champions are traced to Wing Commander.

See Emily Ellen Scharf, *Susanne's Famous Saddle Horses*, vol. 3 (Louisville 1946).

LYNN P. WEATHERMAN

WINN, MATT J. Matt J. Winn, horseman and promoter, was born in Louisville on June 30, 1861, to Patrick J. and Julia (Flaherty) Winn. Winn, who lived his entire live in Louisville, dropped out of school when he was fourteen. He worked as a bookkeeper, a grocery clerk, a traveling salesman, and a tailor. In 1898 Winn was named Louisville's director of safety. In 1902 he was named vice-president and general manager of CHURCHILL DOWNS, after a period of extreme financial difficulties for the track. Mayor Charles F. Grainger, along with Frank Fehr and Louis Seelbach, raised $40,000 to improve the track and rescue it from its financial woes. In the rescue process, Winn bought Churchill Downs' previously leased eighty-one acres of land in 1903 to gain direct control over all aspects of the Downs' dealings.

In 1904 Winn became president of the American Turf Association, serving until 1910. From that position, Winn was able to build a strong foundation for Churchill Downs, and he quickly became a giant in the world of horse racing. Because Kentucky had outlawed auction pools, the bookmaking style of betting used most often in horse racing, Winn developed the pari-mutuel system, making use of machines to stay within the law. Under the new system, track employees set the odds, which changed as more or fewer bets were placed on a particular horse. The system was not only a success at Churchill Downs but also became the popular form of betting elsewhere.

Opposition to gambling among some groups resulted in several attempts to close Churchill Downs while Winn was in charge. The first and most serious attempt came during World War I. Winn feared

that if racing stopped for the war, he would not be able to reopen the track afterward. To help avoid a shutdown, he began growing potatoes in the infield and auctioning off the harvest; the proceeds went to the Red Cross as Churchill Downs' donation to the war effort. Winn had outwitted the opposition.

During Winn's long association with Churchill Downs, he built it into the premier track in the country. In 1920 he lengthened the Kentucky Oaks to a mile and an eighth, but he concentrated on making the Kentucky Derby, then an ordinary horse race, into the most important event for thoroughbreds in the nation. In 1903 only 3,000 people watched Judge Hines win the purse of $4,850. In 1946, after Winn had launched countless fundraisers and publicity campaigns, Churchill Downs was filled by more than 100,000 spectators who watched Assault win the Derby purse of $96,400. Winn had fought to keep the derby running during World War II, and he capped his success with the seventy-fifth running of the derby in 1949, the last Kentucky Derby of his lifetime. He had placed a bet at the very first Kentucky Derby, in 1875. At the time of Winn's death, former Gov. Ruby Laffoon (1931-35) said Winn had "done more than any other man to make Kentucky a household word in the nation." Winn was still the president and manager of Churchill Downs when he died, but he had sold the track for $65,000 in 1945.

He married Rosa Doyle in 1888; they had seven daughters: Ann, Mary, Olive, Elizabeth, Clara, Julia, and Helen. Winn died on October 6, 1949, and was buried in Cave Hill Cemetery in Louisville.

See Matt J. Winn, *Down the Stretch: The Story of Colonel Matt J. Winn* (New York 1945).

WITHERS, GARRETT LEE. Garrett Lee Withers, politician, son of Francis Gooch and Sarah (Imboden) Withers, was born on a farm near Clay in Webster County, Kentucky, on June 21, 1884. He was educated at Province Academy in Webster County and studied law at Southern Normal School (Western Kentucky University) in Bowling Green. Withers taught school for five years before being admitted to the bar in 1908. He practiced law in Webster County from 1911 to 1953. Withers was Webster County circuit court clerk during 1910-12 and master commissioner of the court during 1913-17. Gov. Earle C. Clements (1947-50), a personal friend of Withers, appointed him state highway commissioner in December 1947. When Alben W. Barkley resigned from the U.S. Senate to become vice-president, Governor Clements appointed Withers to the remainder of Barkley's term, from January 20, 1949, to November 26, 1950. Withers then returned to private law practice in Dixon, Kentucky. He reentered politics in 1952, serving in the state House of Representatives. After the death of Rep. John Albert Whitaker in 1952, Withers, a Democrat, was elected to fill Whitaker's position in the U.S. Congress. Withers was then reelected to Congress, serving from August 2, 1952, until his death.

Withers married Mabel Hammack of Webster County in 1912. They had two sons, John and Thomas, and a daughter, Helen. Withers died on April 30, 1953, at Bethesda, Maryland. He is buried in the I.O.O.F. Cemetery in Clay, Kentucky.

WOLFE, NATHANIEL. Nathaniel Wolfe, lawyer, was born in Richmond, Virginia, on October 29, 1808, to Benjamin and Sophia Wolfe. He received a bachelor of law degree from the University of Virginia at Charlottesville and moved to Louisville, where he started his law practice. A highly regarded criminal lawyer, he was involved in several of the well-known cases tried in Louisville courts during his time. Wolfe was a commonwealth's attorney for Jefferson County (1839-1852), a member of the Kentucky Senate (1853-55), and of the Kentucky House (1859-63). Wolfe, a very influential citizen, strongly advocated neutrality for Kentucky in the Civil War. When Wolfe County was formed in 1860, it was named in his honor.

Wolfe married Mary Vernon on October 3, 1838; they had ten children. Wolfe died on July 3, 1865, in Louisville and was buried in Cave Hill Cemetery.

WOLFE COUNTY. Wolfe County, the 110th county in order of formation, is located in eastern Kentucky. It is bounded by Powell, Menifee, Morgan, Magoffin, Breathitt, and Lee counties and has an area of 223 square miles. The county was formed in 1860 from portions of Breathitt, Owsley, and Powell counties, and was named for Nathaniel Wolfe, an eloquent criminal lawyer who represented Jefferson County in the Kentucky legislature (1853-55, 1859-63). The seat of Wolfe County is CAMPTON.

The topography of Wolfe County is hilly and broken terrain. About 14,317 acres in the northwestern part are included in the Daniel Boone National Forest, an area known for its natural sandstone arches and precipitous cliffs. Farms and commercial timberlands make up most of the county. Major products are tobacco, hay, corn, and livestock. Natural resources include timber, oil, and small amounts of coal. Waterways include the Red River and its tributaries and the tributaries of the North Fork of the Kentucky River, which touches Wolfe County's southern boundary in several locations.

Abundant prehistoric remains found under rock ledges give evidence that aboriginal people occupied the area in great numbers. The legendary Jonathan Swift and his "lost silver mine" in the 1760s gave the name to Swift Camp Creek, which flows south to north through the county. Early settlers, many from Lee and Tazewell counties in Virginia, included the Elkins, Days, Richmonds, Cecils, Camples, and Roses. Around 1800 Michael O'Hair and his large family settled at what later became Hazel Green. At about the same time John Lacy settled on Lacy Creek in the same vicinity. In 1810, the county's first water mill, three miles below Hazel Green, was operated by the Cox broth-

ers. Campton was settled at an unknown date by Nim Wills, who named it after an old camp found there.

Hazel Green was incorporated in 1856 as the first city in Wolfe County. When the county was established in 1860, the more centrally located community of Campton was made county seat. During the Civil War, the provisional Confederate government of Kentucky tried unsuccessfully to change Wolfe County's name to honor the late Gen. Felix K. Zollicoffer, who died in battle at Mill Springs on January 19, 1862. The retreating army of Union Gen. George Morgan camped in Hazel Green on September 23, 1862. On June 7, 1864, Gen. John Hunt Morgan's Confederate cavalry passed near Hazel Green.

Wolfe County remained an isolated scattering of agricultural communities for most of the nineteenth century. Pine Ridge, established in 1856, later became a logging center. The pace of timbering picked up in 1898 after the Swan-Day Lumber Company acquired territory in Wolfe and Powell counties. To work the forests in the Red River region, the Mountain Central, a narrow-gauge railroad, was built in 1907 from the Lexington & Eastern in Powell County eastward along Pine Ridge to Campton. With the depletion of the timber, the railroad lingered as a freight and passenger hauler, then ceased operations in 1928. The town of Eastin was established by Swan-Day five miles west of Campton. Eastin flourished as a logging town and by 1900 had thirty-five homes and two hundred people, but when the timber gave out it rapidly became a ghost town.

Wolfe County was known for its resort hotels in the late nineteenth and early twentieth centuries. The El Park Hotel was built between 1890 and 1896 at Torrent, six miles west of Campton. It flourished until the Great Depression and was destroyed by fire in 1935. At Swango Springs near Hazel Green, three hotels and several boardinghouses were in operation by 1895 for those who came to take the mineral waters. Fire destroyed the largest hotel in 1910, but mineral water was bottled and shipped from there until 1943.

Because of Wolfe County's isolation and apparent poverty, several Christian mission societies founded schools there. Hazel Green Academy was founded in 1880 by J.H. Day, G.B. Swango, and W.O. Mize as a college preparatory school. In 1888 the school was taken over by the National Christian Board of Missions. In 1896 Kentucky Wesleyan Academy established a branch of its Winchester campus in Campton, but the school was discontinued in 1912. The Alvan Drew school was started as a Methodist institution in 1913 at Pine Ridge by missionary Mrs. M.O. Everett. The school closed after a 1947 fire, and the property was taken over in 1950 by the Dessie Scott Children's Home.

The U.S. Forest Service acquired 14,178 acres of Wolfe County between 1933 and 1948 for what is now the Daniel Boone National Forest. Small amounts of mining and logging continued there, but by the early 1960s the isolated county was one of Kentucky's poorest. The May 1963 completion of the Mountain Parkway helped to attract some new industry to Campton, and tourists to the Red River Gorge area. Since 1969 the county's largest manufacturing employer has been Campton Electronic, and in 1989 Whiting Manufacturing announced plans to build a bedding supply plant in eastern Wolfe County.

The population of the rural county was 5,669 in 1970; 6,698 in 1980; and 6,503 in 1990.

See Berta K. Cecil, *History of Wolfe County, Kentucky* (Campton, Ky., 1958).

WOLFORD, FRANK LANE. Frank Lane Wolford, lawyer, Union officer, and congressman, was born to John and Mahalia Wolford on September 2, 1817, in Adair County, Kentucky. He studied law under Hiram Thomas, was admitted to the bar in Casey County, and practiced law in Liberty, Kentucky. During the Mexican War, Wolford served under Col. William R. McKee. In 1847 he returned to Kentucky and was elected to the Kentucky House, serving from 1847 until 1849. From 1849 until the outbreak of the Civil War, Wolford earned a reputation as one of the best criminal lawyers in the Green River region.

During the Civil War, Wolford recruited for the 1st Kentucky Cavalry, serving as colonel. He spent most of his time in the 1st Cavalry chasing Gen. John Hunt Morgan of the Confederate cavalry until Morgan's capture in July 1863. In March 1864, Wolford was dishonorably discharged from the army by President Abraham Lincoln after publicly criticizing his presidency and was arrested and jailed several times by Gen. Stephen T. Burbridge until Lincoln intervened and ended the matter in 1865.

On March 4, 1865, Wolford returned to the Kentucky House to represent the Casey-Russell district, serving until 1867. In 1865 and 1869, he was a Kentucky presidential elector, voting for Gen. George B. McClellan and Horatio Seymour, respectively. In 1867 he was appointed adjutant general by Gov. John W. Stevenson (1867-71), serving until 1868. He practiced law in Liberty until 1879 and then in Adair County. He was elected to the U.S. Congress, where he represented the 11th Congressional District, serving two terms (March 4, 1883, to March 3, 1887).

Wolford was married twice: to Nancy Dever on November 2, 1849, and to Elizabeth Bailey on April 6, 1865. He died on August 2, 1895, and was buried in the Columbia, Kentucky, cemetery.

See Hambleton Tapp, "Incidents in the Life of Frank Wolford, Colonel of the First Kentucky Union Cavalry," *FCHQ* 10 (Apr. 1936): 82-100.

WOMEN. Women have played a part in all aspects of the development of Kentucky from the earliest days, but *Women in Kentucky* (1979), by Helen Deiss Irvin, a brief overview, is thus far the only survey. Historians will have to use their skills and imaginations to ferret out materials on women in early Kentucky.

The first women to live in Kentucky were Native Americans, who are not usually included in historical accounts because they left few written records. There are a few written accounts of Native American women in Kentucky by white settlers. Written accounts of the early settlement period tend to focus on a few well-known white women. According to Irvin, Mary Draper Ingles was the first white woman to enter Kentucky, as an Indian captive in 1755; Virginia ("Jenny") Wiley survived kidnapping and imprisonment on the eastern Kentucky frontier in the 1780s. In 1775 Rebecca and Jemima Boone and Esther Whitley were among the first mothers, daughters, and wives migrating in 1775. Molly Logan, an Afro-American slave, braved an Indian attack in Central Kentucky with Esther Whitley in 1777. The Micajah Harrison papers at the Kentucky Historical Society tell of the activities of Charlotte and Milly, slaves from Mt. Sterling, and Milly's husband, a free black.

As Kentucky changed from a raw frontier to a thriving new state, wealthy, well-educated, and well-married women made their marks. Lucretia (Hart) Clay managed her husband's huge estate while he served in the House of Representatives and U.S. Senate. Mary (Austin) Holley, who arrived in Kentucky in 1818 when her husband became president of Transylvania University, wrote about life in Lexington. Margaretta (Mason) Brown, wife of Sen. John Brown, was an astute observer of the Kentucky social and political scene. Elizabeth (Cox) Underwood of Bowling Green ran her husband's businesses, collected his legal fees, and advised him how to vote in Congress.

It is difficult to find accounts of less affluent women. Irvin uses Daniel Drake's story of growing up poor on a farm in Mayslick to show the hard life of his mother, Elizabeth, between 1788 and 1800. The slave narratives collected by the New Deal's Work Projects Administration offer insights into the lives of African-American women in Kentucky before the Civil War. Sophia Ward of Clay County, for example, found many ways of resisting white supremacy. The Gordon family papers at the University of Kentucky and the Underwood papers at Western Kentucky University include letters from former slaves sent to Liberia by the American Colonization Society.

As Irvin's *Women in Kentucky* reveals, religious duty played an important part in the lives of many early Kentucky women. In 1812 the Sisters of Loretto established a motherhouse in Marion County. The Sisters of Charity of Nazareth began near Bardstown about the same time, and another order started at St. Catherine in Washington County in 1822. Women were important in the United Society of Believers in Christ's Second Coming, more popularly known as Shakers. Archival collections from Shaker settlements at South Union and Pleasant Hill are on deposit at the University of Kentucky and Western Kentucky University. Kentucky churches of all denominations contain information on and evidence of women's activities.

Written during the Civil War years, the diary of Mary E. Van Meter of Bowling Green tells how her family fled south when the Union army entered southern Kentucky. The published diaries of Francis Dallam Peter and Lizzie Hardin describe how the war divided Lexington and Harrodsburg society.

As Irvin shows, by January 1865, 3,060 slaves, mostly women and children, had fled to Camp Nelson, a Union training center for black soldiers, only to find harsh conditions and little comfort. The records of the Bureau of Refugees, Freedmen, and Abandoned Lands at the National Archives describe conditions of free black women and men in Kentucky after the Civil War. For Afro-American women in Kentucky, freedom brought neither equal treatment nor opportunities equal to those of white women, much less white men.

In the 1870s the Clay sisters, Laura, Mary Barr, Annie, and Sallie, were early proponents of equal rights for white women. The extensive collection of Laura Clay manuscripts at the University of Kentucky details her activities. The papers of the Louisville Equal Rights Association, formed in the 1880s, are at the Filson Club.

The University of Kentucky first admitted women in 1880. Sophonisba (Preston) Breckinridge, the first woman admitted to the Kentucky bar, became a national leader of educational and social reform. Many other women were involved in reform-minded groups such as the Louisville Charity Organization Society, formed in 1883 and later known as the Family and Children's Agency, whose records are at the University of Louisville.

By 1900, when the United States was becoming more urbanized, more than 44,000 Kentucky women were working in industry, mostly in Louisville, according to Irvin. The Department of Labor's Women's Bureau investigated conditions of working women in Louisville and reported on them in 1911, 1923, and 1937. The studies show that women earned significantly less than men, and that black women, who did the hardest and most dangerous work, received the lowest wages.

Kentucky women were involved in the local, state, and national reforms of the Progressive Era before World War I. Madeline (McDowell) Breckinridge helped win better state laws governing child labor, school attendance, treatment of juveniles, development of parks, and care of poor children, in addition to working for women's suffrage. Katharine Pettit and Frances Beauchamp were active in the Women's Christian Temperance Union and the Federation of Women's Clubs, and Pettit and May Stone founded the Hindman and Pine Mountain settlement schools for eastern Kentucky youth. Papers of women's organizations, such as the Young Women's Christian Association collection at the University of Louisville, reveal much about the activities of less prominent women.

Letters of a young woman who worked for the YWCA in France during World War I are part of the Means family papers at the University of Kentucky. At home, Cora (Wilson) Stewart taught illiterate soldiers and others how to read in her Rowan County moonlight schools. Laura Clay was active in the peace movement. Women in Louisville joined the National League for Women's Service, whose papers are at the Filson Club.

The papers of the Fayette Equal Rights Association at the University of Kentucky show women's struggle for suffrage after the war. Women won the right to vote in 1920, and the papers of the Democratic party at the University of Kentucky reflect their involvement. In 1922, Mary (Elliott) Flanery was the first woman elected to a southern state legislature. More women began working outside the home. The Kentucky Federation of Business and Professional Women was established in 1921; its records are at the University of Louisville.

Reformers such as Linda Neville, Mary Breckinridge, and Alice Lloyd became concerned because many women in rural eastern Kentucky lacked adequate health care, housing, and education. Breckinridge started the Frontier Nursing Service in Leslie County in 1925; the full story of its continuing efforts to provide maternal health care services can be found in the extensive collection at the University of Kentucky. Other perspectives on women in the mountains can be found in the Appalachian Collection at Berea College and at the Kentucky Oral History Commission in interviews with such women leaders as Marie Turner, school superintendent of Breathitt County.

During World War II, ever greater numbers of women in Kentucky, as in other places, went to work outside the home. Mary Edith Engle became a pilot. Ruth (Foxx) Newborg was a radio programming director from 1940 to 1944. After the war, as Harriette (Simpson) Arnow shows in her novel *The Dollmaker* (1954), many women from eastern Kentucky and other parts of the state moved to the industrial Midwest and Northeast to find work. The Kentucky Oral History Commission has sponsored a series of interviews with Appalachian migrant women in the Cincinnati area.

Arnow, a native of East Bernstadt, won national acclaim for her novels about life in Kentucky. Her papers, along with those of other outstanding women writers from the state, like Rebecca Caudill, are at the University of Kentucky. The Kentucky Library at Western Kentucky University houses the manuscripts of Eliza (Calvert) Hill, Emanie Nahm, and Janice (Holt) Giles. The Women Writers Conference, established at the University of Kentucky in 1979 to bring established and aspiring writers together, draws national and international participation. The tradition of outstanding women writers continues with Bobbie Ann Mason of Mayfield, Barbara Kingsolver of Carlisle, Marsha Norman of Louisville, and Louise Natcher Murphy of Bowling Green.

The Kentucky Commission on Women, begun in 1964, was one of the first in the nation to promote the human rights of women. State agencies and universities are making special efforts to recognize the cultural and racial diversity of women in the state. The Kentucky Oral History Commission, established in 1976, encourages the collection of a wide range of oral interviews, including those with Afro-American and minority women. The University of Louisville is building strong collections on women, including Afro-American and Jewish women in Louisville. The University of Kentucky has sponsored oral history projects on blacks in Lexington, including many interviews with women, and on women in eastern Kentucky coal camps.

Women in Kentucky continue to be political leaders at the state and national levels. Gerta Bendl of Louisville, active in city and state politics, left her papers to the University of Louisville. Georgia Powers of Louisville was one of a handful of black women in southern state legislatures. In 1983, Martha Layne Collins was the first women elected governor of the commonwealth. Anne Braden of Louisville is recognized for leadership in civil rights in the South and throughout the nation.

In 1984 the Women's History Coalition of Kentucky was formed to promote the study of women's history in the state and sponsor an annual conference of scholars, teachers, community activists, and others. In 1985 Sallie Bingham, author and philanthropist, established the Kentucky Foundation for Women, dedicated to supporting the work of Kentucky-area women artists and scholars and non-profit organizations composed mostly of women promoting social change. In 1987 Western Kentucky University held the first interdisciplinary women's studies conference, which annually attracts hundreds of participants to southern Kentucky.

Despite these solid accomplishments, a special report, *Women and Poverty in Kentucky*, released in 1988 by the Center for Business and Economic Research at the University of Kentucky, documents that women in the commonwealth continue to suffer from restricted employment opportunities, low earnings, lack of child care and job-protected leave, lack of adequate child support, and insufficient retirement income. The study concludes that reducing high poverty rates will require attention to the specific economic problems of women as well as to the general economic problems of Kentucky.

A complete history of women in Kentucky must include the stories of poor women, rural women, and women of color as well as white women and middle- and upper-class women. Women's studies are being integrated into research and curricula of schools and universities in the state. Archivists, curators, and librarians are developing new collections and rethinking methods of cataloging existing collections to make women's sources more accessible. Researchers are uncovering resources on local women in state agencies, churches, libraries, and historical societies. Editors are including entries on women in published histories of the state.

The University of Kentucky, the University of Louisville, Kentucky State University, Western Kentucky University, and Berea College all have holdings relating to women and are developing ways to find the information sought. There is a helpful guide to the manuscripts of the Kentucky Historical Society, and the Kentucky Oral History Commission has compiled a complete listing of its oral history interviews, including those with women. The Public Records Division of the Kentucky Department for Libraries and Archives has deeds, wills, and marriage certificates relating to women. The Kentucky Guide Project, part of the state Department for Libraries and Archives, is describing and indexing manuscripts and archival collections in 285 public repositories throughout the state. The completed guide will include collections in sixty-six historical societies and museums and ninety-nine public or regional libraries—records of clubs and genealogical societies, letters, diaries, and newspaper clippings concerning women in their communities.

New studies have already begun to appear. Since 1970 excellent biographies and articles on women artists, reformers, and leaders have been written and published. In Kentucky's third century, women are entering the recorded history of the state.

JUDI JENNINGS

WOMEN'S SUFFRAGE. The struggle for equal suffrage in the commonwealth began in the last quarter of the nineteenth century as part of the broader women's rights movement, which sought legal and educational rights as well as political equality. Before full suffrage was achieved with the ratification of the Nineteenth Amendment in 1920, Kentucky women were denied the ballot except under a few exceptional circumstances. The first such exception was school suffrage for unmarried women who owned taxable property in county districts, under a law passed in 1838. It was the first instance of school suffrage on record, and no other state repeated it until Kansas gave its women the school vote in 1861. The limited suffrage extended only to such matters as school bonds and district school trustees. Most women, of course, were not covered by it, and since the right was not widely known or understood, few women in fact voted.

When the commonwealth adopted a new constitution in 1891, the legislature was empowered to extend partial suffrage—in school elections and in municipal and presidential elections—to women. Seizing this opportunity, the Kentucky Equal Rights Association, organized in 1888, persuaded the legislature to pass a school suffrage law in 1894. Unfortunately, the law extended only to women of second-class cities—Lexington, Covington, and Newport—because the General Assembly inexplicably reasoned that since only women of those cities had petitioned for the vote, only they should have it.

In one of the most unusual reversals in suffrage annals, the Kentucky legislature repealed even this limited franchise in 1902. The action was precipitated by the Lexington school board elections of 1901, in which only 662 women registered as

Democrats, while 1,997, many of them black women, joined the Republicans. Although the Democrats won the election, they feared that the black women's vote was threatening their control of the Lexington school system, and they were determined to eliminate it by introducing bills in January 1902 to disenfranchise the women of the second-class cities. After a spirited contest in which several women's organizations lobbied hard to retain the ballot, the bill was repealed. This loss of the vote in Kentucky is the only instance in the history of the American suffrage movement when the franchise, once won, was taken away by the action of a legislature.

Having been victimized once by the central role of race in southern life, Kentucky suffragists decided in post-1902 campaigns to alleviate the fear of the black women's vote by seeking school suffrage with an educational qualification. Since such a bill would enfranchise only literate women, numbering far more whites than blacks, the suffragists hoped to placate the politicians and win quick legislative approval. Despite this concession to racism and despite active campaigning, the women of the commonwealth were denied all forms of the franchise until 1912, when this qualified form of school suffrage was enacted.

Although it is little known, commonwealth women were the beneficiaries of one other partial-suffrage law. Early in 1920, fearing that the Nineteenth Amendment might not be ratified by the states in time for women to vote in the next presidential election, Kentucky suffragists persuaded the legislature both to ratify the federal amendment in January—becoming the twenty-third state to do so—and to grant presidential suffrage by legislative action a few weeks later. The latter provision became redundant in August 1920, when the Nineteenth Amendment was finally added to the Constitution, ending almost fifty years of struggle for political equality in Kentucky.

See Paul E. Fuller, *Laura Clay and the Woman's Rights Movement* (Lexington, Ky., 1975).

PAUL E. FULLER

WOODBURN FARM. The original Woodburn farm in Woodford County totaled 2,000 acres purchased in 1790 by Robert Alexander. By 1990 the acreage had been divided among Airdrie, Binderton, Lanark, and Woodburn farms, all owned by descendants of the original Alexander. Woodburn was brought to national prominence as a thoroughbred breeding operation in the 1850s and 1860s by his son, Robert Aitcheson Alexander, who did more for the cultivation of purebred stock than any other man in America, according to William Warfield as quoted in *Giants of the Turf*. Between 1861 and 1882 the farm dominated the American turf to an unequaled extent. Though breeding less than 5 percent of the nation's thoroughbred foals from 1868 to 1880, it bred 54 percent of the winners of the Belmont, Travers, Saratoga, Jerome, and Dixie stakes in those years.

See Dan M. Bowmar III, *Giants of the Turf* (Lexington, Ky., 1960); James Gill, *Bloodstock* (New York 1977). MARY E. WHARTON

WOODFORD COUNTY. The ninth Kentucky county and the last organized by Virginia prior to Kentucky's separation, Woodford County was created from Fayette on November 12, 1788. It is bordered by Anderson, Fayette, Franklin, Jessamine, Mercer, and Scott counties. The 192-square-mile county was named in honor of Gen. William Woodford, a Virginia officer in the Revolutionary War who died a prisoner of war of the British. VERSAILLES is the county seat.

The topography is gently rolling and deep limestone formations make the soil productive for horses, cattle, and crops. In the antebellum era, agriculture was a combination of small farms and large plantations. Crops included hemp, tobacco, corn, and hay. The slaves that were the labor force of the plantations outnumbered whites by 5,829 to 5,276 in 1860. Thoroughbred farms expanded their operations in the latter half of the nineteenth century, and today horse farms such as Airdrie Stud, Dearborn Vinery Stallions, High Hopes, Hurstland, Pin Oak, Three Chimneys, and Shadwell are dominant forces in the international thoroughbred industry. England's Queen Elizabeth II, who breeds thoroughbreds, has made repeated visits to Lane's End Farm in Woodford County, owned by William S. Farish III. The county's 1989 agricultural receipts ranked second among counties; 82 percent came from livestock and poultry.

Settlers in the 1770s included John Floyd, militia leader and surveyor; Col. William Steele; Joseph Lindsey, who explored Elkhorn Creek; John Lowery; Benjamin Berry, who explored the Falls of the Ohio; James McConnell, later involved in the founding of Cincinnati; and Robert Patterson, who helped settle Lexington. The early settlers clashed with Indians who sought to preserve their hunting grounds. Prehistoric Native Americans lived in what is now Woodford County at Lovedale, where their earthworks and burial sites are found. The county has two incorporated towns, Versailles and Midway, and includes the communities of Duckers, Faywood, Nonesuch, Pisgah, Troy, and Zion Hill.

Pisgah Presbyterian Church was organized in Woodford County in 1784, and its Kentucky Academy became a part of Transylvania University in 1798. James Parrish and Dr. Lewis Pendleton founded a female orphan's school in Midway that became Midway College, the only women's college in the state.

In July 1862 Confederate troops destroyed the Louisville & Nashville (L&N) Railroad line (now CSX Transportation). While the tracks were being torn up, G.A. Ellsworth, a telegraph operator with Gen. John Hunt Morgan, sent false dispatches to Union troops to confuse their movements. Two months later, Confederate forces briefly occupied Versailles. Union troops forced the Confederates out of the county, and Union Gen. Stephen Burbridge executed four guerrillas near Midway in retaliation for a murder by Confederate guerrilla Marcellus Jerome Clarke ("Sue Mundy"). In February 1865 Clarke's men attacked Midway, robbing residents, burning the railroad station, and stealing fifteen of Robert A. Alexander's prized thoroughbreds. After the Civil War, Midway, an L&N development where streets were named for the railroad's board of directors, was rebuilt.

Rand McNally prints books and maps in the county, Texas Instruments makes thermostats and switches there, GTE Sylvania manufactures fluorescent lamps and glass tubing, and the Kuhlman Company produces transformers. Both CSX and the Norfolk Southern railways serve the county, as do U.S. 60, U.S. 62, and the Bluegrass Parkway. Many county residents commute to jobs in Lexington and Frankfort. The thoroughbred horse farms, the rich architectural history of Versailles, and the quaint shopping district on Depot Street in Midway draw visitors to Woodford County, where tourism receipts in 1988 were $3.4 million, a 62 percent increase over the previous year. The county had 14,434 inhabitants in 1970; 17,778 in 1980; and 19,955 in 1990.

See William E. Railey, *History of Woodford County, Kentucky* (Frankfort, Ky., 1938).

RON D. BRYANT

WOODS, BRENT. Brent Woods, awarded the congressional Medal of Honor as a sergeant in the Indian campaigns, was a mulatto born into slavery in Pulaski County, Kentucky, in 1855. Freed at the age of eight, he joined the cavalry ten years later, in 1873. Woods was assigned to Company B of the 9th Cavalry and was stationed in the West to fight in the Indian campaigns (1866-91). During a battle with the Apache Indians led by Chief Nana on August 19, 1881, in Gavilan Canyon, New Mexico, the men of Company B found themselves without a commanding officer when the first in command was killed and the second in command could not be found. Woods rallied the men of his company after taking a group of cowboy civilians, who had joined them the day before, to safety. Woods then led a charge against the Indians, making his way to the top of a ridge where he fought despite a wounded arm until the Indians retreated. A cowboy saved by Woods in the battle said, "If it had not been for him, none of us would have come out of that canyon." Thirteen years later, on July 21, 1894, Woods received the congressional Medal of Honor. The delay is attributed to his race. Woods died on March 31, 1906, and was buried without notice in an unmarked grave in the black section of the First Baptist Church Cemetery at Somerset, Kentucky. He was survived by his wife, Pearl Baker.

Woods went virtually unrecognized until 1982, when Loraine Smith of Somerset began a campaign to mark his grave. On June 20, 1984, Woods's body was moved to Mill Springs Cemetery near Nancy, Kentucky, and on October 28, 1984, with the help of U.S. Rep. Harold Rogers and the Veter-

ans Administration, an official military burial ceremony took place, attended by the secretary of the army, John O. Marsh, Jr. Woods is Pulaski County's only Medal of Honor winner.

See Irvine H. Lee, *Negro Medal of Honor Men* (New York 1969); Patricia D. Wagner and Mary S. Donovan, *Kentucky's Black Heritage* (Frankfort, Ky., 1971).

PEGGY M. BROCK

WOODS, RALPH HICKS. Ralph Hicks Woods, educator, was born in Grant, Grayson County, Virginia, on June 1, 1898, to John W. and Beatrice (Hash) Woods. After completing high school in Virginia, he earned a Ph.B. from Berea College in 1921, a B.S. in 1923 and an M.A. in 1927 from the University of Kentucky, and a Ph.D. in agricultural economics from Cornell University in 1930. Woods was a teacher at La Center High School in Ballard County, Kentucky, in 1923-24, and then became principal there. In 1926 he joined the faculty at the University of Kentucky, where he stayed until November 1, 1945. He was president of the Kentucky Vocational Association during 1934-35.

Between 1939 and 1945 Woods was president of the National Association of State Directors of Vocational Education, director of the War Training Program, member of the National Committee on Vocational War Training, member of the White House Conference on Children, and president of the American Vocational Association. On October 8, 1945, he was elected the fourth president of Murray State Teachers College (now Murray State University), where he served for twenty-three years. In 1948, at the request of the U.S. State Department, Woods set up vocational education in Greece as part of the Marshall Plan. Woods retired on June 30, 1968.

Woods married Elizabeth Harkless, of Wickliffe, on August 6, 1925; they had one daughter, Anne. On September 25, 1973, he died in Murray and was buried in the Harkless family plot in Wickliffe Cemetery.

WILLIAM RAY MOFIELD

WOOLDRIDGE MONUMENTS. The Wooldridge Monuments are a family memorial in the form of a group of statues at Maplewood Cemetery in Mayfield, Kentucky, erected during 1890-99 by Henry Wooldridge, a local horse breeder. The sixteen life-size statues, on a thirty-three by seventeen-foot tract, represent family figures and Wooldridge himself, along with his hunting dogs and his horse. The monuments are listed on the National Register of Historic Places. All of the figures are sandstone and were made in either Paducah or Mayfield, Kentucky, except for the statue of Wooldridge himself, which is marble and was made in Italy. Wooldridge died on May 30, 1899, and was entombed in an above-ground vault. He alone is buried at the memorial.

See Diane Wells and Mary Lou S. Madigan, *Update: Guide to Kentucky Historical Highway Markers* (Frankfort, Ky., 1983).

WOOLEY, AARON K. Aaron K. Wooley, Kentucky state representative and senator, was born in January 1800 in Springfield, New Jersey. He graduated from the U.S. Military Academy at West Point with honors and taught mathematics there for two years. Wooley later studied law with Judge Richard Biddle of Pittsburgh and set up practice in 1823 at Port Gibson, Mississippi. After a visit to Lexington, Kentucky, he was married on October 9, 1827 to Sally Howard Wickliffe, daughter of the prominent lawyer Robert Wickliffe, with whom Wooley became a law partner. Wooley represented Fayette County in the Kentucky House of Representatives from 1832 to 1834 and was a member of the state Senate from 1835 to 1839. After leaving the Senate, he served as judge of the Lexington circuit court and joined the faculty of the Transylvania University Law School (1839). He was a Fayette County candidate for the 1849 state constitutional convention, which addressed the abolition of slavery and the question of appointment versus election of the judiciary. Wooley stumped the county, speaking out against abolition and popular judicial election. He died of cholera on August 3, 1849.

See George Baber, "The Three Woolleys," *Register* 12 (Jan. 1914): 47-49.

WOOLEY, ROBERT WICKLIFFE. Robert Wickliffe Wooley (Woolley), diplomat and soldier, was born in 1829 to Aaron K. Wooley and Sally Howard (Wickliffe) Wooley in Lexington, Kentucky. He attended Centre College, Danville, and the Transylvania University Law School, and practiced law in Lexington with Roger W. Hanson. Nominated in 1855 by the Democratic state convention, Wooley was unsuccessful in a bid for attorney general. He was a nephew to William Preston and in 1858, when President James Buchanan appointed Preston minister to Spain, Wooley became charge d'affaires in Madrid. With the outbreak of the American Civil War, Wooley returned to Kentucky in the early summer of 1861. He joined the Confederate army and served as a captain and lieutenant colonel on the staffs of Gens. William Preston and Simon Bolivar Buckner. Wooley returned to Lexington after the war to practice law. He moved to Louisville after marrying Mary E. Johnston, a Louisville native and the daughter of Dr. James C. Johnston. Wooley died on February 10, 1905, at his Louisville residence and was buried in Cave Hill Cemetery.

WORKMAN, NIMROD. Nimrod Workman, traditional musician, was born in Martin County, Kentucky, on November 5, 1895, the son of Jamce and Henrietta (Jewell) Workman. He was named for his grandfather, a Cherokee who fought in the Civil War. From his grandfather, Workman learned many of the traditional ballads and songs that formed the core of his extensive folk repertoire. When he was fourteen years old, he went to work in the coal mines but was laid off because of physical disabilities. Workman was politically active in early efforts to unionize coal miners. In 1929 he married Mollie Bowens; they have eleven children, including traditional singer Phyllis (Workman) Boyens. Workman, who recorded two albums of folk and original songs, is the subject of the Appalshop film *To Fit My Own Category*. He lives in Chattaroy, West Virginia.   RON PEN

WORLD'S CHAMPIONSHIP HORSE SHOW. The World's Championship Horse Show, held annually during the Kentucky State Fair in Louisville, is an outgrowth of a $10,000 stake for five-gaited saddlebred horses held in 1917. The organizer of the 1917 competition, Curtis P. ("Jumps") Cauthorn of Mexico, Missouri, had raised $5,000 in donations as prize money, to be matched by the state where the competition was held. After the governor of Missouri turned down his proposal, Cauthorn found acceptance from Kentucky Gov. Augustus O. Stanley (1915-19).

The $10,000 in prize money was divided, with $2,500 awarded in each of the three preliminaries—for stallions, mares, and geldings—and $2,500 for the grand championship. The first five-gaited world grand champion was Easter Cloud, owned by Longview farm of Lee's Summit, Missouri, and shown by John T. Hook. The first three-gaited world championship competition was added to the show in 1936, and later the fine-harness world championship. By 1990 the show had grown to 153 classes spread over seven days, with a crowd of about 12,000 for the five-gaited grand championship on the final night.

See Jack Harrison, *Famous Saddle Horses and Distinguished Horsemen* (Columbia, Mo., 1933).

LYNN WEATHERMAN

WORLD WAR II. In October 1939, the authorized strength of the nation's national guards began to increase, and Kentucky's citizen-soldiers, under Adj. Gen. John A. Polin, were reorganized and given additional training. In July 1940 came the announcement of an expansion at the Fort Knox recruit training center and base for armored forces. Washington announced plans to build a large facility near Louisville to manufacture artillery powder—the Indiana Ordnance Works in Charlestown. The Hoosier Ordnance Works and the Louisville Naval Ordnance Plant followed. The Kentucky National Guard in August trained in massive maneuvers in Wisconsin. Later that month the 149th Infantry, the 138th Artillery, and smaller units assumed active duty with the 38th Division. In November the first group drafted under the new Selective Service Act arrived at Ft. Knox.

During 1941 Kentucky cities prepared for air raids, fires, and sabotage. More federal projects were slated—Camp Campbell (in Christian and Trigg counties and parts of Tennessee), an ammunition storage complex (Madison County), and a Signal Corps operation (Fayette County). Symptomatic of the war's industrial nature, "Rubbertown," a congregation of synthetic rubber producers, eventually made Louisville the world's largest source of that commodity. After the attack on Pearl Harbor on December 7, 1941, Kentucky prepared for total war. Polin and J.J. Greenleaf, state director of civilian defense, quickly ordered the Kentucky Active Militia (a substitute for the departed National Guard) and local organizations to intensify crowd control and security measures.

Industries such as Jeffersonville Boat & Machine Company and adjacent Howard Ship Yards held to demanding schedules. Establishment of Louisville's Medical Depot, its huge Nichols General Hospital, and Camp Breckinridge (Union, Henderson, and Webster counties) indicated the accelerating conversion of Kentucky to war support. Air raid drills, war bond drives, salvage drives, blood drives, and other corporate activities promoted the war effort.

In 1944 Kentucky's industries peaked. By then nearly 100,000 jeeps had rolled off the assembly line at Louisville's Ford Motor Company factory. At a similar high pitch, war-related employment statewide surpassed the 100,000 mark. New job opportunities opened for blacks and women, although discrimination against both groups persisted. An increase in crime in some areas and a supposed decline in moral standards were blamed on the social and economic changes wrought by the war. Upon news of Germany's surrender, church services commemorating the event outnumbered wild celebrations; some facilities, like Paducah's Kentucky Ordnance Works, worked on without interruption.

On the battlefield, Husband Kimmel, of Henderson County, led the Pacific fleet and Claude C. Bloch, Butler County, commanded shipyard operations at Pearl Harbor, where seaman Edwin L. Puckett, Glendale, died on the U.S.S. *Arizona*. A few hours later Robert H. Brooks, a black from Sadieville, died in the bombing of Clark Field, Philippine Islands. Sixty-six from Harrodsburg endured Bataan, the Death March, and prisoner-of-war camps. A few months later, George Black, of Elizabethtown, was wounded on Guadalcanal. Offshore, Willis A. ("Ching") Lee, Owenton, commanded a force of battleships and destroyers. On New Guinea, Washington County lost Namon Hood. As American forces marched northward, Earl Davis, Russellville, and the 38th Division aided the reconquest of the Philippines, where the division earned the sobriquet "Avengers of Bataan." As the Allies closed in on Japan, Franklin R. Sousley, Fleming County, helped raise the American flag on Mt. Suribachi, Iwo Jima. At Okinawa, John H.G. ("Skeets") Kelly, Springfield, conned the U.S.S. *Maryland* through a kamikaze attack. Simon B. Buckner, Jr., Munfordville, died on Okinawa while leading a ground force. A few months later near Nagasaki, POW John Sadler, Harrodsburg, witnessed the atomic conclusion of the Pacific war.

North African combat introduced the 106th Coast Artillery, formerly part of a cavalry unit in the Kentucky National Guard, to the European conflict.

In fighting in Italy, Benjamin J. Butler, Trimble County, led an infantry battalion. After Rome fell, Edgar Erskine Hume, Frankfort, served as that city's military governor. In Normandy, Lexington's Walter J. Hillenmeyer, Jr., was aide to the commander of the first division on Omaha Beach. In the Battle of the Bulge, William R. Buster, Burgin, fought in the American counterattack. In the last phase of the European war, Billy Goatley, Washington County, zigzagged under fire across Remagen Bridge, which led into Germany.

These Kentuckians and thousands more fought. The congressional Medal of Honor went to seven. Of the 306,364 Kentuckians in service (2.1 percent of national total), 7,917 died (1.9 percent of national loss). Blacks made up 6.6 percent of Kentuckians who served. Counties with the highest death tolls included Jefferson, 1,121; Kenton, 284; Fayette, 234; Harlan, 216; Campbell, 211; Pike, 210; Boyd, 161; Perry, 158; Daviess, 144; Pulaski, 140; Floyd, 133; Letcher, 130; Whitley, 125; Hopkins, 106; Warren, 105; and Bell, 101. Ten eastern counties, including Knox (88), gave up a total of 1,462 dead, 18.5 percent of Kentucky's total. Sixteen counties each lost more than one hundred soldiers; twenty-seven counties, fifty to one hundred; seventy-seven counties, fewer than fifty. By branch of service, fatalities totaled 6,802 in the army/air corps; navy, 755; marines, 356; and coast guard, 4.

See Richard G. Stone, *Kentucky Fighting Men, 1851-1945* (Lexington, Ky., 1982).

JAMES RUSSELL HARRIS

WRIGHT, WARREN. Industrialist and developer of Calumet farm, Warren Wright was born on September 25, 1875, to William Monroe and Clara Lee (Morrison) Wright in Springfield, Ohio. He was educated in Chicago public schools. In 1890 Wright joined the Calumet Baking Powder Company, founded by his father in 1888, as a stock boy; nine years later he became president of the company. He sold it to General Foods Corporation in 1928 for $40 million. Upon his father's death in 1931, Wright inherited the bulk of the $30 million estate, which included the 1,038-acre Calumet farm on Versailles Road, Lexington, Kentucky. Wright built Calumet into a premier thoroughbred breeding and racing establishment, which produced eight Kentucky Derby winners, seven Preakness winners, two Belmont winners, and two Triple Crown winners— Whirlaway in 1941 and Citation in 1948.

Wright was a director of First National Bank of Chicago, General Foods Corporation, Calumet Chemical Corporation, Paramont Publix, John R. Thompson Company, and Upper Avenue Bank of Chicago. He eventually withdrew from other business interests to devote his entire efforts to Calumet farm. In 1940 he was honored with the ninth annual award of the Thoroughbred Club of America, and he was the leading thoroughbred breeder in 1948. Wright married Lucille Parker of Maysville, Kentucky, on March 25, 1919. They had one son, Warren Wright, Jr. On December 29, 1950, Wright died at his winter home in Miami, Florida, and was buried in Rosehill Cemetery in Chicago.

BETTY B. ELLISON

WYATT, WILSON WATKINS. Wilson Watkins Wyatt, mayor of Louisville and lieutenant governor, was born in Louisville on November 21, 1905, to Richard H. and Mary (Watkins) Wyatt. He graduated from Louisville Male High School and attended the University of Louisville for one year. He graduated from Louisville's Jefferson School of Law and was admitted to the Kentucky bar in 1927. He set up a law practice in Louisville and served as secretary of the Kentucky Bar Association from 1930 to 1934. In 1935 Wyatt started as a junior partner in the law firm of Peter, Heyburn, Marshall and Wyatt, where he became principal counsel for Robert Worth Bingham's *Louisville Courier-Journal* and *Louisville Times*, as well as for the other Bingham family enterprises, including the WHAS radio and television stations.

Elected mayor of Louisville in 1941, Wyatt took office one month after the bombing of Pearl Harbor and immediately undertook regional civil defense planning. Wyatt worked for legislation in the state's General Assembly to modernize and streamline the Louisville city government. He tried to consolidate many city-county functions and created the Louisville-Jefferson County Planning and Zoning Commission. In January 1946 President Harry S. Truman named Wyatt housing expediter in the Office of War Mobilization and Reconversion. Re-turning to Louisville, Wyatt founded the law firm Wyatt and Grafton. He played a key role in the formation of the Americans for Democratic Action, a liberal political action group, serving as the organization's first chairman in 1947. In 1952 he managed the unsuccessful presidential campaign of Adlai Stevenson. He also played a prominent role in Stevenson's 1956 presidential campaign.

In 1959 Wyatt announced his candidacy for governor of Kentucky. Before the primary election, however, he withdrew as a gubernatorial candidate and endorsed Bert Combs's candidacy, running for lieutenant governor on a united ticket with Combs. Combs and Wyatt took office in December 1959. Wyatt served as chairman of the Kentucky Economic Development Commission, created under the new administration. In 1962 Wyatt announced his candidacy for the U.S. Senate, running in the general election against the incumbent, Senator Thruston B. Morton, a fellow Louisvillian. In a hard-fought and often bitter campaign, Morton won reelection. In December 1963 Wyatt established the Louisville law firm Wyatt, Tarrant & Combs. Since leaving public office, Wyatt has worked in a wide variety of civic and cultural activities, both in Louisville and throughout Kentucky. On June 14, 1930, he married Anne Kinnaird Duncan.

See John Ed Pearce, *Divide and Dissent: Kentucky Politics, 1930-1963* (Lexington, Ky., 1987); Wilson W. Wyatt, Sr., *Whistle Stops: Adventures in Public Life* (Lexington, Ky., 1985).

TERRY BIRDWHISTELL

Y

YANDELL, DAVID WENDEL. David Wendel Yandell, physician, was born on September 4, 1826, in Murfreesboro, Tennessee, to Lunsford P. and Susan (Wendel) Yandell. He spent his childhood in Lexington, Kentucky, and in Louisville. Following his 1846 graduation from the Louisville Medical Institute, he studied briefly in Europe. He spent his professional life in private practice in Louisville, teaching surgery at the University of Louisville and writing and editing medical literature. During the Civil War he served as medical director for the Confederate armies of Gen. Albert Sidney Johnston and Gen. Edmund Kirby-Smith and witnessed the shocking consequences of his medical colleagues' inadequate education and ineptness. After the war, Yandell returned to the university and waged a twenty-year campaign to expand the school's medical education facilities. He used his influence to raise professional standards. Yandell's colleagues elected him president of the American Medical Association in 1872 and president of the American Surgical Association in 1886.

In 1851 Yandell married Frances Crutcher of Nashville. They had three children: Allison, Susan, and Maria. Yandell died on May 2, 1898, and was buried in Louisville's Cave Hill Cemetery.

See Nancy D. Baird, *David Wendel Yandell: Physician of Old Louisville* (Lexington, Ky., 1978).

NANCY D. BAIRD

YANDELL, ENID. Enid Yandell, sculptor, was born on October 6, 1869, to Louisville physician Lunsford Yandell, Jr., and Nashville native Louise (Elliston) Yandell. She studied at the Cincinnati Academy of Art and in Paris with Frederick Mac-Monnies and Auguste Rodin. Yandell's first major commission, designing the caryatids for the Women's Building of the 1893 Columbian Exposition at Chicago, earned a gold medal. Yandell is best known for her public statuary, including the Hogan Fountain (1905) and the Daniel Boone statue in Louisville's Cherokee Park, the twelve-foot statue of John Thomas (1907) for Nashville's Centennial Park, and a kneeling figure of Narraganset chieftain Ninigret (1913) in Watch Hill, Rhode Island. The Boone statue in Louisville, originally produced in plaster for the Filson Club to exhibit at the 1893 exposition in Chicago, was cast in bronze in 1906. In the 1960s a copy of the Boone figure was cast for Eastern Kentucky University's campus.

Although most of Yandell's statuary is found in public and private collections along the East Coast, a few of her smaller works are in Kentucky. Plaster busts of John B. Castleman and the "Hunchback of Notre Dame" belong to the Louisville Free Public Library; a bust of James Rucker is on exhibit at Georgetown College; the Filson Club owns her bust of Reuben T. Durrett; and a bust of William Goebel, which Yandell modeled for his cemetery monument, is part of the Kentucky Historical Society collection. Following her death on June 13, 1934, Louisville's J.B. Speed Art Museum received plaster casts for about twenty of Yandell's figurines, bas reliefs, and busts.

Yandell was a member of the National Sculpture Society and the French Academy, and she exhibited her work in at least twenty-seven major shows in the United States and France. She was buried in Cave Hill Cemetery, Louisville.

See Nancy D. Baird, "Enid Yandell: Louisville Sculptor," *FCHQ* 62 (Jan. 1988): 5-32.

NANCY D. BAIRD

YANDELL, LUNSFORD PITTS. Lunsford Pitts Yandell, physician, was born July 4, 1805, in Tennessee. He received a medical degree from the University of Maryland and in 1831 joined the faculty of Transylvania University's medical department in Lexington. Six years later Yandell and several colleagues founded the Louisville Medical Institute (forerunner of the Medical Department of the University of Louisville), where he taught chemistry and materia medica. During his career Yandell also served as editor and contributor of the *Transylvania Journal of Medicine* and the *Western Journal of Medicine and Science* and published scholarly works in other professional periodicals. A charter member of the Kentucky State Medical Association, Yandell served as its eighteenth president. Yandell and his first wife, Susan (Wendel), had three sons—David, Lunsford, Jr., and William—and a daughter, Susan. Yandell died on February 4, 1878, and was buried in Louisville's Cave Hill Cemetery.

NANCY D. BAIRD

YEAMAN, GEORGE HELM. Born on November 1, 1829, in Hardin County, Kentucky, George Helm Yeaman, attorney and diplomat, was the son of Stephen Minor and Lucretia (Helm) Yeaman. He was admitted to the bar in 1852 at Elizabethtown and later moved to Owensboro. He was elected judge of Daviess County in 1854. He was a member of the Kentucky House in 1861, when he was elected as a Unionist to the 37th U.S. Congress to fill the vacancy caused by the death of James S. Jackson. Yeaman was reelected to the 38th Congress (December 1, 1862, to March 3, 1865). He ran unsuccessfully for reelection in 1864.

Yeaman spoke vehemently against the Emancipation Proclamation, echoing many Kentuckians' views on slavery and the nature of the Union. He questioned where President Abraham Lincoln derived the power "to do this great thing," and contended that Kentucky and other border states were being punished for having slaves even though they were Union in allegiance. According to Yeaman, the Proclamation was a "blunder and an injustice" and he protested in the name of the "*loyal people of the Rebel States.*"

He was appointed by President Andrew Johnson in 1865 as minister to Denmark. He resigned in 1870 and moved to New York City, where he practiced law and became a lecturer on constitutional law at Columbia University. Author of several books, pamphlets, and articles, he was president of the Medico-Legal Society of New York. Yeaman died in Jersey City, New Jersey, February 23, 1908, and was buried in Webb Memorial Chapel, Madison, New Jersey.   ALOMA WILLIAMS DEW

YELLOW BANKS. The yellowish clay formation on the south bank of the Ohio River in the great bend bordering Daviess County was called the Yellow Banks. It is now the site of OWENSBORO. The settlement of the area may go back as far as 1775. There was a trading post at the Yellow Banks, which apparently existed until the signing of the Treaty of Greenville in 1794. In 1811 John Melish noted the existence of the village of Yellow Banks on his map of Kentucky. Zadoc Cramer described the region's general appearance in his book *The Navigator* (1814). The Yellow Banks post office was established July 1, 1806. The name was changed to Owensboro in March 1816.

THOMAS D. CLARK

YELLOW FEVER EPIDEMIC. Spread by a mosquito native to Kentucky, yellow fever struck the state during the late summer and fall of 1878 despite assurances that it could not be spread so far north. Bowling Green and Louisville reported thirty-five to fifty deaths. At Hickman, yellow fever reached epidemic proportions. Despite the medical efforts of Dr. Luke Blackburn of Louisville and several out-of-state volunteers, "yellow jack" killed more than one-tenth of Hickman's residents and crippled trade and commerce in the area. Most of the epidemic's victims lie in unmarked graves in the Hickman cemetery.   NANCY D. BAIRD

YOUNG, ALBERT W. Albert W. ("Allie") Young, state senator and attorney, was born in Elizaville, Fleming County, on December 29, 1865, to Col. Zachary T. and Amelia (O'Bannon) Young. He attended public schools in Fleming and Rowan counties, where the family moved in 1875. Most of his education was obtained by reading in his father's law office. Young was first elected to public office as Rowan County attorney in 1886. He was appointed master commissioner in Montgomery County, and was circuit judge of Rowan County for twelve years before resigning to enter private law practice. He was elected to the state Senate in 1923 and served until his death. He acted as Democratic floor leader and is credited with establishing the state teacher training school in Morehead, where he resided and practiced law. Legislation he introduced set up and extended the primary road system in the eastern section of the state. He was one of a number of political bosses who dominated in the 1920s.

Young married Eliza Flora Johnson on November 9, 1885; he married Mary F. Foley on March 15, 1901. There were eight children of the second mar-

riage. Young died February 18, 1935, in Louisville and was buried in the Macphelah Cemetery in Mt. Sterling, Kentucky.

See Juanita Blair and Fred Brown, Jr., *Days of Anger, Days of Tears: Rowan County, Kentucky 1884-1887* (Morehead, Ky., 1984).

CLARA KEYES

YOUNG, BENNETT HENDERSON. Bennett Henderson Young was a Jessamine County, Kentucky, native best known for leading the Confederacy's northernmost action, a raid across the Canadian border on St. Albans, Vermont, in October 1864. Born May 25, 1843, to Robert and Josephine (Henderson) Young, he attended Bethel Academy in Jessamine County and Centre College in Danville before enlisting with John H. Morgan's cavalry in 1863. He married Mattie R. Robinson, daughter of Louisville clergyman Stuart Robinson, in 1866, while still in Canada. The Canadian government had charged him with leading the St. Albans raid as a renegade, rather than as a member of the Confederate army. He was cleared of the charge. Young completed his education in voluntary exile in Ireland, at Queen's University, and in Scotland, at the University of Edinburgh.

He settled in Louisville in 1868, where he became one of the city's foremost courtroom attorneys, an entrepreneur, and a civic leader. He was instrumental in developing the Monon Railroad, the Kentucky and Indiana Bridge, and the Louisville Southern Railway. Young worked for revision of the Kentucky constitution in 1890-91 and was an influential member of the Brigadier faction of the Democratic party. His eloquent speeches and his philanthropy helped establish numerous Presbyterian and other educational and charitable institutions, and revived the debt-ridden Louisville Free Public Library. Young was the principal promoter of the Kentucky Confederate Home, located in eastern Jefferson County, and the Jefferson Davis Monument in Fairview. His leadership of the United Confederate Veterans Association won Young the title of honorary commander-in-chief for life.

Young was the author of *History and Texts of the Three Constitutions of Kentucky* (1890), *Prehistoric Man in Kentucky* (1910), and other books and articles on the Civil War, agriculture, and religion. He married Eliza T. Sharp in 1895; they had two children, Lawrence and Eliza. Young died February 23, 1919, and was buried in Cave Hill Cemetery, Louisville.

See Oscar A. Kinchen, *General Bennett H. Young: Confederate Raider and a Man of Many Adventures* (West Hanover, Mass., 1981).

SHERRILL REDMON

YOUNG, CHARLES. Charles Young, soldier, was born into slavery in a log cabin near Mayslick, Kentucky, on March 12, 1864, the only child of Gabriel and Armintie (Bruen) Young. He graduated from the U.S. Military Academy at West Point in 1889, only the third black to do so and the last until 1941. His distinguished military career included stints in the American West (1889-94, 1909-12), the Philippines (1901-02, 1908), and Liberia (1912-16, 1919-22), as well as many years of service in Ohio, including time at Wilberforce College. In Haiti in 1903, he was the first black to serve in the role of a military attaché to a foreign state; during the Mexican campaign, he was the first officer to lead troops using the maneuver of overhead machine-gun cover in a rescue. While in Africa, he was noted for his road-building and mapmaking achievements.

Racism hampered Young's career most significantly when this highest-ranking black officer was relieved of duties at the outbreak of World War I, ostensibly for medical reasons. To prove his fitness, Young rode horseback from Ohio to Washington, D.C., but to no avail; the military command did not want a black officer leading troops and perhaps commanding white subordinates. Young later was returned to active duty, and he died January 12, 1922, in Lagos, Nigeria, while in service. His body was interred in Arlington National Cemetery in 1923.

See Robert E. Greene, *The Early Life of Colonel Charles Young, 1864-1889* (Washington, D.C., 1973).   JOHN KLEE

YOUNG, JOHN CLARKE. John Clarke Young, educator, was born on August 12, 1803, in Greencastle, Pennsylvania, the youngest child of the Rev. John and Mary (Clarke) Young. He graduated from Dickinson College in Ohio in 1823 and from Princeton Theological Seminary four years later. In 1828 Young became pastor of McChord Presbyterian Church in Lexington, Kentucky, and in 1830 was named president of CENTRE COLLEGE in Danville. During his twenty-seven-year presidency, enrollment increased from thirty-three to 225, the endowment grew to more than $100,000, and the college's reputation for excellence spread. Young was twice the moderator of the Synod of Kentucky, the moderator of the national Presbyterian General Assembly, and the founder of Danville Theological Seminary. He married Frances Breckinridge in 1829; after her death in 1837 he married Cornelia Crittenden. One of his ten children, William C. Young, became president of Centre College in 1888. Young died in Danville on June 23, 1857, and was buried there.

See Walter A. Groves, "Centre College—The Second Phase (1830-1857)," *FCHQ* 24 (Oct. 1950): 311-34.   CHARLES R. LEE, JR.

YOUNG, WHITNEY MOORE, JR. Whitney Moore Young, Jr., civil rights leader, son of Laura (Ray) and Whitney M. YOUNG, Sr., was born at Lincoln Ridge, Shelby County, Kentucky, on July 31, 1921. His father was an instructor at and later president of Lincoln Institute, in Shelby County. Young graduated from Lincoln Institute as valedictorian in 1936. In 1940 he received a premedical degree from Kentucky State College (now Kentucky State University), graduating at the head of his class. Young then taught mathematics and coached at Rosenwald High School in Madison-

ville. In 1941 he enlisted in the army and was sent to the Massachusetts Institute of Technology, where he studied electrical engineering for two years. He then became a first sergeant in the 369th Regiment Anti-Aircraft Artillery Group. While serving in this all-black unit under white officers, Young decided to make race relations his life's work.

Denied admission to the University of Kentucky, Young attended the University of Minnesota during 1944-47 and helped organize a chapter of the Congress of Racial Equality. After he received a master's degree in social work, he went to work for the Urban League chapter in St. Paul, Minnesota, as director of industrial relations. He was promoted to president of the chapter in Omaha, Nebraska, in 1950 and served until 1954. In January 1954 he moved to Atlanta University to become the dean of the School of Social Work, a position he held until he became executive director of the National Urban League on August 1, 1961.

As director, Young guided the Urban League away from traditional social work and into more progressive programs. An advocate of equal employment opportunity, improved housing, and education as the means for social and economic equality for blacks, Young drew upon corporate, government, and foundation support to advance the league's programs. His goal was economically strong black communities that would be integrated into the general society through nonviolent direct action and political lobbying.

During the 1960s, Young emerged as a national leader of the civil rights movement. He served on seven presidential commissions during the Kennedy and Johnson administrations (1961-69) and was president of both the National Conference on Social Welfare and the National Association of Social Workers. He wrote a syndicated weekly newspaper column. His book *To Be Equal* (1964) called for a "domestic Marshall Plan" to deal with black poverty, and in *Beyond Racism: Building an Open Society* (1969), Young outlined sweeping programs to create an egalitarian society. He started the "New Thrust" program of the Urban League in 1968 to move into ghettos to attack the causes of minority deprivation, inadequate housing, poor health, and educational disadvantage; he did not want to focus on the symptomatic statistics of joblessness. Young was awarded the Medal of Freedom in 1969 by President Lyndon B. Johnson.

Young married Margaret Buckner of Campbellsville, Kentucky, on January 2, 1944. She became a teacher and an author of children's books about black history and civil rights. They had two children, Marcia and Laurene.

Young died in Lagos, Nigeria, on March 11, 1971, in a swimming accident while attending a conference to increase understanding between races. He was buried in Lexington's Greenwood Cemetery; later the body was reburied in New Rochelle, New York.

See Alice A. Dunnigan, *The Fascinating Story of Black Kentuckians: Their Heritage and Traditions* (Washington, D.C., 1982).

YOUNG, WHITNEY MOORE, SR. Whitney Moore Young, Sr., educator, was born in Paynes Depot, Shelby County, Kentucky, on September 26, 1897, to Taylor and Annie Young. He attended Zion Hill Public School, Male Underwood School in Frankfort, and the Chandler Normal School in Lexington. He was among the first entrants when the LINCOLN INSTITUTE opened in 1912. He graduated in 1916 and moved to Detroit to work for the Ford Motor Company. During World War I, he joined the U.S. Army and served in France. After the war Moore returned to Ford to work as an electrical engineer. When President A. Eugene Thomas of Lincoln Institute offered Young a job in 1920, he left his higher paying position at Ford and accepted sixty-eight dollars per month to become head of the engineering department. He was promoted to dean of the institute and in 1935 became education director, the first black to head Lincoln Institute. With the school $10,000 in debt and on the verge of closing, Young initiated successful fund raising and student recruiting campaigns. Under his leadership, Lincoln Institute became the leading black college preparatory school in Kentucky. When the school closed in 1964, Young retired and moved to Louisville.

Young continued his own education while heading the school. In 1938 he graduated from Louisville Municipal College and in 1944 received an M.A. from Fisk University in Nashville. An honorary doctor of education degree was awarded in 1955 by Monrovia College in Liberia. Young served twice as president of Kentucky's Negro Education Association during the 1950s. In 1964 he served on President Lyndon B. Johnson's committee to implement the new civil rights law. Young likewise held positions on the Kentucky Commission on Human Rights, the Black History Committee, the Chief Justice's Housing Commission, and the State Vocational Advisory Board.

In 1918 Young married Laura Ray of Lebanon, Kentucky. They had three children: Anita, who became a professor at the University of Louisville and one of its first black deans; Whitney (YOUNG), Jr., the well-known civil rights leader; and Eleanor, a professor at the University of Chicago who was also active in social work. Young died on August 18, 1975, and was buried in Lexington's Greenwood Cemetery.

WILLIAM T. YOUNG. William T. Young, entrepreneur and philanthropist, was born in Lexington, Kentucky, on February 15, 1918, to Willis S. and Margaret (Thompson) Young. He graduated from Lexington's Henry Clay High School in 1935 and received a B.S. degree in mechanical engineering from the University of Kentucky in 1939. He worked as an engineer for Bailey Meter Company (a subsidiary of General Electric) until 1941, then served as an officer in the Ordnance Department of the U.S. Army (1941-46).

After World War II, Young founded W.T. Young Foods in Lexington to manufacture peanut butter. He sold the company to Procter & Gamble in June 1955 and headed P&G's Jif peanut butter subsidiary for the next two years. In 1958 he founded W.T. Young Storage and related warehousing and trucking companies in Lexington. During 1966-84 Young was chairman of the board of Royal Crown Companies of Atlanta.

In 1966 Young joined the Transylvania University board of trustees, which he has chaired since 1977. The university in 1980 awarded Young the Transylvania Medal for significant contributions by a non-alumnus. He is the founder and principal supporter of the William T. Young Scholarship Program at Transylvania, which since 1983 has awarded four-year, merit-based scholarships to twenty-five freshmen students each year. Young's friends funded Transylvania's W.T. Young Campus Center in his honor. He holds an honorary doctorate of laws degree from the university. Among the other charitable and civic projects with which Young is associated are the Lexington Opera House Fund, the Kentucky Center for the Arts, the Lexington Center Corporation, and the Triangle Foundation.

Young married Lucy Hilton Maddox of Blakely, Georgia, in 1945; they have two children, William T., Jr., and Lucy (Young) Ruspoli.

YOUTH ORCHESTRAS. In 1990 there were three youth orchestras in Kentucky. The first, the Central Kentucky Youth Symphony Orchestra in Lexington, was organized in 1947 by Howard Pence; its feeder group, the Central Kentucky Youth Concert Orchestra, was started in 1968. The second, the Louisville Youth Orchestra, was founded in 1958 by Rubin Sher, William H. Sloane, and Robert B. French, sponsored by the Louisville Academy of Music. In 1960 the Louisville Youth Orchestra became independent. The third, the Owensboro Youth Orchestra, was formed in 1970 under the sponsorship of the Owensboro Symphony Orchestra; a feeder group, the Cadet Orchestra, was added later. A fourth group, the Barren River Area Youth Orchestra, performed from 1975 to 1984 in Bowling Green.

See "The Academy Youth Orchestra," *Bluegrass Music News* (February 1959).

ROBERT BRUCE FRENCH

Z

ZOLLICOFFER, FELIX KIRK. Felix Kirk Zollicoffer, Confederate general, was born in Maury County, Tennessee, on May 19, 1812. Starting in the newspaper printing business at age sixteen, he rose to prominence as editor of several influential papers and journals, including the *Nashville Republican Banner*. He served as a lieutenant in the Second Seminole War in 1836, then as comptroller of the Tennessee state treasury (1845-49), state senator (1849-52), and member of the U.S. Congress from 1853 to 1859. A powerful Whig politician, Zollicoffer was highly instrumental in carrying the state of Tennessee for the Whig candidate for president, Winfield Scott, in 1852. A strong advocate of states' rights, he hoped for compromise in the sectional struggle, supported John Bell for president in 1860, and was a member of the Washington Peace Conference in 1861.

Appointed a brigadier general in the Confederate Army July 9, 1861, Zollicoffer was sent to strongly pro-Union east Tennessee. On September 9, 1861, he advanced into Kentucky and later fortified the Cumberland Gap. On September 19 his troops engaged the Home Guards at Barbourville. Zollicoffer participated in the unsuccessful battle of Wildcat Mountain on October 21 and then withdrew to Cumberland Ford. On November 29 he moved his army to Mill Springs and camped on the south side of the Cumberland River. Against the advice of Gen. Albert Sidney Johnston, and in advance of the arrival of his immediate superior, Maj. Gen. George B. Crittenden, Zollicoffer moved his army to the north side of the Cumberland River near Somerset, Kentucky, in December 1861, and prepared for winter encampment.

With the approach of Union troops under Brig. Gen. George H. Thomas, Crittenden faced the choice of withdrawing Zollicoffer's army back across the Cumberland River from its poor position or advancing to engage the Union army before reinforcements joined Thomas's troops. On January 19, 1862, Crittenden engaged the Union troops at MILL SPRINGS at dawn in a surprise attack. In a foggy rain, the nearsighted Zollicoffer rode into a Federal unit that day and was killed; his military career ended too early for any real appraisal of his talents. Zollicoffer was buried in the Old City Cemetery in Nashville.

See C. David Dalton, "Zollicoffer, Crittenden, and the Mill Springs Campaign: Some Persistent Questions," *FCHQ* 60 (Oct. 1986): 463-71; Raymond E. Myers, *The Zollie Tree* (Louisville 1964).

D. WARREN LAMBERT

BIBLIOGRAPHIC ESSAY

The Kentucky Encyclopedia represents the work of more than five hundred authors, whose research relied on the following primary and secondary materials. The available sources vary in both quality and quantity depending upon topic and era. In 1982, in an article entitled "Clio in the Commonwealth: The Status of Kentucky History," James C. Klotter called Kentucky history a "place of few settlements and much mystery," like Daniel Boone's first view of the "wonderful level of Kentucke" as described by John Filson. New monographs and biographies have been published in the past decade, but Klotter's observation remains valid; the commonwealth has not produced as much scholarly writing on its history as our professed interest in the past would indicate.

In part this situation may be due to the scarcity of primary source materials. Only in the mid-twentieth century did Kentucky begin a systematic collection of political documents. Records were either never kept, or destroyed (many in courthouse fires), or otherwise lost.

Available in major state libraries are published primary sources. These include:

Kentucky General Assembly. *Acts*. Frankfort, Ky., 1792- .

Kentucky House of Representatives. *Journal*. Frankfort, Ky., 1792- .

Kentucky Senate. *Journal*. Frankfort, Ky., 1792- .

Kentucky Superintendent of Public Instruction. *Reports*. Frankfort, Ky., 1838-1983.

Kentucky Court of Appeals. *Reports*. Frankfort, Ky., 1785-1951.

South Western Reporter, St. Paul, Minn., 1886- .

Kentucky Bureau of Agriculture, Horticulture, and Statistics. *Reports*. Frankfort, Ky., 1878-1910.

Proceedings and Reports in Convention (Constitutional), 4 vols. Frankfort, Ky., 1890.

Kentucky Documents. Frankfort, Ky., 1839-1943.

Kentucky State Maps. Frankfort, Ky.: Kentucky Geological Survey, 1924, 1927, 1928.

Report of the Debates and Proceedings of the Convention for the Revision of the Constitution of the State of Kentucky, 1849. Frankfort, Ky., 1849.

Hasse, Adelaide R. *Index of Economic Material in Documents of the States of the United States: Kentucky, 1792-1904*. Washington, D.C.: Carnegie Institution of Washington, 1910.

Hening, William W. *Virginia: Laws, Statutes, Etc*. Richmond, Va.: Samuel Pleasants, Jr., 1809-1823.

Hopkins, James F., et al., eds. *The Papers of Henry Clay*, 11 vols. Lexington, Ky.: University Press of Kentucky, 1959-1992.

Little, William, and Jacob Swigert, eds. *A Digest of the Statute Law of Kentucky*, 2 vols. Frankfort, Ky.: Kendall and Russell, 1822.

Manuscript collections are a second source of primary materials. *The Guide to Kentucky Archival and Manuscript Repositories* (Frankfort, Ky.: Department for Libraries and Archives, 1986) contains listings for 285 archival and manuscript repositories open to the public. Barbara Teague has edited *The Guide to Kentucky Archival and Manuscript Collections*, vol. 1 (Frankfort, Ky.: Department for Libraries and Archives, 1988), which describes materials held in twenty-eight of those repositories. The second volume, published in 1991, describes an additional thirty-four collections. Only a few of those collections can be listed here.

In Frankfort the Kentucky Department for Libraries and Archives is authorized as the central depository for public records created by government agencies in Kentucky. It also accepts nonpublic materials that amplify records in its custody. For over a century, the Kentucky Historical Society has collected manuscripts, maps, and photographs to document the commonwealth's history. Its holdings are predominantly private in nature. While materials collected in earlier days focus on Frankfort and the Bluegrass region, current acquisitions reflect a statewide approach. Mary Margaret Bell's *Manuscripts of the Kentucky Historical Society* (Frankfort, Ky.: Kentucky

Historical Society, 1991) is a guide. The Military Records and Research Library of the Kentucky Department of Military Affairs has material on military history, in particular that of the Kentucky National Guard and other Kentucky units.

In Louisville the Filson Club has collected material, especially personal and family history, on early Kentucky, with particular attention to Louisville. Found there are photographs, maps, broadsides, and a large manuscript collection. The J.B. Speed Art Museum's research library contains files relating to the Louisville art scene and art in general.

In northern Kentucky the Kenton County Public Library collects materials related to the political, economic, and cultural development of the region. In each county of Kentucky, both the public library and the courthouse are good sources of local primary and secondary materials. Some counties have museums that offer more tangible evidence of their history.

Each of the public universities and many private colleges have documents and manuscript collections. Among these:

Alice Lloyd College collects photographs, oral history, and documents dealing with central Appalachian culture and society, particularly in eastern Kentucky and Knott County.

Berea College's Appalachian Center and Appalachian Museum house the Appalachian Folklife Project, which collects recordings, photographs, and manuscripts. The Berea College library has a strong manuscript collection relating to the history of the college.

Bellarmine College documents Roman Catholic history in Kentucky. It houses the Thomas Merton Study Center, which contains information on the life, writings, and death of the monk of Gethsemani.

Eastern Kentucky University's library has the John Wilson Townsend Room, containing manuscript collections and genealogical material of local interest. The university archives contain records of the university and the region it serves.

Kentucky State University has materials relating to Afro-Americans in Kentucky and to Afro-American and African history in general.

Morehead State University collects materials relating to the history and culture of eastern Kentucky.

Murray State University focuses on the Jackson Purchase region and has the manuscripts of many political figures. Its Forrest C. Pogue Oral History Institute includes interviews with leaders in Kentucky government and politics.

Northern Kentucky University holds materials pertaining to regional history. Oral history interviews with persons who have been active in campaigns against organized crime in Newport since the 1950s are available.

Transylvania University preserves documents from the early days of Transylvania and related institutions. They include the papers of prominent political and educational leaders such as Henry Clay and Horace Holley and the collection, both papers and books, of local historian J. Winston Coleman, Jr. The medical collection, 1799-1859, includes papers and memorabilia that document the medical college's history.

The University of Louisville, in addition to documents relating to Louisville in general, has special materials on art and music in Kentucky and files of the School of Medicine. The photographic archives document the history of Louisville through photography. Rare books, oral history tapes, and special collections are found as well. A guide to the manuscript collection is entitled *A Place Where Historical Research May Be Pursued: An Introduction to Primary Research Sources in the University of Louisville Archives, William F. Ekstrom Library* (Louisville: University of Louisville, 1981).

University of Kentucky holdings concern Kentucky and the Ohio River Valley and include specialty concentrations, such as Appalachia and modern Kentucky politics. Photographs, oral history, and audiovisual materials are found there. It contains the largest manuscript collection in the state. For details, see Jeanne Slater Trimble, *Guide to Selected Manuscripts Housed in the Division of Special Collections, Margaret I. King Library, University of Kentucky* (Lexington, Ky.: University of Kentucky, 1988). The Kentucky Newspaper Project, which has inventoried, cataloged, and preserved newspapers held within the commonwealth, is housed in the library. As of January 1991, 4,965 bibliographic records and 11,829 holdings records had been entered by the project in the National Newspaper Union List of the Online Computer Library Center Inc.

Western Kentucky University has materials relating to south-central Kentucky, particularly in the period 1830-1900. Its folklife archives contain oral history tapes about life in that region. Included in the holdings of the Kentucky Library are maps, atlases, newspapers, travelers' accounts, and Shaker materials.

Many of these institutions collect oral histories. The Kentucky Oral History Commission in Frankfort has sponsored numerous individual and institutional projects for nearly two decades, and copies of many of these interviews can be found at the Kentucky Department for Libraries and Archives. A guide to the collection is Cary C. Wilkins, ed., *The Guide to Kentucky Oral History Collections* (Frankfort, Ky.: Oral History Commission, 1991).

GENERAL STUDIES

Much of the information contained in this encyclopedia was gathered from secondary source materials. Listed below are some of the most important general studies on the history of the state of Kentucky. None of these is of recent date, but all remain valuable for a number of the area studies. The best source on Kentucky historiography remains J. Winston Coleman, Jr.'s *A Bibliography of Kentucky History* (Lexington, Ky.: University of Kentucky Press, 1949), unfortunately now quite outdated. *The Register of the Kentucky Historical Society* has published a "Subject Index, 1903-1988," 87 (Summer 1989): 199-383.

Allen, William B. *A History of Kentucky*. Louisville: Bradley & Gilbert, 1872.

Battle, J.H.; William Perrin; and G.C. Kniffin. *Kentucky: A History of the State*. Louisville and Chicago: F.A. Battey & Co., 1885. Reprinted in 1979.

Bodley, Temple, and Samuel M. Wilson. *History of Kentucky*. 4 vols. Chicago and Louisville: S.J. Clarke Publishing Co., 1928.

Butler, Mann. *A History of the Commonwealth of Kentucky*. Louisville: Wilcox, Dickermann & Co., 1834. Reprinted in 1968.

Channing, Steven A. *Kentucky: A Bicentennial History*. New York: W.W. Norton Company, 1977.

Clark, Thomas D. *A History of Kentucky*. New York: Prentice-Hall, 1937. Reprinted in 1978.

Collins, Richard H., and Lewis C. Collins. *Historical Sketches of Kentucky*. 2 vols. Covington, Ky.: Collins & Co., 1874. Reprinted in 1966.

Connelley, William E., and E.M. Coulter. *History of Kentucky*. Edited by Charles Kerr. 5 vols. Chicago and New York: American Historical Society, 1922.

Filson, John. *The Discovery, Settlement and Present State of Kentucke*. Wilmington, Del.: James Adams, 1784. Reprinted in 1962.

Marshall, Humphrey. *The History of Kentucky*. 2 vols. Frankfort, Ky.: G.S. Robinson, 1824.

McElroy, Robert M. *Kentucky in the Nation's History*. New York: Moffat, Yard and Co., 1909.

Shaler, Nathaniel Southgate. *Kentucky: A Pioneer Commonwealth*. Boston: Houghton, Mifflin Co., 1884. Reprinted in 1888.

Smith, Zachariah F. *The History of Kentucky*. Louisville: Courier-Journal Job Printing Co., 1886. Reprinted in 1901.

Wallis, Frederick A., and Hambleton Tapp. *A Sesqui-Centennial History of Kentucky*. 4 vols. Hopkinsville, Ky.: Historical Record Association, 1945.

AREA STUDIES

The following list is highly selective, but many of the references include bibliographies that can guide the interested reader to further sources. Many were suggested by the consulting editors, who were asked to recommend sources of additional information within their fields of expertise.

AFRO-AMERICAN

Dunnigan, Alice A. *The Fascinating Story of Black Kentuckians*. Washington, D.C.: Associated Publishers, 1982.

Howard, Victor B. *Black Liberation in Kentucky: Emancipation and Freedom, 1861-1884*. Lexington, Ky.: University Press of Kentucky, 1983.

Donovan, Mary S., and Patricia Wagner. *Kentucky's Black Heritage*. Frankfort, Ky.: Kentucky Commission on Human Rights, 1971.

Wright, George C. *Life Behind a Veil: Blacks in Louisville, Kentucky, 1865-1930*. Baton Rouge, La.: Louisiana State University Press, 1985.

———. *Racial Violence in Kentucky, 1865-1940*. Baton Rouge, La.: Louisiana State University Press, 1990.

AGRICULTURE

Axton, William. *Tobacco and Kentucky.* Lexington, Ky.: University Press of Kentucky, 1975.

Clark, Thomas D. *Agrarian Kentucky.* Lexington, Ky.: University Press of Kentucky, 1977.

Gray, Lewis C. *History of Agriculture in the Southern United States to 1860.* 2 vols. Washington, D.C.: Carnegie Institution of Washington, 1933. Reprinted in 1941.

Hopkins, James F. *A History of the Hemp Industry in Kentucky.* Lexington, Ky.: University of Kentucky Press, 1951.

Nall, James O. *The Tobacco Night Riders of Kentucky and Tennessee, 1905-1909.* Louisville: Standard Press, 1939.

Smith, J. Allan. *College of Agriculture of the University of Kentucky, Early and Middle Years, 1865-1951.* Lexington, Ky.: Kentucky Agricultural Experiment Station, 1981.

ART AND ARCHITECTURE

Carpenter, John W., and William B. Scott, Jr. *John W. Carpenter's Kentucky Courthouses.* London, Ky.: J.W. Carpenter, 1988.

Jones, Arthur F., and Bruce Weber. *The Kentucky Painters.* Lexington, Ky.: University of Kentucky Art Museum, 1981.

Lancaster, Clay. *Antebellum Houses of the Bluegrass.* Lexington, Ky.: University of Kentucky Press, 1961.

————. *Vestiges of the Venerable City.* Lexington, Ky.: Lexington-Fayette County Historic Commission, 1978.

Newcomb, Rexford. *Old Kentucky Architecture.* New York: W. Helburn, Inc., 1940.

Oberwarth, C. Julian, and William B. Scott, Jr. *A History of the Profession of Architecture in Kentucky.* Frankfort, Ky.: The Board, 1987.

Price, Samuel W. *The Old Masters of the Bluegrass.* Louisville: J.P. Morton & Co., 1902.

Whitley, Edna T. *Kentucky Ante-Bellum Portraiture.* Paris, Ky.: 1956.

COAL AND ECONOMICS

Caudill, Harry M. *Night Comes to the Cumberlands.* Boston: Little, Brown, 1963.

Harvey, Curtis E. *Coal in Appalachia: An Economic Analysis.* Lexington. Ky.: University Press of Kentucky, 1986.

Hevener, John W. *Which Side Are You On?: The Harlan County Coal Miners, 1931-39.* Urbana, Ill.: University of Illinois Press, 1978.

Inspector of Mines. *Annual Report.* Washington, D.C.: U.S. Department of Mines and Minerals, 1885- .

Kentucky Economy: Review and Perspective. Lexington, Ky.: University of Kentucky, 1977- .

Kincaid, R.L. *The Wilderness Road.* Indianapolis, Ind.: Bobbs-Merrill, 1947. Reprinted in 1966.

United Mine Workers Journal. Indianapolis, Ind.: United Mine Workers of America, 1891-.

Verhoeff, Mary. *The Kentucky Mountains: Transportation and Commerce, 1750-1911.* Louisville: J.P. Morton & Co., 1911.

COMMUNICATIONS

Birchfield, James D., and William J. Marshall. "A Preliminary Bibliography of Kentucky Printing History," in *A Kentucky Hundred: Landmarks of Kentucky Printing.* Lexington, Ky.: University of Kentucky Libraries, 1987.

Evans, Herndon. *The Newspaper Press in Kentucky.* Lexington, Ky.: University Press of Kentucky, 1976.

Perrin, William H. *The Pioneer Press of Kentucky.* Filson Club Publication No. 3. Louisville: J.P. Morton & Co., 1888.

Wilson, Samuel M. "The *Kentucky Gazette* and John Bradford Its Founder," *Papers of the Bibliographical Society of America* 31 (1937): 102-32.

EDUCATION

Hackensmith, C.W. *Out of Time and Tide: The Evolution of Education in Kentucky.* Lexington, Ky.: College of Education, University of Kentucky, 1970.

Hamlett, Barksdale. *History of Education in Kentucky.* Frankfort, Ky.: Kentucky Department of Education, 1914.

Hartford, Ellis. *The Little White School House.* Lexington, Ky.: University Press of Kentucky, 1977.

Lewis, Alvin F. *History of Higher Education in Kentucky.* Washington, D.C.: U.S. Government Printing Office, 1899.

McVey, Frank L. *The Gates Open Slowly.* Lexington, Ky.: University of Kentucky Press, 1949.

FLORA AND FAUNA

Barbour, Roger W. *Amphibians and Reptiles of Kentucky.* Lexington, Ky.: University Press of Kentucky, 1971.

—— et al. *Kentucky Birds: A Finding Guide.* Lexington, Ky.: University Press of Kentucky, 1973.

—— and Wayne H. Davis. *Mammals of Kentucky.* Lexington, Ky.: University Press of Kentucky, 1974.

Beal, Ernest O., and John W. Thieret. *Aquatic and Wetland Plants of Kentucky.* Frankfort, Ky.: Kentucky Nature Preserves Commission, 1986.

Cranfill, Ray. *Ferns and Fern Allies of Kentucky.* Frankfort, Ky.: Kentucky Nature Preserves Commission, 1980.

Wharton, Mary E., and Roger W. Barbour. *A Guide to the Wildflowers and Ferns of Kentucky.* Lexington, Ky.: University Press of Kentucky, 1971.

——. *Trees and Shrubs of Kentucky.* Lexington, Ky.: University Press of Kentucky, 1973.

FOLKLIFE

Clarke, Kenneth W., and Mary Clarke. *The Harvest and the Reapers: Oral Traditions of Kentucky.* Lexington, Ky.: University Press of Kentucky, 1974.

Dorson, R.M., ed. *Handbook of American Folklore.* Bloomington, Ind.: Indiana University Press, 1983.

Montell, W.L., and Michael Morse. *Kentucky Folk Architecture.* Lexington, Ky.: University Press of Kentucky, 1976.

Wolfe, Charles K. *Kentucky Country: Folk and Country Music of Kentucky.* Lexington, Ky.: University Press of Kentucky, 1982.

GEOGRAPHY

Bladen, Wilford. *A Geography of Kentucky.* Dubuque, Iowa: Kendall-Hunt Publishing, 1984.

Clark, Thomas D. *Historic Maps of Kentucky.* Lexington, Ky.: University Press of Kentucky, 1979.

Karan, P.P., ed. *Kentucky: A Regional Geography.* Dubuque, Iowa: Kendall-Hunt Publishing, 1973.

—— and Cotton Mather, eds. *Atlas of Kentucky.* Lexington, Ky.: University Press of Kentucky, 1977.

Withington, William A. *Kentucky in Maps.* Lexington, Ky., 1980. Reprinted in 1987.

GEOLOGY

McDowell, Robert C., ed. *The Geology of Kentucky.* Washington, D.C.: U.S. Government Printing Office, 1986.

McFarlan, Arthur C. *The Geology of Kentucky.* Lexington, Ky.: University of Kentucky Press, 1943.

Jillson, Willard Rouse. *The Geology and Mineral Resources of Kentucky.* Frankfort, Ky.: Kentucky Geological Survey, 1928.

Miller, Arthur M. *The Geology of Kentucky.* Frankfort, Ky.: Kentucky Department of Geology and Forestry, 1919.

Schwalb, Howard R.; Vivian S. Hall; and Juanita Smith. *Bibliography of the Kentucky Geological Survey, 1839 through 1978.* Lexington, Ky.: Kentucky Geological Survey, 1980.

GOVERNMENT AND LAW

Goldstein, Joel, ed. *Kentucky Government and Politics.* Bloomington, Ind.: College Town Press, 1984.

Jewell, Malcolm E. *The Kentucky Legislature.* Lexington, Ky.: University Press of Kentucky, 1988.

LITERATURE AND POETRY

Day, Bess A., ed. *Biographical and Critical Materials Pertaining to Kentucky Authors.* Louisville: Louisville Free Public Library, 1941.

Kentucky Council of Teachers of English. "Literary Landmarks of Kentucky," *Kentucky English Bulletin* 11 (Fall 1961): 1-48.

Rubin, Louis D., Jr. *The History of Southern Literature.* Baton Rouge, La.: Louisiana State University Press, 1985.

Thompson, Lawrence, and Algernon D. Thompson. *The Kentucky Novel.* Lexington, Ky.: University of Kentucky Press, 1953.

Townsend, John Wilson. *Kentucky in American Letters*, vols. 1 and 2. Cedar Rapids, Iowa: Torch Press, 1913.

—— and Dorothy Edwards Townsend. *Kentucky in American Letters*, vol. 3. Georgetown, Ky.: Georgetown College Press, 1976.

Ward, William S. *A Literary History of Kentucky*. Knoxville, Tenn.: University of Tennessee Press, 1988.

LOCAL HISTORY

Gaventa, John. *Power and Powerlessness: Quiescence and Rebellion in an Appalachian Valley*. Urbana, Ill.: University of Illinois Press, 1980.

Ireland, Robert M. *The County Courts in Antebellum Kentucky*. Lexington, Ky.: University Press of Kentucky, 1972.

——. *The County in Kentucky History*. Lexington, Ky.: University Press of Kentucky, 1976.

——. *Little Kingdoms: The Counties of Kentucky, 1850-1891*. Lexington, Ky.: University Press of Kentucky, 1977.

Lyons, W.E. *The Politics of City-County Merger*. Lexington, Ky.: University Press of Kentucky, 1977.

Share, Allen J. *Cities in the Commonwealth: Two Centuries of Urban Life in Kentucky*. Lexington, Ky.: University Press of Kentucky, 1982.

Wade, Richard C. *The Urban Frontier*. Chicago: University of Chicago Press, 1967.

MEDICINE

Ellis, John. *Medicine in Kentucky*. Lexington, Ky.: University Press of Kentucky, 1977.

Packard, Francis R. *History of Medicine in the United States*. 2 vols. New York: Paul B. Hoeber, Inc., 1931.

Pickard, Madge E., and Carlyle Burley. *The Midwest Pioneer, His Ills, Cures, and Doctors*. Crawfordsville, Ind.: R.E. Banta, 1945.

Rogers, Lewis. *Facts and Reminiscences of the Medical History of Kentucky*. Louisville: John P. Morton & Co., 1873.

Works Progress Administration. *Medicine and its Development in Kentucky*. Louisville: Standard Printing Co., 1940.

MILITARY HISTORY

Hammack, James W., Jr. *Kentucky and the Second American Revolution: The War of 1812*. Lexington, Ky.: University Press of Kentucky, 1976.

Harrison, Lowell H. *The Civil War in Kentucky*. Lexington, Ky.: University Press of Kentucky, 1975.

Rice, Otis. *Frontier Kentucky*. Lexington, Ky.: University Press of Kentucky, 1975.

Stone, Richard. *A Brittle Sword: The Kentucky Militia, 1776-1912*. Lexington, Ky.: University Press of Kentucky, 1977.

——. *Kentucky Fighting Men, 1861-1945*. Lexington, Ky.: University Press of Kentucky, 1982.

POLITICAL HISTORY

Baird, Nancy D. *Luke Pryor Blackburn, Physician, Governor, Reformer*. Lexington, Ky.: University Press of Kentucky, 1979.

Caudill, Harry. *Night Comes to the Cumberlands*. Boston: Little, Brown, 1963.

Chinn, George. *Kentucky Settlements and Statehood, 1750-1800*. Frankfort, Ky.: Kentucky Historical Society, 1975.

Clark, Thomas D. *Kentucky: Land of Contrast*. New York: Harper & Row, 1968.

Cotterill, Robert. *The Old South*. Glendale, Calif.: Arthur H. Clark Co., 1936.

Davenport, F. Garvin. *Antebellum Kentucky: A Social History 1800-1860*. Oxford, Ohio: Mississippi Valley Press, 1943.

Drake, Daniel. *Pioneer Life in Kentucky*. Cincinnati: R. Clarke & Co., 1870. Reprinted in 1948.

Jewell, Malcolm, and Everett W. Cunningham. *Kentucky Politics*. Lexington, Ky.: University of Kentucky Press, 1968.

Kirwan, Albert D. *John J. Crittenden: The Struggle for the Union*. Lexington, Ky.: University of Kentucky Press, 1962.

Klotter, James C. *William Goebel: The Politics of Wrath*. Lexington, Ky.: University Press of Kentucky, 1977.

McGann, Agnes G. *Nativism in Kentucky in 1860*. Washington, D.C.: Catholic University of America, 1944.

Pearce, John Ed. *Divide and Dissent: Kentucky Politics, 1930-1963*. Lexington, Ky.: University Press of Kentucky, 1987.

Stickles, Arndt M. *The Critical Court Struggle in Kentucky, 1819-1829*. Bloomington, Ind.: Graduate Council, Indiana University, 1929.

Tapp, Hambleton, and James C. Klotter, *Kentucky: Decades of Discord, 1865-1900*.

Frankfort, Ky.: Kentucky Historical Society, 1977.

Webb, Ross A. *Kentucky in the Reconstruction Era*. Lexington, Ky.: University Press of Kentucky, 1979.

RECREATION

Federal Writers' Project of the Work Projects Administration. *Kentucky: A Guide to the Bluegrass State*. New York: Harcourt, Brace, 1939. Reprinted in 1954.

RELIGION

Arnold, William E. *A History of Methodism in Kentucky*. Louisville: Herald Press, 1935.

Boles, John B. *Religion in Antebellum Kentucky*. Lexington, Ky.: University Press of Kentucky, 1976.

――――. *The Great Revival, 1787-1805*. Lexington, Ky.: University Press of Kentucky, 1972.

Crews, Clyde F. *An American Holy Land: A History of the Archdiocese of Louisville*. Wilmington, Del.: M. Glazier, 1987.

Crimson, Leo., ed. *Baptists in Kentucky, 1776-1976*. Middletown, Ky.: Kentucky Baptist Convention, 1975.

Posey, Walter B. *Religious Strife on the Southern Frontier*. Baton Rouge, La.: Louisiana State University Press, 1965.

Weeks, Louis. *Kentucky Presbyterians*. Atlanta: John Knox Press, 1983.

SCIENCE

Bruce, Robert V. *The Launching of Modern American Science, 1846-1876*. New York: Knopf, 1987.

Layton, Edwin T., Jr. *Technology and Social Change in America*. New York: Harper & Row, 1973.

Marcus, Alan I., and Howard P. Segal. *Technology in America: A Brief History*. San Diego: Harcourt, Brace, Jovanovich, Inc., 1989.

Numbers, Ronald L., and Todd Savitt, eds. *Science and Medicine in the Old South*. Baton Rouge, La.: Louisiana State University Press, 1989.

Rosenberg, Charles E. *No Other Gods: On Science and American Social Thought*. Baltimore: Johns Hopkins University Press, 1976.

Shine, Ian, and Sylvia Wrobel. *Thomas Hunt Morgan: Pioneer of Genetics*. Lexington, Ky.: University Press of Kentucky, 1976.

SPORTS

Embry, Mike. *Basketball in the Bluegrass State: The Championship Teams*. New York: Leisure Press, 1983.

McGill, John. *Kentucky Sports*. Lexington, Ky.: Jim Host & Associates, 1978.

Nelli, Humbert. *The Winning Tradition: A History of Kentucky Wildcat Basketball*. Lexington, Ky.: University Press of Kentucky, 1984.

TRANSPORTATION

Clark, Thomas D. *The Beginning of the L&N*. Louisville: Standard Printing Co., 1933.

Coleman, J. Winston, Jr. *Stage-coach Days in the Bluegrass*. Louisville: Standard Press, 1935.

Curry, Leonard P. *Rail Routes South: Louisville's Fight for the Southern Market, 1865-1872*. Lexington, Ky.: University of Kentucky Press, 1969.

Hunter, Louis C. *Steamboats on the Western Rivers*. Cambridge: Harvard University Press, 1949.

Kincaid, R.L. *The Wilderness Road*. Indianapolis, Ind.: Bobbs-Merrill, 1947. Reprinted in 1966.

Sulzer, Elmer G. *Ghost Railroads of Kentucky*. Indianapolis, Ind.: V.A. Jones Co., 1967.

Verhoeff, Mary. *The Kentucky River Navigation*. Louisville: John P. Morton, 1917.

WOMEN

Fuller, Paul E. *Laura Clay and the Woman's Rights Movement*. Lexington, Ky.: University Press of Kentucky, 1975.

Irvin, Helen D. *Women in Kentucky*. Lexington, Ky.: University Press of Kentucky, 1979.

Klotter, James C. *The Breckinridges of Kentucky, 1760-1981*. Lexington, Ky.: University Press of Kentucky, 1986.

LOCAL HISTORIES

Many of the county and town entries depend on a few sources that should be identified here. John Clements, *Kentucky Facts* (Dallas: Clements Research, 1990), is divided according to county and emphasizes contemporary conditions, particularly economic. Robert M. Rennick, *Kentucky Place Names* (Lexington, Ky.: University Press of Kentucky, 1984), was consulted to determine the origins of place names. John W. Carpenter and William B. Scott, Jr., *John W. Carpenter's Kentucky Courthouses* (London, Ky.: John W. Carpenter Publishers, 1988), was our source on the many structures in which local government has been conducted. Other information was gathered from Dianne Wells and Lou S. Madigan, *Update: Guide to Kentucky Historical Highway Markers* (Frankfort, Ky.: Kentucky Historical Society, 1983); Federal Writers' Project of the Work Projects Administration, *Kentucky: A Guide to the Bluegrass State* (New York: Harcourt, Brace 1939); and Lloyd G. Lee, *A Brief History of Kentucky and Its Counties* (Berea, Ky.: Kentucke Imprints, 1981).

Some entries dealing with Louisville subjects are indebted to George H. Yater, *Two Hundred Years at the Falls of the Ohio: A History of Louisville and Jefferson County* (Louisville: Heritage Corporation, 1979), and those with northern Kentucky to Jim Reis, *Pieces of the Past* (Covington, Ky.: The Kentucky Post, 1988). Lexington entries owe much to John D. Wright, Jr., *Lexington: Heart of the Bluegrass* (Lexington, Ky.: Lexington-Fayette County Historic Commission, 1982).

Many counties and some cities have been the object of research and publication. These works vary greatly in the quality of their scholarship; many tend to be concerned with genealogy or the recording of prominent local families. Three good standards against which to judge the quality of county histories are

William E. Ellis, H.E. Everman, and Richard Sears, *Madison County: 200 Years in Retrospect* (Richmond, Ky.: Madison County Historical Society, 1985); Thomas D. Clark, *A History of Laurel County* (London, Ky.: Laurel County Historical Society, 1989); and William Lynwood Montell, *Monroe County History, 1820-1970* (Tompkinsville, Ky.: Tompkinsville Lions Club, 1970).

BIOGRAPHICAL REFERENCES

Many of the biographical sketches gathered information from several secondary sources. These include:

Biographical Cyclopedia of the Commonwealth of Kentucky. Chicago and Philadelphia: John M. Gresham Co., 1896. Reprinted in 1980.

Biographical Directory of the United States Congress, 1774-1989. Washington, D.C.: U.S. Government Printing Office, 1989.

Biographical Encyclopaedia of Kentucky. Cincinnati: J.M. Armstrong & Co., 1878.

Coleman, J. Winston, Jr. *Kentucky's Bicentennial Family Register*. Frankfort, Ky.: America's Historic Records, 1977.

Dictionary of American Biography. 11 vols. New York: Scribner, 1958-1964.

Harrison, Lowell H., ed. *Kentucky's Governors, 1792-1985*. Lexington, Ky.: University Press of Kentucky, 1985.

McKerns, Joseph P., ed. *Biographical Dictionary of American Journalism*. New York: Greenwood Press, 1989.

Porter, David. *Biographical Dictionary of American Sports: Basketball and Other Indoor Sports*. New York: Greenwood Press, 1989.

Powell, Robert A. *Kentucky Governors*. Frankfort, Ky.: Kentucky Images, 1976.

INDEX

The index is a guide to locating the subjects and names you want to find among the individual articles in the *Kentucky Encyclopedia*. The titles of the articles and the pages on which they begin are in boldface print. Lightface names and phrases (and lightface page numbers) indicate where in the text you may find related information. The letter *a* or *b* following a page number indicates the column in which the reference falls. (The left-hand column is *a*, the right-hand column is *b*.) "*See*" references send you to another listing in the index that includes information on the topic you have consulted. "*See also*" references send you to additional information on an index entry's subject matter.

Civil War (*continued*)
 effect on state economy 281a
 effects on Kentucky University 515b
 effects on Shaker communities
  812b-813a
 Fort Heiman 344b
 great hog swindle 389a
 Home Guard 192b, 438a, 513a,
  670b, 690a
 ironclads 454b-455a
 Lady Polk cannon 528b
 Mary (Todd) Lincoln 556b
 National Guard split 670b
 Newport Barracks 680b
 Republican party 767b
 Union army
  Alexander McCook 194a, 718a
  Benjamin H. Bristow 123b-124a
  Charles Cruft 772b-773a
  Charles Gilbert 718a
  Cyrus L. Dunham 662a
  Don Carlos Buell 137b
  E.A. Paine 384b
  Edward H. Hobson 435a
  George Thomas 639a
  George W. Morgan 193b
  Green C. Smith 830a
  Jefferson C. Davis 193b-194a,
   357a
  Jeremiah T. Boyle 109b
  John Buford 138b
  John M. Palmer 708b
  John Marshall Harlan 407a
  John T. Wilder 194a, 661b-662a
  Louisville Legion 583b
  Lovell H. Rousseau 783a
  Mahlon D. Manson 193b,
   772b-773a
  Richard Taylor Jacob 462a
  Robert Anderson 21b
  Samuel W. Price 740a
  Silas Adams 169a
  Stephen G. Burbridge 142a
  Stephen Hicks 706a
  Theophilus T. Garrard 364b
  Thomas Crittenden 17a, 194a
  William A. Ward 387b
  William Nelson 676a
Civil War Round Table (Lexington)
 891a
Clack, Dixon (Rowan County settler)
 784a
Clack, George (Cedar Creek settler)
 949a
Claiborne, Jerry (UK football coach)
 340b
Claiborne (horse farm) 883a
Clark, Dorothy Park, writing as
 Clark McMeekin 600a
Clark, Francis 194, 631b-632a,
 764a
Clark, George, family (Logan's Sta-
 tion settlers) 569b
Clark, George Rogers 195, 345a,
 352b, 705a, 728a
 frontier militia commander 228a,
  344a, 495b, 506b, 574b, 713b
 leg amputation 314a
 opposition to Transylvania Company colony 894b
Clark, James 196, 707a

Clark, John (Fort Harrod settler)
 344a
Clark, Lewis (escaped slave), source
 of information for *Uncle Tom's
 Cabin* 905a
Clark, M. Lewis, Jr. (Churchill
 Downs founder) 189a,
 496b-497a
Clark, Thomas Dionysius 196,
 225b, 434a, 446b, 579a
Clark, William 76a, **197**, 705a
Clark County 197, 729a, 858a, 960a
Clarke, Charles Julian 198
Clarke, Kenneth and Mary (folk-
 lorists) 337a
Clarke, Lewis (fugitive slave) 827b
**Clarke, Marcellus Jerome ("Sue
 Mundy") 198**, 623a, 823b,
 967a
Clarke and Loomis (architecture
 firm) 198b
Clark family (Edmonton settlers)
 285a
Clarks River 199, 875a
Clarksville-Hopkinsville metropolitan
 area 729a
Classical Revival architectural style
 Louisville Water Co. Pumping Sta-
  tion No. 1 672a
Classics in Context Festival 1b, 666b
Claude (trotter) 845b
Clay, Brutus Junius 199
Clay, Cassius Marcellus (emancipa-
 tionist) **199**, 280b, 602b, 828a,
 947b
 Lexington True American publisher
  902a
 relations with John Fee 71b, 313a
Clay, Cassius Marcellus (boxer) *see*
 Ali, Muhammad
Clay, Green 200, 299b, 602b, 929b
 Greenville and Clay County named
  for 204a, 606b
Clay, Henry 37a, **200**, 549b, 622a
 American System 19b
 as moderator, Campbell-Rice de-
  bate 155b
 monument in Lexington cemetery
  645b
 as owner of Estill Springs 298b,
  299a
 shorthorn cattle 747a
 slavery dispute with Birney 82b
Clay, James B. (politician) 822b
Clay, Laura 202, 550b
 Kentucky Equal Rights Association
  119a, 498b, 964a
Clay, Lucretia (Hart) 203, 963b
Clay Ashland (capital of Kentucky in
 Liberia) 494a
Claybrook v. Owensboro 203
Clay County 204, 606b
 Baker-White feud 315a
Clay industry 205, 639a, 640a,
 695b, 784b
Clay's Ferry Bridge 205
Clayton, E.R. (coal mine operator)
 211a
Clayton, Francis (Benton settler) 70b
Clayton (original name of Butler)
 715a

Clay Wildlife Refuge 953b
Clean Air laws (federal) 640a
**Clear Creek Baptist Bible College
 206**
Clearfield (community) 784a
Cleburne, Patrick (Conf. gen.) 773a
Clements, Earle Chester 206, 261b,
 758b, 770a
Clergy (ministers) 744b, 745a
 antislavery movement 765a,
  827b-828a
Clifford, John D. (merchant) 752a,
 752b
Clifton, Joe (McCracken County resi-
 dent) 593b
Climate 207, 368b-369a
Clinton (city) **207**, 427a, 614a
Clinton College 207b, 208
Clinton County 208
Clogging, precision 334b
Clooney, Betty 208b
Clooney, Rosemary 208, 464a
Clotel: or, the President's Daughter
 (Brown) 131b-132a
Clothing manufacture 505b, 817a
 in Mayfield 384b, 619b-620a
Clouds of Joy (band) 519b
Coal, as mineral resource 471a,
 501b, 502a, 639a
Coal Availability Project 639b
Coalition for Mental Health 626b
Coal Miner's Daughter (film) 317a,
 587a, 666a
Coal Miners Health and Safety Act
 (federal) 640b
Coal mining 209
 Bell County 69a, 634b, 635a
 Big Sandy Valley 77a
 Breathitt County 116a
 Carter County 167b
 Caudill's books 173a
 coal operators associations 211a,
  528a
  Kentucky Coal Association
   492b-493a
 company towns 210a, 221b, 468a,
  476a, 546b, 586b
 Cumberland Gap 35a
 Cumberland Plateau 248a
 Daviess County 95b, 254b
 Eastern Coal Field region 277a
 Elliott County 292a, 292b
 Floyd County 330b-331a, 739b
 Greenup County 390a
 Hancock County 402a, 419a
 Harlan County 409a
 Hopkins County 258a, 440a, 603a
 Johnson County 476a, 708a
 Kentenia Corporation 487b
 Knott County 523a
 Laurel County 536b-537a
 Lawrence County 537b-538a, 574a
 Letcher County 546b-547a
 Lynch coal camp 586b
 McCreary County 594b
 Magoffin County 604b
 Martin County 613a
 miners *see* Miners
 Muhlenberg County 176b-177a,
  391a, 659b, 660a
 Ohio County 872a

National Folk Festival 522b
Nimrod Workman 968a
Sarah Gunning 394b
Southern Harmony singing 835b
Folk narrative 336
Folk-Songs of the Kentucky Mountains (McGill) 665b
Fontaine, Aaron (ferry landing owner) 338a
Fontaine Ferry Park 338
Foodways 338, 898b
Football 339, 843a
  Albert D. Kirwan 520a
  Blanton L. Long, coach 214a
  Centre-Harvard games 178b
  Charles B. Moran, coach 647b-648a
  George A. McAfee 589a
  George F. Blanda 86a
  George Ratterman 755b
  Howard L. Schnellenberger 799a
  John Simms Kelly 485a
  Johnny Unitas 908b
  Paul ("Golden Boy") Hornung 442a
  Paul William ("Bear") Bryant 134b
  Phil Simms 822a
  Robert Gain 362a
  Roy L. Kidd 516b
  Vito Parilli 709b
  Wallace ("Wally") Chambers 178b
Foote, Andrew H. (flag officer) 455a
Forbes, Hugh (Mt. Sterling proprietor) 657b-658a
Ford, Arthur Younger 341, 913a
Ford, Laura Catherine 341
Ford, Thomas Benton 341
Ford, Wendell Hampton 342
Ford, Whitey ("Duke of Paducah") (country music performer) 531a, 767a
Ford Motor Company assembly plants 342
Forest Retreat Tavern (Carlisle) 163b
Forests, Kentucky State 294b, 343, 738a
Forgy, James (Butler County pioneer) 147a
Forks of Elkhorn (Franklin County community) 355a
Forks of Licking (Falmouth's original name) 305b
Forrest, Nathan B. (Conf. gen.) 194b, 705b, 706a-706b
Forrest C. Pogue Oral History Institute 697b, 727b
Forrest C. Pogue Special Collections Library 664b
Fort Ancient culture 735b, 814b
Fort Boone *see* Boonesborough
Fort Boonesborough *see* Boonesborough
Fort Boonesborough State Park 711a
Fort Campbell 343, 687a
Fort Donelson 455a, 477a, 534b
Fort Harrod 344, 597a, 756b, 780b, 846a
  reconstruction 627a, 712a
Fort Heiman 153a, 344
Fort Jefferson 45a, 345

Fort Knox 140d, 345, 623a, 752a, 910a
  segregated conditions during World War II 582b
Fort Lexington 549b
Fort Logan *see* Logan's Station; Stanford
Fort Massac 346
Fort Mitchell (city) 346
Fort Nelson 347
Forts, stations distinguished from 851b
Fort Stanwix, Treaty of 347, 815a, 865b
Fort Thomas (city) 347
Fort Thomas (military post) 155a
Fort Vienna (settlement) 599b
Fort Wright (city) 347
Forward in the Fifth (organization) 348
Fossils 76a, 348
Foster, Hart (newspaper publisher) 552a
Foster, Jacob (miller) 871b
Foster, John M. (Black Patch War) 84b
Foster, Stephen Collins 349, 665b
Foster, William Forrester 350
Foster Music Camp 665b
Foundation for the Tri-State Community 709b
Fountain Run (Jim-Town) (Monroe County settlement) 643b
Fourteenth Amendment, U.S. Constitution 78b, 462a, 757a
Fourteenth Street Bridge *see* Louisville Bridge
4th Kentucky Infantry Regiment (CSA) 622a
4th Kentucky Volunteers, Scott-Colson battle 805a
4th Regiment, Kentucky Foot Volunteers (Mexican War) 633b
40th Kentucky Infantry Regiment (Union) 385a
Fowler, Charles Wesley (military institute superintendent) 506a
Fowler, John 350
Fowler family (Jackson County settlers) 460a
Fox, Arthur (Washington area settler) 934a
Fox, Fontaine Talbot, Jr. 350
Fox, Frances Barton 351
Fox, J. Francke (radio station operator) 125b
Fox, John, Jr. 244b, 351, 546b, 561a, 867a
Fox, Mary Ignatius (Nazareth Academy director) 675b
Fox Farm Village (archaeological site) 27a
Fox hunting *see* Hunt clubs
Frakes, Hiram Milo 352, 425a
Franchising 469a, 796b
Francis family (Knott County settlers) 523a
Francophilia, in early state history 359a
Frank, Stephen (Frankfort's possible namesake) 352b, 355a

Frankfort (city) 352, 355a, 646a, 672a, 688a
  capitol buildings 160b-161a
  First Presbyterian Church 737a
  flood of 1937 328a
  Kentucky Historical Society home 503b-504a
  murals 662b
  Old State Arsenal 695a
  theater 878a
Frankfort & Cincinnati Railroad 353b
Frankfort Cemetery 354, 645a-646a
Frankfort Commonwealth (newspaper) 131a, 436a
Frankfort Emancipation Convention 828b
Frankfort Resolutions of 1819, on Relief crisis 763a
Franklin (city) 354, 823a
Franklin County 354, 453b, 820b
Franklinville (projected town) 588b
Franklyn, Ezra T. (college president) 907b
Frank's Ford (Frankfort site) 352b, 355a
Frazer, Alexander and Robert (silversmiths) 821a
Frazer, Oliver 33a, 356
Frazer, Patterson T. (college president) 441b
Frazier, Robert (spa owner) 618a
Frazier, Thomas (Princeton settler) 741b
Frederick, Adolphus (Warsaw area settler) 934a
Frederick (village) 630b
Frederick L. Van Lennep Arena, in Kentucky Horse Park 504b
Frederick's River (Walker's name for Licking River) 554b
Fredricksburg (Warsaw's original name) 934a
Freedmen's Bureau 356, 756b-757a, 757b
Freedmen's schools 357
Freemasonry 350b, 357, 572a, 864a
  Masonic University 615a
Free Methodist Church 631b
Free silver policy, Democrats divided by 679a
Free South (newspaper) 356, 680a
Free Will Baptists 49b-50a
French, James (Richmond trustee) 772a
French, Katherine (Jackson) 358
French, Richard, Frenchburg named for 358b
French and Indian War (1755-63) 96b
Frenchburg (city) 358, 625a
French conspiracy, in early state history 359a
French-Eversole feud 315b
French settlement 358, 469a, 819a
Friedman, Joseph L. 359
Friends of Constitutional Reform 828b
Friends of Kentucky Libraries 98b, 359
  bookmobile project 96a, 496a, 554a
Friends of Public Education in Kentucky 746a

Hanna, John H. (Frankfort antebellum leader) 353a
Hannah, Ebenezer (Salyersville area settler) 795a
Hanson, Charles S. (Union col.) 539a
Hanson, Roger Weightman 402
"Happy Pappies" 403, 930b
Harberson, James (Boyle County settler) 110a
Harbut, Will, (caretaker of Man O' War) 607b
Hardee, William (Conf. gen.) 718a
Hardin, Benjamin, Jr. 403, 693a, 702b
Hardin, John 94a, **403**
Hardin, Martin D. John 403
Hardin, Parker Watkins 404, 666b-667a
Hardin, Silas, Battle of Blue Licks 93a
Hardin, William (Breckinridge County settler) 122a, 405a
Hardin (town) 611b
Hardin County 290a, **404**, 674b-675a, 752a
Harding, Chester (artist) 33a
Harding, Duncan (politician) 776b
Harding family (Edmonton settlers) 285a
Hardinsburg (city) 121b, **405**
Hardin's Creek Meeting House 539a
Hardin Village (archaeological site) 814b
Hard Labour, Treaty of 405, 566a
Hardwick, Elizabeth 405
Hargis, James A., Hargis-Cockrill feud 406a
Hargis, James F. 406
Hargis, Thomas F., Rowan County War 784b-785a
Hargis-Cockrill Feud 406
Hargis-Marcum feud 116a, 406a
Harlan, Elijah (Fort Harrod settler) 344a
Harlan, Jacob (Crab Orchard Springs owner) 238b
Harlan, James 406
Harlan, John Marshall 258b, **407**, 768a, 808a
Harlan, Silas 408
Harlan (city) **408**
Harlan Boys Choir 408, 665b
Harlan County 26a488a, **408**, 408a
coal mining 210a, 528a, 578b, 579b, 586b
Pine Mountain Settlement School 719a, 724a, 810a
Harlan County Coal Operators Association 211a
Harlan Hospital 443b
Harm, Ray 409
Harman, Mathias ("Tice") (Harman's Station leader) 410a, 708a
Harman, Pete, first Kentucky Fried Chicken franchise 796b
Harman's Station 410
Harmon, Adam (settler) 452b
Harmon (Hermann), Matthias (German settler) 372b
Harness racing 500a, 669a

Harney, Benjamin Robertson (musician) 666a
Harpe Brothers 174b, 268a, **410**
Harpending, Asbury, Jr. 410
Harper, Frederick (builder) 593b
Harper, Matthew (McConnell's Station settler) 592a
Harper, Nathaniel R. 411
"Harper Valley PTA" (song, Hall) 399b
Harris, Credo (WHAS's first manager) 946b
Harris, James (Floyd County settler) 330b
Harrison, Benjamin 411, 412b
Harrison, Burr (Logan's Station settler) 569b
Harrison, Carter Henry 411
Harrison, Ida Withers (Disciples of Christ leader) 187b
Harrison, William B. 412
Harrison, William Henry, as general, War of 1812 877a, 929a-930a
Harrison County 249b, **412**, 786b
Harrison family (Jackson County settlers) 460a
Harris v. City of Louisville 135b
Harrod, James 413, 571a, 894b
militia officer 495b, 670a
settlements 95a, 110a, 344a
Harrodsburg (city) 64a, **414**, 627a
Old Mud Meeting House 694b
original Kentucky University site 515b
Harrodsburg Springs (spa) **414**, 840a
Harrodsburg Tankers 415
Harrod's Creek (town) 466a
Harrodstown (original name of Harrodsburg) 344b, 413b
Harry Innes's Station (Franklin County) 355a
Hart, George (Fort Harrod settler) 344a, 780b
Hart, Joel Tanner 198a, **415**
Hart, Marvin (boxer) 843b
Hart, Nathaniel Gray Smith 100b, **415**, 668a, 894a
Hart, Thomas (spa owner) 299a, 696a
Hart County 416, 456a, 661b
Hartford (city) **416**, 689b, 783a
Harvest and the Reaper, The (Clarke) 337a
Harvie, John (banker) 47a, 161a
Haskins, Clem 417
Hatcher, Mildred (folklorist) 337a
Hatfield, Anderson ("Devil Anse"), Hatfield-McCoy feud 417b-418a
Hatfield, Ellison, Hatfield-McCoy feud 417b
Hatfield, Floyd, Hatfield-McCoy feud 417b
Hatfield, Johnse, Hatfield-McCoy feud 417b
Hatfield-McCoy Feud 315b, **417**
Havern, Ann, Sisters of Loretto 824b
Haw, James (Methodist missionary) 632a
Hawes, James Morrison 418
Hawes, Richard 222b, **418**

Hawes, Richard (Hancock County landowner) 419a
Hawes-Cooper Act of 1929 743a
Hawesville (city) 401b, **419**
Hawken, Jacob (gunsmith) 395a
Hawkes, Richard (Conf. gov.) 194a
Hawkings, Martin, Kentucky River navigation 352b
Hawkings, Uncle Jim (William Houchens) (country music performer) 231b
Hawkins, James (Carrolton settler) 166a
Hawkins, Joseph and Littleberry (Texas colony promoters) 877a
Hawkins, Richard (Morehead land donor) 649a
Haycraft, Samuel (Hardin County settler) 404b
Hayd, Isaac *see* Hite, Isaac
Hayden, Basil, Sr. (Marion County settler) 609a
Hayden, Basil (basketball player) 58a
Hayden, Lewis (fugitive slave) 827b
Hayden Company (Jessamine County builders) 469b
Hayden family (Marion County settlers) 780b
Hayes family (Knott County settlers) 523a
Haynie, Hugh Smith 419
Hays, Anderson, feud with Clabbe Jones 433a
Hays, William S. (college president) 13b
Hays, William Shakespeare 419, 666a
Hazard (city) **420**, 717a
Hazard Baptist Institute 420
Hazard Coal Operators Association 211b
Hazard Community College 717b
Hazel Green (city) 962b
Hazel Patch (village) 101b, **420**
Hazelrigg, James G. (Morgan County official) 652b
Head, Jesse (minister) 391a, 844b
Headley, George (artist-designer) 421a
Headley-Whitney Museum 421
Healers (folk medicine practitioners) 336b
Heard, Daniel (Greenville Springs owner) 391a
Hearon, Shelby (Reed) 421
"Heartbreak Highway" (Churchill Downs main track) 189a
Heart of Aresthusa, The (Fox) 351a
Heaton, Jonah (Cox's Creek Station settler) 237b
Hebrew Union College (Cincinnati) 72b
Heinrich, Anthony Philip (musician) 665b
Heinzen, Karl (German settler) 372b
Helechawa (Wolfe County) 726a
Hell-Fer-Sartin Creek 545a
Hell's Angels: A Strange and Terrible Saga (Thompson) 880a

Hell's Half Acre (early name for Mt. Olivet) 657a
Helm, Benjamin Hardin 421
Helm, Harvey (attorney) 846b
Helm, John Larue 421
Helm, Thomas (Hardin County settler) 404b
Helm's Station 846b
Hemp industry 7a, 198a, **422**, 469a, 644b
 Fayette County 310b, 383b, 549b
 Pleasant Hill Shaker community 812a
 Shelby County 816a
 state economy 280b, 281b
 use of prison inmates 742b
 use of slaves 827a
 water-retting method of processing 667b-668a
Henderson, H.A.M. (educator) 746a, 799b
Henderson, Richard 96b, 100a, 152a, **422**
 Transylvania Company 865a, 894a
Henderson, Robert (Carter County settler) 167b, 695a
Henderson, Thomas (Choctaw Academy teacher) 184a
Henderson, William T. (surveyor) 424b-425a
Henderson (city) 423
Henderson County 423a, **424**, 463a, 641a, 729a
Henderson line 424
Henderson Settlement School 352a, **425**, 810a
Henry, Patrick 425
Henry Clay Memorial Foundation (museum) 37a
Henry Clay Monument 645b
Henry College 831b
Henry County 425, 677b-678a
Henry Ridge Farmers Association 304a
Hensley, Barton, Sr. (settler) 426a
Hensley Settlement 426
Henson, Josiah 426, 827b, 905a, 905b
Herbs, use in folk medicine 336a, 338b, 339a, 812b
Hermann (Harmon), Matthias (German settler) 372b
Hermany, Charles 427
Herndon, Lake 659a
"Hero of the Derne, The," Presley N. O'Bannon known as 687b
Herrington Lake 532a
Hert family (Hurstbourne residents) 448b
Hesler, Jacob (Owenton area settler) 702a
Hesser, Paul (Lakeside Park landowner) 533a
Heublein, Inc., Kentucky Fried Chicken ownership 796b
Hiatoga (trotter) 845b
Hickman, Paschal 427, 428a
Hickman (city) 360b, **427**
Hickman County 207b, **427**
Hickman County Democrat (newspaper) 208a

Hickok, Wild Bill, Jack McCall as killer of 590b-591a
Hicks, Amanda Melvina (educator) 208a
Hicks, Stephen (Union col.) 706a
Hiestand, Ferdinand J. (Campbellsville settler) 156a
Hie to the Hunters (Stuart) 859a
Higgins, William M. (newspaper editor) 505a
Higginson-Henry Wildlife Refuge 953b
Higginson v. United States 157b
High Bridge 428, 511a, 836a
High Bridge (town), formerly Newmarket 268a
High Bridge Group Palisades 708b
Highland Heights (city) 429, 684b
Highlands region *see* Appalachia
High schools 105a, 746b, 860a
 athletics 340b, 843b
 basketball 57b, 473b, 923b
Hightower, William (union leader) 301a
High Victorian Gothic architectural style 30a
Highway development 92a, 310b, 353a, **429**, 892b
 effect on railroads after 1920 754b
 Kentucky Turnpike 515a
 Louisville and Nashville Turnpike 580a
 Mayo Trail 621a
 Mt. Sterling–Pound Gap Road 658a
 Murphy Toll Bridge Act 663b
Hill, John, Evans-Hill feud 315b, 365a
Hill, Mildred J. (composer) 431a, 666a
Hill, Patty Smith 431, 666a
Hill, Sam (college president) 372a
Hillerich and Bradsby Company, Inc. 133a, **431**
Hill-Evans feud 315a, 315b, 365a
Hillsboro Bridge (covered bridge) 235b
Hill's Grand (Owensboro theater) 878a
Hilltoppers 432
 basketball team 58b, 432b
Hillview (city) 141a, **432**
Hilton, Martin Toby (Ashland planner) 36b
Himlerville (Himmlerville) (town) 433, 613a
Himmler, Martin (coal operator) 613a
Hinchcliffe, John (*Weekly Miner* publisher) 640b
Hindman (city) 433, 523a
Hindman Settlement School 433, 523a, 719a, 810a, 857a
 Ann Cobb as staff member 211b
 James Still as librarian 856a
 Lucy Furman as teacher 361b
 Mary Wheeler as music instructor 947a
Hines, Duncan 433
Hines, Thomas Henry 434, 586a
Hinkston, John (Harrison County settler) 249b, 786b

Hinkston's Station *see* Ruddell's Station
Hinton, John T. (Paris mayor) 104b
Historical, Geographical, Commercial, and Philosophical View . . . , A (Winterbotham) 690b
Historical fiction 561a, 562a, 599b-600a
Historical Records Survey (WPA) 434
Historical Sketches of Kentucky (1847, Collins) 214b, 926b
Historical Sketches of Kentucky (1874, Collins) 215b, 253b, 268b
Historic Commission (Lexington) 551a
Historic document storage site, Fort Knox 910b
Historic period, Native-Americans 734a, 735b-736a
Historic sites 434
Historic Sites Act of 1935 (federal) 671a
History of Corporal Fess Whitaker (Whitaker) 947b
History of Kentucky (Kerr) 293a, 554b
History of Kentucky (Marshall) 610a, 610b
History of Lexington (Ranck) 755a
History of Muhlenberg County (Rothert) 782b
History of the Trial of Delia Webster (Webster) 939b
Hite, Abraham (German settler) 372b
Hite (Hayd), Isaac (early surveyor) 318b, 372b
Hite family (Jefferson County settlers) 468a
Hobbs, Edward D. (Jefferson County estate owner) 466a
Hobson, Edward Henry 387b, **436**
Hocker, James (Hamilton College founder) 400b
Hocker Female College (Lexington) 550a
Hodge, W.J. (minister) 766b
Hodgen, Robert (Hodgenville area settler) 435b
Hodgenville (city) 436, 536a
Hodges, Albert G. (Frankfort antebellum leader) 353a, 354a
Hodges, Albert Gallatin 436
Hoeing, Joseph B. (state geologist) 502a
Hoffman, Charles Fenno, on Louisville 575a
Hogan, Richard (Fort Harrod settler) 344a
Hogg, Hiram, Jr. (Booneville tannery owner) 102b
Hogg, James (Transylvania colony representative) 423a
Hogg, Stephen Hiram (Whitesburg land owner) 948a
Hogs 338b
 breeding 8a, 8b, 804b
 trail drives 307a, 892a
Holbert, Jack (quarryman) 161b

James, Ollie Murray 462
James B. Beam Distillery 677a
James C. Ellis Park (racecourse) 463, 882b
James Harrod Station *see* Boiling Springs Settlement
Jameson, Thomas (Elkton settler) 291a
Jamestown (city) 463, 789b
Jansen, William Hugh (folklorist) 337a, 446a
Japan
   investment in state economy 282a
   Paul Rusch's work 788a
Jasper, Nicholas (Pulaski County resident) 748a
Jay's treaties 463
   with Great Britain 464a, 610a
   proposed Jay-Gardoqui Treaty 463a-463b, 839a-839b
Jazz 464, 665b-666a
   Andrew D. Kirk 519b
   Helen Humes 446a
   James E. Raney 755a
   John H. Smith 830b
   Ricky Skaggs 825a
   Robert Elliott Jones 480a
Jazzers, Joseph (football) 340b
J.B. Speed Art Museum 464, 481b, 577a
J.D. Crowe and the New South 243b, 825a
Jefferson, Thomas, Kentucky Resolutions 508b
Jefferson County 448a, 464, 566b, 729a, 844b-845a
   adult reading program as model 560b
   Long Run massacre 571a
   Mann's Lick 607a
   state nature preserves 674a, 675a
Jefferson County courthouse 465b, 467, 820b-821a
   financing of construction 465b
Jefferson Davis State Historic Site 434b
Jeffersonian Republicans 453a, 464a, 475a, 508b
Jefferson National Forest Wildlife Refuge 954b
Jefferson Seminary 467
Jefferson's Nephew: A Frontier Tragedy (Merrill) 628a
Jeffersontown (city) 465a, 468
Jeffersonville (Ticktown) 644a, 644b
Jellico Field Association 211a
Jenkins, George C. (coal operator) 468a
Jenkins, Samuel H. (Wickliffe courthouse donor) 951b
Jenkins, William (Webster County settler) 268a, 744a, 939b-940a
Jenkins (city) 222a, 468
Jenning, Daniel (Greenville Springs owner) 391a
Jennings, Will, Howard-Turner feud 444a
Jenny Wiley State Resort Park 711b, 739b
Jeptha Knob 468, 631a
Jerrico Inc. 468

Jerry's Restaurants 469a
Jessamine County 469, 682a, 729a
Jessamine Female Institute 469, 469b
Jesse Stuart Foundation 859a
Jesse Stuart (W-Hollow) State Nature Preserve 674a, 674b, 859a
Jesuits (Society of Jesus) 781a
Jewish Community Center (Louisville) 470b, 665b
Jewish Hospital (Louisville) 23b, 72b
Jews 470, 705b, 764b, 765b, 766a
   anti-semitism 23b
Jillson, Willard Rouse 471, 502a, 890a
Jim Crow laws 719b, 808a
Jim Porter's Tavern 730a
Jim Scudder State Nature Preserve 674b-675a
Jim-Town (Fountain Run) (Monroe County settlement) 643b
Jockey Club (American) 471
Joe Creason Community Center (Benton) 71a
John A. Kleber Wildlife Refuge 953b
John C.C. Mayo College 620a
John G. Weisiger Memorial Park (Danville) 252b
John James Audubon Memorial Museum 41a
John James Audubon State Park 424b, 711b
John James Audubon State Park Nature Preserve 675a
John Major's Station (Franklin County) 355a
John Pope house 471
Johnson, Adam Rankin 472
Johnson, Albert M. (insurance executive) 805a
Johnson, Ben 261a, 472
Johnson, Bushrod Rust (military institute president) 944a
Johnson, Cave 475b
Johnson, Darrin W. (insurance executive) 220a
Johnson, Ellis 58b, 473
Johnson, George W. (Afro-American minister) 750b
Johnson, George W. (Conf. gov.) 222b, 473
Johnson, James 310b, 473, 475a
Johnson, Jemima (Scott County settler) 805a
Johnson, Joseph (Whitley County area settler) 949b
Johnson, Keen 474, 668b, 679a
Johnson, Lyman Tefft 263a, 286b, 474
Johnson, Reggie (jazz musician) 464a
Johnson, Richard Mentor 184a, 474, 476a, 622b
   cemetery monument 354b, 645b
   War of 1812 877a, 929b
Johnson, Robert 102b-103a, 143b, 389a, 475
   stations 76b, 805b
Johnson, Thomas, Jr. (author) 560b, 726b
Johnson, Thornton (Bacon College founder) 43a

Johnson, Thornton F. (Western Military Institute founder) 944a
Johnson, Weisiger and Company (stagecoach line) 473b
Johnson County 476, 708a
Johnson Creek Bridge (covered bridge) 236a
Johnson's Station *see* Great Crossing
Johnson v. University of Kentucky (1949) 78b
Johnston, Albert Sidney 476, 934b
Johnston, Annie (Fellows) 477, 616a, 694b
Johnston, Josiah Stoddard, Sr. 105b, 478
Johnston, William Preston 478
John Thomas Association (Free Will Baptists) 50a
Joiner, Charles Harvey 33b, 478
Jolas, Maria (McDonald) 479
Jonas, Abraham (Jewish settler) 470a
Jones, "Casey" *see* Jones, John Luther
Jones, Daniel J. 479, 502a
Jones, David Allen 182a, 445a, 479
Jones, David (Calloway County settler) 152b
Jones, Gabriel (Fort Harrod settler) 344b
Jones, Gayle (author) 562a
Jones, James C. ("Clabe") (feudist) 433a, 907b
Jones, John Luther ("Casey") 361a, 479
Jones, Jonah (jazz musician) 464a
Jones, Joshua (surveyor) 645a, 938b
Jones, Louis Marshall ("Grandpa") 479
Jones, Loyal 229b, 480
Jones, Robert Elliott 480
Jones, Samuel (Pendleton County settler) 714b
Jones, Thomas (Cox's Creek Station settler) 237b
Jones, Wallace (basketball) 303a
Jones, Walter L., Jr. (Churchill Downs board chairman) 189a
Jones, William B. (union leader) 301a
Jones Brothers (steamboat builders) 599b
Jones family (Knott County settlers) 523a
Jones-Keeney Wildlife Refuge 953b
Jordan, William J. (early radio station operator) 125b
Jorris, Anne E. (Grider) 480
Jory, Jon (Actors Theatre director) 1a
Joseph Seagram and Son distillery 466b
Jost, Christian (Prestonsburg resident) 739a
Jouett, James E. 480
Jouett, John 480
Jouett, Matthew Harris 32b, 86b, 393b, 481
Journal, Swift's, on lost silver mines 863b-864a
Judaism *see* Jews
Judd, Naomi and Wynonna 481

Macauley, John T. (theater manager) 590a

Macauley's Theatre 589, 878a
  Kentucky Opera Co. use 507a, 507b

McBrayer, Paul S. 58b, **590**

McBride, William, Battle of Blue Licks 93a

McCall, Duke K. (theological seminary president) 834b

McCall, Jack 590

McCarthy, Joe (baseball manager) 582a

McChord, James (college president) 177b

McClanahan, Edward Poage 562a, **591**

McClean (McLean), George, John, and Leonard (saltpeter miners) 605b

McClellan, Henry B. (headmaster) 799a

McClelland, John (Georgetown area settler) 371a, 591a, 805b

McClelland's Station 76b, **591**, 713b, 805b

McCloskey, William George (Catholic bishop) 68b, 781b

McClung, John Alexander 591

McClure, Charles King, III, Bernheim Research Forest 73a

McCollum, John (Independence settler) 451b

McConnell, Addison Mitchell 592

McConnell, Francis and William (Fayette County settlers) 592a, 888a, 310a

McConnell, James (Woodford County settler) 966b

McConnell, John Ed (folk humor collector) 446b

McConnell's Stations 592, 888a

McCook, Alexander (Union gen.) 194a, 718a

McCormack, Arthur Thomas 592

McCormack, Joseph Nathaniel 512b, **592**, 624a

McCormack's Meetinghouse (Lincoln County) 557b-558a

McCoun, James, Jr., and family (Mercer County settlers) 589a, 627a

McCoy, Randolph ("Ranell"), Hatfield-McCoy feud 417b-418a

McCoy, Roseanna, Hatfield-McCoy feud 417b

McCoy, Sam and Paris, Hatfield-McCoy feud 417b

McCoy, Selkirk, Hatfield-McCoy feud 417b

McCracken, Hugh (Benton site settler) 70a

McCracken, Virgil 593, 593a

McCracken County 543b, **593**, 593a, 705a
  Metropolis Lake State Nature Preserve 675a

McCreary, James Bennett 559b, **594**, 594b, 758a, 772a

McCreary County 77a, **594**, 674b, 949a
  coal industry 209a, 210a

McCreery, Charles (physician) 689b

McCreery, Thomas Clay 595

McCulloch, James (Fort Harrod settler) 344a

McCullom, Isaac (Cadiz settler) 149a

McCullum, Horace (Radcliff settler) 752a

McDonald Brothers (architects) 216b

McDowell, Ephraim 17b, 239b, 252a, **595**, 671b
  home (national historic landmark) 671a, 688a

McDowell, Robert Emmett, Sr. 596

McDowell, Samuel (judge) 252b, 267b

McDowell, William (Falmouth area settler) 305b

McElroy, Hugh (Springfield resident) 844a, 844b

McFadden, Andrew (Warren County settler) 933a

McFarlan, Arthur Crane 502a, **596**

McFarland, Lester 231b-232a, **596**

McGarvey, John William 186a, 553a, **596**

McGary, Daniel (Madisonville land donor) 603a

McGary, Hugh 93a, 344a, **597**, 756b

McGee, John (Methodist preacher) 389b, 632a

McGee, William (Fayette County settler) 310a

McGee family (McAfee Station settlers) 627a

McGee's Station (Clark County) 197b

McGill, Josephine (musician) 665b

McGready, James 389a, 568b, **597**

McGuffey, William Holmes 597, 710a

McGuffey Readers 597b-598a

McGuire, Neely (Floyd County settler) 330b

Machen, Willis Benson 598

McHenry, Henry D. (Rosine settler) 782b

McHenry, Jenny (Taylor), Rosine as pen name 782b

McIntire, John (Floyd County settler) 330b

McKee, George R. (Jackson County judge) 598b

McKee, William (Frankfort businessman) 353a

McKee (city) **598**

McKiernan, John E. (labor leader) 528a

McKinney, Stephen (Metcalfe County settler) 630b

McKinney, William (jazz musician) 464a

McLain, Raymond (university president) 896a

McLaughlin, Lennie Lee (Walls) 598

McLean, Alney 599, 599a

McLean, Archibald (minister) 836a

McLean, Ephraim (Presbyterian minister) 248b

McLean (McClean), George, John, and Leonard (saltpeter miners) 605b

McLean College *see* South Kentucky Institute

McLean County 151a, **599**, 599a, 693a

McMeekin, Clark 562a, **599**

McMeekin, Isabel McLennan (writing as Clark McMeekin) 600a

McMeekin, Robert W. (architect) 671b

McMillan, Gideon (Episcopal minister) 296a

McMillin, Alvin Nugent ("Bo"), Centre-Harvard football game 178b, 340b

McMurtry, John (architect) 759a, 947b-948a

McNitt's company (Whitley County area settlers) 949b

McNitt's Defeat 600

McQueen family (Jackson County settlers) 460a

Macrae, Nathaniel (Newport Barracks commandant) 680b

McReynolds, James Clark 600

McRoberts (company town) 468b, 546b

McVey, Frank LeRond 600, 601a, 618b, 912b

McVey, Mary Frances (Jewell) 601

Madden, John Edward 601

Madden, Thomas (Florence area settler) 329a

Maddentown, original name of Florence 329a

Madison, Gabriel (Hartford area landowner) 416b

Madison, George 601, 774a

Madison County 71a, **602**, 723b, 771b

Madison Female Institute 772a

Madison Male Seminary 602b, 772a

Madisonville (city) 439b, **603**

Maes, Camillus P. (Catholic bishop) 170a, 781b

Magoffin, Beriah 192b, 513a, **603**, 604a, 777a

Magoffin County 554a, **604**, 693a, 795a

Magruder, Henry C. (Conf. guerilla) 198b

Mail-order houses 627b

Major, Samuel I.M. (Frankfort antebellum leader) 353a

Maker's Mark (Star Hill) Distillery 609a, 672b

Malcom, Howard (college president) 372a

Malone, Lake 532b, 659a, 711b

Mammals 604

Mammoth Cave 175a, 176a, 285a, 368b, 715b
  archaeological excavations 27b
  blindfish habitat 320b
  development by the CCC 678a
  early travel to 897a

Miller, John (Hartford area settler) 416b

Miller, John (Richmond area settler) 602a, 772a

Miller, Joseph (Jacob) and family (Lee County settlers) 541b, 602b

Miller, Mahlon A. (college president) 907b

Miller, Mary Millicent (Garretson) 638

Miller, Richard W. (state representative) 278a

Miller, Samuel Freeman 51a, **638**

Miller, William (Garrard County settler) 365a

Millersburg (town) 516a, 638a, 638b

Millersburg College 638, 638b

Millersburg Military Institute 105a, **638**

Millerstown (city) 385b

Million Dollar Factory Fund 577a

Mills, Benjamin (judge) 693a

Mills, Isaac (Elizabethtown postmaster) 290a

Mills, James (Hickman settler) 427a

Mills, Robert (college president) 372b

Mills 795a, 871b
grist 338b
at Shippingport 819a
water-powered 812a

Mill Springs, Battle of 193a, **638**, 748a, 938b

Mineral resources 639 *see also*
Building stone industry; Clay industry; Coal mining; Fluorspar industry; Iron industry; Limestone; Oil and gas industry
Black Mountain area 863a
David D. Owen's surveys 699b–700a
dolomite 639a, 639b–640a, 708b
nutrients for horses 442b
Kentucky Geological Survey information on 501b–502b
Knott County 523a
Middlesborough area 634b
recognized by William W. Mather 615b

Mineral rights
under the broad form deed 126b, 620b
John C.C. Mayo's buying 620a

Miners
battle of Evarts 301a
convict labor 209b, 742b
immigrants 209a, 210a
labor organizations 459a, 527b, 528a *see also* Miners' unions, early; United Mine Workers
slaves 209b

Miners' safety and health 523a, **640**, 716b
deterioration during 1920s 527b
fund for negotiated by UMW 528a
mine disasters 204b, 210a, 210b, 640b
mine inspection laws 209b, 210a

Miners' unions, early 209a, 527b, **640**, 939a

Mingled Yarn (Ethridge) 300b

Miniature painting 33a

Minimum Foundation Program 613a, **641**

Minimum-security prisons 743a

Minimum wage legislation 528a, 528b, 678b

Ministers *see* Clergy

Minter, Charles (Booneville mill owner) 102b

Mint julep 641

Mission–style architecture 30b

Mississippian culture 568b, 572a, 735b

Mississippi Plateau 715b, 738b

Mississippi River 461a, 491a, 774b
Spanish Conspiracy 839a

Mississippi Steamboat Navigation Company 679b

Mobile & Ohio Railroad (M&O) 753a, 753b

Modrel, Robert (settler) 642a

Modrel's Station 641, 952b

"Mollie Darling" (Hays) (song) 419b–420a

Moloney, Richard Patrick 642

Monarch butterflies 454a

Monitor (warship) 454b

"Monkey Bill," antievolution legislation 23a

Monkey's Eyebrow 642

Monon Railroad 580a

Monroe, Alexander L. (Falmouth minister) 305b

Monroe, Burt L., Sr., bird collections 81b

Monroe, Charlie (bluegrass performer) 642b

Monroe, Thomas B. (Monroe County landowner) 889b

Monroe, William Smith ("Bill") 90a–91a, 232a, **642**, 690a, 6661

Monroe County 643, 694b–695a, 889b

Montell, Lynwood (folklorist) 337a

Monterrey, Battle of (Mexican War) 633a

Montgomery, John (settler) 187b, 889a

Montgomery, Richard, Montgomery County named for 644a

Montgomery, Sanders (Morgan County official) 652b

Montgomery, William (Stanford area settler) 846a

Montgomery County 644, 657b

Montgomery's Mill (Greensburg) 388b

Monticello (city) **644**, 938b

Monumental Classicism, architectural style 29a

Monuments 645, 660a, 967b

Moody, Dwight L. (evangelist) 737b, 765b

Moody, William R. (Episcopal minister) 296b

Mooney, Ambrose (Dixon landowner) 268a

Moonlight schools 559b–560a, **646**, 784b, 855b, 964b

Moonshine 267a, 534b, 588b, **646**, 647a
Coe Ridge (Zeketown) 213a

Moore, Alexander (woodwright) 312b, 950b

Moore, C.B. (archaeologist) 671b

Moore, Charles Chilton 90a, **647**

Moore, Clarence B. (archaeologist) 27b

Moore, Davey (boxer) 843b

Moore, Elias (Booneville settler) 102a

Moore, Frederick (Lawrence County settler) 537b, 574a

Moore, George and Robert (Warren County settlers) 106a, 933a

Moore, James (Episcopal minister) 295b

Moore, James, Sr. (Booneville settler) 102a, 703a

Moore, John M. (Butler County resident) 147b

Moore, Richard (university president) 894b–895a

Moore, Robert (Bowling Green settler) 106a

Moore, Samuel (Fort Harrod settler) 344a

Moore's Station (Owsley County) *see* Boone's Station

Mooresville Bridge (covered bridge) 236a

Moran, Charles B. 178b, 340a, **647**

Morehead, Charles Slaughter 176b, 524a, **648**

Morehead, James Turner 141a, **648**, 649a

Morehead (city) **648**, 784a

Morehead State Normal School and Teachers College 504b, 649a, 850b, 873a

Morehead State University 649
accreditation 649b–650a
football 822b
music department 851a
presidents 650a
A.D. Albright 10b, 650a
Adron Doran 269b–270a, 649a, 650a

Morgan, Daniel, Morgan County and Morganfield named for 652b, 653a

Morgan, Garrett Augustus 650

Morgan, George W. (Union gen.) 193b

Morgan, John Hunt 2b, 539a, 546b, 586a, **650**
Battle of Cynthiana Bridge 250b
capture of steamboats in Meade County 623a
closing of the L&N at Muldraugh Hill 660b
raids by 193a, 194b, 198b, 290a, 371a

Morgan, Louis 651

Morgan, Thomas Hunt 651, 802b

Morgan County 652, 762b, 945b

Morganfield (city) **653**, 908a

Morgan Springs (nucleus of Morganfield) 653a

Morgantown (city) 147a, **653**

Mormonism 654

Nickel, Thomas (Morgan County justice of the peace) 652b
Nick of the Woods (Bird) 81a, 561a
Niehaus, Charles H. (sculptor) 162a, 646a
Night Comes to the Cumberlands (Caudill) 172b, 210b
'night, Mother (Norman) 684b, 878b
Night riders 149b, 441a, **682**
  Black Patch War 85a, 143b, 885a, 889a
Niles, John Jacob 683
Nineteenth Amendment, U.S. Constitution 203a, 288b, 538b, 966a
Nobel Prize recipients
  Thomas H. Morgan 652a, 802b
  William N. Lipscomb 559b, 802b
Noble, Thomas K., freedmen's schools 357b
Noble, Thomas Satterwhite 683
Noble family (Breathitt County settlers) 115b
Noe, James Thomas Cotton 561a, **683**, 717a
Noel, Silas Mercer (Baptist minister) 48a, 371b
Nolin River 684
Nolin River Lake 532b
Nolon, Lou (Elsmere developer) 293a
Norfleet, Morris (university president) 650a
Norfolk Southern Railway 754b, 836a
  land ownership in Martin County 613a
Norfolk Western Railway 613a, 836a
Normal School Bill (1906) 278a
Norman, Marsha (Williams) 562a, **684**, 878b
Norris, George (Nebraska senator) 585b
North American Christian Convention 186a
Northeast Coal Company 476a
Northern Coal & Coke Company 620b-621a
Northern Kentucky University 429a, 680b, **684**, 851a
  law school 538a, 685a, 685b, 851a
  National Academy of Criminal Justice 851a
Northwest Ordinance 744b
Norwood, Charles (geologist) 502a, 640a, 640b
Notes on Kentucky (newspaper column) 111b
Nuclear waste disposal facilities, Maxey Flats 325a, 617a
Nunn, Louie Broady 685, 769a, 868b
Nursing care, isolated areas 119b
Nutt, John (McConnell's Station settler) 592a

Oakdale (city) **687**
Oak Grove (city) **687**
Oakland Race Course 687
Oakley, John S. (Morgan County justice of the peace) 652b

Oakwood Training Center for mentally retarded 833b
O'Bannon, Presley Neville 653a, **687**
Obenchain, Eliza Carolina (Calvert) 688
Oberwarth, Clarence Julian 688
Ode to the Confederate Dead (Tate) 727a
O'Donnell, William Francis (university president) 279a
Oelsner's Colonial Tavern (Fort Wright) 348a
Office of Economic Opportunity (OEO) 930b-932a
Ogden, Benjamin (Grayson County settler) 543b
Ogden, Robert W. (Ogden College benefactor) 688b
Ogden College 688, 943a
O'Hair, Michael (Wolfe County settler) 962a
O'Hara, Theodore 560b-561a, 571a, **689**, 726b
Ohio & Big Sandy Railroad 109a
Ohio & Kentucky Railroad 116a
Ohio Company 689
Ohio County 689, 693a, 734b
Ohiopiomingo (projected town) **690**
Ohio River 461a, 521b, **690**, 774b-775a, 909b *see also* Falls of the Ohio
  Big Sandy River 537b-538a
  bridges 579a, 581a
    Roebling Suspension Bridge 488b, 627a, 779b
  charts in *The Navigator* 608a
  flood of 1937 328a, 577a, 731a
  Kentucky History Museum 504a
  Licking River 554b, 728a
  Lock and Dam No. 35 used as biological station 880a
  Rafinesque's survey of fish in 752b
  steamboats 852a, 853a
  used by migrants from Virginia to Kentucky 636b
Ohio River Modernization Project 692a
Ohio v. Kentucky (state boundary) 103b
Ohio Valley Conference (OVC) (athletics) 39a, 340a
Oil and gas industry 471a, 479a, 639a, 639b, **692**
  Ashland Oil, Inc. 37a
  Campton 159a-159b
  Clinton County 208b
  Cumberland Plateau 248a
  Daviess County 254b
  Elliott County 292b
  Green County 387b
  Kentucky Geological Survey information 501b, 502b
  Lawrence County 538a
  McCreary County 595a
  Martin County 613b
  Menifee County 625b
  Pike County 722a
  Russell County 789b
  Webster County 940a

Okolona (suburb) 466a
Old-age pension law (1940s) 528a
Old Bank of Louisville (Louisville Bank of Kentucky) 1a, 672b
Old Capitol grounds (Frankfort) 695a
Old Court–New Court controversy 56a, 57a, **693**, 709a, 763b
  George M. Bibb 75a
  George Robertson 776a
  James T. Morehead 648b
  John Boyle 110a
  Joseph Desha 264a
  William Owsley 702b
  William v. Blair 196a
Old Covered Bridge series (Sawyier) (etchings) 798b
"Oldest Man in the World, The," John Shell dubbed 817a
Old Fort Harrod State Park 712a
Old Governor's Mansion 555a
Oldham, William 694
Oldham County 530a, **694**, 729a
Oldham family (Jefferson County settlers) 468a
Old Heaven Hill Distillery 677a
Old Henderson Homes and Buildings (Merrill, ed.) 628a
Old Morrison, Transylvania University 672b-673a, 820b
Old Mud Meeting House 627a, **694**
Old Mulkey Meeting House 434b, **694**
"Old Pepper Whiskey" 266b
Old Rosebud (racehorse) 497b
Old South, The (Cotterill) 229a
Old State Arsenal 695
Old State House Annex
  Kentucky History Museum 504a
Old Talbott Tavern (Bardstown) 662a
Oldtown Bridge (covered bridge) 236a
Old Wadesboro (capital of Jackson Purchase) 461a
Olive Hill (city) **695**
Oliver, Yelverton (racing entrepreneur) 687a
Olympian Springs (spa) 60b, **695**, 840a, 897a
Olympia State Forest 343a, 954b
Oneida Baptist Institute 204b, **696**
One-room schools 696, 800a, 801b, 856a
Oral history 697, 727b
Oral History Commission 698a
Ordovician period
  dolomites 369b
  rock formations 369a, 468b, 510a
Organized Crime Drug Enforcement Task Force 647a
Organized crime (northern Kentucky) 698, 755b
  Newport 680a, 698a
  Southgate 74b, 836b
Orleans, Duc d' *see* Louis-Philippe
Orphan Asylum of Lexington 383a
Orphan Brigade 670b, **698**
Orthodox Judaism 470b
Osborne Brothers 699
Oswald, John W. (university president) 912a
Other South, The (Degler) 24b
Ottenheim (town) 557b-588a, **699**

Violence 654b, 682b, 742a, 885a, **921** *see also* Feuds
  Bloody Monday 88b, 524a, 576a, 764b
  Regulator uprising 762a-762b
Virginia 54b, 423a, 707b, 861b
  academy movement 744b
  boundary settlement 102b-103a, 475b
  enabling acts 293b-294a
  General Assembly
    creation of Jefferson County 464b
    creation of Lincoln County 557a
  Kentucky County created within 495a
  land law of 1779 534b
  Long Hunters 570b
  militia system copied 506b
  separation from *see also* Statehood conventions
    Humphrey Marshall's opposition 610a
    procedures for 848b-849b
    as subject of Spanish Conspiracy 839a
    support for Kentucky Resolutions 508b, 509a
  survey laws in Kentucky 862a
  Treaty of Sycamore Shoals land claims 865a
Virginia Compact of 1789 294a, 620b, **922**
Virginia Mourning Over Her Son (Il Penseroso) (Hart) (scupture) 415b
Visalia (city) 155b
Vital Statistics, State Bureau of 512b
Vocational education 706a, 716b, **923**, 967b
Vocational Education Act (1963) 923b
Volk, Paul Joseph (Mount St. Joseph Academy founder) 657b
Von Steuben, Friederick Wilhelm, Hopkins County area land grant 439b-440a
Von Zedwitz heirs, Bowman Field land 107b
Voorhees, Daniel W. (attorney) 882a
Voting methods, under state constitutions 289a

Wade, Stephen IV (racism victim) 111a
Wadesboro (settlement, Calloway County) 152b
Wadlington, Thomas (Cadiz settler) 149a
Wadsworth Watch Case Company (Dayton) 259a
Wagner Act, constitutionality 761a
Wagon manufacturing 701b-702a
Wainscott, G.L. (Ale-8-One developer) 11a
Wait, Cyrenius (Pulaski County businessman) 748a
Walam Olum (Native-American epic) 752b
Walcott Bridge (covered bridge) 235b

Walden, Elisha and Tommy (Harlan county area explorers) 409a
Walker, Daniel, Danville named for 252a
Walker, David (Lyon County settler) 283b, 588a
Walker, Francis (land company director) 585b
Walker, George 925
Walker, Moses Fleetwood (baseball player) 581b
Walker, Thomas 925
  explorations 69a, 268b, 541b, 554b, 949a
  Cumberland area 246b, 247a, 247b, 249a
  Loyal Land Co. directorship 585a
  state boundaries survey 84b, 102b, 491a
Walker, William, *Southern Harmony* 70b, 835b
Wallace, Caleb 839a, **925**
Wallace, Earl Dickens 813a, 813b-815a, **925**
Waller, John (Falmouth area settler) 305b
Waller, John Lightfoot 926
Waller, William T., private lottery claim 572b
Wallerstein, Herman L. 926
Wallis, Frederick A. 926
Walton, Matthew (Washington County settler) 844a, 862b, 935a
Ward, Charles 927
Ward, Henry Thomas 927
Ward, James (Episcopal rector) 295b
Ward, Junius (Ward Hall owner) 928a
Ward, Matthews, trial 928
Ward, Sallie 927
Ward, Sophia 963b
Ward, William A. (Union gen.) 387b
Ward, William S. (author) 73b, 562a
Warders, Jesse (civil rights legislator) 192a
Ward Hall (historic house) 29a, 547b, **928**
Ware, James (carpenter, second statehouse) 161a
Ware, Orie S. 928
Warfield, Elisha, Jr. (racehorse owner) 551b
Warfield, Elisha (Fayette County settler) 311a
Warfield (town) 452a
War of 1812 928 *see also* River Raisin, Battle of
  Battle of Thames 728a, 877a, 929b
  Benjamin F. Graves 384a
  cannonball production 455b
  Isaac Shelby 815b
  James and Richard Johnson 473b, 475a
  James M. Meade 622b
  James Wilkinson 955b
  James Winchester 960a
  John E. King 518b
  John M. Edmonson 284b
  John Simpson 823a

  Joseph Allen 15a
  Kentucky militia 506b, 670b
  Leslie Combs 219a
  Lexington Light Infantry 553a
    memorial 645b
  Nathaniel Hart 415b-416a
  Paschal Hickman 427a
  Robert Breckinridge McAfee 589b
  saltpeter production 605b-606a, 794b
  Solomon Brandenburg 470b
  William Orlando Butler 146a
  William Russell 788b
War on Poverty 26a, 716b, **930**
Warren, Robert Penn 345b, 561b, 727a, **932**
Warren College 688b, **932**
Warren County 106a, 692b-693a, **932**
Warriors' Path 101b, 246b, 460a, 630b, **933**
  use by Daniel Boone 96b, 97a
Warsaw (city) 76b, 362b, **934**
Washington, Bushrod, *Green v. Biddle* opinion 390a
Washington, George (Grayson County area landowner) 385b
Washington (community) 614b, **934**
Washington (steamboat) 853a
Washington County 844a, **934**
Washington Globe (newspaper) 85b
Wasioto & Black Mountain Railroad 36a, 409a
"Wasteland, The" (Cawein) (poem) 176b
Watauga, Treaty of *see* Sycamore Shoals, Treaty of
Watches of the Night (Caudill) 173a
Watchmen of the Republic 655a
Waterfield, Harry Lee 208a, 278a, **935**
Water Pollution Control Commission 692b
Watkins, Hays T. 936
Watson, J.C. (Monroe County settler) 889b
Watson, Samuel (Calloway County settler) 152b
Watson's Store (Monroe County settlement) 643b, 889b
Watterson, Henry 398b, 468a, 757b, 882a, **936**
  founder, *Courier-Journal* 233a
  on the Spanish-American War 839a
Watts, John Clarence 937
Watts, William Courtney 938
Watts family (Breathitt County settlers) 115b
Watts iron furnace 456a
WAVE (early radio/television station) 125b, 126a
Waveland (historic site) 311a, 434b, **938**
Wayne County 644b-645a, 692b, **938**
WCKY (early radio station) 125b, 959a
WCMI (early radio station) 125b
Weatherford, Willis D. (college president) 72a

Weaver, Daniel (union organizer) 640b

Weaver, Jim ("Red"), Centre-Harvard football game 178b

Webb, Benjamin (Letcher County settler) 546a

Webb, Brenda Gail (Crystal Gayle) 939

Webb, Nehemiah M. (journalist) 657a

Webb, William Clarke 640b-641a, 908b, **939**

Webb, William S. (archaeologist) 27b-28a, 572a, 671b

Webster, Delia Ann 702b, 765a, **939**
underground railroad 901a, 905b

Webster County 268a, 692b, 744a, **939**

Weddington family (Floyd County settlers) 330b

Weekly Miner 640b

Weil, Meyer 705b, **940**

Weir, James 667b, **940**

Weisiger, Daniel (commissioner, second and third statehouses) 161a

Weissinger, George W. (newspaper publisher) 583a

Weissinger Act 940

Welbourn, W.G. (academy principal) 157a

Welby, Amelia B. (Coppuck) 941

Wells, Edmund (Morgan County official) 652b, 945b

Wells, Elizabeth, Sisters of Charity of Nazareth 824a

Wells, T.N. (college president) 208a

Welsh, William (muralist) 34a

Wendell, Thomas W. 941

Werner, Judith (horsewoman) 19a

Wernwag, Louis 941

West, Edward 821a, **941**

West, Isaac (Wayne County area settler) 938b

Western Baptist Theological Institute 942

Western Citizen (newspaper) 104a

Western City (newspaper) 104b

Western Coal Field (region) 639b, 692b, 738b, 892a, **942**
fossil deposits 349a
geographic area 368a
geological composition 370a

Western Kentucky Conservation Association 211b

Western Kentucky University 943
basketball 58b, 432b
Center for Robert Penn Warren Studies 727a
establishment as normal school 181b, 504b, 850b, 873a
Hilltoppers 432a
Kentucky Library and Museum 505b
Ogden College 688b-689a
oral history program 697b, 851a
presidents 881b, 943a-944b

Western Military Asylum 840a

Western Military Institute 944

Western Recorder (newspaper) 48b, 765b, **944**

Western State Hospital 626a, **944**

Western World (newspaper) 145a

West Kentucky Coal Operators Association 211b

West Kentucky Industrial College 945

West Kentucky State Wildlife Refuge 954a

West Liberty (city) 652b, **945**

Westport (community) 694b

West Virginia
border feuds 315a, 315b, 417a, 418b
migration to Kentucky from 636b

Wetherby, Lawrence Winchester 210b, 642a, 747a, **945**

Wetlands 461a, 738a

Weygold, Frederick, J.B. Speed Art Museum donation 464b

WFIW (early radio station) 125b

Whallen, John Henry and James Patrick 576b, **946**

WHAS radio 125b, 127b, **946**
Bingham family's interest 78b-79a, 80b, 946b
Cawood Ledford as sports announcer 539b
country music 232a, 531a
ecumenical programs 283a

What I Saw in California (Bryant) 134b

Wheeler, Ellen P.T. (Berea instructor) 71b

Wheeler, Joseph (Conf. gen.) 194a

Wheeler, Mary 947

Wheelwright (Inland Steel company town) 222a

Whelan, Maurice (Catholic priest) 780b

Whig party 201b, 523b, 575b

Whiskey *see also* Bourbon; Distilling
as theme in Kentucky literature 562a

Whiskey Rebellion 540b, 646b

Whisman, John (Eastern Kentucky Regional Planning Commission) 278a

Whitaker, Fess 947

Whitaker, Peter (Letcher County settler) 546a

White, David (Barry Report committeeman) 56b

White, James and Daugherty (Manchester residents) 606b

White, John 947, 948a

White, John D. (judge) 606b

White, T. Gilbert (muralist) 662b

White, Willis ("Father") (founder, Clinton College) 208a

White City Wildlife Refuge 954a

White Hall (historic site) 435a, **947**

Whitehaven (historic house) **948**

White Oak Spring Station 100b

Whitesburg (city) 546a, **948**

Whitestone, Henry 198b, 363a, **948**

White Tavern Shoppes 468b

Whitley, Edna Talbout (art historian) 33a

Whitley, Esther (pioneer) 963b

Whitley, William 558a, 569b, **949**

Whitley City 594b, 595a, **949**

Whitley County 949, 957a

Whitney, Robert Sutton 584a, **950**

Whitney Hall, Kentucky Center for the Arts 507b

Whitney M. Young, Jr. College of Leadership Studies, Kentucky State University 515a

Whitney M. Young, Jr., Memorial House 673a

Whitsett, William (Martin's Station settler) 613b

Whitsitt, William H. (theological seminary president) 661a, 765b, 834a

Whittaker, Bill (college president) 206a

WHLN (early radio station) 125b

W-Hollow Nature Preserve *see* Jesse Stuart State Nature Preserve

Whyte, Zach (jazz musician) 464a

Wickland (historic house) 780b, **950**

Wickliffe, Charles Anderson 950, 950b

Wickliffe, Robert 138b, 383b, 390b, **951**
Old Court–New Court controversy 693a, 693b

Wickliffe (city) 45a, **951**

Wickliffe Mounds 45a, **952**

Widener, Joseph E. (Elmendorf farm owner) 293a

Wild Birds, The (Berry) 73b

Wildcat Mountain, Battle of 952

Wilder, John T. (Union col.) 194a, 661b-662a

Wilderness Road 242b, 429a, 570a, 892b, **952**
Squire Boone 99a
stations as defense posts 642a
used by migrants 636b

Wildlife *see* Birds; Buffalo; Cave animals; Fish; Insects; Mammals

Wildlife preservation 673a-675a, 898b, **953**

Wiley, James (Fort Harrod settler) 344a

Wiley, Virginia (Sellards) ("Jenny") 410a, 708a, **954**, 963b
Jenny Wiley State Resort Park named for 711b

Wilgreen Lake 533a

Wilgus, D.K. (folklorist) 337a

Wilkins, Charles (saltpeter dealer) 605b

Wilkinson, James 7a, 268b, 352b, 552b, **955**
home as first state legislature 160b
Spanish Conspiracy 839a, 849b
statehood proposals 294a

Wilkinson, Wallace Glenn 354a, 573b, **956**

Willard, William R. (physician) 624b, 912a

William, Roger (hunt club founder) 447b

Williams, Cratis D. 956

Williams, Daniel (Morgan County settler) 652b, 945b

Williams, David (Fort Harrod settler) 344a

Williams, Evan (distiller) 266b

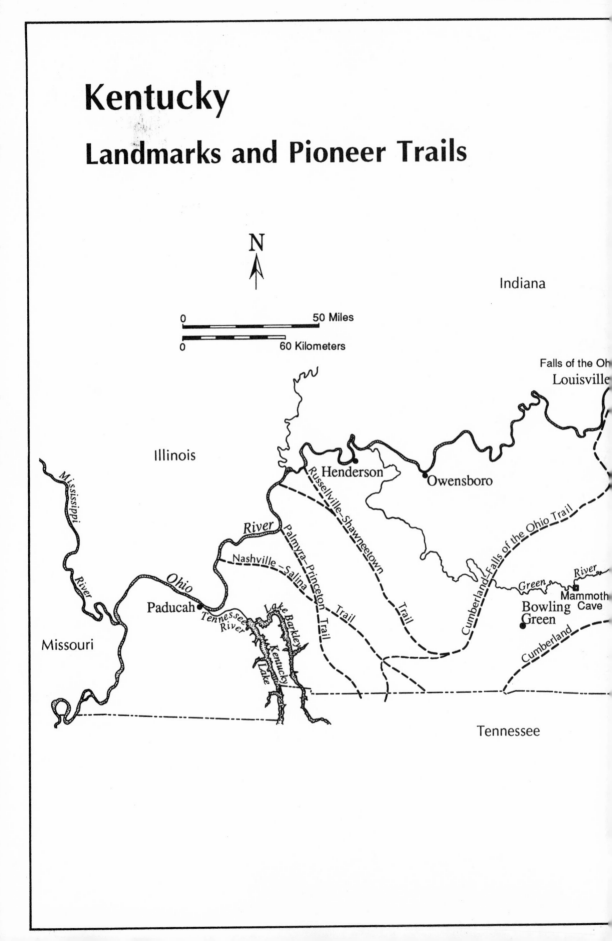

Kentucky

Landmarks and Pioneer Trails

N

0 — 50 Miles

0 — 60 Kilometers

Indiana

Illinois

Mississippi River

Missouri

Ohio River

Paducah

Tennessee River

Lake Barkley

Kentucky Lake

Nashville–Salina Trail

Palmyra–Princeton Trail

Russellville–Shawneetown Trail

Henderson

Owensboro

Falls of the Oh[io]

Louisville

Cumberland–Falls of the Ohio Trail

Green River

Mammoth Cave

Bowling Green

Cumberland

Tennessee